HANDBOOK OF RESEARCH
ON TEACHER EDUCATION

HANDBOOK OF RESEARCH ON TEACHER EDUCATION

A Project of the Association of Teacher Educators

W. ROBERT HOUSTON

EDITOR

MARTIN HABERMAN

JOHN SIKULA

ASSOCIATE EDITORS

MACMILLAN PUBLISHING COMPANY

A Division of Macmillan, Inc.
New York

Collier Macmillan Publishers
London

Macmillan Publishing Company
866 Third Avenue, New York, N.Y. 10022

Collier Macmillan Canada, Inc.

Library of Congress Catalog Card Number: 89-34152

Printed in the United States of America

printing number
1 2 3 4 5 6 7 8 9 10

Library of Congress Cataloging-in-Publication Data

Handbook of research on teacher education / W. Robert Houston,
editor
    Martin Haberman, John Sikula, associate editors.
        p.   cm.
    "A project of the Association of Teacher Educators."

    1. Teachers—Training of—United States.   I. Houston, W.
    Robert.
    II. Haberman, Martin.   III. Sikula, John P.   IV. Association of
    Teacher Educators.
    LB1715.H274   1990
    370'.71'072073—dc20   89-34152
                                                  CIP

CONTENTS

Preface ix

Section
A
TEACHER EDUCATION AS A FIELD OF INQUIRY

Section
B
GOVERNANCE OF TEACHER EDUCATION
---

v

Section

C

CONTEXTS AND MODELS OF TEACHER EDUCATION

Section

D

PARTICIPANTS IN TEACHER EDUCATION

Section

E

CURRICULUM OF TEACHER EDUCATION

Section
F
PROCESSES OF TEACHER EDUCATION

Section
G
EVALUATION AND DISSEMINATION

Section
H
TEACHER EDUCATION IN THE CURRICULAR AREAS

Section

I

BROADENED PERSPECTIVES OF TEACHER EDUCATION

PREFACE

Criticisms of teaching and teacher education occur on a cyclical basis. A new cycle was initiated with the publication of *A Nation at Risk* by the U.S. Department of Education in 1983. Not evident in that report, or the hundreds of national commission and state reports that followed it, was the fact that staff development and teacher education had made tremendous strides toward identifying a research base in the preceding decade. As legislators attempted to solve societal problems through education, and educational problems by political means, the profession was itself engaged in programs of study based on research and evaluated practice.

Schools can never be more effective than the quality of their teachers. Since the 1950s, a number of federal initiatives have sought to make schools more effective while circumventing teacher development by relying on textbooks, curriculum packages, television, school reorganization, parental involvement, testing, and instructional processes that were supposed to be teacherproof. Although hundreds of millions of dollars were expended in developing such resources and strategies, attempts to improve schools are only now refocusing on the quality of teachers and teaching.

This volume is committed to the belief that the improvement of teacher education is integral to the improvement of schools. It was conceptualized and developed to provide a basis for improving the education of teachers at every level, from initial preparation, through the induction of beginners, to continued development as career professionals. The *Handbook* is dedicated to and designed for those persons responsible for preservice and inservice teacher education who would benefit from a critical synthesis and careful interpretation of research to improve their own practice. Finally, the context in which this research is presented is clearly derived from the American experience. The practices, directly and indirectly implied by contributors, can only be judged when it is understood that the *Handbook* helps to define teacher education not only as a scholarly field of inquiry but also as a normative pursuit, dedicated to the education of a free people in a democratic society.

TEACHER EDUCATION RESEARCH AND DEVELOPMENT

As we edited the wealth of information included in the *Handbook*, several conclusions about the current state and potential future of teacher education have emerged. *First*, the conceptual and research base for decisions about teacher education has never been as strong as it is today. *Handbook* authors cite research findings primarily from the last decade. Important studies of previous decades have been incorporated into current work, refined, and applied to the present conditions of education.

Second, there has been notable recent progress, but the research basis for such important work as educating the nation's teachers is still extremely thin. Although the importance of research is being espoused, little progress is being made. Several conditions lead to this conclusion.

1. Few faculty in the nation's nearly 1,400 institutions that prepare teachers ever conduct research beyond their doctoral disserations; given the numerous educational specializations, only a portion of this effort is directed at teacher preparation.

2. Many findings are based solely on perceptions typically drawn from questionnaires or surveys, with conclusions that exceed the limits and power of those instruments.

3. Variables studied tend to be those most easily identified and measured, rather than those with the greatest promise of making a difference.

4. Accounts of proposed and current teacher education programs clog the literature, but few systematic studies report evaluations of the results of these efforts. Glowing accounts of what might be are substituted for actual findings about specific outcomes.

5. Most studies are independent, individual research in which idiosyncratic definitions, instrumentation, and conclusions are difficult to relate to findings of others in the same field.

6. The complexity of teaching and teacher education is sometimes ignored by researchers drawing on inappropriate research paradigms and frequently limited by researchers' lack of vision and practical classroom experience.

7. Few schools, universities, educational service centers, and state agencies are committed to using research as one basis for making policy in teacher education.

8. There is a tradition in teacher education, accurately reflecting the preceding conditions, that each teacher-preparing institution rediscovers its own best way of educating teachers with little or no attention to either other institutions or the research literature.

Finally, we need to base research and practice on what we currently know about teacher education, in order to implement an agenda for consistent, continued development of the field. Until we begin to build on the conceptual constructs and research findings of other scholars and to pursue a line of inquiry in depth, teacher education will continue as a cult practice, with wide differences among schools of education and professors, unable to evaluate or replicate specific practice.

HANDBOOK DEVELOPMENT AND CONTENT

This *Handbook* represents the effors of over 200 people from 34 states and 5 foreign countries who contributed as editors, editorial board members, research advisory council members, authors, and critical reviewers. That it was completed in 3 years is a tribute to the professional competence and dedication of all those involved in meeting quality standards and adhering to tight schedules.

After several weeks of dialogue between the Association of Teacher Educators and Macmillan leadership, ATE agreed in March 1987 to sponsor the *Handbook of Research on Teacher Education*. Janet L. Towslee, ATE president, asked W. Robert Houston to serve as editor of the *Handbook*. After conferring with educational leaders across the country, he recommended, and President Towslee appointed, Martin Haberman and John Sikula as associate editors and a seven-person editorial board composed of distinguished researchers including Dean Corrigan, Walter Doyle, Sharon Feiman-Nemser, Carl Grant, Chris Pipho, Alan Tom, and Janet L. Towslee. The editors and editorial board met for 3 days during May 1987 in Houston to review the preliminary work of the editor, discuss the thrust of the *Handbook*, outline chapter titles, draft brief scope statements for chapters, and nominate recognized authorities in each area as authors and alternates to be invited to prepare chapters.

The Research Advisory Council was named by the editor following further consultation nationally with educators. The Council's purpose was to provide breadth to the deliberations of the editorial board because of the wide experience of its members in teacher education and staff development. The council reviewed the proposed outline of the *Handbook*, scope descriptions for each chapter, and proposed authors and made a number of recommendations that were subsequently incorporated in the development of the *Handbook*.

Authors were contacted personally by the editor, who described the *Handbook*, its goals, and its time lines. A letter of invitation specified in greater detail the dimensions of the *Handbook* and the responsibilities of authors. Authors were requested to use the scope statements as initial guidelines for their chapters, but they were encouraged to draw upon their own expertise. Authors were asked not only to synthesize the most important research in their areas, but also to place it in a conceptual framework, to analyze trends, to summarize new directions, and to evaluate the potential for future research. At least two persons knowledgeable in the field reviewed each chapter and made recommendations on several occasions.

The *Handbook* is divided into 48 chapters organized in nine sections. Section A, "Teacher Education As a Field of Inquiry," explores the bases and issues in teacher education research, as well as its philosophical contexts, historical approaches, and futurist studies. Section B, "Governance of Teacher Education," examines research on governance, standards, policy-making, and fiscal affairs in teacher education. Section C, "Contexts and Models of Teacher Education," considers models of preservice and inservice teacher education, and Section D, "Participants in Teacher Education," analyzes the people involved in teacher education: teachers—their knowledge, development, and socialization—and university-based teacher educators. Section E, "Curriculum of Teacher Education, examines the content of teacher-preparation programs including teachers' knowledge of professional education and the subjects they teach, their educational foundations, and their preparation for teaching diverse pupils. The hidden teacher education curriculum, often unconsidered in designing programs, also is explored.

Section F, "Processes of Teacher Education," analyzes the research in training, technology, student teaching and school experiences, induction, and supervision. Section G, "Evaluation and Dissemination," examines assessment of individual teachers and teacher education programs, as well as strategies for institutional change. Section H, "Teacher Education in Curricular Areas," the largest section, highlights research in teacher education for teachers of mathematics, science, social studies, reading, English language arts, music, visual arts, physical education, vocational education, and business education. It also presents a chapter on teaching language minority students. Finally, Section I, "Broadened Perspectives of Teacher Education," examines teacher education within the larger context of different professions, adult learning, and education in three other English-speaking countries.

ACKNOWLEDGMENTS

Many persons have contributed to the successful completion of this *Handbook*. Lloyd Chilton, executive editor of Macmillan, first conceptualized this *Handbook*, approached ATE leadership, and encouraged us to broaden and strengthen its content. The production staff at Macmillan Publishing Company, directed by Michael Sander, drew upon their skill and experience in transforming manuscripts into a published volume.

A publication of this scope requires the professional services of many individuals. All persons involved in this effort did so voluntarily and for the benefit of the profession rather than for personal gain or compensation. To each we are grateful.

The editors wish to acknowledge particularly the contributions of the Editorial Board that shaped chapter content and organization and the Research Advisory Council, which provided perspective for the project. Their names and particular contributions have been previously identified. The prodigious efforts of authors, who ultimately are responsible for the quality of chapters in the *Handbook*, deserve special attention. Our telephone queries and requests for additional information and further revisions were responded to expeditiously. The critical reviewers, acknowledged at the beginning of each chapter, made numerous suggestions for improving the manuscript.

The editors wish to express appreciation to the leadership of ATE, including Janet L. Towslee, president in 1987–1988;

Billy G. Dixon, 1988–1989; and John Sikula, 1989–1990, who contributed not only in their official capacities but also as individual professionals. Robert J. Stevenson, executive director of ATE, supported the project in many ways through his personal encouragement, handling of contracts and finances, and publicity concerning the *Handbook's* progress.

Gwen Hodgkins coordinated the handling of the many iterations of manuscripts, correspondence with authors and others, and management of this project. Susanne Gauthier and Hilary Ford carefully checked references against citations and original sources. Their careful attention to detail eliminated hundreds of typographical errors and led to more accurate references. Finally, the editors wish to recognize the encouragement and support of Michelle, Nicole, Adam and Daniella Sikula, Florrie Haberman, and Elizabeth Houston.

W. Robert Houston, Editor
Houston, Texas

Martin Haberman, Associate Editor
Milwaukee, Wisconsin

John Sikula, Associate Editor
Long Beach, California

HANDBOOK OF RESEARCH
ON TEACHER EDUCATION

TEACHER EDUCATION AS A FIELD OF INQUIRY

•1•

THEMES IN TEACHER EDUCATION RESEARCH

Walter Doyle

UNIVERSITY OF ARIZONA

Teacher education consists of a loosely coordinated set of experiences designed to establish and maintain a talented teaching force for our nation's elementary and secondary schools. The simplicity of this description belies, however, the complexities and contradictions that beset teacher education as an activity of enormous size and diversity. The enterprise encompasses preservice, induction, and inservice levels of membership in the teaching profession. Each level, in turn, has several components. The content of the preservice level includes general education in the liberal arts and sciences, specialized education in content areas to be taught, and professional education in the disciplines that inform professional practice (e.g., educational psychology) and in pedagogy, including a large component of clinical practice in school settings. Preservice teacher education also includes an assessment component for the selection of candidates to enter programs, the evaluation of graduates, and the certification of eligible teachers by state education agencies.[1] Proposals have recently been made to highlight induction as a key phase in the education of teachers and to encourage the development of assistance and evaluation activities for this level. Finally, inservice teacher education consisting of workshops, conferences, formal courses, and supervisory services is provided to maintain and extend the professional knowledge and skills of practicing teachers.

Teacher education moved to the center of public discussion in the reform-minded climate of the mid-1980s. In both the popular and professional press, questions have frequently been raised, albeit not for the first time, about the purposes of teacher education, the content and pedagogy of professional programs, the quality of teacher education students, the orientations and preparation of teacher educators, and alternative institutional arrangements for entry into the profession. In responding to issues such as these, teacher educators have often turned to research to ground their proposals and decisions (see, e.g., Howsam, Corrigan, Denemark, & Nash, 1976; B. O. Smith, Cohen, & Pearl, 1969; D. C. Smith, 1983). As a result, teacher educators have increasingly become both producers and consumers of research on a wide range of topics and issues related to the selection, preparation, and evaluation of preservice and inservice teachers.

In choosing questions to study or findings to utilize, teacher educators rely on their subjective understandings and assumptions about the nature of the teacher education enterprise itself, the character of the problems it faces, and the types of knowledge that are most important to those who make decisions and carry out functions within its boundaries. The purpose of this chapter is to make explicit the underlying assumptions—the taken-for-granted knowledge and beliefs—that shape knowledge production and, especially, utilization in teacher education. The focus, in other words, is on the often implicit thinking that underlies the relationship between research and teacher education.

To achieve this purpose, it is necessary to sweep across the broad types of inquiry that are commonly perceived to have a bearing on teacher education. In making this sweep, no attempt is made to review the substantive or methodological details within each of these areas. Indeed, the rest of this *Handbook* is devoted to the task of describing and evaluating research findings. The emphasis here is on the thematic content of research (see Holton, 1973), that is, the subjective and usually unstated assumptions and understandings about teaching and teacher education that are used to define legitimate problems, to formulate studies, to identify relevant research domains, and to interpret data.

Few previous attempts have been made to examine the implicit themes that underlie the role of research in teacher edu-

Virginia Richardson (University of Arizona) and Lee S. Shulman (Stanford University) served as editorial consultants for this chapter. The author is grateful to Kathy Carter, Tom Good, Mary Rohrkemper, Jill Keller, Stefinee Pinnegar, and Barbara Morgan for assistance in clarifying many of the ideas presented here but accepts full responsibility for all opinions and errors.

cation. For the most part, reviewers have tended to concentrate on findings and their implications for policy and practice in teacher education (see Peck & Tucker, 1973; D. C. Smith, 1983). Some commentators have attempted to draw broad maps of the terrain of teacher education research. B. O. Smith (1971) defines research on teacher education as "the systematic study of problems that arise in the course of carrying it on" and examined issues related to four problem domains in which research was needed: "(1) training in skills, (2) teaching of pedagogical concepts and principles, (3) developing relevant attitudes, and (4) teaching the various subject matters of instruction" (p. 2). Turner (1971, 1975) seeks to order research on teacher education by defining highly structured models of instruction and evaluation as a guide to investigators. Similar charts of the components of teacher education have been developed. Cruickshank (1984) identifies five clusters of "explanatory variables" that might account for the outcomes of the teacher education enterprise: teacher educators, teacher education students, contexts of teacher education, content or curriculum, and instruction and organization. Katz and Raths (1985) constructed a matrix of 11 variable clusters or "parameters"—goals, characteristics of candidates, characteristics of staff, content, methods, time/timing, ethos, regulations, resources, evaluation, and impacts of the program—which they used to order existing studies and generate new questions for inquiry.

Charts such as these arrange variables and studies and serve as work sheets for planning analyses. The charts typically give only passing attention, however, to the underlying conceptions or platforms that drive inquiry in teacher education. At the platform level, two notable attempts have been made to capture aspects of the thematic content of teacher education. Joyce (1975) analyzes the various orientations toward teacher education that have evolved historically with the development of schools and teacher education: economic, progressive, academic, personalistic, and competency. Similarly, Zeichner (1983) identifies the competing paradigms that underlie controversies about the appropriate focus for teacher education programs. These analyses do not, however, focus directly on relationships between research and teacher education.

Lack of attention to implicit themes reflects, in part, the widespread consensus that existed for many years about the nature of teacher education and the contributions research can make to the resolution of problems that arise in carrying it out. This framework, referred to most recently as technical rationality (see Schon, 1983; Smyth, 1987), holds that teacher education is fundamentally a process of training candidates "to conform to acceptable patterns" of teaching behavior (B. O. Smith, 1971, p. 2). Research, in turn, serves teacher education by (a) identifying acceptable patterns, (b) validating training methods that achieve durable conformity, and (c) devising valid and reliable procedures for continuing assessment of teaching competence (see Darling-Hammond, Wise, & Pease, 1983; Gage & Winne, 1975; F. J. McDonald, 1973; Medley, Coker, & Soar, 1984; Peck & Tucker, 1973). In this framework, the research into practice continuum is remarkably coherent, a kind of unified field theory in education. The same form of description and analysis is used to study teaching, to design and test

teacher education training practices, and to formulate teacher assessment instruments. Over the years this technical view has dominated research and development in teacher education and has recently gained prominence as a guide to reforms in teacher education and evaluation.

Consensus around a strictly technical view of teaching has been eroding, however, for several years. Since the mid-1970s, major critiques of process–product research have been written and a variety of alternative approaches to understanding teaching have been pursued (see Doyle, 1978; Shulman, 1986a). Similarly, within teacher education, serious questions have been raised about the nature of pedagogical knowledge and the contexts in which this knowledge is learned and practiced (see K. Carter & Doyle, 1987; Lanier & Little, 1986; Shulman, 1986b; Smyth, 1987; Tom, 1984; Zumwalt, 1982). Clearly there are competing understandings of teaching and the teacher education process, and the differences among these perspectives have significant implications for how research is formulated and utilized in the field. It is time, therefore, for an analysis of the conceptual underpinnings of research in teacher education.

The chapter begins with a description of the common features of teacher education: the size and complexity of the enterprise and general conceptions of its purposes, substance, and problems. Ordinary knowledge such as this provides a backdrop against which research questions take form. Attention then turns to the search for quality control and effectiveness, a preoccupation that appears to have driven much of the research production and utilization in teacher education. Particular notice in this analysis is given to the unified model of content, pedagogy, and evaluation that has grown out of this search for effectiveness. The third major section of the chapter is devoted to analysis of the emerging emphasis on teacher knowledge and empowerment, an emphasis that appears to be leading to a fundamental thematic shift in teacher education. The chapter concludes with an attempt to pull together the themes and patterns to construct, insofar as possible, a coherent picture of the research territory in teacher education and a guide to the directions the field appears to be taking.

COMMON FEATURES OF TEACHER EDUCATION

Much of what we know about teacher education is common, that is, accumulated from ordinary portrayals and familiar experiences. Such knowledge is seldom codified or examined directly, yet it shapes in fundamental ways our understanding of what teacher education is and what its problems are. A rendering of this knowledge is essential, therefore, to begin a thematic analysis of research production and utilization in teacher education. Common knowledge about teacher education is discussed here from the perspectives of the shape, substance, and contexts of the enterprise.

The Shape of Teacher Education

The sheer size of the teacher education enterprise is sobering. In the United States, nearly 500,000 preservice teachers are enrolled each year in teacher education in over 1,200 institutions in a large variety of specializations from general elementary teaching to secondary core subjects and specializations in art, music, health, physical education, and vocational areas. In addition, approximately 150,000 teachers are inducted into professional practice in classrooms every year, and over 2 million practicing teachers are served in some fashion by staff development.

A large variety of specialists in several contexts play a role in conducting teacher education. Preservice teacher educators include professors in schools or departments of education and those in academic disciplines (although few of the latter see themselves in this light), as well as classroom teachers and school system administrators and supervisors. In addition, the education of teachers is governed by academic committees and codes, school district policies, and state regulations. As students move from preservice to induction, the core of teacher education activity shifts from the university to the school and school district. Central participants in induction include mentor teachers, other colleagues, school principals, district supervisors, and university professors. Beginning teachers also participate with their more experienced colleagues in staff development provided by fellow teachers, district specialists, and outside consultants. In addition, inservice teachers often return to colleges or universities to take formal courses leading to advanced degrees in academic areas or professional specializations such as counseling, supervision, or administration. Finally, some practicing teachers participate as teacher educators for early field experiences, student teaching, and induction.

In sum, teacher education encompasses multiple components operating at separate locations to provide a wide range of training and evaluation services to a large and heterogeneous collection of professionals. This general description only hints at the inherent complexity of the enterprise. In the next section, this complexity is examined from the perspective of the themes and issues that radiate through the field.

The Substance of Teacher Education

Ideally, teacher education exists to produce and maintain a continuous supply (or perhaps a slight oversupply) of highly talented and motivated teachers for the nation's classrooms. Beyond this general level of agreement, however, there are numerous conceptions of what preservice teachers should be prepared to do and how this preparation should be conducted. In this section some of the dominant conceptions of the purposes and functions of teacher education, as reflected in the character of the ideal graduate, are reviewed. Zeichner (1983) argues that these conceptions have the force of *paradigms*, which is to say, they define for specific groups the core meaning of the enterprise itself. Knowledge and progress in one paradigm can be viewed as superstition and retrogression in another. Conflicts over the merits of proposals for content, pedagogy, and standards in teacher education often reflect differences among such paradigms.

Building upon analyses by Zeichner (1983) and Joyce (1975), it is possible to identify five major paradigms or themes that underlie proposals for teacher education.

1. The Good Employee. According to this paradigm, effective teacher education prepares candidates in the prevailing norms and practices of classrooms and schools. The ideal teacher, in this framework, is one who can efficiently cope with the "real world" of schooling. The emphasis is on training and socialization for the job of teaching as it exists. A successful graduate of preservice teacher education would, therefore, be able to slip easily into the teacher's role and be skillful in enforcing the rules, in managing classrooms, and in carrying out the standard forms of instruction and evaluation with a minimum amount of supervision. Teacher education for these purposes is technical and experiential. That is, preparation focuses on the technical skills of teaching and rests heavily on field experience and apprenticeship with a master teacher. Evaluation is based on the demonstration of specific competencies and on the judgments of experienced school practitioners. This view of the nature and function of teacher education is commonly held by school administrators and many experienced teachers.

2. The Junior Professor. According to this paradigm, the foundation of effective teaching is knowledge in the core disciplines of the university curriculum, in other words, the liberal arts and the sciences (Bestor, 1953). Improvement of the quality of teaching, therefore, requires an increase in academic coursework. Advocates of this position are suspicious of the substance and rigor of pedagogical courses in education departments. They want teacher education in the hands of academic professors rather than educationists and maintain that an apprenticeship with a skilled teacher is sufficient to learn how to teach. They often point to news accounts of teachers' illiteracy to illustrate the detrimental consequences of time spent in pedagogical training and are distressed by reports on the intellectual quality of teacher education students. Within this framework, then, teacher education is selective, rigorous, and academic. That is, the emphasis is on high standards for entry and on disciplined academic preparation. This view of teacher education is widely held by members of the academic community and by many state and federal legislators.

3. The Fully Functioning Person. According to this paradigm, teacher education is best when it facilitates personal development (Combs, 1965; Fuller & Bown, 1975; Sprinthall & Thies-Sprinthall, 1983). The emphasis in this personalized approach is on coming to terms with one's self, maximizing a sense of self-efficacy, clarifying one's values, and discovering one's own personal meaning and style in teaching. In addition to personal understanding, knowledge of human development and of processes for creating supportive learning environments to promote growth are considered to be at the heart of teacher education. Prospective teachers are encouraged to seek their own self-knowledge, and psychological maturity is the bench mark of success. This view of teacher education is often held by specialists in developmental and counseling psychology, and it strikes a responsive cord among many education professors, especially elementary teacher educators.

4. The Innovator. According to this paradigm, teacher education should be a source of renewal and innovation for schools.

Rather than accommodating to the so-called realities of schooling, teacher education should be proactive. Teachers should not be prepared in the standard forms of teaching but rather in the latest designs incorporating the most recent research and theory. Within this framework, teacher education can be quite technical and prescriptive, with a focus on training in and evaluation on specific competencies to be used in the classroom. Field experiences and apprenticeships in conventional classrooms are viewed with caution, however, because these settings are seen to socialize prospective teachers into the mores of traditional practice. Learning to teach in field settings, it is argued, most often means learning to survive, and survival engenders conventional modes of thinking and behaving among teachers and resistance to new ideas and innovative practices (see Joyce & Clift, 1984). Clinical training should take place, rather, in laboratory settings in which candidates can be exposed to preferred models and given the chance to master innovative practices so that they can resist influences toward traditional teaching in schools. This perspective on teacher education is common among social and behavioral scientists, educational researchers, and many teacher education professors.

5. The Reflective Professional. According to this paradigm, teacher preparation should foster reflective capacities of observation, analysis, interpretation, and decision making (Duckworth, 1987; Richardson, 1989; Schon, 1983; Zeichner & Liston, 1987; Zumwalt, 1982). Professionally trained teachers, in other words, should first and foremost be able to inquire into teaching and think critically about their work. The knowledge base for the preparation of reflective professionals includes personal knowledge, the craft knowledge of skilled practitioners, and propositional knowledge from classroom research and from the social and behavioral sciences. Within this framework, research and theory do not produce rules or prescriptions for classroom application but rather knowledge and methods of inquiry useful in deliberating about teaching problems and practices. Along similar lines, teaching skills are seen as an important part of teacher education, but they must be embedded in a conceptual framework that enables teachers to decide when to use different skills. In addition, competencies in teaching are to include inquiry skills as well as classroom behaviors. Evaluation in this framework focuses on inquiry processes rather than standard modes of behavior and emphasizes description and feedback rather than summative judgments. This view of teacher education is held primarily by education professors with a qualitative or phenomenological orientation to research and theory.

These frameworks should not be read as absolute categories. The brief descriptions given here do not adequately reflect the diversity within perspectives. In addition, individuals (and programs) are often eclectic, so rationales fall within more than one framework. Nevertheless, these five approaches provide a perspective on debates about purposes and goals in teacher education and illustrate the enormous complexity of the interpretive environment in which decisions about content, time allocations, pedagogical practices, and assessment in teacher education are made. Moreover, demands and expectations for research can vary sharply across these frameworks.

Thus a change in approach often results in a change in the perceived relationship between research and teacher education.

The Contexts of Teacher Education

Teacher education is popularly depicted as an establishment. But in reality the content, governance, and contexts of teacher education are severely fragmented (see Clark, 1986; Clark & Marker, 1975). Over 1,200 teacher education programs exist in the United States, representing a wide range of institutions from small private colleges to large public universities. Because of fundamental differences in size, orientation, and resources among these institutions, conflicts within the teacher education community are not uncommon, and professional associations and accrediting organizations often lack a coherent base of support for setting directions or promoting improvement.

Internally, the curriculum in teacher education is a composite of general undergraduate education, specialized study in academic departments, professional courses in departments or schools of education, and clinical experiences in elementary or secondary classrooms and schools. Policies affecting curriculum are set by state officials, universitywide committees, school district personnel, and individual instructors or cooperating teachers. Beliefs and commitments often differ substantially across these groups, and relationships are sometimes antagonistic. The total group of teacher educators, in other words, is extraordinarily heterogeneous. As students move through the circuitous routes from entry to certification, then, the contexts, that is, the settings, actors, and norms for acting, can change dramatically. Such disjointedness can easily weaken the total effect of preparation for teaching.

Preservice teacher education is typically rooted in a college or university context (see Woodring, 1975). This arrangement, however, has always been problematic for at least two reasons. *First*, the form of most professional coursework is indistinguishable from the rest of undergraduate education. And, especially for secondary teachers, the total professional component is only a small part of the preparation for teaching and must compete for attention with a student's major field of concentration. As a result, there is unlikely to be a strong sense of entry into or identity with the profession until student teaching, which is done in a field setting.

Second, undergraduate teacher education has an uncertain status in higher education. Even in colleges and universities that evolved from normal schools, teacher education is a low-prestige and low-expenditure program, and those who work closest to teachers in training typically have the lowest status and pay (Clark, 1986; Lanier & Little, 1986). And many of the most prestigious universities do not even have teacher education programs. This status affects the ability of teacher education programs to recruit talented students and engender a strong sense of identity with teaching. In addition, the low prestige of teacher education lessens the chances that teacher educators can effectively represent professional interests in university forums.

For most campus and field-based teacher educators, the preparation of teachers is typically not their primary responsibility. Professors in academic departments identify with their disciplines rather than teacher preparation and are frequently antagonistic toward teacher education programs and students. In addition, the status and the reward structures of higher education often work against a professional commitment to teacher education by faculty in departments or schools of education. Many education professors are unwilling to call themselves teacher educators or to spend their time working in teacher education programs. They would prefer, rather, to affiliate with a more prestigious specialization, such as educational psychology or sociology, and seek assignments in graduate programs for school administrators, supervisors, psychologists, or researchers.

In schools, teacher education has an equally uncertain status. The main business of schools is to teach students rather than teachers. As a result, school personnel are likely to view teacher education as an added responsibility to their regular duties as classroom teachers or instructional supervisors.

Teacher education is driven in other indirect but important ways by school districts. The size of the enterprise is determined by the demand for new teachers in the nation's schools, and this demand can fluctuate markedly over time. If the supply of graduates is greater than the demand, teacher education faces cutbacks and often the loss of its best candidates. If the demand is greater than the supply, teacher education is circumvented by emergency certification provisions, so that there will be a sufficient number of teachers to fill classrooms. In the long run, the supply of candidates for teacher education is affected in large measure by the salaries, working conditions, and career opportunities available in schools. Thus, school conditions affect the size and the quality of the talent pool teacher education can draw upon in achieving its mission.

In addition, schools shape the form and substance of teacher education by the way curricula are organized in elementary and secondary schools and by the character of the students who attend. But, given the large diversity among schools and school districts, it is difficult to build site-specific relevance into programs. Thus, teacher education continually runs the risk of not adequately preparing students for the immediate problems of beginning a teaching career.

In sum, there are powerful centrifugal forces that pull the enterprise of teacher education apart. Indeed, the epicenter of teacher education lies somewhere between the university and the school systems, and at this point there is little glue to hold the components together. These structural problems are not, of course, unique to teacher education. All university-based professional education is torn between the academy and the practitioner community. Nevertheless, the structural features of teacher preparation make planning and program operation cumbersome and often confer marginal status on those in universities or school systems who function as teacher educators.

This summary of common knowledge about teacher education is obviously incomplete. Nevertheless, it establishes some of the themes that affect thinking about teacher education programs and that drive research investments: competence, improvement, status, and fragmentation. It provides, in other words, a context for understanding what questions are asked about teacher education and who is interested in the answers.

QUALITY CONTROL: A CORE THEME

The relationship between teacher education and research has been largely dominated by the theme of quality control. Teacher educators have, in other words, defined as their core problem the search for ways to assure or guarantee the quality of programs and the effectiveness of graduates. As a result, the major questions in teacher education have centered around selection criteria for entry into teaching, indicators of appropriate content for the curriculum, efficacy of training methods, and procedures for evaluating candidates and programs. This view of the problems of teacher education has fundamentally shaped both the production and utilization of research in the field. Indeed, over the past several years, the content and pedagogy of teacher education and the evaluation of graduates have been increasingly integrated into a model grounded in conceptions of effective teaching practices.

In this section, the nature and consequences of this preoccupation with quality control are analyzed. Particular attention is given to the fact that the emphasis on quality assurance and effectiveness is deeply enmeshed in issues of status and control that emerged in the development of schooling in the United States.

The Concept of Profession

The question of effectiveness, that is, who are the best teachers or what is the best way to teach, usually takes the form of a statement or claim about the relationship between (a) teacher characteristics or teaching practices and (b) the attainment of some valued educational objective (see Doyle, 1978). It is difficult to talk about teaching for very long without drifting into statements about effectiveness. Thus, effectiveness was a theme in the earliest literature on teaching (e.g., Page, 1847; Payne, 1875). The effectiveness question took on special significance, however, in the formation of a universal system of public schooling in the United States in the late nineteenth and early twentieth centuries (see Doyle, 1976). To understand the preoccupation with effectiveness, then, it is necessary to clarify the intellectual context within which this theme took root and developed. To discover this context, it is necessary to begin with the concept of *profession*.

A profession is conventionally defined as an occupation whose members are reputed to possess high levels of knowledge, skill, commitment, and trustworthiness (see Lieberman, 1956). At the core of this definition is the idea that a profession bases its practices on a body of specialized technical knowledge. There are two major components of this body of knowledge: (a) validated practices, that is, those that have been systematically tested by tradition or science; and (b) propositions, including theoretical models and descriptions of specific indicators, that guide the application of these practices to particular cases. Professionals, in other words, are equipped through specialized and prolonged preparation to use validated practices and to apply them intelligently.

Compared to the established professions of medicine and law, teaching is generally considered to fall short of being a profession, to be at best a semiprofession (Dreeben, 1970; Etzioni, 1969; Howsam et al., 1976). In large measure this assessment is grounded in the charge that teaching lacks a core of specialized, technical knowledge. The role of research is to build this technical core so that teaching will eventually become a profession (see Medley, 1984).

There is an alternative to this standard view of the nature of a profession. Freidson (1970) contends that emphasis on the competence and moral dispositions of members of a profession misses an important aspect of the professionalization process. Professionals might or might not be morally superior or more technically proficient than members of other occupations, but a profession enjoys a preeminence in a division of labor to the extent that it "gains control over the determination of the substance of its own work" (Freidson, 1970, p. xvii). A profession, in other words, monopolizes its sphere of practice.

This dominance is achieved and maintained through social and political processes designed to secure wide social acceptance of an occupation's claims to technical and moral superiority. All occupations make such claims; a profession is an occupation whose claims are in fact believed by the general public, or at least by influential segments of that public, and supported by government policy. The key to professional status is not simply the existence or even the validity of such claims, but rather, public acceptance of the legitimacy of what the occupation asserts about itself. The professional ethic of exemplary skill and virtue serves, therefore, not to define a profession but to aid in the processes of "establishing, maintaining, defending, and expanding the legal or otherwise political advantage of the occupation" (Freidson, 1970, p. 200).

The achievement of professional dominance also depends upon two additional beliefs. *First*, the work of the occupation must be seen as having significant, far-reaching, and proximal social consequences. *Second*, the public must perceive that it is unable to conduct this work on its own or to evaluate adequately the available options within this sphere. These beliefs set the conditions for identifying an occupational group that appears to have the moral and technical qualities necessary to handle public affairs in a particular domain. Occupational groups, in turn, bid for this special status by claiming to possess these qualities.

The Professionalization of Schooling

The issue of professional status is certainly prominent in the research in teacher education (see Lanier & Little, 1986). Studies of governance and institutional structures in teacher education have focused largely on problems of the status of teacher educators among academicians (see Clark, 1986; Clark & Marker, 1975; Clifford & Guthrie, 1988; Ducharme, 1986; Judge, 1982). In Ducharme's words, "Teacher educators are among the least welcome guests at the educational lawn party of the establishment of higher education" (1986, p. 39). In like manner, Lanier & Little (1986) observe that, the closer one

actually works with teachers, the less prestige one holds in the status hierarchy of higher education. As a result, many who work in departments of education shun the label *teacher educator*.

A similar emphasis on status is apparent in studies of the talent pool in teaching. Investigators generally conclude that the average academic qualifications of those who enter teacher education is lower than that of other professions and that the higher qualified graduates of teacher education programs are less likely to accept a teaching position or remain for very long in the occupation (see Book, Freeman, & Brousseau, 1985; Lanier & Little, 1986; Schalock, 1979; Schlechty & Vance, 1983; Weaver, 1979). In the face of these findings, professional status has become a fundamental theme in the reform agenda in teaching and teacher education (Holmes Group, 1986).

This conventional focus on teachers and teacher educators in discussions of the education profession diverts attention away from an extraordinary event in the history of American education: During the nineteenth and twentieth centuries, schooling professionalized. That is, public elementary and secondary schools came to monopolize the domain of education. As a result, the terms *schooling* and *education* became virtually synonymous, and one's level of education is typically defined in units of schooling. Similarly, schooling is frequently linked with social mobility, vocational success, and equality of opportunity, and schools are seen as key instruments for eradicating social ills and securing national prestige and defense.

The story of how schools came to dominate education is instructive (see Doyle, 1976). Social order in the nineteenth century was threatened by industrialization, urbanization, immigration. Private and philanthropic initiatives were no longer seen as adequate mechanisms for counteracting these forces. Free, universal, public schooling—the common school—became the instrument for achieving social control and preserving traditional values. According to Wiebe:

In the spirit of the 19th century evangel, the reformers crusading for common schools in the 1830's and 1840's preached a ritualistic sermon of sin, promise and salvation. The American experiment—perhaps all humanity—had entered a critical phase, they began, with dangers threatening on every side. The trusts and traditions that only a generation ago had cemented society were disintegrating before the rush of the masses. (1969, p. 147)

These moral sentiments set the stage for the growth of schooling, but the eventual achievement of professional dominance in education was propelled by the schooling professionals' claim that they had control over the means of education. These claims were substantiated, in part, by the development during the last half of the nineteenth century of a professional literature and occupational specialization in curriculum, administration, and teaching. This effort was enlarged in the late nineteenth and early twentieth centuries to include scientific research on problems of curriculum, teaching, and supervision, to justify policy decisions regarding education. In keeping with the practices of other professional groups striving for power in the late nineteenth century, superintendents relied on science to substantiate their claims to superior qualifications for controlling the means of education (see Hays, 1972). For example, Cubberley, an influential professor of educational administration, saw in standardized tests a valuable tool for the superintendent because "it means the changing of school supervision from guesswork to scientific accuracy, and the establishment of standards of work by which he may defend what he is doing" (as quoted in Buros, 1977, p. 10). In ways such as this, the trappings of science became powerful symbols of the objectivity and rationality necessary to conduct the affairs of schooling for society.

There are two key points to this story of professionalization in education. *First*, schooling professionalized, that is, it came to dominate education, and the key actors in this process were school superintendents rather than teachers. Administrators, in other words, were the focal group around which the issues of power and control in the education of American youth were resolved. *Second*, knowledge about the processes of schooling—administration, supervision, curriculum, and teaching—grew in part as a resource for substantiating administrators' claims to have control over the means of educating America's children. So the knowledge of most worth, that is, practical knowledge, tended to be that which administrators could use to control how schooling was conducted.

The Effectiveness Question

Emphasis on knowledge for control is especially apparent in the growing concern for scientific information about teaching effectiveness in the early decades of the twentieth century. At that time, school administrators faced a special challenge because of the tradition of lay control in education. Control by local boards extended to the level of hiring and firing teachers, and personnel practices were deeply enmeshed in the patronage system of local politics (see Tyack, 1974). As a result, superintendents did not always have the power to decide who would be allowed to teach: The ward boss's niece might have to be given a job regardless of her qualifications. Under such conditions, it was difficult for superintendents to claim that they had command of the means of education.

A scientific basis for determining teachers' qualifications was unquestionably needed. Jesse Sears (1921), a leading figure in school administration, argues:

What a saving in energy would be effected, what financial waste would be checked, what an amount of justice would be established, and what a professional stimulus would result, if we had tests or instruments of measure by means of which we could predict the success of an applicant for teacher training or for a teaching position, measure the rate of progress of the teacher in training, and evaluate the work of teachers in service. (p. 82)

A scientific answer to the effectiveness questions would, in Cubberley's words, change school administration "from a job depending on political control and personal favors to a scientific service capable of self-defense in terms of accepted standards and units of accomplishment" (as quoted in Joncich, 1968, p. 227).

Effectiveness indicators had, in other words, important symbolic value in establishing the technical qualifications of administrators to control the work force in school systems and thus manage the affairs of education for society. If clear indicators of teacher effectiveness could be identified, superintendents could gain control of the work force in their school systems, link their actions directly to the outcomes of schooling, and validate their claim to be able to control the quality of the service schools provided.

The fact that the search for such generalizable indicators of effectiveness was not always successful did not diminish the importance of the question or discourage attempts to answer it. In the absence of scientific cures, professions, justified their special competence by calling attention to the amount of effort being expended to solve a problem (see Burnham, 1972). The existence of teaching-effectiveness research was important, then, in legitimizing claims to professional competence. Research had value, in other words, "as an activity expected of an expert group, and not [necessarily] for its substantive contribution to either theory or practice" (Joncich, 1968, p. 559).

ANSWERING THE EFFECTIVENESS QUESTION

Answers to the effectiveness question have always been plentiful. Across the centuries, a wide variety of teaching methods have been proposed by such philosophers and educators as Plato, Cicero, Comenius, Froebel, Pestalozzi, Herbart, and Montessori (see Broudy, 1963; Seguel, 1978). More recently, Nuthall and Snook (1973) identify three broad classes of teaching models: (a) a behavior control model based on laboratory studies of learning by Skinner and others; (b) a discovery–learning model based on the cognitive theories of Bruner and others; and (c) a rational model derived from philosophically oriented analyses of cognition and learning. Joyce and Weil (1972) catalogued 16 models of teaching including the social interaction models of Thelen, Massialas and Cox, and the National Training Laboratories; the information-processing models of Bruner, Ausubel, and Piaget; the therapeutic models of Rogers, Glasser, and Schutz; and the behavior modification model of Skinner and others. Other approaches have been based on learning styles (Witkin, Moore, Goodenough, & Cox, 1977), cognitive differences (Klausmeier, Rossmiller, & Saily, 1977), levels of conceptual functioning (Hunt, 1976), and so on. There is a rich heritage, in order words, to prepare teachers to be innovators in school settings. Yet, methods is clearly an embattled field today, and many observers have argued that teaching still lacks an adequately validated technology (Dreeben, 1970; Dunkin & Biddle, 1974).

To comprehend this paradox of simultaneous plenitude and deficiency, one must understand how the themes of status and control shaped the criteria for an acceptable answer to the effectiveness question.

Knowledge and Status

Instruction in methods has a long history in teacher education. University appointments in pedagogy and textbooks on methods began to appear in the United States in the mid-1800s (see Woodring, 1975). As an applied field based largely on philosophy or on personal experience and insight, methods have always lacked scientific and academic respectability, and the claims of methods to space in the higher education curriculum have always been suspect. In contrast, psychology, especially after the early work of such figures as Thorndike (1913), came to play an ever-expanding role as a university discipline and as foundational knowledge in the education of teachers.

From the perspective of status, the affiliation of education with psychology was quite advantageous. Psychology brought to education theoretical knowledge about learning, development, motivation, personality, and intelligence, and it thus appeared to address many of the issues of learning and achievement embedded in discussions of methods. In addition, psychology introduced tools of measurement, experimentation, and statistical analysis and replaced philosophy and ideology with the authority of science. Thus, teaching and teacher education achieved what seemed to be a powerful intellectual foundation and a set of tools to insure efficacy. Teaching methods, stripped of their philosophical and curricular trappings, could be studied as generic processes or treatments in experimental designs, for example, lecture versus discussion or inquiry versus expository teaching. Teachers could be observed and their teaching measured by scientifically derived category and rating systems and related to measures of effectiveness. In addition, discourse about teaching was now possible with the language of psychology, with the result that teacher education could enhance its position as a legitimate academic specialty. Indeed, as Clifford and Guthrie (1988) note, many professors of education, especially in the prestigious research universities, received their preparation in social science disciplines and have avoided contact with applied issues of teaching and teacher education. At the same time, educational psychologists gained advantage from the association with schooling. As perceptions of the foundational knowledge for teaching shifted toward educational psychology, this discipline assumed a central role in a significant arena of social policy and power, namely, the education of children. It is not surprising that educational psychology became the primary foundational or theoretical knowledge in the teacher education curriculum.

Knowledge and Control

Aside from perhaps conferring status on teacher education in the academy, knowledge from educational psychology did not immediately provide a satisfactory answer to the effectiveness question. Numerous attempts have been made, of course, to derive or extrapolate prescriptions for practice from psychological findings and theories. In addition to the more general approaches cited earlier, considerable effort has been invested in formulating specific practices from laboratory studies of contingencies of reinforcement or verbal learning and memory (e.g., learning strategies, behavior modification techniques, programmed instruction) and testing their effectiveness under controlled conditions. In the 1960s, Bruner and others used concepts from psychology to devise inquiry- or discovery-oriented curricula in mathematics and the natural and social sciences (see the discussion of these alphabet curricula, such as

School Mathematics Study Group [SMSG] and Man: A Course of Study [MACOS], in Lazerson, McLaughlin, McPherson, & Bailey, 1985).

To understand why these prescriptions for practice do not answer the effectiveness question, it is necessary to examine the knowledge demands of the original model of administrative control. From the perspective of administrative control, an acceptable answer to the effectiveness question must have at least four key features. *First*, the question was essentially about teachers. If one is faced with the problem of making decisions about teachers, then one is interested primarily in information about teacher characteristics or behaviors. Information about other possible causes of outcomes, such as curriculum, instructional materials, even student background experiences or aptitudes, is relevant only if it can be translated into statements about teachers.

Second, the question was cast in the form of a search for evaluative criteria. If one is required to make decisions about teachers, then one is interested not simply in what teachers commonly do but also in what qualities or actions of teachers are the best, which is to say, predict some valued educational outcome. And the most direct route to this information is to identify good and poor teachers and then describe only those characteristics that distinguished between these two groups.

Third, the findings must be usable in the normal contexts of schools. If one is making decisions about a large number of teachers for an entire school or school system, then indicators of effectiveness need to be few in number, easily applied, and highly generalizable across teaching situations. If several observations are needed to apply an indicator or if many different indicators must be applied to different teaching areas, the answers are not practical.

Finally, the answers had to be indisputable. Because the decisions that administrators make about teachers have large personal and professional consequences, the closer that an answer to the effectiveness question approximated immutable law, the better.

In sum, the effectiveness question was originally designed primarily to generate context-free and scientifically grounded indicators for evaluating teachers. Knowledge in educational psychology and the models and frameworks derived from it were not simply about teachers and were not available in the form of indicators. Such knowledge does not provide direct guidance for observation and judgment. Moreover, the scientific status was not direct. The mode of argument in educational psychology is largely one of extrapolation. Knowledge developed to account for phenomena in one setting, the psychologist's laboratory, is recommended for application to analogous circumstances in schools. Efficacy is claimed on the grounds of the knowledge used to construct the model in the first place rather than being tested directly. It is in this sense that the prescriptions are research-based. Such claims were often seen as untested presuppositions or commitments about teaching effectiveness (see Dunkin & Biddle, 1974) that had no true scientific character. In some instances methods were tested experimentally, but such "horse races" between methods typically generated ambiguous information about effectiveness (see Gage, 1976; Walker & Schaffarzick, 1974).

Recent exceptions to the general failure of teaching models to be accepted tend to prove the rule and suggest conditions under which a model can answer the effectiveness question. Madeline Hunter's (1982) widely adopted program on the "essential elements of instruction" is largely a derivation from psychological research. There is little clear evidence that her model is in fact effective in classrooms (see, e.g., Stallings & Krasavage, 1986). In contrast with most derivational models, however, Hunter's framework can be reduced to a finite set of indicators (establishing set, checking for understanding) and scripts that define how these indicators are manifested in classrooms. It is in this form that the model is widely used primarily as a uniform prescription for practice and an evaluation tool, despite Hunter's (1985) disapproval.

Mastery learning (Block & Burns, 1976; Bloom, 1976) and cooperative learning (see Slavin, 1983) are also widely used in schools and school districts. These models cannot be reduced to indicators. However, considerable evidence was garnered by advocates to support the claim that these models increase student achievement, a major social indicator of school effectiveness. In other words, there were direct tests of the models' validity as an effective school practice. Moreover, the models are essentially generic structures applicable to a wide range of contents and contexts, and procedures for using the models in classrooms are exceptionally well defined. They can easily be used, therefore, to standardize practices across teachers.

This analysis suggests that models extrapolated from psychology will be widely used if they arrive at the door of practice in a form that directly addresses control, either as criteria for evaluation or as a uniform system for teaching practice that promises to improve achievement scores.

Direct Studies of Teaching Effectiveness

In addition to derivations from basic research in psychology, considerable effort has been expended in attempts to answer the effectiveness question directly. An examination of this research tradition and its applications to teaching and teacher education provides further insights into the knowledge demands associated with the themes of status and control.

Teaching-effectiveness research began in the 1920s and continued with remarkable vigor for over 50 years (see Dunkin & Biddle, 1974; Gage, 1985). In the initial framing of this research, the administrative perspective was prominent. Many of the early figures in the field either were school administrators or began their careers in that field. For instance, Barr (1929), who played a key role in defining the first 30 years of effectiveness research, was a school supervisor in Detroit when he first attempted to answer the effectiveness question. As teaching-effectiveness research matured, there was a drift away from these administrative origins. The group of investigators attracted to effectiveness research (e.g., Berliner, Brophy, Evertson, Gage, Good, McDonald, Rosenshine, Soar and Soar, and Stallings) were typically trained in educational psychology, and many had no teaching or administrative experience in elementary and secondary schools. As a result, they had little in common with school administrators and were, for the most part, less preoccupied with the practical problems of personnel selection and evaluation than their predecessors. At the same time, these investigators had little familiarity with curriculum and methods of teaching or the complexities of life in elementary and secondary classrooms. And they adopted the form of the question as framed in the administrative context. Indeed, the initial framing of the question as a search for indicators has endured, and the shift to new paradigms in research on teaching has been recent and gradual (see Doyle, 1978). Even the early studies of teacher thinking show a clear family resemblance to effectiveness research (see Shulman, 1986a), as do some more recent conceptions of expert–novice differences in teaching (e.g., Berliner, 1988).

Most studies in the effectiveness tradition have used one of two categories of teaching variables: (a) teachers' characteristics such as personality dimensions, beliefs, attitudes, intelligence, preparation, academic achievement, and the like (see Getzels & Jackson, 1963); or (b) teaching behaviors, measured by either high-inference rating scales (e.g., clarity, enthusiasm, warmth) or low-inference categories (e.g., frequency of praise, number of product questions per class session). Outcomes in teaching effectiveness studies have been measured by either subjective ratings from principals or supervisors or by objective tests of student achievement or attitudes (see Gage, 1963).

Teacher-Selection Research. Studies of teachers' characteristics produce information useful primarily in selecting individuals for preparation programs or teaching positions (see Howey & Strom, 1987; Pugach, 1984; Schalock, 1979). At issue is the relationship of qualities of prospective teachers (e.g., ability, personal traits, beliefs, prior experience, knowledge, and skill) to on-the-job performance as a teacher. The research problem is to identify the predictive value of measures of teachers' characteristics. The task of predicting success is a very real one: Decisions must be made about who to admit to teacher education programs, who to certify as competent, and who to hire for teaching positions. All such decisions involve predictions about the performance of a candidate at some future time. Selection decisions have important implications for status insofar as the quality of candidates chosen for preparation is associated with the prestige of an occupation. Selection criteria also help to substantiate claims to at least indirect control over the quality of the teaching force.

The record of research on teacher selection is discouraging. Surprisingly little research has been done on many basic issues related to selection, such as the factors leading to the choice of teaching as a career or the consequences of the selection practices in various teacher education programs and school districts (see Schalock, 1979; Wise, Darling-Hammond, & Berry, 1987; Wise et al., 1987). Moreover, the existing body of research is not always very informative. Over the years the largest number of studies have focused on the predictive value of various teacher characteristics. Getzels and Jackson (1963) conclude from their review of this body of research that few significant effects have been found and that many of the findings are pedestrian. In a more recent analysis, Schalock (1979) asserts that "we do not have empirically verified criteria that can be used to effectively predict success in teaching, especially if success is to include the demonstrated ability to foster desired learning outcomes in children" (p. 408).

The problems of research on teacher selection are formidable. The restricted range on most of the variables of interest makes it exceedingly difficult to obtain either statistically or practically significant correlations between predictors and criteria of success. Moreover, several powerful factors (e.g., effectiveness of training and teaching context) intervene between characteristics and outcomes. How a teacher teaches depends not simply on who the teacher is but also on how the teacher was trained and where the teacher is teaching.

Although external policy initiatives are often directed toward selection, interest in research on teacher selection within the field has been tenuous at best (see Pugach, 1984). Teacher educators are often motivated to concentrate more on maintaining enrollments than on screening out candidates beyond a minimal set of standards (e.g., Grade Point Average [GPA] and interest in becoming a teacher). In times of teacher surpluses, enrollments eventually begin to shrink, and teacher educators often attempt to attract, rather than select, students. In times of shortages, pressures exist to take all applicants. Attention within the field, in other words, tends to be focused on program content and exit testing rather than on selection criteria as a means of guaranteeing quality. This might explain the findings that few candidates are ever denied admission and that most of these who are rejected eventually find their way into the program that rejected them or into another program (Pugach, 1984).

Process–Product Research. Contemporary research on effective teaching has generally followed a process–product paradigm (see Gage, 1963; Rosenshine, 1976). According to this paradigm, an adequate study of effectiveness must relate measures of classroom performance (processes) to objective measures of outcomes (products). In the correlational phase of this research program, processes and products are first measured for a sample of classrooms. Classes are then ranked on the basis of mean achievement (adjusted for initial differences in entering ability), and differences in teaching processes among ranked classes are identified. In the experimental phase, processes derived from correlational research are taught to a sample of teachers, observations are made to determine whether the teachers used the processes in their teaching, and the achievement of these teachers' classes is compared with that of control classes to ascertain whether the intervention had an effect. In other words, process–product research is an attempt to explain between-class differences in achievement in terms of differences in teaching processes. The ultimate hope of this kind of analysis is a list of classroom conditions or characteristics known to affect the outcomes of teaching.

Process–product research has been widely celebrated by researchers as one of their major success stories (see Gage, 1978, 1985). Much of this work was initiated in response to a national concern for equality of educational opportunity and to conclusions from survey research that teachers did not make a difference in students' achievement. Moreover, few tangible results could be extracted from the vast quantity of effectiveness studies that had been completed prior to the 1970s (Dunkin & Biddle, 1974; Rosenshine, 1971). When consistent correlations between teaching variables and achievement were obtained across studies, researchers were understandably elated. Moreover, field experiments demonstrated that principles and models constructed from process–product findings could make a difference in teaching practice and student achievement (see L. M. Anderson, Evertson, & Brophy, 1979; Emmer, Sanford, Evertson, Clements, & Martin, 1981; Good & Grouws, 1979). A major milestone in knowledge about teaching appeared to have been reached. Moreover, results from process–product research were perceived from within the research community to have direct utility for school improvement and the curriculum of teacher education (see Stallings, 1987).

Expectations concerning the practical utility of process–product research have been richly fulfilled. Process–product findings have been broadly accepted in the world of practice, and a nationwide effort has been made to infuse these findings into preservice and inservice teacher education. Moreover, process–product research has become an important foundation for the educational reform movement. The findings are being used by legislators, government officials, and school administrators to justify major policy decisions concerning the content and duration of teacher education and the criteria to be used in evaluating teachers. Process–product research, in other words, has been heartily received as an appropriate answer to the effectiveness question.

The widespread acceptance of process–product findings reflects, in part, a close fit between this research program and the demands of a technology for teacher control. Scores in process–product studies were typically aggregated across teaching occasions (which include curriculum, materials, and students), leading to conclusions about generic competencies that could easily be translated into indicators of effectiveness. Moreover, the findings could be collapsed into a relatively short list of indicators, and observation instruments built on these indicators are reasonably simple to use. Finally, the language conformed to popular notions of science, so that the findings were difficult to dispute. Indicators or models of teaching based on these findings could be used to guarantee results. Research that meets these demands is clearly a practical answer to the effectiveness question, that is, it solves the problems of evaluation and control in schooling and enhances claims by administrators, legislators, and government officials, in a time of public concern, that they are doing something to improve education. Thus, the good-employee conception of the outcome of teacher education prevails.

The Legacy of Quality Control

In the context of emphasis on quality control, trust is placed in procedures to train and evaluate teachers rather than in teachers and their ability to make appropriate decisions. Research, in turn, is used to generate a technology for the management of teachers rather than to provide knowledge that teachers might use to inform their own practice. In this scheme, teacher education becomes one of the mechanisms through which the means of schooling are controlled.

This analysis of the quality-control theme reveals the origins of a technical view of teaching and teacher education and of knowledge use in these domains. The remote control of teaching requires a small set of generic indicators that can be applied uniformly across a broad range of teaching situations. The search for such indicators inexorably leads to a minimizing of information, a condensing and simplifying of knowledge, and an economy of expression and deliberation. In this process, teaching is stripped of its particulars. When knowledge of teaching is reduced to indicators, it is all too easy to adopt a fragmented view of teaching and assume that learning from teaching occurs in a unidirectional and mechanistic way as a cumulative effect of particular stimuli. When indicators are used to define the content of teacher education and the evaluative criteria for judging teaching performance, as has been done in some state reform initiatives, one can easily be misled to conclude that little needs to be known to teach effectively and that teaching competence can be reduced to a set of discrete skills.

It is not surprising that expectations for knowledge within teacher education have continued to reflect a quality-control perspective. The question is deeply lodged in the enterprise of school itself and in public discourse about schooling and criteria for government funding of educational research (see J. P. McDonald, 1988). Moreover, most teacher educators are former schoolteachers and administrators who carry many of the norms of schooling with them into higher education (see H. Carter, 1984; Ducharme, 1986). The theme has not faded, because the question of effectiveness and the issue of control remain important within education and within social expectations about the utility of research. To the extent that effectiveness dominates, the window for research production and utilization is narrow and applications are likely to shape findings to fit the practical demands of control.

Over the past decade, reaction against the knowledge assumptions and power relations implicit in this technical view of teaching and teacher education has grown (see Doyle, 1978; Garrison, 1988; Shulman, 1986a; Zumwalt, 1982, 1988). Indeed, some process–product researchers have expressed dismay at some of the ways in which findings from these studies have been applied (see especially Brophy, 1988; Good & Mulryan, in press). Even Hunter (1985) complains that most applications of her framework do not accurately represent what she intended. These investigators and developers saw research as a tool to enrich the teacher education curriculum, to sensitize teachers to dimensions of teaching that needed to be considered in planning effective strategies, and to help teachers make decisions. But precisely the opposite has frequently happened. Findings from process–product research are being used by administrators, legislators, and government officials to narrow the content of the curriculum, reduce the amount of time needed to complete teacher preparation, and impose inflexible structures and formats on teachers. Moreover, despite strong words of caution from some of the leading investigators (see especially Brophy & Good, 1986), process–product research has become the basis of the many teacher assessment plans being developed by states and school districts throughout the nation.

Two central themes underlie the reaction against the quality-control perspective: knowledge and empowerment. Empha-

sis is being placed on the complex intellectual processes involved in teaching and learning to teach and on the essential role of teachers as owners of their knowledge and their destinies. The focus, that is, centers on knowledge that teachers can use to conduct their practice rather than on knowledge administrators can use to control teachers. It now appears, for reasons that are not altogether clear (see J. P. McDonald, 1988), that teachers are being viewed separately from administrators as agents of professionalization and school improvement (see Carnegie Forum on Education and the Economy, 1986; Holmes Group, 1986). And with this separation, teachers are being seen as the primary users, if not the owners, of research and knowledge about teaching.

This movement signals a fundamental shift in conceptions of the relation of research to the education of teachers. In the next section, the underlying dynamics of this shift in the thematic content of research on teaching and teacher education are examined.

KNOWLEDGE AND EMPOWERMENT

The confluence of the themes of knowledge and empowerment has led some writers to emphasize a highly personalistic and phenomenological view of teaching and teacher education (see Connelly & Clandinin, 1986; Smyth, 1987). In this view, teaching practice is seen as largely artistic and intuitive, created on the spot, as it were. To achieve this artistic creation, teachers rely on their personal understanding of a situation and their own purposes, values, and associations. Practitioner knowledge, it is argued, is highly tentative, situational, idiosyncratic, intuitive, and embedded in the particulars of practice. The emphasis in teacher education, therefore, is on processes that stimulate personal reflection, such as action research (Carr & Kemmis, 1986) or life histories (Woods, 1987), methods that start from a teacher's own understandings and construction of meaning. The knowledge resulting from these processes is complex, tentative, and subjective.

Taken to an extreme, this personalistic orientation can lead to rejection of all generalized propositions about teaching practice. Tom (1987), for example, argues that most forms of pedagogical knowledge, whether based on craft experience, disciplined inquiry, or artistic sources, are essentially flawed, of limited utility to teachers, and void of concern for the normative components of teaching. He would replace pedagogical knowledge with pedagogical questions derived from a conception of teaching as a moral endeavor. Such questions (e.g., "How can I both move the classroom group along and respond to the interests of particular individuals?" [p. 14]) would then form the basis of a problem-based professional curriculum in teacher education. Others, who share Tom's distrust of generalized pedagogical knowledge, argue that the content of teacher education should be grounded in historical, philosophical, social, and moral knowledge that helps teachers clarify their own perspectives and the connections between classroom practice and larger social and cultural issues and values. Beyer (1987) argues, for example, that teacher education should foster "practical reason that can help reconstruct a world dominated by inequality and alienation" and thus produce teachers who can contribute to the development of "more responsive, socially just institutions and involvements" (p. 30).

Rejection of a technical view that emphasizes context-free, generic indicators of teaching quality does not necessarily lead, however, to rejection of research-based propositions about teaching. The technical perspective is lodged in the fabric of schooling and shapes how knowledge is received and used, but it is not an essential characteristic of research. It is possible to argue for theoretical knowledge about teaching in classrooms without accepting a technical view of teaching and teacher education. Systematic inquiry can, in other words, generate knowledge about classroom practices, explicate the patterns and regularities of classrooms and the events that occur in these settings, and lead to a better understanding of teachers' knowledge structures and comprehension processes (see K. Carter, in press; K. Carter & Doyle, 1989). Classroom processes are knowable, such knowledge can be codified and systematized, and knowledge in this form is useful to teachers.

This emerging work on knowledge structures for teaching is characterized, however, by appreciation of both the value and the limits of generality in talking about teaching. In contrast with the search for indicators of quality, it is recognized that information about teaching cannot be easily stripped of its particulars without distorting the knowledge one is attempting to create. At the same time, analytical knowledge, that is, knowledge lifted up from but not stripped of its particulars, can provide powerful constructs to guide teachers in interpreting classroom scenes and inventing means for resolving dilemmas. There has also been a shift in the criteria for the validity of knowledge claims. Traditionally, research findings have been judged on degree of experimental and statistical rigor and/or congruence with basic psychological propositions or laws. To an increasing extent, these criteria have been supplanted by concern for ecological verisimilitude or plausibility, as judged by teachers and students who participated in the settings being studied.

Theoretical knowledge about teaching in classrooms is only beginning to be developed, so it is not possible to give a finished account here. Moreover, other chapters in this volume are addressed to aspects of this emerging knowledge (see Carter, in this volume). In the following discussion, this work is summarized in broad strokes around three categories of knowledge about teaching that appear to represent different approaches to research related to teacher education—knowledge about practices, content knowledge, and curriculum-enactment knowledge. Special attention in this discussion is placed on basic themes and issues that guide inquiry and application.

Knowledge About Teaching Practices

One clear strand emerging within research on teaching is the study of teaching practices and their effects. Here the focus is primarily on what happens when particular clusters of teachers' actions or action systems are used in classrooms. In the broadest sense, a practice can be defined at the level of curriculum or program (e.g., a whole-language approach to literacy or activity-based science), although research at this level is of-

ten unproductive (see Bredderman, 1983; Walker & Schaffarzik, 1974). Examples of relatively large-scale practices include cooperative learning in its various forms (Slavin, 1983) and mastery learning designs (Block & Burns, 1976). Reciprocal teaching (Palinscar & Brown, 1984) is a good example of a smaller scale practice for helping students learn comprehension strategies. Finally, practices can be conceptualized in more narrow terms, such as the use of praise (Brophy, 1983).

Many process–product researchers interpreted their findings as practices, especially when they wrote manuals for their field experiments (e.g., L. M. Anderson et al., 1979; Emmer et al., 1981). There are, however, fundamental conceptual and methodological differences between the study of teaching practices and research on process-product relationships. In the process–product tradition, one enters a field setting with observational categories to record indicators of teaching. Differences in practices or approaches, such as inquiry versus expository teaching or whole-language versus basals, are reduced to a common set of indicators, and scores are aggregated across observations for statistical purposes. The processes are variables (e.g., "allocated time" or "stopping misbehavior appropriately") that are used as independent correlates or predictors of achievement. In several respects, these variables are not processes at all because the action is stopped when scores are aggregated within and across observations. They are, at best, characteristics of a teacher's typical processes over time. Within this framework, the teaching process itself is fragmented into discrete elements that presumably affect student achievement in some mechanistic or additive way. In addition, teaching is rendered simplistically generic by stripping it of context and curriculum content. Basic theoretical questions of how teaching effects occur are seldom examined explicitly, and even the complex issues involved in a leap from variables to competencies or practices are ignored.

In the study of teaching practices, the emphasis is on the practice itself, that is, on larger units (e.g., pacing of curriculum or interventions to stop misbehavior) that organize and integrate several types of teacher actions. In many cases, an experimental approach is used in which the practice is introduced into a laboratory or classroom setting, so that its particular effects can be examined. In addition, the practice is described on its own terms rather than in the language of discrete categories or indicators.

As research on practices develops, four important trends appear to be emerging. *First*, the practices themselves are becoming more sophisticated and more richly and thoroughly delineated. As a result, it is becoming easier to know what the practice actually is. *Second*, there is a greater concern for ecological validity, in other words, for the ways in which practices are actually used in classroom and school contexts. Thus, it is becoming easier to imagine how the practice can be utilized in and adapted to particular circumstances. *Third*, the emphasis in research is shifting from a simple horse race between methods to see which one has the greatest effect on achievement to an interest in multiple consequences and in context and curriculum specific effects. It is possible, therefore, to ascertain the conditions under which the practice might be appropriate or inappropriate. *Finally*, investigators are more interested in developing principles for practice (e.g., active teaching) and predictive knowledge about particular practices that teachers can use as guides than in promulgating uniform prescriptions for teaching in all classrooms (see Brophy, 1988). The focus, in other words, is on helping teachers know what they might do once they have figured out what needs to be done rather than on devising a blueprint all teachers should follow regardless of circumstances. In all of this there is also growing concern for the particulars of practice.

One limitation of research on teaching practices is that little attention is given to the knowledge structures and comprehension processes teachers use to interpret classroom scenes and plan strategic actions. The next two areas of knowledge about teaching are more directly concerned with these comprehension and interpretive processes as they relate to curriculum, pedagogy, and classroom processes.

Content Knowledge

In recent years there has been a substantial increase in attention to the subject-matter knowledge of teachers and, in particular, the pedagogical content knowledge teachers need to represent and convey subject matter to students (see C. Anderson, 1989; Leinhardt & Smith, 1985; Shulman, 1986b; 1987; Wilson, Shulman, & Richert, 1987). The emphasis in this work is on the management of ideas in classrooms rather than simply on the management of pupil conduct or the interpersonal processes that occur between teachers and students.

There are two important strands in this work. The first is focused on the key role of content knowledge itself. To teach at all, Shulman (1987) argues, a teacher must

understand the structures of subject matter, the principles of conceptual organization, and the principles of inquiry that help answer two kinds of questions in each field: What are the important ideas and skills in this domain? and How are new ideas added and deficient ones dropped by those who produce knowledge in this area? That is, what are the rules and procedures of good scholarship or inquiry? (p. 9)

The second strand is focused on pedagogical content knowledge: "the capacity of a teacher to transform the content knowledge he or she possesses into forms that are pedagogically powerful and yet adaptive to the variations in ability and background presented by the students" (Shulman, 1987, p. 15). This capacity, which lies at the juncture between content and pedagogy, distinguishes a teacher from a nonteaching content specialist. Merely knowing biology is not sufficient to know how to represent it to students in a particular classroom setting.

One of the key components of pedagogical content knowledge is the ability to represent subject matter to students.

Representation involves thinking through the key ideas in the text or lesson and identifying the alternative ways of representing them to students. What analogies, metaphors, examples, demonstrations, simulations, and the like can help to build a bridge between the teacher's comprehension and that desired for the students? (Shulman, 1987, p. 16)

Shulman also argues that, because of the diversity of students, multiple forms of representation are required of the effective teacher. One also suspects that multiple understandings of the content itself are required to comprehend different students' interpretations.

The study of teachers' content knowledge is based, for the most part, on richly detailed cases of beginning and experienced teachers. Although there is a clear interest in general knowledge about teaching, the analyses are full of the particulars of teaching.

Curriculum-Enactment Knowledge

The third type of knowledge about teaching consists of formulations about the structures and processes in classrooms that shape the enactment of curriculum (see K. Carter & Doyle, 1989; Doyle, 1983, 1986; Westbury, 1973). Enactment knowledge is constructed in answer to two basic questions: How do classrooms work? (i.e., what are the patterns and rhythms that constitute and shape life in classrooms) and How do teaching effects occur? (i.e., what processes connect what teachers do with what students learn).

Research on structures and processes that affect enactment in classroom flourished in the 1970s and 1980s. Much of this work grew out of the ecological, ethnographic, and linguistic traditions in social research (see Cazden, 1986; Erickson, 1986; Gump, 1982; Kounin & Gump, 1974; Stodolsky, 1988; Yinger, 1982), and it has been directed in large measure to issues of classroom organization and management (see Doyle, 1986; Kounin, 1970). The central premise underlying this work is that a classroom is a behavior setting, an ecobehavioral unit composed of segments that surround and regulate thought and action. The central research task, then, is to explicate the texture of these segments and how they influence thinking and acting.

Two important lines of inquiry have emerged from the study of classroom contexts. The first line consists of studies of *classroom activities*. In this work, the activity is considered to be the basic unit of classroom organization. Activities are relatively short segments of classroom time, usually 10 to 20 minutes, during which students are arranged in a particular way. Common types of activities include seatwork, recitation, presentation, discussion, and small groups. Activities are defined by (a) their temporal boundaries, including duration and pace; (b) the physical milieu, including the shape of the site, the number and types of participants, the arrangement of participants in the available space, and the available materials; (c) the behavior format or program of action for participants, such as turn taking for public responses in discussions versus independent work in silence during seatwork; and (d) the focal content of the segment. Changes in any of these features usually signal a change in the nature of the context in classrooms.

The key element in an activity is the *program of action* for participants, which is the sequence or structure of appropriate behaviors and the direction and momentum of action for the situation at hand. A program of action is a vector or trajectory that pulls events and participants along their course. Programs of action are, in part, social, having to do with participation structures: who talks to whom, how turns at talk are selected or secured, and what different participants are to say (see Erickson & Shultz, 1981). In addition, an action program is substantive, or curricular, in that it involves an ability to accomplish the task operating at the moment. To participate in a recitation, for example, a student must know not only how to gain a turn but also what the answer to the question is.

The second line of research on classroom contexts has focused on *classroom tasks* (see Blumenfeld, Pintrich, Meece, & Wessels, 1982; Doyle, 1983; Doyle & Carter, 1984; Erickson, 1982). Tasks, which are embedded in classroom activities, define the work students are to do in classrooms by specifying what products they are held accountable for (answers to questions, written documents) and what resources (notes, consultation with peers) are to be used to generate these products. Classroom tasks define the character of students' contacts with the school curriculum and organize their thinking about subject matter. Research on tasks, by capturing the curriculum in use, has provided insight into how teaching effects occur in classroom settings and how subject matter is shaped by classroom events.

From an enactment perspective, then, teachers must achieve the cooperation of students in classroom activities as they simultaneously carry them through a curriculum by designing academic work and engaging them in the intellectual processes required to understand and do that work.

Answers to enactment questions are largely theoretical, rather than prescriptive or procedural. The emphasis, in other words, is on constructs and propositions that enable teachers to interpret classroom scenes and, thus, invent solutions to common pedagogical problems. The mode of inquiry, in other words, is not causal in the sense of a search for the predictors of successful enactments. The emphasis, rather, is on making explicit the implicit knowledge teachers deploy in interpreting classroom scenes and in bringing knowledge of content, pedagogy, and management to bear in the enactment of curriculum (see K. Carter, in press). It is this knowledge that enables teachers to carry out curriculum plans and teaching practices in the complex environments of classrooms. Such knowledge can inform practice without determining in some mechanical or uniform sense what that practice should be.

Interconnections Among Knowledge Domains

These three categories of knowledge about teaching are not, of course, mutually exclusive, even though they represent different analytical and interpretive emphases. Pedagogical content knowledge encompasses knowledge about teaching practices to the extent that curriculum and instruction are at some point inseparable. An instance of curriculum enactment is also seen to include content (as represented in materials and tasks), instructional practices, and management of classroom action systems. Thus pedagogical content knowledge and enactment knowledge overlap at several points, although emphasis in the latter is on classroom knowledge rather than subject matter, that is, on the knowledge associated with comprehending classroom events rather than the structure and pedagogical representations of disciplines. Similarly, knowledge about practices is closely related to knowledge about the contexts in which practices are enacted. Yet the study of enactment does not necessarily yield explicit procedures or practices.

Enactment research is also similar in several respects to research on personal practical knowledge, in that knowledge is built from the study of thought and action in classroom settings rather than from external sources and what teachers know is assumed to be particularistic and event structured. Within the enactment framework, however, the emphasis leans toward the general and analytical rather than the private and idiosyncratic, toward a common language about classrooms that can inform practical deliberation and problem solving among teachers, even though the application of that knowledge to specific instances is likely to be quite personal and particularistic.

It is interesting to note that these domains of knowledge about teaching connect in several ways with the program paradigms in teacher education delineated in the first section of this chapter. Knowledge about teaching practices and classroom enactment informs conceptions of the good employee and the innovator by enriching our knowledge of what standard practices are and how they can be used successfully in classroom settings. Similarly, the work on pedagogical content knowledge represents a major resource for transforming our understanding of the connections among academic disciplines, school curriculum, and the representation of content in classroom events.

Summary

It is argued here that there is codifiable knowledge about teaching in at least three areas: teaching practices, content, and classroom enactment. A knowledge base for teaching derived from categories of research such as these is substantially richer than any that can be derived from process–product research. It is also argued, in the context of the earlier discussion of professionalization, that teacher empowerment, at least from an occupational perspective, requires such knowledge. Society is more likely to place confidence in the knowledge an occupation holds in common than in the personal attributes of the people who choose to enter it.

One issue raised by advocates of personal knowledge, however, still needs to be addressed: the clear role of individual meaning, insight, and invention in teaching and teacher education. The existence of a knowledge base does not rule out personal understanding, just as the importance of personal meaning does not obviate the value of codified knowledge. But where does personal knowledge fit in the spectrum of teaching and teacher education?

An answer to this question lies in part in the realization that the critique of the technical view of teaching was directed not only to the nature of the knowledge generated about teaching but also to the way in which that knowledge is used to control teachers. The latter domain is essentially about the conceptions that underlie teacher education itself. In the following section, teacher knowledge is discussed in the context of teacher education pedagogy.

Because it's relatively easy to do

EMERGING CONCEPTIONS OF TEACHER EDUCATION PEDAGOGY

As noted earlier, teacher education has largely been dominated by emphasis on direct training in teaching skills. Teacher education methods and procedures—courses, laboratory and field experiences, student teaching, staff development programs—are generally viewed as means of conveying effective practices to teacher education candidates or experienced teachers. The most commonly asked question of teacher education pedagogy, then, concerns its effectiveness in training teachers to perform ably. In this framework, there is little room to incorporate knowledge about content or classroom enactment.

Most of the research on teacher education pedagogy has focused on training in specific teaching skills through feedback from focused observations or direct laboratory training (see Peck & Tucker, 1973). In general, these studies have demonstrated immediate training effects: Candidates acquire the targeted skills. Findings concerning transfer or use of skills over the long term in classrooms are mixed, however. It appears that skill utilization requires both a favorable context in the classroom and an understanding of the occasions in which the skill can be used (see Copeland, 1977; Gliessman, 1984; Wagner, 1973).

Some research has also been done on the effectiveness of field experiences and student teaching (see Applegate, 1987; Feiman-Nemser & Buchmann, 1986; Griffin, 1986; Watts, 1987; Waxman & Walberg, 1986; Zeichner, 1987). In many of these studies, the focus has been on dispositions and socialization into the profession. As a result, outcomes are typically measured by attitudes or perspectives of the participants rather than specific teaching skills, knowledge structures, or achievements of pupils in the candidates' classes. Most reviewers comment on the paucity of research in this area and caution that very little is known about effects. At the same time, reviewers often conclude that, despite the widespread popularity and endorsement of field work and student teaching in the education of teachers, the consequences of these experiences are as much negative (e.g., the development of conservative attitudes toward discipline and pupil control) as they are positive.

There is an even greater paucity of research on staff development. Nonetheless, important work in this area was done in conjunction with field experiments based on findings from process–product studies of teaching. Good and Grouws (1979) for example, constructed a model format for fourth-grade mathematics lessons that specified the order and approximate time allocations for such activities as review, development of new concepts, guided practice, seatwork, and homework. Emmer et al. (1981) made specific suggestions for organizing rooms, communicating rules and procedures, managing student work, and maintaining appropriate student behavior. L. Anderson et al. (1979) wrote 22 specific principles for teaching first-grade reading groups (e.g., "The teacher should have the children repeat new words and sounds until they are said satisfactorily"). The results of these field experiments demonstrated that guidelines for practice based on research findings could

be communicated to experienced teachers and the teachers could use this knowledge to modify practices in their classrooms. Griffin et al. (1983) extended this work to show that findings from research on teaching effects, when combined with knowledge about effective school leadership and change, could be used successfully by staff developers to help teachers change practices.

In interpreting these experiments, it is important to remember their limitations. *First*, the studies demonstrated only that experienced volunteers were able to use some of the information contained in the treatment materials to modify their practices. *Second*, the experiments did little to illuminate the processes by which teachers in experimental groups used the information provided in treatment materials.

This analysis suggests the need for a theory of teacher education that addresses both how teachers learn about teaching and how knowledge about teaching is used to interpret and solve teaching dilemmas. Important insights along these lines can be derived from a constructivist theory of learning and understanding (see Resnick, 1987). According to this theory, meaning and understanding are constructed in particular circumstances by individuals according to their distinctive conceptual and emotional biographies. One comes to know, in other words, by inventing understanding, and this invention involves an interaction of past knowledge with the experience of the moment. This constructive perspective emphasizes the importance of direct experience and the gradual accumulation of knowledge structures from reflection on that experience over time. This constructivist perspective underlies Schon's (1983) analysis of knowledge in action, or, the special knowledge that comes to be during practice, as teachers interpret scenes and discover dilemmas.

Along quite similar lines, Fenstermacher (1986) has developed a conception of how teachers translate knowledge into action. His basic argument is that teachers use information about teaching to activate their own deliberations about events in their classrooms and to modify the practical reasoning that underlies their actions. Indeed, he argues that "the benefit of educational research to educational practice is realized in the improvement of practical arguments, not in programs of performance deduced from the findings of research" (p. 43, emphasis removed). This perspective emphasizes the extent to which knowledge use in teaching is dependent upon a teacher's comprehension or interpretation of his or her classroom situation. If, for example, a teacher understands classroom management in terms of the effectiveness of reprimands rather than as a process of guiding a complex activity system through time and space, information about the consequences of different activity structures for classroom order is likely to be seen as irrelevant to management success (see K. Carter, in press).

These formulations underscore the importance of both propositional knowledge and personal understanding in learning to teach and in applying knowledge to practical situations. In the language of the program paradigms defined earlier in this chapter, teachers are both fully functioning persons and reflective professionals who bring knowledge to bear on cases. From this perspective, the task of teacher education is to foster event-structured knowledge and a practical sense of purposes, tasks, and order in the classroom. To do so, teacher educators must understand how practitioners come to know and navigate practice settings, which are always particular. Such an emphasis is an attractive alternative to the traditional concentration on prescriptions and skill training and represents a powerful foundation on which to build teacher education programs around such practices as cases, simulations, action research, and reflection. But acknowledging the key role of personal conceptions in learning and the use of knowledge does not mean that personal understandings are the only legitimate form of knowledge about teaching. The lesson, rather, is that all learning is constructive, even the learning of academic skills, subject matter, pedagogy, and classrooms. The issue for teacher education is fundamentally curricular: how to represent knowledge about teaching in ways that enable teachers to come to their own understanding of what it means.

CONCLUSION: THEMES AND DIRECTIONS

The purpose of this chapter was to map the conceptual and methodological terrain of research production and use in teacher education. The features of greatest interest in this terrain were the themes that appeared to shape how research is understood and applied. In this final section, the analysis of these themes is summarized and conclusions are drawn concerning directions for theory, research, and practice in teacher education.

Major Themes

At an institutional level, thinking about teacher education programs is driven by an ambivalence toward standard classroom practice. Teacher educators hope to produce graduates who are qualified to teach, who can, that is, function effectively in school settings. Yet there is often a dissatisfaction with how teachers teach and a strong sense that school practice must be changed by preparing teachers to adopt innovative practices. This ambivalence enormously complicates relationships between teacher educators and schools. This complexity is exacerbated by the structural discontinuities and centrifugal forces that characterize the teacher education enterprise itself as it stretches across academic departments, professional programs, and school settings. Given the size of the enterprise, it is not surprising that teacher education is not easy to understand or reform.

Although the search for a knowledge base for the teacher education curriculum has often been in vain, this issue accounts for a large portion of what is considered research in teacher education. This search is dominated by themes of quality control and effectiveness. The effectiveness question (who are the best teachers or what is the best way to teach) is enmeshed in the issues of status and control at the core of the professionalization of education. An important stage of this process was achieved in the late nineteenth century: Schooling professionalized at the level of school administrators. A significant part of this process involved claims by administrators to be able to control the means of education, including teachers, through scientifically validated knowledge and practices.

An examination of the available answers to the effectiveness question revealed the impact of status and control on the legitimacy of knowledge about teaching. Frameworks for understanding teaching have always been plentiful. Indeed, within teacher education there are at least five broad perspectives—the good employee, the junior professor, the innovator, the fully functioning person, and the reflective professional—that suggest domains of knowledge that can be used in the preparation of teachers. Yet only a limited range of information has been deemed satisfactory. The analysis of the professionalization of schooling suggests that knowledge about teaching is considered suitable if it (a) enhances the status of schooling or (b) provides procedures that can be used to control teachers. The first criterion explains the acceptance of educational psychology as a legitimate slot in the teacher education curriculum and the continuing support of academic courses, rather than methods, in the preparation of teachers. The second criterion accounts for the emphasis on knowledge that can be translated readily into evaluative indicators or uniform prescriptions for teaching practice. The form and substance of process–product research was especially suited to these core themes in schooling and the education of teachers.

The search for a technology of teaching was initially framed, then, as a search for practical indicators of effectiveness that would empower administrators to control schooling. Since at least 1980, there has been a growing reaction against the knowledge and power claims that underlie this view of teaching and the control of teachers. The strongest criticism of the traditional view is grounded in an emphasis on the personal practical knowledge of teachers, the idiosyncratic and particularistic conceptions teachers have of the meaning and significance of their work. Taken to an extreme, the argument for personal practical knowledge would reject all generalized knowledge about teaching and, thus, eliminate a role for research in teacher education. Between the technocratic and personal viewpoints, there is a growing body of work on teaching practices, content knowledge, and enactment knowledge. This work is based on the premise that effective teaching requires specialized knowledge structures related to classroom action systems and subject matter. Teachers use these knowledge structures to interpret situations, identify relevant information resources, plan appropriate strategies, and enact these strategies in classrooms. Such knowledge is seen to be generative (see Wittrock, 1974): It enables teachers to recognize unencountered instances and create novel solutions to problems. In addition, this knowledge is richly particularistic and situational, thus enabling teachers to connect what they know to specific circumstances.

This, then, is the basic line of argument advanced here concerning the thematic shifts taking place in teacher education research. In the concluding section, some of the implications of these shifts are examined.

Directions for Teacher Education Research

Several important conceptual and methodological directions for research production and utilization would seem to be emerging from the intellectual turbulence in teacher education. Some of the major directions are discussed briefly here as suggestions for further analysis and inquiry.

Intellectual Foundations for Teaching and Teacher Education. Traditionally, the concepts and methods of educational psychology have been considered the primary foundation for research on teaching and teacher education and for the teacher education curriculum. There are several clear indicators, however, that the disciplinary foundation for teachers and teacher education is shifting. This shift can be seen, for example, in the emphasis on understanding contexts and situations rather than simply individual behavior and in the concern for examining domain-specific knowledge structures rather than general cognitive processes. The constructs and methods necessary for these new interests and questions do not reside in the individualistic theories and quantitative methods that have typically characterized educational psychology. Investigators have adopted, rather, theories and interpretive methods from a variety of disciplines—anthropology, linguistics, sociology, literary criticism—to capture the richness and complexity of teaching practices, classroom life, and teachers' knowledge. In addition, attention has turned to curriculum and to the disciplines the teachers are teaching as an important knowledge source for practice. Finally, there is a growing body of work that is distinctly grounded in classroom conceptions rather than derivations from external disciplines. This depsychologizing of teaching and the development of a language of classroom research is a sign of increasing maturity in the field and supports cautious optimism for progress in the study of teaching and teacher education in the immediate future.

A reappraisal of the role of educational psychology in knowledge production and utilization is likely to have consequences for the teacher education curriculum. As noted earlier, educational psychology enjoys a widely accepted slot in the education of teachers and has evolved into an omnibus course in many programs. This state of affairs is likely to change as new disciplines and new bodies of knowledge make compelling claims as foundations that inform teaching practice. The point is not, of course, that educational psychology has no place in teacher education. To enact curriculum, teachers need a rich understanding of learning, development, and motivation. But space will have to be made for knowledge, both declarative and procedural, that is more situational in character, tied closer to the particulars of curriculum, and framed in ways that capture the event structures of classrooms.

Research Styles and Frameworks. It has become increasingly clear that process–product research has severe limitations as a knowledge base for teaching and teacher education. In part, the problem is that this research tradition is entangled with the technocratic mentality and external control mechanisms of schooling, so that the findings, despite the best intentions of researchers, are likely to be misappropriated in ways that undermine the professional status, autonomy, and judgment of teachers.

In addition, the knowledge generated in process–product studies is not really about teaching at all but about indicators. Process–product research does not account for teaching but rather for student achievement as a function of discrete characteristics of teachers' performances. In essence, such indicators are not skills, processes, or practices. They are, instead, arbitrary fragments stripped of the particulars of purpose, subject matter, context, and understanding. Such knowledge is of quite limited utility to teachers and teacher educators; one gains little understanding of teaching from reading a list of teaching variables derived from process–product research. Moreover, the use of this research base for making curriculum decisions or evaluating teachers is likely to be misleading.

Some researchers have used process–product findings as a basis for constructing teaching practices. This transformation certainly improves the quality of the information that can be extracted from process–product studies. At the same time, there are alternative sources of information in the content fields, in cognitive studies, and in research on pedagogical-content knowledge and enactment knowledge that are much richer than process–product findings for conceptualizing practices that can be studied systematically.

Practicality and Effectiveness. Research on teaching has always been seen, from both within and outside the research community, as a pragmatic enterprise intended to improve teaching and teacher education rather than simply describe or understand it (see Gage, 1966). Thus, issues of practicality and effectiveness will always be central to knowledge production and utilization in this field. From the perspective of technical rationality, practicality and effectiveness are fairly simple matters. Practical knowledge is that which empowers outsiders (e.g., administrators, state officials, or legislators) to control teaching, and effectiveness is assumed by prescribing uniform practice in the classroom and monitoring indicators to enforce compliance. With the thematic shift from status and quality control to knowledge and empowerment, new definitions of practicality and new conceptions of how to insure effectiveness are needed. Although this issue can hardly be resolved here, there are some indications of directions that might be taken.

New understandings emerging from classroom research clearly suggest that practical knowledge for teaching is interpretive and/or procedural rather than simply prescriptive. That is, knowledge that teachers find useful enables them either to (a) understand classroom events (including curriculum, management, and instruction) so that practices can be invented or, if already known, connected to particular situations; or (b) know how to carry out a practice in the typical contexts in which teaching occurs. Thus prescriptions such as "ask higher order questions" or "check for understanding" are virtually useless if a teacher does not already know the procedures implied by these directives and the events in which they might be appropriate. The implication here is that practical knowledge must be event structured and richly descriptive, in other words, framed in the natural units of classroom experience and embedded in the particulars of these situations.

Increasing knowledge about how teaching effects are mediated by tasks, contexts, and participants' understandings suggest that classroom events are not tightly linked to outcomes. Teacher effects are, in other words, situational and elusive (see Lazerson et al., 1985). Different practices adapted to different circumstances can be equally effective, and one can never guarantee effectiveness by imposing uniform practice across classrooms. The alternative is not, however, absolute relativism and blind faith in the wisdom of the practitioner. Although the judgments of many, if not most, teachers are remarkably accurate, not all decisions or practices are necessarily appropriate. What the thematic shift in the field implies is that quality control be based not on a system of external control but on the available knowledge about content and about practices and their enactments in classrooms. The accountability question then becomes, Is the appropriate knowledge being used in this situation? rather than, Is a practice deemed effective on external criteria being used? In the end, the teaching profession must establish trust in its knowledge.

Directions for Research. The final issue is the research agendas that might address the emerging knowledge and practice requirements of teacher education. Much of what has been written in this chapter about emerging research on practices, content, and enactment has a family resemblance to the language of what has traditionally been called *methods*. Historically, discourse about teaching methods encompassed purposes, theories of the content to be taught, learning and motivation processes, conceptions of how teaching events influence learning, and illustrative cases. With the psychologizing of teaching, methods fell on hard times. Teaching was detached from its curricular and philosophical contexts and redefined as generic behaviors or processes such as lecture, discussion, concept teaching, problem solving, inquiry (see Gage, 1976). Teaching was translated, that is, into treatments that could be studied with the conventional constructs and tools of psychology. Eventually, the word *method* virtually disappeared from research on teaching, and the intellectual foundations of method stagnated.

Modern trends in research suggest that something was lost when method was dropped from the vocabulary of research on teaching. It might be useful, therefore, to revisit many of the issues in discussions of method, in part to avoid the pitfalls of previous eras and also to frame research in ways that are intellectually productive and useful.

A resurgence of interest in method must be accompanied by a fundamental shift in the character of research. Traditionally research on teaching has been preoccupied with causality and quantification and has relied on statistics as the basic language of analysis and theory construction. Thus, facets of teaching, even those represented by such constructs as teachers' expectations, metacognitions, decisions, and knowledge structures, have often been viewed essentially as treatment variables, that is, as characteristics of teachers that have significance only as predictors of achievement. This preoccupation with causality has impeded the development of structural explanations (see Culler, 1981) in which events and actions are understood within contexts of purpose and meaning rather than as autonomous entities apart from the system of relations in which they are embedded. From this perspective, the study of teaching practices, for instance, shifts from a search for only treatment effects to an explication of how a practice works and what meaning it has to teachers and students in a particular context.

As a framework for the study of teachers' knowledge, the approach being outlined here combines both context and thought, in an attempt to make explicit the rules and conventions that make meaning or intelligibility possible. The emphasis, in other words, is not simply on what particular teachers think or believe or even on how experts differ from novices. Rather, the purpose is to understand how meanings are constructed in classroom settings. To do this kind of analysis, one must have a powerful language to describe both *events* and the *interpretations* made of these events. It is not assumed that all entities have the same meaning to everyone; indeed the meaning of most objects and actions in the complex environments of classrooms is often indeterminant. The assumption is made, however, that analytical knowledge about the interpretive process is possible. Research along these lines generates not indicators but frameworks about what teachers know, how they act, and what judgments they make in solving teaching dilemmas.

Conclusion

After a history of relatively unremarkable productivity and progress, teacher education research has become an exciting arena for asking questions about classrooms, subject matter, and teachers and for devising strategies to generate sensible answers. If quality control remains the dominant theme in teacher education, it is likely that the connection between research and practice will remain narrow and findings from research will be of interest primarily as indicators for skill training and evaluation. But the signs are clear that there is a readiness within the research and teacher education communities to enlarge the vision of what teacher education can be and what knowledge can inform the enterprise. It now appears that the field is vigorous and that fundamental issues of curriculum and pedagogy can be addressed. This is not an easy agenda, but it is essential, and the prognosis for the coming years is strong.

References

Anderson, C. (1989). The role of education in the academic disciplines in teacher preparation. In A. Woolfolk (Ed.), *Research perspectives on the graduate preparation of teachers* (pp. 88–107). Englewood Cliffs, NJ: Prentice-Hall.

Anderson, L. M., Evertson, C. M., & Brophy, J. E. (1979). An experimental study of effective teaching in first-grade reading groups. *Elementary School Journal, 79*, 193–223.

Applegate, J. (1987). Early field experiences: Three viewpoints. In M. Haberman & J. Backus (Eds.), *Advances in Teacher Education* (Vol. 3, pp. 74–93). Norwood, NJ: Ablex.

Barr, A. S. (1929). *Characteristic differences in the teaching performance of good and poor teachers of the social studies.* Bloomington, IL: Public School Publishing.

Berliner, D. C. (1988). *The development of expertise in pedagogy.* The Charles W. Hunt Memorial Lecture presented at the annual meeting of the American Association of Colleges for Teacher Education, New Orleans.

Bestor, A. (1953). *The restoration of learning.* New York: Alfred A. Knopf.

Beyer, L. (1987). What knowledge is of most worth in teacher education? In J. Smyth (Ed.), *Educating teachers: Changing the nature of pedagogical knowledge* (pp. 19–34). London: Falmer.

Block J., & Burns, R. (1976). Mastery learning. In L. S. Shulman (Ed.), *Review of research in education* (Vol. 4, pp. 3–49). Itasca, IL: F. E. Peacock.

Bloom, B. S. (1976). *Human characteristics and school learning.* New York: McGraw-Hill.

Blumenfeld, P. C., Pintrich, P. R., Meece, J., & Wessels, K. (1982). The formation and role of self perceptions of ability in elementary classrooms. In W. Doyle & T. L. Good (Eds.), *Focus on teaching* (pp. 182–201). Chicago: University of Chicago Press.

Book, C., Freeman, D., & Brousseau, B. (1985). Comparing academic backgrounds and career aspirations of education and non-education majors. *Journal of Teacher Education, 36*(3), 27–30.

Bredderman, T. (1983). Effects of activity-based elementary science on student outcomes: A quantitative synthesis. *Review of Educational Research, 53,* 499–518.

Brophy, J. E. (1983). Teacher praise: A functional analysis. *Review of Educational Research, 51,* 5–32.

Brophy, J. E. (1988). Research on teacher effects: Uses and abuses. *Elementary School Journal, 89,* 3–21.

Brophy, J. E., & Good, T. L. (1986). Teacher behavior and student achievement. In M. C. Wittrock (Ed.), *Handbook of research on teaching* (3rd ed., pp. 328–375). New York: Macmillan.

Broudy, H. S. (1963). Historical exemplars of teaching method. In N. L. Gage (Ed.), *Handbook of research on teaching* (pp. 1–43). Chicago: Rand McNally.

Burnham, J. C. (1972). Medical specialists and movement toward social control in the progressive era: Three examples. In J. Israel (Ed.), *Building the organizational society: Essays on associational activities in modern America* (pp. 19–30). New York: Free Press.

Buros, O. K. (1977). Fifty years in testing: Some reminiscences, criticisms, and suggestions. *Educational Researcher, 6*(7), 9–15.

Carnegie Forum on Education and the Economy. (1986). *A nation prepared: Teachers for the 21st century.* New York: Author.

Carr W., & Kemmis, S. (1986). *Becoming critical: Education, knowledge and action research.* London: Falmer.

Carter, H. (1984). Teachers of teachers. In L. G. Katz & J. D. Raths (Eds.), *Advances in teacher education* (Vol. 1, pp. 125–143). Norwood, NJ: Ablex.

Carter, K. (in press). Teacher comprehension of classroom processes. *Elementary School Journal.*

Carter, K., & Doyle, W. (1987). Teachers' knowledge structures and comprehension processes. In J. Calderhead (Ed.), *Exploring teachers' thinking* (pp. 147–160). London: Cassell.

Carter, F., & Doyle, W. (1989). Classroom research as a resource for the graduate preparation of teachers. In A. E. Woolfolk (Ed.), *Research perspective on the graduate preparation of teachers* (pp. 51–68). Englewood Cliffs, NJ: Prentice-Hall.

Cazden, C. B. (1986) Classroom discourse. In M. C. Wittrock (Ed.), *Handbook of research on teaching* (3rd ed., pp. 432–463). New York: Macmillan.

Clark, D. L. (1986). Transforming the structure for the professional preparation of teachers. In J. D. Raths & L. G. Katz (Eds.), *Advances in teacher education* (Vol. 2, pp. 1–19). Norwood, NJ: Ablex.

Clark D. L., & Marker, G. (1975). The institutionalization of teacher education. In K. Ryan (Ed.), *Teacher education* (74th yearbook of the National Society for the Study of Education, Part II, pp. 53–86). Chicago: University of Chicago Press.

Clifford, G. J., & Guthrie, J. W. (1988). *Ed school: A brief for professional education.* Chicago: University of Chicago Press.

Combs, A. W. (1965). *The professional education of teachers: A perceptual view of teacher education.* Boston: Allyn & Bacon.

Connelly, F. M., & Clandinin, D. J. (1986). On narrative method, personal philosophy, and the story of teaching. *Journal of Research in Science Teaching, 23,* 293–310.

Copeland, W. D. (1977). Some factors related to student teacher classroom performance following microteaching training. *American Educational Research Journal, 14,* 147–157.

Cruickshank, D. R. (1984). Toward a model to guide inquiry in preservice teacher education. *Journal of Teacher Education, 35*(6), 43–48.

Culler, J. (1981). *The pursuit of signs: Semiotics, literature, deconstruction.* Ithaca, NY: Cornell University Press.

Darling-Hammond, L., Wise, A. E., & Pease, S. R. (1983). Teacher evaluation in the organizational context: A review of the literature. *Review of Educational Research, 53,* 285–328.

Doyle, W. (1976). Educational for all: The triumph of professionalism. In O. L. Davis, Jr. (Ed.), *Perspectives on curriculum development 1776–1976* (1976 Yearbook, pp. 17–75). Washington, DC: Association for Supervision and Curriculum Development.

Doyle, W. (1978). Paradigms for research on teacher effectiveness. In L. S. Shulman (Ed.), *Review of research in education* (Vol 5, pp. 163–198). Itasca, IL: F. E. Peacock.

Doyle, W. (1983). Academic work. *Review of Educational Research, 53,* 159–199.

Doyle, W. (1986). Classroom organization and management. In M. C. Wittrock (Ed.), *Handbook of research on teaching* (3rd ed., pp. 392–431). New York: Macmillan.

Doyle, W., & Carter, K. (1984). Academic tasks in classrooms. *Curriculum Inquiry, 14,* 129–149.

Dreeben, R. (1970). *The nature of teaching.* Glenview, IL: Scott, Foresman.

Ducharme, E. (1986). Teacher educators: Description and analysis. In J. D. Raths & L. G. Katz (Eds.), *Advances in teacher education* (Vol. 2, pp. 39–60). Norwood, NJ: Ablex.

Duckworth, E. (1987). *"The having of wonderful ideas" and other essays on teaching and learning.* New York: Teachers College Press.

Dunkin, M. J., & Biddle, B. J. (1974). *The study of teaching.* New York: Holt, Rinehart & Winston.

Emmer, E. T., Sanford, J. P., Evertson, C. M., Clements, B. S., & Martin, J. (1981). *The Classroom Management Improvement Study: An experiment in elementary school classrooms* (R & D Rep. No. 6050). Austin: University of Texas, R & D Center for Teacher Education.

Erickson, F. (1982). Taught cognitive learning in its immediate environment: A neglected topic in the anthropology of education. *Anthropology and Education Quarterly, 13,* 149–180.

Erickson, F. (1986). Qualitative methods in research on teaching. In M. C. Wittrock (Ed.), *Handbook of research on teaching* (3rd ed., pp. 119–161). New York: Macmillan.

Erickson, F., & Shultz, J. (1981). When is a context? Some issues and methods in the analysis of social competence. In J. L. Green & C. Wallat (Eds.), *Ethnography and language in educational settings.* Norwood, NJ: Ablex.

Etzioni, A. (Ed.). (1969). *The semi-professions and their organization: Teachers, nurses, social workers.* New York: Free Press.

Feiman-Nemser, S., & Buchmann, M. (1986). The first year of teacher preparation: Transition to pedagogical thinking? *Journal of Curriculum Studies, 18,* 239–256.

Fenstermacher, G. D. (1986). Philosophy of research on teaching: Three aspects. In M. C. Wittrock (Ed.), *Handbook of research on teaching* (3rd ed., pp. 37–49). New York: Macmillan.

Freidson, E. (1970). *Profession of medicine: A study in the sociology of applied knowledge.* New York: Dodd, Mead.

Fuller, F. F., & Bown, O. H. (1975). Becoming a teacher. In K. Ryan (Ed.), *Teacher education* (74th yearbook of the National Society for the Study of Education, Part II, pp. 25–52). Chicago: University of Chicago Press.

Gage, N. L. (1963). Paradigms for research on teaching. In N. L. Gage (Ed.), *Handbook of research on teaching* (pp. 94–141). Chicago: Rand McNally.

Gage, N. L. (1966). Research on the cognitive aspects of teaching. In Center for the Study of Instruction, *The way teaching is* (pp. 29–44). Washington, DC: Association for Supervision and Curriculum Development and the National Education Association.

Gage, N. L. (Ed.). (1976). *The psychology of teaching methods* (75th yearbook of the National Society for the Study of Education, Part 1). Chicago: University of Chicago Press.

Gage, N. L. (1978). *The scientific basis of the art of teaching.* New York: Teachers College Press.

Gage, N. L. (1985). *Hard gains in the soft sciences: The case of pedagogy.* Bloomington, IN: Center on Evaluation, Development, and Research, Phi Delta Kappa.

Gage N. L., & Winne, P. H. (1975). Performance-based teacher education. In K. Ryan (Ed.), *Teacher education* (74th yearbook of the National Society for the Study of Education, Part II, pp. 146–172). Chicago: University of Chicago Press.

Garrison, J. W. (1988). Democracy, scientific knowledge, and teacher empowerment. *Teachers College Record, 89,* 487–504.

Getzels J. W., & Jackson, P. W. (1963). The teacher's personality and characteristics. In N. L. Gage (Ed.), *Handbook of research on teaching* (pp. 506–582). Chicago: Rand McNally.

Gliessman, D. H. (1984). Changing teaching performance. In L. G. Katz & J. D. Raths (Eds.), *Advances in teacher education* (Vol. 1, pp. 95–111). Norwood, NJ: Ablex.

Good, T., & Grouws, D. (1979). The Missouri Mathematics Effectiveness Project: An experimental study in fourth grade classrooms. *Journal of Educational Psychology, 71,* 355–362.

Good, T. L., & Mulryan, C. (in press). Teacher ratings: A call for teacher control and self-evaluation. In J. Millman & L. Darling-Hammond (Eds.), *Handbook of Teacher Evaluation* (2nd ed.). Newbury Park, CA: Sage.

Griffin, G. A. (1986). Issues in student teaching: A review. In J. D. Raths & L. G. Katz (Eds.), *Advances in teacher education* (Vol. 2, pp. 239–273). Norwood, NJ: Ablex.

Griffin, G. A., Barnes, S., O'Neal, A., Edwards, S., Defino, M. E., & Hukill, H. (1983). *Changing teacher practice: Final report of an experimental study* (R & D Rep. No. 9052). Austin: University of Texas, R & D Center for Teacher Education.

Gump, P. V. (1982). School settings and their keeping. In D. L. Duke (Ed.), *Helping teachers manage classrooms* (pp. 98–114). Alexandria, VA: Association for Supervision and Curriculum Development.

Hays, S. P. (1972). The new organizational society. In J. Israel (Ed.), *Building the organizational society: Essays on associational activities in modern America* (pp. 1–15). New York: Free Press.

Holmes Group. (1986). *Tomorrow's teachers.* East Lansing, MI: Author.

Holton, G. (1973). *Thematic origins of scientific thought: Kepler to Einstein.* Cambridge, MA: Harvard University Press.

Howey K. R., & Strom, S. M. (1987). Teacher selection reconsidered. In M. Haberman & J. M. Backus (Eds.), *Advances in teacher education* (Vol. 3, pp. 1–34). Norwood, NJ: Ablex.

Howsam, R. B., Corrigan, D. C., Denemark, G. W., & Nash, R. J. (1976). *Educating a profession.* Washington, DC: American Association of Colleges for Teacher Education.

Hunt, D. E. (1976). Teachers' adaptation: "Reading" and "flexing" to students. *Journal of Teacher Education, 27,* 268–275.

Hunter, M., (1982). *Mastery teaching.* El Segundo, CA: TIP Publications.

Hunter, M. (1985). What's wrong with Madeline Hunter? *Educational Leadership, 42*(5), 57–60.

Joncich, G. (1968). *The sane positivist: A biography of Edward L. Thorndike.* Middletown, CT: Wesleyan University Press.

Joyce, B. (1975). Conceptions of man and their implications for teacher education. In K. Ryan (Ed.), *Teacher education* (74th yearbook of the National Society for the Study of Education, Part II, pp. 111–145). Chicago: University of Chicago Press.

Joyce, B., & Clift, R. (1984). The phoenix agenda: Essential reforms in teacher education. *Educational Researcher, 13*(4), 5–18.

Joyce, B., & Weil, M. (1972). *Models of teaching.* Englewood Cliffs, NJ: Prentice-Hall.

Judge, H. (1982). *American graduate schools of education: A view from abroad.* New York: Ford Foundation.

Katz, L. G., & Raths, J. D. (1985). A framework for research on teacher education programs. *Journal of Teacher Education, 36*(6), 9–15.

Klausmeier, H. J., Rossmiller, R. A., & Saily, M. (Eds.). (1977). *Individually guided elementary education: Concepts and practices.* New York: Academic Press.

Kounin, J. S. (1970). *Discipline and group management in classrooms.* New York: Holt, Rinehart & Winston.

Kounin, J. S., & Gump, P. V. (1974). Signal systems of lesson settings and the task related behavior of preschool children. *Journal of Educational Psychology, 66,* 554–562.

Lanier, J. E., & Little, J. W. (1986). Research on teacher education. In M. C. Wittrock (Ed.), *Handbook of research on teaching* (3rd ed., pp. 527–569). New York: Macmillan.

Lazerson, M., McLaughlin, J. B., McPherson, B., & Bailey, S. (1985). *An education of value: The purposes and practices of schools.* Cambridge: Cambridge University Press.

Leinhardt G., & Smith, D. (1985). Expertise in mathematics instruction: Subject matter knowledge. *Journal of Educational Psychology, 77,* 247–271.

Lieberman, M. (1956). *Education as a profession.* Englewood Cliffs, NJ: Prentice-Hall.

McDonald, F. J. (1973) Behavior modification in teacher education. In C. E. Thoresen (Ed.), *Behavior modification in education* (72nd yearbook of the National Society for the Study of Education, Part I, pp. 41–76). Chicago: University of Chicago Press.

McDonald, J. P. (1988). The emergence of the teacher's voice: Implications for the new reform. *Teachers College Record, 89,* 471–486.

Medley, D. M. (1984). Teacher competency testing and the teacher educator. In L. G. Katz & J. D. Raths (Eds.), *Advances in teacher education* (Vol. 1, pp. 51–94). Norwood, NJ: Ablex.

Medley, D. M., Coker, H., & Soar, R. S. (1984). *Measurement-based evaluation of teacher performance: An empirical approach.* New York: Longman.

Nuthall G., & Snook, I. (1973). Contemporary models of teaching. In R. M. W. Travers (Ed.), *Second handbook of research on teaching* (pp. 47–76). Chicago: Rand McNally.

Page, D. P. (1847). *Theory and practice of teaching.* New York: Barnes & Burr.

Palinscar, A. S., & Brown, A. L. (1984). Reciprocal teaching of comprehension-fostering and monitoring activities. *Cognition and Instruction, 1,* 117–175.

Payne, W. H. (1875). *Chapters on school supervision.* Cincinnati: Van Antwerp, Bragg.

Peck, R., & Tucker, J. (1973). Research on teacher education. In R. M. W. Travers (Ed.), *Second handbook of research on teaching* (pp. 940–978). Chicago: Rand McNally.

Pugach, M. C. (1984). The role of selective admissions policies in the teacher-education process. In L. G. Katz & J. D. Raths (Eds.), *Advances in teacher education* (Vol. 1, pp. 145–169). Norwood, NJ: Ablex.

Resnick, L. B. (1987). *Education and learning to think.* Washington, DC: National Academy Press.

Richardson, V. (1989). The evolution of reflective teaching and teacher education. In R. Clift, W. R. Houston, & M. Pugach (Eds.), *Encouraging reflective practice: An examination of issues and exemplars.* New York: Teachers College Press.

Rosenshine, B. (1971). *Teaching behaviours and student achievement.* Windsor, England: National Foundation for Educational Research in England and Wales.

Rosenshine, B. (1976). Classroom instruction. In N. L. Gage (Ed.), *The psychology of teaching methods* (77th yearbook of the National Society for the Study of Education, Part 1, pp. 335–371). Chicago: University of Chicago Press.

Schalock, D. (1979). Research on teacher selection. In D. C. Berliner (Ed.), *Review of research in education* (Vol. 7, pp. 364–417). Washington, DC: American Educational Research Association.

Schlechty, P. C., & Vance, V. S. (1983). Recruitment, selection, and retention: The shape of the teaching force. *Elementary School Journal, 83,* 469–487.

Schön, D. (1983). *The reflective practitioner: How professionals think in action.* New York: Basic Books.

Sears, J. B. (1921). The measurement of teaching efficiency. *Journal of Educational Research, 4,* 82–96.

Seguel, M. L. (1978). *Conceptualizing method: A history.* Paper prepared for the Society for the Study of Curriculum History, Toronto.

Shulman, L. S. (1986a). Paradigms and research programs in the study of teaching: A contemporary perspective. In M. C. Wittrock (Ed.), *Handbook of research on teaching* (3rd ed., pp. 3–36). New York: Macmillan.

Shulman, L. S. (1986b). Those who understand: Knowledge growth in teaching. *Educational Researcher, 15,*(2) 4–14.

Shulman, L. S. (1987). Knowledge and teaching: Foundations of the new reform. *Harvard Educational Review, 57,* 1–22.

Slavin, R. (1983). *Cooperative learning.* New York: Longman.

Smith, B. O. (1971). Introduction. In B. O. Smith (Ed.), *Research in teacher education: A symposium* (pp. 1–9). Englewood Cliffs, NJ: Prentice-Hall.

Smith, B. O., Cohen, S. B., & Pearl, A. (1969). *Teachers for the real world.* Washington, DC: American Association of Colleges for Teacher Education.

Smith, D. C. (Ed.). (1983). *Essential knowledge for beginning educators.* Washington, DC: American Association of Colleges for Teacher Education.

Smyth, J. (Ed.). (1987). *Educating teachers: Changing the nature of pedagogical knowledge.* London: Falmer.

Sprinthall, N., & Thies-Sprinthall, L. (1983). The teacher as an adult learner: A cognitive-developmental view. In G. Griffin (Ed.), *Staff development* (82nd yearbook of the National Society for the Study of Education, Part II, pp. 13–35). Chicago: University of Chicago Press.

Stallings, J. A. (1987). Implications from the research on teaching for teacher preparation. In M. Haberman & J. M. Backus (Eds.), *Advances in teacher education* (Vol. 3, pp. 57–74). Norwood, NJ: Ablex.

Stallings J. A., & Krasavage, E. M. (1986). Program implementation and student achievement in a four-year Madeline Hunter Follow Through project. *Elementary School journal, 87,* 117–138.

Stodolsky, S. S. (1988). *The subject matters: Classroom activity in math and social studies.* Chicago: University of Chicago Press.

Thorndike, E. L. (1913). *Educational psychology: The original nature of man* (Vol. 1). New York: Columbia University, Teachers College.

Tom, A. R. (1984). *Teaching as a moral craft.* New York: Longman.

Tom, A. R. (1987). Replacing pedagogical knowledge with pedagogical questions. In J. Smyth, (Ed.), *Educating teachers: Changing the nature of pedagogical knowledge* (pp. 9–17). London: Falmer.

Turner, R. L. (1971). Conceptual foundations of research in teacher education. In B. O. Smith (Ed.), *Research in teacher education: A symposium* (pp. 10–36). Englewood Cliffs, NJ: Prentice-Hall.

Turner, R. L. (1975). An overview of research in teacher education. In K. Ryan (Ed.), *Teacher education* (74th yearbook of the National Society for the Study of Education, Part II, pp. 87–110). Chicago: University of Chicago Press.

Tyack, D. B. (1974). *The one best system: A history of American urban education.* Cambridge, MA: Harvard University Press.

Wagner, A. C. (1973). Changing teacher behavior: A comparison of microteaching and cognitive discrimination training. *Journal of Educational Psychology, 64,* 299–305.

Walker, D., & Schaffarzick, J. (1974). Comparing curricula. *Review of Educational Research, 44,* 83–111.

Watts, D. (1987). Student teaching. In M. Haberman & J. M. Backus (Eds.), *Advances in teacher education* (Vol. 3, pp. 151–167). Norwood, NJ: Ablex.

Waxman, H. C., & Walberg, H. J. (1986). Effects of early field experiences. In J. D. Raths & L. G. Katz (Eds.), *Advances in teacher education* (Vol. 2, pp. 165–184). Norwood, NJ: Ablex.

Weaver, W. T. (1979). The need for new talent in teaching. *Phi Delta Kappan, 61,* 29–46.

Westbury, I. (1973). Conventional classrooms, "open" classrooms and the technology of teaching. *Journal of Curriculum Studies, 5,* 99–121.

Wiebe, R. H. (1969). The social functions of public education. *American Quarterly, 21,* 147–164.

Wilson, S. M., Shulman, L. S., & Richert, A. E. (1987). "150 different ways" of knowing: Representations of knowledge in teaching. In J. Calderhead (Ed.), *Exploring teachers' thinking* (pp. 104–124). London: Cassell.

Wise, A. E., Darling-Hammond, L., & Berry, B. (1987). *Effective teacher selection: From recruitment to retention.* Washington, DC: The RAND Corporation.

Wise, A. E., Darling-Hammond, L., Berliner, D., Haller, E., Schlechty, P., Berry, B., Praskac, A., & Noblit, G. (1987). *Effective teacher selection: From recruitment to retention—case studies.* Washington, DC: The RAND Corporation.

Witkin, H. A., Moore, C. A., Goodenough, D. R., & Cox, P. W. (1977). Field-dependent and field-independent cognitive styles and their educational implications. *Review of Educational Research, 47,* 1–64.

Wittrock, M. C. (1974). Learning as a generative process. *Educational Psychologist, 11,* 87–95.

Woodring, P. (1975). The development of teacher education. In K. Ryan (Ed.), *Teacher education* (74th yearbook of the National Society for the Study of Education, Part II, pp. 1–24). Chicago: University of Chicago Press.

Woods, P. (1987). Life histories and teacher knowledge. In J. Smyth, (Ed.), *Educating teachers: Changing the nature of pedagogical knowledge* (pp. 121–135). London: Falmer.

Yinger, R. J. (1982). A study of teacher planning. In W. Doyle & T.

L. Good (Eds.), *Focus on teaching* (pp. 239–259). Chicago: University of Chicago Press.

Zeichner, K. M. (1983). Alternative paradigms of teacher education. *Journal of Teacher Education, 34*(3), 3–9.

Zeichner, K. M. (1987). The ecology of field experience: Toward an understanding of the role of field experiences in teacher development. In M. Haberman & J. M. Backus (Eds.), *Advances in teacher education* (Vol. 3, pp. 94–117). Norwood, NJ: Ablex.

Zeichner, K. M., & Liston, D. P. (1987). Teaching student teachers to reflect. *Harvard Educational Review, 57,* 23–48.

Zumwalt, K. K. (1982). Research on teaching: Policy implications for teacher education. In A. Lieberman & M. McLaughlin (Eds.), *Policy making in education* (81st yearbook of the National Society for the Study of Education, Part I, pp. 215–248). Chicago: University of Chicago Press.

Zumwalt, K. K. (1988). Are we improving or undermining teaching? In L. N. Tanner (Ed.), *Critical issues in curriculum* (87th yearbook of the National Society for the Study of Education, Part I, pp. 148–174). Chicago: University of Chicago Press.

·2·

ISSUES IN RESEARCH ON TEACHER EDUCATION

Sam J. Yarger and Philip L. Smith

UNIVERSITY OF WISCONSIN-MILWAUKEE

Although there are an extensive body of research and several well-developed programs of research on the teaching–learning process (e.g., the Canterbury studies [Hughes, 1973; Nuthall & Church, 1973; Wright & Nuthall, 1970] and Soar studies [Soar, 1968, 1977; Soar & Soar, 1979]), there are major gaps in what has been studied and in recommendations regarding what should be studied about the teacher education process. It has been noted by Ryan (1979) that the process of teacher education is rarely if ever driven by theory. Most often, it is speculated that teacher education programs expose students to an array of research and theories whose emphasis depends upon the individual instructor (Champion, 1984). Lortie (1975) concludes that the thousands of hours that teachers have spent as students have a much more powerful effect on their socialization as teachers than their brief exposure to teacher education curriculum.

This comes as little surprise to those who understand that no such theory or finite groups of theories exist for teacher education (or professional education in general). It is also understandable in that the social and psychological phenomena operating in the classrooms have served as a formidable impediment to those wishing to solidify and/or legitimize a knowledge base in teacher education through scientific investigation driven by theory.

Rationale of Chapter

The impetus for this chapter comes from the teacher educator's desire to know how to educate individuals to become effective teachers. Like education in all professional fields, the process of teacher education is often guided by belief, historical tradition, and intuition. The same can be said for the recent proliferation of calls for reform in teacher education and the suggested direction for this reform.

Take, for example, the current Holmes Group (1986) recommendations and guiding principles. Although the development of these principles was guided by the feelings and experience of several highly respected individuals involved in teacher education, they are at best only tenuously based on a solid foundation of research. Rather, some are based on loose constructs and beliefs, whereas others are based on the fact that most other feasible options have already been attempted with no discernible effect, so why not try something else? For example, the Holmes Group's recommendation that eliminating undergraduate teacher education will somehow lead to a better prepared teacher has no foundation in fact, but rather was constructed through a general belief that such a procedure would better ground teachers in traditional liberal studies, which would in turn lead to more effective classroom performance.

The need for this chapter stems from both the fact that educators themselves know very little about any rules and constructs of professional education that might exist and the logical premise that educators of educators should be able to provide leadership and guidance in professional education. To this end, this chapter seeks to specify a future direction for research in teacher education, given that no definitive guiding theory or set of theories exists for educating teachers. In doing so, we set forth an organizational framework for research on teacher education that we feel has potential for payoff. We do this by specifying a paradigm for research on teacher education that will help guide what is, in our opinion, worthwhile and high-potential research in teacher education. Because no unified theory of teacher education exists, research in this area must be viewed as exploratory rather than confirmatory. We make no apologies that this framework is not theory based. Only after sufficient exploratory work has been done should those involved in research in teacher education consider a confirmatory posture.

The authors thank reviewers David Berliner (Arizona State University) and James Cooper (University of Virginia) for their helpful suggestions.

It is true that a substantial amount of exploratory work has been done on certain aspects of the teacher education process. Quality aside, confirmation of rules and constructs even in these areas is premature without consideration of the linkages of these aspects with other, less thoroughly researched, aspects of an overall theoretical perspective.

This is not to say that teacher educators should seek a single unifying theory; research in other areas has taught us that such a goal is much too ambitious. Competing theories are healthy and will eventually lead to a greater knowledge base in teacher education. The focus of this chapter is on a general paradigm from which research can, in the foreseeable future, lead to theoretical perspectives. In our opinion, it is a paradigm that would be universal to any theory or set of theories that might emanate from the research.

Scope of Chapter

Our definition of teacher education is somewhat restricted. By *teacher education* we mean the context and process of educating individuals to become effective teachers or better teachers. Following this definition, our discussion focuses on research in the education of teachers, not on the behavior of the teacher or students in the classroom. As detailed later, this definition includes only those variables and activities that somehow influence the education of teachers. Teacher-effectiveness research is relevant only to the extent to which such research and the associated variables are used to measure the impact of our teacher education programs and to which dissatisfaction with teacher effectiveness spurs calls for reform in teacher education. Teacher effectiveness becomes the ultimate dependent variable in the discussion of teacher education research.

In addition, the chapter recognizes that most teacher education research will be decision oriented (Cronbach & Suppes, 1969) or applied. Although the conclusion-oriented (basic) research from fields such as human learning and development is extremely important in guiding and determining options for teacher education, research in teacher education is often action oriented and very applied. This is true because the ecological validity of many teacher education situations must be high if anything practical is to be produced, and, therefore, the rules of appropriate conclusion-oriented research are difficult, if not impossible, to follow. For example, the typical rules of randomization, and the procedures for the construction of a truly equivalent control group, cannot be followed in a field study.

The constraints of basic research in teacher education are known to most. If not obvious already, the reasons should become more obvious once the dimensions and forces on teacher education are further explicated. It should not be inferred from this that no generalizable knowledge is gained through research on teacher education simply because it is applied. Methods such as Glass's meta-analysis (Glass, McGaw, & Smith, 1981) hold much promise for the quasi-experiment and evaluation study that characterizes one aspect of research in teacher education. Indeed, the best we can probably hope for are loose principles, but even these provide a giant step forward, given the state of teacher education research today.

State of Teacher Education Research

Perhaps because of the Holmes group's initiatives and recent national attention to education, calls for research on teacher education proliferated in the late 1980s. Some of these have focused on the state of the art in teacher education research, and others have provided specific frameworks for research on particular topics that the authors consider critical to effective teacher education.

From these studies, reports, and themes one cannot effectively summarize what others consider to be the Achilles' heel of research on teacher education. It seems that the agenda is specific to the individual author; there is no consensus on what research is most important in teacher education or where to begin. Lanier and Little (1986) have correctly characterized teacher education as a field of multidisciplinary inquiry.

Those involved in teacher education have only begun to think about an organized research agenda with a national perspective. Definition of the parameters of this agenda is a logical first step, leaving for later the debate as to what knowledge is worth pursuing and how it should be pursued. One notable effort along these lines is that of Katz and Raths (1985), who provide a framework for research on teacher education programs. Katz and Raths define what they consider the parameters (broad categories of variables that might affect process and outcome) of a teacher education program. These parameters include the goals of teacher education, the characteristics of the candidates, the characteristics of the staff, the content of teacher education, the methods used for teacher education, the duration and sequence of the content and methods, the ethos of the program, the program regulations, the program resources, the program evaluation procedures, the and program effects. A matrix formed by the intersections of each of these parameters defines questions that might be asked about teacher education and teacher education programs. Although the matrix approach makes the complicated and necessarily multivariate nature of research on teacher education look simpler and bivariate, it might provide a useful starting place from which a more complete agenda can be developed.

The framework used for this chapter is both more and less ambitious than the Katz and Raths effort. It is more ambitious in the sense that it seeks to define a paradigm of research on teacher education that might be worth pursuing and goes beyond this by suggesting methodological alternatives and pitfalls in the conduct of this research. It is less ambitious in that it does not attempt to define potential areas of teacher education research in anything other than general terms. It is up to the reader to fit a local or national research agenda into the framework presented.

Organization of Chapter

A major premise of this chapter is that most teacher education research focuses on one or more of the following components and their linkages: antecedent conditions, process, and outcomes. These components and their linkages form a major organizational dimension for this chapter. In particular, our discussion of the state of research on teacher education will focus on each of these domains because the state varies from area to area. *Antecedent conditions* refers to those environmental conditions that set the context for teacher education (e.g., student selection, program structure, student and faculty personalogical characteristics, physical environment, political/ social context).

Process refers to the process of teacher education, to those practices used to educate teachers and prospective teachers. Research that attempts to link antecedents with process will also be discussed.

Outcomes refers to those behaviors exhibited by teachers following participation in an education intervention. In isolation, outcomes are not a major focus of the chapter. Studies of teacher effectiveness, for example, are not necessarily related to research on teacher education, as many such studies focus on the behavioral characteristics of teachers and pupils, with no particular concern for how those teacher behaviors were acquired. Rather, it is the linkages between antecedent and process variables with these outcomes that comprise a major portion of teacher education as defined in this chapter. Outcome variables are a focus in this chapter to the extent that outcomes are viewed as the result of a direct educational intervention in which the teacher participated and are, therefore, linked to antecedents and/or processes.

Such *linking studies* are typically of four varieties: those linking antecedents with processes, those linking antecedents with outcomes, those linking processes with outcomes, and those linking both antecedents and processes with outcomes. Each of these types of studies varies in its prevalence with respect to the teacher education literature. Although the variables examined within each of these domains are likely to differ, depending on whether one is concerned with preservice or inservice teacher education, problems in the conduct of research are similar for both.

The second dimension that defines the lattice used to guide this chapter is the nature of the inquiry or, more specifically, the methodological approach used. The domain of methodological approaches discussed in this chapter will include narrative research, case study research, survey research, correlational research, and causal/experimental research. Both qualitative and quantitative paradigms will be covered within this dimension, although some of the approaches mentioned are more conducive to a qualitative paradigm than others, and vice versa.

Given these two major dimensions, the chapter will be organized as follows. First, a brief description of the various domains of research on teacher education will be provided, along with those additional domains formed by their linkages. Following this will be a discussion of various methodological approaches and options that seem particularly viable for research in teacher education. This discussion also includes a section on measurement issues that directly affect the conduct and interpretation of research in teacher education. Following these discussions, a more detailed look at research in the various inquiry domains will be made. Within each domain, the focus of the discussion will be on aspects of the domain that should be considered in the conduct of research and on the value of research in the domain to the entire paradigm. These discussions will be punctuated with examples of previously completed studies. Each of these discussions is intended to stimulate thought as to the most pressing needs for research in each of the domains. The chapter will conclude with a general discussion of a research agenda for the future. This will include a discussion of specific areas within each domain that have enhanced potential and those that have limited potential for payoff in teacher education.

FOCI OF RESEARCH IN TEACHER EDUCATION

An overly simplistic but instructive way to view the domains of research in teacher education is shown in Figure 2-1. This figure shows three major domains of inquiry: antecedent conditions, processes, and outcomes. Although a portion of research in teacher education has and will focus on each of these three domains (although, as we have argued, studies that focus solely on outcomes are not necessarily teacher education research studies), the bulk of the research in teacher education will focus on relationships among them. We call these *linking studies*, and they are represented in Figure 2-1 by the arrows connecting the three major domains. Linking studies are of four major varieties: those linking antecedents with processes, those linking antecedents with outcomes, those linking process with outcomes, and those linking antecedents with processes, which are in turn linked to outcomes.

These domains and the links associated with them provide a convenient vehicle for discussing the state of the art, the needs, and the appropriate methodology of research in teacher education. Each of the three primary domains is further defined in the following discussion, along with the domains formed by their links.

Antecedents

By antecedents, we mean those conditions and variables that affect teacher education without being directly related to process but, rather, influence or guide that process. This domain is much broader than the personal characteristics that

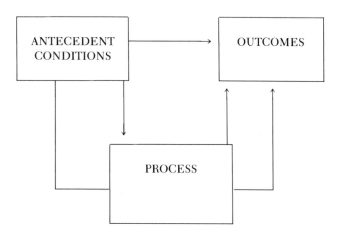

FIGURE 2–1. An Organizational Framework for Research on Teacher Education.

teacher educators tend to think of when the term *antecedent variable* is mentioned. Basically, antecedent variables and conditions are those which in some major respect shape, direct, or dictate the nature of the teacher education process (and therefore perhaps the outcomes), due to their mere presence. This is not to imply that these variables are not manipulatable, although some are not. Examples of variables that clearly fit our definition of antecedent are those such as student, faculty, and institutional characteristics. These are the variables often thought of as antecedents that somehow shape the direction of the process of teacher education.

There are, however, other antecedent variables that are less often thought of, or perhaps considered, in research on teacher education. These include such things as the physical environment of the teacher education setting, the structure of the school or college in which teacher education occurs, the legislative context, the autonomy of institutions from external influences, the state and federal mandates, and the accreditation concerns. It will be argued that antecedents such as these ultimately account for much of the variation in what is possible in teacher education programs—that is, much of teacher education is shaped by outside influences relatively free from the institutions' concern for quality training—and that these areas are a much neglected realm of research because they shape the direction of teacher education.

Processes

By processes, we mean any factor associated with the intervention of a teacher education program (both preservice and inservice). Again, the definition is broader than that normally considered when one thinks of the process of teacher education. Processes would include the actual structure of a teacher education program, the components of the structure, the extent of implementation of various parts, and the methods used for implementation. Processes are those essential aspects associated with the actual delivery of a teacher education experience. For example, studies related to the effective implementation of microteaching or the integration of additional arts and science content into the teacher education curriculum would be examples of process studies.

Outcomes

By outcomes, we mean those learned or provoked behaviors exhibited by the recipients of teacher education that occurred as a direct result of an intervention. This would include both teacher behaviors and student reactions to these behaviors. Teacher effectiveness and classroom performance variables are logical members of this class. Outcome variables, as they are defined here, however, are of interest in this chapter only to the extent that they relate to antecedents and processes. In a real sense, they form a class of dependent variable that are used to judge successes and failures of teacher education efforts. There are however, significant problems in the conduct of teacher education research that are related to outcomes and, therefore, influence the conduct and interpretation of research on teacher education. Many of these problems stem from the inability to define or measure adequately outcome behaviors and the interventions that might have led to these behaviors. For these reasons, a discussion of outcome variables is included in a later portion of the methodology section of the chapter.

Linking Studies

Linking studies are those that tie together or link one of the three aforementioned domains of research on teacher education. As mentioned, these are typically of four varieties: those linking antecedents to processes, those linking antecedents to outcomes, those linking processes to outcomes, and those linking antecedents to processes, which are in turn linked to outcomes. Each of these is discussed briefly.

Antecedent–Process. Antecedent–process studies are linking studies that examine the relationship between antecedent conditions, as defined earlier, and the process of teacher education. Within this domain would fall studies that examine how antecedents influence the process of teacher education, as well as studies that examine the effect of the teacher education process on antecedent conditions. Of course, in some studies, both of these effects are examined simultaneously. An example of such a study would be one that examines how the available resources for teacher education influence the program options (e.g., the availability of funds for paying cooperating teachers influences the extent to which these teachers are involved in the teacher education process).

Antecedent–Outcome. Antecedent-outcome studies are linking studies that examine the relationship between antecedent conditions and outcome behaviors, regardless of process. Most of this domain is dominated by studies that examine the antecedent condition's effects on teacher behavior. However, the domain would also include studies in which teacher behavior, due to some intervention, has somehow, in turn, influenced the antecedent conditions. A study that attempts to link teacher performance with Scholastic Aptitude Test (SAT) results would be an example of this type of study.

Process–Outcome. Process-outcome studies are those that examine the relationship between the process of teacher education and teacher/student behavior following the teacher education intervention. Of traditional research in teacher education, these types of studies are probably the most prevalent, and when one thinks of research in teacher education, this is probably the first type to come to mind. However, studies in this domain are broader than simple process–product research but also include evaluation studies (the applied aspect), which allows one to examine the effects of outcomes on subsequent process. An example of such a study would be one that attempts to show a relationship between initial teaching performance (outcome) and a human relations component of teacher education (process).

Antecedent–Process–Outcome. The domain that is probably less well developed than the others is the one that simultaneously considers antecedents, processes, and outcomes. Typically, this type of study is beyond the scope and budget of most local research projects and tends to be a major national effort. An example of such an effort can be found in the Beginning Teacher Evaluation Study (McDonald & Elias, 1976).

Each of the foregoing domains provides potential research areas that, after integration, could lead to a better understanding (or at least an organized paradigm) with which to consider theories of teacher education. However, the nature of the question asked in each domain can be quite different, and, therefore, research in each domain is likely to be substantially different in terms of both methodology and substance. A mode of inquiry that predominates in one domain will not be equally represented in all domains. What follows is a brief discussion of various methodological approaches that should be considered in the conduct of research in each domain. Our subsequent discussion will focus, in part, on which approaches are likely to predominate in each domain, due to the nature of the questions asked.

METHODOLOGICAL APPROACHES TO RESEARCH IN TEACHER EDUCATION

There is much more to methodology in research on teacher education than selecting the appropriate procedures. Decisions must also be made about the nature of the research question(s), the likely quality of the results, and the assumptions of the research approach. These considerations will all occur within the limitations imposed by the researchers' background and training. A great deal of time and energy in our field is devoted to discussions and debates concerning one's research orientation, one's beliefs and values, and even one's view of the world. No doubt this stems from the diverse backgrounds of educational researchers, and it is reinforced by the great variety of research training programs encountered in the field. Although the debate can be stimulating and enjoyable, it can also be cumbersome and tedious. Unfortunately, too many sound ideas are dismissed because one researcher or another either didn't understand, simply devalued, or plain rejected a colleague's orientation or point of view. In this section, we will attempt to explicate these issues, recognizing that no single analysis will be sufficient and no universal acceptance and understanding of the problem can be expected.

Research Orientation

Talking about one's research orientation is, in and of itself, ambiguous. In research on teacher education, this discussion typically revolves around whether one perceives herself or himself to be a quantitative or qualitative researcher. Sadly, much of the discourse on this topic has generated more heat than light; this might be partially explained by the fact that principals in the debate sometimes lack the depth of knowledge necessary to focus on and explain the critical arguments. Regardless, the terms do have meaning and generally reflect different approaches to scholarly inquiry.

Quantitative approaches to research in teacher education attempt to model the scientific method that has, over the years, been adapted from the natural sciences. Except in the most rigid behavioral research, this adaptation has never been isomorphically implemented and trouble free. Research in teacher education usually takes the investigator to the field, and the realities of field research simply do not allow for complete adoption of a scientific research methodology (random assignment to group, manipulation of variables, equivalent control groups, etc.), although the principles of this approach have certainly served as useful guidelines.

Generally, quantitative research is more narrowly focused than qualitative research and is designed to either test specific hypotheses or address specific questions. Variables are measured in some replicable form, and the results are often represented numerically. It is these numerical representations, taken within the context of the procedures and the limitations imposed by a variety of sources, that provide the basis for the analysis of the data and the resulting conclusions.

One test that is often used to judge the quality of what is referred to as quantitative research is its replicability. Generally, the more readily a quantitative study can be exactly replicated, the more likely it is to be judged to be of sufficient methodological quality, regardless of the content. In practice, particularly in the field of teacher education, replicability has created many problems in such areas as selection of subjects, assignment to treatment, control of variables, and avoidance of the threat of alternative hypotheses. In truth, much of the research that bears the label *quantitative* is, in fact, questionable in its adherence to the basic principles of scientific inquiry.

Because many of the early attempts to use qualitative methodology to study educational phenomena attempted to emulate an ethnographic methodological approach, qualitative inquiry is often identified with the field of anthropology. This, of course, conjures up visions of scholars traveling to distant lands in an effort to learn about exotic cultures. Completing the vision, one finds the open-minded scholar observing everything, interviewing everyone, and sitting up late at night making literally volumes of copiously written field notes. These field notes serve the same function that the numerical representations serve for the quantitative researcher. They form the basis for the analysis and for any conclusions that are to be drawn. In this respect, conclusions drawn from qualitative research are bound to data just as conclusions drawn from quantitative research.

In research on teacher education, qualitative approaches have become as blurred as quantitative approaches. Archival data are frequently utilized, as are questionnaires and other forms of data that require numerical representations.

Thus, one often finds historical and quantitative elements embedded in qualitative research. This moves the research away from the phenomenological orientation that most scholars associate with the approach. Typically, the culture being studied is, in reality, a subculture that is quite familiar to the researcher and is neither foreign nor exotic. Field notes, however, gathered through interview and observation, usually constitute the cornerstone of qualitative research. Obviously, these data pass through the perceptual screen of the researcher. Although this has created controversy in discussions in the field of teacher education, it is likely that these perceptual filtering mechanisms are very similar to the ones used by quantitative researchers as they operationalize their variables, select measurement strategies, and analyze their data.

Qualitative research should probably be viewed as less constricted than quantitative approaches, since it is designed to generate rather than to test hypotheses. It would be convenient to differentiate between quantitative and qualitative approaches as being a difference between the scientific method and the phenomenological and observational experience of a scholar. Unfortunately, that reduces the complexity of the distinction too far. Instead, the critic must consider each research effort individually, must look specifically at what is being done, how it is being done, and what claims are being made. Only then will it be possible to make judgments concerning the adequacy of the research.

The Importance of the Research Question

Nothing is more discouraging to an academic advisor than to have a graduate student report that his or her dissertation will utilize a qualitative approach and will test the merits of two very different instructional strategies in teacher education. It is discouraging because the student has become prematurely wedded to a research orientation, has selected the research orientation prior to the research question, and, most important, has demonstrated a lack of understanding about research. No rule is more rigidly set in concrete than the one that states, "the research question(s) drives the methodology." It is true that one's orientation toward inquiry might affect the question that is posed. Once the question is determined, however, the selection of the appropriate research methodology becomes constrained. In the same way that one probably should not test the relative efficacy of two different instructional strategies using a qualitative approach, one probably should not study the range of emotions in a teacher's lounge using a quantitative strategy. The matching of an important problem to research questions and then to methodology constitutes one of the major issues to be encountered and resolved in the development of a coherent research agenda in teacher education.

It is possible to conceive of the purposes of research in teacher education in three different dimensions that will help us understand this problem. One purpose of research in this broad field, one that has historically been underutilized, focuses on *description*. In this instance, the researcher is interested in knowing what exists. It is, in fact, difficult to conceive of how more analytical research can occur in the absence of a thorough understanding of the phenomenon being studied. Second, one can choose to *explore a familiar condition or phenomenon* in the pursuit of interesting directional conclusions. In this instance, research might be described as "jumping in,"

based on knowledge and familiarity, with the purpose of conducting research directed toward the development of a more thorough understanding. The researcher would be both generating hypotheses and, it is hoped, pursuing a very economical path toward building a body of knowledge. Finally, once a fairly detailed and comprehensive understanding of a condition or phenomenon exists, it then makes sense to raise questions focusing on the *manipulation of that environment* toward specific results. In this case, logical and informed hypotheses would be tested.

This simple three-component framework should lead the prospective researcher to the development of research questions and the selection of an appropriate methodology without having to declare oneself as either a quantitative or qualitative researcher. Mixing and matching of quantitative and qualitative strategies would certainly be employed. Although the elements associated with a quantitative approach are often evident in the third stage, it is entirely probable that both approaches would be evident at some level at all three stages. Remember, one's world view might well influence the questions that are being posed and should lead a researcher in a specific direction. It is not, however, necessary to subscribe to any particular orientation in order to perform important and necessary research in the field of teacher education.

Research Methodologies

We have identified five distinct research methodologies that are commonly used in teacher education. These include *narrative studies, case studies, surveys, correlational studies*, and *causal/experimental studies* (Yarger & Galluzzo, 1983). Interestingly, although the testing of prespecified hypotheses might be the most respected form of research on teacher education, only the latter two methodologies are explicitly designed to achieve that goal. A brief discussion of each methodology and its appropriate uses will make that point more clear.

Narrative Studies. Narrative studies are the most basic kind of research on teacher education. These studies follow no particular format and are not bound to provide evidence concerning the credibility of their findings. No claims are made in narrative studies for reliability of observations, validity, or, for that matter, anything else. In fact, many scholars would not even include narrative studies in a discussion of research on teacher education. They are, however, quite common, typically consisting of program descriptions that are personalized accounts written by participants and/or primary actors in the teacher education activity. The strength of narrative studies is that they provide the reader with a great deal of rich information concerning program ideas and options. In that sense, they are descriptive and they inform. At their very best, they utilize a qualitative approach; at something less than their best, they can become very unstructured and personalized. Unfortunately, narrative studies cannot be replicated and, because they are frequently designed to promote a specific idea or program, are prone to be gilded in some instances.

Case Studies. Case studies differ from narrative studies in that they tend to be more organized and are typically written for a specific purpose. In fact, it is not unusual to find broadly stated research questions associated with case studies. Case studies often offer some glimpse of the methodology that was used, and claims are often made for objectivity, if not for validity and reliability. Some of the data presented in a case study might be represented in numerical fashion, but they typically are not viewed to be quantitative in nature.

Being somewhat more sophisticated than narrative studies, case studies can serve quite well as both descriptive agents and hypothesis-generating activities. At their strongest, case studies can provide the consumer with an in-depth description of some teacher education phenomenon. A great deal of what is commonly referred to as qualitative research in teacher education can be classified as case studies. This is particularly true when the focus of study is on one or a small number of elements within a broader teacher education program. Our definition of a case study has probably been expanded from what has historically been conceived of as being a case study in the broader field of education.

Surveys. Surveys are hybrids in the scheme of research on teacher education in that they are intended to sample large and important populations concerning topics that are pervasive and relevant to these populations. Surveys are distinguished from pseudosurveys by the clear identification of a logical population and adequate sampling procedures. In teacher education, it is not uncommon for pseudosurveys to take little note of the issues of population definition, sampling, instrument design, return rates, response rates, social acceptance, and a host of other important technicalities. Obviously, although important, surveys have distinct limitations in research on teacher education.

Although employing a quantitative methodology, in that the results are represented in numerical fashion, questions, not hypotheses, are posed at the onset of a survey research project. It is possible, however, to pose and test post hoc hypotheses in a well-conducted survey project. Typically, however, surveys are intended to describe specific phenomena, to generate information, and to lead to the development of well-conceived hypotheses.

Correlational Studies. Correlational studies can be defined as attempts to establish relationships between two or more variables deemed important in teacher education. They can grow from surveys, or they can be designed to involve the actual observation of events in a teacher education activity. When appropriately designed, correlational studies can be extended to include the prediction of one variable from another, though causal relationships typically require more sophisticated theory than we customarily find in teacher education.

Obviously, correlational studies utilize a quantitative approach, with the typically desired outcome being the description of some specific phenomena and, perhaps, the generation of hypotheses. Correlational data have the capability to create a great deal of confusion in regard to the power of the results.

It is often difficult to communicate the fact that causal relationships are not evident in correlational research. Knowing, for example, that grade point average and voluntary involvement are positively correlated within a given teacher education program does not answer the question of whether one should select higher achieving students to insure more voluntary involvement or stimulate voluntary involvement to improve grade point average. That finding would, however, promote the explication of a clear testable hypothesis.

Causal/Experimental Studies. Causal/experimental studies represent the most technically sophisticated order of research in teacher education. They are also almost impossible to fully and successfully implement in a field setting. In a causal/experimental study, not only are variables controlled, but also sampling is performed appropriately, subjects are randomly assigned to treatment, and a true experimental manipulation of a variable is required. The causal/experimental study is considered by the quantitative researcher the purist form of the quantitative approach, and it is designed explicitly to test hypotheses. Because most teacher education phenomena cannot be controlled sufficiently to accommodate experimental studies, true experiments most likely occur only in a laboratory setting. And, when that occurs, one must consider the problems of generalizability and the relationship of the experimental to the natural setting.

Having some knowledge of research orientation, methodology, and their relationship is important, but there is at least one other issue that weighs heavily in an understanding of research in teacher education.

Problems with Language

It is no secret that the problems associated with the development of construct validity plague all areas of research in education. For teacher education, the problem is magnified when one considers that the field is relatively short on constructs or theories to underpin and help explain the activities. The need, however, to operationalize constructs and to interpret theories in a variety of ways in the search for theoretical underpinnings is very important, and it should not be underestimated. Further, the diversity of the field makes this a particularly difficult problem in teacher education.

One special aspect of the problem of construct validity in teacher education focuses on words and their meanings. For example, it is difficult to develop techniques to measure *reflective teaching* when there is little or no agreement on what the term means. To some, reflective teaching might focus on the behavior of the teachers and the way they think about their own instructional activities. To others, however, it might well refer to the outcomes of teaching and the behavior that the teachers hope to stimulate in their students. Obviously, once explicated, either approach would be appropriate. However, when both or neither conception of reflective teaching connotes what is in the mind of a particular scholar, then the problems associated with establishing construct validity become insoluble.

What is the difference between a workshop and a seminar? This example presents another kind of problem associated with language that plagues the establishment of construct validity. In fact, a teacher educator might establish a specific kind of instructional activity and call it a workshop if the intended audience is elementary teachers and a seminar if the activity is designed for secondary teachers. Thus, we have a situation where two or more terms can be used to define identical activities. Given this type of problem, it becomes virtually impossible to communicate with precision, unless one develops a standard of long and cumbersome definitions for every term used. Inasmuch as this rarely happens, this problem of language will likely persist, creating the need for ever more vigilance in communication about our research efforts.

The reverse of this linguistic problem also frequently occurs. For example, what is *teacher effectiveness?* Is it characterized by the series of teacher behaviors explicated by Rosenshine and Stevens (1986), or is it those contained in the instructional materials developed by Hunter (1984)? In this instance, we have common language used to connote two totally different and unrelated phenomenon.

Imprecision in language is a special problem associated with the development of construct validity in research on teacher education. By virtue of the fact that research in this area is a new and developing field, the problem is not likely to be resolved in the near future. Thus, it becomes incumbent on researchers to work diligently to improve the precision of their communication and to perhaps become "definers to a fault." The problem will neither be solved soon, nor will it go away.

Other Scholarly Orientations

Although this chapter is focusing on the more contemporary approaches to research on teacher education, the past and future contributions of other scholarly orientations should not be totally ignored. Because much of what transpires in teacher education relates to values and ideology, one cannot ignore the contributions being made in areas such as philosophy, history, and sociology.

It is clear that no *correct* approaches to the training of teachers will ever emerge from either quantitative or qualitative approaches to research in teacher education. Rather, acceptable approaches in the field will emerge from beliefs that people hold concerning how children learn, what should be taught, the role of education in society, and the role of teacher education in the larger enterprise. The necessary discussions will not be held, or at least will not be held efficiently, if sufficient attention is not paid to those scholarly areas that focus on analyzing and understanding the importance and impact of education from a historical, sociological, and philosophical perspective.

Design Considerations for Research in Teacher Education

Given this context, some important guidelines can be developed for the conduct of studies in any of our domains. At a minimum, any study should be accompanied by a fairly detailed analysis of local antecedents that, in the researcher's view, have allowed the phenomena under study to be successful or unsuccessful. The temptation of many researchers is not to do this, however, because a premium is placed on the generalizability of results in the publication of most research literature. In fact, a search of the literature in the domain of *process research*, as we have defined it, shows very little reported in the mainstream literature. Often such studies are seen as having value only at the local level. Teacher educators and those responsible for disseminating research in teacher education must become sensitive to this issue of generalizability. They should begin with the premise that most such studies will not be generalizable but will still have value from the perspective of any research synthesis that might occur in the future. Studies of a local nature should be viewed as case studies from a global prospective, regardless of the methodological approach used. Obviously, the foregoing discussion focuses on the external validity of studies carried out at the local level.

Certain principles of research are universal to any study, regardless of where it falls within our organizational scheme with respect to type of study or type of methodology employed. To avoid redundancy of discussion, it is appropriate at this point to review some of the more salient principles of research design that will then serve as background for the discussion of each general study area.

Much of our analysis regarding research in teacher education, regardless of the area, will focus on the external validity of the studies carried out. Simply stated, external validity refers to the extent to which one can generalize observations or conclusions from one setting to another (even from one cohort group to another cohort group at a single site). Studies conducted in an educational context are often difficult to generalize because of the difficulty of adhering to even the most lenient requirements for external validity. This, of course, is not unique to educational research but is true also for any type of field study.

Specifically, the lack of ability to sample adequately the participants and the interaction of the setting and/or the history of the setting with the intended treatment are impediments to generalization. Studies retain an element of external validity for research synthesis if the setting and history are adequately described. Only if the circumstances under which study is conducted are well understood can one begin to think intelligently about why the results are as they are. If sampling considerations and strict adherence to other design requirements cannot be implemented in a study it must at least be described completely to allow for adequate synthesis, thereby providing a start toward the development of an adequate knowledge base in teacher education.

Internal validity is, of course, another important consideration in the conduct of these studies. Internal validity is important because factors that affect internal validity are those that influence the conclusions that may be drawn from such studies, even at the local level. Regardless of the method of inquiry (*narrative, case study, survey, correlational, causal/experimental*), various factors associated with the subjects and the treatment must be fully described. In particular, it is important to describe the entire history of any intervention through project completion and outcome measurement. Studies that use cross-sectional data bases and that do not focus on interventions per se must provide a clear description of the context leading to the data collection and a clear definition of terms. Rival hypotheses to any treatment effect(s) such as subject maturation, selection, and mortality should also be carefully examined and completely described. In experimental studies, particular attention should be given to the exact nature of experimental and control group differences, in terms of both outcomes and the specific set of treatments used.

It is also important to specify the exact nature of any behavior changes expected or observed when the implementation of a program or program element is the focus of a study. Particularly important to such studies is a thorough definition of the measurement procedures and data collection instruments used. The impression of gains attributable to a particular intervention can be modified considerably with knowledge of how behaviors are measured or recorded. For example, an actual content test of research-based teaching practices is quite different from a self-report of content familiarity on the part of the teacher. Observation of the implementation of such behavior constitutes still another perspective for examining the construct.

Construct validity is of particular importance to teacher education studies if any generalization is to occur through synthesis. In particular, a precise definition of any treatment or process under study is particularly important. Equally important are precise definitions of the variables used to describe interim outcomes of these studies. This would also include a complete description of the subjects (preservice or inservice teachers) who are the focus of the study. Imprecise language in such studies can lead to confusion and conflicting results across studies.

On the surface, it might appear that statistical validation is relevant only to those studies that employ empirical success criteria and focusses on some sort of tangible outcome variable. However, statistical conclusion validity, a concept introduced by Cook and Campbell (1979), actually has many implications for all types of studies, even though statistical techniques are not used. For example, in statistics, the concept of *power* relates to the ability of a statistical test to detect a false null hypothesis (find a real treatment effect). *Power* is directly related to sample size: The larger the sample size, the greater the power. Regardless of whether statistical tests are actually used, one needs to develop some confidence in outcomes and, thus, must insure program or innovation exposure to a reasonable number of participants. A pilot program that focuses on seven or eight students might not be very helpful from this perspective. In addition, investigators of teacher education studies should be concerned with the reliability of the instrumentation used. The conclusions one draws from a study are only as good as the data collected. This is true regardless of how data are collected.

STUDYING ASPECTS OF THE RESEARCH PARADIGM

Having set the stage by providing a brief description of the various elements of our paradigm and a general discussion of methodology and associated concerns, we now turn to a more specific discussion of the nature of research that will likely occur in each domain. Within each of the seven major elements of our paradigm, there are some very special questions that need to be considered about both the nature of the questions asked and the appropriate methodology that needs to be considered. These discussions are next.

Studying Antecedents

As noted previously, antecedent conditions in research on teacher education have been notoriously underdefined. Typically, researchers have focused on personal variables of either teacher education students or their professors. Although helpful, this approach to studying antecedent conditions has limited their importance and has constricted thought in the field concerning the importance of antecedent conditions on the conduct of teacher education. For purposes of this chapter, antecedent conditions are defined as those that have a direct impact on teacher education or that guide or influence the processes of teacher education. Although not including the processes themselves, antecedent can include not only student and faculty characteristics, but also institutional characteristics, state and national legislation and policies, fiscal conditions, and physical environments.

Examples of research on antecedent conditions defined as student and faculty characteristics abound. Although Ryans's (1960) classic work is probably the best known, the Research About Teacher Education (RATE) study (American Association of Colleges for Teacher Education [AACTE], 1987b) is a perfect contemporary example of a study of antecedent factors in regard to both teacher education students and their professors. Ducharme and Agne (1982) have reported in much greater depth concerning the characteristics of school of education faculty members. It would be difficult to find a better example of a study of faculty characteristics as an antecedent factor that most surely influences the conduct of teacher education programs.

Clark and Guba (1976) have devoted a great deal of energy to describing the characteristics of institutions that house teacher education programs. These characteristics include, but are not restricted to, descriptions of work load, professional educational background, salary level, academic productivity, and provide important antecedent characteristics that can and should help form the context for truly understanding teacher education programs.

The American Association of Colleges for Teacher Education annually issues a study of state laws, mandates, and regulations as they affect the conduct of teacher education (AACTE, 1987a). Narrative in nature, this compendium of state regulations provides yet another excellent example of the types of antecedent characteristics that clearly guide or influence teacher education.

Yarger and Mertens (1980) analyzed over 400 teacher-center proposals, comparing the highest rated with the lowest rated. Exploring variables such as level of budget, size of staff, and proposed physical location, this study was, in reality, describing the antecedent conditions under which a federally funded teacher education initiative was going to occur. Although the variables were recognized as important, there was never a follow-up study to attempt to measure the influence these characteristics might have had on the development of programs.

Finally, Peseau and Orr (1979) have, for many years, studied the financial characteristics of schools, colleges, and departments of education. This work examines such characteristics as faculty load, salary, support for summer school, and secretarial support, all within the context of budget allocations. Again, we have examples of a set of important antecedent conditions that cannot help but influence teacher education programs.

The study of antecedent conditions in teacher education is, by definition, descriptive. Consequently, the bulk of the studies of antecedent conditions are either narratives, case studies, or surveys. Virtually all of the examples just presented fall into one of these three categories. Although correlational studies can, and frequently do, use antecedent conditions as one of the variable matrices, they typically correlate these conditions with either process or outcome variables. For example, it would be instructive to know whether a student's age (antecedent) is related to either her or his perception of teacher education program quality (process) or her or his grade point average (outcome). Interestingly, when the analyses are performed, they are typically post hoc in nature, often representing an example of the union of variables of opportunity.

The biggest problem with research on antecedent conditions in teacher education is, with the possible exception of student and faculty personal characteristics, that they simply are not used to provide the important context for more focused inquiry. Part of this problem might be related to the fact that there is no reasonably accepted framework for the conduct of research on antecedent conditions in teacher education. Additionally, because the methodology typically employed is narrative, case study, or survey, this type of research is not as highly valued as it should be. The field of teacher education needs a model of antecedent/contextual variables that precisely describes the conditions under which the enterprise operates and that leads to the tracking of those conditions that influence both the processes and outcomes of programs.

Studies of antecedent conditions in teacher education are often performed for reasons unrelated to the development of a knowledge base. It is not unusual for rather narrow goals to undergird the conduct of this type of research. For example, the Peseau and Orr work concerning fiscal characteristics of schools, colleges, and departments of education mentioned earlier was conducted to provide institutional administrators with comparative financial information that would allow them to lobby more effectively within their institutions for more favorable budget allocations. Although this certainly is a worthwhile goal, it is also suggestive of the problems encountered when no reasonably well explicated and accepted framework exists for the conduct of research on antecedent conditions in teacher education. The importance of antecedent conditions in teacher education has yet to be fully recognized. Until this occurs, the likelihood of examining process and outcome data in the absence of an appropriate analytical context remains.

Studying the Antecedent–Process Link

Study of the antecedent–process link requires investigation of an antecedent condition of teacher education with regard to the process of preparing teachers. Research in this area might address questions of the link between student and/or faculty characteristics and the method in which teacher education programs are implemented. This type of research would be appropriate to explore the effect of state and federal regulations, institutional characteristics, and budget allocations on the actual implementation of teacher education programs. Unfortunately, it is an underdeveloped area in research on teacher education. When examples are found of research exploring the antecedent–process link, the studies tend to be performed with some other goal in mind, only to reveal the antecedent–process link in post hoc analysis. For example, in the Research About Teacher Education study mentioned earlier (AACTE, 1987b), post hoc analysis of the data revealed that, in institutions that do not possess the requirements for research and scholarly productivity one finds in prestigious doctoral institutions, not only does one find fewer refereed publications, but one also finds that professors spend more time both in the classroom and in a field setting. Although crude and nonexplanatory, the fact that lowered levels of pressure for scholarly productivity are linked to more time spent with students both on campus and in elementary and secondary schools is an example of an antecedent–process link. Although we can't know the ultimate effect of that link in this particular instance, there can be no doubt that professors who spend more time with their students in a variety of settings operate differently (process) from the way they otherwise would.

Due to the lack of importance ascribed to antecedent conditions in teacher education programs, there has been insufficient emphasis on this area. A better foundation could be established for the study of teacher education program outcomes if areas such as the effect of state regulations on teacher education processes were better understood. By the same token, it would be equally important to thoroughly understand the effect of fiscal considerations and institutional characteristics on the processes of teacher education. Unfortunately, studies that would illuminate these and similar areas linking antecedent conditions to teacher education processes simply do not exist.

It would be difficult to perform a study exploring the antecedent–process link using a narrative methodology. In this instance, there simply is very little chance that one can establish, in any real and verifiable sense, a link between an antecedent condition and a teacher education program. If sufficient data are available, however, the importance of an antecedent–process link could be studied and explicated in case study form. Survey methodologies are likely to provide a good deal of data that can assist in the establishment of antecedent–process links, with correlational research probably being the most likely methodology of choice for this kind of study.

It would not be outside of the realm of possibility to design causal/experimental studies that would explore the antecedent–process link with more clarity. For example, it would be very helpful to study the impact of physical environment on the actual processes of teacher education. A teacher education program that is field based would be operating in a very different type of environment from one that is housed exclusively on a campus. It is impossible to conceive of this difference in physical setting as neutral in terms of the potential impact on the process of teacher education. This study, however, has never been done. Nor have many others, rendering the antecedent–process link a nearly void cell in research on teacher education.

The problems with studying the antecedent–process link are similar to those associated with investigating antecedent conditions in teacher education. With no conceptual framework to guide researchers in this area, research tends to be unrelated to other aspects of the field, making it difficult to conduct analysis and interpretation. All too often, findings are the result of a post hoc analysis, and they stand isolated from any coherent picture of teacher education.

When antecedent–process links are the result of a post hoc fishing expedition into the data, there is a strong possibility that the results will simply be misleading. For example, if a researcher constructs a 10 by 10 matrix, and orders 45 individual cross-tabulations of antecedent–process variables, the likelihood of some of those variables being significant due to chance alone is very great. If two or three of the 45 correlation coefficients were significant, they are the findings that would likely be highlighted in the literature. With these "significant" correlations constituting only 3 or 4 percent of all those performed, one can speculate that they might, in fact, have occurred merely by chance.

Study of the antecedent–process link is of paramount importance to developing a thorough understanding of teacher education. In fact, making sense of process–outcome research is, to some extent, dependent on understanding the antecedent–process link. This is particularly important if one believes that research should inform the field, leading to productive changes in teacher education programs. It would be one thing to suggest changing a teacher education process simply because teacher educators viewed it as appropriate. It would be quite different, however, if that process were the result of an antecedent condition and, thus, probably more resistant to change. The RATE study that revealed that a more limited demand for scholarly productivity was related to an increase in the amount of time spent with students provides an informative example. It would surely have implications for program developers who wanted to increase the contact between students and faculty, particularly in research-dominated institutions. Although the link is not causal, one can be quite sure that, unless the demand for scholarly productivity were lowered, the contact time between students and faculty would probably not change much.

Studying the Antecedent–Outcome Link

Outcome data are clearly the most valued product of an educational research effort. To many, especially policymakers, the media, and the public, outcome data represent the bottom line in education. All too often, these types of data are gathered without regard to either antecedent conditions or processes,

and they are then used as a report card for educational institutions. The most common example of this can be found when standardized achievement test scores for an identified school, district, or state are released to the media. Quick judgments are made and perceptions are formed without regard for either the conditions or the processes that might have dramatically affected the scores.

In research on teaching, the teacher-effectiveness research provides the best example of outcome data. Although this is not research on teacher education, it exemplifies the generation of outcome data in an attempt to better understand the dynamics of instruction. This line of research has led to a depth of understanding concerning the linkage between teacher behavior and student achievement that otherwise could not have been achieved (Rosenshine & Stevens, 1986).

There has been very little research in teacher education that provides outcome data. When it is found, the outcome data tends to be reported in passive rather than active variables. For example, it is not unusual to find antecedent variables linked with teacher education students' grade point averages or career histories. One typically finds these types of data in follow-up studies of teacher education students. Studies that link antecedent variables to teacher education students' mastery of teaching skills are virtually nonexistent.

The paucity of research linking antecedent conditions to outcomes in teacher education could, in fact, be a blessing. The link is simply not a strong one. Medley provides us with a paradigm that explains this issue quite well (Medley, 1977). Succinctly, it is incumbent upon researchers in teacher education to link antecedent conditions with processes and then to link processes with outcomes. He points out the danger of trying to link antecedent conditions with outcomes. Not only does this strategy ignore the strong likelihood that teacher education programs affect the teaching behavior of students, but it also presents grotesque measurement problems, particularly if one subscribes to the logic of the antecedent–process–outcome continuum (Quirk, 1974).

There is, however, at least one good example of linking antecedent conditions with passive outcome variables. In their study of teachers in North Carolina, Schlecty and Vance (1981) discovered that those teachers with higher SAT scores were more likely to be the ones who abandoned teaching for other careers. Although these data have been questioned because of the novel situation of studying teachers in a single state with a unique organizational structure, they nonetheless cannot be ignored. More importantly, if such a result were pervasive throughout the country, one could still not attribute the fact that certain teachers leave the field of teaching for other careers to the fact that they had higher SAT scores. It would be necessary to explore competing hypotheses, though not necessarily hypotheses that encompassed process factors as a causal condition. Although there is a place for studies that explore the antecedent–outcome link, the results must be interpreted with great care.

The most notable problem in understanding the antecedent–outcome link in education is the lack of research. Although that might be a blessing, it would be better to have some, rather than none, even if such research required very careful interpretation. More importantly, when one does encounter antecedent–outcome research, the outcome data are usually reported in terms of passive behavior (e.g., grade point average, class work) rather than active behavior (e.g., instructional activity). Knowing, for example, that grade point average is not related to success in teaching, though informative, probably raises more questions than it answers.

The most important shortcoming of antecedent–outcome research is that it does not respond to the question of causality. It is difficult to conceive of an experimental design in which antecedent conditions are manipulated in an effort to affect outcome variables. At least it is difficult to conceive of this type of research under the rubric of research in teacher education.

Studying Process

As indicated earlier, *process*, as defined in this chapter, refers to those activities associated with the actual delivery of the teacher education program or, more generally, aspects of how teachers are educated or develop as teachers. As such, research on process is most often focused on particular aspects of a teacher education program and is very applied. Many efforts in this area would be considered evaluation research, necessary for the continuing development and improvement of a teacher education program. Lanier and Little (1986) refer to this type of research as "improvement oriented inquiry," which can be closely identified with the more familiar decision-oriented perspective described by Cronbach and Suppes (1969).

Koehler (1985) found that this category of research comprised the largest body of literature found in the Educational Resources Information Center (ERIC) document retrieval system under teacher education. It is interesting to note that Shulman's (1986) paradigm for studying teaching obscures the role of such inquiry in teacher education by including it as only a very small portion of what he calls research on teacher-training experiences. Much of this category in Shulman's paradigm is dominated by the study of antecedent conditions within teacher training. Shulman's portrayal of process research is not atypical. Even Lanier and Little (1986), in their overview of research in teacher education, do not include process studies as a major category in their "four commonplaces" in teacher education research; the teachers of teacher education students, the students of teacher education, the curriculum of teacher education, and the milieu of teacher education. In the place where one would expect to find research on process, that is, the curriculum, the section focuses more on the antecedents of the curriculum—what content is included, the characteristics of students and faculty, and so on. The lack of attention to process research and its role in the development of a theory or theories of teacher education is curious but, we think, explainable. In short, paradigms for research on teacher education often focus on antecedents and outcomes rather than on process, largely due to the difficulties involved in the external validity of process studies. It is the position here that this *black box* mentality must change if teacher educators expect to dem-

onstrate that some generalizable principles of the education of teaching professionals exist.

Process research, as defined here, focuses solely on the mechanisms used to educate prospective teachers or inservice teachers. The process is the specific intervention that is attempted, and it might or might not be tied to the ultimate goal of teacher education: the production of a better teacher. Process research does not attempt to link this intervention with summative outcomes associated with the act of teaching, but it might link them with interim outcomes. Interim outcomes are those thought to be related to teaching behavior in some fashion, but for which no verified relationship has been established. Examples of interim outcomes include such things as student knowledge of teaching facts or teaching behavior in artificial environments (e.g., microteaching). Thus, some process studies could be thought of as nongeneralizable field studies or experiments, in the sense that a dependent variable exists, although this variable is not considered to be the ultimate goal of the intervention. An interim outcome variable of this sort is not necessary in a process study, however. The overriding concern in this type of research is which processes work best to achieve an interim goal of the teacher education program.

Perhaps the most prevalent type of process study is the narrative report of the conduct or progress of teacher education programs. Such narratives are found quite frequently in the extant literature as descriptions of various attempts at innovation or change within programs. Frequently these narratives are accompanied by loose evaluative data (often perceptually bound and individualistic) regarding the described improvements or changes. Many so-called qualitative studies on specific teacher education programs would fall in this general class as well. For example, ethnographic study of student perceptions as they pass through a teacher education program would provide a narrative that would describe process and prescribe change in the process, but it would be of little value, in isolation, for generalizing beyond the specific set of circumstances addressed in the study (Sears, 1984).

Another useful distinction when considering process studies is that characterized by what we call *dynamic process studies*, versus *static process studies*. Dynamic process studies focus on an actual intervention or planned educational experience for preservice or inservice teachers. Static process studies focus on the development of teaching behaviors, without specific attention to particular interventions. An example of the latter would be Fuller's (1969) work, which focused on, among other things, the survival skills of beginning teachers, in that the most immediate concern of the beginning teacher is survival in the classroom. Only after developing confidence in this survival does the teacher shift attention to predominantly content or curricular concerns.

Guidelines for Conducting Process Studies

Although process studies are typified by the narrative format, quantitative evidence of a particular program component's success or failure may be included. These quantitative results are most frequently in the form of survey (descriptive), correlational, or even experimental studies. The primary focus of Katz and Raths's (1985) framework for research on teacher education described earlier is on process studies and could serve as an organizational schema for such studies. This framework provides a guide to the intersection of various process variables that might be worthy of study within a particular teacher education program and would be conducive to either (or both) qualitative or quantitative investigation. Of even greater importance, if the end to be achieved is generalizable knowledge, is the fact that Katz and Raths's work provides a framework that might be used to guide synthesis of the research literature and generate new research questions. Because most process studies of this sort are characterized by their highly specific nature and lack of generalizability (in most cases even to various cohort groups), such a framework could provide valuable insight into successful and unsuccessful interventions.

In isolation, process studies at the local level do little to help solidify or construct a general theory for teacher education, or even general principles for practice. At best, the narratives provided by descriptive studies of this type help disseminate potential approaches to common problems or experiences in teacher education programs. At the local level, however, studies of this sort can be quite valuable in modifying or reconfiguring certain aspects of a specific teacher education program. The point is that all teacher education programs are rife with nuances that make some processes more effective at some sites than at others.

This is not to say that such studies cannot be useful in the development of a theory or set of theories to guide teacher education. When process studies of similar nature are combined through various research synthesis methods, some generalization can occur, to the extent that experiences are similar across studies. Factors that work against such a strategy are the highly specific nature of most interventions; local process studies cannot often be replicated at a different site due to the specific antecedents at each site. For this reason, antecedent conditions are inextricably linked to process studies, which further points to the importance of studying antecedents. Only after antecedents are well understood can the synthesis of process studies lead to meaningful generalizations.

As might be inferred, we see the primary value of process studies as their contribution to the development of teacher education programs at the local level. Generalizable knowledge from such studies results only through synthesis or combination of these studies. Adequate and meaningful synthesis can occur only if complete description is provided. Even then, only the most global aspects of a theory or theories of teacher education can be extracted.

It seems obvious from this discussion that many process studies are best conducted through a qualitative framework. Often such an approach facilitates the reporting of the situational circumstances that have led to the success or failure of the intervention. This is not to say that quantitative inquiry in process inquiry does not have its place. Clearly, demonstrable effects can be highlighted by precise measurement and the hypothesis-testing approach offered by the latter techniques.

Studying the Process–Outcome Link

Process–outcome studies are distinguished from pure process studies in that the focus of the former is on the link between certain teacher education processes and summative outcomes. A summative outcome is any actual teacher behavior in the classroom that is used as a criterion for performance. As such, various practices and processes in teacher education are linked to teacher outcomes.

Research in this area is fraught with problems. The standard controls and criteria that would ordinarily be expected in process–outcome studies are extremely difficult, if not impossible, to obtain, due to the nature of the teacher education process. Even the design of such a study, which relies heavily on a longitudinal data base, is difficult to implement, in that tracking teachers through a teacher education program (or some aspect thereof) and into a teaching position for some period of time is nearly impossible. Largely due to this problem, many of the studies one can find that focus on the process–outcome link deal with inservice projects in which the participants are captive, the treatment is short, and outcome variables are more easily obtained (e.g., Anderson, Evertson & Brophy, 1979; Good & Grouws, 1981). Dissemination of process–outcome research simply doesn't happen. It is viewed as improvement-oriented inquiry and is seen as having very little value in the overall milieu of teacher education research. In relation to this, Lanier and Little state that "meaningful isolation and control of variables in complex social affairs is rarely, if ever, possible and is not recognized, therefore, as a particularly fruitful line of contemporary inquiry in teacher education" (1986, p. 528).

Often process–outcome studies are conducted as experimental or correlational studies. In addition, many studies of this type are more broadly based than process studies, in that they attempt to look beyond specific teacher education programs. Because of the difficulty of longitudinal study of preservice-to-inservice teachers, such studies often take a reflective perspective, in an attempt to link various preservice practices to current teaching behaviors. Many such efforts focus on student teaching behavior, which could arguably be considered an interim outcome, to the extent that student teaching behavior and actual classroom behavior are not linked. Examples of such studies include those of Tabachnik, Popkewitz, and Zeichner (1979) and Zeichner and Tabachnik (1982), which focus on how university and supervisory staff affected what was learned in field experience.

As with process studies, the issue of variable definition becomes an important consideration in the report of process–outcome studies. A linking study that attempts to report the subject-matter content exposure to teaching effectiveness for secondary teachers must include specific definitions of what is meant by the constructs involved. For example, how is content exposure defined? Is it a question of depth or breadth? In addition, what is meant by teaching effectiveness? It is not the intent of this chapter to discuss the variety of outcome criteria that may be used in studying such phenomena, but it is important that the criteria be fully described. These definitions are quite important in that, once a link (or lack thereof) has been established, one needs to know the exact nature of the link for the knowledge to be meaningfully integrated into a larger picture for teacher education.

A particularly critical issue in the consideration of process–outcome studies is the establishment of causal relationships between the variables under study. In such studies, it is often tacitly assumed that any discovered relationship is causal. For example, a study that has established that fieldwork time during preservice education is positively related to more effective classroom management practices might include the inference that, therefore, more fieldwork experience is desirable to achieve this end. Without appropriate controls and causal models to follow, such inferences could be invalid.

Perhaps the most frequent types of process-outcome studies are those that rely heavily on correlational evidence. Examination of the relationship between a teacher's preservice educational experience (process) and classroom performance is an example. Often such studies do not focus on one particular intervention but examine variation in a preservice variable, such as exposure to research on teaching, as it relates to actual classroom performance.

Studies that take on a more local flavor might examine, from a quasi-experimental perspective, specific treatments in teacher education and the their impact on the behavior of future teachers. For example, Keislar, Fenstermacher, Thayer, and Friedman (1977) examine the effects of various preservice treatments on future classroom behaviors. To conduct such a study, one needs a sizable program, so that adequate treatment groups can be formed. In addition, as with process studies, all conditions must be adequately described.

Studying the Antecedent–Process–Outcome Link

Most linking studies in teacher education would fall into one of the former classes because they involve only a single link. However, linking studies that involve summative outcomes, but only a single link, are weak in the sense that any inferences and/or conclusions drawn from such studies must make extremely strong assumptions. For example, process–outcome studies assume that antecedent conditions play no role or have no direct effect on outcomes (or process if the process is to be generalized). Antecedent–outcome studies assume a black box posture, in that it is assumed that process has no direct link. This is not to say that studies involving a single link are not valuable. To say, for example, that student SAT scores are related to future teacher performance has important policy implications. But certainly such a statement is an overgeneralization, as there are certainly counterexamples. If processes were carefully considered in such an antecedent–outcome study, the place of the counterexamples in a theory of teacher education would likely become more clear.

Regardless, the type of study that would probably have the greatest impact on the development of a theory or set of theories for teacher education is that which would involve a double link among antecedents, processes, and outcomes. In this sense, the antecedents add a covariate to process–outcome studies and recognize that process–outcome relationships are dependent upon inputs. Also, the addition of process to the antecedent–outcome linking study recognizes that teacher ed-

ucation is not a black box and that contradictory findings in such studies can quite likely be traced to alternate processes. Through such an approach, stronger statistical techniques such as path analysis or other causal modeling techniques could be applied to provide a more complete picture of the influences of various characteristics and experiences on teaching ability. Antecedent–process–outcome studies are the *trait-treatment interaction* studies of teacher education. They are necessary to complete understanding of the phenomena under study.

Antecedent–process–outcome studies appear to have significant advantages over single linking studies, but they are clearly exponentially more difficult to implement and analyze than their single-dimension counterparts. This is particularly true when preservice teacher education is the focus. Such studies would require a carefully constructed longitudinal data set to trace the direct and indirect effects of antecedents and process on outcome behavior. Studies of this sort in inservice teacher education are more easily implemented if antecedents are viewed as immediate pre-intervention teacher behaviors. Because of these demands, it is unlikely that antecedent–process–outcome studies will ever dominate the research literature on preservice or beginning teacher education.

The conceptualization of such studies is, perhaps, more important than their implementation, however. That a researcher in teacher education recognizes that the results of a process–outcome study might be highly dependent on antecedents, even if they were not measured, places both the researcher and the consumers of the research in a better position to draw valid inferences from such a study and to place the results of the study more appropriately into the developing solution of a theory (or theories) of teacher education.

Multidimensional studies are subject to the same methodological concerns mentioned earlier for studies involving single links. Most of these studies will be correlational in nature and will not involve a control group or any other normative information. However, methodological developments in path analysis and related techniques can allow these types of studies to take a significant place in the definition of our theories of teacher education.

PUTTING THE PIECES TOGETHER

Rather than trying to prescribe a specific research agenda for teacher education, it is our intent to recommend ways of moving toward a coherent approach to studying teacher education. Our assumption is that, with some coherency in our approach to studying the field, principles or theoretical perspectives will emerge and this will, at some future time, lead to a rational research agenda for teacher education. In the absence of this developmental perspective, the most we can hope for is sporadic work of varying quality, linked together only by the insightfulness of individual researchers and synthesizers.

Summary of Important Highlights

A major point that we have made is that it is imperative that researchers in teacher education pay much more close attention to antecedent conditions in the future than they have in the past. By *antecedents*, we refer to those conditions and variables that affect teacher education, that, while not directly related to process, influence, guide, and even direct that process. In addition to the personal characteristics typically studied, focus on antecedent factors should include such things as the physical setting for a teacher education program, the structure of the school or college in which the program occurs, the legislative context, the autonomy of institutions from external constraints, federal and state mandates, budget allocations, and accreditation concerns.

Individual process studies frequently lack value because relevant antecedent conditions have not been thoroughly catalogued and accurately described. It is only when this occurs that these factors can be linked to the processes under investigation. It is then much more likely that researchers can consider an array of antecedent–process studies and begin to make sense of their meaning. In the absence of this very important linkage, the prospects for moving forward in research in teacher education are quite limited.

Another major point that we have made is that teacher education researchers have a tendency to talk past each other. This imprecision in language has plagued all aspects of educational research for many years, but, due to the underdeveloped nature of the field of research on teacher education, it is currently a greater problem than in many other areas. It is not uncommon for researchers in the field to use the same word or words to mean very different things. By the same token, an identical phenomenon has often been described by two or more labels. Further, except in the most well-developed research projects, important terms are often not defined well enough to permit precise understanding, hence replication. Because of the developmental nature of the field of research on teacher education, researchers must choose their terms carefully, define them fully, and communicate them accurately. Although not insurmountable, this problem of precision in language is likely to be a thorn in the side of research on teacher education for many years to come.

Another major factor inhibiting the development of a framework for study in teacher education is the lack of external validity in most process studies. It has already been noted that probably one reason there is not an abundance of literature on process studies is that reviewers tend to perceive them as relevant only to the local site where the study is performed. Yet it is likely that, if sufficient information were available, particularly in the area of antecedent conditions, some sense could be made of the seemingly large volume of studies in the dissertation and fugitive literature. This is essentially a problem of external validation. The type of synthesis that could occur, possibly in the form of a metastudy, would add immeasurably to the teacher education literature, perhaps paving the way for the development of coherent principles and/or theoretical perspectives. The issue of external validation of research in teacher education cannot be underestimated. Until this problem is confronted, the field is destined to be the benefactor of a largely uncoordinated and incoherent body of research.

Another important point made in this chapter relates to the importance of methodological fit as one goes about designing studies in teacher education. Not only is it crucial that the selected methodology fit the question, but it is also important that the researcher carefully study the paradigm presented in this chapter and fit the methodology to the type of study being performed. As pointed out earlier, it is not necessary to take a firm or restricted position concerning one's research orientation in order to make important inquiries into this very complex field. Rather, it is important to ascertain whether or not the questions being asked and the quality of results being sought are consistent with the specific research methodology being employed. Special consideration given to this problem in the research effort will clearly lead to more coherent and interpretable research results.

Toward Creating a Research Agenda

Because we have elected not to provide a complete research agenda for teacher education, it becomes incumbent on us to at least provide some thoughtful direction. Much of what has been presented in this chapter could be interpreted as suggesting that we believe the field of research in teacher education is in a state of terminal disarray. Actually, nothing could be further from the truth. We believe that the field of research in teacher education is in its infancy, having been born only a few short years ago. In fact, an amazing amount of progress has already been made. It is in the spirit of tackling an exciting future that we conclude this chapter with a few, we hope, logical and certainly important suggestions.

Researchers in teacher education must consider all aspects of the antecedent–process–outcome paradigm each time a research project is planned and implemented. Only by using this framework as a set of conceptual constraints can we avoid the folly of survey research, for example, isolating antecedents that are not linked to anything. Research on antecedent conditions, although important, loses the greater part of its value if not studied in relation to some teacher education process. At the same time, process studies not linked to antecedents suffer the fate of being viewed as important only at the local sites where the studies are performed. Although few would contend that any individual process study is, in and of itself, generalizable to a larger population, at the same time few would deny that, if the appropriate linkages are made with relevant antecedent conditions, a body of research can grow.

Antecedent–outcome studies run the risk not only of being misleading, but also of implicitly assuming that teacher education processes are not accountable for program outcomes. As odd as this sounds, the claim has been made too often, suggesting, for example, that students with certain types of backgrounds or test scores either should or should not be allowed to enter programs. This black box mentality concerning teacher education processes not only denigrates the field but also severely limits the ability of researchers to understand the richness of teacher education programs.

Finally, outcome studies, presented in isolation, are almost surely going to mislead the consumer. Unfortunately, the consumer is too often a newspaper reporter, a public official, a state bureaucrat, or a higher education administrator. Unfortunately, education in general has a long and sad history of using outcome studies to make improper judgments concerning educational programs. Teacher education is in no position to be an exception to this case.

We are not claiming that all studies must be of the antecedent–process–outcome variety. Rather, we are urging researchers to use the paradigm as a context and place their particular work in perspective, to describe it thoroughly and accurately, and to make only the appropriate claims for its value. This adherence to considering all aspects of the paradigm should, in the final analysis, lead to the proliferation of more and more linked studies and, eventually, to the development of important antecedent–process–outcome bodies of literature.

Obviously, each element of the paradigm might not have equal value, particularly in a single study. As we have pointed out, antecedent conditions are really only important when they are linked to processes. These links are what we consider the basic foundation for research in teacher education. Antecedents in isolation are of little value and process studies in isolation are not typically reported. Antecedent–process studies, however, are the key to creating a body of knowledge that

should lead to the development of important principles and theoretical perspectives concerning teacher education.

Finally, and only based on this foundation, does the notion of outcome studies become sensible. Process–outcome studies born from a thorough understanding of the antecedent conditions will provide future researchers with the necessary raw materials to conceive of theoretical positions and to take important steps to validate their hunches. Outcome studies, at this point, become not only comprehensible and important but also crucial. Outcome studies that are linked to processes and then to antecedent conditions become the bottom line of research on teacher education.

We are hopeful! We have watched significant growth in the field of research on teacher education in the last few years, and we sense a readiness for major efforts to occur. If research on teacher education can grow in the same way that research on teaching and learning has grown in the 1970s and 1980s, our optimism will be justified. We hope that this chapter will be helpful in that process.

References

American Association of Colleges for Teacher Education. (1987a). *Teacher education in the states: 50-state survey of legislative and adminstrative actions.* Washington, DC: Author.

American Association of Colleges for Teacher Education. (1987b). *Teaching teachers: Facts and figures.* Washington, DC: Author.

Anderson, L. M., Evertson, C. M., & Brophy, J. E. (1979). An experimental study of effective teaching in first-grade reading groups. *Elementary School Journal, 79*(4), 193–223.

Champion, R. H. (1984). Going beyond lists of research findings: The next challenge to teacher education. *Action in Teacher Education, 6*(1–2), 85–92.

Clark, D. L., & Guba, E. (1976). *Institutional self reports on knowledge production and utilization in schools, colleges, and departments of education* (RITE Occasional Paper Series). Bloomington, IN: Indiana University.

Cook, T., & Campbell, D. (1979). *Quasi-Experimentation: Design and analysis issues for field settings.* Chicago: Rand McNally.

Cronbach, L. J., & Suppes, P. (Eds.). (1969). *Research for tomorrow's schools: Disciplined inquiry for education.* New York: Macmillan.

Ducharme, E. R., & Agne, R. M. (1982). The education professoriate: A research-based perspective. *Journal of Teacher Education, 33*(6), 30–36.

Fuller, F. F. (1969). Concerns of teachers: A developmental conceptualization. *American Educational Research Journal, 6*(2), 207–226.

Glass, G. V., McGaw, B., & Smith, M. L. (1981). *Meta-Analysis in social research.* Beverly Hills, CA: Sage.

Good, T., & Grouws, D. (1981). *Experimental research in secondary mathematics classrooms: Working with teachers* (Final Report). Columbia: University of Missouri. (ERIC Document Reproduction Service No. 219 261)

Holmes Group. (1986). *Tomorrow's teachers.* East Lansing, MI: Author.

Hughes, D. (1973). An experimental investigation of the effects of pupil responding and teacher reacting on pupil achievement. *American Educational Research Journal, 10*(1), 21–37.

Hunter, M. (1984). Using what we know about teaching. In P. L. Hosford (Ed.), *Knowing, teaching and supervising.* Reston, VA: Association for Supervision and Curriculum Development.

Katz, L. G., & Raths, J. D. (1985). A framework for research on teacher education programs. *Journal of Teacher Education, 36*(6), 9–15.

Keislar, E., Fenstermacher, G., Thayer, G., & Friedman, A. (1977). The use of affective outcomes in evaluating a differentiated program of teacher education. *California Journal of Teacher Education, 3*(4), 72–93.

Koehler, V. (1985). Research on preservice teacher education. *Journal of Teacher Education, 36*(1), 23–30.

Lanier, J. E., & Little, J. W. (1986). Research on Teacher Education. In M. C. Wittrock (Ed.), *Handbook of research on teaching* (3rd ed., pp. 527–569). New York: Macmillan.

Lortie, D. (1975). *Schoolteacher: A sociological study.* Chicago: University of Chicago Press.

McDonald, F., & Elias, P. (1976). *Executive summary report: Beginning teacher evaluation study, Phase II.* Princeton: Educational Testing Service.

Medley, D. M. (1977). *Teacher competence and teacher effectiveness: A review of process–product research.* Washington, DC: American Association of Colleges for Teacher Education. (ERIC Document Reproduction Service No. ED 143 629)

Nuthall, G., & Church, J. (1973). Experimental studies of teaching behavior. In G. Chanan (Ed.), *Toward a science of teaching.* London: National Foundation for Educational Research.

Peseau, B. A., & Orr, P. G. (1979). *An academic and financial study of teacher education programs through the doctoral level in public state universities and land grant colleges.* Tuscaloosa, AL: University of Alabama, College of Education.

Quirk, T. J. (1974). Some measurement issues in competency-based teacher education. *Phi Delta Kappan, 55*(5), 316–319.

Rosenshine, B., & Stevens, R. (1986). Teaching functions. In M. C. Wittrock (Ed.), *Handbook of research on teaching* (3rd ed., pp. 376–391). New York: Macmillan.

Ryan, K. (1979). Mainstreaming and teacher education: The last straw. In M. C. Reynolds (Ed.), *A common body of knowledge for teachers.* Minneapolis: University of Minnesota National Support Systems Project.

Ryans, D. G. (1960). *Characteristics of teachers*. Washington, DC: American Council on Education.

Schlecty, P. C., & Vance, V. S. (1981). Do academically able teachers leave education? The North Carolina case. *Phi Delta Kappan*, 63(2), 106–112.

Sears, J. T. (1984). *A critical ethnography of teacher education programs at Indiana University: An inquiry into the perceptions of students and faculty regarding quality and effectiveness*. Unpublished doctoral dissertation, Indiana University.

Shulman, L. S. (1986). Paradigms and research programs in the study of teaching: A contemporary perspective. In M. C. Wittrock (Ed.), *Handbook of research on teaching* (3rd ed., pp. 3–36). New York: Macmillan.

Soar, R. (1968). Optimum pupil–teacher interaction for pupil growth. *Educational Leadership*, 26, 275–280.

Soar, R. (1977). An integration of findings from four studies of teacher effectiveness. In G. Borich & K. Fenton (Eds.), *The appraisal of teaching: Concepts and process*. Reading, MA: Addison-Wesley.

Soar, R., & Soar, R. (1979). Emotional climate and management. In P. Peterson & H. Walberg (Eds.), *Research on teaching: Concepts, findings and implications*. Berkeley, CA: McCutchan.

Tabachnik, B. R., Popkewitz, T. S., & Zeichner, K. M. (1979). Teacher education and the professional perspectives of student teachers. *Interchange*, 10(4), 12–29.

Wright, C., & Nuthall, G. (1970). Relationships between teacher behaviors and pupil achievement in three experimental elementary science lessons. *American Educational Research Journal*, 7(4), 477–491.

Yarger, S. J., & Galluzzo, G. R. (1983). Toward solving the dilemmas of research on inservice teacher education. In K. R. Howey & W. E. Gardner (Eds.), *The education of teachers: A look ahead*. New York: Longman.

Yarger, S. J., & Mertens, S. K. (1980). *A content analysis of the first Teacher Center program proposals*. Washington, DC: ERIC Clearinghouse on Teacher Education (ERIC Document Reproduction Service No. SP 015 397).

Zeichner, K., & Tabachnik, B. (1982). The belief systems of university supervisors in the elementary student teaching program. *Journal of Education for Teaching*, 8(1), 34–54.

·3·

PHILOSOPHICAL INQUIRY IN TEACHER EDUCATION

Robert E. Floden and Margret Buchmann
MICHIGAN STATE UNIVERSITY

> Philosophical discussion is the bringing out of latent opposing forces, like arriving at a decision and not like learning what is behind a closed door or whether $235 \times 6 = 1420$. (Wisdom, 1969, p. 181)

No sharp boundary separates philosophical inquiry in teacher education from other forms of inquiry. Studies that make prominent use of philosophical methods also often draw on other branches of inquiry and knowledge such as the social sciences and common sense. Because writers seldom alert readers to all the types of inquiry or knowledge they draw on, and because much of philosophical method is a refined version of reasoning that all people do, the philosophical component of a study often goes unnoticed. If philosophical dimensions of inquiry remain unnoticed, they are less likely to be critically examined by readers, or improved by writers.

In this chapter, attention is called to philosophical inquiry in writings by both philosophers and nonphilosophers. Examples illustrate philosophical activities such as conceptual and logical analysis, positing and explaining distinctions, evoking shared ideas and values, as well as showing that philosophy plays an important part in arguments not obviously philosophical. Commentary included here on these examples clarifies ways in which people can be moved to do philosophical inquiry, how such inquiry can be carried out, and how its quality can be judged.

A few articles or chapters have appeared in which professional philosophers have written about teacher education as philosophers. Most of these will be discussed, but wider boundaries will be drawn around philosophical inquiry in teacher education to include works by nonphilosophers that contain a significant philosophical component. This chapter is not, however, a comprehensive review of this very broadly defined domain. It is too large to cover thoroughly and too difficult to locate precisely. Because it includes work on a great variety of subjects, standard bibliographic search methods are not of much help. It is possible to identify sets of papers on topics likely to include philosophical inquiry (e.g., work on program purposes), but many of these do not include much philosophical inquiry, and much other work would still be left out. Therefore, only selected papers by nonphilosophers are included, chosen because they provide good examples of the philosophical activities discussed. Analyses of

This work was sponsored in part by the National Center for Research on Teacher Education (NCRTE), College of Education, Michigan State University. The NCRTE is funded primarily by the Office of Educational Research and Improvement, United States Department of Education. The work of the second author was also supported in part by the Institute for Research on Teaching, College of Education, Michigan State University. The opinions expressed in this paper do not necessarily represent the position, policy, or endorsement of any of these sponsors.

David Cohen, Paul Hirst, C. J. B. Macmillan, D. C. Phillips, John Sikula, and Karen Zumwalt provided helpful and, fortunately, consistent comments on an earlier draft, which led to substantial changes in the chapter. Nancy Wiemers provided assistance in locating and selecting literature. We are responsible for all remaining unclarities and errors of fact and judgment.

educational research in its relations to teaching and teacher education are a notable omission. (See, e.g., Buchmann, 1984a; Floden, 1985; Zumwalt, 1982.)

Like any inquiry, philosophical inquiry depends for its quality on aspects of substance as well as method. Indeed, no amount or degree of skill in analysis, for instance, can make up for paucity, thinness, or irrelevance of ideas and questions. Although one can, to some extent, prepare people in the use of methods, it is much less clear how the substantive quality of analyses and proposals might be assured or improved. Recollection and reinterpretation might play at least as important a role in this as invention. In their different ways, most of the essays and chapters discussed remind one of systems and traditions of thought: by drawing attention to the meaning of concepts used in everyday life, by evoking shared ideas and beliefs in human goods, and by renewing connections with works of literature and the philosophy of John Dewey.

HOW PHILOSOPHICAL INQUIRY DIFFERS FROM OTHER FORMS OF INQUIRY

Philosophy is a field whose domain has been gradually narrowed as more and more of its areas broke off into independent disciplines. The natural sciences separated early; the separation of philosophy from psychology is only about a century old. Still, boundaries remain blurred because most disciplines, as well as professions, admit to at least a foundational philosophical component that includes conceptual clarification and ethics. The farther reaches of quantum mechanics could be considered as much philosophy as physics; cognitive science explicitly reunites psychology and philosophy, with the addition of computer science. Similarly, a course on the history of educational thought might easily be classed as a history of educational philosophy. Curriculum theory builds on philosophical categorizations of types of knowledge and the purposes of education.

Despite this blurring of boundaries, two types of work in teacher education seem clearly philosophical. The first is inquiry addressed to normative questions including both specific questions about right and wrong (e.g., Is it right to use physical punishment in schools?) and general questions about the goods teacher education is supposed to advance or its aims (e.g., Should teacher education prepare teachers to change "the system," or to work effectively in existing schools?). Such inquiry often works by reminding people of what they already have in mind, of shared values and ideas, either by analyses of concepts in ordinary language or by reference to texts that are part of a tradition.

To be sure, attempts to answer normative questions often include nonphilosophical inquiry (e.g., finding out what the system is); and they depend for their point, at least in part, on aspects of reality requiring understanding or change (e.g., legality and occurrence of physical punishment in schools). Because philosophical inquiry in teacher education bears on the nested social practices of schooling and teaching teachers, it typically concerns questions that mix facts and values.

A second type of work is inquiry that critically examines the assumptions and logic of some aspect of teacher education thought and practice. One might, for example, go through a recent commission report on teacher education, trying to sort out the arguments (or lack of arguments) behind the report's conclusions, their grounding in facts or reason, their compatibility or incompatibility with one another, and their implicit assumptions. By considering the justification and logic of claims, philosophical inquiry makes a reasoned assessment possible. Likewise, a prevalent practice such as giving teachers field experience might be examined, with one eye to its underlying assumptions and its likely effects and the extent to which these assumptions and consequences are defensible (see, e.g., Feiman-Nemser & Buchmann, 1985; Zeichner, 1980).

Different activities and kinds of background knowledge are required for such analyses. First, philosophical inquiry often relies on analyses of language or concepts. Inquiry focuses on terms that seem to play an important role in an argument or practice, trying to answer the question, What do these words or phrases mean or entail? An answer is not found simply by consulting a dictionary, though the definitions and contexts of usage listed in a good dictionary are often a fruitful starting place.

From that starting place, the inquiry proceeds to examine linguistic intuitions about the term and its associations and implications, then looks at how the term seems to be used in the context of interest and at what that usage suggests for thought and practice. In teacher education, the term *liberal education*, for example, has been a fertile ground for philosophical debate. *Teaching* and *education* are concepts to which philosophers of education have devoted numerous articles and professional meetings. In the following, conceptual analysis will be illustrated with an example from the work of John Wilson.

A second, not unrelated, activity consists of examining the logic and assumptions of an argument, policy, or practice. The basic approach is to identify what might be considered the conclusion of an argument, leading to a principle or practice, then to attempt a reconstruction of that argument, sticking as closely as possible to its presuppositions and the reasons provided by the author, policy maker, or practitioner. These reasons and their connections can then be critically examined, with special attention to logical flaws and the assumptions that might be called into question. Again, assumptions and reasons can bear on facts and values, involving statements about the world and ideas about what is desirable or right. The result of this inquiry might be presented as a critique, a new argument, or a practical proposal; each may refer to the inadequacies of competing lines of thought or practice. A clear example here is Scheffler's (1968) essay on the contributions of theoretical studies of education to the preparation of teachers.

Background knowledge is also important. It concerns both knowledge of the real world—of practices, institutions, policies, and proposals, as well as of their probable or observed consequences—and philosophical and other kinds of literacy. Like all inquiry, philosophical inquiry often works by recognizing the similarities between problems or ideas and exploring how previous understandings might shed light on a current question or situation. Particular situations might be new, but ways to think them through could be strongly suggested by earlier discussions or texts. For instance, proposals for research utilization in teacher education and teaching might be a recent phenomenon. Yet Dewey's critique of a narrow, performance-oriented preparation for teachers, developed from a reasoned conception of the purposes of practice in teaching teachers, dates back to the beginning of the century and can be readily applied to current practices and policies.

The philosophical activities of inquiry into human goods, appeals to shared beliefs, conceptual clarification, criticism of arguments, and establishment of distinctions and category systems are part of all academic fields and everyday life. These activities respond to and express the human need for understanding objects, concepts, and events, and for realizing ideals. Thoughtful politicians might go to some pains to understand exactly what they commit themselves to when they promise not to raise taxes. Did the context make clear that they were only referring to income tax? Is the eliminating of a deduction raising taxes or merely closing loopholes? The patient listening to a doctor's authoritative recommendation for surgery might have the presence of mind to probe the logic that led to the conclusion and the assumptions that the doctor made about how risks should be weighed or how to balance length and quality of life.

Hence, unlike statistical analysis or electrical engineering, philosophical inquiry is not the province of experts. All people ask philosophical questions like, What is the good of this? How do you know? What do you mean? All people practice philosophical inquiry until they have reached *some* clarity or are overtaken by the need to act. "Philosophy is not a body of privileged knowledge, nor a creed, nor a special mode of insight or expertise. . . . It is not an esoteric undertaking, concerned with the solution of logical puzzles mainly or with dramatizing the pathos of life, the anguish, or the despair" (Greene, 1981, p. 34). Philosophical questions "are complex but *informally* complex, like the dilemmas and difficulties of ordinary life and not like problems that yield to well-disciplined formal thought or well-directed observation or experiment" (Bambrough, 1986, p. 65). Philosophical amateurs might not be aware of historical lines of argument, but they often have a clear grasp of the practical contexts that generate philosophical questions and in which some specific resolution must operate.

Philosophical inquiry in teacher education attempts to address informally complex questions by considered reasoning, which appeals to shared ideas and can incorporate empirical evidence, by careful argument, and by analysis or establishment of distinctions in fact or language. Although implying or presenting some substantive position, its mark is also an attitude that acknowledges (in principle, if not always in practice) that no case is immune to challenge.

In the following sections, several articles, chapters, and monographs will be considered in groupings organized according to the role occupied by philosophical activities. In the first set, inquiry is primarily or exclusively philosophical, relying on either linguistic analysis or critical examination of a conclusion or recommendation. In the second set, philosophical inquiry is integrated with empirical claims, so that strengths and weaknesses of the work depend on both the philosophical component and the grounds for assertions about the real world.

In the third set, authors invoke philosophical and other kinds of background knowledge, reminding people of the insights of others (e.g., Dewey) and of shared ideals in the course of making a plea for action. These authors also include empirical claims in their arguments. In the final set, authors establish distinctions, sorting out components of a concept like teacher knowledge (with supposed implications for teaching teachers) or proposing different ways of looking at a practice like giving novices field experience (with different associated goals and likely consequences).

Commentary provided in this chapter points out what it is that the authors seem to be doing and provides some assessment of how well that is being done. These discussions should be helpful in showing what arguments can be mustered on some question in teacher education, how those arguments differ from one another, what they could accomplish, and how they might be examined. The purpose is to increase insight into, and use of, philosophical dimensions of research on teacher education.

PURE PHILOSOPHICAL ANALYSIS

Unpacking the Concept of Teacher Education

John Wilson is a professional philosopher of education who has made frequent use of linguistic analysis to argue for educational practices. When examining the question of what teacher educators ought to do (Wilson, 1975), he asks, What do we mean by *teacher education*? The use of these words, Wilson argues, commits people to some courses of action in preparing teachers and rules out others. The meaning, or logic, of the concepts used provides guidance for action and seeing the world, provided people stop and think what they mean when the talk about doing teacher education.

Wilson's method is a large part of his message; and he associates that method not with academic scholarship and technical language, but with common sense and seriousness, traits that all people are capable of developing. He claims, moreover, that everyday language, with its embedded distinctions, is a "repository" of human interests:

We do in fact have quite a sophisticated "ordinary language." . . . Much of the clarity we need is *already enshrined* in our language, if only we will take its terms and distinctions seriously: it represents important interests and concerns which it has been evolved to describe and identify. . . . The position in education, or indeed the study of human beings generally, is not that we are already quite clear about distinctions made in ordinary language and can move on to new ground: it is rather that we are not clear—not, at least, consciously and explicitly clear—about the concepts and distinctions we already have. (p. 177)

Wilson points out that there is ambiguity already in the term *teacher education*. It can mean the education of teachers *as* teachers or the general education of people who also happen to be teachers; thus he suggests the term *teacher preparation*. Still he thinks that one cannot help bringing in the concept of education, for it is reasonable to assume that teachers are prepared with a view to their purveying education to children, which is the distinctive point of their work. Education can be conceived of plainly as people learning things, with the proviso that the result is an improvement in their state of mind, such as greater rationality and less prejudice or ignorance.

Saying that the class of benefits or goods associated with education has to do with increasing knowledge and understanding is stating the obvious. This reminder, however, helps people to be clear about the crucially important distinction between those goods and ends that are properly educational and those that are related to heterogeneous other agendas such as personal well-being, economic welfare, or social progress. Failure to make this distinction badly serves both educational and other ends. Perhaps the most likely thing to happen is that political or social interests come to dominate educational ones.

In practice, Wilson argues, the question is quite simply *how we view the child*; to be interested in education, he emphasizes, is to view that child, "primarily as a *learner*: to have in mind the process and benefits of learning and understanding and knowledge themselves, rather than other goods—whether or not some of these other goods may be, indirectly, achieved by learning" (p. 44).

The point is not to discredit or disregard more far-flung social and political agendas but to establish some solid conceptual ground for discussing teacher preparation by distinguishing such agendas from the purpose built into the word *teacher*:

It is not conceptually part of "being a teacher" to improve pupils' social or economic chances nor to ensure that they are qualified in various ways to enter various jobs or institutions nor to alter their home background, physical condition, or relationship to "society" nor to dispense particular "social values." (pp. 105–106)

Unless educators are clear about the point of teaching, Wilson warns, they will remain hopelessly muddled. Conversely, identification of the conceptual core of being a teacher provides some well-grounded guidance for teacher education.

In making sense of teacher preparation, one cannot derive its conceptual core from the concept of teaching itself. *Teaching*, which is something everyone does some of the time, is not the same as *being a teacher*. There are other and broader conceptual concerns that come into the picture, for being a teacher entails people (teachers) working in organizations (schools) with other people (pupils) to get these other people to learn something (to be educated). The job of "seeing to it that other people learn things" can, furthermore, be accomplished not only by teaching but also by motivating people or giving them learning materials.

Proceeding to sort out what being a teacher logically requires, Wilson attempts a taxonomy of characteristics that is straightforward, though by no means trivial. The concept of being a teacher entails that people acquire these characteristics to be teachers, though it does not follow that they must be part of formal preparation.

First, there is knowledge of the subject matter. A teacher must be "inside" his or her subject to see to the learning of others:

He must "know his subject" in a way that is most useful for the learning of his pupils; and whilst of course this will usually include possessing a good deal of relevant *information*, we should more naturally stress the idea of having a clear understanding of what it is to make progress in the subject—the type of reasoning involved, its logical structure, the marks of "a good historian" (scientist, mathematician, etc.), and so forth. (p. 111)

Educating others also involves, according to Wilson, displaying and dispensing a serious caring about one's subject. Subject-matter knowledge alone does not suffice for teachers, who are in the business of improving *people*. In other words, the teachers must not only know mathematics or history but also be committed to those forms and pursuits of understanding and get others to share that commitment. This interactional component of what teachers do also presupposes some knowledge of people; and, in general, teaching as getting others to learn requires capacities for personal understanding and dealing with people. It is unlikely that either commitment to one's teaching subjects or knowledge of people can be acquired solely by training; hence the need for teachers to be *educated* follows from all three characteristics that they have to acquire to do their work.

Does the vital practical job of teaching, however, require knowing educational theory or educational research? Wilson maintains that this depends on whether such knowledge, in its given state, focus, or mode of instructional use, helps teachers to be more educated. If it is not sound and related to being a teacher and does not rise above the level of common sense or, worse, obfuscates natural understanding (as a basis for seriousness), such knowledge should be dismissed.

Can the three central characteristics in respect to which teachers need to be prepared by education be acquired through practice in schools? Because teachers cannot "copy" a master teacher's subject knowledge but must acquire it themselves, nor be "apprenticed" to seriousness, nor "imitate" an understanding of people, the answer is clear: Practice is no solution to the problems of teacher preparation either. Although actually being in a classroom does foster the development of the necessary know-how and contextual knowledge, teaching practice in itself does not address the primary educational needs of teachers.

In considering the curriculum of teacher preparation, Wilson concludes, it is not the supposed relation of theory and practice or the allocation of time to either domain, but the development of people who are serious and conceptually alert to educational ideas and practices, that is the problem. Issues of content and modes of teacher learning can be decided after clarifying the prior questions: "What sophisticated *ways of looking at people learning* can we initiate intending teachers into?" or "In what ways can we sharpen their perceptions and understanding for the dispensation of learning (education)?" (p. 127). Wilson's argument illustrates the potential that conceptual analysis contains for employing implicit understandings of the words already used to provide guidance for thought and action. If people say they want to prepare teachers for their work and mean it, then a careful examination of what education means can be revealing. Wilson argues that teacher preparation centrally means getting people to know their subjects and to care about them, to be serious and conceptually alert. And he maintains that the acquisition of these characteristics requires education, rather than training or classroom practice.

These conclusions are reasonably specific and are significantly different from what happens in much of teacher education practice.

One must note, however, that Wilson relies on his own linguistic intuitions to guide him. He has not interviewed teacher educators to find out what they mean. Some common meaning seems reasonable to assume. Lacking it, communication would be difficult. It is less clear how much meaning is shared and whether meanings of specific terms undergirding Wilson's analysis (*knowledge, education*) are stable across time and space. The ambiguity of terms such as *education* might function to allow for superficial agreement about difficult issues, so that people can proceed to act without having to settle all differences in advance. The fact that people can do things vastly different from Wilson's proposals, yet still argue that what they are doing is teacher education, suggests conceptual differences and instabilities in meaning.

The history of science, and of general and professional education, would certainly support the contention that there are multiple meanings, as well as changes of meaning. Concepts also vary across languages, even within the same language groups. German, for instance, has no single conceptual equivalent to *education*, supplying instead at least three ways of talking: instruction, upbringing, and the formative development of the mind (*Bildung*). Each of these concepts suggests different purposes of teacher education.

Still, Wilson could be right, though not because he (or any person) has special access to what words *really* mean. The important task is not to uncover the essence of words, because even that essence can change over time and across social or cultural groups. The important task, rather, is to find ways to make distinctions that will allow wise consideration of various courses of action. Packing the term *education* full of social purposes, for example, makes it difficult to consider how each of many separate, possibly competing, purposes might be achieved and which institutions, or groups, can appropriately be held responsible.

Wilson could also be right in insisting on the importance of meanings that are entrenched in traditional usage. The associations attached to words in use are not easily duplicated (or discarded). If distinctions of importance have been captured in long-established usage, reminding oneself of these distinctions can tap into the tacit convictions and commitments these words call up. Terms newly minted to draw the same distinction are unlikely to match the richness and persuasive power of established terms.

Refuting Skeptical Arguments Against Scholarly Educational Study

Israel Scheffler shares Wilson's skill at unpacking the meanings of educational concepts (see, for example, his analysis of *teaching* in Scheffler, 1960). In the article he most directly addresses to teacher education (Scheffler, 1968), however, his argument is based on uncovering implicit assumptions and the logical flaws in an argument, rather than on analysis of concepts.

In this article, Scheffler considers whether "scholarly and theoretical studies of educational problems" (p. 7) should join practical experience and knowledge of subject matter as a third key component of teacher education. Rather than analyzing a particular paper or policy, Scheffler builds his argument by describing, then criticizing, what he takes to be the arguments of those skeptical about the importance of scholarly studies of education. Scheffler builds a counterargument that not only exhausts the objections of an imaginary skeptic one by one but also shows that the skeptic's position includes assumptions that, if taken seriously, lead to the position Scheffler advocates.

The skeptic's first argument is that the scholarly study of education should not be a part of teacher education, because education is not a science. Until education becomes a science, the skeptic claims, teacher education should concentrate on subject matter and practical experience.

Scheffler is willing to admit that education is not a science, but he points out that the conclusion depends on an implicit assumption that equates the scholarly study of education with the science of education. This assumption is unwarranted. Education can be studied in a scholarly manner by using the methods and materials of established fields such as psychology and history. Although there is, in sum, "no distinctive science or special discipline of education, there are surely multiple modes of analyzing educational problems in a scientific spirit and a disciplined manner. . . . It is . . . the family of university studies, representing the world of science . . . that needs to be brought to bear on the teacher's work" (Scheffler, 1968, pp. 2–3).

The skeptic's second move is to question whether scholarly emphasis is a *necessary* part of teacher education. "Have we not all known teachers of power and resourcefulness, innocent of educational history and philosophy, ignorant of psychology and the social sciences, and yet capable of transmitting their subjects effectively to the minds of their students?" (p. 3).

In response, Scheffler points out that the power of the skeptic's argument depends on the fallacy of equating what is valuable with what is necessary. The skeptic is justified in pointing out that things necessary for teaching (e.g., subject-matter knowledge) should be a part of teacher education. But the skeptic incorrectly extends this argument by assuming that *only* those things necessary to teaching can justifiably be included in teacher education. Surely, Scheffler points out, it is sufficient that scholarly studies enhance the quality of teaching.

Justification is not, as he [the skeptic] supposes, simply a matter of minimal necessity. It is, rather, a matter of desirability, and a thing may be desirable not because it is something we could not do without, but because it transforms and enhances the quality of what we do and how we live. (p. 4)

The skeptic's next challenge is to ask whether the value of theory should not be judged by its potential for improving the practice of teaching, as seen in improvements in teaching techniques and technology. The skeptic is willing to admit theory, provided it really promises to improve instruction.

Again, Scheffler responds by pointing out an implicit, but

debatable, assumption in the skeptic's argument. The skeptic equates improvements in educational quality with technical advances in instruction. Technicians work with materials that do not respond in human ways; in particular, they never ask, Why? Teachers, however, work with pupils, who might raise questions or doubts about what the teacher is doing. Improved techniques might be sufficient for the technician, but the teacher must be able to respond in a way that will encourage pupils to continue to seek understanding. This requires, in addition to technique, "an ability to reflect critically . . . in the face of the searching curiosity of the young" (p. 7). The practical payoff of theoretical study of education comes in enhancing this ability.

The skeptic's final challenge is to reject such notions as the ability to reflect critically as being overly vague. Nothing should be included, continues the skeptic, unless it can be clearly operationalized.

Scheffler counters by pointing out that the skeptic has committed the fallacy of begging the question. Because theoretical study is by its nature general, rather than specific, assuming that knowledge must be specific is simply assuming the conclusion the skeptic wants.

Scheffler employs another philosophical strategy to provide a second response. He points out that the skeptic has earlier advocated strong subject-matter knowledge as part of teacher education. Because such knowledge goes far beyond the content of the school curriculum, the skeptic must be assuming that some general understanding of the subject is also valuable for teaching. If the skeptic makes that admission for subject-matter knowledge, it should also be made for scholarly study of education.

Looking over this entire series of exchanges with the skeptic, Scheffler notes that the skeptic has repeatedly assumed an overly narrow conception of teacher education and teaching, concentrating exclusively on teachers' task to explain their subjects to their pupils. Scheffler counterposes his own view of teaching, in which teachers serve the community as models of the intellectual virtues. For this larger vision of the teaching role, the importance of scholarly study of education is evident.

This article provides clear examples of how philosophical inquiry can raise questions about an argument. Scheffler explicates a version of the arguments dominant in the contemporary discussion, then points out questionable assumptions and logical flaws, particularly flaws produced by taking an unnecessarily narrow view of teaching and teacher education. The strength in Scheffler's approach is that he is explicit about the flaws that he sees and makes clear why he thinks they are flaws.

This article also exemplifies some of the potential weaknesses with this type of philosophical inquiry. *First*, by speaking for both skeptic and advocate, Scheffler might not present the skeptic's best case. Scheffler shows the flaws in his own version of the skeptical argument, but might a real skeptic raise more difficult objections? *Second*, by concentrating on refuting the skeptic, Scheffler devotes less attention to the positive case that needs to be made for giving attention to theory. Scheffler might show that theory could be of value, even though it is not essential. He does not, however, make an overpowering case for including theoretical study in place of some other area that

is also a candidate for the scarce time available in teacher education. Why, for example, should a teacher education program devote time to theoretical study rather than to more field experience or more subject-matter study?

Most important, Scheffler provides little argument for his fundamental assumption that teachers must do more than get worthwhile content across to students. He implies that they have a broader role vital to democracy but provides no argument for that eminently contestable claim. In Scheffler's view, the teacher "should be thought of as a man with a calling or vocation committing him to the values of truth, reason, and the enlargement of human powers, dedicated to raising his voice for them, and to shaping the conditions of his work so that these values may flourish" (p. 11). This is inspirational, but it cries out for the justification and the conceptual unpacking that Wilson does for teacher education.

Arguing from a View of Human Action

Professional philosophers have no corner on philosophical arguments. Though conceptual arguments might most often be made by philosophers, occasionally this way of making a case is taken up by others in teacher education. Rather than exploring meaning or logic, the psychologist Arthur Combs (1965, 1972), for example, bases his recommendation that teacher education eschew teaching skills on a conceptual argument about the relative importance of intention and behavior in human action (Combs, 1965).

He argues (as many philosophers have also argued) that the significant features in human interactions (like teaching) are the interpretations people make, not the specific behaviors they exhibit. A teacher's correction of a child has different effects, depending on whether the child interprets the correction as an expression of kindly feeling or as a reprimand. Combs presents this as a point needing no support. Although it might be taken as an empirical claim, it is more plausibly a conceptual point—an essential part of interpreting something differently is reacting to it differently; hence, differently interpreted actions have different effects.

Combs further argues that teachers' perceptions are more important than their specific behaviors, because the perceptions can guide the selection of action, whereas specific behaviors have only a limited range of appropriateness. Again, though Combs does not seem to think this point requires argument, this appears to be another conceptual point: Specific behaviors have limited appropriateness because they are specific.

Thus, Combs concludes that teacher education should concentrate on perception and interpretation, rather than on teaching skills:

If we can be sure the teachers' ways of perceiving are *[accurate]* and constructive, it may not be necessary to know precisely how he will put his concern into effect. There are thousands of ways to express . . . perceptions in action. The crucial question for teacher education is not which behavior but how to bring about appropriate shifts in perception. (Combs, 1972, p. 288)

Invoking accuracy, Combs's conclusions presuppose that a situation calling for teacher action comes, as it were, with one correct perception. Teacher educators have, accordingly, the task of promoting shifts toward that right interpretation.

Combs's analysis illustrates how focused criticism can lead to strong conclusions about teacher education, without the need to conduct or review empirical studies of teaching or teacher education. Combs draws attention to a shortcoming in any program of teacher education that rests on training in narrowly defined skills. By that narrowness, such skills have a limited range of application, and mere training leaves the crucial question of the appropriateness of action open. Appropriateness, in turn, requires good judgement. Human action is not simply a matter of doing things, but of engaging in correct behavior, in an appropriate manner.

The weakness in Combs's argument is, *first*, that he fails to consider the likely possibility that any one situation is compatible with multiple interpretations (that may be incompatible with one another); this suggests another more complicated task for teacher educators, namely, promoting, beyond accuracy, open-mindedness and flexibility in teacher perceptions. *Second*, he must assume that teachers who have appropriate ways of perceiving are able to come up with some ways of translating perceptions into plans of action and of subsequently carrying out their intentions, plans and means that fit their individual characteristics and the specific situation. The fact that there are thousands of ways to put a concern into effect does not imply that a given teacher will come up with one, or many, or that the teacher will be able to put into practice any of them.

Combs is right in pointing out the narrowness of behavioral approaches to teaching, but narrowness is not the same as worthlessness. Combs is alert to the limits of other positions, but he does not seem to have carefully considered the limits and implicit assumptions that weaken his own argument.

COMBINING CONCEPTUAL ANALYSIS WITH EMPIRICAL CLAIMS

Inquiry in teacher education seldom remains purely conceptual. Teaching teachers is a practical activity; hence, arguments about what to do cannot completely bypass the real world. Many assertions and arguments blend philosophical and empirical dimensions in ways that can obscure one or the other, making it difficult to assess the overall argument or its components. For example, saying that there is too much reliance on the field component of a program combines information about what is happening in the program (and perhaps research findings about the consequences of field experience) with an evaluative statement presupposing normative claims about what it is that teacher education should be trying to accomplish.

Following are two discussions of teacher education, each advocating a particular focus. They combine reference to empirical claims (some with scholarly support, some not) with philosophical arguments concerning meaning, concepts, logic, or values. As in the preceding cases, each argument is traced, to show how it works. This is followed by comments on strengths and weaknesses.

Advocacy for Teaching Techniques

N. L. Gage probably never thought he was engaged in philosophical inquiry when he began this line of work. Gage is one of the most prominent writers on the results of research on teaching that might be used as curricular content in teacher education. His monographs, *The Scientific Basis of the Art of Teaching* (1978) and *Hard Gains in the Soft Sciences: The Case of Pedagogy* (1985), illustrate how his arguments for the relevance of such research combine the philosophical with the empirical.

Hard Gains begins with a quote from Charles Eliot's 1869 address to Harvard College, which signals Gage's intention to highlight teaching methods as a part of teacher education:

The best result of the discussion which has raged so long about the relative educational value of the main branches of learning is the conviction that there is room for them all in a sound scheme, provided that right methods of teaching be employed. . . . *The actual problem to be solved is not what to teach but how to teach.* (p. 1)

Scheffler argues that scholarly study of education must be added to subject matter and teaching practice; Gage wants to make a similar case for scientifically based knowledge about methods of teaching.

Gage recognizes that elevation of teaching method in professional preparation represents a departure from tradition. In fact, a crucial part of his argument for focusing teacher education on pedagogy is the claim that past weaknesses in teacher education stem from neglect of pedagogy. He argues that courses in the foundations of education (perhaps those that Scheffler advocates) do not address students' thirst for knowledge about how to teach and that further study of school subjects is of little value "when the teacher may already know far more about that subject than he or she will ever need in teaching third-graders or even twelfth-graders" (1985, p. 27). He appeals to the reader's common sense to justify the claim that possession of strong subject-matter knowledge does not necessarily lead to good teaching.

Gage's contention is that students should learn about the techniques of teaching and, furthermore, that they should learn techniques whose efficacy has strong empirical support:

Generations of teacher education students have been given inadequate grounding in how to teach. They have not been taught how to organize a course, how to plan a lesson, how to manage a class, how to give an explanation, how to arouse interest and motivation, how to ask the right kinds of questions, how to react to students' responses, how to give helpful correction and feedback, how to avoid unfair biases in interacting with students—in short, how to teach. (1985, pp. 27–28)

In this initial part of his argument, Gage combines a series of empirical claims (e.g., foundations courses do not tell teachers what they wish to know about how to teach, teachers already know much subject matter, teacher education has seldom included adequate attention to general teaching methods) with conceptual arguments (sometimes implicit) about the importance of teaching method and other assumptions. For example, Gage's claim about teachers' overeducation in subject matter presupposes the belief that teachers only need to know whatever subject matter they typically learn in their other college courses. This implies the further assumption that the proper delivery of subject-matter knowledge allows pupils to learn it. (This is an argument that neither Scheffler nor his skeptic would accept; much turns on the meaning of the word *properly* here.) More persuasive is Gage's implicit argument that teachers need to have teaching methods as well as subject-matter knowledge. Gage's argument here is simply an enumeration of the various methods that seem obviously important in getting people to learn in the social context of schools; how to organize a course, plan a lesson, and interact in fair and helpful ways with students.

Gage attributes past failure to concentrate teacher education on techniques in part to the lack of a research base. It might be all right to avoid technique if no one has a strong reason for supposing that a particular way of doing something leads to worthwhile results. Gage argues, not for emphasis on technique in general, but for emphasis on demonstratedly effective techniques. "That is, (a) teacher education should be aimed at producing (b) the kinds of teacher behaviors that have been shown to be related—preferably causally related—to (c) valued kinds of student knowledge, understanding, sensibility, and attitude" (1978, pp. 58–59).

Again, the argument is implicit, though not far below the surface. If you want to produce the educational results you desire, you should prepare teachers who can use the skills that produce, or at least are associated with, these results. Cast in this general way, the argument is sound.

Gage devotes a good portion of both monographs to refuting counterarguments to his advocacy of teaching techniques for teachers. The major objections are that professional preparation should not concentrate on teaching techniques because (a) the empirical base for these techniques is too weak, and (b) teaching is much more than, or at least different from, application of technique. Here Gage is using the same strategy that Scheffler did: describing what he sees as the major objections to his position, then showing the fallacies in arguments behind those objections, drawing on his background knowledge about empirical work in education.

Gage finds two faults with the objection that empirical support is too weak. *First*, he points out that recent research has greatly strengthened the empirical base for singling out certain teaching methods as effective. It might have been true that there was not much to draw on, but the situation has changed.

Second, Gage argues that critics (and even some researchers) refer to empirical associations discovered by research as "weak" or "small," without giving sufficient attention to the criteria employed in using these derogatory labels. Correlations found between teacher behavior and student learning are typically between .2 and .5; these might be small in comparison with other correlations found in educational research, but they might still be large enough to merit attention in teacher education.

Gage argues that it is an error to assess the worth of research findings simply in terms of either the size of the correlation coefficient or the percentage of overall variance explained. The proper basis for assessment is, rather, the benefits likely to be obtained by changes in teaching, as compared with the cost of making those changes. A treatment that reduced bad effects (e.g., dropping out of school) by 33 percent might have a correlation of only .2 with dropping out. If that decline in the dropout rate is worth more than the cost of the treatment, Gage maintains, the treatment would be worthwhile, despite the "low" correlation. He argues that research on classroom management, at least, has already produced results well worth the cost of including them in the teacher education curriculum.

Having dealt with the strength of the empirical base, Gage addresses the objection that teaching is much more than application of technique. Gage's response is to admit the claim but to deny that stress on scientifically grounded teaching techniques is inconsistent with a broader view of teaching. Gage's title, *The Scientific Basis of the Art of Teaching*, alludes to the interplay between instruction in empirically based skills and a view of teaching that includes flexibility, judgment, and intuition.

Gage's argument here resembles Scheffler's ways of dealing with the skeptic who wishes to set a high standard for including something in teacher education, then completely dismisses it if it fails this strict test. Gage thinks that critics of teaching method jump too quickly from the claim that technique is not everything to the conclusion that teaching teachers techniques is irrelevant or miseducative.

Gage agrees with his critics that teaching cannot, in principle, "be reduced to systematic formulas" (1985, p. 4). But he does not agree that this makes learning about empirical regularities unsuitable for teacher education. Even though no formula can tell a teacher exactly what to do in each specific situation, "statistical results can help a teacher know the averages or trends around which individual cases will vary, and such knowledge can aid in understanding the individual" (1985, pp. 4–5). The statistical averages provide the teacher with a place to begin thinking about how this particular case might or might not fit the most common cases. "Applying that scientific basis in the heat of classroom interaction still relies primarily on artistry. But knowledge of the relevant relationships allows teachers to base their artistry on something more than hunch, feeling, intuition, unaided insight, or raw experience" (1985, p. 6).

Gage finds that those who deny the value of research-based teaching techniques have attractive language for describing teaching but provide little help for novice teachers who wish to improve their teaching:

> References to educational imagination, the orchestration of classroom dialogue, and attention to pattern and expressive nuance—all these resounding statements seem to be saying something important. But the teacher or teacher educator who seeks help from such writing comes away empty-handed. It is easy to tell a teacher to be an artist, but teachers who want to know what they should do to reach that height find few answers in rhetoric about artistry, intuition, and insight. (1985, p. 6)

Gage's view of how research results could be incorporated into teacher education is consistent with his view that these results be seen as helpful starting points, not prescriptions to be followed in all circumstances. For both preservice and inservice teacher education,

teachers should be given the full story: how the research-based practices were identified, why they seem reasonable, how they work, and
what questions might be raised about their scientific and moral bases.
Each teacher should be asked to confront the moral issue of whether
these practices can justifiably be rejected on the basis of the teacher's
own experience, intuitions, hunches, or predilections. (1985, p. 58)

Gage's arguments have several strengths. Like Scheffler's
attempting to refute a skeptic, Gage provides a clear description of the position he wants to refute, then makes it easy to
see where the flaws in that position lie. Gage's argument is also
strengthened by his knowledge of the relevant literature, both
that representing his skeptics and that providing the research
base for teaching technique. He uses that knowledge to provide specific examples of teaching technique and why they
would be worth including in teacher education.

The weaknesses in Gage's arguments lie in what his research base entails about what kinds of pupil learning are valuable and, as in Scheffler's case, in possible failure to adequately
represent his skeptic. Gage presents his general argument in
an unexceptionable form: Teachers should acquire the knowledge, skills, and dispositions that promote desirable pupil
learning. But the move to the conclusion that teachers should
learn the skills of effective teaching requires the additional
premises that such skills will lead to the desired learning and
that "effective" teaching is "good" teaching.

Gage has substantial evidence to bring to bear, provided
scores on traditional achievement tests are taken as sufficient
indicators of worthwhile learning and good teaching. Many
people might accept this premise and, hence, Gage's argument. The critics Gage appears to address, however, might see
these tests as too narrow (e.g., Zumwalt, 1982). Emphasis on
skills that promote only these learning goals, they could contend, would lead to a narrowing of the curriculum; gains on
these tests might be offset by reduced attention to other important learning goals (e.g., higher order thinking, creativity,
emotional growth).

Advocates of teaching as an art might also think that Gage's
presentation of their position was weakened by his conviction
about the importance of a scientific basis for teaching. They
might object, for example, to the suggestion that artistry must
be based on either science *or* "hunch, feeling, intuition, unaided insight, or raw experience" (1985, p. 6). Gage's list
makes the bases of artistry seem no more than individual superstition. Advocates of artistry could make a stronger case for
themselves, emphasizing the study and effort that goes into
developing artistic performance and sensibility, as well as the
social bases of artistic standards and traditions.

Advocacy of Subject-Matter Knowledge

Like Gage's monographs, Buchmann's writing about
teacher education combines analysis of meaning and logic with
references to empirical educational research. It is enlightening
to compare the two arguments, because they reach different
conclusions. Gage argues that teachers need more instruction
in teaching techniques, because they already learn more than
enough about the subjects they will teach; Buchmann (1982,

1984b) argues that such subject-matter knowledge has been
neglected in recent American teacher education and that professional preparation puts too much emphasis on techniques
like classroom management.

Neither Buchmann nor Gage bases claims about current
teacher education practices on studies of the teacher education
curriculum. Buchmann, like Gage, relies on what is being emphasized in talks among those in the field. Buchmann cites a
particular example of the neglect of subject matter:

In the 1983 call for papers for the meeting of the American Association
of Colleges for Teacher Education, "Essential Knowledge for Beginning Educators," topics include the evaluation of learning and teacher
evaluation, instructional planning and management, and the influence
of context. Content knowledge is not listed. Who cares for content?
This is a disturbing question. (Buchmann, 1984b, p. 30)

In part, the different conclusions reached by Buchmann and
Gage spring from different (informal) assessments about the
composition of content in current American teacher education.

A more significant basis for disagreement is apparent from
Buchmann's discussion of how much and what teachers need
to know about the subjects they will teach. Recall that Gage
quickly dismisses subject-matter knowledge, with no explicit
argument. He seems to think that current teacher education
provides teachers with more than enough subject-matter
knowledge. Buchmann's explicit arguments lead to quite a different conclusion.

Buchmann begins with a conceptual argument for the priority of subject-matter knowledge as an aim of teacher education.
Drawing on analyses by Green (1971) and Peters (1977), she
points out that knowledge of the subject being taught is logically required for teaching to occur. In other words, it is part
of the meaning of the word *teaching* that teachers have some
knowledge of what is to be taught. "Teachers who never explain or demonstrate anything, who neither answer questions
nor question answers, may be engaged in some useful activity,
but they do not teach. . . . [These] . . . activities of teaching
presuppose subject matter knowledge on the part of teachers"
(1984b, p. 31). This logical requirement, however, indicates
little about how much subject-matter knowledge teachers
should have or about what its substance should be.

To argue that teachers should acquire deep and broad
knowledge of their subjects, Buchmann draws on empirical evidence to remind readers of conceptual points and to supplement her philosophical analysis. Studies of learning have
shown the importance of finding out how pupils understand
subject-matter concepts and of responding appropriately to pupil errors. Buchmann explains that both these tasks logically
require a knowledge of subject matter that includes an elaborated understanding of the various aspects of a content domain,
so that teachers can recognize inconsistencies in pupil responses and can generate hypotheses about what connections
pupils have made incorrectly or appropriately, though deviat-
ing from the textbook.

Teachers who cannot trace student thinking in a subject are
likely to correct specific answers without addressing deeper
confusions; worse still, they might treat appropriate answers or
modes of arriving at them as mistakes. Thus, empirical studies

support the contention that teaching should go beyond presenting the content that pupils should learn. To further student learning, Buchmann concludes, teachers need subject-matter knowledge unlikely to be acquired in current teacher education programs.

Buchmann makes a different assumption than does Gage about what pupils should learn, an assumption that provides a rationale for subject-matter preparation that includes knowledge *about* the subject (e.g., its history, social organization, methods of inquiry), as well as knowledge of the subject as explicit teaching content. Citing agreement with other educational scholars, she asserts that pupils need to get a sense of the evidence and arguments that undergird currently accepted, but possible fallible, interpretations. Teachers need to give pupils "tutored" uncertainty; that gift requires understanding of the bases and processes of knowledge, not merely its conclusions.

Teachers need flexible mastery of their subjects, not merely mastery of the facts and theories that appear in the traditional K–12 curriculum (see, for example, Bromme & Brophy, 1986; Floden & Clark, 1988). The content knowledge of even a typical undergraduate major in a subject is likely to represent the content as a static body of interconnected facts and principles:

Given the pedagogical requirement for flexible control of subject matter, knowledge of epistemology and history of science is a specific preparation for teaching. Content knowledge of this kind and at this level deepens understanding of knowledge and subject matter, encourages the mobility of teacher conceptions, and yields pedagogical knowledge in the shape of multiple and fluid conceptions. It also contributes to a form of classroom life in which all participants are seen and treated as the potential source of thoughts and actions that make sense. (Buchmann, 1984b, p. 46)

Buchmann specifically rejects the idea that teaching methods should be given greater prominence in the teacher education curriculum. In fact, she attempts to show what payoffs for the "how" of teaching can be gained by thorough preparation in teachers' subjects (e.g., having organized understanding is not unrelated to being able to organize one's thoughts; knowing subject matter to teach allows one to go ahead with instruction and avoid pupil boredom; knowing one's subjects flexibly opens up various entry points for different students). She cites empirical literature indicating that teachers and pupils tend to focus their attention on management rather than on the substance of instruction. She suggests that this tendency could be prompted by gaps in content knowledge that lead teachers to see unexpected pupil answers as potential management problems rather than as teachable moments. If pupils are kept engaged in learning content, management problems are less likely to arise; but if the teacher sees instruction only as steps to be followed, minor disruptions can spread (cf. Doyle, 1986; Lampert, 1985). "If the teacher presses forward to new content or responds with care to student understanding, teacher and students will be busy enough with teaching and learning. Under normal circumstances, management is nested in instruction and requires no separate techniques" (Buchmann, 1984b, p. 37).

Buchmann's argument, like Gage's, is strengthened by attention to empirical knowledge about teaching and learning. It is also strong in making explicit the several distinct lines of argument, each of which supports attention to subject-matter knowledge in teacher education for different sets of reasons. With multiple arguments, she might be able to maintain her conclusions, even if one or another argument is shown to be weak or faulty.

Like Gage's argument, this argument depends, however, on debatable assumptions about what sort of learning is most desirable for pupils. Gage's reliance on achievement test scores is not given much defense in his monographs, but he would have little difficulty citing large numbers of citizens, politicians, and school personnel who would endorse his assumption. Buchmann defends her assumption through reference to educational scholars and through appeals to the values of her readers. In both cases, readers who disagree with the assumptions about desired learning would have good cause to question the conclusions.

Buchmann's argument has a further weakness in its reliance on the links between teachers' content knowledge and the learning Buchmann hopes will occur. Though she makes a plausible case for the existence of such links, no research is yet available to provide empirical support. The few studies that have examined the connection have neither conceived of subject-matter knowledge in the way that Buchmann does (they typically merely count the number of completed college courses) nor measured the pupil learning she considers most important.

BASING RECOMMENDATIONS ON APPEALS TO BACKGROUND KNOWLEDGE

The arguments considered in the preceding section drew on empirical studies in building an original philosophical argument. Just as these used empirical work already accomplished, so other arguments draw on philosophical analyses and literature. In both cases, the authors do not pretend to reproduce the complete argument leading up to the conclusions or ideas they invoke. Rather, they remind the reader of these ideas in the course of making a plea for further action.

Bringing Writings on the Human Condition to Bear on Teacher Education

Maxine Greene (1981) draws on the ideas of philosophers, novelists, poets, and others to argue for the importance of foundational studies in teacher education. Her plea for a return to an emphasis on *education* makes extensive use of her broad background knowledge of contributions to thought about the human condition, encompassing both American and European societies.

It is somewhat misleading to call Greene's plea an argument. Though she does provide some reasons for an emphasis on educational foundations, the main force of her essay stems from her evocative reminders of how other thinkers have provided insight into human nature. Throughout the piece, Melville and Whitman share their place with Dewey and Scheffler as supporters of Greene's position. But Greene does not ask the reader to believe anything simply because Dewey or Melville said it. She relies instead on the assumption that her statements about society and education will strike such a responsive chord in the reader's mind that no further argument will be needed. She does not ask the reader to come around to her point of view; she asks the reader to recollect what has been submerged in the press of modern life.

A sketch of Greene's position robs it of some of its power, but such a sketch can be helpful in clarifying how she tries to reach her audience. She thinks that social conditions such as inequality and preoccupation with efficiency make it difficult for people to see what they ought to do. Though education has limited power, schools still "have a particular responsibility when it comes to empowering persons to live in this world. To be an educator is intentionally to move people to what are conceived to be more desirable states of mind, to bring them to care about what is significant and worthwhile" (p. 31). To be such educators, teachers "must be empowered, educated to enter into the discussion of what the schools are for. They must be given the resources they need to articulate and to incarnate the shared norms that ostensibly sustain our society: justice, equality, concern, freedom, mutuality, rationality, decency" (p. 33). The content of educational foundations (e.g., educational psychology, philosophy of education) is well suited to initiate teachers into these resources and ways of thinking; hence, it should be maintained as an important part of teacher education.

Greene lays out this position through a narrative that mixes statements of presumably shared values with examples and quotations from philosophy and literature. The result is a powerful plea for a return to many of the values in education and teacher education articulated by John Dewey and others. Another result is that people might be moved to inquire into their own minds and experiences, which is an aim held by philosophers from philosophy's very beginnings and one that supplies much of the point of ordinary language analysis.

The approach to philosophical writing in Greene's article stands in marked contrast to the pieces considered earlier. Greene makes a case that many will probably find convincing, but she provides little in the way of explicit argument. The power of her case rests rather in the extent to which she is, indeed, able to call on background knowledge, shared with her audience, that makes the case or provides the telling illustration.

To illuminate the importance of posing fundamental questions about education and society, for example, Greene runs through a list of examples of real and fictional characters who have posed such questions: Thomas Jefferson, Horace Mann, Huck Finn, and the ship's officers in *Billy Budd*. It is assumed that the reader recognizes that all these people raised such questions and that they were *right* to do so.

To show that teachers must ask questions about the psychology of the pupils they teach, Greene calls on the reader to imagine the difficulties a teacher without psychological understanding would have with characters from literature: "How are we to release the preferences of the Holden Caulfields we come upon, the Yossarians, the women like Lily Bart in Edith Warton's *House of Mirth*, or the woman desperate to read Chekhov in Tillie Olsen's *Tell Me a Riddle?*" (p. 34).

Perhaps the key to the persuasive power of Greene's article is her own obvious understanding and conviction. She draws on an impressive assemblage of insights in arriving at her position; her tone communicates the feeling and conviction with which she holds that position.

Greene's approach is especially well suited to the difficult philosophical task of helping people recollect the convictions they share. Often, no neat chain of logical argument lies behind these convictions, or the chain of reasons simply ends with them. They are more a matter of common moral intuition and faith, either religious or secular. Because the basis for these convictions is substantive belief, not logic, philosophers cannot use arguments to recall them. Instead, philosophers must do what Greene does: evoke shared ideas or images and point out what the reader already seems to see in them. These ideas or images encapsulate, or gesture at, human wisdom and hope.

Such philosophical writing can be problematic in at least two ways. First, the examples, presumably shared texts and ideas, might not be familiar to the readers, or readers might not find in them what the writer does. Some members of Greene's audience might not remember enough about *Huckleberry Finn* to make the work a persuasive illustration, or they might have no idea about the identity of Holden Caulfield or Yossarian. For those people, the article could fall flat, for it loses its persuasive power. Still, readers not able to interpret every single one of Greene's allusions are not bound to find their reading barren, being moved perhaps by her impassioned tone to some hazy, misty ideas of human truths.

A more fundamental problem is that, because it offers little in the way of argument, it could be difficult to evaluate such writing appropriately. Someone could mount a persuasive case that did not, in fact, invoke shared values. Or the case might be based on attitudes widely shared but pernicious, such as racism or bigotry. Greene is guilty of neither of these evils, but the approach taken in her essay calls for acceptance of her plea, rather than for the further discussion she undoubtedly values. In this kind of philosophical writing, the reader must rely greatly on the good faith of the author, a condition that, of course, must always be met to some extent.

Elaborating Dewey's Vision of Reflective Teaching

Like Greene, Zeichner draws on his background knowledge to call on teacher educators to embrace a vision of their work, a vision he assumes his readers already find appealing. Zeichner and Greene both accept John Dewey as an eloquent spokesman for this vision, but Zeichner draws on educational research, not on literature, to convince his audience that Dewey's ideas merit attempting to use them as guiding principles. Zeichner's use of empirical research makes his approach also similar to that of Buchmann and Gage.

An emphasis on reflection as a central goal of teacher education runs through most of Zeichner's work. Some articles state or assume this position, with little attempt to persuade readers to adopt it. A recent article with Liston in the *Harvard Educational Review*, for example, describes the vision that guides Zeichner's work as a teacher educator. He emphasizes

the preparation of teachers who are both willing and able to reflect on the origins, purposes, and consequences of their actions, as well as on the material and ideological constraints and encouragements embedded in the classroom, school, and societal contexts in which they work. These goals are directed toward enabling student teachers to develop the pedagogical habits and skills necessary for self-directed growth and toward preparing them, individually and collectively, to participate as full partners in the making of educational policies. (Zeichner & Liston, 1987, p. 23)

Zeichner's most explicit argument in support of reflection as a goal of teacher education can be found in his earlier work on field-based experience in teacher education. In "Reflective Teaching and Field-based Experience in Teacher Education" Zeichner (1981–1982) questions the widespread trust in field-based experience in teacher education, stressing that such experience can only be judged by giving careful attention to its purposes. His review of evidence about the effects of field experience shows that it tends to contribute to the development of utilitarian teaching perspectives:

Specifically, as students spend time in the field, getting the class through the required lesson on time in a quiet and orderly manner becomes the major criterion for accepting or rejecting the use of a particular teaching activity. If a technique "works" (that is, solves the immediate problem at hand), it is evaluated as good for that reason alone. (p. 3)

Zeichner then systematically considers the goals of field experience. He uses two approaches to persuade his readers that the typical effects of field experience imply undesirable ends.

First, Zeichner reminds his readers of John Dewey's description of the purposes field experience ought to serve. Zeichner quotes passages from the 1904 article (discussed later in this chapter) in which Dewey characterizes the utilitarian perspective as a danger to be avoided, advocating instead that "practical work should be pursued primarily with reference to its reaction upon the professional pupil in making him a thoughtful and alert student of education" (Dewey, 1965, p. 150). Like Greene, Zeichner uses these passages to help his readers crystalize their own inclination toward an ambitious approach to teacher education. He provides additional reminders of the goals held in common by citing other teacher educators who subscribe to Deweyian aims.

Second, Zeichner elaborates and defends his own adaptation of these goals. Teachers who are thoughtful and alert students of education, Zeichner explains, have both the skills necessary to study and solve classroom problems and the attitudes or qualities of mind that run counter to utilitarian perspectives. Drawing again on Dewey, he describes the desired attitudes as open-mindedness, responsibility, and wholeheartedness; as teacher characteristics, these qualities resemble Wilson's requirement for "seriousness" in learning to teach and learning from teaching.

Zeichner, like Greene, attempts to persuade by evoking and interpreting a vision of teacher education with which the audience is assumed to be familiar and sympathetic. His elaboration suggests how readers might embody Dewey's proposals in their practice.

Zeichner also draws on the empirical literature to convince his readers that bringing this vision to life requires serious effort, yet remains possible. He cites studies showing that the desired attitudes are comparatively rare among experienced teachers; hence, intervention (education, Wilson would claim) is necessary if they are to be learned. "Teachers for the most part do not seem to be especially reflective or analytic about their work. On the contrary, 'reflective conservatism,' the antithesis of reflective thinking, seems to be the central tendency in the profession" (1981–1982, p. 9).

By posing and refuting pessimistic claims that such attitudes either could not be developed or would interfere with teachers' ability to respond to the rapid pace of classroom events, Zeichner attempts to show that the vision is within reach. Reflective teaching is possible because some teachers do it. Furthermore, the fear that reflective teachers would be paralyzed rests on a mistaken interpretation. "To imply that reflection is incompatible with the ecology of the classroom is to distort the true meaning of the reflective process" (1981–1982, p. 10). Most important, objecting to reflection on the grounds that it impedes classroom processes begs the question of the relative merits of reflective and utilitarian perspectives. Reflection is valued *because* it interrupts the smooth flow of events.

Zeichner's argument is, like Greene's, strengthened by his reference to the ideas and conclusions of other scholars. It is also strengthened by his own evident understanding of the concrete details of teacher education. Because he draws on a small set of educational thinkers for ideas about the aims of teacher education, Zeichner can be more assured that his readers will have some familiarity with those he cites, especially with John Dewey. Yet that same restriction keeps Zeichner's essay from having the same depth of insight that affects one in reading Greene's plea. Greene gives the impression of drawing her conviction from fundamental insights into people and society; Zeichner rests his case more on convictions that operate within the practice of education.

Zeichner's approach runs the risks Greene's does. Though he offers rather more in the way of empirical support, he relies heavily on a shared and largely unexamined belief in the validity of Dewey's convictions about education in general and teacher education in particular. He thus has limited power to change the minds of those who might oppose Dewey, and he provides only a limited invitation for readers to continue and redirect the discussion.

ESTABLISHING DISTINCTIONS TO MAKE A POINT

In analytically ordering the world, people draw systematic distinctions. One important philosophical strategy is to point out that what seems to be a straightforward concept can be looked at in different ways or is made of several different elements that might be related but are not interchangeable. One can "unpack" the concept of education to find that it contains ideas of learning coming, so to speak, from the "inside" (maturation, development) and from the "outside" (instruction, training). Such distinctions confer greater clarity and complexity on a situation or question such as, How do we educate teachers? Some of the conceptual elements might be more appropriate or desirable than others, and current practice might take for granted one interpretation to the neglect of others.

Scholastic philosophy has given this strategy a bad name through a proliferation of dry distinctions. It is sometimes not easy to convince people to attend to differences between seemingly similar ideas. Often, therefore, the bulk of an argument positing distinctions lies in persuading the reader that differences are real and significant. To make this case, authors often unpack an idea or practice. Next, two cases are examined: one in which the concept of teacher knowledge is unpacked to show its multiple components, another in which two distinct ways of looking at classroom experience as part of teacher preparation are compared in terms of associated aims and likely outcomes.

Distinctions Within Teachers' Knowledge

Teachers' knowledge of subject matter provides a clear example of an apparently simple idea that can be separated into a variety of distinct components. Buchmann, in the essay discussed earlier (1984b), discusses some such distinctions. Shulman (1986) provides a more extended analysis of this idea. Like Buchmann, he thinks that teachers' subject-matter knowledge should go beyond simple additions to their mastery of the facts and skills of the discipline:

Teachers must not only be capable of defining for students the accepted truths in a domain. They must also be able to explain why a particular proposition is deemed warranted, why it is worth knowing, and how it relates to other propositions, both within the discipline and without, both in theory and in practice. (1986, p. 9)

Shulman does not argue as elaborately as Buchmann for the centrality of content knowledge, relying instead on a combination of its self-evident importance and an analogy to the importance of content knowledge in medicine. But he goes beyond Buchmann in the variety of distinctions he draws within this domain of teachers' knowledge, as well as between this domain and closely related aspects of teachers' knowledge. He then uses these distinctions to argue that the attention of researchers and teacher educators has rested too much on a single aspect of content knowledge.

First, Shulman distinguishes content knowledge per se from *pedagogical* content knowledge and curricular knowledge. The first and last are the familiar knowledge of the subject (including how knowledge is supported and how it changes) and knowledge of the range of methods and programs available for teaching particular domains and topics. Pedagogical content knowledge is the area of knowledge that sets teachers apart from other experts; it is composed of understandings of content related to its teachability. This includes both the

ways of representing content that make others able to understand it—"the most powerful analogies, illustrations, examples, explanations, and demonstrations" (Shulman, 1986, p. 9)—and insights into what makes the learning of specific aspects of a subject easy or difficult (e.g., common misunderstandings and preconceptions).

Within each of these domains, Shulman describes three forms of knowledge: propositional knowledge, case knowledge, and strategic knowledge. Propositional knowledge is the form currently dominant in teacher education; for example, knowledge that direct instruction promotes certain types of learning or that beginning teachers should not smile until Christmas. Shulman suggests that teacher educators should give attention beyond that to the other two other forms of knowledge, case knowledge and strategic knowledge (knowing how to adjudicate when different propositions or cases disagree).

Shulman argues for the importance of these additional forms of knowledge on the grounds that propositional knowledge alone is difficult to remember and difficult to apply in complex and variable settings. Case knowledge aids memory and application by providing examples that vividly illustrate one or more chunks of propositional knowledge. Strategic knowledge is, by definition, the form of knowledge that guides the teacher in resolving the conflicts that inevitably arise in applying several principles, maxims, or norms to a particular situation (e.g., when the principle that unusual student responses should be probed conflicts with the principle that the pace of the lesson should be maintained).

Shulman then goes on to distinguish three types of knowledge in each of these categories, based on whether that knowledge comes from disciplined inquiry, practical experience, or ethical analysis. Thus "don't smile until Christmas" is propositional knowledge derived from experience; detailed knowledge of how an effective teacher begins a typical lesson could be case knowledge that comes from disciplined inquiry.

By using memorable labels for each subcategory of knowledge, Shulman helps the reader keep track of the complex array of types of knowledge by which he has replaced the simple idea of teachers' content knowledge. That knowledge can be sorted into principles, maxims, and norms (all propositional); prototypes, precedents, and parables (all case knowledge); and so on.

Shulman uses this system of categories and subcategories to argue that some aspects of teachers' knowledge (e.g., all forms of case knowledge) have been neglected in research and practice. To make that point understandable, let alone convincing, he has to show that content knowledge is not all of a single type.

The strength of any attempt to make distinctions depends on the extent to which the distinctions appear clear (i.e., the reader must get an idea about what falls into each category, and why) and significant (e.g., that items in different categories highlight different insights or have different consequences). Explanations of the distinctions are of help here, as are good examples. Shulman's case is strong in these regards. The explanations are clear and the examples are consonant with practitioners' knowledge and experience. They also fit clearly into the categories. Take, for instance, his discussion of maxims—propositional knowledge drawn from practice:

The second kind of proposition makes not a theoretical claim, but a practical one. In every field of practice there are ideas that have never been confirmed by research [i.e., are different from the knowledge based on disciplined inquiry] and would, in principle, be difficult to demonstrate. Nevertheless, these maxims represent the accumulated wisdom of practice, and in many cases are as important a source of guidance for practice as the theory or empirical principles. "Never smile until Christmas" would qualify as such a maxim, as would "Break a large piece of chalk before you use it for the first time, to prevent squeaking against the board." (p. 11)

By pointing out that these maxims, although a good source of guidance, are typically overlooked, Shulman makes a good case for his distinction. The distinction makes it possible to identify a valuable, yet neglected, source of knowledge for teaching.

Shulman's argument might be faulted in that some cases seem to fall into more than one category. Propositional knowledge based on scholarly study of the ethics of teaching, for example, seems to fit as both a principle and a norm, because it is based both on disciplined inquiry and ethics. And might not, as Dewey would claim, some practical experience be disciplined? These difficulties might not be very serious; few distinctions are sharp once applied to real cases. Still, when the borderline or ambiguous cases begin to outweigh the paradigm cases, the utility of a distinction is in jeopardy.

More important is the question, Why these distinctions, categories, and subcategories, and not others? Zeichner draws on Dewey's thought, with its comprehensive reconstruction of most ideas and activities people take for granted (e.g., academic knowledge, acting, thinking). Wilson points to ordinary language with its implicit system of relevances and meanings. Shulman bases his distinctions on plain thinking, philosophy, and many studies of teaching and professional decision making. Yet in positing a category *system*, one also needs (theoretical) principles by which distinctions within it are justified. Otherwise, they may simply remain lists of words with definitions and subdivisions, difficult to evaluate.

The power in a distinction, or in a category system, lies in the further insights or arguments it permits. The advantage of Shulman's analysis is that it draws on a variety of different sources, throwing elements of teacher knowledge into relief. It will take further empirical and philosophical work to assess the relative importance of these components and to see what this system still leaves out.

John Dewey: Scientific Thought in Teacher Education

John Dewey's classic essay on teacher education, "The Relation of Theory to Practice in Education" (1965), relies on a distinction rooted in his theory of learning and knowledge. Whereas Shulman makes multiple distinctions to call attention to neglected possibilities in teacher education, Dewey establishes, in essence, one, invoking his whole system of thought about education (and democracy) in so doing.

Dewey describes what he considers the relation of theory to practice in a three-part argument. The first two parts consider practice and theory, respectively, from the vantage point of the distinction between apprenticeship and laboratory approaches to practical work in teacher education. The third part suggests how Dewey's ideas might be put into practice, in the historical context in which he wrote.

The driving distinction opens the section on practice. The question about practice is not, Dewey says, *whether* it should play a part in teacher education, but *what purpose* practical work should serve. He posits two contrasting sets of purposes as two poles of a continuum; these are embodied in his distinction:

Two controlling purposes may be entertained so different from each other as radically to alter the amount, conditions, and method of practice work. On the one hand, we may carry on the practical work with the object of giving teachers in training working command of the necessary tools of their profession; control of the technique of class instruction and management; skill and proficiency in the work of teaching. With this aim in view, practice work is, as far as it goes, of the nature of apprenticeship. On the other hand, we may propose to use practice work as an instrument in making real and vital theoretical instruction; the knowledge of subject-matter and of principles of education. This is the laboratory point of view. (p. 142)

Of course, if teachers were immediately saddled with full responsibility for a class of (in Dewey's times) 30 to 60 pupils, they would have difficulty developing the habits of mind essential to learning from practice.

Though Dewey makes various claims about the consequences of both approaches, he neither provides empirical support for the superiority of the laboratory approach nor claims to analyze ordinary language concepts. The considerable persuasive power of this essay comes instead from a heady mix of vivid imagery and plain thinking, permeated by a sweeping theory of human thought that puts science within the reach of every person wanting to know and act rightly.

For Dewey, scientific thinking is the appropriate model for all thought. He believes that people's minds are impelled by problems motivating inquiry. Outcomes of inquiry provide a basis for tentatively resolving problems and for carrying out further, more systematic, inquiry. Looked at properly, Dewey contends, all scientific knowing can be linked to problems originating in concrete experience. He accordingly believes that teachers can think scientifically about their work and connect it to scholarship as well. Moreover, using scientific methods of thought themselves, teachers can and should teach in ways that can help their pupils practice inquiry.

From this conception of scientific thought comes Dewey's idea of what teaching practice should accomplish and how psychology (as an example of foundational knowledge) and subject-matter knowledge can contribute to these goals. Thus Dewey is no advocate of research utilization as the term is understood in much of current educational usage. Whereas Gage's call for research-based preparation in teaching techniques, for instance, emphasizes the sensible use of externally grounded findings, Dewey's call for a laboratory approach emphasizes intellectual activities that turn teaching practice into science, requiring thought about aims of education and deep knowledge of teaching subjects.

In the section on practice, Dewey lays out three lines of argument for the laboratory approach. *First*, he points out that, historically, more established professions have moved toward the laboratory approach and away from training in specific skills, because professional education can better help people acquire the "scientific foundations" (p. 145) of their work. *Second*, in teacher preparation the apprenticeship approach encourages inordinate attention to classroom management. *Third*, related to this, this approach encourages novices to use whatever methods seem to yield immediate results in limited goals rather than to try to understand how fundamental principles might inform and shape teaching practice over time, in terms of examined and more broadly conceived goals.

In the second part of the essay, Dewey asks, "What must be the aim and spirit of theory in order that practice work may really serve the purpose of an educational laboratory?" (p. 152). He approaches the question by considering how theory might avoid being abstruse and apparently useless, for the laboratory approach cannot rely on practice teaching for motivation and illustrative examples.

Dewey's solution for the example of psychological theory is to link theory to student teachers' own experiences as learners. It is a mistake, Dewey claims, to assume that delaying full-fledged teaching means leaving student teachers without relevant experience. People are learners their whole lives, hence student teachers have "a very large capital of an exceedingly practical sort" (p. 153) that they can draw upon for illustrations of psychological theory.

Dewey thus takes a different view of the importance of psychological theory than do other advocates of the discipline, such as Gage or Scheffler. For Dewey, psychology provides concepts and methods of thought that teachers can learn to use when reflecting on learning, both inside and outside the classroom. For Gage, research provides evidence of the typical causal relationships between teaching and learning, which teachers can use as a starting point for decisions. Dewey thinks that experience is needed to help teachers apply psychological thinking in observing themselves and their students, but Scheffler seems to make the counterintuitive assumption that studying psychology is sufficient—relating scholarship to practice will take care of itself.

For teachers' knowledge of subject matter, Dewey makes a more striking claim: knowledge of subject matter (properly conceived) provides knowledge of teaching method. This is something Buchmann also argues. Again, Dewey's assertion is based on the centrality of having teachers and pupils learn the methods of scientific thought. To argue that subject-matter knowledge is valuable for both intellectual and teaching method, he gives an old argument a new twist.

Everyone knows that some professors are good teachers, though they have never studied pedagogy. The usual conclusion is that knowledge of teaching methods is of little value. Dewey, however, concludes that subject-matter knowledge itself provides *some* knowledge of teaching method and that it is, moreover, a resource that should be tapped more fully:

If it has accomplished so much when working unconsciously and without set intention, have we not good reason to believe that, when ac-

quired in a training school for teachers—with the end of making teachers held definitely in view and with conscious reference to its relation to mental activity—it may prove a much more valuable pedagogical asset than we commonly consider it? (p. 159)

Dewey goes on to explain his view of how method is embodied in subject matter: learning subjects is, at its best, learning the "fundamental mental attitudes and operations—that, indeed, particular scientific methods and classifications simply express and illustrate in their most concrete form that of which simple and common modes of thought-activity are capable when they work under satisfactory conditions" (pp. 161–162). If this is so, then knowledge of teaching subjects brings with it an understanding of how minds ought to work. For Dewey, knowledge of subjects equals knowledge of inquiry *and* knowledge of the educational process as he conceives it.

In the final section of the essay, Dewey considers the feasibility of his proposals, sketching various steps a student teacher might go through in practice teaching, even allowing for some apprenticeship during a final stage. Dewey concludes with an inspirational challenge, laying responsibility for great changes on the shoulders of teacher educators and reminding them that adopting the laboratory approach requires more than mere refinement of current practice: "The thing needful is improvement of education, not simply by turning out teachers who can do better the things that are now necessary to do, but rather by changing the conception of what constitutes education" (p. 171).

By contrasting the laboratory and apprenticeship approaches, Dewey makes one see the experiential component of teacher preparation in a different light, calling into question common practices and assumptions. Rather than accepting a distinction between theory and practice, Dewey unites both in the laboratory image of teacher education. This powerful idea, invoking Dewey's view of the nature and value of science and thought, has affected the thinking of many scholars and practitioners in teacher education.

Much of the appeal of Dewey's argument, communicated specifically in the work of Zeichner and his associates, stems from visualizing teachers' thinking scientifically (in Dewey's sense) and spreading these same habits of mind through classrooms, schools, and, as Greene and Scheffler would join in hoping, through a society thus becoming truly democratic. Perhaps these writers all overestimate the power of schools, even when teeming with reflective teachers, in competition with other institutions and social agencies such as families, the media, and political institutions.

CONCLUSIONS

The philosophical inquiry commented on tells a story. Each partial story responds to ideas and realities, to thought and practice (mostly in the United States), and each looks, as it were, backward and forward—to comprehend or correct past ideas and practices, leading to the present, and to shape new understandings and intentions. Perhaps it is not even true that what eventuates in this dialogue with ideas, social realities, and one's own mind is new as a contribution to the philosophical conversation about teacher education. Rather, there are reminders of elements that seem to have been neglected, parts of the puzzle of teaching teachers that have been temporarily mislaid.

Thus, Wilson calls for taking a hard look at the concepts of education and teaching before one rashly crowds out or distorts educational goods by demanding too much of schooling. In tracing Scheffler's argument, one is taught to consider carefully any narrow view that equates teaching to technical work on unresponsive material. Related to this, Combs's argument drives home the point that teaching is more than a set of effective methods; it is fundamentally human action—cognitive, interpretative, and personal.

Partisans of teaching technique and subject-matter preparation in teacher education, such as Gage and Buchmann, respond to the same historical reality, drawing conclusions that vary according to the educational goals they assume as a starting point. Greene recalls human truths and the hopes of this republic in making her appeal for helping teachers learn to raise fundamental questions. Zeichner reminds teacher educators of the efforts they must make to prepare reflective teachers.

Philosophical inquiry expands and challenges ways of looking at the world by establishing distinctions. Shulman posits a rich variety of ways in which teachers might know their subjects and their work. Based on his distinction between apprenticeship and laboratory views of teaching practice, Dewey argues for a way of seeing teacher preparation in which the distinction between theory and practice vanishes.

Each of the authors' perspectives and arguments illuminates only parts of the puzzle, taking others for granted and leaving out the rest. This could not be otherwise, for examining the normative and conceptual underpinnings of a social practice is like repairing a ship at sea. Only a few parts can be prized out at any one time. The rest must remain in place, even though this means the entire analysis is always in some ways imprisoned by given beliefs and concepts.

Every inquiry has shortcomings and questionable assumptions. Each attempt to understand and reform teacher education is liable to overestimate the importance or trustworthiness of one thing at the expense of others. Is education really something that can be nailed down once and for all by conceptual analysis, or is it, to use Wittgenstein's (1958) image, more like a slowly shifting riverbed? Does it make sense to saddle teachers with the burden of being the prime representatives of intellectual and civic virtues, or should this task be shared with other groups? Perception is surely important in teaching, but specific behaviors most certainly also affect pupils, and situations are never susceptible to only one interpretation.

The presence of weaknesses in all arguments is well exemplified by the partisan arguments we have reviewed; of course, both the "how" and "what" of teaching matter, and preoccupation with one or the other can put thought and action on a false scent. In particular, one must consider what is entailed for educational goals by emphasis on technique in teacher preparation, and one must not ignore the fact that school learning is not just an effect of teachers' subject knowledge but a *social* production, accomplished by teachers and students acting and thinking in concert with one another.

When drawing on background knowledge to evoke a vision and make recommendations, the question is not only to what extent the knowledge or vision is, in fact, shared, but also to what extent it is justified by reason or evidence. Intersubjective agreement does not guarantee truth or rightness, and visions, just as evidence, may be questioned. Likewise, when conceptual distinctions are posited, one needs to comprehend not only definitions but also the theoretical principles of generation accounting for their point, and for the whole framework.

This chapter provides illustrations of how philosophy enters into inquiry in teacher education. Its tools and questions are no privileged possession. Philosophical inquiry allows for a variety of partial views, activities, and kinds of knowledge. But neither are all perspectives of equal merit nor all views of teaching and teacher education equally defensible.

The authors reviewed were all, in their different ways, trying to argue for their insights and proposals in responsible ways, respecting their readers' right to be given reasons for beliefs or actions. They varied in the kinds and mix of reasons they offered for consideration (invoking concepts, logic, common sense, empirical evidence, shared ideas), and they varied, similarly, in their use of philosophical methods or strategies of persuasion. All of the arguments left the reader with more questions to be asked and with uncertainties yet to be resolved.

These philosophical analyses show that the argumentative ladder on fundamental questions has no end. In thinking about teacher education, direction always remains to some extent unclear, and any one decision or perspective could dissolve on the adding of further theoretical, factual, or value premises. If one looks at a situation in a different light (theory) or brings other facts and values to bear on it, one will come up with a different practical answer, or a different idea might suggest itself. However, the argumentative ladder on teacher education is placed somewhere and cannot be shifted around at will or whimsy, for the teaching of teachers has to do with education and teaching youngsters in schools. It is thus committed in conceptual and institutional terms. This should function to orient and bound discussion.

Importantly, these analyses are a reminder of the very special place teachers have in thoughts about how to promote social, not just educational, goods. But there remain grave uncertainties about how to accomplish the task, central to teaching, of helping people learn.

In teacher education thought and practice, it is ill-advised to be an initiate of one ideological camp or other, to be "for" conceptual analysis, teaching techniques, education of teacher perceptions, or what have you. Doing so only debars one from other valuable insights and from seeing the limits of a given perspective. Good ideas and practices are too scarce in any domain of human endeavor to dismiss any of them lightly.

References

Bambrough, R. (1986). Question time. In S. G. Shanker (Ed.), *Philosophy in Britain today* (pp. 58–71). London: Croom Helm.

Bromme, R., & Brophy, J. (1986). Teachers' cognitive activities. In B. Christiansen, G. Howson, & M. Otte (Eds.), *Perspectives on mathematics education* (pp. 99–140). Dordrecht, The Netherlands: Reidel.

Buchmann, M. (1982). The flight away from content in teacher education and teaching. *Journal of Curriculum Studies, 14*(1), 61–68.

Buchmann, M. (1984a) The use of research knowledge in teacher education and teaching. *American Journal of Education, 92*(4), 421–439.

Buchmann, M. (1984b). The priority of knowledge and understanding in teaching. In L. Katz & J. Raths (Eds.), *Advances in teacher education* (Vol I, pp. 29–50). Norwood, NJ: Ablex.

Combs, A. W. (1965). *The professional education of teachers: A perceptual view of teacher preparation.* Boston: Allyn & Bacon.

Combs, A. W. (1972). Some basic concepts for teacher education. *Journal of Teacher Education, 23*(3), 286–290.

Dewey, J. (1965). The relation of theory to practice in education. In M. L. Borrowman (Ed.), *Teacher education in America: A documentary history* (pp. 140–171). New York: Teachers College Press. (Original work published 1904)

Doyle, W. (1986). Classroom organization and management. In M. C. Wittrock (Ed.), *Handbook of research on teaching* (3rd ed., pp. 392–431). New York: Macmillan.

Feiman-Nemser, S., & Buchmann, M. (1985). Pitfalls of experience in teacher preparation. *Teachers College Record, 87*(1), 53–65.

Floden, R. E. (1985). The role of rhetoric in changing teachers' beliefs. *Teaching and Teacher Education, 1,* 19–32.

Floden, R. E., & Clark, C. M. (1988). Preparing teachers for uncertainty. *Teachers College Record, 89*(4), 505–524.

Gage, N. L. (1978). *The scientific basis of the art of teaching.* New York: Teachers College Press.

Gage, N. L. (1985). *Hard gains in the soft sciences: The case of pedagogy.* Bloomington, IN: Center on Evaluation, Development, and Research, Phi Delta Kappa.

Green, T. F. (1971). *The activities of teaching.* New York: McGraw-Hill.

Greene, M. (1981). Contexts, connections, and consequences: The matter of philosophical and psychological foundations. *Journal of Teacher Education, 32*(4), 31–37.

Lampert, M. (1985). How do teachers manage to teach? Perspectives on problems in practice. *Harvard Educational Review, 55*(2), 178–194.

Peters, R. S. (1977). *Education and the education of teachers.* London: Routledge & Kegan Paul.

Scheffler, I. (1960). *The language of education.* Springfield, IL: Charles C Thomas.

Scheffler, I. (1968). University scholarship and the education of teachers. *Teachers College Record, 70*(1), 1–12.

Shulman, L. S. (1986). Those who understand: Knowledge growth in teaching. *Educational Researcher, 15*(2), 4–14.

Wilson, J. (1975). *Educational theory and the preparation of teachers.* Windsor, England: National Foundation for Educational Research.

Wisdom, J. (1969). *Philosophy and psycho-analysis.* Berkeley, CA: University of California Press.

Wittgenstein, L. (1958). *Philosophical investigations.* New York: Macmillan.

Zeichner, K. M. (1980). Myths and realities: Field-based experiences in preservice teacher education. *Journal of Teacher Education, 31*(6), 51–55.

Zeichner, K. M. (1981–1982). Reflective teaching and field-based experience in teacher education. *Interchange, 12*(4), 1–22.

Zeichner, K. M., & Liston, D. P. (1987). Teaching student teachers to reflect. *Harvard Educational Review, 57*(1), 23–48.

Zumwalt, K. K. (1982). Research on teaching: Policy implications for teacher education. In A. Lieberman & M. McLaughlin (Eds.), *Policy making in education* (81st yearbook of the National Society for the Study of Education, Part I, pp. 215–248). Chicago: University of Chicago Press.

HISTORICAL STUDIES OF TEACHER EDUCATION

Wayne J. Urban
GEORGIA STATE UNIVERSITY

In the light of current assaults on formal teacher education requirements in New Jersey and several other states, it is appropriate to note that, for at least the first 2 centuries of our nation's existence, teachers were not at all educated formally for the occupation they would perform. Of course, it should also be noted that, for most of these 2 centuries, other occupations thought of as requiring prodigious amounts of higher education as a prelude to their practice, for example medicine and law, were also without formal educational experiences as prerequisites for their practice. The anomaly, if there is one, is that, in the twentieth century, when medicine, law, and other occupations with which teaching is often compared have developed extensive and elaborate systems of professional education, teacher education continues to face challenges to its very existence. The contemporary legitimacy crisis is one factor to be kept in mind as the story of teacher education practices and institutional arrangements for these practices is detailed.

Before looking at specific historical studies of teacher education, it is helpful to note that historians of education in the latter half of the twentieth century have ceased to be apologists for the phenomena that they study. Unlike their predecessors, some of whose work will be mentioned in this review, contemporary historians of education do not hesitate to be critical of the ideas and institutions that engage their scholarly attention.

Another characteristic of work in the history of education, as in other fields of history, is that its methodological techniques are not complicated enough to be expressed in language that is unintelligible to nonhistorians. It is not methodological expertise that historical researchers possess uniquely, though they do have procedures that they follow when verifying a source and making an inference from their sources. Few of these procedures are complicated in a technical sense, however. Even historians who use relatively sophisticated statisti-cal techniques in their work feel compelled to relate their ideas in language that can be understood by nonquantitatively oriented colleagues (Urban, 1982).

What distinguishes a historian is mastery of the literature in one or more areas of historical study, combined with the above-mentioned critical stance toward the sources with which she or he is dealing, as well as toward the work of other historians. The application of this critical stance characterizes the work of contemporary historians. In educational history, the critical stance has become the necessary view of scholars in the field. The weaknesses and problems in the educational institutions that are being studied are as significant as the strengths and accomplishments of those institutions. This chapter is offered in that critical tradition.

A helpful orienting mechanism for the materials to be covered herein is to think of the formal, conscious attempts at teacher education that began in the mid-nineteenth century as composed of varying degrees of "liberal" and "technical" studies. These two terms, taken from Borrowman (1956), encompass two poles within which most educational activity for teachers can be conceived. Simply stated, technical concerns are those that impinge directly on the practice of teaching as conceived of by teacher educators. Liberal studies, on the other hand, are those that provide an intellectual context within which teachers can reflect upon their occupational activities for the purposes of analyzing and perhaps even altering their viewpoints of their work. In Borrowman's words, the technical refers to "the necessity to train individuals to perform efficiently the technical tasks assigned to them," whereas the liberal reflects "the need to make certain that each person systematically considers the far-flung implications of his vocational and avocational decisions" (p. vii).

In addition to distinguishing between liberal and technical

The author thanks reviewers John Hardin Best (Pennsylvania State University) and Donald R. Warren (University of Maryland) for their careful reading of the chapter and their suggestions for changes.

orientations in teacher education, Borrowman points out the relationship between general education and professional education. General education refers to the studies that college educated persons take in common with each other, regardless of their field of specialization, whereas professional studies refer to those courses and experiences directly structured to students' intellectual and occupational specialties such as preparing for teaching. He points out that it is largely within the professional sequence that the concerns of liberal and technical studies are addressed. He then proceeds with a chronological look at the shifting relations between liberal and technical studies within the professional education sequence. He begins with the normal school in the mid-nineteenth century, then addresses the development of the study of education in universities in the late nineteenth and early twentieth centuries, looks at collegiate teacher education in the first 3 decades of the twentieth century, and concludes with an account of the 2 decades immediately preceding his book's publication.

Borrowman's categories of liberal and technical, as well as his periodization, will be roughly followed in this chapter. Before beginning with normal school development in the mid-nineteenth century, however, a brief word about teacher education prior to those years is in order.

TEACHER EDUCATION IN THE COLONIAL AND EARLY NATIONAL PERIODS

As already mentioned, teacher education did not exist in any formal or structured way in the first 200 years of American history. This is not to say that teaching did not occur in that era, nor that teachers were not prepared, in some sense, for what they were doing. It is, instead, to say that little, if any, part of any formal educational curriculum was devoted to preparing teachers. Of course, analogous statements could be made about schools in this period. Education in the schools, as well as in teacher preparation, took place in the family, in the town or other community in which the family lived, in the church that family members might have attended, and/or often in apprenticeships and indentures.

The distinction between education and schooling has been elaborated most fully for the colonial period by historians Bernard Bailyn (1960) and Lawrence Cremin (1970). They have also used this distinction to argue for a stance on educational affairs including teacher education, which is less school and teacher focused than many educators would like. To make the point clear in its historical context, the index for Lawrence Cremin's massive history of colonial education *American Education: The Colonial Experience* (1970) contains no page references under the term *teacher*. Instead, it refers the reader to other headings such as *church* and *community as educator*. What this lack of references implies is, not that there were no teachers in colonial America, but that those who taught were usually not individuals who looked on their teaching as their primary role in life, or often, not even as their primary occupational role in life.

Teachers taught in a variety of settings in our nation's early history. Some were employed as tutors for the children of wealthy families. Others, usually mature women, taught the elementary subjects in their homes in what were known as "dame schools" (Cremin, 1970). Still others taught in a variety of other arrangements, some of which were labeled *schools* or *academies*. These latter institutions, which in later years would be called *secondary schools*, functioned as places for the higher branches of learning and sometimes as preparatory institutions for college study. Teachers for this wide variety of colonial educational institutions offered diverse preparation for their activities. Perhaps the highest form of preparation would have been to attend one of the colleges that dotted the colonial landscape. Yet teachers who had such training were usually intent on careers as clergymen. They taught most often in academies during their periods away from the college and generally did not intend to make teaching their life careers. Teachers in other schools often had little preparation for their task other than the demonstrated ability to read, write, and cypher, the tasks for which they were to prepare their pupils. In addition to these qualities, they were also usually expected to be of high moral character and orthodox religious beliefs.

This sort of environment for schooling, in which the processes of learning and teaching were not consistently organized into any one pattern or set of institutions, characterized the educational history of our society until well into the nineteenth century. In New England, however, in the early decades of the nineteenth century, the institution of the common school began to surface. What came to distinguish the common school from its predecessors was its character of being free, universal, and tax supported. Schools before the common school were most often not free, that is, tuition was charged. Neither were they universal. They were not open to blacks, and poor children could go only if their parents signed a document affirming their status as paupers. These schools were not supported completely, though often they were supported partially, by tax funds. The establishment of common schools meant that the principles of free tuition, universal attendance, and tax support became more and more important. With the advent of the common school in New England came an institution devoted to preparation of teachers for those common schools, the public normal school.

TEACHER EDUCATION IN THE NINETEENTH CENTURY

The first public normal school was begun in Lexington, Massachusetts, in 1839. Others followed in that state and in other New England states, and the trend eventually spread to the rest of the nation, though not reaching the South until quite late in the nineteenth century or early in the twentieth century. It is the public normal school that represents the distinctive nineteenth-century approach to teacher education and that will receive the bulk of the treatment in this section of the chapter. Before beginning that discussion, however, it is also appropriate to note that many teachers continued to attend academies as their sole preparation for assuming teaching positions, that others attended teachers' institutes (what we would now call *short courses* or *part-time courses*), that others attended normal courses of study at private schools or normal classes at secondary schools, and that still others had little or no formal preparation for their work.

The Normal School

Normal schools were founded as adjuncts to the common school system in Massachusetts. Common schooling meant or, more correctly, accompanied a considerable increase in enrollment in schools (Kaestle, 1983). This, in turn, required a distinct increase in the number of teachers who would be required to staff the schools. Horace Mann, discussed most comprehensively in Messerli (1971), was the most famous early propagandist for both common schools and normal schools in Massachusetts. Mann served as the secretary of the [Massachusetts] State Board of Education from 1837 to 1848. His fostering of normal schools was part of a larger attempt to systematize schooling and instruction in that state, that is, to bring it under the aegis of the State Board of Education.

Mann was at best partially successful in his attempts at systematization of common schooling. The principle of local or district control survived his movement for state power in schooling. He was, however, to prove eventually to be more successful in bringing normal schooling under the tutelage of the state. The early history of the normal school is an area that has received much attention from educators and, more recently, from historians.

The normal school grew with the common school. Its job was to provide teachers for the common schools. Historical studies of the normal school in the early twentieth century (Pangburn, 1932) provide, at best, an incomplete picture of these institutions. They point out that the normal school was founded as a single-purpose institution, one that would train teachers for the common schools. The preparation of students in the normal school varied widely. A few students had had some high school training, whereas the great majority had attended the elementary schools for which they were preparing to teach. The single purpose of training teachers meant that the curriculum of the normal school would be mainly technical. Yet the relatively uneducated character of the normal school students meant that often the normal school would have to offer academic subjects, so that the teachers would be familiar with what they would be teaching in the schools. This was less of a problem in large cities, where the relative wealth of students who had some high school training or were high school graduates meant that the normal school could concentrate almost completely on technical concerns as embodied in pedagogical studies.

Most of the early normal school students, whether in state or city normal classes, were women. This fact was left relatively unanalyzed in early historical accounts for normal schools. More recent historical studies (e.g., Mattingly, 1975, Tyack & Hansot, 1982), however, have paid closer attention to the gender makeup of students in the normal schools and of the nine-

teenth-century teaching force. These works show that the normal school played a major role in the feminization of the teaching profession that occurred in the nineteenth century. Women, who could be enticed to work for salaries considerably lower than men, were recruited into the ranks of teachers to accommodate the burgeoning enrollments in the common elementary schools.

Mattingly (1975) also chronicles how school leaders, almost completely male, changed their orientation from one of moral and religious exemplar to one of scientific leader of a teaching profession. This change in orientation was accomplished through curricular vehicles like the normal school and teacher institutes, both of which enhanced the image of teaching as a more scientific occupation. At the same time they preserved the image of moral exemplar by enrolling an increasingly female student body. The notion of *scientific* held by nineteenth-century school leaders was quite unlike what we mean by the term in contemporary times. To say that education was scientific was to say that it was a systematic enterprise, organized hierarchically into a logically connected set of experiences. It was this notion of a science of education that dominated the curriculum in the nineteenth-century normal schools.

A major pedagogical component of this science of education was the object teaching approach developed by the Swiss educator, Johann Heinrich Pestalozzi (Gutek, 1968). Object teaching, which stressed that the child's attention needed to be gained by contact with the objects of learning before any genuine education could take place, presented itself as an alternative to the formal educational drill usually employed in the schools and to the view of children as needing continual and forceful disciplining that necessitated the drill. Object teaching's principle that children's motivation was critical to the learning process was in keeping with the culture's conception of women as nurturers as more and more women became elementary teachers (Kaestle, 1983). The ways in which object teaching, at Oswego, New York, and other normal schools, supported the emergence of educational science are detailed by Brauner (1964). Later in the nineteenth century, educational science adopted the viewpoint of another European educator, the theorist Johann Friedrich Herbart (Dunkel, 1970).

Relying on the notion that education developed as a scientific study, early twentieth-century historians of the normal school (Pangburn, 1932) could then describe the process by which the normal school grew into the teachers college as an "evolution." What they meant is that it seemed a natural occurrence for the normal school, which at its beginnings functioned as a post–elementary, quasi-secondary school, to develop into a collegiate-level institution as more and more of its students came with some high school preparation and then with a high school diploma. This development enabled the normal school curriculum to begin at an intellectually higher level, to include progressively more complex analyses of teaching and conceptualizations of teaching, and, thus, to increase its scientific rigor.

It has remained for contemporary historians to question this conception of the normal school as a single-purpose institution evolving to a higher intellectual level. Herbst (1980, 1989) has played a major role in questioning this picture of the normal school. In dealing with the normal school in late nineteenth-century Wisconsin, Herbst downplays the notion of the normal school as a single-purpose institution by viewing it, not from the perspective of the educational leaders who sought to promote the science of education, but rather from the perspective of the state legislators who established the normal schools and of the students who attended them. Herbst shows that the early normal schools did not exist as single-purpose institutions but, rather, were driven by a variety of purposes.

Herbst (1980) argues that, in Wisconsin, state legislators, instead of acquiescing in educators' definition of the normal school as a single-purpose institution for training teachers, redefined the mission of the normal school:

Not only were they to offer instruction in the theory and art of teaching and in all the subjects of a common school education, but also in agriculture, chemistry, husbandry, mechanic arts, constitutional law and citizenship, and . . . medicine, astronomy, and other branches of science and literature. (p. 135)

Herbst goes on to show that the citizens of the state who fought to have the normal schools located in their communities were in sympathy with the legislative definition of the normal school. They sent their children to the normal school to gain post–elementary education similar to that provided in high schools and academies. The normal school was the closest post–elementary school available in rural areas, and many students attended to acquire a secondary education. When high schools later developed throughout the state, this did not mean the end of the normal school but, rather, a shift in the normal school to a post–high school status. Here again, however, the single-purpose teacher training institution was not the reality. Students now attended to obtain the closest, most readily available post–secondary education, which they might use for a variety of purposes. Some might want studies relevant to occupations such as farming. Others might wish to enter the university and use their normal studies as preparation for that objective. Still others might attend simply to attain a post–secondary education in subjects of their interest.

Readers might wonder if the particulars of Herbst's argument were completely unknown to the educators who set up and staffed the early normal schools. Were they totally unaware that many of their students were in attendance for purposes that did not agree with the stated purpose of the normal school? Indications that the institutional leaders were cognizant of this mixture of student motive, and that they at times acted on it, can be found in normal schools outside of the state of Wisconsin.

For example, Lynch (1946) indicates that one early president of the normal school at Terre Haute, Indiana, took the step, for a brief period, of formally acknowledging that courses other than those directly relevant to teacher training could be obtained at the school. Courses in the general branches of knowledge, or what Borrowman (1956) refers to as general education, were publicized as part of the offerings. Lynch (1946) also reports that this acknowledgment of general education as part of the curriculum at this normal school lasted only a year. He does not, however, give reasons either for the acknowledgment of general education or the withdrawal of the acknowl-

edgment. Similarly, Borrowman (1956) notes that in 1888 the St. Cloud (Minnesota) State Normal School promised to its prospective students that "the young man or woman, who may not desire to make teaching a life work, will find himself possessed of a thorough education" when he or she had finished the normal school curriculum, thorough enough to ensure that the student "has a substantial preparation for any vocation" (p. 77).

Although diversity of purpose was evident in early normal school development, at least when this development is considered from the point of view of legislators and prospective students, it must be reiterated that most of what constituted the official curriculum at these schools was devoted to teacher education. It seems appropriate, then, to inquire as to what made up this curriculum.

Pangburn (1932) summarizes the situation in the normal schools as it existed in 1890 and indicates that, at least up to that time, there had been no great change in the normal school curriculum since the institution's founding some 50 years earlier. Work in academic subjects at normal schools was largely in subjects that made up the curriculum of the elementary school. Students needed to show a "mastery of reading, writing, spelling, geography, grammar, and arithmetic for admission to the regular professional courses" (p. 14). Students who did not demonstrate such mastery would study those subjects at the normal school until they had mastered them. Work in the professional sequence "consisted of thirteen weeks in the History of Education, twenty-seven weeks in the Science of Education, thirty-one weeks in Methods in the Elementary Branches, and twenty weeks in Mental Science, a week being defined as forty-five minutes a day for five days" (p. 14). Practice teaching in a school, preceded by significant amounts of observation, was also standard in the normal schools.

From this description of the normal school in 1890, we can conclude that the curriculum was largely technical, in the sense that Borrowman (1956) defines the term, directly related to skills and knowledge that would be needed in actual teaching. Although one might contend that the experience in History of Education represented a liberal study, that is, work that enabled prospective teachers to reflect upon, evaluate, and perhaps even alter the assumptions behind their practice and behavior, Borrowman is dubious about this outcome. After discussing the limitations of the early texts in history of education, he concludes that the possibility that "such materials could have brought significant new meanings to the analysis of educational problems seems doubtful, particularly since the students had so little previous liberal education" (p. 62). What we have then is a largely technical approach to the education of teachers in the nineteenth-century normal school.

On the issue of general education, we have seen that some subject matter was offered in the normal school, primarily that which prepared for teaching school subjects. We also have seen, however, that noneducation-related subject matter was advocated for the normal school by legislators and by prospective students, and that many students attended the normal school and studied its courses with general educational goals or goals of preparing for a profession other than teaching school. Finally, it should be remembered that the normal school until the turn of the twentieth century was basically a post–elementary school that often competed with the high school for enrollment of older students. Thus, some young girls would go to the normal school rather than the high school, intending both to acquire a secondary education and to prepare for teaching in the elementary schools.

The attempt to impose a single, nonacademic curriculum on the nineteenth and twentieth century black normal school is an interesting variation in the history of nineteenth-century teacher education. As described by Anderson (1988), one model of the normal school was prescribed as appropriate for all black teacher education, particularly in the South. The Hampton (Virginia) Institute program, which stressed industrial education as the appropriate curriculum for both black teacher education schools and the black elementary schools in which black teachers would work, was advocated by white philanthropists and southern white educators as the only approach useful for blacks. Black resistance to industrial education was centered in the liberal arts colleges founded shortly after the Civil War by various northern missionary societies (Richardson, 1986). The debate on this issue among black institutions of higher education would continue until well into the twentieth century.

Before leaving the topic of teacher preparation in the nineteenth century, one often overlooked but extremely important fact should be reiterated. As Tyack (1967) reminds us, most elementary teachers were prepared not at all for their position. They simply attended elementary schools, perhaps finishing the course of study, and then returned to those schools as teachers. The hiring patterns of heavily locally oriented boards of education in cities or school trustees in towns and rural areas meant that the major qualification for getting a teaching job was being approved of by the local authority. As late as 1898, Tyack (1967) recounts, the number of public normal schools had reached 127, with a similar number of private ones, yet, "all the normal schools together that year graduated no more than one-quarter of the new teachers" (p. 415). Notions of state licensing and certification were nascent or ritualistic in this period. Only in the twentieth century, and well into that century in most places, would certification requirements be used as a vehicle to upgrade the preparation of teachers.

The University Study of Education

While the normal school was growing in numbers throughout the late nineteenth century, another development was taking place elsewhere in the established educational institutions that related to what was to come in teacher education. The beginnings of departments of education in universities came fairly swiftly after universities themselves were founded in the post–Civil War period. The first chair of pedagogy in a university was established at the University of Michigan in 1879 (H. C. Johnson & Johanningmeier, 1972). The holder of this chair, John Milton Gregory, would later move to the University of Illinois to organize the university study of education at that institution. Because universities at this time were often oriented to advanced study and research, their approach to the study of education would be much less technical than that of the normal school, that is, much less focused on daily problems of keeping a school.

University chairs and departments of pedagogy or education were not, however, impractical. They most often devoted their attention to an attempt to organize and place on a sound intellectual footing the activities of the increasingly various educational institutions that were then developing and vying with each other for students. Academies now found themselves competing with newly developing high schools, and both, in turn, had considerable curricular overlap with the normal schools. The elementary schools had undergone an age grading in the cities and larger towns but still maintained their ungraded, one-room schoolhouse character in rural areas and small towns. Many colleges held to the old-time ideal of the colonial college as an institution with a classical, fixed curriculum, whereas new types of agricultural and technical colleges were founded under the impetus of the Morrill Land Grant Act of the 1860s and the second Morrill act of the 1890s (Rudolph, 1962).

For university professors of education, the task in this context seemed to be to try to provide a science of education, in the sense of a systematic approach to the subject, by which the various schools and colleges might be better organized. Intellectually this meant an approach to education that was related to theoretical subjects such as philosophy, with educational theory often being seen as an offshoot of philosophy. Another common strategy was for education to align itself with newly developing social sciences such as psychology, which still often found itself in tandem with philosophy. These approaches were combined, not in an unusual configuration, at the University of Chicago when John Dewey assumed the chairmanship of the Department of Philosophy, Psychology, and Pedagogy in 1894 (Dykhuizen, 1973).

There were still other motives that lay behind the creation of university departments of education, motives that related to the political problems facing these relatively new institutions as they attempted to establish themselves. These political concerns reflected the reality that the new universities, particularly the state universities, had problems in being perceived favorably by citizens and needed to develop rationales for their own existence that would be accepted by those citizens. Clifford (1986) indicates several of these politically related concerns. First, state university departments of education performed the public relations function of showing citizens who were called on to support them with tax payments that the universities were addressing the educational mission of the public schools, institutions that the citizens did not consider esoteric. Education departments, by expressing interest in issues related to the public schools, might help the new universities attract students at a period when colleges and universities seemed to be overbuilt and were in need of bodies to inhabit their classrooms.

Departments of education could also help universities alleviate their enrollment problems by appealing to prospective women students. This would be accomplished in a way that would allow women to enroll but not spread their presence or their influence across the campuses. Women could be contained in education departments, just as they could be contained in schools of home economics. Enrollment could further be increased by education departments' declaring their interest in preparing high school teachers, thereby affirming a link with the schools, but not one with the low-status, common, elementary school.

This last purpose of preparation for the high school offered a way for university departments of education to distinguish themselves from the normal school, which was consigned the job of preparing elementary teachers. Preparing high school teachers also enabled the university to gain an influential role in what would happen in the high schools as their enrollment grew significantly. The primacy of the academic function could be maintained, at least for a while, and even when other functions were taken on in the high schools in the twentieth century, a pecking order that maintained the academic component of the high school would be affirmed (Krug, 1964). Having moved into the twentieth century with this consideration of the high school, let us now turn our attention completely to the development of teacher education in that era.

TEACHER EDUCATION: 1900–1960

The institutions of the university and the normal school, which were the major players in the education of teachers in the nineteenth century, would continue to play their roles in the twentieth century. One of these institutions, the normal school, would transform itself in order to maintain its role. The normal school would first become what it thought was a higher level institution called *the teachers college* and then adopt a curricular focus broader than teacher education and change its name simply to *college*. In the last half of the twentieth century some normal schools even managed to acquire the name university, along with some of the functions that name implies. Before turning to normal school developments, however, it is appropriate first to focus on the study of education in universities and to highlight the changes that occurred in that arena.

Teacher Education in the Universities

In the first 2 decades of the twentieth century, university departments of education maintained their focus on preparing high school teachers at the undergraduate level. They also began to address the issues related to administering the burgeoning school systems that were being created in the nation's cities. Graduate courses and degrees in school administration became a staple of university departments of education during this period. Some historians such as Callahan (1962) have been harshly critical of the nature of these courses and programs, arguing that they represented a capitulation to the business interests that were intent on containing expenditures on public education and an abandonment of genuinely educational concerns. The success of these courses and programs in fitting in with the developing hierarchy in American public education, and in making sure that university graduates with advanced

degrees in school administration would be at the head of this hierarchy, cannot be denied.

The study of education in the nineteenth century, though devoted nominally to developing a science of education, was carried out in ways that would be changed in the twentieth century. In the earlier period, science, in the sense of systematic study, meant that education relied on the theoretical accounts of the enterprise developed by European thinkers such as Pestalozzi and Herbart. The educational science of the nineteenth century, though theoretical, was not unrelated to the issues of teaching and learning that were important in the schools. In terms of Borrowman's (1956) categories, we might conclude that this approach embodied a notion of liberal studies within education as the key to the science of education and to educational leadership. Several influential twentieth-century American thinkers such as John Dewey, who was beginning to undertake and advocate more laboratory-oriented ways of studying education, did so initially in categories that were fundamentally conditioned by Herbartian categories and concerns (Kliebard, 1986).

The graduate programs in school administration of the early twentieth century, however, marked a significant change in emphasis. They adopted rudimentary statistical procedures as a means of gathering prodigious amounts of data on school affairs, which were then used to legitimate decisions made by administrators as "scientific" (Callahan, 1962). University professors of school administration, most notably George Strayer of Teachers College, Columbia, conducted numerous school surveys that utilized this kind of study as a basis for making recommendations to school systems. The invitations to make these surveys were usually extended by the administrator, who would be charged with implementing the recommendations of the surveys. More often than not, this administrator was a graduate of the program at the university employing the surveyor.

Although one could argue that the kind of science embodied in the notion of survey is related to the practical conduct of the educational enterprise in a policy sense, it is hard to see how it was related to the concerns of teachers. Thus, at the same time that it was touted as being scientific, it clearly was not related to any technical sense of teachers' tasks, as conceived by Borrowman (1956). In fact, this divorce from the classroom served the purpose of the university professors of education of maintaining the distance between themselves and the world of the classroom teacher, particularly the increasingly female world of the elementary teacher.

The advocacy of science, and the concomitant denigration of the school classroom as the appropriate focus of educational study, continued throughout much of the twentieth century. For example, the orientation of Charles Judd as head of education at the University of Chicago was to a science of education related to his own discipline of psychology. This also meant the divorce of education from the school classroom as the focus of its inquiry, a focus that had been part of the program of John Dewey, who preceded Judd (White, 1982). The estrangement between the programs in education at the University of Chicago and the schools also existed at Harvard in the same period

(Powell, 1980), as well as at Teachers College (Columbia), Stanford, and the University of California at Berkeley (Clifford, 1986). The particulars of the relationship might vary slightly from university to university, but the invocation of "science" and the denigration of the school were constants in the development of the study of education at the leading universities.

A prime example of these phenomena was the pursuit of IQ scores as important to work in psychology and education. This trend began in the 1920s and has continued, almost unabated, to the present in the educational and psychological literature, as well as in more popular journals. The obvious gap between measuring IQs precisely and developing educational methods or strategies related to the phenomena these instruments measure has hardly been addressed by the researchers in this field. The popularity of ability grouping among teachers is one evidence of how the work of psychologists has been adopted in education without serious attention being paid to the consequences of its adoption by the psychologists or the teachers.

Other psychologists, such as Edward L. Thorndike, were employed by university schools of education and developed research in areas such as transfer of training, memory, and other topics that eventually evolved into the specialized field of the psychology of learning (Joncich, 1968). This field seemed, at least potentially, more closely related to teachers' tasks, yet these psychologists exhibited a penchant for valuing their research for its own sake, rather than for any practical lessons that it might provide teachers. They specialized their work into more and more minute areas of study that had little relevance to the concerns of teachers. When one considers that the work has been undertaken in the psychology of *learning*, not *teaching*, the lack of fit between the research itself and the occupational or technical concerns of teachers is understandable.

Skepticism over the issue of fit between the psychologically based science of education developed in university departments of education and the concerns of schoolteachers are distinct characteristics of recent historical studies of university departments of education (Clifford & Guthrie, 1988; White, 1982). This is not, however, the view of the educational scientists involved in teacher training, including some who have undertaken historical study of teacher education. For example, Monroe (1952), although acknowledging problems in translating the accomplishments of teaching–learning theory into classroom applications, argues that conditions have improved since 1930 and are likely to improve even more in the years after his book's publication. Events since the publication of Monroe's book, at least as read by this historian, seem to belie his optimism.

Teacher Education in the Normal School

While the university departments of education were carrying on their divorce from the concerns of classroom teachers through the development of educational science, the events taking place in the normal schools were proceeding in a similar direction, although for quite different reasons. As the schooling enterprise became increasingly organized into a hierarchy in the twentieth century, normal schools became concerned about their place in that hierarchy. While universities attempted to monopolize the training of high school teachers, normal schools were unwilling to give up their claim to training that group of teachers alongside their elementary counterparts.

When school systems, headed by university doctoral or other advanced degree holders, were faced with employing university-trained high school teachers with bachelor's degrees or normal school graduates without degrees, their preference for the degree holders is not difficult to understand. This preference, along with the desires of normal school administrators and the citizens in communities where the normal schools were located for the higher status and more diversified opportunities that would come with college status, combined to make the normal schools seek their proper position in the educational hierarchy as teachers *colleges*.

The status anxieties inherent in this situation seem to have escaped the concern of those such as Pangburn (1932) who have chronicled the evolution of normal schools into teachers colleges. Her use of the term *evolution* implies a functional interpretation of the change, which is exactly what she offers. She describes the change from normal school to collegiate-level teacher education as related to issues such as increasing enrollments, accreditation, and centralization of administration in ways that make it seem quite natural and expected. Similarly, she is quite satisfied with the situation in the 1930s when most normal schools had become teachers colleges and had taken their proper place in the educational hierarchy. What her perspective does not prepare her readers for is what happened to these normal schools after they developed into teachers colleges and took the next logical developmental step, the progression into multipurpose colleges with a distinct general-education mission, or liberal arts focus, as part of their mission.

When a normal school became a teachers college, it began to offer bachelor's degrees and to compete realistically with universities as a producer of high school teachers. This degree status meant that normal schools' offerings increased substantially in general education, the academic work preparatory for collegiate-level teacher education. This in turn meant a significant increase in faculty in academic subjects not related to the purpose of training teachers. These academic faculty, many of whom were trained in universities, brought university values from their own disciplines into the teachers college setting, values that did not honor the purpose of preparing teachers as the ultimate goal of their work. Instead, they pushed to get students to major in their subjects, and, even if these students also got a high school teaching certificate, their identity, at least as formed by their subject-matter professors, was not geared to honoring the occupation of schoolteacher but, rather, the field in which the high school teacher might teach. When the teachers colleges became colleges, and students might major in liberal arts subjects without getting a secondary certificate, the campus status of school teaching declined even more.

This diversification of function, and eventual denigration of teaching, can also be seen in the history of black normal schools. Caliver (1933) provides a comprehensive account of the education of black teachers, including the developments in black normal schools, in the 1920s and early 1930s. Urban (1985) chronicles the struggle among teacher training, vocational studies in agriculture and allied fields, and liberal arts education for supremacy in the Fort Valley (Georgia) State College. The title of *state college*, given to the normal school at Fort Valley in 1939, signified both its advance to 4-year, degree-granting status and the eventual rise of non-teacher-oriented study in the arts and sciences to the extent that it would compete with teacher education for primacy in the curriculum of the institution.

In the 1950s, David Riesman (1956) used the metaphor the "academic procession" and characterized its movement as snakelike, to indicate the ways in which normal schools, as well as junior colleges and 4-year colleges, have come to imitate those above them in the hierarchy. Thus colleges, instead of concentrating on their mission of teaching undergraduate students, seek to become universities. Their faculty value research as their university teachers did, and they tend to devalue the problems and issues raised by their undergraduate students, which seldom relate to research issues. Those colleges that had been teachers colleges are intent on forgetting that fact and mission and are eager to embrace the wider academic mission of becoming colleges and, later, universities.

Looking at the normal schools as they developed into colleges and, in some instances, universities, E. Alden Dunham (1969) describes these institutions as colleges of the forgotten Americans. This characterization relates the relatively low status of these institutions in the academic pecking order to the largely working- and lower-middle-class students who attend them. Students often enroll in these colleges because they do not qualify for, or they cannot afford, the tuition or the travel expenses necessary to attend the more prestigious state universities. The push from the liberal arts faculty at these institutions to deemphasize, if not forget, their history as teacher training institutions is also a part of Dunham's story.

Thus, we can see how the normal school evolved from a single-purpose institution devoted to training teachers into the low-status institution of teachers college in an educational hierarchy. Many teachers college faculty wished to forget the purpose that animated their school at its origins, and many teachers college students were there because they could not qualify, academically or financially, for study at higher status institutions. Given the relative success of teachers college liberal arts faculties in devaluing teacher education, and given that the teacher education obtained at these colleges was often an imitation of that offered at universities, we find that the role in teacher education played by the teachers college in the twentieth century did little, if anything, to mitigate the problems developing in university teacher education programs.

While the normal school (teachers college), because of its historic commitment to the training of teachers, might have retained closer ties to schools and to teachers than the universities, these relationships were vulnerable to movements on the teachers college campus to become more academic and less school oriented. Attaining university status, as more and more of these institutions have been able to do since the 1950s, only increased the probability that links to schools and teachers

would disappear as characteristics of the institution. Thus the normal school developed into a pale imitation of the university, doing what the university does, namely research, less well than the university and not wishing to do well what it historically did, prepare teachers.

Given this development in the normal schools, it seems clear that the important things that would happen in teacher education in twentieth-century America would occur, at least first, at the universities. Let us then, turn to the movement in teacher education on the university campus that attempted to deal with the divorce between the educational scientists and the schools, the foundations component in teacher education programs begun at Teachers College, Columbia University, in the 1920s.

The Foundations Movement in Teacher Education

In the late 1920s, a group of faculty at Teachers College began to meet regularly for dinner and discussion of educational issues and the social context in which they were embedded. A mid-century retrospective by one of the founders of the group, Harold Rugg (1952), describes the membership and intellectual direction of these early group meetings. The orientation of the group was to the social and philosophical ideas of John Dewey. It also had a distinct affinity with the educational progressivism of Teachers College professor William Heard Kilpatrick, developer of the project method as a means of organizing teaching and member of the group.

It was from the discussions of this group, and similar ideas being voiced by educational intellectuals such as Boyd Bode at The Ohio State University, that the notion of "foundations of education" as we have come to know it emerged. A fairly recent historical study of that movement by Tozer and McAninch (1986) supplements Rugg's memoir. Together, they provide a comprehensive account of the origins and development of the foundations movement.

It is clear that the founders of the foundations approach were dissatisfied with existing teacher education activities for at least two reasons. *First*, the nonmethods studies in teacher education, mainly history of education, philosophy of education, and educational psychology, particularly the latter, tended to be based on the concerns of the parent discipline from which they were taken rather than on the real problems of teaching. *Second*, teacher education curricula tended to take the existing social reality as a given and attempted to adjust the actions of the teachers and the schools to reflect that reality. Following Dewey, the foundations thinkers reflected much more dissatisfaction with American society and its schools, and they looked for ways to bring them into greater conformity with the democratic thrust and mission that both society and school invoked in much of their rhetoric.

The foundations group eventually developed a two-course, interdisciplinary, graduate sequence at Teachers College, divided basically into courses in the social and the psychological foundations of education. The psychological foundations experience developed in ways that made it little different from its predecessor offerings in educational psychology. The social foundations experience, however, moved the teacher education curriculum a good way along the paths of interdisciplinary rather than disciplinary study and of advocating a distinctly more critical intellectual stance by prospective and practicing teachers toward the social role and ramifications of their work. The economic calamities of the Great Depression, occurring while the social foundations movement was emerging, meant that much of the early social foundations emphasis on democracy involved criticism of capitalism and serious study of non-capitalist societies and educational systems. One can view this early social foundations movement at its strongest in books such as *The Social Foundations of Education*, written at the height of the depression by George S. Counts (1934).

As the depression waned, the overt criticism of American society by social foundations scholars abated somewhat. The impetus for development of the field also shifted from Teachers College, Columbia University, to the University of Illinois (Tozer & McAninch, 1986). The group at Illinois, largely trained at Teachers College, modified the earlier approach in part, focusing more on the relational aspects of democratic decision making in schools and elsewhere and introducing material from emerging disciplines such as anthropology that were less evident in the earlier version of the field, but maintaining the consciously critical analysis of schooling and society as an important objective.

The Illinois group produced a book of readings that often posed contradictory ideas in consecutive excerpts and, with editorial assistance, asked prospective teachers to evaluate the arguments. The editors set forth an orientation that they shared with their Teachers College predecessors and that would likely be used by many who teach social foundations in our current period. They argued that teacher education lacked the dimension of a rigorous study of the relation of the place of the school in society. Not having acquired an understanding of the school–society interaction meant that prospective teachers "may not have been taught to see that choices about what to do in school typically reflect wider choices about what to do in the society for which the school is educating the young" (Stanley, Smith, Benne, & Anderson, 1956, p. 3).

The social foundations approach was widely adopted in many universities and colleges, though separate disciplinary courses such as history of education, philosophy of education, and sociology of education did not completely disappear. In fact, criticism of the foundations approach as excessively hortatory and insufficient in intellectual rigor were often made by more disciplinary-oriented scholars in education (Brauner, 1964). The training of social foundations professors also followed disciplinary lines, meaning that the field as a teaching field offered substantial differences from what those who taught it learned in their own training. Despite these difficulties, social foundations and school and society as an area of study and a course title in teacher education have survived into our own time.

Clearly, the social foundations approach typifies what Borrowman (1956) describes as the liberal element in teacher education studies. In fact, Borrowman's artful conclusion to his volume calls for combining social foundational studies, studies in psychological areas such as learning, and more clearly technical areas such as teaching methods and field experiences into a cohesive, coherent, teacher education program. He also acknowledges in his analysis the diversity of institutional settings in which teacher education takes place: private liberal arts colleges, state teachers colleges and state colleges that were formerly normal schools, and university schools, departments, and colleges of education. His analysis, sophisticated both historically and in its awareness of the variety of forces and factors then impinging on teacher education, could have been taken as providing some confidence that teacher education knew where it had been and where it was going. This confidence, if indeed it was present, was about to be challenged severely.

TEACHER EDUCATION: 1960 TO THE PRESENT

To write about the immediate past in teacher education, or any other subject, for that matter, is a task avoided by most historians. Their motivation for this avoidance is often stated in a phrase such as "it just isn't history." What this means is that the events are too recent to be viewed with any perspective other than that of one who has lived through them. Though there have been some historical accounts of education in the recent past (Ravitch, 1983; Spring, 1976), no studies to date deal specifically with teacher education. What follows, then, is offered with the full confidence that errors of omission or commission will be quickly noted by readers who have lived through the same period but experienced it from different perspectives and view it differently.

Critical Treatises of Teacher Education

The early 1960s saw the publication of two critical analyses of teacher education, one by James D. Koerner (1963), an officer on the Council for Basic Education, and the other by James B. Conant (1963), former president of Harvard University and eminent educational statesman. Both of these volumes decry the low quality of students in teacher education programs and the questionable academic credentials of the professors of education preparing them. The 1960s was not the first time that teacher educators and prospective teachers had been criticized. In the early 1950s, Arthur Bestor (1953), professor of history at the University of Illinois, wrote a scathing analysis of the public schools called *Educational Wastelands*, which included a chapter sharply critical of the professional education of teachers.

What gave the criticisms of teacher education impetus in the 1950s and 1960s, in addition to the standing of authors such as Conant and Bestor, was the nation's concern over the educational deficiency of its students. This concern was partly sparked by the Russians' putting their Sputnik satellite into orbit in 1957, thereby beating Americans into space. As the analyses in Conant (1963), Koerner (1963), and Bestor (1953) indicate, however, skepticism over the qualifications of teacher education students and faculty had existed in the minds of college and university professors of the arts and science disciplines for a long time prior to the writing of their books.

As already suggested, substandard students and professors were the major charge of these critics of teacher education programs. Their solutions varied from outright abolition of education courses and faculties to severe diminution of the offerings in professional education. What they could agree on was the adoption of an all-university approach to teacher preparation in place of locating that responsibility exclusively in the education unit. Conant (1963) and Koerner (1963) both used the lack of any reliable data to support a given approach to teacher education as a considerable part of their argument against teacher preparation controlled by education schools or departments. They also relied on the impressions of teachers and compilations of teachers' opinions about the effectiveness of their preparation programs.

It seems clear that the Conant and Koerner books put teacher educators on the defensive and that recent attacks on teacher education programs seem little more than repetitions of those of the critics of the 1960s. The responses of teacher educators to these criticisms have ranged from ignoring them to attempting to demonstrate, in a variety of ways, that the study of education and the professional training of teachers are endeavors that are distinctly defensible both intellectually and practically. Perhaps the most interesting of these defenses is that of those who continued the long-held quest for a science of education, but this time by actually making teaching and schooling the center of that quest. The effective-schools literature might be seen as one part of the search for the new science of education. The astronomical growth of the American Educational Research Association (AERA) is further evidence of that movement.

A Science of Education

A most interesting part of the new science of education movement is that which actually looked at teaching as a basis for its study. Use of modern video technology to tape teachers at work, analyze the tapes, and develop courses and experiences based on these analyses constituted the bulk of what became known as the movement of micro-teaching. One of the prime movers in micro-teaching was B. O. Smith, who had been active in the Illinois version of the social foundations in the 1950s. In *Teachers for the Real World* (1969), Smith posited 10 teaching skills that should form the basis of any teacher education program. Further, he argued that prospective teachers should learn these skills through practice, as well as, or in place of, theoretical study and that they should be given the opportunity to receive feedback on their teaching skills through audio- or videotapes of their actual teaching.

An approach similar to Smith's animated the Performance Based Teacher Education (PBTE) and the Competency Based Teacher Education (CBTE) movements of the 1970s and early 1980s. These movements were heavily influential in many teacher education programs; in fact, CBTE was adopted as the official approach to teacher education in several states (Hertzberg, 1976).

About a decade after publication of *Teachers for the Real World*, Smith elaborated his analysis to the point that it involved an actual *Design for a School of Pedagogy* (1980). In this latter volume, he specified a program for preprofessional education, as well as what should go into the professional sequence. He then outlined a program of professional teacher preparation based on pedagogical knowledge generated from research findings. Smith was optimistic about both the level of knowledge that had been attained by educational research and the possibility that this knowledge could be organized into a coherent program for preparing teachers. The failure of his design to overtake and transform teacher education could be due to his being overly optimistic about the knowledge base generated by educational research or to the simple recalcitrance of education faculties to change themselves in conformity with Smith's, or anyone else's, externally generated mandate.

Whatever the cause of the inertia, teacher educators in the late 1980s found themselves beset with many of the same problems teacher educators faced for generations. Animosity from arts and sciences faculty had diminished little. Teachers were being prepared in universities, state colleges, and small and large private colleges, though differences in the curricula among these types of institutions had been mitigated to some extent by state accrediting agencies and a private national group, the National Council for Accreditation of Teacher Education (NCATE). The questionable academic qualifications of many teachers had once again been raised, this time with considerable amounts of data gathered, not by outside critics, but by educationists themselves.

In short, one might wonder why the contemporary plans of Governor Kean in New Jersey and governors in other states to bypass teacher education programs were not proposed sooner or with greater frequency. To argue that teacher education has solved its problems is to ignore the reality of the field's own development.

HISTORIANS AND THE PRESENT IN TEACHER EDUCATION

Two recent volumes reflect the continuing interest of educational historians in teacher education. The work by Clifford and Guthrie (1988) is a collaborative effort by a historian and an educational policy analyst to detail the weaknesses in the orientation of the schools of education of 10 or so leading American research universities. The lack of fit between these university schools of education and the teachers and the schools to which they were to provide a service is the major theme of this analysis.

More recently, Warren (1989) has edited a volume of essays for the American Educational Research Association in which a number of leading educational historians present the results of their work. Topics covered in this volume include teacher contracts, teacher workplaces, and teacher education, with separate chapters devoted to the latter topic in both the nineteenth and twentieth centuries. Although it is hard to summarize the views of several contributors to such a volume, it seems fair to conclude that few of them are satisfied with things as they are in all the areas of teachers, teaching, and teacher education.

Since 1985, essays on teacher education have been published that are informed by historical analysis. A look at three of them and the conclusions reached by their authors highlights further the emphasis in contemporary historical work on criticism of the field of teacher education.

In "Learning from Experience: History and Teacher Education" (1985), Donald Warren considers teacher education over the entire time span covered in this chapter. He stresses the lack of formal preparation on the part of most teachers until well into the twentieth century. He also notes the considerable strides that have been taken in providing and requiring formal teacher preparation since the 1930s.

In spite of these advances, Warren concludes his essay with the argument that the continuities in the situation surrounding teacher education in the distant past, more recent past, and present are important, and too often neglected. He stresses three continuities as especially significant. First, and perhaps most important, teacher education has always existed in a context driven by market forces that govern the supply and demand of available teachers. Arguments about a science of education and/or a research base as important for teacher preparation, or proposals stressing the applicability of preparation in some other occupation such as medicine or law as a guide for teacher education, are some recent examples of contemporary points of view offered without taking into consideration the job market for teachers. To use Warren's own words: "The teacher economy continues to function independently of professional judgment about teacher education, as it did in the nineteenth century, and independently of research findings, as it does in our time" (p. 11).

Warren notes the long history of conflict on the issue of whether teacher education programs should be separate from other educational endeavors. From the beginnings of normal schools, teacher education advocates of single-purpose preparation for teachers have faced opposition from colleagues in non–normal school educational settings who have argued that they should have influence on the preparing of teachers and from students in teacher-preparation programs who have not envisioned their enrollment in those programs as confining them to an occupational future as a teacher. These concerns often boil down to issues of academic politics, with faculty competing for dollars, enrollments, and prestige, particularly in the twentieth century, when single-purpose teacher preparation in normal schools became a lost cause.

Most important from the point of view of his analysis, Warren argues that teacher education from the beginning has been hampered by stress on instructional preparation as the entire focus of the endeavor. One outcome of this emphasis is noted by Warren in a way that seems to reprise Borrowman's concern for the importance of the liberal in teacher education. According to Warren, "offered in isolation, preparation for instruction has left teachers unprepared for their more difficult responsibilities, which are to conceptualize, innovate, and analyze disparate educational and policy phenomena" (p. 11). Lack of attention to several aspects of the policy environment in which teachers work has meant that preparation programs continue to innovate, in the expectation that these innovations will alter teacher practice in the schools. What this narrowly focused

zeal for improvement has ignored is that changes in teacher training programs, to be effective, "require improvement in the conditions under which teachers work" (p. 11).

Thus, the major point raised by Warren is that teacher education programs should not exist in intellectual vacuums. They must begin to pay attention to who it is that is coming into the programs and the conditions under which those who finish the program will work if changes in teacher education are to have the desired impact.

Two other articles, published in 1987, also involve historical reflection on teacher education. In one of these, Ginsburg reviews historical studies of teacher education, many of which are also discussed in this chapter, from the point of view of class and gender relations. Ginsburg looks at the social composition of student bodies in normal schools and universities and then in education departments and arts and science departments within universities. He notes various decisions taken by these entities that enforce both the social-class and gender distinctions that have existed and continue to exist in our society. For example, normal schools enrolled largely female students, while universities concentrated on males. Similarly, normal school students came from more ordinary social-class backgrounds than did university students. As the universities developed education departments that prepared teachers, similar class and gender differences existed between students in these departments and students in the arts and science disciplines.

Ginsburg also notes the tendency of university educationists, particularly in their first years of existence, to try to disassociate themselves from the female and lower-class world of the public schools and to train administrators to manage those schools. Even when they adopted teacher preparation as a function, university educationists opted for the more male domain of the high school teacher than for the female-dominated elementary school.

Ginsburg even sees the importance of class and gender relations in the curriculum of teacher education programs. He notes the relation of the early normal-school curriculum to the place of women in the changing social relations of the nineteenth century. He discusses home economics and industrial-education training programs in relation to changes in the economy of the early twentieth century. Similarly, he relates the tendency to emphasize social forces in the early twentieth century, particularly the 1930s, to the social and economic crises of those two eras.

Ginsburg ends his article with a plea to look at contemporary developments in teacher education through the lens of the historically conditioned class and gender relations that have characterized this field. This perspective, he argues, should sensitize one to the potential for how reforms of teacher education deflect attention from problems in the economy that might be involved in creating the problems that teacher education reforms are supposed to solve. He also asks his readers to pay attention to the ways that proposals for differentiation in contemporary teacher education programs—such as proposals to concentrate the education of master teachers in universities and take lower-status school instructors from other programs—might repeat the class- and gender-oriented biases of programs for educating administrators in universities that were developed in university education departments in the early twentieth century. As an alternative to this approach, he advocates developing programs for all educators, instead of compartmentalizing their preparation, in an attempt to mitigate the ways in which teacher preparation reinforces class, gender, and racial distinctions.

The final historical article to be considered here is "Empowering Practitioners: Holmes, Carnegie and the Lessons of History," by William Johnson (1987). In this article, Johnson takes issue with the recommendations of the Holmes Group (1986) and the Carnegie Forum on Education and the Economy (1986) regarding the preparation and practice of contemporary teachers. Johnson begins with a vigorous critique of the claim in the two reports that educational research has provided reliable information on which to base a genuine science of education. He then goes on to use the history of the medical profession to refute the notions of the two reports that a properly differentiated teaching occupation can be built on the science of education.

According to Johnson, medical scientists convinced practitioners to adopt scientific medicine in the early twentieth century because that approach to medicine worked in practice. There is no such convincing link between current educational science and teaching. Johnson, noting the widespread difference in the disciplinary base of most contemporary educational research, shows that education now is most like nineteenth-century medicine as it existed before the alteration of medical practice to adopt the scientific paradigm. He uses the experience of this fractionated medical practice before the adoption of science to show that, to embrace a central licensing examination now, in a similar climate, when educational knowledge is fragmented, will likely result in an intellectually splintered occupation, not the professionally unified group that both Holmes and Carnegie seek.

Still another way in which both the Holmes and Carnegie reports misunderstand the history of medicine is in their assumption of the role that reports like their own can play. Johnson (1987) shows how the 1910 Flexner Report, seen by educational groups as the incident that revolutionized the practice of medicine, did no such thing. Rather, it capped the rising influence of scientific medical practice that had begun 2 decades before its publication.

In addition to his arguments with the Holmes and Carnegie reports over their misunderstanding of the history of medicine, Johnson (1987) also argues that the Holmes Group (1986) ironically misreads the history of the individual for whom it is named, Henry Holmes, dean of the Harvard Graduate School of Education. Although the Holmes report correctly notes that, under Holmes, Harvard abolished all undergraduate teacher training and went to a 2-year EdM as its basic professional teaching degree, it misunderstands the orientation of that degree and of Holmes himself. Rather than basing its master's degree on research, as suggested by the Holmes Group (composed of leading research university schools of education), Holmes and Harvard intended to create a practitioner-oriented, common educational experience for all educators. For Holmes, this experience was to be based on the practical knowledge of teachers, not the dubious research findings of an esoteric educational science. Johnson concludes his article with the point that better teacher education and an improved teaching force will likely come from genuine, as opposed to condescending, contact with practicing teachers.

The three historically oriented articles just described are quite diverse in their orientations, their approaches, and their findings. Yet there seem to be at least two common threads in these studies. *First*, the authors of these articles share with the author of this chapter a critical stance toward much of the contemporary optimism in teacher education reform circles. Knowledge of the history of teacher education evidently prepares one to question a too-easy optimism about the prospects for reform. Historians understand that educational reform is intertwined with societal reform and attempts to change education that ignore the larger context are not likely to succeed.

Second, the authors of these articles also share the belief that reform of teacher education will not be accomplished without reform of the occupation of teaching itself. In fact, it seems fair to say that these authors see the latter as more important than the former. Although this chapter has not dealt specifically with the relationship of teacher education to teaching and teachers, that lack simply reflects the omission of the relationship in most of the historical and other studies of the topic until recently.

All of the historical works discussed in the last section of this chapter, as well as the author of this review, agree that teacher education that is studied, conceptualized, analyzed, and "reformed" without careful and critical attention to the social context in which teacher education exists, as well as the practitioners and the practice of teaching, will quite likely be an empty exercise. This conviction constitutes a challenge that teacher educators would be well advised to answer as they evaluate and reform their programs.

References

Anderson, J. D. (1988). *The education of blacks in the South, 1860–1935*. Chapel Hill, NC: University of North Carolina Press.

Bailyn, B. (1960). *Education in the forming of American society*. Chapel Hill, NC: University of North Carolina Press.

Bestor, A. (1953). *Educational wastelands: The retreat from learning in our public schools*. Urbana, IL: University of Illinois Press.

Borrowman, M. L. (1956). *The liberal and the technical in teacher education: A historical survey of American thought*. New York: Columbia University, Teachers College, Bureau of Publications.

Brauner, C. J. (1964). *American educational theory*. Englewood Cliffs, NJ: Prentice-Hall.

Caliver, A. (1933). *Education of Negro teachers* (Bulletin No. 10). Washington, DC: U.S. Office of Education.

Callahan, R. E. (1962). *Education and the cult of efficiency: A study of the social forces that have shaped the administration of the public schools.* Chicago: University of Chicago Press.

Carnegie Forum on Education and the Economy, Task Force on Teaching as a Profession. (1986). *A nation prepared: Teachers for the 21st century.* New York: Author.

Clifford, G. J. (1986) The formative years of schools of education in America: A five-institution analysis. *American Journal of Education, 94,* 427–446.

Clifford, G. J., & Guthrie, J. W. (1988). *Ed school: A brief for professional education.* Chicago: University of Chicago Press.

Conant, J. B. (1963). *The education of American teachers.* New York: McGraw-Hill.

Counts, G. S. (1934). *The social foundations of education.* New York: Charles Scribner's Sons.

Cremin, L. A. (1970). *American education: The colonial experience, 1607–1783.* New York: Harper & Row.

Dunham, E. A. (1969). *Colleges of the forgotten Americans: A profile of state colleges and regional universities.* New York: McGraw-Hill.

Dunkel, H. B. (1970). *Herbart and the Herbartians: An educational ghost story.* Chicago: University of Chicago Press.

Dykhuizen, G. (1973). *The life and mind of John Dewey.* Carbondale, IL: Southern Illinois University Press.

Ginsburg, M. B. (1987). Teacher education and class and gender relations: A critical analysis of historical studies of teacher education. *Educational Foundations, 2,* 4–36.

Gutek, G. L. (1968). *Pestalozzi and education.* New York: Random House.

Herbst, J. (1980). Beyond the debates over revisionism: Three educational pasts writ large. *History of Education Quarterly, 20,* 131–145.

Herbst, J. (1989). *And sadly teach.* Madison, WI: University of Wisconsin Press.

Hertzberg, H. W. (1976). Competency based teacher education: Does it have a past or a future? *Teachers College Record, 79,* 1–21.

Holmes Group. (1986). *Tomorrow's teachers.* East Lansing. MI: Author.

Johnson, H. C., & Johanningmeier, E. V. (1972). *Teachers for the prairie: The University of Illinois and the schools, 1868–1945.* Urbana, IL: University of Illinois Press.

Johnson, W. R. (1987). Empowering practitioners: Holmes, Carnegie and the lessons of history. *History of Education Quarterly, 27,* 221–240.

Joncich, G. (1968). *The sane positivist: A biography of Edward L. Thorndike.* Middletown, CT: Wesleyan University Press.

Kaestle, C. K. (1983). *Pillars of tradition: Common schools and American society, 1780–1860.* New York: Hill & Wang.

Kliebard, H. M. (1986). *The Struggle for the American Curriculum, 1893–1958.* Boston: Routledge & Kegan Paul.

Koerner, J. D. (1963). *The miseducation of American teachers.* Boston: Houghton Mifflin.

Krug, E. A. (1964). *The shaping of the American high school, 1880–1920.* New York: Harper & Row.

Lynch, W. O. (1946). *A history of Indiana State Teachers College.* Terre Haute, IN: Indiana State Teachers College.

Mattingly, P. H. (1975). *The classless profession: American schoolmen in the nineteenth century.* New York: New York University Press.

Messerli, J. (1971). *Horace Mann: A biography.* New York: Alfred A. Knopf.

Monroe, W. S. (1952). *Teaching–learning theory and teacher education, 1890–1950.* Urbana, IL: University of Illinois Press.

Pangburn, J. M. (1932). *The evolution of the American teachers college.* New York: Columbia University, Teachers College, Bureau of Publications.

Powell, A. G. (1980). *The uncertain profession: Harvard and the search for educational authority.* Cambridge, MA: Harvard University Press.

Ravitch, D. (1983). *The troubled crusade: American education, 1945–1980.* New York: Basic Books.

Richardson, J. M. (1986). *Christian reconstruction: The American Missionary Association and southern blacks, 1861–1890.* Athens, GA: University of Georgia Press.

Riesman, D. (1956). *Constraint and variety in American education.* Lincoln, NE: University of Nebraska at Lincoln.

Rudolph, F. (1962). *The American college and university: A history.* New York: Random House.

Rugg, H. O. (1952). *The teacher of teachers.* New York: Harper & Brothers.

Smith, B. O. (1969). *Teachers for the real world.* Washington, DC: American Association of Colleges for Teacher Education.

Smith, B. O. (1980). *A design for a school of pedagogy.* Washington, DC: U.S. Government Printing Office.

Spring, J. H. (1976). *The sorting machine: National educational policy since 1945.* New York: David McKay.

Stanley, W. O., Smith, B. O., Benne, K. D., & Anderson, A. W. (1956). *Social foundations of education.* New York: Holt, Rinehart & Winston.

Tozer, S., & McAninch, S. (1986). Social foundations of education in historical perspective. *Educational Foundations, 1,* 5–32.

Tyack, D. B. (Ed.). (1967). *Turning points in American educational history.* Waltham, MA: Blaisdell.

Tyack, D., & Hansot, E. (1982). *Managers of virtue: Public school leadership in America.* New York: Basic Books.

Urban, W. J. (1982). Historiography. In H. C. Mitzel (Ed.), *The Encyclopedia of Educational Research* (5th ed., pp. 791–795). New York: Macmillan.

Urban, W. J. (1985). Book and platform over anvil and hoe: Horace Mann Bond and the place of industrial education in the black college curriculum. *Journal of the Midwest History of Education Society, 13,* 90–112.

Warren, D. (1985). Learning from experience: History and teacher education. *Educational Researcher, 14*(10), 5–12.

Warren, D. (Ed.). (1989). *American teachers: Histories of a profession at work.* New York: Macmillan.

White, W. T. (1982). The decline of the classroom and the Chicago study of education, 1909–1929. *American Journal of Education, 90*(2), 144–174.

·5·

NATIONAL COMMISSION REPORTS OF THE 1980s

John Sikula

CALIFORNIA STATE UNIVERSITY, LONG BEACH

The issuance of *A Nation at Risk* in 1983 began a barrage of reports pointing out weaknesses in schooling and teacher preparation. These reports have influenced the direction of educational change and will continue to do so in the years ahead. The recommendations are generally consistent, but conflicting priorities, naivete, and political power struggles characterize their findings.

During the early 1980s, the American mass media frequently focused attention on negative aspects of schooling. Television and newspapers regularly reported declining student test scores, drugs and violence in the schools, deteriorating morale and working conditions, teacher burnout, increases in dropouts, and a host of other related and unrelated problems. The National Commission on Excellence in Education (1983) provided international comparisons of student achievement that revealed that, on 19 academic tests, American students were never first or second; indeed, they were last seven times. For more than a decade, college entrance examination scores had declined. Some 23 million American adults were functionally illiterate (National Commission on Excellence in Education, 1983, p. 8). The lure of television had drawn children away from books. Schools were burdened with driver education, sex education, drug education, and a little of everything else (Kilpatrick, 1983, p. 5).

Despite their essential negativeness, the public outcry and the media criticisms and comparisons brought needed attention to schooling and teacher preparation, compelling the country to reexamine priorities and to reconsider the value placed upon schooling and formal education. The catalyst in this process was a series of special reports issued by national commissions and task forces whose memberships were generally composed of respected and thoughtful citizens and leaders who were not part of the educational establishment. During the 5-year period, 1983–1988, dozens of reports from national, regional, and state groups were published.

The first wave of reports focused on public education. A second wave centered on the redesign of teacher preparation. A selected and representative review of important reports and analyses constitutes the essence of this chapter.

THE FIRST WAVE: FOCUS ON PUBLIC EDUCATION

Several of the more prominent reports recommended changes that reflected views of what schools should be like, what schools should accomplish, and how the nation should proceed to make schools more acceptable.

A Nation At Risk, National Commission on Excellence in Education (1983)

Appointed by the U.S. Secretary of Education, the 18-member National Commission on Excellence in Education issued its report in April 1983, following a 20-month study in which it held public hearings, commissioned papers, examined promising programs, and sought national input on the quality of America's schools and colleges. The tone of the report was sobering. It began with an often-quoted passage:

Our Nation is at risk. Our once unchallenged preeminence in commerce, industry, science, and technological innovation is being overtaken by competitors throughout the world. . . . If an unfriendly foreign power had attempted to impose on America the mediocre educational performance that exists today, we might well have viewed it as an act of war. As it stands, we have allowed this to happen to ourselves. (p. 5)

The author thanks his chapter reviewers for their helpful input: Richard E. Ishler (University of South Carolina) and Howard K. Macauley (Bloomsburg University of Pennsylvania). Also very useful was assistance from W. Robert Houston (University of Houston).

The nation was galvanized by its findings and its tone. The report stimulated national and state commissions and task forces across the country to rethink education. It was the first, and perhaps the most important, of the national reports, and it set the tone for those that followed. Among its recommendations, the commission proposed more rigorous high school studies, higher standards for college admission, a nationwide system of standardized achievement tests, more homework, longer school days and years, increased teacher salaries, career ladders, incentives to attract top students to teaching, and states and localities governing and financing reform efforts.

The report strongly criticized teacher education.

The teacher preparation curriculum is weighted heavily with courses in "educational methods" at the expense of courses in subjects to be taught. A survey of 1,350 institutions training teachers indicated that 41 percent of the time of elementary school teacher candidates is spent in education courses, which reduces the amount of time available for subject matter courses. (p. 22)

Two recommendations related directly to teacher education: (a) "Persons preparing to teach should be required to meet high educational standards, to demonstrate an aptitude for teaching, and to demonstrate competence in an academic discipline. Colleges and universities offering teacher preparation programs should be judged by how well their graduates meet these criteria." (b) "Master teachers should be involved in designing teacher preparation programs and in supervising teachers during their probationary years" (pp. 30–31).

Making the Grade, The Twentieth Century Fund Task Force on Federal Elementary and Secondary Education Policy (1983)

This report of a 12-member task force made recommendations on the role of the federal government in promoting quality education within the context of state and local control. The report called for the federal government to dramatize the need for teaching excellence, to focus national attention on educational quality, and to provide incentives to local schools to improve areas of identified national concern—specifically, quality of teaching and proficiency in English, foreign languages, mathematics, and science.

The report stated that schools should provide the same core components to all students: basic skills of reading, writing, and calculating; technical capability in computers; training in science and foreign language; and knowledge of civics. The federal government should provide for the national security by insuring a strong education system. The report recommended that the federal government emphasize the need for better schools and better education for all. It suggested that a master-teacher program be established to reward teaching excellence. It encouraged the federal government to support and promote proficiency in English for all public school students, including transfer of federal bilingual education funds into other programs for limited English proficient (LEP) children. Public schools should provide an opportunity for all students to acquire proficiency in a second language and go beyond basic

scientific literacy by providing advanced training in science and mathematics. Categorical programs required by the federal government should be supported by federal funds, and programs to assist handicapped and disadvantaged children should be continued. The report recommended that federal impact aid be reformulated to focus on school districts with substantial numbers of immigrant children. The federal government should support data collection on various aspects of the educational system, and federal fellowships for failing students should be awarded to school districts to encourage the creation of small, individualized programs.

Making the Grade proposed a new federal policy on elementary and secondary schooling. The report called for the federal government to state clearly that the most important objective of elementary and secondary education in the United States should be the development of literacy in the English language, and further urged that the government provide support for such programs. The report proposed that federal funds now going to bilingual programs should be used to teach non-English-speaking children how to speak, read, and write English. It also encouraged the availability to every American public school student of opportunities to acquire proficiency in a second language.

Action for Excellence: Comprehensive Plan to Improve Our Nation's Schools, Education Commission of the States, Task Force on Education for Economic Growth (1983)

In another 1983 report, a task force of 41 members, including 13 governors as well as business leaders, educators, and legislators, focused on the national economy and international competition (Education Commission of the States, 1983a). It reported in urgent tones that our national defense, our social stability and well-being, and our national prosperity depended upon our ability to improve education for our citizens. Those responsible at the state and local level were encouraged to change now, so that in the future children would be able to meet the demands of the new era that was already upon us. The report covered K–12 and called for new business–labor–professional alliances to improve schools. It recommended rewarding and professionalizing teaching and suggested intensifying K–12 academic experiences. The report writers wanted school leadership improved, and they recommended better service for underserved students.

According to the report, technological change and global competition were making it imperative to equip students with skills that went beyond the basics. For productive participation in a society that depends heavily on technology, students need more than minimum competence in reading, writing, mathematics, science, reasoning, and the use of computers. The school system needs to be mobilized to teach new skills that will foster economic growth.

Some of the report's recommendations included development and implementation of state plans for improving education in K–12 public schools. School districts should develop similar plans. The task force wanted to create broader and more effective partnerships to improve education in states and communities. It intended to marshal resources for public schools and to improve school management. Members hoped to express a new and high regard for teachers, which should include salary increases and establishment of career ladders. They recommended improving the academic experience by raising standards, enforcing discipline, and strengthening the curriculum. They wanted to provide quality assurance in education. This would include evaluating teachers, revising certification requirements, testing student achievement, and raising college and university admissions standards.

The report encouraged firm, explicit, and demanding homework requirements and urged everyone to work toward reducing student absenteeism and dropouts. the members further wanted state certification rules to be flexible enough to encourage qualified persons from business, industry, the scientific and technical communities, and institutions of higher education to serve in public schools.

Educating Americans for the 21st Century: A Report to the American People and the National Science Board, National Science Foundation (1983)

This report encouraged early experience and improved teaching and learning in mathematics, science, and technology, along with a 12-year timetable for implementation and cost estimates. The report supported the improvement of elementary and secondary school systems throughout America, so that, by the year 1995, they would provide the nation's youth with a level of education in mathematics, science, and technology, as measured by achievement scores and participation levels (as well as other nonsubjective criteria), that not only would be the highest quality attained anywhere in the world but also would reflect the particular and peculiar needs of the nation.

The report recommended that the president immediately appoint a national education council to identify national education goals, to recommend and monitor a plan of action, to insure that participation and progress would be measured, and to report regularly to the American people. The states should establish governors' councils, and local school boards should foster partnerships with business, government, and academia.

Priority should be given to obtaining and retaining high-quality mathematics, science, and technology teachers, as well as to providing them with an appropriate work environment. Also, priority should be given to more and earlier instruction in these fields. Of necessity, the school day, week, and/or year should be extended.

State governments should develop teacher training and retraining programs in cooperation with colleges and universities. These training programs should not necessarily be on college campuses. Teacher retraining programs should be supported in part by the federal government.

The National Science Foundation should provide seed money to develop training programs using new information technologies. States should adopt rigorous certification standards, but not standards that bar qualified persons from teaching. Both elementary and secondary teachers should become computer literate as part of their teacher-preparation program.

Liberal arts colleges and academic departments need to assume a much greater role in training elementary and secondary teachers. Basic education courses need to be revised to incorporate current findings in the behavioral and social sciences. State and local systems should draw upon the staffs of industry, universities, the military, and other government departments to provide sources of qualified teaching assistance.

Every state should establish rigorous standards for high school graduation, including 3 years of mathematics, science, and technology. Higher mathematics and science should be required for college admission. Students should be advised of requirements, and remediation should be made available.

The report suggested that the federal government anticipate an initial investment of approximately $1.5 billion for the first full year of the proposed federal initiative. The federal government should study ways to assure that such funds are not used in lieu of states and local communities' increasing taxes for educational purposes.

Academic Preparation for College: What Students Need to Know and Be Able to Do, College Board EQuality Project (1983)

The report was the result of the educational EQuality Project, a 10-year effort by the College Entrance Examination Board initiated in 1980 that involved hundreds of secondary and postsecondary educators, administrators, counselors, parents, and representatives of professional organizations in consensus-building activities. Recommendations were made for a national standard for academic achievement in secondary education detailing what college-bound students need to know to be successful in college. It was intended as a guide for high schools to use in evaluating and revising academic standards and curricula. The premise of the project was that one of our greatest national achievements in education has been to open higher education to the majority of high school graduates, not just the elite. Yet students are not able to take advantage of this opportunity adequately if they lack the necessary preparation. The report did not attempt to suggest what preparation would be needed by job-bound high school graduates:

Discussions with leaders of business and industry confirm, however, that much of the learning described here also can be valuable to students going directly into the world of work. Moreover, although this learning is needed for college, it can engage and reward students in itself, over and above any other goal. (p. 3)

The report recommended that students be proficient in nine content areas: arts, foreign language, language, mathematics, reading and literature, science, social studies, speaking and listening, and writing. It was influential in changing high school graduation requirements in several states.

Achieving these outcomes in schools would require great effort and creativity. Partnerships to strengthen elementary and junior high education also would be necessary. More than a new curriculum would be needed. Counselors would have to help students relate learning to their future plans. The school environment and stated expectations would have to combine to challenge and encourage students to study and to take responsibility for their own learning. School boards and communities would have to assess their curriculum and provide the financial and moral support quality education required. While raising standards, they would have to guard against the danger of limiting equal opportunity for disadvantaged or minority students.

America's Competitive Challenge: The Need for a National Response, Business–Higher Education Forum (1983)

This report was issued by 16 top corporate executives and university presidents who determined that our society must recognize that industrial competitiveness on a global scale is critical to social and economic well-being. The report called for students to have basic foundations in mathematics, science, and technology. It emphasized college teaching and research, delineating the impact of world trade barriers on U.S. competition and foreign management practices. It called for expanded foreign-language studies and curricular reforms for business, engineering, public administration, and other professional schools.

The report suggested that loans and other incentives be given, to attract engineering students into teaching careers. It called for teachers in secondary mathematics and science to upgrade their skills with the help of support programs from both the state and federal governments. Industry was called upon to provide support for modern equipment, and the public was charged to support university research and to help improve precollege education.

The report was prepared at the request of the president, who is advised in the report to make industrial competitiveness one of the top economic goals of the country. The report called for educational training and retraining for millions of people, to keep them abreast of new job needs. The report had little direct advice regarding the preparation of quality teachers. It did call for tax incentives to stimulate additional investment by industry in training and retraining workers.

Staffing the Nation's Schools: A National Emergency, Council of Chief State School Officers, Committee on Teacher Certification, Preparation, and Accreditation (1984)

The Council of Chief State School Officers in 1984 declared that there was a national emergency in teaching. More compelling incentives were needed, they contended, to attract and retain high-quality teachers. The rewards of teaching are few, morale is low, the best teachers are leaving the profession, and the supply of good recruits is drying up.

Changes were taking place. The South Atlantic states had been leaders in implementing change in teacher education, particularly in the 1970s. There had been slow, more cautious movement in the Middle Atlantic states and westward. The report indicated that further changes were needed in attracting persons to the teaching profession, preparing persons for teaching, licensing teachers, and retraining teachers. The rec-

ommendations in the report are based on analysis of survey data and other related research information (p. 41). The goal was to develop in-depth analyses of some policy statements, strategies, procedures, and legislation.

The recommendations called for more research in many areas, for example:

Research needs to be done to determine the most effective means of measuring the competency of teachers during, or upon completion of, their teacher preparation programs, as well as one year, five years, and ten years after the completion of such programs. . . . With respect to the licensing of teachers, research needs to be done to determine what relationship exists between performance on a teacher competency exam and teacher performance in the classroom. (p. 44)

Educational Reform: A Response from Educational Leaders, Forum of Educational Organization Leaders (1983)

Eleven national groups joined forces as the Forum of Educational Organization Leaders: American Association of Colleges for Teacher Education, American Association of School Administrators, American Federation of Teachers, Council of Chief State School Officers, Education Commission of the States, National Association of Elementary School Principals, National Association of Secondary School Principals, National Association of State Boards of Education, National Congress of Parents and Teachers, National Education Association, and National School Boards Association.

In October 1983, the Forum of Educational Organization Leaders released its response to the recommendations of recent national commission reports on American education. The forum acknowledged the importance of raising academic standards to protect our economic position in the world, yet it asserted that such efforts must not cause repeal of the gains in educational equity and civil rights made over the last 25 years. The forum saw no conflict between the goals of *opportunity* and *excellence* and urged continuation of the agenda of the 1950s and 1960s to make educational opportunities available to students. The forum supported the national reports in their focus on the teacher as the central figure in education. The forum leaders agreed that quality education required quality teachers, who can only be attracted and retained through adequate salaries and amenable working environments. The leaders proposed that the federal government share in the cost of improved schooling.

Some of the forum's specific recommendations were to raise substantially the base-pay scale of all teachers and to establish a career ladder for beginning, experienced, and master teachers. Master teachers should possess advanced degrees, work a 12-month year, and team with university faculty to prepare new teachers. The forum recommended the use of a variety of incentives to recruit and retain as teachers the top 25 percent of college graduates, including year-round employment, rewards and recognition, and forgiveness of student loans after 5 years of service. Leaders wanted to guarantee a safe and orderly school environment through discipline codes and alternative arrangements for disruptive students. They wanted to provide salary incentives "such as the reduction of steps on salary scales" (p. 3) to retain experienced teachers. They asked significant persons (e.g., parents, peers, school counselors) to encourage promising candidates to enter teaching.

The forum supported the concept that states and local school systems should prescribe graduation standards. The forum supported curriculum standards by which all students in the United States would be able to speak, write, read, and listen to English. They suggested that all students should master basic arithmetic, algebra, geometry, and mathematical problem solving as it applies to adult life. College-bound students need advanced algebra, calculus, statistics, and probability. World history, U.S. history, and civics or citizenship should be taught at all grade levels. Beginning with natural science in the elementary grades, science courses, including biology, chemistry, and physics, should be available to all students. Educators should promote access to science education for women and minorities. Computers should be in the curriculum from the early grades, and second-language instruction should be available to all.

Regarding quality use of time, the forum supported better use of currently available schooltime. With due concern for student fatigue and the inappropriateness of simply providing more of the same, the forum suggested exploring options for extending learning time, including increasing the school year up to 220 days, and reviewing each district's homework philosophy and practice. An hour a day for elementary students and 2 or more hours for high school students might promote greater learning.

Regarding testing and evaluation, the forum's position was that testing should provide diagnosis, as well as achievement ratings. Reporting of school test data only in reading and mathematics ignores other valuable school learnings. The forum recommended that tests for promotion, graduation, or college admission be used only in conjunction with other indicators of student performance such as grades and teacher recommendations. Although every prospective teacher should pass tests of subject-matter competency and basic skills, performance in the classroom is the ultimate measure of teacher success. Therefore, tests should be used in the process of screening new teachers, but they should not be the sole criterion for certification or employment.

RESPONSES TO CHALLENGE

The nation responded to the challenges issued in the national reports. Some actions were real and made important changes in school policy and practice; others were nominal and led only to reports and exhortation. The American public demanded and supported action.

The Nation Responds: Recent Efforts to Improve Education, U.S. Department of Education (1984)

One of the first indications of action was The Nation Responds, issued by the United States Department of Education in May 1984. This report to the nation, issued one year after A

Nation at Risk, described national developments in education during the previous year. It summarized state and local efforts to improve education by school districts, postsecondary institutions, associations, organizations, and the private sector.

The Nation Responds provided a state-by-state profile of activities and an informed sampling of significant efforts. The report demonstrated that reform efforts were already "bearing fruit" (p. 8). It reaffirmed that the problems of American education can be both understood and corrected if people and their public officials care enough and are courageous enough to do what is required (p. 8). According to then Secretary of Education T. H. Bell, educators saw in the reform reports an opportunity to advance American education, and they seized the opportunity.

Reaching for Excellence: An Effective Schools Sourcebook, National Institute of Education (1985)

This work, edited by R. M. J. Kyle, documented the involvement of state and local policymakers and practitioners in school improvement. Stronger and healthier partnerships between practitioners and researchers were being forged and developed. More effective schools were developing, to show clearly that public schools that were well organized and managed could make a significant difference in the educational achievement of children (Kyle, 1985, p. v). The Sourcebook identified schools in urban areas where children from low-income families were performing well. It demanded effective classroom practice in elementary and secondary schools and effective district and state-level policies and practices that support effective school management and classroom instruction.

Analyses

Almost every national professional organization and many individuals published either a summary or an analysis of the national reports of the 1980s (see, for example, Earley, 1983; Houston, Clift, Freiberg, & Warner, 1988; Lake, 1984). A sampling is presented here.

The Reports: Challenge & Opportunity, Phi Delta Kappa (1983). This brochure summarized three reports: Education Commission of the States. Action for Excellence (1983a); National Commission on Excellence in Education, A Nation at Risk (1983); and Twentieth Century Fund, Making the Grade (1983). The recommendations of these three reports were compared in terms of curriculum, length of the school day and year, programs for special populations, college entrance requirements, student performance, teachers, leadership and management, fiscal support, suggested federal role, implementation plan, business/education partnerships, sponsorship, and commission membership.

Recommendations for Improving K–12 Schools (1983). This analysis by Edelfelt (1983) included the three reports analyzed by Phi Delta Kappa, PDK plus the College Board report, Aca-

demic Preparation for College (1983). By use of a matrix to compare the recommendations, the report was divided into several categories: sponsor and publisher; group creating the report; members of the group; date of publication; recommendations for regular students in each subject field; programs for special populations; and requirements for other aspects of schooling such as attendance, homework, time, testing, textbooks, graduation, and college entrance. The reports were also compared and analyzed in regard to each one's recommendations for preparing and maintaining high-quality teachers, with attention to recruitment and selection, preparation, conditions of work, evaluation, rewards, and inservice education.

A Summary of Major Reports on Education, *Education Commission of the States (1983).* This report (1983b) reviewed ten 1982–1983 reports. It differed from some other analyses in that it reviewed the reports of prominent authors such as Adler (1982) Boyer (1983), and Goodlad (1984) along with the national commission and task force reports. The analysis summarized recommendations from these reports in several sections, including those about curriculum, teachers and teaching, school organization and management, process and the roles of groups outside the school. Following summary statements about recommendations in each of these areas, the specific recommendations of each report were listed.

A Review and Comment on the National Reports, *National Association of Secondary School Principals (1983).* In this analysis, Sizer (1983) saw the national reports legitimizing the more traditional, back-to-basics trends that emerged in schools in the 1970s, after adverse public reaction to the perceived disorder of the late 1960s. He identified several trends in the 1983 statements about reform.

1. There must be a return to "the basics."
2. The connection between school and the economy needs strengthening.
3. Adults must regain authority in the high schools, and students should have less freedom than they may have had in the 1960s.
4. The principal agent of reform should be state government.
5. Schools and students should be judged on the basis of measurable results of teaching and learning. (p. 1)

Other Accounts: Some Good News

Following the lead of the federal government, professional organizations, prominent authors, state governors, state education agencies, institutions of higher education, local education agencies, and others involved with schooling and education in this country began issuing their own reports and publications about the direction of educational change. Some positive news about schooling and teacher education was published to counteract the negative attention in the mass media.

Articles like "Today's Good News About Teacher Education" (Sikula, 1985) began appearing in the professional education literature. Such good news was in response to the perva-

sive criticism in the mass media. Significant reform efforts at all levels of schooling were underway. National accreditation of teacher education was changing dramatically (National Council for Accreditation of Teacher Education, 1985), as were state certification practices and procedures. Teacher-preparation programs themselves were also improving across the country (Feldmann & Fisher, 1984–1985). Higher demands were being placed upon teacher candidates, and the quality of teachers being prepared began to improve (Cohen, 1984; Nelli, 1984). As Feistritzer observed in *Teacher Education Reports* (September 22, 1988), the demand for teachers and concern for quality were paying off (p. 7). She reported positive signs, including the number of high school students who planned to major in education in college and their scores on the Scholastic Aptitude Test, which were increasing (p. 4). On January 12, 1989, Feistritzer reported in *Teacher Education Reports* that during 1988, 8.8 percent of students entering college said they planned to pursue teaching as a career, up from 8.1 percent in 1987. "The proportion of college freshmen with aspirations to teach was almost double the 4.7 percent level recorded in 1982" (p. 5).

An October 17, 1988, *Newsweek* article titled "Back to the Classroom" pointed out that rising salaries and new respect were helping to restore the luster of teaching: "Increasing pay has helped reverse a 20-year decline in the number of college freshmen planning teaching careers. . . . Battered, bad-mouthed and avoided by savvy job seekers for years, the profession is making a comeback" (p. 74).

The front page of the May 18, 1989, issue of *Teacher Education Reports* reported: "The average salary for teachers across the nation has risen 45 percent in the last six years, representing an annual rate two and three times the annual rate of inflation. Dramatic increases in salaries for teachers since 1982 have occurred in every state" (p. 1). "More important still," the *Newsweek* article reported that "the quality of prospective teachers keeps getting better, helping to erase a stigma that has dogged the profession for years" (p. 74). A Harris poll in 1988 reported that "Teachers' overall satisfaction with their careers is on the rise. In 1988, 50 percent said they were very satisfied with teaching as a career, compared to 40 percent in 1987" (Harris, 1988, p. 12).

Commentary

This sampling of reports demonstrates that in the early 1980s American education was in the midst of a dramatic reform movement, one that was different from previous ones in some basic respects (Finn, 1984). It centered on *excellence* and *economics,* and it was driven at the national level by corporate executives and governmental officials concerned about educational quality. Though it initiated the effort, the federal government had relatively little to do with its progress. Actions that resulted developed mostly at state and local levels. The excellence movement was also different in that laypeople and elected officials, rather than the education profession, were largely responsible for it. Reform often became state centered, with governors and legislative leaders as key players, supported by business round tables, citizens' task forces, newspaper editors, and others (Finn, 1984, p. 16).

Another fundamental difference was that this excellence movement was almost single-mindedly concerned with educational outcomes, not school inputs or processes (Finn, 1984, p. 16). People wanted children to learn more, and the call was for higher standards—of intellectual attainment by students, of intellectual and professional prowess of teachers, and of school leadership.

The public was upset about education, and political action resulted. Elected officials "got the message" (Finn, 1984, p. 17) and realized that there were political rewards for paying attention to school quality and even punishment at the polls for those not addressing the issues. Programs of action were demanded. Agencies concerned with public education were asked to band together to form coalitions to address the problems. The role of the school was reexamined, and attention was focused on those essential tasks and functions for which schools were specifically qualified and uniquely responsible (Griffiths, 1983, p. 9).

In 1986 the state governors gave more attention to schools than ever in the 78-year history of the National Governors' Association (*Time for Results*, p. 6). They championed an agenda to improve schools and teaching, and they subtitled their report *The Governors' 1991 Report on Education*.

THE SECOND WAVE: FOCUS ON TEACHER PREPARATION

The second wave of educational reform in the 1980s was addressed less to public schools and more to teacher preparation. Once again, many reports were issued. Some of the major reports that have already had and will continue to have an impact on teacher preparation for years to come are summarized in this section.

A *Nation Prepared*: *Teachers for the 21st Century*, Carnegie Forum on Education and the Economy, Task Force on Teaching as a Profession (1986)

The Carnegie Forum on Education and the Economy was established in January 1985 to draw America's attention to the link between economic growth and the skills and abilities of the people who contribute to that growth and to help develop education policies to meet the economic challenge ahead. The forum assembled a 14-member task force to examine teaching as a profession.

Issued in May 1986, the report of that task force called for the overhaul of the teaching profession, and argued that, if the changes suggested were not implemented, rapidly and totally, our economy would erode and our standard of living would decline. Like *A Nation at Risk*, it presented a pessimistic view of national economic well-being in the future unless the education process were improved. To assure economic well-being, far more demanding educational standards must be achieved

than have been attempted before. To accomplish this goal, we must create a teaching profession equal to the task.

The report proposed the creation of a National Board for Professional Teaching Standards, organized with a regional and state membership structure, to establish high standards for what teachers need to know and to be able to do and to certify teachers who meet these standards. This national board should include governors, chief state school officers, school administrators, and classroom teachers. The task force hoped that individual states would require board certification and state licensure. This would symbolize the strength of the profession, all on a strictly voluntary-compliance basis.

The report called for restructuring schools to provide a professional environment for teaching and freeing teachers to decide how best to meet state and local goals, yet holding them accountable for student progress. Recommendations were made to restructure the teaching force and to introduce a new category of *lead teachers* with proven ability to provide active leadership in redesigning schools and helping colleagues uphold high standards of learning and teaching.

The report recommended that a bachelor's degree in the arts and sciences be a prerequisite for professional study of teaching. It recommended a new professional curriculum in graduate schools of education leading to a Master in Teaching degree, based on systematic knowledge of teaching and including internships and residencies in schools. The report called for mobilization of the nation's resources to prepare underrepresented students for teaching careers.

On a more controversial note, the task force suggested relating incentives for teachers to schoolwide student performance. Providing schools with the technology, services, and staff essential for teacher productivity was also recommended. The task force viewed teachers as the key to reform. Task force goals were to attract able young people to teaching, to prepare them better, to give them greater powers and responsibilities, and to promise them professional status and corresponding pay incentives.

Tomorrow's Teachers, The Holmes Group (1986)

In 1983, 17 education deans interested in alternative ways of involving major research universities in improving the quality of teacher education convened. As the group continued to meet, its size increased to 23, and it developed and submitted a proposal to philanthropic foundations and the U.S. Department of Education. Following funding in 1984, a report with recommendations was drafted, reviewed, revised, made official in 1985, and distributed a year later (Holmes Group, 1986).

The Holmes Group was organized around the twin goals of the reform of teacher education and the reform of the teaching profession. Five goals were developed: (a) to make the education of teachers intellectually more solid; (b) to recognize differences in teachers' knowledge, skill, and commitment, in their education, certification, and work; (c) to create standards of entry to the profession (examinations and educational requirements) that were professionally relevant and intellectually defensible; (d) to connect institutions of higher education to schools; and (e) to make schools better places for teachers to work and to learn (Holmes Group, 1986, p. 4).

About 126 institutions were subsequently invited to participate as Holmes Group charter members. Invitations were extended to institutions belonging to the American Association of Universities, those with reputations or potential for excellence in research and development in education, and selected others.

The report called for extended programs of teacher education wherein the professional education of teachers would take place in a 2-year, postgraduate, master's degree program following a 4-year baccalaureate. It recommended three tiers of teachers: *instructors*, who would be baccalaureate graduates without professional preparation, permitted to teach under supervision for less than 5 years if they had a sound general education, a strong major or minor in the teaching field, and the basics of pedagogy; *professionals*, who would have completed the full 6-year program and be recommended for certification; and *career professionals*, who would engage in study beyond the master's degree and be responsible for the supervision of instructors. The report called for the improvement of undergraduate instruction, so that potential teachers could study subjects they would teach with exemplary instructors who understood the pedagogy of their subjects. The report recommended more in-depth study of subjects taught by prospective elementary teachers and more study of pedagogy by prospective secondary teachers.

The Holmes Group proposed stronger evaluation of teacher candidates for entry, retention, and licensing. It suggested utilization of expert K–12 teachers in the education of teachers and in the conduct of research, development of more extensive clinical experiences in schools, transformation of schools into places where teacher leadership is apparent, and establishment of *professional development schools* analogous to teaching hospitals. The report called for focus on the use of the knowledge base supporting teaching practice and more extensive research on teaching, teacher education, and the learning of academic subjects. It noted the need for increasing the number and quality of minority candidates in teacher education.

Ninety members joined the Holmes Group in the fall of 1986. Institutions committed themselves to major research-and-development initiatives, paying $4,000 annually for membership. Meetings were held in regions of the country, and annual national conferences were conducted to exchange ideas, reformulate programs, and extend understanding.

A Call for Change in Teacher Education, American Association of Colleges for Teacher Education, National Commission for Excellence in Teacher Education (1985)

The commission report called for a new generation of teachers and teacher education programs and for a nationwide commitment to excellent teacher education and superb schools. Recommendations called for more rigorous academic and performance standards for admission to and graduation from teacher education programs; special programs to attract capable minorities and others into teaching; new teachers to complete induction or internship programs of at least one-year duration, for pay; states to maintain rigorous program review standards; and increased teacher salaries.

The report was organized around five themes: (a) supply and demand for quality teachers, (b) programs for teacher education, (c) accountability for teacher education, (d) resources for teacher education, and (e) conditions necessary to support the highest quality of teaching. The 56-page report resulted from a series of public hearings and commissioned papers, as well as from the study of previously issued national reports.

Improving Teacher Education: An Agenda for Higher Education and the Schools, Southern Regional Education Board (1985)

This report (SREB, 1985) supported statewide admission standards for teacher education programs, tests before certification, and career ladders for teachers. The SREB position was that, until the undergraduate curriculum is revitalized and truly represents college-level work, it is premature to abandon the 4-year teacher education program or to commit funds for longer programs.

The report called for assessment of the liberal arts and education curricula. Requirements should be more rigorous and courses more meaningful. Collaboration with schools was encouraged, including actions such as determining how subject-area majors could better match typical high school teaching assignments and how beginning teacher programs could be supported.

The SREB suggested state financial assistance to colleges and universities that undertook large-scale teacher education reforms. Universities were urged to find ways of giving appropriate credit to faculty for service in schools. Greater use of schools and outstanding school teachers in preparing new teachers was also called for in the report. Evaluation of the results of new models to prepare beginning teachers, including state programs for alternative certification of liberal arts graduates and selected fifth-year programs, should be encouraged. The possible benefits of a national certification board should be weighed against the difficulties of implementing a national approach for what is accepted as a state responsibility.

The SREB encouraged states to grant loans and scholarships to attract better students into teaching careers. These loans were to be forgiven if students taught in public schools.

Analyses

As with the first wave, the second wave of reports on teacher education received considerable attention, particularly in the education literature (Clark, 1987; Ducharme, 1986; Goldberg, 1987; Green, 1987; Hample, 1986; Jacobson, 1986; Kaestle, 1985; King, 1986; Leatherman, 1988; Scully, 1986; Shanker, 1986; Sikula 1986, 1987a, 1987b; Tom, 1987; Wiggins, 1986; Zakariya, 1984). A sampling of these analyses is presented here.

Visions of Reform: Implications for the Education Profession, *Association of Teacher Educators, Blue Ribbon Task Force (1986).* This report was presented in two parts. The first part reviewed and analyzed three proposals for teacher education: (a) the redesign of the National Council for Accreditation of Teacher Education (NCATE, 1985); (b) the Holmes Group report (1986); and (c) Report of the Carnegie Forum on Education and the Economy (1986). The second part drew implications of reform efforts for state education agencies, public schools, and institutions of higher education. A matrix identified common elements in teacher-preparation reform proposals (p. 21). It also included 23 consensus items summarizing the direction teacher preparation might take in the future (pp. 56–57), and it ended with a glimpse of what teacher-preparation programs might be like if they incorporated selected elements from Carnegie, Holmes, NCATE, and other national reports.

The report supported the redesign of NCATE but raised serious questions about the Holmes Group's exclusionary model for preparing teachers. The report also cautioned readers about the Carnegie Forum proposals for a national board to certify teachers and for relating teacher incentives directly to standardized student-product measures.

The ATE Blue Ribbon Task Force included representation from state departments of education, public schools, and public and private colleges and universities.

Teacher Education Quarterly, *California Council on the Education of Teachers (1987).* This winter issue of the journal was devoted to an analysis of the Holmes and Carnegie Forum reports. Nine articles summarized and critiqued the two reports. Five articles described and compared the two proposals, and four others analyzed their importance.

The Next Wave: A Synopsis of Recent Education Reform Reports, *Education Commission of the States (1987).* The commission released this work (Green, 1987) summarizing reports from: Boyer (1983); California Commission on the Teaching Profession (1985); Carnegie Forum on Education and the Economy (1986); Holmes Group (1986); National Governors' Association (1986); U.S. Department of Education (1986); and others. The report began by listing eight common points of agreement (pp. 1–2) and three areas in which issues remained unresolved (p. 2). The recommendations in each of nine reports were summarized.

How Should Teachers Be Educated? An Assessment of Three Reform Reports, *Phi Delta Kappa (1987).* This report (Tom, 1987), was Fastback No. 255 in the series published by the Phi Delta Kappa Educational Foundation. The Carnegie and Holmes reports were assessed, along with the National Council for Accreditation of Teacher Education's *NCATE Redesign* (1985). The framework for analysis focused on five major questions, involving problem definition, solutions proposed, rationale, feasibility, and assumptions. The conclusion urged that people be "both skeptical and very selective about accepting the recommendations from the various teacher education reform reports" (p. 37). Ill-defined questions, incomplete ratio-

nales, questionable solutions, and unexamined assumptions were analyzed.

Commentary

From this sampling and other analyses too numerous to elaborate upon here, it is apparent that the thrust of the major reform themes and concerns in teacher preparation centered around expanding the teacher candidate pool, regulating teacher preparation more rigorously, emphasizing the clinical nature of teacher education, mastering subject-matter knowledge, and extending the formal preparation of fully certified teachers. More involvement with outstanding schools and teachers in teacher preparation is also clearly called for and is developing.

The Holmes and Carnegie reform proposals have served to focus needed attention on teacher preparation and retention. But the Holmes Group report has been as much a source of conflict within higher education as a platform around which the profession has been able to unite. The Teacher Education Council of State Colleges and Universities (TECSCU) praised the nation's leading research universities for their attempt to improve teacher education on their own campuses, but it criticized some of the specific proposals. There is no one right way to prepare teachers. Individual programs need to be analyzed, shaped, and developed around the beliefs and experiences of local participants. More specifically, the Holmes Group's recommendation that undergraduate education majors be abolished is not sufficiently supported to warrant its being the only curricular model to be endorsed. Such a move would exacerbate the shortage of minority students entering teaching. There are "important advantages to prospective teachers if they have early involvement in school settings as active participants" ("State-college Deans," 1986, p. 7). These experiences help students confirm career choices and begin to develop a personal knowledge of the teaching–learning process. To delay such involvement until after the completion of a baccalaureate degree is unwise ("State-college Deans," 1986, p. 7).

Those redesigning teacher education programs must be very careful. Alternatives must be encouraged. All-university commitments need to be examined both sensitively and sensibly, along with modifying or restructuring reward and promotion policies. Teacher certification (licensure) and accreditation (program approval) need to be articulated carefully. Individual candidate assessment and program-approval mechanisms also need careful coordination. Academic subject-matter specialists and professional education methodologists need to work together to prepare skilled teachers.

In August 1988, the American Association of Colleges for Teacher Education (AACTE) released *Commitment to America's Children*, in which recommendations were made on how to further strengthen teacher-preparation programs. This report stressed teacher education as a shared responsibility and provided an agenda for the 1989 U.S. national administration and congress, as well as for governors, state legislators, and state boards of education. The report claimed that "the federal government supports no basic research in education" (p. 10).

It recommended a return to funding for education research and improvement to 1972 constant-dollar levels, initiation of a plan to assist in recruiting and preparing minority teachers, avoidance of policy decisions that compromise the tradition of academic freedom in institutions of higher education, elimination of shortcuts that dilute teacher preparation, review of the impact on teachers of statewide testing policies, and provision of explicit funding for educational research and development activities.

Although we have made progress in redesigning teacher education programs, we must be careful not to overgeneralize about that progress. Some states have made greater progress than others; states like Florida and California continue to design, develop, and implement significant reforms (Sikula, 1987b). Some schools, colleges, and departments of education (SCDEs) are progressing more rapidly than others, but few states and SCDEs are still waiting for the reform movement to pass.

As responses have developed to the criticisms of schools and teacher-preparation programs, one significant trend seems to deserve comment. The fully credentialed candidates graduating from teacher-preparation programs today appear to be better prepared teachers than their predecessors (Evertson, Hawley, & Zlotnik, 1985; Haberman, 1984; Hawk, Coble, & Swanson, 1985). They have a broader background in areas such as reading, computer literacy, multicultural education, classroom management, and mainstreaming of exceptional chil-dren. These are areas often neglected or not even included in former teacher-preparation programs. To accompany broader learning, program graduates today generally have engaged in more field experiences well articulated with university courses. Theory and practice are better coordinated today. The result is fewer surprises for new teachers and better survival skills. Also helping are first-year teacher assistance programs, which were uncommon in the past (Sikula, 1988).

Some critics firmly believe that more radical educational reform is needed. *The Wall Street Journal,* for example, published a special report on March 31, 1989, declaring that schools need retooling and that the system needs a complete overhaul, not just more tinkering (Graham, 1989, p. R1). According to this report, comparing schools to obsolete factories whose pupils are stamped out within a rigid bureaucratic structure, U.S. schools have failed to adjust. In much of the country today the sense of urgency associated with educational reform at all levels is escalating.

In sum, redesigned teacher education programs are developing, and significant educational reform is taking place. As a result, the profession of teaching is much more attractive today than it was in 1983, when the first commission report was issued (Sikula, 1988; Sikula & Roth, 1984). Although improved, schooling and teacher education continue to be closely scrutinized, and there continues to develop a heightened sense that more pervasive reform is needed to keep pace with the improving competition.

References

Adler, M. (1982). *The Paideia proposal: An educational manifesto.* New York: Macmillan.

American Association of Colleges for Teacher Education. (1988). *Commitment to America's children.* Washington, DC: Author.

Association of Teacher Educators, Blue Ribbon Task Force. (1986). *Visions of reform: Implications for the education profession.* Reston: VA: Author.

Back to the classroom. (1988, October). *Newsweek, 112*(16), pp. 74, 76.

Boyer, E. L. (1983). *High school: A report on secondary education in America.* New York: Harper & Row.

Business–Higher Education Forum. (1983). *America's competitive challenge: The need for a national response.* Washington, DC: Author.

California Commission on the Teaching Profession. (1985). *Who will teach our children?* Sacramento, CA: Author.

Carnegie Forum on Education and the Economy, Task Force on Teaching as a Profession. (1986). *A nation prepared: Teachers for the 21st century.* New York: Author.

Clark, V. L. (1987). Teacher education at historically black institutions in the aftermath of the Holmes/Carnegie reports. *Planning and Changing, 18*(2), 74–79.

Cohen, D. (1984). *A study of the academic qualifications of students recommended for basic teaching credentials.* Bakersfield, CA: California State College, Bakersfield, Center for Social and Educational Research.

College Board EQuality Project. (1983). *Academic preparation for college: What students need to know and be able to do.* New York: College Entrance Examination Board.

Council of Chief State School Officers, Committee on Teacher Certification, Preparation, and Accreditation. (1984). *Staffing the nation's schools: A national emergency.* Washington, DC: Author.

Ducharme, E. R. (1986). The professors and the reports: A time to act. *Journal of Teacher Education, 37*(5), 51–56.

Earley, P. M. (1983). *A summary of twelve national reports on education and their implications for teacher education.* Washington, DC: American Association of Colleges for Teacher Education.

Edelfelt, R. (1983). *Recommendations for improving K–12 schools.* Washington, DC: Edelfelt Johnson.

Education Commission of the States, Task Force on Education for Economic Growth. (1983a). *Action for excellence: Comprehensive plan to improve our nation's schools.* Denver: Author.

Education Commission of the States. (1983b). *A summary of major reports on education.* Denver: Author.

Evertson, C. M., Hawley, W. D., & Zlotnik, M. (1985). Making a difference in educational quality through teacher education. *Journal of Teacher Education, 36*(3), 2–12.

Feldman, M. E., & Fisher, R. L. (1984–1985). Trends in standards for admission to teacher education. *Action in Teacher Education, 6*(4), 59–63.

Finn, C. E. (1984). The roots of reform. *Social Policy, 15*(2), 16–17.

Forum of Educational Organization Leaders. (1983). *Educational reform: A response from educational leaders*, Washington, DC: Author.

Goldberg, J. G. (1987). *No more teacher traps—Neither in the name of Holmes nor Carnegie*. New York: Vantage Press.

Goodlad, J. I. (1984). *A place called school: Prospects for the future*. New York: McGraw-Hill.

Graham, E. (1989). Retooling the schools. *Wall Street Journal Reports*, March 31, R1–R36.

Green, J. (1987). *The next wave: A synopsis of recent education reform reports*. Denver: Education Commission of the States.

Griffiths, D. E. (1983). The crisis in American education. *Education Digest*, 48(9), 8–10.

Haberman, M. (1984). *An evaluation of the rationale for required teacher education: Beginning teachers with and without teacher preparation* (Paper prepared for the National Commission on Excellence in Teacher Education). Milwaukee: University of Wisconsin-Milwaukee, Division of Urban Outreach.

Hample, R. L. (1986). The political side of reform: Are conflicts, power struggles likely to occur? *NASSP Bulletin*, 70(494), 55–64.

Harris, L. (1988). *The Metropolitan Life survey of the American teacher*. New York: Louis Harris and Assoc.

Hawk, P. P., Coble, C. R., & Swanson, M. (1985). Certification: It does matter. *Journal of Teacher Education*, 36(3), 13–15.

Holmes Group. (1986). *Tomorrow's teachers*. East Lansing, MI: Author.

Houston, W. R., Clift, R. T., Freiberg, H. J., & Warner, A. R. (1988). Exploring school quality. Chapter 6 in *Touch the Future, Teach* (pp. 127–134). St. Paul, MN: West.

Jacobson, R. L. (1986). Carnegie school-reform goals hailed; Achieving them called "tall order." *Chronicle of Higher Education*, 32(13), 1, 23.

Kaestle, C. (1985). Education reform and the swinging pendulum. *Phi Delta Kappan*, 66(6), 422–423.

Kilpatrick, J. J. (1983). The crisis in our schools. *Nation's Business*, 71(7), 5.

King, J. E. (1986, June). *Holmes, Sweet Holmes*. Paper presented at the meeting of the American Association of State Colleges and Universities, Task Force on Excellence in Education, Bal Harbour, FL.

Kyle, R. M. J. (Ed.). (1985). *Reaching for excellence: An effective schools sourcebook*. Washington, DC: U.S. Government Printing Office.

Lake, S. (1984). *The educator's digest of reform: A comparison of 16 recent proposals for improving America's schools*. Redwood City, CA: San Mateo County Office of Education.

Leatherman, C. (1988). Reforms in education of schoolteachers face tough new challenges. *Chronicle of Higher Education*, 34(32), A1, A30.

National Commission for Excellence in Teacher Education. (1985). *A call for change in teacher education*. Washington, DC: American Association of Colleges for Teacher Education.

National Commission on Excellence in Education. (1983). *A nation at risk: The imperative for educational reform*. Washington, DC: U.S. Government Printing Office.

National Council for Accreditation of Teacher Education. (1985). *NCATE redesign*. Washington, DC: Author.

National Governors' Association. (1986). *Time for results: The governors' 1991 report on education*. Washington, DC: Author.

National Science Foundation. (1983). *Educating Americans for the 21st century: A report to the American people and the National Science Board*. Washington, DC: Author.

Nelli, E. R. (1984). A research-based response to allegations that education students are academically inferior. *Action in Teacher Education*, 6(3), 73–80.

Phi Delta Kappa. (1983). *The reports: Challenge & opportunity*. Bloomington, IN: Author.

Scully, M. G. (1986). Study finds colleges torn by divisions, confused over roles. *Chronicle of Higher Education*, 33(10), 1, 16–23.

Shanker, A. (1986). The Carnegie report: An endorsement for teacher education. *Change*, 18(5), 8–9.

Sikula, J. P. (1985). Today's good news about teacher education. *Professional Educator*, 8(2), 1–4.

Sikula, J. P. (1986). One response to the report of the California commission on the teaching profession. *Teacher Education Quarterly*, 13(1), 1–9.

Sikula, J. P. (1987a). Commentary on reform: Implications for the education profession. *Teacher Education Quarterly*, 14(1), 52–59.

Sikula, J. P. (1987b). Teacher education reform California style. *Educational Horizons*, 65(2), 62–65.

Sikula, J. P. (1988). Teacher certification. In *Encyclopedia of School Administration and Supervision* (pp. 270–271). Phoenix: Oryx Press.

Sikula, J. P., & Roth, R. A. (1984). *Teacher preparation and certification: The call for reform* (Fastback No. 202). Bloomington, IN: Phi Delta Kappa Educational Foundation.

Sizer, T. R. (1983). *A review and comment on the national reports*. Reston VA: National Association of Secondary School Principals.

Southern Regional Education Board. (1985). *Improving teacher education: An agenda for higher education and the schools*. Atlanta: Author.

State-college deans rap Holmes report as a 'source of conflict.' (1986). *Education Week*, 5(33), 7.

Teacher education quarterly. (1987, Winter). 14(1).

Teacher education reports. (1988, September). 10(18), 4, 7.

Teacher education reports. (1989, January). 11(1), 5–6.

Teacher education reports. (1989, May). 11(10), 1.

Tom, A. R. (1987). *How should teachers be educated? An assessment of three reform reports* (Fastback No. 255). Bloomington, IN: Phi Delta Kappa Educational Foundation.

Twentieth Century Fund Task Force on Federal Elementary and Secondary Education Policy. (1983). *Making the grade*. New York: Author.

U.S. Department of Education. (1984). *The nation responds: Recent efforts to improve education*. Washington, DC: U.S. Government Printing Office.

U.S. Department of Education. (1986). *What works: Research about teaching and learning*. Washington, DC: U.S. Government Printing Office.

Wiggins, S. P. (1986). Revolution in the teaching profession: A comparative review of two reform reports. *Educational Leadership*, 44(2), 56–59.

Zakariya, S. B. (1984). Sizer, Boyer, Goodlad compare and contrast the proposals of the preeminent education reformers. *American School Board Journal*, 171(9), 29–31, 44.

·6·

FUTURES RESEARCH AND STRATEGIC PLANNING IN TEACHER EDUCATION

Christopher Dede

UNIVERSITY OF HOUSTON—CLEAR LAKE

Long-range thinking has not been a major activity in teacher education. Although people have speculated about the future since the dawn of civilization, systematic strategies for long-range thinking did not emerge until the 1950s. As these techniques have matured, their utility in commercial and political institutions has been repeatedly demonstrated. Unfortunately, as with many methodologies, the transfer of this expertise into educational practice has been slow. This delay in assimilating futures research and strategic planning is unfortunate, given that educational systems in many countries have repeatedly been criticized for lagging behind society.

In this chapter, the fields of futures research and strategic planning are defined, and their major methodologies are summarized. Illustrations of usage in institutions outside of education are provided, to indicate the potential utility of these approaches. Then the historical application (or absence) of long-range thinking in major teacher education reform initiatives is discussed, with an analysis of consequences for the field. Finally, implications for improving current research and practice are delineated.

This overview is limited in several ways. *First*, only teacher education reforms resulting in a national-level impact are considered. *Second*, the discussion is confined to long-range thinking in teacher education rather than in overall educational practice, although some citations to significant work in general educational futures have been included. *Third*, the examples of teacher education reforms analyzed are mostly from the United States. However, because teacher-preparation approaches are similar in many countries, the conclusions of the chapter generalize to a wide range of settings.

THE FIELDS OF FUTURES RESEARCH AND STRATEGIC PLANNING

How do futures research and strategic planning differ? An oversimplified distinction between these fields would hold that futures research is oriented to coping with the long-range external forces that affect individuals, organizations, and societies; strategic planning deals with internal institutional goal setting, resource allocation, and monitoring of progress for multiyear time horizons. This bifurcation is actually a continuum rather than a dichotomy, and overlaps between these fields will be delineated later. Still, as a heuristic for clarifying overlapping terminology and approaches, the external/internal contrast between the foci of futures research and strategic planning will be used throughout this chapter.

The origins of the futures research field stem from the period immediately after World War II. With the end of the war, economists feared that the Great Depression would return and sought new approaches to forecasting the evolution of the

The author is grateful for the comments and ideas provided by this chapter's reviewers: James Morrison (University of North Carolina at Chapel Hill) and Harold Shane (University of Indiana at Bloomington). Valuable feedback was also provided by participants in a symposium at the 1988 American Educational Research Association national conference (Jerry Freiberg, University of Houston; Harry Judge, Oxford University; Robert McNergney, University of Virginia; and Joan Michael, North Carolina University). The support and encouragement of the editor of this handbook, Robert Houston, has been of great assistance. Any weaknesses that remain in the chapter are the sole responsibility of its author. Partial funding for this study was provided by the Faculty Research and Support Fund, University of Houston—Clear Lake.

economy. The military felt that each war was being fought with the weapons left over from its predecessor and wanted ways to predict when the next war would occur and what weaponry would be used.

In the early 1950s, think tanks such as the RAND Corporation initiated the structured use of methodologies such as scenarios, the Delphi technique, and the cross-impact matrix in preparing these economic and military forecasts. Since then, the application of futures concepts and tools has steadily grown, although the popularity of terminology such as *futures, futures research*, and *futuristics* for describing these activities peaked about the mid-1970s (Marien, 1982). No single descriptor in common use now characterizes the approaches that this chapter groups under the field of futures research; "strategic intelligence" is one term currently in vogue.

Strategic planning has a slightly longer history. Attempts to plan can be found throughout the history of civilization, although most examples before this century were utopian rather than pragmatic. Cope (1981) discusses some intellectual roots of long-range planning in geopolitical theory and field theory. National economic planning, which uses some of the tools and approaches of strategic planning, first evolved in the 1920s.

World War II provided an impetus to develop sophisticated methods for managing large, complex organizations under conditions of uncertainty. Strategic planning methodologies created in the war years began to be widely utilized in the corporate sector around the mid-1950s and have since been adopted by many types of institutions. A wide range of terminologies (e.g., long-range planning, comprehensive planning, integrated planning) have been used to describe the approaches this chapter groups under the descriptor *strategic planning*. At a deeper level of detail than this chapter contains, these types of planning would be differentiated, as each has its own objectives and methods.

A more rigorous way of categorizing futures research and strategic planning in the spectrum of methods for organizational management is through the matrix in Figure 6-1. In this matrix, the "control" dimension reflects the ability of the institution to influence the extent to which an emerging environmental issue develops.

An organization can utilize conventional management information systems to gather data about the impact of forces that are both under its control and predictable with high accuracy (near term events, low amounts of environmental turbulence). For example, a university school of education's administration monitors expenditures to insure that costs for each area of the budget remain within projected guidelines. If one sector is overspending its allotted resources, the dean can anticipate a potential shortfall and take steps to reduce those outlays.

Conventional predictive strategies, such as trend extrapolation, can be used for situations in which an impinging force can be projected with high accuracy, but the institution has little control over whether this trend continues. As an illustration, if demographic factors are eroding school enrollments in a region and reducing demand for new teachers, a teacher education program can plan to cut back on its faculty, target alternative populations for instruction, or lobby the university to reduce class sizes.

		Ability to Control Issue: High	Ability to Control Issue: Low
Time Horizon Relative to Environmental Turbulence (Forecasting Accuracy)	Near (High)	I	II
	Far (Low)	III	IV

I. Management Information Systems
II. Conventional Prediction
III. Strategic Planning
IV. Futures Research

FIGURE 6–1. Typology of Methods for Organizational Management.

Cell III (high control, low accuracy) poses a different type of challenge. For example, a university occasionally changes its chief academic officer; often, little warning is given of such a shift (e.g., a provost resigns to take a new job or is forced out by an unexpected political situation). A school of education can position itself through political alliances so that, whenever such a discontinuity occurs, the dean of education will have a strong hand in choosing the provost's successor. This type of strategic planning unobtrusively minimizes crisis-management situations.

The Cell IV situation of low control and low accuracy (long-range issues, high degree of environmental turbulence) is the most difficult for organizations. As an illustration, teachers are asked to prepare students for their occupational roles as adults, but substantial uncertainty exists about what skills and jobs will be typical of the workplace a generation from now. Teacher educators can neither reduce this uncertainty nor change their mission, so developing adaptive strategies that equip them to prepare students for a wide range of possible vocational environments is essential. Futures research approaches can be very useful in identifying forces whose impact is profound, but uncertain, and in assessing institutional options for response.

In all four types of situations, keeping the responsive capabilities of an organization flexible to unexpected shifts in its environment requires management emphasis on strategic, as well as tactical, objectives. For example, many university teacher education programs have recently experienced rapid, unexpected erosion of their baseline funding due to economic and political discontinuities. Often, this loss of resources has been perceived as a short-term deviation that would soon disappear; the management approach of "cutting everything back equally until the funding returns" was a frequent tactical response.

Such a response fails badly if the resource problems are in

fact a long-term shift to a new revenue baseline. Years of low funding for all programs reduce quality and morale; then, after these sacrifices, sectors of the institution must be eliminated anyway. A better response is anticipatory management that recognizes the situation's uncertainty; options are implemented that flexibly allow either (a) a smooth transition to a potential permanent reduction of costs or (b) a reversible set of cuts, should the revenue decrease be temporary. Management strategies that utilize futures research emphasize flexible policies and practices in those sectors of the organization affected by a turbulent environment.

Overall, futures research and strategic planning are becoming increasingly important for teacher education. The remainder of this century will be a time of high environmental change and uncertainty; this necessitates extensive use of Cell III and Cell IV institutional development approaches. In turn, these link to the conventional prediction and management information systems that organizations routinely employ for directing their tactical activities.

Premises and Assumptions Underlying Long-Range Thinking

The fundamental goal of futures research and strategic planning is to aid individuals and organizations in managing complexity and uncertainty in their external environments over time. In particular, the futures research field acts as an umbrella to link work in environmental scanning, forecasting, impact assessment, policy analysis, and strategic planning (Morrison, Renfro, & Boucher, 1984). Each of these approaches has value in its own right, but futures researchers believe that a sequenced synthesis of these methods is more valuable than their use in isolation.

As will be discussed later, the primary emphasis in futures research is on using methodologies from environmental scanning, forecasting, and impact assessment to analyze external forces for change. This work provides contextual knowledge that organizations can use in their policy analysis and strategic planning.

McClellan (1978) defines a futurist as "one who makes other people's futures more real to them." This definition encompasses several concepts. *First*, the future is seen as plural; alternative futures are possible depending on choices made in the present. *Second*, the field is depicted as a service profession; the practitioner is a professional who aids others in shaping the future, rather than someone who makes a self-determination of what is best and acts as social engineer to create that outcome. *Third*, a sense of empowerment is conveyed; making futures "real" involves moving beyond the presentation of plausible alternatives, to indicate how preferred visions can be achieved. *Finally*, the profession of futurist is defined broadly; many who do not consider themselves practitioners of futures research (teachers, journalists, politicians) might make others' futures more real as part of their work.

Kauffman (1976) presents four common metaphors for the future: a roller coaster, a river, an ocean, and a dice game. Each captures an aspect of many people's perceptions about the future: predestination, the momentum of the past, navigating to a chosen outcome, randomness and uncertainty. While reflecting prevalent beliefs about the nature of the future, these metaphors are contradictory in the message they convey about how to act in the present. The roller coaster and the river communicate an image of reacting to a single dominant future; the ocean, a proactive vision of unlimited choice; the dice game, passive acceptance of chaos. Each strategy is appropriate in some situations, but a richer mental model is needed to form the basis of futures planning.

A deeper metaphor, which can support the definition of futurist as presented, is the future as a tree: one trunk (the past and present) with many branches (alternative futures). Individuals and institutions are like ants crawling up the trunk toward the branches. Decisions made in the present weaken branches (limit possibilities), because the choices not made are constrained as alternatives. By the time present becomes future, only one branch is left (the new trunk).

Three kinds of futures practitioners can be characterized in this model: theoretical, applied, and normative. Theoretical futurists work to explicate the spectrum of branches (the range of plausible alternative futures) and to indicate the forces that create and constrain these possibilities. For example, de Jouvenel (1967) describes two types of factors that determine the presence or absence of branches:

1. *Structural certainties.* Factors shaping the future based on the natural and social orders (e.g., the sun rising, U.S. presidential elections occurring every 4 years).
2. *Contractual assurances.* Factors based on individuals and institutions honoring a pre-arranged agreement (e.g., an institution's granting tenure to an individual meeting its requirements).

The practice of schooling and the certification of a worthy preservice teacher education candidate are other examples of structural certainties and contractual assurances.

However, discontinuous forces introduce uncertainty into these premises about the future. Wild cards (e.g., assassinations, earthquakes, technological breakthroughs such as high temperature superconductivity) are events that are possible but have low probability. Indeterminacies are aspects of the future that are decided by choices of the moment, rather than pre-arranged. A reform movement that rapidly reconfigures the structure of a nation's teacher education system would illustrate how uncertainties disrupt (and create) certainties.

Theoretical futurists study how these forces interact to generate (a) dominant branches with high probabilities of occurrence; (b) twigs that are possible, but not plausible; and (c) gaps where a future is imaginable but very unlikely. The challenge of such research is that, although aspects of the future can be discovered (through measuring the probable effect of a predictable force), ultimately the single future that occurs is invented (through the interaction of structural certainties, contractual assurances, wild cards, human choices, and indeterminacies in the present). This epistemology of futures research makes exact prediction impossible; however, even a partially accurate forecast can empower much better decisions than the default assumption that the future will be like the present.

Applied futurists focus on influencing the future through actions in the present; most strategic planners would classify their activities into this category of futures work. Present plans, policies, practices, and organizational cultures are analyzed to determine how shifts in this pattern of institutional choices could maximize the chances of attaining preferred futures while minimizing the risks and costs of undesirable alternative scenarios. As an illustration, practitioners who apply mathematical modeling to strategic planning can analyze for decision makers the likely future expectations of present actions (McNamara, 1971). Using such an approach, a teacher education institution, fearing a gradual decline in federal funding over a 5-year period, could determine the relative merits of alternative policies by using some game-theoretic decision strategy (e.g., minimize the maximum loss).

Normative futurists take a value-laden stance: They build a case that a particular vision is both desirable and, through a radical shift in decision making, attainable—but that a significantly less preferable future is likely to emerge if current trends continue. The distinction between normative futurists and other groups proselytizing for change is that normative futurists:

1. Seek to empower and motivate others, rather than collecting followers to implement a change through direct leadership.
2. Present a range of alternative futures, delineating how shifts in the external environment are rendering historic patterns of behavior less effective.
3. Indicate that the choice of which vision is desirable could depend on individual values and beliefs, instead of arguing that their preferred future is "right."

This definition implies that many reformers are acting as normative futurists without deliberately practicing this approach.

From a philosophic perspective, Fletcher (1979) delineates five fundamental premises of futures research: alternatives and choice, purposeful action, holism and stakeholders, extended time frames, and guiding images. Purposeful action refers to futures researchers' belief that decisions about the future should be proactive, influencing what will come, rather than reactive to a future image viewed as unalterable. Holism affirms the need for examining higher order consequences of change, given the interconnectedness and complexity of the forces shaping the future. Stakeholders include all human beings who might be affected by an action or event (including coming generations, whose options might be mortgaged by present choices).

One's guiding image is the perception of oneself, the surrounding universe, the relationships between self and context, and one's ability to alter these three elements. A group's guiding image of the future (e.g., the American Dream) is crucial in determining its evolution (Polak, 1973). An individual's self-actualization is also shaped by that person's future-focused role image (Singer, 1974).

Psychological Issues Underlying Long-Range Thinking

So far, this discussion of futures research and strategic planning has dealt with the cognitive aspects of looking ahead. However, one reason why structured approaches to long-range thinking have been slow to be accepted and mixed in their results is that people's attitudes about the future are often laden with unconscious emotional biases. Fundamental psychological stances toward the future include:

1. Indifference (the future is intrinsically unknowable, or cannot be changed, or offers little leverage in solving present problems).
2. Optimism (progress is inevitable; enough money and expertise and technology can solve any problem, because people are basically good and wise).
3. Pessimism (present trends are leading to disaster; collapse can only be averted by dramatic sacrifices and top-down imposition of change, because in a crisis most people behave foolishly).
4. Visionary (trends from the past need not shape the future; a major values shift is coming that will alter the course of civilization and change how people act).

Indifference to the future, which all people feel at times, stems in part from the psychological stability of the present. For example, the author's university, which is located 20 feet above sea level and 3 miles from the Gulf of Mexico, will probably be destroyed by a hurricane sometime during the next 20 years. However, sitting in his office, the author cannot believe this statement emotionally, even though its rational underpinnings are clear. On a larger scale, even in times of very rapid change, one day seems much like the next; those who live through an epochal shift in civilization frequently only realize its magnitude retrospectively. This psychological stability breeds a dangerous indifference to potential future discontinuities.

The day-to-day challenges many professionals confront also contribute to an unwillingness to devote much attention to the future. People often feel that thinking about the future draws attention away from the present; but, as will be discussed later, strategic approaches can provide a perspective from which current issues can be understood and changes empowered. Although present crises are legitimate and urgent, teacher education is unlikely to develop much leverage in resolving its present problems until long-range perspectives on change are adopted.

As for attitudes other than indifference, best-selling futures books tend to fall into one of the latter three types of psychological stances. For example, Naisbitt's *Megatrends* (1982) is an optimistic prediction that ignores negative trends, Jay and Stewart's *Apocalypse 2000* (1988) extrapolates irreversible declines, and Ornstein and Ehrlich's *New World, New Mind* (1989) provides a visionary perspective on a change in human consciousness that will alter the course of civilization. Comparable works written during the 1970s are Kahn, Brown, and Martel's *The Next 200 Years* (1976); Meadows, Meadows,

Randers, and Behren's *The Limits to Growth* (1972); and Reich's *The Greening of America* (1970). Numerous other examples could be given.

Although providing images of the future that reinforce people's fundamental emotional stances might be good for a book's sales, its validity as an objective and complete assessment of external uncertainty is lowered. Optimistic, pessimistic, and visionary attitudes stem partially from tempocentrism (people's personal identification with a state of affairs that existed at a particular time). For example, the Republicans accuse the Democrats of wanting to return to the 1960s, and the Democrats respond by charging the Republicans with longing to go back to the 1920s.

Many people bond to the external state of affairs at a particularly happy time in their lives (e.g., childhood, a period of personal success) and experience nostalgia and anger when civilization evolves to another stage. Others find their lives shaped by external decline and impose that personal pattern on civilization as a whole, becoming pessimists and doomsayers. Tempocentrism manifests psychologically similar symptoms to ethnocentrism (clinging to the assumptions, values, and behavior patterns of one particular culture) and leads to regressive, emotional attitudes about the future (Textor, 1980).

Societal problems with tempocentrism are intensified by another human attribute: fear of the unknown. Even when people rationally understand that a forecast delineating the range of uncertainty is the appropriate output of a futures study, the temptation to demand a prediction (or even a prophecy) can be overwhelming. Organizations are much more comfortable building on future "facts" than on analyses of legitimate uncertainty (e.g., "the teacher shortage in 1995 will be 185,000 people" versus "given the large pool of prospective reentrants to the profession, the number of teachers available relative to demand in 1995 will be shaped by comparative teacher salaries, working conditions, and respect for the profession at that time").

These psychological aspects of the future (indifference, tempocentrism, fear of the unknown) are very important. In any situation, although the cognitive challenges involved in long-range thinking could be profound, the ultimate limits on the effectiveness of structured approaches to planning are likely to be psychological and social. Institutional change management techniques, although not discussed in this chapter, are vital for insuring the adoption and usage of long-range strategies. Good resources in this area include Hickman and Silva (1984), Kanter (1983), Lippitt (1982), Mink (1986), and Wygant and Markley (1988).

Methodologies Central to Futures Research

The types of methods used to forecast alternative possibilities and assess their probable consequences depend on a common set of assumptions about epistemology. Because the future is shaped by events in the continuously changing present, its attributes cannot be measured in advance through the lexicon of scientific research tools. All statements about the future are speculative; the goal of futures research methodologies is to insure that an analysis is as complete, consistent, informed, and realistic as possible.

Although basing decisions on speculation might seem a risky approach, no other alternative is possible. Many present choices intrinsically involve assumptions about the long-range environment. Making those decisions on the basis of a conscious, rigorous model of the future is superior to using unexamined default assumptions about what will come.

Qualitative analysis is much more important in futures research than quantitative methods; a "back-of-the-envelope" forecast with all assumptions correct will be more accurate than an elaborate quantitative model with several assumptions wrong. Quantitative methods are more important in Cell II of Figure 6-1: Conventional Prediction. Helmer (1983) describes strategies used by futures researchers to minimize qualitative epistemological problems. These include proximate criteria (monitoring intermediate events as a way of adjusting the probabilities of competing possibilities), informational reproducibility (checking whether similar results are obtained by different forecasters and alternative methods), and sensitivity analysis (judging the extent to which variations in initial assumptions and data produce major shifts in conclusions).

Futures research methodologies can be grouped into three categories: issues management, forecasting, and impact assessment. Issues management provides a systematic overview of trends and emerging discontinuities, to insure that a futures analysis identifies all the potentially important issues for an institution's evolution. Forecasting projects these trends and events forward, developing alternative scenarios of the institution's environmental context. Impact assessment evaluates the likely consequences of these alternatives for the institution's goals, plans, practices, policies, and culture. In sequence, these methodologies form the futures research process.

The initial stage in this process is issues management, which incorporates processes of environmental scanning and monitoring. Its objectives include (Coates, 1986):

1. Detecting scientific, technical, economic, social, and political interactions important to the organization.
2. Alerting decision makers to trends that are converging, diverging, intensifying, eroding, or interacting.
3. Promoting a futures orientation in the organization.

The types of trends and developments teacher-training institutions must monitor are quite diverse. For example, the future supply of teachers needed in a region depends in part on the ratio of local housing costs to personal income. People with younger children often cannot afford homes above a certain monetary ceiling; in areas where house prices are rising rapidly, school enrollments tend to drop, which in turn affects the hiring of new teachers.

Developing an environmental scanning system capable of monitoring these types of indirect interactions involves a number of steps (Morrison, et al., 1984):

1. Identifying potential information resources (databases, journals, newspapers, agency publications, experts).

2. Selecting which resources to monitor through prioritizing themes of interest to the institution.
3. Identifying criteria by which to scan, focusing on key leverage topics.
4. Developing a continuous scanning and summarizing process.
5. Selecting issues for further action from the outcomes of the scanning process, based on their probability of occurrence and potential impact.

In addition to the resources cited, Brown (1979) and Wygant and Markley (1988) present good summaries of corporate, government, and community strategies for environmental scanning. Discussions of environmental scanning systems for colleges and universities can be found in Callan (1986), Hearn and Heydinger (1985), Lozier and Chittipetti (1986), and Morrison (1987).

Forecasting, the next stage in futures analysis, involves projecting the interaction of structural certainties, contractual assurances, wild cards, trends, events, human choices, and present indeterminacies into probable alternative scenarios. Major methodologies used in forecasting include (Hencley & Yates, 1974):

1. Trend extrapolation, such as time series analysis (exponential smoothing, moving average) and regression analysis.
2. Modeling, including econometric and systems dynamics simulations.
3. Delphi surveys, which iteratively assess expert opinion.
4. Cross-impact analysis, to clarify the relationships and interactions among specific events and trends.
5. Relevance trees, for determining pathways of events leading to goals.
6. Morphological analysis, to systematically elucidate the full range of possibilities.

These techniques fall into three general categories (Kirschling & Huckfeldt, 1980): (a) exploratory methods that develop images of the future based on trends and models, (b) intuitive methods such as the Delphi and cross-impact matrix that rely on human synthesis and deduction, and (c) normative methods such as morphological and relevance approaches that trace goals backwards into sequences of prerequisite actions.

Armstrong (1985) provides a summary and evaluation of long-range forecasting techniques and their use in a variety of institutional settings. Makridakis and Wheelwright (1982) have compiled an exhaustive description of forecasting methodologies that indicates the linkage between short-range and long-range approaches. An illustrative case study detailing how modern business uses multiple scenarios as the basis of strategic planning is presented in Wack (1985a, 1985b). O'Connor (1978) delineates the stages of development required to create such a scenario-oriented forecasting system.

Because the future of teacher education is shaped by a broad spectrum of external forces, forecasting of alternative scenarios for the field can be quite complex. For example, demographic, economic, sociopolitical, and technological factors currently are interacting to determine the likely demand for teachers in the 1990s. Some predictions of teacher shortages naively compare demographic projections of the traditional student population with extrapolations of present teacher-preparation enrollments. Such an approach omits other forces that could create situations ranging from surpluses to shortages (e.g., improvements in the profession's working conditions and respect from the community, economic difficulties leading to surpluses of skilled labor in other occupations, replacement of teachers by technology for some pedagogical tasks). The futures analysis required to chart these competing possibilities and determine their relative probabilities necessitates the use of a variety of forecasting methodologies building on data from systematic environmental scanning.

Assessing the consequences of each alternative future for institutional policies, practices, plans, and culture is the third stage of futures analysis. Impact assessment involves rigorously considering the likelihood and magnitude of the multiple long-range effects of a development. The science fiction writer Isaac Asimov once said that the important thing to forecast is not the automobile, but the parking problem; not the income tax, but the expense account; not the television, but the soap opera.

As an illustration, a crucial issue in the future of teacher education is not how many computers will be in classrooms in 1995, but how these instructional devices will change the relationship of teacher and student, school and society (Dede, 1988). Typically, new information technologies have their impact on societal institutions in four sequential stages (Coates, 1977):

Stage One: The new technology is adopted by an institution to carry out existing functions more efficiently.
Stage Two: The institution changes internally (work roles, organizational structures), to take better advantage of these new efficiencies.
Stage Three: Institutions develop new functions and activities enabled by additional capabilities of the technology. As the roles of different types of institutions expand, new competitive relationships emerge.
Stage Four: The original role of the institution can become obsolete, be displaced, or be radically transformed as new goals dominate the institution's activities.

Instructional technology is just entering Stage One in many schools, but current teacher certification candidates will spend the majority of their professional lives working in Stage Four school situations. An impact assessment of what challenges and opportunities they might face is given in Dede (1988).

Applying technology assessment methodologies in education requires focusing on potential economic, political, and sociocultural impacts of these approaches (Locatis & Gooler, 1975). The tools used in impact identification and assessment are detailed in Porter, Rossini, Carpenter, and Roper (1980); these include brainstorming, expert panels, mini-surveys, Bayesian statistical analyses, social indicators, scaling techniques, and goal analysis. Helmer (1983) presents a summary of overall futures methods that delineates how the results of these assessment techniques link to strategic planning.

Educators can evaluate the utility of futures analyses produced with environmental scanning, forecasting, and impact-assessment methodologies through a variety of measures. For example, internal criteria for judging the likely worth of a futures research product include (a) an explicit statement of premises, purposes, methods, values, outcomes, and time frame; (b) plausibility (completeness, imagination, internal consistency, realism, justification through rational explanation); and (c) effectiveness in guiding action in the present (Amara, 1981).

Plausibility and effectiveness in suggesting current options could be more important than accuracy. Forecasts can be self-determining; a grim scenario that inspires measures in the present to prevent its occurrence is very useful, though eventually inaccurate. Because of self-fulfilling and self-negating effects, compiling a record of forecasters' hits and misses to determine the accuracy of their products is only a partial evaluation of quality.

Moreover, measuring the validity of a statement about the future can be difficult, even retrospectively. Knowing that a Republican won the 1980 U.S. presidential election does not conclusively determine the accuracy of a prediction in 1977 that "A Republican has a sixty percent chance of winning the next presidential election." The validity of the probability estimate is still uncertain, reflecting the fundamental unmeasurability of the future. However, the utility of this prediction can be retrospectively assessed by decision makers through estimating the benefits they gained by including this prediction in their pre-election strategic planning.

Methodologies Central to Strategic Planning

The description in this section will be brief compared with that for futures research methods, as the techniques used in strategic planning are better known. Futures work provides environmental knowledge that institutions can use for strategic planning (including policy analysis). Educational policy analysis is the topic of chapter 9, so a discussion of its methodologies is not repeated here.

Peterson (1980) defines planning as a dynamic, continual process (as opposed to a static view that emphasizes occasional production of a plan) and contrasts alternative formulations of this activity. Purposes of planning can include responding to environmental pressures, delineating critical problems facing the institution, increasing external perceptions of being well managed, improving internal communication, and fostering understanding of the interdependence of different organizational sectors.

Strategic planning links four elements:

1. Assessing probable changes in the long-range environment (a step best accomplished through futures research methodologies but often done intuitively).
2. Determining current institutional strengths, weaknesses, problems, and capabilities.
3. Delineating the values of the organization's varying constituencies.
4. Creating a strategic direction for the institution on the basis of the first three elements, including reconceptualizing the institution's rationale, allocating resources, setting tactical goals, and reframing policies.

Institutional policy issues encompassed by strategic planning include (Cope, 1981) (a) the choice of mission, goals, and objectives; (b) decisions on organizational structure; (c) the acquisition of facilities; (d) the determination of which services should be provided; (e) the establishment of tactical policies on personnel, facilities, and financing; and (f) multiyear budgeting. As Keller (1983) indicates, the initial question of strategic planning is, "Long-range, in what business will this institution be?" The average lifetime of a Fortune 500 corporation is only 40 years; a major reason for early demise is that successful organizations often neglect the implications of a changing environment for their fundamental mission (Janis, 1989). Institutions tend to assume that the services and products that made them productive historically are an automatic blueprint for sustainability and growth.

A classic example is the American railroad. In the early part of this century, U.S. railroad companies made careful, long-range projections that included miles of track needed, advances in engine technology, and passenger demand. However, they only thought of themselves as in the railroad business and, so, missed the impact on these projections of the automobile and the airplane. Strategic planning would have fostered a conception of their mission as the transportation business, with vastly different results. Schools of education could become an anachronism in a short time if they conceive of their business as teacher education rather than improving the competence of teachers.

The basic sequence of steps in strategic planning is:

1. Rethink the mission, role, and scope of the institution, given the environmental changes identified by futures methods (particularly opportunities and threats).
2. Gather data on internal operations, especially their strengths and weaknesses.
3. Match the reconceptualized mission with the strengths in ways that highlight alternative formulations of policy.
4. Use policy analysis to determine the relative effectiveness of each alternative formulation in achieving the mission across the range of probable emerging contexts.
5. Develop planning objectives to implement the most effective set of policies.

Techniques utilized in these stages can range from relatively familiar management tools to moderately exotic methods such as probability-diffusion matrices and value profiles (Cope, 1981).

Each planning objective must meet all the following criteria (Wygant & Markley, 1988):

1. Substantive validity (Will this accomplish what is intended?)
2. Economic validity (Are sufficient resources available for this?)

3. Ecological validity (Is this evolutionary from the current organizational culture?)
4. Political validity (Does this have the support of those with the power to block it?)
5. Motivational validity (Does this have a critical mass of committed change agents?)

Steiner (1979) presents a detailed discussion of alternative approaches to strategic planning, contrasting models for different sizes and types of organizations. McCune (1986) depicts a suggested sequence of stages for long-range educational planning. A more formal method tailored to the needs of higher education has been developed by the Resource Center for Planned Change at the American Association of State Colleges and Universities (Alm, Buhler-Miko, & Smith, 1978). An annotated overview of literature on all types of educational planning has been prepared by the Society for College and University Planning (Norris & Poulton, 1987).

The Utility of Long-Range Methodologies for Institutional Development

A growing body of evidence attests to the effectiveness of futures research and strategic planning in organizational management. Many of the studies cited in the previous methodological sections include retrospective assessments of these approaches' utility in a variety of settings. In addition, multiple researchers have compiled data on the extent of use and the effectiveness of futures research and strategic planning in corporate, governmental, and community settings.

As an illustration, Ascher (1978) assesses the accuracy and utility of long-range forecasts in a number of fields: demographics, economics, energy, transportation, and general technological development. Substantial successes are cited in each of these areas, along with a representative range of failures. His findings confirm the premises and assumptions of long-range thinking discussed earlier: (a) the more distant the time horizon, the less accurate the forecast; (b) the validity of assumptions is essential to the quality of the ultimate product; and (c) a combination of methodologies is more likely to avoid systemic bias than a single approach.

Overall, the accuracy of demographic and technological forecasts tends to be higher than that of economic or sociopolitical predictions. This is unsurprising because, the fewer the variables involved, the more likely that futures assumptions and methods can encompass the complexity of the situation. For example, the advent of a technology can be projected by monitoring the level of research funding available, the rate of progress in that field, and the relative economic advantages of implementing the technology's functionalities.

In contrast, determining the likely victor of a future election rests on the interaction of many more variables. However, the utility of an economic or sociopolitical forecast might still be comparable to a demographic or technological prediction, because the leverage of greater knowledge about fiscal and cultural futures can be very substantial.

As another example of research that assesses the effectiveness of long-range methodologies, around 1980 a series of studies was published on the use of multiple scenarios by U.S. industrial companies. Linneman and Klein (1979) surveyed the application of alternative futures forecasting in Fortune 1000 industrial corporations and found both substantial usage and satisfaction with the results. In follow-up research (Klein & Linneman, 1981), eight case histories of multiple-scenario utilization in corporate planning were compiled. These companies indicated that, as the economic and political environment became increasingly turbulent, futures methods were very helpful in managing this complexity and achieving long-range growth. The major limitation these organizations described was the difficulty and expense of rigorously applying extensive scanning, forecasting, and assessment methods. Zentner (1982) responded by detailing strategies for minimizing the cost and complexity of applying futures methods, illustrating his approach through examples from a major energy corporation.

A constraint on the publication of studies assessing the effectiveness of long-range methods is the proprietary nature of most corporate futures research and strategic planning. Assessments of the long-range environment and its likely internal implications convey substantial competitive advantages to an organization; as corporations have realized this, public availability of their futures work has become increasingly limited. Since the early 1970s, funding for futures work has shifted from the public to the private sector and from external think tanks to internal working groups; these developments have intensified the difficulty of obtaining effectiveness data. Long term, the evolution of the futures field might slow unless better arrangements are made for pooling retrospective evaluations.

How rapidly will the effectiveness of long-range thinking methods continue to progress? Over a decade ago, Hofer (1976) summarized research on strategic planning and presented suggestions for future efforts. Almost simultaneously, in a study sponsored by the National Science Foundation (NSF), a group of prominent professionals assessed the current state of the art in futures research (Boucher, 1977). Both these sets of findings detailed substantial advantages to using long-range methods as central strategies for institutional development. In addition, a major focus of the NSF work was to create a research agenda for improving the utility of futures approaches. High-leverage topics that this group cited include (a) evaluating the adequacy of current theories of social change; (b) devising better methods for measuring the possible significance of future problems; (c) improving methods for forecasting the next crisis; (d) developing more detailed criteria and methods of forecast evaluation; (e) developing better means of identifying nonmonetary social costs and relating them to monetary costs, so that overall systems costs can be estimated; and (f) devising improved methods of communicating forecasts to policymakers, so that the value implications of different possible decisions are fully understood. This agenda is still current, as the list delineates very challenging problems endemic not just to long-range thinking, but also to the social sciences as a whole. The development of methods unique to futures research and strategic planning will continue; but the further evolution of these fields will increasingly be limited by the rate of advance in knowledge about detailed social, political, and cultural dynamics.

Although progress in these areas is slow, researchers are making significant discoveries; and the advent of inexpensive, sophisticated computer modeling applications for the social sciences should speed the evolution of this knowledge. Thus, the already significant utility of long-range methods for organizational development is expected to increase over the next decade. In turn, the costs to institutions of not using these approaches in managing a turbulent environment will continue to grow.

A new proverb says, "in times of rapid change, experience is your worse enemy." The solution that many groups are finding to this conundrum is not to abandon organizational wisdom garnered from the past, but to channel and focus its flexible application through utilizing structured tools from futures research and strategic planning.

HISTORICAL ANALYSIS OF LONG-RANGE THINKING IN TEACHER EDUCATION

Numerous distinguished educators have used futures research and strategic-planning approaches as an intrinsic part of their professional contributions. This chapter makes no attempt to review that extensive literature; its focus is limited to national-level teacher education reform proposals. However, in addition to the references discussed in the methodology sections, illustrative work in general U.S. educational futures is cited briefly to give a historical background on the development of the field. Against this context, the use of long-range thinking in teacher education reform can be charted.

A major group in the evolution of educational futures has been the reconstructionist philosophers such as George Counts, Harold Rugg, and Theodore Brameld. The latter's *The Teacher as World Citizen: A Scenario of the 21st Century* (1976) illustrates the perspective these thinkers bring to issues of teacher preparation. A dominant recent figure is Harold Shane, whose books (1973, 1977, 1981, 1987) and articles have done much to raise the awareness of educators. John Pulliam has also been active in educational futures for 2 decades, including participating in a federally sponsored study of the emerging needs of schools (Pulliam, Kierstead, & Bowman, 1980).

The Educational Policy Research centers at Stanford (Williams, 1973) and Syracuse (Green, 1971) were foci for early work. Around the same period, Richard Hostrup coordinated two compendia of readings in educational futures (1973, 1975). In teacher education, Alvin Eurich has been a pioneer in indicating the utility of planning (1962), as has Joel Burdin for educational futures research (1975). Draper Kauffman, Jr. (1976) and Don Glines (1978a, 1978b, 1978c, 1979) have been influential figures in adapting futures methods to classroom teaching.

Jack Culbertson has participated in many studies in educational futures, including an extensive eight-state project early in the development of the field (Morphet & Ryan, 1967a, 1967b, 1967c; Morphet & Jesser, 1968a, 1968b). Jack Frymier

at Ohio State University has played a similar, seminal role, including cooperative work with the Association for Supervision and Curriculum Development (1973). In the early and mid-1970s, this chapter's author co-founded the first and third graduate programs in futures research in the United States, as well as the Education Section of the World Future Society. This professional association published two collections of leading-edge work (Kierstead, Bowman, & Dede, 1979; Redd & Harkins, 1980), and its conferences serve as a continuing resource for the field. The National Education Association has recently studied how education might be restructured to meet the human resource needs of the emerging global, knowledge-based economy (Reich, 1988).

The purpose of this illustrative, but not exhaustive, set of historical citations for U.S. educational futures research is to indicate the context of long-range perspectives in which American teacher education has been operating. As discussed later, the impact of this substantive and methodological futures environment on teacher education practice and reform has been remarkably small.

Major United States Initiatives in Teacher Education

National efforts advocating extensive revision of teacher education are good indicators of overall practice for several reasons: (a) initiatives for change provide a perspective of teacher education as seen by both its practitioners and external critics; (b) reformers are familiar with the leading edge of practice and often represent advanced perspectives on the field; and (c) attempts to revise teacher education generally encompass all its aspects (e.g., preservice, inservice, education of teacher educators). As such, analysis of national-level reform initiatives provides a better representation of overall leading-edge thinking in the field than examining ephemeral, small-scale, teacher education programs.

The major American teacher education reforms discussed in this section were carefully selected to be a typical sample of these efforts. The documents analyzed were chosen using Association of Teacher Educators (1986), Borrowman (1965), Bush (1987), Kinney (1964), and Tyack (1967). The goal of this selection process was to longitudinally compare the extent and quality of long-range thinking in these reform proposals during the period in which futures research and strategic planning perspectives emerged as major themes in teacher education's environmental context.

Both widely read external calls for teacher education reforms and national-level statements by the profession recommending extensive changes in practice were analyzed. The representative proposals selected were Association of Colleges for Teacher Education (AACTE, 1958); Carnegie Forum on Education and the Economy, Task Force on Teaching as a Profession (1986); Commission on Teacher Education (1946); Conant (1963); Cottrell (1956); Cubberley (1906); Evenden (1933); Holmes Group (1986); Howsam, Corrigan, Denemark, and Nash (1976); Kilpatrick (1933); Koerner (1963); Lindsey (1961); National Commission on Excellence in Education (1983); National Council for Accreditation in Teacher Education (1985);

Silberman (1970); B. O. Smith (1969); and E. R. Smith (1962). All these reforms were analyzed for (a) the use of long-range images to guide the evolution of the profession, and (b) the application of futures research and strategic-planning methodologies to managing change in teacher education as those approaches became widely disseminated.

In particular, types of futures thinking that might enhance the utility of teacher education reform efforts include:

1. Alternative scenarios (or even simple predictions) of the changing societal context; implications for the long-range mission, clients, content, and methods of the school; and assessment of corresponding shifts required in teacher education.
2. Projections of teacher supply and demand, with consequences for teacher-preparation institutions.
3. Normative visions of desirable futures for schooling, with assessments of teacher education's role in reaching this goal.
4. Strategic plans for the structured, gradual evolution of the field, including shifts in mission; analyses of strengths, weaknesses, opportunities, and threats; and delineations of strategic and tactical objectives.

Simple projections and normative visions could have been part of proposals predating the emergence of long-range methodologies after the World War II. Futures research and strategic-planning techniques were being utilized in the environmental context of U.S. teacher education by the late 1960s and could have been incorporated in reform efforts of the 1970s and 1980s.

Many of the reform proposals listed earlier were initiated because of problems of poor anticipation of the future (e.g., periodic shortages and surpluses of teachers, emergence and waning of the industrial workplace, external challenges to U.S. economic prosperity and political independence). Almost all of the documents use titles suggestive of long-range thinking: "Facing the Future," "Future Challenges," "Today's Student for Tomorrow's World," "The Profession in the Decades Ahead," "The Future—Past or Prologue," "Tomorrow's Teachers." Regrettably, however, few of the proposals incorporate significant long-range perspectives, and none utilize sophisticated futures research or strategic-planning methodologies.

The reform initiatives on the earlier list that include a substantial discussion of long range issues are:

1. Carnegie Forum on Education and the Economy, Task Force on Teaching as a Profession, *A Nation Prepared: Teachers for the 21st Century* (1986), which presents a projection of how the American economy might develop, a single scenario illustrating a typical twenty-first century school, and a plan (which incorporates few of the elements of a strategic plan) for creating change.
2. AACTE, *The Future Challenges Teacher Education* (1958), which contains a few studies that scan the external environment for emerging long-range forces and issues, but then lapses into present-centered concerns for the remainder of the document.
3. Kilpatrick, *The Educational Frontier* (1933), a manifesto by educational reconstructionists and pragmatists that presents a vision of how changes in teacher education could lead to long-term improvements in society.

The remainder of the documents, spanning a considerable time, offer a remarkably similar litany of present-centered, context-independent problems and proposed solutions.

The conclusion that major American teacher education reform initiatives have been remarkably duplicative is not surprising; historical analysis confirms the repetitive nature of the problems and suggestions for solutions discussed in these proposals (Keith, 1987). The recurring issues are (a) What is "adequate qualification" for a teacher? (b) what is the place of pedagogy in teacher preparation? and (c) what specialized or general academic content should teachers master? In reform efforts, both external and profession-sponsored, the proper resolution of these issues tends to be seen as fundamentally independent of changes in societal environment, even though each reform proposer might believe that the problems to be redressed have arisen from teacher education's unresponsiveness to prior shifts in educational context. This stance is surprising, given the increasing rate of demographic, economic, sociocultural, political, and technological change.

A number of rationalizations and explanations can be advanced for this general lack of long-range perspectives and methodologies in American teacher education reform:

1. Perennialist and idealistic philosophies of education argue that eternal truth is context independent and that education should not alter in response to changing societal conditions. To the extent that these views have dominated pragmatic or reconstructionist educational philosophies, an indifference to futures thinking would be expected.
2. Advocates of reform might believe that teacher education must first be optimized in the present before an attempt to chart an evolution into the future. Because major structural changes tend to take a considerable time to achieve, this view creates a situation in which teacher education is perceived to be constantly lagging behind society and preparing professionals to function well in outdated settings.
3. The psychological problems of long-range thinking discussed earlier (unconscious emotional biases, tempocentrism, fear of the unknown) could be major impediments to fundamentally altering teacher education. Advocates of change might attempt to finesse this problem by minimizing explicit discussion of the future.
4. Reformers might be so focused on problems in the present that their awareness of long-range perspectives and methodologies is low. This is ironic, in that each new generation of proposals for revision is often triggered by the failure of the prior reform to anticipate environmental shifts.
5. Advocates of reform might believe that the future is unpredictable and that development of teachers' flexibility and adaptability is all that can be done to prepare for change.
6. Preservice teacher educators might believe that preparing practitioners for a changing environment is a lifelong issue to be addressed by inservice teacher educators, who in turn

see their responsibility as developing skills useful in the immediate present.

7. Reformers might feel that emphasis on long-range thinking will erode interest in solving short-range problems. This either–or perspective ignores the possibility of using strategic approaches to empower tactical actions.

These explanations are not mutually exclusive, and other reasons for the omission of long-range thinking can also be formulated.

Although futures research and strategic-planning methods have been extensively used for managing change in other types of organizations, these approaches have been largely ignored by those attempting to alter U.S. teacher education. This is unfortunate because linking desired changes in the field to emerging societal shifts can provide powerful leverage for reform movements to achieve their intended outcomes. The usage of futures research and strategic-planning tools could help move the next generation of reform efforts beyond restating similar issues and finding, after years of revision, the same problems persisting.

Illustrative Recent Reforms Outside the United States

Generally, international research on general educational futures has progressed contemporaneously with U.S. efforts. Examples of representative work are *No Limits to Learning* (Botkin, Elmandjra, & Malitza, 1979), sponsored by the Club of Rome, and *Permanent Education* (Schwartz, 1974), part of the European Cultural Foundation's Project on Educating Man for the 21st Century. A recent summary of educational reform issues from a global perspective is Godet's "Worldwide Challenges and Crises in Education Systems" (1988).

Recent teacher education reforms in most countries, as with those in the United States, have been present centered and context independent, without substantial use of long-range perspectives or methodologies. Intergovernmental efforts, even those targeted at futures issues, have similarly focused solely on current problems and agendas. Illustrative examples are the reports *Teachers for the Schools of Tomorrow* (Thomas, 1968) and *Training Needs of Educational Personnel* (Pauvert, 1986), sponsored by the United Nations Educational, Scientific, and Cultural Organization.

Canada has been a leader in applying futures thinking to teacher education and has produced some innovative regional efforts; an example of applying advanced simulation methodologies is the work of the Commission on Declining School Enrollments in Ontario (1978). Per Dalin, in Norway, has championed educational futures for several decades and is currently heading a School Year 2020 Project (Dalin, 1988). Japan's recent wave of educational reforms is targeted at preparing students to work in the country's economic climate of the early twenty-first century (Shimahara, 1986). Spain has been assessing the implications for education of a changing societal context (MacNair, 1988).

Because the United States has a more decentralized educational policy-setting structure than most countries, many nations make greater use of centralized planning approaches. These efforts are not reviewed here, as their emphasis is more on tactical achievement of preset objectives than on the long-range, contingency-based, strategic approaches this chapter discusses. Interestingly, some nations are beginning to move toward more decentralized policy structures that can facilitate the flexibility in planning requisite to implementing futures methods. One example is China, which views such an educational reform as essential to its economic development (Swanson & Zhian, 1987).

Overall, however, generalizations made about the lack of long-range perspectives in U.S. teacher education reforms apply to most other countries as well. How major a problem does this represent, and what steps are being taken to improve this situation?

IMPLICATIONS FOR IMPROVING RESEARCH AND PRACTICE

Reform movements' formulation of the problems of teacher education in a perennial, context-independent manner is not wrong in any fundamental sense. At the deepest level of analysis, the issues that teacher educators face have an underlying consistency independent of schooling's societal environment. The difficulty is that managing the evolution of the field by thinking about problems and solutions in this manner has lower utility and effectiveness than using long-range approaches to comprehend the dynamics of change in the emerging context.

As an illustration, consider a strategic plan for a major business. One way to formulate this statement of desired changes would be perennial and context-independent: (a) Goals of the business are to make a profit and to serve its customers; (b) employees must be intelligent, able to communicate well, flexible, and innovative; and (c) its products must be of high quality and inexpensive. These statements are legitimate, but they are too general and vague to be useful, and a corporation attempting to implement such a plan would find its effectiveness severely limited. Yet teacher education reform movements repeatedly produce plans of comparable generality.

Better is a context-dependent description of problems, forces for change, and strategic allocation of resources to create a desired future. An illustration of the application of this principle would be to chart probable changes in the definition of *school effectiveness* and to assess the implications of these shifts for current educational practice (Dede & Freiberg, 1986). Of course, this approach will meet with stiff opposition from perennialists, people who believe that the future is unpredictable, and those who fear that long-range thinking detracts from short-range issues.

Futures approaches provide several types of leverage to empower change in the present: (a) Emerging external forces can be harnessed to exert increasing pressure for reform (e.g., the growing societal realization that targeted educational innovation is essential to economic development and competitiveness); (b) futures research and strategic planning methods can be used to make institutional evolution continual and evolutionary (revolutionary revisions tend to be short lived and, without provision for environmental change, rapidly outdated); (c) a mission statement developed by strategic planning is targeted; (d) with present-centered approaches, a reform movement tends to become all things for all people, resulting in an unachievable set of goals (a plethora of societal goals for schooling is one of teacher education's recurrent problems); and (e) fields that anticipate and prepare for change receive increased respect and resources from society, which empowers tactical goals. Properly done, long-range thinking and short-range action are complementary, not competitive.

Even in times of rapid change, people tend to be misled by the psychological stability of the present. Thinking about the future is seen as a luxury to be indulged when current crises permit, rather than as intrinsic to their successful resolution. The mid-range future (5–8 years) for teacher education is very close, yet the dynamics of evolution during this next period can be staggering. Consider an illustrative list of major external impacts on American teacher education over the comparable period historically (1980–1988): the virtual disappearance of the federal role in education, the widespread dissemination of microcomputers, the calamity of AIDS, and economic disruptions caused by the emergence of a global marketplace. Partial anticipation of these developments in the late 1970s would have provided substantial leverage for the evolution of teacher education and would have established respect for the field in society.

Two illustrative, emerging, contextual themes that could empower and guide teacher education reform can be posed as queries: (a) In the workplace, what potential demand for professionals with the skills that teacher education programs develop is being created by long-range demographic, economic, and technological dynamics? (b) How do the changes that information technology and the knowledge-based economy are creating in the workplace affect the knowledge and pedagogical skills needed for those teaching the next generation of students? Practitioners external to teacher education are beginning to use futures research and strategic-planning methods to elucidate these questions; examples are the work of Sweet and Jacobsen (1982) and Elmore (1987). The incorporation of long-range thinking about these themes into current discussions on revising teacher education could be very productive.

CONCLUSION

The theory of natural selection indicates that a rapidly changing, complex environment favors the adaptable and the intelligent. Institutions that use futures research and strategic-planning approaches to be proactive will likely prosper. Organizations whose long-range thinking centers on reacting to easily identifiable external trends will probably muddle through. Using conventional management approaches to operate in a crisis mode guarantees ineffectual floundering.

To provide its students with the foundation needed for decades of professional growth, teacher education must convey a long-range perspective on education's role in emerging social change. To inspire the respect from society needed to improve current difficulties in the profession, teacher educators must demonstrate that they can anticipate coming problems and prospects. To minimize crises in the present, teacher educators must develop a vision for reform that encompasses a future-focused mission; an analysis of the field's internal strengths and weaknesses, external opportunities and threats; and a strategic plan for action.

These agendas will require sophisticated use of emerging methodologies from futures research and strategic planning, rather than perennial restatements of fundamental themes and default assumptions about the long-range context. Otherwise, successive generations of teacher education reform will aspire to be blueprints for tomorrow, only to find that their initiatives are outdated before being achieved.

References

Alm, K. G., Buhler-Miko, M., & Smith, K. B. (1978). _A futures-creating paradigm: A guide to long range planning from the future for the future._ Washington, DC: American Association of State Colleges and Universities, Resource Center for Planned Change.

Amara, R. (1981). The futures field: How to tell good work from bad. _Futurist, 15_ (1), 63–71.

American Association of Colleges for Teacher Education. (1958). _The future challenges teacher education_ (11th yearbook). Washington, DC: Author.

Armstrong, J. S. (1985). _Long-range forecasting: From crystal ball to computer_ (2nd ed.). New York: John Wiley & Sons.

Ascher, W. (1978). _Forecasting: An appraisal for policy-makers and planners._ Baltimore: Johns Hopkins University Press.

Association of Teacher Educators, Blue Ribbon Task Force. (1986). _Visions of reform: Implications for the education profession._ Reston, VA: Author.

Borrowman, M. (1965). _Teacher education in America: A documentary history._ New York: Teachers College Press.

Botkin, J. W., Elmandjra, M. E., & Malitza, M. (1979). _No limits to learning: Bridging the human gap._ Oxford, England: Pergamon Press.

Boucher, W. I. (1977). A statement of research needs. In W. I. Boucher (Ed.), _The study of the future: An agenda for research_ (NSF Publication No. RA-770036). Washington, DC: U.S. Government Printing Office.

Brameld, T. (1976). _The teacher as world citizen: A scenario of the 21st century._ Palm Springs, CA: ETC Publications.

Brown, J. K. (1979). _This business of issues: Coping with the company's environments._ New York: Conference Board.

Burdin, J. (1975). Teacher education in the future: The changing world and its implications for teacher education. In K. Ryan (Ed.). _Teacher Education_ (74th yearbook of the National Society for the

Study of Education, Part II, pp. 295–304). Chicago: University of Chicago Press.

Bush, R. N. (1987). Teacher education reform: Lessons from the past half century. *Journal of Teacher Education, 38* (3), 13–19.

Callan, P. M. (Ed.). (1986). *Environmental scanning for strategic leadership.* San Francisco: Jossey-Bass.

Carnegie Forum on Education and the Economy, Task Force on Teaching as a Profession. (1986). *A nation prepared: Teachers for the 21st century.* Washington, DC: Author.

Coates, J. F. (1977). Aspects of innovation: Public policy issues in telecommunications development. *Telecommunications Policy, 1* (3), 11–23.

Coates, J. F. (1986). *Issues management: How you can plan, organize, and manage for the future.* Mt. Airy, MD: Lomond.

Commission on Declining School Enrollments in Ontario. (1978). *The future for teacher education in Ontario* (Working Paper No. 35). Toronto: Author.

Commission on Teacher Education. (1946). *The improvement of teacher education.* Washington, DC: American Council on Education.

Conant, J. B. (1963). *The education of American teachers.* New York: McGraw-Hill.

Cope, R. G. (1981). *Strategic planning, management, and decision making* (AAHE-ERIC Higher Education Research Report No. 9). Washington, DC: American Association for Higher Education.

Cottrell, D. P. (Ed.). (1956). *Teacher education for a free people.* Washington, DC: American Association of Colleges for Teacher Education.

Cubberley, E. P. (1906). *The certification of teachers* (5th yearbook of the National Society for the Study of Education, Part II). Chicago: University of Chicago Press.

Dalin, P. (1988). *Effective schools in Norway.* Oslo, Norway: International Learning Cooperative.

Dede, C. J. (1988). The probable evolution of artificial intelligence based educational devices. *Technological Forecasting and Social Change, 34,* 115–133.

Dede, C. J., & Freiberg, H. J. (1986). The long range evolution of effective schools. *Educational Forum, 51* (1), 65–80.

de Jouvenel, B. (1967). *The art of conjecture.* New York: Basic Books.

Elmore, R. F. (1987). Reforming the finance and structure of U.S. education in response to technological change. In G. Burke & R. W. Rumberger (Eds.), *The future impact of technology on work and education* (pp. 158–175). New York: Falmer.

Eurich, A. C. (1962). Planning for more effective teaching. In E. R. Smith (Ed.), *Teacher Education: A Reappraisal.* New York: Harper & Row.

Evenden, E. S. (1933). *National survey of the education of teachers: Vol VI. Summary and interpretation* (Bulletin 1933, No. 10, Office of Education, U.S. Department of the Interior). Washington, DC: U.S. Government Printing Office.

Fletcher, G. H. (1979). Key concepts in the futures perspective. *World Future Society Bulletin, 13* (1), 25–32.

Frymier, J. R. (Ed.). (1973). *A school for tomorrow.* Berkeley, CA: McCutchan.

Glines, D. E. (1978a). *Educational futures I: Imagining and inventing.* Millville, MN: Anvil Press.

Glines, D. E. (1978b). *Educational futures II: Options and alternatives.* Millville, MN: Anvil Press.

Glines, D. E. (1978c). *Educational futures III: Change and reality.* Millville, MN: Anvil Press.

Glines, D. E. (1979). *Educational futures IV: Updating and overleaping.* Millville, MN: Anvil Press.

Godet, M. (1988). Worldwide challenges and crises in education systems. *Futures, 20*(3), 241–251.

Green, T. (Ed.). (1971). *Educational planning in perspective: Forecasting and policy-making.* London: IPC Science and Technology Press.

Hearn, J. C., & Heydinger, R. B. (1985). Scanning the university's external environment: Objectives, constraints, and possibilities. *Journal of Higher Education, 56* (4), 419–445.

Helmer, O. (1983). *Looking forward: A guide to futures research.* Beverly Hills, CA: Sage.

Hencley, S. P., & Yates, J. R. (Eds.). (1974). *Futurism in education: Methodologies.* Berkeley, CA: McCutchan.

Hickman, C. R., & Silva, M. A. (1984). *Creating excellence: Managing corporate culture, strategy, and change in the new age.* New York: New American Library.

Hofer, C. W. (1976). Research on strategic planning: A survey of past studies and suggestions for future efforts. *Journal of Economics and Business, 28,* 261–286.

Holmes Group. (1986). *Tomorrow's teachers.* East Lansing, MI: Author.

Hostrup, R. W. (Ed.). (1973). *Foundations of futurology in education.* Homewood, IL: ETC Publications.

Hostrup, R. W. (Ed.). (1975). *Education: Beyond tomorrow.* Homewood, IL: ETC Publications.

Howsam, R. B., Corrigan, D. C., Denemark, G. W., & Nash, R. J. (1976). *Educating a profession.* Washington, DC: American Association of Colleges for Teacher Education.

Janis, I. L. (1989). *Crucial decisions: Leadership in policymaking and crisis management.* New York: Macmillan.

Jay, P., & Stewart, M. (1988). *Apocalypse 2000: Economic breakdown and the suicide of democracy.* Englewood Cliffs, NJ: Prentice-Hall.

Kahn, H., Brown, W., & Martel, L. (1976). *The next 200 years: A scenario for America and the world.* New York: William Morrow.

Kanter, R. M. (1983). *The change masters: Innovation for productivity in the American corporation.* New York: Simon & Schuster.

Kauffman, D. L., Jr. (1976). *Teaching the future: A guide to future-oriented education.* Palm Springs, CA: ETC Publications.

Keith, M. J. (1987). We've heard this song before . . . or have we? *Journal of Teacher Education, 38*(3), 20–25.

Keller, G. (1983). *Academic strategy: The management revolution in higher education.* Baltimore: Johns Hopkins University Press.

Kierstead, F., Bowman, J., & Dede, C. (Eds.). (1979). *Educational futures: Sourcebook I.* Bethesda, MD: World Future Society.

Kilpatrick, W. H. (1983). *The educational frontier.* New York: Appleton-Century.

Kinney, L. B. (1964). *Certification in education.* Englewood Cliffs, NJ: Prentice-Hall.

Kirschling, W. R., & Huckfeld V. E. (1980). Projecting alternative futures. In P. Jedamus & M. W. Peterson (Eds.), *Improving academic management* (pp. 200–215). San Francisco: Jossey-Bass.

Klein, H. E., & Linneman, R. E. (1981). The use of scenarios in corporate planning—eight case histories. *Long Range Planning Journal, 14*(5), 69–77.

Koerner, J. D. (1963). *The miseducation of American teachers.* Boston: Houghton Mifflin.

Lindsey, M. (Ed.). (1961). *New horizons for the teaching profession.* Washington, DC: National Education Association.

Linneman, R. E., & Klein, H. E. (1979). The use of multiple scenarios by U.S. industrial companies. *Long Range Planning Journal, 12*(1), 83–90.

Lippitt, G. L. (1982). *Organizational renewal: A holistic approach to organizational development* (2nd ed.). Englewood Cliffs, NJ: Prentice-Hall.

Locatis, C. N., & Gooler, D. D. (1975). Evaluating second-order consequences: Technology assessment and education. *Review of Educational Research, 45*(2), 327–353.

Lozier, G. G., & Chittipeddi, K. (1986). Issues management in strategic planning. *Research in Higher Education, 24*(1), 3–13.

MacNair, J. M. (1988). *Education for a changing Spain.* Manchester, England: Manchester University Press.

Makridakis, S., & Wheelwright, S. C. (Eds.). (1982). *The handbook of forecasting: A manager's guide.* New York: John Wiley & Sons.

Marien, M. (1982). The two post-industrialisms and higher education. *World Future Society Bulletin, 16*(3), 13–28.

McClellan, J. (1978). What is a futurist? *Futures Information Interchange, 5*(2), 1–2.

McCune, S. D. (1986). *Guide to strategic planning for educators.* Alexandria, VA: Association for Supervision and Curriculum Development.

McNamara, J. F. (1971). Mathematical programming models in educational planning. *Review of Educational Research, 41,* 419–446.

Meadows, D. H., Meadows, D. L., Randers, J., & Behrens, W. W., III. (1972). *The limits to growth.* New York: Universe.

Mink, O. G. (1986). *Developing and managing open organizations.* Austin, TX: OHRD Associates.

Morphet, E. L., & Ryan, C. O. (Eds.). (1967a). *Designing education for the future no. 1: Prospective changes in society by 1980.* New York: Citation Press.

Morphet, E. L., & Ryan, C. O. (Eds.). (1967b). *Designing education for the future no. 2: Implications for education of prospective changes in society.* New York: Citation Press.

Morphet, E. L., & Ryan, C. O. (Eds.). (1967c). *Designing education for the future no. 3: Planning and effecting needed changes in education.* New York: Citation Press.

Morphet, E. L., & Jesser, D. L. (Eds.). (1968a). *Designing education for the future no. 4: Cooperative planning for education in 1980.* New York: Citation Press.

Morphet, E. L., & Jesser, D. L. (Eds.). (1968b). *Designing education for the future no. 5: Emerging designs for education.* New York: Citation Press.

Morrison, J. L. (1987). Establishing an environmental scanning/forecasting system to augment college and university planning. *Planning for Higher Education, 15*(1), 7–22.

Morrison, J. L., Renfro, W. L., & Boucher, W. I. (1984). *Futures research and the strategic planning process: Implications for higher education* (ASHE-ERIC Higher Education Research Report No. 9). Washington, DC: Association for the Study of Higher Education.

Naisbitt, J. (1982). *Megatrends: 10 new directions transforming our lives.* New York: Warner.

National Commission on Excellence in Education. (1983). *A nation at risk: The imperative for educational reform.* Washington, DC: U.S. Government Printing Office.

National Commission for Excellence in Teacher Education. (1985). *A call for change in teacher education.* Washington, DC: American Association of Colleges for Teacher Education.

National Council for Accreditation of Teacher Education. (1985). *NCATE redesign.* Washington, DC: Author.

Norris, D. M., & Poulton, N. L. (Eds.). (1987). *A guide for new planners.* Ann Arbor, MI: Society for College and University Planning.

O'Connor, R. (1978). *Planning under uncertainty: Multiple scenarios and contingency planning.* New York: Conference Board.

Ornstein, R., & Ehrlich, P. (1989). *New world, new mind: Moving toward conscious evolution.* New York: Doubleday.

Pauvert, J. C. (1986). *Training needs of educational personnel.* Paris, France: UNESCO Division of Higher Education.

Peterson, M. W. (1980). Analyzing alternative approaches to planning. In P. Jedamus & M. W. Peterson (Eds.), *Improving academic management* (pp. 113–163). San Francisco: Jossey-Bass.

Polak, F. (1973). *The image of the future* (E. Boulding, Trans.). New York: Elsevier. (Original work published 1954).

Porter, A. L., Rossini, F. A., Carpenter, S. R., & Roper, A. T. (1980). *A guidebook for technology assessment and impact analysis.* New York: North-Holland.

Pulliam, J. D., Kierstead, F. D., & Bowman, J. (1980). Mass media values and the future of education. In Subcommittee on Elementary, Secondary, and Vocational Education, Committee on Education and Labor, U.S. House of Representatives, Ninety-Sixth Congress, Second Session, *Needs of elementary and secondary education in the 1980s: A compendium of policy papers* (pp. 400–416). Washington, DC: U.S. Government Printing Office.

Redd, K. M., & Harkins, A. M. (Eds.). (1980). *Education: A time for decisions.* Bethesda, MD: World Future Society.

Reich, C. A. (1970). *The greening of America.* New York: Random House.

Reich, R. B. (1988). *Education and the next economy.* Washington, DC: National Education Association.

Schwartz, B. (1974). *Permanent education* (Project 1, Educating Man for the 21st Century, Volume 8). The Hague, the Netherlands: Martinus Nijhoff.

Shane, H. G. (1973). *The educational significance of the future.* Bloomington, IN: Phi Delta Kappa.

Shane, H. G. (1977). *Curriculum change toward the 21st century.* Washington, DC: National Education Association.

Shane, H. G. (1987). *Teaching and learning in a microelectronic age.* Bloomington, IN: Phi Delta Kappa.

Shane, H. G., & Tabler, M. B. (1981). *Educating for a new millenium: Views of 132 international scholars.* Bloomington, IN: Phi Delta Kappa.

Shimahara, N. K. (1986). Japanese educational reforms in the 1980s. *Issues in Education, 4*(2), 85–100.

Silberman, C. E. (1970). *Crisis in the classroom: The remaking of American education.* New York: Random House.

Singer, B. D. (1974). The future-focused role-image. In A. Toffler (Ed.), *Learning for tomorrow: The role of the future in education.* New York: Vintage.

Smith, B. O. (1969). *Teachers for the real world.* Washington, DC: American Association of Colleges for Teacher Education.

Smith, E. R. (1962). *Teacher Education: A reappraisal.* New York: Harper & Row.

Steiner, G. A. (1979). *Strategic planning: What every manager must know.* New York: Free Press.

Swanson, A. D., & Zhian, Z. (1987). Education reform in China. *Phi Delta Kappan, 68*(5), 373–378.

Sweet, J. A., & Jacobson, L. A. (1982). Demographic aspects of supply and demand for Teachers. In L. S. Shulman & G. Sykes (Eds.), *Handbook of teaching and policy* (pp. 192–213). New York: Longman.

Textor, R. B. (1980). *A handbook on ethnographic futures research* (3rd ed., Version A). Stanford, CA: Stanford University, Cultural and Educational Futures Research Project.

Thomas, J. (1968). *Teachers for the schools of tomorrow.* Paris: UNESCO.

Tyack, D. B. (Ed.). (1967). *Turning points in American educational history.* Waltham, MA: Blaisdell.

Wack, P. (1985a). Scenarios: Shooting the rapids. *Harvard Business Review, 63*(6), 139–150.

Wack, P. (1985b). Scenarios: Uncharted waters ahead. *Harvard Business Review, 63*(5), 73–89.

Williams, C. (1973). *Anticipating educational issues over the next two decades: An overview of trends analysis* (Research Memorandum 17). Menlo Park, CA: Stanford Research Institute, Educational Policy Research Center.

Wygant, A., & Markley, O. (1988). *Influencing the future: A handbook of information sources for professionals, students, and concerned citizens.* Westport, CT: Greenwood Press.

Zentner, R. D. (1982). Scenarios, past, present and future. *Long Range Planning Journal, 15*(3), 12–20.

GOVERNANCE OF TEACHER EDUCATION

GOVERNANCE OF TEACHER EDUCATION

David L. Clark and Robert F. McNergney

UNIVERSITY OF VIRGINIA

Teacher education in the United States is governed by the 50 states. State governments, typically through state education agencies, establish program requirements for teacher-preparation institutions and certification requirements for teachers; they then approve the programs of preparation and certify the teachers. This is clearly a decentralized, formal, governmental structure. It has led, however, to a uniformity in accreditation, certification, and training that has been noted by every systematic observer of the field. In this chapter, we explore this anomaly while providing information and references on the formal governmental structure of the field and the nongovernmental agencies that exercise influence on the field.

Because teacher education is currently being subjected to extraordinary pressure for reform, we will explicitly examine the disequilibrium being caused by these exogenous shocks to the field and will project the likely impact of this period on future governance in teacher education.

FEDERAL AND NATIONAL ACTION–INFLUENCE NETWORKS

Those who espouse devolution as the most effective pattern of governance in education should be well satisfied with the limited federal role in teacher education. But the preparation of quality personnel for service in the nation's schools is clearly a national concern and has attracted the attention and involvement of the federal government, private foundations, and professional associations. There is even a voluntary control mechanism functioning at the national level to monitor and accredit the quality of teacher education programs in colleges and universities.

The Federal Government

Direct federal involvement in teacher education has been of modest proportion and limited duration. The federal role grew in the 1960s and 1970s in response to specific needs and dissatisfaction with the performance level of training programs and reflected the interventionist tone of that era.

The genesis of federal involvement was the National Defense Education Act of 1958 (NDEA) and the concomitant involvement of the National Science Foundation in the improvement of instruction in mathematics, foreign language, and science. These latter efforts were extended by the United States Office of Education into English and social studies. The comprehensive concern was to update and strengthen curricular materials and bring these improved instructional tools to teachers through inservice summer institutes. Titles III and IX of NDEA provided support for both summer and yearlong institutes for teachers.

The peak involvement of the federal government in teacher education was reached in 1967 with the passage of the Education Professions Development Act (EPDA). This legislative authorization superceded the NDEA. The fulgurant appearance and passing of EPDA is described by Jenkins (1977):

The Education Professions Development Act . . . provided funds for the improvement of teachers in all areas, at all levels. . . . In EPDA the concentration was on professional education personnel instead of the subject matter specialists. . . . Financial support was reduced in 1970 and most of the training complexes did not materialize. As late as 1974, several EPDA projects were still in existence, though funding by that time had been drastically reduced, and much of the training complex activity had evolved into the teacher centers, with the requirement that large portions of their support be provided locally. (pp. 276–277)

The authors wish to thank Richard Kunkel (NCATE) and Charles C. Mackey, Jr. (New York State Education Department) for their reviews and feedback.

The teacher education community held high hopes that the EPDA would signal a new commitment by the federal government to support teacher education. Publicly visible and attractive programs like the Teacher Corps addressed specific areas of national need, and comprehensive efforts such as the Trainers of Teacher Trainers (TTT) were designed to effect improvement and involvement in the education of teachers among professional schools of education, academic departments of universities, public schools, and the community. The last-gasp effort of the United States Office of Education (USOE) and its successor agency the Department of Education in major program involvement in teacher education was lost with the demise of the Teacher Centers Program after 1980. The EPDA belies the assertion that no governmental program can ever be phased out and exemplifies the ambivalent attitude of the federal government toward participation in teacher education.

Since 1980 the Department of Education has focused on exhortative tactics, encouraging states and institutions of higher education to raise standards of teacher preparation and local education agencies to use such devices as career ladders for teachers to improve teacher performance. Congress has reentered the arena by providing support in critical areas of teacher shortage, specifically science and mathematics.

To discover the full impact of the federal government on teacher education, an observer has to turn to the general support offered to higher education primarily through scholarships and fellowships rather than to the sporadic concern manifested through programs triggered by perceived shortages or crises. Federal efforts have been of little consequence in determining the direction of teacher education. The policy of the United States in regard to the education of its teachers is that the matter, governmentally speaking, is best left to the 50 state legislatures.

Private Foundations

Predictably, an area of minimal federal involvement but high national concern attracts the interest of private philanthropy. Teacher education has been irresistible in this regard. In tracing experimentation and reform in teacher education, Paul Woodring (1975) notes:

Many of the innovative programs, including some of the most controversial, received support from philanthropic foundations. In 1951, the Fund for the Advancement of Education, which has recently been established by the Ford Foundation, lent its support to a plan to reorganize teacher education throughout the state of Arkansas—a plan to which the Fund eventually committed nearly three million dollars. The intent of the plan was to provide, for all future teachers, a four-year program of broad liberal education, followed by a period during which an internship would be combined with professional studies. All colleges in the state—state teachers colleges, liberal arts colleges, and the state university—were to participate. (pp. 20–21)

The so-called "Arkansas Purchase" was not one of the marked achievements of the fund. In a relatively short period of time, the evidence of the investment in Arkansas disappeared, but the germ of the ideas promulgated by the 40-year-old experiment is found in the recommendations of the Carnegie Task Force on Teaching as a Profession and the Holmes Group in 1986. The foundations have emphasized the role of arts and sciences in teacher education and pressed toward a teacher education program based on a liberal arts background. Although the total investment of the foundation community in teacher education has been modest, its influence on reform in the field has been notable.

Professional Associations

For over a quarter century, critics of teacher education (Conant, 1963; Koerner, 1963; Silberman, 1970) have attributed substantial power to professional associations in maintaining the status quo in the field. In 1988 Secretary William Bennett viewed the National Education Association (NEA) as "the greatest single threat to education reform" (Wilson, 1988, p. A-29). Charles Silberman (1970) saw education schools controlled by "an establishment [with] a shared outlook and community of interests; the latter is reinforced by a series of interlocking directorates in which all roads lead to the National Education Association" (p. 431).

The core cluster of national associations concerned broadly and directly with the education of teachers includes the NEA, the American Federation of Teachers (AFT), the American Association of Colleges for Teacher Education (AACTE), and the Association of Teacher Educators (ATE). Added to this group are the variety of subject-matter-based teacher groups such as the National Council of Teachers of Mathematics, the National Council for the Social Studies, the National Science Teachers Association, and the National Council of Teachers of English.

The associations attend to the issues surrounding teacher education at both the preservice and inservice levels. They are involved actively in the program accreditation process through participation in the National Council for the Accreditation of Teacher Education (NCATE). In fact, the revised NCATE procedures have strengthened the role of the associations in the establishment of program guidelines. NEA has been pressing for self-governance of the teaching profession for over half a century, and this pattern of governance would involve increased participation in both accreditation and certification at state and national levels. The self-governance model envisions the establishment of a proposed National Standards Board for Professional Educators (National Education Association 1987, pp. 13–14). Both the NEA and the AFT are extending their concern with teacher education into the restructuring of the schools in which the teachers will practice and develop their professional skills (American Federation of Teachers, 1986–1987). The AACTE (1985) and the ATE (1986) have contributed comprehensive recommendations for reform in teacher education, which will be reviewed in detail later in this chapter.

The associations, individually and collectively, undoubtedly wish that they exercised the control over the profession attributed to them by their critics. Their influence is exercised through politics and suasion. Their strongest formal vehicles are the voluntary accreditation processes of the NCATE and representation on state-level boards of professional practices, licensure, and accreditation. Their actual impact, however, is undocumented. Lanier and Little (1986) note:

The teachers' associations are another important part of the milieu in which teacher education operates. Their growth and strength over the past 2 decades have raised additional questions about who speaks for teacher education in the public arena. . . . But, especially compared to the size and widespread influence of these organizations, little research has been conducted on their effects as part of the milieu of teacher education. (p. 564)

Our guess is that control over teacher education by the establishment is considerably less powerful than the critics have contended but strong enough to share a portion of the credit for the progress or blame for the failures of the field. Surely, it is the case that the establishment should not be portrayed as monolithic. The professional associations disagree frequently on directions in teacher education. Although the presidents of the NEA and the AFT were both signatories to the report of the Carnegie Task Force on Teaching as a Profession, at the end of the study period Ms. Futrell, of the NEA, submitted a "statement of support with reservations" (pp. 117–118). Mr. Shanker submitted a companion statement noting "full support" and "overall endorsement to the report" (p. 118). Only in 1988 did the AFT join with the other professional associations as a member of NCATE. The AACTE and the NEA jousted for years over their respective numbers of representatives on the NCATE Board. The NEA's political activity to establish professional practice boards at the state level is eschewed by the federation. There are observable efforts on the part of the associations to influence teacher education policy nationally, but the efforts are not monolithic and their effects are not documented.

National Certification and Accreditation Agencies

No agency has ever functioned nationally to certify teachers. However, such a body, the National Board for Professional Teaching Standards, was called for by the Carnegie Task Force on Teaching as a Profession, has been established, and is in the process of defining what teachers need to know and be able to do. The task of the board is to create valid assessments to see that nationally certified teachers meet these standards. As currently envisioned, the board will issue certificates at a high entry level and at an advanced stage signifying the highest level of teacher competence. This process of national certification will be voluntary and will purportedly complement the system of state certification and licensing of teachers.

National accreditation of teacher education programs has a 60-year history. Bush and Enemark (1975) note that, from 1927 to 1952, accreditation of teacher education programs was controlled by the colleges and universities through the American Association of Teachers' Colleges, a predecessor agency to the AACTE. The first 5 years of the NCATE's history were marked with controversy over the control that should be exercised within the council by its constituent organizations. The arguments about the balance between representatives from the

liberal arts, professional education, and classroom teachers were resolved sufficiently to achieve accreditation by the National Commission on Accreditation in 1957.

The NCATE has had a checkered history. The balance of representation has always been an issue. The effectiveness of voluntary rather than mandatory accreditation has been challenged (even though voluntary accreditation is the norm in other professional fields). The adequacy of the standards is continually under debate. Because the standards are formative rather than summative, institutions have challenged their validity and prestigious universities have withdrawn from the NCATE, apparently with impunity. NCATE accreditation has not been required for either state program accreditation (less than half of the state-accredited programs are accredited by the NCATE) or institutional membership in the AACTE. Consequently, non-NCATE institutions are able to retain claims to legitimacy in teacher preparation. The large number of NCATE-accredited institutions with at least one program (517) has raised questions about the stringency of the NCATE standards and their application by NCATE visiting teams (NCATE, 1987).

The NCATE has recently been in the process of a major overhaul designed, at least temporarily, to quell its critics and swell its ranks of supporters (NCATE, 1985). The new standards are argued to be more rigorous. Members of site visiting teams are trained in the application of the standards. State program approval and regional accreditation continue as preconditions for NCATE consideration. The AFT has joined the NCATE Coordinating Board. NCATE is working more closely with the Council of Chief State School Officers to insure that program approval and national accreditation become self-reinforcing processes. The new standards require a stronger collaborative linkage between higher education institutions and school systems, use of research and knowledge of sound practice in curricular design, explicit attention to recruitment of minority students, and basic-skills testing for admission to teacher education. On balance, the redesign appears to have strengthened the NCATE's support in the teacher education community. The developing linkage between the NCATE and state program approval mechanisms should strengthen the hand of each in the process of accrediting teacher education.

STATE ACTION–INFLUENCE NETWORKS

If Darling-Hammond and Berry are correct and the "governance of the teaching enterprise is up for grabs," players at the state level have been unusually aggressive in their efforts to control the action (1988, p. 73). The decrease in federal categorical programs in the 1980s has further stimulated a marked increase in state legislation and programs in teacher education that began in the 1970s. This devolution of responsibility to the states has resulted in a rush toward excellence that has produced a cacophony of often contrary state-level initiatives. For example, efforts to recognize and reward excellence in teaching among the ranks of the experienced have conflicted with the need to attract and keep a talented pool of neophytes. Balancing both kinds of reforms with concerns about the dwindling pool of minority teachers has presented yet another dilemma. People are coming to understand, sometimes painfully, that pushing the system in one place results in placing pressure on another, a condition unforeseen by many at the outset of reform.

Types of Reforms

Darling-Hammond and Berry (1988) note that state initiatives have been characterized by efforts to establish or modify (a) requirements for entering teacher education programs, (b) programmatic requirements for teacher education, (c) concomitant accreditation procedures for these programs including standards boards, (d) alternative and recertification routes to teacher certification, (e) teacher competency testing, (f) programs for new teachers, and (g) teacher compensation systems.

Admissions. Requirements for admission to teacher education programs have been made on the basis of multiple criteria, but college grade point average, or some other indication of scholastic ability, has been the most important factor in the admission process. Carpenter (1972) found that, of 180 AACTE member institutions, 48 percent used 2.0 (on a 4.0 scale) as the criterion level for admission, and 93 percent of the institutions set admission between 2.0 and 2.5. Predictably, these quite minimal requirements had little salutary effect on programmatic reputations. Ten years later Shields and Daniele (1981) observed that "studies generally support the widely held view in the academic community that teacher training programs admit almost anyone who meets minimum entrance requirements" (p. 17).

Admission reforms of the 1980s concentrated on raising these standards. Most of the changes in grade point average requirements have occurred in doctoral-granting universities (American Council on Education, 1985). In 1985, nearly 60 percent of the secondary programs and 45 percent of the elementary education programs required grade point averages of 2.5 to 2.9—more than twice as many institutions with these requirements as in 1980.

Programmatic Requirements. Once people enter teacher education they are finding programs that are in the process of restructuring requirements to meet new state regulations. In the main, program-approval processes concentrate on reviewing course documents, avoid stipulating in great detail the content of course work, and say little about how courses are to be delivered when faculty and students are face-to-face. Some states are beginning to be more prescriptive about field experiences for teachers, instituting such experiences earlier and/or specifying the use of specially trained clinical faculty along the lines suggested by Smith (1980).

If there has been an identifiable conceptual theme in the changing programmatic requirements for teachers in recent years, it would be one of mastering content. Competence in teaching, particularly at the high school level, is being defined first by the acquisition of knowledge in one's discipline. This is being reflected in program accreditation procedures at the state level by increased emphasis on studies in the liberal arts and sciences and decreased emphasis on professional education. About a dozen states have begun to examine possibilities for making state regulations for program approval compatible with evolving national board certification standards.

When the length of teacher-preparation programs has been assumed to be fixed at 4 years, increased course requirements in the disciplines have been accompanied by fewer courses in education. When longer preparation programs have been considered, programs encompassing 5 years or even 6, two courses of action have been advocated: (a) spread education courses over a longer period of time, or (b) hold education coursework until the end of a teacher's program, in some cases placing these courses at the master's level. Neither alternative, however, is being interpreted to mean that teachers need more coursework in the study of pedagogy.

As Lanier and Little (1986) observe, "The most common argument put forward for the low support accorded teacher education is that its knowledge base is weak and questionable" (p. 558). Professionals know and can do things that others without their training do not know and cannot do. To be considered a professional course of study, it is argued, teacher education must make its unique knowledge public and accessible to its clients—something it has failed to do in the past. Although encyclopedias and handbooks of research on teaching are beginning to provide what is often referred to as the "emerging knowledge base" upon which professionally defensible pedagogical training can be established, state regulations only rarely take this knowledge into account.

Standards Boards. More states have established standards boards for teacher education program approval and for other regulatory actions in recent years. Connecticut and South Dakota are now the only states without such boards. These agencies might have final regulatory authority or might simply advise policymakers. For example, in Alabama there is the State Advisory Committee on Teacher Education and Certification, composed of about 30 members. Constituent groups nominate members and the state superintendent appoints. The committee does not have final regulatory authority, but changes in teacher education and certification must have its approval. In contrast, the composition of the Minnesota Board of Teaching is set by law, having seven teachers, one principal, one representative from higher education, and one lay member. The board has autonomous authority to set certification, entry, and exit standards; it also approves teacher education programs. In 1986–1987 bills were introduced in nine state legislatures with the intent of increasing the autonomy of their respective boards (American Association of Colleges for Teacher Education [AACTE], 1987a).

Alternative Routes to Certification. All but 11 states offer some type of irregular or alternative certification route (AACTE, 1987); thus states have ways not only of applying pressure to teacher education but also of releasing it. All alternative certification routes, however, are meant to offer alternatives to traditional 4-year and 2-year course sequences for aspiring teachers in institutions of higher education.

A fairly recent study of 20 alternative certification and re-training programs suggests that state involvement with these types of programs might be expected to increase (Adelman, 1986):

Alternative certification programs appear to be attracting well-educated individuals with a sincere interest in teaching. . . . In comparison with traditional teacher education programs, alternative certification programs feature more field experience and more intense supervision in the field. . . . Alternative certification programs produce subject area-proficient teachers who are also rated highly on instructional skills in comparison with traditionally prepared beginning teachers. (pp. ii–iv)

If Adelman's perceptions are widely held, and if public school superintendents continue to exercise the power to request and acquire emergency certification for teachers in times of need, there will likely be more interest in creating and preserving these loopholes in governance systems at the state level.

Competency Testing. States have exerted their influence on the conduct of teacher education in recent years via teacher competency testing. There are now 46 states that require some form of competency testing (Sandefur, 1986). These tests serve to check the power of approved programs by providing another perspective on the efficacy of training: if teachers do well, programs may claim some of the credit for identifying and developing talent. The influence of such tests, when administered at the end of programs, might be measured most dramatically, not by counting the numbers of teachers passing and failing, but by examining the tests' effects on teacher education curricula. For instance, in some cases the tests can be expected to make explicit the outcomes of training. When teachers exit their formal education programs they will be expected to demonstrate the skills, attitudes, and knowledge that such tests purport to measure. For programs that continue to operate during and after this era of reform, the pressure will be high to help teachers excel on these measures; that is, the teacher education curriculum will be driven to prepare teachers for the tests. Control of teacher education here is subtle but potentially quite powerful. Unlike in the past, when states relied on schools, colleges, and departments of education to provide evidence of program quality via accreditation, competency tests will serve as another bench mark against which program quality will be judged.

Programs for Beginning Teachers. A more direct approach to shaping and controlling teacher education is to institute programs for new teachers. These were stimulated in the 1980s by the realization of how difficult the induction period for teachers can be. Citing AACTE sources on the emergence of beginning teacher programs at the state level, Darling-Hammond and Berry (1988) note that "policymakers and educators are increasingly concerned about the detrimental effects of the traditional 'sink-or-swim' approach to teacher induction. Failure to provide novice teachers with adequate supervision when they first take on clinical responsibilities results in high attri-tion rates for beginning teachers, suboptimal teacher learning, and impaired tenure decisions" (p. 31). To reduce the chances of these outcomes, 39 states are in some phase of planning or implementing beginning teacher programs.

Compensation Plans. State policymakers exert some of their most powerful control over teacher education by how they choose to spend taxpayers' money. Teachers and, more indirectly, teacher educators have been affected by any number of compensation schemes in recent years, including merit pay or pay for performance, career ladders, and the establishment and manipulation of salary schedules. Various compensation plans are being operationalized in a variety of forms in the states. Each reflects a particular value or philosophy about the profession. Some are highly centralized or designed to control teachers by rewarding for a particular definition of excellence and by punishing for pedagogical failure or incompetence. Schemes that propose to pay teachers on the basis of their students' scores on standardized tests would fall into this category. Other plans share responsibility and authority for awarding financial incentives by having teachers and administrators jointly define criteria for success. Some career ladder or differentiated staffing models reflect this position.

Whether these plans will succeed in raising the financial well-being of a given state's teaching force or in enhancing its image in the public eye is unclear. National estimates of the purported financial gains of teachers in recent years would not leave one sanguine about the prospect of substantially higher salaries. In 1986–1987 the average salary for the nations's 2.2 million public school teachers was $26,704. This was up 33 percent from 1981–1982, or the approximate time the reform movement began. As Darling-Hammond and Berry (1988) note, however, when salaries are adjusted for number of years' experience, teachers are still worse off than their less-experienced counterparts were 15 years ago. Conditions vary, of course, from state to state. The psychological control exerted through the use of different compensation programs also varies, working either to restrain teachers in the performance of their duties or to free them to exercise their professional judgment in making job-relevant decisions.

Even though state policymakers have the power to effect change by manipulating financial rewards, they do not always choose to exercise it. For example, even though reformers have emphasized the importance of recruiting and retaining minority teachers, there is little evidence that states are actually putting money toward attracting and/or retaining minority teachers.

Only six states report programs aimed directly at recruiting minorities into the teaching profession. A total of 22 states indicate no activity whatsoever to reverse a nationwide decline in the number of minorities becoming teachers. Efforts by the remaining 22 states and the District of Columbia vary greatly. They range from a task force on the issue to recruitment of minorities into higher education, though not into teaching specifically. (AACTE, 1987a, p. iii)

State-level Influence in Review. There is great potential for innovation in governance at the state level, more than at any other time in American history save perhaps the mid-to-late nineteenth century. There is also evidence of modest change in the ways teaching and teacher education are being shaped. Yet there is surprisingly little variation among states in the overall structure of teacher education. Teacher education still takes place in SCDEs; programs still tend to be judged or approved on the same kinds of criteria; and state agencies and SCDEs still discuss quality as if it were a function of the number of three-credit courses in particular areas. These conditions, although pronounced at the state level, are even more evident when one examines the governance of teacher education at the local level, for it is there that the potential for diversity exists among the many programs across the nation.

LOCAL ACTION–INFLUENCE NETWORKS

There are about 1,200 schools, colleges, and departments of education throughout the United States operating training programs at the preservice and/or inservice levels. The ease with which organizations get into and out of the teacher education business is nothing short of remarkable. Indeed, although the major suppliers of teachers have remained fairly stable, one of the principal difficulties that Clark and Guba (1977) faced in surveying the field of teacher education was trying to determine who was in and who was out. Programs in institutions of higher education and inservice programs sponsored by local education agencies constitute what is perceived as the major effort to educate teachers at the local level.

Colleges and Universities

As one might imagine with so many institutions of higher education involved in teacher education, there is a great deal of variety in the size of the institutions and the kinds of the programs they offer. These institutions, large and small, must contend with governance issues both internally and externally.

Governance of Teacher Education Within SCDEs. Even though programs have looked remarkably alike through the years—some educational foundations, some methods courses, and student teaching—they have not been governed by a consensual philosophy or vision. According to Gideonse (1986), teacher education programs have reflected four competing themes. There are those who have characterized teaching as artistry, setting about educating teachers to perform creatively with sensitivity and devotion. Others have viewed teachers as moral craftspersons with special responsibilities to pose questions and confront issues with the potential for shaping the character of young people. Many have come to think of teachers as applied scientists who try to implement strategies that have shown some relationship to student learning. And still others have conceptualized teachers as decision makers, thus helping them plan and teach by making decisions based on their predictions about the probable effects on students' ac-

complishment of tasks. These themes or philosophical persuasions, along with an abundance of good advice, have been translated to students in different ways, depending on the proclivities of the translators.

Within institutions there are multiple ways people can become teachers. On the average, colleges and universities offer 8 to 12 distinct teacher education programs, with the number and diversity of programs being greatest in doctoral-granting institutions. About 35 percent of the undergraduate students in education are in elementary education programs. Another 18 percent are enrolled in secondary education, 12 percent in special education, and 7 percent in early childhood. About 28 percent of the students have chosen specialty areas such as reading, physical education, and home economics (AACTE, 1987b).

Elementary education students take considerably more credit hours in professional education than do secondary education students. About one-fifth of a prospective secondary teacher's total program is comprised of education coursework, whereas elementary teachers take about one-third of their work in education. This would lead one to conclude quite reasonably that the responsibility for educating teachers does not rest greatly or even mainly with SCDEs, but rather with arts and sciences faculty, from whom prospective teachers take the majority of their coursework. This condition, as the Holmes Group has been influential in pointing out, is one that universities have been reluctant to recognize.

Governance of Teacher Education Externally. Lanier and Little (1986) argue that, because of the shared responsibility for teacher education and because of the fact that many faculty in education units are not involved with the preparation of teachers, the connotative meaning of the term *teacher educator* is not synonymous with those who hold appointments in education units or with faculty who teach an occasional course in pedagogy. Like others before them (Clark & Marker, 1975), Lanier and Little recognize that there has been a general lack of cohesion at the college and university level among those with teacher education responsibilities. Even at the local level, perhaps especially at the local level, responsibilities for teacher education are confused. Duties are compartmentalized and spread around the institution, with little or no communication among the units assigned to carry out the duties. Although the authority for programmatic decision making is usually placed ceremoniously with the dean of education, for all practical purposes, such authority is nonexistent.

Traditionally, for those teacher educators and teacher education programs located in major research universities, the climate has been less than hospitable. Education schools do not have the academic prestige of law and medical schools.

Their legitimacy is repeatedly challenged because of pedagogy's weak technological underpinnings. They have had to cope as "feminine" agencies in a masculine-dominated world. Consequently, they have been like the mammals in the age of the dinosaurs—small, quiet nocturnal omnivores, coming out after 4:10 P.M. to forage and ruffle their fur a little, reflecting a few rays of the vanishing sun. (Clifford & Guthrie, 1988, p. 325)

Those faculty associated with teacher education who hold appointments outside of education schools have had little if anything to gain professionally from their involvement in teacher education. In some cases they have much to lose, namely, time and energy that might be devoted to other more academically acceptable pursuits such as conducting original research and professing one's discipline in public forums, to name but two. It is small wonder, as Judge (1982) observes, that the position of graduate schools of education in major research institutions is "unclear and uncomfortable" (p. 1).

Some people press from outside of SCDEs to make teacher education more academically respectable, and others at the local level also work from the outside to make it more responsive to life in schools. This latter concern seems especially compelling when one considers teaching in difficult circumstances such as those presented by inner-city schools. Haberman (1987) argues that teacher education has been irrelevant to urban schools for too long.

One view is that all teacher education is irrelevant but that since small-town and suburban schools still have some semblance of discipline and traditional values, a neophyte teacher who is knowledgeable in his or her subject matter is more able to learn on the job than in an urban setting characterized by debilitating conditions. Another view is that many students come to schools of education ready, willing, and able to work in urban schools but are subjected to vacuous courses taught so poorly that their subsequent failure (or lack of staying power) is predestined. A third view is that teacher education programs have never accepted the charge of preparing urban teachers since School of Education faculty believe they are providing generic principles for teaching in all situations, they cannot be held accountable for a goal they have never accepted—preparing urban teachers. Finally, there is a view, common to many professional educators, that urban schools are beyond redemption and rather than participate in "band-aid" efforts to keep dying institutions alive it is better to not help urban schools at all and plan for some sort of a replacement institution. (pp. 21–22)

Local Education Agencies

As Preservice Deliverers. The primacy of local decision making has been a hallmark of American education but not necessarily of teacher education. When *teacher education* is defined as preservice and *local* is defined as district level, there is scarcely any activity. Texas passed legislation allowing individual school districts to establish and maintain their own teacher education programs, which cities such as Houston and Dallas have done. Similar programs operate in California and New Jersey. Efforts are being made by Haberman and his colleagues to establish teacher education programs run by local teacher unions in urban schools. Over the years New York City has operated its own licensing examinations, thus exerting control over teacher education in yet another way. But these are the exceptions, not the rule.

As Partners with Institutions of Higher Education (IHEs). For years the most visible link between local education agencies (LEAs) and IHEs with regard to teacher education has been the student teaching program and related pre–student teach-

ing field experiences. To meet program requirements, students must spend a specified period of time teaching in schools under the direction of a fully certified teacher. For the most part, this has resulted in a situation in which those schools physically closest to an IHE are coaxed into the business of clinical teacher education. Many of these arrangements are marriages of convenience rather than truly collaborative efforts to train professionals; under these conditions LEAs wield little, if any, real influence over preparation programs.

In some instances LEAs and IHEs do work together to shape the clinical components of programs. For example, since the early 1970s the University of Minnesota, in cooperation with school districts in the Twin Cities area, has operated Cooperative Teaching Centers. These centers are public schools, or clusters of schools, that are directed by a person jointly hired and supported by the two organizations. This person works with center directors and with university faculty to define and help deliver instruction for preservice teachers assigned to his or her center.

As Inservice Deliverers. When *teacher education* is defined as inservice, there is a great deal of district-level autonomy and, in some cases, money to initiate and sustain programs. Nonetheless, inservice is often geared to helping teachers meet state-defined requirements for recertification. Courses and workshops offered by traveling consultants that do not meet such requirements are usually billed as a response to a need within the district. These, too, can control or shape teachers to fit someone else's vision of life in the schools. Programs like those sponsored by AFT and NEA (described later) are emerging alongside and, in some cases, in place of the usual bill of fare for inservice. They seem to point a way toward educating practicing teachers that is markedly different from the educational gimmickry of the past.

New Practices and Trends

Primacy of Knowledge Base. Only recently have people begun to argue that teacher education can rely on something approaching a knowledge base. These arguments are advanced in part on the basis of the idea that learning about the connections between teachers' actions in classrooms and children's learning provides evidence to be used in the training and evaluation of teachers (Gage, 1978). But the examination of teacher education itself is beginning to offer yet additional direction for the design and delivery of programs (Berliner, 1985; Evertson, Hawley, & Zlotnik, 1985). The ability to control teacher education at the local level will never again be a simple function of political power or lack thereof; any future governance of the enterprise must account for knowledge of effective practice.

But as Medley (1982) argues, using sound public knowledge to educate teachers is only part of the challenge. Teacher educators in schools, colleges, and departments of education have two tasks to perform: a training task and a gatekeeping task. Training requires making students competent practitioners. Gatekeeping requires that the institutions graduate only those students who are competent. Much to his chagrin, Medley sees teacher educators concentrating heavily on training at the expense of gatekeeping, or of sifting the more from the less competent. Moreover, he contends that the existing evaluation has been dominated by paper-and-pencil tests. These fail to communicate the importance of teachers' being able to solve problems or being able to apply their professional knowledge to help children learn.

The efforts of Medley (1982) and Shulman (see Olson, 1988) to encourage the development of new testing techniques that simulate teaching practice by having people solve instructional problems are more than evaluational ploys to enhance the validity of assessment. These techniques are attempts to govern training, to make it more like the real world of teaching.

AFT/NEA Interactive Research Projects. Teachers' professional organizations are recognizing the need to help local education agencies shape their own inservice efforts in ways that are responsive to teachers and that are publicly defensible. The American Federation of Teachers' Educational Research and Dissemination Program is one example. This program tries to take the work of highly regarded educational researchers and share their findings with public school teachers. The emphasis is on classroom applications of research and learning how findings can be adapted or refined to fit teachers' needs. Pilot tested in four big-city school districts, this program is being implemented throughout the country in AFT-affiliated schools. The National Education Association's Mastery in Learning Program is another example of trying to influence teacher education on the local level through national effort. Compared with the AFT program, it is based less on findings of researchers and more on the idea of trying to encourage teachers to do their own classroom investigations.

Professional Development Schools. There is another idea in the making that could prove to be a useful alternative organizational structure for educating teachers at the local level: the *professional development school* as articulated by the Holmes Group. They view the use of professional development schools as a way of both stimulating research and improving teaching and teacher education on the local level. These schools will serve as settings for teaching professionals to test different instructional arrangements, for novice teachers and researchers to work under the guidance of gifted practitioners, for the university faculty and practitioners to exchange professional knowledge, and for the development of new structures designed around the demand of a new profession (Holmes Group, 1986, p. 67).

Although it is still too early to tell if professional development schools will take root, let alone flourish, the concept seems to hold potential for shaping the course of professional preparation.

INSTITUTIONALIZATION OF TEACHER EDUCATION

The control mechanisms governing teacher education are probably best explained by the gradual institutionalization of this complex field. "Institutionalization involves the process by which social processes, obligations, or actualities come to take on a rule-like status in social thought and action" (Meyer & Rowan, 1977, p. 22). This field has perpetuated itself by ritualistically creating structures and functions with connections to the real work of educating children and teachers best described as symbolic or even mythical. Units of control and operation have been buffered from one another by a logic of confidence that has permeated the system.

The yin and yang of institutionalization are manifested in several ways. Teacher education has made friends and acquired support and legitimacy for many of its organizations and for the people who populate them. Men and women enter the system in colleges and universities, they are educated, and they are hired to run the nation's classrooms. In some ways the system works remarkably well—a bureaucratic sameness makes the process understandable and predictable. But teacher education has also become reified in a form that has caused it to lose support and legitimacy among policymakers, the public, and even its own products, classroom teachers. Politicians assert that parents and students are getting shortchanged by an inadequate corps of teachers. The public rates teaching as a low-status occupation and gives those who prepare teachers even lower marks. In some ways the system does not work at all; teacher education seems either to attract too few with intellectual fire in their bellies or to extinguish the fire in others who venture too near.

People institutionalize practice. In the case of teacher education they promulgate and interpret the rules, defining the field as they go. On a macro level one finds interest groups and confederations of groups among state education agencies (SEAs), LEAs, and SCDEs that are intent on influencing teacher education policy and practice: the Holmes Group, the Carnegie Forum, the National Council for Accreditation of Teacher Education, the American Association of Colleges for Teacher Education, the National Education Association, and the American Federation of Teachers. Many of these groups have played significant roles in defining and, now, redefining the formal structures of teacher education. But the rules shape the people as well, often more subtly.

Reciprocity of people and rules in teacher education is also evident on a micro level. A teacher education program spells out the rules of the game; to wit, objectives or competencies are specified, expectations for acceptable performance are delineated, and means for the attainment of objectives are explicated—the rules are meant to affect the play. But when people apply such rules to their own situations, the rules take on new meanings. Sorenson demonstrated as much when he reported on what student teachers thought it took to succeed in their experiences. When they were asked to "list the things you would tell your best friend to do in order to get a grade of 'A' from your present training teacher," 40 percent of his respondents said "listen very carefully to the supervising teacher's suggestions and follow them without question" (1967, p. 177). What mattered in this situation was not the intent of the law in teacher education program objectives and procedures, but the way the people in the system interpreted the law. In other words, the players affected the rules, and the rules took on a life of their own.

It is the ways people make sense of formal organizations—

how they face and avoid decisions, how they negotiate rules, how they deal with all manner of constraints, and how they relate to one another—that help to explain teacher education governance. Meyer and Rowan (1977) offer six propositions about organizational behavior that can be used to guide our understanding of these phenomena in teacher education.

Institutional Sources of Structure

Proposition 1. As rationalized institutional rules arise in given domains of work activity, formal organizations form and expand by incorporating these rules as structural elements.

The gradual incorporation of performance/competency-based teacher education (P/CBTE) by schools, colleges, and departments of education is an excellent example of the applicability of this proposition to teacher education. In 1968 the U.S. Office of Education funded 10 trial projects around the nation, all designed to promote concepts of P/CBTE. In various ways, these projects and the many that followed were to make explicit (a) the skills, knowledge, and attitudes (viz., competencies) necessary for the competent practice of teaching; (b) the means to acquire these competencies; and (c) the behaviors deemed to be indications of the successful mastery of the competencies (Houston & Howsam, 1972).

Although P/CBTE programs were initially viewed by many as being radical departures from traditional approaches to educating teachers, they gradually took on familiar forms. In the early 1980s about 150 of the 1,200 AACTE-affiliated institutions claimed to have P/CBTE programs (Sandefur & Niklas, 1981). In a national survey of preservice programs, Joyce, Yarger, Howey, Harbeck, and Kluwin (1977) observed that, despite the claims, P/CBTE appeared not to have taken hold.

With respect to competency-based teacher education it appears that the language of behaviorism is common but that few institutions operate programs on CBTE principles. Many courses and programs have behavioral objectives (although not all of them by any means) but only 3.4% use criterion-referenced tests for assessment. . . . Many faculty members have had some experience with CBTE during the last few years, but most of them predict that there will be less emphasis on CBTE in the future. (p. 5)

Several years later Kerr (1983) argued, not that P/CBTE programs had disappeared, but that they were largely indistinguishable from other programs: "it is unclear just how CBTE enthusiasts would distinguish a CBTE program from any other program of teacher preparation that is operating under the same constraints and that might be deemed reasonably relevant to teaching" (p. 134).

Proposition 2. The more modernized the society, the more extended the rationalized institutional structure in given domains and the greater the number of domains containing rationalized institutions.

As states take on more responsibility for shaping and controlling teacher education, they are extending existing governance mechanisms and creating new ones. States are developing competency tests for teachers, increasing teacher education program requirements, initiating assistance programs for new teachers, tightening requirements for credentials to teach specific subjects, and creating and altering incentive systems. These new rules for the practice of teaching and teacher education are attempts to professionalize the education enterprise. Success and survival of teacher education under these conditions could well prove to be a matter of negotiating these structures rather than producing qualitatively better teachers.

Proposition 3. Organizations that incorporate societally legitimated, rationalized elements in their formal structures maximize their legitimacy and increase their resources and survival capabilities.

This tenet of organizational behavior seems unusually prophetic, given the recent flurry of activity surrounding teacher testing (AACTE, 1987a). Only three states (Arkansas, Utah, and Vermont) have no legislative mandate or written examinations for entry into teacher education programs, exit from these programs, and/or certification. There are 25 states that require new teachers to pass a test before entering teacher education programs. More than 40 states require teachers to pass tests before being certified. Eleven states require teachers to demonstrate successful classroom performance before being fully certified. Most states also require students in teacher education programs to maintain a minimum grade point average from 2.2 to 2.5 on a 4.0 scale. Given the lack of predictive validity for such measures one can only assume that these efforts at standard setting and modification are calculated to capture public confidence.

Whether or not such moves enhance the likelihood of increasing resources for teacher education remains to be seen. Peseau's (1986) analysis of the resources and productivity of teacher education programs in 77 public universities suggests that teacher education, regardless of how good it is, has never garnered the financial support it needs and deserves. "The cost per weighted credit hour, and per student academic year by degree level, shows that the teacher education programs in these universities continue to cost less for an undergraduate student than for a public school child" (p. 1). If the financial condition of teacher education improves, one possible reason could be that legitimacy has also been enhanced.

Proposition 4. Because attempts to control and coordinate activities in institutionalized organizations lead to conflicts and loss of legitimacy, elements of structure are decoupled from activities and from each other.

There are numerous examples of this phenomenon in teacher education: appointing an all-university committee with symbolic control of teacher education, chaired by the dean of education; creating an accreditation system that accredits all who apply by arguing that its primary function is program development, not the application of sanctions; translating the measurement of teacher competency for initial certification into counting courses; organizing a school of education into subject-oriented departments by methods instead of by functional units such as teacher education.

As Zeichner and Liston (1985) demonstrate, when issues of governance and control are played out on a microlevel, decoupling of structure and activity can be subtle but pervasive. They examined the discourse of supervisors and teachers in conferences about teaching and found that only about 20 percent of the talk between supervisors and student teachers represented attention to the type of discourse that the program purported to emphasize. Moreover, the substance of the discourse was incongruous with the intent of the program. Like Sorenson, then, Zeichner and Liston suggest that the practice of teacher education can be quite separate from its avowed purpose.

Proposition 5. The more an organization's structure is derived from institutionalized myths, the more it maintains elaborate displays of confidence, satisfaction, and good faith, internally and externally.

Teacher education makes a difference, that is, people can be influenced to acquire and modify certain teaching skills (Gliessman, 1981). But it is unclear how many teacher educators use effective training methods and how much of a difference the methods make. Regardless of what is fact and what is fiction in teacher education, the enterprise relies heavily on formal displays of confidence to effect legitimacy.

> Nowhere is this more visible than in the regulation of teaching via certification. One important social function of teacher certification is to suggest legitimacy, to reassure the public that the teacher is competent, properly trained, and thoroughly reliable. Parents want to believe that the adults to whose care they have entrusted their precious children truly are worthy of that responsibility, and the teaching certificate seems to confer that worthiness. Without this symbolic reassurance, many Americans would keep their children at home or try to withhold that portion of taxes that goes for public school expenses. Teachers, especially new teachers, themselves want personal reassurance of their readiness to teach. However flimsy a piece of paper, the teaching certificate appears to assure "competence" and legal respectability upon the practitioners. (Cronin, 1983, p. 172)

Teacher education program accreditation also promotes legitimacy. As we noted, NCATE evaluation procedures are advanced as a way of discriminating among teacher education programs for the purpose of recognizing quality:

> The mission of the National Council for Accreditation of Teacher Education (NCATE) is twofold: (1) to require a level of quality in professional education that fosters competent practice of graduates, and (2) to encourage institutions to meet rigorous academic standards of excellence in professional education. (NCATE, 1987, p. 1)

Some of the reassuring effects of NCATE accreditation are lost on the nation as a whole, however, by virtue of the fact that only 47 percent of teacher education institutions belong to the NCATE.

If successful, the Carnegie Commission's newly proposed National Board for Professional Teaching Standards will be the capstone of this elaborate display of legitimacy. Board-certified teachers will be held up as examples of professionals to be emulated. In some states it appears that board certification will supplant typical state certification requirements.

Proposition 6. Institutionalized organizations seek to minimize inspection and evaluation by both internal managers and external constituents.

Evaluation of teacher education occurs on several levels: national inspection of programs for purposes of accreditation; state review, again to accredit; and local intra-university and intra-departmental monitoring. Much of what passes for evaluation as summative judgment, however, is little more than ritualistic hat doffing.

Wheeler (1980) argues, for example, that the NCATE has helped people think seriously about the conduct of programs but has fallen short in other ways. The NCATE accreditation teams of days gone by looked to see if programmatic functions were being performed, but they did not try to determine how well such functions were being performed. Evaluation, then, was essentially an activity designed for program development and self-improvement. Program accreditation or approval processes in the states have yielded some 1,200 teacher education programs in operation today, a number so great that issues of quality control seem to overshadow all others. Accreditation has not functioned as a lever to force qualitative differences among programs.

At the institutional level, faculty and the consumers of teacher education, students themselves, evaluate teacher education. This is done more often, according to Braskamp, Brandenburg, and Ory (1984), by using rating systems; "over one-half of the private and public colleges used ratings to evaluate teaching, and at universities student ratings as well as chairman and colleague evaluations received the most weight in evaluating faculty teaching effectiveness" (p. 38). It is interesting to note that, when researchers asked education faculty and students from some 90 AACTE institutions to rate the rigor of teacher education courses, compared with noneducation courses, the majority of both groups thought that education courses were "as rigorous as," or more so than, noneducation courses (AACTE, 1987b).

Meyer and Rowan consider organizations, not as they are formally constituted, but as groups of people seeking to shape and adjust to the reality of organizational life. Leaders of teacher education organizations anticipate a future in which the reality of reform is one of gradual, modest gain, in which some reforms substantively affect the governance of teacher education, others fail completely, and some become isomorphic with the environment.

DISEQUILIBRIUM IN GOVERNANCE

In 1985 and 1986, five major national reports were issued that challenged, and supported, elements of the traditional governance structure of teacher education. Two of the reports were produced by professional associations that represent the teacher education community: *A Call for Change in Teacher Education*, AACTE, 1985; and *Visions of Reform: Implications for the Education Profession*, ATE, 1986. Two were reports of ad hoc groups brought together for the purpose of recommending change in teacher education. One of the two, the Holmes Group, was composed of deans of teacher education in a select subset of universities preparing teachers. Their self-definition notes that they are, "by any commonly accepted standard, the top 10% of American institutions engaged in teacher education, even though in some cases [our] teacher education programs are not among the nation's best" (Holmes Group, 1986,

p. viii). The report from this group, *Tomorrow's Teachers*, takes on the character of a dissident subset of professional teacher educators who are also represented in such regular professional groups as the AACTE and the ATE. *A Nation Prepared: Teachers for the 21st Century* was the report of a task force of the Carnegie Forum on Education and the Economy (1986). The members of the task force were drawn chiefly from outside the field of professional education, although 6 of the 14 members were professional educators. The fifth report, *Time for Results*, was based on a series of task forces organized by the National Governor's Association to answer "the seven toughest questions that can be raised about education in the U.S.A" (p. 2) "for the sole purpose of helping governors be better governors" (1986, p. 4). One of these task forces addresses teacher education directly (pp. 30–48).

The Professional Association Agenda for Change

For the purpose of this chapter, the issue is not to comment on the wisdom of the several reform documents but to analyze the extent to which the recommendations of each challenged the existing governance structure of the field. The recommendations of the professional associations emphasize reform through a strengthening of the operative mechanisms controlling teacher education.

1984—AACTE. The first of the reform reports in teacher education was the result of the work of the National Commission for Excellence in Teacher Education, proposed and initiated in 1984 by the American Association of Colleges for Teacher Education, (AACTE, 1985). The commission was chaired by the president of the University of Missouri. Its 17 members included five administrators of teacher education programs, four college presidents, the presidents of the NEA and the AFT, a governor and a state legislator, a chief state school officer and a local school superintendent, a member of Congress, and the past president of the National School Boards Association. Financial assistance to the commission was provided by the Department of Education and several foundations.

AACTE organized its recommendations around five themes: (a) supply and demand for quality teachers, (b) programs for teacher education, (c) accountability for teacher education, (d) resources for teacher education, and (e) conditions necessary to support the highest quality of teaching.

The recommendations on supply and demand were threefold. *First*, entry and egress from academic programs should be "based upon rigorous academic and performance standards" (p. 8). *Second*, federal and state governments should offer financial incentives for recruitment, states and local school boards should adhere to high-quality standards in the processes of certifying and appointing, and universities should work to upgrade the status of teacher education programs. *Third*, federal and state governments and private philanthropics "should ensure that lack of finances will not bar qualified minority students from entering teacher education programs" (p. 9). None of these recommendations challenged the current governance structure of the field.

The program recommendations illustrate the difficulty the commission encountered in balancing basic structural reform against the possibility of reform within the structure as it exists. The three recommendations called for (a) upgrading the quality of the liberal and professional curricula, (b) requiring a one-year internship of "provisional certification," and (c) encouraging experimental models of teacher education. The commission split on the issue of program requirements. A majority of commission members (9 of 17) felt that "some of the recommendations are not far reaching enough" (p. 15). This group wished that the report had included the requirement of an undergraduate academic major for all teachers and the specific assertion that, "A minimum of four years should be devoted to the liberal arts component of the teacher education program: a minimum of five years to the total program" (p. 15). This recommendation would have challenged the ability of undergraduate teacher education colleges to offer a full program of teacher training.

The recommendations on accountability for teacher education affirmed and strengthened the current system. The commission recommended that certification and program approval continue to be state responsibilities, that both state standards for program review and voluntary national accreditation be raised, and that teacher education programs continue to be located in colleges and universities.

The analysis of resources for teacher education led to the recommendation that, "a National Academy for Teacher Education should be established, to which promising teacher educators could be nominated for post graduate traineeships" (p. 24). The academy was viewed as a symbol of the nation's commitment to teacher preparation, as well as a center for postgraduate study.

Finally, the commission tackled the issue of improving the conditions of teaching. The members recommended increased salaries for teachers, staff development opportunities, differentiated staffing, and incentives to pursue additional college work. Modifications were called for in the daily work life of the teacher: increased autonomy and decision-making authority, time for planning, access to clerical and paraprofessional assistance. The commission encouraged "federal and state governments to provide funds for evaluating staff development programs" (p. 29) and encouraged state boards of education to "set as their top priority for 1985 the improvement of the professional development of teachers" (p. 28). Recognizing the impact principals and superintendents have on creating conditions for professional practice, the commission suggested, "that administrative training programs in higher education be examined and modified to provide for explicit leadership skills in existing and potential administrators" (p. 29).

1986—ATE. The Association of Teacher Educators appointed a Blue Ribbon Task Force of its membership in April 1986 to respond to the various proposals for reforming teacher education.

The task force's 8 members "came from different states and provided the viewpoints of local education agencies, state education agencies, and different types of institutions of higher education" (ATE, 1986, p. v).

The report differs from the AACTE document because its stated intent is not "to direct action as much as it is to encourage the analysis of options and to stimulate thinking through the consequences of various alternatives" (p. v). The task force chose three documents to analyze: the Holmes report, the Carnegie report, and *NCATE Redesign*, a description of the reform of program accreditation through the National Council for Accreditation of Teacher Education. (The latter document is not being reviewed in this chapter because it focuses on program review, rather than on comprehensive reform.)

The ATE task force examined the implications of the Carnegie and Holmes reports for state education agencies, institutions of higher education, and local education agencies. The commentary by the task force is a forthright portrayal of the concerns of practicing teacher educators as they view recommendations that would require structural change:

1. Wholesale adoption of the Holmes and Carnegie model for teacher preparation would eliminate undergraduate teacher education majors. . . . Some educators do not want to eliminate four-year programs on the grounds that teacher salaries and working conditions are not attractive enough to justify the cost of an extra year or two. . . . In a period when minority recruitment is so vital, it simply makes little sense to expand the formal preparation period. . . . Surely we can phase-in extended preparation programs with increased emphasis on subject matter at the undergraduate level. (p. 53)
2. The Task Force viewed the National Board for Professional Teaching Standards proposed by Carnegie as problematic for SEAs, LEAs, and teacher education programs in state colleges and universities. In the latter, for example, they note that the Board recommendation might increase competitiveness among state colleges and universities to produce Board-certified teachers. This factor may, in turn, produce a kind of "teaching for the test" or an undesirable homogenization of preparation programs. (p. 41)

The task force shared a number of reform targets with the Holmes Group and the Carnegie task force, ranging from a strong liberal arts background for teachers and expanded emphasis on developing the knowledge base for professional education, through the development of a comprehensive assessment system in teacher education, to increased salaries for teachers, differentiated staffing in school, and more authority and decision-making responsibilities for teachers.

The task force's vision for the future included:

1. Establishment of a "National Network of States for the Teaching Profession," to determine goals and priorities for the teaching profession, set standards for professional practice, and provide direction and support for the profession.
2. Revision of the professional curriculum for teachers based on a strong liberal arts and subject-matter background. The induction phase into teaching would provide an extended internship and a collaborative relationship between schools and colleges.

3. Three-tiered licensure: instructor, teacher, career teacher. Certification would be separated for early, middle, and secondary levels.
4. Organization and management of schools that would emphasize collegial models, with individualized instruction for students and expanded technological support systems.
5. New approaches to teacher preparation that would emphasize consortial approaches between LEAs and IHEs and across schools of education.
6. Negotiation by a school of education with its college or university on the granting of tenure and promotion of faculty according to criteria appropriate for professors in professional schools.

The Ad Hoc Group Agenda for Change

The two reform reports that have received the widest dissemination are those of the Holmes Group and the Carnegie Task Force. Both were published in 1986, and each challenged basic elements of the status quo in teacher education.

1986—The Holmes Group. To classify the Holmes Group as ad hoc is taking some liberties with the term. Initially the group viewed itself as education deans in research universities attempting to improve teacher education programs in their own universities. As they pursued that end they discovered that, to accomplish their objectives, they needed to concern themselves with "the twin goals of the reform of teacher education and the reform of the teaching profession" (Holmes Group, 1986, p. ix). The overall goals of the Holmes Group became five in number: to make the education of teachers intellectually more solid; to recognize differences in teachers' knowledge, skill, and commitment, in their education, certification, and work; to create standards of entry to the profession—examinations and educational requirements—that are professionally relevant and intellectually defensible; to connect institutions of higher education to schools; and to make schools better places for teachers to work and to learn (p. 4).

If the group had stopped at this level of abstraction, it would have found little disagreement within the profession. But it pushed on to specify a set of necessary reforms to achieve these goals:

1. Establish a three-tier system of teacher licensing: *instructors* (beginning teachers, that is, novices with nonrenewable certificates); *professional teachers* (individuals proven competent at work, through examination, and in their own education); *career professionals* (individuals of demonstrated outstanding achievement as teachers and promise as teacher educators and analysts of teaching).
2. Eliminate the undergraduate major in education.
3. Require all teacher education students to complete an academic major and a program of liberal studies.
4. Reform undergraduate education to achieve greater coherence and dedication to the historic tenets of liberal education.

5. Organize academic course requirements so that undergraduate students can understand the intellectual structure of their discipline.
6. Revise educational studies to focus on the study of schooling as an academic field; knowledge of the pedagogy of subject matter; the skills and understandings implicit in classroom teaching; dispositions, values, and ethics of education; and, finally, the integration of these professional studies with clinical experiences.
7. Establish professional development schools to provide opportunities for teachers and administrators to work with university faculty to improve teaching and learning for students in teacher training.
8. Change the structure and working conditions within schools to make them compatible with the requirements of a new profession.
9. Increase significantly the number of minorities in teacher education programs through recruitment, loan forgiveness, retention, and valid evaluations of professional competence.

1986—Task Force of the Carnegie Forum. The report of the Carnegie Task Force appeared only a month after the Holmes Group recommendations and echoed some of the same themes with, however, much stronger emphasis on the reform of schools and schooling. The following eight elements of the Carnegie reform proposal are quoted directly from the text of the report but have been reordered to conform roughly to the same elements in the Holmes Group report:

1. Restructure the teaching force, and introduce a new category of Lead Teachers with the proven ability to provide active leadership in the redesign of the schools and in helping their colleagues to uphold high standards of teaching and learning.
2. Create a National Board for Professional Teaching Standards, organized with a regional and state membership structure, to establish high standards for what teachers need to know and be able to do, and to certify teachers who meet that standard.
3. Require a bachelor's degree in the arts and sciences as a prerequisite for the professional study of teaching.
4. Make teachers' salaries and career opportunities competitive with those in other professions.
5. Relate incentives for teachers to schoolwide student performance, and provide schools with the technology, services and staff essential to teacher productivity.
6. Develop a new professional curriculum in graduate schools of education leading to a Master in Teaching degree, based on systematic knowledge of teaching and including internships and residencies in the schools.
7. Restructure schools to provide a professional environment for teachers, freeing them to decide how best to meet state and local goals for children while holding them accountable for student progress.
8. Mobilize the nation's resources to prepare minority youngsters for teaching careers. (Carnegie Forum, 1986, pp. 55, 57)

A Public Agenda for Change: National Governors' Association

The National Governors' Association Task Force on Teaching had the benefit of all the foregoing reports as it pondered the recommendations it wished to make. Following are the 11 elements the task force recommended in response to the question, "What do we do to attract and keep the able teachers?"

1. Define the body of professional knowledge and practice that teachers must have.
2. Create a national board to define teacher standards. This board would define what teachers need to know and be able to do, administer a voluntary system to assess professional capacity, and award nationally-recognized certificates to qualified candidates.
3. Rebuild the system of teacher education.
4. Redesign the organization of schools to create more productive working and learning environments.
5. Redesign the structure of the teaching career to provide advancement without moving outside the classroom.
6. Recruit able teacher candidates—including minorities.
7. Improve teacher compensation.
8. Align teacher incentives with schoolwide student performance.
9. Improve teacher mobility.
10. Establish a loose/tight approach to state and local regulation of schools.
11. Establish the concept of educational bankruptcy. States should establish a fair, measured process of review against standards, remedial planning, and additional assistance, but with a final recourse to direct state intervention in the school district. (National Governors' Association, 1986, pp. 38–40)

Analysis and Commentary

There is a dichotomy in the reform movement in teacher education. The professional associations representing teacher educators are adopting an essentially conservative view of how change can be engineered to effect improvement in the field. The prominent reform agencies and the major public political groups that have examined teacher education are adopting a more radical stance toward the restructuring that would be required to ameliorate the problems of the field. There are broad areas of agreement on what needs to be achieved to improve teachers and teacher education: (a) an increase in the supply of high quality teachers, (b) more minorities in teaching, (c) higher quality professional preparation, (d) an increase in liberal arts for future teachers, (e) stronger academic backgrounds for all teachers, (f) differentiated levels of teacher licensure, (g) a required internship for all prospective teachers, (h) higher certification standards for teachers, (i) stiffer accreditation standards for preparation programs, (j) improved conditions of teaching, (k) greater decision-making discretion for teachers, and (l) tight linkage between colleges and universities and schools.

The professional associations have recommended that these changes can be achieve within the basic governance structure that exists or through strengthening elements in the structure, for example, by the redesign of NCATE. The extraprofessional reform proposals have introduced recommendations that are intended, at least in part, to upset the equilibrium of the field. The reform reports of the professionals and the reformers differ, to some degree, on the structural changes needed. These issues involve: (a) eliminating the undergraduate major in education, (b) reducing the number of SCDE training sites, (c) requiring an academic major for all teachers, (d) requiring a liberal arts degree before admission to teacher education, (e) establishing professional development schools to link universities and schools, (f) creating a national board for professional teaching standards, and (g) relating incentives for teachers to schoolwide student performance. These disagreements vary from the AACTE to the ATE, and both associations have had time to reexamine the positions advocated in their reports (in the AACTE's case, nearly 3 years). The important point to note is the differences in approach to reform by the reformers and the reformees. The differences are of sufficient magnitude to predict that the contest between what is and what will be will extend into the 1990s.

FUTURE GOVERNANCE PATTERNS IN TEACHER EDUCATION

In spring 1988, the authors interviewed key figures at the national level who were directly involved in and concerned with the teacher education reform movement. Our general question challenged the likelihood of change: "It is reasonable to predict that most of the current initiatives and the changes that they are proposing will simply fail to be sustained (the field will resume its state of equilibrium). Why shouldn't we predict that this will be the case? Which changes have the best chance for survival? Why?" Follow-up questions focused on specific changes, such as the number of institutions offering teacher education, the modal level of teacher training, the federal involvement in teacher education, and the establishment of professional development schools. The following portrayal of the future of governance in teacher education reflects the views of the respondents as best we were able to interpret them.

Systemic Versus Incremental Change

The most ambitious and comprehensive of the change reports, *A Nation Prepared* (Carnegie Forum, 1986), argues that its recommendations are "not a list of independent strategies. They constitute a whole. None will succeed unless all are implemented" (p. 57). The reason offered was that

Policy makers will be tempted to implement only those features of this plan that cost little in organizational trauma or dollars. That would inevitably defeat the purpose, because the result would be to leave in place the forces that make the current system work the way it does. It

is the entire structure that needs an overhaul, not just a few components. (p. 57)

If that were true, our informants would predict that the current system would survive in substantially its current form. Almost without exception they guessed that changes will occur singly and incrementally, rather than systemically and radically. The respondents who referred to systemic change were clearly not thinking of a comprehensive, a priori package of interlocked recommendations such as the Carnegie or Holmes reports. They defined systemic change as any modification that would affect the state, local (LEA and IHE), federal and national components of the loosely linked system of teacher education governance and their interrelationships. No one believes that any of the current reform proposals is justified by either wisdom or necessity to such an extent that it could overcome, in toto, the logistical, political, fiscal, or professional challenges it will face.

Predicted Incremental Changes

On the other hand, the interviewers predicted change in bits and pieces at all levels of institutional involvement.

At the University. Most informants believe that the overall degree structure for teacher education in the university will change. Specifically, they believe that teachers will be required to obtain a liberal arts undergraduate degree with a subject-matter major. This will necessitate some extended life space for teacher education either through a fifth-year or a 5-year program. This modification will transfer more responsibility within the university to the school or college of education for the professional training of teachers. It will probably set to rest the long-standing argument that teacher education is an all-university responsibility, a contention better supported by accreditation guidelines and committee structures than by experience. For better or worse, the university structure for the professional education of teachers will look more like other professional programs such as nursing and business.

Concomitant with this change is the probability that some institutions operating solely at the baccalaureate level might offer only a limited portion of preeducation training or even abandon education altogether. The respondents did not predict a substantial decrement in the number of colleges offering teacher education. They did not see a shift of power, as some have predicted, from the state college or liberal arts college to the research university.

In the LEA. For a variety of reasons, the informants saw an expanded role for teachers and the local education agency in teacher education. The revised guidelines of the National Council for Accreditation of Teacher Education specify increased involvement of teachers in preparation programs. Both the Carnegie and Holmes reports call for school-based professional development centers. The proposed National Board for Professional Teaching Standards not only is a vehicle for enhancing the status of teachers but also provides a voice for teachers in determining eligibility for board certification. Both the AFT and the NEA are operating local teacher-based programs to link educational research and practice. Reforms in school organization (e.g., school site management), the development of differentiated roles for teachers (e.g., lead teachers), and the increased participation of teachers in school-level decision making suggest the likely involvement of teachers in both preservice and inservice education. All the reform reports emphasized the necessity of clinical professors who can bridge the needed involvement of the college and the school in teacher preparation. The national press for research-based classroom practice suggests that the status of the informed practitioner will require her or his involvement in teacher education.

At the State Level. The states have always assumed a critical role in teacher certification and institutional program accreditation. In the latter 1980s the level of state involvement expanded dramatically. Our informants saw no reason why this trend would not continue. The National Governors' Association is committed to a focus on teaching. State legislators are becoming involved in teacher policy issues that they have previously eschewed. State power in teacher education will be enhanced by emerging linkages among state accreditation and certification, NCATE redesign, and the developing National Board for Professional Teaching Standards. As the effect of teacher education reform based solely on bureaucratic strategies slows down, the states will become more active as a force advocating professional reform.

At the National Level. No one predicted an increased level of federal involvement in teacher education. Everyone predicted a stronger national presence. The most obvious example is a national certification board. Less obvious, but potentially equally important, is a strengthened system of voluntary national program accreditation linked to state accreditation. The national teacher associations are both involved heavily in the development of new roles for teachers and in support of increased teacher involvement in decision making.

Looking at the bits and pieces of recommendations from the reform reports and the actions currently being taken in teacher education, the respondents believed that by 1995 there would be

1. Initial teacher education certification based on the completion of a fifth-year or a 5-year program of preparation. The 5 years will include a baccalaureate degree with an undergraduate subject-matter major.
2. Modest reduction in the number of training sites involved in teacher education.
3. Professional development schools or clinical schools and clinical professors to tighten the linkage between colleges and schools.
4. An increased role for teachers in professional decision making at the school level. This might be based upon some form of differentiated staffing supported by, for example, school-site management.
5. Higher standards for teaching certification at the state level and more rigorous program accreditation, with a link be-

tween the state process of program review and voluntary national accreditation.
6. A national certifying board for teachers.

Promises and Problems

The basis for the relative optimism about significant change in the field was most frequently argued in two ways. *First*, the informants believed that the elevated importance of teachers and teaching would be sustained, because it is reinforced at several points in the "system." The educational media are markedly increasing the coverage of teacher education. Even though the statements from the Department of Education are often negative, the Office of the Secretary of Education reaffirms the vital role of the teacher in school improvement. Educational philanthropy is funding major efforts in the reform of teacher education. Governors' offices and state legislatures show no inclination to withdraw from the field of play. There is in place a new state bureaucracy building up expertise in educational policy related to the education of teachers. There simply seems to be sufficient energy from diverse sources to keep the game moving in the foreseeable future.

Second, the respondents argued that more power to influence teacher education was accumulating at all the operating levels in the system. One can argue with some conviction that (a) LEAs are becoming more involved in teacher education and teachers are assuming a more important role in the practice of educating teachers and in the governance of the field; (b) state governments are more active and influential than ever before; (c) schools of education seem to be taking control of their own destiny through such vehicles as the Holmes Group, which, in turn, has spurred activity by the traditional organizations, the AACTE and the ATE; (d) the federal government has done little to increase its role, but that is certainly not true of the NCATE or the private foundations or the organized teaching profession. This is a unique circumstance in which teacher education policy is being redefined as a field of play not housing a zero-sum game. So far, at least, there is some synergy in this reform effort; all parties are influencing something of importance to them.

But there are problems, dilemmas and points of tension that could modify the long-term effect of the reform effort.

1. The basic reforms are expensive. They assume that teachers will be compensated at higher levels, that more money will be spent on teacher training, and that LEAs will have the resources to participate in teacher education. In counterpoint, the limits on governmental spending are apparent at all levels. The states are hard pressed to fund the school-improvement efforts they have already initiated. Universities, many of whom draw significant portions of their budget from state government, feel they are already pricing themselves out of the market. The federal government is up against the budget deficit. Local school districts are not funded to participate in teacher education. Foundations are not capable of handling the bill over the long haul. The best solution to the budgetary limitations might be to let the current system stand essentially as it is operating.

2. The picture of expanding power for all participants glosses over two points of conflict in the reform movement. The higher education community has not resolved the roles of the Holmes Group institutions (research-oriented universities), on the one hand, and the bachelors-level institutions and state colleges and universities, on the other. The overwhelming number of state-accredited teacher education institutions are in the latter two groups, and they train 90 percent of the nation's teachers. To date, they have exhibited little enthusiasm for either a 5-year or fifth-year program requirement, and they are reluctant to grant either the Holmes Group or the Carnegie Forum leadership roles in the reform of what they perceive to be a field in which they have a legitimate proprietary interest.

Simultaneously, the call for teacher empowerment is causing consternation among some administrators, especially school principals, who were identified in the instructionally effective schools research as pivotal to school improvement. The enthusiasm for lead teachers, for example, seems to some administrative groups to conflict with the apparently equal enthusiasm for the principal as the instructional leader of the school.

3. The current reform documents call simultaneously for an increase in minority-group representation in the next generation of teachers and an increase in standards of entry to teacher education programs and to teaching. With heightened competition for minority-group candidates in all fields of employment, the attracting of disproportionate numbers of the best minority candidates to extended preparation programs is a dilemma yet to be solved.

4. The odds seem to be against change, if the best prediction of future events is the past behavior of actors and agencies. The program accreditation process in teacher education has not, in the past, led to insistence on high-quality programs. No one believes that 1,200 colleges and universities are equipped to offer quality programs in teacher education, but there are roughly 1,200 state-accredited programs. The NCATE has not established itself as a necessary accrediting agency in the field. Yet control over program quality will continue to be vested in the SEAs and the NCATE, the institutions that have, in the past, not been able to police program quality.

Standards for teachers and teaching have been raised in past reform eras, yet emergency certification procedures have always been invoked in periods of shortage, and such a period is upon us in many localities.

Reform efforts within schools of education and their national associations have been worn down by a variety of factors, not the least of which is the preparation of a professional cadre of 2.2 million practitioners.

Teacher education has been an accommodating field, a field in which the most likely change to occur and be sustained is the one least likely to upset the accommodation (a) of students, through easy entry and low investment; (b) of institutions, through low cost and high enrollment; and (c) of client agencies, through a steady flow of new teachers who fit the institutional demands of public education.

5. The effort to reform teacher education is complicated by the joint conditions of low mysticism and low confidence. The general public attitude toward teaching is that anyone with a decent substantive background can step into a classroom and be successful. The field has not cultivated the mystical trappings of many professions, the specialized knowledge claims that make it clear that failure of the uninitiated would be total and devastating. The familiarity of the public with the classroom has also supported a lack of confidence on the part of the public that teachers and teacher educators can reform themselves. This combination of low mysticism and confidence even leads some policymakers to the conclusion that alternative routes to teacher certification that de-emphasize or eliminate requirements for professional education beyond subject-matter preparation are likely to improve the conditions of teaching. A field that is insecure in its relationship with its clients is more likely to be conservative in its efforts at reform.

In Sum

What would we predict on the basis of our examination of the literature of the field and our interviews with leaders in the field? We expect that teacher education is undergoing some governance changes of lasting significance. Nationally, an extrafederal cluster of influential agencies will foster and support change in the field. The processes of certification and accreditation at the national level will both be strengthened. The NCATE, or another agency, will make voluntary accreditation a necessity for teacher-preparation institutions. The strength to do this will be found in the linkage between state and national accreditation procedures, with the support of the organized teaching profession. Some form of national certifying board will provide the final push to national responsibility for upgrading programs of teacher education and teachers.

The states will continue to expand their role in teacher education governance, but whether they will persist in a bureaucratic style of reform by standards manipulation or will move toward a professional reform initiative seems less clear. They might, in fact, play two quite different roles simultaneously. The specific actions at the state level might be more regulations, whereas the states might work collectively with national agencies to support professional reform initiatives. We view the states as the linchpin supporting or subverting professional reform in teacher education. Governors, state legislatures, and state education agencies are in a position to initiate revised certification and accreditation requirements that would ensure the diffusion of a fifth-year teacher education program built upon a liberal arts degree. They could, if they chose to do it, be equally influential in tying state-level program accreditation to a revised, strengthened NCATE program of accreditation.

The states are the best barometer of the long-range progress of the proposed national reforms in teacher education governance. Institutionally, we expect a lengthened period of training in teacher education that uses both fifth-year and 5-year designs. Concomitant with this movement will be a significant decrement in the number of teacher education sites. Most of the decline will occur among the private liberal arts colleges, rather than among the state colleges and universities. The Holmes Group movement will subsume, or be subsumed by, the larger group of state colleges and universities. We are not sanguine about the substantive changes in teacher education curricula and field experiences that will accompany the change in the degree structure and demography of the field. From a governance perspective, however, schools of education should gain autonomy and some status from the concentration of study at the graduate level and a reduction in the competition for program space with colleges of arts and sciences.

The most difficult change to effect is likely to be the elevation in importance of field sites in teacher education. LEAs are not funded to participate in teacher education, however important that might be. They are accustomed to being used as student-teaching sites rather than being engaged as partners in the enterprise. The current system is cost effective, or at least inexpensive, and any alternative currently being pushed would be substantially more costly. To complicate the matter further, teacher education candidates assert consistently that the current bargain-basement student-teaching experience is the most valuable component in their training program. Establishing and sustaining professional development centers in field sites will challenge the exclusivity of expertise now claimed by university professors. Our guess is that the insistence on field involvement in teacher education will result in some changes in the student-teaching experience, but teachers and the teaching profession are more likely to gain influence on teacher education at the state and national levels than at the local level.

By the turn of the century we imagine a world of teacher education in which

1. Students in training are enrolled primarily in fifth-year programs based upon undergraduate liberal arts degrees.
2. Schools of education are being operated in 600 to 700 colleges and universities.
3. A national certifying board offers voluntary certification to beginning and experienced teachers.
4. The states, the national certifying board, and a national accrediting agency have modestly upgraded the quality of recruits and programs in teacher education.
5. Experimentation with new roles for teachers in LEAs is extensive, and this movement has had a small but significant impact on the socioeconomic status of teaching.
6. The content and experiences of teacher education are marked by a stronger commitment to research-based instruction and experientially based practice.
7. The organized teaching profession fills a vital role in determining who shall teach, the content of teacher education, and the maintenance of professional standards in classrooms.

References

Adelman, N. E. (1986). *An exploratory study of teacher alternative certification and retraining programs* (U.S. Department of Education, Data Analysis Support Center, Contract No. 300-85-0103). Washington, DC: Policy Studies Associates.

American Association of Colleges for Teacher Education. (1985). *A call for change in teacher education.* Washington, DC: Author.

American Association of Colleges for Teacher Education. (1987a). *Teacher education in the states: 50-state survey of legislative and administrative actions* (6th ed.). Washington, DC: Author.

American Association of Colleges for Teacher Education. (1987b). *Teaching teachers: Facts and figures.* Washington, DC: Author.

American Council on Education. (1985). *Recent changes in teacher education programs (Higher Education Panel Report No. 67).* Washington, DC: Author.

American Federation of Teachers. (1986–1987). *School restructuring: Resource kit.* Washington, DC: Author.

Association of Teacher Educators. (1986). *Visions of reform: Implications for the education profession.* Reston, VA: Author.

Berliner, D. (1985). Laboratory settings and the study of teacher education. *Journal of Teacher Education, 36*(6), 2–8.

Braskamp, L. A., Brandenburg, D. C., & Ory, J. C. (1984). *Evaluating teaching effectiveness: A practical guide.* Beverly Hills, CA: Sage.

Bush, R. N., Enemark, P. (1975). Control and responsibility in teacher education. In K. Ryan (Ed.), *Teacher education* (74th yearbook of the National Society for the Study of Education, Part II, pp. 265–294). Chicago: University of Chicago Press.

Carnegie Forum on Education and the Economy, Task Force on Teaching as a Profession. (1986). *A nation prepared: Teachers for the 21st century.* New York: Author.

Carpenter, J. A. (1972). *Survey of the criteria for the selection of undergraduate candidates for admission to teacher training.* Bowling Green, KY: Western Kentucky University, College of Education. (ERIC Document Reproduction Service No. ED 070 785)

Clark, D. L., & Guba, E. G. (1977). *A study of teacher education institutions as innovators, knowledge producers, and change agencies.* (National Institute of Education Project No. 4-0752). Bloomington, IN: Indiana University. (ERIC Document Reproduction Service No. ED 139 805)

Clark, D. L., & Marker, G. (1975). The institutionalization of teacher education. In K. Ryan (Ed.), *Teacher education* (74th yearbook of the National Society for the Study of Education, Part II, pp. 53–86). Chicago: University of Chicago Press.

Clifford, G. J., & Guthrie, J. W. (1988). *Ed school: A brief for professional education.* Chicago: University of Chicago Press.

Conant, J. B. (1963). *The education of American teachers.* New York: McGraw-Hill.

Cronin, J. M. (1983). State regulation of teacher preparation. In L. S. Shulman & G. Sykes (Eds.), *Handbook of teaching and policy* (pp. 171–191). New York: Longman.

Darling-Hammond, L., & Berry, B. (1988). *The evolution of teacher policy* (JRE-01). Santa Monica, CA: RAND Corporation.

Evertson, C. M., Hawley, W. D., & Zlotnik, M. (1985). Making a difference in educational quality through teacher education. *Journal of Teacher Education, 36*(3), 2–12.

Gage, N. L. (1978). *The scientific basis of the art of teaching.* New York: Teachers College Press.

Gideonse, H. D. (1986). Guiding images for teaching and teacher education. In T. J. Lasley (Ed.), *The dynamics of change in teacher* education: Vol. 1. Background papers from the National Commission for Excellence in Teacher Education (pp. 187–197). Washington, DC: American Association of Colleges for Teacher Education.

Gliessman, D. H. (1981). Learning how to teach: Processes, effects, and criteria. Washington, DC: National Institute of Education. (ERIC Document Reproduction Service No. ED 200 516)

Haberman, M. (1987). Recruiting and selecting teachers for urban schools. New York: Columbia University, Teachers College, and ERIC Clearinghouse on Urban Education Institute for Urban and Minority Education; and Reston, VA: Association of Teacher Educators.

Holmes Group (1986). Tomorrow's teachers. East Lansing, MI: Author.

Houston, W. R. & Howsam, R. B. (1972). Change and challenge. In W. R. Houston & R. B. Howsam (Eds.), Competency-based teacher education: Progress, problems, and prospects (pp. 1–16). Chicago: Science Research Associates.

Jenkins, W. A. (1977). Changing patterns in teacher education. In J. R. Squire (Ed.), The teaching of English (76th yearbook of the National Society for the Study of Education, Part I, pp. 260–281). Chicago: University of Chicago Press.

Joyce, B. R., Yarger, S. J., Howey, K. R., Harbeck, K. M., & Kluwin, T. N. (1977). Preservice teacher education: Report of a survey of the heads of education units, faculty, and students in United States higher education institutions which prepare teachers. Washington, DC: U.S. Office of Education.

Judge, H. (1982). American graduate schools of education: A view from abroad. New York: Ford Foundation.

Kerr, D. H. (1983). Teaching competence and teacher education in the United States. In L. S. Shulman & G. Sykes (Eds.), Handbook of teaching and policy (pp. 126–149). New York: Longman.

Koerner, J. D. (1963). The miseducation of America's teachers. Boston: Houghton Mifflin.

Lanier, J. E., & Little, J. W. (1986). Research on teacher education. In M. C. Wittrock (Ed.), Handbook of research and teaching (3rd ed., pp. 527–569). New York: Macmillan.

Medley, D. M. (1982). Teacher competency testing and the teacher educator. Reston, VA: Association of Teacher Educators; and Charlottesville, VA: University of Virginia, School of Education, Bureau of Educational Research.

Meyer, J. W., & Rowan, B. (1977). Institutionalized organizations: Formal structure as myth and ceremony. American Journal of Sociology, 83(2), 340–363.

National Commission on Excellence in Education. (1983). A nation at risk: The imperative for educational reform. Washington, DC: U.S. Government Printing Office.

National Council for Accreditation of Teacher Education. (1985). NCATE redesign. Washington, DC: Author.

National Council for Accreditation of Teacher Education. (1987). NCATE standards, procedures, and policies for the accreditation of professional education units: The accreditation of professional education units for the preparation of professional school personnel at basic and advanced levels. Washington, DC: Author.

National Education Association. (1987). Establishing and maintaining standards for the governance of the teaching profession. Report of the NEA Standing Committee on Instructional and Professional Development. Washington, DC: Author.

National Governors' Association. (1986). Time for results: The governors' 1991 report on education. Washington, DC: Author.

Olson, L. (1988, June). Capturing teaching's essence: Stanford team tests new methods. Education Week, 7(37), pp. 1, 20.

Peseau, B. A. (1986). Funding and academic production of teacher education in state universities and land-grant colleges (8th annual study). University, AL: American Association of Colleges & Schools of Education in State Universities & Land-Grant Colleges. (ERIC Document Reproduction Service No. 272 489).

Sandefur, J. T. (1986). State assessment trends. AACTE Briefs (7), 12–14.

Sandefur, W. S., & Nicklas, W. L. (1981). Competency-based teacher education in AACTE institutions: An update. Phi Delta Kappan, 62(10), 747–748.

Shields, J. J., & Daniele, R. (1981). Teacher selection and retention: A review of the literature. Unpublished manuscript, The City College of the City University of New York, School of Education.

Silberman, C. E. (1970). Crisis in the classroom: The remaking of American education. New York: Random House.

Smith, B. O. (1980). A design for a school of pedagogy. Washington, DC: U.S. Government Printing Office.

Sorenson, G. (1967). What is learned in practice teaching? Journal of Teacher Education, 18(2), 173–179.

Wheeler, C. (1980). NCATE: Does it matter? (Research Series No. 92). East Lansing, MI: Michigan State University, Instititue for Research on Teaching.

Wilson, R. (1988, May 4). Bennett notes improvement of schools in past 5 years but paints bleak portrait of U.S. education report. Chronicle of Higher Education, p. A-29.

Woodring, P. (1975). The development of teacher education. In K. Ryan (Ed.), Teacher education (74th yearbook of the National Society for the Study of Education, Part II, pp. 1–24). Chicago: University of Chicago Press.

Zeichner, K. M., & Liston, D. (1985). Varieties of discourse in supervisory conferences. Teaching and Teacher Education, 1(2), 155–174.

· 8 ·

TEACHER EDUCATION STANDARDS

Robert A. Roth

CALIFORNIA STATE UNIVERSITY, LONG BEACH

Chris Pipho

EDUCATION COMMISSION OF THE STATES

The distinction between this chapter on standards and the previous chapter on governance is that this chapter considers measures of quality primarily related to individual teacher competence and program offerings, whereas the chapter on governance reviews the people, entities, and institutions that are setting these higher standards. To the degree possible, the issues will be separate, but action taken on standards lacks meaning without a knowledge of why or who influenced the setting of the standards.

STATE CERTIFICATION STANDARDS

State control over education has increased since the beginning of the reform movement. The report, *A Nation At Risk* (National Commission on Excellence in Education, 1983), triggered a series of national and state task force reports and produced mega reform legislation in 15 to 20 states, with nearly all states taking some action in education reform (Pipho, 1986). The raising of academic standards for students and improvement of the quality of teachers being attracted into, and retrained in, the profession have been given top priority by state policymakers. One vehicle for this action has been state standards. Strengthening of teacher education programs and, especially, certification standards, with mandated tests for entry into the profession and competency testing for initial certification, are common elements of state reform efforts.

States entered the standard-setting arena primarily because of the need to protect the public from "harm." Specifically,

their laws gave the states control over the process of preparing teachers and assuring some semblance of job performance once employed. Teacher certification (giving legal sanction to an individual to teach at a particular grade level or in a certain subject) is the primary process of state control over teaching. Historically, first, local or civil authorities, and later, states displayed an interest in testing and certifying teachers. Until well into the early twentieth century, this process was usually controlled by local officials' giving an oral test to individuals wanting a teaching certificate. Later, paper-and-pencil tests were used (Elsbree, 1939). After the 1850s there was a general movement to add questions on theory and practice. This gradually grew into the awarding of a teaching certificate on the basis of completion of a certified program. The program-approval method slowly took hold during the 1920s and 1930s. By 1952 most states issued certificates on the basis of an approved college program (Huggett & Stinnett, 1956).

The education reform movement which began in the 1980s reemphasized competency testing for certification, usually adding this requirement with either a state-prepared test or a nationally, commercially available test (Hawley, 1986a). Testing programs are usually used at the end of an approved college program, with the exception of basic-skills tests. Even these standards are now being changed, with some states requiring that a certain percentage of an institution's graduates pass the teacher competency test for certification or the institution could lose program approval. Some of the states using test scores for this purpose include Alabama, Alaska, Florida, Georgia, Mississippi, South Carolina, North Carolina, Tennes-

The authors wish to thank Richard Kunkel (NCATE) and Charles C. Mackey, Jr. (New York State Education Department) for their reviews and feedback.

see, Texas, and Virginia. In addition to these changes, alternative certification and emergency certification regulations are also undergoing changes (Roth & Lutz, 1986). The redefinition of teacher education, with stronger state control and local school districts playing a larger role through alternative certification, is a trend that is becoming more evident.

Sources of Certification Standards

The state, through its established education boards and governing authorities, is the legal source of teacher certification standards. State boards of education or professional practices boards (PPBs) consider and adopt these standards. Usually this is in conjunction with advisory groups, staff, and voluntary affiliation with related professional organizations. Knowing what the standards are in each state still leaves a researcher with the central question of source unanswered. If states were using independent research to make decisions about certification standards unique to each state, then significant differences in the certification standards should exist in at least some states. On the other hand, is public opinion about good teaching so universal that common sense guides states to the same certification standards? Does research provide a common base of knowledge for certification standards? To what extent do professional practice boards or state agencies use research?

Proposals to reform teacher education standards are frequently based on assertions that might not support the arguments and standards proposed. Speculating that many of these assertions are really value statements, rather than factual statements, Hawley (1986b) identifies eight assertions often visible in teacher education decisions and speculates on the availability of research to support each. These assertions, paraphrased below, are based on studies summarized in Evertson, Hawley, and Zlotnik (1985) and Hawley (1986b, 1989).

Assertion I—Knowing the subject one is to teach in depth will make one a better teacher. Depending on what one means by depth, there is little evidence to support this assertion. Teacher grade point average or number of courses taken in the subject taught do not appear to correlate with student performance on standardized tests—except in advanced high school classes.

Assertion II—Adding an additional year to preservice teacher education will increase the quality of those pursuing a teaching career. Sketchy evidence and inferences drawn from labor economics suggest that the opposite of this assertion is correct. One may think of a labor market as being in equilibrium with respect to the response of that market to the rewards of a given occupation. If the costs of entry are increased, so must the benefits be increased or the size and quality of the candidate pool will decline. Alternatively, the distribution of potential teachers' motives can change, and this happens in response to changes in the value attributed to a role by the society or because of some other cultural change. Changes in the entry costs of particular programs that are accompanied by increased intrinsic rewards may alter the number of students interested in such programs,

but it is unlikely to affect the overall distribution of motives or the perceived benefits of serving in the profession.

Assertion III—Requiring that new teachers have a master's degree before teaching will increase the status of the teaching profession. There is no evidence to support this claim. As the number of teachers with master's degrees has increased, so has the perception that the status of teaching has declined. Education attained by members of a profession appears to be only loosely correlated with occupational status (measured by attraction of the occupation, deference given to the occupation, and earnings). Other professionals have sought status through graduate study requirements (e.g., librarians and social workers) without effect.

Assertion IV—Teacher education is a waste of time; teaching is an art that can be learned on the job. Research on teaching shows that certain teacher behaviors are consistently related to student achievement. Specific programs aimed at teaching particular behaviors (e.g., asking higher order questions) have been shown to be effective in the short run. Students who graduate from teacher education programs are usually judged to be more effective teachers than college graduates who have had little or no formal exposure to a preservice preparation program.

Assertion V—The more prospective teachers learn about teaching (e.g., the more courses they take) before they begin to teach, the more effective they will be. While students who complete conventional teacher preparation programs are usually more effective teachers than those who do not, the outcomes of different types of preservice programs have not been studied. During the first and second years of teaching, teachers abandon some of their skills that are effective in order to simplify their tasks, conform to school norms, and ensure that they can control their classrooms.

Assertion VI—Increasing the amount of preservice practice in schools that a teacher candidate has will increase teaching effectiveness. Teachers generally report that practice teaching is valuable. But, studies of practice teaching suggest that students seldom learn much they did not already know and often narrow rather than expand their repertoire of strategies. Moreover, no consistent relationship between the number of field-oriented courses taken and teacher effectiveness has been found.

Assertion VII—More study in the liberal arts will make one a better teacher. This issue has not been studied. Studies of the changes in student attitudes or ability to reason resulting from variations in their college experiences are few in number and are inconclusive. Small liberal arts colleges do seem to influence student values in ways consistent with the culture of the particular college.

Assertion VIII—The smarter you are, the better teacher you will be. This intuitively sensible assertion cannot be clearly documented. Within the range of the intellectual abilities of teacher candidates who are hired or who complete their programs (many do not), there appears to be little relationship between teacher effectiveness and scores on the National Teachers Exam, scores on the Scholastic Aptitude Test and American College Test, or grade point averages in college. Some tests of teachers' verbal ability have been found to correlate modestly with student achievement and high teacher evaluations.

Johnson-Moore and Nelson, writing in the *Journal of Educational Policy*, express similar concerns over the source and ease with which state policy is made. They maintain that the education-reform era has brought on a propensity to diagnose and propose remedies. "Measured and disinterested inquiry" is set aside in favor of quick answers. State standards have moved beyond traditional accreditation and certification pronouncements to plans and mandates to implement merit pay, career ladders, salary incentive programs, competency tests for teachers, and revisions of tenure law and alternative certification programs (Johnson-Moore & Nelson, 1987).

Although the point of view that careful and in-depth research should lead the way to standard setting cannot be denied, in practice this might not be the way states proceed. Actions are often based on immediate need, and, if the situation is viewed as perilous, rational thought (e.g., research) usually follows, rather than precedes, actions, if engaged in at all.

This sense of urgency can be noted in many state policy reports. In Massachusetts the introduction to a study on the conditions of teaching conveys some of this urgency:

Throughout our history—from our transition from agrarian to industrial society, through our assimilation of millions of immigrants, to our response to the challenge of Sputnik—our public education system has carried out its mandate: education for all Americans. In each succeeding generation, political leaders, educators, scientists and corporate executives have insisted that universal education was the prerequisite for a prosperous nation and that without successful public education the United States would not become or remain the preeminent industrial democracy in the world.

Profound concern about current public education is therefore understandable. Surveys, articles, commissions and reports paint a bleak picture of our public schools. The question then becomes what to do. Shall we find fault—students, teachers, television, family dislocation? Shall we wistfully hearken back to the way schools used to be and then give up? Blaming and complaining, however emotionally satisfying, will not confront the insistent issue: the future of our public schools. As in previous generations, the public schools are our future.

In 1985, Massachusetts stopped blaming, reminiscing and wishing. Instead of adding to the alarmist rhetoric and pessimistic doubt about public education, we acted. We began a program to improve learning and teaching. (*Leading the Way*, 1987, p. 7)

The use of research to develop state standards is lacking. A survey conducted of state certification officials by the authors on the availability of research studies on this subject produced responses from 30 states, with at least 19 indicating that such research studies were not available. Many others sent recently completed reports and examples of current study commission activity. Few states have conducted any experimental research prior to making needed recommendations. In some reports the preface is similar to one unidentified source that merely said "therefore, the Education Standards Commission was directed to conduct a study and make recommendations" before launching into the proposed recommendations. In one or two instances the reports attempt to give a historical perspective to the proposed changes by telling when and how previous stan-

dards have been established and changed. This background is an attempt to assist the current governing board in understanding the operational setting and probably serving as a deterrent from embarrassingly moving to adopt the same rules that were abandoned in a prior decade.

One example of a consensus-building study is evident in California, where the Commission on Teacher Credentialing (Wright, McKibbin, & Walton, 1987) described in some detail the study conducted by the Commission on Pedagogical Standards to determine what elements of pedagogical knowledge and competence were essential for beginning teachers. This study included a survey of 1,218 randomly selected professional educators in California schools, 1,034 teacher educators, and 506 credential candidates. Also included were 500 school board members and 500 randomly selected registered voters. This group was asked to judge the desirability of each of 50 potential standards of pedagogical knowledge and competence for beginning teachers. More than half of each group of respondents judged 20 of the 50 standards to be "absolutely indispensable or highly desirable." The process eventually produced 12 standards that were used in the first draft of proposed standards. The staff also conducted a survey of program-evaluation policies and practices in other states and recommendations made by other state and national professional associations. The proposed recommendations were then presented to a reaction group of 9 California universities, colleges, and professional associations. The proposed standards were then revised and edited by a 24-member advisory panel and presented at a series of regional conferences. The total process as presented by the California Commission on Teacher Credentialing answers more of the political needs than research needs, but, although lacking in applied research, it appears more ambitious and thorough than many other state reports (California Commission on Teacher Credentialing, 1986).

A number of states, for example, New York, conduct public hearings prior to the development of certification regulations. Teachers, teacher educators, parents, and representatives of business and industry are asked to comment on the proposed standards prior to final adoption.

Status of Standards for Certification

Locating current information on existing state standards in all 50 states and for all levels of education is a problem for most researchers working on teacher certification issues. A number of organizations track and report these data on a periodic basis. One report is The American Association of Colleges for Teacher Education's *Teacher Education in the States: A 50-State Survey of Legislative and Administrative Actions*, 6th edition (AACTE, 1987). Included are 50 sets of data on state standards boards with details on membership and authority. Information from a 50-state survey summarizes data under the following categories: standards, standards boards, incentives, beginning teacher induction, irregular certification routes, program curricula, resources for practitioner inservice, and evidence of maintenance of equity. Four additional categories of state activity were also surveyed: capacity-building services and activities that change the ability of schools, colleges, and departments of education (SCDEs) to deliver services to the field of teacher preparation; state-level activity that funds or mandates professional development for faculty members of SCDEs; information on state activity that requires or funds research, data collection, and dissemination; and/or program evaluation relevant to teacher education.

A second report is the *Manual on Certification and Preparation of Educational Personnel in the United States*, published by the National Association of State Directors of Teacher Education and Certification (NASDTEC) in 1984 (Mastain & Roth, 1984) and 1988 (Mastain, 1988). The fifteen major classifications of state information include certification requirements by state; assignment/misassignment of teachers; discipline of credential holders/applicants; substandard, limited, or emergency credentials; use of examinations for certification or admission to teacher preparation; noneducational and special requirements for teaching certificates; minimum requirements for elementary and secondary certificates; out-of-state institutions offering coursework in each state; reciprocity and acceptance of out-of-state certificates and credits; supply/demand data and reports; teacher education institutions and approved programs; state standards for initial teacher certification; state standards for "second-stage" teacher certification; state standards for continuing education; and state support systems for beginning teachers.

Validity of Standards

Measurement of the relationship of standards to teacher effectiveness is another area in which research is lacking. The 50-state survey of state directors of teacher certification conducted by the authors produced no reference to state agency studies. In part this could be due to the fact that state certification requirements are seldom in force for a sufficient period of time to conduct longitudinal research.

Writings in the professional literature make glancing references to the availability or acceptance of research. Ponzio (1985) introduces a special edition of *Teacher Education Quarterly* on research in teaching by commenting that "day to day teaching generally is unguided and uninformed by research findings." In comparing this situation to other professions, classroom teachers were described as having little faith in the applicability or usefulness of research to their practice.

Beginning in 1983 with the release of *A Nation At Risk*, more than 20 national reports or books on the need for education reform were released. Some duplicated each other in pointing out the declining quality of education. Although there was no sustained analysis of the quality of teaching, most reached the conclusion that it had also gone down (Weis, 1987). In general, state policymakers were often influenced by these reports to take action to raise standards for certification.

Testing for Certification

The appropriate role of testing in the certification process and in teacher education programs is a topic of great concern in teacher education. Acting as if the profession can control the variables long enough for thoughtful researchers to find answers is part of the problem. State policymakers assume that finding the appropriate role of testing is merely a political arena question. Research that can show how political decisions might be improved with better information, and show researchers why the politicians need valid test data, might bring the different camps into some form of workable compromise.

The education reform legislation in Arkansas, Georgia, and Texas that called for the testing of all existing teachers for recertification purposes is a classic case in point. In Texas the test became the pawn in a game destined to give teachers one of the largest salary increases in the history of the state. Governor Mark White promised to work for the salary increase, but conservative legislators had to get something in return. A tax to support the salary increase was needed, and the political motto became "no test, no tax." In this instance, the test to rid the teaching profession of incompetent teachers became the actual reform tool rather than an information-gathering tool to verify some other event or action. Once the decision to test was made, the legislature only needed to hear that a test would be developed and administered on schedule. Research showing that the test was invalid or a poor choice would only upset the political balance of the leveraged trade-off. The fact that the eventually developed Texas Examination of Current Administrators and Teachers (TECAT) lowered teacher morale; that the final passing rate was 99 percent; that the public might have lowered its opinion of teachers as a result of the test; and that, for a total cost of more than $78 million, 1,199 teachers were eliminated and another 1,000 to 2,000 were forced out of the profession, is now information that legislators in other states need to hear about (Shepard & Kreitzer, 1987). The Texas experience could become a classic example of how not to use a test for recertification purposes.

Control over the content, construction, and use of teacher tests is an issue still being debated. The National Education Association has stated that there is a role for fair and judicious use of testing (Futrell & Robinson, 1986) and that this process depends on a codified knowledge base for teaching, a model that defines how testing will and will not be used in the profession, professional control of certification and licensure, and the end of politically expedient teacher-testing policies (S. P. Robinson, 1987). From test developers such as Educational Testing Service, the point of view has been supported that paper-and-pencil tests can provide evidence that prospective teachers have a basic knowledge of the subject to be taught, possess adequate pedagogical knowledge, and can demonstrate certain basic communication skills (Anrig, 1987). Beyond entry into the profession there appears to be consensus that practicing classroom teachers should be judged primarily on the basis of systematic supervision and evaluation of actual teaching performance (Goertz, Ekstrom, & Coley, 1984; Rosenfeld, Skurnik, & Thornton, 1986). The move away from credentialing by program approval and graduating from such a program is creating much interest in the study of how examinations are used in other professions, leading to introspection on the meaning of professionalism (Lareau, 1986; Larsen, 1977). For minorities, the impact of testing has been severe. "Literally thousands of minority candidates have been screened by examinations from the teaching profession over the last decade" (G. D. Smith, 1987, p. 1).

Once the decision is made to use a commercial test such as the National Teacher Examination (NTE) or a state or privately developed test, the issue of how to establish cutoff scores or minimum standards takes on importance. Defending decisions when certificates are to be denied to graduates of programs and possibly defending this action in court place this aspect of teacher testing in a vulnerable position. It is generally conceded that the Angoff, Nedelsky, and Jaeger procedures are options administrators of teacher-testing programs can use in determining cutoff scores. A comparison of the three procedures suggests that the Angoff method, modified to provide some informative feedback, might be the most defensible approach (Cross, Impara, Frary, & Jeager, 1984).

By early 1988 more than 40 states were using some form of test for initial certification. Primarily, the NTE test was being used, but, in more than 10 states, tests were developed by state agencies using contracted or staff assistance (Education Commission of the States, 1987; McCarthy, Turner, & Hall, 1987). As test use expanded for teacher certification, there was also a move to extend the process to school administrators (Hazi, 1985).

The Impact of Standards on Minorities

The shortage of teaching jobs in the 1970s, the layoffs caused by declining student enrollment, and the opening of other career areas to women and minorities are forces affecting the entry of minorities into the teaching profession. At a time when the minority population is increasing, especially in urban areas, and a general teacher shortage is anticipated, the recruitment and selection of minority teachers is expected to reach crisis proportions (Hammond & Green, 1988).

Suggestions for correcting the situation have been presented in some of the national studies (Garibaldi, 1987; Kloosterman, Woods, & Matkin, 1987), but it is likely that the issue will not be solved by states working independently. A national plan for solving this problem might be needed, and organizations such as the Education Commission of the States have started to take steps to bring collections of policy leaders together to address this issue (Holmes, 1988). The problem is being addressed generally, but individual efforts have been directed toward blacks (Baratz, 1986) and to the role that testing is playing in reducing the number of minorities in the teaching profession (Garcia, 1986).

Emergency Certification

Filling the teacher need when no one qualified with a teaching certificate is available causes school officials to look for the best available candidate, followed by a request to the state for emergency certification. Typically, states have a process for awarding a substandard certificate for a specific position for a specified period of time. In most states, if the holder of the certificate is working on college credit courses to achieve regular certification, the substandard certificate can be renewed on a year-to-year basis. NASDTEC, in its occasional manual, gives extensive coverage to state use of substandard, limited, and emergency credentials (Mastain & Roth, 1984; Mastain, 1988).

In 1956 the National Education Association reported that 6 percent of teachers in the United States held temporary certificates and 3 percent held regular certificates that did not meet minimum requirements for the classes they were teaching (National Education Association, 1957). A follow-up poll of 1,291 teachers conducted in 1986 by the National Education Association showed that 17 percent of the teachers said they were misassigned to teach subjects they were unprepared to teach. An earlier NEA poll conducted in 1981 showed that 16 percent of the teachers polled were assigned out of field. A similar 29-state survey conducted in 1986 by the National Association of State Boards of Education revealed that most misassignments were made to fill shortages in mathematics and science. The American Federation of Teachers sponsored a survey, announcing that anecdotal evidence on the misassignment of teachers is readily available but that states do not track the problem of misassignment and rarely hold school districts accountable (V. Robinson, 1985).

The growing use of the term *misassigned* and the less frequent use of the terms *emergency certificate* or *temporary certificate* could be an indication that data on these certificates are not available or that the oversupply of teachers, so visible in the 1970s, indicates that individuals with teaching certificates are available. To fill shortages in critical subject areas or in rural or isolated areas, however, teachers are more likely to be misassigned. There are many aspects of the problem. Roth calls for a national summit meeting to assist state and local officials with the misassigned and the emerging certificate problem. Studies quoted in this article testify to a rapidly growing problem (Roth, 1986a).

Hall predicted, in a 1984 presentation to the American Educational Research Association, that the graying of the teacher population and a student enrollment increase would bring on a teacher shortage. He even predicted that, when the higher standards came into conflict with the decreasing supply of teachers, "loopholes will be created such as emergency certificates, accelerated programs and lower standards in order to provide enough bodies . . . at that point, teachers will likely receive even less pedagogical training than is presently offered" (Hall, 1984, p. 29).

Some of these predictions have since come true. Virginia and Texas enacted legislation in the late 1980s, and California enacted legislation prior to this that puts a statewide cap on the number of education courses that can be required for the teacher education sequence at state colleges and universities. The establishment of a maximum raises questions about sequence of offerings and forces cooperation or conflict between schools of education and other general-studies divisions.

Late in 1987 the Southern Regional Consortium of Colleges of Education was organized. In part, this regional consortium of colleges of education representing 35 institutions in 15 southeastern states was organized to further collaborative research projects aimed at better understanding the growing tendency of state policymakers to regulate teacher education training programs (Buccino, 1987).

Alternative Certification Problems

Beginning in the early 1980s, education reform, teacher shortages in critical areas, and general concern that the profession was not attracting and holding the best individuals as teachers resulted in states' creating alternative certification programs. In general these new programs were established to enable liberal arts graduates to teach in schools by permitting them to earn full certification without following the traditional undergraduate sequence of courses (Cornett, 1988). Some states promoted the program as a way to attract additional persons into teaching, whereas others focused on filling positions in critical shortage areas such as mathematics, science, and foreign languages.

The federal Department of Education, in a white paper (Greer, 1987) on alternative certification, recommends that states and school districts tap the pool of new college graduates and individuals seeking a second career in teaching by means of alternative certification programs. The paper suggests that many of these applicants are unwilling "to contend with the unnecessary barriers that block their way into the teaching profession" and that alternative certification programs are a good strategy for countering the poor academic backgrounds of many prospective teachers, the poor quality of many teacher-training programs, the increasing demand for new teachers, and the state certification requirements that discourage well-educated applicants. The perception that teacher education programs and certification rules are the roadblock to improving the system is also espoused by Rowe (1985). He highlights the issue by saying "In many states, no matter how high your college grades, no matter how much life—or even teaching—experience you've had, you still can't teach in public schools without completing a certification drill of teacher education courses" (p. 17).

This criticism of teacher education programs and certification is not new. In the 1970s, Denemark (1972) referred to teacher education programs as being irrelevant and narrowly focused; Joyce and Clift (1984) said teachers commonly believed that coursework in teacher education was not preparing them adequately for the realities of teaching; and Schuttenberg (1983) pointed out that teacher education faculty were not always effective models for sound teaching methods.

The extent to which the public and members of the profession saw weaknesses in teacher-training programs or in the personnel and certification process as a need for alternative education could be debated. As the alternative certification program was going through the hearing process in New Jersey, Gideonse (1984) offered testimony to the New Jersey State Board of Education that was very critical of both the process and the product of the alternative certification plan. He said, "the alternative route to certification as sketched out . . . is unworkable, professionally irresponsible, and could not hope to achieve its objectives" (p. 9). Part of the criticism leveled at the New Jersey State Board by Gideonse concerned the fact that personnel from colleges of teacher education were presumed to have had a vested interest in the issue and were excluded from the process of developing the alternative certification plan. This same concern was also voiced by Berliner's saying that the trend to downgrade teacher education was coming at the wrong time and that the "recently developed body of knowledge and a fresh set of conceptions on which to base teacher education" should be used to upgrade the profession (1984, p. 94).

The American Association of Colleges for Teacher Education's position statement on alternative certification specified the necessary components that should be included in an alternative teacher-preparation program. One group of educators summarized this position statement by saying that the alternative preparation should "recognize the unique strengths of prospective teachers from non-traditional backgrounds and prepare these individuals to meet the same standards that are established for others who enter the profession" (D. C. Smith, Nystrand, Ruch, Gideonse, & Carlson, 1985, p. 24).

Types of Alternative Programs

The variety of programs created by the states and teacher education institutions has created a confusion over terminology. Many different programs are called *alternative certification*. Two main varieties of alternative certification programs exist: those state-mandated programs that permit school districts to initiate the process or programs and those programs that allow postsecondary institutions to initiate programs. Cornett (1988), writing for the Southern Regional Education Board, makes a third distinction by identifying joint school and university programs that provide training and on-the-job supervision. This distinction, although possibly useful, raises other issues, because many of the alternative certification programs, no matter where they are initiated, eventually involve supervision and training from both the school district and the postsecondary institution.

Roth and Lutz (1986) describe alternative programs as "a state-adopted process by which an individual may acquire a regular (standard) teaching certificate through a nontraditional certification program and which allows the individual to assume full classroom responsibility prior to completion of the preparation program" (p. 4). Further clarification is added by pointing out that nonstandard ways of entering the classroom have been in use for years and that states have called these emergency, limited, temporary, or nonstandard teaching permits. For the most part, these permits have been viewed as temporary or emergency programs that do not usually lead to full certification. The alternative approaches to full certification are those state programs that depart from the traditional teacher-preparation programs. Roth and Lutz go on to say that these programs share several characteristics: (a) They allow the individual to enter the classroom as a teacher prior to completing full preparation (standard requirements); (b) they might not require full preparation (standard requirements) to achieve certification; (c) they accept nontraditional students (those with a bachelor's degree, experience in business and industry, retirees); (d) they bypass traditional preparation programs through nontraditional accelerated programs; and (e) they are established through state policy.

School-Initiated Programs. The New Jersey Provisional Teacher Program was initiated by the Department of Education in 1985. The first announcement invited well-prepared liberal arts graduates without traditional training to teach in one of the 600 school districts of the state. By the beginning of the 1985 school year, 121 individuals had been hired by school districts, and a year later the number had increased to 391 (New Jersey Department of Education, 1986).

Once hired by a district, provisional teachers serve for one year as full-time teachers on full salary. In the school they work closely with a support team that gives advice, encouragement, and supervision. Outside of the building they attend 200 hours of state-sponsored seminar classes on subjects such as the curriculum, the student, and the school setting. Full certification comes at the end of the first school year.

The Council for Basic Education (CBE) (Gray & Lynn, 1988), after completing one of the first follow-up studies of the New Jersey program, reported that the candidates entering the program had higher scores on the NTE than their traditional counterparts and that 20 percent were minority candidates. Of the 121 provisional teachers hired the first year, 105 successfully completed the program, with an attrition rate of 10.6 percent, as compared with a 16.6 percent attrition rate among regular-certified and trained first-year teachers. One of the problems with the program, as identified by Grey & Lynn, was the burden of teaching full time and taking 200 hours of training in the first year. They described this as excessive.

They also pointed out that districts were charged with developing local programs of instruction for provisional teachers and that most, in turn, were sending their provisional teachers on to centers coordinated by the state department of education. By the second year of the program, 13 centers had already been placed in operation, and each was affiliated with a collegiate school or department of education that coordinated the instruction provided by college faculty and personnel hired from local districts. Because most of the classes were on evenings and weekends, some of the provisional teachers complained that the quality of instruction was poor and offered little in the way of practical, day-to-day advice.

The CBE study recommended that the number of hours for training be reduced or extended. Reporting on interviews with principals and administrators who had hired the provisional candidates, they found that the majority said that, all things being equal, they would rather employ a certified teacher than a provisional candidate, primarily because of the expense of the extensive mandated supervisory time. Even the superintendents and administrators who had hired a successful provisional teacher felt the same way. In general, the study found that the caliber of teachers entering the program was higher than that of those being recruited into the regular teacher-training program, and that, overall, the program was a success.

Institution-Initiated Programs. Policy Study Associates (Adelman, 1986), conducting a study for the U.S. Department of Education of 12 alternative certification programs and eight teacher retraining programs, found that the alternative certification programs were responsible and innovative approaches to addressing local and state issues of teacher supply and quality. The study concluded that the quality of applicants was higher than that of the traditional program graduates and that, in all cases, the alternative certification selection process was more selective than traditional teacher-training programs. In general the teacher-quality issue appears to be addressed, but the teacher shortage issue, according to Adelman, was clearly not answered by this program. The study also found that alternative certification candidates had a sincere interest in the teaching profession and that most intended to pursue a career in teaching if employment could be found. The study also found that the programs offered aspiring teachers more classroom experience and more intense supervision than did traditional teacher-preparation programs.

Although the Southern Regional Education Board (Cornett, 1988) identifies more than 20 state-initiated alternative certification programs, Adelman (1986) indicates that the total number of programs nationwide was unknown. In some cases postsecondary institutions have developed variations on the traditional preparation program and have received state approval for these new efforts. In general, these institution-based programs differ widely. In Atlanta, Georgia State University, in conjunction with the Atlanta Public Schools, initiated an alternative certification program designed to attract more academically capable and talented people into the teaching profession (Guyton, 1988). Preliminary findings comparing regular first-year teachers with 2 groups of interns were inconclusive, with only 12 teachers in the 3 groups involved. This project was to continue for another 4 years, and better research information will be available.

In 1983 the California legislature established the teacher trainee program as an alternate route to certification for prospective secondary teachers. Applicants were to hold a degree in the subject to be taught and pass the adopted tests of basic academic skills and subject-matter knowledge for prospective teachers, but they were not required to have professional preparation in teaching by a college or university. One of the most distinctive features of the program was that it required school districts to develop a professional development plan for their trainees, assign a mentor teacher to guide and assist each trainee, and evaluate each trainee's performance annually. After 2 years of teaching with a mentor, the district could recommend the trainee for a clear teaching credential.

Evaluating the program, the California Commission on Teacher Credentialing (1987), in a report issued to the state legislature, found that there were weaknesses in the local district evaluation plans. The study found that many of the local evaluation plans were not always implemented in practice, and many of the procedures used were designed for experienced teachers rather than new teachers. It was also reported that there was little communication between the mentors and other staff members who were to guide the new teachers.

Interviews and classroom observation found that the 82 teacher trainees were teaching at least as effectively as the group of 66 other second-year teachers who were teaching the same subjects in the same schools. The report to the legislature concluded that the program should stay, that the commission should be given responsibility to establish standards of quality for the program, that the legislature should appropriate funds for periodic reviews of the program, that the evaluation portion of the program should be improved, and that the legislature should consider requiring school districts to establish an internship program or a teacher trainee program as a condition for employing any teacher with an emergency teaching certificate.

One of the distinctive features of many of the alternative certification programs is the number of changes made at the internship or induction level. Variations in methodology and practice are evident. Huling-Austin (1988) reviewed the research on teacher-induction programs and points out that one of the problems of conducting successful induction programs is the need to provide people on the school site and the institution site with appropriate resources to fulfill their roles. She points out the need for these programs to be flexible, for the role of the support teacher to be clearly identified at the time of placement, and for the education of the profession as well as the public about teacher-induction methods and needs.

Attracting different groups of potential teachers with alternative certification programs is also an area that is undergoing significant development. The National Executive Service Corporation (Popp & Wallace, 1988) has been working since the late 1970s to help retired men and women with executive and professional experience serve as consulting advisors for public benefit. In 1988 they announced a program for retraining retired military personnel with a 24-week instruction course in classroom observation for mathematics and science teachers. The West Virginia Institute of Technology and West Virginia State College, in conjunction with the Charleston schools, initiated a program to take second-career adults through an accelerated program preparing them to teach in secondary and middle school positions. Most of the participants were coming out of Union Carbide Corporation, which announced extensive layoffs of former science and mathematics majors, who were the primary target of the retraining programs.

Some of the individuals participating in the program were more than 30 years out of their undergraduate and graduate degrees, and although their initial training was undoubtedly useful, applying it to a wide spectrum of courses at the middle school or high school level presented some problems. Although chemistry might have been a major, for example, the accompanying mathematics sometimes needed to be upgraded.

Follow-up studies with the interns indicated that they considered their professional education courses to be valuable and necessary. One intern said "no matter how well you know your subject matter, that does not mean you can go in and teach." All agencies involved in the project agreed that alternative delivery systems were important for attracting talent and experienced individuals into teaching. The follow-up study concluded that more formal assessment of content knowledge was needed prior to the end of the classroom training and that academic and field preparation and professional education were critical in retraining these second-career people for teaching positions (Nicholson, Securro, & Dockery, 1987).

Although alternative certification programs and induction variations seem to be on the increase, there is also some evidence that the area of vocational education has used something similar to alternative credentialing for many years. Bringing people in from business and industry or with other majors to teach in vocational education programs is a common practice. Kapes and Pawlowski (1974) researched the effectiveness of people coming into a vocational education setting from a traditional training program or from business and industry. They found no relationship between the years of industrial work experience and the result in student scores on the Ohio Trade Achievement Test. They did find, however, a positive relationship between the amount of college credit earned by the teacher and student achievement. Another study (Rumpf, 1954) found that teachers with more than 12 years of work experience had a negative correlation with teaching success. He concluded that more work experience did not make a better trade and industrial teacher. He found a positive relationship between the number of college credits earned and the better overall rating given by administrators. A study conducted by the New York State Department of Education (1978) comparing vocational and industrial teachers who had entered the teaching profession under revamped certification guidelines found that supervisors wanted individuals to have more classroom-management and human-relations training. School supervisors found that the nontraditionally trained business, industry, and agriculture teachers were sometimes more reluctant to do lesson plans and other paperwork that was required within the system. Erekson and Barr (1985) found that alternative certification programs in vocational education had greatly increased the need for inservice education programs. Working relationships with school districts and people supervising alternative-certified teachers seem to be a crucial element in both vocational education and traditional programs.

Alternative certification programs might hasten the reform of traditional teacher education programs by providing more cooperative college/school district programs. When school districts carry the responsibility to develop training programs, they often turn to traditional teacher education programs. When teacher-training institutions initiate the programs, they usually focus first on the internship or induction process in a school district. Haberman (1984) maintains "that extensive knowledge of subject matter is a necessary but not sufficient condition for effective teaching; and that teacher education is a legitimate professional preparation which should be improved rather than circumvented" (p. 1). Building the case for improved teacher education programs, says Haberman, will require teacher educators to play a middleman role between the school people who would make teacher training an on-site experience only and the arts and science faculty, who only want to require more courses to improve teaching. Negotiating this middle position will be difficult, but it will possibly be done under the aegis of alternative certification.

Gaps and Issues

Generally the areas of certification and licensure have not been adequately covered in education research. Good comparative data across state lines are missing, and few in-depth studies are evident in the literature. Alternative certification routes, the misassignment of teachers, and the impact of these new developments on traditional teacher-training programs need research attention.

STATE PROGRAM-APPROVAL STANDARDS AND PROCESSES

As early as the beginning of the twentieth century, states were starting to exercise control over those who entered the profession of teaching by approving teacher-preparation programs. This initiated a shift from licensure examinations to certification upon completion of an institution's state-approved teacher-preparation program (Stinnett, 1951). By 1952, only Massachusetts did not issue certificates based on program approval (Huggett & Stinnett, 1956). Although state program approval remains in some form in every state, the resurgence of individual testing has found its way into over 40 states (McCarthy et al., 1987). Thus, both program approval and individual assessment are required in almost all states.

A study of state standards for program approval of teacher education was conducted by the National Association of State Directors of Teacher Education and Certification in 1984 (Mastain & Roth, 1984). This study found that all states except Alaska, Delaware, Rhode Island, and Wyoming had developed their own standards for approval of teacher education programs. In some cases these are based on, or are similar to, NASDTEC standards. Wyoming was the only state reporting that it did not have a system for approval of teacher education programs.

What is the nature of these standards, who determines them, and to what extent are standards derived from research on teaching or teacher education? A survey by Roth (1988) requested state agencies to identify and provide information on these questions. Although each state had a particular process and groups involved, the state procedures were essentially the same.

In general, a group of individuals from across the state are convened to develop program-approval standards. The individuals who serve on these committees are usually representatives of special-interest groups such as the state teachers' associations, teacher education institutions, and school administrators. The California process described previously is somewhat atypical in that it employs a statewide survey, a state advisory panel, and a comprehensive set of activities.

The question of who develops state program-approval standards can be responded to in general as being representatives of education special-interest groups. These are individuals who have some connection with teaching and/or teacher education. They are not necessarily selected on the basis of their special knowledge of the research on teaching or teacher education.

The process of generating standards attempts to address the political dimensions of a state as the major concern. The linkage to research is tenuous at best, nonexistent at worst. The collective wisdom of the advisory groups is the primary basis for generation of program-approval standards. At times, efforts are made to review external sources such as learned societies in specialized areas and NASDTEC standards, and these are incorporated in the process.

A fundamental question is, Why is there an apparent lack of direct use of research on teacher education and teaching in the development of program-approval standards? One reason is that, in terms of research on teacher education standards, very little exists. As will be discussed in a subsequent section, little information is available on the effectiveness or predictive validity of program-approval standards in producing competent teachers. It is little wonder that this research has not played a major role in the development process.

A second reason why research perhaps has not been used to any great extent in the development of approval standards is that it is not a simple task. Translating research on effective teaching is complex, and there are few generalizations that can be made from the research that fit the broad format of program-approval standards.

One such attempt at sensitizing the state directors of teacher education and certification to the state of the art in research on teaching took place in 1982. The 54th Annual Meeting of the National Association of State Directors of Teacher Education and Certification was held in conjunction with the Institute for Research on Teaching at Michigan State University. The title of the conference, "Translating Research into Educational Personnel Development Systems," reflects the nature of this effort.

An important premise of the proceedings was that research cannot necessarily be translated into standards on a one-to-one basis. Research has demonstrated that, frequently, effective instruction is both context and subject specific (Roth, 1983). Instructional strategies might be appropriate to a particular grade range (e.g., K–4) or age range (e.g., ages 6 through 9) and a particular subject area (e.g., mathematics, social studies, reading). Generic program-approval standards are not appropriate to these specific research findings.

It can be argued that program approval should not reflect particular findings on effective teaching because of their specific nature. One strategy used is to require institutions to incorporate research in their programs through instruction and the curriculum. Requiring such evidence accommodates the need to integrate research into the teacher-preparation process; yet it avoids mandating specific findings, which are often inconclusive or of limited application.

Influence of NASDTEC

Although almost all states have developed their own standards, most have been influenced by the standards developed by NASDTEC. Although these are developed through a national association, they are not national standards, in that each state has the prerogative to adapt or adopt these as it deems appropriate. They may actually be viewed as guidelines for development of state standards. Only two jurisdictions, Vermont and the District of Columbia, for example, use NASDTEC standards for purposes of interstate certification. This further reflects the fact that NASDTEC standards are viewed as state standards.

A position statement adopted by NASDTEC reaffirms this premise. "The standards of any regional or national accrediting association, including NASDTEC, serve as guidelines or reference for individual states, not as mandates" (NASDTEC, 1976, p. 1). The 1984 survey by NASDTEC revealed that 29 states used NASDTEC standards or their equivalent (Mastain & Roth, 1984).

The NASDTEC standards are developed through a committee of NASDTEC members. This avoids the political aspects that states experience in their developmental process. An important aspect of the NASDTEC standards procedure is the relationship to learned societies. In the process of writing standards in the content areas (e.g., English, science), NASDTEC has traditionally conferred with the learned societies. This provides an opportunity to obtain input from scholars and practitioners in these fields who are familiar with the best of practice and research. The NASDTEC standards are thus likely to reflect the state of the art in any particular discipline. They are, of necessity, stated in very broad terms.

It should be noted that NASDTEC standards are not written to reflect specific research findings in a particular discipline. They do require, however, that the institution's program incorporate recent research findings in its curriculum. It also should be noted that NASDTEC periodically reviews its standards and updates them to be consistent with the current thinking of the learned societies and the profession at large.

Research on Effectiveness of Standards

In addition to the process of developing program-approval standards, there is the issue of studies on the effectiveness of these standards. What impact have these standards had on the profession and on the effectiveness of graduates? Roth's 1988 survey of states requested data of this nature. Several studies have been conducted on the effectiveness of alternative teacher-preparation and certification programs. These results were reported in the section on certification. Very little other research has been conducted to validate these standards, according to the survey.

A notable exception to the dearth of studies on program approval is the report, *Impact of the Program Approval Process in Maryland,* completed in 1982. This report provides a summary of weaknesses and strengths in programs. Areas of greatest concern include policies on admission, retention, exit, and follow-up of education majors. The most frequent area of concern under administration was the need for a clear, comprehensive statement of program purposes and objectives.

Approximately one-half of the institutions reviewed did not adequately develop systematic strategies for using follow-up data to evaluate and improve teacher education programs. Institutions need to develop means to obtain data from employers and others who work with graduates of the program. Other findings include the need to incorporate current research, to assist students in analysis of teaching behaviors, and to distinguish between development of teaching skills and analysis of teaching skills (Champion, 1982, pp. 9–11). These provide a sample of the types of findings reported in the impact study.

The concluding section of the report also provides insights into the perceptions of leaders in teacher education in that state. Several aspects are cited as having the most impact. The self-study process is cited most often as having a lasting effect on programs. Specific outcomes include increased communication with those outside the education department, formulation of long-range plans, and greater faculty involvement in the whole professional program. Feedback from teams of outside professionals is cited as a positive aspect, but the use of peers could be viewed as the least reliable aspect of the evaluation process. Administrators and faculty in academic departments acquired a better understanding of teacher education and the conditions for approval after the on-site team evaluation provided considerable leverage for programs to obtain resources to become more effective in teacher preparation (Champion, 1982).

Recent Trends and Influence

In a previous section, the movement toward alternative teacher preparation and certification was identified and analyzed. This is, essentially, a move away from professional education programs or to a limited role for university/college teacher education. Program-approval standards also are beginning to reflect this approach. Three states now have some type of limitation on the number of credit units an institution may require in its teacher-preparation program: California, Texas, and Virginia.

These states are not indicative of a national trend, because there are only three with actual limitations. In combination with the alternative route, however, this reflects a movement toward a reduced role for university-based teacher education programs in the preparation of the nation's teachers. This is analyzed in "Teacher Education: An Endangered Species?" (Roth, in press), an article whose title reflects the potential seriousness of the situation.

To some extent, there is a direct link between this movement and research on teaching and teacher education. It may be surmised that much of this activity is politically motivated and is generated by legislators and governors seeking recognition in the reform of education. It also may be concluded that this effort reflects the lack of a body of knowledge in teaching and the apparent lack of evidence on the effectiveness of teacher education programs. The dearth of research on standards has been documented. The research on effectiveness of program graduates will be reviewed later. The authors were unable to locate any research on the impact, either positive or negative, of the limitations on the professional preparation of teachers.

Another current activity in the profession is the effort by the Holmes Group (1986) and the Carnegie Forum on Education and the Economy (1986). The impact of these efforts has yet to be determined, because they are still in the early stages of development. These are both highly research-focused activities, and it is anticipated that the role of research in development of programs and standards will increase, due to these projects. There is the potential influence of the Holmes Group on program approval and of the Carnegie Forum on a national board or state certification, due to the prestige of these groups and due also to the continuing development of their programs and the pressure on states and programs to provide evidence of their effectiveness. A detailed analysis of their possible impact has been developed by the Association of Teacher Educators (1986).

NATIONAL ACCREDITATION STANDARDS

The history of national program-approval standards dates back to the era of normal schools. The American Normal School Association (ANSA) was established in 1858 to improve the normal-school curriculum and standardize admission requirements. In 1885, the association appointed the first committee to formally "prepare a report on the curricula and methods of teaching in the different normal schools and to discover what concerned action the normal schools of the United States should take in order to raise the standards and increase the efficiency of their work" (Frazier, 1935).

In 1899 a committee of the ANSA reported on courses of study for 2-, 3-, and 4-year normal-school programs based upon four requisites that are the minimum requirements for a true normal school which has its place as a professional school (NEA, 1899). In 1923, the American Association of Teachers Colleges (AATC) adopted a list of nine minimum standards for normal schools and teacher colleges (Maxwell, 1923).

In 1946 the NEA created the National Commission on Teacher Education and Professional Standards (NCTEPS) as the official agency of the organized teaching profession to establish standards for teacher-education institutions and bring about the enforcement of those standards (Conference on Accrediting, 1951). In 1951 a meeting was held and attended by representatives of AACTE, NCTEPS, NASDTEC, and the Council of Chief State School Officers (CCSSO). A proposal for the establishment of a National Council for Accreditation of Teacher Education was approved (Conference on Accrediting, 1951).

NCATE standards have been developed through committee processes at the national level. Individuals with specialized expertise in teacher education programs, research on teacher education, and related areas are selected for development of standards. This is particularly true for the *unit accreditation standards* adopted in 1987. The NCATE's purpose statement indicates it provides a mechanism for voluntary peer regulation of the professional education unit (NCATE, 1987).

The current NCATE standards were developed over a 2-year period, between 1983 and 1985:

NCATE's Committee on Standards was expanded to include other educators with relevant research and practitioner expertise. The proposed changes were shared with constituent organizations, associate members, all representatives of NCATE, and accredited institutions for the purpose of study and comment. Professional organizations, institutions, and individuals were encouraged to contribute to the development of these standards. (NCATE, 1987, p. 11).

A description and analysis of the reform of the NCATE can be found in an article by its executive director (Gollnick & Kunkel, 1986).

The NCATE also utilizes a different process for the development (actually acceptance) of standards in the specialty studies (content areas or disciplines). In this instance, NCATE requests learned societies or professional specialty organizations to develop standards for their particular areas. The Specialty Areas Studies Board approves guidelines from these associations for use in the program-approval process. These guidelines are thus developed by individuals with specialized expertise and knowledge of research and the best of practice in their respective fields.

NCATE standards are ostensibly developed on the basis of current knowledge and research. NCATE accreditation indicates that the professional education unit meets standards of excellence that reflect nationally accepted criteria based upon research and recognized professional best practice (NCATE, 1987).

Studies of Accreditation

Only a few major studies of accreditation have been written. These include Timothy Stinnett's *The Accreditation of Institutions for Teacher Preparation* (1951); George Overby's *A Critical Review of Selected Issues Involved in the Establishment and Functioning of the National Council for Accreditation of Teacher Education from its Origin Through 1965* (1966); John Mayor and Willis Schwartz's *Accreditation in Teacher Education: Its Influence on Higher Education* (1965); Chris Wheeler's *NCATE: Does it Matter?* (1980); and Richard Roames's dissertation *Accreditation in Teacher Education: A History of the Development of Standards Utilized by the National Council for Accreditation of Teacher Education* (1987). A study by Roth (1989) on the impact of the NCATE is as yet unpublished.

An issue related to the impact of the NCATE on programs is the extent to which standards are flexible and provide for innovation and flexibility. An analysis of this issue by Thurman provides a distinction between *flexible* and *alternative* programs. An alternative program "has two or more competing programs to prepare teachers to assume the same role," whereas a flexible program "calls for a basic program to be followed by all prospective teachers, with variations built in to allow for particular needs" (Thurman, 1974, p. 6).

Thurman's premise is that institutions are "expected to state in explicit terms the objectives of the programs and to design curriculum to accomplish these objectives . . . thus, the standards support the single program concept, not the multiple program or alternative approach, within an institution" (Thurman, 1974, pp. 6–7). On the other hand, "nothing in the standards precludes an institution from developing flexible approaches for accomplishing stated goals" (Thurman, 1974, p. 7).

The NCATE specifically addresses the issue of diversity in its background statement: "A deliberate attempt has been made in these standards to encourage diversity, imagination, and innovation in institutional planning . . . the NCATE standards as now organized may not provide the best vehicle for assessing a unit that is experimenting and/or undergoing extensive changes" (NCATE, 1987, p. 9).

Policy studies suggest that NCATE does not encourage program alternatives but does provide for flexibility in the means of achieving objectives within programs. Little research examined the extent to which innovation and experimentation have been stifled, allowed to develop, or encouraged by NCATE standards or state standards.

Another issue of interest is the extent to which the NCATE has influenced the states through acceptance of the council for assurance of certificates to out-of-state applicants. This is not the same as reciprocity, in which states agree to accept each other's credentials or approved program graduates through the granting of an initial regular certificate. Two studies provide information on this degree of influence by the NCATE. The NASDTEC manual reports that seven states utilize NCATE standards to some extent for purposes of interstate certification (Mastain & Roth, 1984).

A more recent study by Behling indicates that a

total of twenty-five jurisdictions will either grant automatic certification or grant automatic certification with conditions to an individual who has completed an NCATE-approved teacher preparation program. Seven jurisdictions indicated that they will grant a certificate without transcript analysis of credit count requirements when an individual has completed an NCATE-approved teacher preparation program. . . . Eighteen jurisdictions indicated that they will grant automatic certification under certain conditions. (Behling, 1986, p. 1)

These findings suggest that the NCATE is playing an increasing role in interstate certification. This has important implications for the profession and the influence of the council.

An examination of the contrasting roles of national accreditation (NCATE) and state program approval provides a context for understanding the emerging relationship between the NCATE and the states. The states, of course, have regulatory authority, which supports their program-approval responsibility. The standards they set thus have the effect of law, because they are state regulations and the states have the power to enforce penalties regarding them.

National accreditation, on the other hand, is a voluntary process for purposes of national recognition and program renewal. The NCATE's standards, thus, do not have any enforcement authority or penalties to support them. The NCATE's ability to bring about change emanates from its influence, rather than from any power or authority.

The states have responsibility for the approval of programs that operate within their jurisdictions under public protection laws of their states. Given this, states cannot fully delegate the authority for development and enforcement of standards. They cannot abrogate this responsibility and allow other agencies

such as voluntary accreditation to take its place. States can, however, work collaboratively with the NCATE and even use its process in place of their own. Ultimate decision making, however, resides with the states.

The NCATE has developed a mechanism by which it can work more closely with the states reviewing programs for the preparation of educational personnel. As part of its new structure, the NCATE has created a system whereby states can be *recognized*. If a state is recognized by the NCATE, the institutions within the state that are seeking NCATE accreditation need not have certain content areas (specialized studies) reviewed by NCATE, because state review will suffice. This applies to recognition under types one and two only, as described next.

There are four types of NCATE–state relationships in the state recognition system of the NCATE. These differ in terms of the nature of the standards and teams used.

Option One—Under this option, state program approval is conducted separately but concurrently and cooperatively with the NCATE. The procedure consists of two separate teams: One represents the NCATE and uses its unit standards; the other represents the state and uses state standards for program approval.

Option Two—Option two allows state approval to be conducted by a single team jointly selected by the NCATE and the state. This team votes on state approval, based on state standards, and national accreditation, based on NCATE unit standards.

Option Three—Option three allows state approval and NCATE accreditation to be conducted by a single team with common votes, the team being jointly selected by the NCATE and the state. NCATE unit standards are used for both state approval and NCATE accreditation.

Option Four—Under this option, the state uses NCATE accreditation as a basis for approval for those institutions choosing NCATE accreditation; for those not seeking NCATE accreditation, the states uses NCATE unit standards as the basis for approval of the programs within the state.

The implications of this new element in the NCATE for standards in the profession are becoming more evident. As of fall 1988, 18 states were recognized or had applied to be recognized by the NCATE. In some cases, such as Michigan, the state standards for program approval are almost identical with NCATE standards. In general, NCATE standards have an influence on standards in these states. It is anticipated that the number of states seeking NCATE recognition will continue to increase and to reflect the influence of the NCATE standards.

Effectiveness of the NCATE

A published interview with a former executive director of the NCATE provides some insight into the previous status of NCATE standards and their influence on the profession. According to Lyn Gubser, in 1983 there was a backlash among some land-grant institutions regarding the use of classroom teachers on visitation teams and other issues (Gubser, 1983, p. 17). This threatened the credibility and viability of the NCATE. Research has not been conducted on the role and effectiveness of team members from different constituent groups.

The ease of attaining accreditation is an important factor in assessing the strength of accreditation and the profession. One gauge of this element is the denial rate for accreditation by the NCATE. It is only one factor, because weak institutions might not even apply in the first place. Data reveal that in the mid-1970s fewer than 5 percent of the institutions reviewed by the NCATE were denied accreditation in one or more programs. In 1978 that figure rose to almost 25 percent, and in 1979 the figure slipped back to 5 percent (Gubser, 1983, p. 7). This perhaps reflects the reason for the backlash and a response to it.

In 1984–1985, the NCATE failed to approve one or more programs at 24 percent of the institutions applying for accreditation, more than double the denial rate of 1983–1984, which was 11 percent (Roth, 1986b). The 1982 denial rate was only 6.7 percent.

Part of the recent increase in the denial rate is related to the redesign of the NCATE that began in 1983 and that led to the new standards adopted in 1985. These were first implemented on a pilot basis in 1987. One observer noted in 1985 that, with the standards in the back of their minds, the council was being hard-nosed in applying the current standards (Currence, 1985). There is thus some evidence that the NCATE is beginning to have a greater influence on the profession and is more rigorous in applying its standards.

An area of importance is the nature of findings of NCATE reviews. This provides insights into the nature of teacher-preparation programs, albeit only those seeking national accreditation. A review of the NCATE annual reports in the years preceding the redesign, 1979–1982, provides this information. Data were reported in terms of frequency of weaknesses cited in accreditation denials and the most common weaknesses for all programs, for both basic and advanced programs.

Although program weaknesses varied from year to year, some consistencies are discernible. During this period, the previous standard 6.1 (evaluation of graduates) appeared to be the most frequently cited weakness in programs denied accreditation. It was the most frequent weakness in programs denied and for all programs in 1980, 1981, and 1982. Standard 6.2 (use of evaluation data) appeared to be the second most frequently cited weakness for both those denied and all programs. These findings parallel the data on state program approval reported by Maryland and cited earlier. Other standards often cited as weaknesses include 6.3 (long-range planning), 5.2 (instructional media center), and 5.1 (library). In 1981 and 1982, standard 2.1.1 (multicultural education) often appeared as a weakness in both those denied in some categories and those fully accredited.

Little research has been done on standards for advanced or graduate programs. The NCATE study of weaknesses cited provides some insights into graduate programs in relation to standards. As with basic programs, the most frequently cited weakness is 6.1 (evaluation of graduates), which was cited most frequently in all four years from 1979 through 1982. Standards

6.2 (use of evaluation data) and 6.3 (long-range planning) also appear frequently. Interestingly, multicultural education appeared as the number two weakness and the number one strength in frequency of citation in advanced programs in 1982.

In terms of the redesigned standards, results of the 1987 pilot study revealed the faculty-load standard was the most often unmet by the 14 pilot institutions. At the basic level, other standards unmet by about one-third of the 14 units included design of the curriculum, professional studies, and relationships with graduates. At the advanced (graduate) level, other standards unmet by one-fourth of the units included design of the curriculum, relationships with graduates, and faculty qualifications.

One of the most extensive studies of national accreditation is the 1980 analysis by Wheeler. Some of the strengths cited include the following: (a) NCATE generally uncovers major problems in a program of professional education; (b) NCATE denies accreditation to some of the worst programs of professional education. NCATE denial represents a clear signal to the public that a program is inferior (as judged by NCATE standards); (c) institutions accredited by the Council generally benefitted in that they attempted to modify some parts of their programs in response to NCATE concerns; and (d) denial of accreditation has led to some modifications in programs (Wheeler, 1980, p. 5).

A critical weakness cited is that the team members and the council "generally look to see whether a task or function is being performed at all, not, as the NCATE standards require, whether it is being performed well" (Wheeler, 1980, p. 6). This is referred to as a *presence-or-absence* approach, as opposed to an *in-depth* approach. Concerns relate to vagueness of standards, lack of definition of key terms, and lack of suggestions for evidence needed to demonstrate that standards have been met (Wheeler, 1980, p. 6).

Several serious concerns were raised in the Wheeler study, including the following: (a) many requirements were not evaluated; (b) some standards were interpreted in favor of the institution; (c) standards were applied inconsistently; (d) the presence-or-absence approach resulted in accreditation of some programs as deficient as those denied; (e) whether NCATE's stamp of accreditation is a meaningful indicator of quality was questioned; and (f) NCATE's effect on program quality is very limited. NCATE's power base and professional authority proved weaker than the economic or legal authority exercised by other "levers of power" such as alumni support, legislative action, and institutional competition (Wheeler, 1980, pp. 6–8).

The redesigners of the NCATE, beginning in 1983, have attempted to respond to these concerns. Major changes in the standards, including criteria for compliance and definitions of key terms, have been introduced. The new standards also include substantial requirements in the preconditions. In addition, the NCATE has renewed support from the Council of Chief State School Officers.

The first pilot institutions evaluated under the new standards were visited in spring 1987. Data on the effectiveness of the standards should not be expected for some time. A study by Roth (1989) investigates the impact of the new system on the institutions participating in the pilot study.

Findings reveal 11 categories of outcomes, as follows: (a) program cohesiveness, (b) campus collaboration, (c) comprehensive assessment, (d) increased understanding of program, (e) use of research, (f) faculty team building, (g) increased resources, (h) practitioner linkage, (i) renewal and direction, (j) improved image, and (k) tighter governance and management. Observers of the process indicate that programs are making significant changes as a result of the new standards.

Effectiveness of Standards in Relation to Graduates

Studies of the effectiveness of graduates are indirectly linked to the nature and rigor of standards, both certification and program-approval. Studies of graduates of alternative programs were reported in a previous section.

Some other studies have investigated whether teacher education program graduates are better prepared than those who have not had teacher education. These studies have shown on a variety of measures that those who have teacher education *are* better prepared to teach (Erekson & Barr, 1985; Fisher & Feldmann, 1985; Greenberg, 1983; Haberman, 1984; Hawk, Coble, & Swanson, 1984; Olsen, 1985; Williamson, 1985).

It is evident from this review that research on teacher education standards is quite limited. The limited number of studies is consistent for all categories, certification and program approval/accreditation, state and national. Research has been isolated and disjointed, and there is a lack of a comprehensive research program on standards at the state and national levels. An ethos of inquiry is not prevalent in the community of decision makers who set standards. Studies that have been conducted focus mostly on the overall impact of the standard, rather than on validation of standards in relation to particular areas of competence or outcomes. Although small in number, some studies do reveal several important insights.

NATIONAL CERTIFICATION

An effort by states to maximize the interstate mobility of qualified educational personnel through an interstate certification agreement was initiated in the states in 1965 with federal funding. By 1968, through cooperative agreements, Maryland, Massachusetts, California, and New York had entered into formal agreements of cooperation on certification matters. By 1988 this had increased to 38 states, with interstate education laws on the books permitting them to work with a cooperative certification network, the Interstate Certification Project. For many years this program was funded by the U.S. Office of Education, Teacher Corps, and housed at the New York State Education Department. After federal funding was dropped in 1980, the project was continued as the Interstate Certification Compact. Recently, it has become affiliated with the NASDTEC. In an interview, Helen Hartle, former project director in the New York State Education Department, commented that the need for cooperation in this area was still very much alive and that very little research, if any, had ever been conducted on the process.

In mid-1987, NASDTEC, along with the Contract Adminis-

trators Association of the Interstate Certification Compact, signed an agreement with a holding house for official transcripts entitled ACADEM to establish and maintain a credential status clearinghouse. The objective of the association is to organize a central repository of names of individuals whose applications for state certification/licensure have been denied or whose license/certificates have been revoked/annulled/suspended for cause. Because this effort is in the initial stages, it is not likely that any research has been conducted or surveys made of number of records being tracked by this organization.

The establishment of the National Board for Professional Teaching Standards by the Carnegie Corporation and the subsequent work that will follow on the creation of the national certification examination has many implications for state officials responsible for teacher-training programs and for the states themselves. In New York and Massachusetts there are organized efforts on the part of state legislators to mandate support for the Carnegie recommendations.

The national board idea, along with restructured schools, alternative certification, interstate certification, and reciprocity in general, is void of research studies that can be located, but this arena will undoubtedly be producing serious research efforts. The National Board for Professional Teaching Standards will provide a schedule of research steps and efforts that will be administered by the board, leading to a national teachers' examination. Currently this work involves subcontract activity in California and Connecticut.

CONCLUSIONS AND IMPLICATIONS

In relation to state program approval, the studies that have been conducted show that programs do change as a result of the state program-approval process. The extent and nature of these changes is not very clear, but they do lead to program improvements. The state program-approval process seldom leads to nonapproval, but this is not the only indicator of the impact of the process. A fundamental purpose is to provide for growth and improvement, and there is some evidence of this. For example, leaders in education in Maryland suggested formulation of long-range plans as an important outcome of the process. NCATE reports reveal this as one of the more frequently cited weaknesses; thus, this is an important contribution.

Studies of the NCATE have been somewhat more extensive than those of state program approval. These are basically descriptive studies, although the efforts by Wheeler (1980) and Roth (1989) are impact- and policy-oriented as well. In the past, serious questions have been raised about the effectiveness of the NCATE. The denial rate has increased again in recent years, as one indication of renewed rigor. Study of the impact on programs of the new standards is in its early stages, but preliminary results show positive and significant program revisions. The standard focusing on the knowledge base for programs has been an important element in this revision process.

The influence of standards on programs and the profession may be viewed in terms of impact on quality, on quantity or supply, and on the question of how much control or regulation is needed. The impact on quality has been discussed in preceding sections. The impact on supply has been the subject of some study, but more is needed, particularly as it relates to the recruitment, retention, and graduation from teacher education programs of persons from underrepresented groups in teaching such as blacks and Hispanics. The impact on minorities has been documented, but overall effects of testing on the supply of teachers are not clear. In California, for example, students entering teacher-preparation programs must achieve a grade point average above the mean grade point average in their major area of university study. How has this affected overall supply? What about impact on minorities in this highly multicultural state? The relationships between quality and quantity and the influence of standards warrant further research.

Policy studies might clarify the issue of how much control is necessary. When does regulation stifle creativity and experimentation? Should programs be deregulated and accountable only for outcomes? Should standards avoid relating to inputs and processes and focus on outcomes? Research and policy studies have not provided the profession with much to assist in decision making in this regard.

Another set of questions relates to the linkage between and among standards such as the relationship between state certification regulations and state program-approval standards. Are they complementary or redundant? What are their relative contributions to the development of effective programs and graduates of these programs?

Interesting relationships have developed between the NCATE and the state standards. The NCATE now recognizes specialty-area standards in the same areas as NASDTEC subject area standards. How will this be reconciled, and what will be the effect on programs?

Related is the relationship between NCATE and the state in terms of standards. NCATE now recognizes states and accepts their review of specialty areas as part of the NCATE review. What influence will this have on the development of state standards? Will this lead to greater uniformity or greater quality control?

With the growing movement toward tests for certification and at exit from teacher-preparation programs, the relationship of tests to program approval becomes more interesting. If states have appropriate and effective examinations for certification, what is the purpose of program approval? This is particularly of interest when performance tests are integrated into induction programs for beginning teachers. Are dual standards necessary? Strong arguments can be presented on both sides, but the need and opportunity for research are evident.

The review of studies in this chapter indicates a focus almost entirely on undergraduate teacher-preparation programs. There is very little research on the effectiveness of standards for graduate studies. Reports on results of NCATE reviews provide some insights, but of a very limited scope. With the proposals for advanced preparation of teachers, as provided for in both the Holmes Group and Carnegie forum reports, this area could become of increasing importance in the future.

References

Adelman, N. E. (1986). *An exploratory study of teacher alternative certification and retraining programs* (U.S. Department of Education, Data Analysis Support Center, Contract No. 300-85-0103). Washington, DC: Policy Studies Associates.

American Association of Colleges for Teacher Education. (1987). *Teacher education policy in the states: A 50-state survey of legislative and administrative actions* (6th ed.). Washington, DC: Author.

Anrig, G. R. (1987). Teacher testing in American education: Useful but no shortcut to excellence. *Conference proceedings: What is the appropriate role of testing in the teaching profession?* Washington, DC: National Education Association.

Association of Teacher Educators. (1986). *Visions of reform: Implications for the education profession.* Reston, VA: Author.

Baratz, J. E. (1986). *Black participation in the teaching pool.* Commissioned paper for the Carnegie Forum's Task Force on Teaching as a Profession. Princeton, NJ: Educational Testing Service.

Behling, H. (1986). *The use of NCATE-approved programs for automatic certification.* Baltimore: Maryland State Department of Education.

Berliner, D. C. (1984). Making the right changes in preservice teacher education. *Phi Delta Kappan, 66*(2), 94–96.

Buccino, A. (1987, December 4). News release. Athens, GA: Southern Regional Consortium of Colleges of Education.

California Commission on Teacher Credentialing. (1986). *New designs for professional preparation, recommended redesign of program evaluation.* Sacramento, CA: Author.

California Commission on Teacher Credentialing. (1987). *The effectiveness of the teacher trainee program: An alternative route into teaching in California.* Sacramento, CA: Author.

Carnegie Forum on Education and the Economy, Task Force on Teaching as a Profession. (1986). *A nation prepared: Teachers for the 21st century.* New York: Author.

Champion, R. (1982) *Impact of the program approval process in Maryland.* Baltimore: Maryland State Department of Education.

Conference on Accrediting. (1951, April 27–29). *Minutes of the conference on accrediting.* Washington, DC: National Education Association.

Cornett, L. M. (1988). *Alternative teacher certification programs: Are they working?* Atlanta: Southern Regional Education Board.

Cross, L. H., Impara, J. E., Frary, R. B., & Jaeger, R. M. (1984). A comparison of three methods for establishing minimum standards on the national teacher examinations. *Journal of Educational Measurement, 21*(2), 113–129.

Currence, C. (1985). Teaching training standards: Change and debate. *Education Week, 5* (9), 1.

Denemark, G. W. (1972). Teacher education: Repair, reform or revolution? In P. A. Olson, L. Freeman, & J. Bowman (Eds.), *Education for 1984 and after.* Lincoln, NE: University of Nebraska.

Education Commission of the States. (1987). *States requiring testing for initial certification of teachers.* (Clearinghouse Notes). Denver: Author.

Elsbree, W. S. (1939). *The American teacher.* Boston: American Book.

Erekson, T. L., & Barr, L. (1985). Alternative credentialing: Lessons from vocational education. *Journal of Teacher Education 36* (3), 16–19.

Evertson, C. M., Hawley, W. D., & Zlotnik, M. (1985). Making a difference in educational quality through teacher education. *Journal of Teacher Education, 36*(3), 2–12.

Fisher, R. L., & Feldmann, M. E. (1985). Some answers about the quality of teacher education students. *Journal of Teacher Education, 36*(3), 37–40.

Frazier, B. W. (1935). Establishment and growth of normal schools and departments in colleges and universities, from 1839 to 1865. *National Survey of the Education of Teachers.* Washington DC: U.S. Government Printing Office.

Futrell, M. H., & Robinson S. P. (1986). Testing teachers: An overview of NEA's position, policy and involvement. *Journal of Negro Education, 55*(3), 397–404.

Garcia, P. A. (1986). *A study on teacher competency testing and test validity with implications for minorities and the results and implications of the use of the Pre-Professional Skills Test (PPST) as a screening device for entrance into teacher education programs in Texas* (National Institute of Education, NIE Grant No. NIE-G-85-0004). Edinburg, TX: Pan American University.

Garibaldi, A. M. (1987). Recruitment, admissions and standards: Black teachers and the Holmes and Carnegie reports. *Metropolitan Education,* (4), 17–23.

Gideonse, H. D. (1984). *An analysis of the proposed New Jersey alternative route to teacher certification.* Detailed testimony before the New Jersey State Board of Education. Cincinnati, OH: University of Cincinnati.

Goertz, M. E., Ekstrom, R. B., & Coley, R. J. (1984). *The impact of state policy on entrance into the teaching profession* (Final report, NIE Grant No. G83-0073, submitted to the National Institute of Education, Educational Policy Organization). Princeton, NJ: Educational Testing Service.

Gollnick, D., & Kunkel, R. (1986). The reform of national accreditation. *Phi Delta Kappan, 68*(5), 310–314.

Gray, D., & Lynn, D. H. (1988). *EW teachers, EHER teachers: A report on two initiatives in New Jersey.* Washington, DC: Council for Basic Education.

Greenberg, J. D. (1983). The case for teacher education: Open and shut. *Journal of Teacher Education, 34*(2), 2–5.

Greer, P. R. (1987). *Opening alternative routes to teaching: A strategy for increasing the pool of qualified teachers* (White paper, Office of the Department of Education, Under Secretary for Intergovernmental and Interagency Affairs). Washington, DC: U.S. Department of Education.

Gubser, L. (1983). No one wants to pull the plug on teacher-training programs. *Education Week, 2*(6), 7, 17.

Guyton, E. M. (1988). *Becoming a teacher: Description and comparisons of the first year of teaching for teachers who experienced three different teacher preparation/induction experiences.* Atlanta: Georgia State University, College of Education, Teacher Recruitment and Internship Project for Success.

Haberman, M. (1984). *An evaluation of the rationale for required teacher education: Beginning teachers with and without teacher preparation* (prepared for the National Commission on Excellence in Teacher Education). Milwaukee, WI: University of Wisconsin, Division of Urban Outreach.

Hall, G. E. (1984). *A hindsight analysis of the national agenda for teacher education research for the 1980s* (R&D Report No. 3193). Austin, TX: University of Texas, Research and Development Center for Teacher Education.

Hammond, L. D., & Green, J. (1988, Summer) Teacher quality and education quality. *College Board Review,* (148), 17–23, 39–41.

Hawk, P. P., Coble, C., & Swanson, M. (1984). *Certification requirements and their relationships to mathematics teachers' knowledge, professional skills, and students' achievement.* Greenville, NC: East Carolina University.

Hawley, W. (1986a). A critical analysis of the Holmes Group's proposals for reforming teacher education. *Journal of Teacher Education, 37*(4), 47–51.

Hawley, W. (1986b). *Notes on the redesign of teacher education.* Denver: Education Commission of the States.

Hawley, W. (1989) *Directions of teacher education in the United States.* Paris: Organization for Economic and Community Development.

Hazi, H. M. (1985). *The third wave: Competency tests for administrators.* Denver: Education Commission of the States.

Holmes, B. J. (1988). Why black teachers are essential. *Black Issues in Higher Education, 5*(11), 17–18.

Holmes Group. (1986). *Tomorrow's teachers.* East Lansing, MI: Author.

Huggett, E. J., & Stinnett, T. M. (1956). *Professional problems of teachers.* New York: Macmillan.

Huling-Austin, L. (1988, April). *A synthesis of research on teacher induction programs and practices.* Paper presented at the meeting of the American Educational Research Association, New Orleans.

Johnson-Moore, S., & Nelson, N. C. W. (1987). Conflict and compatibility in visions of reform. *Journal of Educational Policy, 1*(1), 67–80.

Joyce, B., & Clift, R. (1984). The Phoenix agenda: Essential reform in teacher education. *Educational Research, 13,* 5–18.

Kapes, J. T., & Pawlowski, V. (1974). Characteristics of vocational-technical instructors and their relationships to student shop achievement. *Vocational development study series monograph No. 17.* University Park, PA: Pennsylvania State University.

Kloosterman, P., Woods, C. J., & Matkin, J. (1987). Attracting minority teachers in science, mathematics, foreign language and computing. *Metropolitan Education,* (4), 24–29.

Lareau, A. A. (1986). A comparison of professional examinations in seven fields: Implications for the teaching profession. *Elementary School Journal, 86*(4), 553–569.

Larson, M. S. (1977). *The rise of professionalism: A sociological analysis.* Berkeley, CA: University of California Press.

Leading the way—Report of the special commission on the conditions of teaching—Massachusetts responds, empowering schools and teachers. (1987). Boston: Massachusetts State Legislature.

Mastain, R. K. (1988). *Manual on certification and preparation of educational personnel in the United States.* Sacramento, CA: National Association of State Directors of Teacher Education and Certification.

Mastain, R. K., & Roth, R. A. (1984). *Manual on certification and preparation of educational personnel in the United States.* Sacramento, CA: National Association of State Directors of Teacher Education and Certification.

Mayor, J. R., & Schwartz, W. G. (1965). *Accreditation in teacher education: Its influence on higher education.* Washington DC: National Commission on Accrediting.

Maxwell, G. W. (1923). Report of committee on American teachers' colleges. *Addresses and proceedings of the sixty-first annual meeting* (pp. 483–484). Washington, DC: National Education Association.

McCarthy, N. M., Turner, D. D., & Hall, G. C. (1987). *Competency testing for teachers: A status report* (Policy Issues Series No. 2, Consortium on Educational Policy Studies). Bloomington, IN: Indiana University, School of Education.

National Association of State Directors of Teacher Education and Certification. (1976). *Position statement.* Sacramento, CA: Author.

National Commission on Excellence in Education. (1983). *A nation at risk: The imperative for educational reform.* Washington, DC: U.S. Government Printing Office.

National Council for Accreditation of Teacher Education (1987). *NCATE standards, procedures, and policies for the accreditation of professional education units: The accreditation of professional education units for the preparation of professional school personnel at basic and advanced levels.* Washington, DC: Author.

National Education Association, Report of the Committee on Normal Schools. (1899). *Journal of proceedings and addresses of the thirty-eighth annual meeting* (pp. 836–837). Washington, DC: Author.

National Education Association, Research Division. (1957). The status of the American public school teacher. *Research bulletin, 35*(5), 63.

New Jersey Department of Education, Office of Teacher Recruitment and Placement. (1986). *Report to colleges, 1986.* Trenton, NJ: Author.

New York State Department of Education, Bureau of Occupational Education. (1978). *A survey of the employment and performance of non-traditionally trained teachers of agriculture and trade and industrial education: Final report.* Albany, NY: Author. (ERIC Document Reproduction Service No. ED 173 661)

Nicholson, K., Securro, S., & Dockery, R. (1987). *Field-based training program: Final report.* West Virginia Institute of Technology, Montgomery, WV; West Virginia State College, Institute, WV; and West Virginia College of Graduate Studies, Institute, WV.

Olsen, D. G. (1985). The quality of prospective teachers: Education vs. noneducation graduates. *Journal of Teacher Education, 36*(5), 56–59.

Overby, G. R. (1966). *A critical review of selected issues involved in the establishment and functioning of the national council for accreditation of teacher education from its origin through 1965.* Unpublished doctoral dissertation, Florida State University, Tallahassee.

Pipho, C. (1986). States move reform closer to reality. *Phi Delta Kappan, 68*(4), K1–K8.

Ponzio, R. (1985). [Guest editor's introduction to special issue on research in teaching]. *Teacher Education Quarterly, 16*(6).

Popp, A. L., & Wallace, G. W. (1988). *Second career teacher candidates honored at Fort Bragg.* News Release. New York: National Executive Service Corporation.

Roames, R. (1987). *Accreditation in teacher education: A history of the development of standards utilized by the National Council for Accreditation of Teacher Education.* Unpublished doctoral dissertation, University of Akron, OH.

Robinson, S. P. (1987). The NEA perspective on the role of testing in the profession. *Conference proceedings: What is the appropriate role of testing in the teaching profession?* Washington, DC: National Education Association.

Robinson, V. (1985). *Making do in the classroom: The misassignment of teachers.* Washington, DC: Council for Basic Education and the American Federation of Teachers.

Rosenfeld, M., Skurnik, L. S., & Thornton, R. F. (1986). *Analysis of the professional functions of teachers: Relationships between job functions and the NTE core battery.* Princeton, NJ: Educational Testing Service.

Roth, R. A. (1983). Translating research into educational personnel development systems. *Proceedings of the 54th Annual Conference.* East Lansing, MI: National Association of State Directors of Teacher Education and Certification.

Roth, R. A. (1986a). Emergency certificates, misassignment of teachers, and other dirty little secrets. *Phi Delta Kappan, 67*(10), 725–727.

Roth, R. A. (1986b). *Teaching and teacher education: Implementing reform.* Bloomington, IN: Phi Delta Kappa Educational Foundation.

Roth, R. A. (1988). *Evidence of effectiveness and use of research in state certification and program approval standards.* Unpublished manuscript, California State University, Long Beach.

Roth, R. A. (in press). Teacher education: An endangered species? *Phi Delta Kappan.*

Roth, R. A. (1989). *NCATE: Institutional perspectives from the pilot studies.* Unpublished manuscript, California State University, Long Beach.

Roth, R. A., & Lutz, P. B. (1986). *Alternative certification: Issues and perspectives.* Charleston, WV: Appalachia Educational Laboratory.

Rowe, J. (1985, December 27). How one state cleared away roadblocks to the teaching profession. *The Christian Science Monitor,* 17–18.

Rumpf, E. L. (1954). *A basis for the selection of vocational industrial education teachers for employment in Pennsylvania.* Unpublished doctoral dissertation, The Pennsylvania State University, University Park.

Schuttenberg, E. M. (1983). Preparing the educated teacher for the 21st century. *Journal of Teacher Education, 34*(4), 14–18.

Shepard, L. A., & Kreitzer, A. A. (1987). The Texas teacher test. *Educational Researcher, 16*(6), 22–31.

Smith, D. C., Nystrand, R., Ruch, C., Gideonse, H., & Carlson, K. (1985). Alternative certification: A position statement of AACTE. *Journal of Teacher Education, 36*(3), 24.

Smith, G. D. (1987). *The effects of competency testing on the supply of minority teachers.* Washington DC: The National Education Association and the Council of Chief State School Officers.

Stinnett, T. M. (1951). *The accreditation of institutions for teacher preparation.* Unpublished doctoral dissertation, University of Texas, Austin.

Thurman, R. (1974). *Flexibility in program planning and NCATE standards.* Washington DC: ERIC Clearinghouse on Teacher Education.

Weis, L. (1987). [Introduction to the special issue on the crisis in teaching]. *Journal of Educational Policy, 1*(1), 3–8.

Wheeler, C. W. (1980). *NCATE: Does it matter?* (Research Series No. 92). East Lansing, MI: Michigan State University, Institute for Research on Teaching.

Williamson, J. L. (1985). Teacher education/certification does make a difference. *Teacher Education and Practice, 2*(2), 5–10.

Wright, D. P., McKibbin, M., & Walton, P. (1987). *The effectiveness of the teacher trainee program: An alternative route into teaching in California.* Sacramento, CA: Commission on Teacher Credentialing.

· 9 ·

SYSTEMATIC ANALYSIS, PUBLIC POLICY-MAKING, AND TEACHER EDUCATION

Willis D. Hawley

PEABODY COLLEGE
VANDERBILT UNIVERSITY

Public policies adopted in the 1980s have had direct and unprecedented consequences for who will be allowed to teach and how they will be prepared. Although the making of teacher education policy is taking place in the context of multiple reports and studies, and although statistics are called upon frequently to justify the need for public action, it appears that most of the policies being adopted are not burdened by their fit with available knowledge or systematically developed theory. Moreover, the policies being implemented seldom call for experimentation and evaluation that might yield new knowledge. This chapter addresses three general questions. *First*, to what extent has systematic empirical analysis influenced public policy affecting teacher education? *Second*, why has systematic analysis played a relatively small role in shaping public policies affecting teacher education? And, *third*, if one wanted to increase the role of systematic analysis in the development of public policies affecting teacher education, what changes in the methods and presentation of analysis would need to occur? Because little previous research has addressed these questions, this chapter is organized so as to set the stage for further inquiry.

This chapter not only seeks to discover the role of systematic analysis in the development of public policies that directly shape teacher education, it also makes an implicit argument for greater application of such inquiry. Of course, systematic analysis can be misused, and sometimes such misuse is intentional. Moreover, policies that have not employed information and insight derived from systematic analysis can be wise and efficacious. Considerations other than knowledge, systematically derived or not, shape public policy. At its best, public policy is a statement of our values and, as such, often transcends the implication of "facts" or reason. Systematic analysis can help us decide what goals to pursue, but it is most useful in helping to clarify the nature of problems and to decide on the means of achieving the ends we seek.

THE EFFECTS OF SYSTEMATIC ANALYSIS ON TEACHER EDUCATION POLICY

The search for the effects of systematic analysis on teacher education policy requires that one know at least two things: *first*, how to distinguish systematic analysis from other sources of information and insight and, *second*, how to find it. Before turning to these matters, it seems necessary to specify what is meant by the term *teacher education policy* and to identify the public policy arenas and the general sources of influence with which this chapter is concerned.

Public Policies Affecting Teacher Education

The term *policy* describes those rules, statements of intent, and specified strategies that are formally adopted by legitimated individuals or agencies to guide collective action. Teacher education policy seeks to influence who shall teach; what prospective teachers know, are able to do, and value; and how the learning of teacher candidates is structured. The instruments through which policymakers seek to affect these outcomes include financial aid and other recruitment tools, vari-

The author is grateful for the comments of chapter reviewers Robert Egbert (University of Nebraska–Lincoln) and Penelope M. Earley (American Association of Colleges for Teacher Education).

ous screening tests and procedures, curriculum requirements, and mandated learning experiences. Any number of factors influence the decisions made about these matters, but this chapter is concerned with policies that are authoritatively issued by or on behalf of public officials with the purpose of shaping these decisions. Furthermore, the authoritative policies of concern here are those that influence what goes on in that aspect of the education of prospective teachers commonly called *preservice teacher preparation*.

Decision making and behavior by teacher educators, except those efforts teacher educators make to influence the formulation of public policies that affect them, are not dealt with in this chapter. It is important to recognize, however, that policy made is not policy implemented. To the chagrin of policymakers, the policies that are enacted into law or otherwise authoritatively issued are often only remotely reflected in the activities carried out under the name or within the scope of those policies. The reasons for this are many and have been explored extensively elsewhere (Bardach, 1977; Hargrove, 1975; Lipsky, 1980). Applied to teacher education, this proposition means that teacher educators and others whose practices are meant to be shaped by teacher education policy enjoy considerable discretion in how they implement the policies directed at them. This not only influences variations in what and how prospective teachers are taught, but also affects why certain policies are adopted rather than others and the character of those policies.

Because public policy affecting teachers is defined and reinterpreted by teacher educators and because public policy leaves many decisions about education to universities and colleges, which, in turn, leave many decisions to faculty, public policy defines only a small part of the formal learning experiences of prospective teachers. Nevertheless, teacher education is probably the most highly regulated course of study in colleges and universities. The fact that state governments believe that they should control teacher education in ways they do not think are appropriate with respect to other courses of study within universities and colleges tells a great deal about the vulnerability of teacher education both to policymakers and within institutions of higher education. Many teacher educators themselves are ambivalent about their role and the ways they have encouraged practitioners to view them. This vulnerability and these perceptions are important in explaining the politics of teacher education policy.

Policy Arenas and Influences Affecting Teacher Education

If teacher education policy deals with the characteristics and qualifications of who will be allowed to teach, and with the formal specification of what and how teachers are to learn about teaching, one can identify four more or less discreet *arenas* in which most such policies are formulated: state governments, local school systems, higher education governing boards, and the federal government. In addition, court decisions relating to testing, discrimination of various sorts, and other matters also affect teacher education, though usually less directly than other types of public policy.

Figure 9-1 seeks to provide a schematic overview of the

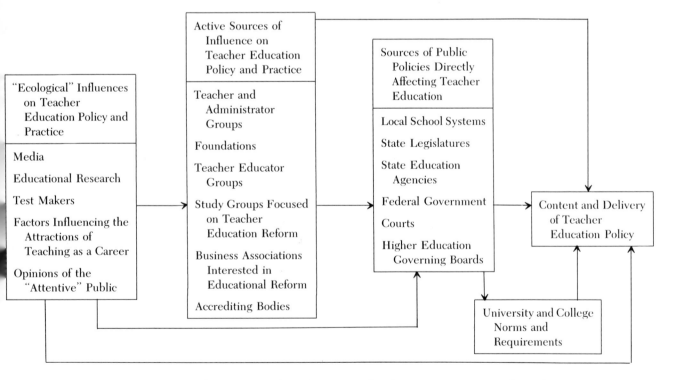

FIGURE 9–1. Patterns of Influence: Public Policies Directly Affecting Preservice Teacher Education

policy arenas and patterns of influence affecting public policies relating directly to teacher education. Although public policies in all of the policy arenas affect the quantity and quality of those who choose to participate in teacher education programs, as well as the content and processes teacher candidates experience, state policies have been the primary force in changing the characteristics of prospective teachers and what they are to know and be able to do before they are allowed to teach (Hawley, Austin, & Goldman, 1988). Thus, this search for the influence of systematic analysis on teacher education policy will focus on state-mandated policies and procedures.

Recognizing Systematic Analysis

Systematic analysis is not a very precise term. It cannot, for example, be found in dictionaries, and it is not a commonly accepted field of inquiry. *Systematic analysis* means empirically based efforts to describe or logically explain why and/or how things do or do not happen or to predict the consequences of a proposed course of action. Education-related policy analysis, which has received considerable methodological attention and has been the focus of inquiry (Mitchell, 1984), is one form of systematic analysis, but it is explicitly aimed at solving problems and evaluating alternatives (MacCrae & Wilde, 1979). This chapter casts its net more broadly.

Preservice teacher education can be thought of as a system of production, the goal of which is the development of beginning teachers who have the knowledge and capabilities that facilitate student learning. In describing and understanding the effects of this system, it would be useful to have information about five types of phenomena:

1. Context—conditions and events outside the system. An example of a contextual influence on the characteristics of teacher education students is changes in teacher salaries.
2. Process—the content, settings, and strategies used to facilitate learning and the characteristics of personnel (e.g., professors and cooperating teachers) that comprise the prospective teachers' learning experiences.
3. Inputs—the number, characteristics, and values of students preparing to teach (as they enter the system).
4. Outputs—the number, knowledge, competencies, and values of students who complete the preparation program.
5. Outcomes—what the new teachers are able to contribute to student learning (i.e., teacher effectiveness).

Ideally, systematic analysis would define the relationship among all five of these sets of factors. At least, systematic analysis provides knowledge about the relationship between processes or inputs, on the one hand, and outputs and/or outcomes, on the other. There do not appear to be studies of teacher education that simultaneously examine context, process, inputs, outputs, and outcomes.

Systematic analysis does not, of course, lead to the utilization of its findings, and evidence that is employed in policymaking is not limited to that derived from systematic analysis. Furthermore, much of the evidence that has been utilized in teacher education reform proposals is not based on studies of the teacher education system. Most obviously, research on teacher effectiveness that can be defined as systematic analysis plays a role in the formulation of policies relating to evaluation of new teachers and the content of the preservice curriculum. But, in itself, the research on effective schools and teaching does not provide direct evidence related to how to achieve preferred outputs or outcomes of teacher preparation, because no study of teacher effectiveness has also examined the effects of variations in preservice teacher education processes on teacher performance or its consequences.

Systematic analysis comes in many forms, including case studies and large-scale analyses of quantitative data. Although the rigor of methods used can vary from one analysis to another, no one form of systematic analysis is an inherently better guide to policy than another, and all methods of systematic analysis have their limitations.

Systematic analysis uses empirical data, but the use of empirical data, in itself, does not represent systematic analysis. For example, almost all reports and studies advocating change in teacher education use (or misuse) descriptive statistics to describe one or more aspects of the teacher education system. In most cases, these statistics are cited to legitimize the need for reform, and the reforms themselves do not follow from the statistics presented.

Systematic, policy-relevant analysis can be thought of as being either retrospective efforts to evaluate the consequences of existing policies or prospective efforts to predict the results of proposed policies. In either case, most systematic analysis applied to teacher education policy is *high inference*, in the sense that the conclusions drawn from the evidence presented are speculative and require one to accept one or more untested (and often unspecified) assumptions. For example, consider the policy goal of increasing the competence of beginning fourth-grade teachers to facilitate their students' learning of mathematics. A low-inference, methodologically rigorous mode of systematic analysis would compare the relationship between two or more different approaches to the training of fourth-grade teachers in mathematics and changes in the achievement levels of the teachers' students, taking into account other factors such as the prospective teachers' intelligence level and their knowledge of mathematics. Such analysis, using student performance as the outcome, has not been reported in what is loosely called the research literature. The way systematic analysis is commonly applied to this type of policy problem is that the instructional strategies of fourth-grade teachers whose students perform well on standardized tests are identified by researchers or by a survey of fourth-grade teachers, and conclusions are drawn that a course on such instructional strategies should be taught to prospective teachers. Even if the research employed is exemplary, its use is based on several unexamined and problematic assumptions including: (a) beginning teachers can learn and implement the strategies employed by expert teachers; (b) methods used by the teachers studied, rather than other teacher characteristics, explain student performance; and (c) courses to be taught to prospective teachers will be taught by persons who not only understand the instructional strategies to be learned but also know how to facilitate the learning of prospective teachers.

The more policymakers rely on teacher education to achieve improvements in student performance, the more they hedge their bets by trying to reduce the contingencies embodied in assumptions like the ones just identified. Thus, policies prescribing course requirements in teaching methods can be accompanied by written tests of teacher candidates' knowledge and various ways of ensuring that prospective teachers learn not only from professors but also from experienced classroom teachers. Of course, each one of these safeguards itself embodies a number of assumptions.

Knowing Where to Look for Systematic Analysis

The most fertile ground for unearthing the effects of systematic analysis on teacher education policy is likely to be state policy arenas, given the outpouring of laws, rules, and regulations from state agencies and legislatures in the 1980s. Although there are a number of studies of state policy-making related to teacher education (Scannell, 1988), only one has focused on the use of systematic analysis (Bull, 1987). Thus, finding systematic analysis, much less its effects, requires some prospecting and no small amount of speculation.

There is considerable debate among scholars as to how systematic analysis influences the thinking and decisions of policymakers generally and under what conditions such influence is greatest. Although the analysts of analysis come to different conclusions, there appears to be considerable agreement that the use of knowledge derived from systematic analysis in policy-making is usually indirect, partial, and selective (see Berg & Theado, 1981; Fullan, 1985; Hall, 1974; Lehman & Waters, 1979; Lindblom & Cohen, 1979; Sabatier, 1978; Useem & Dimaggio, 1978; Weiss, 1977). Further, systematic analysis appears to be more widely used to define or debate the nature of problems than to choose among alternative solutions (Weiss, 1977; Wildavsky, 1979). This makes it difficult to specify the effects of systematic analysis on teacher education policy.

In Figure 9-1, the distinction is made between policymakers and active sources of policy influence. Policymakers talk among themselves and with the legislative and administrative staffs that report to them. No doubt, information and judgments based (or allegedly based) on systematic analysis are exchanged in this way, but there are no studies of this use of systematic analysis. Similarly, individual representatives of *active sources* of policy influence interact with policymakers and their staffs, but the role of systematic analysis in such interactions apparently has gone unrecorded.

Although the extent to which systematic analysis turns up in the deliberations of policymakers remains private information, both policymakers and those who would influence them do go on record when the former produce legislation, rules, and regulations and when the latter issue reports and policy positions. The search for the effects of systematic analysis on teacher education policy can at least begin by examining the extent to which recently proposed or adopted teacher education policy and the assumptions—or definitions of the problems—upon which they are based either fit what can be known from systematic analysis or embody attempts to gain such information as a basis for further policy-making.

There are limitations to this approach to finding systematic analysis and its effects. *First*, identifying a fit between relevant research and the content of teacher education policy might simply identify a coincidence rather than a relationship. *Second*, the assumptions underlying policies must be inferred in most cases. *Third*, because those who engage in systematic analysis do not always agree either on what they find or the implications of their findings, it might be difficult to infer whether systematic analysis played a role in decision making. And, *fourth*, this strategy assumes that the person or persons assessing the use of systematic analysis have a comprehensive knowledge of the relevant information, and this is problematic. To widen the net a bit and to give systematic analysis a better chance to appear in the search for such analysis, the use of theory that is grounded on systematic analysis (such as the recommendation by the Carnegie Forum and others for intensive teacher-induction programs) will be considered evidence of the use of systematic analysis.

THE FIT BETWEEN SYSTEMATIC ANALYSIS AND STATE POLICY

The most significant problem one confronts in talking about state policy is that no two states seem to have approached the reform of teacher education in the same way, and the policies adopted or receiving continuing consideration vary from state to state. Moreover, there are numerous sources of authoritative policy at the state level including legislatures, state education agencies, boards of education, higher education coordinating commissions, and quasi-independent credentialing agencies or professional standards boards. Nonetheless, it does seem possible to identify several major directions in state teacher education policy.

Directions of State Policy Focused on Teacher Education

Since the early 1980s, virtually every state has sought to improve its schools by changing one or more policies related to teacher education. Although dozens of different prescriptions have been seriously considered or adopted in particular states, it seems possible to identify six types of policies that have been of interest to state policymakers throughout the country:

1. Financial incentives, usually in the form of loans that need not be repaid if the recipients teach for specified periods.
2. Various tests or standards relating to intellectual capability and academic achievement, aimed at controlling entry to teacher education and to teaching.

3. Requirements that prospective teachers have a strong grounding in the liberal arts and substantial coursework in the subjects they will teach.
4. Requirements for more field experiences and semester-long practice teaching experiences within the professional education curriculum. A corollary of this policy is that the teachers of prospective teachers are being required in some states to have teaching experience and to go into schools on a regular basis.
5. Induction programs for first-year teachers or special schools for teacher training within public schools systems, to ensure that new teachers are able to put into effect and build upon what they learned about teaching in college.
6. Alternative certification programs that allow individuals to teach without attending conventional preparation programs.

Do the assumptions that seem to underlie these policies and the policies themselves fit evidence available from systematic analysis? Do the policies embody the search for a better understanding of ways to improve teacher education?

Financial Incentives. As of 1988, 38 states offered scholarships, loans, or fellowships to attract new teachers. Most of these programs involve some form of loan that is forgiven in exchange for a specified time spent teaching (AACTE, 1988). In most states, forgivable loan programs have focused on particular fields or geographic areas in which teacher shortages existed or were anticipated (such as mathematics and science). Five states designated minority teachers as a target of financial incentives. The amount of the loans involved typically has been $1,000 to $1,500 a year for one to 4 years, with a year of teaching service resulting in the forgiveness of a year of the support provided.

Such policies have been tried before, the most notable of which was the NDEA loan program begun in 1958 and popular in the 1960s. No studies were done of consequences of the program at that time, and few recent analyses of the program's effects have surfaced. Loan-forgiveness programs assume that the cost of becoming a teacher, rather than the cost of being a teacher, is a major reason why people do not pursue teaching careers. No study of teacher career choices supports this assumption. On the other hand, most analyses of the mathematics and science teacher shortage, which is one usual focus of loan-forgiveness programs, point to the costs of being a teacher—that is, the large differential between the salary of beginning teachers and those of first-year scientists and mathematicians—as the main cause of the long-standing shortages of qualified teachers in these fields (Levin, 1985). If loan-forgiveness programs were to be conceptualized as supplements to beginning salaries, it would be clear that the amounts such loans provide fall far short of the differences in salaries that analysts argue is the major source of the shortage.

Any mathematics and science student with the offer of a higher salary could easily treat a *portion* of the difference between that salary and the salary to be received as a teacher as the way to repay a low-cost loan. Among high-achieving mathematics and science students, this difference would permit the paying off a 4-year loan, and the interest on it, in one year. To the extent that salary differences between teaching and other careers is the problem being addressed, forgivable loans of limited amounts are not likely to make much of a dent in the supply of teachers, because, at the time of career decision, the money will have been spent. If a student has the choice of teaching mathematics for 4 years to pay off the loan or becoming an actuarial for one year to pay off the loan, the student with a choice would rationally choose the insurance industry. Unless, of course, the student really wanted to teach. But those who "really want to teach" might not need financial incentives.

In 1985, the College Board published a study suggesting that loan programs would have little impact on the supply of teachers (Spero, 1985). That study went unnoticed or unheeded. Conversations with officials in several states yield anecdotal evidence about the efficacy of such programs. Invariably, the evidence cited relates to the proportion of appropriated funds spent. Almost never does the evidence available to state officials address the quality of the candidates or the quantity of new teachers actually entering the profession because of the loan program.

In short, systematic analysis was not used to develop loan-forgiveness programs and is not being used to evaluate them. Had systematic analysis been applied, it probably would have yielded conclusions that these programs would need to (a) provide greater financial incentives, (b) target persons who have high achievement in the shortage field (who have other career options), in order to achieve improvement in both quality and quantity. Analysis might also have led to the conclusion that financial incentives at the point of entry to teaching would be more cost effective than incentives during college. North Carolina apparently reached the first two of these conclusions in its deliberations when the state created 20,000 scholarships for academically talented students. The early results are impressive: Large numbers of students, both white and black, in the top 10 percent of their high school classes have applied for the program.

Controlling Entry to Teacher Education and to Teaching. Formal testing and other preservice screening procedures are now widely used to influence the quality of teaching in the United States. For example, by the end of 1987, 45 states required passage of one or more standardized tests of would-be teachers, in addition to those used to determine entry to college (AACTE, 1988). Among the assumptions upon which these policies appear to be based are: (a) a significant proportion of the students who enter teaching in the United States are not very bright or academically able, in comparison with other college graduates; and (b) a prospective teacher's performance on written tests or in college courses is a valid measure of potential teaching effectiveness.

The most widely cited studies from which policymakers draw evidence about the limited academic ability of teachers appear to be those that speak to the poor performance on written tests, especially college entrance examinations, of high school graduates who *say* that they *intend* to teach (Alter, Mc-Cormick, & Joseph, 1984; Feistritzer, 1983; Lyons, 1979; Weaver, 1981).

However, studies that focus on college entrants tell very little about teacher education students, much less about teachers. More than half of the students who initially express interest in teaching never receive a teaching certificate; those college students who transfer into teaching programs from other fields are more able, on the average, than those who drop out; and many of those certified—roughly 30 percent—do not become teachers (Lyson & Falk, 1984).

It is one thing to say that teacher candidates are not as bright as they need to be or that the most academically able tend not to enter the profession (Vance & Schlechty, 1983); it is quite another to develop a host of policies based on the belief that prospective teachers are, generally speaking, from the bottom of the academic barrel.

There are numerous studies that would pass for systematic analysis that have concluded that college students engaged in teacher education, on the whole, appear to be as able academically as other college students (AACTE, 1987, pp. 42–43; Carnegie Foundation, 1987; D. Cohen, 1984; Nelli, 1984; Olsen, 1985 and sources cited there; University of Wisconsin System Task Force on Teacher Education, 1984). These studies, however, have gained limited readership among policymakers.

Do various tests and college grades predict future teachers' performance and effectiveness? Scores on tests of subject-matter knowledge and grades in the subjects a teacher teaches appear to have a small but consistent relationship with teacher performance and student achievement. This relationship is stronger when the courses being taught focus on more sophisticated content matter and learning objectives such as the acquisition of higher order skills (Ashton, Crocker, & Olejnik, 1987; Druva & Anderson, 1983). And there is some reason to believe that scores on tests of teachers' verbal ability are related to student achievement (Hawley & Rosenholtz, 1984: chap. 3). On the other hand, the most widely used tests to screen prospective teachers, the National Teacher Examination and academic aptitude-type tests, seem to have no relationship to teacher performance or student achievement (Ashton, et al., 1987; Evertson, Hawley, & Zlotnik, 1985). In any case, no research on the relationship among measures of academic competence provides evidence that would allow one to conclude that a given passing score reliably divides those more able to teach from those less able to teach.

The quality-assurance measures that could have the greatest effect on teacher education in the long run could be on-the-job tests of beginning teachers' performance. In some states, the performance of new teachers on such measures is tied to state approval of teacher education programs, to teachers' opportunities for certification, or to merit pay. Such performance assessments that are linked to the eligibility of institutions to offer teacher education, which appear to be increasingly popular, especially in southern states (Southern Regional Education Board, 1988b), could be particularly influential in shaping teacher education, because they directly shape the design and content of curricula. Rather than control-

ling the quality of teachers by screening individuals, program-approval strategies based on teacher performance are aimed at eliminating teacher education programs with low standards and/or low capability. In theory, this will lead to a reallocation of both prospective teachers and resources to teacher-preparation programs that graduate well-qualified teacher candidates. The effects of this approach to improving the quality of teacher candidates have not yet been studied, but it seems clear that the approach will have its greatest impact on teacher-preparation programs that historically have produced the largest number of black and Hispanic teachers. In North Carolina, for example, the pass rate on the National Teacher Examination at all ten of the state's historically black teacher-preparation programs falls below state-established standards for program approval in 1990 ("NTE pass rates," 1988).

Many of the measures of teacher effectiveness used in performance-focused policies are derived from systematic analysis of effective teaching practices (for a summary of such analyses, see Good & Brophy, 1986). However, the typical way this research is used by policymakers is flawed in a number of important ways (for an overview critique see M. Smith & O'Day, in press). *First*, the criteria for evaluating teachers often oversimplify the research findings in concluding that the effectiveness of given practices can be generalized from one context to another, are equally important, and are independent of how the teacher uses other related teaching practices. *Second*, the findings that speak to the relationships between teacher behavior and student learning are often based on a narrow range of goals to which many schools aspire, so that the equating of effective teaching with these more easily measured behaviors might trivialize and deprofessionalize teaching (Smith & O'Day, in press). *Third*, the assumption that beginning teachers should be able to do what expert teachers can do is inconsistent with knowledge and theory about how teachers develop and learn (Berliner, 1987), and it leads to low-level standards when the criteria are applied in practice. Although research on teacher effectiveness raises serious questions about the validity of the criteria often used to evaluate teacher performance, research on the processes by which effective teaching is measured raises doubts about the validity of common methods of assessing teaching performance that focus on the frequency with which particular competencies are demonstrated (Darling-Hammond, Wise, & Pease, 1983).

Of particular importance is the research by Barr and Dreeban (1983), Stodolsky (1988), and others that suggests that the decomposition of teaching behaviors into small, presumably observable parts and the specification of effective practices independent of the subject being taught might miss, or even misrepresent, the most important sources of teacher effectiveness.

Stronger Grounding in the Liberal Arts and in Subjects to Be Taught. There appears to be substantial agreement among parties to the debates over teacher education that at least half of a teacher's undergraduate education should be in the liberal arts (though the definition of *liberal arts* is sometimes contested). The assumption underlying this consensus is that such a background will allow teachers to call upon a broad range of knowledge in making judgments in general and in giving context and depth to teaching. There appears to be near consensus that secondary teachers should essentially major for at least a year's worth of courses in the subject to be taught. Although there is much less agreement about whether elementary and middle or junior high school teachers should be required to major in a single subject or in an interdisciplinary major, there appears to be a trend among states to require teacher candidates to major in a field or fields other than, or in addition to, education.

There appear to be four assumptions underlying the idea that teachers should major in a subject other than education. *First*, the more one knows about a topic, the better one can teach it. *Second*, the more a teacher knows about a subject, the easier it is to learn more about that subject. *Third*, learning one subject in some depth is itself a source of intellectual development and gives one confidence that one can gain a sophisticated understanding of a field. *Fourth*, courses in the liberal arts and in a given subject are more challenging intellectually than are education courses. A corollary of this last assumption is that, the less undergraduate coursework in education students have, the better educated they will be (Holmes Group, 1986, p. 93).

A firm grounding in the liberal arts means very different things at different colleges and universities, and the systematic study of the impact of variations in the content and number of liberal arts courses that prospective teachers take on their performance or effectiveness as teachers is virtually nonexistent. There is, however, some evidence that (a) certified secondary teachers who were liberal arts majors perform less well than secondary teachers who majored in education, and (b) teachers with more education courses are more effective and are more likely to stress application than rote learning (McNergney et al., 1988).

The findings from studies that seek to determine the relationship between subject-matter knowledge or background of teachers and their effectiveness in teaching that subject are somewhat inconsistent. It seems reasonable to conclude from the available research that (a) the number of courses one takes in a subject is unrelated to teaching effectiveness, (b) a prospective teacher's grades in a subject taught are weakly related to student achievement, and (c) knowledge of subject matter as measured by written tests is associated with student learning, especially in more advanced courses (Ashton et al., 1987; Evertson et al., 1985). Studies from which these generalizations are derived deal almost exclusively with the teaching and learning of secondary subjects, so there are no helpful lessons here for the redesign of certification programs for elementary school teachers.

The ability to learn more about a topic generally increases as one's store of knowledge of that topic increases. There is, on the other hand, no reason to believe that knowing a given subject well in itself enhances intellectual capacity generally or the ability to transfer expertise in one domain or subject to another (Bransford, 1979).

With respect to the relative rigor of education courses, compared with those in the liberal arts and academic disciplines, no content analyses examine this issue, by whatever standards rigor might be defined. A recent survey of a national sample of teacher education students found that a majority of those preparing for high school teaching ranked their teacher education courses as more time consuming than other courses. When asked to compare the rigor of their methods courses with courses in various content areas, these students saw English and history courses as no more difficult, on average, than methods courses, but a majority saw courses in foreign languages, mathematics, and science as more demanding (AACTE, 1987).

There is reason to believe that prescribing more liberal arts courses might have little effect on the overall rigor of the curriculum in which teacher education students might engage. An extensive study of the transcripts of college students in southern states found that most students took the paths of least resistance in selecting electives or general-education courses (Galambos, Cornett, & Spitler, 1985). Prescribing a greater proportion of upper division courses in the liberal arts apparently would change the patterns of course taking for most teacher education students, but at the expense of breadth. Interestingly, before recent state policies requiring more liberal arts courses were implemented, elementary teaching candidates seem to have taken more liberal arts courses across a broader range of subjects than their peers majoring in liberal arts disciplines (Galambos, et al., 1985).

If it is desirable for students preparing to be teachers to receive a stronger grounding in the liberal arts, so that they can bring what they learn from these courses to their professional performance, one would expect that efforts would be made to integrate, or at least align, liberal arts and education coursework. But few such efforts appear to be under way (Hawley et al., 1988). Moreover, the literature is full of commentary on the reasons why one should expect little commitment to the education of teachers in universities outside teacher education programs themselves (Clifford, 1988; Sykes, 1985)

Increasing the Amount and Quality of Preservice Field-Based Learning Opportunities for Prospective Teachers. Underlying the push for more school-based learning time for teacher candidates is the *belief* that teaching is basically an art and a craft that should be structured less by scientific principles than by intuition, common sense, and lessons derived from experience. For those who subscribe to this assumption, it follows that current teachers have as much or more useful knowledge to share with those learning to teach than do college professors. Therefore, increasing the field-based courses and extending the time for practice teaching should enhance the effectiveness of preservice teacher training.

When asked to choose the most valuable aspect of their preparation for teaching, new teachers more often point to practice teaching and other practical experiences than to their courses in teaching methods, psychology, or other college subjects (see Richardson-Koehler, 1988). This emphasis on practical lessons is greater among elementary than secondary teachers (Killian & McIntyre, 1988).

The available research, however, suggests that practica and practice teaching are often not very effective and even may be counterproductive. On the whole, early (prepractice teaching) field experiences seem to have a small positive effect on teacher candidates' attitudes, and mixed, sometimes negative, effects on their performance. Studies that have focused on the amount of time prospective teachers spend in field-based learning suggest that students taking 1 to 3 courses with field experiences seem to benefit from them. When students are exposed to more than 3 or 4 courses involving a significant field-experience component, desired outcomes may not be affected and may, in fact, decline (Malone, 1985, p. 19). Similarly, in their synthesis of findings from 38 studies on the relationship between early field experiences and prospective teachers' attitudes toward teaching, Samson and his associates (Samson, Borger, Weinstein, & Walberg, 1984) found no consistent effects of the amount of time involved in such experiences (see also Bennie, 1982; Caul & Hahn, 1980; Davis, 1976; Zeichner & Liston, 1987).

There also is not convincing evidence to support the investment of greater time in practice teaching. Some researchers have found that the effectiveness of student teachers increased toward the end of their practice teaching period (Denton & Lacina, 1984; Freeze & Buckner, 1984). However, Feiman-Nemser et al. (1986), Griffin et al. (1983), and others have found that student teachers often unlearn or abandon lessons learned in college courses.

It is possible to derive from available systematic analysis a set of strategies that, if adequately implemented, would increase the productivity of field-based teacher education and practice teaching. But state policies seldom address these problems. One exception to this generalization is found in North Carolina, where the state provided funding for several pilot projects demonstrating different approaches to stronger university–school system collaboration (Stedman, 1988).

Providing for Induction Programs. First-year teachers often have experiences that are unsatisfying professionally and fail to implement much of what they learned in their preservice preparation (Feiman-Nemser & Buchman, 1986; Griffin, 1985; Hall, 1982; Veenman, 1984). It is assumed that induction programs that provide support for new teachers both increase teacher effectiveness and reduce teacher attrition. However, large-scale induction programs have only recently gained attention, and little research links such programs to teacher performance or attrition (see Huling-Austin, 1987). Anecdotal evidence suggests that such programs are making a contribution to a more productive and satisfying transition from college to work for many teachers. At the same time, there is reason to believe that most programs would be more effective if mentor teachers had more time and training to undertake this task and if university faculty had more involvement aimed at linking what is being learned on the job with what is being learned in the classroom. Recent research on teacher mentoring suggests that this role is harder to perform than the legislators who established such programs probably thought, and that it takes time and specific training before most teachers feel comfortable with, and are competent in, the role (Warren-Little, 1988). Research on mentoring in a broad range of settings suggests that claims for it are overrated and that induction pro-

grams should be more formal and structured that those provided for in most state policies (Hurley, 1988). Few state induction programs provide for the collection of data on the efficacy of induction strategies.

Creating Ways to Certify Teachers That Reduce the Time and Specific Requirements Required by College-Based Teacher Certification Programs. Some 25 states allow college graduates who have not been certified through conventional procedures to teach if they participate in some form of alternative certification program (AACTE, 1988). The interest among state policymakers in alternative certification seems motivated by at least three beliefs. *First,* the time, cost, and low status of teacher education programs discourage academically able people from pursuing teaching. *Second,* one can best learn how to teach by learning on the job from outstanding practitioners. *Third,* bypassing state requirements is a way to cope with current inadequacies of certification processes.

Although there appear to be no studies that link variations in teacher education programs with variations in teacher effectiveness, available research shows that those teachers who were certified in traditional programs perform better in classrooms than those who were provisionally certified or not certified at all (Ashton et al., 1987; Evertson et al., 1985). But it is not known whether taking certain education courses or any given number of such courses makes much difference. There is no systematic analysis indicating that the real and anticipated shortages of qualified teachers are traceable to "unnecessary barriers that block [the] way into the teaching profession," as the U.S. Department of Education claims (1987, p. 1), although the fact that there is a market for alternative certification programs suggests that some unknown number of would-be teachers were discouraged from pursuing teaching by conventional university or college-based entry processes. With the exception of New Jersey and some urban districts, alternative certification programs produce only a small proportion of the new teachers hired. They do, however, seem to be gaining in enrollment. Studies of alternative certification programs in North Carolina, Texas, California, and New Jersey conclude that teachers prepared in this way were judged to be as effective in their initial teaching as were teachers prepared in conventional programs. In the California and New Jersey programs, participants had stronger academic records and interest and did somewhat better on written certification tests than those teacher candidates with which they were compared (Rodman, 1988; Southern Regional Education Board, 1988a).

Alternative programs adopted before 1987 were established in the absence of any systematic analysis of the effects of alternative certification on teachers' effectiveness. It is worth noting that, unlike most other state teacher education policies, those calling for alternative certification have sometimes required systematic analysis of outputs and outcomes.

Congruence of State Teacher Education Policies and Systematic Analysis-Summary

Table 9-1 summarizes a number of conclusions about the relationship between teacher education policies and systematic

TABLE 9–1 The Fit Between Typical State Teacher Education Policies and Knowledge Based on Systematic Analysis

A Policy Type	B Nature of Relevant Systematic Analysis (high or low inference)	C Fit of Systematic Analysis with Assumptions (none, weak, good)	D Fit with Prescriptions (none, weak, good)	E Comments - Best Fit/Worse Fit Examples
1. Financial incentive for recruitment	High	None	None	Best: Large amount of money is provided and is linked to high ability of students. Worse: Small amounts are provided, e.g., $1,000 per yr.
2. Screening of teacher candidates based on tests and college Grades				Best: Tests of verbal ability and knowledge of subject matter are used, and high standards are set.
Basic skills	Low	Weak	Good	Worse: Any use of the National Teacher Examinations (NTE).
Subject matter	Low	Weak	Weak	
General knowledge	Low	None	None	
Pedagogical knowledge	Low	None	None	
Pedagogical performance	Low	Weak	Weak	
GPA	Low	None	None	
3. Increased requirements in liberal arts and disciplinary courses				Best: The required content represents advanced-level subject matter. This happens, because of requirements at particular colleges, usually those that educate few teachers.
Liberal arts	None	None	None	
Subject matter[a]	Low	Weak	None	Worse: Requiring more "open electives."
4. More field-based learning to teach				Best: Provisions for funding and evaluating alternative models of collaborative school–university practice teaching.
Field-based courses	Low	None	None	
Practice teaching	Low	Weak	None	Worse: Adding the number of hours required in field-based instruction.
5. Induction programs	High	Good	Weak	Best: Intensive year-long programs with inservice training and trained mentor teams. Worse: Assignment of untrained mentors who receive no release time.
6. Alternative certification	High	Weak	Weak	Best: Collaborative school–university programs coupled with evaluation and selective admission. Worse: Brief, introductory training, school-based seminar, no follow-up.

[a] There might appear to be an inconsistency in conclusions drawn about subject-matter-related policy. Here the focus is on number of courses.

analysis. It is complicated and requires some explanation. The extent to which systematic analysis is used in policy-making is influenced by the availability and nature of the evidence. Column B estimates whether the relevant systematic analysis that is available is of high or low inference. (*Level of inference* refers to the degree to which the evidence speaks directly to the policy or assumptions underlying it.) An example of low-inference analysis would be a study of the relationship between the number of hours spent in practice teaching and the effectiveness of first-year teachers. An example of high-inference analysis would be a study that describes the relationship between academic ability and subsequent income in different occupations and draws inferences about the effects of increases in teacher salaries and the supply of teacher candidates.

No attempt is made to judge the quality of the available systematic analysis. If differences in the methodological sophistication and the volume of systematic analysis explained differences in the extent to which systematic analysis is used, the assessment of quality would be important, however difficult it was to do across so broad an array of studies. However, quality of analysis and level of agreement among analysts seldom seem to shape the outcome of deliberations over alternative public policies (see Berman & McLaughlin, 1978; Hood, 1979; Hood & Blackwell, 1976; Long & Terry, 1986; Nelson & Sieber, 1976; Yin, Heald, Vogel, Fleishaur, & Vladeck 1976, pp. 72–75). Teacher education policy-making seems no exception to this generalization (M. Cohen, 1985).

Columns C and D in Table 9-1 seek to assess the fit between

the evidence from systematic analysis and the assumptions upon which the policies are based. Overall, the fit approximates that experienced by Cinderella's stepsisters.

Column E recognizes that generalization across 50 states is precarious, and an attempt is made to contrast best-fit with worse-fit policies. Most of the policies referred to are composites of actual policies.

No doubt, others would describe the manifestation of systematic analysis in teacher education policy differently. Clearly, there are many exceptions to the overall conclusions drawn here. But it does seem difficult to conclude that recent teacher education policies adopted by states reflect the understanding of problems that could be derived from a synthesis of available systematic analysis or that the prescriptions set forth were those that one would propose if systematic analysis were weighted heavily in formulating the policy.

EXPLAINING THE USE OF SYSTEMATIC ANALYSIS BY POLICYMAKERS

Three sets of conditions might explain why and how systematic analysis is utilized by policymakers: the dynamics of the political process in the context of unusual demands for policy reform, the characteristics of the supply of systematic analysis, and the nature of the demand for information upon which to base policy decisions. These conditions are interactive in the sense that each influences the others. The intent here is not to develop a theory that encompasses these relationships. However, the key variables within each set of conditions are described in ways that facilitate insight and future inquiry.

The Dynamics of the Policy Process

Policy-Making in Normal Times. Most of the time, the outcomes and processes of domestic, as opposed to foreign, policy-making are fairly predictable. Current policy represents the accommodations made to the distribution of power and influence among those interested in any given set of policies. Within each policy arena, expectations have been developed about what is possible with respect to change, and relatively stable alliances and interrelationships among actors have been built. Past policies themselves distribute influence and access and create or lead to rules and routines that, in effect, place limits on change.

Over time, policy arenas—the space in the political system where particular policy is made and implemented—become increasingly populated and built up, and there is, in effect, less and less room for nonincremental change. This results, most of the time, in only modest efforts to change a given set of policies. When these efforts at change are successful, the usual result is amendments to existing policy that reflect small changes in the distribution of influence, fluctuations in the energy of different interests, or changes in environmental conditions that have impact across the groups and influential actors with an active interest in the policy or set of policies involved.

In the context of incremental policy-making, systematic analysis is not in much demand, and its primary use is to fine-tune existing policies in ways that do not redistribute benefits or authority. Systematic analysis might occur, especially if the institutional structures for conducting it were established at some earlier time, but it seldom attracts the best minds. Studies that might, if taken seriously, suggest the need for major changes in policy have a limited audience among policymakers and practitioners. Often, such systematic inquiry is described by potential users as "academic," which the Random House Dictionary defines as "not practical, realistic or directly useful."

This general characterization of the nature of the political process in the United States (and in most democratic nations) helps to explain why public budgets change little from year to year despite the struggles over public expenditures (Wildavsky, 1964), why the reform of welfare or agricultural policies is so difficult to bring about (Lowi, 1969), why the "steady work" of education reform seems to change schools little (Elmore & McLaughlin, 1988), and why would-be reformers usually have a short attention span. It also explains why, until recently, changes in public policy affecting teacher education have seldom been more consequential than changes in course requirements for prospective teachers. But, just as this general picture of stable and predictable policy processes cannot account for the Federal Income Tax Reform Act of 1986, the patterns of normal policy-making that would explain most past public policy affecting teacher education cannot account for the dramatic changes in the volume and character of teacher education policy coming from the states in the 1980s.

Policy-Making in the Context of Reform Movements. Criticisms of teacher education have not been substantially different from earlier periods, and the proposals that have become public policy have been made before (Clifford, 1988; Sykes, 1985). The changes that have come to be described as the *teacher education reform movement* came about because the stable, relatively small, and structurally dense policy arena in which teacher education policy had been formulated was destabilized.

The destabilization of a policy arena occurs when one or both of two circumstances happen: (a) the issues upon which the arena focuses "heat up," in the sense that they receive greater attention from those who have been outside the arena; and (b) the issue is redefined as an important element of a larger set of concerns. Both of these happened to the teacher education policy arena. As the quality of American education came under greater scrutiny, so did teacher education. Greater attention in the media was accompanied, or followed, by greater interest among politicians who had previously been concerned with other issues. Teachers were seen as part of the problem, and the improvement of teaching was defined as a big part of the solution (Passow, 1987). Thus, improvement in the selection and preparation of new teachers was defined as essential to the improvement of teaching (a visible statement of this assumption is the report of the Carnegie Forum on Education and the Economy, 1986).

Generally speaking, the amount of change that can occur in a destabilized policy arena depends on the resistance new actors encounter to particular prescriptions. In the case of teacher education policy, new actors in the arena encountered mainly teacher educators and state civil servants who were no match for state legislators and governors who found educational improvement to be an issue on which voters and influential foundations, among others, expected action. Thus, politicians and those who sought to be responsive to politicians had considerable incentive to put the heat on teacher education and keep it there until they achieved the adoption of new policy to which they could point as evidence of their concern and effectiveness. Teacher education proved to be a policy arena that outsiders could enter easily and demonstrate a capacity to act without incurring political costs. As a report summarizing the conclusions of a study by the Education Commission of the States (1985) put it, "state policy makers—who have been spurred on by the national reports, activities in other states, and the sense that education again can be a politically popular issue—have seized the initiative, taking educators at least partially out of the picture" (p. 3).

During the first stages of the educational reform movement, new policies related to teacher education exceeded in number policies dealing with other aspects of educational improvement, and did so by a large margin. In 1983, the most common *school improvement* policies being proposed by state legislatures were those related to teacher education: loans and scholarships for teacher candidates, higher standards for entry to teacher education, competency testing for teacher certification, and alternative routes for teacher certification. From 1983 to 1985, more than 30 states passed teacher education–related policies whereas only 8 increased salaries for beginning teachers (Education Commission of the States, 1985). The emphasis on teacher education among education reformers has continued.

In retrospect, it is not surprising that teacher education reform attracted so much attention from policymakers, although teacher educators, accustomed to fights over policy changes within their universities and with state certification agencies, appear to have been surprised by the swiftness of the incursions into their policy domain. The pace of the teacher education reform movement is one reason why the systematic analysis that was available did not get used, or was misused. Another is that most demands for reforming teacher education met with little forceful opposition. This affected not only the rate at which policy was made but also the supply of and demand for systematic analysis. The use of systematic analysis or the provision for its development are greater with respect to those proposals that have engendered greater conflict and thus could lead to political costs for policymakers.

One might surmise that opportunities for significant change occur when policy arenas are destabilized. But electoral incentives direct the interests of policymakers to policies that hold prospects for short-run or interim results (McDonnell, 1988). This, in turn, means that policies that are easily implemented and, in themselves, represent clearly understood consequences (such as requirements) are politically attractive. When political victories come easily, the prospects for policies that might bring about more fundamental change are shut down.

There appear to be at least five reasons why teacher educa-tion reform met with relatively little resistance and confronted few of the problems that constrained action on many other reform proposals. *First*, teacher education programs are generally held in low esteem on their own campuses. Thus, not only did few leaders in higher education come to the defense of teacher education programs, or at least oppose regulation of them; a number of prominent academicians joined in the attack. Although these calls for basic reform from within were not prescriptive, they gave implicit support to the premise that intervention by state governments or university governing boards was justified. Moreover, the denigration of teacher education from within universities might have implied that evidence about the efficacy of teacher education was unnecessary.

Second, the perception that college students pursuing teacher education were, in general, very weak academically made it easy to argue that various constraints should be placed on who should be admitted to teacher education and to the profession itself. And the assumption that teacher education students were weak reinforced the belief that teacher education curricula were not very rigorous or worthy of considerable investment of student time.

Third, as the reform movement gained momentum, teacher educators were engaged in extensive self-studies, and those advocating change sought to build support for their proposals by pointing to the weaknesses of conventional strategies for preparing teachers. Although many teacher educators were seeking a place in the reform movement for themselves, there was little agreement about the directions of change, at least little agreement that others could discern. Moreover, the most visible calls for change (Carnegie Forum, 1986; Holmes Group, 1986, National Commission on Excellence in Teacher Education, 1985) directly or indirectly argued for eliminating or diminishing undergraduate teacher preparation, and this led to considerable rancor among teacher educators. This internal division might have confirmed the idea that change from within colleges and universities is unlikely and that, if teacher educators disagreed so greatly, intuition and common sense are probably good bases upon which to make public policy.

Fourth, teacher education was already heavily regulated by states. Most states had specific course requirements for teachers, for example, and had had them for some time (Roth & Mastain, 1984). Indeed, teacher educators themselves regularly advocated, without burdening policymakers with relevant systematic analysis, state policies that would insure that prospective teachers would take the courses they believed were essential to effective teaching and that they, it happens, taught. This, of course, legitimated further prescriptions in the absence of systematic analysis.

Fifth, teacher education reforms did not cost the states much money. Thus, state policymakers could require more or fewer courses, more fieldwork, teacher candidate testing, and other provisions without having to make trade-offs with other reforms. Even if one did not think teacher education reform was a high priority, establishing policies to bring it about seemed to cost less than other ways of expressing a commitment to educational improvement. Scannell (1988) found that the states with the most restrictive regulatory teacher entry policies typically made relatively low investments in public education.

All of this is not to suggest that all of the reform proposals that found their way into policy were imposed on reluctant but impotent teacher educators. One reason for the absence of conflict over teacher education policy and the subsequent enactment of legislation or other state provisions that seemed to ignore the available evidence from systematic analysis is that some policies seemed to please almost everyone. For example, despite considerable evidence that simply increasing the number of field experiences required of preservice teachers would not likely be effective, many states have enacted, or are in the process of enacting, such policies. In this case, policy can change without anyone's changing, and almost everyone involved can feel better. Teacher educators need not change what they do if these newly required courses do not require the elimination of others. Many teacher candidates will almost certainly report that they welcome the extra chance for *practical experience*, and, if some students find such experiences unrewarding, this will be seen as helpful in making career decisions. And teacher organizations will view this policy as confirmation of the importance of experience-based expertise and recognition of their professional status. In such contexts, systematic analysis has no buyers.

Summary. Most of the time, most policy arenas are characterized by incremental policy change, so that systematic analysis plays little role in shaping policy except at the margins and, perhaps, when the influential actors within that arena seek to make greater demands on their environments (i.e., other or larger policy arenas). When, for various reasons, policy arenas are destabilized, the policy process opens up and opportunities exist for systematic analysis to be used by those who want to bring about change. Whether systematic analysis gets used to define the problem in detail or to identify and evaluate and promote alternative policies depends, in addition to the characteristics of the supply and demand for systematic analysis to be discussed, on how quickly such analysis can be mobilized and made relevant and on the amount of political conflict and costs that accompany the alternatives being proposed.

The Supply of Systematic Analysis

Two general aspects of the supply of systematic analysis appear to affect the extent to which it is utilized in the formulation of teacher education policy: the characteristics of the providers and the nature of the product.

The Providers. The supply of quality providers is one problem. Although there are many first-rate researchers and analysts who study teaching and learning, there are relatively few persons in universities or in public agencies who have focused their attention on teacher education. This is one reason why a number of important questions related to teacher education that warrant systematic inquiry have not been studied. There are a number of reasons for this. *First,* until recently, teacher education has not been of much interest to people other than teacher educators and prospective teachers. *Second,* within universities, the education of teachers is not and never has been a high-status enterprise (Clifford, 1988; Ducharme, 1986), and within schools and colleges of education at research universities, teacher education has been a relatively low priority (Bok, 1987; Holmes Group, 1986; Sykes, 1985). Thus, the number of scholars studying teacher education in a sustained way has been small and the quality of their work uneven. It follows that the number of young researchers trained to conduct systematic analysis of teacher education is correspondingly small. *Third,* systematic analysis of teacher education that engages a range of alternative explanations for the effects of teacher education is time consuming and costly. Little money has been available to support such inquiry. The problem is neatly summarized by the fact that the National Institute of Education established a center for research on teacher education in the 1970s and then directed the center's staff to focus attention on teaching strategies and educational innovation.

The credibility of quality providers is a second problem. Policymakers seem to question the reliability of the information they do receive, at least much of it that comes from university-based providers. One source of the lack of confidence is the relatively low status of education professors just noted.

Another is that teacher educators are the source of most systematic analysis related directly to teacher education policy and are personally affected by such policy (Malen, Murphy, & Geary, 1988). Policymakers are accustomed to seeing teacher educators in the role of advocates for or opponents of state rules and regulations that shape the character of teacher education. This last point links to a third likely reason why policymakers have some doubts about the usefulness of systematic analysis; they seldom see teacher educators who are advocating or opposing change utilizing analysis. For example, in presenting its more than 90-page argument for why research universities should play the dominant role in the preparation of new teachers, the Holmes Group (1986), which is comprised of education deans from research universities, cites no systematic analysis to support its position. Further, even those reform-oriented groups that commission considerable systematic analysis seldom explicitly report the results of the analysis (see, for example, the report of the National Commission on Excellence in Teacher Education, 1985). Thus, not only does systematic analysis that is developed not get disseminated, but also the conclusions reached by these and other reports appear to be based on careful judgments, rather than on empirical evidence. Policymakers might reasonably conclude that their judgment is as good as anyone else's.

The fact that teacher educators who advocate changes in teacher education policy do not employ systematic analysis is probably related to what might be called *the reformer's trap.* Bringing about change in a stable policy arena requires that reformers describe problems in stark and dramatic terms and that the solutions to the problems be easily understood by those to be influenced. Careful analysis, however, usually leads to gray, rather than to black and white, pictures. Thus, even reformers who know better tend to oversimplify problems and to suggest solution that promise substantial payoffs for low investment. And, to paraphrase H. L. Mencken, for every complex problem, there is usually a simple solution that is wrong.

When policymakers do look for systematic analysis, they typically turn to people in whom they have confidence. Such confidence usually derives, not from assessments of technical or scientific competence of the individuals, but from personal friendships, close working relationships, and a sense that the person from whom information is being sought both understands the politics of the situation (Cohen, 1985) and has some expertise. Such persons are not likely to be the providers of systematic analysis, and, even when they are teacher educators, they might be unfamiliar with recent research or reduce the research to generalizations that lead to simplistic solutions or to the conclusion by policymakers that what is known by "experts" is "commonsensical" anyway.

Characteristics of the Product. Other reasons why systematic analysis plays little role in teacher education policy have to do with characteristics of the product (i.e., systematic analysis), including the methodological difficulty of developing a link between the processes of teacher education and the outcome, the relevance to policy of much systematic analysis, the unclear language of systematic analysis, and the absence of quality control.

Methodological problems of systemic analysis limit its use. Ideally, systematic analysis related to teacher education policy would establish relationships (or the absence thereof) between the characteristics of teacher candidates and teacher education programs, on the one hand, and outputs and outcomes, on the other. There are at least three major difficulties in demonstrating such linkages. *First,* the characteristics of teacher education students and their experiences vary considerably, so that it is difficult to isolate the effects of differences in inputs and processes. Random assignment of prospective teachers to different learning processes would be one way to address this problem, but there are ethical and procedural difficulties in so doing. *Second,* because many different experiences make up the typical preservice teacher-preparation program, the cooperation and discipline of many different professors and cooperating teachers are necessary. Even if these problems could be resolved, measuring the outcome of teacher education is difficult, as those seeking to develop valid and reliable measures for assessing teaching effectiveness have discovered. *Third,* the accepted test of the effectiveness of teacher education is how teachers teach, rather than what they know and are able to do upon entry to the profession. But when prospective teachers finish their preparation programs, they find positions in many different schools and school systems, so that follow-up is difficult. Moreover, the different settings in which teachers are placed significantly affect their effectiveness. Thus, most studies of the effects of teacher education programs look at the performance or attitudes of teacher candidates while they are practice teaching or are otherwise involved in preservice teaching situations. As noted, there is considerable research that points to the fact that, once they begin teaching, new teachers often do not use much of what they knew and were able to do while they were advanced teacher education students.

The utilization of systematic analysis depends on the perception of relevance. Even if methodological problems like the ones just cited can be addressed, the content of systematic analysis might not be useful to policymakers, either because the information they want most is missing, or because the answer that systematic analysis provides is too complex to be incorporated into public policies. One reason that there is often a poor fit between the information relating to teacher education and the needs of policymakers is that teacher education policy typically provides little money for policy evaluation, and legislative and agency staff members are seldom experts on teacher education. Thus, the systematic analysis that is undertaken is driven by the interests of foundations or, more often, by researchers. Researchers often ask different questions from those asked by policymakers. For example, policymakers often want to know how much different alternatives cost (Cohen, 1985), but cost-effectiveness is almost never studied by university-based researchers, who are the major suppliers of systematic analysis related to teacher education policy. Indeed, some teacher educators seem to find issues of cost-effectiveness offensive because they imply that there is some higher value than teacher education (Gideonse, 1987).

A second limitation to the fit between systematic analysis and the needs of policymakers is the fact that, because many problems are very complicated, systematic analysis related to the improvement of teacher education would point in the direction of complex answers. Such answers seldom translate well into public policy. Consider, for example, the improvement of practical teaching skills through preservice teacher education. It is clear that *simply* increasing the time spent in student teaching is a weak intervention. On the other hand, if legislators sought to formulate policy that would address the problem adequately, the policy would be complex. And, because it would seek to influence the behavior of teachers, school administrators, and school board, as well as teacher educators, it would engender considerably more opposition than simpler but less ambitious policies. Policymakers want to solve problems in straightforward ways. In contrast, researchers, in their roles as researchers rather than advocates, are prone to emphasize the complexity of the problem and to warn that all proposed solutions are uncertain. Indeed, researchers often recommend further research, or at least experimentation, rather than decisive action (Florio, Behrman, & Goltz, 1979).

The flow of information, and therefore the use of information, is often impeded by the language used and lack of clarity (Bardach, 1984; Hosford, 1984; Lieberman, 1980). The problem of language is not just the problem of jargon or esoteric meaning; it is more subtle and elusive. Fenstermacher (1986, p. 45) makes this point eloquently in arguing that research findings seem to rob the processes of teaching and learning of their morality and complexity and to diminish their perceived importance to the welfare of children and society. Thus, he argues, next to the language of experience and faith, the language of research often seems relatively unpersuasive and, indeed, academic. In addition, communication between researchers and policymakers involves connecting with frames of reference and understanding the presuppositions individuals bring to their efforts to communicate (Bolman & Deal, 1983; Marshall, 1988).

The absence of control over the quality of systematic analysis is another problem. There are literally hundreds of publications through which individuals can publish studies, syntheses of research, and expert opinion. The extent to which the quality of the information so published is constrained by careful quality review varies enormously, and much of what passes for systematic analysis is of low quality. Thus, policymakers are often swamped with information that seems to come from reputable sources, but points in different directions. Having little time or expertise to separate the wheat from the chaff, policymakers often decide to use their best judgment or to turn to people with first-hand experience, especially people they know personally.

The Demand for Systematic Analysis: Characteristics of Consumers

This section deals with how characteristics of the policymakers and staff who support them directly affect the extent to which systematic analysis is used in developing teacher education policy. These include the degree to which action is perceived to be politically necessary or expedient, the substantive importance attributed to the potential solution of the problem, the assumptions made about the sources of the problem and alternative remedies, and the experience and expertise of the consumer in using systematic analysis.

Perceptions of the Political Context. Although the level of political demand for reform and the level of conflict over alternative solutions affect the market for systematic analysis, the way individual policymakers respond to these conditions varies. To the extent that they see teacher education as politically expedient (i.e., a low-cost way of responding to political demands), they are not likely to be interested in systematic analysis. Complex answers are difficult to understand and to write into policy that can be passed. This, of course, affects the demand.

In the context of the perceived need for political action, the only answers most policymakers want to hear from analysts are those that are certain and unambiguous. From the point of view of many policymakers, knowledge that there is no adequate solution to a problem is not usable knowledge. If systematic analysis is to be used by policymakers, it must provide direction, not add to uncertainty. Indeed, as policy analysts in government quickly learn, not having answers means not being questioned.

The way testing is dealt with by policymakers illustrates another general proposition related to the type of knowledge they seek. Evidence related to outputs is usually of more interest than knowledge related to outcomes. The relationship between outputs and policy is invariably more certain than the relationship between policy and outcomes. Thus, output data are likely to be seen as useful in justifying a policy in which one has invested, and they not only make one look good, but also suggest that the need for further action is unnecessary. This, of course, affects the willingness of policymakers to fund evalua-

tions, especially those that examine outcomes. Knowledge often acts as a constraint on action, unless the user is the only party in a conflict situation with access to the knowledge.

Values of the Potential Consumer. Independent of their perception of the potential costs of political action, policymakers differ to the extent that they see teacher education policy as substantively important. Although some policymakers turn to teacher education policy in the face of demands for educational reform, because the net political benefit and the symbolic value of this response are high, others believe that improvement in teacher education is an effective solution to the problem. In the latter cases, one would expect policymakers to use systematic analysis more extensively.

Assumptions About Teaching, Teachers, and Teacher Educators. When faced with nonroutine decisions, one may ask whether the search for additional information will improve the efficacy of the decision to be made. One's answer to this question will be based on the assumptions made and the beliefs held about the problem and its causes. Often these assumptions and beliefs are not specific to the particular issue but are applications of more general assumptions that the decision maker has learned are generally correct. For example, when looking for the source of a problem, one might believe that "people make the difference" or, alternatively, that "it is the way things are structured" that really counts. The decisions of policymakers with respect to their searches for and uses of systematic analysis related to teacher education seem to be influenced most by their assumptions about teaching, teachers, and teacher educators.

As countless commentators on the popular view of the requirements for effective teaching have observed, good teaching is often assumed to be the result of a caring disposition, sincere effort, and experience (Sykes, 1985). For those who hold this view, it follows that it should not take much time to learn to teach while in college and that a *real* understanding of teaching is best gained from teachers or, perhaps, from professors with much and recent experience in schools. When personal characteristics and experience are assumed to be the best sources of learning to teach, three conclusions follow: (a) there is no need for systematic knowledge to define problems or point the way to solutions, (b) preservice teacher preparation need not be extensive, and (c) most of the preparation to teach should be field-based.

The view that teaching is an art and a craft with little scientific basis is reinforced by many university professors not involved in teacher education, who, having made a career of doing something for which they received no formal education or training, believe that teaching is something one can do effectively if one is smart, reflective, and willing to learn on the job.

Some teacher educators, especially those active in regional and national organizations, have sought to counter the belief that teaching is largely a matter of common sense and hard work by identifying a knowledge base in clear and specific terms (Egbert & Kluender, 1984; Reynolds, 1989; Smith, 1983). Other teacher educators, however, have argued that it is premature to identify a knowledge base and that teaching is much too complex and uncertain an endeavor to be reduced to a series of propositions (Lanier, 1984; Shulman, 1986). Efforts to convince policymakers that there are scientific reasons to value substantial preservice teacher preparation can have anomalous consequences. The clearer and more specific teacher educators seek to make the lessons they derive from systematic knowledge, the more likely policymakers are to use systematic knowledge. But often this use of knowledge can result in policies that limit teacher education by prescribing certain professional practices and courses as obligatory. On the other hand, those who caution against premature specification of the content of teacher education might lead policymakers who perceive a need for action to conclude that there is no systematic knowledge to which one can turn and that, given the apparent disagreement among those who should know, investments in the future development of systematic knowledge are likely to be unproductive.

Assumptions about the qualifications of teachers also influence policymakers. For those who believe that one does not learn to teach from studying research on teaching, much less from studying educational philosophy, the role of teacher education might be seen as gatekeeping. That is, teacher education and teacher certification can be seen as effective to the extent that they serve as mechanisms for selecting students with the commitment, intelligence, subject-matter knowledge, and values that are appropriate to teaching. The instruments for performing these functions seem to be obvious enough to legislators, or so it seems. Thus, teacher education policy in the 1980s has been dominated by the imposition of tests and by requirements for field experiences during which suitability for teaching might be scrutinized. The fact that some of the measures for screening, including those most commonly used, have no demonstrated validity, apparently bothers few state policymakers. No doubt most policymakers would choose better tests if offered them, but, for reasons noted earlier, it seems clear that the perception that something must be done leads to the conclusion that a bad test is better than no test at all.

Two types of assumptions about teacher educators (as deliverers of services rather than as suppliers of systematic analysis) seem related to the use of systematic analysis to shape teacher education policy. The first of these is the perception previously noted that teachers, rather than teacher educators, are in the best position to provide preservice training. A second assumption that could influence how legislators or other state policymakers use systematic analysis involves beliefs about whether teacher educators can be trusted to pursue the spirit of the policy without constraints or sanctions. In those cases where trust is low, policymakers look, not for the best policies, but for those that are self-implementing or readily monitored, such as specific admission or course requirements and tests. Systematic analysis that relates to outcomes or outputs with multiple causes usually yields complicated prescriptions that rely for their effectiveness on initiatives and discretion on the part of service providers. In other words, *if* policymakers believe that those whose behavior they hope to influence do not share their goals, systematic analysis appears to go unheeded and unwanted, particularly if it would lead to policies that leave options for those who must implement the policy.

The Capacity of Potential Users. The use of systematic analysis depends on the extent to which potential users are familiar with the problem and/or particular policy alternatives and their technical capacity to use the analyses. The more one knows about any given subject, the better one can use information related to that subject (Bransford, 1979; Katz & Lazarsfeld, 1955). This general finding from research on cognition and communication has been reported in studies of how state policymakers use knowledge (Cohen, 1985). Few state legislators have much information about teacher education, and most of what they do know comes from retrospective reports from former or current teachers. Although it is not uncommon, for example, for legislators to tour prisons or even schools, state legislators seldom visit teacher education programs. State education agency personnel are often more knowledgeable about education and are usually better users of analysis than legislators. But it is not just one's knowledge that affects interest in additional knowledge; how one has acquired knowledge affects where one looks for new information. Many state agency personnel are former teachers and school administrators. Their personal experiences and networks are from the world of practice rather than academe. Not surprisingly, they might be more confident of information derived from experience than from systematic analysis.

Information will be used most fully when it and the implications it has for action are within the technical competence of the potential user, or are within the capacity of the organization to absorb new information (Barnard, 1938; Cohen, 1985; Deal, Meyer, & Scott, 1983; Hawley, 1977; Sarason, 1982; Szanton, 1981). Thus, in states where the legislature and/or the agency responsible for developing teacher education policy have staffs with professional expertise in dealing with systematic analysis, such as Connecticut, California, and Florida, the use of systematic analysis in the formulation of new policy has been relatively extensive (on California, see Bissell, 1979; Fuhrman & McDonnell, 1985). Moreover, the interest in evaluating policies that are enacted will be greater when the policymakers have the capacity to make more use of the information that evaluation can provide. Indeed, analysts within government agencies need work to do and answers to provide. Thus, they become advocates for systematic analysis. North Carolina provides a variation on this point. There the legislature entrusted the central university system with the responsibility for developing a plan for reform with the confidence, apparently, that it would insist on bold changes. The policy process in North Carolina made extensive use of systematic analysis, and much of the reform effort reflects the use of the analysis (University of North Carolina Board of Governors, 1986).

INCREASING THE UTILIZATION OF POLICY ANALYSIS

Systematic analysis has not been used extensively in the making of teacher education policy, and the available systematic analysis suggests that many of the policies that have been adopted are unlikely to make much of a difference in the contributions teacher education might make to educational improvement. Would a greater use of systematic analysis enhance the positive effects of public policy on teacher effectiveness? Knowledge is both a stimulus to and a constraint on decision making and, when used wisely, should enhance the prospects of effectively using scarce resources and avoiding harm. This could be particularly important in policy arenas, like teacher education, that are usually characterized by low conflict and low salience, because such arenas are easily invaded by powerful individuals and groups who often use the easy victories gained to avoid action that would involve greater political and economic costs. Every substantial effort at reforming public policy has its manifestation of *symbolic politics* (Edelman, 1964), and teacher education policy has played this role in the educational reform movement of the 1980s.

The conditions that now influence the use of systematic analysis are the product of circumstances and actions largely unplanned and undirected. Suggesting strategies for change seems to imply that there is someone or some organization in a position to act on these proposals. That is not the case with respect to the education of teachers, and no attempt is made to analyze the problems of implementing the proposals made. Moreover, some of the suggestions that follow might lead to the greater use of systematic analysis, but they have other consequences that would be seen as undesirable. These trade-offs are not explored here.

Affecting or Adapting to the Political Context

If systematic analysis is not much in demand when policy domains are stable, that is, in normal times, it is not surprising that the supply of systematic analysis during such periods is not extensive. During these times, the capabilities to provide and the readiness to use systematic analysis within governments, interest groups, and colleges and universities need to be nurtured.

To increase the opportunities to influence policy through systematic analysis during times of reform, several conditions could be encouraged. *First*, because the possibilities of political action engender little use of systematic analysis in the absence of conflict, those concerned with increasing the use of systematic analysis need to anticipate conflict and build coalitions with those with political power, such as teacher organizations, who are likely to be interested in substantive teacher education policy that can be mobilized when the policy domain is stabilized. To the extent that those with a potential interest in teacher education can speak with one voice, at least about the nature of the problems and the inappropriateness of certain policies, the rush to judgment that characterizes reform movements and precludes the use of systematic analysis might be slowed.

Second, if the issues that are likely to motivate an interest in teacher education from outside the conventional policy domain can be anticipated, systematic analysis can be readied. For example, given the interest the media had in teacher competence during the late 1970s and early 1980s, it would not have been difficult to guess that policymakers would become interested in quality control.

Third, if teacher education policy is likely to be substituted for reforms that more directly influence the quality of schools, it would seem important to clarify, through empirical research, the relationship between teacher education and student learning and what it would cost to bring about really meaningful reform in teacher education. It could be that teacher educators and their allies have been their own worst enemies in this respect. They have often claimed too much for teacher education and have been unwilling to acknowledge the full costs, much less the costs relative to other reforms, of the changes they proposed (Hawley, 1987).

Fourth, so long as teacher education is held in low repute, both inside and outside of universities, policymakers will have little reason to turn to systematic analysis. There are at least three ways that those concerned with improving teacher education through systematic analysis might directly address some of the perceptions that lead to the low status of teacher education: objectively describe the effects of teacher education, aggressively attack the myths upon which the low estimates of the quality and efficacy of teacher education are based, and identify reforms that are not self-serving and that are responsive to the perception that there is a need for substantive changes in the way teachers are educated. This last step would seem to require action endorsed by actors or potential actors in the teacher education policy arena, in addition to teacher educators themselves.

Increasing the Volume of High Quality Systematic Analysis

More and better trained providers of systematic analysis are needed. University leaders and college deans can influence the desirability of particular fields of inquiry by the priority they assign to them in allocating rewards and resources. Federal and foundation resources can be focused on research and development related to teacher education, especially on the education and activities of graduate students and junior researchers. A number of fellowship and young-scholar programs explicitly preclude persons whose field is education, much less teacher education. Efforts can be made by those who fund research and development to induce researchers from traditional disciplines to undertake systematic analysis related to teacher education by providing resources and by identifying generic issues, such as organizational change and the cognitive development of adults, that might be pursued in the context of studies of teacher education. The Spencer Foundation's Seed Grant Program of the early 1980s, for example, attracted young researchers from several disciplines to the study of education.

The methodological problems and relatively high cost associated with the study of teacher education outputs and outcomes come with the territory. But these could be diminished by interinstitutional inquiries constrained and directed by common design and measurement of variables. Much of the work of the National Center for Research on Teacher Education at Michigan State University focuses on the resolution of methodological problems in the study of teacher education, and this could lead to increased credibility for research on teacher education. One of the reasons that systematic analysis is not used is that it is often buried by a good deal of other information with which it is confused. Many education journals read like collections of "op-ed" pieces, though they are not labeled accordingly. The federally supported ERIC centers, the primary catalog of information to which policymakers might turn, focuses on the number of items recorded (because of federal funding incentives), rather than the reliability, validity, and importance of the information provided. Even with respect to such screens to information as the definition of research, most ERIC centers are not very rigorous.

Much of the information published about teacher education is not of high quality, but those who engage in systematic analysis related to teacher education are, on the whole, rather polite and constrained in their criticisms of analysis that is weak. Such civility might be traded for professional responsibility. And the use of systematic analysis might be increased if the number of publications that served as outlets for studies of teacher education were reduced by several hundred, or at least, as is the case with respect to other topics of systematic analysis (e.g., economic policy and medical practices), a clear hierarchy with respect to the status accorded to various publications were developed.

In their search for credibility and status within colleges and universities, many teacher education programs are placing greater emphasis on faculty research activity (Hawley, et al., 1988). However, more "research" by more teacher educators is not, in itself, desirable. Given the difficulty of doing good systematic analysis, the weak training many teacher educators receive in research methods, and the labor-intensive nature of teacher education itself, the spread of expectations for research productivity to teacher education programs generally is not likely to lead to further use of systematic analysis in the development of teacher education policy.

The demand for systematic analysis is constrained by doubts about the credibility of the providers and the analysis itself. Indeed, there appears to be a predisposition among policymakers to expect that researchers or experts not chosen by them or their staffs will provide information that is too theoretical or untimely (Hedrick & Van Horn, 1988; McDonnell, 1988). Thus, they tend to look for signs, such as jargon, references to theory or other states, or complicated statistical analysis, to support their expectations and to excuse them from having to examine the information provided. This skepticism might be addressed if teacher educators were more mindful that their actions as advocates often cast them in the roles of interest group members rather than of objective analysts or critics. Advocacy, of course, is perfectly legitimate in itself, but it does undermine the credibility of systematic analysis provided by the advocates, especially when the arguments made in advocacy do not employ systematic analysis or even emphasize the importance of experimentation and evaluation that might generate new knowledge through systematic analysis. Many of those engaged in the provision of systematic analysis have seen their consumers to be other analysts, or at best, practitioners, but not policymakers themselves. In the world of policy-making, familiarity breeds acceptance of ideas. Thus, investments by those who engage in systematic analysis in the development of personal relationships with policymakers and their staffs

would increase the use of information provided by systematic analysis.

More broadly, the providers of systematic analysis need to recognize that policymakers look to intermediaries, such as professional associations, the Education Commission of the States, and the Southern Regional Education Board, both to interpret and to legitimize the information they consider (McDonnell, 1988). The diffusion and use of analysis can be increased if its suppliers map information networks within each state. These are shaped by historical events and political cultures that vary from state to state and affect the significance of different types of political actors in the shaping of education policy (Fuhrman & McDonnell, 1985).

The perceived relevance of systematic analysis might be enhanced if the development of research agendas related to teacher education and the research itself were undertaken in collaboration with policymakers and their staffs. This might make analysis more relevant and might increase the capabilities of potential consumers to use it. Systematic analysis of teacher education needs to involve issues of cost and implementation difficulty, so that it can address the types of questions policymakers most often ask (see Levin, 1988).

Those who engage in analysis most systematically are often very tentative about asserting that their work provides clear answers. Although most policymakers want clear answers, they do not expect certainty, only the reduction of uncertainty. Developing estimates of the "subjective probability" of the validity of findings from systematic analysis might increase their use. Clarity and brevity of presentation would enhance the use of systematic analysis. Those who do systematic analysis would find a better market for their efforts if they tried to package it with knowledge of the assumptions and capabilities policymakers bring to the development of teacher education policy.

Asking the Right Questions

The extent to which systematic analysis would increase the contributions teacher education policy makes to the enhancement of student learning depends on the assumptions made about the purposes of teacher education. That is, what outputs and outcomes are expected of teacher education?

For various reasons, teacher educators have encouraged policymakers and the public to believe that the purpose of teacher education is to prepare people who, in general, are ready to assume the responsibilities of teaching as they enter the classroom to which they are assigned in their first position (AACTE, 1987). Just as a well-manufactured car rolls off the assembly line to drive, the producers of newly certified teachers are prone to claim that their products are ready for the road, rough as it might be. School systems eagerly accept, and even insist upon, this belief because it means that few resources need to be diverted to the special needs of new teachers. Indeed, it is not uncommon to assign new teachers to the teaching positions more experienced teachers have found excessively difficult and unsatisfying. The credibility of current assumptions about what teachers can learn in preservice education is being questioned by recent analyses of how teachers use information (Carter et al., 1987) and the stages of cognitive development through which teachers probably proceed (Theis-Sprinthall & Sprinthall, 1987).

The notion that teacher education can actually produce defect-free, fully functioning teachers is not one on which many teacher educators or school administrators would bet their salaries. The recent movement to establish induction programs for first-year teachers represents a recognition that extra support is needed. But teacher educators persist in asserting that they could do the job expected of them if only the schools would change (Holmes Group, 1986). Almost all induction programs are based on the assumption that new teachers need moral support and practical advice more than they need to develop greater professional skills or to probe more deeply into the fundamental knowledge upon which effective teaching and learning could be based. In short, if the test of the success of teacher education is its direct influence on teacher effectiveness, teacher education is not likely either to be as productive an investment as many other strategies for enhancing teacher effectiveness or to have the same political support as many strategies (e.g., reduced class size).

If not teacher effectiveness, what might the outcome of teacher education be that would more nearly reflect what can and should be done? An answer is that preservice teacher education, in addition to involving the acquisition of transferable knowledge about the subjects to be taught and a good general study of the liberal arts, should be responsible for the readiness and ability of teachers to learn how to teach. This is not a modest goal. Its achievement would require that prospective teachers learn how to learn from experience, how to understand the dynamics of the organizations within which they will work, how to assess student intellectual and social development, and how to include the use of educational technology in basic teaching.

Teacher education viewed in this way rests on the following propositions:

It is unlikely that the conditions under which teachers learn to teach approximate the conditions under which they initially teach.

Teachers' learning on the job is heavily influenced by the nature of their work and the culture of the school in which they first teach (Sarason, 1982).

The first teaching experience is likely, even under the best of circumstances, to be so complex that only a small part of what has been learned can be applied (Zeichner, 1987). It seems probable that much of what is taught in preservice teacher education cannot be understood and internalized with much sophistication until after a person has taught (Academy for Educational Development, 1985).

Teachers learn much of the competencies they most value on the job from personal experience (Bacharach, Bauer, & Shedd, 1986).

Knowledge about teaching is changing rapidly (Reynolds, 1989; Wittrock, 1986, p. 53)

The adoption of public policies to bring about certain outcomes through specific means creates expectations that the intended outcome will result. Public policies assign various roles in the process of teacher preparation and relieve others of the responsibility for promoting the desired outcome. For example, state policies that seek to make teacher candidates more ready to teach by requiring more field-based college courses encourage school systems to invest little in training new teachers. This, in turn, affects the level of investment school systems make in the professional development of experienced teachers. Thus, reformulation of the basic purposes of teacher preparation is important not only for increasing the probability that systematic analysis might yield positive assessments of its efficacy, but also because of its implications for the broader reshaping of teacher policy.

References

Academy for Educational Development. (1985). *Teacher development in schools.* New York: Author.

Alter, J., McCormick, J., & Joseph, N. (1984, September 24). Why teachers fail. *Newsweek*, pp. 64–70.

American Association of Colleges for Teacher Education. (1987). *Teaching teachers: Facts and figures.* Washington, DC: Author.

American Association of Colleges for Teacher Education. (1988). *Compendium of state policies.* Washington, DC: Author.

Ashton, P., Crocker, L., & Olejnik, J. (1987). *Teacher education research: A call for collaboration.* Paper presented at the meeting of the Southern Regional Consortium of Colleges of Education, Nashville.

Bacharach, S. B., Bauer, S. C., & Shedd, J. B. (1986). *The learning workplace: The conditions and resources of teaching.* Ithaca, NY: Organizational Analysis and Practice.

Bardach, E. (1977). *The implementation game.* Cambridge, MA: MIT Press.

Bardach, E. (1984). The dissemination of policy research to policy makers. *Knowledge, 6*(2), 125–144.

Barnard, C. (1938). *Functions of the executive.* Cambridge, MA: Harvard University Press.

Barr, R., & Dreeban, R. (1983). *How schools work.* Chicago: University of Chicago Press.

Bennie, W. A. (1982). Field-based teacher education. A reconsideration. *Teacher Educator, 17*(1), 19–24.

Berg, W. F., & Theado, R. (1981). The utilization of evaluative research in social welfare programs. *Social Service Review, 55*(2), 183–192.

Berliner, D. C. (1987). In pursuit of the expert pedagogue. *Educational Researcher, 15*(7), 5–13.

Berman, P., & McLaughlin, M. W. (1977). *Federal programs supporting educational change: Vol. VII. Factors affecting implementation and continuation.* Santa Monica, CA: RAND Corporation.

Bissell, J. (1979). Use of educational evaluation and policy studies by the California legislature. *Educational Evaluation and Policy Analysis, 1*(3), 29–37.

Bok, D. (1987). *The president's report, 1985–86.* Cambridge, MA: Harvard University.

Bolman, L., & Deal, T. E. (1983). *Modern approaches to understanding organizations.* San Francisco: Jossey-Bass.

Bransford, J. D. (1979). *Human cognition: Learning, understanding and remembering.* Belmont, CA: Wadsworth.

Bull, B. (1988). Confronting reform in teacher preparation: One state's experience. *Educational Evaluation and Policy Analysis, 9*(1), 25–40.

Carnegie Forum on Education and the Economy, Task Force on Teaching as a Profession. (1986). *A nation prepared: Teachers for the 21st century.* New York: Author.

Carnegie Foundation for the Advancement of Teaching. (1987). Prospective teachers: Career choices. *Change, 19*(2), 31–34.

Carter, K., Sabers, D., Cushing, K., Pinnegar, P., & Berliner, D. (1987). Processing and using information about students: A study of expert, novice, postulant teachers. *Teaching and Teacher Education, 3,* 147–157.

Caul, J., & Hahn, K. (1980). *Effects of increasing time allocated to student teaching.* Unpublished doctoral dissertation, University of Michigan, Ann Arbor.

Clifford, G. J. (1988). The professional school and its publics. In P. Jackson (Ed.), *Contributing to educational change* (pp. 1–26). Berkeley, CA: McCutchan.

Cohen, D. (1984). *Memo to the president: New California study belies conventional wisdom on academic qualifications of students enrolled in education programs.* Washington, DC: American Association of State Colleges and Universities.

Cohen, M. (1985). *Meeting the information needs of state education policymakers: Report of a survey of state policymakers.* Washington, DC: State Education Policy Consortium.

Darling-Hammond, L., Wise, A. E., & Pease, S. L. (1983). Teacher evaluation in the organizational context: A review of the literature. *Review of Educational Research, 53*(3), 285–328.

Davis, M. (1976). Eight weeks versus sixteen weeks of student teaching. *Journal of Educational Research, 70*(1), 31–34.

Deal, T. E., Meyer, J., & Scott, W. (1983). Organizational influences on educational innovation. In J. Baldridge & T. E. Deal (Eds.), *Managing change in educational organizations* (pp. 109–132). Berkeley, CA: McCutchan.

Denton, J. J., & Lacina, L. J. (1984). Quantity of professional education coursework linked with process measures of student teaching. *Teacher Education and Practice, 1*(1), 39–46.

Druva, C. A., & Anderson, R. D. (1983). Science teacher characteristics by teacher behavior and by student outcome: A meta-analysis of research. *Journal of Research in Science Teaching, 20*(5), 467–479.

Ducharme, R. J. (1986). Teacher educators: Description and analysis. In J. Raths & L. Katz (Eds.), *Advances in Teacher Education* (Vol. 2, pp. 61–67). Norwood, NJ: Ablex.

Edelman, M. (1984). *The symbolic uses of politics.* Urbana, IL: University of Illinois Press.

Education Commission of the States. (1985). *New directions for state teacher policies* (ECS working paper TR-85-1). Denver, CO: Author.

Egbert, R. L., & Kluender, M. M. (1984). *Using research to improve teacher education* (The Nebraska Consortium). Washington, DC: ERIC Clearinghouse on Teacher Education.

Elmore, R. F., & McLaughlin, M. W. (1988). *Steady work.* Santa Monica, CA: Rand Corporation.

Evertson, C. M., Hawley, W. D., & Zlotnik, M. (1985). Making a difference in educational quality through teacher education. *Journal of Teacher Education, 36*(13), 2–12.

Feiman-Nemser, S., & Buchmann, M. (1986). Pitfalls of experience in teacher preparation. In J. D. Raths & L. G. Katz (Eds.), *Advances in teacher education* (Vol. 2, pp. 61–67). Norwood, NJ: Ablex.

Feiman-Nemser, S., et al. (1986). Student teaching: Following the book or doing your own thing. *IRT Communications Quarterly,* pp. 2, 4.

Feistritzer, C. E. (1983). *The American teacher.* Washington, DC: Feistritzer Publications.

Fenstermacher, G. (1986). Philosophy of research on teaching. In M. C. Wittrock (Ed.), *Handbook of Research on Teaching* (3rd ed., pp. 37–49). New York: Macmillan.

Florio, D., Behrman M., & Goltz, D. (1979). What do policy makers think of educational research and evaluation? *Educational Evaluation and Policy Analysis, 1*(6), 61–87.

Freeze, C. R., & Buckner, S. L. (1984). The length of time spent in student teaching as a factor in student teacher performance evaluation. *Teacher Education and Practice, 1*(1), 47–50.

Fuhrman, S., & McDonnell, L. (1985). *Information networks for state policy-making.* Washington, DC: State Education Policy Consortium.

Fullan, M. (1985). Redefining the development of teachers. In S. Packard (Ed.), *The leading edge: Innovation and change in professional education* (pp. 165–178). Washington, DC: American Association of Colleges for Teacher Education.

Galambos, E. C., Cornett, L. M., & Spitler, H. D. (1985). *An analysis of transcripts of teachers and arts and science graduates.* Atlanta: Southern Regional Education Board.

Gideonse, H. D. (1987). Which way to Millinocket? *American Journal of Education, 95*(1), 309–313.

Good, T. L., & Brophy, J. E. (1986). Teacher behavior and student achievement. In M. C. Wittrock (Ed.), *Handbook of Research on Teaching* (3rd ed., pp. 328–375). New York: Macmillan.

Griffin, G. A. (1985). Teacher induction: Research issues. *Journal of Teacher Education, 36*(1), 42–46.

Griffin, G., Barnes, S., Hughes, R., Jr., O'Neal, S., Defino, M., Edwards, S., & Hukill, H. (1983). *Clinical preservice teacher education: Final report of the descriptive study.* Austin, TX: University of Texas at Austin, Research and Development Center for Teacher Education.

Hall, G. E. (1974). *A concerns-based model: A developmental conceptualization.* Austin, TX: University of Texas at Austin, Research and Development Center for Teacher Education.

Hall, G. E. (1982). Induction: The missing link. *Journal of Teacher Education, 33*(3), 53–55.

Hargrove, E. G. (1975). *The missing link: The study of the implementation of social policy.* Washington, DC: Urban Institute.

Hawley, W. D. (1977). Horses before carts: Developing adaptive schools and the limits of innovation. In S. Gove & F. Wirt (Eds.), *Political science and school politics* (pp. 1–22). Lexington, KY: D. C. Heath.

Hawley, W. D. (1987). The high costs and doubtful efficacy of extended teacher preparation programs: An invitation to more basic reform. *American Journal of Education, 95*(1), 275–298.

Hawley, W. D., Austin, A., & Goldman, E. (1988). *Changing the education of teachers.* Atlanta: Southern Regional Education Board.

Hawley, W. D., & Rosenholtz, S. (1984). Good schools: A synthesis of research on how schools influence student achievement [Special issue]. *Peabody Journal of Education, 4,* 1–178.

Hedrick, B., & Van Horn, C. E. (1988). Educational research information: Meeting the needs of state policymakers. *Theory into Practice, 27*(2), 106–110.

Holmes Group. (1986). *Tomorrow's teachers.* East Lansing, MI: Author.

Hood, P. (1979). *Indicators of educational knowledge production, dissemination and utilization: A conceptual framework.* San Francisco: Far West Laboratory for Educational Research and Development.

Hood, P., & Blackwell, L. (1976). *The education information market study* (Vols. I & II). San Francisco: Far West Laboratory for Educational Research and Development.

Hosford, P. L. (1984). *Using what we know about teaching*. Alexandria, VA: Association for Supervision and Curriculum Development.

Huling-Austin, L. (1987). *Beginning teacher programs: Research, practica and change*. Paper presented at the Professional Development Symposium, Canaan Valley Resort and Conference Center, WV.

Hurley, D. (1988). The mentor mystique. *Psychology Today, 22*(9), 41–43.

Katz, E., & Lazerfeld, P. F. (1955). *Personal influence*. Glencoe, IL: Free Press.

Killian, J. E., & McIntyre, D. J. (1988). Grade level as a factor in participation during early field experiences. *Journal of Teacher Education, 39*(2), 36–41.

Lanier, J. (1984). The preservice teacher education improvement project: A critical review. *Journal of Teacher Education, 35*(4), 24–27.

Lehman, E. W., & Waters, A. M. (1979). Control in policy research institutes: Some correlates. *Policy Analysis 5*(2), 201–221.

Levin, H. (1985). Solving the shortage of math and science teachers (Project No. 85-A2). Stanford, CA: Institute for Research on Educational Finance and Governance.

Levin, H. (1988). Cost-effectiveness and educational policy. *Educational Evaluation and Policy Analysis, 10*(1), 51–69.

Lieberman, A. (1980). Dissemination: The jargon and the reality. In C. Denham & A. Lieberman (Eds.), *Time to learn* (pp. 223–230). Washington, DC: National Institute of Education.

Lindblom, C., & Cohen, D. K. (1979). *Usable knowledge*. New Haven, CT: Yale University Press.

Lipsky, M. (1980). *Street-level bureaucracy: Dilemmas of the individual in public services*. New York: Basic Books.

Long, C., & Terry, P. (1986). *Using telecommunications for principals' professional development*. Paper presented at the annual meeting of the American Educational Research Association, San Francisco.

Lowi, T. (1969). *The end of liberalism*. New York: W. W. Norton.

Lyons, G. (1980). Why teachers can't teach. *Phi Delta Kappan, 62*(2), 108–112.

Lyson, T. A., & Falk, W. W. (1984). Recruitment to school teaching: The relationship between high school plans and early adult attainments. *American Educational Research Journal, 21*(2), 181–193.

MacCrae, D., Jr., & Wilde, J. A. (1979). *Policy analysis for public decision*. North Scituate, MA: PWS Publishers, Duxbury Press.

Malen, B., Murphy, M. J., & Geary, S. (1988). The role of evaluation information in legislative decisionmaking: A case study of a loose cannon on deck. *Theory Into Practice, 27*(2), 111–125.

Malone, M. (1985). *A quantitative synthesis of preservice teacher field-experience*. Paper presented at the annual meeting of the American Educational Research Association, Chicago.

Marshall, C. (1988). Bridging the chasm between policy makers and educators. *Theory Into Practice, 27*(2), 98–105.

McDonnell, L. M. (1988). Can education research speak to state policy? *Theory Into Practice, 27*(2), 91–97.

McNergney, R., et al. (1988). *Should a master's degree be required for all Virginia teachers?* Charlottesville, VA: Commonwealth Center for the Education of Teachers.

Mitchell, D. E. (1984). Education policy analysis: The state of the art. *Education Administration Quarterly, 20*(3), 129–160.

National Commission for Excellence in Teacher Education. (1985). *A call for change in teacher education*. Washington, DC: American Association of Colleges for Teacher Education.

Nelli, E. R. (1984). A research-based response to allegations that education students are academically inferior. *Action in Teacher Education, 6*(3), 73–80.

Nelson, M., & Sieber, S. D. (1976) Innovations in urban secondary schools. *School Review, 84*, 213–231.

NTE pass rates endanger ten North Carolina education programs. (1988, December 22). *Black Issues in Higher Education*, p. 24.

Olsen, D. G. (1985). The quality of prospective teachers: Education vs. noneducation graduates. *Journal of Teacher Education, 36*(5), 56–59.

Passow, H. (1987). *Present and future directions in school reform*. Paper presented at a conference on restructuring schooling for quality education: A new reform agenda, Trinity University, San Antonio, TX.

Reynolds, M. C. (Ed.). (1989). *Knowledge base for the beginning teacher*. Oxford, England: Pergamon Press.

Richardson-Koehler, V. (1988). Barriers to the effective supervision of student teaching: A field study. *Journal of Teacher Education, 39*(2), 28–34.

Rodman, B. (1988, February 24). Alternate route said a success. *Education Week*, p. 7.

Roth, R., & Mastain, R. (Eds.). (1984). *The NASDTEC Manual*. Sacramento, CA: National Association of State Directors of Teacher Education and Certification.

Sabatier, P. (1978). The acquisition and utilization of technical information by administrative agencies. *Administrative Science Quarterly, 23*(3), 396–417.

Samson, G. E., Borger, J. B., Weinstein, T., & Walberg, H. J. (1984). Pre-teaching experiences and attitudes: A quantitative synthesis. *Journal of Research and Development in Education, 17*(4), 52–56.

Sarason, S. B. (1982). *The culture of the school and the problem of change* (2nd ed.). Boston: Allyn & Bacon.

Scannell, M. (1988). *State characteristics associated with policies restricting entry to teaching: Merits and consequences*. Paper presented at the annual meeting of the American Educational Research Association, New Orleans.

Shulman, L. S. (1986). Paradigms and research programs in the study of teaching: A contemporary perspective. In M. C. Wittrock (Ed.), *Handbook of Research on Teaching* (3rd ed., pp. 3–36). New York: Macmillan.

Smith, D. C. (Ed.). (1983). *Essential knowledge for beginning educators*. Washington, DC: American Association of Colleges for Teacher Education.

Smith, M., & O'Day, J. (in press). *Teaching policy and research in teaching*. New Brunswick, NJ: Rutgers University, Center for Educational Policy Research.

Southern Regional Education Board. (1988a). *Alternative teacher certification programs: Are they working?* Atlanta: Author.

Southern Regional Education Board. (1988b). *State-level evaluation of teacher education programs in SREB states*. Atlanta: Author.

Spero, I. K. (1985, July 31). *The use of student financial aid to attract prospective teachers: A survey of state efforts*. Testimony before the Subcommittee on Postsecondary Education, Committee on Education and Labor, U.S. House of Representatives.

Stedman, D. (1988). The preparation and retention of teachers. In R. Haskins & D. MacCrae, Jr., (Eds.), *Policies for America's public schools: Teachers, equity and indicators* (pp. 55–69). Norwood, NJ: Ablex.

Stodolsky, S. (1988). *The subject matters: Classroom activity in math and social studies*. Chicago: University of Chicago Press.

Sykes, G. (1985). Teacher education in the United States. In B. Clark (Ed.), *The school and the university: An international perspective* (pp. 264–290). Berkeley, CA: University of California Press.

Szanton, P. L. (1981). *Not well advised*. New York: Russell Sage Foundation.

Thies-Sprinthall, L., & Sprinthall, N. (1987). Preservice teachers as adult learners: A new framework for teacher education. In M. Haberman & J. Backus (Eds.), *Advances in teacher education* (Vol. 3, pp. 35–56). Norwood, NJ: Ablex.

University of North Carolina Board of Governors. (1986). *The education of North Carolina's teachers: A report to the 1987 North Carolina General Assembly.* Chapel Hill, NC: University of North Carolina.

University of Wisconsin System Task Force on Teacher Education. (1984). *Benchmarks of excellence: Recommendations of the University of Wisconsin System Task Force on Teacher Education 1984.* Madison, WI: Author.

U.S. Department of Education (1987). *Opening alternative routes to teaching: A strategy for increasing the pool of qualified teachers.* Washington, DC: Author.

Useem, M., & Dimaggio, P. (1978). An example of evaluation research as a cottage industry: The technical quality and impact of arts audience studies. *Sociological Methods and Research, 7*(1), 55–84.

Vance, V. S., & Schlechty, P. C. (1982). The distribution of academic ability in the teaching force: Policy implications. *Phi Delta Kappan, 64*(1), 22–27.

Veenman, S. (1984). Perceived problems of beginning teachers. *Review of Educational Research, 54*(2), 143–178.

Warren-Little, J. (1988). *District policy choices and teachers' professional development opportunities.* Paper presented at the annual meeting of the American Educational Research Association, New Orleans.

Weaver, W. T. (1981). Demography, quality, and decline: The challenge for schools of education for the 1980s. In *Policy for the education of educators: Issues and implications* (pp. 50–65). Washington, DC: American Association of Colleges for Teacher Education.

Weiss, C. (1977). Research for policy's sake: The enlightenment function of social resources. *Policy Analysis, 3*(4), 531–545.

Wildavsky, A. (1964). *The politics of the budgetary process.* Boston: Little, Brown.

Wildavsky, A. (1979). *Speaking truth to power: The art and craft of policy analysis.* Boston: Little, Brown.

Wittrock, M. C. (Ed.). (1986). *Handbook of research on teaching* (3rd ed.). New York: Macmillan.

Yin, R. K., Heald, K. A., Vogel, M. E., Fleishaur, P. D., & Vladeck, B. C. (1976). *A review of case studies of technological innovation in state and local services* (pp. 72–75). Santa Monica, CA: RAND Corporation.

Zeichner, K. M. (1987). The ecology of field-experience: Toward an understanding of the role of field experiences in teacher development. In M. Haberman & J. M. Backus (Eds.), *Advances in teacher education* (Vol. 3, (pp. 94–117). Norwood, NJ: Ablex.

Zeichner, K. M., & Liston, D. P. (1987). Teaching student teachers to reflect. *Harvard Educational Review, 57*(1), 23–48.

·10·

FINANCING TEACHER EDUCATION

Bruce A. Peseau
THE UNIVERSITY OF ALABAMA

A major issue in teacher education across the United States concerns the need for program standards and policies that will help insure adequate financing for quality programs. Even in the new National Council for Accreditation of Teacher Education standards, the policy concerning minimally adequate program funding is vague. Historically, the bulk of the research and rhetoric on teacher education focuses on program characteristics and delivery systems, but without direct relationships to funding and resources. Nevertheless, academic program funding, which provides resources for faculty, support staff, facilities, operating costs, and other essentials, strongly influences program quality in any academic discipline. Without definitive guidelines for rigorously enforced program funding standards, generalized quality improvement of teacher education is, at best, wishful thinking.

There is abundant literature on the economic and social benefits of higher education. There is also an extensive body of literature on the concepts and processes of determining and analyzing the financing of academic programs. The research becomes scarce and fragmented as it focuses more specifically on a particular discipline (e.g., engineering, nursing, teacher education). There are, however, sufficient studies to provide a useful base for a beginning understanding of the financial aspects of teacher-preparation programs.

This chapter summarizes the literature on quantitative aspects of teacher education. Concepts and research on the economics of higher education are briefly presented. This introduction provides a framework for understanding more specific aspects of financing higher education, especially teacher education. The economics of higher education includes topics such as the development of human capital, who pays and who benefits, accountability for the use of resources, and the relationship of the college experience to subsequent success in the workplace and the community. Broadly grouped, these categories reflect the breadth of the literature on the economics, value, and outcomes of higher education.

This provides a background for looking at how higher education, especially teacher education, is financed. Seven specific areas of concern are discussed: (a) funding higher education and teacher education, (b) inputs for teacher education, (c) outputs and productivity in teacher education, (d) internal and external financing comparisons, (e) identification of peer programs, f) financing inservice education, and (g) cost-effectiveness and cost benefits of teacher education.

RESEARCH ON THE ECONOMICS OF EDUCATION

The section on the economics of education includes only essential ideas and key research findings. A large body of research exists on this field. The points covered are essential for understanding the methods and results of studies on the finance of academic programs. Benson's (1988) chapter in the *Handbook of Research on Educational Administration* is especially recommended as an important study of the economics of education; it provides the foundation for more specific financial analyses of programs.

The Educational Policies Commission (1940) produced the landmark essay, which explained the influence of education on economic growth. Major contributions to understanding that complex relationship were made by Anderson and Bowman (1965); Becker (1975); Davis and Morrall (1974); Denison (1962); Innes, Jacobson, and Pellegrin (1965); Johns and Morphet (1960); Leftwich and Sharp (1980); Rivlin (1971); Schultz

The author is grateful for the constructive and detailed reviews provided by Deborah Verstegen (University of Virginia) and Richard Wisniewski (University of Tennessee at Knoxville).

(1963); and Solmon (1973). Because educators have traditionally resisted studying their discipline from the perspectives of price and efficiency, efforts at program improvement have tended to be shaped by ideals and concepts of innovation. However, Schultz (1963) points out that "whatever the benefits, costs really matter" (p. 27). Analysis of the price of education does not debase it. Because the rates of return on investment in education are higher than on investment in nonhuman capital, the concept should be a key argument for adequately funded programs. The concept of cost efficiency, however, appears to hold negative connotations for educators. Nevertheless, how effectively academic programs utilize resources is a fundamental policy issue.

Basic research on the economic and financial aspects of academic programs is vital to the creation of realistic and better policies on how teacher education should be financed. Research has contributed to a better understanding of at least four primary issues: the linkages between investment in education and economic development; the direct and hidden costs of education to the student; the payback, or returns, from educational investments; and the relationship between research on educational economics and policy formation.

Schultz (1963) pioneered a framework for understanding the linkages between education and economic development. As a key investment in national growth, education provides significant social benefits by enhancing a person's capabilities as both producer and consumer, in addition to providing individual benefits such as a higher salary, more leisure time, and a better quality of life. From 1929 to 1956, education accounted for 21 to 40 percent of national income growth. Denison (1962) estimates that increased educational attainments per member of the labor force contributed 23 percent to the national income growth rate. Bowman (1964) criticizes the methodologies of these studies and cautions that such findings be interpreted modestly, using them as rough, not precise, explanations. The inputs of education into a complex national economy interact with many other factors such as international competitiveness. Rivlin (1971) acknowledges that strong relationships between education and economic growth seldom show up statistically, even though they exist. Nevertheless, the power of education to individual and national development continues to be widely supported. In addition, Thurow (1977) shows that education changes the differentials between rich and poor, serving as a primary facilitator of economic and social mobility.

Schultz (1963) reasons that both the individual and society should pay for education, because both benefit from the investment. The hidden costs to the individual, such as earnings forgone while attending school, comprise about 60 percent of the total costs of an education. Federal and state investments in education are in the form of grants, loans, and minimum program funding in elementary/secondary education and formula funding in higher education. The Carnegie Commission on Higher Education (1973; 1974) reports that costs of higher education are shared 30 percent by families, 60 percent by taxpayers, and 10 percent by philanthropists. The payback to society is in the form of worker productivity, economic growth, consumerism, and taxes paid. Similar analyses are provided by Cohn (1979), Eckhaus (1973), Johns and Morphet (1960), and Murgo (1972).

Teachers and teacher education faculty do not compare favorably with other professionals on the rate of return on their educational investment. Cohn (1979) attributes this to the employment of teachers primarily in the public sector, where salaries tend to be lower than in the private sector. Schultz (1963) reports the high dropout rate of teachers from the labor force as a factor. Psacharopoulos (1977) presents data from 10 countries; whereas higher education overall returned 1.5 to 5.0 times the investment, it was among the lowest for teachers in the United States, but higher in the United Kingdom. In contrast, Rivlin (1971) reports that vocational rehabilitation education programs have a return ratio of 12 or 13 to 1. However, R. H. Anderson (1980) estimates the return to be negative for teacher education, even through the doctoral level, because most teachers are on the public payroll and because state funding for teacher education programs is only at a marginal, survival level. Duff and Dold (1978) found little relationship between education and economic returns. There was a range of $15,000 among college majors for starting salaries. Market conditions were the determinants of what new college graduates were paid.

In addition to personal and societal benefits (Bowen, 1980; Hartnett, 1971; Pace, 1979; Solmon & Ochsner, 1978), the creation and application of new knowledge are major contributions of education. Bowen (1980) explains the benefits of higher education research and service to economic productivity. Because of the holistic effects of education, such contributions are difficult to measure. They are sufficiently identifiable, however, to significantly influence national policy.

FUNDING HIGHER EDUCATION AND TEACHER EDUCATION

Because investment in education plays such a vital role in social and personal development, how education is funded must be a major concern. The limited resources of the state are shared among higher education institutions and programs through a series of decisions, from the legislature to college and university administrators. Rivlin (1971) criticizes the lack of systematic rationality in decision making about public services. Public aspirations for better social services such as education have shifted from quantity—providing enough for those who need it—to quality. The widespread use of minimum foundations programs for public elementary and secondary education and of formula funding for higher education reflect confidence in the belief that resources influence program quality.

Equity in Program Funding

Equity is one of the foundation concepts undergirding both K–12 and higher education funding. Augenblick (1983), Coons (1980), Guthrie (1980), Jordon and McKeown (1980), and Thomas (1980) describe equity as the expectation that all students have access to programs with reasonably adequate resources. In public higher education, Allen and Topping (1979), Bowen (1980), Halstead (1974), and Lawrence, Weathersby, and Patterson (1970) report studies of cost comparisons between programs, as a means of comparing the equity and adequacy of funding. Because no a priori standard of adequacy is known, most of the concept's rationale is based on past experience, as shown in the pioneering work in Texas (Texas College and University System, 1970) and in more recent studies in Kansas (Downey, Lahey, & Hoyt, 1982). These analyses of historic costs provide the framework for higher education formula funding. Because how much a higher education program of minimally acceptable quality should cost is not known, funding formulas based on past spending patterns have significant flaws built into them. Nonetheless, formula funding can facilitate decision making about a given program's funding because it is based on comparisons with other programs. How equitably resources are shared among programs is another matter; such decisions might be enforced by accountability procedures initiated by the allocating authority, or they might be left largely to trust in the integrity of local decision makers. However, political influence on resource-allocation decisions at the local or institutional level is a powerful force in higher education.

The Need for Standards in Teacher Education

Professional programs often communicate their minimum quality expectations through accreditation standards. C. Gross (1975) and Masoner (1972) describe the imperative need for a national teacher education policy that includes minimum program-financing standards. Gross states that teacher education has failed because educators have not insisted on adequate funding as a vital prerequisite for success. Other researchers (Berliner, 1984; Denton, Peters, & Savage, 1984; Orr & Peseau, 1979; Peseau, 1984, 1986, 1988; Peseau & Orr, 1980) point out the negative consequences of the lack of quantitative resource standards for teacher education. Downey et al. (1982) criticize the continuing claims of better quality in teacher education without more program funding.

Quantitative Indicators and Funding Formulas

Institutional and departmental financial reports explain how funding was distributed among and within academic programs, and several kinds of data reflect what was produced with those resources. Orwig and Jones (1977) reason that better quantitative indicators help higher education become more systematic and accurate in reporting for accountability purposes, although linking data to decisions is still problematic. The Western Interstate Commission on Higher Education (Lawrence et al., 1970) and the National Center for Higher Education Management System (NCHEMS) have led the research on input and output indicators and their relationships. It continues to be a major area of inquiry (Allen & Topping, 1979; Atkinson, 1983; Balderston, 1970; Bowen, 1981; Brinkman & Teeter, 1987; Brown, 1970; Chambers, 1979; Coleman & Bolte, 1977; Dressel & Simon, 1976; Enthoven, 1970; Noe, 1986; Salley, 1977; Vaizey, 1970; Walters, 1981; Wildman, 1976). Leslie and Brinkman (1988) published a meta-analysis of more than 200 studies of resource and productivity indicators in higher education. They found great variation among measures of the indicators, particularly those focusing on costs per full-time equiva-

lent (FTE) student, costs per credit hour, and student–faculty ratios, usually differentiated by academic discipline and level.

Academic program resource indicators are reflected in line-item budget allocations (number of faculty, salaries by faculty rank, support personnel, operating expenses, graduate assistants, and capital outlay). These are translated into FTE personnel positions and support costs. Output or productivity indicators include credit hours produced, class size, number of courses and sections offered, cost per credit hour and per student, student–faculty ratios, and degrees awarded, by level. The relationships between resource and productivity indicators are reported in analytical studies by Denton and Smith (1983), Peseau (1984, 1986, 1988), Peseau and Orr (1980) and Tudor (1988) for teacher education and by Hemp and Brunson (1984) for engineering education.

A consensus exists that the principal academic program productivity data—credit hours produced—must be weighted to differentiate between academic disciplines and levels (undergraduate, master's, and post-master's levels). However, there are substantial interstate differences among weighting formulas. Further, broad-based comparative analyses between institutions must recognize differences in quarter- and semester-based academic calendars and transform credit hours produced, so they are comparable (Peseau, 1984, 1986, 1988). Teacher education also has extensive clinical components and costs, as in nursing and medical education, that must be taken into account (Peseau, Backman, & Fry, 1987). Unfortunately, the differential weights intended to reflect program complexity, that, therefore, infer relative funding differences, are uniformly lowest for teacher education in higher education funding formulas (R. H. Anderson, 1980; F. M. Gross, 1973; Peseau, 1988; Texas Select Committee on Public Education, 1984).

Teacher education is generally considered to be primarily didactic in nature, which results in its being weighted at the lowest cost levels in funding formulas (Allen & Topping, 1979; Downey et al., 1982; F. M. Gross, 1973; Peseau & Orr, 1980; Spence, 1978; Texas College and University System, 1970). These weights are even lower than the typical college programs in English, mathematics, and history. In reality, most teacher education programs require substantial portions of their preparation requirements in clinical form, ranging from classroom observation to student teaching.

Those program components were included by Peseau et al. (1987) in the design of a cost model for clinical teacher education. Based on actual costs for eight university programs in Florida, the clinical activities involved several cost-related functions atypical of didactic courses: (a) program coordination including student placement, travel, and communications; (b) faculty costs budgeted for clinical supervision; (c) support services and materials; (d) simulation and microteaching costs; and (e) payments to cooperating teachers. These added costs ranged from $134 to $934 per clinical course. The study recommended higher weights of 2.0 for clinical observation and 2.5 for clinical practice courses, compared with 1.5 for didactic courses in teacher education; better compensation for cooperating teachers; and at least some clinical experiences in two-thirds of the undergraduate teacher education programs. Such a program would include about 33 percent classroom instruction, 22 percent clinical instruction, and 44 percent clinical practice. Applying the recommended weights to program activities distributed in these proportions, funding of the eight Florida programs would have to be increased by a total of 106 percent. Such a redesign and its much higher costs for clinical preparation reflect, again, the severe underfunding of most teacher education programs.

INPUTS FOR TEACHER EDUCATION

Denton and Smith (1983) and Nash and Ducharme (1983) describe how teacher education reforms focus on program design and ignore fundamental financial requirements. Hawley (1986) criticizes the Holmes Group reform for avoiding the issue of adequate financing.

The outcomes of preparation programs, and ultimately their quality, cannot be judged independent of inputs. The objective of having cost data is to relate costs to program outputs in the form of cost-benefit and cost-efficiency analyses. These data also help in the assessment of the production functions. The inputs for teacher education can be clustered into data on (a) financial resources, (b) faculty, (c) support services, and (d) students. Of course, funding is the engine that drives all other resources.

The identification and use of input indicators is widely supported (Atkinson, 1983; Caruthers & Orwig, 1979; Caulley & Dawson, 1980; Froomkin, n.d.; Huff, 1975; Orwig & Jones, 1977; Rivlin, 1971; Vaizey, 1970; Walters, 1981). Standard cost items, such as for faculty, support staff, operating costs, and fringe benefits, reflect the inputs made available to academic programs. These data must be gathered in standardized form from a broad base of institutions over a long period of time. The relative size of a program—the concept of economies of scale—influences how much it costs to produce something (a graduate, a credit hour, a course). Regional wage markets also influence academic program costs.

Teacher education suffers from a historic lag in understanding what preparation programs cost and what they should cost. A small but growing sector of the research on teacher education explores this issue (Berliner, 1984; Bloom, 1983; D. L. Clark & Marker, 1975; Duff & Dold, 1978; Feldmann & Fisher, 1982; Klitgaard, Siddiqui, Arshad, Niaz, & Khan, 1985; Lanier & Little, 1986; Texas Select Commission on Public Education, 1984). Even fewer sources have produced in-depth studies of the inputs and outputs of teacher education (Denton & Smith, 1983; Peseau, 1982, 1984, 1986, 1988; Tudor, 1988). The American Association of Colleges for Teacher Education annually collects extensive data from member programs (AACTE, 1983), but it is of little practical use beyond developing individual and national descriptive profiles. There has been no attempt to use the massive AACTE data base to identify cost or productivity measures that might serve as bench marks for comparison. Without such comparisons, the reader is left to assume that, whatever resources an institution might provide, its teacher education program is acceptable—clearly not a contribution to stimulating improvements.

Financial Resources

Relatively little is known about the financial resources provided teacher education, though it is a critical determinant of how programs are carried out. The data collected by Peseau (1986) for the Association for Colleges and Schools of Education in State Universities and Land-Grant Colleges (ACSESULGC) were from public universities with teacher education programs through the doctorate; 77 programs from a population of 111 provided data for the 1984–1985 year. The teacher education fiscal year budget from both university and contract and grant sources ranged from $16.3 to $1.46 million. The average annual budget from university sources only was $4.74 million. An average of 59 percent was spent for instructional faculty, 7 percent for research positions, 4 percent for service positions, 7 percent for administration, 9 percent for support personnel, 6 percent for graduate assistants, 7 percent for departmental operating expenses including travel, and 1 percent for capital outlay.

These public universities were financed from three primary sources: state legislative appropriation, contracts and grants, and student tuition. Academic year (1984–1985), university-wide tuition costs ranged from $2,740 in one state to only $120 in another where in-state students were highly subsidized. The national average tuition cost for an academic year was $1,238.

Faculty

Faculty positions accounted for 70 percent of the university-supplied funding. Contract and grant funds tended to be used more for support staff, graduate assistants, and operating costs than for faculty, other than for grant-administration personnel.

The 77 major universities that reported data for the Peseau (1986) study varied greatly, with a range of 229 to 30 headcount faculty; the average was 104. The mean salary for faculty at the full professor rank was $38,413 for the academic year, $30,179 for associate professors, $24,198 for assistant professors, and $18,489 for instructors. The academic year salary ranged from $56,046, for professors in Alaska, to a low of $8,666, for instructors in another state. However, within faculty ranks, the salary range was about 2 to 1, with the exception of instructor-level faculty, where it was more than 4 to 1.

About 85 percent of all faculty were budgeted for instruction, 4 percent for research, 3 percent for service, and 8 percent for administration from university funds. Faculty in those public university, doctoral-granting, teacher education programs predominantly held the PhD (48 percent) as their highest earned degree, 32 percent the EdD, less than 1 percent the EdS, 13 percent the master's, and 6 percent some other degree.

Support Services

Secretarial and technical specialists provide support services to teacher education faculty (Peseau, 1986). Among 77 programs in public universities, there was a ratio of one such support staff position per 3.76 faculty positions. Graduate assistants are employed, usually on a half-time basis, to assist faculty with research, teach undergraduate classes, and supervise clinical experiences. The average number of FTE graduate assistant positions was 21.21, or about 42 headcount graduate assistants on a half-time basis.

Departmental services also include the costs of supplies and materials, communications, and travel. An average of $3,129 was provided each FTE faculty from university financing during 1984–1985.

Students

Data inputs about students include their demographics, numbers, retention rates, sources of financial support, and supply and demand factors influencing enrollment. Research on student demographics, numbers, and flow is typical of the information found in the annual American Association of Colleges for Teacher Education data base on teacher education. Romney and Micek (1977) provide a useful student-flow model that could be applied in teacher education. Teacher supply and demand studies were of great interest in the 1980s. Gifford and Stoddart (1985) estimate that 50 to 75 percent of California teachers would need to be replaced by 1991. However, national estimates of teacher supply and demand vary greatly; Atkinson (1983) points out that educational systems are so diffuse that accurate forecasting is problematic. Successful competition by other academic specializations (business, engineering, law, and medicine) for recruitment of women and minorities has seriously eroded both the quantity and quality of potential teacher education recruits (Burns, 1985; Darling-Hammond, 1984).

Low salaries for teachers also encourage some to opt for other career choices. Gifford and Stoddart (1985) found that California teachers earned only 80 percent as much as social workers and 60 percent as much as engineers. The National Education Association (NEA, 1983) reports that teachers' salaries were only 60 percent of all college-educated professionals'. Roth (1981) compared seven teacher supply and demand studies and concluded that shortages at the elementary school level and in some secondary teaching fields were already substantial. However, most of these market demand studies focus on population demographics (live births projected to school age) and ignore other influential factors. In particular, changes in student–teacher ratios are strongly influenced by general economic conditions and what the public is willing to pay. Further, the supply-and-demand studies do not explore a major related problem: the graying of the teacher work force and the probability of a massive number of retirements of teachers who began their careers with the post–World War II baby boom.

Accurate counts of students enrolled in teacher education programs are not only problematic but also very imprecise. Enrollments in classes and credit hours produced are better data from which to calculate full-time equivalent students. An FTE student is one with a full load of 15 credit hours enrolled for two semesters. Most students, particularly at the undergraduate level, complete only a portion of their studies in teacher education.

Peseau (1986) reports 112,332 FTE students in teacher education in 77 universities for 1984–1985. The headcount number could be more than twice as great. Of course, only 61,180 (55 percent) were enrolled as undergraduates; 33,820 (30 percent) were enrolled at the master's level; and 20,368 (15 percent) were enrolled at the post-master's and doctoral levels. The average of this group of programs was 1,518 FTE students, with a ratio of FTE students to FTE instructional faculty of 15 to 1. Again, the ratio of headcount students to faculty might have been twice as great.

OUTPUTS AND PRODUCTIVITY IN TEACHER EDUCATION

Beyond the important and abstract issue of the quality of graduates produced by teacher education, quantitative data on outputs and productivity help administrators understand and improve preparation programs. Brown (1970) stresses that output measures must be (a) quantifiable, (b) stated in comparable units, (c) equally available and meaningful to different institutions, (d) appropriate for all members of a group, (e) consensually derived, and (f) flexible. Academic program output measures usually focus on student and faculty activity data. Enthoven (1970) and Rivlin (1971) describe the need for output information as an aid to more rational decision making about how resources are shared and how well they were used. Such decisions can lead to fair judgments about the effectiveness of faculty and programs. Because those programs vary greatly within teacher education (Peseau, 1988), data must be broken down to reflect differences in program type, level (undergraduate, master's, and post-master's), and object of expenditure. If data are related to specific programs (cost centers), then cost models can be developed (Peseau et al., 1987). Because academic program demand and productivity change over time, the use of longitudinal and comparative output data should encourage systematic procedures for the allocation and reallocation of resources.

Credit-Hour Production

The teaching of courses typically absorbs most of the financial resources in teacher education. The number of credit hours produced is a principal indicator of productivity and is used for comparisons with other programs. As has been noted, this indicator must be differentially weighted by level (often lower division, upper division, master's, post-master's, and sometimes dissertation research) and by program (engineering, humanities, sciences, teacher education) to reflect differences in program complexity (Allen & Topping, 1979; Balderston, 1970; Enthoven, 1970; F. M. Gross, 1973; Meisinger, 1976; Walters, 1981). Weighting by race, sex, and socioeconomic status of students has also been recommended (Vaizey, 1970), but it has not been widely applied. Teacher education carries the lowest weights of academic disciplines in most state funding formulas. To enhance comparability, credit hours produced at quarter- and semester-based campuses must be equated (Peseau, 1986, 1988). Those weights applied to levels of credit hours produced can be used for both analyzing productivity and defining budget needs (Spence, 1978).

Peseau (1986) created a single indicator, the institutional complexity index, to reflect the internal mix of credit hours produced by level. Among 77 teacher education programs in public universities, the index ranged from 1.22 (mostly undergraduate) to 5.43 (almost entirely post-master's). Interestingly, the cost per weighted credit hour was much higher in predominantly undergraduate programs ($58.23) than in predominantly graduate programs ($15.42).

In one of the teacher education programs in the Peseau study, students paid 74 percent of the direct costs of the program with their tuition, whereas students in another, predominantly advanced, graduate program, paid almost 300 percent of the direct program costs with their tuition.

Feldmann and Fisher (1982) produced a cluster analysis of 179 teacher education programs They found the expenditure per credit hour higher in programs other than teacher education. This reflects the severe underfunding of teacher education.

Credit hours produced during the fiscal year 1984–1985, including the summer term, ranged from 100,091 to 7,674 among 77 teacher education programs reported by Peseau (1986), with an average of 39,658. When these data were transformed using weighting factors to differentiate undergraduate, master's, and post-master's levels, the average more than doubled to 92,044 weighted credit hours (WCH). The direct expenditures per weighted credit hour were calculated to be $50.97. When that cost was multiplied by 30 credit hours (an academic year equivalent) and the undergraduate weight of 1.04, the academic year cost for an undergraduate teacher education student was $1,590.

Faculty Productivity

What faculty produce, at least in terms of their instructional effort and the budgets assigned for that purpose, can be studied in various ways. Walters (1981) points out that the cost per student must include both direct costs of instruction and indirect costs of program support and materials. Smaller programs normally have higher costs, because some costs are fixed and do not show efficiency until a sufficient size, or critical mass, is reached. Henard (1977) used quantitative factors, (credit hours taught, weighted credit hours produced, contact hours, and load factors, which vary with type of instruction), but also suggests the need to provide credit for university and committee service, professional development, scholarly publication, advising, and time spent in departmental governance. Kully (1986) reports the problems of accounting for faculty productivity when the standards for work load change from one budget period to another. The level and mode of instruction directly affect resource needs, because the curriculum becomes more specialized and class sizes are smaller at advanced levels. Much of the quantification of what faculty do ignores the quality of the student–faculty relationship. It is reasonable to posit that the quality of that relationship is directly related to the ratio of students to professors.

The study of faculty productivity in teacher education is an emerging area of interest. Bloom (1983) compared teaching loads in several academic areas in 21 major universities, using 3 years of data. Three levels of instruction were used but were classified as lower division, upper division, and graduate, thereby ignoring the predominantly graduate, and particularly post-master's, makeup of many teacher education programs. Moreover, Bloom used the lowest weights for teacher education; because of those low weights, the results show the productivity of teacher education faculty as consistently low, compared with other disciplines. The use of appropriate weights between disciplines and levels makes a great difference in the results.

The studies by Peseau (1986) under ACSESULGC sponsorship were limited to the internal analysis of faculty productivity in teacher education and comparative analysis between and within states (Peseau, 1988). Peseau (1986) found that 407 credit hours, or 929 weighted credit hours, were produced per FTE faculty in 77 teacher education programs. This number was probably high, because these were predominantly graduate programs. About 57 percent of the unweighted credit hours were produced at the undergraduate level, 28 percent at the master's level, and 11 percent at the post-master's level. However, after raw credit hours were weighted, 32 percent of the weighted credit hours were at the undergraduate level, 30 percent at the master's level, and 38 percent at the post-master's level. The average undergraduate class size was 20, with 11 at the master's, and 8 at the post-master's, level.

Degrees and Certificates Awarded

The AACTE (1983) data base on teacher education includes comprehensive information on degrees and certificates awarded from a broad base of institutions. Although these are interesting indicators for assessing program productivity, they are not as accurate as weighted credit hours produced. Degree completion includes academic components usually provided by colleges and departments other than teacher education. In some states, licensure and certification cannot be tracked easily because it is outside the authority of the state's central education agency. Although Peseau's (1986) studies of teacher education in senior universities included degrees awarded by level as data elements, no attempt was made to separate those credit hours specifically contributing to certification.

Peseau found that 112,332 degrees were awarded by the 77 teacher education programs in his study. Of those, 38,500 (49 percent) were at the baccalaureate level, 14,938 (39 percent) were at the master's level, 784 (3 percent) were at the educational specialist level, and 3,108 (8 percent) were at the doctoral level. However, these data did not account for the substantial amount of coursework and credit hours produced for students in nondegree, certification studies.

Clinical Costs in Teacher Education

In 1972 Masoner urged teacher education to develop national standards that included necessary financial support. Citing the uncoordinated and haphazard way in which preparation programs were funded, he reported that few states recognized the importance of clinical education and provided finances for it. As a result, local cooperating school districts made substantial contributions of their personnel and resources; even with such help, the financing of clinical education was criticized as inadequate. Teacher education suffered not only from insufficient state funding but also from wide variations in financing from one program to another in a given state. A wide range in quality of programs was inevitable.

A very comprehensive national study of student teaching, as an important sector of clinical studies in teacher education, is reported by Johnson and Yates (1981). Financial indicators derived from the summary of institutional data yielded an average budget for student teaching of $42,729 and a cost per student teacher of about $425. Other quantitative information included the length of the student-teaching assignment, the number of college faculty assigned as supervisors, and the number of student teachers per supervisor.

The study of clinical education by Peseau, et al. (1987) was restricted to 8 teacher education programs in public Florida universities. They categorized teacher education into three types: classroom instruction, clinical instruction, and clinical practice. Large variations were found among the eight programs. Clinical courses, both instruction and practice, ranged from 12 to 75 percent of the total credit hours produced. Faculty assigned to clinical studies varied from 20 to 80 percent of the total faculty. Teacher education programs with more graduate-credit-hour productivity had a smaller percent of faculty assigned to the clinical effort. Clinical faculty spent from 1.5 to 7.2 hours per week per course. The support services cost per clinical course varied from $175 to $925, and the cost for producing each clinical credit hour at the undergraduate level ranged from $70 to $160. In Florida, universities awarded vouchers redeemable for college tuition to cooperating teachers. From 150 to 750 vouchers were awarded by the eight teachers education programs in 1984–1985, with a value of from $25,000 to $250,000. Interestingly, the analysis of undergraduate credit hours produced found that 95 percent were at the upper division level. The study concluded with recommendations for greater weighting of teacher education credit hours, especially those of a clinical nature. It recommended that teacher education courses be classified into three types: classroom instruction, clinical instruction, and clinical practice. Classroom instruction courses, which are mostly upper division, would be weighted 1.5 times the cost of university general studies courses. Clinical instruction courses would be weighted 2.0, and clinical practice 2.5, times the general studies courses. Program funding would be based on credit hours produced by course type. This weighting plan would require a funding increase statewide of 106 percent over the 1984–1985 appropriation.

INTERNAL AND EXTERNAL FINANCING COMPARISONS

Higher education institutions collect data because policy requires it. Orwig and Jones (1977) observe that, in the absence of policy, insufficient and random data are gathered for use internal to programs, but usually not shared. Intra-institutional equity of resource distribution is therefore difficult to verify. Clark and Marker (1975) attribute the low-prestige, low-cost status of teacher education in almost all higher education institutions to the comparatively low socioeconomic status of teachers. In turn, the economic treatment of teachers influences the funding of teacher education programs. Teacher education in most public universities is funded at approximately the same level per credit hour as in the undergraduate components of colleges of arts and sciences, schools of communication, and health and physical education.

Downey et al. (1982) and Augenblick and Hyde (1979) recommend the use of comparative studies of resources and productivity as a means to justify plans for program improvement. Requests for funding increases are based on assumptions that funding is related to quality, even though there is not strong evidence to support this assertion, and no single index or criterion of the funding and program quality relationship exists.

Comparative studies of salaries among professional groups consistently show that teachers fare poorly (Cohn, 1979; Duff & Dold, 1978). In-depth and comprehensive studies of financing and productivity in single disciplines have not been systematically compared. The Hemp and Brunson (1984) national studies of engineering education and those by Peseau (1982, 1984, 1986, 1988) of teacher education report similar sets of variables. These include average faculty salaries, instructional costs, cost per credit hour, and financing for operations. Moreover, both sets of studies build on longitudinal data bases.

A single-year comparative analysis of funding and productivity in business administration, engineering, and teacher education is reported by Peseau (1984) for a single university. An underlying assumption was that, after credit hours were normalized by applying differential weighting factors, the cost per weighted credit hour should have been the same for the three disciplines. Instead, the weighted credit hour in teacher education was funded at 5 percent less than in engineering and 14 percent less than in business administration. When that per-credit-hour cost difference was multiplied by the total weighted credit hours produced in the three colleges, engineering received $555,000 more than an equitable sharing of funds would have provided teacher education, and business administration received $972,000 more. Peseau judges that this practice of financial starvation was probably widespread and persistent throughout the nation, seriously eroding attempts to achieve quality teacher education. Berliner (1984) found the same expenditure pattern in a major Arizona university.

Multicampus studies comparing the costs and productivity of teacher education with other professional schools would enhance understanding of the equity and adequacy of funding academic programs. In addition, relatively little is known about the scholarly productivity of teacher education faculty.

Intrastate Financing Comparisons

A key principle underlying formula funding for public higher education is that its intent is to help legislatures make appropriation decisions that treat similar academic programs within a state equitably. Funding formulas are grounded in a core of data reported on the number of credit hours produced for each institution, by major and by level. The principle works reasonably well through the appropriations process, but it breaks down at the institutional level under the guise of autonomy (Orr & Peseau, 1979; Peseau, 1988). Whereas public school systems operate under a framework of accountability and oversight that requires the local district superintendent to show evidence that funds were spent for the purpose appropriated, higher education is generally exempt from such regulation.

Peseau (1988) hypothesizes that, if university administrators had achieved equitability in the apportionment of funds among academic programs, teacher education funding, as measured by the weighted credit hour, should be reasonably consistent within any given state. By normalizing the data collected in the ACSESULGC studies, the basic weighted credit-hour cost was used for intrastate comparisons of teacher education programs in 15 states in three AACTE geographic regions. Large variations were found among teacher education programs within most of the 15 states, as measured by several critical resource variables: funds for operations, total university funds per faculty member, ratio of support staff to faculty, and average graduate assistant salary. Although urban location and program reputation contribute to a teacher education program's accessibility and attractiveness, they only partially explain the second finding: large discrepancies in productivity indicators. Among the teacher education programs in one state, the cost of producing a credit hour was as much as four times greater from one program to another. Student–faculty ratios were as much as four times greater, and students in some programs paid as much as three times the direct cost of their programs through tuition.

Because legislative authorization and state funding for teacher education were based on standard weighted credit hours, these great discrepancies could only result from differences in funding on each campus. The discretion permitted university administrators in deciding how much each program is allocated and the virtual absence of any state oversight for accountability contribute to severe financial deprivation for teacher education. Because of the lack of specific and generally accepted policies, teacher education suffers the consequences of unregulated administrative discretion in most colleges and universities.

Mingle (1983) argues that administrative discretion in funding academic programs was necessary and desirable to enable campuses to adjust better to changing conditions. He reasons that legislative oversight tends to stifle flexibility. Gifford and Stoddart (1985), however, report on findings that teacher education had been "punitively starved" by administrators in a major California university. Huge differences in teacher education financing internal to several states (Peseau, 1988) were attributed to the low value many university administrators place on these programs. Even though the funding for academic programs in a given state derives primarily from state appropriations based on credit hours produced and tuition, there is ample evidence that those funds are not equitably and uniformly distributed at the institutional level. This by no means infers that each teacher education program should be allocated equal amounts; instead, each should receive its fair share as a function of its program size and complexity. The student who elects teacher education as a major suffers greatly from what R. H. Anderson (1980) terms "academic snobbery." The fact is that teacher education students' tuition often pays for more than 100 percent of their program's direct costs.

Bowen's (1981) conclusion that several million students are served by colleges with patently inadequate resources seems to hold true for teacher education. Even though there remains much to be done in clarifying the complex and elusive relationships between resources and program quality, it is clear that financing shapes the quality and output of all academic programs. Equity is served by reasonably equal funding (per weighted credit hour) among teacher education programs in a given state.

Comparison of K–12 and Teacher Education Costs

Comparison of public school costs and those of teacher education in public universities provides another insight into their relative condition. Cost per student is often calculated as direct costs and total costs. Direct costs include instructional and administrative salaries, support costs, and operating expenses, but they do not include bonded indebtedness/capital outlay in school districts or overhead costs in universities. The NEA (1986) reports per-student costs by state for both direct and total-cost categories. Because direct costs are typically 85 to 90 percent of total costs, direct costs per public school student were compared by Peseau (1986, 1988) with direct teacher education costs. The per-credit-hour and per-FTE-student costs in the ACSESULGC studies included only college budgets, not total university costs. Peseau calculated that the direct cost per FTE teacher education student from 1979–1980 through 1984–1985 ranged from only 53 to 81 percent as much as the cost per public school student. In fact, the teacher education student cost in 1984–1985 was the lowest for the 7 years in relation to K–12 costs per student. Burns (1985) reports that the direct cost per K–12 student in California was more than $3,000 in 1984–1985; the cost per undergraduate teacher education student among 77 universities was only $1,590.

IDENTIFICATION OF PEER PROGRAMS

Peer-program analysis of academic programs shows promise for comparing levels of resources and productivity. A group of peer programs will not match perfectly, but analysis serves to identify those programs substantially alike, based on stated criteria. Most peer group identification studies are highly subjective (Astin & Solmon, 1981; Blau & Marguiles, 1974; Cartter, 1966; Roose & Anderson, 1970). They are subject to much criticism because they were primarily dependent on perceptions of reputation (Astin & Solmon, 1981; Fretter, 1977; Hattendorf, 1986, 1987; Webster, 1981). More objective ratings of academic programs were derived from analyses of resource and productivity data (M. J. Clark, Hartnett, & Baird, 1976; Elton & Rose, 1972; Terenzini, Hartmark, Lorang, & Shirley, 1980).

Cross-comparisons between the subjective ratings based on reputation and the objective ratings based on data analysis often found the subjective methods to be legitimate. However, some academic programs were incorrectly judged, based on the raters' perceptions of lower quality of the institutions themselves. Brinkman and Teeter (1987) describe the range of orientations to peer-program identification, from highly judgmental approaches using individual or panel review to quantitatively based approaches using statistical analysis of data. They found cluster analysis to be a very good technique for peer group identification, because the researcher does not introduce bias in selecting the threshold levels that separate groups.

Cluster analysis has been recommended as one defensible statistical approach to the identification of peer academic programs. This technique arranges programs in a sequential order, but not in terms of their relative quality; the criterion is homogeneity of characteristics such as data representing resource and productivity indicators. The technique ignores possible peer relationships that evolve from geographic location, urban or rural population from which students are recruited, or territorial competitiveness. The bias-free identification of peer programs using statistical analysis can serve a useful purpose, providing a base from which the planner and decision maker can project goals. Such refinements to the statistical foundation were used by the Kansas Board of Regents (Brinkman & Teeter, 1987) and in West Virginia (Lane, Lawrence, & Mertins, 1987). The intent of peer analysis should not be to change programs so they become more homogeneous; the goal should be to assess relative strengths and weaknesses as inputs intended to influence planned improvement. Such knowledge is particularly urgent during this period of major changes in enrollment (Sikula, 1987) and program design (Munday, 1976; Watkins, 1983) for teacher education.

Tudor (1988) reports a teacher education peer group identification study using Peseau's (1986) data from 76 programs in major state universities and land-grant colleges in 41 states. Cluster analysis was used to group programs by commonality of characteristics, based on 8 resource and 10 productivity variables. Tudor (1988) used a multistage analytical process. First, a larger set of variables was subjected to correlation analysis. Variables with the highest correlations were identified. This step verified the need to group variables through factor analysis. The 18 resource and productivity variables were then subjected to principal components analysis, which transformed the original data into another set of composite variables that were orthogonal and uncorrelated with one another. Four factors describing the characteristics of teacher education programs emerged. These factors were labeled F1 (large program size), F2 (advanced graduate program orientation), F3 (high financial emphasis), and F4 (predominantly undergraduate programs). Each program's data were processed, and a score on each factor was calculated.

Cluster analysis paired the programs that were most alike, and the programs were separated into five clusters. To test the quality of the clustering results, analysis of variance verified ($p. < .001$) that these four factors were the most useful in distinguishing between clusters, or groupings, or teacher educa-tion programs. In addition, classification analysis was applied to confirm that each program had been optimally placed in its cluster. The results indicated that 88.2 percent were correctly placed. Table 10-1 shows the five clusters of teacher education programs. In this procedure, each program was most like the adjacent ones in a cluster, and those in any cluster were more alike than those in another cluster.

Cluster 1 was characterized by being below average on all but Factor 3, high financial emphasis. These teacher education programs had higher average faculty salaries and more funds for operations, but they were below average in size and graduate orientation. Cluster 2 included only two colleges of teacher education, but they were above average on all four factors. These were very large programs, and they were well above average in headcount faculty, budget resources, weighted semester credit hours (WCH) produced, and number of graduate students. Faculty salaries and budgets for operations were also high. Both programs had large undergraduate and graduate enrollments, but they also were the largest teacher education programs in the United States.

The third cluster was marginally below average on Factors 1, 3, and 4 but highest in Factor 2, advanced graduate orientation. They produced a larger proportion of total credit hours at the post-master's level. Faculty WCH productivity was highest in this cluster. However, the cost per WCH was negatively loaded on Factor 2. In addition, teacher education students in Cluster 3 programs generally paid a larger share of direct program costs from their tuition. These programs were slightly smaller in size and had less that average emphasis on undergraduate programs. Cluster 4 included 13 teacher education programs below average in size, but with greater undergraduate emphasis. These programs were generally not well funded. Cluster 5 was the largest and most diverse group. These teacher education programs were generally larger than average, had less of an advanced graduate orientation, and were lower in program financing and cost per WCH produced.

Cluster analysis adds considerable power to the selection of peer teacher education programs. Because the method is based on the comparison of financially related resource variables and what each program produced with them, it is more bias free than judgmental peer ratings. Peseau and Tudor (1989) describe how, once peer programs are identified, teacher education administrators can compare their program with others by examining the raw data for the variables of concern. Cluster analysis groups programs by their commonalities. If a given teacher education program aspired to become more like another, comparison with resource and productivity variables would be a practical beginning. Characteristics of relative quality might emerge from such a process. Further, these data can be helpful to the profession in the search for more objective standards and policies for general program improvement.

FINANCING INSERVICE EDUCATION

Beyond the initial preparation and continuing-education services provided by teacher education programs, continuing professionalization of the teacher work force is a neglected

TABLE 10–1. Clusters of Teacher Education Programs

CLUSTER 1 ($n = 11$)
State University of New York/Buffalo
University of North Carolina/Chapel Hill
University of Massachusetts
University of Virginia
Virginia Tech University
University of Delaware
Ohio University
Pennsylvania State University
University of Iowa
Oklahoma State University
University of Alaska

CLUSTER 2 ($n = 2$)
University of Georgia
Ohio State University

CLUSTER 3 ($n = 19$)
Rutgers University
University of Maryland
University of Pittsburgh
University of Southern Mississippi
University of Alabama
University of Cincinnati
Florida State University
University of Kansas
University of Missouri/Columbia
University of Houston
University of Florida
University of Kentucky
Kansas State University
College of William and Mary
University of Oklahoma
University of Nevada/Reno
University of North Carolina/Greensboro
University of Arizona
University of South Carolina

CLUSTER 4 ($n = 13$)
State University of New York/Potsdam
Montana State University
University of Montana
Florida Atlantic University
University of Missouri/St. Louis
University of New Orleans
University of Missouri/Kansas City
University of Maine
Oregon State University
University of Alabama/Birmingham
New Mexico State University
University of Louisville
Indiana University

CLUSTER 5 ($n = 31$)
Virginia Commonwealth University
University of Hawaii
Indiana State University
Iowa State University
Memphis State University
Auburn University
University of Wisconsin/Milwaukee
Utah State University
University of Arkansas
Colorado State University
University of South Florida
Miami University of Ohio
Georgia State University
North Carolina State University
Washington State University
Wayne State University
Texas Tech University
University of Wyoming
University of Nevada/Las Vegas
University of Washington
University of Tennessee
Northern Illinois University
University of Texas/Austin
West Virginia University
East Texas State University
New Mexico State University
North Texas State University
Louisiana State University
University of Nebraska
Southern Illinois University
Texas A&M University

Note. From A Typology of Teacher Education Programs in State Universities and Land-Grant Colleges Based on Resource and Production Variables; A Cluster Analysis Approach by R. L. Tudor, 1988, unpublished doctoral dissertation, The University of Alabama, Tuscaloosa, AL, pp. 88–89. Reprinted by permission.

area. School systems and teacher education institutions tend to be myopic; few genuinely cooperative and successful programs exist (Cooley & Thompson, 1986; Cuban, 1972; Howey, 1980; New York State Department of Education, 1981; Seldin, 1981; Swenson, 1981; Warnat, 1980; Yarger & Mertens, 1976).

Cost analysis and cost-benefit studies of inservice education programs have been reported. The annual cost of teacher inservice education was estimated to be about $2 billion, or $1,000 per teacher (Farris & Fluck, 1985). Leighty and Courter (1984) trace the costs of inservice through three levels, from administrators to teachers to students. Lytle (1983) found that the Philadelphia public elementary/secondary schools paid more than $2 million to reimburse teachers for college courses completed in 1980–1981, but they spent only $500,000 for district inservice. The college courses were judged to be most cost effective.

Morelli, Mizell, Horton, Lizer, and Wu (1980) describe a statewide inservice program mandated and funded by the Florida legislature. Inservice was cofunded by local districts and teacher education programs. At the district level, the state appropriated $5.00 per student for staff development. Local districts dedicated $3.00 per student to activities cooperatively planned with teacher education. Each district was required to have an inservice master plan. More than $8 million was budgeted for these purposes in 1980–1981; the carryover of funds to the next fiscal year was allowed.

An evaluation of the Tennessee state plan for inservice was published by Banta and Boser (1981). The state funded 38 percent of the Career Incentive Program, local school districts paid 35 percent, and other sources paid 27 percent. Cost breakdowns for 10 projects were included. New Hampshire teachers developed an inservice program for recertification independent of teacher education participation (Andrew, 1981). Eight thousand teachers were trained in a 50-clock-hour program over 3 years. Most of the costs were borne by teachers, at $300 each, and they favored it 4 to 1 over recertification through college courses.

Comparative studies of public school inservice education programs were reported for Canada and the United States. Fennell (1980) analyzed inservice costs of three alternative programs in Edmonton. Direct costs to the three school districts were $4 million, but indirect costs of teacher salaries for released time and for their substitutes were $24 million. The cost per participant ranged from $38 to $1,070, and 23,867 teachers completed the programs. Costs for inservice in three urban districts in the United States were studied by Moore and Hyde (1981). Six categories of expenditures were included (for consultants, sabbaticals, teacher stipends, substitutes, salary increases, and supplies and materials). Monetary incentives in the form of salary increases and stipends accounted for most of the costs. Kaplan (1980) acknowledges that his analyses of the inservice costs of six countries of INSET (Inservice Education for Teachers) were not comparable, because standard monetary units were not used. Data for the six nations showed the distribution of expenditures to be 62 percent for study days, 16 percent for sabbaticals, 7 percent for program planning, and 5 percent for school management training. Within Kaplan's report, budgets for teacher inservice averaged $13,500 per year for rural and $446,000 for urban school districts in Florida.

Denton and Smith (1983) criticize most financial analyses of teacher inservice programs because they rarely evaluate the quality of the output other than by surveys of teacher satisfaction. An exception is the detailed analysis of inservice program content, costs, and efficiency distributed by the Far West Laboratory for Educational Research and Development (1980). Nash and Ducharme (1983) argue that cost-effectiveness analysis of inservice programs is inappropriate. Quality is an elusive concept in higher education and cannot be compared with that in other sectors of society. Orlich (1982) concludes from his extensive survey that inservice programs are effective for upgrading teachers and contributing to better classroom performance. However, lack of systematic policies that direct either state or national standards has been a serious problem inhibiting broad-scale quality improvement. The Holmes Group effort to reform teacher education has set the establishment of policies and standards as a major objective.

Proposals have been offered that could provide models for more comprehensive, unified, inservice planing. Girhiny (1978) suggests an ambitious plan for Ontario, Canada. From a review of continuing-education activities for teachers throughout eight countries, 40 areas of staff development were described. The funding for the proposed program would come from an annual 6.25 percent salary reduction from teachers, supplemented by 3 percent of the teacher salary base by the Ministry of Education. This funding would pay for the inservice programs, for a 5-month leave of absence for teachers every 5 years, and for the costs of their substitutes during that sabbatical. Jones and Steinbrink (1986) demonstrated how a shared local resource model, derived from experiences in energy education inservice under a NSF grant, could be more generally applied. Cost per participant was only about $22 per day in 13 sites. The low cost was attributed to the use of volunteer resource persons as speakers, the field sites for experiential learning, and the use of publicly available materials in the curriculum. Garrett (1980) recommends the successful staff development model used in Massachusetts, where participants were extensively involved in planning their inservice programs.

COST-EFFECTIVENESS AND COST BENEFIT OF TEACHER EDUCATION

The evaluation of academic program efficiency is not generally accepted in higher education (Hyde, 1974), but public demands for accountability have motivated continuing efforts to justify how well academic programs use resources (Nichols, 1976). The efficiency of educational programs has been defined as being demonstrated by those that (a) give priority to groups or areas in which given inputs produce highest attendance and demand for the programs, (b) optimize the gains in subsequent income in relation to what the education cost, and (c) contribute to increasing per capita income (C. A. Anderson & Bowman, 1965). The evidence consistently confirms that those who select teaching as a profession do not benefit from the latter two criteria. Notwithstanding the intrinsic rewards of the profession, teacher education students and teacher educators are shortchanged of their fair share of the benefits valued by society. Teachers pay a high proportion of the costs of their preparation programs and receive less in career earnings than other professions.

Temple and Riggs (1978) describe the inadequacy of funding formulas, particularly for teacher education, as they tend to perpetuate serious deficiencies of both equity and adequacy. As has been noted, teacher education has the lowest credit-hour weights in most higher education funding formulas, and substantial underfunding from the past is therefore carried over from one year to the next.

In fact, when across-the-board budget increases are made, the difference between a given percentage increase applied to an already underfunded program and to an adequately funded program becomes exacerbated, and inequity perpetuates inadequacy. The consequences of this pattern are program stagnation, faculty overload, low salaries, neglect of clinical education, and generalized mediocrity (Peseau & Orr, 1980). Students in teacher education pay an excessive share of their program costs. More able teachers leave the profession earlier and in larger numbers (Schlechty & Vance, 1981); the relatively poor quality of the preparation program could also contribute to attrition. Teacher education can be considered to be extremely efficient in the use of such meager resources to produce as many graduates as it does.

Teacher education students probably never recover financially from forgone opportunity costs, in comparison with students of other majors. Notwithstanding the intent of student aid (El-Khawas & Bisconti, 1974) to equalize educational access and opportunity, the excessive burden of tuition as a share of program cost, lower salaries in the profession, and debt obligation from loans place teacher education students at a disadvantage that they carry throughout their careers.

MacPhail-Wilcox (1982) shows that the return on investment in teacher education is negative, even through the doctoral level. The average white male with a high school education earns 35 percent more in his working life than a teacher with a bachelor's degree and 18 percent more than one with a doctorate. Average white males in the United States with a high school education earn 89 percent more in their working lives than the average teacher. Only the average white female with a high school diploma or a bachelor's degree earns less than a teacher. Even those teachers in relatively wealthy school districts suffer the same losses of lifetime income. These career income disadvantages, coupled with the disequitably low funding of teacher education programs, clearly reflect the value of teaching and teacher education held by both society and the college and university cultures that perpetuate them.

SUMMARY AND RECOMMENDATIONS

Research on the relationships between academic program resources as inputs and productivity measures as outputs serves two purposes: reporting for accountability and comparison with other similar programs to assess a program's relative condition. The studies reported in this chapter indicate that teacher education has serious and persistent problems. Resources are generally inadequate for what the profession aspires to achieve. The lack of definitive resource standards as benchmark minimums to support reasonably qualitative programs is a major cause of those inadequacies. Such standards should be set by the profession itself, not created by external forces as a result of continuing criticism. If professional preparation programs were to receive their fair share of resources, they could be more specifically accountable for how effectively the resources were used. The research reported here reveals real disparities in the amount of resources available to teacher education programs, even within the same states.

Because the profession has not defined minimum resource standards, each teacher education program is left to compete independently for its fair share of campus resources. This situation contributes to unevenness in quality. Creativity and innovation are essential to the continuing redesign of teacher education. Without the necessary resources to carry out planned program change, teacher education will continue to promise more than it can deliver. Worse, it will fail in its fundamental mission to prepare quality personnel for the nation's schools into the twenty-first century.

References

Allen, R. A., & Topping, J. R. (Eds.). (1979). *Cost information & formula funding: New approaches.* Boulder, CO: National Center for Higher Education Management Systems.

American Association of Colleges for Teacher Education. (1983). *Report to the profession.* Washington, DC: Author.

Anderson, C. A., & Bowman, M. J. (1965). Patterns and variability in distribution and diffusion of schooling. In C. A. Anderson & M. J. Bowman (Eds.), *Education and economic development* (pp. 314–344). Chicago: Aldine.

Anderson, R. H. (1980). Financing of teacher education. *Action in Teacher Education, 2*(3), 31–38.

Andrew, M. D. (1981). Statewide inservice without colleges and universities: New Hampshire's quiet move toward teachers' control. *Journal of Teacher Education, 32*(1), 24–28.

Astin, A. A., & Solmon, L. C. (1981). Are reputational ratings needed to measure quality? *Change, 13*(7), 14–19.

Atkinson, G. B. J. (1983). *The economics of education.* London: Hodder & Stoughton.

Augenblick, J. (1983). *School finance equity.* Denver: Education Commission of the States. (ERIC Document Reproduction Service No. ED 234 507)

Augenblick, J., & Hyde, W. (1979, February). *Patterns of funding, net price and financial need for postsecondary education students: Differences among states, institutional sectors, and income groups.* Denver: Education Commission of the States.

Balderston, F. (1970). Thinking about the outputs of higher education. In B. Lawrence, G. Weathersby, & V. W. Patterson (Eds.), *The outputs of higher education: Their identification, measurement, and evaluation* (pp. 10–16). Boulder, CO: Western Interstate Commission for Higher Education.

Banta, T. W., & Boser, J. A. (1981). *Evaluation of Tennessee state plan for career education.* Knoxville, TN: Tennessee University Bureau of Educational Research & Service. (ERIC Document Reproduction Service No. ED 201 729)

Becker, G. S. (1975). *Human capital* (2nd ed.). Chicago: University of Chicago Press.

Benson, C. S. (1988). Economics of education: The U.S. experience. In N. J. Boyan (Ed.), *Handbook of research on educational administration* (pp. 355–372), White Plains, NY: Longman.

Berliner, D. C. (1984). Making the right changes in preservice teacher education. *Phi Delta Kappan, 66*(2), 94–96.

Blau, P. M., & Marguiles, R. Z. (1974). The reputation of American professional schools. *Change, 6*(10), 42–47.

Bloom, A. M. (1983). Differential instructional productivity indices. *Research in higher education, 18*(2), 179–193.

Bowen, H. R. (1980). *Investment in learning: The individual and social value of American higher education.* San Francisco: Jossey-Bass.

Bowen, H. R. (1981). *The costs of higher education: How much do colleges and universities spend and how much should they spend?* San Francisco: Jossey-Bass.

Bowman, M. J. (1964). Schultz, Denison, and the contribution of "eds" to national income growth. *Journal of Political Economy, 72,* 450–464.

Brinkman, P. T., & Teeter, D. J. (1987). Methods for selecting comparison groups. In P. T. Brinkman (Ed.), *Conducting inter-institutional comparisons* (pp. 5–23). San Francisco: Jossey-Bass.

Brown, D. (1970). A scheme for measuring the output of higher education. In B. Lawrence, G. Weathersby, & V. W. Patterson (Eds.), *The outputs of higher education: Their identification, measurement, and evaluation* (pp. 26–38). Boulder, CO: Western Interstate Commission for Higher Education.

Burns, H. W. (1985). A view of standards in postsecondary education. In W. J. Johnston (Ed.), *Education on trial: Strategies for the future* (pp. 79–102), San Francisco: Institute for Contemporary Studies.

Carnegie Commission on Higher Education. (1973). *Higher education: Who pays? Who benefits? Who should pay?* New York: McGraw-Hill.

Carnegie Commission on Higher Education. (1974). *A digest of reports of the Carnegie Commission on Higher Education.* New York: McGraw-Hill.

Cartter, A. M. (1966). *An assessment of quality in graduate education.* Washington, DC: American Council on Education.

Caruthers, J. K., & Orwig, M. (1979). *Budgeting in higher education* (Higher Education Research Report No. 3). Washington, DC: Clearinghouse on Higher Education, The George Washington University, American Association for Higher Education.

Caulley, D. N., & Dawson, J. A. (1980). Quantitative versus qualitative program evaluation. In L. Rubin (Ed.), *Critical issues in educational policy: An administrator's overview* (pp. 354–362). Boston: Allyn & Bacon.

Chambers, C. M. (1979). What have we learned? In A. W. Astin, H. R. Bowen, & C. M. Chambers (Eds.), *Evaluating educational quality: A conference summary* (pp. 30–31). Washington, DC: Council on Postsecondary Accreditation.

Clark, D. L., & Marker, G. (1975). The institutionalization of teacher education. In K. Ryan (Ed.), *Teacher education* (74th yearbook of the National Society for the Study of Education, Part II, pp. 53–86). Chicago: University of Chicago Press.

Clark, M. J., Hartnett, R. T., & Baird, L. L. (1976). *Assessing dimensions of quality in doctoral education: A technical report of a national study on three fields.* Princeton, NJ: Educational Testing Service.

Cohn, E. (1979). *The economics of education.* Cambridge, MA: Ballinger.

Coleman, D. R., & Bolte, J. R. (1977). A theoretical approach to the internal allocation of academic personnel resources. In R. H. Fenske (Ed.), *Conflicting pressures in postsecondary education* (193–198). Tallahassee, FL: Association for Institutional Research.

Cooley, V. E., & Thompson, J. C., Jr. (1986). *Staff development in varied U.S. geographical regions: A study of attitudes and practices.* Paper presented at the annual conference of the National Council of States on Inservice Education, Nashville, TN. (ERIC Document Reproduction Service No. ED 275 653)

Coons, J. E. (1980). Can education be equal and excellent? In J. W. Guthrie (Ed.), *School finance, policies and practices: The 1980's, a decade of conflict* (First Annual Yearbook of the American Education Finance Association, pp. 131–142). Cambridge, MA: Ballinger.

Cuban, L. (1972). Teaching the children: Does the system help or hinder? In V. Harbrick (Ed.), *Freedom, bureaucracy, and schooling* (pp. 155–159). Washington, DC: Association for Supervision and Curriculum Development.

Darling-Hammond, L. (1984). *Beyond the commission reports: The coming crisis in teaching* (R-3177-RC). Santa Monica, CA: The RAND Corporation.

Davis, J. R., & Morrall, J. F., III. (1974). *Evaluating educational investment.* Boston: D. C. Heath.

Denison, E. F. (1962). *The sources of economic growth in the United States and the alternatives before us.* New York: Committee for Economic Development.

Denton, J. J., Peters, W., & Savage, T. (Eds.). (1984). *New directions in teacher education: Foundations, curriculum, policy.* College Station, TX: Texas A & M University, Instructional Research Laboratory. (ERIC Document Reproduction Service No. ED 253 502)

Denton, J. J., & Smith, N. L. (1983). *Alternative teacher preparation programs: Cost-effectiveness comparison* (Paper and report series #86). Portland, OR: Northwest Regional Education Laboratory. (ERIC Document Reproduction Service No. ED 237 569)

Downey, R. G., Lahey, M. A., & Hoyt, D. P. (1982). *Costs in higher education: Do they make a difference?* Paper presented at the 22nd Annual Association for Institutional Research Forum, Denver.

Dressel, P., & Simon, L. A. K. (1976). *Allocating resources among departments.* San Francisco: Jossey-Bass.

Duff, F. L., & Dold, C. D. (1978). *The relationship between program cost and economic return: The case of one public university.* Paper presented at the 18th Association for Institutional Research Forum, Houston. (ERIC Document Reproduction Service No. ED 161 387)

Eckhaus, R. S. (1973). *Estimating the returns to education: A disaggregated approach* (A Tech. Rep.). Berkeley, CA: The Carnegie Commission on Higher Education.

Educational Policies Commission. (1940). *Education and economic well-being in American democracy.* Washington, D.C: National Education Association and American Association of School Administrators.

El-Khawas, E. H., & Bisconti, A. S. (1974). *Five and ten years after college entry. 1971 followup of 1961 and 1966 college freshmen* (ACE Research Rep. 9, No 1.). Washington, DC: American Council on Education, Office of Administrative Affairs, Division of Educational Statistics.

Elton, C. F., & Rose, H. A. (1972). What are the raters rating? *American Psychologist, 27,* 197–201.

Enthoven, A. C. (1970). Measures of the outputs of higher education: Some practical suggestions for their development and use. In B. Lawrence, G. Weathersby, & V. W. Patterson (Eds.), *The outputs of higher education: Their identification, measurement, and evaluation* (pp. 51–55). Boulder, CO: Western Interstate Commission for Higher Education.

Far West Laboratory for Educational Research and Development. (1980). Educational programs that work (A resource of exemplary educational programs approved by the joint dissemination review panel) (7th ed). Washington, DC: Department of Education. (ERIC Document Reproduction Service No. ED 195 011)

Farris, P. J., & Fluck, R. A. (1985). Effective staff development through individualized inservice. *Action in Teacher Education, 7*(4), 23–27.

Feldmann, M. E., & Fisher, R. L. (1982, February). *The role of cluster analysis in comparing teacher education programs among similar institutions.* Paper presented at the annual meeting of the American Association of Colleges for Teacher Education, Houston.

Fennell, B. H. (1980). Teacher inservice training costs: A staff study. Edmonton, Canada: Alberta Department of Education, Planning and Research Branch. (ERIC Document Reproduction Service No. ED 198 072)

Fretter, W. (1977). The Cartter report on the leading schools of education, law, and business. *Change, 9*(2), 44–48.

Froomkin, J. (n.d.) *Cost/effectiveness and cost/benefit analysis of educational programs.* Washington, DC: Office of Education.

Garrett, S. V. (1980). *Participant planned staff development.* Boston: Massachusetts State Department of Education Dissemination Project (Resources for Schools No. 18). (ERIC Document Reproduction Service No. ED 199 248)

Gifford, B. R., & Stoddart, T. (1985). Teacher education: Rhetoric or real reform? In R. Johnston (Ed.), *Education on trial* (pp. 177–197). Boston: Allyn & Bacon.

Girhiny, J. (1978). Professional development and declining enrollment in Ontario. *Proceedings of the Joint Commission on Declining School Enrollment in Ontario.* Toronto, Ontario: Commission on Declining School Enrollments in Ontario. (ERIC Document Reproduction Service No. ED 197 474)

Gross, C. (1975). Drumbeats of dissonance: Variations on a theme for teachers (Sixteenth Annual Charles W. Hunt Lecture). In American Association of Colleges for Teacher Education, *Strengthening education of teachers. Proceedings of the 27th American Association of Colleges of Teacher Education Annual Meeting.* Washington, DC: AACTE.

Gross, F. M. (1973, December). *A comparative analysis of the existing budget formulas used for justifying budget requirements or allocating funds for the operating expenses of state-supported colleges and universities.* Knoxville, TN: University of Tennessee, Office of Institutional Research.

Guthrie, J. W. (1980). United States school finance policy. In J. W. Guthrie (Ed.), *School finance policies and practices: The 1980's, a decade of conflict.* (First Annual Yearbook of the American Education Finance Association, pp. 3–46). Cambridge, MA: Ballinger.

Halstead, D. K. (1974). *Statewide planning in higher education.* Washington, DC: U.S. Government Printing Office.

Hartnett, R. T. (1971). *Accountability in higher education: A consideration of some of the problems of assessing college impacts.* Princeton, NJ: College Entrance Examination Board.

Hattendorf, L. C. (1986). College and university rankings: An annotated bibliography of analysis, criticism, and evaluation. *RQ, 25*(3), 332–347.

Hattendorf, L. C. (1987). College and university rankings: Part 2—An annotated bibliography of analysis, criticism, and evaluation. *RQ, 26*(3), 315–322.

Hawley, W. D. (1986). A critical analysis of the Holmes Group's proposals for reforming teacher education. *Journal of Teacher Education, 37*(4), 47–51.

Hemp, G., & Brunson, J. (1984). *1982–83 planning factors in engineering education national study. A study for the American Society for Engineering Education.* Gainesville, FL: University of Florida.

Henard, R. E. (1977). An examination of the uses of five measures in determining faculty workload. In R. H. Fenske & P. J. Staskey (Eds.), *Proceedings of the 17th Annual Meeting of the Association for Institutional Research Forum* (pp. 195–199). Tallahassee, FL: Association for Institutional Research.

Howey, K. R. (1980). Current trends in in-service teacher education. In L. Rubin (Ed.), *Critical issues in educational policy. An administrator's overview* (pp. 346–352). Boston: Allyn & Bacon.

Hyde, W. (1974). Proved at last: 1 physics + 1.35 chemistry = 1.66 economics. *Educational Record, 55*(4), 286–290.

Huff, R. A. (1975). *Undergirding program decisions with information and unit costs: An approach to differential funding for statewide systems of postsecondary educational institutions* (Report ot the Education Commission of the States, Inservice Education Programs; State Higher Education Executive Officers Association). Denver: Education Commission of the States. (ERIC Document Reproduction Service No. ED 202 287)

Innes, J. T., Jacobson, P. B., & Pellegrin, R. J. (1965). *Economic returns to education: A survey of the findings.* Eugene, OR: University of Oregon Press.

Johns, R. L., & Morphet, E. L. (1960). *The economics and financing of education: A systems approach.* Englewood Cliffs, NJ: Prentice-Hall.

Johnson, J., & Yates, J. (1981). *A national survey of student teaching programs.* Dekalb, IL: Northern Illnois University. (ERIC Document Reproduction Service No. ED 232 963)

Jones, R. M., & Steinbrink, J. E. (1986). Curriculum institutes for teachers: Utilizing local resources. *Science Education, 70*(2), 105–109.

Jordan, K. F., & McKeown, M. P. (1980). Equity in financing public elementary and secondary schools. In J. W. Guthrie (Ed.), *School finance policies and practices: The 1980's, a decade of conflict* (First Annual Yearbook of the American Education Finance Association, pp. 79–129). Cambridge, MA: Ballinger.

Kaplan, P. (1980). *The cost and efficient utilization of resources* (Synthesis report for the Organization for Economic Cooperation & Development). Paris, France: Center for Education Research & Innovation. (ERIC Document Reproduction Service No. ED 198 097)

Klitgaard, R. E., Siddiqui, K. Y., Arshad, M., Niaz, N., & Khan, A. (1985). The economics of teacher education in Pakistan. *Comparative Education Review, 29*(1), 92–110.

Kully, R. D. (1986). On faculty workload and productivity. *Thought and Action*, 63–72.

Lane, F. S., Lawrence, J. S., & Mertins, H., Jr. (1987). University financial analysis using interinstitutional data. In P. T. Brinkman (Ed.), *Conducting interinstitutional comparisons* (pp. 83–101). San Francisco: Jossey-Bass.

Lanier, J. E., & Little, J. W. (1986). Research on teacher education. In M. C. Wittrock (Ed.), *Handbook of research on teaching* (3rd ed., pp. 527–569). New York: Macmillan.

Lawrence, B., Weathersby, G., & Patterson, V. W. (1970). An accounting structure for outputs of higher education: One proposal. In B. Lawrence, G. Weathersby, & V. W. Patterson (Eds.), *The outputs of higher education: Their identification, measurement, and evaluation* (pp. 112–124). Boulder, CO: Western Interstate Commission for Higher Education.

Leftwich, R. H., & Sharp, A. M. (1980). Economics of higher education: Who benefits and pays? In R. H. Leftwich & A. M. Sharp

(Eds.), *Economics of social issues* (4th ed., pp. 63–91). Dallas: Business Publications.

Leighty, C. A., & Courter, L. (1984). *Focus on effective teaching/staff development: District adoption of the changing teacher practice study* (San Diego Unified School District, CA). Austin, TX: University of Texas, Research Development Center for Staff Development. (ERIC Document Reproduction Service No. ED 246 039)

Leslie, L. L., & Brinkman, P. T. (1988). Educational finance: Higher education. In N. J. Boyan (Ed.), *Handbook of research on educational administration* (pp. 391–435). White Plains, NY: Longman.

Lytle, J. H. (1983). Investment options for inservice teacher training. *Journal of Teacher Education, 34*(1), 28–31.

MacPhail-Wilcox, B. (1982). An analysis of investment in teacher education: The Texas case 1978–79. *Journal of Educational Finance, 7,* 462–472.

Masoner, P. H. (1972). An imperative: A national policy for teacher education. In P. H. Masoner (Ed.), *Address to the 16th Annual Convention of the National Reading Association* (pp. 15–31). Washington, DC: American Association of Colleges for Teacher Education.

Meisinger, R. J., Jr. (1976). *State budgeting for higher education: The uses of formulas.* Berkeley, CA: Center for Research and Development in Higher Education.

Mingle, J. R. (1983). *Management flexibility and state regulation in higher education.* Atlanta: Southern Regional Education Board.

Moore, D. R., & Hyde, A. A. (1981). *Making sense of staff development: An analysis of staff development programs and their costs in three urban school districts.* Chicago: Designs for change. (ERIC Document Reproduction Service No. ED 211 629)

Morelli, L. V., Mizell, M. M., Horton, J. R., Lizer, J. W., & Wu, P. C. (1980). *Statewide teacher education center network.* Paper presented at the annual conference of the National Council of States on Inservice Education, San Diego, CA. (ERIC Document Reproduction Service No. ED 198 137)

Munday, L. A. (1976). *Impact of educational development, family income, college costs, and financial aid in student choice and enrollment in college* (ACT Research Rep. No. 77). Iowa City, IA: The American College Testing Program, Research & Development Division.

Murgo, J. D. (Ed.). (1972). *Readings in the economics of education.* New York: MMS Information Corporation.

Nash, R. J., & Ducharme, E. R. (1983). The paucity of the investment metaphor and other misunderstandings. *Journal of Teacher Education, 34*(1), 33–36.

National Education Association. (1983). *Teacher supply and demand in the public schools, 1981–82.* Washington, DC: Author.

National Education Association. (1986). *Rankings of the states.* Washington, DC: Author.

New York State Department of Education. (1981). *Insuring effective inservice programs.* Albany, NY: Author. (ERIC Document Reproduction Service No. ED 223 556)

Nichols, J. O. (1976). The program productivity ratio: Toward a better measure of academic program efficiency. In R. H. Fenske (Ed.), *Conflicting pressures in postsecondary education* (pp. 29–32). Tallahassee, FL: Association for Institutional Research.

Noe, R. C. (1986). Formula funding in higher education: A review. *Journal of Education Finance, 11,* 363–376.

Orlich, D. C. (1982). In-service education: Fiscal implications for policy-makers. *Planning & Changing, 13* (4), 214–222.

Orr, P. G., & Peseau, B. A. (1979). Formula funding is not the problem in teacher education. *Peabody Journal of Education, 56*(1), 61–72.

Orwig, M. D., & Jones D. P. (1977). Why not "indicators" for postsecondary education? In R. H. Fenske & P. J. Staskey (Eds.), *Proceed-

ings of the 17th Association for Institutional Research Forum. Research and Planning for Higher Education* (pp. 131–133). Tallahassee, FL: Association for Institutional Research.

Pace, C. R. (1979). *Measuring outcomes of college. Fifty years of findings and recommendations for the future.* San Francisco: Jossey-Bass.

Peseau, B. A. (1982). Developing an adequate resource base for teacher education. *Journal of Teacher Education, 33*(4), 13–15.

Peseau, B. A. (1984). *Resources allocated to teacher education in state universities and land-grant colleges.* (Report prepared for the National Commission on Excellence in Teacher Education). University, AL: American Association of Colleges for Teacher Education. (ERIC Document Reproduction Service No. ED 250 297)

Peseau, B. A. (1986). *Funding and academic production of teacher education in state universities and land-grant colleges* (8th annual study). University, AL: Association of Colleges & Schools of Education in State Universities & Land-Grant Colleges. (ERIC Document Reproduction Service No. ED 272 489)

Peseau, B. A. (1988). Funding of teacher education in state universities. In K. Alexander & D. Monk (Eds.), *Attracting and compensating America's teachers* (8th annual yearbook of the Education Finance Association, pp. 179–208). New York: Ballinger.

Peseau, B., Backman, C., & Fry, B. (1987). A cost model for clinical teacher education. *Action in Teacher Education, 9*(1), 21–34.

Peseau B. A., & Orr, P. G. (1980). The outrageous underfunding of teacher education. *Phi Delta Kappan, 62*(2), 100–102.

Peseau, B. A., & Tudor, R. L. (1989). Peer teacher education programs. *Journal of Teacher Education, 40*(3), 42–48.

Psacharopoulos, G. (1977). Family background, education and achievement: A path model of earnings determinants in the UK and some alternatives. In C. Baxter, P. J. O'Leary, & A. Westoby (Eds.), *Economics and educational policy: A reader* (pp. 310–324). London, England: Open University Press.

Rivlin, A. M. (1971). *Systematic thinking for social action.* Washington, DC: Brookings Institution.

Romney, L. C., & Micek, S. S. (1977). Translating goals into measurable objectives: Research studies and practical procedures. In R. H. Fenske & P. J. Staskey (Eds.), *Proceedings of the 17th Association for Institutional Research Forum: Research and planning for higher education* (pp. 93–96). Tallahassee, FL: Association for Institutional Research.

Roose, K. D., & Anderson, C. J. (1970). *A rating of graduate programs.* Washington, DC: American Council on Education.

Roth, R. A. (1981). A comparison of methods and results of major teacher supply and demand studies. *Journal of Teacher Education, 32*(6), 43–46.

Salley, C. D. (1977). Calculating the economic multiplier for local university spending. In R. H. Fenske & P. J. Staskey (Eds.), *Proceedings of the 17th Association for Institutional Research Forum: Research and planning for higher education* (pp. 49–53). Tallahassee, FL: Association for Institutional Research.

Schlechty, P. C., & Vance, V. S. (1981). Do academically able teachers leave education? The North Carolina Case, *Phi Delta Kappan, 63*(2), 106–112.

Schultz, T. W. (1963). *The economic value of education.* New York: Columbia University Press.

Seldin, C. A. (1981). *National study of state universities and land grant colleges: Off-campus inservice activities.* Amherst, MA: University of Massachusetts. (ERIC Document Reproduction Service No. ED 209 944)

Sikula, J. (1987). Teacher education reforms, California style. *Education Horizons, 65*(2), 62–65.

Solmon, L. C. (1973). *Schooling & subsequent success: Influence of ability, background, and formal education* (ACT Research Rep.

#57). Iowa City, IA: The American College Testing Program, Research & Development Division.

Solmon, L. C., & Ochsner, N. (1978). New findings on the effect of college. *Current Issues in Higher Education* (1978 National Conference Series). Washington, DC: American Association for Higher Education.

Spence, D. S. (1978). Formula funding in the SREB states. Atlanta: Southern Regional Education Board, 1–25. (ERIC Document Reproduction Service No. ED 167 048)

Swenson, T. L. (1981). The state-of-the-art in inservice education and staff development in K–12 schools. *Journal of Research & Development in Education, 15*(1), 2–7.

Temple, C. M., & Riggs, R. O. (1978). The declining suitability of formula funding for higher education. *Peabody Journal of Education, 55*(4), 351–357.

Terenzini, P. T., Hartmark, L., Lorang, W. G., & Shirley, R. C. (1980). A conceptual and methodological approach to the identification of peer institutions. *Research in Higher Education, 12*(4), 621–636.

Texas College and University System. (1970, June). *Designation of formulas.* Austin, TX: Author.

Texas Select Committee on Public Education. (1984). *Select Committee on Public Education: Recommendations.* Austin, TX: Texas State Legislature. (ERIC Document Reproduction Service No. ED 259 438).

Thomas, J. A. (1980). Issues in educational efficiency. In J. W. Guthrie (Ed.), *School finance policies and practices: The 1980s, a decade of conflict* (First annual yearbook of the American Education Finance Association, pp. 145–168). Cambridge, MA: Ballinger.

Thurow, L. C. (1977). Education and economic equality. In C. Baxter, P. J. O'Leary, & A. Westoby (Eds.), *Economics and education policy: A reader* (pp. 353–366). London, England: Open University Press.

Tudor, R. L. (1988). *A typology of teacher education programs in state universities and land-grant colleges based on resource and production variables: A cluster analysis approach.* Unpublished doctoral dissertation, The University of Alabama, Tuscaloosa, AL.

Vaizey, J. (1970). The outputs of higher education: Their proxies, measurement, & evaluation. In B. Lawrence, G. Weathersby, & V. W. Patterson (Eds.), The *outputs of higher education: Their identification, measurement, and evaluation* (pp. 18–23). Boulder, CO: Western Interstate Commission for Higher Education.

Walters, D. L. (1981). *Financial analysis for academic units* (Higher Education Research Rep. No. 7, Clearinghouse on Higher Education). Washington, DC: George Washington University; American Association for Higher Education.

Warnat, W. T. (1980). In-service training: Higher education vs. public school system response. In L. Rubin (Ed.), *Critical issues in educational policy. An administrator's overview* (pp. 364–371). Boston: Allyn & Bacon.

Watkins, B. T. (1983). Universities moving to raise quality of education schools. *Chronicle of Higher Education, 27*(2), 1, 14.

Webster, D. S. (1981). Advantages and disadvantages of methods of assessing quality. *Change, 13*(7), 20–24.

Wildman, L. (1976). *Economic assumptions and the future of higher education.* Paper presented at the Economics and the Future of Higher Education Conference. Seattle, WA: Institute for Quality in Human Life and The Washington Commission on the Humanities (pp. 112–113). Boulder, CO: Western Interstate Commission for Higher Education.

Yarger, S. J., & Mertens, S. K. (1976, November). *About the education of teachers: A letter to Virginia.* Paper presented at the conference on quality inservice education, sponsored by the National Council of States on Inservice Education, New Orleans. (ERIC Document Reproduction Service No. ED 199 188)

·11·

THE IMPACT OF FEDERAL FUNDING FOR RESEARCH AND DEMONSTRATION ON TEACHER EDUCATION

Roy A. Edelfelt
UNIVERSITY OF NORTH CAROLINA AT CHAPEL HILL

Ronald G. Corwin
OHIO STATE UNIVERSITY

William I. Burke
UNIVERSITY OF NORTH CAROLINA AT CHAPEL HILL

This chapter could be particularly timely, because the *handbook* of which it is a part is being published near the outset of a new federal government administration. The data, interpretations, ideas, and recommendations should be of value as plans for carrying out the "education president's" agenda take shape. The authors trust that there will be a receptiveness to learn from the experience this chapter reflects, so that federal money and energy will not be expended on relearning some of the lessons of the past 30 or so years.

FEDERAL INFLUENCE ON TEACHER EDUCATION

The story of the transformation of the federal government's role in education is familiar to most teacher educators. In the space of a few years during the 1960s, this formerly neutral observer and benefactor became a concerned, if sometimes directive, manager. Before that decade there were only a few major education programs such as the GI Bill, and the pathbreaking National Defense Education Act of 1958. During the expansion of the 1960s, federal aid to elementary and secondary education surged from $.5 billion to more than $3.5 billion annually. By 1978 the number of federal categorical programs had zoomed from 20 to over 100, scattered throughout more than a dozen autonomous departments and agencies (Graham, 1984).

The task in this chapter is to address several questions. Have these programs worked? How well have they accomplished what they were intended to do? When they have not worked well, why has that been so? What has been learned about federal funding in teacher education?

People want to know the answers to these questions. There are no simple answers, and it is probably impossible to address the questions conclusively. The purpose is to report some impressions from informants, review a small sample of an extensive literature, and raise a few fundamental issues. To make

The authors wish to acknowledge the counsel, criticism, and other assistance of Henry Hermanowicz (Pennsylvania State University), Edward Nussel, James Steffensen, and Meena Wilson (University of North Carolina at Chapel Hill).

173

the views as balanced and objective as possible, a team of authors was composed with very different perspectives on, and broad experience with, federal funding in teacher education.

Background

Teacher education has been criticized, often severely, for being sluggish, unbending, and simplistic. One sometimes gets the impression that teacher education is intended primarily for prospective elementary school teachers, that it is of lesser importance for future secondary school teachers. Actually, teacher education has developed dramatically in the last 100 or so years, from normal-school training in the eighteenth and nineteenth centuries, mainly to prepare elementary school teachers, to college and university study for all levels of public school teachers today. Along the way, there have been substantial changes in the content and length of preparation and in the formal qualifications of teachers. Teachers now have a bachelor's degree that reflects at least 2 years of general or liberal education, a major field of specialization, and professional studies including a practicum (almost always full-time student teaching for 10–16 weeks guided and evaluated by teachers and college professors).

Definitions

The definition of *teacher education* is often restricted to preservice preparation. That definition is too narrow to account for all the education that determines how teachers behave in the classroom and how they become better at what they do. Further, preservice preparation has not been the focus of most of the federal programs in teacher education. A broader definition is essential, because assessing impact requires ascertaining what has changed and whether changes have altered how teachers perform.

Progress in teacher education is a function of advances made in the total enterprise of education. Therefore, the term is used here to include preservice and inservice teacher education and all the elements related to that continuum: recruitment, selection, preservice preparation (general education, specialization in an area of study, and professional education), career-long professional development (encompassing school improvement), teacher certification, and accreditation of undergraduate and graduate teacher education programs.

Approach

In the search for federal influence, the authors used technology, people, and a variety of written sources. Among the several computer data bases tapped were ERIC, Dissertation Abstracts, the National Technical Information Service (NTIS), and the U.S. Government Printing Office (GPO Publications).

People were involved in three ways. *First,* through a questionnaire, information and opinions were sought on the influence of federal funding in teacher education. *Second,* written data were requested from some people in our network that were not available in published form or in data bases. *Third,* the people contacted were queried for the names of others who might have helpful information and data.

The paper chase included a search of the literature (by other than computer means). The *Education Index* was a primary source. Others were (a) bibliographies, (b) reference lists in literature that was retrieved, and (c) indexes to the most relevant journals, for example, the *Journal of Teacher Education,* the *Review of Educational Research,* the *American Educational Research Journal,* the *Educational Researcher,* the *Journal of Staff Development, Action in Teacher Education,* and the *Journal of Research and Development in Education.*

Scope of the Chapter

The focus in this chapter is on the last 30 or so years. Interest is in the influence of federally funded research and demonstration programs supporting teacher education since the advent of substantial federal support in the late 1950s, when Congress enacted the National Defense Education Act. Our interest extends principally to the early 1980s. Much of the research was done prior to 1980. Also, in 1981 a large portion of the funding that influenced teacher education was consolidated into block grants to the states, making it difficult to track. Finally, during the Reagan administration, many programs were curtailed.

The year 1958 is an arbitrary starting point. Yet the date does mark the beginning of major funding for teacher education. Earlier funding was authorized in vocational education legislation—the Smith-Hughes Act of 1917 (PL 64-347), the Vocational Education Act of 1936 (PL 74-673), the George-Barden Act of 1946 (PL 79-586), and others. These early programs are overlooked for three reasons: (a) the base of training was narrow (teachers, supervisors, and directors of agricultural subjects and teachers of trade, industrial, and home economics subjects); (b) not many of the programs funded personnel development expressly and exclusively; and (c) most of the money for personnel development went into state grants, the use of which is not easy to trace.

An exception to the 1958 starting point is the Cooperative Education Research Act of 1956. Another exception is science education funding, which began in 1954 when the National Science Foundation funded its first summer institute for high school teachers.

Some of the policies in force during the 1960s and 1970s have been modified or changed. However, programs must be discussed in the context of the policies that existed when the programs were operative.

INFORMANTS' THINKING ABOUT FEDERAL PROGRAMS IN EDUCATION

The authors surveyed a group of educators selected for their knowledge of, and experience with, federally funded programs. This was done to gain a general understanding of what some individuals who had been closely associated with a few federal programs thought about them. The available data on the topic were limited, and the definition of teacher education appeared to be unclear and narrow. The term *informants* is used to describe the people surveyed, because they were selected to give information on a certain situation about which they had special expertise; it is used in preference to *respondents*, which refers to people who answer a questionnaire.

The selection of people to survey proceeded as follows. First, a list of individuals involved in federally funded programs in teacher education was developed. To expand the list, the authors queried the people on it for the names of others they knew to be knowledgeable. Next, some federal and state department of education staff who had administered or monitored federal programs were chosen. Several of these were former government bureaucrats who, subsequent to government service, were recipients of federal funds; they were classified in terms of their current employment. Third, some deans of education were selected. The final list of subjects included deans, professors, government staff, and miscellaneous personnel, the latter group composed of professional association and union staff, directors of research and development centers and regional laboratories, foundation personnel, teacher center directors, editors of selected publications, personnel in private educational research corporations, and education consultants.

As the selection of informants proceeded, a questionnaire was constructed to elicit (a) impressions of federal funding in teacher education, (b) impact on teaching and on teachers prepared in programs that had received such funding, and (c) impact on teacher education institutions and faculty. Also, some items were designed to elicit reactions to the way in which the Department of Education (formerly the Office of Education) had planned and coordinated its operation, the approaches used to solicit proposals, the procedures followed in selecting recipients, equity in the grants made, the resources provided, and the evaluation and monitoring of programs. Finally, four open-ended questions were included to draw out reactions and opinions that forced-choice items did not permit.

Concurrent with the development of the questionnaire, an ERIC and Dissertation Abstracts search and a review of the literature took place. That experience led the authors to limit the coverage of the questionnaire to eight federal research and demonstration programs that had made major teacher education commitments: National Science Foundation institutes, National Defense Education Act institutes, Teacher Corps, the Career Opportunities Program (COP), Training the Trainers of Teachers, Urban/Rural School Development (URSD), Teacher Centers, and Research and Development Centers/Regional Educational Laboratories. Focusing on eight programs made it necessary to add some names to the list of informants, so that the survey population would represent all of the programs selected.

The process yielded 167 informants (44 deans, 49 professors, 20 government staff, and 54 miscellaneous personnel), to whom a questionnaire was sent in spring 1988. By mid June, 75 responses had been received. Follow-up telephone calls increased the number to 96 (a 57 percent return). Eighty-one of the questionnaires were usable for aggregating data. Fifteen people did not return usable questionnaires but sent written

reactions; these are reflected in the narrative. Others who were queried replied that they were not knowledgeable in teacher education. Their definition of teacher education might have been the narrow version, that is, preservice teacher education.

The questionnaire (available from the authors) consisted of a series of statements with forced-choice responses of Strongly Agree/Agree/Disagree/Strongly Disagree, and Very Adequate/ Adequate/Needs Improvement/Totally Inadequate. Its design was guided by the following questions:

1. How and in what ways have federally funded research and demonstration programs influenced or modified practice, thinking, and direction in teacher education?
2. Have the planning and the continuity of research and demonstration been sufficiently long range to make a difference in educational practice?
3. Have research and demonstration efforts been sufficiently concentrated to yield significant results?
4. Have the time given and the resources provided to a particular research agenda been adequate to gather significant evidence, to disseminate results, and to apply findings?
5. Have sufficient time and resources been provided for demonstration projects, and have the variety of contexts in which demonstrations have been conducted been adequate to draw conclusions about wider use and adaptation?
6. Has research and evaluation been a sufficiently critical component of the federal effort in education?
7. Has there been sufficient emphasis (and resources) on evaluation and research in federally funded projects in teacher education?
8. Have certain types of research and evaluation been more highly prized by the federal education agency?
9. Are procedures for announcing, selecting, and monitoring research and demonstration projects adequate and appropriate?
10. Has the time provided between issuance of requests for proposals (RFPs) and submission of proposals been adequate?
11. Have procedures for securing research and demonstration support favored educators skilled in grantsmanship?
12. Have political influences been used in determining what gets funded and who gets a contract or grant?
13. Are the priorities that federal education department staff give to monitoring and follow-through appropriately balanced?

General Assessment of Program Performance and Impact

Several of the statements presented to the survey population were broad assessments of how well the subject programs had performed. Most of the 81 informants reported generally favorable impressions. Over 70 percent agreed that the programs had been well thought through, based on sound research or wisdom, carefully planned and executed, and responsible for many significant new practices in teacher-preparation programs. As to whether teacher preparation had become more practical because of federal programs, the number concurring was smaller, but it still amounted to a majority (three-fourths of the government employees and 57 percent of the others). Most informants also agreed that programs had been carried out in enough places for valid conclusions to be drawn.

Competence of Project Directors. Of special interest was whether the informants were satisfied with the competence of the individuals most directly responsible for directing the projects, because, presumably, much hinged on their skills and commitment. It is significant, then, that 82 percent of the informants agreed that the project directors selected for awards were technically competent and good scholars. Most (two-thirds) also believed that the directors were very familiar with teaching practice.

Differences of Opinion. However, it would be a mistake to stop with these data, for informants' total scores on the questionnaire revealed no clear consensus on most of the issues. The four choices on questionnaire items—Strongly Agree/Agree/Disagree/ Strongly Disagree, and Very Adequate/Adequate/Needs Improvement/ Totally Inadequate—were assigned values of 3, 2, 1, or 0. The highest possible score across all 74 items, then, was 222. The actual scores, based on 74 items, ranged from a highly favorable 209 to a very critical 56. Thus, for example, 23 of 76 informants disagreed with the proposition that project directors had been sufficiently familiar with classrooms. Eight of 20 deans and 11 of 27 professors rated

them inadequate; 14 challenged their technical and scholarly competence. Twenty-four of 80 informants said that the changes that had occurred had been marginal. Nineteen of 31 professors felt that projects had not been tried out in enough places. The answers of 7 of 20 deans and 9 of 31 professors indicated that they were negative about the ways in which projects had been executed.

Such differences of opinion reflect the fact that the individuals were associated with different programs, at different times and places, and they developed distinct perspectives and personal interests from being identified with particular positions such as college dean, professor, or government staff.

To highlight some of the disagreement further, the 15 persons with the most favorable questionnaire scores were compared with the 15 whose scores were least favorable. The favorable group's responses averaged between *agree* and *strongly agree* on a 4-point scale. The least favorable group's responses averaged midway between *agree* and *disagree*. Differences between these two extreme groups will be mentioned further as seems relevant.

Impact on Teaching Practice and Teachers. Informants were asked to compare teachers prepared in federally funded programs with teachers prepared in regular teacher education programs on many dimensions. Table 11-1 shows the percentage who agreed and disagreed with each statement. The number of informants answering each question is also reported.

On 10 of 23 items, 75 percent or more of the informants agreed that teachers prepared in federally funded programs

TABLE 11-1. Comparison of Teachers Prepared in Federally Funded Programs with Teachers Prepared in Regular Programs

"Compared with teachers prepared in other programs, teachers prepared in federally funded programs—"	Percentage Who		Number of Informants
	Agreed	Disagreed	
Have better abilities to diagnose student needs	65	35	68
Are more likely to experiment with new approaches to teaching	88	12*	72
Have greater knowledge of subject matter	55	45	65
Show keener awareness of student motivation	71	29	66
Use techniques more appropriate to their teaching goals	81	19*	67
Employ wider variety of techniques	82	18*	68
Involve students more in learning	82	18*	67
Are more involved in curriculum decisions	75	25*	64
Have more effective contact with parents	70	30	67
Are more sensitive to culture of school	81	19*	70
Function more effectively in their work situation	73	27	66
Are more involved in community	75	25*	68
Keep more extensive records on progress	48	52	58
Collaborate more effectively with colleagues	69	31	65
Function more effectively with administrators	45	55	58
Are more involved in school policy development	75	25*	61
Appear to have better understanding of children	69	31	65
Are better able to maintain control of their classrooms	52	48	58
Are more knowledgeable about resources	81	19*	70
Are more effective in helping children learn	77	23*	60
Have higher standards for themselves and their students	74	26	66
Elicit more respect from students	63	37	60
Are highly regarded as good teachers by colleagues	71	29	62

* = significant agreement

were better than those prepared in regular programs. The 10 items related largely to teaching techniques, learning, teaching resources, decision making, and sensitivity to context. On the remaining items there was less agreement. On 4—differences in knowledge of subject matter, keeping of student records, functioning with administrators, and maintenance of classroom control—agreement and disagreement were almost evenly balanced.

Impact on Teacher Education Institutions and Faculty. Opinions were also sought on whether colleges and universities receiving federal funds for teacher education had experienced more changes than institutions not receiving such support. These items focused on changes in faculty and improvements in programs.

Informants were significantly positive on only 4 of 10 items: greater faculty involvement in change (85 percent); more faculty involvement with public schools (84 percent); more effective relationships between colleges of education and public schools (83 percent); and improvement in practicum programs (78 percent). Interestingly, all these items deal with factors external to the campus program. Informants were less positive about the improvement in the teaching of faculty (67 percent agreed); the intensified supervision of practicum experience (67 percent agreed); the focus and use of research to improve teacher education (66 percent agreed); and the use of research findings to improve the regular teacher education program (63 percent agreed). Opinion about improvements in advising prospective teachers was more negative than positive (53 to 47 percent). Only half of the informants (51 percent) agreed that there had been more careful selection of cooperating teachers.

Differences Among Informants by Position

Categories of informants (deans, professors, government staff, and miscellaneous personnel) were compared. Using mean composite scores for all questions in Part 1, the authors identified, by code number, the 15 informants who were most positive and the 15 informants who were most negative. The same was done for all questions in Part 2 and for all questions in Parts 1 and 2 combined. The *possible* totals for the tallies of most positives and most negatives were 45 and 45 (15 for Part 1, 15 for Part 2, and 15 for Parts 1 and 2 combined). No one was counted twice. With the duplicates eliminated, the *actual* totals were 27 most positive and 22 most negative. The tallies in both cases fell far short of 45, because the people who were

the most positive (or negative) in one part tended to be the same ones who were the most positive (or negative) overall. The breakdown is shown in Table 11-2.

The results of this analysis (even though the *n* is small) indicated that the government staff and miscellaneous personnel were most positive (7 of 13 and 8 of 15, respectively). The deans and professors were most negative (8 of 21 and 9 of 32, respectively). One might expect government personnel to be more positive because they were closely identified with the programs and responsible for their operation. The miscellaneous group included many people who were participants in funded programs. They might have had a vested interest and emotional commitment to the success of one or more programs and, therefore, probably were more likely to harbor bias.

Among the most negative informants, deans were the least favorable. They were also fairly positive among the most positive informants. This ambivalence may be explained in part by their conflicting interests in federal programs. Additional money provided a chance to experiment and accorded some distinction to a college of education. However, it also created more paperwork and jealousies among the faculty, because project staff had more privileges and license—discretionary money, latitude in schedule and teaching assignments, opportunities to travel, and frequent chances to confer with colleagues around the country.

Professors were probably negative for a number of reasons. Tenured professors often had a broader view of the teacher education scene and could see many of the shortcomings of federally funded programs. In addition, most were not recipients. In some situations they felt put upon to seek federal funds. Writing proposals was a time-consuming, tedious business, and only a few professors had skills in grantsmanship. Success in obtaining grants became part of the reward system, but only a small proportion of those submitting proposals received funding. Adjunct staff were often dominant (and more numerous) in federally funded programs. Thus, nontenured people had a license to experiment and be creative that professors envied.

The Way in Which Federal Funding Operated

In addition to the general assessments of program performance and impact, the authors were concerned with how programs became funded and how they operated, for to improve impact, it is first necessary to improve the procedural aspects of programs. This part of the questionnaire revealed more criticism than the part concerned with impact itself.

TABLE 11-2. Positions of the Most and Least Favorable Informants

27 Most Positive Respondents		Number in Sample	22 Most Negative Respondents	
6	28%	21 deans	8	38%
6	18	32 professors	9	28
7	54	13 government staff	2	15
8	53	15 misc. personnel	3	20
		81 informants		

Note. Based on the composite scores for Parts 1 and 2 of the questionnaire, both taken separately and combined.

In contrast with their generally favorable views reported earlier, the informants were especially critical of some aspects of the implementation process. Fewer than half regarded the procedures used by federal agencies to monitor projects as adequate; significantly, 7 of 13 government employees, who were very close to all phases of the projects, concurred. A bare majority of informants considered the resources and concentration of effort to have been adequate for separate projects. Only two-thirds judged the length of projects and the long-range continuity among them to have been inadequate. There was considerable difference of opinion regarding the desirable length of projects; 60 percent of the government employees were satisfied, whereas only one-fourth of the deans were. Even fewer of the informants (28 percent) were satisfied with the resources available for demonstrations. The select group of 15 who were generally most favorable were more critical of this aspect of programs than of any other.

Coordination. The sample as a whole was most critical about the lack of coordination among federal agencies and among federal, state, and local levels of government. They were less favorable about these two dimensions of coordination than about any other issue. Only 17 percent judged coordination among federal programs to have been adequate, and only 25 percent regarded coordination among levels of government to have been adequate. Again, even the most positive group rated these aspects lower than they rated most other dimensions of programs.

Evaluation. Even informants who were favorable toward other aspects of federal programs were less charitable toward the priority that had been given to evaluation. The mean score for all informants on this question (1.5) hovered between *agree* and *disagree.* Indeed, this is the only item on which there was close agreement between our select groups of positive and negative respondents.

Still, there were important differences of opinion. Ten of 13 (78 percent) of the government employees were satisfied with the role of evaluation within projects, whereas most of the professors were not. Deans were divided on this question. Informants were nearly equally divided on whether resources for evaluations had been adequate; professors were especially concerned about the need for more money for evaluation. But when asked about the degree to which evaluations had been used to guide demonstrations and dissemination efforts, more agreement emerged. Only one-third of the informants were satisfied with the role of evaluation in demonstrations, and still fewer (one-fourth) were satisfied with the use of evaluations to guide dissemination efforts.

The Funding Process. A majority of the informants (60 percent) were satisfied with procedures used by federal agencies to announce new projects and to solicit proposals for funding. The RFP procedure for solicitation was highlighted in the questionnaire. Under this procedure, the Education Department publishes an RFP describing the parameters and requirements for funding, with a specified time line for submission. Proposals are reviewed anonymously and evaluated by panelists (experts in the particular field). The assessments of panelists are reviewed and preliminary decisions made by government staff. A high-level manager (usually the assistant secretary if there is disagreement or a political issue involved) makes the final decision.

Slightly more than half (54 percent) regarded the RFP funding mechanism as adequate for the task. But, again, there were striking differences of opinion on these issues. Seventy-eight individuals responded to this question. Thirty-six (36 percent) said the RFP was not an adequate funding mechanism. Half the deans and government employees were included in this number. And although 11 of 13 government employees (85 percent) and 60 percent of professors thought the proposal-selection process had been adequate, only 8 of 21 deans (38 percent) had positive views about that process.

Informants were especially critical about three aspects of the funding process: the amount of time provided to respond to RFPs and the lack of clarity regarding both the policy issues and the policy options addressed by projects. Roughly two-thirds of the sample were critical of each dimension. Thus, even some of the informants who were generally favorable about the RFP process had reservations about the way it had operated.

Equity and Favoritism. The sample was divided over whether the distribution of awards among individual recipients and institutions had been equitable. Slightly more than one-half of government employees and professors were satisfied with the way in which awards had been distributed among individuals, but only one-third of deans expressed satisfaction with this aspect. And although 83 percent of government employees judged the distribution of awards among institutions to have been adequate, professors were split, and only 40 percent of deans were satisfied. It is not clear from these responses whose estimate is accurate, but the differences in perception between government and university personnel seem to indicate a potential blind spot in the funding process that deserves closer scrutiny.

The informants were also divided over whether federal funding had promoted pet ideas and faddishness. Two-thirds of deans and over half of government employees and miscellaneous personnel, but slightly under half of professors, believed these programs to have promoted fads in education, for example, competency-based teacher education and career ladders.

Did staff members of government agencies require proposers to adopt their pet ideas? Over one-half of deans and professors said yes; about 40 percent of the others concurred. And three-fourths of all informants believed that funding decisions had reflected the political persuasion of the administration in office.

One of the most critical questions concerning the equity of the funding process is reflected in the charge sometimes made (often by losers, to be sure) that competitions are biased and sometimes "wired," that is, that the recipients have been determined before an RFP has been issued. Three-fourths of the informants disagreed with this allegation. However, there were notable differences of opinion here too. Only 15 percent of government employees and 7 percent of miscellaneous personnel conceded that wiring had occurred. However, nearly half of deans and one-quarter of professors thought it had. A total of 18 of the 71 respondents who answered the question suspected wiring. This is a good example of why minority opinion should not be totally discounted. Although all 18 of these individuals could be wrong, at least some might have evidence that some competitions were wired, if not for a particular individual, then for one of a select pool of people. This practice might not have occurred frequently, but even one such incident undermines the credibility of the funding process.

Participation in Decision Making. When asked whether teachers and members of the research and development community had been sufficiently involved in making decisions about who should receive awards, the sample was again divided. Fewer than half (44 percent) considered teachers' level of involvement to have been adequate; only slightly more (52 percent) thought the research community had had an adequate voice.

Informants were especially critical about the lack of opportunities to support ideas initiated by individual research scholars. Two-thirds of the sample regarded this type of support as having been inadequate. The aspects of the funding process already considered could be partly at fault; in particular, the reliance placed on RFPs and other procedures associated with a "product purchase" funding mode. This funding strategy places heavy responsibility for designing and implementing research in the hands of federal employees, rather than in the hands of teachers and researchers.

To sum up, most informants thought government programs had a positive impact on many aspects of teacher practice. Also evaluated favorably were several aspects of higher education, the overall program impact, and the competence of the directors. These dimensions were viewed more favorably than many aspects of implementation were. However, the question of cost-effectiveness was not addressed and must be left to a future study.

AN INTERPRETATION OF SELECTED LITERATURE

Still other perspectives on how federal programs have operated are revealed by published research. The focus here is on literature published by researchers and other outside observers, many of whom have been more critical than the program participants themselves. In reporting this review, the authors have deliberately been selective and interpretive. The interpretation is divided into two parts: (a) an enumeration of tacit assumptions that seem to underlie federal school improvement programs, and (b) a list of problems that reportedly have been associated with such programs.

Tacit Assumptions Underlying Federal School-Improvement Programs

Federal efforts to improve teaching programs share assumptions commonly associated with other programmatic school-improvement efforts sponsored by federal agencies. They cannot be fully understood apart from the generic properties of such programs. Since at least the beginning of the 1970s, these programmatic efforts seem to have been driven by the following tacit assumptions:

1. A perceived national crisis demands immediate attention. The evidence of crisis can be found in illiteracy rates, school-completion rates, riots, poor performance of American students on international comparisons of test scores, competitive disadvantages of U.S. businesses, and more. The notion of crisis further suggests that local schools will be caught up in the movement, will thus be ready for change, and will extend themselves if provided with some additional resources and leadership.

2. Crises must be attacked directly and vigorously. Big problems demand big changes, and big changes in turn call for big, coordinated programs. Accordingly, fragmented, piecemeal, and incremental efforts do not work (Gideonse, 1979; Herriott, 1979).

3. Congress must assume responsibility for initiating and coordinating school-improvement programs, especially because only the federal government has the magnitude of dollars required. Categorical programs in the United States "are mounted with a presumption that the professional educator cannot be trusted and has helped cause the problem through neglect or bad practice" (Kirst, 1983, p. 432). On the other hand, the persons who staff federal agencies presumably are prepared to start and manage these programs. Federal programs help make up for the absence of a nationally centralized educational system in this country (Meyer, 1981).

4. Typically, there is a sense of urgency. Programs are rushed into existence, proposals must be submitted under tight deadlines, and projects should be completed within a few years.

5. The key to a successful program is finding "the right people" and giving them some freedom and resources to carry out their ideas. There are bright people outside federal agencies with good ideas who can help solve the problem; indeed, there is no shortage of people with good ideas. Sometimes they are people who have been involved in other school-improvement efforts and/or are closely identified with the situations that need to be changed. But sometimes they are distinguished citizens totally unconnected with the education establishment. Yet the central actors seldom if ever include classroom teachers, and it is not uncommon to exclude other professional educators not teaching in classrooms.

6. Freedom given recipients must be tempered with guidance from a federal agency. The amount of guidance depends in part on whether the award is a grant or a contract, the grant permitting recipients to exercise more discretion. Regardless of the mix of mandates, grants, dissemination, and technical-assistance strategies that might be used, the primary approach is legal and bureaucratic. Firm guidelines must be established and monitored by federal agencies. After initial plans have been formulated, guide-

lines make it possible to rely on technically proficient people capable of carrying out the plans of others. Their services can be procured through the competitive-bidding process used by industry. Guidelines implicitly presume that some ingredients of the solution are known, for example, citizen participation or a certain approach to curriculum or teaching, such as open education, magnet schools, bilingual education, or ability grouping.

7. Improvement is a product of political and managerial activities (Gideonse, 1979). Political tasks are associated with mixed authority structures, vague goals, and commitments based on negotiated consensus. But management tasks require well-defined goals, clear authority structures, and measurable outcomes. The apparent inconsistencies will work themselves out satisfactorily in the course of the program.

8. When implementation problems are encountered, the fault usually is resistance, rigidity, or ignorance at the local level. The tradition of localism, with attendant suspicion of federal intentions, virtually requires local control. This means that any given program becomes transformed into thousands of separate, different programs run according to the preferences of entrenched local interests (M. W. McLaughlin, 1975). Incentives may be used to secure cooperation, but if they do not work, it might be necessary to compromise the original plans to fit the circumstances (Berman & McLaughlin, 1975).

9. Federal programs should operate as supplementary activities at the margin of local school system programs. Schools can be changed by assigning the additional responsibilities associated with a change effort to personnel already in the school. It usually is not necessary to provide more time, training, materials, or rewards. Any problems that arise will work themselves out as the project matures.

10. Intellectual growth in children is the ultimate objective of school improvement. However, other intermediate outcomes must be accomplished, such as recruiting and retaining better teachers, in order to achieve this objective.

Some Problems Frequently Associated with Federal Programs

The assumptions just outlined have contributed to several problems that various writers have identified with a number of federally supported school-improvement programs. Some of the problems frequently cited are summarized.

Poor Fit Between Program and Context. Top-down programs designed in Washington are usually based on standardized, uniform approaches that rarely match the varied and often unpredictable situations to which they will be applied (Louis & Dentler, 1988). Cohn and Distefano (1984) draw upon case materials to demonstrate that the major recommendations of the *Nation at Risk* report (National Commission on Excellence in Education, 1983) have little relevance to the underlying problems of a district they studied. Yet fiscal requirements often mandate uniform operating standards—for example, that

school districts be the unit of change, that projects work through the state education agency, or that matching funds be provided. Speaking of Title I of the Elementary and Secondary Education Act (ESEA), Bailey and Mosher (1968) ask, "How is it possible for an agency to be specific and strict about fiscal accounting without becoming inflexible with regard to project operations?" (p. 99).

The Experimental Schools program was guided by a philosophy of comprehensive change. Notwithstanding the vagueness of that concept, guidelines for the program were sometimes rigidly enforced, typically without an attempt to fit federal requirements to the major immediate problems of school districts. Gideonse (1979) suggests that, in the zeal to enforce such requirements, the relationship between Washington and local sites amounted to one culture imposing itself on another, rather than collaboration (see also Corwin, 1983.) As one example of the consequences, guidelines for this program stipulated that the school district be treated as the unit of change. But in many districts there were wide differences among schools, which rendered uniform, districtwide approaches inoperable for some schools (Kirst, 1979).

Uniform federal guidelines tacitly suggest that there is one best approach to schooling that is already known. In fact, schools and classrooms are characterized by variation, making a given requirement less appropriate for some settings than for others. Consequently, local sites often comply only superficially with some requirements, in order to obtain resources that they might or might not use to meet other requirements. Many communities included citizen participation in their proposals for the Experimental Schools program, but later ignored it (Kirst, 1979). Speaking of another program, Provus (1975) notes, "The hodgepodge of local activities put together to satisfy national TTT guidelines soon lost direction" (p. 147).

The answer is not necessarily to abandon federal guidelines. If an agency is to be held accountable for the success of the programs it sponsors, as is now the case, it must be able to control the basic parameters of the local projects involved. Federal program officers are criticized for trying to exert too much control over local operations, for promulgating fiscal procedures, reports, and evaluations intended to help them keep programs on track; then, as Timpane observes (1977), they are criticized again when programs fail to produce substantial and effective results. Timpane laments, "As presently conceived, the job of federal program management is probably impossible" (p. 13).

Ambiguous, Inconsistent Designs. Although some writers are quick to attribute implementation problems to characteristics of local sites (Berman & McLaughlin, 1975), others point out that fundamental problems are often virtually guaranteed by ambiguities and inconsistencies in the program design (Corwin, 1983; Williams, 1976). Funding agencies sometimes do not know what they want and speak with several voices. Moreover, there are few checks and balances in the program development process. The decision to launch the $12 million Experienced-Based Career Education program, for example, one of the largest curriculum development efforts ever undertaken, was made by two individuals (Millsap, 1983). No other public constituencies were involved until the proposed regulations were published. By that time comments necessarily had to be restricted to reactive, minor suggestions; there was little room for outsiders to propose alternatives that would restructure the program. Instead, the program evolved from the internal workings of the agency.

Federal programs, therefore, are necessarily a blend of logic and the organizational politics characteristic of a given federal agency (Corwin & Nagi, 1972). As a result, they often embody inconsistent alternatives and vague objectives. Williams (1976) says:

What we are finding over and over again is that program objectives are often so elusive as to be difficult to determine at all, much less define rigorously. Moreover, as we move from broad objectives that are subject to many interpretations to rigorous ones that are not, the likelihood of disagreement rapidly increases. (p. 275)

The compromises necessary to bring programs into existence in the first place continue to plague the participants during the course of implementation. On this point Firestone (1979) reports:

The superintendent remembers dealing with [Experimental Schools] Washington as . . . a very frustrating thing; to say that we have no guidelines and yet to be evaluated on a sub rosa set of guidelines that we didn't know but we found out later they were evaluating on. . . . If they'd just told us that to begin with, it would have been a lot easier than to try to outguess them all the time and wondering if we were getting the right things in. So what was supposed to be a proposal based on our ideas was instead a proposal based on what they wanted. . . . The thing that really bothered me was that we were playing games with each other, rather than just having them say we've got to have this because Congress has said this. . . . Why not just tell us that? (p. 162)

Corwin (1983) writes:

[Communities participating in the Experimental Schools program had agreed to some key] provisions that were not well defined. For example, in principle they agreed that the project should produce "comprehensive" change, but as one program officer admits, "We didn't necessarily think it through, as a group, and come to some sort of consensus on what the behavioral manifestations would be of what we expected." (p. 128)

Another source complained about the awkward position in which this placed the program officer:

I was responsible for going over their drafts and criticizing them from some basis, which really wasn't specified—something to do with "feasibility," and whatever "comprehensiveness" was.. . . . I looked for obvious failure to see how elements in the plan would connect with each other . . . but I thought that some of the kinds of things that were vetoed by the staff here were arbitrary. And I found that I was in the middle of the situation; that I really couldn't explain to a local community why things in their plan weren't acceptable. I found that the most difficult, because I didn't think there was a firm guideline to give them. (p. 128)

One program officer told Corwin (1983):

At the moment, there is almost no reason for the local community to trust the federal government. They're confused about our inclinations; they're confused about our staff assignments; they're confused about our organization; they're confused about personnel; they're confused about direction. We present a chaotic picture. (pp. 154–155)

The beginnings of the Research, Development, and Utilization (RDU) program exemplify the compromise and maneuvering sometimes associated with the birth of new programs. Rather than being able to start with a rational plan, it was necessary to design the guiding concepts and procedures in a way that would not duplicate several other existing programs. Moreover, the program was premised on the need for more effective, formalized linkage between the research and development community and practitioners. However, in the face of potential competition from existing programs, it functioned independently, totally disconnected from several relevant, ongoing programs.

Within this political environment, inconsistencies crept into the program design itself. For example, the objective was to get research and development products into the hands of teachers, but the National Institute of Education also wanted to help schools solve their problems. It was assumed that technical assistance would be needed to help teachers use new research-and-development products. However, it became clear that they needed help in many other areas. The balance of effort shifted from implementing products to helping schools with problems unrelated to the products the agency originally wanted to promote. The projects devoted less time to matching products with problems and much more time to managing interpersonal relationships—organizing decision-making groups, conducting needs assessments, and implementing other "organizational development" types of managerial techniques. As a consequence, the program became almost indistinguishable from other programs within the agency that were already in place when RDU began. "Goal displacement" occurred because of the way the program was designed. Priorities among the variety of strategies used were decided in the marketplace. Ambiguity permits flexible, creative solutions, but local implementors are placed in a potentially confusing position unless the parameters of their latitude are made clear.

The ambiguities and inconsistencies characteristic of federal programs are promoted by the RFP funding mechanism, which is frequently used to award contracts. RFPs can be thought of as mixtures of two radically different funding strategies. They are simultaneously operational plans that explicitly describe what is to be done and flexible guides that permit accommodation and initiative. The problem is that the balance is not always clear. For example, RDU was not set up as an operational plan; nonetheless it suffered much criticism because many people thought of it as one (Corwin & Louis, 1982). Some of the National Institute of Education staff were uneasy about the failure of the RFP to specify and operationalize more explicitly what was to be done and who was to do it. The Contracts Office within the institute was particularly nervous about what it considered to be the looseness in the RDU request for proposals. Some of the experienced staff members in the institute complained that such a wide range of activities was permissible within the RFP that establishing concrete criteria for selecting the winners was difficult. Every proposer wanted to do something different.

One institute staff member asked, "How do programs like this get into existence when the initial idea is little more than an 'inkblot' to which everyone applies his own meanings?" (Corwin, 1983, p. 48). There are several possible answers. Ambiguity capitalizes on the initiative of the proposers, giving them latitude to tailor activities to new ideas and specific situations. Also, as was the case with RDU, ambiguity helps avoid confronting critical policy issues in the interest of launching a program (Corwin & Louis, 1982) and makes it easier to cope with a changing political climate and widely divergent circumstances where a program is going to be installed. However, Sieber (1982) warns, "Vagueness permits federal managers to select proposals that are compatible with their own private expectations on how the program should be conducted and allows leeway later on in defining more sharply the rules of the game" (p. 54).

Overextension. Announced objectives of programs frequently promise more than is possible within the limits of the existing knowledge base, technology, and resources. Indeed, it has been suggested that broad legislative policy solutions are often invoked to solve problems for which the necessary knowledge and expertise are otherwise unavailable (Dreeben & Barr, 1983). Those who promote programs might have high hopes or simply believe it necessary to promise much in order to win support.

In any case, resources, information, and staff capabilities are often overestimated by federal officials who design programs. Wise (1979) calls efforts to exert rational control beyond the bounds of knowledge "hyperrationalization." Title I of the 1965 Elementary and Secondary Education Act, for example, was premised on the belief that, by providing money, solutions would be found to uncharted problems for a population that the schools had never been able to help. However, at best, social science knowledge is tentative. The status of existing technology and theories does not warrant direct attacks on most big problems. On the contrary, from a solely technical viewpoint, it seems that solutions using science must come slowly and incrementally.

In addition to the indeterminate nature of the knowledge base itself, federal agencies sometimes do not even have access to the necessary information and expertise that is available. For example, the federal agency responsible for monitoring the Experimental Schools program in Washington never had adequate information on what was happening in the communities (Kirst, 1979). Similarly, the Teacher Corps program staff in Washington did not fully understand what was happening in the local schools; for example, the director misunderstood the forms of team teaching going on in schools (Corwin, 1972b). A premise of the RDU program was that the federal agency would be able to identify reliable, tested teaching materials worthy of dissemination and then write guidelines for their use. When it became clear that the needed capabilities were not available to the agency, the rationale on which the program rested was destroyed.

Murphy (1971) observes that the Office of Education officials who monitored Title I programs were untrained for the heavy responsibilities involved, understaffed, shaken by reorganizations, and reluctant to enforce the rules. Sizer (1974) accuses government agencies of myopia, caused by lack of understanding of the real needs of children, fostering of impractical ideas, yet impatience for practical answers to complex questions. Gideonse (1979) says bluntly that, although the local school districts in the Experimental Schools program projects were required to spend one year in detailed planning and training for district personnel, nowhere was there reference to the need for similar reflection and training for staff members of the federal agency. The government officials who monitor the performance of federal projects are in a position to exercise vital influence on the nature and quality of relationships that federal agencies establish with local communities (Corwin, 1983). Yet they often have received little special training for this role and are not closely supervised by someone who is an acknowledged expert in such responsibilities.

As well as overextending their own capacities, federal agencies often underestimate the resources required to accomplish even simple objectives. Most programs follow the strategy of funding a few projects rationed among the thousands of eligible sites. Moreover, within a given site, projects are often complex and plans often exceed available resources. In the case of Trainers of Teacher Trainers (TTT), one observer has concluded, "Time and again failure of TTT projects can be traced to lack of resources to satisfy plans" (Provus, 1975, p. 148).

Crisis Management. At birth, federal programs are often cloaked in an aura of urgency. Reporting on the Head Start Planned Variation program, Parelius and Parelius (1987) observe that pressures to get the program into the field were intense. The haste was associated with a number of the later problems that contributed to the program's initial failures, including many conceptual and methodological inadequacies. Writing about the TTT program, Provus (1975) notes, "Something was wrong from the very start" (p. 146). The program had been "rush into birth," "clear programmatic goals had not been set," and that produced "bureaucratic confusion." The Experimental Schools program was never planned in any detail at the federal level, and its operational capability was never reviewed before it was funded. The program was nonetheless launched immediately after the funds were appropriated. There was little time to recruit personnel, select local sites, formulate job descriptions, and develop workable guidelines. This forced the program officers, individually and on their own, to assume responsibility for shaving down broad and vague policy goals into something feasible. Moreover, even though the program required grantees to implement "comprehensive" change efforts, as noted earlier, that term was never defined by the federal agency. Local sites were left with the responsibility of guessing what their project monitors would accept (Corwin, 1983; Firestone, 1979; Herriott, 1979).

The sense of urgency typical of many programs contributes to failures in diagnosing problems properly and in working out effective program designs, even to failure in defining the guiding concepts. There is typically little time to engage in essential diagnostic activities (Gross, 1979). As Gross notes, one reason that new reading programs have frequently proven unsuccessful (Popp, 1975) is the assumption that reading problems can be remedied with better technology, without consideration of the importance of teachers' expectations, training, and ability to diagnose learning problems.

Discontinuities. Instability seems to be a general characteristic of federal programs. Pressman (1975) reports that officials associated with various federal programs change priorities, renege on financial commitments, and yet hold local people responsible for properly administering their projects. Programs in education, in particular, often have been disrupted by fickle political forces. The new curriculum projects devoted to excellence, initiated in the 1960s, were eclipsed by the compensatory education movement, which in turn was overshadowed by desegregation programs, which were for a time stalled by the drive for community control.

Similarly, although perhaps some programs have not changed focus over time, for many, demands vacillate with shifting political currents (Edelfelt & Darland, 1972). As one consequence, fundamental premises, such as the criteria for judging results, often change at midcourse. For example, Provus (1975) observes that, with a change of administration in Washington, new demands were placed on TTT. The critics wanted immediate and tangible results. What had been a "wide-furrowing plow" had to become a "sharp-cutting diamond" (p. 146). The scenario was repeated for the Experimental Schools program in the 1970s. Before it had properly been started, the program had become a part of various power struggles within the executive branch and within OE itself.

The confusion over whether this was primarily a research project, a grant-in-aid, or a demonstration program eventually had a paralyzing impact on the projects. After the program was transferred from one agency to another, what had been conceived as an "experiment" in the loosest sense was suddenly expected to meet the stringent tests of a scientifically controlled design.

Changes in political philosophies are often compounded by rapid turnover in the federal personnel who monitor projects. Several rural communities participating in the Experimental Schools program had been assigned as many as four project monitors within a 5-year period. All projects had to deal with more than one monitor (Corwin & Louis, 1982). Among the consequences were extended delays in funding and idiosyncratic requirements from different monitors. Born largely as the result of the thinking of a few people, the RDU program generated little interest or even much awareness within the agency. None of the individuals who started the program were still with the agency when the final reports were submitted (Corwin & Louis, 1982).

Arbitrary Uses of Discretion. The discretion of federal program officers has already been mentioned. School officials in communities participating in the Rural Experimental Schools program often complained about the vague and sometimes rather arbitrary way in which different program officers interpreted the requirements. Corwin (1983) relates the account of one program officer who believed that another program officer had given some bad advice about a math program:

I discussed this with the superintendent and criticized much of what I saw in the way of the [materials] the teachers had developed. The superintendent went back with this consultant, reworked in-service and spent maybe the last year in trying to improve the quality of those things. (p. 151)

Elsewhere Corwin observes:

One program officer gave the very strong impression to a community that it would not be funded until it independently stumbled into what [Experimental Schools] Washington had in mind all along. This officer gave the impression to local administrators that he knew exactly what was wanted but adamantly refused to say what it was. For example, the program officer required the community to rewrite the entire proposal, to direct it toward a local rather than a professional audience. One school board member responded, "You are the one who is going to write the plan. You know you are. Just tell us what you want. If you want it in red ink, we'll write it in red ink. If you want it in green ink, we'll write it in green ink." (pp. 28–29)

Sometimes program officers chose to operate in subtle ways, as this one confided:

I rarely give a direct order to the projects. . . . I usually try to arrive at things through questions, asking them questions, leading them. And I know that's what I am doing, and I have to assume they know that, too, leading them down a particular path. I usually have an idea of where I want them to end up. (p. 147)

Staff members of federal agencies can choose and sometimes have chosen to play several extremely different roles, depending on the individuals and the circumstances involved: contract monitors, project advisors, or technical-assistance consultants. In the order listed, relationships become more collegial and more intrusive (Corwin, 1983). But the monitoring responsibilities are always present, never in the background. Thus, if a project officer chooses to play an advisory or technical-assistance role, that person is put in a position to persuade and intimidate colleagues to adopt ideas as a condition of receiving or maintaining federal money. One federal program officer in Corwin's (1983) study confided:

I've been particularly cool about their approach to the bilingual education program, and have told them, in fact, that I thought they were not being faithful to what they had agreed to do. . . . [I] pointed out to them that if they couldn't come up with some kind of program that there was some question if they could be eligible for refunding. That's real pressure. (p. 165)

This is the epitome of federal control. There is at best a fragile line between a federal employee who, in the capacity of colleague, offers advice or technical assistance to recipients and one who insists on dictating procedures as a condition of being funded.

Favoritism. The search for talent and technical expertise sometimes creates semiclosed circles, oligarchies of elites who are favored by an agency. For example, Provus (1975) observes that responsibility for changing the training of teachers was assigned to the people who had been doing that job all along. There might be separate circles, one consisting of chosen scholars and another of research contract firms, both with the capabilities of meeting the demanding conditions mentioned earlier, such as the ability to respond to quick deadlines and the readiness to attack big problems using precarious technologies and indeterminate knowledge bases. Thus it is sometimes possible to predict in advance the winners of a proposal competition; more frequently, it is possible to predict that winners will come from a restricted pool of favorites. Frequently too, the scholars who work with contract firms lend their names for legitimacy, rather than provide real intellectual guidance.

SPECULATIONS AND CONJECTURES

Although some of the tenuous assumptions and problems associated with federal programs have been highlighted, this does not imply that federal programs have been entirely ineffective. As informants' responses have indicated, many knowledgeable people, especially those who have been closely associated with these programs, are convinced that programs do have desirable effects on teacher education, even when this was not the primary objective, as was true of some programs included in the survey. The main point is that federal programs are not perfect and can be made more effective than they have been. But they will not improve until there is a better grasp of some basic issues that are often obscured in the literature but must eventually be resolved.

The Impact of Federal Programs

There is no better place to start than with the issue that motivates this chapter: What evidence is there regarding whether federal programs have had some kind of impact? A small sampling of the extensive literature on the subject might help to provide a sense of the perplexing difficulties of answering this question.

On the one hand, some evaluations have been optimistic. For example, a study of the Master of Arts in Teaching (MAT) program, designed to give bright students an opportunity to take academic courses and internships in schools, concluded that it attracted academically able students and was successful in getting its graduates into classroom teaching (Coley & Thorpe, 1985). Eighty-three percent of the graduates entered teaching, most taught at least 5 years, and one-third were still teaching after 20 years, mainly in suburban schools. However, many of the teachers complained that they were not prepared to handle individual differences among students with varying abilities and exceptionalities. Similarly, they felt unprepared to cope with differences among students from different backgrounds, and many did not feel competent to handle discipline problems. Also, it was noted that the success of programs depended heavily on the ability of the supervising teachers and

on close relationships between universities and local education agencies.

Some evaluations have been guarded, seeing impact as variable and conditional, even within a school or a program. For example, Edelfelt, Corwin, and Hanna (1974) found disagreement about whether the Teacher Corps had improved the curriculum of schools. Although most of the respondents thought techniques had changed, many of them thought the changes would be temporary. At best, it was concluded, the program had helped bring some new techniques into at least one school in each school district visited by members of the research team. Likewise, most of the respondents agreed that at least some children were learning more because of the program. Many of the respondents who were most positive were talking about the reduced work loads for teachers due to the presence of interns in the classroom (who disappeared with the termination of the program). At the same time, most of the teachers involved in the program said their attitudes toward teaching and their students had improved.

The picture was equally mixed at the universities. Again, there seemed to be more agreement that professors had been awakened to the problems of the poor and racial minorities and had become more receptive to new ideas, than that concrete behavioral changes had occurred. Although most of the college faculty queried said that there had been new courses, only about half reported changes in classroom techniques during the program, and nearly as many saw no significant changes of this sort.

Many evaluations have been negative about the question of impact. An evaluation of over 300 compensatory-education programs introduced into urban schools in the 1960s concluded that they had had minimal influence on raising student academic achievement (Gordon & Wilkerson, 1966). Reporting on another large-scale assessment of federally financed school-improvement programs, Berman and McLaughlin (1974) found no consistent, significant effect on student outcomes that could be attributed to participation in special programs funded by federal dollars. In many cases, the outcomes that could be identified lacked statistical significance. Berman and McLaughlin identified three outcomes of implementation efforts: nonimplementation, cooptation (in which the fundamental properties of the innovation are lost), and mutual adaptation (in which both innovation and local context change). The incidence of even mutual adaptation was exceedingly rare.

Therefore, there is no simple answer to the issue addressed in this chapter. The answer depends on the programs and the places one has in mind. It also depends on one's definition of impact and one's judgment.

Defining Impact

Obviously, there are many definitions of impact. Some are simple and short-term, for example, Did student test scores improve because of a particular program? Were beginning teachers more effective as the result of a change in the preservice program? Did teacher performance improve when teachers earned a master's degree? Another view of impact might involve change over time or the durability of change. Did the program of teacher education change during federal funding? Was the change sustained after funding terminated? If probed further, these questions open up a whole set of issues about the way in which impact is conceptualized and measured. Examination of such issues can shed light on the nature and extent of the impact of federally funded programs.

Review of issues can be critical, especially because some reviews of the impacts of federal programs have been mixed or discouraging. Such wholesale assessments tend to oversimplify and obscure complex issues inherent in evaluating impact. An observer's judgment about the consequences of teacher education in a school-improvement program depends on the mix of many decisions that, explicitly or implicitly, must be made. Some of the critical issues to consider follow.

1. *Whether an observed change is compared with what was promised or with what existed before the program; and whether the stated objectives are concrete and focused or abstract and evolving.* Because of the complexity of changing any program of teacher education, most programs turn out to be only partially successful, at best. Moreover, objectives can be traded off or negotiated away during the early stages, and those that remain are often blunted by day-to-day problems. Nevertheless, the same program can look different when the results are compared with what existed, rather than with what was promised. For example, recent studies of Title I programs suggest that they have become more effective. The gains are modest, compared with the original promises, but they are positive, considering the earlier negative conclusions. In this connection there is some evidence that, although more project goals are likely to be achieved in small projects, the more ambitious ones are likely to lead to more change in teacher behavior (Berman & McLaughlin, 1977).

2. *Whether there is a single objective or multiple objectives; and whether unintended and intended consequences are considered.* Many minor changes scattered throughout a variety of places could incrementally add up to a substantial overall effect. Speaking of TTT, Provus (1975) concludes that, even though different innovations were tried from place to place and success varied among the different sites, the total effect might have been substantial.

3. *Whether only positive changes are considered or whether net change is calculated.* Net change can be computed in two ways. *First,* because the solution to one problem often creates others, the negative consequences can be deducted from the positive effects. For example, a new textbook might improve information but have a deleterious effect on children's enthusiasm toward the subject. *Second,* improvements can be calculated as the net of the social costs associated with implementing a change, such as role overload or reduced harmony. Suppose, for example, that to make team teaching work most effectively, it is necessary for teachers to double their work load.

4. *Whether a short or long time span is considered.* Synthesizing 13 years of studies of the Elementary and Secondary Education Act's Title I, Kirst and Jung (1980) found that

the regulations were implemented with greater fidelity at the end of a 15-year period than during the early years. The Head Start program received negative evaluations in the first years, but more favorable reviews in later years (Ballentine, 1983). On the other hand, although the adoption of new-math textbooks mushroomed in the first 5 years they were promoted, school districts discontinued them almost as rapidly after that (Stake & Easley, 1978). Over short periods, it is often impossible to distinguish incremental impacts from some fads.

There is some evidence that structural changes are more durable than reforms calling for new skills or added effort on the part of existing staff (Tyack, Kirst, & Hansot, 1980). In particular, adding specialist positions and layers of personnel (e.g., vocational specialists, pupil-service personnel, instructional aides, and remedial reading or bilingual education teachers) often has lasting impact. Kirst (1983) concludes that federal and state aid has been a major force behind the growth of professional subspecialties within the ranks of certified teachers, as well as behind the growth in size and scope of the paraprofessional sector and specialized administrative units (Meyer, 1981). As a consequence of specialization, teachers must cope with tensions and frustrations associated with more complexity and hierarchy, but they can also focus on developing specific skills and competencies, and they have more opportunities for career advancement.

In comparison with structural changes, Tyack et al. (1980) conclude that attempts to modify time spent on specific instructional tasks, curriculum organization, or teaching methods and strategies tend to have low impact, partly because specific teacher behaviors are difficult to monitor. Moreover, because there is no consistent federal policy on teaching methods and content, federal impact in these areas understandably will be ephemeral and cyclical (Kirst, 1983).

5. *Whether all levels of the social system in question are considered or only one; and whether or not changes at both managerial and technical levels are taken into account and treated equally.* Slippages are characteristic of long delivery chains such as the one between a federal agency and a particular classroom. Therefore, even when it is intended that federal funds have an impact on classrooms, they might be diverted to other purposes. A program could affect college administration (e.g., it could require more staff to handle paperwork) without resulting in school district change. Or college programs could change (e.g., they might require more liberal arts courses for teachers) without having a measurable impact on school districts. District offices might change in certain ways without having an impact on schools. And the administrative structure of a school might change without affecting teachers. Even when the quality of available technologies and resources such as textbooks improves, it is problematic whether the improvements have an impact on teaching in the classroom. On this point, a survey of school superintendents indicated general agreement (58 percent) that federal support for curriculum development had improved the quality

of curriculum alternatives, but agreement from only a minority (27 percent) that the national curriculum effort had greatly improved the quality of classroom instruction (Weiss, 1978).

Most of the implementation literature has focused on levels above the classroom; little research has been devoted to changes in teacher behavior or attitudes as a result of implementation (Benson, Medrich, & Buckley, 1980; Kirst, 1983). However, it seems that getting research products into classrooms has generally proven difficult. One reason is suggested by Kirst (1983), who points out that the amount of time explicitly set aside for inservice training of teachers involved with federal programs is surprisingly low. For example, in 1976 only about $100 million of more than $4.5 billion expended by the federal government on elementary and secondary education was for teacher-training programs (Timpane, 1977). But more fundamentally, most school-improvement projects lack tangible relevance to classroom concerns (Fullan & Pomfret, 1975). Teachers often fault innovation projects for insufficient guidance on which teaching strategies, instructional activities, or materials should be used.

6. *Whether second-order changes in attitudes, norms, and value climates are treated on a par with more concrete changes in structures, materials, and behavior.* Even a program that fails in other respects can serve as a source of enlightenment and as a catalyst for other efforts to change. The mistakes made by a program could lay the foundation for improving the chances of success of still other efforts. One effect of Teacher Corps programs was to make college professors more aware of their own deficiencies and more receptive to the need to change, even though they continued to teach as they always had. Some authors suggest that the most significant federal impact might be to provide opinion leadership (Timpane, 1979). Also, according to Meyer (1981), programs can act as symbolic models that ultimately help crystallize a new consensus on national norms and priorities. Meyer suggests that, in a nation such as ours with a decentralized education system, federal initiatives are needed to prod schools into responding to emerging national issues. Even ineffectively enforced federal requirements can help mobilize and support local constituencies in sympathy with federal objectives. Thus, regardless of its shortcomings, the Elementary and Secondary Education Act spotlighted the needs of poor children and fueled the equity movement.

7. *Whether only universally applicable improvements are considered, or whether conditional changes, which produce improvements only under very specific and limited circumstances, are counted.* Improvements are often limited to specific situations. An approach that works in one place could and will often fail in another. The RAND change-agent study documented a range of implementation outcomes in its school-site investigations (Berman & McLaughlin, 1975). Thus, on the whole, compensatory reading programs have, at best, produced only limited improvements in student performance, but, in some places

and for some individuals, there has been more substantial improvement (Thomas & Pelarin, 1976).

Accordingly, assessments of programs usually provide a mixed picture (D. H. McLaughlin, 1977). This variability characteristic of program outcomes is often further confounded by the use of different evaluation procedures and frameworks at different sites within a given program. Early attempts to synthesize the results of locally conducted evaluations of Title I projects were unsuccessful because the data were too divergent in terms of quality, quantity, and focus (Stonehill & Groves, 1983).

8. *Whether different dimensions and forms of change are treated as equivalent or given differential weighting.* A given program could be assessed by (a) gross volume (e.g., the total number of changes of all kinds); (b) magnitude as reflected in iterations and substitutions (e.g., one book replaced by another); (c) magnitude as reflected in structural modifications (e.g., a new position added); (d) magnitude as reflected in altered relationships (e.g., professors working closely with teachers) and authority relations (e.g., cross-age teaching); and (e) scope, as reflected in the number of students, teachers, classrooms, schools, and grade levels within schools affected. A team-teaching approach to new curricula might score high on *(b)*, *(c)*, and *(d)* but, if limited to a few classrooms, low on *(a)* and *(e)*. Or a school might score high on *(a)* but low on *(b)*, *(c)*, *(d)*, and *(e)*.

9. *Whether assessments of impact are limited to quantitative measures and/or to observable criteria that can be validated by independent observers; and whether personal evaluations of participants are used at face value.* In his book, *Legislated Learning*, Wise (1979) speculates that preoccupation with measuring the effects of educational programs and policies has selectively narrowed attention to a few instrumental goals and has simultaneously bureaucratized the American classroom as a means of insuring conformity to the chosen goals, namely, basic and vocational skills. Broader, more ambitious objectives concerned with socialization, character formation, and values have been eclipsed. The search for measurable goals, he charges, is driven by a rationalistic model that is consistently violated by how schools actually operate and by what teachers are actually trying to achieve.

On the other hand, other than by obtaining test scores, it is often difficult to measure impacts objectively, because necessary measurements are not available, time and resources are in short supply, several implementation programs are simultaneously in operation together with myriad other local influences, and a variety of different outcomes are involved in many locations. Often the only information available comes from value-laden personal views of participants, random comments, or accidental discoveries, which produce distorted and often exaggerated claims (Kirst, 1980; Timpane, 1979).

10. *Whether the observer has attempted to distinguish between impact and improvement, and if so, whether there is a high degree of consensus among participants and ob-*

servers about what constitutes an improvement, more important, what constitutes a significant one.

In sum, determining the impact of federal programs is as complex and as fraught with problems as the programs themselves.

Whom to Believe

The answer to how much impact federal funding has had also depends upon who is making the judgment. It became apparent in gathering data for this chapter that at least two categories of federal funding have influenced teacher education. People's opinions about the effects of federal programs seemed to differ, at least to some extent, depending on the category with which they were more closely identified. The two categories are associated with different objectives and procedures for allocating grants or contracts.

One category supports local projects designed to test, demonstrate, or implement a particular or general type of program. Teacher Centers, the Career Opportunities Program, Teacher Corps, and the National Institute of Education programs are examples. The magnitude of grants made by such programs was relatively small, most under $200,000 per year, and almost all of them provided funding at a number of sites (e.g., Teacher Centers made over 100 grants) to a variety of institutions and agencies. Except for Research and Development Centers/Regional Educational Laboratories, all programs included in the questionnaire used to gather data for this chapter qualified for this category. The people in this category were often regularly employed staff of a school system or college. Federal funding enabled them to introduce an innovation in their school, to which they developed a special commitment. The innovation directly influenced their lives. They tended to be more positive about impact.

The second category of funding includes Research and Development Centers/Regional Education Laboratories and other large studies and projects. Usually only one grant was made for each study, type of center, or project in this category. The magnitude of funding in these contracts was far larger, often running into millions of dollars. The Berman and McLaughlin (1974–1980) study of federal programs (ESEA Title I) supporting educational change and the contract for the National Assessment of Educational Progress (first with the Education Commission of the States, currently with the Educational Testing Service), are illustrations. The employment of participants in this category often depended on whether funding was sustained. Their commitment was more to a particular project than to an educational program.

A further differentiation on the point of judgment relates to the formal evaluations of federal programs that have been conducted. Most of the university professors and other researchers conducting and reporting these evaluations have been outside observers. They have been one step removed from the action, and for that reason they have been able to take a broad view of many projects. They have used systematic approaches to appraisal, often relying on a narrower set of criteria for judgment than practitioners. Also, they have paid more attention to the mechanisms of funding and the performance of federal bureaucrats.

The participants in action projects, whether they have been school or higher education personnel or the government employees who monitored projects, have firsthand knowledge (and memories) of one or more projects. They are less objective and more intuitive in both attitude and approach to evaluation, but they know more about the total experience of their programs and thus probably reflect a broader, more holistic view of impact. Whereas researchers are inclined to evaluate against stated goals, participants often make assessments of a developmental nature as projects evolve new goals or produce unintended outcomes. These observations are apparent from the questionnaire and are substantiated further by the preceding analysis.

The Determinants of Organizational Change

An obvious but fundamental fact has often been ignored in school-improvement programs: Individual teachers are part of an organizational system, and their behavior cannot be altered in any permanent way without first changing that system. This means that an intermediate form of impact, organizational change, must precede impact on classrooms, teachers, and students. Conversely, the form and degree of impact will be shaped by organizational structures. There is a considerable literature detailing how changes occur in many types of organizations that can be used to guide school improvement and evaluation designs.

Some important lessons were learned in the early years of the NSF and NDEA institutes. The initial concern of both programs was to improve the teacher's competence in subject matter. Evaluations of institutes demonstrated that subject matter was too narrow a focus (Gross, 1979; Popp, 1975). Even expanding the scope to include techniques of teaching and the use of materials was not sufficient. With further experience, at least some leaders in these programs came to understand that schools as complicated social systems have an ecology; that considering only one element such as the individual teacher might do little to affect the whole; and that it is very difficult to isolate the specific impact of a federally funded program from other events and circumstances associated with particular schools.

The experiences with NSF and NDEA institutes seemed to have considerable influence on subsequent federal programs such as Teacher Corps, TTT, Teacher Centers, and others, all of which included schools, communities, and teacher education institutions in their training models. The directors of one long-term study of the Teacher Corps conclude, "The outcomes were hammered out in the schools and colleges. Consequently, each program varied depending upon the individuals involved and the structures in which they worked" (Edelfelt et al., 1974, p. 42). For example, according to that study, the amount of change in schools depended on who controlled the federal money; the greater the proportion of funds controlled by the schools, the fewer the changes that took place. Also, there were fewer changes in schools where teachers were very concerned about maintaining tight discipline, which presumably restricted opportunities for creativity. Furthermore, contrary to a popular myth, there was less change where teachers took part in writing the proposal for the program, apparently because teachers saw this as a self-serving opportunity to get more help in the classroom, not as a chance to promote fundamental change. For perhaps the same reason, there was more change where decision-making power was centralized in school district offices.

The community environment was also important. There was more change where there had been a history of cooperative projects between schools and groups in the community. Also, schools in large urban centers in the industrialized regions of the country changed the most.

However, it was concluded that the single most crucial factor determining how much change occurred was a viable relationship between a school and a university, provided that the professors and the teachers involved were competent and interested in change (Corwin, 1972a). This finding underscores the critical role played by outside sources of stimulus for change and assistance to carry it out. In short, the ability to understand and improve teaching ultimately hinges on the ability to understand how teachers are affected by factors within schools and school districts.

The Connection Between Impact and the Procedural Aspects of Programs

As observed earlier, informants were more optimistic about the impact that programs had on teachers and universities than about the effectiveness of some of the procedures used to procure and implement programs, such as the short turnaround characteristically allowed to respond to RFPs. Also, many of the criticisms found in the literature review pertain to this procedural dimension. This relationship between procedure and outcome has not been systematically addressed. Although it might be reasonable to assume that outcomes will improve as procedures are improved, it remains to be seen which procedures are most in need of change and precisely which outcomes are most likely to be affected.

There is no simple way to attack this issue empirically. However, informants did provide some clues. In an open-ended question, they were asked to identify, in their own words, the greatest impediments to federally funded projects in teacher education. Over half of the 60 who answered mentioned various forms of discontinuity in the funding process: the turnover among project directors or federal personnel, the short-term nature of most projects, and the lack of institutionalization or follow-through on things that seemed to be working. Fifteen, or one out of every four, mentioned bureaucratic regulations, hasty procurements, or low quality of monitoring. The same number mentioned lack of coordination among programs or an unclear, segmental-focus characteristic of program designs. Eleven of the 60 also mentioned the politics of funding such as favoritism and pet ideas pushed by the agencies.

CONCLUSIONS AND RECOMMENDATIONS

There has been little agreement on what constitutes impact. At best, the evidence is mixed. Generalization is therefore difficult. There is reason to believe that the many individuals associated with some of these programs have become more aware of the need to improve teacher education and more receptive to the idea that they should change. And many have gravitated to positions of greater power. But, at a general level, many people seem to believe that federal funding has not had major influence on redirecting teacher education.

Reasons for the Limited Impact

Failure to Involve a Critical Mass. In most programs a major lack was a critical mass of teachers and administrators. Programs became too fragmented and too narrowly based either to demonstrate an idea conclusively or to allow time for an innovation to become institutionalized.

Teachers were infrequently involved in planning and decision making. They rarely developed ownership of a new project. Too often programs were devised in Washington and were required to be implemented uniformly across the country. There was insufficient attention to local needs. In fact, local needs were seldom ascertained. As a result, programs were often not aimed at the changes teachers felt they needed to improve schools (e.g., involvement in decision making and time to work with colleagues in solving problems, devising schedules and assignments, and improving communication).

Insensitivity to Different Populations. Policymakers and government staff, by virtue of their level of education and income, were largely middle-class. Many had little direct personal experience with ethnic minorities, people in poverty, and adversities of the disadvantaged. They often lacked sensitivity to low-income and minority children and youth. Frequently the accepted measures of achievement were standardized test scores, a yardstick that discriminates against students from disadvantaged backgrounds and against most minorities.

Many programs were of short duration. There was not enough encouragement to fashion changes to fit local circumstances. Rather extravagant expectations existed for the transfer of innovations from one context to another. Breakthroughs that worked in one context (e.g., a suburban school) were expected to be appropriate in any situation (e.g., an inner-city school). Even the language suggested uniformity and a mechanical process of installation—for example, "Programs That Work" and "delivery systems." Programs were not monitored and evaluated sufficiently, and evaluation of program success or failure was seldom used in subsequent funding decisions.

Lack of Follow-Through. Continuity and follow-through in programs were also problematic. Too many programs had only just started when they were terminated. Teacher Centers, TTT, and the URSD programs are illustrative. Other programs went through extensive planning phases and then received no government support for implementation. Under the Model Elementary School effort, for example, 10 institutions were granted over $2 million for planning and designing innovative programs; then not a nickel was allocated to make even one of the plans operational. Another case in point was Teacher Corps. To stay alive, it changed from a preservice teacher-training program for liberal arts graduates to a program that admitted any college graduate. It also shifted its focus from one new idea to the next (competency-based teacher education, multicultural education, community-based education, the exceptional child), losing the original concept.

Insufficient Attention to Chance Outcomes.

Inadequate provision was made in most federally funded programs for recognizing and valuing unintended outcomes, those that occurred fortuitously, coincidentally, serendipitously. Here are examples of serendipity. A teacher who was seeking better ways to teach reading discovered that she could teach a child to read through writing. A school staff attempting to improve human relations in the schools discovered that reading scores and attitudes about reading improved dramatically without any special attention. Teachers in a school serving children from low-income homes visited parents to enlist their support for developing literacy, and, as a result, the teachers began treating children with greater understanding and sensitivity.

Plans have value, but the chance outcome, as in many scientific discoveries, might be more important than the original goal. When progress is achieved by happenstance, it should be acknowledged and valued as forward motion.

Bias in Federal Support.

Considerable negative criticism has been leveled at the procedures for announcing, reviewing, selecting, and monitoring federally funded research-and-demonstration projects. The dominant procedure has been the RFP. The procedure has been criticized as inequitable, partial to entrepreneurs skilled in grantsmanship, most favorable to high-prestige educators and institutions, and subject to political influence. All of these criticisms have been valid for some RFPs over time.

There have also been claims of bias. One sort is favoring or discriminating against certain projects or proposers (Vobejda, 1988). Another is partiality toward a particular individual or institution. In the most extreme cases, the suspicion is that RFPs have been wired, that is, as mentioned earlier that grantees have been selected in advance and that the RFP procedure has been employed to give the appearance of a peer review.

An alternative to the RFP approach has been sole-source contracting, which is selecting a contractor without competition because a particular institution or agency has the singular capability to carry out the project. Sole-source contracting can be criticized as partial to selected contractors and favoring old-boy networks. Contractors might come from an interlocking system of relationships, such as university professors, former doctoral students, and/or erstwhile colleagues. Although often built on respect for competence and admiration of mentors, such networks also promote favoritism toward people with big names and a kind of mutual back scratching. Sole-source contracting depends more than the RFP on judgments made by civil service personnel and staff appointed by the administra-

tion in power, some of whom, particularly at the Office of Educational Research and Improvement, rotate between university and government employment. Sole-source decisions have prompted critics to allege that the pet ideas of federal Education department staff (and their university contacts) and the administration in power have received too much support.

Politics.

The preceding section illustrates a kind of special influence or bias in awarding grants within the Education Department. In the broader political realm, influence exists at two levels. Elected representatives in Congress and in the administration propose and approve legislation and appropriations. These actions are a part of the political process. When legislation becomes too explicit, however, it can dictate the type and the scope of the programs funded, often without sufficient advice from educators and without adequate objectivity about what is most needed. Department personnel further influence decisions within the discretion allowed by the legislation, and sometimes beyond it.

Decisions about who gets money are generally made by appointed Education Department staff after the peer review process. But, not infrequently, there has also been political input—a member of Congress calling the Secretary of Education, an Assistant Secretary, or a bureaucrat to encourage a decision in a constituent's favor. When and how often political influence determines who gets funded has never been explored thoroughly, but it is a fact of life and it carries weight, particularly on big grants or contracts. Insiders at the Education Department report that political influence has become more dominant in recent years.

Role Ambiguity in the Education Department.

At times, federal staff have come under severe criticism. Some are not adequately prepared for the programs they manage or monitor (CPI, 1977). Usually they have been left to educate themselves about a new program to which they are assigned. Rarely is there in-depth staff training when a new program is launched. Bureaucrats (career civil servants) often know less about the program that they oversee than the site-based people whom they monitor (Corwin, 1983).

A number of department personnel are political appointees—in federal jargon, Schedule C personnel—selected by the administration. Some are qualified educators; some are professional managers; others are selected because they have worked for the party in power or have connections to people who have.

The attitude and the skill of department staff in dealing with educators in the field sometimes leave much to be desired. They are often insensitive to how they are perceived by personnel at a local site (Corwin, 1983). First-time or occasional recipients of federal funds are especially impressed with "the people in Washington." At times Education Department staff are perceived as overly impressed with their own importance, and they are arrogant, overbearing, and authoritarian in their behavior. This is not surprising, given that they go largely unmonitored (Corwin, 1983).

Confusion about the role of federal staff is not new. Whether staff are monitors, advisors, observers, consultants, supervisors, or evaluators has never been clear within the department (Corwin, 1982). It should be. Grantees need to know what they can expect from federal staff. There is also rampant criticism of the amount of assistance and monitoring that program officers provide. Most project directors complain of too few site visits, too little support and constructive criticism, and minimal communication between the department and a funded project (current travel restrictions in the department exacerbate the situation).

Broad Policy Recommendations

The continuing issue throughout this chapter has been the need for federal policy on research and demonstration in teacher education. If the federal operation in this arena could be removed one step from the mainstream of legislative decisions, the separation of responsibilities in such a system would see elected representatives setting broad policy and direction, and appointed and career government employees (and the education community at large) carrying out programs within that policy. For example, on the matter of publicly supported research and demonstration on teacher education as it relates to the education of 3- and 4-year-olds, the Congress and administration would set policy for a preschool program, and department staff would work with the various constituencies—state government, professional organizations and unions, higher education, welfare and health agencies—to implement policies, with the Congress and the administration maintaining oversight.

To undertake such an approach, the Congress and the administration should set policies that establish

1. A programmatic research-and-demonstration agenda sufficiently coherent and rigorous to warrant a commitment extending beyond a single administration.
2. A process by which priorities assigned by the federal government can be verified publicly as to their relevance, importance, and feasibility.
3. Procedures that narrow the social and professional distance between federal research projects and practicing teachers. This means insuring communication among teachers, teacher educators, and researchers.
4. A system that recognizes the relevant national organizations with interests and concerns in teacher education and provides the mechanisms for intercommunication, so that such organizations have both the pipeline to attract congressional attention and the responsibility of oversight to insure that federal programs are managed in the way Congress intends.
5. A process to guide the Education Department's management of research funds that insures the quality of research supported by those funds.

Detailed Recommendations

Following are particular suggestions and comments about federal funding for research and demonstration in teacher education that emerge from this chapter.

1. View Reform in Teacher Education as a Long-term Process. There are no quick solutions in teacher education. Improvements usually cannot happen fast. A 10-year period is realistic for the continuity and follow-through needed for fundamental reforms. Changes and improvements depend on and are related to developments in schools. Schools and colleges must develop responsiveness to each other. Being at cross-purposes creates conflict, and change becomes difficult, if not impossible. Transmitting ideas, finding new agreements, and changing operational patterns are not easy when so many people are involved and when habits and tradition are deeply rooted.

2. Create a Linkage Between Teacher Education and Practice in Schools. Keeping preparation and practice closely connected seems essential if preparation is to be more responsive to the real world and if practice is to be in constant touch with the latest and best developments in knowledge. Such a linkage should give teachers (practitioners) and knowledge producers (teacher educators and researchers) more productive roles in upgrading teaching practice and school programs.

3. Broaden the Concept of Teacher Education. Teacher education should be defined to include all the activities in which a teacher participates in learning to teach before and during practice. Teacher education, then, is a career-long endeavor. Initial preparation is only a first step. Learning to teach continues throughout a career; there are constant refinements that teachers achieve through study and work. The concept of a teaching profession that relates responsibility, competence, challenge, and rewards should be promoted. People who stay in teaching should always have new goals to which they can aspire, while experiencing satisfaction and renewal.

4. Promote an Interrelationship Among Research, Training, and Practice. Connecting research, preparation, and practice should provide a cycle of discovery, development of competence, and execution. This relationship can make research more consequential, bring the real problems in schools under scrutiny, and reduce the lag between discovery and practice.

5. Modify the Reward System in Colleges of Education. The typical university criteria for recognizing faculty achievement are not well suited to teacher education faculty. College of education faculty should be able to gain tenure, promotion, and other rewards by satisfying criteria that reflect quality performance in their field and with public schools. If the reward system is not altered, not much is apt to change in most programs that prepare teachers.

6. Support Various Models for Improvement. The size and diversity of the country and the necessity of responding to local and regional needs require a variety of models for teacher education. Uniformity in programs has been endorsed too long in federal funding. There is no one right way to prepare teachers, no one right way to organize and operate schools. An ideal school will not be discovered. Diversity is a democratic virtue and strength. It should be nourished.

7. Recognize that Context Influences Teaching and Curriculum. Each school, class, and student is different, some radically so. Differences should be honored. Teaching and curriculum should be fashioned to fit each context, responding to forces outside the school such as family, neighborhood, community, and socioeconomic and ethnic factors. A great variety of teachers are required to satisfy the diversity of contexts. Some of teacher education should be situation specific, and some should be general (addressing what every teacher needs to know and be able to do).

8. Involve a Critical Mass in Reform. Institution of basic changes in the structure, organization, and operation of schools should involve a large enough group of faculty in a school or college to make an impact on the social system of the institution.

9. Give Attention to Career Patterns in Teaching. A teaching career should have constant challenges and rewards. Growth in competence should be recognized, and continuous development should be encouraged and rewarded. Assignments should be arranged so that greater ability brings more responsibility, additional reward, and higher status.

10. Acknowledge the Complexity of Evaluation. Reforms in teacher education have many consequences—on the curriculum, the students, the school and college personnel, the teaching profession, the social system of schooling, and more. All should be considered when innovations and reform are planned, and they should be assessed again when changes are implemented. The multiple consequences of reform in teacher education must be evaluated if achievement is to be adequately documented.

11. Require Local In-kind Contributions. Little commitment to change has developed when innovation and reform have been funded completely from outside sources. An in-kind contribution increases local involvement and builds ownership. It pledges local responsibility to seeking success and institutionalization. As a project achieves success, its continuance should gradually become more and more a local obligation.

12. Improve Federal Monitoring. Education Department personnel should be well trained in the area of funding they oversee, and skillful and nonthreatening in working with local project directors and personnel. Training and coaching should be provided to federal personnel to insure high-level, effective, empathic performance. Periodic evaluation of federal monitoring should be instituted.

13. Provide Assurance of Continued Funding. There has been too much vacillation and shifting in federal funding in education. The time and commitment required for change and improvement in education have not been adequately understood by federal lawmakers. Institutions and agencies are more apt to pledge their efforts and people to new ventures if they are assured that the federal commitment is strong. Support for reforms should involve a commitment to continue funding for a sufficient time to make change and improvement possible.

14. Reduce Political Influence in Federal Funding. Federal programs will never be apolitical, but they need to be much less subject to political influences. Procedures to protect federal funding of educational research and demonstration should be explored to make the system more objective and less subject to political power plays.

15. Encourage Collaborative Projects Among Federal Departments. Most problems in society are influenced by family, employment, housing, and health. Projects designed to improve the human condition and to address all these aspects of life should get more attention. A broad-based and concerted attack promises more success than one directed at a single dimension of social reform. Such an approach needs the collaborative support of more than one federal agency. The departments of Education, Labor, Housing and Urban Development, and Health and Human Services, for example, should be required to collaborate on reform when complementary efforts are required to make substantial societal improvements.

References

Bailey, S. K., & Mosher, E. K. (1968). *ESEA: The Office of Education administers a law.* Syracuse, NY: Syracuse University Press.

Ballentine, J. H. (1983). *The sociology of education: A systematic analysis.* Englewood Cliffs, NJ: Prentice-Hall.

Benson, C. S., Medrich, E. H., & Buckley, S. (1980). A new view of school efficiency. In J. W. Guthrie (Ed.), *School finance policies and practices: The 1980's, a decade of conflict* (1st annual yearbook of the American Finance Association, pp. 169–204). Cambridge, MA: Ballinger.

Berman, P., & McLaughlin, M. W. (1974–80). *Federal programs supporting educational change* (8 vols., issued annually). Santa Monica, CA: RAND Corporation.

Cohn, M., & Distefano, A. (1984). The recommendations of the National Commission on Excellence in Education: A case study of their value. *Issues in Education, 2*(3), 204–220.

Coley, R. J., & Thorpe, M. E. (1985). *A look at the MAT model of teacher education and its graduates: Lessons for today* [Microfiche]. Princeton, NJ: Educational Testing Service.

Corwin, R. G. (1972a). Strategies for organizational innovation: An empirical comparison. *American Sociological Review, 37,* 441–454.

Corwin, R. G. (1972b). Strategies of organizational survival: The case of a national program for educational reform. *Journal of Applied and Behavioral Science, 8*(4), 451–480.

Corwin, R. G. (1982). The impact of federal program officers on federal–local relationships. In R. G. Corwin (Ed.), *Research in sociology of education and socialization: Vol. 3. Policy research in education* (pp. 151–183). Greenwich, CT: JAI Press.

Corwin, R. G. (1983). *The entrepreneurial bureaucracy: The biographies of two federal programs in education.* Greenwich, CT: JAI Press.

Corwin, R. G., & Louis, K. S. (1982). Organizational barriers to the utilization of research. *Administrative Science Quarterly, 27*(4), 623–640.

Corwin, R. G., & Nagi, S. Z. (1972). The case of educational research. In S. Z. Nagi & R. G. Corwin (Eds.), *The social context of research* (pp. 351–396). New York: John Wiley & Sons.

CPI Associates Inc. (1977). *The role and function of project officers in DHEW Region VI program agencies: Final report.* Unpublished report.

Dreeben, R., & Barr, R. (1983). Educational policy and the working of schools. In L. S. Shulman & G. Sykes (Eds.), *Handbook of teaching and policy* (pp. 81–94). New York; Longman.

Edelfelt, R. A., Corwin, R. G., & Hanna, B. (1974). *Lessons from the Teacher Corps.* Washington, DC: National Education Association.

Edelfelt, R. A., & Darland, D. D. (1972). The fickle frenzy of federal funding [editorial]. *Journal of Teacher Education, 23*(1), 3–4.

Firestone, W. A. (1979). Butte-Angels Camp. Conflict and transformation. In R. E. Herriott & N. Gross (Eds.), *The dynamics of planned educational change: Case studies and analyses* (pp. 150–184). Berkeley, CA: McCutchan.

Fullan, M., & Pomfret, A. (1975). *Review of research on curriculum implementation.* Toronto: Ontario Institute for Studies in Education.

Gideonse, H. D. (1979). Designing federal policies and programs to facilitate local change efforts. In R. E. Herriott & N. Gross (Eds.), *The dynamics of planned educational change: Case studies and analyses* (pp. 298–327). Berkeley, CA: McCutchan.

Gordon, E. W., & Wilkerson, D. A. (1966). *Compensatory education for the disadvantaged.* New York: College Entrance Examination Board.

Graham, H. D. (1984). *The uncertain triumph: Federal education policy in the Kennedy and Johnson years.* Chapel Hill, NC: University of North Carolina Press.

Gross, N. (1979). Basic issues in the management of educational change efforts. In R. E. Herriott & N. Gross (Eds.), *The dynamics of planned educational change: Case studies and analyses* (pp. 20–46). Berkeley, CA: McCutchan.

Herriott, R. E. (1979). The federal context: Planning, funding, and monitoring. In R. E. Herriott & N. Gross (Eds.), *The dynamics of planned educational change: Case studies and analyses* (pp. 49–73). Berkeley, CA: McCutchan.

Kirst, M. W. (1979). Strengthening federal–local relationships supporting educational change. In R. E. Herriott & N. Gross (Eds.), *The dynamics of planned educational change: Case studies and analyses* (pp. 274–297). Berkeley, CA: McCutchan.

Kirst, M. W. (1980). A review of legislated learning. *Administrative Science Quarterly, 25*(4), 705–708.

Kirst, M. W. (1983). Teaching policy and federal categorical programs. In L. S. Shulman & G. Sykes (Eds.), *Handbook of teaching and policy* (pp. 426–448). New York,: Longman.

Kirst, M. W., & Jung, R. (1980). The utility of a longitudinal approach in assessing implementation: A thirteen year view of Title I, ESEA. *Educational Evaluation and Policy Analysis, 3*(5), 17–34.

Louis, K. S., & Dentler, R. A. (1988). Knowledge use and school improvement. *Curriculum Inquiry, 18*(1), 33–62.

McLaughlin, D. H. (1977). *Title I, 1965–1975: A synthesis of the findings of federal studies.* Palo Alto, CA: American Institutes for Research.

McLaughlin, M. W. (1975). *Evaluation and reform: The Elementary and Secondary Education Act of 1965, Title I.* Cambridge, MA: Ballinger.

Meyer, J. W. (1981). *Organizational factors affecting legalization in education.* Stanford, CA: Stanford Institute for Research on Educational Finance and Governance, School of Education.

Millsap, M. A: (1983). Federal regulations writing. An invisible arena of policymaking. *Educational Evaluation and Policy Analysis, 5*(1), 5–12.

Murphy, J. T. (1971). Title I of ESEA: The politics of implementing federal education reform. *Harvard Educational Review, 41*(1), 35–63.

National Commission on Excellence in Education. (1983). *A nation at risk: The imperative for educational reform.* Washington, DC: U.S. Government Printing Office.

Parelius, R. J., & Parelius, A. P. (1987). *The sociology of education.* Englewood Cliffs, NJ: Prentice-Hall.

Popp, H. M. (1975). Current practices in the teaching of beginning reading. In J. B. Carroll & J. S. Chall (Eds.), *Toward a literate society* (pp. 101–146). New York: McGraw-Hill.

Pressman, J. L. (1975). *Federal programs and city politics.* Berkeley, CA: University of California Press.

Provus, M. M. (1975). *The grand experiment. The life and death of the TTT program as seen through the eyes of its evaluators.* Berkeley, CA: McCutchan.

Sieber, S. (1982). Scholarship and contract evaluation research—A problem of integration. In R. G. Corwin (Ed.), *Research in sociology of education and socialization: Vol. 3. Policy research in education* (pp. 45–62). Greenwich, CT: JAI Press.

Sizer, T. R. (1974). On myopia: A complaint from down below. *Daedalus, 103*(4), 332–340.

Stake, R., & Easley, J., Jr. (1978). *Case studies in science education* (2 vols.). Washington, DC: National Science Foundation.

Stonehill, R. M., & Groves, C. L. (1983). U.S. Department of Education policies and ESEA Title I evaluation utility: Changes in attitudes, changes in platitudes. *Educational Evaluation and Policy Analysis, 5,* 65–73.

Thomas, T. C., & Pelarin, S. H. (1976). *Patterns of ESEA Title I reading achievement.* Menlo Park, CA: Stanford Research Institute.

Timpane, M. P. (1977). *Federal education programs and their effect on teacher education.* Santa Monica, CA: RAND Corporation.

Timpane, M. P. (1979). *The federal interest in financing education.* Cambridge, MA: Ballinger.

Tyack, D., Kirst, M. W., & Hansot, E. (1980). Educational reform: Retrospect and prospect. *Teachers College Record, 81*(3), 253–269.

Vobejda, B. (1988, October 20). Education Department grant process assailed. *Washington Post,* p. 20.

Weiss, I. (1978). *Report of the 1977 national survey of science, mathematics, and social studies education.* Research Triangle Park, NC: Research Triangle Institute.

Williams, W. (1976). Implementation analysis and assessment. In W. Williams & R. Elmore (Eds.), *Social program implementation* (pp. 267–292). New York: Academic Press.

Wise, A. (1979). *Legislated learning: The bureaucratization of the American classroom.* Berkeley, CA: University of California Press.

CONTEXTS AND MODELS OF TEACHER EDUCATION

·12·

THE CONTEXT OF TEACHER EDUCATION

Dean C. Corrigan

TEXAS A&M UNIVERSITY

Martin Haberman

UNIVERSITY OF WISCONSIN–MILWAUKEE

System analysis provides a process and a conceptual framework for examining the interactions among separate elements in order to understand their operation within a larger, more complex system. The purpose of this chapter is to clarify the context within which the system of teacher education functions. This will be accomplished by analyzing the research and conceptual foundations of teacher education in terms of the critical elements of a profession. This framework for conceptualizing the context of professional teacher education will then be analyzed with respect to its interactions with other systems of influence.

THE CHARACTERISTICS OF A PROFESSION

Four critical elements of a profession serve as the framework for this analysis: *knowledge base, quality controls, resources,* and *conditions of practice.* They are common elements derived from a wide range of basic studies regarding the nature of all professions (Argyris & Schön, 1974; Etzioni, 1969; Schein, 1972). In addition, these elements have played a central role in debates about teacher *education as a* profession (Howsam, Corrigan, & Denemark, 1985; Lortie, 1975). It is reasonable to anticipate they will continue to be used as significant criteria for defining a profession in future.

Knowledge Base

A profession has a clearly defined body of knowledge and skills that is held in common by practitioners in the field and not generally possessed by the lay public. This body of knowledge is undergirded by theory, research, and a set of professional values and ethics.

Quality Controls

All professions require a system of quality controls. Evaluation processes and instruments are designed to insure that professional candidates possess both the essential knowledge and the required skills for them to be safely placed with clients upon licensing. Some evaluation procedures and policies are related to insuring program quality; others are directed at the means for insuring quality among individual practitioners before and after entry into the profession.

Resources

Adequate resources are necessary for practitioners to perform in a professional manner. Salaries, equipment, and facilities are some of the more obvious examples of critical resources, but other aspects of this dimension that are often overlooked can play an even more important role in actualizing a given profession. In teacher education, time and access to faculty throughout the university and to teachers in appropriate school settings and field sites used for professional laboratory experiences are important attributes. The authority to require courses in university programs of teacher preparation is also a major resource. General university requirements inevitably compete with college of education requirements for a

The authors acknowledge the assistance of their reviewers Dale L. Brubaker (University of North Carolina), Edward Ducharme (University of Vermont), Richard Wisniewski (University of Tennessee, Knoxville), and Leonard Lindstrom for assistance with references and figures.

place in students' programs. The portion of the professional curriculum for which the education faculty is responsible is here referred to as *life space*. It is a critically important resource that refers to the power of a particular professional college to determine how much of the total university curriculum it can control in order to prepare a competent, beginning practitioner.

Conditions of Practice

The conditions of professional practice refer to those elements that must exist in the work setting for a professional to be effective. An occupation does not become a profession by announcing it is, or even by preparing people to function at a high level of competence. A professional must have the autonomy, authority, and resources to act on his or her knowledge in the actual work setting. It is essential that conditions of practice exist that are favorable to, or which at least do not impede, the delivery of professional-level services by the practitioner to the client group and community. With respect to teacher education, these conditions refer to training practices in the

field (student teaching, internship, and the first years of teaching) whereby preservice professionals are inducted into teaching under the guidance of able practitioners demonstrating effective instructional techniques in successful schools.

SPHERES OF INFLUENCE ON TEACHER EDUCATION

Figure 12-1 identifies the enteracting spheres of influence within which the system of professional teacher education must function:

1. The societal sphere (national)
2. The state sphere
3. The university sphere
4. The college of education sphere
5. The school sphere

Figure 12-2 presents the conceptual schema around which this chapter is organized. In reality, all the spheres in Figure

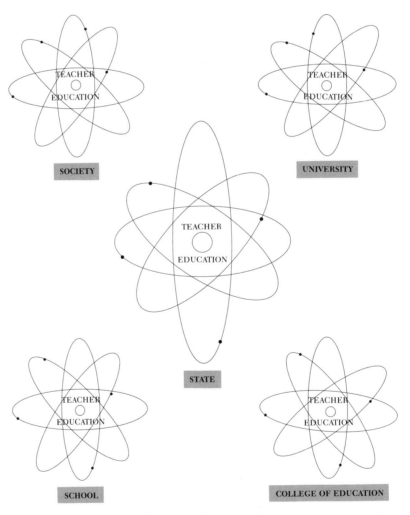

FIGURE 12–1. Spheres of Influence on Teacher Education.

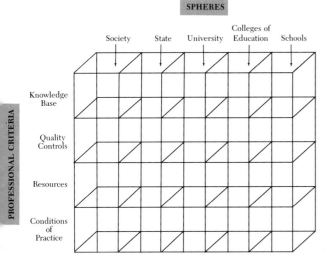

FIGURE 12–2. The Context of Teacher Education: Interaction and Emergence.

12-1 interact as one highly complex system. In combination with the characteristics of a profession, the interactions among the spheres of influence form a dynamic, constantly changing suprasystem defined here as the total context in which teacher education operates. Out of this interaction the educational system and teaching profession of the future emerge.

THE KNOWLEDGE BASE DIMENSION

The Society as a Sphere of Influence on the Knowledge Base

During the 1980s the national reform literature influenced the knowledge base in teacher education across a wide range of issues. Demographic studies, for instance, were frequently used to demonstrate the changing nature of our society in terms of age, ethnicity, race, migration patterns, occupations, income, and education (Hodgkinson, 1987; U.S. Congress, 1977; Weaver, 1981). Numerous surveys summarized the public's great concern with drugs and school discipline (Gallup & Clark, 1987). An entire genre of studies created a catchall category called *at risk* that included dropouts, low achievers, drug users, teenage parents, low-income and most minority students (Levin, 1985; McDill, Natriello, & Pallas, 1985; Natriello, 1986). Studies dealing with desegregation in urban schools were used to supplement this literature (Commission on the Cities, 1988). The changing status of the American family, including the fact that the United States leads the world in teenage pregnancies, was cited frequently (Howe, 1986). Unfavorable comparisons of American students with those in other industrialized nations were also widely cited (Livingstone, 1986; McKnight et al., 1987).

A Nation at Risk and subsequent reports cataloged the decline of the American work force vis à vis other industrialized nations (National Commission on Excellence in Education, 1983). Workers' educational levels, their capability for training and retraining, and their productivity were the focus of numerous studies and reports (Kearns & Doyle, 1988). The shift of the United States into a debtor nation and the negative projections for the Social Security System in the twenty-first century were other recurring themes in the reform literature (Buccino, 1988). Essentially, the reform literature connected societal problems with the failures of elementary and secondary schools. The reform literature's primary impact was to influence the general public to reorder its traditionally broad priorities for public education in such a manner that basic skills clearly emerged as the primary goal of schooling (National Governors' Association, 1986). In former times, the preparation of citizens, the enhancement of individual abilities and talents, the education of professionals needed by society, the intellectual attainment in academic subjects, or even other purposes such as moral development were serious contenders for high priority status (Dewey, 1915; Whitehead, 1929). By the end of the 1980s, however, there was little basis for challenging the popular belief that the teaching of basic skills was the paramount purpose of public schools. Indeed, basic skills were generally assumed to be prerequisite to the achievement of all other goals. The reform literature focused on competing economically with the Japanese, solving welfare issues, providing workers to support the social security system, preparing graduates for the 25 million jobs projected for the year 2000, and resolving the issues of drugs, crime, illiteracy, and teenage pregnancy. A direct line of logic was employed to connect almost every social ill with a need for jobs that, in turn, require minimum basic skills. Job skills have become widely understood and accepted as a knowledge of the three Rs, supported by the attributes of punctuality, ability to cooperate with others, and willingness to follow the rules and directions of a given workplace (Committee for Economic Development, 1985).

The effect of this reform literature on teacher education has been to narrow the broad knowledge base formerly required of teachers to emphasize their preparation with know-how in teaching extremely narrowly defined basic skills. All teacher education programs require at least one course in the teaching of reading for elementary teachers and at least some study in the reading of a particular content area for secondary teachers. Some states mandate as many as 12 credits in reading and language arts courses for elementary teachers. At the same time, few states mandate separate methods courses in science and social studies for elementary teachers. This trend reinforces the perceptions of many who select elementary teaching as a career that the three Rs and good work habits are the primary goals of schooling.

If schools can help solve societal problems by teaching the basics to future jobholders, then teacher education must train teachers who are effective skills trainers. This specific and direct connection between the national reform literature and the curricula of teacher education has been complemented by the connection between the colleges of education and the knowledge base. A small minority of faculty in colleges of education have generated the research in direct instruction that was essentially derived from studies dealing with the achievement of basic skills among disadvantaged, urban, elementary pupils (House, Glass, McClean, & Walker, 1978). This literature now comprises a substantial portion of what is referred to as the knowledge base in teacher education. In this example, then, the national sphere of influence and the college of education sphere of influence have combined to emphasize the need for basic skills and the benefits of direct instruction; this axis exerts a strong influence on the context in which teacher education operates.

In a similar but less dramatic way, it is possible to trace societal concerns with shifts in the knowledge base of future and practicing teachers. For example, societal concerns regarding racism, sexism, and ethnic discrimination have led to the incorporation of multicultural components in most teacher education programs. Also, the economic benefits of cooperative activity in the workplace undergird the increasing emphasis on cooperative learning as a teaching strategy in teacher education programs (Johnson & Johnson, 1985; Slavin, 1987). Similarly, societal concerns with law and order vis à vis child abuse, drugs, crime, and absenteeism help to maintain the continuing emphasis on discipline, classroom management, and even school law in the curricula of teacher education (Karnes, Black, & Downs 1983). The influence of such issues on the knowledge base is apparent in the research and demonstration projects funded by both public and private sources. By identifying and defining the problems deemed most critical, it becomes inevitable that research-and-demonstration support are directed at those issues.

The national literature has also effected public awareness and support for teachers and teacher education. Numerous studies have described future teachers as among the lowest achieving students on various tests (Nelli, 1984; Weaver, 1983). Other studies examined whether or not education courses make a difference (Nelli, 1981). Numerous follow-up studies of first-year teachers' perceptions strongly support the contention that their training is unrelated to practical demands (Veenman, 1984).

By providing various forms of data, as well as interpretations, this national literature supports the view that American society is under grave economic and social threat, if not already disintegrating, and that a major cause of the deterioration is directly attributable to inferior schooling, less able students who become teachers, and irrelevant teacher education. There can be little doubt that the national reform literature, by constantly defining and reiterating the constituencies deemed to be "at risk," the treatments they need, and the bases for evaluating effective school learning, has influenced the knowledge base of teaching. Because national reports frequently derive goals from particular forms of problem definition (e.g., at-risk students) and then identify specific treatments (e.g., public schools of choice), this literature is used as a rationale for requiring specific policies or components in teacher education programs. Many of these policies have actually been counterproductive for the target groups they have been proposed to serve (Bing & Wheelock, 1986; Brown, 1986; Pellicano, 1987).

The State as a Sphere of Influence on the Knowledge Base

Examination of the state as a sphere of influence on the knowledge base overlaps that of the national level. Indeed, the case might well be made that the national reform literature, by affecting the state sphere of influence, which, in turn, mandates specific controls over teacher education programs, has had a greater impact on teacher education than any research or evaluation generated from within the profession itself (National Governors' Association, 1986). Essentially the state's role is to define the minimum standards of what teachers need to learn in their accredited university programs and what they need to demonstrate on state tests of licensure. In the process of overseeing what might appear to the naive as bureaucratic trivia, the state actually identifies the essence of future teachers' required knowledge. The state can mandate admission requirements to teacher education programs, as well as the particular course content to be included in these programs. In addition, the content that the state chooses to test as exit or license criteria also exerts strong control over the actual content of teacher education programs. For example, as the state requires competence in direct instruction or experiences in multicultural settings as necessary teacher knowledge, it has, in effect, exerted strong and direct curriculum influence on university programs of teacher education. Even more, the state has identified selected aspects of the knowledge base as the minimum essentials for beginning teachers.

Every state has enacted laws requiring universities to make specific additions to their teacher education programs. For instance, strongly supported by the national sphere, it has been the state level of influence that has institutionalized the mainstreaming of handicapped children as a necessary area of teacher knowledge (Grosenick & Reynolds, 1978). Similar state mandates frequently deal with school discipline, at-risk students, bilingual education, and the educational applications of computers (Pipho, 1986).

These are not benign regulations. In most cases state laws or administrative codes define the nature of a particular societal problem, including who is to be served and what treatment is to be applied. They then mandate what teachers specifically need to be taught to ameliorate the situation. Because there is little room in teacher education programs for adding requirements, state minimums inevitably become transformed into maximums.

The University as a Sphere of Influence on the Knowledge Base

The influence of the total university on the knowledge base of teachers highlights the ongoing controversy among university requirements in a specific teaching field, in liberal studies, and in pedagogy. Knowledge of the specific discipline in which the teacher is prepared to teach competes for time and other resources with the general-education and professional-education components of teacher preparation (King, 1987). Underlying this controversy are different views regarding what knowledge is of most worth to the educated citizen in general and to the future teacher in particular.

There are several areas within the social sciences and humanities disciplines that are acknowledged as contributing to the knowledge base of teachers (Bigelow, 1971; Denton, 1987). For example, there can be no debate that the overwhelming thrust of pedagogic studies derives from psychological constructs: concepts such as motivation, transfer, reward, readiness, and achievement and ability testing are now generally accepted in the field of education. More recently, concepts from emerging fields such as linguistics, systems theory, computer science, and metacognition have been added, but these are minimal additions that do not challenge the hegemony of the constructs from educational psychology. And although there is continuing debate on the role and extent of philosophy, sociology, anthropology, history, and ethics in the knowledge base of teachers, such cultural foundations have been de-emphasized for some time (Smith & Street, 1980).

The College of Education as a Sphere of Influence on the Knowledge Base

A large portion of the knowledge base in teacher education has emanated primarily from faculty in schools and colleges of education. Examples of this literature are the studies dealing with effective schools (Block, 1983; Edmonds, 1982; Robinson, 1985; Squires, 1983) and direct instruction (Walberg & Waxman, 1983). Some argue that the nature of these research findings is such that they cannot be directly translated into applications of what future teachers need to know and do (Doyle, 1981). More recently, schools and colleges of education have begun to emphasize biography, case studies, exemplars, and ethnography as ways to build the knowledge base for future teachers (Feiman-Nemser, 1983). Added to this mélange are the continuing advocacies of those who would prepare the teacher as a moral guide, a self-actualized personality, or a socializing agent of society (Cruickshank & Callahan, 1983; Henjum, 1983; Ryan, 1986). These additions to the knowledge base are sometimes derived empirically on the basis of what teachers actually do in practice (Arlin, 1984; Evertson, Hawley, & Zlotnik, 1984; Good & Grouws, 1977). More frequently, these contents represent ideologies and advocacies of the roles future teachers should perform and, therefore, how they should be prepared (American Association of Colleges for Teacher Education, 1983; National Commission on Excellence in Teacher Education, 1985).

The Schools as a Sphere of Influence on the Knowledge Base

The final sphere of influence on the knowledge base comes from the practitioners themselves: their teaching behaviors, perceived problems, and analyses of their daily activities (Cruickshank, 1985). This literature includes the problems encountered by beginning teachers, teachers under stress, teach-

ers with burnout, and teachers in physical danger (Alschuler, 1980, Dworkin, 1987; Kyriacou, 1987). The research on teacher efficacy and the impact of the school bureaucracy on teachers' feelings of efficiency are critical dimensions of this literature (Dembo & Gibson, 1985). Another important aspect is the continuing dialogue among teachers through informal problem solving and action research (Biott, 1983; Ross, 1984). The problems discussed in this literature have evolved into what has become known as the craft knowledge of the practitioner (Eble, 1988; Tom, 1984).

Craft knowledge is generally regarded by classroom teachers as the most relevant aspect of the knowledge base of their practice. These perceptions are supported by innumerable follow-up studies in which teachers cite student teaching and internship as the most useful part of teacher preparation (Roth, 1983). Researchers, however, find that practice teaching in the preparation of teachers could well be overrated, because the most extensive study yet conducted indicates that little change occurs in student teachers' performance as a result of their direct experiences (Griffin et al., 1983).

Summary of the Knowledge Base Dimension

Several generalizations follow directly from an examination of the combined impact of the five spheres of influence on the knowledge base in teacher education: (a) there are several knowledge bases being emphasized by different spheres of influence; (b) some of the influences being exerted by different spheres complement each other, whereas others appear to be working in opposition; (c) the diversity of these spheres makes their impact on teacher education more complex than representatives from any one sphere seem willing to recognize or able to comprehend.

By the end of the 1980s, the knowledge base in teacher education emphasized the content and processes needed for preparing teachers to teach job-related and basic skills. At the same time, the university sphere of influence did not support this drive to prepare teachers as skills trainers and markedly broadened the academic disciplines that it regarded as fundamental for all educated citizens, including teachers. At the university level, the social sciences in general, as well as several new and emerging areas of inquiry, sought to demonstrate the relevance of their basic concepts to the work of the teacher, although psychology retained its dominance as the parent discipline.

Space in the teacher education program continued to be keenly competed for by disciplines within the university and the college of education. Although the total credit hours in teacher preparation programs have generally remained stable, there has been a shift of credits within the professional sequence from foundations to field experiences (Smith & Street, 1980). Educational foundation studies were broadened to include moral development, organizational science, and metacognition, as well as the traditional studies of history, philosophy, sociology, and psychology, but did not increase in share of the teacher education curriculum. All of these studies competed with the research base on effective schools and direct instruction for space in the preservice program. Finally, the pressure from teachers and schools for preparation programs to depict more accurately and to analyze the work of the classroom teacher intensified (Feiman-Nemser, 1983). Ethnography, case studies, and biography transformed narrow perceptions of teaching as a series of skills that are learned on the job through imitation to a legitimate body of research and theory involving reflection and analysis as a guide to practice. The difficulty of defining and offering a cohesive professional teacher education program in which the advocacies of all of the spheres of influence are reconciled is quite apparent.

THE QUALITY CONTROLS DIMENSION

The Society as a Sphere of Influence on Quality Controls

Recent studies of school improvement have included recommendations to restructure schools, in order to provide more professional environments; to require new forms of bachelor's and master's degrees for beginning teachers; to markedly upgrade teacher salaries; to prepare more minorities to become teachers; and to make teachers more accountable for pupil learning. At the same time, there is an active effort to create a national certification board to establish higher standards regarding what genuinely professional teachers need to know and be able to do (Carnegie Forum on Education and the Economy, 1986).

Concomitant efforts are directed at upgrading the quality of programs offered future teachers in colleges of education. The National Council for the Accreditation of Teacher Education periodically revises its standards of program approval and serves as the professional counterpart of national accrediting bodies in other professions (Gollnick & Kunkel, 1986). The motivation undergirding these efforts has, in part, derived from the assumption that teacher education is at a crisis point and, to a marked degree, is responsible for the inadequate quality of schools nationwide.

In addition to the national reports, the creation of a system of national board certification for teachers, and the NCATE accreditation procedures, there are several other societal influences on quality control in teacher education. *First* are the studies cited earlier that support the contention that teacher education students are not as competent as other students. *Second* are the studies that show a national need for urban teachers and for teachers in selected specialties such as mathematics, science, and bilingual and special education (Darling-Hammond, 1984). *Third* are studies that have been critical of teacher-preparation programs for over a century (Conant, 1963; Damerell, 1985; Koerner, 1963). *Fourth* are studies of why able students choose other professions upon graduation and why practicing teachers quit (Haggstrom, Darling-Hammond, & Grissmer, 1988). *Fifth* are studies of teachers practicing without a license, with emergency certificates, and prepared through alternative certification programs (Adelman, 1986; California Commission on the Teaching Profession,

1985). In addition, the accreditation of teacher education institutions is a voluntary process allowing over 1,340 colleges and universities to continue to prepare teachers whether or not they are nationally accredited. The national association that enrolls most of the institutions that prepare most of the nation's teachers, the American Association of Colleges for Teacher Education, does not require accreditation by the National Council for the Accreditation of Teacher Education (NCATE) as a condition of membership. These conditions create a national climate in which teacher education is viewed as a low-status field of substandard institutional programs with little or no quality control when compared with other professions.

The State as a Sphere of Influence on Quality Controls

The influence of the state over teacher education in terms of quality control is clear and direct. *First* is the state's power to accredit teacher education programs. Through this process the state establishes specific criteria for program standards, which the universities must meet. *Second*, the state establishes specific licensure requirements for individuals to be certified, including mandated tests. *Third*, almost all states require individuals to pass tests of basic skills before they can even be admitted to university teacher education programs (American Association of Colleges for Teacher Education [AACTE], 1986). It is important to note that no state confines itself only to professional requirements. They all have mandates related to what studies future teachers must complete in general–liberal education and in academic teaching fields. At the same time, states institutionalize their perceptions of quality through the tests and coursework they require of future teachers. All states have legislation or regulations that permit exceptions to licensing requirements on an emergency or out-of-license basis. Although these exceptions have traditionally been aimed at helping remote rural districts and large urban schools cover staffing needs in the absence of fully certified teachers, they have, in effect, undermined the states' own mandated university requirements. In many states, emergency teachers can be hired at 80 percent (or less) of the salary paid beginning certified teachers. Shortages of teachers are dealt with at the school level through loopholes that exist in law and practice by hiring people who are not licensed in a particular subject matter, grade, or specialization.

Some states are beginning to address the question of teacher competency by passing legislation requiring that parents of children who are taught by unlicensed individuals must be notified. At the same time, to circumvent the requirements of regular university teacher education programs, several states have directly enacted laws or administrative codes to facilitate alternative certification programs, especially in high-need fields such as science, mathematics, special education, and bilingual education (AACTE, 1986). Some universities have developed alternative certification programs on their own, while other alternatives have been offered by the school districts themselves, especially in large urban centers where shortages are most severe. In the typical alternative-certification program, liberal arts graduates are hired and trained on the job after they have been employed as teachers. Every state maintains a degree of latitude for its major urban areas to employ some form of emergency teacher, whether an alternative-certification program exists or not. Typically, in remote rural and urban areas, the poorer the school clientele, the more likely the teachers are less than adequately prepared and less than fully certified.

Emergency certified teachers mainly differ from those in alternative programs by virtue of not having a mentor or supervisor and not being required to work toward some form of university-based, academically designed certification plan. In effect, many states operate two distinct and conflicting worlds of teacher education. The first is comprised of an ever-increasing set of state requirements placed on universities and colleges of education that seek to maintain their approved programs. In this world quality and excellence are the watchwords. The second world is a system in which expediency and exceptions facilitate urban schools' meeting their continuous need for new teachers and poor rural schools' meeting their ordinary staffing patterns. Except in the very few states that have professional licensing boards, teachers have no control over the employment or licensure of beginning teachers (AACTE, 1987). The inconsistencies in the state's influence over teacher education is manifested by the haphazard nature of reciprocity among the states with regard to teacher certification. Although it is common for an experienced teacher who is fully licensed in one state to be able to begin teaching in another state, it is also common for such a teacher to be required to complete additional university coursework and even a written examination to become fully certified in the new state.

There is no question that, as a sphere of influence, state requirements exert the greatest degree of control over the nature and quality of teacher education. Teacher education, like the public schools, is primarily a state function.

The University as a Sphere of Influence on Quality Controls

The university exerts its influence on quality in at least four ways. *First,* the university controls the admission criteria of all entering students. *Second,* the university sets the general education requirements. *Third,* the university defines what constitutes an area of specialization (major). *Fourth,* the university establishes the requirements for graduation that will directly affect all students including those in teacher education. The university directly controls and teaches approximately two-thirds of the elementary teacher's and four-fifths of the secondary teacher's curriculum. The university also sets the criteria for hiring, rewarding, and promoting faculty and deans in colleges of education. All of these contextual elements essentially reflect the university culture and are unrelated to the needs of elementary and secondary schools.

The College of Education as a Sphere of Influence on Quality Controls

Schools, colleges, or departments of education overlay an additional set of their own entrance requirements and exit criteria on top of those established by the university (Rudner et al., 1987). These criteria can relate to proficiencies (e.g., communications skills and mathematics proficiency), grade point average, specific course requirements, personal interviews, or additional proficiency examinations of various kinds. College of education requirements are almost always stated in the form of other traditional university requirements (i.e., course requirements, grade point average, and examination scores), rather than as proficiencies or functions that must be performed by practicing teachers.

The Schools as a Sphere of Influence on Quality Controls

University education majors select their teaching specialties, whereas elementary and secondary schools typically have needs for teachers that do not match self-selection patterns of university students. The continuing critical needs in lower schools for teachers of special education, of bilingual education, of science, of mathematics of early childhood, and of middle schools evidence the marked degree of this mismatch. Nowhere is this difference more pronounced than in comparing the need for urban teachers with the predominance of middle-class young women attending universities with the goal of preparing to teach in suburban and small-town schools. Nevertheless, the need for particular types of teachers in elementary or secondary schools does exert a modest degree of influence over programs offered in colleges of education. Early childhood, for example, is an area in which the need for teachers has, with a lag of 20 years, influenced *some* universities to hire a *few* more faculty, in an effort to produce more early-childhood teachers. The critical point, however, is the fact that the primary university client is the college student. The needs of the elementary and secondary schools for teachers with particular specializations has very little effect on the choices made by college youth. Furthermore, universities define demand in terms of student preferences rather than school needs.

Summary of the Quality Controls Dimension

The pressures that emanate from national and societal spheres for upgrading the quality of teachers and teacher education programs are sometimes supported by states. At other times, states, in response to local districts, facilitate the circumvention of their own stated standards. Recently states have become more restrictive of university programs and simultaneously less restrictive regarding alternative-certification programs offered by school districts, thus accentuating the two distinct patterns of teacher education.

The university sphere continues to be characterized by influences derived from the traditional disciplines comprising the liberal arts. More academic course requirements are automatically equated with higher quality, with little reference to any thoughtful argument or evidence that the problems of teachers and lower schools can be ameliorated by such additions. The unreflected-upon assumption is that, if children do not meet achievement expectations, it is because their teachers do not know enough subject matter. The subject-matter knowledge their teachers are assumed to need is more–liberal studies and less pedagogy (Southern Regional Education Board, 1986).

Colleges of education are caught between the demands of practitioners in the schools, the requirements of the university, the mandates of the state, and the special interests of the education faculty. The national reports tend to define educational quality in terms of the economy's ability to compete with other industrialized nations. The state views teacher competence as synonymous with scores on its licensure examinations. The university typically views quality in terms of the student's grade point average in liberal arts courses. The college of education regards quality as the completion of its certification requirements. The lower schools view quality as teachers' on-the-job performance. There are no societal or institutional mechanisms for reconciling these different criteria of quality.

THE RESOURCE DIMENSION

The Society as a Sphere of Influence on Resources

Less money is spent on educating a typical prospective teacher in a public university than is spent on educating a child for one year in an elementary or secondary school. Comparative studies have consistently shown that teacher education is underfunded, when compared with other units of the university (Ornstein, 1984; Peseau, 1982; Peseau & Orr, 1980).

Federal funding of teacher education has been characterized by shifting levels of financial support and shifting priorities. In 1958 the National Defense Education Act provided funds for training teachers of science, mathematics, and foreign language. The National Teacher Corps of 1965 and other teacher education programs formerly supported by the Bureau of Educational Personnel Development are no longer in existence. In the 1970s, the Triple-T Project aimed at the training of teacher trainers, while teacher centers were established for classroom teachers to help each other improve their skills. These approaches have been replaced by block grants to the states. In the 1980s, special education was the major funded program for university teacher education at the national level. The National Science Foundation increased its funding for science and mathematics teachers to upgrade their knowledge, but in subject-matter disciplines, not pedagogy (Carnegie Foundation for Advancement of Teaching, 1987).

Private foundation grants for teacher education continue to be awarded for national projects, but at decreased levels. In former times, the Ford Foundation supported the Master of Arts in Teaching programs to prepare individuals with baccalaureate degrees to teach. In the 1980s, the Carnegie Foundation and other major foundations specifically targeted support for the creation of a national licensing and examination board, research and development to reform teacher education in selected disciplines, and initiatives to reexamine the arts and science portion of teacher education. Some federal funding continues to be provided for one or two research laboratories or for the study of teaching and teacher education. There is also funding for a few technical assistance centers and ERIC clearinghouses.

The Holmes Group, a consortium of 96 research-oriented universities, was organized in 1986 to work on several goals: (a) the improvement of the intellectual preparation of teachers in the arts and sciences and in education; (b) more flexible approaches to improving the quality of teacher education assessment and evaluation; (c) more effective collaboration among colleges of education, arts and sciences, and public schools; and (d) improvement of the conditions in schools in which teachers work, practice, and learn. Funding for the group comes from a $4,000 per institution dues structure, as well as from the Ford Foundation (Holmes Group, 1986).

Some major areas of potential new funds for teacher education are tied to the recruitment and retention of minority teachers. Other targeted programs relate to child care and preschool education, in an effort called *even start*. A proposal that recurs regularly is the human services plan for some form of urban teacher corps. Leading educators frequently advocate utilizing the talents of arts and sciences graduates, people from other careers, or ex-military personnel in a new form of National Teacher Corps. Advocates of these types of services propose that such teachers be paid through an arrangement similar to the GI Bill. *Star schools*, a proposal to bring outstanding teachers and experts, particularly in the fields of mathematics and science, to rural schools through interactive satellite television, is an example of another federal program indirectly related to teacher education.

Since 1962, national leaders within the profession have called for extended teacher education programs with little success (Denemark, 1962; Denemark & Nutter, 1980; Howsam, Blackburn, Burnham, Scannell, & Gant, 1981). Is a 5-year, sequentially integrated model or a fifth-year model with completion of a baccalaureate program as a prerequisite the best approach? In large part, the answer to this question is arrived at operationally, as competing university constituencies seek to control their graduation requirements, and not empirically in terms of which programs produce the most effective teachers. Every major national report on the reform of education (Carnegie Forum on Education and the Economy, 1986; Holmes Group, 1986) recommends 5-year of fifth-year teacher education programs, yet most teachers are still prepared in 4-year programs.

One of the arguments made by advocates of 5-year programs is that all teachers ought to be as well educated as other college graduates. In former times, teachers were among the best educated citizens in their communities. This is no longer true; yet the public has come to expect such a standard. All the major national reports recommend that teachers ought to have completed a baccalaureate degree with an academic major and be professionally educated in addition to such specialization.

Whether the public will provide support for the teacher education programs to produce and maintain the cadre of professionally committed, well-educated, career teachers they are demanding remains to be seen. Several states, such as Florida and California, have mandated 5 years of preparation for beginning teachers. Other states, such as Oklahoma, require a year of successful practice in an induction program before certification. Beyond these states, however, very few 5-year programs have become the established pattern. Reports cited earlier provide examples of model 5-year programs in operation and explain why colleges of education have lagged behind calls of professional groups such as the American Federation of Teachers to move to extended programs. Since 1967, the National Education Association has also called for 5-year programs with built-in internships (National Education Association, 1984).

The State as a Sphere of Influence on Resources

State funding for teacher education is usually part of an overall formula whereby the states provide various levels of support to universities for students engaged in particular fields of study. In some states, the decisions regarding particular levels of support are reached internally within the university after the state has set the total budget. In almost all state formulas, however, a student credit hour in engineering, for example, typically receives more funding than a credit hour in education or even liberal arts. In most formulas, student credit hours are also weighted in relation to whether they are undergraduate, master's, or doctoral study. Special considerations are also given to the method of instruction. Laboratory work or supervised field experiences might receive additional funding in the formula. Typically, teacher education credit hours are funded at lower levels than any other professional program in the university, with medical education usually receiving the highest allocations (Peseau & Orr, 1980).

In many states, two different agencies are involved in funding and setting requirements for teacher education. Higher education agencies or boards of higher education oversee the total public university system and set the funding formulas, whereas the state education agencies or boards usually set the standards for lower schools and approve standards, program policies, and procedures for evaluating teacher education programs. At times, the two agencies disagree on policies related to teacher education.

Beyond the basic formula funding, publicly supported institutions that prepare teachers can usually submit proposals for funding certain teacher education improvement projects. The amount of state funding for research-and-development projects in teacher education is minimal, compared with state funding available to other professions such as agriculture or engineering. Because research and development in teacher education falls within the province of two state agencies (higher education and public education), neither considers it its primary responsibility, resulting in little commitment from either.

Funding mechanisms such as experiment and extension agencies in agriculture and engineering simply do not exist in elementary, secondary, or teacher education. The concept of a system of teacher centers or regional research-and-development units similar to the agricultural and engineering extension model has yet to be developed in teacher education. Inservice education is typically funded by school districts or service centers run by state education departments rather than by coordinating boards of higher education departments. Because university budgets for teacher education are most directly influenced by the number of student credit hours generated, very few resources or mechanisms are available for assigning university personnel to inservice or staff-development functions in schools. In return, schools are reluctant to advocate an increase in teacher education resources.

The teaching profession is limited primarily to internal constituencies advocating for their own resources; universities advocate for preservice funds and public schools for inservice funds. Teacher groups lobby for state education funds, and universities lobby higher education agencies. This gives such advocacy a self-serving quality. The college of education is caught between advocating for the public schools it serves and for the university from whom it derives its budget. Should a college of education seek to enhance its own budget by advocating the improvement of the university and, thereby, secure these resources at the expense of the public schools; or, should the college of education argue against funds for the university, in an effort to secure more resources for public schools? Colleges of education in this highly competitive, fixed-sum context typically choose to operate as part of the university constituency and not as allies of the public schools. This is a high-stakes competition, because the budget for both public schools and state universities inevitably exceeds 50 percent of the total of most state budgets.

The University as a Sphere of Influence on Resources

Among the approximately 3,000 universities in the United States, 1,340 offer some form of teacher education. Larger institutions usually have a unit called a school or college of education. Smaller institutions often locate teacher education as a department within a larger academic unit such as a college of arts and science. In some institutions teacher education is merged with related academic disciplines.

Teacher education does not ordinarily enjoy the planning and budgetary autonomy of other units on campus. In the case of other campus units, unless there are serious questions of quality, impropriety, financial problems, or similar serious issues, the unit determines its own priorities. This is not the case for teacher education units. There are very few institutions in which teacher education units enjoy privileges of self-determination equal to other units'. Some explanations for this lack of self-determination include (a) the low status of colleges of education; (b) the tendency of education colleges to have the greatest proportion of the institution's graduate students, thereby threatening the "balance" of the institution; (c) the state mandates; and (d) the fact that colleges of education are dependent on arts and science units for offering the academic major and general-education components of the teacher-preparation program. Teachers are the only professional group prepared in university programs who continue to study in the arts and science colleges after completion of their general education studies and even after their initial licensure.

Teacher education students are advised by the faculty in both the arts and science and teacher education. Each unit, in effect, seeks hegemony over baccalaureate degree requirements because of budgetary rewards (i.e., more new faculty, research and teaching assistants, and assorted faculty perquisites). Teacher education units are supported in this battle for control of the curriculum by the increasing state mandates, the perceptions of practitioners in schools who point to gaps in the beginning teacher's performance, and the expanding knowledge base in pedagogy. The fact that university budgets are based upon, or weighted to, student credit hours intensifies this tension between professional schools and arts and science colleges.

Universities have the capability to resolve the problem of giving teacher education higher priority internally, but they are unlikely to do so on their own initiative. To attain additional resources, the teacher education units appeal to state agencies and national accreditation bodies, demanding greater university investment to meet higher education standards of state certification and national accreditation. The threat of losing national accreditation was an effective growth strategy for colleges of education between World War II and 1970, before all other professional groups started to make similar demands on limited university budgets. Given a choice between responding to calls for reform, which many universities realize can only be achieved by investing additional resources in their colleges of education, or ignoring calls for change in their teacher education programs, most universities have opted to maintain the status quo (Hawley, Austin, & Goldman, 1988).

The teaching profession itself is also increasing its advocacies related to the control of professional programs. For instance, most organizations support some form of alternative teacher certification. These types of programs, however, directly impact on the *total* university through the loss of the tuition produced by significantly fewer education students generating fewer credit hours.

The College of Education as a Sphere of Influence on Resources

Within the college of education, the preparation of classroom teachers competes for resources with other professional programs preparing a wide array of specialists including curriculum supervisors, special education experts, counselors, administrators, and school psychologists. In many of the larger, more prestigious, research universities, undergraduate education enrollments provide the support base for more expensive graduate student programs and assistantships. Through such support, professors get graduate research and teaching assistants. In many of these universities, graduate assistants teach and supervise the preservice teachers. The undergraduate teacher education program occupies a low budget priority within the college of education, and the more prestigious the college of education, the greater this exploitation of undergraduate preservice programs. A few large research-oriented universities have colleges of education that actually use their undergraduate teacher education programs as a training laboratory for preparing future professors of education and for generating usable research about teacher education, but these

are notable exceptions (Clark, 1987). Recognizing this situation, the primary goal of the Holmes Group is to make the study and practice of teacher education a high priority in the major research universities (Holmes Group, 1986).

The separation of administrators from teachers in the public school is also reinforced within the college of education. Educational administration departments are typically set apart from curriculum and teaching departments. Few courses are taken by both the curriculum and teaching students and the future administrators who will be their school leaders.

The relationship that exists in the public schools also seems to exert an analogous effect on the relationship among the college departments that prepare educational specialists such as school psychologists and counselors. Because teacher education still deals primarily with undergraduate education and the preparation of administrators and other education specialists is primarily a graduate-level activity, teaching loads are heavier for teacher education faculty.

Within the various teacher education faculty groups there also seem to be status gradients related to perceived university roles. Those teacher education faculty who specialize in fields such as the history of education, tests and measurement, and learning theory take on the characteristics and expectations of many of the faculty in their parent academic disciplines in the arts and science colleges. Similarly, those faculty who work primarily with pedagogy and school curriculum tend to take on the values, work habits, and expectations of the school practitioners with whom they associate. Because university promotion and tenure committees more readily recognize high-quality faculty performance if it appears to be traditional research rather than applications of knowledge, these differences in faculty culture are significant determinants of the reward system in colleges of education (Schwebel, 1985).

The Schools as a Sphere of Influence on Resources

The aspect of teacher education that is perceived to be most meaningful to teacher education candidates is their direct experience. Such positive perceptions, however, result from comparing direct experience with traditional courses. Professional laboratory experiences (i.e., fieldwork, student teaching, and internships) are aspects of the teacher education program in need of the most improvement. The involvement of classroom teachers and schools is still as junior partners in university programs. Professional laboratory experiences for future teachers are also underfunded. The number of visits provided by underpaid college supervisors and the resources provided for coaching of future teachers by on-site teacher-mentors are also inadequate.

Very few situations exist in which teachers are inducted into their profession in their beginning year with a reduced class load and a supervisory support system to make their first year of teaching an educative, professional, growth experience (Johnston & Ryan, 1980). In recent years, a few states have passed legislation to provide these types of professional, career development patterns, but they have not provided sufficient funds to implement the programs. Funds to maintain even these sporadic efforts seem difficult to maintain across legislative sessions (Hall, 1982).

Another of the central factors that impacts on the resource question is the fact that women make up 75 percent of the teaching force in elementary and secondary schools. In American society, women have traditionally filled low-paying, essential, service roles that require some degree of higher education. In a very real sense, the degree to which the women's rights movement achieves equity in salary for comparable work will, in large measure, determine the future status of the teaching profession, as well as the success or failure of the women's rights movement itself.

Summary of the Resources Dimension

No new methods of directly funding teacher education have been proposed by any sphere of influence to attain increased quality. No significant new federal initiatives or strategies, such as special components of the former Higher Education Act, are currently being proposed for teacher education, despite the spate of national reform literature calling for improved teachers and schools, although it has become popular to support some reincarnation of the National Teacher Corps.

In the future, the most significant influence on teacher education funding could well result from the belief that the best way to improve schools is to improve the quality of teachers. What makes such a future scenario a possibility is that all the major proposals for improving schools place high priority on some form of incentive system to keep good teachers in the classroom, (i.e., career ladders, merit pay, and merit school plans). *Indirectly*, what happens in relation to the status of classroom teachers and their salaries could be the single most important factor in providing more resources to universities functioning as the training arm of the profession. Resources to produce quality at one end of the system (in the schools) could be the factor that generates more resources and quality at the other end of the system, in the colleges of education and the universities.

Even though the future of teacher education is inextricably interwoven with the future of the teaching profession, education professionals in universities and in settings outside of school have done little to help improve the conditions under which classroom teachers work or the rewards teachers receive. In fact, many college professors have made notable careers attacking public schools. Members of the professoriate have not generally considered themselves partners in a common enterprise with teachers, and they certainly have not been active advocates for teachers in the legislative process.

Collaboration built around mutual interests might be the motivating force that brings the training, research, and practice arms of the profession together; however, there is no historical precedent for such an expectation. Historically, there has been an ever-widening gulf between the organizations representing classroom teachers and the associations of researchers from colleges of education (Travers, 1983). A turnaround in the current situation is necessary. Teacher education will

receive support from the public in direct relationship to improvement of the conditions for professional practice. If teachers are treated like professionals instead of executors of somebody else's orders, the status and funding of teacher education will improve. Every aspect of teacher education is influenced by the public view of the importance of teaching.

THE CONDITIONS OF PRACTICE DIMENSION

The Society as a Sphere of Influence on Conditions of Practice

A significant development reflected in national reports is the concept of *teacher empowerment* (Yonemura, 1986). Professional groups have shifted from concern with only welfare issues to proposals for improving the profession of teacher education (Shanker, 1985). What is yet to be determined is the degree of teacher control over conditions of professional training and practice.

After a number of waves of reform at the national level, the concept of the professional teacher as the key to educational improvement now appears to be widely accepted. The first reforms following *A Nation at Risk* were characterized by efforts to raise the achievement level of students. Reform through regulation was the major strategy. Intensification of existing practices was assumed to be the solution. Lack of attention to the problems of school force-outs and dropouts, especially among disadvantaged students, and a decline in teacher morale revealed the limitations of this phase. Forty-five states raised graduation requirements between 1983 and 1987 (Association for Supervision and Curriculum and Development, 1985). Teacher education was little affected by this phase. It soon became apparent that these proposals were inadequate and, in some respects, counterproductive.

The second wave of reform shifted the attention to teachers and teacher performance. Teacher testing was emphasized, and teacher supervision, appraisal, and accountability were increased. The second wave called for teachers to be accountable, individually and collectively, for the effectiveness of their teaching (Ornstein, 1986). Classroom teachers argued that, because they played no major role in teacher education, lacked autonomy, had no peer review or involvement in hiring practices, did not choose their own administrators, and did not control the conditions of practice, the call for teacher accountability was an ill-conceived movement. If teachers were to be accountable, they expected to be significant players in setting and implementing the reform agendas.

The third wave of reform challenged the schools to provide conditions more favorable to teacher professionalization. A great many influential, well-financed groups became involved in this wave of reform. Unlike earlier efforts, this phase of reform challenged the organization, management, and structure of the schools as they existed. The stated goal was to gain professional status for classroom teachers by changing both university programs and the conditions for teaching and learning.

The State as a Sphere of Influence on Conditions of Practice

Teachers' practices are directly influenced by state law and state administrative codes in a wide variety of ways. The number of school days, the subjects in the curriculum, the number of minutes devoted per week to the teaching of each subject, and the nature of state mandates for student progress and graduation are examples of the direct controls exerted by the state on the conditions of teacher practice. Indeed, it might very well be argued that, although teachers are employees of particular school districts, it is the state that exerts the most pervasive controls over their practice (Shulman, 1983).

The sphere of state influence over conditions of practice is also obvious when one considers the process of licensure. Every state has a licensing system in which the dominant pattern continues to emphasize the beginning teacher as a fully functioning practitioner completely capable of doing what an experienced master teacher can do. The process of state licensure is the legal underpinning that continues to permit school districts to assign first-year and experienced teachers comparable teaching loads. Indeed, the practice of giving beginning teachers the most difficult assignments would not be possible were it not the traditional state practice of licensing the novice as fully competent.

The state, by controlling the content of teacher education programs, also defines the minimum levels of how much and what beginning teachers must know and be able to do. Inevitably, minimum requirements become maximum requirements. By controlling the content of teacher certification programs, the state is directly influencing how well the beginning teacher will function in the schools in response to the real world's conditions of practice. The state maintains its dominance by also defining the amount and nature of inservice work required for teachers to retain particular forms of licensure. These state requirements interact with the conditions of practice in schools that might or might not be relevant to the real, day-to-day work of the teacher (Yarger, 1982).

On the one hand, the state has a set of mandates that relate directly to the operations of public schools and the conditions under which they operate. At the same time, the state has a set of mandates related to the knowledge and skills required for teacher licensure. For example, a state might require schools to offer instruction in "Safety and Protective Behavior" but have no requirement for this content to be offered in its teacher education programs. States are not organized to analyze their own separate sets of mandates to determine the degree to which they agree with or contradict each other.

Every state has other powerful ways of influencing the conditions of professional practice in addition to those cited. Whether or not to have kindergartens, and their length; minimum salary for beginning teachers; maximum number of pupils permitted in a classroom; tests and standards required for promotion or graduation; degree and nature of mainstreaming handicapped children, criteria for selecting state-adopted texts; provision of special funds for at-risk populations; and licensure requirements of supervisors and principals are additional examples of state influences on the conditions of professional practice. The state prescribes requirements for degrees, approves courses, and decides what credits will be given and which courses can be taught on and off campus and the way they will be delivered.

The state serves more than a regulatory role in overseeing licensure and minimum standards for schools. Through its power to tax and allocate, every state creates situations in which the conditions for professional practice vary widely among the school districts. Finally, the state has the power to accredit and, thereby, directly controls various aspects of the conditions of practice.

The bureaucratic style of the state must also be taken into account for a full understanding of the state's impact on conditions of practice in the local schools. It is ponderous and formalistic, and, although it seems to focus on the short term because state budgets pass in annual or 2-year cycles, the actual relationship of local schools to the state and the effects of state policies are long-term in nature.

States have increasingly pursued standards of equity and excellence at the expense of local districts. Every state enacts and enforces new laws and rules for its schools without providing additional state funding. This trend requires schools to perform continuously expanding functions. The state is more vulnerable than local districts to the demands of diverse constituencies; it is also more accessible than the federal government. This, in part, explains why state practices exert the strongest influence in shaping the conditions of professional practice in public schools.

The University as a Sphere of Influence on Conditions of Practice

Universities are comprised of faculties that represent the arts and science disciplines, on the one hand, and professional schools, on the other. Although sharing the basic values of the university, the two groups have different emphases in their academic missions. Each group has a university subculture of its own that is highly functional.

Teacher education has not been able to shed the image of marginal academic respectability, a carryover from its normal school past, or to convince the academic community that it is or could be a genuine profession (Clifford & Guthrie, 1988). Consequently, colleges of education have existed in a no-man's-land between the demands of public schools for relevance and the demands of academic disciplines for traditional forms of research. Education faculty are pressured to make their scholarship more useful for solving problems faced by classroom teachers and, at the same time, to make the knowledge they deal with more scholarly in terms of criteria used by graduate schools. Operationally, this presents education faculty with the dilemma of deciding which sphere of influence to satisfy.

The reasons for the continuing low status and lack of acceptance of teacher education as a legitimate field of study on the university campus are varied.

1. If university faculty were to admit that entrance to the teaching profession requires an understanding of a specific professional and pedagogical knowledge base, as well as demonstrated competence under supervision prior to approval to practice, they would have to admit that they were unprepared to perform their roles as teachers.
2. Because the academic community regards off-campus teaching as less valuable than on-campus teaching, instruction in general as less valuable than research, and applied research as less valuable than basic research, some teacher education faculty must inevitably be low status.
3. Many university-wide faculty insist on defining teaching as an art rather than as an art and science; an art requires selection of talented individuals more than it involves the formal study of pedagogy.
4. University faculties, particularly those in arts and science, do not view themselves as instruments for implementing public policy and social reforms. Equalizing of opportunities (and other societal missions of schoolteachers) are not conceived of as the primary mission of university faculty engaged in generating new knowledge.
5. Teacher education has failed to explain its uniqueness to the public or to develop a distinctive presence on campus.
6. State mandates for coursework give university-wide faculty the impression that education faculty are not professionals who are capable of determining the content they teach.
7. No forces or constituencies outside the university sphere are sufficiently concerned with university programs to advocate significantly greater resources for professional education.

The College of Education as a Sphere of Influence on Conditions of Practice

As difficult as it might be for most of the 45,000 professors of education to accept, there are few practices in schools that can be directly traced to the theories and research taught in colleges of education. Yet the knowledge base actually exceeds current practice (Brophy, 1988). The major exception to this general lack of university influence is the development and use of norm-referenced tests in schools. Also, as one examines the advocacy and research related to teaching those with handicapping conditions, some connections can be clearly made between the principles and skills taught in colleges of education and the conditions of practice in public schools. Much of the learning theory undergirding the training of exceptional education teachers is also manifested and observed in schools.

When typical practices in elementary and secondary schools are examined, it becomes difficult to connect school practitioners' (teachers, specialists, others) daily operations with the research and knowledge offered in university programs. There is some evidence that teachers' childhood school experiences are much more likely to explain their teaching behavior than the content of their courses in pedagogy (Zeichner & Tabachnick, 1981). Specific mandates of a particular school district and the precise demands imposed by administrators in specific school buildings, rather than any college of education advocacy, research, or theory, overwhelmingly influence conditions of school practice. One might even make the case that lay persons (parents, businessmen, legislators) have significantly more influence on school practices than the education professoriate.

Summaries of research conclude that the value of basic research in education is severely limited (Ebel, 1982). The area of reading, which has been one of the most heavily researched specializations, is still another example of this lack of impact on school practice. An extensive review of the reading literature covering over 170 books and articles between 1967 and 1987 concluded that this vast body of research has not provided clearcut answers to such questions as when to begin to teach children to read, how they learn, or what are the best methods (Barbour, 1987).

In considering the gap between educational research and school practice, there are clearly some notable examples of influence. The principles espoused in the more effective schools research literature, for example, are now commonly understood and widely accepted (Edmonds, 1982). Specific practices are also identifiable that can be connected to research conducted on direct instruction and time on task. The opposite case, however, might be made for the research on heterogeneous versus homogeneous grouping, mastery learning, cooperative learning, and individual differences. In these areas there is not only a lack of widespread adoption but also an aggressive resistance to the research literature by many schools and practitioners. In other areas, notably discipline, there are active controversies within and among faculty in colleges of education, with some being more successful than others at having their advocacies, ostensibly based on research, adopted by practitioners.

The issue of applicability is best made by leading researchers themselves (Goodlad, 1984). Many argue that the findings of research cannot, and should not, be expected to translate directly into what teachers do or are taught to do. In sum, there are mixed responses to the question of how much schools of education have influenced conditions of practice in public schools. It might very well be that faculty in colleges of education have influenced more school practices by their discursive writings, theories of instruction, consultations, and problem-solving activities than they have by their research. Finally, the influence of college faculty in continuing to offer inservice courses and workshops cannot be ignored.

Any in-depth, comprehensive study of school practices, however, will inevitably reveal that the overwhelming majority of school practices reflect the results of bureaucracy, norm-referenced testing, school culture, financial resources, state laws, community demands, pupil expectations, and a host of traditions more than they reflect the influence of any college of education or the professional knowledge base. The legal and widespread use of corporal punishment in all but 11 states provides dramatic evidence of the sanctioning of unprofessional practice. There is no knowledge base that supports, or college of education that officially advocates, the use of corporal punishment (Cryan, 1981). The influence of the training arm of the profession on practice is much less than might be assumed in any real profession (Doyle, 1981; Howsam, 1976).

The Schools as a Sphere of Influence on Conditions of Practice

Literature on teacher efficacy or, more accurately the studies that catalog the lack of it, continue to increase. Unlike practitioners in other professions, teachers function in complex, hierarchically organized, social systems. It would be more accurate to refer to practicing teachers as bureaucratic functionaries than as professional practitioners. The lack of efficacy that teachers report is a consequence of their not being able to control the conditions of practice they regard as germane to their work: who their students are, the number of students in a given class, the content to be taught, the methods employed, the materials utilized, the purposes of the course, and the assessment of student achievement.

Added to this real and perceived lack of efficacy among teachers are the conditions that exist in schools that directly impinge on teaching and learning. The high frequency of classroom interruptions, for instance, is seen by teachers as an indicator of the low value placed on their work. The staffing of schools places classroom teachers near the bottom of the status hierarchy; specialists in various instructional areas, guidance people, testers, supervisors, administrators, social workers, and school nurses pursue activities that can interrupt the work of classroom teachers. Other conditions such as the transportation schedule, which controls the ability of teachers to provide after-school tutoring or extracurricular activities, reinforce teachers' feelings of low efficacy.

Research has identified a number of factors present in the workplace that demoralize even the most dedicated teachers (McLaughlin, Peifer, Swansen-Owens, & Yee, 1986). Large class size, supervision of study halls and cafeterias, inadequate instructional materials, administrative decisions that undermine teacher efficacy, isolation from colleagues, low pay, decrepit buildings, incessant paperwork, parental complaints, and lack of input into the decision-making process of the school convince teachers that they are held in low esteem. Teachers frequently need to moonlight at second jobs in order to afford a college education for their own children. And the most disturbing factor is that many teachers are apologetic about what they do for a living. Policy implications of teacher criticisms of the workplace suggest systemic rather than single-issue reforms.

Summary of the Conditions of Practice Dimension

The national sphere of influence has clearly emphasized upgrading the conditions under which teachers practice. States have exerted a regulatory role, identifying teachers as the targets to be upgraded rather than the victims of unprofessional working conditions. The university sphere ignores conditions in the schools and focuses on insuring quality in the individual teacher's knowledge of subject matter. The college of education sphere provides mixed influences. Some faculty are sensitive to the negative conditions of practice; others regard classroom teachers as inadequate and the cause of school problems.

CONCLUSIONS

Given the systems model used in this chapter, important change will occur in teacher education when one or more of the spheres of influence dominate the others. But, if the preceding analysis is correct, the present power of each sphere appears to be too effective at maintaining its existing authority to be significantly redirected. In effect, for any comprehensive change to occur, there must be agreement within and among the five spheres of influence.

It is reasonable and understandable that political organizations, social institutions, and educational bureaucracies pursue their own agendas. It might be inevitable that these five spheres will never function in mutually supportive ways. The unlikelihood of a shared vision developing among the five spheres of influence acts as a deterrent to change. Because no one sphere can control the manner in which the four critical dimensions of a profession are practiced, it is unlikely that comprehensive change will occur. In this sense, the contradictory thrusts among the five spheres of influence serve a stabilizing, or homeostatic, function. Of course, other change scenarios are possible.

One possible change scenario, given this systems analysis, is that some spheres of influence would be substantially weakened as other spheres assume their functions. For example, given the critical shortage of urban teachers, it is possible that school-based alternative teacher certification programs might grow and become more significant in the 1990s. This would substantially weaken the college of education and university spheres. The public school sphere would then legitimately deal directly with the state sphere and be more susceptible to influences from the societal sphere. In this scenario, the college of education and university roles in teacher education might not be eliminated but be relegated to secondary, rather than primary, roles.

Another change scenario might be a marked increase in federal or state mandates, so that the university and college of education roles in teacher education become matters of simply following directives. By marked redistribution of the balance of power among the spheres, change in the entire system becomes possible. This analysis assumes that the current balance among the five spheres must be altered in some major way for comprehensive change to occur in teacher education.

It is also possible to conceive of a positive, collaborative scenario in which American schools are restructured to meet the challenges of the twenty-first century. In this scenario, the reform of education at all levels is made urgent by the dropout problem, the impending shortage of youth prepared to enter the work force, and the increase in the number of elderly on social security. The states, federal agencies, educational organizations, national reform groups, universities, and schools come together to support reforms in the schools and teacher education that emphasize the need for highly educated teachers who understand pedagogy, how children learn, and the content they teach. Americans recognize that they can no longer afford school dropouts or push-outs. Employed, fully functioning, high school graduates are needed to help pay the social security of an ever-increasing elderly population, as well as their own. The public realizes that if young people, especially minorities who drop out at a rate of 50 percent, go on welfare or into prison instead of entering the work force, few will be able to retire at even a fraction of current levels. As more Americans realize they are interdependent economically and socially, the schools and schoolteachers are viewed as performing an essential professional service. Economic self-interest may motivate those who up to now have been unmoved by human rights arguments for supporting equal educational opportunity.

Political leaders, as well as educators, recognize and admit that the schools must educate all students, regardless of income, race, or handicapping conditions. To meet the special learning needs of all children, professional teachers for the future are expected to be competent in teaching different knowledges, skills, and values, as well as in teaching them in more effective ways, ways that engage students of all backgrounds and all ability levels. The need for a comprehensive knowledge base for teachers is demonstrated as the public observes that professionally educated teachers can successfully teach children with complex learning needs.

Quality controls such as accreditation, selection, certification, induction, and licensing are established by the profession itself to insure competency in teaching. As a result, the public gains confidence in the quality of teachers, and this trust trans-lates into a greater willingness to pay salaries that are competitive with other professions requiring advanced levels of education. Taxpayers understand the importance of providing the resources to create the conditions for professional practice as well as professional study. The concept of the *empowered teacher* becomes a reality. The public schools attract and keep highly qualified teachers because they are treated as professionals. The teaching profession accepts accountability for the learning of children and youth because of its involvement in and accountability for school reform.

Education-minded parents and teachers, the largest professional work force in the nation, comprise a political constituency that coalesces and exerts a powerful influence on national, state, university, college, and school spheres. Teacher education is given a high priority on everyone's agenda, because the public finally realizes that America's aspirations can rise no higher than the quality of America's teachers.

These particular scenarios might or might not become reality. At any point in time teacher education is defined by the interaction and emergence of various events and policy changes. The characteristics of the teaching profession identified here, as well as many of the other characteristics germane to an understanding of the teaching profession, will be affected by the action, reaction, and confluence of various forces within and across each sphere of influence.

What this chapter has presented is a conceptual framework for analyzing teacher education. If the present rate of change continues, many new developments will have to be included when this conceptual framework is used again to update and synthesize research on the context of teacher education.

References

Adelman, N. E. (1986). *An exploratory study of teacher alternative certification and retraining programs.* Washington, DC: Policy Studies Associates.

Alschuler, A. S. (Ed.). (1980). *Teacher burnout.* Washington, DC: National Education Association.

American Association of Colleges for Teacher Education. (1983). *Educating a profession: Profile of a beginning teacher.* Washington, DC: Author.

American Association of Colleges for Teacher Education. (1986). *Teacher education policy in the states: A 50-state survey of legislative and administrative actions* (Entering, Exit and Certification Examinations). Washington, DC: Author.

American Association of Colleges for Teacher Education. (1987). *Teacher education policy in the states: A 50-state survey of legislative and administrative actions* (State Standards Boards or Like Bodies). Washington, DC: Author.

Argyris, C., & Schön, D. A. (1974). *Theory in practice: Increasing professional effectiveness.* San Francisco: Jossey-Bass.

Arlin, M. (1984). Time variability in mastery learning. *American Educational Research Journal, 21*(1), 102–120.

Association for Supervision and Curriculum Development. (1985). *With consequences for all: A report from the ASCD task force on increased high school graduation requirements.* Alexandria, VA: Author.

Barbour, N. H. (1987). Learning to read. In C. Seefeldt (Ed.), *The early childhood curriculum: A review of current research* (pp. 107–140). New York: Teachers College Press.

Bigelow, D. N. (1971). *The liberal arts and teacher education: A confrontation.* Lincoln: University of Nebraska Press.

Bing, S. R., & Wheelock, A. (Eds.). (1986). Students at-risk and the schools they go to: An advocate's bibliography. *Equity and Choice, 3*(1), 12–13.

Biott, C. (1983). The foundations of classroom action-research in initial teacher training. *Journal of Education for Teaching, 9*(2), 152–60.

Block, A. W. (1983). *Effective schools: A summary of research.* Arlington, VA: Educational Research Service.

Brophy, J. E. (1988). Educating teachers about managing classrooms and students. *Teachers and Teacher Education, 4*(1), 1–18.

Brown, R. (1986). State responsibility for at-risk youth. *Metropolitan Education, 2,* 5–12.

Buccino, A. (1988). Redefining competitiveness and national well-being: Reaction paper #1. In D. C. Corrigan (Ed.), *Purposes of American education today: Conceptions of schooling* (pp. 21–32). College Station, TX: Texas A&M University, College of Education.

California Commission on the Teaching Profession. (1985). *Who will teach our children? A strategy for improving California schools.* Sacramento, CA: Author.

Carnegie Forum on Education and the Economy, Task Force on Teaching as a Profession. (1986). *A nation prepared: Teachers for the 21st century.* New York: Author.

Carnegie Foundation for Advancement of Teaching. (1987). The ups and downs of federal funding for R & D. *Change, 19*(6), 35–39.

Clark, D. (1987). Transforming the structure for the professional preparation of teachers. In J. D. Raths & L. Katz (Eds.), *Advances in teacher education* (Vol. 2, pp. 1–19). Norwood, NJ: Ablex.

Clifford, G., & Guthrie, J. W. (1988). *Ed school: A brief for professional education.* Chicago: The University of Chicago Press.

Commission on the Cities. (1988). *Report of the national advisory commission on civil disorders.* New York: New York Times.

Committee for Economic Development. (1985). *Investing in our children: Business and the public schools.* New York: Author.

Conant, J. B. (1963). *The education of American teachers.* New York: McGraw-Hill.

Cruickshank, D. R. (1985). Uses and benefits of reflective teaching. *Phi Delta Kappan, 66*(10), 704–706.

Cruickshank, D. R., & Callahan, R. (1983). The other side of the desk: Stages and problems of teacher development. *Elementary School Journal, 83*(3), 250–258.

Cryan, J. R. W. (1981). *Corporal punishment in the schools: Its use is abuse.* Toledo: University of Toledo, College of Education and Allied Professions.

Damerell, R. G. (1985). *Education's smoking gun: How teachers colleges have destroyed education in America.* New York: Freundlich.

Darling-Hammond, L. (1984). *Beyond the commission reports: The coming crisis in teaching* (R–3177–RC). Santa Monica, CA: RAND Corporation.

Dembo, M. H., & Gibson, S. (1985). Teachers' sense of efficacy: An important factor in school improvement. *Elementary School Journal, 86*(2), 173–184.

Denemark, G. W. (1962). Encouraging expertness through extending the period of professional preparation beyond four years. In *Professional Imperatives: Expertness and Self Determination* (Report of the NCTEPS Fort Collins conference, pp. 163–172). Washington DC: National Education Association.

Denemark, G. W., & Nutter, N. (1980). *The case for extended programs of initial teacher preparation.* Washington, DC: ERIC Clearinghouse on Teacher Education.

Denton, J. J. (1987). Factors influencing quality in teacher education: Program, faculty, and productivity. *Teacher Education & Practice, 4*(1), 7–34.

Dewey, J. (1915) *The school and society* (rev. ed.). Chicago: University of Chicago Press.

Doyle, W. (1981). Research on classroom contexts: Toward a knowledge base for policy and practice in teacher education. In G. A. Griffin & H. Hukill (Eds.), *Alternate perspectives for program development and research in teacher education* (pp. 75–94). Summary of Proceedings of an Invited Symposium for the Annual Meeting of the American Educational Research Association, Los Angeles.

Dworkin, A. G. (1987). *Teacher burnout in the public schools: Structural causes and consequences for children.* Albany, NY: State University of New York Press.

Ebel, R. (1982). The future of educational research, Part I. *Educational Researcher, 11*(8), 18–19.

Eble, K. E. (1988). *The craft of teaching: A guide to mastering the professor's art.* San Francisco: Jossey-Bass.

Edmonds, R. R. (1982). Programs of school improvement: An overview. *Educational Leadership, 40*(3), 4–11.

Etzioni, A. (1969). *The semi-professions and their organization: Teachers, nurses, social workers.* New York: Free Press.

Evertson, C., Hawley, W. O., & Zlotnik, M. (1984) *The characteristics of effective teacher education programs: A review of research.* Nashville: Vanderbilt University, Peabody College.

Feiman-Nemser, S. (1983). *Learning to teach.* East Lansing, MI: Institute for Research on Teaching.

Gallup, A. M., & Clark, D. L. (1987). The 19th annual Gallup Poll of the public's attitudes toward the public schools. *Phi Delta Kappan, 69*(1), 17–30.

Gollnick, D. M., & Kunkel, R. C. (1986). The reform of national accreditation. *Phi Delta Kappan, 68*(4), 310–314.

Good, T., & Grouws, D. (1977). Teaching effects: A process product study in fourth-grade mathematics classrooms. *Journal of Teacher Education, 28*(3), 49–54.

Goodlad, J. I. (1984). *A place called school: Prospects for the future.* New York: McGraw-Hill.

Griffin, G. A., Barnes, S., Hughes, R., O'Neal, S., Defino, M., Edwards, S., and Hukill, M. (1983). *Clinical preservice teacher education: Final report of descriptive study.* Austin, TX: University of Texas, Research and Development Center for Teacher Education.

Grosenick, J. K., & Reynolds, M. C. (1978). *Teacher education: Renegotiating roles for mainstreaming.* Reston, VA: Council for Exceptional Children.

Haggstrom, G. W., Darling-Hammond, L., & Grissmer, D. W. (1988). *Assessing teacher supply and demand* (R–3633–ED/CSTP). Santa Monica, CA: RAND Corporation.

Hall, G. (1982). Induction: The missing link. *Journal of Teacher Education, 33*(3), 53–55.

Hawley, W. D., Austin, A. E., & Goldman, E. S. (1988). *Changing the education of teachers.* Atlanta: Southern Regional Education Board.

Henjum, A. (1983). Let's select "self-actualizing" teachers. *Education, 104*(1), 51–55.

Hodgkinson, H. L. (1987). Changing society, unchanging curriculum. *National Forum: Phi Kappa Phi Journal, 67*(3), 8–11.

Holmes Group. (1986). *Tomorrow's teachers.* East Lansing, MI: Author.

House, E. R., Glass, G. V., McClean, L. D., & Walker, D. F. (1978). No simple answer: Critique of the follow through evaluation. *Harvard Educational Review, 48*(2), 128–160.

Howe, H., II. (1986). The prospect for children in the United States. *Phi Delta Kappan, 68*(4), 191–196.

Howsam, R. B. (1976). *Now you shall be real to everyone* (The 17th Annual Charles W. Hunt Lecture). Washington, DC: American Association of Colleges for Teacher Education.

Howsam, R. B., Blackburn, J., Burnham, R., Scannell, D., & Gant, J. (1981). *Final report of the task force on quality standards for extended programs.* Washington, DC: Association of Colleges and Schools of Education in State Universities and Land-Grant Colleges.

Howsam, R. B., Corrigan, D. C., & Denemark, G. W. (1985). *Educating a profession.* Washington, DC: American Association of Colleges for Teacher Education.

Johnson, R. T., & Johnson, D. W. (1985). Student-student interaction: Ignored but powerful. *Journal of Teacher Education, 36*(4), 22–26.

Johnston, J. M., & Ryan, K. (1980). *Research on the beginning teacher: Implications for teacher education.* Columbus: The Ohio State University. (ERIC Document Reproduction Service No. ED 209 188)

Karnes, E. L., Black, D. D., & Downs, J. (1983). *Discipline in our schools: An annotated bibliography.* Westport, CN: Greenwood Press.

Kearns, D. T., & Doyle, D. P. (1988). *Winning the brain race.: A bold plan to make our schools competitive.* San Francisco: Institute for Contemporary Studies Press.

King, J. (1987). The uneasy relationship between teacher education and the liberal arts and sciences. *Journal of Teacher Education, 38*(1) 6–10.

Koerner, J. (1963). *The miseducation of American teachers*. Boston: Houghton Mifflin.

Kyriacou, C. (1987). Teacher stress and burnout: An international review. *Educational Research*, 29(2), 146–152.

Levin, H. M. (1985). *The educationally disadvantaged: A national crisis:* Philadelphia: Public/Private Ventures.

Livingstone, I. D. (1986). *Second international mathematics study: Perceptions of the intended and implemented mathematics curriculum*. Washington, DC: U.S. Department of Education.

Lortie, D. C. (1975). *Schoolteacher: A sociological study*. Chicago: University of Chicago Press.

McDill, E. L., Natriello, G., & Pallas, A. M. (1985). Raising standards and retaining students: The impact of the reform recommendations on potential dropouts. *Review of Educational Research*. 55(4), 415–433.

McKnight, C. C., et al. (1987). *The underachieving curriculum: Assessing U.S. school mathematics from an international perspective*. Champaign, IL: Stipes.

McLaughlin, M. W., Peifer, R. S., Swansen-Owens, D., & Yee, S. (1986). Why teachers won't teach. *Phi Delta Kappan*, 67(6), 420–426.

National Commission on Excellence in Education. (1983). *A nation at risk: The imperative for educational reform*. Washington, DC: U.S. Government Printing Office.

National Commission on Excellence in Teacher Education. (1985). *A call for change in teacher education*. Washington, DC: American Association of Colleges for Teacher Education.

National Education Association. (1984). *An open letter to America on schools, students, and tomorrow*. Washington, DC: Author.

National Governors' Association. (1986). *Time for results: The governors' 1991 report on education*. Washington, DC: Author.

Natriello, G. (Ed.). (1986). *School dropouts: Patterns and policies*. New York: Teachers College Press.

Nelli, E. R. (1981). Five myths in need of reality. *Action in Teacher Education*, 3(4), 1–6.

Nelli, E. R. (1984). A research-based response to allegations that education students are academically inferior. *Action in Teacher Education*, 6(3), 73–80.

Ornstein, A. C. (1984). The changing federal role in education. *American Education*, 20(10), 4–7.

Ornstein, A. C. (1986). Teacher accountability: Trends and policies. *Education and Urban Society*, 18(2), 221–29.

Pellicano, R. R. (1987). At risk: A view of "social advantage." *Educational Leadership*, 44(6), 47–49.

Peseau, B. A. (1982). Developing an adequate resource base for teacher education. *Journal of Teacher Education*, 33(4), 13–15.

Peseau, B. A., & Orr, P. (1980). The outrageous underfunding of teacher education. *Phi Delta Kappan*, 62(2), 100–102.

Pipho, C. (1986). States move reform closer to reality: Kappan special report. *Phi Delta Kappan*, 68(4), K1–K8.

Robinson, G. E. (1985). *Effective schools research: A guide to school improvement*. Arlington, VA: Educational Research Service.

Ross, D. D. (1984). A pratical model for conducting action research in public school settings: Focus on research. *Contemporary Education*, 55(2), 113–117.

Roth, R. A. (1983). *The status of the profession: Selected characteristics of teacher education and teaching*. (ERIC Document Reproduction Service No. ED 233 988)

Rudner, L. M., et al. (1987). *What's happening in teacher testing: An analysis of state teacher testing practices*. Washington, DC: Office of Educational Research and Improvement.

Ryan, K. (1986). The new moral education. *Phi Delta Kappan*, 68(4) 228–233.

Schein, E. H. (1972). *Professional education.: Some new directions*. New York: McGraw-Hill.

Schwebel, M. (1985). The clash of cultures in academe: The university and the education faculty. *Journal of Teacher Education*, 36(4) 2–7.

Shanker, A. (1985). *The making of a profession*. Washington DC: American Federation of Teachers.

Shulman, L. S. (1983). Autonomy and obligation. In L. S. Shulman & G. Sykes (Eds.), *Handbook of Teaching and Policy*. New York; Longman.

Slavin, R. E. (1987). *Cooperative learning: Student teams. What research says to the teacher (2nd ed.)*. Washington, DC: National Education Association.

Smith, D., & Street, S. (1980). The professional component in selected professions. *Phi Delta Kappan*, 62(2), 103–107.

Southern Regional Education Board. (1986). Major reports on teacher education: What do they mean for states? *Regional Spotlight*, 15(1).

Squires, D. A. (1983). *Effective schools and classrooms: A research-based perspective*. Alexandria, VA: Association for Supervision and Curriculum Development.

Tom, A. R. (1984). *Teaching as a moral craft*. New York: Longman.

Travers, R. M. W. (1983). *How research has changed American schools: A history from 1840 to the present*. Kalamazoo, MI: Mythos Press.

U.S. Congress, subcommittee on elementary, secondary, and vocational education of the committee on education and labor, House of Representatives, Ninety-Fifth Congress, First Session on H.R. 15. Part I. (1977). *General issues in elementary and secondary education* (Hearing). (ERIC Document Reproduction Service No. ED 150 223)

Veenman, S. (1984). Perceived problems of beginning teachers. *Review of Educational Research*, 54(2), 143–178.

Walberg, H. J., & Waxman, H. C. (1983). Teaching, learning, and the management of instruction. In D. C. Smith (Ed.), *Essential knowledge for beginning educators* (pp. 50–65). Washington, DC: American Association of Colleges for Teacher Education.

Weaver, W. T. (1981). Demography, quality, and decline: The challenge for schools of education for the 1980s. In *Policy for the education of educators: Issues and implications*. Washington, DC: American Association of Colleges for Teacher Education.

Weaver, W. T. (1983). *America's teacher quality problem: Alternatives for reform*. New York: Praeger.

Whitehead, A. N. (1929). *The aims of education and other essays*. New York: Macmillan.

Yarger, S. J. (1982). *Inservice education*. Washington, DC: National Commission on Excellence in Education.

Yonemura, M. (1986). Reflections on teacher empowerment and teacher education. *Harvard Educational Review*, 56(4), 473–480.

Zeichner, M., & Tabachnick, B. R. (1981). Are the effects of university teacher education washed out by school experience? *Journal of Teacher Education*, 32(3), 7–11.

·13·

TEACHER PREPARATION: STRUCTURAL AND CONCEPTUAL ALTERNATIVES

Sharon Feiman-Nemser

MICHIGAN STATE UNIVERSITY

This chapter focuses on different ways of conceiving and carrying out teacher preparation. It examines some of the ideas that Americans have had about how teachers should be prepared and offers some frameworks for looking at distinctive approaches and alternatives. The chapter also discusses the state of the art concerning programs of initial teacher preparation and indicates where conceptual, empirical, and practical work are needed.

The organization of the chapter reflects a basic distinction in the professional literature and public debate. In discussing needed changes in teacher preparation, people tend to emphasize either structural or conceptual issues. Many of the current reforms, for example, call for adding a fifth year, increasing the amount of field experience, limiting the number of credit hours in education, creating alternative routes to teaching by providing on-the-job training for liberal arts graduates. Tied to policy mandates and questions of supply and demand, these structural alternatives reflect political and economic considerations more than clear thinking about what teachers need to know or how they can be helped to learn it.

At the same time, one can hardly pick up a professional journal or attend a professional meeting these days without encountering the terms *reflective teaching* and *teacher education*. Fifteen years ago, the same would have been true of the terms *competency-based* and *performance-based teacher education*. These conceptual alternatives reflect different views of teaching and learning to teach and suggest different orientations to the preparation of teachers.

Distinguishing between structural alternatives and conceptual orientations provides a way to highlight some of the major efforts that have dotted the teacher education landscape. At the same time, the need for such a strategy underscores the immature state of a field in which different forms of teacher preparation are only loosely tied to explicit traditions of thought, and conceptual orientations lack well-developed traditions of practice. Instead of mandates and models, we need to learn from the past, experiment with alternatives, and clarify what is entailed in helping people in different settings learn to teach.

The chapter begins with a brief overview of historic traditions that have influenced our ways of thinking about teacher education and learning to teach. Next comes a discussion of what is known about different institutional arrangements and program structures. The third section examines various conceptual orientations that have shaped the professional sequence. The chapter closes with a brief introduction to promising research-in-progress designed to illuminate different ideas about and approaches to preparing teachers.

HISTORIC TRADITIONS IN PREPARING TEACHERS

Today most teachers enter teaching by means of a 4-year undergraduate program. There was a time, however, when few believed that elementary teachers needed a college education,

This research was supported in part by the National Center for Research on Teacher Education, Michigan State University. The NCRTE is funded primarily by the Office of Educational Research and Improvement, United States Department of Education. The opinions expressed herein are those of the author and do not necessarily reflect the position, policy, or endorsement of the OERI/ED. (Grant No. OERI-G-86-0001)

The author expresses appreciation to the following people for their helpful comments on an earlier draft of this chapter: Margret Buchmann, Robert Houston, Susan Melnick, Michelle B. Parker, Michael Sedlak, Alan Tom, Ken Zeichner, and Karen Zumwalt.

that high school teaching required professional preparation, or that teacher education was a fit undertaking for a major research university. To appreciate how teacher preparation acquired its characteristic shape and where some of the major ideas about learning to teach have come from, we need to know something about the history of teacher education.

Three historic traditions have influenced ideas about and approaches to teacher preparation. Each tradition can be linked to a different institution offering a different kind of preparation to a different group of clients (see Table 13-1). The liberal arts tradition had early ties to the preparation of secondary teachers in liberal arts colleges. The normal-school tradition was intimately connected with the preparation of elementary teachers. The tradition of professionalization through graduate preparation and research was promoted by the modern university, which sought to prepare educational leaders.

The Normal-School Tradition

The idea of teacher education as a special kind of academic training did not exist before there were normal schools. Prior to their appearance in the second quarter of the nineteenth century, few elementary teachers had any specific instruction for their work. Figuring out what kind of training to offer was the central challenge.

The early normal schools provided a brief course of study to help students master the subjects they would teach and acquire some techniques for managing instruction. With the spread of secondary education, normal schools began to require a high school diploma for admission and to offer a 2-year course of study. The typical curriculum consisted of reviews of elementary subjects (e.g., reading, spelling, arithmetic), some secondary academic subjects (e.g., geometry, philosophy), and pedagogical subjects (e.g., history of education, psychology, teaching methods, observation and practice) (Monroe, 1952).

TABLE 13–1. Historical Traditions in Teacher Preparation

Institution	Elements/Themes	Clientele
Normal schools and teachers colleges	▶ institutional autonomy ▶ professional esprit de corps ▶ professional treatment of subject matter ▶ art and science of teaching	Elementary teachers
Liberal arts colleges	▶ liberal arts as preparation for teaching ▶ education as liberal art ▶ intellectual values, knowledge, and skills ▶ common learnings	Secondary teachers
University schools of education	▶ research ideal ▶ education as applied social science ▶ professionalization through graduate study ▶ devaluing of experience	Educational leaders

When students had barely completed elementary school, it made sense to review the common branches. Once normal schools required a high school diploma, some leaders felt that they should not duplicate academic instruction available in secondary schools and colleges. Rather, normal schools should offer a strictly professional curriculum. There were two approaches to this goal. One school of thought emphasized the professional treatment of subject matter; the second emphasized training in special methods (Cremin, 1953).

Professional Treatment of Subject Matter. Proponents of professional treatment believed that a teacher's knowledge of subjects differed from academic knowledge. This idea was promoted at Indiana State Normal, where faculty developed a distinctive kind of instruction in which the method of the subject became the main object of attention. Subject-matter courses modeled principles taught in professional courses on the psychology of learning. Methods courses engaged students in reflection on their own experience as learners of school subjects, as a way of sensitizing them to problems their pupils might encounter (Borrowman, 1956; Randolph 1924). In this way, the entire program was organized around the professional goal.

Technical Theory and Methods. The second approach to creating a strictly professional curriculum emphasized technical theory and training in method. Edward Sheldon, president of Oswego Normal and Training School, developed a philosophy and methodology called *object teaching* based on ideas about the dignity and worth of children and the role of the senses in learning. Under this system, students learned special rules for teaching various subjects and practiced them in the training school.

Sheldon considered the training school the heart of the professional program. Here students could observe model lessons and practice approved methods under close supervision. Recognized as part of the necessary equipment for training teachers, the practice school fostered close ties between pedagogical theory and practice.

Object teaching was replaced by a second general method developed by the Herbartians. Also influenced by European pedagogical theory, the Herbartians emphasized technical competence. They believed that good teaching consisted of 5 steps: preparation, presentation, association, generalization, and application. These ideas, which sound like contemporary models of direct instruction, were popular during the last quarter of the nineteenth century (Woodring, 1975).

Although we tend to associate normal schools with narrow training, this judgment ignores the historic context in which they evolved and their hard-won gains in differentiating professional from liberal arts education. Commenting on their contribution, Clifford and Guthrie (1988) write:

Although, in fact, the nineteenth century normal schools were never the single-minded and essential teacher education centers that their supporters had wished, their disappearance took with it two professional assets: first, the ideal of the autonomous professional school devoted solely to the exalted preparation of teachers and second, a dominating concern with "practical pedagogy." (p. 61)

Normal schools had a clear sense of their mission. They championed the idea of teaching as a noble calling or vocation and fostered a professional esprit de corps. Unlike modern-day schools of education, with their fragmented mission and defensive posture, normal schools knew that their major purpose was to serve the profession by educating practitioners. They "formed" their students more effectively than the large university schools and departments of education that replaced them (Powell, 1980, p. 159)

They also "glorified and supported the ideal of superb craftsmanship" (Borrowman, 1956, p. 19). The normal-school curriculum gave explicit attention to pedagogical training and supervised practice, and practice schools, at least in the stronger normal schools, fostered close ties between theory and practice (Clifford & Guthrie, 1988).

The Liberal Arts Tradition

The older, liberal arts tradition predates any thought of teacher preparation as a special kind of schooling. Linked in the nineteenth century with the preparation of secondary teachers, the liberal arts tradition highlights the unique relationship between liberal education and teaching. According to this tradition, "to be liberally educated and to be prepared to teach are equivalent" (Borrowman, 1965, p. 1). The problem is, of course, that we have no clear idea of what liberal education entails.

The Closed Circle. In the nineteenth century, liberal arts colleges and secondary schools formed a closed circle. The colleges offered a classical education to a select group of students who mostly entered the higher professions and became leaders in the community. A few taught in secondary schools, which were elite, college preparatory institutions (Borrowman, 1956; Church & Sedlak, 1976).

The expansion of secondary education brought a more diverse student population and the need to adapt the high school curriculum to a broader set of purposes. Still, liberal arts colleges kept their distance from school reform and persisted in the view that a liberal arts program was the best preparation for teaching, especially at the secondary level (Borrowman, 1956; Church & Sedlak, 1976; Cremin, 1953).

Liberal Aims for Professionals. The idea that liberal and useful knowledge were incompatible dominated collegiate education for a long time. Harking back to the Greeks, who reserved the liberal arts for free citizens, supporters of the classical curriculum believed that liberal study was only possible when students were not preoccupied with the immediate demands of vocational preparation (Borrowman, 1956).

Although not designed with vocational goals in mind, the traditional college program served both liberal and professional aims. It introduced students to a common body of knowledge embodied in traditional texts. It fostered intellectual habits and skills deemed necessary for continued learning. It sought to develop humane values and a sense of social responsibility. At the same time, the classical curriculum exposed students to the best available thinking about education. Texts encountered in courses on mental and moral philosophy such as Aristotle's *Ethics* and Cicero's *Orations* discussed the meaning of a good life, the role of education in society, the nature of learning and human development, even the methods of teaching.

Challenging the Liberal Ideal. The modern university challenged the classical curriculum. By the end of the nineteenth century, the notion that only certain subjects were inherently liberal came under attack. New disciplines like the natural sciences were developing, and some university leaders thought they should be taught.

The rejection of the classical curriculum inspired various experiments in general education during the early decades of the twentieth century. Designed to balanced the traditional liberal arts ideal of a common course of study with growing specialization, these experiments typically involved a prescribed curriculum in the first 2 years, designed to insure breadth of exposure and understanding, and opportunities for electives in the last 2 years to respond to students' specialized interests. While the liberal arts tradition represents a defense against early specialization, both academic and professional, it became increasingly difficult in the twentieth century to preserve this value in the university and even in the liberal arts college.

The Liberal Legacy. The liberal arts tradition speaks to the education of teachers as individuals and citizens, but it does not prescribe a particular course of study. Each generation must define the nature of that education for its own time. Kimball (1986) argues that the idea of liberal education embraces two contradictory traditions—the tradition of the philosophers with their commitment to reason and the tradition of the orators with their commitment to tradition and community. Historically the liberal arts college endorsed the orators' emphasis on language and texts, while the modern research university allied itself with the philosophers' pursuit of knowledge. Our challenge is to recover elements from both traditions and link them with the theme of democracy (Featherstone, 1988).

The liberal arts tradition also underscores the special ties that link intellectual arts, academic content, and teaching. Some people associate a liberal arts education for teachers with subject-matter preparation, but this interpretation misses the larger message. What makes the relationship between liberal arts education and teacher education unique is the fact that the goods intrinsic to liberal education—humane values, critical thinking, historic perspective, broad knowledge—are central to teaching (Travers & Sacks, 1987).

Finally, the liberal arts tradition construes education itself as a liberal art. "The study of education," writes Silberman (1970), "is the study of almost every question of importance in philosophy, history, and sociology . . . there can be no concept of the good life or the good society apart from a concept of the kind of education needed to sustain it" (p. 384). From this perspective the academic study of education belongs at the center of a liberal arts curriculum.

Professionalizing Education Through Scientific Research and Graduate Preparation

The creation of university schools of education at the turn of the century was part of a larger movement to professionalize various occupations. Like their counterparts in law and medicine, educators sought to place teacher education in the modern research university, hoping that the new location would dignify education as a career, lead to the development of a specialized knowledge base, and support the professional preparation of educational leaders (Clifford & Guthrie, 1988; Powell, 1976).

Graduate Preparation for Careers in Education. Early on, leading university schools of education bypassed the preparation of new teachers, concentrating instead on graduate programs for experienced teachers interested in careers outside the classroom. Previous efforts to transform high school teaching into a respected profession through graduate-level programs proved unrealistic and inappropriate in the face of mass secondary education. The unanticipated growth of secondary schools created a need for administrators, supervisors, and specialists, and schools of education found a new social mission in training experienced, male teachers for these roles (Powell, 1976).

Education faculty recognized that gender played a part in the low esteem in which many people held teaching and teacher education. They sought to overcome the stigma by focusing on career opportunities for ambitious schoolmen. Unfortunately, by increasing the status of those leaving the classroom, they lowered the status of those who remained (Clifford & Guthrie, 1988, p. 119).

The Research Ideal. Although fields like law and theology found the codification of experience a useful strategy for creating a knowledge base, schools of education adopted the approach of the natural sciences. Developing a *science of education* through research became an overriding concern.

The science of education movement embraced experimental and quantitative methods. Psychologist Edward Thorndike of Teacher's College discovered general laws of learning through laboratory experiments and led the development of intelligence and achievement tests. The new fields of administration and supervision eagerly applied the tools of quantitative measurement to problems of school organization and pupil classification.

As the number of education faculty with social science training and research interests increased, the focus shifted from psychology and measurement. A growing confidence in the capacity of social science research to solve broad social problems led to a new wave of research that rarely addressed problems confronting teachers in classrooms.

The emphasis on research and academic specialization had a fragmenting effect on the curriculum. Courses, organized along disciplinary or occupational lines, proliferated. Even courses for practitioners treated students as though they were preparing to do research (Powell, 1976).

Devaluing Experience. In searching for a special expertise that could not be supplied by experience, education faculty cut themselves off from models of good practice. Though early schools of education often drew inspiration from medical education, the idea of the teaching hospital as a setting for experimental treatment, research, and professional training did not transfer. Even the label *laboratory school* applied to some campus or affiliated schools was an empty promise. Educational researchers were not interested in studying classroom problems, supervision of practice teaching carried little status, and developing exemplary training sites required considerable resources (Clifford & Guthrie, 1988, pp. 109–121).

A Mixed Legacy. The historic distinctions between the normal school and the liberal arts traditions did not disappear when teacher education took up residence in the modern university. Rather they increased, as schools of education found themselves caught between pressures from the university and pressures from the field. During their formative period, leading schools of education accommodated to these academic and professional pressures by ignoring initial teacher preparation and concentrating instead on graduate training and research. These policies might help to explain why Borrowman (1956) characterizes the opening decades of the twentieth century as a time when the purposes of teacher education received little serious attention.

Still, the leading schools of education did bequeath a mixed legacy that continues to influence the character of teacher preparation and proposals for its improvement. That legacy includes the precedent of professionalization through graduate training, the ideal of scientific research as the key to an authoritative knowledge base, the devaluing of experience, and the continuing estrangement from teachers in the field and academic colleagues in the university (Judge, 1982).

STRUCTURAL ALTERNATIVES

3 + 2 programs will become the more likely professional pattern among innovative programs by the middle of the 1990s and the 3 + 3 teaching program . . . will evolve from the integrated five-year programs and will probably be rather common within another generation. (Monahan, 1984, p. 43)

The 4 + 1 model creates a relatively inexpensive program of short duration which can be subsidized if necessary when shortages become critical. (Wise, 1986, p. 39)

Our experience suggests that the two-year, post-baccalaureate Teacher Corps model is superior to the one-year MAT program and also to the four-year undergraduate model. (Bush, 1977, p. 6)

These three passages reflect a particular way of thinking about teacher preparation. They describe programs in terms of their general organization, specifying the length of the two main components. They imply that 4-year, undergraduate programs are inadequate and should be replaced by a different model. They give the impression that this kind of general description is a meaningful way to characterize different approaches to teacher preparation.

The passages also reflect the escalation of credentials that has characterized the field. From the days of the normal schools to the present, reformers have sought to improve the status and quality of teaching and teacher preparation by lengthening programs and adding requirements. The tendency to impose structural changes in the hope that substantive changes will follow or to link quality with particular institutional arrangements is all too familiar.

This section examines what is known (or believed) about different institutional arrangements for preparing teachers. Most teachers enter teaching by way of a 4-year, preservice program. The object of much criticism, undergraduate teacher education is the norm against which various structural alternatives have been proposed. One alternative involves extending the undergraduate program to 5 years. A second involves shifting or delaying professional studies until the graduate level. A third involves bypassing professional studies completely in favor of on-the-job training. Designed to address various limitations associated with undergraduate teacher preparation, these alternative structures differ in the extensiveness of the preparation they offer and in the ways they define the boundaries of their responsibility.

Undergraduate Programs

Despite considerable variation among the institutions that offer undergraduate programs, many people assume that such programs, like Gertrude Stein's proverbial rose, are all pretty much the same. Certainly common ways of talking give the impression that there is such a thing as a typical program. Four-year programs are so uniform, notes Kerr (1983), that "a Trollope would surely mistakenly believe that a national curriculum has been imposed" (p. 133).

The impression of sameness in content, organization, and structure is reinforced by surveys of preservice preparation (American Association of Colleges for Teacher Education [AACTE], 1987; Joyce, Yarger, & Howey, 1977). For example, the Preservice Teacher Education Study (Joyce et al., 1977; Yarger & Howey, 1977), which surveyed faculty, students, and heads of education units in a random sample of 238 institutions preparing teachers, found limited variation in programs across the country. Commenting on the findings, Howey (1983) observes: "Initial training or teacher preparation programs across the country tend to appear quite similar at least in terms of the number and general type of experiences they afford students and the structure and framework in which these are organized" (p. 11).

A "Plain Vanilla" Program. When people talk about a traditional preservice program, they have in mind a 4-year program in which the first 2 years are devoted to general education and the last 2 to professional studies. The modern formula of breadth plus depth defined in terms of three or four grand divisions of knowledge (humanities, social sciences, natural sciences, fine arts) and calculated in courses and credits shapes general education requirements for teachers. Secondary education students major in an academic field close to their teaching subject; elementary majors construct a collection of academic minors supposedly related to the elementary school curriculum.

The professional sequence is also differentiated by teaching level. For elementary teachers, it consists of some sort of introduction to education; a course in educational psychology; six or seven methods courses for teaching reading, social studies, arithmetic, science, art, and music; and student teaching. For secondary teachers, it involves a course in adolescent psychology, a general methods course, a subject-specific methods course, and student teaching (Clark & Marker, 1975; Howey, Yarger, & Joyce, 1978). Typically the sequence begins with more theoretical courses, often accompanied by some form of field experience, and culminates in practice teaching (AACTE, 1987).

In terms of time, which many see as a major constraint, elementary education students complete an average of 50 of their 125 hours of credit in the education unit, compared with secondary education students, who average only 26 hours of credit in education (AACTE, 1987, p. 12).

Russell's Paradigm: Spirit or Letter? Where did this familiar structure come from? Cremin (1978) attributes the "present day paradigm of professional training in education" to James Earl Russell, dean of Teachers College (1894–1927), and his colleagues at Teachers College. According to Cremin, this model emerged at the turn of the century alongside different models in other fields as a response to widespread dissatisfaction with professional training at that time (e.g., apprenticeships for lawyers, proprietary schools for doctors, academies and normal schools for teachers).

In Russell's terms, a proper curriculum for teachers should contain four components: general culture, special scholarship, professional knowledge, and technical skill. Cremin (1978) summarizes what Russell had in mind:

By general culture, he meant . . . the kind of preparation that would enable the student to see the relationships among the various fields of knowledge. . . . By special scholarship, he meant not only further academic study but the kind of reflective inquiry that would equip an aspiring teacher to select different sequences of material and adapt them to the needs of different students. . . . By professional knowledge, he implied . . . systematic inquiry into the theory and practice of education in the United States and abroad. . . . And, by technical skill, he implied . . . expert ability in determining what to teach and by what methods, when and to whom. Technical skill would be acquired in an experimental or model school, serving as a laboratory for pedagogical inquiry and a demonstration center for excellent practice. . . . [T]he teachers in the school would be critic-teachers, capable of exemplifying first-class reflective pedagogy at the same time that they oversaw the training of novices. (pp. 10–11)

Although we can discern the basic structure of Russell's curriculum in the familiar components of the typical undergraduate program, it is the letter, not the spirit, of the proposal that stands out. The dominance of the general-education sequence reflects widespread agreement about its importance. In practice, however, general education is more like a supermarket where students make independent choices from a wide array of offerings. Rarely does it provide broad cultural knowledge or deep and flexible subject-matter understanding.

Organizationally and conceptually, general education and professional education are separate and distinct. This makes it difficult to orient the study of academic content around problems of teaching and learning, despite the fact that such an orientation might be as helpful to students who do not intend to teach as to those who do.

In the professional sequence, the balance between what Borrowman (1956) calls the liberal and the technical seems tilted in the direction of the technical. Methods courses dominate, taught not by master teachers but by university professors. Foundational knowledge comes mostly from educational psychology. The development of technical skills is limited to a brief stint of student teaching. In short, the typical undergraduate program seems more like an organizational compromise, the offspring of an unhappy union between the normal school and the liberal arts traditions.

Critics. From their beginnings, undergraduate programs have been the object of intense criticism. Academics (e.g., Bestor, 1953; Conant, 1963; Koerner, 1963) charge that education courses lack rigor; teachers claim they lack practical relevance (Lortie, 1975). Despite the fact that faculty in the arts and sciences provide most of the undergraduate courses that future teachers take, criticism about teacher preparation has often meant criticism of the professional sequence.

Some researchers blame structural features in the undergraduate context for constraining programs and undermining improvement efforts. They point to persistent underfunding, second-class status, the diffuse nature of program responsibility and accountability (Clark, 1986; Clark & Marker, 1975; Kerr, 1983; Peseau, 1982). Although future teachers take most of their undergraduate courses in academic departments, for example, these units are organized with little attention to their teacher education function (Lanier & Little, 1986). Until teacher education is removed from the undergraduate context, the argument goes, it will not be able to overcome these barriers.

Recent studies in higher education have focused on the need to improve the overall quality of undergraduate education (Association of American Colleges, 1985; Boyer, 1987; U.S. Department of Education, 1984). From the standpoint of teacher preparation, the criticism is timely. Still, the prospects for genuine reform are unclear. As Tom (1986) points out, the real task is to rethink general education and subject-matter preparation, not to simply expand requirements in these areas, because "the problem with general education is its quality and coherence, not its length" (p. 31).

Supporters. Not all critics of undergraduate teacher preparation question its viability. Even a harsh critic like Conant (1963), whose study of American teacher education became a best-seller, thought teachers could be adequately prepared for initial employment in 4 years, provided they had a good high school education and an appropriate balance of general education, academic concentration, and professional studies. Conant outlined programs for elementary and secondary teachers that emphasized broad academic studies, minimal professional education, and a combination of methods instruction and practice teaching supervised by a clinical professor, an expert teacher with high university rank.

Contemporary supporters of baccalaureate approaches to teacher preparation agree that the present size of the preservice curriculum is sufficient, given the current status of pedagogical knowledge. They also claim that undergraduate programs allow for the integration of general and professional education, capitalize on the youthful idealism of students, provide a more cost-effective alternative than postbaccalaureate programs, and support a developmental curriculum. Combined with a careful induction program for first-year teachers, undergraduate teacher preparation is a viable option (Hawley, 1986; Tom, 1986).

Extended (5-Year) Programs

In an extended, or 5-year, program, students begin their professional work as undergraduates and continue through a fifth year of professional study and supervised internship. Most extended programs culminate in a master's degree and certification, but some end only in certification. Supporters argue that the 5-year structure offers a more flexible framework and results in better integration of theory and practice. The extended time frame allows the possibility of greater emphasis on academic preparation and fieldwork and has encouraged some rethinking of the professional sequence (Denemark & Nutter, 1984; Scannell, 1987; Weinstein, 1988).

Some extended programs try to improve on conventional undergraduate programs by avoiding the proliferation of methods courses. At the University of Virginia, for example, separate methods courses have been replaced by six-credit blocs in language skills (reading, language arts, children's literature, creative arts) and reasoning skills (mathematics, science, social studies, and creative arts) (Weinstein, 1988). The reduction of subject-specific methods courses tends to reinforce a generic view of teaching.

Another common feature is the emphasis on field experience that begins early, continues throughout the undergraduate years, and culminates in a semester of student teaching or a fifth-year internship. Compared with an undergraduate or a graduate-level program, an extended program offers the possibility of gradual induction into the study and practice of teaching.

Sometimes the promise of the 5-year structure is compromised when a significant number of students transfer in as juniors or fifth-year students or cannot meet the requirements for graduate study (Zeichner, 1988c). Moreover, the graduate status of integrated programs could also be questionable if fifth-year courses do not build on prior knowledge and experience and offer greater intellectual challenge than undergraduate courses (Weinstein, 1988).

Graduate-Level Programs

Since the turn of the century, graduate-level preservice programs have been associated with efforts to professionalize teaching (Wise, 1986). Popular during times of teacher shortage, graduate programs are supposed to attract stronger candidates, offer more rigorous instruction, and carry greater prestige than undergraduate programs. Supporters claim that having students spend 4 years acquiring a liberal arts education before they undertake professional studies means they will be better educated and have a stronger grounding in their teaching subjects. Two types of postbaccalaureate preservice programs can be discerned: an academic model emphasizing academic knowledge and practical experience and a professional model combining professional studies with guided practice.

Academic Model. The MAT program originated in the 1930s when James Conant, president of Harvard University, proposed a new kind of teacher preparation for secondary teachers that would help bridge the gap between education and the arts and sciences (Powell, 1980). The program combined advanced study of a scholarly discipline with a sequence of professional seminars and an internship. The program attracted few students, but it provided the prototype for MAT programs that flourished in the 1950s and 1960s with support from the Ford Foundation (Cogan, 1955; Stone, 1968; Woodring, 1957).

Recruitment of liberal arts students into teaching was an overriding goal. The foundation supported programs at Ivy League institutions and directed resources toward elaborate recruiting schemes. The emphasis on a scholarly curriculum and the creation of a new academic degree were also designed to lure students wary of traditional education courses (Powell, 1980; Woodring, 1957).

Stone (1968) offers the following description of a typical MAT program:

The graduate student arrives at the university in June. The first week of the summer, he (approximately two-thirds of the students were women) enrolls in six to eight units of education courses at the same time assisting in teaching high school classes on campus or at a public school. During the second six weeks of the summer session he takes regular academic courses. Then the MAT candidates are divided, half beginning full-time teaching internships at nearby schools and the other half continuing on campus as full-time graduate students. At the end of the fall semester, the two groups reverse their activities. By the following June, candidates are eligible for the Master of Arts in Teaching degree and have qualified for their teaching credentials. (p. 96)

Although MAT programs succeeded as a recruiting strategy (Coley & Thorpe, 1985; Stone, 1968; Zeichner, 1988a), they did not lead to new conceptualizations of subject-matter knowledge or pedagogical understanding and skill (Clifford & Guthrie, 1988; Powell, 1980). Students took regular academic courses, designed for potential researchers and scholars, and most programs relied on a disciplinary approach to educational foundations. When external funding ran out and the teacher shortage ended, many programs disappeared. Although MAT programs left behind good ideas about financing internships and using summer school as a laboratory for demonstrating pedagogy, they did not advance our understanding of how to institutionalize such practices.

Professional Model. The professionally oriented, preservice, master's degree program represents a contrast with the academically oriented MAT approach. The idea has been promoted by educators who believe that the key to upgrading the quality of teaching lies in professional education, not recruitment.

One such educator was Henry Holmes, Dean of the Harvard Graduate School of Education in the 1920s, who vigorously promoted the EdM as the highest practitioner degree in professional education. Influenced by other professional schools at Harvard, Holmes advocated a 2-year, professional-preparation sequence that would follow the completion of a liberal arts college course. The goal was to train educators rather than craftsmen, professionals who could interpret issues, policies, and decisions in terms of their impact on educational goals (Powell, 1980).

The success of this "radical adventure" depended on the development of a curriculum that would transform novices into educators. Holmes envisioned an intense, prolonged, integrated experience that would fuse knowledge, understanding, skills, and outlook into an active whole (Powell, 1980, p. 159). Holmes sought, but never succeeded in identifying, a set of fundamental principles around which to organize the professional curriculum. After a decade of trying, he sadly concluded that the problem seemed to lie in the state of the field (Powell, 1980).

It is fitting and a bit ironic that a major national effort to reform teaching and teacher education today should carry Holmes's name (Holmes Group, 1986). The Holmes Group, a consortium of education deans and chief academic officers from nearly 100 research universities, is dedicated to the improvement of teacher education and the construction of a genuine profession of teaching. Like its namesake, the Holmes Group advocates the elimination of undergraduate degrees in education in favor of graduate-level programs; however, the Holmes Group's emphasis on scientific knowledge and research and its endorsement of a hierarchy of teacher roles reflect different values from those advocated by Holmes himself (Johnson, 1987).

The group's first report, *Tomorrow's Teachers*, calls for a rethinking of liberal arts education including the design of more coherent majors, graduate-level professional studies, better articulation between pedagogical and clinical studies, creation of exemplary training sites along the lines of a teaching hospital, and establishment of a new career structure in teaching based on different kinds of professional preparation. The report claims that "a vital program of professional studies" can now be designed, because scientific research has produced a body of professional knowledge helpful to teachers. According to the report, the "science of education promised by Dewey, Thorndike and others" is on the horizon. If this were so, a central problem that has plagued teacher education since its inception—the lack of a specialized knowledge base derived from neither the academic disciplines nor experience alone—would be solved.

Both critics and supporters of the Holmes Group point out that such claims are excessive and imply a devaluing of teachers' practical knowledge (Jackson, 1987; Zumwalt, 1987). Holmes himself emphasized practitioner training over scientific research, because he saw how the university's emphasis on research widened the gap between researchers and practitioners and created a hierarchy in the education profession, with researchers at the top and teachers at the bottom (Johnson, 1987).

The Holmes Group's proposals call for the redesign of every aspect of teacher preparation and require collaboration among groups that have historically not worked well together. It is too soon to tell what kinds of structural and conceptual changes will result from this latest effort at promoting graduate-level teacher preparation as part of a comprehensive reform effort (Woolfolk, 1988a, 1988b).

Alternative Certification Programs

Alternative certification programs are designed to increase the supply of teachers in areas of critical need during times of teacher shortage. A form of nontraditional teacher preparation, alternative certification programs provide on-the-job training to college graduates with no previous education background.

Supporters claim that alternative certification programs attract talented people who might otherwise not go into teaching by avoiding certain features of traditional teacher preparation. For example, the traditional undergraduate program requires an early commitment (e.g., junior year), consumes a third of one's college education, and offers little or no financial assistance. Alternative certification programs do not require an early commitment, and they reduce the costs of training by shortening the time frame and paying a salary (Carey, Mittman, & Darling-Hammond, 1988).

Alternative certification programs rely on teacher's undergraduate programs to provide a good general education and an adequate grounding in subject matter. The actual program emphasizes learning by doing and the wisdom of practice. Sponsored by school districts and state education departments, alternative certification programs are oriented toward helping new teachers learn their jobs in particular contexts. The distinction between preservice and inservice teacher education disappears as alternative certification candidates learn to teach while teaching.

The typical program includes some formal instruction and work with an experienced teacher. Offered in the evenings, on weekends, and during the summer, the formal instruction often focuses on practical how-to topics (Adelman, 1986). Support and advice are provided by mentors, usually classroom teachers, who receive a stipend for their work.

For example, the New Jersey Provisional Teacher Program requires 200 hours of formal instruction, 80 during the first 6 weeks of the program and the rest throughout the year. Offered in regional training centers managed by a school of education, the training addresses broad topics mandated by the state: curriculum and instruction, classrooms and schools, student learning and development.

The local school district assumes responsibility for the practical aspects of the training. Each teacher is assigned a three-member support team consisting of a principal, an experienced teacher, and another educator. In the first phase of the clinical component, the provisional teacher works for a month with an experienced teacher, undergoing a gradual introduction to the classroom. Phase Two lasts 10 weeks. During this time, the provisional teacher is supervised at least once a week by one member of the support team, usually the experienced teacher. At the end of Phase Two, the first formative evaluation is performed by the principal, who solicits feedback from other members of the support team. Phase Three includes the remaining 20 weeks of the academic year. During this time the provisional teacher must be supervised at least once a month, and two more evaluations are carried out. A final summative evaluation occurs after the thirtieth week of full-time teaching (Natriello, 1988).

Because alternative certification programs are new, we know relatively little about the kind of preparation they offer and the sort of teaching they promote. Clearly their success hinges on the caliber of the recruits and the quality of the supervision. In terms of recruitment goals, however, they seem to be attracting strong candidates from a variety of labor market pools (Adelman, 1986; Carey et al., 1988; Natriello, Zumwalt, Hansen, & Frisch, 1988).

Many policymakers regard the use of alternative certification programs as a promising strategy for balancing the competing demands of quantity and quality (Carey et al., 1988; Oliver & McKibbin, 1985). In the last few years, 23 states have enacted provisions for alternative certification (Feistritzer, 1986). But critics argue that such programs undermine efforts to professionalize teaching. At a time when the work of teachers is becoming increasingly complex, alternative certification programs allow people to teach with little formal preparation.

Discussion

Reforms in teacher education tend to pit one set of institutional arrangements against another—normal schools versus teachers colleges in the past, undergraduate programs versus graduate or alternative certification programs in the present. In fact, we know relatively little about what goes on inside these different program structures.

The forms of teacher preparation discussed in this section differ in the extensiveness of the preparation they offer, in the way they define the boundaries of their responsibility, and in their location on the preservice–inservice continuum. Four- and 5-year programs encompass both general and professional education; graduate and alternative route programs assume that candidates will come with a solid liberal arts background and adequate grounding in their teaching subjects. The widespread criticism of general education, however, raises questions about the adequacy of teachers' academic preparation, whether or not it falls inside or outside the boundaries of the program's responsibility.

In terms of professional education, all forms must confront the question of what teachers need to know and how they can be helped to acquire and develop that knowledge. Except for alternative certification programs, which take a clear stand on the matter, none of the other program forms is uniquely associated with a particular point of view. All must determine what counts as "knowledge for teaching" and decide how to embody it in a preservice curriculum.

Obviously differences in the time frame and the timing of the professional sequence affect what is possible. Four- and 5-year programs, for example, allow for a spiral curriculum and a staged induction into the study and practice of teaching. Fifth-year programs do not, especially when they are largely taken up with an internship. Four-year programs fit completely within the preservice phase of learning to teach; 5- and fifth-year programs might bridge the preservice–inservice continuum. Because alternative certification programs provide on-the-job training to novice teachers, they could technically be considered a form of inservice. Quality programs require adequate time, but time alone does not guarantee quality. The important question is how that time is spent. Such a question cannot be answered by focusing on the structure alone.

Reformers debate the relative merits of one form over another, but the dominance of a given program structure at a particular historic moment depends as much on compelling social forces as it does on the demonstrated strengths or weaknesses of the form itself. There are several contemporary trends that might influence the popularity and availability of different forms of teacher preparation. These include efforts by state legislators to limit undergraduate credits in education, availability of alternative certification programs, challenge to vocationalism at the undergraduate level by the reform movement in liberal arts education, and increase in the number of at-risk students in schools (Wilkinson, 1988). Ironically, as the work of teaching is becoming more complex and challenging, suggesting the need for more extensive preparation, forces are in operation that permit college graduates to begin teaching with minimal preparation.

Finally, the history of teacher education suggests the importance of institutional norms in shaping the character and quality of preservice programs (Rhoades, 1985). As Clark & Marker (1975) observe, "The critical variance in teacher education programs among institutions is more a function of overall variance by institutional types than a systematic variation attributable to the professional training itself" (p. 58). Although an undergraduate program in a liberal arts college might have the same components as an undergraduate program in a state university, what goes on inside the components can be very different (Howey & Zimpher, 1989; National Center for Research on Teacher Education, 1988a). To some extent, the impression of sameness among 4-year programs could be an artifact of survey research that focuses on surface features and ignores institutional variation.

CONCEPTUAL ORIENTATIONS

This section surveys five conceptual orientations in teacher preparation: (a) academic, (b) practical, (c) technological, (d) personal, and (e) critical/social. An orientation refers to a set of ideas about the goals of teacher preparation and the means for achieving them. Ideally, a conceptual orientation includes a view of teaching and learning and a theory about learning to teach. Such ideas should give direction to the practical activities of teacher preparation such as program planning, course development, instruction, supervision, and evaluation.

Unlike structural alternatives, conceptual orientations are not tied to particular forms of teacher preparation. They can shape a single component or an entire professional sequence and apply to undergraduate or graduate level programs. Nor are the conceptual orientations mutually exclusive. By design or default, they can, and indeed do, exist side-by-side in the same program.

Since the mid-1970s, several frameworks for examining conceptual variations in teacher education have been proposed (Hartnett & Naish, 1980; Joyce, 1975; Kennedy, 1987; Kirk, 1986; Zeichner, 1983; Zimpher & Howey, 1987). A comparison of these typologies reveals considerable overlap in the theoretical perspectives, models, and paradigms discussed. Of the six typologies identified for this review, all include something re-

TABLE 13–2. Conceptual Orientations in Teacher Education

	Critical/ Social	Personal	Technological	Practical	Academic
Joyce (1975)	progressive	personalistic	competency	traditional	academic
Hartnett & Naish (1980)	critical		technological	craft	
Zeichner (1983)	inquiry	personalistic	behavioristic	craft	academic
Kirk (1986)	radicalism		rationalism		
Zimpher & Howey (1987)	critical	personal	technical	clinical	
Kennedy (1987)			applications of skills; applications of principles and theories	deliberate action; critical analysis	

sembling the critical, technological, and practical schools of thought; three acknowledge a personal tradition; and two reveal an academic orientation (see Table 13-2).

The major difference between the present formulation and previous ones is the treatment of the practical and academic orientations. By linking the practical orientation with a more respectful stance toward the wisdom of practice, and the academic orientation with new research on subject matter pedagogy, both categories are extended beyond their traditional associations.

Reflective Teaching as a Generic Professional Disposition. Some readers might wonder about the absence of a reflective orientation. Analyzing various descriptions of reflective teacher education programs (e.g., Beyer, 1984; Cruickshank, 1987; Feiman, 1979; Goodman, 1984; Noordhoof & Kleinfeld, 1987; Posner, 1985; Zeichner & Liston, 1987) and considering recent attempts to distinguish different versions of reflective teacher education (Clift, Houston, & Pugach, in press; Liston & Zeichner, 1988b; Tom, 1985; Valli & Taylor, 1987) led to the conclusion that reflective teacher education is not a distinct programatic emphasis but rather a generic professional disposition. This position is supported by the fact that many of the programs described in this section explicitly endorse the goal of reflection, even though they embody different conceptual orientations.

What differentiates advocates of reflective teaching and teacher education are their substantive goals, which suggest different levels or foci for reflection (Van Manen, 1977). For example, a technological orientation might focus reflection on the most effective or efficient means to achieve particular instructional objectives, whereas a practical orientation might encourage reflection on practical dilemmas or tensions among competing goals in particular situations.

Describing Orientations. Each orientation has a focus or thesis that highlights certain aspects of teaching, learning, and learning to teach; directs attention to a central goal of teacher preparation; and manifests itself in particular practices. Although the orientations do not have uniform and explicit positions on each of these dimensions, it is possible to summarize what supporters have to say about the teacher's role, teaching and learning, knowledge for teaching, and learning to teach.

To illustrate the practical expression of different orientations, programs or components are described. These brief sketches, based mostly on efforts by faculty to explain, document, and evaluate their own work, often reflect the espoused, rather than the enacted, curriculum. Still, the descriptions reveal some of the diversity within each orientation and provide a basis for thinking about the value and limitations of describing teacher preparation in terms of conceptual orientations.

The Academic Orientation

The academic orientation in teacher preparation highlights the fact that teaching is primarily concerned with the transmission of knowledge and the development of understanding. Tra-

ditionally associated with liberal arts education and secondary teaching, the academic orientation emphasizes the teacher's role as intellectual leader, scholar, and subject-matter specialist. Supporters of the academic tradition, even those skeptical of teacher preparation, have always stressed the importance of teachers' academic preparation, but there is a growing appreciation that the kind of subject-matter knowledge teachers need is not likely to be acquired through academic study alone.

The academic orientation embraces various images of good teaching, ranging from didactic instruction to Socratic inquiry. In terms of general goals, proponents talk about inducting students into different ways of knowing and thinking, teaching the "structures of the disciplines," fostering "meaningful" understanding of academic content. Different interpretations of these goals yield different ideas about how particular subjects should be taught.

In the area of mathematics education, for example, there are at least three competing views of effective teaching. One view emphasizes student performance and mastery of mathematical rules and procedures; a second stresses students' grasp of mathematical concepts and processes; and a third focuses on students' personal construction of mathematical ideas. These views imply different ideas about what knowing, learning, and teaching mathematics entail (see, e.g., Ball, 1988a; Good & Grouws, 1977; Lampert, 1986).

Because teacher educators have not been responsible for teachers' subject-matter preparation, they have tended to ignore the question of what teachers need to know about their subjects to teach them effectively and where that knowledge is acquired. In the case of elementary teaching, many assume that the content is easy to learn or already familiar, because prospective teachers have had it in school themselves. In the case of secondary teaching, majoring in one's teaching field as an undergraduate is supposed to provide adequate subject-matter background.

Research on Subject-Matter Pedagogy. Conceptual and empirical research on teachers' subject-matter knowledge challenges these assumptions and provides a beginning knowledge base for the academic orientation. Besides clarifying what it means to know one's subjects for the purposes of teaching them, investigators are exploring how teachers' ideas of and about their subjects interact with other kinds of knowledge to influence teaching and learning in classrooms (see, e.g., Ball, 1988b; Brophy, in press; Leinhardt & Smith, 1985; McDiarmid, Ball, & Anderson, in press; Shulman, 1986, 1987; Stodolsky, 1988).

Subject-matter, or content, knowledge includes knowledge of the facts, concepts, and procedures that define a given field and understanding of how these pieces fit together. It also includes knowledge about knowledge—where it comes from, how it grows, how truth is established (Anderson, 1988; Buchmann, 1984; Schwab, 1978).

Teachers need more than content knowledge. They need a special blend of content and pedagogy that Shulman (1986) has labeled *pedagogical content knowledge.* The unique province of teachers, pedagogical content knowledge includes useful ways to conceptualize and represent commonly taught topics in a given subject, plus an understanding of what makes learning those topics difficult or easy for students of different ages and backgrounds (Wilson, Shulman, & Richert, 1986).

The academic orientation turns the attention of teacher educators back to the "professional treatment of subject matter" theme associated with the normal-school tradition. It challenges the familiar division of labor between arts and science faculty and teacher educators and suggests the need for new conceptualizations and new institutional arrangements.

The MAT programs of the early 1960s, with their emphasis on disciplinary rather than professional knowledge, illustrate one version of the academic orientation. The Academic Learning Program at Michigan State University illustrates another. Designed as a 2-year sequence, the Academic Learning Program represents a serious effort to work out some of the conceptual and organizational problems associated with the academic orientation at the undergraduate level.

The Academic Learning Program. The Academic Learning Program is centrally concerned with helping elementary and secondary teachers learn to teach school subjects in ways that promote conceptual understanding. To prepare for that kind of teaching, the program emphasizes three areas of understanding: (a) broad understanding of the disciplinary roots of school subjects, (b) knowledge about how pupils learn in different subject areas, and (c) knowledge of effective teaching strategies and learning environments that promote conceptual understanding. The faculty also aim to prepare teachers who will "reflect on their own learning and teaching practice" (Rosaen, Lanier, & Roth, 1988).

The program consists of an integrated sequence of core courses and ongoing field experiences. The first two core courses, Learning of School Subjects and Curriculum for Academic Learning, draw on concepts from cognitive psychology, philosophy of science, and curriculum to explore the major themes of the program: knowledge is socially constructed, learning is an active process of making meaning, and good teaching depends on a thorough understanding of disciplinary knowledge and a repertoire of ways to represent key ideas in the teachers' fields (Amarel, 1988).

At the beginning of the program, students are paired with a local teacher (mentor teacher). Each term they visit their mentor teacher's classroom to carry out field assignments and, in the second year, to student teach. The field assignments are designed to help students link concepts taught in university courses with classroom practice. For example, students analyze how knowledge is represented in lessons and curricular materials and interview pupils to discover how they make sense of particular lessons.

Elementary education majors are also required to take a specially designed, three-course mathematics sequence taught by a mathematics professor and a mathematics educator. The first course focuses on number theory, the second on geometry, and the third on statistics. The sequence emphasizes conceptual understanding and actively engages students in making sense of mathematical situations. The course was motivated by the realization that elementary teachers cannot teach for understanding when they themselves have never been taught to understand the conceptual foundations of school mathematics.

Preliminary findings on the impact of the first course suggest that students were beginning to understand for the first time why rules and procedures they had memorized years ago really worked. Still, at least half remained skeptical about whether instructional processes that had enabled them to reach such understanding, such as group problem solving, were realistic in elementary classrooms (Schram, Wilcox, Lanier, & Lappan, 1988).

The Practical Orientation

The practical orientation focuses attention on the elements of craft, technique, and artistry that skillful practitioners reveal in their work. It also recognizes that teachers deal with unique situations and that their work is ambiguous and uncertain. Long associated with apprenticeship systems of training, the practical orientation endorses the primacy of experience as a source of knowledge about teaching and a means of learning to teach.

Advocates of the practical orientation do not necessarily share the *same* image of good teaching. They would, however, agree on its essential character. Both researchers (e.g., Jackson, 1968, 1986; Lortie, 1975) and practitioners (e.g., Kohl, 1976; Lampert, 1985; McDonald, 1986) have described the localized, uncertain, often conflicting nature of teaching, with its concomitant demand for personal artistry, adaptability, and invention.

Lampert's (1985) analysis of her own teaching practice, for example, reveals how these characteristics affect teachers' work. In trying to solve many common pedagogical problems, she argues, teachers have to balance a variety of interests. Often this results in *practical dilemmas*, situations that present equally important but conflicting alternatives. Rather than resolving these dilemmas, teachers "manage" them, inventing and improvising a succession of temporary responses.

Schön's (1983) insights about the nature of professional practice further illuminate ideas about teaching associated with the practical orientation. Schön discusses the kind of artistry or tacit "knowing-in-action" that competent practitioners reveal in their work. Highlighting those situations in which established theory and codified technique do not apply, he describes how thoughtful practitioners engage in on-the-spot reflection and experimentation. In these internal conversations with the situation, they consider different interpretations or courses of action, drawing on a repertoire of images, theories, and actions to construct an appropriate response.

Apprenticeship Learning. From this general view of teaching, it follows that learning to teach comes about through a combination of firsthand experience and interaction with peers and mentors about problematic situations. Through these experiences, the novice is inducted into a community of practitioners and a world of practice.

The apprenticeship is the standard mode of learning associated with the practical orientation. Working with a master over a period of time, the apprentice acquires practical skills and learns what works in real situations. Ever since Dewey (1904) distinguished the *laboratory* view of practice work, with its emphasis on intellectual methods, from the *apprenticeship* view, with its focus on technical proficiency, the apprenticeship has received bad press in teacher education circles. Apprenticeships, say the critics, encourage imitation rather than understanding and foster maintenance of existing standards and practices (Arnstine, 1975; J. Wilson, 1975). Certainly research on student teaching confirms these outcomes.

The apprenticeship model does encourage novices to learn the practices of the master, but it does not necessarily preclude consideration of underlying principles or the development of conceptual understanding (Ball, 1987; Tom, 1984). Collins, Brown, & Newman (in press) have coined the term *cognitive apprenticeship* to describe experiential learning situations in which teachers think aloud so that learners can not only observe their actions but also "see" how their teachers think through particular problems or tasks.

Using the architectural design studio as his prototype, Schön (1987) proposes the idea of a *reflective practicum* as an important element in professional education. In contrast with an apprenticeship, a practicum provides a simplified, or protected, encounter with the world of practice.

In a practicum situation, students would engage in activities that simulate or simplify practice or they would take on real-world projects under the guidance of a senior practitioner. To support the goals associated with the practical orientation, the focus would have to be on helping prospective teachers think through situations in which there are no right answers. By trying out multiple interpretations and considering alternative courses of action, prospective teachers would be helped to recognize and even accept the endemic uncertainties of teaching (Floden & Clark, 1988).

The Teachers for Rural Alaska program (TRA), located at the University of Alaska in Fairbanks, prepares teachers to work in situations of extreme ambiguity and uncertainty. Perhaps this explains why the program directors were drawn to ideas about teaching and learning to teach that are associated with the practical orientation.

The Teachers for Rural Alaska Program. The TRA program prepares liberal arts graduates to work in rural Alaskan high schools. In these small, isolated communities, teachers are expected to teach many subjects and grade levels and assist communities faced with complicated political, social, and economic challenges.

Initially attracted to the rhetoric of reflective inquiry, the program developers found the concept too general to provide direction to staff and students.

We wanted to stress the problematic nature of practice and to orient our students to the complexities of the kinds of situations they could encounter. As we came to see it, however, the term "reflective inquiry" doesn't help much in talking about *what* it is to be reflected upon, *how* that reflection is to occur, and to *what ends* it is directed. (Noordhoff & Kleinfeld, 1987, p. 6)

Instead of reflective teaching, they adopted the metaphor of teaching as a design activity.

To give students practice in deliberating about uncertain situations, the staff developed three major case studies based on the experiences of rural Alaskan teachers. Each case study describes a problem situation familiar to rural teachers in cross-cultural and multicultural communities: native students' feelings about being "dumb" in a class with middle-class Caucasian students, a rural teacher's experiences in a community where alcoholism is rampant, a teacher's being harassed by a village and told to leave. Students analyze the cases from different vantage points, imagining a range of possible actions and their consequences.

Students also complete a series of design projects during the professional seminar, which meets daily on campus during the fall term. For example, students are given information about a particular context and culture (e.g., a village economy based on salmon fishing, parental ambivalence about sending children to college) and descriptions of individual students (e.g., seven Yupik Eskimo children of varying ages). Their job is to design a biology curriculum, formulating goals, exploring curricular materials, developing an instructional plan, and justifying it on the basis of knowledge about students, subject, and setting.

The practical wisdom of expert teachers has a prominent place in the TRA program. During the planning summer, five master teachers, selected by their colleagues, help the project staff identify problems and dilemmas that teachers in rural settings face. Linked to the teaching of particular subjects, these problems provide the framework for the professional seminar that students take during the fall term. Master teachers also serve as mentors during a 6-week, afternoon apprenticeship and a semester of student teaching.

The TRA program seems oriented to fostering the capacity for what Kennedy (1987) calls *deliberate action*, a form of professional expertise that enables teachers to choose among alternative goals that are sought in a given situation. Like critical analysis, deliberate action recognizes multiple ways of interpreting situations, but it goes beyond analysis to action.

The Technological Orientation

The technological orientation focuses attention on the knowledge and skills of teaching. The primary goal is to prepare teachers who can carry out the tasks of teaching with proficiency. Learning to teach involves the acquisition of principles and practices derived from the scientific study of teaching. Competence is defined in terms of performance.

The technological orientation goes hand-in-hand with the search for a scientific basis of teaching. Proponents believe that the future of teaching as a profession rests on improvements that will come from the accumulation and application of scientific knowledge (Berliner, 1985; Gage, 1978; Lortie, 1975).

The productive research on teaching effectiveness done in the 1980s has yielded a technology that can be taught to prospective teachers. It consists of generic teacher behaviors and strategies associated with student achievement. (For a recent summary of the research, see Brophy & Good, 1986). Based on studies of mathematics and reading instruction in conventional classrooms, the findings cohere around a direct instructional model of teaching.

How should this research-based technology be used by teacher educators? Some proponents regard effective teaching behaviors as content for teacher training and criteria for the assessment of teaching competence. Others believe that findings from teacher-effectiveness research should be taught as principles and procedures to be used by teachers in making decisions and solving problems. The former suggests the metaphor of teacher as technician; the latter, teacher as decision maker. In both cases, professional knowledge is basically procedural knowledge: ways to achieve specified goals and solve familiar problems.

Training Model. The technological orientation is primarily associated with a training model of learning to teach. Joyce and Showers (1980, 1984) outline the components of effective teacher training. *First*, teachers should learn about the theory or rationale behind a given strategy or procedure. *Second*, they should see a demonstration. *Third*, teachers need a chance to practice and get feedback on their performance. Ideally this should initially take place in a relatively safe environment where they can concentrate on mastering skills and concepts without having to deal with all the complexities that arise in real classrooms. *Finally*, teachers need help transfering the new behaviors to the classroom from a coach who can detect errors in application and point out correct responses.

Teacher as Decision Maker. The rational, decision-making version of the technological orientation is captured by a description of an educational psychology course in an undergraduate preservice program. The description comes from an exploratory study of what was taught and learned in two contrasting preservice programs (Feiman-Nemser, 1987; Feiman-Nemser & Buchmann, 1989).

The course focused on instructional decision making from a systems perspective. Students received an instructional packet containing an overview of the course, a list of terminal behaviors, and a description of the projects they would complete to demonstrate their attainment of the course objectives.

The course was organized around five topics: goals and objectives, task analysis, evaluation, information, and practice. The instructor presented a format for daily lessons: introduction, instruction, practice and feedback, daily evaluation, and application. Students were told that, if they planned systematically and their plans reflected empirically validated principles of motivation and instruction, they could be reasonably certain that their pupils would learn what they were trying to teach.

The course exemplifies the training-model approach. The instructor explained and demonstrated the elements in lesson planning. Students had an opportunity to practice each step separately and then to put them together in designing an instructional unit. Students were also expected to transfer their newly acquired planning skills to the field. All term they developed and taught mini lessons. Field instructors reinforced the systematic approach to planning by using the lesson plan framework as a basis of classroom observation and feedback.

Competency-Based Teacher Preparation. No discussion of the technological orientation is complete without a reference to competency-based teacher education. The reform movement of the late 1960s and 1970s, competency-based teacher education requires that teacher educators state explicitly the competencies students will acquire in their program and the criteria by which they will be assessed. Typically, a competency-based program consists of instructional modules, sets of learning activities designed to help students achieve specific objectives (Elam, 1971; Houston, 1974; Houston & Howsam, 1972). Students' rates of progress through the program are determined by demonstrated competence rather than course completion.

In 1969 the U.S. Office of Education funded the design of nine comprehensive, competency-based, elementary, preservice models (Burdin & Lanzillotti, 1969). Although the project stimulated considerable talk about CBTE, lack of funding and an inadequate research base kept the idea from becoming much of a reality.

Currently, competency-based teacher preparation is getting a boost from state legislatures, who have mandated performance assessments of beginning teachers on the basis of generic teaching principles. To help graduates meet the teaching competencies identified by the state, some universities have revised their preservice programs.

PROTEACH, a five-year preservice program at the University of Florida at Gainesville, provides an interesting case in point. Adopted in 1983 in response to the expanding knowledge base in teaching and state mandated assessments of beginning teachers, PROTEACH aims to prepare professional teachers who make instructional decisions based on research and clinical insights (Smith, 1984). Widely publicized for its attention to teacher-effectiveness research, the PROTEACH program actually embraces multiple commitments. Thus, it illustrates some of the problems of trying to classify a program in terms of a single orientation.

Statewide use of the Florida Performance Measurement System (FPMS) has influenced the PROTEACH program. Based on generic research on teaching, the FPMS is organized into six domains: (a) instructional planning, (b) management of student conduct, (c) instructional organization, (d) presentation of subject matter, (e) communication, and (f) testing. Each domain consists of specific behaviors grouped into sets of competencies. Overall, the six domains include 128 behaviors organized into 28 competency categories. The faculty are committed to helping students understand and become proficient in the performance domains of the FPMS.

At the same time, faculty want students to view the FPMS as only one of many sources that professional teachers draw on in making instructional decisions and to use it intelligently, not mechanically (Zeichner, 1988c). A core group of faculty have adopted the term *reflective teaching* to express the stance they are trying to promote in the PROTEACH program. They have also created program components that stress the role of teachers as producers, not simply consumers, of classroom research (Ross & Kyle, 1987).

For purer examples of competency-based programs, see case studies of programs at the University of Toledo (Howey & Zimpher, 1989) and the University of Houston (Ginsburg, 1988).

The Personal Orientation

The personal orientation places the teacher–learner at the center of the educational process. Learning to teach is construed as a process of learning to understand, develop, and use oneself effectively. The teacher's own personal development is a central part of teacher preparation.

"A good teacher," writes Combs (1965), "is first and foremost a person, a unique personality" striving for self-fulfillment (p. 6). Students also share this basic drive toward self-adequacy and enhancement. It follows that teaching is less a matter of prescribing and molding and more a matter of encouraging and assisting. The teacher is a facilitator who creates conditions conducive to learning. To do this, teachers must know their students as individuals. With this knowledge they can select materials or set learning tasks that respond to individual interests, needs, and abilities.

Advocates of the personal orientation favor classrooms in which learning derives from students' interests and takes the form of active, self-directed exploration. They emphasize concepts like readiness and personal meaning and appreciate the interconnections of thinking and feeling. Just as teachers must come to know students as individuals, so students are allowed to know each of their teachers as a person (Combs, 1982).

The general description of teaching and learning set forth here also applies to learning to teach, which advocates of the personal orientation describe as a process of becoming or development. Teacher educators in preservice preparation attach various meanings to these phrases. For some, becoming a teacher means making a psychological shift from the partly dependent role of student to the fully responsible role of teacher (Biber & Winsor, 1967), For others, it means developing a personal psychology and finding one's own best ways of teaching (Combs, 1965; Combs, Blume, Newman, & Wass, 1974). Still others focus on helping prospective teachers make the transition from early concerns about self-adequacy to more mature concerns about pupils and their learning (Fuller & Bown, 1975).

Different versions of the personal orientation draw their rationale and guiding principles from developmental, humanistic, and perceptual psychology. From these sources, proponents derive content for the preservice curriculum, such as dynamic concepts of learning and development and theories of human behavior and potential. They also draw ideas about the kinds of enabling conditions that promote meaningful learning on the part of prospective teachers.

Most proponents talk about creating a supportive atmosphere in which preservice students feel safe to take risks and discover personal meaning. They advocate field experiences, in which students can learn what they need to know and try their wings in encounters with real professional problems. They stress the importance of personal interactions with teacher educators, who function as counselors or facilitators, helping prospective teachers explore problems, events, themselves, and others (e.g., Combs, 1978; Fuller & Bown, 1975).

One dilemma facing advocates of the personal orientation is how to balance openness to individual teaching styles with commitment to particular values. Can a personally oriented preservice program promote a view of good teaching and, at the same time, encourage students to develop their own theories and discover methods that work for them? The programs described next illustrate two resolutions to this question.

Personalized Teacher Education. The Personalized Teacher Education Program (PTEP) at the University of Texas was an effort to make teacher preparation more relevant by gearing the curriculum to the developmental concerns of preservice students. The program grew out of research on teacher concerns conducted by Frances Fuller and her associates at the Research and Development Center for Teacher Education.

Fuller (1969) discovered not only that prospective teachers have common concerns, but also that their concerns emerge in a fairly regular sequence. The sequence goes from early concerns about self to later concerns about pupils and their learning. If teacher educators want to engage the interests of their preservice students, Fuller concludes, they should start with content related to concerns about the self as teacher, such as how to control a class, and hold off on content related to concerns about educational goals, instructional design, and pupil evaluation.

The PTEP was designed to help undergraduate students resolve concerns about themselves as teachers, so they could move toward concerns about pupils. To arouse teaching concerns early in the program, for example, students were required to plan and teach a 15-minute lesson to a real class. This early teaching experience, which was videotaped, did not allay concerns about self-adequacy, but it certainly elicited teaching-related concerns (Newlove, 1969). Although the program succeeded in moving students from concerns about self to concerns about teaching, few undergraduates made the transition to concerns about pupils that Fuller regarded as the most difficult, yet most important, transition teachers ever make (Fuller, 1970).

The PTEP seems to give teacher educators a clear message about where they should put their energies: in helping prospective teachers make a transition from concerns about self to concerns about students. In fact, a descriptive model of teacher concerns can never tell teacher educators what to do unless they first endorse the implicit goal of teacher development (Feiman-Nemser & Floden, 1981).

The Advisement Program at Bank Street College. Whereas the PTEP seems to regard teacher development as an end in itself, the advisement program at Bank Street College in New York views it as a vehicle for promoting a particular way of working with children. Since its founding in 1931, Bank Street College has been dedicated to "a clear system of values about education" and "a model of teaching excellence deemed essential to that system of values" (Biber & Winsor, 1967, pp. 115–117). The advisement program was conceived as an analogue to that system of values and model of teaching. It allows students to experience on an adult level the kinds of learning opportunities and personal relationships that they, in turn, will share with their pupils (Shapiro, 1988).

Shapiro (1988) describes the advisement program as "the intersection of learning in coursework, in fieldwork, in informal exchange with peers, and in the development of a personal style of teaching" (p. 10). Advisors help students integrate the different parts of the program and reflect on what they are learning and how they are changing (p. 29).

Advisors work with students in three settings: field placements, weekly group conferences, and individual sessions. Advisors help students function in the field and relate experiences there with what they are learning in courses. As students try on the role of teacher, they discover questions and problems to raise in conference groups and individual sessions. The conference group is an occasion for learning from and with peers, a forum for group problem solving and reflection. The content comes from the students, but the advisor guides the discussion and summarizes the salient points. Personal material is typically discussed in individual sessions in which advisors function like counselors. Advisors recognize that the quality of their relationship with students is the key. Shapiro (1988) characterizes that relationship as "personal but not intimate, supportive but not maternal, non-didactic but not laissez-faire. It is, at base, a relationship of teacher and student, based on mutual trust and respect" (p. 28).

Advisors must balance their commitment to a particular view of good teaching with their wish to help students find their own teaching styles. Shapiro (1988) quotes an advisor who tells her students, "I don't want you to become a 'Bank Street teacher' but the best teacher you can be" (p. 12). Still, this openness to individual styles is bounded by the larger ethos of the institution.

The Critical/Social Orientation

The critical orientation in teacher preparation combines a progressive social vision with a radical critique of schooling. On the one hand, there is an optimistic faith in the power of education to help shape a new social order; on the other, a sobering realization that schools have been instrumental in preserving social inequities. Just as the teacher plays an important role in social reform, so teacher education is part of a larger strategy to create a more just and democratic society.

The teacher is both an educator and a political activist. In the classroom, the teacher creates a learning community that promotes democratic values and practices through group problem solving. In the school, the teacher participates in curriculum development and policy-making. In the community, the teacher works to improve school conditions and educational opportunities through community involvement and political activity. Ginsburg (1988) offers the following rationale:

As educators of teachers, we must . . . operate as activists in broader struggles for social transformation . . . because these broader structural and ideological struggles are . . . dialectically related to the struggles within teacher education, because we need to be models for the people we seek to educate as teachers; and because becoming involved

in such political activity will help us to establish relations with others whose lives are similiarly enabled by these broader structures. (p. 214)

Contemporary proponents of the critical orientation in teacher preparation speak about "progressive education," "critical pedagogy," "emancipatory teaching," and "student empowerment," but they rarely translate these terms into concrete classroom practices. There is a general consensus about the importance of promoting democratic values, helping students find their voice and develop their identity, linking schooling with students' experiences in the larger community. Still, it is easier to visualize the kind of teaching that supporters reject than the kind of teaching they seek to promote through teacher preparation. The discourse about critically oriented teacher preparation is often quite theoretical, and ways to achieve particular purposes have not been clearly articulated.

There are discussions of the sorts of issues and topics that a critically oriented preservice curriculum should address and examples of the kinds of teacher education practices that promote critical analysis and action. Giroux and McLaren (1986) recommend the critical study of such themes as language, history, culture, and power. They also stress the value of direct experience in helping teachers understand the relationships and forces that influence their pupils. For example, they suggest that student teachers compile oral histories of the communities in which they teach or work and analyze the roles of different community agencies. Such experiences would help them develop curricula around the traditions, histories, and forms of knowledge that are often ignored within the dominant school culture.

The literature also contains descriptions of how individual methods courses, curriculum courses, and field experiences have been designed to promote critical analysis and critical pedagogy (e.g., Goodman, 1986a, 1986b; Zeichner & Liston, 1987). From such work, Zeichner (1987) identified five instructional strategies used by teacher educators associated with the critical tradition: ethnographic studies, journal writing, emancipatory supervision, action research, and curriculum analysis and development. Of course, it is not the strategies themselves, but the purposes to which they are put, that justify the link with the critical orientation.

The description of New College, an unorthodox experiment in teacher preparation mounted at Teachers College, Columbia University, between 1932 and 1936 illustrates the continuity of the critical orientation with earlier progressive reforms. The description of the student teaching program at the University of Wisconsin illustrates the more analytic practices associated with contemporary expressions of the critical orientation.

The New College Experiment. The New College program attempted to integrate general education, professional education, and laboratory experiences. The entire program was shaped around a definition of the teacher as a social leader. The faculty believed that "teachers should view their work against the background of world events and conditions and regard community involvement and leadership as a professional responsibility" (New College, 1936, pp. 29–30).

In their first 2 years, New College students attended a central seminar organized around broad problem areas, supplemented by divisional seminars in philosophy, natural sciences, the arts, and human relationships. New York City served as a natural laboratory for developing general cultural understandings.

In their last 2 years, the emphasis shifted from general cultural background to professional preparation. The central seminar took up educational implications of persistent social problems, and divisional seminars focused on particular teaching specializations. New College students were also required to spend time in the New College Community, a student-run farm in North Carolina, and to study and travel abroad for at least a summer.

Student teaching provided contacts with many phases of the teacher's work. In addition to opportunities for curriculum development, child study, and instructional planning, it provided student teachers with a chance to survey local resources and needs and take part in various community activities.

The faculty continually tried to encourage political activity among the students. For example, in 1937 the director announced that two scholarships would be awarded to students "who go furthest beyond 'academic neutrality' in active participation in life outside the walls of the university" (Cremin, Shannon, & Townsend, 1954, p. 226).

Student Teaching at the University of Wisconsin. The activist stance of the New College program, with its varied opportunities for direct experience, contrasts with the analytic stance of the University of Wisconsin student-teaching program. Designed by teacher educators closely identified with the critical orientation, student teaching at Wisconsin is designed to foster critical reflection and pedagogy.

Earlier statements of the program's rationale stressed the need for teachers to reflect on the moral and political implications of school structures and pedagogical practices and to participate in curriculum development and educational policy-making (e.g., Zeichner, 1981–1982); recent refinements call for teachers to add the role of political activist outside the classroom to their primary role as educators. The underlying metaphor of the program is *liberation* (Liston & Zeichner, 1988a; Zeichner & Liston, 1987).

The curriculum for the student-teaching semester has five elements. The first is a teaching component that combines the gradual assumption of classroom responsibilities with curriculum development. The second is an inquiry component that focuses attention on the culture of schools and classrooms and their relationship to the larger political milieu. Students are required to carry out some investigation related to their own practices or the settings in which they work. For example, students have analyzed the assumptions in various curricular materials, studied pupils' perceptions of school, and experimented with different grouping strategies and their effects on pupil involvement. The third component, a weekly seminar, is designed to help students "broaden their perspectives on teaching, consider the rationale underlying alternative possibilities for classrooms and pedagogy, and assess their own developing perspectives toward teaching" (Zeichner & Liston, 1987, p. 32). Journals, the fourth component, encourage student teachers to reflect systematically on their own development and their actions in classrooms and in the school. Finally,

supervisory conferences emphasize analysis of classroom instruction, focusing on student teachers' intentions and beliefs, the social context of teaching, the content of instruction, and the hidden curriculum.

Studies of the student-teaching component at Wisconsin suggest partial implementation of goals (Zeichner, Mahlios, & Gomez, 1988) but limited impact on student teachers' perspectives (Tabachnick & Zeichner, 1985; Zeichner & Grant, 1981).

Discussion

A plurality of orientations and approaches exists because people hold different expectations for schools and teachers and because, in any complex human endeavor, there are always more goals to strive for than one can achieve at the same time. Teacher educators cannot avoid making choices about what to concentrate on. Thus deliberation about worthwhile goals and appropriate means must be an ongoing activity in the teacher education community.

These deliberations would be aided by a conceptual framework that identifies central tasks of teacher preparation, those core activities that logically and practically belong to the preservice phase of learning to teach. Examples of central tasks include helping teachers to examine their preconceptions about teaching and learning; to learn about transforming subject-matter knowledge for purposes of teaching; and to develop a commitment to teach all children. Such a framework could provide guidance to teacher educators in program development and evaluation by identifying issues or tasks that programs should address, whatever their orientation. In a field like teacher education, which has been shaped by external factors more than by a clear sense of purpose, this kind of conceptual clarity is essential.

Some of the orientations discussed in this section focus on essential tasks of teacher preparation, but collectively they do not represent a set of equally valid alternatives from which to choose. Rather, they constitute a source of ideas and practices to draw on in deliberating about how to prepare teachers in a particular context. Each orientation highlights different issues that must be considered, but none offers a fully developed framework to guide program development.

The personal orientation reminds us that learning to teach is a transformative process, not just a matter of acquiring new knowledge and skills. Because prospective teachers are no strangers to classrooms, resocialization is necessary, especially if new ways of teaching are to be fostered.

The critical orientation highlights the teacher's obligations to students and society, challenging teacher educators to help novices learn to align school practices with democratic principles of justice and equality. The critical orientation also underscores the need to develop the habit of questioning taken-for-granted assumptions about teaching, learning, knowledge, schooling, and so on.

The technological and practical orientations represent different ideas about the nature and sources of knowledge about teaching and how it can be acquired and developed. The former stresses scientific knowledge and systematic training; the latter, the wisdom of practice and learning from experience.

Clearly both have a contribution to make to the content and processes of teacher preparation.

Finally, the academic orientation focuses attention on the distinctive work of teaching. What distinguishes teaching from other forms of human service is its concern with helping students learn worthwhile things they could not pick up on their own. It follows that preparing people to teach means helping them develop ideas and dispositions related to this goal (Buchmann, 1984; Feiman-Nemser & Buchmann, 1989; J. Wilson, 1975).

The academic orientation has been a missing paradigm in teacher education. Historically viewed as someone else's responsibility, preparing teachers to teach academic content has rarely been a central concern of teacher educators. The current reform movement, with its concern for improving the academic quality of teaching, and the new research emphasis on the role of subject-matter knowledge in teaching provide the impetus to give serious attention to this neglected aspect of teacher preparation.

STUDYING DIFFERENT APPROACHES AND ALTERNATIVES

Many contemporary proposals for reforming teacher preparation echo earlier efforts. Still, the lack of systematic data makes it difficult to learn from past experience. Existing data do not permit clear portraits of the explicit preservice curriculum in different settings (Lanier & Little, 1986). Nor do they help us understand the relative effects of selection, compared with socialization, or the relationship between opportunities to learn and learning outcomes in different types of preservice programs.

In a recent review of research on graduate-level preservice programs since the early 1950s, for example, Zeichner (1988a) laments the paltry findings despite millions of dollars spent on program development. Although various studies do show that the quality of teaching displayed by MAT graduates was superior or comparable to that of teachers from undergraduate programs, there is no way of telling whether this outcome reflected the kinds of students recruited or the sort of preparation offered.

To consider the relative strengths and limitations of alternative approaches to teacher preparation, we need at least three kinds of research: program studies that examine what different programs are like as educational interventions, implementation studies that examine the factors promoting the success or failure of various programmatic reforms, and impact studies that explore the effects of particular program components and learning opportunities on teachers' ideas and practices.

Research-in-Progress

Recently several large-scale investigations have been undertaken that seek to address this need. Designed to generate information about different approaches to teacher preparation in different types of institutions, these studies promise to yield a body of information and insight that can inform the work of policymakers and practitioners. Although they differ in their scope and purpose, research design, and methodology, the projects all use teacher education programs as a major unit of analysis.

Research About Teacher Education (RATE). The Research About Teacher Education project is on ongoing data collection project of the American Association of Colleges for Teacher Education. Launched in 1985, the project is designed to generate a national data base about the substance of teacher education programs and the perceptions of faculty and students. Each year 90 programs, stratified according to the highest degree offered, are sampled from the membership of 713. One person at each site fills out an institutional questionnaire, and 10 faculty and students complete a faculty or student survey that focuses on a specific program component (e.g., foundations, secondary methods).

The RATE project can be helpful in documenting program trends within and across different types of institutions. Two reports (AACTE, 1987, 1988) provide a variety of facts and figures concerning the preparation of teachers. This kind of research is less effective in exploring issues related to program quality. For example, the 1987 report tells us that both faculty and students consider secondary education methods courses to be "as rigorous as" or "more rigorous than" comparable courses in English and history, but "less rigorous than" science and mathematics courses. Because we know nothing about the criteria people used to reach this judgment or the courses they had in mind, this kind of finding does not illuminate the quality of teacher education (Zeichner, 1988b).

Case Studies of Elementary Teacher Preparation. In conjunction with the first RATE survey, Howey and Zimpher conducted field studies of six elementary education programs. Their goal was to provide in-depth, personal accounts of initial teacher preparation as it is carried out in different institutions of higher education. Six research sites in the Midwest were chosen because they represent major types of institutions preparing teachers (research universities, comprehensive state universities, liberal arts colleges) and because their programs were nominated as distinctive and/or exemplary. Besides generating descriptions of the lived experience of teacher education in particular settings, researchers sought conditions and practices worthy of emulation. Influenced by the school-effectiveness literature that identifies schoolwide characteristics associated with a particular view of effective schools, they hypothesized that similar dimensions of program quality might exist for preservice programs.

During brief visits to the sites, researchers talked with program participants, observed various activities, and collected documents. From these data they have produced a set of case studies describing how teacher preparation is carried out in quite different settings (Howey & Zimpher, 1989). They have also generated a list of conditions and practices that appear to contribute to coherent or effective preservice programs. Examples include a clear conception of teaching/schooling, use of student cohorts, high expectations, curriculum articulation, and adequate life space.

The portraits help fill a void in the descriptive literature, and the conceptualization of effective program features provides one framework for thinking about potentially desirable practices. It would be a mistake, however, to assume that the features of effective programs were derived from the data itself. Rather they reflect the researchers' views about what makes for a coherent teacher education program. Like any other normative concept, *coherence* must be defined and justified as a desirable quality in a preservice program.

Studying the Education of Educators (SEE). Values provide an explicit starting point for the SEE project, which is looking at the preparation of teachers (and principals) in 29 institutions of higher education. Researchers are seeking evidence about the extent to which current practices fit the project's working assumptions about the ideal features of a good teacher education program.

Starting from an explicit vision of what teaching and schooling should be like, researchers formulated a set of postulates regarding a well-conducted teacher education program. For example, one postulate says: "Teacher preparation programs will admit the number of candidates for whom they can guarantee exposure to and participation in at least six different modes of exemplary teaching actually practiced in available school settings" (Goodlad, 1988, p. 110). Such a criterion seeks to remedy casual selection of sites for student teaching and encourage colleges and universities to collaborate with school districts in creating exemplary settings. Differences between what the postulate recommends and what researchers find will determine the project's recommendations regarding student teaching.

A sample of 29 institutions, located in 8 states, was chosen to maximize the diversity of educational programs across a range of institutional types (Sirotnik, 1988). Drawing on multiple sources of data gathered over three 2-day site visits during the 1987–1988 academic year, researchers produced information-based portraits of each institution. They described trends across institutions or trends moderated by such institutional factors as size, history, and student population.

As John Goodlad (1988), director of the study, points out, the research is not designed to address such matters as "whether the education of educators should be a graduate or undergraduate enterprise, whether all teachers should have masters degrees . . . or similar matters that crop up frequently in the current rhetoric of reform" (p. 111). Rather, the project is interested in broader issues of institutional commitment, faculty support, program philosophy, and so on. By studying a set of representative programs within an explicit normative framework, researchers hope to generate ideas about improving teacher preparation that go beyond piecemeal programatic changes.

Teacher Education and Learning to Teach (TELT). The National Center for Research on Teacher Education, located at Michigan State University, is studying the role of teacher education in teacher learning (National Center for Research on Teacher Education, 1988b). The center's work combines case studies of different teacher education programs with longitudinal studies of teachers' learning. The two-part design allows the center to describe the purpose and character of different programs, to determine whether and how teachers' ideas and practices change as they participate in programs and move into teaching, and to explore the relationship between opportunities to learn and learning outcomes.

Eleven programs representing important ideas in contemporary teacher education and different types of learning opportunities serve as settings for the research. The sample includes preservice, induction, inservice, and alternative-route programs, so that the center can explore questions about teachers' learning at different stages of their careers.

A distinguishing feature of the work is the focus on teacher learning in relation to two subject areas, mathematics and writing. Within each site, the center is following a sample of teachers over time, tracking changes in knowledge, skills, and dispositions as teachers move through teacher education and into independent teaching (Ball & McDiarmid, 1988). The overall goal of this project is to uncover the reasoning behind different ways of helping teachers learn to teach and to describe their impact on teachers' learning.

Informing Policy and Practice. Collectively these projects will provide the field with a rich body of information about different approaches and alternatives to teacher preparation. They will also contribute various conceptual frameworks for thinking about issues of program quality and teacher learning. A major strength of this work-in-progress is the effort to supplement what people say by observing what they do. In at least three of the projects, researchers are collecting observational data in classes and field experiences. Although the intensity of the effort varies across the projects, there is a clear recognition that claims about the character and quality of programs must ultimately be grounded in observations of teacher education practices, not simply in self-reports.

The projects also reflect appreciation for the fact that programs are nested within larger institutional, historical, geographical, and policy contexts. By reporting insights and information in the form of program case studies, researchers will be telling stories about how and why programs have taken on their particular shape and character. This kind of information is essential in understanding the impact of various policy initiatives designed to improve teacher education.

Finally, at least one project is exploring the issue of program effects. Many people believe that teacher education is a weak intervention incapable of overcoming the powerful influence of teachers' own personal schooling or the impact of experience on the job. In addition, various claims have been made about the strengths and limitations of different program structures. By generating systematic data about the impact of different kinds of programs on teachers' ideas and practices, the National Center for Research on Teacher Education will enable the field to test these and other claims against some real evidence.

The research will inform and enrich the debate about how teachers should be prepared for their work. It will also provide a data base and a set of frameworks for thinking about different approaches and alternatives to teacher preparation. As a result, when the Association of Teacher Educators undertakes its next *Handbook of Research on Teacher Education*, there should be a more robust body of research to draw on in discussing structural and conceptual alternatives in teacher preparation.

References

Adelman, N. (1986). *An exploratory study of teacher alternative certification and retraining programs.* (Data Analysis Support Center Contract No. 300-85-0103). Washington, DC: Policy Studies Associates.

Amarel, M. (1988). *Site report: Academic Learning Program.* Michigan State University, National Center for Research on Teacher Education, East Lansing. Unpublished manuscript.

American Association of Colleges for Teacher Education. (1987). *Teaching teachers: Facts and figures.* Washington, DC: Author.

American Association of Colleges for Teacher Education. (1988). *Teaching teachers: Facts and figures.* Washington, DC: Author.

Anderson, C. (1988). The role of education in the academic disciplines in teacher education. In A. Woolfolk (Ed.), *Research perspectives on the graduate preparation of teachers* (pp. 88–107). Englewood Cliffs, NJ: Prentice-Hall.

Arnstine, D. (1975). Apprenticeship as the miseducation of teachers. *Philosophy of Education 1975: Proceedings of the 31st Annual Meeting of the Philosophy of Education Society* (pp. 113–123). San Jose, CA: Society for Studies in Philosophy and Education.

Association of American Colleges. (1985). *Integrity in the academic curriculum.* Washington, DC: Author.

Ball, D. (1987, April). *"Laboratory" and "apprenticeship": How do they function as metaphors for practical experience in teacher education?* Paper presented at the meeting of the American Educational Research Association, Washington, DC.

Ball, D. (1988a). *Research on teaching mathematics: Making subject matter knowledge part of the equation* (Research Rep. No. 88-2). East Lansing: Michigan State University, National Center for Research on Teacher Education.

Ball, D. (1988b). *The subject matter preparation of prospective mathematics teachers: Challenging the myths* (Research Rep. No. 88-3). East Lansing: Michigan State University, National Center for Research on Teacher Education.

Ball, D., & McDiarmid, W. (1988). Research on teacher learning: Studying how teachers' knowledge changes. *Action in Teacher Education, 10*(2), 17–24.

Berliner, D. (1985). Laboratory settings and the study of teacher education. *Journal of Teacher Education, 36*(6), 2–8.

Bestor, A. (1953). *Educational wastelands.* Urbana, IL: University of Illinois Press.

Beyer, L. (1984). Field experience, ideology, and the development of critical reflectivity. *Journal of Teacher Education, 35*(3), 36–41.

Biber, B., & Winsor, C. (1967). An analysis of the guidance function in a graduate teacher education program. In *Mental health and teacher education* (46th yearbook of the Association for Student Teaching, pp. 81–119). Dubuque, IA: William C. Brown.

Borrowman, M. (1956). *The liberal and technical in teacher education: A historical survey of American thought.* New York: Columbia University, Teachers College, Bureau of Publications.

Borrowman, M. (1965). Liberal education and the professional preparation of teachers. In M. L. Borrowman (Ed.), *Teacher education in America: A documentary history* (pp. 1–53). New York: Teachers College Press.

Boyer, E. (1987). *College: The undergraduate experience in America.* New York: Harper & Row.

Brophy, J. (in press). *Advances in research on teaching: Vol. 2. Teachers' subject matter knowledge and classroom instruction.* Greenwhich, CT: JAI Press.

Brophy, J., & Good, T. (1986). Teacher behavior and student achievement. In M. C. Wittrock (Ed.), *Handbook of research on teaching* (3rd ed., pp. 328–375). New York: Macmillan.

Buchmann, M. (1984). The priority of knowledge and understanding in teaching. In L. Katz & J. Raths (Eds.), *Advances in teacher education* (Vol. 1, pp. 29–50). Norwood, NJ: Ablex.

Burdin, J., & Lanzillotti, K. (1969). *A reader's guide to the comprehensive models for preparing elementary teachers.* Washington, DC: American Association of Colleges for Teacher Education.

Bush, R. (1977). We know how to train teachers: Why not do so! *Journal of Teacher Education, 28*(6), 5–9.

Carey, N., Mittman, B., & Darling-Hammond, L. (1988). *Recruiting mathematics and science teachers through nontraditional programs: A survey.* Santa Monica, CA: RAND Corporation, Center for the Study of the Teaching Profession.

Church, R., & Sedlak, M. (1976). *Education in the United States: An interpretive history.* New York: Free Press.

Clark, D. L. (1986). Transforming the structure for the professional preparation of teachers. In L. Katz & J. Raths (Eds.), *Advances in teacher education* (Vol. 1, pp. 1–19). Norwood, NJ: Ablex.

Clark, D., & Marker, G. (1975). The institutionalization of teacher education. In K. Ryan (Ed.), *Teacher education* (74th yearbook of the National Society for the Study of Education, Part II, pp. 53–86). Chicago: University of Chicago Press.

Clifford, G., & Guthrie, J. (1988). *Ed school: A brief for professional education.* Chicago: University of Chicago Press.

Clift, R., Houston, W. R., & Pugach, M. (Eds.). (in press). *Encouraging reflective practice: An examination of issues and exemplars.* New York: Teachers College Press.

Cogan, M. (1955). Master of arts in teaching at Harvard University. *Journal of Teacher Education, 6*, 135–142.

Coley, R., & Thorpe, M. (1985). *A look at the MAT model of teacher education and its graduates: Lessons for today* (Final report sponsored by the Ford Foundation) Princeton: NJ: Educational Testing Service, Division of Education Policy Research and Services.

Collins, A., Brown, J., & Newman, S. (1989). Cognitive apprenticeship: Teaching the craft of reading, writing and mathematics. In L. B. Resnick (Ed.), *Knowing, Learning, and Instruction* (pp. 453–494). Hillsdale, NJ: Lawrence Erlbaum.

Combs, A. (1965). *The professional education of teachers: A perceptual view of teacher education.* Boston: Allyn & Bacon.

Combs, A. (1978). Teacher education: The person in the process. *Educational Leadership, 35*, 558–561.

Combs, A. (1982). *A personal approach to teaching.* Boston: Allyn & Bacon.

Combs, A., Blume, R., Newman, A., & Wass, H. (1974). *The professional education of teachers: A humanistic approach to teacher education.* Boston: Allyn & Bacon.

Conant, J. (1963). *The education of American teachers.* New York: McGraw-Hill.

Cremin, L. (1953). The heritage of American teacher education. Part I. *Journal of Teacher Education, 4*(2), 163–170.

Cremin, L. (1978). *The education of the educating professions* (The 19th Charles W. Hunt Lecture). Chicago: American Association of Colleges for Teacher Education.

Cremin, L., Shannon, D., & Townsend, M. (1954). *A history of Teachers College.* New York: Columbia University Press.

Cruickshank, D. (1987). *Reflective teaching: The preparation of students of teaching.* Reston, VA: Association of Teacher Educators.

Denemark, G., & Nutter, N. (1984). The case for extended programs of initial preparation. In L. Katz & J. Raths, (Eds.), *Advances in teacher education* (Vol. 1, pp. 203–246). Norwood, NJ: Ablex.

Dewey, J. (1904). The relation of theory to practice in education. In C. A. Murry (Ed.), *The relation of theory to practice in the educa-*

tion of teachers (3rd yearbook of the National Society for the Scientific Study of Education, Part I, pp. 1–30). Chicago: University of Chicago Press.

Elam, S. (1971). *Performance based teacher education.* Washington, DC: American Association of Colleges for Teacher Education.

Featherstone, J. (1988). A note on liberal learning. *NCRTE Colloquy,* 2(1), 1–8.

Feiman, S. (1979). Technique and inquiry in teacher education: A curricular case study. *Curriculum Inquiry, 9,* 63–79.

Feiman-Nemser, S. (1987). *Talking to prospective teachers: Lessons from educational psychology.* Paper presented at the meeting of the American Educational Research Association, Washington, DC.

Feiman-Nemser, S., & Buchmann, M. (1989). Describing teacher education: A framework and illustrative findings from a longitudinal study of six students. *Elementary School Journal, 89,* 365–377.

Feiman-Nemser, S., & Floden, R. (1981). A critique of developmental approaches in teacher education. *Action in Teacher Education,* 3(1), 35–38.

Feistritzer, E. G. (1986). *Profile of teachers in the U.S.* Washington, DC: National Center for Education Information.

Floden, R., & Clark, C. (1988). Preparing teachers for uncertainty. *Teachers College Record, 89,* 505–524.

Fuller, F. (1969). Concerns of teachers: A developmental conceptualization. *American Educational Research Journal, 6,* 207–226.

Fuller, F. F. (1970). *Personalized education for teachers: One application of the teacher concerns model.* Austin, TX: University of Texas, Research and Development Center for Teachers.

Fuller, F. F., & Bown, O. (1975). Becoming a teacher. In K. Ryan (Ed.), *Teacher education* (74th yearbook of the National Society for the Study of Education, pp. 25–52). Chicago: University of Chicago Press.

Gage, N. (1978). *The scientific basis of the art of teaching.* New York: Teachers College Press.

Ginsburg, M. (1988). *Contradictions in teacher education and society: A critical analysis.* Philadelphia: Falmer.

Giroux, H., & McLaren, P. (1986). Teacher education and the politics of engagement: The case for democratic schooling. *Harvard Educational Review, 56,* 213–238.

Good, T., & Grouws, P. A. (1977). Teaching effects: A process–product study in fourth-grade mathematics classrooms. *Journal of Teacher Education,* 28(3), 49–54.

Goodlad, J. (1988). Studying the education of educators: Values-driven inquiry. *Phi Delta Kappan, 70,* 105–111.

Goodman, J. (1984). Reflection and teacher education: A case study and theoretical analysis. *Interchange,* 15(3), 9–26.

Goodman, J. (1986a). Making early field experience meaningful: A critical approach. *Journal of Education for Teaching, 12,* 109–125.

Goodman, J. (1986b). Teaching preservice teachers a critical approach to curriculum design: A descriptive account. *Curriculum Inquiry, 16,* 179–201.

Hartnett, A., & Naish, M. (1980). Technicians or social bandits? Some moral and political issues in the education of teachers: Explorations in the sociology of the school. In P. Woods (Ed.), *Teacher strategies* (pp. 254–274). London: Croom Helm.

Hawley, W. (1986). A critical analysis of the Holmes Group's proposals for reforming teacher education. *Journal of Teacher Education,* 37(4), 47–51.

Holmes Group. (1986). *Tomorrow's teachers.* East Lansing, MI: Author.

Houston, W. R. (Ed.). (1974). *Exploring competency based teacher education.* Berkeley, CA: McCutchan.

Houston, W. R., & Howsam, R. (1972). *Competency-based teacher education: Progress, problems and prospects.* Chicago: Science Research Associates.

Howey, K. (1983). Teacher education: An overview. In K. R. Howey & W. E. Gardner (Eds.), *The education of teachers* (pp. 6–37). New York: Longman.

Howey, K. R., Yarger, S. J., & Joyce, B. K. (1978). *Improving teacher education.* Reston, VA: Association of Teacher Educators.

Howey, K., & Zimpher, N. (1989). *Profiles of preservice teacher education: Inquiry into the nature of programs.* Albany, NY: State University of New York Press.

Jackson, P. (1968). *Life in classrooms.* New York: Holt, Rinehart & Winston.

Jackson, P. (1986). *The practice of teaching.* New York: Teachers College Press.

Jackson, P. (1987). Facing our ignorance. *Teachers College Record, 88,* 384–389.

Johnson, W. (1987). Empowering practitioners: Holmes, Carnegie, and the lessons of history. *History of Education Quarterly,* 27(2), 221–240.

Joyce, B. (1975). Conceptions of man and their implications for teacher education. In K. Ryan (Ed.), *Teacher education* (74th yearbook of the National Society for the Study of Education, Part II, pp. 111–145). Chicago: University of Chicago Press.

Joyce, B., & Showers, B. (1980). Improving inservice training: The message of research. *Educational Leadership, 37,* 379–385.

Joyce, B., & Showers, B. (1983). *Power in staff development through research on training.* Alexandria, VA: Association for Supervision and Curriculum Development.

Joyce, B., Yarger, S., & Howey, K. (1977). *Preservice teacher education.* Palo Alto, CA: Booksend Laboratory.

Judge, H. (1982). *American graduate schools of education: A view from abroad.* New York: Ford Foundation.

Kennedy, M. (1987). Inexact sciences: Professional education and the development of expertise. In E. Rothkopf (Ed.), *Review of Research in Education* (Vol. 14, pp. 133–167). Washington, DC: American Educational Research Association.

Kerr, D. H. (1983). Teaching competence and teacher education in the United States. In L. S. Shulman & G. Sykes (Eds.), *Handbook of teaching and policy* (pp. 126–149). New York: Longman.

Kimball, B. (1986). *Orators and philosophers.* New York: Teachers College Press.

Kirk, D. (1986). Beyond the limits of theoretical discourse in teacher education: Towards a critical pedagogy. *Teaching and Teacher Education, 2,* 155–167.

Koerner, J. (1963). *The miseducation of American teachers.* Baltimore: Penguin Books.

Kohl, H. (1976). *On teaching.* New York: Schocken Books.

Lampert, M. (1985). How do teachers manage to teach? Perspectives on problems in practice. *Harvard Educational Review, 55,* 178–194.

Lampert, M. (1986). Knowing, doing, and teaching multiplication. *Cognition and Instruction, 3,* 305–342.

Lanier, J., & Little, J. (1986). Research on teacher education. In M. C. Wittrock (Ed.), *Handbook of research on teaching* (3rd ed., pp. 527–569). New York: Macmillan.

Leinhardt, G., & Smith, D. (1985). Expertise in mathematics instruction: Subject matter knowledge. *Journal of Educational Psychology, 77,* 247–271.

Liston, D., & Zeichner, K. (1988a, April). *Critical pedagogy and teacher education.* Paper presented at the meeting of the American Educational Research Association, New Orleans.

Liston, D., & Zeichner, K. (1988b). Reflective teacher education and moral deliberation. *Journal of Teacher Education,* 38(6), 2–8.

Lortie, D. (1975). *Schoolteacher: A sociological study.* Chicago: University of Chicago Press.

McDiarmid, G. W., Ball, D. L., & Anderson, C. (1989). Why staying ahead one chapter just won't work: Subject-specific pedagogy. In M. Reynolds (Ed.), *Knowledge base for beginning teachers* (pp. 193–205). Washington, DC: American Association of Colleges for Teacher Education.

McDonald, J. P. (1986). Raising the teacher's voice and the ironic role of theory. *Harvard Educational Review, 56,* 355–378.

Monahan, W. (1984). *Teacher education in the '90's: A working paper.* Charleston, NC: Appalachia Education Laboratory.

Monroe, W. (1952). *Teaching–learning theory and teacher education: 1890–1950.* Urbana, IL: University of Illinois Press.

National Center for Research on Teacher Education. (1988a). *Dialogues in teacher education* (Issue Paper 88-4). East Lansing: Michigan State University, National Center for Research on Teacher Education.

National Center for Research on Teacher Education. (1988b). Teacher education and learning to teach: A research agenda. *Journal of Teacher Education, 39*(6), 27–32.

Natriello, G. (1988). *Site report: New Jersey Provisional Teacher Program.* Michigan State University, National Center for Research on Teacher Education, East Lansing. Unpublished manuscript.

Natriello, G., Zumwalt, K., Hansen, A., & Frisch, A. (1988, April). *Who is choosing different routes into teaching?* Paper presented at the meeting of the American Educational Research Association, New Orleans.

New College. (1936). *Teachers College Record, 38*(1), 1–73.

Newlove, B. W. (1969). *The fifteen minute hour: An early teaching experience* (Report Series No. 23). Austin, TX: University of Texas, Research and Development Center for Teacher Education.

Noordhoff, K., & Kleinfeld, J. (1987, October). *Rethinking the rhetoric of "reflective inquiry": What this language came to mean in a program to prepare rural teachers.* Paper prepared for the Reflective Inquiry Conference, Houston.

Oliver, B., & McKibbin, M. (1985). Teacher trainees: Alternative credentialing in California. *Journal of Teacher Education, 36*(3), 20–23.

Peseau, B. A. (1982). Developing an adequate research base for teacher education. *Journal of Teacher Education, 33*(4), 13–15.

Posner, G. (1985). *Field experience: A guide to reflective teaching.* New York: Longman.

Powell, A. (1976). University schools of education in the twentieth century. *Peabody Journal of Education, 54*(1), 3–20.

Powell, A. (1980). *The uncertain profession: Harvard and the search for educational authority.* Cambridge, MA: Harvard University Press.

Randolph, E. (1924). *The professional treatment of subject matter.* Baltimore: Warwick & York.

Rhoades, G. (1985). *The costs of academic excellence in teacher education* (Working Paper #5). Los Angeles, CA: University of California, Graduate School of Education, Comparative Higher Education Research Group.

Rosaen, C., Lanier, P., & Roth, K. (1988, April). *Educative field experiences: The faculty perspective.* Paper presented at the meeting of the American Association of Colleges for Teacher Education, New Orleans.

Ross, D., & Kyle, D. (1987). Helping teachers learn to use teacher effectiveness research. *Journal of Teacher Education, 38*(2), 40–44.

Scannell, D. (1987). Fifth year and extended programs. In M. Haberman & J. Backus (Eds.), *Advances in Teacher Education* (Vol. 3, pp. 168–180). Norwood, NJ: Ablex.

Schön, D. (1983). *The reflective practitioner: How professionals think in action.* New York: Basic Books.

Schön, D. (1987). *Educating the reflective practitioner.* San Francisco: Jossey-Bass.

Schram, P., Wilcox, S., Lanier, P., & Lappan, G. (1988). *Changing mathematical conceptions of preservice teachers: A content and pedagogical intervention* (Research Rep. No. 88–4). East Lansing: Michigan State University, National Center for Research on Teacher Education.

Schwab, J. (1987). Education and the structure of the disciplines. In I. Westbury & N. Wilkof (Eds.), *Science, curriculum, and liberal education: Selected essays* (pp. 229–272). Chicago: University of Chicago Press.

Shapiro, E. (1988). *Teacher: Being and becoming.* New York: Bank Street College.

Shulman, L. (1986). Those who understand: Knowledge growth in teaching. *Educational Researcher, 15*(2), 4–14.

Shulman, L. (1987). Knowledge and teaching: Foundations of the new reform. *Harvard Educational Review, 57,* 1–22.

Silberman, C. E. (1970). *Crisis in the classroom: The remaking of American education.* New York: Random House.

Sirotnik, K. (1988). Studying the education of educators: Methodology. *Phi Delta Kappan, 70,* 241–247.

Smith, D. (1984). PROTEACH: Teacher preparation at the University of Florida. *Teacher Education and Practice, 1*(2), 5–12.

Stodolsky, S. (1988). *The subject matters.* Chicago: University of Chicago Press.

Stone, J. (1968). *Breakthrough in teacher education.* San Francisco: Jossey-Bass.

Tabachnick, T., & Zeichner, K. (1985). *The development of teacher perspectives: Final report.* Madison, WI: University of Wisconsin, Center for Education Research.

Tom, A. (1984). *Teaching as a moral craft.* New York: Longman.

Tom, A. (1985). Inquiring into inquiry-oriented teacher education. *Journal of Teacher Education, 36*(5), 35–44.

Tom, A. (1986). *The case for maintaining teacher education at the undergraduate level.* St. Louis: Washington University, Coalition of Teacher Education Programs. (ERIC Document Reproduction Service No. ED 267 067).

Tom, A. (Ed.). (n.d.). *Teacher education in liberal arts settings: Achievements, realities and challenges.* Washington, DC: American Association of Colleges for Teacher Education and American Independent Liberal Arts Colleges for Teacher Education.

Travers, E., & Sacks, S. (1987). *Teacher education and the liberal arts: The position of the consortium for excellence in teacher education.* Swarthmore, PA: Swarthmore College.

U.S. Department of Education. (1984). *Involvement in learning: Realizing the potential of American higher education.* Washington, DC: National Institute of Education.

Valli, L., & Taylor, N. (1987). *Reflective teacher education: Preferred characteristics for a content and process model.* Paper prepared for the Reflective Inquiry Conference, Houston.

Van Manen, M. (1977). Linking ways of knowing with ways of being practical. *Curriculum Inquiry, 6,* 205–228.

Weinstein, C. (1988). Case studies of extended teacher preparation. In A. Woolfolk (Ed.), *Beyond the debate: Research perspectives on the graduate preparation of teachers* (pp. 30–50). Englewood Cliffs, NJ: Prentice-Hall.

Wilkinson, L. (1988). Prospects for graduate preparation of teachers. In A. Woolfolk, (Ed.), *Research perspectives on the graduate preparation of teachers* (pp. 352–369). Englewood Cliffs, NJ: Prentice-Hall.

Wilson, J. (1975). *Educational theory and the preparation of teachers.* Windsor, England: National Foundation for Educational Research.

Wilson, S., Shulman, L., & Richert, A. (1986). "150 different ways" of knowing: Representations of knowledge in teaching. In J. Calderhead (Ed.), *Exploring teachers' thinking* (pp. 104–124). London, England: Cassell.

Wise, A. E. (1986). Graduate teacher education and teacher professionalism. *Journal of Teacher Education, 37*(5), 36–40.

Woodring, P. (1957). *New directions in teacher education.* New York: Fund for the Advancement of Education.

Woolfolk, A. (1988a). Graduate preparation of teachers: The debate and beyond. In A. Woolfolk (Ed.), *Research perspectives on the graduate preparation of teachers* (pp. 1–11). Englewood Cliffs, NJ: Prentice-Hall.

Woolfolk, A. (Ed.). (1988b). *Research perspectives on the graduate preparation of teachers.* Englewood Cliffs, NJ: Prentice-Hall.

Yarger, S., & Howey, K. (1977). Reflections on preservice preparation: Impressions from the national survey. *Journal of Teacher Education, 28*(6), 34–37.

Zeichner, K. (1981–1982). Reflective teaching and field-based experience in teacher education. *Interchange, 12,* 1–22.

Zeichner, K. M. (1983). Alternative paradigms of teacher education. *Journal of Teacher Education, 34*(3), 3–9.

Zeichner, K. (1987). Preparing reflective teachers: An overview of instructional strategies which have been employed in preservice teacher education. *International Journal of Educational Research, 11,* 565–575.

Zeichner, K. (1988a). Learning from experience in graduate teacher preparation. In A. Woolfolk (Ed.), *Research perspectives on the graduate preparation of teachers* (pp. 12–29). Englewood Cliffs, NJ: Prentice-Hall.

Zeichner, K. (1988b). *Understanding the character and quality of the academic and professional components of teacher education* (Research Rep. No. 88–1). East Lansing: Michigan State University, National Center for Research on Teacher Education.

Zeichner, K. (1988c). University of Florida, Gainesville, Elementary PROTEACH and Secondary English PROTEACH: Site Report. In National Center for Research on Teacher Education, *Dialogues in Teacher Education* (Issue Paper 88-4, pp. 55–81). East Lansing: Michigan State University, NCRTE.

Zeichner, K., & Grant, C. (1981). Biography and social structure in the socialization of student teachers. *Journal of Education for Teaching, 1,* 198–214.

Zeichner, K. M., & Liston, D. P. (1987). Teaching student teachers to reflect. *Harvard Educational Review, 57,* 23–48.

Zeichner, K., Mahlios, M., & Gomez, M. (1988). The structure and goals of a student teaching program and the character and quality of supervisory discourse. *Teaching and Teacher Education, 4,* 349–362.

Zimpher, N., & Howey, K. (1987). Adapting supervisory practice to different orientations of teaching competence. *Journal of Curriculum and Supervision, 2*(2), 101–127.

Zumwalt, K. (1987). Tomorrow's teachers: Tomorrow's work. *Teachers College Record, 88,* 423–431.

14

MODELS OF STAFF DEVELOPMENT

Dennis Sparks

NATIONAL STAFF DEVELOPMENT COUNCIL

Susan Loucks-Horsley

THE REGIONAL LABORATORY FOR EDUCATIONAL IMPROVEMENT OF THE NORTHEAST AND ISLANDS

The research on staff development has an interesting history. In the early 1970s, growing concern about the effectiveness of inservice education resulted in a spate of studies to determine the attitudes of educators about their inservice programs (Ainsworth, 1976; Brim & Tollett, 1974; Joyce & Peck, 1977; Zigarmi, Betz, & Jensen, 1977). The findings indicated nearly unanimous dissatisfaction with current inservice but strong consensus that inservice was critical if school programs and practices were to be improved (Wood & Kleine, 1987).

During the late 1970s and early 1980s, several major studies and reviews contributed to our understanding of the characteristics of effective staff development, focusing not on attitudes, but on actual practices (Berman & McLaughlin, 1978; Kells, 1981; Lawrence, 1974; Yarger, Howey, & Joyce, 1980). The resulting list of effective practices, well known by now, included (a) programs conducted in school settings and linked to schoolwide efforts; (b) teachers participating as helpers to each other and as planners, with administrators, of inservice activities; (c) emphasis on self-instruction, with differentiated training opportunities; (d) teachers in active roles, choosing goals and activities for themselves; (e) emphasis on demonstration, supervised trials, and feedback—that is, training that is concrete and ongoing over time; and (f) ongoing assistance and support available on request.

Staff development came of age in the 1980s. It was the focus of countless conferences, workshops, articles, books, and research reports. State legislators and local school district administrators considered staff development a key aspect of school-improvement efforts. Many school districts initiated extensive staff-development projects to improve student learning. Research on these projects and craft knowledge generated by staff developers have substantially advanced our understanding of effective staff-development practices beyond the overview studies of the early 1980s.

In spite of this current, intense, widespread interest in staff development, much remains to be learned about the process by which staff development occurs. This chapter organizes what is known about effective staff development into several models being espoused and used by staff developers in an effort to promote good staff-development practice. A review of the supporting theory and research on these models is followed by a description of what is currently known about the organizational context required to support successful staff-development efforts. The conclusion discusses what can be said with confidence about effective staff-development practice and what remains to be learned. First, however, are definitions of the key terms and a description of the literature that is used throughout the chapter.

Definitions

Staff development is defined as those processes that improve the job-related knowledge, skills, or attitudes of school

---

The authors wish to thank reviewers Susan Ellis [Greenwich Public Schools] and Fred Wood [University of Oklahoma] for their thoughtful and helpful suggestions.

The work of Susan Loucks-Horsley on this chapter was supported by The Regional Laboratory for Educational Improvement of the Northeast and Islands, funded by the U.S. Department of Education's Office of Education Research and Improvement. The opinions expressed are those of the authors.

employees. Although participants in staff-development activities can include central office administrators, principals, and noncertified staff, this chapter focuses on staff development for teachers. In particular, it examines what is known about staff development that is intended to improve student learning through enhanced teacher performance. The narrow focus represents a particular bias on the part of the authors: the most important purpose of staff development is to enhance student learning, and the individuals most responsible for this are teachers. The models discussed herein have all been used for staff other than teachers, and with similar effects, but the authors have chosen to use examples and illustrations of teacher-focused activities.

Two uses of the word *model* have been combined in this chapter, in an effort to both conceptualize staff development and make the conceptualization useful to staff developers. Borrowing from Ingvarson's (1987) use of the term, a model is seen here as a design for learning that embodies a set of assumptions about first, where knowledge about teaching practice comes from, and second, how teachers acquire or extend their knowledge. Models chosen for discussion in this chapter differ in their assumptions. Also adapting Joyce and Weil's (1972) definition of a model of teaching, a staff-development model is a pattern or plan that can be used to guide the design of a staff-development program. The models selected for this chapter have an individual teacher orientation—they describe different ways teachers can engage in their own growth and development. Thus, what some call *district* or *state models* of staff development have not been included. The structures, policies, and procedures established at the district or state level are, instead, viewed as supports for different teacher-oriented models. They are referred to in the section on organizational context.

Each staff-development model presented is discussed in terms of its theoretical and research underpinnings, its critical attributes (including its underlying assumptions and phases of activity), and illustrations of its impact on teacher growth and development. The literature supporting these models is of several types. *First*, for each model, the theoretical and research bases that support its use in improving teachers' knowledge, skills, or attitudes are considered. The question asked was, Why should one believe that this model *should* affect teachers' classroom behavior? *Second*, program descriptions were reviewed in which these models were applied. The question asked was, Why should one believe that this model can be implemented by staff developers in schools and school districts? *Third*, evidence about outcomes was sought. The question asked was, What evidence indicates that this model makes a difference in teacher performance?

Overview

This chapter presents five models of staff development. *Individually guided staff development* is a process through which teachers plan for and pursue activities they believe will promote their own learning. The *observation/assessment* model provides teachers with objective data and feedback regarding their classroom performance. This information may be used to select areas for growth. Involvement in a *development/improvement process* engages teachers in developing curriculum, designing programs, or engaging in a school-improvement process to solve general or particular problems. The *training* model, which could be synonymous with staff development in the minds of many educators, involves teachers in acquiring knowledge or skills through appropriate individual or group instruction. The *inquiry* model requires teachers to identify an area of instructional interest, collect data, and make changes in their instruction on the basis of an interpretation of those data.

This chapter also examines the organizational context required to support these models. Our discussion includes organizational climate, leadership and support, district policies and systems, and participant involvement.

The final section of this chapter looks for gaps in the knowledge base, identifying areas about which there is still more to learn and areas that as yet remain unexplored by researchers. The hope is that this chapter will serve both as a signpost for how far we have come in the past 20 years in our understanding of effective staff-development practices, and as a springboard for future research in this vital area.

INDIVIDUALLY GUIDED STAFF DEVELOPMENT

Teachers learn many things on their own. They read professional publications, engage in discussions with colleagues, and experiment with new instructional strategies, among other activities. All of these occur with or without the existence of a formal staff-development program.

It is possible, however, for staff-development programs to promote individually guided activities. The actual activities can vary widely, but the key characteristic of the individually guided staff-development model is that the learning is designed by the teacher. The teacher determines her or his own goals and selects the activities that will result in the achievement of those goals. Perhaps a sense of this model is best represented in a *New Yorker* advertisement for the Great Books Foundation that read: "At 30, 50, or 70, you are more self-educable than you were at 20. It's time to join a Great Books reading and discussion group."

Underlying Assumptions

This model assumes that individuals are capable of self-direction and self-initiated learning and that they can best judge their own learning needs. It also assumes that adults learn most efficiently when they initiate and plan their learning activities, rather than spend their time in activities that are less relevant to them than those they would design. (It is, however, true that, when individual teachers design their own learning, there is much "reinventing of the wheel," which might seem inefficient to some.) The model also holds that individuals are most motivated when they select their own learning goals on the basis of personal assessment of their needs.

Theoretical and Research Underpinnings

Theory supporting the individually guided model can be found in the work of a number of individuals. Rogers's client-centered therapy and views on education (1969) are based on the premise that human beings will seek growth, given the appropriate conditions. "I have come to feel," Rogers wrote, "that the only learning which significantly influences behavior is self-discovered, self-appropriated learning" (p. 153).

The differences among people and their needs are well represented in the literature on adult learning theory, adult development, learning styles, and the change process. Adult learning theorists (Kidd, 1973; Knowles, 1980) believe that adults become increasingly self-directed and that their readiness to learn is stimulated by real-life tasks and problems. Stage theorists (Levine, 1988) hold that individuals in different stages of development have different personal and professional needs. Consequently, staff development that provides practical classroom-management assistance to a 22-year-old beginning teacher might be inappropriate for a 62-year-old teaching veteran approaching retirement.

Researchers in learning styles (Dunn & Dunn, 1978; Gregorc, 1979) argue that individuals are different in the ways they perceive and process information and in the manner in which they learn most effectively (e.g., alone or with others, by doing as opposed to hearing about). Research on the Concerns-Based Adoption Model (CBAM) (Hall & Loucks, 1978) indicates that, as individuals learn new behaviors and change their practice, they experience different types of concerns that require different types of responses from staff developers. For instance, when first learning about a new instructional technique, some teachers with personal concerns require reassurance that they will not be immediately evaluated on the use of the strategy, whereas teachers with management concerns want to learn specifically how this technique can be used in the classroom.

Taken together, these theorists and researchers recognize that the circumstances most suitable for one person's professional development can be quite different from those that promote another individual's growth. Consequently, individually guided staff development allows teachers to find answers to self-selected professional problems using their preferred modes of learning. Lawrence's (1974) review of 97 studies of inservice programs determined that programs with individualized activities are more likely to achieve their objectives than those providing identical experiences for all participants.

Phases of Activity

Individually guided staff development consists of several phases: (a) identification of a need or interest, (b) development of a plan to meet the need or interest, (c) learning activity(ies), and (d) assessment of whether the learning meets the identified need or interest. These phases might be undertaken informally and almost unconsciously, or they might be part of a formal, structured process. Each phase is next explained in greater detail.

Identification of a Need or Interest. In this phase the teacher considers what he or she needs to learn. This assessment can be done formally (e.g., through the completion of a needs assessment process or as a consequence of evaluation by a supervisor) or occur more spontaneously (e.g., through a conversation with a colleague or reflection upon an instructional problem). The need or interest could be remedial (e.g., "I've really come to dislike my work because of the classroom-management problems I'm having") or growth oriented (e.g., "I'm intrigued by recent research on the brain and want to improve my understanding of its implications for student learning").

Development of a Plan to Meet the Need or Interest. Having identified the need or interest, the teacher selects a learning objective, which could be quite vague or precisely defined, and choses activities that will lead to accomplishing this objective. Activities might include workshop attendance, reading, visits to another classroom or school, and initiation of a seminar or similar learning program.

The Learning Activity. The learning activity can be a single session (e.g., attendance at a workshop on new approaches to reading in the content areas) or be spread over time (e.g., examination of the research on retaining students in grade). Based on the individual's preferred mode of learning, it can be done alone (e.g., reading or writing) or with others (e.g., a seminar that considers ways of boosting the self-esteem of high school students).

Assessment. In more formal individually guided processes the teacher might be asked to make a brief written report to the funding source or an oral report to colleagues. In other instances the teacher might simply become aware of a better understanding of something. It is not uncommon that, as a result of this assessment phase, the teacher realizes how much more there is to be learned on the topic or is led to a newly emerging need or interest.

Illustrations and Outcomes

Individually guided staff development can take many forms. It can be as simple as a teacher's reading a journal article on a topic of interest or doing library research to determine what the experts have to say about a particular question. Similarly, a teacher might attend a workshop or conference related to her or his subject area or an instructional concern.

Other forms of individually guided staff development are more complex. For instance, teachers might design and carry out special professional projects supported by incentive grants such as the competitive teacher excellence fund promoted by Boyer (1983) or the mini grants described by Mosher (1981). Their projects could involve research, curriculum development, or other learning activities. Evidence of outcomes for such programs is thin, but there are indications that they can empower teachers to address their own problems, create a sense of professionalism, and provide intellectual stimulation (Loucks-Horsley et al., 1987). This strategy proved effective in

New York City and Houston, where teachers were supported to develop and disseminate their own exemplary programs through Impact II grants. They reported changes in their classroom practices, as well as increases in student attendance, discipline, and motivation (Mann, 1984).

Teacher evaluation and supervision can feed into individually guided staff development. McGreal (1983) advocates that teacher evaluation promote the setting of goals as its principal activity. Supervisors would assist in the establishment of those goals, based on the motivation and ability of the teacher. Goals for teachers, the activities they engage in to meet the goals, and the amount of assistance provided by supervisors would differ from teacher to teacher, based upon developmental level, interests, concerns, and instructional problems.

Similarly, Glatthorn's (1984) differentiated supervision calls for self-directed development as one form of assistance to teachers. Self-directed development is a goal-based approach to professional improvement in which teachers have access to a variety of resources for meeting their collaboratively identified needs.

Research on teacher centers also demonstrates the value of individually guided staff development. Hering and Howey (1982) summarize research conducted on 15 teacher centers from 1978 to 1982. They conclude that "the most important contribution of teachers' centers is their emphasis on working with individual teachers over time" (p. 2). Such a focus on individual teachers is absent from many traditional staff-development programs, which teacher centers appear to complement quite effectively.

Hering and Howey (1982) report that mini grants of up to $750 provided by the St. Louis Metropolitan Teacher Center were used to fund a variety of classroom-oriented projects. Interviews with participants found that teachers made extensive use of the ideas and products they developed. Some of these projects eventually affected not only an individual classroom but also a school or an entire district. Regarding this project, Hering and Howey conclude:

As would be expected, teachers who were given money and support reported high levels of satisfaction and a sense of accomplishment. Also not surprisingly, they developed projects anchored in the realities of the classroom and responsive to the needs and interests of their students. Perhaps most important, however, is the strong suggestion that they can, indeed, influence change and innovation in other classrooms, as well as their own, through projects they design at minimal costs. (p. 6)

Hering and Howey (1982) also report the findings of a study on individualized services provided at the Northwest Staff Development Center in Livonia, Michigan. Even though these awards rarely exceeded $50, 78 percent of the recipients reported that they had considerable control over their own learning and professional development. Almost 85 percent of the recipients thought that these services had made a substantive difference in their classrooms. In summarizing the value of individualized services, the researchers wrote, "Individual teacher needs and concerns have to be attended to, as well as school-wide collective ones, or enthusiasm for the collective approach will quickly wane" (p. 6).

Although there are many illustrations of an individualized approach to staff development in the literature and many more in practice, research on its impact on teaching is largely perceptual and self-report. Perhaps as more resources are directed to supporting this strategy, particularly in the form of incentive grants to teachers, more will be learned about its contribution to teacher, as well as student, growth.

OBSERVATION/ASSESSMENT

"Feedback is the breakfast of champions" is the theme of Blanchard and Johnson's (1982) popular management book *The One Minute Manager*. Yet many teachers receive little or no feedback on their classroom performance. In fact, in some school districts teachers are observed by a supervisor as little as once every 3 years, and that observation/feedback cycle is perfunctory in nature.

Observation/assessment can be a powerful staff-development model, but in the minds of many teachers it is associated with evaluation. Because the process often has not been perceived as helpful (Wise & Darling-Hammond, 1985), teachers frequently have difficulty understanding the value of this staff-development model. However, once they have had an opportunity to learn about the many common forms this model can take (for instance, peer coaching and clinical supervision, as well as teacher evaluation), it might become more widely practiced.

Underlying Assumptions

One assumption underlying this model, according to Loucks-Horsley and her associates (1987), is that "Reflection and analysis are central means of professional growth" (p. 61). Observation and assessment of instruction provide the teacher with data that can be reflected upon and analyzed for the purpose of improving student learning.

A second assumption is that reflection by an individual on his or her own practice can be enhanced by another's observations. Because teaching is an isolated profession, typically taking place in the presence of no other adults, teachers are not able to benefit from the observations of others. Having "another set of eyes" gives a teacher a different view of how he or she is performing with students.

Another assumption is that observation and assessment of classroom teaching can benefit both involved parties—the teacher being observed and the observer. The teacher benefits by another's view of her or his behavior and by receiving helpful feedback from a colleague. The observer benefits by watching a colleague, preparing the feedback, and discussing the common experience.

A final assumption is that, when teachers see positive results from their efforts to change, they are more apt to continue to engage in improvement. Because this model can involve multiple observations and conferences over time, it can help teachers see that change is possible. As they apply new strategies, they can see changes in both their own and their students' behavior. In some instances, measurable improvements in student learning are also observed.

Theoretical and Research Underpinnings

Theoretical and research support for the observation/assessment model can be found in the literature on teacher evaluation, clinical supervision, and peer coaching. Each of these approaches is based on the premise that teaching can be objectively observed and analyzed and that improvement can result from feedback on that performance.

McGreal's (1982) work on teacher evaluation suggests a key role for classroom observation but expresses a major concern about reliability of observations. The author points to two primary ways to increase the reliability of classroom observations. The first is to narrow the range of what is looked for by having a system that takes a narrowed focus on teaching (for instance, an observation system based on the Madeline Hunter approach to instruction) or by using an observation guide or focusing instrument. The second way is to use a pre-observation conference to increase the kind and amount of information the observer has prior to the observation. Glatthorn (1984) recommends that clinical supervisors (or coaches) alternate unfocused observations with focused observations. In unfocused observations the observer usually takes verbatim notes and makes observer's comments on all significant behavior. These data are used to identify some strengths and potential problems, which are discussed in a problem-solving feedback conference. A focus is then determined for the next observation, during which data are gathered that relate to the identified problem.

Glickman's (1986) work suggests that the type of feedback conference provided teachers should be based on their cognitive levels. Teachers with a "low-abstract" cognitive style should receive directive conferences (problem identification and solution come primarily from the coach or supervisor); "moderate-abstract" teachers should receive collaborative conferences (an exchange of perceptions about problems and a negotiated solution); and "high-abstract" teachers should receive a nondirective approach (coach or supervisor helping the teacher clarify problems and choose a course of action).

Peer coaching is a form of the observation/assessment model that promotes transfer of learning to the classroom (Joyce & Showers, 1982). In peer observation, teachers visit one another's classrooms, gather objective data about student performance or teacher behavior, and give feedback in a follow-up conference. According to Joyce and Showers (1983):

Relatively few persons, having mastered a new teaching skill, will then transfer that skill into their active repertoire. In fact, few will use it at all. Continuous practice, feedback, and the companionship of coaches is essential to enable even highly motivated persons to bring additions to their repertoire under effective control. (p. 4)

Joyce (in Brandt, 1987) says that up to 30 trials might be required to bring a new teaching strategy under "executive control." Similarly, Shalaway (1985) found that 10 to 15 coaching sessions might be necessary for teachers to use what they have learned in their classrooms.

Phases of Activity

The observation/assessment model, whether implemented through evaluation, clinical supervision, or peer coaching, usually includes a pre-observation conference, observation, an analysis of data, a postobservation conference, and, in some instances, an analysis of the observation/assessment process (Loucks-Horsley et al., 1987). In the pre-observation conference, a focus for the observation is determined, observation methods are selected, and any special problems are noted. According to Acheson and Gall (1980), observation techniques include verbatim recordings (based on the goals established at this time), or they might be based on seating charts or checklists.

During the observation, data are collected using the processes agreed upon in the pre-observation conference. The observation can be focused on the students or on the teacher and can be global in nature or narrowly focused. The analysis-of-data phase involves both the teacher and the observer in considering the lesson. Data are related to the goals for the observation established during the pre-observation conference. Patterns found during instruction could become evident. Hunter (1982) recommends three points of analysis: (a) behaviors that contribute to learning, (b) behaviors that interfere with learning, and (c) behaviors that neither contribute nor interfere but use time and energy that could be better spent.

In the postobservation conference both the teacher and the observer reflect on the lesson, and the observer shares the data collected. Strengths are typically acknowledged and areas for improvement suggested, either by the teacher or the observer, depending upon the goals established in the pre-observation conference. The analysis of the supervisory-process phase, although not necessarily included in all forms of this model, provides both participants an opportunity to reflect on the value of the observation/assessment process and to discuss modifications that might be made in future cycles.

Illustrations and Outcomes

Acheson and Gall (1980) report a number of studies that have determined that the clinical-supervision model is accepted by teachers when they and their supervisors are taught systematic observation techniques. They further note that this process is viewed as productive by teachers when the supervisor uses indirect behaviors (e.g., accepting feelings and ideas, giving praise and encouragement, asking questions). Although the authors report that trained supervisors helped teachers make improvements in a number of instructional behaviors, they were unable to find any studies that demonstrated student effects.

The most intensive and extensive studies of the impact of observation/assessment on learning come from the work of Showers and Joyce. Discussed in more detail in the training section, these authors and their associates have found powerful contributions to be made to student learning when the training of teachers in effective instructional practices is followed by observations and coaching in their classrooms (Joyce & Showers, 1988). In a study of the source of coaching, Sparks (1986) contrasted a workshop-only approach with peer coaching and with consultant coaching. The findings indicated that peer coaching was most powerful in improving classroom performance.

The research, then, provides some reason to believe that teacher behaviors can be positively influenced by the use of an observation/assessment model of staff development. However, it still remains to be learned whether this model must be combined with particular kinds of training if student learning is to be enhanced.

DEVELOPMENT/IMPROVEMENT PROCESS

Teachers are sometimes asked to develop or adapt curriculum, design programs, or engage in systematic school-improvement processes that have as their goal the improvement of classroom instruction and/or curriculum. Typically these projects are initiated to solve a problem. Their successful completion might require that teachers acquire specific knowledge or skills (e.g., curriculum planning, research on effective teaching, group problem-solving skills). This knowledge or skills could be acquired through reading, discussion, observation, training, and/or trial and error. In other instances, the process of developing a product itself might cause significant learnings (e.g., through experiential learning), some of which could have been difficult or impossible to predict in advance. This model focuses on the combination of learnings that result from the involvement of teachers in such processes.

Underlying Assumptions

One assumption on which this model is based is that adults learn most effectively when they have a need to know or a problem to solve (Knowles, 1980). Serving on a school-improvement committee might require that teachers read the research on effective teaching and that they learn new teaming and interpersonal skills. Curriculum development might demand of teachers new content knowledge. In each instance, teachers' learning is driven by the demands of problem solving.

Another assumption of this model is that people working closest to the job best understand what is required to improve their performance. Their teaching experiences provide guidance to teachers in framing problems and recognizing and/or developing relevant solutions. Given appropriate opportunities, teachers can effectively bring these unique perspectives to the tasks of improving their schools and their teaching.

A final assumption is that teachers acquire important knowledge or skills through their involvement in school-improvement or curriculum-development processes. Such involvement could cause alterations in attitudes or acquisition of skills, as individuals or groups work toward the solution of a common problem. For instance, teachers might become more aware of the perspectives of others, more appreciative of individual differences, more skilled in group leadership, or better able to

solve problems. Although the learnings can be unpredictable in advance, they are often regarded by teachers as important.

Theoretical and Research Underpinnings

We have chosen to represent curriculum development and school improvement as types of staff development; mere involvement in these processes nurtures teachers' growth. Others see staff development (perhaps viewed more narrowly as training) as a key component of effective curriculum development and implementation. As Joyce and Showers (1988) write, "It has been well established that curriculum implementation is demanding of staff development—essentially, without strong staff development programs that are appropriately designed a very low level of implementation occurs" (p. 44).

Whichever perspective one has, staff development and the improvement of schools and curriculum go hand in hand. Glickman (1986), who argues that the aim of staff development should be to improve teachers' ability to think, views curriculum development as a key aspect of this process. He believes that the intellectual engagement of curriculum development requires teachers not only to know their content but also to acquire curriculum planning skills. He recommends that curriculum development be conducted in heterogeneous groups composed of teachers of low, medium, and high abstract reasoning abilities. According to Glickman, the complexity of the curriculum-development task should be matched to the abstract reasoning ability of the majority of teachers in the group.

Glatthorn (1987) describes three ways in which teachers can modify a district's curriculum guide. They might operationalize the district's curriculum guide by taking its lists of objectives and recommended teaching methods and turning them into a set of usable instructional guides. Or they might adapt the guide to students' special needs (e.g., remediation, learning-style differences). Finally, teachers might enhance the guide by developing optional enrichment units. Glatthorn recommends that these activities be done in groups, believing that, in doing so, teachers will become more cohesive and will share ideas about teaching and learning in general, as well as those focused on the development task at hand.

The involvement of teachers in school-improvement processes, although similar in its assumptions and process to curriculum development, finds its research and theory base in other literature. General approaches to school improvement come from the literature on change and innovation. For example, Loucks-Horsley and Hergert (1985) describe seven action steps in a school-improvement process that are based upon research on implementation of new practices in schools (Crandall & Loucks, 1983; Hall & Loucks, 1978; Louis & Rosenblum, 1981). The research on effective schools underpins other approaches to school improvement (Cohen, 1981). Finally, an approach to school improvement through staff development developed by Wood and his associates was derived from analysis of effective staff-development practices as represented in the research and in reports from educational practitioners (Thompson, 1982; Wood, 1988). The result is a five-stage RPTIM model (Readiness, Planning, Training, Implementation, and

Maintenance) widely used in designing and implementing staff-development efforts (Wood, Thompson, & Russell, 1981). As a result of involvement in such improvement efforts, schools (and the teachers within them) might develop new curricula, change reporting procedures to parents, enhance communication within the faculty, and improve instruction, among many other topics.

Phases of Activity

This model begins with the identification of a problem or need by an individual, a group of teachers (e.g., a grade-level team or a secondary department), a school faculty, or a district administrator. The need might be identified informally through discussion or a growing sense of dissatisfaction, or through a more formal process such as brainstorming or use of a standardized instrument (such as a school-improvement survey or needs assessment), or through examination of student achievement or program-evaluation data.

After a need has been identified, a response is formulated. This response can be determined informally or formally. In some cases, the response becomes immediately evident (e.g., the need for new lunchroom rules). At other times, teachers might need to brainstorm or search out alternatives, weigh them against a set of predetermined criteria, develop an action plan, and determine evaluation procedures. This process can take several sessions to complete and can require consultation with a larger group (e.g., the schoolwide staff-development committee might receive feedback on the tentative plan from the entire faculty).

Typically, it becomes evident during this phase that certain knowledge or skills are required to implement the response. For instance, the faculty might decide that it wants to study several discipline systems before implementing the new lunchroom-management system. The improvement of students' higher-order thinking might suggest the selection of new textbooks, requiring that committee members better understand which features to look for in a textbook, to support this goal. The development or selection of a new elementary science curriculum might require study of the latest research on science teaching and examination of other curricula.

At this point the plan is implemented or the product is developed. This process can take several days, several months, or several years. As a final step, the success of the effort in meeting the original need is assessed. If teachers are not satisfied with the results, they return to an earlier phase (e.g., acquisition of knowledge or skills) and repeat the process.

Illustrations and Outcomes

Teachers have long been involved in curriculum development, but little research on the impact of their experiences on their professional development has been conducted. The research that has been conducted has assessed the impact of such involvement on areas other than professional development, for example, job satisfaction, costs, and commitment to the organization (Kimpston & Rogers, 1987). Similarly, al-

though the engagement of teachers in school-improvement processes increased in the 1980s, little research was conducted on the effects of that involvement on their development. There are, however, a multitude of examples illustrating the variations schools and districts have used to enhance teacher growth by engaging them in developmental work.

In the late 1980s, many state education agencies supported implementation of state-initiated reforms through the encouragement (and sometimes mandating) of school-improvement processes. For example, the Franklin County (Ohio) Department of Education used a staff-development process to assist five school districts in meeting mandated state goals (Scholl & McQueen, 1985). Teachers and administrators from the districts learned about the state requirements and developed goals and planning strategies for their districts. A major product of the program was a manual that included a synthesis of information and work sheets that could be used to guide small-group activities in the five districts.

School districts were also initiating programs involving teachers in the planning of school improvement. In the Hammond (Indiana) Public Schools, decision making was school based (Casner-Lotto, 1988). School-improvement committees (each composed of 15 to 20 members including teachers, administrators, parents, students, and community members) received training in consensus building, brainstorming, creative problem solving, and group dynamics. After this training, each committee developed a "vision of excellence" for its school. As a result, schools have initiated projects in individualized learning, peer evaluation, cross-grade-level reading, and teacher coaching/mentoring.

Sparks, Nowakowski, Hall, Alec, and Imrick (1985) report on two elementary school-improvement projects that led to large gains on state reading tests. The first school's staff decided to review the reading curriculum and to investigate alternative instructional approaches. Teachers task-analyzed the six lowest scoring objectives, studied effective instructional techniques, and participated in self-selected professional growth activities. In 2 years students who scored above the average rose from 72 percent to 100 percent. In the second school, teachers adopted a new reading series, revised the kindergarten program, and created a booklet that included practice test items and effective instructional practices for improving student achievement. The percentage of students achieving the reading objectives increased almost 20 percent in 3 years.

The Jefferson County (Colorado) School District has long involved teachers in curriculum development and adaptation (Jefferson County Public Schools, 1974). A process that includes needs assessment, curriculum-objective statements, curriculum writing, pilot testing evaluation, field testing evaluation, and districtwide implementation has been used to cycle through the major content areas on a regular basis. Teachers involved in writing and pilot test teams hone their skills as curriculum planners and developers and as masters of the new techniques incorporated into the curriculum (including such strategies as cooperative learning and individualized instruction). They often take on roles as teacher trainers for the districtwide implementation that follows pilot and field tests (Loucks & Pratt, 1979).

E. J. Wilson High School in Spencerport, New York, is one of many across the country that has implemented elements of effective schools through a systematic school-improvement process. Teachers in the school participate with building administrators on a Building Planning Committee that spearheads the achievement of ideal practices within the school through a seven-step process that engages the entire faculty in assessment, planning, implementation, and evaluation. As a result, the school climate and student achievement has improved, as have the knowledge, skills, and attitudes of the teachers involved. This school's outcomes represent those of many who have sought to implement similar improvement processes (Kyle, 1985).

These state-, school-, and district-level efforts illustrate the wide variety of ways this model of staff development is being used. Although the research and evaluation evidence of impact on teacher knowledge and skills is thin, there is research to support many of the factors that improve the probability of success, including: commitment to the process by school and building administrators, which includes giving authority and resources to the team to pursue and implement its agenda; development of knowledge and skills on the part of teacher participants; adequate quality time to meet, reflect, develop, and so on; adequate resources to purchase materials, visit other sites, hire consultants to contribute to informed decision making; leadership that provides a vision, direction, and guidance but allows significant decision making on the part of teacher participants; and integration of the effort into other improvement efforts and into other structures that influence teaching and learning in the school (Loucks-Horsley et al., 1987). When these factors are present, some research data and considerable self-report data indicate clearly that the desired outcomes of staff development are achieved.

TRAINING

In the minds of many educators, training is synonymous with staff development. Most teachers are accustomed to attending workshop-type sessions in which the presenter is the expert who establishes the content and flow of activities. Typically, the training session is conducted with a clear set of objectives or learner outcomes. These outcomes frequently include awareness or knowledge (e.g., participants will be able to explain the five principles of cooperative learning) and skill development (e.g., participants will demonstrate the appropriate use of open-ended questions in a class discussion). Joyce and Showers (1988) cite as additional outcomes changes in attitudes and transfer of training and executive control (the appropriate and consistent use of new strategies in the classroom). It is the trainer's role to select activities (e.g., lecture, demonstration, role playing, simulation, microteaching) that will aid teachers in achieving the desired outcomes.

Whatever the anticipated outcomes, the purpose of all training is to improve teachers' thinking. According to Showers, Joyce, and Bennett (1987):

The purpose of providing training in any practice is not simply to generate the external visible teaching "moves" that bring that practice to

bear in the instructional setting but to generate the conditions that enable the practice to be selected and used appropriately and integratively . . . a major, perhaps the major, dimension of teaching skill is cognitive in nature. (pp. 85–86)

Underlying Assumptions

One assumption that undergirds the training model of staff development is that there are behaviors and techniques worthy of replication by teachers in the classroom. This assumption can certainly be supported by the large number of research-based effective teaching practices that have been identified and verified in the 1970s and 1980s (Sparks, 1983).

The other assumption underlying this model is that teachers can change their behaviors and learn to replicate behaviors in their classroom that were not previously in their repertoire. As Joyce and Showers (1983) point out, training is a powerful process for enhancing knowledge and skills. "It is plain from the research on training," they say, "that teachers can be wonderful learners. They can master just about any kind of teaching strategy or implement almost any technique as long as adequate training is provided" (p. 2).

Certain types of knowledge and skills lend themselves particularly well to training processes. In addition, because of a high participant-to-trainer ratio, training is usually a cost-efficient way for teachers to acquire knowledge or skills. For instance, many instructional skills require teachers to view a demonstration of their use to fully understand their implementation. Likewise, certain instructional techniques require for their classroom implementation that teachers have an opportunity to practice them with feedback from a skilled observer. Training could be the most efficient means for large numbers of teachers to view these demonstrations and to receive feedback as they practice.

Theoretical and Research Underpinnings

The theoretical and research underpinnings of the training model come from several sources, but the most recent and intensive research and development efforts have been conducted by Joyce and Showers (1988). They have determined that, depending upon the desired outcomes, training might include exploration of theory, demonstration or modeling of a skill, practice of the skill under simulated conditions, feedback about performance, and coaching in the workplace. Their research indicates that this combination of components is necessary if the outcome is skill development. In fact, they have determined that the size of the combined effect of all the components except coaching is .39; with the addition of coaching, the effect size is 1.68.

In addition to those components identified by Joyce and Showers (1988), Sparks (1983) cites the importance of discussion and peer observation as training activities. She notes that discussion is useful both when new concepts or techniques are presented and as a problem-solving tool after teachers have had an opportunity to try out new strategies in their classrooms. Sparks also points out that peer observation as an adjunct to training benefits not only the observed teacher, but also the observer who analyzes the lessons of a colleague. Training sessions that are spaced one or more weeks apart so that content can be "chunked" for improved comprehension and teachers have opportunities for classroom practice and peer coaching have been shown to be more effective than "one-shot" training (Loucks-Horsley et al., 1987; Sparks, 1983).

Sparks (1983), Wu (1987), and Wood and Kleine (1987) point out the value of teachers as trainers of their peers. Sparks indicates that teachers can learn as much from their peers as from expert trainers. She also argues that school districts can afford the type of small-group training that she recommends when peers are used instead of more expensive external consultants. Wood and Kleine found, in reviewing the research, that teachers preferred their peers as trainers. Wu's review of the research confirmed this, finding that when their peers are trainers, teachers feel more comfortable exchanging ideas, play a more active role in workshops, and report that they receive more practical suggestions. Other research, however, indicates that expert trainers who have the critical qualities teachers value in their peers, (e.g., a clear understanding of how a new practice works with real students in real classroom settings) can also be highly effective (Crandall, 1983).

Phases of Activity

According to Joyce and Showers (1988), "Someone has to decide what will be the substance of the training, who will provide training, when and where the training will be held and for what duration" (p. 69). Although training content, objectives, and schedules are often determined by administrators or by the trainer, Wood, McQuarrie, and Thompson's (1982) research-based model involves participants in the planning of training programs. Participants serve on planning teams that assess needs (using appropriate sources of data), explore various research-based approaches, select content, determine goals and objectives, schedule training sessions, and monitor implementation of a program.

Joyce and Showers (1988) point out that there are specific "learning-to-learn" skills that teachers posses or can develop to aid the training process. They cite persistence, acknowledgement of the transfer problem (the need for considerable practice of new skills in the classroom), teaching new behaviors to students, meeting the cognitive demands of innovations (developing a "deep understanding" of new practices), productive use of peers, and flexibility. The authors list several conditions of training sessions that foster these aptitudes and behaviors: adequate training, opportunities for collegial problem solving, norms that support experimentation, and organizational structures that support learning.

Sparks's (1983) review of staff-development research suggests that a diagnostic process such as detailed profiles of teaching behaviors based upon classroom observations is an important first step in the training process. Depending upon the nature of the objectives, training activities can include exploration of theory, demonstrations, practice under simulated conditions, feedback, and discussion (Joyce and Showers, 1988).

Sparks (1983) underscores the importance of small-group discussion and problem solving during training, to aid learning and promote transfer to the classroom.

After training, in-classroom assistance in the form of peer observation and coaching is critical to the transfer of more complex teaching skills (Joyce & Showers, 1988). The process of data gathering and analysis that accompanies most forms of peer observation is valuable to the observer as well as to the observed teacher (Brandt, 1987; Sparks, 1986).

Illustrations and Outcomes

The power of training to alter teachers' knowledge, attitudes, and instructional skills is well established. Its impact on teachers, however, depends upon its objectives and the quality of the training program. Joyce and Showers (1988) have determined that, when all training components are present (theory, demonstration, practice, feedback, and coaching), an effect size of 2.71 exists for knowledge-level objectives, 1.25 for skill-level objectives, and 1.68 for transfer of training to the classroom. "We have concluded from these data," write Joyce and Showers (1988), "that teachers can acquire new knowledge and skill and use it in their instructional practice when provided with adequate opportunities to learn" (p. 72). Research on coaching and peer observation cited earlier in the observation/assessment model also supports the effects of training.

Wade (1985) found in her meta-analysis of inservice teacher education research that training affected participants' learning by an effect size of .90 and their behavior by .60. An effect size of .37 was found for the impact of teacher training on student behavior. Wade also concluded that training groups composed of both elementary and secondary teachers achieved higher effect sizes than did those enrolling only elementary or only secondary teachers.

Gage (1984) traced the evolution of research on teaching from observational and descriptive studies to correlational studies, to nine experiments based on these findings that were designed to alter instructional practices. "The main conclusion of this body of research," Gage writes, "is that, in eight out of the nine cases, inservice education was fairly effective—not with all teachers and not with all teaching practices but effective enough to change teachers and improve student achievement, or attitudes, or behavior" (p. 92).

Numerous specific illustrations of training programs are available that have demonstrated impact on teacher behavior and/or student learning. For instance, studies indicate that teachers who have been taught cooperative learning strategies for their classrooms have students who show higher achievement, display higher reasoning and greater critical thinking, have more positive attitudes toward the subject area, and like their fellow students better (Johnson, Johnson, Holubec, & Roy, 1984).

Good and Grouws (1987) describe a mathematics staff development program for elementary teachers. In this 10-session program teachers learned more about mathematics content and about instructional and management issues. As a result of the training, the researchers measured change in teachers' classroom practice and improved mathematics presentations. Student mathematics performance was also improved.

Kerman (1979) reports a 3-year study in which several hundred K–12 teachers were trained to improve their interactions with low-achieving students. The five-session training program included peer observation in the month between each session. The researchers found that low-achieving students in experimental classes made significant academic gains over their counterparts in control groups.

Rauth (1986) describes an American Federation of Teachers training program that brought research on teaching to its members. Teacher Research Linkers (TRL's) first determined which aspects of the research would be most valuable in their teaching. Between sessions they carried out implementation plans in their own classrooms. TRL's were then taught how to effectively share this research with their colleagues. A study of this program indicated that teachers made significant changes in their practice and that, in addition, their morale and collegiality increased dramatically.

Robbins and Wolfe (1987) discuss a 4-year staff-development project designed to increase elementary students' engaged time and achievement. Evaluation of the training program documented steady improvement for 3 years in teachers' instructional skills, student engaged time, and student achievement in reading and math. Although scores in all these areas dropped in the project's fourth and final year, Robbins and Wolfe argue that this decline was due to insufficient coaching and peer observation during that year.

As these illustrations of the training model of staff development and reports of their effectiveness indicate, there is a much more substantial research literature on this model than on the others discussed earlier. Under the appropriate conditions, training has the potential to change significantly teachers' beliefs, knowledge, and behavior and the performance of their students.

INQUIRY

A high school teacher wonders if an alteration in her lesson plan for first period will produce improved student understanding in her second-period class. A brief written quiz given at the end of the class indicates that it did. A group of teachers gathers weekly after school for an hour or two at the teacher center to examine the research on ability grouping. Their findings will be shared with the district's curriculum council. Several elementary teachers study basic classroom research techniques, formulate research questions, gather and analyze data, and use their findings to improve instruction in their classrooms.

Teacher inquiry can take different forms. It can be a solitary activity, be done in small groups, or be conducted by a school faculty. Its process can be formal or informal. It can occur in a classroom or at a teacher center or result from a university class. In this section teacher inquiry is explored as a staff-development model.

Underlying Assumptions

Inquiry reflects a basic belief in teachers' ability to formulate valid questions about their own practice and to pursue objective answers to those questions. Loucks-Horsley and her associates (1987) list three assumptions about a teacher inquiry approach to staff development: (a) teachers are intelligent, inquiring individuals with legitimate expertise and important experience; (b) teachers are inclined to search for data to answer pressing questions and to reflect on the data to formulate solutions; and (c) teachers develop new understandings as they contribute to and formulate their own questions and collect their own data to answer them. The overarching assumption of the model is that

the most effective avenue for professional development is cooperative study by teachers themselves into problems and issues arising from their attempts to make their practice consistent with their educational values. . . . [The approach] aims to give greater control over what is to count as valid educational knowledge to teachers. (Ingvarson, 1987, pp. 15,17)

Theoretical and Research Underpinnings

The call for inquiry-oriented teachers is not new. Dewey (1933) wrote of the need for teachers to take "reflective action." Zeichner (1983) cites more than 30 years of advocacy for "teachers as action researchers," "teacher scholars," "teacher innovators," "self-monitoring teachers," and "teachers as participant observers."

More recently, various forms of inquiry have been advocated by a number of theorists and researchers. Tikunoff and Ward's (1983) model of interactive research and development promotes inquiry into the questions teachers are asking about their teaching through close work with researchers who help with methodology and staff developers who help them create ways of sharing their results with others. Lieberman (1986) reports on a similar process, in which teachers serving on collaborative teams pursued answers to school, rather than classroom, problems. Watts (1985) discusses the role of collaborative research, classroom action research, and teacher support groups in encouraging teacher inquiry. Simmons and Sparks (1985) describe the use of action research to help teachers relate research on teaching to their unique classrooms.

Glickman (1986) advocates action research in the form of quality circles, problem-solving groups, or school improvement projects, as the means to develop teacher thought. Cross (1987) proposes classroom research to help teachers evaluate the effectiveness of their own teaching. Glatthorn (1987) discusses action research by teams of teachers as a peer-centered option for promoting professional growth. Loucks-Horsley and her colleagues (1987) discuss teachers as researchers as a form of teacher development that helps narrow the gap between research and practice. Sparks and Simmons (1988) propose inquiry-oriented staff development as a means of enhancing teachers' decision-making abilities.

One of the important tenets of the inquiry approach is that research is an important activity for teachers, although they rarely participate in it other than as subjects. Gable and Rogers (1987) "take the terror out of research" by describing ways in which it can be used as a staff-development tool. They discuss both qualitative and quantitative methodology, providing specific strategies that teachers can use in their classrooms. They conclude by saying "the desire to and ability to do research is an essential attribute of the professional teacher of the Eighties" (p. 695).

Phases of Activity

Although the inquiry model of staff development can take many forms, all have a number of elements in common. First, individuals or a group of teachers identify a problem of interest. They explore ways of collecting data that can range from examining existing theoretical and research literature to gathering original classroom or school data. These data are then analyzed and interpreted by an individual or the group. Finally, changes are made, and new data are gathered and analyzed to determine the effects of the intervention.

This process is adapted to the unique needs of a particular approach to inquiry. For instance, Hovda and Kyle (1984) provide a 10-step process for action research that progresses from identifying interested participants, through sharing several study ideas, to discussing findings and considering having the study published or presented. Glatthorn (1987) describes a four-step process for action research. Collaborative research teams (a) identify a problem, (b) decide upon specific research questions to be investigated and methodology to be used, (c) carry out the research design, and (d) use the research to design an intervention to be implemented in the school.

Watts (1985) describes "reflective conversation," in which teachers carefully observe and thoughtfully consider a particular child or practice. Using a standard procedure, the group shares observations, reviews previous records and information, summarizes their findings, and makes recommendations. As a final step, the group reviews the process to assess how well it went, looking for gaps and identifying ideas to repeat in future conversations.

Throughout the phases of an inquiry activity, organizational support and/or technical assistance might be called for. Organizational support can take the form of structures such as teacher centers or study groups or resources such as released time or materials. Technical assistance can involve training in research methodologies, data-gathering techniques, and other processes that aid teachers in making sense of their experiences.

Illustrations and Outcomes

The forms that inquiry as a staff-development model can take are limited only by the imagination. Simmons and Sparks (1985) describe a Master of Arts in Classroom Teaching degree designed to help teachers meet their individually identified improvement goals. Teachers in this program learn about educational research, identify and analyze classroom problems, pursue topics of professional interest, and improve their overall teaching ability. These authors report evidence of change

in participant knowledge (e.g., concerning effective teaching–learning), thinking (e.g., enhanced problem-solving skills, increased cognitive complexity), and patterns of communication and collegiality.

Watts (1985) identifies a number of ways in which teachers act as researchers. She discusses collaborative research in teacher centers funded by the Teachers' Center Exchange (then located at the Far West Laboratory for Educational Research and Development) that was conducted in the late 1970s and early 1980s. Fourteen projects were funded in which teachers collaborated with researchers on topics of interest to the individual teachers' center. Watts also describes ethnographic studies of classrooms conducted collaboratively by teachers and researchers. In addition, she provides examples of classroom action research and teachers' study groups as forms of inquiry. She concludes from reports of all three approaches that they share several outcomes: As a result of learning more about research, teachers make more informed decisions about when and how to apply the research findings of others; teachers experience more supportive and collegial relationships; and teaching improves as teachers learn more about it, being better able to look beyond the immediate, the individual, and the concrete.

The outcomes of the teacher inquiry model of staff development can reach beyond the realm of the individual teacher participant and the group to which the participant belongs. An example of schoolwide impact comes from the report of a high school team convened to reflect on a lack of communication and support between teachers and administrators (Lieberman & Miller, 1984). When teachers and administrators worked together to define the problem, learn each other's perspectives, gather evidence, and formulate solutions, they began addressing important school problems collaboratively and increased expectations for student attendance. A substantial overlap exists between this kind of "school-based" inquiry and some of the school-improvement processes discussed earlier in the model described as development/improvement process.

Although the research base related to the inquiry approach to staff development is as scanty as that of other approaches, there are some indications that more than teacher development can be expected by increasing and enhancing teachers' opportunities to reflect alone or with their colleagues on matters of concern to them.

ORGANIZATIONAL CONTEXT

Teacher development in school districts does not take place in a vacuum. Its success is influenced in many ways by the district's organizational context (McLaughlin & Marsh, 1978; Sparks, 1983). Key organizational factors include school and district climate, leadership attitudes and behaviors, district policies and systems, and involvement of participants.

Staff development fosters the professional growth of individuals, but organizational development addresses the organization's responsibility to define and meet changing self-improvement goals (Dillon-Peterson, 1981). Consequently, effective organizations have the capacity to continually renew themselves and solve problems. Within this context, individuals can grow.

In earlier sections of this chapter, five models of staff development were discussed that have solid foundations in research and/or practice and are being used in increasingly robust forms throughout the country today. Although each model requires somewhat different organizational supports to make it successful, research points to a common set of attributes of the organizational context without which staff development can have only limited success (Loucks-Horsley et al., 1987). In organizations where staff development is most successful:

1. Staff members have a common, coherent set of goals and objectives that they helped formulate, reflecting high expectations of themselves and their students.
2. Administrators exercise strong leadership by promoting a norm of collegiality, minimizing status differences between their staff members and themselves, promoting informal communication, and reducing their own need to use formal controls to achieve coordination.
3. Administrators and teachers place high priority on staff development and continuous improvement of personal skills, promoting formal training programs, informal sharing of job knowledge, and a norm of continuous improvement applicable to all.
4. Administrators and teachers make heavy use of a variety of formal and informal processes for monitoring progress toward goals, using them to identify obstacles to such progress and ways of overcoming them, rather than using them to make summary judgments regarding the competence of particular staff members (Conley & Bacharach, 1987).
5. Knowledge, expertise, and resources including time are drawn on appropriately, yet liberally, to initiate and support the pursuit of staff-development goals.

Organizational Climate

Little (1982) found that effective schools are characterized by norms of collegiality and experimentation. Simply put, teachers are more likely to persist in using new behaviors in schools where collaboration and professional risk taking (and its occasional failures) are encouraged. Fullan (1982) reports that the degree of change is strongly related to the extent to which teachers interact with each other and provide technical help to one another. "Teachers need to participate in skill-training workshops," Fullan wrote, "but they also need to have one-to-one and group opportunities to receive and give help, and more simply to converse about the meaning of change" (p. 121).

Joyce and Showers (1983) point out that "in a loose and disorganized social climate without clear goals, reticent teachers may actually subvert elements of the training process not only for themselves but also for others" (p. 31). Other research has shown that, when there are clear goals and a stable organizational structure, change that is introduced where there is not initial commitment by all teachers can still be successful. Miles

(1983) found that teacher–administrator harmony was critical to the success of improvement efforts, but that it could develop over the course of an improvement effort. Initially, working relationships between teachers and administrators had to be clear and supportive enough that most participants could "suspend disbelief," believing that the demands of change would be dealt with together (Crandall, 1983). In their study of school-improvement efforts that relied heavily on staff development for their success, these authors found that, in projects in which a mandated strategy caused some initial disharmony between teachers and administrators, the climate changed as the new program's impact on students became clear. When a new program was selected carefully and teachers received good training and support, most who were initially skeptical soon agreed with, and were committed to, the effort. Showers et al. (1987) support the position that, at least initially, teachers' ability to use a new practice in a competent way is more important than commitment.

Few would disagree with the importance of a school and district climate that encourages experimentation and supports teachers to take risks, that is, establishes readiness for change (Wood et al., 1981). Yet a supportive context consists of more than good feelings. The quality of the recommended practices is also critical. Research conducted by Guskey (1986) and Loucks and Zacchei (1983) indicates that new practices developed or chosen by or for teachers to implement need to be effective ones, either by virtue of evaluation results offered by the developer or by careful testing by the teachers who have developed them. These researchers found that only when teachers see that a new program or practice enhances the learning of their students will their beliefs and attitudes change in a significant way.

Leadership and Support

According to the RAND Change Agent Study (McLaughlin & Marsh, 1978), active support by principals and district administrators is critical to the success of any change effort.

The RAND research sets the role of the principal as instructional leader in the context of strengthening the school improvement process through team building and problem solving in a "project-like" context. It suggests that principals need to give clear messages that teachers may take responsibility for their own professional growth. (p. 92)

Stallings and Mohlman (1981) determined that teachers improved most in staff-development programs in which the principal supported them and was clear and consistent in communicating school policies. Likewise, Fielding and Schalock (1985) reported a study in which principals' involvement in teachers' staff development produced changes that lasted longer than when principals were not involved.

In their discussion of factors that affect the application of innovations, Loucks and Zacchei (1983) wrote "administrators in successful improvement sites take their leadership roles seriously and provide the direction needed to engage teachers in the new practices" (p. 30).

According to Huberman (1983), teachers' successful use of

new skills often occurs when administrators exert strong and continuous pressure for implementation. He argues that "administrators, both at the central office and building levels, have to go to center stage and stay there if school improvement efforts are to succeed" (p. 27). Although administrator presence is important, administrators must also act as gatekeepers of change, so that "innovation overload" can be avoided (Anderson & Odden, 1986).

Although much research points to administrators as key leaders in staff development and change, others can take leadership and support roles, and they might, in fact, be better placed to do so. Research on school improvement indicates that a team approach can help orchestrate leadership and support functions that can be shared by administrators (building and district level), district coordinators or staff developers, teachers, and external trainers and consultants (Loucks-Horsley & Hergert, 1985). For example, Cox (1983) reports that, although principals seem to play an important role in clarifying expectations and goals and stabilizing the school organization, central office coordinators, who often know more about a specific practice, can effectively coach teachers in their attempts to change their classroom behavior. Coordinating leadership and support can also help avoid such situations as a school's textbooks and curriculum not being matched to the instructional models teachers are being taught to use (Fielding & Schalock, 1985).

District Policies and Systems

Staff development activities occur within the context of a school district's staff-development program. According to Ellis (1988), a comprehensive staff-development program includes a philosophy, goals, allocation of resources, and coordination. The philosophy spells out beliefs that guide the program. District, school, and individual goals (and their accompanying action plans) direct staff-development efforts. Resources need to be allocated at the district, school, and individual levels, so that these goals have a reasonable chance of being achieved. Staff-development programs need to be coordinated by individuals who have an assigned responsibility for this area. Ellis also supports the use of a district-level staff-development committee to aid in coordination of programs.

The selection, incorporation, or combination of the models of staff-development described in this chapter is the responsibility of the district's staff-development structure. Decisions about their use need to match the intended outcomes if they are to be effective (Levine & Broude, 1988), but these decisions are also influenced by state and/or community initiatives aimed at the improvement of schools and/or teaching (Anderson & Odden, 1986).

Participant Involvement

Research clearly indicates that involvement of participants in key decisions about staff development is necessary for a program to have its greatest impact. According to Lieberman and Miller (1986), a supportive context for staff development requires both a top-down and a bottom-up approach. The top-down component sets a general direction for the district or school and communicates expectations regarding performance. The bottom-up processes involve teachers in establishing goals and designing appropriate staff-development activities.

Common goals are important to the success of staff-development efforts (Ward & Tikunoff, 1981). Odden and Anderson's (1986) research indicates that a clearly defined process of data collection, shared diagnosis, and identification of solutions to problems must be employed during the planning phase. Collaboration, from initial planning through implementation and institutionalization, is a key process in determining these goals and in influencing lasting change (Lambert, 1984; McLaughlin & Marsh, 1978; Wood et al., 1981).

Lortie (1986) argues that, when teachers perceive that they can participate in important school-level decisions, the relationship between the extra efforts required by school improvement and their benefits becomes clearer. Following this argument, he recommends that schools be given relatively little detailed supervision but be monitored, instead, for results based on explicit criteria.

Others report that when teachers cannot be involved in initial decisions regarding staff development, such as when the staff-development program is mandated by state legislation or when it supports use of a districtwide curriculum, teachers' involvement in decisions about the hows and whens of implementation can be important to success. Furthermore, their involvement in developing curriculum and as trainers for staff-development programs can contribute in important ways to the success of an effort (Loucks & Pratt, 1979).

Concluding Thoughts

Odden and Anderson (1986) capture the reciprocal relationship between organization and individual development in this discussion of their research: "When instructional strategies, which aim to improve the skills of individuals, were successful, they had significant effects on schools as organizations. When school strategies, which aim to improve schools as organizations, were successful, they had significant impacts on individuals" (p. 585).

The importance of paying attention to the context of staff development is underscored by Fullan (1982). When told by educators that they cannot provide the elements that support change (e.g., supportive principals, a 2- or 3-year time period for implementation), he responded,

Well don't expect much implementation to occur. . . . I say this not because I am a cynic but because it is wrong to let hopes blind us to the actual obstacles to change. If these obstacles are ignored, the experience with implementation can be harmful to the adults and children directly involved—more harmful than if nothing had been done. (p. 103)

CONCLUSION

Staff development is a relatively young science within education. In many ways the current knowledge base of staff development is similar to what was known about teaching in the early 1970s. During the 1970s and early 1980s research on teaching advanced from descriptive to correlational to experimental studies (Gage, 1984). With the exception of research on training, much of the staff-development literature is theoretical and descriptive, rather than experimental, but it is quickly moving in the latter direction. The remaining two sections describe what can be said with some confidence about the research base for the staff-development models and what is still left to be learned.

What Can Be Said with Confidence

Staff development possesses a useful craft knowledge that guides the field. This craft knowledge includes ways to organize, structure, and deliver staff-development programs (Caldwell, 1988). It has been disseminated in the 1980s through publications such as *Journal of Staff Development, Educational Leadership,* and *Phi Delta Kappan* and through thousands of presentations at workshops and conventions. As a result, in the 1970s and 1980s hundreds of staff-development programs were established in urban, suburban, and rural school districts throughout the United States and Canada. This craft knowledge serves another useful purpose: It can guide researchers in asking far better questions than could have been asked in the 1970s.

Of the five models discussed in this chapter, the research on training is the most robust. It is the most widely used form of staff development and the most thoroughly investigated. As a result, it is possible to say with some confidence which training elements are required to promote the attainment of specific outcomes. Likewise, research on coaching has demonstrated the importance of in-classroom assistance to teachers (by an expert or by a peer) for the transfer of training to the classroom.

The consensus of expert opinion is that school improvement is a systemic process (Fullan, 1982). This ecological approach recognizes that changes in one part of a system influence the other parts. Consequently, staff development both influences and is influenced by the organizational context in which it takes place. The impact of the staff-development models that have been discussed depends upon not only their individual or blended use but also the features of the organization in which they are used.

Although this appears to relate to the art of making staff development work (i.e., the judgement with which one combines and juggles the various organizational interactions), considerable science can be drawn on when organizational supports are necessary for effective staff development. Study after study confirms the necessity of (a) schools with norms that support collegiality and experimentation; (b) district and building administrators who work with the staff to clarify goals and expectations and actively commit to and support teachers' efforts to change their practice; (c) efforts that are strongly focused on changes in curricular, instructional-, and classroom-management practices with improved student learning as the goal; and (d) adequate, appropriate staff-development experiences with follow-up assistance that continues long enough for new behaviors to be incorporated into ongoing practice.

Interestingly enough, it appears that these factors apply to a wide variety of school-improvement and staff-development efforts. Hard research data on some of the models discussed are sparse, but most, if not all, of these factors will certainly continue to be important, regardless of what is learned about other models.

What We Need to Learn More About

Although the work of staff-development practitioners during the 1980s has been grounded in theory and research from various disciplines (e.g., adult learning, organization development, training), the scientific base of their own practice is quite thin (with the exception of training and coaching). Unfortunately, the systematic study of some of the models discussed earlier is difficult, because their use is not widespread or because they have been implemented only recently as part of comprehensive staff-development programs. Listed next are areas for further study.

1. *We need research to determine the potency of the models described (with the exception of training).* We need to learn which models are most effective for which outcomes with which teachers. For instance, we might ask: How effective is individually guided staff development for knowledge-level outcomes for self-directed experienced teachers? Or how effective is an inquiry approach in helping beginning teachers learn their craft?

2. *We need a better understanding of the impact on student learning of nontraining staff-development models.* Do nontraining models alter teacher knowledge or skills in a way that improves student learning?

3. *We need to know more about the impact on teachers of blending the models in a comprehensive staff-development program.* How are teachers' attitudes, knowledge, and skills altered when they choose among and blend various models as the means of reaching one or more "growth" goals? For instance, what would be the result if a teacher blended individually guided staff development (e.g., reading research on tracking), observation/assessment (e.g., peer observation), and training (e.g., in cooperative learning) as a means of altering classroom practices that are viewed as disadvantageous to a subgroup of students?

4. *We need a systemic view of comprehensive staff development at the district level.* Most districts provide a variety of staff-development opportunities for teachers. Some purposely support individual, school-based, and district-based activities. We need descriptive studies of what these look like, both from the overall, coordination point of view and from the individual teacher's point of view. We need to know: How are goals set and coordinated? How are resources allocated? How equitable are opportunities for individual teachers? How do different contextual factors (e.g., resources, state mandates) influence success?

5. *We need to understand more about the relative costs of different staff-development models and combinations of the models.* Moore and Hyde (1978, 1981) have conducted some useful analyses of how many school district resources actually are used for staff-development purposes. But more microanalyses would be useful to an understanding of the cost-effectiveness of relatively labor-intensive models (e.g., coaching), versus those that rely on teacher activity only (e.g., individually guided staff development).

6. *Finally, we need to examine staff development as it contributes to teacher professionalism and teacher leadership.* These are terms that many believe must characterize our education systems in the future if those systems are to survive. Yet there are as many different definitions of the terms as there are ideas of how to implement them. One role of staff-development research is to help identify and clarify the various meanings given to them. Then we need descriptive studies of staff development's contributions to these efforts, with special attention to how these efforts influence the conduct of staff development.

It is possible that future research will contradict current craft knowledge (this has occurred, for example, with the learning that attitude change does not always have precede behavior change); or, as is likely, future research will support current practice. Many questions about effective staff development remain unanswered. The need is great for well-designed long-term studies of school-improvement efforts based on staff development. The field of staff development seeks a solid base that moves beyond description and advocacy to a better understanding of those factors that support and improve classroom practice.

References

Acheson, K., & Gall, M. (1980). *Techniques in the clinical supervision of teachers.* New York: Longman.

Ainsworth, A. (1976). Teachers talk about inservice education. *Journal of Teacher Education, 27*(2), 107–109.

Anderson, B., & Odden, A. (1986). State initiatives can foster school improvement. *Phi Delta Kappan, 67*(8), 578–581.

Berman, P., & McLaughlin, M. (1978). *Federal programs supporting educational change: Vol. 8. Implementing and sustaining innovation.* Santa Monica, CA: RAND Corporation.

Blanchard, K., & Johnson, S. (1982). *The one minute manager.* New York: William Morrow.

Boyer, E. (1983). *High school: A report on secondary education in America.* New York: Harper & Row.

Brandt, R. (1987). On teachers coaching teachers: A conversation with Bruce Joyce. *Educational Leadership, 44*(5), 12–17.

Brim, J., & Tollett, D. (1974). How do teachers feel about inservice education? *Educational Leadership, 31*(6), 521–525.

Caldwell, S. (Ed.). (1988). *Staff development: A handbook of effective practices.* Oxford, OH: National Staff Development Council.

Casner-Lotto, J. (1988). Expanding the teacher's role: Hammond's school improvement process. *Phi Delta Kappan, 69*(5), 349–353.

Cohen, M. (1981). Effective schools: What the research says. *Today's Education, 70,* 466–496.

Conley, S., & Bacharach, S. (1987). The Holmes Group report: Standards, hierarchies, and management. *Teachers College Record, 88*(3), 340–347.

Cox, P. (1983). Complementary roles in successful change. *Educational Leadership, 41*(3), 10–13.

Crandall, D. (1983). The teacher's role in school improvement. *Educational Leadership, 41*(3), 6–9.

Crandall, D., & Loucks, S. (1983). *A roadmap for school improvement.* Executive summary of *People, policies, and practices: Examining the chain of school improvement.* Andover, MA: NETWORK.

Cross, P. (1987). The adventures of education in wonderland: Implementing education reform. *Phi Delta Kappan, 68*(7), 496–502.

Dewey, J. (1933). *How we think: A restatement of the relation of reflective thinking to the educative process.* Lexington, MA: D.C. Heath.

Dillon-Peterson, B. (1981). Staff development/organizational development—perspective 1981. In B. Dillon-Peterson (Ed.), *Staff development/organization development.* Alexandria, VA: Association for Supervision and Curriculum Development.

Dunn, R., & Dunn, K. (1978). *Teaching students through their individual learning styles: A practical approach.* Reston, VA: Reston.

Ellis, S. (1988). Putting it all together: An integrated staff development

program. In S. Caldwell (Ed.), *Staff development: A handbook of effective practices.* Oxford, OH: National Staff Development Council.

Fielding, G., & Schalock, H. (1985). *Promoting the professional development of teachers and administrators.* Eugene, OR: ERIC Clearinghouse on Educational Management.

Fullan, M. (1982). *The meaning of educational change.* Toronto: OISE Press.

Gable, R., & Rogers, V. (1987). Taking the terror out of research. *Phi Delta Kappan, 68*(9), 690–695.

Gage, N. (1984). What do we know about teaching effectiveness? *Phi Delta Kappan, 66*(2), 87–93.

Glatthorn, A. (1984). *Differentiated supervision.* Alexandria, VA: Association for Supervision and Curriculum Development.

Glatthorn, A. (1987). Cooperative professional development: Peer-centered options for teacher growth. *Educational Leadership, 45*(3), 31–35.

Glickman, C. (1986). Developing teacher thought. *Journal of Staff Development, 7*(1), 6–21.

Good, T., & Grouws, D. (1987). Increasing teachers' understanding of mathematical ideas through inservice training. *Phi Delta Kappan, 68*(10), 778–783.

Gregorc, A. (1979). Learning/teaching styles: Their nature and effects. In *Student learning styles: Diagnosing and prescribing programs* (pp. 19–26). Reston, VA: National Association of Secondary School Principals.

Guskey, T. (1986). Staff development and the process of teacher change. *Educational Researcher, 15*(5), 5–12.

Hall, G. E., & Loucks, S. (1978). Teacher concerns as a basis for facilitating and personalizing staff development. *Teachers College Record, 80*(1), 36–53.

Hering, W., & Howey, K. (1982). Research in, on, and by teachers' centers (Occasional Paper No. 10). San Francisco: Teachers' Center Exchange, Far West Laboratory for Educational Research and Development.

Hovda, R., & Kyle, D. (1984). A strategy for helping teachers integrate research into teaching. *Middle School Journal, 15*(3), 21–23.

Huberman, A. (1983). School improvement strategies that work: Some scenarios. *Educational Leadership, 41*(3), 23–27.

Hunter, M. (1982). *Mastery teaching.* El Segundo, CA: TIP Publications.

Ingvarson, L. (1987). *Models of inservice education and their implications for professional development policy.* Paper presented at a conference on Inservice Education: Trends of the Past, Themes for the Future, Melbourne, Australia.

Jefferson County Public Schools. (1974). *Report of the task force to define the process of developing curriculum.* Lakewood, CO: Author.

Johnson, D., Johnson, R., Holubec, E., & Roy, P. (1984). *Circles of learning.* Alexandria, VA: Association for Supervision and Curriculum Development.

Joyce, B., & Peck, L. (1977). *Inservice teacher education project report II: Interviews.* Syracuse, NY: Syracuse University.

Joyce, B., & Showers, B. (1982). The coaching of teaching. *Educational Leadership, 40*(1), 4–10.

Joyce, B., & Showers, B. (1983). *Power in staff development through research on training.* Alexandria, VA: Association for Supervision and Curriculum Development.

Joyce, B., & Showers, B. (1988). *Student achievement through staff development.* New York: Longman.

Joyce, B., & Weil, M. (1972). *Models of teaching.* Englewood Cliffs, NJ: Prentice-Hall.

Kells, P. (1981). Quality practices in inservice education. *The Developer* (1–6). Oxford, OH: National Staff Development Council.

Kerman, S. (1979). Teacher expectations and student achievement. *Phi Delta Kappan, 60*(10), 716–718.

Kidd, J. (1973). *How adults learn.* Chicago: Follett.

Kimpston, R., & Rogers, K. (1987). The influence of prior perspectives, differences in participatory roles, and degree of participation on views about curriculum development: A case study. *Journal of Curriculum and Supervision, 2*(3), 203–220.

Knowles, M. (1980). *The modern practice of adult education.* Chicago: Follett.

Kyle, R. H. J. (Ed.). (1985). *Reaching for excellence: An effective schools sourcebook.* Washington, DC: U.S. Government Printing Office.

Lambert, L. (1984). *How adults learn: An interview study of leading researchers, policy makers, and staff developers.* Paper presented at the meeting of the American Educational Research Association, New Orleans.

Lawrence, G. (1974). *Patterns of effective inservice education: A state of the art summary of research on materials and procedures for changing teacher behaviors in inservice education.* Tallahasee: Florida State University, Div. of Elementary and Secondary Education. (ERIC Document Reproduction Service No ED 176 424)

Levine, S. (1988). *Promoting adult growth in schools: The promise of professional development.* Lexington, MA: Allyn & Bacon.

Levine, S., & Broude, N. (1988). Designs for learning. In S. Caldwell (Ed.), *Staff development: A handbook of effective practices.* Oxford, OH: National Staff Development Council.

Lieberman, A. (1986). Collaborative research: Working with, not working on. *Educational Leadership, 43*(5), 28–32.

Lieberman, A., & Miller, L. (1984). *Teachers, their world and their work: Implications for school improvement.* Alexandria, VA: Association for Supervision and Curriculum Development.

Lieberman, A., & Miller, L. (1986). School improvement: Themes and variations. In A. Lieberman (Ed.), *Rethinking school improvement: Research, craft, and concept.* New York: Teachers College Press.

Little, J. W. (1982). Norms of collegiality and experimentation: Workplace conditions of school success. *American Educational Research Journal, 19*(3), 325–340.

Lortie, D. (1986). Teacher status in Dade county: A case of structural strain? *Phi Delta Kappan, 67*(8), 568–575.

Loucks, S., & Pratt, H. (1979). A concerns-based approach to curriculum change. *Educational Leadership, 37*(3), 212–215.

Loucks, S., & Zacchei, D. (1983). Applying our findings to today's innovations. *Educational Leadership, 41*(3), 28–31.

Loucks-Horsley, S., Harding, C., Arbuckle, M., Murray, L., Dubea, C., & Williams, M. (1987). *Continuing to learn: A guidebook for teacher development.* Andover, MA: Regional Laboratory for Edu-

cational Improvement of the Northeast and Islands/National Staff Development Council.

Loucks-Horsley, S., & Hergert, L. (1985). *An action guide to school improvement.* Alexandria, VA: Association for Supervision and Curriculum Development/Andover, MA: NETWORK.

Louis, K., & Rosenblum, S. (1981). *Linking r & d with schools: A program and its implications for dissemination and school improvement policy.* Washington, DC: National Institute of Education.

Mann, D. (1984). Impact II and the problem of staff development. *Educational Leadership, 42*(4), 44–45.

McGreal, T. (1982). Effective teacher evaluation systems. *Educational Leadership, 39*(4), 303–305.

McGreal, T. (1983). *Successful teacher evaluation.* Alexandria, VA: Association for Supervision and Curriculum Development.

McLaughlin, M., & Marsh, D. (1978). Staff development and school change. *Teachers College Record, 80*(1), 69–94.

Miles, M. (1983). Unraveling the mystery of institutionalization. *Educational Leadership, 41*(3), 14–19.

Moore, D., & Hyde, A. (1978). *Rethinking staff development: A handbook for analyzing your program & its costs.* Chicago: Designs for Change.

Moore, D., & Hyde, A. (1981). *Making sense of staff development: An analysis of staff development programs and their costs in three urban school districts.* Chicago: Designs for Change. (ERIC Document Reproduction Service No. 211 629)

Mosher, W. (1981). *Individual and systemic changes mediated by a small educational grant program.* San Francisco: Far West Laboratory for Educational Research and Development.

Odden, A., & Anderson, B. (1986). How successful state education improvement programs work. *Phi Delta Kappan, 67*(8), 582–585.

Rauth, M. (1986). Putting research to work. *American Educator, 10*(4), 26–31.

Robbins, P., & Wolfe, P. (1987). Reflections on a Hunter-based staff development project. *Educational Leadership, 44*(5), 56–65.

Rogers, C. (1969). *Freedom to learn.* Columbus, OH: Charles E. Merrill.

Scholl, S., & McQueen, P. (1985). The basic skills articulation plan: Curriculum development through staff development. *Journal of Staff Development, 6*(2), 138–142.

Shalaway, L. (1985). Peer coaching . . . does it work? *R & D Notes.* Washington, DC: National Institute of Education.

Showers, J., Joyce, B., & Bennett, B. (1987). Synthesis of research on staff development: A framework for future study and a state-of-art analysis. *Educational Leadership, 45*(3), 77–87.

Simmons, J., & Sparks, G. (1985). Using research to develop professional thinking about teaching. *Journal of Staff Development, 6*(1), 106–116.

Sparks, G. (1983). Synthesis of research on staff development for effective teaching. *Educational Leadership, 41*(3), 65–72.

Sparks, G. (1986). The effectiveness of alternative training activities in changing teaching practices. *American Educational Research Journal, 23*(2), 217–225.

Sparks, G., Nowakowski, M., Hall, B., Alec, R., & Imrick, J. (1985). School improvement through staff development. *Educational Leadership, 42*(6), 59–61.

Sparks, G., & Simmons, J. (1988). Inquiry-oriented staff development: Using research as a source of tools, not rules. In S. Caldwell (Ed.), *Staff development: A handbook of effective practices.* Oxford, OH: National Staff Development Council.

Stallings, J., & Mohlman, G. (1981). *School policy, leadership style, teacher change, and student behavior in eight schools, final report.* Washington, DC: National Institute of Education.

Thompson, S. (1982). *A survey and analysis of Pennsylvania public school personnel perceptions of staff development practices and be-*

liefs with a view to identifying some critical problems or needs. Unpublished doctoral dissertation, The Pennsylvania State University, University Park.

Tikunoff, W., & Ward, B. (1983). Collaborative research on teaching. *Elementary School Journal, 83*(4), 453–468.

Wade, R. (1985). What makes a difference in inservice teacher education? A meta-analysis of research. *Educational Leadership, 42*(4), 48–54.

Ward, B., & Tikunoff, W. (1981, September). The relationship between inservice training, organizational structure and school climate. *Inservice,* 7–8.

Watts, H. (1985). When teachers are researchers, teaching improves. *Journal of Staff Development, 6*(2), 118–127.

Wise, A., & Darling-Hammond, L. (1985). Teacher evaluation and teacher professionalism. *Educational Leadership, 42*(4), 28–33.

Wood, F. (1988). Organizing and managing school-based staff development. In S. Caldwell (Ed.), *Staff development: A handbook of effective practices.* Oxford, OH: National Staff Development Council.

Wood, F., & Kleine, P. (1987). *Staff development research and rural schools: A critical appraisal.* Unpublished manuscript, University of Oklahoma, Norman.

Wood, F., McQuarrie, F., & Thompson, S. (1982). Practitioners and professors agree on effective staff development practices. *Educational Leadership, 40,* 28–31.

Wood , F., Thompson, S., & Russell. F. (1981). Designing effective staff development programs. In B. Dillon-Peterson (Ed.), *Staff development/organization development.* Alexandria, VA: Association for Supervision and Curriculum Development.

Wu, P. (1987). Teachers as staff developers: Research, opinions, and cautions. *Journal of Staff Development, 8*(1), 4–6.

Yarger, S., Howey, K., & Joyce, B. (1980). *Inservice teacher education.* Palo Alto, CA: Booksend Laboratory.

Zeichner, K. (1983). Alternative paradigms of teacher education. *Journal of Teacher Education, 34*(3), 3–9.

Zigarmi, P., Betz, L., & Jensen, D. (1977). Teachers' preferences in and perceptions of inservice education. *Educational Leadership, 34*(7), 545–551.

15

RESEARCH ON PROFESSIONAL DEVELOPMENT SCHOOLS

Jane A. Stallings

UNIVERSITY OF HOUSTON

Theodore Kowalski

BALL STATE UNIVERSITY

Professional development schools have existed in many forms since the late nineteenth century. In this chapter, the professional development school is defined as a school setting focused on the professional development of teachers and the development of pedagogy. Laboratory schools embedded in schools of education were the earliest forms of professional development schools. John Dewey (1896) compared the need for a teachers' professional development laboratory to that of scientists and medical practitioners. With accordionlike dimensions, the laboratory school movement has expanded and contracted from that time until today. In the late 1960s and 1970s, professional development schools took the form of portal schools. Portal schools were located within the public school system and focused on developing and field-testing new curriculum, teacher preparation, and inservice education in public school settings. In the 1980s, such schools were called school–college partnerships or professional-practice schools; some have originated from school districts and others from colleges of education. This chapter describes the mission and the structure of several efforts to join college and school resources in providing professional development opportunities for educators. Most of the research in this area is descriptive rather than empirical.

LABORATORY SCHOOLS

As long ago as 1896, John Dewey (p. 422) argued that the teaching laboratory bears the same relation to the work of pedagogy that a laboratory bears to biology and physics. Like any such laboratory, it has two main purposes: first, to exhibit, test, verify, and criticize theoretical statements and principles; second, to add to the sum of facts and principles in its special line.

During the 1980s, Dewey's idea was rekindled, as schools of education sought improvements and more rational solutions to the myriad problems plaguing elementary and secondary education. Once again, the brave dream of a truly experimental school chronicled by Van Til (1969) was being resurrected. The vision was of a school where faculty are master teachers demonstrating their skills in the art and science of teaching, carrying forward research and experimentation with children and youth. Observers and participants would be introduced to the best possible educational theory and practice. In this dream, the development of significant research was a shared responsibility among the faculties of the experimental school and the university.

No aspect of the laboratory school produced higher expecta-

The authors thank reviewers Dick Aarons (University of Maryland), John Sikula (California State University, Long Beach), and Robert Houston (University of Houston). Thanks also to Yvonne Cavitt (University of Houston) and David Markham (MITRE Corporation).

tions and more disappointments than the area of research. In the midst of arguments that teacher education ought to be based upon a body of research (e.g., Berliner, 1985), the potential of campus laboratory schools to contribute to knowledge deserves careful consideration. Presented here is an overview of the history of laboratory schools, findings from the available research, and recommendations for making laboratory schools effective environments for research related to teaching and teacher education. For the purpose of this chapter, the name laboratory school is synonymous with campus school; it is a school located on or near a college campus and administered by the college of education solely or in cooperation with the local school district.

Laboratory Schools' Historical Basis

Two of the more prominent laboratory schools established in this country illuminated research as an essential goal. The Horace Mann School at Teachers College, Columbia University, established in 1887, and the Laboratory School at the University of Chicago, established by John Dewey around the turn of the century, focused upon research activities designed to improve teaching and the experiences of those who were preparing to enter the profession (Page & Page, 1981).

The prominence of these two schools contributed to a broad mission for all laboratory schools. There was a common expectation for research to occur in laboratory schools, and it did through the 1930s. During the war years of the 1940s, there is little evidence that sponsoring institutions provided resources for research. McGeoch (1971), taking a historical perspective, noted that by 1971 experimentation and research were more talked about than practiced in laboratory schools. The two primary purposes she identified were to provide an on-campus environment in which prospective teachers could observe prevailing methods and to provide a setting where student teaching could be completed. Lumpkins and Parker (1986) confirm this, noting that most campus schools continued to serve as convenient sites for pre–student teaching and student teaching experiences. Thus, it appears that 100 years after the inception of the Horace Mann School, those in charge of laboratory school agendas had given up the research mission.

From their beginning in 1887, the number of laboratory schools increased until their peak in 1964, when, according to Kelley (1964), the National Association of Laboratory Schools (NALS) had 212 schools on its roster. This number diminished to 208 by 1969. A more recent report of NALS indicated the number of laboratory schools had dwindled to 95 in 1988. Factors influencing these shifts are reported in the following research studies.

Research on Laboratory Schools

Research about laboratory schools is sparse; however, studies have been conducted periodically to examine their primary functions. One study completed in the early 1940s found that the fundamental use of laboratory schools was almost exclusively for student teaching (Williams, 1942). Another con-

ducted in 1952 established that 85 to 90 percent of 185 campus schools identified observation, participation, demonstration, and student teaching as their major functions. This same study indicated that little more than one-third of the schools even professed to be engaged in any form of research (Rucker, 1952).

Because the primary purpose of most laboratory schools, historically, was to service teacher education, many educators believed that the schools should duplicate as closely as possible the conditions students would meet in the field (e.g., Harper, 1939). A majority of the schools adhered to this recommendation. As teacher education programs began to swell in enrollment, however, it became necessary to place student teachers in the public schools, as well as in the laboratory schools. Administrators in laboratory schools were slow to react to the implications of this unavoidable decision. If students could complete their student teaching in regular classrooms, was a laboratory school really necessary? And because such great effort had been made to assure that the campus school reflected the real world, was there any substantial difference between the environment of the campus school and the public school? Slowly but surely the public schools became the focus of student teaching and participation (Van Til, 1985). Once they had abandoned the research mission and relinquished the preparation of student teachers, the validity of laboratory schools was questioned.

In 1948, the School and Community Laboratory Experiences Committee of the American Association of Teachers Colleges (AATC) advocated decreasing the emphasis on student teaching in laboratory schools. At the same time, the committee called for laboratory schools to place greater emphasis on experimentation. Student teaching in laboratory schools was reduced, so that laboratory schools served primarily as sites for observation, participation, and curriculum development. The AATC's recommendation that research and experimentation be increased was not followed (Lumpkins & Parker, 1986).

Twenty-two years after the AATC report, Hunter (1970) identified critical problems similar to those cited by the AATC that needed to be addressed by laboratory schools. The first issue examined was an ever-widening gap between findings from research on teaching and the continuing practice in laboratory school classrooms. The second was a critical need for experimental labs to field-test educational innovations. Studies completed in the 1980s revealed that the problems identified by the AATC and Hunter had not been addressed; in fact, laboratory schools were seriously declining, and little research was being conducted.

Jackson (1986) concludes that existing laboratory schools were vulnerable for several reasons. First, although the six commonly stated functions of laboratory schools (educate children, develop innovative practices, conduct research, prepare new teachers, provide inservice practice, and disseminate innovations) are not incompatible, functions considered less important are likely to be inconsistently implemented. Indeed, laboratory school faculties most often have differing beliefs regarding the importance of the six functions; very few place research at the top of their list. For successful operation, laboratory schools need university and school district support.

Incongruence in expectations and values has made it difficult to secure the desired level of support. Consequently, laboratory schools have been on the decline since 1969.

To examine the priorities, mission, and motivation of laboratory school faculties, F. M. Page and Page (1981) sent a questionnaire to the 123 schools listed in the 1981–1982 National Association of Laboratory Schools Directory. Fifty-seven schools responded. Based upon this input, the following conclusions were drawn.

1. Increased costs in higher education are a contributing factor to the closing of laboratory schools.
2. Many laboratory schools are attempting to broaden their missions and to maximize support for operations.
3. There is some indication that research is gaining in importance, but it is not viewed as a primary function.
4. Promotion, tenure, and continued employment appear to be the greatest extrinsic motivators with regard to laboratory school faculties' conducting research.
5. Faculty in laboratory schools have limited time to conduct research.

In a follow-up study, Page (1983) found that laboratory school faculty reported spending as much as 13.7 percent of the time in research-related activities. This is equal to the amount of time reported by faculty in research-focused colleges of education. In a survey of college of education professors, Ducharme (1987) found time spent in research differed according to the type of institution. He found that, on the basis of a typical 44-hour week, professors in small 4-year colleges reported spending 4 hours per week on research. In big state colleges offering the master's degree, professors spent 5 hours a week. In research-focused institutions offering the doctorate, professors reported spending 6 hours a week (14 percent of their time) on research activities.

Employing the same list of laboratory schools used by Page and Page in 1981, Kowalski, Glover, and Krug (1988) surveyed the 95 remaining laboratory schools regarding their research activities. Their sample reported use of only 3 percent of the time on research activities. This is approximately 10 percent less time spent on research than that reported by Page in 1983. The classification for time utilization was not identical, and these differences could explain the variance in the findings for the two studies. In the Kowalski et al. (1988) study, those few institutions reporting research activity described the foci of their research efforts as follows: teaching methods—35 percent; curriculum—18 percent; teacher education—9 percent; learning/development—35 percent; other—31 percent.

Although laboratory schools have been conceptualized as special environments in which the joining of theory and practice can be explored, 61 percent of the schools surveyed reported little or no collaboration between college and laboratory school faculties (Kowalski et al., 1988).

Unlike previous survey studies, Kowalski et al. also conducted a data-base search (*Psychological Abstracts* and ERIC for 1986) in an attempt to verify the level of laboratory school activity related to research. This search identified 168 journal articles, convention papers, and occasional papers authored by individuals affiliated with laboratory schools in the United States. When convention papers (the majority given at state and regional meetings) and articles in the *National Association of Laboratory Schools Journal* were subtracted from this total, only 32 remained. Of the 32 articles, only one had appeared in a journal sponsored by the American Educational Research Association, the American Psychological Association, or the American Association of Colleges for Teacher Education. These results support the conclusion that laboratory schools and their faculties, in general, have contributed very little to the development of theory in the field of teacher education.

The Future of Laboratory Schools

The national attention accorded to education in the 1980s presented a rare opportunity for laboratory schools to achieve what Van Til (1985) describes as Dewey's dream of a laboratory school that is truly a laboratory. If laboratory schools are to become that dream, priorities must change. *First*, university and laboratory school faculties must make a philosophical commitment to collaborate in developing a research mission for the laboratory school. For example, models to develop teachers who are reflective about the teaching–learning process are desperately needed. Models are needed for developing teachers who can teach with sensitivity and knowledge the 55-percent-multicultured nation of children predicted for the twenty-first century. To develop new models and to conduct controlled experiments of their effects, research-oriented faculty needed to be recruited to work with or in laboratory schools. Faculty working in laboratory schools also need cooperative working skills, so that the needs and attributes of participants are recognized and growth opportunities are supported.

Second, the agenda of the laboratory school should be to ask and answer important educational questions. Research-and-development efforts should result in visible products of value to elementary and secondary schools, as well as to teacher education programs. The research-and-development activities should address the needs specified by stakeholders in the laboratory school community, including the service commitments of the university and college of education.

Third, incentives for working in laboratory schools need to be clearly delineated. Nielsen (1986) states that, if the desired changes in laboratory schools are to come about, instructors recruited for campus schools must have full university faculty status including rank, access to tenure, sabbaticals, and related professorial roles. Research by Page and Page (1981) indicates that, if laboratory schools are to prosper, the administration must systematically illuminate and reward research efforts that occur within the laboratory schools. The infusion of adequate fiscal resources permitting appropriate teaching loads for those engaging in research is also required. It is unrealistic to expect faculty to assume teaching loads similar to those in the public schools and to simultaneously perform research activities.

Other fiscal considerations must include the support necessary to sustain research efforts. Support must include material, equipment (e.g., computers), travel monies, and reimbursement for publication costs. Research support, however, also includes human resources (e.g., secretaries, graduate assistants, aides) that allow laboratory school faculty the time to do research.

Effective research in teacher education cannot be done in a vacuum. It needs to occur in settings where there are real children, real adults, and effective teaching (Van Til, 1985). Research models must be validated with real classroom events and produce studies useful to practitioners in education (Ornstein, 1985). The achievement of realistic research goals, therefore, is most probable in an environment where classroom teachers also become researchers. Those who control university and public school budgets must be convinced that experimentation and applied research are important to teacher education and that the laboratory school is a feasible environment for conducting such activities.

PORTAL SCHOOLS

The label of *portal school* appeared first in the literature describing the teacher education process in the *Florida State University Model for the Preparation of Elementary School Teachers* as described by Sowards (1969). The portal school is broadly described by its name. "It is a school in a district selected as a point of entry for promising new curricula and practices. It is for new or experienced teachers who wish to improve learning for children" (Chambers & Olmstead, 1971, p. 2).

To provide a sense of history, early in 1970 President Nixon addressed the crisis in education (as have succeeding presidents):

There comes a time in any learning process that calls for reassessment and reinforcement. It calls for new directions in our methods of teaching and new understanding of our ways of learning, for fresh emphasis on our basic research. We must improve education in those areas of life outside the school where people learn so much or so little. (Bradley, 1971, p. 1)

Although Bradley mentions the shortage of teachers in the 1950s and 1960s, the more profound problem then, as now, was the quality of education:

While there are more teachers now, little has been done to change the way in which they are prepared, especially for the inner-city public schools. New teachers are graduated who lack field experience. Inservice training is limited and university teacher trainers are isolated from the public schools in which they are preparing their students to teach. (p. 2)

These words have a familiar ring; the problems of educating teachers in the 1970s sound similar to problems identified in the late 1980s, with possibly similar solutions being proposed.

The portal schools grew out of the perceived need for improving the quality of education at all levels. The portal school concept provided for a process of self-renewal to take place within the school system, so that the education of teachers and children would become more relevant to the world in which they lived. The concept was designed to orchestrate the discrete elements of public school education (universities, public school administrators, teachers, professional organizations, and the community). A unified educational focus was expected to improve the total learning environment and build the process for self-renewal into the system itself. Joyce (1972) wrote:

Massive infusion of funds into the educational system can do little to change it unless teachers become agents of change. Teacher education must be rooted in commitment to educational change. Young teachers need to be prepared—not by socializing them to the existing pattern of the school—but by preparing them to participate in the re-creation of educational forms and substance. (p. 10)

The portal schools were regular schools in a district selected as a point of entry for promising new curricula and practices. It was for new or experienced teachers who wished to improve learning for children. According to Chambers and Olmstead (1971), the portal school served as a focal point for interaction with the university in specifying those teaching competencies needed to create and sustain innovative practices that had proven to be effective. The portal school was a dissemination point or point of exit into other schools in the district for tested curricula and for teams of retrained teaching personnel.

Considerable support for the portal school idea came from the Council of the Great City Schools. The council was committed to a need for systematic change, new curricula in the schools, relevant teacher education, and relevant inservice education. Portal school models were developed at Florida State University, Temple University and the Philadelphia Public Schools, University of Georgia and the Atlanta Public Schools, and the Wisconsin Research and Development Center. Teacher Corps and the American Federation of Teachers also embraced the portal school concept. Through Teacher Corps grants, there was some federal funding for Portal School network activities.

Although each model was different in its response to the needs of the community in which it was located, there were elements common to portal schools, including:

An advisory council established at the beginning with representatives from each group (i.e., teachers' bargaining agent, students in pre-service training, administration, community, university). This council acted in an advisory capacity to the building principal, who retained chief administrative responsibility.

Selection of portal schools made with firm support from the teachers and administrators in the schools, as well as the top administrations of the university and school system.

Planning time provided for developing projected goals and for designing programs to meet those goals. This planning involved teachers, union, community, college faculty, and school system staff from the beginning.

Agreements made among the schools, colleges, state departments of education, community, and teachers for the administration, evaluation, and revision of education programs. (Lutonsky, 1972a, p. 8)

Existing university and school system programs for pre- and inservice training and curriculum development were concentrated in portal schools. With enough programs per building, the university was able to justify financing a full-time professor per school to assist in the development and coordination of portal school programs. These programs provided more professional staff per school, resulting in more programs for pupils. This staff was available for a variety of consultative, testing, workshop, staff, program development, and material-construction purposes at no additional cost to the school.

Each group recognized that this concept relied upon equal sharing of responsibility for the development of portal school programs. A written agreement was drawn up and signed by all cooperating agencies and was effective for at least 3 years; one year for planning and development and 2 years for implementation.

Competency-based educational learning experiences were available in portal schools so that (a) future teachers could develop and demonstrate professional skills in the field, (b) their professors could return to the field to test and refine their expertise, and (c) both professors and coordinating teachers could assess students' professional growth and the effectiveness of curricula and instructional skills in a real-life context.

It was the interaction of these processes that defined the uniqueness of a portal school and served as a strategy for self-renewal (Lutonsky, 1972a, p. 11). Although the mission, essential elements, objectives, and implementation stages of the portal schools were clearly defined in their monthly newsletters (Lutonsky, 1972b), evaluation or systematic assessment of the program or projects were not mentioned in any of the portal school literature. Innovators of portal schools seemingly did not design research to see whether objectives were met. Research methodology to assess expected or unexpected changes in teacher education or student outcomes was not included in their plans. Perhaps the lack of information regarding the effectiveness of the portal schools led to their lack of funding and subsequent demise. By 1980 the portal school terminology had dropped from the literature, and schools and colleges of education were once again isolated in their attempts to improve teacher education.

CURRENT REFORM EFFORTS IN PROFESSIONAL DEVELOPMENT SCHOOLS

The plummeting test scores of students in the 1970s were dramatically presented to the American people through the popular press. Not only did the achievement-test scores of the traditionally lower achieving segments of the population drop, but also the college-bound students were mastering less in academic subjects than their counterparts in previous decades. These events brought components of the education system under close scrutiny. Congress and private foundations commissioned assessments of our nation's educational system. Forthcoming were arousing, quotable indictments such as the opening words in A *Nation At Risk* by the National Commission on Excellence in Education (1983): "If an unfriendly foreign power had attempted to impose on America the mediocre educational performance that exists today, we might well have

viewed it as an act of war" (p. 5). In John Goodlad's book, *A Place Called School* (1984), the first sentence reads "American schools are in trouble." In his book *High School: A Report on Secondary Education in America*, Ernest Boyer (1983) added his voice to the battle cry for educational change. The effect of these reports was to propel stakeholders in education to a frenzied examination of the goals and conditions of schools in their own locales. The subsequent education reform movement in the 1980s created state and local commissions of excellence that have functioned to recommend legislation and mandate change in school curricula, graduation standards, teacher certification, and teacher assessment.

After the first wave of responses to the challenge for excellence, a more in-depth analysis identified goals for schools that were much broader than gains on achievement-test scores. The leaders of business and industry declared a need for employees who had basic skills but who were flexible learners who could transfer knowledge from one task to another. They needed employees who were responsible, who had high work standards, and who had the social skills necessary for cooperative tasks. With rapidly exploding information and technology, workers in the 1990s and the twenty-first century are likely to change occupations three or four times during their lives. Given the expected changes, employees will need learning to learn skills. Such outcomes of schooling require a different structure of schools and classroom instruction. To develop the type of citizenry required for the twenty-first century, schools must be different, principals must be different, teachers must be different, and colleges of education must be different.

Two major reports have driven the reconceptualization of teacher education toward a model of professional-school partnerships linking colleges of education and schools. These are the Carnegie Forum's report and the Holmes Group report.

The Carnegie Forum on Education and the Economy (1986) recommended the development of a National Board for Professional Teaching Standards. This board would have created a set of assessments of teachers' subject-matter knowledge, pedagogical understandings, and application of this knowledge in simulated classrooms. Specifying a high standard of professionalism in teaching would enhance the prestige of the occupation and would enable the recruitment of more academically able candidates. To prepare teachers to meet these standards, the Carnegie Task Force recommended the establishment of *clinical schools*. Clinical schools would link faculties in elementary and secondary schools, colleges of education, and colleges of arts and science to provide the best possible learning environment for teacher preparation. The forum recommended a 2-year graduate course, the first year spent in coursework and internship, the second year in residency, working under supervision in a *clinical school*. The clinical school was seen as analogous to a teaching hospital. This design called for teachers in outstanding public schools to work closely with colleges of education in the clinical school. *Lead teachers* would hold adjunct appointments at the university. They would serve on the instructional staff of the Masters in Teaching Degree Program. Participants in this partnership would have opportunities to reflect upon teaching and learning within the clinical school environment. "The clinical schools should exemplify the collegial, performance-oriented environment that newly certified teachers should be prepared to establish" (Carnegie Forum on Education and the Economy, 1986, p. 77.).

Professional development schools are described in the Holmes Group report (1986) as institutions that would connect colleges of education with schools in a manner similar to that described by the Carnegie Forum report. The Holmes Group report also recommended that professional development schools be analogous to teaching hospitals in the medical profession. The partnership among practicing teachers, administrators, and university faculty would be based on the following principles: (a) reciprocity, or mutual exchange and benefit, between research and practice; (b) experimentation, or willingness to try new forms of practice and structure; (c) systematic inquiry, or the requirement that new ideas be subject to careful study and validation; and (d) student diversity, or commitment to the development of teaching strategies for a broad range of children with different backgrounds, abilities, and learning styles.

These schools would serve as settings for teaching professionals to test different instructional arrangements for novice teachers and for researchers to work under the guidance of gifted practitioners, for the exchange of professional knowledge between university faculty and practitioners, and for the development of new structures designed around the demands of a new profession (Holmes Group, 1986, p. 67).

Another term for professional development schools was used by Wise et al. (1987) in the RAND study. They promoted the idea of an *induction school*. Although Wise et al. believed that universities should provide a sound knowledge base, they also believed that a teacher can become fully prepared only through extensive, supervised, classroom experience. In the induction school, new teachers would be supervised frequently by expert teachers. Recognizing the difficulty of recruiting and keeping good teachers in inner-city schools, the RAND study recommended that the induction school be located in an inner-city neighborhood. The rationale for this proposal was that senior tenured teachers would be more likely to stay in such schools, given the benefits and chances to advance through opportunities to serve as expert teacher trainers. Heavy staffing to allow frequent supervision of the novice teachers would be a key feature of this program. Expected benefits include (a) supervision for beginning teachers with eased entry to teaching, better preparation for teaching, and reduced attrition; (b) an attractive assignment for senior teachers that recognizes and uses their talent and experience; (c) a setting where first-year teachers could be efficiently and effectively evaluated, and (d) more resources and more stable teaching for disadvantaged children (Wise et al., 1987, p. 96).

Although differing somewhat in conceptualization, the goal of the professional-development schools described are similar. Each recommends partnerships that join teachers, administrators, and college faculties in an effort to restructure the preparation and the induction of teachers into the teaching profession. The goal of this collaborative effort is to develop schools and colleges where participants will acquire essential (a) subject-area knowledge; (b) reflective, analytic, problem-solving skills; and (c) social skills, so that the educational needs of soci-

ety now and in the twenty-first century are met. The resultant structure of such consortiums is schools where administrators, teachers, student teachers, and college faculty can grow professionally.

Although these reports have conceptualized specific types of professional development schools requiring extensive restructuring of schools and colleges, in 1988 such schools were more in the planning stage than a reality. There were many forms of school–college partnerships and a few experiments whose purpose was to explore the possibilities of professional development schools in a wide range of contexts. Two fairly recent directories of school–college partnerships, both authored by Wilbur, Lambert, and Young (1987, 1988), describe partnerships in the form of institutes, academies, academic alliances, residencies, and induction teams.

Programs selected to be described met the following criteria: (a) the program must be in existence now, not just a twinkle in the developer's eye; (b) there must be some form of evaluation, either descriptive or empirical; (c) the project must involve some type of ongoing professional development program, even though the school campus might be floating or invisible. Based on these criteria, a broad definition of professional development schools was determined. The examples included here range all the way from single schools to complex statewide networks and include schools addressing preservice preparation and induction. For some, lengthy research findings are available; for others, the findings are very meager. Because more information is available, those programs reporting their impact on participants are reviewed more extensively.

Professional Development Schools Focused on Inservice Teachers

Yale University and New Haven Public Schools. In a joint effort to strengthen teaching and learning in the community's middle and high schools, Yale University and the New Haven Public Schools established the *Teachers Institute*. The institute has become a place where Yale faculty members and school teachers join in interschool, interdisciplinary forums. At the institute, teachers work together on new curricula. Participants can become institute fellows if they responsibly complete the subjects the institute offers. Fellows must participate fully in the program by attending talks and seminar activities. They must research the seminar topic and the unit topic, using their data to develop curriculum units. Finally, they must submit a thoughtful written evaluation of the program. All of these assignments must be submitted on time. Fellows who meet these expectations become members of the Yale community with library and other university privileges. Evaluations by fellows and research studies of the program indicate an increase in teacher preparation in their subject areas, higher teacher morale, higher expectations of students, and higher student performance. Combinations of these outcomes have influenced teachers to remain in teaching in New Haven. Demographic information indicates that the attrition rate of institute fellows is considerably lower than that in most urban schools.

Oberlin Teachers Academy. The purpose of the Oberlin Teachers Academy is to make its resources available to Cleveland area secondary teachers and administrators. The academy offers summer institutes and weekend workshops in such areas as English, biology, chemistry, computer science, French, mathematics, Soviet and American relations, and Japanese history and culture. Oberlin College credit is awarded for summer seminars and week-long workshops. Teachers who participate in academy programs over an extended period of time and perform at a consistently high level of excellence are given the title Fellow of the Oberlin Teachers Academy. A high level of excellence includes a significant project that makes a contribution to the field of pedagogy or curriculum. Several hundred teachers have participated in academy activities. Since its inception in 1986, two candidates have qualified for status as fellows.

University of Maryland–College Park/Teaching Associates. In a partnership with Montgomery County Public Schools, the University of Maryland–College Park has offered secondary school teachers in mathematics, chemistry, and physics an opportunity to become *teaching associates* at the university. The purpose of the program is to improve science and mathematics instruction in secondary schools. Associates are selected for the year-long leave by a joint committee of school and university faculty. Teaching associates take graduate-level courses, help teach in a first-year course, supervise laboratories, and help with lectures and discussions. Another requirement is to complete a subject-relevant project acceptable to the Montgomery County Schools and the university. Upon return to the school, the project is shared with fellow teachers. Survey evidence indicates that the program has built closer university–school ties, has helped update and enrich the background knowledge of teachers, and has contributed substantially to the mathematics and science curricula. It has also helped university and school instructors understand shared problems such as student learning difficulties.

Maryland Teaching Effectiveness Network (TEN). TEN is a professional development program for teacher education faculty, principals, and supervising teachers. The goal of TEN is to create and maintain a continuum between campus-based courses and school-based field experiences in preservice teacher education programs. TEN is a three-phase process started in 1984. Its objectives include: (a) to facilitate the connection between preservice programs and school observation sites; the intent is to provide teacher models and mentors who use the same terminology and learning principles as used in college educational psychology and methods courses; (b) to support the development of supervision and coaching skills by college/university supervisors and LEA supervising teachers so that they will reinforce a common core of learning principles through analyzing teaching and labeling behaviors; (c) to support the ongoing training of institution of higher education (IHE) teacher educators and LEA supervisors; and (d) to coordinate the collection of data for evaluating the TEN program improvement and training process and the teacher education graduates' competence (Arends & Murphy, 1986, p. 20).

This project is interesting in that the first year's evaluations focused on college faculty. Interviews were held with 25 of the 28 college faculty involved in TEN. These interviews consisted of three sections: (a) the focused Levels of Use—an interview structured after Hall's Concerns Based Adoption Model (Hall & Loucks, 1978); (b) a learning-activities questionnaire (Arends, 1982); and (c) questions aimed at participant reaction to various components of the project and staff-development events.

Participants were asked to list staff-development activities in which they had participated during the past 2 years. Activities listed by teacher educators in this project consisted of seminars or colloquia, most often on topics associated with mainstreaming and multicultural education.

Participants were also asked how much financial support they had received for professional development activities. Most professors said they had received less that $100 per year for professional development. This is consistent with an analysis of budgets in Maryland that shows that less than $100 per year is spent on each faculty member's travel or professional development. This can be compared with the reported public school figure of $1,000 to $1,700 spent annually per teacher for staff development.

The 28 faculty participants basically had favorite reports of their inservice experiences. If funding (cost of training), leadership, and appropriate staff-development designs are present, teacher education faculty respond to the challenge of growth, just as do their colleagues in elementary and secondary schools (Arends & Murphy, 1986, pp. 17–22).

Preservice and Induction Professional Development Schools

Professional school partnerships described in this section focus upon the preparation of teachers. Those with research evidence have been given priority in reporting. Many of these are reported in the *National Directory of School-Partnerships* (Wilbur et al., 1987) and in *School College Partnerships: A Look at the Major National Models* (Wilbur et al., 1988).

University of Oregon Resident Teacher Program. The University of Oregon's Resident Teacher Master's Degree Program combines graduate study with a year of full-time teaching in a public school. The resident teacher is under the direction of jointly appointed school district faculty and faculty from the university's College of Education. This induction program was developed to provide the beginning teacher with the support needed to succeed in the first year of teaching. The program includes five critical components: (a) the Program is under joint governance by the university and each cooperating school district; (b) a liaison between the educating bodies is provided by the director of the program and a jointly appointed clinical professor for each school district; (c) teacher education and peer support are provided by weekly seminars designed by clinical professors where theory and practice are integrated and teachers learn from teachers; (d) on-site classroom supervision is provided by a school district appointed supervisor/cooperating teacher and the clinical professor; and (e) effective teaching in the first-year teacher's classroom is implemented by monitoring the beginning teacher's abilities and reinforced as needed, while advanced teaching techniques learned in the seminars can be applied immediately to the classroom setting (Wilbur et al., 1988, p. 18).

In a 13-year follow-up study of randomly selected Resident Degree Program graduates, the University of Oregon found that the majority of graduates have continued in education and plan to remain. This program was named as one of the four Exemplar Induction Programs by Educational Testing Service (1980).

University of Wisconsin at Whitewater. The University of Wisconsin at Whitewater has established a professional school Teacher Induction Team approach (Varah, Theune, & Parker, 1986). The team includes the administrator of a local school; a mentor teacher who is teaching in the same subject/grade level as the inductee; and a university consultant who is a specialist in the teaching methodology of the subject/grade of the inductee. The Teacher Induction Program requires admission to the university's graduate school, where students enroll for three to six graduate credits per semester. A personal development plan is prepared in consultation with mentor faculty at weekly conferences. Monthly seminars are held for induction team members, with topics including classroom management, management of student behavior, parent conferences, student evaluation, teacher evaluation, and lesson plans for slow and accelerated learners.

An experimental design involving 12 inductees and a control group of 12 first-year teachers who did not participate in the program was developed to evaluate the program. All the inductees completed the 1984–1985 academic year, whereas only 10 of the 12 control group teachers completed the first year of teaching. Seventy-five percent of the inductees indicated that they planned to be teaching in 5 years, whereas only 25 percent of the control group indicated that they had the same plans.

Other significant findings of the program are: (a) participating first-year teachers view teaching from a student/learner-centered approach, while the nonparticipants view teaching from a more global point of view; (b) administrators reported fewer problems with first-year teachers in the program as compared with those not in the program, indicating there were fewer discipline referrals and staff member and parent complaints; and (c) mentor teachers indicated they would work in the program and on subsequent research and indicated that the program has been beneficial to them because of the professional challenge, renewal, and recognition. Mentors reported the seminars were of special help to them (Varah et al., 1986, p. 33).

Northern Arizona University Center for Excellence in Education. The university has collaborated with Flagstaff Public Schools to provide undergraduate college students with an on-site preservice program for sophomore and junior students that precedes student teaching. Students attend seminars taught by university and local school faculty teams in the mornings. They are assigned in pairs to teach in classrooms in the afternoons

for 8 weeks. Partners are able to observe each other and to discuss the experiences they are having. At the end of 8 weeks, they are assigned new partners and new supervising teachers. This design allows students to have a variety of classroom experiences. The university reports many positive outcomes of the program, including the facts that: (a) participating students are successful in their academic learning and their teaching competencies; (b) students gain a clear-eyed view of their potential as teachers and four students have decided not to become teachers as a result of their experience; (c) students' self-concepts and sense of personal power have been enhanced; (d) most students emerge from the experience more idealistic and dedicated to teaching; and (e) teamwork, sharing, and professionalism are learned naturally (Wilbur et al., 1988, p. 16).

Cleveland State University. The purpose of the Teacher Training Center established by Cleveland State is to provide effective early field placement for preservice teachers. The plan evolved from a pattern of scattered placements into a structured program that places students in one of six centers. There are two inner-city and four suburban centers. The centers are governed by a coordinating committee of university faculty, classroom teacher educators (CTE), building principals, and central office personnel. This committee controls the funds granted by the college of education.

The field-service program relies upon the use of CTEs who have been trained at the university to work with preservice students, methods students, or student teachers. CTEs have a special contract and have agreed to have students placed continuously in their classrooms throughout the year. In addition, CTEs function as resource teachers for other teachers in their building who have field-experience students but who are not themselves CTEs. CTEs occasionally teach university supervision or methods classes.

The main goals of the program are (a) congruence between university instruction and classroom practice; (b) communication between school and university, including shared decision making; (c) a corps of committed classroom teachers who view participation in field experience as an opportunity for growth; and (d) effective supervision of students' field experience (Wilbur et al., p. 16).

Evaluations of the CTE system and the new center organization indicate that each of these four goals is being met. Questionnaire data give evidence that CTE placement students perceived their field-placement experiences to be more valuable than those students who had the traditional placement experience.

University of Maryland's Teacher Education Centers. A partnership was formed between the University of Maryland's College of Education and cooperating school systems in the mid-1960s to improve professional education.

Four to six geographically close schools are usually identified for a Teacher Education Center. These schools serve as sites for preservice and inservice professional development. The school administration and faculty voluntarily join the center after discussions of its goals and responsibilities.

Each center has a coordinator appointed jointly by the cooperating school district in which the center is located and the college of education. The coordinator provides the link between the school system and the college and facilitates the on-site program.

The coordinator is assisted by center staff members, who work as cooperating teachers, curriculum developers, and observers. Faculty and staff from the college of education serve as workshop leaders, consultants, course instructors, and members of joint committees. Each center includes a beginning teacher seminar that incorporates the crucial elements of nonthreatening, nonevaluative, instructional support. The support group includes peers who share and grow through reflective attention to their common experiences. Centers also support action research among student teachers and their supervising teachers (Levinson, 1981).

Four years after its inception, the Beginning Teacher Seminar Project was evaluated in 1985. The purpose of the study was to compare the beginning teacher seminar members with teachers who had not participated in the seminar. Data were "gathered by regularly observing the seminar, by interviewing the beginning teachers in their classrooms, and by analyzing assignments completed by the course" (McCaleb, 1984, p. 5). Results indicate that (a) teachers from the seminar changed from an average of 5.3 to 7.8 on a 10-point principal rating scale. Teachers not in the seminar dropped from 7.5 to 6.7 on average; (b) on the same 10-point scale, teachers in the seminar rated themselves at a 5.3 average, while those not in the seminar gave themselves an 8.3 average. Since both sets of beginning teachers were seen as comparable by principals and observers, the lower self-ratings by those in the seminar suggest an increased awareness of how much they still had to learn about teaching. Such an awareness might motivate continuing development; and (c) when visited in their classrooms near the end of the year, the beginning teachers from the seminar and those not in the seminar received comparable scores on pupil engagement (McCaleb, 1984, p. 5).

The purpose of the project was to offer a focus for the development of analytic capabilities and then create a template of problem-solving steps in the mind of the preservice teacher.

It was found that when a problem shared by the cooperating teacher and student teacher was analyzed and a solution technique was introduced by the student teacher, there were several results: the specific problem was usually alleviated, evidence of which appeared in achievement score increases or in the student teacher assessment of improved class tone; the student teacher reported feeling empowered to solve future problems using the problem-solving pattern; and the cooperating teacher was made aware of the techniques which "work" and of a process for assessing them. (Davie & Lyman, 1985, p. 9)

These results indicate that this project has enabled both preservice and inservice teachers to gain the skills for solving their classroom problems through the use of action research. They have become more reflective professionals. This project received the Maryland ASCD Award in 1985 for collaborative research.

Collaborative Teacher Education Program. The Virginia Commonwealth University and the Richmond City Public Schools have established a Collaborative Teacher Education Program (CoTEEP). The CoTEEP 3-year pilot program was initiated in 1984 to establish and document a collaborative approach integrating preservice and inservice teacher education.

Involved in this partnership are Richmond public schools central office personnel, 6 Richmond elementary and middle schools, university faculty members and administrators, elementary education undergraduates, and representatives from the Virginia Department of Education.

In the CoTEEP program, students move from the earliest preservice experiences, through provisional certification as beginning teachers, to being certified teachers. This program design supports the concept of teacher education as an ongoing developmental process. Students are assigned to work with teachers who are working with university faculty in a sequence of supportive school-based leadership experiences. Teachers who complete the program earn the title *mentor-lead teacher*. Mentor-lead teachers may then work with preservice students, beginning teachers, and peer teachers who have not yet achieved the mentor-lead teacher status.

There is something for everyone in the CoTEEP program. For preservice students, the program provides a collaboratively planned and supervised sequence of field experiences. For inservice teachers, there is a sequence of innovative, on-site, workshops–seminars carrying prepaid university credits. For the schools, the program brings consultation and resource services. For university faculty members, there are opportunities to field-test ideas in classroom demonstrations and to develop innovative inservice approaches. The CoTEEP has a comprehensive evaluation design that includes documentation of inservice approaches.

Zaret (1988) reports that, since its inception, the project has been modified in response to formative and summative evaluation data. Involvement in a collaborative program commands an enormous amount of time, willingness on the part of participants to respect the contributions that others can make, and willingness to give up traditional lines of authority in the decision-making process that normally governs policies and programs for the given agency.

Houston Teaching Academy. In Spring 1987 the University of Houston College of Education and the Houston Independent School District became partners in creating the Houston Teaching Academy. The academy school focuses on the preparation and renewal of teachers for inner-city schools. Urban cities need teachers prepared to teach successfully in schools serving a wide variety of cultural groups and economic levels. Colleges of education need field-service placements in supportive environments where their students can develop the skills, sensitivity, and wisdom to work in inner-city schools. The goal is to decrease the attrition of teachers in inner-city schools. In Houston, as in other large cities, there is a nearly 60 percent loss of new teachers by the end of the first year.

The school selected for the academy serves kindergarten through eighth-grade children and also houses a magnet music and fine arts school. This school was selected because of its multiethnic and multieconomic student population. It has early childhood, bilingual, and special education programs.

Functionally, the academy provides a school site where 10 to 20 student teachers are placed each semester. This concentration of student teachers in one location allows university supervisors to reduce their travel time and to spend more time at this site. To reduce the variance between what the supervising teacher and the college supervisor expect of the student teacher, the triad (student teacher, supervising teacher, and university supervisor) are required to attend a weekly 3-hour seminar. The teacher receives college credit or career ladder credit, and the student teacher substitutes the school-based seminar for the campus seminar required of other student teachers.

The self-analytic model used in the seminars is the third phase of the university's Reflective Inquiry Teacher Education (RITE) program. The basic philosophy is that people learn best in a supportive environment where it is safe to try new ideas, evaluate the results, modify, and try again. Early in the semester, student teachers and teachers are observed and receive profiles of how they manage time, behavior, and interactions. The participants analyze their own profiles according to established criteria (Sparks, 1983). The triad discusses plans for change and sets goals. During the seminars, student teacher panels and supervising teacher panels meet to discuss problems and solutions with peers. The agendas for the seminars are modified or changed as recommended by the panels. The content of the seminars focuses upon those issues of greatest concern to student teachers, such as managing student behavior, planning and adjusting lessons, grading, and working with parents. Other seminars focus on cooperative grouping, questioning strategies, and higher order thinking skills. Seminars held early in the semester focus on the culture of the school and community.

Formative and summative evaluations were a part of the program design each semester. The following evaluation questions were asked when data were collected in school year 1987–1988.

1. Do Experimental Student Teachers (ESTs) improve their behavior management skills and interactive instructional strategies more than do Control Student Teachers (CSTs) during the student teaching semester?
2. Are there observable differences in the teaching performance of ESTs who participated in Phases I and II of the RITE program and those who participated in the postbaccalaureate credentialing program?
3. Is a modeling effect observed between the supervising teachers and their student teachers' instructional behavior?
4. Does the academy school prepare the ESTs so that they are more likely to choose to teach in an inner-city school than are CSTs? Do academy school teachers choose to remain in the academy? (Stallings, 1988, p. 3)

The sample included 20 ESTs. Fifteen ESTs had baccalaureates in subjects other than education and returned to complete courses required for certification. Ages ranged from 22 to 59, with only 3 under 25.

The 20 CSTs were selected from those who volunteered to be observed as a part of the study and were matched for grade level and subject area. Because student teachers are not typically assigned to inner-city schools, all but 3 CSTs were placed in suburban schools. Ages of CSTs ranged from 22 to 40.

The 22 supervising teachers ranged in age from 25 to 61. Their experience in years of teaching ranged from 3 to 41 years. Only 2 had previously supervised student teachers at other times during their teaching careers.

Both qualitative and quantitative data were collected to use in evaluating the program, including objective observations used in a pretest/posttest design, questionnaires, interviews, and journals. An ethnographer was employed and was on site one day each week.

To measure classroom behavior change, the Stallings Observation Instrument (SOI) was used. The SOI provides a time sample of how teachers spend their classroom time, how students spend their time, and the nature of classroom interactions (Stallings, 1986). Each teacher and student teacher in the study was observed at the beginning and end of each semester for 3 days during the same class period, so that change could be measured. Substitute teachers and doctoral students were trained in a 7-day session to reliably use the SOI.

The first-year evaluation was designed to examine the student teachers' and teachers' changes in the specific instructional strategies and management skills addressed in the seminars. Of particular interest to the student teachers was behavior management. Indicative of poor classroom management is a high student off-task rate and a low percentage of academic interactions (Stallings & Krasavage, 1986). Five variables were selected for preliminary analysis: off-task behavior, academic instruction, higher level questions, praise/support, and guided corrections. These variables were compared in the following ways: (a) ESTs versus CSTs, (b) secondary postbaccalaureate certification ESTs versus elementary-major ESTs, and (c) ESTs versus their supervising teachers.

Off-task behavior was recorded whenever students were disruptive, sleeping, or uninvolved in the lesson in ways expected by the teacher. Analysis of the off-task data yielded some interesting findings (see Table 15-1). These findings can be summarized as follows.

CSTs' students averaged 10 percent off-task on the first observation (the range was 0 to 21 percent); this increased by 1 percent during the semester. Nine of the 20 CSTs had students increase their off-task rates.

ESTs' students had very high off-task rates at the beginning

TABLE 15–1. Percentage of Off-Task Observation Findings

Variables	Pre (%)	Post (%)	Difference (%)
Off-Task (Criterion 6%)			
Control Student Teachers	10	11	+1
Experimental Student			
Teachers total	22	15	−7
Elementary	17	15	−7
Secondary	28	21	−7
Teachers total	10.5	7.5	−3
Elementary	6.8	4	−2.8
Secondary	14.4	10.5	−3.9

of the semester. The range for off-task was from 11 to 64 percent. At the end of the semester, 14 ESTs had reduced their off-task rates; the average reduction was 7 percent.

A comparison of student teachers and their teachers indicated a modeling effect. The highest off-task rate for a teacher group was matched by the highest off-task rate for a student teacher. Similarly, the two lowest off-task rates for teachers were matched by the two lowest off-task rates for student teachers.

Approximately 900 teacher–student interactions were recorded for pre- and postobservations. Four interaction variables have been analyzed for percentage of occurrence and compared across CSTs, ESTs, and supervising teachers. The results of the interaction analysis indicate that the ESTs improved their interactive instruction on the 5 variables analyzed. Although gains were small, they were consistent. This finding is contrasted with the CSTs, who consistently started higher than ESTs and decreased their percentage of interactions on these variables. Again the decrease was small but consistent (see Table 15-2).

As a group, the supervising teachers met the criterion of 80 percent academic interactions at pre- and postobservations. Eleven of the 20 increased their use of supportive statements and positive corrective feedback, variables found to be related to student achievement (Stallings, 1975). Interestingly, the supervising teachers asked fewer higher level questions than did their ESTs. An analysis of individual teachers' profiles revealed that only 1 of the 22 supervising teachers met the criterion of 3 percent for higher level questions, whereas 3 of the 11 ESTs were above that level. None of the CSTs were as high as 1 percent in higher level questions. It appears that the seminars, in conjunction with RITE, affected the frequency of higher level questions for the ESTs.

An interesting relationship was found in the rank order of supervising teachers' use of academic interactions and the ESTs. Teacher rank order after the first observation matched nearly perfectly the rank order of ESTs at the second observation ($r = .84$). This finding suggests a strong modeling effect of teachers on their student teachers. Teachers, for the most part, did not shift ranks from the pre- to postobservation, but the ESTs did.

In an exit interview each semester, student teachers were

TABLE 15–2 Interaction Variables

Variables	Fall			Spring		
	Pre (%)	Post (%)	Difference (%)	Pre (%)	Post (%)	Difference (%)
Academic statements (criterion 80%)						
CST*	78	75	−3	82.51	80.56	−2.0
EST† total	74	81	+7	76.29	69.82	−6.47
Elementary	74	79	+5	72.76	70.42	−2.33
Secondary	74	82	+8	79.83	69.23	−10.61
Teachers total	80	80	0	77.64	81.94	+4.30
Elementary	80	77	−3	74.28	81.24	+6.95
Secondary	81	83	+2	83.52	83.16	+.36
Higher order questions (criterion 3%)						
CST	.93	.22	−.71	2.42	1.47	−.95
EST total	.36	1.55	+1.19	.88	2.03	+1.14
Elementary	.14	2.0	+1.86	.59	1.80	+1.21
Secondary	.58	1.11	+.53	1.16	2.26	+1.10
Teachers total	.86	.58	−.28	.89	.48	−.41
Elementary	.36	.26	−.10	.24	.38	+.14
Secondary	1.36	.89	−.47	1.34	.81	−.31
Praise support (criterion 6%)						
CST	6.6	5.8	−.82	6.32	5.81	−.51
EST total	5.8	6.8	+1.0	5.38	6.37	+1.00
Elementary	6.6	7.8	+1.2	7.79	7.89	+.10
Secondary	5.0	5.75	+.75	2.98	4.75	+1.77
Teachers total	7.8	7.5	−.3	7.64	8.39	+.75
Elementary	8.0	8.0	0	8.42	8.57	+.15
Secondary	7.6	6.9	−.7	6.29	8.07	+1.78
Correct with guidance (criterion 4%)						
CST	2.5	1.8	−.71	1.78	1.43	−.35
EST total	1.8	2.46	+.66	2.38	2.75	+.38
Elementary	2.45	3.2	+.79	2.56	2.94	+.38
Secondary	1.15	1.72	+.57	2.19	2.56	+.37
Teachers total	2.71	3.31	+.60	2.05	2.65	+.60
Elementary	1.98	2.75	+.77	2.13	3.20	+1.07
Secondary	3.45	3.87	+.42	1.90	1.68	−.21

*Control Student Teachers ($n = 10$, fall; $N = 10$, spring)
†Experimental Student Teachers ($n = 11$, fall; $n = 9$, spring)

asked if they would teach in an inner-city school if offered the opportunity. Eighteen out of 20 ESTs said yes. None of the CSTs answered affirmatively. In the fall of 1988 follow-up interviews were conducted with all ESTs and CSTs who could be contacted. All but 2 of the 20 former Houston Academy School student teachers are now employed as teachers. Fifteen are employed in schools with students from low-income families, representing a variety of cultural groups. Two are employed at the Houston Teaching Academy. The two ESTs who are not employed as teachers have returned to technical work in industry; they did not adapt to the school environment or develop an understanding of the students they served. The behavior of adolescents confused and annoyed them. Missing from their preparation was prior field experience with adolescents.

Ninety percent of the student teacher population of 40 was over 25 years of age and came to teaching from other professions. Given this population, it is imperative that their certifications require exposure to students and classrooms and in-depth coursework in child development, adolescent development, and reading in the content area prior to student teaching.

Of the 6 student teachers who earned master's degrees in education, no differences in their favor could be found in teaching performance when compared with those who earned a baccalaureate degree. Essentially, these data suggest that student teachers developed and maintained more effective instructional strategies in the academy school environment than in the conventional setting with one teacher, a traveling college supervisor, and large-group, university-based seminars. Further, it appears that time and experience with children and classrooms prior to student teaching are important to successful student teaching.

CONCLUSION

In the summer of 1988 many promising plans for professional development schools originated from school–college partnerships. Some emanated from school districts, others from colleges of education. Several grant request proposals to the federal government and private foundations focused on the development of such schools. During the 1990s more of these plans can be expected to become reality and to provide research evidence of their effectiveness. Longitudinal evaluations of several models of preparation are needed to study the long-range effects upon teacher placement and retention. Findings from research projects in the Maryland Teacher Education Centers and from the University of Wisconsin at Whitewater and preliminary findings from the Houston Teaching Academy suggest that experiments are badly needed to examine differences in effect of professional development schools on undergraduate, graduate, elementary, and secondary preparation and credentialing before undergraduate programs are too hastily eliminated. Also needed are experiments in several models of preparing and inducting teachers through professional development schools. These experiments must report the longitudinal impact of teacher-preparation models on teachers and students. In lieu of substantive research findings, teacher-preparation and certification policies are being made by state legislatures on the basis of passionately held philosophical beliefs and guesses.

Review of the literature on professional development schools suggests that the laboratory schools became too far removed from the mainstream of school life to be credible, and the portal schools spent too much time designing elaborate relationships between schools and colleges that never really got started before their window of opportunity closed. The designers of laboratory and portal schools paid little attention to evaluation or to reporting the effects of their efforts upon teachers or students; thus, little but rhetoric remains to indicate their value. In the 1980s there were many conceptualizations of professional development schools, and, at the time of this writing, only a few have been implemented. Only 3 could be found to have collected systematic qualitative and/or quantitative baseline data, so that they could estimate changes resulting from model intervention. Such evaluations must be planned and carried out if there is to develop a body of knowledge about teacher preparation through professional development schools.

References

Arends, R. (1982). Beginning teachers as learners. *Journal of Educational Research, 76*(4), 235–242.

Arends, R., & Murphy, J. (1986). Staff development for teacher educators. *Journal of Teacher Education. 37*(5), 17–22.

Berliner, D. C. (1985). Laboratory settings and the study of teacher education. *Journal of Teacher Education, 36*(6), 2–8.

Boyer, E. (1983). *High school: A report on secondary education in America.* New York: Harper & Row.

Bradley, B. (1971, May 13). *Rationale and definition of the portal school concept.* Unpublished memorandum to Portal School Project Steering Committee. Washington, DC: Council of the Great City Schools.

Carnegie Forum on Education and the Economy, Task Force on Teaching as a Profession. (1986). *A nation prepared: Teachers for the 21st century.* New York: Author.

Chambers, M., & Olmstead, B. (1971). Teacher corps and portal schools. *Portal Schools, 1*(1), 7–8.

Davie, A. R., & Lyman, F. T. (1985). *Action research: A problem-solving approach to teacher education.* Howard County, MD: University of Maryland, Office of Laboratory Experiences, Southern Teacher Education Center.

Dewey, J. (1896). The university school. *University Record, 5,* 417–442.

Ducharme, E. (1987). Teaching teachers facts and figures. *Education Professorate.* Washington, DC: American Association of Colleges for Teacher Education.

Educational Testing Service. (1980). *Study of induction programs for beginning teachers.* Princeton, NJ: Author.

Goodlad, J. I. (1984). *A place called school: Prospects for the future.* New York: McGraw-Hill.

Hall, G. E., & Loucks, S. F. (1978). Teacher concerns as a basis for facilitating and personalizing staff development. *Teachers College Record, 80*(1), 36–53.

Harper, C. A. (1939). *A century of public teacher education.* Washington, DC: American Association of Teachers Colleges.

Holmes Group. (1986). *Tomorrow's teachers.* East Lansing, MI: Author.

Hunter, M. (1970). Expanding roles of laboratory schools. *Phi Delta Kappan, 21*(1), 14–19.

Jackson, C. L. (1986). *Status of laboratory schools.* Jacksonville, FL: Florida Institute of Education. (ERIC Document Reproduction Service No. ED 277 691)

Joyce, B. (1972). The teacher innovator: A program for preparing educators. In B. Joyce & M. Weil (Eds.), *Perspectives for reform in teacher education* (pp. 4–22). Englewood Cliffs, NJ: Prentice-Hall.

Kelley, I. H. (1964). *College centered laboratory schools in the United States.* Washington DC: American Association of Colleges for Teacher Education.

Kowalski, T. J., Glover, J. A., & Krug, D. (1988). The role of the laboratory school in providing a research base for teacher education. *Contemporary Education, 60*(1), 19–22.

Levinson, N. S. (1981). *School–university collaboration supporting school improvement: Vol. 11. The Eastern State Case.* Washington, DC: Knowledge Transfer Institute.

Lumpkins, B., & Parker, F. R. (1986). *The inservice roles fulfilled by campus laboratory schools.* Paper presented at the annual conference of the National Council of States on Inservice Education, Nashville, TN. (ERIC Document Reproduction Service No. ED 275 665)

Lutonsky, L. (1972a). *Portal Schools.* Washington, DC: Council of the Great City Schools.

Lutonsky, L. (1972b). Toward a definition of "Portal Schools." *Portal Schools, 1*(3), 1–19.

McCaleb, J. L. (1984). *An investigation of on-the-job performance of first-year teachers who are graduates from the University of Maryland, from December 1982 to August 1983.* College Park, MD: University of Maryland, Department of Curriculum and Instruction.

McGeoch, D. M. (1971). *The campus laboratory school: Phoenix or dodo bird.* Washington, DC: National Center for Educational Communication. (ERIC document Reproduction Service No. ED 050 046)

National Commission on Excellence in Education. (1983). *A nation at risk: The imperative for educational reform.* Washington, DC: U.S. Government Printing Office.

Nielsen, R. A. (1986). *Laboratory schools: Blue print for success.* Paper presented at the annual convention of the National Association of Laboratory Schools, Chicago. (ERIC Document Reproduction Service No. ED 273 626)

Ornstein, A. C. (1985). Research on teaching: Issues and trends. *Journal of Teacher Education, 36*(6) 27–31.

Page, F. M., & Page, J. A. (1981). *The development of research as a role in laboratory schools.* Farmville, VA: National Association of Laboratory Schools. (ERIC Document Reproduction Service No. ED 212 628)

Page, J. A. (1983). Laboratory schools: Update or outdated? *Education, 103,* 372–374.

Rucker, W. R. (1952). *A critical analysis of current trends in student teaching.* Unpublished doctoral dissertation, Graduate School of Education, Harvard University, Cambridge, MA.

Sowards, W. (1969). Florida State University model for the preparation of elementary school teachers. *Journal of Research and Development in Education, 2*(3), 22–30.

Sparks, G. (1983). *Inservice education: Training activities, teacher attitude, and behavior change.* Unpublished doctoral dissertation, Stanford University, Palo Alto, CA.

Stallings, J. A. (1975). Implementation and child effects of teaching practices in follow-through classrooms. *Monographs of the Society for Research in Child Development, 40* (Serial No. 163).

Stallings, J. A. (1986). Effective use of time in secondary reading programs. In J. Hoffman (Ed.), *Effective teaching of reading: Research and practice* (pp. 85–106). Newark, NJ: International Reading Association.

Stallings, J. A. (1988). *The Houston teaching academy: A professional development school.* Paper presented at the meeting of the American Educational Research Association, New Orleans.

Stallings, J. A., & Krasavage, E. M. (1986). Program implementation and student achievement in a four-year Madeline Hunter follow-through project. *Elementary School Journal, 87*(2), 117–138.

Van Til, W. (1969). *The laboratory school: Its rise and fall?* Terre Haute, IN: Indiana State University, School of Education.

Van Til, W. (1985). *Laboratory schools and the national reports.* Paper presented at the annual convention of the National Association of Laboratory Schools, Denver.

Varah, L. J., Theune, W. S., & Parker, L. (1986). Beginning teachers: Sink or swim? *Journal of Teacher Education, 37*(1), 30–34.

Wilbur, F. P., Lambert, L. M., & Young, M. J. (1987). *National directory of schools partnerships.* New York: American Association for Higher Education.

Wilbur, F. P., Lambert, L. M., & Young, M. J. (1988). *School college partnerships: A look at the major national models.* Washington, DC: National Association of Secondary School Principals.

Williams, E. I. (1942). *The actual and potential use of laboratory schools in state normal schools and colleges* (Contribution to Education, No. 846). New York: Columbia University, Teachers College, Bureau of Publications.

Wise, A. E., Darling-Hammond, L., Berry, B., Berliner, D., Haller, E., Praskac, A., & Schlechty, P. (1987). *Effective teacher selection: From recruitment to retention* (R-3462-NIE/CSTP). Santa Monica, CA: RAND Corporation.

Zaret, E. (1988). *The collaborative teacher education program.* Richmond, VA: Virginia Commonwealth University.

PARTICIPANTS IN TEACHER EDUCATION

· 16 ·

TEACHERS AND TEACHING: SIGNS OF A CHANGING PROFESSION

Linda Darling-Hammond

The occupation of teaching is changing, and, as it does, so will the nature of the teaching force. Female-dominated since the mid-nineteenth century, teaching in elementary and secondary schools has struggled to achieve professional status in terms of salaries, standards, and prestige. Though strides have been made over more than a century, that status has not yet been entirely won. Recent reforms, however, are likely to dramatically change both who teaches and what teaching is, as a job, an occupation, and a profession. This chapter examines teaching and teachers from this vantage point, exploring their current and potential status in light of political, social, and economic trends.

THE TEACHING OCCUPATION

In a wide-ranging historical overview of teaching, Sedlak and Schlossman (1986) observe that:

Teaching has become a far more desirable occupation during the twentieth century. Teachers today enjoy more freedom and autonomy than did their nineteenth-century predecessors, and they are saddled with fewer arduous burdens in their daily work. Nevertheless, it has always been difficult to recruit talented teachers and to retain those willing to give teaching a try. Despite brief periods of surplus, there has usually been a shortage of willing and qualified teachers. (p. vii)

The recent teacher surplus in the 1970s was one of these exceptions; it is now quickly being replaced by growing shortages once again.

Occupational Features

The general state of teacher undersupply is the result of several attributes of teaching: financial compensation consistently lower than that earned by the other similarly educated workers; a flat career structure, with few opportunities for advancement; and relatively poor working conditions, when compared with other professional lines of work. That elementary and secondary school teaching is largely regarded as "women's work" has perhaps helped to maintain these characteristics of the occupation. The fact that women now have many more career opportunities available could likewise change the characteristics of teaching.

Among the legacies of the feminization of teaching since the middle 1900s is the unstaged career structure, allowing intermittent and "seasonal" employment compatible with child rearing. Clearly, salaries have been greatly influenced as well, for, though lower than those paid to men in other fields, they have been competitive with the lower wages offered women in the other feminized occupations. Some scholars argue that "the prevalence of women in classrooms has contributed to pressure to strengthen bureaucratic controls over teaching and has given teaching the image of a lower-skilled profession" (Sedlak & Schlossman, 1986, p. viii).

But as new opportunities for both women and minorities (also historically overrepresented in teaching) reduce the captive labor pool for teaching, its occupational attractions will have to increase. That is already occurring. At the same time, heightened demands of the educational system are requiring

Portions of this chapter rely on data and analyses reported in two recent RAND documents (Darling-Hammond & Berry, 1988; Haggstrom, Darling-Hammond, & Grissmer, 1988), whose co-authors are gratefully acknowledged. This chapter was also greatly strengthened by comments from its reviewers: Henrietta Schwartz, John Sikula, and Robert Houston. Of course, none of these are responsible for any shortcomings that remain.

more productivity of schools and teachers. This push, reflected in the education reform movement of the 1980s, is encouraging steps toward further professionalization of teaching.

Professional Features

Professionalization is not a dichotomous event or a state of grace into which an occupation clearly falls or not. Rather, it describes points along a continuum representing the extent to which members of an occupation share a common body of knowledge and use shared standards of practice in exercising that knowledge on behalf of clients. It incorporates conditions of specialized knowledge, self-regulation, special attention to the unique needs of clients, autonomous performance, and a large dose of responsibility for client welfare.

The first American reforms to professionalize teaching occurred over a century ago, when Horace Mann established the first state normal school for the training of teachers in 1839. Mann argued tirelessly that educational improvement depended on both increased public support, including state involvement, and the careful selection, advanced training, and improved status and authority of teachers.

At the turn of the century the progressives took up the charge to support universal education, pressing for professional schools of education analogous to those in law, medicine, and the applied sciences. Their establishment in many universities, albeit with less status than those they sought to emulate, is, according to historian Lawrence Cremin (1965), "one of the leading educational developments of the twentieth century." "But," he notes, "they have always been under attack from faculties of arts and sciences, and in recent years that attack has grown sharper" (p. 104).

Meanwhile, the progressives also argued for a restructuring of schooling to replace the factory approach to knowledge production, with "its passivity of attitude, its mechanical massing of children, its uniformity of curriculum and method" (Dewey, 1900/1968, p. 34), with a more child-centered approach. The criticisms of the second wave of reformers, in the 1980s, are virtually identical with those of the progressives at the turn of the century and of the 1960s: our schools provide most children with an education that is too rigid, too passive, and too rote oriented to produce learners who can think critically, synthesize and transform, experiment and create. Indeed, with the addition of a few computers, the Carnegie report's scenario for a twenty-first century school is virtually identical with John Dewey's account of the twentieth century ideal.

Then, as now, the notion was advanced that professionalization of teaching is linked to provision of universal, high-quality education. But these earlier attempts at reform failed to take hold in any substantial way. Cremin (1965) argues that progressive education demanded infinitely skilled teachers and failed because they could not be recruited in sufficient numbers. In each of its iterations, progressivism gave way to standardizing influences: in the efficiency movement of the 1920s, in the teacherproof curricular reforms of the 1950s, and in the back-to-basics movement of the 1970s.

Nonetheless, over the course of the twentieth century, teaching has continued to move toward professionalization. The educational requirements for teachers have continued to rise, as have their salaries, though in fits and starts during times of teacher shortages and public attention (Sedlak & Schlossman, 1986). On the other hand, increasing public regulation of teaching has decreased the control of teachers over what is taught and how it is taught, lessening their professional responsibility and autonomy. And standards for entry into the profession have continued to fluctuate when the demand for teachers exceeds the readily available supply.

Professionalization

Occupations that have become professions have substituted professional accountability systems for bureaucratic accountability systems. The bargain entails rigorous, professionally determined standards for education, internship, and licensure, to guarantee that all members of the profession are competent to exercise good judgment, in exchange for professional control over the structure and content of the work, monitored through peer review of practice. Members of the profession are held to professional standards of practice but not to uniform treatment of all clients. Indeed, the latter, because it would be inappropriate to clients' needs, would constitute unprofessional practice. Democratic oversight occurs through public representation on such bodies as licensing boards and hospital boards, where public input into professional standard-setting processes occurs; technical decisions are delegated to the members of the profession themselves.

Professionalizing policies seek to protect the public by ensuring that (a) all individuals permitted to practice in certain capacities are adequately prepared to do so responsibly; (b) where certainty about practice does not exist, practitioners, individually and collectively, continually seek to discover the most responsible course of action; and (c), as the first two points suggest, practitioners pledge their first and primary responsibility to the welfare of the client.

The first of these goals—that *all* individuals permitted to practice are adequately prepared—is absolutely crucial to attaining the conditions for and benefits of professionalism. So long as anyone who is not fully prepared is admitted to an occupation in which autonomous practice can jeopardize the safety of clients, the public's trust is violated.

This is a key issue in teaching, where 46 states maintain emergency licensure procedures and 23 have recently sanctioned a double standard for entry by adopting alternative certification provisions (Darling-Hammond & Berry, 1988). These allowances are deemed necessary to insure an adequate supply of teachers, but by failing to distinguish the roles and responsibilities that special entrants are qualified to assume, they fundamentally undermine the presumption that all professionals holding the same office share common knowledge and commitments. They permit autonomous practice by those who have not satisfied the prerequisites for public trust.

This is a situation in which the alternatives available within the current structure of teaching seem constrained to distasteful trade-offs. If one admits untrained teachers to full membership in the occupation, the risk of uninformed practice, and student mistreatment, is high. If one does not, and a shortage of teachers results, the alternatives are also suboptimal: enlarged class sizes, constricted program offerings, misassignment of current teachers. This bind occurs because current school and teaching structures do not yet envision diversity of service-delivery structures and roles, and they do not foster professional supervision.

In other professions, differentiated roles and responsibilities have gradually emerged as a means of balancing the requirements of supply and qualifications. Those not fully certified or less extensively trained are limited to performing tasks for which they have been prepared, and they practice under supervision. Complex decisions are reserved to those certified to make such judgments. The Holmes Group's suggestion that untrained college graduates be hired only as instructors who practice under the supervision of certified teachers is a step toward protecting the public interest (Holmes Group, 1986).

The second and third goals—that professionals continually seek to discover what is the most responsible course of action and that their first obligation be to the client's welfare—suggest that norms of inquiry and ethical conduct are extremely important. But because knowledge is constantly expanding and problems of practice are complex, ethical dilemmas result. These cannot be satisfied by codifications of knowledge, prescriptions for practice, or unchanging rules of conduct.

On the one hand, appropriate practice cannot be reduced to rules and lodged in concrete, but on the other hand, there must be means for reaching a common definition of inappropriate practice and for encouraging the pursuit of "what's right," even when that is not a routine judgment. Although standardized practice is not adequate, it is also not true that *any* practice is equally appropriate. What is sought cannot be achieved through more precise legislation of practice or by total discretion for teachers. Instead, we are seeking to vest in members of the profession a common set of understandings about what is known *and* a common commitment to test and move beyond that knowledge for the good of individual students and the collective advancement of the profession. Both common and uncommon practice must be guided by considerations of what is known and what serves the welfare of students.

Professions seek to accomplish these goals by creating structures and processes by which standards of professional practice and norms of professional conduct are defined, transmitted, and enforced. Training and socialization processes such as preparation programs, supervised internships, and continuing-education requirements are the primary vehicles for transmitting standards. Professional bodies such as professional standards boards and accrediting agencies are the primary vehicles for articulating and enforcing standards. Norms of responsibility for the welfare of clients are buttressed by peer control over preparation and entry and by peer review of practice. These norms require a certain convergence of knowledge, view, and purpose among those who set and enforce standards, those who train practitioners, and those who practice.

Shared knowledge and shared commitment to extend that knowledge depend in large part on shared membership in a group that articulates and supports their pursuit. Here, the structure of the profession is critical, for it defines the group's boundaries and its reach. Teaching has suffered from the lack of such a professional structure—a community within the community (Sykes, 1984)—by the balkanization of the occupation.

There is no single institution for teaching, such as the analog to a bar association, medical board, or architectural institute, that can lay claim to representing or enforcing the common claims of members of the profession to knowledge and standards of conduct. Teachers' unions represent the employment interests of those individuals called teachers, who arrive at this title by various routes; administrator unions do likewise for those teachers who have been "promoted" by school boards. Other professional associations for teachers require no prerequisites for membership. State licensing bodies represent the lay public as its views are given voice through legislatures and state boards of education. Teacher educators need not meet the lay public's standards for licensure.

Most organizing rubrics for group membership are based on employment status, acquired through variable means, or on self-selection by claims of interest in the education enterprise. Because no common structure or standard exists for defining entry into the *profession* (and such standards as do exist do not govern rights to practice), occupational status becomes the predominant mode of organization. Furthermore, the associations that represent the interests of those people employed as schoolteachers, principals, supervisors, superintendents, and teacher educators do not consider themselves members of a common profession with common understandings and purposes; much of the time they view themselves as engaging in competing claims to authority by virtue of role rather than expertise.

However, various teaching associations are now making efforts to create structures that define professional membership by virtue of knowledge. A National Board for Professional Teaching Standards was established in 1987 to create an assessment structure for professional certification of teachers, much as the National Board of Medical Examiners certifies physicians in their specialty areas. More states are joining the handful that have delegated licensure decisions to professionally constituted standards boards. Organizations such as the National Science Teachers Association are creating their own standards for certifying members. The Holmes Group of education school deans is considering what knowledge constitutes a fully professional course of preparation and how that should be delivered. These efforts are buttressed by a recent major revision of the standards used by the National Council for Accreditation of Teacher Education for evaluating teacher-preparation programs.

At the same time, state regulation of teaching has also increased. By the late 1980s, virtually all the states had changed their requirements for teacher certification. By 1988, 27 states regulated admission to teacher education; most had made changes in course requirements for certification; and standards for state approval of teacher education programs had also become more highly specified. Forty-one states had imposed tests for inital teacher licensure, and three had imposed tests for continuing licensure. Twenty-five states had created programs for the supervision of beginning teachers, in most cases tied to the acquisition of a continuing teaching license (Darling-Hammond & Berry, 1988).

These changes indicate real efforts to regulate entry into the occupation of teaching, one of the important prerequisites for establishing a profession. However, the changes have largely come from legislatures and state agencies, and they do not reflect a consensual view either within the profession or across states of what a prospective teacher ought to know and be able to do. Most of the tests are basic skills examinations; existing tests of general or professional knowledge tap very little of what might be called a knowledge base for teaching (Darling-Hammond, 1986; Macmillan & Pendlebury, 1985; Shulman, 1987).

These first-generation "standards" have served political purposes well, imposing screens to justify greater investment in teacher salaries, but they have not yet been brought to serve professional purposes. Most of the discourse about the measures has focused on pass rates and cutoff scores, rather than on content. Preparation requirements and examinations are a major means by which a profession makes an explicit statement about what is worth knowing and how it should be known and demonstrated. This statement exerts a powerful influence on training and practice independent from cutoff scores or pass rates.

When candidates prepare to take the bar examination, for example, they know they will have to study constitutional law, torts, contracts, tax law, criminal law, and so on. Regardless of the pass rate for their exam in a given year, candidates know they will have to demonstrate their knowledge of these topics in particular ways. Not only will they need to be able to identify facts about legal rules and cases, but also they will have to apply this knowledge in essays responding to case scenarios. The examination provides an explicit standard of knowledge that influences legal training and practice in important ways, regardless of the vertical standards used to determine who will be licensed.

Professional tests are designed and controlled by the members of a profession. Teacher tests currently are not. They are purchased by state departments of education from test developers who respond to different imperatives. By and large, the tools that have thus been developed give little support to the notion that a knowledge base for teaching, grounded in an appreciation of how children learn and how content is transformed into understanding, exists or needs encouragement.

This situation perpetuates an already acute problem: The public does not trust the standards it has set for teachers. Although states have long regulated the content of teacher preparation and the requirements for licensure, there is so little public confidence in these standards that many believe better teachers might be had by eliminating or skirting these requirements altogether. Alternative certification and other loopholes are the results of this lack of trust. The curious outcome is that tests that avoid pedagogical problems are seen as a substitute for pedagogical preparation.

Until the content of standards becomes the subject of debate and transformation by members of the profession, the standards will serve only short-term political goals. In the long term, professional standards must demonstrate to educators and the public that they, in fact, produce improvements in the quality of education. For this to occur, many of the policies currently controlled by political bodies must come to be shared with teachers.

COMPOSITION OF THE TEACHING FORCE

Characteristics of Current Teachers

In 1984, the average teacher was 39 years old, had 4.9 years of college education, worked 42.9 hours per week, and earned $20,649 per year (U.S. Bureau of the Census, 1984). More than two-thirds of teachers were women. Thirteen percent were members of minority groups, and 54 percent lived in metropolitan areas. Compared with the general population of college-educated workers, teachers are older, have completed more years of college, earn less, and are more likely to be female or to be a member of a minority group (see Table 16-1).

The majority of teachers in the United States now have over 15 years of teaching experience, and more than one-quarter have over 20 years of experience, a sharp increase since 1976, when the mean experience level was only 10 years (see Table 16-2). The median experience level in 1986 was higher than it had ever been in the last quarter century.

This is due to both the increased proportion of highly experienced teachers and the dramatic decline in the proportion of new teachers (with less than 5 years of experience) from about 30 percent in the years 1961 through 1976 to only 8 percent in 1983.

The rise in experience level of teachers has been associated with an increase in the average age of teachers. The median age of teachers increased from 35 in 1971 to 41 in 1986 (National Education Association [NEA], 1987). Over 11 percent of U.S. elementary and secondary school teachers were age 55 or older (Table 16-3). Another 22 percent were between 45 and 54 years of age. Given that average ages at retirement have been declining, we can expect that one-third of all current teachers will be retiring by the turn of the century.

Many of today's teachers entered the profession during the period of rapid expansion of the teaching force to accommodate the baby boom. This expansion, which began in the mid-1950s and lasted through the early 1970s, was followed by a signifi-

TABLE 16–1. Characteristics of Teachers and Nonteachers in the College-Educated U.S. Workforce: 1984

Characteristic	Teachers	Nonteachers
Percent female	67.5%	33.8%
Percent minority	12.6	10.0
Age	39.2	37.17
College education	4.9	4.5
Percent urban	54.4	72.8
Annual earnings	$20,649	$27,525
Weekly hours	42.9	42.9

Note. Compiled from U.S. Bureau of the Census, 1984 Current Population Survey, unpublished tabulations.

TABLE 16–2. Distribution of Teachers by Experience, Public Elementary and
Secondary Schools: 1961–1983

Years Experience	Percent Distribution of Teachers						
	1961	1966	1971	1976	1981	1983	1986
1 to 2	14.3	18.4	16.8	11.3	5.3	3.2	4.6
3 to 4	13.2	14.4	15.6	16.0	8.2	5.1	4.8
5 to 9	19.4	21.7	24.0	28.9	26.2	22.4	17.7
10 to 14	15.1	14.2	15.6	17.3	23.0	25.7	22.3
15 to 19	10.4	9.8	9.7	12.5	15.4	17.4	23.1
20 or more	27.6	21.4	18.3	14.1	21.9	26.1	27.7
Mean years of experience	13	12	11	10	13	15	15
Median years of experience	11	8	8	8	12	13	15

Note. Compiled from National Education Association, *Status of the American Public School Teacher*, 1985–1986 (NEA, 1987); and NEA, *National Teacher Opinion Poll*, 1983 (NEA, 1983).

cant decline in enrollments during the 1970s and early 1980s, accompanied by some retrenchment in the size of the teaching force. Staff reductions in force during the late 1970s and early 1980s fell disproportionately on younger teachers. Because so many of today's teachers were hired in the late 1950s and 1960s, whereas relatively few were hired in subsequent years, a disproportionate share are now reaching retirement age. As demand for teachers increases once again, we can expect to see more hiring of younger teachers to replace those who will be retiring throughout the 1990s. The beginnings of this trend can be seen in the slight increase in the number of inexperienced teachers from 3.2 to 4.6 percent between 1983 and 1986 (Table 16-2).

Other changes in the composition of the teaching force since the early 1960s are notable. Although the breakdown be-

TABLE 16–3. Age Distribution of Employed Teachers: 1984

Age Group and Characteristic	Percentage of Teachers		
	1976–1977	1983–1984	1985–1986
All teachers			
20 to 24	10.2	4.5	2.7
25 to 34	43.0	32.9	23.1
35 to 44	21.4	35.3	40.6
45 to 54	15.9	17.4	22.1
55 and over	9.5	9.9	11.5
Elementary teachers			
20 to 24	11.2	5.0	2.6
25 to 34	42.3	32.5	27.3
35 to 44	20.3	34.7	36.6
45 to 54	16.0	17.6	21.7
55 and over	10.2	10.1	11.8
Secondary teachers			
20 to 24	9.0	3.9	2.6
25 to 34	43.8	32.9	19.7
35 to 44	22.6	36.2	44.3
45 to 54	15.7	17.1	22.7
55 and over	8.8	9.9	10.9

Note. Compiled from National Center for Education Statistics, *Condition of Education* (1985a), Table 3.7, p. 156; NEA, *Status of the American Public School Teacher*, 1985–86 (NEA, 1987), p. 152.

tween women and men has remained stable, at roughly two-thirds and one-third respectively, the proportion of teachers who are black decreased steadily from over 8 percent in 1971 to under 7 percent in 1986 (Table 16-4). The proportion of other nonwhite teachers dipped sharply from 3.6 percent in 1971 to 0.7 percent in 1981, but it increased again to over 3 percent by 1986. The decreases in the numbers of minority teachers could have been caused partly by attrition. They certainly also reflect the dramatically reduced numbers of minority college graduates entering teaching since the early 1970s, a trend discussed more fully in the next section.

Fewer teachers are likely to be single now than in 1961, and all—both males and females—are substantially more likely to have employed spouses. This certainly reflects the general social trend toward two-wage-earner families, as well as the increased average age of teachers over these years. Because teacher salaries declined in purchasing power throughout the 1970s, it might also reflect the need for supplemental income for individuals who remained in teaching.

Although the teaching force has become more experienced and stable over time, some characteristics have not changed. Most public school teachers (over 80 percent) are first-generation college graduates, and about 60 percent come from working-class families. These proportions have remained fairly stable since 1961 (NEA, 1981, 1987). About 30 percent of public school teachers are teaching in the community where they grew up; another 50 percent teach in a community where they have spent much of their adult life (NEA, 1981).

These characteristics suggest that teaching has been an avenue of upward mobility for working-class families and that labor markets for teachers have been largely local. As more college students are second-generation college attenders, they are less apt to opt for teaching than for other higher status occupations. This would be a factor contributing to the dwindling supply of new teachers. At the same time, teacher shortages are exacerbated by the localism of teacher labor markets. Lack of mobility contributes to supply-and-demand imbalances and could also constrain competition that would drive up wages (Wise, Darling-Hammond, & Berry, 1987).

TABLE 16–4. Selected Characteristics of Public School Teachers:
1961–1986 (in Percentages)

	1961	1966	1971	1976	1981	1986
Gender						
Male	31.3	31.1	34.3	32.9	33.1	31.2
Female	68.7	69.0	65.7	67.0	66.9	68.8
Race/ethnicity						
White	—	—	88.3	90.8	91.6	89.6
Black	—	—	8.1	8.0	7.8	6.9
Other	—	—	3.6	1.2	0.7	3.4
Marital status						
Single	22.3	22.0	19.5	20.1	18.5	12.9
Married	68.0	69.1	71.9	71.3	73.0	75.7
Widowed, divorced, separated	9.7	9.0	8.6	8.6	8.5	11.4
Percent with employed spouses						
All teachers	49.5	51.0	54.4	57.1	62.3	65.4
Male	32.4	35.7	44.9	47.6	58.9	65.5
Female	57.3	57.9	59.4	61.9	64.2	65.4

Note. From NEA, *Status of the American Public School Teacher,* 1985–1986 (NEA, 1987).

Educational Attainment

The greater experience level of the teaching force is also reflected in higher levels of educational attainment, as most teachers continue to gain education throughout their years in teaching. The educational-attainment level of teachers has increased dramatically in recent years. According to the most recently available data, 51.4 percent of all public school teachers held at least a master's degree in 1986. This represents an increase from only 38 percent in 1976 and 23 percent in 1966. Although 15 percent of teachers had less than a bachelor's degree in 1961, by 1986 the proportion was only 0.3 percent (see Table 16-5).

Private school teachers have, overall, lower levels of educational attainment than public school teachers. In 1986, only 30 percent of private school teachers had more than a bachelor's degree, whereas 4 percent had less than a bachelor's degree (Center for Education Statistics [CES], 1987a, p. 54). This might reflect, in part, the fact that private school teachers also had less teaching experience, with 29 percent having had fewer than 5 years of experience and fewer than half having had 10 or more years of experience. Private school teachers are also exempt from licensing regulations requiring public school teachers to acquire master's degrees in some states.

Although educational attainment of the current teaching force has clearly increased, some evidence suggests that the academic ability of entrants to teaching declined during the 1970s. A study commissioned by the Council of Chief State

School Officers (1984, p. 1) noted that education majors have usually ranked below other college majors on measures of academic ability but that the gap widened between 1972 and 1980, when the average verbal SAT scores of education majors declined by 29 points and their mathematics SAT scores fell by 31 points. During the same period, the average SAT scores of the general student population fell by approximately 20 points. In 1980 the SAT verbal scores of education majors were 35 points below the average for all U.S. college students, and their SAT mathematics scores were 48 points below the average (Council of Chief State School Officers, 1984). A 1984 study of education majors at 17 colleges in the South found that SAT scores of education majors averaged 70 points below those of students in the arts and sciences divisions (Galambos, 1985, p. 34).

Of course, education majors are not the only college graduates who enter teaching; of the recent college graduates who entered teaching in 1985, over 30 percent majored in fields other than education (CES, 1987a). However, other evidence (Vance & Schlechty, 1982) indicates that during the 1970s both education majors and other entrants to teaching were disproportionately drawn from the lowest groups of SAT scorers and that the most academically able were least likely to enter teaching if they majored in education or to stay in teaching if they entered.

Test scores are not clear evidence of quality or lack of quality. What we mean by teacher quality should be more influenced by what teacher candidates learn after they enter college

TABLE 16–5. Educational Attainment of Public School Teachers:
1961–1986

Highest Degree Held	1961	1966	1971	1976	1981	1986
Less than a bachelor's	14.6	7.0	2.9	0.9	0.4	0.3
Bachelor's	61.9	69.6	69.6	61.6	50.1	48.3
Master's or 6-year diploma	23.1	23.2	27.1	37.1	49.3	50.7
Doctorate	0.4	0.1	0.4	0.4	0.3	0.7

Note. From NEA, *Status of the American Public School Teacher 1985–1986* (NEA, 1987), p. 16.

than by the entrance examination scores they presented at matriculation. The likeliest interpretation of the test score trends during the 1970s is that teaching became a less attractive career option to many college students facing alternative opportunities. These trends stem from a variety of complex forces that might be changing.

Teacher Certification and Training

In an effort to insure the qualifications and quality of the teacher work force, most states enacted changes in teacher certification and training policies in the 1980s (American Association of Colleges for Teacher Education [AACTE], 1985). These changes included establishment of teacher testing as a part of the training and certification process in 46 states, additions to the course requirements for students in teacher-preparation curricula, and establishment of minimum academic achievement standards for admission to teacher-preparation programs (Darling-Hammond & Berry, 1988).

In support of efforts to improve the qualifications of the teacher work force, 70 percent of teacher education programs now have minimum grade requirements that must be met before a student can be admitted. Half also require that students pass a proficiency test before completing the program, a number that has doubled since 1980 (Holmstrom, 1985).

In some cases the adoption of higher admission standards or of higher academic-performance standards for students in teacher-training programs has been the initiative of an individual institution. In many instances, however, the adoption of such policies has been mandated by stated education authorities as an extension of teacher certification requirements. Seventeen states have prescribed admissions tests for entry into teacher-training programs, and 13 states have enacted minimum grade point standards for program admissions (Goertz, 1985, p. 20).

Most states have also adopted modifications in specific teacher certification requirements. The most notable of these have been increases in required hours of college credit in a subject area for secondary certification, evaluation of classroom performance for beginning teacher certification, and continuing-education requirements for recertification. However, state requirements for teacher certification, and the nature of recent changes, vary so substantially that a teacher certified in one state is unlikely to meet the certification requirements in another.

Although national data on the effects of these recent changes on the composition of the teaching force are not available, we can piece together information from a variety of sources that indicates important changes in who enters and remains in teaching.

WHO ENTERS AND STAYS IN TEACHING

Trends in Education Degrees

The most obvious observation about who is entering teaching is that there are fewer of them now than in the early 1970s. Between 1972 and 1985 the number of college students receiving bachelor's degrees in education declined precipitously, from over 194,000 to about 88,000. Male and female participation declined at about the same rate, with women earning about 75 percent of these degrees throughout this time (see Table 16-6). The decreasing numbers, however, reflect a major shift in the career choices of women college students. Although the proportion of men choosing education majors has always been relatively low (just under 10 percent of male degrees in 1975 and about 5 percent in 1985), teaching was not long ago the predominant field of choice for women attending college.

As recently as 1975, 30 percent of all bachelor's degrees awarded to women were in education, by far the largest single field of study. By 1985, only 13 percent of women's bachelor's degrees were awarded in education. During this decade, business degrees jumped from 5 percent to over 20 percent of women's total degrees, and women's degrees in fields like engineering and computer sciences increased 10-fold (CES, 1986b, p. 40).

Similar patterns are apparent for minority college students. Although the number of education bachelor's degrees awarded to white students decreased by half between 1975 and 1985, the number awarded to black students declined by nearly two-thirds (see Table 16-7). The steady increase in education degrees awarded to Hispanics from 1975–1976 through 1980–1981 was sharply reversed in subsequent years. Overall, the share of education degrees awarded to minority candidates dropped from 13 to 10 percent during this time. Although edu-

TABLE 16–6. Earned Degrees in Education: 1972–1985

Degree	1972–1973	1976–1977	1980–1981	1984–1985	% increase/decrease
Bachelor's	194,229	143,722	108,309	88,161	−55
Men	51,441	39,941	27,076	21,264	−59
Women	142,788	103,781	81,233	66,897	−53
Master's	105,565	126,825	98,938	76,137	−28
Men	44,128	43,288	28,256	20,945	−53
Women	61,437	83,537	70,682	55,192	−10
Doctor's	7,318	7,963	7,900	7,151	−2
Men	5,504	5,189	4,164	3,419	−38
Women	1,814	2,774	3,736	3,732	+106

Note. From Center for Education Statistics, *Digest of Education Statistics*, 1987 (1987b), Table 167, p. 204.

TABLE 16–7. Bachelor's Degrees in Education, by Race and Ethnicity:
1975–1976 to 1984–1985

	1975–1976	1978–1979	1980–1981	1982–1983	1984–1985
White	135,514	108,984	93,750	81,663	77,531
Black	14,229	11,538	9,517	6,826	5,456
Hispanic	4,447	4,763	5,192	3,499	2,533
Asian	836	832	767	689	770
American Indian	742	645	569	476	483
Total minority	20,254	17,778	11,490	11,490	9,242

Note. Compiled from Office for Civil Rights, *Data on Earned Degrees Conferred by Institutions of Higher Education by Race, Ethnicity, and Sex, Academic Years 1975–76, 1978–79, 1980–81, and 1982–83* (OCR, 1975–76, 1978–79, 1980–81, 1982–83); Center for Education Statistics, *Racial/Ethnic Data for 1984 Fall Enrollment and Earned Degree Recipients for Academic Year 1984–85* (Center for Education Statistics, 1986a).

cation had once been a predominent field of choice for minority students (accounting for one-third of all black female degrees in 1976, for example), by 1984–1985, education accounted for only 10 percent of bachelor's degrees to both blacks and Hispanics; 11 percent to Native Americans; and 3 percent to Asians.

The trends among minority college students toward other choices of major were equally dramatic. At the bachelor's level, sharp declines in education and social science degrees were accompanied by equally sharp increases in business, engineering, the health professions, and biological, physical, and computer sciences. As with women generally, these shifts were most pronounced for black and Hispanic women.

Significant but less dramatic declines occurred in the number of master's degrees awarded in education (Table 16-6). There was an overall decrease in total master's degrees during this time, which can be attributed almost entirely to decreased participation in education programs. Doctor's degrees in education dipped only slightly, but women increased their share of these degrees substantially, outnumbering men for the first time in 1984–1985 in doctoral degrees earned.

Trends in Entry to Teaching

Only about 60 percent of all education majors enter teaching immediately after college (CES, 1987a, p. 48). There are many reasons for this. For the cohort who graduated with bachelor's degrees in education in 1983–1984, about half of those not teaching in 1985 were unable to find employment in their teaching field; the other half decided to pursue other options. Of the nonteachers employed full-time, about half worked in nonprofessional jobs such as sales or clerical work, and the remainder were employed in a variety of other professional jobs.

On the other hand, education majors are not the only entrants to teaching. There are at least three other sources of new teacher supply: (a) bachelor's degree recipients who majored in noneducation fields but took education courses for certification; (b) individuals who became qualified to teach through a master's degree program; and (c) individuals who enter teaching without having completed coursework necessary for certification. Although the overwhelming majority of newly gradua-

ted teachers are undergraduate education majors, a number of signs suggest that this is changing.

Other Degree Recipients Qualified to Teach. A small proportion of new teachers receive their preparation in master's degree programs. In 1983–1984, about 6 percent of degree recipients who were newly qualified to teach had received master's degrees (see Table 16-8).

Although most bachelor's candidates newly qualified to teach in 1983–1984 had majored in education (76 percent), at the master's degree level, only 26 percent of those newly qualified to teach had received education degrees. Among the bachelor's degree recipients, 7.4 percent had majored in the humanities and 5.8 percent in the social sciences. The health professions and biological sciences combined contributed another 4.8 percent. Among master's degree recipients, though a much smaller number overall, graduates with degrees in the health professions constituted 23 percent of those newly qualified to teach. Thirteen percent had degrees in the humanities; 9 percent, in public affairs and social service fields; and just over 4 percent each, in psychology and quantitative fields (mathematics, computer, and physical sciences). These data suggest a somewhat larger pool of potential teachers than is indicated by earned degrees in education, but many of those who prepare to teach do not enter teaching.

Table 16-9 shows the number of recent bachelor's degree recipients who were newly qualified to teach and who were teaching full-time in 1981 and 1985. In 1981, of those newly qualified to teach, about 85 percent applied for teaching jobs and about 60 percent were teaching full-time. (Another 4 percent were teaching part-time.) In 1985, only about 74 percent of those newly qualified to teach applied for teaching jobs, and just under 50 percent ended up teaching full-time. More striking, only 38 percent of the newly qualified minority candidates entered teaching full-time.

Other Entrants to Teaching. An interesting story about the flow of individuals into and out of teaching is told by the certification and employment status of these recent college graduates. Table 16-10 indicates that, for the 1983–1984 cohort of bachelor's degree recipients, about 9 percent of those who entered teaching in 1985 were not certified. A much greater number of individuals were certified but not teaching (about

TABLE 16–8. Fields of Study for Newly Qualified to Teach Recent Graduates: 1983–1984

	Bachelor's		Master's	
	Number	%	Number	%
Total newly qualified to teach	98,658	100	6,373	100
Professional fields	74,666	75.7	3,652	57.3
Business & management	1,180	1.2	0	0
Education	70,406	71.4	1,659	26.0
Engineering	357	.4	0	0
Health professions	2,287	2.3	1,440	22.6
Public affairs/social service	437	.4	553	8.7
Arts & sciences fields	18,825	19.1	1,372	21.5
Biological science	2,459	2.5	0	0
Math, computer, & physical science	1,753	1.8	265	4.2
Social science	5,705	5.8	0	0
Humanities	7,260	7.4	819	12.9
Psychology	1,648	1.7	288	4.5
Other fields	5,166	5.2	1,349	21.2

Note. Compiled from unpublished tabulations, Recent College Graduates Survey, 1985, by National Center for Education Statistics.

60 percent more than the number teaching). Blacks and Native Americans were least likely to be teaching without certification, whereas blacks and whites were most likely to be certified but not teaching.

Virtually all of the 1983–1984 master's degree recipients who were in teaching were also certified. The total number of certified individuals at this level also surpassed the number teaching by about 40 percent. The vast majority of these certified nonteachers were employed in jobs outside of teaching. Among master's degree recipients with certification, about three-quarters of blacks, Hispanics, and Asians were still teaching, as compared with just under 60 percent of whites.

What is most striking about these data is that the number of recent degree recipients certified to teach but not teaching is much greater than the number teaching (with or without certification) or the number newly qualified to teach. This suggests that many of these certified individuals had gone back to school to obtain degrees in other fields and did not reenter teaching; others became certified but opted to take other jobs or pursue further education. This was particularly true for minority degree recipients. For example, whereas 14,600 black degree recipients were certified to teach, only 8,500 of them were actually teaching; for Hispanics, of 4,100 certified recent graduates, only 2,700 were employed in teaching. The rest had taken other jobs or had gone on in school.

TABLE 16–9. Racial/Ethnic Distribution of Recent Bachelor's Degree Recipients, Newly Qualified to Teach, and Teaching Full-Time: 1981 and 1985

	All Recent Bachelor's Recipients		Recent Bachelor's Recipients Newly Qualified to Teach		Recent Bachelor's Recipients Teaching Full-Time	
	1981	1985	1981	1985	1981	1985
Total	905,700	955,275	132,200	98,658	79,800	49,078
White	824,200	851,472	119,800	89,850	73,000	45,693
	(91%)	(89.1%)	(90.7%)	(91.1%)	(91.6%)	(93.1%)
Black	47,100	51,332	8,400	5,574	4,000	1,887
	(5.2%)	(5.4%)	(6.4%)	(5.6%)	(5.0%)	(3.8%)
Hispanic	15,400	23,202	2,300	1,744	1,900	807
	(1.7%)	(2.4%)	(1.7%)	(1.8%)	(2.4%)	(1.6%)
Asian	16,300	25,351	1,300	890	600	288
	(1.8%)	(2.7%)	(1.0%)	(.9%)	(.7%)	(.6%)
Native American	2,700	3,918	300	601	200	404
	(.3%)	(.4%)	(.2%)	(.6%)	(.3%)	(.8%)

Note. Compiled from National Center for Education Statistics, The Condition of Education, 1983 Edition (NCES, 1983), and unpublished tabulations, Recent College Graduates Survey, 1985, by National Center for Education Statistics.

TABLE 16–10. 1985 Employment Status of Recent College Graduates
Certified to Teach or Teaching

Bachelor's Degrees	White	Black	Hispanic	Asian	Native American	Total
Total teaching	73,594	4,924	2,308	1,138	527	82,491
Newly qualified	89,850	5,574	1,744	890	601	98,658
Total certified	120,029	8,208	3,011	1,557	723	133,528
Teaching	67,719	3,848	1,910	1,077	527	75,081
Not teaching	31,812	2,434	400	230	61	34,937
Not in labor force	18,009	1,516	517	204	135	20,382
Unemployed	2,489	410	184	46	0	3,128
No response	785	297	0	0	0	1,082
Master's Degrees						
Total teaching	55,033	4,728	830	1,645	0	62,236
Newly qualified	5,797	288	0	288	0	6,373
Total certified	93,862	6,398	1,106	2,216	0	103,582
Teaching	53,694	4,728	830	1,645	0	60,897
Not teaching	30,973	1,118	276	571	0	32,937
Not in labor force	8,367	552	0	0	0	8,919
Unemployed	828	0	0	0	0	828
No response	552	0	0	0	0	552

Note. Compiled from unpublished tabulations, Recent College Graduates Survey, 1985, by National Center for Education Statistics.

Trends in Mobility and Attrition

As noted earlier, teacher experience and education increased during the period from the late 1960s to the early 1980s, as the veteran teaching force became more stable. There are several indicators of increased stability over the course of this 15-year period, including fewer breaks in service for teachers, decreased mobility, and evidence of lower attrition. However, the conditions that might have encouraged lower turnover in the recent past are likely to change in the near future.

About 70 percent of public school teachers in 1981 had no breaks in their continuous teaching service, up from about 62 percent in 1966. Although more female teachers had breaks in service than men (37 percent versus 16 percent), primarily for maternity and child rearing, the proportion of women teachers taking leaves from teaching declined steadily from 1966 to 1981 (NEA, 1981). A slight increase in the proportion of teachers taking service breaks occurred between 1981 and 1986 (NEA, 1987), but the traditional view that teaching is an occupation in which women make frequent, temporary exists for homemaking is less true than it once was.

Teacher mobility also appears to have declined over the years from 1966 to 1981, with only 2 percent of public school teachers in 1981 having moved from another school system in the previous year and an equal number planning to move in the following year, as compared with 6 to 7 percent 15 years earlier (Table 16-11). Because mobility is an important compo-

TABLE 16–11. Activities for Previous and Following School Years for All Teachers: 1966–1981 (in Percent)

Activity	1966		1971		1976		1981		1986	
	Last Year	Next Year	Last Year	Next Year	Last Year	Next Year	Last Year	Next Year	Last Year	Next Year
Teaching full-time	87.4	91.3	88.2	89.4	90.8	91.2	94.5	89.1	94.7	92.8
Same system	80.5	85.6	83.9	84.6	88.3	87.3	92.5	87.3	92.3	89.6
Another system	6.9	5.7	4.3	4.8	2.5	3.9	2.2	1.8	2.4	3.2
Attending college full time	8.5	1.7	7.0	1.4	4.5	1.3	1.0	0.9	0.9	0.4
serving in the military	0.2	0.0	0.3	0.0	0.2	0.0	0.0	0.1	0.0	0.0
Working in nonteaching position	1.1	1.5	1.4	2.1	1.2	1.9	0.9	2.4	0.8	1.7
Homemaking/childraising	1.6	2.9	2.0	3.2	1.7	2.1	1.2	2.4	1.5	1.2
Unemployed and seeking work	0.2	0.4	0.3	0.3	0.4	1.1	0.2	1.1	0.1	0.7
Retired	0.0	1.5	0.1	2.2	0.0	1.5	0.1	1.7	0.0	1.4
Other	0.9	0.8	0.8	1.3	1.4	0.9	2.1	2.3	2.0	1.7

Note. From NEA, *Status of the American Public School Teacher,* 1985–1986 (NEA, 1987).

nent of turnover at the district and state levels, this decline is part of the reduced turnover described later. The decline in mobility might be partly caused by the decrease in new teacher demand during the 1970s, as mobility is easier when many positions need to be filled. However, in 1981, for the first time, a larger percentage of teachers was teaching during the previous school year than planned to teach the following year (NEA, 1981), a sign that turnover might once again increase.

Other data suggest that turnover declined throughout the 1970s and early 1980s, but that it is likely to increase into the 1990s (Grissmer & Kirby, 1987). This is to be expected from the demographic shifts within the teaching profession during this period. During the 1960s and early 1970s, a higher proportion of teachers were young and inexperienced—and subject to higher levels of turnover. This younger force, which resulted from the strong demand for new teachers caused by the baby boom of the 1960s, had become by the 1980s a predominantly stable, midcareer teaching force, causing low overall turnover levels. As these teachers reach retirement age and are replaced by younger attrition-prone recruits, turnover will rise, keeping the demand for teachers high.

Life Cycle Career Patterns for Teachers. Patterns of participation in the teaching profession tend to follow a life cycle theory of participation and attrition from occupations (Grissmer & Kirby, 1987; Haggstrom, Darling-Hammond, & Grissmer, 1988). Attrition rates follow a U-shaped pattern, with high attrition for individuals early in their careers, very low attrition during the mid-career phase, and increasing attrition once retirement eligibility is achieved. Early attrition could be caused by dissatisfaction with teaching, a decision to start a family, or attractive outside opportunities. For a number of reasons, transfers to other occupations are generally easier at this early phase of the career, as salaries are lower and occupation- and location-specific human capital investments are not high. In addition, teachers with less seniority are most apt to be dismissed when school districts must reduce the size of their teaching forces due to declining student enrollments.

It is also probable that the career decisions of younger teachers are more sensitive to school- and district-specific policies and the institutional environment than at later points in their careers. Incoming teachers are often given the least desirable assignments, spend more time preparing for classes, and often lack an established support network. School and teaching conditions might influence their decisions about remaining in the profession, as well as about continuing in a particular job.

The probability of attrition falls with age and years of teaching experience; those teachers who survive to the mid-career phase of teaching (defined roughly as 10–25 years of teaching experience) have very low attrition rates. This is partly due to the self-selection process: Teachers who survive have a higher "taste" for teaching. That is, they have survived in part because they like teaching. If they did not leave earlier in their careers, they are less likely to leave later. There are also other barriers to departure in mid-career. It is harder to find alternate jobs with matching salaries for those who lack the kinds of skills or training that could command equivalent salaries in other occupations. Individuals at this career stage are also less likely to

be able to accept lower entry-level salaries in other occupations because of family responsibilities and debt obligations.

Late-career attrition is dependent on the structure of the retirement system. Eligibility for retirement ordinarily depends on two factors: age and years of experience. A typical system might require the attainment of age 55 with at least 20 years of teaching in the system. Staying beyond these minimum requirements, typically to age 62 or 65, enhances the retirement pension. Attrition rates increase when teachers attain the minimum requirements for eligibility and continue to increase through mandatory retirement age.

Reasons for Leaving. Life cycle factors are important reasons for teacher attrition. Many teachers leave temporarily or permanently on the occasion of childbirth, household moves, retirement, and related events. But occupational factors are also important. For those teachers who leave for other occupations, the most prevalent single reason is financial; 60 percent of recent former teachers surveyed in 1985 said they left due to teaching's low salaries. The same answer was given by over 60 percent of current teachers considering leaving (Metropolitan Life, 1985). Working conditions and administrative factors, especially lack of input and independence, lack of administrative support, and extent of nonteaching duties, were cited by two-thirds of leavers and by as many potential leavers. Student factors were mentioned by 30 percent of former teachers.

Disturbingly, a recent survey found that 41 percent of minority teachers reported that they are likely to leave teaching within the next 5 years, as compared with 25 percent of nonminority teachers (Metropolitan Life, 1988). This included 55 percent of minority teachers with less than 5 years' experience and 31 percent of nonminority teachers with similar experience. The normally high early attrition suggested by these data is exacerbated in the case of minority teachers by the more difficult working conditions found in the inner-city schools in which they are overrepresented. Thus, dwindling recruitment of minority teachers is likely to be accompanied by increased attrition.

These conditions that cause attrition can vary to some degree from one school or district to another, causing higher turnover in some places than others. But teachers also compare the overall salary levels and working conditions in teaching with those in other occupations; their relative attractiveness influences the probability that potential teachers will enter or reenter the occupation and how long they will stay. The extent to which teaching can compete with other occupations for new entrants is one of several labor market factors that shape the teaching force at different points in time.

Labor Market Conditions and Teaching

Trends toward lower teacher turnover rates and higher stability in the teaching force from the late 1960s through the early 1980s might be explained by a combination of factors:

Declining enrollments, resulting in less hiring and less opportunity for mobility within the profession.

Reluctance to leave teaching, especially for short periods, because of a higher risk of not gaining reemployment in teaching.

Selection of individuals into teaching who were more likely to stay longer.

A tight labor market outside of teaching, reducing opportunities for teachers to move from teaching to other occupations.

Improvements in pay, benefits, or teaching conditions.

A major factor influencing the teaching force between the late 1960s and the early 1980s was the decline in student enrollments, producing lower demand for new teachers at a time when there was also an oversupply of college graduates seeking work in other sectors of the economy. Relatively steady increases in the unemployment rate from the 1960s through 1983, especially among persons with 4 or more years of college, and steady increases in the proportion of women in the labor force, produced substantial competition among college graduates for jobs. The oversupply of prospective teachers in the 1970s who could not easily find alternative employment resulted in salary levels that did not keep pace with increases in other fields and in more selectivity on the part of school administrators in teacher hiring. The recessions in the early 1980s, and their aftermath of unusually high unemployment for college graduates in 1982–1983, undoubtedly influenced the observed decline in teacher turnover rates during the early part of the 1980s. Virtually all of these factors, however, can be expected to change in the years ahead.

Individuals and employing institutions behave differently in a labor market characterized by rapid growth than in one characterized by stable or contracting size. Other things being equal, the ready availability of jobs encourages individuals to enter the profession who might have made less informed, and more easily reversed, decisions about the suitability of teaching for them. At the same time, school districts have to be less selective in hiring during times of high demand for new teachers. Greater selectivity can mean hiring more experienced and able teachers, rather than new college graduates, or choosing individuals displaying characteristics associated with longevity and commitment to the profession. As demand for new teachers grows, school districts must reach deeper into the pool of applicants, which usually means accepting teachers who might otherwise not have been hired.

There has been an additional change in the pool of entering teachers in recent years that might have led to lower attrition. This change is the greater proportion of entering teachers with either previous teaching experience or previous work experience outside the profession. Both of these characteristics lead to lower attrition. Two conditions created this pool of more experienced individuals. A surplus of education majors unable to get teaching jobs occurred in the 1970s as the demand for new teachers declined rapidly. Some of these individuals took other jobs and waited to enter teaching until opportunities became available. At the same time, reductions in force were occurring in some areas, creating a pool of teachers with experience who would later reenter teaching. The presence of these

pools in the early 1980s meant that school districts were less dependent on more attrition-prone, new college graduates.

These trends are displayed in Table 16-11. From 1966 to 1986 the proportion of new entrants (those who were not teaching in the previous year) declined from 13 percent to 5 percent of the total teaching force. Meanwhile, the proportions of these new entrants who had been attending college the previous year declined from 67 percent (or 8.5 percent of the total teaching force) in 1966 to 17 percent (or 1 percent of the total teaching force) in 1986. Thus, new graduates had become a small portion of all teachers hired in that year. In 1986, about 15 percent of new entrants had been working in nonteaching positions during the previous year; 28 percent had been homemakers; 2 percent had been unemployed or retired; and the remainder (38 percent) were engaged in other pursuits.

It thus seems likely that the new teachers hired in the late 1970s and early 1980s were more highly selected and more experienced than those selected in the 1960s and early 1970s. This is consistent with evidence suggesting that districts' ability to be selective in hiring teachers is dependent on demand conditions (Murnane & Phillips, 1981).

Another factor driving high turnover in the profession in times of growth is the relative ease of movement among teaching jobs. Decisions to move among schools, districts, and states are less risky when jobs are readily available than they are in tighter labor markets. It is also easier to stop teaching to return to school, raise children, or try another job knowing that teaching jobs will be available if one decides to return. The presence of teacher reductions in force in the late 1970s and 1980s reinforced the risk associated with leaving teaching jobs.

Real increases in teacher pay, benefits and working conditions relative to closely competing occupations would result in increased teacher retention. Although such salary increases occurred in response to shortages during the 1960s, salaries subsequently declined in real-dollar terms throughout the 1970s (see Table 16-12). Increases since 1981 have just barely returned average teacher salaries to their real-dollar level of 1971. Looking ahead, we can anticipate that, with greater competition for college-educated workers in the labor market, teacher recruitment and retention will be more difficult, unless

TABLE 16–12. Average Teacher Salaries: 1956–1986

Year	Current Dollars	1986 Dollars	Adjusted for Teacher Experience (1986) dollars
1956	4,055	16,564	—
1961	5,275	19,575	21,410
1966	6,485	22,184	24,818
1971	9,269	25,408	29,060
1976	12,591	24,554	28,698
1981	17,364	21,203	23,085
1986	25,240	25,240	25,240

Note. Computed from American Federation of Teachers, *Salary Trends, 1986: Survey and Analyses* (AFT, 1986), Tables II-1 and II-2, pp. 18, 21.

salaries increase in real-dollar terms to a level more closely comparable to those of competing occupations.

Alternative Career Opportunities. One of the labor market factors having the greatest effect on the teaching profession is the growth in career opportunities available to women and minorities. Women have traditionally comprised the large majority of the teaching force, and they still do. However, academically talented women, in particular, are increasingly pursuing other occupations. Between 1970 and 1981, the proportion of women receiving bachelor's degrees in education decreased by more than half, from 36 percent to 17 percent. During that decade, women's professional options expanded enormously. Women's occupational choices shifted from education, English, and the social sciences to business and commerce and the health professions. The same pattern is evident for minority students (Darling-Hammond, 1984). Since then, these trends have only grown more pronounced.

The range of expanded options available to talented women and minorities today means that schools now have to compete with other occupations and industries for talent. This has affected teacher production and might affect the size of the reserve pool too. The number of college students opting to teach has declined from over 200,000 annually (or about one-fifth of all college graduates) during the early 1970s to just over 100,000 annually in the mid-1980s. In addition, those leaving teaching might be less likely to return to the profession. As the number of college-age students declines in coming years, and competition for college graduates increases from other sectors of the labor market, the former traditional pools of teachers might become harder to tap.

Educational policymakers are just beginning to assess whether working conditions that used to be a plus for a heavily female teaching force might now be a minus for some of the women they want to attract. Traditionally, women entered teaching both because they had few other professional opportunities and because its work schedule was more consistent with family responsibilities than that of many occupations. It also did not require organizational and labor force continuity; individuals could move in and out of school districts and/or the labor force almost at will. Consistent with this flexibility has been a lack of career ladders and fairly flat wage profiles. Teacher salaries have also lagged relative to those of comparable occupations, and their competitive position deteriorated throughout the 1970s. Although the compatibility of teaching with family responsibilities is probably still an attraction for many women, as women's labor force patterns increasingly approximate those of men's, many professional women can be expected to seek the same payoffs from their labor force activity that men seek, such as promotion opportunities and professionally competitive salaries.

The changes in women's initial occupational choices are also mirrored in changes in their labor force participation. Since the early part of this century, women's labor force participation rates have steadily increased (Waite, 1981). Starting with the cohort born about 1935–1945, each succeeding cohort remained out of the labor force for less time during the childbearing period, and a higher percentage went back to work after their children had entered school. The baby boom and subsequent cohorts (born since 1946) have shown high initial labor force participation rates (over 50 percent for the 1946–1966 group and nearly 70 percent for the post-1955 group) and a steady increase in these rates, even through the childbearing years. The overall labor participation rate for all women is now over 50 percent, including married women and women with children.

As the teaching force is still predominantly female and the job is structured in many ways on the basis of the premise that this will continue to be so, these dramatic changes in the occupational and labor force decisions of women have important implications for teaching. On the one hand, more career-oriented younger women might be less willing to settle for low salaries and flat careers for the accommodations that teaching has allowed with child rearing. On the other hand, some women who have remained out of the labor force to raise children (many now in their late 30s to mid-40s) might, in seeking entry or reentry to the labor force, consider teaching as a job option, thus expanding the potential pool of teachers. These women, some of whom might have prepared to teach years ago, could be part of the reserve pool for teaching, an increasingly important source of supply. Access to this reserve pool, though, might be limited by recent changes in certification standards, which make reentry to teaching more difficult.

In addition to these labor force changes affecting the primary pool of traditional teachers, a number of recent policy changes are likely to influence the nature of teaching as a career and, hence, the types of individuals who will enter teaching and the amount of time they will stay.

Changes in the Teaching Occupation

The recognition of problems facing the teaching occupation has led to a series of policy initiatives and changes by state legislatures, governors, state and local school boards, and colleges involved in teacher preparation. These changes have tried to increase teacher supply, improve teacher quality, and improve productivity in schools.

The reform initiatives include efforts to attract more qualified individuals into teaching through improved teacher salaries, student aid programs, and innovations in teacher licensing policies; efforts to upgrade teacher-training programs and tighten teacher certification requirements; and programs to recognize and reward outstanding teachers, to improve teacher working conditions, and to increase public awareness of the pivotal role of teachers in shaping the nation's future.

Teacher Compensation. In the late 1980s, teacher salaries increased in every state. Much attention was focused on beginning teacher salary levels, because the entry salary seems critical to attracting new entrants. Across-the-board salary increases were also enacted in some states.

In 1985–1986, the average public elementary and secondary school teacher's salary was $25,240, up 31 percent from

1981–1982, but just equivalent to the real value of average teacher salaries in 1971–1972. When salaries are adjusted for years of experience, the more experienced teaching force now is, on average, still about 15 percent worse off than their less-experienced counterparts were in the early 1970s. In recent years, salaries for beginning teachers have risen steeply. These increases have both benefits and disadvantages. They have reduced, but not eliminated, the gap between the entry-level wages of beginning teachers and those of college graduates in other fields, a gap that still averages between 25 and 30 percent.

Thirty states have mandated minimum compensation levels. Nineteen states have also established statewide salary schedules on which teachers advance, usually one step for each year of experience. During the 1980s, states mandated statewide minimum or overall salaries for the first time. Although creating a statewide compensation system might increase teachers' pay within a state, on average the salaries of teachers in states with mandated schedules are somewhat lower than those in states without such schedules. Typical schedules are flat and guarantee smaller increases as years of experience mount. This flat compensation structure is one of the factors that has given rise to proposals for career differentiation and performance-based compensation.

In 29 states, laws have been enacted creating career ladder, merit pay, or incentive pay systems. Some are statewide, others are to be locally developed and piloted before adoption is considered (Southern Regional Education Board, 1986). In addition to raising earnings, it is presumed that such plans will make teaching more attractive to capable individuals who expect to be rewarded for their achievements. The ultimate outcomes of these plans have yet to be determined, though, since some have met with substantial opposition and others have been tabled for lack of funding (Darling-Hammond & Berry, 1988).

Other Efforts to Increase Teacher Supply. Besides the increase in teacher salaries, a number of other innovations have been adopted to encourage a greater supply of teachers. Almost every state has recently adopted some form of aid for college students who prepare to enter teaching. These programs range from scholarships for academic achievement to forgivable student loans for those who complete a minimum period of teaching service (AACTE, 1985). In some states these programs are directed only toward candidates for teaching positions in areas of critical need such as mathematics and science. Increasingly, though, the trend is toward incentives in all teaching fields. A fairly recent report cited evidence that 25 percent of all teacher-preparation programs in the nation now offer some form of scholarship or loan program to recruit high academic achievers into teaching (Holmstrom, 1985).

To insure an adequate supply of teachers, many states have employed teachers with emergency credentials or have allowed teachers to teach out of field. In 1983, 46 states allowed substandard, limited, or emergency certification, and 27 of these states allowed these certificates to be issued to teachers who did not hold a bachelor's degree. Although virtually all states had provisions for temporary or emergency certification before 1983, some have added additional provisions to allow individuals who have not taken education courses to teach or have created new classes of emergency certificates.

Another innovation to encourage greater teacher supply has been the adoption of alternate teacher certification routes in 23 states. Alternative programs generally offer inservice and limited university training for graduates of liberal arts programs who have not completed traditional teacher-preparation curricula. Candidates take fewer education courses than traditional entrants. Following a brief orientation seminar (usually 4–6 weeks), candidates assume full-time teaching responsibilities. They are to receive on-the-job supervision while completing education courses after school hours. These initiatives, though useful for boosting supply quickly, operate in tension with simultaneous state moves to increase regular certification requirements.

By 1986, 46 states had mandated teacher competency tests in basic skills, subject matter, or professional knowledge as a requirement for admission to teacher education, or for certification, or both. Of the three most prevalent types of competency tests, basic-skills tests have been most readily enacted and implemented in states. In recent years, a few states have added on-the-job performance assessments of first-year teachers as a requirement for continuing certification. Of the 25 states that have determined the structure of their beginning teacher programs, 18 have chosen to require that their beginning teachers pass a formal performance assessment before receiving full certification. Six other states have chosen to emphasize only the support component of their beginning-teacher programs.

Until recently, most states had few, if any, requirements for teachers to satisfy once they were initially certified. However, states are disallowing the "life" certificate—requiring teachers to continuously renew their credentials with additional formal college coursework or inservice training. Thirty-two states now require teachers to renew their certificates on a continuing basis.

Over the last few years, the trend has been to enact more stringent recertification standards. In the past, many states have not specified the quality or nature of the courses required. More states are now requiring teachers to successfully complete courses in content areas applicable to their teaching field. In three states, Arkansas, Texas, and Georgia, experienced teachers have to pass competency examinations to be recertified. In two of these, the tests are basic-skills assessments. In the third, teachers are tested in their subject-matter areas and are required to pass a performance assessment before they can be recertified.

Changes in Incentives, Working Conditions, and Status. Recent discussions of the problems facing the teaching profession have to recognize that the solutions to the lessened attractiveness of teaching must go deeper than pay raises and competency testing. Large and increasing numbers of teachers are dissatisfied with the working conditions and social status of teaching. They regret having chosen to become teachers. Between 1966 and 1981 the proportion of teachers saying they would not choose teaching as a career if they had it to do over again increased from under 10 percent to 36 percent (Darling-Hammond, 1984). Attention to teachers' salaries and status during the early 1980s might have contributed to some improvement in attitudes by 1986, when the proportion claiming they would not choose teaching again dipped slightly, to 31 percent (NEA, 1987). Still, this is not a promising sign for the profession or its future, as many teachers who now regret their career decisions might discourage their own students from considering teaching as a career (Berry, 1985).

The causes of alienation among teachers can be traced to a number of factors including working conditions, organizational patterns, salary policies, and public attitudes. Working conditions that have been identified as sources of teacher dissatisfaction include crowded classrooms, inadequate preparation time, and lack of time and energy for teaching because of the burden of clerical, custodial, and disciplinary duties. Teachers have difficulty perceiving of themselves as valued, competent professionals when their work environments lack the kind of clerical support and facilities that they observe are available to other professionals.

Organizational patterns have also been cited as sources of disaffection. A bureaucratic approach to administration tends to strip teachers of decision-making authority and the ability to be creative and innovative in their teaching. Lack of control by teachers over the structure and content of their work reduces the motivation for performance.

Salary policies are important influences on teacher morale in two ways. *First,* the general inadequacy of teacher salary levels has been interpreted as a measure of our society's true regard for the value of teaching and of teachers. This is to be expected in a society that often relates social status and prestige to economic status. *Second,* the standardized nature of most teacher pay scales—in conjunction with a flat career structure—provides little motivation or reward for outstanding performance. Teachers' social status has also declined as the general population has become more educated and as dissatisfaction with school performance has increased.

Efforts to improve teacher status and working conditions include a variety of teacher-recognition programs, increased funding for teacher aides and clerical assistance, and relief from nonteaching duties. Reallocation of decision-making authority to give voice to teachers' views has been much discussed but little implemented, as it threatens established organizational patterns and presumes norms of collegiality and shared knowledge not yet widely prevalent in many schools.

Over time, the development of policy reforms that might change the occupational structure of teaching will influence who enters and who stays in the profession. The ways in which current education reforms are managed and implemented will interact with labor market factors in the 1990s to shape the supply and demand for teachers.

TEACHER SUPPLY AND DEMAND

The teacher labor market has been characterized by seemingly abrupt shifts between shortage and surplus, with lagged responses on the part of training institutions and policymakers to current conditions. These responses in turn have produced the next boom-or-bust cycle, because adequate methods for projecting their effects in the context of changing labor market conditions have not been applied. Approaching is one of these volatile periods, produced in part by the policy responses to teacher surpluses in the 1970s—then projected to continue for some time. Other societal factors, though, have had independent effects on the teacher labor market. These, too, must be understood when interpreting current projections of teacher supply and demand.

Educational policy decisions that will affect the demand for teachers include new course requirements for students and pressures for school improvement that could lead to lower student–teacher ratios. Teacher supply will be affected by changes in certification standards, levels of compensation, and working conditions. Besides these factors, which are affected by educational policy decisions, there are factors outside the control of policymakers, such as changing wages in other occupations, availability of alternate careers (especially for women), and changes in basic family formation and labor force participation patterns that reflect when and how individuals marry, have children, and work.

From a national perspective, the teacher market appears to be shifting from a state of surplus to shortage. In the late 1980s, at least spot shortages were reported in certain teaching areas, particularly in secondary school specialties such as mathematics, physics, computer programming, chemistry, data processing, bilingual education, special education, earth science, and biology (Association for School, College, and University Staffing, 1984; Howe & Gerlovich, 1982). The shortages in mathematics and the physical sciences seem particularly severe and, some evidence suggests, endemic (Levin, 1985; National Science Board, 1985), but other teaching areas that formerly showed surpluses seem to be joining the list.

National projections suggest that the shortages of specialized teachers could expand to a more general shortage of qualified teachers during the 1990s. After a decade of declining enrollments in elementary and secondary schools, a baby boomlet that began in the early 1980s has led to enrollment increases starting in 1985. At the same time, the college-age population from which many potential teachers are drawn will continue to decline through the remainder of the decade. The proportion of college students choosing a major in education has been declining since 1970 (NEA, 1983). Although a slight upsurge in the percentage of college freshmen expressing interest in education majors and careers has been noted since 1983, the numbers are still much smaller than a decade earlier, and it is not yet clear how many of these students choose teaching. Astin et al. (1987) note:

Education careers have experienced the greatest decline in student interest since 1966. Between 1966 and 1985 there was a 71 percent decline in the proportion of freshmen planning to pursue elementary or secondary teaching careers (from 21.7 to 6.2 percent). . . . (E)ven with the recent slight increase, student interest in education careers is still far below the levels recorded in previous decades and falls far short of anticipated needs for the 1990s. (pp. 17–18)

Projections from the National Center for Education Statistics (NCES, 1985b) based on current trends in the school-age population and data on prospective entrants to the teaching profession indicate that the supply of new teacher graduates will satisfy only about 75 percent of the demand for additional teachers between 1988 and 1992.

There are good reasons to believe that imbalances between supply and demand will be distributed unevenly across regions and types of school districts. Population trends, access to pools of potential teachers, and policies affecting supply and demand all vary across regions, states, and localities. Prospects of encountering and resolving shortages also differ across districts. Salary adjustment and increased recruiting intensity are likely in higher income areas; these districts are not only likely to win the competition for new teachers, but also might pull existing teachers out of districts with lower salaries and less attractive working conditions.

However, these projections and perceptions of current shortages do not adequately describe the state of the teacher labor market in a way that is predictive of future events or useful for policy formulation. What is critical for describing the teacher labor market is an understanding of (a) those factors that influence individuals' decisions to offer their services to teaching and then to remain in teaching (in particular fields and locations), and (b) those factors that determine which of these individuals will be deemed qualified to teach. In the first category one must consider attributes of the pool of potential teachers and attributes of teaching as an occupation relative to other alternative occupations open to similarly qualified individuals. In the second category one must consider state and local certification policies and hiring practices as these interact with other policies and conditions that create teacher demand.

State-level policymakers have begun to respond in two different ways to emerging indications of teacher shortages and declines in the measured academic ability of those entering teaching. On the one hand, they have been raising standards for entry to teaching by requiring examinations at various points along the pipeline to becoming a teacher. On the other hand, they have responded to shortages by relaxing requirements to allow those not trained as teachers to enter teaching. School administrators, faced with an increasing demand for teachers in some areas and a shrinking supply of qualified teachers, must either hire inexperienced teachers with minimal qualifications or entertain stopgap changes in course offerings, teacher reassignments, and field-switching among continuing teachers. These responses to imbalances in the supply and demand for teachers affect both the composition of the teaching force and the educational offerings available to students.

Factors Affecting Teacher Supply

State and district personnel policies regarding teacher certification, compensation, hiring, and retention mediate between the demand for teachers and the supply of potential teachers to produce the characteristics of the teaching force at any given point in time. These policies (along with individuals' occupational choices affected by labor market conditions and the relative attractiveness of teaching) influence which members of the potential pool of teachers are likely to offer their services to

teaching and which are selected to teach. The policies themselves do not remain immune from supply and demand forces; in times of high demand or relatively short supply, the policies often change to allow most positions to be filled (e.g., increases in salary, relaxation of certification requirements, changes in hiring practices).

When shortages or budgetary problems occur, other staffing and scheduling changes might be used to alleviate unfilled or partially filled vacancies. These include reassigning some courses to other teachers who do not have a full teaching load, changing course offerings, and adjusting class sizes or teaching loads. These responses artificially alter the demand for teachers of certain types and affect the character of teacher supply in ways that can only be inferred from examination of hiring and assignment practices.

Because there are potentially important interactions between the supply and quality of teaching candidates, estimates of supply must take into account the qualifications of current and potential members of the teaching force. The quality distribution of each element of the supply pool is a critical characteristic of supply, because much of the adjustment to sharp changes in demand occurs in terms of the qualifications of teachers hired, rather than the quantity.

Shortages and Standards. Although data are not available to demonstrate conclusively how qualifications-related measures of supply and demand would affect estimates of shortages, some sense of the possible magnitude of differences in estimates derived from alternative assumptions can be gained from fairly recent surveys. The 1983–1984 NCES estimates of teacher shortage, based on a measure of unfilled vacancies reported by a sample of school districts, indicate overall shortages in the neighborhood of only 1.6 per thousand current teachers (or 19 per 1,000 vacancies), with field-specific shortages ranging from .4 per thousand teachers for reading to 8.8 per thousand for bilingual education (NCES, 1985a). This range may reflect supply as it interacts with the outer bounds of teacher substitutability in different fields. That is, a number of individuals might well be viewed as capable of teaching reading, but the potential supply of bilingual education teachers is limited to individuals who are, in fact, bilingual themselves, aside from the application of any credentialing standards. On the other hand, the number of unfilled vacancies in a particular field might also reflect a view that some courses are more dispensable than others; in these fields, difficult-to-fill vacancies could be left unfilled rather than filled with uncertified candidates. Thus, if all students must take high school English, vacancies cannot be left unfilled; however, an upper level mathematics course might simply be cancelled if a teacher cannot be found.

Applying a standard other than unfilled vacancies leads to quite different estimates of shortage. For example, the same 1983–1984 survey provided estimates of the proportion of total and newly hired teachers not certified in their principal field of assignment; these amounted to 3.4 percent of all teachers and 12.4 percent of all newly hired teachers. If one assumed that no certified applicants could be found to fill the vacancies filled by uncertified teachers and added these 26,300 positions to the count of unfilled vacancies, the estimate of shortages would increase by more than 10-fold, to 12.3 per 1,000 current teachers and over 14 percent of all vacancies. If one further assumed that the positions filled by teachers assigned outside their fields of certification could not have been filled by certified applicants, the estimates would skyrocket further.

Applying still more rigorous standards yields predictably larger estimates. Because certification is not a perfect measure of preparation, one might want to know what proportion of teachers are teaching classes outside their fields of preparation who might otherwise be counted as evidence of shortage. (Admittedly, this requires inferences about hiring and staffing and disallowances of substitutions or economies that are not entirely realistic, given current staffing practices.) A 1980–1981 NEA survey of teachers indicates that 16 percent of all teachers teach some classes outside their field of preparation, and 9 percent spend most of their time teaching "out of field" (NEA, 1981); the *High School and Beyond* special survey supplement of 10,000 teachers indicates that, among high school teachers, 11 percent teach primarily outside their area of state certification and 17 percent have less than a college minor in the field they most frequently teach (C. D. Carroll, 1985).

To be sure, one does not know the degree to which such out-of-field assignments are actually inappropriate according to various standards, or the degree to which they impair teaching quality; nor does one know the extent to which the discontinuation of some of these types of hiring and assignment practices would influence teacher demand or shortage. Some of these practices are undoubtedly the result of capitalizing on teachers' individual uncredentialed abilities and interests; some result from district attempts to continue to employ senior teachers when demand in their particular teaching fields declines; some are probably supported by inservice training that upgrades teachers' skills. On the other hand, misassignment as a response to teacher shortages might also result in poor teaching and, in any event, produces a distorted picture of teacher supply.

It is probably fair to say that there is currently little agreement on how various types of personnel policy changes will affect the supply and quality of teachers and little consensus on the usefulness of the standards that currently exist. Thus, one sees states both tightening and loosening certification and entry standards (sometimes both simultaneously) and making various adjustments in compensation at different junctures in the teaching career, with little ability to predict how these changes will affect the supply of teachers or the composition of the teaching force.

At least two competing theories are now offered for the presumed declines in teacher supply and quality during the 1970s. Weaver (1978), for example, has argued that decreased demand for teachers during the 1970s led to a decline in the quality of supply as colleges of education attempted to maintain enrollments by lowering their standards. If this theory were correct, increased demand should of itself increase the supply of potential candidates, and tighter certification and entry standards should increase quality. In contrast, Schlechty and Vance (1981) argue that expansion of nonteaching employment opportunities for "traditional" prospective teachers has caused a decrease in the supply and quality of teaching candidates, as many have been lured away to other fields with greater financial and nonpecuniary attractions. If this theory were correct, the only way to increase teacher supply without lowering standards (or to maintain standards without further decreasing supply) would be to increase the attractions to teaching.

Factors Affecting Entrance. In the past, most new teachers were recent bachelor's degree recipients who had completed an approved teacher education program or accumulated the requisite college courses for initial certification. However, the proportions of teacher education graduates who do not initially enter teaching vary substantially over time and across teaching fields. In 1976–1977 the NCES estimated that the proportion of newly qualified graduates seeking teaching positions was 77 percent, with only 60 percent ultimately accepting teaching positions. In 1981, the estimate of those seeking full-time positions was 85 percent, with 64 percent ultimately accepting such positions. Differences among teaching fields are also substantial. In 1981, for example, only 30 percent of prospective health teachers accepted full-time teaching jobs, as compared with 75 percent of prospective special education teachers (NCES, 1983).

The second major component of the flow of college graduates into teaching includes persons who are not qualified to teach upon graduation but who enter a postbaccalaureate program that leads to qualification; this might be a year of graduate education or a sequence of undergraduate courses, depending on state requirements. Although, in the past, the vast majority of masters' degrees were awarded to existing teachers, this could change as states open up new routes to certification for liberal arts graduates and as some teacher education programs move to a 5-year model.

Many college graduates who are qualified to teach take nonteaching jobs or remain unemployed for a year or more before they enter teaching. Others who initially enter nonteaching occupations or pursue homemaking careers seek teaching credentials several years after leaving college. Although late entrants from the nonteaching sector might not have constituted a large proportion of new teachers in the past, college graduates in nonteaching occupations and homemaking constitute a relatively large population of individuals who might consider a career in teaching at some time in the future, given appropriate inducements or adverse employment experiences in other fields.

Another large group of college graduates who are possible candidates for teaching constitute the reserve pool of former teachers who are currently in nonteaching jobs, unemployed, or out of the labor force as homemakers and/or students. The size of the real reserve pool depends on what proportion of these individuals would consider reentering teaching under various conditions. This can depend on labor market conditions, as well as on barriers to or incentives for reentry.

Though information from some states and districts suggests that the reserve pool, however defined, is an increasingly important current source of teacher supply (Raizen, 1986), there is no way of knowing how much of the pool has already been tapped, how near is the bottom of the pool, or what it would take in terms of changes in the occupation to expand the pool or increase the propensities of members of various sectors to enter teaching.

Like other components of teacher supply and demand, it is undoubtedly true that the size, composition, and potential availability of the reserve pool varies among locations (and for different fields), depending on characteristics of the local population (age, education, and employment) and economy, degree of transiency in the population, and current and past school personnel practices. Districts that laid off teachers in the early 1980s, for example, might still be rehiring members of their former teaching staffs. Districts with lenient hiring practices might find it easier to tap the reserve pool than those that apply stringent certification, education, or testing requirements. States and districts with more attractive teaching conditions—higher salaries, better working conditions, good benefits—and those that can offer full credit on the salary scale for prior teaching experience might tap more competent sectors of the reserve pool.

Factors Influencing Turnover. Teacher turnover is an important determinant of future supply, as it defines the number of continuing teachers. In addition, teacher turnover is the largest component of new teacher demand and is probably the most unstable component over time and across schools. There are a number of reasons to believe that teacher attrition rates are not static. *First,* the age composition of the teaching force changes over time; hence, the proportion of the force nearing retirement also changes. *Second,* recent data from a number of states and school districts suggest that annual attrition rates are especially high for inexperienced teachers during the first few years (cf. Grissmer & Kirby, 1987; Mark & Anderson, 1985; Vance & Schlechty, 1982). Thus, the experience composition of the teaching force is an important (and changing) variable. *Third,* labor market forces in teaching and in the general economy undoubtedly influence turnover. When teaching positions are scarce, temporary exits might be fewer, due to expected difficulty in reentering; when other opportunities are plentiful, career changes are more likely.

Finally, policy variables influence attrition rates. Incentives for early retirement, for example, became widespread in school districts during the 1970s, when declining enrollments required reductions in force. These incentives might now begin to work, ironically, to produce shortages. Current policy initiatives such as internships for beginning teachers and merit pay or career ladders for veterans, along with other changes in salary levels, are intended to influence attrition rates. Perhaps they will. Suffice it to say that attrition will change with the shape of the teaching force, with the health of other sectors of the economy, and perhaps even with changes in policy affecting teachers.

Factors Affecting Teacher Demand

Teacher demand is determined by enrollment changes and changes in pupil–teacher ratios. Although the components of teacher demand are fairly clear-cut, they do not add up in a straightforward manner to produce an exact count of teachers needed from year to year. Enrollment changes, for example, generally produce lagged and nonlinear effects on the demand for teachers. An increase or decrease in enrollment does not usually translate immediately into a corresponding proportional increase or decrease in the number of teachers. Adjustments are made to pupil–teacher ratios to smooth the effects of rapid enrollment changes, to accommodate established school staffing patterns and budgets, and to take into account existing contractual agreements with teachers. For example, as enrollments decline, teacher organizations and school boards might be willing to forgo salary increases or other instructional supports to keep current teachers employed; when enrollments increase, teacher–pupil ratios might fall, to support higher salaries or because of hiring lags (Cavin, Murnane, & Brown, 1985).

Teacher demand is also affected by state and local district policies, which mediate the effects of school enrollments on the numbers and types of teachers needed by specifying class sizes, teaching loads, program and course requirements, and staffing requirements. These demand-related policies are a blend of legal requirements and less formalized practices, which can vary among districts and schools, depending on state statutes or regulations and on the choices made by local districts.

A school district's teacher–pupil ratio is determined in the course of a complex budget-allocation process. School district budgets are based upon the community's perceptions of its educational needs, its abiity and willingness to allocate funds to meet those needs, and the amount of state and federal aid received. The school district, in turn, allocates its budget among various school inputs: teachers, aides, supplies, and so on. Teacher–pupil ratios depend on the costs of purchasing or hiring the various school inputs (e.g., teacher salaries), district commitments (e.g., contracts with teachers, tenure policies, agreements with suppliers of purchased inputs), and the ways in which it organizes instructional activities (S. J. Carroll, 1973).

Pupil–teacher ratios are influenced by a number of factors in addition to school budgets and enrollments. The mix of programs and courses offered to students often dictates different levels of staff resources. Special education courses, for example, require a lower pupil–teacher ratio than others; districts or schools serving a large number of students in such courses tend to have lower pupil–teacher ratios overall. Similarly, as program and staffing patterns change for school systems as a whole, attendant changes can be expected in the total demand for teachers, as well as in the demand for particular types of teachers. The introduction of nearly universal kindergarten, the mandated provision of special education and bilingual education services, and the proliferation of auxiliary teaching staff (e.g., counselors, librarians, school psychologists, and resource teachers) are all examples of changes in program and staffing arrangements during the 1970s and 1980s that affected demand for particular types of teachers and, in some cases, also influenced overall pupil–teacher ratios.

The distribution of enrolled children between public and private education and the related need for teachers at specific grade levels, are other factors influencing demand. Although the proportion of students in private education is small (about 13 percent) and the current difference between public and private teacher–pupil ratios is not large, the number of teachers in private schools increased by 45 percent between 1970 and 1983, from 10 percent of all K–12 teachers to nearly 14 percent. This is not only due to growth in the private sector over these years but also to sharper declines in pupil–teacher ratios in private schools than in public schools. Between 1965 and 1983, overall pupil–teacher ratios declined by 27 percent. This same rate of decrease in public elementary schools' pupil–teacher ratios was matched by a 46 percent decrease in private elementary ratios during the same period.

Demand for particular types of teachers also varies from school to school and from district to district, both as a function of community wealth, which influences overall demand, and as a function of community preferences for different types of education. For example, suburban college-preparatory districts evidence higher demand for elementary mathematics, science, and art teachers and secondary arts and humanities teachers, whereas urban and rural districts have a higher demand for vocational education teachers (Crane, 1982). Factors such as community education levels, poverty, and receipt of federal education aid are even stronger predictors of the type of teacher demand than are locational characteristics of districts.

Finally, when relative demand for teachers shifts among fields, as has occurred in recent years (e.g., less demand for teachers in home economics, physical education, vocational education, and business education, concurrently with increased demand for mathematics and science teachers), school systems often tend to shift senior teachers from low-demand courses to high-demand courses, rather than hiring newcomers trained in these fields (Johnson & Aldridge, 1984). If a subject-area vacancy is only part-time (e.g., two sections of biology to be covered and three of physical education), the incentive to "cross-assign" is very strong. Thus "misassignment" is a product of both market shortage and district personnel policies regarding staffing and teacher assignment, as well as the fact that demand does not always occur tidily by subject area.

The Influence of Teaching Structure

The composition of the teaching force and the nature of teaching work that result from these factors have important implications for supply and demand in future years. For example, a teaching force heavily weighted toward very old or very young teachers will produce higher attrition in subsequent years, thus increasing demand and reducing the supply of continuing teachers. Furthermore, the same curricular and staffing policies that partially determine the nature of teacher demand also affect the nature of teaching as an occupation. Determinations about what will be taught and who will teach it (and how other staff time will be spent) exert a powerful influence on teaching practices and views of the teaching profession, which in turn influence both the retention of current teachers and the attractiveness of teaching to potential new entrants.

The nature of the teaching occupation is a structural factor that interacts with other demographic, economic, and social conditions to produce changes in both the quantity and quality of teacher supply. Among the relevant descriptors of the teaching occupation at present are the following:

Relatively low beginning salaries and a flat wage and career structure (both of which are beginning to change, but not yet sufficiently to be competitive with most alternative occupations open to college graduates).
Low levels of autonomy and decision-making responsibility. Little opportunity for advancement or variability in job functions, important to individuals who value opportunities for growth, challenge, and change in their work.
Low, but possibly increasing, community regard for the occupation of teaching.
Relatively unattractive working conditions with respect to physical facilities, access to office space and equipment, and opportunity for collegial exchange.

These are not entirely new features of teaching, but they occur in the context of other societal changes. Changes in lifestyles, changes in technology, and changes in career opportunities for college graduates, especially women, minorities, and individuals in scientific and technical fields, have combined to alter the traditional patterns of supply and demand. What once sufficed to attract new entrants looks less appealing in comparison with other alternatives now available.

CRITICAL ISSUES

Supply and Distribution of Teachers

Throughout the twentieth century, teacher shortages have been common, and they have provided an impetus for upgrading salaries and standards within the profession. Shortages following World War I and World War II, and again in the 1960s, propelled substantial real increases in teacher salaries, accompanied by increases in the educational requirements for teaching. As Sedlak and Schlossman (1986) note:

Contrary to what many modern-day educators tend to assume, teacher shortages have been commonplace throughout the twentieth century. Nonetheless, it has proved possible, time and again, to raise certification standards during periods of protracted shortage. Not only has the raising of standards not exacerbated teacher shortages, it may even—at least where accompanied by significant increases in teachers' salaries—have helped to alleviate them (and, at the same time, enhanced popular respect for teaching as a profession). (p. 39)

Their research demonstrated that teacher shortages generally followed periods of decline in real income for teachers and that, in most instances, the shortages produced both salary gains and heightened standards for teaching.

The 1980s mirrored past experiences with teacher shortages and changes in compensation and certification. Following the wage declines of the 1970s, which, along with widely publicized surpluses, dramatically decreased the supply of teachers in training, emerging teacher shortages led to a 35 percent increase in nominal salaries between 1981 and 1986, and certification standards were raised by virtue of required licensure tests in most states (Darling-Hammond & Berry, 1988). These salary hikes, though helpful, just returned average teacher salaries to the level they had reached in 1972, following the shortages of the 1960s. More important, salaries in other occupations remained well ahead of those in teaching, averaging about 30 percent higher in other occupations requiring 4 years of college.

Shortages and Loopholes

Even as certification standards have ostensibly been raised, however, current shortages have been addressed by certification loopholes including increased use of emergency certificates to fill vacancies and the creation of alternative routes to certification that lessen the preparation requirements for teaching. Counting just the small sample of states who keep records on emergency and temporary licenses, over 30,000 were issued in 1985 alone (Feistritzer, 1986). Although recent attention to teaching has stimulated an increase in the number of college freshmen reporting interest in education as a major or a career (Astin, Green, & Korn, 1987), their numbers would have to more than double to satisfy the demand for new teachers in coming years.

The dilemma, then, is that, although teacher shortages have created a political climate within which standards and salaries might be raised, they have also created conditions that work against the continuation of these initiatives. The effect of having standards, however high, with large loopholes available to satisfy demand pressures is that salaries always remain somewhat depressed. In the past, although teacher salaries have always increased in times of short supply, they have never reached comparability with those of other professions requiring similar training, and they have tended to slip again when the supply crisis was "solved." If no substantial improvement occurs in the attractions to teaching, it will be difficult to improve overall teacher quality because the pool of potential candidates who can meet the standards will not be sufficiently enlarged. In circular fashion, the failure to attract sufficient numbers of well-qualified teachers will lessen teachers' claims for professional responsibility and autonomy and will increase the press for regulation of teaching, thus further decreasing the attractions to teaching for professionally oriented candidates.

It is interesting to note that this process of standard raising and nearly simultaneous undermining of those standards has occurred over the last century in other occupations, such as law and medicine, that sought to become professions. In those cases, currently in teaching, the loopholes were created by state governments, who established statutory exemptions to certification requirements. In some cases, the states were encouraged by college faculties or employers, who had greater incentives to insure an adequate supply of students or practitioners than to insure the quality of that supply (see e.g., Starr, 1982). It was not until members of these occupations

organized themselves to promulgate and enforce their own standards through professionally controlled licensure and examination boards that standards could be used as a determinant of permission to practice. Teaching now is alone in the granting of substandard licenses. The American Association of Colleges for Teacher Education Task Force on Teacher Certification has been unable to discover any other state-licensed occupation for which "emergency certification" exists (Bacharach et al., 1985). And most of the untrained recipients of such certificates are hired to teach in disadvantaged schools, where recruitment is most difficult (Darling-Hammond, 1988). Thus, the children in these schools bear the brunt of the teacher-supply problem.

Shortages and Equity

Teacher shortages are most acute and underqualified entrants to teaching are most numerous in central-city schools, where poor and minority children are increasingly concentrated.

- In 1983, the most recent year for which national information is available, shortages of teachers, as measured by unfilled vacancies, were three times greater in central cities than in rural areas or suburbs (NCES, 1985a).
- More than 14 percent of all newly hired teachers in central-city school districts in 1983 were uncertified in their principal field of assignment, nearly twice the proportion experienced by other types of districts.
- The most severe shortages of teachers occurred in such fields as bilingual education and special education, fields that are in especially great demand in central cities; these fields are also among those with the highest proportions of uncertified teachers.
- A survey of high school teachers in 1984 found that the schools where uncertified teachers were located were disproportionately central-city schools with higher than average percentages of disadvantaged and minority students (Pascal, 1987, p. 24).
- In 1985, at least 5,000 teachers were hired on emergency certificates in New York, Los Angeles, and Houston alone. Many of these districts' vacancies were not filled when schools opened that fall (Darling-Hammond, 1987). Each year since then, large urban districts have encountered similar problems in recruiting teachers.

Teacher shortages subvert the quality of education in a number of ways. They make it hard for districts to be selective in the quality of teachers they hire, and they often result in the hiring of teachers who have not completed (or sometimes even begun) their pedagogical training. In addition, when faced with shortages, districts must often hire short- and long-term substitutes, assign teachers outside their fields of qualification, expand class sizes, or cancel course offerings. No matter what strategies are adopted, the quality of instruction generally suffers.

The elimination of this particular form of inequality can

come only by a large and sustained boost in the supply of well-trained teachers, coupled with incentives for many of these teachers to train in shortage fields and to locate in shortage areas. Though federal initiatives to boost the supply of teachers in fields like mathematics and science are now being considered, no analog to the distributional incentives of the 1958 National Defense and Education Act for teachers has yet become available to address this acute problem. The NDEA provided forgivable loans to college students who entered teaching, with an added incentive for those who entered teaching in urban districts. Similarly, the National Medical Manpower Act and the Health Professions Educational Assistance Act for physicians have, since the 1960s, provided forgivable loans to medical students who practice in underserved rural and central-city locations.

Such initiatives must be launched soon if the severe teacher shortfall anticipated over the coming years is to be even partially averted. Special efforts will be needed to avert the additional tragedy of a teaching force that no longer represents the racial and ethnic diversity of society. Recent substantial drops in the number of minority entrants to teaching could bring the proportion of minority teachers down from over 10 percent to less than half that number by the turn of the century.

Current shortages of minority candidates in teaching are partly the result of teacher tests, which influence entrance at the point of certification, but they are mainly the result of the defections of academically able minority students to other careers and professions. Enrollment of minority students in teacher education programs plummeted sharply prior to 1981, when most teacher tests were just beginning to be enacted, and they have continued to drop since. Education has been replaced as a field of choice by other careers, many of which require graduate education and licensure testing. The sharp changes in minority students' social opportunities and career preferences since the late 1960s are reflected in the astounding fact that in 1985 only 8,800 minority students who had received bachelor's degrees in the previous year entered teaching, whereas over 30,000 were enrolled in first professional degree programs (Darling-Hammond, Pittman, & Ottinger, in press). Ultimately, improvements in the attractiveness of teaching are key to resolving the problem of shortages for majority and minority candidates alike.

Short of a total overhaul of the teaching occupation and the structure of schooling, there are a number of strategies that can be pursued to increase the attractions to teacher preparation. First, and most obvious, lowering the financial costs of acquiring teacher preparation will sharply improve recruitment, particularly for minority students. Offering scholarships and forgivable loans to prospective teachers ought to be at the top of the federal and states' agenda throughout the 1990s.

There are also ways in which teacher preparation can be made more accessible to candidates who do not choose to enroll in an education major in their junior year of college. Graduate-level teacher education programs can succeed in attracting an entirely different pool of recruits: those who were unable or unwilling to commit to teaching at a very early point in their academic careers during undergraduate school and those who are interested in changing careers but are unwilling to return to undergraduate school to do so. Without diluting requirements for teacher preparation, colleges of education can lower the transaction costs of attendance by creating more time-efficient and flexibly scheduled programs than most undergraduate programs typically allow. Indeed, recently created programs designed to attract (and fully certify) nontraditional recruits to mathematics and science teaching have succeeded in maintaining standards for preparation while attracting recent bachelor's degree recipients and mid-career candidates to graduate-level programs targeted at their career needs and schedules. In many cases, these programs also attract much larger numbers of minority candidates than traditional undergraduate teacher-preparation programs (Carey, Mittman, & Darling-Hammond, 1988; Darling-Hammond, Hudson, & Kirby, 1989).

Once graduated from teacher-preparation programs, though, candidates must be persuaded to enter and stay in teaching at rates higher than currently pertain. Ultimately, having an adequate supply of well-trained teachers over the coming years will depend on (a) increasing the initial attractions to teaching, primarily its wage competitiveness with other occupations requiring similar training; (b) stemming the high early attrition of new entrants; (c) creating an occupational structure and job conditions that will encourage retention of talented veterans. Achieving these conditions rests in turn on the extent to which teachers are educated, and consequently viewed and treated, as skilled and knowledgeable professionals.

Importance of Teacher Preparation

American school policy has often started with the assumption that teachers are conduits for policy or curricula rather than active agents in the production of learning. Consequently, many reform initiatives have emphasized improving schools by changing curricula, programs, tests, textbooks, and management processes rather than by improving the knowledge and capacity of teachers. Indeed, American policymakers sometimes seem to doubt whether there is anything that a teacher brings to the classroom other than the state's or school district's mandated materials, procedures, and regulations. They question whether teacher preparation is necessary and seem to believe that unprepared teachers are as safe and effective as well-trained teachers. These beliefs support the myth that allows teaching expertise to be unequally distributed, the myth that all teachers and classrooms are equal.

Since the late 1960s, educational research has exploded the myths that any teaching is as effective as any other and that equally trained and experienced teachers are equally advantageous to students. Those who are well prepared to teach do indeed teach more effectively. Researchers are now identifying what it is that expert veterans do in the classroom that distinguishes their teaching from that of novices (see e.g., Berliner, 1986; Shulman, 1987). Much of this research also demonstrates the importance of teacher education for the acquisition of knowledge and skills that, when used in the classroom, improve the caliber of instruction and the success of student learning (see e.g., Berliner, 1984; Evertson, Hawley,

& Zlotnik, 1985; Haberman, 1984; Hawk, Coble, & Swanson, 1985).

Professionalism starts from the proposition that knowledge must inform practice; its major goal is to ensure that all individuals permitted to practice are adequately prepared. Yet school reform has rarely focused on the support and improvement of teacher preparation.

In most universities, colleges of education get the fewest resources. Even during those periods of intense interest in improving education that seem to occur about once a generation, and that is currently the case, neither the federal government nor most states nor most school systems seem inclined to spend much money or attention on preparing teachers well. As Berliner (1984) observes:

It is time for creative thinking on how to revitalize teacher preparation programs. It is also time for budgetary allocations for such programs. Currently, we do not have much of either. At my own institution, the University of Arizona, we have found that it costs the state about $15,000 to educate a liberal arts undergraduate in, say, comparative literature, history, or psychology. To educate an individual for the vitally important profession of teaching, the state pays $2,000 less. . . . I am afraid that Arizona, like the 49 other states engaged in teacher preparation, gets precisely what it pays for. (p. 96)

One reason for this lack of support is a deeply felt ambivalence. Is there knowledge about teaching that makes some teachers more effective? If so, teachers ought to learn it. Or is teaching something that anyone can do, without any special preparation? If so, anything that purports to be preparation is certainly not worth supporting. Clearly, the tension between these two points of view, unresolved for the past 200 years, continues today as policymakers override educational standards to keep classrooms filled.

A profession is formed when members of an occupation agree that they have a knowledge base, that what they know relates directly to effective practice, that being prepared is essential to being a responsible practitioner, and that unprepared people will not be permitted to practice. Until members of the profession band together to articulate and enforce standards, the debate will continue.

As noted earlier, the federal government has supported the efforts of medical schools to develop the capacity to produce and transmit knowledge. It has provided support for building particular programs in high-need areas, for strengthening existing programs, and for improving teaching hospitals where clinical training is pursued. It has provided scholarships and loans for medical students. Now that the United States has perhaps the finest system of medical education in the world, the great debates of 80 or so years ago have lost all but historical interest. The acute shortages of 20 years ago seem a dim memory, as an ongoing substantial supply of well-trained physicians now seems assured.

But before medicine coalesced into a profession, back when people thought the doctor-to-be might as well learn what she or he could just by following a doctor around, the debate raged. Was medical education necessary and desirable? Or should medical training be dispensed with in favor of the follow-me-around-in-the-buggy approach? The decision to formalize and strengthen medical education has brought tremendous advances in knowledge. But perhaps the greatest benefit of setting standards of competence in medicine has been that even the people least well served by doctors are now much better protected from quacks and charlatans and incompetents.

To general considerations of improving the preparation of teachers one must add at least a consideration that relates directly, though not exclusively, to improving education for minority students. For many reasons, increasing the supply of well-prepared teachers who are themselves members of minority groups is vital. Teaching ought to reflect the population, as should all parts of society; yet as the proportion of minority students in public schools is increasing, the proportion of minority teachers, especially black teachers, is declining rapidly. Yet the colleges of education in historically black colleges and universities, from which most black teachers have graduated, are, for various reasons, facing great difficulties. Never well financed for the most part, these institutions now face great financial difficulties. Their education programs are in even greater jeopardy in the several southern states that seek to tie pass rates on teacher certification tests to approval of teacher education programs.

A distinction needs to be drawn here that is often ignored. The distinction is that supporting the institutions that prepare teachers and supplying particular support for the ones that characteristically train most minority teachers is one policy, and testing teachers is another. For all the talk about the central importance of good teaching to good education, the first policy remains essentially untried. Supporting teacher education has simply not been a strategy that policymakers have yet been willing to adopt.

Federal support for historically black colleges, and for minority student scholarships generally, will be needed to open up again the pipeline to teaching (and other professions) that has narrowed in recent years as minority students' college-going rates have declined. Enlarging the pipeline of college-educated workers is critical to solving the teacher-supply problem, because competition among occupations is expected to be fierce throughout the 1990s, as the number of entering workers declines and the number of jobs increases.

Similarly, stemming the flow of teachers, especially new entrants, out of teaching will be more difficult, as opportunities in other fields will be plentiful. Yet reducing attrition will be even more imperative to keep pace with demand and to avoid squandering investments in teacher training. For both practical and professional reasons—to increase teacher effectiveness and reduce turnover—teacher preparation will need to extend through initial clinical training and induction.

Teacher Induction

Consistent with a professional view of teaching knowledge and practice, serious and intensive induction of new teachers is necessary before they can be allowed or expected to teach without supervision. This major departure from the current sink-or-swim approach to beginning teaching is crucial for two equally important reasons: (a) because teaching knowledge is complex and requires judgment in its application, it cannot be fully acquired in a classroom setting; and (b) because a teaching profession is first and foremost committed to the welfare of students, inexperienced practitioners cannot be allowed to learn on the job without guidance. Furthermore, supportive and sustained induction is necessary to stem high attrition rates of new teachers and to provide equity to students.

The current lack of support experienced by beginning teachers is exacerbated by typical school district placement policies. As McLaughlin, Pfeifer, Swansen-Owens, and Yee (1986) note:

New teachers are often given those students or courses with which experienced teachers do not wish to deal. Instead of giving beginning teachers a nurturing environment in which to grow, we throw them into a war zone where both the demands and the mortality rate are excessively high. It is really not surprising that one-third of teachers leave the profession within their first five years of teaching. (p. 424)

The placement of beginning teachers in the most difficult assignments is encouraged by district internal-transfer policies that allow successful senior teachers to move to schools of their choice. Schools with high turnover rates, which also tend to be schools serving the most disadvantaged students in the most challenging teaching conditions, hire new teachers to fill their vacancies. When a vacancy arises in a desirable school, senior teachers tend to transfer away from the more difficult schools. Consequently, these schools are more likely to be staffed with disproportionate numbers of new and inexperienced teachers and are less likely to maintain an adequate cadre of expert, experienced teachers who can assist these novices. Thus, beginning teachers are presented with the most difficult educational problems and with little assistance. As a result, many experience frustration and leave the profession. Not incidentally, the students of these neophytes, those who most need expert teaching, are continually subjected to instruction by persons who are just learning, or perhaps not learning, how to teach (Wise, Darling-Hammond, & Berry, 1987).

Ultimately, the creation of professional-development schools, analogous to teaching hospitals, in which expert teachers join with university faculty to provide a structured internship experience for new teachers would be a most effective means of inducting new teachers. Such schools would be exemplars of good practice, would produce and transmit knowledge of teaching to new entrants, and would provide high-quality education to those students who in many cases now receive some of the lowest quality schooling. In much the same way that federal support for medical internships and residencies, and for the establishment and improvement of teaching hospitals themselves, has helped to improve the caliber of clinical practice, so the launching of such training grounds for teachers can improve teacher skill, retention, and teaching equity.

It is true that an all-out effort to improve the preparation of teachers would cost far more than the current strategy of simply testing teachers. But discussions of cost could more usefully be discussions of cost effectiveness. In education each suggestion for reform is generally viewed as discrete, as a program to add on here, a requirement to add on there, an allocation to add to the already large sums of money being spent. But if one were, instead, to examine carefully each reform strategy, one might see that the money spent recruiting and preparing teachers adequately is money that would not need to be spent thereafter to patch up the problems created by inadequate investment in teachers.

References

American Association of Colleges for Teacher Education. (1985). *Teacher education in the states: 50-state survey of legislative and administrative actions.* Washington, DC: Author.

American Federation of Teachers. (1986). *Salary trends, 1986: Survey and analyses.* Washington, DC: Author.

Association for School, College, and University Staffing (1984). *Teacher supply/demand.* Madison, WI: Author.

Astin, A. W., Green, K. C., & Korn, W. S. (1987). *The American freshman: twenty year trends.* Los Angeles, CA: American Council of Education, Cooperative Institutional Research Program.

Bacharach, S. B., et al. (1985). *Teacher shortages, professional standards, and "hen house" logic.* Ithaca, NY: Organizational Analysis and Practice.

Berliner, D. C. (1984). Making the right changes in preservice teacher education. *Phi Delta Kappan, 66*(2), 94–96.

Berliner, D. C. (1986). In pursuit of the expert pedagogue. *Educational Researcher, 15,* 5–13.

Berry, B. (1985). *Understanding teacher supply and demand in the southeast: A synthesis of qualitative research to aid effective policy-making.* Research Triangle Park, NC: Southeastern Regional Council for Educational Improvement.

Carey, N. B., Mittman, B. S., & Darling-Hammond, L. (1988). *Recruiting mathematics and science teachers through nontraditional programs: A survey* (N-2736-FF/CSTP). Santa Monica, CA: RAND Corporation.

Carroll, C. D. (1985). *High school and beyond tabulations: Background characteristics.* Washington, DC: National Center for Education Statistics.

Carroll, S. J. (1973). *Analysis of the educational personnel system: III. The demand for educational professionals* (R-1308-HEW). Santa Monica, CA: RAND Corporation.

Cavin, E. S., Murnane, R. J., & Brown, R. S. (1985). School district responses to enrollment changes: The direction of change matters! *Journal of Education Finance, 10*(4), 426–440.

Center for Education Statistics. (1986a). *Racial/ethnic data for 1984 fall enrollment and earned degree recipients for academic year 1984–85.* Washington, DC: U.S. Department of Education.

Center for Education Statistics. (1986b). *Trends in bachelors and higher degrees, 1975–1985.* Washington, DC: U.S. Department of Education.

Center for Education Statistics. (1987a). *The condition of education, 1987.* Washington, DC: U.S. Department of Education.

Center for Education Statistics. (1987b). *Digest of education statistics, 1987.* Washington, DC: U.S. Department of Education.

Council of Chief State School Officers. (1984). *Staffing the nation's schools: A national emergency.* Washington, DC: Author.

Crane, J. (1982). *Teacher demand: A socio-demographic phenomenon.* Washington, DC: U.S. Department of Education, Center for Education Statistics.

Cremin, L. (1965). *The genius of American education.* New York: Vintage.

Darling-Hammond, L. (1984). *Beyond the commission reports: The coming crisis in teaching* (R-3177-RC). Santa Monica, CA: RAND Corporation.

Darling-Hammond, L. (1986). Teaching knowledge: How do we test it?" *American Educator, 10*(3), 18–21, 46.

Darling-Hammond, L. (1987). What constitutes a "real" shortage of teachers? Commentary. *Education Week, 6,* 16.

Darling-Hammond, L. (1988). Teacher quality and educational equality. *College Board Review, 148,* 16–23, 39–41.

Darling-Hammond, L., & Berry, B. (1988). *The evolution of teacher policy* (JRE-01). Santa Monica, CA: RAND Corporation.

Darling-Hammond, L., Hudson, L., & Kirby, S. N. (1989). *Redesigning teacher education: Opening the door for new recruits to science and mathematics teaching.* Santa Monica, CA: RAND Corporation.

Darling-Hammond, L., Pittman, K. J., & Ottinger, C. (in press). *Career choices for minorities: Who will teach?* Paper prepared for the National Education Association and Council of Chief State School Officers.

Dewey, J. (1968). *The school and society.* Chicago: University of Chicago Press. (Original work published 1900)

Evertson, C. M., Hawley, W. D., & Zlotnik, M. (1985). Making a difference in educational quality through teacher education. *Journal of Teacher Education, 36*(3), 2–12.

Feistritzer, C. E. (1986). *Teacher crisis: Myth or reality?* Washington, DC: National Center for Education Information.

Galambos, E. C. (1985). *Teacher preparation: The anatomy of a college degree.* Atlanta: Southern Regional Education Board.

Goertz, M. (1985). *State educational standards: A 50 state survey.* Princeton, NJ: Educational Testing Service.

Grissmer, D., & Kirby, S. N. (1987). *Teacher attrition: The uphill climb to staff the nation's schools.* Santa Monica, CA: RAND Corporation.

Haberman, M. (1984). *An evaluation of the rationale for required teacher education: Beginning teachers with and without teacher preparation* (Paper prepared for the National Commission of Excellence in Teacher Education). Milwaukee, WI: University of Wisconsin—Milwaukee, Division of Urban Outreach.

Haggstrom, G. W., Darling-Hammond, L., & Grissmer, D. W. (1988). *Assessing teacher supply and demand* (R-3633-ED/CSTP). Santa Monica, CA: RAND Corporation.

Hawk, P. P., Coble, C. R., & Swanson, M. (1985). Certification: It does matter. *Journal of Teacher Education, 36*(3), 13–15.

Holmes Group. (1986). *Tomorrow's teachers.* East Lansing, MI: Author.

Holmstrom, E. I. (1985). *Recent changes in teacher education programs.* Washington, DC: American Council on Education.

Howe, T. G., & Gerlovich, J. A. (1982). *National study of the estimated supply and demand of secondary science and mathematics teachers.* Ames, IA: Iowa State University.

Johnston, K. L., & Aldridge, B. G. (1984). The crisis in science education: What is it? How can we respond? *Journal of College Science Teaching,* 20–28.

Levin, H. M. (1985). Solving the shortage of mathematics and science teachers. *Educational Evaluation and Policy Analysis, 7*(4), 371–382.

MacMillan, J. B., & Pendlebury, S. (1985). The Florida performance measurement system: A consideration. *Teachers College Record, 87*(1), 67–78.

Mark, J. H., & Anderson, B. D. (1985). Teacher survival rates in St. Louis, 1969–1982. *American Educational Research Journal, 22*(3), 413–421.

McLaughlin, M. W., Pfeifer, R. S., Swansen-Owens, D., & Yee, S. (1986). Why teachers won't teach. *Phi Delta Kappan, 67*(6), 420–426.

Metropolitan Life Insurance Co. (1985). *Former teachers in America.* New York: Author.

Metropolitan Life Insurance Co. (1988). *The American teacher 1988: Strengthening the relationship between teachers and students.* New York: Louis Harris and Associates.

Murnane, R. J., & Phillips, B. R. (1981). Learning by doing, vintage, and selection: Three pieces of the puzzle relating teaching experience and teaching performance. *Economics of Education Review, 1*(4), 453–465.

National Center for Education Statistics (1983). *The condition of education, 1983 edition.* Washington, DC: U.S. Department of Education.

National Center for Education Statistics (1985a). *The condition of education, 1985 edition.* Washington, DC: U.S. Department of Education.

National Center for Education Statistics. (1985b). *Projections of education statistics to 1992–93.* Washington, DC: U.S. Department of Education.

National Education Association. (1981). *Status of the American public school teacher, 1980–1981.* Washington, DC: Author.

National Education Association. (1983). *National teacher opinion poll, 1983.* Washington, DC: Author.

National Education Association. (1987). *Status of the American public school teacher, 1985–1986.* Washington, DC: Author.

National Science Board. (1985). *Science indicators: The 1985 report.* Washington, DC: U.S. Government Printing Office.

Office for Civil Rights. (1975–76, 1978–79, 1980–81, 1982–83). *Data on earned degrees conferred by institutions of higher education by race, ethnicity, and sex, academic years 1975–76, 1978–79, 1980–81, and 1982–83.* Washington, DC: Author.

Pascal, A. (1987). *The qualifications of teachers in American high schools.* Santa Monica, CA: RAND Corporation.

Raizen, S. A. (1986). *Estimates of teacher demand and supply and related policy issues.* Paper presented at the annual meeting of the American Educational Research Association, San Francisco.

Schlechty, P. C., & Vance, V. (1981). Do academically able teachers leave education? The North Carolina case. *Phi Delta Kappan, 63*(2), 106–112.

Sedlak, M., & Schlossman, S. (1986). *Who will teach? Historical perspectives on the changing appeal of teaching as a profession* (R-3472). Santa Monica, CA: RAND Corporation.

Shulman, L. (1987). Knowledge and teaching: Foundations of the new reform. *Harvard Educational Review, 57*(1), 1–22.

Southern Regional Education Board. (1986). *Incentive programs for teachers and administrators: How are they doing?.* Atlanta, GA: Author.

Starr, P. (1982). *The social transformation of American medicine.* New York: Basic Books.

Sykes, G. (1984). The Conference [Mimeograph]. Stanford, CA: Stanford University.

U.S. Bureau of the Census. (1984). *1984 current population survey.* Washington, DC: Author.

Vance, V. S., & Schlechty, P. S. (1982). The distribution of academic ability in the teaching force: Policy implications. *Phi Delta Kappan, 64*(1), 22–27.

Waite, L. (1981). *U.S. women at work* (R-2824-RC). Santa Monica, CA: RAND Corporation.

Weaver, W. T. (1978). Educators in supply and demand: Effects on quality. *School Review, 86,* 553–593.

Wise, A. E., Darling-Hammond, L., & Berry, B. (1987). *Effective teacher selection: From recruitment to retention* (R-3462-NIE/CSTP). Santa Monica, CA: RAND Corporation.

·17·

TEACHERS' KNOWLEDGE AND
LEARNING TO TEACH

Kathy Carter

UNIVERSITY OF ARIZONA

The question of how teachers learn to teach is clearly basic to the enterprise of teacher education. Only recently, however, have researchers begun to systematically frame and study this question. For the most part, attention in teacher education has traditionally been focused on what teachers need to know and how they can be trained, rather than on what they actually know or how that knowledge is acquired. The perspective, in other words, has been from the outside, external to the teachers who are learning and the processes by which they are educated.

Although the phrase "learning to teach" rolls easily off the tongue, research in this field has, to date, been largely unproductive (see reviews by Feiman-Nemser, 1983; Feiman-Nemser & Floden, 1986; Zeichner, 1987). One suspects that the core problems are conceptual. The phrase itself is not used consistently. Sometimes it refers globally to the entire enterprise of teacher education, or it is a substitute for such constructs as teacher development or teacher socialization. Moreover, the phrase subsumes and sometimes masks key assumptions about (a) *outcomes*, that is, what teachers are or should be learning; (b) *treatments or settings*, that is, what effects can be attributed to programs, program components, or experience in various sites; and (c) *learning*, that is, how change occurs in teaching. As a result, a study focused on the effects of field experiences or student teaching on occupational perspectives and one directed to changes in personal concerns during preservice teacher education are both considered to be about learning to teach, even though the results are not comparable.

Although the manifest purpose of this chapter is to review the state of research on learning to teach, another compilation of discouraging findings was deemed unnecessary and unhelpful. Instead, an attempt was made to construct an intellectual context within which the learning-to-teach process could be framed and understood. To this end, Zeichner (1986, 1987) argues for improved conceptualizations of what goes on in teacher education settings and how individual characteristics interact with these setting features. Although Zeichner's argument is certainly reasonable, it still bypasses issues of the substance of what teachers know or how that knowledge is acquired. In the present chapter, therefore, emphasis is placed on emerging conceptions of teachers' knowledge. In the past, researchers have focused attention primarily on teachers' skills and dispositions. Recently, however, investigators, armed with the new conceptual and methodological tools of cognitive science and interpretive research, have begun to examine the character and substance of teachers' knowledge. Although clearly in its infancy, this line of inquiry is generating lively discussions about theory, research methodology, and teacher education practices. It also seems to be a promising framework, establishing focus and coherence in research on how teachers learn to teach.

To distinguish the chapter from others in this volume, the focus here is primarily on knowledge related to or grounded in classroom practice. The chapter is based, in other words, on a knowledge conception of teaching, and the phrase "learning to teach" is taken to mean the acquisition of knowledge directly related to classroom performance. This definition excludes

The author thanks reviewers Mary Rohrkemper (Bryn Mawr College) and Robert Yinger (University of Cincinnati). Walter Doyle was generous with his help, comments, and suggestions. Conversations with Virginia Richardson, Mary Rohrkemper, and Stefinee Pinnegar have been helpful in clarifying the issues presented in this chapter, but the opinions and errors are the responsibility of the author.

studies specifically focused on teachers' formal subject-matter knowledge (see the chapter by Ball and McDiarmid), teachers' institutional and occupational perspectives (see the chapter by Zeichner and Gore), and the professional knowledge base for teaching (see the chapter by Tom and Valli).

The chapter is directed, then, to questions of what teachers know and how that knowledge is acquired. Three broad categories of teachers' knowledge are examined: (a) teachers' information processing, including decision making and expert–novice studies; (b) teachers' practical knowledge, including personal knowledge and classroom knowledge; and (c) pedagogical content knowledge, that is, the ways teachers understand and represent subject matter to their students. Within each of these categories, implications for conceptualizing research on learning to teach are considered, and specific studies, where available, are reviewed. The chapter opens with an analysis of the assumptions about outcomes, treatments, and learning that are implicit in research on learning to teach. This analysis provides a background for the subsequent review of knowledge domains in teaching. The chapter concludes with an analysis of common themes in this research literature, directions for further inquiry, and implications of this work for designing teacher education practices.

It is important to note that much of the work on teachers' knowledge and learning to teach is in an early, formative stage. As a result, many studies are still in progress, and the emphasis in available reports is as much conceptual as it is empirical. Investigators are in the process of collecting data, often in the form of extensive and detailed case analyses, but the focus at this point is often on the refinement of concepts and method, rather than on the report of findings. This review reflects these characteristics of inquiry in the field.

THE LEARNING-TO-TEACH QUESTION

This section contains a brief survey of research that has been seen to have a bearing on the question of how teachers learn to teach. The purpose of this survey is to clarify the assumptions concerning outcomes, treatments, and learning that have been implicit in this field.

Early Studies of Teachers' Experience

Over the years, investigators have occasionally been interested in the effects of experience on teachers. Within a psychological tradition, there are two major approaches to research on experience. In the first approach, investigators generally focused on the effects of training, feedback, and field experiences on observable behaviors or skills, rather than on knowledge or cognition (see Gliessman, 1984; Peck & Tucker, 1973; Watts, 1987; Waxman & Walberg, 1986). The assumptions were, in other words, that teachers needed to know certain basic teaching skills and that such skills were best learned through directed laboratory practice and extensive practical experience in "real" settings.

Three interesting studies in this area indicate, however,

that the effects of training on classroom performance are mediated by cognitive processes and contexts. Wagner (1973) compared a microteaching treatment, in which preservice teachers learned *how* to perform teaching skills, with a second treatment, cognitive-discrimination training. In the latter treatment, the teachers learned *when* skills were appropriate but did not practice them. Wagner found that cognitive-discrimination training had greater effects on classroom performance than microteaching. Along similar lines, Gliessman, Pugh, and Bielat (1979) found that learning teaching skills as concepts, without practice, increased their use in classrooms, and, indeed, the greater the concept mastery, the greater the skill use. Practice without concept acquisition did not affect classroom performance (see Gliessman & Pugh, 1981). Finally, Copeland (1977) found that acquisition of teaching skills in a laboratory setting did not predict their use by student teachers in classrooms. The use of skills was dependent, rather, on the ecology of the classroom in which the student teacher taught. One important dimension of this ecology was prior use of the skills by the cooperating teacher, so that pupils in the classes were familiar with them. As will be seen, these issues of cognition and setting eventually moved to the center of research on teachers' knowledge and learning to teach.

The second cluster of studies is based on personality or development perspectives and focused on attitudes, motives, and concerns. Hoy (1968), for example, examined the effects of teaching experience on pupil-control ideologies and found that, with experience, beginning teachers acquired a more "custodial" attitude toward pupils. Wright and Tuska (1968) devised an elaborate Freudian conception of teacher personality development and utilized the theory to construct semantic differential questionnaires to study the attitudes and recollections of 508 beginning women teachers during student teaching and their first year of experience. They attempted to discover how the resolution of relationships with early authority figures (mother, father, and teacher) influenced the choice of elementary, middle school, or high school careers and shaped their unconscious motives during teacher education. The authors argue that their theory predicted career choices well and explained the personal struggles many candidates experienced during preparation. They also found that the women they studied experienced considerable disillusionment as they moved from their "dream" of becoming a teacher to actual teaching during their first year. In contrast with elementary candidates, the women preparing to be high school teachers began to be disillusioned during student teaching. Finally, Fuller (1969), in widely cited research on teacher development, mapped the concerns of teachers, from the early focus on survival and practical techniques to the later emphasis on curriculum and student learning, arguing that these concerns shaped the readiness of teacher education students and practicing teachers to learn about different aspects of teaching.

Research on the occupational and institutional aspects of teaching has concentrated on how teachers are socialized into the norms and perspectives of the profession. Particular attention in this tradition has been given to the familiarity of teaching—prospective teachers have spent a large amount of time as students in classrooms and thus acquire preconceptions of standard classroom practices and solutions to teaching problems—and to the effects of informal contacts between experienced and novice teachers during student teaching and the beginning years of experience (see Dreeben, 1970; Eddy, 1969; Hoy & Woolfolk, 1989; Lortie, 1975; Zeichner, 1986). Familiarity and school-based socialization, it is argued, account for the stability of classroom practices, the conservatism of teachers, and the low impact of teacher education.

Recent Developments

These early studies of teachers' experience have shaped in major ways the current research on learning to teach. Attention to the biographies of teacher candidates, their developing attitudes and concerns, and their professional orientations and perspectives is quite apparent in recent studies in this area. Representative studies are described subsequently to suggest the direction of this influence. Reading these studies, one is encouraged to find that the person in teaching is no longer quietly tucked away in tables of aggregated data. Moreover, these studies represent improvements in the way program effects are described. For example, they put to rest the assumption that programs with the same general goal statements and course guidelines are likely to have similar effects. Rather, they demonstrate that program effects must be described with reference to the actual representation of teacher education content in teacher education classrooms. On the other hand, findings from these studies often appear impoverished, for they tell us little about the actual learning processes of beginning teachers and provide only sketchy information about the substance of the knowledge they acquire.

Entering Dispositions. Work at the National Center for Research on Teacher Education at Michigan State University is focused in part on the levels of disciplinary knowledge in mathematics and writing that prospective teachers possess when they enter teacher education. These researchers use questionnaires with large samples of prospective teachers to determine how respondents understand and would use knowledge of their content in classroom settings and how they view the learner with respect to such content. In addition, extensive interviews are used with smaller samples to uncover respondents' views about common tasks of teaching in these content areas.

Ball (1988), for example, has recently used these methods to explore prospective teachers' understandings of a particular mathematics topic: division with fractions. The questionnaire for this study required respondents to select a story problem that represented a particular division statement from among a limited set of choices. Interviews focused on prospective teachers' backgrounds in learning about the division of fractions and also asked them to discuss their ideas about how they might represent a particular division problem to students. Ball argues that findings from this study were somewhat discouraging, suggesting that the majority of prospective teachers who would be teaching mathematics to both elementary and secondary students had limited knowledge of division with fractions; indeed, most were unable to select the correct representation of the

problem posed to them. Interview results helped to explain the phenomenon, suggesting that most prospective teachers' knowledge of mathematics was rule-bound. Few appeared to have a substantive understanding of the underlying principles of this key mathematical concept.

Gomez (1988) asked 90 students enrolled in the first course of their professional sequence to provide written responses to a number of questions directed at obtaining an understanding of prospective teachers' backgrounds in learning writing, at securing information about their reasons for nominations of persons they considered to be good at writing, and the aspects of writing they enjoyed or disliked. The picture that emerged from this study is one of diversity, in terms of both students' backgrounds in learning to write and their stated preferences for different aspects of the composing process. One particularly interesting finding was that most of these teacher candidates held their college coursework in low esteem in terms of helping them increase their ability to write or their knowledge of writing processes in general. Importantly, Gomez concluded from the respondents' comments about good writers that their judgments were based on questionable indices (many had never even seen the writing of those they nominated as good writers) and that their responses suggested that these teachers had limited knowledge about what good writing, in fact, was. Moreover, Gomez interviewed a different set of teachers, in an attempt to ascertain the kind and quality of their responses to an example of student writing provided to them. She found that prospective teachers at both the elementary and secondary level attended mostly to the surface features of the text in the student example, suggesting limited ways that these teachers had of conceptualizing various features of the writing process.

Paine (1988) explored prospective teachers' orientations toward diversity. Using questionnaires and interviews, Paine attempted to analyze respondents' views concerning the meaning of diversity, as well as what their notions of diversity meant when translated to their thoughts about teaching. Paine's analyses led her to conclude that entering candidates' orientations toward diversity were often superficial; their ability to talk about student differences in thoughtful, comprehensive ways was often limited; and their thinking about its pedagogical implications was often quite problematic. For example, these prospective teachers seemed to share the sense that student differences should be taken into account, but they were often unsure about how to think about those differences in terms of planning and arranging academic work. Their discussions of diversity were often contradictory, at one moment uncomplicated conceptually and at another moment quite complicated. For instance, these teachers felt that fairness was the key to successfully attending to student diversity, but their projected mechanisms for dealing with diversity could often be judged to be quite inequitable. One student argued, for example, that all students should be treated the same, but when presented with scenarios of specific differences students might bring with them, she suggested that applying different standards to these students would be appropriate. Paine argues that pretraining teachers' views of diversity are, comparatively, more coherent in the abstract than in the context of specific scenes and situations, yielding a prepractice view of diversity that is, in large measure, divorced from contexts and concomitantly static.

Amarel and Feiman-Nemser (1988) also used questionnaires and interviews to assess pretraining teachers' views concerning what they needed to know to teach successfully. Students' responses to inquiries around this question indicated that their primary concerns were about management and about feeling at ease in front of students. Moreover, many students simply felt that what they most needed was practical experience in teaching. Students rarely mentioned subject-matter knowledge or enhanced understanding of student learning in their responses and, in general, appeared to devalue what might be learned in professional coursework in advance of their formal study in it. In their study, Amarel and Feiman-Nemser traced closely, in written cases, two pretraining teachers' views of necessary knowledge for teaching to their own remembered school experiences, illustrating how the views articulated by these teachers inhered in their individual experiences as students and as people. Along similar lines, Weinstein (1988) found that candidates prior to student teaching had "unrealistic optimism" about their ability to solve teaching problems in classrooms. They agreed that many experienced teachers had problems in areas of management, discipline, and instruction, but they felt that they would not have these problems. With such an orientation, it is unlikely that these student teachers expected to learn very much from experienced teachers.

Changes in Orientations and Perspectives. Another major focal point for research on learning to teach is the nature of change in orientations, commitments, and perspectives of teacher candidates. Investigators have carefully attempted to unpack orientations through extensive conversations with and observations of candidates. For example, Ball and Noordhoff's (1985) study demonstrated that students' prior dispositions about the use of textbooks were affected, not from a single source, but from several sources, both formal and informal. Ball and Noordhoff followed eight elementary education students in two programs that differed in their structure, ideology, and content. One program, the Academic Program, was characterized by its emphasis on and understanding of disciplinary knowledge and theoretical propositions. The other program, the Decision-making Program, focused on a generically based approach to knowledge of teaching and aimed at improving students' reflective capacities and decision-making skills. Although both programs seemed to convey through coursework a negative view of reliance on the textbook, they differed in the stance toward how to deal with these students, who, during their student teaching and because of various factors (e.g., the cooperating teacher's influence and the lack of other instructional materials) used textbooks heavily. The Decision-making Program continued to suggest strongly the negative aspects of reliance on the textbook, whereas the Academic Program took a more passive approach to this practice. Ball and Noordhoff developed rich cases of two prospective teachers, Danielle and Sarah, to illustrate how programs, persons, and setting affect teachers' orientations to the textbook and, in so doing, suggest that knowledge outcomes from professional preparation are largely characterized by unique features in all three of these aspects.

Hollingsworth (1988) attempted to investigate changes in preservice teachers' knowledge and beliefs before, during, and after a fifth-year teaching program. Hollingsworth developed baseline profiles of 14 elementary and secondary preservice teachers as they entered the teacher education program and, using a constant comparative process involving analysis of interview and observational data, tracked the patterns of their intellectual change over the course of a year. Although the focus was on studying global changes in teachers' knowledge and beliefs, their changing knowledge of reading instruction was also highlighted, in an attempt to relate general knowledge of teaching to content knowledge. By the use of existing taxonomies of cognitive processing and change (e.g., those of Doyle, 1983, and Rumelhart & Norman, 1978), preservice teachers' profiles taken at different points along the year were analyzed for consistency with or deviation from baseline profiles. Patterns emerging from these data led Hollingsworth to develop a model to illustrate that prior beliefs of teachers play a critical part in the process of learning to teach. The model suggests that preprogram beliefs about teaching potentially interact dynamically with program content and classroom opportunities to produce different levels of teaching knowledge. Hollingsworth contends that patterns of knowledge growth suggest a number of themes about the learning-to-teach process:

> *pre-program beliefs* served as filters for processing program content and making sense of classroom contexts; *general managerial routines* had to be in place before *subject specific content and pedagogy* became a focus of attention; and that interrelated managerial and academic routines were needed before teachers could actively focus on *students; learning from academic tasks in classrooms*, while pre-program interest students as individuals and a program-developed interest in subject pedagogy were needed to provide the motivation to do so. In turn, each new level of knowledge affected changes in pre-program beliefs. (p. 9)

Hollingsworth has developed descriptive cases of these teachers that illustrate the movement described in this model.

Zeichner and Tabachnick (1985) followed 13 preservice teachers through their student-teaching experience and a small subset of these teachers into their first year of teaching. Their study attempted to assess preservice teachers' perspectives on the teacher's role, teacher–pupil relationship, student diversity, and knowledge and curriculum. Importantly, student teachers in this study were able to participate in the selection of their field placements. This might have contributed to the finding that little alteration in students' original perspectives in the areas just mentioned was apparent during the practicum. However, individual knowledge "journeys" were observed for the four teachers who were studied during their first year of teaching. Based on their analyses, Zeichner and Tabachnick argue that the knowledge path looks quite different for different individuals and with different contexts for learning. They suggest that there needs to be debate about how to recognize the personal experience of learning to teach and how to promote preparatory experiences that allow individuals to reach their knowledge potential.

Similarly, Feiman-Nemser and Buchmann (1986) were interested in looking at the interactions among classroom setting, professional coursework, and persons on prospective teachers' pedagogical thinking during the student-teaching experience. In terms reminiscent of Fuller (1969), these researchers hoped to track students' movement from daily preoccupations with sustaining pupils' cooperation to thinking about pupils' learning. The two teacher candidates they studied entered the program with limited understandings of teaching. They spent the time and performed the tasks necessary to feel they learned from their student-teaching experience and to get positive evaluations from their cooperating teachers, and yet Feiman-Nemser and Buchmann illustrate in their case studies that neither was able to acquire the kind of pedagogical thinking that they argue is central to teaching, that is, an understanding of how to recognize, evaluate, and implement activities with pupils' learning in mind. Through these case studies, Feiman-Nemser and Buchmann reveal how both coursework in two separate programs and aspects of the settings for student teaching differentially and negatively influenced chances for students' acquisition of critical knowledge of teaching.

Calderhead's (1987) study echoes many of the same themes. The purpose of this study was to determine the kinds of interpretative frameworks student teachers use in their thinking about classroom practice and to study how these frameworks are affected by students' professional development and student-teaching experience. Calderhead found that there were aspects of the student-teaching experience that negatively affected what and how students learned about teaching. Student teachers entered their student-teaching experience with conceptions of teaching that were incomplete and often dysfunctional (e.g., teacher as "guide" and "friend"). But, although their early experiences in student teaching appeared to help them acquire improved knowledge about planning and instructional activities, midway through their student teaching they had reached a plateau in their learning. Interviews with student teachers suggested that they had comparatively more difficulty citing new knowledge or understandings at this point than they had had earlier in their student-teaching experience. Calderhead's analysis of student teaching suggests that, as it often presently exists, it is a sort of "driving test" for students; this experience does not provide for much experimentation, for valid assessment of student teachers' teaching from supervisors, or for student teachers' own chances to reflect and accurately assess their teaching. Here, the themes of the recent research echo the concerns expressed in earlier discussions of the student-teaching experience (see, for example, Griffin, 1986; Richardson-Koehler, 1988; Zimpher, 1987).

Summary and Conclusions

This brief and quite selective survey illustrates well the problems of research on learning to teach. Aside from a few broad generalizations about complexity and multiple interactions, few conclusions can be drawn from these studies. Feiman-Nemser's (1983) appraisal still stands: "With few exceptions, the existing research tells us very little about the actual conduct of teacher preparation . . . [or] about the job of learning" (p. 151). Moreover, there is a distinct lack of coherence across studies. Outcomes are designated in a variety of ways: attitudes, dispositions, orientations, perspectives, knowledge, concerns, or commitments, and, despite apparent differences in meaning, these terms are often used interchangeably. Settings are sometimes only loosely defined and vary widely across studies. Attempts to isolate the relative contributions of program components or experiences (if such isolation is, in fact, an appropriate research goal) are futile under these circumstances. Perhaps most importantly, except for vague references to development, change, and growth, investigators are largely silent about the nature of the learning process in teacher education. Given this conceptual diversity and ambiguity, it is not surprising that cumulative findings are scarce.

One important lesson that can be drawn from this analysis is that the learning-to-teach question might well be unanswerable at a global level. What is needed, instead, are frameworks that focus more explicitly on *what* is learned and that specify more fully how that knowledge is acquired. In an attempt to search for such frameworks, attention in this chapter is directed to recent research on teachers' knowledge.

RESEARCH ON TEACHERS' KNOWLEDGE

The study of teachers' knowledge has emerged only quite recently in educational research. In the behaviorist tradition that dominated the study of teaching and teacher education, knowledge and thinking were generally considered too "mentalistic" for serious research attention, so the focus was primarily on observable behaviors or skills (see Peck & Tucker, 1973). The emergence of systematic research on teachers' knowledge and its acquisition signaled a substantial shift from a preoccupation with behavior and with what teachers need to do to a concern with what teachers know and how that knowledge is acquired through formal training and classroom experience.

The emphasis on cognition in teaching was stimulated, in large measure, by the growing concern for cognition and text in the social sciences and by the appearance in the late 1960s of qualitative or interpretive studies of classroom teaching. By generating richly detailed portraits of the demands of classroom environments and the ways in which teachers struggled to cope with these demands, this tradition had a powerful influence on the development of research on teachers' knowledge and its acquisition. As the study of cognition became more widely acceptable in the social and behavioral sciences, educational researchers turned to the study of teachers' cognitive processes and thinking (see Shavelson, 1983).

In one of the seminal qualitative studies, Jackson (1968) describes life in elementary classrooms in evocative detail. As part of this study, he interviewed 50 elementary teachers nominated by their administrators as outstanding and examined the ways in which they talked about their work. The interviews focused on the teachers' self-evaluations, their conceptions of institutional authority-relationships, and the satisfactions they derived from their work. Jackson identified four recurrent themes in the interviews: immediacy, informality, autonomy, and individuality. The teachers reported that they watched for immediate and spontaneous signs of involvement and enthusiasm to tell how things were going. Formal tests of students' achievement, on the other hand, were distrusted, because the teachers felt that pupil performance was atypical on tests and that the tests measured native ability rather than teaching effectiveness. The teachers also described their style of interacting with students as informal, within the limits of institutional responsibility and authority. Autonomy, they felt, was threatened by curricular constraints and by administrators' intrusions for evaluation, both of which reduce spontaneity and insult professional pride. Finally, seeing an individual child make progress, especially one who was unresponsive or unlikely to succeed, was their greatest source of satisfaction or joy in teaching.

In one of the more controversial parts of this analysis, Jackson (1968) characterizes the teachers' language and thought as conceptually simple and lacking in technical vocabulary. Caught up with the here and now and in emotional ties with pupils, they had, he argued, a simple and uncomplicated view of causality, they adopted an intuitive rather than a rational approach to classroom events, they were quite opinionated about their classroom practices, and they had narrow working definitions of abstract terms (e.g., motivation and intellectual development). His assessment of these characteristics was quite mixed. He deplored the particularity, impulsivity, conservatism, and myopia of their talk and their technical naivete, in comparison with psychologists.

Jackson was not the first to use psychologists as the standard for judging the adequacy of teachers' knowledge. In a widely cited classic, Wickman (1928) reports substantial differences between the attitudes of teachers and those of mental health experts concerning the significance of children's behavior. Teachers tended to rank disruptive behavior, violations of rules, and sexual transgressions as the most serious behavior problems; clinicians, on the other hand, saw passivity and withdrawal as more serious than acting out. Jackson also acknowledges that what teachers knew was perhaps appropriate to the complexity and unpredictability of the settings in which they worked. He speculates that a rational and deliberative style might be more prevalent in the "preactive" phase of teaching, during which teachers planned for teaching, rather than in the "interactive" phase, in which teachers faced the uncertainty and confusion of classroom events.

A similar emphasis on knowledge was evident in Smith's microethnographic study of a seventh-grade teacher in an urban classroom (see Smith & Geoffrey, 1968). Smith carefully describes how Geoffrey established classroom procedures and routines, built relationships with students, orchestrated classroom activities, and conducted lessons. With Geoffrey's help, Smith also mapped the working theories that accounted for these teaching actions.

Finally, Kounin (1970) published the results of an extraordinary research program directed at fundamental questions in classroom management and discipline. Kounin began his work on the practical problems of classroom discipline by focusing on "desists" (what teachers do to stop misbehavior after it occurs) and "ripple effects" (how desists affect nontarget students

in the class). After only modest success in accounting for students' work involvement, Kounin turned to an ecological analysis of over 250 videotaped lessons to learn how teachers managed classroom groups. He found that four clusters of actions—withitness, overlapping, group focus, and movement management—were associated with high levels of work involvement. Kounin's clusters clearly imply cognitive processes, that is, awareness and divided attention.

These early qualitative studies underscored the cognitive dimensions of teaching practice and made specific contributions to subsequent work on teachers' thinking and knowledge. Jackson's distinction between preactive and interactive thinking shaped research on teachers' decision making, and his emphasis on teacher's naive knowledge, along with Smith and Geoffrey's ideas of working theories, stimulated research on teachers' implicit understandings of teaching. Finally, Kounin's cognitive-related formulations of classroom management, as well as his ecological approach to inquiry, had a direct bearing on conceptions of teachers' classroom knowledge.

Within the broad field of research on teachers' knowledge, several distinct but overlapping approaches have evolved, approaches that represent different assumptions, emphases, theoretical frameworks, and methodological commitments and yet share many common themes. For purposes of this review, three approaches have been identified: (a) information-processing studies, which have tended to focus on decision making and contrasts between experts and novices; (b) studies of teachers' practical knowledge, or what teachers know about actual practice and the navigation of complex classroom settings; and (c) studies of pedagogical content knowledge, or what teachers know about subject matter and its representation to students.

Information-processing studies are typically framed in the technical language of psychology and often use controlled laboratory settings and/or standardized tasks and data collection procedures. The focus in such studies is typically on the cognitive processes or operations teachers use in thinking about teaching. Research on practical knowledge includes studies of teachers' personal knowledge and implicit theories, as well as ecological studies of the demands of classroom environments and their effects on the thoughts and actions of participants. Personal knowledge studies are typically grounded in a phenomenological perspective, use qualitative or interpretive methods consisting of extensive observations and interviews of one or a few teachers, and express findings in a language that reflects the expressions of the teachers who were participants in the research. The emphasis in these studies is often on idiosyncratic perspectives, interpretations, intentions, or beliefs that influence the sense teachers make of classroom situations. Ecological studies also rely on qualitative methods but focus on how thought and action are organized by situational tasks. Thus, formal, analytic descriptions of environmental structures are considered useful approximations of what participants know and how they comprehend actions and events. Finally, studies of pedagogical content knowledge employ information processing and qualitative methods to construct cases but focus on subject matter and the structure of explanations as key features of teachers' knowledge.

In the following sections, each of these frameworks is described, and implications for the formulation of research on learning to teach are delineated. Where possible, studies of learning to teach that relate to a framework are reviewed.

Information Processing

Information-processing approaches to teachers' knowledge have as their focus operations inside the minds of teachers, that is, the mental processes teachers use to identify problems, attend to cues in the classroom environment, formulate plans, make decisions, and evaluate alternative courses of action. Early studies on teacher planning and decision making were based largely on psychological frameworks and often used decision-tree structures to model processes in teachers' minds. The goal of the research was to determine the points and parameters of teachers' choices about their actions. Later, studies of expert and novice differences in teaching emerged, studies that attempted to unravel in a more complex fashion what was in the minds of different teachers as they taught. These studies were still focused primarily on internal processes, but some investigators attempted to focus on common pedagogical problems derived from classroom settings, as opposed to more artificially constructed laboratory tasks. These two related, but distinct, areas are summarized next.

Teacher Planning and Decision Making. Beginning in the 1970s, considerable interest was devoted to the study of teachers' planning and decision making, using a variety of interview, think-aloud, and observational strategies. This literature has been extensively reviewed by Clark and Peterson (1986) and will only be summarized briefly here.

Following Jackson's (1968) distinction cited earlier, decision-making research is divided between preactive or planning studies and interactive studies. For a time, greater attention was given to planning than to interactive thinking. This occurred partly because of the immediate interest in knowledge use and decision-making processes and partly because methods for engaging in studies of planning were comparatively more available and accommodating. Much of the planning research focused on the types of teacher planning (yearly, unit, weekly, daily), the topics around which planning occurred (objectives, activities, content, students), the cognitive processes teachers used in planning (forming mental images, problem finding and formulation), and the effect of planning on classroom performance.

Research on interactive decision making, which was much less common, tended to focus on the topics around which decisions were made (learners, classroom management, instruction), the frequency of decisions, and the effectiveness of different patterns of decision making. The primary research tool for interactive studies was the stimulated-recall interview, in which teachers viewed a videotape of their teaching and were asked to tell what they were thinking about during the lesson. This method has been strongly criticized recently on grounds that it generates accounts of the videotaped segment rather than an accurate report of what the teacher was thinking about

at the time of the original event (see Ericsson & Simon, 1980; Yinger, 1986).

One of the major conclusions from this research tradition was that prior assumptions about teachers' decision making were often inaccurate. Investigators found, for instance, that teachers seldom followed formal Tylerian models of planning and that, during interaction, teachers seldom made logical choices among several different alternatives. Rather, their actions seemed to be largely governed by rules and routines, with decision making in a studied, deliberative sense taking a minor role in their interactive thinking.

Some attempts have been made to examine planning and interactive teaching in a learning-to-teach framework. For example, Borko, Lalik, and Tomchin (1987) and Borko, Livingston, McCaleb, and Mauro (1988) explored novice teachers' thoughts about planning and specific instructional events. The investigators followed students through the final year of professional preparation and the first year of teaching. Through interviews, analyses of journals, on-site observations, and videotaped records of teaching, contrasts were made between weaker and stronger student teachers in terms of their developing understandings about instruction and planning. Both strong and weak student teachers had similar initial conceptions of successful lessons, views that did not appear to become markedly different over the year-long field experience. However, their views about unsuccessful lessons and about planning did differ over time. Moreover, stronger teachers apparently came to engage in comparatively more complex planning activities than did weaker novices. They planned in more detail, anticipated events that might affect their written plans, and developed solution strategies to deal with such problems. Rohrkemper's (in press) work suggests a plausible explanation for differences in teachers' development of teaching knowledge. It could be that teachers who developed richer and more efficient understandings about teaching learned well from unsuccessful lessons and failure situations.

Expert–Novice Studies. Beginning in the mid-1980s, information-processing researchers turned their attention to studies designed to account for differences in thinking between expert teachers and candidates in initial teacher-preparation programs. The study of expert–novice contrasts in teaching drew upon a relatively new, but well established, body of work in cognitive psychology on expert–novice differences (see Chi, Glaser, & Farr, in press).

Carter, Sabers, Cushing, Pinnegar, and Berliner (1987), using a simulated teaching task that required subjects to prepare to take over a class in midyear, examined expert–novice differences in processing and using information about students. One major finding from this study was that the routines that experts reported for organizing and managing instruction were comparatively more rich than those of novices. Protocols obtained in the study suggested that experts, when preparing to assume responsibility for a class that had been previously taught by another teacher, gave considerable attention to getting the students "to work." Experts were anxious to "start fresh" with the class and to organize the group of students so that they could move through the curriculum. In coming to understand what

needed to be done, experts were also able to make clear inferences about the previous teacher's practices. Much of this expert thinking was guided by routines and action plans drawn
from their prior experience in the classroom. Novices were
much less specific in interpreting what the previous teacher
had done and in describing changes they might want to make
in class routines and assignments.

In a task designed to uncover expert and novice differences
in visual information processing, Carter, Cushing, Sabers,
Stein, and Berliner (1988) discovered a related focus on classroom work systems. Indeed, "work" appeared to be a salient
organizing concept for experts as they viewed a series of classroom slides presented to them. Their comments suggested that
they saw classrooms as moving systems and that they reacted
quickly to visual stimuli indicating whether or not students
were "working" well within that system. Novices' protocols did
not reveal the same level of attention to work-related actions
of students but rather described the physical appearance of the
students.

In this study, experts also showed a sense of "typicality"
about classroom scenes and individual students' behavior.
Once experts assessed a situation as typical, they had little
more to say. If situations or behaviors depicted in the slides
appeared to be unusual, however, experts spent considerable
time attempting to make sense of anomalies. It appears, then,
that experts' responses to management-related visual stimuli
in classrooms are driven, at least in part, by their perceptions
of what is typical, versus atypical, in classroom scenes. As
might be expected, this sense of typicality was notably rare in
novice protocols.

In another study designed to examine expert–novice differences in teaching, Housner and Griffey (1985) found that expert physical education teachers constructed elaborate managerial plans for implementing activities and tasks for their
students. Novices, in contrast, planned logically well-formed
activities for teaching motor skills or exercise routines, but
they gave considerably less attention than experts to how these
events would be carried out under classroom conditions.

Peterson and Comeaux's (1987) study of experienced and
novice secondary social studies teachers sought to explore differences in teachers' recall, representation, and analysis of
classroom problem situations. In this study, teachers were
shown videotapes of three different 4-minute scenes in social
studies classrooms. One scene portrayed an episode in which
a teacher was handing back essay tests students had previously
taken. In this scene, a number of related interactions and
events occurred (e.g., students complained about grades and
the teacher chided students for their lack of effort). The second
videotaped scene portrayed a classroom discussion about the
Civil War (within which a number of distracting student behaviors occurred and teacher attempts to desist such behaviors
took place). The third and final classroom episode revolved
around students cheating on a test and the simultaneous instances that occur when the teacher attempts to discuss the
infraction with students. Each of these scenes contained 17 actions, either verbal or physical, that were notable and of nearly
the same duration.

Participants in this study were initially shown one of these
three videotaped scenes and asked to recall as many events as
they could after this initial viewing. The videotape was then
shown again to participants, but this time they were asked to
discuss points at which the teacher might have made a different
decision that would have positively affected subsequent occurrences and to describe alternative decisions to the ones the
videotaped teacher made at those points. This pattern of viewing and questioning was repeated for each of the three videotaped episodes.

Participants were given recall scores, based on the number
of events they remembered from the first viewing of the videotape. In addition, their discussions about alternative decisions
were rated for the level of knowledge that seemed to characterize their responses. Responses were coded as *Level 1* if they
appeared to focus on surface or literal characteristics of classroom events and *Level 2* if they suggested knowledge of underlying principles and procedures for managerial or instructional
tasks. Results from these analyses suggested that experienced
teachers had significantly greater recall of classroom events
than did novice teachers. Moreover, experienced teachers' discussions of alternate decisions and their potential impact on
the course of classroom events suggested that they had richer
knowledge of the underlying structures or meaning of teaching
and learning events. Peterson and Comeaux argue that it is
probably these comparatively more complex understandings
that assist experienced teachers in accurately perceiving and
appropriately responding to interactive teaching events.

Ropo (1987) used a combination of interviews and observations to examine the differences in three expert and four novice
mathematics teachers. Ropo focused on teachers' conceptions
of interaction in the classroom and on the nature of interactions
observed for these teachers during the last 2 months of the
school year. Analysis of both the interview and observational
data suggested that one salient difference between expert and
novice teachers was their knowledge of students and the impact of that knowledge on the form and substance of their interactions. In comparison with novices, experts focused more on
concrete examples of interactions to bring about student learning and on the importance of analyzing students' responses to
the work, in order to plan future instructional interactions and
actions. In addition, experts discussed the need, and exhibited
the ability to change the plan for the lesson, dependent on
contextual and situational factors.

Borko and Livingston (in press) also examined expert and
novice differences in mathematics teachers. Specifically, they
explored differences in expert and novice teachers' planning,
teaching, and postlesson reflections. Using interviews and observations, these researchers uncovered a number of differences in teachers' planning and enactment of mathematics instruction. Not surprisingly, they found that the planning of
novices was comparatively less efficient than that of experts
and that the enactment of lessons was comparatively more
problematic for novices when unexpected events obstructed
the scripted actions they had for their instruction. Moreover,
novices' postlesson reflections ranged across a wider host of
concerns than experts' and were noticeably more dependent
upon the events of the day. Borko and Livingston explain these
differences in terms of experts' more complex, connected, and

easily accessed schemata for classroom events and upon their concomitant abilities to use these schema to improvise in the face of surprising circumstances.

In summary, these studies suggest that expert teachers, in contrast with novices, draw on richly elaborated knowledge structures derived from classroom experience to understand teaching tasks and interpret classroom events. Expert teachers know the common forms of activities (recitations, seatwork, discussions) and academic assignments as classroom occurrences. They are familiar with typical behaviors, interactions, and situations associated with such events. This event-structured knowledge appears to help experts make highly accurate predictions about what might happen in a classroom.

Contributions of Information-Processing Studies. L. Shulman (1986) notes that research on teacher planning and decision making, by focusing on a few characteristics of teachers' thinking, has closely resembled process–product research in its search for predictors of teaching effectiveness. Given this framework, investigators have typically examined a narrow range of topics that teachers might be required to think about. Other than calling attention to the types and frequencies of teachers' thoughts or decisions, then, information concerning teachers' knowledge or learning remains sparse. The focus, in other words, has been on cognitive processes, rather than on the knowledge teachers use to interpret situations or formulate plans and decisions.

In many respects, a similar criticism can be made of research on contrasts between experts and novices. These studies have tended to focus on a few topics about which teachers think and on the character or quality (e.g., efficiency or accuracy) of their thinking. And some investigators have been tempted at times to revert to process–product formulations and, thus, treat these characteristics of experts' thinking as criteria for judging teaching effectiveness. This level of generality is a potential hazard in the design of expert–novice studies. Any attempt to account for differences between novices and experts is likely to lead only to broad generalizations about the quality of those differences. But simply knowing that there are qualitative differences between novices and experts is not especially helpful in understanding what teachers know. Moreover, without actually tracing the processes by which novices become experts, nothing is learned about how experts' knowledge is acquired.

At the same time, expert–novice studies have provided a useful framework for beginning to examine teachers' knowledge and the path to expertise. There are, in fact, three important implications for teachers' knowledge that can be drawn from the teaching studies and other studies in semantically rich domains such as medical diagnosis (Patel, Frederiksen, & Groen, 1984); political cognition (Fiske, Kinder, & Larter, 1983); physics problem solving (Champagne, Gunstone, & Klopfer, 1983; Chi & Glaser, 1982, Larking, McDermott, Simon, & Simon, 1980); and games such as chess or bridge (Chase & Simon, 1973; Engle & Bukstel, 1978). *First,* experts' knowledge is *specialized and domain specific.* Experts are not simply more efficient in general problem-solving skills (e.g., problem analysis and hypothesis formulation and testing). Ex-

pertise appears, rather, to be based on highly specialized knowledge in a particular domain. Expert teachers have richly elaborated knowledge about classroom patterns, curriculum, and students that enables them to rapidly apply what they know to specific cases. *Second,* experts' knowledge is *organized.* Their stored knowledge of scenes, patterns, and procedures is organized around interpretative concepts and propositions that reflect the task environments in which they operate. Novices, on the other hand, often focus on discrete objects or surface features of events and problems. *Finally,* much of what experts know is *tacit* knowledge. Such knowledge does not readily lend itself to formalization and direct instruction, but rather it is constructed or invented from repeated experience accomplishing tasks in a domain (Simon, 1979). As a result, it takes considerable time to become an expert. Simply telling novices what experts know will not produce expertise.

These features of expertise suggest the need for better conceptions of the substance and organization of teachers domain-specific knowledge and the processes by which that knowledge is acquired. Without these conceptions, the path from novice to expert is difficult to trace or guide. The focus, in other words, must be on what experts know and not just what distinguishes them from novices. Moreover, as Clift (1989) notes, it is insufficient simply to attribute differences to experience, without a conception of how expertise is acquired from experience. Finally, present conceptions of teaching knowledge might wrongly imply that expertise in teaching is acquired through repeated, successful experiences, and it might fail to take into account growth that occurs through experiencing, and learning from, failure (see Rohrkemper, in press, for a more comprehensive discussion of this view). The following reviews of teachers' practical and pedagogical content knowledge represent important movements toward better understandings of knowledge and learning in teaching.

Practical Knowledge

Studies framed in the information-processing tradition, by opening up inquiry into cognition in teaching, were important precursors to research on teachers' knowledge. Subsequent research has focused more specifically on the substance and organization of that knowledge. For present purposes, the research on the domain-specific knowledge of teachers is divided into two broad categories: practical knowledge and pedagogical-content knowledge.

In this section, research on teachers' practical knowledge is reviewed. Practical knowledge refers broadly to the knowledge teachers have of classroom situations and the practical dilemmas they face in carrying out purposeful action in these settings. Included in this review are studies of teachers' personal practical knowledge and implicit theories, ecological studies of classroom knowledge structures and comprehension processes, and emerging theories of how teachers use knowledge to plan and carry out instruction. In contrast with the more deliberative focus of the previously discussed studies of planning and information processing, the emphasis in the study of classroom knowledge is clearly on the complexities of interactive teaching and thinking-in-action.

Personal Practical Knowledge. As the label implies, research on teachers' personal practical knowledge focuses on the personal understandings teachers have of the practical circumstances in which they work (see Feiman-Nemser & Floden, 1986). Investigators in this area argue that practical rationality is fundamentally different from the technical rationality that dominates academic conceptions of professional knowledge (see Schön, 1983). Under technical rationality, research leads to generalizations about the nature of things, and practitioners are to apply this objective, scientific knowledge to solve problems and achieve effective outcomes. But the realities of practice are quite different. Professionals make complicated interpretations and decisions under conditions of inherent uncertainty (Doyle, 1986), and to do this they engage in practical thinking that leads to an action appropriate to the particular situation. The knowledge required for practice under these circumstances is experiential, that is, it evolves out of "reflection-in-action" (Schön, 1983) as professionals deal with the complexity and uncertainty. Moreover, practical knowledge is shaped by a professional's personal history, which includes intentions and purposes, as well as the cumulative effects of life experience. Such knowledge must be expressed, therefore, in all of its rich particulars and in a language close to that of the practitioners themselves.

Investigators in this area argue further that conventional research on teaching is based on technical rationality and ignores the practical knowledge and personal intentions of teachers. Such conventional research has, therefore, limited utility for practice and imposition of findings from such research deskills teachers (see, for example, Richardson, 1989; Schwille & Melnick, 1987; Woods, 1987). From the perspective of practical rationality, the knowledge base for teaching resides as much within the ranks of teachers as it does in outside, research-derived principles for practice (Elbaz, 1987). Some scholars, arguing from a feminist perspective, suggest, in fact, that prevailing conceptions of what professional knowledge is have often silenced the voices of teachers and prevented professional growth (Richert, 1987). As Atwell (1988) suggests, "life in schools for teachers and students is too often a performance of either cheery or grudging subordination of the ego to a positivistic, idealist world of science or the arts" (p. 4).

Although there are often substantial differences across research programs, studies of personal practical knowledge have generally consisted of intensive case analysis, and in some instances self-analyses, of classroom episodes. By staying very close to the action of classrooms, investigators have tended to focus inquiry on the images, metaphors, and tacit theories teachers use to make sense of specific events in classrooms. The following review of the major research programs illustrates the general properties of inquiry in this area.

Implicit theories. Some investigators, in early studies of planning and decision making, attempted to account for the decisions teachers were making by constructing, often in close conjunction with them, implicit theories, that is, conceptions of the personal values, beliefs, and principles that seemed to guide action. Janesick (1977), for example, concluded that the sixth-grade teacher she studied intensively was primarily committed to creating and sustaining a stable and cohesive class-room group. Marland (1977) derived five principles of practice from stimulated-recall interview transcripts of six elementary teachers: compensation (favoring shy, low-achieving, or impoverished students); strategic leniency (ignoring infractions by students who needed special help); power sharing (attempting to use peer power to influence the group); progressive checking (inspecting and helping during seatwork); suppressing emotions (avoiding expressions of their own emotions, so as not to excite students and create management problems).

Elbaz. Through a case study of a high school English teacher called Sarah, Elbaz (1983) attempted to define the character of practical knowledge in teaching. She identified five broad domains of practical knowledge: (a) self, (b) the milieu of teaching, (c) subject matter, (d) curriculum development, and (e) instruction. She also identified three levels of generality in the organization of practical knowledge. The first level consists of *rules of practice*, which are statements of what actions to take in particular situations when purposes are clear. The second level consists of *practical principles*, which are broader statements for use in reflecting upon situations and selecting from among practices those which apply to specific circumstances. The third level consists of *images*, which are general orienting frameworks. "The teacher's feeling, values, needs, and beliefs combine as she forms images of how teaching should be, and marshals experience, theoretical knowledge, and school folklore to give substance to these images" (Elbaz, 1983, p. 134).

Elbaz's study provides insights into the overall scope and organization of teachers' knowledge and the connection of that knowledge to practical conditions of teaching. At the same time, the focus tends to be on the characteristics, rather than the substance, of what teachers know.

Lampert. In case analyses of two elementary teachers and of her own teaching, Lampert (1985) examined the personal knowledge teachers use to manage dilemmas in teaching. The emphasis in these analysis was on how knowledge of self, especially of personal values and intentions, and knowledge of students was used to handle competing goals such as the desire to work with an individual student and the need to deal with groups of students. Lampert's work gives a useful perspective on the choices teachers face in classrooms and the personal meaning these choices have.

Munby and Russell. Munby and Russell have grounded their work in Schön's (1983) explication of the epistemology of practice, especially the notions of nonpropositional knowledge (i.e., knowledge that is not easily expressed in rules, maxims, or prescriptive principles), reflection-in-action, and the effects of problems and surprises on the development of professional understandings (see Munby, 1986, 1987, 1989; Russell, 1989; Russell & Johnston, 1988; Russell, Munby, Spafford, & Johnston, 1988). In working closely with a sample of preservice, beginning, and experienced teachers, they have concentrated especially on the metaphors in teachers' accounts of their practical knowledge about instruction and curriculum and on the changes across time that occur in these metaphors. They argue that the study of teachers' metaphors could be a powerful way of uncovering how teachers frame and solve classroom problems. Further, these authors suggest that metaphors might provide a window into the levels and types of professional knowledge held by different teachers.

Russell and Johnston's (1988) case studies of four teachers illustrate the kind of work that these authors do to explore teachers' professional knowledge. The focus of the analysis was on the extent to which these four teachers reframed the events of practice and acted on their new understandings in subsequent teaching events. Moreover, they examined how these teachers' images of teaching constrained or unlocked possibilities for teachers to learn from their experiences in teaching. For example, the teacher who appeared to be constrained the most by her image of teaching and learned the least from her experience was Wendy, a high school science teacher who saw herself as a transmitter of knowledge. During her first 2 years of teaching, she came to explore methods of helping students participate more fully in classroom work, but she was not able to reframe her experience in ways that resulted in notable changes in her teaching actions. She did modify and improve a number of her teaching techniques, but her teaching stayed largely consistent with the transmitter view, despite her expressed wish to change. Russell and Johnston argue that Wendy appeared to view teaching through a "conduit" metaphor, a metaphor that describes her prevailing view of teaching as carrying students through the curriculum.

In contrast, Roger, a fifth-year science teacher of seventh and eighth grades, came to teaching with a strongly held belief in the inquiry approach, but he learned from watching his students that, although they enjoyed working with science in this fashion, their *learning* of the content and concepts of science was sometimes questionable. Roger began to read criticisms of the inquiry approach to teaching that he had supported, but he initially greeted these criticisms with anger and resentment. Later he experimented by using his own blend of inquiry and content knowledge in science, and, seeing that his students were constructing much-improved meaning about the subject of science, he altered his original view of teaching and continued to construct his own interpretation of teaching from his classroom experiences and from his reading of theory about how children learn. Russell and Johnston illustrate how Roger's metaphors for teaching revolved around students and their understandings of science and conveyed a view of teaching that was focused on attending to how students learn from the activities that he enacted with them in classrooms.

In their studies of professional knowledge, these investigators have been especially sensitive to patterns of development in teachers' awareness of practice events. Initially, teachers become aware of the strategies with which they are comfortable. With more experience, they fine-tune these strategies. The researchers argue that, at these two levels, teachers strive to maintain a coherent framework and tend to ignore back talk from their classes. At the next level of awareness, teachers become attentive to students' reactions, reflect on puzzling situations, and start to reframe their view of their practice. They now begin, in other words, reflection-in-action, a process through which practice changes, although teachers might not always be able to express their reframed view analytically.

Clandinin and Connelly. The work of Clandinin and Connelly is, in many ways, the most clearly personalistic in this tradition (see Clandinin, 1985; Clandinin & Connelly, 1986; Connelly & Clandinin, 1985, 1986). These investigators concentrate on specific teaching episodes in a teacher's classroom and on the personal practical knowledge defined as an account of how the teacher knows this situation. They reject Schön's (1983) focus on problems in favor of an emphasis on regularities and patterns, that is, practical rules and principles, routines, rituals, habits, cycles, rhythms, and images. Image is especially important as a type of knowledge that "draws both the past and the future into a personally meaningful nexus of experience focused on the immediate situation that called it forth" (Connelly & Clandinin, 1985, p. 198).

These investigators further reject Schön's conceptual understanding of teachers' thinking in favor of an experiential understanding found in the narrative unities of practitioners:

> Narrative unity is a continuum within a person's experience which renders life experiences meaningful through the unity they achieve for the person. What we mean by unity is a union in a particular person in a particular time and place of all that has been and undergone in the past and in the past of the tradition which help to shape him. (Connelly & Clandinin, 1985, p. 198)

From the perspective of method, a study in this research program involves the preparation of narrative accounts of field notes and interviews. The narrative accounts are the first formal step in the interpretive process. They are written in the first person and are addressed as letters from the researcher to the teacher as a way of initiating discussion of developing notions of the teacher's personal practical thinking. The interaction enables a researcher to uncover a teacher's personal philosophy of teaching, as well as the historical, personal and professional experience that allows the teacher to reconstruct narrative unities.

These researchers used fragments of teaching episodes as a basis for working with the teacher to uncover the narrative unity. In one case study (Kroma, 1983), for example, these teaching episodes included a note-taking activity in science in which scientific terms were to be recorded verbatim, a discussion of botany in which the teacher downplayed technical language, and the teacher's use of slang when he was holding a snake and preparing to show a biology film. Through narrative method, these seemingly unconnected fragments of teaching were woven together through a researcher and teacher's dialogue in ways that revealed the teacher's reasonably coherent set of practical understandings. This dialogue suggested that this teacher placed importance on having students confronted with various forms of language in the classroom and on ultimately being asked to improve their use of standard language. In this method, teaching episodes are not easily "horribilized" by outsiders, because the episodes are connected to a teacher's understanding of how the curriculum interacts with such things as the constraints and cycles of the school year and to an overall instructional plan.

In recent studies, Clandinin (n.d.) has begun to focus on novice teachers' personal experiences in classroom settings and the impact of that experience on how they understand their work. For example, Clandinin describes the case of Stewart, a beginning kindergarten teacher who cared greatly about relating to children and spending time interacting with them individually. As Stewart's first year of teaching progressed, the tensions between his desires to spend quality time interacting with students about academic matters and the stops, starts, and surprises of the school calendar surfaced in ways that caused him, over time, to gain a rhythmic sense of teaching. Reconstructing knowledge about classrooms was quite uncomfortable for Stewart at first, but by the spring of the year, he had come to understand the school cycle, so that he could operate within the demands of his particular workplace. On the basis of this case study, Clandinin argues that the acquisition of teaching knowledge is not adequately portrayed as the obtaining and practicing of a set of skills. Instead, "Learning to teach involves the narrative reconstruction of a teacher's experience as personal practical knowledge is shaped through its expression in practical situations" (p. 22).

Summary. Research on teachers' personal knowledge, by focusing primarily on idiosyncratic forms and expressions of knowing and acting, tells more about the characteristics of teachers' knowledge than about what teachers know. The results of this inquiry do not add up to a codified body of teaching knowledge. Indeed, some investigators (e.g., Clandinin and Connelly) explicitly reject this level of general conceptual understanding in favor of an experiential understanding of teaching that does not separate knowledge from the knower. By staying very close to the particulars of practice, however, this tradition does provide a rich picture of the effects of experience and the conditions under which teachers use their knowledge to make sense of a complex, ill-structured, classroom world of competing goals and actions. It furnishes, in other words, a theory of how teachers learn by teaching and how teachers use their knowledge, rather than a generalized conception of what teachers know.

In many respects, this personalized view of teachers' knowledge is implicit in much of the research on learning to teach, especially that which has focused on such outcomes as attitudes, beliefs, orientations, and perspectives (e.g., Zeichner, 1987). In these studies it is assumed, in other words, that knowledge at the level of classroom practice is, at the core, personal and idiosyncratic. The issue then becomes one of how settings affect the development of personal perspectives, rather than of how teachers learn a defined body of knowledge about practice.

This personal conception of practical knowledge is not, however, the only way of describing what experienced teachers know about teaching. In the next section, one alternative, research on classroom knowledge, is considered.

Classroom Knowledge. Research on classroom knowledge is based on the assumption that, although there is wide variation among classrooms, teachers, and students, it is possible to codify in a general sense what teachers know that enables them to navigate within these settings (see Carter & Doyle, 1987). The construction of such knowledge is based on two frameworks: (a) an ecological perspective that focuses on the demands of environments and the impact of these demands on the thoughts and actions of participants, and (b) a schema-theoretic approach to the organization of knowledge and the comprehension processes by which that knowledge is connected to ongoing events in the environment. The convergence of these two perspectives leads to the assumption of a functional congruence between the structure of situations and the structure of knowledge that persons have of those situations. As a result of this assumption, classroom knowledge, therefore, is not a body of propositions or prescriptions derived from external disciplines or process–product studies, but, rather it is "situated" (see, for example, Morine-Dershimer, 1989) and is by conceptions grounded in the common experience of classroom events.

According to Doyle (1983), the central construct in the study of classroom knowledge is "task." Doyle suggests that a task has three basic elements: a goal to be achieved, a set of circumstances or "givens" under which the goal is to be achieved (i.e., a problem space), and a set of resources that can be used to reach the goal. Tasks are accomplished by interpreting the problem space (e.g., discovering what the problem of achieving order is in a particular class) and organizing resources (activities, rules, physical space) in ways that "fit" or account for the features of that problem space. Tasks organize situations for individuals and thus shape cognition and the organization of knowledge. They are, in other words, the medium through which persons intersect with their environments. They, therefore, define the "work" people must do (i.e., what they must think about), as well as the "treatments" embedded in situations. One learns about the world, that is, from what one does in accomplishing tasks. This task framework, then, becomes a theory of both knowledge and its acquisition.

The tasks of teaching. Studies of classroom knowledge have focused primarily on two key teaching tasks: (a) creating and sustaining order in classrooms, and (b) moving students through the curriculum. Doyle (1988) has recently integrated these two lines of inquiry into the concept of teaching as curriculum enactment.

Research on classroom order has concentrated primarily on the creation and maintenance of *work systems* consisting of (a) activities that organize students for working, that is, large group presentations and recitations, small group discussions, and seatwork segments; and (b) rules and procedures that specify actions for routine events such as obtaining materials, sharpening pencils, and turning in assignments (see Doyle, 1986; Leinhardt & Greeno, 1986). The most important feature of a work system for a class is the *program of action* that defines the character of order for particular segments of time and pulls students along specified paths (Doyle, 1986). For example, during whole-class presentations, students are typically supposed to attend to the explanation, respond to occasional questions, and take notes. During discussions, in contrast, students are to attend to one another, as well as to the teacher, and take appropriate turns at talking. When a program of action is not established or breaks down because of disruptions, orderliness has no situational foundation, and attempts to restore order are unlikely to be successful for more than a few moments.

A teacher's role in management has at least three dimensions. *First,* successful managers, defined by indicators of work involvement and achievement, *design* sensible and context-sensitive work systems for their classes. In other words, they prepare in advance for how students will be organized to accomplish work and what rules and procedures will govern movement around the room and routine access to resources and materials. *Second*, successful managers *communicate* their work systems clearly to students through explanations, examples, practice, and feedback. *Finally*, successful managers *monitor* classroom events to make sure that the work system, including the curriculum flow (see Putnam, 1987), is operating within reasonable limits and to notice early signs of potential disruptions. By monitoring the flow of classroom activity, they reduce the need for frequent reprimands and other interventions to restore order and maximize the opportunity for students to engage in working with the curriculum (see, for example, Good & Brophy, 1987).

It is interesting to note that investigators in the information-processing and personal-knowledge traditions have reported a similar emphasis on rituals, routines, and principles of action in their studies of teachers' thinking.

Ecological studies of instruction and curriculum in classrooms have focused on the academic work, or tasks, students accomplish (see Blumenfeld, Mergendoller, & Swarthout, 1987; Doyle & Carter, 1984; Doyle, Sanford, Schmidt-French, Emmer, & Clements, 1985). In these studies it was found that assignments with different cognitive and procedural complexity for students were enacted in very different ways in classrooms. Familiar, routinized, and simple work was accomplished with ease. Explanations were clear and precise, students' misunderstandings were minimal, and work began quickly and proceeded efficiently. Moreover, there was high congruence between the announced work and the final products students handed in, and the teachers' criteria for evaluating products were consistently and often rigorously applied. On the other hand, complex assignments, in which students encountered novel information or problems and were required to make decisions in order to generate products, were much more difficult to enact. Explanations were longer, students frequently failed to grasp key points, and work sessions seldom flowed smoothly. Moreover, assignments drifted, that is, over time, the teacher often became more explicit about product specifications and the scope of students' decisions was narrowed. In writing assignments, for example, teachers often introduced model sentences or paragraphs for students to emulate when they had difficulty generating acceptable essays on their own. As a result, the announced work and the work students actually accomplished were often quite different.

Grant (1987, 1988) explored teachers' knowledge and understandings of the means to teach critical thinking tasks to students. By interviewing and observing teachers who were nominated for their successes in teaching critical reasoning, Grant described the organizational strategies teachers used to sustain tasks that were intended to promote critical thinking in their classrooms. Teachers in these studies shared a number of conventional strategies in teaching critical thinking (e.g. using writing to learn, discussing major topics thoroughly, interjecting humor to lighten otherwise serious work, responding supportively to student comments, ignoring incongruous student responses, and correcting erroneous thinking), but they also possessed unique strategies that seemed to emanate from teachers' organizing images about the demands of classroom work. For example, the imagery of the teacher in Grant's (1988) study (e.g., that learning in classrooms is an extended and difficult pilgrimage for students) appeared to help her to travel with students through the work in ways that promoted critical thinking. Importantly, engaging students in the intellectual risk taking of critical reasoning often meant a journey that was, according to Grant, "bumpy, circuitous, and unpredictable."

Teachers' comprehension processes. These studies of classroom order and academic work give a broad outline of teachers' knowledge. Additional work in the ecological tradition has concentrated on teachers' comprehension processes, that is, the processes by which teachers use their knowledge to interpret tasks and events. In an early study of teachers' comprehension, Doyle and Ponder (1977/8) examined the "practicality ethic" by which experienced teachers appeared to decide whether to use suggestions for classroom practice. They concluded that suggestions that were judged to be practical were framed in an instrumental language (i.e., describing a procedure, rather than a principle or ideal), were congruent with the circumstances and personal conceptions of the teachers, and involved a reasonably large return for the amount of energy and time invested. They also argued that these factors in teachers' judgments were shaped by the situational demands they faced in classrooms.

Pinnegar (1988) attempted to uncover the meaning of the phrase "with me" (e.g., "My students were really 'with me' today") in the language commonly used by teachers. Pinnegar conducted interviews with 40 experienced teachers who had recently served in the role of cooperating teacher. She asked the teachers to imagine they were talking to a student teacher and then explain how they knew a class was or was not "with" them and what meaning such cues had for their subsequent actions. Pinnegar's analysis suggested that the term described an important area of teacher knowledge. With this knowledge, teachers could react to subtle cues of boredom, disinterest, or fatigue and could redirect their own actions, change the pace of the lesson, or take other actions to engage students in work at hand.

Carter (in press-a, in press-b) examined detailed narrative records of classes taught by junior high school English teachers who differed on indicators of classroom-management success. The focus in these studies was on constructing interpretive frameworks or metaphors to account for how teachers appeared, through their comments and actions, to comprehend the problem of order in classrooms. The studies have suggested that experienced and effective teachers understood the problem of classroom order as one of guiding or steering the flow of action around potential obstacles. Managers who had difficulty sustaining order, on the other hand, often stopped the action to attend to misbehavior or build personal bonds with individual students. These comprehension studies are interesting in that they provide evidence of alternative ways in which teachers understand classroom events and connect those understandings to different consequences for the task of teaching.

Learning to teach. The task framework in research on classroom knowledge, by directing attention to how situations and thinking interact, has provided a rich ground for studies of learning to teach. In an early study framed in ecological terms, Doyle (1977) traced the processes by which student teachers learned to cope with the multidimensionality, simultaneity, immediacy, and unpredictability of the classroom environment. He noted that student teachers who successfully coped with classroom demands appeared to develop cognitive strategies such as rapid judgment, chunking, and differentiation that enabled them to simplify classroom complexity and accurately interpret events that occurred in front of them.

More recently, Pinnegar (1989) studied how teachers' knowledge and thinking about their students develop. The study involved extensive interviews with 12 secondary science teachers (four student teachers, four first-year teachers, and four experienced teachers with greater than 7 years of teaching experience) at five points in the semester (before school started, after 3 days, after 3 weeks, at the end of the first grading period, and at the end of the semester). The initial interview focused on obtaining information from the teacher about the image he or she projected or had of the class, the "personality" the teacher ascribed to the class, the nature of thought about the teacher's class when he or she was planning, and the typical kinds of interactions the teacher carried out with students. In addition, Pinnegar asked teachers to tell her about any advice they would give to a substitute teacher or to her if she were to decide to teach the class in the future. Beginning with the third interview, teachers were asked to talk about specific students they had nominated and who contrasted in terms of teachers' views of their ability.

Pinnegar's intensive work with these teachers suggested that knowledge and thinking about students takes on a different character with experience. Although all teachers tended to focus on information about student cooperation, experienced teachers appeared to have much more finely tuned cognitive skills in identifying resisters to cooperation and in talking about ways to engage them in classroom work. Student teachers' responses suggested that they thought cooperation was best achieved by developing good relationships with students. First-year teachers argued that it was important to know which students were likely to block progress, but they were not sophisticated at seeking out information about students that would help channel them into the curriculum. As one first-year teacher said, "You can only hope to sit on them." Experienced teachers, in contrast, thought often about students who resisted involvement and seemed to make clear distinctions between those who "could not" and those who "would not" do the work. They had a repertoire of strategies for using their knowledge to engage students in the work and to acquire new knowledge from students that could be used to sustain their interest.

Gonzalez (in progress) is attempting to examine the acquisition of "event-structured knowledge" (see Carter & Doyle, 1989) through extensive interviews, observations, and supervisory conferences with 15 student teachers. By tracking well-remembered events of these students and their reflections about them, Gonzalez is developing frameworks to describe this kind of knowledge growth. The work is preliminary, but she has found that student teachers' differential responses to particularly problematic events early in the student-teaching semester affect subsequent understandings of classroom events and might lead to a "ballooning" of dysfunctional interpretations of the *meaning* of student behavior and classroom episodes.

Points of Convergence. At their extremes, the personal and the ecological views represent clearly different stances on the form that knowledge of what teachers know can take. For extreme personalists, each person's knowledge is unique and cannot be codified across individuals without damaging important nuances of meaning. For the extreme ecologist, situations program what individuals think and do. Between these opposites, however, there is considerable overlap, with personalists stressing idiosyncratic variations close to the action of teaching and ecologists emphasizing common patterns and themes across situations. But both are interested in what teachers know and in how that knowledge is influenced by situations.

This sense of convergence of the personal and the ecological frameworks is apparent in two perspectives on teachers' knowledge use. Fenstermacher (1986) posits that teachers use information about teaching, regardless of its origins, not as a blueprint for acting, but as a resource for the practical arguments that undergird their actions. This concept of practical arguments acknowledges the personal voice of the teacher and of her or his individual interpretations of classroom events, but it incorporates general knowledge about content, students, learning, and classrooms. Information about the association between time and achievement, for example, can sensitize teachers to how time is spent in their classrooms and guide them in inventing ways to maintain or increase the quality of students' use of time. Morine-Dershimer (1988), in a reanalysis of stimulated-recall data from eight student teachers, concluded that uncovering practical arguments and then improving them by providing research knowledge could, theoretically speaking, be quite useful but, practically speaking, be both time consuming and difficult. Some optimism for the approach, however, is seen in Driscoll and Stevens's (1985) study. These authors found that experienced teachers used knowledge about teaching effectiveness as analytical categories for thinking about their teaching, rather than a guidelines for acting. Further attempts are currently underway to explore the nature of teachers' practical arguments and how these change with additional information (see, for example, Richardson & Anders, 1988; Richardson-Koehler & Fenstermacher, 1988).

Yinger has recently formulated a conception of teachers' knowledge use in interactive teaching (Yinger, 1986, 1987; Yinger & Villar, 1986). This conception is framed around the idea of improvisation. Yinger argues that teachers have a rich store of knowledge that enables them to make sense of immediate scenes and bring past experiences to bear on these scenes to invent, virtually on the spot, actions that fit these circumstances. He emphasizes that this knowledge, which encompasses past experiences and personal intentions and understandings, is "holistic and patterned" and might be inseparable from action in a situation. Thus teachers cannot necessarily talk analytically about what they do in specific situations, because what they know is whole actions connected to situational frames. The trick in learning to teach is to acquire sufficient experience to develop a patterned language of practice with which to recognize what situations mean and how they might be responded to in particularistic ways.

These convergences of personal and ecological frameworks are promising. In particular they suggest that investigators interested in learning to teach should begin to tie knowledge to situations. This can be done by examining the tasks of teacher education, how these tasks are interpreted by those who are accomplishing them, and what can reasonably be expected to result from task accomplishment.

Pedagogical Content Knowledge

The final approach to studying teacher knowledge represents an attempt to determine what teachers know about their subject matter and how they translate that knowledge into classroom curricular events. There has been recent concern that the disciplinary knowledge that beginning and many experienced teachers possess poorly equips them for this transformation process (see, for example, Anderson 1989; Ball, 1988; Buchmann, 1984; Gomez, 1988). The process, to be sure, is multifaceted and complex. L. Shulman and Sykes (1986) suggest that pedagogical content knowledge includes:

understanding the central topics in each subject matter as it is generally taught to children of a particular grade level and being able to ask the following kinds of questions about each topic: what are core concepts, skills and attitudes which this topic has the potential of conveying to students? . . . What are the aspects of this topic that are most difficult to understand for students? What is the greatest intrinsic interest? What analogies, metaphors, examples, similes, demonstrations, simulations, manipulations, or the like, are most effective in communicating the appropriate understandings or attitudes of *this topic* to students of particular backgrounds and prerequisites? What students' preconceptions are likely to get in the way of learning? (p. 9)

Tamir (1988) suggests that additional aspects of what he terms "subject matter specific" pedagogical knowledge include a teacher's knowledge of students' interest and motivation to learn *particular* topics within a discipline, a teacher's understanding of how to make outside-school settings (e.g., museums and laboratories) quality learning environments for special content areas, and a teacher's discipline-based knowledge of special needs for testing and evaluating students' work (e.g., practical laboratory tests in science).

Inquiry into teachers' pedagogical content knowledge has been particularly active since about 1985, and yet it is important to preface a review of representative studies by saying that the work is still in its early stages. General statements about what teachers know about content in their fields and its transformation into forms accessible to students is clearly premature. But what has been learned to date has signaled concern about the limited pedagogical content knowledge of new teachers and has enlivened the present debates concerning the redesign of teacher education programs (see, for example, Grossman & Richert, 1988; L. Shulman, 1986, 1987).

Studies to date of teachers' pedagogical content knowledge have addressed some, but certainly not all, of the different dimensions described above. These studies have examined teachers' pedagogical content knowledge in several different disciplines.

Mathematics. Representative studies in the area of mathematics include the work of Carpenter, Fennema, Peterson, and Carey (1988); Leinhardt and Smith (1985); and Steinberg, Haymore, and Marks (1985). Carpenter et al. investigated the pedagogical content knowledge of 40 first-grade teachers. Specifically, these researchers focused on teachers' knowledge of distinct types of addition and subtraction problems, their understandings about the strategies children use to solve different problems, their abilities to predict the manner and success of their own students in solving different problem types, and the relationship between these aspects of teachers' pedagogical content knowledge and their students' achievement. Multiple measures and techniques were employed to assess teachers' knowledge, including tasks requiring teachers to represent different problem types, to determine the relative difficulty of pairs of problems presented to them, to use information presented to them vis-à-vis videotapes to predict students' problem-solving strategies, and to predict how a small sample of their own students would solve different addition and subtraction problems.

Although teachers had little trouble making distinctions among different kinds of problems, this knowledge did not appear to be logically linked to their considerations when deciding on the relative difficulty of different problems. Nor did teachers' general knowledge of problem difficulty appear to be related to their ability to predict their own students' success in solving different problems. However, teachers' ability to predict whether their own students could solve different kinds of problems was significantly related to student achievement. These authors suggest that one possible explanation for teachers' inability to make coherent connections among the different aspects of pedagogical knowledge they studied was their lack of exposure to an existing, rich, knowledge base for how students solve addition and subtraction problems.

Other studies in the content area of mathematics have looked more directly at how subject-matter knowledge is translated into curricular events in classrooms. Leinhardt and Smith (1985), for example, not only investigated teachers' knowledge of mathematical computational procedures that they taught, but also assessed their knowledge of lesson structure and teaching routines. Leinhardt and Smith videotaped classroom lessons on fractions, obtained teachers comments on these lessons, and ultimately mapped complex relationships between teachers' subject-matter knowledge and their strategies and routines for engaging students in the content.

Similarly, Steinberg, et al. (1985) used interviews and observations to explore possible links between four new secondary teachers' differing levels of knowledge of mathematics and the ways they structured instructional tasks for their students. These researchers collected information about teachers' intellectual biographies; their perspectives on and personal understandings of their discipline; their sense of the organization, crucial topics, and relative difficulty of concepts in algebra; and their general and subject-specific ideas about teaching. Results from this work suggested a relationship between the quality of an individual's knowledge of mathematics and the kind and quality of lessons carried out in classrooms. Specifically, a relationship existed between greater knowledge of mathematics and, for example, the use of more conceptual teaching strategies, the instructional practice of identifying relationships among concepts inside and outside the mathematics discipline, and the ability to engage students in active problem-solving activities.

Social Studies and English. Cases of pedagogical content knowledge have been conducted in other content areas as well. These studies include a focus not only on the substantive knowledge of teachers and its ties to transformation of content but also on the disciplinary perspectives, orientations, and beliefs of individuals. Wilson and Wineburg (1988), for example, studied four novice social studies teachers who differed widely in the focus of their academic studies. One teacher viewed history from the preparatory lens of anthropology, one from international relations and political science, one from American studies, and one from American history. Cases developed through extensive interviews and observations with these teachers indicated that these varied backgrounds held great sway on their conceptions of the role of factual knowledge, the place of interpretation, the significance of chronology and continuity, and the meaning of causation in history, and, ultimately, the processes and content of their instruction.

Similarly, Grossman's (1987) work with two beginning English teachers revealed that different orientations to subject matter influenced how they planned to carry out content in their classrooms. Grossman's extensive interviews with and observations of these two teachers as they were learning to teach suggested that they had very different motivations for becoming teachers and possessed quite different orientations to the subject matter of English. These differences surfaced in planned strategies and focus areas of their lessons. For example, Colleen, whose first love was the text and texture of the English language itself, focused her instruction on powerful passages, reading of words, and attention to detail in literature. Martha, in contrast was less enamored with stressing detail in the literature than with using literature to elicit student reactions and responses about the human condition. Grossman found that these teachers' differences in orientation affected their instructional strategies for teaching writing as well and, importantly, to some extent shaped the impact of their professional preparation.

Gudmundsdottir's (in press) four case studies of veteran teachers of history and English echo themes similar to those that surfaced in the studies described above. Interviews with and observations of teachers, as well as the graphic pedagogical models of their disciplines constructed by these teachers, suggested strongly that their disciplinary backgrounds, orientations, substantive knowledge, and beliefs affected their planning and instruction, the goals they set for themselves and their students, the organization they developed for different units of study, and the means of communicating their own ideas and values about the content to students.

Learning to Teach Content. Although learning to teach subject matter is a priority in this research program, only a few studies in this area have actually been completed. Studies in this tradition by Ball (1988) and by Gomez (1988) were reviewed earlier in this chapter as representative of learning to teach research. Additional studies with a subject-matter focus include those of Duffy and Roehler (1986) and their colleagues (see Michelson, 1985, 1987; Roehler et al., 1987) on changes in teachers' knowledge structures during course instruction in reading methods. Using techniques that result in graphic representations of an individual's ordering of concepts and their relationships in an area (e.g., semantic mapping and ordered-tree techniques), these researchers asked reading-methods students to create representations of their content knowledge prior to their methods instruction, during methods instruction, and after such instruction had been completed. These products were rated for their arrangements, relationships, and integrations and were analyzed for their levels of complexity at different times.

Although the degree of change was found to be unique to the student, these investigators have described trends in the kinds of knowledge changes made at the various points of assessment. For example, between baseline and second maps, there tended to be a "spreading" of students' understanding of their discipline. Students appeared to have added to their baseline knowledge and to have been differentially successful in developing some new frameworks for their content. At the next interim point, students' maps, in general, were more cohesively connected and seemed to indicate that they had gone through a process of reconceptualizing their content. At the final point of assessment, after students had completed their methods course, further development in knowledge structures occurred for some students, although at this stage the degree and nature of the growth was much more difficult to capture and describe.

Summary. Taken together, these studies suggest that differences in teachers' disciplinary knowledge, background, experiences, and orientations have a significant impact on how teachers organize instruction and represent the substance of the curriculum to students. This line of inquiry is important in that is focuses on a neglected aspect of knowledge about teaching and attempts to capture the collective understandings and traditions of the profession about how subject matter is to be represented in classrooms.

From a learning-to-teach perspective, pedagogical content knowledge is a domain distinct from, but not unrelated to, practical knowledge. The major difference is that pedagogical content knowledge is to a greater extent grounded in disciplines and in formulations related to school curriculum and the collective wisdom of the profession than practical knowledge. It is, in other words, more formal than personal and situational knowledge. The learning-to-teach problem, therefore, is more one of translating knowledge from one form to another, from propositional to procedural, than of unraveling the meaning of complex experiences. At the same time, curricular goals, as well as forms of representation and modes of instructing, are often quite personal and must be understood, if they are to be enacted at all, as classroom events. It might well be that pedagogical content knowledge and classroom knowledge are not ultimately that different for the learning teacher.

A final note: One suspects that teachers, especially at the secondary level, are more familiar with pedagogical aspects of teaching from their apprenticeship as students than they are with the practical knowledge gained primarily from experience as a teacher. This differential familiarity is likely to affect how preconceptions and expectations operate in learning to teach.

CONCLUSIONS AND RECOMMENDATIONS

Throughout the chapter issues of findings, implications, and methods have been discussed in conjunction with specific research domains and studies. In this final section, some of the broader themes raised by this review are addressed.

This survey would seem to have demonstrated the value of considering knowledge and learning in studies of learning to teach, as well as the clear interdependency of these two fields. How one frames the learning-to-teach question depends a great deal on how one conceives of what is to be learned and how that learning might take place. At the same time, an understanding of teachers' knowledge is enhanced by probing more deeply the question of how that knowledge is obtained or changes over time. It is likely, therefore, that these fields will move forward together.

There are also indications in this literature that greater clarity on issues of both knowledge and learning is needed for productive research on learning to teach. There is still a tendency in studies of teachers' knowledge to focus on characteristics of what teachers know (e.g., their knowledge is complex, diverse, idiosyncratic, rich, holistic, personal) or on topics about which they think (e.g., they know about routines, students, images, curriculum). Less attention is given to the substance of that knowledge, to what teachers actually know or need to know about classrooms, content, and pedagogy and how that knowledge is organized. The latter task is considerably more difficult but is likely to be quite productive.

Similarly, greater thought needs to be given to a theory of learning in teaching. There are clear and promising signs of an interest in constructivist theories of learning, but the formulations are still primitive. More discussion needs to be directed to what it means to learn to teach, rather than simply to what is learned in which settings.

The final message of this review is twofold. *First*, the range and complexity of what is learned in teacher education are enormous. Unraveling knowledge and learning in teaching will be a very difficult task. *Second*, progress along the lines sketched here will lead to radical reforms in teacher education both in the conceptions of what the knowledge base for teaching is and in approaches to curriculum and pedagogy (see, for example, Woolfolk, 1989). Whatever the future holds for inquiry, it is now evident that teachers' knowledge is not highly abstract and propositional. Nor can it be formalized into a set of specific skills or preset answers to specific problems. Rather it is experiential, procedural, situational, and particularistic. It will be necessary, therefore, to develop forms of representation that capture these essential features of what teachers know with a high degree of situation and task validity.

This characterization of teachers' knowledge does not mean that teaching can only be learned by apprenticeship in field settings. "Natural" settings can be quite confusing (Smylie, 1989), and novices might well direct their attention to irrelevant aspects of the stream of action. Constructed and guided experiences designed on the basis of an analytical understanding of teaching events are often more instructive than natural settings, because the essential cognitive dimensions are more easily accessible. Such experiences, in turn, provide the cognitive foundation for knowledge construction in more natural environments.

Processes used to deliver teacher education content to novices must not only reveal pedagogical problems but also bring out ways of thinking about these problems and provide opportunities for novices actually to practice problem solving. Several observers (e.g., Brophy, 1988; Carter, in press-a; Carter & Richardson, 1988; J. Shulman & Nelson, 1989) have recently suggested that the use of cases holds promise for achieving these ends. But it is important to note that evolving a case literature to capture the complexities and contingencies of classroom life and to convey the kinds of knowledge necessary to teach successfully is likely to be an expensive and labor-intensive enterprise (see Carter & Unklesbay, in press). The 1990s should speak to our capacity to support a commitment to a reconceptualized teacher education process.

References

Amarel, M., & Feiman-Nemser, S. (1988). *Prospective teachers' views of teaching and learning to teach.* Paper presented at the meeting of the American Educational Research Association, New Orleans.

Anderson, C. (1989). The role of education in the academic disciplines in teacher preparation. In A. Woolfolk (Ed.), *Research perspectives on the graduate preparation of teachers* (pp. 88–107). Englewood Cliffs, NJ: Prentice-Hall.

Atwell, W. (1988). *Strengthening the dialectical relationship between teachers' personal knowledge and their professional knowledge through autobiography and object relations.* Paper presented at the Conference on Reflective Inquiry, Orlando, FL.

Ball, D. L. (1988, April) *Prospective teachers' understandings of mathematics: What do they bring with them to teacher education?* Paper presented at the meeting of the American Educational Research Association, New Orleans.

Ball, D. L., & Noordhoff, K. (1985). *Learning to teach by the book: The influence of persons, program, and setting on student teaching.* Paper presented at the meeting of the American Educational Research Association, Chicago.

Blumenfeld, P. C., Mergendoller, J. R., & Swarthout, D. W. (1987). Task as a heuristic for understanding student learning and motivation. *Journal of Curriculum Studies, 19,* 135–148.

Borko, H., Lalik, R., & Tomchin, E. (1987). Student teachers' understandings of successful teaching. *Teaching and Teacher Education, 3,* 77–90.

Borko, H., & Livingston, C. (in press). Cognition and improvisation:

Differences in mathematics instruction by expert and novice teachers. *American Education Research Journal.*

Borko, H., Livingston, C., McCaleb, J., & Mauro, L. (1988). Student teachers' planning and post-lesson reflections: Patterns and implications for teacher preparation. In J. Calderhead (Ed.), *Teachers' professional learning* (pp. 55–83). London: Falmer.

Brophy, J. (1988). *Educating teachers about managing classrooms and students. Teaching and Teacher Education, 4,* 1–18.

Buchmann, M. (1984). The priority of knowledge and understanding in teaching. In L. Katz & J. Raths (Eds.), *Advances in teacher education* (Vol. I, pp. 29–50). Norwood, NJ: Ablex.

Calderhead, J. (1987). *Cognition and metacognition in teachers' professional development.* Paper presented at the meeting of the American Educational Research Association, Washington, DC.

Carpenter, T., Fennema, E., Peterson, P., & Carey, D. (1988). Teachers' pedagogical content knowledge of students' problem-solving in elementary arithmetic. *Journal for Research in Mathematics Education, 19,* 385–401.

Carter, K. (in press-a). Contrast cases of teacher comprehension of classroom management. In J. Shulman (Ed.), *The Teacher Educator's Casebook.*

Carter, K. (in press-b). Teacher comprehension of classroom processes. *Elementary School Journal.*

Carter, K., Cushing, K., Sabers, D., Stein, P., & Berliner, D. (1988). Expert–novice differences in perceiving and processing visual classroom information. *Journal of Teacher Education, 39,* 25–31.

Carter, K., & Doyle, W. (1987). Teachers' knowledge structures and comprehension processes. In J. Calderhead (Ed.), *Exploring teachers' thinking* (pp. 147–160). London: Cassell.

Carter, K., & Doyle, W. (1989). Classroom research as a resource for the graduate preparation of teachers. In A. E. Woolfolk (Ed.), *Research perspectives on the graduate preparation of teachers* (pp. 51–68). Englewood Cliffs, NJ: Prentice-Hall.

Carter, K., & Richardson, V. (1988). Toward a curriculum for initial year of teaching programs. *Elementary School Journal, 89,* 405–419.

Carter, K., Sabers, D., Cushing, K., Pinnegar, S., & Berliner, D. C. (1987). Processing and using information about students: A study of expert, novice, and postulant teachers. *Teaching and Teacher Education, 3,* 147–157.

Carter, K., & Unklesbay, R. (in press). Cases in teaching and law. *Journal of Curriculum Studies.*

Champagne, A. B., Gunstone, R. F., & Klopfer, L. E. (1983). *A perspective on the differences between expert and novice performance in solving physics problems.* Pittsburgh: University of Pittsburgh, Learning Research and Development Center.

Chase, W. G., & Simon, H. A. (1973). Perception in chess. *Cognitive Psychology, 4,* 55–81.

Chi, M. T. H., & Glaser, R. (1982). *Knowledge and skill differences in novices and experts.* (Tech. Rep. No. 7). Pittsburgh: University of Pittsburgh, Learning Research and Development Center.

Chi, M. T. H., Glaser, R., & Farr, M. (in press). *The nature of expertise.* Hillsdale, NJ: Lawrence Erlbaum.

Clandinin, D. J. (n.d.) *Developing rhythm in teaching: The narrative study of a beginning teacher's personal practical knowledge of classrooms.* Unpublished manuscript.

Clandinin, D. J. (1985). *Classroom practice: Teacher images in action.* London: Falmer.

Clandinin, D. J., & Connelly, F. M. (1986). Rhythms in teaching: The narrative study of teachers' personal practical knowledge of classrooms. *Teaching and Teacher Education, 2*(4), 377–387.

Clark, C., & Peterson, P. (1986). Teachers' thought processes. In M. C. Wittrock (Ed.), *Handbook of research on teaching* (3rd ed., pp. 255–296). New York: Macmillan.

Clift, R. (1989). Unanswered questions in graduate teacher preparation. In A. E. Woolfolk (Ed.), *Research perspectives on the graduate preparation of teachers* (pp. 179–193). Englewood Cliffs, N.J.: Prentice-Hall.

Connelly, F. M., & Clandinin, D. J. (1985). Personal practical knowledge and the modes of knowing: Relevance for teaching and learning. In E. Eisner (Ed.), *Learning and teaching the ways of knowing* (84th yearbook of the National Society for the Study of Education, Part II, pp. 174–198). Chicago: University of Chicago Press.

Connelly, F. M., & Clandinin, D. J. (1986). On narrative method, personal philosophy, and narrative unities in the story of teaching. *Journal of Research in Science Teaching, 23*(4), 283–310.

Copeland, W. D. (1977). Some factors related to student teacher classroom performance following microteaching training. *American Educational Research Journal, 14,* 147–157.

Doyle, W. (1977). Learning the classroom environment: An ecological analysis. *Journal of Teacher Education, 28,* 51–55.

Doyle, W. (1983). Academic work. *Review of Educational Research, 53,* 159–199.

Doyle, W. (1986). Classroom organization and management. In M. C. Wittrock (Ed.), *Handbook of research on teaching* (3rd ed., pp. 392–431). New York: Macmillan.

Doyle, W. (1988). *Curriculum in teacher education.* Paper presented at the meeting of the American Educational Research Association, New Orleans.

Doyle, W., & Carter, K. (1984). Academic tasks in classrooms. *Curriculum Inquiry, 14*(2), 129–149.

Doyle, W., & Ponder, G. (1977). The practicality ethic in teacher decision-making. *Interchange, 8*(3), 1–12.

Doyle, W., Sanford, J., Schmidt-French, B., Emmer, E., & Clements, B. (1985). *Patterns of academic work in junior high school science, English, and mathematics classes: A final report* (R&D Rep. No. 6190). Austin: University of Texas, Research and Development Center for Teacher Education.

Dreeben, R. (1970). *The nature of teaching.* Glenview, IL: Scott, Foresman.

Driscoll, A., & Stevens, D. (1985). *Classroom teachers' response to the research on effective instruction.* Paper presented at the meeting of the American Educational Research Association, Chicago.

Duffy, G., & Roehler, L. (1986). *The evolving knowledge structures of five preservice teachers of reading.* Unpublished manuscript, Michigan State University, East Lansing, MI.

Eddy, E. (1969). *Becoming a teacher: The passage of professional status.* New York: Teachers College Press.

Elbaz, F. (1983). *Teacher thinking: A study of practical knowledge.* New York: Nichols.

Elbaz, F. (1987). Teachers' knowledge of teaching: Strategies for reflection. In J. Smyth (Ed.), *Educating teachers: Changing the nature of pedagogical knowledge* (pp. 45–53). London: Falmer.

Engle, R. W., & Bukstel, L. (1978). Memory processes among bridge players of differing expertise. *American Journal of Psychology, 91,* 673–689.

Ericsson, K., & Simon, H. (1980). Verbal reports as data. *Psychological Review, 87,* 215–151.

Feiman-Nemser, S., (1983). Learning to teach. In L. Shulman & G. Sykes (Eds.), *Handbook of teaching and policy.* New York: Longman.

Feiman-Nemser, S., & Buchmann, M. (1986). *When is student teaching teacher education?* (Research Series No. 178). East Lansing, MI: Michigan State University, Institute for Research on Teaching.

Feiman-Nemser, S., & Floden, R. (1986). The cultures of teaching. In M. C. Wittrock (Ed.), *Handbook of research on teaching* (3rd ed., pp. 505–526). New York: Macmillan.

Fenstermacher, G. D. (1986). Philosophy of research on teaching

Three aspects. In M. C. Wittrock (Ed.), *Handbook of research on teaching* (3rd ed., pp. 37–49). New York: Macmillan.

Fiske, S. T., Kinder, D. R., & Larter, W. M. (1983). The novice and the expert: Knowledge-based strategies in political cognition. *Journal of Experimental Social Psychology, 19*, 381–400.

Fuller, F. F. (1969). Concerns for teachers: A developmental conceptualization. *American Educational Research Journal, 6*, 207–226.

Gliessman, D. H. (1984). Changing teacher performance. In L. G. Katz & J. D. Raths (Eds.), *Advances in teacher education* (Vol. 1, pp. 95–111). Norwood, NJ: Ablex.

Gliessman, D. H., & Pugh, R. C. (1981). Developing teaching skills through understanding. *Action in teacher education, 3* (1), 11–18.

Gliessman, D. H., Pugh, R. C., & Bielat, B. (1979). Acquiring teaching skills through concept-based training. *Journal of Educational Research, 72*, 149–154.

Good, T. L., & Brophy, J. E. (1987). *Looking in classrooms* (4th ed.). New York: Harper & Row.

Gomez, M. (1988). *Prospective teachers' beliefs about good writing: What do they bring with them to teacher education?* Paper presented at the meeting of the American Educational Research Association, New Orleans.

Gonzalez, L. (in progress). *Learning about classroom events: A study of student teachers' developing understandings about teaching.*

Grant, G. (1987). *Transforming content knowledge into work tasks: Teaching reasoning in four subject areas.* Paper presented at the meeting of the American Educational Research Association, Washington, DC.

Grant, G. (1988). *Teacher knowledge and classroom organization: Managing critical thinking tasks.* Paper presented at the meeting of the American Educational Research Association, New Orleans.

Griffin, G. (1986). Issues in student teaching: A review. In J. Raths & L. Katz (Eds.), *Advances in teacher education* (Vol. 2, pp. 239–273). Norwood, NJ: Ablex.

Grossman, P. (1987). *A tale of two teachers: The role of subject matter orientation in teaching.* Paper presented at the meeting of the American Educational Research Association, Washington, DC.

Grossman, P. & Richert, R. (1988). Unacknowledged knowledge growth: A reexamination of the effects of teacher education. *Teaching and Teacher Education, 4*, 53–62.

Gudmundsdottir, S. (in press). Pedagogical models of subject matter. In J. Brophy (Ed.), *Advances in research on teaching.* Greenwich, CT: JAI Press.

Hollingsworth, S. (1988). *Toward a developmental model of learning to teach reading.* Paper presented at the meeting of the American Educational Research Association, New Orleans.

Housner, L. D., & Griffey, D. C. (1985). Teacher cognition: Differences in planning and interactive decision-making between experienced and inexperienced teachers. *Research Quarterly for Exercise and Sport, 56*, 45–53.

Hoy, W. (1968). The influence of experience on the beginning teacher. *School Review, 76*, 312–323.

Hoy, W., & Woolfolk, A. (1989). Supervising student teachers. In A. E. Woolfolk (Ed.), *Research perspectives on the graduate preparation of teachers* (pp. 108–131). Englewood Cliffs, N.J.: Prentice-Hall.

Jackson, P. (1968). *Life in classrooms.* New York: Holt, Rinehart & Winston.

Janesick, V. (1977). *An ethnographic study of a teacher's classroom perspective.* Unpublished doctoral dissertation, Michigan State University, East Lansing.

Kroma, S. (1983). *Personal practical knowledge of language in teaching: An ethnographic study.* Unpublished doctoral dissertation, University of Toronto, Toronto.

Kounin, J. S. (1970). *Discipline and group management in classrooms.* New York: Holt, Rinehart & Winston.

Lampert, M. (1985). How do teachers manage to teach? Perspectives on problems in practice. *Harvard Educational Review, 55*, 178–184.

Larkin, J., McDermott, J., Simon, D. P., & Simon, H. A. (1980). Expert and novice performance in solving physics problems. *Science, 208*, 1335–1342.

Leinhardt, G., & Greeno, J. G. (1986). The cognitive skill of teaching. *Journal of Educational Psychology, 78*, 75–79.

Leinhardt, G., & Smith, D. (1985). Expertise in mathematic instruction: Subject matter knowledge. *Journal of Educational Psychology, 77*(3), 247–271.

Lortie, D. (1975). *Schoolteacher: A sociological study.* Chicago: University of Chicago Press.

Marland, P. (1977). *A study of teachers' interactive thoughts.* Unpublished doctoral dissertation, University of Alberta, Edmonton, Canada.

Michelson, S. (1985). *A descriptive study of preservice teachers' conceptual change during reading methods instruction.* Unpublished doctoral dissertation, Michigan State University, East Lansing.

Michelson, S. (1987). *Evolving patterns of preservice teachers' knowledge structures.* Paper presented at the meeting of the American Educational Research Association, Washington, DC.

Morine-Dershimer, G. (1988). Premises in the practical arguments of preservice teachers. *Teaching and Teacher Education, 4*, 215–229.

Morine-Dershimer, G. (1989). *Peer teaching model lessons and free-style lessons.* Paper presented at the annual meeting of the American Educational Research Association, San Francisco.

Munby, H. (1986). Metaphor in the thinking of teachers: An exploratory study. *Journal of Curriculum Studies, 18*, 197–209.

Munby, H. (1987). Metaphor and teachers' knowledge. *Research in the Teaching of English, 21*, 377–397.

Munby, H. (1989). *Reflection in action and reflection on action.* Paper presented at the meeting of the American Educational Research Association, San Francisco.

Paine, L. (1988). *Prospective teachers' orientations towards diversity.* Paper presented at the meeting of the American Educational Research Association, New Orleans.

Patel, V. L., Frederiksen, C. H., & Groen, G. J. (1984). *Differences between experts and novices in a complex verbal task in a medical domain* (Report No. CME 84-3). Montreal: McGill University, Centre for Medical Education.

Peck, R. F., & Tucker, J. A. (1973). Research on teacher education. In R. M. W. Travers (Ed.), *Second handbook of research on teaching* (pp. 940–978). Chicago: Rand McNally.

Peterson, P., & Comeaux, M. (1987). Teachers' schemata for classroom events: The mental scaffolding of teachers' thinking during classroom instruction. *Teaching and Teacher Education, 3*, 319–331.

Pinnegar, S. (1988). *Throwing a hard ball into a stack of cotton: An examination of the term "with me."* Paper presented at the meeting of the American Educational Research Association, New Orleans.

Pinnegar, S. (1989). *Teachers' knowledge of students and classrooms.* Unpublished doctoral dissertation, University of Arizona, Tucson.

Putnam, R. T. (1987). Structuring and adjusting content for students: A study of live and simulated tutoring of addition. *American Educational Research Journal, 24*, 13–48.

Richardson, V. (1989). The evolution of reflective teaching and teacher education. In R. Clift, W. R. Houston, & M. Pugach (Eds.), *Encouraging reflective practice: An examination of issues and exemplars.* New York: Teachers College Press.

Richardson, V., & Anders, P. (1988). *A study of teachers' research-based instruction of reading comprehension.* Paper presented at the meeting of the American Educational Research Association, New Orleans.

Richardson-Koehler, V. (1988). Barriers to the effective supervision of student teachers: A field study. *Journal of Teacher Education, 39*(2), 28–34.

Richardson-Koehler, V., & Fenstermacher, G. (1988). *The use of practical arguments in staff development.* Paper presented at the annual meeting of the American Association of Colleges of Teacher Education, New Orleans.

Richert, A. (1987). *The voices within: Knowledge and experience in teacher education.* Paper presented at the conference of the American Educational Research Association Special Interest Group for Women and Education, Portland, OR.

Roehler, L., Duffy, G., Conley, M., Hermann, B., Johnson, J., & Michelson, S. (1987). *Exploring preservice teachers' knowledge structures.* Paper presented at the meeting of the American Educational Research Association, Washington, DC.

Rohrkemper, M. (in press). Self-regulated learning and academic achievement: A Vygotskian view. In D. Schunk & B. Zimmerman (Eds.), *Self-regulated learning and academic achievement: Theory, research, and practice.* New York: Springer-Verlag.

Ropo, E. (1987). *Teachers' conceptions of teaching and teaching behavior: Some differences between expert and novice teachers.* Paper presented at the meeting of the American Educational Research Association, Washington, DC.

Rumelhart, D. E., & Norman, D. A. (1978). Accretion, tuning, and restructuring: Three modes of learning. In J. W. Cotton & R. L. Klatzky (Eds.), *Semantic factors in cognition.* Hillsdale, NJ: Lawrence Erlbaum.

Russell, T. (1989). *The roles of research knowledge and knowing-in-action in teachers' development of professional knowledge.* Paper presented at the annual meeting of the American Educational Research Association, San Francisco.

Russell, T., & Johnston, P. (1988). *Teachers' learning from experiences of teaching: Analysis based on metaphor and reflection.* Paper presented at the meeting of the American Educational Research Association, New Orleans.

Russell, T., Munby, H., Spafford, C., & Johnston, P. (1988). Learning the professional knowledge of teaching. In P. Grimmett & G. L. Erickson (Eds.), *Reflection in teacher education.* Vancouver: Pacific Press.

Schön, D. (1983). *The reflective practitioner: How professionals think in action.* New York: Basic Books.

Schwille, S., & Melnick, S. (1987). *Teachers' professional growth and school life: An uneasy alliance.* Paper presented at the meeting of the American Educational Research Association, Washington, DC.

Shavelson, R. (1983). Review of research on teachers' pedagogical judgments, plans and decisions. *Elementary School Journal, 83,* 392–413.

Shulman, J., & Nelson, L. (Eds.). (1989). *Case methods in teacher education.* San Francisco: Far West Laboratory for Educational Research and Development.

Shulman, L. (1986). Those who understand: Knowledge growth in teaching. *Educational Research, 15,* 4–14.

Shulman, L. (1987). Knowledge and teaching: Foundations of the new reform. *Harvard Educational Review, 57*(1), 1–21.

Shulman, L., & Sykes, G. (1986). *A national board for teaching? In search of a bold standard: A report for the task force on teaching as a profession.* New York: Carnegie Corporation.

Simon, H. A. (1979). Information processing models of cognition. *Annual Review of Psychology, 30,* 363–396.

Smith, L. M., & Geoffrey, W. (1968). *The complexities of an urban classroom.* New York: Holt, Rinehart & Winston.

Smylie, M. (1989). Teachers' views of the effectiveness of sources of learning to teach. *Elementary School Journal, 89,* 543–548.

Steinberg, R., Haymore, J., & Marks, R. (1985). *Teachers' knowledge and structuring content in mathematics.* Paper presented at the meeting of the American Educational Research Association, Chicago.

Tamir, P. (1988). Subject matter and related pedagogical knowledge in teacher education. *Teaching and Teacher Education, 4,* 99–110.

Wagner, A. C. (1973). Changing teacher behavior: A comparison of microteaching and cognitive discrimination training. *Journal of Educational Psychology, 64,* 299–305.

Watts, D. (1987). Student teaching. In M. Haberman & J. M. Backus (Eds.), *Advances in teacher education* (Vol. 3, pp. 151–167). Norwood, NJ: Ablex.

Waxman, H. C., & Walberg, H. J. (1986). Effects of early field experiences. In J. D. Raths & L. G. Katz (Eds.), *Advances in teacher education* (Vol. 2, pp., 165–184). Norwood, NJ: Ablex.

Weinstein, C. (1988). Preservice teachers' expectations about the first year of teaching. *Teaching and Teacher Education, 4,* 31–40.

Wickman, E. K. (1928). *Childrens' behavior and teachers' attitudes.* New York: Commonwealth Fund.

Wilson, S., & Wineburg, S. (1988). Peering at history through different lenses: The role of disciplinary perspectives in teaching history. *Teachers College Record, 89* (4), 525–539.

Woods, P. (1987). Life histories and teacher knowledge. In J. Smyth (Ed.), *Educating teachers: Changing the nature of pedagogical knowledge* (pp. 121–135). London: Falmer.

Woolfolk, A. (1989). Graduate preparation of teachers: The debate and beyond. In A. E. Woolfolk (Ed.), *Research perspectives on the graduate preparation of teachers* (pp. 1–11). Englewood Cliffs N.J.: Prentice-Hall.

Wright, B., & Tuska, S. (1968). From dream to life in the psychology of becoming a teacher. *School Review, 76*(3), 253–293.

Yinger, R. (1986). *Examining thought in action: A theoretical and methodological critique of research on interactive teaching.* Paper presented at the meeting of the American Educational Research Association, San Francisco.

Yinger, R. (1987). *By the seat of your pants: An inquiry into improvisation in teaching.* Paper presented at the meeting of the American Educational Research Association, Washington, DC.

Yinger, R., & Villar, L. (1986). *Studies of teachers' thought-in-action: A progress report.* Paper presented at the meeting of the International Study Association on Teacher Thinking, Leuven, Belgium.

Zeichner, K. (1986). Individual and institutional influences on the development of teacher perspectives. In J. Raths & L. Katz (Eds.), *Advances in teacher education* (Vol. 2, pp. 135–163). Norwood, NJ: Ablex.

Zeichner, K. (1987). The ecology of field-experience: Toward an understanding of the role of field experiences in teacher development. In M. Haberman & J. M. Backus (Eds.), *Advances in teacher education* (Vol. 3, pp. 94–117). Norwood, NJ: Ablex.

Zeichner, K., & Tabachnick, B. (1985). The development of teacher perspectives: Social strategies and institutional control in the socialization of beginning teachers. *Journal of Education for Teachers, 11,* 1–25.

Zimpher, N. (1987). Current trends in research on university supervision of student teaching. In M. Haberman & J. M. Backus (Eds.), *Advances in Teacher Education* (Vol. 3, pp. 118–150). Norwood, NJ: Ablex.

·18·

TEACHER DEVELOPMENT

Paul R. Burden

Knowledge of the characteristics of teachers is important to teacher education for three reasons. It can provide a foundation upon which teacher educators can diagnose needs and abilities, offer a guide for ways to support teachers, and help select teacher developmental objectives that focus on short-term or long-term personal growth (McNergney & Carrier, 1981, p. 120). Knowledge of teachers' personal and professional developmental changes can help teacher educators understand the needs and abilities of teachers at different points in their careers and can serve as a basis for planning interventions to promote developmental growth.

TEACHERS' CAREER DEVELOPMENT

Development generally refers to the phenomenon of change in form over time. This change usually is from relatively simple to complex forms; it often proceeds through stages, and transitions between stages are frequently viewed as relatively irreversible. The forces behind the changes are believed to be maturational factors within the individual and interactional factors between personal characteristics and environmental stimulation (Charlesworth, 1972). The terms *phase* and *stage* are very similar. A phase is any stage in a series of changes, as in development. A stage is a period in a process of development.

Although adult development is not a fully articulated concept, an increasing amount of information has been generated about phases of adult life and adult developmental characteristics. Those who select teaching as a career exhibit these phases and developmental characteristics, as do all other adults. In addition, teachers express different professional skills, knowledge, behaviors, attitudes, and concerns during their careers. Taken together, this information can help teacher educators understand the needs and abilities of teachers as they advance through their careers.

Adult Development

As individuals move through life from youth to old age, changes constantly take place within them, as well as within the setting in which they live and work. To understand teacher development, it is important to understand the interaction of physiological, psychological, and social aspects of human development.

Baltes and Goulet (1970) and A. K. Chickering (1974) divide adult-development theorists into two basic groups: (a) developmental-age theorists, who examine sections of the age span; and (b) developmental-stage theorists, who examine various psychological processes related to age. Actually, the distinction between age and stage theorists is not totally discrete. Rather, age is the major variable for some theorists, whereas stages in the structure of thinking are the major variable for others.

Developmental Ages. In reviewing adult-development literature, Bents and Howey (1981) state that age theorists are interested in determining if there are concerns, problems, and tasks common to most or all adults at various times in their lives. A. K. Chickering (1974) notes that some researchers take chronological age as a major variable and search for general orientations, problems, developmental tasks, personal concerns, or other characteristics associated with particular ages or times. These researchers are also concerned with explaining why certain concerns, problems, and tasks loom more prominently at one time of life than another and how these affect adult behavior. Age theorists discuss adult development in such terms as life periods, passages, stages of life, and periods of transition.

Recent reviews of literature attempt to identify different types of developmental-age theorists. Oja (1980) notes that age-related developmental task models are suggested by (a) life-age theorists such as Gould, Levinson, and Sheehy, who consider roles, tasks, and coping behaviors needed at certain times of life; and (b) life-cycle theorists such as Erikson, Neu-

The author thanks reviewers Peter J. Burke (University of Wisconsin—Madison) and John M. Johnston (Memphis State University).

garten, and Havinghurst, who emphasize the experiences adults encounter through various ages and cycles of life.

Age-linked developmental periods have been proposed by many theorists. Levinson, Darrow, Klein, Levinson, and McKee (1978) identified periods of transition in the lives of men and described the timing of typical life events. Gould (1972, 1978) detailed a similar set of stages of life. Sheehy (1976) popularized these concepts of age-linked behavior as she described passages in adults' lives.

The general pattern of adult development that Levinson, Gould, and Sheehy described begins with the transition in the late teens and early twenties from adolescence to adulthood. The mid-twenties is a period of provisional adulthood in which first commitments to work, marriage, and family, and to other adult responsibilities are lived out. These initial commitments are reexamined and their meaning questioned in another transitional period in the late twenties and early thirties. At that time, long-range implications of continuing with current work, spouse, community, and life-style become apparent. Changes must be made in some cases; reaffirmation and renewed commitment occur in others. The thirties are a time for settling down, for achievement, and for becoming one's own person. Time becomes more finite in the forties. The limits of success and achievement become apparent, and mid-life transition is at hand. Major questions concerning priorities and values are examined. Friends, relatives, and spouse become increasingly important as restabilization occurs during the late forties and fifties. Personal interests receive more attention. Mellowing and an increasing investment in personal relationships characterize the fifties.

Krupp (1981), deeply influenced by Levinson, describes adult growth as a sequence of overlapping stages. Each of these periods can be stable or transitional. Krupp notes that individuals make key decisions in stable periods and that, in transitional periods, individuals question, reappraise, explore possibilities, and move toward new commitments. According to Krupp, stable and transitional periods alternate throughout life.

Bernice Neugarten has elaborated the roles of age and the timing of life events in adult development more than any other theorist (A. W. Chickering, 1976, p. 65). She has examined adult life in terms of development of the personality, age norms, sociology, and psychology. She stated that time, rather than age, is the critical variable in adult development. When normal events such as children's leaving home were "on time," they were not experienced as crises. Therefore, the timing of life events provides some of the most powerful cues to adult personality and behavior.

Erikson (1959, 1963), a life-cycle theorist, charted the course of personality development by proposing eight universal stages of psychosocial growth for the human life span. Each stage represented a major crisis—a challenge or a turning point—faced in the normal course of life that dealt with the needs to trust, to assert independence, to resolve guilt, to form bonds with others, to find solitude, to produce, to work with strength and conviction, and to know oneself. The last three stages typically occur in adulthood. Each crisis is considered to be salient at a particular age period, and optimal development is characterized by a sequence of eight successful resolutions. Although the sequence forms a logical series of stages, the stages are not hierarchial and can occur at any time in life. Although they are not necessarily related to particular ages, Erikson indicated general time periods when the crises occur (e.g., adolescence, early adulthood, middle adulthood).

Developmental Stages. Stage theorists focus on distinct or qualitative differences in modes of thinking at various points in development that are not necessarily age related. The different structures, or ways of thinking, form an invariant sequence or progression in individual development. Bents and Howey (1981) note that these structural changes provide insight into what information individuals tend to use, how they use information, and the types of interactions they might have with the environment.

Drawing upon Piaget's writing, Kohlberg (1973) describes characteristics of stages: (a) Stages imply distinct or qualitative differences in structures (modes of thinking) that perform the same function (e.g., intelligence) at various points in development; (b) different structures form an invariant sequence in individual development. Although factors might accelerate, slow, or stop development, the sequence does not change; (c) each of these different and sequential modes of thought forms a structural whole; (d) stages are hierarchial integrations. Higher stages reintegrate the structures found at lower stages. Kohlberg's notion of stage involves changes in quality, competence, and form as one moves from one stage to another, rather than changes in quantity, performance, and content. Structural change tells less about *what* information people process but more about *how* they use that information; less about *what* people are performing but more about *how* they are performing; and less about *what* they are thinking but more about *how* they are thinking (Willie & Howey, 1980, p. 29).

Piaget, Kohlberg, Loevinger, Hunt, and Perry are among the stage theorists who view adult development in individuals as a definite progression from concrete, undifferentiating, simple, unstructured patterns of thought to more abstract, differentiating, and complex patterns of thought. Table 18-1 displays these theorists and the domains of developmental stages of human growth.

Piaget's (1963) framework provides a means of understanding cognitive growth and how people understand the physical world of time, space, and causality. Kohlberg (1969) emphasizes moral development as people change in their orientations toward authority, others, and self when making decisions. Loevinger (1966) examines ego development and describes how adults pass through stages as they try to understand themselves. Adults move from conformity to emotional independence and, finally, to a state in which individuals reconcile inner conflicts, renounce the unattainable, cherish individuality, and find their identity. Hunt (1971) reports that more advanced conceptual systems have been associated with creativity, a greater cognitive flexibility, a wider range of coping behaviors, and a greater tolerance for stress.

Perry (1970) describes stages of intellectual and ethical development in which individuals move from dualistic thinking with a right-or-wrong perspective, to relativistic thinking in

TABLE 18–1. Domains of Developmental Stages

Theorist	Piaget (1963)	Kohlberg (1969)	Loevinger (1966)	Hunt (1971)	Perry (1970)	Selman (1980)
Domains	Cognitive	Value/Moral	Ego/Self	Conceptual	Epistemological Ethical	Interpersonal Development
Stages	Sensori-motor	Obedience–Punishment (1)	Presocial Impulsive	Unsocialized Impulsive		Unilateral relations
	Preoperational	Naively Egotistic (2)	Self-protective	Concrete Dogmatic		Bilateral relations
	Concrete	Social Conformity (3)	Conformist	Dependent Abstract	Dualist	Homogeneous relations
	Formal Substage I	Authority-Maintaining (4)	Conscientious		Relativist	
	Formal Substage II	Principles Reasoning (5 and 6)	Autonomous	Self-directed Abstract	Committed-Relativist	Pluralistic relations

Note. Adapted from "The Teacher as an Adult Learner: A Cognitive-Developmental View," by N. A. Sprinthall and L. Thies-Sprinthall (1983). In G. A. Griffin (Ed.), Staff Development (Eighty-second yearbook of the National Society for the Study of Education, pp. 13–35). Chicago: NSSE, 1983. Copyright 1983. Reprinted by permission.

which the world of knowledge is seen as relativistic and uncertainty becomes legitimate, and, finally, to the point at which individuals make choices to define their identity.

Harvey, Hunt, and Schroeder (1961) developed a cognitive-stage model that dealt with the pattern of beliefs, attitudes, and values through which one interprets experience. Four conceptual stages were proposed, in which individuals (a) are viewed as basically self-centered, with an orientation toward external causality and the primacy of concrete rules; (b) can examine themselves apart from external standards and conditions; (c) move to an even more personal introspection; and (d) achieve a more integrated and truly independent set of internal standards that might or might not coincide with cultural norms and external pressures. Selman (1980) describes four stages of interpersonal development: (a) unilateral relations, (b) bilateral relations, (c) homogeneous relations, and (d) pluralistic relations.

Effects of Adult Development on Teaching Performance. A comprehensive set of studies concerning adult teachers was conducted in natural settings by David Hunt (1971) and associates at the Ontario Institute for Studies in Education. Teachers who were assessed at more advanced developmental stages (in terms of their conceptual level) were more effective as classroom teachers. For example, teachers at higher stages of development functioned in the classroom at a more complex level. They were more adaptive in their teaching style, more flexible, and more tolerant. These teachers also were more responsive to individual differences and used a variety of teaching models such as lectures, small group discussions, inquiry, and role playing. They were more emphatic, in that they could more accurately read and respond to the emotions of their students. Overall, they provided a wide and varied learning environment for their students.

Additional studies have established the relationship between conceptual level and teaching style. Research by Harvey, Hunt, Joyce, and colleagues suggests that teachers at higher conceptual levels are more flexible, more tolerant of stress, and more adaptive than teachers at lower levels (Harvey 1966, 1967, 1970; Hunt, et al., 1974). Furthermore, teachers at higher stages might be able to assume multiple perspectives, to use a wide variety of coping behaviors, to employ a broader repertoire of teaching models, and, consequently, to be more effective with a wider range of leaning styles and with students from diverse cultural backgrounds (Harvey, Prather, White, & Hoffmeister, 1968; Hunt, 1966, 1975).

Hunt and Joyce (1967) found significant positive correlations between indexes of reflective teaching (use of learner's frame of reference to plan, initiate, and evaluate performance) and conceptual level. Teachers at higher conceptual levels could create a great variety of learning environments and use a variety of teaching approaches. High conceptual teachers also were more helpful to students in evaluating information and generating hypotheses than low conceptual level teachers. Joyce, Weil, and Wald (1973) also report that a teacher's ability to use a variety of educational environments is positively correlated with higher conceptual level scores.

Studies by Tomlinson and Hunt (1971) and Gordon (1976) revealed that low conceptual level preservice teachers preferred to teach using a rule–example order (general principles or rules stated first and then examples given), whereas high conceptual level teachers preferred using an example–rule order (first providing an example and then determining a rule or principle to govern the example). Other studies reported that high conceptual level teachers are more stress tolerant (Suedfeld, 1974), better able to look at a problem from multiple perspectives (Wolfe, 1963), and function best with discovery types of learning (McLachlan & Hunt, 1973).

Recognizing the relationship between higher conceptual levels and effective teaching performance, Sprinthall and Thies-Sprinthall (1980b, 1983a, 1983b) also effectively assert that a theoretical framework must be established for educating teachers for continued cognitive development and that consideration must be given in the training model to the teacher as an adult learner.

Teacher Development

Teacher career development deals with changes that teachers experience throughout their careers in (a) *job skills, knowledge, and behaviors* in such areas as teaching methods; discipline techniques; curriculum; lesson plans; rules and procedures; and relationships with students, colleagues, supervisors, parents, and other members of the school community; (b) *attitudes, expectations, and concerns* in such areas as attitudes toward self and others; images of teaching; professional confidence and maturity; commitment to teaching; and satisfactions, beliefs, and concerns; and (c) *job events* in such areas as changes in grade level, school, or district; breaks in service; involvement in additional professional responsibilities such as serving on committees or in teacher associations or as department head; involvement in professional development programs; entry into and retirement from teaching; and achieving honors, titles (e.g., master teacher), or other forms of recognition.

Reports of Teachers' Developmental Stages. A number of research studies provide descriptions of various aspects of teacher development. Motivated by a desire to make teacher education more relevant, Frances Fuller and her associates at the University of Texas at Austin (Fuller, 1969; Fuller & Bown, 1975; Fuller, Parsons, & Watkins, 1973; George, 1978) examined the nature of teacher concerns. In the original work, Fuller (1969) presents the results of two of her studies and reviews the results of a number of related studies conducted by other researchers. When drawing conclusions about all of these reports, she proposes a four-stage developmental model of teacher concerns in the process by becoming a teacher. First was the preteaching phase of no concerns, second was the early teaching phase of concerns about self, and third was the late phase of concerns about pupils. Based on subsequent data gathering and analysis, these stages were revised and explained by Fuller and Bown (1975) as a developmental sequence of concerns. For preteaching concerns in the first stage, preservice teachers identify realistically with pupils but only in fantasy with teachers. In the second stage, there are early concerns about survival in which idealized concerns are replaced by concerns about their own survival as teachers and concerns with class control and mastery of content to be taught. For the third stage, teachers have concerns about their teaching performance, about limitations and frustrations of the teaching situation, and about demands being made on them. In the fourth stage, teachers have concerns about the learning, social, and emotional needs of the pupils and about their own ability to relate to pupils as individuals. Fuller and Brown said

these "stages" are described mainly in terms of what the teachers are concerned about, rather than what they actual accomplish. Whether the stages were distinct or overlapping has not been established.

The theories of Fuller and her associates have been further investigated in studies (e.g., Adams, 1982; Adams, Hutchinson, & Martray, 1980; Briscoe, 1972/1973; Pataniczek, 1978/1979; Ryan et al., 1980) designed to document the actual concerns of teachers and how these vary according to a teacher's year of service or according to grade level of the teaching assignment. Adams (1982) reports that the results of a 5-year longitudinal study generally support Fuller's early stages of concern about self and about instructional tasks. But Adams suggests that there might be an error in Fuller's theory about impact or pupil concerns, because his study indicated no significant differences in impact concerns across years of experience. Adams also reports significant differences between elementary and secondary teachers for the stages of concern about self, about instructional tasks, and about pupil impact. In each case, elementary teachers reported greater concerns.

Sitter and Lanier (1982) report that their research on student teachers supports the work of Frances Fuller in that "commonalities" of concern were expressed by people engaged in the process of learning to teach. In contrast with the results of the Fuller research, however, the commonalities did not occur in clusters and did not occur sequentially. Concerns about self, survival, teaching tasks, pupil learning, materials, and curriculum development occurred simultaneously and were dealt with concurrently by the student teachers. They perceived the student-teaching experience as a time to consolidate and integrate these concerns into a whole, a time to "put it all together."

Other studies on the process of becoming a teacher have identified stages of development. Sacks and Harrington (1982) label six stages as students prepare for and move through student teaching: (a) anticipation, (b) entry, (c) orientation, (d) trial and error, (e) integration/consolidation, and (f) mastery. From this study of student teachers, Sacks and Harrington conclude that identification of the stages and the associated student behaviors and feelings would make early remediation of problems possible. They recommend intervention strategies for seminars and individual conferences appropriate to each stage. These strategies would start with a focus on details of the student-teaching assignment and end with a focus on specific teaching behaviors.

Based on his work with student teachers in seminars and on his reading of student logs, Caruso (1977) discusses phases of feelings that student teachers had about themselves and about their experiences as they continued in student teaching. These feelings affected the development of the student teachers' personal and professional identities. Caruso notes that the phases were not mutually exclusive and that there was much overlap. He gave these phases the following labels: (a) anxiety/euphoria, (b) confusion/clarity, (c) competence/inadequacy, (d) criticism/new awareness, (e) more confidence/greater inadequacy, and (f) loss/relief.

Research by Iannaccone (1963) indicates that student teaching is a transitional period in the making of a teacher. Three stages of this transition are identified in terms of the social distance between the student teacher and the cooperating (critic) teacher. Changes in the student teachers' perceptions concerning classroom management and levels of expectations were also identified.

Burden (1979/1980a, 1980b) reports experienced elementary teachers' perceptions of their personal and professional development for their entire careers. Limitations of the study include the fact that the data were self-selected by the teachers as they recounted the events in their careers, that the sample included only teachers with certain demographic characteristics (e.g., elementary teachers in suburban school districts), and that only teachers who had continued to teach were interviewed. In spite of the limitations, the study contributes to an understanding of teachers' professional development by providing details of teachers' experiences. Teachers reported that they passed through three stages in their teaching careers. Stage 1, a *survival stage*, occurred during the first year of teaching. Teachers reported their limited knowledge of teaching activities and environment: They were subject centered and felt they had little professional insight; they lacked confidence and were unwilling to try new methods; and they found themselves conforming to their preconceived image of "teacher." Stage 2, an *adjustment stage*, occurred for these teachers in the second through fourth years. The teachers reported that during this period they were learning a great deal about planning and organization and about children, curriculum, and methods. They started to see children's complexities and sought new teaching techniques to meet the wider range of needs they found. The teachers became more open and genuine with children and believed they were meeting pupils' needs more capably. The teachers gradually gained confidence in themselves. Stage 3, the *mature stage*, comprised the fifth and subsequent years of teaching. Teachers in this stage felt they had a good command of teaching activities and the environment. They were more child centered, felt confident and secure, and were willing to try new teaching methods. They found that they had gradually abandoned their former image of "teacher," had gained professional insight, and thought they could handle most new situations that might arise. Because teachers who dropped out of teaching were not included in the study, it is possible that they had followed a different developmental pattern than those who continued to teach.

Field (1979) interviewed teachers and found three identifiable stages in their development. For each stage, broad descriptions were provided in each of the following dimensions: planning the day, arranging the classroom, planning for large groups, diagnosis, record keeping, parent conferences, unstructured time, behavior of children, self-evaluation, and self-concept. The detailed descriptions included changes in skills and perceptions. Stage 1 was characterized by day-to-day survival, hit-or-miss solutions to problems, and intense feelings of inadequacy. In Stage 2, teachers expressed increased self-confidence and feelings of self worth. Success provided them with some appropriate and reliable solutions to problems, and teachers in stage 2 extended the boundaries of their planning beyond one day at a time to weeks in advance. At Stage 3, teachers viewed learning as a whole process, not as something

to be divided into subjects or blocks of time. Teachers felt at home in the classroom and saw children as people, not just pupils. Field indicates that transition from one stage to another is not clear; new problems might cause teachers to have feelings of regression to an earlier stage, whereas successes could have a reverse effect. The descriptions of the stages were meant to serve as a continuum for identifying where teachers are and where they are going.

Anthony Gregorc (1973) and the leadership team at University High School in Urbana, Illinois, studied the behavior of teachers to determine patterns of development. They identified four stages—becoming, growing, maturing, and the fully functioning professional—and provided a detailed chart of the teachers' professional behaviors, knowledge and techniques, and values, beliefs, and needs at each stage. Teachers in the *becoming stage* demonstrated an ambivalent commitment to teaching. They began to develop initial concepts about the purposes of education, the nature of teaching, the role expectations in the educational process, and the role of the school as a social organization. They had limited perceptions of the complexity of the work environment and felt that their job was to share knowledge with students, get through the book, do what the principal said, and be protective of their students. The level of commitment for teachers in the *growing stage* tended to be based on their minimal expectations of the school and the school of them. Their basic concepts and stereotypes of the educational process, of their discipline, and of their responsibilities were forming. Teachers had increased knowledge about students, curricula, materials and equipment, and themselves. Gregorc suggests that teachers who reach this stage and stop developing might reject new experiences, whereas others might progress to advanced stages. Teachers in the *maturing stage* had made a strong commitment to education, functioned beyond minimum expectations, and drew upon and contributed to the varied resources of the school. Teachers reconsidered instructional objectives and altered teaching techniques, materials, and attitudes about roles played in the educational process. They reexamined concepts about education, themselves, others, subject matter, and the environment. This period of reexamination can be stressful, yet it can also be exhilarating as new insights are gained. Teachers at the *fully functioning professional stage* had made a definite commitment to the education profession, were immersed in the process of education, and tried to realize their full potential as individual teachers and as contributing members of the profession. They constantly tested and restructured their concepts and beliefs.

Newman (1978/1979) interviewed 10 public school teachers who ranged in teaching experience from 19 to 31 years, to obtain their perceptions of their career development. Several stages emerged from the teachers' experiences in this cross-sectional study in the dimensions of work history, graduate study, teaching, professional membership, and satisfaction. Newman used 10-year periods of time in teaching to discuss changes that the teachers reported. The first 10 years of teaching involved several changes in schools, levels, and subjects taught. Many women took breaks in service to raise families. Graduate study was done, and there was reconsideration and reaffirmation of the decision to teach. The teachers were highly satisfied and had achieved a feeling of professional maturity. The second 10 years of teaching found most teachers settled in one school system, grade level, and subject. They experienced highs and lows in their satisfactions. Toward the end of the second 10 years of teaching, some felt themselves getting into a rut and changed schools and/or grade levels in an attempt to revitalize themselves. Several experienced a decline in satisfaction. The third 10 years of teaching brought a continuation of the stability in the work situation, but the teachers felt moderately dissatisfied. As they looked back over their careers, they realized they had become more personal in their relationships with students, more flexible in their dealings with student behavior, and less energetic. They were thoughtful and troubled as they faced the early retirement decision. The teachers saw their careers being significantly affected by contemporary history.

Peterson (1978/1979) used a structured interview with 50 retired secondary school teachers to find out how teachers' attitudes and outlooks changed throughout their careers. From the personal changes the teachers described, Peterson said the teaching career could be divided into three phases. The first phase, from the approximate age of 20 to 40, involved considerable shifts in commitment to teaching, job morale, and other outlooks. Teachers were in the process of establishing themselves in their careers, finding the optimal school environment, and beginning and raising their families. This period of ups and downs for teachers appeared to end when they found a school that gave them the chance to put down roots and begin a phase of professional commitment and growth. Teachers in the second phase, ages 40 to 55, seemed to be at their professional peak, as they exhibited high morale and commitment to teaching. The final phase, from age 55 to retirement, was marked by withdrawal from the teaching profession as energy and enthusiasm faded. Teachers were able to maintain high job morale but were aware of the effects of biological aging.

Based on their experiences with teachers and teacher education, Yarger and Mertens (1980) describe a continuum of career stages that teachers experience. These career stages were identified on the basis of analysis of working conditions that teachers meet throughout their career, including the need to be evaluated, credentialed, and tenured and the need to adjust to new policies, procedures, and innovations in both teaching and organization.

Yarger and Mertens (1980) also provide a detailed description of inservice programming that would be appropriate to meet the needs at each professional stage. The preeducation student, at Stage 1, examines the teaching career but is not yet committed. The education student, at stage 2, typically a junior or senior student, has made a conscious decision and a commitment to become a teaching professional and develops basic teaching skills. In the first year of teaching, the initial teacher, at stage 3, moves from the relative security of a training program to the demands of the teaching profession. Concerns about classroom discipline, further development of pedagogical skills, and receiving specific, immediate feedback characterize this stage. The developing teacher, at stage 4, during the second and third year of teaching, still has initial concerns, but new concerns also emerge about content and gaps in previous training. These teachers start to recognize that the teaching environment continually changes. The practicing teacher, at stage 5 (3–8 years of experience), is more stable. At this stage teachers are apt to have completed requirements for advanced certification, tenure, and even advanced degrees. Content expertise is a high priority, as well as preparation for a new professional role such as department chairperson, team leader, or administrator. At stage 6, teachers with at least eight years of experience are labeled experienced teachers by Yarger and Mertens. These teachers had already carved out their areas of particular strength and expertise and therefore had different needs for professional activities.

Katz (1972), on the basis of her work with preschool teachers, proposes that there might be at least four developmental stages for the professional growth of teachers. As she describes the characteristics of teachers, Katz also identifies the type of training assistance that would be appropriate at each stage. The length of time teachers spend in each stage can vary greatly. Teachers in stage 1, the *survival stage*, are mainly concerned about surviving, as they realize the discrepancy between their anticipated success and classroom realities. This stage could last throughout the first year of teaching, and teachers might feel inadequate and unprepared. On-site support and technical assistance would be appropriate at this stage. Teachers in stage 2, the *consolidation stage*, consolidate the gains made in the first stage, begin to focus on individual children, and differentiate specific tasks and skills to be mastered next. This stage can occur during the second year and continue into the third year. On-site assistance would be appropriate at this stage, with access to specialists and advice from colleagues, consultants, and advisors. Teachers in the *renewal stage*, stage 3, during the third or fourth years of teaching, might tire of doing the same things and want to look for innovations in the field. Training needs could be achieved through conferences, visits to demonstration projects, teachers' centers, journals, films, and critiques of their videotaped lessons. Katz suggests that some teachers might reach the *maturity stage*, the fourth one, within 3 years, whereas others might need 5 years or more. Teachers come to terms with themselves as teachers and ask deeper and more abstract questions. Training needs at this stage are met by seminars, institutes, courses, degree programs, books, journals, and conferences.

After reviewing the literature on teacher career development, Watts (1980) describes three stages of teacher development. The survival, or beginning, stage is characterized by the teacher's struggling with problems of personal and professional competence. Teachers in the middle stage show an increased sense of comfort and shift toward more child-centered activities. In the mastery stage, they function smoothly within the context of the school and their own experiences.

Based on their experience working with teachers, Unruh and Turner (1970) suggest that there are four periods of professional growth for teachers: (a) the *preservice period*—preparation at the high school and college level; (b) the *initial teaching period*—one to 6 years of service similar to the probationary period, though it can vary in length; (c) the *security period*—roughly 6 to 15 years of service, building upon the early years

TABLE 18–2. Preservice Teachers' Developmental Stages

Theorist	Fuller and Bown (1975)	Caruso (1977)	Yarger and Mertens (1980)	Sacks and Harrington (1982)
Stages	Preteaching Concerns	Anxiety/euphoria	Preeducation student	Anxiety
	Early concerns about survival	Confusion/clarity	The education student	Entry
	Teaching situation concerns	Competence/inadequacy		Orientation
	Concerns about pupils	Criticism/new awareness		Trial and error
		More confidence/ greater inadequacy		Integration/ consolidation
		Lost/relief		Mastery

of service; and (d) the *maturity period*—a continuing increase in competence and effectiveness.

Unruh and Turner indicate that some teachers could remain in the initial teaching period for many years, whereas others progress rapidly toward the maturity period. Teachers in the initial teaching period often have problems with discipline, routine and organization, scoring and marking papers, and curriculum development, while, at the same time, they are trying to gain acceptance from the rest of the staff. Teachers in the security period find security in their convictions and commitments. In this period, teachers are also devoted to seeking excellence in instruction, and they often seek ways to improve their background and to increase their personal knowledge. Teachers in the maturity period usually exhibit considerable depth in most phases of the professional life and are likely to be highly competent and feel quite secure in the performance of teaching duties. The attitude of the mature teacher permits change to be accepted as the dominant process of life rather than as a threat. The teachers recognize and accept the concept that a teacher never actually arrives.

McDonald (1982) suggests four stages in the professional development of a teacher: (a) the *transition stage*, during which there is a low sense of efficacy and there is elemental teaching, learning about pupils, and learning basic skills of managing and organizing; (b) the *exploring stage*, in which there is a sense of efficacy in using basic skills of teaching

and instruction is effectively managed; (c) the *invention and experimenting stage*, in which the teacher tries major strategies, invents new strategies and techniques, seeks opportunities for development, and is developing critical judgment; and (d) the *professional teaching stage*, when the teacher has problem-solving skill and is able to teach other teachers to be creative.

Summaries of many of these reports concerning stages of teachers' careers are displayed in Tables 18-2 and 18-3.

Critique of Stage Models

Helpful summaries and critiques of teacher-development literature are provided by Feiman and Floden (1980a, 1980b, 1981) and Floden and Feiman (1980, 1981a, 1981b). They identify three approaches to, or conceptions of, teacher development. The first, based largely on the work of Frances Fuller and her colleagues at the Research and Development Center for Teacher Education at the University of Texas at Austin, involves attempts to construct theories of teacher development. Based on the theory, training programs would use a diagnostic–prescriptive approach to match the intervention to the teacher's current concerns. The second approach involves efforts to apply existing cognitive-development theories to teacher development. Training programs would be built

TABLE 18–3. Inservice Teachers' Developmental Stages

Theorist	Unruh and Turner (1970)	Katz (1972)	Gregorc (1973)	Peterson (1978/1979)	Burden (1979/1980)	Yarger and Mertens (1980)	McDonald (1982)
Stages	Initial teaching	Survival	Becoming	First attitudinal phase (age 20–40)	Survival stage	The initial teacher	Transition stage
	Security	Consolidation	Growing	Second phase (age 40–55)	Adjustment stage	The developing teacher	Exploring stage
	Maturing	Renewal	Maturing	Third phase (age 55–retirement)	Mature stage	The practicing teacher	Invention and experimenting stage
		Maturity	The fully functioning professional			The experienced teacher	Professional teaching stage

around a disequilibrium model that seeks an optimal mismatch between the teacher's current and desired stages of development. The third approach contains descriptions of practices and efforts to justify them in developmental terms. Training programs would emphasize certain enabling conditions that support self-directed learning (Feiman & Floden, 1980a, 1980b).

Despite their differences, all three approaches emphasize certain aspects of teacher education generally underestimated in conventional programs and approaches. *First*, they acknowledge the reality of individual differences among preservice and inservice teachers and the necessity for more individualized training opportunities. *Second*, they focus on changes in teachers over time, which calls for interventions and support spread over time. *Third*, they take into account teachers' present needs and interests in developing appropriate interventions (Feiman & Floden, 1980a, p. 16).

Floden and Feiman (1981a, p. 6) note that two types of descriptions are needed to explain developmental theory for teacher change. The first is a description of the sequence of changes leading up to the end state, and the second is a description of the process or mechanism by which change is brought about. They conclude that most developmental theories are weakest in the descriptions of the mechanism for change (Feiman & Floden, 1980b). Floden and Feiman (1980, p. 22) also found weaknesses in the defenses of the criteria for all three approaches to teacher development. They raise questions about weaknesses in developmental-stage models and lack of clarity in the descriptions. The implied relationship between higher developmental stages and more effective instruction is also questioned.

Floden and Feiman (1981a, pp. 18–24) identify a number of uses of a theory of teacher development while recognizing that there is no single approach to development. A theory of teacher change could indicate what should be done to reach goals in a teacher education program. The theory could provide a description of the changes individuals must go through and the mechanism by which change occurs. The theory could also be used by teacher educators when arranging instructional content and sequence.

PROMOTING DEVELOPMENTAL GROWTH

When designing programs to promote teacher development, it is important to recognize how adults learn, how they prefer to learn, and what they want to learn. Principles of adult learning must be considered as aspects of instruction are developed. Furthermore, it is important to be able to assess teacher development over time.

Goals for Promoting Growth

Based on her study of ages and stages of the adult development of teachers, Oja (1980) proposes that staff-development programs be designed to allow for adult development in ego maturity, principled moral and ethical reasoning, and increased conceptual complexity.

Similarly, Howey (1985) indicates that there are six purposes of staff development: (a) continuing pedagogical development, (b) continuing understanding and discovery of self, (c) continuing cognitive development, (d) continuing theoretical development, (e) continuing professional development, and (f) continuing career development (p. 59).

Factors Affecting Teacher Career Development

Teacher career development is influenced by factors in both the personal and professional settings. As one result of a collaborative action research effort involving school-based and university personnel, Oja and Pine (1988) report that the teachers involved were positively affected in their views of school context, collegiality, and teacher skills and attitudes as action researchers. Collaborative action research stimulated adult cognitive development and was a process for linking theory with practice (Oja & Pine, 1983).

Fessler (1985) examined the dynamics of the teacher life cycle and identified three major spheres of influence: (a) the personal environment, (b) the career cycle, and (c) the organizational environment (see Figure 18-1).

Pedagogical Considerations

As efforts are made to promote teachers' developmental growth, adult learning principles and various aspects of instruction need to be considered. Furthermore, it might be useful to determine teachers' stages of development as instructional decisions are made.

Principles of Adult Learning. There are some generally accepted principles for facilitating adult learning, regardless of one's stage of development, that need to be considered in relation to promoting teacher development. These principles are based on the recognition that adults exhibit characteristics and learning needs significantly different from children's. According to Knowles (1978), these principles constitute "the foundation stones of modern adult learning theory":

1. Adults are motivated to learn as they experience needs and interests that learning will satisfy; therefore these needs and interests are appropriate starting points for organizing adult learning activities.
2. Adult orientation to learning is life-centered; therefore, the appropriate units for organizing adult learning are life situations, not subjects.
3. Experience is the richest resource for adult learning; therefore, the core methodology of adult education is the analysis of experience.
4. Adults have a deep need to be self-directed; therefore, the role of the teacher is to engage in a process of inquiry with adult learners rather than to transmit knowledge to them and then evaluate their conformity to it.
5. Individual differences among people increase with age; therefore, adult education must make optimal provision for differences in style, time, place, and pace of learning. (p. 31)

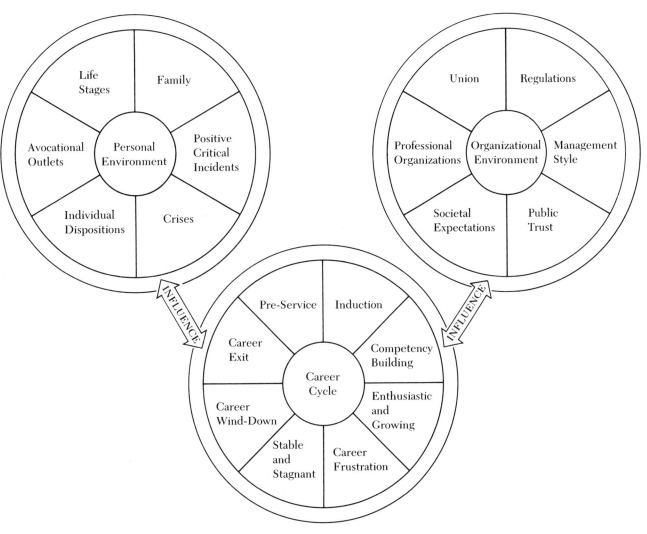

FIGURE 18–1. Dynamics of the Teacher Career Cycle

Note. From "A Model for Teacher Professional Growth and Development," by R. Fessler, 1985. In P. J. Burke and R. G. Heideman (Eds.), Career-Long Education (pp. 181–193), Springfield, IL: Charles C Thomas. Copyright 1985 by Charles C Thomas, Publisher. Reprinted by permission.

Some of Knowles's statements should be qualified, because teachers can vary in the degree of self-directedness, the ability and desire to work collaboratively, and the competence to deal with conceptual problems and universal principles, as well as practical concerns. Furthermore, teachers' orientation for professional development should be centered on professional performance.

In a study for the Ontario Institute for Studies in Education, Brundage and MacKeracher (1980) identify 36 principles of learning with respect to adults. For example, adults are more concerned that what they study fit with their idealized self-concept than with standards and objectives set by others; unlike children, they want assistance and support, not pressure or demands, from instructors or other learners. They learn best when their study is relevant to their experience and concerns. Factors such as stress, anxiety, and even physical aging also affect an adult's ability to learn. A similar report, prepared by

the Adult Learning Potential Institute (1980) at American University, provided an overview of training practices related to adult learning, including teacher training.

In a review of principles of adult learning, Wood and Thompson (1980) conclude that there is support for training programs to include both experiential learning and informal learning situations in which social interaction can take place among learners. They describe experiential learning, or learning by doing, as including (a) an initial limited orientation, followed by participation activities in a real setting, to let learners experience and implement what is to be learned—the skill, concept, or strategy; (b) an examination and analysis of the experience, in which learners identify the effects of their actions; (c) an opportunity to generalize and summarize, in which learners develop their own principles and identify applications of those principles; and (d) an opportunity to return to try out the principles in the work setting and develop confidence in what is learned. On the basis of these concepts, Wood and Thompson then propose guidelines for effective staff development for adult teachers.

Andrews, Houston, and Bryant (1981, p. 11) assert that educational programs are not properly designed for adults and that adult learning principles are often not applied. The Adult Learning Potential Institute (1980, p. 10) emphasized that adult learners are consistently approached as a homogeneous group in which every member is expected to participate and respond in like fashion.

Aspects of Instruction. Hunt (1978) notes that the developmental level of a child, adolescent, or adult is not necessarily a permanent classification but, instead, is a current preferred mode of functioning. Hunt further states that one of the greatest challenges facing educators is to create programs designed to stimulate development to a higher mode of functioning.

Programs proposed by educators to stimulate this development seem to have several common features: (a) guiding teachers' reflection of their experience, (b) matching training programs to teachers' skills and needs, (c) enabling teachers to anticipate further development, (d) providing a supportive yet challenging environment during instruction, (e) emphasizing the individual teacher rather than large group instruction, and (f) involving teachers in planning and direction.

Newman, Burden, and Applegate (1980) assert that teachers' understandings and interpretations of their own development could be a positive influence on their further development. They propose that programs be designed to help teachers reflect on their development and anticipate future developmental stages. A number of methods are suggested to meet these objectives. *First,* teachers could examine their own careers, through activities such as writing autobiographies, charting their careers in terms of stages or experiences, and comparing present and past attitudes and behaviors. *Second,* teachers could view other teachers' careers, through activities such as befriending an experienced teacher and reading about other teachers' experiences and teacher career development. *Third,* teachers could compare personal and professional development, including reading about stages of adult lives and considering lifelong learning needs.

Watts (1982) used staff-development programs in teacher centers as the context for discussing some of Kohlberg's suggestions for promoting developmental growth. These included association with ideas or people whose thinking is slightly ahead of one's own; practical experience; and the opportunity to reflect on one's own experience, talk it over, and develop greater understanding and new insights.

Feiman and Floden (1981, pp. 27–28) suggest that helping teachers reflect on their experiences and providing support during times of change could be effective practices in promoting development, regardless of the developmental status of the learner. They further suggest that it makes sense to pay attention to what teachers are motivated to learn when determining the appropriate starting point for learning.

Devaney (1977) identifies four conditions that summarize what practitioners believe teachers need in order to develop and what teachers' centers try to provide: warmth, concreteness, time, and thought. Warmth means a responsive, nonjudgmental setting that promotes sharing, a sense of community, and support for the risks of change. Concreteness refers to the hands-on, real-life curricular material that teachers explore and construct in center workshops. Thought means increased understanding of children and the subject matter that is required for curricular decision making. Development takes time, and teachers' centers structure activities to give teachers time to discover their own needs and their students' needs.

Kelly and DeMarte (1981) investigated the effects of reflective writing on the personal and professional development of inservice teachers. Although the changes in professional development on most scales were not statistically significant, Kelly and DeMarte conclude that the reflective writing helped create a supportive environment for development. After reviewing their own research and the literature on reflective writing, they assert that those responsible for staff development, teacher education, and supervisory functions must be trained in ways of establishing supportive, challenging environments to promote teachers' developmental growth.

When considering aspects of instruction, it is useful to look at two additional issues: the cognitive complexity of the teachers and the concept of matching teachers to appropriate training models.

First, a number of researchers have addressed the issue of cognitive complexity. After reviewing developmental-stage theory, Willie and Howey (1980, p. 30) conclude that teacher education should focus on instructional designs to promote more psychological growth in terms of increased cognitive complexity.

Sprinthall and Thies-Sprinthall (1980a) examined how adult development theory could be used to help prepare adults for new roles as teachers. They conclude that behavior modification, skills training, and academic acquisition training models each appear to be inadequate, single-variable solutions to complex training needs for trying to promote development. They further indicate that training programs should focus on the teachers' cognitive development. This training approach is based on Dewey's contention that a central goal of education is to promote developmental growth, with psychological maturity as a primary indicator of this development. Developmentally mature humans can perform the requisite complex tasks of adulthood, whereas less mature, less complex adults process experience and behave less adequately. Sprinthall and Thies-Sprinthall strongly urged tryouts of a developmental instructional model for adults, even though all the answers are not yet in from basic research. Tryouts or field-based experiments are themselves basic research. Interaction of theory and practice were suggested as going hand-in-hand.

On the basis of their review of the developmental literature, Sprinthall and Thies-Sprinthall (1983b, pp. 27–31) identify and discuss elements of training programs that are designed to stimulate developmental-stage growth. The elements of the training programs for preservice and inservice teachers were (a) role-taking experiences—requiring direct and active experience in a variety of professional roles (such as cross-role teaching and internships); (b) qualitative role taking—matching the level of complexity in the role to the level of development in the students; (c) guided reflection—teaching how to ask questions and examine one's experience from a variety of views, through structured learning; (d) guided integration—providing a balance between real experience and discussion/reflection/teaching; (e) continuity—arranging for continuous programs that extend over at least a one-year period; (f) personal support and challenge—providing for both support and challenge during instruction; and (g) assessment level—identifying an individual's level of development through a variety of test instruments.

This section on aspects of instruction deals with matching teachers to the most appropriate training model for promoting their development. Teachers at different stages in their careers have different skills, concerns, and needs and might operate at different conceptual levels, which would affect what they learn in training programs. Therefore, matching of training programs to individual developmental needs and specific learning styles has been proposed by a number of educators (e.g., Burden & Wallace, 1983; Christensen, Burke, & Fessler, 1983; Joyce, 1980; Krupp, 1981; Wilsey & Killion, 1982; Yarger & Mertens, 1980). Based on their research with adult teachers, Hunt (1971) and Hunt and Sullivan (1974) propose a matching model to facilitate adult learning and enhance developmental growth. They demonstrate that less developmentally mature individuals—those at more concrete levels—profit most from highly structured training environments. More developmentally mature individuals at more abstract levels can profit from either highly or lowly structured environments. Bents and Howey (1981, pp. 21–27), drawing upon Santmire, consider the theoretical treatment of matching teachers' conceptual level to training programs, and they translate that into the kinds of orientations found in teachers' day-to-day experience. Drawing from Joyce (1980) and Bents and Howey (1981), Wilsey and Killion (1982) identify four distinct stages of adult development and provide a detailed description of the training environment appropriate at each stage.

For each of the six stages they identify in a teacher's career, Yarger and Mertens (1980) describe the training programs in terms of appropriate content and delivery. They further recommend a model for integrating stages of teachers' careers, program agenda types (content), and program development issues (authority, credibility, finance, and governance) in teacher education.

In a similar way, Burden and Wallace (1983) propose a three-dimensional model for teacher training in staff-development programs that integrates teachers' developmental stages with different types of content and different delivery approaches. In the model, the plane for teachers' developmental stages represents stages through which teachers might advance (i.e., from an early survival stage to an advanced mature stage, or from a low to a high conceptual level). The content plane represents the content that would be offered in staff-development programs (e.g., programs on microcomputers, gifted students, or classroom management). The plane for the delivery mode represents the type of supervisory or administrative approach that would be used in delivering the staff-development program. This approach might range from a directive to a collaborative to a nondirective supervisory or administrative

style. In an effort to be responsive to the various instructional preferences of teachers at different developmental levels, Burden and Wallace recommend that programs be offered with a variety of delivery modes, so that teachers can select the type of delivery mode best suited to them.

When considering the three stages of development that she describes, Watts (1980) indicates that the formal and traditional forms of inservice programs decreased in value as teachers increased in mastery. Workshops and how-to courses were valuable to most first- and second-stage teachers but helpful only occasionally for third-stage teachers.

Techniques for Determining Teachers' Stages of Development. In the effort to match the complexity or the content of an instructional program to the teacher, it is important to first determine the teacher's stage of development. Sprinthall and Thies-Sprinthall (1980a, p. 48) indicate that indexes of psychological development should form an important core of the selection procedure. They suggest that assessment might range from very informal measures such as open-ended question interviews as proposed by Hunt and Perry, to formal measures such as Hunt's Conceptual Levels test, Loevinger's Ego Development test, or Kohlberg's Moral Judgment test.

McNergney and Carrier (1981, pp. 154–176) also propose using both informal and formal assessment of teacher characteristics and provide a detailed review of the measuring instruments developed by others. Brief descriptions of the instruments they reviewed are listed.

1. Embedded Figures Test—measures field dependence; involves the identification of simple geometric figures embedded within complex figures.
2. Paragraph Completion Test—measures conceptual level; involves the completion of six open-ended topic stems (Hunt, Greenwood, Noy, & Watson, 1973).
3. Washington University Sentence Completion Test—measures ego development; involves the finishing of 36 sentence completion items (Loevinger & Wessler, 1970).
4. Defining Issues Test—measures moral judgment development; involves six stories and the multiple-choice rating and ranking of responses in relation to the stories (Rest, 1974).
5. Minnesota Teacher Attitude Inventory—measures attitudes that predict how well teachers will get along with pupils and the degree of satisfaction with teaching as a vocation; involves the completion of 150 items with a 5-point rating scale.
6. Teacher Preference Scale—measures an individual's unconscious motivations for teaching; involves the completion of 200 items with a 6-point rating scale.
7. Manifest Anxiety Scale—measures anxiety; involves the true or false rating of 50 anxiety-related items.
8. Teaching Anxiety Scale—measures anxiety directly related to teaching; involves the completion of 29 items with a 5-point rating scale.
9. Stages of Concern About an Innovation Questionnaire—measures teachers' concerns about change; involves the completion of 35 items on an 8-point rating scale.

10. Role Construct Repertory Test—measures the complexity of an individual's system for describing other people; involves the identification and comparison of people in 12 different roles.

In assessing inservice teachers' developmental growth, Kelly and DeMarte (1981) used the Loevinger Sentence Completion Test, Hunt's Conceptual Systems test, and George's (1974) Teacher Concerns Checklist.

Another method of gathering development-related information is through the analysis of questions received at teacher centers. Apelman, cited in Feiman and Floden (1980b), observed that teachers' developmental stages are reflected in types of requests for curriculum aid: first, for immediate, practical help; second, for how-to-use aid when exposed to new curricular materials; and third, self-initiated questions for aid in curriculum development and enhancement.

On the basis of a review of literature (Christensen et al. 1983) of adult development, teacher development, and inservice education, Burke, Fessler, and Christensen (1983) developed a 60-item instrument to identify stages of teacher growth. The next phase of their research is to test the importance of items or categories in the instrument to individuals in certain career stages. With reliable measures of teachers' professional development, Burke et al. suggest, planners of staff-development programs could begin to individualize such programs.

IMPLICATIONS OF THE CAREER-STAGE MODEL

Developmental-stage theory growth appears to hold promise for (a) improving preservice teacher education programs, (b) providing induction programs, (c) improving staff-development programs, (d) improving the supervision of teachers, (e) providing a longitudinal framework for teachers to make decisions about their careers, (f) helping in institutional planning, and (g) providing the basis for making decisions about differentiated staffing plans or career ladder plans for teachers.

Preservice Programs

Information on teacher career development could be used to improve preservice teacher education programs by (a) serving as the basis for revising instructional content and learning experiences to better meet preservice teachers' developmental needs and to promote further growth, and (b) providing preservice teachers with information on how teachers change throughout their careers.

Revising Instructional Content and Procedures. Preservice teachers go through several stages of development in the process of becoming a teacher (e.g., Caruso, 1977; Fuller & Bown, 1975; Sacks & Harrington, 1982). Fuller and Bown (1975) suggest that teacher educators could use this developmental information to select appropriate training content and learning experiences for preservice teachers at a given developmental stage, to meet their current needs and to promote further development.

Because research on teacher career development provides details about the unique needs and problems of first-year teachers, teacher educators could revise content to better prepare preservice teachers to meet these needs (Burden, 1982b). For instance, more emphasis could be placed on such topics as classroom management, discipline, time management, and evaluation and record keeping. In a review of the stages and problems of teacher development, Cruickshank and Callahan (1983) indicate that novices can be helped to make the transition from students to teachers. Cruickshank and Callahan further suggest that preservice teachers "can anticipate and cope successfully with the stages of teacher development and with the problems of practice, thus achieving personal satisfaction as well as student achievement and satisfaction" (p. 257).

Sprinthall and Thies-Sprinthall (1983a, pp. 93–94) propose a theoretical framework for educating teachers that uses a cognitive-developmental perspective. They suggest that a series of differentiated learning environments and different supervision techniques be applied to groups of student teachers according to their entry developmental level. The initial training stage would represent the individual's current preferred style. Matching the general instruction (content and process) to the initial training level would be nothing more than Dewey's original dictum of starting where the learner is. Readings, homework assignments, and even examinations could represent different developmental levels and could be selected to be congruent with the developmental level of the student. With careful assessment through formative evaluation, the preservice training program could continually be refined.

Including Content on Teacher Career Development. There are several advantages to including content in preservice programs on how teachers change throughout their careers. *First*, preservice teachers would have more information about teachers and the teaching career on which to base a career decision. With this additional information on teacher career development, some preservice teachers might choose to switch majors before finishing college training. Those who continue in the teacher education program would presumably be more certain of their career selection and have more commitment. The dropout rate in the early years of service would likely be lower. *Second*, detailed information on teacher career development would present preservice teachers with a realistic view of various aspects of the job and the teaching career, consequently helping to minimize the disequilibrium that many first-year teachers experience. *Third*, this career development information would provide a foundation for the preservice teacher's self-assessment of professional skills. Areas of weakness would be identified and corrected before entry into the public classroom.

To obtain this information on teacher career development, preservice teachers could conduct interviews with experienced teachers, and readings could be assigned to help students recognize changes that teachers experience throughout their careers (Burden, 1983a). Readings might include career descriptions written by teachers themselves, research reports, and brief career descriptions on teacher development. Sources for the readings could include authors such as Fuller and Bown,

Burden, Gregorc, Newman, Katz, Yarger and Mertens, Ryan and others, Loevinger, Hunt, and Perry.

Induction Programs

Information about characteristics of beginning teachers can be useful as teacher-induction programs are developed. A number of useful references are available including Brooks, 1987; Elias, Fisher, and Simon, 1980; Galvez-Hjornevik, 1986; Johnston and Ryan, 1983; Lasley, 1986; McDonald and Elias, 1980; and Veenman, 1984.

Staff-Development Programs

The premise that the stages of teacher development are important in planning effective professional-development programs is well accepted in the literature (e.g., Andrews et al., 1981; Bents & Howey, 1981; Brundage & MacKeracher, 1980; Burden, 1982a; Hall & Loucks, 1978). In these reports there are many similarities in the recommendations to match staff-development content and delivery modes to the teacher's stage of development. In general, teachers in the early stages need much assistance with the technical skills of teaching and would benefit most from a highly structured, directive, staff-development program. Practical information and applications would be most useful. Teachers who are a little more advanced developmentally would seek information to add variety to their teaching and would prefer a collaborative approach to staff development and supervision. Teachers at the highest developmental levels would focus on more complex and cross cutting concerns and would prefer more team types of arrangements and staff-development programs that are nondirective. Tailoring staff-development programs to individual developmental needs and specific learning styles has the potential for making teachers more effective (Bents & Howey, 1981, p. 20).

Applications of the conceptual systems theory as described by Bents and Howey (1981), Joyce (1980), and Wilsey and Killion (1982) provide useful guidelines for matching learning environments in staff-development programs to teachers at different developmental stages. Krupp's (1981) handbook on adult development also provides useful guidelines for designing staff-development programs based on the stages of adults' lives.

In an effort to provide optimal environments for teacher growth, Yarger and Mertens (1980) describe teachers' career stages, with matching content and program types for training. Burke, Fessler, and Christensen (1984) examined teacher career-stage information and recommended several implications for the teacher-career-cycle model. They propose that traditional inservice activities focusing on instructional techniques should be used at particular points in the career cycle, that staff development and professional development should be broadened to include personal needs and concerns of teachers, that organizational policies should be related to providing support for teachers throughout their career cycle, and that approaches to staff development and professional development should emphasize personalized, individualized support systems. They discuss these issues in several other reports (Burke, Christensen, Fessler, McDonnell, & Price, 1987; Burke & Heideman, 1985).

Supervision of Teachers

One responsibility of school administrators and supervisors is to help classroom teachers improve their instruction and facilitate their development. With knowledge of teacher career development, supervisors could provide different types of supervisory assistance and vary their supervisory strategies with teachers at different developmental levels.

After examining teacher-development studies, Glickman (1981) suggested developmental supervision as a means for helping teachers at various points in their careers. He proposes three orientations to the supervision of teachers, each with differing degrees of teacher and supervisor responsibility when meeting the objectives of the supervision. *First*, with the directive approach, the supervisor assumes a high degree of responsibility when delineating standards. Definite, immediate, and concrete assistance is provided when the supervisor demonstrates, clarifies, directs, and reinforces teacher behaviors. *Second*, the collaborative approach includes supervisory behaviors such as listening, presenting, problem solving, and negotiating. The end result would be a mutually agreed-upon contract by supervisor and teacher that would delineate the structure, process, and criteria for subsequent instructional improvement. *Third*, the nondirective approach rests on the premise that teachers are capable of analyzing and solving their own instructional problems. The supervisor helps channel the teacher toward self-discovery.

Supervisors can assess an individual teacher using two variables: (a) level of teacher commitment, drawing largely from the literature on adult development and teacher career development, and (b) level of abstraction, based largely on cognitive development theory (Glickman, 1981, p. 47). The assessment is accomplished by a simple paradigm with two intersecting lines, one for the line of commitment and one for the line of abstraction. Then the teacher can be matched to the supervisory approach most suited to him or her, using the paradigm.

Because many teachers' changes in job skills, knowledge, behaviors, attitudes, and concerns appear to follow a developmental sequence, Burden (1982a) suggests one developmental line representing stages of teacher career development to be used for assessment in developmental supervision rather than the two intersecting lines proposed by Glickman. Using three stages of teacher career development (Burden, 1980b), Burden (1982a) proposes that teachers at State 1, concerned with self-adequacy, might profit most from a directive supervisory approach that would include modeling, directing, and measuring by the supervisor. Teachers at Stage 2, concerned with improving the learning environment for their students, might be approached using the collaborative supervisory model that would include presenting, interacting, and contracting by the supervisor. Teachers at Stage 3, concerned with helping other students and teachers, might need only the minimal influence of a nondirective supervisory approach in which the supervisor would listen, clarify, and encourage.

Teachers' Career Decisions

Knowledge of teacher career development can help teachers recognize where they are in terms of their development and serve as a basis for making professional growth plans.

Information on teacher career development provides a reference point for teachers to compare their development with that of other teachers. Field (1979) states that her description of teachers' career stages were "meant to provoke a sense of community for the teacher who often feels so very much alone" (p. 2). First-year teachers, for instance, might feel that they are the only ones experiencing problems with planning, discipline, or time management. They might feel more at ease knowing that the problems they experience are common for first-year teachers, that they will develop and refine their teaching skills, and that the initial problems will be overcome.

Teachers with a knowledge of teacher career development can be aware of and anticipate changes they might experience. Field (1979) describes the stages in the teaching career as a continuum for identifying where one is and where one is going. Taking it one step further, Gregorc (1973) says this career perspective could be used in professional-development goal setting.

The concept of career stages can help teachers think more clearly about not only what they should be doing and learning at their current level of development but also what they should do if they want to continue their development.

Institutional Planning

School districts could use information on teacher career development to aid in planning a differentiated program for assisting teachers in their professional development. To meet teachers' needs and learning styles at different points in their careers, these programs should include a variety of topics and be conducted in learning environments ranging from high to low structure. Planning for financial support for professional-development programs would be simplified if details of the programs had been identified.

Differentiated Staffing and Career Ladders

Because of limitations in salary, status, gains, recognition, job responsibilities, and growth possibilities, many competent and knowledgeable teachers leave teaching and go into administration or other occupations. In an effort to address these issues and promote teacher retention, differentiated staffing plans (Dempsey & Smith, 1972; English & Sharpes, 1972), and career ladder plans (Association of Teacher Educators, 1985) have been proposed that provide promotion opportunities for teachers. These plans offer a variety of stages in the teaching career, with different duties and possibly different pay at each stage. As teachers climb the career ladder, they might become eligible to become involved in curriculum development, staff development, and departmental leadership. Information on teachers' developmental needs and abilities could be used to

aid school districts in determining criteria and duties for each step of the career ladder.

Burden (1987) provides a number of guidelines for establishing career ladders in schools districts. The career ladder concept has also been adapted into a career lattice, as a means of personalizing staff development (Christensen, McDonnell, & Price, 1988).

FUTURE DIRECTIONS FOR RESEARCH

Additional research could be conducted to define and clarify many aspects of teacher development. Research strategies should be selected carefully to meet the objectives of the investigations, and researchers should publish results to add to the data base in this area.

Research Topics

One desirable result of the investigation of teacher development is increased efforts to promote teacher development. With that objective in mind, research efforts should focus on (a) changes teachers experience, (b) influences on teacher changes, and (c) ways to promote teacher development.

Changes Teachers Experience. There are many possible areas of investigation that would help define and clarify teachers' changes. Some of the most useful topics include:

1. Changes in teachers' cognitive, conceptual, ego, moral, and ethical development
2. Changes in teachers' professional behaviors, attitudes, and job events
3. Effects of personal and professional changes on teacher behavior and teacher effectiveness
4. Effects of reassignment or relocation to new schools on teacher development
5. Differences in development for elementary, middle school, junior high, and high school teachers; men and women teachers; and teachers of different ethnic and cultural backgrounds
6. Relationships between teachers' developmental characteristics and student outcomes
7. Comparisons of developmental and career patterns of those who quit teaching and those who continue teaching
8. Relationships between adult development and teacher development

Influences on Teacher Changes. The forces that affect teacher change are complex. Research could explore cognitive and intellectual development of teachers, effects of career development and the career cycle, influences by the organization, factors related to adult and personal development, and other related areas.

Ways to Promote Teacher Development. Teacher development could be positively influenced in a variety of ways. Some useful areas for research include the following items:

1. Content, instructional approach, and timing of training programs for preservice and inservice teachers
2. Effects of supervision on teacher development
3. Effects of various incentives and rewards on development

Research Approaches

A multifaceted research approach is needed for examining teacher development. The ultimate aim of hypothesis-generating research designs (often using ethnographic and qualitative approaches) is to seek meaning and to generate hypotheses. Hypothesis-testing research designs (often using experimental, quasiexperimental, correlational, or survey methods) are used to test the truthfulness or accuracy of predetermined hypotheses. These two approaches help answer different types of questions and serve different purposes. In terms of teacher development, the use of hypothesis-generating designs can lead to descriptions and hypotheses of teachers' developmental char-

acteristics and influences. Further testing could be conducted with hypothesis-testing research designs (Burden, 1983b).

SUMMARY

On the understanding that adult development and teacher development are not fully articulated concepts, teachers' personal and professional characteristics were described in this chapter. Acceptance of the premise that teachers are different in some important ways is a prerequisite to differentially supporting their development. A number of strategies were discussed to promote teacher development, but it is clear that much work needs to be done before a fully articulated education program for teacher development will be ready for implementation. Training programs should have continual developmental evaluation. There needs to be clarification of the nature of teacher changes and the process by which this change is brought about.

References

Adams, R. D. (1982, March). *Teacher development: A look at changes in teacher perceptions across time.* Paper presented at the meeting of the American Educational Research Association, New York.

Adams, R. D., Hutchinson, S., & Martray, C. (1980, April). *A developmental study of teacher concerns across time.* Paper presented at the meeting of the American Educational Research Association, Boston.

Adult Learning Potential Institute. (1980). *Overview of training practices incorporating adult learning: Adult learning in inservice training and staff development.* Washington, DC: Author. (ERIC Document Reproduction Service No. ED 198 365)

Andrews, T. E., Houston, W. R., & Bryant, B. L. (1981). *Adult learners (A research study).* Washington, DC: Association of Teacher Educators.

Association of Teacher Educators. (1985). *Developing career ladders in teaching.* Reston, VA: Author.

Baltes, P. B., & Goulet, L. R. (1970). Status and issues of a life-span developmental psychology. In L. R. Goulet & P. B. Baltes (Eds.), *Life-span developmental psychology: Research and theory.* New York: Academic Press.

Bents, H. R., & Howey, K. R. (1981). Staff development: Change in the individual. In B. Dillon-Peterson (Ed.), *Staff development/organizational development.* Alexandria, VA: Association for Supervision and Curriculum Development.

Briscoe, F. G. (1973). The professional concerns of first year secondary teachers in selected Michigan public schools: A pilot study (Doctoral dissertation, Michigan State University, 1972). *Dissertation Abstracts International, 33,* 4786A.

Brooks, D. M. (Ed.). (1987). *Teacher induction: A new beginning.* Reston, VA: Association of Teacher Educators. (ERIC Document Reproduction Service No. ED 279 607)

Brundage, D. H., & MacKeracher, D. (1980). *Adult learning principles and their application to program planning.* Toronto: Ontario Institute for Studies in Education. (ERIC Document Reproduction Service No. ED 181 292)

Burden, P. R. (1980a). Teachers' perceptions of the characteristics and influences on their personal and professional development (Doc-

toral dissertation, The Ohio State University, 1979). *Dissertation Abstracts International, 40,* 5404A.

Burden, P. R. (1980b). *Teachers' perceptions of the characteristics and influences on their personal and professional development.* Manhattan, KS: Author. (ERIC Document Reproduction Service No. ED 198 087)

Burden, P. R. (1982a, February). *Developmental supervision: Reducing teacher stress at different career stages.* Paper presented at the meeting of the Association of Teacher Educators, Phoenix, AR. (ERIC Document Reproduction Service No. ED 218 267)

Burden, P. R. (1982b). Implications of teacher career development: New roles for teachers, administrators, and professors. *Action in Teacher Education, 4*(4), 21–25.

Burden, P. R. (1983a). Confidence in career choice: Preservice teachers interview experienced teachers. *Teacher Educator, 18*(4), 19–23.

Burden, P. R. (1983b). Research designs used to examine teacher development. *College Student Journal, 17*(2), 116–120.

Burden, P. R. (Ed.). (1987). *Establishing career ladders in teaching: A guide for policy makers.* Springfield, IL: Charles C Thomas.

Burden, P. R., & Wallace, D. (1983, October). *Tailoring staff development to meet teachers' needs.* Paper presented at the Association of Teacher Educators Mini-Clinic, Wichita, KS. (ERIC Document Reproduction Service No. ED 237 506)

Burke, P. J., Christensen, J. C., Fessler, R., McDonnell, John H., & Price, J. R. (1987, April). *The teacher career cycle: Model development and research report.* Paper presented at the meeting of the American Educational Research Association, Washington, DC.

Burke, P. J., Fessler, R., & Christensen, J. (1983, April). *Teacher life-span development: An instrument to identify stages of teacher growth.* Paper presented at the meeting of the American Educational Research Association, Montreal.

Burke, P. J., Fessler, R., & Christensen, J. C. (1984). *Teacher career stages: Implications for staff development.* Bloomington, IN: Phi Delta Kappa.

Burke, P. J., & Heideman, R. G. (Eds.). (1985). *Career-long teacher education.* Springfield, IL: Charles C Thomas.

Caruso, J. J. (1977). Phases in student teaching. *Young Children*, 33(1), 57–63.

Charlesworth, W. R. (1972). Developmental psychology: Does it offer anything distinctive? In W. R. Looft (Ed.), *Developmental psychology: A book of readings.* Hinsdale, IL: Dryden Press.

Chickering, A. K. (1974, December). *The educational needs of new learners: Implications for liberal arts colleges.* Paper presented at the East Central Colleges Consortium Conference on New Learners.

Chickering, A. W. (1976). Developmental change as a major outcome. In M. Keeton & Associates (Eds.), *Experiential learning: Rationale, characteristics, and assessment.* San Francisco: Jossey-Bass.

Christensen, J., Burke, P., & Fessler, R. (1983, April). *Teacher life-span development: A summary and synthesis of the literature.* Paper presented at the meeting of the American Educational Research Association, Montreal.

Christensen, J. C., McDonnell, J. H., & Price, J. R. (1988). *Personalizing staff development: The career lattice model.* Bloomington, IN: Phi Delta Kappa.

Cruickshank, D. R., & Callahan, R. (1983). The other side of the desk: Stages and problems of teacher development. *Elementary School Journal*, 83(3), 250–258.

Dempsey, R. A., & Smith, R. P., Jr. (1972). *Differentiated staffing.* Englewood Cliffs, NJ: Prentice-Hall.

Devaney, K. (1977). Warmth, concreteness, time, and thought in teachers' learning. In K. Devaney (Ed.), *Essays on teachers' centers.* San Francisco: Teachers' Center Exchange, Far West Laboratory for Educational Research and Development.

Elias, P, Fisher, M. L., & Simon, R. (1980). *Helping beginning teachers through the first year: A review of literature.* Princeton, NJ: Educational Testing Service.

English, F. W., & Sharpes, D. K. (1972). *Strategies for differentiated staffing.* Berkeley, CA: McCutchan.

Erikson, E. H. (1959). *Identity and the life cycle.* New York: International Universities Press.

Erikson E. H. (1963). *Childhood and society* (2nd ed.). New York: W. W. Norton.

Feiman, S., & Floden, R. E. (1980a, April). *Approaches to staff development from conceptions of teacher development.* Paper presented at the meeting of the American Educational Research Association, Boston.

Feiman, S., & Floden, R. E. (1980b). *What's all this talk about teacher development?* (Research Series No. 70). East Lansing, MI: Michigan State University, Institute for Research on Teaching. (ERIC Document Reproduction Service No. ED 189 088)

Feiman, S., & Floden, R. E. (1981). *A consumer's guide to teacher development* (Research Series No. 94). East Lansing, MI: Michigan State University, Institute for Research on Teaching. (ERIC Document Reproduction Service No. ED 207 970)

Fessler, R. (1985). A model for teacher professional growth and development. In P. J. Burke & R. G. Heideman (Eds.), *Career-long teacher education* (pp. 181–193). Springfield, IL: Charles C Thomas.

Field, K. (1979). *Teacher development: A study of the stages in development of teachers.* Brookline, MA: Brookline Teacher Center.

Floden, R. E., & Feiman, S. (1980, April). *Basing effectiveness criteria on theories of teacher development.* Paper presented at the meeting of the American Educational Research Association, Boston, MA.

Floden, R. E., & Feiman, S. (1981a). *A developmental approach to the study of teacher change: What's to be gained?* (Research Series No. 93). East Lansing, MI: Michigan State University, Institute for Research on Teaching.

Floden, R. E., & Feiman, S. (1981b). *Problems of equity in developmental approaches* (Research Series No. 91). East Lansing, MI: Michigan State University, Institute for Research on Teaching.

Fuller, F. F. (1969). Concerns of teachers: A developmental conceptualization. *American Educational Research Journal*, 6, 207–226.

Fuller, F. F., & Bown, O. H. (1975). Becoming a teacher. In K. Ryan (Ed.), *Teacher education*, (74th yearbook of the National Society for the Study of Education, Part II, pp. 25–52). Chicago: University of Chicago Press.

Fuller, F. F., Parsons, J. S., & Watkins, J. E. (1973). *Concerns of teachers: Research and reconceptualization.* Austin, TX: University of Texas, Research and Development Center for Teacher Education.

Galvez-Hjornevik, C. (1986). Mentoring among teachers: A review of literature. *Journal of Teacher Education*, 37(1), 6–11.

George, A. (1974). *Analysis of five hypothesized factors on the teacher concerns checklist, form B.* Austin, TX: University of Texas, Research and Development Center for Teacher Education.

George, A. (1978). *Measuring self, task, and impact concerns: A manual for the use of the teacher concerns questionnaire.* Austin, TX: University of Texas, Research and Development Center for Teacher Education.

Glickman, C. D. (1981). *Developmental supervision: Alternative practices for helping teachers improve instruction.* Alexandria, VA: Association for Supervision and Curriculum Development.

Gordon, M. (1976, April). *Choice of rule–example order used to teach mathematics as a function of conceptual level and field dependence–independence.* Paper presented at the meeting of the American Educational Research Association, San Francisco.

Gould, R. (1972). The phases of adult life: A study in developmental psychology. *American Journal of Psychiatry*, 129, 521–531.

Gould, R. (1978). *Transformations.* New York: Simon & Schuster.

Gregorc, A. F. (1973). Developing plans for professional growth. *NASSP Bulletin*, 57, 1–8.

Hall, G. E., & Loucks, S. F. (1978). Teacher concerns as a basis for facilitating and personalizing staff development. *Teachers College Record*, 80(1) 36–53.

Harvey, O. J. (1966). *Experience, structure, and adaptability.* New York: Springer.

Harvey, O. J. (1967). Conceptual systems and attitude change. In C. W. Sherif & M. Sherif (Eds.), *Attitude, ego-involvement, and change.* New York: Wiley.

Harvey, O. J. (1970, December). Beliefs and behavior: Some implications for education. *Science Teacher*, 37, 10–14, 73.

Harvey, O. J., Hunt, D. E., & Schroeder, H. (1961). *Conceptual systems and personality organization.* New York: John Wiley.

Harvey, O. J., Prather, M., White, B., & Hoffmeister, J. (1968, March). Teachers' beliefs, classroom atmosphere, and student behavior. *American Educational Research Journal*, 5 151–166.

Howey, K. R. (1985). Six major functions of staff development: An expanded imperative. *Journal of Teacher Education*, 36(1), 58–64.

Hunt, D. E. (1966). A model for analyzing the training of training agents. *Merrill-Palmer Quarterly of Behavior and Development*, 12, 137–156.

Hunt, D. E. (1971). *Matching models in education.* Toronto: Ontario Institute for Studies in Education.

Hunt, D. E. (1975). Person–environment interaction: A challenge found wanting before it was tried. *Review of Educational Research*, 45 209–230.

Hunt, D. E. (1978). In-service training for persons in relation. *Theory Into Practice*, 17, 239–244.

Hunt, D. E., Greenwood, J., Noy, J. E., & Watson, N. (1973, June). *Assessment of conceptual level: Paragraph completion method*

(*PCM*). Toronto: Toronto Institute for Studies in Education. (mimeographed)

Hunt, D. E., & Joyce, B. R. (1967). Teacher trainee personality and initial teaching style. *American Educational Research Journal, 4*, 253–259.

Hunt, D. E., Joyce, B. R., Greenwood, J. A., Noy, J. E., Reid, R., & Weil, M. (1974). Student conceptual levels and models of training: Theoretical and empirical coordination of two models. *Interchange, 5*(3), 19–30.

Hunt, D. E., & Sullivan, E. V. (1974). *Between psychology and education.* Hinsdale, IL: Dryden Press.

Iannaccone, L. (1963). Student teaching: A transition stage in the making of a teacher. *Theory Into Practice, 2*, 73–81.

Johnston, J. M., & Ryan, K. (1983). Research on the beginning teacher: Implications for teacher education. In K. R. Howey & W. E. Gardner (Eds.), *The education of teachers: A look ahead.* New York: Longman.

Joyce, B. R. (1980). Learning how to learn. *Theory Into Practice, 19*, 15–27.

Joyce, B. R., Weil, M., & Wald, R. (1973). The teacher–innovator: Models of teaching as the core of teacher education. *Interchange, 4*, 47–59.

Katz, L. G. (1972). Developmental stages of preschool teachers. *Elementary School Journal, 73*(1), 50–54.

Kelly, M. K., & DeMarte, P. J. (1981). *Reflective writing: An effective look for the professional and personal development of teachers.* Paper presented at the meeting of the American Educational Research Association, Los Angeles.

Knowles, M. S. (1978). *The adult learner: A neglected species.* Houston, TX: Gulf.

Kohlberg, L. (1969). Stage and sequence: The cognitive developmental approach to socialization. In D. Croslin (Ed.), *Handbook of Socialization Theory and Research* (pp. 347–380). New York: Rand McNally.

Kohlberg, L. (1973). Continuities in childhood and adult moral development revisited. In P. B. Baltes & K. W. Schaie (Eds.), *Life-span developmental psychology: Personality and socialization* (pp. 179–204). New York: Academic Press.

Krupp, J. A. (1981). *Adult development: Implications for staff development.* Manchester, CT: Author.

Lasley, T. J. (Ed.). (1986). Teacher induction: Programs and research [Special issue]. *Journal of Teacher Education, 37*(1).

Levinson, D. J., Darrow, C. N., Klein, E. B., Levinson, M. H., & McKee, B. (1978). *The seasons of a man's life.* New York: Alfred A. Knopf.

Loevinger, J. (1966). The meaning and measurement of ego development. *American Psychologist, 21*, 195–206.

Loevinger, J., & Wessler, R. (1970). *Measuring ego development.* San Francisco: Jossey-Bass.

McDonald, F. J. (1982, March). *A theory of the professional development of teachers.* Paper presented at the meeting of the American Educational Research Association, New York.

McDonald, F. J., & Elias, P. (1980). *Study of induction programs for beginning teachers* (Vol. 1). Princeton, NJ: Educational Testing Service.

McLachlan, J. F. C., & Hunt, D. E. (1973). Differential effects of discovery learning as a function of student conceptual level. *Canadian Journal of Behavioral Science, 5*, 152–160.

McNergney, R. F., & Carrier, C. A. (1981). *Teacher development.* New York: Macmillan.

Newman, K. K. (1979). Middle-aged experienced teachers' perceptions of their career development (Doctoral dissertation, The Ohio State University, 1978). *Dissertation Abstracts International, 39*, 4885A.

Newman, K. K., Burden, P. R., & Applegate, J. H. (1980). Helping teachers examine their long-range development. *Teacher Educator, 15*(4), 7–14.

Oja, S. N. (1980). Adult development is implicit in staff development. *Journal of Staff Development, 1*(2), 7–56.

Oja, S. N., & Pine, G. J. (1983). *A two year study of teacher stages of development in relation to collaborative action research in schools: Final report.* Washington, DC: National Institute of Education. (ERIC Document Reproduction Service No. ED 248 227)

Oja, S. N., & Pine, G. J. (1988). Collaborative action research: Teachers' stages of development and school contexts. *Peabody Journal of Education, 64*(1).

Pataniczek, D. (1979). A descriptive study of the concerns of first year teachers who are graduates of the secondary pilot program at Michigan State University (Doctoral dissertation, Michigan State University, 1978). *Dissertation Abstracts International, 39*, 5916A.

Perry, W. (1970). *Forms of intellectual and ethical development during the college years.* New York: Holt, Rinehart & Winston.

Peterson, A. R. (1979). Career patterns of secondary school teachers: An exploratory interview study of retired teachers (Doctoral dissertation, The Ohio State University, 1978). *Dissertation Abstracts International, 39*, 4888A.

Piaget, J. (1963). *Psychology of intelligence.* Totowa, NJ: Littlefield, Adams.

Rest, J. (1974). *Manual for the defining issues test: An objective test of moral judgment.* Minneapolis: University of Minnesota.

Ryan, K., Newman, K. K., Mager, G., Applegate, J. H., Lasley, T., Flora, V. R., & Johnson, J. (1980). *Biting the apple: Accounts of first year teachers.* New York: Longman.

Sacks, S. R., & Harrington, G. N. (1982, March). *Student to teacher: The process of role transition.* Paper presented at the meeting of the American Educational Research Association, New York.

Selman, R. L. (1980). *The growth of interpersonal understanding.* New York: Academic Press.

Sheehy, G. (1976). *Passages: Predictable crises of adult life.* New York: E. P. Dutton.

Sitter, J. P., & Lanier, P. E. (1982, March). *Student teaching: A stage in the development of a teacher or a period of consolidation?* Paper presented at the meeting of the American Educational Research Association, New York.

Sprinthall, N. A., & Thies-Sprinthall, L. (1980a). Adult development and leadership training for mainstream education. In D. C. Corrigan & K. R. Howey (Eds.), *Concepts to guide the education of experienced teachers.* Reston, VA: Council for Exceptional Children.

Sprinthall, N. A., & Thies-Sprinthall, L. (1980b). Educating for teacher growth: A cognitive developmental perspective. *Theory Into Practice, 19*(4), 278–286.

Sprinthall, N. A., & Thies-Sprinthall, L. (1983a). The need for theoretical frameworks in educating teachers: A cognitive-developmental perspective. In K. R. Howey & W. F. Gardner (Eds.), *The education of teachers.* New York: Longman.

Sprinthall, N. A., & Thies-Sprinthall, L. (1983b). The teacher as an adult learner: A cognitive-developmental view. In G. A. Griffin (Ed.), *Staff development* (82nd yearbook of the National Society for the Study of Education, Part II, pp. 13–35). Chicago: University of Chicago Press.

Suedfeld, P. (1974). Attitude manipulation in restricted environments: Conceptual structure and response to propaganda. *Journal of Abnormal and Social Psychology, 68*, 242–247.

Tomlinson, P. D., & Hunt, D. E. (1971). Differential effects of rule–example order as a function of learner conceptual level. *Canadian Journal of Behavioral Science, 3*, 237–245.

Unruh, A., & Turner, H. E. (1970). *Supervision for change and innovation.* Boston: Houghton Mifflin.

Veenman, S. (1984). Perceived problems of beginning teachers. *Review of Educational Research, 54*(2), 143–178.

Watts, H. (1980). *Starting out, moving on, running ahead, or how the teachers' center can attend to stages in teacher's development.* San Francisco: Far West Laboratory for Educational Research and Development. (ERIC Document Reproduction Service No. ED 200 604)

Watts, H. (1982). Observations on stages in teacher development. *MATE Viewpoints, 4*(1), 4–8.

Willie, R., & Howey, K. R. (1980). Reflections on adult development: Implications for inservice teacher education. In W. R. Houston & R. Pankratz (Eds.), *Staff development and educational change* (pp. 25–52). Reston, VA: Association of Teacher Educators.

Wilsey, C., & Killion, J. (1982). Making staff development programs work. *Educational Leadership, 40*(1), 36–38, 43.

Wolfe, R. (1963). The role of conceptual systems in cognitive functioning at varying levels of age and intelligence. *Journal of Personality, 31,* 108–123.

Wood, F. H., & Thompson, S. R. (1980). Guidelines for better staff development. *Educational Leadership, 37*(5), 374–378.

Yarger, S. J., & Mertens, S. K. (1980). Testing the waters of school-based teacher education. In D. C. Corrigan & K. R. Howey (Eds.), *Concepts to guide the education of experienced teachers.* Reston, VA: Council for Exceptional Children.

·19·

TEACHER SOCIALIZATION

Kenneth M. Zeichner and Jennifer M. Gore

UNIVERSITY OF WISCONSIN—MADISON

Teacher socialization research is that field of scholarship that seeks to understand the process whereby the individual becomes a participating member of the society of teachers (Danziger, 1971). This chapter reviews that research, but, rather than simply describing in a chronological, cumulative, or even thematic way studies that have been conducted since Lortie's (1975) classic work *Schoolteacher: A Sociological Study*, the intention is also to examine competing explanations of teacher socialization that have arisen from different intellectual traditions. In addition, the chapter will address issues of the relation of the research to teacher education practice and issues related to the social relations of the research process itself.

INTELLECTUAL TRADITIONS IN TEACHER SOCIALIZATION RESEARCH

The three main traditions in teacher socialization research can be identified as functionalist, interpretive, and critical. Each is characterized by a theoretical orientation that shapes the questions that are asked, the way the research is conducted, and the interpretation of the data collected. Given their distinctiveness, we might go so far as to call these *paradigms* in teacher socialization research. However, it is rare to find articulation of these paradigms in the teacher socialization literature. Too often, research methods precede research questions, and the questions themselves are narrowly construed.

To examine a research paradigm critically, to see it clearly, to begin to assess its contribution, one needs to step back from the particular paradigm and consider its location in a broader context. Because teacher socialization research exists as part of a larger body of research on occupational socialization, the paradigms in teacher socialization research have clear links

with particular forms of sociological study. In the first section of the chapter, we illustrate the links between teacher socialization and occupational socialization research and trace that work back to its origins in particular schools of intellectual thought. Such a task could easily take all of this chapter but would prevent us from pursuing our other purposes. Consequently, the following discussion reduces the complexity and contradiction within the traditions and simplifies the links between the intellectual paradigms and occupational and teacher socialization. We have done this for purposes of analysis, clarity, and conservation of space.

The term *socialization* as it is used in teacher socialization research is relatively new. Clausen (1968) and Danziger (1971) trace the current usage of the term to Dollard (1939), Park (1939), Ogburn and Nimkoff (1940) and Sutherland and Woodward (1937) and point out that it emerged at around the same time in sociology, anthropology, and psychology. As Danziger (1971) comments: "in view of the rare occurrence of the term in earlier writings in the three disciplines, its sudden emergence to prominence suggests the operation of a powerful undercurrent of ideas" (p. 13). He describes that undercurrent as a shift from social philosophy to positivistic social science.

The Functionalist Approach to Socialization

The oldest and still most pervasive approach to teacher socialization, functionalism, is one rooted in the tradition of sociological positivism that arose in France (e.g., Comte, 1853; Durkheim, 1938). The functionalist paradigm holds a view of the social world that "regards society as ontologically prior to man [sic] and seek[s] to place man and his activities within that wider social context" (Burrell & Morgan, 1979, p. 106).

We would like to express our thanks to the following people for their helpful comments and criticisms of an earlier draft of this chapter: Niels Brouwer, Nedra Crow, Sharon Feiman-Nemser, Mark Ginsburg, Sandra Hollingsworth, Karl Jordell, Gary Knowles, Judith Little, Bob Tabachnick, and Alan Tom.

Functionalism is a view characterized by a concern with providing explanations of the status quo, social order, consensus, social integration, solidarity, need satisfaction, and actuality. It approaches those general sociological concerns from a standpoint that tends to be realist, positivist, determinist, and nomothetic (Burrell & Morgan, 1979, p. 26). Functionalism is based on a conception of science that emphasizes the possibility of objective inquiry capable of providing true explanatory and predictive knowledge of an external reality. Functionalists tend to assume the standpoint of the observer, attempting "to relate what *they* observe to what *they* regard as important elements in a wider social context" (Burrell & Morgan, 1979, p. 107).

Within the functionalist paradigm several schools of thought can be identified, such as structural functionalism (Malinowski, 1923, 1936; Radcliffe-Brown, 1952), systems theory (von Bertalanffy, 1956), social action theory (Parsons, 1949; Weber, 1947), integrative theory (Merton, 1968), and behaviorism (Skinner, 1953). Although important within the paradigm, for our purposes, the differences between these schools of thought are best seen as differences of degree rather than of fundamental perspective (Burrell & Morgan, 1979, p. 108).

Some of the earlier occupational socialization research arose out of this tradition. The best known study is unquestionably that of Merton, Reader, and Kendall (1957), published as *The Student Physician*. In this account of medical student socialization, the medical school was seen to infuse students with the orientations, the knowledge, and the skills fundamental for living the life of a physician (Wentworth, 1980, p. 52). Socialization was seen as "a smooth change in absolute personal qualities" (p. 54).

The link between Merton's work and teacher socialization research is often made quite self-consciously, even though the links to functionalism and positivism are not. For example, Hoy and Rees's (1977) study on the bureaucratic socialization of student teachers drew on Merton's notion that bureaucratic structures might have the capacity to modify personality types. They measured students' custodialism, bureaucratic orientation, and dogmatism before and after a 9-week period of student teaching, and they found that "secondary school teachers become substantially more bureaucratic in orientation as a result of student teaching" (p. 25).

If we consider Hoy and Rees's work in relation to the characteristics of the functionalist paradigm, it can be seen to corroborate Burrell and Morgan's description of the paradigm. It is realist in attempting to explain the status quo; positivist in the methods employed and in the predictive intent; determinist, in that schools are seen as determining the orientations of student teachers, who are viewed as passive or plastic; and nomothetic in that lawlike statements are made (e.g., "secondary schools in general began almost immediately to mold neophytes into roles devised to maintain stability" (Hoy & Rees, 1977, p. 25).)

The functionalist paradigm emphasizes reproduction of existing arrangements and assumes that socialization produces continuity (Wentworth, 1980, p. 53). It is "geared to providing an explanation of the regulated nature of human affairs" (Burrell & Morgan, 1979, p. 107) and, in so doing, focuses on central tendencies and de-emphasizes complexity, contradiction, and human agency.

The Interpretive Approach to Socialization

The interpretive paradigm is rooted in the German idealist tradition of social thought (e.g., Dilthey, 1976; Husserl, 1929; Kant, 1876; Schutz, 1967; Weber, 1947). "It challenges the validity of the ontological assumptions which underwrite functionalist approaches to sociology" (Burrell & Morgan, 1979, p. 32). As with the functionalist paradigm, there are several schools of thought within the interpretive paradigm, such as hermeneutics (Dilthey, 1976; Gadamer, 1975), phenomenology (Husserl, 1929; Sartre, 1948; Schutz, 1967), and ethnomethodology (Garfinkel, 1967). Nevertheless, there is a common effort to understand the fundamental nature of the social world at the level of subjective experience. Interpretive approaches seek explanation "within the realm of individual consciousness and subjectivity, within the frame of reference of the participant as opposed to the observer of action" (Burrell & Morgan, 1979, p. 28). The descriptors used by Burrell and Morgan to characterize the paradigm are that it is nominalist, anti-positivist, voluntarist, and ideographic (p. 28). An outline of an occupational socialization study and a teacher socialization study that are interpretive in orientation will be helpful in understanding these descriptors.

Of the occupational socialization research, Becker, Geer, Hughes, and Strauss's (1961) study of medical students, titled *Boys in White*, is the best known and most commonly cited, often in juxtaposition to Merton's study (e.g., Battersby, 1983; Olesen & Whittaker, 1970; Wentworth, 1980). Becker's research team attempted to get inside, and understand from within, the students' experiences of medical school. Students were attributed considerable agency and were understood as being able to turn themselves into the kinds of persons the situation demanded (Becker, 1964). Socialization was, therefore, viewed as a more complex and problematic process than implied in the functionalist paradigm.

C. Lacey's (1977) study of teacher socialization in the United Kingdom is consistent with Becker's work. The study was designed in part to illustrate some of the perceived flaws of functionalist socialization theory, a feature that highlights the emergence of the interpretive paradigm in opposition to functionalism as a way of understanding teacher socialization. Lacey's study "aimed at developing a model of the socialization process that would encompass the possibility of autonomous action by individuals and therefore the possibility of social change emanating from the choices and strategies adopted by individuals" (C. Lacey, 1985, p. 4076). Participant observation and questionnaire data were collected, in an attempt to understand the experiences of student teachers.

Although Lacey and Becker both acknowledge structural elements or institutional constraints within the context in which socialization occurs, as seen in their use of terms like *situational adjustment* (Becker et al.) and *strategic redefinition* (C. Lacey), their emphasis is on subjective meanings of participants. The studies are nominalist in terms of seeing the social world as largely existing through the names, concepts, and laels used by participants; antipositivist in that they reject the view that human affairs can be studied in the manner of the natural sciences; voluntarist in that individuals are viewed as making choices and capable of "autonomous action"; and ideographic in their emphasis on subjective accounts.

Functionalist and interpretive approaches to the study of teacher socialization are fundamentally distinct, with quite different assumptions regarding the ontological status of the social world (Burrell & Morgan, 1979). Nevertheless, there are similarities between the two approaches. Both are concerned with "sociology of regulation," "a concern to provide explanations of society in terms which emphasize its underlying unity and cohesiveness" (Burrell & Morgan, 1979, p. 17). Both view socialization as an overarching process whereby the individual engages in role learning that results in the situational adjustment (passive or active) of the individual to the culture of the profession (Battersby, 1983, p. 327). Neither challenges the status quo, operating as they do from a value-neutral research stance. The functionalist paradigm demonstrates greater concern for explanation than the interpretive paradigm, which aims for understanding. From a critical perspective (the third paradigm), neither of these research aims is sufficient; they are merely moments in the transformative process" (Carr & Kemmis, 1986, p. 156). As will be further discussed, the critical tradition emphasizes transformation.

The Critical Approach to Socialization

As with the functionalist and interpretive paradigms, the critical tradition encompasses several schools of thought including those deriving from Marxism and from the Frankfurt School philosophy. Furthermore, as Wexler (1987) observes, "the meaning of critical theory is changing" (p. 100). Nevertheless, two main approaches can be identified in the critical paradigm, one emphasizing reproduction (e.g., Althusser, 1971; Bernstein, 1979; Bourdieu, 1977; Bowles & Gintis, 1976) and another emphasizing production (e.g., Giroux, 1981, 1983; Willis, 1977). The view in this chapter of the critical paradigm acknowledges both production and reproduction, agency and structure. Weiler (1988) summarizes the concerns of such a position in her own conclusions about critical educational theory:

It is important to acknowledge the intended role of schools as apparatuses of social reproduction and sites of cultural reproduction at a high level of theoretical abstraction; we need to keep in mind the relationship of schools to the wider society and to recognize the realities of class and gender [and race] relationships in terms of power and control. But at the same time, the acts of resistance, negotiation, and contestation of individuals in the production of meaning and culture must also be recognized. (p. 24)

"People must be considered as both the creators and the products of the social situations in which they live" (Bolster, 1983, p. 303).

Burrell and Morgan (1979) characterize what we refer to as the critical paradigm (which they refer to as "radical humanism") as being concerned with totality, consciousness, alien-

ation, and critique. A central purpose of critical approaches is to bring to consciousness the ability to criticize what is taken for granted about everyday life. Class, gender, and race relations become key foci, given the historical and contemporary alienation of particular groups. A vital concern of those operating within the critical paradigm is social transformation aimed at increasing justice, equality, freedom, and human dignity. Reality is viewed as socially created and sustained. Research professing to be critical must ideally be participatory and collaborative. Underlying the critical paradigm is a reflexivity not found in the other paradigms, particularly, as Gouldner (1976) says, "when at its best." It

eschews all temptations to claims of moral elitism and superiority, as well as all posturings of innocence. It never imagines—when at its best—that its own self-understanding can be taken at face value, or that its commitments are lacking in ambiguities or even contradictions. . . . Affirming human emancipation as a goal, it never allows itself to intimate—when at its best—that it itself has already achieved that emancipation and never allows itself to forget that it, too, possesses a repressive potential. . . . Knowing it will win no easy victories, relying upon its continual work and struggle, . . . critical theory seeks to understand itself as well as serving the world, and it suspects—as self-serving and sycophantic—all offered conceptions of itself that bring it no painful surprises. When it is at its best. (pp. 293–294)

In the functionalist and interpretive traditions, we found it relatively straightforward to trace clear links between the teacher and occupational socialization literature and the intellectual paradigms from which they emerged. The same is not true in the critical tradition. One reason for the difficulty we encountered is that the term *socialization* arose out of the very positivism that critical theorists reject. Wexler's (1987) deconstruction of the term illustrates the problem:

The category of socialization affirms the powerlessness of the individual against a reified collectivity, a system which purportedly reproduces itself. . . . The concept of socialization surrenders in advance the capacity for collective appropriation and transformation, to a system view, in which individuals are merely structural supports. (p. 100)

Critical theorists tend to relate the term to its functionalist origins and, hence, reject it. However, as was seen with the interpretive paradigm, alternative conceptions of socialization exist and still others are possible. Part of the aim of this chapter is to present a reconception of socialization and to demonstrate that it warrants closer intellectual treatment by those who profess concern for critical educational theory and practice. This reconception will be elaborated as the chapter progresses.

In the occupational socialization literature, there is no exemplary critical study of medical students to contrast with the studies of Merton and Becker. However, many studies have been conducted that address power relations in medical school. One example is Shapiro's (1978) *Getting doctored: Critical reflections on becoming a physician*. Drawing on Marx's theory of alienation and Fromm's writings on authoritarianism, Shapiro traces socialization from acceptance into medical school to work on hospital wards. He argues that alienation and authoritarianism are rooted in an oppressive social order and that change in medicine "can only come as part of a more general transformation of society itself" (p. 205).

More generally in the occupational socialization literature, there is attention to the fact that, until recently, the sociology of occupations was a sociology of men's occupations. Thus, recent research tends to focus on the experiences of women (e.g., M. McNeil's (1987) *Gender and Expertise*) and to highlight class, gender, and race relations as elements in the formation of work relations.

A critical approach to teacher socialization would also address these elements. For example, when we recognize that teaching is largely women's work (Apple, 1987; Mattingly, 1987), gender issues cannot be neglected. One possible reason for such neglect by researchers in the other paradigms is that they tend to focus on the event rather than to view socialization as located in a broader history. One does not have to look at too many events, or cycles of history (Braudel, 1980), to see that teacher socialization is a process in which men (teacher educators, school principals, administrators) exercise power over women and that teacher socialization research is an enterprise traditionally designed and conducted by men on women.

Few empirical studies of teacher socialization can be located within the critical paradigm. Ginsburg's (1988) work best exemplifies the approach articulated. He conducted a 2-year ethnographic study of preservice teacher socialization, "the process of formally preparing to become a teacher" (Ginsburg, 1988, p. 1). The study was contextualized by addressing the historical development of teacher education in the United States, as well as the development of the specific teacher education program that provided the site for the study. Employing the concept of contradiction, Ginsburg tied the specific experiences of individuals to class, race, and gender relations within society and within education. His transformative intent is made explicit in the concluding chapter of his book, which is titled "What Is to Be Done? Critical Praxis by Educators of Teachers."

As this review of the teacher socialization literature continues, readers might consider the research reported here in light of the preceding analysis. Identification of the intellectual traditions from which particular lines of research have arisen facilitates understanding of the questions that have been asked, the methodologies that have been employed, and the results that have been presented.

The following analysis of the teacher socialization literature will be organized around stages of teachers' careers. Specifically, it will review influences on teacher socialization (a) prior to formal teacher education, (b) during preservice teacher education, and (c) during the inservice years of teaching. Within that framework three layers of social context will be addressed: interactive, institutional, and cultural. Works published in English from a number of countries (Australia, Canada, the United Kingdom, and the United States) will be included in this analysis. Problems of generalizing across countries will be discussed later in the chapter.

The discussion of the extant literature will be critical and analytic, rather than merely descriptive: to assess the degree to which particular generalizations are supported by empirical evidence, the ways in which certain commonsense generalizations might need to be modified in light of the empirical evidence now available, and to identify alternative explanations of the same event that are plausible, given the current state of knowledge. The chapter will also identify areas in which further research is needed. Following the analysis of the literature, a final section of the chapter will summarize that which has been concluded about the extant empirical literature and will highlight central issues and concerns in teacher socialization research and their implications for practice in teacher education.

THE TEACHER SOCIALIZATION LITERATURE

Influences on Teacher Socialization Prior to Formal Teacher Education

Given the widely accepted view that students come to any learning situation with previously constructed ideas, knowledge, and beliefs, and with certain capabilities acquired through prior experience that affect the ways in which they interpret and make use of new information (e.g., Posner, Strike, Hewson, & Gertzog, 1982), it is not surprising that teacher socialization research has paid considerable attention to influences on teacher learning that predate entry into a formal program of teacher education. Dan Lortie (1975) argues in his highly influential work on the sociology of teaching, *Schoolteacher*, that students' predispositions stand at the core of becoming a teacher, exerting a much more powerful socializing influence than either preservice training or later socialization in the workplace. The apparent persistence of particular forms of pedagogy over time (e.g., see Cuban, 1984; Sirotnik, 1983) is frequently explained by the failure of school reform initiatives, staff development, or preservice teacher education to alter the predispositions of teachers.

There have been several major explanations in the literature of pretraining influences on teacher socialization. Feiman-Nemser (1983) summarizes the arguments related to three of the most prevalent explanations of these influences. First, Stephens (1967) proposes an evolutionary theory to account for the socialization of teachers and emphasizes the role of primitive spontaneous pedagogical tendencies in explaining at least some of the reasons why teachers act as they do. According to this view;

Human beings have survived because of their deeply ingrained habit of correcting one another, telling each other what they know, pointing out the moral, and supplying the answer. These tendencies have been acquired over the centuries and are lived out in families and classrooms. Thus, children not only learn what they are told by parents and teachers, they also learn to be teachers. (Feiman-Nemser, 1983, p. 152)

In addition to these spontaneous communicative tendencies, Stephens (1967) also discusses the role of spontaneous manipulative tendencies in determining teaching practices. Here the focus is on a set of playful tendencies that have little immediate utility but that over time, have had tremendous survival value for the human race (e.g., making marks on rocks, playing with echoes). Stephens's theory of spontaneous schooling and his evolutionary account of teacher socialization stress those common aspects of teaching practice that exist apart from the deliberate rational actions of teachers or the specific contextual conditions in particular schools and communities. According to this view, teachers bring to teacher education a set of predispositions that are present in all individuals to varying degrees. Although Stephens's work has been largely ignored by scholars of teacher socialization, he presents a convincing case for the argument that at least some aspects of teaching cut across individuals and contexts.

A second position outlined by Feiman-Nemser (1983) is the psychoanalytic explanation found in the work of Wright (1959) and Wright & Tuska (1967, 1968). This line of work suggests that teacher socialization is affected to a considerable extent by the quality of relationships teachers had as children with important adults (e.g., mother, father, teachers) and that becoming a teacher is, to some extent, a process (sometimes unconscious and sometimes deliberate) of trying to become like significant others in one's childhood or trying to replicate early childhood relationships. According to this view, early relationships with significant others are the prototypes of subsequent relationships throughout life, and the kinds of teachers that education students become are governed by the effects of this early childhood heritage on their personalities (Wright & Tuska, 1967).

These studies offer empirical data in support of this "childhood romance theory of teacher development," including statements written by teachers that illustrate the significance of conscious identification with a teacher during childhood (Wright, 1959). Although recent teacher socialization research has not explicitly pursued the psychoanalytic orientation of Wright and his colleagues, there are several very striking examples in recent studies of the effects of early childhood relationships on teacher practices.

One vivid example of this influence is found in Knowles's (1988a) case study of Cynthia, a student teacher who experienced failure in a graduate teacher education program. Here a number of learned behaviors that were important to Cynthia's survival at home during childhood (e.g., being quiet spoken and unassertive) were also important in explaining her student-teaching failure in a junior high school. Connell (1985) also provides evidence of teachers reproducing parent–child relationships experienced in their own childhood in their interactions with children.

A third viewpoint on the role of pretraining influences on the socialization of teachers emphasizes the influence of the thousands of hours spent by teachers as pupils in what Lortie (1975) refers to as an "apprenticeship of observation." According to this view, teacher socialization occurs largely through the internalization of teaching models during the time spent as pupils in close contact with teachers. According to Lortie, the activation of this latent culture during formal training and later school experience is a major influence in shaping teachers' conceptions of the teaching role and role performance. Formal teacher education is viewed as having little ability to alter the cumulative effects of this anticipatory socialization.

Lortie's argument is based, in part, on several studies in which teachers attested to the tangential role of their formal training and in which they frequently referred to the continuing influence of their earlier mentors. Recent work has shown that student teachers and teachers do indeed draw upon models provided by teachers that were experienced during the "apprenticeship of observation." These experiences provide them with both positive and negative role models. For example, Colleen, a secondary student teacher in a graduate teacher education program (Crow, 1987), discusses the continuing positive influence of her seventh-grade English teacher;

Miss Smoot, a 7th grade English teacher. She was extremely knowledgeable about literature and grammar. She stimulated me to want to know more . . . I wanted to read and read and understand . . . she was always an English teacher and we (the class) all liked it . . . she had quite an influence on me. . . . I definitely will use a lot of different things like she did. (p. 10)

On the other hand, Ross (1987) cites several cases in which previous teachers served as negative role models for secondary social studies teacher education students; for example:

To tell you the truth, some of the worst teachers I had were my history teachers in high school. They were the most boring teachers I ever had. Everything came straight from the book. . . . It was just so dull. They just basically said "turn to chapter eight, read section one, answer the questions at the end." I don't want to be like that. (p. 234)

Closely related to the influence of positive and negative role models provided by former teachers are cases in which prospective teachers and teachers focus more directly on their own learning as pupils and deliberately seek to create in their own teaching those conditions that were missing from their own education. For example, Jack, a teacher in an action research seminar at the Horace Mann Institute, recalls:

When I think back to my own experience in school, I remember that I was a retarded reader. I was retained in the first grade. The reason—reading handicap. I could never understand how a teacher could do it to a first grader. I was injured. In the fourth grade, I suddenly caught up and saw the light. I did it on my own. No one handled me and my problem on an individual basis. As far as they were concerned, I could sink or swim. When I chose teaching for a profession, I guess the strongest point in its favor was that I wanted to do for children things that were not done for me. This is the sort of thing that inspires me in my educational work. (Shumsky, 1958, p. 75)

Ross (1987) argues that this process of modeling former teachers is a highly selective and deliberate process in which student teachers and teachers pick and choose the various attributes and practices they observed as pupils and synthesize them into the model they would like to become. Although the teacher socialization literature tends to support this view of modeling as selective rather than as global (LeCompte & Ginsburg, 1987; Zeichner, 1979), this position does not account for any of the more subtle influences that prior school experience and former teachers might have had on individuals. The case study of the elementary teacher Rachel (Zeichner, Tabachnick, & Densmore, 1987) clearly illustrates how deeply ingrained and partly unconscious feelings and dispositions developed as a pupil (in this case regarding issues of authority) exert a continuing influence on teacher activity.

These three explanations of pretraining influences on teacher socialization (evolutionary, psychoanalytic, and apprenticeship of observation) have been discussed in the literature for many years. Recent work has expanded upon and/or elaborated on these original explanations and has brought into focus other pretraining influences that have received little attention from researchers. For example, as a result of changing demographics in U.S. teacher education institutions, many nontraditional students are now entering teacher education programs. At least some of these students now coming into teacher education have had previous teaching, other work experience, and/or experience in parenting. Even many of the so-called traditional teacher education students come to teacher education with prior experience in such activities as camp counseling, baby-sitting, and teaching Sunday school, (Lanier & Little, 1986). To date, only a few studies have explored the influence of these kinds of experiences on teaching conceptions and practices (e.g., Bullough, 1989; Crow, 1987; Feiman-Nemser & Buchmann, 1986). Much more attention needs to be given to this issue in the future.

The use of various life history methodologies offers much promise for capturing the socializing influence of the full range of life experiences or "architecture of self" (Pinar, 1986) that individuals bring to teacher education programs and teaching (Goodson, 1980; Woods, 1987). In recent years studies in a number of different countries, (especially in Canada, have employed a variety of biographical, autobiographical, and life history methodologies to understand the development of teachers' knowledge. These include autobiography (Grumet, 1980; Pinar, 1986); collaborative autobiography (Butt & Raymond, in press; Butt, Raymond, & Yamagishi, 1988); narrative inquiry (Connelly & Clandinin, 1987); repertory grid techniques (Ingvarson & Greenway, 1984); diary interviews (Burgess, 1988); and the combined use of biographical and ethnographic methods in the same study (Raymond & Surprenant, 1988). These interpretive and critical studies have begun to provide us with rich information about the ways in which teachers' perspectives are rooted in the variety of personal, familial, religious, political, and cultural experiences they bring to teaching (also see Casey, 1988; Knowles, in press).

One aspect of what students bring to teacher education programs (and teachers to teaching) that has received very little attention until recently is knowledge of and about subject matter and the teaching of subject matter and one's affective dispositions toward subject matter. Following Lee Shulman's (1986) influential critique of the absence of subject matter in studies of teaching and learning to teach, at least two groups of researchers have begun to focus on the subject-matter knowledge and disciplinary perspectives of teachers as factors in the teacher socialization process. One group of researchers at the National Center for Research on Teacher Education plans, in the future, to track the continuing influence of subject-matter knowledge on socialization into teaching (D. Ball & McDiarmid, 1987). To date, only the entering conceptions of preservice teachers have been reported by this research group (e.g.,

D. Ball, 1988; Gomez, 1988; Neufeld, 1988). The knowledge Growth in a Profession Project at Stanford University has also reported work on the subject-matter conceptions and intellectual histories of preservice teachers. This research group has already been able to document the continuing influence of subject-matter knowledge on teaching conceptions and teacher behavior (e.g., Ringstaff & Haymore, 1987; Wilson & Shulman, 1987; Wilson & Wineburg, 1988). Grossman (1987), for example, demonstrates how both the depth and the character of a beginning English teacher's subject-matter knowledge influenced her classroom teaching.

Although more attention to the issue of subject matter is clearly warranted, there are also other conceptions that students bring to teacher education programs that need to be addressed. For example, researchers have suggested that prospective teachers' entering expectations regarding teacher education (Book, Byers, & Freeman, 1983) and their conceptions of the process of learning to teach (Amarel & Feiman-Nemser, 1988) could be important keys to understanding the socializing influence of subject-matter knowledge, prior teaching experiences, and whatever else students bring to teacher education programs.

Several researchers have also shown that the nature of an individual's commitment to teaching as a career could be important to consider. Studies conducted by D. S. Anderson (1974) and C. Lacey (1977) revealed two broad orientations or types of commitment to teaching (radical and professional) that emerge early in the period of anticipatory socialization and that can be traced through the training period into the early years of teaching. This research suggests that there are distinct patterns of socialization experienced by individuals committed to a career as a classroom teacher (professional) and by those committed primarily to a set of ideals that might be realized in or outside of the classroom (radical).

One major problem with almost all of the research that has focused on the role of pretraining influences on teacher socialization (functionalist and interpretive) is that they have focused almost exclusively on the individual characteristics, conceptions, skills, and dispositions that students bring to teacher education programs and have ignored the collective aspects of socialization into teaching.

Feiman-Nemser & Floden (1986) describe various ways in which the teaching force is segmented. Teachers are not just individuals possessing various knowledge, skills, and dispositions, but they are also gendered subjects who are members of particular generations, races, social-class groups and who teach particular subjects at specific levels in the system of schooling. Almost none of the existing research on teacher socialization has taken into account patterns of socialization into teaching that are related to the characteristics that segment the occupational group.

One area that has received at least some attention in relation to the collective aspects of teacher socialization is gender. Here several researchers have focused on the influence of traditional and atypical socialization and gender-identification patterns for both males and females on teaching conceptions and practices (e.g., Barrows, 1978; Freedman, Jackson, & Boles, 1986; Goodman, 1988; McCarthy, 1986). In the example of Cynthia cited earlier, the fact that Cynthia was female was of no small consequence in her being taught to be unassertive and unassuming. Knowles (1988a), however, focuses exclusively on Cynthia's individual life history and ignores the role of gender in shaping that history. It is very clear that race, class, and gender in particular are related to different life chances and educational outcomes for individuals (e.g., Delone, 1979; Weis, 1988). These issues need to receive much more attention in explanations of teacher socialization.

One way to approach this issue is to do comparative studies of different groups of prospective teachers, each of which shares some collective attribute. For example, studies could be conducted on differences in socialization experienced by groups of male and female teachers, elementary and secondary teachers, teachers who teach different subjects, and teachers who have different social-class backgrounds. Cross-national studies could also be conducted on how the socialization process differs for particular groups of teachers across national and cultural boundaries. The socialization of minority teachers is another area that has been totally neglected in the literature to date.

Another group characteristic that warrants particular attention is the notion of subject subculture. Consistent with Bernstein's (1971) argument that induction into a subject is also induction into a subject culture or community that represents particular assumptions about knowledge and the nature of teaching and learning, both C. Lacey (1977) and Yaakobi and Sharan (1985) have identified distinct differences in teachers' theories of knowledge, beliefs, practices, and, in Lacey's case, patterns of socialization into teaching that are related to particular academic disciplines. Although the notion of subject subculture does not give enough weight to variations within subjects (S. Ball & Lacey, 1980) or to how beliefs about subjects and within subject areas change over time (Goodson, 1983), this area has been identified as one of the key determinants of teacher actions (Hargreaves, 1988). Distinct patterns of socialization into teaching have also been identified for primary and secondary teachers (Gibson, 1972).

In summary, the key role of pretraining influences in understanding the socialization of teachers has been stressed for many years now. Studies in several countries have documented the continuing influence of teachers' predispositions during their training and into later school experience. Examples of these include studies conducted by Hogben and Petty (1979a, 1979b), Petty and Hogben (1980), and Hogben and Lawson (1983, 1984) in Australia; by Mardle and Walker (1980) and Hanson and Herrington (1976) in the United Kingdom; and by Zeichner and Grant (1981), Zeichner, et al. (1987), Crow (1987, 1988), Ross (1987, 1988), Knowles (1988a, 1988b), Hollingsworth (in press), and Ginsburg (1988) in the United States.

Early studies that stressed the role of these formative experiences in the socialization process (e.g., Lortie, 1975) were largely functionalist and adopted a very deterministic view of the influence process. In the minds of many, little could be done to overcome the powerful effects of prior experience. Most recent work, however, has stressed a more interactive view of the socialization process in which formative experiences exert some influence but do not totally determine socialization outcomes (e.g., Hollingsworth, in press; Ross, 1988; Zeichner et al., 1987). The level at which the analysis of data is conducted is particularly crucial in this regard. When the focus is on central tendencies in groups of individuals, little change in predispositions is noted. This approach, however, masks a great deal of individual variation that can be detected when the development of specific individuals is traced (Hogben & Lawson, 1984; C. Lacey, 1977; Pearson, 1987; Power, 1981). The shift from a deterministic to a more interactive view of the role of formative experiences in teacher socialization is a consequence, in part, of changes in data collection and analysis procedures employed by researchers, which are, in turn, related to the increasing influence of the interpretive tradition in guiding teacher socialization research.

Crow (1987) and Knowles (1988b) have proposed a Biographical Transformation Model to explain the processes by which formative experiences are modified and effectively enacted in teachers' practices. This model seeks to show the linkages among early childhood experiences with significant others, teacher role identity (a construct used to depict entering conceptions and dispositions), and subsequent actions in the classroom. Although Knowles (1988a) cites some theoretical support for this model in his own study of Cynthia and in studies conducted by Crow (1987) and Bullough (1987), he also admits that the model is still largely speculative. The work of Nias (1986), Sikes, Measor, and Woods (1985), and Spencer (1986), and the Canadian work using life course methodologies (e.g., Butt & Raymond, in press) suggests that Knowles's focus on teacher role identity might provide too narrow a lens for viewing what teachers bring to teacher education and the development of teachers over time. This work suggests the need for a much broader focus on a teacher's personal identity and on a teacher's role identity as one component of self-identity. And, as previously noted, this focus on what individuals bring to teacher education, whether narrowly or more broadly defined, ignores the collective character of how teachers are socialized into their ideas. Jordell (1987) argues that the role of formative life experiences in the teacher socialization process diminishes as time goes on and individuals experience teacher education programs and careers in schools. Nias (1986) has shown, on the other hand, that teachers continue to draw on their personal experiences as pupils even after up to 9 years of teaching experience. This difference in perspective regarding the longevity of pretraining influences leads to a consideration of the role of formal teacher education and later work experience on teacher socialization.

The Socialization Role of Preservice Teacher Education

There are three major components in preservice teacher education programs that can potentially exert influence on the socialization of teachers: (a) general education and academic specialization courses, completed outside schools, departments, and colleges of education; (b) methods and foundations courses, usually completed within education units; and (c) field-based experiences, usually completed in elementary and secondary school classrooms. In addition to the influence of these specific elements of programs, there are also the effects that stem from participation in the general life of the college or university in which the teacher education program is housed.

Since the 1950s, a very substantial literature has emerged that focuses on the effects of colleges and universities on the cognitive, moral, political, and affective development of students. These studies have consistently shown a clear link between college attendance and a general liberalization of personality and values, increases in the sophistication with which students reason about moral issues, and increases in verbal, mathematical, and general knowledge and various measures of cognitive development such as intellectual flexibility and reflective judgment (Feldman & Newcomb, 1969; Nucci & Pascarella, 1987; Pascarella, 1985). Despite these changes, which have been identified for college students in general, this literature also shows very clearly that not all students change in the same ways after they enter college. Astin's (1977) study of 200,000 students over a 10-year period, for example, identified several factors that mediate the socializing impact of the college on students. These included a student's age, gender, race, ability (as measured by college admissions tests), social-class background, religious background, and degree of active participation in the life of the institution (also see K. L. Anderson, 1988). Very little attention has been paid by researchers to these issues in relation to the problem of teacher socialization.

The literature also suggests that at least some of the variation that exists in socializing experiences among students is a result of differences in the institutional environments of colleges and universities. Clark & Marker (1975) argue that these institutional differences are the major source of variation among teacher education programs:

> Given the range of institutional settings, it is simply not reasonable to argue that one finds a common teacher education program wherever one looks. Institutional climates vary markedly and these variances affect the nature of the student population, the expectations held for student productivity, the background and activities of the faculty and the availability of physical and cultural resources. Such variances are not to be dismissed lightly. They affect all aspects of the relationship between the institution and its students, including the professional preparation of students in teacher training. Thus the critical variance in teacher education programs among institutions is perhaps more a function of variance by institutional types than by a systematic variance attributable to professional training itself. . . . Similarity in course structure does not mean identical content of instruction within courses. (pp. 58–59)

Studies of teacher socialization have rarely taken into account the character and quality of the institutions in which teacher education programs exist. At most, we might be told the size (e.g., large), funding source (e.g., state), and geographical location (e.g., Midwest) of an institution, but little more. Even those who have carefully described the goals and priorities of teacher education programs under study (e.g., Feiman-Nemser & Buchmann, 1986; Ginsburg, 1988; and Hollingsworth, in press) have paid little attention to the intellectual, social, and political character of institutions. Studies on undergraduate education (e.g., Nucci & Pascarella, 1987; Pascarella, 1985) have suggested several different dimensions of institutions that could be taken into account by teacher socialization researchers, such as the frequency of student–faculty interactions, the degree of curricular flexibility, the intellectual challenges of the academic program, and the strength of cultural facilities. Because of the evidence suggesting a number of distinguishable subenvironments in any institution (Lacy, 1978) and the mediation of institutional effects by a variety of individual characteristics such as gender (K. L. Anderson, 1988), it is important for teacher education researchers to incorporate institutions into future studies, by examining the different institutional environments that exist for particular students and groups of students under study. Although Clark & Marker (1975) are correct in asserting that the character and quality of teacher education institutions need to be taken into account in attempts to assess the impact of teacher education programs, to do so at the level of the global campus environment might be unproductive (see Pascarella, 1985, p. 23).

Despite many recent reports that have addressed the quality of undergraduate education in the United States (e.g., Boyer, 1987; U.S. Department of Education, 1984), there is a clear lack of empirical data about the impact of particular academic courses on students (Tom, 1987; Trow, 1987). Furthermore, although there have been repeated regarding the need to increase the period of time that prospective teachers spend in subject-matter preparation, there is very little empirical evidence about how the amount of coursework in academic subjects contributes to teacher effectiveness (Ashton & Crocker, 1987). Generally, this whole area regarding the socializing impact of specific academic courses and patterns of academic preparation is in need of further exploration. Both the Knowledge Growth in Teaching Project at Stanford (Grossman, 1987) and the National Center for Research on Teacher Education (Zeichner, 1988) are currently involved in attempts to assess the contribution of particular kinds of academic preparation and coursework on how teachers learn to teach particular subjects.

When we examine the socializing role of the professional component of preservice teacher education programs, we need to distinguish between campus-based and field-based elements, because they represent different, and often competing, notions of the process of learning to teach (Feiman-Nemser, 1983). First, with regard to the methods and foundations courses, there is much evidence that the knowledge, skills, and dispositions introduced to students in these courses have little influence on their subsequent actions, even during initial training (Grant, 1981; Hodges, 1982; Katz & Raths, 1982). There is very strong evidence, for example, that, when attempts are made to train prospective teachers in the performance of specific teaching skills through microteaching and other systematic procedures, the continued use of the skills by prospective teachers outside of the laboratory is highly dependent upon whether the ecological conditions in specific classrooms are conducive to the use of the skills. Copeland's (1980) work suggests that the impact of education courses cannot be assessed apart from these ecological conditions. Students come into these courses with very low expectations about what can be learned from professional courses about teaching (Book, e al., 1983), and, typically, they evaluate the contribution of these courses to their professional development as minimal after the courses are completed (Yamamoto et al., 1969).

Consistent with Mardle & Walker's (1980) thesis that teacher education courses do little to alter, and in all probability confirm and reinforce, what students bring with them, many researchers have concluded that teacher education has a weak impact on at least some of the values, beliefs, and attitudes that students bring with them into their teacher education programs (Britzman, 1986; Bullough, 1989; Connell, 1985; Crow, 1987; Ginsburg & Newman, 1985; Knowles, 1988a; Ross, 1987).

Several explanations are offered in the literature for the apparent low impact of preservice teacher education courses on the socialization of students into teaching. First, there is the argument that formal teacher education is impotent because of the strong and enduring effects of the kinds of pretraining influences discussed earlier. Crow (1988), for example, documented how the teacher role identities brought into teacher education programs were still the major driving forces for two teachers after 3 years of teaching. Closely related to this argument is the position that the impact of preservice teacher education is diffused because of the segmentation within teacher education programs and the mixed messages that are sent to students as a result (Atkinson & Delamont, 1985).

As case studies of students moving through teacher education programs have begun to accumulate in recent years, it has become more and more common to find examples of students interpreting the messages of teacher education courses in ways that reinforce the perspectives and dispositions they bring to the program, even when these interpretations involve a distortion of the intentions of teacher educators. One very striking example of this process is found in Feiman-Nemser & Buchmann's (1986) case study of Janice. In this example, Janice construes a critique posed in one of her course readings of the unequal distribution of knowledge according to social class as an argument for the way things ought to be. Other examples of this inversion process can be found in Ginsburg's (1988) studies.

Various challenges have been raised regarding this commonly accepted view that professional education courses have little impact on teacher education students. Recent studies of teacher education students, for example, have shown that students attribute worth and influence to their professional education courses (Grossman & Richert, 1988; Zeichner, 1988). Recent studies have also shown that it makes little sense to talk about the socializing influence of teacher education courses without accounting for the particular focus of the courses in relation to the perspectives that students bring to the courses. Crow and Kauchak (1988), D. Ball and Noordhoff (1985) and Hollingsworth (in press) all provide examples of cases of a varied responses to the same teacher education program by different individuals.

Also, teacher education programs are not all alike. Several attempts have been made to describe the diversity of approaches that exist (Hartnett & Naish, 1980; Kirk, 1986; Zeichner, 1983a). Several recent studies have shown that the particular focus of the professional education component of a program is related to the occurrence of certain kinds of changes in students. Grossman & Richert's (1988) study of knowledge growth in two teacher education programs, for example, shows that one program's focus on subject matter was related to particular kinds of changes in secondary teacher education students' conceptions of subject matter. These changes were not present for the students who participated in a teacher education program that emphasized things other than subject matter. Other researchers have begun to identify certain key elements in courses or in the relationship between courses and students' latent perspectives that seem to enhance the socializing impact of professional education courses. D. Ball and Noordhoff (1985), Goodman and Adler (1985) and Hollingsworth (in press) spell out some of these key elements. Hollingsworth concludes from a study of 14 preservice teachers in one fifth-year preservice program that some teacher education factors were more effective than others in preparing the preservice teachers to manage classrooms, teach reading, and understand student learning. She argues, for example, that matched pairings of like-minded cooperating teachers and student teachers (a common practice in the United States) actually hinders knowledge growth and that exposing students to contrasting viewpoints is more helpful in clarifying the complex aspects of classroom life when also accompanied by "expectation and support for preservice teachers to try out their own and program-related ideas" (p. 27).

Another challenge to the position that professional education courses have a weak socializing impact on students comes from those who consider the hidden curriculum of these courses. Ginsburg and Clift (1990), for example, describe how the hidden curriculum in teacher education sends messages to students concerning such issues as teachers as an occupational group (their status and power); the theory and practice of teaching; the nature of the curriculum and the teacher's role in making curriculum decisions; and the relationship of inequalities in society to the role of the school in terms of those inequalities. They argue that the hidden curriculum constitutes the core of teacher socialization.

Ginsburg & Clift (1989) identify certain dominant messages that teacher education programs send to students. They also recognize, however, that contradictory messages exist within programs and that there is the possibility of various responses from students to any messages sent through the hidden curriculum. (Also, see Ginsburg, 1988).

The studies of Dale (1977a, 1977b) and Bartholomew (1976) in the United Kingdom are representative of the work in this area. Dale conducted a content analysis of typical British courses on the psychological, sociological, and philosophical foundations of education and concluded that initial teacher training fosters a cognitive style of liberal individualism that predisposes prospective teachers to see the world in particular ways, to become conscious of its having particular properties and possibilities, and to reject or never recognize other properties or possibilities. Dale (1977a) specifically argues that this cognitive style directs teachers to seek the source of their problems in individuals (e.g., pupils) and not in the institutions in which they work.

Bartholomew analyzes other aspects of the hidden curriculum of preservice teacher preparation (the pedagogical prac-tices and social relations in programs and the social organiza-tion of programs) and concludes that, despite the fact that teacher education programs encourage students to use liberal phrases and to affirm liberal slogans in places other than the university, the facts of socialization within the university (e.g., the separation of theory and practice) encourage the develop-ment of objectivist conceptions of knowledge, fragmented views of curriculum, and views of learners as passive recipients of officially approved knowledge. According to Bartholomew and others such as Giroux (1980), and Ginsburg (1988), Pop-kewitz (1985), the real impact of preservice preparation lies in these images of teacher, learner, knowledge, and curriculum, which are subtly communicated to prospective teachers through the covert processes of the hidden curriculum of teacher education programs. Thus, despite the existence of many studies suggesting that teacher education courses have a low socializing impact, one must be cautious in accepting their findings.

Generally, arguments related to the impact of the hidden curriculum of preservice teacher education programs have been offered on logical and theoretical grounds, with very little supporting empirical evidence. With the exception of Gins-burg's studies on the development of teacher perspectives to-ward professionalism (e.g., Ginsburg, 1988; Ginsburg & New-man, 1985) and the evidence provided by Connell (1985) of the psychologization of social relations by teachers, we do not have very strong empirical evidence confirming the fact that teach-ers actually incorporate elements into their perspectives in ways consistent with the theoretical arguments. In fact, we know very little about what goes on inside teacher education courses at all beyond what students or faculty tell us or what foundation-sponsored studies report on the basis of the same sort of secondhand reports (Zeichner, 1988). Clearly, more direct study of the formal and hidden curriculum of teacher education courses and of the ways in which the messages of these courses are received and interpreted by students is needed.

Another aspect of preservice teacher preparation that has received much attention in the literature in relation to the is-sue of teacher socialization is the field-experience or practicum component. Those who have analyzed the empirical literature have consistently characterized the knowledge base related to the socializing impact of these experiences as weak and ambig-uous (Griffin et al., 1983; McIntyre, 1983; Watts, 1987; Zeichner, 1980). Today, despite the existence of numerous in-dividual studies that have suggested specific effects of field ex-periences on the development of teachers, there continues to be a great deal of debate about the actual role they play.

Generally, with few exceptions (e.g., Tabachnick, 1980), studies on the socializing role of field experiences have not at-tended to the quality or substance of these experiences, which often differ from program intentions (Calderhead, 1988a), and have not identified the particular kinds of field programs and components within programs (e.g., characteristics of place-ment sites) that are related to different socialization outcomes for different students.

Circumstances in individual schools influenced the experiences of stu-dents on Introductory School Experience and the impressions they developed or had confirmed about the nature of teaching—the extent to which school policy required teachers to follow the textbook, for example, as opposed to providing freedom to construct or amend the curriculum, or the extent to which other classrooms in the school were accessible, or the level of collegiality and discussion that was evident amongst teachers affected the nature of the learning experience for student teachers. (Calderhead, 1988b, p. 82)

Recent studies have suggested several factors that serve as obstacles to teacher learning during field experiences, such as the norms regarding the process of learning to teach that exist in many placement settings (e.g., see D. Ball & Noordhoff, 1985; Calderhead, 1988b; Feiman-Nemser & Buchmann, 1987; Koehler, 1988). More studies are needed that attend to the complex set of interactions existing among program fea-tures, dimensions of school contexts and individual classrooms as settings for learning to teach, and the characteristics and dispositions that individual students bring to the experience. The currently dominant practice of attempting to explain the socializing role of field experiences, in general, has not been very productive to date, nor is it likely to become more so in the future (Zeichner, 1986a).

In summary, the question of the socializing impact of pre-service teacher education programs has several dimensions. Studies of the influence of the formal curriculum of programs suggest that preservice programs are not very powerful inter-ventions. On the other hand, studies of the influence of the hidden curriculum of programs suggest, with little supporting empirical evidence, that the impact of preservice preparation might be far greater than has been thought. Studies of field-based experiences indicate that these experiences have differ-ential effects on teachers, but we are only beginning to gain an understanding of the specific factors that affect the course of teacher learning. Finally, research on undergraduate educa-tion has begun to illuminate some of the consequences of at-tending a college or university for the cognitive, moral, affect-ive, and political development of students, but we still know very little about how the character and quality of particular kinds of institutions and of various subenvironments within in-stitutions affect student development in general and the devel-opment of teachers in particular. There is a critical need for more empirical work regarding the impact of both academic and professional courses on students. To date, there has been very little direct study of specific courses and their impact on prospective teachers.

Socialization in the Workplace and Culture

Pollard's (1982) conceptual model describing three levels of social contextualization is helpful in understanding the socializ-ing influence of the workplace subsequent to preservice prepa-ration. According to Pollard, teachers' actions represent active and creative responses to the constraints, opportunities, and dilemmas posed by the immediate contexts of the classroom and the school, and it is through these immediate contexts that the wider structure of the community, the society, and the state have their impact on teachers.

At the interactive level within the classroom, Pollard (1982) describes several different kinds of influences on teachers. Two of these influences; the socializing role of pupils and the influence of the ecology of the classroom, will be considered here. First, the position emphasizing the significant role of pupils on the socialization of teachers is supported both on logical grounds and by empirical evidence. Doyle (1979) and Haller (1967) argue, for example, that the important role of pupils in teacher socialization is understandable, given the typical isolation of teachers from their colleagues and supervisors and given the transitory and invisible nature of the learning process. These and other logical explanations of the importance of pupils in the occupational socialization of teachers are consistent with now widely accepted bidirectional models of childhood socialization (e.g., Baumrind, 1980; Drietzel, 1973) and are supported by a substantial number of empirical studies on the nature of classroom influence (e.g., Blase, 1985, 1986; Brophy & Evertson, 1981; L. McNeil, 1983; Riseborough, 1988). According to Doyle (1979), the influence of students ranges from effects on the general teaching approach and patterns of language used by teachers in classrooms to the type and frequency of specific teaching methods utilized by teachers. Furthermore, the individual characteristics of both teachers and students seem to affect the ways in which pupils influence teacher development. Larson (1986) argues that the socializing role of pupils becomes increasingly greater as teachers gain experience and become more aware of and concerned with pupils.

As a result of these classroom studies, as well as studies on teacher socialization (e.g., Grant & Sleeter, 1985; Hammersley, 1977a, 1977b; Jordell, 1987; Metz, 1988; Tabachnick & Zeichner, 1985), there is little question that classroom influence is reciprocal in nature and that teachers' perceptions of pupils' characteristics, expectations, and behaviors influence the nature of teacher development. Despite this general knowledge, however, there is currently very little understanding of how the specific characteristics of teachers and pupils mediate the processes of teacher socialization.

Doyle (1979) argues that pupil effects are just one facet of the larger question of the effects of classrooms on teachers. Copeland (1980) and Doyle (1977, 1979) have emphasized the role of the ecology of the classroom in teacher socialization. Doyle and Ponder (1975) define the ecological system of the classroom as "that network of interconnected processes and events which impinge upon behavior in the teaching environment" (p. 183). Doyle (1986) identifies six distinctive features of classrooms that he feels are crucial in shaping the course of teacher development: multidimensionality, simultaneity, immediacy, unpredictability, publicness, and history. Others such as Connell (1985), Dale (1977a, 1977b), Denscombe (1980, 1982), Dreeben (1973), Sharp and Green (1975), and Westbury (1973) all discuss various factors related to the material conditions and social organization of the classroom and how they affect teachers' work. Among these are teacher–pupil ratios, declining levels of resources, and limited time.

According to this view of classrooms as ecological environments, learning to teach involves "learning the texture of the classroom and the sets of behaviors congruent with the environmental demands of that setting" (Doyle, 1977, p. 31). The environmental demands posed by current classroom arrangements establish limits on the range of teacher behaviors that can be successful in particular settings and show that successful teachers must learn a set of coping strategies appropriate to particular settings. These classroom conditions, however, not only act as constraints on the actions of teachers, but they also exert positive pressures to act in certain ways. In any case, the actions of teachers, according to Hargreaves (1988), are closely tied to environmental circumstances:

Teachers do not just decide to deploy particular skills because of their recognized professional worth and value, or because of their own confidence and competence in operating them. Rather they make judgements about the fit between particular skills, constraints, demands, and opportunities of the material environment of the classroom; about the appropriateness of particular styles or techniques for present circumstances. (p. 219)

Although there seems to be little doubt at present that the characteristics of the classroom need to be closely examined in any attempt to understand teacher socialization, the analysis cannot remain at the level of the classroom, because these ecological conditions are themselves products of policy decisions, political actions, and other influences at levels beyond the classroom.

At the institutional level of analysis (Pollard, 1982), socializing influences related to schools as workplaces come into focus. Fenstermacher (1980) argues that teachers' experiences with the institutional characteristics of schools are the most potent determinants of their perspectives toward teaching. In a similar vein Dreeben (1973), Gitlin (1983) and Larkin (1973) have written about how certain organizational properties of schools (e.g., internal spatial arrangements and authority relationships) have implications for the character of teachers' work. Two aspects of school-level socializing influences will be considered here: the influence of teaching colleagues and the influence of evaluators.

There is little question that the influence of colleagues needs to be taken into account in attempts to understand teacher socialization, despite the existence of an ethos of privacy and individualism within many schools (Denscombe, 1980; Eddy, 1969; Nigris, 1988). Given that teachers in a given school work under generally similar conditions, collegial influence is probably closely tied to the common circumstances that teachers face in the structural characteristics of schools and in the ecological conditions of classrooms. It is also clear, however, as studies by Carew and Lightfoot (1979) and Metz (1978) have shown, that several diverse teacher cultures often exist, even in a single school, and that teachers often face conflicting pressures by colleagues to influence them.

Edgar and Warren (1969) challenge this view of the strong socializing role of colleagues and argue that colleagues per se and the contextual effects of the workplace are less important in explaining teacher socialization than are the attitudes of significant evaluators, those having power over teachers in terms of their ability to potentially apply organizational sanctions. However, despite the existence of this one study that addressed the socialization of teachers with regard to their perspectives on autonomy in the teachers' role, the empirical literature does not generally confirm the view that teachers' superordinates contribute substantially to teacher socialization. On the contrary, there is overwhelming evidence that teachers generally receive very little direct assistance and advice from their superiors (Zeichner, 1983b) and that teachers can insulate themselves from at least some of the directives and sanctions of significant evaluators when they choose to do so (Zeichner & Tabachnick, 1985). This is not to say that the classroom is an impregnable sanctuary where teachers are free from administrative influence. The literature does suggest, however, that it is more through the structural imperatives of the job than through the influence of individual administrators that teaching perspectives are developed and maintained over time. Studies conducted by, Connell (1985) and Zeichner and Tabachnick (1985) indicate that there is a great deal of variation both among and within schools in the degree to which significant evaluators influence teachers' work.

At the cultural level of analysis (Pollard, 1982), attempts have been made to link the perspectives of individual teachers and groups of teachers, as well as the microlevel of the classroom, both to the immediate local community of the school and to ideologies, practices, and material conditions at the macrolevel of society (e.g., inequalities in wealth and power).

First, drawing on the work of Arfwedson (1979) and his notion of the "local social context," Hatton (1987) challenges the position that it is the classroom context that is the chief socializing influence on teachers. She presents data from a study conducted in one high-status, state, primary school in Australia that shows parental power to be a significant determinant of pedagogical practices. According to Arfwedson (1979)

There is no such thing as a common working situation of all teachers. On the contrary, the working conditions of a teacher are strongly linked to the kind of school in which he serves. Consequently, the occupational socialization of teachers varies according to the school conditions which are, in turn, dependent on the local society surrounding the school. . . . (p. 93)

According to this view, schools that serve high and low socioeconomic populations can be thought of as providing quite distinct working situations for teachers, and parents can be seen as exerting either direct or indirect influence on teachers. In high-status schools, the influence is seen to be exerted directly by parents, whereas in low-status schools, it is thought to be carried most frequently through the agency of the children as representatives of their families, their social class, and its interests. In any case, parental pressure (from the most influential parents in a community) is seen as a basic mechanism for the socialization of teachers into the traditions of a school community. Teachers do not necessarily passively conform to these pressures, but they must take them into account in some way as they go about their work. Since Waller's (1932) seminal analysis, which initiated the modern era of teacher socialization

research, local social context or community pressure has repeatedly surfaced in studies of teaching as a salient socializing influence (e.g., Carew & Lightfoot, 1979; Gracey, 1972; McPherson, 1972; Metz, 1978, in press).

Once we move beyond the immediate community of the school to consider forces and influences in the broader society, two main types of analysis can be found. First, those such as Apple (1983, 1987), Gitlin (1983), and Wise (1979) have explored how practices and policy initiatives outside of the school have affected the material resources available to teachers and the character of teachers' work. According to this view, teacher actions represent active and creative responses to constraints and opportunities determined externally at a societal level and mediated through institutional structures and processes. Studies have clearly documented how such factors in a society as the bureaucratization of work, the deskilling of labor, the social division of labor, and the stereotypes and discrimination against women (S. Ball & Goodson, 1985; Feiman-Nemser & Floden, 1986) have affected the circumstances of teachers' work, although the frequently alleged linkages to the perspectives of individual teachers have not been well documented empirically. Some progress has been made, though, in general occupational socialization studies in understanding how various structural conditions of an occupation (e.g., closeness of supervision and degree of routinization) affect various worker attitudes and dispositions (e.g., intellectual flexibility and self-directedness of orientation) (see Kiecolt, 1988). Teacher socialization research could benefit from more attention to this sociological literature.

A second type of analysis of the relationship between cultural forms and teacher socialization has attempted to link the perspectives of individual teachers to forms of meaning and rationality that are dominant in a society. Dale's (1977a, 1977b) arguments related to the development of a cognitive style of liberal individualism, Giroux's (1980) analysis of the development of a technocratic rationality, and Popkewitz's (1985) thesis regarding the socializing influence of the professionalization of knowledge and the ideology of professionalism are examples of recent attempts to demonstrate the effect of cultural codes on the development and nurturance of individual teachers' perspectives. As was argued earlier, however, there is currently very little, if any, empirical evidence available that substantiates these claims and that documents that individual teachers' actually incorporate forms of meaning and modes of rationality into their perspectives in ways consistent with the macrolevel theories. In one interesting study involving teachers' interpretations of teacher actions in another culture, Spindler & Spindler (1987) are able to demonstrate the impact of deeply held and culturally determined values and beliefs on teaching perspectives.

Generally, the cultural level of analysis has received the least attention of the three levels in relation to teacher socialization (Atkinson & Delamont, 1985). Although many of the analyses at a macrolevel are very persuasive on logical grounds and although some definite influences have been amply documented regarding the link between the cultural and institutional contexts, much work remains to be done regarding empirical substantiation of theories of the influence of cultural codes and the material conditions of a society on the socialization of teachers.

In summary, this analysis of workplace and cultural influences on teacher socialization at three different levels has revealed some evidence in the literature supporting the view that pupils, the ecology of the classroom, colleagues and institutional characteristics of schools all play significant roles in the socialization of teachers. The specific nature of these influences was described (e.g., the informal and contradictory nature of colleague influence), together with areas in which more research is particularly needed. It was also concluded that research has not generally confirmed Edgar Warren's claim that significant evaluators play a substantial role in teacher socialization. Finally, it was also concluded that, although some evidence has been accumulated relating to the socializing influence of various factors in the culture as a whole on the conditions of teachers' work, the links between these cultural factors and the socialization of individual teachers have not been firmly established, with the exception of the influence of parents and the local social context.

DISCUSSION

Thus far, we have outlined three intellectual traditions in teacher socialization research, as well as several alternative explanations of how teachers are socialized at various points in their careers. Until recently, the study of teacher socialization was dominated by functionalist studies, which depicted teachers as either prisoners of their pasts (e.g., of anticipatory socialization during childhood) or prisoners of the present (e.g., of pressures emanating from the workplace). In the years since C. Lacey's (1977) highly influential study in England and the increasing influence of interpretive perspectives in educational research generally, numerous interpretive accounts of teacher socialization have emerged in the United States, the United Kingdom, Canada, and Australia that portray the socialization process as much more partial and incomplete than did many of the earlier functionalist studies. There is a growing consensus in the field about the highly interactive nature of the socialization process and about the constant interplay between choice and constraint in the process of learning to teach. The critical tradition, on the other hand, has had very little influence on work in this area. As was mentioned earlier, many of the alleged influences on teacher socialization emanating from the broader society have not been documented in empirical studies, and, generally, the collective aspects of socialization, particularly with regard to the issues of race, social class, and gender, have not received adequate attention from researchers.

Functionalist studies, by focusing on the description of central tendencies in teacher development, fail to illuminate the diversity present in individual stories of teacher development. Although the recent shift to interpretive accounts of socialization has resulted in much more attention being given to the unique elements of each teacher's socialization, this research has caused us to lose sight of many of the more collective aspects of the socialization process, of patterns in teacher social-

ization for particular subgroups of teachers, and of the social and political contexts within which the socialization process occurs (Atkinson & Delamont, 1985). The socialization stories of teachers of a particular gender, and of those who represent certain social-class backgrounds, generations, races, and so on, and of teachers who teach in particular kinds of settings will have many things in common despite the unique aspects of each account. In our view, researchers need to pay attention to both uniqueness and commonality in the socialization of teachers. More attention to the collective aspects of socialization and to the kinds of structural issues raised by studies conducted in the critical tradition could help correct the imbalance that has developed in the literature from overemphasis on individual stories of socialization and the lack of attention to institutional and cultural contexts in which socialization occurs. More attention, in particular, needs to be devoted by researchers to the ways in which race, social class, and gender mediate the socialization process and establish socialization patterns for particular groups of individuals who teach in particular kinds of schools.

One consequence of viewing teacher socialization as an interactive process is that teachers influence and shape that into which they are being socialized at the same time that they are being shaped by a variety of forces at many levels. This chapter has concentrated on presenting a variety of explanations regarding how teachers are influenced by structural and personal factors. The emphasis has continually been on how teachers have been influenced and not on how the structures into which they are being socialized have been shaped and recreated by the teachers. An adequate account of teacher socialization must attend to both sides of this issue. Much of the work related to how schools and the contexts in which they exist are maintained and/or altered by the actions of teachers can be found in the sociological literature on social and cultural production and reproduction (see Weiler, 1988). Although much of this literature has not been discussed in the current chapter, an important task for researchers in the future is to address the reciprocal nature of the agency–structure relationship in any given piece of research; that is, how are teachers shaped by, and in turn influence, the structures into which they are socialized?

Another problem that needs attention in the future is that of interpreting research findings that have been generated in a number of countries. This chapter has dealt with research in the United States, the United Kingdom, Canada, and Australia without much attention to the different traditions and pressures that exist in these countries with regard to schooling, teaching, and teacher education. Furthermore, substantial bodies of teacher socialization research completed in many non-English-speaking countries have not been dealt with (e.g., see Jordell, 1987). Tabachnick (1988) has warned researchers about the dangers of transporting research generated in one country to another and has stressed the importance of accounting for the particular conditions and traditions in a country when interpreting research. One must be extremely cautious in interpreting the research on teacher socialization, even when studies from several countries appear to converge around particular explanations of the socialization process, as was the case in several instances in this chapter. For example, in this chapter studies from several countries that discussed the impact of the student-teaching experience or practicum on prospective teachers were cited. What has to be kept in mind is that student teaching/practicum has a very different meaning in Australia and in the United States. For example, spending a full university semester working in a single classroom, as is common in the United States, provides a very different learning context from spending several shorter practicums in different settings, as is common in Australia. To discuss the socializing role of any specific aspect of this experience (e.g., cooperating teachers) across cultures without taking into account the specific nature of the practicum experience in different countries is potentially misleading. And, as was mentioned previously, differences in teacher education programs also need to be taken into account in the interpretation of research findings.

This issue of how the cultural context of research influences the interpretation of research findings raises the more general question of the meaning of teacher socialization research for teacher education practice, regardless of the similarity between the context of the research and the context of the practice. In our view, there is not a direct link between teacher socialization research and practice in teacher education programs, even within the same site in which a research study has been conducted. We agree with those who have stressed the point that the links between research and practice are always mediated by particular moral frameworks and that the same research findings can lead to a variety of implications for practice, depending upon one's view of the purposes of teacher education, the role of the teacher in the school and society, and other considerations (Buchmann, 1987).

For example, studies that illuminate the ways in which various factors interact in their influence on the formation of teaching perspectives can be used to either enable teacher educators to exert tighter controls over the socialization process (an instrumental view of the research–practice relationship) or empower prospective teachers to be more aware of and, hence, more in control of the direction of their own education for teaching (an educative view of the research–practice relationship). Neither course of action is implied by a particular set of findings that enlighten us about the mysteries of the socialization process.

It is our belief that research on teacher socialization should be used by teacher educators and policymakers in ways that further the roles of teachers as extended professionals who play a significant part in the making of educational policies at the classroom and school levels within democratic school environments (Zeichner, 1989). This research should also be used in a manner that helps teachers establish more control over their education for teaching by making them more aware of the nature of their socialization into teaching. This position is similar to the one advocated by various researchers with regard to the proper relationship between research on teaching and teachers (e.g., Fenstermacher, 1980; Zumwalt, 1982). One way this can happen is for teacher educators to use accounts of socialization that are produced for research purposes as part of the curriculum of their teacher education programs. Examples of this will be discussed shortly.

This concern with the empowering potential of teacher socialization research raises a number of critical issues related to the social relations of the research process itself. In recent years a rapidly growing literature has emerged that has questioned the traditional hierarchical relationships existing between university researchers and either teachers or student teachers (see Bolster, 1983; Noddings, 1986; Reinharz, 1988; Roman & Apple, 1988; Wexler, 1987). The major points raised in these critiques are concerned with ethical dimensions of the research process, such as whose perspectives are represented in the research and who benefits from the research. A great deal of concern has been expressed in this literature about the wronging of persons that could result from existing research practices. Teacher education students, teachers, and teacher educators are often portrayed in a negative way in these studies, sometimes without having an opportunity even to read and respond to researchers' interpretations of their work. Research concerned with teaching and teacher education has rightly been criticized at times for being research on rather than for the people who are studied.

These criticisms of research practices are applicable to all three of the intellectual traditions that underlie teacher socialization research, for, as Lather (1986) points out, even critical studies, with their transformative intent, have not necessarily redressed the unequal power relations between researchers and researched. Furthermore, as Noffke & Zeichner (1987) argue, this is also the case for some of the studies researchers label collaborative. We believe that work on teacher socialization must begin to explore and practice ways of democratizing the research process if the empowering potential of the research is to be realized.

One way to begin this democratizing process is to insure that, at minimum, those whose practices are studied in teacher socialization research have an opportunity to read and react to researchers' portrayals. If there are disagreements between researchers and researched about some aspect of the socialization account, then either these differences should be negotiated until some agreement is reached or the perspectives of those who are studied should be published along with the researchers' accounts. Ideally, there would be mutual constructions of the socialization portrayals by the researchers and the researched.

It needs to be emphasized that the socialization research that has been reviewed in this chapter has largely been conducted on female teachers, oftentimes by male university researchers. There is burgeoning interest in feminist methodology in social science research, which, in part attempts to redress the inequitable relationships that typically exist between researcher and researched and to correct the distortions of women's experiences that are sometimes a consequence of these relationships. Recent work on feminist methodology (e.g., Belenky et al., 1986; Scott, 1985) serves to remind us that we need to be more responsive to the fact that many of those who are portrayed in teacher socialization studies are women and that there is a need to develop new and more interactive methods of conducting research that illuminate teachers' perspectives of their own development.

A final issue is concerned with the question of who benefits from the kinds of teacher socialization studies that have been reviewed in this chapter. Although the academic researchers who conduct these studies usually benefit from public reports of the work by receiving traditional academic rewards of promotion, tenure, further research grants, and peer recognition, little is typically done with research to better the life circumstances of those students, teachers, and teacher educators who are studied (e.g., Schneider, 1987). We feel that this state of affairs is morally unacceptable. A priority in teacher socialization research (in addition to its value in increasing our collective understanding of the processes of teacher socialization) needs to become one of finding ways to use our research studies to enhance the lives of those who open themselves up to us in these studies.

Knowles's (1988a) study of the failure of Cynthia provides one example of the kind of stance we feel is important for researchers to adopt. This study illustrates how it is possible for a preservice teacher to benefit directly from a researcher's account of her socialization into teaching. After Cynthia withdrew from her student-teaching experience, Knowles continued to meet with her in a series of debriefing sessions to discuss his interpretations of her experiences. Over a period of time and through these interactions, Cynthia gradually developed new understandings of her experience and "from a potentially devastating experience she was able to attain a new personal understanding" (p. 32). Knowles's commitment to helping Cynthia benefit in a concrete way from his research labors and his genuine concern for her plight are exemplary, and they serve as a model for the kind of moral commitment to teacher education that we feel needs to become an integral part of teacher socialization research. Some of the recent work using various forms of life history methodologies (e.g., Butt, 1984, in press; Butt & Raymond, in press; Quicke, 1988; Tripp, 1987) also clearly illustrates the educative and emancipatory potential of research that seeks to understand the development of teachers' knowledge.

In addition to benefiting from researchers' accounts of their own socialization experiences, teacher education students, teachers, and teacher educators can also benefit from reading and reflecting on research accounts of the experiences of others. It is common practice, for example, for supervisors of student teachers in the program with which we are both associated to use case studies of individual student teachers or research accounts of common patterns in student teacher socialization (e.g., Feiman-Nemser & Buchmann, 1983) as part of the curriculum in the student-teaching seminars. Student teachers read and discuss these accounts of teacher socialization and relate them to their own experiences in learning to teach and potentially gain greater insights into and control over their own socialization.

At a different level, it is also important for teacher education programs to benefit from studies of teacher socialization as reports of research are fed back into program-development efforts. As discussed, these studies would not provide solutions,

or even directions, for teacher educators to adopt. These will come from the interplay of the research with the moral frameworks and commitments of teacher educators. What the research can do, however, is challenge our thinking and help us think more clearly about the consequences of our work for those we seek to educate. Ultimately, the questions that must be resolved are moral ones, and teacher socialization research needs to become part of a process of moral and political deliberation about the purposes and goals of teacher education and schooling.

Finally, the teacher socialization literature clearly demonstrates that interventions at the level of individual students or teacher educators such as the ones stressed here are inadequate by themselves for altering the course of teacher education programs. Studies that have focused on the institutional and cultural levels of analysis have clearly shown, for example, that various ideological and material conditions within teacher education institutions, schools, and societies serve to establish limits on the range of options available to both teacher education students and teacher educators. Teacher educators must, in addition to their efforts to shape the curricular and instructional practices within programs, work to alter the institutional, social, and political contexts and the principles and practices of authority, legitimacy, and control underlying them (Liston & Zeichner, 1988; Popkewitz, 1985). The literature in teacher education is filled with examples of how external contexts of teacher education programs have undermined the intentions and hopes of program reformers and, in many cases, have served to sustain the very practices that are the foci of reform initiatives (Zeichner, 1986b). Only by our attention to these issues of institutional and social change will our hopes for the betterment of individual lives and the improvement of teacher education programs be realized.

A Brief Note on the Use of the Term *Socialization*

As pointed out in the beginning of the chapter, the term *socialization* is commonly defined too narrowly. Such definitions as Danziger's (1971), with which this chapter began, legitimize only functionalist studies and lack the element of reciprocity that characterizes much interpretive work. Other definitions, which support interpretive studies, allow for tension in the socialization relationship and emphasize interaction rather than internalization (e.g., Wentworth, 1980), but the focus is still on the individual in interaction. At various points in this chapter, we have emphasized a critical view of socialization that depicts the socialization process as contradictory and dialectical, as collective as well as individual, and as situated within the broader context of institutions, society, culture, and history. We have also argued that socialization research conducted from a critical perspective must seek to redress the unequal power relations between researchers and the researched. Thus, rather than rejecting the term *socialization* as inherently limiting, we have taken the position that meaning is always open to challenge and redefinition (Weedon, 1987) and have tried to demonstrate that an alternative conception of the term exists.

References

Althusser, L. (1971). *Lenin and philosophy and other essays.* New York: Monthly Review Press.

Amarel, M., & Feiman-Nemser, S. (1988). *Prospective teachers' views of teaching and learning to teach.* Paper presented at the meeting of the American Educational Research Association, New Orleans.

Anderson, D. S. (1974). *The development of student teachers; A comparative study of professional socialization.* Paris: Organization for Economic Cooperation & Development.

Anderson, K. L. (1988). The impact of colleges and the involvement of male and female students. *Sociology of Education, 61,* 160–177.

Apple, M. (1983). Curricular form and the logic of technical control. In M. Apple & L. Weis (Eds.), *Ideology and practice in education.* Philadelphia: Temple University Press.

Apple, M. W. (1987). *Teachers and texts: A political economy of class and gender relations in education.* London: Routledge & Kegan Paul.

Arfwedson, G. (1979). Teachers' work. In U. Lundgren & S. Patterson (Eds.), *Code, context and curriculum processes.* Lund, Sweden: Gleerup.

Ashton, P., & Crocker, L. (1987). Systematic study of planned variations: The essential focus of teacher education reform. *Journal of Teacher Education, 38*(3), 2–8.

Astin, A. (1977). *Four critical years.* San Francisco: Jossey-Bass.

Atkinson, P., & Delamont, S. (1985). Socialization into teaching: The research which lost its way. *British Journal of Sociology of Education, 6*(3), 307–322.

Ball, D. (1988). *Prospective teachers' understandings of mathematics: What do they bring with them to teacher education?* Paper presented at the meeting of the American Educational Research Association, New Orleans.

Ball, D., & McDiarmid, B. (1987). *Understanding how teachers' knowledge changes.* East Lansing, MI: National Center for Research on Teacher Education.

Ball, D., & Noordhoff, K. (1985). *Learning to teach by the book: The influence of persons, program, and setting on student teaching.* Paper presented at the meeting of the American Educational Research Association, Chicago.

Ball, S., & Goodson. (1985). *Teachers' lives and careers.* London: Falmer.

Ball, S., & Lacey, C. (1980). Subject disciplines as the opportunity for group action: A measured critique of subject subcultures. In P. Woods (Ed.), *Teacher strategies* (pp. 149–177). London: Croom Helm.

Barrows, L. (1978). *Student teaching and success: A field study of four male elementary school student teachers.* Unpublished doctoral dissertation, University of Wisconsin—Madison.

Bartholomew, J. (1976). Schooling teachers: The myth of the liberal college. In G. Whitty & M. Young (Eds.), *Explorations in the politics of school knowledge.* Driffield, England: Nafferton.

Battersby, D. (1983). The politics of teacher socialization. In R. K. Brown & L. E. Foster (Eds.), *Sociology of education* (3rd ed.). Melbourne, Austrialia: Macmillan.

Baumrind, D. (1980). New directions in socialization research. *American Psychologist, 35,* 639–652.

Becker, H. S. (1964). Personal change in adult life. *Sociometry, 27,* 40–53.

Becker, H. S., Geer, B., Hughes, E. C., & Strauss, A. L. (1961). *Boys in white.* Chicago: University of Chicago Press.

Belenky, M. F., et al. (1986). *Women's ways of knowing: The development of self, voice, and mind.* New York: Basic Books.

Bernstein, B. (1971). On the classification and framing of educational knowledge. In M. Young (Ed.), *Knowledge and control.* London: Collier-Macmillan.

Bernstein, B. (1979). *Class, codes and control* (Vol. 3). London: Routledge & Kegan Paul.

Blase, J. (1985). The socialization of teachers: An ethnographic study of factors contributing to the rationalization of the teacher's instructional perspective. *Urban Education, 20*(3), 235–256.

Blase, J. (1986). Socialization as humanization: One side of becoming a teacher. *Sociology of Education, 59*(2), 100–113.

Bolster, A. S. (1983). Toward a more effective model of research on teaching. *Harvard Educational Review, 53*(3), 294–308.

Book, C., Byers, J., & Freeman, D. J. (1983). Student expectations and teacher education traditions with which we can and cannot live. *Journal of Teacher Education, 34*(1), 9–13.

Bourdieu, P. (1977). *Outline of a theory of practice.* Cambridge, England: Cambridge University Press.

Bowles, S., & Gintis, H. (1976). *Schooling in capitalist America.* New York: Basic Books.

Boyer, E. (1987). *College: The undergraduate experience in America.* New York: Harper & Row.

Braudel, F. (1980). *On history.* Chicago: University of Chicago Press.

Britzman, D. (1986). Cultural myths in the making of a teacher: Biography and social structure in teacher education. *Harvard Educational Review, 56*(4), 442–472.

Brophy, J., & Everston, C. (1981). *Student characteristics and teaching.* New York: Longman.

Buchmann, M. (1987). Reporting and using educational research: Conviction or persuasion. In J. Goodland (Ed.), *The ecology of school renewal.* Chicago: University of Chicago Press.

Bullough, R. (1987). First-year teaching: A case study. *Teachers College Record, 89*(2), 39–46.

Bullough, R. V., Jr. (1989). *First-year teacher: A case study.* New York: Teachers College Press.

Burgess, R. (1988). Examining classroom practice using diaries and diary interviews. In P. Woods & A. Pollard (Eds.), *Sociology and teaching.* London: Croom Helm.

Burrell, G., & Morgan, G. (1979). *Sociological paradigms and organizational analysis.* London: Heinemann.

Butt, R. L. (1984). Arguments for using biography in understanding teacher thinking. In R. Halkes & J. Olson (Eds.), *Teaching thinking* (pp. 95–102). Lisse, Holland: Swets and Zeitlinger.

Butt, R. L. (in press). An intergrative function for teacher's biographies. In B. Milburn (Ed.), *Reinterrupting curriculum research: Images and arguments.* London: Falmer.

Butt, R., & Raymond, D. (in press). Studying the nature and development of teachers' knowledge using collaborative autobiography. *International Journal of Educational Research.*

Butt, R., Raymond, D., & Yamagishi, L. (1988). Autobiographical praxis: Studying the formation of teachers' knowledge. *Journal of Curriculum Theorizing, 7*(4), 87–164.

Calderhead, J. (1988a). The contribution of field experience to student primary teachers' professional learning. *Research in Education, 40,* 33–49.

Calderhead, J. (1988b). Learning from introductory school experience. *Journal of Education for Teaching, 14*(1), 75–83.

Carew, J., & Lightfoot, S. L. (1979). *Beyond bias: Perspectives on classrooms.* Cambridge, MA: Harvard University Press.

Carr, W., & Kemmis, S. (1986). *Becoming critical: Education, knowledge and action research.* London: Falmer.

Casey, K. (1988). *Teacher as author: Life history narratives of contemporary women teachers working for social change.* Unpublished doctoral dissertation, University of Wisconsin—Madison.

Clark, D., & Marker, G. (1975). The institutionalization of teacher education. In K. Ryan (Ed.), *Teacher education* (74th yearbook of the National Society for the Study of Education, Part II, pp. 53–86). Chicago: University of Chicago Press.

Clausen, J. A. (Ed.). (1968). *Socialization and society.* Boston: Little, Brown.

Comte, A. (1853). *The positivist philosophy* (Vol. 1). (H. Martineau, Trans.). London: Chapman.

Connell, R. W. (1985). *Teachers' work.* Sydney, Austrialia: George Allen and Unwin.

Connelly, F. M., & Clandinin, D. J. (1987). On narrative method, biography and narrative unities in the study of teaching. *Journal of Educational Thought, 21*(3), 130–139.

Copeland, W. (1980). Student teachers and cooperating teachers: An ecological relationship. *Theory Into Practice, 18,* 194–199.

Crow, N. (1987). *Preservice teacher's biography: A case study.* Paper presented at the meeting of the American Educational Research Association, Washington, DC.

Crow, N. (1988). *A longitudinal study of teacher socialization: A case study.* Paper presented at the meeting of the American Educational Research Association, New Orleans.

Crow, N., & Kauchak, D. (1988). *Teacher socialization: A quasi-experimental case study.* Paper presented at the meeting of the American Educational Research Association, New Orleans.

Cuban, L. (1984). *How teachers taught: Constancy and change in American classrooms: 1890–1980.* New York: Longman.

Dale, R. (1977a). Implications of the rediscovery of the hidden curriculum for the sociology of teaching. In D. Gleason (Ed.), *Identity and structure: Issues in the sociology of education.* Driffield, England: Nafferton.

Dale, R. (1977b). *The structural context of teaching.* Milton Keynes, England: Open University Press.

Danziger, K. (1971). *Socialization.* Baltimore: Penguin.

Delone, R. (1979). *Small futures.* New York: Harcourt Brace Jovanovich.

Denscombe, M. (1980). The work context of teaching: An analytic framework for the study of teachers in classrooms. *British Journal of Sociology of Education, 1,* 279–292.

Denscombe, M. (1982). The hidden pedagogy and its implications for teacher training: An ecological analysis. *British Journal of Sociology of Education, 3,* 249–265.

Dilthey, W. (1976). In H. P. Rickman, (Ed.), *Selected writings.* Cambridge: Cambridge University Press.

Dollard, J. (1939). Culture, society, impulse and socialization. *American Journal of Sociology, 45*(1), 50–63.

Doyle, W. (1977). *Learning the classroom environment: An ecological analysis. Journal of Teacher Education, 28,* 51–55.

Doyle, W. (1979). Classroom effects. *Theory Into Practice, 18,* 138–144.

Doyle, W. (1986). Classroom organization and management. In M. C. Wittrock (Ed.), *Handbook of research on teaching* (3rd ed., pp. 392–431). New York: Macmillan.

Doyle, W., & Ponder, G. (1975). Classroom ecology: Some concerns about a neglected dimension of research on teaching. *Contemporary Education, 46,* 183–188.

Dreeben, R. (1973). The school as a workplace. In R. Travers (Ed.), *Second handbook of research on teaching.* Chicago: Rand McNally.

Dreitzel, H. P. (1973). *Childhood and socialization.* New York: Macmillan.

Durkheim, E. (1938). *The rules of sociological method.* Glencoe, IL: Free Press.

Eddy, E. (1969). *Becoming a teacher: The passage to professional status.* New York: Teachers College Press.

Edgar, D., & Warren, R. (1969). Power and autonomy in teacher socialization. *Sociology of Education, 42,* 386–399.

Feiman-Nemser, S. (1983). Learning to teach. In L. Shulman & G. Sykes (Eds.), *Handbook of teaching and policy.* New York: Longman.

Feiman-Nemser, S., & Buchmann, M. (1983). Pitfalls of experience in teacher education. In P. Tamir, A. Hofstein, & M. Ben-Peretz (Eds.), *Preservice and inservice education of science teachers.* Philadelphia: Balaban International Science Services.

Feiman-Nemser, S., & Buchmann, M. (1986). The first year of teacher preparation: Transition to pedagogical thinking. *Journal of Curriculum Studies, 18*(3), 239–256.

Feiman-Nemser, S., & Buchmann, M. (1987). When is student teaching teacher education? *Teaching and Teacher Education, 3*(4), 255–273.

Feiman-Nemser, S., & Floden, R. (1986). The cultures of teaching. In M. C. Wittrock (Ed.), *Handbook of research on teaching* (3rd ed., pp. 505–526). New York: Macmillan.

Feldman, K., & Newcomb, T. (1969). *The impact of college on students.* San Francisco: Jossey-Bass.

Fenstermacher, G. (1980). On learning to teach from research on teacher effectiveness. In C. Denham & A. Lieberman (Eds.), *Time to learn.* Washington, DC: U.S. Department of Education.

Freedman, S., Jackson, J., & Boles, K. (1986). *The effect of teaching on teachers.* Grand Forks, ND: North Dakota Study Group on Evaluation.

Gadamer, H. G. (1975). *Truth and method.* London: Sheed and Ward. (Original work published 1965.)

Garfinkel, H. (1967). *Studies in ethnomethodology.* Englewood Cliffs, NJ: Prentice-Hall.

Gibson, D. R. (1972). Professional socialization: The effects of a college course upon role conceptions of students in teacher training. *Educational Research, 14,* 213–219.

Ginsburg, M. (1988). *Contradictions in teacher education and society: A critical analysis.* New York: Falmer.

Ginsburg, M., & Clift, R. (1990). The hidden curriculum of preservice teacher education. In W. R. Houston (Ed.), *Handbook of research on teacher education.* New York: Macmillan.

Ginsburg, M., & Newman, K. (1985). Social inequalities, schooling, and teacher education. *Journal of Teacher Education, 26,* 49–54.

Giroux, H. (1980). Teacher education and the ideology of social control. *Journal of Education, 162,* 5–27.

Giroux, H. (1981). *Ideology, culture and the process of schooling.* Philadelphia: Temple University Press.

Giroux, H. (1983). *Theory and resistance in education: A pedagogy for the opposition.* South Hadley, MA: Bergin & Garvey.

Gitlin, A. (1983). School structure and teachers' work. In M. Apple & L. Weis (Eds.), *Ideology and practice in education.* Philadelphia: Temple University Press.

Gomez, M. (1988). *Prospective teachers' beliefs about good writing: What do they bring with them to teacher education?* Paper presented at the meeting of the American Educational Research Association, New Orleans.

Goodman, J. (1988). Masculinity, feminism, and the male elementary school teacher: A case study of preservice teachers' perspectives. *Journal of Curriculum Theorizing, 7*(2), 30–60.

Goodman, J., & Adler, S. (1985). Becoming an elementary school social studies teacher: A study of perspectives. *Theory and Research in Social Education, 13*(2), 1–20.

Goodson, I. (1980). Life histories and the study of schooling. *Interchange, 11*(4), 62–76.

Goodson, I. (1983). *School subjects and curriculum change*. London: Croom Helm.

Gouldner, A. W. (1976). *The dialectic of ideology and technology*. London: Macmillan.

Gracey, H. (1972). *Curriculum or craftsmanship*. Chicago: University of Chicago Press.

Grant, C. (1981). Education that is multicultural and teacher preparation: An examination from the perspectives of preservice students. *Journal of Educational Research, 75*, 95–101.

Grant, C., & Sleeter, C. (1985). Who determines teacher work? *Teaching and Teacher Education, 1*(3), 209–220.

Griffin, G. A., Barnes, S., Hughes, R., O'Neal, S., Defino, M., Edwards, S., & Hukill, H. (1983). *Clinical preservice teacher education: Final report of a descriptive study*. Austin, TX: University of Texas, Research & Development Center for Teacher Education.

Grossman, P. (1987). *Colleen: A case study of a beginning English teacher*. Stanford, CA: Stanford University, School of Education.

Grossman, P., & Richert, A. (1988). Unacknowledged knowledge growth: A re-examination of the effects of teacher education. *Teaching and Teacher Education, 4*(1), 53–62.

Grumet, M. (1980). Autobiography and reconceptualization. *Journal of Curriculum Theorizing, 2*(2), 155–158.

Haller, E. (1967). Pupils' influences in teacher socialization: A sociolinguistic study. *Sociology of Education, 40*, 316–333.

Hammersley, M. (1977a). *Teacher perspectives*. Milton Keynes, England: Open University Press.

Hammersley, M. (1977b). *The social location of teacher perspectives*. Milton Keynes, England: Open University Press.

Hanson, D., & Herrington, M. (1976). *From college to classroom*. London: Routledge & Kegan Paul.

Hargreaves, A. (1988). Teaching quality: A sociological analysis. *Journal of Curriculum Studies, 20*(3), 211–231.

Hartnett, A., & Naish, M. (1980). Technicians or social bandits? Some moral and political issues in the education of teachers. In P. Woods (Ed.), *Teacher strategies* (pp. 254–274). London: Croom Helm.

Hatton, E. (1987). Hidden pedagogy as an account of pedagogical conservatism. *Journal of Curriculum Studies, 19*(5), 457–470.

Hodges, C. (1982). Implementing methods: If you can't blame the cooperating teacher, whom can you blame? *Journal of Teacher Education, 33*, 25–29.

Hogben, D., & Lawson, M. (1983). Attitudes of secondary school teacher trainees and their practice teaching supervisors. *Journal of Education for Teaching, 9*, 249–263.

Hogben, D., & Lawson, M. (1984). Trainee and beginning teacher attitude stability and change: Four case studies. *Journal of Education for Teaching, 10*(2), 135–153.

Hogben, D., & Petty, M. (1979a). Early changes in teacher attitude. *Educational Research, 21*, 212–219.

Hogben, D., & Petty, M. (1979b). From student to primary school teacher: Attitude stability and change. *South Pacific Journal of Teacher Education, 7*, 92–98.

Hollingsworth, S. (in press). Prior beliefs and cognitive change in learning to teach. *American Educational Research Journal*.

Hoy, W., & Rees, R. (1977). The bureaucratic socialization of student teachers. *Journal of Teacher Education, 28*(1), 23–26.

Husserl, E. (1929). Entry on "Phenomenology." *Encyclopedia Brittanica* (14th ed.).

Ingvarson, L., & Greenway, P. (1984). Portrayals of teacher development. *Australian Journal of Education, 28*(1), 45–65.

Jordell, K. (1987). Structural and personal influences in the socialization of beginning teachers. *Teaching and Teacher Education, 3*(3), 165–177.

Kant, I. (1876). *Critique of pure reason* (J. M. D. Meiklejohn, Trans.). London: Bell & Daldy.

Katz, L., & Raths, J. (1982). The best of intentions for the education of teachers. *Action in Teacher Education, 4*, 8–16.

Kiecolt, K. J. (1988). Recent developments in attitudes and social structure. *Annual Review of Sociology, 14*, 381–403.

Kirk, D. (1986). Beyond the limits of theoretical discourse in teacher education: Towards a critical pedagogy. *Teaching and Teacher Education, 2*, 155–167.

Knowles, J. G. (1988a). *The failure of a student teacher: Becoming educated about teachers, teaching, and self*. Paper presented at the meeting of the American Educational Research Association, New Orleans.

Knowles, J. G. (1988b). *Models for understanding preservice and beginning teachers' biographies: Illustrations from case studies*. Paper presented at the meeting of the American Educational Research Association, New Orleans.

Knowles, J. G. (in press). A beginning English teacher's experience: Reflections on becoming a teacher. *Language Arts*.

Koehler, V. (1988). Barriers to the effective supervision of student teaching. *Journal of Teacher Education, 39*(2), 28–35.

Lacey, C. (1977). *The socialization of teachers*. London: Methuen.

Lacey, C. (1985). Professional socialization of teachers. In T. Husen & T. N. Postlethwaite (Eds.), *The international encyclopedia of education*. Oxford: Pergamon Press.

Lacy, W. (1978). Interpersonal relationships as mediators of structural effects. *Sociology of Education, 51*, 201–211.

Lanier, J., & Little, J. (1986). Research on teacher education. In M. C. Wittrock (Ed.), *Handbook of research on teaching* (3rd ed., pp. 527–569). New York: Macmillan.

Larkin, R. (1973). Contextual influences on teacher leadership styles. *Sociology of Education, 46*, 471–479.

Larson, S. (1986). Learning from experience: Teachers' conceptions of changes in their professional practice. *Journal of Curriculum Studies, 19*(1), 35–43.

Lather, P. (1986). Research as praxis. *Harvard Educational Review, 56*(3), 257–277.

LeCompte, M., & Ginsburg, M. (1987). How students learn to become teachers: An exploration of alternative responses to a teacher training program. In G. Noblit & W. Pinle, *Schooling in social context: Qualitative studies*. Norwood, NJ: Ablex.

Liston, D., & Zeichner, K. (1988). Critical pedagogy and teacher education. *Journal of Education, 169*(3), 117–137.

Lortie, D. (1975). *Schoolteacher: A sociological study*. Chicago: University of Chicago Press.

Malinowski, B. (1923). *The meaning of meaning*. New York: Harcourt Brace & World.

Malinowski, B. (1936). *The sexual life of savages in northwestern Melanesia; An ethnographic account of courtship, marriage and family life among the natives of the Trobriand Islands, British New Guinea*. New York: Halcyon House.

Mardle, G., & Walker, M. (1980). Strategies and structure: Critical notes on teacher socialization. In P. Woods (Ed.), *Teacher strategies* (pp. 98–124). London: Croom Helm.

Mattingly, P. H. (1987). Workplace autonomy and the reforming of teacher education. In T. S. Popkewitz (Ed.), *Critical studies in teacher education: Its folklore, theory and practice* (pp. 36–56). London: Falmer.

McCarthy, C. (1986). Teacher training contradictions. *Education and Society, 4*(2), 3–15.

McIntyre, D. J. (1983). *Field experiences in teacher education*. Washington, DC: Foundation for Excellence in Teacher Education and ERIC Clearinghouse on Teacher Education.

McNeil, L. (1983). Defensive teaching and classroom control. In M. Apple & L. Weis (Eds.), *Ideology and practice in schooling*. Philadelphia: Temple University Press.

McNeil, M. (1987). *Gender and expertise*. London: Free Association.

McPherson, G. (1972). *Small town teacher*. Cambridge, MA: Harvard University Press.

Merton, R. K. (1968). *Social theory and social structure*. New York: Free Press.

Merton, R. K., Reader, G. G., & Kendall, P. L. (Eds.). (1957). *The student physician: Introductory studies in the sociology of medical education*. Cambridge, MA: Harvard University Press.

Metz, M. (1978). *Classrooms and corridors*. Berkeley, CA: University of California Press.

Metz, M. (1988). *Teachers' ultimate dependence on their students*. Madison, WI: National Center on Effective Secondary Schools.

Metz, M. (in press). How social class differences shape the context of teachers' work. In M. McLaughlin & J. Talbert (Eds.), *The secondary school workplace*. New York: Teachers College Press.

Neufeld, B. (1988). *Why do I have to learn that? Prospective teachers' ideas about the importance of the subjects they will teach*. Paper presented at the annual meeting of the American Educational Research Association, New Orleans.

Nias, J. (1986). *Teacher socialization: The individual in the system*. Geelong, Australia: Deakin University Press.

Nigris, E. (1988). Stereotypical images of schooling: Teacher socialization and teacher education. *Teacher Education Quarterly, 15*(2), 4–19.

Noddings, N. (1986). Fidelity in teaching, teacher education, and research for teaching. *Harvard Educational Review, 56*(4), 496–510.

Noffke, S., & Zeichner, K. (1987). *Action research and teacher thinking*. Paper presented at the meeting of the American Educational Research Association, Washington, DC.

Nucci, L., & Pascarella, E. (1987). The influence of college on moral development. In J. Smart (Ed.), *Higher education: Handbook of theory and research* (Vol. 3, pp. 271–325). New York: Agathon Press.

Ogburn, W. F., & Nimkoff, M. F. (1940). *Sociology*. Boston: Houghton Mifflin.

Olesen, V., & Whittaker, E. W. (1970). Critical notes on sociological studies of professional socialization. In J. A. Jackson (Ed.), *Professions and professionalization* (pp. 179–221). Cambridge, England: Cambridge University Press.

Park, R. E. (1939). Symbiosis and socialization: A frame of reference for the study of society. *American Journal of Sociology, 45*(1), 1–25.

Parsons, T. (1949). *The structure of social action*. Glencoe, IL: Free Press.

Pascarella, E. (1985). College environmental influences on learning and cognitive development: A critical review and synthesis. In J. Smart (Ed.), *Higher education: Handbook of theory and research* (Vol. 1, pp. 1–61). New York: Agathon Press.

Pearson, J. (1987). The problems experienced by student teachers during teaching practice: A review of research studies. *Journal of Teaching Practice, 7*(2), 1–20.

Petty, M., & Hogben, D. (1980). Explorations of semantic space with beginning teachers: A study of socialization into teaching. *British Journal of Teacher Education, 6*, 51–61.

Pinar, W. (1986). *Autobiography and the architecture of self*. Paper presented at the meeting of the American Educational Research Association, Washington, DC.

Pollard, A. (1982). A model of classroom coping strategies. *British Journal of Sociology of Education, 3*, 19–37.

Popkewitz, T. (1985). Ideology and social formation in teacher education. *Teaching and Teacher Education, 1*(2), 91–107.

Posner, G. J., Strike, K. A., Hewson, P. W., & Gertzog, W. A. (1982). Accommodation of a scientific conception: Towards a theory of conceptual change. *Science Education, 66*, 211–227.

Power, P. (1981). Aspects of the transition from education student to beginning teacher. *Australian Journal of Education, 25*(3), 288–296.

Quicke, J. (1988). Using structured life histories to teach the sociology and social psychology of education. In P. Woods & A. Pollard (Eds.), *Sociology and teaching*. London: Croom Helm.

Radcliffe-Brown, A. (1952). *Structure and function in primitive society*. London: Cohen & West.

Raymond, D., & Surprenant, M. (1988). *Investigating teachers' knowledge through ethnographic and biographic approaches: A case study*. Paper presented at the meeting of the American Educational Research Association, New Orleans.

Reinharz, S. (1988). *Social science methods: Feminist voices*. London: Pergamon.

Ringstaff, C., & Haymore, J. (1987). *The influence of subject matter background on planning and instruction*. Paper presented at the meeting of the American Educational Research Association, Washington, DC.

Riseborough, G. (1988). Pupils, recipe knowledge, curriculum, and the cultural production of class, ethnicity, and patriarchy: A critique of one teacher's practices. *British Journal of Sociology of Education, 9*(1), 39–54.

Roman, L., & Apple, M. (1988). *Is naturalism a move away from positivism? Materialist and feminist approaches to subjectivity in ethnographic research*. Paper presented at the Qualitative Inquiry Conference, Palo Alto, CA.

Ross, E. W. (1987). Teacher perspective development: A study of preservice social studies teachers. *Theory and Research in Social Education, 15*(4), 225–243.

Ross, E. W. (1988). Preservice teachers' responses to institutional constraints: The active role of the individual in teacher socialization. *Educational Foundations, 2*(1), 77–92.

Sartre, J.-P. (1948). *Existentialism and humanism* (P. Mairet, Trans.). London: Methuen.

Schneider, B. (1987). Tracing the provenance of teacher education. In T. Popkewitz (Ed.), *Critical studies in teacher education* (pp. 211–241). New York: Falmer.

Schutz, A. (1967). *The phenomenology of the social world* (G. Walsh & F. Lehnert, Trans.). Evanston, IL: Northwestern University Press.

Scott, S. (1985). Feminist research and qualitative methods. In R. Burgess (Ed.), *Issues in educational research: Qualitative methods* (pp. 67–85). London: Falmer.

Shapiro, M. (1978). *Getting doctored: Critical reflections on becoming a physician*. Ontario, Canada: Between the Lines.

Sharp, R., & Green, A. (1975). *Education and social control*. London: Routledge & Kegan Paul.

Shulman, L. (1986). Those who understand: Knowledge growth in teaching. *Educational Researcher, 15*(2), 4–14.

Shumsky, A. (1958). *The action research way of learning*. New York: Teachers College Bureau of Publications.

Sikes, P., Measor, L., & Woods, P. (1985). *Teacher careers: Crises and continuities*. London: Falmer.

Sirotnik, K. (1983). What you see is what you get: Consistency, persistency, and mediocrity in classrooms. *Harvard Educational Review, 53*, 16–31.

Skinner, B. F. (1953). *Science and human behavior*. New York: Appleton-Century-Crofts.

Spencer, D. A. (1986). *Contemporary women teachers: Balancing school and home*. New York: Longman.

Spindler, G., & Spindler, L. (1987). Cultural dialogue and schooling in Schoenhausen and Roseville: A comparative analysis. *Anthropology and Education Quarterly, 18*(1), 3–16.

Stephens, J. (1967). *The processes of schooling*. New York: Holt, Rinehart & Winston.

Sutherland, R. L., & Woodward, J. (1937). *Introductory sociology.* New York: J. B. Lippincott.

Tabachnick, B. R. (1980). Intern-teacher roles: Illusion, disillusion and reality. *Journal of Education, 162,* 122–137.

Tabachnick, B. R. (1988). *Research on teacher education in the future: Naturalistic research that is culturally responsive.* Paper presented at the First Asia-Pacific Conference on Teacher Education, Bangkok, Thailand.

Tabachnick, B. R., & Zeichner, K. (1985). *The development of teacher perspectives: Final report.* Madison, WI: University of Wisconsin, Center for Education Research.

Tom, A. (1987). A critique of the rationale for extended teacher preparation. *Educational Policy, 1*(1), 43–56.

Tripp, D. (1987). Teachers, journals and collaborative research. In J. Smyth (Ed.), *Educating teachers: Changing the nature of pedagogical knowledge* (pp. 179–191). London: Falmer.

Trow, M. (1987). The national reports on higher education: A skeptical view. *Educational Policy, 1*(4), 411–428.

U.S. Department of Education. (1984). *Involvement in learning: Realizing the potential of American higher education.* Washington, DC: Author.

von. Bertalanffy, L. (1956). General system theory. *General Systems, 1,* 1–10.

Waller, W. (1932). *The sociology of teaching.* New York: John Wiley.

Watts, D. (1987). Student teaching. In M. Haberman & J. M. Backus (Eds.), *Advances in teacher education* (Vol. 3, pp. 151–167). Norwood, NJ: Ablex.

Weber, M. (1947). *The theory of social and economic organization* (A. Henderson & T. Parsons, Eds. & Trans.). New York: Free Press.

Weedon, C. (1987). *Feminist practice and poststructuralist theory.* Oxford: Basil Blackwell.

Weiler, K. (1988). *Women teaching for change: Gender, class and power.* South Hadley, MA: Bergin & Garvey.

Weis, L. (1988). *Class, race and gender in American education.* Albany, NY: State University of New York Press.

Wentworth, W. M. (1980). *Context and understanding: An inquiry into socialization theory.* New York: Elsevier North Holland.

Westbury, I. (1973). Conventional classrooms, open classrooms, and the technology of teaching. *Journal of Curriculum Studies, 5*(2), 99–121.

Wexler, P. (1987). *Social analysis of education: After the new sociology.* London: Routledge & Kegan Paul.

Willis, P. (1977). *Learning to labour:* How working class kids get working class jobs. Farnborough, England: Saxon House.

Wilson, S., & Shulman, L. (1987). 150 different ways of knowing: Representations of knowledge in teaching. In J. Calderhead (Ed.), *Exploring teachers' thinking.* London: Cassell.

Wilson, S., & Wineburg (1988). Peering at history through different lenses: The role of disciplinary perspectives in teaching history. *Teachers College Record, 89*(4), 525–539.

Wise, A. (1979). *Legislated learning: The bureaucratization of the American classroom.* Berkeley, CA: University of California Press.

Woods, P. (1987). Life histories and teacher knowledge. In J. Smyth

(Ed.), *Educating teachers: Changing the nature of pedagogical knowledge* (pp. 121–135). London: Falmer.

Wright, B. (1959). Identification and becoming a teacher. *Elementary School Journal, 59*(7), 361–374.

Wright, B., & Tuska, S. (1967). The childhood romance theory of teacher development. *School Review, 75*(2), 123–154.

Wright, B., & Tuska, S. (1968). From dream to life in the psychology of becoming a teacher. *School Review, 76*(3), 253–293.

Yaakobi, D., & Sharan, S. (1985). Teacher beliefs and practices: The discipline carries the message. *Journal of Education for Teaching, 11*(2), 187–200.

Yamamoto, K., Pederson, D., Opdahl, R., Dangel, H., Townsend, C., Paleologos, M., & Smith, A. (1969). As they see it: Culling impressions from teachers in preparation. *Journal of Teacher Education, 20*(4), 465–475.

Zeichner, K. (1979). *The dialects of teacher socialization.* Paper presented at the meeting of the Association of Teacher Educators, Orlando, FL.

Zeichner, K. (1980). Myths and realities: Field-based experiences in preservice teacher education. *Journal of Teacher Education, 31,* 45–55.

Zeichner, K. (1983a). Alternative paradigms of teacher education. *Journal of Teacher Education, 34,* 3–9.

Zeichner, K. (1983b). Individual and institutional factors related to the socialization of beginning teachers. In G. Griffin & H. Hukill (Eds.), *First years of teaching: What are the pertinent issues?* Austin, TX: University of Texas, Research & Development Center for Teacher Education.

Zeichner, K. (1986a). The practicum as an occasion for learning to teach. *South Pacific Journal of Teacher Education, 14*(2), 11–28.

Zeichner, K. (1986b). Social and ethical dimensions of reform in teacher education. In J. Hoffman & S. Edwards (Eds.), *Clinical teacher education* (pp. 87–108). New York: Random House.

Zeichner, K. (1988). *Understanding the character and quality of the academic and professional components of teacher education* (Research Rep. No. 88-1). East Lansing, MI: Michigan State University, National Center for Research on Teacher Education.

Zeichner, K. (1989). Preparing teachers for democratic schools. *Action in Teacher Education 11*(1), 5–10.

Zeichner, K., & Grant, C. (1981). Biography and social structure in the socialization of student teachers. *Journal of Education for Teaching, 1,* 198–214.

Zeichner, K., & Tabachnick, B. R. (1985). The development of teacher perspectives: Social strategies and institutional control in the socialization of beginning teachers. *Journal of Education for Teaching, 11,* 1–25.

Zeichner, K., Tabachnick, B. R., & Densmore, K. (1987). Individual, institutional, and cultural influences on the development of teachers' craft knowledge. In J. Calderhead (Ed.), *Exploring teachers' thinking* (pp. 21–59). London: Cassell.

Zumwalt, K. (1982). Research on teaching: Policy implications for teacher education. In A. Lieberman & M. McLaughlin (Eds.), *Policy making in education* (81st yearbook of the National Society for the Study of Education, Part I, pp. 215–248). Chicago: University of Chicago Press.

PROFESSORS AND DEANS OF EDUCATION

Kenneth R. Howey and Nancy L. Zimpher

THE OHIO STATE UNIVERSITY

This chapter reviews studies of professors and deans of education. The first section of the chapter addresses studies of professors of education. It begins with a historical perspective and proceeds to an overview of the current context in which the education professoriate engages in its critically important work. This current context includes a brief review of studies of the larger academy across the range of institutions of higher education in this country. Then education professors are reviewed in terms of their social demography and background characteristics. Next, the authors examine studies of career patterns, work load, and various indexes of productivity. This section of the chapter also provides an overview of efforts to enhance faculty vitality and productivity and concludes with an examination of issues and unstudied problems, with suggestions for future research.

The second section of this chapter follows a similar outline. Sociodemographic studies of the deanship are reviewed, as is inquiry that examines the role and function of deans. Where possible, effectiveness of impact is analyzed. A case is made for studying deans from an ecological perspective as they interact with faculty and other significant actors in various organizational and cultural contexts. Suggestions for pursuing new and needed lines of inquiry are advanced.

PROFESSORS OF EDUCATION

Historical Perspective

By the mid-1870s public elementary schools had spread across the nation. Teachers for these common schools, however, were largely being prepared, to the extent they were prepared, either in normal schools or on the job by superintendents empowered to certify teachers. Teacher education in a college or university context, as such, did not exist in the early development of the common elementary school, and, even as late as 1930, a college education was not a prerequisite for elementary school teachers. As an example, E. S. Evenden (1933), in a survey of American teachers, found that only a little more than one in 10 elementary teachers (12.1 percent) had 4 or more years of college.

It was shortly after the country's centennial that the first pedagogical chair in the country was established, at the University of Michigan (Hazlett, 1989; Johanningmeier & Johnson, 1975). According to Johanningmeier and Johnson, prior to 1890, pedagogy was at best a branch of moral philosophy. After 1890, historians are somewhat able to trace the succession of attempts to establish pedagogy as a discipline of study. Hazlett reports that, by 1890, there were 31 professors of education in the country. By the turn of the century it was possible to pursue a doctorate in the subject at a few universities (Johanningmeier & Johnson, 1975). Thus, one can trace the establishment of the American educational professoriate to shortly before the turn of the century.

The historiography of how the American education professoriate has evolved since that time is still in its formative stage. There are only a few biographies of early professors of education (Allison, 1989) and but a few institutional histories (Cronbach & Suppes, 1969; Lynch, 1946; Powell, 1980; Sizer & Powell, 1969).

It is not until the 1960s that one finds texts devoted to studies and analyses of the professoriate in education. Examples include *The Professorship in Educational Administration*, edited by Willower and Culbertson (1964), and *To Be a Phoenix: The Education Professoriate*, edited by Counelis (1969). Perhaps the most notable collection of writings attempting to conceptualize the conditions in which professors of education work was compiled by Bagley (1975) for the Society of Professors of

The authors wish to recognize Frederick R. Cyphert (professor emeritus, The Ohio State University) for his critical reviews of this chapter.

Education in 1975. More recent is the text titled *The Professors of Teaching: An Inquiry*, edited by Wisniewski and Ducharme (1989).

In the last quarter century there have been more studies of the education professoriate. Hazlett (1989) observes that studies and analyses of the professoriate tend to fall into three major genres: those that focus on the characteristics of the professoriate, those that seek to define the field, and those that deal more with conceptualizing the field. Each of these types of studies of the education professoriate is reviewed in this chapter after a context and a perspective for interpreting them are provided.

The Broader Professoriate and Education Professors

It seems appropriate to examine, however briefly, the current context in which the professoriate in general toils, in order to place analyses of the education professoriate in perspective. There appears to be a general decline in work conditions today from those of the late 1960s and early 1970s, when the condition of faculty in American institutions of higher education appeared in many respects to have reached its zenith. At that time there was a considerable expansion in the numbers of professors generally, including education professors. This was also a time of considerable programmatic development in teacher education; the widespread efforts to implement the competency-based teacher education programs at that time are an example. Economists have recorded that faculty compensation, after adjustment for inflation, reached its peak during this time, in 1973. More importantly, by the early 1970s the professoriate had achieved substantial influence over both the curriculum and matters of selection and promotion.

Schuster and Bowen (1985), in a study of 38 diverse colleges and universities wherein they conducted over 500 interviews with rank-and-file faculty members and academic administrators, document problems and issues that have evolved since that period. For example, since the early 1970s. there have been relatively few faculty positions available in education and most other academic units. They conclude from their study that the strong buyer's market reflected in campus after campus has been the catalyst for a move to aggressively upgrade the importance of scholarly productivity as a criterion for academic personnel decisions. To be sure, this situation is not all, or even largely, negative. Clearer expectations for the conduct of various forms of scientific inquiry and more attention to criteria for assessing the quality of this work remain challenges in a still evolving field such as teacher education. Further, a number of basically teaching institutions, attempting to alter both their image and their mission, have been able to hire young scholars during this buyer's market. Where research had previously been a low priority, with effective teaching the dominant criterion for promotion and tenure, expectations in a number of these institutions are changing.

The downside of this condition, however, according to Schuster and Bowen, is its effects on how faculty have chosen to accommodate these altered or higher expectations. As a result of their interviews, they suggest that junior faculty, especially, view themselves as under considerable pressure. These investigators portray "a privatized, isolated junior faculty 'grinding' away in laboratories or library stacks, boring their way toward tenure, unable and/or unwilling to participate fully in campus life. Anxiety and stress predominate in their professional lives" (p. 18).

They further suggest that the negative consequences of these altered expectations, or at least perceptions of altered expectations, are not limited to professors at the assistant level. They found many faculty members at the associate professor level, referred to by them as mid-careerists, caught in the middle of these changing standards. They characterize these faculty as

enjoying the benefits of tenure and more-or-less secure, but continuously looking over their shoulders where they see a new breed of better-prepared, younger faculty performing at levels of "productivity" heretofore rarely encountered on their campuses. When these associate professors look the other way, they find perched in the higher rank faculty who were tenured under the old reward system and who are now safely ensconced in the highest pay grades. (p. 18)

The morale problem they portray does not escape even the most senior faculty. Schuster and Bowen concluded from their interviews that many full professors were

angry, embittered, and feeling devalued and abandoned. They often expressed outrage about market-driven compensation and differential pay policies to recruit new faculty which they considered unjust, even humiliating. From the viewpoint of some senior faculty members, such compensation policies not only skew rewards in favor of the new faculty, but also favor the high-demand academic fields. (p. 19)

The extent to which one can generalize about such conditions is constrained by the major differences both across and within the many institutions of higher education that prepare teachers in this country, and these need to be underscored in terms of setting a context. In a counterscenario developed by B. Clark (1985) on the basis of interviews with over 170 professors in 16 institutions representing 6 different types of institutions, the "good life" is portrayed, as opposed to the problems just identified. He notes that, in leading universities, especially in resource-rich fields, professors frequently teach as little as one course at a time, often at the graduate level: "Life in this context is centered upon research, with light teaching following in its trial" (p. 38). These respondents indicated that they never got bored, were surrounded by stimulating colleagues, and were heavily involved in their research and the amenities that go with it. They referred to academic life at the top as exuding a cosmopolitan excitement, where, in one's speciality, according to the view from on high, one "runs with the best." They continue, "this high cosmopolitanism is even found in the upper reaches of the not-so-rich humanities, where a conference on structuralism one week in New York for the academic jetset might be followed by a conference on post-structuralism the following week in Stockholm or Bellagio" (p. 39).

To underscore the differences in professorial life-style, contrast Clark's scenario with the following excerpt from an interview with an education professor who chairs a department in what can be characterized as a regional, state-supported, teaching-oriented university. Howey and Zimpher (1989), in their study of teacher education faculty, share the following quote:

I tell them [new faculty] if you come here you're going to work. These are all people who have recently been in college and in Ph.D. programs and typically in a large university where their major professors have two hours of class a week. And I tell them, look you're going to be here at 7 : 30 or 8 : 00 every morning and you're not going to leave until 4 : 30 or 5 : 00. You're going to be flooded with students all day long. If you're not supervising, you're going to have students in your office, so you're not going to be able to do any extended preparation during the day. You're not going to be able to check any papers during this time. If you think you're going to do research, you're going to have to do that on Saturdays and Sundays. I tell them this is the kind of institution we are. Don't come here if you think you're going to have the kind of life you've seen in a large university because you may not even have time to eat dinner some days. (p. 107)

Certainly there is great diversity across the more than 1,300 institutions that prepare teachers. Cosmopolitans, if you will, can be found among these as surely as those whose academic life at best resembles that of their counterparts in secondary schools, at times in the same institution. Likely, morale problems similar to those uncovered by Schuster and Bowen exist in several instances among education professors. What limited data exist regarding the education professoriate suggest such a condition might not be pervasive. Nussel, Wiersma, and Rusche (1988) surveyed a stratified sample of 426 teacher educators in 39 public and 25 private institutions to examine job satisfaction. They developed their survey instrumentation on the basis of the conceptual work of Herzberg, Mausner, and Snyderman (1959) and Kalleberg (1977). However, an interpretation of these data by the researchers raises another major concern. They conclude:

With the extensive criticism of teacher education that we discussed at the outset of this report, lower levels of satisfaction were anticipated. However, the results indicate a rather high level of satisfaction, with certain administrative factors contributing to a decrease in satisfaction. It appears that teacher educators derive a great deal of satisfaction in working with students and colleagues.

One might argue that because senior faculty are more satisfied than younger, non-tenured professors, they have distanced themselves from the reform debate because their jobs are not in jeopardy. Could it be that education faculty members continue to do what they have been doing all along and are oblivious to the ferment in the profession? If this is so, serious questions need to be addressed as to how education faculty relate to change. Nevertheless, they remain satisfied with the work itself, and the factors of satisfaction and dissatisfaction as identified by Herzberg, seem applicable to professors of education. (1988, p. 50)

These findings and, especially, the interpretation of them are provocative, as are the studies of Schuster and Bowen and B. Clark of the broader professoriate. The contrasting perspectives, however, underscore the need to study faculty carefully at various stages of their careers and the multiple effects of movement across professorial rank. Beyond this, the obvious need to study faculty in what are dramatically different cultures and subcultures cannot be overemphasized. qualitative research is badly needed, as are quantitative studies that incorporate inter- and intra-institutional strata and that are longitudinal in nature.

Efforts to define and describe similarities and differences in the teacher education professoriate are further complicated by the changing missions and expectations in many larger state colleges today. B. Clark (1985) observes:

Generally the state college of today was a teachers college in the recent past, and is now somewhere midstream between that blighted shore and the promised land of university status. The midstream location may be nigh-permanent, however, since existing universities have already pre-empted the high ground on the far shore and state plans insist that the newcomers stay out of the way of Ph.D. programs for major research. Some respondents referred to an inchoate institutional character—"the place has not come to terms with itself—" that confuses their own professional culture. (p. 40)

This is a time of ferment and tension. During a period when there is call for major "reform" in the arts, sciences, humanities, and teacher education, Schuster and Bowen (1985) conclude that four factors strongly influence the condition of the faculty: declining compensation, deteriorating work environment, tight labor market, and shaky faculty morale. Thus, at the same time that a variety of forces point to a major effort by education faculty to engage in more collegial, programmatic development and to more and better research into those very programs—a type of research rarely engaged in by most academicians—these scholars identify a variety of conditions that militate against this.

In summary, studies of the education professoriate need to both better acknowledge historical evolution and attend to the current contexts in which these professors work. Likewise, the understanding of deans, their roles, functions, and indexes of productivity, also needs to be derived from examining how they interact with such tensions.

Contextual Variation

At a time when the call for reform is pervasive, decontextualized sociodemographic data about the professoriate provide little guidance. Therefore, one has to differentiate contexts along dimensions that have potency for not only describing professorial behavior but also predicting it. Degree of professorial autonomy is one obvious construct that might have explanatory power. Baldridge, Curtis, Ecker, and Riley (1978) provide a framework for conceptualizing differences across and within institutions of higher education in this regard. They examined six dimensions of faculty autonomy: (a) the extent to which faculty employment contracts explicitly specify work to be performed or are relatively open ended; (b) the extent to which professional travel is tightly regulated; (c) the locus of control over faculty teaching assignments; (d) the extent to which faculty are evaluated by their professional colleagues, rather than by administrators; (e) the locus of control over faculty hiring—departmental versus administrative; and (f) the locus of control over tenured positions—departmental versus administrative.

They found considerable variation in terms of professional autonomy across these six dimensions. As might be expected, faculty at different types of institutions manifested very different levels of professional autonomy, with autonomy tending to be highest at research universities, followed in descending order by private liberal arts and public comprehensive colleges and universities. Further research or a chain of inquiry employing conceptual frameworks such as this is needed to better understand how specific dimensions of institutional context effect the life-style and productivity of professors. Howey and Zimpher's (1989) case studies of the nature and character of teacher education *programs* in different institutional contexts is one modest effort in this regard.

Assessments of the productivity of the education professoriate also need to be interpreted in terms of the particular external challenges they are faced with, as opposed to those of other academics. The relationship of their inquiry to major social problems confronting our nation's schools is a problem that will receive increasing attention. Schwebel (1989) elaborates on the quandary facing education faculty: "to perhaps become mired in finding ways to make the schools work for larger proportions of children, or to follow a safer, more traditional academic path. If education faculty are to 'make it' under the new priorities in the university, and if their research is to be useful to the schools, they must choose the riskier course" (p. 64).

It appears that scientific inquiry by many education faculty in schools and colleges of education in prestigious institutions has been conducted largely apart from the context of K–12 schools. Rather, research by these faculty has emulated norms of scholarship for graduate faculty in other disciplines, as aptly characterized by Judge (1982). How this tension is addressed should guide future research into professors, and again there are also major implications for studying the deanship in the midst of altered missions and evolving organizations.

Formative Experiences of Education Faculty. Let us turn now from contexts that suggest directions for future research to a review of past research and what this suggests for further inquiry. Lanier and Little (1986) build a rationale for examining the effects of social class on the propensities of education faculty. They draw on the work of Kohn (1969) and Kohn and Schooler (1982), who have demonstrated the considerable influence of social class on orientations to and involvement in education. Constructs of social class typically include patterns of child rearing, formal education, and occupation. For example, conformist values appear to be stressed in child rearing in the lower segments of social class, especially for females. An instrumental, rather than intellectual, orientation to schooling is stressed. Job conditions have also been found to correlate with psychological functioning, and Lanier and Little hypothesize that teacher educators, because of their common, often considerable, prior experience in rule-oriented K–12 schools, have had limited opportunities to promote occupational self-direction and ideational flexibility. Thus, because there are data to indicate that many present education faculty have lower

social-class origins, these scholars develop a profile of a conformist, other-directed, more instrumental, and less intellectually oriented education professoriate than the professoriate in general.

Their hypothesis is provocative and calls for further study. First, better baseline data are needed. The demographic data upon which they base their case are both somewhat dated and limited in terms of social-class origins (Ducharme & Agne, 1982; Fuller & Bown, 1975; Prichard, Fen, & Buxton, 1971). Data on the number of years of education faculty experience in elementary and secondary schools are more widely and recently documented, as in the 1987 RATE study (American Association of Colleges for Teacher Education, 1987), wherein it is reported that over 80 percent of methods faculty had at least 4 to 6 years of experience in schools; 65 percent, at least 7 to 9 years; and 35 percent, at least 10 years. The nature of these experiences and the variety of school types in which professors were engaged are less clear, however, although the constraining effects of many K–12 schools are widely chronicled (Goodlad, 1984).

If more recent and more representative sociodemographic data, including sampling by institutional strata, support the lower social-class origins premise, then the education professoriate could well differ from the larger professoriate. Finkelstein (1984) reports that, as a group, the broader professoriate tends to come from families that stress intellectual pursuits and school achievement. Professors as a whole are twice as likely to have fathers who were college graduates (nearly one-fourth do), and they are nine times more likely to have fathers who engaged in graduate work. He reports that 40 percent of the faculty come from professional, semiprofessional, or managerial families, and another 20 percent come from business backgrounds. Only one-fourth are characterized as having grown up within the working class.

It would first be helpful to clarify better the extent to which at least segments of education faculty are different from the broader professoriate. A number of other questions can be raised that suggest further study. First, to what extent are there social-class differences across geographic regions, different institutional types, and different disciplines and departments within schools and colleges of education? To what extent are they apparent across rank and gender? When and where a lower socioeconomic status profile does prevail, again what factors appear to contribute to this?

Finally, how much of the variance in faculty activity and productivity can be accounted for by these basically presage variables, as opposed to the context variables enumerated earlier? Institutional mission and faculty autonomy are but two central context factors that contribute to variability. Roemer and Martinello (1982) suggest, for example, that the relatively unique organizational pattern of the educational academy deserves further study in explaining faculty propensities. These scholars find it curious, at least, that those who research and teach in the disciplinary and functional studies of education are commonly grouped together in the same academic unit. They point out that the general practice of academic organization is rather to separate disciplinary and practical studies. For example, schools of medicine are separate from departments of chemistry and biology, schools of engineering are separate from departments of mathematics and physics, and engineering is becoming increasingly theoretical and removed, for example, from studies of design and construction. In education, however, the disciplinary study of education is conducted alongside the study of educational practice. Thus, Roemer and Martinello (1982) posit: "the question occurs whether education is an enlightened example of how unity can be achieved between disciplines and practice or whether, by forcing incompatible studies together, education is a field in which academic misunderstanding is endemic" (p. 204).

These alternative idiographic and nomothetic perspectives suggest *lines* of inquiry about a largely unstudied population as it interacts with a variety of contexts and cultures. The norms, values, and behaviors, as manifested in case type institutions and programs, need to be examined, as well as their formative experiences, if a better understanding of the education professoriate is to develop.

Graduate Training. Although data regarding the social-class origins of the educational professoriate and the nature and quality of their formative educational experiences in K–12 schools are incomplete, even less is known about the nature and extent of graduate training. In perhaps the most comprehensive study of productivity of educational faculty, Guba and Clark (1977) surveyed almost 3,000 faculty (of the almost 35,000 schools, colleges, and departments of education faculty members throughout the country) and found that "in general, SCDE faculty are trained at a higher degree level then their academic counterparts in other departments. This finding was especially surprising in view of the stereotype held by many academics of SCDE personnel as conceptually weak and heavily practitioner-oriented" (p. 711).

More recent data raise questions. For example, Barrow (1984) found a *lack* of correlation between the graduate programs in which science educators were prepared and the preservice education courses they subsequently taught. Likewise, in the 1988 RATE study it appeared that a large percentage of faculty teaching social, philosophical, and historical foundations did not appear to have substantive academic preparation in these disciplines (AACTE, 1988).

In terms of studies of the nature and quality of doctoral preparation, one has to go back to the data reported by Buswell, McConnell, Heiss, and Knoll (1966). They examined PhDs who had had research assistantships in their doctoral training in terms of their eventual scholarship. As might be expected, Buswell and colleagues found that, in general, professors who had had research assistantships had published twice as much as those who had not. More recently, Adams (1986), in a study of the vitae of faculty of education, found that faculty who had published during their doctoral studies eventually had a higher publication rate than those who had not. Research assistantships reside largely in research-oriented institutions, which are much more likely to have research funds and, in turn, have faculty qualified for and committed to scholarly inquiry. However, there is considerable variation across departments or program units even within research-oriented institutions. Scientific study of doctoral training, al-

though basically virgin, is not without direction. Program review and accreditation are long standing and offer indexes of program quality that might have explanatory power. Graduate training could be changing generally. As indicated, there are data that strongly suggest that new faculty entering the ranks of the general professoriate are both able and disposed to devote considerable energies to scholarly inquiry. It appears that some faculty pursue research to the extent that there are pernicious effects in terms of both the constraints to their overall responsibilities and development and the creation of morale problems for at least some senior faculty (Schuster & Bowen, 1985). Schwebel (1985) and, more recently, Ducharme and Agne (1989) also provide some evidence that new professors entering the education ranks are more oriented to scholarship generally. Schuttenberg, Patterson, and Sutton, in their study of 391 college of education faculty members from 38 institutions, underscored once again the primacy of teaching over scholarly productivity generally. They discovered, however, that "scholarship was found to be an important component, especially among the younger faculty members, who also rated their future scholarship potential higher than their older colleagues" (1985, p. 4).

Education Professors and Experience in K–12 Schools

Numerous studies have attested to the experience of education faculty in schools: Darter (1980); Ducharme and Agne (1982); Howey, Yarger, and Joyce (1978); and, more recently, the 1987 and 1988 AACTE RATE studies. Although there are several types of education faculty, with varying kinds of school experience, the nature and quality of these experiences, their consonance with present assignments, and the effects of these on various indexes of productivity, including scholarship, are far less clear.

Howey (1977), in attempting to interpret data on the education professoriate from a large-scale survey study, drew two contrasting scenarios in an effort to underscore the equivocal nature of the data. These alternative interpretations appear appropriate more than a decade later.

Scenario One: Professors generally are familiar with the daily activity, the curriculum issues, and problems of schools. Students generally are able to work in classroom situations throughout their initial preparation. These same students at the completion of their programs generally are satisfied. They perceive themselves as competent to begin teaching. In spite of common retrenchments in personnel and resources, individual faculty are continuing to refine and even expand curricular offerings to accommodate changes in the schools.

Scenario Two: For all their prior experience and current familiarity in schools, professors generally appear to influence but minimally those changes they often call for. For all their experiences in schools, student teachers receive but periodic and general feedback about their development. For all their confidence the high attrition rate of beginning teachers suggests many may well have a false sense of security. The beginning teacher may be ready to teach in the suburban school; his or her readiness to assume responsibility in many schools in the core of our major cities is more questionable. Beginning teachers generally appear neither well prepared nor especially interested in confronting those problems attendant to the economically disadvantaged or culturally different. While the professor does spend more time in counseling, advising, and teaching than generally given credit for, there is little individual or collective effort to study current practice; the empirical data to support what is done in preservice training are minimal. Coherent and comprehensive program reform, such as that initiated by many institutions under the competency-based umbrella has rarely been achieved, and it appears that momentum for such effort has been lost. (p. 26)

It can only be hoped that the conclusion about program development espoused by CBTE advocates will be different in this more recent round of reform efforts.

Professors of Education: Reasons for Pursuing These Roles

The career development literature is informative in terms of when and why people pursue a career in K–12 teaching (Harren, 1976; Strom, 1980). What might one learn about when and why a person decides to become an education professor? Where can one turn for data? Scholars who have conducted survey research of the education academy reveal but modest insights into the motivations of faculty. Ducharme and Agne (1982) are among the few scholars who have engaged in this type of inquiry. They conducted a number of interviews with education faculty and raised the question of what led them to pursue a position in higher education–teacher education. They report that:

Some individuals thought higher education the next logical step from where they were; others saw it as a way of "reaching" more young people by teaching future teachers, administrators, and counselors; others could not remember. We encountered no one who responded initially in terms of wanting to do research, wanting to be part of the frontiers of knowledge, or wanting to lead and assist doctoral students in their research. We do not doubt that there are such people; we simply have not found them yet. What we have most commonly found is a group of people who have gone to one place—higher education—in order to have a direct impact on the place from which, in general, they have come—the lower schools. (p. 34)

Again, more adequate sampling is needed to reflect possible differences across institutional programs and types, and more interview and observational data are called for in future research designs. One would assume those in major research-oriented institutions would indicate a greater propensity for research, yet there are substantial numbers of faculty with orientations other than research in these institutions. Guba and Clark (1977) report from their study that "research was perceived by a significant number of the faculty as of central importance only in the research center institutions—the A-Public and A-Private institutions. Even here, however, the majority of the faculty of public doctoral-institutions (A) did not name research as primary: fewer than 50 percent gave it this status" (p. 712). This diversity *within* institutions raises key questions of just who is defined as a teacher educator and how relationships with schools define their role and functions.

Education Faculty: Institutional Demographics

The 1987 and 1988 RATE studies report that over 90 percent of the education faculty was white. Approximately 5 percent was black, and another 4 percent was Asian or Pacific Islander. Almost three-quarters (72 percent) of the faculty were males. Consistent with the larger professoriate, they were largely tenured and resided heavily at the upper ranks—conditions understandably related to their age and experience in higher education. Some 44.7 percent of the foundations faculty surveyed in 1986 were at the level of full professor, with another 29.6 percent at the associate professor rank and 20.4 percent at the assistant professor rank. There were differences in terms of rank between these faculty and the slightly larger sample of secondary faculty surveyed the previous year. Only 38.6 percent of those teaching secondary methods courses were at the full professor rank, with 27 percent at the assistant level.

Such aggregate profiles point the way to further inquiry. Within case studies of institutional and program type, the potential effects of imbalance in faculty rank and age on a number of critical variables could be examined, such as the disposition, or lack thereof, to engage in programmatic research and development, a possibility suggested by Nussel and his colleagues (1988). The potential for faculty "misassignments" as the result of relatively few new faculty positions over time could also be examined. From a budgetary perspective, the effects of a higher paid, disproportionate-in-numbers cohort of senior professors could be undertaken in terms of its relationship to funds available for a number of other critical endeavors.

There were some notable differences when the 1988 RATE faculty data were examined by gender. Females constituted almost 28 percent of these faculty, but only 19 percent of these women were at the full-professor rank, compared with 55 percent of the males who had achieved this rank. Likewise, 45 percent of the women were reported as holding assistant professorships, compared with only 10 percent of the males. Once again, these data are difficult to interpret without more fine-grained study. One interpretation is that recent affirmative action has had some impact, considering the number of women at the assistant level. On the other hand, historical inequities with regard to race, ethnicity, and gender need to continue to be addressed. Some of the inequities in gender by rank appear to be related to the problems female faculty have being socialized into the academy. In a number of instances, strong female models, let alone mentors, are lacking to assist women at the assistant level. More study is needed in terms of understanding gender differences, especially in terms of morale, productivity, and career advancement.

Education Faculty and Distribution of Responsibilities

Ducharme and Agne (1982) report:

Teaching is the commonly shared task of the education professoriate. In our study, 14 percent report spending three hours or less per week in the classroom, while 56 percent spend from four to nine hours and 25 percent spend from ten to 15 hours. For the most frequently recorded faculty classroom contact hour load of four to nine hours per week, the percentage of each rank engaged in actual teaching was professors 61 percent; associate professors 61 percent; assistant professors 51 percent; and instructors, lecturers or other designations, 30 percent. (p. 33)

Academic life in research-oriented institutions has traditionally been shared among teaching, scholarship, and service responsibilities. The 1987 RATE survey probed these distributions in some detail with secondary education methods faculty. Their results indicated that 60 percent of those professors' time was devoted to teaching, with 22 percent devoted to various types of service and 15 percent devoted to scholarship. There were differences across strata in terms of the number of courses taught, with faculty in bachelors institutions teaching the equivalent of about seven and a half courses a year during an academic year; those in masters institutions teaching about eight courses; and those in PhD-granting institutions teaching slightly more than five courses a year.

In the 1987 RATE study, faculty reported that, during a typical week, they spent the greatest amount of time in either preparing to teach or teaching itself. Faculty in this study, even at doctoral institutions, devoted a good deal of time to instructing undergraduate students (8 hours per week). Beyond teaching, faculty time appeared to be distributed uniformly among performing administrative tasks, supervising field experience, advising students, and working on committees.

The RATE report concludes that faculty from all three strata taught more than they believed their institutions desired and more than they thought would be ideal. They devoted less time to scholarly activities than they would have liked and less than they believed their institutions desired of them. Finally, they spent more time providing service to the institution and to the profession than they believed their institutions would like but less time than they considered ideal (1987, p. 28).

The majority of secondary methods professors in all three institutional types in the study indicated that they supervised student teachers, and more than a third of the faculty reported that they were also involved in the conduct of early field experiences. More methods faculty in PhD-granting institutions spent more time in K–12 schools in a variety of functions than their counterparts in masters and bachelors institutions. For example, about one in five faculty who taught methods in the doctoral institutions in the sample reported that they devoted time to research in K–12 schools, with only 9 percent of the faculty in masters institutions and 3 percent in bachelors institutions indicating this to be the situation.

Differences in publication rate as a measure of scholarship are apparent across strata in the 1988 RATE studies. To the point in their careers when they were surveyed, faculty in bachelors institutions reported 2 articles published in refereed journals; those in masters-granting institutions, 3 articles; and those in doctoral institutions, 13. More than half of the faculty in bachelors and masters institutions had no published refereed articles; 40 percent of those in PhD institutions reported at least 11 publications.

Again the question must be raised, what does one make of these studies of distribution of time and effort? It is necessary to proceed beyond describing differences to understanding why they exist and what they mean. For example, the compatibility and efficacy of engaging in a research role while teaching have been the subject of long-standing debate. To what extent is a single individual able to perform both functions well? What conditions are necessary to enable this? What difference does it make? Does scholarship inform or detract from teaching? Finkelstein (1984) reviews a number of hypotheses in this regard. Two of his hypotheses assume an intrinsically positive relationship between research productivity and teaching effectiveness, and two assume an intrinsically negative relationship (although they represent very different lines of reasoning), and a final hypothesis assumes no interrelationship whatsoever. These hypotheses are as follows:

1. Faculty who are productive researchers keep abreast of the latest developments in their field and therefore are likely to display a higher degree of interest and expertise in their subject—this makes them better teachers.
2. Both research productivity and teaching effectiveness reflect a general ability factor—therefore, good researchers tend to be good teachers and vice versa.
3. Faculty who are productive in research tend to spend more time in research and concomitantly less time in teaching—this lesser amount of time and effort expended presumably results in poorer quality teaching.
4. Researchers and teachers are different sorts of people—teaching effectiveness might depend on personality attributes that are inversely correlated with those associated with high research productivity.
5. Research productivity and teaching effectiveness are totally independent traits and are randomly distributed throughout the population.

Finkelstein attempted to synthesize and interpret the scant research that exists with regard to studying this question in terms of the larger professoriate. He concludes:

What status does the evidence accord the five latent hypotheses that have undergirded the debate? In the first place, the proposition of the total independence of research productivity and teaching effectiveness appears not quite on the mark. To the extent that judgments of teaching effectiveness are based largely on its intellectual competence dimension (and this appears to be the preferred criterion of faculty), then research productivity and the expertise that it engenders or the general ability that it signals does bear a fairly small, but consistently positive relationship to good teaching. To the extent that judgments of teaching are based on socioemotional aspects of the learning situation (and students appear more disposed to this criterion), then the expertise developed via research activity appears a largely irrelevant factor. That good research is both a necessary and sufficient condition for good teaching, then, is not resoundingly supported by the evidence. Resoundingly disconfirmed, however, is the notion that research involvement detracts from good teaching by channeling professorial time and effort away from the classroom. Harry and Goldner (1972) found that the extra time faculty devote to research activity tends to be taken from their leisure and family activities and not from their teaching.

Indeed, they report that the time a faculty member devotes to research is positively associated with the intellectual competence dimension of teaching effectiveness and not associated with the socioemotional component one way or the other. Similar findings are reported by McDaniel and Feldhusen (1970). (p. 126)

If research does not necessarily detract from good teaching and, in fact, can contribute to it, why do faculty, even where research is an expectation, tend not to engage in it? Finkelstein (1984) identifies three plausible explanations that could shed light on the variation in faculty allocation of effort. These include differential reward systems, differential work assignments, and differential faculty selection. Other factors can be added; for example, the nature and type of graduate training. Also, both formal or informal mentoring when one is first socialized into the academy can have an effect (Myers & Mager, 1983). The type of research called for in terms of specific disciplines or the magnitude of social and school problems can considerably influence the nature of research. Also the extent of publication outlets is a factor.

Finally, there have been studies conducted in major research-oriented institutions (Borland, 1970; DeVries, 1975) focusing on the faculty at large, which indicated that an individual faculty member's self-expectations were the best predictor of distribution of time. DeVries concluded that self-expectations explained between 30 percent and 43 percent of the variance in time allocation among the three core role components of teaching, research, and administration (p. 93). This finding would appear to have major implications for further studies of *when* and *how* these self-expectations are formed or altered.

Gideonse (1989), in a pilot study with 27 faculty from three teacher education institutions, examined weekly logs in an attempt to discern in a more fine-grained manner how faculty spend their time. What is especially helpful from his study are the various categories he identified for beginning to describe the nature of how faculty distribute their time. For example, his categories include amount of time devoted to preparation for class, travel associated with supervision of practicum experiences (as well as amount of time devoted to these experiences themselves), governance in academic units, and a variety of ceremonial responsibilities. The inclusiveness of these categories is most helpful. Again, further exploration of time allocation with a broader sample is in order. This line of inquiry might uncover, among other matters, why such a large proportion of teacher education faculty report that they devote considerable portions of their time to administrative and managerial matters.

Nature of Teaching. If teaching is understandably a primary activity of the professoriate, research into it is not. There have been a few studies that address the diversity of various teaching technologies and methodologies employed in the classroom. Howey, Yarger, Harbeck, Kluwin, and Joyce (1977) report limited use of modern technologies from their survey of teacher educators. Katz and Raths (1982) report similar findings in a study of 88 teacher education social studies instructors working with preservice students. They report that the dominant instructional methodology was discussion followed by student reports and lecture. In the 1987 RATE studies of secondary methods professors, however, fairly frequent utilization of general pedagogical methods was reported. Although lecture and group discussion remain the staples of faculty instruction, the methods professors in this study reported common use of such activities as role playing and simulations, microteaching, and use of case studies of critical incidents. Little is known, however, about the appropriateness of these various instructional tactics or methods relative to the goals set forth for prospective teachers and, more fundamentally, their effects on students.

Out-of-Class Interactions with Students. Attempts to study the effects of the education professoriate are not confined to the four walls of the classroom. The effects of a college education, including that of the education of a teacher, go far beyond what occurs in classrooms. The selective institutions studied by Astin (1977) indicate that the broader student experience in research universities and top liberal arts colleges promotes positives effects on students generally.

Faculty interactions with students occur in formal and a variety of informal settings. For example, the 1988 RATE study reported that foundations faculty in bachelors institutions reported almost 10 hours per week reserved for office hours, masters institutions reported 11 hours; and doctoral institutions reported about $7\frac{1}{2}$ hours a week. In their case studies, Howey and Zimpher (1989) found across all institutional types a surprising amount of time given over to students by faculty in elementary teacher education programs. The faculty member's sentiment that follows was not atypical in the many interviews conducted:

We're not investing in a program—we're investing in the students in a very, very personal way. I don't think there's a single student that goes through our program that doesn't have a friend on the faculty. I'm not saying that some wouldn't have two or three friends on the faculty but they choose somebody they can go to and can cry on a shoulder and they can share the things they do and get advice. I had students in Special Education—who are in a different major—who come to me and say they are having this problem. And they come to me as a *person*, not as a professor—certainly not as one of their major professors—simply because we hit it off. We can interact in that way. But everybody is the same way and there are people that come to them. (p. 120)

Ducharme and Agne (1982), in their studies of the education professoriate, also report that SCDE faculty invest significant amounts of time and commitment in the advisement and teaching of their undergraduate students.

Again, conceptual frameworks exist to guide study of the extent and quality of these myriad interactions and their impact on students. The research of Gaff and Wilson (1975) uncovered three closely interrelated variables that appear to differentiate faculty members in higher education in general in terms of the frequency of their contact with students. These variables include faculty beliefs about the intrinsic importance of such interaction to the educative process, the types of faculty instructional practices employed in the classroom that carry over outside of the classroom, and sheer physical availability, as in the case of posted office hours (p. 117). Finkelstein (1984) notes, however, that the predictive power of this triumvirate of variables is related to the type of student–faculty contact under consideration and that the basic purposes of these interactions need more attention. Purposes for student–faculty contacts include, among others, one-on-one instruction, career advice, personal counseling, discussion of campus issues, and personal friendship. After an analysis of studies of out-of-class contacts, finkelstein (1984) concludes: "It would appear, then that a faculty member's interaction with students, although broadly sensitive to institutional context, is a function of internal standards of performance no less than are his or her general activity patterns, productivity and research, and teaching practices" (p. 118).

Thus, it appears that, to design more well-conceived studies of the nature and impact of out-of-class faculty and student interactions, the types of *goals* or *purposes* faculty embrace are critical not only within their formal instruction but also in a broader educational sense. Also, the extent to which they view these interactions as important by some *personal* standard is critical, apparently more so than institutional expectations.

Broader Life-style

The broader academic community appears associated with a distinctive life-style. The professoriate generally shows consistent differences from the general population in terms of nature of work–family relationships, friendship patterns, religious involvement, strength of ethnic ties, and political allegiances (Finkelstein, 1984, p. 174). Finkelstein suggests that these dispositions were formed largely before graduation from college and that the academic role is chiefly by selection, rather than by socialization. Socialization might selectively reinforce extant predispositions, but, typically, they are resisted when institutional norms run counter to them. Do professors of education, especially teacher educators, vary from their academic counterparts in terms of socialization and life-style? If so, why? How have they been socialized? Certain aspects of life-style appear especially pertinent in assessing the impact of teacher educators. The extent to which they manifest a global, or catholic perspective; their degree of civic responsibility; and their political activism would, for example, appear to be of some consequence as they relate to students, given the well-documented parochial nature and conservative posture of many students enrolled in programs of teacher education.

Also, one could study the nature and character of education faculty with regard to their possible involvement in myriad consulting activities, as embedded in the broader notion of service, as this is a major aspect of the lives of many education professors. The possible negative aspects of consulting have been well articulated in terms of their potential conflicts with other institutional responsibilities that are perceived as more central functions.

There are also, of course, many positive consequences of consulting including benefits to the individual in terms of her or his own enlightenment and professional growth; benefits of several types to the university in terms of external visibility and potential support; and, perhaps most obvious, benefits of various types to those who are the recipients of these services and who are clients of education. The life-style of more cosmopolitan faculty contrasts sharply with those who view their responsibilities almost exclusively attached to institutional maintenance and renewal. Tension between such faculty types is common. Faculty of "star" status are able to buttress already higher salaries with myriad opportunities for further consulting. This leads to a further bifurcation of roles and role relationships between faculty with fundamentally different conceptions of what their primary responsibilities are, including not only teaching, as opposed to research and teaching, but also national networking and consulting, as opposed to the primacy of institutional functioning. Given the considerable diversity in terms of allocation of time among educational faculty in various academic programs and units, more well-conceived studies are in order, such as those outlined by S. Clark and Lewis (1985), which examine both the positive and negative consequences of consulting and the role relationships between faculty with clearly different dispositions.

Research Productivity

It is clear that education faculty productivity, at least as measured in terms of publication rate of journal articles and books, varies considerably across institutional type. This profile of variability across institutional types is similar to differences in the broader professoriate. One of the first priorities in terms of further inquiry is to determine the validity of assessments of faculty scholarly productivity. Surely publication rate is one barometer by which to measure this, but, as in the case of the perennial examination of faculty vitae in terms of tenure and promotion decisions, counting publications has obvious limitations. Sound scholarship and scientific inquiry acquire many forms and can result in a variety of products, of which publication in journals is but one.

A second area calling for more inquiry is the variety of factors that limit education faculty involvement in research and related activities. S. Tucker (1981) elaborates:

Heavy teaching loads as a function of a clinical, instructional model; the need to coordinate with field sites; consistent pressures for curriculum revision, and low status in the parent institution. To these must be added; a prejudice in the Federal establishment *against* the encouragement of active involvement on the part of SCDEs. The prejudice seems born of an attitude that the "educational establishment" is precisely where the competence does not lie to generate the kinds of understandings and innovations that will correct the problems and difficulties confronting the educational systems of the nation. (p. 14)

There are other constraining factors as well. For example, Rodrigues and Uhlenberg (1978) underscore the problem of the deluge of manuscripts submitted to the limited number of professional journals that exist in many fields. They report that, not only is the rejection rate dismally pessimistic at over 90 percent with many journals, "but that authors must wait and worry up to twelve months for acceptance or rejection slips" (p. 64).

Mitra (1974) and Judge (1982) have underscored another problem historically associated with social science and education research: a tendency to imitate the physical sciences. Mitra's comments are especially indicting in this regard: "in the field of education one would like to see a systematic study of significant problems, rather than a scientific study of insignificant problems" (p. 234). Similarly, Schwebel (1989) calls for educational research and development that address the major challenges facing our schools, especially in light of a number of larger social issues. Productivity, as measured in terms of publication rate, likely drives the unfortunate scenario shared by Schuster and Bowen at the outset of this chapter wherein faculty distance themselves to produce—to write, whatever the quality or nature of the manuscript. The very term *productivity* connotes quantity rather than quality. Thus, a central concern is how the scholarly inquiry of educational faculty across a variety of institutions can be not only increased but also balanced appropriately so that it addresses problems of social significance. Guba and Clark (1977) further point out the magnitude of the problem:

From the point of view of the planner attempting to devise means of increasing knowledge production and utilization (KPU) activities—all those other than teaching—in SCDEs, this situation is none too heartening. The majority of SCDE faculty have already received the doctoral degree, so the possibility of additional training is minimal; SCDE faculties are comprised of higher-ranking tenured personnel, so the impact of the reward system on them is lessened, and staffing flexibility is decreased; the proportion of faculty in SCDEs who still must confront promotion and tenure decisions is relatively small (although the absolute numbers are still large); teaching loads are heavy, so time allocated by the institution to the faculty member for KPU is minimal. (p. 712)

What can be done to promote more harmonious faculty collaboration and faculty and K–12 interactions and, at the same time, increase needed research and development? First, better understanding of present teacher education contexts in terms of both constraining and enabling factors is needed to point the way for how to study faculty scholarship in the future. More accurate assessments of the *quality*, as well as quantity, of present research undertaken in different contexts and with different purposes in mind is but needed baseline data. Obviously, this is a complex interactive problem that calls for leadership of a variety of types, not the least of which is that provided by deans of schools and colleges of education.

Career and Professional Development

Differences among professors at various stages of their careers in the larger professoriate were sketched briefly at the outset of this chapter. A few scholars have attempted to look at education faculty at various stages of their careers as well. Myers and Mager (1983), in a series of studies, followed 191 doctoral graduates from the 14 highest-ranked institutions in graduate education into their careers. They found as a consistent theme among new professors the inability to find and manage time, to do all the work called for, and to set priorities and balance divergent demands. A second common theme they found was the inability to deal harmoniously with peers and to respond effectively to the culture and norms of the institution. A quote from one of the new professors in their study illustrates this:

Applying for promotion and tenure (currently) has brought out the stark reality that what is "expected" as usual responsibilities has little effect on the decision in actuality! It is extremely difficult to publish (or even write) with four individual course preparations each semester, office hours, and committee assignments. (p. 10)

Ducharme (1986) reminds us that the problems associated with meeting diverse expectations are hardly limited to beginning professors and that additional problems and challenges come with middle age and higher rank. He suggests that this latter period might well be one calling for more adjustment to personal changes than earlier periods in one's career. The effects of aging and its relationship to various indexes of productivity have been studied in the larger professoriate and are informative. Bayer and Dutton (1977) employed the 1972–1973 American Council on Education data for over 5,000 doctoral teaching faculty from 7 scientific fields to assess the relationship between stage in career and 8 measures of productivity. Their indexes of productivity included recent articles, lifetime articles, books, number of works cited in the science citation index, pure research orientation, time spent in research, number of journal subscriptions, and time spent consulting. This appears to be at least a start in terms of a more differentiated perspective of productivity. Blackburn (1982), in analyzing these studies, found, perhaps predictably, that productivity does not show a simple, negative relationship with age. Among the groups studied, the first of the two plateaus tended to occur about 10 years after the PhD, and the second occurred as scientists neared retirement age. Scientists, whose productivity does not recover from a midcareer slump, tended to shift into nonresearch positions or to retire early (although early retirements are uncommon among doctoral scientists). Although Bayer and Dutton (1977) conclude that it is apparent that there are differences in terms of orientation and productivity that are somewhat generalizable across various faculty types at various stages of their careers, in order to understand these they have to be assessed in concert with a number of mediating variables. A variety of these constraints were identified earlier. Conceptual frameworks such as the one these scholars employed help point the way research designs might assist in understanding the interaction between education faculty activity and contributions of various types and career development over time.

Data in terms of research into faculty development are also very limited. This is due largely to a lack of conceptualizing and fully implementing comprehensive schemes of continuing faculty professional development. Numerous authors have described *types* of faculty development, such as Bergquist (1978). He reviews a variety of models such as the use of a student evaluation to guide faculty workshops, formalized forms of instructional diagnosis and clinical supervision, use of instructional methods training, and organizational development and team planning. These are simply not common. Also, it would indeed be a mistake to construe faculty development only, or even largely, in terms of the limited number of *formal* staff-development efforts that exist. Tough (1978) has engaged in numerous studies to identify and describe largely self-initiated learning projects by people from different walks of life. He has included faculty members in his sample and reports that they typically engage each year in a large number of self-initiated learning projects. Given the life-style and independent nature of many faculty, such self-initiated development efforts need to be examined more carefully. An orientation toward understanding faculty development largely embedded in the ongoing work of faculty is needed. Howey (1985) articulates various types of *job-embedded* professional development and outlines a typology of interacting dimensions that could guide more comprehensive and coherent professional development, as well as studies of this phenomenon.

Looking to the Future

There are major issues that need to be addressed to enable future research into the education professoriate. *First*, the variety of professorial roles and functions within the education academy needs to be more fully delimited and defined in order to communicate more clearly who assumes what type of function, especially in terms of teacher education. The perennial discussion of the differences in orientation between the disciplinists and the functionalists has proven to be of limited utility. There are, for example, growing numbers of education faculty who have made major contributions through their research representing multidisciplinary perspectives, especially of the complex ecology of schools and classrooms. Thus, there are at least two major groups in terms of the study of pedagogy represented at present: those who are discipline embedded and those concerned with more transcendent pedagogical and schooling processes. Further, it would appear that long-overdue attention is finally being given to the nature of laboratory and clinical training, with a focus on the central question of how one learns to teach in a variety of *controlled* settings with and without students. The contributions of such scholars as Berliner (1985) and Shulman (1986) have been most helpful in this regard. Although both discipline-specific and more general orientations are represented in laboratory and clinical faculty, these faculty are distinguished primarily by their assignment to scholarship and instruction in specific contexts for much of their time, as in teaching laboratories and school sites. When studying teacher educators one needs to better define who they are, in terms not only of their specific functions, but also and especially their relationships with the field, the context in which they work, the corpus of knowledge they draw upon, and the outcomes for which they are responsible.

Second, considerable conceptual work and hypothesis-generating inquiry is needed to better explicate both key *personal* and *contextual* factors that interact to enable or constrain faculty effectiveness.

Third, and as an example of the presage and personal dimensions, more inquiry is needed into faculty motives and self-expectations in terms of both why they pursue the professoriate and what they do once they are in it. The inquiry of Finkelstein (1984) and DeVries (1975) concerned with self-expectations and that of Ducharme and Agne (1982) that focused on motives of teacher educators suggest factors that might be predictive of faculty functioning.

Fourth, the socialization and acculturation of faculty are little understood, regardless of what presage and personal factors appear to mediate these conditions and processes. Given the formative-years construct developed by Lanier and Little (1986) and the fact that a large number of education faculty teach in K–12 schools for a considerable period before pursuing or completing a doctorate, the matter of how education professors are socialized both in graduate training and in the critical early years on the job deserves major attention. Further, inquiry into role relationships and role expectations and their genesis is needed. The apparent problems of many beginning professors, females in particular, need to be studied, especially where formal, structured interventions designed to mentor and assist these professors might exist.

Fifth, given the provocative inquiry of such scholars as B. Clark (1985), Myers and Mager (1983), and Schuster and Bowen (1985), academic rank and the criteria and procedures for achieving promotion, including the political dimensions, should be considered a major area in need of further analysis.

Sixth, more research is needed to understand the *range* of activities faculty engage in and the *motivation* behind these. The projected increase of faculty consulting to compensate for declining institutional compensation suggests an area ripe for study.

Seventh, the effects of changing institutional missions and major programmatic initiatives need to be better understood. A prime illustration is the movement toward norms more consistent with a professional school than a graduate school. A second example is the continued evolution of larger state institutions to some research emphasis, and a third is the move toward the development of more coherent programs demanding considerable faculty cooperation.

The study of professorial scholarship is limited. More applied research in school sites, more consonant with the most pressing problems and more commonly undertaken cooperatively with those in schools, suggests dimensions of *critical* research (as in critical theory). The processes of negotiating and conducting joint research in schools and the multiple formative findings and benefits associated with these will undoubtedly demand a rethinking of productivity in the future.

DEANS OF EDUCATION

The deanship surfaced in the 1860s when most universities and colleges had no more than four administrative officers and when universities were comparable in size to contemporary departments (McGrath, 1938; Rudolph, 1965). Bevan (1967) also suggests a humble beginning and observes "that the deanship was born out of the servile tasks which the registrar no longer had time to perform and the faculty regarded as unworthy of the time needed to assemble for deliberation" (p. 344). A more prevalent view is that, in their emergent history, deans were viewed as extentions of the presidency and were called upon to preside at faculty meetings in the president's absence and administer disciplinary matters, to handle petitions of students, and generally to supervise the clerical and administrative business of the college. By 1900 fewer than 20 percent of all universities had deans (W. Dill, 1980). As recently as 1947 faculty typically still were not involved in the selection of deans. However, by 1960 deans were common in university settings. As William Dill further observes, "there were more on some campuses than there had been faculty members a century earlier" (p. 264). By 1977 D. Clark and Guba identified 1,367 education units, the majority of which were presided over by deans. This relatively recent growth in the dean's position led eventually to its study, but, again, only recently.

Limitations to Studying the Deanship

Perhaps the first comprehensive study of the education deanship was that by Cyphert and Zimpher (1976). This study was published in what is to date the most inclusive treatment of the education deanship, *The Dilemma of the Deanship*.

The editors of this volume, Griffiths and McCarty (1980), claim that, prior to the publication of this text, "there had been so little theoretical, conceptual, or research literature published on the deanship as to constitute an embarrassment to both the practitioners and scholars of higher education" (p. v). Doi further observes:

Colleges and university administrators still remain untouchable as objects for systematic research on role perception and conflict, personality characteristics, value orientation, status seeking behavior, and identification with institution. Published works about administrators, of which there is no dearth, are mainly anecdotal or advisory. (1965, p. 352)

Coladarci (1980) shared this pithy observation of his preparation for the deanship:

In the guilty realization that I was assuming a role for which I was most unprepared, I set about to locate and study the accumulated knowledge and wisdom bearing on employment as dean of a school of education. I found, with Adamic surprise, that the literature addressing this honorable estate could be read comfortably between a late breakfast and an early lunch—and that the dearth in volume was not compensated for by substance. It appears that educational researchers, even those given to extended fits of intemperate empiricism, essentially have been disinterested in examining a role that, in their own profession, is rumored to be consequential but is charged frequently to be ineffective. (p. 125)

Thus, the University Council for Educational Administration's interest in studying the deanship was long overdue. Citing the need for research in order to establish a body of knowledge on which the deanship could rest, Culbertson (1980) questioned whether the field of study possessed (a) symbolic generalizations that function as laws and definitions for the field, (b) shared beliefs including heuristic models to develop

analogies and metaphors to describe role and function, and (c) scientific values needed to assess the adequacy of theories that would inform and even predict actions of deans. On all criteria he concluded that "in higher education, including higher education management and leadership, there is very little use of laws, models and scientific values" (p. 10). Thus, he placed the study of the academic deanship, particularly in schools, colleges, and departments of education in a preparadigmatic stage of development (Kuhn, 1970).

More fundamentally, Cyphert and Zimpher (1980) describe the litany of unknowns that impede our ability to adequately prepare educators for the dean's role:

We know virtually nothing about the goals of incumbents in these leadership positions; where they come from, what their backgrounds are, what their personal characteristics are. Neither do we know who might be potential candidates for these administrative positions. We know more about the proficiencies by which these individuals are selected than we do about the survivors of this screening process. We are not knowledgeable about the career aspirations of incumbents in leadership positions. In addition, we know very little about why recent deans have left their positions. Likewise, we have no knowledge about the characteristics of future deans. . . . And finally, although we are currently giving some consideration to institutional differences, we do not know what effect these differences have on the leaders in these institutions. (p. 92)

Thus, this section of the chapter reviews essentially only a decade of studies on the deanship, including a personal/professional (or demographic) profile of deans; perceptions of the dean's role and function, including a limited number of impact studies; and studies attempting to examine interactions of the individual and the organization. The chapter concludes by looking at the implications of the literature, particularly with regard to significant questions warranting further study.

A Personal/Professional Profile of Deans

According to Cyphert and Zimpher (1980), two profiles emerged from their national stratified random sample of deans of schools, colleges, and departments of education. One is of the personal posture of the dean:

Personally, American deans of education today are most commonly healthy and energetic, middle-aged, married, male, white, protestant, democratic, and from a relatively non-college educated, lower middle class, non-professional–managerial, native-born, small town, multi-child family background. (p. 117)

They acknowledge that there are few surprises to be found in this analysis. There is also much commonality between this demographic profile of deans and that of the professoriate, surely in part because deans generally move to their positions from the faculty. The second profile that emerged is that of the professional attributes of deans:

Professionally, American deans of education today normally hold the doctorate degree, have had some training in educational administration, entered the profession through public school experiences, adanced from there to the university faculty, and took the deanship directly from a position in higher education. Despite their administrative duties, they manage to engage in as much research and writing as do their professorial colleagues. They find that the deanship does constrain both their personal and professional activities, however. They do belong to several national and regional professional associations, and acknowledge the need for professorial self improvement, even though they engage in relatively little of it. (p. 118)

Many deans graduated from programs of higher education administration, and more than one in four earned their doctorate in educational administration. Another 34 percent of deans in this survey earned their doctorate in teacher education (elementary and secondary education, the teaching of a specific subject area, and/or general instruction). Similar proportions were found by Anderson and King (1987) wherein the same percentage of deans (25 percent) majored in curriculum and instruction as majored in educational administration.

A comparison of 8 other common variables from the personal/professional profiles of deans developed by Cyphert and Zimpher and by Anderson and King reflects little difference in the typical age of the dean (about 50), the dean's ethnicity (except for an increase of 6 percent more black deans in the latter study, deans are still about 90 percent Caucasian), possession of the terminal degree (most hold PhDs), or relative tenure status (the great majority are tenured as faculty members). What has changed in the professoriate as well as in the deanship, is the shift in gender. Whereas 84 percent of the deans in 1976 were male, 33 percent of the deans in 1987 were female.

With regard to career path, in the Cyphert and Zimpher study, 89 percent of the deans took their positions from previous positions held within higher education (57 percent from the very same institution). Nearly 70 percent of the respondents had had over 3 years of teaching experience, with 94 percent of the Anderson and King respondents citing the same. Thus, the lineage from classroom teacher to professor to dean seems to be supported by these 2 studies.

One myth that can be disspelled, however, is the notion that deans take positions as the result of a pattern of appointments, first as a professor, then as a chair, and then as associate or assistant dean, prior to the deanship. This contention, for example, is made by Morris (1981). Only 27 percent of deans in the Cyphert and Zimpher study, however, held prior administrative positions; 12 percent as chairs, 12 percent as associate or assistant deans, and 3 percent as both. Further, less than 1 percent of the population had held another deanship prior to assuming their current deanships. Deans also reported that it had been less than 2 years from the time they first thought about taking the deanship to the time they ultimately assumed it. Interestingly, the range was 2.2 years for male and 6 months for female aspirants. Thus, deans often appear to come to the role with less than optimum prior administrative experience in higher education, though they come from within higher education, and with little time to prepare for the role, once making the decision to pursue it.

Another dimension of the Cyphert and Zimpher study examines deans' scholarship. Some question the ability of deans to pursue scholarship as one means of providing academic lead-

ership among their colleagues in the face of the considerable managerial responsibility required of the deanship (Ciardi, 1962; Lee, 1959). Nonetheless, the data show that 50 percent of the deans report some ability to sustain scholarly inquiry, having published books and monographs while in the role, with 80 percent of those in doctoral institutions doing so. It should be underscored, however, that 73 percent reported that they published articles regularly prior to assuming the deanship and that the rate of publication declined significantly afterward.

In terms of the tenure of deans, the Cyphert and Zimpher study shows that respondents had held their position for 70 months (nearly 6 years) and that their predecessors had served an average of 8 years in the deanship. Deans in this study expected to serve 4 to 6 more years; chairpersons anticipated remaining in the role for only one to 3 more years. In the Anderson and King study, exactly half the respondents had been deans for 5 years or less, 30 percent between 6 to 10 years and 10 percent between 11 to 15 years. The investigators found an inverse relationship between years of service as a dean and size of the institution, noting that, in general, the length of service as dean at very large institutions is relatively short.

Over time, cross-sectional studies such as this will allow the charting of major shifts by gender, ethnicity, age, and preparation, as well as by scholarly productivity and professional interests and contributions. But to understand more fundamentally the motivation, behavior, and effectiveness of deans, inquiry at this level needs to be much more diversified and conceptually grounded. Studies of personality and persuasion, cognitive ability, coping skills, ethical and moral propensities, and sense of efficacy are noticeably absent. As more robust profiles are produced, correlational and predictive studies could be possible. These should be developed and supported with case studies linking critical personal and professional dispositions to various types of impact. To date, no such analyses are available.

Perceptions of Deans' Role, Function, and Impact

There are understandable differences in what deans do as well as in their beliefs about what they should do. Expectations are often high. William Dill invokes Reisman's (1956) view that deans are "the chief remaining force for innovation and constructive change in large university systems" (W. Dill, 1980, p. 264). Salmen (1971) calls deans "the most important group of administrators in the whole of higher education" (p. 21). From an analysis of a handful of extant studies on self-perceived role and function and from a few conceptual pieces on the impact and effectiveness of deans, a composite picture of deans' functions can be drawn.

Perceptions of Deans' Functions. In the Cyphert and Zimpher study, a category system was used to portray deans' perceptions of a series of functions including (a) their observations on the need for prior training in these areas; (b) the amount of free time they would choose to invest in these areas should they have additional working hours available during the week; (c) the degree to which they experienced success or failure, satisfaction or frustration in the role; and (d) the degree of expertise they believed they held in each area. A view of these functions was also solicited from the deans' immediate superordinates, in most cases the views of an academic vice president or provost. Their data suggest a preponderance of activity with regard to program development, budgeting, staff development; the general administrative aspects of organizing, executing, and decision making; and the general administration of the education unit. Provosts also viewed these as the top-ranking functions with regard to areas of deans' success and failure.

Morsink's (1987) study of 70 educational administrators, 36 of whom were SCDE deans or chairpersons, reveals an interesting array of functions for deans. She reviewed the literature on critical functions of administrators from studies of business and industry (Peters & Waterman, 1981), effective schools (Purkey & Smith, 1985), and higher education (Grosnick & Reynolds, 1978; Norton, 1978, 1980; Sivage, Bryson, & Okum, 1982; A. Tucker, 1984). In this analysis the critical functions of communicating goals and mission, involving people on a team to fulfill these goals, and supporting the efforts of staff and encouraging innovations generally followed the standard tasks of administration. As a result of Morsink's analysis, two critical functions were identified across the population: (a) administrators provide leadership for their unit to focus on its mission, particularly in the specification of educational goals and ways to achieve these; and (b) administrators provide support that allows personnel to perform effectively, including assistance in generating resources for activities and modeling behaviors that support goal attainment.

In a third study of the functions of the deanship and self-perceptions of incumbents, Dejnozka (1978) attempted to isolate role *norms*, which he defined as "specific observable behaviors which an office holder is apt to exhibit when facing a particular recurrent situation" (p. 81). Those several functions that received the greatest priority from respondents with regard to role orientation were rewarding effective teaching, maintaining equitable work loads, interviewing likely candidates, terminating the unqualified or the weak, meeting regularly with chairpersons, involving faculty in policy-making, seeking faculty opinions of chairpersons, participating in professional conferences, rewarding research and scholarly writing, and overseeing reviews of courses and programs. In contrast, among the lowest-ranking responses were reviewing professor course outlines and observing faculty in classrooms. The results of the study further revealed that faculty, chairs, and other administrators generally agree on role expectations for the education deanship. Between-group differences were not of a magnitude to suggest that there were major differences in perception of role.

Dejnozka observed:

All groups, faculty and department chairpersons especially, tend to view the dean as the college's advocate rather than as its policeman. Faculty members expect fairness, an open system, free reign and participation, and consultation and involvement in matters effecting the policy of the unit. The practice of assigning "final say" responsibilities to the dean is one which wins but average support from all groups. To a limited extent, deans apparently are more inclined to assume such "final say" authority than any of the three remaining groups surveyed would want. (p. 84)

Further, one major paradox was reflected in the responses to the study that, by Dejnozka's attribution, would puzzle most laypersons who observe how colleges and universities function:

Specifically, deans are expected to reward outstanding faculty members and to terminate those who are weak or unqualified. In so doing, however, the dean is dissuaded from employing some of the primary sources which could help with the carrying out of this mandate: observing faculty at their work in classrooms or reviewing their course outlines and grade sheets. (p. 84)

In a survey of 19 deans of schools and colleges of education in the University of Tennessee system, Fullerton (1978) sought to examine two major dimensions of the deanship: issues related to education from a dean's point of view and issues related to the role of dean. Accordingly, a list of possible issues was rated by respondents and an open-ended section requested the enumeration of five role functions they felt were most important for the deanship. Top-ranking educational issues among dean respondents included maintenance and improvement of the quality of programs, allocation of resources for academic needs, uncertainty of continued support from state legislatures, leveling effect of state funding patterns, and inability to secure adequate resources commensurate with enrollment. Those issues recorded by deans in terms of their role, in rank order, were cultivation and promotion of progressive ideas among faculty and students, lack of time to write and publish, lack of leisure time for relaxation, lack of adequate secretarial help, and lack of sufficient administrative help. In the open-ended responses the largest number of items dealt with the development of programs, the leadership function of the dean, and the concerns related to public relations with internal and external constituents.

Throughout these studies, which are largely the perceptions of deans tempered by responses of other administrators and faculty, there is some confluence of perspectives on role and function. Certainly, deans are occupied with decision making; leadership and management functions; concerns over faculty development, rewards, selection, retention, and dismissal; and, to a great extent, budgetary concerns. Still these studies largely constitute self-perceptions of function and, as a consequence, are descriptive in nature, with only modest validation of appropriateness or significance by others.

Perceptions of Impact. Several studies on the effectiveness of deans are discussed here, as are a cluster of studies having to do with criteria appropriate for the selection of deans. In a study by Lasley and Haberman (1987), a questionnaire consisting of 20 items was distributed to vice presidents or vice chancellors of academic affairs regarding criteria for assessing deans. A brief summary of the data reveals that the top-ranking evaluative criteria were (a) the dean chooses and supports quality faculty; (b) the dean maintains quality standards in his or her recommendations for promotion; (c) the dean, as a developmental leader, seeks to improve and initiate programs, rather than manage the status quo; (d) the dean stimulates faculty productivity; and (e) the dean is equitable in making merit decisions.

Cole (1983) focused on two important aspects of a dean's role: that of administrative effectiveness generally and effectiveness of deans of education specifically. Surveyed were 27 institutions in Texas, including chief academic officers, deans, chairs, and a random sample of faculty. Administrative effectiveness was defined as "that quality of a decision which produces a definite or desired result, with qualitative efficiency which implies skill as well as economy of energy or resources in producing the desired result" (p. 48). Cole used five categories to divide decisions among instructional program, research, student affairs, faculty affairs, and financial affairs. In rank order, respondents viewed the importance of critieria for assessing deans to be effectiveness in managing faculty affairs, followed by administration of financial affairs, instructional programs, student affairs, and research. Deans were viewed by faculty not as effective in program matters as in other endeavors, and almost no one viewed deans as effective in support for research activities. Perhaps surprisingly, deans were viewed as solidly effective by all in exerting administrative effectiveness on financial affairs.

The Rooney and Clark (1982) study developed a somewhat different perspective on the deanship in that it projects a period of initial appointment (called, not surprisingly, the honeymoon period) wherein deans are viewed as able to make more gains in terms of the management of programs and faculty than in their later tenure. They report that, "the overall results of the survey were unambiguous . . . in six areas a statistically significant relationship existed which substantiated more positive perceptions held about the new dean" (p. 47). The major variables or attributes about which faculty were queried included expectations held for the dean in terms of both institutional impact (e.g., Can the new dean change the mission of the school to obtain more financial support?) and individual success (e.g., Can the dean help me achieve success in my own teaching, research, and service activities)? Areas in which new deans were perceived by faculty as significantly more influential than longer tenured deans included the following: (a) garnering federal financial support for the SCDE, (b) changing the mission emphasis of the SCDE, (c) promoting research and scholarly productivity, (d) promoting SCDE faculty activities in research, (e) effecting changes generally within the SCDE, and (f) acquiring resources.

The Rooney and Clark study was designed essentially as an outgrowth of 20 site studies by D. Clark and Guba (1977) wherein they conclude: "Faculty, subordinant administrators, (and) constituents hold unrealistic expectations for newly appointed deans . . . with little in the way of new support. They attribute to the dean the ability to overcome long standing constraints in the institutional environment" (pp. vii–18). As a consequence, Rooney and Clark suggest that "new deans can expect that faculty will be largely positive about their work, anticipating positive change and supporting most of their new initiatives. Conversely, the dean had better expect that each passing day will establish a more realistic perception of what can and cannot be achieved by the administration" (p. 49).

Heald (1982) takes a slightly different direction but adds additional information to the understanding of the functions engaged in by education deans. He inventoried institutions engaged in searches for education deans and studied the list of criteria published in the *Chronicle of Higher Education*, and he ultimately categorized them into 7 general categories: general demonstrated skills, focused demonstrated skills, institutional eligibilities (forms of appointment), personal attributes, professional commitments to education, professional experiences, and professional sensitivities. Heald asked chairs of search committees and newly hired deans to reflect on the importance of these variables in both the *selection* of the dean and the *functioning* of the dean. For all responses, there was no statistically significant difference between the responses of deans and search committee chairs. With regard to focused demonstrated skills, of highest ranked importance were decision-making ability, program development, and planning and evaluation activities. With regard to more general demonstrated skills, there was also congruence from the respondents on the top three criteria, noted as leadership ability, ability to deal with faculty, and human relations generally. There was some variability, however, between rankings with regard to attributes deemed important for selection versus function: leadership ability was the highest criterion for selection and only third for functioning. This raises questions, because Mangieri and Arnn (1984) underscore that the integrity of a dean's search is related to the match between espoused values and critical functions in role, or, taking the "guessing and wishing" out of leadership selection.

In a case study of deans' impact, Arends, Reinhard, and Sivage (1981) analyzed the impact of education deans by examining behaviors associated with the implementation of special projects. Two kinds of descriptions were provided relating to the behavior of deans: (a) categories of behaviors formed by faculty that appeared to influence what happened in these projects; and (b) the respondents' judgment of the degree to which specific deans' behaviors facilitated or restrained the progress of the projects that faculty and staff were attempting to implement.

The researchers were able to identify 244 supportive and over 30 nonsupportive behaviors across the 10 sites. This collectively represents an interesting finding in and of itself. Ultimately, these latter behaviors were clustered into 3 major categories. Choreographic behaviors were those activities related to building and maintaining a temporary support system for a project, acquiring and allocating resources, and negotiating conflicts. In much the same way a choreographer manages dance, music, and design to bring about a unified performance, deans created the overall composition, the structure, and the processes that guided the activities of a project and helped maintain the consistent warmth that was created.

Advocacy behaviors occurred when deans acted as promoters of the projects. To some extent, these activities involved the process of performing ceremonial duties, including the dean's physical presence, guest speeches and lunches, and cosigning of certain memoranda. Deans also acted as persuaders at faculty meetings, as spokespersons in college addresses, and as providers of social and political rapport for the project faculty and coordinators. As the researchers observe:

Support could vary from a pat on the back during a difficult time, a wink during an important meeting, or public acknowledgement and recognition for work done well . . . this kind of support, particularly when it was made public, was considered very helpful; failing to "compliment" or taking a "stand offish" position were behaviors viewed as undesirable and unhelpful. (p. 18)

A third category of behaviors included communication behaviors with both internal people and external clients, including serving as a liaison with outsiders and as a disseminator. The researchers found a high level of involvement of deans in these projects.

This study explored particularly the behaviors deans use that support or hinder curriculum change in higher education and found striking similarities in their behaviors across sites. Although this study does not provide documentation on the quality of projects that emerged, it does begin to identify relationships between the deans' behaviors and the perceived complementarity of these behaviors to fostering project success.

In a parallel vein, Swanson (1983) conducted a single case analysis of a successful curriculum change effort in one school of education and, as a result, suggests that certain precepts about change might well be myths. These, briefly stated, are as follows: *Myth 1*, any departmentwide change effort must begin with a common goal; *Myth 2*, all staff and faculty in the department must plan together if a lasting change is to occur; *Myth 3*, the dean must initiate, or at least actively support, an innovation for it to meet with success; and *Myth 4*, successful implementation of an innovation requires acceptance and uniform action from all faculty. Contrary to any visible or even behind-the-scenes leadership role, the dean in this case study had relatively little involvement. The dean was communicated with by those who championed the curriculum innovation and was described as offering verbal support, but was not credited with behaviors that either enhanced or stifled the innovation that took place. More specifically, Swanson observes "a staff that waits for the dean to initiate change or actively direct change misunderstands the dynamics of a certain, forward-moving organization. While active leadership from the dean may be desirable, this support is not critical to the success of curriculum innovation. A few energetic faculty and staff can make innovation happen" (p. 28). This is a view somewhat contrary to that observed in the 10-site study initially described by Arends and others. Nevertheless, it brings to bear the critical question of the dean's involvement in curriculum innovation.

To summarize findings drawn from the studies reviewed, first, no one category system appears sufficient for analyzing the dean's role. Nonetheless, it is clear that the functions identified by deans themselves, as well as others, appear common across a number of institutional settings. There are alternative notions of leadership associated with the deanship, and there is also something in the role of deans that speaks to leadership, choreography, and organization, as well as to administrivia. Mutual decision making, shared governance, and collegiality are viewed as critical to the success of deans. Also, the communicative abilities of deans appear critical in a number of the studies described. There is clear support for the dean's involvement in faculty or staff development, program develop-

ment, and, to some extent, garnering support for faculty research. There is also common support for the dean's involvement in changing the SCDE mission, presumably for the better. And, finally, there is considerable support for the dean's role with regard to financial management.

Although there appears to be general agreement about the various roles, functions, and expectations for deans in schools, colleges, and departments of education, there are critical questions left unanswered. Some hinge on the nature of the substantive issues surveyed, and others call for more sophisticated research methodology to more validly and reliably interpret what was asked. The Cyphert and Zimpher study provides some attention to different personal, career, and role attributes, for example, by institutional type. Yet in most of the studies reviewed, no stratification of the sample occurred, a problem repeatedly noted in studies of the professoriate. It is reasonable to expect that the roles and functions of deans do in fact vary across institutional types and, probably, even within degree-granting classifications. Yet little of the initial research has taken into account major context differences. The studies reviewed make little mention of institutional context and organizational milieu. Thus, one cannot generalize from this meager sample of available studies on the deanship about deans across institutional types and across settings. There does seem to be some commonality in role expectation and function, but with little linkage either to the type of institution served or to the specific nature of substantive outcomes as a result of or related to the dean's leadership. Only in a few instances are there case studies that speak more qualitatively to a dean's functioning, but only modestly to measures of the impact of that functioning.

The Organizational Context for Deans

Bok (1986) observes that professional schools serve many different callings and come in many sizes and shapes. Schools, colleges, and departments of education are certainly no exception. Thus, it is important to look particularly at institutional hallmarks and variations peculiar to SCDEs, because there is no guarantee of organizational structures in higher education that are isomorphic to SCDEs. Specifically, D. Clark and Guba (1980) make several observations about SCDEs and about the dean's role. As they observe, the predominant governance pattern in higher education is collegial, but no one is specifically trained to engage in and foster collegiality. Few can initiate change unilaterally. A rational, bureaucratic, decision-making model does not appear especially consistent with the particularly fluid nature of many SCDEs. Also, as Rooney and Clark (1982) found, deans are often expected to overcome long-standing social and organizational constraints in the SCDE. Often there is a predictable shortfall in their performance because many of their faculty colleagues are not willing to invest much in organizational renewal. Possible periods of change in SCDEs are often a result of unfounded hopes for new deans, and the tenure of deans is so abbreviated that innovation in schools, colleges, and departments of education moves in a process of fits and starts (D. Clark & Guba, 1980).

If neither a bureaucratic nor a collegial leadership model

necessarily prevails, what is appropriate to a better understanding of SCDEs as organizations and to the effectiveness of deans therein? How have SCDEs been described, and, as a consequence, how might deanships be studied in light of these characterizations? David Dill (1980) discusses the nature of schools of education as complex organizations or as systems composed of subsystems. The subsystems he refers to are a compilation of goals and values, technology, structural dynamics, and psychological and managerial considerations. He provides a series of propositions, or hypotheses, that could inform the study of the dean's role in diverse organizations. Particularly, he posits these propositions. Schools of education are essentially open systems affected by and dependent on other systems. They are contained in diverse settings. They can change, but they are composed of differing layers of control and autonomy. However, the higher the level of (central) authority, or the greater the level of authority in an SCDE, the lower the degree of innovation. More autonomy and more idiographic behavior among faculty precipitate more innovation and more activity. Conversely, the greater the complexity, the less the centralization. Even though more organization might be more efficient, it fosters less job satisfaction. These are attributes that Dill hypothesizes are particularly germane to SCDEs. Dill evokes three primary models for analyzing the decision-making process in SCDEs that could apply to the *study* of schools of education as complex organizations and the study of the dean's role within these organizations. Essentially, these models derive from classical studies of organizational development.

The *rational-actor* model is "a derivative of Weber's conception of bureaucracy as an organization rationally designed to pursue a given goal" (D. Dill, 1980, p. 203). Here an explicit relationship between cause and effect and means and ends exists. In this model, individuals, groups, and organizations make choices between means to a given end because the organization assumes that relationships between means and ends are predictable and rational. The touchstone of bureaucratic organization is forming objectives, searching for alternatives, comparing consequences, ranking alternatives, and verifying the consequences that flow from a given alternative.

A second conception assumes that organizational characteristics affect more fully the decision-making processes; thus, the bureaucratic or rational-actor model is seriously circumscribed. It assumes that organizations are characterized by uncertainty, by pressing problems that take priority over long-range goals. Often the search for alternatives must be limited, because means and ends are not necessarily predictable. Such a view of organizations is posited by Cohen, March, and Olsen (1972), who ultimately refer to university governance as organized anarchy wherein a "garbage can" model of decision making (a model of limited rationality and predictability) often works.

A third model assumes that the outcome of the decision-making process is not so much the product of analytical procedures as of political forces that influence or affect the SCDE. Most notably, this model is explicated by Baldridge (1971) and gives significant weight to an analysis of the social structure or organizational characteristics of the system. Its distinctive features are its focus upon *political* bases used in the analysis of decision making and its assumption that interest-group values

predominate in that process. Obviously, aspects of each of these views of organizations pertain in the multiple realities of any complex organization. These models serve, at the very least, however, as departure points for future research.

McCarty and Reyes (1987) attempt to explain deans' behavior in academic colleges at a major research-oriented university through a variation of the organizational models just discussed. First, the "most venerable" perspective depicts colleges and universities as a collegium (Goodman, 1962; Millett, 1962; Parsons, 1956). In this model of consensus decision making between faculty members and administrators, the authors reference Perkins's observation of deans as "first among equals in an organization of professionals" (McCarty & Reyes, 1987, p. 3). A second model is that of the academic bureaucracy modeled after the rational-organizational structure, where coordination is achieved through superordination and subordination of persons and groups (Hall, 1977; Weber, 1947). In this model, as portrayed by Etzioni (1975), the dean is an authoritative figure "who stands at the top of the bureaucracy pyramid and wields much of the organization's power through budgetary controls" (McCarty & Reyes, 1987, p. 3). A third organizational orientation views colleges and universities as political systems in which powerful actors build coalitions and dominate the organization through intentional political actions (Karpik, 1978). As such, the dean's role is to function as a mediator (Baldridge, 1971; Baldridge, et al., 1978). Finally, as referred to earlier, Cohen et al. (1972) portray the university as organized anarchy wherein the organization is "a collection of choices looking for problems, issues, and feelings looking for decision situations in which they may be aired, solutions looking for issues to which they might be the answer, and decision makers looking for work" (p. 81). In this latter, rather eclectic view of universities, the dean's role is "to keep track of useful solutions and pursue them in whatever context they happen to occur" (McCarty & Reyes, 1987, p. 3).

As a result of the analysis of interview data from 55 department chairs, McCarty and Reyes draw conclusions about organizations and the dean's role within them. First, chairs do *not* see deans as powerful and bureaucratic administrative figures. Rather, they view deans as somewhat distant from departments and responding primarily to departmental initiatives. In this portrayal deans control such resources as budget and space and exercise a considerable amount of authority, largely through veto power and not necessarily through initiation. Neither do chairs consider deans the intellectual leaders of the academic unit. However, whether deans provide much initiation or are primarily responsive, some perceive their role negatively: "For the dean, it is sort of a 'catch twenty-two.' If he provides leadership, he is going to get resistance; if he doesn't provide leadership, then people will wish he did. I'm not sure how any one individual can resolve that" (p. 5).

With regard to a collegial model of academic administration, several observers suggest that colleges really are bureaucratic but masked by collegial ideology. Still collegiality continues to be an article of faith in most SCDEs. Obviously, many schools and colleges are not basically Weberian. Deans do not wholly control budgets, they do not wholly select faculty, but they have veto power over appointments, the assigning of space, and the approving of proposals. Although they appear to be in a hierarchical position, they rarely exercise personalized and arbitrary rule.

Problematic too is the model of organizations as anarchies, wherein decisions seem extremely random and frenzied. Particularly in the research-oriented university studied by McCarty and Reyes (1987), organizations were unified around a common belief in the primacy of research that did not appear to allow for the kind of randomness proposed by the view of institutions as organized anarchies. The esprit de corps established by an orientation toward and respect for scholarly inquiry reinforces collegiality and counters the self-interests of colleges, departments, and individuals. In the final analysis, the collegium appears to be a powerful enough organizer to incorporate the features of the other three models:

We assumed that the type of college, the personality and leadership style of the dean, and the predisposition of the department chairperson might be significant. It did not turn out that way. . . . Nearly every member of the institution who is selected for an administrative role, regardless of college, individual personality, or previous position seemingly becomes captured by the prevailing ethos. To think otherwise would be to become disloyal. (p. 6)

Although the prevailing ethos might be one of collegiality, the authors conclude that deans, as a matter of fact, govern in a host of ways reflecting each of these four models. For example, rational bureaucracy allows administrators to orchestrate rational decision making when appropriate. There are also many formal patterns of friendship, group coalitions, and hidden powers that play a role in the political ideology of the organization. At times, the diffuseness of quasi-autonomous departments borders on anarchy. This aptly illustrates the point that future study of the deanship should be grounded in the institutional context and its various nuances.

Burnham (1987) identifies a series of paradoxes that could be helpful as perspectives for viewing the dean's ability to affect the nature of organizations and the goals organizations pursue. For example, there is the struggle between the view of the dean as a leader and the view of the dean as a manager. Managers, Burnham contends, maintain existing order. Leaders are concerned with establishing the paradoxes of change. There is for the dean and all who function in such an organization the contrast of fear and hope; fear of destroying the present and hope for renewal of the organization. In a case study, Burnham describes the risk-taking behaviors and courage necessary to move ahead on reform agendas and the defensiveness inherent in admitting that a crisis might exist in the organization.

In any new perspective on organizations, old stereotypes must fall. D. Clark's (1984) analysis of the "entrenched paradigm" of bureaucratic administration emanates from Weber's (1947) and Parsons' (1956) view of bureaucracy as a normative pattern of organizations. Such a pattern rests on the fundamental assumption of legal authority. Here the derivative language has strong linguistic and metaphorical overtones. "It is materialistic, mechanistic, sexist, capitalistic, western and rationalistic" (p. 11). It is in conflict with contemporary notions of organizational function gleaned from the study of major corporate enterprises that reward (a) a bias for action; (b) getting close to the customer; (c) autonomy and entrepreneurship; (d) productivity through people; (e) hands-on, value-driven activities; (f) sticking to the knitting; (g) simple form and lean staff; and (h) simultaneous loose–tight properties (Peters & Waterman, 1981).

Although analyses contribute to an understanding of alternative perspectives on organizations, they also reveal characteristics of appropriate leadership by deans within alternative organizational structures. They chronicle a propensity to rationalize the behavior of deans within organizational models. In search of new paradigms for studying the deanship, Coladarci (1980) believes that researchers should assume a posture of "agnosticism" about explanations of behavior; that is, there is no administrator for all seasons. Thus, Coladarci argues for a proliferation of studies about administrators in situ. These studies of "deans-and-deanships-in-context" could be done in comprehensive case analyses with a more ethnographic posture, thus introducing the opportunity for more interpretation about the interplay of role and context. Coladarci argues that the multivariate reality of administrative roles is underestimated and oversimplified. Thus, correlational studies tend to be trivialized if researchers do not recognize major differences across institutions. D. Clark (1984) acknowledges the dominance of the bureaucratic paradigm in past study of leadership, wherein the field moved from trait studies of leaders, to style and behavior, and, ultimately, to situational factors, largely because it could not relate independent personal variables to success in organizations. He concludes that these studies have made limited contributions largely because "the inquirers cannot proceed beyond certain critical bounds without denying the root paradigm" (p. 34). Thus Clark challenges earlier rational hierarchial assumptions and supports more recent theorists who suggest a departure from linear causality to mutual causality. The bureaucratic orientation to goals, rationality, sequence, causality, and purposive behavior has moved toward a cultural orientation to organizations in terms of the dialectic of conflict, contradiction, domination, power, and class.

Implications for Future Research

Given the combined views of leadership as a more consensual and horizontal enterprise, embedded in a cultural milieu of authority exchanges, the view of how to study the impact of deans needs to be altered as well. Rather than an attempt to isolate critical administrative functions as a linear set of skills and attitudes exercised by deans upon others, there is a need to study the *interactive* capacities of deans. To what extent do their planning modes acknowledge the autonomy of the professionals for whom they serve as academic head? To what extent do leaders balance the need to initiate with consideration of member needs? To what extent do leaders appropriately rely on others? To what extent do deans provide rewards and incentives to encourage action, rather than acting to discourage participation? Not only do these dimensions suggest new lines of study, but they might also help redefine what institutions judge as the outcomes of their labor. Certainly the creation of new programs, the increase of staff and budgets, and the initiation of new priorities will continue to be standard measures of productivity. So, however, should be various measures of organizational well-being as this relates to leadership capabilities of deans.

In summary, much of the study of deans in organizations has been a case of finding what we were looking for; that is, what deans do in terms of conventional task analysis. Even when researchers depart from this form of descriptive study to some measures of impact, they retain limited views of task and organization, drawing primarily on somewhat collegial, but often more bureaucratic, frameworks for analysis. Emerging views portray faculty members as autonomous, idiographic, and individually determined entities and deans largely as the facilitators of individual effort toward a collective goal.

Our path in this analysis of deans has been essentially to understand the nature of extant studies on the deanship, essentially divided into categories of personal and professional demography, perceptions of role and function (by deans and those with whom they work), studies of the impact of organizational context on deaning, and, finally, a brief review of literature enunciating new conceptions of leadership and organizations. This path has led to a series of observations about deans and studying the deanship. Advances in studying the deanship necessarily depend on adjusted views of the role itself; thus, the link between how one views what the dean does and how the role is studied.

Traditional notions of organizations as rational, authoritative bureaucracies suggest that the members or the followers in these organizations often want to be led by a person in a dean's role and that leadership is to a large degree a matter of hierarchial decision making, authority, and influence. More recent and more in-depth analyses of schools and colleges of education suggest that they are more complex organizations, often anti-bureaucratic and understandably culturally embedded. These attributes suggest that leadership is more of a shared phenomenon; that all individuals experience tension and paradox as organizations change; that change requires the deterioration of stability and the creation of disequilibrium, which is equally difficult for those in leadership positions and those construed as followers. Thus, a constructionist focus on the transactive nature of deans and faculty in schools, colleges, and departments of education is critical to future study.

To summarize suggested future research on deans, longitudinal baseline studies are needed to acknowledge the changing personal/professional profile of deans. Studies of deans need to acknowledge what can be major differences in institutional mission, organization, ethos, and culture. Conceptions of leadership and organization embedded in alternative theoretical frameworks need to guide case study, cases in which there is both a match with more contemporary notions of leadership and more historical and orthodox views.

Most fundamental to an understanding of leadership, especially in terms of major change initiatives, the shared, *distributed* nature of leadership needs to be examined. This calls for study of the relationships not only between deans and faculty but also between deans and a variety of others in administrative and leadership positions and between those in *informal* and formal leadership and managerial roles.

Given the considerable challenges of providing leadership, let alone effective management in complex organizations, more study is needed of how deans are selected, by whom, and for what reasons. There are many paradoxes embedded in the institutional functioning of institutions of higher education, and it would be fallacious to assume, for example, that aggressive leadership in terms of institutional renewal constitutes a major criterion for selection and support of deans, either by faculty or by superordinates to the deans, such as provosts.

In this latter regard, little attention has been given to the role and functioning of deans beyond the context of significant endeavors undertaken with the faculty. The more singular interactions with such key agents external to the school or college as presidents and provosts have not been systematically studied. Surely, direction and support for schools and colleges of education, often characterized as low within the institutional pecking order, are influenced by these critical transactions. What can we learn in terms of successful and not so successful efforts here? If researchers are to advance the studies of role expectation and role conflict from earlier social-systems theory, then the roles of the dean have to be examined in well-designed case studies as they interact with a variety of key people.

Finally, well-conceived studies of deans in different contexts should be complemented by more well-conceived personal profiles that portray the motivations, aspirations, wants and needs, successes and failures of real people in real places. To provide guidance in the selection and, it is hoped fuller preparation and support of persons in these key roles, one needs to move from citing abstract principles of organizational change and leadership to rich descriptions of theory in practice and practicing new theory. A person-in-context perspective calls for, just as in studies of faculty, thoughtful selection of key presage and personal factors or variables as these interact with organizational and cultural ones.

References

Adams, R. (1986, February). *The teacher education professorate.* Paper presented at the annual meeting of the American Association of Colleges for Teacher Education, Chicago.

Allison, C. (1989). Early professors of education: Three case studies. In R. Wisniewski & E. Ducharme (Eds.), *The professors of teaching: An inquiry* (pp. 53–93). Albany, NY: State University of New York Press.

American Association of Colleges for Teacher Education. (1987). *Teaching teachers: Facts and figures.* Washington, DC: Author.

American Association of Colleges for Teacher Education. (1988). *Teaching teachers: Facts and figures.* Washington, DC: Author.

Anderson, D., & King, J. (1987). A dean of education: A demographic analysis. *Journal of Teacher Education, 38*(5), 9–13.

Arends, R., Reinhard, D., & Sivage, C. (1981). The educational dean: An examination of behaviors associated with special projects. *Journal of Teacher Education, 32*(5), 14–20.

Astin, A. (1977). *Four critical years.* San Francisco: Jossey-Bass.

Bagley, A. (Ed.). (1975). *The professor of education: An assessment of conditions.* Minneapolis: University of Minnesota Press.

Baldridge, J. (1971). *Academic governance.* Berkeley, CA: McCutchan.

Baldridge, J., Curtis, D. , Ecker, G., & Riley, G. (1978). *Policy making and effective leadership.* San Francisco: Jossey-Bass.

Barrow, L. (1984). *Demographic survey of New England teacher educators of elementary science methods courses.* Orono, ME: University of Maine. (ERIC Document Reproduction Service No. ED 255 354)

Bayer, A. E., & Dutton, J. (1977). Career age and research-professional activities of academic scientists. *Journal of Higher Education, 48*(3), 259–282.

Bergquist, W. (1978). Relationship of collegiate professional development and teacher education. *Journal of Teacher Education, 24*(3), 18–24.

Berliner, D. C. (1985). Laboratory settings and the study of teacher education. *Journal of Teacher Education, 36*(6), 2–8.

Bevan, J. (1967). The deanship. *Liberal Education, 3*(3), 344.

Blackburn, R. (1982). Career phases and their influence on faculty motivation. In J. Bess (Ed.), *Faculty motivation to teach effectively* (pp. 95–98). San Francisco: Jossey-Bass.

Bok, D. (1986). *Higher learning.* Cambridge, MA: Harvard University Press.

Borland, D. (1970). *The university as an organization: An analysis of the faculty rewards system.* Unpublished doctoral dissertation, Indiana University, Bloomington.

Burnham, A. (1987). *The paradox of reform.* Paper presented at the symposium of the schools of education in research universities, American Educational Research Association, Washington, DC.

Buswell, G. T., McConnell, T. R., Heiss, A. M., & Knoll, A. M. (1966). *Training for educational research.* Berkeley, CA: University of California Center for the Study of Higher Education.

Ciardi, J. (1962). To the damnation of deans (A prejudice). *Saturday Review, 45*(12), 31.

Clark, B. (1985). Listening to the professoriate. *Change, 17*(4), 37–43.

Clark, D. (1984). *Emerging paradigms in organizational theory and research.* Unpublished manuscript, University of Kansas, School of Education and Center for Public Affairs, Lawrence.

Clark, D., & Guba, E. (1977). *A study of teacher education institutions as innovators, knowledge producers, and change agencies* (NIE Project No. 4-0752) Bloomington, IN: Indiana University. (ERIC Document Reproduction Service No. ED 139 805)

Clark, D., & Guba, E. (1980). Schools, colleges and departments of education: Demographic and contextual features. In D. Griffiths & D. McCarty (Eds.), *The dilemma of the deanship* (pp. 67–90). Danville, IL: Interstate Printers and Publishers.

Clark, S., & Lewis, D. (1985). *Faculty vitality and institutional productivity.* New York: Teachers College Press.

Cohen, M., March, J., & Olsen, J. (1972). A garbage can model of organizational choice. *Administrative Science Quarterly, 17*(1), 1–25.

Coladarci, A. (1980). Some notes on deans as individuals and the role of the dean. In D. Griffiths & D. McCarty (Eds.), *The dilemma of the deanship* (pp. 125–131). Danville, IL: Interstate Printers and Publishers.

Cole, B. (1983). Administrative effectiveness of deans of education on decisions affecting teacher education. *Journal of Teacher Education, 34*(4), 48–51.

Counelis, J. (1969). (Ed.). *To be a phoenix: The education professoriate.* Bloomington, IN: Phi Delta Kappan Educational Foundation.

Cronbach, L., & Suppes, P. (Eds.). (1969). *Research for tomorrow's schools: Disciplined inquiry for education.* New York: Macmillan.

Culbertson, J. (1980). Programmatic research on the deanship: Rationale and strategy. In D. Griffiths & D. McCarty (Eds.), *The dilemma of the deanship* (pp. 3–20). Danville, IL: Interstate Printers and Publishers.

Cyphert, F., & Zimpher, N. (1976). *The education deanship: Who is the dean?* Paper presented at the meeting of the American Educational Research Association, San Francisco.

Cyphert, F., & Zimpher, N. (1980). The education deanship: Who is the dean? In D. Griffiths & D. McCarty (Eds.), *The dilemma of the deanship* (pp. 91–122). Danville, IL: Interstate Printers and Publishers.

Darter, C. (1980). *Qualifications of professional education faculty.* Washington, DC: ERIC Clearinghouse on Teacher Education. (ERIC Document Reproduction Service No. ED 198 084)

Dejnozka, E. (1978). The dean of education: A study of selected role norms. *Journal of Teacher Education, 29*(5), 81–84.

DeVries, D. (1975). The relationship of role expectations to faculty behavior. *Research in Higher Education, 3*(1), 111–129.

Dill, D. (1980). Schools of education as complex organizations. In D. Griffiths & D. McCarty (Eds.), *The dilemma of the deanship* (pp. 177–216). Danville, IL: Interstate Printers and Publishers.

Dill, W. (1980). The deanship: An unstable craft. In D. Griffiths & D. McCarty (Eds.), *The dilemma of the deanship* (pp. 261–284). Danville, IL: Interstate Printers and Publishers.

Doi, J. (1965). Organization and administration, finance and facilities. *Review of Educational Research, 35*(4), 352.

Dreeben, R. (1970). *The nature of teaching.* Glenview, IL: Scott, Foresman.

Ducharme, E. R. (1986). Teacher educators: What do we know? *ERIC Digest 15.* Washington DC: ERIC Clearinghouse on Teacher Education.

Ducharme, E. R., & Agne, R. M. (1982). The education professoriate: A research-based perspective. *Journal of Teacher Education, 33*(6), 30–36.

Ducharme, E. R., & Agne, R. M. (1989). Professors of education: Uneasy residents of academe. In R. Wisniewski & E. Ducharme (Eds.), *The professors of teaching: An inquiry* (pp. 121–152), Albany, NY: State University of New York Press.

Etzioni, A. (1975). *A comparative analysis of complex organizations.* New York: Free Press.

Evenden, E. S. (1933). *National survey of the education of teachers: Vol. VI. Summary and interpretation* (Bulletin 1933, No. 10, Office of Education, U.S. Department of the Interior). Washington, DC: U.S. Government Printing Office.

Finkelstein, M. J. (1984). *The American academic profession.* Columbus: Ohio State University Press.

Fuller, F., & Bown, O. (1975). Becoming a teacher. In K. Ryan (Ed.), *Teacher education* (74th yearbook of the National Society for the Study of Education, Part II, pp. 25–52). Chicago: University of Chicago Press.

Fullerton, N. (1978). Issues in the role of the dean. *Journal of Teacher Education, 29*(5), 23–25.

Gaff, J. G., & Wilson, R. C. (1975). Faculty impact on students. In R. C. Wilson, J. G. Gaff, E. R. Dienst, L. Wood, & J. L. Bavry (Eds.), *College professors and their impact on students* (pp. 27–41). New York: John Wiley & Sons.

Gideonse, H. D. (1989). The uses of time: Evocations of an ethos. In R. Wisniewski & E. Ducharme (Eds.), *The professors of teaching: An inquiry* (pp. 214–238). Albany, NY: State University of New York Press.

Goodlad, J. (1984). *A place called school: Prospects for the future.* New York: McGraw-Hill.

Goodman, P. (1962). *The community of scholars.* New York: Random House.

Griffiths, D., & McCarty, D. (1980). From here to there. In D. Griffiths & D. McCarty (Eds.), *The dilemma of the deanship* (pp. 285–294). Danville, IL: Interstate Printers and Publishers.

Grosnick, J., & Reynolds, R. (1978). *Teacher education: Renegotiating roles for mainstreaming.* Reston, VA: Council for Exceptional Children.

Guba, E., & Clark, D. L. (1977). Knowledge production and use in schools, colleges, and departments of education. *Phi Delta Kappan,* 58(9), 711–713.

Hall, R. (1977). *Organizations: Structure and process.* Englewood Cliffs, NJ: Prentice-Hall.

Harren, V. (1976). Assessment of career decision-making. Unpublished progress report, Southern Illinois University, Carbondale.

Harry, J., & Goldner, N. (1972). Null relationships between teaching and research. *Sociology of Education,* 45(1), 47–60.

Hazlett, J. (1989). Education professors: The centennial of an identity crisis. In R. Wisniewski & E. Ducharme (Eds.), *The professors of teaching: An inquiry* (pp. 17–48). Albany, NY: State University of New York Press.

Heald, J. (1982). *Report to the profession 1982 American Association of Colleges for Teacher Education.* Washington, DC: American Association of Colleges for Teacher Education. (ERIC Document Reproduction Service No. ED 216 010)

Hertzberg, F., Mausner, B., & Snyderman, B. (1959). *The motivation to work.* New York: John Wiley & Sons.

Howey, K. R. (1977). Preservice teacher education: Lost in the shuffle? *Journal of Teacher Education,* 28(6), 26–29.

Howey, K. R. (1985). Six major functions of staff development: An expanded imperative. *Journal of Teacher Education,* 36(1), 58–64.

Howey, K., Yarger, S., Harbeck, K., Kluwin, T., & Joyce, B. (1977). *Preservice teacher education.* Washington, DC: U.S. Office of Education. (ERIC Document Reproduction Service No. ED 146 210)

Howey, K. R., Yarger, S. J., & Joyce, B. R. (1978). *Improving teacher education.* Reston, VA: Association of Teacher Educators.

Howey, K. R., & Zimpher, N. L. (1989). *Profiles of preservice teacher education: Inquiry into the nature of programs.* Albany, NY: State University of New York Press.

Johanningmeier, E. V., & Johnson, H. C. (1975). The educational professoriate: A historical consideration of its work and growth. In A. Bagley (Ed.), *The professor of education: An assessment of conditions* (pp. 1–18). Minneapolis: University of Minnesota, College of Education, The Society of Professors of Education.

Judge, H. (1982). *American graduate schools of education: A view from abroad.* New York: Ford Foundation.

Kalleberg, A. L. (1977). Work values and job rewards: A theory of job satisfaction. *American Sociological Review,* 42(1), 124–143.

Karpik, L. (Ed.). (1978). *Organization and environment: Theories, issues and reality.* London: Sage.

Katz, L., & Raths, J. (1982). The best of intentions for the education of teachers. *Action in Teacher Education,* 4(1), 8–16.

Kohn, M. L. (1969). *Class and conformity: A study of values.* Homewood, IL: Dorsey Press.

Kohn, M. L., & Schooler, C. (1982). Job conditions and personality: A longitudinal assessment of their reciprocal effects. *American Journal of Sociology,* 87(6), 1257–1286.

Kuhn, T. (1970). *The structure of scientific revolutions.* Chicago: University of Chicago Press.

Lanier, J., & Little, J. (1986). Research on teacher education. In M. C. Wittrock (Ed.), *Handbook of research on teaching* (3rd ed., pp. 527–569). New York: Macmillan.

Lasley, T., & Haberman, M. (1987). How do university administrators evaluate education deans? *Journal of Teacher Education,* 38(5), 13–17.

Lee, W. (1959). *God bless our queer old dean.* New York: G. P. Putnam and Sons.

Lynch, W. (1946). *A history of Indiana State Teachers College, 1865–1945.* Terre Haute, IN: Indiana State Teachers College.

Mangieri, J., & Arnn, J. (1984). Finding a dean: Minimizing the guesswork. *Journal of Teacher Education,* 35(5), 56–57.

McCarty, D., & Reyes, P. (1987). Organizational models of governance: Academic deans' decision-making styles. *Journal of Teacher Education,* 38(5), 2–9.

McDaniel, E., & Feldhusen, J. (1970). Relationships between faculty ratings and indices of service and scholarship. *Proceedings of 78th annual American Psychology Association convention* (pp. 63–80). Washington, DC: American Psychology Association.

McGrath, J. (1938). *The evaluation of administrative offices in institutions of higher education in the United States from 1860 to 1933.* Chicago: University of Chicago Press.

Millett, J. (1962). *The academic community.* New York: Random House.

Mitra, S. R. (1974). A brief note on American education research. *American Educational Research Journal,* 11(2), 41–49.

Morris, V. (1981). *Deaning.* Urbana, IL: University of Illinois Press.

Morsink, K. (1987). Critical functions of the educational administrator: Perceptions of chairpersons and deans. *Journal of Teacher Education,* 35(5), 17–22.

Myers, B., & Mager, G. (1983). *Choices in academic careers.* Paper presented at the meeting of the American Educational Research Association, Montreal.

Norton, M. (1978). A study of the department chairperson in colleges of education. *Research and Services Bulletin 37.* Tempe, AZ: Arizona State University, College of Education.

Norton, M. (1980). *Academic department chair: Tasks and responsibilities.* Tempe, AZ: Arizona State University, College of Education, Department of Administration.

Nussel, E. J., Wiersma, W., & Rusche, P. J. (1988). Work satisfaction of education professors. *Journal of Teacher Education,* 39(3), 45–52.

Parsons, T. (1956). A sociological approach to the theory of organizations. *Administrative Science Quarterly,* 1(1), 63–85.

Perkins, J. (Ed.). (1973). *The university as an organization.* New York: McGraw-Hill.

Peters, T., & Waterman, R. (1981). *In search of excellence.* New York: Harper & Row.

Powell, A. G. (1980). *The uncertain profession: Harvard and the search for educational authority.* Cambridge, MA: Harvard University Press.

Prichard, K., Fen, S., & Buxton, T. (1971). Social class origins of college teachers of education. *Journal of Teacher Education,* 22(2), 219–228.

Purkey, S., & Smith, M. (1985). School reform: The district policy implications of the effective schools literature. *Elementary School Journal,* 85(3), 353–390.

Reisman, D. (1956). *Constraint and variety in American higher education.* Lincoln, NE: University of Nebraska Press.

Rodrigues, R. J., & Uhlenberg, D. M. (1978). Publish? Or perish: The thought? *Journal of Teacher Education,* 29(4), 64–66.

Roemer, R., & Martinello, M. (1982). Divisions in the educational professoriate and the future of professional education. *Educational Studies,* 13(2), 203–223.

Rooney, P., & Clark, D. (1982). New deans, old deans: A test of the "honeymoon period." *Journal of Teacher Education,* 33(5), 47–49.

Rudolph, F. (1965). *The American college and university*. New York: Vintage Books.

Salmen, S. (1971). *Duties of administrators in higher education*. New York: Macmillan.

Schuster, J., & Bowen, H. (1985). The faculty at risk. *Change, 17*(4), 13–21.

Schuttenberg, E., Patterson, L., & Sutton, R. (1985). *Self-perceptions of productivity of education faculty: Life phase and gender differences*. Washington, DC: American Association of Colleges for Teacher Education. (ERIC Document Reproduction Service No. ED 257 807)

Schwebel, M. (1985). The clash of cultures in academe, university, and the education faculty. *Journal of Teacher Education, 36*(4), 2–7.

Schwebel, M. (1989). The new priorities and the education faculty. In R. Wisniewski & E. Ducharme (Eds.), *The professors of teaching: An inquiry* (pp. 94–120). Albany, NY: State University of New York Press.

Shulman, L. (1986). Paradigms and research programs in the study of teaching: A contemporary perspective. In M. C. Wittrock (Ed.), *Handbook of research on teaching* (3rd ed., pp. 3–36). New York: Macmillan.

Sivage, C., Bryson, J. & Okum, K. (1982). *Politics, power and personality: The role of deans in dean's grant projects*. Washington, DC: American Association of Colleges for Teacher Education.

Sizer, T. R., & Powell, A. G. (1969). Changing conceptions of the professor of education. In J. S. Counelis (Ed.), *To be a Phoenix: The education professoriate* (pp. 61–76). Bloomington, IN: Phi Delta Kappan Educational Foundation.

Strom, S. (1980). Post high school career management tasks. In W. Tennyson, L. Hansen, M. Klaurens, & M. Antholtz (Eds.), *Career development education: A program approach for teachers and counselors*. St. Paul, MN: National Vocational Guidance Association for the Minnesota Department of Education.

Swanson, E. (1983). Four common myths about change in schools of education. *Journal of Teacher Education, 34*(5), 26–29.

Tough, A. (1978). Major learning efforts: Recent research and future directions. *Adult Education, 28*(4).

Tucker, A. (1984). *Chairing the academic department: Leadership among peers*. New York: Macmillan.

Tucker, S. (Ed.). (1981). *Increasing the research capacity of schools of education: A policy inquiry*. Washington, DC: American Association of Colleges for Teacher Education. (ERIC Document Reproduction Service No. ED 211 453)

Weber, M. (1947). *The theory of social and economic organization* (A. Henderson & T. Parsons, Eds. & Trans.). New York: Free Press.

Willower, D., & Culbertson, J. (1964). *The professorship in educational administration*. Columbus, OH: University Council for Educational Administration.

Wisniewski, R., & Ducharme, E. (Eds.). (1989). *The professors of teaching: An inquiry*. Albany, NY: State University of New York Press.

· E ·

CURRICULUM OF TEACHER EDUCATION

·21·

PROFESSIONAL KNOWLEDGE FOR TEACHERS

Alan R. Tom
UNIVERSITY OF ARIZONA

Linda Valli
THE CATHOLIC UNIVERSITY OF AMERICA

There is broad consensus that the teacher education curriculum should be composed of three areas of study: general education, subject matter specialization, and professional education. This chapter discusses only the professional education of teachers, emphasizing the knowledge that ultimately becomes the substance of the professional curriculum. However, the focus is not on the substance of professional knowledge, but rather on several epistemological traditions by which professional knowledge is derived and on the characteristic way knowledge from each tradition is related to practice. In short, professional knowledge for teachers is examined in terms of underlying epistemological and theory–practice issues.

The authors of several related *Handbook* chapters examine how teachers acquire professional knowledge and explore the intentional and unintentional impact of teacher education curricula on preservice and inservice teachers. What is not systematically addressed in these chapters on learning to teach, teacher socialization, and models of teacher education are the various epistemological traditions from which professional knowledge is derived and the contrasting perspectives from which it is viewed as being linked to teaching practice. To sharpen the focus on these two topics, this chapter poses these issues as an interrelated set of questions: (a) What do we mean by knowledge when we talk about professional knowledge for teachers? (b) How has professional knowledge been portrayed as being related to practice? (c) What is the basis for portraying the knowledge–practice relationship in diverse ways? These three questions direct attention to epistemological considera-

tions and to the connection of professional knowledge and practice, all within the context of professional education for teachers.

OVERVIEW OF CHAPTER

Because what counts as knowledge is vigorously contested, it is important to explore the contrasting epistemologies of professional knowledge and how these formal epistemologies—positivistic, interpretive, and critical—direct our attention to differing professional knowledge. Another tradition—craft knowledge, or what Schön (1983, 1989) calls the epistemology of practice—is less systematically developed and is therefore examined in less detail in this chapter, though all four traditions are addressed in section one. Teacher educators, however, rarely generate a curriculum design from a favored epistemological stance. Indeed, epistemological issues usually remain latent in the professional curriculum. The reason for explicating alternative epistemologies is to provide a template to facilitate understanding of why professional knowledge is so varied in its purposes and forms. What constitutes knowledge, as well as its purposes and forms, depends largely on underlying epistemological assumptions. Exploring these assumptions, we make an attempt to answer the first question: What do we mean by knowledge when we talk about professional knowledge?

The second section of this chapter moves from the problem-

The authors thank reviewers Hilda Borko (University of Maryland), Sharon Feiman-Nemser (Michigan State University), Hendrik Gideonse (University of Cincinnati), Mark Ginsburg (University of Pittsburgh), and Thomas Lasley (University of Dayton). The opinions expressed herein are those of the authors.

atic issue of what constitutes professional knowledge to the equally problematic issue of the relationship between knowledge and practice. There has long been disagreement about the relationship of knowledge and teaching practice, but this issue has become an object of close scrutiny and careful analysis only in recent years. The key question in this section, of how professional knowledge has been portrayed as being related to practice, is addressed in two steps. To gain perspective on the range of possible knowledge–practice interrelationships, we briefly review several typologies that outline various ways knowledge and practice can be seen as connected. To better understand the dynamics of the knowledge–practice relationship, we examine four distinct points of view concerning how knowledge and practice ought to be connected. In the discussion of the four points of view, professional knowledge is by turns considered as a source of schemata for altering how teachers view educational phenomena (Clark, 1988; Fenstermacher, 1982), as a source of rules for determining effective teaching behaviors (Gage, 1978, 1985), as in need of linking premises before ties can be made between this knowledge and teaching practice (Phillips, 1978, 1980), and as the basis of emancipatory actions for empowering oppressed groups (Giroux & McLaren, 1986). These four points of view differ both in the extent to which knowledge entails practice and in the purpose for which knowledge is employed.

The third section of this chapter addresses the last question: What is the basis for portraying the knowledge–practice relationship in such diverse ways? To answer this question, we explore two considerations. On the one hand, each epistemological orientation has a distinctive warrant for practice, that is, the nature of the knowledge has implications for its legitimate use in practice. On the other hand, as one adopts a particular point of view on the relating of knowledge and practice, one is also implicitly taking a position on the relative status of the realms of knowledge and practice. Thus, the relating of knowledge and practice requires cognizance of its epistemological orientation and entails deciding whether one sees practice as derived from knowledge (the rule approach), dependent on knowledge (the schemata approach), independent of knowledge (the linking premises approach), or superior to knowledge (the emancipatory approach).

KNOWLEDGE

Is there a substantial body of professional knowledge? This issue is frequently the topic of discussion among researchers who study teaching and teacher education. Although many bodies of knowledge are pertinent to teacher education, research on teaching is generally believed to be the major source of professional knowledge for teachers. On the one hand, many scholars and policymakers point with pride to what they see as a growing body of research literature on teaching (e.g., Brophy & Good, 1986; Gage, 1978, 1985; Gideonse, 1982; Holmes Group, 1986; B. O. Smith, 1980, 1983). Others assert that disciplined inquiry has not yielded much insight into the nature of teaching (e.g., Cronbach, 1975; Ebel, 1982; Jackson, 1970, 1987a, 1987b; Sanders, 1978, 1981). Opinions on the size of

the knowledge base for effective teaching are not only widely divided but also hotly contested.

But the debate over the size of the body of professional knowledge has been less than informative. For example, this debate has not led to agreement on some points and clarification of others; on the contrary, the tone of the debate is often strident, and the arguments and counterarguments tend to be presented in the form of incantations. Moreover, the issue itself, the size of the body of professional knowledge, does not seem to be as critically important as it once did. Those who proclaim most loudly that teacher education has a substantial knowledge base often appear to be interested not only in establishing the intellectual basis of professional education but also in proving that teaching is a profession and that teacher education deserves professional-school status (Holmes Group, 1986; Tom, 1987; Wise, 1986).

More important than the quantity of professional knowledge is its validity, especially to teacher educators, staff developers, and others who continually confront the issue of how knowledge and teaching practice are interrelated. If we aspire to have professional knowledge inform or guide practice, this knowledge must be epistemologically sound. Although having valid knowledge is not a sufficient basis for linking knowledge to teaching practice, for reasons explored later in this chapter, such knowledge is certainly a necessary premise of the reasoning that links it to practice. Thus, teacher educators must be keenly attuned to the epistemological underpinnings of professional knowledge; that is, what do we mean by knowledge when we refer to professional knowledge for teachers?

A single answer does not exist for this question because professional knowledge can be generated through more than one epistemological tradition. In the remainder of this section we examine four traditions: positivist, interpretive, critical, and craft. For each epistemological tradition, we identify the characteristic form and purpose of knowledge, as well as the distinctive role that values play in it. As indicated earlier, our treatment of the craft tradition is less complete than that of the other three traditions.

Positivism

In the 1960s the concern for epistemological issues related to the generation of professional knowledge was largely restricted to the methodology of so-called process–product research (Dunkin & Biddle, 1974; Rosenshine & Furst, 1973). The emphasis then was on increasing methodological rigor, based on the assumption that prior research on teaching was insufficiently precise and inadequately controlled (Berliner, 1976). Careful attention to the methodology of studying the effects of teachers' behaviors on students' achievement would be rewarded by a better understanding of what behaviors made teachers effective in promoting student learning.

Although much of the process–product work, even to this day, is correlational, scholars in this tradition have aspired to do experimental studies in order to make causal claims about the relationship of teachers' behaviors and students' achievement (Gage, 1985; Gage & Giaconia, 1981; Rosenshine &

Furst, 1973). Causal knowledge seems to have such obvious implications for practice that the complexities of the knowledge–practice linkage are rarely explored by process–product researchers (for an exception, see Gage, 1983, 1985, pp. 25–40).

Rooted in psychological behaviorism, process–product research is an example of a methodological orientation commonly labeled *positivism*. Positivists believe that the social sciences ought to emulate the natural sciences, especially in the latter's detachment of the observer from the object of inquiry and in the pursuit of "laws" by which the social system operates (Bredo & Feinberg, 1982; J. K. Smith, 1983). Because social phenomena are presumed to exist naturally rather than be socially constructed, knowledge of how social variables affect one another is cumulative; thus, the concept of a knowledge base (or knowledge bases) fits comfortably in the professional vocabulary of educational positivists. Moreover, the emphasis on deriving a professional knowledge base meshes well with the implicit orientation of positivism to the prediction and control of human behavior. The actual linkage between knowledge and practice, however, is deeply influenced by the logical distinction positivists make between fact and value. They view "empirical generalizations as a map describing the connections between what is and values as determining where one wants to go" (Bredo & Feinberg, 1982, p. 16).

Professional knowledge from a positivistic orientation, therefore, is as lawlike as possible, is cumulative, and is sharply distinguished from values (Popkewitz, 1980; J. K. Smith, 1983). Positivists believe that the collection of generalizations resulting from positivist inquiries can be brought to bear on the improvement of teaching for a variety of purposes, depending on the values held by the educators who work in any given setting. Process–product researchers, as do other positivists, see this specification of values as falling outside the realm of methodological rigor and thus embodying an arbitrary decision, variously framed as "a matter of definition" (Brophy & Good, 1986, p. 328) or as an issue of personal choice (Gage, 1978, 1985). Educational positivists attend carefully to the generation of context-independent generalizations and presume that these generalizations are enduring and useful.

But are context-free generalizations attainable for the human sciences? Many social scientists think not. The fundamental problem for social-scientific positivism lies in the conflict between the drive for lawlike generalizations, spurred on by the attendant assumptions of prediction and control, and the reality that humans act with will and purpose, including the ability to act stupidly or inconsistently (Fenstermacher, 1986). Moreover, positivism in the natural sciences has been under attack. Studies of the scientific community such as Kuhn's (1962) *The Structure of Scientific Revolutions* suggest that the development of science was governed not so much by a logical model as it was by the dominance of a particular paradigm. Paradigms, or theoretical ways of seeing, influence our observations so that we can no longer contend that our observations are completely independent of our theories (Bredo & Feinberg, 1982). Facts, although not necessarily subjective, are theory laden, or, to put it another way, they are relative to the theoretical constructs used in observations. The positivist

belief that knowledge can be completely objective and that this knowledge can adequately explain and predict human behavior has come under severe attack in recent years.

Interpretivism

Many social scientists responded to the growing loss of faith in positivism by turning their attention away from a "laws-and-instances ideal of explanation toward a cases-and-interpretations one" (Geertz, 1980, p. 165). The focus of interpretive explanation is on what "institutions, actions, images, utterances, events, customs, all the usual objects of social-scientific interest, mean to those whose institutions, actions, customs and so on they are" (p. 167). Explanation has not been abandoned by those social scientists who have turned to what is often termed *interpretation*, but explanation no longer entails pursuing lawlike, context-free generalizations, with the ultimate goal of developing a unified science of humanity. Rather, interpretive scholars seek the meaning that humans attach to the interpersonal and social aspects of their lives, with this meaning being viewed as context dependent (Mishler, 1979; Popkewitz, 1980; J. K. Smith, 1983).

Interpretivists are much more intimately involved with the object of inquiry than are social-scientific positivists in that they attempt to understand another's character or culture by comparing its consistency with their own characterological or cultural patterns. The interpretivists' patterns become a sounding board, a way of detecting differences between these patterns and those under study. Thus, in interpretive study the knower and the known are closely intertwined, because "one must use oneself or one's culture to understand others" (Bredo & Feinberg, 1982, p. 6). Even though an interpretivist tries to understand others in their own terms, this understanding is rooted in the interpretivist's own conceptual system.

Nevertheless, the interpretivist's use of theory-laden constructs in studying social life does not mean that the resultant analyses are completely subjective. On the one hand, the interpretive researcher is a member of a scientific community and must meet the methodological conventions of a particular discipline, though some interpretivists might not attend carefully enough to questions concerning the validity of knowledge (Phillips, 1987). On the other hand, the meanings an individual (or a group) attributes to a particular social action depend heavily on the social conventions of the society under study. For example, the meaning a teacher attaches to individual academic achievement is influenced by societal context, and a researcher's interpretation of this meaning must conform to the canons of sociology or some other social science discipline. However, many positivists believe that interpretive understanding and explanation are insufficiently rigorous because the focus is on case study analysis rather than on generalizations across cases and also because interpretivists are unwilling to rigorously separate facts from values as personally held meanings are explored (e.g., Borman, LeCompte, & Goetz, 1986; Brophy, 1986; Gage, 1985, pp. 53–56; J. K. Smith, 1983).

The differences between positivists and interpretivists can

probably be traced to the different purposes of the two research orientations. Educational positivists (especially process–product researchers) do desire, as suggested by a prominent practitioner of interpretive research, "to make statements about the general effectiveness of various teaching practices" (Erickson, 1986, p. 158). In contrast, interpretivists believe they share with teachers a concern for the "specifics of local meaning and local action," a shared concern enabling these researchers to propose to teachers "useful suggestions about the practice of teaching" (pp. 156, 158). However, the extended case study format of these useful suggestions makes the suggestions difficult for teachers to process and use, a theme developed in the next section of this chapter.

But the problem of making practical use of interpretive knowledge extends beyond its length and detail. A further complication is the relativism inherent in interpretive scholarship. Because interpretive inquiry is an attempt to understand others in their own terms, this inquiry accepts implicitly the values of those being studied. That is, in the process of exploring local meanings and of placing these meanings in the context of social conventions, the interpretivist also implicitly accepts the values that underlie local actions and societal conventions. If multiple actors exist in a local setting and if they appeal to conflicting value systems, a likely possibility in a pluralistic society, then the interpretivist must empathetically understand all of these value systems. The result is relativism, the inability of interpretive research to offer any form of critical commentary on the values that ultimately give meaning to the individuals or groups under study. An appeal to disciplinary canons and an attempt to embed local meanings in societal conventions might help increase the validity of interpretive knowledge, but moral relativism is not thereby excluded.

Ironically, even though educational positivism and interpretivism differ fundamentally in the form and purpose of knowledge (generalizations/improve teaching effectiveness, as opposed to cases/provide suggestions that teachers see as useful), both epistemological traditions have trouble addressing the issue of values. Positivism attempts to rigorously separate fact and value and, thus, places values outside the realm of systematic inquiry. Values, acknowledged to be pivotal in identifying the goal of effective teaching, become an arbitrary matter of definition or of personal choice. Interpretivism melds values and facts together in an attempt to understand the meanings that various actors construct out of educational and other social encounters. The interplay of fact and value at once yields empathetic understanding and moral relativism.

Critically Oriented

In recent years, some researchers have moved values to the center of their inquiries. In general these researchers have argued that institutionalized education is sexist, racist, and/or class biased, characteristics also attributed to the larger society. These researchers are motivated above all by an explicit commitment to particular values, namely equality and justice, but also, in some cases, freedom, self-determination, and other values in the liberal democratic tradition. The label *critical*

theory is often used to capture certain aspects of this epistemological orientation, but those who conduct scholarship aimed at emancipatory goals have variously called themselves Marxists, feminists, Marxist feminists, radicals, or even liberals, as well as critical theorists. What is common to such diverse scholars is a conviction that current educational and social arrangements are unjust and unequal and thus need to be reformed (Popkewitz, 1980). There is also general agreement among critically oriented scholars, ranging from liberals to Marxists, that current educational practice is overly technical and puts excessive emphasis on efficiency and value neutrality. Interpretivists often share this concern about the technical nature of education, yet they would be uneasy adopting a specific value stance (Popkewitz, 1980). Positivists, of course, believe neither in integrating values with scholarship nor in abandoning a technical approach to education (Brophy, 1986, 1988; Gage, 1978, 1985; Schön, 1983, 1989).

Beyond the shared conviction among critically oriented scholars that education and society must be reformed and that education is overly technical are a series of lively intramural debates. Placing values at the heart of educational inquiry does not necessarily result in adherence by all to the same values. Equity and justice seem central to many critically oriented scholars, especially Marxists; however, other critically oriented but non-Marxist scholars have directed attention to such diverse values as caring (Noddings, 1984, 1988) and cultural diversity (Sleeter & Grant, 1987).

Not only is there no consensus on the normative basis for reforming education and society, but in addition critically oriented scholars take varying positions concerning the power of dominant institutions, especially economic institutions, to influence the development of schools. Some (e.g., Bowles & Gintis, 1976) argue that the structure, processes, and norms of schooling inevitably mirror the way those same characteristics are manifested in our bureaucratically and hierarchically organized economic institutions. In contrast with this correspondence theory grounded in economic determinism, most critically oriented scholars (e.g., Apple, 1982; Giroux & McLaren, 1986; Valli, 1986; Willis, 1977) have a more dialectical conception of power relationships. Schools and other social institutions are viewed as semiautonomous institutions; moreover, humans are seen as capable of resisting the pressure of dominant social and economic institutions. Although shaped and limited by these institutions, people are, at the same time, able to act upon and transform institutional arrangements. The differing assessments of the validity of correspondence theory are important, because the ontological status of professional knowledge is weakened by any form of economic or societal determinism. Why even bother with the curricular implications of professional knowledge if this knowledge is merely a reflection of broad social or economic forces? If educational arrangements correspond to social and economic institutions, then the reform of these institutions is the only logical approach to educational reform.

Nevertheless, the status of professional knowledge is questionable even for those who have a dialectical conception of power relationships. If values are central to critical inquiry, then what role is there for empirical knowledge? Is not the critical scholar an ideologue, an advocate of particular values, someone whose motive for action is independent of a knowledge of relationships among educational variables or of the meanings held by participants in a given educational setting? Positivists and interpretivists might well answer yes to this question, and there are those in the critical tradition who argue that the foundations of radical theories need further evidential substantiation and ethical justification (Liston, 1988). Even when critically oriented scholars assert that all knowledge claims are tied to some value position, they are not thereby released from evaluating the validity of the empirical claims at the base of critical analyses of education and society. In principle, scholars can rigorously assess explanatory claims in a way that would allow both a Marxist and a non-Marxist to agree on the soundness of the assessment (Liston, 1984, 1986).

An empirical tradition within critical inquiry is directed toward the explanatory issue of whether our society and its schools are indeed unjust. This tradition includes such diverse inquiries as the study of whether textbook content is biased in favor of those who are rich and powerful (Anyon, 1979) or the examination of the impact of early field experiences on prospective teachers' conceptions of teaching (Goodman, 1985). Because these studies are initiated from a critical perspective, one that presumes a moral or political stance, critically oriented researchers often conclude their inquiries with recommendations for action such as, to revise textbook content to eliminate social class "distortions" (Anyon, 1979, p. 385) or to put students in field placements that encourage "instructional and curricular experimentation" (Goodman, 1985, p. 47). Other scholarship in the critical tradition is analytic and calls for rethinking taken-for-granted role relationships or educational practices, such as the rethinking of the concept of teacher as detached professional, in favor of a more nurturing stance (Freedman, 1987) or the addition of a political dimension to the traditional teacher focus on craft issues (Kohl, 1976).

Yet the centrality of values to critical inquiries, both to the recommendations emanating from such inquiries and to the origins of these inquiries, is likely to continue to raise questions about the role of knowledge in improving practice. Is it not possible that the value commitments of critically oriented scholars both lead to distorted empirical findings and essentially render such findings unnecessary, because values are perceived by critical researchers as at the heart of educational practice? Perhaps all we need do to improve educational practice is be clear about our values and then act on them to alter the socially constructed reality around us, presuming we have the power to do so. However, the arguments of Lather (1986), of Liston (1984, 1986, 1988), and of Sears (1988) provide a rationale and an approach for carefully assessing the knowledge claims of critically oriented scholarship. Nevertheless, some critical scholars seem not to recognize the need for such assessment when they characterize knowledge as a social construction and therefore open to change (Adler & Goodman, 1986) or employ the Habermasian notion that all knowledge is connected to specific interests to conclude that the key epistemological question is which knowledge serves which interests (Giroux, 1983; also see Habermas, 1971, for the original text). Within the critical tradition, attention needs to be addressed not only to how knowledge is used by dominant interests but also to the validity of the underlying radical analyses of education and society.

Craft

The three orientations toward professional knowledge examined thus far represent established epistemological traditions (Bernstein, 1978; Bredo & Feinberg, 1982; Fay, 1975). Positivism has long been the dominant orientation in educational research. Interpretivism has recently gained considerable recognition, but critically oriented approaches, including critical theory, have received much less acceptance. A fourth orientation is outside recognized epistemological traditions yet is generally acknowledged to be the dominant orientation among both classroom teachers and teacher educators. Within this fugitive though popular orientation, teaching is considered a craft and teacher education is often viewed as an enterprise of traditionalism and apprentice training (Hartnett & Naish, 1980; Kirk, 1986; Zeichner, 1983).

The criticisms of the craft view of teaching and teacher education are legion. In discussing teaching as a practical art analogous to cooking or coaching, Scheffler (1960) echoes the concerns of many about the craft, or practical arts, tradition. This tradition, he notes, generates rules of practice out of knowledge that is derived from "the heritage of common sense, or folklore, or the accumulated experience of practitioners" (p. 73). Though Scheffler grants that many rules for teaching are currently grounded in such craftlike sources as common sense and folklore, he argues that we need a scientific basis for teaching so that we can increasingly "judge and choose procedures on the basis of theoretical understanding, rather than their mere conformity to cookbook specifications embodied in the lore transmitted by previous generations" (p. 74). Positivists and some interpretivists focus their critique of the craft orientation on its antiscientific epistemology (Broudy, 1956; Gage, 1985), whereas critically oriented researchers stress the conservatism inherent in reliance on the wisdom of past practice (Kirk, 1986; Zeichner, 1983).

Ironically, although there abounds spirited criticism of the trial-and-error nature of craft knowledge and of the dire political consequences of basing teacher education on craft knowledge, there is in reality little consensus on what is meant by craft knowledge. Scheffler (1960) talks about rules that guide practice, observing that these rules embody commonsense knowledge. Shulman (1986) argues that practical experience gets codified in the form of maxims such as the classic advice of never smiling before Christmas. Tom (1984) believes craft involves not only technical skill but also analytic knowledge and the ability to apply this analytic knowledge to teaching situations. Kohl (1976) interprets teaching craft as a series of practical problems, ranging from "making transitions" to "dealing with fatigue"; one learns to cope with these problems through the personal experience of teaching and through studying the practice of superb teachers. Numerous authors (e.g., Arnstine, 1975; Brauner, 1978; Broudy, 1956; Hartnett & Naish, 1980; Zeichner, 1983) identify teaching craft with copying or imitating the practice of master teachers. Does craft knowledge therefore consist of imitating expert practice, developing responses to dilemmas or practical problems, analyzing and acting upon teaching situations, relating maxims to practice, or employing rules to guide practice? Or is craft knowledge some combination of these varied purposes and forms of knowledge?

The great confusion over how craft knowledge ought to be construed, a confusion considerably more baffling than the varied approaches lodged under the banner of *critically oriented*, leads us to exclude craft knowledge from the next two sections of this chapter. What is currently most needed are thoughtful attempts by scholars and teachers to describe and conceptualize craft knowledge and its relationship to teaching practice. Initial attempts at such analysis do exist (e.g., Blumberg, 1989; Buchmann, 1987; Clandinin & Connelly, 1987; Elbaz, 1983; Kohl, 1976; Lampert, 1985; Schön, 1983, 1989), but the task of coming to terms with the nature of teachers' craft knowledge has barely begun, and even less attention has been devoted to the interconnections of craft knowledge and practice. In the concluding section of this chapter, we return to craft knowledge and explore ways in which this tradition might be strengthened so it can become a legitimate orientation to professional knowledge.

Summary

This section began by posing the question, What do we mean by *knowledge* when we talk about professional knowledge for teachers? That question was addressed by examining three epistemological traditions: positivism, interpretivism, and varied approaches grouped under the label of critically oriented. These three traditions differ radically in the form and purpose of professional knowledge: generalizations, lawlike if possible, designed to improve teaching effectiveness (positivism); cases, designed to reveal meaning in context (interpretivism); and varied forms of knowledge, designed to expose ways in which favored values are prevented from being realized (critically oriented). The three orientations to knowledge also contrast in their approaches to values: value neutral (positivism), value relative (interpretivism), value centered (critically oriented). After a brief review of various ways of specifying the purpose and conceptualizing the form of craft knowledge, further discussion of craft knowledge was delayed until the conclusion of this chapter.

KNOWLEDGE AND PRACTICE: LINKAGES AND PURPOSES

The reader might well expect that the next step in the analysis of professional knowledge would be to elaborate how each epistemological orientation leads to a distinct conception of the relationship between knowledge and practice. In fact, several scholars do attempt to link ways of knowing with ways of acting. May and Zimpher (1986), for example, contend that most approaches to supervision are rooted in the perspectives of positivism, phenomenology, and critical theory. Van Manen (1977) argues that empirical-analytic science, interpretive inquiry, and critical theory each entails a distinctive view of the practical, that is, the practical as instrumental reasoning (focus on efficiency), the practical as analysis of individual and social experiences (focus on meaning), and the practical as critical reflection (focus on ethical principles).

However, most attempts by educators to conceptualize the interrelationship of educational knowledge and practice do not give prominent attention to the epistemological roots of that knowledge. Instead, educational theorists emphasize the nature and strength of the link between knowledge and practice, without much regard to the origins and characteristics of this knowledge.

The next section of the chapter illustrates how the epistemological orientation of educational knowledge does help clarify the knowledge–practice relationship. This section, however, does not address the three epistemological orientations, but rather the literature that directly speaks to the question of how professional knowledge has been portrayed as being related to practice. One major thrust of this literature involves the development of typologies of the knowledge–practice relationship. These typologies attempt to outline the varieties of this relationship. Starting with the applied research-basic research distinction, the section reviews several typologies that try to account for alternative conceptions of the impact of research on practice. Two of these typologies, the ones proposed by Fenstermacher (1982) and Clark (1988), go beyond identifying the types of impact that knowledge can have on practice to try to outline the dynamics of this knowledge–practice relationship.

Typologies, however, do little more than provide an overview of the alternative conceptualizations of the knowledge–practice relationship. Detailed exploration of this relationship is dependent upon there being systematically developed points of view of how knowledge ought to be related to practice. The latter part of this section introduces and critically analyzes four such points of view: (a) Fenstermacher's concept of schemata that can alter how practice is perceived, (b) Gage's concept of research-based generalizations for directing how practice ought to be organized, (c) Phillips's concept of linking premises that are the necessary condition for creating any link between knowledge and practice, and (d) Giroux and McLaren's concept of the teacher as a transformative intellectual who employs knowledge to help realize the practice of favored values. This analysis focuses attention on how each of these four conceptualizations both construes the strength of the knowledge–practice relationship and identifies the purpose to be served when relating knowledge to practice.

Knowledge–Practice Typologies

Perhaps the oldest typology entails the distinction between basic and applied research. In this typology, the fundamental difference is between the search for theories or fundamental structures that underlie and explain the processes of teaching, learning, and other aspects of educational practice and the attempt to study the effectiveness of educational practices directly. The basic–applied research typology is grounded in two assumptions: (a) the possibility that discovering theories or fundamental structures has implications, often indirect, for educational practice; and b) the possibility of devising empirical studies to determine whether one form of educational practice is superior to others. A reformulation of the basic–applied categorization is the distinction Cronbach and Suppes (1969) make between conclusion-oriented and decision-oriented inquiry, the former being directed to the understanding of particular phenomena and the latter being guided by the information needs of a decision maker. Both the applied–basic and the conclusion–decision distinctions presume a positivist epistemology, in that the focus is on alternative ways of discovering systematic knowledge applicable to the solution of problems of practice (Schön, 1989).

Not only have researchers uncovered few fundamental structures or theories in education, but also there is wide recognition that "fundamental knowledge . . . does not prescribe a suitable practice"(Cronbach & Suppes, 1969, p. 123), an insight James (1899/1902) elegantly formulated nearly a century ago when he noted that "psychology is a science, and teaching is an art; and sciences never generate arts directly out of themselves. An intermediary inventive mind must make the application, by using its originality" (pp. 7–8). At the same time, the concept of applied research has lost much of its appeal, due to the growing belief among decision makers that educational problems are extraordinarily complex and often value laden (Howe, 1976) and due to the growing belief among researchers that applied research "does not ordinarily lead to understanding of the complex phenomena behind educational practice" (Kerlinger, 1977, p. 7). Thus applied research is seen as inconclusive, practically speaking, and often superficial, whereas basic research is frequently viewed as distant or even disconnected from the problems of practice. Is it any wonder that the applied–basic distinction is rarely used anymore, especially by those who are interested in the link between knowledge and practice?

At the same time that educational researchers and policymakers were losing interest in the applied–basic distinction, especially in its relevance to clarifying the relationship of knowledge and practice, others were attempting to identify the diverse ways that research does affect practice. Krathwohl (1977), for instance, elaborates a typology of several ways that research changes practice: namely, by helping us see educational phenomena in new ways, by legitimating educational movements through the development of new concepts and techniques, and by challenging educational movements through the documentation of unforeseen problems. These forms of impact are neither breakthroughs nor are they permanent; rather they are "slow, unobtrusive, adoptions of frameworks or conceptualizations" (p. 11). Jackson and Kieslar (1977) outline a similar set of indirect ways by which research affects practice. Research can influence what the practitioner views as real, believes to be achievable, knows how to do, and decides to do. These four forms of influence are offered as "a substitute for the conventional stereotype of omniscient scientists telling teachers how to teach" (p. 16). The actual dynamics of influence are believed by Jackson and Kieslar to be "opaque and mysterious" (p. 17). Although the Jackson and Kieslar typology, as well as that of Krathwohl, includes the interpretive knowledge of cases, both typologies also appeal to the positivist knowledge of generalizations.

Krathwohl, as well as Jackson and Kieslar, identifies specific types of research influence on practice, but the actual processes by which research affects practice are left unanalyzed. Instead, research is portrayed as lava creeping down the side of the mountain of practice, inevitably altering the mountain, slowly and unpredictably. Krathwohl and Jackson and Kieslar seem more interested in tempering our enthusiasm for the practical potency of knowledge than in clarifying the processes by which educational knowledge can be linked to practice.

But is there a characteristic link (or links) by which knowledge does affect (or should affect) practice? Fenstermacher is one educational philosopher who has given considerable attention to this question. In addressing how a teacher might make use of the research results from teacher-effectiveness studies, Fenstermacher (1982) contends there are at least three ways that bridges can be built between research on teaching and teacher practices: rules, evidence, and schemata. When rules are used to bridge the gaps between educational research and practice, "the results of research are converted to imperatives for teachers to follow" (p. 7). Thus, a principal could convert a particular teacher-effectiveness finding into a rule and act to see that teachers follow this rule. Rule-based bridging could be seen as the rigid application of the findings from an applied research study to other comparable settings. Bridging with evidence occurs when "the results of research are used to test the beliefs that practitioners hold about their work" (p. 8). Teachers do indeed have assumptions and theories about what constitutes effective teaching, and research findings can be employed to evaluate how reasonable these beliefs are. Lastly, schemata, that is, representations of educational phenomena, can be used by teachers to see their work in new ways. For example, time-related schemata, including the concepts of allocated time, engaged time, and wait time, can lead practitioners to rethink the organization of their teaching activities. Schemata derived by researchers sometime appear unrelated to the realities of practice, but many schemata can provide "the means to interpret and evaluate our experience, and to do so in a manner that allows us to become more rational and moral in our actions" (p. 10). Thus, research can affect practice in dramatically different ways: as a source of prescriptions for teachers (rules), as a check on the validity of teachers' assumptions (evidence), and as a source of insight for teachers (schemata).

Similar to this typology is one proposed by Clark (1988), who believes that research on teaching can be related to teacher education and teacher educators in one of three ways. *First*, there might be no relationship if researchers pursue narrow and parochial interests and avoid discussing the practical implications of their inquiries. *Second*, research might be directly related to practice if teacher educators are seen as training prospective teachers "to behave in the ways that research has shown to be most effective in producing achievement gains in students" (p. 5). This second direct linkage is very similar to Fenstermacher's (1982) concept of bridging by rules. *Third,* Clark (1988) sees the linkage as indirect and occurring not so much between research and practice as between researcher and practitioner (in this case, a teacher educator). The researcher acts as a consultant to several teacher educators as they attempt to rethink and redesign their program. As teacher educators identify desired changes, the consultant–researcher, operating from the perspective of a "sympathetic insider," tries to provide "food for thought" (p. 6) from the research findings that seem to be pertinent to the concerns of teacher educators. These teacher educators then decide whether the research findings are relevant and how the findings might, in some modest way, help in the rethinking of a teacher education program. Clark's researcher–consultant role roughly unites Fenstermacher's alternatives of bridging with evidence and bridging with schemata.

Points of View on the Knowledge–Practice Link

Although Clark (1988) and Fenstermacher (1982) both provide a typology of alternative types of research influence on practice, each of them has a preferred conceptualization. Fenstermacher supports the concept of bridging with evidence but is even more enthusiastic about bridging with schemata, whereas Clark endorses the researcher–consultant approach to relating research to practice.

Moreover, both of them have similar reasons for believing one alternative is superior to the others. Fenstermacher (1982) contends that the concept of teaching implicit in a rule-based approach to bridging presumes that "teaching is exclusively a skill the characteristics of which are well defined" (p. 11), whereas he believes that teaching is not only a skill amenable to guidance by rules but also an activity requiring teacher judgments grounded in professional knowledge. Similarly, Clark (1988) believes there will never be a direct link between research on teaching and teaching practice, a link some researchers mistakenly believe could be grounded in "quasi-experiments and other tough-minded designs from which prescriptions will flow for how teachers ought to think, plan, and decide" (p. 5). Instead, the real importance of research on teaching is that it can help practitioners concretely understand the "complexity, artistry, and demandingness of classroom teaching" (p. 11). Thus Fenstermacher and Clark agree that a ruled-based (or direct-link) approach oversimplifies the nature of teaching. They also agree that a ruled-based approach for relating knowledge to practice represents a top-down model in which researchers inappropriately tell practitioners what to do. Fenstermacher (1982, 1983) is especially critical of the top-down model, contending that it fails to give teachers an opportunity to grow as professionals; furthermore, a top-down management approach, researcher to teacher, is a bad model if we want teachers to encourage independent and creative thinking in their pupils.

Using very similar reasoning, Fenstermacher and Clark arrive at a preference for a knowledge–practice linkage that they believe both honors the complexity and sophistication of teaching and presumes that the teacher (or teacher educator) is a practitioner who legitimately has broad responsibility for professional decision making. Fenstermacher's favored stance of bridging with schemata is somewhat similar to Clark's image of the practitioner calling upon a researcher–consultant. Both see research as a source of insight, a way of transforming how the practitioner perceives teaching and other educational phenomena. In the end, the decision on which knowledge to use and how to relate this knowledge to practice is seen by both Clark and Fenstermacher as being a decision rightfully made by the practitioner. This general stance seems consistent with the interpretive emphasis on providing "useful suggestions" for practitioners (Erickson, 1986), but neither scholar argues for restricting the source of these suggestions to knowledge derived from the interpretive tradition.

Although neither Fenstermacher nor Clark speaks of the impact of knowledge on practice as being an "opaque and mysterious" process (Jackson & Kiesler, 1977, p. 17), they are both vague about how knowledge actually alters, or possibly transforms, the perceptions of the practitioner. Fenstermacher gives examples of ideas (e.g., the concepts related to time on task) that could have such transformational power; Clark suggests questions a teacher educator might pose in the context of program planning. Nevertheless, both seem more interested in establishing the practitioner's right to decide whether some finding has practical implications than in understanding the process of deriving implications. Clark (1988), for instance, concludes: "Particular changes and improvements made in the content and process of teacher preparation ought to be invented, tested, and adapted by teacher educators themselves" (p. 6). Fenstermacher (1983) is even more direct; "Instead of asking how the implications shall be used, we might ask who is to decide what the implications of research for practice are" (p. 498). To make the central issue the empowerment of the practitioner is to divert attention away from understanding the process for drawing implications. Thus the dynamics of altering practitioner perceptions remain cloudy; we can only acknowledge that the influence of knowledge on practice is indirect, because the practitioner mediates between these two arenas.

Questioning this conception of an indirect or mediated impact of knowledge on practice, a number of researchers have formulated rule-oriented approaches that focus on converting research findings directly into practice. In reviewing the case for this conversion approach, we will refer back to several of the criticisms Fenstermacher and Clark make of rule-making approaches to linking knowledge and practice.

The work of N. L. Gage is closely associated with both the process–product tradition and the attempt to convert research findings from this tradition into teaching practices. What constitutes the scientific basis of pedagogy and how this scientific basis can be applied to practice are questions that have occupied his attention for a number of years (Gage, 1963, 1978, 1983, 1984, 1985). Gage's focus on developing a scientific basis for pedagogy places him squarely in the positivist research tradition, a tradition that emphasizes the development of context-free generalizations.

As process–product researchers seek to discover teacher behaviors and instructional patterns that are effective in producing student learning, these researchers proceed with the conviction that these effective behaviors and patterns should become the curriculum of teacher education. All that is needed is a second round of studies to discover effective training procedures for instructing teachers in the behaviors or instructional patterns that in turn are effective in producing student learning, usually measured by tests of student achievement (Gage, 1978, 1985; Griffin & Barnes, 1986). Thus, if a study concluded that superior student achievement in reading was a result of ordered turn taking, as opposed to random or voluntary turn taking (Anderson, Evertson, & Brophy, 1979), the second round of study should focus on discovering effective means for training teachers in the importance and the mechanics of implementing ordered turn taking. The goal in this two-step research process is to discover effective training procedures for teaching the research-based rule, in this case, that ordered turn taking yields higher student achievement than does random or voluntary turn taking.

The internal logic of this approach for converting knowledge into practice is compelling. One works backward from student achievement to teacher actions to effective teacher training procedures. Thus, accountability in terms of results (student achievement) seems assured (Brophy, 1986, 1988; Gage, 1985). Moreover, the rule—those teacher behaviors or patterns that are empirically proven to be linked to student achievement—is not presumed to be invariably true; rather, the rule merely represents a statistical relationship between teacher behavior and student learning variables. Researchers do not make extravagant claims about the potency of the rules, perhaps requiring only that a correlation exist on the order of .2 to .5 (Gage, 1984). Finally, the research-based rules have appeal because they are sometimes counterintuitive to the practical wisdom of practitioners, as in the case of the rule on turn taking. When asked how to allocate turns in a primary reading group, teachers would probably opt for a random approach that can both maintain student attention and create an optimum level of anxiety (Shulman, 1987). Yet research findings support the superiority of ordered turn taking in which some kind of system is followed.

So why is it not sensible to require the practitioner to implement research-based generalizations, some of which run counter to the wisdom of practice? Three types of objections have been raised to using research-based rules for linking knowledge to practice. Two of these objections have already been reviewed in the discussion of Clark's and Fenstermacher's ideas of relating knowledge and practice. On the one hand, specific and separable rules do not do justice to either the complexity of classroom phenomena or the judgment involved in teaching. On the other hand, the use of rules fosters top-down management of teachers, thereby limiting their ability to grow as professionals and implicitly encouraging their use of a similar top-down approach with their students.

A third criticism, which will be evident shortly, is the product of Gage's response to the criticisms of oversimplification and top-down control. What Gage does is imply that neither criticism is valid, because he recognizes that teaching is a practical art. As such, it entails "intuition, creativity, improvisation, and expressiveness—a process that leaves room for departures from what is implied by rules, formulas, and

algorithms. . . . The classroom teacher uses judgment, sudden insight, sensitivity, and agility to promote learning" (Gage, 1978, p. 15). Gage, perhaps justifiably, can argue that, far from oversimplifying the task of teaching and controlling the teacher, his portrait of the teacher as a practical artist acknowledges the sophisticated nature of teaching and the professional autonomy of the teacher. Indeed, Gage might say, the research-based rules actually empower the teacher by replacing trial-and-error teaching with teaching grounded in well-established principles, a claim explicitly made by Brophy (1988).

But Gage's interpretation of a practical art brings up a third problem. In no instance does Gage provide guidance for the on-the-spot decisions to be made by the teacher–practical artist. If research findings are not to be viewed as rules—that is, the teacher can legitimately use professional judgment and insight in deciding when to apply findings—then how does the teacher know when to apply a finding? What student cues or classroom events or other contextual factors form an appropriate basis for the teacher to respond differently on Monday than on Tuesday, first hour than third, or to Tim than to Lois? This guidance cannot come from the findings themselves, because these findings are stated in the form of generalizations, and generalizations focus on the relationships among variables without sensitivity to variations in context (Gage, 1983). In fact, to introduce contextual considerations is to violate the conditions under which such research-based generalizations were derived, because these generalizations result from applying a treatment across all cases in a population. Thus, for a teacher to act according to some element of context is to sacrifice the authority of any knowledge cast in the form of generalizations.

As a result, Gage, and those who favor a conversion approach to the knowledge–practice linkage (e.g., Brophy, 1986, 1988; Gideonse, 1986; Griffin & Barnes, 1986; Guskey, 1986), confront a dilemma. If Gage holds to a practical-arts conception of teaching, he is less vulnerable to criticisms of oversimplification and top-down control; yet he is at the same time endorsing a conception of teaching in which research generalizations lose their authority. But, if he converts generalizations into rules that are consistent with the context-free conditions under which the generalizations were derived, then he is open to criticisms of oversimplification and top-down control. Neither resolution of the dilemma is a satisfactory basis for deciding how to relate research-derived generalizations to practice. Further analysis of the proper use of positivist generalizations as rules is contained in the next section.

In contrast with the indirect perceptual approach of Fenstermacher and Clark and the direct conversion approach of Gage is a third approach, proposed by Phillips (1978, 1980), in which knowledge is seen as not necessarily having any implications for practice. Instead, Phillips believes there is a logical gap between knowledge and practice, resulting from the failure of this knowledge to contain appropriate, everyday terms, terms pertaining to a specific teacher or classroom and to particular curriculum content. Therefore, to move from knowledge to practice, "links of some sort have to be established" (Phillips, 1980, p. 19). For example, it must be demonstrated that the content of the finding is relevant to the specific situation and that other factors are less important than this finding in deciding how to act in the situation. Phillips (1978, 1980) identifies such considerations as relevance and importance as "linking premises," which, he believes, are often suppressed or unarticulated. He appears to distinguish between empirical premises, which stress the relevance of a finding to a particular situation, and value premises, which stress the educational importance of a finding.

An example might help explicate both the function of linking premises and the need for at least one value premise whenever a prescriptive course of action, or a *should* statement, is to be derived from knowledge, or an *is* statement. Consider a hypothetical situation in which Piagetian ideas are to be applied to teaching practice:

Suppose that a psychologist of Piagetian orientation found that the concepts involved in understanding the National Anthem could not be mastered by children until they reached the "formal operations" period of development (approximately at the age of 11). What would be the "educational implication" of this psychological discovery?

It might be thought that the implication is clear cut: that the National Anthem should not be taught until children are about 11. But this conclusion is *not* implied by the psychological discovery taken by itself. Certainly it is *compatible* with the discovery, but the policy of not teaching the National Anthem follows from the psychological discovery only if it is assumed (hidden value premise) that children should only be taught what they can understand—that they should never be required to memorize material that is meaningless to them. . . . Now it is clear that the value or linking premise in this argument is one that can be challenged, and it is possible for other linking premises to be substituted in its place, leading to different "educational implications." Thus, many people feel that the benefits of knowing the words of the National Anthem (such as the emotional thrill of participating in singing it, or the social cohesion that it produces) far outweigh the fact that young children will not understand the words. (Phillips, 1980, pp. 19–20)

Explicit value judgments are essential to the satisfactory linking of *is* and *ought* statements; moreover, different prescriptive courses of action result from the same research findings when a key value premise is altered.

Elements of Phillips's position are reminiscent of James's (1899/1902) contention that several forms of the art of teaching might be generated from any particular science (for James, psychology was the appropriate science). James insisted, however, that every form of teaching so derived "must *agree* with the psychology" (p. 9) because "a science . . . lays down lines within which the rules of the art must fall" (p. 8). Here James and Phillips part company. Phillips asserts that, although a course of pedagogical action might be empirically compatible with research-based knowledge, such compatibility is not essential. A linking value premise might yield a pedagogical course of action that many would see as incompatible with relevant research findings, as in the hypothetical Piagetian example.

Phillips's reliance on linking premises, especially value premises, for determining a practical course of action from research findings is very similar to the thinking of Best (Best, 1967; Phillips, 1971, p. 18). Another related approach to linking knowledge and practice is that of practical reasoning, a concept that Fenstermacher (1986, 1987) borrows from Green

(1976) and defines as fairly coherent reasoning that starts with a desired end state and proceeds through premises to an intention to act in a particular way. According to Fenstermacher, research findings can become evidence to help teachers evaluate the accuracy of the empirical premises in their practical arguments.

In opposition to Phillips's assertion that there exists a logical gap between knowledge and practice, a gap that at minimum requires value premises to be closed, Giroux and McLaren (1986) presume that an intimate connection exists between knowledge and practice. As with the case of other critically oriented scholars, Giroux and McLaren ground their inquiries in favored values that they want to see actualized in practice. The role of knowledge is to identify the emancipatory actions needed to realize the practice of these favored values, a linkage that essentially interrelates knowledge with practice.

Giroux and McLaren appeal to democratic values, never clearly delineated, but apparently focused on "equity and justice" (1986, p. 218). They view the schools and the wider social setting as environments in which democratic principles and practices are inadequately actualized. To remedy this situation, they argue that teachers should be prepared to be "transformative intellectuals." Such teachers engage in intellectual and pedagogical practices that "insert teaching and learning directly into the political sphere by arguing that schooling represents both a struggle for meaning and a struggle over power relations" (p. 215). Thus, teachers should not attempt to be neutral agents but, rather, should become partisans who ground their efforts in "moral and ethical discourse exhibiting a preferential concern for the suffering and struggles of the disadvantaged and oppressed" (p. 215). The role of teachers as transformative intellectuals stresses their engagement in the fostering of democratic procedures and principles, both within the school and within the larger society.

Because Giroux and McLaren ground their inquiries in a prior commitment to democratic values, they presume a more intimate relationship between knowledge and practice than is the case with Phillips (1978, 1980); Phillips also stresses the role of values but employs empirical and value linking premises to cross the gap between knowledge and practice. For Giroux and McLaren (1986) there is no necessary logical gap between knowledge and practice. Rather, knowledge is in part the elaboration of how dominant groups have maintained their position over oppressed ones and in part the identification of ways by which current school and social practices can be transformed to better realize democratic values. Thus knowledge is appropriately seen as a source of emancipatory action, either by exposing the dynamics of oppression or by pointing the direction toward the actualization of democratic schooling within the context of broader social reform.

For Giroux and McLaren, teachers as transformative intellectuals ought to be educated in preparation programs that are "self-consciously guided by political and moral considerations" (p. 223). As a starting point, prospective teachers should be educated in "the languages of critique and possibility" so that they might have:

The critical terminology and conceptual apparatus that will allow them not only to critically analyze the democratic and political shortcomings of schools, but also to develop the knowledge and skills that will advance the possibilities for generating curricula, classroom social practices, and organizational arrangements based on and cultivating a deep respect for a democratic and ethically-based community. (p. 223)

Addressing this broad normative mandate requires conceiving of teacher education as cultural politics, a conception that construes school life as an arena of conflict among competing social, political, and economic viewpoints.

The teacher education curriculum for cultural politics must concurrently expose the interests and ideologies that help socialize students in the beliefs of the dominant culture (the language of critique) and suggest alternative teaching practices that help empower students outside as well as inside the schools (the language of possibility). Giroux and McLaren (1986) believe the curriculum for cultural politics needs to address the topics of power, language, culture, and history. In the case of power, for example, knowledge is seen not merely as a reproduction of reality but also as "an ideological construction linked to particular interests and social relations" (p. 230). Thus, school knowledge frequently reflects the interests of powerful groups within society. Similarly, historical knowledge often focuses on the dominant perspective of white, middle-class males, downplaying the role of women, minority groups, and indigenous peoples. In these and related ways, school knowledge serves the interests of the powerful, and prospective teachers need to examine how knowledge is used to sustain dominant groups. In contrast with this relatively specific discussion of the language of critique, Giroux and McLaren have relatively little to say concerning the language of possibility, a shortcoming that is common within the critical tradition (Britzman, 1988).

The central role of democratic values in the inquiries of Giroux and McLaren leads knowledge to be seen both as the exploration of how these values have been incompletely realized in practice and as the source of alternative practices for better achieving these values. This kind of knowledge serves to emancipate oppressed groups and has an obvious link to practice. In a sense, the practice desired by Giroux and McLaren requires knowledge, emancipatory knowledge, or this democratic practice can never be fulfilled.

The positions of Giroux and McLaren, Phillips, Gage, Clark, and Fenstermacher (the latter's original focus on schemata, not his recent emphasis on practical reasoning) represent diverse portrayals of the relationship between professional knowledge and practice. As has been seen, they differ on how strongly knowledge is connected to practice. For Gage, the ideal relationship results from an experimental inquiry that establishes direct links between knowledge and practice, though the linking generalizations are statistical statements rather than laws. For Clark and for Fenstermacher, the relationship between knowledge and practice is indirect, both in that the connection is mediated by the practitioner and in that the mediation process cannot be specified in advance. For Phillips, the tie between knowledge and practice is problematic, involving no necessary connection between knowledge and practice but, rather, being contingent on the systematic reasoning of the practitioner. For Giroux and McLaren, knowledge is required to actualize the practice of democratic values, so that knowledge is embedded in practice. Thus these four positions involve knowledge–practice relationships that can be characterized as direct, indirect, problematic, and embedded.

Purposes of the Knowledge–Practice Link

How knowledge is to be used to alter or improve practice also differs widely, depending on whether the linkages are based on rules, schemata, linking premises, or emancipation. In the case of rules, the key is in establishing experimental evidence linking teacher behaviors and student outcomes, as well as in developing potent training procedures for producing these teacher behaviors. Little attention is paid to how the research-based rules are employed during teaching, other than to note that they can be used flexibly (as in the case of a practical art). The emphasis is on the research soundness of the rules, with the intention of increasing the productivity of conventional classroom teaching. Schrag (1981) considers this method of improving practice an "effective" use of knowledge, an attempt to achieve practical ends more efficiently without substantially changing the means to those ends. Researchers in this effectiveness tradition thus insist that educational scholarship focus on preset and specific instructional objectives, outcomes related to the preset objectives, realistic student–teacher ratios, and other factors related to typical classroom settings (Brophy, 1986, 1988; Gage, 1985, pp. 48–50).

In addition to viewing knowledge as a source of effectiveness, Schrag (1981) notes that knowledge can also be used in a way that is "generative," so that knowledge leads to the achievement of practical ends by suggesting novel means to their attainment. Therefore, a generative use of knowledge "may provide the basis for an entirely new way of doing things" (p. 255). This generative use of knowledge is precisely what schemata achieve under ideal conditions (Clark, 1988; Fenstermacher, 1982). Schrag (1981) makes the interesting point that a theory need not be true for it to have generative value. In fact, he suggests that psychological theories that are invalid overall (e.g., those of Erickson and Skinner) could have more generative power than generally sound theories (e.g., Piagetian theory). This irony results from the difficulty in deriving novel strategies from Piagetian theory "due precisely to its general validity" (p. 258); whereas other theories that are invalid overall, such as those of Skinner and Erickson, might present the "opportunity . . . for interpreting human behavior within schemas that are notably discrepant from those we would normally employ" (pp. 262–263). In this way, theories lacking in overall validity could well have schemata that are both valid in restricted circumstances and capable of fostering counterintuitive analyses of those circumstances. Thus, Schrag observes that behaviorist theory fails as an overall interpretation of human behavior but can help us understand how the action of a parent striking a child for being aggressive toward a sibling can be interpreted by that child as providing a reward, an interpretation at variance with the normal way of understanding a child's behavior.

Phillips (1978, 1980) presents an alternative to using knowledge in an effective or a generative sense. In this instance, knowledge becomes just one of many factors influencing the conduct of practice. Phillips devotes special attention to the linking premises, normative and empirical, in deciding whether and how knowledge might be employed to alter practice. In a similar way, Fenstermacher (1986, 1987) sees the use of knowledge as dependent on practical arguments that entail empirical and situational premises, as well as the identification of desirable (normative) end states. The role of knowledge is important to practical arguments, but it is restricted to evaluating the accuracy of the empirical premises of such arguments.

In contrast with the logical gap Phillips and Fenstermacher maintain between knowledge and practice, Giroux and Mc-Laren (1986) conceive of knowledge as intertwined with practice. Because they focus on the analysis of current practice in light of favored values, knowledge becomes both a justification for new practices (the critique) and the outline of new practices consistent with democratic values (the possibilities). On the one hand, the critique of current practice amounts to claiming that these practices are ineffective for realizing democratic values. On the other hand, the possibilities for reformed practices are an appeal for a generative use of knowledge, because the focus is on suggesting novel means to the achievement of the practical end of democratic values.

Summary

Although many typologies attempt to specify how knowledge affects practice, these typologies often do nothing more than outline the various types of impact knowledge has on practice, such as the distinction basic–applied research and the typologies of Krathwohl and of Jackson and Kieslar. The processes by which educational knowledge is linked to practice are somewhat better addressed by several recently developed typologies: the typologies created by Fenstermacher and by Clark.

But the most systematic treatments of how knowledge is related to practice seem to occur when a scholar takes a personal position on the nature and purpose of this relationship. Thus knowledge has been portrayed as related to practice in at least four diverse ways: (a) as a source of rules (Gage) that specify a direct tie between knowledge and practice, a link that can increase the effectiveness of conventional classroom teaching; (b) as a source of schemata (Fenstermacher, Clark) that can alter the perception of the practitioner, who then generates novel means of achieving practical ends; (c) as a source of empirical linking premises (Phillips) or of evidence to evaluate empirical premises (Fenstermacher), in both cases these premises being only one element of the reasoning by which practitioners establish a connection between knowledge and practice; and (d) as a basis for emancipatory action (Giroux and McLaren), partly by establishing that current practices are ineffective for realizing democratic values and partly by generating new practices that are more consistent with these values.

KNOWLEDGE AND PRACTICE: WARRANTS AND STATUS

Although we have made some critical comments about the four positions on the knowledge–practice relationship, further exploration of the grounds for various knowledge–practice ties does seem wise, as these positions differ in such fundamental ways. Why are there widely varying positions on a fundamental issue in teacher education? What assumptions do people make as they choose one position on the proper knowledge–practice link over others? Addressing these issues brings into focus a third major question: What is the basis for portraying the knowledge–practice relationship in diverse ways?

To address this overarching question, we will examine two interrelated considerations. On the one hand, attention is directed to the epistemological orientation that particular professional knowledge represents. Here the presumption is that the three systematically developed orientations toward knowledge carry with them distinctive types of warrants (or justified uses) for practice; each warrant involves consideration of the conditions under which knowledge is generated when relating this knowledge to practice. To be aware of the epistemological origins of knowledge, therefore, is to know, in part, how that valid knowledge can legitimately be related to practice.

On the other hand, more than epistemology is at issue when the knowledge–practice connection is addressed. As one determines whether to develop rules, to locate schemata, to reason with linking premises, or to seek emancipation, one is in effect taking a stand on the relative status of the realms of knowledge and practice. We will argue that practice can be seen as derived from knowledge (the rule approach), dependent on knowledge (the schemata approach), independent of knowledge (the linking premises approach), or superior to knowledge (the emancipatory approach).

We will first examine the three orientations toward knowledge and their associated warrants for practice; we then turn our attention briefly to the four alternative views on the knowledge–practice relationship and their correlated positions on the relative status of the realms of knowledge and practice.

Knowledge Warrant: Positivism

What does it mean to say that differing types of knowledge have differing warrants for practice? Basically, the concept of a *knowledge warrant* suggests that the conditions under which knowledge is generated, including the form in which it is cast, place restrictions on how it can legitimately be used. A return to the earlier discussion of Gage's (1978) conception of teaching as a practical art should help clarify the warrant of positivist knowledge. Gage, like other positivists, is interested in correlations between variables because these correlations reveal "central tendencies in the relationship between the variables" (1985, p. 51), that is, generalizations. These generalizations come from the study of many individual contexts, such as a sampling of first-grade classrooms from all Missouri school districts. Consequently, a particular research-derived generalization does not reflect the variations within these first-grade rooms, thereby leading to the creation of a weak generalization. Nevertheless, a hypothetical research finding is potentially valid for all classrooms from the sampled population, weak though the overall relationship among the variables is.

Because this hypothetical finding was derived across a set of contexts, first-grade classrooms in Missouri, the finding can be generalized only to that population of classrooms. Here there is little controversy; generalization of results ought not go beyond the original population. At the same time, however, whenever possible the generalization of results ought not be selective within the original population, an outcome that would occur if a particular teacher decided to follow Gage's advice and apply a finding in some cases but not others. The problem is that the teacher has no assured way of knowing whether a particular case represents an instance of a positive, neutral, or even negative correlation of variables, not only because the teacher's analysis of the relevance of a specific finding to an individual student can be mistaken but also because the teacher can be systematically wrong about an entire class of students (some positivistic knowledge is indeed counterintuitive). Thus, when the practitioner chooses to substitute her or his analysis of individual students for the research-derived correlations across students (generalizations), the warrant for the positivistic generalizations no longer applies to the given teaching situation.

Certainly, a teacher has every right to rely upon personal analysis of a student to determine individualized treatment, and many researchers believe responding differentially to individuals is the essence of good teaching (e.g., Hunt, 1976, 1987). However, once the teacher uses professional judgment to decide how to act, the authority for that action is the professional judgment rather than the positivistic generalization. This generalization becomes, at best, a hypothesis in service of professional judgment; the generalization no longer can be said to represent a knowledge claim for the teacher, because the sampling conditions accompanying its derivation are not being honored when it is being applied in practice.

To many, the argument that the teacher must apply positivistic knowledge to all instances of the original population is less than convincing. After all, the findings in positivistic educational science are statistical; thus, the universal application of a finding to all accessible instances of the original population does not guarantee success in every case. The issue here, however, is not one of certainty but of whether the positivistic knowledge establishes a direct, albeit weak, link to practice. This presumption of linkage can be lost by inconsistent application of results, as well as by inconsistent sampling or some other error in research methodology. Thus, Gage cannot contend that scientific knowledge has direct implications for practice and in the same breath argue that scientific knowledge provides "the rules, even if they are only weak generalizations, by which *artistry* [italics added] can operate in dealing with the unique classroom full of unique students" (1985, p. 6).

Another way of viewing the practical warrant of positivistic knowledge is to note that Gage proposes employing knowledge in what amounts to an interpretive sense. When Gage recommends that teachers use their "intuition, creativity, improvisation, and expressiveness," as well as their "judgment, sudden insight, sensitivity, and agility" (1978, p. 15), the perception and analytic ability of teachers has become paramount. This approach to teaching approximates the conception of the practical that van Manen (1977) argues is consistent with interpretive knowledge; namely, that the practical involves "the process of analyzing and clarifying individual and cultural experiences, meanings, perceptions, assumptions, prejudgments, and presuppositions, for the purpose of orienting practical actions" (p. 226). Gage does not stress the cultural dimen-

sion of practical thinking, but he does give considerable emphasis to the individual dimension of van Manen's interpretive orientation toward knowledge. On the other hand, Gage's description of the art of teaching is more expansive than is van Manen's conception of the practical associated with positivism. For the positivist (van Manen uses the term *empirical-analytic*), "the practical refers to the technical application of educational knowledge and of basic curriculum principles for the purpose of attaining a given end" (van Manen, 1977, p. 226). The positivist position posits the practical, not as artistic implementation, but as the application of basic principles in a rule-like way. Therefore, Gage's conjoining of the teacher-as-artist conception with positivist knowledge entails relating knowledge to practice in a way that is inconsistent with the warrant of positivist knowledge.

Knowledge Warrant: Interpretivism

Issues related to the appropriate use of interpretive knowledge are even more complex than in the case of positivistic knowledge. This complexity results partly from the confidence interpretivists have that their perspective, with its emphasis on meaning and classroom context, has implications for the everyday life of teachers (Bolster, 1983; Erickson, 1986). Having spent considerable effort criticizing the absence of context and purpose in positivistic knowledge, interpretivists see little need to defend the relevance of their context-sensitive and meaning-oriented scholarship to the complex, interactive events of the classroom. Indeed, so few interpretivists take time to question how the results of interpretive scholarship are useful to teaching that the raising of this question is the cause for special discussion. For example, when Cazden (1986) asks "how the understandings of researchers help the practice of teachers" and "who should select the research questions and who can make the best use of the answers" (p. 458), Jackson (1987b), in his review of the handbook in which Cazden's article appears, observes that these rarely asked questions deserve analysis.

Erickson (1986), writing in the same handbook, discusses the practical utility of educational scholarship in the interpretive tradition. He argues that "the results of interpretive research are of special interest to teachers" because the localistic perspective of interpretive inquiry is "the stuff of life in daily classroom practice" (p. 156). Convinced that the interpretivist and the teacher share similar concerns, Erickson contends that interpretivist research, "while it does not claim to speak in a voice of univocal, positive truth, can make useful suggestions about the practice of teaching" (p. 158). The nature of these useful suggestions is not discussed, for, as with most analyses by researchers of the utility of knowledge for practice, this discussion comes in the last few paragraphs of the paper. In fact, these "useful suggestions" can be seen as a throwaway, because they are diminished by his quite modest truth claims for interpretive knowledge. Erickson makes the unusual assertion that "the *chief* [italics added] usefulness of interpretive research for the improvement of teaching practice may be its challenge to the notion that certain truths can be found" (p. 158). Do we really need interpretive scholarship to know that truth is elusive? Classroom teachers do not, and positivistic researchers have long since abandoned the optimism of E. L. Thorndike, Elwood Cubberley, and other early twentieth-century proponents of a science of education.

Besides illustrating that "certain truths" are unlikely to be found, Erickson (1986) sees a second "chief usefulness" of interpretive research. This research is a "call to reconstrue fundamentally our notions of the nature of the practical in teaching" (p. 158). Thus, "interpretive research on teaching . . . is not only an alternative method, but an alternative view of how society works, and of how schools, classrooms, teachers, and students work in society" (p. 158). The warrant that interpretivism is a representation of practice, a warrant that recalls the enthusiasm associated with the early positivist claims that the laws of learning were just around the corner, is an example of what Jackson (1987b) refers to as "new paradigm optimism."

But apart from whether interpretivism represents a dramatic reconceptualization of teaching practice, Erickson (1986) also asserts that part of interpretivism's warrant is normative. Interpretivism, he believes, is antithetical to the top-down management of teachers, policies that are grounded in positivist research about what works across classrooms. Interpretive scholarship, however, has "theoretical orientations" and "a growing body of empirical findings" that suggest the appropriateness of giving "more autonomy to front-line service providers in the system" (p. 158). Here Erickson seems to go beyond the legitimate warrant of interpretivism, because interpretive inquiry does not necessarily serve the interests of any group. Many instances of interpretive scholarship could be cited in which sympathetic treatment was accorded teachers and other "front-line" practitioners, but interpretivism also has documented conflicts between parents and teachers (e.g., Gold & Miles, 1981) and ways in which education professionals have inflicted harm upon students (Heath, 1982; Henry, 1955, 1957; Page, 1987; Rist, 1970). Thus, for Erickson to contend that interpretive scholarship supports the interests of teachers vis-à-vis managers and policymakers is to take, unconsciously, a normative stance, when interpretivism is in reality a relativistic form of inquiry. Individual interpretive scholars, of course, can formulate research questions consistent with their particular value commitments (e.g., Heath, 1982, 1983), but the research tradition itself is not embedded in a particular value orientation.

The relativism of interpretive thought is brought into sharp focus by Cazden's (1983) query: Can ethnographic research go beyond the status quo? This inquiry was prompted by a sign alleged to have been posted in a state department of education: We Don't Need Any More Anthropological Explanations of School Failure. Cazden observes that "there can be no direct derivation of advice for change from any descriptive account— no matter how rich" (p. 38), a position that reaffirms the inability to derive improved educational programs from scholarship in which all values are accepted but none are affirmed. Kleinfeld (1983) not only concurs that anthropology fails to recommend ideas for educational improvement but also contends that anthropological findings often do harm. She argues that anthropology often both diverts attention from pedagogical problems and proposes cultural differences as a reason for school failure, thus providing teachers "with facile rationaliza-

tions for giving up" (p. 285). Interpretive scholarship, therefore, can lead the practitioner to become an apologist for the status quo, for the constellation of dominant values in a society.

To identify the relativistic potential of interpretive scholarship or to highlight the possibility of the interpretive scholar's unconsciously imposing personal values on findings is not to suggest that either normative stance is a legitimate warrant for interpretive knowledge. Acceptance of the status quo or the positing of an alternative value stance is a decision ultimately made by the person seeking to relate interpretive knowledge to practice. Neither stance is defensible without some kind of appeal to values external to the research itself. Interpretive scholarship, as well as other forms of knowledge, carries no prescriptive warrant, either in support of a particular role such as the teacher or in support of an educational solution such as making the school environment congruent with the students' culture (Kleinfeld, 1984; Kleinfeld, McDiarmid, Grubis, & Parrett, 1983; Zeuli & Floden, 1987).

If interpretive scholarship has no prescriptive warrant, then what kind of legitimate warrant remains? Apparently, there are two possibilities, both raised by Erickson (1986) and introduced earlier in this discussion. One is for interpretive research, with its emphasis on the specifics of meaning and action in social life, to serve as a view of practice, a model of how school and society operate. The problem with this model is that the practitioner cannot remain the detached observer; relativism within the classroom is not possible because teaching inevitably entails making curricular choices that reflect normative priorities (Tom, 1984). Thus, seeing practice as an instance of interpretivism inappropriately limits the conception of practice.

The second possibility raised by Erickson (1986) is that interpretive scholarship can provide useful suggestions for teachers. Here the enthusiasm for interpretive scholarship is sparked by its promise "to reveal aspects of teaching that have never before been known or understood" (Jackson, 1987b, p. 508). Because interpretive inquiry follows a case study format, the warrant for these newly revealed complexities is limited in scope and in authority. These limitations are imposed not only because validity is a complex issue for interpretive scholarship (Peshkin, 1988; Phillips, 1987) but also because generalization from case study material to a broader population is perilous. This conclusion, however, presumes that the ostensible purpose of interpretive scholarship is to increase the effectiveness of teaching practices, whereas a generative approach would be a more appropriate use of this scholarship. Revealing the underlying complexities of teaching is generative in the sense that these revealed complexities can suggest novel means for teachers to achieve practical ends. Of course, interpretive scholarship is restricted in its generative possibilities by the universe of alternatives that have been systematically examined, as well as by the access of teachers to these studies.

This latter issue of disseminating interpretive scholarship to teachers deserves special mention. There is little to suggest that teachers would find generative potential in certain forms of interpretive scholarship. To the extent that this scholarship adopts a teacher perspective and stresses localist meanings, the teacher–reader is likely to see this scholarship as belaboring the obvious and, therefore, not worth the time to read it. Portrayals of practice in terms that are familiar to teachers are likely to have little if any generative potential (Schrag, 1981).

Thus, the interpretive scholarship with the greatest potential for generative use by teachers is scholarship that reveals aspects of teaching that have been hidden from the typical teacher. In particular, teachers might find generative possibilities in accounts of school-based student culture or student culture within the larger societal context (e.g., Canaan, 1987; Cusick, 1973; Heath, 1982; Weis, 1985). Moreover, teachers might discover generative possibilities in the examination of the teacher role when this analysis occurs in a novel setting, for example, urban teachers reading interpretive accounts of teaching in small towns (e.g., McPherson, 1972; Peshkin, 1978). A third instance would be the reexamination of taken-for-granted notions of teaching (e.g., Henry, 1955, 1957; Page, 1987; Valli, 1986). In the end, therefore, the most defensible warrant for interpretive findings seems to be a generative use of this knowledge. Although positivist scholarship can also be employed in a generative way, especially when it represents counterintuitive findings, the typical warrant for positivist knowledge focuses on improving the effectiveness of teaching practices.

Knowledge Warrant: Critically Oriented

Considerably problems arise when analyzing the warrant for critically oriented scholarship, perhaps because we have grouped a variety of perspectives under this category, liberal as well as Marxist and feminist, critical theory as well as more conventional approaches to knowing and understanding. About the only unifying theme of this critically oriented scholarship is a commitment to specific values, a commitment that precedes empirical study. However, even though equality is widely embraced by critically oriented scholars, there is by no means universal adherence to this particular value.

As a result, the identification of the warrant for knowledge coming out of the critical tradition appears to be difficult. Not only is there no agreement on values among critical scholars, but, in addition, much of the scholarship in this tradition is aimed at analyzing the corruption of the present system and, therefore, might not have specific implications for improving practice, except perhaps in a generative sense. Yet a generative use of knowledge is quite appropriate when the issue is using knowledge to identify practices that might foster the achievement of favored values. Moreover, lack of consensus on values is not necessarily damaging to the critical tradition, if a defining characteristic of the tradition is the prior commitment to values, rather than agreement on a particular value or values. That is, commitment to diverse values often leads to prescriptions for practice that differ in substance, but the process for relating knowledge to practice could well be a shared process when inquiries are conducted by scholars who all have a priori value commitments. Moreover, the stress here has been on the diversity of the critical tradition, without simultaneous acknowledgment that diversity is also a characteristic of the positivist and interpretive traditions (Atkinson, Delamont,

& Hammersley, 1988; Jacob, 1987, 1988; Zeichner & Gore, 1990).

When critically oriented scholars discuss the relationship of knowledge and practice within the context of teacher education, they tend to emphasize the need for prospective teachers to be active inquirers, not the passive recipients of knowledge. Ginsburg (1988), for example, argues that teacher education students need "the requisite analytical skills and conceptual tools to critically reflect and inquire about their own and the broader experiences of school and society" (p. 211). Students should not only examine "issues relevant to social class, gender and race relations" in school and society but, in addition, subject the teacher education curriculum itself to critical examination, both the "formal curriculum" and the "'hidden' curriculum . . . constituted by the social relations of the teacher education program, the university, and school/communities" (pp. 211, 212).

According to Ginsburg (1988), one purpose of this broad-ranging critical inquiry is understanding; however, the key purpose of such inquiry is to cause teachers to act collaboratively to correct the inequalities embedded in schools and the social system. Thus, Ginsburg sees critical inquiry as a means of becoming conscious of the complex dynamics of educational and social inequality, but he also approvingly quotes Shor (1986) to the effect that "only political movements can transform inequality" (p. 213). Other critically oriented teacher educators share this dual focus on examining current inequalities in education and society and on making the case for political action to alter educational and social institutions (e.g., Beyer & Zeichner, 1987; Giroux & McLaren, 1986; Kohl, 1976; Leck, 1987; Maher, 1987; Weiler, 1988).

In the critical tradition, knowledge is viewed less as a received product than as an active process of analysis by which the contradictions and shortcomings of educational and social institutions are revealed. As a result many critically oriented teacher educators want future teachers to generate their own critical analyses of institutions, a position consistent with the widely held view among such teacher educators that analyses should not be imposed upon anyone. Yet an underlying commitment to a particular value, or set of values, is often presumed to be the starting point for student-conducted critical analyses. Does the prescription of a moral starting point entail inculcation because "other defensible moral positions exist" besides "viewing schools as harbingers of injustice" (Liston & Zeichner, 1987, p. 120)? Or is the prescription of a moral starting point for critical analyses essential, if these analyses are to focus on the unjust aspects of schooling and society, not merely serve the interests of dominant groups?

In this chapter we cannot resolve the dispute among those in the critical tradition who see a radical perspective as the only conceivable stance, as opposed to those who believe a variety of stances are justifiable. This argument is an old one, having last been center stage in the 1930s when Boyd Bode and John Childs debated whether the social reconstructionist platform entailed indoctrination (Chambliss, 1963; Kliebard, 1986). Our critically oriented category is broadly construed to also include people falling outside Marxism and feminism, thereby further complicating the issue of how much concerning values is contestable within the critical tradition. Nevertheless, all scholars in what we have termed the critical tradition believe that values are central to inquiry, even if they do differ on when and how values enter into inquiry.

The emphasis on values therefore binds together "factions" of critically oriented scholarship and also suggests that such scholarship might in fact, represent a social theory as well as an epistemological orientation. On the one hand, critically oriented scholars do not appeal to a unique set of standards and procedures for generating knowledge; instead, these scholars borrow research techniques from the other two traditions. Some critical scholars draw heavily on positivist techniques and assumptions (e.g., Bowles & Gintis, 1976), whereas others appeal to interpretive techniques and assumptions (e.g., Willis, 1977). On the other hand, the core of critical scholarship concerns an interrelated set of empirical and value claims concerning how schools and society should be reorganized, a social theory of institutional life.

The warrant for knowledge in the critical tradition is intimately wrapped up in its accompanying social theory, because that social theory both activates epistemological inquiry and establishes goals to guide this inquiry. Because the validity of any particular social theory can be contested, the warrant of its companion knowledge is equally at issue. One way to respond to an ambiguous warrant is to engage prospective teachers in personal reflection and study of their educational and social situations, as Ginsburg (1988) recommends. If such personal reflection and study treats as problematic the underlying social theory and the knowledge about practices instrumental to realizing this social theory, the ambiguous nature of the warrant for knowledge from the critical tradition would seem to have been honored.

But can we not consider the warrant of knowledge from the critical tradition apart from its coordinate social theory? This possibility seems particularly appealing if the knowledge at issue meets the standards of one of the other two epistemological traditions. Certainly such separate consideration can be pursued, so long as the knowledge so considered has its warrant reviewed in light of the appropriate epistemological tradition. However, knowledge generated out of the critical tradition obtains part of its significance from its coordinate social theory. In the critical tradition, not only is knowledge creation stimulated by social values, as embodied in a social theory, but also this knowledge is seen as having the purpose of identifying practices instrumental to achieving these values. Therefore, the separation of knowledge from its coordinate social theory has the effect of tearing this knowledge out of the context that provides its meaning and direction.

Relative Status of Knowledge and Practice

Besides the varying warrants implicit in differing orientations to knowledge, a second underlying factor that is correlated with variations in the knowledge–practice relationship is differing conceptions of the status of knowledge and practice. Here we return to the four ways examined earlier of relating professional knowledge to practice: rules, schemata, linking

premises, and emancipation. This discussion is speculative and brief because conceptions of the relative status of knowledge and practice are usually latent. Moreover it is unclear whether particular conceptions of the relative status of knowledge and practice ought to be seen as major causes of varying positions on the relationship of knowledge and practice or whether each of these positions entails a particular view of the relative status of knowledge and practice.

To see the improvement of practice as involving the creation of rules grounded in the findings of scientific research is to see the realm of practice as being derived from knowledge. Knowledge, that is, scientific knowledge, is presumed to be the basis for improving practice, and practice is presumed to be both the proper context for such studies and an object that can be molded to conform to findings of these studies. In the positivist literature on applying rules to practice, one finds literally no discussion of the realm of practice other than as an object of reform (e.g., Gage, 1983; Garrison & Macmillan, 1984; B. O. Smith, 1983).

On the surface, the use of schemata in a generative sense suggests a considerably higher status for practice, as it is the teacher who decides which professional knowledge might be of interest and then determines how to relate that knowledge to practice (Fenstermacher, 1983). However, note that the origin of the ideas is outside practice and that this external origin suggests that a dependency relationship exists between knowledge and practice (for a related set of arguments, see Confrey, 1987). The greatest degree of dependency probably occurs when interpretivism is seen as a model of practice, because practice in such a situation has no logical standing independent of an interpretive epistemology.

There is logical independence when knowledge is related to practice through linking premises. Phillips (1978, 1980) is quite explicit on this point when he notes that the practical actions determined through the use of reasoning—reasoning that employs empirical as well as value premises—do not necessarily have to be consistent with the pertinent professional knowledge. Value considerations can override empirical consistency, as in the hypothetical instance of the application to practice of Piagetian ideas. In Fenstermacher's (1987) closely related approach based on practical reasoning there is a clear distinction between research and practice. Research is the source of scientific knowledge, and that knowledge is one source of the reasoning practitioners can use to think through practical issues. Thus, for both Phillips and Fenstermacher, there is properly a logical disjunction between knowledge and practice.

In the case of the emancipatory approach of relating knowledge to practice, new actions consistent with the favored values are to be achieved through knowledge. Giroux and McLaren (1986) refer to such knowledge as the language of possibility, clearly suggesting that this knowledge obtains its justification from its ability to foster new actions on the part of teachers. Practice, therefore, can be seen as having higher status than knowledge, because knowledge is of interest only if it helps bring about the emancipatory actions that lead to the desired forms of practice. Practice, in revised form, is viewed as dominant over knowledge.

Summary

In this section we have focused on the epistemological origins of knowledge as one way to understand why the knowledge–practice relationship is portrayed in differing ways. The central idea is that knowledge from each of the three epistemological orientations carries a characteristic warrant for practice. In the case of positivistic knowledge, careful attention ought to be given to the population to which the knowledge is to be applied. The effectiveness warrant for this knowledge lies with statistical correlations between variables, not with the professional judgment of the teacher. The teacher's contribution to implementing positivistic knowledge is to provide the value judgments about what instructional goals are important, so that the statistically based rules can be directed toward a particular target. The major legitimate warrant for interpretive knowledge involves a generative use of knowledge, though a normative perspective is at times intertwined with interpretive knowledge in an inappropriate manner. Critically oriented scholarship is more explicit about normative commitments, but its strength lies in its generative possibilities, if the teacher–reader shares the particular value commitments or social theory in which the knowledge is embedded.

At the same time as the three epistemological orientations raise differing issues about knowledge's warrant for practice, the relative status of knowledge and practice also differs for each of the four distinctive positions on the knowledge–practice relationship. The rule approach is correlated with practice being derived from knowledge; the schemata approach, with practice being dependent on knowledge; the linking premises approach, with practice being independent of knowledge; and the emancipatory approach, with desired forms of practice being superior to knowledge.

CONCLUSION

The term *knowledge base* has become an extremely popular concept in teacher education, even to the point of having a cluster of knowledge-base standards included in the most recent revision of accreditation standards (National Council for Accredition of Teacher Education [NCATE], 1987; Gideonse, 1988). The presumption in these accreditation standards is that a knowledge base, actually knowledge bases, exist and that every faculty ought to attend carefully to the knowledge bases that underlie its teacher education program. The NCATE standards recognize two types of knowledge bases: "the traditional forms of scholarly inquiry as well as theory development related to professional practice" (NCATE, 1987, p. 37).

This chapter briefly considered the craft knowledge that is grounded in the wisdom of practice but explores in some detail knowledge derived from the traditions of positivism, interpretivism, and critically oriented scholarship. Knowledge from these three traditions varies in its purposes and forms, and typologies have been developed to portray contrasting ways knowledge can be seen as related to practice. Special attention was given in this chapter to four conceptions of the knowledge–practice relationship: rules, schemata, linking premises, emancipatory action. These four points of view differ in both the extent to which knowledge entails practice and the purpose for which knowledge is used. Selecting one of these points of view also involves taking a position on the relative status of knowledge and practice.

Intricacies of the four points of view and of the three epistemological traditions were explored in the chapter and were summarized periodically. These conclusions are not repeated here. However, interconnections between the four conceptualizations of the knowledge–practice relationship and the three epistemological traditions were not made explicit earlier. For the most part, these interconnections are obvious, as there is essentially a one-to-one correspondence between a positivist epistemology, with its emphasis on generalizations, and a focus on rules that specify a direct tie between knowledge and practice; between an interpretive epistemology, with its stress on the case knowledge of meaning in context, and a focus on schemata that can alter a teacher's perception; between a critical epistemology (perhaps more accurately described as a social theory), with its a priori commitment to particular values, and a focus on emancipatory actions to bring about new practices more consistent with these values. These three pairings, however, leave the approach of linking premises without a corresponding epistemology, and there might well be no appropriate pairing for the linking premises approach. Central to the linking premises approach is the idea that practice is independent of knowledge, thereby making it logical that knowledge from all three traditions could be employed when using linking premises to relate knowledge and practice.

Much of the content of this chapter might aptly be described as cautions about drawing implications from knowledge for practice. The section on knowledge warrants addressed this topic directly, but the entire chapter bore upon the difficulties of making links between knowledge and practice. Thus we believe that the issue of knowledge bases for teacher education is much more complex than locating knowledge about teaching, about students, about schooling, or about the social context of schooling. To have a knowledge base (or bases) for professional education means to have not only knowledge but also insight into how this knowledge is properly related to practice.

But that which can be done is not necessarily that which ought to be done. That is, the identification of possible professional knowledge, including considerations of the knowledge–practice relationship, is not the same process as the identification of the professional curriculum for teacher education. Constructing a professional curriculum requires judgments about what a teacher must know and be able to do. Professional knowledge is one source of the content for such a curriculum, but the ultimate justification for curricular decision making in professional education is normative: a conception of a set of desirable understandings, skills, and dispositions. In this chapter we have not addressed the issue of curriculum making, preferring instead to investigate the characteristics of professional knowledge and of the knowledge–practice relationship. Professional knowledge, or knowledge bases for professional education, are extremely complex terrain; the professional curriculum is equally complex, but different, terrain. Both need more exploration.

Among researchers interested in teacher education, and teacher educators generally, there is a strong preference for construing professional knowledge in terms of one (or more) of the three systematic epistemological traditions. Although the critical tradition receives less recognition than the other two traditions, all three traditions are seen as more reputable than craft knowledge. Yet classroom practitioners and some teacher educators continue to rely upon a craft conception of professional knowledge; they seem to find little of generative or effective value in knowledge derived from the standard epistemological traditions. The reasons for their rejection of knowledge from the conventional traditions are unclear, but such rejection, along with the complexities of knowledge bases from these traditions, suggests that the tradition of craft knowledge needs continued attention from researchers, teacher educators, and teachers, not necessarily in that order.

The questions we believe should be at the base of this continued attention are complicated and not necessarily internally consistent. Is it possible to conceive of the craft tradition in analytic and self-critical terms, as well as in terms of imitation and traditionalism? If so, why has the more conservative variant of the craft orientation been dominant? In what ways can tacit knowledge from the craft tradition be codified? Which forms of codification make this knowledge accessible to other practitioners? Or is the codification of craft knowledge, knowledge sensitive to various contexts and to contrasting conceptions of good teaching, a contradiction in terms? Is the very idea of codification, that is a knowledge base, appropriate only in the case of positivism, an orientation that presumes practice to be derived from knowledge? Can craft knowledge ever be viewed as a systematic way of knowing, with its characteristic methods of inquiry, rules of evidence, and forms of knowledge, so that we can talk about an epistemology of craft knowledge? What is the warrant for craft knowledge? These and related questions would focus attention on craft knowledge in a way that might secure its position as a legitimate fourth tradition.

References

Adler, S., & Goodman, J. (1986). Critical theory as a foundation for methods courses. *Journal of Teacher Education, 37*(4), 2–8.

Anderson, L. M., Evertson, C. M., & Brophy, J. E. (1979). An experimental study of effective teaching in first-grade reading groups. *Elementary School Journal, 79,* 193–223.

Anyon, J. (1979). Ideology and United States history textbooks. *Harvard Educational Review, 49*(3), 361–386.

Apple, M. (1982). *Education and power.* Boston: Routledge and Kegan Paul.

Arnstine, D. (1975). Apprenticeship as the miseducation of teachers. *Philosophy of education 1975: Proceedings of the 31st annual meeting of the Philosophy of Education Society* (pp. 113–123). San Jose, CA: Society for Studies in Philosophy and Education.

Atkinson, P., Delamont, S., & Hammersley, M. (1988). Qualitative research traditions: A British response to Jacob. *Review of Educational Research, 58,* 231–250.

Berliner, D. C. (1976). A status report on the study of teacher effectiveness. *Journal of Research in Science Teaching, 13,* 369–382.

Bernstein, R. J. (1978). *The restructuring of social and political theory.* Philadelphia: University of Pennsylvania Press.

Best, E. (1967). The suppressed premiss in educational psychology. In B. P. Komisar & C. J. B. Macmillan (Eds.), *Psychological concepts in education* (pp. 1–13). Chicago: Rand McNally.

Beyer, L. E., & Zeichner, K. (1987). Teacher education in cultural context: Beyond reproduction. In T. S. Popkewitz (Ed.), *Critical studies in teacher education* (pp. 298–334). London: Falmer Press.

Blumberg, A. (1989). *School administration as a craft.* Boston: Allyn & Bacon.

Bolster, A. S. (1983). Toward a more effective model of research on teaching. *Harvard Educational Review, 53*(3), 294–308.

Borman, K. M., LeCompte, M. D., & Goetz, J. P. (1986). Ethnographic and qualitative research and why it doesn't work. *American Behavioral Scientist, 30,* 42–57.

Bowles, S., & Gintis, H. (1976). *Schooling in capitalist America: Educational reform and the contradictions of economic life.* New York: Basic Books.

Brauner, C. (1978). Accustoming: The hidden concept in training. *Philosophy of education 1978: Proceedings of the 34th annual meeting of the Philosophy Education Society* (pp. 162–172). San Jose, CA: Society for Studies in Philosophy and Education.

Bredo, E., & Feinberg, W. (Eds.). (1982). *Knowledge and values in social and educational research.* Philadelphia: Temple University Press.

Britzman, D. P. (1988). On educating the educators. *Harvard Educational Review, 58*(1), 85–94.

Brophy, J. (1986). Where are the data?–A reply to Confrey. *Journal for Research in Mathematics Education, 17,* 361–368.

Brophy, J. (1988). Research on teacher effects: Uses and abuses. *Elementary School Journal, 89,* 3–21.

Brophy, J. E., & Good, T. L. (1986). Teacher behavior and student achievement. In M. C. Wittrock (Ed.), *Handbook of research on teaching* (3rd ed., pp. 328–375). New York: Macmillan.

Broudy, H. S. (1956). Teaching—Craft or profession. *Educational Forum, 20,* 175–184.

Buchmann, M. (1987). Teaching knowledge: The lights that teachers live by. *Oxford Review of Education, 13,* 151–164.

Canaan, J. (1987). A comparative analysis of American suburban middle class, middle school, and high school teenage cliques. In G. Spindler & L. Spindler (Eds.), *Interpretive ethnography of education: At home and abroad* (pp. 385–406). Hillsdale, NJ: Lawrence Erlbaum.

Cazden, C. B. (1983). Can ethnographic research go beyond the status quo? *Anthropology and Education Quarterly, 14,* 33–41.

Cazden, C. B. (1986). Classroom discourse. In M. C. Wittrock (Ed.), *Handbook of research on teaching* (3rd ed., pp. 432–463). New York: Macmillan.

Chambliss, J. J. (1963). *Boyd H. Bode's philosophy of education.* Columbus, OH: Ohio State University Press.

Clandinin, D. J., & Connelly, F. M. (1987). Inquiry into schooling: Diverse perspectives. *Journal of Curriculum and Supervision, 2,* 295–313.

Clark, C. M. (1988). Asking the right questions about teacher preparation: Contributions of research on teacher thinking. *Educational Researcher, 17* (2), 5–12.

Confrey, J. (1987). Bridging research and practice. *Educational Theory, 37,* 383–394.

Cronbach, L. J. (1975). Beyond the two disciplines of scientific psychology. *American Psychologist, 30,* 116–127.

Cronbach, L. J., & Suppes, P. (Eds.). (1969). *Research for tomorrow's schools: Disciplined inquiry for education.* London: Macmillan.

Cusick, P. A. (1973). *Inside high school: The student's world.* New York: Holt, Rinehart & Winston.

Dunkin, M. J., & Biddle, B. J. (1974). *The study of teaching.* New York: Holt, Rinehart & Winston.

Ebel, R. (1982). The future of educational research. *Educational Researcher, 11*(8), 18–19.

Elbaz, F. (1983). *Teacher thinking: A study of practical knowledge.* New York: Nichols.

Erickson, F. (1986). Qualitative methods in research on teaching. In M. C. Wittrock (Ed.), *Handbook of research on teaching* (3rd ed, pp. 119–161). New York: Macmillan.

Fay, B. (1975). *Social theory and political practice.* London: Allen & Unwin.

Fenstermacher, G. D. (1982). On learning to teach effectively from research on teacher effectiveness. *Journal of Classroom Interaction, 17*(2), 7–12. Reprinted from C. Denham & A. Lieberman (Eds.). (1980). *Time to learn* (pp. 147–168.). Sacramento, CA: California Commission for Teacher Education and Licensing.

Fenstermacher, G. D. (1983). How should implications of research on teaching be used? *Elementary School Journal, 83*(4), 496–499.

Fenstermacher, G. D. (1986). Philosophy of research on teaching: Three aspects. In M. C. Wittrock (Ed.), *Handbook of research on teaching* (3rd ed, pp. 37–49). New York: Macmillan.

Fenstermacher, G. D. (1987). Prologue to my critics. A reply to my critics. *Educational Theory, 37,* 357–360, 413–421.

Freedman, S. (1987). Teachers' knowledge from a feminist perspective. In J. Smyth (Ed.). *Educating teachers: Changing the nature of pedagogical knowledge* (pp. 73–81). London: Falmer Press.

Gage, N. L. (1963). Paradigms for research on teaching. In N. L. Gage (Ed.), *Handbook of research on teaching* (pp. 94–141). Chicago: Rand McNally.

Gage, N. L. (1978). *The scienticfic basis of the art of teaching.* New York: Teachers College Press.

Gage, N. L. (1983). When does research on teaching yield implications for practice? *Elementary School Journal, 83,* 492–496.

Gage, N. L. (1984). What do we know about teaching effectiveness? *Phi Delta Kappan, 66*(2), 87–93.

Gage, N. L. (1985). *Hard gains in the soft sciences: The case of pedagogy.* Bloomington, IN: Phi Delta Kappa.

Gage, N. L., & Giaconia, R. (1981). Teaching practices and student achievement: Causal connections. *New York University Education Quarterly, 12* (3), 2–9.

Garrison, J. W., & Macmillan, C. J. B. (1984). A philosophical critique of process–product research on teaching. *Educational Theory, 34,* 255–274.

Geertz, C. (1980). Blurred genres: The refiguration of social thought. *American Scholar, 49,* 165–179.

Gideonse, H. D. (1982). The necessary revolution in teacher education. *Phi Delta Kappan, 64*(1), 15–18.

Gideonse, H. D. (1986). Blackwell's commentaries, engineering's handbooks, and Merck's manuals: What would a teacher's equivalent be? *Educational Evaluation and Policy Analysis, 8,* 316–323.

Gideonse, H. D. (1988). *Relating knowledge to teacher education: Responding to NCATE's knowledge base and related standards.* Washington, DC: American Association of Colleges for Teacher Education.

Ginsburg, M. B. (1988). *Contradictions in teacher education and society: A critical analysis.* London: Falmer Press.

Giroux, H. A. (1983). *Theory and resistance in education: A pedagogy for the opposition.* South Hadley, MA: Bergin & Garvey.

Giroux, H. A., & McLaren, P. (1986). Teacher education and the politics of engagement: The case for democratic schooling. *Harvard Educational Review, 56*(3), 213–238.

Gold, B. A., & Miles, M. B. (1981). *Whose school is it, anyway? Parent–teacher conflict over an innovative school.* New York: Praeger.

Goodman, J. (1985). What students learn from early field experiences: A case study and critical analysis. *Journal of Teacher Education, 36*(6), 42–48.

Green, T. F. (1976). Teacher competence as practical rationality. *Educational Theory, 26,* 249–258.

Griffin, G. A., & Barnes, S. (1986). Using research findings to change school and classroom practices: Results of an experimental study. *American Educational Research Journal, 23*(4), 572–586.

Guskey, T. R. (1986). Staff development and the process of teacher change. *Educational Researcher, 15*(5), 5–12.

Habermas, J. (1971). *Knowledge and human interests.* Boston: Beacon Press.

Hartnett, A., & Naish, M. (1980). Technicians or social bandits? Some moral and political issues in the education of teachers. In P. Woods (Ed.), *Teacher strategies: Explorations in the sociology of the school* (pp. 254–274). London: Croom Helm.

Heath, S. B. (1982). Questioning at home and at school: A comparative study. In G. Spindler (Ed.), *Doing the ethnography of schooling: Educational anthropology in action* (pp. 102–131). New York: Holt, Rinehart & Winston.

Heath, S. B. (1983). Research currents: A lot of talk about nothing. *Language Arts, 60,* 999–1007.

Henry, J. (1955). Docility, or giving teacher what she wants. *Journal of Social Issues, 11*(2), 33–41.

Henry, J. (1957). Attitude organization in elementary school classrooms. *American Journal of Orthopsychiatry, 27*(1), 117–133.

Holmes Group. (1986). *Tomorrow's teachers.* East Lansing, MI: Author.

Howe, H. (1976). Education research—The promise and the problem. *Educational Researcher, 5*(6), 2–7.

Hunt, D. E. (1976). Teachers' adaptation: "Reading" and "flexing" to students. *Journal of Teacher Education, 27*(3), 268–275.

Hunt, D. E. (1987). *Beginning with ourselves: In practice, theory, and human affairs.* Cambridge, MA: Brookline.

Jackson, P. W. (1970). Is there a best way of teaching Harold Bateman? *Midway, 10*(4), 15–28.

Jackson, P. W. (1987a). Facing our ignorance. *Teachers College Record, 88,* 384–389.

Jackson, P. W. (1987b). Research on teaching: Quo vadis? [Review of *Handbook of research on teaching* (3rd ed.)]. *Contemporary Psychology, 32,* 506–508.

Jackson, P. W., & Kieslar, S. B. (1977). Fundamental research and education. *Educational Researcher, 6*(8), 13–18.

Jacob, E. (1987). Qualitative research traditions: A review. *Review of Educational Research, 57,* 1–50.

Jacob, E. (1988). Clarifying qualitative research: A focus on traditions. *Educational Researcher, 17*(1), 16–19, 22–24.

James, W. (1902). *Talks to teachers on psychology.* New York: Henry Holt. (Original work published 1899)

Kerlinger, F. N. (1977). The influence of research on education practice. *Educational Researcher, 6*(8), 5–12.

Kirk, D. (1986). Beyond the limits of theoretical discourse in teacher education: Towards a critical pedagogy. *Teaching and Teacher Education, 2,* 155–167.

Kleinfeld, J. (1983). First do no harm: A reply to Courtney Cazden. *Anthropology and Education Quarterly, 14,* 282–287.

Kleinfeld, J. (1984). Some of my best friends are anthropologists. *Anthropology and Education Quarterly, 15,* 180–184.

Kleinfeld, J., McDiarmid, G. W., Grubis, S., & Parrett, W. (1983).

Doing research on effective cross-cultural teaching: The teacher tale. *Peabody Journal of Education, 61*(1), 86–108.

Kliebard, H. M. (1986). *The struggle for the American curriculum 1893–1958*. Boston: Routledge and Kegan Paul.

Kohl, H. (1976). *On teaching*. New York: Schocken.

Krathwohl, D. (1977). Improving educational research and development. *Educational Researcher, 6*(4), 8–14.

Kuhn, T. S. (1962). *The structure of scientific revolutions*. Chicago: University of Chicago Press.

Lampert, M. (1985). How do teachers manage to teach? Perspectives on problems in practice. *Harvard Educational Review, 55*(2), 178–194.

Lather, P. (1986). Research as praxis. *Harvard Educational Review, 56*(3), 257–277.

Leck, G. M. (1987). Review article—Feminist pedagogy, liberation theory, and the traditional schooling paradigm. *Educational Theory, 37*, 343–354.

Liston, D. P. (1984). Have we explained the relationship between curriculum and capitalism? An analysis of the selective tradition. *Educational Theory, 34*, 241–253.

Liston, D. P. (1986). On facts and values: An analysis of radical curriculum studies. *Educational Theory, 36*, 137–152.

Liston, D. P. (1988). *Capitalist schools: Explanation and ethics in radical studies of schooling*. New York: Routledge, Chapman & Hall.

Liston, D. P., & Zeichner, K. M. (1987). Critical pedagogy and teacher education. *Journal of Education, 169*(3), 117–137.

Maher, F. A. (1987). Toward a richer theory of feminist pedagogy: A comparison of "liberation" and "gender" models for teaching and learning. *Journal of Education, 169*(3), 91–100.

May, W. T., & Zimpher, N. L. (1986). An examination of three theoretical perspectives on supervision: Perceptions of preservice field supervision. *Journal of Curriculum and Supervision, 1*(2), 83–99.

McPherson, G. (1972). *Small town teacher*. Cambridge, MA: Harvard University Press.

Mishler, E. G. (1979). Meaning in context: Is there any other kind? *Harvard Educational Review, 49*(1), 1–19.

National Council for Accreditation of Teacher Education. (1987). *NCATE standards, procedures, and policies for the accreditation of professional education units: The accreditation of professional education units for the preparation of professional school personnel at basic and advanced levels*. Washington, DC: Author.

Noddings, N. (1984). *Caring*. Berkeley, CA: University of California Press.

Noddings, N. (1988). An ethic of caring and its implications for instructional arrangements. *American Journal of Education, 96*(2), 215–230.

Page, R. (1987). Lower-track classes at a college-preparatory high school: A caricature of educational encounters. In G. Spindler & L. Spindler (Eds.), *Interpretive ethnography of education: At home and abroad* (pp. 447–472). Hillsdale, NJ: Lawrence Erlbaum.

Peshkin, A. (1978). *Growing up American: Schooling and the survival of community*. Chicago: University of Chicago Press.

Peshkin, A. (1988). In search of subjectivity—One's own. *Educational Researcher, 17*(7), 17–22.

Phillips, D. C. (1971). *Theories, values and education*. Carlton, Victoria, Australia: Melbourne University Press.

Phillips, D. C. (1978). A skeptical consumers' guide to educational research. *Andover Review, 5*(2), 39–53.

Phillips, D. C. (1980). What do the researcher and the practitioner have to offer each other? *Educational Researcher, 9*(11), 17–20, 24.

Phillips, D. C. (1987). Validity in qualitative research: Why the worry about warrant will not wane. *Education and Urban Society, 20*(1), 9–24.

Popkewitz, T. S. (1980). Paradigms in educational science: Different meanings and purpose to theory. *Journal of Education, 162*(1), 28–46.

Rist, R. C. (1970). Student social class and teacher expectations: The self-fulfilling prophecy in ghetto education. *Harvard Educational Review, 40*(3), 411–451.

Rosenshine, B., & Furst, N. (1973). The use of direct observation to study teaching. In R. M. W. Travers (Ed.), *Second handbook of research on teaching* (pp. 122–183). Chicago: Rand McNally.

Sanders, J. T. (1978). Teacher effectiveness: Accepting the null hypothesis. *Journal of Education Thought, 12*(3), 184–189.

Sanders, J. T. (1981). Teacher effectiveness and the limits of psychological explanation. *McGill Journal of Education, 16*(1), 67–75.

Scheffler, I. (1960). *The language of education*. Springfield, IL: Charles C Thomas.

Schön, D. A. (1983). *The reflective practitioner: How Professionals think in action*. New York: Basic Books.

Schön, D. A. (1989). Professional knowledge and reflective practice. In T. J. Sergiovanni & J. H. Moore (Eds.), *Schooling for tomorrow: Directing reforms to issues that count* (pp. 188–206). Boston: Allyn & Bacon.

Schrag, F. (1981). Knowing and doing. *American Journal of Education, 89*, 253–282.

Sears, J. T. (1988, October). *The glass bead game of curriculum theorizing: Reconceptualism and the new orthodoxy*. Paper presented at the conference on Curriculum Theory and Classroom Practice, Dayton, OH.

Shor, I. (1986). Equality is excellence: Transforming teacher education and the learning process. *Harvard Educational Review, 56*(4), 406–426.

Shulman, L. S. (1986). Those who understand: Knowledge growth in teaching. *Educational Researcher, 15*(2), 4–14.

Shulman, L. S. (1987). The wisdom of practice: Managing complexity in medicine and teaching. In D. C. Berliner & B. V. Rosenshine (Eds.), *Talks to teachers: A festschrift for N. L. Gage* (pp. 369–386). New York: Random House.

Sleeter, C. E., & Grant, C. A. (1987). An analysis of multicultural education in the United States. *Harvard Educational Review, 57*, 421–444.

Smith, B. O. (1980). *A design for a school of pedagogy*. Washington, DC: U.S. Government Printing Office.

Smith, B. O. (1983). Some comments on educational research in the twentieth century. *Elementary School Journal, 83*(4), 488–492.

Smith, J. K. (1983). Quantitative versus qualitative research: An attempt to clarify the issue. *Educational Researcher, 12*(3), 6–13.

Tom, A. R. (1984). *Teaching as a moral craft*. New York: Longman.

Tom, A. R. (1987). A critique of the rationale for extended teacher preparation. *Educational Policy, 1*(1), 43–56.

Valli, L. (1986). *Becoming clerical workers*. Boston: Routledge & Kegan Paul.

van Manen, M. (1977). Linking ways of knowing with ways of being practical. *Curriculum Inquiry, 6*(3), 205–228.

Weiler, K. (1988). *Women teaching for change: Gender, class and power*. South Hadley, MA: Bergin & Garvey.

Weis, L. (1985). *Between two worlds: Black students in an urban community college*. Boston: Routledge & Kegan Paul.

Willis, P. E. (1977). *Learning to labour: How working class kids get working class jobs*. Farnborough, England: Saxon House.

Wise, A. E. (1986). Graduate teacher education and teacher professionalism. *Journal of Teacher Education, 37*(5), 36–40.

Zeichner, K. M. (1983). Alternative paradigms of teacher education. *Journal of Teacher Education, 34*(3), 3–9.

Zeichner, K. M., & Gore, J. (1990). Teacher socialization. In W. R. Houston, (Ed.), *Handbook of research on teacher education*. New York: Macmillan.

Zeuli, J. S., & Floden, R. E. (1987). Cultural incongruities and inequities of schooling: Implications for practice from ethnographic research. *Journal of Teacher Education, 38*(6), 9–15.

·22·

FOUNDATIONS OF EDUCATION IN
TEACHER EDUCATION

Kathryn M. Borman

UNIVERSITY OF CINCINNATI

The place of the foundations of education in teacher education has never been as important or as uncertain as it is today. The importance of a foundations perspective for students in teacher education can be illustrated by one of the issues confronting them at the moment. In the debate surrounding the reform of teacher education fueled by the succession of national, regional, and state commission reports, several models of teacher education have emerged. These models range from a strongly behaviorist, narrow conception of competency-based teacher education to a view of teacher education as primarily a means to empower and involve teachers fully in all phases of their own instruction, including the classroom- and school-based research that informs it (Beyer & Zeichner, 1982; Bowers, 1982; Garrison, 1988; Tom, 1986). Whatever model students are encouraged to adopt not only influences their classroom instruction but also affects their orientations to career, colleagues, and supervisors. A foundations perspective encourages reflective discussion of these implications (Pink, 1988).

The uncertainty of a foundations perspective is illustrated by the ferment in many institutions carrying out widespread change of their teacher education programs, primarily motivated by the Holmes initiative. Most Holmes Group institutions are in their second, third, or fourth years of full-scale, universitywide discussion of the specific coursework, interdepartmental arrangements, and alliances with arts and sciences faculty that are designed to lead to changed curricula by the early 1990s. It is not at all clear what benefits or costs will accrue to foundations perspectives and faculty who teach from these perspectives as a result of these changes.

A prevailing metaphor in many Holmes Group campus discussions is that of the teacher education student as apprentice to the experienced teacher. A particularly disturbing aspect of this image is its narrow focus on the classroom. The *student as apprentice* metaphor is a continuation of a long-prevailing vocational orientation toward teacher preparation in the United States, an orientation often highly valued by some for its supposed ideological neutrality (Beyer & Zeichner, 1982; Greene, 1976). However, education is more than the process of schooling in the classroom; its practice involves teachers in critical evaluations of the web of cultural, political, and social structures that surrounds them (Berlak & Berlak, 1981). To understand the process of schooling, students in teacher education must also come to understand the nexus of societal, school, and community influences that impinge upon classroom instruction.

As important in the preparation of teachers as classroom observation and other forms of apprenticeship might be, activities such as observing school board meetings, mapping community resources, and researching local job markets are equally imperative if students are to comprehend the forces influencing the outcome of the schooling process. Yet both the Holmes Group's 1986 report and the other recent major reform document, issued by the Carnegie Forum on Education and the Economy (1986), largely ignore the role of educational foundations in teacher education. Although the Holmes Group emphasizes the implications for the teacher education curriculum of the scientific study of teaching processes, the Carnegie Task Force extols the wisdom of practice as the primary source of content for the professional curriculum. Both of these emphases suggest models such as the teacher apprentice for

The author thanks reviewers William T. Pink (National College of Education) and Steve Tozer (University of Illinois). The author acknowledges the additional help of editor W. Robert Houston and editorial board member Alan Tom.

teacher education that might be limited in their scope and vision to an image of the teacher as a technical expert whose knowledge base has application only to the classroom.

A foundations curriculum in teacher education provides the tools for prospective teachers to determine the strengths and weaknesses of these and alternative images or models of teaching. It is also the vehicle for other kinds of knowledge and understanding. This chapter is organized to provide answers to the following questions. What is educational foundations? What are the demographics of courses in the field (e.g., Where are they taught? Who teaches them? Who takes them?) In considering the current context of educational foundations, the important questions center on two concerns. The first is directly linked to the current climate of educational reform and the reconstruction of teacher education in the wake of the Holmes initiative and the Carnegie report. Is the reorganization of schools of education and the portended takeover of teacher education by the liberal arts a threat to educational foundations? Or, on the contrary, do the winds of change promise to breathe new life into educational foundations in its role in teacher education (Clifford & Guthrie, 1988)?

The second concern is the particular focus of discussions among academic associations such as the American Educational Studies Association (AESA), which advance the political interests of educational foundations scholars. Not all faculty who instruct courses in foundations have had extensive graduate training in the field or are affiliated with those national organizations currently advocating an important place for educational foundations in teacher education. It is important to examine the role of professional organizations, particularly the AESA and its sister associations, the John Dewey Society, the Society of Professors of Education, the Philosophy of Education Society, and the History of Education Society. All of these groups have taken strong, activist roles in strengthening and maintaining the position of educational foundations in teacher education. What policies to strengthen the field are currently being put forward by these organizations? Do these policies show promise of contributing to the strengthening of teacher education, or are these organizations simply intent upon their own survival needs?

EDUCATIONAL FOUNDATIONS DEFINED

Although some observers might initially see the field of foundations of education as sprawling and incoherent, perhaps because foundations scholars cross disciplinary lines in their work, those who identify themselves as foundations scholars can quite clearly describe their areas of professional activity. They do so especially with reference to the particular perspectives informing their work. These interpretive, normative, and critical perspectives, more so than a strictly disciplinary orientation, set foundations scholars apart from their other colleagues. However, this emphasis on *perspectives* rather than *disciplines* must be qualified.

Historically, during its early development beyond the normal school, in the 1890s, teacher education in 4-year colleges and universities emphasized the scientific base of teaching

methods *and* studies in the so-called foundational disciplines of comparative education, history, philosophy, sociology, and psychology of education (Tozer & McAninich, 1986). In these early years, foundational studies viewed the field through an uncritical, normative lens, seeing education as adjustment and adaptation, as opposed to perceiving education as challenge and critique of the existing social order. It was not until the late 1920s through the 1940s that the "critical questioning of the social and educational order" encouraged a cross-disciplinary, integrated approach to educational and social processes, ideas, and institutions (Tozer & McAninich, 1986, p. 9).

The clearest current statement defining the field of educational foundations is, not surprisingly, found in a publication of the seven-member Council of Learned Societies in Education, composed of the following national organizations: the American Educational Studies Association, the Comparative and International Society, the History of Education Society, the John Dewey Society, the Philosophy of Education Society, the Society for Educational Reconstruction, and the Society of Professors of Education. These associations have been a loosely constructed confederacy since 1982. Their collective interest is served by the publication and enforcement of a set of *Standards for Academic and Professional Instruction in Foundations of Education, Educational Studies, and Educational Policy Studies* (Council of Learned Societies in Education, 1986), first published by AESA in 1975, well before the current reform movement in teacher education was underway. It is clear that the AESA has been the major impetus behind the effort to establish a set of uniform standards, or criteria, to define the role of educational foundations in teacher education. The *Standards* are an important manifestation of that mission.

According to the *Standards*, the foremost characteristic of educational foundations is that it is "broadly conceived" and cross-disciplinary and "derives its character and fundamental theories from a number of academic disciplines, combinations of disciplines, and area studies: history, philosophy, sociology, anthropology, religion, political science, economics, psychology, comparative and international education, educational studies, and educational policy studies" (Council of Learned Societies in Education, 1986, p. 3). Study in these areas and disciplines as part of teacher education accompanied the shift from 2-year normal-school education and the move from a merely technical orientation for teachers to current 4-year teacher education degree programs at around the turn of the century. The *Standards* consider the relationship between educational foundations and both teacher educators and scholars whose work is discipline based and whose academic homes are usually departments and programs in the liberal arts. The orientation of foundations faculty to the education of teachers, as opposed to their own particular disciplines is problematic. Also at issue is the question of whether foundations courses and scholarship should target social problems or should more directly aim at specific theoretical concerns in one or another of the foundations disciplines. The *Standards* back away from a position that is supportive of one scholarly orientation or another and simply acknowledge that "there are distinguished advocates for all approaches" (p. 3). Rather than deriving from incoherence in the field of educational foundations, these debates and tensions are grounded within the debates of the parent disciplines themselves and, thus, are present in the structure of sociology of education, anthropology of education, philosophy of education, and the other foundational disciplines in this post-Kuhnian era.

What holds foundations scholars together despite the diversity in their disciplinary allegiances? According to the *Standards*, the common credo is a strong commitment to "the development of interpretive, normative and critical perspectives on education" including nonschooling enterprises. And, although there are a number of historians among the ranks of foundations scholars, a "strong concern for present circumstances, events and conditions" (Council of Learned Societies in Education, 1986, p. 4) underscores and augments the field's roots in the social reconstructionism of the 1930s. Not surprisingly, foundations faculty have been quick to rally around the major social concerns of the day, usually advocating the elimination of elitist tendencies in educational institutions at all levels. The career of Maxine Greene at Teachers College presents a notable example. Her work has resolutely entered into the thicket of important social considerations and reflects her ongoing concerns, as a foundations scholar, with all the major issues, most recently literacy (Borman, 1986; Greene, 1986).

Thus, in reference to current debates about directions in the reform of teacher education, foundations scholars generally serve as advocates for the empowerment of teachers. They reject models of competency-based teacher education, for example, because these frameworks reduce the teacher's role to that of technician, as opposed to major social actor and professionally empowered and autonomous decision maker. Generally, they oppose the perceived elitism of the Holmes Group consortium of research universities, and argue strenuously for a perspective in teacher education that "sharpens students' abilities to examine and explain educational proposals, arrangements, and practices and to develop a disciplined sense of policy-oriented educational responsibility" (Council of Learned Societies in Education, 1986, p. 5). These attributes are developed through the interweave of the interpretive, normative, and critical perspectives mentioned previously.

Three perspectives undergird all inquiry and instruction offered in the name of educational foundations scholarship. *The interpretive perspectives* use theories and resources from the humanities and the social and behavioral sciences to explain education in different contexts. These contexts and their underlying belief structures can be perceived differently from various historical, philosophical, cultural, and social-class perspectives. Thus, the ultimate goal of the interpretive perspectives in teacher education is to equip practitioners with resources, incentives, and skills necessary to achieve a deeper level of understanding and comprehension of educational thought and practice.

The normative perspectives assist students in examining and explaining education in light of value orientations. Normative and ethical references on educational development, thought, and practice and policy-making are probed. The ultimate goal of the normative perspectives is to encourage students in teacher education to develop their own value positions on the basis of critical study and reflection.

Finally, *the critical perspectives* assist students in examining and explaining education in light of its origins, major influences, and consequences. The critical perspectives are particularly important in enabling students to examine equality and inequality in the distribution of educational opportunity and outcomes, patterns of past and present exclusion in education, causes of exclusion and inequality, and educational needs and aspirations of excluded minorities. The ultimate goal of these perspectives is to encourage the development of policy-making perspectives and skills in searching for resolutions to educational problems and issues.

Thus, educational foundations as a field has the unique role in teacher education of encouraging both knowledge about current societal issues related to education and understanding of how these are related to classroom processes. The foundational perspectives also fuel active engagement in educational policy formation. The acquisition of these skills is interdisciplinary and rooted in the use of the humanities and the social and behavioral sciences as the fundamental tools for achieving them.

EDUCATIONAL FOUNDATIONS COURSEWORK AND TEACHER EDUCATION

Given the diversity of orientations within the field of educational foundations, it follows that no single focus for an introductory course or courses for students in teacher education prevails. In fact, development of a consensus within a department of educational foundations, educational studies, or educational policy studies is likely to present in microcosm the national debate among foundations scholars. Foundations scholars are, however, at least according to the *Standards*, uniformly guided by their orientation to the normative, interpretive, and critical perspectives on educational institutions, including formal and informal schooling and educational processes. Nonetheless, what constitutes foundations coursework for students in teacher education is problematic.

There have been several attempts to compile information about what is taught in educational foundations courses. For example, Bartos and Souter (1982) reviewed syllabi for introductory courses in educational foundations from 81 institutions across the country. In addition, they obtained data on the amount of time devoted to particular topics included in these courses from 46 of their respondents. Fifteen topics were mentioned on the syllabi analyzed for this study. "Current issues" and "history of education" were the 2 most frequently mentioned topics, appearing in 10 percent of the syllabi. Those responding to the questionnaire indicated that the largest percentage of time in the course (13 percent) was allocated to each of these topics. Together, then, history and current issues took up more than 25 percent of instructional time in the introductory course, according to Bartos and Souter's respondents. Overall, the authors conclude that "there is agreement that the topics of history, current issues, the teaching professional, the school organization and administration, educational philosophy and society and culture should be included in the course content of an introductory education course" (p. 46).

These topics seem well chosen to fulfill the role of educational foundations coursework in teacher education to provide the knowledge and understanding of the social forces surrounding education, informed by the humanities and social and behavioral sciences. However, it is not the topics themselves that define the educational foundations enterprise. Rather, it is the critical, normative, and interpretive methodological approaches that distinguish a foundations approach from a mere introduction to education.

The Lucas and Cockriel Study. In another more comprehensive study of courses in foundations of education in teacher preparation, Lucas and Cockriel (1981) surveyed 380 schools, colleges, and departments of education. One purpose of their study was to investigate the effect of climate on course offerings. By climate, Lucas and Cockriel meant the location of a particular unit in a public or private institutional context. Their measure of climate also included size. Small institutions were those with less than 500 enrolled students; those in the middle range had between 500 and 1,499 students; and large units had more than 1,500 full-time students in education. Almost half (49 percent) of their sample was representative of small, private colleges with departments of education, whereas the smallest percentage (2 percent) represented large, private institutions. Almost equal numbers of public institutions were represented across the three dimensions. The median number of students enrolled in a unit was 475 undergraduates majoring in education.

Interestingly, size had no particular effect on the amount of coursework required for the baccalaureate degree in education. The range was from 120 to 139 semester hours, with an average of 124 hours. In addition, the number of credit hours for coursework in educational foundations hardly varied across the public and private units surveyed in this study. Overall, both types demanded close to 5 credit hours, a rather small portion of the 124 hours required on average for completion of the degree. As opposed to either of the two institutional variables that had no appreciable effect, student status as an elementary or secondary education major *did* make a difference in the amount of required coursework in educational foundations at the baccalaureate level. On average, almost one-fifth of all program hours acquired by undergraduates majoring in secondary education were courses in educational foundations. In contrast, elementary education majors invested only 15 percent of their time in foundations studies.

In their focus on the content of curricula in courses offered under the rubric of educational foundations, Lucas and Cockriel (1981) used four statements from the *Standards* as options from which their respondents could select the description characterizing undergraduate coursework in educational foundations at their respective institutions. As noted previously, the *Standards* suggest four possibilities: (a) "Concepts and/or issues"; (b) "concerns. . . . [that] transcend specific discipline-based approaches"; (c) a discipline-based approach; and (d) a curriculum based on "the concepts, problems and concerns of teacher-educators across the field of education" (Council of Learned Societies in Education, 1986, p. 13).

Lucas and Cockriel (1981) learned that the *concepts and issues* approach was the most frequently mentioned, particu-

larly by respondents in private institutions. Forty-three pe cent overall selected this option. Ranked second among t four choices was the *interdisciplinary and generalist* approac selected by 22 percent of the respondents. The remaining tw options were ranked rather similarly, with approximately 1 percent of the respondents selecting either the *discipline-or ented* or the *teacher educator–oriented* options.

When Lucas and Cockriel (1981) provided their respo dents a list of 24 course topics or organizational framework for foundations coursework at the undergraduate level, the obtained some rather interesting results, allowing them to di cuss course content with greater specificity. Fourteen of the 2 options were cited by 10 percent or more of those responding Introduction to education was mentioned by 60 percent those responding. As should now be apparent, introduction t education courses might or might not reflect a foundations per spective. Philosophy of education, one of the perennial founda tional disciplines, followed closely, with 58 percent indicatin such a course. History of American education, curriculum the ory, (humanistic) psychology of education, and issues an trends in education were closely grouped together, all men tioned by approximately 35 percent of those responding. I the next tier, selected by between 25 and 29 percent of those surveyed, were school law, social foundations of education, multi-cultural education, and school organization and manage ment. In the bottom sector, with between 15 and 22 percen selecting them, were comparative education, human relation in education, sociology of education, and history of educationa thought.

In an effort further to refine knowledge about the actual curricular contents of courses in educational foundations, Lu cas and Cockriel (1981) subsequently analyzed specific instruc tional approaches used in courses at the introductory level in teacher education having an educational foundations content. Their sample included a group of 55 institutions selected as representative of the full taxonomy of institutional control (i.e., public or private) and size dimensions. In summarizing the findings from this portion of their research, the authors state:

First, in . . . [programs requiring] only one foundations course, proba-bilities favor its being an omnibus, multipurpose survey of the field of education. Secondly, general foundations courses tend to be organized around issues, trends or concepts in education; this approach predomi-nates over all others. Thirdly, the teaching of philosophy of education still reflects in the greatest percentage of cases a "school of thought" approach utilizing labels such as Idealism, Realism, Pragmatism and so forth. . . . Finally, the term "foundations of education" or its equiv-alent is a rubric for describing *one component* of courses, each of which may differ from others significantly in terms of subject matter of con-tent, objectives, organization, and instructional approaches. (p. 359)

Among their rather disturbing conclusions overall, in view of the coursework in teacher education mandated by the *Stan-dards*, was the finding that only a relatively small percentage of those responding (less than a third) indicated that students devoted as much as 16.6 percent of their credit hours to courses in foundations. By far, the majority of these students (75 percent) fulfilled the requirement by enrolling in a single course during their undergraduate careers.

The Bauer and Borman Study. In a more recent study, Bauer and Borman (1988) undertook a systematic review of current U.S. college and university catalogs to determine the nature of course offerings in teacher education in the field of educational foundations. The investigation focused upon curricula and mission statements for colleges, departments, and programs offering coursework in educational foundations.

The initial selection of public and private institutions was made from the standard reference on higher education, *American Universities and Colleges* (American Council on Education, 1987). An effort was made during this initial selection process to identify a public and a private institution offering a degree in teacher education in each of the 50 states. However, two states (Nevada and Wyoming) have no private college or university offering such a program. Ultimately, 49 private and 51 public colleges and universities representing the 50 states were selected. Across these institutions, a total of 508 courses in educational foundations were identified in the catalogs examined during the course of the study. In their earlier study, Lucas and Cockriel (1981) had identified introduction to education and philosophy of education as the courses most frequently offered in the undergraduate teacher education curricula described by their respondents. In the current results, shown in Table 22-1, multicultural education, ranked a distant ninth in the earlier study, was, along with the traditional front-runner, philosophy of education, the most frequently listed course in the materials reviewed.

Another contrast to the earlier study was an apparent decline in the status of school law courses. Ranked seventh in the Lucas and Cockriel survey, a highly ranked newcomer in our

study was sociology of education. Others, including trends in education, foundations of education, and school and society, were all as frequently present in course listings as they had been in the earlier study. Although they comprised only a fraction (less than 5 percent) of the courses listed, human relations and education, urban education, and sociology of sex roles/gender issues, all absent from the earlier rankings, *did* appear in the catalogs reviewed in 1988. These courses have in common with each other, and with multicultural education, a concern with equity issues and issues related to social problems. Thus, it could be concluded that, during the decade of the 1980s, educational foundations as a field became more involved with educational equity issues in coursework offered to students in teacher education. This emphasis contrasts with the earlier apolitical, more strictly disciplinary and academic, focus during the late 1970s, as reported by Lucas and Cockriel (1981).

EDUCATIONAL FOUNDATIONS COURSES

Although the nature of educational foundations coursework in teacher-preparation programs varies from one institution to the next, the likelihood that students will encounter such coursework at some point in their undergraduate careers is relatively great. As is clear from the surveys of faculty and institutions discussed previously, at least one course in the undergraduate sequence is offered in each program examined by each set of researchers whose findings were analyzed in the previous section. Further evidence suggests that it is likely to be required coursework (Jones, 1988).

TABLE 22–1. Undergraduate Foundations of Education Courses

Courses	Rank Order	Number of Courses Listed	Percentage of Total
Philosophy of education	1	63	12.4
Multicultural education	1	63	12.4
History of American education	2	58	11.4
Issues and trends in education	3	47	9.25
Sociology of education	4	43	8.5
Foundations of education	5	36	7.5
School and society	6	32	6.3
Special topics, readings	7	18	3.5
Comparative education	8	16	3.1
Human relations and education	8	16	3.1
Urban education	9	15	3
School organization, management	10	14	2.75
Curriculum theory	11	11	2.2
Sociology of sex roles/gender issues	12	10	2
Education in other countries	12	10	2
Economics/politics of education	13	8	1.6
School law	14	7	1.4
Humanistic psychology of education	15	5	1
School policy	15	5	1
Educational anthropology	15	5	1
Total Courses		508	

Courses listed two times or less: seminar in athletic education; learning principles for school and environment; religion and education.

Note: Compiled from catalogs for 100 U.S. public and private universities and colleges offering courses in foundations of education.

Students and Educational Foundations Courses

This section focuses on the response of students to course-work in educational foundations. The question here is, To what extent do students in teacher education value the instruction they receive in educational foundations courses? In an initial study of 652 junior and senior students in teacher education at Ball State University, Birkel (1983) reported an overall high regard for courses in educational foundations expressed by these students. Specifically, students valued the sociological aspects of educational foundations, placing least value on the historical and philosophical dimensions. This pattern of findings held for students whether or not they had completed a student-teaching experience. In a subsequent study of a similar group of 367 secondary education students, Birkel (1983) found that the same high regard for educational foundations was also apparent.

In examining 18 specific dimensions of coursework in educational foundations, Birkel asked respondents to indicate to what extent they valued a range of insights and perspectives drawn from among historical, philosophical, and sociological foundations of education. Among the 18 items, those most valued by students were either the ones most closely tied to current equity issues or, to a lesser extent, the ones allowing a more general appraisal of the purpose of education. Thus, the highest ranked item ("An awareness of differing patterns and values among different social classes") was accorded "much value" by 70 percent of the students responding. Ranked second and third, with approximately 60 percent placing "much value" on the items, were the following: "A consideration of such questions as school integration and equality of opportunity" and "An inquiry into the purpose of education." The lowest ranked item, with fewer than 17 percent according it "much value," was "A study of various recognized systems of thought that influence our current educational practice, such as essentialism, pragmatism, and existentialism." Based on his review of these findings, Birkel recommends that, although sociological concerns in education might arguably form the most compelling substantive content for coursework for students in teacher education, philosophical questions to examine these social concerns could be integrated into the curriculum, and historical aspects of the issues might be offered as background material in analyzing the contemporary issues of value to students. In other words, according to the student responses he received, Birkel recommends coursework in foundations that is cross-disciplinary, organized to include a focus on current social issues such as equity and educational excellence, and framed with sociological concepts.

In another, more recent, study of students' views, Dawson, Mazurek, and DeYoung (1984) surveyed a total of 615 students attending two large universities. Survey forms were distributed to them during the course of their upper-year foundations coursework. The researchers noted that in both universities a variety of courses was offered under the rubric of educational foundations; however, all courses offered at these two institutions were designed to promote "the cultivation of analytic skills which are perceived to facilitate teachers' abilities to evaluate educational policy decisions constructively and critically, and to allow future teachers a fuller participation in the establishment and direction of policies" (p. 248). This, the authors acknowledge, is "a long term and subtle pedagogical goal" (p. 248).

To assess students' perceptions of the strengths and importance of educational foundations courses in their teacher-training programs, these researchers requested their respondents to indicate the extent to which they agreed or disagreed with a number of statements regarding the importance of foundational studies for their future careers. Overall, approximately two-thirds of the students surveyed agreed that foundations courses (a) "have given me a better understanding of modern education," (b) "were valuable for all prospective teachers," and (c) "were a necessary and desirable element in our teacher training program." Moreover, there was general agreement among those responding that the content of educational foundations courses is not adequately covered in other educational courses.

Given these results, together with those from the two Birkel studies, it seems appropriate to conclude that coursework in educational foundations is well regarded and valued by those undergraduate students in teacher education surveyed in these reports. Evidence from recent AESA syllabi sessions at that organization's annual meetings over the last 5 years also suggests that these courses are highly rated by students. Such courses, especially when their contents highlight current social issues and sociological concepts, are seen as particularly informative and valuable.

Faculty and Educational Foundations Courses

The faculty who teach foundations courses and the nature of texts that they are likely to include in their undergraduate instruction are important dimensions. Not surprisingly, most research examining the quality of faculty and course materials has been conducted by scholar advocates for a foundations perspective in teacher education. These researchers are guided by a concern to educate others in the field of foundations from the perspectives of normative, interpretive, and critical inquiry and to provide a platform for designing policies to benefit its development (Jones, 1988).

In their study of faculty offering instruction in educational foundations courses, Shea and Henry (1986) were concerned to "develop a composite profile of personnel teaching social foundations courses" (p. 11). In addition, they concluded their research report with a strong set of policy recommendations. To investigate the credentials of foundations faculty, Shea and Henry surveyed 753 foundations faculty from the AESA mailing list. It was assumed that these individuals had strong professional identities tied to the field. Of the 753 social foundations faculty contacted, 242 responded with usable information. Among the important findings was the fact that 67 percent of those responding had earned doctoral degrees in the traditional social foundations concentrations. Specifically, 19 percent had obtained degrees in history of education; 16 percent in philosophy of education; 10 percent in educational foundations; 8 percent in comparative education, and 6 percent in educational administration. Of the 242, 19 percent had obtained the advanced degree (PhD or EdD) in an educationally related field, and 11 percent had doctorates in noneducation fields. These numbers contrasted with the 98 percent of chemistry instructors in higher education also surveyed by Shea and Henry who held doctorates in the cognate field in which they taught.

The importance of so many nonfoundations specialists and the quality of their courses warrants further systematic research. There is no mandate that introduction to education courses be wedded to either a disciplinary or a cross-disciplinary emphasis or to a set of perspectives grounded in the interpretive, normative, and critical analyses of schools and society. Critics such as Diane Ravitch and others before her have railed against teacher education curricula that feature " 'Mickey Mouse' courses in educational theory" (1985, p. 94). These courses may in fact be taught by individuals whose backgrounds are not solidly informed by study in the foundational disciplines. As we have seen, courses in the foundations are highly valued by those whose instructors are, in fact, foundations specialists.

When Shea and Henry examined the background coursework completed by their respondents during their graduate careers, interesting cohort patterns emerged. For those who had been in the field for 15 years or less, preparation was more focused on coursework in the traditional foundations areas such as history of education, sociology of education, comparative education, and social foundations of education than for cohorts with more years' experience following the award of the doctoral degree.

Finally, in examining institutional differences in the kinds of courses and the amount of coursework completed in the various foundations subject areas, Shea and Henry considered contrasts between public and private institutions and Catholic universities. Those who had attended public or private institutions for their doctoral work reported greater investment in courses in policy analysis, educational administration, research, and urban education than those with degrees from Catholic universities. In turn, the latter, as a group, took an average of 10 courses in philosophy of education, while those from the other programs averaged less than four courses in this area.

In summary, from what we know about students enrolled in courses in educational foundations and their instructors, we can conclude that at least some undergraduate students are generally enthusiastic about and value the contents of these courses, courses they believe cover a unique set of topics of current social concern. Although students express quite positive responses to their coursework in educational foundations, it should be kept in mind that the great majority of those in teacher education are required to take only a single course in this area. On average, this represents an investment of as little as 5 percent of their coursework overall. Finally, those who teach educational foundations courses are likely to have had doctoral training in one of the related foundations disciplines. Approximately 60 percent of those responding in the Shea and Henry study reported background training of this kind, but the remainder, close to 40 percent, were not so educated. Given these data, it is imperative that textbooks in the field be structured and arranged to assist faculty without a strong foundations background to work effectively with the major concepts in the field as they instruct foundations courses.

Texts in Educational Foundations Courses

Unfortunately, it appears that the textbooks in foundations available for undergraduate courses in teacher education present a problem. In their analysis of social foundations texts, Tozer and McAninich (1986) determined that the market is dominated by a highly inadequate set of texts. The authors framed their discussion of current texts in the field in a useful analysis of the genesis and development of educational foundations as an area of graduate study and scholarship. In this and in a subsequent analysis more closely focused on the field of educational foundations per se, they adopted Harold Rugg's (1952) framework for evaluating the evolution of teacher education and the place of educational foundations in those developments. Rugg saw the field of teacher preparation and the role of educational foundations as having two distinct phases. During the first period (1890–1920), coursework in the foundations field was strongly connected to the disciplines, specifically to philosophy, history, psychology, and sociology of education. Tozer and McAninich argue that, through a curriculum of this nature, future teachers learned "to take their places as preservers of the social order" as opposed to "critical students of the social order" (1986, p. 7). The textbooks of the times mirrored the accepted norms in teacher education, which emphasized maintenance of the status quo and acceptance of a conservative social and political order.

A much stronger social and political critique emerged during the period identified by Rugg (and also by Tozer & McAninich, 1987, p. 22) as the Second Draft (1920–1950). Textbooks developing a deeper understanding of social foundations perspectives were framed by faculty and scholars in the newly emergent programs in educational foundations at three of the major graduate training centers in the field at that time: Columbia's Teachers College, The Ohio State University and the University of Illinois. These texts emphasized a cross-disciplinary analysis of social problems, such as the effect of the depression on economic, political, and social institutions, and urged major reform of education and schools, along with massive social changes across all institutions.

The fervor of social reconstructionism was, of course, ultimately replaced in the postwar years by the grey-flannel suited organization man, "the lonely crowd," and other parallel images depicting the dilemma of the individual in mass society. During this period, according to Tozer and McAninich, instruction in educational foundations and the curriculum of the leading texts "encouraged a considerable amount of inquiry into fundamental issues concerning distribution and uses of social and economic power" (Tozer & McAninich, 1986, p. 15). In addition, many authors explicitly encouraged values reminiscent of the social reconstructionism of the 1930s in such influential texts as Stanley, Smith, Benne, and Anderson's edited volume, *Social Foundations of Education* (1956). These texts activated students' development within the parameters set by liberal democratic values and ideals of cooperative, social-scientific problem solving and of their own analyses and normative evaluations of the aims and processes of American education and society (Tozer & McAninich, 1986, p. 15).

Most of the textbooks currently available for use in undergraduate educational foundations courses tend to provide superficial analyses of social and historical phenomena, presenting the sweep of black history, for example, in two or three sentences. Tozer and McAninich conclude that the major problem with current texts is that their authors lack an understanding "of the unique possibilities and responsibilities social foundations of education can claim as its conceptual territory in undergraduate education" (Tozer & McAninich, 1986, p. 31). If their analysis is correct, the problem of nonfoundations specialists teaching in the field is compounded by the lack of well-conceived texts for undergraduate instruction.

STRENGTHENING THE ROLE OF EDUCATIONAL FOUNDATIONS IN TEACHER EDUCATION

Educational foundations has historically fared well as a field during periods of reform and change in teacher education. There is no reason why current reform efforts should not launch a Fourth Draft similar to the period at the turn of the century, when teacher education moved from the circumscribed and highly technical orientation of the normal school to a burgeoning knowledge base grounded in the disciplines and sufficiently broad and complex to require a 4-year degree program.

Paradoxically, perhaps, today's reforms call for *both* an increase in the number of years of preprofessional studies, with postponement of focused study in the field of education until the fifth year, *and* a closer alliance with practitioners. In their candid account of developments in the nation's ranking colleges of education, *Ed School*, Clifford and Guthrie (1988) argue persuasively for a set of changes that would promote alliances with teachers and others in the field at the same time that placement in the field would be delayed until after the undergraduate degree had been achieved. Their model is cautiously drawn to correspond to the professional education of physicians and lawyers; Cautiously drawn because they clearly desire that education as a field neither attempt to apologize for itself nor be organized to gain status as a full profession.

If the reforms that are underway *do* change the face of teacher education programs both by reorienting them to practitioners (and away from the more academic side of higher education) and by lengthening and reorganizing the educational program for students of teacher education, what, then could we expect the role of educational foundations to be? Before this question can be answered, it is crucially important to acknowledge the deep and highly public criticism of educational foundations that circulates in the community of educational researchers and scholars. These are issues that foundations scholars themselves must begin to address if they wish to make their bid for greater inclusion in programs of teacher education.

First, it is not clear that full knowledge of the foundations perspectives enhances the effectiveness of classroom teachers. Put another way, foundations coursework in teacher education does not easily link up with improved efficiency and achievement in the classroom setting on the part of students instructed by those who have had such coursework. Most foundations scholars reject an experimentalist orientation to the question of whether or not a background in educational foundations promotes more effective classroom instruction and management, greater student achievement and the like. These, it is argued, are the wrong outcomes to be evaluated in the first place. Rather, what is more to the point is whether teachers versed in foundations are indeed sharper and more knowledgeable in their critique of educational issues, policies, and institutions and if, in turn, their students are more socially aware and more fervently activist in their orientations to these same matters.

The impact of coursework in educational foundations on attitudes, beliefs, and behaviors might be, as foundations scholars assert, virtually impossible to measure. Nonetheless, there will always be critics such as B. O. Smith and Diane Ravitch who assert that "academic pedagogical knowledge . . . seldom yields teaching prescriptions" or that "theory has value in the art of teaching only if 'theory' is used to mean empirical clinical knowledge" (B. O. Smith, 1980, p. 89). In other words, the highly technical model of the student teacher as apprentice to the experienced journeyman classroom teacher continues to be valued by some of educational foundations' harshest critics. The unfortunate consequence is that this perspective negates and devalues the image of the reflective, autonomous, and empowered teacher.

Second, the problem of aligning teacher education coursework in foundations with the disciplinary departments in universities, as contrasted with creating stronger ties with practitioners in the field, is far from resolved. The Clifford and Guthrie formula for altering these arrangements emphasizes closer ties to practitioners and seems also to relegate foundations as a field to the dustbin of higher education. Clifford and Guthrie seem to equate developments in the field of foundations with a suicidal orientation to the academic disciplines, in part because their discussion of educational foundations programs is limited to Teachers College, Columbia (Clifford & Guthrie, 1988, pp. 232–237). At Teachers College and at other ranking schools of education during the 1960s and 1970s, foundations departments were frequently merged with programs in educational administration and often reoriented toward policy studies, perhaps to attract a greater flow of federal grant monies. The consequence of this organizational shift and the rise of revisionist scholarship in the 1970s served to splinter and weaken educational foundations as a field, according to Clifford and Guthrie's account. Revisionism, in fact, drove the final nail into the coffin of foundations of education because its "expose of schools and schoolmen [sic] linked the foundations disciplines more closely with university scholarship, especially New Left historiography and sociology—hardly a development calculated to appeal to most teachers and other school professionals" (Clifford & Guthrie, 1988, p. 236). This seems a partial and weak analysis of both revisionist scholarship and the highly exaggerated reports of the death of foundations as a field due to its removal from alliances with practitioners. In fact, as we have seen, foundations courses flourish in hundreds of teacher education programs and are highly regarded by many students. Moreover, in his recent survey of deans, directors, and chairs at member institutions of the American Association of Colleges for Teachers Education, Jones (1988) determined that the preponderant number of those responding indicated support for both the national accreditation standards requiring study in the social foundations of education and the *Standards* by the Council of Learned Societies in Education.

If a Fourth Draft alters the organization and substance of teacher education and if educational foundations emerges with a crucial role in these changes, we could logically expect a model of teacher empowerment and autonomy to be at the center of a foundations perspective. This claim is based both on the historical record of foundations scholarship and teaching and the direction undertaken by those currently doing work in the field. Most of these foundations faculty are on campuses of colleges and universities throughout the broad midsection of the country. Indeed, there seems to be a "coastal bias" against educational foundations; the field is weakest on the West Coast, as gauged by AESA membership rolls and the absence of foundations departments in most West Coast colleges and universities.

On those campuses where educational foundations faculty appear to form a critical mass, there is opportunity to build a coherent foundations core curriculum in teacher education and, on the graduate level, to construct doctoral programs in concert with faculty in related arts and sciences disciplines. From the institutional point of view, these arrangements make good economic sense. Resources can be shared across academic units, interdisciplinary studies can be undertaken, and joint course offerings can be made. In fact, this profile is currently present in some form at the University of Illinois, the University of Cincinnati, the State University of New York—Buffalo, the University of Minnesota, the University of Kentucky, the University of Tennessee, the University of Virginia, the University of Wisconsin, and Washington University, among others. However, smaller colleges and universities such as Miami University (Ohio) and Ohio University, with committed, vocal faculties can also exert serious influence on the field and on teacher education on their own campuses.

At Ohio University, for example, Wood has forged a strong network of classroom teachers, foundations scholars, and students in teacher education through the Institute for Democracy in Education (IDE). Far from exemplifying the New Left scholar alienated from practitioners, Wood's career illustrates the new foundations concerns, present since the 1970s, with critiquing the classist (racist and sexist) biases inherent in the school curriculum and social organization of schooling, especially, in the latter case, the consequences of academic tracking arrangements.

The link to John Dewey is apparent in both the IDE's name and mission. In the institute's publication, ("*The* magazine for classroom teachers") *Democracy and Education*, the following Statement of Purpose appears:

IDE is a partnership of all participants in the educational process—teachers, administrators, parents and students—who believe that democratic school change must come from those at the heart of education.

IDE promotes educational practices that provide students with experiences through which they can develop democratic attitudes and values. Only by living them can students develop the democratic ideals of equality, liberty and community.

IDE works to provide teachers committed to democratic education with a forum for sharing ideas with a support network of people holding similar values and with opportunities for professional development. (Institute for Democracy in Education [IDE], 1988, p. 1)

The familiar themes in foundations scholarship of antielitism, equalitarian social relations in all institutional spheres, and *communitas* are visible in the institute's mission. If all this sounds utopian, recall that foundations' roots are still quite strong in the social reconstructionism of the 1930s and the challenge to dare to build a new social order through the schools.

However, the major impetus to create the Institute for Democratic Education has been concern to counter the damaging criticism of teachers in reports such as *A Nation at Risk* (National Commission on Excellence in Education, 1983) and the even more forcible Holmes and Carnegie reports. In an editorial entitled "A Voice for Progressive Change," Wood declares that, as critics demanded that classroom teachers engage in more testing, more homework assignments and "more everything," the "single-minded pursuit of higher standardized test scores crushed the idealism of those who became teachers to help young people become active and inquisitive participants in democracy" (IDE, 1988). It, therefore, became the task of the institute to create a network of support and encouragement by linking practitioners in the field with academics at the university.

The journals put out by the institute illustrate the close connection between practitioners and foundations scholars in higher education, suggesting a model of the teacher as researcher. Indeed, the thrust of the institute's work and, by extension, the work of foundations faculty everywhere, is to engage in collaborative research and reflective study in exploring problems and issues of concern to practitioners. In the publication's first appearance as a journal, articles, most of them written by classroom teachers, focused on how students could play an active role in their own learning (as described by Eliot Wigginton, founder of the *Foxfire* program); how classroom teachers could deal with racism and sexism in early childhood education; and alternatives to ability grouping.

By developing normative, interpretive, and critical perspectives on the teaching and learning process and on institutional patterns and societal practices more generally, foundations scholars and teachers can and do play an important role in teacher education. This chapter has attempted to illustrate the ways this has been true historically, as well as the manner in which problems have beset the field, most of them resulting from lack of understanding of the unique structure of foundational studies constructed by both the disciplines and the normative, interpretive, and critical perspectives. In the frenzied attempt to professionalize teacher education, current reformers of teacher education must take into account the less easily measured outcomes educational foundations curricula have historically espoused. It is not enough to attend to the scientific knowledge base from the psychological side, even though this might appear somehow to be more discrete and, therefore, easier to lecture about or somehow more scientific and, therefore, easier to measure in its impact on practice.

References

American Council on Education (1987). *American universities and colleges.* New York: Walter de Gruyter.

Bartos, R., & Souter, F. (1982). What are we teaching in educational foundations? *Journal of Teacher Education, 33*(2), 45–47.

Bauer, L., & Borman, K. (1988). *A review of educational foundations courses offered in U.S. colleges and universities.* Unpublished manuscript: University of Cincinnati.

Berlak, A., & Berlak, H. (1981). *Social Change.* London: Methuen.

Beyer, L. E., & Zeichner, K. M. (1982). Teacher training and educational foundations. A plea for discontent. *Journal of Teacher Education, 33*(3), 18–23.

Birkel, L. I. (1983). How students view foundational studies in education. *Teacher Education, 5,* 79–87.

Borman, K. M. (1986). An ethnography of the American Educational Studies Association: A collective insider's perspective on the organization (AESA Presidential Address). *Educational Studies, 11,* 337–363.

Bowers, C. A. (1982). The reproduction of technological consciousness: Locating the ideological foundations of a radical pedagogy. *Teachers College Record 83,* 529–557.

Carnegie Forum on Education and the Economy, Task Force on Teaching as a Profession (1986). *A Nation prepared: Teachers for the 21st century.* New York: Author.

Clifford, G. J., & Guthrie, J. W. (1988). *Ed school: A brief for professional education.* Chicago: University of Chicago Press.

Council of Learned Societies in Education. (1986). *Standards for academic and professional instruction in foundations of education, educational studies and educational policy studies.* Ann Arbor, MI: Prakken.

Dawson, D., Mazurek, K., & DeYoung, A. J. (1984). Courses in the social foundations of education: The students' view. *Journal of Education for Teaching, 10*(3), 242–248.

Garrison, J. W. (1988). Democracy, scientific knowledge and teacher empowerment. *Teachers College Record, 89,* 487–503.

Greene, M. (1976). Challenging mystification: Educational foundations in dark times. *Educational Studies, 7*(10), 9–29.

Green, M. (1986). Toward possibility: Expanding the range of literacy. *English Education 18,* 231–243.

Holmes Group. (1986). *Tomorrow's Teachers.* East Lansing, MI: Author.

Institute for Democracy in Education. (1988). *Democracy and Education, 3*(1).

Jones, A. R. (1988). *The individual and the scholarly community in the social foundations of education: Some political propositions.* Presidential address to the meeting of the American Educational Studies Association, Toronto.

Lucas, C., & Cockriel, I. (1981). The foundations of education in teacher preparation: A national assessment. *Educational Studies, 11,* 337–363.

National Commission on Excellence in Education. (1983). *A nation at risk: The imperative for educational reform.* Washington, DC: U.S. Government Printing Office.

Pink, W. T. (1988). The new equity: Competing visions. In C. Shea, E. Kahane, & P. Sola (Eds.), *The new servants of power* (pp. 123–134). New York: Greenwood Press.

Ravitch, D. (1985). *The troubled crusade.* New York: Basic Books.

Raywid, M. A., Tesconi, C. A., & Warren, D. R. (1984). *Pride and promise: Schools of excellence for all the people.* Westbury, NY: American Educational Studies Association.

Rugg, H. (1952). *The teacher of teachers.* New York: Harper and Brothers.

Shea, C. M., & Henry, C. A. (1986). Who's teaching the social foundations? *Journal of Teacher Education, 37*(2), 10–15.

Smith, B. O. (1980). *A design for a school of pedagogy.* Washington, DC: U.S. Government Printing Office.

Stanley, W. O., Smith, B. O., Benne, K. D., & Anderson, A. W. (1956). *Social foundations of education.* New York: Dryden.

Tom, A. R. (1986). The Holmes Report: Sophisticated analyses, simplistic solutions. *Journal of Teacher Education, 37*(4), 44–46.

Tozer, S., & McAninich, S. (1986). Social foundations of education in historical perspective. *Educational Foundations, 1,* 3–32.

Tozer, S., & McAninich, S. (1987). Four texts in social foundations of education in historical perspective. *Educational Studies, 14,* 13–33.

·23·

PREPARING TEACHERS FOR DIVERSITY

Carl A. Grant and Walter G. Secada

UNIVERSITY OF WISCONSIN–MADISON

The current demographic makeup of our student and teaching populations, as well as of the projections for the future, shows a striking discontinuity between teacher and student diversity. In 1976, 24 percent of the total student enrollment in U.S. schools was nonwhite; by 1984, the figure had risen to 29 percent. In the 20 largest school districts, the respective figures were 60 percent and 70 percent (Center for Education Statistics [CES], 1987a, p. 64). By the year 2000, between 30 and 40 percent of the total school enrollment will be of color (Hodgkinson, 1985). One in four students is poor (Kennedy, Jung, & Orland, 1986, p. 71); one in five students lives in a single-parent home (CES, 1987b, p. 21); and one in seven students is at risk of dropping out of school (Hodgkinson, 1985).

The intercorrelation among these various demographic characteristics has been well documented. For example, poverty and race are correlated. Of white children who were between one and 3 years old in 1968, 25 percent experienced some period of poverty over the next 15 years. For black children, the same statistic was 78 percent. The experience of poverty is more intense for black children. Of white children experiencing poverty, 20 percent lived in poverty for more than 4 years of their childhood; among black children similarly situated, the comparable statistic was 59 percent (Kennedy, et al., 1986, p. 45).

Increasing numbers of children from minority language backgrounds are entering school with little or no competence in the English language (O'Malley, 1981). Though Spanish is the predominant first language for most of these children, and is likely to remain so into the next century, increasing numbers of children are entering school with non-Spanish language

backgrounds including Arabic, Chinese, Hmong, Khmer, Lao, Thai, and Vietnamese (Oxford-Carpenter, Pol, Gendell, & Peng, 1984).

DISCONTINUITY BETWEEN TEACHER AND STUDENT DIVERSITY

In contrast with an increasingly diverse student population, this nation's teaching force is homogeneous, and it is projected to become increasingly more so into the next century. Though the current school population is 29 percent nonwhite, only 12 to 14 percent of the current teaching force is nonwhite; and it is 67 percent to 68 percent female (CES, 1987a, p. 54; 1987b, p. 60). The median age for teachers steadily rose from 33 to 37 to 39 years in 1976, 1981, and 1983 (CES, 1987b, p. 60). Sixty-eight percent of all teachers have had 10 or more years of experience (CES, 1987a, p. 54).

These teachers will be replaced by an increasingly female and white cohort. In 1983, 67 percent of public school teachers in the United States were women, yet in 1980–1981, 1982–1983 and 1983–1984, 75 percent, 76 percent, and 76 percent, respectively, of bachelor's degrees in education were awarded to women (CES, 1987b, pp. 60, 195, 183, 175). In Illinois, during the 1985–1986 school year, 70 percent of all teachers were women; however, 79 percent of those completing and 77 percent of those entering degree-granting teacher-training programs during the 1984–1985 school year were women (Illinois State Board of Education [ISBE], 1987, p. 19). In Illinois, 15 percent of all public school teachers were nonwhite in 1985–

Thanks to Elizabeth Fennema (University of Wisconsin—Madison), Edward D. Fuentes (Office of Bilingual Education and Minority Language Affairs), Donna Golnick (National Council for Accreditation of Teacher Education), and Martin Haberman (University of Wisconsin—Milwaukee) for their criticisms and comments on an earlier draft of this chapter. Their suggestions proved very helpful as we worked on it. Shortcomings and flaws remain our responsibility.

The preparation of this chapter was supported in part by the Wisconsin Center for Education Research, School of Education, University of Wisconsin—Madison.

1986. Yet only 10 percent of those completing and 10 percent of those entering teacher education programs during the 1984–1985 school year were from minority groups (ISBE, 1987, p. 19). Moreover, the use of tests for teacher certification is expected to reduce the certification rate for teachers of color even more (Cole, 1986; Darling-Hammond, 1988; Garcia, 1986; Gifford, 1986).

Not only is minority group representation in the teaching force dropping, but also its composition seems to be changing. Though 13.1 percent of all Illinois schoolteachers during the 1985–1986 school year were black, only 7.4 percent of those completing and 7.3 percent of those entering teacher education programs in 1984–1985 were black. In contrast, though 1.5 percent of public school teachers were Hispanic, 2.2 percent of those completing and 2.1 percent of those entering were Hispanic (ISBE, 1987, p. 19).

For the foreseeable future the teaching force will be predominantely white and female. Schools of education, themselves predominantely white and male, will be required to prepare this increasingly homogeneous teaching force to teach a student population that is becoming increasingly diverse in terms of race, class, language, and sex-role socialization patterns. The multiple discontinuities—between student population and teaching force demographics and between teaching force and teacher educator demographics—should elicit a broad range of responses among researchers, policymakers, members of the teaching profession, and others who are concerned about the education of our children.

Focus of this Chapter

Because current teacher education efforts to prepare all teachers to teach all students have, thus far, been inadequate, we sought to systematically answer the question, What does empirical research on demographic diversity and teacher education tell us? As two teacher educators and researchers who belong to different minority groups, we focused on the demographic discontinuity between student populations and the teaching force.

We envisioned possible responses, and allied research, as being located at three points in the teacher education process: the recruitment of teachers; the precertification education of teachers; and the inservice staff development of teachers. Cutting across each of these points in the process are three broad content domains in which teachers have received education and in which research questions have been investigated: multicultural education, sex equity, and second-language concerns. These domains might also be thought of as separating themselves on the basis of the equity of race, gender, and national origin.

Paucity of Research

We conducted a search of the ERIC data base using descriptors based on race, gender, and ethnic group membership, as well as on teacher education, effectiveness, and standards. We orginally turned up over 500 journal and 700 ERIC citations from 1964 to June 1988. After reviewing descriptors and abstracts for evidence that each document was an empirical research study, we excluded papers that might be described as opinion pieces, descriptions of programs, or exhortations about the virtues of particular efforts without some external objective support for the claims of program impacts. We looked for operationalization of constructs, for use of empirical measures, for existence of treatment versus (quasi-) control groups; in other words, we looked for the empirical validation of claims about the effectiveness of specific efforts. The original set of documents was thereby decreased to fewer than 100. Next, we obtained complete documents and continued the winnowing process. We supplemented this set with manuscripts from recent conferences reporting studies not widely available.

Using these criteria and this process, only 23 books, journal articles, AERA paper presentations, and other, fugitive, literature remained as the core set of studies for review. No empirical studies focused on the recruitment of a diverse teaching force; 16 studies addressed preservice teacher education; and 7 dealt with inservice teacher education. In contrast, 17 of the studies were concerned with multicultural education; 7, with gender equity; and one, with second-language issues. Three studies overlapped on multicultural and gender issues.

We note this paucity of research of two reasons. *First*, it suggests the marginal status and low importance that has been given to research on the preparation of teachers to work with diverse student populations. The general population has known of the educational barriers and challenges facing different student populations at least since the time of the Coleman Report (Coleman et al., 1966). Research in teacher education has been slow to address those challenges. Indeed, most of the journal articles we found were not in what would be considered mainstream, professional outlets. At best, this suggests great insensitivity among those engaged in the peer-review process for such journals. At worst, there is blatant bias against research efforts involving teacher education predicated on the existence of diverse student populations.

Second, though we looked for research to answer our basic question, we found ourselves having to struggle with gaps in the field, with the lack of cumulative findings in programs of inquiry, and with the failure of studies to develop conceptual distinctions that would seem to be critical in the development of such chains of inquiry. Though we found some commonalities, and we report them here, we found ourselves creating a wish list of issues around which a range of research agendas could be developed.

Organization of this Chapter

We have organized this chapter in terms of the critical points in the teacher education process: recruitment of a diverse teaching force, preservice education of student teachers, and inservice staff development of current teachers. For each point, we drew from the three content domains of multicultural education, sex equity, and second-language issues. We recognize the traditions within each of these domains as classically understood. The overarching theme of student diversity is so critical that we purposely did not organize this review in terms of race, gender, class, or language, but integrated these studies into the narrative.

RECRUITMENT AND EDUCATION OF A DIVERSE TEACHING FORCE

We found no empirical studies that investigated how different recruitment models for a diverse teaching cadre might vary in their impact. We found survey reports, recruitment and retention studies, and very thoughtful position papers indicating (a) the trends toward an increasingly white and female teaching force and why people of color are not entering the teaching profession as they once did; (b) the need to recruit a diverse teaching force; (c) the financial costs, especially to poor students, of the increased time required to complete teacher education programs; and (d) the threat of excessive testing (see, for example, Baratz, 1986; Darling-Hammond, 1984; Gordon, 1987; G. P. Smith, 1984; Witty, 1983.) Many of these issues seem not to be researchable, others are. We did locate a relatively large body of survey research on issues related to supply and demand for certified specialist teachers to work with students of limited English proficiency (LEP).

Need for Teachers of LEP Students

A subset of students from minority language groups have limited proficiency in the English language. Though there has been a long and oftentimes acrimonious debate about the best way to educate such students (see, for example, K. Baker, 1987; Secada, 1987b; Willig, 1987), there is a research-based, as well as a legal, consensus that LEP students do require some special educational services. The two major classes of supplementary educational services are bilingual education (BE), which entails using both English and the child's native language as media of instruction, and English as a second language (ESL), which entails providing instruction in the English language. Typically, BE and ESL services are provided in concert, though in some cases just one is provided, usually ESL. In 24 states, legislation either requires or encourages BE and/or ESL (National Clearinghouse for Bilingual Education, 1986, p. 7). Many school districts, in response to mandates, local needs, parental pressure, legal actions, funding enticements, or some combination of these influences, have hired increasing numbers of specially trained teachers to provide these services.

A total of 37 states and the District of Columbia provide certification or endorsement in BE and/or ESL. (Certification refers to a stand-alone license to teach in a specific content area. An endorsement gives the holder a license to teach in the area but is attached to another, stand-alone certificate.) Seven states provide certification in both; 11 provide endorsements. Three provide certification only in BE; 3, only in ESL. An additional 5 states provide endorsement only for ESL. Six states provide certification in ESL and endorsement in BE.

Utah provides either certification or endorsement in ESL and endorsement in BE. Texas offers all four options: certification and/or endorsement in BE and/or ESL (McFerren, 1988).

Research on teacher training for working with diverse minority language populations is driven in large part by issues related to the education of a group of specialists who seek licensure for their specialization. Kaskowitz, Binkley, and Johnson (1981), Macias (1986), O'Malley and Waggoner (1984), Reisner (1983), Waggoner (1979), and Waggoner and O'Malley (1984) report survey studies that describe some combination of (a) the number of teachers who have LEP students in their classrooms; (b) the intensity of their work with LEP students; (c) the qualifications in terms of language proficiency, coursework, and certification of BE and/or ESL teachers to provide specialized services; and (d) the need for additional teachers to fill specialized teaching roles.

How need was defined varied from study to study. Macias, for example, used estimates of the country's total LEP population and divided the student–teacher ratio estimates. His result was a need for between 100,000 and 200,000 BE teachers. In contrast, Kaskowitz et al. (1981), "under what [they] considered to be plausible assumptions estimated a need in public elementary school for 24,300 qualified BE teachers and a maximum supply of 17,700 such teachers. If projections [for the increased LEP student population] prove to be true, then the shortage of qualified BE teachers will be even larger in the year 2000" (pp. xiv–xv). Relying on assumptions concerning teacher certification requirements, acceptable teacher–student ratios in self-contained classrooms versus pull-out programs, and use of teacher aides, Reisner (1983, p. 186) arrived at an estimated need for between, 49,000 and 103,000 BE teachers. Furthermore, "of the 42,000 teachers using a second language in instruction, only 13,000 could be considered minimally qualified to do so" (p. 190).

Waggoner (1979) reports the major results of the Teachers Language Skills Survey, conducted in 1976–1977. Of more than 2.1 million public school teachers, an estimated 77,000 taught only ESL; another 22,000 taught ESL and BE; 20,000 taught BE only. Of the overall teaching population in the United States, 6 percent had had some coursework related to bilingual children; for teachers teaching only ESL, both BE and ESL, and BE only, the respective rates were 29 percent, 59 percent, and 35 percent. As coursework increased in complexity, the rates of completion dropped precipitously (Waggoner, 1979, Table 1). Finally, 86 percent of the teachers who were expected to use the child's native language during instruction, that is, taught BE, with or without ESL, reported having knowledge of that language.

In a 1980–1981 follow-up to the Teachers Language Skills Survey, Waggoner and O'Malley (1984) report that, of over 2.2 million teachers in the United States, 103,000 taught ESL only; 26,000 taught both BE and ESL; 30,000 taught only BE. However, 367,000 teachers had LEP students who were not receiving any supplementary services in their classrooms. Proportionately more teachers than in 1976 reported having received minimal and more advanced training. Waggoner and O'Malley conclude: "Fewer than one in four teachers teaching bilingually in 1980–81 had the basic academic or non-academic qualifications and language skills to do so. Another approximately 20 percent had the necessary language skills and had taken minimal course work in the relevant teaching techniques" (p. 40).

Waggoner and O'Malley (1984) provide a detailed breakdown of teaching assignments for the 1980–1981 school year, based on teacher preparation and qualifications to teach bilingually but not based on student language group. In 1980–1981, 24,000 teachers were qualified (i.e, could speak a non-English language) and had been prepared to teach bilingually; 32,000 more were qualified and had been minimally prepared (pp. 33, 39); another 3,000 seemed to be qualified and to have received sufficient inservice training to be minimally prepared for teaching. Of these 59,000 certified teachers, 40,000 were *not* in a bilingual assignment, though an additional 9,000 were teaching ESL. Waggoner and O'Malley suggest that "the reasons why these teachers were not using bilingual skills or teaching ESL should be investigated to determine whether they in fact can be used in the future to respond to the need for teachers of LEP students" (p. 40).

Two studies reported by Merino, Politzer, and Ramirez (1979) suggest that bilingual teachers' proficiency in Spanish is positively correlated with Hispanic bilingual children's academic achievement in both English and Spanish. This study is noteworthy in that the language proficiencies of both teachers and their bilingual aides were assessed, in an effort to obtain as complete information as possible about language proficiency for each classroom's total teaching staff. They conclude: "it would seem that requiring Spanish proficiency of prospective teachers of limited and non-English-speaking children is a legitimate concern" (p. 35).

Though a study by Binkley et al. (1981) provided descriptive information about federally funded BE teacher-training projects, we were unable to find any study that tied such descriptions to programmatic impact. Nor could we find even descriptive studies of ESL programs.

Discussion

Though we could not find research that investigated different recruitment and retention models for a diverse teaching cadre, these survey studies on BE and ESL teacher supply and demand provide examples of the sorts of issues that should be investigated.

Why There Should Be a Diverse Teaching Population. Articles about the increasing homogenization of the teaching force contain the tacit assumption that, "of course, such an event is undesirable." We agree with that view. However, agreement should not preclude empirical inquiry about that assumption. Why is it so bad? Similarly, how does one respond to the frequently asked question; Is there empirical evidence that having teachers of color will positively effect the achievement scores of students of color and help white students to have more positive attitudes toward people of color? Perhaps the teaching force simply should be diverse. That it is predominantly white shows that our society has not succeeded in insur-

ing the full and complete participation of all its members in its various careers. This reason is a belief and does not seem open to empirical scrutiny. Other views might be.

At the start of this chapter, we noted the discontinuity between the teaching force and the school populations. We believe, as do many others, that there is some link between the composition of the two. The existence and nature of that link is subject to research and scholarly scrutiny. For example, the makeup of the two populations is linked by the hypothesis that teachers of color understand the cultural backgrounds of diverse learners better than do whites; hence, they can adapt instruction to meet those differences. What the source of such understanding is, how it might be demonstrated, and how that understanding actually translates into practice and student outcomes are all empirical questions. That teachers of color serve as role models for students of color to emulate is another belief that can be empirically investigated.

Though beliefs such as these might be true, we need to investigate their conceptual and empirical limits. At the extreme, such beliefs could lead to the segregation of students. Attempts to match teachers and students on the basis of similar backgrounds could exclude teachers and their students from experiencing people from other backgrounds. Moreover, such beliefs might serve to excuse white teachers from their own obligations to teach all students, because, after all, they would not be expected to succeed, due to their students' dissimilar backgrounds.

Finally, beliefs such as these might set differential standards for teachers of color that white teachers would not have to meet. That students are better understood by teachers most like them could be used to set up teachers of color. They could be held to higher standards of success than white teachers in terms of their abilities to work with students of color. Given the well-documented educational challenges that many students of color pose, such a standard is clearly unrealistic. A similar point could be made about the belief that teachers of color are better role models for students of color.

Another reason for linking teacher and student diversity could be that students of diverse backgrounds should interact with teachers from all backgrounds. According to this view, diversity is good for everyone to experience. Children need experiences in which people from diverse backgrounds work together and in which they share positions of power and authority.

Diversity Versus Quality. Various beliefs and arguments can be found that set concerns about increasing the diversity of the teaching force in opposition to policies designed to improve the quality of that force. Among these are beliefs concerning the role of teacher competency tests for certification, opposition to special programs for increasing the pool of minority teacher candidates, and specialized licenses that create niches within the teaching profession that are not easily filled by nonminority candidates.

Some policy analysts have stated that BE is a jobs program for Hispanics or for other minority language groups (Epstein, 1977; M. Smith, 1988). By implication, teacher education in BE becomes a job-training program for individuals who could not otherwise become teachers. Though 15,000 of 42,000 certified teachers who taught bilingually in 1976–1977 were Hispanics, Waggoner (1979) reports that very few of them had actually received even a little preservice training related to BE or ESL. Rather, the large majority of these teachers had been certified prior to being assigned to teach bilingually. Their assignments as bilingual teachers were due to their language skills, not the reverse. Waggoner and O'Malley's (1984) data are not presented by ethnicity; yet, given the low level of non-English language skills reported by the respondents, it seems highly unlikely that the picture is that much different from Wagonner's earlier survey. More surveys similar to those conducted by O'Malley and Waggoner might help dispel similar myths about the larger teaching force.

Diversity and Teacher Marginalization. Marginalization here refers to the concept of preparing certain teachers, in this case teachers of color, at only those times when special needs are perceived and not on a regular, continuing basis. The educational needs associated with students of color, and the discontinuity between teaching and student populations, might lead to limits on the career opportunities and the marginalization of teachers from such groups. This danger was alluded to in our discussion of the belief that teachers should match students' demographic characteristics. Arguments related to this concern are put forth by Reisner (1983) and Waggoner and O'Malley (1984); they report that there is a latent pool of bilingual personnel not teaching bilingual learners who should be encouraged to work with LEP students. The pressing need to educate diverse learners might lead to the marginalization of career entries and the limitation of opportunities for teachers from underrepresented groups. We need research on this possibility.

Development of Teachers from Diverse Backgrounds. We need more information about students from diverse backgrounds as they go through teacher education programs. If these students are recruited into teaching because they have something special to contribute, do the programs they enter acknowledge and develop those skills? Do they neglect the skills and understandings that these students bring? Worse yet, do teacher education programs attempt to socialize their students to norms that essentially invalidate the reasons they were sought out in the first place? We need more information about students who enter teaching. What are their understandings about the student populations they hope to (and actually will) encounter? These students seem to prefer to teach in the suburbs (American Association of Colleges for Teacher Education [AACTE], 1987).

A basic tenet of instruction is that it should build on what students know. We have minimal understanding of what students of color and BE and/or ESL students in teacher-training programs actually know that is pedagogically relevant or how such knowledge develops. Hence, we are unable to design programs that build on student knowledge. However, research can be designed that takes into account students' backgrounds in terms of class, gender, ethnicity, language, and race. These factors and their interactions affect how younger students react to their educational experiences (Grant & Sleeter, 1986) and should not be ignored in teacher education.

Need for Validated Information. We need to determine empirically and to validate the knowledge, skills, and beliefs that teacher education programs seek to impart, as well as those that are requirements for certification. Recommended competencies from guidelines for the development of BE (Center for Applied Linguistics, 1974) and ESL (Teachers of English to Speakers of Other Languages, 1975) teacher certification programs can be found, in one form or another, in many state licensure requirements and many teacher-training programs. The Center for Applied Linguistics *Guidelines* lists desirable personal qualities and minimal competencies in language proficiency, linguistics, culture, instructional methods, curriculum, assessment, school–community relations, and student-training experiences. With the exception of the studies reported by Merino et al. (1979), there seems to be no empirical validation for such a set of guidelines (see Richards, 1987, for a discussion of ESL.)

Finally, what models of teacher recruitment and retention have been successful in obtaining a teaching force sensitive to the needs of diverse students? Over the last years, the recruitment and retention of students of color to predominately white institutions of higher learning have received varying levels of attention. Different methods and procedures have been used to attract and retain these students. Have any program models been successful? What factors seem to account for success and failure in these models?

A TYPOLOGY FOR CLASSIFYING STUDIES

Grant and Sleeter (1985); Grant, Sleeter, and Anderson (1986); and Sleeter and Grant (1987, 1988) note that authors writing about multicultural education use different terms synonymously: bicultural education, biracial education, multiracial education, intercultural education, ethnic education, multiethnic education, and multiracial education, to name a few. Moreover, regardless of the term used, the educational, social, and political meanings advocated also vary. Banks (1977) additionally notes contradictions and inconsistencies with theory and research in the behavioral sciences. Various authors also differ regarding the characteristics of the term *multicultural*. For example, Gay (1983) observes that the original aim of multiethnic–multicultural education was to provide information about the life-styles and heritages of American ethnic groups in school programs. She acknowledges that the experience and issues regarding women, the handicapped, the aged, and the poor are legitimate areas of study and clearly intertwined with ethnicity. But, she argues, "including them under the conceptual umbrella of multiethnic or multicultural education may tend to divert attention away from ethnicity" (p. 563).

However, Gollnick and Chinn (1983), among others, argue for broader conceptualization of multicultural education that includes race, class, and gender. To provide a basis for using multicultural education in this chapter, we have adapted the Grant and Sleeter (1985) typology to include the education of diverse learners and those with second languages. Race, class, gender, and language are the ascribed characteristics included in the definition of multicultural education used in this typology. This extended typology includes five different conceptions of multicultural education: teaching the different child, human relations, single-group studies, multicultural approaches, and education that is multicultural and social reconstructionist (EMC).

Teaching culturally different or exceptional children helps fit people into the existing social structure and culture. Dominant traditional educational aims are taught by building bridges between the students and the school. The curriculum is made relevant to the students' background; instruction builds on students' learning styles and is adapted to their skill levels. Teaching culturally different or exceptional children accommodates such students by altering regular teaching strategies to match student learning styles through use of culturally relevant materials or remedial teaching strategies that would otherwise be used in a pull-out program. Education that prepares teachers for teaching culturally different children would, by extension, not question the dominant culture's traditional aims. Rather, the emphasis would be on techniques for building the bridges between children and school and for helping students adapt to the norms of the dominant culture. The problem of cultural discontinuity remains the students'.

Human relations attempts to foster positive affective relationships among individual members of diverse racial and cultural groups, and/or between males and females, to strengthen student self-concept and to increase school and social harmony. The human relations curriculum includes lessons about stereotyping and individual differences and similarities. Instruction includes using cooperative learning. Teacher education from a human relations perspective prepares teachers to honor diverse student backgrounds and to promote harmony among students. Real conflicts between groups are often glossed over in this effort.

Single-group studies promote social structural equality for, and immediate recognition of, an identified group. Commonly implemented in the form of ethnic studies or women's studies, these programs assume that knowledge about particular oppressed groups should be taught separately from conventional classroom knowledge, in either separate units or separate courses. Single-group studies seek to raise people's consciousness concerning an identified group, by teaching its members and others about the history, culture, and contributions of that group, as well as how it has been oppressed by or worked with the dominant groups in our society.

Multicultural approaches to education promote social equality and cultural pluralism. The curriculum is organized around the contributions and perspectives of different cultural groups, and it pays close attention to gender equity. For example, with the multicultural approach, teachers attend to how gender-biased socialization and oppression get transmitted in their own teaching practices, and they pay attention to how males and females from different ethnic backgrounds are socialized. Multicultural approaches to education build on students' learning styles, adapt to their skill level, and involve students actively in thinking and analyzing life situations.

These approaches also encourage school staffing patterns to include diverse racial, gender, and disability groups in nontraditional roles.

Education that is multicultural and social reconstructionist extends the previous approaches by teaching students to analyze inequality and oppression in society and by helping them develop skills for social action. EMC promotes social structural equality and cultural pluralism and prepares citizens to work actively toward social structural equality.

The Grant and Sleeter typology grew out of the way classroom teachers teach multicultural curriculum and the way multicultural education is discussed in the professional literature. In the present usage, it provides a broad base on which to analyze studies of teacher education and research that look at race, class, language, ethnic background, and gender socialization. Sleeter and Grant (1987) observe that, "originally linked only to concerns about racism in schooling, it [multicultural education] has expanded to address sexism, classism, and handicappism" (p. 421).

Similar analyses are possible for second-language concerns. Bilingualism and its relationship to minority-language-group education has been the focus of struggle since the beginnings of the American common school (Perlman, 1987; Stein, 1987). Within that history and in current practice, examples can be found that fit Grant and Sleeter's (1985) typology. For example, teacher education focused on the best techniques for adapting instruction to children's language-based needs could fall under the rubric of either teaching the different child or single-group studies, again depending on the goals of the program. Alternatively, teacher education focused on empowering one's students (Cummins, 1986) and on the struggles of various linguistic minorities to obtain educational opportunity (Skutnabb-Kangas & Cummins, 1988; Stein, 1986) is EMC. Hence, we extend the Grant and Sleeter (1985) typology to provide a framework for organizing the 23 core studies in this review (Table 23-1). Four studies were based on teaching the different child; two, on human relations; four, on single-group studies; nine, on multicultural approaches to education; and one, on EMC. We could not classify three.

PRECERTIFICATION EDUCATION OF STUDENT TEACHERS FOR DIVERSITY

We found 16 studies, published between 1973 and 1988, on preservice teacher education related to multicultural education, broadly defined. Of these, Sleeter (1985) analyzed 6, the only ones she could locate. Since Sleeter's analysis, 10 additional studies that investigate the impact of multicultural education on preservice education students have been reported.

Teaching the Different Child

Henington (1981) assessed the effect of multicultural and nonsexist instruction on the knowledge, attitudes, and personal values of student teachers. The student teachers received this instruction for 11 hours over the course of 4 days. The

TABLE 23–1. Classification of Core Studies According to Grant and Sleeter Typology

	Preservice	Inservice
Teaching the different child	Henington, 1981 Mahan, 1982	Calderon, cited in Macias, 1986
Human relations	Moultry, 1988 Lambert & Rohland, 1983	
Single-group studies	C. T. Bennett, 1979 Sadker & Sadker, 1981	Baty, 1972 Fennema, Wolleat, Pedro, & Becker, 1981
Multicultural approaches to *education*	Bennett, 1988 Contreras, 1988[a] Mills, 1984 Wayson, 1988[a] Grant, 1981 Grant & Koskela, 1986 Koppelman & Martin, 1988 Sleeter, 1988	Washington, 1981 Fleming & Sutton, 1987
EMC		Grant & Grant, 1985
Could not tell	Baker, 1973 Baker, 1977	Cross, Deslone, & Ziajka, 1978

[a]Contreras's and Wayson's meanings for multicultural education were determined by examination of their instrumentation.

results were mixed. Immediately after instruction, there was a significant increase in multicultural and nonsexist knowledge and more positive attitudes on the part of the teachers. However, just 26 days after instruction, only knowledge gains remained; attitude gains were lost.

Mahan (1982) immersed 291 student teachers in the Navajo and Hopi cultures. Prior to their field placements, students had completed on-campus cultural preparation through seminars, workshops, films, readings, and interviews. Each student teacher spend 17 weeks working, teaching, and living with American Indian students in their communities. The results from this study were positive in every area that was investigated: student attitude, involvement, employment success, and supervising teacher evaluation. Mahan concludes:

Follow-up data clearly indicates that these teachers, culturally prepared on Indian Reservations, are highly employable both in Native American settings and back home in mainstream settings. The positive data collected over nine years from this Native American focused project should encourage other institutions to replicate similar cultural immersion projects in Native American or other ethnic minority communities. (p. 110)

Human Relations

Moultry (1988) surveyed student teachers in the college of education at Ohio State University to determine their attitudes about minority populations and issues related to minorities in the United States. He reports that:

One can draw the following conclusions for about 30 percent to 40 percent of the student teachers and the preparation they had received:

Students showed a lack of empathy with minority problems in regard to institutional racism; Students demonstrated a lack of knowledge about indirect, non-proximate causes for human actions; Students expressed a lack of confidence in education and politics as sources for change in the way in which people think and act relative to pluralistic values. (p. 11)

Based on the results of his study, Moultry recommended to the Ohio State University Senate Committee that all students in the College of Education take one course whose content would specifically address different cultural groups; that multicultural inservice programs be provided for the faculty; that field experiences for students include multicultural settings and populations; and that faculty be rewarded for work on multicultural education (pp. 12–13).

Lambert and Rohland (1983) attempted to determine whether preservice teachers needed to be taught about sexrole stereotyping and whether a general or specific teaching approach would be more effective in decreasing or eliminating sex-role stereotyping by the 50 students that made up the experimental and control groups. The results of the study documented the need to teach about sex-role stereotyping. Specific teaching was more effective, especially if students were familiar with the issues being considered. The authors argue that students today, because of media and public sensitivity in general, enter discussions about sex-role socialization with a higher level of awareness. Therefore, discussion should start at that level, and it should focus on issues with which students are familiar. But then, instruction should "probe deeper into [the] causes and reasons for perpetuation [of stereotyping], and [it should] help students to analyze and problem-solve for solution to classroom situations" (p. 21).

Single-Group Studies

In C. T. Bennett's study (1979), students were sensitized to social forces that lead to negative assumptions regarding racial and cultural groups and were required to select and focus on one of the following racial and/or cultural groups: black Americans, Japanese Americans, Jewish Americans, American Indians, and Spanish-speaking Americans. Compared with students in a control group, students in the experimental group were more positive in their attitudes toward members of ethnic groups in general and toward Jewish, Japanese, American Indian, and Spanish-speaking Americans specifically. No group differences were found between experimental and comparison groups on their perceptions of black Americans. Bennett concludes:

The use of an experimental model which emphasized a multiethnic and multicultural approach for teaching pre-service teachers to instruct within a pluralistic society does have a valid and fruitful potential. This study has demonstrated that a comparative multiethnic methods course can enable preservice teachers to develop a comparative perspective to combat racial and cultural indifference. (p. 235)

Sadker and Sadker (1981) provided 10 demonstration sites with a total of six nonsexist teacher education units designed for elementary and secondary students. Results were mixed. Though "students in 20 of 27 field classes (74 percent) showed an increase in their perception of the importance of sex equity as measured by [changes on] the pre-test/post-test attitude survey" (p. 2), they still listed Equal Opportunity for Men and Women as the third most important issue behind Teenage Drinking and Drugs and Developing New Energy Sources on an attitude scale. Whether such a rank ordering represents more general debates among competing social concerns, or whether it represents a lack of impact by the training effort, remains an open question.

W. Smith (1978) used 12 instructional modules—Analysis of Textbooks and Classrooms for Sex Discrimination, Interpreting Written Materials, etc.—with an elementary education class, to promote sex blindness and prevent sex-role stereotyping. Pre- and posttests were given to an experimental and three comparison groups. Once again, results were mixed. Both the pretest and posttest data indicated that all four group of students were neither clearly traditional nor clearly nontraditional in their attitudes toward sex roles, measured on a 5-point Likert scale of agreement or disagreement. Also, posttest results did not indicate that the experimental group differed in attitude from the control groups after treatment. However, members of the experimental group did demonstrate a greater growth in sex equity teaching behavior; they developed lesson plans that more often encouraged and supported their students' considering and trying out nontraditional career roles. Nevertheless, as Smith points out, "Preservice elementary teachers may have been willing to focus on these roles in instruction, but they did not seem ready to advocate any change in traditional family role patterns" (p. 9).

Multicultural Approaches to Education

Eight studies based on multicultural approaches to teacher education were examined: C. Bennett (1988), Contreras (1988), Grant (1981), Grant and Koskela (1985), Koppelman and Martin (1988), Mills (1984), Sleeter (1988), and Wayson (1988).

Grant (1981) followed 17 students through their preservice program, after providing them with baseline information about education that is multicultural and social reconstructivist (EMC), to discover (a) whether students would receive (and recognize when they did receive) additional instruction in EMC in their other coursework; (b) whether students would incorporate EMC into their class assignments or projects; (c) whether other university faculty would try to help them learn how to incorporate EMC into their classroom planning during their field experiences; (d) whether student teachers would adapt different teaching strategies to their own students' learning styles; and, finally, (e) whether student teachers felt comfortable with EMC. Grant and Koskela (1985) replicated but extended Grant's study to include comparison of the responses received from the education students with the response received from the methods instructors, cooperating teachers, and university supervisors. They also observed the teaching behavior of a subsample of the population in the classroom.

Both studies produced similar, and mixed, results. Students did receive additional information in EMC; however, the information seemed mostly related to an awareness and understanding of EMC concepts. Very little attention was given to the use of EMC within the classroom curriculum. Grant (1981) and Grant and Koskela (1985) found an absence of EMC in the classroom environment, although in both studies the students reported feeling comfortable working with EMC. The reasons given by students, in both cases, were the same. They did not have enough time and/or they were teaching in predominately white classrooms and, therefore, did not see a reason to use EMC. Grant and Koskela argue:

Students seem to include EMC mostly when it is promoted by someone in charge. Those aspects of EMC that are more frequently integrated into the curriculum relate to individualizing for skill-related needs of children rather than for issues of race, class, and gender. . . . In order to help students to transfer campus learning to their classroom teaching, not only must they be given information, they must be shown how to put that information into practice in the daily curriculum. (p. 203)

Mills (1984) attempted to explore the feasibility of a joint teacher-training activity in multicultural education between a historically black university (Grambling State) and a historically white university (Louisiana Tech). Student teachers worked together in short-term seminars. Students from both colleges reported overall satisfaction with their training experiences and felt the need for more cross-cultural training earlier in their college careers. However, Mills reports that "the student teachers were less certain about whether the recent training would improve their relations with the culturally different" (p. 21).

Sleeter (1988) studied what teachers with preservice coursework in multicultural education, as required by the State of Wisconsin's Human Relations Code, reported doing in their classrooms and the extent to which specific features of the preservice program related to what they did. Sleeter analyzed 24 teaching behaviors (e.g., the use of multiracial materials, teaching about women, teaching about social class) in relationship to the number of human relations credits required in Wisconsin's 32 preservice teacher education programs. Sleeter found that the average teacher certified by a program requiring more than 4 credits in human relations reported engaging in 12 of the 24 behaviors more frequently than the average teacher certified by a program requiring 1 or 2 credits. For example, one-fourth of the teachers with 1 or 2 human relations credit, versus two-thirds of those teachers with 4 or more credits, reported using multiracial and nonsexist materials, teaching lessons about stereotyping, and trying to reduce social barriers between students of different races more than once a week. On the other 12 items, Sleeter found no appreciable relationship between the number of credits in human relations required by a teacher's preservice program and the frequency with which a teacher reported engaging in a behavior. More than two-thirds of the teachers reported doing things like reteaching concepts as needed, adapting teaching to reading levels, and teaching the same behavior and skills to both sexes. Not too surprisingly, teachers certified by programs requiring 1 or 2 credits who worked in an urban area reported more multicultural teaching than teachers certified by programs requiring 3 or 4 credits who did not work in an urban area. However, teachers certified by programs requiring more than 5 credits reported engaging in the most multicultural teaching.

Preservice students were more likely to complete a field experience with minority people when it was required than when it was not. Of seven curricular areas investigated, only one produced measurable differences in teaching behavior: the examination and use of instructional materials. In the conclusion to her study, Sleeter offers the following observation:

Including a relatively small amount of multicultural education training in students' preservice programs probably does not have much impact on what they do. It may give them a greater repertoire of teaching strategies to use with culturally diverse students, and it may alert them to the importance of maintaining high expectation. For significant reform of teaching to occur, however, this intervention alone is insufficient. (p. 29)

C. Bennett (1988), Contreras (1988), and Wayson (1988) were part of a unified effort to assess the effectiveness of multicultural approaches to education among students at Indiana and Ohio State universities. Bennett reported that the common goals for multicultural education included development of historical perspectives and cultural consciousness; development of intercultural competence; eradication of racism, prejudice, and discrimination; and successful teaching of multicultural students.

Bennett analyzed the immediate impact of a required multicultural education course on the attitudes and knowledge of the preservice students, as well as the long-range influence of the course on the attitudes, knowledge, and classroom behavior of a smaller subsample. Her study examined the relationship between the students' attitudes and knowledge held when they entered the course. Her study traced changes in those attitudes and knowledge as the course progressed. She reports mixed results. The multicultural course had an initial positive impact on students' attitudes and knowledge. Gains were lost a year later. She argues that initial gains were not maintained because the students had not received additional instruction in multicultural education after they had completed the original course. Bennett concludes:

Some of the findings lend support to the charge that we know how to reach the already convinced, but do little to reach the others. It is important to note that typically we provide similar/identical educational experiences for the already convinced and the others. Different experiences are most likely needed, experiences matched with the individual's level of readiness for multicultural education. For example, students who hold greater amounts of stereotyped knowledge might benefit from training in critical thinking. (p. 30)

Contreras (1988) assessed what a sample of beginning secondary education students knew about "the multicultural youth that will predominate schools and how they feel about these student populations" (p. 3). Wayson (1988) assessed a sample of student teachers to determine: (a) the degree of proficiency that advanced students felt they had attained relative to a set of competencies considered important for educating minority populations effectively; (b) the students' ability to answer correctly a selected set of questions concerning the history of minority populations in the United States; and (c) whether these respondents would teach classes that contained minority and low socioeconomic children. Wayson also assessed the students' attitudes toward "ethnic and social class groups and social policies and practices for providing better education and economic conditions for those groups" (p. 3). Contreras and Wayson used four instruments to assess student attitudes about minority populations and issues related to minorities in the United States, the competencies needed for effective teaching among multicultural populations, and student knowledge about ethnic history and culture: the Multicultural Opinion Survey, the Ethnic History and Culture Awareness Survey, the Desire to Teach Minority Children Survey, and the Multicultural Teaching Scale.

For both studies, results were mixed. Contreras reports that, based on the Multicultural Opinion Survey, "the respondents believed that teachers can make a difference if they feel that minority children can learn and manifest this by expecting high academic performance of students of color" (p. 10). However, on this same survey, respondents felt strongly that not all minority children can do well and appreciate receiving help. The Ethnic History and Culture Awareness Survey produced the following kinds of mixed results: 65 percent knew that the first man to die in the revolutionary war was a black man, Crispus Attucks; 52 percent knew that the Supreme Court Case of *Brown v. Topeka Board of Education* (1954) reversed legal doctrines that had allowed blacks and whites to be educated in separate schools; and 58 percent knew that most Germans who immigrated to the United States in the late 1800s came to escape the draft. The Desire to Teach Minority Children Survey revealed that "the majority of respondents were willing to teach in a class of ethnically diverse students; however, there were some who would only consider teaching students of color if no other employment opportunity were available" (p. 13). In conclusion, Contreras argues,

Teacher educators continue to assume that teacher education students will pick up the necessary knowledge, skills and attitudes that will help them teach classes of socioculturally diverse students without any direct instruction and planned experience. Moreover, teacher educators assume that most of the schools will continue to be monocultural and monosocial, therefore, there is no obligation to commit time and resources to preparing teachers to teach children who are at risk of being miseducated and undereducated. (p. 14)

Wayson also reports mixed results. His results from the Multicultural Teaching Scale revealed that 75 percent felt very competent to provide multicultural instruction, 77 percent felt they could present cultural groups as real people, and 74 percent felt they could help build mutual respect for different cultures. However, "at least 60 percent of these same respondents did not feel sure of their knowledge about how various cultures contribute to American society and 75 percent weren't confident about their knowledge of the history of minority groups in America" (p. 11). The Knowledge About Ethnic History and Culture Survey revealed that very few of the respondents knew elementary facts about the history or culture of ethnic groups they were likely to come into contact with in American schools (p. 16). Wayson concludes:

Since many students are graduating without basic skills, attitudes and knowledge for promoting equal educational opportunity and teaching students to participate effectively in a just and fair society, professors and other instructors bear responsibility for developing and /or redesigning courses and activities to insure that students learn those skills, attitude and knowledge. . . . Clearly, it is faulty to assume that the undergraduate (or graduate) programs are developing competence for delivering effective multicultural education. . . . Effective preparation seemed to require, at a minimum, *direct contact* with students from cultures other than the prospective teacher's combined with translation and interpretation gained from *discussion* with a knowledgeable and sensitive supervisor, professor, critic teacher or other tutor. . . . Yet, college faculty appear to have little interest in correcting the situation. At Ohio State, all but one of the practices reported to meet NCATE standards . . . had been abandoned by Spring, 1986. (p. 17)

Koppelman and Martin (1988) conducted a study to determine the impact of a human relations/multicultural education course on the attitudes of prospective teachers regarding issues of race, class, and gender. The course included weekly lectures accompanied by a 2-hour group discussion. In the discussion group, students' responses and work based on reading assignments, media presentations, and moral dilemmas raised in the weekly lecture were critiqued. The data were collected, over six semesters, from 876 students, 565 females and 312 males. The results reported were: (a) students' attitudes regarding race, class, and gender showed a significant, positive increase. (b) Female students showed greater sensitivity toward gender issues than did male students. There were no differences between male and female students' attitudes regarding classism for five of the six semesters, but, in one semester, females showed greater sensitivity toward classism issues. There was no significant difference between the male and female students on the racism category in four of the six semesters, but, in the other two, women indicated more sensitivity than men regarding racism issues. (c) The data from each semester of the study indicated no significant difference between the changes in male and female students' attitudes toward sexism and racism. However, for one of the six semesters, male and female students did show a change in attitude related to issues of classism, the change for women being stronger than for men. The authors conclude their study by noting that the human relations course had had a positive impact on heightening student sensitivity toward gender, race, and class issues but that no conclusion can be drawn about any long-term effects of this training or whether these attitude changes would have an impact out of the classroom once the students started their teaching.

Education that is Multicultural and Social Reconstructionist

None of the studies we reviewed seemed to be of programs in which students were exposed to curriculum and instruction practices that taught them to develop and teach social action and empowerment skills throughout their preservice experience. Grant (1981) and Grant and Koskela (1986) point out that students in these studies were given baseline instruction in EMC, but this effort was not continued after the initial class; therefore, these studies were placed in the multicultural education approach.

Additional Studies

Two studies by G. Baker (1973, 1977) do not provide enough information to determine how multicultural education was defined. Therefore, they are treated separately. In her first study, Baker (1973) found that, although perceptions concerning some ethnic groups, mainly Jewish-Americans, held by student teachers enrolled in a multicultural workshop could be altered, perceptions concerning others, such as blacks, were quite resistant to change. No statistically significant differences between pre- and posttests were found on the black anti-irrational or pro-irrational subscales. Baker, therefore, concludes that "the change in perceptions of Blacks held by the students remained fairly constant" (p. 307). This result is consistent with C. T. Bennett's (1979) finding that the single-group-studies approach could change perceptions concerning some ethnic groups, and minorities in general, but that changing student–teacher perceptions concerning blacks was more difficult.

In her second study, G. Baker (1977) extended her line of inquiry. Believing that multiethnic training can alter students' perceptions of ethnic groups, she sought to determine whether a workshop requirement or a course requirement in multicultural education would produce the greater effect. Baker discovered the multicultural course requirement to be more effective. In her conclusion, Baker argues "that both time and intensity produce more desirable outcomes" (p. 33).

Discussion

Geographic, Conceptual, and Programmatic Isolation. Thirteen of these 16 studies were conducted in the Midwest, and only 3 (Baker, 1973, 1977; C. T. Bennett, 1979) were conducted prior to 1980. Race was the dominant theme for conceptualizing and operationalizing multicultural education in most of these studies. Three studies examined gender (Lambert & Rohland, 1983; Sadker & Sadker, 1981; W. Smith, 1978) but failed to consider social class jointly with gender. This omission is particularly important, because women of color are often more affected by sex-role stereotyping and other forms of gender bias than are white women. Studies by Grant (1981), Grant and Koskela (1986), Koppelman and Martin (1988), and Sleeter (1988) included race, social class, and gender; Henington (1981) included race and gender. Mills (1984) included religious differences. Thirteen of these studies focused on individual programs. Mills (1984) looked at two different university programs and C. Bennett (1988), Contreras (1988), and Wayson (1988) examined programs at two different universities. Sleeter (1988) was the only one to examine multiple programs other than her own.

Assessment of Outcomes. Most of these studies did not define multicultural education, equity, or other similar terms. Dolce (1973), among others, argues that the vagueness associated with multicultural education makes it difficult to relate such programs effectively to the real world. Researchers seem to assume that their readers understand their meanings. Yet Grant and Sleeter's (1985) typology, as extended here, provides five meanings for the term *multicultural education*; Secada (1989) and Grant (1989) discuss similar problems of how equity is defined.

Program effectiveness was determined mainly by use of attitude surveys. In at least half of the studies, the researchers developed their own attitude scales. However, G. Baker (1973, 1977), C. Bennett (1988), C. T. Bennett (1979), and Henington (1981) used attitude scales already familiar to the educational community.

Of the sixteen studies, only C. Bennett's (1988) assessed attitude, knowledge, and behavior. Contreras (1988), Henington (1981), Moultry (1988), and Wayson (1988) assessed both attitudes and knowledge, but not behavior. Mills (1984) assessed satisfaction with the course and knowledge. Grant (1981), Grant and Koskela (1985) and Sleeter (1988) assessed behavior, though their concern for coursework could be considered a proxy for knowledge. G. Baker (1973, 1977), C. T. Bennett (1979), and Koppelman and Martin (1988) assessed only attitude. Mahan (1982) assessed attitude and also external indicators of success such as involvement, employment, and ratings by supervising teacher.

Preservice students' reactions to multicultural education were assessed in four of the studies and was measured by self-report, interviews, and observations. Only Sleeter (1988) as-

sessed the impact of the preservice experience on teaching behavior after certification.

Six studies used a pretest/posttest design (G. Baker, 1973; C. Bennett, 1988; C. T. Bennett, 1979; 1988; Henington, 1981; Koppelman & Martin, 1988; Mahan, 1982); the others used a posttest only. In more than half the studies a self-report instrument was used (C. Bennett, 1988; Contreras, 1988; Grant, 1981; Grant, & Koskela, 1986; Mills, 1984; Moultry, 1988; Sleeter, 1987; Wayson, 1988).

Mahan's (1982) was the only study to report clear positive results, and he argues, "Follow-up data clearly indicate that these teachers, culturally prepared on Indian Reservations, are highly employable both in Native American settings and back home in mainstream settings" (p. 110). The remaining studies report mixed results.

Recommendations. One of the more positive aspects of this research is that individuals who are responsible for multicultural education, or who play a major role in the teaching of it at their institutions, are interested in discovering its effectiveness. All of the authors seem to be advocates of some form of multicultural education and strongly recommend that universities and schools of education prepare student teachers to use the concept in their teaching. They also did this research without the benefit of what we would consider appropriate research support money. The downside of the research reviewed here, like so much research in education, is that it does not offer enough detail or conclusive enough evidence to argue that these are effective ways of offering multicultural preservice education. We can use this information to speculate about good multicultural teaching, preservice program design, preservice course content, inservice needs of college faculty, and field experiences and placements. But we still need more information about the scope of effective educational practice and the combinations of practice that will result in optimal outcomes.

Sleeter (1985) offers nine recommendations for multicultural education research. With minor changes, they are included here, because they address this issue in a comprehensive and thoughtful manner.

1. More studies that assess the effectiveness of preservice programs for educational equity should be undertaken and reported in the literature. These studies are particularly needed in regions of the United States outside the Midwest.
2. Program conceptualizers should clearly state what they hope to see teachers do in the classroom. It would be helpful if these statements were articulated within a framework such as the typology used earlier.
3. Programs should experiment with different kinds of field experiences, wherever possible. These programs seem to produce better gains than those without field experiences, although the optimal length and intensity of field experiences have not been determined.
4. Programs should be assessed with measures that capture what preservice students actually do when they get into the classroom. At the least, we need to know whether attitude surveys like those used in these studies actually differenti-

ate those who affirm educational equity when teaching from those who do not.

5. Measures of assessment should be sensitive to how preservice students perceive and respond to specific groups within general target populations, such as black Americans, as opposed to minorities, or blind people, as opposed to the handicapped.

6. More data need to be collected on the effectiveness of different plans for coursework Baker (1977) found a course more effective than a workshop; Sleeter (1988) found that more coursework was more effective than less. Some institutions require more than one course; others require only that certain topics or competencies be included in existing courses. There need to be more data regarding the impact of how much is included and how it is packaged.

7. Insights from studies of single programs should be used to design studies of the same variables in multiple programs. The 16 studies reviewed here have limited generalizability because programs were different, outcome measures were different, and, in many cases, settings were different. There need to be studies conducted across many programs in which, for example, the same approach to preparing students to affirm equity is used and the same kinds of outcomes are assessed. The concerted effort by C. Bennett (1988), Contreras (1988), Moultry (1988), and Wayson (1988) shows some promise in this regard.

8. Program impact should be judged on its ability to produce lasting results. This might encourage teacher educators to overhaul their treatment of equity issues programwide, because the research here suggests that one separate course is not enough to make lasting gains.

9. Teacher educators in the areas of mainstreaming and multicultural education should attempt more collaboration. This should not mean attempting to treat both areas within a single course previously reserved for one area. It should mean more dialogue about common concerns in teacher education and more collective effort to build educational equity into preservice programs.

EDUCATING CERTIFIED TEACHERS TO TEACH DIVERSE STUDENT LEARNERS

We located six research studies that examined multicultural education at the inservice level (Calderon, cited in Macias, 1986; Cross et al., 1978; Fennema et al., 1981; Fleming & Sutton, 1987; Grant & Grant 1985; Washington, 1981). We will begin with the first approach from the extended typology.

Teaching the Different Child

Macias (1986) cites research conducted by Margarita Calderon in 1984 that was intended to help bilingual teachers improve their teaching of LEP students. Calderon's efforts were drawn from other, more general, research on staff development. The elements of the teachers' training consisted of (a) 5–10 hours of theory and background information, (b) 10–15 hours of demonstrations for each teaching model, (c) 15–20 hours of practice with feedback for each model, (d) 10–15 hours of practice giving technical and informal feedback among peers, and (e) weekly peer observations and coaching session at the school site during the first 2 months of classroom implementation.

Macias provided Calderon's data, comparing four levels of training intensity: (a) theory only; (b) theory and demonstrations; (c) theory, demonstrations, practice, and peer feedback; and (d) theory, demonstrations, practice, peer feedback, and peer coaching. Outcome measures included the degree of skill development and accurate and continuous use in the classroom. (Exactly how these were operationalized and measured is not clear; neither is the specific content of the training presented.) Adding demonstration to theory, that is, moving from level (a) to level (b) of intensity, resulted in an increase from 5 percent to 50 percent in skill development. The addition of practice and peer feedback—moving to level (c)—resulted in another jump in skill development to 90 percent. However, when the outcome measure was actual classroom use of the information, only level (d), which included coaching, increased classroom use from 5 percent to the range of 75 percent to 90 percent.

Rodriguez (1980) attempted to validate a series of competencies as necessary for successful bilingual instruction. She interviewed 20 elementary school bilingual teachers who had been nominated by their supervisors as being either superior or simply competent. Teachers were asked to retell stories concerning successful and unsuccessful teaching and other episodes involving them and their children and families. Cues were used to elicit as complete a retelling of each episode as possible. Protocols were analyzed in terms of whether or not they contained evidence of six competencies that effective teachers were hypothesized to possess. Three of the six competencies differentiated the two groups: self-confidence, nonauthoritarianism, and communication skills (with parents and children). Nonsignificant group differences, which nonetheless were in the expected directions, were found in terms of positive regard, use of varied teaching methodologies, and cultural knowledge (p. 9).

Single-Group Studies

Two studies were identified that followed a single-group approach. Both examined teacher attitudes. Baty (1972) examined teachers' attitudes toward a racial group, and Fennema et al., (1981) examined teachers' attitudes toward gender.

Baty conducted a pretest–posttest control-group design study to determine the effect of 10 three-hour evening meetings that exposed teachers to the historical, cultural, and social heritage of Mexican-Americans. The format of the meetings was as follows: lecture, discussion, and answer session and discussion groups. One goal of the course was to help teachers become aware of their cultural blinders; a second goal was to help teachers learn how to increase their Mexican-American students' self-esteem. The study examined two areas of teacher attitudes: tolerance and optimism. On the dimension of optimism, teachers with one to 6 years of experience working in the school district, who also had over one year of experience with culturally different students, had significantly higher scores than beginning teachers or teachers with 7 or more years of experience. Also, contact with Mexican-American students in the classroom proved to be sufficient to increase teacher optimism about pupil-achievement potential. Exposure to members of the Mexican-American group did positively affect the teachers' tolerance toward them and helped the teachers become better able to identify with the students' learning problems. In the conclusion to his study, Baty notes,

This increased empathy together with a greater understanding of ways in which the school system acts to remove the child from his/her culture increases the teacher's propensity to change her/his approach and to have changes introduced in the school system, in the form of greater experimentation and more deliberate attempts to harness the potential contribution of Mexican-American children to the classroom. (p. 73)

Fennema et al. used a series of videotapes entitled "Multiplying Options, Subtracting Bias" in a pretest-intervention-posttest study that was designed to increase females' selection of high school mathematic courses. Of the study's two assumptions, the second is of particular interest to this chapter: "since females' attitudes are influenced by their social environment, the attitude toward females as learners of mathematics held by significant others [including teachers] would also need to be changed if females' attitudes were to be changed" (p. 3). As a group, teachers in the experimental group did not change more than control-group teachers did after viewing the videotape prepared for teachers. However, near-ceiling pretest scores of the 19 female mathematics teachers might have attenuated the impact of the program. Data for the 45 male teachers, whose pretest scores were below ceiling, were analyzed separately. The male teachers showed significant increases on their level of information on sex-related differences and on other videotape content. Moreover, pretest-to-posttest differences approached significance on two variables, Knowledge, and Usefulness—Girl.

Multicultural Approaches to Education

Washington (1981) reports the results from a 5-day multicultural workshop with 49 elementary school teachers in North Carolina. In the workshop, teachers were exposed to films, audiotapes, and group dynamics designed to explore racism, white consciousness, the ideological basis for multicultural education, school desegregation, children's racial knowledge and identities, and multicultural materials and method. A survey instrument was used to collect data regarding the teachers' multicultural attitudes and behavior. Washington concludes that: "The 5-day antiracism/multicultural education training failed to affect these elementary teachers' attitudes or classroom behavior. . . . Generally, the attitudinal and behavioral changes were extremely negligible, remained relatively constant, or declined slightly" (p. 190).

Fleming and Sutton (1987), as part of a larger study, assessed teachers' attitudes and beliefs toward teaching problem solving, the importance of problem solving for low-achieving children, and teachers' beliefs about racial and gender equity in society and their own schools. After the teachers had had a 5-day intervention workshop, they felt more comfortable and had more skills to teach problem solving, and their beliefs about the importance of problem solving for low-achieving children increased. Teachers' beliefs about racial and gender equity in society did not change, but teachers did report being more aware of sex discrimination in their own schools.

Education that is Multicultural and Social Reconstructionist

Grant and Grant (1985) report mixed results from a 2-week inservice institute for teachers and principals. The 30 participants were in teams comprised of two teachers and an administrator. Each team was drawn from a different Teacher Corps Project across the United States. Five questions gave direction to this multicultural inservice program:

1. To what extent would an inservice institute on EMC influence the participants' attitudes and opinions about age, class, gender, handicap, and race?
2. To what extent would the inservice institute prepare the participants to eliminate stereotyping and to analyze and modify their curriculum from a multicultural perspective?
3. To what extent would the institute participants implement EMC concepts in their classrooms and schools after attending the institute?
4. What impact would inservice using a buddy system—two teachers and an administrator from the same school—have on the implementation of a sensitive education concept?
5. To what extent would the three-phase inservice model of awareness, acceptance, and affirmation be useful in training institute participants about EMC?

Participants demonstrated changed attitudes concerning age, class, gender, handicap, and race on the posttest. Concerning stereotyping (Question 2, above), only 3 of the 30 participants negatively stereotyped minority group members on the posttest. Although all the participants demonstrated considerable improvement with EMC curriculum analysis and modification, the degree of success depended on how complicated the material was, how extensive participants' knowledge about the concept had been, and how much knowledge they had about EMC implementation.

Concerning the third question, Grant and Grant used a 35-item, open-ended, self-report questionnaire to collect information in the following 15 areas: personal awareness, display materials, curriculum, lesson plans, resource materials, resource people, field trips, special events, teaching strategies, faculty utilization of materials, school–community relationships, inservice meetings, school goals, comfort level, and barriers to and facilitating factors of multicultural implementation. The majority of the participants indicated positive results in most areas for implementing EMC in their classrooms. However, they pointed out that, because basic skills were a school priority, there was difficulty in trying to get other colleagues to work with EMC and to see the relationship between EMC and basic skills. The other two major factors hindering the implementation of EMC were lack of materials and time. The three most important facilitating factors for implementing EMC concepts were attending the institute, having EMC materials, and feeling support from the administration.

Schools where the buddy system comprised the principal and two teachers were more successful in implementing EMC than were schools where the buddies were two teachers and some other administrator, the school counselor, or an assistant principal. Knowledge of EMC and support of it as a school goal by the principals who attended made the difference. Grant and Grant conclude:

This study has demonstrated that the three stage inservice concept—awareness, acceptance, and affirmation—is successful in helping a group of educators understand and implement an educational concept—EMC—in their schools. Educators can grow in their awareness, as demonstrated by subjects' changes of attitudes, increased ability to identify curriculum bias, and continuous attempts to increase their awareness of race, sex, age, handicap, and class after the Institute. Educators can learn to accept and affirm EMC . . . as shown by subjects' increased ability to write lesson plans and make curriculum modifications, and by their high degree of comfort in working with the concept in school. (p. 17«

Grant and Grant (1985) included a separate analysis for issues of sex equity. Institute participants were better able to modify curriculum materials and eliminate sex-role bias and stereotyping. On the sexism subscale of the Education That Is Multicultural Attitude Instrument, institute participants showed growth from pretest to posttest. On the basis of follow-up self-reports and a collected sample of instructional materials, Grant and Grant conclude that institute participants paid attention to issues of gender equity in their teaching.

Additional Studies

Cross et al. (1978) don't provide enough information to determine where their study fits in the typology. They used a pretest-treatment-posttest design to assess the impact of a multicultural inservice program on 82 elementary teachers from five school districts in southern California. Unfortunately, neither the content nor the duration of the inservice program was given. Results from the study were obtained from a self-report questionnaire. The 82 teachers reported that they did not perceive the multicultural inservice training as useful and that the training had had little effect on their acquisition of knowledge about minorities, their understanding of racism and sexism in schools and society, and their insights into minority-group needs and problems. Also, there was no increase in the quality of teachers' relationships with students, and few teachers felt the need to revise their teaching strategies and/or curriculum as a result of inservice programs (p. 103). In the conclusion, Cross et al. argue that "Those interested in change, a change that might make a difference, [must] understand that public schools are intensely political. Unless these politics are understood, multicultural education and other approaches are at best cosmetic" (p. 104).

Because Waggoner and O'Malley (1984) report that one in four teachers has had some LEP students in his or her classroom, we expected there to be some research on inservice training for these teachers. Unfortunately, we could not find any published research results pertaining to inservice education for teachers in general who are engaged in the education of LEP students, regardless of whether or not they were in BE or ESL programs. However, since 1976, the federal government, first through the Office of Bilingual Education in HEW and then through the Office of Bilingual Education and Minority Language Affairs in the Department of Education, has funded a series of training and technical assistance centers whose mission is to help school districts improve their programs for the education of LEP students. These centers provide training through a variety of vehicles such as workshops, institutes, seminars, conferences, and on-site coaching. Typically, these activities include participant evaluations. To outline some possibilities for research on this topic, we reviewed information from annual reports for three such centers (Midwest Bilingual Education Multifunctional Resource Center, 1986; Midwest Bilingual Education Multifunctional Support Center, 1985; and, Secada, 1987a).

All three centers, which operated in consecutive years, tried to conduct training at central sites and to draw participation from surrounding school districts. Typically, inservice training involved a workshop lasting anywhere from one hour to a full day. Training activities for the third report (Secada, 1987a) were often tied to a full day of on-site classroom visits by the trainer the day before the workshop. These visits helped the trainer learn more about the program, schools, and district in which she or he was conducting training. Training evaluations included asking participants to write about what they had learned from the activity that would be helpful to them in their jobs.

Responses to questions about personal learning indicated that there is some fidelity between the workshop topic and what participants think they have been exposed to. Comments about personal learning indicated changes in participant affects, beliefs, knowledge, and potential behaviors. Respondent comments tended to be more positive and more detailed when the trainer had actually visited the schools prior to conducting the workshop. This result could be interpreted as due to bias, but it also might speak to the deeper issue of teacher isolation. One teacher wrote to a particular presenter:

You told me that you thought I was good, and I really appreciate hearing that. It is not often that teachers hear anything which approaches good. I know that I said, "I know." Flip comments come easily to people who rarely receive compliments on their life's work. . . . When I listened to people talking today, I realized how close we all are to major burnout—everyone was talking privately about how we have to think of ways to keep going. . . . Thank you very much for spending these days with us. It is not apparent to you that our moods are lifted for a while and that our teaching improves visibly for a while. I know how good it felt to have you tell me that I was good. If you feel half as good, hearing that you are good, you get through the week painlessly. (personal communication)

Inservice staff development allows teachers to reflect on what they are doing, to regroup, and to compare notes. This sense of recharging oneself, as communicated by the writer just quoted, was a constant theme in participant comments. Comments about personal learning also included general statements about the gist of the session. This could be interpreted as participants' having obtained a superficial understanding of the material or their already being familiar with the major points of the topic being covered. Teachers would respond in ways such as "I already knew this, but it was a good review." Also, we found responses indicating that teachers had not realized how important a given topic had been. Whether and how such realizations transferred into classroom practice remains an open question. Finally, some few participant responses about personal learning included very detailed reports about the content and some specific ways in which that content could be applied in the teachers' classroom.

Secada (1987a) included a follow-up survey to participants to workshops lasting a minimum of half a day. They were asked to respond within a month and to report what they had tried and how well it had worked. Response to the follow-up survey was very low, but the few follow-up responses received indicated that, at least on some occasions, teachers did, in fact, try out what had been discussed. Initially cautious, they were surprised that they were frequently successful at implementation.

Discussion

These studies were all short-term efforts to change teachers' attitudes and/or behaviors regarding multicultural education. Two studies, by Baty (1972) and Grant and Grant (1985), found positive results. Baty attributes his positive results to greater awareness, empathy, and understanding on the part of teachers regarding how schools affect culturally different students. Grant and Grant believe that positive results might have resulted from the fact that these teachers were recruited from Teacher Corps programs and were already committed to the goals of helping the poor and students of color. Another explanation might be the intense nature of the institute. Members of different ethnic groups roomed together; study teams were composed of participants of differing races, genders, and ages; and discussions were held to investigate and analyze participants' philosophies about race, class, and gender issues. Fleming and Sutton (1987) also note an increase in the comfort level regarding race and gender equity and greater skills in teaching problem solving.

Grant and Grant provided a definition of multicultural education, and Washington (1981) suggests multicultural goals for the workshop. Only three of the studies examined more than one ascribed characteristic. Cross et al. (1978), Grant and Grant (1985), and Fleming and Sutton (1987) included race and gender in their efforts; Grant and Grant also included class, age, and handicap in their study.

Grant and Grant found that institute participants had more difficulty working with classism than with any of the other isms. Although only two of the studies produced somewhat mixed positive results, all of the studies indicated strong support and commitment to multicultural education, and they recommend more research in the area. In other words, the researchers do not fault the method, procedures, and treatment in their studies for their results, but they argue, instead, that people's attitudes and behaviors about multicultural education are not easily changed and that extended training is necessary. Washington's (1981) concluding statement makes this point:

The impact of antiracism/multicultural education training programs on elementary school teachers' attitudes and classroom behaviors may benefit from extended exposure to the concepts presented. . . . An extended training program should include opportunities for discussion and peer learning among teachers of similar content area or grade level. A critical feature of training would be opportunities for work within the classroom setting, including the provision of multicultural materials, examples of models or alternative instructional methodology, and assistance in observing, identifying and capitalizing on the unique strengths of individual learners. (p. 191)

All seven studies report some success at changing teacher attitudes with their treatment. However, all the studies used only short-term intervention programs, and only Grant and Grant (1985) followed the participants over time.

It is important to note that, by situating and discussing the studies that only examine gender equity within our typology, we could be critiquing them in a way that the authors might not have imagined or would consider fair. Perhaps more important than a critique of the strengths and weaknesses of these efforts is to note what they collectively do: They point to the need for research on inservice teacher education related to gender equity. There is much that we do not know about how teacher education for gender equity affects classroom life. Grant and Sleeter, as well as many others involved in issues of gender equity, have found that teachers treat children differently as a function of gender. The critical issue to remember, however, is that sometimes such differential treatment is appropriate (Brophy, 1986). We need to understand when treatment should be the same, when it should different, and how to communicate these conditions to inservice teachers.

Sanders (1989) discusses her own work as a developer of programs, the resistance in many schools to implementing and maintaining gender equity initiatives, and some of the traps into which equity trainers fell:

Our passion and our anger at the injustice came through clearly to the teachers who were required to attend these inservice sessions. With hindsight, the result was predictable. No one likes to be yelled at or blamed for oppressing poor defenseless little girls, teachers who had been neutral about sex equity distanced themselves from it, and teachers who had been actively sexist found in their resentment justification for being so. (p. 163)

The studies by Calderon (in Macias, 1986) and Rodriguez (1980) are provocative but far from conclusive. In Calderon's research involving bilingual teachers, it is not clear whether the data were drawn from the same group of teachers as they progressed through their training sessions or whether four groups of teachers were given different treatments. If the former, it is necessary to disentangle the effects of increased familiarity with the material from the actual delivery model. In addition, other elements and combinations might be tried. Might coaching by itself be sufficient, given the fact that, without coaching, classroom use of the material was minimal? For example, would 25 hours of theory tied to in-class discussion about how that theory relates to the teacher's own situation have resulted in outcomes similar to those found at intensity level (b): 50 percent skills development and 5 percent classroom use.

An alternative model of inservice training, with slightly different measures, might reveal different outcomes. Carpenter, Fennema, Peterson, Chiang, and Loef (1988) conducted a 3-week summer workshop for first-grade teachers on the principles of Cognitively Guided Instruction. They took about as much total time during their workshop as did Calderon; yet their workshop was organized much differently. A week was used in presenting research on the development of addition and subtraction problem solving (Carpenter & Moser, 1983) and in showing teachers how to interview children who are solving those problems. The remaining time was used by the teachers to discuss the research among themselves and engage in curriculum development. Time, reference books, and materials were all that was provided. After the researchers were sure that the teachers had understood the core body of research, the teachers worked on their own. Not only did the research team not provide any demonstrations, practice, feedback, or coaching, but they also did not even enterpret the research in terms of its classroom implications, beyond telling the teachers that problem solving is important and that they should assess children's understanding.

When the research team conducted classroom observations 5 or 6 months after the workshop had ended, they found 20 different teaching interpretations of the research. Some teachers were using direct instruction (Good & Grouws, 1979); others did more open-classroom type of teaching. Compared with 20 control classrooms, what Carpenter et al. found in the experimental teachers' classrooms were a range of teaching strategies focused more on problem solving and less on basic skills; enhanced student performance on problem solving, with no loss of basic skills; enhanced teacher beliefs about the importance of problem solving; and students more sure of their own ability to solve problems. Fennema has suggested (verbal communication) that, in classrooms where teachers had gone through training, she found less gender-biased interaction patterns during instruction than in control classrooms. Case studies of selected classrooms are currently under way.

Though Carpenter and his associates went against current recommendations for inservice staff development, their results are suggestive. If we provide inservice teachers with a coherent body of research results and if we encourage them to interpret that research, they might actually apply it.

The generic competencies reported by Rodriguez (1980) actually contained content more specifically tied to the teaching of bilingual learners. Selecting teachers by nomination is somewhat problematic, as is the fact that protocols were scored as either containing or not containing the trait in question. Finally, the retelling of stories without some external validation raises the possibility of incorrect self-reports.

GENERAL DISCUSSION

We started working on this chapter believing that research would tell us many things about how to prepare teachers for diverse learning populations. Several of our beliefs have changed, and some general tentative conclusions now seem possible.

Some Tentative Results

Experiences with representatives from diverse populations are worthwhile for teachers. Grant and Grant (1985) mixed inservice teachers from various backgrounds together; Mills (1984) did the same for preservice teachers. Not surprisingly, Sleeter (1985) and, to some extent, Baty (1972) report that teachers who are in multicultural settings are more likely to focus on issues of race, class, and gender in a reconstructive manner than teachers who are not. Finally, Mahan's experiences with preservice teacher placements are also important. All these results, however, seem predicated on the students' and teachers' having support mechanisms and some contexts within which to interpret their experiences. It seems important for the participants to have some external motivation for their efforts.

Barriers to using what has been learned include not enough time in the classroom, or at least that perception (Grant & Grant, 1985; Grant & Koskela, 1986); homogeneous classrooms or schools (Grant & Koskela, 1980; Sleeter, 1985); and a basic skills orientation to teaching that seems to render multicultural concerns superfluous (Grant & Grant, 1985).

The more intense the exposure and the more time spent learning the content, the more likely learning will be successful. Calderon (in Macias, 1986) found that a combination of theory, demonstration, practice, and coaching resulted in greatest use of specific classroom strategies. G. Baker (1977) found coursework to be more effective than workshops. Sleeter (1985) found that more coursework resulted in greater use of what had been learned.

The actual content for these studies is not provided in enough detail for us to recommend specific content for specific types of pre- and inservice education. Nevertheless, all these studies show that the curriculum must somehow address issues of race, class, gender, and language ethnicity in areas as diverse as history, ideology, culture, stereotyping, politics, psychology, and economics. Another result is that teacher attitudes and behaviors must be understood and, it is hoped, changed. We would venture a calculated hunch that most of these studies were conducted in populations in which whites were a majority. Because most of these studies reported mixed results, and because the discontinuity between student and teaching populations will increase, the attitudes and behaviors of educators should continue to receive research attention.

Possible Research Directions

A final barrier to the success of these programs was not necessarily discussed in the reports, but it became obvious after we read the entire collection of papers and reviewed *Teaching teachers: Facts and figures* (AACTE, 1987). Programs that stress human diversity—multicultural education, nonsexist education, bilingual–bicultural education—do not typically receive the formal and informal support from university faculty needed to make them successful. We hypothesize that this is due to the composition and biographies of the education professorate. The education professorate is 93 percent white; it is 70 percent male; and its faculty is aging. Professors average 53 years of age, associates average 47 years, and assistants average 42 years. These demographics suggest that the education faculty in universities did not receive multicultural education. It is difficult to teach, and maybe even to support, what one really does not know. Lortie (1975) argues that biography and formal training are strong influences on what one is qualified to teach. Peters's (1977) observation on teachers of teachers is important: "The effect of training programs on the practice of teachers in the classroom is negative compared with the influence of models in their past with whom they identify and of demands springing from their own personalities" (p. 162). Research should be conducted to investigate how teacher educators of different races, classes, and gender influences future teachers.

Beyond Behaviorist Conceptions of Knowledge. The bulk of the research focused on changing either teacher beliefs or teacher behaviors. In view of the large body of research on teacher expectancies (Dusek, 1985) and the process–product research on teacher behaviors (Brophy & Good, 1986), this is not surprising. We agree that attitudes and behaviors are important.

However, research should go beyond such conceptions of the teacher and of teacher education for diverse student populations. Though we know that teacher attitudes are important, we need to know more about how they are formed and the functions they serve. for example, teachers often expect less of students of color and of females than they do of whites and of males. Yet we have not asked what function such beliefs serve. If they organize the teacher's world and reduce the complexity of instructional decisions, then race, gender, family background, and similar characteristics might serve as initial proxies for needed knowledge about student ability. By the time a teacher has gathered direct evidence about students' different abilities, individual students might have already lived down (or up) to those expectations. Hence, the bias is strengthened. If this characterization is true, then removing such biases would make the teacher's initial task much more difficult. Research should focus on three interrelated issues: (a) the roles that teacher expectations play in helping organize the teacher's classroom management and instructional preparation, (b) how biases about different student populations can be reduced, and (c) how biased student expectations might be replaced with more direct methods of accessing student abilities. In this regard, the research by Carpenter et al. (1988) is suggestive, because teachers who had been taught how to access student cognition directly seemed to engage in less gender-biased patterns of behavior.

A basic tenet of education is that instruction should follow development. Yet we have no maps of how teacher cognitions,

beliefs, and skills with respect to the teaching of diverse student populations actually develop. We do not know what a beginning teacher really knows versus what successful, experienced colleagues might know about the teaching of diverse student populations. If we could map how teachers move from the former to the latter, we might be able to plan teacher education programs to help teachers develop these skills. As suggested in our discussion about the recruitment of a diverse teaching population, a reasonable starting point for beginning this work might be mapping what teachers from diverse populations know that makes a difference in their teaching of students from similar backgrounds.

Validation of Target Knowledge. We discussed how teacher certification programs and requirements have not been empirically validated. Though there are some things that we all agree are desirable to know and to do, it is far from clear that we have enough information to specify such domains on the basis of empirical evidence. A similar observation applies to preservice and inservice teacher education as well. It is likely that this knowledge will be contingent and based on particular teaching situations. For example, the literature on teacher effectiveness indicates that effective teachers keep lessons moving at a brisk pace (Brophy, 1986); yet the literature on wait time shows that many minority children, especially older males, refuse to participate in lessons as a form of resistance to the classroom (Grant, 1989). Communicating both types of information to a pre- or inservice teacher could result in confusion. What seems to be needed is some sense of contingency. Identifying this type of information and how it should be communicated to various teachers in teacher education programs will be a major challenge.

Distribution of Knowledge. We need more careful analyses of how knowledge about the teaching of diverse student populations should be disseminated within schools. Too often we assume that every teacher needs to know everything about every topic. Resnick (1987) provides an analysis of how real-world knowledge differs from school knowledge. Analyzing how complex tasks are allocated among different crew members on a ship, she discusses how knowledge is distributed among the various players. Certainly schools are more complex than ships, and the teaching of children is different in many ways. Yet schools are also cooperative ventures; this is one critical message from the effective-schools movement. A necessary response to the increasing diversity in the student population might be for instructional staff to have access to specialized bodies of knowledge at times when they need such access. Hence, cooperation among teachers could become an increasingly important skill. An intriguing possibility is provided by a school in Seattle in which the principal abolished special programs and their attendant labels. All special teachers were assigned to teach regular subjects, resulting in smaller classes, without sacrificing the specialized forms of knowledge they could bring to the school (Olson, 1988).

Moreover, different schools might devise different responses, based on the ecology of their own populations. For example, Brookover and Lezotte (in Good & Brophy, 1986) compare effective black and white schools with ineffective ones. In the effective white school there was no ability grouping. Though the effective black school grouped students by ability, it was solely for the purpose of moving students out of the lower groups into the more advanced groups as quickly as possible. On the other hand, ineffective schools, both black and white, used grouping as a means of writing off large numbers of students. More research is needed to determine whether the effective black school's actions represent valid knowledge.

We need to inquire about the sense in which teachers who fail to use content from their courses are making valid responses to their situations. For example, in Grant and Koskela (1986) and Sleeter (1985), student teachers and teachers report that they did not use what they had learned about multicultural education in situations involving predominantly white students. Were these decisions based on the belief that such information was to be used only in the case of diversity? If so, it might be necessary to reconceptualize how similar content is presented to teachers.

Transfer of Knowledge to the Classroom. As the mixed results from most of the studies indicate, and as graphically demonstrated by Calderon's research (in Macias, 1986), teachers might know content they do not use. We need to create models about why teachers use, or fail to use, the information we think they know. The Carpenter et al. (1988) study suggests that this could, in part, result from researchers not recognizing a variety of responses in the classroom. There might also be other reasons.

Creation of Teacher Expectations As a Function of Initial Teaching Experiences. In the discussion on bilingual and ESL teacher preparation, we noted the danger of not preparing sufficient numbers of bilingual teachers in the name of student need. Teachers who teach lower level courses or populations who are seen to need special services are typically perceived of as having low status in their schools. Beginning teachers are often assigned classrooms that other teachers do not want, such as the remedial classes. Because many low-skills classrooms are densely populated with students of color, we need to investigate how teachers in these situations develop their beliefs about the children they teach. It is ironic to note that, after teachers have learned their craft with students who can ill afford to be experimented on, they move on to teach other, more capable, students. Teachers who do not move on are frequently felt to have lower status. How these two practices might interact to develop teacher beliefs about diverse learners seems to be important.

Concluding Comments

There is much that we do not know about how to prepare teachers to teach an increasingly diverse student population. We think that new responses are called for in teacher recruitment, preservice education, and inservice education. Given the paucity of empirical research that we have found in this area, we believe that a major research effort is called for. More than scattered studies, more than studies that seek to document and to correlate deficiencies, we need programs of research that acknowledge what is lacking but that also provide a vision and hope for what might be done. It is a challenge that must be met.

References

Ada, A. F. (1986). Creative education for bilingual education teachers. *Harvard Educational Review* [Special issue: Teachers, teaching, and teacher education], 56(4), 386–394.

American Association of Colleges for Teacher Education. (1987). *Teaching teachers: Facts and figures.* Washington, DC: Author.

Baker, G. (1973). Multicultural training for student teachers. *Journal of Teacher Education,* 24(4), 306–307.

Baker, G. C. (1977). Multicultural education: Two preservice training approaches. *Journal of Teacher Education,* 28(3), 31–33.

Baker, K. (1987). Comment on Willig's "A meta-analysis of selected studies in the effectiveness of bilingual education." *Review of Educational Research,* 57, 351–362.

Banks, J. A. (1977). The implications of multicultural education for teacher education. In F. H. Klassen & D. M. Gollnick (Eds.), *Pluralism and the American teacher* (pp. 1–34). Washington, DC: American Association of Colleges for Teacher Education.

Baratz, J. C. (1986). Black participation in the teacher pool. *Carnegie Forum's task force on teaching as a profession.* Princeton, NJ: Educational Testing Service.

Baty, R. M. (1972). *Re-educating teachers for cultural awareness.* New York: Praeger.

Bennett, C. (with Okinaka, A., & Xiao-yang, W.). (1988, April). *The effects of a multicultural education course on preservice teachers' attitudes, knowledge, and behavior.* Paper presented at annual meeting of the American Educational Research Association, New Orleans.

Bennett, C. T. (1979). The preparation of pre-service secondary social studies teachers in multiethnic education. *High School Journal,* 62, 232–237.

Binkley, J. L., Johnson, D. M., Stewart, B. L., Abrica-Carrasco, R., Naja, H. G., & Thorpe, B. (1981). *A study of teacher training programs in bilingual education:* Vol. I. Program descriptions (RMC Report No. UR-474.). Mountain View, CA: RMC Research Corporation.

Brophy, J. E. (1986). Teaching and learning mathematics: Where research should be going. *Journal for Research in Mathematics Education,* 17, 323–346.

Brophy, J. E., & Good, T. L. (1986). Teacher behavior and student achievement. In M. C. Wittrock (Ed.), *Handbook of research on teaching* (3rd ed., pp. 328–375). New York: Macmillan.

Brown v. Topeka Board of Education, 347 U.S. 483 (1954).

Carpenter, T. P., Fennema, E., Peterson, P. L., Chiang, C., & Loef, M. (1988, April). *Using knowledge of children's thinking in classroom teaching: An experimental study.* Paper presented at the meeting of the American Educational Research Association, New Orleans.

Carpenter, T. P., & Moser, J. M. (1983). The acquisition of addition and subtraction concepts in grades one through three. *Journal for Research in Mathematics Education,* 15, 179–202.

Center for Applied Linguistics. (1974). *Guidelines for the preparation and certification of teachers of bilingual-bicultural education.* Washington, DC: Author.

Center for Education Statistics. (1987a). *The condition of education.* Washington, DC: U.S. Government Printing Office.

Center for Education Statistics. (1987b). *Digest of education statistics.* Washington, DC: U.S. Government Printing Office.

Cole, B. P. (1986). Black educator: An endangered species. *Journal of Negro Education, 55*(3), 326–346.

Coleman, J. S., Campbell, E. Q., Hobson, C. J., McPartland, J., Mood, A. M., Weinfeld, F. D., & York, R. L. (1966). *Equality of educational opportunity.* Washington, DC: U.S. Government Printing Office.

Contreras, A. R. (1988, April). *Multicultural attitudes and knowledge of education students at Indiana University.* Paper presented at annual meeting of the American Educational Research Association, New Orleans.

Cross, D. E., Deslone, M. A., & Ziajka, N. (1978). The impact of teacher inservice programs on attitudes toward multicultural education. *Education Research Quarterly, 2*, 97–105.

Cummins, J. (1986). Empowering minority students: A framework for intervention. *Harvard Educational Review, 56*(1), 18–36.

Darling-Hammond, L. (1984). *Beyond the commission reports: The coming crisis in teaching* (R-3177-RC). Santa Monica, CA: RAND Corporation.

Darling-Hammond, L. (1988). *Equality and excellence: The educational status of Black Americans.* New York: College Entrance Examination Board.

Dolce, C. J. (1973). Multicultural education: Some issues. *Journal of Teacher Education, 24*, 282–284.

Dusek, J. B. (Ed.). (1985). *Teacher expectancies.* Hillsdale, NJ: Lawrence Erlbaum.

Educational Researcher. (1986). [Special issue: The new scholarship on women in education], *15*(6).

Epstein, N. (1977). *Language, ethnicity, and the schools.* Washington, DC: George Washington University.

Fennema, E., Wolleat, P. L., Pedro, J. D., & Becker, A. D. (1981). Increasing women's participation in mathematics: An intervention study. *Journal for Research in Mathematics Education, 12*(1), 3–14.

Fleming, E., & Sutton, R. (1987). *Equals at Cleveland State University: 1985–86 evaluation report.* Cleveland, OH: Cleveland State University, College of Education.

Garcia, P. A. (1986). The impact of national testing on ethnic minorities: With proposed solutions. *Journal of Negro Education, 55*, 347–357.

Gay, G. (1983). Multiethnic education: Historical developments and future prospects. *Phi Delta Kappan, 64*(8), 560–563.

Gifford, B. R. (1986). Excellence and equity in teacher competency testing: A policy perspective. *Journal of Negro Education, 55*(3), 251–271.

Gollnick, D., & Chinn, P. (1983). *Multicultural education in a pluralidetic society.* St. Louis: C. V. Mosby.

Good, T. L., & Brophy, J. (1986). School effects. In M. C. Wittrock (Ed.), *Handbook of research on teaching* (3rd ed., pp. 570–603). New York: Macmillan.

Good, T. L., & Grouws, D. A. (1979). The Missouri mathematics effectiveness project: An experimental study of fourth-grade classrooms. *Journal of Educational Psychology, 71*, 355–362.

Gordon, B. (1987). *Newsletter of the Special Interest Group: Research Focus on Black Education.* American Educational Research Association annual business meeting, Washington, DC.

Grant, C. (1981). Education that is multicultural and teachers preparation: An examination from the perspective of preservice students. *Journal of Educational Research, 75*(2), 95–99.

Grant, C. (1989). Equity, equality, and classroom life. In W. G. Secada (Ed.), *Equity in education* (pp. 89–102). London: Falmer Press.

Grant, C., & Grant, G. (1985). Staff development and education that is multicultural: A study of an inservice institute for teachers and principals. *British Journal of Inservice Education, 2*(1), 6–18.

Grant, C., & Koskela, R. (1986). Education that is multicultural and the relationship between preservice campus learning and field experiences. *Journal of Educational Research, 79*, 197–203.

Grant, C., & Sleeter, C. (1985). The literature on multicultural education: Review and analysis. *Educational Review, 37*(2), 97–118.

Grant, C., & Sleeter, C. (1986). Race, class, and gender effects in education: An argument for integrative analysis. *Review of Educational Research, 56*, 195–211.

Grant, C., Sleeter, C., & Anderson, J. (1986). The literature on multicultural education: Review and analysis. *Educational Studies, 12*, 47–71.

Henington, M. (1981). Effect of intensive multicultural non-sexist instruction on secondary student teachers. *Educational Research Quarterly, 6*(1), 65–75.

Hodgkinson, H. L. (1985). *All one system: Demographics of education—kindergarten through graduate school.* Washington, DC: Institute for Educational Leadership.

Illinois State Board of Education, Office of Management and Policy Planning. (1987). *A study of teacher trends and traits.* Springfield, IL: Author.

Kaskowitz, D. H., Binkley, J. L., & Johnson, D. M. (1981). *A study of teacher training programs in bilingual education: Vol. 2. The supply of and demand for bilingual education teachers* (RMC Report No. UR-487). Mountain View, CA: RMC Research Corporation.

Kennedy, M. M., Jung, R. K., & Orland, M. E. (1986). *Poverty, achievement, and the distribution of compensatory education services* (An interim report from the National Assessment of Chapter 1). Washington, DC: U.S. Government Printing Office.

Koppelman, K., & Martin, R. (1988, April). *A longitudinal study of the impact of a human relations/multicultural education course on attitudes of prospective teachers regarding issues of race, class, and gender.* Paper presented at the meeting of the American Educational Research Association, New Orleans.

Lambert, V., & Rohland, G. (1983). *The feasibility of teaching about sex-role stereotyping in a pre-service teacher training setting: A pilot study.* Paper presented at the ninth annual midyear conference of the AERA/SIG: Women and Education, Tempe, AZ.

Lortie, D. (1975). *Schoolteacher: A sociological study.* Chicago: University of Chicago Press.

Macias, R. F. (1986). Teacher preparation for bilingual education. In *A report of the compendium of papers on the topic of bilingual education of the Committee on Education and Labor, House of Representatives* (Serial No. 99-R, pp. 41–56). Washington, DC: U.S. Government Printing Office.

Mahan, J. (1982). Native Americans as teacher trainers: Anatomy and outcomes of a cultural immersion project. *Journal of Educational Equity and Leadership, 2*(2), 100–110.

McFerren, M. (1988). *Certification of language educators in the United States* (CLEAR Educational Report Series No. ER 11). Los Angeles: University of California, Center for Language Education and Research.

Merino, B. J., Politzer, R., & Ramirez, A. (1979). The relationship of teachers' Spanish proficiency to pupils' achievement. *NABE Journal, 3*(2), 21–37.

Midwest Bilingual Education Multifunctional Resource Center. (1986). *Annual report: 1985–1986* (Contract no. 300850188). Rosslyn, VA: InterAmerica Research Associates.

Midwest Bilingual Education Multifunctional Support Center. (1985).

Final report: 1984–1985 (Contract no. 300830217). Arlington Heights, IL: Northwest Educational Cooperative.

Mills, J. (1984). Addressing the separate-but-equal predicament in teacher preparation: A case study. *Journal of Teacher Education, 35*(6), 18–23.

Moultry, M. (1988, April). *Multicultural education among seniors in the College of Education at Ohio State University.* Paper presented at the meeting of the American Educational Research Association, New Orleans.

National Clearinghouse for Bilingual Education. (1986). *Forum, 9*(3). Wheaton, MD: Author.

Olson, L. (1988, April 13). A Seattle principal defies the conventional wisdom. *Education Week, 1,* 22–23.

O'Malley, J. M. (1981). *Children's English and services study: Language minority children with limited English proficiency in the United States.* Rosslyn, VA: InterAmerica Research Associates, National Clearinghouse for Bilingual Education.

O'Malley, J. M., & Waggoner, D. (1984). Public school teacher preparation and the teaching of ESL. *TESOL Newsletter, 18*(3).

Oxford-Carpenter, R., Pol, L., Gendell, M., & Peng, S. (1984). *Demographic projections of non-English-background and limited-English-proficient persons in the United States to the year 2000 by state, age, and language group.* Rosslyn, VA: InterAmerica Research Associates, National Clearinghouse for Bilingual Education.

Perlman, J. (1987, December). *Bilingualism and ethnicity in American schooling before 1960: An historical review.* Paper presented at the Harvard University Institute on Bilingual Education; Research to Policy to Practice, Cambridge, MA.

Peters, R. S. (1977). *Education and the education of teachers.* London: Routledge & Kegan Paul.

Reisner, E. R. (1983). The availability of bilingual education teachers. In K. A. Baker & A. A. DeKanter (Eds.), *Bilingual education: A reappraisal of federal policy* (pp. 175–203). Lexington, MA: Lexington Books.

Resnick, L. B. (1987). Learning in school and out. *Educational Researcher, 16*(9), 13–20.

Richards, J. C. (1987). The dilemma of teacher education in TESOL. *TESOL Quarterly, 21*(2), 209–226.

Rodriguez, A. M. (1980). Empirically defining competencies for effective bilingual teachers: A preliminary report. *Bilingual Education Paper Series, 3*(12). (ERIC Document Reproduction Service No. ED 224 662)

Sadker, D., & Sadker, M. (1981). The development and field trial of a non-sexist teacher education curriculum. *High School Journal, 64,* 331–336.

Sanders, J. (1989). Equity and technology in education: An applied researcher talks to the theoreticians. In W. G. Secada (Ed.), *Equity in education* (pp. 158–179). London: Falmer Press.

Secada, W. G. (1987a). *Annual report. Year 1: 1986–1987* (Contract no. 300860050). Madison WI: University of Wisconsin–Madison, Wisconsin Center for Education Research, Upper Great Lakes Multifunctional Resource Center.

Secada, W. G. (1987b). This is 1987, not 1980: A comment on a comment. *Review of Educational Research, 57,* 377–384.

Secada, W. G. (1989). Equity in education versus equality of education: Toward an alternative conception. In W. G. Secada (Ed.), *Equity in education* (pp. 68–88). London: Falmer Press.

Skutnabb-Kangas, T., & Cummins, J. (1988). *Minority education: From shame to struggle.* Clevedon, Avon, England: Multilingual Matters.

Sleeter, C. (1985). A need for research on preservice teacher education for mainstreaming and multicultural education. *Journal of Education Equity and Leadership, 5*(3), 205–215.

Sleeter, C. (1988). *Preservice coursework and field experience in multicultural education: Impact on teacher behavior.* Unpublished manuscript.

Sleeter, C. & Grant, C. (1987). An analysis of multicultural education in the United States. *Harvard Educational Review, 57,* 421–444.

Sleeter, C., & Grant, C. (1988). *Making choices for multicultural education: Five approaches to race, class, and gender.* Columbus, OH: Charles E. Merrill.

Smith, G. P. (1984). The critical issue of excellence and equity in competency testing. *Journal of Teacher Education, 35*(2), 6–9.

Smith, M. (1988, April). *Comments made in response to "Bilingual education research and policy: The debate continues"* (A symposium) at the meeting of the American Educational Research Association, New Orleans.

Smith, W. (1978, March). *Evaluation of modules on sex role stereotyping integrated into preservice elementary teacher education.* Paper presented at the meeting of the American Educational Research Association, Toronto.

Stein, C. B. (1986). *Sink or swim: The politics of bilingual education.* New York: Praeger.

Teachers of English to Speakers of Other Languages. (1975). *Guidelines for the certification and preparation of teachers of English to speakers of other languages in the United States.* Washington, DC: Author.

Waggoner, D. (1979). Teacher resource in bilingual education: A national survey. *NABE Journal, 3*(2), 53–60.

Waggoner, D., & O'Malley, J. M. (1984). Teachers of limited English proficient children in the United States. *NABE Journal, 9*(3), 25–42.

Washington, V. (1981). Impact of antiracism/multicultural education training on elementary teachers' attitudes and classroom behavior. *Elementary School Journal, 81*(3), 186–192.

Wayson, W. (1988, April). *Multicultural education among seniors in the College of Education at Ohio State University.* Paper presented at the meeting of the American Educational Research Association, New Orleans.

Willig, A. C. (1987). Examining bilingual education research through meta-analysis and narrative review: A response to Baker. *Review of Educational Research, 57,* 363–374.

Witty, E. P. (1983). *Prospects for Black teachers: Preparation, certification, employment.* Washington, DC: ERIC Clearinghouse on Teacher Education. (ERIC Document Reproduction Service No. ED 213 659)

·24·

EDUCATING TEACHERS FOR SPECIAL EDUCATION STUDENTS

Maynard C. Reynolds

UNIVERSITY OF MINNESOTA

Ideas are tested at their margins, and so are schools and even teacher education. Many students learn quite adequately with only minor assistance from teachers, but this is not so for those at the margins. As Smith (1980) puts it, "The test of helping professions is whether they can serve those who cannot get along without them rather than those who can proceed or make progress without them" (p. 25). In this chapter the focus is on teacher preparation in the field of special education, which is addressed to the needs of exceptional students.

The term *exceptional* is used frequently to refer to children whose marginality comes on the gifted and talented side, as well as to those who are disabled. In this chapter attention will be given only to disabled students, omitting even on that side the important subfields of speech–language disorders and severe–profound disabilities. It will be enough to look critically at teacher education programs relating to mild levels of disabilities including mental retardation, learning disabilities, emotional and behavioral problems, sensory disorders, and various physical handicaps. Because trends are moving strongly toward serving handicapped students in regular education environments, with help from special educators, school psychologists, and other support staff, some attention will be given to the preparation of "regular" teachers. In 1986–1987, more than 92 percent of special education students received their education in regular education buildings (U.S. Department of Education, 1988).

Very little research has been directed specifically to the preparation of special education teachers. More research has been conducted on characteristics and needs of exceptional students, which of course indicate important elements needed in teacher preparation. A theme developed in this chapter is that much of the relevant research shows that there are few qualitative differences in the teaching practices useful to mildly handicapped and nonhandicapped students. It is possible, however, to point out aspects of teacher preparation that seem especially important in serving handicapped students. The intent is to challenge teacher educators to match the very large and growing challenge now faced by schools in trying to teach handicapped and at-risk students.

SPECIAL EDUCATION STUDENTS

On December 1 of every school year, all school districts of the nation report the numbers of children enrolled in special education by categories. For the 1986–1987 school year, summary data were as reported in Table 24-1.

The total of 4.4 million pupils enrolled in special education programs falls short of the 8 million estimated to need special education and related services at the time of the congressional hearings leading to Public Law 94-142. It is to be noted that 4.4 million is the figure representing students served on a particular day. If data were available on the numbers of students in school served in special education, past or present, the fig-

The writing of this chapter had the advantage of early reviews of drafts by Catherine Morsink (University of Florida) and Naomi Zigmund (University of Pittsburgh). The help is gratefully acknowledge, but they cannot be held accountable for the final manuscript.

TABLE 24–1. Children Ages 0–21 Served in Special Education Programs in the 1986–1987 School Year

Category	Number Enrolled in Special Programs	% of Total Served
Learning disabled	1,926,097	43.6
Speech impaired	1,140,422	25.8
Mentally retarded	664,424	15.0
Emotionally disturbed	384,680	8.7
Deaf and hard of hearing	66,761	1.5
Multihandicapped	99,416	2.2
Orthopedically impaired	58,328	1.3
Other health impaired	52,658	1.2
Visually handicapped	27,049	0.6
Deaf–blind	1,766	0.04
Total	4,421,601	100.0

Note: From *Tenth Annual Report to Congress on the Implementation of the Education of the Handicapped Act* (p. 9), U.S. Department of Education, 1988, Washington, DC: Author.

ure might well approach 8 million. At least 75 percent, possibly as many as 90 percent, of students enrolled in special education programs, according to Algozzine and Korinek (1985), are *mildly handicapped* as that term is used in this chapter.

As we look to the future and consider what might be required of special education, it is clear that the numbers and proportions of children with extraordinary needs are increasing in our society. The challenge this presents to the schools and, specifically, to special education will be very great for the foreseeable future. In brief, these are some of the trends:

An increasing general school population (U.S. Bureau of the Census, 1983)

An increasing number of children living in poverty (National Center for Health Statistics, 1981)

Increasing numbers and proportions of children with learning problems (Child Trends, 1985)

Increasing rates of survival of low-birth-weight children who then show relatively high disability rates (Zill, 1985)

Increasing numbers and proportions of children involved with drug addiction, alcoholism, child neglect, and child abuse.

Each of these factors predicts increases in the numbers and proportions of students likely to be referred to special education. However, the rising public debt and aversion to tax increases makes the continued expansion of high-cost special education programs unlikely. The estimated expenditure for special education, considering only special funding by state and federal governments (not including basic or formula aids given for all students), is about $18 billion per school year (Moore, Strang, Schwartz, & Braddock, 1988). Already, several state legislatures have put caps on special education expenditures. There is a rising call for programs to serve at-risk students, but how these will relate to traditional special education programs and be funded is unclear. Passage of PL 99-457 in 1986, which mandates services to handicapped children down to age 3 and creates incentives for providing education for such children even down to infancy, added additional pressures for expansion of special education programs. Providing teachers to meet these expanding needs is a very large chal-

lenge. The changes required could go beyond incremental moves to structural changes.

SPECIAL EDUCATION TEACHERS

A breakdown of the number of special education teachers employed by category is given in Table 24-2 for the 1985–1986 school year. The 291,954 special teachers represent about one out of eight of the total number of K–12 teachers employed in the nation. If one adds the additional 107,368 professional staff employed primarily in special education programs (e.g., school psychologists and social workers), the total rises to about 400,000 professional special education staff (U.S. Department of Education, 1988). Also included in Table 24-2 are the estimated numbers of teachers, as reported by all school districts of the nation, required to fill vacancies and replace noncertified staff. Considering all categories, it appears that "additional teachers needed" approaches about one-tenth of the total employed.

Notably, Table 24-2 does not include a *noncategorical* entry for teachers, which might well have been the most rapidly growing category in recent years. A 1985 report showed that, in a one-year period, from the 1981–1982 to the 1982–1983 school years, the number of noncategorical teachers employed in special education programs in the United States rose from 16,177 to 25,305 (U.S. Department of Education, 1985). In percentage terms, that was a higher gain in a short period than for any other category considered.

In thinking forward about likely developments and needs for special education teachers, it might be useful to look briefly to the past and for trends that have significance. The history of special education can be summarized in two words: *progressive inclusion*. Children with disabilities have been accepted into the schools in gradually increasing numbers and proportions. Since enactment of Public Law 94-142, the Education for All Handicapped Children Act in 1975, we have neared the end of a long journey, in the sense that virtually all disabled children are now enrolled in a school program of some kind. They now have the right to free and appropriate education. There is

TABLE 24–2. Teachers Employed in Special Education in the 1985–1986 School Year

Handicapping Condition	Number Employed	Estimated Number of Additional Teachers Needed[a]
Learning disabled	111,427	10,785
Mentally retarded	61,411	5,014
Emotionally disturbed	32,774	4,701
Speech or language impaired	39,747	3,504
Hard of hearing and deaf	8,200	679
Multihandicapped	9,078	868
Orthopedically impaired	4,681	446
Other health impaired	3,376	230
Visually handicapped	3,261	342
Deaf–blind	298	46
Total	291,954	27,474

Note: Data from *Tenth Annual Report to Congress on the Implementation of the Education of the Handicapped Act* (pp. 34–35), U.S. Department of Education (1988), Washington, DC: Author.

[a]To fill vacancies and to replace noncertified staff.

still much debate, however, about how inclusive or integrated the arrangements should be within a school.

The legal requirements are that instruction be provided in the *least restrictive environment*, which creates a bias toward mainstreaming, but programs must also be *appropriate*, which makes the situation ambiguous and the cause of much debate. Many strong advocates propose that even severely disabled pupils should be enrolled in *mainstream* classes (Lipsky & Gartner, 1989). Others are opposed to, or at least cautious about, the so-called *regular education initiative*, which calls for more initiatives by teams of special and regular teachers to provide mainstream instruction for mildly disabled students (Kauffman, Gerber, & Semmel, 1988; Will, 1986). The assumption made here is that the story for the future, as well as for the past, will be one of *progressive inclusion*. This suggests that all teachers need to be prepared to help accommodate disabled students in regular school environments and that special education teachers need to be prepared for consultation and teaming functions, as well as for direct teaching functions.

The attrition rate of special educators is relatively high (Morsink, 1982). In part, this could be because the attrition rate is relatively high for new teachers of all kinds, and special education has been growing, thus employing more new teachers than most other fields. Smith-Davis, Burke, and Noel (1983) estimate, on the basis of interviews with special education leaders in all states (plus four territories), that about 25,000 special education teachers leave the field annually, whereas the supply of new special educators in 1983–1984 was about 22,000. Uncertainties exist about these estimates, but it appears that rates of attrition and new entry in special education teaching were approximately in balance in 1983, even though much unevenness in supply and need existed for particular states and localities. Attrition rates were found to be especially high in rural districts and inner-city schools. National data for 1985–1986 indicated that the percentage of college students enrolling in teacher education programs had stabilized after more than a decade of decline, a trend that could be helpful in special education (U.S. Department of Education, 1987).

Teacher demand in the field of special education is influ-

enced by rate of turnover, and one factor in rate of turnover is so-called *burnout*. Freudenberger (1977) defines *burnout* as the condition of being exhausted from excessive demands on energy, strengths, or resources. Special education teachers, especially those who work with students showing difficult behavior problems (Morsink, 1982), tend to be highly vulnerable to burnout. Similarly, minority-group teachers are prime candidates for burnout. Zabel and Zabel (1983) suggest that more experienced, highly trained, and older teachers are less at risk for burnout than others.

Possible approaches to preventing and reducing burnout among special education teachers include developing stronger support systems, more completely preparing themselves in anticipation of burnout, including consideration of personal strategies for coping, and recycling special education teachers to regular classrooms on a periodic basis (assuming they have dual teacher certification).

THE ATI ASSUMPTION

Special education is based on an aptitude-treatment-interaction (ATI) assumption. That is, it is assumed that there are variations in characteristics of the learners (aptitudes) and in available treatments (instruction and curriculum) that need to be matched in particular ways to improve learning outcomes; otherwise, everyone could be taught in the same way, with no special arrangements of any kind.

The ATI assumption in special education has implications of considerable depth. It is assumed, not only that children having certain characteristics in common require distinctive forms of instruction, but also that the teachers who offer such instruction need to be prepared in special ways and work in special places with the selected children. Thus, one often sees "learning disability" teachers instructing "learning disabled" children in "learning disability resource rooms," or teachers of educable retarded students teaching EMR children in classes for EMR pupils.

The extreme manifestations of the ATI assumption and the

related structuring of special education programs are cast into considerable doubt these days. For example, Hobbs (1975, 1980) led a major study of the classification system used in special education and concluded that it has become a barrier to efficient services to handicapped children and their families. A panel created by the National Academy of Sciences (Heller, Holtzman, & Messick, 1982) also raised serious questions about classification and placement practices in special education. A recent summary of research, led by Wang, Reynolds, and Walberg (1987, 1988) again revealed major problems in classification processes.

ATIs are of two types, ordinal and disordinal. It is apparent that some parts of the special education enterprise present disordinal interactions. Children who are blind cannot read in ordinary ways by using sight; for such students special materials and nonvisual procedures for reading have been invented (using braille mainly, but some other approaches as well). Thus, for children who are blind, very distinctive approaches to reading are required, and, to an extent, the teachers who teach these special approaches can be described as special education teachers. This example is *disordinal* because there is a definite crossover such that one approach (braille) is superior for reading by blind pupils, and other approaches (print) are better for seeing pupils. There are some partially seeing children for whom the decision about using braille or print materials is ambiguous and difficult, depending perhaps on a child's prognosis for better or worse vision in the future, but at extremes there is a clear disordinal interaction. In a similar way, distinctive educational procedures are required for students who cannot hear. These relate to communication without audition and to the serious language-development problems associated with deafness. Severely and profoundly handicapped students, those with extremely attenuated cognitive abilities, require curricula that are discontinuous with those of nonhandicapped students; so, again, the interaction is disordinal.

It appears that, for most handicapped students, however, mainly those with milder degrees of deviation, the ATIs are ordinal. Such students require, not a different kind of instruction, nor a totally different curriculum, but only more time, more intensive forms of teacher involvement, closer monitoring, more deliberate efforts at strategic approaches to learning and generalization, and the like.

In a summary paper concerning research on disadvantaged students, but with frequent references to special education as well, Brophy (1986) concludes that research has provided very little evidence of a need for qualitatively different forms of instruction for exceptional students; but he makes it clear that some students need more instruction than others. To teach mildly handicapped students, teachers appear not to need qualitatively different preparation from that of regular teachers, but they require situations in which they can work at high density with children who otherwise show poor progress in school. To achieve such teaching it might not be necessary to move children and teachers to special places; and not all functions necessarily require fully trained teachers. Possibly some of the necessary instruction can be provided by technical staff working under the supervision of highly professional regular and special education teachers.

A further distinction when considering ATIs is that one can teach for development of aptitudes that have importance or one can teach in ways that circumvent inaptitude (Corno & Snow, 1986). In the first case the term *remedial* is often used; in the latter case, the terms *compensatory* and *short circuiting* are used. Special education involves all of these approaches.

In summary, the evidence is that, for mildly handicapped students, ATIs are ordinal. There are no unique methods to be taught to special education teachers, as contrasted with what is included in the preparation of regular teachers. However, we can expect special education teachers to work in situations where they offer high-density instruction to individuals or small groups of children who need extra time and help. Through experience, special education teachers can be expected to become especially competent in highly intensive forms of instruction.

THE KNOWLEDGE BASE

The term *knowledge base* is used here to refer to the wide range of constructs, principles, skills, and dispositions that support the teaching of handicapped students. What is presented here is surely not unique to the teaching of handicapped students; the ideas here represent only what is judged to be especially important in such teaching. Included are theory and empirical knowledge from several disciplines, ethical and moral principles, rules of law and regulations, and maxims developed and tested through practical experience, all of which taken together represent a basis for teaching. It is assumed that, through teacher education and experience, the knowledge base (know that) is matched with procedural knowledge (know how) and conditional knowledge (know when). Further, it is assumed that teaching is complex and ambiguous work, requiring thoughtful deliberation and judgment by highly informed professional teachers. The belief is that the knowledge base is constantly changing and growing, so that teachers must be expected to keep up with developments, just as the public is correct in expecting teachers to be constantly engaged in improving their understanding and skills.

Special Considerations About the Knowledge Base

A number of preliminary considerations warrant attention before moving directly to statements about the knowledge base for special education teaching.

Teaming Arrangements. It probably is useful to conceptualize the knowledge base as comprised of a general pool or large store of knowledge relevant to teaching. Mastery of that knowledge goes beyond what one could consider appropriate for any one profession or person. Thus, although there might not be distinct or unique domains of knowledge relevant to teaching handicapped students, it is possible to consider the preparation of teachers for complementary roles. Teaming and consulting arrangements are common in serving handicapped pupils in the schools. Together, teams can encompass the knowledge pool quite thoroughly, but individuals cannot.

Dispositional Analysis. There has been a tendency in special education to engage in what could be called an *order of disposition analysis* (Meehl, 1972; Reynolds & Birch, 1988). For example, when a child is not learning to read at an acceptable rate, there is often a turn to psychologists, who then study the child to estimate the rate at which one might predict or expect the child to learn to read. This involves a step away from the level of the curriculum or the *level of the lesson.* Often it results in the classification of the child as learning disabled (LD) or EMR. It focuses on certain conditionals or dispositions. This process often becomes complex, involving discussion of details of cognitive abilities, personality traits, or more, all removed by some distance from the level of the lesson. In the case of learning disabilities, the definition proposed by federal authorities (U.S. Office of Education, 1977) calls for evidence of "disorder in one or more basic psychological processes involved in understanding or in using language" (p. 42478). Thus, the very definition of the problem involves dispositional analysis.

The analysis can go a further step in removal from the level of the lesson; for example, in hypothesizing that medical factors are predispositional. One leading special educator has said that learning disabilities are "essentially and almost always the result of perceptual problems based on the neurological system" (Cruickshank, 1972, p. 383). In this case, attention has shifted two orders of disposition away from the level of the lesson.

Instruction planned in terms of analyses one or more orders of disposition removed from the level of the lesson often results in teaching targeted at such objectives as more proficient auditory sequencing, visual perception, or sensory integration. The knowledge claims about the value of teaching at such levels and the assumptions about transfer to reading abilities or other common curricular objectives are very complex and, so far, not well validated (Arter & Jenkins, 1979). Also, such teaching tends to cause a loss of time in teaching essential topics at the level of the lesson (Leinhardt, Zigmond, & Cooley, 1981). There is a strong turn against diagnosis, classification, and instruction based on remote dispositional analysis. Instead, one sees increasing emphasis on curriculum-based assessment and on principles of instruction as applied directly in classroom situations.

Special Educators and Other Professionals. Special educators, more than teachers of any other kind, tend to have close working relations with representatives of other professions such as medicine, psychology, and social work. This brings colleagues and assistance to special education teachers, but it can also be problematic. Frequently, the preparation of special education teachers has involved heavy medical components in the knowledge base. Historically, special education was created by physicians, but often with limiting, and even misleading, ideas about education. The so-called *medical model* has been a burden to special education, even in recent years, as in the high orientation to neurology in approaching learning problems. Actually, one learns very little, at the present state of knowledge, about the teaching of reading or other subjects from the neurologist or neuropsychologist. Coles (1988), in an unusually thorough review of research conducted at the boundaries of medicine and education, concludes that "after decades of re-

search, it has still not been demonstrated that disabling neurological functions exist in more than a minuscule number of these [learning disabled] children" (p. xii).

It has been a special problem that educators so often give to psychologists or physicians a major voice in classification functions and in the placement of children for special education purposes. All too often in the past, psychologists have contributed IQ testing and grand predictions about children's development, but little to practical management of instruction. That is changing for the better these days, with more psychological research focused on manipulable variables and instructional effectiveness. In any case, it is to be recognized that the knowledge base for special education crosses boundaries with several other prominent professions, and not always critically.

Special Education Referrals. Most referrals of children to special education are for reasons of poor progress in basic literacy skills and/or unacceptable social behavior. Children do not get referred because they are progressing poorly in learning to play the flute or failing in courses on biology or woodworking. They get referred because they are not learning to read or because they are disturbing other students and teachers.

When considering the knowledge base for special education teachers, it is important to hold in mind why referrals are made. Special educators must be especially expert in the "cultural-imperative" curricular domains. These imperatives are the basic tools of our culture—such as language (in all forms) and social skills—in contrast with the so-called cultural electives. It is for reasons of failure to progress in these essential areas, the cultural imperatives, that society has been willing to create and fund a high-cost supplementary or second system of education, including special education.

The Knowledge Base for Teachers in Special Education

Following is a set of topics believed to be essential for special education teachers. Actually, most of these domains could well be included in the preparation of all professional teachers. However, they are especially important for teachers who focus on serving handicapped children. In listing topics separately, one runs the danger that readers will see them as discrete elements in planning and conducting instruction and as topics to be covered in separate courses or modules for teachers in preparation. Nothing like that is intended. This sketch of relevant knowledge is but a starting point. How to teach the knowledge and how and when to apply it are other very complex matters, open to various approaches. The several topics should be treated in an interactive way in teacher preparation and be thoroughly coordinated in practicums.

Legal and Ethical Principles. The schooling of handicapped children is circumscribed by a variety of laws and regulations, some guaranteeing rights and others prescribing procedures to be followed. The trends in law have been to offer rights of education to all children, to move instruction progressively toward mainstream placements, to involve parents as coequals with educators in planning individualized programs, and to require recurring accountability reviews of educational processes and outcomes for individuals. Particulars of law and regulation vary somewhat from one political entity to another and from time to time, but they can be ascertained quite readily. The Council for Exceptional Children, the major professional organization of special educators, is a steady source of information about laws, policies, regulations, and professional codes (Ballard, Ramirez, & Weintraub, 1982). Beyond matters of law, ethical issues of deep importance to pupils, families, and teachers often arise in special education. For example, what should be done about a child who quite frequently disrupts regular class routines and good order? The problems could be only marginal for most pupils in the class; if the child causing the disturbance is removed and sent to a special class or school, that experience could be catastrophic for child and family. Should marginal gains for the many be sought even at the cost of catastrophic losses for one child and his or her family? Teacher preparation should include consideration of such ethical dilemmas, suggesting how teachers can approach such problems in principled ways.

Curriculum. Teachers of special education need to have broad knowledge of curricula and how to make modifications in curriculum and materials for instruction to meet individual needs. With other team members and parents, they must be capable of contributing to assessment and educational diagnosis and to developing short- and long-range objectives for individual pupils. They should be especially creative in representing knowledge from the various content areas, to connect with the schemas of students who might be unusually lacking in experience, skill, and understanding. To the maximum extent feasible, it is desirable that the curricula followed by special education students be basically the same and yet as varied as those followed by nonhandicapped pupils.

Educational Theories and Systems. Special educators need to be knowledgeable about a variety of theories and systems of teaching and to use them in planning instruction. Discussed next are several of the important approaches.

Direct instruction. As advanced by Engleman and associates at the University of Oregon, direct instruction emphasizes small-group, face-to-face, highly scripted instruction using carefully sequenced lessons (Becker, 1977; Engleman, 1967; Engleman & Carnine, 1982). It represents an extreme form of high structure by teachers. In fact, even the behavior of the teacher is highly structured. Use of direct instruction procedures, such as in the Direct Instructional System for Teaching Arithmetic and Reading (DISTAR) program, might be a good beginning activity for novice teachers, assuming they have a view of teaching and of their own development that will gradually open to them a broader range of theoretical and practical approaches.

Evaluations of direct instruction have shown highly positive results (Abt Associates, 1977). Low-achieving students tend to profit more than others from instruction that is highly structured; DISTAR and kindred procedures satisfy that criterion to an extraordinary degree (Engleman & Carnine, 1982). One limitation of highly structured teaching could be that it be-

comes an extreme prosthetic, with the teacher doing for handicapped children what they cannot easily do but should learn to do for themselves and, as a result, failure on the part of students to learn self-management procedures (Corno & Snow, 1986).

A notable feature of direct instruction is that, because it can be so highly scripted, it can be used at times by paraprofessionals working under the supervision of professional teachers. This kind of teaming and differentiation of roles seems likely to be common in the future as a way of meeting personnel needs and as an aspect of differentiation in the roles of educators (Holmes Group, 1986).

Effective instruction. Recent research concerning effective instruction and schools focuses on variables that are manipulable by teachers, some of them illustrated in direct instruction, but the orientation is broader (Rosenshine, 1987; Walberg, 1984; Walberg & Wang, 1987). Some of these variables are environmental characteristics, including high expectations and high teacher directedness; instructional characteristics such as high academic learning time (ALT—meaning time spent on tasks the student can perform at a high rate of success), frequent and systematic monitoring, and systematic feedback and reinforcement; and curricular adaptations linking instruction to the present levels of knowledge and skill of pupils.

Many of the effectiveness variables can be understood and dealt with at a classroom level; expert teachers exhibit the principles in smooth operation day-by-day. But the same variables can be thought of and used in reference to individual pupils and their special education (Reynolds & Birch, 1988). For example, some children are extremely inattentive in school, off task, and low on ALT. In such cases, an analysis is required, not just of the situation in the class, but also of the particular student's problem and what can be done to solve it. Perhaps a school psychologist or special education teacher, working with regular teachers, can design a plan to help the student learn to be more attentive over longer periods of time. Similarly, some students have learned to expect little of themselves and need extraordinary attention to increase motivation, positive self-concepts, and achievement expectations.

Most basic of all considerations in effective instruction is detailed understanding of the present status of exceptional pupils concerning what they know and can do (their knowledge and skills), in order to plan the next steps in instruction. Such understanding of the present developmental levels of the individual disabled student is one element in forming individualized educational programs (IEPs) as required by PL 94-142.

Special educators share with all educators the need to know and use effectiveness principles; in addition, they need practical skill in application of these principles in work with individual students whose status in the class or group is marginal in one or more significant ways.

Behavioral principles. Special education teachers should be well informed and practiced concerning behavioral analysis and operant principles (Haring, 1975; Lindsley, 1972; Lovitt, 1978; Rusch, Rose, & Greenwood, 1988). In Walberg's (1984) summary of meta-analyses in education, no factor rated higher in *effect size* than systematic use of reinforcement principles. Special educators should be able to pinpoint behaviors that need to be either accelerated or decelerated and to help devise operant procedures for making the necessary changes. It is hoped that special educators are not rigidly confined just to behavioral methods, but this is one of the domains in which they should show competence.

Classroom management. Along with other teachers, special educators need to be well informed and capable in classroom-management procedures. When classes lack good order, pupils who are marginal in some way tend to become problems to both themselves and their classmates. At least five aspects of classroom management are important, as follows:

1. Establishment of a good climate for learning (Fox, 1974; Walberg, 1987)
2. Good ecological management, in the sense of demonstrating "withitness," high rates of pupil alertness, well-managed transitions, and so on, as researched by Kounin (1970) and transformed for teacher education by Borg, Langer, and Wilson (1975)
3. Clear teaching of rules, expectations, and other aspects of classroom behavior (Evertson et al., n.d.)
4. Application of behavioral principles in managing both group and individual behavior (Rusch et al., 1988)
5. Crisis management; that is, managing situations in which extremely aggressive or otherwise unacceptable behavior occurs (Morse, Ardizzone, MacDonald, & Pasick, 1980; Wood, 1980).

Teaching basic literacy skills. Special education teachers are challenged to be especially resourceful in teaching basic academic skills such as reading and arithmetic. It is failure to learn these subjects that drives many referrals to special education. Progress can be made with many exceptional students by intensive reteaching of the skills, with much support and use of principles of good teaching.

Beyond lessons structured by teachers, it is critically important that students who have fallen behind in reading actually read a great deal. That might appear to be a simplistic principle; but, in fact, it is of major importance and difficult to implement. One of the great problems of students who fall behind in reading is that they tend to read progressively less and less than their classmates, a phenomenon referred to by Stanovich (1986) and Walberg and Tsai (1983) as the *Matthew Effect*. This follows the biblical statement (Matthew 25:29): "For unto every one that hath shall be given and he shall have in abundance; but from him that hath not shall be taken away even that which he hath." Stanovich reports that low-ability readers might be reading only one-tenth as many words per day as top-group readers at middle elementary school level. School programs that permit Matthew Effects to occur are contributing to inequity problems among pupils. The solution is to provide massive practice in reading for those who have fallen behind, and that requires very special arrangements and effort.

Some of the experiences required by exceptional pupils are of routine kinds, as in building up *automaticity* in word recognition or mastery of basic number combinations in arithmetic. But it is increasingly being recognized that even the traditional three Rs are very complex and require teaching far beyond demonstration and drill. Emphasis is being given increasingly to matters of comprehension and problem solving, and special education teachers need awarenesses in these domains (Chipman, Segal, & Glaser, 1985).

The attention of special educators is being drawn to means by which they can facilitate early childhood experiences, in cooperation with parents, to help more children to succeed in basic skills and fewer to fail. The review work of Stanovich (1986), suggesting that *phonological awareness* is a key factor in early success in reading, is helpful as a guide to early education activities, both at school and at home. In sum, the special education teacher needs to be able to extend the work of the best of regular teachers in teaching the basic literacy skills.

Teaching for self-regulation and strategic behavior. An emerging and very important development of recent years has been the emphasis on teaching for self-regulatory behavior. The aim is to teach every student how to manage herself or himself in school and beyond. This requires that self-regulation be made a regular part of the curriculum and that students who show particular difficulty in this aspect of the curriculum be given intensive extra help. For example, in the Adaptive Learning Environments Model (ALEM) developed by Wang, elementary school pupils are gradually taught to make small, then larger, decisions about how they will organize their school day (Wang, Reynolds, & Schwartz, 1988). They are taught to understand the materials of the classroom, the scheduling procedures, and the accountability system of the class. In effect, they join their teachers as managers of the classroom. These procedures provide very practical ways of teaching self-management as a deliberate aspect of the curriculum.

In a somewhat different vein is the work on metacognition, showing how students can learn to be aware of their own awareness and take a degree of command over how they learn (A. L. Brown, 1980). For example, students can learn to plan their own studies in respect to place, purposes, and self-checking or monitoring. Evidence supports the effectiveness of metacognitive procedures, especially for low-achieving students. Palincsar (1987); Schumaker, Deshler, Allen, and Warner (1983); Deshler and Schumacher (1986); and others have been active in researching the use of metacognitive procedures in the teaching of reading to students who have fallen behind in skill and comprehension. So-called cognitive-behavioral methods, in which students are taught to manage their own behavior by deliberate processes, are a self-regulatory procedure of emerging importance in special education (Gerber, 1987).

Interactive teaching for cognitive change. Increasing attention is being given these days to teaching that involves detailed understanding of the present knowledge, concepts, and misconceptions held by students in various subject-matter fields and the necessary active transformations of knowledge by teachers to assist students in gradually reshaping toward maturity the schemas they use to structure their views of the world. It assumes that learning is not just cumulative, but also involves conceptual transformations of emerging complexity and maturity and that teachers mediate in the changing cognitive processes linking pupil understanding and subject-matter knowledge. Instructional theories relating to conceptual change have their origins mainly in cognitive science, with much debt to Piaget. Lampert (1986) and Scardamalia, Bereiter, and Steinbach (1984) have provided examples of how the research in the field can be applied in real-world classroom situations.

Because special education teachers often have opportunities to work with individuals or small groups of pupils, there is more than the usual opportunity for intimate interactive teaching directed to cognitive change. Many pupils referred to special education are very low achievers and burdened with inaccuracies or very immature levels of understanding in areas of the school curriculum. Busy, unassisted, regular classroom teachers can easily overlook or bypass the intensive contacts with exceptional pupils required for interactive teaching directed to cognitive change. This is an area of deep, complex, and growing challenge for special education teachers.

Positive interdependencies among handicapped and non-handicapped students. When forming small groups for instruction, traditionally teachers have tended to create homogeneous groups. Separate *good, average,* and *low* groups in reading achievement are still common in primary school classrooms. Sending those with extremely low abilities to resource rooms or special classes has been part of a larger tracking system. In grading practices and in many other ways, students are expected to be competitive with one another; if they interact with one another it could be considered to be cheating.

Lately, however, a number of researchers have shown the advantages of using deliberately formed heterogeneous groups, including handicapped and nonhandicapped students, who are taught and expected to be useful to one another (Johnson & Johnson, 1975). Pupils are expected to interact with one another, not to compete, but in positive ways. The situation calls for group work by pupils, teaching them to be mutually helpful, and evaluation of how well cooperative behavior is performed. In such situations, students become aware of individual differences, but in a framework that is positive and supportive. Meta-analyses of research comparing such cooperative approaches with individualistic and competitive procedures have produced positive effect sizes approximating three-quarters of a standard deviation on academic achievement, as well as important gains on affective and social variables (Johnson, Johnson, & Maruyama, 1983). Advantages accrue for students at all ability levels.

Another approach involving deliberately formed interactions of handicapped and nonhandicapped students is through peer tutoring (Jenkins & Jenkins, 1981; Hawryluk & Smallwood, 1988). Used expertly and in selected ways, peer teaching can have good effects on all participants and on both academic and social outcomes.

A variety of helpful materials is now available for use in teaching nonhandicapped students about handicapping conditions and how exceptional students prefer to be treated. These include children's books about handicapped persons and guides for teachers (Bookbinder, 1978; Cohen, 1977; Madsen, 1980; Sapon-Shevin, 1982, 1983; Shaver & Curtis, 1981). Expert teachers know and use these materials as part of planned approaches to creating healthy classroom climates and pupil-to-pupil relationships.

Social skills. Since about the late 1950s a remarkable transformation has been observed in serving children who are emotionally disturbed or who present behavioral problems. The change is in the buildup of school and teacher involvement in treating the problems. The territory is no longer owned exclusively by medical and other clinical personnel. Teachers now offer social-skills training and self-control curricula (Morse, et al., 1980). All special education teachers need background on the systematic approaches now being advanced in this important field.

One example of the approaches now being taken is shown in the work of Quay (1972) and of Goldstein, Sprafkin, Gershaw, and Klein (1980). Quay describes four patterns of unacceptable social behavior: conduct disorder (aggression), personality disorder (withdrawal), immaturity, and socialized delinquency. The work of Goldstein et al. follows from Quay's analysis and makes the assumption that, just as unacceptable behavior has been learned, so it can be corrected through learning. They devised systems for teaching preferred forms of social behavior using a prosocial skills checklist covering areas such as beginning social skills, dealing with feelings, dealing with stress, and planning skills. Specific lessons have been constructed for detailed aspects of each of the several domains. Special education teachers, school psychologists, and school social workers can be expected to conduct lessons in the area or to assist regular teachers in doing so. Research and evaluation of programs for teaching social skills are still at rudimentary stages, meaning that this area of work needs to be presented with tentativeness and caution.

Working with parents. Under PL 94-142, parents and educators are full partners in planning individualized special education programs. All parties need preparation for this collaboration. Teachers need preparation to understand parents, families, and communities that might be quite different from their own and to develop skills to communicate effectively with parents on the deeply sensitive topic of their own children (Kroth, 1975; Turnbull & Turnbull, 1985). Parents now have rights to participate in planning educational programs for their children. If parental rights have to be demanded, there can be loss of trust between educators and parents; legal procedures might be used to insist on matters such as due process. By all possible means, teachers should be prepared to use their work with parents as an opportunity to build trust and to create better school programs, not as an occasion for antagonism and loss of trust.

Communication and consultation. Special education teachers are members of teams and need to be sensitive and effective listeners and communicators. Increasingly they are called upon to work on problems indirectly through consultation with other teachers, parents, and school principals. They need to know about and be skilled in the processes of indirect work, both as consultants and as consultees (Bergan, 1977; Caplan, 1970; Curtis & Meyers, 1988; Idol-Maestas, 1983; Knight, Meyers, Paolucci-Whitcomb, Hasagi, & Nevin, 1981).

Increasing numbers of schools are organizing formal systems for prereferral interventions (Graden, Casey, & Bonstrom, 1985) and for use of teacher assistance teams (Chalfant, ysh, & Moultrie, 1979); they involve expert communications and consultation. Both approaches appear to be useful in reducing rates of problem behavior in classes and referrals to special education programs. Special education teachers should be prepared to lead the way in establishing such programs.

Assessment. Special education teachers must be expert in assessment, particularly as applied to decisions about the instruction of individual students. In the past, much of the assessment of individual students was oriented to making grand predictions about the likely achievements of students. IQ tests were validated for use in schools by how well they predicted school learning, not by how useful they were in arranging instruction that would improve such learning. In her book telling of the general turn of psychology toward individuality, Tyler 1978) says of teachers that they are "being challenged to find out how each individual learns most readily rather than just how much he or she learns in a standard situation" (p. 237).

An emerging trend is to emphasize curriculum-based assessments as integral parts of instruction (Deno & Mirkin, 1977; Salvia & Ysseldyke, 1988). Relatively short, simple measures of reading, arithmetic, spelling, and writing are proving to be of value in frequent measuring of academic progress, which makes them valuable in making decisions about the worth of various approaches to instruction and as motivational devices for students (Tucker, 1985).

It is important that special education teachers be prepared to undertake assessments relating to affective and social behavior, as well as to academic progress. Observation procedures, such as those described by Deno and Mirkin (1977), are useful, as are rating scales such as the Walker-McConnell Scale of Social Competence and School Adjustment (Walker & McConnell, 1988).

Technology. Special education teachers have been deeply involved in the use of prosthetic devices such as wheelchairs, communications boards, individual electronic hearing aids, and low-vision aids. Lately they have been advancing into the use of computer-assisted instruction (Blackhurst, MacArthur, & Byrom, 1987). For example, computers can be used to permit pupils to "touch" unknown words while reading and have them "spoken," thus improving the rates and amounts of their independent reading (McConkie & Zola, 1985). Videodisc technology is also highly promising for special education (Hofmeister & Thorkildsen, 1981). Since 1978 videodisc programs have been under development and test at a special media center at the University of Nebraska. Colleges and universities have generally been slow in developing teacher-preparation sequences relating to technology, but progress has been quite notable in a number of places such as the University of Kentucky, the University of Maryland, the Pennsylvania State University, the University of Indiana, and Utah State University. Through Project RETOOL, organized by the Teacher Education Division of the Council for Exceptional Children, training in the uses of technology has been offered to professors of special education from many parts of the nation (Byrom, 1986).

In addition to the previous topics proposed as the core of the preparation for special education teachers, one would need to add special topics for teachers of children with visual impairments (e.g., teaching of braille, use of residual vision, mobility, and orientation). To teach hearing-impaired pupils, teachers need strong backgrounds in language development and specialized skills in visual forms of communication (e.g., American Sign Language, lipreading, "total" communication, and specialized forms of oral-speech training). To work with severely handicapped students, those with extreme cognitive limitations, teachers need orientation to the teaching of "persistent life needs" elements of curricula and to "criteria of ultimate functioning" (L. Brown, Nietupski, & Hamre-Nietupski, 1976). The references here are to the most basic abilities needed to survive and live meaningfully in open, normalized, community life.

MODELS AND ISSUES IN SPECIAL EDUCATION TEACHER PREPARATION

Special education teachers are employed in a wide variety of settings, sometimes involving responsibility for the full curriculum of exceptional children (as in full-day special classes and schools) and sometimes for only highly specialized components of a child's program (as in part-time resource-room teaching of reading or in after-school mobility training of a pupil who is blind). Sometimes teachers serve only children in one category of exceptionality; others serve diverse groups in cross-categorical or noncategorical classes. Discussed next are some of the models for and associated issues concerning special education teacher preparation.

Undergraduate Versus Graduate Preparation

Some colleges prepare special education teachers at an undergraduate level, whereas others admit and prepare such teachers only at a graduate or postbaccalaureate level. No research has tested the superiority of one approach over the other. However, the movement to professionalize teaching, represented, for example, in the proposals of the Holmes Group (1986), is causing much debate. The knowledge base for teaching appears to require more academic space than is available in undergraduate programs. At minimum, the specialized components in undergraduate programs have consisted of three parts: (a) studies of characteristics and needs of exceptional pupils, usually emphasizing just one category; (b) curriculum, methods, and materials for teaching in the special area; and (c) a related practicum. More advanced programs include a wider range of components such as those discussed under the Knowledge Base heading earlier in this chapter.

Single Versus Dual Preparation

Should special education teachers always qualify for certification of two kinds, one in regular education and the other in special education? In the past, such dual-certification programs have been common. If programs of regular teacher preparation are extended to the fifth year, as proposed widely, will special education preparation then require a sixth year? Or, might there be a trend away from dual certification and toward a narrower and shorter version of special education teacher preparation, leading only to specialized certification? If this narrower and more separate version of special education teacher preparation becomes common, it will run counter to the progressive inclusion trend.

Categorical Versus Noncategorical (or Cross-Categorical) Preparation

There appears to be a growing belief that children at the mild levels in the several categories of exceptionality are not distinctive enough in needs to justify teacher preparation separately by category. Some special education teachers work directly with exceptional pupils in regular classes in a teaming arrangement with regular teachers; this can involve pupils of several special education categories, plus Chapter I (for disadvantaged) children, children from migrant families, and others. Reynolds, Wang, and Walberg (1987) argue for such broadly coordinated programs, believing that the needs across the various categories are not clearly distinctive and that treating them organizationally as different causes excessive *disjointedness* and wasteful *proceduralism* in the schools and in teacher preparation. The latter term refers to situations in which the categorizing of pupils and managing of separateness in accordance with many tracks for program eligibility, funding, and accountability become so complex that mere procedural norms tend to take over the system and limit its productivity.

In a summary of the research, Morsink, Smith-Davis, and Thomas (1987) observe that the same methods of instruction are used successfully with students in the categories of emotional disturbance, educable mental retardation, and learning disabilities. In one of the few studies testing whether teachers with different categorical licenses actually achieved higher results with students in the same categories, Marston (1987) found the results to be negative. Morsink et al. note, as do others (Marston, 1987), that the categories are used so unreliably and differently in various places as to make research findings in the area noncumulative and of doubtful significance. Morsink et al. (1987) conclude their review cautiously, feeling that, if noncategorical classes contain students from several categories and individual differences become very extensive, it might become impossible for teachers to provide appropriate instruction.

The National Academy of Science panel (Heller et al., 1982) proposed the following policy on classification of children, which has implications for the categorical versus noncategorical issue: "it is the responsibility of the placement team that labels and places a child in a special program to demonstrate that any differential label used is related to a distinctive prescription for educational practices . . . that lead to improved outcomes" (pp. 101–102). That standard, considered in conjunction with evaluative studies, suggests that much of the categorizing and special placing of children and the preparation of teachers by categories is unjustified by any present evidence (Heller et al., 1982).

Chafey, Pyszkowski, and Trimarco (1985) report that about half the states now issue noncategorical teaching certificates as one type of special education teaching credential and that 70 percent of the respondents in their study indicated that they would choose a noncategorical approach for the future. The trend toward organizing teacher preparation and certification in noncategorical or cross-categorical ways confirms a prediction in a 1973 Delphi study (Reynolds, 1973), although it is moving more slowly than anticipated by study participants.

K–12 Versus Separate-Level Preparation

In some areas of special education it is common to offer preparation of a broad K–12 kind. For example, a teacher who specializes in visual impairments might be expected to be competent in working with parents of a newborn child who is blind and also with a teenager who has limited vision and needs special help to maintain braille skills. In contrast, it is quite common to prepare special teachers of preschool handicapped children who will be considered unqualified to work at middle school or high school levels. Decisions need to be made in the colleges about how they will approach issues in this domain. It appears that any one of several approaches might be desirable, depending upon local school practices in deployment of specialists, the extent to which the special teachers carry responsibility for the full curriculum of students or just specialized aspects of the curriculum, and the size of the districts in which graduating teachers are employed. In small districts, specialists are likely to be called upon to offer consultation and assistance over a wider range of school levels than those employed in large districts that have more specialists and can limit the kinds of functions assigned to individuals.

Direct Versus Indirect Services

In the past, most special education teachers were prepared to teach directly the exceptional students assigned to them and who came to them in special classes, in special schools, or in resource rooms. Increasingly, however, special education teachers work indirectly with children by consulting with their regular classroom teachers and parents. In such cases the relationships can be described as triadic (the *special education teacher* consults with the *regular teacher* to improve services for a *child*). Ownership of the problem remains with the regular teacher, and the child remains in the regular class. In each teacher-preparation program it is necessary to consider the extent to which special education teachers will be prepared for indirect work, as well as for direct teaching. In a few instances such as at the University of Vermont, programs have been conducted strictly on an assumption of total indirect practice (Knight et al., 1981). In this case it is assumed that special education will be conducted totally (or mainly) in regular education environments.

A LOOK TO THE FUTURE

This final section presents one possible view of where teacher education in special education might go in the future, taking into consideration a number of the issues and trends cited earlier in this chapter. Obviously this is highly speculative territory that will invite disagreement. It is presented seriously but with intent to stir healthy debate. The summary view is begun with a set of assumptions about the future.

1. That teacher education in special education should be linked closely with progressive efforts to professionalize regular teacher education. Under the best circumstances the professional special education teacher should be certifiable in both regular and special education and be able to exchange positions occasionally.

2. That the preparation program for professional, regular, and special education teachers should overlap almost completely, the difference coming mainly in the greater emphasis on procedures for individualized assessments and teaching in the case of special education.

3. That much wider and more frequent use should be made of paraprofessionals who perform routine supportive duties and highly scripted instruction under the supervision of professional teachers. Included here are persons who might be prepared to provide some technical services (e.g., preparing materials for and correcting braille lessons, providing language interpretation between teachers and deaf pupils, offering on-the-street mobility and orientation training for blind pupils). All of these functions require regular practice to be effective; they also represent long-term employment opportunities. Paraprofessional work can also be entry jobs for people who decide, after some experience, to become fully prepared professional teachers. Persons who enter special education through these technical-level positions would correspond to the instructor-level entry positions envisioned in the Holmes Group report (1986). Many professional groups have recognized the growing need for differentiated staffing; there are too many children with problems and too few certified specialists to help them.

4. That it will be important to keep special education teachers fully in touch on a continuing basis with relevant knowledge bases for their work. This will require employment of a cadre of career professionals in special fields such as parent consultation and education, teaching of literacy skills, dealing with severe behavior problems, audiology, adaptations for blind and partially sighted pupils, and training in social skills. Such career professionals would have advanced graduate preparation and work with educators of all kinds to keep them up-to-date on relevant knowledge and skills. This proposal corresponds with the highest level of career professionals advanced by the Holmes Group (1986).

Large school systems might well employ their own cadre of such career professionals; in smaller districts and rural areas one would look to cooperative agreements or regional structures to employ them. By implication, this suggestion proposes that all special educators come under the administrative leadership of regular school principals and superintendents. The career professionals in special education might often interchange their positions with college teacher education staff, reflecting their dual orientation to research and development and to the practical world of the schools.

5. That most special education will be delivered in mainstream educational environments in which it will be common for one or more regular teachers to be working in a teaming arrangement with a special education teacher skilled and practiced in individualized assessment and intensive individualized teaching. Further, it is assumed that teams would be assisted by at least one paraprofessional, who would work under their supervision and have the support (through consultation and training) of career professionals as described.

Putting all of these assumptions together in a practical format for teacher education would result in a strong move toward a noncategorical program to serve at least the mildly handicapped pupils. These are the students about whom Brophy says there is no need for a different kind of instruction nor a markedly different curriculum but there is need for truly expert and intensive teaching over longer periods of time. Bereiter (1985) makes much the same point when referring to educationally disadvantaged children:

For any sort of learning, from swimming to reading, some children learn with almost no help and other children need a great deal of help. . . . Why they need such help is open to all sorts of explanation. But suppose that, instead of reopening that issue, we simply accept the fact that youngsters vary greatly in how much help they need and why. (p. 54)

In addition, strong efforts would be made at two levels that, so far, have not had high priority in special education: first, the preparation of paraprofessionals; secondly, the preparation at an advanced-specialist (post-master's-degree) or doctoral level of a cadre of highly specialized consultants/trainers.

Little has been said in this chapter about the fields of vision and hearing. It could be that quite separate programs of teacher preparation are needed in these fields. Certainly we do need to have experts in language development and audiology who serve in school programs for the hearing handicapped. On the other hand, it can be equally a mistake to turn over too much of education to such specialists. The children require special modes of communication, but in many fundamental ways (learning to read, compute, behave acceptably in the community) *what* they require is not greatly different from that of other students. Children with sensory disabilities might profit from instruction provided by professional regular teachers who have the support of specialists in communications. This is likely to be a highly arguable topic; and it should be, for what has been delivered so far by special educators to deaf and blind pupils is not all that impressive. One recent review suggests, for example, that deaf pupils read no better than they did in the early days of this century (Quigley & Paul, 1988).

It is proposed here that we come down to just four teacher education programs in special education: one in noncategorical teaching for mildly handicapped pupils, one for students with severe and multiple handicaps, one in vision, and one in hearing. That would take us to a far simpler structure of teacher education in special education than exists now. Such simplification would issue a very large challenge to provide high-quality teacher preparation for both regular and special teachers and to create structures in which they could work together. That would be consonant with the theme of progressive inclusion that continues to be a major trend in all of education; that is, becoming more inclusive in the mainstream, serving there children who have special needs, along with all others. Separate is not equal in special education for children or for their teachers.

References

Abt Associates. (1977). *Education as experimentation: A planned variation model* (Vol IV). Boston: Author.

Algozzine, B., & Korinek, L. (1985). Where is special education for students with high prevalence handicaps going? *Exceptional Children, 51,* 388–397.

Arter, J. A., & Jenkins, J. R. (1979). Differential diagnosis–prescriptive teaching: A critical appraisal. *Review of Educational Research, 49*(4), 517–555.

Ballard, J., Ramirez, B., & Weintraub, F. J. (Eds.). (1982). *Special education in America: Its legal and governmental foundations.* Reston, VA: Council for Exceptional Children.

Becker, W. (1977). Teaching reading and language to the disadvantaged: What we have learned from field research. *Harvard Educational Review, 47,* 518–543.

Bereiter, C. (1985). The changing face of educational disadvantagement. *Phi Delta Kappan, 66*(8), 538–554.

Bergan, J. R. (1977). *Behavioral consultation.* Columbus, OH: Charles E. Merrill.

Blackhurst, A. E., MacArthur, C. A., & Byrom, E. M. (1987). Microcomputing competencies for special education professors. *Teacher Education and Special Education, 10*(4), 153–160.

Bookbinder, S. R. (1978). *What every child needs to know about disabilities.* Providence: Rhode Island Easter Seal Society.

Borg, W. R., Langer, P., & Wilson, J. (1975). Teacher classroom management skills and pupil behavior. *Journal of Experimental Education, 44,* 52–58.

Brophy, J. (1986). Research linking teacher behavior to student achievement: Potential implications for instruction of Chapter I students. In B. I. Williams, P. A. Richmond, & B. J. Mason (Eds.), *Designs for compensatory education: Conference proceedings and papers* (pp. 121–179). Washington, DC: Research and Evaluation Associates.

Brown, A. L. (1980). Metacognitive development and reading. In R. J. Spiro, B. L. Bruce, & W. F. Brewer (Eds.), *Theoretical issues in reading comprehension.* Hillsdale, NJ: Lawrence Erlbaum.

Brown, L., Nietupski, J., & Hamre-Nietupski, S. (1976). Criterion of ultimate functioning. In M. A. Thomas (Ed.), *Hey, don't forget about me.* Reston, VA: Council for Exceptional Children.

Byrom, E. M. (1986). Project RETOOL: *Training in advanced microcomputer applications in special education for postdoctoral personnel.* Reston, VA: Council for Exceptional Children.

Caplan, G. (1970). *The theory and practice of mental health consultation.* New York: Basic Books.

Chafey, G. D., Pyszkowski, I. S., & Trimarco, T. A. (1985). National trends for certification and training of special education teachers. *Teacher Education and Special Education, 8*(4), 203–208.

Chalfant, J. L., Pysh, M. V., & Moultrie, R. (1979). Teacher assistance teams: A model for within-building problem solving. *Learning Disabilities Quarterly, 2,* 85–96.

Child Trends. (1985). *The school aged handicapped* (NCES 85-400). Washington, DC: U.S. Government Printing Office.

Chipman, S. S., Segal, J. W., & Glaser, R. (Eds.). (1985). *Thinking and learning skills: Vol. 2. Research and open questions.* Hillsdale NJ: Lawrence Erlbaum.

Cohen, S. (1977). *Accepting individual differences.* Allen, TX: Developmental Learning Materials.

Coles, G. (1988). *The learning mystique.* New York: Pantheon.

Corno, L., & Snow, R. E. (1986). Adapting teaching to individual differences among learners. In M. C. Wittrock (Ed.), *Handbook of research on teaching* (3rd ed., pp. 605–629). New York: Macmillan.

Cruickshank, W. M. (1972). Some issues facing the field of learning disability. *Journal of Learning Disabilities, 5,* 380–383.

Curtis, M. J., & Meyers, J. (1988). Consultation: A foundation for alternative services in the schools, In J. L. Graden, J. E. Zins, & M. J. Curtis (Eds.), *Alternative educational delivery systems: Enhancing instructional options for all students* (pp. 35–48). Washington, DC: National Association of School Psychologists.

Deno, S. L., & Mirkin, P. K. (1977). *Data-based program modification: A manual.* Reston, VA: Council for Exceptional Children.

Deshler, D. D., & Schumacher, J. B. (1986). Learning strategies: An instructional alternative for low-achieving adolescents. *Exceptional Children, 52*(6), 583–590.

Engleman, S. (1967). Teaching formal operations to preschool children. *Ontario Journal of Educational Research, 9*(3), 193–207.

Engleman, S., & Carnine, D. (1982). *Theory of instruction: Principles and applications.* New York: Irvington.

Evertson, L. M., Emmer, E. T., Clements, B. S., Sanford, J. P., Worsham, M. E., & Williams, E. L. (n.d.). *Organizing and managing the elementary school classroom.* Austin, TX: University of Texas Research and Development Center for Teacher Education.

Fox, R. S. (1974). *School climate improvement: A challenge to the school administration.* Bloomington, IN: Phi Delta Kappa.

Freudenberger, J. J. (1977). Burnout: Occupational hazard of the child care worker. *Child Care Quarterly, 6,* 90–98.

Gerber, M. M. (1987). Application of cognitive-behavioral training methods to teaching basic skills to mildly handicapped elementary school students. In M. C. Wang, M. C. Reynolds, & H. J. Walberg (Eds.), *Handbook of special education: Research and practice* (Vol I, pp. 167–186). Oxford: Pergamon Press.

Goldstein, A. P., Sprafkin, R. P., Gershaw, N. J., & Klein, P. (1980). *Skill-streaming the adolescent.* Champaign, IL: Research Press.

Graden, J. L., Casey, A., & Bonstrom, O. (1985). Implementing preferral intervention system: Part II. The data. *Exceptional Children, 5*(1), 487–496.

Haring, N. G. (1975). Application of behavior modification techniques to the learning situation. In W. M. Cruickshank & D. P. Hallahan (Eds.), *Psychoeducational practices* (Vol. 1). Syracuse, NY: Syracuse University Press.

Hawryluk, M. K., & Smallwood, D. L. (1988). Using peers as instructional agents: Peer tutoring and cooperative learning. In J. L. Graden, J. E. Zins, & M. J. Curtis (Eds.), *Alternative educational delivery systems: Enhancing instructional options for all students* (pp. 371–390). Washington, DC: National Association of School Psychologists.

Heller, K. A., Holtzman, W. H., & Messick, S. (1982). *Placing children in special education: A strategy for equity.* Washington, DC: National Academy Press.

Hobbs, N. (1975). *The futures of children.* San Francisco: Jossey-Bass.

Hobbs, N. (1980). An ecologically oriented service-based system for the classification of handicapped children. In S. Salzinger, J. Antrobus, & J. Glick (Eds.), *The ecosystem of the "sick" child: Implications for classification and intervention for disturbed and mentally retarded children.* New York: Academic Press.

Hofmeister, J. M., & Thorkildsen, R. J. (1981). Videodisc technology and the preparation of special education teachers. *Teacher Education and Special Education, 4*(3), 34–39.

Holmes Group. (1986). *Tomorrow's teachers.* East Lansing, MI: Author.

Idol-Maestas, L. (1983). *Special educators' consultation handbook.* Rockville, MD: Aspen Systems Corp.

Jenkins, J. R., & Jenkins, L. M. (1981). *Cross-age and peer tutoring: Help for children with learning problems.* Reston, VA: Council for Exceptional Children.

Johnson, D. W., & Johnson, R. T. (1975). *Learning together and alone.* Englewood Cliffs, NJ: Prentice-Hall.

Johnson, D. W., Johnson, R., & Maruyama, G. (1983). Interdependence and interpersonal attraction among heterogeneous and homogeneous individuals: A theoretical formulation and meta-analysis of the research. *Review of Educational Research, 53*(1), 5–54.

Kauffman, J., Gerber, M., & Semmel, M. (1988). Arguable assumptions underlying the regular education initiative. *Journal of Learning Disabilities, 21,* 6–11.

Knight, M. F., Meyers, H. W., Paolucci-Whitcomb, P., Hasagi, S. E., & Nevin, A. (1981). A four-year evaluation of consulting teacher service. *Behavior Disorders, 6*(2), 92–100.

Kounin, J. S. (1970). *Discipline and group management in classrooms.* New York: Holt, Rinehart & Winston.

Kroth, R. L. (1975). *Communicating with parents of exceptional children.* Denver: Love.

Lampert, M. (1986). Knowing, doing, and teaching multiplication. *Cognition and Instruction, 3,* 305–342.

Leinhardt, G., Zigmond, N., & Cooley, W. W. (1981). Reading instruction and its effects. *American Educational Research Journal, 18,* 343–361.

Lindsley, O. R. (1972). From Skinner to precision teaching: The child knows best. In J. B. Jordan & L. S. Robbins (Eds.), *Let's try doing something else kind of thing: Behavior principles and the exceptional child* (pp. 2–11). Reston, VA: Council for Exceptional Children.

Lipsky, D. K., & Gartner, A. (Eds.). (1989). *Beyond separate education.* Baltimore, MD: Brooks.

Lovitt, T. C. (1978). *What research and experience say to the teacher of exceptional children: Managing inappropriate behaviors in the classroom.* Reston, VA: Council for Exceptional Children.

Madsen, J. M. (1980). *Please don't tease me.* Valley Forge, PA: Judson Press.

Marston, D. (1987). Does categorical teacher certification benefit the mildly handicapped child? *Exceptional Children, 53*(5), 423–431.

McConkie, G. W., & Zola, D. (1985). *Computer aided reading: An environment for developmental research.* Paper presented at the meeting of the Society for Research in Child Development, Toronto.

Meehl, P. (1972). Specific etiology, psychodynamics and therapeutic nihilism. *International Journal of Mental Health, 1,* 10–27.

Moore, M. T., Strang, E. W., Schwartz, M., & Braddock, M. (1988). *Patterns in special education service delivery and cost.* Washington, DC: Precision Resources Corporation.

Morse, W. C., Ardizzone, J., MacDonald, C., & Pasick, P. (1980). *Affective education for special children and youth.* Reston, VA: Council for Exceptional Children.

Morsink, C. V. (1982). Changes in the role of special educators: Public perceptions and demands. *Exceptional Education Quarterly, 2*(4), 15–25.

Morsink, C., Smith-Davis, J., & Thomas, C. (1987). Noncategorical special education programs: Process and outcomes. In M. C. Wang, M. C. Reynolds, & H. J. Walberg (Eds.), *Handbook of special education: Research and practice* (Vol. 1, pp. 287–312). Oxford: Pergamon Press.

National Center for Health Statistics. (1981). *Final natality statistics, monthly vital statistics report.* Washington, DC: Author.

Palincsar, A. (1987). Metacognitive strategy instruction. *Exceptional Children, 53,* 118–24.

Quay, H. C. (1972). Patterns of aggression, withdrawal and immaturity. In H. C. Quay & J. S. Werry (Eds.), *Psychopathological disorders in children.* New York: John Wiley & Sons.

Quigley, S. P., & Paul, P. V. (1988). English language development. In M. C. Wang, M. C. Reynolds, & H. J. Walberg (Eds.), *Handbook of special education: Research and practice* (Vol. III, pp. 3–21). Oxford,: Pergamon Press.

Reynolds, M. C. (1973). *Delphi survey.* Reston, VA: Council for Exceptional Children.

Reynolds, M. C., & Birch, J. W. (1988). *Adaptive mainstreaming.* White Plains, NY: Longman.

Reynolds, M. C., Wang, M. C., & Walberg, H. (1987). The necessary restructuring of special and regular education. *Exceptional Children, 53*(5), 391–398.

Rosenshine, B. (1987). Direct instruction. In M. J. Duncan (Ed.), *The international encyclopedia of teaching and teacher education* (pp. 257–262). Oxford: Pergamon Press.

Rusch, F. F., Rose, T., & Greenwood, C. R. (1988). *Introduction to behavior analysis in special education.* Englewood Cliffs, NJ: Prentice-Hall.

Salvia, J., & Ysseldyke, J. (1988). *Assessment in special and remedial education* (4th ed.). Boston: Houghton Mifflin.

Sapon-Shevin, M. (1982). Mentally retarded characters in children's literature. *Children's Literature in Education, 13*(1), 19–31.

Sapon-Shevin, M. (1983). Teaching children about differences: Resources for teaching. *Young Children,* 24–32.

Scardamalia, M., Bereiter, C., & Steinbach, R. (1984). Teachability of reflective processes in written composition. *Cognitive Science, 8,* 173–190.

Schumaker, J. B., Deshler, D. D., Alley, G. R., & Warner, M. M. (1983). Toward the development of an interaction model for learning disabled adolescents: The University of Kansas Institute. *Exceptional Children Quarterly, 4*(1), 45–74.

Shaver, J. P., & Curtis, C. K. (1981). *Handicapism and equal opportunity: Teaching about the disabled in social sciences.* Reston, VA: Council for Exceptional Children.

Smith, B. O. (1980). On the content of teacher education. In G. E. Hall, S. M. Hord, & G. Brown (Eds.), *Exploring issues in teacher education: Questions for future research* (pp. 3–34). Austin, TX: University of Texas, Research and Development Center for Teacher Education.

Smith-Davis, J., Burke, P., & Noel, M. (1983). *Personnel to educate the handicapped in America: Supply and demand from a programmatic viewpoint. Executive summary.* College Park, MD: University of Maryland, Institute for the Study of Exceptional Children and Youth.

Stanovich, K. E. (1986). Matthew effects in reading: Some consequences of individual differences in the acquisition of literacy. *Reading Research Quarterly, 21*(4), 360–407.

Tucker, J. A. (1985). Curriculum-based assessment [Special issue]. *Exceptional Children, 52*(3).

Turnbull, A., & Turnbull, H. (1985). *Parents speak out: Then and now.* Columbus, OH: Charles E. Merrill.

Tyler, L. E. (1978). *Individuality.* San Francisco: Jossey-Bass.

U.S. Bureau of the Census. (1983). Projections of the populations of the United States: 1982 to 2050. *Current Population Reports,* Series P25 No. 922. Washington, DC: Author.

U.S. Department of Education, (1985). *Seventh annual report to Congress on implementation of P.L. 94-142.* Washington, DC: U.S. Government Printing Office.

U.S. Department of Education. (1987, December). *Bulletin OERI.* Washington, DC: U.S. Government Printing Office.

U.S. Department of Education. (1988). *Tenth annual report to Congress on the implementation of the education of the handicapped act.* Washington, DC: Author.

U.S. Office of Education. (1977). Implementation of Part B of the Education of the Handicapped Act. *Federal Register, 42,* 42474–42518.

Walberg, H. (1984). Improving the productivity of America's schools. *Educational Leadership, 41*(8), 19–30.

Walberg, H. J. (1987). Psychological environment. In M. J. Dunkin (Ed.), *The international encyclopedia of teaching and teacher education* (pp. 553–558). Oxford: Pergamon Press.

Walberg, H. J., & Tsai, S. (1983). Matthew effect in education. *American Educational Research Journal, 20,* 359–373.

Walberg, H. J., & Wang, M. C. (1987). Effective educational practices and provisions for individual differences. In M. C. Wang, M. C. Reynolds, & H. J. Walberg (Eds.), *Handbook of special education: Research and practice* (Vol. 1, pp. 113–128). Oxford: Pergamon Press.

Walker, H. M., & McConnell, S. R. (1988). *The Walker-McConnell Scale of Social Competence and School Adjustment: A Social Skills Rating Scale for Teachers.* Austin, TX: PRO-ED.

Wang, M. C., Reynolds, M. C., & Schwartz, L. L. (1988). Adaptive instruction: An alternative educational approach for students with special needs. In J. L. Graden, J. E. Zins, & M. J. Curtis (Eds.), *Alternative educational delivery systems: Enhancing instruction and options for all students* (pp. 199–220). Washington, DC: National Association of School Psychologists.

Wang, M. C., Reynolds, M. C., & Walberg, H. (1987, 1988). *Handbook of special education: Research and practice* (Vols. I–III). Oxford: Pergamon Press.

Will, M. (1986). *Educating students with learning problems: A shared responsibility.* Washington, DC: U.S. Department of Education.

Wood, F. H. (Ed.). (1980). *Teachers for secondary students with serious emotional disturbance: Content for training programs.* Minneapolis: University of Minnesota, Department of Educational Psychology.

Zabel, M. K., & Zabel, R. H. (1983). Burnout among special education teachers: The role of experience, training and age. *Teacher Education and Special Education, 6*(4), 255–259.

Zill, N. (1985, June 25). *How is the number of children with severe handicaps likely to change over time?* Testimony prepared for the Subcommittee on Select Education of the Committee on Education and Labor, U.S. House of Representatives.

·25·

THE SUBJECT-MATTER PREPARATION OF TEACHERS

Deborah Loewenberg Ball and G. Williamson McDiarmid

MICHIGAN STATE UNIVERSITY

If anything is to be regarded as a specific preparation for teaching, priority must be given to a thorough grounding in something to teach. (Peters, 1977,
p. 151)

That subject matter is an essential component of teacher knowledge is neither a new nor a controversial assertion. After all, if teaching entails helping others learn, then understanding what is to be taught is a central requirement of teaching. The myriad tasks of teaching, such as selecting worthwhile learning activities, giving helpful explanations, asking productive questions, and evaluating students' learning, all depend on the teacher's understanding of what it is that students are to learn. As Buchmann (1984) points out: "It would be odd to expect a teacher to plan a lesson on, for instance, writing reports in science and to evaluate related student assignments, if that teacher is ignorant about writing and about science, and does not understand what student progress in writing science reports might mean" (p. 32).

Although subject-matter knowledge is widely accepted as a central component of what teachers need to know, research on teacher education has not, in the main, focused on the development of teachers' subject-matter knowledge. Researchers specifically interested in how teachers develop and change have focused on other aspects of teaching and learning to teach, for example, changes in teachers' role conceptions; their beliefs about their work; their knowledge of students, curricu-

lum, and teaching strategies. Yet to ignore the development of teachers' subject-matter knowledge seems to belie its importance in teaching and in learning to teach.

The focus of this chapter is the subject-matter preparation of teachers: what subject-matter preparation entails, where and when it occurs, and what outcomes it produces. Because research on teachers' learning of subject matter is a relatively new domain of inquiry in teacher education, the literature is scant. The purpose of this chapter, therefore, is to offer a framework that can contribute to future research in this area. The chapter is organized in three parts. To lay a foundation for the argument, the first section examines the concept of subject-matter knowledge, for, although the claim that teachers must know what they are teaching appears self-evident, agreement does not exist about what is included in the idea of knowing subject matter for teaching. The second section offers a framework for the sources and outcomes of teachers' subject-matter learning. In the third section, this framework is used to consider extant evidence about teachers' subject-matter preparation. The chapter concludes with a discussion of issues raised in earlier sections that suggest directions for future work on the subject-matter preparation of teachers.

This research was supported in part by the National Center for Research on Teacher Education, Michigan State University. The NCRTE is funded primarily by the Office of Educational Research and Improvement, United States Department of Education. The opinions expressed herein are those of the authors and do not necessarily reflect the position, policy, or endorsement of the OERI/ED (Grant No. OERI-G-86-0001).

We would like to acknowledge David K. Cohen for his helpful comments and suggestions on an earlier draft of this chapter.

THE ROLE OF SUBJECT-MATTER KNOWLEDGE IN TEACHING

Helping students learn subject matter involves more than the delivery of facts and information. The goal of teaching is to assist students in their development of intellectual resources that enable them to participate in, not merely to know about, the major domains of human thought and inquiry. These include the past and its relation to the present; the natural world; the ideas, beliefs, and values of our own and other people; the dimensions of space and quantity; aesthetics and representation; and so on. Understanding entails being able to use intellectual ideas and skills as tools to gain control over everyday, real-world problems. Students should see themselves, either alone or in cooperation with others, as capable of figuring things out—of using mathematics to define and reason through a problem, of tracking down the origins of current social policy, of interpreting a poem or story, of understanding how physical forces operate, of re-creating in writing a feeling, idea, or experience. They should be both able and inclined to challenge the claims in a politician's speech, to make sense of and criticize presentations of statistical information, and to write an effective letter to an editor. A conceptual mastery of subject matter and the capacity to be critical of knowledge itself can empower students to be effective actors in their environment.

Philosophical arguments, as well as common sense, support the conviction that teachers' own subject-matter knowledge influences their efforts to help students learn subject matter. Conant (1963) writes that "if a teacher is largely ignorant or uniformed he can do much harm" (p. 93). When teachers possess inaccurate information or conceive of knowledge in narrow ways, they may pass on these ideas to their students. They may fail to challenge students' misconceptions; they may use texts uncritically or alter them inappropriately. Subtly, teachers' conceptions of knowledge shape their practice—the kinds of questions they ask, the ideas they reinforce, the sorts of tasks they assign.

Although early attempts to validate these ideas, to demonstrate empirically the role of teachers' subject-matter knowledge, were unsuccessful (e.g., Begle, 1979), recent research on teaching and on teacher knowledge is revealing ways in which teachers' understandings affect their students' opportunities to learn (e.g., Ball, in press b; Grossman, 1988; Lampert, 1986; Leinhardt & Smith, 1985; Roth & Anderson, in press; Shroyer, 1981; S. M. Wilson, 1988; Wineburg & Wilson, 1988). This research is proving fruitful, in part, because of the researchers' conceptual work on dimensions of subject-matter knowledge, work that is moving the field beyond the counting of course credits as a measure of teacher knowledge. Shulman's (1986) three categories of content knowledge—subject-matter content knowledge, pedagogical content knowledge, and curricular content knowledge—are at the heart of much of the current inquiry. This chapter focuses on the first, on what Shulman (1986) calls "subject matter content knowledge."

What teachers need to know about the subject matter they teach extends beyond the specific topics of their curriculum. Shulman (1986) argues that "teachers must not only be capable of defining for students the accepted truths in a domain. They must also be able to explain why a particular proposition is deemed warranted, why it is worth knowing, and how it relates to other propositions" (p. 9). This kind of understanding encompasses a knowledge of the intellectual fabric and essence of the subject matter itself. For example, English teachers need to know about particular authors and their works, about literary genres and styles, but they also need to know about interpretation and criticism (Grossman, in press). A history teacher needs detailed knowledge about events and people of the past but must also understand what history is: the nature of historical knowledge and what it means to find out or know something about the past. Scheffler (1973) writes that this kind of subject-matter understanding "strengthens the teacher's powers and, in so doing, heightens the possibilities of his art" (p. 89).

Lampert (in press), writing about her own teaching of fifth-grade mathematics, provides a vivid picture of the role this kind of subject-matter knowledge plays in teaching. She describes a series of lessons in which her students were learning to compare numbers written as decimal fractions: Which is greater—.0089 or .89—or are they equal? Part of her goal was for her students to develop conceptual understanding of place value with decimal numbers, but she also had another aim: "My wish [was] to present mathematics as a subject in which legitimate conclusions are based on reasoning, rather than on acquiescing to teacherly authority. . . . I wanted to enable the students themselves to question their own assertions and test their reasonability within a mathematical framework" (p. 24). Concretely, this means that Lampert chose not to teach her fifth graders the familiar algorithm: "Add zeroes after the digits to the right of the decimal points until the numbers you are comparing have the same number of decimal places. Now ignore the decimal point and see which of the numbers is larger" (p. 4). This common approach—"line up the places and add zeroes"—is not essentially mathematical: Students arrive at an answer "through a combination of trust in authority, memory, and mechanical skill" (p. 5).

Lampert's own understanding of the substance of mathematics, as well as its nature and epistemology, shape what she is trying to help her students learn. When a student in her class asserted that .0089 is a negative number, for example, Lampert interpreted his claim as a conjecture whose validity could be judged by the classroom mathematical community rather than as a misconception that she should correct. Because she conceives of mathematics as a system of human thought rather than as a fixed body of procedures, she believes that students must have experience in developing and pursuing mathematical hunches and learning to make mathematical arguments for their ideas within the context of a discourse community. Orchestrating this in a fifth-grade classroom requires that the teacher draw simultaneously on her substantive understanding of mathematics, in this case, place value and decimal numeration, and on her knowledge about the discourse, activities, and epistemology of mathematics. This knowledge of mathematics is necessary but not sufficient. Good teaching demands that teachers know a lot of other things, for example, about learning, about their students, and about the cultural, social, and political contexts within which they work.

That teachers may hold such goals for student learning that grow out of their study of subject matter does not, however, dictate a particular pedagogy. In helping students develop such understandings, teachers play a variety of roles and draw on a variety of knowledge and skills. Teaching styles and the manner in which teachers organize their classrooms also vary. Wineburg and Wilson (1988) describe two very different but equally excellent high school history teachers, Mr. Price and Ms. Jensen, teaching their students about the American Revolution:

The juxtaposition of Price and Jensen offers a study in contrasts. Watching Price, we see what Cuban has called "persistent instruction"—whole group recitation with teacher at the center, leading discussions, calling on students, and writing key phrases on the chalkboard. Jensen's classroom, on the other hand, departs from the traditional: cooperative small groups replace whole-group instruction; student debate and presentation overshadow teacher recitation; and the teacher's voice, issuing instructions and dispensing information, is largely mute. (p. 56)

Despite differences in their pedagogy, these teachers conceive of history and of what is important for students to learn about history in similar ways. Both want their students to understand that history is fundamentally interpretive: Learning history means studying accounts of the past that have already been constructed, as well as learning about alternative accounts of the same phenomenon and how such accounts are constructed. In Scheffler's (1973) terms, these teachers' knowledge of history underlies their power and strength as pedagogues.

Whether or not they intend to, teachers in all subjects influence students through their own engagement in ideas and processes. Teachers' intellectual resources and dispositions largely determine their capacity to engage students' minds and hearts in learning. For instance, Lampert's deep interest in numbers and their patterns is contagious. And her understanding of mathematics as an active domain of human interest and inquiry leads her to orchestrate opportunities for learning that differ from those found in many mathematics classes (Ball, in press b; Stodolsky, 1988). Similarly, describing his decision to challenge the conventional wisdom that students must be of high school age to tackle Shakespearean tragedy, Herbert Kohl (1984) writes of his own involvement with the play that he later staged with the 45 elementary and middle school students who attended his summer school:

During the winter I thought about Macbeth occasionally, but it wasn't until I encountered an ad in the New York Times that read "Macbeth lives on in the story, but Cawdor Castle lives on in fact," and had a photo of Hugh Vaughn, sixth earl of Cawdor, posed in front of Macbeth's Cawdor Castle, that I began to work seriously on planning the play. The photo of the castle made Macbeth's world come alive for me as it did for my student actors during the summer. It gave a scale and shape to Macbeth's world. I began gathering resources as well as reading and rereading Shakespeare's play to prepare for writing my own shortened version. (p. 145)

In history, teachers who from time to time challenge the textbook's account of events demonstrate that history is not merely a matter of fact but also of interpretation; learning history involves developing the tools to assess various interpretations of the past. S. M. Wilson (1988), in her study of expert and novice history teachers, reports the description of a graduate seminar in history offered by one of her expert teachers: "It was a revelation to me. And this has always been reflected in my teaching. The idea, for instance, of the American Revolution as being two events: a war of independence and an internal revolution" (p. 137). In explaining the emphasis he places on the interpretative nature of history in teaching, this teacher says:

I have always put a heavy emphasis on interpretations in history. Not necessarily because I wanted to make them junior historians. But interpretations are useful to me because they help me create a frame of reference for kids in which they can realize their own frame of reference. I want them to understand that all of history is an interpretation. I want kids to confront their mindsets. . . . But most important on the high school level, interpretations show that different approaches yield different answers to the same problem. (p. 309)

This teacher's engagement with history as a way of making sense of our past is part of what he communicates to his students.

The next section examines where and how teachers acquire the understandings of mathematics, literature, history, and science that they draw upon in their teaching. First, the sources of teachers' subject-matter knowledge are discussed, and, then, before discussing some of the research on what is actually learned, a tripartite scheme for examining the outcomes of subject-matter study is presented.

SOURCES AND OUTCOMES OF TEACHERS' SUBJECT-MATTER LEARNING

Where "Subject-Matter Preparation" Takes Place

Critics of teacher education tend to overlook the fact that prospective teachers take most of their courses, not in much-maligned colleges of education, but in liberal arts departments. The professional training they receive in colleges of education is also not centrally concerned with their subject-matter knowledge. Elementary teachers take half or more of their courses in the liberal arts. Recent policy initiatives, in states such as New Jersey, California, Illinois, Texas, and Virginia, have drastically curtailed or have eliminated the education courses that prospective teachers can take. Secondary teachers have, for many years, taken as few as four or five teacher-preparation courses in addition to student teaching. Yet few critics or researchers concerned with teachers' ability to help their pupils learn subject-matter knowledge have shown a broad philosophical interest in the liberal arts component of teacher education (see, for example, Bigelow, 1971).

Although secondary teachers usually major in a discipline, elementary teachers take a range of survey and introductory courses in a variety of disciplines: history, English, sociology, biology, psychology, and art. What students actually learn about subject matter from their college and university liberal arts courses is both an open and a critical question. This chapter, therefore, examines what is learned in university courses.

Yet to limit the exploration of prospective teachers' subject-matter preparation to their university education would be to miss the point. Teachers usually spend 13 years in school prior to entering college. During this period, they take English, mathematics, science, and social studies. What is the contribution of this precollegiate experience to teachers' subject-matter understanding? A central premise of this chapter is that teachers' understandings are shaped significantly through their experiences both in and outside of school and that a major portion of teachers' subject-matter learning occurs prior to college. Consequently, this exploration of the subject-matter preparation of teachers examines what children learn in school about science, mathematics, social studies, and writing, assuming that prospective teachers were once themselves such children.

Although learning to teach begins long before formal teacher education, it also continues for years thereafter (Feiman-Nemser, 1983). Therefore, this chapter looks to practice as an additional source of teachers' subject-matter learning, for teachers may learn content from teaching it. Because of a student's question, a particular textbook activity, or an intense class discussion, teachers often report that, for the first time, they came to really understand an idea, a theme, or a problem that heretofore they had just known as information. How does this learning from practice contribute to the subject-matter preparation of teachers?

Outcomes of Subject-Matter Learning

What is learned through studying a subject, whether at the elementary, secondary, or college level? On the one hand, this might seem an obvious question. Mathematics classes teach students to add and subtract fractions, factor equations, construct deductive proofs, and solve story problems; social studies classes provide them with information about our nation's past, cultures different from their own, and world geography. In English, students learn to write the five-paragraph essay, to construct grammatical sentences, and to spell and punctuate correctly; in science they learn about electricity, gravity, and the ecosystem. An abundance of evidence belies these easy assumptions about what students learn from subject-matter study; we take a closer look at this later in this chapter.

On the other hand, what is learned from studying a subject entails much more than what can be inferred from examining course syllabi or curricular goals and objectives. Paradoxically, although students seem to learn less of the substance of the subject matter—the facts, concepts, procedures, information, and skills—than we often assume, they also learn more than the substance. Seldom the focus of research on student learning, these other outcomes contribute to students' ideas about the nature of the subject, their dispositions toward the subject, and their assumptions about the teaching and learning of the subject. Three dimensions of what students learn from subject-matter study are discussed next: substantive knowledge of the subject, knowledge about the subject, and dispositions toward the subject.

Substantive Knowledge of the Subject. The first dimension is what is conventionally thought of as subject-matter knowledge.

Every subject-matter field, although continually changing and growing, includes specific information, ideas, and topics. This information and these ideas and topics can be subject to disagreement and different interpretations based on competing perspectives within the field. Still, no conception of subject-matter knowledge can exclude attention to substantive knowledge. The very stuff of a subject, its components and the terms used to classify it, differ from one subject to another. Knowledge of mathematics includes specific concepts, definitions, conventions, and procedures (e.g., what a rectangle is, how to find the maximum value of a function). Historical knowledge focuses on differing accounts of people, societies, and events and on explanations of factors that influence the course, sequence, and relationship of events (e.g., what contributed to the Great Depression or to the suffrage movement in the United States and other countries). Biology includes knowledge of organisms, their functions and relationships (e.g., respiration and photosynthesis), and the nomenclature that signifies systemic differences. Knowledge of writing includes conceptual, propositional, and procedural knowledge about language, syntax, grammar, audience, and text genres (e.g., construction of a persuasive argument or a compelling narrative).

Knowledge About the Subject. Substantive knowledge, knowledge of the ideas, facts, and theories of a subject, is but one aspect of subject-matter knowledge. Subject-matter knowledge also includes a host of understandings *about* the subject, for example, the relative validity and centrality of different ideas or perspectives, the major disagreements within the field (in the past and the present), how claims are justified and validated, and what doing and engaging in the discourse of the field entails. Whether or not such understandings are explicit goals of instruction, students develop ideas about the subjects they study. Beers (1988) argues that, although epistemological issues are rarely made explicit in classrooms, they are implicitly represented in the organization and content of curriculum, in the interaction between teachers and students, and in the nature of classroom activity and discourse.

The issues critical to knowledge about the subject vary. In mathematics, for example, a critical dimension of knowledge about the subject is the distinction between convention and logical construction. That positive numbers run to the right on the number line or that we use a base-ten system of numeration is arbitrary. That division by zero is undefined or that any number to the zero power (e.g., 8^0) is equal to one is not. Critical knowledge about mathematics also includes relationships within and outside of the field: understanding the relationship among mathematical ideas and topics and knowing about the relationship between mathematics and other fields. Knowing the fundamental activities of the field—looking for patterns, making conjectures, justifying claims and validating solutions, and seeking generalizations, for example—is yet another aspect of knowledge about mathematics.

Knowledge about history has both parallels with and differences from knowledge about mathematics. Because history is fundamentally interpretive, distinguishing fact from conjecture is critical, just as distinguishing convention from construction is in mathematics. And, as with mathematics, knowledge about discovery and discourse in the field—what is entailed in doing history—is an important aspect of knowledge about the field. On the other hand, historical knowledge, as interpretation, grows out of alternative perspectives that evolve from different, sometimes conflicting, theoretical orientations. Moreover, historians' different perspectives lead not only to different interpretations of the same phenomena but also to the pursuit of entirely different questions or to different phenomena. S. M. Wilson (1988) writes that: "Historians . . . can tell qualitatively different stories about the same past, depending on the questions they find interesting and the frameworks they use to make sense of the world" (p. 216). Wilson points out that some historians, for instance, focus on issues of gender or power, others ask economic questions, and still others use sociological or psychological theories and constructs. Although these perspectives are not wholly separable when seeking knowledge about the past, a historian's orientation shapes his or her account of particular phenomena. For example, Eric Foner (1988) views black officeholders in the South after the Civil War as thoughtful, independent politicians who sought, partially through their alliance with so-called carpetbaggers from the North, to improve the lot of their people. His account of Reconstruction, as a consequence, differs markedly from those of earlier historians. Foner's account is different, less because of his reliance on previously unexamined evidence, than because of the weight he gives to certain types of evidence and his orientation to black history: He rejects as biased the view that postbellum southern black politicians were, by definition, passive, ignorant, and pliable.

Knowledge about science and knowledge about writing complement substantive knowledge in mathematics and history. What do scientists do? What is the interplay between theory and empiricism in scientific inquiry (Kuhn, 1962; Phillips, 1985; Popper, 1958; Schwab, 1978)? How does this vary with the focus and nature of particular scientific inquiry? And, as with mathematics and history, understanding the nature of particular knowledge, fact or theory, is essential. Writing, in many ways a different kind of field, nevertheless embodies critical epistemological issues. For example, writers, like historians, construct their texts according to their purposes and orientations. Mystery writing differs substantially from sports journalism, personal letters, and persuasive essays. Within and across kinds of writing, what standards govern the use of language and mechanics and how do conventions interplay with style? How does audience influence text design and construction?

Some of the ideas students develop about the subjects they study may not accord with the ways in which scholars who work in these fields think about their subjects. For example, students may come to view history as a factual account of the past or mathematics as a domain of clearly right and wrong answers. Students' beliefs about the nature of the subjects they study constitute a critical element of their subject-matter knowledge that also influences their substantive understandings. A student who thinks that poems must rhyme and that good writing is signaled by mechanical correctness is unlikely to appreciate or understand Ezra Pound or e. e. cummings. A student who believes that the meaning of history is a matter of debate is more likely to interrogate accounts of the past.

Dispositions Toward the Subject. In addition to understandings of the substance and nature of the subjects they study, students also develop dispositions toward those subjects. They acquire tastes and distastes for particular topics and activities, propensities to pursue certain questions and kinds of study and to avoid others. Students develop conceptions of themselves as good at particular subjects and not at others. For example, 65 percent of third graders think they are good at mathematics; by the end of high school this proportion has dropped to roughly half (Dossey, Mullis, Lindquist, & Chambers, 1987). And college students tend to juxtapose being good at mathematics with being good at writing (Ball, 1988). Such dispositions toward subject matter, though well known, are often overlooked in considering what students learn from studying subject matter.

THE PRECOLLEGE CURRICULUM AND TEACHERS' SUBJECT-MATTER PREPARATION

Prospective teachers have been studying mathematics, science, social studies, and writing long before they enter a university. Their precollege education forms a much bigger chunk of their formal education than does the relatively brief period of college study. Not only is the precollege phase of subject-matter study longer than the college period, but also the content studied in elementary and high school classes is often closer to that that prospective teachers actually teach.

The subject-matter preparation of English teachers reveals perhaps the closest correspondence between what is studied in college and what teachers teach in elementary and high school. High school English teachers study literature in their college courses; the works they read and what they learn about literary interpretation may contribute to the understandings upon which they draw in teaching. Still, high school English teachers also teach grammar, spelling, and writing, topics rarely explicitly central to the college major. Thus, English teachers must often draw ultimately on what they learned when they themselves were in school.

The centrality of the teacher's own precollege education is clearer yet in the case of mathematics teachers. High school mathematics teachers teach about exponents, division, slope, topics they will not have revisited since high school themselves. Thus, their own understanding of these ideas is the product of their own high school mathematics experience, an experience that is likely to have been focused on an algorithmic approach to mathematics (Davis & Hersh, 1981; Goodlad, 1984; Madsen-Nason & Lanier, 1987; Wheeler, 1980) and unlikely to have contributed to conceptual understanding (Ball, in press a). In a longitudinal study of undergraduate teacher education candidates at five institutions, researchers at the National Center for Research on Teacher Education explored the understandings of mathematics held by 252 prospective elementary and secondary mathematics teachers. Concepts on the questionnaire and interviews included place value, slope, multiplication and division, zero, and perimeter and area. Researchers found that both elementary and secondary majors had difficulty remembering particular ideas and procedures. Moreover, many were unable to make conceptual sense of the mathematics they had learned to perform. In seeking to explain "particular mathematical concepts, procedures, or even terms, the prospective teachers typically found loose fragments—rules, tricks, and definitions. Most did not find meaningful understanding" (Ball, in press a).

Other studies that examine prospective teachers' understandings of school mathematics content have yielded similar findings. More research has focused on elementary teacher candidates' subject-matter knowledge (e.g., Graeber, Tirosh, & Glover, 1986; Mansfield, 1985) than on the understandings of students intending to teach high school. A notable exception is Even's (1989) cross-institutional study of mathematics majors' understandings of functions. Although the concept of function is central to both mathematics and the high school curriculum, many students had limited and inaccurate knowledge of functions.

Science and social studies teachers face a common problem unlike that faced by English or mathematics teachers. Because of the way in which school subjects are organized, the courses these teachers become responsible to teach are frequently well beyond the scope of their college disciplinary specialization. Science teachers teach earth science, physical science, biology, health; social studies teachers teach civics, geography, economics, sociology, and history. Yet, as university students, prospective science and social studies teachers major in a single science—chemistry, physics, or biology, for example—or in a single social science such as anthropology, political science, sociology, or history. As teachers, what they understand about topics outside their areas of specialization is likely to be based on what they remember from elementary and high school classes. For example, in science, Hashweh (1987) compared the subject-matter knowledge of science teachers, focusing on topics from physics and biology. He found that teachers, not surprisingly, had more detailed knowledge of topics and were able to make more connections to higher order principles and unifying disciplinary concepts within their areas of specialization. Outside the area, knowledge was often inaccurate and thin. Two of the biology teachers, for example, held commonsense notions about work and force; similarly, some of the physics teachers misunderstood cellular respiration.

Research conducted by Wilson and Wineburg (1988) suggests that, in the case of social studies teaches' background knowledge, the issues are subtler still. They suggest that the perspectives developed as a result of their college disciplinary specialization may dominate, inappropriately, their representation of other areas:

What is interesting about our findings is the way in which our teachers' undergraduate training influenced their teaching. The curriculum they were given and the courses they subsequently taught were shaped by what they did and didn't know. Thus Fred's U.S. history course became the study of political science . . . organized around [political] themes. . . . In much the same way, Cathy used her knowledge of the structures of anthropology and archaeology to make sense of the social sciences she was simultaneously learning and teaching. (pp. 534–535).

The authors argue that these teachers' "disciplinary lenses" at times skewed and misrepresented the content they were teaching. Failing, for example, to appreciate the role of context in interpreting events of the past, nonhistory majors overgeneralized across distinctly different time periods.

Although the outcomes of college study are relatively undocumented, what students learn in elementary and high school classes is a question more commonly explored; inferences about the outcomes of prospective teachers' precollege studies are possible, based on these data. In mathematics, for example, data from the most recent National Assessment of Educational Progress (Dossey, et al., 1987) show that, although students are able to perform routine arithmetic calculations, many have difficulty with moderately complex procedures and reasoning. Only about half the 17-year-olds were successful with problems such as calculating the area of a 6×4 cm rectangle or solving a simple algebraic equation. Most high school seniors (94 percent) were unable to solve multistep problems: "Suppose you have 10 coins and have at least one each of a quarter, a dime, a nickel, and a penny. What is the *least* amount of money you could have?" On the basis of these data, which suggest that students leave high school with little more than basic whole-number computational skills, Dossey et al. (1987) argue that many students "are unlikely to be able to match mathematical tools to the demands of various problem situations that permeate life and work" (p. 41).

Data on what students learn in their science and social studies classes, on what they learn about writing, reveal a similar, although possibly more variable, picture. Furthermore, students also acquire ideas about the meaning of knowledge and of knowing in their elementary and secondary classes. When mathematics consists of memorizing rules and formulas, history means knowing dates and names, science means reading a text or carrying out scripted laboratory experiments, and writing consists of spelling, grammar, and the five-paragraph essay, students are not likely to think of knowledge as constructed and uncertain or of themselves as bona fide participants in these domains. Evidence abounds, too, that the representations of knowledge embodied in many classrooms are jointly negotiated between teachers and students. Cusick (1983) studied the relationships among students, teachers, and administrators in urban high schools and found that, in the effort to keep students in school, the subject matter of the curriculum was often transformed or even abandoned. Powell, Farrar, and Cohen (1985) report similar results in their 5-year study of U.S. high schools. They describe student resistance to complex intellectual tasks and a widespread air of indifference. In response, they found, teachers seemed to negotiate implicitly with students, arriving at treaties that made classroom life more harmonious. As the researchers observed classes, they saw a predominance of so-called discussions that consisted of teachers asking convergent questions that demanded only one-word answers. Similarly, some teachers, despite their initial commitment to having students write regularly, gave up assigning writing in favor of fill-in-the-blank work sheets, because of problems entailed in getting students to do the writing. These treaties between teachers and students about the nature of classroom activity and discourse served, in many cases, to narrow and distort the subject-matter content and, consequently, to limit students' learning opportunities.

Whether prospective teachers' precollege learning has a greater influence on their subject-matter understandings than do their subsequent formal college studies is an open and empirical question. Some evidence suggests that the formal period of preservice teacher education is a relatively weak influence on what teachers know and believe. This has often been explained in terms of the powerful effect of the school culture once teachers begin teaching (e.g., Hoy & Rees, 1977; Zeichner & Tabachnik, 1981), but the powerful effect of the school and wider cultures on prospective teachers before they enter a university seems an equally plausible explanation (Ball, 1988).

THE COLLEGE CURRICULUM AND TEACHERS' SUBJECT-MATTER PREPARATION

What about teachers' college study of subject matter? Two somewhat competing perspectives on the role of liberal arts courses in preparing to teach are evident in the literature. In the first, subject-matter study is thought to provide the teacher with an understanding of the content she or he is to teach (e.g., Anderson, 1988). From this perspective, recommendations for the improvement of teachers' subject-matter preparation tend to focus on which subject-matter courses elementary and secondary teachers ought to take to be qualified to teach. Should the major for the prospective teacher include the same requirements as that for the future mathematician, physicist, or historian? What mathematics should prospective elementary teachers study? Number theory? Calculus? Algebra? What literature should they study? Shakespeare? Modern contemporary poets?

A second perspective conceives of liberal education itself as preparation for teaching (e.g., Buchmann, 1984; Dewey, 1904; Kaysen, 1974; Peters, 1977; Scheffler, 1973; J. Wilson, 1975). A liberal education, according to this perspective, provides the intellectual resources, the essential cultural capital, and the knowledge. It fosters a spirit of inquiry, as well as critical intellectual dispositions and skills. To engage and help students develop their minds, teachers must themselves be well educated:

Subjects should be taken to represent, not hard bounds of necessity which confine the teacher's training, but centers of intellectual capacity and interest, radiating outward without assignable limit. Anything that widens the context of the teacher's performance, whether it extends his mastery of related subject matter or, rather his grasp of the social and philosophical dimensions of his work has a potential contribution to make to his training. . . . We accordingly conceive of the education of teachers not simply as the development of a class of individual classroom performers, but as the development of a class of intellectuals vital to a free society. (Scheffler, 1973, pp. 89, 92)

A liberal education conceived of as preparation for teaching is, of course, in some ways a contradiction in terms. A liberal education, after all, is education not for any specific end but for its own sake. Still, because teachers' work is centrally involved with knowledge and the life of the mind, their own intellectual qualities are critical. Teachers must care about knowing and about inquiry. They must be able to grapple with fundamental questions about ideas and ways of knowing, to know the kinds of questions and problems on which different disciplines focus. Being liberally educated means, ideally, being a "veteran of encounters within the community of discourse" (King & Brownell, 1966, p. 121) of particular disciplines—having participated in critical analyses of literary texts, having compared and disputed competing accounts of historical phenomena, having constructed and defended an argument in support of a mathematical conjecture. In this way, liberal education marshals against the "misleading dichotomy of the scholarship of a field or subject and the teaching and learning of the field" (King & Brownell, 1966, p. 68) and is, therefore, in spite of itself, ultimately practical as preparation for teaching.

Whether one assumes the first or second perspective on the contribution of liberal arts to teacher education, what students actually learn about subject matter from their college and university liberal arts courses remains a critical question. What do we know about what prospective teachers have an opportunity to learn in liberal arts courses? If one assumes that course descriptions and syllabi provide an adequate account of what is learned, we could claim to know a lot. If, however, we look at studies of what actually seems to be learned, instead of what faculty claim to teach, the picture that emerges is sketchy (Lanier with Little, 1986) and, for those concerned about the education of teachers, worrisome.

The two subject-matter areas in which researchers have studied both what undergraduates are taught and what they actually learn are physics and mathematics. Those who teach undergraduate physics have been puzzled for years by recurring student misunderstandings about mechanics. Physics students, even those in their second physics course, persist in believing that motion implies a constant force in the face of numerous examples to the contrary. That is, for an object such as a pendulum to remain in motion, it must be acted upon by a constant force that causes the motion. Through interviews, researchers have determined that students tend to draw on their own experience of the physical world in developing an implicit theory about bodies in motion. Students are in good company: Aristotle, based on his experience of the world and common sense, concluded similarly that motion implies a force. Until Newton, the few people who chose to think about such matters took Aristotle's word for it, as nothing in their experience contradicted this belief. McDermott (1984) describes research on students' understanding of force and motion conducted by Laurence Viennot at the University of Paris that has led him to evolve a model of student conceptions. According to Viennot (1979), students may hold both Newtonian and non-Newtonian ideas of force; the pedagogical circumstances in which they confront representations of force determine which conception they draw upon to make sense of the situation. When instructors subsequently develop representations of motion, velocity, and acceleration that directly address students' naive conceptions, students could compare their implicit theories with physicists' understandings of motion and force (see McDermott, 1984, for a review of research on undergraduates' naive theories and common misconceptions in mechanics; see Champagne, Gunstone, & Klopfer, 1985, for an example of instruction that targets specific misunderstandings in mechanics.)

In mathematics, research on students' understanding has produced similar findings. A number of studies in this decade (Clement, 1982; Clement, Lochhead, & Monk, 1981; Maestre, Gerace, & Lochhead, 1982; Maestre & Lochhead, 1983) have demonstrated the inability of undergraduates majoring in science and engineering to represent correctly a simple algebraic relationship between two variables, to wit, the famous "student–professor" problem: "Write an equation using the variables S and P to represent the following statement: 'There are six times as many students as professors at this university.' Use S for the number of students and P for the number of professors" (Maestre & Lochhead, 1983). Typically, students who offer an incorrect equation reverse the variables: $6S = P$. Clement and his colleagues (1981) report that over one-third of the engineering students they tested and nearly 6 out of 10 nonscience majors could not offer an appropriate representation. It appears that many students, even when they have mastered the mechanics of the subject, fail to develop an understanding of the underlying meanings. Ball (1988) reports that, whereas mathematics majors planning to teach produced more correct answers for division involving fractions, zero, and algebraic equations than did elementary education majors, the math majors frequently struggled in "making sense of division with fractions, connecting mathematics to the real world, and coming up with explanations that go beyond restatement of the rules" (p. 39). Schoenfeld (1985) reports on his undergraduates, most of whom had previously done well in college calculus and in secondary school geometry, and their efforts to solve fairly simple geometric problems. The students, working as a whole group, could solve the problems, but they struggled to explain why the solutions worked: "My class spent a week (at the college level) uncovering the reasons for two constructions that they had been able to produce from memory in less than two minutes" (p. 376).

In both physics and mathematics, evidence is mounting that all students, not just those intending to be teachers, can meet the expectations for satisfactory work without developing a conceptual understanding of the subject matter, the lack of which, we have argued, seriously inhibits teachers' capacities to help school pupils learn in ways that are meaningful. In other subject-matter areas, particularly history and composition, researchers seem to have paid less attention to the difficulties of undergraduates in understanding the conceptual foundations of these fields. The literature consists more often of exhortations about what should be included in the study of the subject, based on the theoretical orientations of various schools within the field, than about attention to learners and the understandings they bring with them. (For a review of research on writing, see Hillocks, 1986.) As Bartholomae (1980) writes of students in basic college writing courses, "We know little about their performance as writers, beyond the bald fact

that they fail to do what other, conventionally successful writers do" (p. 253).

In writing, exceptions exist, such as in Coleman's (1984) ethnographic study of five undergraduates in her basic writing course. Through the use of specific pedagogical devices such as learning logs and peer-response groups, she both documents and facilitates her students' evolution from writers who viewed revision as fixing mistakes to writers who conceived of revision as clarifying meanings. Drawing on Perry's (1970) conjectured epistemological development of college students as his theoretical frame, Ryan (1984) finds a relationship between students' belief that knowledge is "an array of interpreted and integrated propositions"—as opposed to a view of knowledge as "an unorganized set of discrete and absolute truths"—and their ability to produce coherent text. In these studies, the researchers have examined college students' conceptions as a basis for thinking about instruction. Research of this type parallels the work of Britton, Burgess, Martin, McLeod, and Rosen (1975) with precollege learners. Britton and his colleagues found that students write for their teachers with the purpose of reporting what they know.

Our review of the literature on history failed to turn up research on college students' understanding of history. S. M. Wilson (1988) describes the historical understanding of novice, developing, and expert teachers and, in so doing, delineates the differences in the kinds and amounts of knowledge that teachers in each of these categories exhibit. Missing from the literature are investigations of the evolution of learners' understandings of critical historical concepts such as causation, sequence, and development and their notions of what doing history means.

As we have argued, students' encounters with the disciplines in liberal arts courses likely shape their notions of the *nature* of subject matter, as well as their disposition to think about and find out more about ideas in a given field. Imagine the difference between prospective teachers who experience history as an argument about what happened in the past and why, and those who encounter history as what is represented in a textbook. And yet, with the exception of the types of studies described earlier, researchers tend to ignore the intellectual constructions in which college students are involved and focus instead on instructional issues, such as the relative advantages of lecture or discussion approaches to teaching (see Dunkin & Barnes, 1986). As a result, we understand far too little about what prospective teachers learn from their college study of specific subject areas.

LEARNING SUBJECT MATTER FROM TEACHING IT

As we have seen, most prospective teachers have few, if any, opportunities in school, college, or the wider culture to come to understand the substance and nature of their subject matter or to develop dispositions that would enable them to teach in ways that enable their students, in turn, to develop meaningful and connected understandings. Another potential source of subject-matter knowledge is the experience of teaching in the classroom. The experience of coming to understand, for example, the division of fractions, or the causes of the American Civil War, or the meaning of "In a Station at the Metro" while actually teaching is probably fairly common. Yet neither teachers themselves nor those who study teaching appear to have written enough about such subject-matter epiphanies to help us understand the conditions that produce them.

Recently, however, the Knowledge Growth in Teaching Program at Stanford University has set as its goals exploring and better understanding beginning teachers' subject-matter knowledge (Wilson, Shulman, & Richert, 1987). On the basis of intensive data on 12 beginning secondary teachers whom they began to follow in their teacher-preparation programs, Wilson and her colleagues (1987) propose a model of pedagogical reasoning that is posited on teachers' comprehension of their subject matter:

Teachers must critically understand a set of ideas, a piece of content, in terms of both its substantive and syntactic structure. History teachers should understand the causes of the American Civil War. English teachers should be able to do analyses of the themes and characters in to *Kill a Mockingbird*. Teachers should also understand the relationships between that piece of content and other ideas within the same content as well as ideas in related domains. Math teachers should understand the relationships between fractions and decimals. English teachers need to have some knowledge of the Bible in order to understand the symbolism in *Moby Dick*. (p. 119)

Such understanding of the subject matter, these researchers argue, is a precondition for students to come to understand their subject matter in a new way for teaching. As they struggle to teach their subject in ways that make it meaningful to the students, the beginning teachers in the Stanford study draw on their growing knowledge of students, of the context, of the curriculum, and of pedagogy. In short, they evolve a new understanding of the content, informed by their new knowledge, that Shulman (1986) terms *pedagogical-content knowledge*.

The case studies that have come out of the project provide evidence of the transformation of teachers' extant subject-matter understanding in teaching; however, evidence is lacking that teachers' personal knowledge of the substance and structure of the subject matter has grown (Grossman, 1987a, 1987b; Reynolds, 1987; Reynolds, Haymore, Ringstaff, & Grossman, 1986; Wilson et al., 1987; Wineburg & Wilson, 1988). Whether the absence of data on growth in the teachers' subject-matter knowledge is because such growth did not seem to occur or because the researchers focused on pedagogical-content knowledge is not clear. One exception to the generalization that novice teachers' substantive knowledge and knowledge about the subject matter do not appear to change is the case of a first-year teacher described by Wineberg (1987) who began teaching social studies from the perspective of her undergraduate major, physical anthropology, and moved toward a broader view under the influence of the social studies textbook. One could argue, in this case, that this teacher's understanding of the nature of the subject matter, as well as her substantive knowledge, were increased by her practice.

Ball and Feiman-Nemser (1988), writing about prospective elementary teachers, also offer examples of learning from textbooks. For instance, one of the student teachers they studied, Sarah, unsuccessful in developing her own unit to teach fifth graders about numeration and place value, discovered the conceptual essence of the topic by working through the textbook. At the beginning of the unit, she dismissed the approach taken by the textbook. She could see no reason why the text asked students to expand numerals, for instance, 74 as "seven tens and four ones." Sarah spent over 3 weeks working on place value with her class and, during this time, gradually came to see position and value as critical conceptual features of numeration. She observed, "I had to really think about what place value *is*. Last week, if you'd asked me what place value was, I don't *know* . . . [But] like today, I thought of that example of 1263 and 2163 on the spot to get them to see about *places*" (p. 419).

That teachers may learn about the substance and nature of their subject matter from textbooks may, however, be viewed as problematic, given the ways in which disciplinary knowledge is misrepresented in many school textbooks (see, for example, Bettelheim & Zelan, 1982; Fitzgerald, 1979; Gagnon, 1988; Hashweh, 1987; Jenkinson, 1979; Kantor, Anderson, & Armbruster, 1983; Romberg, 1983; Schmidt, Caul, Byers, & Buchmann, 1984; Smith & Anderson, 1984; Sykes, 1985). History texts, for example, tend to portray accounts of the past as factual and finding out about the past as a process of looking up information. History texts are also notably silent on the histories of minority peoples and have been criticized for the particular accounts they choose to include (Fitzgerald, 1979). In mathematics, textbooks often foster an algorithmic approach to the subject, for example, "To divide by a fraction, just multiply by the reciprocal" (*Mathematics Around Us*, 1978, p. 147). Stodolsky's (1988) analysis of elementary mathematics textbooks suggests that concepts and procedures are often inadequately developed, with just one or two examples given and an emphasis on "hints and reminders" to students about what to do. Mathematical thinking, when it is addressed at all, is often portrayed as a linear step-by-step process. With an emphasis on the substance of mathematics, the texts also tend to stress calculational skill and to give short shrift to other central aspects of mathematics. Similar criticisms exist of the ways in which texts misrepresent both the substance and the nature of science and writing (or composition). In short, learning from textbooks, although it may help to illuminate subject-matter concepts for teachers (as in the case of Sarah), may also contribute to the perpetuation of thin or inaccurate representations of subject matter.

Teachers' subject-matter knowledge may also be affected by the attitudes and expectations their students bring to the classroom. As was discussed, if teachers face learners who rebel against uncertain or complex intellectual tasks, they may feel pulled to simplify content, to emphasize algorithms and facts over concepts and alternatives (Cohen, in press; Cusick, 1983; Powell, et al., 1985).

Not surprisingly, teachers' capacity to increase, deepen, or change their understanding of their subject matter for teaching depends on the personal understandings of the subject matter they bring with them to the classroom (e.g., Wilson & Wineburg, 1988). Although teachers' knowledge about learners, the curriculum, pedagogy, and the context seems to increase with their practice, whether they will learn enough about their subject matter from their teaching to shore up inadequate knowledge and understanding is unclear. There is some research that has contributed to our understanding of what teachers can learn about their subject matter from practice, but this has not been a focus of most research on the development of experienced teachers' knowledge. We need to understand more about the conditions that contribute to teachers' learning of subject matter from teaching it.

CONCLUSIONS

Until a few years ago, the subject-matter knowledge of teachers was largely taken for granted in teacher education and in research on teaching. Recent research, focused on the ways in which teachers and teacher candidates understand the subjects they teach, reveals that they often have misconceptions or gaps in knowledge similar to those of their pupils (e.g., Mansfield, 1985; McCloskey, 1983). This chapter argued that, as teachers are themselves products of elementary and secondary schools, in which, research has shown, pupils rarely develop a deep understanding of the subject matter they encounter, we should not be surprised by teachers' inadequate subject-matter preparation.

Although the perspective taken in this chapter is an expansion of the traditional one that assumes that subject-matter preparation is what occurs as part of prospective teachers' general college education, it is still a relatively narrow view. Understandings of subject matter are acquired in significant ways outside of schools; to assume that teachers' subject-matter preparation is confined to experiences of formal schooling would be to ignore a major source of teachers' learning and ideas. People construct understandings of phenomena from their everyday experiences: from their activities in their environment, from what they see adults around them doing, from messages they receive from others in the community (Cohen, in press). In addition to understandings of particular concepts, people also develop notions about knowledge itself. Ideas about knowledge as objective fact, as authoritative truth, have roots deep in Western intellectual traditions (Cohen, in press). It is not just as a consequence of schooling that most people view mathematics as a set of arbitrary rules, indisputable and fixed, or think history books tell the truth about what really happened. In short, everyday experience and cultural traditions are a significant and often overlooked source of people's subject-matter knowledge. In fact, Cohen (in press) argues that "family and community influences on children's learning are more powerful than the schools' influences." Future research on teachers' subject-matter preparation should consider the relative impact of nonformal sources.

A second issue worthy of consideration has to do with what teachers learn from subject-matter study. Subject-matter classes usually aim to help students acquire substantive knowledge—specific information, ideas, and topics—of the subject. Yet there is a hidden curriculum in subject-matter classes, a curriculum that is especially important for the education of teachers. Students, spending thousands of hours in subject-matter classrooms, also develop ideas about teaching and learning particular subjects (Lortie, 1975). Watching their teachers, they acquire specific scripts for teaching particular topics (Putnam, 1987) and develop views about what teachers should and should not do, beliefs about what contributes to academic success, and notions about what makes a good class (Feiman-Nemser, McDiarmid, Melnick, & Parker, in press). They also form ideas about testing and evaluation, as well as about how to interest students in the subject. These conceptions of subject-matter study appear when young children play school; they also constitute the standards against which older students judge their teachers and courses. To regard physics or English classes exclusively as sites for learning about force or Mark Twain is to underestimate their potential impact.

The central question for research on teachers' subject-matter preparation is, How can teachers and prospective teachers increase their knowledge of the subjects they teach? What kinds of experiences seem to make a difference in teacher candidates' knowledge of mathematics, science, or writing? Researchers need to search out and investigate the various efforts to provide more effective subject-matter preparation: courses, workshops, and thematic programs. Such research should track the changes in teachers' and prospective teachers' understandings over time as they participate in these experiences. The experiences themselves also need to be documented to provide knowledge about approaches that may be effective in improving the understanding with which many students, on their way to becoming elementary and secondary teachers, leave high school and college.

A related question is whether and what teachers learn about subject matter *from* their own practice. According to common belief, graduating teacher candidates lack adequate subject-matter preparation, but they will develop deeper knowledge as a result of having to explain it to others. In fact, we have little evidence to support this assumption. *Does* this happen? If so, how and under what circumstances? How do teachers' understandings of their subjects change as they teach? Are some aspects of subject-matter knowledge (e.g., knowledge of facts or procedures) more likely to change than others (e.g., understandings about the nature of knowledge in the discipline)? Do certain approaches to or conditions of teaching foster teachers' subject-matter learning more than others?

New research in this area should attend to how to change and deepen teachers' subject-matter knowledge. Continued documentation of the inadequacy of subject-matter preparation will not help to improve the problems we face in teacher education and teaching, for the contributing views of knowledge, teaching, and learning are deeply rooted in educational institutions and in the wider culture. Altering these patterns will not be easy. We should turn our future efforts and attention to the difficult task of improving teachers' subject-matter preparation.

References

Anderson, C. (1988). The role of education in the academic disciplines in teacher education. In A. Woolfolk (Ed.), *Research perspectives on the graduate preparation of teachers* (pp. 88–107). Englewood Cliffs, NJ: Prentice-Hall.

Ball, D. L. (in press a). The mathematical understandings that prospective teachers bring to teacher education. *Elementary School Journal.*

Ball, D. L. (in press b). Research on teaching mathematics: Making subject matter knowledge part of the equation. In J. Brophy (Ed.), *Advances in research on teaching* (Vol. 2). Greenwich, CT: JAI Press.

Ball, D. L. (1988). *Knowledge and reasoning in mathematical pedagogy: Examining what prospective teachers bring to teacher education.* Unpublished doctoral dissertation, Michigan State University, East Lansing.

Ball, D. L., & Feiman-Nemser, S. (1988). Using textbooks and teachers' guides: A dilemma for beginning teachers and teacher educators. *Curriculum Inquiry, 18,* 401–423.

Bartholomae, D. (1980). The study of error. *College Composition & Communication, 31,* 253–269.

Beers, S. (1988). Epistemological assumptions and college teaching: Interactions in the college classroom. *Journal of Research and Development in Education, 21*(4), 87–94.

Begle, E. G. (1979). *Critical variables in mathematics education: Findings from a survey of empirical literature.* Washington, DC: Mathematics Association of America and the National Council of Teachers of Mathematics.

Bettelheim, B., & Zelan, K. (1982). *On learning to read: The child's fascination with meaning.* New York: Vintage.

Bigelow, D. N. (1971). *The liberal arts and teacher education: A confrontation.* Lincoln, NE: University of Nebraska.

Britton, J. N., Burgess, T., Martin, N., McLeod, A., & Rosen, H. (1975). *The development of writing abilities (11–18).* London: Macmillan.

Buchmann, M. (1984). The priority of knowledge and understanding in teaching. In L. G. Katz & J. D. Raths (Eds.), *Advances in Teacher Education* (Vol. 1, pp. 29–48). Norwood, NJ: Ablex.

Champagne, A. B., Gunstone, R. F., & Klopfer, L. E. (1985). Effecting changes in cognitive structures among physics students. In L. H. T. West & A. L. Pines (Eds.), *Cognitive structure and conceptual change* (pp. 163–187). New York: Academic Press.

Clement, J. (1982). Students' preconceptions in introductory mechanics. *American Journal of Physics, 50,* 66–71.

Clement, J., Lochhead, J., & Monk, G. S. (1981). Translation difficulties in learning mathematics. *American Mathematical Monthly, 8,* 286–290.

Cohen, D. K. (1988). Teaching practice: Plus ça change . . . In P. W. Jackson (Ed.), *Contributing to educational change: Perspectives on research and practice* (pp. 27–84). Berkeley, CA: McCutchan.

Coleman, E. (1984). *An ethnographic description of the development of basic writers' revision skills.* Charleston, SC: Baptist College at Charleston. (ERIC Document Reproduction Service No. 283 151)

Conant, J. (1963). *The education of American teachers.* New York: McGraw-Hill.

Cusick, P. (1983). *The egalitarian ideal and the American high school: Studies of three schools.* New York: Longman.

Davis, P., & Hersh, R. (1981). *The mathematical experience.* Boston: Houghton Mifflin.

Dewey, J. (1904). The relation of theory to practice in education. In R. Archambault (Ed.), *John Dewey on education* (pp. 313–338). Chicago: University of Chicago Press.

Dossey, J., Mullis, I., Lindquist, M., & Chambers, D. (1987). *The mathematics report card: Are we measuring up? Trends and achievement based on the 1986 National Assessment.* Princeton, NJ: Educational Testing Service.

Dunkin, M. J., & Barnes, J. (1986). Research on teaching in higher education. In M. C. Wittrock (Ed.), *Handbook of Research on Teaching* (3rd ed., pp. 754–777). New York: Macmillan.

Even, R. (1989). *Prospective secondary mathematics teachers' knowledge and understanding about mathematical functions.* Unpublished doctoral dissertation, Michigan State University, East Lansing.

Feiman-Nemser, S. (1983). Learning to teach. In L. S. Shulman & G. Sykes (Eds.), *Handbook of teaching and policy* (pp. 150–170). New York: Longman.

Feiman-Nemser, S., McDiarmid, G. W., Melnick, S., & Parker, M. (in press). Changing beginning teachers' conceptions: A study of an introductory teacher education course. *Journal for the Education of Teachers.*

Fitzgerald, F. (1979). *America revised.* Boston: Beacon Press.

Foner, E. (1988). *Reconstruction: America's unfinished revolution, 1873–1877.* New York: Harper & Row.

Gagnon, P. (1988, November). Why study history? *Atlantic Monthly,* pp. 43–66.

Goodlad, J. I. (1984). *A place called school: Prospects for the future.* New York: McGraw-Hill.

Graeber, A., Tirosh, D., & Glover, R. (1986, September). *Preservice teachers' beliefs and performance on partitive and measurement division problems.* Paper presented at the eighth annual meeting of the North American chapter of the Study Group for the Psychology of Mathematics Education, East Lansing, MI.

Grossman, P. L. (1987a). *Conviction—that granitic base. Martha: The case study of a beginning English teacher.* Paper presented at the meeting of the American Educational Research Association, Washington, DC.

Grossman, P. L. (1987b). *A tale of two teachers: The role of subject matter orientation in teaching.* Paper presented at the meeting of the American Educational Research Association, Washington, DC.

Grossman, P. L. (1988). *Sources of pedagogical content knowledge in English.* Unpublished doctoral dissertation, Stanford University, Stanford, CA.

Grossman, P. L. (in press). Subject matter knowledge and the teaching of English. In J. Brophy (Ed.), *Advances in research on teaching* (Vol. 2). Greenwich, CT: JAI Press.

Hashweh, M. (1987). Effects of subject matter knowledge in the teaching of biology and physics. *Teaching and Teacher Education, 3,* 109–120.

Hillocks, G., Jr. (1986). *Research on written composition.* Urbana, IL: ERIC Clearinghouse on Reading and Communication Skills and the National Conference on Research in English.

Hoy, W., & Rees, R. (1977). The bureaucratic socialization of student teachers. *Journal of Teacher Education, 28*(1), 23–26.

Jenkinson, E. B. (1979). *Censors in the classroom.* Carbondale, IL: Southern Illinois University.

Kantor, R., Anderson, T., & Armbruster, B. (1983). How inconsiderate are children's textbooks? *Journal of Curriculum Studies, 15,* 61–72.

Kaysen, D. (1974). What should undergraduate education do? *Daedalus* [Special issue: American education: Toward an uncertain future], *1,* 180–185.

King A., & Brownell, J. A. (1966). *The curriculum and the disciplines of knowledge: A theory of curriculum practice.* New York: John Wiley & Sons.

Kohl, H. (1984). *Growing minds: On becoming a teacher.* New York: Harper & Row.

Kuhn, T. (1962). *The structure of scientific revolutions.* Chicago: University of Chicago Press.

Lampert, M. (1986). Knowing, doing, and teaching multiplication. *Cognition and Instruction, 3,* 305–342.

Lampert, M. (in press). Choosing and using mathematical tools in classroom discourse. In J. Brophy (Ed.), *Advances in research on teaching: Teaching for meaningful understanding* (Vol. 1). Greenwich, CT: JAI Press.

Lanier, J. E., & Little, J. W. (1986). Research on teacher education. In M. C. Wittrock (Ed.), *Handbook of research on teaching* (3rd ed., pp. 527–569). New York: Macmillan.

Leinhardt, G., & Smith, D. (1985). Expertise in mathematics instruction: Subject matter knowledge. *Journal of Educational Psychology, 77,* 247–271.

Lortie, D. (1975). *Schoolteacher: A sociological study.* Chicago: University of Chicago Press.

Madsen-Nason, A., & Lanier, P. (1987). *Pamela Kaye's general math class: From a computational to a conceptual orientation* (Research Series No. 172). East Lansing, MI: Michigan State University, Institute for Research on Teaching.

Maestre, J. P., Gerace, W. J., & Lochhead, J. (1982). The interdependence of language and translational math skills among bilingual Hispanic engineering students. *Journal of Research in Science Teaching, 19,* 339–410.

Maestre, J. P., & Lochhead, J. (1983). The variable-reversal error among five culture groups. In J. C. Bergeron & N. Herscovics (Eds.), *Proceedings of the fifth annual meeting of the North American Chapter of the International Group for the Psychology of Mathematics Education* (pp. 181–188), Montreal, Canada.

Mansfield, H. (1985). Points, lines, and their representations. *For the Learning of Mathematics, 5*(3), 2–6.

Mathematics around us (gr. 8). (1978). Glenview, IL: Scott, Foresman.

McCloskey, M. (1983). Intuitive physics. *Scientific American, 248*(4), 122–130.

McDermott, L. C. (1984), July). Research on conceptual understanding in mechanics. *Physics Today,* 24–32.

Perry, W. G., Jr. (1970). *Forms of intellectual and ethical development in the college years: A scheme.* New York: Holt, Rinehart & Winston.

Peters, R. S. (1977). *Education and the education of teachers.* London: Routledge & Kegan Paul.

Phillips, D. C. (1985). On what scientists know and how they know it. In E. Eisner (Ed.), *Learning and teaching and the ways of knowing,* (84th yearbook of the National Society for the study of Education, pp. 37–59). Chicago: University of Chicago Press.

Popper, K. (1958). *Conjectures and refutations: The growth of scientific knowledge.* New York: Harper & Row.

Powell, A., Farrar, E., & Cohen, D. (1985). *The shopping mall high school: Winners and losers in the educational marketplace.* Boston: Houghton Mifflin.

Putnam, R. (1987). Structuring and adjusting content for students: A study of live and simulated tutoring of addition. *American Educational Research Journal, 24,* 13–48.

Reynolds, A. (1987). *"Everyone's invited to the party": Catherine: A case study of a beginning teacher.* Palo Alto, CA: Stanford University, Knowledge Growth in Teaching Project.

Reynolds, A., Haymore, J., Ringstaff, C., & Grossman, P. (1986, April). *Subject matter knowledge and curricular materials: Which influences which as secondary teachers begin to teach?* Paper presented at the meeting of the American Educational Research Association, San Francisco.

Romberg, T. (1983). A common curriculum for mathematics. In G. Fenstermacher & J. Goodlad (Eds.), *Individual differences and the common curriculum* (82nd yearbook of the National Society for the Study of Education, pp. 121–159). Chicago: University of Chicago Press.

Roth, K., & Anderson, C. W. (in press). Meaningful learning of science. In J. Brophy (Ed.), *Advances in research on teaching: Teaching for meaningful understanding* (Vol. 1). Greenwich, CT: JAI.

Ryan, M. P. (1984). Conceptions of prose coherence: Individual differences in epistemological standards. *Journal of Educational Psychology, 76*(6), 1226–1238.

Scheffler, I. (1973). *Reason and Teaching.* New York: Bobbs-Merrill.

Schmidt, W., Caul, J., Byers, J., & Buchmann, M. (1984). Content of basal text selections: Implications for comprehension instruction. In G. Duffy, L. Roehler, & J. Mason (Eds.), *Comprehension instruction: Perspectives and suggestions* (pp. 144–162). New York: Longman.

Schoenfeld, A. (1985). Metacognitive and epistemological issues in mathematical understanding. In E. A. Silver (Ed.), *Teaching and learning mathematical problem-solving: Multiple research perspectives.* Hillsdale, NJ: Lawrence Erlbaum.

Schwab, J. J. (1978). Education and the structure of the disciplines. In I. Westbury & N. Wilkof (Eds.), *Science, curriculum, and liberal education: Selected essays* (pp. 229–272). Chicago: University of Chicago Press.

Shroyer, J. (1981). *Critical moments in the teaching of mathematics: What makes teaching difficult?* Unpublished doctoral dissertation, Michigan State University, East Lansing.

Shulman, L. (1986). Those who understand: Knowledge growth in teaching. *Educational Researcher, 15*(2), 4–14.

Smith, E. & Anderson, C. W. (1984). *The planning and teaching of intermediate science: Final report* (Research Series No. 147). East Lansing, MI: Michigan State University, Institute for Research on Teaching.

Stodolsky, S. (1988). *The subject matters: Classroom activity in math and social studies.* Chicago: University of Chicago Press.

Sykes, G. (1985, March). *Teaching higher order thinking skills in today's classrooms: An exploration of some problems.* Testimony presented to the California Commission on the Teaching Profession, Claremont, CA.

Viennot, L. (1979). *Le raisonnement spontané en dynamique élémentaire.* Paris: Hermann.

Wheeler, David, (1980). An askance look at remediation in mathematics. *Outlook, 38,* 41–50.

Wilson, J. (1975). *Educational theory and the preparation of teachers.* Windsor, England: National Foundation for Educational Research.

Wilson, S. M. (1988). *Understanding historical understanding: Subject matter knowledge and the teaching of U.S. History.* Unpublished doctoral dissertation, Stanford University, Stanford, CA.

Wilson, S. M., Shulman, L. S., & Richert, A. E. (1987). '150 different ways' of knowing: Representations of knowledge in teaching. In J. Calderhead (Ed.), *Exploring teacher thinking* (pp. 104–124). London, England: Cassell.

Wilson, S. M. & Wineburg, S. (1988). Peering at history through different lenses: The role of disciplinary perspectives in teaching history. *Teachers College Record, 89,* 525–539.

Wineburg, S. S. (1987). *From fieldwork to classwork—Cathy: A case study of a beginning social studies teacher.* Palo Alto, CA: Stanford University, Knowledge Growth in Teaching Project.

Wineburg, S. S., & Wilson, S. M. (1988). Models of wisdom in the teaching of history. *Phi Delta Kappan, 70*(1), 50–58.

Zeichner, K., & Tabachnik, B. (1981). Are the effects of university teacher education washed out by school experience? *Journal of Teacher Education, 32*(3), 7–11.

·26·

THE HIDDEN CURRICULUM OF PRESERVICE
TEACHER EDUCATION

Mark B. Ginsburg
UNIVERSITY OF PITTSBURGH

Renee T. Clift
UNIVERSITY OF HOUSTON

Our purpose in this chapter is to seek out the hidden messages in the preservice teacher education curriculum. Although these messages might not have been originally or deliberately hidden (Lynch & Plunkett, 1973; Popkewitz, 1987; Vallance, 1983), they are not currently made explicit in that curriculum. These implicit messages accompany the publicly stated and intended goals of teacher education, possibly communicating a stronger and more persuasive set of ideas about teaching as occupation, pedagogy, curriculum, and society. Through the identification of these ideas it is possible to examine them and evaluate their impact before they subtly influence prospective teachers in an unrecognized and possibly undesirable manner.

The literature reviewed here includes empirical studies in which the concept of the hidden curriculum was employed explicitly in analyzing teacher education (e.g., Bartholomew, 1976; Crow, 1987a; Dale, 1977; Efland, 1977; Ginsburg, 1986, 1987b, 1988; Ginsburg & Newman, 1985; Horton, 1972; Hursh, 1987; Mardle & Walker, 1980; J. Parsons & Beauchamp, 1985; Zeichner & Tabachnick, 1981) and also those studies providing relevant insights without explicit reference to the term *hidden curriculum*. Research that has employed both qualitative and quantitative designs will be identified, and contemporary and historical analyses of preservice teacher education in the United States and other societies will be in-

cluded. Finally, because of the inherent difficulty in studying a phenomenon as elusive as hidden curriculum, more reflective and speculative analyses of the implicit messages in teacher education curricula, based less on systematic data collection and more on inference and reasoning, will be included. The chapter begins with a discussion of the term *hidden curriculum* as it applies to teacher education, followed by the elaboration of four major themes derived from our review of literature. The last section of this chapter will discuss the implications of our analysis for further investigations of both the explicit and implicit messages within preservice teacher education curricula.

THE CONCEPT OF A HIDDEN CURRICULUM

The term *hidden curriculum* was first coined by Jackson (1968) in his discussion of the demands on students and teachers that "may be contrasted with the academic demands" (pp. 33–34), although others discuss the notion of a hidden curriculum (e.g., Dreeben, 1968; Henry, 1955; Illich, 1970; Overly, 1970; T. Parsons, 1959; Waller, 1932). Various definitions of the hidden curriculum exist, and it has been analyzed from different theoretical perspectives (Apple, 1979; Chiang; 1986;

Our sincere appreciation is expressed to Thomas Lasley, Thomas Popkewitz, Alan Tom, and Linda Valli, who provided constructive criticisms and helpful editorial suggestions on an earlier draft of this chapter. We would also like to thank Donnie Booker, Susan Cooper, Yvonne Jones, Sarath Menon, and Rajeshwari Raghu for their assistance in this project.

for example

Giroux, 1983). Nevertheless, all discussions of the hidden curriculum contrast it with the stated or *explicit* curriculum; that is, a course or a series of experiences designed to accomplish educational goals (Eisner, 1985). For example, hidden curriculum has been defined as "those nonacademic but educationally significant consequences of schooling that occur systematically but are [no longer] made explicit at any level of the public rationales for education" (Vallance, 1983, p. 11) and as "the outcomes or by-products of schools or of non-school settings, particularly those states that are learned yet are not openly intended" (Martin, 1983, p. 124). Although these definitions highlight many of the key issues surrounding the concept, there is a problem with defining the hidden curriculum in terms of consequences or outcomes. In so doing an important set of issues is glossed over: Under what circumstances do hidden curricular messages have what effects on which people?

More generally we want to counter the claim that the concept of a hidden curriculum "is now dead" (Chiang, 1986, p. 9) and to break from approaches to studying hidden curricula that "have reached their theoretical limits" (Giroux, 1983, p. 42). Thus, we conceptualize a hidden curriculum as the content of the messages "that are transmitted to students through the underlying structure of meaning in both the formal content as well as the social relations" (Giroux & Penna, 1983, p. 102) of teacher education programs beyond that conveyed by the stated curriculum. Messages of a hidden curriculum of teacher education are transmitted from within and between departments or colleges of schools of education, other university or college programs, and elementary and secondary (field-site) schools. These sources of hidden curricular messages include the institutional and broader social contexts in which teacher education operates and the structure and processes of the teacher education program, including pedagogical techniques and texts and materials within the program. Messages are also sent by the bureaucratic, social, and interpersonal relationships that exist between the numerous groups who might be considered to be educators of teachers (Clift, 1988).

IMPLICIT MESSAGES IN PRESERVICE TEACHER EDUCATION

Our review of literature is organized around four major themes. The first theme, teaching as an occupation, refers to messages about the status and power of teachers as an occupational group. The second and third themes refer to the work of teaching, specifically messages about pedagogy and about curricular knowledge and decision making. The last theme, messages about society and the relationships between society and schooling, highlights teaching as it relates to social issues and social change. Use of these themes as a framework for organizing the discussion does not imply that they are exhaustive. This organization, however, does provide a sense of the range of messages that can be conveyed through the hidden curriculum of preservice teacher education.

TEACHING AS AN OCCUPATION

Status

It has been suggested that the low status of teacher education is due in part to the low status of the profession (e.g., Clifford, 1986; Ginsburg, 1987c; Peters, 1977); that is, the university educational hierarchy reflects the social hierarchy. We would also assert the reverse position, that prospective teachers receive messages about the status of teaching as an occupation from the institutional placement of teacher education within the education system.

Such messages about the teacher's status are not uniform or constant across time and place. From a historical perspective, the status of teaching has been enhanced insofar as the professionalization strategies of locating teacher education at the university (or higher education) level have been successful in the United States (Clifford & Guthrie, 1988; Ginsburg, 1987c; Mattingly, 1975; Popkewitz, 1987; Powell, 1976); England (Cook, 1984), France, and Germany (Lynch & Plunkett, 1973); Prussia (LaVolpa, 1980); and the Soviet Union (Popkewitz, 1982). This trend has involved moving from no formal preparation through teachers' institutes, normal schools, and other precollegiate institutions, none of which have been accorded the status associated with higher education (Beggs, 1965; Borrowman, 1965; Bullough, 1982; Elsbree, 1939; Harper, 1939; Mattingly, 1975; Snarr, 1946; Spring, 1986), to colleges of education and then to university colleges and schools of education. In some cases, historically (Powell, 1980) and more recently (McCaleb, Borko, Arends, Garner, & Mauro, 1987; Weinstein, 1988), the movement to implement graduate-level programs in preservice teacher education transmits messages of increased status for teachers.

But this has not been a linear trend (e.g., Reid, 1986) nor one without considerable struggle on the part of teacher educators (e.g., Borrowman, 1956; Clifford & Guthrie, 1988; Cremin, Shannon, & Townsend, 1954; Haberman, 1986; Haberman & Stinnet, 1973; H. Johnson & Johanningmeier, 1972; Woodring, 1975). Even after having achieved university status, teacher preparation has sometimes been demoted from higher education, as was the case in China during the Cultural Revolution (1966–1976) (Paine, 1985; Tucker, 1981) and is now in the United States with the current emphasis on alternative certification. Consequently, the hidden curriculum of institutional location, depending on the historical and social context, sends messages that label teaching as either a high- or a low-status profession.

The status of teaching as an occupation has been undermined, relative to other occupations requiring preservice preparation experiences in higher education, because of the low standing of education and teacher education in such institutions in the United States (Clifford, 1986; Clifford & Guthrie, 1988; Ginsburg, 1987c; Sears & Henderson, 1957; Schneider, 1987; Warren, 1985); in China (Paine, 1985); and in England, Germany, and France (Lynch & Plunkett, 1973). The messages about the low standing of teacher education in universities originate from several sources, one being the relatively low level of funding that education tends to receive, compared with other-discipline departments and professional schools (e.g., Clark & Marker, 1975; Ginsburg, 1987b; Howey, 1986; H. Johnson & Johanningmeier, 1972; Judge, 1982; Peseau, 1980; Reid, 1986; Spillane & Levenson, 1976). This inequity is mirrored in the relatively low salaries of education faculty, compared with these in other fields; for example, in 1987–1988 the average salaries of assistant professors and full professors in education departments were ranked seventeenth and twentieth, respectively, out of 21 fields (American Association of University Professors, 1988, p. 6).

A second signal about education's lowly place in the university hierarchy is the tacit lower status characteristics of its faculty and students. The status of the former has been diminished by perceptions of their "inferior intellectual quality" (Koerner, 1963), and the lower academic ability and achievement test scores of students have been noted in the United States (Lanier & Little, 1986), China (Paine, 1985; Tucker, 1981), and the Soviet Union (Popkewitz, 1982). Further, enrollment in education courses includes higher proportions of faculty and students from lower status or socially disadvantaged groups: women and lower social classes (Clifford, 1986; Cremin et al. 1954; Ginsburg, 1987c; Lanier & Little, 1986; Spring, 1986).

Other sources of messages communicating the low status of schools of education and, hence, the low status of teaching as an occupation, include (a) perceptions of the "ease of access, low standards, and lack of rigor" in programs in education in the United States (e.g., Bullough, 1982; Howey, 1986, 1987; Sears, 1987; Spillane & Levenson, 1976), Germany, and Norway (Schwarzweller & Lyson, 1978); (b) the limited scholarly productivity of education faculty in the United States (Howey, 1986; Schneider, 1987; Yarger, Howey, & Joyce, 1977) and China (Tucker, 1981); and (c) uncertainty about the importance and the purpose of formal, university-based teacher education communicated by faculty (Borrowman, 1956; Powell, 1980; Woodring, 1975) and students (Book, Beyers, & Freeman, 1983; Grossman & Richert, 1988; Lanier & Little, 1986; Weinstein, 1988).

Institutional arrangements that communicate the low status of teaching are reinforced by the reward system in the general university context, wherein responsibilities and achievements in teaching are seldom rewarded to the same extent as scholarly productivity (Ginsburg & Spatig, 1985; H. Johnson & Johanningmeier, 1972; Palmer, 1984). And even though, "education professors make teaching appear to be an attractive profession . . . [and] see their primary mission as teaching" (Yarger et al., 1977, pp. 35–36), they are at the same time sending mixed signals. For instance, when the institutions and faculty that consistently receive top ratings are those involved in research or preparation programs for educators other than schoolteachers (Clifford, 1986; Ginsburg, 1987c; Howey, 1987; Judge, 1982; Lanier & Little, 1986; Powell, 1980; White, 1982) or when most graduate offerings in education encourage students to pursue training that would take them out of classroom teaching responsibilities (Palmer, 1984), the messages in the hidden curriculum do not exactly glorify teaching.

Finally, the "semiprofessional status" of schoolteachers in various societies (e.g., Dutt, 1970; Ginsburg & Chaturvedi, 1988; Lortie, 1975; Ozga & Lawn, 1981; Paine, 1985) and expressions of dissatisfaction from teachers and former teachers (Clifford & Guthrie, 1988) could mean that, during field experiences, preservice teachers are exposed to similar messages concerning the relatively low status of teaching as an occupation.

Power

Helsel and Krchniak (1972, p. 90) argue that the official curriculum of formal teacher preparation describes teachers as "autonomous practitioners," as opposed to less autonomous "employed professionals" working in bureaucratic settings. If this is (or was) accurate, the hidden curriculum sends an opposite message. Indeed, the dominant message of the hidden curriculum of teacher education seems to echo what Henry (1955) describes as the experience of elementary school students: learning to be "docile" and to give those in charge "what they want" (Ginsburg, 1987b; Horton, 1972; Mardle & Walker, 1980; Pruitt & Lee, 1978).

Messages about the power of teaching as an occupation emanate from all departments within the university and from the field-site schools. The first source of messages involves the relations between faculty and administrators in education and others within the university. Although the messages are clearly mixed (Ginsburg, 1987b), the historical examples in the United States of faculty and administrators in education being denied funding, positions, and buildings by university administrators are legion (e.g., H. Johnson & Johanningmeier, 1972; Powell, 1980). Similar research also points to the limited amount of power some education faculty members exercised vis-à-vis their own deans even during periods when faculty governance structures were established (e.g., Ginsburg & Spatig, 1985).

University faculty members' relations with national, state, and local governments, as well as with economic elites, often signal a message about the lack of power of teachers as an occupational group. Academic social scientists have been described as "servants of power" (Silva & Slaughter, 1984). And there are many examples of government intervention in the affairs of teacher educators in China (Paine, 1985; Tucker, 1981); England (McNamara & Desforges, 1978; Reid, 1986; Whitty, Barton, & Pollard, 1987); Spain (Morgenstern de Finkel & Pereyra, 1987); the Soviet Union (Popkewitz, 1982); the United States (e.g., Clark & Marker, 1975; Ginsburg, 1987b; Pangburn, 1932; Tyack, 1967); and Uruguay in the post-1973 period (Otero, 1981). The point here is not whether such state intervention is justified or whose interests it serves but, rather, that preservice teachers might receive a message that even teachers in higher education, let alone schoolteachers (see Spillane & Levenson, 1976, p. 435), are subject to the dictates of political elites regarding number of students, funding, length of programs, and curricular content in teacher education. Moreover, during field observation and practice-teaching assignments in schools, preservice teachers in many societies probably encounter messages concerning the limited power and autonomy of schoolteachers (e.g., Ginsburg & Chaturvedi, 1988; Ginsburg, Wallace, & Miller, 1988; Grace, 1987; Tabachnick, Popkewitz, & Zeichner, 1978; Whitty et al., 1987; Zimpher, Nott, & deVoss, 1980).

We note, however, that not all hidden curricular messages undermine the power of individual teachers or the occupational group. For instance, by their use of "scientific" discourse in analyzing educational issues, teacher educators "offer a legitimating machinery that enables the new teacher to uphold the symbols of mystery and power of the occupation" (Popkewitz, 1979, p. 16), signaling that "teachers are not servants of the state" (Hartnett & Naish, 1978a, p. 24). Moreover, prospective teachers undoubtedly receive messages from the practice of university-based and school-based teacher educators that teachers do and should exercise some measure of control, not only over whether other adults enter the classroom (Altenbaugh, 1987; Lortie, 1975), but also over what occurs behind classroom doors. But the prevailing messages in the hidden curriculum of teacher education could communicate "that teachers only hold power over students, and are subordinated to administration, university professors, and politicians," as J. Parsons & Beauchamp (1985, p. 55) claim from their analysis of a student-teaching evaluation form at the University of Alberta.

PEDAGOGY

One of the frequently cited areas of hidden curriculum in teacher education concerns pedagogy, the theory and practice of teaching. For example, Peck and Tucker (1973, p. 955) argue that "'Do as I say, not as I do' is [the formula that] . . . teacher education has largely followed . . . for centuries" (see also Tuckman, 1987). Thus, prospective teachers learn about pedagogy through the official curriculum *and* the hidden curriculum.

We argue that the messages in the latter, whether encountered in university settings (Bartholomew, 1976; Wideen, Holborn, & Desrogiers, 1987; Zeichner & Tabachnick, 1981) or in school settings (Cohen, 1968; Perry, 1969; Renshaw, 1971), tend to effectively contradict the messages in the former. Nevertheless, not all messages in the hidden curriculum of either the school-based or university-based components of all teacher education programs contradict the messages in the official curriculum. For example, Weisbeck and Buchman (1981) report that a Michigan State University mathematics education instructor modeled in his classroom action that was consistent with what he taught students to do, and Gallmeier and Poppleton (1978) note that, in a postgraduate certificate of education program at the University of Sheffield (England), school field sites were selected on the basis of their exemplifying the practices stressed in the university courses.

This section of the chapter will discuss two examples of such contradiction: messages related to the degree of emotional involvement with one's students and messages related to the degree to which teachers are encouraged to engage in reflective practice.

Emotional Engagement Versus Emotional Detachment

Connell (1985) contends that there are two contradictory sets of demands made of teachers: (a) emotional engagement, or closeness associated with efforts to motivate, persuade, and influence, and (b) emotional detachment, or social distance linked to strategies of exercising power and control over students. How are these two different forms of gender-related emotional labor (see Hochschild, 1983) emphasized in the hidden curriculum of teacher education? Until recently, the official curriculum of teacher education focused little attention on classroom management and control (Ginsburg, 1986; Yarger et al., 1977). During field experiences, however, preservice teachers in the United States and in England learn to emphasize the detached form of emotional work related to control and management (Hoy, 1967, 1968; Hoy & Rees, 1977; Lanier & Little, 1986; Popkewitz, 1979; Pruitt & Lee, 1978; Tabachnick et al., 1978; Zeichner & Tabachnick, 1984; Zimpher et al., 1980). For example, Wehlage (1981) reports that Teacher Corps interns "became less concerned with personal and social development of the children. They felt a need to have greater social distance from the children [and] . . . indicated a much greater desire to become proficient with a stock of teaching techniques which would aid in controlling children" (p. 106).

This desire for control and an emotionally detached, socially distant form of teacher–student relations can be explained in part by what Denscombe (1982, p. 256) labels the "hidden pedagogy" of schooling; that is, the messages transmitted by the limited time and material resources and the reality of pupil–teacher ratios combined with compulsory-attendance laws. However, as Bartholomew (1976) astutely reminds us, hidden curricular messages pertaining to emotional involvement with students can also emanate directly from college and university settings. For instance, the finding that many teacher education programs apparently have not met the needs, emotional or otherwise, of their students (Fuller & Bown, 1975; Spillane & Levenson, 1976) would appear to indicate that at least in the United States emotional engagement is not being modeled by university-based teacher educators. Similarly, in the United Kingdom, McNamara and Desforges (1978) found that instructors in colleges of education have little knowledge about their students because of the number of students they work with and the time constraints they face. University instructors also maintain emotional detachment through "impersonal grading in written quantitative form" and their "obsession with sophisticated schemes of evaluation and measurement" (Noddings, 1988, pp. 222 and 226).

The extent of extraclassroom interaction with faculty available to students in teacher education programs varies by size of program and institution (Cohen, 1968). As Tuckman (1987) observes, in some foundations courses "prospective teachers are lectured about sensitivity, caring, and personal attention. . . . But when a student tries to see the professor after class, he [or she] is nowhere to be found" (p. 26). This observation obviously applies throughout the university, but it should be qualified with reference to Howey's (1987) finding that, although a majority of teacher education students involved in a recent AACTE survey reported that they rarely received out-of-class help from faculty, over 75 percent of them indicated that "their faculty are often or nearly always available" (p. 6).

The types of instructional strategies employed by faculty in the university and schools should be examined as a source of hidden curricular messages about emotional engagement in teaching. For example, "the overuse of lecture without discussion" signals an attempt "to avoid caring occasions" (Noddings, 1988, p. 222). In this regard, Tuckman's (1987) observation, that teacher educators "lecture when claiming the need for student involvement" (p. 26) is supported by a variety of forms of research in the United States (e.g., W. Johnson, 1987; Katz & Raths, 1982; Yarger et al., 1977); Canada (J. Parsons & Beauchamp, 1985); and England (Dale, 1977), France, and Germany (Lynch & Plunkett, 1973). Similar observations of the dominance of the lecture and recitation instructional strategies have been made about school classrooms in the United States (Cuban, 1984; Dreeben, 1988; Spring, 1986) and in England (Dale, 1977), possibly indicating reinforcement of pedagogical strategies to avoid emotionally engaged, caring occasions.

Nevertheless, these messages are not universal. For instance, Howey (1987) reports that, although lectures and student presentations predominate in education classes, a considerable amount of discussion, albeit sometimes in large groups, is employed as an instructional strategy (see also Ginsburg, 1988; Hursh, 1987). Likewise, historical accounts of teacher-preparation programs in the United States emphasize that some programs are (and were) characterized more by interactive (and presumably more emotionally engaged) teaching and learning than might be surmised by the comments about the dominance of lecturing (e.g., Altenbaugh, 1987; Borrowman, 1956).

Reflective Practitioner Versus Technician

In recent years there has been a considerable interest in defining teaching as reflective practice (Clift, Houston, & Pugach, in press; Schön, 1983) and in emphasizing reflection in the preparation of prospective teachers (Holmes Group, 1986; Schön, 1987; Zeichner, 1979). And there is evidence of school-teachers' being reflective decision makers, as well as operating like technicians (Borko, 1984). But what messages are signaled in the hidden curriculum of teacher education about teachers' being reflective practitioners concerned with ethnical and political dimensions, in contrast with teachers' being technicians concerned primarily with the use of technical skills? Because there is a lack of "consensus . . . over what it means to be a reflective practitioner" (Hursh, 1987, p. 13), we note that we draw on Gitlin's (1982) distinctions between "activism" (action without reflection) and "verbalism" (reflective discourse without action) to clarify our discussion (see also Van Manen, 1977). *Reflection* as used here refers to the systematic and concerted synthesis of theory and practice—praxis.

Traditionally, teacher-preparation programs in the United States have neither encouraged nor modeled the notion of instructors as reflective practitioners (Borrowman, 1956; W. Johnson, 1987; Mattingly, 1975; Woodring, 1975). Similarly, early training programs for urban elementary teachers in En-

gland did not offer students "the means for theoretical engagement with issues connected with their future roles, nor . . . much opportunity for intellectual (or indeed any other) reflection" (Cook, 1984, p. 273). Nevertheless, although some argue that the hidden curriculum of competency-based teacher education programs is especially likely to promote a "technical" mind-set, rather than setting "the mind free to question and probe" (Horton, 1972, p. 30), the clinical emphasis of the early federally funded (CBTE) "models" programs at Syracuse University, University of Massachusetts, and Michigan State University did give prominence to reflecting, proposing, and doing (Apple, 1972). We should also note that teacher education programs have been seen to vary in the extent to which they promote reflective practice in their official and hidden curricula (Hartnett & Naish, 1978a, 1980; O'Shea, 1983; Zeichner, 1985). And, in China, Paine (1985) informs us, teacher education programs since 1949 have tended to shift their focus in a dialectical fashion between a technocratic, or "expert", model and a political, or "red", model of the practice of teaching.

In programs designed specifically to develop reflective practitioners (Clift et al., in press; Clift, Marshall, & Nichols, 1987; Crow, 1987a; Hursh, 1987) and in school-based components of teacher education in England (Perry, 1969; Renshaw, 1971), the rhetoric of reflection has not always matched the reality. The lack of importance given to theory in education, especially as it informs and is informed by practice, can signal that theory is antithetical to the realities of practice. Crow (1987a, 1987b) comments that the separation of theory (university-based) and a trial-and-error, experience form of practice (school-based) clearly transmits such a message (see also Bullough, 1982; Watts, 1987). And others have commented on students' low expectations for theoretical knowledge about pedagogy (Book et al., 1983; Grossman & Richert, 1988; Lanier & Little, 1986; Thies-Sprinthall & Sprinthall, 1987).

The strong antitheoretical bias (Crittenden, 1973) and the lack of an explicit epistemology (Wideen et al., 1987) in teacher education contributes to the perceived duality of theory and practice. One might also question how much reflection, as opposed to verbalism, is evidenced in the foundations of education courses (see Greene, 1978, p. 59) and the arts and science department courses that preservice teachers take.

Another signal undermining the idea of teaching as reflective practice is provided by instructors who operate in isolation from each other, as opposed to working in professional, communal settings (Cinnamond & Zimpher, in press). In schools the dominant model is that of the eggcrate school, with teachers working in isolation from each other most of the day (Dreeben 1987, 1988; Eddy, 1969; Lortie, 1975). Finding time for collective reflection on practice requires maximal efforts from teachers (Wildman & Niles, 1987). Thus, during field observation and practice-teaching experiences in at least Canada, England, and the United States, perservice teachers encounter messages contradicting a view of teachers engaged in practice together, whether reflective or otherwise (Yarger et al., 1977; Wideen et al., 1987).

Although student teaching might seem to provide at least the possibility of collective reflection involving the student teacher, the school-based teacher educator, and the university-based teacher educator or supervisor (Lacey, 1977), the twin roles of advisor and supervisor preclude reflective practice (Hoy & Woolfolk, 1988). This problem is exacerbated by the absence of articulation and definition of the roles for each member of the student-teaching triad (Applegate, 1987; Clark & Marker, 1975; Watts, 1987), the limited amount of time available for collective reflection, and the lack of sustained contact, especially involving university faculty members (American Association of Colleges for Teacher Education [AACTE], 1987; Wildman & Niles, 1987).

Indeed, the strongest message about teaching as a reflective, rather than a technical, activity is communicated in university and field sites by the amount of time, the level of material resources, and the size of classes in which teachers work. Both Crow (1987a) and Hursh (1987) stress these constraints on opportunities to reflect for both instructors and the prospective teachers observing them (see also Pangburn, 1932, p. 97; Noordhoff & Kleinfeld, in press). This point is also highlighted in England by Hartnett and Naish (1978b), who note that, in the face of a declining birthrate, the national government opted to maintain class sizes and the number of teaching periods in schools or colleges of education "rather than [giving] those who teach . . . time for . . . reflection and study" (p. 20).

CURRICULUM KNOWLEDGE AND DECISION MAKING

Until recently, epistemological and social analyses of curricula have not been stressed historically in teacher-preparation programs in England, France, or Germany (Lynch & Plunkett, 1973, p. 118) or given much attention in more contemporary programs in the United States (Ginsburg, 1986, 1988). In contrast, the hidden curriculum of teacher education has continued to be full of messages on these topics. In this section we review literature regarding messages in the hidden curriculum of teacher education about the nature of curriculum knowledge and the teacher's role in deciding what knowledge should be included and how it should be organized in the curriculum. To structure our discussion we draw on Berlak and Berlak's (1981) dilemma language of schooling to focus on three dilemmas or contradictions concerning curriculum knowledge: public versus personal knowledge, knowledge as molecular versus holistic, and knowledge as given versus problematic (see also Ginsburg, 1986, 1988).

Public Versus Personal Knowledge

Berlak and Berlak (1981) distinguish between a view of knowledge as "accumulated traditions [that] have value external and independent of the knower" (public) (p. 144) and a view of knowledge as worthwhile to the extent that it is "established through its relationship to the knower" (personal) (p. 145). Eisner (1985) makes a similar distinction between two of his five identified orientations to teaching: respectively, an academic rationalist orientation, stressing a view of curriculum knowledge defined by tradition and agreed upon as an important set of facts and concepts, and a personal-relevance orienta-

tion, emphasizing a view of curriculum knowledge as needing to be tailored to individual needs.

Generally, the literature we reviewed indicates that the hidden curriculum of teacher education communicates a conception of knowledge as public, rather than personal, in both university- and school-based components of preparation programs. As Bartholomew (1976) notes: "In both kinds of institutions the main form in which curriculum knowledge appears is as a corpus, as predefined 'worthwhile activities' existing in theory separately from teachers and learners" (p. 120).

A number of scholars have commented on how a public conception of curriculum knowledge is signaled strongly in competency-based teacher education programs (e.g., Apple, 1972; Ginsburg, 1986). For example, Horton (1972) observes that a dominant message in the hidden curriculum of CBTE programs is that the curriculum or "educational experiences can be prescribed in terms of precise conditions rather than based on the individual's assimilation of his [or her] own experiences" (p. 7).

A similar point has been made about other teacher-preparation programs, in both university settings (Crow, 1987a; Sears, 1983) and school-based field settings (Tabachnick, 1983). That the content of university coursework in teacher education in the United States, at least until recently, has been remarkable similar across institutions (Joyce, Howey, & Yarger, 1977), despite the variations in student populations served (AACTE, 1987), provides a clear message stressing a public conception of knowledge. This message is further reinforced by state legislation that specifies the content of preparation programs (Clift, 1989) and certification tests of both subject-matter preparation and professional knowledge (Eissenberg & Rudner, 1988). Judge (1982) also seems to make this point when he describes "elite" graduate schools of education in the United States as the fount of educational knowledge that is then distributed to instructors and their students at other institutions. Prospective teachers are also likely to encounter messages about a public conception of knowledge during their field experiences in at least Australia, Brazil, England, and the United States. Writers from these countries have stressed how worthwhile school- or university-level knowledge, rather than being defined in relation to the learners, is often treated as a product, or commodity, produced outside of the teaching–learning context and then transferred through the activities of teachers to students (Apple, 1979; Bloom, 1987; Connell, 1985; Freire, 1970; Young, 1971).

Nevertheless, we should be aware that, within a given program, there could be messages contradicting this dominant one of a public conception of knowledge (Ginsburg, 1986) and that the hidden curriculum of inquiry-oriented and personalistic types of programs (compared with behaviorist and tradition/craft types) might give more voice to a conception of knowledge as personal (Zeichner, 1985).

Knowledge as Molecular Versus Holistic

Here the dilemma, or contradiction, "represents contrasting ways of organizing and teaching school subjects" (Berlak & Berlak, 1983, p. 278). The distinction, following Bernstein

(1975), is (a) between a conception of curriculum knowledge as being fragmented or strongly bounded and having clearly distinguished content areas (molecular) and (b) a view of knowledge as being integrated or having weak boundaries separating subjects or topics within subjects (holistic). Overall, the literature we reviewed characterized the hidden curriculum of teacher education as communicating a molecular, or fragmented, conception of curriculum knowledge. This is the case whether based on (a) historical analyses (e.g., Lanier & Little, 1986; W. Johnson, 1987) or more contemporary survey research and ethnographic studies in the United States (e.g., Ginsburg, 1986; Howey, 1987; Howey & Zimpher, 1987; Sears, 1983; Spillane & Levenson, 1976); or (b) investigations conducted in Canada (Wideen et al., 1987), England (McNamara & Desforges, 1978), and Spain (Morgenstern de Finkel & Pereyra, 1987). Some exceptions are noted, namely in teacher education programs in the United States (Altenbaugh, 1987; Lather, 1984), China (Tucker, 1981), England (Bowden, 1972), France and Germany (Lynch & Plunkett, 1973), and the USSR (Popkewitz, 1982). These programs presented a holistic, or integrated, view of curriculum knowledge. More often, however, most agree with Pruitt and Lee (1978) that the "teacher training curriculum is composed of numerous, unrelated courses, forcing the students to make connections or bridges between them" (p. 70).

The view of curriculum knowledge as molecular or fragmented is communicated first by the boundaries between academic subject and professional knowledge, organized literally and symbolically by the division between the arts and sciences departments and schools of education (Bell, 1981; Bullough, 1982; Burgess, 1977; Cole & McCormick, 1987; Ginsburg, 1986; Judge, 1982; Lynch & Plunkett, 1973; McNamara & Desforges, 1978; Monroe, 1952; Pangburn, 1932; Reid, 1986; Renshaw, 1971; Whitty et al., 1987). This view is reinforced by the boundaries between the various subject departments within the arts and sciences (Ginsburg, 1986; Popkewitz, 1987; Tucker, 1981) and by the division within many teacher education programs into educational psychology, social foundations, and methods courses (Ball & Lacey, 1980; Howey, 1986; Lacey, 1977; Lynch & Plunkett, 1973; Monroe, 1952; Pangburn, 1932; Snarr, 1946). A molecular, or fragmented, conception of curricular knowledge is also communicated during field experiences by elementary and secondary school curricula (e.g., Ginsburg, 1986; Tabachnick et al., 1978; Zeichner, & Tabachnick, 1984), textbooks (Newman, 1982), professional associations (Lynch & Plunkett, 1973), and some student-teaching evaluation forms (J. Parsons & Beauchamp, 1985). See Borrowman (1956), though, for a historical analysis of effects by "harmonizers" and "integrators" (versus, "purists") to break down these boundaries between academic subjects and professional knowledge and skill in normal schools, teachers colleges, and universities in the United States.

Knowledge as Given Versus Problematic

Berlak and Berlak (1981) posit a dilemma between a conception of curriculum knowledge as *given*—objective, absolute, and uncontroversial—and a view of curriculum knowledge as *problematic*—"constructed, provisional, tentative, subject to political, cultural and social influences" (p. 147). Implicit in this dilemma is the issue of what role teachers play in conceptualizing, designing, and implementing a curriculum. To the extent that teachers take curriculum knowledge as given, they are more likely to implement the curriculum bureaucratically as knowledge formally defined by others and less likely to adapt the curriculum functionally or to take an independent role in defining it (Tabachnick, Zeichner, Densmore, Adler, & Egan, 1982).

With few exceptions (Beatty, 1987; Ginsburg, 1986; Lather, 1984), the literature reviewed indicates that the hidden curriculum of teacher education communicates a conception of knowledge as given (e.g., Crow, 1987b; Giroux, 1981; Sears, 1983; Tabachnick et al., 1978). This point has been made specifically in reference to competency-based teacher education programs (Apple, 1972; Efland, 1977; Ginsburg, 1986; Horton, 1972). More generally, Cornbleth (1987) argues that one of the myths embedded in the organization and practice of teacher education is "right answerism," that one should always seek the single "right" answer (see also Tabachnick et al., 1978). Teacher education "rituals" (Popkewitz, 1979), field-based experiences (Zeichner, 1979), textbooks used in university liberal arts and teaching-methods courses (Popkewitz, 1983, 1987), and school textbooks (Newman, 1982) often communicate a view of knowledge as unproblematic and unambiguous, as a "thing" or a commodity that can be accumulated and distributed (Sears, 1983).

Other sources of messages about knowledge as given are the tendencies in some programs to employ evaluation procedures when considering students' admission, course achievements, and practice teaching performances (e.g., Efland, 1977; Horton, 1972; Howey & Zimpher, 1987; Noddings, 1988; J. Parsons & Beauchamp, 1985), as well as faculty members' scholarly merit (DeYoung, 1985), thus emphasizing a preference for easily measurable products over less tangible processes inherent in a more problematic conception of knowledge. A SAT score, a letter grade or a grade point average, and a count of published articles become meaningful only if one assumes that knowledge is objective and absolute and not subject to political, cultural, and social influences.

The given conception of curriculum knowledge is reinforced by the idea that teachers are curriculum-delivery service workers, at least in the United States, Canada, and Australia (Ginsburg, 1986; J. Parsons & Beauchamp, 1985; Pittman, 1987). Lynch and Plunkett (1973) explain why teacher education programs in England, France, and Germany focus so little attention on the problematic nature of curriculum knowledge: "For as long as teaching could be considered a craft concerned with the efficient transmission of knowledge there was no need for a training component that raised philosophical questions about the status of school curricula in terms of epistemological assumptions and the social justifications for the selection and classification of their content" (p. 118).

Epistemological and other issues about curriculum decision making are sometimes afforded space in the official curriculum of preservice preparation programs (Bullough, 1982; Ginsburg, 1986; Giroux, 1981; Lanier & Little, 1986; Tyack, 1967; White,

1982), but the hidden curricular messages generally communicate the idea that curriculum decision making is not a central part of the teacher's role (Horton, 1972). A similar statement is made by teacher educators who help develop teacherproof curricula for use in schools (Palmer, 1984, p. 16). Once again, we should note that programs vary in the extent to which they portray teachers as curriculum deliverers of decision makers (Hartnett & Naish, 1978a, 1980; Zeichner, 1985).

The model of the teacher as curriculum deliverer is often reinforced by the activity of teachers in field-site schools, many of whom are perceived as having been deskilled in this respect by curriculum packages, state- or district-mandated curricula, or their own defensive strategies (Apple, 1983, 1986; Beyer, 1983; Beyer & Zeichner, 1987; Borko, 1984; Buswell, 1988; Densmore, 1987; Gitlin, 1982; Lynch & Plunckett, 1973; McNeil, 1983; Tabachnick et al., 1978). This message might be conveyed by the assignment of substitute (and other) teachers to classes for which they have limited subject-knowledge preparation (Lanier & Little, 1986) and by teachers' manuals and textbooks that do not require teachers to construct their own curricula (Newman, 1982).

Similarly, teacher educators, and, less frequently, other educators of teachers in higher education institutions, have been described as being deskilled or in some other fashion restricted in their role as curriculum decision makers in the United States (Katz & Raths, 1982; Lather, 1984; Tyack, 1967); China (Tucker, 1981); England (McNamara & Desforges, 1978; Spillane & Levenson, 1976; Whitty et al., 1987); France and Germany (Lynch & Plunkett, 1973); and the Soviet Union (Popkewitz, 1982). The message signaled by this dynamic's affecting teacher educators might be particularly strong in competency-based teacher education programs, where the curriculum can consist of modules designed by experts and assigned to professors to be delivered or presented to students in the program (Ginsburg & Spatig, 1985; Gitlin, 1982; Tom, 1977). That faculty members individually or collectively can resist such pressures, and thus model a role of teacher as curriculum decision maker, means that the dominant message is at least sometimes contradicted, even in CBTE programs (Ginsburg, 1988; Ginsburg & Spatig, 1985).

SOCIETY AND ITS RELATION TO SCHOOLING

Some education and other university courses address issues of society and its relation to schooling in the official curriculum (Ginsburg, 1988; Ginsburg & Newman 1985; Hursh, 1987; Lather, 1984; Popkewitz, 1983, Powell, 1980) Nevertheless, the limited attention in the explicit university curriculum for preservice teachers to social issues such as class, gender, and race conveys and message that these issues are unimportant for prospective teachers (Britzman, 1986; Burgess, 1977; Butts, 1983; Ginsburg, 1988; Ginsburg & Newman, 1985; Giroux & McLaren, 1986, 1987; Goodman, 1984; Lather, 1984; Reid, 1986; Spring, 1986; Tabachnick et al., 1982). For example, in the United States only 18 percent of the teacher education programs surveyed in the mid-1970s gave any curricular attention to sex-role stereotyping (McCune & Mathews, 1975), and less

than 1 percent of the material in more recently analyzed textbooks used in teacher education programs focused on racial- or gender-equity issues (Sadker & Sadker, 1980).

When society and its relation to schooling are discussed in teacher education, the hidden message is that existing institutions and social relations are natural, neutral, legitimate, or just given (Beyer & Zeichner, 1987; Bowden, 1972; Britzman, 1986; Burgess, 1977; Dale, 1977; Ginsburg, 1988; Kelly, 1987; McNamara, 1972; Popkewitz, 1983, 1985). Again, this can vary across programs (Cook, 1984; Gitlin, 1982; Zeichner, 1985), but those involved in the education of teachers generally "transmit, often tacitly, benign or neutral visions of social reality [that encourage] uncritical acceptance of meritocratic arrangements, of stratification and hierarchies" (Greene, 1978, p. 56). This might be the case for many school-based teacher educators as well (e.g., Grace, 1978; Lee, 1987), although some schoolteachers, and some of their counterparts in higher education, (see Bullough, 1982; Ginsburg, 1987a), adopt a critical stance and are engaged in political activity to challenge unequal social relations (e.g., Clifford, 1987; King, 1987; LaVolpa, 1980).

A major source of messages legitimizing the existence of social stratification originates in the process of education itself, which sorts and selects individuals (and groups) for future positions in the occupational hierarchy (Mardle & Walker, 1980; Popkewitz, 1987). For example, the hidden curriculum of university-based teacher education is filled with messages that reinforce the evaluation and stratification of students, because grades and grade point averages dominate a number of teacher education programs (Gallmeier & Poppleton, 1978; Ginsburg, 1988; Ginsburg & Newman, 1985; LeCompte & Ginsburg, 1987; Noddings, 1988; Zimpher et al., 1980) and university settings more generally (Becker, Geer, & Hughes, 1968). Currently, these messages are being further reinforced in England and the United States through reform efforts to institute standardized tests for evaluating future teachers at points of entrance into and exit from preservice programs (Ginsburg, 1988; Reid, 1986). Field experiences also expose prospective teachers to messages about stratification in both education and society. Grading, testing, and tracking practices, in addition to differences in funding and curriculum across schools and school districts, communicate the pervasiveness and legitimacy of existing social stratification (Bowles & Gintis, 1976; Ginsburg, 1988; Ginsburg & Newman, 1985).

Teacher education programs have also been described as experiences through which future teachers learn about hierarchy and authority relations in education (Dale, 1977; Giroux, 1981; Horton, 1972; Popkewitz, 1979; Tabachnick et al., 1978). These hidden messages are communicated in various societies through the hierarchy of institutions organized to train primary, secondary, and college teachers (Bergen, 1988; Borrowman, 1956; Danielsson, Proppe, & Myrdal, 1987; Ginsburg, 1987c; Harper, 1939; Lacey, 1977; Lynch & Plunkett, 1973; Morgenstern de Finkel & Pereyra, 1987; Popkewitz, 1982; Snarr, 1946) and by the different types of educational institutions "serving" different racial and ethnic groups and, more generally, people coming from and heading toward different locations in the social structure (Ginsburg & Newman, 1985;

Grace, 1978; Kamens, 1977; Lee, 1987). The creation of key (i.e., elite) and nonkey normal universities in China in the post-Mao era has provided a strong message about social stratification (Paine, 1985). Another source of these messages is the higher status of educational administration and educational research, as opposed to teacher education, within schools of education (Bullough, 1982; Clifford, 1986; Ginsburg, 1987a; Lanier & Little, 1986; Powell, 1980; Spring, 1986; White, 1982). Explicit ranking systems of university faculty members and hierarchical relationships among administrators, faculty, and staff in schools and universities communicate a sense of stratification as the legitimate status quo (Ginsburg, 1988).

We turn now to more specific messages about unequal class, race, and gender relations. Except in China during the Great Leap Forward and the Cultural Revolution (Paine, 1985; Tucker, 1981), teacher-preparation programs have been designed so that prospective teachers are educated, not by adult workers and peasants, but by a credentialed, higher status group. Moreover, prospective teachers encounter these inequalities during field experiences in school settings that reflect social class and racial segregation (Ginsburg, 1988). And, although it might be true that elite graduate schools of education have been "important engines for assisting the advancement of . . . blacks" (Judge, 1982, p. 47), relatively few members of racial and ethnic minorities populate the student body of faculties of education (AACTE, 1987) or of universities more generally (Lanier & Little, 1986; White, 1982). Similarly, at least in the mid-1970s, few teacher educators in the United States spoke a language other than English (Yarger et al., 1977).

Another line of scholarship has focused on the hidden messages related to gender. The message that males are dominant is expressed by the fact that, although most teacher education students are women, most faculty members in education and in the total university are men (Clifford, 1986; W. Johnson, 1987; Lanier & Little, 1986; McCune & Matthews, 1975; White, 1982; Yarger et al., 1977). These messages are reinforced by the fact that, when women are members of the faculty, they tend to occupy lower ranks, to work in less prestigious programs, and to hold no administrative appointments in either universities (Lather, 1984; McCune & Matthews, 1975; Sears, 1983) or school settings (Apple, 1986; Connell, 1985; Grumet, 1981; King, 1987; Schmuck, 1987; Strober & Tyack, 1980).

Hidden curricular messages about gender relations are also transmitted by teacher and counselor expectations, as well as by messages in textbooks in school-based (McCune & Matthews, 1975) and university-based teacher education programs (Lather, 1984; Maher & Rathbone, 1986; Sadker & Sadker, 1980). Finally, in education, and in the academy more generally, classroom discourse tends to reflect masculine language (Lewis & Simon, 1986), analyses of educators and other workers tend to be based on models of male experience (Acker, 1983; Schmuck, 1987), and the dominant orientation is that of "masculine intellectualism: abstractionism and consequentialism . . . [versus] compassion and caring" (Noddings, 1986, p. 499). The dominance of masculine intellectualism in higher education could help explain why "an incipient professional culture of teaching possessed by female primary teachers was ig-

nored by male professors in the 19th century normal schools who stressed academic learning and by the 20th century university schools of education who stressed scientific instruction and school management" (W. Johnson, 1987, p. 43). This throws a different light on Lortie's (1975) comment regarding the lack of a "technical culture" of teaching (see also Acker, 1983).

IMPLICATIONS

The research on hidden curriculum in teacher education does not support definitive conclusions regarding content or effects at this time. It should be emphasized that the content of hidden curricula can vary within and across programs, over time, and cross-nationally. Some hidden curricular messages have been reported consistently by scholars using a variety of research techniques (e.g., historical, survey research, and ethnographic approaches) and focusing on a range of societal contexts, but other findings indicate contrasting messages. The broadly defined, relevant literature reviewed here does not point up all the messages contained in even one program, let alone all the possible messages transmitted in the variety of settings that might be investigated. Clearly, there is a need for additional research examining the content of hidden curricula in teacher education programs in a variety of institutional, societal, and historical contexts (Atkinson & Delamont, 1985; Crow, 1987b; Popkewitz, 1982).

Such investigations could involve a variety of research approaches, but we believe that employing experimental or quasi-experimental designs along with input–output, black-box conceptualizations of courses and programs (Wideen et al., 1987) hampers researchers in illuminating the content of both the hidden and official curricula of teacher education. Tindall's (1975) description of a research program for the hidden curriculum of sport is illustrative of the type of research that, in our opinion, is most likely to reveal both the content of implicit messages and the impact of those messages on the diverse groups who receive them.

In this review we have focused mainly on the content of messages, rather than on the impact they might have on specific individuals and groups in a particular setting at a given time (as urged by Martin, 1983, p. 125). We tend to agree that the hidden curriculum "constitutes the core of teacher socialization" (Mardle & Walker, 1980, p. 106) and that "the chief impact of colleges, like that of the schools they serve, comes from the hidden curriculum" (Dale, 1977, p. 51). As we noted in the introduction to this chapter, however, we want to leave open the possibility that at least some messages transmitted through a hidden curriculum will not be received either consciously or unconsciously, let alone internalized, by all individuals who experience them (Atkinson & Delamont, 1985; Mardle & Walker, 1980; Popkewitz, Tabachnick, & Zeichner, 1979; Ross, 1988; Spatig, Ginsburg, & Liberman, 1982; Thielens, 1977; Thies-Sprinthall & Sprinthall, 1987; Zeichner, 1985). This possibility is due in part to the conception of human thought and action as relatively independent of the cultural and structural levels comprising the sources of a hidden curriculum (see Giddens, 1976). It cannot be assumed that the messages of the hidden curriculum are consistent. Indeed, messages tend to be contradictory. Future research should be directed toward examining the effects of different kinds of hidden curricular messages on students of different social class, gender, and racial groups who participate in a range of teacher education programs and plan to work in various school–community settings in different countries.

Furthermore, given the potential for contradictions within both the hidden curriculum and the official curriculum, we do not conclude that the relation between these two curricula will be one of "lack of correspondence" as Crow does (1987a, p. 3). We are not surprised that the hidden curricular messages that contradict the "official" curricular messages are most likely to attract the attention of teacher educators and researchers. But additional research is needed to clarify under what conditions various types of hidden curricular messages contradict those in the official curriculum and what effects such contradictory or reinforcing messages have on individual preservice teachers and teacher educators.

The question of the effects of hidden curricula on society is similarly problematic, even assuming students receive (and internalize) hidden curricular messages. Although we concur with Vallance's (1983) statement that many of the messages are likely to reinforce the status quo because, in a sense, the messages are reflections of current social relations and culture, we do not want to suggest that social and cultural reproduction are the only logical or natural consequences of a hidden curriculum (see also Apple, 1979; Giroux, 1981, 1983). *First*, we have presented some evidence of hidden curricular messages that seem to communicate alternative or contradictory images of teachers, schooling, and society. *Second*, as we will suggest, those of us involved in the education of teachers have some, but not total, control over the kinds of hidden curricular messages we help to send, as well as over what we do to enable prospective teachers to recognize, critically reflect upon, and act upon the extant messages.

Given such tentative conclusions, why concern ourselves with the hidden curriculum in teacher education? Surely, trying to understand and develop the official curriculum and organizational structures in teacher education are sufficient challenges. The point is that these issues cannot be considered independently. We have attempted to illustrate that both the official curriculum and the organization of university-based and school-based teacher education programs are sources of hidden curricular messages. Although we do not and, perhaps, cannot know (in some positivistic, scientific sense) the content and effects of all messages in the hidden curricula of teacher education, that certainly does not prevent us from examining them in a variety of settings, including those in which many of us work. Nor does it preclude us from consideration of the content and effects of hidden curricular messages that are transmitted by proposed reforms in teacher education (see Ginsburg, 1988).

For example, the teacher education reform agenda (e.g., Carnegie Forum on Education and the Economy, 1987; Holmes Group, 1986; Joyce & Clift, 1984; National Commission for Excellence in Teacher Education, 1985) includes plans to (a) make entry into and exit from teacher education more selective; (b) extend the length of preservice teacher preparation; (c) make programs academically more demanding; (d) increase the involvement of faculty outside education; (e) further stratify the educational work force by creating a formal hierarchy of teaching positions associated with different kinds and amounts of training; and (f) restructure school organizations so that (some) teachers have greater autonomy and receive greater remuneration. The issue for us here is not whether such reforms would produce more effective or respected teachers, but rather what are likely be the hidden curricular messages transmitted in the reformed teacher education programs.

The first three proposals represent part of a long-standing professionalization strategy (Feinberg, 1987) and, to the extent they are successfully implemented, would tend to convey messages that would elevate the status of teaching as an occupation. At the same time, however, the reforms might reduce the percentage of preservice and inservice teachers from ethnic-minority and working-class backgrounds, thus, perhaps, communicating more clearly than ever the legitimacy of inequality in schooling and society.

The proposal to more systematically involve educators of teachers in university arts and sciences departments in the planning and implementing of a teacher-preparation program has the potential to (a) send the message that learning to teach represents a wholistic synthesis of knowledge, as opposed to a fragmented patchwork; and (b) present a model of teaching that is more reflective than technical. In addition, instructors might have greater power, in that the intervention of administrators and state officials might be limited by cross-university collaboration of faculty members. Nevertheless, the increased involvement of noneducation faculty in program design might be interpreted as reducing the influence of education faculty, thus further diminishing the status and power of teaching as an occupation. And, as Martin (1987) stresses, teacher educators should be sensitive to gender and class-biased messages contained in the liberal arts: divorcing of head from hand, production from reproduction, and reason from emotion, the latter dualism having pedagogical implications as well.

The institution of proposals (f) and (g) would also send mixed messages. The *career professional teacher's* role (cf. Holmes Group, 1986) would seem to communicate a conception of teachers as high-status professionals, reflective practitioners, and curriculum decision makers. Nevertheless, the majority of teachers would be at the lower rungs of the ladder, signaling the opposite message, much as the creation of the principal teacher did in the United States (Dreeben, 1988; Ginsburg, 1988; Raywid, 1987; Sedlak, 1987; Shive & Case, 1987; Tom, 1987; Zumwalt, 1987). Depending on the class, race, and gender of teachers occupying these roles, the messages would either reinforce or challenge existing inequalities; in any case, stratification would be conveyed as a normal and necessary aspect of human existence (Futrell, 1987; Ginsburg, 1988; Judge, 1987).

No reform of education or of teacher education will eliminate undesirable messages in the hidden curriculum. Because of the dynamic and dialectical nature of society, the messages will likely remain contradictory or mixed. Thus, it will always be important for professors, teachers, and prospective teachers to engage in dialogue and critical reflection about hidden curricula (Beyer & Zeichner, 1987; Ginsburg, 1988; Lather, 1984; Lynch & Plunkett, 1973; J. Parsons & Beauchamp, 1985; Sears, 1983). As Martin (1983) encourages; "When we find a hidden curriculum, we [should] show it to those destined to be its recipients. Consciousness raising . . . [should focus on] counteracting the hidden curriculum of settings we are not now in a position to change or abolish" (p. 136).

Some evidence indicates that preservice teachers can learn to confront the messages in the hidden curriculum and, thus, avoid being accidentally influenced by them (Gitlin, 1982; Hursh, 1987; Zeichner & Tabachnick, 1984). But we must go beyond merely identifying hidden messages to critically analyzing the political and economic interests that might be served by their being effectively transmitted. Moreover, we need to engage in broader social struggles, as well as to partake in ideological critique, at least as such activity connects with our concerns about a hidden curriculum of teacher education (Beyer, 1988; Ginsburg, 1988; Giroux, 1983; Liston & Zeichner, 1987).

The task is not an easy one, considering the various roles we occupy as intellectuals in schools, universities, and society (Popkewitz, 1985, 1987), but it is one we must undertake. Thus, no matter whether we are educational researchers or other educators of teachers in universities and schools, our inquiry and teaching must attend to the hidden curriculum of teacher education. We must all collaborate in a continuous effort to produce educational institutions that live up to their own stated values or bear the consequences of institutions that might, in effect, be working against the causes of equity, justice, and peace.

References

Acker, S. (1983). Women in teaching: A semi-detached sociology of a semi-profession. In S. Walker & L. Barton (Eds.), *Gender, class and education* (pp. 123–139). London: Falmer Press.

Altenbaugh, R. (1987, April). *Professional socialization gender? The case of the Frick (Pittsburgh) training school for teachers, 1912–1937*. Paper presented at the meeting of the American Educational Research Association, Washington, DC.

American Association of Colleges for Teacher Education. (1987). *Teaching teachers: Facts and figures*. Washington, DC: Author.

American Association of University Professors. (1988). Mastering the academic market place: The annual report on the economic status of the profession. *Academe 74*(2), 3–16.

Apple, M. (1972). Behaviorism and conservatism: The educational views in four of the "systems" models of teacher education. In B. Joyce & M. Weil (Eds.), *Perspectives for reform in teacher education* (pp. 237–262). Englewood Cliffs, NJ: Prentice-Hall.

Apple, M. (1979). *Ideology and curriculum*. Boston: Routledge & Kegan Paul.

Apple, M. (1983). Curricular form and the logic of technical control. In M. Apple & L. Weis (Eds.), *Ideology and practice in schooling* (pp. 143–166). Philadelphia: Temple University Press.

Apple, M. (1986). *Teachers and text*. Boston: Routledge & Kegan Paul.

Applegate, J. (1987). Early field experiences: Three viewpoints. In M. Haberman & J. Backus (Eds.), *Advances in teacher education* (vol. 3, pp. 75–93). Norwood, NJ: Ablex.

Atkinson, P., & Delamont, S. (1985). Socialization into teaching: A research which lost its way. *British Journal of Sociology of Education*, *6*(3), 307–322.

Ball, S., & Lacey, C. (1980). Subject disciplines as the opportunity for group action: A measured critique of subject subcultures. In P. Woods (Ed.), *Teacher strategies* (pp. 149–177). London: Croom Helm.

Bartholomew, J. (1976). Schooling teachers: The myth of the liberal college. In G. Whitty & M. Young (Eds.), *Explorations in the politics of school knowledge* (pp. 114–124). Driffield, England: Nafferton.

Beatty, B. (1987, April). *Teacher training for women in New England: The preparation of women teachers at Wheelock School and at Wellesley College, 1888–1914*. Paper presented at the meeting of the American Educational Research Association, Washington, DC.

Becker, H., Geer, B., & Hughes, E. (1968). *Making the grade: The academic side of college life*. New York: John Wiley & Sons.

Beggs, W. (1965). *The education of teachers*. New York: Center for Applied Research in Education.

Bell, A. (1981). Structure, knowledge and social relationships in teacher education. *British Journal of Sociology of Education*, *2*(1), 3–24.

Bergen, B. (1988). Only a schoolmaster: Gender, class, and the effort to professionalize elementary teaching in England, 1870–1910. In J. Ozga (Ed.), *School work: Approaches to the labour process of teaching*. Milton Keynes, England: Open University Press.

Berlak, A., & Berlak, H. (1981). *Dilemmas of schooling: Teaching and social change*. New York: Methuen.

Berlak, A., & Berlak, H. (1983). Toward a nonhierarchical approach to school inquiry and leadership. *Curriculum Inquiry*, *13*(3), 267–294.

Bernstein, B. (1975). On the classification and framing of educational knowledge. In *Class, codes and control* (pp. 85–115). London: Routledge & Kegan Paul.

Beyer, L. (1983). Aesthetic curriculum and cultural reproduction. In M. Apple and L. Weis (Eds.), *Ideology and practice in schooling*. (pp. 89–113). Philadelphia: Temple University Press.

Beyer, L. (1988). *Knowing and acting: Inquiry, ideology and educational studies*. London: Falmer Press.

Beyer, L. E., & Zeichner, K. (1987). Teacher education in cultural context: Beyond reproduction. In T. Popkewitz (Ed.), *Critical studies in teacher education: Its folklore, theory and practice* (pp. 298–334). London: Falmer Press.

Bloom, A. (1987). *The closing of the American mind*. New York: Simon & Schuster.

Book, C., Beyers, J., & Freeman, D. (1983). Student expectations and teacher education traditions with which we can and cannot live. *Journal of Teacher Education 34*(1), 9–13.

Borko, H. (1984). Teachers as decision makers vs. technicians. In J. Nile & L. Harris (Eds.), *Changing perspectives on research in reading, language processing and instruction*. (33rd yearbook of the National Reading Conference, pp. 124–131). Rochester, NY: American Reading Conference.

Borrowman, M. (1956). *The liberal and the technical in teacher education: A historical survey of American thought*. New York: Columbia University, Teachers College, Bureau of Publications.

Borrowman, M. L. (Ed.). (1965). *Teacher education in America: A documentary history.* New York: Teachers College Press.

Bowden, T. (1972). On the selection, organization and assessment of knowledge for teachers: A case study. *Education for Teaching, 89,* 3–28.

Bowles, S., & Gintis, H. (1976). *Schooling in capitalist America: Educational reform and the contradictions of everyday life.* London: Routledge & Kegan Paul.

Britzman, D. (1986). Cultural myths in the making of a teacher: Biography and social structure in teacher education. *Harvard Educational Review, 56*(4), 442–456.

Bullough, R. (1982). Professional schizophrenia: Teacher education in confusion. *Contemporary Education, 53,* 207–212.

Burgess, R. (1977). Sociology of education courses for the intended teachers: An empirical study. *Research in Education, 17,* 41–62.

Buswell, C. (1988). Pedagogic change and social change. In J. Ozga (Ed.), *Schoolwork.* Milton Keynes, England: Open University Press.

Butts, R. F. (1983). Teacher education and the revival of civic learning. In A. Bagley (Ed.), *Civic learning in teacher education* (pp. 8–13). Washington, DC: Society of Professors of Education.

Carnegie Forum on Education and the Economy, Task Force on Teaching as a Profession. (1987). *A nation prepared: Teachers for the 21st century.* New York: Author.

Chiang, L. (1986, September) *Is our understanding of the hidden curriculum hidden from us?* Paper presented at the meeting of the Philosophy of Education Society of Australia, Armidale. (ERIC Document Reproduction Service No. ED 285 256)

Cinnamond, J. H., & Zimpher, N. C. (in press). Reflectivity as a function of community. In R. T. Clift, W. R. Houston, & M. C. Pugach (Eds.), *Reflective practice: An examination of issues and exemplars.* New York: Teachers College Press.

Clark, D., & Marker, G. (1975). The institutionalization of teacher education. In K. Ryan (Ed.), *Teacher Education* (74th yearbook of the National Society for the Study of Education, pp. 53–86). Chicago: University of Chicago Press.

Clifford, G. (1986). The formative years of schools of education in America: A five-institution analysis. *American Journal of Education, 94,* 427–446.

Clifford, G. (1987). Lady teachers and politics in the United States, 1850–1930. In M. Lawn & G. Grace (Eds.), *Teachers: The culture and politics of work* (pp. 3–30). London: Falmer Press.

Clifford, G., & Guthrie, J. W. (1988). *Ed School: A brief for professional education.* Chicago: University of Chicago Press.

Clift, R. T. (1989). Unanswered questions in graduate teacher preparation. In A. Woolfolk (Ed.), *Beyond debate: Research perspectives on the graduate preparation of teachers* (pp. 179–193). Englewood Cliffs, NJ: Prentice-Hall.

Clift, R. T., Houston, W. R., & Pugach, M. (Eds.). (in press). *Reflective practice: An examination of issues and exemplars.* New York: Teachers College Press.

Clift, R. T., Marshall, F., & Nichols, C. (1987). *Turning opportunities into problems: Anger and resistance in teacher education.* Paper presented at the annual meeting of the American Educational Research Association, Washington, DC.

Cohen, L. (1968). Colleges and the training of teachers. *Educational Research, 11,* 14–24.

Cole, D., & McCormick, T. (1987). *Infusion of international perspectives into undergraduate teacher education programs.* Paper presented at the annual meeting of the Educational Studies Association, Chicago.

Connel, R. (1985). *Teachers' work.* Sydney: Allen and Unwin.

Cook, C. (1984). Teachers for the inner city: Change and continuity. In G. Grace (Ed.), *Education and the city: Theory, history and contemporary practice* (pp. 269–291). London: Routledge & Kegan Paul.

Cornbleth, C. (1987). The persistence of myth in teacher education and teaching. In T. Popkewitz (Ed.), *Critical studies in teacher education: Its folklore, theory and practice,* (pp. 186–210). London: Falmer Press.

Cremin, L., Shannon, D., & Townsend, M. (1954). *A history of Teachers College.* New York: Columbia University Press.

Crittenden, B. (1973). Some prior questions in the reform of teacher education. *Interchange, 4*(2–3), 1–11.

Crow, N. (1987a, April). *Hidden curriculum in a teacher education program: A case study.* Paper presented at the annual meeting of the American Educational Research Association, Washington, DC.

Crow, N. (1987b, April). *Preservice teachers' biography: A case study.* Paper presented at the annual meeting of the American Educational Research Association, Washington, DC.

Cuban, L. (1984). *How teachers taught: Constancy and change in American classrooms 1890–1980.* New York: Longman.

Dale, R. (1977). Implications of the rediscovery of the hidden curriculum for the sociology of teaching. In D. Gleason (Ed.), *Identity and structure: Issues in the sociology of education.* Driffield, England: Nafferton.

Danielsson, B., Proppe, O., & Myrdal, S. (1987, October). *Teacher education in Iceland: Historical and institutional development.* Paper presented at the Conference on the Six Country Study of Teacher Education, Wingspread Center, Racine, WI.

Denscombe, M. (1982). The "hidden pedagogy" and its implications for teacher training. *British Journal of Sociology of Education, 3*(3), 249–265.

Densmore, K. (1987). Professionalism, proletarianization and teacher work. In T. Popkewitz (Ed.), *Critical studies in teacher education: Its folklore, theory and practice* (pp. 130–160). London: Falmer Press.

DeYoung, A. J. (1985). Assessing faculty productivity in colleges of education: Penetration of the technical thesis into the status system of academe. *Educational Theory, 35*(4), 411–21.

Dreeben, R. (1968). *On what is learned in school.* Reading, MA: Addison-Wesley.

Dreeben, R. (1987). Comments on tomorrow's teachers. *Teachers College Record, 88*(3), 359–365.

Dreeben, R. (1988). The school as a workplace. In J. Ozga (Ed.), *Schoolwork: Approaches to the labour process of teaching* (pp. 21–36). Milton Keynes, England: Open University Press.

Dutt, S. (1970). Towards a true profession of teaching. In S. Ruhela (Ed.), *Sociology of the teaching profession in India* (pp. 3–11). New Delhi: National Council of Educational Research and Training.

Eddy, E. (1969). *Becoming a teacher: The passage to professional status.* New York: Teachers College Press.

Efland, A. (1977). Competence and the hidden curriculum. In N. MacGregor (Ed.), *Competency and art education: A critique* (pp. 15–19). Columbus, OH: Ohio State University, Department of Art Education.

Eisner, E. (1985). *The educational imagination.* New York: Macmillan.

Eissenberg, T. E., & Rudner, L. M. (1988). State testing of teachers: A summary. *Journal of Teacher Education, 39*(4), 21–22.

Elsbree, W. (1939). *The American teacher: Education of a profession in democracy.* New York: American Book Company.

Feinberg, W. (1987). The Holmes Group report and the professionalization of teaching. *Teachers College Record, 88*(3), 366–377.

Freire, P. (1970). *The pedagogy of the oppressed* (M. Ramos, Trans.). New York: Seabury Press.

Fuller, F. F., & Bown, O. H. (1975). Becoming a teacher. In K. Ryan (Ed.), *Teacher education* (74th yearbook of the National Society for the Study of Education, Part II, pp. 25–52). Chicago: University of Chicago Press.

Futrell, M. (1987). The Holmes Group report: A Teacher perspective. *Teachers College Record*, 88(3), 378–383.

Gallmeier, T., & Poppleton, P. (1978). A study of early school experience in the PGCE course at the University of Sheffield. *British Journal of Teacher Education*, 4(2), 125–135.

Giddens, A. (1976). *Central problems in social theory*. Berkeley, CA: University of California Press.

Ginsburg, M. (1986). Reproduction, contradictions and conceptions of curriculum in preservice teacher education. *Curriculum Inquiry*, 16(3), 283–309.

Ginsburg, M. (1987a). Contradictions in the role of professor as activist. *Sociological Focus*, 20(2), 111–122.

Ginsburg, M. (1987b). Reproduction, contradictions and conceptions of professionalism. In T. Popkewitz (Ed.), *Critical studies in teacher education: Its folklore, theory and practice* (pp. 86–129). London: Falmer Press.

Ginsburg, M. (1987c). Teacher education and class and gender relations. *Educational Foundations*, 2, 4–36.

Ginsburg, M. (1988). *Contradictions in teacher education and society: A critical analysis*. London: Falmer Press.

Ginsburg, M., & Chaturvedi, V. (1988). Teachers and the ideology of professionalism in India and England. *Comparative Education Review*, 32(4), 465–477.

Ginsburg, M., & Newman, K. (1985). Social inequalities, schooling, and teacher education. *Journal of Teacher Education*, 26, 49–54.

Ginsburg, M., & Spatig, L. (1985, March). *The proletarianization of the professorate: The case of producing a competency based teacher education program*. Paper presented at the annual meeting of the American Educational Research Association, Chicago. (Also chap. 3 in M. Ginsburg (Ed.). [1988] *Contradictions in teacher education and society: A critical analysis*. London: Falmer Press.)

Ginsburg, M., Wallace, G., & Miller H. (1988). Teachers, economy and the state. *Teaching and teacher education*, 4(4), 1–21.

Giroux, H. (1981). Teacher education and the ideology of social control. In H. Giroux (Ed.), *Ideology, culture, and the process of schooling* (pp. 143–162). Philadelphia: Temple University Press.

Giroux, H. (1983). Schooling and the politics of the hidden curriculum. In H. Giroux (Ed.), *Theory and resistance in education* (pp. 42–71). South Hadley, MA: Bergin & Garvey.

Giroux, H., & McLaren, P. (1986). Teacher education and the politics of engagement: The case for democratic schooling. *Harvard Educational Review*, 56(3), 213–238.

Giroux, H., & McLaren, P. (1987). Teacher education as a counter public sphere: Notes toward a redefinition. In T. Popkewitz (Ed.), *Critical studies in teacher education: Its folklore, theory and practice* (pp. 266–297). London: Falmer Press.

Giroux, H., & Penna, A. (1983). Social education in the classroom: The dynamics of hidden curriculum. In H. Giroux & D. Purpel (Eds.), *The hidden curriculum and moral education: deception or discovery?* (pp. 100–121). Berkeley, CA: McCutchan.

Gitlin, A. (1982, March). *Reflection and action in teacher education programs*. Paper presented at the annual meeting of the American Educational Research Association, New York.

Goodman, J. (1984). *Masculinity, feminism, and the male elementary school teacher: A case study of preservice teachers perspectives*. Paper presented at the Curriculum Theory and Practice Conference, Dayton, OH.

Grace, G. (1978). *Teachers, ideology and control: A study in urban education*. London: Routledge & Kegan Paul.

Grace, G. (1987). Teachers and the state in Britain: A changing relation. In M. Lawn & G. Grace (Eds.), *Teachers: The culture and politics of work* (pp. 193–228). London: Falmer Press.

Greene, M. (1978). The matter of mystification: Teacher education in unquiet times. In M. Greene, *Landscapes of learning* (pp. 53–73). New York: Teachers College Press.

Grossman, P., & Richert, A. (1988). Unacknowledged knowledge growth: A re-examination of the effects of teacher education. *Teaching and Teacher Education*, 4(1), 53–62.

Grumet, M. (1981). Pedagogy for patriarchy: The feminization of teaching. *Interchange*, 12(2–3), 165–184.

Haberman, M. (1986). An evaluation of the rationale for required teacher education: Beginning teachers with and without teacher preparation. In T. Lasley (Ed.), *Issues in teacher education 2* (pp. 7–54). Washington, DC: American Association of Colleges for Teacher Education.

Haberman, M., & Stinnet, T. (1973). *Teacher education and the new profession of teaching*. Berkeley, CA: McCutchan.

Harper, C. (1939). *A century of public teacher education: The story of state colleges as they evolved from normal schools*. Westport, CT: Greenwood Press.

Hartnett, A., & Naish, M. (1978a, September). *Cloning or educating? Some issues about skepticism, ideology and the education of teachers*. Paper presented at the Social Science Research Council Conference on Teacher and Pupil Strategies, St. Hilda's College, Oxford, England.

Hartnett, A., & Naish, M. (1978b). Educational theory: Bromide and barmecide. *Journal of Further and Higher Education*, 1(3), 63–75.

Hartnett, A., & Naish, M. (1980). Technicians or social bandits? Some moral and political issues in the education of teachers. In P. Woods (Ed.), *Teacher strategies: Explorations in the sociology of school* (pp. 254–274). London: Croom Helm.

Helsel, A., & Krchniak, S. (1972). Socialization in a heteronomous profession: Public school teaching. *Journal of Educational Research*, 66(2), 89–93.

Henry, J. (1955). Docility, or giving teacher what she wants. *Journal of Social Issues*, 2(2), 33–41.

Hochschild, A. (1983). *The managed heart*. Berkeley, CA: University of California Press.

Holmes Group (1986). *Tomorrow's teachers*. East Lansing, MI: Author.

Horton, L. (1972). *The hidden curriculum of competency based teacher education*. Unpublished manuscript. (Eric Document Reproduction Service No. ED 080 511)

Howey, K. (1986). The next generation of teacher preparation programs. In T. Lasley (Ed.), *The dynamics of change in teacher education 1* (pp. 161–185). Washington, DC: American Association of College for Teacher Education.

Howey, K. (1987, April). *AACTE national survey: Teacher education programs*. Paper presented at the annual meeting of the American Educational Research Association, Washington, DC.

Howey, K., & Zimpher, N. (1987, April). *Case studies of elementary teacher Preparation programs in six schools and colleges of education: Preliminary study findings*. Paper presented at the annual meeting of the American Educational Research Association, Washington, DC.

Hoy, W. (1967). Organizational socialization: The student teacher and pupil control ideology. *Journal of Educational Research*, 61(4), 153–155.

Hoy, W. (1968). The influence of experience on the beginning teacher. *School Review*, 76, 312–323.

Hoy, W., & Rees, R. (1977). The bureaucratic socialization of student teachers. *Journal of Teacher Education*, 28(1), 23–26.

Hoy, W. K., & Woolfolk, A. E. (1988). Supervising student teachers. In A. Woolfolk (Ed.), *Beyond the debate: Research perspectives on the graduate preparation of teachers* (pp. 108–131). Englewood Cliffs, NJ: Prentice-Hall.

Hursh, D. (1987, October). *Becoming reflective teachers: Preservice teachers' understanding of school and society.* Paper presented at the meeting of the Midwest Educational Research Association, Chicago.

Illich, I. (1970). *Deschooling society.* New York: Harper & Row.

Jackson, P. (1968). *Life in classrooms.* New York: Holt, Rinehart & Winston.

Johnson, W. (1987, April). *Teacher training in Maryland, 1850–1915.* Paper presented at the meeting of the American Educational Research Association, Washington, DC.

Johnson, H., & Johanningmeier, E. (1972). *Teachers for the prairies: The University of Illinois and the schools, 1868–1945.* Urbana, IL: University of Illinois Press.

Joyce, B., & Clift, R. (1984). The Phoenix agenda: Essential reform in teacher education. *Educational Researcher, 13*(4), 5–18.

Joyce, B., Howey, K., & Yarger, S. (1977). *Preservice teacher education.* Palo Alto, CA: Booksend Laboratories.

Judge, H. (1982). *American graduate schools of education: A view from abroad.* New York: Ford Foundation.

Judge, H. (1987). Another view from abroad. *Teachers College Record, 88*(3), 394–399.

Kamens, D. H. (1977). Legitimating myths and educational organization: The relationship between organizational ideology and formal structure. *American Sociological Review, 42,* 208–219.

Katz, L., & Raths, J. D. (1982). The best of intentions for the education of teachers. *Action in Teacher Education, 4*(1), 8–16.

Kelly, T. (1987, April). *Teacher education and democratic empowerment.* Paper presented at the annual meeting of the American Educational Research Association, Washington, DC.

King, S. (1987). Feminists in teaching: The national union of women teachers, 1920–1940. In M. Lawn & G. Grace (Eds.), *Teachers: The culture and politics of work* (pp. 31–49). London: Falmer Press.

Koerner, J. (1963). *The miseducation of American teachers.* Boston: Houghton Mifflin.

Lacey, C. (1977). *The socialization of teachers.* London: Methuen.

Lanier, J. E. & Little, J. N. (1986). Research on teacher education. In M. C. Wittrock (Ed.), *Handbook of research on teaching* (3rd ed., pp. 527–569). New York: Macmillan.

Lather, P. (1984, April). *Women's studies as counter hegemonic work: The case of teacher education.* Paper presented at annual meeting of the American Educational Research Association, New Orleans.

LaVolpa, A. (1980). *Prussian school teachers: Profession and office.* Chapel Hill, NC: University of North Carolina Press.

LeCompte, M., & Ginsburg, M. (1987). How students learn to become teachers: An exploration of responses to teacher training programs. In G. Noblit & W. Pink (Eds.), *Schooling in social context: Qualitative studies* (pp. 3–22). New York: Ablex.

Lee, J. (1987). Pride and prejudice: Teachers, class and an inner-city infants school. In M. Lawn & G. Grace (Eds.), *Teachers: The culture and politics of work* (pp. 90–116). London: Falmer Press.

Lewis, M., & Simon, R. (1986). A discourse not intended for her: Learning and teaching within patriarchy. *Harvard Educational Review, 56*(4), 457–472.

Liston, D., & Zeichner, K. (1987). Critical pedagogy and teacher education. *Journal of Education, 169*(3), 117–133.

Lortie, D. C. (1975). *Schoolteacher: A sociological study.* Chicago: University of Chicago Press.

Lynch, J., & Plunkett, H. (1973). *Teacher education and cultural change: England, France and West Germany.* London: Allen and Unwin.

Maher, F., & Rathbone, C. (1986). Teacher education and feminist theory: Some implications for practice. *American Journal of Education, 94*(2), 214–235.

Mardle, G., & Walker, M. (1980). Strategies and structure: Some critical notes on teacher socialization. In P. Woods (Ed.), *Teacher strategies* (pp. 98–124). London: Croom Helm.

Martin, J. (1983). What should we do with a hidden curriculum when we find one? In H. Giroux & D. Purpel (Eds.), *The hidden curriculum and moral education: Deception or discovery?* (pp. 122–140). Berkley, CA: McCutchan.

Martin, J. (1987). Reforming teacher education, rethinking liberal education. *Teachers College Record, 88*(3), 406–410.

Mattingly, P. (1975). *The classless profession: American schoolmen in the nineteenth century.* New York: New York University Press.

McCaleb, J. L., Borko, H., Arends, R. A., Garner, R., & Mauro, L. (1987). Innovation in teacher education: The evolution of a program. *Journal of Teacher Eduction, 38*(4), 57–64.

McCune, S., & Matthews, M. (1975). Eliminating sexism: Teacher education and change. *Journal of Teacher Education, 26*(4), 294–300.

McNamara, D. (1972). Sociology of education and the education of teachers. *British Journal of Educational Studies, 20*(2), 137–147.

McNamara, D., & Desforges, C. (1978). The social sciences, teacher education and the objectification of craft knowledge. *British Journal of Teacher Education, 4*(1), 17–36.

McNeil, L. (1983). Defensive teaching and classroom control. In M. Apple & L. Weis (Eds.), *Ideology and practice in schooling* (pp. 114–142). Philadelphia: Temple University Press.

Monroe, W. (1952). *Teaching–learning theory and teacher education: 1890–1950.* Urbana, IL: University of Illinois Press.

Morgenstern de Finkel, S., & Pereyra, M. (1987, October). *Teachers' education in Spain: A reform postponed.* Paper presented at the Conference on the Six Country Study of Teacher Education, Wingspread Center, Racine, WI.

National Commission on Excellence in Teacher Education (1985). *A call for change in teacher education.* Washington, DC: American Association of Colleges for Teacher Education. (ERIC Document Reproduction Service No. ED 252 525).

Newman, K. (1982, November). *The hidden curriculum of a textbook: What books teach about reading.* Paper presented at the meeting of the Reading Association, San Diego.

Noddings, N. (1986). Fidelity in teaching, teacher education, and research for teaching. *Harvard Educational Review, 56*(4), 496–510.

Noddings, N. (1988). An ethic of caring and its implications for instructional arrangements. *American Journal of Education, 96*(2), 215–230.

Noordhoff, K., & Kleinfeld, J. (in press). Rethinking the rhetoric of reflective inquiry: What this language came to mean in a program to prepare rural teachers. In R. T. Clift, W. R. Houston, & M. C. Pugach (Eds.), *Encouraging reflective practice: An examination of issues and exemplars.* New York: Teachers College Press.

O'Shea, D. (1983). *Teacher education: An empirical study of problems and possibilities.* Los Angeles: University of California at Los Angeles, Graduate School of Education Research Report.

Otero, M. (1981). Oppression in Uruguay. *Bulletin of Atomic Scientist,* 29–31.

Overly, N. (Ed.). (1970). *The unstudied curriculum: Its impact on children.* Washington, DC: Association for Supervision and Curriculum Development.

Ozga, J., & Lawn, M. (1981). *Teachers, professionalism and class: A study of organized teachers.* London: Falmer Press.

Paine, L. (1985, April). *The teaching of teachers: Technocracy and politics in China.* Paper presented at the meeting of the Comparative and International Education Society, Stanford University.

Palmer, J. (1984). The failure of the schools of education. *Texas Humanist,* 15–17.

Pangburn, J. (1932). *The evolution of the American teachers college.* New York: Columbia University, Bureau of Publications.

Parsons, J., & Beauchamp, L. (1985). *The hidden curriculum of student teaching evaluation*. Unpublished manuscript. (Eric Reproduction Service Document No. ED 261 983).

Parsons, T. (1959). The school class as a social system. *Harvard Educational Review, 29*, 297–308.

Peck, R., & Tucker, J. (1973). Research on teacher education. In R. M. Travers (Ed.), *The second handbook of research on teaching* (pp. 940–978). Chicago: Rand McNally.

Perry, L. (1969). Training. *Education for Teaching, 79*, 3–9.

Peseau, B. A. (1980). The outrageous underfunding of teacher education. *Phi Delta Kappan, 62*(2), 100–102.

Peters, R. S. (1977). *Education and the education of teachers*. London: Routledge & Kegan Paul.

Pittman, A. (1987, October). *Reform of teacher education in Victoria [Australia]*. Paper presented at the Conference of the Six Country Study of Teacher Education, Wingspread Center, Racine, WI.

Popkewitz, T. (1979, April). *Teacher education as socialization: Ideology of social mission*. Paper presented at the annual meeting of the American Educational Research Association, San Francisco.

Popkewitz, T. (1982). The social/moral rise of occupational life: Teacher education in the Soviet Union. *Journal of Teacher Education, 33*(3), 38–44.

Popkewitz, T. (1983). Methods of teacher education and cultural codes. In P. Tamir, A. Hofstein, & M. Ben-Peretz (Eds.), *Preservice and inservice training of science teachers*. Philadelphia: Balaben International Science Services.

Popkewitz, T. (1985, April). *Curriculum studies, knowledge and interest: Problems and paradoxes*. Paper presented at the annual Meeting of the American Educational Research Association, Chicago.

Popkewitz, T. (1987). Ideology and social formation in teacher education. In T. Popkewitz (Ed.), *Critical studies in teacher education: Its folklore, theory and practice* (pp. 2–34). London: Falmer Press.

Popkewitz, T. S., Tabachnick, R. B., & Zeichner, K. (1979). Dulling the senses: Research in teacher education. *Journal of Teacher Education, 30*(5), 52–59.

Powell, A. (1976). University schools of education in the twentieth century. *Peabody Journal of Education, 54*(1), 3–20.

Powell, A. G. (1980). *The uncertain profession: Harvard and the search for educational authority*. Cambridge, MA: Harvard University Press.

Pruitt, K., & Lee, J. (1978). Hidden handcuffs in teacher education. *Journal of Teacher Education, 29*(5), 69–72.

Raywid, M. (1987). Tomorrow's teachers and today's schools. *Teachers College Record, 88*(3), 411–418.

Reid, I. (1986). Hoops, swings and roundabouts in teacher education. *Journal of Further and Higher Education, 10*(2), 20–26.

Renshaw, P. (1971). The objectives and structure of a college curriculum. In J. Tibble (Ed.), *The future of teacher education* (pp. 53–67). London: Routledge & Kegan Paul.

Ross, E. W. (1988). Preservice teachers' responses to institutional constraints: The active role of the individual in teacher socialization. *Educational Foundations, 2*(1), 77–92.

Sadker, M., & Sadker, D. (1980). Sexism in teacher-education texts. *Harvard Educational Review, 50*(1), 36–45.

Schmuck, P. (1987). *Women educators: Employees of schools in western countries*. Albany, NY: State University of New York Press.

Schneider, B. (1987). Tracing the provenance of teacher education. In T. Popkewitz (Ed.), *Critical studies in teacher education: Its folklore, theory and practice* (pp. 211–241). London: Falmer Press.

Schön, D. A. (1983). *The reflective practitioner: How professionals think in action*. New York: Basic Books.

Schön, D. (1987). *Educating the reflective practitioners*. San Francisco: Jossey Bass.

Schwarzweller, H., & Lyson, T. (1978). Some plans to become teachers: Determinants of career specification among rural youth in Norway, Germany and the United States. *Sociology of Education, 51*, 29–43.

Sears, J. (1983). *Peering into the black box of teacher training*. Unpublished doctoral dissertation, Indiana University.

Sears, J. (1987, April). *The political economy of teacher training: Attracting high-ability persons into teaching: A Critique*. Paper presented at the annual meeting of the American Educational Research Association, Washington, DC.

Sears, J., & Henderson, A. (1957). *Cubberly of Stanford and his contribution to American education*. Stanford, CA: Stanford University Press.

Sedlak, M. (1987). Tomorrow's teachers: The essential arguments of the Holmes Group report. *Teachers College Record, 88*(3), 314–325.

Shive, R., & Case, C. (1987). Differentiated staffing as an educational reform response. *Educational Policy, 1*, 57–66.

Silva, E., & Slaughter, S. (1984). *Serving power: The making of the academic social science expert*. Westport, CT: Greenwood Press.

Snarr, O. (1946). *The education of teachers in the middle states: A historical study of the professional education of public school teachers as a state function*. Moorehead, MN: Moorehead State Teachers College.

Spatig, L., Ginsburg, M., & Liberman, D. (1982). Ego development as an explanation of passive and active models of teacher socialization. *College Student Journal, 16*(4), 315–325.

Spillane, R., & Levenson, D. (1976). Teacher training: A question of control not content. *Phi Delta Kappan, 57*(7), 435–439.

Spring, J. (1986). *The American Schools, 1642–1985*. New York: Longman.

Strober, M., & Tyack, D. (1980). Why do women teach and men manage? *Sighs, 3*, 494–503.

Tabachnick, B. R. (1983, April). *The development of teacher perspectives*. Paper presented at the annual meeting of the American Educational Research Association, Montreal.

Tabachnick, B. R., Popkewitz, T., & Zeichner, K. (1978, March). *Teacher education and the professional perspectives of teachers*. Paper presented at the annual meeting of the American Educational Research Association, Toronto.

Tabachnick, B. R., Zeichner, K., Densmore, L., Adler, S, & Egan, K. (1982, March). *The impact of the student teaching experience on the development of teacher perspectives*. Paper presented at the annual meeting of the American Educational Research Association, New York.

Thielens, W. (1977). Undergraduate definitions of learning from teachers. *Sociology of Education, 50*, 159–181.

Thies-Sprinthall, L., & Sprinthall, N. (1987). Preservice teachers as adult learners: A new framework for teacher education. In M. Haberman & J. Backus (Eds.), *Advances in teacher education* (Vol. 3, pp. 35–56). Norwood, NJ: Ablex.

Tindall, B. A. (1975). Ethnography and the hidden curriculum of sport. *Behavioral and Social Science Teacher, 2*(2), 5–25.

Tom, A. (1977). A critique of performance based teacher education. *Educational Forum, 42*(1), 77–87.

Tom, A. (1987). The Holmes Group report: Its latent political agenda. *Teachers College Record, 88*(3), 430–435.

Tucker, J. (1981). Teacher education policy in contemporary China: The socio-political context. *Theory and Research in Social Education, 8*(4), 1–13.

Tuckman, B. W. (1987). Teacher education needs a Lee Iacocca to make the case for effective reforms. *Chronicle of Higher Education 33*(26), 7.

Tyack, D. (1967). The education of teachers and the teaching of education. In D. Tyack (Ed.), *Turning points in American educational history* (pp. 412–465). Waltham, MA: Blaisdell.

Vallance, E. (1983). Hiding the hidden curriculum: An interpretation of the language of justification in nineteenth century educational reform. *Curriculum Theory Network, 1,* 5–21.

Van Manen, M. (1977). Linking ways of knowing with ways of being practical. *Curriculum Inquiry, 6*(3), 205–228.

Waller, W. (1932). *The sociology of teaching.* New York: Wiley.

Warren, D. (1985). Learning from experience: History and teacher education. *Educational Researcher, 14*(10), 5–12.

Watts, D. (1987). Student teaching. In M. Haberman & J. Backus (Eds.), *Advances in teacher education* (Vol. 3, pp. 151–167). Norwood, NJ: Ablex.

Wehlage, G. (1981). Can teachers be more reflective about their work? A commentary on some research about teachers. In R. Tabachnick, T. Popkewitz, & B. Szekely (Eds.), *Studying teaching learning trends in Soviet and American research* (pp. 101–113). New York: Praeger.

Weinstein, C. (1988). Case studies of extended teacher preparation. In A. Woolfolk (Ed.), *Beyond the debate: Research perspectives on the graduate preparation of teachers.* Englewood Cliffs, NJ: Prentice-Hall.

Weisbeck, C., & Buchmann, M. (1981). *Learning the lessons of experience: A field study in teacher education* (Research Series No. 96). East Lansing, MI: Michigan State University, Institute for Research and Teaching.

White, W. T. (1982). The decline of the classroom and the Chicago study of education, 1909–1929. *American Journal of Education, 90*(2), 144–174.

Whitty, G., Barton, L., & Pollard, A. (1987). Ideology and control in teacher education: A review of recent experience in England. In T. Popkewitz (Ed.), *Critical studies in teacher education: Its folklore, theory and practice* (pp. 161–184). London: Falmer Press.

Wideen, M., Holborn, P, & Desrogiers, M. (1987, April). *A critical review of a decade of Canadian research on teacher education.* Paper presented at the meeting of the American Educational Research Association, Washington, DC.

Wildman, T. M., & Niles, J. A. (1987). Reflective teachers: Tensions between abstractions and realities. *Journal of Teacher Education, 38*(4), 25–31.

Woodring, P. (1975). The development of teacher education. In K. Ryan (Ed.), *Teacher education.* (74th yearbook of the National Society for'the Study of Education, Part II, pp. 1–24). Chicago: University of Chicago Press.

Yarger, S., Howey, K., and Joyce, B. (1977). Reflections on preservice preparation: Impressions from the national survey. *Journal of Teacher Education, 28*(6), 34–37.

Young, M. (1971). An approach to the study of curricula as socially organized knowledge. In M. Young (Ed.), *Knowledge and control* (pp. 19–46). London: Collier-Macmillan.

Zeichner, K. (1979, April). *Reflective teaching and field-based experience in teacher education.* Paper presented at the annual meeting of the American Educational Research Association, San Francisco.

Zeichner, K. (1985, April). *Content and contexts: Neglected elements in studies of student teaching as an occasion for learning to teach.* Paper presented at the annual meeting of the American Educational Research Association, Chicago.

Zeichner, K., & Tabachnick, B. R. (1981). Are the effects of university teacher education washed out by school experience? *Journal of Teacher Education, 32*(3), 7–11.

Zeichner, K., & Tabachnick, B. R. (1984, April). *Social strategies and institutional control in the socialization of teachers.* Paper presented at the annual meeting of the American Educational Research Association, New Orleans.

Zimpher, N., Nott, D., & deVoss, G. (1980, February). *A multiple perspective ethnographic account of the student teaching experience: Preliminary data summary.* Paper presented at the annual meeting of the American Educational Research Association, Washington, DC.

Zumwalt, K. (1987). Tomorrow's teachers: Tomorrow's work. *Teachers College Record, 88*(3), 436–441.

PROCESSES OF TEACHER EDUCATION

·27·

TRAINING WITHIN TEACHER PREPARATION

Donald R. Cruickshank

THE OHIO STATE UNIVERSITY

Kim Kenneth Metcalf

SOUTHWEST MISSOURI STATE UNIVERSITY

MEANINGS AND RELATIONSHIPS OF EDUCATION, TRAINING, AND SKILLS

Education and Training

The difference between education and training is blurred (Glaser, 1962; Gliessman, 1984; Hills, 1982), and dictionaries regularly comingle the terms (e.g., Webster's *New World Dictionary of the American Language*, 1980). However, Billings (1981) and Robertson (1987) provide a distinction useful here. The former notes that education permits us to be informed, to know about something, whereas training permits us to do something. Robertson agrees, stating, "The focus of training is on knowing-how rather than knowing-that" (p. 16). Be that as it may, Billings notes, "In one learning system, we can find elements of both" (p. 273).

To gain a more precise meaning of the term *train*, Webster's *Third New International Dictionary of the English Language Unabridged* (Gove, 1971) was consulted. Therein the following notations were extracted from many as the most suitable for consideration here:

3 a: to instruct or drill in habits of thought or action: shape or develop the character of by discipline or percept . . . **b(1):** to teach or exercise (someone) in an art, profession, trade, or occupation: direct in attaining a skill . . . (2): to cause (as judgement) to be disciplined: cultivate: . . . develop skill or habits in . . . **2a:** to undergo instruction, discipline, or drill. . . . (Gove, 1971, 2424)

Thus, literally, it would seem possible to train persons in quite a variety of behaviors: habits of thought (how to think), attitudes and dispositions (what to think), actions (what to do), skills (how to do) and taste (what is good). Hills (1982) primarily agrees, defining training "as a process . . . to modify attitudes, knowledge or skill behavior so as to achieve effective performance" (p. 273). (When the intention is to modify habits of thought such as attitudes, training seems to bear a resemblance to indoctrination.) Hinnrichs (1976, p. 833) concurs, noting that training can be directed toward any behavior: motor skills, cognitive skills, or interpersonal (affective) skills.

Training, then, connotes the development of a variety of behaviors depicting know-how across a wide spectrum of human activity. Unfortunately, training is delimited by some to mean only how to do physical or manual activities.

Skills

The term *skill* is often associated with training and would seem to be an outcome of it. As with the term *train*, the most appropriate meanings for use here were taken from Webster's (Gove, 1971):

(2): The ability to use one's knowledge effectively and readily in execution or performance: technical expertise: PROFICIENCY . . . **b:** dexterity, fluency, or coordination in the execution of learned physical or mental tasks . . . : technical competence without insight or understanding or the ability for further elaboration or development . . . : a developed or acquired aptitude or ability . . . : a craft requiring the use of

The authors wish to express their thanks to David H. Gliessman (Indiana University) and E. Dale Doak (University of Tennessee) for their critical reviews of this chapter.

related skills . . . **c:** a coordinated set of actions become smooth and integrated through practice. . . . (p. 2133)

Examination of the usage of the term *skill* seems to indicate that: it is related to training ("being able to use knowledge"); skills encompass both the intellect and the physical (unfortunately like *train*, the term often conjures up only motor development); skill attainment or at least skill refinement, requires practice; and, like training, skill attainment devoid of education is craftlike. Because skills are acquired as a result of training and since training can appropriately be done with regard to a variety of behaviors (intellectual, affective, and physical), the use of the term *skill* as an adjective or modifier of training is, on the one hand, needlessly redundant and, on the other hand, wrongheaded, in that it incorrectly qualifies and limits the term. As we have seen, skill does not equate vis-à-vis with a particular type. To use the two terms *skill and training* together, yet another more precise adjective is required, perhaps *problem-solving skill training* or *classroom-routines skill training*. Thus, if used concurrently, the two terms should have a more precise modifier.

Lower order skills can be gained and refined through practice and are mostly self-taught. As the nature of skill becomes of a higher order, a greater amount of education is required. For example, the lower order teaching skill of writing on the chalkboard is mastered with little accompanying education. Next, consider a higher order skill, teaching spelling. This skill is gained through having knowledge or understanding of what we know about spelling, perhaps through planned observations of others, as in the instance of demonstration lessons, and through putting into practice what we know. Finally, consider a yet higher order skill, classroom problem solving. Here, if the skill is to be gained, teachers need a great deal of education as part of their training. Among other things, they need knowledge of problem solving and problem-solving strategies or regimens that can be followed, knowledge of the generic types of problems teachers face and variations on the theme, and knowledge of each generic type such as knowledge about classroom control. Certainly they need practice in applying knowledge of problem solving and classroom control to problem situations.

Training efforts in teacher education mostly attempt to promote the acquisition of medium to higher level skills and, therefore, require provision of knowledge, plus practice. Gliessman and Pugh (1987) make a strong case for insuring that teacher training be knowledge or conceptually based. They even suggest that knowledge of a skill by itself might be sufficient to insure trainee skill acquisition "if concepts about skills are mastered, skills are highly likely to follow" (p. 562).

Skill Acquisition

Tillema and Veenman (1987) summarize Norman's (1980) view of how the development of skills occurs and how it depends on existing knowledge, its expansion, its restructuring, and its fine-tuning:

In the acquisition of skills [Norman] recognized three different [situations]. In the case of learning new skills, already existing knowledge

structures are gradually adapted and expanded with new information in a process called "accretion"—a slow learning process in which misconceptions about correct performance are frequent. A more advanced stage is the restructuring of knowledge. Based upon greater experience with what is already known, new insights into performance components become possible. The expert stage consists of finely tuning the existing knowledge in order to perform more automatically, even to a degree in which the knowledge is not explicitly available at the time of performance. (pp. 520–521)

Conceptualizations of Training Outcomes

A number of scholars provide potential organizing frameworks for educational and training learning outcomes. They are considered *cognitive*, or *intellectual*, as in the case of comprehension, application, analysis, synthesis, and evaluation (Bloom, Englehart, Furst, Hill, & Krathwohl, 1956); *affective*, as in the case of affections, or feelings and emotions, expressed as interests, attitudes, appreciations, values, and emotional sets and biases (Krathwohl, Bloom, & Maria, 1964); or *psychomotor* muscular or motor skills, expressed as perception, set, guided response, mechanism, complex overt response, adaptation and origination (Simpson, 1972). Other categories include Gagne's (1985) intellectual skills, cognitive strategies, verbal information, problem solving, motor skills, and attitudes; Guilford's (1962) cognitive memory, convergent thinking, divergent thinking, and evaluation; and Plowman's (1971) academic, cognitive, creative, craftsman, and leadership skills.

CONNOTATIONS OF TRAINING IN TEACHER PREPARATION

Opponents of training in teacher preparation hold a narrow definition of the term and mostly equate it with conditioning or indoctrinating teachers, so that they become mindless and are not aware of why they are doing what they are doing (Silberman, 1970). Their arguments include the following: Training is vocational in nature and has no place on a university campus; teaching cannot be reduced to principles and techniques; emphasis on training significantly curtails preservice teacher interest in becoming educated; and training has resulted in teachers being treated as hired hands (see Beyer, 1986; Beyer & Zeichner, 1982; Dawe, 1984; Finklestein, 1982; Lucas, 1985). At least in part, such criticisms result from equating or confusing training in a profession with training for a trade, competition for education students, and perhaps failure to recognize that training, according to its definition, takes on many guises. Some opposed to training could unknowingly be engaged in it themselves, particularly those who "instruct or drill in habits of thought" (Gove, 1971).

Advocates consider training integral to professional preparation. Zahorik (1986) exhorts that one goal of teacher preparation must be to help teachers become more skillful and thoughtful about their work. Medley (1984) expresses the thought that, "Fewer teachers fail because they are ignorant [of professional knowledge than fail] because they cannot apply what they know" (p. 81). Relatedly, Gliessman (1986) notes that teachers cannot be expected to infer the skills implied in the body of knowledge about education (p. 12). Gage (1972) agrees, declaring that the "traditional approach has been to assume that once [scholars] have done their work . . . practitioners [will put their ideas and findings] into practice" (pp. 191–192). This approach has not worked. D. Allen and Ryan (1969) call for a method of bridging the gap between instruction in education and classroom practice, and they suggest that such a method should provide teachers with training in specific skills and strategies (p. 61). Borg, Kelly, Langer, and Gall (1970) make a strong logical case for training:

How much confidence . . . would you have in a surgeon if you knew that he had never perfected his techniques . . . and never practiced under the guidance of an expert the specific skills needed in a given operation—if, in fact, he had learned surgery by listening to lectures given by someone who had not performed an operation . . . and had been graduated from medical school largely on the basis of ability to pass multiple-choice tests. (p. 24)

In professional preparation, prospective teachers gain general knowledge (general education), academic knowledge of their teaching discipline (e.g., science) or disciplines, and professional knowledge of such things as child development, effective teaching, and classroom management through education. On the other hand, training prepares them to do something with what they have come to know, that is, to put knowledge into practice. For example, teachers learn *how* to teach science, to use principles of child development, to teach effectively, to prevent disruptive behavior. Thus, teacher preparation can be thought of as having two, hand-in-glove parts: *teacher education*, wherein preservice or inservice teachers gain knowledge-about; and *teacher training*, wherein they gain skill-in its application.

Both education and training are widely accepted as requisite to professional preparation. After Borg et al. (1970), we want neither well-educated but poorly trained nor well-trained but poorly educated physicians, lawyers, or teachers.

Ideally, training in a profession implies having knowledge of some phenomenon and being instructed with regard to how to use it. Medley (1984) defines professional skill as the ability to use professional knowledge in the solution of professional problems. When individuals gain knowledge and understandings of their actions, when they know why they are doing what they are doing, they move toward an educated state. Thus, the skills of teaching may be thought of as the professional application of knowledge about teaching to the conduct of a teacher's classroom on a day-to-day basis. These skills are implemented and utilized, whether or not they have been firmly grounded in professional knowledge and whether or not they have been developed at a level befitting the label *professional skills*.

Although training conveys a negative image to some in teacher-preparation circles, that ought not to be the case. Its proper use within teacher preparation focuses on helping preservice and inservice teachers gain higher level skills that require prerequisite, and at times considerable theoretical, knowledge (concepts, definitions, facts, and conditional propositions), in order for the learner to know why, how, and when to initiate a certain action. Therefore, training within teacher preparation more closely mirrors training in the professions.

TYPES OF TRAINING IN TEACHER PREPARATION

Holding to our definition that training implies gaining know-how instrumental to putting knowledge-of and knowledge-that to work, what should we train for? What that comes to be known (or should come to be known) through educative processes requires teacher training, skill-in? Both teachers in preparation and in service demand a great deal by way of an answer and are quick to criticize aspects of their academic work that come up short in their eyes by failing to show them what to do with, or precisely how to apply, what they are learning (Medley's 1984 earlier-mentioned fault).

Several sources exist to which we can turn for direction with regard to requisite teacher-preparation training and, relatedly, educational needs. They include surveys to identify precisely what the activities, needs, and problems of teaching are, that is, what teachers do that requires know-how (Dick, Watson, & Kaufman, 1981; Huberman, 1985); pronouncements of individual scholars on teacher training; and findings of field studies that reveal effective K–12 teaching programs, effective teaching, and effective schooling practices.

National Surveys

The most notable efforts to determine training needs of teachers were through surveys sponsored by a private foundation and the federal government. The *Commonwealth Teacher Training Study* (Charters & Waples, 1929) was a national survey to determine the actual duties of K–12 teachers, undertaken to give direction to the "teacher-training curricula" (p. v). Approximately 12,000 specific teacher activities were obtained and, consequently, classified as follows:

I. Teachers' activities involved in classroom instruction
   A. Teaching subject matter
   B. Teaching pupils to study
II. Teachers' activities involved in school and class management (exclusive of extra-curricular activities)
   A. Activities involved in recording and reporting facts concerning pupils
   B. Activities involving contacts with pupils
III. Activities involving supervision of pupils' extraclassroom activities (exclusive of activities involved in school and classroom management)
IV. Activities involving relationships with personnel of school staff
V. Activities involving relations with members of school community
VI. Activities concerned with professional and personal advancement
VII. Activities in connection with school plant and supplies (p. 21)

One hundred and seventy pages are devoted to an elaboration of activities under each of these seven divisions.

The Comprehensive Elementary Teacher Education model program (Cruickshank, 1970), a forerunner of performance- and competency-based teacher education (PBTE and CBTE), was the U.S. Office of Education's effort to improve preservice teacher preparation. It required successful bidders to describe the teacher-preparation curriculum in terms of teacher competencies. A direct outgrowth of these two efforts were assorted catalogs of teacher competencies, the best-known being the

Florida Catalog of Teacher Competencies (Dodl et al., 1972). Therein 1,119 competencies (behaviors) are subsumed under the following rubrics: assessing and evaluating student behavior, planning instruction, conducting and implementing instruction, performing administrative duties, communicating, developing personal skills, and developing pupil-self (p. 6).

In another catalog, Turner (1973a) categorized teaching skills: generic, early childhood, socialization and classroom management, language arts in the elementary school, English, social studies, mathematics, and science. Missing were teaching skills related to music, art, and physical education. Taken together, the Commonwealth Teacher Training Study (Charters & Waples, 1929) and U.S. Office of Education fostered efforts to provide an extraordinary treasury of training (and, of course, educational) objectives.

Scholars

Individual scholars and groups promote particular kinds of training as follows: Broudy (1972)—test construction, materials selection, classroom management; Broudy (1978)—instruction, classroom management, decision making; Chaukin & Williams (1984)—parent relationships, human relationships; Collins (1978)—enthusiasm; Cruickshank et al. (1980)—problem solving, affiliation, control, parent relationships, student success, time management; Cruickshank (1987)—reflection; Dunkin (1987)—assessing pupil needs, monitoring one's own teaching, analyzing the requirements of subject matter and educational objectives; Flanders (1963a)—verbal influence; Gage (1972)—information processing, social interactions, technical skills of teaching, such as structuring, soliciting, responding, reacting; Gliessman (1986)—questioning, direct influence, verbal structuring, behavior management; Jackson (1965)—planning, arranging classrooms, analyzing pupil information; Joyce & Showers (1983)—collaboration, teaching styles; Medley (1984)—decision making; Turney, Clift, Dunkin, and Traill (1973)—motivation, presentation and communication, questioning, small-group and individual instruction, development of pupil thinking skills, evaluation, classroom management; and Zahoric (1986)—presentational skills, checking (monitoring, reflecting).

Research

A third source of training needs derives from research on effective teaching techniques and programs, teaching, and schooling. In the first instance, teaching techniques and programs, a report by Ellson (1986) is exemplary. When he reviewed comparative studies of teaching techniques, he found 125 that met his criterion (one of the two or more methods compared was at least 100 percent better than either the other or both in bringing about greater K–12 pupil learning or in being cost effective [p. 84]). Among the many promising techniques are the following, which cover a wide range of academic content: College-Bound Project Method, Fernold Method, R-3 Program, Montessori Method, Enriched Curriculum, Diagnostically Based Curriculum, Success Environment, Youth Teaches Youth Program, Language Stimulation Method, programmed learning, Direct Instruction Method, and Meleragno's Early Reading.

Walberg's (1984) study of effective educational practices is noteworthy. He identifies certain alterable variables influencing school learning. Clearly having implications for training, they are use of reward/reinforcement, provision of advanced activities for pupils with outstanding test scores, adjustment of reading speed and techniques to the purpose of reading, help to pupils in noticing important cues and provision of corrective feedback, use of cooperative or team learning, use of personalized and adoptive instruction, tutoring, and use of diagnostic prescriptive methods. Joyce and Showers (1988) also point out some research supporting effective teaching techniques or programs, including cooperative learning, advanced organizers, mnemonics, synectics, and DISTAR.

In the second instance, a good bit of research on what constitutes effective teaching has been undertaken, accumulated and summarized by, among others, Berliner (1984), Brophy and Good (1986), Cruickshank (1976, 1986b), Denham and Lieberman (1980), Dunkin and Biddle (1974), Medley (1977) Rosenshine (1971), Rosenshine and Berliner (1978), and Stallings (1982). These compilations of research findings provide considerable support for teacher training in such things as planning and managing lessons (e.g., selecting curriculum activities, maximizing opportunity to learn, maintaining a businesslike and cooperative work setting, and responding to pupil deviancy); conducting lessons (e.g., being clear and enthusiastic; structuring goals, directions, and pupil expectations; and pacing); and evaluating learning (e.g., monitoring pupil achievement, providing corrective feedback, testing, and grading).

In the third instance, summaries of research on what constitutes effective schooling are available from, among others, Averch, Carol, Donaldson, Kiesling, & Pincus (1974); Bickel (1983); Cruickshank (1986c); Good and Brophy (1986); Purkey and Smith (1983); and Rowan, Bossert, and Dwyer (1983). Results provide support for teacher training in holding and encouraging high expectation for and in pupils, in basic skills advocacy and focus, in providing clear instructional goals, in monitoring learning, in maintaining orderly classrooms, in efficiently using classroom time, in using teacher assistants, in increasing the quality of parent involvement, in employing diagnosis and evaluation of pupil work, in providing corrective feedback, in showing enthusiasm, in selecting content at an appropriate level of difficulty, in establishing flexible grouping arrangements, in utilizing homework effectively, and in using strategies that avoid nonpromotion.

From such documentation it is clear that there certainly is no dearth of ideas regarding teacher-training needs. As scholarship regarding teaching has progressed, more and more of the subtleties and intricacies of teaching practice and related skills are being identified. Further, analysis of the proposal prompts several reactions. *First*, teachers as professionals require both education (knowledge-of and knowledge-that) and training (know-how) with regard to these activities, competencies, needs, and phenomena. *Second*, these activities, competencies, and needs are primarily generic. They are requisite of teachers, regardless of academic specialty and grade level taught. *Third*, they are fairly specific in nature and, as such, are not much like the actual content of professional education courses nor of requirements called for by accreditation or state program-approval agencies or professional societies (e.g., NCATE, NASDTEC, NCTE). *Fourth*, the training activities, competencies, and needs are distributed across the entire aforementioned training spectrum: training in habits of thought (reflection, problem solving, decision making), in attitudes and dispositions (high expectations, enthusiasm, human relationships), in actions (pupil needs assessment, cooperative learning use), in skills (how to be clear, to pace, to react to pupil responses), and in what is good (development of pupil thinking skills, monitoring of one's own teaching). Obviously, training in professional preparation includes much more than acquisition of simple motor or behavioral skills. It would seem professionally advantageous for teacher educator scholars to create some unifying conceptualization or taxonomy of teacher-training needs, to provide a map of the territory that might guide curricular and instructional efforts.

TRAINING

Because training is an integral part of preparation for a profession and because it is possible to identify training needs, it becomes incumbent upon teacher preparation units and individuals therein to develop and implement appropriate training regimens (Gliessman, Pugh, & Bielat, 1979). As Glaser (1962) notes: "The process of behavior modification called training and education should be built upon the findings and consequent technological implications brought about by research in psychological science" (p. 1). Glaser acknowledges that much of this research has been done for and by the military but argues, nevertheless, that the results are relevant to civilian use.

Systems of Training

There is no such thing as a complete, universally accepted, identifiable, and verifiable psychology of training. Any description of training practices is invariably a mishmash of different frames of reference reflecting how the field has evolved without direction or unifying theory (Hinnrichs, 1976, p. 831).

When looking for such regimens to follow, one is struck by the fact that they all seem to be variations on a theme called a *systems approach*. That approach was particularly noteworthy in teacher preparation during the late 1960s and early 1970s. LeBaron (1969) uses the term as follows:

In its briefest form, "system analysis" is an orderly process for first, defining and describing a universe of interest (and the significant factors and their interrelationships within the universe); and, second, determining what changes in the universe will cause a desired effect. (p. 12)

He lists six steps in the process of systems analysis: conceptualizing the system or the problem universe, defining the subsystems, stating the objectives of the system, developing alter-

native procedures for accomplishing the objectives, selecting the best alternative, and implementing the system (pp. 20–24). Described in such a way, systems analysis is very akin to problem solving.

More specifically, as it relates to education and training, LeBaron notes that systems analysis has been applied to the design of learning systems, particularly learning modules that include objectives, criterion measures, information or necessary resources and experiences, and prerequisites (p. 40).

Generally, the literature on the systems approach (Cicero, 1976; Goldstein, 1986; Hinnrichs, 1976; Houston, 1987; Peck & Tucker, 1973) implies a regimen, or procedure, consisting of four parts: instructional objectives, controlled learning experiences, performance criteria, and evaluation.

Central to this approach is the determination and definition of instructional objectives. Once what the teacher needs to have know-how in is identified, that skill is analyzed to determine specific behaviors the teacher must attain. Suppose teachers need to know how to be clear. This skill comprises several related yet discrete teacher subskills or behaviors: informing pupils of learning objectives, presenting content in a logical manner, using simple explanations, checking for understanding, repeating as required, teaching at an appropriate pace, and so on. (Cruickshank & Kennedy, 1986). Thus, to be clear, teachers must be able to do these things, which, in that light, become known as instructional objectives, perhaps behaviorally stated; that is, precisely stated in terms of what the learner will be able to do (Mager, 1962).

To gain the skill, teachers must accomplish each instructional objective. Hence, carefully controlled learning experiences are necessary. Hinnrichs (1976) suggests a variety of strategies: cognitively oriented (lecturing, audiovisuals, programmed instruction), process oriented (role playing, sensitivity training), and mixed (conference–discussion, case study, simulation, on-the-job training).

Performance criteria are often stated as part of the instructional objective, as in the case of behavioral objectives (Mager, 1962). These criteria establish an observable, acceptable level of learner performance. Take teacher-clarity training again. Teachers would be expected to perform the mentioned subskills under prespecified conditions, at appropriate times, and to a certain degree.

As Goldstein (1986) notes, "Training programs are never finished products; they are continually adaptive to information that indicates whether the program is meeting its stated goals" (p. 15). Thus, a systems approach provides for the collection and use of information regarding its efficiency and effectiveness—efficiency meaning accomplishment of its objectives, and effectiveness meaning satisfaction of learners with the process.

As mentioned, most training uses a variation on the theme of a systems approach. The spiral model, after Turner (1973b), emphasizes extensive practice within the controlled learning experiences portion of the system. Moreover, this practice of the skills to be learned occurs in increasingly realistic phases. For example, preservice teachers might learn about teacher clarity in a tertiary setting. They would gain knowledge of the skill (concepts, definitions, facts) that would lead to verbal or written descriptions and the ability to recognize examples of clarity, perhaps in transcripts of activity in K–12 classrooms. Second, teachers would observe performance of the skill by others. Finally, teachers would perform and refine the skill in natural classrooms. The self-instructional model described by Hudgins (1974) also proposes that the controlled learning experience occur in increasingly realistic contexts. First, he advocates clear, cognitively oriented instruction through written materials. Skill descriptions, explanations, examples, and recognition tests are emphasized. This is followed by isolated practice and then practice in real-world contexts as performance of the skill warrants.

Latham and Saari's (1979) variation of the systems approach emphasizes the delineation of points to be learned during modeling. They promote introducing the learner to the skill verbally. Learners are then presented with a model of the skill on film, with specific learning points presented immediately before and after skill demonstration. Following that, learners discuss the effectiveness of the skill demonstration. Finally, learners practice the skill in the training setting, and peers share perceptions regarding the effectiveness of the performer.

Tillema and Veenman (1987) review training proposed particularly for teacher preparation by Joyce and Showers (1980, 1981, 1983, 1988). According to Tillema and Veenman, these regimens are intended to move the learner from initial awareness of the skill and its uses, through conceptual understanding and implementation of the skill into practice, to the level of problem solving wherein skills are transferred to the teacher's active behavioral repertoire. (p. 523)

Tillema and Veenman support regimens suggested by Joyce and Showers, which emphasize five components:

1. Presentation of theory or description of skill or strategy;
2. Modeling or demonstration of skills . . .;
3. Practice [of the skills] in simulated and natural classroom settings;
4. Structured and open-ended feedback (providing information on performance);
5. Coaching for application (hands-on, in classroom assistance with the transfer of the skill). (p. 524)

More recently, Joyce and Showers (1988) suggest that training regimens include an explanation of theory, multiple demonstrations of processes and content to be mastered, and opportunities for practice with factual, nonevaluative feedback (p. 77).

Research Findings Usable in Training Regimens

Principles of training seem to include the following:

1. Establish clear performance goals and communicate them to learners (Glaser, 1962; Goldstein, 1986; Ribler, 1983).
2. Insure that learners are aware of the requisite level of skill mastery (Glaser, 1962; Goldstein, 1986).
3. Determine learners' present skill level (Glaser, 1962).
4. Introduce only a few basis "rules" during the early learning stages (J. Anderson, 1980, 1984; Gagné, 1984; Kieras & Bovair, 1986; Latham & Saari, 1979).

5. Build upon learners' present skill level during early learning stages (Goldstein, 1986; Ross, 1984; Wong & Iwata, 1978).
6. Ensure during the initial acquisition stage, a basic, essential conceptual understanding of the skill to be learned and when and why it is used (Gliessman & Pugh, 1984, 1987; Harding, 1965; Hudgins, 1974; Kieras & Bovair, 1986).
7. Demonstrate during the initial acquisition stage what final skill performance should look like, drawing attention to salient features of the skill or subskills, as in the case of clarity (Goldstein, 1986; Harding, 1965; J. Putnam & Johns, 1987; Wade, 1985). Provide sufficient opportunity to learn and apply the feature labels to the demonstration (Ellis, 1965, cited in Goldstein, 1986; Friedman & Yarbrough, 1985; Latham & Saari, 1979).
8. Provide opportunity for learners to discuss the demonstration (Swenson & Kulhany in Friedman & Yarbrough, 1985).
9. Provide sufficient, spaced, skill practice after understanding of the skill has been developed, in both subskill and cumulative whole-skill acquisition (Fitts, 1962; Gagné, 1984; Goldstein, 1986; Halding, 1965; Hudgins, 1974; Lung & Dominowski, 1985; Naylor, 1968, cited in Goldstein, 1986; O'Sullivan & Pressley, 1984). Hudgins (1974) suggests that preservice teachers practice on their own and that "amounts of practice normally necessary to attain the required level and smoothness of the skill" be made known (p. 52).
10. See that practice of the skill is followed by knowledge of results (Chhoker & Wallin, 1984; Goldstein, 1986; Harding, 1965; Hudgins, 1974; Komaki, Heinzman, & Lawson, 1980).
11. Provide frequent knowledge of results early in the learning process which is more effective if given with less emphasis on response quantity than on quality (Lung & Dominowski, 1985; Sturgess, 1972; Waldrop, Justen, & Adams, 1986). With increased mastery, less knowledge of results should be provided, to encourage self-evaluation and intrinsic motivation (Hayes et al., 1986).
12. Provide knowledge of results after incorrect performance of a skill, which is most important (Waldrop et al., 1986; Wyer & Frey, 1983).
13. Delay knowledge of results when the learner is beyond the initial stage of learning, which can be as effective as immediate knowledge of results when performance is correct or good. (Lung & Dominowksi, 1985; Waldrop et al., 1986).
14. Provide for transfer of training that is enhanced by maximizing similarity between the training and the natural environment, overlearning salient features of the skill, providing extensive and varied practice, using delayed feedback, and inducing reflection and occasional testing (Baer, Williams, Osner, & Stoker, 1984; Ellis, 1965, cited in Goldstein, 1986; Hagman & Rose, 1983; Kemler-Nelson, 1984; Nairne, 1986).
15. Provide full support and reinforcement for use of the skills in natural settings (Copeland, 1975, 1977; Joyce & Showers, 1988).

Differing perceptions exist regarding the relative importance of each of these principles. A number of investigators have produced a body of literature providing moderate but consistent support for *conceptually based* or *conceptually oriented* training (Gliessman, 1986; Gliessman & Pugh, 1981, 1984; J. J. Koran, 1969, 1970, 1971; M. S. Koran, Snow, and McDonald, 1971; Santiesteban & Koran, 1977; Wagner, 1973). Conceptually based training emphasizes trainee conceptual understanding of a skill developed through "filmed or videotaped (less frequently, audiotaped or written) models or examples of the teaching skills to be acquired," generally eliminating practice components (Gliessman & Pugh, 1981, p. 14). Pegg (1985) essentially agrees when he reports that "practice [is] not an essential requirement for skill acquisition in [my study]" (p. 227). Berman and McLaughlin (1975), Joyce and Showers (1988), and Sharan and Hertz-Lazarowitz (1982) place high emphasis on on-the-job coaching of the skill.

EXTENT OF TRAINING IN TEACHER PREPARATION

Given that true professional preparation consists of education (knowledge-of) and training (skill-in), it might be assumed that both would be highly visible. Such, normally, is not the case. The vast majority of what passes for teacher preparation makes little effort directly or indirectly to provide preservice or inservice teachers with precise professional intellectual, affective, or psychomotor skills called for in surveys, by scholars, or as a result of research on teaching. Teachers simply are not much trained. This situation is lamented by many including D. Allen and Ryan (1969); Berliner (1985); Charters and Waples (1929); Cruickshank (1986a, 1987); Gage (1972, 1985); Gliessman (1984, 1986); Gliessman, et al. (1979); Howsam, Corrigan, Denemark, and Nash (1976); Joyce and Showers (1988); Medley (1984); Nolan (1982); Smith, Cohen, and Pearl (1969); and Smith, Silverman, Borg, and Fry (1980).

Even the segment of teacher education intended to be most pragmatic and practical, school-based experience including student teaching, is suspect. These experiences provide practice, but of what? In addition to being given knowledge of some significant teaching activity, teaching technique, educational practice, teacher behavior, or competency prior to or during field experiences, are novices directly trained in them by any conception of the term? Not so, say many including Smith et al. (1969), who would eliminate student teaching and substitute systematic training in training complexes. We must ask ourselves whether, for the most part, field experiences are more akin, by way of analogy, to swimming preparation, wherein learners are given general conceptual knowledge about the complexity of swimming and then substantial knowledge and practice with each of its elements, or to swimming preparation, wherein, following a description of the general conceptual knowledge (for example they are told to "be clear"), learners are thrown into the pool with the charge, "Now let's see if you can do it?" Exhortation (do it!) seems to take precedence over real training (here's how).

UTILIZATION AND OUTCOMES OF TRAINING IN TEACHER PREPARATION

Examples of Training Within Teacher Preparation

Over the past several decades there have been isolated, yet discernible, efforts to train teachers in selected, called-for skills. They have been facilitated by naturalistic events, scholarly breakthroughs, enlightened funding, and supportive workplaces.

Descriptions of some of the better known efforts to help teachers gain a variety of skills follow. These efforts focus on training teachers to (a) change the deviant behavior of pupils, (b) use inquiry or discovery teaching, (c) observe and analyze classroom verbal communication, (d) enact teaching skills with a basis in the psychological literature, (e) internalize and use educationally significant concepts, (f) become more reflective, (g) become better classroom problem solvers, and (h) use the results of teacher-effectiveness research. Trainers have utilized a variety of instructional procedures, including behavior modification, heuristics, interaction analysis, protocols, microteaching, reflective teaching, simulation, or combinations thereof.

Training teachers via behavior modification to change deviant pupil actions. Children generally, and K–12 pupils specifically, can behave in ways deemed by others to be undesirable. At times such behavior is severe enough to warrant professional attention, as in the case of children who suffer from hyperactivity, autism, or enuresis. Classroom teachers encounter such children and a markedly larger number of others who engage in actions that are disconcerting to life in classrooms or detrimental to their own learning. These children could be disorderly, be noisy, use obscenities, fail to attend to or complete learning activities and so forth. Teachers are being helped to change such negative child behavior to positive child behavior through a strategy called *behavior modification.*

Behavior modification assumes that the maladaptive behaviors children engage in "are learned ways of dealing with the world that are themselves problems" (Liebert, Wicks-Nelson, & Vail, 1986, p. 442). Advocates of the training of teachers in behavior modification suggest that teachers follow a general process when working with such children. The process includes observation and assessment of the actual behavior of a child; development and implementation of a specific, detailed intervention plan intended to change the target behavior; and continuation or modification of use of the plan, depending upon whether the desired behavior change is occurring.

Hall (1971) suggests a detailed process for training teachers in behavior modification. His proposal recommends 2 or 3 hours of inservice training for 16 consecutive weeks. During that time, subjects would gain an understanding of basic learning theory, become acquainted with the experimental literature on operant conditioning, become prepared to observe and record target behavior, engage with a pupil to modify a target behavior, and discuss that effort with others.

A yet more comprehensive plan specifically addressed to teacher preparation is presented by Novak (Cruickshank et al.,

1980). His particular regimen would have teachers learn to analyze events that precede, accompany, and follow problem behavior; use positive techniques for managing behavior (reinforcing approximations of desirable behavior, using teacher behavior associated with positive pupil behavior, etc.); use punishment appropriately and sparingly; and teach students to manage their own behavior (pp. 117–149).

Research on training teachers in behavior modification has been synthesized by C. T. Allen and Forman (1984). Individual studies wherein teachers were trained to employ behavior modificationlike modes are reported among others by Andrews (1970); Bowles and Nelson (1976); J. C. Brown, Montgomery, and Barclay (1969); Cooper, Thomson, and Baer (1970); Cossairt, Hall, and Hopkins (1973); Horton (1975); Johnson and Sloat (1980); Ringer (1973); Sloat, Tharp, and Gallimore (1977); Thomson and Cooper (1969); and Woolfolk and Woolfolk (1974).

Allen and Forman (1984). These reviewers identify 17 studies in which teachers had been prepared to use behavior modification techniques and sought to report on the efficacy of the techniques. Several observations are reported. *First,* nearly all the training efforts made use of some kind of didactics: lectures, manuals, books, or handouts. C. T. Allen and Forman indicate that didactic training of and by itself might not be sufficient to change teacher behavior. Studies reporting beneficial effects of didactic-only training of teachers are seen to be flawed, in that the positive results are based on teacher perceptions rather than on measured pupil behavior.

Second, in three studies teachers were cued during actual teaching precisely when to use a particular principle or principle of behavior modification. Relatedly, reviewers report that, even though teachers might be able to use principles of behavioral modification when cued to do so by observers who give them signals, there is no evidence that the teacher behaviors persist without such second-party prompting. *Third,* it is reported that, when demonstration or modeling of target behavioral principles and/or role plays were used as part of the training regimen, training was generally more effective. Finally, observer feedback provided to trainees increased or maintained their use of target behavioral principles. However, following training, mixed results emerged regarding the subjects' continued use of such behaviors.

Andrews (1970). The objective of the study was to judge the effectiveness of a relatively short-term training program intended to prepare K–4 teachers in classroom use of behavioral principles. Volunteer subjects were used and provided with training during four $1\frac{1}{2}$ hour sessions that instructed them in observing and measuring the frequency of occurrence of a target behavior by one of their pupils, provided them with knowledge of behavioral principles (extinction, reinforcement, reinforcement schedules, baseline data, etc.), and discussed results of using the behavioral principles in modifying the target behavior. Subjects reported that training resulted in decreases in pupil target behaviors.

Bowles and Nelson (1976). This investigation sought to compare the interaction of two training modes for behavior modification. Subjects were volunteer teachers. Experimental subjects completed a six-session workshop that included discussion of problems occurring in subjects' classrooms, presentation of selected target pupil behaviors and opportunity to observe them in skits (role plays) and on videotape, presentation of behavior modification concepts and skills (reinforcement, punishment, extinction etc.), discussion of antecedents of target pupil behaviors and how to control them, discussion of how to use behavioral techniques in the classroom; and review of all points covered. Following the workshop, subjects were randomly subdivided. One subgroup received a second treatment, BIE (bug-in-ear). They received 2 hours of training, during which a radio receiving device was placed in their ears so that when they taught they could be cued or prompted with regard to what behavioral principles they should apply. The second subgroup received no BIE treatment. Investigators report no significant differences in training effects on teachers classroom use of behavioral principles.

Brown et al. (1969). The objective of the study was to gauge the effects of the experimenter's use of social reinforcements with teachers on teachers' subsequent use of similar social reinforcements with a target pupil. Subjects were an elementary teacher and an aide who was an undergraduate education student. Both were reinforced (smiles, nods, verbal praise) for 7 days; then reinforcement was removed for 5 days and, finally, reinstated for 3 days. Results indicate that teachers' use of the target behaviors increased during the period of reinforcement but declined in its absence.

Cooper et al. (1970). This study attempted to increase teachers' attention to desirable student responses by providing them with feedback regarding their own performances. Two preschool teachers in separate schools were selected as subjects. After an initial baseline condition was established, the investigators began providing each teacher with feedback regarding that teacher's attention to appropriate student behavior. Feedback consisted of a description of the appropriate student behaviors and the percentage of time the teacher spent attending or not attending to each of them. Observers found that both teachers' percentages of time spent attending to student behavior increased significantly during the treatment condition. During a later 4-day probe in which no teacher feedback was administered, the percentage of teacher attending behavior remained above that observed before training began.

Cossairt et al. (1973). The purpose here was to study the individual effects of two experimental conditions on use of teacher praise for student attending behavior. Three elementary teachers were selected as subjects. After baseline data had been collected, two of the teachers entered a 17-day period in which appropriate use of teacher praise was explained, subjects were instructed to praise students who were attending, and they were reminded daily of the positive effects of praise. During the next 8 days each teacher was provided daily feedback regarding her use of teacher praise. The final training condition lasted approximately 20 days and combined feedback with experimenter praise of appropriate teacher behavior. The third teacher was simultaneously introduced to all experimental conditions. Feedback combined with praise of the teachers' behavior was consistently found to result in greater use of praise.

Horton (1975). The objective of this study was to find out if training teachers in the use of "behavior-specific praise" as a reinforcer in reading, language arts, and mathematics instruction would result in teacher use of that behavior when other subjects were being taught. Subjects were two elementary teachers randomly selected from eight volunteers. In Phase 1 subjects were trained to use the target behavior by reading about it, discussing it, viewing a videotape of a teacher using it (discriminating examples from nonexamples of its use), and graphing its occurrence during an audiotaped reading lesson. Subjects were then asked to use behavior-specific praise in their own teaching, which was monitored and provided with feedback. After a period of no feedback, Phase 2 began, in which teachers were given specific training in the use of the target behavior in language and mathematics instruction. Follow-up observations revealed that subjects' use of the target behavior modification skill was confined primarily to the specific academic subject areas used during training.

Johnson and Sloat (1980). The intention here was to study the effects of a five-part training regimen on teachers' classroom use of positive reinforcement. Subjects were elementary teachers enrolled in a 16-hour, 16-week, university extension course. Reading assignments, activity assignments, discussion, audiovisual materials, and practice were used during each phase of training. Phase 1 was devoted to providing conceptual knowledge of reinforcement. During Phase 2 teachers were instructed to practice reinforcement in their classrooms. Phase 3 provided the trainees with demonstrations and modeling of reinforcement techniques, followed by guided practice in peer groups and in natural classrooms. The next phase required subjects to learn, practice, and master a system of student and teacher behavior coding. The final phase of training provided daily feedback to teachers regarding their use of positive reinforcement in the classroom. Throughout training, observers recorded teachers' classroom use of reinforcement. Teachers exhibited more use of praise and less use of negative behavior at the conclusion of training. Phases 1 and 2 resulted in no measurable changes in teacher behavior, whereas guided practice and feedback produced the most substantial increases in use of positive reinforcement.

Ringer (1973). The investigator sought to determine whether, if he provided token reinforcement to pupils for behaving appropriately while their teacher was teaching, the teacher would gradually be able to take over and apply the reinforcements herself. This single-subject study followed a regimen that included establishment of baseline data regarding subject's use of reinforcement, cooperative development by the subject and experimenter of a token reinforcement program, experimenter distribution of tokens to pupils during 10 sessions while the teacher taught, intermittent experimenter–subject discussion of the system's use, and gradual assumption by the subject of the experimenter's task of distributing the tokens. Results seem to indicate the training was not effective. The teacher's use of the system rapidly diminished when the experimenter withdrew.

Sloat et al. (1977). As in the Johnson and Sloat study (1980), the purpose was to field-test a training regimen for enabling teachers to apply principles of behavior modification in their classrooms. Subjects were elementary teachers who, over 16 weeks, were observed to gain baseline data on their use of

praise, given conceptual knowledge of behavioral analysis principles, taught to identify when other teachers used the principles, given opportunity to practice the principles via role play, expected to use principles when teaching in their own classrooms, provided with in-class coaching (prompting and cuing), given graphic information regarding their use of behavioral principles, and, finally, given goals to be reached. Results seem to support the fact that most improvement over baseline data occurred in association with subjects' practicing the principles during role playing and when they were given video or graphic feedback of their performance with regard to goals to be reached.

Thomson and Cooper (1969). The purpose here was to study the effects of providing teachers with two types of feedback on their attention to appropriate pupil behavior. Two multiple-baseline studies were conducted. In the first study, two Head Start teachers were provided with feedback on their classroom use of attending techniques at 10-minute intervals. The second study provided two student teachers with immediate feedback on their use of the behavioral principles via a radio receiver worn by them. Both intermittant and instantaneous methods of providing feedback were found to produce increased use of the target behaviors.

Woolfolk and Woolfolk (1974). The investigators compared the effects of 2 1/2 hours of training to nontraining on elementary teachers' reinforcement of pupil attending behavior. Four teachers were randomly assigned to the training condition, and the remaining teachers served as a control. Experimental subjects received presentations, participated in discussions, and practiced techniques of reinforcement through role playing. The results of observations following training indicate no significant differences between trained and untrained teachers.

In summary, behavior modification has been used to train teachers to change the behavior of deviant pupils and to increase certain pupil actions related to school learning such as their attending behaviors. In either instance, teachers are given knowledge-of psychological principles related to human learning and extinction and skill-in their application. Reviews of such literature (C. T. Allen & Forman, 1984; Patterson, 1971) suggest that training regimens for behavior modification can be characterized as using a combination of didactic, or direct, instruction; cuing, or prompting; demonstrations, or modeling; role plays, or practice in natural classrooms; and feedback, or knowledge of results. Further reviewers note that most researchers describe positive results, in that teachers can learn and will use behavior modification principles. Most disconcerting, however, is that use seems to diminish after the training period is over.

Training teachers via interaction analysis to consider the appropriateness of verbal communication in the classroom. Teacher preparation in the late 1950s and throughout the 1960s and 1970s was characterized by development and substantial training in the use of classroom observational systems. Early systems are presented in Simon and Boyer (1968). Impetus for such activity grew from the work of, among others, Bellack, Davitz, Kliebard, and Hyman (1963); Flanders (1963a); Gallagher (1965); Smith and Ennis (1961); Smith,

Meux, Coombs, and Szoke (1962); Taba, Levine, and Elzey (n.d.); and Withall (1949). Medley and Mitzel in Gage (1963) is a basic reference for the early period, and Rosenshine and Furst in Travers (1973) and Evertson and Green in Wittrock (1986) bring us up-to-date. According to Dunkin and Biddle (1974), they were designed for use in observing "the emotional content of teacher-pupil exchange, problems of classroom management, classroom ecology, the logic and ideas exchanged in lessons, and on and on" (p. 71).

Flanders's interaction-analysis system for observing, recording, and analyzing classroom teacher and pupil verbal exchanges is best known for its relative simplicity and the availability of accompanying training materials (Amidon & Flanders, 1963). After studying audiotapes of lessons in natural classrooms, he determined that classroom discourse can be thought of as falling into 10 categories, 7 for teacher talk (accepts and clarifies the feelings of pupils, praises or encourages pupils, accepts or uses pupil ideas, asks questions, lectures, gives directions or orders, and criticizes pupils or justifies the teacher's authority), 2 for pupil talk (talk in reply to the teacher and talk initiated by pupils), and one category where there is either confusion about who is talking or silence exists.

Preservice and inservice teachers were expected to become conceptually knowledgeable about these 10 categories of classroom communication, to know how to analyze their own teaching in terms of them, and to reflect upon their intentions in relation to their performance. Generally, to learn to utilize interaction analysis, the following regimen has been promoted. Teachers are introduced to the notion of analysis of teaching and encouraged to value it as a means of professional self-improvement. Then they are taught the 10 categories and given discrimination training using examples and nonexamples of each. Once low-inference understanding and the accompanying ability to recognize occurrence of the 10 categories is established, teachers learn how to transfer observed occurrences to a matrix and how to quantify and analyze the recorded data. Next, teachers listen to audiotapes of teaching and practice making matrixes of the teacher–pupil exchanges. Penultimately, they either tape-record lessons they teach or have trained colleagues observe them and make a matrix of the verbal discourse. Finally, teachers reflect upon the results, asking themselves, Is actual discourse in my classroom in keeping with what I wish it to be?

Studies in which teachers were trained in interaction analysis are reported, among others, by Bondi (1970); Flanders (1963b); Furst (1967); Hough and Amidon (1967); Hough, Lohman, and Ober (1969); Hough and Ober (1966); Kirk (1967); Langer and Allen (1970); Lohman, Ober, and Hough (1967); Luebkemann (1965); and Sandefur, Pankratz, and Couch (1967).

Bondi (1970). Bondi wanted to determine the effect of an interaction-analysis training treatment on subjects' subsequent teaching behavior. Subjects were randomly selected, pre-student-teaching elementary education majors. All were trained in interaction analysis. All were repeatedly observed during student teaching. Half, the experimental subjects, were given interaction-analysis feedback regarding how they had used verbal discourse. The remaining teachers did not receive feed-

back. When observed near the conclusion of student teaching, the experimental group differed significantly from its non-feedback-receiving cohort in terms of greater use of praise and acceptance and use of pupil ideas.

Flanders (1963b). This study was designed to determine how teachers who themselves used direct or indirect teaching styles would be affected by training in interaction analysis delivered to them either directly or indirectly. Subjects were voluntary secondary teachers. Half of those who used direct teaching styles were assigned to learn interaction analysis via direct instruction. The rest received indirect instruction. In parallel fashion, those who used indirect teaching styles were split and assigned to direct and indirect treatments. Results support the fact that teachers who used indirect teaching styles prior to training in interaction analysis became even more indirect, regardless of whether that training was provided directly or indirectly.

Furst (1967). This investigator wanted to know whether interaction-analysis training would be more effective if provided before or during student teaching. Subjects were English and social studies student teachers. Three treatment groups were established. One group was trained in interaction analysis prior to student teaching, a second group was trained concurrently with student teaching, and the third group was not trained at all. Subjects were observed in student teaching after training was completed, using an instrument similar to Flanders's interaction-analysis system. Results indicate that both trained groups exhibited significantly more teacher acceptance of pupil ideas and total acceptance of behavior than did control teachers. Further, slight differences favored teachers trained prior to student teaching.

Hough and Amidon (1967). The student-teaching performance of 20 subjects previously trained in interaction analysis was compared with that of untrained student teachers. Training was conducted in an educational psychology course. Students in the class received training in interaction analysis and practiced recording and coding classroom interaction during weekly peer teaching sessions in an on-campus setting. Upon completion of the course, subjects began semester-long student teaching. A control group of 20 student teachers was selected to resemble the training group. Observations of all subjects during student teaching revealed that trained teachers made more use of indirect teacher behaviors than untrained teachers.

Hough et al. (1969). The investigators compared two groups of preservice teachers to find out how one trained in interaction analysis would differ in subsequent teaching behavior from one not so trained. Subjects in Group 1 learned interaction analysis and then practiced more indirect teacher behaviors both during on-campus, microteaching-like sessions and in natural classrooms. Subjects in Group 2 listened to audiotapes of classroom interactions, discussed teacher verbal behavior, and taught in microteaching-like sessions and natural classrooms, but they did not learn a formal observation or coding system. During posttraining microteaching-like sessions, all subjects were observed and their behavior coded, using Flanders's system. Teachers who were trained in interaction analysis evidenced more indirect teaching behaviors: more praise and encouragement, more acceptance and clarification of student ideas, fewer directions, and less criticism and corrective feedback. Subsequent observations of randomly selected trained teachers at 4 and 12 months after training indicated continued use of more indirect teacher behaviors.

Hough and Ober (1966). The investigators studied the effects of training in human relations and interaction analysis on subsequent verbal behavior of preservice teachers. Classes of preservice secondary teachers enrolled in a teaching methods course were assigned to treatments. All subjects received human relations training either by use of case studies or through readings, lectures, and discussions of human relations. Additionally, randomly selected classes learned and practiced coding teacher verbal behavior, using Flanders's system, and then practiced indirect verbal behaviors in microteaching-like sessions. Remaining classes listened to audiotapes of classroom incidents, discussed teacher verbal behavior, and practiced in microteaching-like sessions. All subjects' verbal behavior was observed and coded, using an adapted version of Flanders's system during posttraining peer teaching sessions. Hough and Ober report that subjects trained in Flanders's system exhibited significantly more indirect teacher behavior than teachers who were not.

Kirk (1967). The research question was, Would knowledge of interaction analysis cause changes in the performance of student teachers? Fifteen student teachers were selected to be trained in interaction analysis. An additional 15 student teachers judged to be comparable in age, experience, personality, and attitude were selected as a control group. Experimental subjects were given 5 hours of training in interaction analysis, observed weekly thereafter while in student teaching, and provided with feedback by a college instructor. Control teachers received no training or feedback. Using posttraining observations of each student teacher, trained teachers were found to use less continuous lecture, their classrooms had more spontaneous pupil talk, and their pupils more often interjected talk into the lecture.

Langer and Allen (1970). The purpose here was to determine the effectiveness of a program designed to teach interaction analysis and find out if users' teaching behaviors were subsequently modified. Volunteer teachers were instructed in Flanders's system of interaction analysis and practiced indirect patterns of verbal behavior. When compared with their pretraining performance, the 10 teachers completing training were reported as showing significantly increased use of indirect methods during posttraining videotaped lessons.

Lohman et al. (1967). Here the intention was to determine the training effect of interaction analysis on subsequent student-teaching behavior. Two groups of subjects were selected. One group consisted of student teachers who had previously received formal training and practice using Flanders's system. A second group consisted of student teachers who had informally discussed teacher verbal behavior, with no formal analysis system provided. Formally trained student teachers were observed to differ from those informally trained in the following behaviors: they used less direct teacher talk, did less lecturing, gave fewer directions, exhibited less extended teacher talk and more indirect teacher talk, more often accepted and clarified student talk, and generally used more indirect teacher verbal behaviors.

Luebkemann (1965). The investigator studied the effects of three methods of instruction in interaction analysis on subsequent student teacher classroom behavior. All subjects were enrolled in a weekly seminar during student teaching. During this seminar, Group 1 subjects learned about interaction analysis through "descriptive discussions," required reports, and panel discussions. Group 2 also received interaction-analysis instruction through discussion, but it was not required to complete reports or participate in panel discussions on the subject. Group 3 did not receive instruction in interaction analysis. Only student teachers in the more extensive instruction group were observed to demonstrate increased skill in their use of indirect behaviors.

Sandefur et al. (1967). This study examined the effects of training in Flanders's system on preservice teachers' attitudes toward engaging in classroom observations. Seven hundred and seventy-eight subjects from 16 teacher-preparation units participated in the study. Subjects from selected institutions received 2 hours of classroom instruction in interaction analysis and were encouraged in its use during classroom observation. All subjects then observed 24 classroom situations via videotaped recordings and were questioned about this experience. Preservice teachers who had received interaction-analysis instruction reported being more positive toward the observation experience.

In summary, considerable effort was made to train teachers to observe and to analyze a number of classroom phenomena, among them the verbal exchanges between teacher and pupils. These efforts were facilitated by several things. *First,* some of the observational systems were rather carefully constructed. The units for analysis, target behaviors, or events to be observed were fairly independent and of a low-inference nature, therefore measurable and quantifiable. *Second,* timing was right. Analysis of teaching was on the ascendance and evaluation of teaching was on the decline. *Third,* newer technology for use in training, audio and visual, was more readily available and touted.

Implicit in such training was that teachers so trained would improve. Not only would they know how to record and analyze classroom phenomona, but they would also see the errors of their ways. Thus, for example, teachers trained in interaction analysis would see that they needed to become more pupil centered or indirect, that is encourage and use more pupil talk and less teacher-centered or direct talk, that is tone down teacher talk. Results provide support for this training expectation.

Preparing teachers via inquiry training to habituate pupils to developing inquiring, scientifically oriented mental habits. Inquiry training became particularly ascendant during the 1950s and 1960s with the introduction of K–12 curricular changes in the form of "new" math, science, social studies, and so forth. All were concerned with enhancing pupils' higher level thinking abilities. Events probably contributing directly to this emphasis included the 1956 publication by Bloom and his associates of the *Taxonomy of Educational Objectives* and the launching of the Soviet Sputnik the following year. Accordingly, rote learning was out and inquiry was in. "Analysis" and "discovery" became catchwords, and programs to enhance pupil inquiry skills flourished. Consequently, teachers were to be taught to use inquiry as an instructional strategy.

According to Joyce and Showers (1988), teachers intending to teach inductively, that is to help pupils process information, generate the development of concepts, and foster causal thinking, require intensive training:

Teachers need to study the substance of a lesson . . . and develop a rich array of instructional materials that can be explored by children. They have to guide concept formation activities and help the students become more sophisticated in the making of categories and inferences. The flow of instruction emerges, depending upon the thinking of the students, and the environment has to be adjusted to the developing lesson. Knowledge of both substance and process appear to be critical. (p. 39)

Studies in which teachers were trained to use inquiry are reported by Cotten, Evans, and Tseng (1978); George and Nelson (1971); Hurst (1974); Lombard, Konicek, and Schultz (1985); Porterfield (1974); and Zevin (1973).

Cotten et al. (1978). The purpose was to field-test written self-instructional materials that had been developed to enhance inquiry (process) skills of teachers. Elementary teachers were to learn these skills themselves and teach them to their pupils. The design did not make use of random assignment or an equivalent control group. Reported results note that experimental subjects, when observed in their classrooms, used more inquiry-oriented strategies such as higher order and probing kinds of questions and less lecture.

George and Nelson (1971). This study was intended to determine the effects of training on the ability of 12 elementary science teachers to use techniques of inquiry. The training began with a special workshop in which subjects were taught science through an inquiry approach. During the following school year, subjects were visited in their classrooms and helped to implement inquiry methods. The following summer, subjects concluded training with an additional 6-week workshop using an inquiry approach. Results suggest that less experienced teachers are more likely to use principles of inquiry in their teaching.

Hurst (1974). This investigator designed instructional modules intended to develop inquiry skills in preservice subjects. Each module contained rationale, overview, objectives, preassessment instruments, learning activities, and postassessment instruments. In a pretest–posttest control-group design, 60 elementary education majors were randomly assigned to one of three treatment groups. Group 1 engaged with the modules independently as an out-of-class activity, group 2 used the modules in a specially arranged course that met for 10 hours and in which group discussion of the materials was encouraged, and group 3 received no related instruction. The results of written evaluations revealed that both instructional treatments were equally effective in promoting knowledge and understanding of inquiry teaching methods.

Lombard et al. (1985). These investigators examined the effects of a yearlong inservice program intended to help teachers make better use of inquiry methods in their teaching. Joyce and Showers' (1980) training regimen was followed. In workshops conducted throughout the year, inquiry skills were first explained, described, and modeled. Then teachers were instructed to practice the skills in their own classrooms. During the subsequent workshops, teachers discussed their attempts to implement the skills. These workshops were supplemented by having teachers make on-site observations of one another and by coaching in the use of inquiry strategies. According to the investigators, although subjects were enthusiastic about incorporating inquiry approaches, they were not observed to do so in any significant way. The lack of a sufficient degree of coaching necessary for transfer is identified by the investigators as a potential weakness of this training effort.

Porterfield (1974). The purpose of this study was to determine the influence of inquiry–discovery science instruction on the level of classroom discourse. Experimental subjects were eight second- and eight fourth-grade teachers. Controls were 16 untrained teachers selected for comparison. Experimental subjects were instructed in using the Science Curriculum Improvement Study (SCIS) method of instruction. Following treatment, trained subjects were observed to use significantly less recognition and recall, or lower level questions, and more higher level questions soliciting attitudes, values, and opinions.

Zevin (1973). The investigator wished to determine what differences in inquiry teaching behavior would result from exposure of K–12 teachers to instructors who regularly use inquiry methods, as opposed to instructors who talk about using inquiry but do not engage in it. Social studies teachers participating in an 8-week summer workshop were assigned to one of three instructors and conditions. Some were assigned an instructor who selected material related to inquiry-oriented teaching and utilized these methods in his teaching. A second group received instruction in inquiry, but from an instructor who did not incorporate inquiry methods into his teaching. A third group served as a control. In the comparison of pre- and postworkshop observations of each teacher, only the teachers receiving instruction and modeling showed significant changes toward more inquiry-oriented teaching behaviors.

To summarize, even though inquiry is a highly touted instructional strategy, as Zevin (1973) notes, little has been done to train teachers systematically in its use. Perhaps as well as any example, it makes evident the chronic dichotomy between exhorting teachers regarding what they should do and giving them knowledge-of and, particularly, skill-in those things.

The training efforts presented here would seem to indicate most success in getting teachers to use more inquiry-oriented strategies, that less experienced teachers are more affected by training, and that modeling of the target skills facilitates their acquisition and use by subjects.

Training teachers via microteaching to gain skill in teacher behaviors based in the psychological literature. Microteaching, often referred to as *technical-skill training*, is operationally defined as:

A brief teaching encounter in which preservice teachers teach five to twenty-minute lessons in their subject field . . . to a small group of pupils who are usually peers. The purpose of microteaching lessons is to [give] practice [in each] specific technical skills of teaching until the preservice teacher reaches an acceptable level of performance. (Cruickshank, 1986a)

The training regimen proceeds as follows. *First*, the subject is given, or chooses, a single technical skill of teaching to learn about and subsequently to practice. *Second*, the subject reads about the skill in one of several pamphlets (D. Allen & Ryan, 1969). *Third*, the subject observes a master teacher demonstrating the skill on film or videotape. *Fourth* and *fifth*, the learner prepares a 3- to 5-minute lesson to demonstrate the skill and teaches it to a small group of peers, and the episode is videotaped. *Sixth*, the subject, the instructor, and the subject's peers critique the lesson, using the videotape to judge the adequacy of skill performance. At this point the subject is asked to either reteach the skill or prepare to learn and teach a new one from a set of about 18 arranged into five clusters: response repertoire, creating student involvement, questioning skills, increasing student participation, and presenting skills.

As MacLeod (1987) notes, "What remained constant [in microteaching] was the opportunity to practice teaching in a simplified environment, simplified usually in three ways: class size, lesson length and task complexity" (p. 532). Research on training in microteaching has been assembled and reported by, among others, Copeland (1982); MacLeod (1987); and Turney, Clift, Dunkin, and Traill (1973).

MacLeod (1987) suggests that microteaching training efforts have been of four kinds. In the first:

Microteaching was seen within a general training paradigm: concepts from psychology like modeling and reinforcement were freely borrowed; the emphasis was upon "what worked"; the decisions as to what skills should be developed . . . were not made in light of any set of rules about what good teaching consists of or what teachers need to know, but resulted from the discussions and debates of the [Stanford] microteaching staff (D. Allen & Ryan, 1969, p. 14)

In the second kind of effort, advocated by Stanford's McDonald, behavior modification is the training methodology of choice, because the "teaching skills are but sets of behavior that may be acquired" through application of classical, well-established, behavior modification procedures" (MacLeod, 1987, p. 537).

G. Brown (1975), cited in MacLeod, views teaching skills as analogous to perceptual and motor skills and supports the social-skills training model of Argyle (1969). Brown's training preference is to focus on "selection of aims, selective perception of relevant cues, motor responses or practice, and feedback or correction" (p. 537).

MacLeod (1987) and MacLeod and McIntyre (1977) propose the fourth microteaching training strategy that "facilitates long-term changes in [teachers'] thinking about teaching rather than short term changes in their teaching behavior" (MacLeod, 1987, p. 537). Herein analysis of classroom life is emphasized in a way, as in reflective teaching, which will be described later.

Among the individual studies reported are: Ajayi-Dopemu and Talabi (1986); Borg (1972); Borg, Kallenbach, Morris, and Friebel (1969); Borg, et al. (1970); Copeland (1975, 1977); Copeland and Doyle (1973); Jenson and Young (1972); Kallenbach and Gall (1969); Katz (1976); MacLeod (1987); Perrott (1987); Peterson (1973); Raymond (1973); Reed, Van Mondfranz, and Smith (1970); Saunders, Nielson, Gall, and Smith (1975); and Yeany (1978).

Ajayi-Dopemu & Talabi (1986). In an attempt to determine the effect of the videotape feedback component of microteaching training, Nigerian student teachers were randomly assigned to either an experimental or a control group. Both groups participated in 3 weeks of microteaching training directed at the development of questioning and visual presentation skills. Training followed a suggested microteaching format including use of written materials, preparation of lessons, peer teaching, and instructor evaluation of skill demonstration. Experimental, but not control group, teachers were videotaped during their peer teaching lessons and viewed this recording with their instructor upon completion of the lesson. Posttraining tests revealed significant improvement in experimental-group teachers' conceptual understanding of the skills; however, the investigators did not assess trainee use of skills.

Borg (1972). The purpose here was to evaluate the effectiveness of a minicourse training in questioning, to determine whether it had both short- and long-term effects. The minicourse regimen was developed at the Far West Laboratory for Educational Research and Development and incorporates and expands the microteaching format. Minicourse training combines the technical-skills approach, audiovisual recording of trainee practice, structured feedback of microteaching with extensive written descriptions and exercises, and recorded demonstrations of skills to be mastered. Further, each minicourse program generally includes a cluster of one to three related specific skills that are developed through repeated microteaching sessions. Subjects in this single-group design study were inservice teachers. The treatment included studying questioning skills conceptually; learning to discriminate among types, using examples and non-examples; and viewing the demonstration of skills on film. Next, subjects practiced using the skills with small groups of pupils in their respective classrooms. Videotapes made before training, at the end of training, and 4 and 39 months later were compared. Reported findings include the fact that of the 12 target questioning skills were significantly more evident following training and remained evident 39 months later.

Borg et al. 1969). The investigators compared the effects of varying minicourse training methods on teacher behavior. Student teachers participated in one of four training groups. Group 1 received training as described in Borg (1972). Group 2 participated in similar training but with no videotape feedback. Group 3 was provided only with written descriptions and examples and viewed filmed demonstrations of the skills. A fourth group received no training. At the conclusion of training, observers analyzed pre- and posttraining videotaped lessons that had been made of each student teacher. Borg and his associates report that subjects provided with more extensive training did not consistently make more or greater changes in teaching behavior than did subjects in the conceptual or non-training groups.

Copeland (1975). This study was undertaken to determine the effects of microteaching skill training on later student-teaching behavior. Subjects were pre-student-teaching elementary education majors randomly assigned to treatment, no-treatment groups. The former were trained in the use of higher order and probing questions following the earlier described microteaching training regimen. The latter received no training. Following the training period, half the subjects in each group were videotaped as they taught a brief microteaching lesson. Observation of the trained and untrained subjects during student teaching revealed no significant differences between experimental and control group members.

Copeland (1977). As a result of the disappointing findings of his 1975 training effort, the researcher wanted to determine the influence of the cooperating teacher with regard to whether or not student teachers who were trained would exhibit target skills during the practicum experience. In this study, only experimental subjects were trained in skills related to "completeness of communication" and asking "probing questions." Additionally, randomly selected cooperating teachers were trained in observation and problem resolution for use in systematically helping student teachers improve their teaching skills. Observation revealed that whether or not student teachers used skills in which they were trained seemed to be a function of the use and reinforcement of these skills by cooperating teachers.

Copeland and Doyle (1973). This study was intended to determine the influence of microteaching training on the classroom performance of social-studies student teachers. Prior to student teaching, subjects were randomly assigned to groups for 6–8 weeks of training. Experimental-group teachers engaged in microteaching training in questioning skills, whereas control teachers learned and practiced unrelated skills in a less structured, less formal laboratory setting. Immediately after training, the teachers began student teaching. In the sixth week of student teaching, all subjects were audiotaped under the guise of an unrelated study. Blind raters found no significant differences between control and experimental-group teachers in their use of questioning skills. Copeland and Doyle point out that microteaching alone might be insufficient to facilitate skill acquisition among teacher trainees.

Jensen and Young (1972). To determine the effects of microteaching training on the teaching performance of student teachers, preservice teachers enrolled in an educational methods course were randomly assigned to an experimental (microteaching) or a control (no-microteaching) group. With the exception of microteaching training, classroom activities were identical for both groups. After completion of the methods course, all subjects began an 8-week period of student teaching during which each was observed on three separate occasions. The investigators state that student teachers who participated in microteaching exhibited more positive personality traits and more warmth, created better general classroom atmospheres, and made more meaningful lesson presentations than control teachers. They further indicate that these differences between experimental and control subjects became greater over the student-teaching period.

Kallenbach and Gall (1969). The purpose of this study was to compare prolonged training in microteaching skills with an equivalent amount of normal participation in student teaching. Subjects were graduate students enrolled in a postdegree teacher certification program. All subjects were taught selected teaching skills in the areas of lesson planning and presentation, measurement of pupil learning, and community and professional participation, followed by related discrimination training. Then about half of them, as experimental subjects, received 7 weeks of microteaching training, and the remaining subjects (controls) were assigned to school field experiences. All subjects were later observed during their first year of teaching. The investigators report that they saw no indication that the experimental treatment resulted in greater manifestation of the skills learned during treatment.

Katz (1976). This study was intended to determine whether subjects trained in skills related to improving children's oral language would differ in their use of the skills. Subjects were student teachers in special education classrooms. Experimental subjects were trained in the skills via the minicourse regimen and then practiced them during student teaching. Control subjects were given only brief, written, conceptual knowledge of the skills. Persons who observed all subjects following training reported that experimental subjects used only 2 of the 14 skills significantly more often than controls.

Peterson (1973). This investigator wished to see whether technical-skill training prior to student teaching would have a discernible effect on use of the skills during student teaching. Subjects were elementary pre–student teachers, all of whom received a treatment that provided conceptual knowledge of the skills, discrimination training, and the opportunity to observe films and identify the skills in appropriate use. At this point, randomly selected experimental subjects were provided the opportunity to practice the skills in the microteaching manner, whereas controls were permitted only a single peer-teaching opportunity without feedback. During subsequent student teaching, observers reported no difference between the two groups in their use of questioning skills.

Reed et al. (1970). Again, to determine the effects of different kinds of training for skill enhancement, three groups were formed and provided separate treatments. Subjects were preservice teachers in an educational psychology course. Group 1 received lectures on the teaching skills. Group 2 learned the skills during microteaching sessions. The third, a control group, received lectures unrelated to the skills. All subjects then taught a small group of peers a lesson in which they were to demonstrate the target skills. Observers reported that the group that learned the skills during microteaching was significantly more able to demonstrate "lesson-ending" and "lesson-evaluating" skills than were lecture groups.

Saunders et al. (1975). The investigators wanted to see if differences in usage of higher order questioning skills would exist among three groups of education majors who were differentially prepared. In each of three consecutive academic terms, subjects enrolled in an education course were divided into two groups. Each term one group participated in microteaching with junior high students. Training for the other groups varied for each term. One term the comparison group participated in microteaching with peers. Another term the comparison group learned about the target skills only through lecture and discussion, with no practice of skills provided. The remaining term, the comparison group received conceptual knowledge of the skills and observed in classrooms. Observations of pre- and posttraining peer-teaching lessons revealed no significant differences among the six treatment groups.

Yeany (1978). This investigator wished to know which of three training regimens that varied feedback provided to the learner was most likely to beget improved skill performance. Subjects were preservice teachers in a methods course. Training Regimen 1 consisted of teaching, videotaped feedback, and reteaching. Regimen 2, in addition to videotaped feedback, also provided for learner self-evaluation. The third regimen provided videotape feedback, self-evaluation, and feedback from the college instructor. Yeany reports that the conditions utilizing either self-evaluation or instructor evaluation resulted in significantly higher ratings of teacher performance than training without this provision.

In conclusion, training in microteaching was and still is popular. That popularity is a function of several things: Preservice teachers want to practice teaching and value any and all such opportunities; they enjoy the cosmetic benefits of being videotaped; television is readily available in most education units; and the application of technology to teacher education continues to be supported (American Association of Colleges for Teacher Education, 1987).

Popular though microteaching is, training studies reported here make clear that it is difficult to modify the behavioral repertoire of preservice and inservice teachers to include the so-called microteaching skills. Only one variation on these training regimens presents a finding not fully or partially disputed, that being Copeland's (1977). He found that such training is facilitated when it provides for learners to see significant others (cooperating teachers) using the target skill or skills or when cooperating teachers recognize and reward learners' use of them.

MacLeod (1987), himself a scholar in this area, has been able to review considerably more studies and reports favorably but cautiously that microteaching training efforts are enhanced when they use modeling more suitably (use visual rather than written examples of the skill to be learned and label examples and nonexamples of the skill during discrimination learning). With regard to the provision of practice during training, he is sanguine about the probability that practice is even necessary to skill acquisition, that discrimination training might suffice or even be superior (this would of course change microteaching dramatically). On the topic of feedback, MacLeod supports self-viewing or self-confronting the teaching skill episode, although this position is not supported explicitly by the studies he reviews. Finally, he admits, "Despite the enormity of research endeavor, there are few definite conclusions which can be drawn about the . . . effectiveness of microteaching" (p. 538).

Training teachers via protocols to use critical concepts when teaching. In its original sense, a *protocol* was to be an audiovisual or written record or recording of a naturally occurring classroom or school event or phenomenon (Smith et al., 1969). For example, assume "cheating" is such an event or phenomenon. A camera would be placed in a classroom with the hope that its occurrence might be captured naturally. In actual use, however, a protocol was to become mostly a recording of a contrived classroom or school event that illustrated a concept teachers should know and put to use. For example, assume "clarity" is such a phenomenon. A staged and recorded example of clear (or unclear) teaching would be made.

Studies in which teachers were trained via protocols are reported by Borg (1973, 1975); Borg, Langer, and Wilson (1975); Borg and Stone (1974); Gliessman and Pugh (1976, 1978); Kleucker (1974); and Rentel (1974). These studies are presented and extensively and critically reviewed elsewhere (Cruickshank & Haefele, 1987).

Borg (1973). Six self-instructional modules, each dealing with one concept of teacher language (clarity, emphasis, encouragement, extension, feedback, and organization), were used in training preservice teachers in two educational psychology classes, one each at Utah State University and the University of Colorado. Modules required subjects to read a description of a particular concept such as clarity. Next, subjects were required to read a transcript of a classroom recitation and to identify instances of teacher clarity. Another, similar, task was undertaken, this time with an imposed time limit. Fourth, subjects viewed a filmed protocol of a classroom and again were called upon to identify instances when the teacher was clear according to the original description. Finally, given a transcript, subjects were required to fill in omitted teacher remarks that would be illustrations of clear teacher behavior. Borg felt the training regimen would cause the trainees to recognize the occurrence of the clarity concept in both transcripts and a filmed protocol and to use it, that is, apply it appropriately to contrived, written transcripts. According to the report, more than 80 percent of the subjects reached mastery level on all six modules, and they were "generally favorable" toward their use as training vehicles. Ninety percent of them regarded their content as equal or better than the teacher content of education courses, and 88 percent reported the modules to be as, or more, interesting.

Borg (1975). In another study, Borg tried out four of the same modules, in part to see if subjects so trained would later be able to demonstrate the behaviors in natural classrooms when teaching a predetermined lesson. This time subjects were volunteer Utah fourth-, fifth-, and sixth-grade teachers. First, they were involved in training wherein they were taught 12 concepts and were able to identify them in use by other teachers in transcripts and filmed protocols. Next, subjects themselves were expected to demonstrate the 12 concepts during two 50-minute social studies lessons taught in their own classrooms. Borg reports that subjects who had undergone such training demonstrated significantly more of 4 of the 12 behaviors than did the control group who had not received training.

Borg et al. (1975). A partial purpose of this study was to determine whether teachers trained with four Utah State University Management Protocol Modules would exhibit greater frequency of use of the target concepts. Experimental subjects were teachers enrolled in an extension class on classroom management at the University of Colorado. They were trained, as in the earlier Borg studies, through engaging with and completing modules, this time on "transactions, learner accountability, group alerting, and withitness" (p. 53). Following training, the investigators report that subjects failed to exhibit significant behavior change from pretest to posttest in using the concepts in their classrooms.

Borg and Stone (1974). Here, two of the aforementioned (Borg, 1973) six self-instructional modules were used to determine whether subjects trained with them would increase the frequency of use of the target concepts. Subjects were volunteer fourth-, fifth-, and sixth-grade Utah teachers. Before training, subjects were videotaped while teaching, to capture baseline data. The training methodology was essentially the same as Borg's (1973), with one exception. The subjects, as in Borg (1975), concluded by teaching lessons in their classrooms, so that observation could determine the extent to which they increased their use of the target concepts compared with baseline data. Borg reports that use of "specific praise," one target concept, increased significantly, as did "use of student ideas, prompting, further clarification and refocusing" (p. 37).

Generally, and at first glance, with the exception of Borg et al. (1975), the Borg studies provide support for the premise that teachers, when shown how to behave desirably through training, catch on and can change their teaching performance in the desired ways. Careful inspection of the studies' conduct, however, weakens the claims (Cruickshank & Haefele, 1987).

Gliessman and Pugh (1976). More modestly, Gliessman and Pugh returned to determining the value of using protocols in concept acquisition. Subjects were education students in a graduate course in educational psychology. Three filmed protocols were used to illustrate three pairs of matched concepts: "approving-disapproving, probing-informing, and reproductive-productive questioning." Six different films then showed the concepts in use in classrooms (patterns). A test film showing 30 instances of the concepts was used to see if they could be identified by the subjects. Investigators report that use of the three concept and six pattern films resulted in significant gains in concept acquisition and that, in another study they conducted, subjects in 15 college classrooms reacted favorably to their use.

Gliessman and Pugh (1978). In the two studies reported herein, investigators compared four different regimens for acquiring the previously discussed six concepts: the concept names, definitions of the concept, and filmed examples (NDE); only names and definition; (ND) merely names (N), and; names and examples (NE). In Study 1, graduate students in an elementary education methods course randomly received one of three treatments. The fourth treatment group contained subjects from another elementary education course who received the NE treatment. In Study 2, graduate students in an educational psychology course were randomly given NDE or E (example only) treatments. Over the two studies investigators re-

port that, "The exemplification of concepts in protocol films . . . apparently contributes significantly to concept acquisition" (p. 89).

Although the Gliessman and Pugh studies are often thought of as training, they probably are more akin to education in that the emphasis is on knowledge-of or knowing-that rather than knowing-how.

Kleucker (1974) compared the effects of three treatments on subjects' ability to recognize, categorize, and demonstrate two teaching skills: exposure to the skills (as concepts) through protocol materials, exposure and practice via microteaching, and a combination of the two. Skills were "probing questions" and "offering acceptable reactions." Subjects were preservice teachers in an educational psychology class. Kleucker reports that the combined treatment including both efforts at concept acquisition and opportunity to practice was a consistently and significantly more effective technique than either procedure employed alone.

Rentel (1974). The investigator carried out a study to determine whether five linguistic concepts (phonology, syntax, morphology, semantics, and functions) could be taught better to preservice teachers at The Ohio State University using traditional lecture combined with direct observation of children's language or via protocol materials. Both lecture and protocol cohorts read a summary of research about each concept and then engaged in discussion. Following that, lecture-treatment subjects spent 2 hours observing children, whereas protocol subjects were given behavioral objectives they were to accomplish, were shown protocol films depicting the target concepts as they occur in children's language, and were asked to make records of the occurrence of the concepts. The investigator reports that neither treatment group was superior in its ability to respond to an achievement test on children's language, although, as in Borg (1973), protocol users were positive about the experience and reported that the materials were interesting, attractive, well-organized, and clear and contained worthwhile knowledge. Again, as with the Gliessman and Pugh studies, this one seemed to address knowledge-of rather than know-how.

In summary, protocols can be used to do several things. *First*, as proposed by the originators, they can be used to present recorded events or phenomena that teachers should be aware of *and* understand. No examples of such use are found in the research literature. *Second*, they can and have been used as a procedure for concept acquisition (Borg, 1973, 1975; Borg et al., 1975; Borg & Stone, 1974; Gliessman & Pugh, 1976, 1978; Kleucker, 1974; Rentel, 1974). *Finally*, they can be a vehicle for both concept acquisition (knowledge-of) and training (knowing-how) (Borg, 1975; Borg et al., 1975; Borg & Stone, 1974). When used for the purposes of concept acquisition, skill teaching, or both, protocols, for the most part, are reported to be effective, although, as noted by two reviewers (Cruickshank & Haefele, 1987), many of the studies had considerable shortcomings.

From the studies described here it can be assumed that persons trained through the use of protocols find the experience pleasurable, learn the target concepts, are able to demonstrate only some of the learned concepts when teaching, and benefit most when training includes both concept acquisition and practice. Still at issue is the purpose of protocol materials: Should they illuminate events and phenomena of special significance to teachers, help teachers acquire concepts important to teaching, provide practice in teaching skills, or achieve some combination thereof? Should protocol materials be used for education and/or training?

Training teachers via reflective teaching to become more thoughtful and wise. Reflective teaching has become a generic term referring to a range of efforts intended to prepare teachers to be more thoughtful. These efforts differ with regard to purposes and means. Some advocates hope to engage teachers in becoming more thoughtful about the educational–cultural context, with the assumption that teachers are or should be agents of social change. Others wish to focus teachers' thoughts on the act of teaching, in the hope that, through inspection, introspection, and analysis, teaching can be enhanced. The second way reflective teaching efforts differ is in their means. Some advocates are cautious about putting forth exact strategies by way of enhancing teacher reflection; others are willing to be more specific (Zeichner, 1987). The concept and descriptions of several programs are given in Clift, Houston, and Pugach (in press) following a national conference on reflective inquiry.

Herein the concept's use will be limited to efforts related to work at The Ohio State University. This limitation seems to be judicious, because this particular reflective-teaching formulation is explicit and clear about its purposes and means and has resulted in a few formal training efforts.

The Ohio State University notion of reflective teaching is presented in Cruickshank (1987). The purpose is stated therein to be to prepare students of teaching. Operationally, behaviorally such teachers would reflect on teaching and become, in practice, thoughtful and wise teachers. "Rather than behaving according to technique, impulse, tradition, and authority, they [would] deliberate on their teaching" (p. 3). Several instructional alternatives are named that could be used as vehicles for promoting reflection on teaching: classroom diaries or journals, observational systems (including interaction analysis), problem-solving-based simulations, protocols as first described by Smith et al. (1969), and reflective teaching itself.

The Ohio State University regimen for reflective teaching consists of a number of exact procedures: (a) Learners are assigned to groups of four to six members; (b) one member is appointed the "designated teacher"; (c) designated teachers from each group are given common reflective-teaching lessons (RTLs) that provide the objectives of the lesson and appropriate related lesson content information; (d) designated teachers decide how to teach the lesson so as to maximize both learning and satisfaction; (e) designated teachers teach the lesson to their small groups; (f) at the conclusion of a prearranged time period, the lessons, if not completed, are halted, the learners are tested in relationship to the lesson's purposes, and they are asked to complete a "learner satisfaction form"; (g) utilizing the results of the posttest, comments on the "learner satisfaction form", and, mostly, the teaching–learning experience, all in the small group, guided by a series of questions,

consider what has happened with what consequences; and (h) all groups are merged to share individual and subgroup experiences and to consider what has been learned or rediscovered about teaching and learning.

Research on training for reflective teaching (following The Ohio State University model) is presented by Beeler, Kayser, Matzner, and Saltmarsh (1985); Cruickshank, Kennedy, Williams, Holton, and Fay (1981); McKee (1986); and Troyer (1988).

Beeler et al. (1985). These researchers trained participants in an educational psychology course in reflective teaching. Methodology is not described. Findings reported included the facts that, for training purposes, a small group size of 5–8 persons is optimal, persons in the group should be balanced in terms of likelihood of active participation, the first RTL used should be interesting and enjoyable; the first designated teacher should be predictably forthcoming; small-group membership should be rotated over RTLs; and immediate and nonthreatening feedback is highly beneficial.

Cruickshank et al. (1981). The purpose here was to examine whether (a) reflective teaching would promote preservice teachers' ability to think and, hence, express themselves in a complex manner when discussing the act of teaching; (b) subjects would be able to identify a greater number and wider variety of variables extant during teaching; and (c) subjects' attitudes toward student teaching might change. Subjects were enrolled in four sections of a first course on pedagogy. Sections were randomly assigned to treatments. Experimental subjects received 6 hours of reflective teaching, during which time each subject taught one RTL and was a small-group learner the other 5 hours. Control subjects received unrelated instruction. Thus, experimental subjects reflected on their teaching and learning, whereas controls reflected on teaching more generally. Results of training supported the fact that reflective teaching significantly prompted experimental subjects' ability to think and, hence, express themselves in a complex manner when writing posttest compositions, "When I think about teaching" and "When I think about learning."

McKee (1986). The purpose of the third reported study intended to train teachers in reflective teaching was to determine whether such training would be more successful than microteaching as a means of developing and refining basic skills in lesson preparation, delivery, and evaluation. Subjects were Technical and Further Education teachers undergoing an initial (inservice) diploma in teaching at Newcastle College of Advanced Education, Australia, where reflective teaching was used with modification over three summers. The modifications were that all lessons were videotaped; designated teachers were required to engage in self-viewing and self-rating within five categories; designated teachers were rated by their learners on 10 items; and a summary of the "main discoveries about teaching and learning" was distributed after each reflective-teaching session. When current students' responses to reflective teaching were compared with previous students' responses to microteaching, the former indicated a much higher level of satisfaction."

Troyer (1988). The investigator wished to determine whether preparation of teachers to be reflective following The

Ohio State University regimen described earlier would be improved by providing subjects with enhanced theoretical knowledge prior to engagement in reflective teaching. Preservice teachers enrolled in seven intact sections of an education class were randomly assigned to one of three treatment conditions—(a) ordinary reflective teaching, (b) augmented reflective teaching, or (c) a control—and to one of two levels, pretested or not pretested. In pre- and posttests, subjects observed two videotapes of teaching and were then asked to write an essay analyzing the teaching. Condition 1 subjects participated in reflective teaching over three class periods, or 6 hours. Condition 2 subjects participated in reflective teaching and were given an additional $1\frac{1}{2}$-hour theoretical session to provide them with an understanding of the concept of reflectivity and its benefits. Condition 3 subjects participated in regular course activities. Results are numerous and positive and include the fact that both treatment conditions have substantial effects on preservice teachers' reflectivity in analyzing classroom teaching. Ordinary reflective teaching has a greater effect on explanatory/hypothetical ability than on justificatory and critical ability. Augmented reflective teaching has a positive effect on all three reflective abilities, with the greatest impact on critical.

Because the generic notion of reflective teaching is quite new, or at the least newly revisited, reports of training endeavors are scant. The few available that result from the work at Ohio State suggest it is a promising regimen for bringing about the intended main effect, reflection resulting in higher order thinking about teaching. Additionally, its use suggests that modifications might be in order to further satisfy trainers and subjects who seem to find it compelling.

Training teachers via simulations to become improved classroom problem solvers. Simulation is an instructional alternative whereby elements of real situations are presented to learners, to provide them with awareness and an opportunity to learn and practice responses. It is an instructional alternative used for a wide variety of purposes in teacher preparation (Cruickshank, 1988): preparing teachers for problems encountered during student teaching, beginning teaching, regular teaching, and teaching in desegregated schools; teaching teachers to use the informal reading inventory; acquainting student teachers with pupil diversity; improving teachers' skills in behavior modification; improving teachers' ability to identify learning-disabled pupils; diagnosing and treating teachers' questioning deficiencies; improving teachers' abilities to diagnose pupil errors; and providing practice in teaching spelling.

Because the literature is both diverse and vast (Cruickshank, 1988), focus here will be limited to its use in promoting enhanced teacher problem-solving skills. Several simulations have been developed related to this goal (Cruickshank, 1969; Cruickshank, Broadbent, & Bubb, 1967; Kersh, 1962; Morine-Dershimer, 1987; Twelker, 1970). In common, they provide preservice or inservice teachers with background information about a hypothetical school, classroom, and/or pupils they will teach. Following such orientation, participants assume the role of student teacher or teacher and confront various problems of practice. Next, participants act to resolve each problem. Fi-

nally, according to simulation type, participants either receive knowledge of results, that is, of the goodness of their solution, or are engaged in group discussion wherein effort is made to increase their problem-solving skills, thereby raising their cognitive understanding of the complexity of life in classrooms. Examples of the two somewhat distinct types might make them more clear.

Kersh (1962) and Twelker (1970) more or less follow a behavior modification mode of training. In the Kersh Classroom Simulator a participant reacts in a contrived classroom setting to a filmed classroom situation such as pupils entering the classroom in a disorderly manner. Depending upon the participant's reaction, the experimenter projects a filmed consequence showing how pupils or the class respond to such teacher behavior. The participant does not receive a passing grade on an incident until until he or she responds in a way that has been prejudged to be most appropriate. Thus, the intention is to modify participant's behavior in a predetermined way that reflects presumed good practice. Morine-Dershimer's (1987) simulation seems to be a variation on that theme. Her Simulators of Teacher Decision Making cause teachers to make decisions about pupils at the beginning of a school year; for example, how should they be grouped for reading instruction? Given substantial available data, teachers perform the grouping task and indicate their decision rules. Feedback enables them to modify the groupings they have made. Finally, participants are given a predetermined probable best placement for each pupil, based upon the judgment of an experienced teacher. Participants are encouraged and challenged to think, but, in the end, a correct answer is provided.

Cruickshank et al. (1967) and Cruickshank (1969) intend to improve generic teacher problem-solving ability. Their simulations also cause participants to react to classroom events and to make instructional decisions. However, there are no predetermined correct responses in them. Rather, participants work individually and then collectively to resolve the problems or complete the activities, utilizing the orientation materials, related theoretical knowledge, and a problem-solving regimen. Significant in the regimen were the questions, Were participants clear about problem ownership, their goals (What do they want to happen that is not happening?), obstacles to goal achievement, and alternatives for goal achievement, and Were they able to choose one or more alternatives most likely to gain the goal with the fewest negative side effects?

Early studies in which teachers were trained to become better problem solvers are reported in detail by Cruickshank (1971).

Kersh (1963). In this study the purpose was to compare two training regimens, to assess which was more effective in helping subjects respond correctly to the aforementioned filmed situations. The variable of main interest was realism or fidelity in the presentation of the classroom problems. A two-way factorial design was employed, and subjects, comprising two intact college classes of juniors and seniors, were assigned to one of four treatment groups. Factors investigated were the size of the classroom problem image visually presented (small versus large) and whether it was moving or still (motion picture versus slides). Thus, Group 1 was shown large screen images utilizing motion pictures, group 2 was shown small screen images using motion pictures, group 3 was shown large screen images of single frames (stills) of the motion pictures, and Group 4 was shown small screen images of single frame stills. Kersh reports mild support for the training regimen utilizing small still projection.

Vlcek (1966). This study investigated the effect of use of a replica of the Kersh Classroom Simulator in providing subjects with experience in identifying and solving classroom problems, the transfer value of the experience, and the effect of the experience on self-confidence in teaching. A two-way factorial design provided subjects, who were junior level elementary education majors divided into high and low grade point average groups, with simulation versus no-simulation training. After the training period, both groups were tested in the simulator. Vlcek reports that experimental subjects were significantly better at being aware of and using principles of classroom management. In a follow-up study, all subjects were observed during student teaching, but no differences were seen between experimental and control subjects either in their awareness of existing problems or in their effectiveness in coping with them. Finally, the investigator reports strong support that experimental subjects expressed greater self-confidence in ability to teach.

Twelker (1970). Here the purpose was to develop a less expensive, less labor-intensive, Kersh-like simulation. Two sets of materials were developed, one presenting problems of classroom management, the other focusing on discovery teaching. Cruickshank and Broadbent (1969) describe the former:

Teaching Research's "low cost" simulation is geared toward helping participants become more effective classroom managers and thus better teachers. The two phases of the simulation are intended to teach certain principles of classroom management and to exercise the application of the principles in the simulation. The simulation contains a variety of feedback. In Phase I, using an exercise book and a film-tape presentation on an Audascan projector, participants react to the way a teacher handles classroom management. Seeing two teaching episodes, the participant must choose which teacher behavior is preferable and state why in the exercise book. The participant receives feedback as he compares his written response with one contained on the following page of the book. During the final part of Phase I, feedback a-la-Kersh is used; that is, participants see a film of how the class would respond according to the two teaching strategies employed. Phase II gives the participant . . . an opportunity to practice . . . application of principles (learned in Phase I). In this Phase participant responses to filmed incidents are compared with responses to the same incident made by "expert teachers." Finally a third section of the film depicts how children would probably respond to the "expert teachers'" behavior. Ultimately feedback is obtained as the participant compares his response with that of the expert. (pp. 29–30)

The Twelker materials were evaluated by a variety of persons including instructors, instructional systems experts, subject-matter experts, and preservice teachers. They were field-tested under somewhat differing circumstances. "For the most part, field trial site representatives were responsible for deciding how the materials would be used" (Twelker, 1970, p. 19). Results reported include the fact that the "'Classroom Management Series' left little to be desired in the way of timeliness

and credibility . . ." but "that use of the materials did not cause all students to achieve proficiency" (p. ii).

Cruickshank and Broadbent (1968). This study was an effort to judge the effectiveness of simulation in presenting teacher problems and whether or not exposure to them would have observable effects on trainees' behaviors during subsequent student teaching. Would they have fewer problems, generally perform better, be more confident, or be able to assume full-time classroom responsibilities sooner? A randomized pretest–posttest control-group design was used during two independent field tests in which experimental subjects who were K–9 preservice teachers undertook 2 weeks' preparation in the simulator, described earlier, in lieu of the first 2 weeks of student teaching. According to the researchers, subjects became highly involved and stimulated, and, during student teaching, the experimental subjects were reported by their cooperating teachers to have fewer classroom problems.

Morine-Dershimer (1987). Almost 2 decades passed before another effort was made to help teachers become better problem solvers. This effort, described earlier, seems to have been spurred by the advent of the microcomputer, "What we are attempting to accomplish [is] developing computer simulations for training teachers in preactive decision making" (pp. 27–28). One field test used 18 elementary education majors enrolled in a professional education course who completed the Grouping for Instruction in Reading Task. Some also completed the second task, "Allotting Time for Instruction. Results reported include these facts:

In general, student reactions to the simulations were quite favorable . . . In general, students did revise their initial decisions [about reading groupings] after receiving additional data . . . that the revised decision led to more appropriate placement of the data bank pupils . . . and, the feedback was [not] totally effective in changing preservice teachers' beliefs about the value of certain instructional practices. (p. 35)

Eighteen of the 23 experimental subjects completed both tasks. They were compared on posttests with 17 other students in the class who were not elementary education majors and who did not receive a training treatment. Performance on the measures used showed no significant differences between trained and untrained students in ability to see problems or general planning skills and academic success in the course.

Doak, Keith, Emmer, and Turner (1988). The developers of this newer simulation provided trainees with experience in effective classroom-management procedures that was appropriate for the initial 2 weeks of the school year. Four simulated activities utilized written materials, work sheets, and videotape recordings of classroom situations to develop understanding of planning classroom organization, establishment of reasonable expectations for pupil talk and pupil movement, and development of activities-appropriate rules and procedures. The simulations could be completed independently in small groups or as a total class, each taking approximately 4 hours. No research is yet available on the effectiveness of these materials.

Among more recent simulations developed for the purpose of improving problem solving in specific subject areas or along more specific themes are Copeland (1987) (handling deviancy and overlappingness); Lunetta (1985) (classroom management). Pankratz, Martray, Becker, and Law (1983) (behavior management and discipline); R. Putnam (1983, 1987) (diagnosis of arithmetic errors); and Strang, Badt, and Kauffman (1987) (teaching spelling).

In summary, several efforts have been made to help teachers increase their problem-solving abilities through engagement in simulations that re-create selected conditions of classroom life. They can be thought about as being media versus computer-based, providing for group versus individual instruction, using operant conditioning versus open-ended, and being simplistic versus complex. The earlier versions were all media based, relying heavily on visual images of classrooms and their attendant problems. Individual instruction is the method of choice for Kersh and Twelker. Cruickshank and Broadbent utilized small- and large-group problem solving and Morine-Dershimer had her subjects work in pairs.

Many of the emphases of these programs were on the extensive and complex development of the simulations, seemingly leaving less time and care for studying their effectiveness as training devices. Consequently, reports of the validity or lack of validity of these particular simulations and, in fact, simulations used in teacher education generally must be accepted with caution.

The results of studies reported here seem to support the facts that simulation training devices need not have a high degree of verisimilitude or one-to-one correspondence to reality, subjects can be reinforced to respond appropriately to problems during training, subjects and users find the devices timely and believable, and subjects are perceived by others as having fewer classroom problems following their training.

Training teachers to bring about pupil learning by instilling teacher-effectiveness behaviors in them. During the 1960s, 1970s, and 1980s, the momentum for conducting inquiry on what constitutes effective teaching practice when the outcome measure is pupil academic achievement was generated by several events. First, Mitzel (1960) analyzed the types of research on teaching that had to be and could be done and pointed out the independent and dependent variables. Next, a bevy of scholars led by Flanders (1963b) and others (Simon & Boyer, 1968) constructed observation instruments capable of measuring the variables (for a description of one instrument see the preceding section on Interaction Analysis). During this time, preparation in research methodology was establishing a foothold in graduate education programs and computers were becoming ubiquitous. Another event that clearly was advantageous was the publication of a number of syntheses of research on teaching (see the earlier section on kinds of training) With the increased residue of research on teaching and the growing confidence in it by such powerful stakeholders as the American Association of Colleges for Teacher Education, the American Educational Research Association, the Association of Teacher Educators, the National Association of State Directors of Teacher Education and Certification and the National Council for Accreditation of Teacher Education, the larger teacher edu-

cation community, although in part reluctant, was swayed to consider its use. Consequently, persons became immersed in developing programs wherein preservice or inservice teachers could become knowledgeable-of and skilled-in selected teacher behaviors that researchers had shown were by association or causally linked with K–12 pupil learning.

A number of studies are available in which teachers were trained in teacher effectiveness behaviors. Such studies are reported by L. M. Anderson, Evertson, and Brophy (1979); Borg and Ascione (1982); Colodarci and Gage (1984); Crawford, Gage, Corno, Stayrook, and Mitman (1978); Denight and Gall (1989); Emmer, Sanford, Clements, and Martin (1982); Emmer, Sandford, Evertson, Clements, and Martin (1981); Gliessman, Pugh, Brown, and Archer (1989); Good and Grouws (1979, 1981); Griffin and Barnes (1986); Harris (1989); Klesius, Searls, and Zielonka (1989); Metcalf (1989); and Stallings, Needels, and Stayrook (1979).

Anderson et al. (1979). These investigators examined the effects of engaging teachers in a training program intended to improve small-group reading instruction in grade one. Subjects were volunteer elementary teachers randomly assigned to experimental and control groups. Experimental teachers were asked to read a brief manual describing 22 research-based principles of effective small-group instruction in early grades. Then they met once with the investigator to discuss the principles. No further training or coaching was provided. Control teachers received no training. Observations of all teachers during reading instruction revealed inconsistent use of the principles. Principles observed to be implemented most consistently by experimental, but not control, teachers were specifically described during training and related to behaviors already familiar to the teachers and had a rationale based on other classroom processes or student outcomes that made sense to the teachers.

Borg and Ascione (1982). The purpose of this work was to determine the effect of a training program in classroom management on teacher use of the target skills in natural classrooms. Subjects were elementary teachers assigned randomly to experimental or control groups. Experimental subjects were afforded a training regimen that included presentation of knowledge about a set of research-supported classroom-management skills, exercises in skill recognition, skill practice in their classrooms, and videotaping and discussion of a skill demonstration with a fellow trainee. Control subjects received training in skills related to developing student self-concepts, via a similar training regimen. Borg and Ascione report that experimental teachers exhibited significantly more of the target behaviors than did control teachers.

Colodarci and Gage (1984). This study sought to find out the value of a "minimal" training intervention in causing teachers to use behavior supported by research on effective classroom management. Subjects were volunteer elementary teachers who were observed before and after training, to determine their level of use of the target skills. Randomly assigned experimental subjects were mailed training packets; controls were not. Packets contained knowledge about classroom management and instructional strategies drawn from teacher-effectiveness research, including descriptions, definitions, examples, and specific suggestions for implementing the practices. Observations revealed no differences between treatment and control teachers in use of target practices.

Crawford et al. (1978). The purpose was to determine the effects of three levels of teacher training in the use of effective methods of reading instruction. Subjects were elementary teachers randomly assigned to one of three training regimens. The minimal training group received training via printed materials and a self-test on the target teaching skills that related to classroom management, instructional methods, questioning, and feedback. The maximal training group received these materials and discussed them. Additionally, they saw demonstrations of the target skills, acted them out during role plays, and practiced them in workshops. The no-training group served as a control. All teachers were observed regularly before, during, and after training. The investigators report that both training conditions resulted in significantly greater use of the teaching skills and neither training condition was deemed to be more successful in changing teacher behavior. Teachers in the maximal group reported greater satisfaction with training.

Denight and Gall (1989). This study investigated the effects of enthusiasm training on teachers' classroom behavior. Twenty volunteer secondary teachers participated and were matched by subject area between training and control groups. First, all teachers were videotaped while teaching a lesson of their choice. Next, training-group teachers received training in enthusiasm, which consisted of group discussion of teacher enthusiasm, practice lessons taught to peer and then actual students, and follow-up discussion of teacher enthusiasm. Control-group teachers received no training. Then, all teachers were again videotaped teaching a lesson of their choice. Observers rated trained teachers as significantly more enthusiastic than untrained teachers.

Emmer et al. (1981). The investigators studied the effects of providing training in 11 research-based classroom-management techniques before the beginning of school, at midyear, or not at all on teachers' classroom behavior. Volunteer elementary teachers were paired by age, experience, and grade level. Then members of each pair were randomly assigned to experimental or control groups. Experimental-group teachers received training prior to the first day of school. Half of the so-called control group received training in early December, and the remaining control-group teachers were not trained. Training included a manual with a rationale, description, and implementation guidelines for each of the techniques, and two half-day workshops to discuss the manual and answer questions. Observations of all teachers were conducted from August through February. Emmer et al. report that teachers trained at the beginning of the year implemented the techniques to a significantly greater degree than teachers receiving midyear or no training.

Emmer et al. (1982). Again, the purpose was to validate a regimen intended to train teachers in the use of classroom-management skills derived from research. Subjects were volunteer junior high school teachers who were randomly assigned to treatment and control groups. The training regimen for experimental subjects consisted of providing them with in-

formation about the skills and their applications via a manual and two half-day workshops. Posttraining observation of all teachers revealed that trained teachers made greater use of the management skills than did untrained teachers.

Gliessman et al. (1989). The investigators report the results of a three-phase study that examined the effect of conceptual training on teacher use of six components of instructional clarity. Subjects were preservice teachers enrolled in an educational psychology course. In phase one, subjects were randomly assigned to either extended conceptual training, limited conceptual training, or no-training groups. All trained teachers received 45 minutes of instruction in clarity, which included information about teacher clarity and a videotaped demonstration. Teachers in the extended training group received an additional hour of similar training. Results indicate that subjects in both training groups performed better than untrained subjects on written tests of clarity knowledge.

In phase two, extended training group teachers were randomly assigned to instruction/application or instruction/no application groups. Instruction/application teachers worked in pairs to plan a short lesson in which they were to optimize their use of the clarity skills. Instruction/no application teachers received no further training. All teachers then taught a short lesson to a small group of peers. Trained observers found no significant between-group differences in use of the desired skills.

In phase three, 15 subjects from the instruction/application group were randomly assigned to receive further training. All subjects were afforded additional peer-teaching practice. Next, 6 subjects were helped by the investigator to prepare a lesson to be taught in a natural classroom. Remaining teachers prepared lessons without assistance. Then, all teachers taught their lessons. Observation revealed that teachers who were helped to prepare their lessons used the 6 components of clarity significantly more frequently than teachers who prepared lessons without assistance.

Good and Grouws (1979). Here the investigators' purpose was to field-test a training regimen for preparing teachers to teach arithmetic, utilizing the results of teacher-effectiveness research in that subject. Subjects were volunteer fourth-grade teachers randomly assigned to treatment or no-treatment groups. Experimental subjects followed a regimen that included hearing a 90-minute explanation of the program, reading a 45-page training manual containing knowledge-of the target skills and knowledge-about how to implement them during teaching, and participating in a meeting for the purpose of providing necessary clarification. Following training, all subjects were observed over 4 months. The investigators report that experimental subjects exhibited significantly more target skills.

Good and Grouws (1981). This study sought to compare the effects of two training regimens in bringing about changes in the subjects' use of target skills, in this case mathematics skills derived from research on effective mathematics instruction. Subjects were volunteer junior high mathematics teachers randomly assigned to one of two treatment groups or to a control group. Group 1, termed a "partnership group", met with the investigators to consider and modify the training regimen to be used. This group was combined with Group 2 and followed the training procedure, which consisted of receiving an explanation of the program and reading the training manual (see Good & Grouws, 1979). Posttraining observations revealed that teachers in both training groups were following the training recommendations to a greater extent than control teachers and that neither Group 1 nor Group 2 training proved significantly more effective.

Griffin and Barnes (1986). The purpose here was to train staff developers to change subordinates' teaching practices so that they mirrored the findings from teacher-effectiveness research. Subjects were nominated staff developers and two elementary teachers selected by each. Staff developers were randomly assigned to treatment or control conditions. The experimental treatment consisted of one week of staff-developer training prior to the opening of school that focused on acquainting the subjects with findings of research on teaching and school effectiveness via lecture, written material, and videotape. Discrimination training was emphasized, and the investigators modeled target skills when possible. At the conclusion of training, experimental-group staff developers prepared school-specific staff-development plans. During the period of the study, September through January, all staff developers and the pair of elementary teachers working with them maintained structured journals of all staff-development contacts, formal and informal. Additionally, teachers were observed, using a 10-category rating scale consisting of effective teaching behaviors, and pupil on-task behavior was estimated. The investigators report that this training resulted in significant differences between experimental and control staff developers, between the teachers associated with each, and between those teachers' pupils as follows. Experimental staff developers demonstrated significantly more of 4 of the 10 desired behaviors. Their teachers, contrasted with the control group's teachers, exhibited significantly more target skills in planning and preparation, presentation, organizing the classroom and presenting rules and procedures.

Harris (1989). The investigator reports the results of four studies that examined the effectiveness of a training regimen on teachers' use of classroom time. In these studies, elementary student teachers were observed and then assigned to experimental or control groups. Members of the experimental group received 5 weeks of training in the Stallings Effective Use of Time (EUOT) staff development program. Training included discussion, practice with peer observation, and feedback about their teacher-student interactions and student off-task behavior. Control teachers participated in seminar groups focused on their student teaching experiences. All teachers were observed at the conclusion of student teaching. Results indicate that trained teachers used desired behaviors more frequently than untrained teachers, although this was statistically significant in only 2 of 11 areas. Further, in one study, teachers who were not trained but received feedback regarding their use of classroom time were found to improve their performance more significantly than teachers receiving the complete EUOT program.

Klesius et al. (1989). This study investigated the effect of training delivered either conventionally or by videotape on el-ementary teachers' reading instruction. Preservice elementary teachers were randomly assigned to each of two treatment groups. Both groups received training in conducting a Directed Reading Activity (DRA). All subjects were provided with written materials, a teachers' manual for a basal reading series, a suggested lesson plan, step-by-step instructions for conducting a DRA, and discussion of the observation form by which teaching performance was to be evaluated. Teachers in one group also viewed a videotaped demonstration of a Directed Reading Activity. Post-training observations revealed no significant differences in ability to conduct a DRA between teachers who viewed the demonstration and teachers who had not.

Metcalf (1989). This study sought to determine the efficacy of a research-based regimen of training in helping teachers improve the clarity of their instructional presentations. Subjects were preservice teachers enrolled in 4 sections of a general methods course. Sections were randomly selected and assigned to training or control conditions. All sections provided regular course content and activities that included didactic instruction in general aspects of teaching, and peer and natural classroom teaching experiences. Additionally, sections in the training condition incorporated *The Clarity Training Program* (Cruickshank & Metcalf, 1989) into course activities. Clarity training utilized an extensive manual, videotaped and written demonstrations, skill discrimination exercises, guided practice in laboratory and natural classroom settings, and performance-specific feedback regarding use of behaviors associated with clear teaching. At the conclusion of the 10-week course, all teachers prepared and taught short lessons to small groups of peers while being videotaped. Observation revealed significant between-group differences in the frequency with which teachers used desired behaviors and in global ratings of teachers' overall instructional clarity that favored clarity-trained teachers.

Stallings et al. (1979). The investigators report two studies. In the first the purpose was to assess the power of a training regimen intended to cause teachers to use research-based skills related to the teaching of basic reading. Subjects were junior and senior high school teachers who were observed prior to training and then assigned to training or no-training groups. Training consisted of five 2-hour inservice workshops wherein subjects received materials describing the target skills and discussed them. Posttraining classroom observation revealed that trained teachers showed greater improvement in the target skills.

In the second study, three methods of training were compared. Volunteer junior and senior high teachers were selected for participation and assigned to one of three groups. Group 1 received instruction directly from the investigators using the workshop format as in the earlier study. Group 2 received similar instruction but from teachers trained in the earlier study rather than the investigators. Group 3 received only written materials explaining the instructional processes. The investigators report that teachers in both training groups showed greater positive change in target behaviors than teachers receiving only written materials. Training by previously trained teachers was deemed successful.

In summary, these efforts to prepare teachers to use skills derived from research on effective teaching were mostly favorable. Some of these studies would seem to support the previously mentioned contention of Gliessman that practice might not be required, at least for the initial demonstration of a target skill.

Other Training Efforts Within Teacher Preparation

At least two additional training efforts deserve mention because of their seriousness of purpose and the receptivity of them. *First* is the inservice training conducted by Hunter (Hunter Teacher Decision-making Model or Instructional Theory Into Practice Model). This effort is well described and documented elsewhere by Stallings and Krasavage (1986), Robbins (1986), Porter (1986), Slavin (1986), and Hunter herself (1986) in five articles in the November 1986 *Elementary School Journal*.

Second is training conducted by Joyce and others (Models of Teaching). A synthesis of related research on training effects resulting from use of some of these models is reported in Joyce, Showers, and Rolheiser-Bennett (1987). Joyce and Showers (1988) refer to research on training per se and provide some interesting normative data regarding the efficacy of various training components (p. 70). Unfortunately, they do not provide information regarding the suitability of their particular training regimen, although they note that its use has been evaluated by several school districts (see pp. 123–126).

RELATIONSHIP BETWEEN THEORY AND PRACTICE OF TRAINING

The examples described in preceding sections make clear that the target skills of teaching may be drawn from a variety of sources. They are generally complex skills (e.g., teacher clarity) rather than discrete behaviors and are mostly of a higher cognitive order. As a result, development of these skills requires learners to gain both knowledge-of the skill and skill-in its application. Most notably, the examples indicate that these skills *can* be learned and mastered by preservice and inservice teachers.

Literature on the conduct, objectives, and effectiveness of training in teacher education is sparse. Due to confusion of terms, misconceptions of the uses of training and skill development, lack of agreement regarding desirable teacher behavior, and numerous other factors, skill development efforts have been relatively infrequent and disjointed. The examples suggest that trainers have operated in isolation from each other, seemingly unguided by a common frame of reference or model with regard to either use of training as a phenomenon or a systematic, coordinated effort to use training within professional teacher preparation.

At least two recurring weaknesses of training efforts in teacher education can be identified. First, such efforts do not explicitly account for the alterations of training required by differential levels of learner entry behavior or the systematic evaluation of discrete components of the training regimen. Training efforts have generally emphasized only the evaluation of learner exit behavior. A second weakness is the failure to pursue long-term, continued development of successful training regimens. Training efforts, even those producing desirable results (e.g., training in interaction analysis), have been short lived. Training programs have been developed, often at great expense of both time and money, and implemented to varying, though usually limited, degrees, sometimes validated through research and then abandoned. Few training efforts in teacher education have maintained long-term usage, research, or development.

SOME FINAL THOUGHTS

Given the historic brouhaha over training in teacher preparation, it would be expected that a considerable available related literature would exist. Such is not the case. The topic is notable by its near absence of mention in the *Encyclopedia of Educational Research* and the several editions of the *Handbook of Research in Teaching*. Relatedly, there seems to be no guru in the field. Thus, teacher preparers are, for the most part, unguided, or possibly misguided, if and when they aspire to skill development.

Literature that does exist indicates that training *can* produce positive changes in the behavior of teachers. Both preservice and inservice teachers benefit from programs that provide them not only with knowledge-of but also with skill-in using desirable teaching practices. The relative effectiveness of the examples cited in this chapter is an encouraging indication that teacher education, when it includes training, can produce teachers capable of skillful and consistent professional practice.

In spite of this, problems abound. Among the obvious are the need for greater conceptual clarity with regard to nomenclature such as *training* and *skills*; the related need to establish the idea that teaching skills are mostly intellectual and affective, rather than motor; the need to make evident in teacher preparation the fact that, although education can be separated from training, the reverse is not true; the need to establish hierarchies of training goals and the related need to study the phenomenon of training and apply its principles; the need to recognize and accept that little that presently passes as a proxy for training is such (including the vast majority of student teaching); relatedly, the need to establish training centers on campus and in the field (see Smith et al., 1969); the need for teacher preparers to be readied to conduct training and education; and, importantly, the need for related coordinated scholarship and inquiry into effective training in teacher preparation.

If we are not sanguine that these indeed are justifiable ends and that they can be realized, then the professional preparation of teachers will continue to be incomplete and faulty. An aggregate of teachers without significant and consistent teaching skills simply will never be respected in a culture that demands that professionals have both clinical knowledge and ability.

References

Ajayi-Dopemu, Y., & Talabi, J. K. (1986). The effects of videotape recording on microteaching training techniques for education students. *Journal of Educational Television, 12*(1), 39–44.

Allen, C. T., & Forman, S. G. (1984). Efficacy of methods of training teachers in behavior modification. *School Psychology Review, 13*, 26–32.

Allen, D., & Ryan, K. (1969). *Microteaching*. Reading, MA: Addison-Wesley.

American Association of Colleges for Teacher Education. (1987). The challenge of electronic technologies for colleges of education. *Journal of Teacher Education, 38*(6), 25–29.

Amidon, E. J., & Flanders, N. A. (1963). *The role of the teacher in the classroom: A manual for understanding and improving teachers' classroom behavior*. Minneapolis: Amidon.

Anderson, J. (1980). *Cognitive psychology and its application*. San Francisco: W. H. Freeman.

Anderson, J. (1984). *The acquisition of complex skills*. Hillsdale, NJ: Lawrence Erlbaum.

Anderson, L. M., Everston, C. M., & Brophy, J. E. (1979). An experimental study of effective teaching in first-grade reading groups. *Elementary School Journal, 79*(4), 193–223.

Andrews, J. K. (1970). The results of a pilot program to train teachers in the classroom application of behavior modification techniques. *Journal of School Psychology, 8*, 37–42.

Argyle, M. (1969). *Social interaction*. London: Methuen.

Averch, H., Carol, S., Donaldson, T. S., Kiesling, H., & Pincus, J. (1974). *How effective is schooling? A critical review of research*. Santa Monica, CA: RAND Corporation.

Baer, A., Williams, J., Osner, P., & Stoker, T. (1984). Delayed reinforcement as an indiscriminable contingency in verbal/nonverbal correspondence training. *Journal of Applied Behavioral Analysis, 17*(4), 429–440.

Beeler, K., Kayser, G., Matzner, K., & Saltmarsh, R. (1985). Reflective teaching. Reflections on college classroom experience. *Educational Journal, 18*(1), 4–8.

Bellack, A., Davitz, J., Kliebard, H., & Hyman, R. (1963). *The language of the classroom: Meanings communicated in high school teaching*. New York: Columbia University, Teachers College, Institute of Psychological Research.

Berliner, D. (1984). The half-full glass: A review of research on teaching. In P. Hosford (Ed.), *Using what we know about teaching* (pp. 51–81). Alexandra, VA: Association for Supervision and Curriculum Development.

Berliner, D. C. (1985). Critical needs in teacher education. *Journal of Industrial Teacher Education, 22*(4), 5–11.

Berman, P., & McLaughlin, M. (1975). *Federal programs supporting educational change: Vol IV. The findings in review*. Santa Monica, CA: RAND Corporation.

Beyer, L. E. (1986). Beyond elitism and technicism: Teacher education as practical philosophy. *Journal of Teacher Education, 37*(2), 37–41.

Beyer, L. E., & Zeichner, K. M. (1982). Teacher training and educational foundations: A plea for discontent. *Journal of Teacher Education, 33*(3), 18–23.

Bickel, W. (1983). Effective schools: Knowledge, dissemination and inquiry. *Educational Researcher, 12*(4), 3–4.

Billings, T. A. (1981). Knowing about and knowing how to do. *Phi Delta Kappan, 62*(8), 596–597, 610.

Bloom, B., Englehart, M., Furst, E., Hill, W., & Krathwohl, D. (1956). *Taxonomy of educational objectives: The classification of educational goals: Handbook I. Cognitive domain*. New York: David McKay.

Bondi, J. C. (1970). Feedback from interaction analysis: Some implications for the improvement of teaching. *Journal of Teacher Education, 21*, 189–196.

Borg, W. (1972). The minicourse as a vehicle for changing teacher behavior: A three year follow-up. *Journal of Educational Psychology, 63*(6), 572–579.

Borg, W. (1973). Protocols: Competency-based teacher education modules. *Educational Technology, 13*(10), 17–20.

Borg, W. (1975). Protocol materials as related to teacher performance and pupil achievement. *Journal of Educational Research, 69*(1), 23–30.

Borg, W. R., & Ascione, F. R. (1982). Classroom management in elementary mainstreaming classrooms. *Journal of Educational Psychology, 74*, 85–95.

Borg, W. R., Kallenbach, W., Morris, M., & Friebel, A. (1969). Videotape feedback and microteaching in a teacher training model. *Journal of Experimental Education, 37*(4), 9–16.

Borg, W. R., Kelly, M. L., Langer, P., & Gall, M. (1970). *A microteaching approach to teacher education*. Beverly Hills, CA: Macmillan Educational Services.

Borg, W. R., Langer, P., & Wilson, J. (1975). Teacher classroom management skills and pupil behavior. *Journal of Experimental Education, 44*(2), 52–58.

Borg, W., & Stone, D. (1974). Protocol materials as a tool for changing teacher behavior. *Journal of Experimental Education, 43*(1), 34–39.

Bowles, P. E., Jr., & Nelson, R. O. (1976). Training teachers as mediators: Efficacy of a workshop versus the bug-in-the-ear technique. *Journal of School Psychology, 14*(1) 15–25.

Brophy, J. E., & Good, T. L. (1986). Teacher behavior and student achievement. In M. C. Wittrock (Ed.), *Handbook of Research on Teaching* (3rd. ed., pp. 328–375). New York: Macmillan.

Broudy, H. S. (1972). *The real world of the public schools*. New York: Harcourt Brace Jovanovich.

Broudy, H. S. (1978). *Faculty Study in a Second Discipline*. Urbana, IL: University of Illinois, Advisory Committee on Interdisciplinary Programs.

Broudy, H. S. (1984). The university and the preparation of teachers. In L. G. Katz & J. D. Raths (Eds.), *Advances in teacher education*, (Vol. 1, pp. 1–8). Norwood, NJ: Ablex.

Brown, G. (1975). *Microteaching: A programme of teaching skills*. London: Methuen.

Brown, J. C., Montgomery, R., & Barclay, J. R. (1969). An example of psychologist management of teacher reinforcement procedures in the elementary classroom. *Psychology in the Schools, 6*, 336–340.

Charters, W. W., Waples, D. (1929). *The commonwealth teacher training study*. Chicago: University of Chicago Press.

Chaukin, N. F., & Williams, D. L. (1984). *Guidelines and strategies for training teachers about parent involvement* (Executive summary of the final report). Austin, TX: Southwest Educational Development Laboratory. (ERIC Document Reproduction Service No. ED 274 411)

Chhoker, J., & Wallin, J. (1984). A field study of the effect of feedback frequency on performance. *Journal of Applied Psychology, 69*(3), 524–530.

Cicero, J. P. (1976). Instructional systems. In R. L. Craig (Ed.), *Training and development handbook: A guide to human resource development* (pp. 12.1–12.10). New York: McGraw-Hill.

Clift, R. T., Houston, W. R., & Pugach, M. (Eds.). (in press). Reflective practice: An examination of issues and examplars. New York: Teachers College Press.

Collins, M. L. (1978). Effects of enthusiasm training on preservice elementary teachers. *Journal of Teacher Education*, 29(1), 53–57.

Colodarci, T., & Gage, N. L. (1984). Effects of a minimal intervention on teacher behavior and student achievement. *American Educational Research Journal*, 21, 539–555.

Cooper, J., Hanson, J., Martorella, P., Morine-Dershimer, G., Sadker, D., Sadker, M., Sokolove, S., Shostak, R., Tonbrink, T., & Weber, W. (1977). *Classroom teaching skills.* Lexington, MA: D. C. Heath.

Cooper, M. L., Thomson, C. L., & Baer, D. M. (1970). The experimental modification of teacher attending behavior. *Journal of Applied Behavioral Analysis*, 3, 153–157.

Copeland, W. (1975). The relationship between microteaching and student teacher classroom performance. *Journal of Educational Research*, 68, 289–293.

Copeland, W. (1977). Some factors related to student teacher classroom performance following microteaching training. *American Educational Research Journal*, 14, 147–157.

Copeland, W. D. (1982). Laboratory experiences in teacher education. In H. E., Mitzel (Ed.), *Encyclopedia of Educational Research* (pp. 1008–1019). New York: Free Press.

Copeland, W. (1987). Teacher information processing in the management of classrooms. In E. Doak, T. Hipple, & M. Keith (Eds.), *Simulation and clinical knowledge in teacher education* (pp. 47–61). Knoxville, TN: The University of Tennessee, College of Education.

Copeland, W. D., & Doyle, W. (1973). Laboratory skill training and student teacher classroom performance. *Journal of Experimental Education*, 42, 16–21.

Cossairt, A., Hall, R. V., & Hopkins, B. L. (1973). The effects of experimenters' instructions, feedback and praise on teacher praise and student attending behavior. *Journal of Applied Behavior Analysis*, 6, 89–100.

Cotten, D. R., Evans, J. J., & Tseng, M. S. (1978). Relating skill acquisition to science classroom teaching behavior. *Journal of Research in Science Teaching*, 15, 187–195.

Crawford, J., Gage, N. L., Corno, L., Stayrook, N., & Mitman, A. (1978, March). *An experiment on teacher effectiveness and parent-assisted instruction in third grade.* Paper presented at the annual meeting of the American Educational Research Association, Toronto. (ERIC Document Reproduction Service No. ED 160 648)

Cruickshank, D. (1969). *Inner-city simulation laboratory.* Chicago: Science Research Associates.

Cruickshank, D. (1970). *Blueprints for teacher education: A review of phase II proposals for the U.S.O.E. comprehensive elementary teacher education models program.* Washington, DC: U.S. Department of Health, Education and Welfare. (ERIC Document Reproduction Service No. ED 013 371)

Cruickshank, D. (1971). Teacher education looks at simulation. In P. Tansey (Ed.), *Educational aspects of simulation* (pp. 185–203). New York: McGraw-Hill.

Cruickshank, D. (1976). Synthesis of selected research on teacher effects. *Journal of Teacher Education,* 27(1), 57–60.

Cruickshank, D. (1986a). *Models for the preparation of America's teachers.* Bloomington, IN: Phi Delta Kappa.

Cruickshank, D. (1986b). Profile of an effective teacher. *Educational Horizons*, 64(2), 80–86.

Cruickshank, D. (1986c). A synopsis of effective schools research. *Illinois School Research and Development*, 22(3), 112–127.

Cruickshank, D. (1987). *Reflective teaching: The preparation of students of teaching.* Reston, VA: Association of Teacher Educators.

Cruickshank, D. (1988). The uses of simulations in teacher preparation: Past, present and future. *Simulations and games*, 19(2), 133–156.

Cruickshank, D., Applegate, J., Holton, J., Mager, G., Myers, B., Novak, C., & Tracey, K. (1980). *Teaching is tough.* Englewood Cliffs, NJ: Prentice-Hall.

Cruickshank, D., & Broadbent, F. (1968). *The simulation and analysis of problems of beginning teachers* (Final report, Project No. 5-0798) Washington, DC: U.S. Department of Health, Education and Welfare.

Cruickshank, D., & Broadbent, F. (1969). *Simulation in preparing educational personnel.* Washington, DC: U.S. Office of Education, Bureau of Research. (ERIC Document Reproduction Service No. ED 036 470)

Cruickshank, D., Broadbent, F., & Bubb, R. (1967). *Teaching problems laboratory.* Chicago: Science Research Associates.

Cruickshank, D., & Haefele, D. (1987). Teacher preparation via protocol materials. *International Journal of Educational Research*, 11(5), 543–554.

Cruickshank, D., & Kennedy, J. (1986). Teacher clarity. *Teaching and Teacher Education*, 2(1), 43–67.

Cruickshank, D., Kennedy, J., Williams, J., Holton, J., & Fay, D. (1981). Evaluation of reflective teaching outcomes. *Journal of Educational Research*, 75(1), 26–32.

Cruickshank, D., & Metcalf, K. (1989). The clarity training program: Instructor's manual. In K. Metcalf, *An investigation of the efficacy of a research-based regimen of skill development on the instructional clarity of preservice teachers* (pp. 387–528). Unpublished doctoral dissertation, The Ohio State University, Columbus, OH.

Dawe, H. A. (1984). Teaching: A performing art. *Phi Delta Kappan*, 65, 548–552.

Denham, C., & Lieberman, A. (Eds). (1980). *Time to learn.* Washington, DC: National Institute of Education.

Denight, J., & Gall, M. (1989). *Effects of enthusiasm training on teachers and students at the high school level.* Paper presented at the annual meeting of the American Educational Research Association, San Francisco, CA.

Dick, W., Watson, K., & Kaufman, R. (1981). Deriving competencies: Consensus versus model building. *Educational Researcher*, 10(8), 5–10.

Doak, E. D., Keith, M., Emmer, E. T., & Turner, T. (1988). *Classroom management: The first two weeks.* Knoxville, TN: University of Tennessee, College of Education, Teaching Simulation Laboratory.

Dodl, N., Elfner, E., Becker, J., Halstead, J., Jung, H., Nelson, P., Purinton, S., & Wegele, P. (1972). *Florida catalog of teacher competencies.* Tallahassee, FL: Florida State University.

Dunkin, M. (1987). Technical skills of teaching. In M. Dunkin (Ed.), *International Encyclopedia of Teaching and Teacher Education* (pp. 703–706). Oxford: Pergamon Press.

Dunkin, M., & Biddle, B. J. (1974). *The study of teaching.* New York: Holt, Rinehart & Winston.

Ellis, H. C. (1965). *The transfer of learning.* New York: Macmillan.

Ellson, D. (1986). Improving productivity in teaching. *Phi Delta Kappan*, 68(2), 111–124.

Emmer, E. T., Sanford, J. P., Clements, B. S., & Martin, J. (1982). *Improving classroom management & organization in junior high schools: An experimental investigation.* Washington, DC: National Institute of Education. (ERIC Document Reproduction Service No. ED 261 053)

Emmer, E. T., Sanford, J. P., Evertson, C. M., Clements, B. S., & Martin, J. (1981). *The classroom management improvement study: An experiment in elementary school classrooms.* Austin, TX: University of Texas, Center for Teacher Education. (ERIC Document Reproduction Service No. ED 178 460)

Finkelstein, B. (1982). Technicians, mandarins, & witnesses: Searching for professional understanding. *Journal of Teacher Education, 33*(3), 25–27.

Fitts, P. M. (1962). Factors in complex skill training. In R. Glaser (Ed.), *Training research & education* (pp. 177–197). New York: John Wiley & Sons.

Flanders, N. A. (1963a). *Helping teachers change their behavior* (Project numbers 1721012 & 7-32-0560-171.0) Washington, DC: U.S. Office of Education.

Flanders, N. (1963b). Intent, action and feedback. *Journal of Teacher Education, 14*(2), 251–260.

Friedman, P. G., & Yarbrough, E. A. (1985). *Training strategies: From start to finish.* Englewood Cliffs, NJ: Prentice-Hall.

Furst, N. (1967). The effects of training in interaction analysis on the behavior of student teachers in secondary schools. In E. J. Amidon & J. B. Hough (Eds.), *Interaction analysis: Theory, research & application* (pp. 315–328). Reading, MA: Addison-Wesley.

Gage, N. L. (Ed.). (1963). *Handbook of Research on Teaching.* Chicago: Rand McNally.

Gage, N. L. (1972). *Teacher effectiveness and teacher education: The search for a scientific basis.* Palo Alto, CA: Pacific Books.

Gage, N. L. (1985). *Hard gains in the soft sciences: The case of pedagogy.* Bloomington, IN: Phi Delta Kappa.

Gagné, R. (1984). Learning outcomes and their effects. *American Psychologist, 37*(3), 377–385.

Gagné, R. (1985). *The conditions of learning* (4th ed.). New York: Holt, Rinehart & Winston.

Gallagher, J. (1965). *Productive thinking in gifted children* (Cooperative research project No. 965). Urbana, IL: University of Illinois, Institute for Research on Exceptional Children.

George, K. D., & Nelson, M. A. (1971). Effect of an inservice science workshop on the ability of teachers to use the techniques of inquiry. *Science Education, 55,* 165–169.

Glaser, R. (Ed.). (1962). *Training research and education.* Pittsburgh: University of Pittsburgh Press.

Gliessman, D. H. (1984). Changing teacher performance. In L. G. Katz & J. D. Raths (Eds.), *Advances in teacher education* (Vol. 1, pp. 95–111). Norwood, NJ: Ablex.

Gliessman, D. H. (1986). *Laboratory methods in teacher training: Rationale and use* (An information analysis prepared for the coalition of teacher education programs). Bloomington, IN: Indiana University. (ERIC Document Reproduction Service No. ED 268 114)

Gliessman, D. H., & Pugh, R. (1976). The development and evaluation of protocol films in teacher education. *AV Communications Review, 24*(1), 21–48.

Gliessman, D. H., & Pugh, R. (1978). Research on the rationale, design, and effectiveness of protocol materials. *Journal of Teacher Education, 29*(6), 87–91.

Gliessman, D. H., & Pugh, R. (1981). Developing teaching skills through understanding. *Action in Teacher Education, 3*(1), 11–18.

Gliessman, D. H., & Pugh R. (1984). Conceptual variables in teacher training. *Journal of Education for Teaching, 10,* 195–208.

Gliessman, D. H., & Pugh, R. (1987). Conceptual instruction and intervention as methods of acquiring teaching skills. *International Journal of Educational Research, 11*(5), 555–563.

Gliessman, D. H., Pugh, R., & Bielat, B. (1979). Acquiring teaching skills through concept-based training. *Journal of Educational Research, 72,* 149–154.

Gliessman, D., Pugh, R., Brown, L., & Archer, A. (1989). *Research-based teacher training: Applying a concept teaching model to the development and transfer of a learning-related teaching skill.* Pa-

per presented at the annual meeting of the American Educational Research Association, San Francisco, CA.

Goldstein, I. L. (1986). *Training in organizations: Needs assessment, development, and evaluation.* Monterey, CA: Brooks/Cole.

Good, T. L., & Brophy, J. (1986). School effects. In M. Wittrock (Ed.), *Handbook of research on teaching* (3rd ed., pp. 570–604). New York: Macmillan.

Good, T. L., & Grouws, D. A. (1979). The Missouri Mathematics Effectiveness Project: An experimental study in fourth-grade classrooms. *Journal of Educational Psychology, 71,* 355–362.

Good, T. L., & Grouws, D. A. (1981). *Experimental research in secondary mathematics classrooms: Working with teachers.* Columbia: University of Missouri. (ERIC Document Reproduction Service No. ED 219 261)

Gove, P. B. (Ed. in chief.). (1971). *Webster's third new international dictionary of the English language unabridged.* Springfield, MA: G & C Merriam.

Griffin, G., & Barnes, S. (1986). Using research findings to change school and classroom practices: Results of an experimental study. *American Educational Research Journal. 23*(4), 572–586.

Guilford, J. (1962). Creativity: Its measurement and development. In S. Parnes & H. Harding (Eds.), *A sourcebook for creative thinking* (pp. 151–168). New York: Charles Scribner's Sons.

Hagman, J., & Rose, A. (1983). Retention of military tasks: A review. *Human Factors, 25*(2), 199–213.

Halding, D. H. (1965). *Principles of training.* New York: Pergamon Press.

Hall, R. V. (1971). Training teachers in classroom use of contingency management. *Educational Technology, 11*(4), 33–38.

Harding, D. (1965). *Principles of training.* New York: Pergamon Press.

Harris, A. (1989). *A search for sources of treatment effects in a teacher effectiveness training program.* Paper presented at the annual meeting of the American Educational Research Association, San Francisco, CA.

Hayes, S. C., Munt, E. D., Korn, Z., Welfert, E., Rossenfarb, I., & Zettle, R. D. (1986). The effect of feedback and self-reinforcement instructions on studying performance. *Psychological Record, 36*(1), 27–37.

Hills, P. J. (1982). *A dictionary of education.* London: Routledge and Kegan Paul.

Hinnrichs, J. R. (1976). Personnel training. In M. D. Dunnette (Ed.), *Handbook of industrial and organizational psychology* (pp. 237–249). Chicago: Rand McNally.

Horton, G. O. (1975). Generalization of teacher behavior as a function of subject matter specific discrimination training. *Journal of Applied Behavior Analysis, 8,* 311–319.

Hough, J. B., & Amidon, E. J. (1967). Behavioral change in student teachers. In E. J. Amidon & J. B. Hough (Eds.), *Interaction analysis: Theory, research & application* (pp. 307–314). Reading, MA: Addison-Wesley.

Hough, J. B., Lohman, E. E., & Ober, R. (1969). Shaping and predicting verbal teaching behavior in a general methods course. *Journal of Teacher Education, 20,* 213–224.

Hough, J. B., & Ober, R. (1966). *The effect of training in interaction analysis on the verbal teaching behavior of preservice teachers.* Paper presented at the meeting of the American Educational Research Association, Chicago. (ERIC Document Reproduction Service No. ED 011 252)

Houston, W. R. (1987). Competency-based teacher education. In M. J. Dunkin (Ed.), *International encyclopedia of teaching and teacher education* (pp. 86–96). Elmsford, NY: Pergamon.

Howsam, R. B., Corrigan, D., Denemark, J., & Nash, R. (1976). *Educating a profession.* Washington, DC: American Association of Colleges for Teacher Education.

Huberman, M. (1985). What knowledge is of most worth to teachers: A knowledge use perspective. *Teaching and teacher education, 1*(3), 251–262.

Hudgins, B. (1974). *Self-contained training materials for teacher education: A derivation from research on the learning of complex skills.* Bloomington, IN: Indiana University, National Center for the Development of Training Materials in Teacher Education.

Hunter, M. (1986). Comments on the Napa county, California, follow-through project. *Elementary School Journal, 87,* 173–180.

Hurst, J. B. (1974). Competency-based modules & inquiry teaching. *Journal of Experimental Education, 43*(2), 35–39.

Jackson, P. (1965). The way teaching is. *NEA Journal, 54*(8), 10–13.

Jensen, L. C., & Young, J. I. (1972). Effect of televised simulated instruction on subsequent teaching. *Journal of Educational Psychology, 63,* 368–373.

Johnson, J. L., & Sloat, K. C. M. (1980). Teacher training effects: Real or illusory? *Psychology in the Schools, 17*(1), 109–115.

Joyce, B., & Showers, B. (1980). Improving inservice training: The messages of research. *Educational Leadership, 37*(5), 379–385.

Joyce, B., & Showers, B. (1981). Transfer of training: The contribution of coaching. *Journal of Education, 163,* 163–172.

Joyce, B. R., & Showers, B. (1983). *Power in staff development through research in training.* Alexandria, VA.: Association for Supervision and Curriculum Development. (ERIC Document Reproduction Service No. ED 240 677)

Joyce, B., & Showers, B. (1988). *Student achievement through staff development.* New York: Longman.

Joyce, B., Showers, B., & Rolheiser-Bennett, C. (1987). Staff development and student learning: A synthesis of research on models of teaching. *Educational Leadership, 45*(2), 11–23.

Kallenbach, W. W., & Gall, M. D. (1969). Microteaching versus conventional methods in training elementary intern teachers. *Journal of Educational Research, 63,* 136–141.

Katz, G. (1976). Use of minicourse instruction with student teachers of educable mentally retarded children. *Journal of Educational Research, 69,* 355–359.

Kemler-Nelson, D. (1984). The effect of intention on what concepts are acquired. *Journal of Verbal Learning and Verbal Behavior, 23*(6), 734–759.

Kersh, B. (1962). The classroom simulator. *Journal of Teacher Education, 13,* 109–110.

Kersh, B. (1963). *Classroom simulation: A new dimension in teacher education, final report* (Title VII, Project Number 886, National Defense Education Act of 1958, Grant Number 7-47-0000-164). Washington, DC: U.S. Department of Health, Education and Welfare.

Kieras, D., & Bovair, S. (1986). The acquisition of procedures from text: A production-system analysis of transfer of training. *Journal of Memory and Language, 65*(3), 507–524.

Kirk, J. (1967). Elementary school student teachers & interaction analysis. In E. J. Amidon & J. B. Hough (Eds.) *Interaction analysis: Theory, research & application* (pp. 299–306). Reading, MA: Addison-Wesley.

Klesius, J., Searls, E., & Zielonka, P. (1989). *The effectiveness of the direct instruction model for training preservice teachers.* Paper presented at the annual meeting of the American Educational Research Association, San Francisco, CA.

Kluecker, J. (1974). Effects of protocol and training materials. In L. D. Brown (Ed.), *Acquiring teaching competencies: Reports and studies* (No. 6) (pp. 6–33). Bloomington, IN: Indiana University, National Center for the Development of Training Materials in Teacher Education. (ERIC Reproduction Service No. ED 144 926)

Komaki, J., Heinzman, A., & Lawson, L. (1980). Effect of training and feedback: Component analysis of a behavioral safety program. *Journal of Applied Psychology, 65*(3), 261–270.

Koran, J. J. (1969). The relative effects of classroom instruction and subsequent observational learning on the acquisition of questioning behavior by pre-service elementary science teachers. *Journal of Research in Science Teaching, 6,* 217–223.

Koran, J. J. (1970). A comparison of the effects of observational learning and self-rating on the acquisition and retention of a questioning behavior by elementary science teacher trainees. *Science Education, 54,* 385–389.

Koran, J. J. (1971). A study of the effects of written and film-mediated models on the acquisition of a science teaching skill by preservice elementary teachers. *Journal of Research in Science Teaching, 8,* 45–50.

Koran, M. S., Snow, R. E., & McDonald, F. J. (1971). Teacher aptitude and observational learning of a teaching skill. *Journal of Educational Psychology, 62,* 219–228.

Krathwohl, D., Bloom, B., & Maria, B. (1964). *Taxonomy of educational objectives: The classification of educational goals: Handbook II. Affective domain.* New York: David McKay.

Langer, D., & Allen, G. E. (1970). *The minicourse as a tool for training teachers in interaction analysis.* Paper presented at the annual meeting of the American Educational Research Association, Minneapolis. (ERIC Document Reproduction Service No. ED 037 393)

Latham, P., & Saari, M. (1979). Application of social learning theory to training supervisors through behavior modeling. *Journal of Applied Psychology, 64,* 239–246.

LeBaron, W. (1969). *Systems analysis and learning systems in the development of elementary teacher education models.* Washington, DC: U.S. Department of Health, Education and Welfare.

Liebert, R., Wicks-Nelson, R., & Vail, R. (1986). *Developmental psychology* (4th ed.). Englewood Cliffs, NJ: Prentice-Hall.

Lohman, E. E., Ober, R., & Hough, J. B. (1967). A study of the effect of pre-service training in interaction analysis on the verbal behavior of student teachers. In E. J. Amidon & J. B. Hough (Eds.), *Interaction analysis: Theory, research and application* (pp. 346–359). Reading, MA: Addison-Wesley.

Lombard, A. S., Konicek, R. D., & Schultz, K. (1985). Description and evaluation of an inservice model for implementation of a learning cycle approach in the secondary science classrooms. *Science Education, 69,* 491–500.

Lucas, C. J. (1985). Why teacher education needs educational foundations courses. *Education Digest, 50*(5), 48–49.

Luebkemann, H. H. (1965). *The effects of selected student teaching program variables on certain values and certain verbal behaviors of student teachers.* Unpublished doctoral dissertation, Pennsylvania State University.

Lunetta, V. (1985). School transactions. *Conduit.* Ames, IA: University of Iowa.

Lung, C., & Dominowski, R. (1985). Effects of strategy instructions and practice on nine-dot problem solving. *Journal of Experimental Psychology: Learning, Memory and Cognition, 11*(4), 804–811.

MacLeod, G. R. (1987). Microteaching: Modeling. In M. J. Dunkin, (Ed.), *The international encyclopedia of teaching and teacher education* (pp. 720–722). Oxford: Pergamon.

MacLeod, G., & McIntyre, D. (1977). Towards a model for microteaching. In D. McIntyre, G. MacLeod, & R. Griffiths (Eds.), *Investigations of microteaching* (pp. 253–263). London: Croom Helm.

Mager, R. (1962). *Preparing objectives for programmed instruction.* San Francisco: Fearon Press.

McKee, A. (1986). *Reflective teaching as a strategy in TAFE teacher education.* Paper presented at the South Pacific Association of Teacher Education Conference, Perth, Australia.

Medley, D. M. (1977). *Teacher competence and teacher effectiveness: A review of process–product research*. Washington, DC: American Association of Colleges for Teacher Education. (ERIC Document Reproduction Service No. ED 143 629)

Medley, D. M. (1984). Teacher competency testing and teacher education. In L. G. Katz & J. D. Raths (Eds.), *Advances in teacher education* (Vol. 1, pp. 51–94). Norwood, NJ: Ablex.

Metcalf, K. (1989). *An investigation of the efficacy of a research-based regimen of skill development on the instructional clarity of preservice teachers*. Unpublished doctoral dissertation, The Ohio State University, Columbus, OH.

Mitzel, H. (1960). Teacher effectiveness. In C. Harris (Ed.), *Encyclopedia of educational research* (pp. 1481–1485). New York: Macmillan.

Morine-Dershimer, G. (1987). Creating a recycling center for teacher thinking. In E. Doak, T. Hipple, & M. Keith (Eds.), *Simulation and clinical knowledge in teacher education*. Knoxville: University of Tennessee, College of Education.

Nairne, J. (1986). Active and passive processing during primary rehearsal. *American Journal of Psychology*, 99(3), 301–314.

Nolan, J. (1982). Professional laboratory experiences: The missing link in teacher education. *Journal of Teacher Education*, 33(4), 49–53.

Norman, D. (1980). Cognitive engineering and education. In D. T. Tuma & F. Reif (Eds.), *Problem solving in education: Issues in teaching and research* (pp. 97–107). Hillsdale, NJ: Lawrence Erlbaum.

O'Sullivan, J., & Pressley, M. (1984). Completeness of instruction and strategy transfer. *Journal of Experimental Child Psychology*, 38(2), 275–285.

Pankratz, R., Martray, C., Becker, J., & Law, S. (1983). *Interactive video: A unique tool for development of behavior management skills*. Paper presented at the meeting of the American Association of Colleges for Teacher Education, Detroit.

Patterson, G. R. (1971). Behavioral intervention procedures in the classroom and in the home. In A. E. Bergin & S. L. Garfield (Eds.), *Handbook of psychotherapy and behavior change* (pp. 751–775). New York: Wiley.

Peck, R., & Tucker, J. (1973). Research on teacher education. In R. M. W. Travers (Ed.), *Second handbook of research on teaching* (pp. 940–978). Chicago: Rand McNally.

Pegg, J. (1985). *The effect of practice on the acquisition of teaching skills*. Unpublished doctoral dissertation, University of New England, Armidale, Australia.

Perrott, E. (1987). Minicourses. In M. J. Dunkin (Ed.), *The International encyclopedia of teaching and teacher education* (pp. 764–772). Oxford: Pergamon Press.

Peterson, T. L. (1973). Microteaching in the preservice education of teachers: Time for a reexamination. *Journal of Educational Research*, 67, 34–36.

Plowman, P. (1971). *Behavioral objectives*. Chicago: Science Research Associates.

Porter, A. (1986). From research on teaching to staff development: A difficult step. *Elementary School Journal*, 87, 159–165.

Porterfield, D. (1974). Influence of inquiry-discovery science preparation on questioning behavior of reading teachers. *Reading Teacher*, 27, 589–593.

Purkey, S., & Smith, M. (1983). Effective schools: A review. *Elementary School Journal*, 83(4), 427–452.

Putnam, J., & Johns, B. (1987). The potential of demonstration teaching as a component for teacher preparation and staff development programs. *International Journal of Educational Research*, 11(5), 577–587.

Putnam, R. (1983). *A computer simulation for studying teachers' diagnoses and decisions*. Paper presented at the meeting of the American Educational Research Association, Montreal.

Putnam, R. (1987). Structuring and adjusting content for students: A study of live and simulated tutoring of addition. *American Educational Research Journal*, 24(1), 13–48.

Raymond, A. (1973). The acquisition of nonverbal behaviors by preservice science teachers and their application during student teaching. *Journal of Research in Science Teaching*, 10, 13–24.

Reed, C. L., Van Mondfranz, A. D., & Smith, T. M. (1970). *The effect of microteaching, directive, and nondirective lectures on achievement and attitudes in a basic educational psychology course*. Paper presented at the meeting of the American Educational Research Association, Minneapolis. (ERIC Document Reproduction Service No. ED 037 390)

Rentel, V. (1974). A protocol materials evaluation: The language of children. *Journal of Teacher Education*, 25, 323–329.

Ribler, R. (1983). *Training development guide*. Englewood Cliffs, NJ: Prentice-Hall.

Ringer, V. M. J. (1973). The use of a "token helper" in the management of classroom behavior problems and in teacher training. *Journal of Applied Behavior Analysis*, 6, 671–677.

Robbins, P. (1986). The Napa-Vacaville follow-through project: Qualitative outcomes, related procedures, and implications for practice. *Elementary School Journal*, 87, 139–158.

Robertson, E. (1987). Teaching and related activities. In M. J. Dunkin (Ed.), *International encyclopedia of teaching and teacher education* (pp. 15–18). Oxford: Pergamon Press.

Rosenshine, B. (1971). *Teaching behaviors and student achievement*. London: National Foundation for Educational Research.

Rosenshine, B., & Berliner, D. (1978). Academic engaged time. *British Journal of Teacher Education*, 4(1), 3–16.

Ross, B. (1984). Reminders and their effects in learning a cognitive skill. *Cognitive Psychology*, 16(3), 371–416.

Rowan, B., Bossert, S., & Dwyer, D. (1983). Research on effective schools: A cautionary note. *Educational Researcher*, 12(4), 24–31.

Sandefer, J. T., Pankratz, R., & Couch, J. (1967). *Observation and demonstration in teacher education by closed-circuit television and video-tape recordings* (Final report, research project no. 5-1009, title III-A, NPEA, PL. 85-864). Emporia, KS: Kansas State Teachers College. (ERIC Document Reproduction Service No. ED 014 904)

Santiesteban, A. J., & Koran, J. J. (1977). Acquisition of science teaching skills through psychological modeling and concommitant student learning. *Journal of Research in Science Teaching*, 14(3), 199–207.

Saunders, W., Nielson, E., Gall, M. D., & Smith, G. (1975). The effects of variations in microteaching on prospective teachers' acquisition of questioning skills. *Journal of Educational Research*, 69, 3–8.

Sharan, S., & Hertz-Lazarowitz, R. (1982). Effects of an instructional change program on teachers' behavior, attitudes, and perceptions. *Journal of Applied Behavior Science*, 18(2), 185–201.

Silberman, C. E. (1970). *Crisis in the classroom: The remaking of American education*. New York: Random House.

Simon, A., & Boyer, E. (1968). *Mirrors for behavior: An anthology of classroom observation instruments*. Philadelphia, PA.: Temple University, Center for the Study of Teaching.

Simpson, E. (1972). The classification of educational objectives in the psychomotor domain. In *The Psychomotor Domain: A resource book for media specialists* (Vol. 3, pp. 43–56). Washington, DC: Gryphon House.

Slavin, R. (1986). The Napa evaluation of Madeline Hunter's ITIP: Lessons learned. *Elementary School Journal*, 87, 165–172.

Sloat, K. C. M., Tharp, R. G., & Gallimore, R. (1977). The incremental effectiveness of classroom-based teacher training techniques. *Behavior Therapy, 8,* 810–818.

Smith, B. O., Cohen, S. B., & Pearl, A. (1969). *Teachers for the real world.* Washington, DC: American Association of Colleges for Teacher Education.

Smith, B., & Ennis, R. (1961). *Language and concepts in education.* Chicago: Rand McNally.

Smith, B., Meux, M., Coombs, D., & Szoke, R. (1962). *A study of the logic of teaching* [mimeo]. Urbana, IL: University of Illinois.

Smith, B. O., Silverman, S., Borg, J., & Fry, B. (1980). *A design for a school of pedagogy.* Washington, DC: U.S. Department of Education.

Stallings, J. (1982). Effective strategies for teaching basic skills. In D. Wallace (Ed.), *Developing basic skills programs in secondary schools* (pp. 1–19). Alexandria, VA: Association for Supervision and Curriculum Development.

Stallings, J., & Krasavage, E. (1986). Program implementation and student achievement in a four-year Madeline Hunter follow-through project. *Elementary School Journal, 87,* 117–138.

Stallings, J., Needels, M., & Stayrook, N. (1979). *How to change the process of teaching basic reading skills in secondary schools: Phase II & phase III* (Grant No. NIE-G-77-0001). Washington: DC: National Institute of Education. (ERIC Document Reproduction Service No. ED 210 670)

Strang, H. R., Badt, K. S., & Kauffman, J. M., (1987). Microcomputer-based simulations for training fundamental teaching skills. *Journal of Teacher Education, 38*(1), 20–26.

Sturgess, P. T. (1972). Information delay and retention: Effect of information in feedback and tests. *Journal of Educational Psychology, 63,* 32–43.

Taba, H., Levine, S., & Elzey, F. (n.d.). *Thinking in elementary school children* (Cooperation Research Project No. 1574). San Francisco: San Francisco State College.

Thomson, C. L., & Cooper, M. L. (1969). *The modification of teacher behaviors which modify child behaviors* (Tech. Research Rep. No. 19). Lawrence, KS: Head Start Evaluation and Research Center. (ERIC Document Reproduction Service No. ED 042 499)

Tillema, H., & Veenman, S. (1987). Conceptualizing training methods in teacher education. *International Journal of Educational Research, 11*(5), 519–529.

Travers, R. M. W. (Ed.) (1973). *Second handbook of research on teaching.* Chicago: Rand McNally.

Troyer, M. (1988). *The effects of reflective teaching and a supplemental theoretical component on preservice teachers' reflectivity in analyzing classroom teaching situations.* Unpublished doctoral dissertation, The Ohio State University, Columbus.

Turner, R. (1973a). *A general catalog of teaching skills.* Bloomington, IN: Indiana University.

Turner, R. (1973b). *Generic teaching skills in teacher skills training.* Bloomington, IN: Indiana University, National Center for the Development of Training Materials in Teacher Education.

Turney, C., Clift, J., Dunkin, M., & Traill, R. (1973) *Microteaching: Research, theory and practice.* Sydney, Australia: Sydney University Press.

Twelker, P. (1970). *Development of low-cost instructional simulation materials for teacher education* (U.S. Department of Health, Education and Welfare, Office of Education, Cooperative Research Project No. 5-0916). Monmouth, OR: Oregon State System of Higher Education, Teaching Research. (ERIC Document Reproduction Service No. ED 045 553)

Vlcek, C. (1966). *Assessing the effect and transfer value of a classroom simulator technique.* Unpublished doctoral dissertation, Michigan State University.

Wade, B. (1985), Teacher development: The challenge of the future. *Journal of Teacher Education, 36*(1), 52–57.

Wagner, A. C. (1973). Changing teacher behavior: A comparison of microteaching and cognitive discrimination training. *Journal of Educational Psychology, 64,* 299–305.

Walberg, H. (1984). Improving the productivity of America's schools. *Educational Leadership, 41*(8), 19–30.

Waldrop, P., Justen, E., & Adams, E. (1986). A comparison of three types of feedback in a computer assisted instruction task. *Educational Technology, 26*(11), 43–45.

Withall, J. (1949). The development of a technique for the measurement of social-emotional climate in classrooms. *Journal of Experimental Education, 17,* 347–361.

Wittrock, M. C. (Ed.). (1986). *Handbook of research on teaching* (3rd ed.). New York: Macmillan.

Wong, S., & Iwata, B. (1978). *Training behavioral contractors to conduct initial assessment interviews.* Paper presented at the annual convention of the Association for Behavioral Analysis, Dearborn, MI. (ERIC Document Reproduction Service No. ED 178 787)

Woolfolk, A. E., & Woolfolk, R. L. (1974). A contingency management technique for increasing student attention in a small group setting. *Journal of School Psychology, 12,* 204–212.

Wyer, R., & Frey, D. (1983). The effect of feedback about self and others on the recall and judgments of feedback relevant information. *Journal of Experimental Social Psychology, 19*(6), 540–559.

Yeany, R. H. (1978). Effects of microteaching with videotaping and strategy analysis on the teaching strategies of preservice science teachers. *Science Education, 62,* 203–207.

Zahoric, J. A. (1986). Acquiring teaching skills. *Journal of Teacher Education, 37*(2), 21–25.

Zeichner, K. (1987). Preparing reflective teachers: An overview of instructional strategies which have been employed in preservice teacher education. *International Journal of Educational Research, 11*(5), 565–575.

Zevin, J. (1973). Training teachers in inquiry. *Social Education, 37,* 310–316.

·28·

TECHNOLOGY AND TEACHER EDUCATION

Douglas Brooks
MIAMI UNIVERSITY

Thomas W. Kopp
MIAMI UNIVERSITY

A chapter focusing on the presence and effectiveness of technology in the training of teachers is timely in professional education. The authors have been able to reference major reports by the U.S. Congress, Office of Technology Assessment (1988), and the National Task Force on Educational Technology (1988); special issues of respected journals devoted to the instrumentation of the information age and its relationship to education (McClintock, 1988); international reviews of the field (Fauquet, 1986); reviews focusing on specific instructional applications of technology (Frager, 1985); and vendor product initiatives.

Technology is maturing quickly in the information age. The computer industry has made important strides in user-friendly hardware and software. The cost of hardware is decreasing and storage capabilities are geometrically increasing. University and K–12 environments are being recognized as important socialization zones for life long computer use and have become the object of vendor support. Funding structures such as interest-free university loans are being recommended to facilitate the acquisition of technology in its various forms. Product designers are becoming more imaginative in their design of software. Application of the computer to the management of video data bases is becoming increasingly refined. Perhaps most exciting of all, the hardware and software for implementing and applying computer networks to the learning process could transform institutionally based learning as currently supported, funded, and known. "In its broadest sense, a frontier is

what is crossed when an irreversible action has been initiated" (McClintock, 1988, p. 345). A new frontier for teaching and learning interactions has been entered with a distinctive ecology of videocassette recorders (VCRs), computer graphics, videodiscs, laser pointers, laser disks, projection pads, and computer networks.

The purpose of this review is to provide a document that increases the probability of focused research and development on the applications and outcomes of technology in teacher education. Glaser and Cooley (1973) define technology "in its broadest sense, as the application of science to practice". They suggest that "a new and exciting development that could hasten progress is the recognition that scientific principles can be designed into teaching instruments and systems which can then become available to the teacher to use in guiding the learning of students" (p. 833). Thus, as in their conceptualization, this chapter seeks to review and describe ways in which instrumentation and the application of instructional technology might facilitate the distribution of scientific information in undergraduate teacher education programs. To stimulate increased focus and activity, the review developed in the following ways and is limited to:

1. Reports that have reviewed or made recommendations on the application of technology to the training of teachers. This body of research naturally breaks down into preservice and inservice categories. Not included are studies that re-

The authors wish to thank David Jonassen (University of Colorado), Walter Wager (Florida State University), Hal Lawson and Allen Berger (Miami University of Ohio), and Hans Klinzing (University of Tübingen, West Germany) for their external reviews and comments on this manuscript. Particular thanks goes to John Sikula for his patient editing. The authors wish to thank Marilyn Vankat for her diligent and thorough library research assistance and Kim Miley for her organizational and word-processing skills.

port the application of technology to the teaching of K–12 or university students, other than students in teacher education programs or teachers in inservice training programs.

2. Investigations that report the effects of a particular technological treatment effect within a teacher-training program. This review is not of the field of instructional technology. Not referenced are the myriad of studies that lament the negative effects of technology.

This review concludes that an alarming state of the art currently exists. Undergraduate teacher-training institutions are not taking a convincing or focused leadership role in identifying solid evidence about the applications of technology to teacher training. The best and most consistent exposure for teachers to classroom-relevant technologies is often at the inservice or private sector level. In short, the information age has yet to significantly influence teacher training.

CHAPTER ORGANIZATION

Howey and Zimpher (1987) recommend a thematic approach to undergraduate teacher education program design as a characteristic of excellent undergraduate programs. Thus, although other approaches to a review of technology in teacher education were possible, a thematic analysis seemed particularly promising. Brooks, Moore, and Ziegler (1987) report a comprehensive undergraduate teacher education program structure referred to as the Information Management Model that features 16 entry-level professional-development statements. The 16 entry and related exit performance statements serve as program themes for organizing the professional knowledge base within the program. The 16 program themes permit the development of a systems approach to undergraduate teacher training as suggested by Parker, Varnell, and Rinewalt (1983).

Applied within the Miami University undergraduate teacher education program, the 16 themes are statements of programmatic intent and curricular responsibility. The statements of professional development are introduced to entering teacher education candidates. These statements are directly related, in vocabulary and curricular commitment, to exit-level performance expectations for student teaching. The statements are sequenced deliberately from fundamental information on learner characteristics to the important concern for long-term professional development. They are designed to develop teaching candidates' abilities and skills, from simple identification and comprehension to complex requirements for analysis, synthesis, performance, and problem solving. As these statements evolve, they require the capacity to recall, comprehend, and apply prior knowledge included in preceding statements.

Each program theme includes topic areas of knowledge, skills, attitudes, and values that define it. The topic list following each theme is not intended to be inclusive or exclusive of topics or content; rather, it provides examples of potentially related curricular information. The same topic approached from different perspectives or different levels could become eligible for inclusion in several professional-development statements. The same topic at various levels of performance expec-

tation becomes eligible for spiraling across several courses or experiences within the program. A "Statement of Desired Exit Performance" is listed for each of the 16 themes. The purpose is to suggest a domain of possible expectations for exiting student teachers.

Research studies meeting review criteria were categorized by themes and then assigned to one of the six levels of cognition within Bloom's Taxonomy (Bloom, Engelhart, Furst, Hill, & Krathwohl, 1956). This categorization strategy permitted examination of a study's cognitive level of application, as well as of its application to a programmatic theme. For each citation the level of application of the study taxonomically is indicated using the following symbols: (K)nowledge, (C)omprehension, (AP)plication, (AN)alysis, (S)ynthesis, and (E)valuation. For example, Strang, Kauffman, Badt, Murphy, and Loper (1987: AN) was placed in the theme "Implements Individual and Group Management Skills." It has been assigned the analysis level in Bloom's cognitive domain (AN). The sequence of categorization for a reference (AN, AP) suggests the dominance of one cognitive level over another and acknowledges the breadth of the study. The studies cited within each theme are referenced in chronological order, with the most recent studies listed first. The date-of-publication format, as distinct from the more standardized alphabetical format, permits chronological comparisons of research focus and frequency within and between program themes.

Three questions were applied to every study reviewed:

1. Was the study intended to examine the acquisition of undergraduate or inservice teacher knowledge, skills attitudes, or values using technology as the treatment effect?
2. Which of the 16 programmatic themes does the study appear to address?
3. Which level of cognition within Bloom's Taxonomy does the study suggest or require?

The program theme approach to this review was extended by creating a section under each theme entitled "Potential Applications of Technology to Obtain This Performance." This section within each of the 16 program themes is intended to be realistic inside emerging technologies and is recommended to address multiple levels of Bloom's cognitive domain.

The review structure of programmatic themes, levels of cognition, exit performance statements, and potentials for application should encourage teacher educators to classify their courses or program assignments within particular programmatic themes. Once having identified them, teacher educators can more easily begin to systematically investigate the applications of technology to teacher training.

PROGRAM THEMES FOR TEACHER EDUCATION

1. Identifies Learner's Emotional, Social, Physical, and Intellectual Characteristics for the Purpose of Instruction

This statement of programmatic intention is included to address topics and experiences in the general area of identity;

self-concept; emotional problems; moral judgment; value development; physical growth; psychophysical development; family; peers; school relations; and vocational interests. No studies were identified within this program theme.

Statement of Desired Exit Performance

1. Demonstrate an ability to use the vocabulary of pupil traits and characteristics.
2. Relate a knowledge of pupil traits and characteristics to explanations for professional behavior.

Potential Applications of Technology to Obtain This Performance

1. Develop videotaped examples of how various learner characteristics manifest themselves in school settings, to give students a visual portrayal of what textbook descriptions look like in reality.
2. Let students try diagnostic work with computerized profiles from simulated school records. Students could then try to recommend instructional strategies based on the documents, with the computer evaluating the success of these efforts.
3. Design interactive computer systems whereby vignettes of typical learner behavior are presented, with students' reactions related to probable antecedents for such behavior.
4. Develop, conduct, and videotape for discussion role-playing simulations wherein students take on the roles of students with specific emotional, social, and intellectual characteristics.
5. Use computer-graphics generation and storage to create, for analysis by students, artifacts of special learner characteristics such as drawings from emotionally disturbed children.
6. Use computer networks that link field sites with university supervisors to carry curricular information on learner characteristics to preservice teachers.
7. Develop with learners with special needs or characteristics collections of audiotaped or videotaped interviews on what the schooling process is like for them. Interviewees could be learning disabled, emotionally disturbed, physically handicapped, or merely the smallest child in the class, the early maturing girl, or the extremely shy pupil.

Conclusions and Recommendations. The most glaring conclusion is that no research studies conformed to the criteria and demonstrated the effects of a technological enhancement to address the broad range of learner characteristics. The simple knowledge level of preservice student cognitive activity may be addressed by the standard lecture on Piaget's stages of intellectual development. When the lecture becomes difficult to recall in student teaching, a computer network could facilitate access to the original information.

The field experience might send untrained eyes and suspect memories to the context of the classroom. Preservice students are likely to see what they want to see or focus on less significant events. They return to the regular university classroom with selective memories of events but no common frame of reference. However, the more advanced levels of student cognitive activity such as analysis, synthesis, and problem solving might better be served with professor-led analyses of student characteristics on a videotape complemented with classroom discussion. Systematic study of the applications of technology to the identification of learner characteristics for the purpose of instruction must begin.

2. Identifies and Provides a Rationale, Goals, and Objectives in Curricular Planning

This statement of programmatic intention is included to address topics and experiences in the general area of curricular models, needs assessments, instructional models, behavioral objectives, stages of instruction, and taxonomies. Studies reported within this program theme are Henrie and Whiteford (1972: AP) and Judy (1969: K).

Statement of Desired Exit Performance

1. Write clearly stated objectives appropriate to expectations.
2. Use instructional plans consistently.
3. Modify plans in response to pupil achievement.
4. Provide pupils with performance expectations.

Potential Applications of Technology to Obtain This Performance

1. Computer simulations can be used to show hypothetical outcomes of the planning process, with students modifying plans and observing resultant changes in a simulated classroom.
2. Computer networks, with the appropriate software, would permit the exchange of preliminary lesson plans between student teacher and university supervisor. The editing could be stored and used for prerequisite class examples.
3. Simulations and games could be used in group settings to give highly interactive, simulated experience in the planning process.
4. Videotaped examples of unsuccessful class activities could be analyzed by students for possible errors and oversights in the planning process.
5. Professional-development audiocassettes could be produced, as in the corporate sector, to help teachers come to view such planning as a key to professional happiness and success.

Conclusions and Recommendations. The authors found two references to technologically enhanced preservice training that addressed the basics of curricular planning. This area of professional teacher training is often cited by undergraduates and inservice classroom teachers as the segment that is least motivating and most detached from the reality of the undergraduate curriculum. The courses are sometimes included with foundations courses and, by virtue of their early program timing or sequence, are further removed from the realities of classroom application. It is the absence of the opportunity to observe the consequences of a particular plan that fuels preservice student malaise with this content. By not learning the consequences of good and bad planning, preservice students might learn not to value effective planning. Systematic study of the applications of technology to curricular planning that increases the motivation to plan must begin now.

3. Designs Instructional Methodology in Media and Technology Appropriate to Instructional Goals and Objectives

This statement of programmatic intention is included to address topics and experiences in the general area of instructional models for basic skill acquisition, social attitudes, personal development, problem solving, and critical thinking. Central to this statement would be instructional systems such as audio-media demonstration, film, audio tutorials, lecture, mastery, television, text, discussion, projects, computer-assisted instruction, contract learning, videodisc technology, interactive video, and teleconferencing. Studies identified within this program theme include Forcheri and Molfino (1986: AN, AP); Connett (1985: AP); McBride (1985: AP); M. K. Johnson & Amundsen (1983: AP); Snyder & Anderson (1980: AP); Yelon (1980: AP); Bonar (1976: AP); Rosenshine (1977: AP); Meierhenry (1970: AP); and Meierhenry (1976: AP).

Statement of Desired Exit Performance

1. Select an instructional system appropriate to the instructional goal.
2. Match instructional models to appropriate goals.
3. Evaluate the appropriateness of curricular organization.
4. Use media and technology effectively.

Potential Applications of Technology to Obtain This Performance

1. Help students develop a commitment to instructional media usage by conducting units that begin with the most comfortable media such as snapshot cameras and Walkmans, and, after gaining confidence with this layer of media complexity, gradually move to progressively higher forms of instructional technology.
2. Videotape case studies of teachers who have successfully used media interventions in classes and use them to model effective instructional technology use.
3. Help preservice teachers begin to anticipate the range of problems and constraints that can occur during media use by developing computer simulations of planning and conducting a mediated lesson.
4. Use media to create some exciting, entertaining, and highly effective learning experiences. Videotapes of such performances can be made to show the full potential of this form of instructional presentation.

Conclusions and Recommendations. Ten studies are reported in the theme area of designing instruction for preservice

teacher training using media and technology. These are studies in which a technological treatment effect was applied in a university teacher-training context to test the effects of technological enhancement on preservice student achievement. Studies are not being done in sufficient enough numbers or with sufficient enough frequency to establish a need to do the research, let alone test the effects of the technological enhancements on preservice training. Freestanding media courses should service professors and students. Advanced technologies should be visible to undergraduates in every course in the professional curriculum. Preservice teachers need to see the technologies being used confidently by instructors. This modeling will announce the value of the technological applications in their own classrooms.

4. Selects and Adopts Curricular Resources Including Media and Technology Appropriate to Identified Instructional Goals and Objectives

This statement of programmatic intention is included to address topics and experiences in the general area of media utilization, community, school and regional resources, and curricular classification systems such as basic text series and visual curricular systems associated with specific technology. No studies were identified within this program theme.

Statement of Desired Exit Performance

1. Select and secure curricular resources.
2. Produce materials and systems of good quality.
3. Use and adapt curricular resources, media, and technology creatively.

Potential Applications of Technology to Obtain This Performance

1. Video briefings and tours of educational agencies and facilities such as museums and zoos can give students insight into making use of the instructional potential of such community resources.
2. Computerized curricular resource indices and data bases, such as ERIC, can give students experience with information retrieval. Scaled-down computer networks could provide preservice experience with curriculum access, storage, and retrieval.
3. Teacher guides, lesson plans, and other such stock curricular resources can be given to students in the form of word-processed documents. In such form, students can then easily practice modifying them for use with specific groups of learners.

Conclusion and Recommendations. Instructional methods designed to include media and technology need to be tested for their applications in teacher-training contexts. Films, computers, and videotapes used in instruction need to be tested for the effects of their usage on student achievement of the objectives of the teacher education program. A section of preservice students could be sent to a field experience using the standard format of multiple placements, cars, appointments, and debriefings. Another section of students could analyze, on campus, a videotape of a typical classroom, with the benefit of rewind, pause, volume control, a laser pointer, the instructor's insights, and group discussion. The effects of one experience over the other could be measured. Recommendations enhancing teacher training could be suggested, if it were proven that one type of experience was more productive than the other in accomplishing the same program objective.

5. Develops Curricular Materials That Reflect a Culturally Diverse Society

This statement of programmatic intention is intended to address topics and experiences in the general area of evaluating, selecting, and developing curricular materials with positive references to examples, models, and methods for diverse cultures. Topics might include multicultural unit development, text evaluation, and evaluation of materials for a sexist, ethnic, or cultural bias. No studies were identified within this program theme.

Statement of Desired Exit Performance

1. Demonstrate a knowledge of ethnic and cultural groups.
2. Plan instruction to include contributions of ethnic/cultural groups.
3. Adapt curricular materials and plan units to include ethnic/cultural groups.

Potential Applications of Technology to Obtain This Performance

1. Collect and view video recordings of the customs, foods, and life-styles of other cultures. Public and instructional television can be valuable resources in locating these recorded experiences.
2. Use computer networks in cross-cultural, problem-solving activities, to allow students to examine cultural differences, their own ethnicity, and any attitudes or misconceptions they might harbor toward others of differing ethnic/cultural backgrounds.
3. Use satellite broadcasts from abroad to give students the chance to interact with other cultures.
4. Use video interviews with actual schoolchildren to help reveal the kinds of cultural, ethnic, and racial stereotypes and misconceptions that are innocently or otherwise harbored. Video interviews can sensitize new teachers to a side of learners that is often difficult to assess accurately.

Conclusions and Recommendations. No studies could be found that tested technological enhancements in preservice teacher training to assist students in developing curricular materials reflecting a culturally diverse society. Systematic study of the application of technology in preparing preservice teachers to develop culturally diverse curricular materials must begin.

6. Develops Curricular Materials and Instructional Methodologies to Enhance the Learning of Culturally Different Pupils

This statement of programmatic intention is included to address topics related to maintaining high expectations for culturally different students, honoring and valuing cultural alternatives, using cross-cultural communication, employing appropriate tests and testing strategies, giving attention to learning styles and environment, and checking for cultural bias in tests. No studies were reported within this program theme.

Statement of Desired Exit Performance

1. Respond positively to culturally different students.
2. Communicate effectively with culturally different students.
3. Foster interaction among students in a multicultural setting.

Potential Applications of Technology to Obtain This Performance

1. Videotaped interviews could be developed featuring people from other cultures who have gone through a different educational system. Students in groups or as individuals can react to this commentary and develop improved instructional strategies for more sensitive instruction with these groups.
2. Videotapes of effective teachers interacting in critical incidents with culturally different students could be viewed and discussed in class contexts.
3. Videodiscs could be used to store thousands of examples of cultural events and artifacts that could be programmed into instructional presentations to offer some alternative examples when explaining instructional concepts, processes, and principles.

Conclusions and Recommendations. No studies are reported that tested technological enhancements in preservice teacher training for the purpose of developing curricular materials and instructional methodologies that enhance the learning of culturally different pupils. Systematic study of the application of technology to preparing preservice teachers for developing instructional methods with culturally diverse curricular materials and students must begin.

7. Develops Curricular Materials and Instructional Methodologies to Enhance the Learning of Exceptional Pupils

This statement of programmatic intention is included to address topics and experiences in the general area of exceptionality, learning disabled, emotionally disabled, developmentally delayed children; physical impairments; communication disorders; visual impairments; gifted and talented children teacher behaviors toward exceptional children; adaptive environments; and testing. Studies reported within this program theme include Wood, Combs, and Swan (1986: AP); Frick, Rieth, and

Polsgrove (1984: AN, AP); M. K. Johnson and Amundsen (1983: AP).

Statement of Desired Exit Performance

1. Identify the characteristics of exceptional children.
2. Respond positively to exceptional children.
3. Adapt instructional resources to exceptional students.
4. Adapt instructional strategies to exceptional students.

Potential Applications of Technology to Obtain This Performance

1. Given videotaped vignettes of exceptional children at work or play, students could identify behaviors indicative of such pupils, as well as the reactions of other children to them. The opportunity to specify how the teacher should intervene could be a part of this exercise.
2. The computer can be used to simulate classroom life from the perspective of the exceptional learner. As the student, for instance, types a passage into the computer, it can produce the sounds that the speech-impaired student, for instance, would make in speaking the words to the student's classmates.
3. Videotaped case study comparisons of before and after training for learners with such problems as handicaps could show new teachers the kinds of improvements that can be reasonably expected, instilling the hope and optimism that is so necessary when working with these children.
4. Computer networks could facilitate immediate feedback from university or private sector specialists to student teachers who have exceptional students in their classes.
5. Comparison videotapes could be developed wherein exceptional children are viewed in the classroom or at play, with their teachers then offering commentary on what it is like to adjust to the special characteristics and challenges these children provide.
6. Word-processed, standard classroom materials could be modified and remodified by students for use with exceptional children. These materials could then be used to practice the process of analysis and revision of curricular materials.

Conclusions and Recommendations. Three studies were found that tested technological enhancements in preservice teacher training for the purpose of developing curricular materials and instructional methodologies to enhance the learning of exceptional children. Systematic study of the application of technology to the development of curricular materials and instructional methods for exceptional children must be expanded.

8. Incorporates Instruction in Reading, Critical Thinking, Problem Solving, and Study Skills to Enhance Pupils' Learning

This statement of programmatic intention is included to address topics and experiences in the general area of reading, writing, and study skills; comprehension; time management; problem-solving strategies; critical-thinking techniques; test taking, determining reading ability; adapting content materials; and developing vocabulary and comprehension skills. One study was identified within this program theme: Caskey and Trang (1980: AN).

Statement of Desired Exit Performance

1. Demonstrate a knowledge of reading, writing, critical-thinking, problem-solving, and study skills.
2. Adapt classroom materials to match learner characteristics.
3. Enhance student performance in content areas by way of these skills.

Potential Applications of Technology to Obtain This Performance

1. Simulations, both simple and elaborate, could be used to teach almost any of the skills contained in this category. For example, problem-solving skills taught by means of computer simulation not only provide valuable instruction in methods of solving problems but also model the process.
2. Rough drafts of documents could be programmed into word-processing software for students to edit and refine. Computers could then rate the thoroughness of the performance.
3. Audio or video interviews could be conducted with pupils of different ages and gender, to collect and present an image of how learners study, use time, or solve problems. This mediated survey of actual learner habits and traits could be useful to preservice teachers as they prepare to work within the diverse atmosphere of the classroom.
4. Learners and their parents could be interviewed, with the tapes played back in a side-by-side, split-screen format as they comment on the use of time, study skills, and other learning factors that depend to a certain degree on the influence of the home environment. This kind of comparison video format facilitates analysis of such issues as parental influence and the intellectual development of learners.
5. Before and after tapes could be made to document the effects of study skills and oral reading training. Such an approach could help preservice teachers see the efficacy of such efforts.
6. Walkman-type equipment, drill, and practice tapes for vocabulary and spelling skills could be developed for use in portable audiocassette players.
7. "Talk-aloud" videotapes could be made wherein learners give a running commentary on just what they are thinking and doing as they solve a given problem or work at an instructional task.

Conclusions and Recommendations. One study was found that tested technological enhancements in preservice teacher training designed to incorporate instruction, reading, writing, problem-solving, and study skills to enhance pupil learning. Professional organizations like the Association for Supervision and Curriculum Development dedicate complete journal issues to the teaching of critical thinking. One study was found that tested the effects of a technologically enhanced preservice experience designed to develop student critical-thinking skills. Systematic study of the application of technology to the development of critical-thinking, problem-solving, and study skill classroom methods needs to begin.

9. Organizes a Positive Classroom Environment to Enhance Instruction

This statement of programmatic intention is included to address topics and experiences in the general area of classroom and school physical arrangements, learning spaces, adapting educational environments, change strategies, and administrative effects on classroom organization. One study was identified within this program theme: Wellington (1986: AP).

Statement of Desired Exit Performance

1. Create a visually stimulating classroom environment.
2. Arrange the classroom environment to promote learning.

Potential Applications of Technology to Obtain This Performance

1. A typical classroom floor plan could be created on graphic software, so that students would have the experience of trying different seating plans or creating locations for learning centers. A computer network would permit university supervisors and student teachers to exchange preliminary and improved plans.
2. A computer simulation based on such research as needs for stimulation or boredom susceptibility could be used to demonstrate the individual and cumulative effects of using certain seating arrangements with different types of learners. Such effects as the proximity of certain learners to the teacher related to outcomes of attention and motivation, for instance, could be traced and recorded.
3. A video gallery of classrooms with teachers giving tours, answering questions, and sharing insights on the creation of classroom environments could give preservice teachers more exposure to the possibilities for classroom design than ever before.

Conclusions and Recommendations. One study was found that tested the technological enhancement of undergraduate preservice teacher training in organizing a positive classroom environment to enhance instruction. Although the capacity of videotape and computer simulation abounds in this theme, the area of technologically enhanced room design and school planning experiences remains virtually unexplored and untested in the undergraduate curriculum. This needs to begin.

10. Uses Effective Patterns of Communication in the School and Community

This statement of programmatic intention is included to address topics and experiences in the general area of principles of communication, models of communication, verbal behavior, nonverbal behavior, effective modeling, information-processing models, and capacity to evaluate and improve communication in school environments. Studies reported within this program theme include Young (1969: AN); Fauquet (1978: AN); Gillis (1975: K); Mertz (1972: AP).

Statement of Desired Exit Performance

1. Communicate effectively with pupils.
2. Communicate effectively with peers and other adults.

Potential Applications of Technology to Obtain This Performance

1. Learners' verbal and nonverbal behaviors could be videotaped as they perform some task or interact in the classroom. They could then be interviewed as they watch themselves on tape, to share what was going on in their minds as they were being taped. Students could use such narrated tapes to gain insight into what certain verbal and nonverbal behaviors mean as they seek to understand these patterns of communication within a classroom.
2. Standard models of communication could be programmed to interact with videotapes of actors as they conduct common classroom interactions. Students could provide alternative message content and responses, with the computer retrieving from either disk- or tape-filmed examples of what could result under these revised circumstances.
3. Audiotape microteaching could be conducted simply to document and analyze the use of speech in instruction. Teachers could come to recognize their voice mannerisms, inflections, and volume as they attempt to refine this critical aspect of classroom communication.
4. Sample videotapes of effective verbal–nonverbal behavioral expression within naturally occuring classroom activities could be filmed and collected for instruction and inspiration.

Conclusions and Recommendations. Four studies were found that tested technological enhancement of the undergraduate preservice curriculum designed to have students use effective patterns of communication in the school and community. Many professionally produced videotapes exist that demonstrate effective communication among teachers, students, and principals. These tapes are available through professional organizations for rent or purchase. University instructors purchase these films and often show them to their classes. But the next step toward validation of their utility is rarely if ever taken. The missing step includes studies that test the effects of seeing these films on the performance of student teachers and entry-year teachers.

11. Implements Individual and Group Management Skills

This statement of programmatic intention is included to address topics and experiences in the general area of individual and group management systems, task and activity analysis, reality therapy, assertive discipline, logical consequences, management principles, cuing and reinforcing, getting and holding attention, responding to inattention and misbehavior, responding to prolonged or disruptive behavior, serious adjustment problems, first days and weeks of school, and teacher-induction needs for management skills. Studies reported within this program theme include Evans (1988: AP); Strang et al., (1987: AP); Zuckerman (1979: AP); Kaczkowski, Lieberman, and Schmidt (1978: AN, AP); and Nias (1974: AN).

Statement of Desired Exit Performance

1. Demonstrate a knowledge of individual and group management systems.
2. Implement specific individual and group management skills.
3. Establish and maintain task orientations and cooperation during instructional activities.

Potential Applications of Technology to Obtain This Performance

1. Computerized explanations of the principles of classroom management could be followed by computer-coordinated video examples of the principles in action. Both examples and suitable nonexamples could be used to demonstrate operation of the principles.
2. Computers have a tremendous capability to depict the give-and-take within such dynamic arenas as classroom management. Interactive video programs could be developed and tested that permit data and decisions to be entered by students as they watch the critical events in any classroom unfold.
3. Computer networks could facilitate immediate feedback "between classes" from the university supervisor on incidents that could potentially threaten the entire day or field experience.
4. Microteaching could be conducted to help teachers learn to manage progressively more difficult forms of disruptive behavior. This could be conducted with either actors posing as the disruptive learners or videotape clips of actual learners edited into a format appropriate for discussion and analysis.
5. Simple, straightforward audio- or videotaped interviews with students who chronically misbehave could be produced, in an attempt to isolate and analyze possible reasons for and potential solutions to the misbehavior problems.

Conclusions and Recommendations.
Six studies were found that tested a technological enhancement of preservice students' capacity for individual student and large-group classroom management. The use of videotapes designed with expert–novice comparisons within critical incidents or naturally occurring classroom activities brings important instructional modeling to the preservice environment. Over time one would expect the video-treatment effect to show up in overall student perceptions of competence and performance in student teaching. The promise to novice teachers of computer networks' facilitating immediate access to multiple suggestions for effective management is considerable.

12. Implements Instructional Methodologies to Complement Goals and Objectives

This statement of programmatic intention is included to address topics and experiences in the general area of learning, theory, associationists, social learning, cognitive models, humanistic models, instructional theory, verbal learning, serial learning, paired associate learning, concept, process, and principal approximations and applications of learning and instructional theory to instructional goal-setting methods and evaluation. One study is reported within this program theme: Ramani (1987: AN).

Statement of Desired Exit Performance

1. Demonstrate a knowledge of principles of instruction.
2. Match strategies with objectives.
3. Sequence learning activities effectively.
4. Exhibit variability in instructional strategies.

Potential Applications of Technology to Obtain This Performance

1. A collection of videotaped and multimedia samples/models of a central set of learning and instructional theories could be developed for use in teacher-preparation classes, to facilitate the identification and analysis of various theories in operation in the classroom.
2. Sample instructional units could be entered in a word-processor system that would allow students to practice the critical skill of sequencing. These units could be created, exchanged, and edited by supervisors and returned to student teachers through the application of computer networks to teacher training.
3. Basing all examples on the same lesson, videotaped examples of how various schools of theory would handle the lesson could be produced for use with preservice personnel.
4. Classroom video vignettes could be shown to students for their analysis and estimation of the theories and accompanying methodologies being expressed.

Conclusions and Recommendations.
One study was found that tested the effect of a technological enhancement during preservice training, focusing on the implementation of instructional methodologies that complement instructional objectives. Reliance on lectures of learning theory and instructional theory, independent of commonly shared visual or curricular data-base frames of reference, might limit the impact of these important topics. Investigations in which technology is applied to the teaching of instructional theory and learning theory must begin in earnest.

13. Demonstrates a Repertoire of Appropriate Teacher Skills and Behaviors

This statement of programmatic intention is included to address topics and experience in the general area of teacher interpersonal skills, expectation effects, motivational behaviors, self-concept enhancement, crisis intervention, preinstruction skills such as planning, instructional skills such as establishing a set, frames of reference, closure achievement, attention getting, reinforcing, participation control, repetition and practice, illustrating, questioning skills, wait time, induction, deduction, and lecturing. The studies reported within this program theme included Azbell (1988: AP); Gebhard, Gaitan, and Oprandy (1987: AN); Ramani (1987: AN, AP); Strang et al. (1987: AP); Strang, Badt, and Kauffman (1987: AP); Ajayi-Dopemu and Talabi (1986: K); Fauquet (1986: AN); Klinzing and Leuteritz (1986: AP); Greis (1986: E); Volker, Gehler, Howlett, and Twetten (1986: E); Loper, Strang, Richards, and Badt (1985: AP); Strang and Loper (1985: AP, AN); Hargie and Bamford (1984: AP); Klinzing, Kunkel, Schiefer, and Stieger (1984: AP); Strang & Loper (1984: AP); Strang & Loper (1983: AP); G. Anderson, Frager, and Boling (1982: AP); Leith (1982: AP); McConnell and Fages (1981: AN); Copeland (1981: AP); Caskey and Trang (1980: AN); Madike (1980: AP); Moritz and Martin-Reynolds (1980: AN); Schade and Bartholomew (1980: AP, AN); Zuckerman (1979: AP); Sharan, Hertz-Lazarowitz, and Reiner (1978: AP); Bradley (1978: AP, AN); Ephraty (1978: AP); Stanton (1978: AP); Moore (1977: AP, K); Rabozzi (1977: AP); Yorke (1977: AP); Gurau (1976: AN); Perrott (1976: AP); Gillis (1975: K); Fuller and Manning (1973: AN); Llewellyn (1973: AP); Henrie and Whiteford (1972: AP); Cotrell and Doty (1971: AP); Affleck (1971: AP); Judy (1969: K); and Young (1969: AN, AP).

Statement of Desired Exit Performance

1. Have realistic expectations for all pupils.
2. Enhance pupil self-concept.
3. Motivate students to achieve instructional goals.
4. Exhibit effective crisis intervention skills.
5. Demonstrate a broad range of instructional skills.

Potential Applications of Technology to Obtain This Performance

1. Microteaching, in all its various forms, could be used on practically any area of this category of teaching performance.
2. Discussion tapes of various examples of teaching behavior could be produced and distributed.
3. Simulated classroom crises could be developed, with the student intervening via the computer, with feedback on one's actions developed in return.
4. Sample audio- or videotapes of model teaching behavior could be collected and shared. Computer networks could facilitate supervisor-friendly, on-screen reinforcement more immediately than the more common university supervisor visit.
5. Computer software that operationalizes classroom analysis systems with videotaped teaching performance could help teachers objectively and systematically self-evaluate their teaching.

Conclusions and Recommendations. This review found 42 studies that used a technological enhancement to demonstrate a repertoire of appropriate teacher skills and behaviors. The dominant enhancement was video recorders and taped playback in its various stages of maturity, from reel-to-reel to videocassette. Interactive videodisc technology is an emerging format for course instruction (Azbell, 1988). The developmental stage of this computer-video format continues to be emergent and expensive, but it is exciting and promising. The usual location for the microteaching experience was instructional methods courses. Videos and films have been used to show students classroom segments ranging from "How to respond to student questions" to "What does a full classroom session look like?" In summary, these studies suggest that, if preservice students are given an opportunity to review nonperishable video records of their instructional performance, they become aware of their performance and are likely to alter that performance in the direction of improved behavioral expression.

The analysis of personal videotapes during student teaching is an exciting area for future studies and development. The microteaching literature reviewed here provides considerable evidence of the impact on student insight into classroom initiations, routines, responses, and habits. Comparative tapes recorded between the first weeks of student teaching and the final weeks might imprint a preservice student with a positive image of how to professionally develop and encourage long-term professional analysis of performance. Tested research on questions like "What is the impact of VCR experiences on willingness to develop professionally?" are not abundant.

14. Designs and Implements, for Diagnostic and Prescriptive Purposes, Student Evaluation Instruments and Strategies

This statement of programmatic intention is included to address topics and experiences in the general area of purposes of evaluation (formative, diagnostic, summative, placement, norm-referenced, criterion-referenced, self-referenced, classroom-testing, individual-testing, test-planning); test-item construction, scoring, and grading; achievement tests; aptitude tests; state tests of student performance; test and item analysis; interpretation of test results; and decision making with test results. Studies reported within this program theme included Azbell (1988: AP); and D. L. Johnson, Willis, and Danley (1982: AP).

Statement of Desired Exit Performance

1. Demonstrate a knowledge of evaluation systems.
2. Select evaluation systems that complement instruction.
3. Design evaluation tools appropriate to instructional and student ability.

4. Administer evaluation appropriately.
5. Interpret test results responsibly.

Potential Applications of Technology to Obtain This Performance

1. Computer software could be created that would allow students to develop test questions, administer them to a simulated sample of students with given characteristics, see the results of test and item analyses of these questions, and revise and readminister until a satisfactory testing experience had been achieved.
2. Computer networks that link university supervisors with student teachers could facilitate the exchange and editing of tests and test-item "drafts" before poor questions or tests caused major interpersonal classroom problems for the student teacher.
2. Video demonstration of proper and improper test-administration practices could be produced for analysis and instruction.
3. Printouts of test or evaluation results, which the student could analyze in conjunction with course objectives, could allow practice in the key area of teaching the objectives–instructional strategies–evaluation continuum.

Conclusions and Recommendations. Two studies were found that examined the effect of a technological enhancement on the ability of preservice students to diagnose and prescribe evaluation procedures consistent with policies, goals, objectives, and strategies. Either there is no place for technological enhancements in this programmatic area, or much more needs to be done to establish the potential of technology. Faculty need to pursue the enormous potential of computers, computer networks, videos and interactive videodiscs to enhance the diagnostic and prescriptive components of teacher education programs.

15. Demonstrates Ability to Synthesize and Evaluate the Structure, History, Philosophy, Governance, and Current Issues in Education

This statement of programmatic intention is included to address topics and experiences in the general area of philosophy and education, history and education, culture and education, school law, school finance, constitutional teacher and student rights and responsibilities, state and federal governments roles, boards of education roles, citizens' groups and teacher associations roles, organization and structure of education, and current issues and trends in education. No studies were reported within this program theme.

Statement of Desired Exit Performance

1. Clarify and explain the relationship between teaching activities and philosophical positions.
2. Analyze the relationship between teaching activities and the structure and governance of education.

3. Explain the relationship between teaching activities and social, historical, and cultural concepts.

Potential Applications of Technology to Obtain This Performance

1. A video forum of noted spokespersons could be produced to present some of the current views and philosophies of education, using such resources as public broadcasting systems' video files.
2. Computer networks could facilitate the resolution of the often noted antagonism that occurs when university theory is applied to real classroom settings. Daily conflicts between theory and reality could be addressed by supervisors and made immediately available to all student teachers on the network.
3. The dynamic nature of the system by which the United States provides support for and control of education would lend itself very well to the capabilities of computer simulation.
4. Video documentaries could be produced in a case study format to demonstrate how parent groups have worked to bring about change in their local school districts.
5. Videotapes of the critical events of daily school governance and operation could be produced for observation and analysis. Scenarios might include a school board meeting, a hearing, or a teacher association meeting.
6. Computer simulations that allow a student to interact with a school budget could be developed. Students would have the opportunity to manipulate factors and decisions that comprise the budget system of a school and then watch the aftermath, which might include layoffs, cutbacks of extracurricular activities, or the curtailing of school bus service.
7. Computers could also be used to simulate the dynamics of collective bargaining within a school district. Students, acting alone or as opposing members of the school community, could observe the politics, conflict, and negotiation.

Conclusions and Recommendations. No studies were found that demonstrate the application of technology to the development of preservice students' ability to evaluate the structure, history, philosophy, governance, and current issues in education. No doubt videos and films are shown to undergraduates in an effort to stimulate their interest and vocabulary in professional education issues. But it would appear that these applications have rarely, if ever, been researched to determine their impact and relationship to program or course objectives.

16. Demonstrates a Willingness and Ability to Evaluate and Improve Instructional and Professional Effectiveness

This statement of programmatic intention is included to address topics and experiences in the general area of teacher personal traits, process variables, and structural/ecological behaviors; characteristics of effective classrooms, curriculas, and schools; qualitative and quantitative methods of teacher analysis; clinical supervision; videotape analysis; microteaching; teacher induction; staff development; continuing education; professionalism; professional organizations; interviewing, applications, résumés, certification, and accreditation. Studies reported within this program theme included Meierdiereks (1981: AN, E); Moritz and Martin-Reynolds (1980: AN); Menges (1979: AP); Pietras (1978: AN); Martin (1977: AP, AN); Bowles and Nelson (1976: K, AP); and Legge and Asper (1972: AN).

Statement of Desired Exit Performance

1. Demonstrate a willingness and capacity to self-analyze professional behavior.
2. Respond positively to professional feedback.
3. Demonstrate a willingness to develop professionally.

Potential Applications of Technology to Obtain This Performance

1. Engage in videotaping and sharing of lessons with student teachers and colleagues. These sessions would permit a common frame of reference for the introduction of the effective teaching literature.
2. Develop video descriptions of the missions and memberships of professional organizations.
3. Create simulations in which students have the opportunity to develop, organize the logistics, and conduct an inservice workshop on a critical topic for the teachers of a given school district.
4. Use interactive computer simulation of the interview process to help preservice teachers prepare for the rigors of obtaining a teaching job.
5. Develop multimedia packages of résumés, application forms, and letters of application to use as models and discussion starters in the process of preparing to find a position in the teaching profession.
6. Create and edit videotaped examples of teaching feedback to help students adjust to the sometimes uncomfortable process of performance evaluation, critique, and feedback.
7. Edit together excellent classroom lessons and provide student teachers with demonstration tapes of their instructional abilities. Micro floppy disks could be developed to store undergraduate curricular information. Student teachers could then take the disk sets with them to their first professional assignments.

Conclusions and Recommendations.

Six studies were found in the theme area of willingness and ability to evaluate and improve instructional and professional effectiveness. There is some overlap between this theme area and the professional-development statement "Demonstrates a repertoire of appropriate teacher skills and behaviors." The process of viewing a videotape inevitably produces evaluative responses. The insight derived from video replay can be very influential in modifying classroom behavior and providing the justification for it.

The future is bright, as the professional vocabulary of instructional effectiveness matures and is integrated into video replays of preservice teacher performance. Preservice social-

ization to video analysis could set the stage for more receptivity by inservice faculty to use of the video medium for long-term professional development. The permanent storage on floppy disks of undergraduate curricular information could ease the transition into the first year of teaching. Videotape records of excellent teaching could serve to remind entry-year teachers of prior excellent performances and give them much-needed confidence as they start their first day of classroom teaching.

FACTORS INFLUENCING PRESENCE AND EFFECT OF TECHNOLOGY IN TEACHER TRAINING

Referencing the evolution of major technical systems like the telephone, television, automobiles, and air transportation, McClintock (1988) concludes that "technical systems of substantial complexity require one to two hundred years for the development of their full potentials" (p. 347). The information age is no more than 50 years old. The year 1990 sits on the cusp of an industrial and information age "overlap." The dominance of the former is yielding to the necessity of the later. Teacher educators have a professional responsibility to experiment with technology. This inquiry should be well planned and could be coordinated, but such is not the case. Many factors are currently affecting the directions and support for research.

Planning

The Information Age may require a more creative form of planning than is typical in higher education. Most preservice and inservice teacher education programs have not come to grips with what it is that they should be trying to accomplish. Often there are as many descriptions of what a program is trying to accomplish as there are faculty members and administrators associated with the program. Very often the justification for technology is based on idiosyncratic faculty demand, not designed program need. One must ask a new set of questions as educators plan for the application of technology to teacher education programs. Some of the questions are:

What are the major themes of the teacher education program that could be enhanced by technology?
What research has been generated on the effects of this technology in service to this theme?
How will this technology stimulate or support purposeful research agenda inside the program theme?
What is the developmental stage of the technology? Has it matured to being user friendly? What software support complements teacher preparation? What is the quality of the software? What research has been done on the software?
What are the competitive model options available to the user? How competitive is the service system? What are the repair ratios for particular models? How stable is the product line? What do the vendors anticipate from their research-and-development group in the next 5 years?

What plans have been made to introduce and encourage faculty members in the applications of the technology?

What support is available to extend the capabilities of the technology or repair it when (not if) it breaks?

Will preservice or inservice exposure to this technology increase teacher confidence, competence, and creativity in designing instructional environments?

What are the organizational rewards for experimenting or applying the technology? Will the technology carry a faculty member outside the reward system?

What is the tenure status of the faculty member most likely to make application of the technology?

What is the extent of faculty commitment to the presence of technology as an instructional tool?

Costs

The report of the National Task Force on Educational Technology (1988) offers several suggestions for addressing the high cost of integrating technology into teacher training. The report recommends (a), grants and loans for students entering teacher education programs; (b), funds for schools of education, to support the purchase of equipment; (c), grants to support the workshops and courses, to upgrade the technology skills of education faculty; (d), demonstration grants for innovative internships where electronic networks connect the student teacher to the education school; and (e) grants for research on methods of training teachers to use technology and funding for the dissemination of promising practices. Funding agencies that support education will have to be increasingly sensitive to the need for supporting equipment expenditures in grant proposals.

Funding Priorities

In professional education, equipment dollars are often allocated after everything else has been funded. This priority system is a carryover from the agrarian and industrial ages. It remains partly because of the belief that the teacher without technology can still cover the content and that students will still learn something. Every piece of standardized test data available to educators and overwhelming public opinion attest to the naïveté of this belief. When the perceived value of something is low (even if the culprit is a lack of experience with the information age), the priority that technology receives is low. Low priorities are not competitive for funds. Higher priority funding for technology, to transform classroom environments in the information age, can be a tough sell.

Faculty Development

The National Governors Association Task Force on Technology recommends that:

All prospective teachers should learn about effective and emerging uses of technology in their respective curriculum areas. This training might exist as part of university-based courses or internships in ele-

mentary and secondary schools that have made good use of technology or during training by private vendors, or some combination of the two. Every university teacher education department should develop relationships with as many schools that use technology as possible, in order to bring together as many educational professionals at all levels to share ideas on the most effective use of technology, to use outstanding district administrators as adjunct faculty, and to provide internships for the undergraduate and graduate college students. (Sununu, 1986, p. 221)

In a report by the Corporation for Public Broadcasting entitled "Faculty Perspectives on the Role of Information Technologies in Academic Instruction," 250 college faculty members were surveyed from 15 colleges and universities. Faculty reported that lack of funding is the greatest obstacle to the instructional use of information technologies in higher education. Service support is hard to come by and is not adequate compensation for the extra effort they are forced to make (Barbour, 1986). There is another side to the reality of limited faculty models in the application of technology. A report by Naron and Estes (1985) notes:

Perhaps one of the strongest reasons that teacher training is approached in a more haphazard way in colleges and universities than in the public schools is that faculty members in higher education hold sacred a high degree of autonomy. Many do not voluntarily choose to upgrade their skills in a new area, whereas teachers in the elementary and secondary schools are mandated, or at least given strong motivation from pay or credit, to do so. (p. 19)

Semantics

The vocabulary of technology is not currently the vocabulary of teacher training. The discipline of teacher education struggles with its own knowledge base of valid and reliable terminology. The language of high technology is new, complex, constantly changing, and often distinct from the discipline-oriented language of professional educators. Reading and applying an operating manual or user's guide can be an exercise in total frustration. In the context of high technology, it is difficult to ask questions intelligently, not to mention form comprehensive schemata for processing new terms. Acquiring the language of technology takes time and energy, resources that faculty might not have very much of with their existing work loads.

CONCLUSION

There are many journal articles, papers, and books on the subject of technology and its implications for teacher training, of which the following are only a sample (Allen, 1980; C. A. Anderson, 1983; Cobb & Horn, 1986; Dennis & Standiford, 1984; Frager, 1985; Friedman, 1983; Glenn, 1984; Hoffman, 1984; Hunter, 1983; Meutsch, 1988; Nelson & Waack, 1985; Reiser, 1986; Rhodes & Azbell, 1987; Singletary, 1987; Stevens, 1984; Stevenson, 1983; Stolovitch, 1980; Tetenbaum & Mulkeen, 1986; Uhlig, 1983; Woodrow, 1987; and Zuckerman, 1983).

Seventy-two research articles were categorized within the 16 program themes, with some studies placed in more than one theme. These same 72 studies were categorized into the six levels of Bloom's Taxonomy of the Cognitive Domain, with some studies being placed in more than one domain: Knowledge/7 studies; Comprehension/0 studies; Application/53 studies; Analysis/26 studies; Synthesis/0 studies, and Evaluation/3 studies. Seventeen studies were categorized in more than one domain.

The program themes most deficit in reported studies of technological enhancements are important, preservice teacher education, program-content and experience themes (see Figure 28-1). They include the themes of learner characteristics (Theme 1/0 studies), instructional goal setting (Theme 2/2 studies), curriculum adaptation (Theme 4/0 studies), cultural diversity (Theme 5/0 studies), adaptation of materials for culturally diverse populations (Theme 6/0 studies), methods and materials for exceptional student populations (Theme 7/2 studies), critical thinking and problem-solving skills (Theme 8/1 study), organization of classroom environments (Theme 9/1 study), patterns of communication (Theme 10/4 studies), classroom-management techniques (Theme 11/5 studies), instructional and learning theory (Theme 12/1 study), design and implementation of diagnostic and evaluation procedures (Theme 14/2 studies), and structure, history, philosophy, and governance of professional education (Theme 15/0 studies). The presence of more research activity can be found in the theme area "Designs Instructional Methodology in Media and Technology Appropriate to Instructional Goals and Objectives" (Theme 3/9 studies). The research evidence in theme area "Demonstrates

a Repertoire of Appropiate Teacher Skills and Behaviors" (Theme 13/42 studies) suggests impact and direction focused on microteaching experiences. Technological enhancement does not appear to be frequently researched at the knowledge, comprehension, synthesis, and evaluation levels of the professional curricular knowledge base. Important preservice program themes do not appear to be targeted for research exploring the potential for technological enhancement.

Forty of the 72 studies in this review were reported within two significant periods of research activity. Both periods were dominated by research on the effects of microteaching experiences. The years between 1976 and 1980, and then again between 1986 and 1987, appear to have been the most active in reported research on technological enhancements to undergraduate programs.

There are exciting and forward-looking initiatives in curricular information presentation, storage, and retrieval. Azbell (1988) reports an interactive videodisc project that seeks to improve preservice reading teacher training. Computer network projects that connect student teachers with university sites are emerging as network technologies mature. Swift and Coxford (1988) report on a network project, MICH: EdCorps, at The University of Michigan. Perry and Brooks (1988) report a computer network project EDTNet at Miami University in Oxford, Ohio, that links student teachers and instructional supervisors with electronic mail, undergraduate curricular-content storage, and a bulletin board update. EDTNet also links School of Education and Allied Professions faculty with faculty from the College of Arts and Science and public school sites. University supervisors are networked from home sites, as well as their

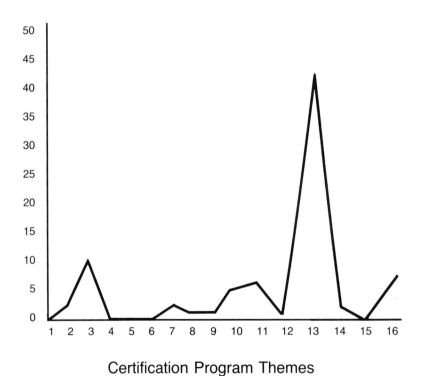

Certification Program Themes

FIGURE 28–1. Frequency of Reported Studies of Technological Enhancements Within Sixteen Certification Program Themes

offices. Merseth (1988) reports on the development of an "electronic community" for first-year teachers at the Harvard Graduate School of Education.

The application of current technologies and information formats to teacher training is behind schedule. If first-year teachers are expected to be creative and facile with technology, they deserve exposure to technogical enhancements at all levels of the preservice curriculum. Enhanced entry-year teacher competence with technological enhancements to instruction begins with faculty research and instructional modeling of technological enhancements throughout the preservice curriculum.

References

Affleck, M. (1971). Producing and using videotapes in preservice education. In N. B. Smith (Ed.), *Reading methods and teacher improvement* (pp. 178–183). Newark, DE: International Reading Association.

Ajayi-Dopemu, Y., & Talabi, J. K. (1986). The effects of videotape recording on microteaching training techniques for education students. *Journal of Educational Television, 12*(1), 39–44.

Allen, D. W. (1980). Microteaching: A personal review. *British Journal of Teacher Education, 6*(2), 147–151.

Anderson, C. A. (1983). Computer literacy: Changes for teacher education. *Journal of Teacher Education, 34*(5), 6–9.

Anderson, G., Frager, A., & Boling, C. (1982). Developing instructional competence in field-based programs: Videotape protocols versus role-play simulations. *Teacher Educator, 18*, 16–25.

Azbell, J. (1988, February). *Video discs in the preparation of teachers.* Paper presented at the seventh annual Instructional Technology Fair, Columbus, OH.

Barbour, A. (1986). Institutional support for technology falls short. *Electronic Learning, 6*(2), 16–18.

Bloom, B., Engelhart, M., Furst, E., Hill, W., & Krathwohl, D. (1956). *Taxonomy of educational objectives: The classification of educational goals: Handbook I: Cognitive domain.* New York: David McKay.

Bonar, J. R. (1976). Developing and implementing a systems-design training program for academic advisors. *Journal of College Student Personnel, 17*(3), 190–198.

Bowles, P. E., Jr., & Nelson, R. O. (1976). Training teachers as mediators: Efficacy of a workshop versus the bug-in-the-ear technique. *Journal of School Psychology, 14*(1), 15–25.

Bradley, C. H. (1978). Program VITAL: Characteristics, concepts and derived learnings. *Journal of Industrial Teacher Education, 16*(1), 57–67.

Brooks, D., Moore, R., & Ziegler, J. (1987, April). *The information management model: A systems approach to teacher education.* Paper presented at the Ohio Conference of Teacher Education Organizations Spring Conference, Columbus.

Caskey, O. L., & Trang, M. (1980). Videotape in instructional improvement: Using interpersonal process recall. *Educational Technology, 20*(10), 44–47.

Cobb, H. B., & Horn, C. J., Jr. (1986). Planned change in special education technology. *Journal of Special Education Technology, 8*(2), 18–27.

Connett, J. H. (1985). Satellite technology: Application for high schools. *NASSP Bulletin, 69*(484), 29–32.

Copeland, W. D. (1981). Clinical experiences in the education of teachers. *British Journal of Teacher Education, 7*(1), 3–16.

Cotrell, C. J., & Doty, C. R. (1971). *An analysis of face-to-face video and remote audio feedback techniques* (Report No. R & D-Ser-49). Columbus, OH: The Center for Vocational and Technical Education. (ERIC Document Reproduction Service No. ED 052 325)

Dennis, J. R., & Standiford, S. N. (1984). The computer and the teacher-educator: Or should it be vice versa? *Educational Perspectives, 22*(4), 27–31.

Ephraty, N. (1978). The use of VTR systems in instructional situations in pedagogy in a teachers' college. *British Journal of Educational Technology, 9*(1), 71–76.

Evans, A. (1988, February). *An interactive video approach for teaching discipline techniques in a teacher preparation program.* Paper presented at the seventh annual Instructional Technology Fair, Columbus, OH.

Fauquet, M. (1978). Example of a multi-media package for use in teacher training. *Educational Media International, 3*, 19–24.

Fauquet, M. (1986). The development of video training: The ICEM Survey. *Educational Media International, 23*(4), 167–177.

Forcheri, P., & Molfino, M. T. (1986). Teacher training in computers and education: A two-year experience. *Computers and Education, 10*(1), 137–143.

Frager, A. M. (1985). Video technology and teacher training: A research perspective. *Educational Technology, 25*(7), 20–22.

Frick, T., Rieth, H., & Polsgrove, L. (1984). Use of microcomputers in training special education teachers. *Peabody Journal of Education, 62*(1), 77–86.

Friedman, D. (1983). The impact of educational computing on teacher education. *Journal of Teacher Education, 34*(5), 14–18.

Fuller, F. F., & Manning, B. A. (1973). Self-confrontation reviewed: A conceptualization for video playback in teacher education. *Review of Educational Research, 43*(4), 469–528.

Gebhard, J. G., Gaitan, S., & Oprandy, R. (1987). Beyond prescription: The student teacher as investigator. *Foreign Language Annals, 20*(3), 227–232.

Gillis, D. (1975). *Teaching as a performing art.* Columbia, SC: South Carolina University, School of Education. (ERIC Document Reproduction Service No. ED 117 093)

Glaser, R., & Cooley, W. (1973). Instrumentation for teaching and instructional management. In. R. Travers (Ed.), *Second handbook of research on teaching* (pp. 832–857). Chicago: Rand McNally.

Glenn, A. D. (1984). Computer literacy among college of education faculty. *Educational Perspectives, 22*(4), 24–26.

Greis, N. (1986). Self evaluation in practice teaching. *Foreign Language Annals, 19*(3), 231–236.

Gurau, P. K. (1976). Time lapse videography in teacher training. *Educational Technology, 16*(8), 34–35.

Hargie, O., & Bamford, D. (1984). A comparison of the reactions of pre-service and in-service social workers to microtraining. *Vocational Aspect of Education, 36*(95), 87–91.

Henrie, H. H., & Whiteford, E. B. (1972). *The teleconference: A supervisory procedure in educational clinical experiences.* Minneapolis, MN: Minnesota Research Coordinating Unit for Vocational Education. (ERIC Document Reproduction Service No. ED 160 761)

Hoffman, R. I. (1984). Recommended changes in the teacher preservice program to reflect computer technology and its impact on education. *Educational Perspectives, 22*(4), 21–23.

Howey, K., & Zimpher, N. (1987, April). *Case studies of elementary teacher preparation programs in six schools and colleges of education; preliminary study findings.* Paper presented at the annual meeting of the American Educational Research Association, Washington, DC.

Hunter, E. (1983). What's the low-down on high tech?: Some questions for teacher educators. *Journal of Teacher Education, 34*(5), 26–28.

Johnson, D. L., Willis, J., & Danley, W. (1982). A comparison of traditional and computer based methods of teaching students to administer individual intelligence tests. *AEDS Journal, 16*(1), 56–64.

Johnson, M. K., & Amundsen, C. (1983). Distance education: A unique blend of technology and pedagogy to train future special educators. *Journal of Special Education Technology, 6*(3), 34–45.

Judy, S. (1969). *A study of the production and use of videotaped materials in the training of in-service and pre-service teachers of English: Final report* (Contract No. OE-5-10-029). Urbana, IL: Illinois Statewide Curriculum Study Center in the Preparation of Secondary English Teachers. (ERIC Document Reproduction Service No. ED 030 671)

Kaczkowski, H., Lieberman, L., & Schmidt, L. (1978). The critical incident as a teaching strategy. *Counselor Education and Supervising, 18*(1), 74–77.

Klinzing, H., Kunkel, K., Schiefer, H., & Stieger, S. (1984). *The effects of nonverbal behavior training on teacher clarity, interest, assertiveness, and persuasiveness during microteaching.* Paper presented at the annual meeting of the American Educational Research Association, New Orleans.

Klinzing, H. & Leuteritz, A. (1986). *The effects of training teachers using improvisational methods on nonverbal sensitivity, nonverbal expressiveness and on the clarity and interest of the presentation.* Paper presented at the annual conference of the Australian Association for Research in Education, Melbourne, Australia.

Legge, W. B., & Asper L. (1972). The effect of videotaped microteaching lessons on the evaluative behavior of pre-student teachers. *Journal of Teacher Education, 23*(3), 363–366.

Leith, G. O. M. (1982). The influence of personality on learning to teach: Effects and delayed effects of microteaching. *Educational Review, 34*(3), 195–204.

Llewellyn, G. C. (1973). Using exchange tapes in the preparation and training program for student teachers. *Educational Technology Systems, 1*(4), 323–328.

Loper, A. B., Strang, H. R., Richards, F., & Badt, K. (1985). Use of a microcomputer-based simulation to enrich teacher training. *Educational Technology, 25*(12), 36–37.

Madike, F. U. (1980). Teacher preparation and student achievement: An experimental comparison of microteaching with a traditional approach. *Journal of Educational Psychology, 72*(6), 866–874.

Martin, J. (1977). *A study of the effects of a self-evaluation model on the focus reaction of student teachers during split-screen videotape feedback.* Unpublished doctoral dissertation, Bowling Green State University, Bowling Green, OH.

McBride, R. E. (1985). STTM—A systematic teacher training model. *Education Canada, 25*(1), 22–25.

McClintock, R. O. (1988). Marking the second frontier. *Teachers College Record, 89*(3) 345–351.

McConnell, A., & Fages, S. (1981). Videotaped feedback in physical education methods class. *Journal of Physical Education and Recreation, 51*(5), 64–65.

Meierdiereks, K. (1981). Supervision and the videotape recorder. *NASSP Bulletin, 65*(448), 38–41.

Meierhenry, W. C. (Ed.). (1970). *Mediated teacher education resources.* Washington, DC: American Association of Colleges for Teacher Education. (ERIC Document Reproduction Service No. ED 044 389)

Meierhenry, W. C. (1976). Development of multimedia teacher education materials: A case study. *Journal of Teacher Education, 27*(3), 235–237.

Menges, R. J. (1979). Raising consciousness about college teaching: Rationale and effects of college classroom vignettes. *Educational Technology, 19*, 14–18.

Merseth, K. (1988). Project at Harvard Graduate School of Education. *Education Week, 7*,(32), 1.

Mertz, D. C. (1972). *The effects of split-screen videotaping as a vehicle to encourage teacher self-analysis.* Unpublished doctoral dissertation, University of Toledo, Toledo, OH.

Meutsch, D. (1988, April), *Television-processing: Preliminaries to a theory of knowledge acquisition with audio-visual materials.* Paper presented at the annual meeting of the American Educational Research Association, New Orleans.

Moore, G. E. (1977). *Providing instructional feedback to students in education classes.* West Lafayette, IN: Purdue University. (ERIC Document Reproduction Service No. ED 173 309)

Moritz, W., & Martin-Reynolds, J. (1980). Split-screen videotaping: The genie in the bottle. *Educational Leadership, 37*(5), 396–399.

Naron, N. K., & Estes, N. (1985). *Technology in the schools: Trends and policies.* Chicago: American Educational Research Association. (ERIC Document Reproduction Service No. ED 262 775)

National Task Force on Educational Technology (1988). *Transforming American education: Reducing the risk to the nation: A report to the Secretary of Education.* Washington, DC: U.S. Department of Education.

Nelson, P., & Waack, W. (1985). The status of computer literacy/computer-assisted instruction awareness as a factor in classroom instruction and teacher selection. *Educational Technology, 25*(10), 23–26.

Nias, J. (1974). Beyond microteaching: Other uses of video recording in teacher training. *Visual Education, 18*, 223–226.

Parker, W. C., Varnell, R. C., & Rinewalt, J. R. (1983). Building a computer-managed teacher education curriculum. *Journal of Teacher Education, 34*(5), 10–12.

Perrott, E. (1976). Individualized teacher training programmes involving the use of television. *Educational Broadcasting International, 9*(2), 61–65.

Perry, B, & Brooks, D. (1988). *Department of Teacher Education project evaluation report, EDTNet: Computer network grant.* Oxford, OH: Miami University Graduate School and Apple Inc.

Pietras, T. P. (1978). Modification of preservice teacher attitudes through analysis of films. *Peabody Journal of Education, 55*(2), 127–130.

Rabozzi, M. D. (1977). Microteaching/videotaping experiences in the methods course. *Social Education, 41*(3), 229–231.

Ramani, E. (1987). Theorizing from the classroom. *ELT Journal, 41*(1), 3–11.

Reiser, R. A. (1986). Some questions facing academic programs in instructional technology and some means for answering them. *Journal of Instructional Development, 8*(3), 20–23.

Rhodes, D. M., & Azbell, J. W. (1987). The CAIV syndrome: Treatment and prevention. In E. E. Miller (Ed.), *Educational Media and Technology Yearbook* (Vol. 13, pp. 47–56). Littleton, CO: Libraries Unlimited.

Rosenshine, B. (1977). A national teaching contest. *Journal of Teacher Education, 28*(5), 19–21.

Schade, W. R., & Bartholomew, R. B. (1980). Analysis of geology teaching assistant reaction to a training program utilizing videotaped teaching episodes. *Journal of Geological Education, 28*(2), 96–102.

Sharan, S., Hertz-Lazarowitz, R., & Reiner, T. (1978). Television for changing teacher behavior. *Journal of Educational Technology Systems, 7*(2), 119–131.

Singletary, T. J. (1987). Programming for leadership. *Journal of Teacher Education, 38*(3), 26–30.

Snyder, K. J., & Anderson, R. H. (1980). Leadership in teacher education: A systems approach. *Journal of Teacher Education, 31*(1), 11–15.

Stanton, H. E. (1978). Self-concept change through a microteaching experience. *British Journal of Teacher Education, 4*(2), 119–123.

Stevens, D. J. (1984). Why computers in education may fail. *Education, 104*(4), 370–376.

Stevenson, C. (1983). Microcomputers and macrocautions. *Journal of Teacher Education, 34*(5), 23–25.

Stolovitch, H. D. (1980). Instructional technology and its challenges to teacher training. *NSPI Journal, 14*(6), 17–19.

Strang, H. R., Badt, K. S., & Kauffman, J. M. (1987). Microcomputer-based simulations for training fundamental teaching skills. *Journal of Teacher Education, 38*(1), 20–26.

Strang, H. R., Kauffman, J. M., Badt, K. S., Murphy, D. M., & Loper, A. B. (1987). Acquisition of fundamental behavior management skills with microcomputer-simulated pupils. *Journal of Special Education Technology, 8*(3), 14–28.

Strang, H. R., & Loper, A. B. (1983). Microcomputer-based simulation in training elementary teachers. *Educational Technology, 23*(10), 30–31.

Strang, H. R., & Loper, A. B. (1984). A microcomputer-based simulation of classroom interaction. *Journal of Educational Technology Systems, 12*(3), 209–219.

Strang, H. R., & Loper, A. B. (1985). Microcomputer support of teacher–pupil dialogue. *Journal of Educational Technology Systems, 14*(2), 119–128.

Sununu, J. H. (1986). Will technologies make learning and teaching easier? *Phi Delta Kappan, 68*(4), 220–222.

Swift K., & Coxford, A. (Spring, 1988). Computer network for student teachers. *Innovator.* Ann Arbor: University of Michigan, School of Education, *19*(3), 1, 5.

Tetenbaum, T. J., & Mulkeen, T. A. (1986). Computers as an agent for educational change. *Computers in the Schools, 2*(4), 91–103.

Uhlig G. (1983). Dimensions of technology literacy in teacher education. *Journal of Teacher Education, 34*(5), 2–5.

U.S. Congress, Office of Technology Assessment. (September, 1988). *Power on! New tools for teaching and learning* (OTA-SET-379). Washington, DC: U.S. Government Printing Office.

Volker, R., Gehler, D., Howlett, W. P., & Twetten, A. (1986). Using interactive video to assess teaching behaviors. *Educational Leadership, 43*(6), 59–61.

Wellington, J. J. (1986). Providing in-house teaching experience: A case-study of its value and possibilities. *Journal of Education for Teaching, 12*(1), 47–51.

Wood, M. M., Combs, C., & Swan, W. W. (1986). Computer simulations: Field testing effectiveness and efficiency for inservice and preservice teacher preparation. *Journal of Educational Technology Systems, 14*(1), 61–74.

Woodrow, J. E. J. (1987). Educators' attitudes and predispositions towards computers. *Journal of Computers in Mathematics and Science Teaching, 6*(3), 27–37.

Yelon, S. L. (1980). Instuctional technology at teacher training courses. *NSPI Journal, 14*(6), 20–21, 24–25, 28.

Yorke, D. M. (1977). Television in the education of teachers: A case study. *British Journal of Educational Technology, 8*(2), 131–141.

Young, D. B. (1969). The modification of teacher behavior using audio videotaped models in a micro-teaching sequence. *Educational Leadership, 26*(4), 394–403.

Zuckerman, R. A. (1979). Simulation helps pre-service students acquire pragmatic teaching skills. *Journal of Teacher Education, 30*(4), 14–16.

Zuckerman, R. A. (1983). Computers and teacher training. *AEDS Journal, 16*(2), 123–130.

·29·

STUDENT TEACHING AND SCHOOL EXPERIENCES

Edith Guyton
GEORGIA STATE UNIVERSITY

D. John McIntyre
SOUTHERN ILLINOIS UNIVERSITY

Student teaching and related school experiences have emerged as an entrenched and widely accepted component of teacher preparation. Noted educators such as Conant (1963) and Andrews (1964) have described school experiences as the most important element in professional education and student teaching as the most universally approved education course. These assertions are supported by teachers' consistently high ratings of student teaching as the single most beneficial segment of their teacher education program (Appleberry, 1976; Haring & Nelson, 1980; Nosow, 1975). In addition, the recent educational reform movement has resulted in some legislatures and state boards of education increasing the number of school experiences required of teacher candidates.

Given the apparent esteem accorded student teaching, one might assume that it is grounded in a sound theoretical foundation, with general agreement concerning its structure and activities. Despite knowledge of research on teaching, learning, and educational psychology, many critics have charged that student teaching has failed to evolve much beyond the medieval apprenticeship training model, has not developed a sound theoretical basis, and has no uniform or standard structure.

LACK OF A THEORETICAL BASE FOR FIELD EXPERIENCES

As early as 1964 Andrews argues that student teaching was beginning to be viewed with great concern and that its effectiveness was being questioned. LaGrone (1965) stressed the fact that teacher education programs were taking a highly randomized approach to field experiences and were expressing this quantitatively, rather than with any substance. The attitude of teacher educators was one of uncertainty about what they wanted to happen during field experiences. Rivilin (1965) attacked the prevalent apprenticeship model by asserting that teaching is much more than a skilled trade, and, unless experience is related to theory, the tricks students learn will be only tricks.

More recently, McIntyre (1983) argues that the major void in the field-experience literature is lack of emphasis on the theoretical basis for fieldwork. Field experience evolved from early apprenticeship programs without examination of their purposes, nature, or length. Watts (1987) and Zeichner (1987) state that there is no agreed-upon definition of the purpose and goals of school experiences or student teaching and that much variety exists in the ways these experiences are conceptualized, organized, and actually implemented, even within the same institution.

Dussault (1970) explains that the field of education has no common scholarly language about science, scientific inquiry, or theory and theory building, so that one who undertakes to develop an educational theory might feel the need to state a personal position with regard to these matters. Dussault's work might place the quest for a theoretical foundation for student teaching and school experiences in proper perspective. He states that there are two major stages in the life history of an empirical science: the *natural history stage* and the *stage of theory*. Researchers at the natural history stage are interested in a systematic description of their world as it currently exists.

The authors thank reviewers Jane Applegate (Kent State University) and Allen R. Warner (University of Houston).

514

The scientific, searching mind is not content with knowing reality but further seeks to explain the reality. When a science reaches the explanatory stage, it reaches maturity, the stage of theory. In essence, science at the natural history stage searches for regularities in phenomena, whereas, at the stage of theory, it investigates, manipulates, and explains the form of regularities whose existence is already recognized.

Given the current state of research in student teaching and school experiences, the field is establishing a firmer natural history foundation that promotes transition to the theory stage. The research summarized in this chapter not only describes the reality of student teaching but also begins to explain that reality.

HISTORICAL OVERVIEW

Although schools have existed for over 4,000 years, formal teacher education has existed for less than 300 years. Until the late seventeenth century, there was little interest in specialized teacher training. At that time, Jean Baptiste de la Salle, the Father of Student Teaching, established the first normal school at Rheims, France (Johnson, 1968a). Prior to de la Salle's efforts, the earliest method of preparing teachers was the apprenticeship model in the Middle Ages.

Student teaching slowly evolved from the apprenticeship model until normal schools emerged in this country during the mid-1800s. At that time, student teaching consisted of imitation and repeated practice of a particular method taught by the normal-school professor and demonstrated in the classroom by the model teacher. These courses in student teaching predate the development of educational psychology, the testing movement, and research on child development and teacher effectiveness. As a result, the early student-teaching component developed prior to knowledge that would have provided a more sound theoretical base and that might have preempted the development of a system narrow in both its conception and practice (Andrews, 1964).

Until the 1920s, student teaching remained a vocational, practically oriented course required for prospective elementary teachers. Secondary teachers were, however, graduated from liberal arts colleges with no professional teacher preparation. From 1920 to 1940, most states began requiring student teaching and professional courses as prerequisites to certification.

This period was noteworthy for two developments. First, professional organizations began to exert considerable influence on student teaching (Andrews, 1964). The American Association of Teachers Colleges (AATC), now the American Association of Colleges for Teacher Education (AACTE), was established in 1917. In 1928 it required member institutions to set a minimum of 90 clock hours for student teaching. Later, AACTE published *School and Community Laboratory Experiences in Teacher Education* (Flowers, Patterson, Stratemeyer, & Lindsey, 1948), one of the first documents not only to report existing practice and suggest standards, but also to argue for an image of what ought to be included in a good program. Whereas AATC/AACTE was an association of institutions, student-teacher directors formed an association in 1920 for individuals, the Association for Student Teaching (AST), later renamed the Association of Teacher Educators (ATE) with a broadened focus. Over the past 70 years AST/ATE has published over 40 yearbooks and a considerable number of books, bulletins, research reports, and newsletters that have contributed to the advancement of student teaching (Johnson, 1968a).

The second major development of this 20-year period was the increase in campus laboratory schools (McCarrel, 1933). The purpose of laboratory schools was not only to provide a site for student teaching but also to serve as centers for the study of teaching (Lindsey, 1969). Prior to student teaching, teacher candidates observed and worked in laboratory schools as part of their coursework. Following World War II, the large number of student teachers and the special conditions of laboratory schools that made them dissimilar to public schools caused many universities to begin using the public schools for clinical sites.

Recently, student teaching and school experiences have undergone several major developments. *First*, early field experiences have been greatly expanded, so that teacher education students spend as many as 300 contact hours in classrooms prior to student teaching (McIntyre, 1983). *Second*, many universities have developed the center concept as the means for organizing their school experience component. Twenty to forty students complete student teaching in a school district that might be hundreds of miles from the university; a university faculty member based in the center coordinates and supervises the experiences and serves as a liaison between the university and the school district. *Third*, fifth-year programs and internships have been adopted by several universities and have been proposed as a means for improving teacher education (Carnegie Forum on Education and the Economy, 1986; Holmes Group, 1986). *Fourth*, there is renewed interest in the preparation of student teacher supervisors, at both the university and the public school level (Killian & McIntyre, 1986b; McIntyre & Killian, 1987). *Finally*, research in student teaching and school experiences has become more naturalistic, so that current researchers are examining more closely what is occurring during student teaching.

The history of student teaching and school experiences has evolved from the medieval apprenticeship system to a more structured, expanded series of experiences that integrates modern technology and related fields of study and often begins at matriculation and extends beyond graduation.

CURRICULUM AND ORGANIZATION

Although student teaching is the most widely accepted component of teacher preparation, it is criticized for lacking a theoretical and conceptual framework, for lacking commonly espoused goals, and for not fulfilling its potential. Nowhere is this contradiction more evident than in the curriculum and organization of student teaching and school experience programs.

The fragmentation and lack of articulation within student teaching mirrors a similar dilemma throughout most teacher education programs. Wisniewski (1978) charges that the content and articulation of professional courses are determined more by departmental and professorial interest than by their relevance to an intensive preparation process. Similarly, many institutions add hours to their student teaching and school experiences component without examining what occurs during these experiences.

Curriculum Orientation and Models

Four orientations have been identified that direct teacher education programs and, subsequently, the student teaching component (Zeichner, 1983). The first, the *behavioristic* orientation, emphasizes the development of specific and observable skills of teaching related to pupil learning. The second major orientation, *personalistic*, seeks to promote the psychological maturity of student teachers and emphasizes the reorganization of perceptions and beliefs over the mastery of specific skills and knowledge. The third, prevalent at many institutions, is the *traditional-craft* orientation. This approach encourages student teachers to view teaching as a craft and learning to teach as traditional initiation into this craft, viewing student teaching as a process of apprenticeship. In an effort to address these concerns about the apprenticeship model, the *inquiry-oriented* approach emerged as another viable option for teacher education programs. Zeichner (1983) describes this orientation as one that prioritizes the development of inquiry about teaching and about teaching contexts. This approach does not devalue technical teaching skill but values it as a means to objectives, not as an objective itself. Feiman (1979) stresses the fact that this orientation views student teachers in an active, rather than passive, sense and assumes that the more teachers are aware of the origins and consequences of their actions and of the realities that might constrain these actions, the greater the likelihood they can control and change both actions and constraints.

Zeichner (1983) suggests that, as student teachers carefully examine the origins and consequences of their actions and of the settings in which they work, the following questions become of central importance:

What knowledge should be taught and to whom? How should a teacher allocate time and resources among different children? To what extent should the personal knowledge that children bring to school be considered a legitimate part of the school curriculum? How much control do (and should) teachers exert in determining what is taught, how it is to be taught, and how it is to be evaluated? (p. 6)

Student teaching seminars within this context would not ignore the how-to questions but would focus on the what and why questions, reflecting the complex nature of improving schooling and teacher education by offering a perspective that would challenge existing instructional patterns and belief systems and promote reflection upon fundamental, substantive questions of education, ethics, and the social implications of schooling (Goodman, 1983).

If teacher education institutions are to succeed in providing prospective teachers with skills and knowledge needed for effective performance, as Applegate and Lasley (1982) stress, the experiences provided in the classroom must correspond to the goals established for the entire teacher education program. Congruence between the on-campus courses and the experiences of student teaching is important. Cruickshank and Armaline (1986) state that student teaching experiences should derive from the total teacher education curriculum and that "each education unit should indicate specifically what parts of that curriculum can best be attained via teaching experiences in the field and, in addition, what prerequisites on campus teaching experiences are necessary" (p. 37).

Many teacher education programs exhibit on-campus programs and field experiences that lack articulation, function independently, and probably even conflict with each other (H. Barnes, 1987; Watts, 1987). In these programs, learning to teach is viewed as an experiential, craft-oriented process that is guided indirectly, if at all, by theory (Feiman-Nemser & Buchmann, 1983). This incongruence model fosters the development of student teachers who eventually deny allegiance to education courses, fail to understand any theoretical foundation behind their own or their pupils' actions, and claim that student teaching is the only beneficial aspect of the teacher education program.

One model that attempts to integrate theory and practice is the course-specific model (Elliott & Mays, 1979). Most common for early field experience, this model links school experiences to a teacher education course and allows students to observe theory learned at the university applied almost simultaneously in the school classroom. Research on this curriculum is scarce. Hill (1986) found that the integration of theory and practice encouraged reflective thought and discussion about the language development of young children. Heath and Cyphert (1985) discovered that more elementary education courses are associated with field experiences than are secondary education courses. Applegate (1987) explains that many introductory education courses include early field experiences as a means of developing career commitment. Although it is not clear how early field experiences contribute to self-knowledge, it is clear that many students view knowledge about themselves as a primary outcome of early field experiences. A study by Sunal (1980) indicated that increased involvement in early field experiences improves a preservice teacher's performance of the specific behaviors modeled in the methods course. Denton (1982) found that early field experiences seem to have an effect on subsequent course achievement, rather than on courses of which the field experiences are a part.

A second type of curriculum model, described by H. Barnes (1987), is the thematic model. Often closely aligned with inquiry orientation, this model emerged from the awareness that learning to teach requires building schemata that are well organized and capable of directing one's actions as a teacher. Barnes explains that the cornerstone of a thematic program is its conceptual framework. McCaleb, Borko, Arends, Garner and Mauro (1987) discuss a program that revolved around resolving issues regarding four interrelated themes: identity, nonpassivity, control, and curriculum. Although not all thematic programs incorporate the same themes or kinds of activities to achieve their goals, each develops experiences that are extensions of the program's theme. In a thematic program, school experiences are planned through the curriculum that will reflect the basic theme. If real-world examples are not available, role playing and simulations are utilized to aid in the transference of theory to practice. Also, field experiences in thematic programs are monitored closely by instructors who share an understanding of the program's theme and implications for practice (H. Barnes, 1987).

Little is known about the effectiveness of the various models for the delivery of field experience programs. All too often, models for student teaching and school experiences are developed out of convenience or tradition. Often, little thought is given to the most powerful or effective means for linking campus and field-based programs or to reinforcing the goals of the teacher education program while students are practicing their craft in the schools. Better research is needed to determine the most effective models for field experience programs.

Content and Structure

A major decision for teacher educators is the content to be included in student teaching and school experiences. Studies in this area have been few.

Table 29–1 summarizes findings regarding the organization and structure of early field experiences (EFEs), which have become an established, if variant, component of teacher education programs. The consistency of the findings (Puckett, 1985; Webb, Gehrke, Ishler, & Mendoza, 1981) indicates reliability in the reporting of data, but surveys addressing institutional

TABLE 29–1. Structure and Organization of Early Field Experiences

Component of student teaching	Study	Subjects	Findings
Occurences	Flowers et al. (1948)	AACTE member institutions	EFEs uncommon
	Webb, Gehrke, Ishler, & Mendoza (1981)	AACTE member institutions	99% with EFEs
	Puckett (1985)	AACTE member institutions	99% with EFEs
Time spent in EFE	Webb et al. (1981)	AACTE member institutions	Average number of hours in EFEs from 63 to 150 for different programs
	Puckett (1985)	AACTE member institutions	Range of 5 to 85 hours for different programs
Activities	Webb et al. (1981)	AACTE member institutions	Most common activities: observing, tutoring, writing reports of experiences, completing noninstructional tasks, operating media, assessing student activity and characteristics, designing instructional materials
	Puckett (1985)	AACTE member institutions	Most common activities: observing, tutoring, assessing student characteristics and behavior, designing instructional materials, planning instruction, instructing small groups, operating instructional media, noninstructional tasks, and writing reports of experiences
Organization	Webb et al. (1981)	AACTE member institutions	Most common arrangement: linking EFE teaching education courses and increasing responsibility as student progresses through program. Percentage of institutions having EFEs at different levels: 40%, freshman; 82%, sophomore; 91%, junior; 69%, senior, and, 17% graduate
School sites	Webb et al. (1981)	AACTE member institutions	88% < school sites for EFEs; 95% < 25 nonschool sites for EFEs (day-care centers, hospitals, etc.)
	Puckett (1985)	AACTE member institutions	95% using public schools; 55% using private schools; 50%, 66%, and 63%, respectively, using rural, urban, and suburban schools

EFE practices have many limitations. Most schools, colleges, or departments of education have multiple programs, and, when limited to one answer per category on the survey, respondents' answers probably reflect average numbers or typical practices. The lack of comparative studies is a gap in the research; research that is program specific would generate findings more useful and conducive to comparisons.

One study that compared tutoring and observation programs (Ross, Raines, Cervetti, & Dillon, 1980) finds no significant differences in the number of activities performed by each group. In addition, 6 percent of students in the observation group did not observe and 16 percent in the tutoring group did not tutor. Other studies have indicated that EFE students are engaged in the following types of activities: observing instruction, tutoring, operating media, assessing student characteristics, planning lessons, designing instructional materials, engaging in small- and large-group teaching (Heath & Cyphert, 1985; Ishler & Kay, 1981; Killian & McIntyre, 1988). These studies indicate that a sequence of experiences does exist in many early field experience programs. This sequence, however, appears to focus more on the amount of time a student spends in a given activity during a particular semester than on proceeding from less to more difficult or involved classroom activities. In a longitudinal study of field experiences, Killian and McIntyre (1986a) discovered that, throughout the early field component, elementary students were significantly more involved in a variety of teaching activities than were their secondary counterparts. However, there were few differences in the types of activities engaged in by both elementary and secondary student teachers. Bischoff (1988) found that although there were few differences in teaching opportunities in full and half-day early field experiences, students preferred a full day. Most descriptions of the structure of early field experiences report only the intentions of programs, and often recommendations are made only from descriptive survey research. Current policy does not inform best practice. Research that accurately and richly describes practice and deals with the outcomes of practice is needed to inform decisions about EFEs.

Student Teaching

Tabachnick, Popkewitz, and Zeichner (1979) discover that student teachers were involved in a narrow range of classroom activities over which they had little control. Their interactions with pupils were brief and usually related to the task at hand. Their teaching was routine and mechanical and became equated with moving children through prescribed lessons in a given period of time. In addition, Griffin (1986) finds that research on teacher and school effectiveness was not included in the knowledge base that supports student teaching. His data indicated that student teaching content was based primarily on situation-specific phenomena of individual classrooms.

Table 29-2 displays findings regarding the organization and structure of student teaching. Most student teaching takes place in public schools and is a full-time experience for 10–12 weeks. This basic organizational framework is nearly universal

in the United States; Yates (1981) found a different pattern in England.

Additional research in this area is vital. One must study not only what is occurring but also what should be occurring in the student teaching curriculum. What activities are appropriate for the various levels of field experiences? How should these activities be sequenced and evaluated? Where should they occur? What strategies can be implemented to encourage student teachers to be students of teaching and reflective about their behavior and surroundings? These are but a few of the questions to be addressed by educational researchers.

Context

It is impossible to discuss thoroughly the student teaching curriculum without also examining its context, or ecology: the public school system and its classrooms. Zeichner (1986) argues that researchers have not paid enough attention to the impact of particular types of classrooms, schools, and communities or the relationship between student teaching and teacher development. Copeland (1977) suggests that the major influence on a student teacher's acquisition of skills is the ecology of the school, by which the pupils, physical environment, curriculum, community, and other school-related variables support and promote a student teacher's performance.

The available research in this area does not present the school context as a positive influence on student teacher development. Often the performance of cooperating teachers a teacher educators–supervisors (Boothroyd, 1979; Grimmett & Ratzlaff, 1986) and the socializing pressures of field sites (Seperson & Joyce, 1973; Zevin, 1974) are negative influences regarding context. The context of the public school classroom cannot always be viewed positively as a means of promoting program's orientation or goals. Richardson-Koehler (1988) finds that, within 2 weeks, student teachers discounted the influence of their pedagogical instructor, attributing most of their practices to the cooperating teacher. Copeland (1981), Denemark and Nutter (1984), and Watts (1987) suggest that the quality of student teaching programs depends too much on specific classroom sites, which are not designed to prepare student teachers and are beyond the control of the institution.

The implementation of inquiry-oriented teacher education is an example. Goodman (1983) describes the difficulty of implementing an inquiry-oriented seminar because student teachers were placed in classrooms that reflected conservative attitudes and practices and the curriculum and instruction were highly structured, predetermined, and mechanistic. Zeichner, Liston, Mahlios, and Gomes (1987) discuss the dilemma of conducting an inquiry-oriented supervisory program in schools where teacher education was not a priority, where the university supervisor lacked any authority to influence the classrooms in which students were placed, and where cooperating teachers were asked to assume the role of teacher educator in addition to full teaching loads. Zeichner and Liston (1987) claim that most schools do not actively encourage teachers to engage in the practices that inquiry-oriented teacher ed-

TABLE 29–2. Structure and Organization of Student Teaching

Component of student teaching	Study	Subjects	Findings
Length of student teaching	Johnson (1968b)	AACTE member institutions	Average length of student teaching: 12 weeks 65% have full-time elementary student teaching 60% have full-time secondary student teaching 62% place only in public schools, 2% only in private schools, 30% in both, and 17% only in laboratory school
	Yates (1981)	All teacher education institutions in England	Average length of student teaching: 17 weeks over a 3-year period
	Johnson & Yates (1982)	902 teacher education institutions in the United States	Length of student teaching: from 5 to 19 weeks Average length of student teaching: approximately 12 weeks
	Simbol & Summers (1984)	All teacher education institutions in Ohio, Indiana, Illinois, and Missouri	Length of student teaching: from 7 to 16 weeks Average length of student teaching: approximately 10 weeks
Activities in student teaching	Johnson & Yates (1982)	902 teacher education institutions in the United States	Average % of time spent observing, 14%; participating, 26%; teaching, 60%
	Griffin et al. (1983)	Student teachers in 2 teacher education institutions	Classroom teacher usually involved in instruction or mentoring even when student teacher nominally in charge; student teachers and classroom teachers demonstrated little variation in teaching practice; typical pattern was small group, teacher-led instruction followed by seatwork; emphasis was on basic skills.
	Richardson (1987)	Survey of 300 student teaching teams: Student teacher, classroom teacher, college supervisor, and building administrator	98% of student teachers communicated with students; 71% participated in extracurricular activities
Student teaching sites	Johnson (1968b) Johnson & Yates (1982)		90% provide opportunity to work in disadvantaged areas. Most student teaching placements (92–94%) are off campus. Most assignments of student teachers are done by student teaching office (62%), staff of the cooperating school (14%), or college supervisor (19%). 76% never place more than one student student teacher in a classroom.

ucation programs attempt to promote. Regardless of the university or public school, student teaching tended to be similar in all settings (O'Neal, Barnes, & Edwards, 1986). Thus, the predominant strategy of seeking to alter the form and content of student teaching within its current conceptualization might not be possible (Zeichner et al., 1987).

To reform the contexts of student teaching and school experiences, Zeichner and Teitelbaum (1982) suggest that the amount of time students spend in actual teaching be greatly reduced and that a greater proportion be allocated to studying the culture of the school and its relationship to the surrounding community through participant observation. This approach would eliminate the school as a place merely to practice one's craft and, instead, would modify it into a social laboratory, it-

self an object of scrutiny and challenge. Copeland (1986) states that teacher education programs must ensure that the context within which a student teacher is placed is one that supports the student's professional development. He insists that schools that do not offer sound educational experiences for pupils are simply not appropriate settings for field experience.

One model utilized as a means of enhancing the professional development of students and teachers and as a means of having better control over the student teaching context is the teaching center, a school within a school district to which many preservice students report for field experiences. A university faculty member assigned full- or part-time to the center is responsible, not only for the preservice program, but also for developing or facilitating a staff-development program for teachers.

Gardner (1979) cites several advantages to using teaching centers: (a) The placing of relatively large numbers of interns in schools dramatically alters the teacher–pupil ratio and makes possible classroom activities that otherwise would be different; (b) the enriched student–teacher mix frees teachers for planning, evaluating, or other tasks during the school day; and (c) the presence of university faculty provides extra skill and knowledge, as well as access to campus resources. McIntyre (1979) suggests that field experiences based in teaching centers facilitate the integration of theory and practice by meshing preservice and inservice programs. McIntyre and Vickery (1979) found that teaching centers seem to reduce student anxiety because they are observed by university faculty better known to them.

Some evidence exists that the preparation of cooperating teachers for their roles is effective in developing a more positive context. When cooperating teachers were prepared for inquiry-oriented/reflective supervision, student teachers showed less movement in a conservative direction (Zeichner & Liston, 1985) and evidenced positive attitude changes (Corrigan & Griswold, 1963; Perrodin, 1961). Classroom teachers with special preparation showed positive changes in cognitive-development growth, in active listening, in use of different teaching models (Thies-Springthall, 1984), in increased self-knowledge, sense of autonomy, and self-direction (Thies-Sprinthall, 1986), and in supervision skills (Nagel, Berg, Malian, & Murphy, 1988). Supervision education also improved communication between cooperating teachers and student teachers (Painter & Brown, 1979) and improved the quality of early field experiences (Killian & McIntyre, 1986b; McIntyre & Killian, 1987). Wheeler (1989) found that trained cooperating teachers provided a more stable field experience, more specific feedback, and a more positive affective experience. Classroom teachers themselves supported the notion of preparation in supervision (Drummond, 1980; Guyton, 1986, 1987; Hauwiller, Abel, Ausel, & Sparapini, 1988–1989; Houston, Cooper, & Warner, 1976; Twa, 1984).

Several educators urge more school interaction by advocating the reemphasis of professional teaching laboratories. Cruickshank (1984) states that, although student teaching has the necessary conditions to become a laboratory activity, it currently is not, because student teachers are not viewed as students of teaching involved in discovering, testing, reflecting, and modifying. As a result, Berliner (1985) argues pedagogy must become a laboratory-based field of study and real laboratories must be created to educate teachers by providing environments where students can experiment with producing cognitive and affective change in children. However, a most important product of the laboratories would be a newly created norm for teaching, because the orientation of the teacher would change from the practical to the analytic.

Lindsey (1969) suggests that successful professional laboratories must remain centers where students and their supervisors are engaged in continuous study of teaching, rather than practice and testing centers for researchers. Andrews (1964) goes so far as to suggest that if the public refuses to support quality professional teaching laboratories adequately, then the institution should eliminate its teacher education curriculum. Whatever the outcome, teacher educators must examine the impact of the context in which student teaching occurs and develop a strategy for gaining more control of the curriculum within that context.

The framework, articulation, and integration of the curriculum of student teaching and school experiences are vital to the success of this component. Most decisions concerning the curriculum of field experience are based on expediency and tradition, rather than on a data-based or theoretical framework. Future research needs to investigate the impact of various orientations, models, contexts, contents, and methods on the development of prospective teachers.

ADMINISTRATION OF FIELD EXPERIENCES

Almost all schools, colleges, and departments of education establish an office to organize and manage field programs.

Administrator of Field Experiences

Information regarding the administrator of field experiences has been limited to results of descriptive survey research. The most extensive and most recent national studies were conducted by Johnson and Yates (1982) and by Morris et al. (1982). Johnson (1968b) and the Association for Student Teaching's Committee on Research (1968) conducted earlier studies. Descriptions of field experience administrators have varied little over the years. A composite profile of the typical administrator was developed from these four sources. He is male, about 50 years old, and the Director of Student Teaching or Field Experiences. He holds a doctoral degree, has teaching experience, and has been a college supervisor but not a cooperating teacher. The Director of Field Experiences has professional rank and tenure. His work is supported by one or two secretaries and by student assistance.

About 50 percent of his work load is classified as administrative, and most of the load not so classified is instructional. The director's duties include (a) preparing the student teaching budget; (b) selecting, orienting, and providing inservice for college supervisors and cooperating teachers; (c) determining eligibility of and placing student teachers; (d) maintaining records and preparing reports; (e) developing handbooks and forms used in student teaching; (f) handling public relations; (g) setting up seminars for and handling supervision of student teachers; and (h) making final decisions regarding student teachers. If he is at a public institution, his duties are also likely to include initiating and carrying out research and experimental programs. The director is highly satisfied with his role but is likely to feel dissatisfied with the qualifications and training of cooperating teachers and college supervisors.

The administrator of field experiences has been a neglected participant in the student teaching process; no research goes beyond surface-level descriptions of the administrator's characteristics and responsibilities, and no in-depth analyses of the role exist. Research needs to be conducted on administrators' performance of duties, impact on field programs, and relationships to other parties.

Policies Governing Field Experiences

Flowers et al. (1948) found few self-imposed standards regulating the conduct of student teaching and almost no commonalities among different schools, colleges, and departments of education (SCDEs), a finding supported by Johnson (1986b). Although they found more policies internal to individual SCDEs, later studies confirmed great variations in policies and practices among different institutions (Johnson & Yates, 1982; Simbol & Summers, 1984). The greatest commonalities occurred in admission requirements to student teaching; over one-half of the SCDEs required a specific grade point average, English proficiency, speech and voice screening and advisor recommendations (Johnson & Yates, 1982).

Policies regarding field experiences have been developed by several external sources. The most influential and pervasive are those of the National Council for Accreditation of Teacher Education. The most comprehensive set of external standards are the Guidelines for Professional Experiences in Teacher Education (Association of Teacher Educators [ATE], 1986), developed by the National Field Directors Forum of ATE. Most of the provisions of both NCATE and ATE standards are sufficiently general to support great diversity among programs. The one exception is that both have a specific provision regarding preparation for college supervisors, something seldom provided by SCDEs (Beswick, Harman, Elsworth, Fallan, & Woock, 1980). It could be that supervision skills can alter the pattern of lack of college supervisor impact on the behavior of student teachers (McIntyre, 1983), because preparation in supervision does seem to have a meritorious effect on cooperating teachers (Corrigan & Griswold, 1963; Killian & McIntyre, 1988; Thies-Sprinthall, 1984; Zeichner & Liston, 1985).

Morris, Pannell, and Houston (1985) reviewed state standards relating to professional field experiences. The most common practice relating to the collaborative framework for field experiences was the requiring of a written agreement (17 states). Thirty-five states had standards pertaining to pre–student teaching experiences. Student teaching is required by all states; common regulations pertain to substitutes for student teaching, design and length of student teaching, grade level/field of assignments, supervision, evaluation, and criteria for selection of a school/district. Eighteen states provided criteria for being a cooperating teacher, but only five provided criteria for college supervisors. Almost no states provided for the evaluation of the cooperating teacher and the college supervisor.

The literature on field experience policies illuminates the serious problem of extreme diversity in policies and practices. Certainly, strict standardization is not desirable, but justification probably does not exist for such variances as from 5 to 19 weeks of student teaching and institutional ratios of college supervisors to student teachers of from 1/1–9 to 1/26–30 (Johnson & Yates, 1982). As Morris et al. (1985) point out, standards "have been derived primarily from practice and not research" (p. 76).

Costs of Educational Field Programs

Very little is known about the costs of educational field programs. In the Johnson and Yates (1982) and Johnson (1968b) studies, only 32 percent of the institutions responded to an item regarding budgets; for those institutions, the average total budget was $38,000 (1968) and $42,000 (1982) and cost per student teacher was $314 (1968) and $424 (1982). If these averages are representative, they would indicate that, although programs are expanding with the increase of pre–student teaching experiences, the overall budgets for the programs, when inflation is taken into account, have decreased considerably.

Legal Aspects of Field Experiences

Very few lawsuits and court cases have grown out of student teaching conflicts (Johnson, 1968b; Swalls, 1976; Yates & Johnson, 1982b). The most common causes of lawsuits are injury to a child by the student teacher, denial of entry to student teaching, negligence, and the grade given in student teaching. Issues center around student teacher conduct in schools and SCDE policies governing student teaching (Yates & Johnson, 1982b). States vary greatly in statutory regulation of student teaching and protection of student teachers through legal status, certification, liability insurance, and/or save-harmless statutes (Swalls, 1976).

Considering the small number of lawsuits and even smaller number of court cases arising from student teaching, tort issues do not seem to be the most compelling legal aspects of field experiences. Morris and Curtis (1983) point out that, although more and earlier field experiences are required, legal support systems relating to quality in field experiences are minimal. They assert that issues such as certification of cooperating teachers are more germane than tort issues to the interests of SCDEs. Also SCDEs are required by law or by state standards to conduct student teaching experiences in teacher education programs. Yet local education agencies are not required to participate, which sets up an interesting paradox. State provisions for incentives for LEAs and cooperating teachers and for mandates that compel LEA participation could enhance the quality of field programs. Where such arrangements do exist, research on the effects would be useful and would provide helpful information.

Relationships Between SCDEs and LEAs

The ATE field experience guidelines (ATE, 1986) call for collaborative organizational structures (p. 7) and cooperative decision making (p. 9). If such structures exist, they often are superficial and exist mainly on paper for the 46 percent of SCDEs that do have written contracts with cooperating schools (Johnson & Yates, 1982). Field experiences involve very complex arrangements and processes, yet, of all the people involved, generally only the director of field experiences and the student teacher have field experiences as a major responsibility. And the director works with large numbers of LEAs, student teachers, cooperating teachers, and college supervisors. It is not surprising that Griffin et al. (1983) found few instances of policy, practice, or personal relationships between SCDEs and LEAs, or that Cope (1973) found that English cooperating teachers described contacts with SCDEs as pleasant but not constituting a genuine working relationship.

A case study of 14 cooperating-school arrangements throughout Australia (Turney, 1977) found a number of factors basic to the development of cooperative relationship, including collaboratively formulated and communicated objectives, explicit role expectations, collaborative program development, constant monitoring, and abundant formal and informal channels of communication. Given the current administrative and organizational structure of field programs, these conditions are not likely to exist.

Applegate (1985) asserts that institutional dilemmas are recurring in field programs. Institutional dilemmas include logistics, politics, personnel, sites, travel, hours, course and program organization, SCDE–LEA contacts, and legal responsibility (p. 62). Student teaching is an institutional, as well as an individual, process. Being a process, its essence is not easily captured by survey research. For example, when an institutional representative states that placements are made by the student teaching office, the following questions are left unanswered. Is this true for all programs in the SCDE? Who in the office makes the placement decisions and with input from whom? How many institutions and people are involved in making a placement? Is this arrangement the most effective for securing the best placements?

Research on the organization of student teaching has not addressed institutional and power issues. Close examination of field programs and interviews with and observations of key people (e.g., director of student teaching, school system contact person, principal) could lead to an understanding that informs practice. Otherwise, many student teaching organizational patterns are likely to remain as static as the findings indicate they now are. More student teaching innovations were reported in 1968 (Johnson, 1968b) than in 1982 (Johnson & Yates), and most reported in 1982 had been reported in 1968. The innovations reflected unilateral decision making by the SCDE; did not affect organizational arrangements with schools; and related to the entire teacher education program more than to student teaching specifically. Should this type of situation persist, variances that do occur will remain idiosyncratic, and lists of characteristics of "best student teaching programs" (Johnson & Yates, 1982, pp. 3–4) will continue to be ungrounded in research.

PEOPLE INVOLVED IN FIELD EXPERIENCES: THE TRIAD

A typical student teaching experience brings together three people who are expected to work together for common purposes: a student teacher, a cooperating teacher, and a college supervisor. The working relationship is a well established and accepted one, and the work context and conditions are similar for the thousands of triads in existence at any given time.

Perspectives on Roles

Roles and responsibilities for each member of the triad are outlined in SCDE handbooks, state requirements, and national guidelines. Although the NCATE standards state that "The roles and responsibilities of education students, college-based supervisors and field-based supervisors are delineated in negotiated written agreements" (National Council for Accreditation of Teacher Education, 1986, p. 6), no formal comparative studies have been conducted, so it is difficult to discuss differences and similarities in stated expectations. An examination of the one set of national guidelines (ATE, 1986) uncovers very general descriptions of responsibility such as "Establish and maintain open channels of communication between the college and university and affiliated components" (p. 15). A section of the guidelines entitled Qualifications and Responsibilities of Affiliated Supervisory Personnel lists no specific responsibilities of cooperating teachers (p. 17). The SCDEs are more specific in enumerating roles and responsibilities, but written statements are somewhat general, especially regarding the cooperating teacher, over whom the SCDE has no authority. This situation fosters an environment in which statements are freely interpreted by the triad members who bring with them role expectations of themselves, of the other triad members, and of the student teaching experience.

Agreement among triad members regarding roles and responsibilities is not prevalent. Among cooperating teachers and college supervisors in Australian SCDEs, there was a shared frame of reference regarding the purposes of the practicum experience but divergence in role interpretations (Beswick et al., 1980). Garland (1965) and Kaplan (1967) also reported conflicting expectations of the cooperating teacher, and Kapel and Sadler (1978) found that cooperating teachers and college supervisors had different views on the cooperating teacher's role in decision making and policy formation. Disagreement was also found regarding the student teacher's role in the schools (Gettone, 1980), and interview data indicated that student teachers' self-perceived roles shifted throughout the student teaching experience (Calderhead, 1987).

Grimmett and Ratzlaff (1986) compared the findings from their Canadian study of the expectations regarding the cooperating teacher's role with the findings from two American studies (Castillo, 1971; Copas, 1984). Both Castillo (1971) and Grimmett and Ratzlaff (1986) found conflicting ideas among the triad regarding the role of the cooperating teacher, but the studies were not similar in their specific findings. Grimmett and Ratzlaff compared the three studies and found more similarities between their own findings and Copas's than between the two American studies, and they suggest that proximity of time has more influence than context. A major difference was the articulated expectation in the more recent studies that the cooperating teacher would take an active teacher educator role.

Expectations for Field Experiences

Studies also indicate conflict among triad members regarding expectations for field experiences. Tittle (1974) found that student teachers and cooperating teachers thought that developing self-confidence was most important, whereas college supervisors and administrators considered application of theory most important. Student teachers thought experimentation important, but the other three groups did not. Perspectives on benefits of student teaching were also divergent.

Applegate and Lasley (1985) obtained descriptions of what students expected to learn in early field experiences and developed a checklist of expectations. Using the same instrument, Martin and Wood (1984) found that cooperating teachers' expectations were different from EFE students' expectations and that students were not able to gain experiences compatible with their levels of expectation. Campbell and Williamson (1983) found significant differences in several areas between cooperating teachers' expectations and reality. Griffin (1983) found that for student teachers, expectations were fulfilled, but cooperating teachers' and college supervisors' expectations varied and were global and general, and "Attention to the particulars of either research-derived or craft knowledge was conspicuous by its absence" (p. 18).

Problems Regarding Field Experiences

Problems expressed by triad members are indications of unfulfilled expectations and desires. Communication is a recurring problem. Yates (1981) reports that cooperating teachers in England and Wales were unsure of what was expected of them and expressed a need for better communication. American studies confirm the fact that lack of communication is a problem for cooperating teachers, as well as for college supervisors, student teachers, and EFE students. Problems center around unclear expectations, university–school communications (particularly flowing from the university or college supervisor to the school or cooperating teacher), and interpersonal exchanges among triad members (Beswick et al., 1980; Southall, 1984; Thompson & Ellis, 1984). Lack of time and lack of training and experience in supervision also create difficulties for cooperating teachers and college supervisors (Beswick et al., 1980; Martin & Wood, 1984). The most common problems do not relate specifically to teaching, although problems with field experience students' skills, behaviors, and attitudes were reported (Applegate & Lasley, 1982; Martin & Wood, 1983; Southall, 1984). Triad members also evidenced a lack of understanding of each other's problems in the discrepancies between self-reported problems and problems each group perceived for the other (Beswick et al., 1980).

Tittle (1974) found divergence and tendencies of triad members to blame each other when problem areas were examined. The college supervisor and the student teacher saw the cooperating teacher's lack of modeling as a serious problem, and the cooperating teachers and administrators viewed insufficient help from the college supervisor as one. School personnel saw preparation of the student teacher and lack of information from the SCDE as serious problems, and college supervisors viewed lack of control over the practical experience as one for the college. The one point of agreement for the groups was that finding and retaining good cooperating teachers was a problem for the college.

Triad Attitudes Toward Each Other

The members of the triad bring role conceptualizations and expectations of each other to the student teaching experience that are often divergent and/or confused. Boothroyd (1979) found that even though there was a fair amount of within- and between-triad group agreement as to the importance of different student teaching objectives, perceived concordance was lower than actual, and "the three classes of subjects had less positive attitudes toward each other than warranted" (p. 247). Even when contacts among the triad were pleasant, the relationship did not constitute a genuine working partnership and evidenced some wariness and distrust between college and school staff (Cope, 1973).

From the beginning to the end of student teaching, triad members become more negative toward each other, especially college supervisors and student teachers, and triad relationships are more competitive than cooperative (Yee, 1967). Barrows (1979) characterizes the triad as a very unbalanced relationship, with the teacher exercising inordinate power and authority in determining student teacher success. Student teacher dissatisfaction with the role of the college supervisor is prevalent (Funk et al., 1982; Griffin et al., 1983), and student teachers seek legitimization of their roles as professionals and indicators of success more from pupils than from cooperating teachers and almost never from college supervisors (Friebus, 1977).

Cognition and Behavior

The members of the triad experience intra- and interpersonal role confusion during student teaching, uncertainty about their own and others' roles, and divergent role expectations of themselves and others. These phenomena contribute to the disappointing outcomes of the student teaching experience and the lack of achievement of objectives, particularly objectives desired by the SCDE. Three people involved in a common experience cannot always share the same frame of reference, but convergence, rather than divergence, can be fostered. The key is communication, but a simplistic view of the concept will not facilitate cohesion. Student teaching is a complex process, and one of its most abstruse components is the cognitive complexity of the triad members.

An easy solution requires more detailed and better explicated guidelines, role definitions, and instructions. But these probably would help only minimally. Those that currently exist are based on tradition and practice, rather than on a theoretical or an empirical base, and are very individualistic. The research in this section informs about what roles and expectations are, but not about what they ought to be. Also, individuals interpret and act on written and verbal symbols, and it is only through eliciting internal responses to and interpretations of the external framework that facilitative communication can occur. Several studies that focus on college supervisors illustrate the need for exploring cognitions that influence behaviors and attitudes. The utility of these studies is based on two criteria: (a) they go beyond survey data, that is, the research techniques include interviews and/or observation; and (b) they deal with how college supervisors think and actually act in their roles, not just with what they think their roles are and which ones they think are most important.

Zimpher, DeVoss, and Nott (1980) found that college supervisors did not carry out their formal roles and that they believed they had little impact on student teacher methods. This second finding was supported by Koehler (1984), who also found that if college supervisors held clinical supervision as one of their primary responsibilities, they felt little satisfaction with or accomplishment in their roles. If they considered their primary responsibility one of support for the student teacher, they felt a strong sense of role satisfaction and efficacy.

Interviews uncovered three different belief systems operating for college supervisors who saw themselves as practicing clinical supervisors, who identified the goal of helping student teachers become more reflective in and analytical about their teaching, and who had similar patterns of supervisory practices (Zeichner & Tabachnick, 1982). Similarly, Zahorick (1988) found three goal clusters operating for college supervisors for whom the mechanics of supervision were alike in terms of number of visits, observation instruments, and conference format. Two of the three categories of college supervisor behavior found in each study were alike, and each study had a distinct third category. One category emphasized teaching techniques and classroom management. Another focused on broader issues such as human relations, political influence, and the nature of schools. Zahorick's third category was goals oriented toward the development of problem-solving ability, whereas Zeichner and Tabachnick found a focus on personal growth.

Conclusions

The studies cited in this section are generally helpful to persons developing field programs. It seems clear that roles and responsibilities of triad members and goals of field experiences need to be clearly explicated and that there should be mutual understanding of them. Beyond specific written statements regarding functions, though, college supervisors, cooperating teachers, and student teachers need opportunities to discuss among themselves and with field experience administrators the personal meanings they attach to role descriptions. The research indicates that planned, purposeful talking with each other about roles and objectives might alleviate contradictions and the frustrations that flow from them.

Current research indicates little about what explicated roles and responsibilities of the triad members should be or which ones can be implemented effectively. Just because most people think that a major responsibility of the college supervisor is to hold conferences with the student teacher does not mean that holding conferences is an important function. College supervisors' time might be better spent in group seminars. The assumption that college supervisors should have a major impact on student teacher teaching behavior is prevalent, but if the college supervisor cannot have any discernible effect in this area under the current student teaching structure, it might be an inappropriate expectation. The studies that relied on data from interviews and observations indicated that role behaviors

are influenced greatly by the way one conceptualizes or thinks about that role. Qualitative research provides better access to thinking and behavior and holds more promise of generating information about appropriate roles, responsibilities, and goals. Three components are necessary for research to uncover such information: written role definitions of triad members and goals for student teaching in teacher education programs, interpretations of triad members regarding roles and goals, and implementation of roles. Given these data, it can be determined if triad members are able to carry out stated and/or internal roles and responsibilities and what functions facilitate achievement of teacher education program goals.

PROCESSES OF THE STUDENT TEACHING EXPERIENCE

Some research on student teaching has been of the "black box" variety. Data are collected prior to and after student teaching and compared, without any information about what goes on during student teaching. Thus, the student teaching experience becomes a black box, an undefined and mysterious variable. This phenomenon has been unrecognized when researchers used psychometric research paradigms that inferred that student teaching was a known quantity and a singular experience, regardless of participants, processes, and contexts. Pretest–posttest research creates a situation in which student teaching is a treatment, but it is not an operationalized variable, so changes and outcomes cannot be related specifically to the treatment. The knowledge thus produced is akin to the quantum theory of physics; we know what goes in (e.g., the attitude toward teaching) and what comes out (e.g., a more negative attitude), but not what occurs in the interim.

Conferences

The conference is the situation in which much of the formal supervision of student teachers occurs; it takes place when the student teacher sits down with the cooperating teacher and/or the college supervisor to discuss teaching and the student teaching experience. Evidence indicates that, although conferences are common (Yates & Johnson, 1982a), they are not frequent (Tittle, 1974), especially with college supervisors (Flowers et al., 1948), and they cluster more at the end of the student teaching experience (Killian & McIntyre, 1988).

Conferences have been analyzed functionally and substantively. Heidelbach (1969) developed three functional categories of cooperating teacher verbal behavior from conference tapes of student teacher–cooperating teacher dyads. Most (67 percent) operational talk was descriptive, 17 percent was prescriptive, and 16 percent was focusing (calling attention to a particular substantive area). Heidelbach also found that conferences of college supervisors focused on particular substantive issues more than cooperating teacher conferences and that, although given slightly different emphasis, the major substantive issues of conferences were the same for the both groups.

Tabachnick et al. (1979) intensively studied student teaching experiences using interviews and observations of conferences, seminars, orientations, and workshops. Student teachers assumed a passive role in their interactions with cooperating teachers. Directions, procedural issues, and classroom management were predominant cooperating teacher activities and topics, with no serious reflection on or analysis of teaching. College supervisor–student teacher conferences also emphasized teaching techniques and classroom management. What was to be taught and for what purposes was seldom discussed. Not evident were program goals for student teachers: to be reflective, autonomous, self-fulfilled, and actively involved.

O'Neal and Edwards (1983) conducted a complex analysis of cooperating teacher–student teacher conferences. Teachers dominated conferences, doing 72 percent of the talking, reviewing classroom events or student teacher activities and giving directions. Student teacher talk mainly addressed classroom events, student teacher activities, and acknowledgements of supervisor talk. The great majority of conferences focused on specific teaching events, rather than on teaching in general. They focused on the methods and materials of instruction and were devoted to the cognitive domain. The authors conclude that "there was no evidence of an articulated knowledge base regarding either the context or process of teaching or the content or process of training the student teacher" and that "craft knowledge" and "common sense" are the basis of most discussions regarding specific clinical experiences (p. 35). Research conducted by Richardson-Koehler (1988) confirmed these findings.

Most conferences involve a dyad rather than the triad. Conferences are dominated by cooperating teachers and student teachers take a passive role. Conferences involve low levels of thinking: descriptions and direction-giving interactions predominate. Analysis and reflection on teaching are not common; the substantive issues of conferences tend to focus on teaching techniques, classroom management, and pupil characteristics. Craft and experiential knowledge and efficiency are rationales for most recommendations.

Seminars

Whereas the conference can be characterized as an individualized experience in student teaching, the seminar is a group process, usually involving one college supervisor and a number of student teachers. Conferences between student teachers and college supervisors tend to focus on an episode of teaching observed by the college supervisor, whereas the focus of seminars is more general.

Although seminars in field experiences are quite common (Johnson, 1968b), very little research has focused on them. Although seminars have been advocated as facilitators of reflective teaching (Armaline & Hoover, 1989; Liggett, Fulwiler, Clarke, & Hood, 1988), seminars are like conferences in that they encourage an emphasis on mastery of technique and classroom management, rather than on theory and reflection (Lanier & Little, 1986). Zeichner and Tabachnick (1982) found that, although most college supervisors said they used semi-

nars "to rise broader issues of teaching and learning, about school and education," most focused on concrete teaching incidents. Tabachnick et al. (1979) confirmed that seminars were not issue oriented and that they were "eclectic collections of responses to immediate classroom demands" (p. 21); critical thought, analysis, and reflection were not facilitated. Liggett et al. (1988) did find that frequent seminars promoted reflection in student teachers.

Goodman (1983) studied five seminar groups through observations, individual and group interviews, and teacher education program literature. The seminar's role did not depend on the formal statements of its purpose but on the ways the statements were interpreted. Seminars played three roles. In the liberalizing role, the seminar was organized to create a liberal, open learning environment and was characterized by informality, attention to student concerns, freedom for student teachers to criticize the seminar leader, and a liberal review of teaching in which there was no one right answer. In the collaborating role, the seminar supported practices and beliefs found in schools and was characterized by a focus on management problems, a sharing of techniques, an emphasis on what worked, and no questioning of assumptions. In the inquiring role, seminars focused on more substantive issues and encouraged student teachers to think more deeply about schools, education, pupils, and their own roles as teachers. The inquiring role was infrequent, and the collaborating role predominated.

Seminars are removed from the school setting, in terms of time and usually place, but participants do not seem to take advantage of the opportunity to step back from teaching and emphasize broader issues. The focus of seminars is narrow and seems to reflect the immediate needs and concerns of student teachers. The group process becomes an extension of the individualized processes of conferencing.

Feedback and Evaluation

Evaluation of student teachers is an integral part of teacher education programs. A structure of formative and summative evaluation is developed to serve several purposes. Gatekeeping, or control of entry to the profession, is one of the major functions. Final evaluations, in particular, purport to distinguish among competent and incompetent, effective and less effective, talented and less talented, outstanding, average, and below-average students regarding their potential as teachers. Assessing student teachers in terms of the goals of the teacher education program is another purpose that serves as a validating device for the program, as well as a source of feedback for program modifications. Feedback and evaluation are also a mechanism for helping the student teacher identify strengths and weaknesses in order to improve teaching. These processes have been part of a relatively large number of studies of student teaching.

Evaluation Criteria. It is a well-established educational premise that the criteria used for evaluation should be explicit and that the stated standards should be the actual standards utilized. These phenomena, particularly the latter, do not appear to be operating in field-experience programs. Both cooperating teachers and college supervisors tend to base evaluations on a single, overall affective impression rather than on distinct professional competencies (Griffin et al., 1983; Wheeler & Knoop, 1982). Even when explicit behaviors were defined and evaluated, cooperating teachers made few discriminations (Phelps, Schmitz, & Wade, 1986). Turney et al. (1982), reviewing Australian literature on student teaching, stated that evaluation is subjective and impressionistic, using " 'hidden' criteria which are more concerned with the personality and social acceptability of the students than with their teaching ability" (p. 26). Motivation and personal characteristics such as flexibility and commitment are considered more important student teacher qualities than knowledge of subject matter and instructional skills (Koehler, 1984). Martin (1988) found differences between least and most effective student teachers related to pupils' perceptions and teaching behaviors, indicating that objective criteria could be applied successfully.

Yee (1967) examined differences in evaluations of student teachers who had different relationships with and expectations of cooperating teachers. Affectively oriented student teachers were more concerned with warmth and support of cooperating teachers, and cognitively oriented student teachers were more concerned with cooperating teachers' general abilities as leaders. Many more cognitively oriented student teachers received a lower grade than affectively oriented student teachers, who almost exclusively received grades of A or B.

In other words, the student teachers who indicated they wanted to learn how to be more effective teachers received lower grades and criticisms for being uncommitted to teaching and uninterested in children. The student teachers who indicated they wanted the leaders' social-emotional aid and sympathy rather than instructional guidance received high grades and favorable comments concerning their commitment to teaching and interest in children. (p. 113)

In early field experiences, attitudes and interpersonal skills, personal appearance, and emotional and psychological factors are used as evaluation criteria by more SCDEs than are instructional skills, content knowledge, intellectual skills, and leadership (Webb et al., 1981). This phenomenon could be somewhat intentional, because the purposes of early field experiences are different and often focus on suitability and compatibility with the profession, but developing objective evaluations based on these dimensions is difficult.

Reliability and Validity of Evaluations. Because student teacher evaluations can serve as the major screening device for entry to the profession, they assume a great degree of importance, and reliability and validity of evaluations become key issues. Interrater reliability between college supervisor and cooperating teacher and intrarater reliability, particularly for the college supervisor, seem to be minimal requirements. The cooperating teacher and college supervisor should be using similar standards for evaluation, and the college supervisor should be using the same standards for all student teachers. The issue of validity in student teaching evaluation has two components: the establishment of criteria for evaluation that are related to

effective teaching and to program goals (criterion-related validity) and the determination that what is stated to be measured is what is actually measured (construct validity). Studies lend credence to neither reliability nor validity in student teaching evaluation.

College supervisors give more evaluative feedback to student teachers than do cooperating teachers (O'Neal, 1983; Zimpher et al., 1980). Boothroyd (1979), Reiff (1980), and Yee (1967) report discrepancies between cooperating teacher and college supervisor evaluations, but Mahan and Harsle (1977) found agreement among cooperating teachers, college supervisors, and student teachers regarding who is and who is not a professionally effective student teacher. When discrepancies exist between the cooperating teacher and the college supervisor evaluations, student teachers tend to lend more credence to cooperating teacher evaluations (Yates, 1981; Zimpher et al., 1980). When rating instruments have been compared, analytic methods using specific criteria seem to be more reliable than profile or global scales (Allison, 1978; Povey, 1975; Turney et al., 1982).

Bias can be fairly easily introduced into the evaluative process (Reavis, 1979) and is somewhat common (Turney et al., 1982; Yee, 1967; Zimpher et al., 1980). Differences in cooperating teachers' and student teachers' conceptual levels of thinking and moral reasoning can foster bias, as there is evidence that these differences lead to incongruencies between cooperative teacher subjective evaluations and objective performance measures (Thies-Sprinthall, 1980).

Hattie, Warwick, and Cole (1982) found that training sessions increased the reliability of cooperating teachers' evaluations, and Siedentop (1981) reported that educating cooperating teachers, college supervisors, and student teachers regarding observation and feedback on a given set of competencies resulted in positive student teacher behavior change.

Evidence of inflated grades in student teaching is related to the validity of student teacher evaluations. Evaluations tend to have a limited range in the upper levels of rating scales and do not make adequate discriminations among more effective and less effective student teachers, regardless of criteria used (Defino, 1983; Funk et al., 1982; Haviland & Haviland, 1981).

Final Evaluations of Student Teachers. The ultimate evaluation of a student teacher is the grade in student teaching. The most common type is a letter grade (55 percent), although 38 percent of SCDEs use pass–fail or satisfactory–unsatisfactory grading systems. In most cases (67 percent) the college supervisor determines the grade, but directors of student teaching (29 percent) and cooperating teachers (12 percent) also have responsibility in some cases (Johnson & Yates, 1982). Failure in student teaching is uncommon. Fifteen percent of SCDEs never fail student teachers, 50 percent fail less than 1 percent, and 15 percent fail 1 percent. Failure is attributed more to motivational and classroom-management problems than to instructional ones (Johnson & Yates, 1982; Koehler, 1984). The issue of whether the low failure rate is attributable to failure or dropout in early field experiences or to being counseled out by teacher education faculty has not been addressed through research. Knowles (1988) found that student teacher failure was a very complex issue and that SCDEs had few effective ways of preventing or dealing with failure.

Linkages in Student Teaching Processes: Promising Research Practices

Studying the processes of student teaching is one way of defining and operationalizing student teaching. Yet many studies fail to yield information about student teaching supervision that can inform practice and move research on field experiences from a descriptive to an explanatory stage. It is interesting to know that cooperating teachers dominated conferences and that a particular topic was most often discussed, but if such information is isolated and not linked to a larger framework, its value is limited. Descriptions of what occurs in seminars enrich knowledge about student teaching but do little to inform about how seminars should be conducted for particular purposes. This section will attempt to illustrate a framework, shown in Figure 29-1, that produces research on student teaching that informs practice.

A major premise of this framework is that supervision processes are what make up the event called student teaching. Other factors, such as activities engaged in and classroom context, surely have an effect on student teaching, but they are not peculiar to student teaching and are likely to affect student teaching experiences in ways similar to their effects on teaching. To learn about student teaching, one needs to know what occurs in student teaching, and the most significant occurrences center around supervision processes. For the purposes of this chapter, the processes of student teaching (supervision) have been limited to conferences, seminars, and evaluations, with full knowledge that they are representative, and not exhaustive, categories. Even though context is not explicit in the model, its effects on supervision processes are acknowledged.

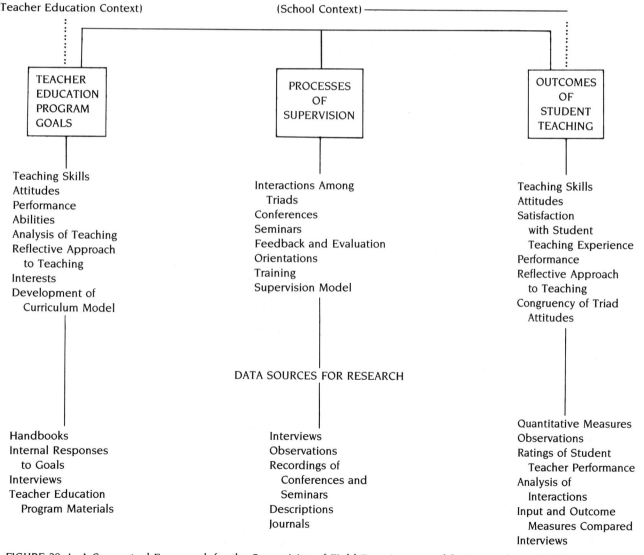

FIGURE 29–1. A Conceptual Framework for the Supervision of Field Experiences and for Research on Field Experiences

Research has indicated that student teaching and the supervisory processes are separate activities, disconnected from the rest of the teacher education program (Griffin et al., 1983). Even when a supervision model is connected to the goals of the teacher education program (e.g., developing reflective, autonomous teachers), supervisors' actual activities are individual interpretations, and often distortions, of the goals (Tabachnick et al., 1979).

Research on field experiences has suffered from the same disconnected nature. Until very recently, it often focused on an isolated piece of the student teaching experience. Teacher educators have been left feeling hopeless about having any effect on student teaching outcomes. Given the research methodologies, epistemologies, and frameworks, it is no wonder that the editor of *The Journal of Teacher Education* would lament in a preface to a review of English research on student teaching, "student teaching problems are unchanging, persistent and universal. . . . The problems are unsolvable" (Yates, 1981, p. 44).

Creating and maintaining linkages among the dimensions of student teaching, including teacher education goals and/or the outcomes of field experiences, can develop more useful knowledge. Some research on student teaching has established strong linkages between at least two of the three dimensions of student teaching. This research will be reviewed to show how the linkages were established, what knowledge was developed due to these relationships, and how even better linkages might be established to create a more solid knowledge base for student teaching.

A fairly well-developed area of research considers the effect of particular supervision models on outcomes of student teaching. A number of studies have focused on the effects of the clinical supervision model and have reported positive outcomes of using the model, such as increased internal control (Armstrong & Ladd, 1975), positive self-assessment (Cook, 1976), improved supervision (Shuma, 1973), improved teaching and attitude toward teaching (Krajewski, 1976), and generation of preferred behaviors (Reavis, 1978). Studies also have focused on student teacher attitude toward direct or indirect supervisory approach (Copeland, 1980; Copeland & Atkinson, 1978; Reavis, 1977) and on positive effects of combinations of direct and indirect supervision (Sanders & Merritt, 1974). Other studies have reported that horizontal evaluation facilitated student teacher analysis and reflection (Gitlin, Ogawa, & Rose, 1982); a reflective teaching supervision model promoted more complex analyses of teaching and more favorable attitudes toward student teaching (Cruickshank, 1987); the teaching clinic facilitated improved communication and increased feedback (Buttery & Michalak, 1975); and developmentally based supervision had a positive effect on student teachers' psychological development (Glassberg & Sprinthall, 1980).

The studies connect supervision processes with outcomes. Though more helpful than studies of an isolated dimension of student teaching, these studies have typical handicaps in that the supervision model focuses on procedural rather than substantive aspects of supervision. No linkages with program goals are made. The substance of supervision, the what that goes with the how, is not a component of the research. When that connection is made, research on student teaching can be more meaningful.

Goodman (1985) linked all three dimensions of field experiences. The goals of a pre–student teaching block were explicated (creativity and high level of reflection). Efforts were made to influence cooperating teachers' supervisory behavior (supervision processes). Based on students' coursework and evaluations, Goodman concluded that students were able to link theory and practice and had an enhanced sense of professional autonomy and creativity (outcomes).

Zeichner and Liston (1985) also conducted research exemplary of the linkages among goals, supervision, and outcomes. They studied college supervisors and their student teachers in a program designed to foster inquiry, reflection, and analysis among student teachers, as well as an awareness of the problematic nature of teaching (goals). Findings regarding how college supervisors implemented the program goals (processes) led the authors to conclude that program goals were partially implemented. They also reported that student teacher perspectives became better articulated without becoming more custodial or negative (outcomes). This study indicates that articulation of goals and preparation for implementing these goals can have some effect on supervision processes and the realization of goals. The findings would be even more informative if student teacher outcomes for individual college supervisors were analyzed to determine the effects of different goal-implementation strategies.

S. Barnes and Edwards (1984) conducted a study in which the connections between supervision and outcomes were explicit. In a secondary analysis of data from a comprehensive study of student teaching, they identified cooperating teacher–student teacher dyads as most and least effective (outcomes). Then they analyzed the interactions of those dyads (supervision processes) to determine what, if any, differences existed between the more and less effective dyads. Effective student teaching experience was defined as that "in which the acquisition of technical skills of teaching was accompanied by the development of a concomitant ability to make appropriate judgments with regard to the application of those skills" (p. 2). Data sources were taped conferences, journals, interviews, observation, and 10 quantitative measures. The qualitative data uncovered a large number of differences between the more and less effective cooperating teachers. All of the teachers held a common set of beliefs, but teachers in the more effective experiences functioned in a more open and conditional exercise of these beliefs. More effective cooperating teachers responded to student teacher inadequacies by adjusting instruction and expectations and treating them as mistakes or omissions that could be corrected. Less effective cooperating teachers were confused and complained, responded with very general directives, and justified failure in terms of inadequacies. The more effective cooperating teachers treated the student teacher and the school administration more as colleagues. They also were more willing to share materials and help the student teacher and had a more questioning attitude about the meaning, use, and effects of grading pupils. Less effective cooperating teachers accepted grades as objective evidence of pupil ability or performance level. The S. Barnes and Edwards (1984) study is exemplary of the usefulness of information derived from studies that link student teaching processes to outcomes of student teaching. If the linkage had not been made, the knowledge that communication and other patterns of cooperating-teacher behavior differ would be interesting, but it would not inform practice.

AN EMERGING PARADIGM FOR RESEARCH ON FIELD EXPERIENCES

The phenomenon of the atheoretical nature of field experiences that has existed for many years can be attributed partly to the imposition of a scientific research paradigm on situations that are not compatible with the methods, purposes, philosophy, epistemology, or assumptions of the paradigm. This paradigm adopted the scientific methods of the natural sciences. A major breakthrough in the 1980s was the emergence of a new paradigm for research on field experiences, a naturalistic approach. This new paradigm has generated more meaningful results than the old and, if continued, could lead to substantive and procedural changes in the way field experiences are conceptualized and structured.

Guba (1978) compared the two paradigms, and Table 29-3 summarizes the major characteristics of each. Guba refers to the new paradigm as naturalistic; it also has been called ethnographic, sociological, anthropological, qualitative, interpretive, phenomenological, and constructivist (Erickson, 1986; Lutz & Ramsey, 1974: Magoon, 1977; Popkewitz, Tabachnick,

& Zeichner, 1979; Wilson, 1977; Zeichner, 1978). For research on field experiences, this approach has produced several outcomes. Naturalistic inquiry regards field experiences as a process rather than as a variable. This systemic approach acknowledges the complexity of field experiences. Also, more naturalistic inquiry has included subjects' frames of reference, particularly those of the triad. Traditionally, studies have ignored the meanings actors bring to the experience, rather than viewing them as integral components of the experience. Another outcome is that research has moved from the more restrictive pretest–posttest design studying predetermined variables and from descriptive survey data to a discovery mode in which concepts and categories emerge from the data. Field experiences are abstruse processes, making it difficult to identify a priori the important variables, particularly given the limited knowledge base.

Naturalistic inquiry is appropriate for the natural history stage of science (Dussault, 1970). This stage is the descriptive stage of looking, seeing, naming, describing, and classifying. Dussault asserts that if these processes are not given sufficient consideration, the result of scientific inquiry is "immature, half-baked, dogmatic, and worthless" (p. 15). Where exceptions to this characterization do exist in research on field experiences, the critical factor usually is that the research paradigm is naturalistic and incorporates descriptive knowledge. Quantitative, correlational, psychometric research designs have been premature and have hindered the development of cumulative knowledge about field experiences.

Science produces four basic kinds of knowledge that are not

TABLE 29–3. Comparisons of Conventional and Naturalistic Inquiry

Characteristic	Conventional	Naturalistic
Philosophical base	Seek facts or causes of social phenomena with little regard for subjective states of individuals	Concerned with understanding human behavior from actors' frames of reference
Inquiry paradigm	Scientific method	Ethnographic
Purpose	Test hypotheses; verification	Discovery
Stance	Reductionist; seek data to answer preformulated questions or to test preformulated hypotheses	Expansionist; exploratory; open-minded; seeking
Framework/design	Preordinate, fixed design	Emergent and variable designs
Style	Intervention on variables	Selection of vaiables
Reality manifold	Single, objective reality	Changing, subjective reality
Value structure	Value-free	Multiple value positions; researcher's values part of inquiry
Setting	Laboratory	Natural
Context	Render context unrelated through control of variation	Try to understand context to assess its meaning for and impact on elements of study
Conditions	Control conditions	Open inquiry to uncontrolled conditions as much as possible to understand how events occur in the "real world"
Treatment	Important to inquiry	No treatment
Scope	Limited by range of variables	Unlimited range of variables
Methods	Objectivity through intersubjective agreement	Objectivity through confirmation, agreement among a variety of information sources

Note. Compiled with permission from *Toward a Methodology of Naturalistic Inquiry in Educational Evaluation* (pp. 11–18) by E. G. Guba, 1978, Los Angeles: University of California, Los Angeles, Center for the Study of Evaluations. Copyright 1978 by the Center.

mutually exclusive but are cumulative stages; a higher stage is difficult if not impossible to reach unless the prerequisite knowledge is attained (Dussault, 1970). The progression of knowledge is from

DESCRIPTION→UNDERSTANDING→
EXPLANATION→PREDICTION.

Different kinds of knowledge can be gained from a single research study, but higher levels (explanation, prediction) are dependent upon some basic foundation of lower levels of knowledge (description, understanding). Yet for some time research on field experiences persisted in trying to produce explanatory and predictive knowledge (e.g., What student teacher attitudes predict success in student teaching? Does the cooperating teacher or college supervisor influence the attitudes and behavior of student teachers?) without an adequate grasp of the "dynamic social event" (Tabachnick, 1981) that is student teaching. This situation is analogous to meteorologists attempting to predict the weather without any knowledge about or understanding of clouds, atmosphere, temperature, or airflow patterns.

It is not necessary, though, to isolate description from explanation, understanding from prediction, in research designs. Glaser and Strauss (1967) advocate the discovery of grounded theory, research processes that produce rich descriptions and also categories and concepts for theories. Many of the studies that fit into the new paradigm for research on field experiences cite the work of Glaser and Strauss as bases for the research. Dussault (1970) claims that theory is generated logically from the knowledge accumulated in the natural history stage of a science. His theory of supervision is a logico-deductive theory. In contrast, grounded theory is generated from data systematically obtained and analyzed in research (Glaser & Strauss, 1967, p. 5). This phenomenological approach to theory involves an elaborate process of theoretical sampling, "the process of data collection for generating theory whereby the analyst jointly collects, codes, and analyzes his data and decides what data to collect next and where to find them" (p. 45). Also involved is constant comparison of incidents and emerging categories and their properties (pp. 101–115). Conceptual categories are the building blocks of grounded theory, and these categories and their properties emerge from the data. The concepts are the descriptive knowledge used to generate theory, explanatory and predictive knowledge. The generation of grounded theory combines the natural history and theoretical stages described by Dussault (1970) through a research paradigm characteristic of what Guba (1978) calls naturalistic inquiry.

Research on field experiences cited in this chapter provides evidence of the emergence of this new paradigm. More recent studies have qualities of naturalistic inquiry, lay a natural historical groundwork by focusing on descriptions of processes in field experiences, and allow concepts to flow from the data rather than be determined logically and verified empirically. A characteristic of these studies is the use of qualitative methods, particularly interviews and observations; concepts are developed from data produced by these methods. Other characteristics are (a) focus on cognitions of actors and their frames of reference, (b) multiple perspectives on one issue, (c) multiple measures, (d) attention to processes (e.g., supervision), (e) relation of processes to goals, (f) collection of longitudinal data, and (g) critical stance toward the status quo of field experiences and teaching. These characteristics are consistent with Guba's characteristics of naturalistic inquiry, although several create additional, but not contradictory, categories.

Studies using a naturalistic research paradigm have generated more useful knowledge about student teaching. One of the most extensive studies made of student teaching (Griffin et al., 1983) provides a stark example of the capacity of a naturalistic research paradigm to produce more meaningful findings than a psychometric paradigm. Quantitative and qualitative research methods were employed in a study of triads from two state universities. Ten quantitative measures were administered to triad members two or three times during the student teaching experience. Qualitative data, gathered from an intensive sample of 20 triads, came from journals, observations, interviews, conference records, and program descriptions.

The major findings from the study are reported in other sections of this chapter (S. Barnes & Edwards, 1984; Koehler, 1984; O'Neal, 1983; O'Neal & Edwards, 1983) and represent a significant contribution to the knowledge on student teaching. Most of these findings were products of the qualitative data, and where quantitative data were useful, they were considered in conjunction with qualitative data. It was the use of research methodology consistent with naturalistic inquiry that generated description, understanding, and explanation of the processes of student teaching and that demonstrated the efficacy of the new paradigm for research on field experiences.

This chapter has emphasized research exhibiting characteristics of the new paradigm, research that takes a systems approach to field experiences and includes the processes of the experience, as well as the cognitions and interactions of the actors in the experience. Haberman (1983) points out that no common practices have been dropped from student teaching programs on the basis of research evidence. The static, craft-oriented nature of field experiences could shift to more dynamic, knowledge-based programs as current research produces richer descriptions and deeper understanding to inform practice. Cumulative studies using the naturalistic research paradigm hold promise for further developing the natural history stage of research on field experiences and facilitating the development of explanation and grounded theory regarding field experiences. These eventualities could have a powerful influence on the structure and conceptualization of field experiences and could lead to a situation in which teacher educators fulfill their "primary responsibility" to their students.

A primary responsibility of educators is that they not only be aware of the general principle of the shaping of actual experience by environing conditions but that they also recognize in the concrete what surroundings are conducive to having experiences that lead to growth. Above all, they should know how to utilize the surroundings, physical and social, that exist so as to extract from them all that they have to contribute to building up experiences that are worth while. (Dewey, 1938, p. 35)

References

Allison, H. K. (1978). *Rating scale format as it affects ratings in student teaching*. Paper presented at the annual meeting of the American Educational Research Association, Toronto.

Andrews, L. O. (1964). *Student teaching*. New York: Center for Applied Research in Education.

Appleberry, M. (1976). What did you learn from student teaching? *Instructor*, 85(6), 38–40.

Applegate, J. H. (1985). Early field experiences: Recurring dilemmas. *Journal of Teacher Education*, 36(2), 60–64.

Applegate, J. (1987). Early field experiences: Three viewpoints. In M. Haberman & J. M. Backus (Eds.), *Advances in teacher education* (Vol. 3, pp. 75–93). Norwood, NJ: Ablex.

Applegate, J. H., & Lasley, T. J. (1982). Cooperating teachers' problems with preservice field experience students. *Journal of Teacher Education*, 33(2), 15–18.

Applegate, J. H., & Lasley, T. J. (1985). Students' expectations for early field experiences. *Texas Tech Journal of Education*, 12(1), 27–36.

Armaline, W. D., & Hoover, R. L. (1989). Field experiences as a vehicle for transformation: Ideology, education, and reflective practice. *Journal of Teacher Education*, 40(2), 42–48.

Armstrong, E., & Ladd, G. (1975). *Rotating peer supervision: Implementation & evaluation of its effects on the inner-direction and internal control constructs of teacher trainees*. Paper presented at the annual meeting of the National Association for Research on the Science of Teaching, Los Angeles.

Association for Student Teaching, Committee on Research. (1968). *The director of student teaching: Characteristics and responsibilities*. Washington, DC: Author.

Association of Teacher Educators. (1986). *Guidelines for professional experiences in teacher education: A policy statement*. Reston, VA: Author.

Barnes, H. L. (1987). The conceptual basis for thematic teacher education programs. *Journal of Teacher Education*, 38(4), 13–18.

Barnes S., & Edwards, S. (1984). *Effective student teaching experience: A qualitative–quantitative study* (Report No. 9060). Austin, TX: University of Texas at Austin, Research and Development Center for Teacher Education.

Barrows, L. K. (1979). *Power relationships in the student teaching field*. Paper presented at the annual meeting of the American Educational Research Association, San Francisco.

Berliner, D. C. (1985). Laboratory settings and the study of teacher education. *Journal of Teacher Education*, 36(6), 2–8.

Beswick, D. G., Harman, G. S., Elsworth, G. R., Fallon, B. J., & Woock, R. R. (1980). *Australian teacher educators and education policy: A national study of the views and characteristics of academic staff and practicing teachers who contribute to teacher education*. Melbourne, Australia: University of Melbourne, Center for the Study of Higher Education.

Bischoff, J., Farris, P., & Henniger, M. (1988). Student perceptions of early field experiences. *Action in Teacher Education*, 10(3), 22–25.

Boothroyd, W. (1979). Teaching practice supervision: A research report. *British Journal of Teacher Education*, 5(3), 243–250.

Buttery, T. J., & Michalak, D. A. (1975). The teaching clinic: A peer supervision process. *Education*, 95(3), 263–269.

Calderhead, J. (1987). *Cognition and metacognition in teachers' professional development*. Paper presented at the annual meeting of the American Educational Research Association, Washington, DC.

Campbell, L. P., & Williamson, J. A. (1983). Supervising the student teacher: What is really involved? *NASSP Bulletin*, 67(465), 77–79.

Carnegie Forum on Education and the Economy, Task Force on Teaching as a Profession. (1986). *A nation prepared: Teachers for the 21st century*. New York: Author.

Castillo, J. B. (1971). *The role expectations of cooperating teachers as viewed by student teachers, college supervisors, and cooperating teachers*. Unpublished doctoral dissertation, University of Rochester.

Conant, J. B. (1963). *The Education of American Teachers*. New York: McGraw Hill.

Cook, G. E. (1976). *Supervisors for the classroom: A study of the professional growth of educational supervisors in a program of clinical training*. Unpublished doctoral dissertation, Howard University, Washington, DC.

Copas, E. M. (1984). Critical requirements for cooperating teachers. *Journal of Teacher Education*, 35(6), 49–54.

Cope, E. (1973). School experience and student learning. In D. E. Lomax (Ed.), *The education of teachers in Britain* (pp. 243–261). London: Wiley.

Copeland, W. (1977). *The nature of the relationship between cooperating teacher behavior and student teacher classroom performance*. Paper presented at the annual meeting of the American Educational Research Association, New York.

Copeland, W. D. (1980). Affective dispositions of teachers in training toward examples of supervisory behavior. *Journal of Educational Research*, 74(1), 37–42.

Copeland, W. (1981). Clinical experiences in the education of teachers. *Journal of Education for Teaching*, 7(1), 3–16.

Copeland, W. (1986). The RITE framework for teacher education: Preservice applications. In J. Hoffman & S. Edwards (Eds.), *Reality and reform in teacher education* (pp. 25–44). New York: Random House.

Copeland, W., & Atkinson, D. (1978). Student teachers' perceptions of directive and nondirective supervisory behavior. *Journal of Educational Research*, 71(3), 123–127.

Corrigan, D., & Griswold, K. (1963). Attitude changes of student teachers. *Journal of Educational Research*, 57(2), 93–95.

Cruickshank, D. (1984). *Models for the preparation of American's teachers*. Bloomington, IN: Phi Delta Kappa.

Cruickshank, D. (1987). *Reflective teaching: The preparation of students of teaching*. Reston, VA: Association of Teacher Educators.

Cruickshank, D., & Armaline, W. (1986). Field experiences in teacher education: Considerations and recommendations. *Journal of Teacher Education*, 37(3), 34–40.

Defino, M. E. (1983). *The evaluation of student teachers: A description of practice*. Paper presented at the annual meeting of the American Educational Research Association, Montreal.

Denemark, G., & Nutter, N. (1984). The case for extended programs of initial teacher preparation. In L. Katz & J. Raths (Eds.), *Advances in teacher education* (Vol. 1, pp. 203–246). Norwood, NJ: Ablex.

Denton, J. (1982). Early field experience influence on performance in subsequent coursework. *Journal of Teacher Education*, 33(2), 19–23.

Dewey, J. (1938). *Experience and education*, New York: Macmillan.

Drummond, R. (1980). *The impact of a model of student teaching supervision on cooperating teachers and field supervisors*. Portsmouth, NH: New England Teacher Corps Network. (ERIC Document Reproduction Service No. ED 189 092)

Dussault, G. (1970). *A theory of supervision in teacher education*. New York: Teachers College Press.

Elliott, P., & Mays, R. (1979). *Early field experiences in teacher education* (Fastback 125). Bloomington, IN: Phi Delta Kappa Foundation.

Erickson, F. (1986). Qualitative methods in research on teaching. In M. C. Wittrock (Ed.), *Handbook of research on teaching* (3rd ed., pp. 119–161). New York: Macmillan.

Feiman, S. (1979). Technique and inquiry in teacher education: A curricular case study. *Curriculum Inquiry, 9*(1), 63–79.

Feiman-Nemser, S., & Buchmann, M. (1983). *Pitfalls of experience in teacher education* (Occasional Paper #65). East Lansing, MI: Michigan State University, Institute for Research on Teaching.

Flowers, J. G., Patterson, A. D., Stratemeyer, F. B., & Lindsey, M. (1948). *School and community laboratory experiences in teacher education*. New York: American Association of Teachers Colleges.

Friebus, R. J. (1977). Agents of socialization involved in student teaching. *Journal of Educational Research, 70*(5), 263–268.

Funk, F. F., Hoffman, J. L., Keithley, A. M., & Long, B. E. (1982). Student teaching program: Feedback from supervising teachers. *Clearinghouse, 55*(7), 319–321.

Gardner, W. (1979). Dean's perspective of support for teachers in the beginning years. In K. Howey & R. Bents (Eds.), *Toward meeting the needs of the beginning teacher* (pp. 95–110). Minneapolis: Midwest Teacher Corps Network and the University of Minnesota/St. Paul Schools Teacher Corps Project.

Garland, C. B. (1965). *An exploration of role expectations for student teachers: Views of prospective student teachers, cooperating teachers, and college supervisors*. Unpublished doctoral dissertation, University of Rochester.

Gettone, V. G. (1980). Role conflict of student teachers. *College Student Journal, 14*(1), 92–100.

Gitlin, A., Ogawa, R. T., & Rose, E. (1982). Horizontal evaluation: Its impact in three case studies. *CCBC Notebook, 3*(11), 1–13.

Glaser, B. G., & Strauss, A. L. (1967). *The discovery of grounded theory: Strategies for qualitative research*. Chicago: Aldine.

Glassberg, S., & Sprinthall, N. A. (1980). Student teaching: A developmental approach. *Journal of Teacher Education, 31*(2), 31–38.

Goodman, J. (1983). The seminar's role in the education of student teachers: A case study. *Journal of Teacher Education, 34*(3), 44–49.

Goodman, J. (1985). *Making early field experiences meaningful: An alternative approach*. Paper presented at the annual meeting of the American Educational Research Association, Chicago.

Griffin, G. A. (1983). *Expectations for student teaching: What are they and are they realized?* Paper presented at the annual meeting of the American Educational Research Association, Montreal.

Griffin, G. (1986). Issues in student teaching: A review. In J. D. Raths & L. G. Katz (Eds.), *Advances in teacher education* (Vol. 2, pp. 239–273). Norwood, NJ: Ablex.

Griffin, G. A., Barnes, S., Hughes, R., O'Neal, S., Defino, M., Edwards, S., & Hukill, H. (1983). *Clinical preservice teacher education: Final report of a descriptive study*. Austin, TX: University of Texas, R & D Center for Teacher Education.

Grimmett, P. P., & Ratzlaff, H. C. (1986). Expectations for the cooperating teacher role. *Journal of Teacher Education, 37*(6), 41–50.

Guba, E. G. (1978). *Toward a methodology of naturalistic inquiry in educational evaluation*. Los Angeles, CA: University of California, Los Angeles, Center for the Study of Evaluation.

Guyton, E. (1986). *Incentives for working with student teachers*. Paper presented at the summer workshop of the Association of Teacher Educators, Flagstaff, AZ.

Guyton, E. (1987). Working with student teachers: Incentives, problems, and advantages. *Professional Educator, 10*(1), 21–28.

Haberman, M. (1983). Research in preservice laboratory and clinical experiences: Implications for teacher education. In K. R. Howey & W. E. Gardner (Eds.), *The education of teachers: A look ahead* (pp. 98–177). New York: Longman.

Haring, M., & Nelson, E. (1980). *A five year follow-up comparison of recent and experienced graduates from campus and field based teacher education programs*. Paper presented at the annual meeting of the American Educational Research Association, Boston.

Hattie, J., Warwick, O., & Cole, B. (1982). Assessment of student teachers by supervising teachers. *Journal of Educational Psychology, 74*(5), 778–785.

Hauwiller, J. G., Abel, F. J., Ausel, D., & Sparapani, E. F. (1988–1989). Enhancing the effectiveness of cooperating teachers. *Action in Teacher Education, 10*(4), 42–46.

Haviland, C. P., & Haviland, M. G. (1981). Student teacher evaluations and inflation. *Journal of College Placement, 42*(1), 67–69.

Heath, P., & Cyphert, F. (1985). *A report of the curriculum of early field experiences in selected teacher education programs in Ohio*. Paper presented at the annual meeting of the American Educational Research Association, Chicago.

Heidelbach, R. (1969). The cooperating teacher as teaching tutor. In M. Lindsey (Ed.), *Inquiring into teaching behaviors of supervisors in teacher education laboratories* (pp. 109–166). New York: Teachers College Press.

Hill, S. E. (1986). Language education and field experiences. *Journal of Teacher Education, 37*(3), 56–59.

Holmes Group. (1986). *Tomorrow's teachers*. East Lansing, MI: Author.

Houston, W. R., Cooper, J. M., & Warner, A. R. (1976). *School based teacher educator project: Report of first year activities, 1975–76*. Houston, TX: University of Houston Teacher Center. (ERIC Document Reproduction Service No. ED 131 041)

Ishler, P., & Kay, R. (1981). A survey of institutional practice. In C. Webb, N. Gehrke, P. Ishler, & A. Mendoza (Eds.), *Exploratory field experiences in teacher education* (pp. 15–22). Reston, VA: Association of Teacher Educators.

Johnson, J. (1968a). *A brief history of student teaching*. Dekalb, IL: Creative Educational Materials.

Johnson, J. A. (1968b). *A national survey of student teaching programs*. Baltimore: Multi-State Teacher Education Project.

Johnson, J., & Yates, J. (1982). *A national survey of student teaching programs*. DeKalb, IL: Northern Illinois University. (ERIC Document Reproduction Service No. ED 232 963)

Kapel, D. E., & Sadler, E. J. (1978). *How much involvement in student teaching: A study of cooperating teachers*. Paper presented at the annual meeting of the Association of Teacher Educators, Las Vegas.

Kaplan, L. (1967). *An investigation of the role expectations for college supervisors of student teaching as viewed by student teachers, supervising teachers, and college supervisors*. Unpublished doctoral dissertation, University of Rochester.

Killian, J. E., & McIntyre D. J. (1986a, February). *The differences between the field experiences of elementary and secondary preservice teachers*. Paper presented at the annual meeting of the Association of Teacher Educators, Atlanta.

Killian, J. E., & McIntyre, D. J. (1986b). Quality in the early field experiences: A product of grade level and cooperating teachers' training. *Teaching and Teacher Education, 2*(4), 367–376.

Killian, J. E., & McIntyre, D. J. (1988). Grade level as a factor in participation during early field experiences. *Journal of Teacher Education, 39*(2), 36–41.

Knowles, J. G. (1988). *The failure of a student teacher: Becoming educated about teachers, teaching, and self*. Paper presented at the annual meeting of American Educational Research Association, New Orleans.

Koehler, V. (1984, April). *University supervision of student teaching*. Paper presented at the annual meeting of the American Educational Research Association, New Orleans.

Krajewski, R. J. (1976). Clinical supervision: To facilitate teacher self-improvement. *Journal of Research and Development in Education, 9*(2), 58–66.

LaGrone, H. (1965). Teaching: Craft or intellectual process? In C. Lauby (Ed.), *Theoretical bases for professional laboratory experiences in teacher education* (44th yearbook, pp. 93–104). Washington, DC: Association for Student Teaching.

Lanier, J. E., & Little, J. W. (1986). Research on teacher education. In M. C. Wittrock (Ed.), *Handbook of research on teaching* (3rd ed., pp. 527–569). New York: Macmillan.

Liggett, A., Fulwiler, L., Clarke, J., & Hood, K. (1988). *Supervisory experience as a means of reflection: Policy implications for schools of inventories*. Paper presented at the annual meeting of the American Educational Research Association, New Orleans.

Lindsey, M. (1969). *Inquiring into teaching behaviors of supervisors in teacher education laboratories*. New York: Teachers College Press.

Lutz, F., & Ramsey, M. (1974). The use of anthropological field methods in education. *Educational Researcher, 3*(10), 5–9.

Magoon, J. A. (1977). Constructivist approaches in educational research. *Review of Educational Research, 47*(4), 651–693.

Mahan, G., & Harsle, J. (1977). *Professional judgment as a criterion variable in preservice teacher education research*. Paper presented at the annual meeting of the American Educational Research Association, New York.

Martin, D. V. (1988). *A study of the longitudinal behavior development of more or less effective student teachers*. Paper presented at the annual meeting of the American Educational Research Association, New Orleans.

Martin, R. E., & Wood, G. H. (1983). *Two perspectives of early field experiences: Inservice and preservice teachers*. Paper presented at the meeting of the Association of Teacher Educators, Orlando.

Martin, R. E., & Wood, G. H. (1984). *Early field experiences: Unifications of cooperating teachers' and teacher education students' diverse perspectives*. Paper presented at the meeting of the American Educational Research Association, New Orleans.

McCaleb, J. L., Borko, H., Arends, R. A., Garner, R., & Mauro, L. (1987). Innovation in teacher education: The evolution of a program. *Journal of Teacher Education, 38*(4), 57–64.

McCarrel, F. (1933). *The development of the training school*. Nashville, TN: George Peabody College for Teachers.

McIntyre, D. J. (1979). Integrating theory and practice via a teaching center. *Contemporary Education, 50*(3), 146–149.

McIntyre, D. J. (1983). *Field experiences in teacher education: From student to teacher*. Washington, DC: Foundation for Excellence in Teacher Education and the ERIC Clearinghouse on Teacher Education.

McIntyre, D. J., & Killian, J. E. (1987). The influence of supervisory training for cooperating teachers on preservice teachers' development during early field experience. *Journal of Educational Research, 80*(5), 277–282.

McIntyre, D. J., & Vickery, T. R. (1979). Differential observer effects on student teacher verbal behavior. *College Student Journal, 13*(3), 263–264.

Morris, J. E., et al. (1982). *The director of student teaching/field experiences: Characteristics and responsibilities*. Unpublished manuscript, National Field Directors Forum, Association of Teacher Educators Research Committee, Reston, VA.

Morris, J. E., & Curtis, J. F. (1983). Legal issues relating to field-based experiences in teacher education. *Journal of Teacher Education, 34*(2), 2–6.

Morris, J. E., Pannell, S. K., & Houston, W. R. (1985). Standards for professional laboratory and field experiences: Review and recommendations. *Action in Teacher Education. 7*(3), 73–78.

Nagel, A., Berg, M., Malian, D., & Murphy, D. (1988). *Changing supervisory performance through training intervention*. Paper presented at the annual meeting of the American Educational Research Association, New Orleans.

National Council for Accreditation of Teacher Education. (1986). *Standards for the accreditation of teacher education*. Washington, DC: Author.

Nosow, S. (1975). Students' perceptions of field experience education. *Journal of College Student Personnel, 16*(6), 508–513.

O'Neal, S. F. (1983). *Supervision of student teachers: Feedback and evaluation*. Austin: University of Austin, R&D Center for Teacher Education. (ERIC Document Reproduction Service No. ED 240 106)

O'Neal, S., Barnes, S., & Edwards, S. (1986). Clinical teacher preservice education. In J. Hoffman & S. Edwards (Eds.), *Reality and reform in clinical teacher education* (pp. 135–139). New York: Random House.

O'Neal, S., & Edwards, S. (1983). *The supervision of student teaching*. Paper presented at the meeting of the American Educational Research Association, Montreal.

Painter, L. H., & Brown, W. K. (1979). Developing competent cooperating teachers. *Improving College Education and University Teaching, 27*, 13–15.

Perrodin, A. (1961). In support of supervising teacher education programs. *Journal of Teacher Education, 12*(1), 36–38.

Phelps, L. A., Schmitz, C. D., & Wade, D. L. (1986). A performance-based cooperating teacher report. *Journal of Teacher Education, 37*(5), 32–35.

Popkewitz, T. S., Tabachnick, R. B., & Zeichner, K. M. (1979). Dulling the senses: Research in teacher education. *Journal of Teacher Education, 30*(5), 52–59.

Povey, R. N. (1975). A comparison of three methods of evaluating teaching performance in a college of education. *British Journal of Educational Psychology, 45*(3), 279–285.

Puckett, E. H. (1985). *A national survey of field experiences in elementary teacher preparation programs*. Paper presented at the meeting of the Association of Teacher Educators, Las Vegas.

Reavis, C. A. (1977). A test of the clinical supervision model. *Journal of Educational Research, 70*(6), 311–315.

Reavis, C. A. (1978). Clinical supervision: A review of the research. *Educational Leadership, 35*(7), 580–584.

Reavis, C. A. (1979). A study of the effects of prefatory remarks on teacher evaluations. *Journal of Educational Research, 72*(3), 173–177.

Reiff, J. C. (1980). Evaluating student teacher effectiveness. *College Student Journal, 14*(4), 369–372.

Richardson, R. C. (1987). *What really transpires during the supervision of student teachers: A role function analysis*. Paper presented at the meeting of the Association of Teacher Educators, Houston.

Richardson-Koehler, V. (1988). Barriers to effective supervision of student teaching. *Journal of Teacher Education, 39*(2), 28–34.

Rivilin, H. (1965). Theory underlying professional laboratory experiences. In C. Lauby (Ed.), *Professional laboratory experiences in teacher education*. Washington, DC: Association for Student Teaching.

Ross, S. M., Raines, F. B., Cervetti, M. J., & Dillon, D. A. (1980). Field experiences for teacher candidates: A comparison between tutorial and apprenticeship programs on student activities and attitudes. *Journal of Teacher Education, 31*(6), 57–61.

Sanders, J. & Merritt, D. L. (1974). *Relationship between perceived supervisor style and teacher attitudes*. Paper presented at the annual meeting of the American Educational Research Association, Chicago.

Seperson M., & Joyce, B. (1973). Teaching styles of student teachers as related to those of their cooperating teachers. *Educational Leadership Research Supplement, 31*(2), 146–151.

Shuma, K. (1973). *Changes effected by a clinical supervising relationship which emphasizes a helping relationship and a conference format made congruent with the establishment and maintenance of this helping relationship.* Unpublished doctoral dissertation, University of Pittsburgh.

Siedentop, D. (1981). The Ohio State supervision research program summary report. *Journal of Teaching in Physical Education,* Introductory Issue, 30–38.

Simbol, M. A., & Summers, J. A. (1984). *Administrative policy and supervisory load for student teaching programs in Ohio, Indiana, Illinois, and Missouri.* Muncie, IN: Indiana Unit of the Association of Teacher Educators.

Southall, C. (1984). *Critical incidents in student teaching.* Paper presented at the meeting of the Association of Teacher Educators, New Orleans.

Sunal, D. (1980). Effect of field experiences during elementary methods courses on preservice teacher behavior. *Journal of Research in Science Teaching, 17*(1), 17–23.

Swalls, F. (1976). *The law on student teaching in the United States.* Terre Haute, IN: Interstate Printers and Publishers.

Tabachnick, B. R. (1981). Teacher education as a set of dynamic social events. In B. R. Tabachnick, T. S. Popkewitz, & B. B Szekely (Eds.), *Studying, teaching and learning: Trends in Soviet and American research* (pp. 76–86). New York: Praeger.

Tabachnick, B. R., Popkewitz, T. S., & Zeichner, K. M. (1979). Teacher education and the professional perspectives of student teachers. *Interchange, 10*(4), 12–29.

Thies-Sprinthall, L. (1980). Supervision: An educative or miseducative process? *Journal of Teacher Education, 31*(4), 17–20.

Thies-Sprinthall, L. (1984). Promoting the developmental growth of supervising teachers: Theory, research, programs and implications. *Journal of Teacher Education, 35*(3), 53–60.

Thies-Sprinthall, L. (1986). A collaborative approach for mentor training: A working model. *Journal of Teacher Education, 37*(6), 13–20.

Thompson, M. L., & Ellis, J. R. (1984). *Identifying anxieties experienced by student teachers: A twenty year follow-up.* Paper presented at the meeting of the Association of Teacher Educators, New Orleans.

Tittle, C. K. (1974). *Student teaching: Attitude and research bases for change in school and university.* Metuchen, NJ: Scarecrow Press.

Turney, C. (1977). *Innovation in teacher education: A study of the directions, processes and problems of innovation in teacher preparation with special reference to the Australian content and to the role of co-operating schools.* Sydney, Australia: Sydney University Press.

Turney, C., Cavins, L. G., Eltis, K. J., Hatton, N., Thew, D. M., Towler, J., & Wright, R. (1982). *The practicum in teacher education: Research, practice, and supervision.* Sydney, Australia: Sydney University Press.

Twa, J. (1984, June). *Teacher associate perceptions of the effectiveness of the clinical supervision workshop.* Paper presented at the annual meeting of the Canadian Society for the Study of Education, Ontario. (ERIC Document Reproduction Service No. ED 269 855)

Watts, D. (1987). Student teaching. In M. Haberman & J. M. Backus (Eds.), *Advances in teacher education* (Vol. 3, pp. 151–167). Norwood, NJ: Ablex.

Webb, C. D., Gehrke, N., Ishler, P., & Mendoza, A. (1981). *Exploratory field experiences in teacher education: A report of the commission on exploratory field experiences of the Association of*

Teacher Educators. Reston, VA: Association of Teacher Educators. (ERIC Document Reproduction Service No. ED 205 482)

Wheeler, A. E., & Knoop, H. R. (1982). Self, teacher and faculty assessments of student teaching performance. *Journal of Educational Research, 75*(3), 178–181.

Wheeler, P. J. R. (1989). *Cooperating teachers as instructional supervisors: Student teacher perceptions of training effects.* Paper presented at the annual meeting of the American Educational Research Association, San Francisco.

Wilson, S. (1977). The use of ethnographic techniques in educational research. *Review of Educational Research, 47*(1), 245–265.

Wisniewski, R. (1978). *Credibility gaps in teacher education.* Keynote speech delivered at the meeting of the Association of Teacher Educators, Las Vegas.

Yates, J. W. (1981). Student teaching in England: Results of a recent survey. *Journal of Teacher Education, 32*(5), 44–47.

Yates, J. W., & Johnson, J. A. (1982a). *A national survey of student teaching programs: Innovations in student teaching programs* (Supplemental Report #4). Dekalb, IL: Northern Illinois University.

Yates, J. W., & Johnson, J. A. (1982b). *A national survey of student teaching programs: Lawsuits growing out of student teaching* (Supplemental Report #1). Dekalb, IL: Northern Illinois University.

Yee, A. H. (1967). *The student teaching triad: The relationship of attitudes among student teachers, college supervisors, and cooperating teachers.* Austin, TX: University of Texas, College of Education.

Zahorik, J. A. (1988). The observing-conferencing role of university supervisors. *Journal of Teacher Education, 39*(2), 9–16.

Zeichner, K. M. (1978). *The student teaching experience: A methodological critique of the research.* Paper presented at the meeting of the Association of Teacher Educators, Las Vegas.

Zeichner, K. M. (1983). Alternative paradigms of teacher education. *Journal of Teacher Education, 34*(3), 3–9.

Zeichner, K. M. (1986). Content and contexts: Neglected elements in studies of student teaching as an occasion for learning to teach. *Journal of Education for Teaching, 12*(1), 5–25.

Zeichner, K. (1987). The ecology of field experience: Toward an understanding of the role of field experiences in teacher development. In M. Haberman & J. M. Backus (Eds.), *Advances in teacher education* (Vol. 3, pp. 94–117). Norwood, NJ: Ablex.

Zeichner, K. M., & Liston, D. P. (1985). *Theory and practice in the evolution of an inquiry-oriented student teaching program.* Paper presented at the meeting of the American Educational Research Association, Chicago.

Zeichner, K. M., & Liston, D. (1987). Teaching student teachers to reflect. *Harvard Educational Review, 57*(1), 23–48.

Zeichner, K., Liston, D., Mahlios, M., & Gomes, M. (1987). *The structure and goals of a student teaching program and the characteristics and qualities of supervisory discourse.* Paper presented at the meeting of the American Educational Research Association, Washington, DC.

Zeichner, K. M., & Tabachnick, R. (1982). The belief systems of university supervisors in an elementary student teaching program. *Journal of Education for Teaching, 8*(1), 34–54.

Zeichner, K. M., & Teitelbaum, K. (1982). Personalized and inquiry-oriented teacher education: An analysis of two approaches to the development of curriculum for field-based experiences. *Journal of Education for Teaching, 8*(2), 95–117.

Zevin, J. (1974). *In thy cooperating teacher's image: Convergence of social studies student teachers' behavior patterns with cooperating teachers' behavior patterns.* Paper presented at the meeting of the American Educational Research Association, Chicago.

Zimpher, N. L., DeVoss, G. G., & Nott, D. L. (1980). A closer look at university student teacher supervision. *Journal of Teacher Education, 31*(4), 11–15.

·30·

TEACHER INDUCTION PROGRAMS AND INTERNSHIPS

Leslie Huling-Austin

SOUTHWEST TEXAS STATE UNIVERSITY

Teacher induction has been defined as the transition from student of teaching to teacher (Griffin, et al., 1983). In the past, this transition has often been quite abrupt. In the teaching profession, beginners are expected to do essentially the same job on their first day of employment as 20-year veterans. In addition, because teachers spend the majority of their workday isolated from their peers, the natural induction process that occurs in most professions (i.e., beginners receiving ongoing direction and assistance from more experienced colleagues) is prevented from occurring. Concern both within the profession and from external sources about beginning teachers and their induction into the profession has in recent years prompted the development of teacher induction programs and internships.

TEACHER INDUCTION: BACKGROUND AND HISTORY

In this introductory section, teacher induction will be examined first as a part of the larger teacher education continuum. The focus and organization of the chapter will be explained, definitions of induction programs and internships will be presented, and the rationale for teacher induction programs and internships will be examined. This section will conclude with a brief overview of the historical development of teacher induction programs.

Following this introductory section, the chapter will be organized into four sections. The next three sections will relate to the current state of the scene in the areas of policy, practice, and research. The final section, "Summary and Conclusions"

will identify both consensus and controversy in the field of teacher induction and will suggest needed next steps in the areas of policy, practice, and research.

Part of a Continuum

Teacher induction is best understood in the larger context of teacher education, which is often described as a continuum, represented as follows.

Preservice---Induction---Inservice

Viewed in this context, it becomes clear that programs to address the induction period (i.e., induction programs and internships) need to function both as logical extensions of the preservice program and as entry pieces in a larger career-long professional-development program. Induction programs acknowledge that beginning teachers have recently completed teacher-preparation programs and still need supervision and support similar to that which was available in the student phase. Such support enables beginners to continue to develop their teaching skills while confronting the adjustment difficulties of the first years. From this transition stage, the teacher can then proceed to a staff-development program that provides opportunities for continued professional growth.

Induction Programs and Internships Defined

The focus of this chapter is on teacher induction programs and internships, not on the broader phenomena of teacher induction as a socialization process. Broadly defined, an induc-

The author would like to acknowledge and thank Sandra Odell (University of New Mexico), Peggy Ishler (Bowling Green State University), and Mary Marockie (West Virginia Regional Education Service Agency) for the assistance they provided in shaping this chapter through their critical reviews of several drafts of the manuscript.

tion program is a planned program intended to provide some systematic and sustained assistance, specifically to beginning teachers for at least one school year (Zeichner, 1979). It is important to clarify that, for purposes of this chapter, for a beginning-teacher program to be considered an induction program it must contain some degree of *systematic and sustained assistance* and not merely be a series of orientation meetings or a formal evaluation process used for teachers new to the profession (or state or district). Internships are also induction programs, but they usually serve persons who are entering the profession through some other route than the traditional preservice teacher education program. As such, internships often involve uncertified teachers on limited contracts who have reduced teaching responsibilities and increased support and supervision. For example, the Lyndhurst Fellowship Program offered at Memphis State University is a 9-month program for certifying teachers for secondary schools. This program strongly emphasizes the mentoring of interns by both university faculty and classroom teachers (Butler, 1987). Another internship program, the Master of Arts in Teaching Program at the University of Pittsburgh, is designed for college graduates and is built upon extended practical experience in the university's laboratory school (Creek & Vollmer, 1984). To summarize, internships often include many of the same features as induction programs, but they are likely to focus more heavily on *training* than more traditional teacher induction programs, which tend to emphasize *transition* from student of teaching to teacher. Furthermore, the role and responsibilities of the intern typically are substantially different from those of the first-year teacher. These distinctions serve as a general rule, and certainly exceptions can be found among both induction and internship programs.

Finally, it is important to clarify that induction programs can serve both beginning teachers and teachers new to a district or school, as well as new educational personnel including administrators, and can vary in length from one semester to 3 years. For purposes of this chapter, the primary focus will be on programs for teachers in their first year of teaching.

Rationale for Induction Programs and Internships

As explained earlier, the unique nature of the teaching profession in many ways hinders the natural induction process that takes place in many other professions. In most professions, beginners gradually assume job responsibilities over a period of months (or even years) and have ready access to experienced colleagues to get help as problems arise. Because this is not the case in education, beginning teachers frequently resort to learning by trial and error (Lortie, 1975) and to developing "coping" strategies that help them survive in the classroom. Unfortunately, these strategies could actually prevent effective instruction from occurring. An example of such a case is reported by Huling-Austin, Barnes, & Smith (1985), who describe a beginning teacher having difficulty controlling students during class discussions. The teacher's response was to eliminate class discussions from her repertoire of teaching activities. Such case study examples lend credence to the hypothesis that if beginning teachers are not provided with support and assistance during their early years, these early coping strategies can crystalize into teaching styles that will be utilized throughout entire careers (McDonald, 1980). Sandefur (1982) points out that unassisted entry-year teachers often shift from a progressive teaching style practiced in preservice training to a traditional style. Unassisted beginning teachers can also develop negative teaching behaviors in which they perceive themselves as authoritarian, dominating, and custodial in their treatment of students (McArthur, 1978).

Another more easily documented effect of not providing beginning teachers with support during their first year(s) in the classroom is observed in the attrition rate of beginning teachers. It is well documented in the literature that without induction support and assistance, many potentially good teachers become discouraged and abandon their teaching careers (Ryan et al., 1980). Schlechty and Vance (1983) estimate that approximately 30 percent of beginning teachers leave the profession during their first 2 years, compared with the overall teacher turnover rate of 6 percent per year. The turnover rate of new teachers does not level out to the overall rate of 6 percent until the fifth or sixth year. Of all beginning teachers who enter the profession, 40%–50 percent leave during the first 7 years of their careers, and over two-thirds of these do so in the first 4 years of teaching. In some states the statistics are even more alarming. For example, in Indiana a statewide needs assessment reported that 26.5 percent of Indiana teachers who entered teaching dropped out within 2 years and that 62 percent dropped out within 5 years (Summers, 1987). The retention rates of beginning teachers are especially depressing in light of evidence suggesting that those teachers who are the most academically talented leave in the greatest numbers (Schlechty & Vance, 1981).

Another reason why induction programs are needed relates to the personal and professional well-being of beginning teachers. Although not all beginning teachers experience personal and professional trauma during their first year, many do. In many cases, beginning teachers have been known to lose self-confidence, experience extreme stress and anxiety, and question their own competence as teachers and people. Such cases are documented by Hawk (1984), Hidalgo (1986), Huling-Austin and Murphy (1987), Ryan et al. (1980), and others.

Historical Development of Induction Programs

The history of teacher induction programs in the United States is really quite brief. Prior to 1980, only a few isolated induction programs, most of which were initiated by local districts or individual schools, were in operation in the United States. One early forerunner of induction programs in this country that was a large-scale effort was a 3-year experimental demonstration project on the Induction of Beginning Teachers sponsored by the National Association of Secondary School Principals (Swanson, 1968). In general, however, prior to 1980, most educators who were writing about teacher induction were from other countries, namely Great Britain and Australia.

In 1980 Florida was the only state that had a mandated induction program. The movement toward induction programs grew dramatically in the 1980s, due to the educational reforms that swept this country in the mid-1980s and in anticipation of future severe teacher shortages. By the late 1980s, at least 31 states plus the District of Columbia had either implemented or were piloting/planning teacher induction programs (Hawk & Robards, 1987).

The educational literature is also reflective of the increasing popularity of the topic of teacher induction. For example, several major journals have devoted entire issues to the topic, including *Action in Teacher Education* (Winter, 1987), *Educational Leadership* (November, 1985), *Journal of Teacher Education* (January–February, 1986), *Kappa Delta Pi Record* (Summer, 1986) and *Theory Into Practice* (Summer, 1988). The ERIC Clearinghouse for Teacher Education produced three digests in 1986 related to beginning teachers: "Components of Induction Programs," "Current Developments in Teacher Induction Programs," and "Teacher Mentoring." Other noteworthy writings in the field include two monographs published by the Association of Teacher Educators (Brooks, 1987; Huling-Austin, Odell, Ishler, Kay, & Edelfelt, 1989), a selected annotated bibliography, *The Knowledge Base of Teacher Induction*, compiled by Johnston (1988), and a set of background papers entitled *The First Years of Teaching* commissioned by the Illinois State Board of Education (Griffin & Millies, 1987).

Annual meeting programs of various educational organizations including the Association of Teacher Educators, American Association of Colleges for Teacher Education, American Educational Research Association, and National Staff Development Council, to name a few, also indicate that increasing numbers of sessions are being devoted to the topic of teacher induction. Several national conferences focusing totally or partially on teacher induction have recently been sponsored by the Research and Development Center for Teacher Education (R&DCTE) at the University of Texas at Austin and have resulted in publications of conference proceedings (Griffin & Hukill, 1983; Hord, O'Neal, & Smith, 1985; Huling-Austin, Putman, Edwards, & Galvez-Hjornevik, 1985).

A national Teacher Induction Network consisting of persons working in the field of teacher induction from local school districts, colleges, and universities; state departments of education; regional educational service agencies; and national professional organizations was launched by R&DCTE in 1983. This network currently operates out of the LBJ Institute for the Improvement of Teaching and Learning at Southwest Texas State University.

Further, the Association of Teacher Educators sponsored a 3-year national Commission on the Teacher Induction Process from 1985 to 1988. In addition to the monograph on teacher induction (Brooks, 1987), the commission jointly produced, along with the national Teacher Induction Network, a national Directory of Teacher Induction Programs (Huling-Austin, 1986a). The ATE Commission on the Teacher Induction Process in 1988 formed a special interest group (SIG) on teacher induction that continues to operate in the association. In addition, a subsequent 3-year Commission on the Training of Mentor Teachers was appointed by ATE in 1988.

In summary, compared with the 1970s, there is a great amount of interest and activity related to teacher induction. Furthermore, an increasing body of literature on the topic of teacher induction is providing the field with both direction and intriguing questions to investigate. The following sections focus on the current scene of induction, seen from the perspectives of policy, practice, and research.

POLICY: CURRENT DEVELOPMENTS

Policy related to teacher induction stems primarily from recommendations from national reports produced by panels, boards, and commissions and from the actions of state legislatures. In both of these areas, recent activity related to teacher induction has been vigorous.

National Reports

A number of national reports from the mid-1980s have addressed the issue of teacher induction and internships. Among teacher educators, probably the best known of these are the National Council for Accreditation of Teacher Education's *NCATE Redesign* (1985); the Holmes Group report, *Tomorrow's Teachers* (1986); and the Carnegie Forum report, *A Nation Prepared: Teachers for the 21st Century* (1986). All three reports recommend a supported induction period for beginning teachers. For example, in Standard Two (Relationship to the World of Practice) of the *NCATE Redesign*, it is stated that the teacher education institution will maintain and develop relationships with its graduates and will provide assistance to first-year teachers when needed. The Holmes Group proposes that beginning-teacher support systems be carried out through an induction year consisting of a year-long, paid, and well-supervised internship. The Carnegie Forum report recommends the development of a new professional curriculum in graduate schools of education leading to a Master in Teaching degree, based on systematic knowledge of teaching, *including internships and residencies in the schools*.

In the Association of Teacher Educators' Blue Ribbon Task Force report, *Visions of Reform: Implications for the Education Profession* (1986), an explicit recommendation related to teacher induction was made:

Upon successful completion of their undergraduate program, candidates would enter the induction phase. The induction phase would:
a. bridge the preservice and inservice phases of the professional curriculum;
b. be collaboratively developed and administered by the colleges/universities and the schools;
c. provide a post-baccalaureate, protracted period of study and practice with an imbedded internship; This post-baccalaureate protracted period of study and practice (1–2) years would be prior to accepting full-time employment, and prior to being initially (even provisionally) certified;
d. provide an opportunity and a vehicle to develop and monitor a sequential approach to the assumption of professional responsibility based upon demonstrated readiness and competence;

e. provide a program of clinical practice and professional development; This program would include micro-teaching, simulations and coaching as well as multiple options for supervised practice. Provision for these would draw upon the resources and expertise of both the training arm at the university and the practicing arm in the schools (as well as others);

f. provide for a continuous monitoring and tracking system that would supply regular feedback, developmental data, and clinical assistance on a personal basis for each individual candidate. (p. 62)

The ATE Induction Commission, chaired by Peggy Ishler, a national group that focused on teacher induction for a 3-year period from 1985–1988, made the following five policy recommendations in their monograph (Brooks, 1987):

1. Induction programs are necessary in every school district to assist beginning teachers in making the transition from novice to experienced professional.

2. Induction programs must be based on the needs of the individuals as they adjust to their particular professional context.

3. The experienced professionals who serve as sources of help to beginning teachers should receive training and support to facilitate their assistance, including reduced teaching loads.

4. Support personnel should be concerned with the professional development of individual beginning teachers and be separated from the evaluation role of a district.

5. The training of teachers should be recognized as an ongoing educational process from pre-service to retirement requiring cooperative financial and programmatic support from those involved including the local district, higher education, and state departments of education. (p. v)

It is clear from the national reports highlighted that the issue of teacher induction is firmly planted in the national spotlight of educational reform. This being the case, it is not surprising that teacher induction also has appeared as a major feature in state legislative educational-reform packages across the nation.

State Legislation

Even though four national surveys of state legislative activity related to teacher induction have been conducted since 1985, it is still difficult to obtain up-to-date information because the field is changing so rapidly. The surveys were sponsored by the ATE Induction Commission (Hawk & Robards, 1987), the Illinois State Board of Education (Eastern Illinois University, 1986), the American Association of Colleges for Teacher Education (Neuweiler, 1987), and the National Association of State Directors of Teacher Education and Certification (Mastin, 1988).

The data provided by the Illinois report indicate that, of the 50 states and the District of Columbia (treated as a state unit), 17 states had induction programs in the piloting or implementation stages, 14 states had programs in the study/planning/development stages, and 20 states had no programs or current

planning for such programs. Of the states with operating programs, virtually all were established by state mandate (either legislation or state agency regulations). In the 1988 NASDTEC report, 12 states were identified as having programs linked to certification. In regard to characteristics of state programs, state policies for induction programs generally specify a particular person or agency to be responsible for the support of the beginning teachers and frequently include evaluation as part of the plan. In addition, state programs linked to certification generally provide some measures for training of support personnel (Mastin, 1988).

In data compiled by AACTE in December, 1987, only three states reported that there was no activity at the state level related to teacher induction (Neuweiler, 1987). This information indicates that concern about teacher induction is sweeping the entire nation, making it one of the fastest growing educational movements in recent history.

PRACTICE: CURRENT STATE OF THE SCENE

To examine current practice related to teacher induction it is important to consider certain factors including the sources of programs, the goals of programs, and the components of programs. In addition, this section will conclude with a brief discussion of conceptual paradigms and teacher induction programs and internships.

Sources of Programs

A most powerful testimony to the importance of teacher induction is the increasing number of teacher induction programs being implemented across the country. Various educational agencies including local school districts, colleges and universities, regional educational service agencies, and state departments of education are involved in designing and implementing teacher induction programs. Some of the most recent partners in the teacher induction enterprise are professional organizations (Ishler & Kester, 1987). Many teacher induction programs are collaborative in nature and involve two or more sponsoring agencies representing different branches of the teacher education enterprise.

Currently there are hundreds of teacher induction programs operating across the country. Among those that have received the most national attention through the scope of the programs and through being the recipients of national awards are the Kentucky Beginning Teacher Internship Program, the California Mentor Teacher Program, the Georgia Teacher Certification Program, the Florida Beginning Teacher Program, the Virginia Beginning Teacher Assistance Program, the North Carolina Initial Certification Program, the Oklahoma Entry-Year Assessment Program, the University of New Mexico–Albuquerque Public Schools Program, the Regional Education Service Agency VI/Ohio County Public Schools (Wheeling, West Virginia) program, the Indiana State University Multiple Support Program, and the Memphis State University Integrative Approach Program.

Goals of Programs

Goals of specific induction programs and internships vary greatly. However, working from the underlying rationale for teacher induction programs, one can identify five goals that are typically included, explicitly or implicitly, in most induction programs or internships, including:

1. To improve teaching performance
2. To increase the retention of promising beginning teachers during the induction years
3. To promote the personal and professional well-being of beginning teachers by improving teachers' attitudes toward themselves and the profession
4. To satisfy mandated requirements related to induction and certification
5. To transmit the culture of the system to beginning teachers

These are not the only appropriate goals for inclusion in induction programs but rather are generic or foundation goals addressed by most programs.

Before leaving this discussion of rationale and goals, it is important to again point out that some programs, especially some internship programs, are not so much focused on helping beginning teachers with the transition into the role of classroom teacher, as they are attempting to provide a substantially (sometimes radically) different training program for teachers entering the profession. Although these programs generally also deal with the five goals stated, some of the programs are, in essence, offering "a different mousetrap" in teacher education. For example, the Brackenridge Internship in Teaching Program being conducted by Trinity University in San Antonio, Texas, is a 16-year model program for recruiting, training, and retaining high-ability high school students as elementary and secondary school teachers (Marshall, 1987). Therefore, it is important for the reader to be aware that some internship programs more strongly emphasize training than transition aid.

Components of Programs

As can be expected, the comprehensiveness and quality of teacher induction and internship programs across the nation vary greatly. Some programs are elaborate and others are modest. Among the components that can be found in teacher induction programs are the following (Huling-Austin, 1986b):

a. printed materials of employment conditions and school regulations
b. orientation meetings and visits
c. seminars on curriculum and effective teaching topics for beginning teachers
d. training sessions for mentor teachers and other support personnel
e. observations by supervisors/peers/assessment teams and/or videotaping of the beginning teacher in the classroom
f. follow-up conferences with observers
g. consultations with experienced teachers

h. support (helping/buddy/mentor) teachers
i. opportunities to observe other teachers (in person or through subject-specific videotapes)
j. released time/load reduction for beginning teachers and/or support teachers
k. group meetings of beginning teachers (for emotional support)
l. assignment to a team teaching situation
m. credit courses for beginning teachers (university and/or local credit)
n. beginning teacher newsletters and other publications designed to provide helpful teaching tips for the novice teacher. (p. 2)

It is unlikely that any single program would contain all of these features, but these components represent the building blocks of most programs, and most programs contain some variation of these features. Of course, programs vary greatly across sites, depending upon the priorities and resources of their sponsoring agencies.

As to which components are most common, Marshall (1983) attempted to identify induction program components by surveying 72 districts across the nation. She found that 85 percent of the programs offered meetings or workshops focused on beginning-teacher needs prior to the opening of school; 57 percent assigned an experienced fellow teacher as a "buddy" to the beginning teacher; and 44 percent provided a handbook containing such items as school or district philosophy, practices, and procedures. On the other hand, only 18 percent provided ready access for the beginning teacher to a nonevaluating facilitator.

Conceptual Paradigms

In the field of teacher education, basic paradigms have been identified. For example, Zeichner (1983) identifies four basis paradigms: (a) behavioristic, (b) personalistic, (3) traditional-craft, and (d) inquiry-oriented. Others have identified different, yet highly similar, paradigms for teacher education (Hartnett & Naish, 1980; Mitchell & Kerchner, 1983).

It is conceivable that teacher induction programs could be more effective if they, too, were structured around conceptual paradigms. Different programs could have different foci relating to the specific paradigms upon which they are based. Currently, to talk about conceptual paradigms in teacher induction is perhaps a bit like discussing "the emperor's new clothes." To date, conceptual paradigms in teacher induction programs relate simply to the identification of different underlying philosophies of programs. For example, some programs have a strong *assistance* emphasis and others have a strong focus on *assessment* (Nemser, Odell, & Lawrence, 1988). Some programs are built around the idea of *transition into teaching*, whereas others assume more of a *training* role. Still other programs strongly emphasize *socialization* into the profession and the workplace. Although these different approaches to teacher induction could be the beginnings of future conceptual paradigms, it is premature to identify clear conceptual paradigms on basis of current practice. Readers can anticipate the development of such paradigms as the field of teacher induction matures.

RESEARCH: CURRENT KNOWLEDGE

Progress was made in certain areas of teacher induction research in the late 1980s. In this section, the early beginning-teacher research will be highlighted, and some of the more recent larger studies related to teacher induction will be discussed. The final part of this section will highlight findings from a recent synthesis of research on teacher induction (and internship) programs and practices.

Preliminary Work in the Field

Until recently most of the research on beginning teachers focused on the study of the needs and concerns of beginning teachers, or what Griffin (1985) refers to as "the adjustment phenomena"—investigations of the degree to which new teachers fit into their new role and context. Among studies that investigated the needs and concerns of beginning teachers are Bolam, Baker, McMahon, Davis, and McCabbe, 1977; Grant and Zeichner, 1981; Howey and Bents, 1979; Huling-Austin, Barnes and Smith, 1985; McCaleb, 1984; McDonald, 1980; Newberry, 1977; Ryan, 1970; Tisher, 1978; and Zeichner, 1983. Veenman (1984) synthesized a total of 91 studies focused on the self-reported concerns of beginning teachers. The concerns, in the order of frequency mentioned, included: classroom discipline, motivating students, dealing with individual differences, assessing students' work, relations with parents, organizing class work, insufficient materials and supplies, and problems of individual students. This early body of research has significantly advanced understanding of new teachers and the problems they face in their first years of teaching. It is important, however, to note that most of this early work on beginning-teacher concerns and problems was conducted on teachers not involved in formal induction programs, and recent research has indicated that beginning teachers in induction programs experience needs and concerns somewhat different from those of teachers not in induction programs (Odell, 1986b; Odell, 1988).

Major Studies on Teacher Induction

In the 1980s, several large studies focusing on beginning teachers and teacher induction programs were conducted. One of the largest of these was by McDonald and Elias (1982). Their work provides an analysis of the characteristics of both internship and induction programs, as well as an examination of the problems of beginning teachers. Another major study, the Teacher Induction Study (Hoffman, et al. 1985; Hoffman, Edwards, O'Neal, Barnes, & Paulissen, 1986) was a policy-into-practice study of two state-mandated induction programs. In this study, researchers traced the implementation of state leg-islative mandates through local districts and into schools and classrooms. A third major research effort involved a large, national, collaborative study of teacher induction in diverse contexts, which was conducted in the 1985–1986 school year by members of the Teacher Induction Network. In this study, researchers from 26 sites across the nation collected data in their own settings to document induction practices and effects and contributed it to a national data base at the Research and Development Center for Teacher Education at the University of Texas at Austin (Huling-Austin & Murphy, 1987; Murphy & Huling-Austin, 1987).

A Synthesis of Research on Teacher Induction Programs and Practices

In 1988, in order to clarify the research base on teacher induction programs and practices, Huling-Austin attempted to identify those studies that focused on beginning teachers in induction programs. To be included in the synthesis, studies must have been (a) data-based (i.e., data must have been systematically collected and analyzed); (b) focused on beginning teachers in an induction program (i.e., teachers must have been receiving some type of formal induction assistance; studies of beginning teachers not in an induction program were not included); and (c) reported since 1977. With these criteria, 17 studies were identified. Findings were organized around five, commonly accepted goals of induction programs. In addition, other noteworthy findings that did not directly relate to any specific goal were included in a final section. Highlights from this synthesis are presented here.

Goal #1: To Improve Teaching Performance. The only study identified that attempted to compare student achievement of first-year teachers in an induction program with first-year teachers not receiving induction support found no significant differences between the student achievement of control and experimental teachers (Blackburn, 1977). This study did, however, find significant differences in how principals rated the teaching competency of experimental and control teachers. The teaching competency of experimental teachers who had cooperating teachers assigned to them on a one-to-one basis were rated significantly higher than that of "nonsupported" first-year teachers.

Another controlled study was conducted by Project CREDIT (Certification Renewal Experiences Designed to Improve Teaching), a teacher induction program sponsored by Indiana State University and funded through the Indiana Teacher Quality Act (PL 102-1985). This study indicated that first-year teachers participating in the project showed specific and significant measurable changes when compared with the control group (Summers, 1987). The evaluation report indicated:

CREDIT interns demonstrated (1) a significant gain in the use of mastery learning and mastery learning theory, (2) increased motivation to understand and use higher order questions, (3) increased inclination to teach critical thinking skills, (4) increased awareness of state and local curriculum guides, (5) enhanced ability to communicate with parents, and (6) improved ability to communication with the public at large. (pp. 33–34)

In an evaluation of the Oklahoma Entry-Year Assessment Program (Elsner, 1984), committee members including entry-year teachers, teacher consultants, school administrators and higher education representatives were asked to rate beginning teachers' knowledge, skills, and competencies in 10 areas at the beginning of the school year and again at the end. Data from this sample of more than 200 respondents indicated that first-year teachers in the state program made significant progress in planning skills, handling class discussions, preparing unit and lesson plans, managing discipline problems, and being able to teach or train others.

Goal #2: To Increase Retention of Promising Beginning Teachers During the Induction Years.

Just how much teacher induction programs have influenced the retention of beginning teachers is not well documented. However, from the evidence that is available, it appears that at least some induction programs are having the desired effects on retention of beginning teachers. For example, Project CREDIT reported that, after one year of operation, all 21 participating first-year teachers indicated a desire to return to teaching the following year. This compares with figures from a statewide needs assessment indicating that 26.5 percent of Indiana teachers who entered teaching dropped out within 2 years and that 62 percent dropped out within 5 years (Summers, 1987, p. 34).

Similarly impressive results have been reported by the University of Alabama–Birmingham First-Year Teacher Pilot Program (Blackburn, 1977). In this effort, data were collected from 100 first-year teachers receiving induction support and 100 first-year teachers in a control group not receiving support. Of the 100 teachers in the experimental group, all but 4 taught the following year; 20 of the control teachers did not teach the second year (p. 9).

In the fall of 1983, Doane College in Nebraska instituted an induction program as one component of its teacher education program. In 1987, the program reported that 24 of the 25 teachers participating in the induction program remained in the teaching profession (Hegler & Dudley, 1987).

Goal #3: To Promote the Personal and Professional Well-Being of Beginning Teachers.

Many beginning teachers experience personal and professional trauma during their first year without the support of an induction program. For example, Hidalgo (1986), in studying emergency credentialed teachers in the Los Angeles Unified School District, found that teachers had persistent personal and management preoccupations that "obstructed, and even paralyzed their progress toward more sophisticated use of teaching knowledge" (p. 78). In several case studies he described in detail their anxieties, insecurities, and frustrations.

Teacher induction programs can serve as one avenue of personal and professional support to beginning teachers, and many studies have reported positive outcomes in this area.

One such example is provided by Huffman and Leak (1986) and is related to the mentor teacher component of the North Carolina Beginning Teacher Program. "Mentor teachers were found to have provided 'positive reinforcement,' 'guidance and moral support,' 'patience and understanding,' and even 'a shoulder to cry on'" (p. 23). Brooks (1986), in his work with the Richardson Independent School District (ISD) (Texas) New Teacher Induction Program, found that beginning teachers in the program reported increased feelings of competence, motivation, belonging, support, and attention as a result of their experiences in the program.

Huling-Austin and Murphy (1987) studied groups of beginning teachers across the country who were and were not participating in teacher induction programs. Using a questionnaire designed to measure the beginning teacher's perception of effectiveness and the desirability of the teaching profession, they found that "Responses from sites that had no formal induction program in operation were noticeably less positive than the other sites" (p. 33). Summers (1987) found a similar situation in Project CREDIT. Control-group comparisons revealed that intern teachers completed the year with significantly healthier attitudes and perceptions about teaching than did a similar group of beginning teachers who did not have the CREDIT support program. Control-group data revealed that nonsupported beginning teachers reported deteriorating attitudes or teaching perceptions in 88 of 98 surveyed variables (pp. 33–34). The findings from these two studies suggest that when beginning teachers are not supported, they begin to question their own effectiveness and their decisions to become teachers.

Interestingly, although beginning teachers often report that the emotional support they received was the most beneficial aspect of their teacher induction program, Odell (1986a) found in analyzing categories of support provided to first-year teachers that emotional support accounted for only a small percentage of the assistance provided. She wrote, "Although emotional support was of considerable importance across semesters, clinical support teachers generally offered more assistance with the formal teaching processes to new teachers than emotional support" (p. 28). This suggests that emotional support is very important and without it beginning teachers have difficulty dealing with other matters. However, once emotional support is established, beginning teachers do not require large amounts of such support but, rather, can move on to deal with instructional matters.

Goal #4: To Satisfy Mandated Requirements Related to Induction and Certification.

Once a mandated program is implemented, in one sense at least the mandate has been satisfied, but a more important question is to what degree the initial intent of the mandate is actually being addressed. While some researchers have found evidence that mandated state induction programs are working (Blackburn, 1977; Elsner, 1984), others are concerned that most studies to date have focused on how programs have been implemented and the factors influencing implementation, but have not examined the extent to which programs have fulfilled the original intent of "improving the quality of teaching" (Friske & Combs, 1986).

This concern was addressed by researchers in a study of two state-mandated teacher induction programs (Hoffman et al., 1986).

> At the school level, our analyses of implementation focused on the work of the support teams with the beginning teacher. It is useful to draw a distinction at this level between procedural compliance and substantive implementation of program requirements. Procedurally, the teams included in our sample accomplished all of the required activities in terms of observing, conferring, completing necessary forms, and so on. Substantively there was great variance in terms of how the program was carried out. . . . In cases where no strong team leadership appeared, the induction program seldom rose above the procedural compliance level. (p. 19)

These same researchers also noted an interesting point related to the gatekeeping function of teacher induction programs. Data secured from interviews with state officials in the two states indicated that nearly all of the teachers statewide enrolled in both programs were recommended for certification. They comment, "Such patterns would seem to call into question either the gate-keeping capacity of such programs or the real need for such programs in the first place on the grounds of controlling for the quality of entering teachers" (p. 18).

Goal #5: To Transmit the Culture of the System to Beginning Teachers. It appears that this goal is less prevalent in many programs than the other four. Although it is true that many programs recognize that one program function is to socialize beginning teachers and to familiarize them with the workplace norms, the majority of programs stop far short of defining and transmitting the culture of the system. It can be speculated that locally developed programs more often tend to emphasize this culture goal than state-mandated programs, in that local agencies are more likely to "own" a common culture that they want to transmit to the beginning teacher. In any case, the two studies that addressed this goal most directly were both locally developed programs.

The Ohio County School Teacher Induction Program in Wheeling, West Virginia, had as one of its objectives the development by teachers of a sense of ownership and bonding to an excellent system (Marockie & Looney, 1988). The evaluation report on the program stated:

> Results of evaluation of the Teacher Induction Program indicated that the program was extremely successful in guiding inductees in becoming bonded to the system and adopting the goals of the system. Through a positive interaction between central office personnel and new teacher as well as principal and new teacher, ownership began to develop. (pp. 2–3)

A similar phenomenon was described by Brooks (1986) in his work with the Richardson ISD (Texas) induction program. He wrote, "Beginning teacher reports of increased feelings of competence, motivation, belonging, support and attention combine to produce an overwhelming perception of district competence and motivation to assist and develop entry year professionals" (p. 7). From this observation it can be inferred that the Richardson program has attempted to address the goal of transmitting the culture of the district to beginning teachers and has indeed accomplished this goal to a reasonably high degree.

Other Noteworthy Findings. Huling-Austin (1988) notes that there are four additional points clearly present in these studies that do not relate to program goals: the need for flexibility in induction programs, the important role of the support teacher, the importance of placement in promoting beginning-teacher success, and the need to educate both the profession and the public about teacher induction.

1. *The need for flexibility in induction programs.* Because beginning teachers are individuals, they experience their first year of teaching and the induction process in individual, personal ways. In a study of the Virginia Beginning Teacher Assistance Program (Wildman, Niles, Magliaro, McLaughlin, & Drill, 1987), considerable attention was given to this point. These researchers argue that it is important to consider beginning teachers individually because their sources of problems, their ways of reacting, and their aspirations for teaching can vary dramatically from person to person (p. 9).

Grant and Zeichner (1981) acknowledge the personal nature of teaching by noting that the problems and concerns experienced by the beginning teachers in their study were extremely diverse:

> As Lewis (1980) argues, blanket statements about what to provide for first-year teachers are not very helpful. While general conclusions can be drawn about the necessity of more in-school support and better orientations, our data seem to indicate that the most useful thing that can be done with regard to induction is to personalize and individualize this support and gear it to the needs of the specific beginning teachers. (p. 110)

Huling-Austin, Putman, and Galvez-Hjornevik (1986) recommend that induction programs should be structured flexibly enough to accommodate the emerging needs of participants:

> A prepackaged, "canned" program determined in advance will not be flexible enough to meet the variety of needs that are likely to emerge. . . . It is important to closely monitor the specific emerging needs and concerns of participants and to select appropriate interventions accordingly. (pp. 52–53)

2. *The important role of the support teacher.* Probably the most consistent finding across studies is the importance of the support teacher (sometimes called the mentor teacher, the helping teacher, the peer teacher, or the buddy teacher). Huling-Austin, Putman, and Galvez-Hjornevik (1986) contend that, "The assignment of an appropriate support teacher is likely to be the most powerful and cost-effective intervention in an induction program" (p. 50). Most of the beginning teachers in their study reported that having a support teacher was the single most helpful aspect of the program because it gave them someone to turn to on a daily basis as problems arose.

The role of the support teacher, or mentor teacher, has been carefully studied by the staff of the Center of Excellence in Teacher Education at Memphis State University. Butler

(1987) outlines a number of personal factors that appear to support the development of a positive mentor–protégé relationship including, (a) prior experiences in assisting student teachers and novice teachers in understanding and mastering the responsibilities of teaching; (b) years of experience as a classroom teacher; (c) willingness to commit time to the protégé early in the relationship so that both have opportunities to come to know and respect each other; (d) ability to conceive of the relationship in developmental terms, with sensitivity to the need to modify the mentor role as the protégé progressed; and (e) high status within the school and within the profession, such as attainment of higher rank on the state's career ladder program (pp. 3–4). Odell (1987) provides a similar list of important mentor teacher characteristics including successful teaching experience, demonstrated success in working with adults, close proximity, sensitivity and responsiveness to the ideas of others, receptivity to learning new information about the process of teaching, and capacity for empathy.

Regarding exactly what mentors do, the list of responsibilities and activities is considerable. Huling-Austin and Murphy (1987) found that first-year teachers in their study reported receiving help from their support teachers in 14 different areas. Areas most frequently mentioned included "someone to talk to/listen to," followed by "locating materials" and "help with clerical work related to district policies and procedures." Other areas frequently mentioned were "lesson planning," "classroom organization," and "discipline" (p. 33). Because the role of the support teacher is so extensive, Huling-Austin and Murphy recommend that support teachers receive training in how to provide assistance in a variety of areas and in how to work with another adult in a supportive manner. They should also be compensated for their participation in induction programs (pp. 34–35).

In regard to what should be included in mentor training, a number of authors and programs provide direction in this area. Odell (1987) suggests that content for mentor training programs should be derived from the literature pertaining to teacher development, new teacher needs and concerns, effective teaching, supervision, induction, and adult professional development. The Leadership Resource book for the State of Ohio designed to assist the entry-year teacher (Gordon, 1987) contains the following topics to be included in mentor training: effective classroom management—research and alternative models of classroom management; effective instruction—knowledge base, effective schools research, learning-style theories and models of teaching; adult learning and development; observation systems; diagnostic skills; conferencing skills; and a framework for ongoing support activities including systems information, videotaping and audiotaping, and coaching skills.

The North Carolina Trainer's Manual for the Mentor/Support Team Training Program (North Carolina Department of Public Instruction, 1986) includes many of the same topics centered around the major areas of technical assistance skills; adult learner information; and support skills including effective communication, helping relationships, role establishment; effective teacher training; and performance appraisal training.

Kilgore and Kozisek (1988) concluded from their study, in which mentors were provided with neither training nor com-

pensation, that the envisioned role of the mentor teacher was not fulfilled, primarily because mentors were not provided with support for assuming the duties of a mentor (e.g., extra pay, recognition, training). They stated that "The school as an organization has to come to grips with how they see mentors or career teachers helping those working their way into the system" (p. 12).

3. *The importance of placement in promoting beginning-teacher success.* Beginning teachers are often placed in teaching assignments that would challenge even the most skillful veteran teachers. These difficult assignments can take several forms including teaching in a subject area for which the teacher is not certified, having numerous class preparations, "floating" from classroom to classroom, working with low-ability or unmotivated and disruptive students, and being responsible for demanding or time-consuming extracurricular activities.

Hidalgo (1986) recently completed a study of first-year teachers in difficult settings. His case studies give vivid accounts of novice, emergency-credentialed teachers assigned to teach high-demand subjects in low-income, overcrowded, junior high schools while they were still enrolled in teacher-preparation classes. Although Hidalgo's subjects certainly were in extremely challenging assignments, even less extreme circumstances can have major effects on the induction process, according to a number of different teacher induction researchers who have noted the importance of teaching assignment as it relates to beginning-teacher success.

For example, in their study of two state-mandated programs, Hoffman and his colleagues (1986) note:

The programs appeared to work best when the teaching context was appropriate to the talents and interests of the first year teacher. The programs did not provide sufficient support to overcome inappropriate placements or stressful work conditions. And, in fact, in such situations the programs only serve to further antagonize and exacerbate negative feelings. (p. 20)

In a later study, Huling-Austin, Putman, and Galvez-Hjornevik (1986) came to a similar conclusion:

Placement of first-year teachers may well be the most influential variable in first-year teaching success. Which classes a first-year teacher is assigned to teach will be extremely influential in how successful a year that teacher is likely to have. The interventions supplied in the project were not sufficiently powerful enough to resolve the types of problems beginning teachers will experience in a difficult teaching assignment. (p. 48)

4. *The need to educate the profession and the public about teacher induction.* It is easy to assume that, because more legislatures are mandating induction programs and programs are rapidly increasing in number across the nation, there must be general concensus in the profession at large about the need for and potential benefits of teacher induction programs. However, the reality of the situation is that beginning-teacher induction is probably not viewed by many practitioners as a pressing need.

Kilgore and Kozisek (1988) comment on this issue, "For the most part, school personnel are not aware of the literature or effects they have on first-year teachers. Simply stated, principals and teachers treat novice teachers like they were treated, and have had no reason to think that things should be any different" (p. 11).

Friske and Combs (1986) discuss the problem of trying to bring about improvement without first obtaining the commitment of those expected to implement the reforms:

Improving the quality of education can not merely be legislated. On paper requirements can be met, and still not effect true educational reform. . . . Without the commitment to the quality with which each (school practitioner) fulfills responsibilities to the beginning teacher and the teacher induction program, new teachers will merely be socialized into the existing system. (p. 72)

Summary of Findings. There is research data to support the fact that induction programs can be successful in achieving each of the five stated goals. In addition, the studies collectively include important findings about four other points: (a) the need for flexibility in induction programs, (b) the important role of the support teacher, (c) the importance of placement in beginning-teacher success, and (d) the need to educate the profession, as well as the public, about teacher induction. However, although there is evidence to suggest that induction programs can be successful, it is important for those who develop and implement programs to realize that desired outcomes will rarely be achieved by accident just because a program exists. For the goals to be achieved, program activities specifically targeted at identified outcomes must be carefully designed and appropriately implemented.

SUMMARY AND CONCLUSIONS

Currently, there is extensive interest across the nation in teacher induction programs and internships. Furthermore, a large amount of writing and activity has been produced on the topic in the past few years, so much so that it is becoming increasingly difficult at any point in time to determine what the knowledge base and the research base are saying to the field. To try to help identify what is currently known related to teacher induction, this final section will suggest areas of both consensus and controversy. The chapter will conclude with a brief discussion of needed next steps in the areas of teacher induction policy, practice, and research.

Consensus and Controversy

Even though the field of teacher induction is quite young, already there are clearly defined areas of both consensus and controversy. Points of agreement and disagreement are emerging from the experience of practitioners and the work of researchers. In some instances, the points of consensus and controversy are related, as is the case when there is agreement on the *what* but disagreement on the *how*. Here general points of agreement related to teacher induction are highlighted along with unresolved issues that remain to be addressed.

Consensus. Based upon a survey of the existing literature and research bases, agreement appears to exist on the following points:

1. The general needs and concerns of beginning teachers such as classroom management, student evaluation, individual student differences, parents (see Veenman, 1984), and the need for induction programs to include assistance to address these areas
2. The need for induction programs to remain flexible enough to accommodate the individual, context-specific concerns of beginning teachers as they experience them
3. The important role of the support (mentor/peer/buddy) teacher
4. The need for various agencies (institutions of higher education, state education agencies, local education agencies, professional organizations, and service agencies) to collaborate in providing support and assistance to beginning teachers
5. The need for beginning teachers to be placed in assignments that will allow them to succeed, as opposed to extremely difficult placements that will promote their failure

Controversy and Unresolved Issues. Just as there are areas of consensus related to the field of teacher induction, there are also areas of controversy. The following are some of the unresolved issues in the field:

1. What is a realistic definition of a "successful beginning teacher"? It is unrealistic to expect the beginning teacher to perform as well as the 20-year veteran at the end of one year of teaching, regardless of how effective the teacher induction program is. Even so, in many programs the same evaluation criteria are being used for beginning teachers that are being used for experienced professionals at other phases of their careers.
2. What are the best ways of accommodating the assistance and assessment functions of induction programs? Because there are much data to support the fact that beginning teachers are hesitant to seek assistance from persons responsible for conducting their formal assessments, most educators agree on the need to separate the assistance and assessment roles of program facilitators. However, in practice, many programs have the same persons fulfilling both assessment and assistance roles.
3. How should programs be structured?
   What is the best combination in structuring programs to provide for both predetermined/assumed needs and emergent needs?
   Should program activities be required or voluntary?
4. How should the support teacher role be structured?
   How much release time is necessary for support teachers to be effective?
   How much training is necessary to prepare support teachers to successfuly fulfill their role?
   What is reasonable compensation for support teachers?
5. What responsibilities should be filled by the various agencies involved in the induction process (institutions of higher

education, state education agencies, local education agencies, etc.)?

6. How can induction programs be financed, and what program expectations are realistic given limited or no funding?
7. How should induction programs be evaluated?

Needed Next Steps

Considering the brief history of teacher induction programs in this country, considerable progress has been made. However, in the future there is a clear need to sharpen the focus of efforts in the areas of policy, practice, and research.

Policy. It is important that increasing numbers of legislators and other policymakers understand that teacher induction is one of several powerful influencing factors when it comes to attracting and retaining a quality teaching force. Other related factors include teacher salaries, status of the teaching profession, work conditions in the school, and opportunities for advancement within the profession. If one is serious about attracting and retaining a quality teaching force, it is imperative to do a better job of inducting teachers into the profession, as well as addressing these other issues. Until improved induction processes are widely implemented across the country, many talented persons who have chosen to become teachers will undoubtedly leave the profession prematurely, due to problems encountered in their first years in the classroom. Furthermore, one can only speculate on the number of interested, qualified persons who decide not to enter the profession because of what is told by former beginning teachers who experienced failure due to inadequate support during the induction period. Addressing the issue of teacher induction alone will not solve the overall problem of attracting and retaining a quality teaching force, but the problem most assuredly will not be solved until better, more systematic induction processes for beginning teachers are provided.

If teacher induction efforts are to succeed, policymakers need to become more realistic about providing adequate funding for these efforts. Funding levels reported by the states vary from no money allocated, to a high of $5,000 (Eastern Illinois University, 1986). Inadequately funded induction programs typically not only provide limited support to beginning teachers, but also compound problems for experienced educators involved with the program who are already overloaded with other job responsibilities.

Finally, policymakers need to be aware of and guided by research findings that have policy implications. For example, research has indicated that, when programs need large amounts of procedural requirements and record keeping, they are often not implemented beyond the level of procedural compliance. Another example of a research finding with policy implications is related to the support teachers. Research has indicated that when support teachers are not provided with adequate training and compensation, their role is seldom fulfilled successfully.

In conclusion, it is essential that increasing numbers of policymakers recognize the broader importance of teacher induction programs as they relate to attracting and retaining a quality teaching force. In addition, it is imperative that policymakers provide adequate financing for induction programs and that they be responsive to research findings with policy implications.

Practice. Although it is certainly encouraging that increasing numbers of induction programs are being implemented nationwide, there is a need for ongoing program improvement that acknowledges the transition role of induction between preservice and inservice. Currently many induction programs operate as discrete and isolated entities. Practitioners need to operationalize induction programs that function as both a logical extension to the preservice teacher-training program and an entry piece to a larger career-long professional-development program for teachers.

Practitioners from the various role groups concerned about teacher induction (institutions of higher education, state education agencies, local education agencies, professional organizations, and service agencies) need to explore better ways of collaboratively addressing the concerns of beginning teachers. If teacher induction programs are to function as part of the teacher education continuum, it is crucial that those groups representing the various parts of the continuum play a substantive role in designing, implementing, and evaluating such programs

Practitioners also need to remain abreast of what is being learned from induction research in order to apply and integrate these findings into practice. For example, as a result of teacher induction research, the types of teaching assignments that create problems for beginning teachers are known. In addition, there is general agreement about what should be included in the overall content of teacher induction programs. Furthermore, a large body of research is becoming available about the important role and function of support personnel in induction programs. Practice could be greatly improved if what is already known from induction research is applied. The need exists for practitioners to contribute to the research base on teacher induction programs by becoming involved in research on their own programs.

Finally, an induction program could potentially be more effective if it were built around a specific conceptual paradigm. Just as conceptual paradigms have evolved in the field of teacher education (see Zeichner, 1983), it is possible for induction programs to be designed around these same paradigms or a new set of paradigms specific to teacher induction programs. In either case, it is likely that if program developers and facilitators could agree on the specific conceptual focus of the program, program activities could be structured more coherently and could be targeted toward more specific outcomes.

Research. Much progress was made in teacher induction research in the 1980s, yet many questions remain unanswered. A number of educators have identified future avenues to be explored through teacher induction research. Among these are Griffin (1985), who has provided a lengthy list of stimulating research questions and pressing research issues: McCaleb (1985), who has pointed out the need to investigate the effects of specific induction interventions, as well as the cumulative effects of specific induction programs; and Zeichner (1982), who has argued that there is a critical need to investigate the influence of specific contexts in which beginning teachers function. Collectively, these recommendations are extremely valuable in determining both direction and focus for future research efforts related to teacher induction.

A key question is: What induction practices work best under what conditions? Although there has been important progress in documenting the effects of induction programs in a number of areas, it is still not clear from induction research what specific practices or combination of practices are achieving what outcomes. To determine this, it will be necessary for researchers not only to investigate the effects of induction programs, but also to do a much better job of documenting the specific components and practices included in programs, as well as the contexts within which these programs operate, and then to compare effects across similar and different programs and contexts. It is also extremely important to investigate to what degree legislative mandates are achieving their original intents. This difficult task of determining what works will require careful attention on the part of individual researchers studying specific programs, as well as a concerted effort on the part of other researchers who are willing to tackle the task of analyzing and synthesizing findings across studies.

Finally, some of the most intriguing questions of all will undoubtedly be some of the most difficult to answer. Some of these questions are:

1. To what degree do teacher induction programs change teacher attitudes about professional development and the desirability of the teaching profession?
2. What are the long-range effects of attitude changes on teacher retention, teacher effectiveness, and efforts to recruit new talent into teaching?

If these and other important questions are to be addressed, it will be imperative that a variety of research methodologies be used to investigate in greater depth the highly complex phenomena of teacher induction. Griffin (1985) makes this point when he writes:

To understand the interactions around and within complex contexts such as schools, I believe it is absolutely necessary that we make much more vigorous use of methodologies that blend and explain, that answer and provide needed detail, and that name and describe. This blend is only possible when complementary although basically different conceptions of scientific inquiry can be used in tandem. (p. 45)

Finally, as the body of research on teacher induction programs and internships grows, there is an increasing need for researchers to translate their findings into formats that are useful to policymakers and practitioners and to develop improved strategies for communicating these findings. If the art and science of inducting new teachers is to advance, it is essential to continue to push forward the boundaries of knowledge. Policymakers, practitioners, and researchers must work together toward providing better programs for inducting new teachers into the profession.

References

Action in Teacher Education. (Winter, 1987). 8(4).

Association of Teacher Educators, Blue Ribbon Task Force. (1986). *Visions of reform: Implications for the education profession.* Reston: VA: Author.

Blackburn, J. (1977). *The first-year teacher: Perceived needs, intervention strategies and results.* Paper presented at the annual meeting of the American Educational Research Association, New York. (ERIC Document Reproduction Service No. ED 135 768)

Bolam, R., Baker, K., McMahon, A., Davis, J., & McCabbe, C. (1977). *The 1977 national conference on teacher induction.* Bristol, England: University of Bristol, School of Education.

Brooks, D. M. (1986). *Richardson new teacher induction program: Final data analysis and report.* Richardson, TX: Richardson Independent School District. (ERIC Document Reproduction Service No. ED 278 627)

Brooks, D. M. (1987). *Teacher induction: A new beginning.* Reston, VA: Association of Teacher Educators. (ERIC Document Reproduction Service No. ED 279 624)

Butler, E. D. (1987, February). *Lessons learned about mentoring in two fifth-year teacher preparation–induction programs.* Paper presented at the annual meeting of the Association of Teacher Educators, Houston.

Carnegie Forum on Education and the Economy, Task Force on Teaching as a Profession. (1986). *A nation prepared: Teachers for the 21st century.* New York: Author.

Creek, R. J., & Vollmer, M. L. (1984). *The educational internship: A teacher training model for the nineties.* Pittsburgh, PA: University of Pittsburgh. (ERIC Document Reproduction Service No. ED 261 006)

Eastern Illinois University. (1986). *Final report for initial year of teaching study.* Chicago: Illinois State Board of Education.

Educational Leadership. (November, 1985). 43(3).

Elsner, K. (1984, January). *First year evaluation results from Oklahoma's entry-year assistance committees.* Paper presented at the annual meeting of the Association of Teacher Educators, New Orleans. (ERIC Document Reproduction Service No. ED 242 706)

ERIC Digest. (1986a). *Components of teacher induction programs.* Washington, DC: ERIC Clearinghouse on Teacher Education.

ERIC Digest. (1986b). *Current developments in teacher induction programs.* Washington, DC: ERIC Clearinghouse on Teacher Education.

ERIC Digest. (1986c). *Teaching mentoring.* Washington, DC: ERIC Clearinghouse on Teacher Education.

Friske, J., & Combs, M. (1986). Teacher induction programs: An Oklahoma perspective. *Action in Teacher Education, 7*(2), 67–74.

Gordon, S. P. (1987). *Assisting the entry-year teacher: A leadership resource.* Columbus, OH: Ohio Department of Education, Inservice Education.

Grant, C., & Zeichner, K. (1981). Inservice support for first-year teachers: The state of the scene. *Journal of Research and Development in Education, 14*(2), 99–111.

Griffin, G. A. (1985). Teacher induction: Research issues. *Journal of Teacher Education, 36*(1), 42–46.

Griffin, G. A., Barnes, S., Defino, M., Edwards, S., Hoffman, J. V., Hukill, H., & O'Neal, S. (1983). *Teacher induction: Research design for a descriptive study.* Austin, TX: University of Texas at Austin, R & D Center for Teacher Education.

Griffin, G. A., & Hukill, H. (1983). *First years of teaching: What are the pertinent issues?* (Report No. 9051). Austin, TX: University of Texas at Austin, R & D Center for Teacher Education.

Griffin, G. A., & Millies, S. (Eds). (1987). *The first years of teaching: Background papers and a proposal.* Chicago: Illinois State Board of Education.

Hartnett, A., & Naish, M. (1980). Technicians or social bandits? Some moral and political issues in the education of teachers. In P. Woods (Ed.), *Teacher strategies: Explorations in the sociology of school* (pp. 254–274). London: Croom Helm.

Hawk, P. P. (1984). *Making a difference: Reflections and thoughts of first year teachers.* Greenville, NC: East Carolina University.

Hawk, P., & Robards, S. (1987). Statewide teacher induction programs. In D. Brooks (Ed.), *Teacher induction: A new beginning* (pp. 33–44). Reston, VA: Association of Teacher Educators.

Hegler, K., & Dudley, R. (1987). Beginning teacher induction: A progress report. *Journal of Teacher Education, 38*(1), 53–56.

Hidalgo, F. (1986). The evolving concerns of first-year junior high school teachers in difficult settings: Three case studies. *Action in Teacher Education, 8*(4), 75–79.

Hoffman, J., Edwards, S., O'Neal, S., Barnes, S., & Paulissen, M. (1986). A study of state-mandated beginning teacher programs. *Journal of Teacher Education, 37*(1), 16–21.

Hoffman, J. V., Griffin, G. A., Edwards, S. A., Paulissen, M. O., O'Neal, S. F., & Barnes, S. (1985). *Teacher induction study: Final report of a descriptive study* (Report No. 9063). Austin, TX: University of Texas at Austin, R & D Center for Teacher Education.

Holmes Group. (1986). *Tomorrow's teachers.* East Lansing, MI: Author.

Hord, S. M., O'Neal, S. F., & Smith, M. L. (Eds.). (1985) *Beyond the looking glass: Papers from a national symposium on teacher education policies, practices and research* (Report No. 7203). Austin, TX: University of Texas at Austin, R & D Center for Teacher Education.

Howey, K. R., & Bents, R. H. (Eds.). (1979). *Toward meeting the needs of the beginning teacher.* Minneapolis: Midwest Teacher Corps Network.

Huffman, G., & Leak, S. (1986). Beginning teachers' perceptions of mentors. *Journal of Teacher Education, 37*(1), 22–25.

Huling-Austin, L. (Ed.). (1986a). *Directory of teacher induction programs* (Report No. 7216). Austin, TX: University of Texas at Austin, R & D Center for Teacher Education and the ATE Commission on the Teacher Induction Process.

Huling-Austin, L. (1986b). What can and cannot reasonably be expected from teacher induction programs. *Journal of Teacher Education, 37*(1), 2–5.

Huling-Austin, L. (1988). A synthesis of research on teacher induction programs and practices. *Centering Teacher Education 6*(1), 19–28.

Huling-Austin, L., Barnes, S., & Smith, J. (1985). *A research based staff development program for beginning teachers.* Paper presented at the annual meeting of the American Educational Research Association, Chicago.

Huling-Austin, L., & Murphy, S. C. (1987). *Assessing the impact of teacher induction programs: Implications for program development.* Paper presented at the annual meeting of the American Educational Research Association, Washington, DC. (ERIC Document Reproduction Service No. ED 283 779)

Huling-Austin, L., Odell, S., Ishler, P., Kay, R., & Edelfelt, R. (1989). *Assisting the beginning teacher.* Reston, VA: Association of Teacher Educators.

Huling-Austin, L., Putman, S., Edwards, S., & Galvez-Hjornevik, C. (1985). *MTIP satellite conference proceedings* (Report No. 7209). Austin, TX: University of Texas at Austin, R & D Center for Teacher Education.

Huling-Austin, L., Putman, S., & Galvez-Hjornevik, C. (1986). *Model teacher induction project study findings* (Report No. 7212). Austin, TX: University of Texas at Austin, R & D Center for Teacher Education.

Ishler, P., & Kester, R. (1987). Professional organizations and teacher induction: Initiatives and positions. In D. Brooks (Ed.), *Teacher induction: A new beginning* (pp 61–68). Reston, VA: Association of Teacher Educators.

Johnston, J. M. (1988, February). *The knowledge base of teacher induction: A selected annotated bibliography.* Paper presented at the annual meeting of the Association of Teacher Educators, San Diego.

Journal of Teacher Education. (January–February, 1986). *37*(1).

Kappa Delta Pi Record. (Summer, 1986). *22*(4).

Kilgore, A. M., & Kozisek, J. A. (1988, February). *The effects of a planned induction program on first-year teachers: A research report.* Paper presented at the annual meeting of the Association of Teacher Educators, San Diego.

Lewis, C. (1980). Some essential characteristics of programs to support teachers in the beginning years. In K. Howey & R. Bents (Eds.), *Toward meeting the needs of the beginning teacher.* Minneapolis: Midwest Teacher Corps Network.

Lortie, D. C. (1975). *School teacher: A sociological study.* Chicago: University of Chicago Press.

Marockie, M., & Looney, G. E. (1988, February). *Evaluating teacher induction in Ohio County Schools, Wheeling, West Virginia.* Paper presented at the meeting of the Association of Teacher Educators, San Diego.

Marshall, F. G. (1983). Perceived effectiveness of induction practices by beginning teachers in public school districts in the greater Houston area (Doctoral dissertation, University of Houston). *Dissertation Abstracts International, 43,* 7.

Marshall, J. D. (1987). *The Brackenridge internship in teaching program: Acknowledging research as a component of teacher education reform.* San Antonio, TX: Trinity University. (ERIC Document Reproduction Service No. ED 277 679)

Mastin, R. K. (Ed.). (1988). *The NASDTEC Manual.* Sacramento, CA: National Association of State Directors of Teacher Education and Certification.

McArthur, J. T. (1978). What does teaching do to teachers? *Educational Administration Quarterly, 14*(3), 89–103.

McCaleb, J. L. (1984). *An investigation of on-the-job performance of first-year teachers who are graduates from the University of Maryland, from December 1982 to August 1983.* College Park, MD: University of Maryland, Department of Curriculum and Instruction.

McCaleb, J. L. (1985). *Summary of research on induction.* Paper presented at the Forum of Teacher Education, Virginia Beach, VA.

McDonald, F. (1980). *The problems of beginning teachers: A crisis in training: Vol. 1. Study of induction programs for beginning teachers.* Princeton, NJ: Educational Testing Service.

McDonald, F. J., & Elias, P. (1982). *The transition into teaching: The problems of beginning teachers and programs to solve them. Summary report.* Berkeley, CA: Educational Testing Service.

Mitchell, D., & Kerchner, C. (1983). Labor relations and teacher policy. In L. Shulman and G. Sykes (Eds.), *Handbook of teaching and policy* (pp. 214–238). New York: Longman.

Murphy, S., & Huling-Austin, L. (1987, February). *The impact of context on the classroom lives of beginning teachers.* Paper presented at the annual meeting of American Educational Research Association, Washington, DC. (ERIC Document Reproduction Service No. ED 283 780).

National Council for Accreditation of Teacher Education. (1985). *NCATE redesign*. Washington, DC: Author.

Nemser, S., Odell, S, & Lawrence, D. (1988). Induction programs and the professionalization of teachers: Two views. *Colloquy, 1*(2), 11–19.

Neuweiler, H. B. (1987). *Teacher education policy in the states: 50-state survey of legislative and administrative actions*. Washington, DC: American Association of Colleges for Teacher Education.

Newberry, J. M. (1977). *The first year of experience: Influences on beginning teachers*. Paper presented at the annual meeting of the American Educational Research Association, New York.

North Carolina Department of Public Instruction. (1986). *North Carolina mentor/support team training program. Trainer's manual*. Raleigh, NC: Division of Program Approval, Personnel Services Area.

Odell, S. J. (1986a). Induction support of new teachers: A functional approach. *Journal of Teacher Education, 37*(1), 26–29.

Odell, S. J. (1986b). Functional approach to identification of new teacher needs in an induction context. *Action in Teacher Education, 8*(4), 51–57.

Odell, S. J. (1987). Teacher induction: Rationale and issues. In D. Brooks (Ed.), *Teacher induction: A new beginning* (pp. 69–80). Reston, VA: Association of Teacher Educators.

Odell, S. J. (1988). *Characteristics of beginning teachers in an induction context*. Paper presented at the annual meeting of the American Association of Colleges for Teacher Education, New Orleans.

Ryan, K. (Ed.). (1970). *Don't smile until Christmas: Accounts of the first year of teaching*. Chicago: University of Chicago Press.

Ryan, K., Newman, K. K., Mager, G., Applegate, J. H., Lasley, T., Flora, V. R., & Johnston, J. (1980). *Biting the apple: Accounts of first year teachers*. New York: Longman.

Sandefur, J. T. (1982). What happens to the teacher during induction? In G. E. Hall (Ed.), Beginning teacher induction: Five dilemmas (pp. 41–46). Austin, TX: University of Texas at Austin, R & D Center for Teacher Education.

Schlechty, P., & Vance, V. (1981). Do academically able teachers leave education? The North Carolina case. *Phi Delta Kappan, 63*(2), 106–112.

Schlecty, P., & Vance, V. (1983). Recruitment, selection, and retention: The shape of the teaching force. *Elementary School Journal, 83*(4) 469–487.

Summers, J. A. (1987). *Summative evaluation report: Project CREDIT*. Terre Haute, IN: Indiana State University, School of Education.

Swanson, P. (1968). A time to teach—and a time to learn: The beginning teacher. *National Association of Secondary School Principals Bulletin, 52*(330), 74–84.

Theory Into Practice. (Summer, 1988). 27(3).

Tisher, R. (Ed.). (1978). *The induction of beginning teachers in Australia*. Melbourne, Australia: Monash University.

Veenman, S. (1984). Perceived problems of beginning teachers. *Review of Educational Research, 54*(2), 143–178.

Wildman, T. M., Niles, J. A., Magliaro, S. G., McLaughlin, R. A., & Drill, L. G. (1987). *Virginia's colleague teacher project: Focus on beginning teachers' adaptation to teaching*. Paper presented at the annual meeting of the American Educational Research Association, Washington, DC.

Zeichner, K. (1979). *Teacher induction practices in the United States and Great Britian*. Madison, WI: University of Wisconsin, Department of Curriculum and Instruction.

Zeichner, K. (1982). *Why bother with induction?*. Paper presented at the annual meeting of the American Educational Research Association, New York.

Zeichner, K. (1983). Individual and institutional factors related to the socialization of teaching. In G. Griffin & H. Hukill (Eds.), *First years of teaching: What are the pertinent issues?*. Austin, TX: University of Texas at Austin, R & D Center for Teacher Education.

·31·

SUPERVISION

Carl D. Glickman and Theresa M. Bey

UNIVERSITY OF GEORGIA

This chapter reviews research on supervision in both inservice and preservice settings. Because the roles, responsibilities, and contexts of supervision in service and before service are dissimilar, each dimension is analyzed separately.

INSERVICE SUPERVISION

"Good morale and the routine of people working harmoniously together as part of an efficient system meant that both *supervision* and *support* [italics added] were available to teachers in a way which was absent in less successful schools" (Rutter, Maughan, Mortimore, Ouston, & Smith, 1979, p. 184). This statement is from one of the most extensive studies ever conducted on secondary schools. The literature on successful schools is replete with references to ongoing, close, and professional interactions among administrators and teachers, with a focus on instruction (Little, 1982; Rosenholtz, 1985).

The terms *assistance, monitoring, observing,* and *dialogue* are parts of the concept of instructional supervision, which is generally defined as the function or process of working with teachers to improve instruction (see Glickman, 1985; Harris, 1985; Oliva, 1988; Sergiovanni, 1982). That the supervision of instruction is vital to school success appears nondebatable. The provision of focus, structure, and time for teachers to discuss and plan actions for helping students learn is a penetrating force against the inertia of isolation, invisibility, and lack of intellectual discourse that is prevalent in many unexceptional schools (Boyer, 1983; Brookover, Beady, Flood, Schweiter, & Weisenbaker, 1979; Goodlad, 1984).

If one accepts the premise that supervision of instruction is vital to school success, the specification of the particular kind of supervision, conducted by whom, for whom, toward what end, and within what organizational context assumes major importance. It is in specifying the details of instructional supervision that much confusion arises. For example, most writers of supervision textbooks agree that it is a process of working with teachers to improve instruction; however, they disagree as to which particular process or model of supervision is most effective, what constitutes instructional improvement, and who should be responsible for supervision (Bolin, 1987; N. E. Hart, 1979; May & Zimpher, 1986). Furthermore, the organizational context of schools mediates the support, resources, and training allocated for implementing supervisory approaches. As a result, before the research on instructional supervision can be reviewed, it is necessary to note several important limitations.

Supervision encompasses tasks that create instructional dialogue and planning. Such endeavors as curriculum development, staff development, action research, program evaluation, and group development activities can be logically viewed as components of a comprehensive program of instructional supervision. Many authors of supervision books also include any school process that stimulates teachers' intellectual inquiry regarding instruction as part of the process of supervision. The definition of instructional supervision in school settings is much broader than the definition of supervision in preservice settings, which tends to be limited to a university supervisor and cooperating teacher working with a student teacher. Space constraints prevent a review of the much broader concept of instructional supervision. For purposes of this review, the supervision studies included are those that focus narrowly on direct, one-to-one instructional work with teachers and will be referred to as *direct supervision.*

A further limitation is that direct supervision needs to be

In acknowledgement, Dale Rogers, Barbara F. Lunsford, and Nancy Quintrell deserve a special word of thanks for their excellent assistance on this project. Gillian Cook deserves recognition for her comprehensive review of previous drafts. For their valuable help in manuscript preparation Louise F. Seagrave, L. Ann Seagraves, and Linda M. Edwards also receive our gratitude.

viewed as a function performed by many persons in various positions, for example, principals, assistant principals, lead teachers, department heads, mentor teachers, peer teachers, central office supervisors. Because there is no one definition of a supervisor, in practice or in research, the role can best be established by examining the actions of those who supervise. Broad generalizations about the attitudes, approaches, and outcomes across different supervisory positions are problematic and must be viewed with skepticism.

Another caution is that research in direct supervision does not seem to cumulate. The field has been marked by theoretic development derived from researching organizations, human psychology, curriculum, and instruction, more than by research on direct supervision per se. The preponderance of research studies are doctoral dissertations. As a result, few investigators have conducted more than a single study on a given topic. There is no replication of studies using similar models, methods, or populations, nor are there longitudinal studies utilizing the same treatment of samples over several years. What exists in the research on direct supervision is a scattering of isolated, onetime studies that have little coherence among themselves. Generalizations across such studies become largely speculative.

This review of direct supervision research will be reported in terms of (a) philosophy and history; (b) purposes and outcomes; (c) survey of existing supervision practices; (d) variables, behaviors, attitudes, and approaches of those who supervise; (e) nature of feedback; (f) training; (g) particular models; and (h) organizational considerations.

Philosophy and History

The history of instructional supervision in the United States parallels periods of organizational and industrial management. Inspectorial, scientific management, democratic, humanistic, competency-based, and neoscientific periods have been explained in Lucio and McNeil (1979) and Tanner and Tanner (1987). Each period is marked by the predominance of a particular type of supervision, with other concurrent forms of supervision gaining or losing momentum. A review of historic documents (Blumberg, 1985) and a comparison of past textbooks with current ones (Bolin, 1987) reveal that philosophical debates about the nature and purpose of supervision are enduring.

Philosophical issues in education deal with such matters as the goals of the school, the nature of the learner, the knowledge that is of most worth, and the role of the teacher. In supervision, such concerns focus on the nature of teaching, the sources of knowledge about instruction, and the role of the supervisor vis-à-vis the teacher.

It is possible to classify approaches in terms of how they deal with the content of supervision, the structure or procedures of supervision, the locus of control for making instructional improvement decisions, and the ultimate purposes of supervision. Varying views can be detected in the adjectives with which authors define their models, such as clinical supervision, differentiated supervision, developmental supervision, human

resources supervision, supervision for intelligent thinking, and scientific supervision. There are those who take the position that scientifically derived elements, behaviors, and competencies about instruction should be the focus of observation, feedback, and future planning with teachers. In this view, the supervisor has a greater understanding of what teachers need to do to be more effective and can help teachers understand and use this essential information. Therefore, the process of supervision involves observing teachers by utilizing predetermined observation guides and conferring with teachers on how to plan and use essential teaching elements more wisely and judiciously.

Opposite to this view is a concept of supervision that views knowledge about teaching as derived from the individual teacher, making the focus of supervision a process of eliciting the teacher's own thinking and planning. In this approach the supervisor has no preconceived system to use with teachers but, instead, utilizes various ways of interacting and communicating with teachers to facilitate their self-determined growth.

The middle position is an orientation to supervision that focuses on experimentation and mutual agreements about ways to improve classroom instruction. Here, the supervisor is free to use or abandon methods of observing, conferring, and teaching, in order to reach workable agreements with teachers. These approaches, supported by ideological positions related to supervision, have been described as essentialism, experimentalism, and existentialism by Glickman (1985) and as positivism, phenomenology, and critical theory by May and Zimpher (1986). Lively debates have ensued in the public arena about the focus, structure, and use of supervision (see Garman, Glickman, Hunter, & Haggerson, 1987). Without a grasp of the philosophical premises underlying particular supervision theories and practices, an attempt to determine success becomes obscured. For example, one might view a particular supervision program as not working because research treatment did not lead to gains in teachers' self-analytical abilities, whereas another study might view the supervisory treatment as highly successful because teachers demonstrated more frequent use of effective teaching practices.

Purposes and Outcomes

Why should teachers be supervised? Why use one supervision program instead of another? If the ultimate outcome of supervision is to improve instruction, what do researchers mean by improved instruction? Answers to such innocent questions are vital to interpreting various research findings in supervision. Researchers utilize different outcomes when determining the success or failure of a particular supervisory program. An analysis of the various outcome measures brings the underlying perspectives of supervision to the surface. For example, Russell and Spafford (1986) argue that supervision must be aimed at producing a climate for teachers to *reflect in action* about their own practices; thus, to use supervision for the more traditional purposes of implementing particular teaching behaviors or raising student achievement is inappropriate and will yield disappointing results. On the other hand, Gage and

Giaconia (1981) argue that, because research on improving teaching should use causal process and product research with which gains are measured in student achievement and attitudes, supervision should seek to implement teaching behaviors derived from research that has been linked to student achievement.

Research in supervision uses varying criteria of success and includes outcomes such as (a) increased reflection and higher order teacher thinking; (b) improved collegiality, openness, and communication; (c) increased teacher retention, anxiety, and burnout; (d) greater teacher autonomy, self-growth, and personal efficacy; (e) improved teacher attitudes; and (f) improved student achievement and attitudes.

Increased Reflection and Higher Order Thinking. Russell and Spafford (1986) used a personal account of a beginning teacher to explain how a supervisory process can influence teachers' reflection and understanding of teaching, as well as their working relationships with peers. Goldhammer (1966), one of the original developers of clinical supervision, analyzed the training of the initial Harvard-Lexington pilot program and found that trainees were more successful in analyzing teaching behavior than in changing it. Grimmett and Crehan (1988) and Gordon (1989) have studied conceptual thought interactions among supervisors and trainees to determine how supervision is influenced by the cognitive structures of participants and the value, productivity, and planning that occur in supervisory conferences. Continuing research (Phillips, 1989) uses conceptual thought and levels of higher order thinking as dependent measures to test changes in teachers involved in peer supervision. Phillips found that supervision can stimulate teachers to move into higher stages of thinking.

Improved Collegiality, Openness, and Communication. In a study of two cycles of supervision with elementary school teachers, Coe (1985) found that the lasting benefit might be the new, professional respect that teachers gain from each other. He explains that self-analysis, self-improvement, improved teaching practice, and improved student achievement are of less significance than an improved school climate of collegial respect and assistance. Similarly, Sparkes and Bruder (1987), in a study of peer coaching using videotapes to observe and provide feedback, measured the outcomes of the project in terms of "greater communication about and experimentation with teaching techniques" (p. 12). Reavis (1977) contrasted a clinical supervision model with traditional supervision models and studied the improvements in communication between supervisors and teachers. Davie (1986) analyzed the discrepancy of perceptions between teachers and principals about the importance of instructional supervisory activities in schools using a clinical process versus schools not using such a process. Using Likert-type scales, he found that teachers and principals were in much closer alignment regarding support, observation, agreement, and feedback in schools using clinical supervision. Simone (1986) found a relationship of common technical language and a public agenda between teacher and supervisor related to interpersonal trust. These findings seem to indicate that supervision has value in promoting a common language between teachers, peers, and supervisors.

Increased Teacher Retention, Anxiety, and Burnout. Parker (1986) studied two groups of 12 first-year teachers in Wisconsin. The experimental group received a formal program of supervision and the control group received no such support. The major outcomes of the study were that (a) attrition occurred in the control room, and (b) a majority of experimental-group teachers, but a minority of control teachers, planned to remain in teaching over the next 5 years. A major conclusion was that teacher retention was influenced by the provision of direct assistance. K. E. Cook (1983) examined the relationship of high school teacher perceptions of supervisory behavior and teacher burnout. Supervisory behavior was measured in the two domains of consideration and structure. Some significant findings were that supervisory consideration was inversely related to emotional exhaustion and depersonalization, and consideration was directly related to teachers' personal accomplishments. The case was made that perceptions by teachers of supervisory consideration relates to less burnout and less stress. In a similar study, Stein (1985) examined the relationship between elementary school teachers' burnout and the discrepancy between teacher and supervisor perceptions of the supervisor's behavioral style. Among the findings, teacher anxiety was related to the discrepancy between teacher and supervisor preferences for the ideal supervisory style, and burnout was related to teachers who received few supervisory visits.

Greater Teacher Autonomy, Self-Growth, and Personal Efficacy. Outcome measures of several supervision studies have been teacher autonomy, self-growth, and personal efficacy. S. C. Smith (1985) explored the effects of supervision on teachers' growth towards autonomy and awareness of productive relationships. She found that there were significant differences in self-actualization and self-acceptance, as well as in productive relationships. Teachers who saw themselves engaged in productive supervisor–teacher conferences also saw themselves growing in autonomy, competence, and self-regard.

Ellis (1986) analyzed the relationships among job design, supervisory behaviors, and motivation of 207 teachers. Her findings supported the utilization of a supervision process based on adult learning, which would meet the needs of high growth and achievement-oriented teachers and keep them in the profession. A previous study by Osterman (1984) also supported Ellis's findings. Osterman found, in a study of six middle schools with 181 teachers, that, in most of the schools where supervision was neglected, teachers saw themselves as having little influence on school practice. In those schools where supervision was practiced, teachers showed greater satisfaction, productivity, and commitment to improving the school. An individual study of a teacher over a 5-year span (Kilbourn, 1982) revealed how a direct supervision process helped the teacher develop abilities of autonomy, self-examination, and confidence.

Improved Teacher Attitudes. Do supervision programs change teachers' attitudes toward the concept of supervision?

Historically, the concept of supervision has held negative connotations for teachers (see Blumberg, 1985). Researchers have looked to see if particular supervision procedures and interventions improve teacher attitudes. Pavan (1983) reviewed 23 studies of clinical supervision and found that 8 used an attitude measure, when comparing clinical supervision with typical or traditional supervision. The findings were that more positive attitudes occurred with clinical supervision. Examples of such studies can be found in the work of Powell (1982) and Mattes (1983). Powell studied 621 teachers in 44 schools and compared the teachers in schools that had implemented clinical supervision with teachers in schools where there was no implementation. Although no significant overall differences in teacher attitudes were found in the two samples, in the single school district where the highest degree of implementation had occurred, teachers had significantly more positive attitudes toward supervision and its value.

Mattes conducted a comparative study of middle school and high school supervisors, 12 who were clinical supervisors and 12 who were traditional. One hundred eighty-three teachers were surveyed, and the conclusion was that teachers were more positive toward clinical supervision than they were toward traditional supervision. An abundance of such studies can be found in a previous review of research by Sullivan (1980).

Improved Student Achievement and Student Attitudes. What occurs in classrooms in regard to teacher behaviors and student outcomes has been measured in several supervision studies. The rationale is that, as supervisors work with teachers on acquiring certain instructional practices and providing appropriate supervisory feedback, the transfer of such skills will be lasting, and student achievement, as measured by criterion-referenced or norm-referenced tests of basic skills, will rise. The first part of this equation has been studied in several contexts by Joyce and Showers (1980). Where classroom supervision (referred to as coaching) provided teachers with training in instructional skills, the results were clear changes in teacher behaviors (Showers, 1983). Mohlman (1982) conducted a study of three different inservice models. The first contained inservice activities followed by no classroom feedback, the second contained inservice activities followed by classroom feedback by the trainer, and the third contained inservice activities followed by classroom feedback by peers. In the acquisition of teaching skills, those teachers who received peer feedback ranked first, those who received trainer feedback ranked second, and those who received no classroom feedback ranked last.

Gibson (1985) contrasted training in specific teacher behaviors through self-guided, multimedia material with supervisor-guided training with classroom feedback. The measures of teacher–student contact, divergent and convergent questions, and teacher praise showed some positive, but not statistically significant, changes.

Stallings (1985, 1987) reported on a longitudinal study comparing elementary schools using a supervision model that combined a particular instructional program with staff development with schools using no such model. The findings, over a 4-year implementation period, were that gains in teacher practices and student engagement rate did not correlate with achievement gains, and, although the achievement scores of students in the treatment school indicated a modest total gain, the achievement scores of students in the nontreatment schools were higher.

Few large-scale assessments of programs and schools have correlated ongoing supervision processes with measures of student achievement. The District of Columbia Public Schools (1981a) reported on a project to improve instruction through implementing a deliberate supervisory support service to teachers. Teachers and administrators were both trained in supervision. Statistically significant differences were found between one group of students who were with the project-trained teachers, compared with students with nontrained teachers in areas of social maturity, self-security, and test scores. Grande (1979) and Vak (1979) attempted to establish whether time spent on supervision correlated with student cognitive and affective gains. Both Grande's study of elementary schools and Vak's study of secondary schools found no significant relationship. Guditis (1979), however, argued that the aggregation of data in both of these studies masked individual differences. He proceeded to analyze the studies according to disaggregated measures and groups of students. He found a statistically significant relationship between the amount of time spent on supervision in elementary schools and student scores on measures of self-esteem, mathematics, and verbal skills. At the secondary level, Guditis found a significant relationship between schools that spent more time in supervision of teachers and above-average student scores in verbal skills. In schools involved extensively with supervision of teachers with below-average students, test scores increased in areas of self-esteem, verbal skills, and interest in school.

It can be concluded that research on supervision has been tied to varying outcome measures ranging from teacher retention, levels of thinking, and sense of efficacy to the transfer of teacher behaviors and student achievement. Although no unequivocal claims can be made, it appears that direct supervision can contribute to diverse and, indeed, competing purposes.

Survey of Existing Supervision Practices

Survey research as to perceptions of supervision practices has been a topic of considerable study (Cawelti & Reavis, 1980; Goldsberry & Hoffman, 1984; Jones, 1986; Rogers, 1986). One difficulty with survey research is the time frame for reporting. The literature on school improvement has been replete with calls for greater attention to supervision. New supervisory procedures and programs are constantly being adopted and developed at school, district, state, and regional levels. As a result, it is impossible to state with any conviction that a survey of even the past year is indicative of the present situation. To make sense of survey research, it is necessary to analyze recurring themes and contexts.

The adequacy of supervisory assistance to teachers appears

in some part to be a function of context. Supervision in Nigeria is infrequent and irregular, with over 80 percent of teachers reporting zero to one classroom observation during a 5-year period (Okwuanaso, 1983). A study in the Geelong region of Victoria, Australia (Strachan, 1981), reported that teachers do not value the traditional supervision provided to them and that classroom observation was not a widespread activity. D. M. Taylor (1986) looked at small, isolated, Alaskan schools and found that teachers desired more supervisory assistance and did not see the person in their school with formal supervisory responsibilities as a source of teaching improvement.

Blankenship and Irvine (1985) surveyed experienced teachers in Georgia and found that more than 50 percent of them had never been observed for instructional-improvement purposes (as distinct from teacher evaluation for contract renewal purposes) and 80 percent had never experienced any peer supervision. Calhoun (1984) studied elementary schools in a medium-sized, wealthy district in Georgia and found a relatively high perception among teachers of available supervisory services including observations and conferences about instruction. Generally, the more remote, smaller, and poorer in resources a school district is, the less supervision is available to teachers.

Available supervision services, however, do not necessarily equate with teacher usage. In a study of 15 school districts in 12 states, Rogers (1986) found no correlation between degree of supervisory services available to teachers and utilization of such services. This study concluded that there appeared to be a tacit agreement between teachers and supervisors. Supervisors were to be available to provide more assistance to teachers than was minimally required, but teachers were not expected to seek out their assistance, nor were supervisors expected to initiate extra assistance. This state of détente might be explained by a previous survey study in which W. K. Smith (1979) found that teachers and supervisors held differing perceptions about the meaning and purpose of direct supervision. Teachers believed that supervision should involve them in making decisions about the what and why of conferences and observations. Yet, in reality, these teachers felt that most classroom observations were seen as evaluative by themselves and by supervisors. Cawelti and Reavis (1980) found that those who supervise see their work as being more valuable than teachers do.

S. M. Taylor (1984) found in a case study that where a supervisor and three experienced secondary teachers made a commitment to work closely with each other for 10 weeks, changes occurred in teacher perceptions about supervision. Their initial perceptions of the uselessness of supervision changed to seeing supervision as important. In fact, these initially reluctant teachers recommended at the end of the treatment period that this type of close-working supervisory relationship be extended to all teachers.

Survey research seems to suggest that there is a wide disparity among services available to teachers, yet even when those services are available, teachers and supervisors do not tend to initiate their delivery. As a result, wide misperceptions continue to exist about the role and importance of supervision.

Variables, Behaviors, Attitudes, and Approaches of Those Who Supervise

The work of Blumberg and Amidon (1965) focused on the interactions between supervisor and teachers. Blumberg (1980), in summarizing this work, states that "supervisors seem to be saying that they want to spend more time doing what their clients (the teachers) consider to be relatively useless" (1980, p. 13). Blumberg refers to interpersonal relations between supervisors and teachers as a "private cold war." Since then, much has been learned about the personal attributes of supervisors that promote a positive and productive relationship with teachers.

Phares (1981) studied teachers in an urban area of Alabama (10 teachers from 52 elementary schools and 14 high schools) who participated in supervisory conferences. He compared the productivity of such conferences with demographic variables of supervisors. The findings were that age, sex, race, degree level, and professional experience of supervisors had no relationship to the value of conferences.

In place of correlations with demographic attributes, a more fruitful approach has been the interpersonal, perceptual, and conceptual attributes of those who supervise. For example, Ritz and Cashell (1980) studied 143 supervisors and found that ratings of supervisory effectiveness were strongly related to interpersonal skills. Al-Duaij-Abdulaziz (1986) examined effective supervisory styles with secondary teachers in Kuwait and found that, regardless of the particular communication style (high direct or high indirect), the critical factor for teachers was their perception of the supervisors' care and consideration for them. In a similar manner, the matching or mismatching of perceptions about the purpose of supervision explains a great deal about teachers' perceptions regarding its value. Brande (1980), in a study of New York City school districts, found that teacher participants viewed supervision as important when understood as a formative process for growth rather than as a summative process of evaluation. Burke and Kray (1985), in a study of 100 teachers, found the same need to understand supervision as a formative process. Chunn (1985), in a study of 100 teachers and supervisors in elementary and secondary schools in Mississippi, and Bauer (1986), in a study of 234 elementary school teachers and supervisors concerning effective supervision cycles, both uncovered the same confusions and differences in perception among teachers and supervisors. Without a clear agreement as to the purpose of supervision and an understanding of its practices, it is quite difficult to develop the supportive relationship between supervisor and teacher that is critical to success. Kottkamp (1982), in investigating supervisory authenticity, communication, productivity, and loyalty of 173 classroom teachers concluded with a statement that comes close to the conflict and misunderstanding about supervision:

The study supports the assumption that means such as frontal assault, imposition of heavy doses of formal authority and close, task oriented and directive supervision are not likely to lead to improvement of instruction if teachers have anything to say about it. And they have a good deal to say about it—especially, No! (p. 26)

Does the general communicative style or approach of the supervisor in a supervisory conference make a difference in teachers' perceptions of value, growth, and change? Already mentioned was the Al-Duaij-Abdulaziz study (1986) that supported previous studies reported by Blumberg and associates (Blumberg, 1980) that found that a style of high direct and high support or high indirect and high support, were better received by teachers than high direct and low support or high indirect and low support.

In a different conceptualization of supervisory approaches labeled *nondirective*, *collaborative*, and *directive* (Glickman, 1981, 1985), several studies were conducted to determine the influence of each approach. Ginkel (1983), Konke (1984), and Rossicone (1985) found in their studies that approximately two-thirds of experienced teachers preferred a collaborative approach, one-third preferred a nondirective approach, and the remaining small percentage preferred a directive approach. Ngugi (1984) studied secondary teachers and supervisors, with similar results, finding that older teachers preferred that principals be more non-directive in providing materials and facilities than younger teachers did. Rossicone (1985) reports that "as professional training increased, teachers preferred a non-direct style but perceived their supervisor to be more inclined to a collaborative approach" (abstract). He concluded that, overall, the approach that teachers preferred was not the approach that they received.

Blackbourn (1983), in a study of 338 elementary and secondary teachers, found that teachers with the most positive perceptions of supervisory conferences received more collaboration from their supervisors and less nondirectiveness. On the other hand, Williams (1986), in a replication of Blackbourn's study with 120 secondary teachers, found that positive attitudes toward conferences were independent of any particular approach.

It could well be that the particular supervisory style or behavior used with teachers cannot be studied independently of the interpersonal milieu of shared understandings, clear purpose, and sensitivity to individual needs of teachers. After studying 150 teachers in Kansas, Lyman (1987) explained that factors of confidentiality, involvement, consideration, appreciation, and respect establish a milieu in which authentic supervision can occur irrespective of the particular supervisory behaviors, styles, or approaches used.

Studies of supervisors' thoughts, judgments, and decisions have been the focus of study by Glickman (1985), Gordon (1989), Grimmett and Housego (1983), Hunt (1987), and Simmons, Moon, and Niedermeyer (1987). The research attempted to understand either the in-act supervisor decisions involved in communicating with teachers that enhance or impede discussion or the supervisor's level of conceptual thought (i.e., fluency and flexibility) in processing and using information about approaches in a supervisory conference (Gordon, 1989; Grimmett & Housego, 1983). From their limited studies, these researchers imply that supervisors' thought could be a more critical factor in determining success than the use of a particular set of supervisory behaviors or approaches. The ability to read a teacher's needs, to be aware of the prior history of the relationship, and to determine the course of discussions showed promise of explaining successful supervision.

Nature of Feedback

How feedback is organized and given in supervisory conferences that precede or follow classroom observations has attracted the attention of several researchers. A study in Pennsylvania found that teachers perceived supervisory feedback as helpful when it stimulated their thinking about teaching. "When teachers recognize and discuss potential improvements in practice as part of the supervisory process, they are much more likely to report that supervision is helpful in improving teaching" (Goldsberry & Hoffman, 1984, p. 14).

Such a finding is consistent with the work of Jonas and Blumberg (1986) and Pajak and Glickman (1984). Jonas and Blumberg interviewed teachers in New York and found that positive teacher–supervisor relationships depended upon supervisors' gaining psychological access to teachers by (a) being available, (b) recognizing teacher expertise, (c) giving immediate and nonpunitive feedback, (d) using active listening, and (e) using a problem-solving, collaborative approach. Pajak and Glickman conducted a study in which 30 teachers were assigned to three treatment groups, and each was asked to view videotapes of simulated supervisor feedback. Teachers rated highest the supervisory conference in which the supervisor communicated information about the classroom observation and followed with specific suggestions that might help them. The second highest rated conference was one in which the supervisor gave only information about the classroom observation, without making suggestions. The lowest rated conference was one in which the supervisor gave feedback on the classroom observation, followed by directives as to what the teacher should do to improve. It can be surmised from these studies that teachers generally preferred descriptive feedback about their teaching, followed by discussion of interpretations and future goals, culminating in collaborative suggestions and decisions about future instructional actions.

The research of Squires (1978) and Little and Galagaran (1984) provides insights into the sequence of productive feedback. Squires used a phenomenological method to investigate the work of supervisors and concluded that there were five phases to a positive supervisory relationship. *Entrance* related to reducing the initial anxiety of supervisor and teacher by discussing and understanding each other's expectations. *Diagnosis* involved engaging the teacher in reflection upon his or her professional behavior, self-assessed needs, and history with previous supervision. *Technical success* involved planning and implementation with the teacher of specific actions to change behavior patterns and increase skills. *Examination of meaning for self* involved helping the teacher clarify underlying beliefs and long-term educational goals held for students. The last phase, *reintegration*, involved reviewing knowledge gained and performance and required self-examination by both the supervisor and the teacher, thereby setting the conditions for greater mutual trust and openness toward the next sequence of supervisory interactions.

Little and Galagaran studied 10 teacher advisors and their supervision of 14 teachers. The researchers collected videotapes of conferences and transcribed them for analysis. They found the first 2 minutes of a supervisory conference to be crucial. Within those 2 minutes, the successful supervisor, free of distractions, attended to the setting and prepared notes and other materials to convey a message of clear purpose to the teacher. The supervisory behaviors that followed in those first few minutes included inviting to participate, checking out boundaries, keeping it equal, reviewing agreements on topics, making explicit suggestions about procedure, inviting the teacher to go first, reciprocating (we're in this together), or showing a commitment to new learning, sharing the obligations and the risks, and giving due credit. As Little and Galagaran write:

The conferences, finally, are very human events. Advisors and teachers act toward one another with tact, good will and good humor. They laugh with each other, become excited together and confused together. There are occasional moments of strain and many more of genuine enjoyment. (1984, p. 57)

What is apparent about the nature of feedback in supervision is that two dimensions are attended to simultaneously: (a) focus on the task at hand for conveying and discussing classroom observations leading to future goals, actions, and reflections; and (b) focus on the interpersonal dimension for promoting open discussion, care, and consideration for each other.

Training

There seem to be personal attributes and conditions of feedback that relate to supervisory success. Are these attributes and conditions parts of a given personality or can they be learned? The answer from research is that they can be learned. The following are samples of studies in which particular training has been found to transfer into new knowledge and supervisory behaviors.

G. E. Cook and Skipper (1986) assessed a clinical-supervision training program of department coordinators conducted over a 4-year period in six high schools and nine middle schools in Texas. They found that training improved classroom observations, self-analysis of instruction, and skills in listening, reflecting, and problem solving. In a districtwide study of training and implementing new supervision skills in secondary schools in Alberta, Townsend (1984) surveyed 117 teachers and 16 administrators. Both teachers and supervisors considered the changes to be improvements.

In an evaluation of a 1977–1979 training project intended to improve instruction instruction through supervision in the District of Columbia schools, it was concluded that the training led to improved practice (District of Columbia Public Schools, 1980, 1981a, 1981b). The study involved 39 schools. Training in supervision was provided to both teachers and administrators. The trained personnel implemented the supervisory model in their work with teachers, used supervisory techniques in a more positive manner than an untrained group, and demonstrated better understanding of concepts and strategies. Snyder (1982) surveyed 412 school district administrators and compared the participants who had received more training in supervision with others who had received less training. The group with more training used preconferences more appropriately, practiced more conference follow-through, and used instructional models more effectively.

In related studies (Johnston, 1987; Johnston, Galluzzo, & Kottkamp, 1986), it was found that training in Transactional Analysis (TA) techniques had a significant effect on supervisors' behaviors in conferences with teachers. In the first study (Johnston et al., 1986), 52 teachers were placed in experimental and control groups. Both groups participated in a graduate course in supervision, but the experimental group received specific training in Transactional Analysis. There was a significant difference in the trained groups' use of productive responses in simulated conferences, compared with the untrained groups. In the second study, Johnston (1987) found that, when the training moved to actual supervisory conferences, the differences were significant in that the trained group made more productive responses. Although training had a real transfer effect, other factors contributed to a supervisor's ability to communicate constructively. Previously, Lombardo (1980) had conducted a small-scale study using TA training and studied long-term supervision. He concluded that such training stimulated change, growth, and improvement of practice.

Although the training of skills has been shown to be important to positive supervision transfer, Grimmett and Housego's (1983) study linking the conceptual, or thinking, level of supervisors to productive supervision is a compelling one. In their examination of videotapes of four supervisors in conducting 14 actual conferences with teachers, they found that:

The two more abstract functioning supervisors seemed able to "read" their supervisees' needs and the situational constraints in a way that enabled them to "flex" upwards or downwards in their verbal communication, to the "pull" of supervisee initiative. The two more concrete functioning supervisors . . . seemed unable to do this." (p. 4)

These data support the contention that conceptual level, as well as training in specific skills, is related to success.

Particular Models

What is the research evidence in support of any particular model of direct supervision? Names are used in the literature to refer to particular models as *clinical, developmental, human resources, diagnostic, differentiated,* and *walk-through* supervision. The overwhelming number of research studies of direct supervision refer to the clinical-supervision model. Many of the studies reviewed in previous sections of this chapter are studies of some version or variation of clinical supervision. However, to complicate matters, there is no standard definition as to what constitutes clinical supervision, and most models of direct supervision can be construed as variations or extensions of clinical supervision.

Books about clinical supervision generally outline a sequence of preconference, observation, postobservation analysis, postconference, and critque (see Acheson & Gall, 1987; Cogan, 1973; Glickman, 1985; Goldhammer, 1966; Goldhammer, Anderson, & Krajewski, 1980). However, even this sequence is challenged by writers who define clinical supervision as a concept, rather than a format (Garman, 1986; Smyth, 1988). The debate about conflicting conceptions of clinical supervision is quite apparent (see Garman et al., 1987). Garman sees clinical supervision as a concept of collegiality and inquiry; Glickman sees it as a tool for promoting teacher thinking, commitment, and autonomy in instruction; and Hunter sees it as steps for providing teachers with feedback on the use of elements of effective teaching to improve student achievement. Because there have been several reviews of studies of clinical supervision, it is unnecessary to review each study in detail. Instead, a summary of the reviews on general clinical supervision and selective studies on the specific Glickman and Hunter versions will be reported; the Hunter model because of its widespread use in American schools and the Glickman model because many recent studies have been conducted on it. Other models, although prominent in the literature, such as differentiated supervision, human resources supervision, diagnostic supervision, and walk-through supervision, do not appear frequently as research topics.

Research studies in clinical supervision are generally surveys, case studies, and quasi-experimental studies that compare clinical with traditional supervision. *Clinical* is usually defined as a formative evaluation process involving a preconference, observation, and postconference cycle, whereas *traditional* is defined more loosely as whatever usually occurs between teachers and supervisors. The traditional approach is assumed to utilize a summative evaluation process that is typically infrequent, random, and lacking in follow-through.

Sullivan (1980), in the first widely recognized attempt to review studies on clinical supervision, looked at 21 studies from 1971 to 1978. She states that:

Taken together, these studies yield some findings in support of the clinical supervision model. . . . Changes in the teacher's classroom behavior occurred in directions designated as "desirable." . . . There was evidence of teacher growth. . . . While findings and indications can be summarized, no general conclusions can be drawn. (pp. 22–23)

Adams and Glickman (1984), in a later review, analyzed 18 studies from 1978 to 1981 and conclude: "According to this review, the clinical model has a positive effect on teacher attitudes towards supervision, effects changes in teacher behavior, and promotes better working relationships between teachers and supervisors" (p. 27).

Pavan (1983), in a review of 25 studies from 1973 to 1983, was more cautious in her conclusions. She notes a variety of methodological errors, poor instrumentation, lack of clear definitions, short time durations, and inadequate or incomplete samplings of populations. She concludes:

At this time it is clear that there is no definitive answer to the title question, "Clinical Supervision: Does It Make a Difference?" In none of the four areas: attitudes towards supervision, training effects, characteristics of professional staff, or student achievement; has research been complete which answers that question. (p. 11)

A more detailed analysis of the research into the two clinical-supervision models might explain Pavan's reservations about conclusive evidence.

Glickman established a theory of developmental supervision (Glickman, 1981, 1985; Glickman & Gordon, 1987) that, in part, discusses how those involved in supervision can diagnose the stages of conceptual thought and commitment of an individual teacher in regard to instructional improvement. The supervisor can then match one of three approaches, nondirective, collaborative, or directive, to the teacher's current stage of development and then, over time, use other approaches that increase the teacher's choice and responsibility for making her or his own decisions.

Many empirical questions have been generated by this theory, and studies have been conducted to test various dimensions of it. For example, both Konke (1984) and Ginkel (1983) found that nearly two-thirds of experienced teachers preferred a collaborative approach, one-third a nondirective approach, and relatively few a directive approach. Whether age or experience is a factor in one's preference for particular approaches is unclear. Humphrey (1983) found that entry-year teachers overwhelmingly preferred a collaborative approach (92 percent); however, they also perceived themselves to be at the highest stages of development. When studying a population of secondary school teachers at various levels of experience, Ngugi (1984) found that older teachers preferred their supervisors to be more nondirective in providing materials. Similarly, Rossicone (1985) found, in a study of 259 secondary teachers in 16 high schools, that "As professional training increased, teachers preferred a non-directive style but perceived their supervisors to be more inclined to a collaborative approach" (p. 1). Akinniyi (1987), in a study of 70 secondary principals and 288 secondary teachers in Wisconsin, found that, as teachers gained experience and expertise they preferred more input, choice, and control in supervision situations. She concludes, "Considering Glickman's (1985) view on when to utilize the collaborative approach, this study tends to support the same idea" (p. 117). Survey research on teachers and preferred supervisory approaches tends to support the need for a variety of supervisory approaches, with some studies indicating that, with experience, teachers tended to want less supervisory control. However, the main approach preferred by most teachers was the collaborative one.

Another class of studies deals with field treatment; that is, the training offered supervisors to help them to learn to diagnose developmental levels of individual teachers and be able to match and flex with different approaches. Waters (1985) conducted a study of 23 beginning vocational teachers and university supervisors and found no differences between teacher reactions to trained or untrained supervisors. However, Wright (1987) reported on a yearlong case study of elementary school teachers trained to use and implement developmental supervision when observing and holding conferences with each other. Teachers listed numerous benefits including new insights about teaching, new approaches to problem solving, and willingness to experiment with new ideas. Benefits identified by students were improved attitudes toward work, more time on task, improved behavior, extra help from the teacher, and more dynamic student-to-student interactions. Glickman (1987) trained secondary and junior high school assistant principals in developmental supervision in an urban school district and collected pre and post data on more than 400 teachers who were supervised over the year by these assistant principals. The results were increases in teachers' perceptions of the value of supervision on 8 of 10 measures and a significant gain in teachers' perceptions of "supportive and helpful assistance."

Gordon (1989) conducted a training program with 16 supervisors and analyzed their subsequent work with 48 teachers. He found that 44 percent of supervisors could successfully diagnose levels of teacher thinking, 87 percent of the time supervisors could flex and use various approaches consistent with their diagnosis, and teachers perceived such supervision as vastly superior to previous supervision. Finally, Phillips (1989) reports significant gains in teachers' conceptual thought by those involved in peer coaching using developmental supervision. Does developmental supervision work? The answer, as of now, is that the exactness of the model is suspect; yet field treatments appear to improve working relationships between supervisors and teachers. In analyzing any model of supervision, the intricacies of connecting what is measured, how it is measured, with whom, and over what time period make definitive conclusions about any supervisory model tentative.

The Hunter Model of Clinical Supervision is interrelated with the Hunter instructional model of seven essential elements of instruction (anticipatory set, objective, input, modeling, checking for understanding, guided practice, and independent practice). The focus of clinical supervision is to help teachers understand these elements, received feedback on their use, and critique, suggest, and plan ways to become more adept in their usage. The model is used in training administrators, supervisors, and teachers in numerous districts and states and has various labels. It has come under intense attack by critics who claim it is overly prescriptive in its applications and lacks research to support its claims (Gibboney, 1987). It is noteworthy that Hunter's model has no less a research base than most other supervisory models that are not criticized on this basis. One reason for the intensity of criticism is clearly that her model is having much wider application and influence than others.

Relatively few studies have been published on what happens to teachers and students when the Hunter clinical model is used. Pavan (1985a, 1985b) could find seven studies reported in the research literature, all inconclusive. Two studies (Congdon, 1979/1980; Spaulding, 1983/1984) found either no significant performance gains or inverse gains in student achievement. One study by Mayfield (1983) found a significant gain in reading comprehension of students. Hunter (1987) responded to the question of research by citing two studies, one unpublished and conducted in Los Angeles and the other recently completed in Napa Valley. The unpublished study, using the model in a Los Angeles inner-city school, was reported by Hunter: "students doubled and in some cases quadrupled, their previous learning gains. Discipline and vandalism were dramatically reduced and students' self concepts as learners . . . became more positive" (Hunter, 1987 p. 51).

The second study in Napa Valley is one of the most thorough longitudinal studies of any supervision model (Stallings, 1987). The study was conducted from 1981–1985 on two target schools with a high concentration of Chapter I students. Teachers and supervisors were trained according to the Hunter model. Standardized achievement tests in reading and mathematics, time on task, and teacher behaviors were measured. Two comparable schools not involved in the training were used as a control group. The findings were that achievement did improve in the target schools over 4 years but, unexpectedly, took a dramatic drop in year 4. To complicate matters further, Stallings reported, "The sobering fact is that during the four years of the study the project school did not achieve higher scores than did children in the control schools in either reading or mathematics" (1987, p. 62). The control group with no training exceeded the treatment schools, in which $400,000 had been spent on the program.

Because the main outcome of the Hunter model is aimed at improving student achievement, how should this study be interpreted? One explanation is that the model did not work very well. It is necessary, however, to note the comprehensive and longitudinal nature of the Hunter model study. Readers should not conclude that this model did not work on the basis of comparison with other supervision models tested and deemed successful on very limited study. For example, many supervision studies do not utilize any comparison or control group. If the Napa Valley study had not had a comparison group, the treatment would have shown definite student gains and been judged a success. In addition, many studies of supervisory effects are of a treatment period of no more than one school year. If the Napa Valley study had stopped at 3 years, the Hunter model would have been judged a success, because the dramatic drop that occurred in the fourth year would have remained unknown. In effect, the Hunter model was subjected to much longer and rigorous scrutiny than any other supervision study cited in this chapter. If all supervision models were studied in the same depth as the Hunter model, there would be a more valid basis for making comparative assessments.

Organizational Considerations

Direct supervision of teachers is a function and process conducted within a particular school, district, and state organization. There are norms and values shared by teachers and administrators that can support or interfere with classroom observations, conferences, and ongoing discussions about instructional improvement. Similarly, there are policies and regulations about the nature and purpose of observations and conferences in a school that can create either defensiveness or receptivity among participants. Studies by Hallinger and Murphy (1987) and Little and Bird (1987) have pointed out differences in supervision in various secondary schools. In some schools, time, rewards, recognition, and resources are provided by administrators to support the supervisory process. Such added costs symbolize to teachers that analyzing, talking about, and planning instructional improvement are an important part of their daily work. On the other hand, there are schools that use the language of supervision in manuals and guidelines, but resources are not allocated and supervision is not seen as a valued part of a teacher's work.

In a rather vitriolic series of reports and retorts, McFaul and Cooper (1984) write about the failure of a peer supervision process in an elementary school, as traced to the larger organization. McFaul and Cooper write:

> In general, the goals, assumptions and procedures of this highly acclaimed model were found to be incongruent with this particular urban school setting. . . . It became impossible to foster trust equality, an openness and reflective behavior in an environment where survival necessitated the opposite. (1983, p. 13)

Clarke and Richardson (1986) came to a similar conclusion in their study of 11 elementary teachers. Supervision programs fared best in schools where collegial relationships were already established and status leaders actively supported the process. Hart (1985) found that the success of supervision conducted by teacher mentors was dependent on organizational clarity in separating formative from summative evaluation of teachers. Grimmett (1987) analyzed the extent to which district-level initiatives enable administrators, supervisors, and teachers to work together in supervision settings. He concluded that the reason supervision programs do not work in particular schools was the fact that "By far the most telling omission on the part of the district personnel was the lack of careful, detailed planning for the project's operation. Therefore, implementation at the district level appeared to proceed in a happenstance fashion" (Grimmett, 1987, p. 9).

An analysis of research on organizational support for supervision inevitably leads researchers and practitioners to the need for greater clarity in specifying the philosophy, purpose, and outcomes of such supervision. Is supervision aimed at changing particular teacher behaviors? Is it to improve short-term student achievement? Is it intended to implement an instructional model? Is it to increase teacher reflection and critical analysis? Is it to improve general satisfaction with teaching? Is it to evaluate teachers for competence, against some district-wide standards? Or is its purpose assisting teachers in enhancing their own perceptions of professional growth? It is only through greater clarity of a supervisory model's purpose that consumers of research will be able to choose the procedures, training, roles, resources, and schedule to implement a particular model.

PRESERVICE TEACHER EDUCATION

The research literature on preservice supervision is substantially smaller than that on inservice supervision. Instead of categorizing research by themes, the analysis that follows will focus on roles that appear constant throughout preservice studies. The activities and processes of preservice supervision are linked to a triad (student teacher, cooperating teacher, and university supervisor), which enables student teachers to apply the information learned in teacher preparation courses (Yee, 1969).

The one supervisory process that has continued to serve as a framework for supervision in preservice teacher education is the cycle of *clinical supervision* developed by Goldhammer (1966) and Cogan (1973). Various versions are found in the literature and research on teacher education that addresses the student teacher, the cooperating teacher, and the university supervisor relationship.

This review will deal specifically with research on the cooperating (classroom) teacher, the student teacher, and the university supervisor. Throughout the research, names applied to members of the student-teaching triad differ, but for purposes of clarity the following terms will be used consistently: *cooperating teacher*, *student teacher*, and *university supervisor*.

Cooperating Teacher

The cooperating classroom teacher's role has been cited as influential, important, and essential to the teaching experience of student teachers (Copeland, 1980; Koehler, 1984; Seperson & Joyce, 1973; Yee, 1969). Cooperating teachers' perceptions of their roles as supervisors have shown concern for guiding student teachers toward competence in classroom management, lesson planning, and lesson delivery (O'Neal, 1983a). Drummond (1980) reports that cooperating teachers tended to be highly concerned with being proper role models, anxious about their performance, introspective, and analytical about their behavior. Primarily, they were concerned about their effectiveness in helping student teachers become teachers. Kuehl (1976) found the one competency considered important by both teachers and administrators was that cooperating teachers be exemplary models of good teachers.

Grimmett and Ratzlaff (1986) compared findings from both a study in the United States and a study in Canada on the expectations held by student teachers, cooperating teachers, and university supervisors about the role of cooperating teachers. In both studies, teachers were expected to hold conferences regularly with the student teacher and to take a direct role in teaching skills of presentation and classroom management. Such expectations placed the classroom teacher in the active role of practicing supervisor. As role models, cooperating teachers were expected to observe and to provide feedback as to the effectiveness of performance. The supervisory training of the cooperating teacher has been shown to affect the quality of early field experiences (Killian & McIntyre, 1985, 1986). Trained teachers had more interactions with their field-experience students and were more likely to offer feedback concerning their performance than nontrained teachers. This finding demonstrated the need to train cooperating teachers in supervision. Training for cooperative teachers had a positive impact on the classroom teacher's work with field-experience students.

The need to establish a helping relationship between the cooperating teacher and the student teacher and to improve the supervisory skills of the teacher in data collection, observation, and conference conducting was a strong recommendation from many studies. Koehler (1986) proposes that such training needs to emphasize observation, analysis of behavior, and feedback. When cooperating teachers were trained in supervisory techniques consistent with clinical supervision, the techniques remained in use in real school settings (Hill, 1977). In Drummond's (1980) study, cooperating teachers reported that training in supervision helped their work with student teachers. Twa (1984) found, at the University of Lethbridge in Canada, that cooperating teachers valued their clinical-supervision training. As a result of the training, they were more eager to accept student teachers, their supervisory skills improved, and they felt more comfortable as supervisors.

When cooperating teachers were trained in Cogan's model of clinical supervision, their conference behavior changed (Thorlacius, 1980). Supervisory behavior moved more toward the collegial approach and away from the directive approach, and supportive behavior increased in both cooperating teachers and student teachers.

Chandler (1971) found that, without training, cooperating teachers dominated over 60 percent of the talk in conferences. Higher level categories such as divergent or evaluative dialogue accounted for little of the total time. Changler found that the teacher's level of thinking, as exhibited during the conference, was reciprocated by the student teacher. In other words, the cooperating teacher's level of cognition tended to influence the level of thought of the student teacher.

O'Neal (1983b) studied supervisory conferences and found that 79 percent of the talk between cooperating teachers and student teachers focused on classroom events or activities. During conferences, cooperating teachers clearly dominated the verbal interaction, whereas the student teacher's talk simply acknowledged what the cooperating teacher had said.

Actual analysis of the student teacher's instruction was seldom the major thrust of a conference discussion. Koehler (1986) found that conference dialogue focused on noninstructional tasks and classroom occurrences, rather than on analysis of instruction. The feedback provided to the student teacher by the cooperating teacher tended to be particularistic and not tied to research and general aims about teaching.

Bradley (1966), in an investigation of cooperative relationships between teachers and student teachers, found that, regardless of the type of information and feedback discussed during a conference, for a cooperative relationship to exist between the teacher and the student teacher there had to be give-and-take exchange. In addition, cooperating teachers had to provide time during the teaching day for discussion with student teachers. Survey findings have shown that additional demands are placed on the teachers' time when they are assigned a student teacher (Campbell & Williamson, 1983). Therefore, cooperating teachers must find and spend extra time planning lessons and communicating with student teachers about the instructional process, in order to develop a positive relationship. Western, Zahorik, Kritek, and Smith (1987) found that, with more experience, teachers tended to be more proactive. It was evident that the more experience individuals had had supervising student teachers, the more they allowed verbal interaction with student teachers. The quality of interaction was influenced by the way cooperating teachers and student teachers viewed themselves, their workplace, and the world in general (O'Neal, 1983a).

Generally, if cooperating teachers wanted to increase motivation of student teachers, the conference provided an opportunity for doing so. A study of supervisory conferences revealed that cooperating teachers affected student teachers' motivational growth to a greater extent than did university supervisors (Cuff, 1978). Cooperating teachers have significant impact on the behavior of their student teachers (Copeland, 1982). Research has shown that the attitude and behavior of student teachers has been influenced by the cooperating classroom teacher and the type and extent of supervision used.

Student Teacher

Historically, student teachers have been expected by the university supervisor and the cooperating teacher to comply with university regulations for practice teaching. Therefore, they have found their role to be predetermined. Consequently, cooperating teachers' and university supervisors' performance ratings for student teachers tended to reflect differences based on expectations (Sentz, 1981).

When differences or conflicts concerning a student teacher's performance occurred, it was suggested that the cooperating teacher might be operating in the pragmatic mode and the university supervisor in a theoretical mode, and the student teacher, drawn by the demands of each, was somewhere in between (Tanner, 1986). The cooperating teacher was identified by student teachers as the major source of conflict in Webb's (1979) study. Student teachers reported that conflict occurred most frequently with the cooperating teacher in the area of classroom management and with the university supervisor in the area of teaching skills.

The effectiveness and productivity of student teaching is related to the help provided by the cooperating teacher and the university supervisor. Dean (1971) ascertained that help provided by cooperating teachers was more adequate than that provided by university supervisors. More time was spent with the cooperating teacher than the university supervisor throughout the teaching experience. However, students were not likely to be dissatisfied with the help received from university supervisors. In a survey of 421 student teachers from 10 states in the western United States to determine the helpfulness of supervisory practices of university supervisors, Johns and Cline (1985) found that student teachers were satisfied, and the supervisory practices they favored most were ability to clarify their concerns, sufficient length of observation at each visit, ability to diagnose learning problems, and frequency of feedback.

As for supervisory methods, student teachers favored cooperating teachers who used clinical supervision. Whitehead (1984) found that student teachers rated cooperating teachers who had clinical supervision training more positively than those who had not. Specifically, trained teachers were rated higher than untrained teachers in the following practices: use of freeing, rather than binding, interpersonal behaviors; use of an indirect, rather than a direct, supervisory style; emphasis on information, rather than opinion, in feedback; and provision of solicited, rather than unsolicited, feedback.

In evaluating the effectiveness of the clinical-supervision model, Berg, Harders, Malian, and Nagel (1986) found, in general, that clinically supervised student teachers had more positive and effective internships than student teachers who were not clinically supervised. Dawson (1982) found no significant difference in the self-actualization of student teachers who had been supervised by cooperating teachers trained in clinical supervision and those supervised by teachers not trained in clinical supervision.

The use of different types of supervision and the effects on the student teacher's attitude were examined by Thompson (1978). Three groups of student teachers were supervised in three different ways: (a) peer groups trained in clinical supervision, (b) peer groups not trained in clinical supervision, and (c) no peer groups and no training, only the traditional university supervision. The peer group trained in clinical supervision had significantly higher posttest scores than the other two groups.

Another supervisory model that has been studied is the *instructional supervision process* (ISP). The ISP is intended to help student teachers assess their own teaching. It was developed at the University of California at Santa Barbara to train cooperative teachers to work with student teachers (Boyan & Copeland, 1974). With the ISP, emphasis was placed on the relationship between supervising teacher and student teacher moving, from a supervisor-dominated arrangement to a collegial arrangement that supported a cooperative and nonthreatening relationship.

Studies have shown that student teachers initially were inclined to favor the directive approach over the nondirective approach of supervision (Copeland, 1980; Copeland & Atkinson, 1978). Findings inferred that student teachers felt they lacked the experience to resolve their instructional problems under nondirective supervision. A direct supervisory approach in which the cooperating teacher or university supervisor targeted the problem and offered concrete solutions for day-to-day difficulties was more appealing.

In a follow-up study, Copeland (1982) reports that student teachers' initial preference for directive supervision gave way to a more nondirective approach as their experience increased. Vukovich's (1976) research concluded that the student teacher's self-concept influenced his or her preference for direct or indirect supervision. Results showed that the directive method was more effective for low-self-concept student teachers and the indirective method was more effective for high-self-concept student teachers. Overall, research indicates that no one supervisory approach is effective for all students. Student teachers, in general, have rated supervisors as more credible when they used a directive, over a nondirective, supervisory style (Desrochers, 1982).

University Supervisor

The role of the university supervisor has been characterized as overlapping the role of the cooperating teacher. The duplication of supervisory tasks in assisting the student teacher was evident throughout the research. Nevertheless, the student teachers' perception of the tasks they expected the university supervisor to perform related to the regularity and nature of supervisory visits and the specific assistance supervisors were able to provide (J. E. Morris & Chissom, 1975). Research on the perceptions of the university supervisor's role revealed discrepancies among student teachers, cooperating teachers, and university supervisors (Ortiz-Vega, 1982; Page, 1979; Stewig, 1970).

Even though there was a lack of consensus concerning the supervisor's role, supervisors were likely to be satisfied with their jobs. However, the level of satisfaction they experienced in their role differed significantly according to affiliated institution. Koehler's (1984) research showed that university supervisors at private higher education institutions viewed themselves as professional educators. They were extremely satisfied with their jobs, they felt successful and efficacious. In contrast, university supervisors at a large state university considered themselves to be university faculty members, but in lower status positions than other faculty. They were frustrated in their clinical role, due to the need for more time to do an effective job of supervision.

A difference exists among supervisors concerning the time spent visiting student teachers. Supervisors who were generalists had been assigned more student teachers than those who were specialists, and they spent more time working with student teachers than did specialists (Herbster, 1976; Spivey, 1974). Koehler (1984) contends that the clinical functions of supervisors, such as observation, data collection, and feedback, were devalued, because there was so little time to observe and communicate with students. In terms of clinical support, supervisors felt they contributed very little to the student teacher's classroom experience. Short observations and feedback sessions with student teachers once every 2 weeks failed to provide enough time for adequate supervision, particularly clinical supervision. The number of visits required for a university supervisor to observe student teachers was established by a majority of institutions. Bowman (1978) found that supervisory visits typically involved 30 to 90 minutes per student per week, over an 8-week period.

From a total of 570 cooperating teachers, 55 percent rated university supervisors good to excellent in the amount of time spent observing student teachers. However, the overall rating of university supervisors was not impressive (Funk, Hoffman, Keithley, & Long, 1978). In rating the effectiveness of university supervisors, both student teachers and cooperating teachers perceived little difference between those with classroom experience and those without classroom experience (Lamb & Montague, 1982). In addition, differences in the effectiveness and supervisory performance of tenured faculty, university supervisors, and temporary graduate assistants were minimal. Lamb and Montague support the view that graduate assistants, when carefully selected, provide valuable supervision to student teachers through classroom observations, feedback conferences, and evaluation conferences. Furthermore, when their academic and supervisory loads are reasonable, graduate assistants function effectively as supervisors.

Elsmere and Daunt (1975), in a comparison of the effectiveness of supervisors working with large and small groups of students, found that, in large groups of 30 or more student teachers, the supervisor was viewed as simply a troubleshooter. A large number of student teachers affected the supervisor's performance. The sporadic visits were not of high benefit to student teachers. In fact, J. R. Morris (1974) found no significant difference between the performance and adjustment of student teachers who had a university supervisor and those who did not; the supervisor who supervised on an occasional basis had little effect on the student teacher's experience.

In studying the effective and ineffective behaviors of university supervisors as perceived by secondary school cooperating teachers, Rothman (1981) found two major areas of conflict. The university supervisor and cooperating teacher disagreed, first, over the goal of student teaching and, second, over the task expectations of the supervisor. To solve this conflict, it was recommended that expectations and professional goals be agreed upon in conference with members of the student teaching triad prior to the beginning of the student teacher's assignment. Failure to resolve conflicts reflected negatively on the university supervisors themselves and on the university (Koehler, 1984). Conferences tended to be held at the convenience of the supervisor and not according to the needs of the cooperating teacher or the student teacher. Consequently, the cooperating teacher spent little time communicating with the university supervisor (Funk et al., 1978).

An examination of audiotaped conferences showed no clear link between the supervisors' verbal styles and the quality of their interpersonal relationships with student teachers (Cryan, 1972). However, a study on verbal behaviors in the relationship between university supervisors and student teachers by White (1977) found that supervisory training in supportive verbal communication skills was needed. Clark, Smith, Thurman, and Baird (1984) examined the written feedback on 275 observation reports filled out on 63 student teachers, selected at random from 22 supervisors. Eighty-five percent of the comments were about strengths of the student teacher, 11 percent were suggestions, and 4 percent mentioned weaknesses. Because there were relatively few comments offering suggestions or mentioning weaknesses, the researchers concluded that university supervisors perceived their function as nurturing and supportive and demonstrated a commitment to the use of positive reinforcement as an aid in teacher development.

The creative ability of the university supervisor affects the kind of diagnostic feedback given the student teacher. Cicirelli's study (1969) revealed that the more creative supervisors tended to observe and diagnose classroom performance of student teachers differently from less creative supervisors. More creative supervisors encouraged student teachers to explore a full range of teaching behaviors and tended to use broad, general factors in assessing student performance, rather than specific, detailed ones.

Other research showed that university supervisors were eclectic in their supervisory role. In one study (Shahzade, 1983), 37 university supervisors, indicated that they altered their supervisory styles as needed to be effective with particular student teachers. Half of the group indicated that they used the collaborative style half the time. Two-thirds of the supervisors reported they were directive one-fourth to one-third of the time. More than 50 percent indicated they were nondirective in their style of supervision about half the time. All the supervisors had been assessed as functioning at high conceptual levels of thought. High conceptual thought was marked by flexibility and adaptability in using various styles.

SUMMARY

Inservice studies of direct supervision have demonstrated positive change in teacher reflection and higher order thought; collegiality, openness, and communication; teacher retention, anxiety, and burnout; teacher autonomy, self-growth, and personal efficacy; teacher attitudes; teacher behaviors; student achievement; and student attitudes. Surveys of existing supervisory practice indicate, in general, that teachers receive little supervisory support (rather, what they receive is mostly evaluative in nature), and, even in districts where it is readily available, teachers do not initiate supervision. Those who do supervise successfully tend to function on a high conceptual level, use mostly collaborative and nondirective approaches, and they provide feedback that stimulates teachers' thinking rather than controls teachers' actions. Studies of training programs in supervision show that supervisors learn and improve their skills in observing, listening, reflecting, and problem solving. No one model of supervision is supported for generic application by the research. In all cases, the actual results of using a particular model are mixed. Finally, organizational consideration of providing time, rewards, recognition, and resources for implementing a direct supervision program appears essential to its success.

Research in preservice supervision has been sporadic, with many areas still uncovered. There has been little attention to comparing the organization and governance of supervision of student teaching. The question of whether responsibilities reside mainly with cooperating teachers at the local school site or with university supervisors at the institutional level remains unresolved. Nor has there been great attention to studying outcomes of different supervision delivery systems, such as comparing formal supervision on a frequent basis with drop-in visits on an occasional basis or comparing the outcomes of various supervision programs with different underlying philosophical assumptions about teaching and teachers.

Research has shown the need to provide supervision training to both university supervisors and cooperating teachers; to carefully select cooperating teachers according to their potential influence as role models and their previous supervisory experience; to attend to supervisory styles and match these with the self-concept and conceptual level of the student teacher; and to clearly delineate responsibilities and expectations among university supervisors, cooperating teachers, and student teachers. The need to develop a reward structure of resources and time allocations that reflects a higher university priority on supervision of student teachers has been clearly demonstrated.

References

Acheson, K. A., & Gall, M. D. (1987). *Techniques in the clinical supervision of teachers* (2nd ed.). New York: Longman.

Adams, A., & Glickman, C. (1984). Does clinical supervision work? A review of research. *Tennessee Educational Leadership, 11,* 38–40.

Akinniyi, G. O. (1987). *Perceptions and preferences of principals' and teachers' supervisory behavior.* Unpublished doctoral dissertation, University of Wisconsin, Madison.

Al-Duaij-Abdulaziz, D. M. (1986). A study of the impact of supervisory style on teachers' job satisfaction in the secondary schools in Kuwait (Doctoral dissertation, Western Michigan University). *Dissertation Abstracts International, 48,* 12A.

Bauer, L. K. (1986). Teacher attitudes toward supervisory practices of elementary school principals (Doctoral dissertation, Arizona State University). *Dissertation Abstracts International, 47,* 1540A.

Berg, M., Harders, P., Malian, I., & Nagel, A., (1986, February). *Partners in supervision: A clinical supervision program, San Diego State University.* Paper presented at the annual meeting of the Association of Teacher Educators, Atlanta. (ERIC Document Reproduction Service No. ED 271 436)

Blackbourn, R. L. (1983). The relationship between teachers' perceptions of supervisory behaviors and their attitudes toward a post-evaluative conference (Doctoral dissertation, Mississippi State University). *Dissertation Abstracts International, 45,* 694A.

Blankenship, Jr., G., & Irvine, J. J. (1985). Georgia teachers' perceptions of prescriptive and descriptive observations of teaching by instructional supervisors. *Georgia Educational Leadership, 1,* 7–10.

Blumberg, A. (1980). *Supervisors and teachers: A private cold war* (2nd ed.). Berkeley, CA: McCutchan.

Blumberg, A. (1985). Where we came from: Notes on supervision in the 1840's. *Journal of Curriculum and Supervision, 1*(1), 56–65.

Blumberg, A., & Amidon, E. (1965). Teacher perceptions of supervisor-teacher interaction. *Administrator's Notebook, 14*(1).

Bolin, F. S. (1987). Perspectives and imperatives on defining supervision. *Journal of Curriculum and Supervision, 2*(4), 368–380.

Bowman, N. (1978). Student teacher supervision, practices, and policies. *Action in teacher Education, 1,* 62–65.

Boyan, N. J., & Copeland, W. D. (1974). A training program for supervisors: Anatomy of an educational development. *Journal of Educational Research, 68*(3), 100–116.

Boyer, E. L. (1983). *High school: A report on secondary education in America.* New York: Harper & Row.

Bradley, R. C. (1966). Clarifying the supervising teachers role. *Teachers College Journal, 38,* 92–94.

Brande, R. T. (1980). Supervisory behaviors which contribute to the improvement of instruction: An analysis of teacher and supervisor perceptions (Doctoral dissertation, Hofstra University). *Dissertation Abstracts International, 41,* 4897A.

Brookover, W., Beady, C., Flood, R., Schweiter, J., & Wisenbaker, J. (1979). *School social systems and student achievement: Schools can make a difference.* New York: Praeger.

Burke, P. J., & Kray, R. (1985). *Experienced and inexperienced teachers' attitudes toward supervision and evaluation.* Paper presented at the annual meeting of the American Educational Research Association, Chicago.

Calhoun, E. F. (1984). *Teacher utilization of supervisory services.* (ERIC Document Reproduction Service No. ED 264 237)

Campbell, L. P., & Williamson, J. A. (1983). Supervising the student teacher: What is really involved? *NASSP Bulletin, 67*(465), 77–79.

Cawelti, G., & Reavis, C. (1980). How well are we providing instructional improvement services? *Educational Leadership, 38*(2), 236–240.

Chandler, B. (1971, February). *Levels of thinking in supervisory conferences.* Paper presented at the annual meeting of the American Educational Research Association, New York. (ERIC Document Reproduction Service No. ED 049 186)

Chunn, G. F. (1985). Perceptions of teachers and principals concerning behaviors and attitudes that contribute to an effective supervisory cycle (Doctoral dissertation, University of Mississippi). *Dissertation Abstracts International, 46,* 2494A.

Cicirelli, V. G. (1969). University supervisors' creative ability and their appraisal of student teachers' classroom performance: An exploratory study. *Journal of Educational Research, 62,* 375–381.

Clark, D. C., Smith, R. B., Thurman, R. A., & Baird, J. E. (1984). *Supervisors' feedback to student teachers.* (ERIC Document Reproduction Service No. ED 257 794)

Clarke, C., & Richardson, J. A. (1986, November). *Peer clinical supervision: A collegial approach.* Paper presented at the annual conference of the National Council of States on Inservice Education, Nashville.

Coe, D. E. (1985). *Toward collegial inquiry: A case study in clinical supervision.* (ERIC Document Reproduction Service No. ED 281 847)

Cogan, M. (1973). *Clinical supervision.* Boston: Houghton Mifflin.

Congdon, C. J. (1980). A study of the role of the principal in clinical supervision (Doctoral dissertation, United States International University, 1979). *Dissertation Abstracts International, 40,* 4819A.

Cook, G. E., & Skipper, B. L. (1986, March). *Bridge over troubled waters: Training for department level supervisors.* Paper presented at the annual meeting of the Association for Supervision and Curriculum Development, San Francisco.

Cook, K. E., Jr. (1983). The relationship between teacher perceptions of supervisory behavioral style and perceived teacher burnout (Doctoral dissertation, University of Connecticut). *Dissertation Abstracts International, 44,* 925A.

Copeland, W. D. (1980). Affective dispositions of teachers in training toward examples of supervisory behavior. *Journal of Educational Research, 74*(1), 37–42.

Copeland, W. D. (1982). Student teachers' preference for supervisory approach. *Journal of Teacher Education, 33*(2), 32–36.

Copeland, W. D., & Atkinson, D. R. (1978). Student teachers' perceptions of directive and nondirective supervisory behavior. *Journal of Educational Research, 71*(3), 123–127.

Cryan, J. R. (1972, April). *Supervisor verbal style. as related to the quality of interpersonal relations.* Paper presented at the annual meeting of the American Educational Research Association, Chicago. (ERIC Document Reproduction Service No. ED 062 663)

Cuff, W. A. (1978). Indirect versus direct influence in supervisory conferences and student teachers' levels of needs (Doctoral dissertation, New York University). *Dissertation Abstracts International, 39,* 4877A.

Davie, G. S., Jr. (1986). Teachers' and principals' perceptions of the performance and importance of instructional supervisory behaviors of the principal in schools using or not using clinical supervision (elementary) (Doctoral dissertation, University of San Francisco). *Dissertation Abstracts International, 47,* 1944A.

Dawson, J. L. (1982). Clinical and nonclinical supervision of student teachers (Doctoral dissertation, University of Idaho). *Dissertation Abstract International, 43,* 2638A.

Dean, K. (1971). *Supervision of student teachers: How adequate?* (ERIC Document Reproduction Service No. ED 079 256)

Descrochers, C. G. (1982). *Relationships between supervisory directors and justification in the teacher–supervisor conference and teachers' perceptions of supervisor credibility.* Unpublished doctoral dissertation, University of California.

District of Columbia Public Schools. (1980). *Improving instruction through supervision* (E.S.E.A. Title IV-C Final Evaluation Report). Washington, DC: Author. (ERIC Document Reproduction Service No. ED 182 865)

District of Columbia Public Schools, Division of Research, Planning, and Evaluation. (1981a). *Improving instruction through supervision: Developing supervisory support for teachers* (E.S.E.A. Title IV-C Final Evaluation Report, 1979–80). Washington, DC: Author. (ERIC Document Reproduction Service No. ED 201 707)

District of Columbia Public Schools, Division of Quality Assurance. (1981b). *Improving instruction through supervision: Developing supervisory support for teachers* (E.S.E.A. Title IV-C Final Evaluation Report, 1980–81). Washington, DC: Author. (ERIC Document Reproduction Service No. ED 213 799)

Drummond, R. (1980). *The impact of a model of student teaching supervision on cooperating teachers and field supervisors.* Washington, DC: American Association of Colleges for Teacher Education. (ERIC Document Reproduction Service No. ED 189 092)

Ellis, N. H. (1986). An andragogical model of educational supervision, job design, and teacher motivation (Doctoral dissertation, Fordham University). *Dissertation Abstracts International, 47,* 2390A.

Elsmere, R. T., & Daunt, P. D. (1975). *Effects of the size of the student teacher group on the supervisory program.* (ERIC Document Reproduction Service No. ED 132 120)

Funk, F. F., Hoffman, J. L., Keithley, A. M., & Long, B. E. (1978). *The influence of feedback from supervising teachers on a student teaching program.* (ERIC Document Reproduction Service No. ED 211 492)

Gage, N. L., & Giaconia, R. (1981). Teaching practices and student achievement: Causal connections. *New York University Education Quarterly, 12*(3), 2–9.

Garman, N. B. (1986). Clinical supervision: Quackery or remedy for professional development. *Journal of Curriculum and Supervision, 1*(2), 48–57.

Garman, N. B., Glickman, C. D., Hunter, M., & Haggerson, N. L. (1987). Conflicting conceptions of clinical supervision and the enhancement of professional growth and renewal: Point and counterpoint. *Journal of Curriculum and Supervision, 2*(2), 152–177.

Gibboney, R. A. (1987). A critique of Madeline Hunter's teaching model from Dewey's perspective. *Educational Leadership, 44*(5), 46–54.

Gibson, R. J. (1985). The effectiveness of clinical supervision in modifying teacher instructional behavior (Doctoral dissertation, University of Montana). *Dissertation Abstracts International, 46,* 2499A.

Ginkel, K. (1983, April). *An overview of a study which examined the relationship between elementary school teachers' preference for supervisory conferencing approach and conceptual level of development.* Paper presented at the annual meeting of the American Educational Research Association, Montreal.

Glickman, C. D. (1981). *Developmental supervision: Alternative practices for helping teachers improve instruction.* Alexandria, VA: Association for Supervision and Curriculum Development.

Glickman, C. D. (1985). *Supervision of instruction, a developmental approach.* Newton, MA: Allyn & Bacon.

Glickman, C. D. (1987). Unpublished evaluation of supervision training to the Richmond County (Augusta, Georgia) School District.

Glickman, C. D., & Gordon, S. P. (1987). Clarifying developmental supervision. *Educational Leadership, 44*(8), 64–68.

Goldhammer, R. (1966). *Clinical supervision: Special methods for the supervision of teachers.* New York: Holt, Rinehart & Winston.

Goldhammer, R., Anderson, R. H., & Krajewski, R. J. (1980). *Clinical Supervision.* New York: Holt, Rinehart & Winston.

Goldsberry, L., & Hoffman, N. E. (1984, April), *A comparison of teachers' perceptions of supervisory practices and their consequences with those of their supervisors.* Paper presented at the annual meeting of the American Educational Research Association, New Orleans.

Goodlad, J. I. (1984). *A place called school: Prospects for the future.* New York: McGraw-Hill.

Gordon, S. P. (1989). *Developmental supervision, supervisor flexibility and the post-observation conference.* Unpublished doctoral dissertation, University of Georgia.

Grande, A. (1979). *The relationship between teacher supervision and the Pennsylvania educational quality assessment inventory (elementary).* Unpublished doctoral dissertation, Lehigh University.

Grimmett, P. P. (1987). The role of district supervisors in the implementation of peer coaching. *Journal of Curriculum and Supervision, 3*(1), 3–28.

Grimmett, P., & Crehan, P. (1988, April). *Conferencing strategies used by supervisors of high conceptual level interacting with teachers of low conceptual level and effects on classroom management practices.* Presentation to the annual meeting of the American Educational Research Association, New Orleans.

Grimmett, P. P., & Housego, I. E. (1983, May). Interpersonal relationships in the clinical supervision conference. *Canadian Administrator, 22,* 8.

Grimmett, P. P., & Ratzlaff, H. C. (1986). Expectations for the cooperating teacher role. *Journal of Teacher Education, 37*(6), 41–50.

Guditis, C. W. (1979, November). *Supervisors improving the quality of teaching.* Presentation to the meeting of the Council of Professors of Instructional Supervision, Athens, Georgia.

Hallinger, P., & Murphy, J. (1987). Instructional leadership in the school context. In W. Greenfield (Ed.), *Instructional leadership concepts, issues, and controversies* (pp. 179–203). Newton, MA: Allyn & Bacon.

Harris, B. M. (1985). *Supervisory behavior in education* (3rd ed.). Englewood Cliffs, NJ: Prentice-Hall.

Hart, A. W. (1985, March–April). *Formal teacher supervision by teachers in a career ladder.* Paper presented at the annual meeting of the American Educational Research Association, Chicago.

Hart, N. E. (1979). *The philosophical bases of instructional supervision, identification and classification.* Unpublished doctoral dissertation, University of Georgia.

Herbster, D. L. (1976). Generalists versus specialists in the supervision of student teachers. *Teacher Educator, 11*(3), 32–34.

Hill, R. D. (1977). A study of the effects of joint laboratory training on the supervisory conference, the teacher–intern relationship and the intern's teaching practices (Doctoral disseration, University of Oregon). *Dissertation Abstracts International, 39,* 238A.

Humphrey, G. L. (1983). The relationship between orientations to supervision and the developmental levels of commitment and abstract thinking of entry-year teachers (Doctoral dissertation, University of Tulsa). *Dissertation Abstracts International, 44,* 1644A.

Hunt, D. E. (1987). *Beginning with ourselves: In practice, theory, and human affairs.* Cambridge, MA: Brookline Books.

Hunter, M. C. (1987). Beyond rereading Dewey . . . what's next? A response to Gibboney. *Educational Leadership, 44*(5), 51–53.

Johns, K. W., & Cline, D. H. (1985, October). *Supervisory practices and student teacher satisfaction in selected institutions of higher education.* Paper presented at the annual meeting of North Rocky Mountain Educational Research Association. (ERIC Document Reproduction Service No. ED 267 037)

Johnston, C. (1987, April). *TA training in supervisory international communication: Two tests of the effect*. Paper presented at the annual meeting of the American Educational Research Association, Washington, DC.

Johnston, C., Galluzzo, G. R., & Kottkamp, R. B. (1986, April). *The effects of training in transactional analysis on supervisory interpersonal communication*. Paper presented at the annual meeting of the American Educational Research Association, San Francisco.

Jonas, R. S., & Blumberg, A. (1986, March-April). *The concept of access in supervisor–teacher relationships*. Paper presented at the annual meeting of the American Educational Research Association, San Francisco.

Jones, J. W. (1986). *A data collection system for describing research-based supervisory practices for promoting instructional improvement in a local school district*. Unpublished doctoral dissertation, University of Georgia.

Joyce, B., & Showers, B. (1980). Improving inservice training: The messages of research. *Educational Leadership, 37*(5), 379–385.

Kilbourn, B. (1982). Linda: A case study in clinical supervision. *Canadian Journal of Education, 7*(3), 1–24.

Killian, J. E., & McIntyre, D. J. (1985, April). *The influence of cooperating teachers' supervisory training and experience on teacher development during early field experiences*. Paper presented at the annual meeting of the American Educational Research Association, Chicago. (ERIC Document Reproduction Service No. ED 257 810)

Killian, J. E., & McIntyre, D. J. (1986). Quality in the early field experiences: A product of grade level and cooperating teachers' training. *Teaching and Teacher Education, 2*(4), 367–376.

Koehler, V. (1984, April). *University supervision of student teaching* (National Institute of Education Report No. 9061). Austin, TX: University of Texas, R & D Center for Teacher Education. (ERIC Document Reproduction Service No. ED 270 349)

Koehler, V. R. (1986, April). *The instructional supervision of student teachers*. Paper presented at the annual meeting of the American Educational Research Association, San Francisco. (ERIC Document Reproduction Service No. ED 271 430)

Konke, K. (1984, April). *A study of the relationship of teacher conceptual level with perceptions of teachers in regard to staff development, curriculum development, and instructional improvement*. Paper presented at the annual meeting of the American Educational Research Association, New Orleans.

Kottkamp, R. B. (1982, March). *Supervisory authenticity, communication, productivity and subordinate loyalty*. Paper presented at the annual meeting of the American Educational Research Association, New York.

Kuehl, R. (1976). *A taxonomy of critical tasks for supervising teachers* (A research study). (ERIC Document Reproduction Service No. ED 179 507)

Lamb, C. E., & Montague, E. J. (1982, February). *Variables pertaining to the perceived effectiveness of university student teaching supervisors*. Paper presented at the annual meeting of the Southwest Educational Research Association, Austin. (ERIC Document Reproduction Service No. ED 212 613)

Little, J. W. (1982). Norms of collegiality and experimentation: Workplace conditions of school success. *American Educational Research Journal, 19*(3), 325–340.

Little, J. W., & Bird, T. (1987). Instructional leadership "close to the classroom" in secondary schools. In W. Greenfield (Ed.), *Instructional leadership concepts, issues, and controversies* (pp. 118–138). Newton, MA: Allyn & Bacon.

Little, J. W., & Bird, T. (1987). Instructional leadership "close to the classroom" in secondary schools. In W. Greenfield (Ed.), *Instructional leadership concepts, issues, and controversies* (pp. 118–138). Newton, MA: Allyn & Bacon.

Lombardo, B. J. (1980, February). *The effects of supervision employing interaction analysis on the teaching behavior of selected physical education teachers*. Paper presented at the Eastern District Association Convention of the American Alliance for Health, Physical Education, Recreation and Dance, Lancaster, PA.

Lucio, W. H., & McNeill, J. D. (1979). *Supervision: A synthesis of thought and action* (3rd ed.). New York: McGraw-Hill.

Lyman, L. (1987, March). *Principals and teachers: Collaboration to improve instructional supervision (building trust, fostering collaboration, encouraging collegiality)*. Paper presented at the annual meeting of the Association for Supervision and Curriculum Development, New Orleans.

Mattes, R. G. (1983). A comparative study of teachers' perceptions of teacher development and supervisory practices under clinical and traditional supervision practices in selected Colorado schools (Doctoral dissertation, University of Colorado). *Dissertation Abstracts International, 44*, 940A.

May, W. T., & Zimpher, N. L. (1986). An examination of three theoretical perspectives on supervision: Perceptions of preservice field supervision. *Journal of Curriculum and Supervision, 1*(2), 83–99.

Mayfield, J. E. (1983). The effects of clinical supervision on pupil achievement in reading (Doctoral dissertation, Wayne State University). *Dissertation Abstracts International, 44*, 940A.

McFaul, S., & Cooper, J. (1984). Peer clinical supervision: Theory versus reality. *Educational Leadership, 41*(7), 4–9.

Mohlman, G. G. (1982, March). *Assessing the impact of three inservice teacher training models*. Paper presented at the annual meeting of the American Educational Research Association, New York.

Morris, J. E., & Chissom, B. S. (1975). *An investigation of the effectiveness of graduate assistants and faculty serving as university supervisors of student teachers*. (ERIC Document Reproduction Service No. ED 182 274)

Morris, J. R. (1974). The effects of the university supervisor on the performance and adjustment of student teachers. *Journal of Educational Research, 67*, 358–362.

Ngugi, N. (1984). The relationships between Mississippi public senior high school principals' perceptions of their actual supervisory behaviors and teachers' perceptions of actual and preferred principals' supervisory behaviors (Doctoral dissertation, Mississippi State University). *Dissertation Abstracts International, 46*, 319A.

Okwuanaso, S. I. (1983). Perceptions of supervisory process: A study of Anambra (Nigeria) selected secondary school teachers and principals (Doctoral dissertation, Michigan State University). *Dissertation Abstracts International, 44*, 3565A.

Oliva, P. F. (1988). *Supervision for today's schools* (3rd ed.). New York: Longman.

O'Neal, S. (1983a, April). *An analysis of student teaching cooperating teacher conferences as related to the self-concept, flexibility, and teaching concerns of each participant*. Paper presented at the annual meeting of the American Educational Research Association, Montreal. (ERIC Document Reproduction Service No. ED 234 030)

O'Neal S. F. (1983b). *Supervision of student teachers: Feedback and evaluation*. Austin, TX: University of Texas at Austin, R & D Center for Teacher Education. (ERIC Document Reproduction Service No. ED 240 106)

Ortiz-Vega, J. (1982). Role expectations of university supervisors as expressed by participants in teacher training programs in Puerto Rico (Doctoral dissertation, New York University). *Dissertation Abstracts International, 43*, 2320A.

Osterman, K. F. (1984). Supervision in public schools: An examination of the relationship between supervisory practices of principals and organizational behavior of teachers (Doctoral dissertation, Washington University). *Dissertation Abstracts International, 46*, 572A.

Page, F. P., Jr. (1979). The college supervisor's role as perceived by college supervisors, cooperating teachers, and student teachers (Doctoral dissertation, Mississippi State University). *Dissertation Abstracts International, 40,* 3243A.

Pajak, E. F., & Glickman, C. D. (1984, April). *Teachers' discrimination between information and control in response to videotaped simulated supervisory conferences.* Paper presented at the annual meeting of the American Educational Research Association, New Orleans.

Parker, L. S. (1986). The efficacy of a teacher induction program in providing assistance and support to first-year teachers (retention, supervision, Wisconsin) (Doctoral dissertation, University of Wisconsin). *Dissertation Abstracts International, 47,* 872A.

Pavan, B. N. (1983, November). *Clinical supervision: Does it make a difference?* Paper presented at the annual meeting of the Council of Professors of Instructional Supervision, DeKalb, IL.

Pavan, B. N. (1985a, April). *Clinical supervision: Research in schools utilizing comparative measures.* Paper presented at the annual meeting of the American Educational Research Association, Chicago. (ERIC Document Reproduction Service No. ED 255 516)

Pavan, B. N. (1985b, November). *Hunter's clinical supervision and instruction models: Research in schools utilizing comparative measures.* Paper presented at the annual meeting of the Council of Professors of Instructional Supervision, Washington, DC.

Phares, D. R. (1981). Teachers' perceptions of the supervisory conference following classroom observation as affected by selected demographic variables of principals (Doctoral dissertation, Mississippi State University). *Dissertation Abstracts International, 42,* 4675A.

Phillips, M. (1989). *A case study evaluation of the impact on teachers of the implementation of a peer coaching training program in an elementary school.* Unpublished doctoral dissertation, University of Georgia.

Powell, N. D. (1982). The relationship existing between clinical supervision and certain teacher attitudes (Doctoral dissertation, University of Southern California). *Dissertation Abstracts International, 43,* 3177A.

Reavis, C. A. (1977). A test of the clinical supervision model. *Journal of Educational Research, 70*(6), 311–315.

Ritz, W. C., & Cashell, J. G. (1980). "Cold War" between supervisors and teachers. *Educational Leadership, 38*(1), 77–78.

Rogers, M. G. (1986). Teacher satisfaction with direct supervisory services (Doctoral dissertation, University of Georgia). *Dissertation Abstracts International, 47,* 4260A.

Rosenholtz, S. J. (1985). Effective schools: Interpreting the evidence. *American Journal of Education, 93,* 352–388.

Rossicone, G. A. (1985). The relationship of selected teacher background versus preferences for supervisory style and teacher perceptions of supervisory style of supervisors (Doctoral dissertation, St. John's University). *Dissertation Abstracts International, 46,* 321A.

Rothman, L. S. (1981). Effective and ineffective supervisory behaviors of college supervisors as perceived by secondary school cooperating teachers (Doctoral dissertation, University of Florida). *Dissertation Abstracts International, 42,* 2086A.

Russell, T. L., & Spafford, C. (1986, April). *Teachers as reflective practitioners in peer clinical supervision.* Paper presented at the annual meeting of the American Educational Research Association, San Francisco.

Rutter, M., Maughan, B., Mortimore, P., Ouston, J., & Smith, A. (1979). *Fifteen thousand hours: Secondary schools and their effects on children.* Cambridge, MA: Harvard University Press.

Rentz, E. I. (1981). An analysis of the relationships between supervising teachers' self-perceived leadership styles and performance and attitudes of student teachers (Doctoral dissertation, University of Northern Colorado). *Dissertation Abstracts International, 42,* 179A.

Seperson, M. A., & Joyce, B. (1973). Teaching styles of student teachers as related to those of their cooperating teachers. *Educational Leadership Research Supplement, 31*(2), 146–151.

Sergiovanni, T. J. (Ed.). (1982). *Supervision of teaching* (1982 yearbook). Alexandria, VA: Association for Supervision and Curriculum Development.

Shahzade, J. B. (1983). The match of style and conceptual level of university supervisors with student teachers in relationship to supervisor effectiveness (Doctoral dissertation, University of the Pacific). *Dissertation Abstracts International, 44,* 2449A.

Showers, B. (1983, April). *Transfer of training.* Paper presented at the meeting of the American Educational Research Association, Montreal.

Simmons, J. M., Moon, R. A., & Niedermeyer, R. (1987, April). *A critique of recent methods and variables used to research the thinking and evaluative decision making of instructional supervisors.* Paper presented to the annual meeting of the American Educational Research Association, Washington, DC.

Simone, M. A. (1986). Uses of common technical language and public agenda in the supervisory process and their relationship to trust of the supervisor and teacher efficacy (Doctoral dissertation, Rutgers University). *Dissertation Abstracts International, 47,* 2838A.

Smith, S. C. (1985). The effects of clinical supervision on teachers' autonomy and perceptions of productive relationships (Doctoral dissertation, University of Idaho). *Dissertation Abstracts International, 46,* 3003A.

Smith, W. K. (1979). A study of supervisory practices with reference to classroom observations and conferences as perceived by teachers, principals, and supervisors in elementary schools in an urban school district in southeast Louisiana (Doctoral dissertation, University of New Orleans). *Dissertation Abstracts International, 41,* 53A.

Smyth, J. (1988). A critical perspective for clinical supervision. *Journal of Curriculum and Supervision, 3*(2), 136–156.

Snyder, K. J. (1982, February). *The implementation of clinical supervision.* Paper presented at the annual meeting of the Southwest Educational Research Association, Austin, TX.

Sparks, G. M., & Bruder, S. (1987, April). *How school-based peer coaching improves collegiality and experimentation.* Paper presented at the annual meeting of the American Educational Research Association, Washington, DC.

Spaulding, J. W. (1984). A study of the implementation of a clinical supervision model in the Santee (California) School District (Doctoral dissertation, Northern Arizona University, 1983). *Dissertation Abstracts International, 44,* 2948A.

Spivey, G. D. (1974). *The subject area specialist approach versus the generalist approach in the supervision of student teaching.* Unpublished doctoral dissertation, University of Tennessee.

Squires, D. A. (1978). *A phenolmenological study of supervisors' perceptions of a positive supervisory experience.* (ERIC Document Reproduction Service No. ED 195 031)

Stallings, J. (1985, April). *Under what conditions do children thrive in the Madeline Hunter Model? A report of Project Follow Through, Napa, California.* Paper presented at the annual meeting of the American Educational Research Association, Chicago.

Stallings, J. (1987). For whom and how long is the Hunter-based model appropriate? Response to Robbins and Wolfe. *Educational Leadership, 44*(5), 62–63.

Stein, R. D. (1985). The relationship between principal supervisory behavior and teacher burnout (Doctoral dissertation, University of Illinois). *Dissertation Abstracts International, 46,* 577A.

Stewig, J. W. (1970). What should college supervisors do? *Journal of Teacher Education, 21,* 251–257.

Strachan, J. L. (1981). Instructional supervision and teacher development. *Australian Administrator, 2*(2).

Sullivan, C. G. (1980). *Clinical supervision: A state of the art review.* Alexandria, VA: Association for Supervision and Curriculum Development.

Tanner, D. E. (1986, February). *Do university supervisors, cooperating teachers and student teachers agree about the student teachers performance?* Paper presented at the annual meeting of the Association of Teacher Educators, Atlanta. (ERIC Document Reproduction Service No. ED 272 507)

Tanner, D., & Tanner, L. N. (1987). *Supervision in Education.* New York: Macmillan.

Taylor, D. M. (1986). Perceptions of teachers in small, isolated Alaskan schools regarding supervision received compared to supervision preferred (rural education) (Doctoral dissertation, University of Montana). *Dissertation Abstracts International, 47,* 2411A.

Taylor, S. M. (1984). Teachers' perceptions of intensive supervisor/teacher relationships (phenomenology) (Doctoral dissertation, University of Pittsburgh). *Dissertation Abstracts International, 46,* 953A.

Thompson, J. C., IV. (1978). An assessment of the effects of peer supervision in attitudes, appraisals, and classroom control of student teachers (Doctoral dissertation, Pennsylvania State University). *Dissertation Abstracts International, 39,* 16082A.

Thorlacius, J. (1980, April). *Changes in supervisory behavior resulting from training in clinical supervision.* Paper presented at the annual meeting of the American Educational Research Association, Boston. (ERIC Document Reproduction Service No. ED 211 506)

Townsend, D. G. (1984). The first year of implementation of a new policy of teacher supervision and evaluation in five secondary schools of Lethbridge School District No. 51 (Educational Change; Alberta, Canada) (Doctoral dissertation, University of Oregon). *Dissertation Abstracts International, 45,* 3509A.

Twa, J. (1984, June). *Teacher associate perceptions of the effectiveness of the clinical supervision workshop.* Paper presented at the annual meeting of the Canadian Society for the Study of Education, Ontario. (ERIC Document Reproduction Service No. ED 269 855)

Vak, S. M. (1979). *The relationship between teacher supervision and the Pennsylvania educational quality assessment inventory (secondary).* Unpublished doctoral dissertation, Lehigh University.

Vukovich, D. (1976, April). *The effects of four specific supervision procedures on the development of self-evaluation skills in pre-service teachers.* Paper presented at the annual meeting of the American Educational Research Association, San Francisco. (ERIC Document Reproduction Service No. ED 146 224)

Waters, R. G. (1985). *An evaluation of the beginning teacher supervision program conducted by the Department of Agricultural and Extension Education at The Pennsylvania State University* (Final Report). University Park, PA: Pennsylvania State University.

Webb, M. S. (1979). Conflict in the supervisory triad of college supervisor, cooperating teacher and student teacher (Doctoral dissertation, University of Oregon). *Dissertation Abstracts International, 40,* 5012A.

Western, R., Zahorik, J., Kritek, W., & Smith, P. (1987, April). *A study of cooperating teachers' instructional roles.* Paper presented at the annual meeting of the American Educational Research Association, Washington, DC.

White, P. L. (1977). The relationship between student teacher perceptions of the effective environment in supervision and their supervisors' participation in a workshop designed to foster supportive verbal communication skills (Doctoral dissertation, Temple University). *Dissertation Abstracts International, 39,* 2204A.

Whitehead, R. (1984, June). *Practicum students' perceptions of teacher associates' supervisory behaviors.* Paper presented at annual meeting of the Canadian Society for the Study of Education, Guelph, Canada. (ERIC Document Reproduction Service No. ED 269 856)

Williams, R. E. H. (1986). The relationship between secondary teachers' perceptions of supervisory behaviors and their attitudes toward a post observation supervisory conference (Doctoral dissertation, Mississippi State University). *Dissertation Abstracts International, 47,* 1976A.

Wright, L. V. (1987). A program for improving teacher decision making through peer coaching and reflection. *Journal of Staff Development, 8*(3), 54–57.

Yee, A. (1969). Do cooperating teachers influence the attitudes of student teachers? *Journal of Educational Psychology, 60*(4), 327–332.

EVALUATION AND DISSEMINATION

ASSESSMENT OF TEACHING

Theodore E. Andrews

OFFICE OF THE SUPERINTENDENT OF PUBLIC INSTRUCTION, WASHINGTON

Susan Barnes

SOUTHWEST TEXAS STATE UNIVERSITY

Rapidly developing national, state, and local assessment programs have the greatest potential for immediately and forever impacting on teacher education practices. Prospective teachers are now being tested prior to entry into teacher education programs for their knowledge of basic skills; at the end of preparation, they might be assessed for knowledge of pedagogy and the content they are certified to teach; and, in some states, beginning and experienced teachers are being asked to demonstrate their teaching competency in the classroom.

The variety in these extensive testing efforts is documented in other publications such as *Teacher Assessment* (Association of Teacher Educators, 1988), and *What's Happening in Teacher Testing* (U.S. Department of Education, 1987). The emphasis in this chapter is on only one aspect of these efforts, the area of greatest challenge and greatest potential, the assessment of teaching.

Assessment programs affect curriculum decisions. Teacher educators, reluctantly or joyfully, are and will be revising preparation programs on the basis of state assessment systems. States have committed millions of dollars in developmental costs and additional funds to the administration of their programs. They have addressed every issue teacher educators need to consider. More important, state efforts in Georgia and Florida, for example, have changed the assessment procedures used by colleges and universities throughout the United States.

Legislative mandates have driven many of the state programs, focusing the states' efforts while, at the same time, politicizing policies that most teacher educators would prefer to see addressed in a university setting.

BACKGROUND ISSUES

This chapter is designed for (a) teacher educators who are interested in the assessment of teaching, especially those developing or improving their own assessment systems or those who will be developing such systems in the future; and (b) administrators, supervisors, and teachers who are demanding to know more about assessment policies that are strongly influencing roles and responsibilities. There is a significant body of literature on the development of observation systems and the selection of the teaching behaviors included in those systems, which will not be reviewed here. Rather, this chapter synthesizes the available literature addressing the purposes for teacher evaluation, considers the methodological issues related to teacher evaluation, and describes state and university assessment programs. These examples illustrate how varying purposes and methodological issues have been addressed in different assessment systems.

Much of the available information on these programs comes from internal studies, completed by an institution or a state, that are available upon request but unknown to the average educator. These studies provide an untapped resource for any-

A number of people assisted in obtaining materials and reviewing drafts of this chapter. In particular we wish to acknowledge the contributions of Lester Soloman (Georgia Department of Education), Don Peterson (University of South Florida), Roger Pankratz (Western Kentucky University), Jack Beal (University of Washington), Donald Medley (University of Virginia), and William Capie (University of Georgia).

one interested in teacher assessment. They provide answers to a number of questions. What has been learned about how these systems work? Have revisions been made and why? If the organizations were starting over today, what would they do differently? Literally, what can be learned from someone else's efforts?

Purposes: Formative and Summative

Two conflicting positions most commonly encountered in the teacher assessment literature relate to the relative weight given to formative and summative evaluation. Formative evaluation is defined as process evaluation and summative evaluation as product evaluation. Process evaluation provides "in-flight" information to teachers, so they can make appropriate adjustments during the year or the life of an educational program; placing a value on the teacher's performance is not included at this point in the process. With summative evaluation, value is placed on performance or whatever product is being evaluated, and the value can be used in a decision-making process for certification, contract renewal or assignment to a career ladder, or an award of incentive pay.

Formative evaluation has much in common with clinical supervision, with its associated interactions between teacher and evaluator, provision of feedback to the teacher, and focus on the professional growth of the individual teacher. Summative evaluation provides those in decision-making positions with information for accountability and for differentiation among teachers. Programs designed to differentiate between and among teachers require more legally defensible assessments (Shaw, 1985). McGreal (Brandt, 1987b) advocates separation of supervisory behavior from administrative or summative behaviors, but he maintains some support for assessment of a teacher's skill against a minimum performance level and against the set of skills that every teacher ought to be able to perform, essentially the skills identified by the line of research known as research on teaching. He cautions that the criteria should not be too narrow: higher order teaching skills are often not included in evaluation systems because of the narrowness of the research base and the difficulty of evaluating these areas. In his opinion, these skills, rather than simple discrete behaviors, should be used to measure the highest levels of skill in teaching.

Others hold the view that the two basic functions of evaluation—accountability and professional development—are incompatible and that one system cannot perform both functions simultaneously and effectively. Stiggins (1986) states that these two functions differ in four ways: (a) purposes of the systems, (b) impact on teachers, (c) evaluation mechanisms used, and (d) potential limitations and benefits. Systems that serve accountability, or summative purposes, focus on evaluating teacher performance based on predetermined goals; those that serve formative purposes have as their goal improvement of teacher performance. Both summative and formative evaluations should have as their ultimate goal improvement of student learning. Accountability systems are used to identify the

incompetent teacher and the outstanding (merit) teacher. As a consequence, they affect only a small number of poor teachers, whereas professional-development systems have the capability to affect growth in all teachers, even experienced career professionals. The data used to evaluate the teacher in the accountability system must sustain intense scrutiny, because dismissal is a likely consequence of an evaluation that does not meet minimum standards of performance. For growth systems, the evaluation process can be individualized to meet the needs of the particular teacher, with data and the nature of the evaluation process varied accordingly (Peterson, 1984).

Stiggins describes the limitations of both accountability and growth systems. The limitations of the accountability system include (a) a relatively narrow definition of good teaching necessary to define standard performance criteria; (b) a reliance on a small sample of teacher performance, usually in one or two classroom observations; (c) the potential for bias, due to primary reliance upon the teacher's supervisor and a limited number of other observers; and (d) the relatively limited effects on few teachers. Among the limitations associated with growth systems are (a) the potential for role conflict when the supervisor acts as both the formative and summative evaluator, and (b) the inadequacy of financial resources committed to opportunities for teacher growth and improvement (Stiggins, 1986).

Appraisal systems that focus on the professional development of the teacher are based on several assumptions. According to Barber and Klein (1983), such systems assume that teachers are professionals who can evaluate their own worth, strive for excellence in their teaching, and participate in not only their own evaluations but also those of their peers. Further, not only are they good people but they are also perceived to be people of worth to the community, so that the community is willing to support further growth with financial resources. When these assumptions are not met, the validity and usefulness of the evaluation process can be seriously questioned.

The purposes of teacher evaluation are often described as dichotomies between *assessment* and *assistance* orientations, *formative* and *summative* evaluation, *employment* and *dismissal* decisions, and *qualifying* and *not qualifying* for merit pay or career ladder advancement. These purposes are overarching in their importance and influence on teachers. Teachers tend to support systems that primarily support professional growth and do not force comparative decisions. On the other hand, less support and acceptance are evident when the system provides information for career ladder placement and incentive pay decisions (Darling-Hammond, Wise, & Pease, 1983). This is the context within which much appraisal is currently occurring, and the effects of that context should not be minimized. According to Darling-Hammond et al., the process of teacher evaluation will strike a balance at some point between a standardized, tightly administered approach and a teacher-oriented approach to evaluation and professional development. That balance point has profound implications for teacher professionalism and teacher evaluation.

The first lesson to be learned from this discussion is the importance of clarifying the purpose, or adequately balancing the multiple purposes, of the evaluation system. According to

Wise, Darling-Hammond, McLaughlin, and Bernstein (1984), clarifying the purpose of the evaluation is important in determining what data are examined for evaluation and which processes are used for gathering and sharing information.

Criteria

For each evaluation system, certain criteria can be advanced to judge the success of the evaluation system itself. According to Medley, each system must be objective, reliable, valid, and practicable (1982). These criteria are similar to those proposed by Carey (1984) as a means of evaluating state-level policies. She identifies fairness, equity, utility, and feasibility as guideposts for evaluating the effectiveness of a policy. Once again a balancing process is required. Given limited resources, each of these criteria must be balanced against the others; to maximize one may minimize another. The credibility of an assessment system is often based on the extent to which the stakeholders believe that it works.

Medley (1982) provides a schema for conceptualizing points at which the teacher may be evaluated and identifies contextual factors that must be considered in interpreting evaluation results. Teacher characteristics that could be measured include (a) personal traits, (b) competence, (c) performance, (d) learning experiences provided to students, and (e) student learning outcomes. According to Medley it is critical to identify which outcomes can be attributed to the actions of the teacher and which are affected by contextual factors. Medley also makes a useful set of distinctions among teacher competence, teacher performance, and teacher effectiveness. In his view, teacher competence is defined as the repertoire of professional knowledge, skills, and values held by the teacher. Teacher performance is the behavior of the teacher on the job, and teacher effectiveness is the teacher's impact on students. Each of these constructs is assessed in a different manner to accurately evaluate the teacher.

Most evaluation systems in current use focus on teacher performance as observed in the classroom or within the school or community setting. Some systems also attempt to evaluate teacher competence by the examination of portfolios, teaching materials, and other documents; by surveys; and by interviews with knowledgeable persons. A few systems are also attempting to assess teacher effectiveness by examining student achievement, as measured by gains on test scores or other evidence of student progress. In assessing each of these constructs, appropriate attention must be paid to the extraneous factors that could affect teacher performance and effectiveness. If the purpose is to evaluate teacher performance, then direct observation of student learning experiences provides the best estimate of teacher performance effects, according to Medley 1982); if the purpose is to evaluate teacher competence, then direct observation of teacher behavior provides the best estimate of teacher competence, given the teacher's specific classroom setting. Although most existing teacher assessment programs focus on teacher behavior, Oregon is implementing revised certification standards that include demonstrations of student growth.

Philosophy

The focus of teacher evaluation is also guided by the predominant view of the teacher as technician, professional, or some compromise between these two views. Soar, Medley, and Coker (1983) discuss the implications of these distinctions and conclude that the basic differences in the job responsibilities of technicians and professionals should be reflected in the type of evaluation (level of accountability) to which they are held. Specifically, technicians face problems that are less complicated and have known solutions. The test of their competence is to select the most appropriate solution from a collection of known solutions. The professional is expected to operate on problems that have no known solutions, that require the application of a new combinations of skills and knowledge to estimate a probable success. As a consequence, the professional should be held accountable, not for specific outcomes from the application of known prescriptions (as is the technician), but for using *best practice*, or engaging in a defensible process in reaching a solution to a problem.

Because the distinction between teacher as technician and teacher as professional is so crucial to teacher evaluation, professionalism in the larger sense bears examination. Professionalism has often been defined as the possession of a unique knowledge base and the situational life space to exercise decision-making skills (Darling-Hammond et al., 1983). Medley further characterizes professionalism as a combination of professional knowledge, professional skill or ability, and professional attitudes or value positions.

Professional skill, or the ability to use professional knowledge in the solution of professional problems, is subcategorized into perceptual skills, performance or implementation skills, and decision-making skills. Professional skill in decision making is the ability of a teacher, once a problem has been diagnosed, to call upon professional knowledge to prescribe an experience for the learner that can be supported by the resources available and that can be defended as following approved practice. Because of the limitations of the knowledge base for teaching, the concept of best practice or approved practice becomes fundamental to teacher evaluation. Approved practice is practice consistent with research, evolving theory, and generally accepted standards. Most of the newly developed evaluation systems discussed in this chapter attempt to balance attention to performance skills, perceptual skills, and decision-making skills by using multiple sources of information about teacher performances in systematic ways.

Another philosophy that assumes a more direct relationship between teaching and learning is reflected in the Florida Performance Measurement System. In the view of Smith, Peterson, and Micceri (1987), "Learning is the product of teaching." The teacher is not held accountable for factors beyond her or his influence, but the teacher is held accountable for using valid methods of diagnosis and research-based teaching methods.

Whatever its purpose, a critical issue in teacher evaluation is the accuracy and fairness of the evaluative judgment, and much has been written about the methodological issues that should be addressed to insure minimum standards of quality and to provide evaluations acceptable to those being evaluated. As Peterson (1984) points out, teacher evaluation takes place within *political* and *social* contexts, and, within these contexts, decisions are made to evaluate in some way the teacher's application of skills and knowledge and to use the results for some purpose. Ignoring the social and political contexts invites the risk of implementing an evaluation system that does not function as designed (Peterson, 1984). More important, the social and political contexts shape the evaluation design (some would say restrict, narrow, or subvert the original intent of the evaluation system).

METHODOLOGICAL ISSUES

Methodological issues usually translate into questions of what to measure, how to measure, what evidence to consider, and what to do with the results. These are merely convenient subdivisions of a complex topic and should not be interpreted as disconnected questions; in fact, each is intimately connected to the other questions and is affected by the constraints associated with the answers to the other questions. The uses of assessment data are of great importance in determining what to measure and how the measurements will be made (Capie, 1983; Wise et al., 1984).

Measurement and Evaluation: Definitions

Measurement, or assessment, is defined as the accurate, objective description of performance relative to the construct of interest; *evaluation* is placing value upon what has been measured. Evaluation by definition is subjective and reflects the values placed on something within a social and political context. Differing options exist regarding the balance sought between rigorous, objective measurement and the role of professional judgment in teacher evaluation. Medley, Coker, and Soar (1984) advocate separation of measurement and evaluation by stressing the use of low-inference-data records during classroom observation and then evaluating the data against scoring keys established by expert opinion and statistical investigation of the data obtained. Popham (1987) does not embrace this distinction so strongly and has spoken in favor of more subjectivity in the evaluation process; in his terms, *judgment-based evaluation* through the pooled professional judgments of trained evaluators.

Readers need to be sensitive to the reality that no measure is totally objective (judgment always exists to some extent). Low-inference systems *are* more objective, and high-inference systems *are* more subjective; the differences in the systems are a matter of degree, however, not of kind. Capie, Ellett, and Cronin (1985) argue that the distinctions are more a matter of data recording or scoring than of inference level.

Within the teacher evaluation systems currently in use, examples are available to illustrate both of these views. The COKER system (Medley et al., 1984) represents the observation of discrete teaching behaviors within a teaching format

and is described as a low-inference system. The systems in use in North Carolina (Holdzkom, 1987; North Carolina State Department of Public Instruction, 1986) and Texas (Barnes, 1987) for career ladder decisions depend upon the professional judgments of trained evaluators. However, teacher acceptance of either type of system is problematic. A pilot system developed for the state of Alabama, based upon the COKER, met resistance from teachers and has yet to be implemented (Southern Region Education Board, 1987). On the other hand, teachers' criticisms of the Texas system focus heavily upon the consistency of judgments made by appraisers in determining the quality of teaching performance (Barnes, 1987).

What to Measure

Assumptions. Teacher evaluation is based upon certain assumptions (and assumptions *do* vary). The basic assumption underlying work in this field is that good teaching behavior is identifiable, stable, and consistent in its effects upon students across contexts (Medley, 1985; Stodolsky, 1985). Evaluation systems reflect these competencies and focus on teacher performances presumed to be related to teacher effectiveness in terms of student learning outcomes. Teacher evaluation systems assume that certain generic essential skills exist and that those who desire to call themselves professional teachers should be able to demonstrate and apply those skills in appropriate situations. However, Shulman argues that there are no generic skills, that all teaching skills are subject and situation specific (Shulman, 1988). Fundamentally, the validity of the evaluation system depends upon the accuracy of the underlying beliefs about effective teaching (Soar et al., 1983).

The validity of a teacher evaluation system also depends upon the ability of that system to measure accurately the teacher's behavior and effectiveness while taking into account other factors possibly influencing the teacher's performance score. When making inferences about teachers' performances, the system must demonstrate that differences detected between two teachers are true differences in levels of skill and not differences that would disappear if the teachers traded classes or subjects. Teacher evaluation in this sense assumes that different levels of skills are evident in the teacher's behavior or in the teacher's effects upon student learning across contexts and that these differences can be accurately measured. This assumption is challenged by Shulman, however.

The assumption that good teaching can be defined relates to the assumption that teaching effectiveness is stable, repeated by a teacher over time and in different instructional contexts. Some support for the stability of teacher effects was found in studies conducted at the Research and Development Center for Teacher Education (Brophy, 1972; Emmer, Evertson, & Brophy, 1979) and by Shavelson and Russo (1977). Brophy examined teacher effects on student achievement in reading and mathematics, as evidenced by gains on standardized tests administered to the teachers' classes each year for a 3-year period. He found that (a) teachers were more consistent in producing gains within curricular areas over the 3 years than across the curricular areas, (b) teachers did not differ in their effects on the achievement of girls and boys within their classes, (c) teachers were consistent across years, (d) student cohort or class effects were independent of the teachers' consistency over the years. Consistently over the 3 years for both girls and boys, teachers were more effective in one curricular area than in the other, and with their classes in some years than in others. A further analysis that examined the achievement data for these teachers over a 5-year period showed slightly higher stability measures (Veldman & Brophy, 1974), producing more support for the stability of these teacher effects. In the Emmer et al., study (1979), adjusted achievement effects and measures of student attitudes were examined for two classes of mathematics teachers and for two classes of English teachers. For mathematics teachers, the effects of the teachers were moderately stable for both adjusted achievement and student attitudes; for English teachers, only effects on student attitudes were stable. In their review of studies of teacher effectiveness, Shavelson and Russo (1977) found moderately consistent and stable effects for teachers teaching the same lesson to similar students. In contrast, teachers teaching different lessons to the same or similar students produced much less consistent results.

Medley (1982) reports that the average correlation between measures on the same teacher for different classes is .30, reflecting instability in teacher effectiveness across classes. Medley also reports that teachers shown to be effective with high-ability students, in terms of student achievement, do not exhibit the same behaviors as teachers shown to be most effective with low-ability students. In addition, a report of the pilot study for the master teacher program in Florida also documented a relationship between teacher performance scores and different instructional formats (Teacher Evaluation and Assessment Center, 1985), where higher performance scores were systematically related to certain instructional formats.

Recognizing that the fundamental assumption in teacher evaluation is the stability of teacher effects, the paucity of support found in the literature is not comforting. Stodolsky (1985) raises serious questions about the consistency and stability of measures of classroom observation. An objective, reproducible, measurement situation is *necessary*, but it is not *sufficient* to guarantee stable estimates of teaching behavior across observations. Stability can only be seen across occasions if teaching is actually consistent across teaching situations.

Support for the stability of scores of teacher behaviors across contexts is seen in the Shavelson, Webb, and Burstein review (1986) and in the series of generalizability studies conducted by Capie and associates for teacher evaluation systems in Georgia (University of Georgia, 1987); Dade County, Florida (Performance Assessment Systems, Inc., 1986); and Texas (Texas Education Agency, 1987a). In these studies much of the variation in teacher scores was attributable to differences among teachers demonstrating desired behaviors, regardless of the subject taught, the type of observer, and the other factors examined.

If one accepts the assumptions that those teacher behaviors sampled by the system are associated with teaching effectiveness and that teacher behaviors are stable, classroom observation takes a central role in assessment and evaluation. The

teaching behaviors included in the teacher evaluation should be those that can be validated against student achievement. According to Medley (1982), the only generic set of skills stable enough across situations to make an adequate research base possible is that which addresses the maintenance of a learning environment. Other reviewers have been less restrictive and produced compendiums of teaching behaviors considered by experts, practicing professionals, and policymakers to be of value in the classroom (Brouillet, Marshall, Andrews, & Hunt, 1987a, 1987b; Office of Teacher Education, 1983; Texas Education Agency, 1987a).

Other limitations of structured observational systems as measures of teacher effectiveness include observer bias, insufficient sampling of teacher performance across subjects or other influential factors and inappropriately broad (or inappropriately narrow) focus in an instrument, making it impossible to report accurately performance for the intended evaluation purpose.

Validity. The primary, fundamental concern of an evaluation system is whether it is valid for making the kinds of decisions required. Because these decisions affect licensure, certification, retention, promotion, and incentive pay, the most rigorous guidelines should be followed. The concepts of external and internal validity that have been applied to experimental and quasi-experimental studies (Campbell & Stanley, 1966), appear to have more general applicability to other measurement situations. When evaluating the performance of teachers and attributing differences among teachers to differences in skills, rather than to extraneous variables, concern for the validity of an evaluation system is vital. Criteria are meant to ensure that any testing is job related, accurately represents the job to be performed, and can be used to estimate the likelihood of the candidate's success in the job. Because performance evaluation has similar impacts on the individual, these same criteria can provide yardsticks against which teacher evaluation systems can be measured.

External validity. This is a relative measure of the generalizability of the results of a study to other areas of interest. In terms of teacher evaluation, external validity can refer to the generalizability of a teacher's performance in a given period, class, and subject area to the teacher's performance in other periods, classes, and subject areas. If the evaluation of the teacher's effectiveness varies in different settings, with different students, or with different content, the evaluations cannot be used as a generalized estimate of the teacher's performance. Snow (1974) presents the following three dimensions of external validity, which have immediate implications for teacher evaluation.

Ecological validity refers to the degree to which the items studied represent the larger population of items; the more representative the sample, the more generalizable the results from the sample to the population. Ecological validity in respect to teacher evaluation would be satisfied when the teacher was observed or otherwise provided samples of work for evaluation in a manner accurately representing the entire domain of teaching. The assessment system should adequately sample the teacher's performance related to student development in cognitive, affective, and psychomotor domains, and to subject areas appropriate to the teaching assignment.

Population validity refers to the generalization from one sample to the larger population and usually depends on an appropriate description of the sample and population of interest (Snow 1974). In teacher evaluation, this means that the students in the observed class should be similar to students in other classes in the school or to other classes that the teacher teaches. This means that an accurate, complete description of the students must be available and used in the evaluation. Variations from the norm should be noted and adjustments made. For example, the classroom with a large number of mainstreamed special education students would be more likely to present a complex teaching situation than other classes in the school in which this was not the case. Evaluations of teacher effectiveness should take into account information about the classroom and school context.

Finally, *referent generality* refers to the "range of pervasiveness of possible experimental outcomes measured" in the study (Snow, 1974, p. 273). Much of current teacher evaluation is based upon behaviors identified by teacher-effectiveness research, and, as a consequence, other teaching behaviors are absent from evaluation instruments. Especially notable are the limited number of items to evaluate teacher effects in the affective domain, and almost complete absense of items to evaluate the psychomotor domains and in higher order thinking skills, as well as teaching behaviors associated with models of instruction other than direct instruction. Outcome measures in teacher evaluation should provide adequate samples of the range of teacher effects through a variety of measures, criterion- and norm-referenced tests or attitudinal surveys.

The Equal Employment Opportunity Commission's (EEOC) *Uniform Guidelines on Employee Selection Procedures (1978)* (1983) establish requirements for three types of validity that can have application in employee evaluation: content, construct, and criterion validity.

Content validity relates to the particular set of skills assessed in the evaluation and is often established by asking a representative sample of knowledgeable people in the field of interest to verify that a particular set of behaviors or skills is critical to success as a practicing professional in that field. This set of behaviors becomes the sample of performance indicators for which the group of professionals can be held accountable (Equal Employment Opportunity Commission, 1983). The political importance of establishing the job relatedness of the skills contained in a teacher evaluation system justifies an in-depth examination of the teaching process.

Establishment of both job relatedness and role delineation is fundamental to the content validity of an evaluation system, according to D'Costa (1985). The describing of job relatedness will result in a systematic delineation of functions of a particular job in terms of information needed to do the job, people encountered in the job, and resources used on the job. The description should identify major and minor functions and differentiate that job from other, related jobs. D'Costa states that roles are differentiated in terms of the (a) types of functions performed in the job, (b) level of responsibility associated with the job, (c) level of resources and specialized skills learned

through education or experience and used in the job, and (d) context or setting in which the job is performed.

Job delineation is a process of several steps. From an examination of literature, information about the job is located and used to present a tentative picture of the job. Often a survey instrument is developed, and individuals currently performing the job are asked to respond to the items in terms of how frequently the skill or behavior is used on the job, how important the skill or behavior is in job performance, and whether the skill or behavior represents an acceptable level of responsibility for those in the job. The results of such a survey are examined to insure that skills are appropriately clustered and that discrepancies between the literature review and job incumbents' descriptions are identified and resolved. D'Costa suggests that the next step in the development of role delineation is to secure the consensus of the leaders of the profession in making a judgmental validation of the major responsibilities and specific functions associated with each major grouping resulting from the survey. The product is a description of a competent professional: "A competent professional is one who performs her/his job functions/responsibilities with sensitivity to the job context/situation and at a level of sophistication commensurate with his/her education, experience, and resources available" (D'Costa, 1985, p. 9).

The recognition of the importance, from legal, technical, political, and social perspectives, of establishing content validity for teacher evaluation systems has been one of the major recent developments in the field of evaluation. Studies in Connecticut (Streifer & Iwanicki, 1985) and Texas (Barnes & Dodds, 1986) report on the development processes used to establish the job relatedness of evaluation systems in those states.

Construct validity. This demonstrates that the underlying factor, or construct, being measured by the evaluation instrument is the one intended. Construct validity is demonstrated when the decisions of multiple, trained observers judging multiple sources of relevant information on the basis of criteria and processes specified in the assessment system converge to define the underlying construct, or factor, being measured (Borich, 1977). Common processes used to investigate construct validity include factor analysis (Texas Education Agency, 1987a) and studies correlating results from an instrument that measures teaching performance and an instrument that measures a different construct (Campbell & Stanley, 1966).

Criterion validity. To establish criterion validity, the results of the evaluation must demonstrate that the decisions based upon the information gathered accurately reflect distinctions among individuals. One method for establishing criterion validity is to test the results obtained through the assessment process against the results from another instrument that measures the same skills. Assuming that both instruments are accurately measuring the underlying construct, the correlation between the teacher's scores on both measures will be high when other variables are equal. Where comparable measures do not exist, the collective judgment of representatives of the teaching profession may serve as the criterion. *In essence this means that those teachers considered to be competent or expert in the judgment of their peers should also be identified by the evaluation system as such* (Capie, Ellett, & Cronin, 1985; Texas Education Agency, 1987a). Whether or not teachers considered to be expert are in fact more effective in promoting important educational goals remains an unanswered question. There is little evidence that peer judgment of teacher effectiveness is predictive of student learning. Another method of measuring criterion or predictive validity is to relate teacher performance measures to measures of student outcomes (Smith, Peterson, & Micceri, 1987).

How To Measure: Data Collection and Scoring

Another fundamental question related to teacher evaluation is the reliability of the scores used to assess teacher performance. Once the focus of the evaluation has been determined, the data collection and scoring methods that are the most consistent across repeated occasions, across different observers, and, if overall performance is being assessed, across different teaching situations should be identified and employed. The consistency of evaluations is affected by many things, among them the data sources chosen to provide evidence for the assessment, the qualifications and training of the observers, the conditions established for the assessment, the level of inference required of the observers, and the scoring procedures chosen to report the assessment.

What Evidence to Consider. If the teacher's performance is the focus of evaluation, certain sources of information are more likely to provide useful, accurate information than others. The best sources of information should be used, but the assessment of some data sources is more difficult than others and requires more training for appraisers, which, of course, has implications for total program costs. Because of the limitations of various lines of evidence (Peterson, 1984) or data sources taken individually, the common practice has become to resort to multiple lines of evidence. The assumption is that a more representative picture of the teacher's performance can be secured by examining more than one source of information. Multiple lines of evidence using multiple methods gathered across multiple settings are required to generalize accurately from the samples of behavior to overall performance (McDonald, 1979; McLarty, Furtwengler, & Malo, 1985; Peterson, 1984; Shavelson et al., 1986).

In systems that use multiple lines of evidence, data sources are combined, in part or whole, in prearranged ways to maintain consistency of measurement across teachers. Among the data sources commonly used are classroom observations, informal visits by adminstrators, portfolios, interviews with teachers, peer evaluations, teacher tests, principal ratings, pupil evaluations of teacher performance, and evidence of student growth (Furtwengler, 1987; Peterson, 1984; Popham, 1987). According to Bolton (1986), such multiple lines of evidence, when used to establish a score in order to make a decision, increase the generalizability of the evaluation. However, when multiple lines of evidence are used, the appraisers' task becomes more complex and the training process more difficult. In some cases, the same teacher characteristic is measured in multiple ways; in other systems multiple lines of evidence are used to measure different but related characteristics. Tennessee uses a complex system of data sources, including low-inference observations, in the career ladder evaluation system; therefore, evaluators were required to complete a month-long training program in the initial year of implementation (McLarty et al., 1985). State evaluator training programs (e.g., in Georgia, Texas, South Carolina) include structured practice sessions and require the passage of observation exercises using predetermined criteria that insure higher levels of reliability for state-approved observers. As long as teacher performance is the focus of evaluation, classroom observation will constitute a major data source, if only because the public and the profession expect and support what appears on the surface to be the logical method of securing information for teacher evaluation.

Use of Multiple Evidence Sources. Special attention must be given to making the assessment technically reliable and valid to insure fair and equitable treatment to individuals. Training must be designed not only to provide information about the process to be used in the assessment of portfolio materials, for example, but also to include sample portfolios to score, followed by comparisons of results among trainees and retraining until acceptable levels of agreement are achieved. Furthermore, each line of evidence must be validated and data collection and interpretation procedures tested for reliability.

When student progress data are presented for evaluation, the evaluators must be able to assess the appropriateness of the measures employed to demonstrate growth (Brandt, 1987a). When the teacher is responsible for the choice of measures, the evaluator must assess whether the teacher chooses appropriate measures to assess student growth, given the learning goals and objectives, the curriculum, and the instructional strategies employed by the teacher. When the teacher does not have the option to choose the measures used to document student growth, the evaluator must also be able to take this constraint into consideration when judging the success of the teacher. It is readily apparent that advanced levels of evaluation skills are required for evaluators when multiple lines of evidence are used in teacher evaluation (McLarty et al., 1985).

Another consideration involves the amount of administrative paperwork and time required of both teachers and evaluators as multiple lines of evidence are included in the system. Portfolios can quickly become paperwork nightmares, and several evaluation systems have dropped the original versions of the portfolio and moved assessment of the targeted skills to another instrument or restructured the portfolio to meet these concerns (Barnes, 1987; Furtwengler, 1987; Georgia Department of Education, 1985). The interviewing processes included in the Georgia and Tennessee systems were time consuming and produced information of questionable value from a psychometric viewpoint. Both systems have been revised to eliminate or revise the interview as originally implemented (Furtwengler, 1987; University of Georgia, 1987).

Observers. The new role of the state in teacher evaluation has given questions of reliability, practicality, and usability more importance. Because of the impact of teacher evaluations, the qualifications and training of observers or appraisers have become questions of interest for the teacher. The consistency of appraisers becomes a paramount concern in any state-mandated system that provides information for certification or career ladder decisions. In fact, teachers' perception of the qualifications and skills of appraisers could be the most potent factor in their acceptance of the system (Barnes, 1987).

That principals have not been accurate judges of teacher performance has been well documented. It appears that they are either unable or unwilling to recognize differences in the effectiveness of their own teachers. According to Medley and Coker (1987), the correlations between the average principal's ratings of teacher performance and direct measures of teacher effectiveness are, on average, near zero. Principals judged their teachers to be far superior to teachers in other schools; they reported that 87 percent of their teachers were above average in providing experiences that resulted in students' acquisition of fundamental knowledge, and they judged 85 percent of the teachers to be above average in providing learning experiences that lead to good citizenship, personal satisfaction, and self-understanding (Medley & Coker, 1987). This bunching of scores for teachers at the high end of the distribution is consistent with another study of administrator evaluations (Wheeler & Knoop, 1982), which found that the correlation between principals' ratings and expected achievement gains for students in the teachers' classes was .20. The fact that principals did not vary significantly in their ability to judge teacher performance when student achievement was used as the measure of teacher success suggests that few of this group were able to rank teachers in effectiveness.

Increasing emphasis on administrator accountability has also affected the development of teacher evaluation systems. According to Buttram and Wilson (1987), administrators are increasingly being held accountable for the quality of teacher evaluation. These pressures have resulted in more structured requirements for training local administrators and more commitment of administrators' time to observing and documenting evidence of teacher performance, with concomitant effects of these new requirements and commitments on the administrators' work load (Ellett, 1985).

Others have questioned the use of principals as observers and appraisers because of the high potential for bias and their limited expertise in the varieties of instructional models used in classrooms (Scriven, 1981). In reporting the results of a locally developed teacher evaluation system in Utah, Peterson (1987) found that, compared with pupil reports, parent surveys, and tests of the teachers' general and specialized knowledge, reports by administrators were lenient, negatively skewed (bunched toward high scores), and characterized by low correlations with the other lines of evidence.

The decision to use external (off-site) observers or a combination of external and internal (on-site) observers has been one response to the question of using principals as evaluators. The decision to use external observers has implications for program costs and acceptance of the evaluation system by both teachers and administrators. As a consequence, several states have put in place evaluation systems that involve the local principal in the observation and evaluation process (e.g., Texas, Oklahoma, Georgia, Florida). Determining the optimal mix of external and internal observers involves both practical and measurement issues. In Georgia, where a team consisting of an on-site administrator, an on-site peer, and an off-site evaluator is used a number of studies of team composition have been done. Capie, Cronin, and Yap (1985) report that external observers scored more rigorously and more consistently than did school-site observers. However, although the addition of a second external observer to the team tended to raise the reliability, the effects were not substantial.

Although concerns about the principal as evaluator are not without merit, when large numbers are to be evaluated, the expense of outside evaluators must be weighed against other demands for resources. In some cases, teachers have expressed the desire to be evaluated by the principal because that person is more aware of the teaching situation, the school context, and the students in the teachers' classes. In fact, recommendations for revisions to the Tennessee career ladder system included the addition of the teacher's principal to the evaluation team (Rodman, 1988).

Conditions of Measurement

Among the issues to be decided for any evaluation system using classroom observation are the conditions under which observations occur and how the data are analyzed. Because the state of the art for performance evaluation is not as highly developed as for other standardized test procedures, much of the information available has been generated by states and local districts as they develop and implement systems to meet legislative mandates. Decisions about the number of observations, the number of observers, observer consistency, and announced or unannounced observations become important as states establish the conditions under which the teacher will be evaluated.

Observer reliability is an essential feature in any system used to assess teaching. Reliability relates to the accuracy of measuring any phenomenon and the extent to which differences can be determined accurately and repeatedly (Shavelson et al., 1986). The reliability of the system is determined by the consistency displayed by observers over observation conditions, and this consistency is affected by the number of observations and observers. One of the most common methods of assessing the consistency of observers over observations is to determine the level of interobserver agreement. High reliability, or consistency, depends upon high agreement among observers; however, high agreement does not guarantee high reliability. According to Shavelson et al., (1986), reliability coefficients are low, despite a high level of interobserver agreement, if there is little variation among performances of teachers being evaluated or if the teachers' behavior varies greatly from one observation to another.

Little empirical evidence exists to guide policymakers in determining either the number of observations or the number of observers required to reach an acceptable level of reliability for decision-making purposes (Rosenshine & Furst, 1973, p.

169). At issue are the conditions for gathering information that will give an accurate, consistent picture of teacher performance. A common solution is to conduct multiple observations of different content areas for each teacher over a period of time (Shavelson et al., 1986).

Bolton (1986) reports no evidence that observation periods of more than 30 minutes provided more valid or reliable data. Observation periods of less than 30 minutes did not provide as valid and reliable information as data collected in 30-minute observations. Rowley (1978) recommends increasing the number of observations, over increasing the length of the observation (from 30 to 50 minutes), when attempting to increase reliability of classroom observations. Likewise, increasing the number of observations was more effective than increasing the number of observers in a study by McGaw, Wardrop, and Bunda (1972). In a generalizability study by Yap and Capie (1985), multiple observers observing the same teacher on separate days produced higher generalizability coefficients than multiple observers observing the same teacher on the same day.

A related question concerns other conditions of observation, namely, whether observations should be announced. Several patterns are seen in systems in place within different states; in the Tennessee career ladder system, the visit of the first evaluator is announced, whereas the visits of the second and third evaluators are unannounced (Furtwengler, 1987). In the Texas career ladder assessment, as originally implemented, only the first observation by the second appraiser (who might be an external observer) was required to be scheduled by date and time. Other observations were to be scheduled at local discretion, and local definitions of "scheduled" varied from exact date and time to a broad 2-week window. In a study of the Texas Teacher Appraisal System, Andrews Associates (1987) found a relationship between the final evaluation scores of teachers and whether districts chose to schedule the remaining required observations and how the district chose to define scheduled. The more observations scheduled and the more closely the announcement of scheduling to exact date and time, the higher the district means for teacher evaluations.

In general, it appears that multiple observers observing on different days would be a supportable set of procedures. Although the answers to these questions have technical import, nothing generates more interest and emotion among teachers during the development of an evaluation system than these issues (Barnes, 1986).

Instruments, Scoring Procedures, and Standard Setting. Professional opinion regarding the best metric or measurement system to use is characterized by diversity. Generally, systems can be categorized as high or low inference, when high inference means that a system requires the evaluator to operate at a high level of abstraction. An example of an instrument at a high level of inference is the rating scale commonly used in locally developed evaluation systems. Rating scales combine statements about the quality of teaching performance with statements about the consistency of the teacher's performance at those levels. Rating scales are criticized for the vagueness with which their scale points are described, their lack of valid-

ity, and their susceptibility to observer bias (Soar et al., 1983). Much of the concern focuses on the assumption that the rating scale is "evaluation with measurement," because a separate data record is not usually produced. However, some significant improvements have been made to rating scales by the addition of behavioral anchors that clearly describe minimally acceptable teaching behaviors and provide examples of those behaviors (Capie, 1983; North Carolina State Department of Public Instruction, 1986).

Several states use a dichotomous decision-making process in which observers observe a class, produce an anecdotal data record, and later score the observation using a checklist of behaviors to make a judgment, based upon a preponderance of evidence, that the desired behaviors were present and performed at or above a minimum level. This type of instrument was pioneered by Georgia in its beginning-teacher program in the late 1970s. The purpose of the instrument was to provide information for certification decisions within a criterion-referenced decision-making setting. The instrument or adaptions of it have been adopted by several other states and are currently in use. Studies of the validity and reliability of the original instrument and its revisions have been reported (University of Georgia, 1987).

Two other types of instruments used in various states include the tally system developed for the Florida Performance Measurement System, described elsewhere, and the system used in Virginia's Beginning Teacher Assistance Program. The Virginia system is an adaption of the COKER instrument and uses the snapshot approach to classroom observation: the observer marks each behavior that has been observed during a 3-minute period. The process is repeated until seven snapshots have been recorded during one class period. The records are scored against scoring keys that combine various behaviors and assign weights to different combinations of behaviors.

The debate between those advocating low-inference and those advocating high-inference instruments focuses on the difference in the demands placed upon the observer. With low-inference instruments specific behaviors are defined, and observers are trained to recognize and to record their occurrence (McLarty & Rakow, 1986). Scoring occurs later by comparing individual teacher scores to scores of a representative sample of teachers or by matching the discrete observed behaviors (teacher asks lower order question) to more global concepts (teacher actively engages students in learning activities).

The decision of which discrete behaviors to collapse to create the more abstract concept itself is a judgmental process. The advantage of this process is that it can be reversed and each score on a concept broken down mechanically into its separate parts (Soar et al., 1983). This same advantage is perceived by some as a disadvantage, in that teaching may be trivialized to a meaningless level (Popham, 1987). The focus is limited to a numerical characterization of teaching, ignoring its quality aspects (how well the particular teacher demonstrated the various behaviors). The validity of these criticisms may be tested by studying the degree to which performance scores from low-inference systems predict student outcomes. Another concern is the nonpublic scoring key, which is similar to the answer key for a test. If the key is made public, teachers include desirable behaviors in desirable patterns to secure the best possible scores. This is desirable providing the scores remain valid. The problem is that if observers know the scoring key, the halo effect is likely to reduce the system to a rating scale that does not differentiate among levels of teaching effectiveness. If the keys are kept confidential, teachers are not likely to trust the system, which produces results through an unknown formula. Because of these kinds of concerns, the state department in Tennessee decided to make public the criteria upon which teachers were being scored after the first year of implementation (Furtwengler, 1987).

A similar issue involves the complexity of the scoring system. As the system increases in complexity, it becomes more difficult to explain to teachers, the public, and policymakers; and teachers are less likely to approve of the system. Several states implemented more complex scoring systems, only to revise and simplify them in response to voiced concerns (Furtwengler, 1987; Texas Education Agency, 1987b). It should perhaps be noted that it is even more difficult to explain how raters arrive at their scores. Curiously enough, this does not generally disturb teachers, the public, or the policymakers. Nor do they seem to perceive that the process of teaching is too complex to be scored validly by a simple approach.

With the prevalence of multiple lines of evidence used by several evaluation systems, aggregating data gathered from multiple observers or through multiple data sources presents another set of challenges. The nature of the decisions requires that guidelines be established to insure fair and equitable treatment of individuals. In addition, scoring procedures are affected by the kinds of instruments used for the evaluation process (Capie, 1983). For example, the FPMS uses tallies of teaching behaviors and scoring procedures that involve aggregating points for effective behaviors and deducting for ineffective behaviors. A total score is based upon the frequency and distribution of normed item scores on the effective and ineffective sides of the instrument. This allows the teacher to perform poorly in some areas and compensate by performing very well in others. In contrast, the 1985 revision of Georgia's Teacher Performance Assessment Instrument (TPAI) limits compensation in several ways (Cronin & Capie, 1985). Observers score descriptors, which are then aggregated to make indicator scores. These, in turn, are aggregated to make competency scores. Thus, for each competency, there are several indicator subscores generated by each observer. The first level of assurance occurs because teachers must demonstrate satisfactory scores in a number of competency areas (e.g., "Maintains appropriate classroom behavior" and "Communicates with learners"). A second level of assurance is provided because a teacher must receive acceptable scores for at least 83 percent of the indicator scores within a competency. An indicator is scored acceptable if a required number of descriptors is demonstrated (typically, three of four descriptors must be demonstrated). A third level of assurance is provided by the designation of some descriptors as "essential" (for acceptable performance on indicator). With a poor performance on an essential descriptor, a teacher cannot receive an acceptable score for the indicator, even though all other descriptors might have been satisfactory. With this data-aggregation procedure, a teacher can fail to demonstrate some essential descriptors and fail to earn satisfac-

tory scores on some indicators and still master a competency. The consequences are that teachers who have minor weaknesses in a number of competency areas are likely to master all competencies, whereas those with weaknesses concentrated in specific areas are not.

Few discussions describing standard-setting procedures are available to guide policymakers. A basic decision must be made, nonetheless, about whether to implement a criterion-referenced decision process or a norm-referenced process (see Capie, Ellett, & Cronin, 1985). Norm-referenced situations have no preset standard for making decisions, whereas criterion-referenced situations do have. For norm-referenced decisions, scores are usually ranked, and those teachers who compose a specified percentage are selected for recognition or reward. This procedure is often needed for incentive pay programs when a finite amount of money is available for distribution. This was the procedure used in Florida, where the percentile scores were used on the FPMS (or two other approved alternative observation instruments) in combination with subject knowledge tests to select a small group of teachers recognized as master teachers. For criterion-referenced decisions, the teacher's score is compared with the preset standard, and the teacher is automatically selected if the standard is surpassed. This decision is essentially a "go, no-go" situation and is most useful for decisions about certification, employment, and dismissal. This has been the procedure used for certification decisions based upon the TPAI. In a series of studies based on generalizability theory (Brennan, 1980; Cronbach, Gleser, Nanda, & Rajaratnam, 1972), Capie, Ellett, and Cronin (1985) state that the estimates of reliability for the evaluation system depend upon whether the model is criterion- or norm-referenced and present analyses that address both models.

A word of caution should be given here. Standard-setting activities that use pilot data, as opposed to data gathered when conditions are real and consequences are in place, can be flawed. Capie, Ellett, and Johnson (1982) found that data gathered under real conditions displayed higher mean scores and decreased variance than data gathered in a pilot study. These changes resulted in lowered dependability coefficients, which means an increased likelihood of misclassifying teachers.

Berk (1986) examined the most defensible methods for standard-setting for various purposes. Although a detailed discussion of that work is beyond the scope of this chapter, attention to standard-setting procedures is a critical and often misunderstood component of the evaluation process. Unfortunately, Berk does not address standard setting with the complex scoring procedures associated with many performance assessment systems. Further work is needed to develop guidelines for defensible standard-setting procedures that will enhance the evaluation system legally, politically, and technically.

Implications

Whether the system is norm referenced or criterion referenced has widespread implications for the philosophy, focus, conditions of measurement, instrumentation, scoring, and evaluation within the system. If recognition and reward of, for example, only the top 5 percent of teachers is the purpose of the evaluation (e.g., a state's establishing a merit pay system), several considerations follow: (a) The evaluation results should be normed, so that all teachers can be ranked according to the variables of interest and the top 5 percent identified; (b) the evaluation process can be measurement driven, with more attention to objective, standardized assessment and less attention to feedback and interaction between teacher and evaluator; and (c) the data sources can be those shown to be most discriminating and focused upon those skill areas in which differences can be efficiently detected in a cost-effective manner.

On the other hand, if the purpose is more heavily directed toward instructional improvement (the major concern of colleges and universities and often of school districts), other considerations are primary: (a) The evaluation results for an individual may be compared with either norm- or criterion-referenced standards of performance providing that the standards have been shown to be associated with measures of teacher effectiveness; (b) the evaluation process must be diagnostic, because the skills being evaluated are valued and are themselves subject to instruction (i.e., with appropriate, specific feedback the teacher will improve, given the opportunity to practice and the resources needed); and (c) the data sources should be broadly representative of the field of teaching, with enough depth to accurately identify strengths and weaknesses for the purpose of remediation, as well as to accurately estimate the level of the teacher's performance.

Although these comparisons are certainly not exhaustive, they do serve to illustrate the point that scoring systems do not operate in isolation and should serve the overall philosophy of the evaluation system.

An assessment system must be conceptualized with a well-understood purpose and a scoring system that supports that purpose. With that intention, the next concern is the practical: Can the system be implemented, given the limits of dollars and people's patience? The next concerns are reflections of the scores. The scores derived with the assessment system must be valid, not just validated by being literature based or having great face validity. The scores must be validated. Similarly, the scores must be reliable. It is insufficient to have objective agreement on whether or not a teacher has asked a question; the scores derived from the tallies of questioning behavior must be reliable. Finally, the results and the process must be credible. Care must be taken that the system is not abused or implemented poorly, so that the results are trustworthy. Furthermore, the outcomes should mesh with a commonsense knowledge of the candidates or applicants. Weak teachers should be so identified, and strong teachers should, too. No matter how much literature is incorporated, or how many validity coefficients are calculated, or what false denial probability is computed, if educators perceive the results to be capricious, the assessment program will fail.

EXISTING ASSESSMENT PROGRAMS

Existing assessment of teaching programs can best be understood by considering a series of related questions (Shulman, 1988). What does a teacher need to know? What does a teacher need to know how to do? What does a teacher need to know

how to do to teach fractions? What does a teacher need to know how to do to teach fractions to youngsters in an urban setting who have limited language skills?

Four major state and national approaches to teacher assessment policies have shaped, are shaping, and will continue to shape the development of programs in the 1990s. First were the efforts of the Educational Testing Service, with its development of pedagogical and subject-matter written tests designed to answer the question, What does the teacher need to know?

Next, the Georgia Department of Education added the assessment of performance (What does the teacher need to know how to do?) by developing an observation instrument containing competency statements derived from the literature and validated on the basis of surveys of Georgia educators and through numerous criterion-related validity studies. The Florida Performance Measurement System, developed in the early 1980s, only included behavioral indicators that had been validated in research studies on teacher effectiveness. Since that time the competency statements and skill descriptors in teacher assessment systems can be traced to either validated research studies or the consensus recommendations of educators, or to both. The Georgia and Florida systems are based on an assumption that certain generic skills include behaviors that all teachers should be expected to demonstrate in any course and with students of any age or ability.

The Georgia and Florida state programs have had a major impact on student-teaching and school-district assessment programs in their states and throughout the country. The TPAI has been emulated or adopted in statewide programs in South Carolina, Texas, and Mississippi and has been translated for use in Portugal, Spain, and Taiwan. College faculty and school-district principals and supervisors in Kentucky, Colorado, Washington, the Virgin Islands, England, and Portugal have received training in FPMS.

The fourth major effort is underway at Stanford University where the Teacher Assessment Project is developing prototype measures of teacher effectiveness (Shulman, 1987). Supported by the Carnegie Foundation, this effort is more comprehensive than the state efforts and is attempting to integrate the concept of instructional effectiveness with specific teaching topics and with specific students in specific situations (adding questions three and four to previous efforts).

Communication

Despite these major efforts, state agencies, colleges and universities, and school districts interested in the assessment of teaching have yet to develop a consistent way of communicating what is being learned about evaluation in one system to others who are interested or are developing their own evaluation systems. The priorities of testing companies, state agencies, colleges and universities, and school districts vary greatly, contributing to the lack of consistent procedures being used to assess teachers.

A small cadre of educators working full-time in this field have developed an effective, informal network. The American Educational Research Association at its annual conference and the Education Commission of the States at its Annual Assessment Conference bring many of these people together, and the papers presented there often represent the latest information on the assessment of teaching. These papers, however, seldom become part of the literature on teacher education, adding to the communication gap between those who are directly involved in teacher evaluation and those who are becoming involved.

In this section, assessment procedures reported at these conferences will be reviewed. With the exception of Shulman's work, which is still developmental, structured observation instruments are being used to assess prospective teachers, beginning teachers, and/or experienced teachers. Some of these agencies have already sponsored studies of their programs and have or will be making needed revisions. It is these efforts that need to be understood by anyone interested in developing a teacher assessment system.

Georgia

Georgia was the pioneer. Beginning in the early 1970s, the Georgia State Education Agency funded a series of developmental projects and, in 1976, awarded a major contract to the University of Georgia to develop the Teacher Performance Assessment Instrument.

The Georgia certification model, which became fully operational in 1980, requires the passage of a criterion-referenced subject-matter examination and an on-the-job demonstration of required competencies during the first 3 years of practice. The development of a state certification system based in part on successful performance in the classroom also forced Georgia to address from the beginning the possibility of legal challenges to its system. Because some people were ultimately to be de-

TABLE 32–1. Summary of TPAI Organization

Planning	Observation	Observation
I. PLANS INSTRUCTION TO ACHIEVE SELECTED OBJECTIVES 1. Specifies or selects learner objectives for lessons 2. Specifies or selects learning activities 3. Specifies or selects materials and/or media 4. Plans activities and/or assignments that accommodate learner differences	IV. ORGANIZES TIME, SPACE, MATERIALS, AND EQUIPMENT FOR INSTRUCTION 8. Attends to routine tasks 9. Uses instructional time efficiently 10. Provides a physical environment conducive to learning	VI. DEMONSTRATES APPROPRIATE INSTRUCTIONAL METHODS 19. Uses instructional methods acceptably 20. Matches instruction to learners 21. Uses instructional aids and materials during lesson observed 22. Implements activities in a logical sequence
II. OBTAINS INFORMATION ABOUT NEEDS AND PROGRESS OF LEARNERS 5. Specifies or selects procedures or materials for assessing learner performance on objectives 6. Uses systematic procedures to assess all learners	11. Assesses learner progress *during the lesson observed*	VII. MAINTAINS POSITIVE LEARNING CLIMATE 23. Communicates personal enthusiasm 24. Stimulates learner interest 25. Demonstrates warmth and friendliness 26. Helps learners develop positive self-concepts
III DEMONSTRATES ACCEPTABLE WRITTEN AND ORAL EXPRESSION AND KNOWLEDGE OF SUBJECT 7. Uses acceptable written expression	12. Uses acceptable written expression with learners 13. Uses acceptable oral expression 14. Demonstrates command of school subject being taught	VIII. MAINTAINS APPROPRIATE CLASSROOM BEHAVIOR 27. Maintains learner involvement in instruction 28. Redirects learners who are off task 29. Communicates clear expectations about behavior 30. Manages disruptive behavior
	V. COMMUNICATES WITH LEARNERS 15. Gives explanations related to lesson content 16. Clarifies explanations when learners misunderstand lesson content 17. Uses learner responses or questions regarding lesson content 18. Provides information to learners about their progress throughout lesson	

nied a certificate on the grounds that they had not demonstrated a minimum level of competency, the state knew that the system would face legal challenges. Standards for validity and reliability in teacher assessment systems were developed at that time and have formed the basis of other state systems.

Other states followed Georgia's lead, some adopting the Georgia model and others adapting it to their own needs. Georgia, however, was not content with its initial work. A number of studies of its system were completed, and a major revision of the TPAI was instituted in 1985 (University of Georgia, 1987). What changes were made? Why? To answer these questions, it is necessary to examine both the 1980 and the 1985 TPAI.

The 1980 TPAI included five data collection instruments: Teaching Plans and Materials (five competencies defined by 15 indicators); Classroom Procedures (six competencies and 20 indicators); Interpersonal Skills (three competencies and 10 indicators); Professional Standards (two competencies and 6 indicators) (pp. 8–9); and Student Perceptions. The use of these last two instruments was optional.

The 1985 TPAI replaced the first three instruments with the Planning/Observation Instrument, divided into the Planning Section and the Observation Section and containing eight competencies and 30 indicators.

Data are collected by examination of a lesson plan portfolio and ancillary material and from classroom observation as the plans are implemented. The organization is summarized in Table 32-1, in which each block represents one competency. The numbered statements are indicators that define the competencies. Each competency is defined by three or four indicators. Indicators 1–7 are scored on the basis of information reflected in the portfolio. The remaining indicators are scored on the basis of classroom observation. One competency includes indicators that reflect only planning elements. Five competencies reflect only instructional elements. The remaining two competencies reflect both planning and instructional elements (Georgia Department of Education, 1985, pp. 13–14).

The Professional Standards and the Student Perceptions instruments were retained; however, neither were at any time part of the certification process. Although the number of competencies was reduced, much of the original content was incorporated into the 1985 version. For example, competencies VI and VIII in the 1980 edition appear as competency VI in the 1985 version (University of Georgia, 1987, p. 12). Because of revisions in the discrete descriptors and the designation of essential descriptors, the number of ideas and the criteria in the 1985 version are greater than the total in the 1980 TPAI.

The major change in the instrument has been in the descriptive statements that follow each indicator and in the scoring key. In the 1980 version, the indicators were originally designed to be scored on a 5-point scale. The descriptors were intended to establish the scale points for each indicator (see Table 32-2).

Hierarchical descriptors were included in the initial development of the instrument. It was quickly learned, however, that some of the descriptors were not suited to a hierarchical framework, and early versions of TPAI began the conversion to discrete descriptors. The 1985 TPAI completed that conver-

TABLE 32–2. Sample Indicator and Descriptors from the 1980 TPAI

Indicator 7. Provides feedback to learners throughout the lesson
1. Accepts learner comments or performance without feedback about their adequacy.
2. Responds to negative aspects of student work, but few comments are made about positive aspect.
3. Informs students of the adequacy of their performance. Few errors pass by without being addressed.
4. Helps learners evaluate the adequacy of their own or each other's performance.
5. In addition to 4, the teacher probes for the source of misunderstandings which arise.

Note: From TPAI, *Administration and Technical Manual, Preliminary Partial Draft* (pp. 7–8), 1987. Athens, GA: University of Georgia, Center for Performance Assessment. Reprinted by permission.

sion (Center for Performance Assessment, 1987, p. 15). Every indicator has four descriptors. Typically, demonstration of three is required for a minimally acceptable performance on the indicator. Any essential descriptor in a set must be demonstrated before minimum performance level is reached (Table 32-3).

Five goals were pursued in developing the revised TPAI:

1. The competencies should be essential for effective teaching.
2. They should have a strong logical, practical and statistical basis.
3. They should be defined by three or four indicators so that the influence of each indicator is similar, regardless of the competency in which it is located.
4. Critical areas (particularly acceptable written and oral expression) should be elevated to competency status so that they would make the desired contribution to the certification decision.
5. The total number of competencies should not be a critical issue as long as these other concerns could be met (University of Georgia, 1987, p. 16).

Scoring. The 1980 TPAI included two types of indicators, hierarchical and discrete. For each indicator, a minimum acceptable level of performance was established (e.g., 4). Each

TABLE 32–3. Sample Indicator and Descriptors from the 1985 TPAI

Indicator 18: Provides information to learners about their progress.
a. Expectations about learner outcomes are communicated at the onset of activity (ies).
b. Specific feedback is provided to learners when their performances are inadequate ***or*** there are no inadequacies.
c. Specific feedback is provided to learners when their performances are adequate.
d. Suggestions for improving performances are provided to learners ***or*** none are needed.
Descriptors (a) and (b) are essential.

Note: From TPAI, *Administration and Technical Manual, Preliminary Partial Draft* (p. 18), 1987. Athens, GA: University of Georgia, Center for Performance Assessment. Reprinted by permission.

teacher was observed by three observers: an external data collector, an administrator, and a peer teacher (University of Georgia, 1987, p. 44). The percentage of the three data collectors' scores at or above the minimum level was established. Scores at or above the minimum were tallied as acceptable; those below the minimum were not. All indicator scores were expected to be at or above the minimum level for each competency. To compensate for observer error and possible inconsistencies in the teaching performance, Georgia required each teacher to demonstrate the minimum acceptable level on 75 percent of the indicators for any competency (p. 47).

The 1985 TPAI maintains the same approach to scoring, with the exception that all hierarchical items have been eliminated. Credit is given when each of the essential descriptors is demonstrated. "The 1985 TPAI was designed to improve clarity and reduce ambiguity, is more consistent with recent teacher effectiveness research, more complete in its assessment of instructional performance, fairer to teachers, more diagnostic, and easier to score" (University of Georgia, 1987, p. 12).

One major change in data collection was made between the 1980 and the 1985 TPAI: elimination of the interview. In the original edition, scoring for the Teaching Plans and Materials Instrument included the examination of an extensive lesson plan portfolio and an interview with the teacher being assessed. Revisions in the 1985 TPAI developed competencies and indicators that were not dependent upon an interview for scoring. Validity issues related to the structure of interviews were in part responsible for the revisions.

Extensive studies led to the development of the TPAI, and numerous studies of the existing instruments have been completed. A content validation study of the 1985 TPAI, completed by Capie, Howard, and Cronin in 1986 (University of Georgia, 1987, pp. 73–86), which surveyed 1,500 educators, supported its structure and scoring procedures.

Prior to implementation in 1980 there were numerous criterion-related validity studies of the TPAI that demonstrated a relationship between competency scores and learner achievement on measures such as teacher-made tests and California Achievement Tests. In addition, numerous generalizability analyses were conducted in field-test years and continued annually as the program was implemented. The generalizability studies were used to assess interobserver agreement, temporal stability, and internal consistency, along with their effects on false denial probabilities.

Concern for validity and reliability continued with the development of the 1985 TPAI. In a study conducted in 1986, Capie and Cronin (University of Georgia, 1987) examined the relationship between 1985 TPAI scores and learner achievement (criterion-related validity) in 40 seventh-grade science classes in a large Georgia school district. Differences in learner ability were corrected with a pretest, and the class mean of residualized gain scores was used as the achievement index. In regression analyses, every competency except one correlated significantly with achievement ($p < .05$). The authors conclude that "while not every descriptor had a significant validity coefficient, having multiple criteria enhances the likelihood of better prediction of achievement" (p. 155). This study is noteworthy

because of its careful design and the fact that instrument scores were related to learner achievement.

Noteworthy dimensions of the Georgia program, including the regional assessment centers, the use of external observers, the careful monitoring of implementation, the provisions for appeal, the large body of research done with the TPAI, and the provision for infusion of new ideas into the TPAI, have not been addressed in this review. The emphasis in this section is not on an individual program, per se, but rather on its contributions to what is now known about the assessment of teaching.

Implications. The Georgia revisions might offer direction to others who wish to develop assessment programs:

1. Interviews were eliminated as part of the formal data collection process.
2. Discrete, not hierarchical, indicators are now being used.
3. Only some indicators appear to be clearly related to student achievement. All but one competency did correlate with achievement.

Florida

No individual shall be issued an initial regular certificate until he has successfully completed a yearlong beginning teacher program or has demonstrated successful instructional performance on a department approved instructional personnel performance evaluation system. (Florida Beginning Teacher Program, Section 231.17 Florida Statutes, quoted in Florida Coalition for the Development of a Performance Measurement System, 1984, p. 32)

In 1981, a group of Florida educators formed a coalition consisting of Florida Department of Education officials, school district representatives, and a research team from the University of South Florida to develop a Florida Performance Measurement System to implement the Florida state law just quoted. Members of the coalition recognized that, without some direction, each district could implement its own system for first-year teacher evaluation, which could create chaos and confusion as a variety of standards were developed. The coalition addressed this potential problem as a challenge.

Fundamental to its efforts was the development of the volume, *Domains: Knowledge Base of the Florida Performance Measurement System* (Office of Teacher Education, 1983), which documents 121 teacher behaviors that have been demonstrated through research on teacher effectiveness to be directly related to increased student achievement and improved classroom conduct (p. 1). This volume was the first successful attempt to link research findings to teacher behaviors and then to the development of both formative and summative observation instruments. The low-inference summative instrument contrasts examples of effective and ineffective teacher behaviors identified in the review of research (see Figure 32-1).

The volume categorizes the research into six domains: Planning; Management of Student Conduct; Instructional Organization and Development; Presentation of Subject Matter; Communication: Verbal and Nonverbal; and Evaluation. Each domain contains sections on *principles of effective instruction*

Number of Students Not Engaged
1 ☐ 2 ☐ 3 ☐ 4 ☐

DOMAIN	Tot. Freq	Frequency	Frequency	Effective Indicator	Tot. Freq	Frequency	Frequency	Concern
3.0 Instructional Organization and Development				1. Begins instruction promptly				1. Delays
				2. Handles materials in an orderly manner				2. Does not organize materials systematically
				3. Orients students to classwork/maintains academic focus				3. Allows talk/activity unrelated to subject
				4. Conducts beginning/ending review				4.
				5. Questions: academic comprehension/lesson development — a. single factual (Domain 5.0)				5a. Allows unison response
				b. requires analysis/reasons				5b. Poses multiple questions asked as one
								5c. Poses nonacademic questions/nonacademic procedural questions
				6. Recognizes response/amplifies/gives correct feedback				6. Ignores students or response/express sarcasm, disgust, harshness
				7. Gives specific academic praise				7. Uses general, nonspecific praise
				8. Provides for practice				8. Extends discourse, changes topic with no practice
				9. Gives directions/assigns/checks comprehension of homework seatwork assignments/gives feedback				9. Gives inadequate directions on homework/no feedback
				10. Circulates and assists students				10. Remains at desk/circulates inadequately
4.0 Presentation of Subject Matter				11. Treats concepts - definition/attributes/examples nonexamples				11. Gives definition or examples only
				12. Discusses cause-effect/uses linking words/applies law or principle				12. Discusses either cause or effect only/uses no linking word(s)
				13. States and applies academic rule				13. Does not state or does not apply academic rule
				14. Develops criteria and evidence for value judgment				14. States value judgment with no criteria or evidence
				15. Emphasizes important points				15.
5.0 Communication: Verbal and Nonverbal				16. Expresses enthusiasm verbally/challenges students				16.
				17.				17. Uses vague/scrambled discourse
				18.				18. Uses loud-grating, high pitched, monotone, inaudible talk
				19. Uses body behavior that shows interest - smiles, gestures				19. Frowns, deadpan or lethargic
2.0 Management of Student Conduct				20. Stops misconduct				20. Delays desist/doesn't stop misconduct/desists punitively
				21. Maintains instructional momentum				21. Loses momentum - fragments nonacademic directions, overdwells

Observer's Notes: _____

FIGURE 32–1. Florida Performance Measurement System Screening/Summative Observation Instrument

583

TABLE 32–4. Principles of Effective Teaching (Research-Based), Florida Performance
Measurement System

Planning

Principles

If teachers attend to content, instructional materials, activities, learner needs, and goals in their instructional planning, then the resulting preparedness can increase the probability of effective classroom performance.

If teachers plan, then they experience more confidence, direction, and security in their performance in the classroom.

If teachers attend to elements such as arrangement of the physical setting, selection of basic texts and materials, and familiarity with social and academic development of their students early in the year, then a framework for future planning is established for the year.

Management of Student Conduct

Principles

If the teacher clearly specifies classroom rules, explains them, provides practice, enforces them and gives positive consequences for compliance, then disruptive behavior will decrease, on-task time will increase, and achievement will increase.

If the teacher demonstrates awareness of disruptive student behavior, selects the correct target, and stops it before it spreads, and offers alternative behaviors, then disruptive student behavior decreases.

If the teacher handles overlapping situations without becoming preoccupied with one of them alone, then withitness is enhanced.

If a teacher uses angry, punitive desists, then the deviant student may stop his or her misconduct but the ripple effect on other students will cause an increase in emotional tension and disruptive conduct.

If the teacher keeps the group alerted and focused on the lesson by creating a degree of suspense before calling on students to recite, selecting varied strategies for recitation and informing nonperformers they may be called on, then deviant behavior will decrease, and students will become more work involved.

If jerkiness in the flow of classroom work is minimized in recitation settings, then disruptive behavior is decreased if momentum is maintained and disruptive behavior is decreased.

Presentation of Subject Matter

Principles

If concepts are taught by providing definitions, examples and non-examples, and by identifying criterial [sic] attributes, then students are more likely to acquire complex concepts than if taught other ways.

If teachers analyze causal conditions and their effects, then students are more likely to comprehend cause-effect relationships.

If teachers use linking words to connect the conditional part of a principle to the consequent part, then student achievement in explanatory content will be higher than if the connection is made with conjunctions such as "and" or, even less effective, not made at all.

If teachers make applications of laws or law-alike principles, then student achievement in explanatory knowledge will increase.

If teachers direct students in using academic rules by describing rule circumstances and by providing rule practice, then students are more likely to comprehend rule situations and follow appropriate rules.

If teachers perform in keeping with the schema of evaluation and are rigorous in treating criteria and their application, then students will likely learn to be systematic in considering value questions and more likely to reach defensible value judgments.

Communication: Verbal and Nonverbal

Principles

If teacher discourse is thematically connected, vague terms minimized, and questions are asked singly and exactly, then student achievement will increase.

If marker expressions and techniques are used and main points are repeated in spaced intervals, then students will be aware of important elements of content and achievement will be increased.

If the teacher is zestful and challenges the students when moving from one task to another, then the students become more work oriented and less disruptive.

If the teacher's speech characteristics including volume, pitch, rate, etc. are not extreme, then student achievement may not be adversely affected.

If the teacher demonstrates positive non-verbal (body) communication, then students react favorably and achievement may be increased.

If slow-down of movement in class activities is avoided in recitations, then disruptive behavior decreases and student involvement in class activities increases. In seat work settings, avoidance of slowdown decreases deviancy but has no effect on work involvement.

If the teacher uses praise in the primary grades, even if it is general, noncontingent, or otherwise flawed, then children will be encouraged and their good conduct increased.

If the teacher uses praise in the higher grades and high school then it will tend to correct misconduct provided it is specific, low key, sincere or used contingently.

Instructional Organization and Development

Principles

If the teacher is efficient in the use of class time, then students will spend a high proportion of class time engaged in academic tasks and achievement will likely be higher.

If reviews are conducted at the end of the lesson and at weekly intervals (or occasionally longer ones), then retention as well as the amount of learning will be increased.

If the teacher begins lessons by providing orientation and direction and sustains the lesson momentum by providing clear explanations, checking for student comprehension of explanations, maintaining direction by transitions from one part of the lesson to another and providing practice in unison where it is appropriate, then learning will be increased.

If low order questions are used by teachers of low SES students, then achievement is likely to be higher than if high order questions are used.

If the teacher acknowledges and amplifies student responses, uses their ideas, but organizes the lesson around the teacher's questions, and maintains academic focus, then learning is increased.

If academic feedback is specific, evaluative, and/or provides corrective information, then achievement will increase.

If students are prepared in class for assigned homework so they understand how to do it, the assignments are short, students are held accountable, and corrective feedback is provided, then achievement can increase.

If students understand what they are to do at seatwork and how they are to do it; and if the teacher monitors their work, provides corrective feedback, and holds them responsible, then learning will be enhanced.

If practice exercises of appropriate length and spacing are provided and students are held accountable for on-task behavior, then learning will be enhanced.

Evaluation

Principles

If the teacher informs students of the purpose of the test, how the results will be used and why the results are relevant to them personally, then their test performance will likely improve.

If the teacher instructs students in utilizing the characteristics and formats of tests and/or test-taking situations to receive higher scores, then the tests will be more valid measures of what they are intended to measure.

If tests are administered in a physical setting which is comfortable and free of distractions and opportunities to cheat, by an examiner who is positive and encouraging, then students will have a fair chance to demonstrate what they know and the teacher will more likely obtain a valid measure of their achievement.

If the teacher is aware of the anxiety caused by tests in some students and refrains from using tests as a threat or from emphasizing the negative consequences of poor performance, then high anxious students will suffer less anxiety and perform better on tests.

If the teacher provides feedback to students on their tests, then motivation, learning, and retention will increase, and the teacher will be more able to adjust instruction to the needs of the classroom group.

(see Table 32-4) and *supportive evidence*, the research that forms the basis for the principles. Descriptions of the research studies include information on when the studies were completed, by whom, the number of students or teachers in the studies, and the levels of statistical significance obtained. In addition, a section on *extension exceptions* describes studies that do not support the principles. As a result, this report is a valuable tool for anyone wishing to learn what research studies on effective teaching have or have not revealed.

Scoring. Trained observers record data on the summative instrument by making a check each time a behavior is seen, with the exception of "Begins instruction promptly," which can only be checked once. A general rule applies that repeated behaviors in the same category are not checked until an intervening behavior occurs. The summative instrument can be used to evaluate the overall effectiveness of the teacher, but it can also be used to identify areas in which formative observations and feedback may be most beneficial to the improvement of performance. The FPMS is not scored by the observer; scoring is done by a central agency on the basis of normal distributions. Florida has completed major norming studies revealing the number of behaviors found among certain teaching populations

(e.g., beginning teachers, experienced teachers, teachers identified as superior). These norms can be used to assist beginning teachers in the state program in comparing their performance with that of one or more normed groups and can also be used to develop a scoring key.

Studies. Because this system was built on validated research findings, the FPMS may be assumed to have content validity; nonetheless, several studies have been completed on the system. Smith, Micceri, and Peterson (1987) report a metaanalysis of 5 FPMS validity studies conducted at elementary and secondary levels in science, mathematics, social studies, and language arts. Findings across these 5 studies show a positive and significant relationship between FPMS scores and student achievement and student task engagement.

An external review of the FPMS (Kay, Evertson, & Mitzel, 1984) notes four premises that underlie its development:

1. The system is based *solely* on what is known about demonstrably effective teacher performance: those teaching behaviors that have been shown through research to be associated with or able to bring about desired student learning and/or conduct.

2. Instructional behavior is the sole focus of the system.
3. With the FPMS there is no established or implied sequence or order in which the identified instructional behaviors are to be either performed or observed.
4. The system addresses competencies at a generic rather than subject or grade specific level. (pp. 2–3)

The review team strongly supported FPMS and recommended that the knowledge base and score norms be continually updated. They also added cautions about the use of the "Effective" and "Ineffective" indicators:

A separate but related matter about the setting of standards is important. There is a good bit of evidence to support the idea that the two scales of the FPMS are not equivalent scales and that cut scores should be set separately for each of the scales. The scales are not conceptually equal. One contains indicators of effective teaching and the other of ineffective teaching, and the items on either side of the scale are not necessarily the opposite of one another. Furthermore, it is not likely that the scores on the two scales will discriminate equally well between teachers who are effective and those who are not. The X (positive) scale scores seem to be better at doing this than the Y (negative) scale scores. In addition, it is likely that with training the Y scale behaviors will drop out of teaching repertoires, leaving, in effect, only one scale on which decisions will be based. It will be important, therefore, to monitor the standards to continue to insure that they are reasonable and valid. It will be easier to make adjustments and seems to make good sense to set cut scores for the two scales separately. (Kay et al., 1984, pp. 12–13)

Implications. The Florida efforts lead to the following possible considerations:

1. Continued research should be conducted on FPMS to maintain the recency of the content base and to monitor norms and standards used in the formative and summative evaluation of teachers.
2. The essential teacher's skills measured by FPMS should be studied in relation to higher order teaching skills once instrumentation is available to measure the latter.

Kentucky

In 1985, the Kentucky Department of Education initiated the Kentucky Beginning Teacher Internship Program and adopted the Florida Performance Measurement System as the instrument to collect data on first-year teachers. Two studies of the program have been completed, the first by Western Kentucky University and the University of South Florida for the 1985–1986 school year, and the second by Western Kentucky University in the fall of 1987. Several of the questions that were investigated are of direct concern to educators interested in the assessment of teaching (Pankratz, Leopold, & Metze, 1987):

1. How did the performance of elementary, middle and high school interns compare? Data for the interns were compiled by developing ratios for comparing effective teacher behaviors to total behaviors. Interns in grades K–4, (elementary) had the highest performance

ratios while interns in 9–12 (high school) had the lowest performance ratios. The high school interns made greater improvement during the school year so that by the end of the first year the differences between the elementary and high school interns were less pronounced. (p. 2)

The report suggests the following explanation.

The lower grade teachers begin their internship with considerably more professional education training then their colleagues in the upper grades. Thus, they would be expected to initially demonstrate a higher level of teaching skills in the classroom. The interns from the higher grades, on the other hand, may enter their internship year at a lower level of classroom performance, but due to the concentrated focus on the specific skills identified in the FPMS are able to show a marked improvement. (p. 11)

2. How did the performance of successful interns compare to the performance of unsuccessful interns as measured by the FPMS Summative Observation Instrument? A question often asked is "Can the Summative instrument help identify teacher strengths and weaknesses and can the instrument identify the potentially weak intern?" The Kentucky study clearly answers that question with a "Yes" (p. 13). Unsuccessful interns had performance ratios that averaged .31 lower than the average of successful interns. Successful interns improved their performance ratios over the intern year in 13 categories; unsuccessful interns showed improvement in some categories and actually decreased in effectiveness in many categories. (Pankratz et al., pp. 13–15)
3. What is the relationship of first-year teacher's academic performance to their classroom teaching performance? Scores on the National Teacher Examination (NTE) General Knowledge, Professional Knowledge, and Specialty Area tests were compared to scores on the classroom teaching performance ratios. Kentucky concluded that there is little evidence that a candidate's scores on such tests predict how the intern will perform in the classroom. The report cautions that the results do not support the conclusions that academic achievement is not important; only that achievement in one area is not related to the other. If both are important, then both need to be measured separately. (p. 15)

Additional studies completed on the Kentucky Career Ladder Pilot Project were designed to test the feasibility of operating the proposed career ladder and to provide a basis for making decisions about the future operations of a teacher career incentive program (Kentucky Career Ladder Commission, 1988, p. I-1). Based in part on the Florida Performance Measurement System. Kentucky developed a list of behaviors and indicators (Table 32-5) and completed a Domain handbook that included more recent research findings consistent with the Kentucky model. The low-inference data collection instrument requires the observer to tally the frequency with which the teacher demonstrates 23 interactive teaching behaviors (pp. III-12–III-14).

The pilot project in Kentucky reported several additional facts about the assessment of teaching. The coding of content included in the FPMS was eliminated because the data proved too unreliable. The remaining sections of the observation instrument revealed 14 scores that appear to be reflective of effective teaching behaviors: Questioning, Responses, Praise, Communication, Management, Time Management, Seatwork

TABLE 32–5. List of Behaviors And Indicators For The Kentucky Career Ladder
Observation Instrument

1.0	PLANNING
1.1	Identifies the content, activities, learner needs, resources, and goals to be covered
1.1.1	Teacher states one or more skills, concepts, facts, rules, principles, laws, or value statements to be taught
1.1.2	Teacher states the order and component parts for a series of activities
1.1.3	Teacher statements which focus on students' ability or achievement, background, or needs as a group
1.1.4	Teacher names the specific text pages and other resources to be used
1.1.5	Teacher states the expected learner outcome(s) of the instruction
1.2	Structures plans
1.2.1	Plans in phases
1.2.2	Prepares written instructional plans
1.2.3	Plans for short, lower-level activities
2.0	MANAGEMENT/STUDENT CONDUCT
2.1	Management
2.1.1	Promotes student attentiveness
	— alerts the group about possible performance
	— tells students to be thinking of an answer
	— alerts non-performers they may be called on next
2.1.2	Minimizes classroom management time
	— is involved in transitions from one activity to another
	— monitors procedures and routines
	Extends classroom management time
	— teacher is uninvolved in transitions
	— fragments the directions into a series of procedures rather than one set of functional directions
	— teacher engages in discussion beyond what is necessary for the students to understand
2.1.3	Manages overlapping events
	— teacher attends to the academic activity already underway and an intrusion by an outsider without becoming overly engaged in either one
	— teacher maintains the flow of the activity and successfully stops misconduct in another part of the classroom
2.2	Student conduct
2.2.1	Promptly stops misconduct in a positive manner
	— teacher stops deviancy from spreading to other students
	— issues a timely, accurate, clear and firm desist to deviant student(s)
	— suggests an alternative behavior
	— states consequences for continued deviant behavior
	Does not stop misconduct or stops misconduct in a negative manner
	— allows misconduct to continue
	— makes statement which invites student retort
	— expresses anger or impatience
	— implies feelings for the students
2.2.2	Uses authentic praise to reinforce desired conduct
	— praises student(s) for desired behavior
	— praises student(s) for compliance with classroom rules
	— issues contingent praise for completion of an obligation
3.0	INSTRUCTIONAL ORGANIZATION AND LESSON DEVELOPMENT
3.1	Efficient use of time
3.1.1	Attends to classroom organization routines
	— attends to routines with dispatch
3.1.2	Begins instruction promptly
3.1.3	Has learning materials organized and ready for use
3.1.4	Signals transitions from one topic to another
3.2	Establishes academic focus
3.2.1	Begins the lesson with a review of previous content/skills
3.2.2	Begins the lesson by going over the homework assignment
3.2.3	Provides an overview of the new content/skills to be taught
3.2.4	States the objective(s) for the lesson
3.3	Presents the new content/skill
3.3.1	Focuses on one point/skill at a time
3.3.2	Checks student comprehension before proceeding
3.3.3	Models the skill (if necessary)
3.3.4	Provides varied and specific examples
3.4	Provides student practice

TABLE 32–5. (*Continued*)

3.4.1	Asks academic questions
3.4.2	Corrects errors or misunderstandings
3.4.3	Praises specific superior performance
3.4.4	Praises group performance
3.4.5	Involves all learners
3.5	Provides independent practice
3.5.1	Provides clear directions for seatwork/homework
3.5.2	Circulates during seatwork
3.5.3	Asks student about or to show his/her progress
4.0	PRESENTATION OF SUBJECT MATTER
4.1	Presentation of concept
4.1.1	Provides definition only
4.1.2	Provides examples only
4.1.3	Tests the concept
4.1.4	Identifies attributes
4.1.5	Distinguishes related concepts
4.2	Presentation of laws and cause-and-effect relationships
4.2.1	States the causal relationship using linking words
4.2.2	Actively explains the cause
4.2.3	Actively explains the effect
4.2.4	States and applies the law
4.3	Presentation of academic rules
4.3.1	Describes the academic rule
4.3.2	Provides student practice
4.4	Presentation of value knowledge
4.4.1	Poses a puzzling situation or value
4.4.2	Develops criteria for evaluation
4.4.3	Gathers data for evaluation
4.4.4	Tests the value judgment
5.0	COMMUNICATION: VERBAL AND NON-VERBAL
5.1	Academic material is organized and understandable
5.1.1	Clarity of presentation
5.1.2	Vague words/discourse
5.2	Teacher enthusiasm
5.2.1	Smiles/gestures
5.2.2	Frowns
5.2.3	Lethargic
5.2.4	Monotone vocal delivery
5.3	Emphasis
5.3.1	Verbal expressions which indicate the importance of a particular point or skill
5.3.2	Non-verbal and visual techniques which convey to the students the importance of a particular point or skill
5.4	Challenges students
5.4.1	Verbal statements which pique student interest in completing a task
6.0	EVALUATON
6.1	Uses evaluative procedures to assess student progress
6.1.1	Uses in-class questioning to determine individual student progress
6.1.2	Uses in-class observation to determine individual student progress
6.1.3	Uses subjective judgment to evaluate the students
6.1.4	Uses test questions to evaluate student progress
6.1.5	Grades and uses homework and other daily work as a part of the evaluation process
6.2	Maintains accurate records of student progress
6.2.1	Uses records to assess skill and weaknesses of the students
6.2.2	Uses records to evaluate classroom planning and strategies
6.2.3	Keeps students informed of their individual progress
6.3	Uses student assessment data in future planning
6.3.1	Uses collected data to assess student placement
6.3.2	Uses collected data to diagnose and remediate individual student problems
6.3.3	Uses collected data to analyze and modify course goals
6.4	Reviews prior to major tests
6.4.1	Encourages students to have realistic self-expectations
6.4.2	Reinforces confidence in the students with positive reactions
6.4.3	Provides practice before a test

TABLE 32–5. (*Continued*)

6.4.4	Provides test-taking strategies for the students
6.4.5	Makes efforts to reduce anxiety among the students
6.5	Test administration procedures
6.5.1	Provides seating arrangements during testing session
6.5.2	Takes steps to keep distractions to a minimum during testing session
6.5.3	Monitors the class during the testing session to minimize cheating
6.6	Provides formative feedback of written assignments and tests
6.6.1	Provides feedback in a timely manner
6.6.2	Provides corrective discussions for incorrect responses
6.6.3	Provides feedback in a positive manner/avoids negativism
6.6.4	Provides praise during feedback

Note: From *Research Report on the 1986–87 Pilot Program* (Appendix III-D) by Kentucky Career Ladder Commission, 1988. Bowling Green KY: Western Kentucky University. Reprinted by permission.

Begins Promptly, Academic Focus, Present New Content, Effective Questioning Techniques, Provided Clear Directions, Was Involved, and Was Enthusiastic.

Kentucky also experienced restraints in establishing criterion validity (e.g., the degree to which results on the observation instrument are related to student achievement scores). The first problem had to do with selecting which teachers could be included in the criterion validity study. Statewide, only 36 percent of Kentucky's teachers work in classrooms without students who are identified as special education or gifted students. The percentage of teachers acceptable for the study was even less: only 63 of the 337 teachers in the study, or 19 percent, met the criteria for inclusion: (a) Teachers had to teach in a self-contained classroom; (b) their classrooms could not contain specialized students who, by policy, would be excluded from state testing programs; (c) teachers had to be responsible for teaching mathematics and reading skills, because the reading and mathematics subsections of the Kentucky Essential Skills Test are the only two for which the scoring has remained consistent over the 2-year period; and (d) teachers had to teach at the second-grade level or higher, because gain scores cannot be calculated for first-grade students (Kentucky Career Ladder Commission, 1988, p. ix-2).

The study of this limited sample found that the 63 teachers in the study who demonstrated "academic praise" in their interactions with students tended to have students who demonstrated positive gains in reading and mathematics. Students' mathematics gains were negatively related to teachers who demonstrated positive response behaviors. No explanation for this finding is apparent, other than the difficulty of using standardized examinations to measure teacher effectiveness (Redfield, 1987, p. 47). Kentucky concluded, however, that the Classroom Observation and Dialogue Instrument possessed content validity. The pilot study also revealed that the evaluation system was able to identify teachers of high quality and produce a range of scores to rank teachers from lowest to highest (Pankratz et al., 1987, p. 15).

Finally the Kentucky pilot project contained a special project on student achievement. "Steps three and four of Kentucky's Career Ladder Plan call for the evaluation of a teacher 'regarding the achievement of his/her students . . . based on a determination of whether or not the students have been achieving at the expected level' " (Kentucky Career Ladder Commission, 1988, pp. ix-2, ix-3). This project was designed to focus on outcome measures other than standardized tests. The study found:

1. That experienced teachers want a variety of student outcomes (e.g., outcomes specific to a subject matter area, such as mathematics facts; academic outcomes that cut across curriculum areas, such as writing; and nonacademic outcomes peculiar to a particular teacher, such as tooth brushing; and nonacademic outcomes valued by most teachers, such as self-confidence and self-discipline).
2. That there are desired outcomes common across subject matter areas and grade levels as well as outcomes that are unique to each.
3. That teachers use a variety of methods to assess these outcomes when standardized tests are not available. (pp. ix–4, ix–5)

Kentucky concluded that the student achievement project has the potential to develop a teacher evaluation system that includes student achievement data (pp. ix–8, ix–9). Whether that can be accomplished remains to be seen. The data reported, however, appear to have an impact on formative evaluation systems that will be of direct concern to local school-district administrators and teachers.

Implications. The Kentucky efforts support the following considerations:

1. Academic measures are separate and not (or at best are slightly) related to performance measures of teacher effectiveness (supported also by studies at the University of Washington).
2. One problem with using standardized test scores to validate teacher observation systems is the small percentage of teachers (in Kentucky, 36 percent) who teach in self-contained classrooms without either special education or gifted students.
3. The concept of teacher outcomes needs to be expanded and might be able to be incorporated into teacher assessment systems.

4. The domain "Presentation of Subject Matter" on the FPMS might not provide valid measures of teacher performance in the Kentucky field tests.

Texas

With the passage of reform legislation in 1984, a four-step career ladder program was established for teachers, with advancement based upon experience, additional training or education, and performance appraisal. The legislation, known as House Bill 72, requires that criteria and processes be adopted to appraise the performance of teachers and that the criteria be observable and job related. Each teacher was to be appraised by no fewer than two appraisers twice each year, and each teacher would be appraised by the same criteria and in the same manner, regardless of career ladder level. The legislation also required that the appraisal provide detailed categories and that ratings be provided for each category. At the end of the year, the teacher receives a rating ranging from 1 (Unsatisfactory) to 5 (Clearly Outstanding). A conference is required each year, and appraisers must complete a uniform training program and be certified.

The Texas Education Agency was charged with the development of a teacher appraisal system to be used for career ladder decisions, staff development, and contract renewal. During the fall of 1984, agency staff conducted a review of literature and surveyed other states where statewide appraisal systems were in place or in the development stage. Districts within the state were randomly selected to participate in a survey to establish the state of the art in Texas. An advisory committee was established to make recommendations to the State Board of Education and to the commissioner regarding the content, processes, and measurement procedures for the evaluation system. From

these sources a job-relatedness survey, which served as the basis of the content validation for the system, was constructed and distributed to a statewide sample of teachers. Items that were affirmed by the sample (n = 16,000) as being observable, frequently used, and important to success as a teacher were retained for the pilot study conducted in six school districts with 1,600 teachers and 96 administrators trained as appraisers. Items were also subject to a bias review by a group of minority teachers (Barnes & Dodds, 1986).

The appraisal system assumes that:

Teaching is an intentional act which has as its goal student growth. Teaching includes, but is not limited to, "planning, delivering, evaluating, and reporting of student learning of the essential elements" as required by statute and regulation. Although classroom teaching is the primary focus of the performance appraisal, no single model of teaching is mandated by the statewide teacher appraisal system. (Texas Education Agency, 1987a)

Appropriate teaching behavior varies according to the learning goals and the objective of the lesson. The system then assumes that some common teaching behaviors that can serve as areas of evaluation occur across grade levels and subject areas.

Scoring. For statewide implementation in school year 1986–1987, the appraisal system contained five domains: (a) Instructional Strategies, (b) Classroom Management and Organization, (c) Presentation of Subject Matter, (d) Learning Environment, and (e) Growth and Responsibilities (see Table 32.6). Each domain contained subsections called *criteria*, and each criterion contained subsections called indicators. For each indicator, a decision was made about whether the teacher had demonstrated the behavior, based upon observable evidence, at an acceptable level of quality and in sufficient quan-

TABLE 32–6. Texas Teacher Appraisal Instrument

Domain I. Instructional Strategies
  Criterion 1. Provides opportunities for students to participate actively and successfully.
    Indicator a. appropriately varies activities
        b. interacts with students in group formats as appropriate
        c. solicits student participation
        d. extends students' responses/contributions
        e. provides ample time for students to respond to teacher questions/solicitations *and* to consider content as it is presented
        f. implements instruction at an appropriate level of difficulty
  Criterion 2. Evaluates and provides feedback on student progress during instruction
    Indicator a. communicates learning expectations
        b. monitors students' performances as they engage in learning activities
        c. solicits responses or demonstrations from specific students for assessment purposes
        d. reinforces correct responses/performances
        e. provides corrective feedback/clarifies, or none needed
        f. reteaches, or none needed
Domain II. Classroom Management and Organization
  Criterion 3. Organizes materials and students
    Indicator a. secures student attention, or students are attending
        b. uses administrative procedures and routines which facilitate instruction
        c. gives clear administrative directions for classroom procedures or routines, or none needed
        d. maintains seating arrangements/grouping appropriate for the activity and the environment
        e. has materials, aids, and facilities ready for use

TABLE 32–6. (*Continued*)

Criterion 4. Maximizes amount of time available for instruction
  Indicator a. begins promptly/avoids wasting time at the end of the instructional period
    b. implements appropriate sequence of activities
    c. maintains appropriate pace
    d. maintains focus
    e. keeps students engaged
Criterion 5. Manages student behavior
  Indicator a. specifies expectations for class behavior, or none needed
    b. uses techniques to prevent off-task behavior, or none needed
    c. uses techniques to redirect/stop inappropriate/disruptive behavior, or none needed
    d. applies rules consistently and fairly, or none needed
    e. reinforces desired behavior when appropriate

Domain III. Presentation of Subject Matter

Criterion 6. Teaches for cognitive, affective, and/or psychomotor learning
  Indicator a. begins instruction/activity with an appropriate introduction
    b. presents information in an appropriate sequence
    c. relates lesson content to prior or future learning
    d. provides for definition of concepts and description of skills and/or attitudes and interests
    e. provides for elaboration of critical attributes of concepts, skills, and/or attitudes and interest
    f. stresses generalization, principle, or rule as a relationship between or among concepts, skills, or attitudes/interests
    g. provides opportunities for application
    h. closes instruction appropriately
Criterion 7. Uses effective communication skills
  Indicator a. makes no significant errors
    b. explains content and/or learning tasks clearly
    c. stresses important points and dimensions of content
    d. uses accurate grammar
    e. uses accurate language
    f. demonstrates skill in written communication

Domain IV. Learning Environment

Criterion 8. Uses strategies to motivate students for learning
  Indicator a. relates content to student interests/experiences
    b. emphasizes the value/importance of the activity or content
    c. reinforces/praises learning efforts of students
    d. challenges students
Criterion 9. Maintains supportive environment
  Indicator a. avoids sarcasm and negative criticism
    b. establishes climate of courtesy and respect
    c. encourages slow and reluctant students
    d. establishes and maintains positive rapport with students

Domain V. Professional Growth and Responsibilities

Criterion 10. Plans for and engages in professional development
  Indicator a. shows progress in completing professional growth requirements as agreed upon with appraiser(s), or none needed
    b. stays current in content taught
    c. stays current in instructional methodology
Criterion 11. Interacts and communicates effectively with parents
  Indicator a. initiates communications with parents about student performance and/or behavior when appropriate
    b. conducts parent–teacher conferences in accordance with local district policy
    c. reports student progress to parents in accordance with local district policy
    d. maintains confidentiality unless disclosure is required by law
Criterion 12. Complies with policies, operating procedures, and requirements
  Indicator a. follows statutory and Texas Education Agency regulations
    b. follows district and campus policies and procedures
    c. performs assigned professional duties
    d. follows district promotion/retention policy and procedures
Criterion 13. Promotes and evaluates student growth
  Indicator a. participates in campus goal-setting for student progress
    b. plans instruction in accordance with district requirements
    c. documents student progress
    d. maintains accurate records
    e. reports student progress at appropriate intervals

tity, given the effects upon student behavior and the apparent success of the students in learning activities. For some indicators, additional points were given for exceptional performance. If credit was denied or exceptional quality points awarded, the appraiser was required to record the evidence for that decision on the observation record. Points were aggregated within the five domains for four observations and converted to the 5 point scale required in statute.

For school year 1987–1988, several changes in scoring were made by the State Board of Education. Exceptional quality points were moved to the next level of organization, from the indicator level to the criterion level, on the recommendation of a panel established to review the first semester of implementation. In addition, instead of accumulating points within a domain and then averaging across domains, the board approved a total instrument score based upon the generalizability studies conducted with a sample of fall data. These studies indicated that reliability would be increased with this change (Barnes, 1987).

In a special session of the legislature in the summer of 1987, the minimum number of observations was reduced from four to two per year for teachers on career ladder level two or higher whose most recent appraisal at least exceeded expectations or a rating of (4). Each subsequent legislative session has resulted in revisions, both major and minor, in the appraisal system.

Studies. Major results of a pilot study were:

1. Although overall scores were very high, no substantial differences were detected between subgroups of ethnicity, gender, teaching assignment, teaching field or years experience.
2. The factor analysis confirmed the organizational structure of the pilot instrument.
3. Interobserver agreement achieved during training ranged from 87.5 for field practice to 81.5 for videotape practice.
4. Based upon the results of generalizability studies, each domain appeared to be suitable for differentiating teachers against a high performance standard when using multiple observers.
5. The pilot instrument was able to differentiate among teachers considered master teachers (based upon peer nomination) and other teachers.
6. At the direction of the State Board of Education, a quality dimension was added to the pilot instrument to answer the concern that the dichotomous scoring procedure did not allow sufficient ceiling to differentiate among teachers for career ladder decisions. (Texas Education Agency, 1987a)

During the pilot study a work sample was assessed, which provided evidence of the teacher's ability to plan and evaluate student learning and consisted of 2 weeks of lesson plans, samples of student work, and evidence of student progress. During the pilot study, the testimony given by participating administrators and teachers convinced the board to eliminate the work sample from the system prior to statewide implementation in 1986–1987. Criticism centered upon the paperwork involved

and the excessive time needed to produce and assess a work sample of anywhere from 10 to 200 pages. Based on the pilot study, several procedures were also altered by the State Board of Education. In addition to formal observations, the teacher's supervisor may make informal observations and document anything that would influence the teacher's appraisal. An additional domain was added to measure job responsibilities. In this domain the teacher receives credit automatically for the indicators unless the appraiser documents deficiencies. Finally, instead of equally weighting the observations of the teacher's supervisor and the other appraiser (who might be an external observer by district choice), the board decided to assign 60 percent to the teacher's supervisor.

In the fall of 1986, a reliability study (Texas Education Agency, 1987a) was conducted in five school districts with 28 teachers who were each observed by a team of three appraisers on three occasions. Based upon a generalizability study, reliability coefficients ranged from .85 to .88 when domains were the bases of the score and .90 when the total instrument was the basis of the score.

In the summer of 1987, the board funded three research studies of the Texas Teacher Appraisal System (TTAS). In a study conducted by Andrews Associates no differences were found among teacher scores on the bases of teaching assignment or teaching field; however, statistically significant differences were found among districts. In a follow-up interview, it was determined that differences could be consistently related to the scheduling of observations and to additional training for observers, usually by outside consultants. The more closely scheduled the observations and the more outside training, the higher the scores given in the district (Andrews Associates, 1987). A study conducted by Humble Independent School District investigated the relationship between residualized gain scores in reading for fourth-grade students and teacher scores on the TTAS (Humble Independent School District, 1987). No significant relationship was found; however, approximately one-half of the observations were conducted in classes other than reading, which could account for the lack of relationship. However, significant relationship was found between teacher score on the TTAS and teacher completion of training in the lesson-cycle model of instruction. Finally, a descriptive study of the teacher self-appraisal instrument concluded that teachers were generally unable to state measurable student learning objectives or match appropriate measures of student learning, or to describe reasonable procedures to enhance reliable and valid measurement of classroom learning (MGT Consultants, 1987).

Implications. The Texas efforts support the following considerations:

1. If a statewide system is to be implemented, a commitment must be made to conduct continuous research and development and to make appropriate adjustments after input from knowledgeable individuals in the field.
2. An instrument that requires trained appraisers to make subjective judgments about the quality of teacher performance can produce reliable results.

3. The conditions under which observations are conducted directly influence scores and the information available for decision making.
4. An appropriate balance must be established between the demands of the appraisal system and the demands of running a school; administrators need time to administer and teachers need time to teach, and neither has spare time to devote to extraneous paperwork that produces information of questionable value for evaluation.

University of Washington

The previously described state efforts have had a major impact on college and university training programs in their states. The development of research-based observation systems is also influencing college and university programs in other states. The Ohio State University and the University of Washington are examples of higher level institutions that are adapting their programs on the basis of what is being learned about the assessment of teaching.

Influenced initially by the work in Georgia, the University of Washington Teacher Assessment System (UWTAS) was first used in 1984 and revised in 1986 following a validation study. The UWTAS (Beat, Foster, & Olstad, 1985) is a low-inference observation instrument that includes three components: planning, instruction, and professional responsibilities. It provides data on 11 skill areas that are further broken down into 47 indicators. Four descriptors are provided for each indicator (Beal, Betza, Foster, Marrett, & Olstad, 1986).

The instrument was developed to make diagnostic, training, certification, hiring, and placement decisions about preservice teachers and for program research and evaluation (Beal et al, 1986, p. 5). Local school districts are also adopting or adapting UWTAS for their use. The handbook describing the system includes an annotated bibliography of supporting research studies. The scoring key asks the observer to make qualitative decisions. Individual scores can be reported as totals on the entire instrument or by each of the 11 skill areas. The system provides a computer-generated student teacher profile and can be used to evaluate both individuals and programs on the major components or skill areas.

Three studies utilizing UWTAS have been completed that add to what is being learned about teacher assessment. One considered the relative importance of the 11 skills deemed essential for good teaching. Three questions guided the study: (a) Do differences of perceived importance exist among the 11 teaching skills in the UWTAS instrument? (b) Do teachers, principals, supervisors, and professors view the perceived importance of the 11 teaching skills similarly in the context of hiring beginning teachers? (c) Do educators (teachers, principals, supervisors, and professors) responsible for different levels (elementary and secondary) perceive the relative importance of the 11 teaching skills similarly for all grade levels? (Beal et al., 1986, p. 2)

Two hundred and fifty educators were asked to group the most and the least important of the 11 teaching skills and also to select the single most important skill for the successful first-year teacher (Beal et al., 1986, p. 12). The 11 skill areas were not perceived as equally important. Three areas were identified as less important: Uses Evaluation Procedures, Maintains Professional Standards, and Engages in Professional Self-Development (p. 13). The raters' consensus was less strong for the most important skills, with five skills being identified: Reinforces and Encourages Learner Involvement, Organizes Instruction Effectively, Communicates with Learners, and Exhibits Appropriate Interpersonal Behavior. In selecting the most important behavior, the participants focused on affective behaviors that have consistently been difficult to measure. In addition, the respondents, irrespective of their roles, agreed on the relative importance of the skills, suggesting that a generic student-teaching assessment system can describe successful teaching behavior at different grade levels (p. 14).

The UWTAS also allows the university to compare other aspects of students' programs and assessments to the competencies demonstrated during student teaching (Olstad, Beal, & Marrett, 1986). To determine the importance of academic achievement in predicting teacher effectiveness, the university compared students' scores on UWTAS to their scores on the California Achievement Test and on the NTE Science Specialty tests. Student grade point averages were also considered. No correlation was found between any of the academic measures and the UWTAS score (p. 5). It is impossible to tell if the lack of correlation is a result of the selection of students for the College of Education's program or an actual lack of relationship, but this study again supports the belief of many educators that academic achievement and teaching effectiveness are different and that separate measures of each must be developed.

The UWTAS also provided an opportunity to examine the extent to which the skills included on the instrument were actually being taught in the classroom (Beal, Betza, & Olstad, 1987). A questionnaire was sent to all instructors in the teacher certification program during 1985–1986 for each course they taught. They were asked to rate the amount of coverage they gave to each of the indicators (p. 1). Two of the responses raise questions about the generalizability of the data (one person rated all items zero and wrote a note complaining about the incomprehensibility of the survey; the other person rated every item 3). Nonetheless, the elementary faculty appear to address the skills more consistently than do the secondary faculty; only 3 of the 38 indicators had a mean elementary rating lower than 3 (moderate coverage), whereas 42 percent of the responses from secondary faculty were rated lower than a three (p. 3).

Implications. These three modest studies suggest several concerns that are troubling:

1. All competencies and skill behaviors are not perceived to be, and might not be, equally important.
2. Admission criteria to a teacher education program based on academic achievement could have little relationship to classroom teaching performance.
3. Differences in performance between elementary and secondary student teachers (and, subsequently, in classroom

teaching) on these competencies might be related to differences in the opportunity to learn provided by the training institutions.

Stanford Teacher Assessment Project

The Teacher Assessment Project is developing prototype assessments of teachers in two areas: the teaching of fractions to elementary students, and the teaching of the American Revolution to high school students. These prototypes are designed to assist and shape the certification decisions of the National Board of Professional Teaching Standards funded by the Carnegie Foundation. The project is designed to move discussion about the assessment of teaching to a new level.

Our program . . . rests on a set of conceptions of teaching, teacher education, and teacher assessment. The research program centers on a conception of teaching as an activity that is more than behavior, more than the generic skills of pedagogy, and more than can be observed in any single setting.

The key words in our critique of existing forms of teacher assessment are content, context, and cognition. Most current evaluations of teachers grow out of a heavily behavioral and generic view of teaching. This view draws heavily on the effective-teaching literature, which has tended to be interpreted by policy makers and practitioners as asserting teaching skills are generic across ages and school subjects. Moreover, this literature has defined teaching skill almost exclusively in terms of observable classroom behavior. . . . Our research strongly disputes the sufficiency of this position. We argue that teaching typically occurs with reference to specific bodies of content or specific skills and that modes of teaching are distinctly different for different subject areas. The particular kinds of learners and the character of the setting also influence the kind of instruction that takes place. Finally, we believe that teaching involves reasoning as well as acting; it is an intellectual and imaginative process, not merely a behavioral one. (Shulman, 1987, p. 41)

The assumptions underlying the Teacher Assessment Project are that (a) there is a knowledge base for teaching; (b) we assume teachers use knowledge of learners and learning and curriculum and content in their teaching; (c) we do not assume that it is completely codified; (d) we do not assume that one can go to the disciplines and say, Tell us what teachers need to know; (e) we do not assume that one can go to researchers and say, Tell us what teachers need to know and that we will get answers; (f) we do assume that those people are smart about some of the things we have to consider; and (g) we do assume that we have to go to teachers and find out what wise teachers know (Wilson, 1988). And we know that is a very complicated issue.

Shulman describes the prototypes as follows:

Each assessment prototype includes between 10 and 15 distinct exercises, requiring from 45 minutes to three hours to administer. Each of these prototype exercises can potentially yield both a general pass/fail judgment and a series of discrete scores in the areas of content, process, skill, and disposition. Some of these exercises may be generalizable to other teaching areas; others will be quite domain-specific. Some exercises will deal with fairly generic teaching skills and understandings; others will focus on a particular subject. Thus a prototype is

far more than a single instrument; it is a set of about a dozen exercises designed to assess the content knowledge and pedagogical understandings and skills of candidates as these relate to the teaching of particular topics within particular subject areas. (Shulman, 1987, p. 43)

Shulman's work is in its preliminary stage. It is estimated that $50,000,000 in developmental funds will be needed to develop the first National Board assessment. Shulman draws a distinction between licensure, the state function called *certification* by most state agencies, and certification, which is a board function. The analogy can be drawn between the person who serves as an accountant and the one who serves as a Certified Public Accountant (CPA). The CPA status is reserved for accountants who can demonstrate additional knowledge and skills. Board certification would function in the same manner. Shulman also believes that the Carnegie-sponsored efforts will lead to reforms in teacher education and teaching. Undoubtedly, these efforts will have an impact; whether the reforms will occur is difficult to predict.

Implications. Shulman's work prompts the following thoughts:

1. Teaching effectiveness is subject and student specific. The state and university systems previously described assume that it is generic.
2. National Board certification and state licensure might not remain separate and distinct. If states accept board certification as an essential element in their licensure procedures, the mix of state politics and board certification could compromise Shulman's efforts.
3. These efforts will lead to needed reforms in teacher education and in teaching. One could argue about needed reforms, but present state certification efforts have altered teacher education programs and teacher assessment policies; the potential impact of Shulman's efforts would be greater than the efforts of any one state.

Conclusion

Developmental efforts in assessment and evaluation continue to evolve rapidly, so that what is state of the art today could be anachronistic tomorrow, and efforts to establish evaluation standards are already occurring (Joint Committee on Standards for Educational Evaluation, 1988). What will not change are some basic questions that should be used to review any assessment system that is developed.

1. What Is the Purpose of the Assessment? An understanding of the purpose(s) of an assessment system is fundamental to the consideration of any evaluation design, because the purposes of evaluation vary (e.g., to promote staff improvement, to eliminate incompetent teachers, to reward outstanding teachers).

2. What Is the Vision/Definition of Teaching Upon Which the System Is Being Built? To assess teaching, one should begin with a vision/definition of teaching. That definition is both personal and professional and can vary greatly from person to person or system to system, depending on the basis used for its foundation. That definition will not only be based on a set of beliefs about teaching but will also be shaped in part by a set of beliefs about evaluation.

3. Are the Assumptions Public? The development of an assessment system should begin with assumptions (about teaching, scoring, data collection, etc.). The system should be built to reflect those assumptions. An exercise that has considerable merit is to ask a group of educators, not experts in the assessment of teaching, to review the instrument being proposed and report the assumptions they believe were in the minds of the developers. There could well be differences between what was intended and what has been produced. This is an important element, because observation instruments used to collect data about effective teaching might take on a life of their own, existing for decades and being used by persons or agencies that have no idea about the original purposes and assumptions. To guard against this, assumptions should be presented, agreed upon, and disseminated with the instrument.

4. What Forms of Assessment Best Serve the Stated Purpose? *Summative assessments* lead to decisions, include the potential for passing or failing, place value on a particular action or combination of actions, and reflect the values of those who develop the system. Because these systems could lead to career-threatening decisions, the procedures must meet legal challenges. Careful consideration must be given to the number of observations, the number of observors, the length of observations, the management of the data collected, and the training of the data collectors. *Formative assessments* give feedback useful for the improvement of instruction. As a result, formative systems can be developed and implemented that do not address the legal challenges facing the summative systems.

5. How Will Data Be Collected? To assess teaching, some form of data collection system must be established. The most commonly used systems either provide a narrative description of the activities in the classroom or use a data collection instrument that is filled out by the observer.

6. What Is the Basis for the Behaviors Included in the Data Collection Instrument? Research findings have become the standard for determining what items to include in the data collection instruments. Although research studies have identified teacher behaviors that are linked to student growth, the research base is limited. Behaviors that are difficult to evaluate are also difficult to investigate in the classroom and, subsequently, difficult to incorporate into the research base. A limited sample of teacher behaviors results.

7. What if Teaching Behaviors Are Not Generic? If teaching behaviors are not generic (all teachers need to demonstrate a particular behavior with all students irrespective of the age of the students or the subject taught), the existing data collection instruments might be irrelevant. If, in fact, the behaviors included on the instruments are the wrong behaviors for some students in some classes, then the instruments could have a negative impact on student performance.

8. Does the Assessment System Include Some Measure of Student Growth? Teacher assessment systems that do not include some measure of student growth will always be suspect by policymakers. Most existing systems do not use measures of student growth. Educators can now describe, measure, and evaluate much of what a teacher does in a classroom. The extent to which a behavior has a direct impact on student learning, attitude, or affect is still being studied. What is known is that the same teacher behavior can have a positive impact on one student and a negative impact on another. Until the link between teacher behavior and impact on students is forged, the assessment of teaching will remain a developmental science.

9. Who Will Be Evaluated? Summative evaluations based on state-developed data collection instruments could provide valued assistance to beginning teachers but have a negative impact on experienced teachers. The skills and abilities of experienced teachers provide so much depth and range of possibility that the constraints placed on their behavior by a system designed for beginning teachers is not only an insult to a professional but also a force for limiting the professional growth opportunities of experienced teachers.

10. Who Will Evaluate and What Should Be Their Qualifications? New systems often require new skills from appraisers. When administrators have traditionally served as teacher evaluators, they have used systems chosen or developed by the local school district. These evaluators received little training for these systems. The new state mandates have included requirements for extensive staff training of evaluators. For any system to be successfully used, qualified and committed evaluators are necessary.

11. How Is Feedback Given to the Teacher? The most important aspect of any teacher assessment system is the impact on the teacher being assessed and, consequently, on the quality of instruction and learning that result. The effectiveness of the feedback is important if teachers are to accept and use evaluation results. Teacher assessment has tremendous potential for positive or negative impact on instruction. A 1988 report from the Arlington School District, Washington, on its Model Evaluation Project, addressed this issue:

> There are many commercially available teacher evaluation programs on the market and in use by school districts. Most of the systems used by districts for teacher evaluation ultimately can be reduced to some form of checklist or narrative statement. The critical component thus becomes the interface between the evaluator and the evaluatee. Trust and fear therefore become an issue between these two people, and it is at this level that a better evaluation system/process can be achieved. (Arlington School District, 1988)

It is that connection between trust and fear that ultimately determines whether the teacher assessment system has value.

A Final Thought

The assessment efforts since the late 1970s are now being challenged by the developmental work of Lee Shulman at

Stanford University. Rating scales (high-inference) were replaced by low-inference instruments, only to be replaced by a combination of performance measures including professional judgment (often very high inference). A research-based knowledge domain has been established and is expanding. Validity studies show at least some relationship between teacher behaviors and student achievement. Shulman's work focuses on the integration or links between teaching behaviors and the content taught and the context in which the teaching occurs. Although this work is exciting, it is too early to predict whether prototype assessment models will be able to be developed in any or all appropriate fields, whether the cost and politics of implementing the models will abort these efforts, whether the measurement knowledge and skills exist to complete this task, and, most important, whether the will to persist in a task that could well take 20 years will be there.

Assessment developments are, however, not limited to Shulman's efforts. The Educational Testing Service has announced plans for radically different tests to license new teachers. The new examinations, to be available by 1992, will assess (a) knowledge of basic skills after the student's sophomore year, (b) knowledge of subject matter and principles of teaching at the completion of the teacher-preparation program, and (c) ability to teach a subject in the classroom. In addition to traditional paper-and-pencil examinations, the assessment formats could include "live exercises, computer simulations, in-class observations of the candidate's performance, and portfolios documenting the teacher's work" (Olson, November 2, 1988).

Written assessments of pedagogical knowledge also need to move beyond the ability to answer multiple-choice questions. Connecticut is developing videotapes of teaching sequences to use in its state testing program. Washington and Minnesota will include essay examinations (comparable to those used on the bar examination) to determine the extent to which prospective teachers are able to integrate their knowledge into the analyses of simulated teaching problems.

It is too easy to forget that assessment of teaching occurs daily in schools across the United States, with little consideration given to all that has been learned in the efforts discussed in this chapter. A major task is to bring these two efforts together. Knowledge about the assessment of teaching has grown enormously since the late 1970s. Only with time will educators know whether they have taken the first step or traveled the first mile. In either case, more work lies ahead than behind.

References

Andrews Associates. (1987). *A study of the effects of school level, subject taught, and other characteristics on the domain and criterion scores of the Texas Teacher Appraisal System.* Olympia, WA: Author.

Arlington School District, #16. (1988). *Model evaluation programs report of the Arlington Instructional Model.* Arlington, WA: Author.

Association of Teacher Educators. (1988). *Teacher assessment.* Reston, VA: Author.

Barber, L., & Klein, K. (1983). Merit pay and teacher evaluation. *Phi Delta Kappan.* 65(4), 247–251.

Barnes, S. (1986). Assessment issues in initial year of teaching programs. In G. Griffin & S. Milles (Eds.), *The first years of teaching: Background papers and a proposal* (pp. 115–128). Chicago: University of Illinois at Chicago.

Barnes, S. (1987 April). *The development of the Texas teacher appraisal system.* Paper presented at the annual meeting of the American Educational Research Association, Washington, DC.

Barnes, S., & Dodds, J. (1986, April). *Establishing content validity through a job-relatedness survey.* Paper presented at the annual meeting of the American Educational Research Association, San Francisco.

Beal, J. L., Betza, E., Foster, C. D., Marrett, V., & Olstad, R. G. (1986). *Relative importance of basic teaching skills* (Research Report 87-1). Seattle: University of Washington.

Beal, J. L., Betza, R. E., & Olstad, R. G. (1987). *Survey of faculty on coverage of University of Washington teacher assessment system indicators* (Research Report 87-4). Seattle: University of Washington.

Beal, J. L., Foster, C. D., & Olstad, R. G. (1985). *Handbook and users manual (2nd ed.).* Seattle: University of Washington.

Berk, R. (1986). A consumer's guide to setting performance standards on criterion-referenced tests. *Review of Educational Research, 56,* 137–172.

Bolton, D. (1986). *Review of research and literature concerning teacher evaluation process.* Seattle: University of Washington, Center for the Assessment of Administrative Performance.

Borich, G. (1977). *The appraisal of teaching: Concepts and process.* Reading, MA: Addison-Wesley.

Brandt, R. (1987a, April). *Improving the quality of student outcome data used in career ladder promotion decisions.* Paper presented at the annual meeting of the American Educational Research Association, Washington, DC.

Brandt, R. (1987b). On teacher evaluation: A conversation with Tom McGreal. *Educational Leadership.* 44(7), 20–24.

Brennan, R. L. (1980). Applications of generalizability theory. In R. A. Berk (Ed.), *Criterion-referenced measurement: State of the art.* Baltimore: Johns Hopkins University Press.

Brophy, J. (1972). Stability of teacher effectiveness. *American Educational Research Journal, 10,* 245–252.

Brouillet, F., Marshall, C., Andrews, T., & Hunt, W. (1987a). *Teaching and learning in the affective domain: A review of the literature.* Olympia, WA: Superintendent of Public Instruction.

Brouillet, F., Marshall, C., Andrews, T., & Hunt, W. (1987b). *Teaching and learning in the cognitive domain: A review of the literature.* Olympia, WA: Superintendent of Public Instruction.

Buttram, J., & Wilson, B. (1987). Promising trends in teacher evaluation. *Educational leadership.* 44(7), 5–6.

Campbell, D., & Stanley, J. (1966). *Experimental and quasi-experimental designs for research.* Chicago: Rand McNally.

Capie, W. (1983, April). *Methodological issues in combining teacher performance data for decision-making.* Paper presented at the annual meeting of the American Educational Research Association, Montreal.

Capie, W., Cronin, L., & Yap, K. C. (1985, April). *The influence of observer type on the assessment decision and its reliability.* Paper presented at the annual meeting of the American Educational Research Association, Chicago.

Capie, W., Ellett, C., & Cronin, L. (1985). *Assessing meritorious* teacher performance: Reliability, decision-making and standards setting procedures. Paper presented at the annual meeting of the American Educational Research Association, Chicago.

Capie, W., Ellett, C., & Johnson (1982, March). *The effects of assessment demand characteristics on the dependability of teacher performance measures.* Paper presented at the annual meeting of the American Educational Research Association, New York.

Carey, L. (1984). *State-level teacher performance evaluation policies.* Syracuse, NY: Syracuse University, School of Education, National Dissemination Center.

Cronbach, L. J., Gleser, G. C., Nanda, H., & Rajaratnam, N. (1972). *The dependability of behavioral measurements: The theory of generalizability for scores and profiles.* New York: Wiley.

Cronin, L., & Capie, W. (1985, April). *The influence of scoring procedures on assessment decisions and their reliability.* Paper presented at the annual meeting of the American Educational Research Association, Chicago.

D'Costa, A. (1985, April). *Documenting the job-relevance of certification and licensure examinations using job analysis.* Paper presented at the annual meeting of the American Educational Research Association, Chicago.

Darling-Hammond. L., Wise, A., & Pease, S. (1983). Teacher evaluation in the organizational context: A review of the literature. *Review of Educational Research, 53,* 285–328.

Ellett, C. (1985). Emerging teacher assessment practices: Implications for the instructional supervision role of school principals. In W. Greenfield (Ed.), *Instructional leadership: Concepts and controversies* (pp. 302–327). Boston: Allyn & Bacon.

Emmer, E., Evertson, C., & Brophy, J. (1979). Stability of teacher effects in junior high classrooms. *American Educational Research Journal, 16,* 71–75.

Equal Employment Opportunity Commission. (1983). Uniform guidelines on employee selection procedures (1978). *Federal Register, 29,* Sec. 1607, 150–177.

Florida Coalition for the Development of a Performance Measurement System (1984). *Handbook for the beginning teacher's support staff.* Tallahassee, FL: Office of Teacher Education, Certification and Inservice Staff Development.

Furtwengler, C. (1987). Lessons from Tennessee's career ladder program. *Educational Leadership, 44*(7), 66–69.

Georgia Department of Education. (1985). *Teacher performance assessment instruments.* Atlanta: Author.

Holdzkom, D. (1987). Appraising teacher performance in North Carolina. *Educational Leadership. 44*(7), 40–44.

Humble Independent School District. (1987). *Relationship between the progress of fourth grade students in reading and the TTAS scores of their teachers* (Final report submitted to the Texas Education Agency, Austin, Texas).

Joint Committee on Standards for Educational Evaluation. (1988). *The personnel evaluation standards.* Newbury Park, CA: Sage.

Kay, P. M., Evertson, C., & Mitzel, H. (1984). *Review of the Florida performance measurement system* (Report prepared for the Office of Teacher Education, Certification, and Inservice Staff Development. Tallahassee, FL).

Kentucky Career Ladder Commission. (1988). *Research report on the 1986–87 pilot program* (Submitted to Governor Martha Layne Collins). Bowling Green, KY: Western Kentucky University.

McDonald, J. (1979). Evaluation of teaching: Purpose, context, and problems. In W. Duckett (Ed.), *Planning for the evaluation of teaching.* Bloomington, IN: Phi Delta Kappa.

McGaw, B., Wardrop, J. L., & Bunda, M. A. (1972). Classroom observation schemes: Where are the errors? *American Educational Research Journal, 9,* 13–27.

McLarty, J., Furtwengler, C., & Malo, E. (1985). *Using multiple data sources in teacher evaluation.* Paper presented at the annual meeting of the National Council on Measurement in Education, Chicago.

McLarty, J., & Rakow, E. (1986). *Low-inference observation in the evaluation of Tennessee's career ladder teachers.* Paper presented at the annual meeting of the National Council on Measurement in Education, San Francisco. (ERIC Document Reproduction Service No. ED 274 671)

Medley, D. M. (1982). *Teacher competency testing and the teacher educator.* Charlottesville, VA: University of Virginia, Bureau of Educational Research.

Medley, D. (1985, April). *Issues and problems in the validation of teaching and teacher professional behaviors.* Paper presented at the annual meeting of the American Educational Research Association, Chicago.

Medley, D., & Coker, H. (1987). The accuracy of principals' judgments of teacher performance. *Journal of Educational Research, 80,* 242–247.

Medley, D., Coker, H., & Soar, R. (1984). *Measurement-based evaluation of teacher performance: An empirical approach.* New York: Longman.

MGT Consultants. (1987). *Evaluation of teacher self-appraisal practices* (Final report submitted to the Texas Education Agency, Austin, Texas).

North Carolina State Department of Public Instruction. (1986). *Teacher performance appraisal system: The standards and processes for use.* Raleigh, NC: Author. (ERIC Document Reproduction Service No. ED 271 453)

Office of Teacher Education, Certification and Inservice Staff Development (1983). *Domains: Knowledge base of the Florida performance measurement system* (p. 8). Tallahassee, FL: Author.

Olson, L. (1988, November 2). Different tests of teaching skill planned by firm. *Education Week,* 1, 27.

Olstad, R. G., Beal, J. L., Marrett, A. V. (1986). *Predictive validity of GPA, CAT, and NTE science specialty tests on scores of a performance based student teaching evaluation instrument* (Research Report 86-2). Seattle: University of Washington, Teacher Education Research Center.

Pankratz, R., Leopold, G., & Metze, L. (1987). *The classroom performance of Kentucky beginning teacher interns: A research report.* Prepared by the Kentucky Department of Education with the assistance of Western Kentucky University. Bowling Green, KY: Western Kentucky University.

Performance Assessment Systems. (1986). *Teacher assessment and development assistance: Administration and technical manual* (pp. 59–68). Athens, GA: Author.

Peterson, K. (1984). Methodological problems in teacher evaluation. *Journal of Research and Development in Education, 17*(4), 62–70.

Peterson, K. (1987). Teacher evaluation with multiple and variable lines of evidence. *American Educational Research Journal, 24,* 311–317.

Popham, J. (1987) The shortcomings of champagne teacher evaluations. *Journal of Personnel Evaluation in Education, 1,* 25–28.

Redfield, D. L. (1987). *Special project on expected student achievement: Technical report.* Bowling Green, KY: Western Kentucky University.

Rodman, B. (1988, February 10). Tennessee may drop part of career ladder system. *Education Week,* 10–11.

Rosenshine, B., & Furst, N. (1973). The use of direct observation to study teaching. In R. M. W. Travers (Ed.), *Second handbook of research on teaching* (pp. 122–183). Chicago: Rand McNally.

Rowley, (1978). The relationship of reliability in classroom research to the amount of observation: An extension of the Spearman-Brown formula. *Journal of Educational Measurement, 15*(3), 165–180.

Scriven, M. (1981). Summative teacher evaluation. In J. Millman (Ed.), *Handbook of teacher evaluation* (pp. 244–271). Beverly Hills, CA: Sage.

Shavelson, R., & Russo, N. (1977). Generalizability of measures of teacher effectiveness. *Educational Research, 19*, 171–183.

Shavelson, R. I., Webb, N. M., & Burstein, L. (1986). Measurement of teaching. In M. C. Wittrock (Ed.), *Handbook of research on teaching* (3rd ed., pp. 50–91). New York: Macmillan.

Shaw, F. W., III. (1985). A summary of legal implications of teacher evaluation for merit pay and a model plan. *Educational Administration Quarterly, 21*, 51–69.

Shulman, L. (1987). Assessment for teaching: An initiative for the profession. *Phi Delta Kappan, 69*(1), 38–44.

Shulman, L. (1988, March). Speech presented at the meeting of the New Teacher Assessment and Support Consortium, Stanford, CA.

Smith, B. O., Micceri, T., & Peterson, D. (1987). *Florida performance measurement system predictive validity report: A meta analysis of five predictive validity studies.* Tampa, FL: University of South Florida.

Smith, B. O., Peterson, D., & Micceri, T. (1987). Evaluation and professional improvement aspects of the Florida performance measurement system. *Educational Leadership, 44*, 16–19.

Snow, R. (1974). Representative and quasi representative designs for research on teaching. *Review of Educational Research, 44*,(3) 265–291.

Soar, R. S., Medley, D. M., & Coker, H. (1983). Teacher evaluation: A critique of currently used methods. *Phi Delta Kappan, 65*(4), 239–246.

Southern Region Education Board. (1987). *Career ladder clearinghouse.* Atlanta: Author.

Stiggins, R. (1986). Teacher evaluation: Accountability and growth system—different purposes. *NASSP Bulletin, 70*(490), 51–58.

Stodolsky, S. (1985). Teacher evaluation: The limits of looking. *Educational Research, 13*(9), 11–18.

Steifer, P. A., & Iwanicki, E. (1985, April). *The validation of beginning teacher competencies in Connecticut.* Paper presented at the annual meeting of the American Educational Research Association, Chicago. (ERIC Document Reproduction Service No. ED 265 148)

Teacher Evaluation and Assessment Center. (1985). *Report for 1984-85.* Tampa, FL: University of South Florida. (ERIC Document Reproduction Service No. ED 266 089)

Texas Education Agency. (1987a). *Final report of the pilot study for the Texas teacher appraisal system.* Austin, TX: Author.

Texas Education Agency. (1987b). *Texas teacher appraisal system Teacher orientation manual.* Austin, TX: Author.

University of Georgia, Center for Performance Assessment. (1987). *TPAI, administration and technical manual, preliminary partial draft.* Athens, GA: Author.

U.S. Department of Education, Office of Educational Research and Improvement. (1987). *What's happening in teacher testing.* Washington, DC: Author.

Veldman, D., & Brophy, J. (1974). Measuring teacher effect on pupil achievement. *Journal of Educational Psychology, 66*, 319–324.

Wheeler, A., & Knoop, H. (1982). Self, teacher and faculty assessments of student teaching performance. *Journal of Educational Research, 75*, 178–181.

Wilson, S. (1988, April). *New forms of assessment.* Paper presented at the annual meeting of the American Educational Research Association, New Orleans.

Wise, A., Darling-Hammond, L., McLaughlin, M., & Bernstein, H. (1984). *Teacher evaluation: A study of effective practices.* Santa Monica, CA: RAND Corporation.

Yap, K. C., & Capie, W. (1985, April). *The influence of same day or separate day observations on the reliability of assessment data.* Paper presented at the annual meeting of the American Educational Research Association, Chicago.

·33·

EVALUATION OF PRESERVICE TEACHER
EDUCATION PROGRAMS

Gary R. Galluzzo and James R. Craig
WESTERN KENTUCKY UNIVERSITY

Historically, teacher educators have used subjective judgments to make decisions regarding the effectiveness of the programs they offer to prospective teachers. However, beginning with the publication of *An Illustrated Model for the Evaluation of Teacher Education Graduates* (Sandefur, 1970), interest in gathering objective data about students and programs in teacher education began to gain momentum. Since 1970 there has been a small but growing interest among teacher educators in collecting data on their programs. The purpose of this chapter is to describe the rise of educational evaluation and its applications and contributions to teacher education.

This is not a chapter on evaluation methodology or data analysis. Rather, the intent here is to review the current state of practice in the application of evaluation methods to programs of preservice teacher education. The scope of the chapter is limited to preservice teacher education because the lion's share of the work conducted to date has focused on the preservice curriculum. However, our comments about preservice teacher education program evaluation also apply to graduate programs, and the reader is encouraged to consider the implications for evaluating graduate programs in teacher education. There are obvious connections.

NECESSARY DEFINITIONS

In an attempt to "draw attention to its full range of functions," Cronbach (1963) defined evaluation as "the collection and use of information to make decisions about an educational program" (p. 672). Eighteen years later, in its volume, *Stan-

dards for Evaluations of Educational Programs, Projects, and Materials, The Joint Committee on Standards for Educational Evaluation (1981) detailed the expression "to make decisions" by defining evaluation as "the systematic investigation of the worth or merit of some object" (p. 12). Within the evaluation community, worth and merit have become accepted concepts. Worth is defined by Scriven (1981) as the contribution that an object (or educational program) makes to its system, or, its external value. Merit is defined as the intrinsic value the object (or educational program) engenders (Scriven, 1981). Therefore, in current practice, evaluation is a data collection process wherein the focus is on making decisions about the degree to which educational programs, projects, or materials are valuable to the participants they are intended to serve and to the system in which evaluation operates. In teacher education, the worth of a program would be the degree to which the school administrators who hire recent graduates are satisfied with the quality of the program from which the beginning teacher graduated. In this instance, merit is the degree to which the students and faculty within the program value its experiences and processes. In educational evaluation both perspectives are important in the design and utility of an evaluation.

Stufflebeam and Webster (1988) boldly state that "evaluation is a conceptual activity" (p. 570). They assert that an essential attribute of evaluation is the extent to which evaluators and their clients conceptualize the evaluation process from purpose, to questions, to data collection methods, to data analyses, to conclusions and recommendations, to utilization of results. Performing these tasks certainly is conceptualizing an evaluation, but they also connote that evaluation is a social activity.

The authors thank their reviewers, Jon Denton (Texas A&M University) and Don Freeman (Arizona State University), for their invaluable suggestions; however, the authors assume complete responsibility for the form and content of this chapter.

Evaluators and their clients must engage in a social process, the results of which yield the evaluation design conceptualized to meet the needs of the evaluator and the clients. One of the key contributing factors to the use of an evaluation is the degree of ownership felt by the clients. If the conceptual and social process with which the evaluation begins garners the support of the clients, as well as improved instruments and procedures, then time spent on the planning process is time well spent.

MODELS, APPROACHES, AND PERSUASIONS

Anderson, Ball, and Murphy (1975) and Caro (1971) trace the broad array of programs to which evaluation methods were applied in the New Deal era. However, as Popham (1975) notes, the initial applications of evaluation to education began during the 1950s and 1960s and grew because of four forces pressuring the education enterprise: (a) dissatisfaction with the performance of public education; (b) increased federal money allocated for education, especially the title monies associated with the Elementary and Secondary Education Act of 1965, coupled with the requirement for receiving funds that local education agencies must inquire into (i.e., evaluate) the effectiveness of the funded programs; (c) shrinking financial support for education at the local level and demand for assessment of the relative effectiveness of education programs; and (d) decentralization (i.e., the effects of late 1960s rethinking concerning the contributions of the consolidated school district). During these years, there were few heuristics to provide practitioners with direction in determining the effects of their programmatic endeavors.

The use of terms has not been consistently clear in the evaluation literature. The term used most often to describe "a conception or approach or sometimes even a method of doing evaluation" (Scriven, 1981; pp. 97–98) is *model*. This term is used to identify a variety of practices, philosophical stances toward evaluation practice, data-gathering technique, or even a graphic representation of an evaluation plan. Borich (1983) characterizes the problem of describing precisely what is included in an evaluation model. He cites the work of Stake (1981), who suggests that evaluation models or approaches are really persuasions, that is, value-laden guides for conducting an evaluation. As Borich summarizes, evaluation models are heuristics that help the evaluator decide what types of data will be collected, from whom, and how. Given the foregoing problem of common nomenclature, we briefly describe some of the most visible approaches to evaluation in the literature.

Objectives-Based Evaluation

Prior to the 1960s, evaluation in concept and practice was limited to objectives-based measurement—what Popham (1975) has labeled *goal attainment*. The role of an evaluator was to determine whether the stated obejctives of a program were achieved, and the quality of the evaluation depended on the clarity with which the objectives of the program were communicated. This model of evaluation follows most closely the influential work of Ralph Tyler. With this approach, a program is judged successful when the goals, actually the behavioral objectives derived from the goals, are achieved. The Tylerian goal-attainment model, designed in the 1930s and applied in the classic Eight-Year Study, dominated conceptual thought about educational evaluation. However, by the late 1960s, two writers of immense importance to the development of educational evaluation were rethinking the concept of evaluation. Michael Scriven, a philosopher of science, and Robert Stake, a psychometrician, were preparing treatises that challenged goal attainment, or objectives-based approaches to evaluation, and each began from the precept that evaluating is one part valuing.

Formative–Summative and Goal-Free Evaluation. Scriven made significant contributions to the evaluation literature. He introduced educators to the distinction between formative and summative evaluation (1967). In formative evaluation, the evaluator is working to improve a project, program, or set of materials still under development. In summative evaluation, the evaluator is seeking to assess the merit, by Scriven's analysis, of a completed program, project, or set of materials. Another contribution by Scriven is the concept of goal-free evaluation (Scriven, 1972). In goal-free evaluation, the evaluator intentionally avoids any direct contact with the goals of the program the planners might have stated. He or she collects evaluation data on the goals of the program, both intended and unintended, to make judgments about its merit. Thus, the evaluator is not predisposed to look for the anticipated expectations of the program and is more free to seek (blindly) any and all information that can be used to discuss the worth and merit of the program. The formative–summative distinction and goal-free evaluation are two contributions to the literature that provided the first competing visions for evaluation practice.

Countenance Model. At the same time as Scriven, Stake was preparing an alternate perspective on evaluation practice. In what has come to be called the Countenance Model, Stake (1967) emphasizes two critical elements of evaluation: description and judgment. He argues that evaluations should be rich descriptions, or portrayals, of three phases of a program: the preexisting conditions, or the antecedents; the processes of the program, or the transactions; and the effects, or the outcomes. He then divides each of these three phases into a description matrix that includes intents and observations. He also includes a judgment matrix comprised of standards and judgments. Stake's conception of evaluation is presented in Figure 33-1.

Popham (1975) categorizes the approaches advocated by Scriven and Stake as "judgment models using extrinsic criteria" (p. 15). That is, in each of these approaches, the evaluator seeks to make judgments based on criteria external to the program. Popham terms his other category of evaluation models that has implications for teacher education *decision-facilitation models*.

Decision-Facilitation Models of Evaluation

With the decision-facilitation model the goal is "toward servicing educational decision-makers" (Popham, 1975, p. 33.

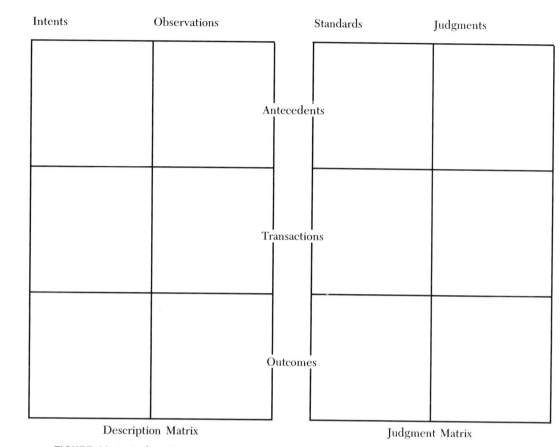

Intents   Observations   Standards   Judgments

Rationale

Antecedents

Transactions

Outcomes

Description Matrix   Judgment Matrix

FIGURE 33–1. Stake's Countenance Model. From "The Countenance of Educational Evaluation" by R. E. Stake, 1967, *Teachers College Record*, *68*, p. 529. Copyright 1967 by Teachers College Record. Reprinted by permission.

That is, the evaluator acts as a collector of data that she or he then organizes and presents to the decision makers of the program, so they can make their own judgments from the data. In other words, judgments about the worth and/or merit of a program are outside the responsibility of the evaluator and rest with the program planners, a point of contention among the various evaluation perspectives. Should the evaluator make judgments from the evaluation data and, therefore, make recommendations about the program? Or should judgments and recommendations be the province of the program planners? The decision of which role the evaluator will play in the evaluation process is a local one, and the reader should consult the debates on the evaluator role presented in current evaluation texts (e.g., Stufflebeam & Shinkfield, 1985; Worthen & Sanders, 1988).

CIPP Model of Evaluation. Probably the most widely known decision-facilitation model is the CIPP model designed by Stufflebeam and Guba and presented by Stufflebeam et al. (1971). CIPP is an acronym for four types of evaluation: context, input, process, and product evaluation. Stufflebeam (1982) applied the CIPP to teacher education and defined evaluation in a rather omnibus manner, demonstrating the evaluator's role in helping program planners make informed deci-

sions: "Evaluation is the process of delineating, obtaining, and applying descriptive and judgmental information about the worth or merit of some program's goals, design, implementation, and impact in order to promote improvements, serve needs for accountability, and foster understandings" (p. 138). This definition represents a consideration of the work of Tyler and the goal-attainment approach, but it limits evaluation to the presentation of information essential for making judgments to guide decision making. The underlying principle of the CIPP Model is that "the purpose of evaluation is *not* to prove but to improve" (p. 1).

The introduction of the CIPP Model into the evaluation literature grandly changed the definition of what program evaluation could be. The goal-attainment model that had dominated evaluation design was expanded to include a broader range of questions including goals, design, implementation, and impacts. Stufflebeam and his associates proffered a model as comprehensive as most programs in teacher education. They infused evaluation into the program as a conceptual and social process that seeks to build the ownership of the participants as informants and decision makers.

The four types of evaluations that comprise the CIPP are (a) context evaluation, (b) input evaluation, (c) process evaluation, and (d) product evaluation. Each is described next.

A context evaluation provides a rationale for the identification of educational objectives. Its purpose is to describe the processes and events leading to the program or project being implemented. In evaluating the context of an educational program, the evaluator identifies the target population, conducts needs assessments, and provides information for judging whether the objectives are responsive to the assessed needs. For the most part, the methods of data collection for context evaluation are descriptive and include, among others, systems analyses, surveys, and interviews. Context evaluation is roughly analogous to Stake's antecedents. In each instance, the evaluator collects data regarding the preexisting conditions.

In input evaluation the evaluator seeks to determine whether the program has the resources to insure the successful completion of the program. Evaluators work to identify strategies for implementation that resonate with the human, fiscal, logistical, and temporal resources available. In this regard, input evaluation should inform the decision makers of potential problem areas in implementation. Methods for collecting input-evaluation data include such things as assessing the human resources and the life space for the program and conducting pilot tests and cost-accounting studies.

A process evaluation is conducted once the program has been established and is operating. The purpose of conducting a process evaluation is to locate any flaws in the procedures or processes in the implementation of the program. The role of the process evaluator is to identify aspects of the program that might need adjustment. Methods for collecting process data include noting and describing the process as it actually occurs, interviewing key participants, and observing their routine behavior. Process evaluation is analogous to Stake's transactions.

Product evaluation is similar to goal attainment under the Tyler model or to Stake's outcomes. The purpose of product evaluation is to collect data on the outcomes of the program, to relate them to the contexts, inputs, and processes, and to interpret their worth and merit. In this type of evaluation the evaluator helps the program planners decide whether the program should be continued, revised, or terminated. In product evaluation, the evaluator operationalizes the stated objectives of the program and collects either quantitative or qualitative data that measure the extent to which the objectives of the program have been achieved.

Additional Alternatives. There are many models for evaluation that could be employed. Stake (1981) argues that we should recognize the value-laden contributions and limitations of each. For a more complete treatment of the various evaluation models, one should read Madaus, Scriven, and Stufflebeam (1983).

PROGRAM EVALUATION IN TEACHER EDUCATION

Obscurity

Much has been written about program evaluation in many other fields, but little has been written about it in teacher education. As Galluzzo (1986) notes, current practice in teacher education program evaluation can not yet be characterized as a field of inquiry. There is very little analysis of past practice, few position papers on method, and only a handful of theoretical papers inquiring into the purpose and results of program evaluation studies in teacher education. Previous attempts to describe program evaluation in teacher education are best described as site-specific, idiosyncratic models designed for particular applications at individual institutions.

Cooper (1983), in attempting to characterize and summarize what is known about program evaluation in teacher education, was limited to describing efforts at individual institutions to build an evaluation agenda. He labels these "lighthouse" efforts amidst "relative darkness." He names a handful of institutions where evaluation is an ongoing component of program development. For example, Reiff (1980) describes the features of the model for the University of Georgia. Yeany (1980) calls for alternate models based on varying perspectives on data gathering. Benz and Newman (1986) call for the use of both quantitative and qualitative data to provide a more complete picture of the transaction and outcomes. Zimpher and Loadman (1986) describe a documentation and assessment system that is being used to monitor programs at Ohio State University. However, one cannot review literature on program evaluation in teacher education and avoid the conclusion that more is known about designing models than about implementing them. Reading the literature, one gets the impression that program evaluation is teacher education's orphan. There are no outlets for evaluation studies. There are no professional associations that consistently recognize the contributions that can be made toward understanding teacher education through evaluation. There is no network for communication. Manuscripts submitted to professional journals are probably rejected, because the methodology is typically not very sophisticated, or the problems are narrowly conceived, or the subjects are narrowly defined, or the results are not generalizable.

Visibility

As early as 1944 an important volume was prepared by Troyer and Pace on the application of evaluation methods to teacher education. The two authors documented the methods used at a variety of teacher education institutions to evaluate programs in terms of the general education component, the professional education sequence, student teaching, and follow up studies. In retrospect, practice in teacher education program evaluation is only slightly more sophisticated some forty years later, one-shot mailed surveys dominate the practice of teacher program evaluation (Adams & Craig, 1983).

Perhaps the main reason for the continued reliance on follow-up studies can be traced to Sandefur's (1970) monograph on a model for program evaluation. Between the publication of Troyer and Pace's volume and Sandefur's monograph, little else was written regarding the application of evaluation methods to teacher education. Although Troyer and Pace (1944) described a variety of methods for assessing the skills, attitudes, and understandings of preservice teachers, Sandefur describes a product-oriented, competency-based approach. A program was evaluated by measuring the degree to which graduates could demonstrate selected competencies that served as the objectives of the program (Sandefur, 1970). With minor exceptions, those empowered to conduct program-evaluation studies have continued to employ product-oriented follow-up studies without inquiring into their relative advantage over other evaluation methods. The continued use of product-oriented evaluations has recently been assured by the National Council for Accreditation of Teacher Education in its revised standards (National Council for Accreditation of Teacher Education, 1987). The new NCATE guidelines define evaluation in teacher education as assessing the degree to which students achieve the objectives of the program.

Although Sandefur did not intend his explication of a model to be limited to follow-up studies, the net effect was to forestall the development of alternative approaches. Interpretations of his monograph nurtured a reliance by many institutions on following the path of collecting quantifiable product data. The monograph had the effect of moving our understanding of evaluation in teacher education ahead, but it also had the effect of impeding continued growth. Both reactions notwithstanding, Sandefur's monograph opened the door to visibility and to treating program evaluation more seriously.

More recently, the goal-attainment, or outcomes-based, perspective on evaluating a teacher education program was offered by Medley (1977). According to Medley, program evaluation is defined as the extent to which "the training experiences produce the competencies defined as objectives of the training program" (p. 69). If the student teachers in a teacher education program or the recently graduated beginning teachers can demonstrate the "competencies" or "objectives" of a program, the program is evaluated as being effective (see Figure 33-2). Like Sandefur's model, Medley's approach requires the program planners to specify the expected outcomes of the program and to design a data collection system around the stated outcome. In each of these applications of evaluation to teacher education, the authors rely on the goal-attainment orientation to evaluation. Medley embraces the notion that program evalu-

ation in teacher education should examine the degree to which teachers exhibit the objectives of the teacher education curriculum. However, since the publication of these two documents, definitions of program evaluation for teacher education have been reconsidered to include more than the outcomes-based orientation.

Alternate Perspectives

Rejecting the product assessment/measurement orientation outlined by Sandefur (1970), de Voss and Hawk (1983) challenge what had become conventional thinking and argue that outcome assessment is a rather narrow definition of program evaluation for teacher education. Employing the inquiry methods of anthropology, deVoss and Hawk describe a program-evaluation effort that relies more on documentation than on assessment. With their approach, the student becomes an informant, rather than a subject, and capturing the processes or transactions of the program are as essential as describing the outcomes. The students' perceptions, their attitudes, and their dispositions upon entry into the teacher education program, during the program, and after the program are all important explanations of other outcome data that need to be considered when conducting a complete program evaluation. Consistent with deVoss and Hawk's position (de Voss & Hawk, 1983), Reed (1978) stresses that the reliance on natural and behavioral science models of inquiry unthinkingly limits what one can learn about a teacher education program. Also, deVoss and Hawk (1983) and Reed (1978) advocate the inclusion of data-gathering methods drawn from anthropology. The recent trend in program evaluation literature and practice is toward greater acceptance of qualitative methods (Guba, 1987), and evaluation in teacher education could soon follow.

Zimpher and Loadman (1986) further our understanding of alternate methods of data collection. In their monograph describing the Ohio State University Student Information Sys-

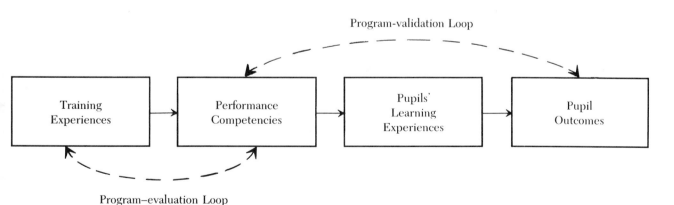

FIGURE 33–2. Levels of Assessment of Teacher Competence in Teacher Education. From *Teacher Competence and Teacher Effectiveness: A Review of Process–Product Research* (p. 68) by D. M. Medley, 1977, Washington, DC: American Association of Colleges for Teacher Education. Copyright 1977 by American Association of Colleges for Teacher Education. Reprinted by permission.

tem, these two authors present a comprehensive model for collecting, recording, analyzing, and reporting a wide variety of quantitative and qualitative data that can be used to assess the worth and merit of a program. What sets this model apart is the application of the model to practice. The authors not only describe a comprehensive model, but they also demonstrate its utility. They include detailed descriptions of instrument design, faculty involvement, data collection, data analysis, and implications for program revision.

Another example is Nelli and Nutter's (1984) application of Stake's Countenance Model to teacher education. They present a model for program evaluation that provides in-depth analysis of the antecedents, transactions, and outcomes. Throughout their monograph, Nelli and Nutter build evaluation around questions that a program faculty would want to ask of evaluation data to provide a "portrayal" of the curriculum. What might separate this volume from most of the work in teacher education program evaluation is the insistence on considering the antecedents of a program. As will become evident later, program evaluation often has had limited utility in program revision, due to failure to consider the contexts in which a program operates.

In an effort to advance practice across the board in the evaluation of teacher education programs, Hord, Savage, and Bethel (1982) compiled a set of papers presented at an invitational conference sponsored by the Research and Development Center for Teacher Education at the University of Texas. This monograph includes descriptions of the characteristics of program evaluations designed to meet the needs of different audiences. In this monograph, Sandefur (1982) reflects on 10 years' work in evaluation and its effects on program development at Western Kentucky University. Gardner (1982) analyzes the role of evaluation as it relates to accreditation and professionalizing teacher education from the perspective of NCATE. Erly (1982), operationalizing the evaluation of worth, delineates the assurances local education officials would like from a program faculty as they seek new teaching candidates. Roth (1982), writing from the perspective of a state department official, offers recommendations to teacher educators for state program evaluation. And Galluzzo (1982) outlines how the CIPP model could profitably be applied to teacher education. The entire monograph broadens our understanding of program evaluation and the particular needs of the various audiences.

Validity

The literature on program evaluation includes a point–counterpoint analysis of the validity and usefulness of data collected from follow-up surveys of graduates. Katz, Raths, Mohanty, Kurachi, and Irving (1981), from a review of 26 follow-up studies, raise issues about subject selection/identification, representativeness of the sample in relation to the target population, conclusions drawn from program-evaluation data, and times when most program-evaluation data are collected. In this article, Katz et al. also introduce the feed-forward principle into the literature on program evaluation. Feed-forward,

in contrast with feedback, questions the validity of graduates' responses in follow-up studies. Katz et al. define feed-forward as the "resistance from the student at the time of exposure to given learnings and, later, protestations that the same learning had not been provided, should have been provided, or should have been provided in stronger doses" (p. 21). In reviewing these 26 studies, Katz et al. were unimpressed by the state of the art in follow-up studies. They found sampling biases in response rates and obvious and global recommendations for change, which, given the vague and general nature of the recommendations, would not and *could* not be addressed by the faculty in the program. Katz et al. concluded that, under current conditions, there is little reason for conducting program-evaluation studies using follow-up questionnaires. They suggest that enough rival hypotheses and explanations could be generated from a teacher education follow-up study to render it virtually useless as an instrument for program change and development. They further suggest a rethinking of the methods for conducting follow-up studies, to increase the reliability and validity of the resultant data.

In counterpoint, Adams, Craig, Hord, and Hall (1981) agree with Katz et al. (1981) on one point and disagree on two others. Both groups of writers agree that practice in teacher education program evaluation is narrowly conceived; however, Adams and his colleagues argue that, by focusing solely on follow-up studies, Katz and her colleagues present a distorted view of the variety of methods employed in program evaluation. Adams and his colleagues further argue that using review methods and standards in the Katz et al. analysis was more appropriate for education research than for program evaluation. Consequently, Adams et al. find the critique by Katz et al. to be a "straw-man" argument. Regardless of which group of writers makes the most cogent argument, there is still agreement that the lack of experimental evaluation methods limits what is known about the effectiveness of teacher education programs.

A survey of all institutions affiliated with the American Association of Colleges for Teacher Education was conducted by Adams & Craig (1983) to ascertain normative practice in teacher education program evaluation. Eighty-six percent of these institutions reported conducting program-evaluation studies. The dominant data collection method was the mailed questionnaire follow-up study; other methods included interviews and direct observations. The areas typically addressed included teaching skills, knowledge of subject matter, relationships with students, and relationships with colleagues. On the one hand it is encouraging that about four hundred institutions reported gathering evaluation data. On the other hand, judging from the methods used and the focus of the studies, one can only wonder for what purposes these evaluations were conducted and how the data were used.

In sum, program evaluation in teacher education has a rather checkered history. If examined closely enough, the lack of a distinct field of program evaluation in teacher education parallels the lack of a prominent research literature in teacher education. As the research literature on teaching and teacher education increases, one can speculate that the future of inquiry in teacher education will also improve.

PURPOSES OF TEACHER EDUCATION PROGRAM EVALUATION

Why should teacher educators engage in evaluation of their programs? There are four purposes for conducting evaluation studies in teacher education: (a) accountability, (b) improvement, (c) understanding, and (d) knowledge production. On the face of it, each is probably obvious and not worth belaboring; however, "it is precisely because evaluation has a purpose that the way it is carried out becomes important" (Troyer & Pace, 1944, p. 367) and demands that each of the four purposes be examined in more detail.

Accountability

Accountability is the degree to which an evaluation is conducted to meet external accreditation standards. As noted earlier, NCATE historically has included a standard on program evaluation. Many states and regional accreditation associations also require that a program faculty routinely collect evaluation data intended to be used for decision making. Adams and Craig (1983), in their study of program-evaluation practice, did not conclude that evaluations were conducted primarily for accountability purposes. But, given the facts that almost 400 institutions reported conducting evaluations and that there are comparatively few evaluation reports in the literature, it appears that concerns about accountability motivate a considerable number of teacher educators to collect evaluation data. Once the evaluation has been used to meet the requirements of accountability, the report has served its purpose and it is not submitted for publication. An example of an evaluation conducted to demonstrate accountability would be a report submitted to an accreditation agency. Stufflebeam and Webster (1988) briefly describe the curriculum audit approach to evaluation, wherein representatives from an agency to which the institution is accountable conduct a site visit to assess the strengths and weaknesses of the curriculum. Program evaluations can also be driven by accountability, but the reason might not always be positive (Suchman, 1972). For example, an evaluation might be conducted solely to make a program look good and to cover or soft pedal any deficiencies.

Improvement

The second purpose of conducting an evaluation is to improve the program under scrutiny. This purpose is consistent with most of the scholarly writing in educational evaluation. To improve a program, the audience for an evaluation shifts from an external agency to the program participants themselves. Evaluations should be conducted because they can inform participants of the strengths and weaknesses of the program in all respects. The information needed by the participants to make informed decisions about the teacher education curriculum is not different from the information needed to meet the accountability purpose (e.g., systematically collected teaching performance data or students' performances on designated paper-and-pencil measures or some other desired outcomes). In regard to this purpose, one is concerned with how the data are interpreted, reported, and used. An analysis of the items on selected competency measures could yield information valuable to program faculty seeking to make adjustments in the curriculum. For example, Medley (1982) advocates that program evaluation serve a gate keeping function, controlling who successfully completes a teacher education program. Such a practice places the responsibility for quality control with the teacher education faculty and not with the state office of teacher certification. In this way, program evaluation becomes a statement from the profession that teacher educators are confident of the qualities of their graduates.

Borich (1979) suggests that the improvement purpose can be accomplished through discrepancy evaluation, in which "what is" is compared with "what should be." With the discrepancies made apparent, a program faculty can act to make improvements in the curriculum. In this regard, evaluation is a process that can help teacher educators ask the best questions, collect and analyze the most relevant data, and design more efficient and responsive programs.

Understanding

As the program-improvement purpose follows from the accountability purpose, a third purpose follows directly from the first two: understanding. Conducting an evaluation for understanding is potentially a more intrinsically useful purpose for conducting program-evaluation studies. Simply put, the more clearly the stakeholders understand the experiences of preservice teachers, the more likely they will operate from a set of shared perceptions and the more capable they will be to make decisions about the continuation, modification, or termination of the program. The process of conducting systematic evaluations for understanding provides a common language among the stakeholders. The growth of any of the sciences is measured by the degree to which the practitioners use a vocabulary of key concepts readily understood by all practitioners. An evaluation conducted to meet the understanding purpose probably is indistinguishable from most other evaluations. The essential trait of an evaluation with a purpose to develop a common vocabulary among the stakeholders is the degree to which the stakeholders are involved in the process. In this regard, evaluation is a social process that can have at its heart the explicit goal of inviting the participation of as many stakeholders as possible. From another perspective, understanding can also be considered ownership. Borich (1982) emphasizes the role of the social process in fostering useful evaluations. As will be discussed later, one of the greatest obstacles to the use of evaluation data is a feeling of detachment on the part of the stakeholders. Thus, although the methods used to gather evaluation data to address this purpose might not be different from the methods used to address the accountability or improvement purposes, the way in which the evaluation plan is designed and implemented is as important to an evaluation as are the resultant data and recommendations. Developing a broad-based understanding of the program is an essential step in facilitating the faculty's ownership of the evaluation and its successful implementation.

Knowledge

The fourth purpose of conducting an evaluation is to contribute to the knowledge about teacher education. As noted, there is a historic tendency for evaluation reports to be used to meet accountability concerns and not to add to a body of literature on practice or measurement in teacher education. Generalizing from one evaluation at one institution to other settings is difficult at best (Galluzzo, 1986). The findings from one institution might or might not ring true at another institution; however, until the faculty at the latter institution collects similar data, there is little reason to ascribe external validity to the findings from the former institution. Perhaps what is most generalizable from program evaluation in teacher education are the methods and techniques used to answer a set of unique questions, not the findings.

Overarching Purpose

The goal of a program-evaluation effort should be to develop a comprehensive knowledge-production effort about the relationships among a program's contexts, inputs, processes, and products. Although evaluations conducted solely to be accountable might contribute little to our understanding of a program, the converse is not necessarily true. Evaluations designed to address understanding and knowledge production should also satisfy the accountability and improvement purposes. An institution's evaluation effort should include the development of a long-range plan for program evaluation. The plan should actively involve the various stakeholders and should be designed to improve the overall program. To define program evaluation narrowly as product evaluations or follow-up studies fails to address the essential features of a total evaluation effort. Teacher education program evaluation encompasses a commitment to inquiring into practice, to facilitating communication, to improving how teacher education is practiced, to advancing what is known about teacher education, and to raising important questions about issues and practices that need to be addressed (Freeman, 1987). Each of the purposes discussed in this section of the chapter will be reflected throughout the remainder of this chapter as examples of various evaluation efforts are discussed.

Regardless of the purpose, however, the basic assumption underlying education in the first place is the belief that examined behavior is better than unexamined behavior. That is, the hope of the education system rests on the belief that we learn from inquiry. How we change and how we improve should be based on the answers to a set of questions that are systematically and objectively investigated. Subsequently, evaluation studies, properly designed, should ask questions that need to be answered to inform our thinking. Therefore, regardless of the purpose of conducting an evaluation, the premise of the education system is being addressed.

THE SOCIAL CONTEXT OF PROGRAM EVALUATION IN TEACHER EDUCATION

Program evaluation in any field must be recognized as being a social process as much as a data collection process. The social context in which an evaluation is conducted sets the parameters within which decisions regarding resources and operations can be made. There are four key features of the social context in which teacher education programs operate that individually or collectively influence the way in which evaluations are conducted.

First, program evaluation in teacher education is conducted within a political atmosphere in which different groups and individuals "relate to each other from different positions of power, influence, and authority" (Banner, Doctors, & Gordon, 1975, p. 2). The reality of the interplay among the various players is that, for political reasons, the conditions under which an evaluation is conducted might be less than ideal, and, therefore, the evaluation might be less effective and less useful in some contexts than in others.

Second, the personal and professional relationship between the program operator and program evaluator is a key feature, if, in fact, they are different people. Ideally, program operation and program evaluation should be relatively independent but function together to create, operate, and refine the best program possible. The two, program operation and program evaluation, truly go hand in glove.

Third, the social context in which teacher education programs operate changes over time and, therefore, what was appropriate and acceptable at one time might not be at another. For instance, laws could be passed requiring additional courses or modified course content and, hence, change the requirements for completion of a teacher education program. For example, a state might introduce the requirement that all teachers receive instruction regarding AIDS, necessitating a revision of the program of study and the development of instructional materials to meet the new requirement.

Fourth is the values held by the various audiences for which the evaluation is intended. Values are positive and negative feelings that people have and project onto other people, objectives, and situations (Williamson, Swingle, & Sarget, 1982). As such, values are relatively permanent cognitive structures that have a pervasive effect on an individual's behavior. In the context of program evaluations, values are a major force in the formation, operation, and evaluation of programs (Wortman, 1975) and in the interpretation of evaluation and program outcomes (Gorry & Goodrich, 1978). Because values are relatively resistant to change, they tend to determine the direction and operation of a program, regardless of the nature and extent of the evaluation information made available. For example, in public school education:

equality can be enforced through quotas, busing, location of new schools, etc., or by "freedom of choice" in incorporating "educational vouchers" . . . in which every family has the same amount of money to spend on a child's schooling and gives this voucher to the school of their choice. (Wortman, 1975, p. 567)

Which of these various alternatives individuals choose is based largely on values they hold and not necessarily on which procedures result in the greatest student achievement. This means that, although both administrators and faculties aspire to the Dogma of the Immaculate Perception (Kaplan, 1964), that is, conducting value-free inquiry during the program-evaluation process, in reality it is not possible to do so. As Bickman (1987) points out, "the initial casual beliefs of key stakeholders can affect their cooperation in implementing an evaluation and their reactions to evaluation findings that do not fit their initial theory of the program" (p. 14). Recognition of the preeminent role that values play in the evaluation process provides a basis for understanding the social context in which teacher education programs must operate and be evaluated (Conrad & Miller, 1987).

PROGRAM EVALUATION AUDIENCES

Teacher education programs, as do all programs, operate in relation to a number of individuals and groups, each of which influences the nature of the programs and how they are operated. Wortman (1975) generically identifies these groups as being (a) the treatment administrator (e.g., program director) and staff, which will be referred to as the teacher education administrators and faculties; (b) the respondents (e.g., community), which will be referred to as the preservice students and practicing teachers; (c) the initiator or sponsor (e.g., government agency or foundation), which will be referred to as the accrediting agencies; (d) the research designer or researcher (e.g., the evaluator), which will be referred to as the program evaluator; and (e) the clients (e.g., society, politicians, special interest groups), which will be referred to as the public.

All of these groups have vested interests in teacher education programs and, based on their individual and collective value systems, attempt to influence the operation and evaluation of teacher education programs in a variety of ways.

Teacher Education Administrators and Faculties

The administrators and faculties associated with teacher education programs in higher education have, in the past, typically not been concerned with (i.e., have not valued) evaluating their programs except in some very general ways. Their concerns have focused more on recruiting and retaining faculty, conducting and publishing research, maintaining enrollments, teaching classes, and so on. In some instances, a few individuals have expressed program-evaluation concerns, have collected evaluation data, and have attempted to introduce programmatic change based on the evaluation data, but that number has been relatively small (Cooper, 1983).

Preservice Students and Practicing Teachers

Preservice students and practicing teachers are the "products" of teacher education programs, and they tend to judge the worth or merit of those programs on a personal level in terms of their experiences while completing the program and include such things as (a) whether the program is difficult, (b) whether there are particular instructors they liked, and (c) whether they received particular instruction that makes their job easier. For the practicing teacher, continuing education in the form of inservice training and/or pursuit of graduate degrees is usually judged in terms of time commitment and difficulty rather than in terms of timeliness and relevance.

Accrediting Agencies

Accrediting agencies (such as state departments of education and professional associations like NCATE) exercise considerable control over education programs in that they are charged with translating the outcomes of the legislative process into action. The resulting regulations and the manner in which they are monitored and enforced place restrictions on content and structure of programs and specify, at least to some degree, program outcomes. Accrediting agencies value conformance to regulations and statutes. As a result, they have typically monitored the number of credit hours teacher education graduates collect in particular content and professional courses and, only relatively recently, have required scores on certification tests such as the National Teachers Examination (Sandefur, 1987) or internships in which teaching performance is assessed (Galluzzo, 1987).

The Program Evaluator

The program evaluator, if one even exists in association with the teacher education program, is charged with collecting and interpreting information. For effective program evaluation to occur, program evaluators and program administrators and faculties must value the evaluation effort and be willing to share information with each other. If such interdependence does not exist, program-evaluation data might be collected but will rarely, if ever, be used to modify, change, or improve programs. In short, unless program administrators and faculties value the information and value using the information in making decisions about the program, program evaluation will be little more than window dressing. Program faculties cannot charge infringement of academic freedom when evaluation data indicate that their particular courses are not producing the outcomes desired. Likewise, the program evaluator cannot cry foul when program faculties want to collect additional data and/or interpret evaluation data differently.

The Public

With respect to teacher education programs, the public consists of a variety of political constituencies: politicians, school administrators, school board members, parents, and, ultimately, students. Each of these groups in one form or fashion is the consumer of the products of teacher education programs. Yet each has relatively little power to influence those programs except through elected representatives and the pressure they can generate during the legislative process. And it is here that the public has stated with a rather clear voice what they want: better teachers. The public clearly wants prospective teachers who are minimally competent in their ability to read and write, as well as in their ability to teach. The program evaluator's dilemma is to identify what those minimum levels are and how those skills are best assessed.

LIMITING FACTORS IN THE EVALUATION OF TEACHER EDUCATION PROGRAMS

This section will focus on a variety of factors that limit what is known about teacher education as derived from program evaluations. Simply stated, methodological concerns plague evaluation practice. In that regard there are three basic issues: (a) identification of criterion variables, (b) identification of independent variables, and (c) evaluation design.

Identification of Criterion variables

There is little evidence available to support the assumption that a program faculty can state the specific expectations of a program, such as teaching skills, interpersonal skills, and subject-matter competence. A search of the literature unearthed no lists of specific program expectations that were not compiled or mandated by accreditation agencies. With the exception of outcome lists generated for competency-based teacher education programs, stating the expectations for a program seems to comprise the null set. The expectations of a teacher education program are typically defined by the identification of measurement devices such as tests, observation instruments, attitude/belief inventories, and interview protocols that capture in general ways the processes or effects of the program. Criterion, or dependent, variables represent the widest possible array of areas including (a) general, professional, and subject-matter knowledge; (b) teaching behaviors/skills; (c) attitudes and dispositions; and (d) perceptions of preparation. Institutions have defined each of these criterion variables in ways that meet their own needs for evaluation data. However, each is not without its problems.

Knowledge. The knowledge possessed by teacher education students is commonly considered a general category of outcome variables of a teacher education program. Even though it is considered an outcome, it is not measured in any systematic way by most institutions. One study that attempted to measure the knowledge possessed by students prior to, during, and after completing their teacher education program was conducted by Galluzzo (1984). Nineteen preservice teachers were administered the National Teachers Exam to assess their knowledge of general studies and their professional knowledge upon entering the teacher education program and at annual intervals thereafter. The results indicated no significant differences in knowledge of general studies over the 4 years of teacher preparation. In contrast, data did show significant differences in mean scores on the professional education compo-

nent of the NTE, suggesting that these students attended college to be something, but it was not necessarily to be liberally educated. The main difficulty with studies such as this one is that a general standardized test was used to measure what students are expected to know as a result of completing a teacher education program. The degree to which the test is consistent with the content taught in the courses a student takes is problematic. There is no reason to believe that the NTE is a content-valid measure of the general or professional education components at any given institution. To learn the degree to which prospective teachers possess the knowledge expected by a program faculty, it would seem most appropriate to design measures that assess subject-matter and professional knowledge. Institutions resist preparing such measures because of the cost involved in developing a test and, possibly more important, because of their inability to reach a consensus on what should be assessed. Therefore, teacher educators are virtually at the mercy of testing corporations, state departments of education, and other groups that have narrowly defined teacher knowledge as performance on a standardized test. With the tests and testing procedures currently available, it is difficult to separate the influences of the person, such as innate intellectual abilities, from the effects of the program.

Perhaps the greatest impediment to measuring knowledge is the lack of consensus as to what a prospective teacher needs to know. The most promising work in this area is still in the future. Alternate methods of assessing knowledge must be developed before measuring cognitive attainment becomes routine in evaluating teacher education programs. We are encouraged by the work of Shulman (1986) and his colleagues as they build assessment procedures that emphasize knowledge production over reproduction of knowledge. At this point, beginning teachers are being inappropriately tested or not tested at all, and teacher educators are not building convincing arguments about the shortcomings of current practice. The selection of tests for evaluation is usually determined by the tests available rather than by deciding what to evaluate and then locating or designing measures consistent with expectations.

Teaching Behavior/Skills. The development of effective teaching skills is another common expectation in all teacher education programs. Similar to the expectations for knowledge, institutional assessment of teaching skills is slowly being replaced by state departments of education in the form of internships and performance assessments of beginning teachers (Galluzzo, 1987). The premise upon which a performance assessment system is founded is that there are selected behavioral outcomes that students of a teacher education program should be able to demonstrate in the classroom.

The work of Ayers (1986) represents perhaps the longest commitment to using performance data for program evaluation. Employing a modified Flanders observation instrument, Ayers began assessing the teaching skills of preservice teachers at Tennessee Technological University. According to this investigator, teacher education at Tennessee Technological University has undifferentiating effects on the teaching skills of preservice teachers, regardless of whether the candidates are typical undergraduate students or master's degree students seeking initial certification. Longitudinal observation data for each group of teachers indicates that the teaching skills of the program's graduates improved during each of the first 3 years of teaching.

The premise that assessment of teaching behavior can form the basis for program modification and instructional improvement has been demonstrated by Dickson and Wiersma (1985). These researchers measured the teaching skills of preservice teachers, using two instruments to observe interaction and transactions in the classroom: (a) Teacher Performance Assessment Instrument (Capie, Anderson, Johnson, & Ellet, 1980), a high-inference instrument; and (b) Classroom Observation Keyed for Effectiveness Research (COKER) (Coker & Coker, 1982), a low-inference instrument. Dickson and Wiersma report that the COKER, in particular, was especially sensitive to classroom processes and revealed suggested areas of improvement to the faculty at the University of Toledo. For example, the student teachers at Toledo typically did not (a) make use of pupils' viewpoints, (b) ask pupils to elaborate on a point, or (c) use reinforcement patterns regularly. This type of information, which is neither vague nor general, illustrates what program evaluations could reveal.

Future program evaluators might resist the use of any of the instruments used in the Ayers (1986) or Dickson and Wiersma (1985) studies. Such a reaction should be expected as the field develops. The essence of these two efforts is that basic behavioral competence is important to these institutions. Both studies demonstrate that, through concerted faculty development and the use of observation systems tied to the expectations of the program, teaching performance can be assessed and the resultant data can be used for program improvement. Following Medley's (1977) definition, each of these evaluation efforts has found ways to measure the degree to which students can demonstrate the competencies of the program.

When performance assessments of teaching skills are being conducted, sampling remains a prepotent issue. Stodolsky (1984) presents data indicating that elementary school teachers have differential expectations for pupil attentiveness across content areas. For instance, the expectation for attentiveness during mathematics might be different from the expectation for attentiveness during social studies. In other words, the context in which observations take place can influence the degree to which the teacher demonstrates the expected outcomes of the program. In the main, for teacher education program evaluation, time and event sampling are concerns that must be considered in the design of the evaluation plan.

Attitudes and Dispositions. When teacher educators think of the expectations of the program, the words *skills, knowledges,* and *attitudes* typically come to the fore. In an effort to clarify our understanding of skills, knowledges, and attitudes, some teacher educators have concerned themselves with the dispositions teachers hold toward their roles as teachers (Katz & Raths, 1986a, 1986b). A disposition is a cognitive orientation, as opposed to an affective attitude, and is operationalized as the tendency of a teacher to act in a consistent manner, demonstrating a habit of the mind. Dispositions include what and how preservice teachers think about the professional, technical, student, procedural, intellectual, and value concerns of their craft. Teacher educators have long argued that teachers not only are good technicians but also make complex decisions and possess the tendency to act in certain and consistent manners. Dispositions represent a powerful and new interpretation concerning the effects of teacher education programs and can become a separate domain of program outcomes.

Measuring teacher attitudes has historically been a demanding and inconclusive effort. The measures "often suffer from inadequate predictive validity" (Borich, 1977, p. 14) and have been reduced to global measures that offer little insight into program effects (Zeichner & Tabachnick, 1981). As Borich (1977) notes, "relationships between attitude and teacher performance in the classroom are commonly low and nonsignificant" (p. 14). The measurement of attitudes, however, is a significant problem, which can be traced to the faculty's inability to agree upon a set of attitudes it would like to address. Thus, an instrument such as the Minnesota Teacher Attitude Inventory (Cook, Leeds, & Callis, 1951) remains the most overused instrument in the study of program effects and yields little information that teacher educators can use to improve their programs.

There is precedence for linking knowledge, teaching behavior, dispositions, and attitudes in teacher education. All are equal and legitimate expectations from any instructional interaction (Berliner, 1976). However, studies of teacher preparation have neglected to link these distinct sets of criterion variables. The frequency at which expected behaviors are demonstrated in the classroom is important in any program evaluation effort, and how a beginning teacher organizes subject matter for teaching (Shulman, 1986) is equally important. The relationship of attitudes and, specifically, dispositions and how they relate to teacher knowledge and performance is virtually unexamined. Yet, by examining skill and knowledge in relationship to attitudes or to dispositions, evaluators create a more complete portrayal of the expectations of their programs. Students are asked to explain the use of selected behaviors as they are demonstrated in various settings (e.g., primary and intermediate classrooms, low and high socioeconomic classrooms). Students' attitudes or dispositions and how well these correlate with or explain other data are essential to understanding the outcomes of a teacher education program.

Perceptions of Preparation. If any area of criterion measure has been developed for site-specific evaluation studies, it is students' perceptions obtained via mailed follow-up questionnaires. The survey method persists because it is probably the easiest data collection technique in the teacher education program-evaluation arsenal. We seem to have succumbed to Kaplan's Law of the Instrument (Kaplan, 1964); that is, because we know how to do follow-up mail questionnaires, we attempt to use them regardless of what we want to know. Rather, we should first pose our questions and *then* identify the best available methodology that will provide the answers we need (Raths, 1987).

The available data, however, present a fragmented picture regarding graduates' perceptions. Adams (1987) concludes that beginning teachers' perceptions of their preparation appear to be very unstable during the first years of teaching, with stability not occurring until somewhere around the fifth year of teaching. Across programs, the areas in teacher education programs that are highly rated typically include the preactive phases of teaching such as planning, selecting materials, and sequencing learning activities, whereas weaknesses include interactive aspects of teaching, particularly classroom management and discipline.

Identification of Independent Variables

The central issue impeding the advancement of program evaluation in teacher education relates directly to the inability of the faculty to reach consensus on what the essential attributes of their teacher education program are. It is rare to find a program outlined with a knowledge base, conceptions of teaching, processes for importing the knowledge base, and appropriate assessment techniques for program evaluation. Unless there is a curriculum design, the measurement of expectations is diminished. Thus, the program as an independent variable is a central issue in conducting useful evaluations. Simply stated, what is a teacher education program? Is a program a treatment? Raths (1987) argues that the slow development of the field of teacher education program evaluation is a direct result of the inability of teacher educators to describe the essential attributes of a program.

In the preceding discussion, the argument was advanced that teacher educators rarely agree on the characteristics of the competent beginner. Teacher educators in a given program must also agree upon a body of knowledge or, as it is currently labeled, a knowledge base: skills, understandings, and dispositions they want to develop in the preservice teacher. Teacher educators must provide curricular wholeness in terms of course content, instructional process, field experiences, clinical experiences, and modeling. A program must be something more than a "dog's breakfast," or a mere collection of "restricted general electives," from which students can sample a variety of areas in which depth is compromised for breadth. Much of what passes as a program in teacher education is a subjectively arranged sequence of courses from which the preservice teacher is expected to uncover themes the faculty have not yet identified and labeled. The development of a stated knowledge base with goals and benchmarks and expectations is necessary to design a useful program-evaluation effort. Teacher educators need to address the issues raised by the questions, What do we want our graduates to know, feel, do, and think as a result of completing our program?, How do we want our graduates to act in given contexts?, and How do we structure experiences that promote achievement of these expectations? It is safe to state that, without a collection of purposeful processes on which the faculty members have reached consensus, there can be no program evaluation that has meaningful implications for program improvement, understanding, and knowledge production.

Problems in Evaluation Design

Beyond the issues of defining, operationalizing, and characterizing a program, teacher educators who conduct program evaluations must also wrestle with the issue of designing a method for collecting and analyzing data. A problem for any researcher, determining an evaluation design is a particular problem for an evaluator. The proprietary nature of program-evaluation efforts forces evaluators to locate or create measurement devices that appeal specifically to the potential audience (the program faculty). Given the paucity of research literature in teacher education, many teacher educators are not familiar with most of the data collection instruments and how and when data should be collected. Borich (1978) and Cooper (1983) each offer a compendium of instruments that could help bring a program-evaluation effort to fruition. Decisions about whether to conduct longitudinal studies, follow-up surveys, or experimental designs must be the consensus of the program faculty, based upon the questions that the evaluation is designed to address and not based upon what is "best" from a research-design perspective. If the data are not valued by the program faculty, then it does not matter whether the data are best. It is incumbent upon a program evaluator to communicate regularly with the program faculty in planning the data collection effort. To do otherwise undercuts three of the four purposes outlined earlier in this chapter, specifically, improvement, understanding, and knowledge production.

RECENT BENCHMARK TEACHER EDUCATION PROGRAM EVALUATION EFFORTS

Koehler (1985) notes in her discussion of teacher education research that there are many studies in the literature, and, considering issues in design, one can draw some observations on more effective practice. The same statement can be made concerning evaluation in teacher education. Although there are factors that limit evaluation practice, there are also methodological concerns that have been addressed in selected exemplary studies and from which useful results can be gleaned. Evaluation studies designed to address the problems of method are described next to provide a picture of what has been and can be learned through teacher education program evaluation.

Program evaluation in teacher education tends to be a hit-and-miss operation in which little effort is made to collect information from a variety of sources about tightly conceived program outcomes. According to Adams and Craig (1983), program evaluation in teacher education has typically not been valued at the institution level, because budget allocations for evaluation of teacher education programs are small. Across a vast majority of institutions offering teacher education, program evaluation is a covert operation maintained by but a few dedicated educators. However, to revisit Cooper's (1983) analogy, there are a few more "lighthouse efforts" on the horizon.

In preparing this chapter, we hoped to demonstrate that program evaluation is widely practiced, with the use of common instruments building toward a body of identifiable knowledge. Although that is really not the case, we are able to identify and describe a collection of innovative efforts to chart new avenues of inquiry in teacher education. The benchmark studies to be described are those that have been useful in (a) demonstrating the robustness of data collection methods, (b) demonstrating the range of evaluation foci, and (c) adding to our understanding of teacher education. As was discussed earlier, what is generalizable across most program-evaluation efforts are the methods used. Substantive findings are also important but only as they echo the results of other studies.

A follow-up questionnaire is the most commonly used data collection procedure for obtaining information from program graduates and practicing teachers. Typically, the questionnaire is sent one year after the student has graduated from the teacher education program, to collect data on the perceptions of recent graduates regarding their assessments of the merits of particular aspects of the program including course content and related experiences (Adams & Craig, 1983). The survey method has been manipulated in various ways. The vast majority of the surveys are one-shot events, but groups of researchers at four institutions have attempted to gain more than a general picture from the follow-up studies.

In their review of follow-up studies, Katz et al. (1981) cited the failure of many program evaluators to identify accurately the target population. They found that follow-up questionnaires are sent to all graduates, regardless of whether the graduate is teaching. Thus, a questionnaire designed to elicit the perceptions of preparation for teaching is sent to nonteaching teacher education graduates. Katz et al. assert that the resultant data can be biased by the responses of a subset of the sample that has been inappropriately surveyed. Pigge (1978) addressed this concern by using the directory of the Ohio Department of Education to locate graduates of Bowling Green State University who actually took a teaching position. He then drew his sample from this group of employed teachers and avoided errors in data analysis and interpretation that would result from using nonteaching graduates as respondents. The focus of Pigge's study was to determine the beginning teachers' responses to 26 selected competencies of interest to the program faculty. The graduates rated their need for each of the competencies in the classroom, their reported skill in using each competency, their proficiency in using each competency, and where they believed they had developed proficiency. Among the findings Pigge reported were (a) a relatively high correlation between the teachers' perceived needs to use a competency and their proficiency at it, (b) a tendency to rank competencies for which they expressed a high need as being developed on the job and not during the teacher education program, and (c) a tendency to credit the teacher education program with developing proficiency in competencies they did not need on the job. This study remains exemplary because of the comprehensive nature of the questions asked. Points of leverage become much clearer and commitment to change becomes much easier when the questions guiding an evaluation are specific.

A second variation on the survey method addresses two important features of teacher education program-evaluation follow-up studies: (a) the need for baseline information from first-year teachers, and (b) the need to interpret the effects of experience on the development of beginning teachers. Hummel and Strom (1987) examined the relationship between graduates' perceptions of their preparation and the number of years the graduates had been teaching. Their first finding echoes a finding reported by Adams (1978) that graduates with no teaching experience view their preparation more positively than experienced teachers, particularly in the area of working with developmental differences among students and students with handicapping conditions. Hummel and Strom also found that teachers who had 2 years' experience were significantly less positive in their attitudes toward teaching than were those who had taught for one year.

The study conducted by Hummel and Strom (1987) makes a contribution to the literature because it elevates the dialogue about what can be learned from program-evaluation studies. Program evaluators soon learn that, with continued investigation, the sophistication of the questions improves, the methods for collecting data improve, and the likelihood of achieving the four purposes outlined earlier (accountability, improvement, understanding, and knowledge production) increases. As a result of this study, not only do the program faculty know more about their programs, but they also (a) are in better positions to consider changes in their programs, (b) have added to the body of knowledge about program-evaluation methodology, and (c) have addressed the effects of experience on the self-report perceptions of graduates.

Denton, Tsai, and Chevrette (1985) manipulated the follow-up method in a study designed to increase the percentage of returned questionnaires. The study was conducted with two purposes: (a) to test the effects of incentives, and (b) to acquire the perceptions of graduates from Texas A&M University from 1980 to 1984. Three hundred students were sent follow-up questionnaires concerning their perceptions of how much emphasis selected content and skills should receive in a teacher-preparation program. To encourage a higher response rate, 40 subjects from the total sample also received a token monetary incentive (a quarter) to complete the questionnaire. The results of this portion of the study revealed that the monetary incentive did not produce proportionally more returns than did routine reminders mailed 3 and 6 weeks after the initial mailing. The data indicate a trend toward higher response rates from students who had recently graduated. The respondents suggested more emphasis on classroom management, instructional methods, and legal and ethical aspects of teaching.

These findings are common in program evaluation. Teacher education programs are evaluated as less effective in the interactive functions of teaching, such as classroom management, instructional methods, asking questions, and giving praise, and are evaluated more effective in the preactive functions of teaching, such as planning and selection of materials. It seems that graduates would like professional programs that anticipate most of the problems beginning teachers encounter and training in how to solve them. In a sense, program graduates give the knowledge base for teacher education far more credit than it presently deserves. The deficiencies that graduates attribute to their programs could be just the teachers' deficiencies in studying the complex environment of the classroom and then having a set of heuristics available to make the appropriate decisions. In other words, the perceptions of these graduates might be no more than their response to the unpredictable and multidimensional nature of the classroom, as described by Doyle (1986), and the inability of novice teachers to interpret the complex environment they encounter. The literature review for this chapter uncovered no studies in which the respondents were asked to characterize their classrooms on a variety of dimensions such as socioeconomic status of the students, number of students taught in a day or a class, aptitude(s) of the group, and whether the students are grouped according to ability. Without such data, which provide contexts for the ratings and opinions of the graduates, much of the evaluation data necessarily remains nonspecific and lacking direction for the revision of a program.

In another unique approach to program evaluation, Krajcik and Penick (1987) compared the skills of recent graduates in science education at the University of Iowa to a group of experienced science teachers attending a summer Honors Workshop in science education. The measurement instrument was the National Survey of Science and Mathematics Education, a questionnaire about instructional practices in the teaching of science and mathematics. Data were collected from 40 Honors Workshop teachers and 37 University of Iowa graduates in science education. The data indicated that the recent graduates compared favorably with the Honors Workshop teachers on many dimensions. The beginning teachers and the Honors Workshop teachers had similar course objectives, employed similar teaching strategies, used similar materials and equipment in much the same way, and allocated class time similarly. From these data, Krajcik and Penick conclude that science education at the University of Iowa provided a quality teacher-preparation program. They also include a few recommendations to the program faculty for making selected revisions.

One of the criticisms of the program-evaluation literature raised by Galluzzo (1986) was the lack of studies comparing a standard program to an alternative program. One study that has reported such a comparison was conducted by Denton and Smith (1985), who conducted a cost-effectiveness study of alternate teacher education programs. One program was the standard program for individuals majoring in education and the other was a certification-only program for noneducation majors. The essential difference between the two programs was 12 hours of professional coursework. Using data collected from 82 secondary student teachers and 9,001 secondary school learners and an analysis of costs including faculty, equipment, materials, facilities, and services, Denton and Smith used the pupil-achievement data to relate pupil learning to the cost of delivering a teacher education program. They found that education majors accomplished a 10 percent higher increase in pupil achievement but that it cost $73 more per semester per education major enrolled to effect that 10 percent gain. Thus, they conclude that the certification-only track was more cost-effective than the education-major route.

Perhaps the most consistent institutional effort toward incorporating evaluation into program development is the work conducted at Michigan State University with respect to their elementary education programs. Rather than offer one traditional and monolithic program in elementary education, the faculty developed four alternate programs organized around themes concerning the purposes of schools. The themes are entitled (1) Learning Community, (2) Academic Learning, (3) Multiple Perspectives, and (4) Teaching in Heterogeneous Classrooms. Each course in the professional sequence within each program seeks consistency with all other professional courses within the program theme. For example, the subject area methods class in the Learning Community program is designed to increase preservice teachers' abilities to make decisions about curriculum and instruction that enhance the social and academic skills of their pupils (Little, 1984; Barnes, 1987).

The primary characteristic of this work is a detailed response to Raths's (1987) call for a definition of *program* in teacher education. The faculty members who teach in each of the four alternate programs have defined what is distinct about their programs. The contexts, inputs, processes, and outcomes are more clearly delineated. Thus, it becomes more meaningful to implement a large-scale, longitudinal, and meaningful evaluation such as that described by Freeman (1986) and highlighted in Book, Byers, and Freeman (1983), Book and Freeman (1986), and Brousseau and Freeman (1988). Consider that many of the essential features of a program-evaluation effort are included in this approach. The faculty have designed the intents and processes of the program. They have generated the specified outcomes toward which they are teaching and participated in the design of the evaluation instruments and procedures. Program development through program evaluation is enhanced once there is delineation of the concepts of beginning teacher, how he or she will be prepared, and what data will serve as evidence of effectiveness. Barnes (1987) indicates that graduates of the revised, thematic programs are more able to attribute their proficiency with specific teaching skills precisely to professional learning activities in the preservice program, rather than to on-the-job experiences. She suggests that the evaluation data indicate a greater likelihood of students' transferring their skills from the practice setting to the classroom.

In an attempt to bring some commonality to a field heretofore marked by the idiosyncratic use of evaluation practices at individual institutions, an effort was begun under the auspices of the National Center for Research on Teacher Education at Michigan State University (Freeman, 1989). A group of program evaluators from ten institutions developed a common questionnaire for follow-up studies that could be used by institutions nationwide. Entitled the National Database for Teacher Education Program Follow-up, the project has been field-testing a rather extensive follow-up questionnaire. Preliminary results reported by Loadman (1989) suggest that the questionnaire has the potential to link faculty members at both similar and dissimilar institutions as they undertake a program evaluation effort. This project represents the first attempt to assist institutions in conducting meaningful program evaluations, and establishes the framework for a network of teacher education program evaluators.

USING EVALUATION RESULTS

Since the late 1960s, program evaluators (Chelimsky, 1987a; Mathis, 1980; Weiss, 1972) have become increasingly aware that evaluation is not "method bound" but, rather, bound by the sociopolitical context within which evaluations are conducted and data are used. Ideally, evaluation data are used to make objective program decisions regarding program development, modification, operation, effectiveness, and the like. However, program evaluation data are rarely used in such a direct, straightforward manner (Chelimsky, 1987b; Patton, 1978). Part of the problem in determining the nature and extent of use lies with the definition of *use* itself.

The definition typically advanced in the past has been that use occurs when evaluation data are directly employed in objective, observable ways in program modification and operation (Cohen, 1977; Mathis, 1980; Patton, 1978). However, such a definition naively does not take into account the sociopolitical context in which programs operate and are evaluated, nor does it acknowledge that program-evaluation data constitute just one of several bits of information (e.g., governmental statutes, personal gain) that enter into program decision making, especially in teacher education. A more realistic view is that use of evaluation data in program decision making is almost always diffuse in nature and not always (if ever) directly observable (Patton, 1978); use is an iterative process that focuses on the assimilation of evaluation information into the decision-making process and not a determination of it (Craig & Adams, 1981).

How then can program-evaluation systems be structured to more efficiently use the data the system provide? The answer to that question seems to be to develop program-evaluation systems for teacher education in which the emphasis from the outset is on building mechanisms to increase the systematic inclusion of evaluation data in program decision making, a suggestion advanced by evaluators working in a variety of settings (e.g., Akpom, 1986; Covert, 1987; Craig & Adams, 1981; Mowbray, 1988; Nowakowski, 1985; Smith, 1988). First and foremost, policymakers, administrators, and program personnel at all levels must be actively involved in the organization and implementation of the evaluation. This starts with the chief administrative officer responsible for the program (usually the dean) but extends to all individuals who are involved in the program and have a stake in its operation. The particular procedures by which this involvement is accomplished can vary (e.g., Havelock & Lindquist, 1980), but the outcome should be that all involved have the opportunity to conduct a preliminary overview of the evaluation and an analysis of its various ramification where the intent is to identify their perceptions of (a) the present institutional and program circumstances, (b) the ideal program, (c) the need to conduct an evaluation, (d) the possible options for implementing the evaluation, (e) the possible program implications that might be suggested by different evaluation data, and (f) the resource restrictions within which the evaluation must be conducted (Craig & Adams, 1981). The objective is not to establish the form and substance of what the evaluation should be, but to provide the individuals involved with an understanding of how the evaluation process can operate and of its possible outcomes. This process will allow individuals to (a) set the parameters within which the evaluation can realistically function, (b) develop a commitment to the evaluation process, and (c) identify possible program decisions that could result. That is, the process will facilitate the use of program-evaluation data in program decision making.

Traditional definitions of evaluation require feedback of the data to the identified audiences. Indeed, recent writings about program evaluation in teacher education emphasize the utilization of results as an essential attribute of a complete program-evaluation effort (e.g., Freeman, 1987). And although there is some debate about how this is best accomplished, the evaluation literature does provide a number of recommendations regarding how evaluators can stimulate evaluation use (e.g., Mowbray, 1988; Smith, 1988). The strategies range from reporting findings in terms familiar to the intended users to designing problem-solving activities based upon the data collected during the evaluation, to stating recommendations as questions or goals that should be addressed rather than as delineated specific courses of action (Freeman, 1987; Smith, 1988). A major weakness of virtually all of the teacher education program-evaluation models we found is that knowledge utilization is not considered an essential ingredient. An evaluation in which useful and usable data are collected and that meets the criterion of internal logic is doomed to failure unless knowledge utilization is considered at every evaluation decision point.

A FINAL WORD

It is difficult to assess the overall impact evaluation has had in program development in teacher education because the scope of problems addressed through evaluation is unconnected. This chapter presented many reasons for the inchoate nature of program evaluation including vague and general notions of outcomes, difficulty in accurately identifying audiences, lack of network for sharing program-evaluation practice and data, variety of methodological issues, inability of teacher educators to present a unified definition of what a teacher education program is, historic lack of inquiry by teacher educators, and absence of a recursive system for program evaluation in schools, colleges, and departments of education in which utilization is an essential feature. For practice in teacher education to be informed by data about the field, program administrators in schools, colleges, and departments of education need to allocate resources and qualified personnel to an evaluation that enfranchises the faculty to become active participants at all stages of the process. Program evaluation in teacher education as a practice has hardly been tested for its potential. Our conclusion is that most institutions are committed to program evaluation insofar as it relates to accountability. It is our opinion that such a narrow conception of program evaluation always relegates evaluation to a reoccurring temporary system within a larger structure. It does not have the credibility of the faculty or the administration and it makes insignificant impacts on the total program.

Each of the shortcomings described in this chapter is not new and neither is the solution. To overcome the program-evaluation obstacles identified, teacher educators need to adopt an attitude of inquiry. In our estimation, the best scenario is that program evaluation become a collection of small, loosely coupled studies conducted by a variety of faculty members, all of which are designed to gain a clearer understanding of the contexts, inputs, processes, and outcomes of the teacher education program. These studies would focus on the natural processes of the program and would not necessarily include studies that have interventions. The key feature of any program-evaluation effort is the degree to which it addresses the purposes outlined earlier in this chapter. As the purposes focus more internally on the program, the faculty, and the students, there is an increased likelihood the evaluation effort will serve useful and important functions.

Lest the picture be deemed to be too bleak, we do feel the situation is improving. During the 1980s more writers and more institutions considered the contributions well-designed evaluations could make to a program (Felder, Hollis, & Hous-

ton, 1981; Raths, 1987). At an increasing number of institutions, evaluation is becoming an essential component in a complete program. By examining the behavior of the program through evaluation, the efforts at these institutions can help program faculty approach consensus on the roles of teachers and schools and how beginning teachers should be prepared. We are hopeful that we have prepared a chapter that advocates program evaluation as an essential characteristic in program development in teacher education.

References

Adams, R. D. (1978). Western Kentucky University follow-up evaluation of teacher education graduates. In S. M. Hord & G. E. Hall (Eds.), *Teacher education program evaluation and follow-up studies: A collection of current efforts* (pp. 11–35). Austin, TX: University of Texas, R&D Center for Teacher Education.

Adams, R. D. (1987). Follow-up studies of teacher education graduates. In M. Haberman & J. M. Backus (Eds.), *Advances in teacher education*, (Vol. 3, pp. 181–201). Norwood, NJ: Ablex.

Adams, R. D., & Craig, J. R. (1983). A status report of teacher education program evaluation. *Journal of Teacher Education, 34*(2), 33–36.

Adams, R. D., Craig, J. R., Hord, S. M., & Hall, G. E. (1981). Program evaluation in teacher education: A response to Katz et al. (1981). *Journal of Teacher Education, 32*(5), 21–24.

Akpom, K. (1986). Planning program evaluation to meet management information needs. *Evaluation Practice, 7*(4), 35–37.

Anderson, S. B., Ball, S., & Murphy, R. T. (1975). *Encyclopedia of educational evaluation*. San Francisco: Jossey-Bass.

Ayers, J. B. (1986). *Teacher education program evaluation: A case-study past and future*. (ERIC Document Reproduction Service No. ED 275 669)

Banner, D. K., Doctors, S. I., & Gordon, A. C. (1975). *The politics of social program evaluation*. Cambridge, MA: Ballinger.

Barnes, H. L. (1987). The conceptual basis for thematic teacher education programs. *Journal of Teacher Education, 38*(4), 13–18.

Benz, C. R., & Newman, I. (1986). *Qualitative–quantitative interaction continuum: A model and application to teacher education evaluation*. (ERIC Document Reproduction Service No. ED 269 406)

Berliner, D. C. (1976). Impediments to the study of teacher effectiveness. *Journal of Teacher Education, 27*(1), 5–13.

Bickman, L. (1987). The functions of program theory. In L. Bickman (Ed.), *New directions for program evaluation: Using program theory in evaluation* (Number 33, pp. 5–18). San Francisco: Jossey-Bass.

Book, C., Byers, J., & Freeman, D. J. (1983). Student expectations and teacher education traditions with which we can and cannot live. *Journal of Teacher Education, 34*(1), 9–13.

Book, C., & Freeman, D. J. (1986). Differences in entry characteristics of elementary and secondary teacher candidates. *Journal of Teacher Education, 37*(2), 47–51.

Borich, G. D. (1977). *The appraisal of teaching: Concepts and process*. Reading, MA: Addison-Wesley.

Borich, G. D. (1978). *The evaluation of teaching: A sourcebook of instruments*. Reading, MA: Addison-Wesley.

Borich, G. D. (1979). *Three models for conducting follow-up studies of teacher education and training*. Austin, TX: University of Texas, R&D Center for Teacher Education.

Borich, G. D. (1982). Building program ownership: A collaborative approach to defining and evaluating the teacher training program. In S. M. Hord, T. V. Savage, & L. J. Bethel (Eds.), *Training education networks: Toward usable strategies for teacher education program evaluation* (pp. 81–100). Austin, TX: University of Texas, R&D Center for Teacher Education.

Borich, G. D. (1983). Evaluation models: A question of purpose not terminology. *Educational Evaluation and Policy Analysis, 5*(1), 61–64.

Brosseau, B. A., & Freeman, D. J. (1988). How do teacher education faculty members define desirable teacher traits? *Teaching and Teacher Education: An International Journal of Research and Studies, 4*(3), 267–273.

Capie, W., Anderson, S. J., Johnson, C. E., & Ellet, C. D. (1980). *Teacher performance assessment instruments: A handbook for interpretation*. Athens, GA: Teacher Assessment Project.

Caro, F. G. (1971). *Readings in evaluation research*. New York: Russell Sage Foundation.

Chelimsky, E. (1987a). The politics of program evaluation. In D. S. Cordray, H. S. Bloom, & R. J. Light (Eds.), *New directions for program evaluation: Evaluation practice in review* (Number 34, p. 5–21). San Francisco: Jossey-Bass.

Chelimsky, E. (1987b). What have we learned about the politics of program evaluation? *Evaluation Practice, 8*(1), 5–21.

Cohen, L. H. (1977). Factors affecting the utilization of mental health evaluation research findings. *Professional Psychology, 8*(4), 526–534.

Coker, J. G., & Coker, H. (1982). *Classroom observations keyed for effectiveness research*. Atlanta, GA: Georgia State University, Carroll County Teachers Corps Project.

Conrad, K. J., & Miller, T. Q. (1987). Measuring and testing program philosophy. In L. Bickman (Ed.), *New directions for program evaluation: Using program theory in evaluation* (Number 33, p. 19–42). San Francisco: Jossey-Bass.

Cook, W. W., Leeds, C. H., & Callis, R. (1951). *The Minnesota teacher attitude inventory*. New York: Psychological Corporation.

Cooper, J. M. (1983). Basic elements in teacher education program evaluation: Implications for future research and development. In K. R. Howey & W. E. Gardner (Eds.), *The education of teachers: A look ahead* (pp. 118–135). New York: Longman.

Covert, R. W. (1987). Ways of involving clients in the evaluation process. *Evaluation Practice, 8*(4), 83–87.

Craig, J. R., & Adams, R. D. (1981, February). *Use-oriented evaluation*. In S. M. Hord & R. D. Adams (Eds.), *Teacher education program evaluation, 1981: Theory and practice* (pp. 38–49). Austin, TX: University of Texas, R&D Center for Teacher Education.

Cronbach, L. J. (1963). Course improvement through evaluation. In A.

A. Bellack & H. M. Kliebard (Eds.), *Curriculum and evaluation*. Berkeley, CA: McCutchan.

de Voss, G., & Hawk, D. (1983). Follow-up models in teacher education. *Educational Evaluation and Policy Analysis, 5*(2), 163–171.

Denton, J. J., & Smith, N. L. (1985). Alternative teacher preparation programs: A cost-effectiveness comparison. *Educational Evaluation and Policy Analysis, 1*(3), 197–205.

Denton, J. J., Tsai, C., & Chevrette, P. (1985). Perceptions of former students on degree of emphasis to place on pedagogical topics. College Station, TX: Texas A & M University. (ERIC Document Reproduction Service No. ED 261 997)

Dickson, G. E., & Wiersma, W. (1985). *Empirical measurement of teacher performance*. Toledo, OH: University of Toledo, College of Education.

Doyle, W. (1986). Classroom organization and management. In M. C. Wittrock (Ed.), *Handbook of research on teaching* (3rd ed., pp. 392–431). New York: Macmillan.

Erly, M. C. (1982). A practitioner's perception regarding programs. In S. M. Hord, T. V. Savage, & L. J. Bethel (Eds.), *Toward usable strategies for teacher education program evaluation* (pp. 39–50). Austin, TX: University of Texas, R&D Center for Teacher Education.

Felder, B. D., Hollis, L. Y., & Houston, W. R. (1981). *Reflections on the evaluation of a teacher education program: The University of Houston experience*. Washington, DC: American Association of Colleges for Teacher Education.

Freeman, D. J. (1986). *Overview: Program evaluation in the College of Education at Michigan State University* (Program Evaluation Series No. 10). East Lansing, MI: Michigan State University, College of Education. (ERIC Document Reproduction Service No. ED 281 830)

Freeman, D. J. (1987, October). *Issues and strategies for using program evaluation findings in teacher education at Michigan State University*. Paper presented at the American Evaluation Association, Boston.

Freeman, D. J. (1989). *A compendium of items for follow-up surveys of teacher education programs*. East Lansing, MI: National Center for Research on Teacher Education.

Galluzzo, G. R. (1982). Program evaluation in teacher education: From admissions to follow-up. In S. M. Hord, T. V. Savage, & L. J. Bethel (Eds.), *Toward usable strategies for teacher education program evaluation* (pp. 67–80). Austin, TX: University of Texas, R&D Center for Teacher Education.

Galluzzo, G. R. (1984, March). *An evaluation of a teacher education program*. Paper presented at the annual meeting of the American Educational Research Association, New Orleans.

Galluzzo, G. R. (1986). Teacher education program evaluation: Organizing or agonizing? In J. D. Raths & F. G. Katz (Eds.), *Advances in teacher education* (Vol. 2, pp. 222–237). Norwood, NJ: Ablex.

Galluzzo, G. R. (1987). Assessment of the teaching skills of beginning teachers. In L. M. Rudner (Ed.), *What's happening in teacher testing* (pp. 39–42). Washington, DC: U.S. Department of Education.

Gardner, W. E. (1982). NCATE accreditation: Issues, problems, and needed research. In S. M. Hord, T. V. Savage, & L. J. Bethel (Eds.), *Toward usable strategies for teacher education program evaluation* (pp. 51–66). Austin, TX: University of Texas, R&D Center for Teacher Education.

Gorry, G., & Goodrich, T. J. (1978). On the role of values in program evaluation. *Evaluation Quarterly, 2*, 561–571.

Guba, E. G. (1987). Naturalistic evaluation. In D. S. Cordray, H. S. Bloom, & R. J. Light (Eds.), *New directions for program evaluation: Evaluation practice in review* (Number 34, pp. 23–43). San Francisco: Jossey-Bass.

Havelock, R. G., & Lindquist, J. (1980). A conceptual framework for increasing the impact. In J. Lindquist (Ed.), *Increasing the impact of social innovations funded by grantmaking organizations* (pp. 5–19). Battle Creek, MI: W. K. Kellogg Foundation.

Hord, S. M., Savage, T. V., & Bethel, L. J. (1982). *Toward usable strategies for teacher education program evaluation*. Austin, TX: University of Texas, R&D Center for Teacher Education.

Hummell, T. J., & Strom, S. M. (1987). The relationship between teaching experience and satisfaction with teacher preparation: A summary of three surveys. *Journal of Teacher Education, 38*(5), 28–36.

Joint Committee on Standards for Educational Evaluation. (1981). *Standards for evaluations of educational programs, projects, and materials*. New York: McGraw-Hill.

Kaplan, A. (1964). *The conduct of inquiry: Methodology for behavioral science*. San Francisco: Chandler Publishing.

Katz, L. G., & Raths, J. D. (1986a, July). *Dispositional goals for teacher education: Problems of identification and assessment*. Paper presented at the International Conference on Education for Teaching, Kingston, Jamaica.

Katz, L. G., & Raths, J. D. (1986b). Dispositions as goals for teacher education. *Teaching and Teacher Education, 1*(4), 301–307.

Katz, L., Raths, J., Mohanty, C., Kurachi, A., & Irving, J. (1981). Follow-up studies: Are they worth the trouble? *Journal of Teacher Education, 32*(2), 18–24.

Koehler, V. (1985). Research on preservice teacher education. In S. M. Hord, S. F. O'Neal, & M. L. Smith (Eds.), *Beyond the looking glass* (pp. 67–84). Austin, TX: University of Texas, R&D Center for Teacher Education.

Krajcik, S. S., & Penick, J. E. (1987). *Evaluation of a model science teacher education program*. Unpublished manuscript, University of Iowa, Iowa City.

Little, T. H. (1984). *Course design within the context of a thematic teacher education program: A case study* (Program Evaluation Series No. 6). East Lansing, MI: Michigan State University. (ERIC Document Reproduction Service No. ED 265 095)

Loadman, W. E. (1989). Developing a national database for preservice teacher education follow-up studies. Paper presented at the meeting of the American Association of Colleges for Teacher Education, Annaheim, CA.

Madaus, G. F., Scriven, M. S., & Stufflebeam, D. L. (1983). *Evaluation models: Viewpoints on educational and human services evaluation*, Boston: Kluwer-Nijhoff.

Mathis, W. (1980). Evaluating: The policy implications. *Phi Delta Kappa CEDR Quarterly, 13*(2), 3–6, 22.

Medley, D. M. (1977). *Teacher competence and teacher effectiveness: A review of process–product research*. Washington, DC: American Association of Colleges for Teacher Education. (ERIC Document Reproduction Service No. ED 143 629)

Medley, D. M. (1982). *Teacher competency testing and the teacher educator*. Charlottesville, VA: University of Virginia, School of Education, Bureau of Educational Testing.

Mowbray, C. T. (1988). Getting the system to respond to evaluation findings. In J. A. McLaughlin, L. J. Weber, R. W. Covert, & R. B. Ingle (Eds.), *New directions for program evaluation: Evaluation utilization* (Number 39, p. 47–58). San Francisco: Jossey-Bass.

National Council for Accreditation of Teacher Education. (1987). *Standards for the accreditation of teacher education*. Washington, DC: Author.

Nelli, E., & Nutter, N. (1984). *A model for evaluating teacher education programs*. Washington, DC: American Association of Colleges for Teacher Education.

Nowakowski, J. (1985). Evaluation for strategy setting. *Evaluation Practice, 6*(4), 57–61.

Patton, M. Q. (1978). *Utilization-focused evaluation.* Beverly Hills, CA: Sage.

Pigge, F. L. (1978). Teacher competencies: Need, proficiency, and where proficiency was developed. *Journal of Teacher Education, 29*(4), 70–76.

Popham, W. H. (1975). *Educational evaluation.* Englewood Cliffs, NJ: Prentice-Hall.

Raths, J. D. (1987). An alternative view of the evaluation of teacher education programs. In M. Haberman & J. M. Backus (Eds.), *Advances in teacher education* (Vol. 3, pp. 202–217). Norwood, NJ: Ablex.

Reed, H. B. (1978). *The accuracy–meaning tensions in teacher education evaluation.* Paper presented at the F. G. Watson Festschrift Conference, Cambridge, MA. (ERIC Document Reproduction Service No. ED 205 524)

Reiff, J. C. (1980). Program evaluation based on faculty/student responses. *College Student Journal, 14*(3), 237–246.

Roth, R. A. (1982). Requirements of a data base for effective program evaluation. In S. M. Hord, T. V. Savage, & L. J. Bethel (Eds.), *Toward usable strategies for teacher education program evaluation* (pp. 23–38). Austin, TX: University of Texas, R&D Center for Teacher Education.

Sandefur, J. T. (1970). *An illustrated model for the evaluation of teacher education graduates.* Washington, DC: American Association of Colleges for Teacher Education.

Sandefur, J. T. (1982). Teacher education's evaluation of graduates: Where are we going and how do we know when we get there? In S. M. Hord, T. V. Savage, & L. J. Bethel (Eds.), *Toward usable strategies for teacher education program evaluation* (pp. 9–22). Austin, TX: University of Texas, R&D Center for Teacher Education.

Sandefur, J. T. (1987). Historical perspective. In L. M. Rudner (Ed.), *What's happening in teacher testing: An analysis of state teacher testing practices* (pp. 11–14). Washington, DC: U.S. Government Printing Office.

Scriven, M. (1967). The concept of evaluation. In M. W. Apple et al. (Eds.), *Educational evaluation analysis and responsibility* (pp. 39–63). Berkeley, CA: McCutchan.

Scriven, M. (1972). Prose and cons about goal-free evaluation. *Evaluation Comment, 3*(4), 1.

Scriven, M. (1981). *Evaluation thesaurus* (3rd ed). Inverness, CA: Edgepress.

Shulman, L. S. (1986). Those who understand: Knowledge growth in teaching. *Educational Researcher, 15*(2), 4–14.

Smith, M. F. (1988). Evaluation utilization revisited. In J. A. McLaughlin, L. J. Weber, R. W. Covert, & R. B. Ingle (Eds.), *New directions for program evaluation: Evaluation utilization* (Number 39, p. 7–19). San Francisco: Jossey-Bass.

Stake, R. E. (1967). The countenance of educational evaluation. *Teachers College Record, 68*(7), 523–540.

Stake, R. E. (1981). Persuasions, not models. *Educational Evaluation & Policy Analysis, 3*(1), 83–84.

Stodolsky, S. (1984). The evaluation of teaching: The limits of looking. *Educational Researcher, 13*(9), 11–18.

Stufflebeam, D. L. (1982). Explorations in the evaluation of teacher education. In S. M. Hord, T. V. Savage, & L. J. Bethel (Eds.), *Toward usable strategies for teacher education program evaluation* (pp. 131–168). Austin, TX: University of Texas R & D Center for Teacher Education.

Stufflebeam, D. L., Foley, W. J., Gephart, W. J., Guba, E. G., Hammond, R. L., Merriman, H. O., & Provus, M. M. (1971). *Educational evaluaton and decision-making.* Itasca, IL: F. E. Peacock.

Stufflebeam, D. L. & Shinkfield, A. J. (1985). *Systematic evaluation: A self-instructional guide to theory and practice.* Boston: Kluwer-Nijhoff.

Stufflebeam, D. L., & Webster, W. J. (1988). Evaluation as an administrative function. In N. Boyan (Ed.), *Handbook of research on educational administration* (pp. 569–601). New York: Longman.

Suchman, E. A. (1972). Action for what: A critique of evaluative research. In C. H. Weiss (Ed.), *Evaluating action programs: Readings in social action and education* (pp. 113–129). Boston: Allyn & Bacon.

Troyer, M. E., & Pace, C. R. (1944). *Evaluation in teacher education.* Washington, DC: American Council on Education.

Weiss, C. H. (1972). *Evaluation research: Methods for assessing program effectiveness.* Englewood Cliffs, NJ: Prentice-Hall.

Williamson, R. C., Swingle, P. G., & Sarget, S. S. (1982). *Social Psychology.* Itasca, IL: F. E. Peacock.

Worthen, B. R., & Sanders, J. R. (1988). *Educational evaluation: Theory and practice.* Worthington, OH: Charles A. Jones.

Wortman, P. M. (1975). Evaluation research: A psychological perspective. *American Psychologist, 30*, 562–575.

Yeany, R. H. (1980). Redefining process and product in teacher training: Alternative modes for evaluating teacher training programs. *Journal of Research in Science Teaching, 17*(5), 383–386.

Zeichner, K. M., & Tabachnik, B. R. (1981). Are the effects of university teacher education washed out by school experience? *Journal of Teacher Education, 32*(3), 7–11.

Zimpher, N. L., & Loadman, W. E. (1986). *A documentation and assessment system for student and program development.* Washington, DC: American Association of Colleges for Teacher Education.

·34·

CHANGING TEACHER EDUCATION

H. Jerome Freiberg and Hersholt C. Waxman

UNIVERSITY OF HOUSTON

Change in its broadest view is the modification of existing conditions in response to present forces or future needs. The history of human experience is one of change. From the grasslands of southern Africa hundreds of thousands of years ago to the high technology cities of the twenty-first century, change is part of our everyday existence. Change is a cumulative process, with each new successful modification building upon previous efforts to form a new strata of efforts, ideas, processes, and products. The rate of change increases or decreases depending on human and world events. Many would see the Dark Ages (A.D. 400–1500) as a time of limited change, yet the cumulative efforts made during this time exploded into the Renaissance (A.D. 1500–1600), when social, political, and technological change forged the structure of Western civilizations that exist today.

Numerous theories about change relate to organizations both small and large and to individuals, but one outcome is certain: Institutions exist at the discretion of society. If the institution fails to respond to the needs of society, it loses its support and ultimately ceases to exist. An understanding of the processes and forces of change enable teacher educators to better initiate and respond to challenges and demands being placed on the profession by external and internal sources.

This chapter analyzes the issues of change from both a *macro* and a *micro* perspective. The macro perspective examines broad influences of change and their implications for teacher education. The chapter includes, under the macro analysis, the role of the federal government as change agent and seven global factors that inhibit or support change in teacher education. A micro-level analysis examines the role that field experiences, innovative teaching tools (e.g., microteaching), and feedback approaches have played in changing teacher education. A *meso*, or institutional, level, where there

is collaboration between and within institutions (e.g., academy schools and induction programs), is explored as a possible link between the macro and micro levels of change.

The final section of the chapter includes a discussion of change strategies using a model developed by Chin and Benne (1969), which examines change from three perspectives: rational-empirical, normative-reeducative, and power-coercive. The three strategies are examined within the context of change in teacher education in the 1980s. The final section presents recommendations for change strategies and a research agenda that could be explored into the 1990s.

A MACRO VIEW OF CHANGE

There have been several key players in the evolution of the teaching profession and the subsequent development of teacher education, from the first public normal school in 1837 (Haberman, 1982) to the nearly 1,400 United States teacher-preparation programs in 1989. One of the least prominent historically has been the federal government. Due in part to the states' sovereignty over education, the federal government has played a limited role since the Department of Education was established in 1867 to serve the states as a data gatherer and dissemination source (Howsam, Corrigan, Denemark, & Nash, 1976). Although the federal government has played a limited role historically, during the 1960s it extended and reshaped its responsibilities in education and teacher education.

The Federal Government As Change Agent

The federal government's strategy for educational change since the beginning of the 1960s has been to move American

We wish to thank Gene Hall (University of Colorado in Greeley) and Michael Fullan (University of Toronto) for their guidance and feedback on the initial draft of this chapter; to express our appreciation to Tessa J. Shokri for her diligence in typing the chapter against pressing timelines; and to thank W. Robert Houston for his guidance and feedback on subsequent drafts of the chapter.

education from an exclusive educational system, which was evident through most of American history, to an inclusive system through both equality of opportunity for students and a new multicultural cohort of teachers. The government provided resources to school districts to improve instruction and learning through new curriculum and staff development and to colleges and universities to expand the pool of potential teachers to reflect the ethnic and racial composition of the schools and to improve the quality of teacher preparation. Equality in the 1960s was a direct result of increased federal involvement through legislative acts. This period was characterized by federal legislation as part of Lyndon Johnson's Great Society (Burns, 1968). Key legislative acts included the Civil Rights Act of 1964, incorporating Title VI, which was designed to end segregation by prohibiting the use of federal funds to support racially segregated schools. The Elementary and Secondary Act of 1965 included Title I and Head Start programs and was designed to improve opportunities and education for the disadvantaged. Some federal legislation predates the Great Society period including the National Defense Education Act of 1958, which supported programs to improve the quality of science and mathematics instruction in the public schools through new curriculum and teacher training. Public Law 94–142, Education for All Handicapped Children Act, passed in 1975, continued the emphasis on equality of educational opportunity for all children by providing for the least restrictive learning environment. The Teacher Corps legislation, enacted in 1965, was intended to be the cornerstone of change in teacher education.

Teacher Corps

Teacher Corps attempted to parallel the successful Peace Corps model (which was designed to improve the quality of life of people in developing countries) by improving the quality of education for low-income students in the nation's urban schools. Teacher Corps legislation was designed to affect teacher education through improving the quality of teachers entering the profession. Over 13,000 black, Hispanic, Asian, Native American, and white liberal arts college graduates were recruited into Teacher Corps projects during its first 10 years of operation, and nearly 70 percent remained in teaching or education (Freiberg, 1981a). Teacher Corps was designed to change the way colleges of education prepared teachers by providing resources to develop innovative practices and linking school districts, colleges, and communities, to provide more meaningful clinical experiences and change the way decisions were made about teacher education.

Bush (1987) calculates that the federal government expended during the life of the Teacher Corps "over a half billion dollars, the largest single effort in teacher education ever made" (p. 15). The Teacher Corps programs, which lasted from 1965 through 1982; signaled the entry of the federal government as a change agent into teacher education (see Bush, 1977; Fox, 1975; Freiberg, 1981a; Marsh, 1979). Teacher Corps became a pioneer in developing and supporting educational change and innovations in schools and teacher-preparation institutions, including, "team teaching, flexible grouping of students, individualized and personalized instruction, bilingual and multicultural education, competency-based teacher education, alternative schools, collaborative planning and decision-making, field-based teacher training, community-based teacher education, and diagnostic and prescriptive teaching" (Freiberg, 1981a, p. 232).

Teacher Corps utilized two major strategies in changing teacher education. The first, beginning in 1965 and concluding in 1975, could be called the *preservice* phase. It emphasized the recruitment of from 50 to 100 teacher education interns per project. Often they were minorities, and all were committed to changing schooling, primarily of disadvantaged students. In the process of preparing a new generation of prospective teachers, Teacher Corps leadership hoped to change the content and approach used in teacher education.

The second, or *inservice*, phase began in 1976 with the reduction of intern recruits to four per project. The emphasis was placed on enriching the quality of veteran teachers in the public schools through staff development and structural changes by improving school climate (see for example, Pyper, Freiberg, Ginsburg, & Spuck, 1987). In each project, a pyramid of schools (a high school and its feeder schools) was targeted for special attention and additional resources. The change to an inservice phase was necessitated by a tightening of the job market for new teachers (W. L. Smith, 1975) and a realization that inexperienced interns had little credibility for enacting change with their veteran counterparts (Fox, 1975).

The longevity of Teacher Corps was unique in federal efforts to change teacher education. The extent to which Teacher Corps processes and products were disseminated to other non–Teacher Corps sites is an open question. The last initiative (1978–1983) had a fifth year designed exclusively for dissemination of project results. The funds and the program were eliminated in the fourth year, before large-scale dissemination could occur.

Teacher Corps was evaluated more than most education programs in the 1960s and 1970s. However, only a handful of studies met the criteria for quality research or objective evaluation. The following studies are reviewed to assess the effectiveness of Teacher Corps as a change agent for teacher education.

Colleges and School Districts. Teacher Corps programs attempted to change the status quo in colleges of education through professional-development activities for teacher education faculty. These activities included support for conference travel to national meetings, special seminars on current research and practice, and team curriculum-planning and curriculum-development activities for teacher education interns. Fox (1975), however, found that Teacher Corps had mixed results in his analysis of nine studies (from 1968–1974) of Teacher Corps as a change agent for schools or universities conducted during the preservice phase. Fox concludes that Teacher Corps was effective in recruiting minority interns with backgrounds that were uniquely different from traditional teacher education students. However, the interns were not effective change agents in the schools. He found that colleges and universities (institutions of higher education) were less flexible than school districts, and few changes were made in teacher education curriculum, instructional procedures, or basic organizational arrangements. This lack of change was due in part, according to Fox, to the ability of colleges and universities to isolate Teacher Corps projects from other teacher-preparation components. Additionally, IHEs were not geared to coordinating effectively with school districts and communities. He concludes that greater school-district involvement inhibited innovation and, the more service directed the project, the less curricular and instructional change. Compared with other federal programs, however, Fox considers Teacher Corps successful in achieving its inservice objectives.

Bush and Bock (1982) conducted a study of the institutionalization of change in colleges of education in four program sites in 1980–1981 as a result of their participation in the 1978 and 1979 Teacher Corps program cycles. Using a case study methodology, the authors conclude:

In one way or another, all of the schools of education studied made substantial changes along the following lines:
(1) Strengthened and expanded their attention to inservice education.
(2) Expanded and enriched the field-based aspects of their training programs.
(3) Brought themselves and the local schools into a more collaborative relationship.
(4) Increased the prominence of community participation in educational personnel development programs.
(5) Brought inservice education and preservice education into a closer relationship.
(6) Modified departmental organizations and operations.
(7) Dropped old courses, added new courses, and changed the content, emphasis, and methods of existing courses.
(8) Increased emphasis in such substantive areas as multicultural education, the education of gifted and talented students, special education, and the teaching of reading and mathematics.
(9) Altered the understandings, attitudes, and behaviors of faculty and students, causing them to be more sensitive to the needs of children from homes of minorities and the poor.
The evidence is that such changes have already taken place in the schools and departments of education studied and are likely to last beyond the federal funding period. (p. xxii)

The discrepancy between the Fox review of Teacher Corps and the Bush and Bock studies could be a function of methodologies and the period when the studies were conducted. The Fox review summarizes the results of nine studies conducted prior to 1975, during the preservice phase when Teacher Corps was changing its mandates for colleges of education and public schools. The Bush and Bock study directly examined on-going projects near the end of the Teacher Corps cycle and might reflect a change process built upon previous knowledge and experiences in improving teacher education.

Student Interns. Marsh (1979) conducted a 3-year national study of the effects of teacher-preparation programs on the instructional skills of 82 graduates of the Sixth Cycle Teacher Corps program during their first year of full-time teaching (1973–1974). The graduates were compared with a matched sample of new teachers (grades 2–6) who did not receive their preparation from Teacher Corps programs. Classroom performance in the two groups was measured by observations, using the Stallings Observation System (Stallings & Kaskowitz, 1974), the Metropolitan Achievement Test, and the Piers-Harris Self-Concept Scale. A teacher questionnaire was also included, to gather information about the teacher's actions as a change agent, the utilization of community resources, the development of new curricular materials, and the perceptions of problems related to schooling. Marsh concludes that the Teacher Corps graduates during their first year of teaching were most different from the control-group beginning teachers in (a) developing culturally relevant curricula, (b) using community resources in teaching and initiating contact with parents, and (c) holding positive attitudes about reading development and causes of poverty in the society. These variables reflect graduates' special concerns about low-income and minority-group children.

A second difference between Teacher Corps graduates and control teachers was the teachers' attitudes about reading development and causes of poverty. Teacher Corps graduates believed they had more control over pupils' reading development. Teacher Corps graduates were more likely to blame poverty on the failure of the society to provide good education for low-income students; the control group considered poverty to be the result of lack of effort by the poor. Marsh, however, found no differences between the two groups of teachers in either their perceptions of the importance of change or their ability to bring about change in the schools. Students in the fourth and sixth grades (10–12-year-olds) had positive changes in self-concept that were significantly greater with Teacher Corps graduates. However, no differences were observed in instructional variables in the classroom. Marsh concludes his study by stating:

Thus, rather clear and consistent differences between Teacher Corps graduates and controls on such things as the introduction of culturally relevant materials or the use of community resources did not generalize to such areas as being a change agent in the school or the interaction between teacher and pupils in the classroom as assessed by the teacher performance measures used in the study. (1979, p. 28)

The findings by Marsh indicate that Teacher Corps graduates did not receive unique observable teaching skills, but they did bring attributes that had a direct effect on the self-concept of some students. There is little evidence that the curricular models, instructional strategies, or intergration of university, school, and community evident in the Teacher Corps programs had a lasting effect on teacher education.

Education Professions Development Act

The Education Professions Development Act (EPDA, Public Law 90-35), enacted on June 29, 1967, was another attempt by the federal government to change the agenda for teacher education. According to Wilkerson (1979), Congress hastily enacted the legislation with little debate and no conference, because Teacher Corps funding was to expire on June 20, 1967. The Education Professions Development Act lasted until 1976 and funded "26 national programs with nearly 3,000 projects, involving the participation of more than 300,000 persons" (see

Table 34-1) at a cost of nearly $800,000,000 (p. xi). The EPDA's dominant goal was to unify the layers of the educational system and provide educational and social reform, with efforts directed at changing the system "on all levels of education" (p. viii).

The EPDA was designed to improve the quality of educational personnel generally, improve education for the disadvantaged, meet other critical personnel needs, and develop educational leadership. It drew upon some of the most innovative thinking of its time to make comprehensive changes in education; for instance, programs like the *Training of Teacher Trainers* Program (Triple T), established to improve the quality of staff and inservice development; *Training Complexes*, which brought together school districts and universities to benefit teacher education students; *New Careers in Education*, designed to meet the shortage of qualified teachers; and *Educational Leadership* programs, designed to improve the quality of administrative personnel in the schools. A litany of macro-level initiatives from EPDA funding resulted in limited change. Wilkerson concludes that few of the EPDA programs

TABLE 34–1 Education Professions Development Act Programs

A. Programs to Improve Educational Personnel Generally
   Basic Studies Program
   Training of Teacher Trainers Program
   Protocol and Training Materials Program
   Competency-Based Education Program
   School Personnel Utilization Program
   Training Complexes (forerunner of the Teacher Centers Program)
   Teacher Centers Program
B. Programs to Improve Education for the Disadvantaged
   Career Opportunities Program
   Urban/Rural School Development Program
   Targeting Resources on the Educational Needs of the Disadvantaged Program
   Teacher Corps
C. Programs to Meet Other Critical Personnel Needs
   Early Childhood Education Program
   Exceptional Children Program
   New Careers in Education Program
   State Grants Program (to attract and qualify personnel to meet critical teacher shortages)
   Pupil Personnel Services Program
   Vocational Education Program (general personnel training)
   Bilingual Education Program
   Indian Teacher Education Program
   Volunteers in Education Program
   Teacher Training in Developing Institutions Program
   Media Specialists Program
D. Programs to Develop Educational Leadership
   Vocational Education Leadership Development Program
   Educational Leadership Program
   Fellowships for the Management of Educational Change Program
   Project Open

Note. From *The Education Professions Development Act: In Congress, in the Office of Education, and in the Field* (p. xii) by D. A. Wilkerson, 1979, Westport, CT: Mediax Associates. Reprinted by permission.

and projects yielded "comprehensive and systematic evidence on program outcomes, in terms of changes in teacher behavior and/or student learning" (p. xiii).

Comprehensive Teacher Education Models

In 1968, the U.S. Office of Education, through the Bureau of Research, funded nine *Comprehensive Models for Preparing Elementary Teachers* (Burdin & Lanzillotti, 1969). The change strategy was to provide teacher-preparation institutions with models of preparation and materials for their implementation, thus increasing the effectiveness of such programs. Eight models were subsequently funded for feasibility studies in 1969 (seven of the original nine, plus one additional model). Small amounts were allocated to the models over the following decade, but the federal initiative was never completed because of lack of funds; priorities changed and the emphasis was more on creating new programs than refining old ones.

Competency-Based Teacher Education

The Comprehensive Teacher Education Models projects evolved into the Competency-Based Teacher Education movement (CBTE) in the early 1970s (see, for example, Franc, 1978; Hall & Jones, 1976; Houston & Howsam, 1972; Rosner, 1972). The competency- or performance-based teacher education movement emphasized mastery by the learner of specific observable teaching behaviors or competencies. "The [teacher education] student must either be able to demonstrate his ability to promote desirable learning or exhibit behaviors known to promote it" (Elam, 1971, p. 2). "Competency-based programs demand explicitness of objectives and of assessment criteria" (Houston & Howsam, 1972, p. 7). The teacher education student was required to master a series of competencies. This was in contrast to the traditional mode of learning, in which a student took a series of courses and received grades for mostly paper-and-pencil learning. The CBTE approach emphasized individualized instruction, usually through instructional modules containing media and print information. The student was held accountable for mastering the one set of modules before moving on to another set. The role of the teacher was changed from information giver to manager of the instructional process. There was less concern for entrance requirements and greater emphasis on exit tests. The variable of time was considered unimportant, because students would exit at different times, based on their ability to master predetermined competencies.

The competency-based teacher education movement peaked in the late 1970s. The highly visible association of self-paced modules with CBTE presented several problems that had profound implications for those involved in change efforts. Faculty who directed energies toward the development of modules were rarely rewarded by their institutions for their efforts. Hall (personal communication, 1988) cites one major CBTE institution where all six junior faculty who provided module development and leadership did not receive tenure. The variable of time become a management, as well as a philosophical, problem. Although teacher education programs moved to a module system of learning, the universities in which they resided continued with the course approach to learning. Additionally, faculty had difficulty keeping track of and evaluating student mastery on hundreds of discrete behaviors and activities. A research review by Roth (1976) of CBTE programs in 56 colleges and universities was inconclusive regarding changes in teacher education. Roth indicates that one of the difficulties in reaching conclusions about CBTE programs was the lack of generally accepted definitions for competency-based teacher education across programs. The problem of a common frame of reference in federal programs (including definitions for the operation of programs) has inhibited the ability of researchers to measure change and of policymakers to determine which programs should be continued (Berman & McLaughlin, 1978).

The remnants of CBTE, however, can be found in the technologies perfected during the CBTE era, including microteaching, classroom observation analyses, and extended field experiences with video- or audiotaping for later feedback (Freiberg, 1987b). The use of objectives in lesson plans, exit tests for prospective teachers, and performance-based standards for new and veteran teachers using observable criteria (through classroom observations) also have its roots in competency-based teacher education. In the late 1980s school districts in Arizona and Utah were using *outcome-based education programs* to allow students who had received less than a B on tests or assignments to have additional time and tutoring without being penalized with a lower grade (Mitgand, 1988).

Research Centers

Lack of a strong, comprehensive knowledge base was considered a major problem in changing education; thus, the federal government initiated a massive effort to expand the knowledge base of teacher education and included the funding of research centers through the National Institute of Education and, more recently, the Office of Educational Research and Improvement (OERI).

Hall (1974, 1979) and his colleagues (Hall & Hord, 1984, 1987; Hall & Loucks, 1978, 1981; Hall, Loucks, Rutherford, & Newlove, 1975; Manning, 1973; Wallace, 1973) at the Research and Development Center for Teacher Education at The University of Texas in Austin examined the implementation of changes from a developmental or *concerns-based adoption model* (CBAM). They (a) identified and described phases and steps involved in innovation adoption in education institutions, (b) developed assessment methods for predicting successful adoption, and (c) developed measurement procedures for assessing the developmental stages and levels of individuals involved in the innovation.

In their framework for analyzing innovative adoption, Hall and his colleagues found eight levels of use of the innovation: (a) nonuse—taking no action to learn about the innovation; (b) orientation—seeking information about the innovation; (c) initial training—preparing to use the innovation; (d) mechanical—using the innovation in an awkward, mechanical manner; (e) routine—doing a good job with the innovation; (f) refine-

ment—varying the use of the innovation; (g) integrated—sharing with others what has been learned; and (h) renewing—seeking more effective alternatives. Most innovations in teacher education do not reach the renewal level.

Studies conducted on the transfer of staff development to teachers' classrooms (Freiberg, Buckley, & Townsend, 1983; Freiberg, Townsend, & Buckley, 1982) found high levels of agreement between separate ethnographic data collection and the Level of Use of an Innovation (Hall & Loucks, 1978). The Level of Use of an Innovation was able to track teachers' use of the innovations from nonuse to renewal. In these studies, half of the teachers were at the refinement and integration stages of use. The Level-of-Use data provided verification for the changes teachers were experiencing in transferring staff-development materials to their classrooms.

Hall and his colleagues found that the actual implementation of innovations in teacher education can be enhanced by using one or more of several adoption strategies and not using others. In his evaluation of a competency-based teacher education program, for example, Hall (1974) found at least 11 adoption strategies (for which he provided creative labels) that have been extensively employed: (a) the bootstraps approach, (b) the decree strategy (c) the God-bless-you approach, (d) the intensive pretraining approach, (e) the sabbatical strategy, (f) the superstar strategy, (g) the experimental units strategy, (h) the blanket adoption strategy, (i) the outside collaboration strategy, (j) the Pennsylvania contingent strategy, and (k) the good time workshop strategy. The bootstraps approach is one in which an individual or entire group within an institution decides to develop or use a new product, learns how to use it, and collects the necessary resources for using it without outside help. The decree strategy exists when a decision maker within the institution announces that the innovation will begin at a particular time. The God-bless-you approach features an innovative representative or consultant working with the institution for a short time when the innovation is first adopted. The intensive pretraining approach is being used when individuals are introduced to the innovation through workshops or retreats and then begin using the innovation. The sabbatical strategy exists when an individual takes off for an extended period of time to be trained in using the innovation. The superstar strategy has the institution bringing in a recognized expert as a full-time member of the institution. The experimental units strategy features a smaller group of individuals using the innovation on a trial basis. The blanket adoption strategy is being used when the innovation is adopted for everyone in the institution at the same time. The outside collaboration strategy is in place when the institution collaborates with an outside resource system for a long-term relationship. The Pennsylvania contingent strategy comes being when a new group of administrators is added to the institution. Good time workshops are typically designed to entertain individuals and not show a real commitment to the innovation or its adoption.

These different adoption strategies illustrate the problems that have been encountered when some teacher education institutions have tried to adopt innovations and change their programs. The R&D Center for Teacher Education at The University of Texas was one of the few institutions that systematically assessed problems or concerns with change in teacher education.

Reflection in Teacher Education

The Office of Educational Research and Improvement has also funded colleges and universities (1985–1988) in the redesign of their teacher education programs (see Waxman, Freiberg, Vaughan, & Weil, 1988). Reflective-oriented teacher education programs have become an important focus in teacher education, because they try to enable preservice teachers to progress through these developmental stages so that they have (a) technical competence in instruction and management, (b) ability to analyze teaching, (c) awareness that teaching has ethical and moral consequences, and (d) sensitivity to the needs of students with diverse intellectual, racial, physical, and social characteristics (Tom, 1985; Waxman, Freiberg, Vaughan, & Weil, 1988; Zeichner, 1983; Zeichner & Liston, 1987). In the late 1980s several studies examined the effect of inquiry-oriented, or reflective-oriented, teacher education programs on prospective teachers' cognitive-developmental stages (Waxman, Freiberg, Clift, & Houston, 1988; Waxman & Sexton, 1988). Some of the preliminary research and theoretical work in this area suggests that this approach could facilitate appropriate changes in prospective teachers. The initial results indicate that participating projects have changed their teacher-preparation programs and, in specific projects, have had an effect on how student teachers teach in the classroom (Freiberg & Waxman, 1988), but it is too early to determine long-term impact of the OERI projects. If past events are a predictor of future change, the OERI initiative in teacher reflection was too short lived to have a significant impact on the other teacher education programs that were not directly involved in the projects.

Reforms in Teacher Education

Efforts to reform teacher education through the development of professional organizations, reports, and commissions sponsored by federal, state, and local organizations are not new to the profession. Most professions including medicine, law, and divinity (Starr, 1982) have undergone reform efforts as part of their development into recognized professions. Teacher education has had its share of reform efforts throughout this century. The teaching profession evolved into a national movement from the founding of the Department of Education in 1867 and the organizing of the American Association of Teacher Colleges in 1918 through the development of testing procedures initiated by the Pennsylvania Study of Higher Education, the involvement of the Ford Foundation in the development of the Master of Arts in Teaching in the 1950s, and the recent reform efforts by such as the Carnegie Forum on Education and the Economy's Task Force on Teaching as a Profession (1986), the Holmes Group (1986), and the National Council for Accreditation of Teacher Education (NCATE). The various commission reports put forth different strategies for creating a climate for change related to teaching and teacher education.

A Nation at Risk (National Commission on Excellence in Education, 1983) and other commission reports by leaders of business and industry and politicians was to bring about change by making explicit the shortcomings of educational outcomes, creating public awareness, and fermenting local and state efforts to change teaching and teacher education. One strategy of the Carnegie Forum was to initiate a national certification program through a national teaching standards board, which would certify teachers who had demonstrated the highest level of professional competence. The teaching profession would take responsibility for the testing and certifying of teachers. This task is currently the responsibility of the states and is delegated to various governmental agencies. The Holmes Group's strategy for change was to draw upon the total university to educate prospective teachers and link together the major research universities to expand the knowledge base of teaching and teacher education. Both Holmes and Carnegie have proposed eliminating the undergraduate teacher education degree and extending formal preparation and certification periods as a strategy for changing teacher education (Soltis, 1987).

States have directed their efforts at changing teacher education through legislative intervention. Over 1,000 pieces of legislative action were directed at the preparation of teachers during the 1980s (Darling-Hammond & Berry, 1988). The states have used several paths to enact change in teacher education, including strengthening entry and exit requirements for prospective teachers through mandated basic skills tests; increasing preteaching field experiences and limiting the teacher education curriculum (Texas, Virginia, New Jersey, and California have placed limits on the number of education credit hours students may take); and creating alternative paths for receiving certification. Cornbleth (1986) indicates, however, that reform activity should not be confused with change.

WHAT CHANGE?

Factors Inhibiting Change

In looking at the impact of change on teacher education at the macrolevel, we are confronted with a lack of significant differences in how teachers have been prepared for their profession since the 1930s. Despite change efforts, it can still be argued that there have been no fundamental or substantive changes in teacher education during the past several decades (Ashton & Crocker, 1987; Bush, 1987; Keith, 1987; B. O. Smith, 1969, 1980; Sykes, 1984; Tyler, 1985). Furthermore, some critics maintain little optimism that significant changes will occur in teacher education, based on its dismal history (Romanish, 1987; Sykes, 1984). One of the reasons for the lack of change is the view that teaching and teacher education are semiprofessions. The lack of full professional status has inhibited teaching and teacher education from realizing its full potential.

Profession or Semiprofession?

The American Association of Colleges for Teacher Education Bicentennial Commission Report (Howsam et al., 1976) traces the evolution of teacher education from a nonprofession at its inception in the 1830–1840s to a semiprofession in the 1970s. Howsam et al. identify 12 characteristics of a profession, ranging from the possession by the profession of a unique body of knowledge to agreed-upon standards of admissions and performance. They conclude that teacher education is, in fact, a semiprofession lacking key elements of the older professions of medicine, law, and theology. Howsam et al. quote Etzioni, who notes of semiprofessions: "Their training is shorter, their status is less legitimated, their right to privileged communication less established, there is less of a specialized body of knowledge, and they have less autonomy from supervision or social control than 'the' professions" (Etzioni, 1969, p. v). Lortie (1975) identifies the lack of a common professional language and culture in teaching, which inhibits the ability to form a true profession. One of the criteria of a profession is the ability to establish authority over the decision-making process that affects its members.

Based on Bush's (1987) article on reform in teacher education, five additional problems, or areas of concern, contribute to the lack of change in teacher education: (a) little change in schools, (b) diffusion of control, (c) insufficient resources, (d) faulty design problems, and (e) lack of commitment to research. The status of colleges of education and institutional commitment to change in teacher education are being added to this list as impediments to reform.

Little Change in Schools

Because teaching in schools and teacher education programs are interrelated, one explanation for the lack of change in teacher education programs is that there has been little change in the ways pupils have been taught in schools (Bush, 1987). Bush summarizes the relationship between change in teacher education and teaching: "If teachers continue to teach in traditional ways, why should teacher education change? . . . This lack of change in how students are taught in schools partly explains why teacher education has not fundamentally changed. Teaching in schools and teacher education in colleges and universities are inevitably interrelated" (p. 15). Teacher-directed instructional approaches that are textbook driven have been the predominant method used in most schools since the 1930s (Bush, 1987). Studies and reviews beginning in the 1960s of teacher–student classroom interactions by Brophy and Good (1986), Cuban (1984), Flanders (1965), Freiberg (1976), Goodlad (1984), and Sirotnik (1983) indicate a historical pattern of high amounts of teacher talk (70 percent plus), mostly lecture, and low levels of student involvement, particularly in secondary schools. Furthermore, the history of public schooling is marked by resistance to change on the part of teachers and administrators (Cuban, 1984, 1988). Teachers have generally worked within a curriculum they did not devise, used instructional materials they did not like, and accepted a schedule that contained little flexibility or adequate time to prepare lessons (Cohen, 1988). These conditions have restricted opportunities for teachers to change their instruction. This lack of change in schools explains, in part, why teacher education has made only limited changes.

Diffusion of Control

Another explanation for the lack of change is that there has been no locus of power in the control of teacher education, and the resulting calls for reform in teacher education have resulted in contradictions in the direction of change (Cornbleth, 1986). Bush (1987) identifies different centers of control including state, regional, and national accreditating agencies; state licensing agencies and certification boards; and governance structures of colleges and universities that regulate teacher education through course and program approvals. Other agencies add to this diffusion of control over the profession: national, regional, and local teacher organizations; teacher education professional organizations including the Association of Teacher Educators [ATE], the American Association of Colleges for Teacher Education [AACTE], and, more recently, Division K of the American Educational Research Association [AERA]); discipline-related organizations such as the National Council of Teachers of English; and college and university coordinating boards.

Since the late 1970s, private foundations such as the Carnegie Forum on Education and the Economy, state legislatures, and governors have directly entered the arena of teacher education policy and regulation. The popularization of education has expanded the base of interest and support for teaching, but it has also eroded the authority of teacher educators to determine the entry and exit requirements and course of study of teacher education. There has been such a diverse degree of opinion among these groups and organizations as to the types and magnitude of changes needed in teacher education that, as a result, conflicting strategies have emerged for enacting change (Bush, 1987; Cornbleth, 1986).

Creation and Dissemination of Knowledge

Denton, Tsai, and Cloud (1986) cite two results of Clark and Guba's (1976) study: faculty from over 56 percent of teacher education programs in the United States did not contribute to education journals or to the ERIC Clearinghouse, and doctoral-degree-granting institutions were the primary source of scholarship in teacher education (p. 12). The dissemination patterns identified by Clark and Guba continued into the 1980s. Denton, Tsai, and Cloud examined teacher education faculty productivity through paper presentations at three teacher education professional organizations, including ATE, AACTE, and AERA, and publications in the *Journal of Teacher Education* and *Action in Teacher Education*. A total of 35.6 percent of the 1,367 teacher-preparation programs in the United States were represented at national conferences (86.1 percent) or in one of the two journals (13.9 percent) between 1980 and 1984 (p. 14). They conclude that the number of institutions that share their inquiry through national teacher education associations and journals is limited. The dominant source of dissemination continues to be the doctoral-granting institutions (p. 15). The dearth of dissemination of knowledge might indicate insufficiency of both time and resources to study new areas and report them to the profession.

Insufficient Resources

Lack of resources has been frequently cited as a contributing factor for the little change in teacher education (Bush, 1987; Lanier & Little, 1986). Colleges and universities have traditionally spent far less on teacher education than on training in other fields (Bush, 1987). Black's (1980) study on the practices of compensating supervising teachers in the 50 states, for example, found that states generally do not provide funding for field-based experiences in teacher education programs. Consequently, educators like Berliner (1985) argue that teacher education needs additional resources like video equipment and money to analyze the performances of prospective teachers to the extent to which athletic coaches receive resources to analyze their student athletes.

Howsam et al. (1976) cite the Study Commission on Undergraduate Education and the Education of Teachers report *Teacher Education in America* (1975), which indicates that, in 1972–1973 teacher education received $1,300 to $1,500 per full-time equivalent undergraduate student in education. In a study conducted by Peseau (1982) of land-grant colleges and universities in 1981–1982, $1,406 was being expended on undergraduate teacher education students, whereas $1,966 was being spent per student in public schools. Teacher education is receiving two-and-one-half times less support than other professional schools at most colleges and universities, and the prospects for greater financial support in the 1990s are slight. Although the decline in prospective teachers during the 1970s resulted in a decrease in faculty in colleges of education, current increases in students have occurred without a corresponding increase in faculty positions.

Faulty Design Problems

One of the important concerns relating to factors that influence change in teacher education is the current design of teacher education programs. Bush (1987) cites three specific faulty design problems: (a) insufficient time, (b) failure to relate different parts of teacher education to each other, and (c) the notion of one best design, which has prevented change from occurring. Teacher education also provides less time for its preprofessional program than other professions (Houston, 1983).

The failure of teacher education programs to relate the different parts of the program (e.g., methods courses, foundation courses, general education, field experiences) to each other has led to isolation of courses, incongruencies, and prevention of meaningful change (Bush, 1987). Research and development has tended to seek the one best way to teach and to train teachers; for example research on effective teaching; models of elementary teacher education, or CBTE.

Lack of Commitment to Research

A fifth explanation for why there has been little change in teacher education is the lack of commitment to educational research, which occurs at two levels: (1) the limited amount and quality of research in the area of teacher education, and (2) the failure of research to have an impact on educational practices.

A number of sweeping statements about the quality and quantity of research on teacher education have been made by reviewers in the mainstream, as well as by those outside the field (Ashton & Crocker, 1987; Cruickshank, 1984; Lanier & Little, 1986; Waxman & Walberg, 1986). Lanier and Little point out that the lack of a body of research knowledge in teacher education is one of the major obstacles that has prevented us from changing or improving teacher education. Ashton and Crocker highlight some of the methodological weaknesses that pervade research studies in teacher education, as well as the decline in the number of studies in the 1970s and 1980s.

Some critics have argued that research cannot solve the problems of teacher education (Tom, 1980), but others maintain that teacher education can solve some of the problems of educational research by facilitating, critically reviewing, synthesizing, summarizing, collaborating, and sharing research findings with classroom teachers (Fisher & Berliner, 1979; Huling, Trang, & Correll, 1981; Justiz, 1984; Lanier & Glassberg, 1981; Vaughan, 1984). Before teacher educators can translate research into practice, however, they must make sure that teachers are secure in their understanding of educational research. Unless teachers have the prerequisite skills necessary to understand research, the chance of their utilizing research is remote. To facilitate change in schools and in teacher education, more emphasis should be placed on providing preservice and inservice teachers with the appropriate skills to help them understand educational research studies, and on applying research findings in the classroom.

Status of Colleges of Education

Another factor inhibiting change in teacher education is the status of colleges of education (Goodman, 1988). The lack of resources for teacher training constitutes a serious problem and, consequently, requires most institutions to use either part-time instructors, graduate students, or junior faculty to supervise field experiences and student teaching (Goodman, 1988). Furthermore, colleges of education generally suffer from low status within the university structure (Clark & Marker, 1975; Goodman, 1988; Judge, 1982; Lanier & Little, 1986; Schlechty, George, & Whitford, 1978). There are few incentives for faculty in colleges of education to work with preservice teacher education students (Goodman, 1988; Lanier & Little, 1986). Consequently, many education faculty members try to "distance [themselves] from the world of teacher education" (Judge, 1982, p. 9). Similarly, there are even status distinctions among those few faculty who are actually involved in preservice teacher education programs. As Joyce and Clift (1984) point out, the closer one gets to supervising field experiences, the lower the status.

Because those individuals who are most often involved in preservice teacher education programs have low rank and status, they also "have the least amount of formal power within the university culture to implement the types of organizational alterations needed to significantly change people's roles, relationships, and responsibilities" (Goodman, 1988, p. 48). Finally, there is serious concern that more prestigious research-oriented universities will eliminate their preservice teacher education programs because they will find it difficult to attract students to their programs who meet the general university standards required of all students (Schlechty & Vance, 1983). Consequently, teacher education would continue to lose status in our society.

Institutional Commitment

A study commissioned through the Southern Regional Education Board, entitled *Changing the Education of Teachers* (Hawley, Austin & Goldman, 1988), concludes that standards have been tightened at most southern colleges and universities that are responsible for teacher preparation, but few programs have revamped their curriculum. Entry requirements have been raised and exit requirements for certification have been made more rigorous. The study found that most of the changes in teacher education in the 15 southern states were initiated by state legislators or state boards of education, rather than by colleges and universities. The authors cite a lack of institutional commitment to teacher education, with few college or university presidents and other academic leaders involved in educational reform.

The federal role in changing teacher education has had some limited short-term successes (Bush & Bock, 1982; Freiberg, 1981a), but the long-term picture has not been encouraging. Those who study the federal role in educational change (Berman & McLaughlin, 1978; Moore & Hyde, 1981; Radin, 1977) have indicated that the long-term results usually end when the funds are terminated.

The federal agenda for change in teacher education at the macrolevel has not been achieved. Since the late 1950s, millions have been spent to reform the way teachers are taught; however, positive changes in teacher attitudes, behaviors, and learner success have been elusive. A federal agenda with good intentions has not received a parallel response from those who are charged with implementing change. The absence of macro-change is due in part to lack of ownership, which would be evident from both financial and political support necessary to continue successful federal programs. Although the scope of federal intervention has been broad, it is evident that a small percentage of the nearly 1,400 teacher-preparation institutions have changed as a result of federal support.

Extensive studies conducted on the federal government as change agent by Berman and McLaughlin (1978) and on the use of federal funds for staff development by Hyde and Moore (1982) suggest that little thought is given to financial requirements or the political support necessary to continue the efforts of program developers. Although few of the programs reviewed in the macrosection have undergone extensive evaluation or research, the absence or existence of hard data seems to have little to do with program continuance. The federal government has cut dissemination activities for training and research grants. Project proposals are rarely required to delineate specifically how project ideas and findings will be communicated to others or what evaluative strategies will be used to determine if dissemination activities transfer. Low expectations for dissemination are generally followed by equally low levels of activity once the grant is completed. The National Diffusion Network (NDN), which is funded by the U.S. Department of Education, is designed to disseminate exemplary educational programs that have been reviewed by the Joint Dissemination Review Panel, based on reasonably rigorous outcome criteria for teaching and teacher education. In the 1985 NDN catalog *Educational Programs That Work* (National Dissemination Study Group, 1985), of the hundreds of programs listed, only one is identified as serving teacher education. The federal government may have had more impact in its indirect role in education, evident in the reporting and disseminating of national educational data, the providing of funds for local initiatives, and the mirroring of national concerns of which *A Nation at Risk* (National Commission on Excellence in Education, 1983) is a prime example.

A MICRO VIEW OF CHANGE: CHANGING THE TEACHING PERFORMANCE AND ATTITUDES OF PROSPECTIVE TEACHERS

Although preservice teacher education is a critical part of the professional development of teachers, there is a dearth of research studies indicating the impact that different approaches or types of program components have had on changing the prospective teacher's teaching performance and attitudes (Goodman, 1988; Howey, 1977; Lanier & Little, 1986; Zeichner, 1980; Zeichner & Liston, 1987). One of the major concerns among teacher educators is that practices are often based on unexamined assumptions (Tabachnick, Popkewitz, & Zeichner, 1980; Zeichner & Liston, 1987).

There have, however, been a number of studies that examined specific aspects of preservice teacher education. Although results in some of the areas researched, like early field experiences, are based on studies conducted in the mid-1970s, results in other areas such as feedback from classroom observation systems are based on studies conducted during the late 1980s. The following sections describe some of the areas in which an accumulation of studies describe factors that change the teaching performance and attributes of prospective teachers. These are (a) early field experiences, (b) microteaching, and (c) feedback approaches such as audiotape analysis, classroom observation systems, and pupil feedback. In addition to changing the teaching performance and attributes of prospective teachers, these three areas have also all changed the content of teacher education programs, and the extent of their impact can be seen in the sections that follow.

Early Field Experiences

Early field experiences have had a great impact on programmatic changes in teacher education. Some educators, for example, argue that this area now constitutes a serious national concern, because there are several proposals for reducing the number of pedagogy courses offered in teacher education programs and increasing the number of field experiences (i.e., internships in school settings) for prospective teachers (Waxman & Walberg, 1986).

Several studies conducted in the 1970s found that early field experiences influenced positively the teaching performance and attitudes of prospective teachers (Benton & Osborn, 1979; Marso, 1971; Peck & Tucker, 1973; Sandefur, 1970; Veldman, Menaker, & Newlove, 1970; Yarger, Howey, & Joyce, 1977). As a consequence, many teacher education institutions incorporated more early field experiences into their preservice teacher education programs and eliminated some pedagogy courses. This practice is even more common today as some state legislatures begin to mandate the maximum number of pedagogy courses that teacher education institutions can offer.

Some teacher educators, however, challenge the widespread belief that field experiences help prospective teachers become more effective teachers. Although it is maintained that they give future teachers a taste of reality, it is also claimed that they can foster bad habits and narrow vision (Goodman, 1986; Nemser, 1983; Zeichner & Liston, 1987). Some are concerned that extended field experiences and more pedagogy courses will not improve the quality of teaching in our nation's schools. Sykes (1983), for example, indicates that adding "more college and university course work would increase the initial costs of becoming a teacher beyond what the market might bear and fails to answer students' demands for more practical experience" (p. 105). Cronin (1983) similarly maintains that "the cost will discourage the economically disadvantaged and many minority candidates in particular from teaching careers" (p. 184). Tabachnick, Popkewitz, and Zeichner (1980) are also critical of extending field experiences, because they contend that "proposals which 'solve' problems of teacher education by scheduling more student time in classrooms rest upon the apparently untenable assumption that more time spent in that way will automatically make better teachers" (p. 28).

The area of early field experiences has had a great impact on teacher education programs. The ambiguous findings regarding the research on the effects of field experiences on the prospective teacher's performance and attitudes has allowed teacher educators and non–teacher educators (such as legislators) to propose changes in programs without adequate evidence to support their points of view.

Microteaching

The evolution of video technology in the 1970s and 1980s enabled teacher educators to focus on specific teaching behaviors for both research analysis and training. Since the development of microteaching (Allen & Fortune, 1966; Bush & Allen, 1964) the use of simulated teaching has become a part of many teacher education programs (D. S. Lewis, 1987; Macleod, 1987; Perlberg, 1987).

The videotaping of teaching has enabled researchers, for example, to develop stimulated recall methodologies and to analyze the thinking and subsequent actions of neophyte teachers. The same technology has enabled teacher educators to create opportunities for student teachers to use videotaped lessons for later analysis and reflection (Freiberg & Waxman, 1988).

The microteaching format includes a process in which a preservice student learns and then employs a series of teaching behaviors (e.g., nonverbal cues; wait time for questioning, motivation and facilitation of set inductions, and higher level questioning skills). These skills are usually demonstrated to preservice teachers during methods-related coursework. Later the students are asked to teach a group of five to six other preservice students for 10 to 20 minutes. During the early development of microteaching and with the access of laboratory schools, five or six elementary or secondary level students participated in the miniteach. The minilesson was videotaped, and the student received feedback from the instructor or a graduate student. The feedback was provided while the student and the instructor watched the videotape of the minilesson and, using a checklist in many instances, determined which previously identified behaviors were being exhibited. In some teacher education programs, students were then graded on their ability to perform a specific teaching behavior during the microteaching lesson. Both students and educators, however, questioned the appropriateness of this summative use of microteaching, due to the contrast with natural classroom settings (Good, Biddle, & Brophy, 1975). Although data were provided to the teacher education student, the opportunity for reflection was not part of the simulated learning experience. Students were expected to perform specific teaching behaviors, from which a grade would be determined.

The summative environment of many microteaching situations provided minimal opportunities for either exploration or reflection. Recent modifications of the microteaching process, however, have provided opportunities to use a reflective tool. Rather than simulated teaching's being a summative occurrence, the opportunity exists for formative feedback, peer feedback, and self-assessment during microteaching experiences. Building in the opportunities and providing the encouragement and climate for reflection both individually and collectively in cohort groups increases the chance for professional growth. The combination of experiences and reflection equals growth (Posner, 1985). Consequently there has been a recent revival of the application of this technology, with more and more institutions incorporating microteaching activities in their teacher education programs.

Feedback Approaches

It is difficult for preservice teachers to change their performance and attitudes toward teaching when they are unaware of their effectiveness during simulated or student teaching and often lack information about the nature of their interactions with classes or individual students. This might explain why student teacher self-perceptions about teaching effectiveness have generally been found to be incongruent with their academic or field supervisors (Briggs, Richardson, & Sefzik, 1986; Wheeler & Knoop, 1982) and with their students (Waxman & Duschl, 1987).

Specific approaches such as collaborative conferencing

(Hoover & O'Shea, 1987), reflective peer group teaching (Cruickshank, 1987), reflective teaching lessons (Korthagen, 1985), situational teaching experiences (Cohn, 1981), and seminars (Hill, 1986) have been designed to encourage preservice teachers to think critically about their instruction and to facilitate change. These methods, however, only provide external sources of information to student teachers about their teaching. Consequently, they have not been widely adopted by many teacher education programs. Change in teaching requires more than information originating from others; it necessitates the ability to be introspective and to be able to generate one's own sources of information.

Several recent studies have found that self-assessment procedures enhance the teacher's ability and willingness to be reflective about classroom instruction (Freiberg & Waxman, 1988; Freiberg, Waxman, & Houston, 1987; Koziol, Bohn, & Moss, 1983; Koziol & Burns, 1986). One key to effective self-assessment is the provision of accurate and valid tools for preservice teachers to examine and assess their teaching.

One approach that has been found to facilitate change in prospective teachers is the use of audiotape analyses. Self-assessments from *audiotape analyses* of classroom lessons have been found to help student teachers and classroom teachers improve their classroom instruction (Freiberg et al., 1987; Hoover & Carroll, 1987). The use of *systematic classroom observation* is another approach that has been found to facilitate change in the teaching performance of prospective teachers (Freiberg & Waxman, in press).

A third approach to providing prospective teachers with accurate feedback about their classroom performance is the use of *pupil judgment*, or rating instruments. They can be used to obtain feedback and have several advantages: (a) They are relatively inexpensive to administer, (b) they can be administered at a convenient or relevant time during the class, (c) they can be standardized, (d) they can be designed to maintain anonymity, (e) they are the product of observation of the prospective teacher on many occasions under normal conditions, and (f) they can pick up a wealth of data in a very short time (B. J. Fraser & Walberg, 1981; Waxman, 1984). Such instruments can assess, for example, students' perceptions of the prospective teacher's instructional skills and strategies, learning environment, and attitudes toward teaching.

Only a few studies have examined the effect of student feedback on altering student teacher behavior. Although M. Lewis and Bartholomew (1984) found that neither student teacher self-analysis with student feedback nor self-analysis alone increased the frequency of select teaching practices, Lacy, Tobin, and Treagust (1984) found that providing feedback to preservice teachers regarding their classroom learning environments helped assist them in changing their teaching in ways that students perceived to be improvements. Furthermore, Tuckman and Oliver (1968) also found that students' feedback improved student teachers' instruction.

The three feedback approaches help prospective teachers become aware of their own behavior in the classroom. This feedback is intended to create what Heider (1958) would call an "imbalance" in preservice teachers' perceptions of their own instruction. Posner, Strike, Hewson, and Gertzog (1982) would call this a "conceptual change" in a teacher's central commit-

ments. This imbalance or conceptual change occurs whenever student teachers find out their attitudes or perceptions of their instruction differ from that of systematic feedback. Student teachers in such a state of imbalance are motivated to do something about their behavior, in order to restore themselves to a balanced condition (Gage, 1972). Thus, the use of systematic and credible data sources is a valuable link in changing preservice teachers' performance and attitudes. These feedback approaches have changed the practice of teacher education to the extent that many institutions are now moving to more systematic data collection in their programs.

A MESO VIEW OF CHANGE: COLLABORATION AND PARTNERSHIPS IN TEACHER EDUCATION

The meso view of change (Fullan, personal communication, 1988) in teacher education focuses on the linkages or partnerships between and within institutions. Collaborative projects, or partnerships, between local education agencies and teacher-training institutions have been recommended for improving educational excellence (Maeroff, 1983; National Commission on Excellence in Education, 1983). These types of projects and partnerships, however, can also be viewed as means of changing teacher education.

Some public school and university collaborative projects such as academy schools, teacher centers, induction programs (Burke & Notar, 1986), and "adopt-a-school" programs (see e.g., J. L. Fraser, 1986; Ishler & Leslie, 1987) have been successful. On the other hand, other partnerships have failed because university professors and school-district personnel often have divergent perspectives on what should be done and how it should be done (Parish, Underwood, & Eubanks, 1987). In reviewing the research on collaboration, Houston (1980) points out several of the pitfalls that teacher education institutions encounter when they work with others within their own institution, as well as when they work with public schools, business establishments, social agencies, and other institutions. One major pitfall is that the reward systems of the two groups are different. University faculty are rewarded through research and scholarly publications, whereas school personnel are rewarded for school efficiency and effectiveness. Furthermore, another problem with collaboration is that working on school-based service projects is typically not rewarded in colleges of education, and collaborative work is usually viewed as extra duty by school-district personnel.

According to S. D. Smith and Auger (1986), there are four key elements to successful partnerships in teacher education: (a) timeliness, (b) mutuality or co-ownership of the collaborative program among all participants, (c) trust, and (d) results that benefit each cooperating group. In an era of scarce resources for education, relationships among local education agencies and teacher-training institutions need to be reexamined (Wallace, 1987). These partnerships could form the linkages needed to change teacher education.

Cooperative Teacher Center Networks are one example of successful collaborative programs between schools and teacher education institutions (Clift & Houston, 1988; O'Dell, 1985). These centers usually provide teacher education institutions with the opportunities for training prospective and first-year teachers. In some cases, like the University of New Mexico and the Albuquerque Public Schools, experienced classroom teachers work as clinical faculty in the university's teacher education program (O'Dell, 1985). These types of partnerships have the potential to change the size and type of faculty that currently exist in teacher education institutions.

University and business partnerships have also provided a vehicle for change in teacher education. The Chevron Corporation, for example, formed a partnership with San Francisco State University, the University of Houston, and the University of New Orleans to retrain former engineers and geologists as science and math teachers (Clift & Houston, 1988). These types of collaborative projects allow teacher education institutions to meet the needs of both schools, by providing them with teachers in critical areas, and businesses that need to retrain employees who would otherwise be unemployed.

The Schenley High School Teacher Center in Pittsburgh is another example of a successful collaborative project between public schools and universities (Wallace, 1987). School-district staff and representatives from the University of Pittsburgh, Duquesne University, and Carnegie-Mellon University developed a plan for inservice training for all secondary teachers in the district. One unique feature of this program is that all secondary teachers in the district received an 8-week minisabbatical from their classroom and attended training sessions at Schenley, where they participated in (a) seminars with peers, center staff, and university and business personnel; (b) clinical experiences related to teaching, and (c) activities related to an individualized study plan (Wallace, 1987). Projects of this nature can have a great impact on changing teacher education, because they suggest that the training of teachers be done collaboratively *and* take place in the schools rather than in the university.

CHANGE STRATEGIES

Several strategies for change with potential applications in teacher education have been historically used in education and other professions. A selected review of the literature (see Argyris, 1964; Bennis, Benne, & Chin, 1969; Berman & McLaughlin, 1978; Carnegie Foundation for the Advancement of Teaching, 1988; Darling-Hammond & Berry, 1988; Etzoni, 1964; Fullan, 1982; Fuller, 1969; Hall & Loucks, 1978; Herriott & Gross, 1979; Hersey & Blanchard, 1972; Lewin, 1951; McGregor, 1960; Miles, 1964; Owens, 1987; Owens & Steinhoff, 1976; Radin, 1977; Rogers, 1962; Soltis, 1987; Starr, 1982) indicates that change is a multidimensional force that occurs in planned and unplanned states and affects individuals, groups, and the organizations they design. Some change efforts and outcomes are planned; others are unplanned and often unanticipated. Unplanned change, for example, can be initiated by natural disasters like the Great Plague during the Middle Ages, which created labor shortages in Europe and ended a system of servitude that had existed for centuries. Another example of unplanned change is economic recessions and depressions, which have reduced or redistributed wealth. A final example

of unplanned change is wars, which have both ravaged and enhanced the development of civilizations throughout history. Analysis and provision for unplanned change in the twentieth century have resulted in the field of futures study. Planned changes in teacher education are intentional, deliberate, and projected with some consideration for resources as they affect teacher education.

Chin and Benne (1969) outline a model of change expanded by Owens (1987), which describes three frameworks of change: (a) rational-empirical, (b) normative-reeducative, and (c) power-coercive. These have important implications for teacher educators, providing a framework for the current reform movement that is reshaping teacher education.

Rational-Empirical Change

The rational-empirical approach examines the historical roots of the country and traces the evolution of change as a function of reason based on knowledge and logic rather than on untested assumptions. Chin and Benne liken this approach to change as enlightenment and scientific thought and investigation. The rational-empirical approach to planned change includes six strategies for change: (a) basic research and dissemination of knowledge through universal educational opportunities, (b) personnel selection and replacement, (c) scientific management, (d) applied research and linkage systems for diffusion, (e) visionary thinking, and (f) clarification of language.

The use of research to create new knowledge and enlist basic education to diffuse the knowledge to the general public has been a strategy for change used by both the federal government and private agencies to solve societal problems (see Bush & Bock, 1982; Carnegie Foundation for the Advancement of Teaching, 1988; Fullan, 1982; Hall, 1979; Radin, 1977; Soltis, 1987). The funding by the federal government of the Research and Development Center for Teacher Education at The University of Texas at Austin (Hall, 1979) and at Michigan State University, initiation of the Teacher Corps programs to recruit liberal arts graduates into the teaching profession, and development of newsletters (*Teacher Education Reports*, 1988; and *Holmes Group Forum*, Devaney, 1988) to disseminate findings to both the education community and selected members of the general public are examples of attempts to create change through research and development.

Personnel selection and replacement as a change strategy is predicated on the assumption that the right person is needed to interpret and apply knowledge to the task and job. The emphasis is on screening applicants, assessing their work, and replacing them, if necessary, as a means of improving education. This strategy is evident in the screening of new members entering the teaching profession. Currently, 25 states require their teacher-training institutions to test prospective education students prior to admission, and 41 states require written examinations from the program certifications and exits into the profession (American Association of Colleges for Teacher Education [AACTE], 1988b).

Unintended consequences of change efforts must also be considered. Although the screening process has assured the public that new teachers have passed basic-skills tests, written tests have reduced minority students both entering teacher education programs (AACTE, 1988a; G. P. Smith, 1987) and passing written tests. A study of 123 teacher education institutions in 15 southern states conducted for the Southern Regional Education Board (Hawley et al., 1988) found that "only 22 percent of the colleges in the survey indicated an increase in enrollments among non-white students; 44 percent indicated a decline" (p. 10). A study of test results in 19 states commissioned by the Council of Chief State School Officers and the National Education Association conducted by Smith in 1987 and reported by the *Chronicle of Higher Education* (Fields, 1988) indicates that 38,000 members of minority groups failed mandated tests for entrance into the teaching profession. This comes at a time when enrollments of black, Hispanic, and Asian students are increasing in all urban school districts. Nearly 100 urban school districts currently categorize more than half their students as minority. Perhaps it is a misnomer to continue calling black, Hispanic, and Asian students minorities when they represent a majority in these school districts.

Chin and Benne (1969) point to the Binet and other tests that business and industry have used to screen applicants. This strategy is limited in its vision of change and, generally, supports the existing organization.

Scientific management is a change strategy with which the resources of the organization are marshaled to make the organization more efficient. Systems analysts and consultants are brought into an organization to "create a science of management which could be applied to everyday problems in the organization" (Owens, 1987, p. 269). The Beginning Teacher Evaluation Studies (BTES), conducted in the mid 1970s (Fisher et al., 1978) and reported in *Time to Learn* (Denham & Lieberman, 1980), consisted of a series of studies that examined the use of instructional time or academic learning time in the classroom and its implications for academic achievement. Bush (1987), in his review of educational reform, indicates that the BTES studies funded by the National Institute of Education in collaboration with the California Commission for Teacher Preparation and Licensing are more widely used by the teacher education community than almost any research effort; it is still influencing teacher education practices at both the pre- and inservice levels" (p. 15). The use of scientific methodologies in the gathering of the BTES data and the use of actual classroom settings for the studies added credibility to the findings for teachers and administrators and teacher educators.

Applied research and linkage systems for diffusion present a change strategy with roots in the land-grant colleges and universities where basic science was translated and disseminated for use in agriculture and engineering (Chin & Benne, 1969). This model's effectiveness depends on the ability of developers and consumers to establish two-way communication. The lack of significant change during the era of the teacher-proof curriculum in the early 1960s, particularly in science, could be traced to a lack of basic communication between the scientists who were designing the materials and the teachers who were responsible for implementing programs. The historical assumption for diffusion of ideas (Rogers, 1962) has been based on an active disseminator and a passive receiver. Effective dissemination requires interaction including feedback from the consumer to the developer (Freiberg, 1981b).

In teacher preparation, new teachers, or "consumers," have indicated lack of confidence in their undergraduate teacher education programs. Studies of teacher satisfaction have found a consistent theme of inadequate preparation for teaching. Teachers indicate lack of preparation for interpreting and applying educational research to their classrooms (Freiberg, Waxman, & Knight, 1986). Over 63 percent of 159 teachers surveyed in one school district indicated that their undergraduate professors did not adequately prepare them to translate research into classroom practice (Freiberg et al., 1986).

Although teacher education programs have begun, since the mid-1980s, to respond to the needs of their students, a cohort of teachers remain who continue to express disdain for teacher education. This negative response on the part of teacher education's consumers has translated itself into legislative actions for four states (Texas, California, New Jersey, and Virginia) that limit the number of education courses for teacher preparation while holding the institutions accountable for the quality of their graduates. Such action at the macrolevel leads to important changes in programs set up primarily on political grounds.

Visionary thinking as a strategy for change is reflected in most of the reports on teacher education, beginning with the Commonwealth Teacher Training Study (Charters & Waples, 1929) and continuing with the Commission on Teacher Education report (Bigelow, 1946), Conant's study of teacher training in 1963, the Carnegie Study reported by Silberman in 1970, and, more recently, the AACTE report *A call for change in teacher education* (National Commission on Excellence in Teacher Education, 1985). The reports have a common vision of those outcomes of teacher education that are valued and those shortcomings of practice. To understand the potential of such reports for change in professional practice, consider the field of medicine.

A profession establishes itself through a relationship with its constituency that is based on expertise and knowledge about the profession that is greater than that available to the nonprofessional, trust by the nonprofessional in professional competence, consistency from one professional to another, higher standards than those for nonprofessionals, and a level of sovereignty over both entry and exit of its membership. Only in the majority of the twentieth century has the practice of medicine been considered a profession by its constituency. It was common knowledge at the turn of the century that one went to a hospital to die and home remedies were better than those of the physician. The professionalization of medicine began with physicians' creating a scientific base of knowledge for their profession that was greater than the knowledge to the ordinary citizen. Starr (1982), in his historical analysis of the medical profession *Social Transformation of American Medicine*, explains how Abraham Flexner, representing the Carnegie Foundation for the Advancement of Teaching, embarked on a study requested by the American Medical Association to examine the quality of medical schools in 1906. The Flexner report (1910) indicates that medical science had progressed, but medical education was lagging far behind. The report proposes that the best schools be strengthened, the middle range of schools be supported, but the majority of medical schools (most of which were privately operated, as trade schools are today), which fell into the bottom category, be eliminated. The report, coming from outside the profession, speeded the demise of many medical schools that were financially marginal, consolidated the remaining schools, and, ultimately, strengthened the medical profession.

Clarification of language as a strategy for change provides a semantic basis upon which to communicate more effectively (Chin & Benne, 1969). The need for a clear, concise form of language is reinforced by Lortie (1975). The lack of a common language and culture in teaching and teacher education has resulted in teaching's remaining a semiprofession (Howsam et al., 1976).

Normative-Reeducative Change

The second part of the Chin-Benne model examines change as a function of the interaction among members of the organization, in order to both increase the problem-solving abilities of the system and release and encourage the growth of the persons who form the system to be changed. These components of the change model emphasize organizational development through direct intervention of training, staff development, or other supports that enhance the change efforts. "The goals of OD (organizational development) include both the quality of life of individuals as well as improving organizational functioning and performance" (Fullan, Miles, & Taylor, 1978, p. 14).

In teacher education, there has been little effort to improve the quality of the teacher educator's life or organizational function. The need for staff development and its relationship to student achievement is well documented (Joyce & Showers, 1988). The need for application of research findings through staff development to K–12 classroom teachers has been consistently supported in the literature (Gage, 1984; Griffin, 1984; Huling & Johnson, 1983; Justiz, 1984; Vaughan, 1984); however, there is even less development for teacher educators themselves. In an analysis of funds expended on staff development in three school districts between 1976–1978, Moore and Hyde (1981) estimate the range was $1,000–$1,700 per teacher each year. A report from the American Association of Colleges for Teacher Education (AACTE, 1988b) indicates that 10 states have some limited form of faculty development. It is evident from the report summaries that the programs are underfunded, given the number of faculty involved in teacher preparation (p. 139).

Arends, Murphy, and Christensen (1986) conclude, in a study of the Teaching Effectiveness Network, that the staff development of teacher educators has been neglected in terms of both faculty support and research. Arends et al. found, on average, in five teacher-training institutions in Maryland that $163 per year for each teacher education faculty was allocated mostly for travel and professional development. School districts allocate nearly 10 times the resources to teacher development that universities provide for teacher education faculty development. If this strategy is to be utilized in changing teacher education, the reform of teacher education will require a staff development undertaking equal to or greater than the staff-development efforts provided to teachers in K–12 classrooms.

Change that occurs through a normative-reeducative strategy (Chin & Benne, 1969) must take into consideration the political forces that shape society. Chin and Benne view the exercise of power as a basic human function. Power is gained through knowledge, and the reeducation strategy would provide a level of personal power. Networking increases the range of personal power. The forces that have begun to reshape teaching and teacher education have been more political than educational.

Power-Coercive Change

Power-coercive approaches to effecting change as a strategy include the use of political institutions to achieve change. This strategy incorporates power based on political and economic sanctions, rather than on personal power through reeducation or empherical-rational strategies. The current evolution of educational reform efforts has been a case study in political power from federal and, particularly, state levels (AACTE, 1988b; Carnegie Foundation for the Advancement of Teaching, 1988; Darling-Hammond & Berry, 1988; Freiberg, 1985, 1987a; Association of Teacher Educators [ATE], 1986; Soltis, 1987). The first wave of commission reports, starting with *A Nation at Risk* in 1983, prepared the groundwork for both the legislative response and the second wave of reports highlighted by *Tomorrow's Teachers* (Holmes Group, 1986) and *A Nation Prepared: Teachers for the 21st Century* (Carnegie Forum on Education and the Economy, 1986). There have been numerous analyses of these two commission reports (see Ashton & Crocker, 1987; ATE, 1986; Keith, 1987; Soltis, 1987). Organizations can function in different segments in the Chin and Benne model. The Carnegie Foundation, acting at the request of the American Medical Association in 1906, gave the association the impetus and vision to make needed changes. The Holmes Group and the Carnegie Forum reports have been used by state legislatures to justify mandated changes. The reports propose empowering teachers and improving the quality of pedagogy for teacher education (not eliminating it); the legislative acts, however, have had the effect of limiting teacher initiative and minimizing the life space of teacher preparation. A survey conducted by the Associated Press of all 50 states in 1988 indicates that many states are beginning to loosen their regulatory grip on reform efforts and return some of the initiative back to the teaching profession (Mitgang, 1988). The second wave of reports emphasized the need to change the teaching profession by improving the status and power of teachers and by altering the structure of teacher education. The states have mandated changes in teacher education admissions standards, alternative certification, certification, curriculum, incentives, and initial certification. Teacher education is controlled in most states by state boards who enforce the laws passed by state legislatures. The creation of linkages with the political establishment through dissemination of research findings and evaluation of programs creates a basis for dialogue that is currently missing and is perceived by state legislatures as self-serving, once the political process has begun to enact legislation. The Chin and Benne model places in perspective some of the strategies and implications of the strategies for change in teacher education. Based on their model and our review of the literature, the final section addresses some possible future directions for significant changes in teacher education.

CONCLUSIONS AND RECOMMENDATIONS

One is confronted with the uncomfortable reality that there have been some significant changes in the education of teachers in the twentieth century, but these changes pale in the face of the needs placed on teaching and teacher education by American society. Teaching and teacher education continues to be semiprofessional, constantly responding to the demands and needs of others, responsible for educating the nation's teachers without the authority to implement change beyond an immediate sphere of influence.

Teacher education has a low status on many college and university campuses, and it is inadequately funded to prepare teachers to effectively respond to the changing needs and demographics of public school populations into the next century. Teacher education faculty receive one-tenth of the financial support of classroom teachers for professional growth and development, and inquiry and the dissemination of knowledge remains in the hands of a relatively few researchers.

Although medicine progressed dramtically from a semiprofession to a profession in the twentieth century, initiated by self-examination of its role and the quality of medical education, teacher education and teaching have remained relatively unchanged and, perhaps, unwilling to undertake self-examination in light of changing societal needs. We recommend that teacher educators and members of the teaching profession go beyond mandated blueprints for those issues raised in this chapter and this handbook. Specifically, the following areas are presented for consideration:

1. *Multidimensional strategies.* Many of the reformers of teacher education consider the process unidimensional. Change in teacher education should be directed at the macro, micro, and meso levels. Several different strategies at each of the three levels need to be incorporated to meet the diversity of conditions in which teachers are ultimately expected to teach.

2. *Federal efforts.* Changing teacher education will require a long-term federal commitment that builds from those most directly involved in preparation of teachers. The lack of long-term commitment by the federal government to its programs only creates expectations that are rarely realized. The federal government should also provide technical support for dissemination at the beginning of each new project. Future funding for teacher education might need to include predetermined and supported cluster sites to insure adequate dissemination and diffusion. Creating a national network of teacher educators who could share information, research, and program development with each other and members of the teaching profession would greatly enhance change efforts.

3. *Faculty development.* The lack of teacher education faculty development needs to be addressed at the college, university, state, and national levels. Funding for faculty development should be equal to or greater than that provided for classroom teachers. Private foundations, as well as public agencies and legislative bodies, need to make faculty development a high priority. Teacher education faculty will continue to lose the ability to respond to the needs of current and future teachers without understanding of and participation in a growing knowledge base of the profession.

4. *Noncoercive change strategies.* States and institutions of higher education should learn from past efforts to reform teacher education. Coercive models circumvent the same people who are then asked to implement change. Models emphasizing rational-empherical and normative-reeducative strategies for change allow for the collaboration and participation necessary for lasting effects.

5. *Increased research opportunities.* Federal, state, and institutional support for research in teacher education is a necessity, if we are going to learn about factors influencing teacher training. Many teacher educators in recent years have become overloaded with organizational and instructional tasks. Building a profession requires a continuous growth of the knowledge base. Greater emphasis needs to be placed on local networks that link schools and teacher-preparation programs, to expand the base of inquiry and establish a cumulative system for testing programs and establishing criteria and conditions for effective programs.

6. *Self-efforts.* Teacher educators can always point to nonsupportive conditions and others as the source of their problems, but, in the final analysis, change must be instituted from within. A network like the Holmes Group is an important first step, but their membership represents less than 8 percent of the teacher-preparation programs. Teacher education will only be as viable as its members, and change occurs from proactive rather than reactive positions. Teacher educators must take the initiative and provide an agenda for change to policymakers who support and finance these changes. Having both the responsibility and authority over one's profession should be the collaborative goal of teacher educators and other members of the teaching profession.

This chapter began with the statement that institutions serve at the mandate of society. Failure to respond to the mandate of providing the best education to future and current teachers will result in further weakening and, ultimately, the demise of teacher preparation as a function of higher education. The increase since the mid-l980s in alternative routes to teaching in 23 states indicates a serious lack of confidence in the ability of colleges and universities to prepare the next generation of teachers. Constructive change is possible, if the profession, including teachers and teacher educators, is willing to take the leadership and make difficult decisions about the directions of teacher preparation into the twenty-first century.

References

Allen, D., & Fortune, J. (1966). An analysis of micro teaching: New procedures in teacher education. In *Microteaching: A description.* Stanford, CA: Stanford University Press.

American Association of Colleges for Teacher Education. (1988a). *Teacher education pipeline: SCDE enrollments by race and ethnicity.* Washington, DC: Author.

American Association of Colleges for Teacher Education. (1988b). *Teacher education policy in the states: A 50-state survey of legislative and administrative actions.* Washington, DC: Author.

Arends, R. I., Murphy, J., & Christensen, P. (1986). Faculty development for teacher educators. *Journal of Teacher Education, 37*(5), 17–22.

Argyris, C. (1964). *Integrating the individual and the organization.* New York: John Wiley & Sons.

Ashton, P., & Crocker, L. (1987). Systematic study of planned variations: The essential focus of teacher education reform. *Journal of Teacher Education, 38*(3), 2–8.

Association of Teacher Educators. (1986). *Visions of reform: Implications for the education profession.* Reston, VA: Author.

Bennis, W. G., Benne, K. D., & Chin, R. (Eds.). (1969). *The planning of change* (2nd ed.). New York: Holt, Rinehart & Winston.

Benton, S. E., & Osborn, J. (1979). Early field based experiences in an education curriculum. *Southern Journal of Educational Research, 13,* 119–125.

Berliner, D. C. (1985). Laboratory settings and the study of teacher education. *Journal of Teacher Education, 36*(6), 2–8.

Berman, P., & McLaughlin, M. W. (1978). *Federal programs supporting educational change: Vol. 8. Implementing and sustaining innovation.* Santa Monica, CA: RAND Corporation.

Bigelow, K. W. (1946). *The improvement of teacher education.* Washington, DC: American Council on Education.

Black, D. (1980). *Cooperating teacher remuneration: Where are we?* Reston, VA: Association of Teacher Educators.

Briggs, L. D., Richardson, W. D., & Sefzik, W. P. (1986). Comparing supervising teacher ratings and student teacher self-ratings of elementary student teaching. *Education, 106,* 150–159.

Brophy, J., & Good, T. L. (1986). Teacher behavior and student achievement. In M. C. Wittrock (Ed.), *Handbook of research on teaching* (3rd ed., pp. 328–375). New York: Macmillan.

Burdin, J. L., & Lanzillotti, K. (Eds.). (1969). *A reader's guide to the comprehensive models for preparing elementary teachers.* Washington, DC: American Association of Colleges for Teacher Education. (ERIC Document Reproduction Service No. SP 003 421)

Burke, P., & Notar, E. E. (1986). The school and university: Bridging the gap in teacher induction. *Action in Teacher Education, 7*(4), 11–16.

Burns, M. J. (1968). *To heal and to build.* New York: McGraw-Hill.

Bush, R. N. (1977). We know how to train teachers: Why not do so? *Journal of Teacher Education, 38*(2), 148–149.

Bush, R. N. (1987). Teacher education reform: Lessons from the past half century. *Journal of Teacher Education, 38*(3) 13–19.

Bush, R., & Allen, D. (1964). *Controlled practice in the training of teachers.* Paper presented at the Ford foundation conference on teacher education, Santa Barbara.

Bush, R. N., & Bock, J. C. (1982). *Institutionalization of educational change: Case studies of Teacher Corps' influence on schools of education.* Special in-depth study II. *Teacher Corps national evaluation* (Contract No. 300-78-0289). Menlo Park, CA: U.S. Department of Education, Office of Dissemination and Professional Development.

Carnegie Forum on Education and the Economy Task Force on Teaching as a Profession. (1986). *A nation prepared: Teachers for the 21st century.* New York: Author.

Carnegie Foundation for the Advancement of Teaching. (1988). *An imperiled generation: Saving urban schools* (A special report). Princeton, NJ: Author.

Charters, W. W., & Waples, D. (1929). *The commonwealth teacher training study.* Chicago: University of Chicago Press.

Chin, R., & Benne, K. D. (1969). *General strategies for effecting changes in human systems in the planning of change* (2nd ed.). New York: Holt, Rinehart & Winston.

Clift, R. T., & Houston, W. R. (1988). The medusa, the snail, and educational practice. *Professional Educator, 11*(1), 40–44.

Clark, D. L., & Guba, E. G. (1976). *Studies of productivity in knowledge production and utilization by schools, colleges and departments of education* (RITE Occasional Papers). Bloomington, IN: Indiana University, Research on Institutions of Teacher Education.

Clark, D., & Marker, G. (1975). The institutionalization of teacher education. In K. Ryan (Ed.), *Teacher education* (74th yearbook of the National Society for the Study of Education, part II, pp. 53–86). Chicago: University of Chicago Press.

Cohen, D. K. (1988). Teaching practice: Plus que ça change. In P. W. Jackson (Ed.), *Contributing to educational change: Perspectives on research and practice* (pp. 27–84). Berkeley, CA: McCutchan.

Cohn, M. (1981). A new supervision model for linking theory to practice. *Journal of Teacher Education, 32*(3), 26–29.

Conant, J. B. (1963). *The education of American teachers.* New York: McGraw-Hill.

Cornbleth, C. (1986). Ritual and rationality in teacher education reform. *Educational Researcher, 15*(4), 5–14.

Cronin, J. M. (1983). State regulation of teacher preparation. In L. S. Shulman & G. Sykes (Eds.), *Handbook of teaching and policy* (pp. 171–191). New York: Longman.

Cruickshank, D. R. (1984). Toward a model to guide inquiry in preservice teacher education. *Journal of Teacher Education, 35*(6), 43–48.

Cruickshank, D. (1987). *Reflective teaching: The preparation of students of teaching.* Reston, VA: Association of Teacher Educators.

Cuban, L. (1984). *How teachers taught: Constancy and change in American classrooms: 1880–1980,* New York: Longman.

Cuban, L. (1988). Constancy and change in schools (1880s to the present). In P. W. Jackson (Ed.), *Contributing to educational change* (pp. 85–106). Berkeley, CA: McCutchan.

Darling-Hammond, L., & Berry, B. (1988). *The evolution of teacher policy.* Santa Monica, CA: RAND Corporation.

Denham, C., & Lieberman, A. (Eds.). (1980). *Time to learn.* Washington, DC: National Institute of Education.

Denton, J. J., Tsai, C. Y., & Cloud, C. (1986). Productivity of faculty in higher education institutions. *Journal of Teacher Education, 37*(5), 12–16.

Devaney, K. (Ed.). (1988). *The Holmes Group Forum, 3*(1).

Elam, S. (1971). *Performance-based teacher education: What is the state of the art?* Washington, DC: American Association of Colleges for Teacher Education.

Etzioni, A. (1964). *Modern organizations.* Englewood Cliffs, NJ: Prentice-Hall.

Etzioni, A. (1969). *The semi-professions and their organization: Teachers, nurses, social workers.* New York: Free Press.

Fields, C. M. (1988). *Chronicle of Higher Education.*

Fisher, C. W., & Berliner, D. C. (1979). Clinical inquiry in research on classroom teaching and learning. *Journal of Teacher Education*, 30(6), 42–48.

Fisher, C. W., Berliner, D. C., Filby, N. N., Marliave, R., Cahen, L. S., Dishaw, M. M., & Moore, J. E. (1978). *Beginning teacher evaluation study: Technical report series*. San Francisco: Far West Laboratory.

Flanders, N. (1965). *Teacher influence, pupil attitudes, and achievement* (Cooperative Research Monograph No. 12). Washington, DC: U. S. Office of Education.

Flexner, A. (1910). *Medical education in the United States and Canada* (Bulletin No. 4). New York: Carnegie Foundation for the Advancement of Teaching.

Fox, G. T., Jr. (1975). Who is being evaluated? *Journal of Teacher Education*, 26(2), 141–142.

Franc, L. H. (1978). *Competency-based education: Toward improving patterns of instruction*. Durham, NH: New England Teacher Corps Network.

Fraser, B. J., & Walberg, H. J. (1981). Psychosocial learning environment in science classrooms: A review of research. *Studies in Science Education*, 8, 67–92.

Fraser, L. A. (1986). The Atlanta adopt-a-school program: Innovative interactions. *Action in Teacher Education*, 7(4), 17–22.

Freiberg, H. J. (1976). An investigation of the effects of verbal teacher–student interaction of similar and different ability groups in secondary classrooms. *Classroom Interaction Newsletter*, 11(2), 34–45.

Freiberg, H. J. (1981a). The federal government as a change agent—fifteen years of the Teacher Corps. *Journal of Education for teaching*, 7(3), 231–245.

Freiberg, H. J. (1981b). Three decades of the Flanders Interaction Analysis System. *Journal of Classroom Interaction*, 16(2), 1–7.

Freiberg, H. J. (1985). Master teacher programs: Lessons from the past. *Educational Leadership*, 42(4), 16–21.

Freiberg, H. J. (1987a). Career ladders: Messages gleaned from experience. *Journal of Teacher Education*, 38(4), 49–56.

Freiberg, H. J. (1987b). Teacher self-evaluation and principal supervision. *NASSP Bulletin*, 71(498), 85–92.

Freiberg, H. J., Buckley, P., & Townsend, K. (1983). Improving a school through field-based clinical instructors. *Journal of Staff Development*, 4(1), 78–93.

Freiberg, H. J., Townsend, K., & Buckley, P. (1982). Does inservice make a difference? *British Journal of In-Service Education*, 8(3), 189–200.

Freiberg, H. J., & Waxman, H. C. (1988). Alternative feedback approaches for improving student teachers' classroom instruction. *Journal of Teacher Education*, 39(4), 8–14.

Freiberg, H. J., & Waxman, H. C. (in press). Reflection and acquisition of technical teaching skills. In R. T. Clift, W. R. Houston, & M. Pugach (Eds.), *Encouraging reflective practice: An examination of issues and exemplars*. New York: Teachers College Press.

Freiberg, H. J., Waxman, H. C. & Houston, W. R. (1987). Enriching feedback to student teachers through small group discussion. *Teacher Education Quarterly*, 14(3), 71–82.

Freiberg, H. J., Waxman, H. C., & Knight, S. (1986, February). *Using research knowledge to improve teacher education: Teachers' perspective of the value of educational research*. Paper presented at the annual meeting of the Association of Teacher Educators, Atlanta. (ERIC Document Reproduction Service No. ED 267 031)

Fullan, M. (1982). *The meaning of educational change*. New York: Teachers College Press.

Fullan, M., Miles, M. B., & Taylor, G. (1978). *OD in schools: The state of the art: Vol. 1. Introduction and executive summary*. (Final report to the National Institue of Education, Contract No. 400-77-0051-0052). Toronto: Ontario Institute for Studies in Education.

Fuller, F. F. (1969). Concerns of teachers: A developmental conceptualization. *American Educational Research Journal*, 6, 207–226.

Gage, N. L. (1972). *Teacher effectiveness and teacher education: The search for a scientific basis*. Palo Alto, CA: Pacific Books.

Gage, N. L. (1984). What do we know about teaching effectiveness? *Phil Delta Kappan*, 66, 87–93.

Good, T., Biddle, B., & Brophy, J. (1975). *Teachers make a difference*. New York: Holt, Rinehart & Winston.

Goodlad, J. I. (1984). *A place called school: Prospects for the future*. New York: McGraw-Hill.

Goodman, J. (1986). Making early field experience meaningful: A critical approach. *Journal of Education for Teaching*, 12(2), 109–125.

Goodman, J. (1988). University culture and the problem of reforming field experiences in teacher education. *Journal of Teacher Education*, 39(5), 45–53.

Griffin, G. A. (1984). Why use research in preservice teacher education? *Journal of Teacher Education*, 35(4), 36–39.

Haberman, M. (1982). Research needed on direct experience. In D. C. Corrigan, D. J. Palmer, & P. A. Alexander (Eds.), *The future of teacher education: Needed research and practice* (pp. 69–84). College Station, TX: Texas A&M University, College of Education, Dean's Grant Project.

Hall, G. E. (1974). Implementation of CBTE:Viewed as a developmental process. In W. R. Houston (Ed.), *Competency, assessment, research and evaluation* (pp. 252–269). Washington, DC: American Association of Colleges for Teacher Education.

Hall, G. E. (1979). The concerns-based approach for facilitating change. *Educational Horizons*, 57, 202–208.

Hall, G. E., & Hord, S. M. (1984). Analyzing what change facilitators do: The intervention taxonomy. *Knowledge: Creation, Diffusion, Utilization*, 5, 275–307

Hall, G. E., & Hord, S. M. (1987). *Exploring issues in teacher education: Questions for future research*. Austin, TX: University of Texas at Austin, R&D Center for Teacher Education.

Hall, G. E., & Jones, H. L. (1976). *Change in schools: Facilitating the process*. Ithaca, NY: University of New York Press.

Hall, G. E., & Loucks, S. F. (1978). Teacher concerns as a basis for facilitating and personalizing staff development. *Teachers College Record*, 80, 36–53.

Hall, G. E., & Loucks, S. F. (1981). Program definition and adaptation: Implications for inservice. *Journal of Research and Development in Education*, 14(2), 46–58.

Hall, G. E., Loucks, S. F., Rutherford, W. L., & Newlove, B. (1975). Levels of use of the innovation: A framework for analyzing innovation adoption. *Journal of Teacher Education*, 24, 52–56.

Hawley, W. D., Austin, A. E., & Goldman, E. S. (1988). *Changing the education of teachers*. Atlanta: Southern Regional Education Board.

Heider, F. (1958). *The psychology of interpersonal relationships*. New York: Holt, Rinehart & Winston.

Herriott, R. E., & Gross, N. (Eds.). (1979). *The dynamics of planned educational change: Case studies and analyses*. Berkeley, CA: McCutchan.

Hersey, P., & Blanchard, K. H. (1972). *Management of organizational behavior* (2nd ed.). Englewood Cliffs, NJ: Prentice-Hall.

Hill, S. E. (1986). Language education and field experiences. *Journal of Teacher Education*, 37(3), 56–59.

Holmes Group. (1986). *Tomorrow's teachers*. East Lansing, MI: Author.

Hoover, N. L. & Carroll, R. G. (1987). Self-assessment of classroom instruction: An effective approach to inservice education. *Teaching and Teacher Education*, 3, 179–181.

Hoover, N. L., & O'Shea, L. J. (1987, April). *Effects of collaborative conferencing and feedback on student teachers' perceptions and performance.* Paper presented at the annual meeting of the American Educational Research Association, Washington, DC.

Houston, W. R. (1980). Collaboration—see "treason." In G. E. Hall, S. M. Hord, & G. Brown (Eds.), *Exploring issues in teacher education: questions for future research* (pp. 331–348). Austin, TX: University of Texas at Austin, R&D Center for Teacher Education.

Houston, W. R. (1983). *Improving Texas teacher education: Recommendations to the Governor's Select Committee on Public Education.* Houston, TX: University of Houston, College of Education.

Houston, W. R., & Howsam, R. B. (Eds.). (1972). *Competency-based teacher education: Progress, problems, and prospects.* Chicago: Science Research Associates.

Howey, K. R. (1977). Preservice teacher education: Lost in the shuffle? *Journal of Teacher Education, 28*(6), 26–28.

Howsam, R. B., Corrigan, D. C., Denemark, G. W., & Nash, R. J. (1976). *Educating a profession.* Washington, DC: American Association of Colleges for Teacher Education.

Huling, L. L., & Johnson, W. L. (1983). A strategy for helping teachers integrate research into teaching. *Teacher Educator, 19*(2), 11–18.

Huling, L. L., Trang, M., & Correll, L. (1981). Interactive research and development: A promising strategy for teacher educators. *Journal of Teacher Education, 32*(6), 13–14.

Hyde, A., & Moore, I. (1982). *Making sense of staff development: An analysis of staff development programs and their costs in three urban school districts.* Washington, DC: U.S. Government Printing Office.

Ishler, R. E., & Leslie, E. C. (1987). Bridging the gap between a public school system and a university. *Phil Delta Kappan, 68,* 615–616.

Joyce, B., & Clift, R. (1984). The Phoenix agenda: Essential reform in teacher education. *Educational Researcher, 13*(4), 5–18.

Joyce, B., & Showers, B. (1988). *Student achievement through staff development.* New York: Longman.

Judge, H. (1982). *American graduate schools of education: A view from abroad.* New York: Ford Foundation.

Justiz, M. (1984). Improving teacher education through research. *Journal of Teacher Education, 35*(4), 2.

Keith, M. J. (1987). We've heard this song . . . Or have we? *Journal of Teacher Education, 38*(3), 20–25.

Korthagen, F. A. J. (1985). Reflective teaching and preservice teacher education in the Netherlands. *Journal of Teacher Education, 36*(5), 11–15.

Koziol, S. M., Jr., Bohn, S., & Moss, P. A. (1983, April). *Composition instruction in four suburban school districts: Grades 3–6.* Paper presented at the meeting of the American Educational Research Association, Montreal.

Koziol, S. M., Jr., & Burns, P. (1986). Teachers' accuracy in self-reporting about instructional practices using a focused self-report inventory. *Journal of Educational Research, 79,* 205–209.

Lacy, T., Tobin, K. G., & Treagust, D. F. (1984). *Development, validation and reliability of the Elementary Science Learning Environment Inventory.* Paper presented at the conference of the International Association for Student Assessment, Perth, Australia.

Lanier, J. E., & Glassberg, S. (1981). Relating research in classroom teaching to inservice education. *Journal of Research and Development in Education, 14,* 22–33.

Lanier, J. E., with Little, J. W. (1986). Research on teacher education. In M. C. Wittrock (Ed.), *Handbook of research on teaching* (3rd ed., pp. 527–569). New York: Macmillan.

Lewin, K. (1951). *Field theory in social science: Selected theoretical papers.* New York: Harper & Brothers.

Lewis, D. S. (1987). Microteaching: Feedback. In M. J. Dunkin (Ed.),

The international encyclopedia of teaching and teacher education (pp. 722–726). Oxford: Pergamon Press.

Lewis, M., & Bartholomew, R. (1984). The effectiveness of pupil feedback and self-analysis in changing selected science teaching practices. In L. J. Bethel (Ed.), *Research and curriculum development in science education.* Austin, TX: University of Texas, Science Education Center.

Lortie, D. (1975). *Schoolteacher: A sociological study.* Chicago: University of Chicago Press.

MacLeod, G. R. (1987). Microteaching: Effectiveness. In M. J. Dunkin (Ed.), *The international encyclopedia of teaching and teacher education* (pp. 726–729). Oxford: Pergamon Press.

Maeroff, G. (1983). *School and college.* Princeton, NJ: Carnegie Foundation for the Advancement of Teaching.

Manning, B. A. (1973). *The "Trouble-Shooting" Checklist: A manual to aid educational change agents in the prediction of organizational change potential.* Austin, TX: University of Texas, R&D Center for Teacher Education.

Marsh, D. D. (1979). The classroom effectiveness of Teacher Corps graduates: A national assessment. *Journal of Classroom Interaction, 15*(1), 25–33.

Marso, R. N. (1971). Project interaction: A pilot study in a phase of teacher preparation. *Journal of Teacher Education, 22,* 194–198.

McGregor, D. (1960). *The human side of enterprise.* New York: McGraw-Hill.

Miles, M. B. (Ed.). (1964). *Innovation in education.* New York: Teachers College Press.

Mitgang, L. (1988, Sept. 4). Benefits of school reform may not be seen for years. *Houston Chronicle,* p. 4A.

Moore, D. R., & Hyde, A. A. (1981). *Making sense of staff development: An analysis of staff development programs and their costs in three urban school districts.* Chicago: Designs for Change. (ERIC Document Reproduction Service No. ED 211 629)

National Commission on Excellence in Education. (1983). *A nation at risk: The imperative for educational reform.* Washington, DC: U.S. Government Printing Office.

National Commission on Excellence in Teacher Education (1985). *A call for change in teacher education.* Washington, DC: American Association of Colleges for Teacher Education.

National Dissemination Study Group. (1985). *Educational programs that work: A collection of proven exemplary educational programs and practices* (11th ed.). Longmont, CO: Sopris West.

Nemser, S. F. (1983). Learning to teach. In L. S. Shulman & G. Syke (Eds.), *Handbook of teaching and policy* (pp. 150–170). New York: Longman.

O'Dell, S. J. (1985). A collaboration model for teacher induction. Unpublished manuscript, University of New Mexico, Albuquerque.

Owens, R. G. (1987). *Organizational behavior in education* (3rd ed.). Englewood Cliffs, NJ: Prentice-Hall.

Owens, R. G., & Steinhoff, C. R. (1976). *Administering change in schools.* Englewood Cliffs, NJ: Prentice-Hall.

Parish, R., Underwood, E., & Eubanks, E. E. (1987). We do not make change: School–university collaboration. *Metropolitan Education, 3,* 44–55.

Peck, R. F., & Tucker, J. A. (1973). Research on teacher education. In R. M. W. Travers (Ed.), *Second handbook of research on teaching* (pp. 940–978). Chicago: Rand McNally.

Perlberg, A. (1987). Microteaching: Conceptual and theoretical bases. In M. J. Dunkin (Ed.), *The international encyclopedia of teaching and teacher education* (pp. 715–720). Oxford: Pergamon Press.

Peseau, B. A. (1982). Developing an adequate resource base for teaching education. *Journal of Teacher Education, 33*(4), 13–15.

Posner, G. J. (1985). *Field experience: A guide to reflective teaching.* New York: Longman.

Posner, G. J., Strike, K. A., Hewson, P. W., & Gertzog, W. A. (1982). Accommodation of a scientific conception: Toward a theory of conceptual change. *Science Education, 66,* 211–227.

Pyper, J., Freiberg, H. J., Ginsburg, M., & Spuck, D. (1987). School climate questionnaires. In H. J. Freiberg, A. Driscoll, & S. Knight (Eds.), *School climate* (pp. 87–96). Bloomington, IN: Center on Evaluation, Development, Research, Phi Delta Kappa.

Radin, B. A. (1977). *Implementation, change, and the federal bureaucracy: School desegregation policy in H.E.W., 1964–1968.* New York: Teachers College Press.

Rogers, E. M. (1962). *Diffusion of innovations.* New York: Free Press.

Romanish, B. (1987). A skeptical view of educational reform. *Journal of Teacher Education, 38*(3), 9–12.

Rosner, B. (1972). *The power of competency-based teacher education: A report.* Boston: Allyn & Bacon.

Roth, R. A. (1976). *A study of competency based teacher education: Philosophy, research, issues, models.* Lansing, MI: Department of Education, Teacher Preparation and Professional Development Services.

Sandefur, J. T. (1970). Kansas State Teachers College experimental study of professional education for secondary teachers. *Journal of Teacher Education, 21,* 386–395.

Schlechty, P. C., George, J., & Whitford, B. L. (1978). Reform in teacher education and the professionalization of teaching. *High School Journal,* 61, 313–320.

Schlechty, P. C., & Vance, V. S. (1983). Do academically able teachers leave education? The North Carolina case. *Phi Delta Kappan,* 63(2), 106–112.

Silberman, C. (1970). *Crisis in the classroom: The remaking of American education.* New York: Random House.

Sirotnik, K. A. (1983). An inter-observer reliability study of a modified SRI observation system. *Journal of Classroom Interaction, 19*(1), 28–38.

Smith, B. O. (1969). *Teachers for the real world.* Washington, DC: American Association of Colleges for Teacher Education.

Smith, B. O. (1980). Pedagogical education: How about reform? *Phi Delta Kappan,* 62(2), 87–91.

Smith, G. P. (1987). *The effects of competency testing on the supply of minority teachers.* Unpublished report commissioned by the Council of Chief State School Officers and the National Education Association.

Smith, S. D., & Auger, K. (1986). Conflict or cooperation? Keys to success in partnerships in teacher education. *Action in Teacher Education,* 7(4), 1–9.

Smith, W. L. (1975). Facing the next ten years. *Journal of Teacher Education,* 26(2), 150–152.

Soltis, J. F. (Ed.). (1987). *Reforming teacher education: The impact of the Holmes Group Report.* New York: Teachers College Press.

Stallings, J. A., & Kaskowitz, D. (1974). *Follow through classroom observation evaluation, 1972–1973.* Menlo Park, CA: Stanford Research Institute.

Starr, P. (1982). *The social transformation of American medicine.* New York: Basic Books.

Study Commission on Undergraduate Education and the Education of Teachers. (1975). *Teacher education in America.* Lincoln, NE: University of Nebraska.

Sykes, G. (1983). Public policy and the problem of teacher quality: The need for screens and magnets. In L. S. Shulman & G. Sykes (Eds.), *Handbook of teaching and policy* (pp. 95–125). New York: Longman.

Sykes, G. (1984). Teacher education and the predicaments of reform. In C. Finn, Jr., D. Ravitch, & R. T. Fancher (Eds.), *Against mediocrity. The humanities in America's high schools* (pp. 172–194). New York: Holmes & Meier.

Tabachnick, B. R., Popkewitz, T. S., & Zeichner, K. M. (1980). Teacher education and the professional perspectives of student teachers. *Interchange,* 10, 12–29.

Teacher Education Reports. (1988). 10(23), 2.

Tom, A. R. (1980). The reform of teacher education through research: A futile quest. *Teacher College Record,* 82, 15–29.

Tom, A. R. (1985). Inquiring into inquiry-oriented teacher education. *Journal of Teacher Education,* 36(5), 35–44.

Tuckman, B. W., & Oliver, W. S. (1968). Effectiveness of feedback to teachers as a function of source. *Journal of Educational Psychology,* 59, 297–301.

Tyler, R. W. (1985). What we've learned from past studies of teacher education. *Phi Delta Kappan,* 65, 682–684.

Vaughan, J. (1984). Knowledge resources for improving the content of preservice teacher education. *Journal of Teacher Education,* 35(4), 3–8.

Veldman, D. J., Menaker, S. L., & Newlove, B. (1970). *The Porter Project: Teacher aides in a secondary school. A preliminary report.* Austin, TX: University of Texas, R&D Center for Teacher Education.

Wallace, R. C. (1973). *Each his own man: The role of adoption agents in the implementation of personalized teacher education.* Austin, TX: University of Texas, R&D Center for Teacher Education.

Wallace, R. C. (1987). Establishing partnerships between schools and teacher training institutions. In C. P. Magrath & R. L. Egbert (Eds.), *Strengthening teacher education* (pp. 150–162). San Francisco: Jossey-Bass.

Waxman, H. C. (1984). Utilizing student feedback to improve reading instruction. *Reading Improvement,* 21, 126–127.

Waxman, H. C., & Duschl, R. (1987). Using student perception data to improve preservice teachers' instruction and classroom environment. In B. F. Fraser (Ed.), *Study of learning environments* (Vol. 2, pp. 77–79). Bentley, Australia: Western Australian Institute of Technology.

Waxman, H. C., Freiberg, H. J., Clift, R. T., & Houston, W. R. (1988, February). *The development of reflective inquiry in teacher education.* Paper presented at the meeting of the Association of Teacher Educators, San Diego.

Waxman, H. C., Freiberg, H. J., Vaughan, J. C., & Weil, M. (Eds.). (1988). *Images of reflection in teacher education.* Reston, VA: Association of Teacher Educators.

Waxman, H. C., & Sexton, W. W. (1988, January). *Investigating cognitive-developmental changes in preservice teachers' perceptions of teaching.* Paper presented at the meeting of the Southwest Educational Research Association, San Antonio.

Waxman, H. C., & Walberg, H. J. (1986). Effects of early field experiences. In J. D. Raths & L. G. Katz (Eds.), *Advances in teacher education* (Vol. 2, pp. 165–184). Norwood, NJ: Ablex.

Wheeler, A. E., & Knoop, H. R. (1982). Self, teacher, and faculty assessments of student teaching performance. *Journal of Educational Research,* 75(3), 178–181.

Wilkerson, D. A. (1979). *The education professions development act: In Congress, in the Office of Education, and in the field.* Westport, CT: Mediax Associates.

Yarger, S. J., Howey, K., & Joyce, B. (1977). Reflections on preservice preparation: Impressions from the national survey. *Journal of Teacher Education,* 28(6), 34–37.

Zeichner, K. M. (1980). Myths and realities: Field-based experiences in preservice teacher education. *Journal of Teacher Education,* 31(6), 45–55.

Zeichner, K. M. (1983). Alternative paradigms of teacher education. *Journal of Teacher Education,* 34(3), 3–9.

Zeichner, K. M., & Liston, D. P. (1987). Teaching student teachers to reflect. *Harvard Educational Review,* 57(1), 23–48.

TEACHER EDUCATION IN THE CURRICULAR AREAS

·35·

MATHEMATICS TEACHER EDUCATION

Stephen I. Brown
STATE UNIVERSITY OF NEW YORK AT BUFFALO

Thomas J. Cooney
UNIVERSITY OF GEORGIA

Doug Jones
UNIVERSITY OF GEORGIA

Many forces influence practice and research in mathematics teacher education. Some are external (or at least perceived as such by many) to the field of mathematics education in that they involve matters of a more general nature regarding broader concerns of teacher education, as well as political, economic, and sociological interests that link education to society at large. The spate of reports following publication of *A Nation at Risk* (National Commission on Excellence in Education, 1983) constitutes one such force. These reports indirectly influenced teacher education through the discussions they fostered that provided a basis for defining excellence in terms of increased and more extensive exposure to subject matter. More recently, the reports of the Holmes Group (1986) and the Carnegie Forum on Education and the Economy (1986) have provided a sharper focus on pedagogical and social considerations that impinge upon and redefine the professional life of teachers.

Accrediting agencies shape teacher education programs, as do the historical contexts of the institutions in which individual teacher education programs are created. Forces from within the educational community consist of the collective wisdom of teacher educators, a general sense of what constitutes good teaching, and various research findings on effective teaching and effective methods of training teachers. These general educational influences are renegotiated as they are articulated by constituents of the mathematics education community, sometimes more finely honed, sometimes ignored.

Fully aware of the general, though pervasive, nature of such external forces, we turn now to a brief historical perspective on the more mathematically oriented influences on research in mathematics teacher education. Against this backdrop, we will consider two research perspectives for mathematics teacher education, one based primarily on quantitative methodologies that are often rooted in positivism, the other oriented toward more qualitative methodologies in which interpretation and meaning are of paramount importance.

In describing the conceptions of mathematics and the assumptions underlying each of the paradigms, we continue to be reminded of the fact that no paradigm is value free; embedded in an epistemology of mathematics and of research is a view of mind and human nature. It is our hope that an explicit recognition of the epistemelogical foundations of both research and mathematics can precipitate a discussion of some of the factors that motivate research.

The authors thank reviewers Paul Cobb (Purdue University), Jack Easley (University of Illinois), Magdeline Lampert (Michigan State University), Marilyn Nickson (Essex Institute of Higher Education), Lynn Steen (St. Olaf College), and Robert Underhill (Virginia Polytechnic Institute and State University) for helpful comments on an earlier draft. The authors also thank Heinrich Bauersfeld (Universität Bielefeld) for criticism of related material recently published by the authors that contributed to the development of this chapter.

Teaching method – discovery [handwritten]

HISTORICAL PERSPECTIVE ON MATHEMATICS EDUCATION

Numerous programs have been proposed and implemented since the late 1940s, their major goal being improvement in the teaching and learning of mathematics. These programs have had various implications for mathematics teacher education, although they rarely served as a basis for conducting research in this area.

One of the earliest influences stemmed from the research of Brownell, who provided a sharp contrast to the essentially behavioristic model of learning prevalent at the time (Brownell 1944, 1945, 1947). He rejected the associationist view of learning mathematics that focused more on performance than on meanings underlying performance. Brownell proposed a meaning theory of arithmetic that was based on a conception of rationality as giving reasons to justify procedures rather than on the mechanistic mastery of procedures that often characterized the associationist perspective on learning mathematics. Brownell suggested that meaning was derived from within the connectedness of mathematics itself, for instance, explaining why 4 times 5 is 20 on the basis of what is known about the meaning of those numbers and on the nature of multiplication as repeated addition.

At about the time that Brownell was proposing his meaning theory, progressive education was in its heyday and began to influence curriculum. Dewey's focus upon the social context of education and upon the need for the entire curriculum to be understood as a connected, rather than a disjointed enterprise, had begun to influence educators to view mathematics as a subject best understood in relation to other subjects (Dewey, 1896, 1898; Dewey & McLellan, 1895). That movement devised curricula that focused less on mathematics as a self-contained and self-justifying activity and more on its relatedness to other fields of activity. Once again, rationality was invoked as a neglected category of importance; however, this time it did not mean searching for reasons to justify procedures, but rather seeking connectedness in a cloth that was woven of many different fabrics.

Many of the proposals since the late 1950s for defining what mathematics education ought to be can be seen to have evolved from these two strands of structure and connectedness. The *new mathematics* of the late 1950s and 1960s arose in part because of a perceived need to produce more mathematically sophisticated students in the post-Sputnik era and had two very different themes. The more dominant theme was based on the view that curricula in the schools should be revised to emphasize the axiomatic and structural aspects of mathematics, rather than its applications. This view was supported by such research mathematicians as Edward Begle and Edwin Moise, who played significant roles in the development of the curriculum of the *School Mathematics Study Group* (SMSG). People such as Jerome Bruner supplied a psychological rationale for approaching mathematics as the study of structure. The approach was believed to be superior not only because it portrayed the nature of mathematics but also because

Structure of the discipline approach [handwritten]

the emphasis on structure would aid memory, understanding, and a deep sense of transfer of training (Bruner, 1960, 1966).

An important pedagogical dimension that accompanied the structure movement was that of *teaching by discovery*, a method in which students could learn mathematics as if much of what they were learning were being discovered for the first time (Davis, 1967). Max Beberman was perhaps the most eminent spokesman for revising the curriculum and teaching mathematics in such a way that its structure was emphasized through discovery methods (1958). For those who subscribed to Beberman's philosophy, the value of studying mathematics was based not only on the richness with which mathematics could solve real-world problems but also on the intrinsic beauty of the subject, which could be appreciated by students at both the elementary and secondary levels. Beberman and Vaughan collaborated in producing a curriculum known as the *University of Illinois Committee on School Mathematics* (UICSM), which provided a counterpoint to the SMSG program.

Thus, in the 1960s there was not only an overhauling of school curricula through the development of SMSG, UICSM, and other curriculum projects but also a proposed revolution in the teaching of mathematics through the discovery method. Debates raged over philosophies of mathematics that emphasized either applications or axiomatics (Kline, 1958; Meder, 1958) and over the advantages and disadvantages of teaching by discovery (Shulman & Keislar, 1966). During the 1960s numerous summer and inservice institutes funded by the National Science Foundation attempted to upgrade teachers' mathematical backgrounds. The rationale for the programs was the premise that teachers needed additional mathematical training to effectively teach modern mathematics. The dominant view was that the primary emphasis in teacher education should be on increasing the mathematical knowledge of teachers. Little evidence emerged, however, to suggest a relationship between the amount of mathematics studied by a teacher and student learning (Begle, 1968; Eisenberg, 1977). Although pedagogy was the subject of theoretical debate, it was a secondary consideration in pragmatic national initiatives.

A second stream of the new mathematics movement was more closely associated with the elementary school. Although mathematical content was one of the foci, the primary thrust of the movement was emphasis on using concrete materials and models such as Cuisenaire rods, geoboards, and multibase blocks to promote children's development of mathematical meaning. Various projects such as the Madison Project, the University of Maryland Mathematics Project, the University of Illinois Arithmetic Project, the Greater Cleveland Mathematics Program, and the Minnesota Mathematics and Science Teaching Project contributed to a focus on the use of manipulatives that complemented the already established movement focused on structure and learning by discovery (Nichols, 1968). These projects stressed the teaching of elementary school mathematics in a meaningful way, much as Brownell had emphasized, through exploration and use of concrete materials. This position was strengthened by the influence of Piaget and the Genevan school of psychology, which held that learning i

Hands-on math [handwritten]

a function of one's active experiences. Mathematics educators' preoccupation with Piaget's developmental stages encouraged many to design activities that would accommodate students' mathematical maturity (e.g., Piaget, 1952; Piaget, Inhelder, & Szeminska, 1960). Some teacher education programs embraced the Genevan notion of the clinical interview as a technique for teachers to better understand how students construct mathematical knowledge. Although considerable research has been conducted using Piaget's theory to demonstrate its effect on children's learning of mathematics, little research exists on the role or influence of Piaget's theory or the use of concrete materials more generally on mathematics teacher education programs.

In the 1970s one of the emerging modes of mathematics teacher education programs, particularly at the elementary level, was the notion of *competency-based teacher education*, which was rooted in behaviorism and emphasized behavioral objectives and accountability. McKillip (1980) defines a competency as "a teaching performance observed in a selection of appropriate situations together with the supporting knowledge and attitudes which enable the teacher to describe how, when, with whom, and for what outcomes to use it" (p. 25). Embedded in the context of mathematics teacher education, competencies were the organizing agent for methods classes and involved students' mathematical, psychological, and pedagogical outcomes.

Advances in quantifying the teaching act and subsequent process–product studies also enhanced the notion of competency-based teacher education. Research on teacher effectiveness in the 1970s generated considerable analysis and debate (e.g., Dunkin & Biddle, 1974; Heath & Nielsen, 1974; Magoon, 1977) and with it the question of whether it produced an adequate knowledge base for constructing viable competency-based teacher education programs. The movement was in contrast with the Genevan school and with the legacy of both Brownell and Dewey.

More recently, mathematics education has emphasized problem solving and applications. In the National Council of Teachers of Mathematics' (NCTM) *Agenda for Action* (1980), problem solving was proclaimed as the first priority for school mathematics in the 1980s. Problem solving may be viewed as a further extension of Brownell's program, although its more explicit roots lie with George Polya and his enormous contributions (Polya, 1945, 1962, 1965). Fine-tuning the rationality theme once again, problem solving is viewed by many mathematics educators as an effort to learn and appropriately invoke heuristics to deal with not only what is already known (as was the case with Brownell) but also what is unknown. The heuristic approach focuses on efforts such as understanding what a problem is asking of the student, what a student already knows, and how that knowledge can be put to use in coping with what is not known.

The current emphasis on applications in mathematics education is in some sense an extension of Dewey's program, although its immediate impetus is a perceived overemphasis on the structural aspects of mathematics. Efforts are made to relate mathematics to science in the secondary school curriculum

and to the real world at the elementary school level. At the secondary level, the emphasis on applications reinforces the position that Kline (1958) expresses when debating the advent of the new mathematics, which is that the emphasis in mathematics should be on its relationship to physics and other application-oriented subjects, rather than on teaching mathematics as a self-contained field of inquiry.

The most recent proclamation on the teaching and learning of mathematics appears in the *Curriculum and Evaluation Standards for School Mathematics* developed by the NCTM (1989). These standards were written, at least in part, as a response to a growing concern about the status of school mathematics as presented in the *Underachieving Curriculum* (McKnight et al., 1987) and in various National Assessment of Educational Progress reports on mathematics (e.g., C. A. Brown et al., 1988a, 1988b; Carpenter, Corbitt, Kepner, Lindquist, & Reys, 1980; Carpenter, Lindquist, Matthews, & Silver, 1983; Kouba et al., 1988). In a sense, the book on standards represents a call for reform motivated in part by a perceived loss of an international economic competitive edge somewhat reminiscent of the post-Sputnik era. That book assumes the availability of calculators for all students and a computer, for at least demonstration purposes, for every classroom. In addition to highlighting problem solving and mathematic reasoning, it picks up the progressive view of the classroom as a forum for social interaction.

Mathematics teacher education has not been untouched by these various historical thrusts; however, the effects have stemmed more from a reasoned accommodation than from a research perspective. Consider, for example, the elementary and secondary components of the new-math movement in the 1960s and 1970s. It was a time in which experienced teachers at all levels were paid to attend institutes (many of which were funded by the National Science Foundation) to learn new conceptions of mathematics and of teaching mathematics. Despite the fact that such teacher education programs were deeply entrenched in the mathematics education community, relatively little research per se investigated the effectiveness of such programs. Furthermore, the models of education implicit in those programs were few in number and, with considerable hindsight, lacking in imagination. Many of the courses tended to focus on the learning of the new math in a way that separated it from concern for pedagogy. In some cases, there was an effort to engage teachers in pedagogical matters, by either having them experience such phenomena as discovery learning firsthand or informing them of its potential in the classroom. Institutes that focused on the education of elementary school teachers sometimes provided models of good teaching by having teachers observe content and pedagogical principles in action with "real kids" or, in a more vicarious way, by having them see films of such teaching.

Given that the most highly funded mathematics teacher education program in the history of the United States was not viewed seriously from a research perspective, we know very little about the variety of teacher education approaches and even less about long- or short-range impacts of different styles of teacher education. The folk wisdom of many mathematics educators, however, is that, despite the fact that there was a change in curriculum (and even the extent of that change is difficult to document) as a result of massive teacher education programs, there was a relatively insignificant change in the manner in which mathematics was taught. One can conjecture that, because the movement was basically top-down and largely dominated by mathematicians who rewrote curriculum, which was perceived by some teachers as being foisted upon them, it should not be surprising that teachers approached the new material cautiously, with minimal attention to changes in teaching style (Cooney, 1988; Sarason, 1982).

RESEARCH PERSPECTIVES

Having given a broad overview of the field of mathematics education in the past half century or so, we turn now to research on teacher education as it relates to some of the curriculum and instruction themes we developed in the previous section. To aid reflection upon various types of research, we will consider a typology of research proposed by Mitroff and Kilmann (1978) that captures and elucidates research ranging from the interpretation of individual meanings to the generation of quantifiably based generalizations. Mitroff and Kilmann identify four types of research perspectives, personified as the analytic scientist, the conceptual theorist, the conceptual humanist, and the particular humanist. Their scheme is derived from Jung's personality categories, which dichotomize how people "take in" the world (primarily through the senses or through an act of intuition) and how they process it (through thinking or feeling). The four research types are derived by placing each of the dichotomies orthogonally to each other. We will focus on two research perspectives, the *analytic perspective* and the *humanist perspective*, as we consider different paradigms for research in mathematics teacher education. We see this classification as deeper than the standard quantitative–qualitative split, though that designation might be helpful as a first approximation.

Mitroff and Kilmann dscribe the *analytic scientist* as one who tends to emphasize the value-free nature of science. The analytic scientist (sensing, thinking) maintains a certain distance between herself or himself and the object being studied. It is assumed that knowledge is discovered through carefully prescribed procedures that embody as much objectivity as the context and instrumentation allow. Further, the analytic scientist conceives of research as being generalizable to broader populations than the particular one(s) under study.

Alternately, the authors describe a *humanistic researcher* (Mitroff and Kilmann's third and fourth categories) as one who defines a problem by reference to the concept of one's being and whose appreciation of the uniqueness of individuals is often expressed through the presentation of case studies. These researchers make sense of the world through intuition and process it through feeling. Mitroff and Kilmann's notion of a humanistic orientation to research emphasizes the belief that knowledge is personal and is revealed through processes that promote intimacy of communication between researcher and the individual being studied.

It is important to appreciate that, though the humanistic perspective has existed in research in education for a while, it has only recently emerged in mathematics education per se. Hence, we would like to briefly indentify four characteristics that we think contrast this more recently accepted humanistic perspective with the more established analytic perspective. *First*, humanistic-based research tends to take into account the political, social, historical, and philosophical contexts within which research takes place. Hence, the research tends to be more holistic and experientially based. *Second*, although analytic-based research tends to cast the investigator as a neutral observer with efforts made to minimize investigator bias, the humanistic researcher attends less to minimizing bias and more to recognizing and accounting for bias when analyzing data. *Third*, the analytic researcher tends to produce generalizations that are quantifiable and replicable, whereas the humanistic researcher is more content to produce naturalistic generalizations in which generality is a function of shared meanings among individuals (Stake & Easley, 1978). *Fourth*, in contrast with the analytic perspective, research in the humanistic mode tends to be less driven by an effort to verify or falsify a priori hypotheses and is more concerned with the creation of categories of analysis as part of the on-going research experience, rather than as a final act of reflection. Our analysis of research will take into consideration these various aspects of analytic and humanistic research.

It would be a mistake to convey the notion that either perspective is all of one cloth. Each research tradition is multifaceted in terms of its potential to address researchable questions. Nevertheless, we focus on this dichotomy with the realization that the sharpening of distinctions can enable us to better unravel assumptions inherent in each of the perspectives as they are manifested in various research programs. The issue is one that transcends methodology and reaches to the researcher's hard core (Lakatos, 1978), that is, to how research is conceived and what one values in the research enterprise. For example, a researcher might use aspects of qualitative methodologies, but do so with the intention of generating hypotheses and findings that could drive more quantitatively oriented studies in which scientifically generated knowledge about teaching and learning would be identified. Such a researcher is operating from a basically analytic perspective, despite the fact that the research initially used qualitative methodologies.

The following sections focus on research that reflects the analytic and humanistic perspectives. We do not offer an exhaustive review of this research, for those reviews are elsewhere (e.g., Brophy & Good, 1986; Lampert, 1986; Romberg & Carpenter, 1986), but we shall highlight selected topics, in order to consider the nature and implications of research based on the two perspectives.

RESEARCH BASED ON THE ANALYTIC PERSPECTIVE

In this section we will provide a brief analysis of analytic-based research that has been reported since the late 1970s with respect to elementary teachers (we found virtually nothing of a similar sort on secondary mathematics teachers) and research on effective teaching, expert–novice teachers, and research involving aspects of teacher education.

Elementary Teachers' Knowledge and Attitudes

One type of research related to mathematics teacher education focuses on the knowledge and attitudes of elementary teachers. Research since the late 1970s has provided a glimpse of elementary teachers' knowledge about different mathematical topics. Research of this type leaves the distinct impression that preservice elementary teachers do not possess the level of mathematical understanding necessary to teach elementary school mathematics as recommended in various proclamations from professional organizations such as NCTM. For example, Wheeler and Feghali (1983) concluded that elementary preservice teachers have an inadequate concept of zero, given that 15 percent of the preservice teachers studied did not think it was a number and that approximately 75 percent of the teachers did not respond correctly to the question, "What is zero divided by zero?" Graeber, Tirosh, and Glover (1986) found that preservice elementary teachers have difficulty selecting an appropriate operation for solving arithmetic story problems and, in particular, tend to conceive of division only in its partitive (sharing) representation, overlooking the quantitative (measurement) representation. Fisher (1988) found that many teachers have an inadequate understanding of proportion and of direct and inverse variation. Mayberry (1983) found that elementary preservice teachers do not have a level of geometric understanding supportive of a formal study of deductive geometry, despite the fact that more than two-thirds studied high school geometry. Battista, Wheatley, and Talsma (1982) conclude that elementary teachers' spatial ability improves after a semester course in geometry. The gain is approximately four times greater for the group below the median on an initial spatial visualization test than for those who score above the median.

Interestingly, Ginther, Pigge, and Gibney (1987) found that, although twice as many elementary teachers who were trained during the period 1983–1985 had 4 or more years of high school mathematics than did their counterparts from the 1967–1969 era (31 percent versus 16 percent) and that the percentage of teachers taking three or more college mathematics courses increased from 4 percent to 23 percent from these same eras, their understanding of mathematics decreased. If these results are replicated, we might conclude that mathematics courses alone do not address the apparent mathematical deficiencies that seem to characterize many elementary teachers.

Another area of research has focused on various aspects of training elementary teachers to use certain pedagogical strategies. Eastman and Barnett (1979) studied preservice teachers' use of manipulatives and found that the experimental group, which used manipulatives, did not perform better than the control group, which observed the use of manipulatives with respect to either a paper-and-pencil test or a demonstrated ability to use manipulatives. The authors suggest, however, that attitudinal differences might exist in favor of the experimental group. Charles (1980) reports success in training preservice elementary teachers to use specific techniques for teaching certain geometric concepts.

Attitudes of elementary teachers toward mathematics have also been the focus of research from an analytic perspective. The intent of some of the research is to describe existing attitudes of elementary teachers (e.g., Becker, 1986) or to examine attitudes in conjunction with other aspects of mathematics education, for example, with respect to performance on computational estimation and the effects of instruction and practice activities on estimation skills (Bestgen, Reys, Rybolt, & Wyatt, 1980). Bitter (1980) reports that teachers can become more positively disposed to use calculators when they become familiar with their potential use in teaching elementary school mathematics.

Galbraith (1984) studied the attitudes of both postgraduates enrolled in mathematics teacher education courses and undergraduates enrolled in first-year university mathematics courses. He found that, the more students studied mathematics, the less they liked it. More than half of the prospective teachers in his study had, at best, a lukewarm attitude toward mathematics. Galbraith also found that the prospective teachers had more positive recollections of their high school mathematics experiences than did the undergraduates. However, they tended to see school mathematics as significantly different from university mathematics. Galbraith raises the following question: "If mathematics is not seen as a continuum . . . then for the teacher which is the real mathematics?" (p. 684).

Although this research embraces an analytic perspective, it does not share a common theoretical foundation, with the exception that the research on attitudes sometimes shares some of the same literature. It seems fair to say that the research essentially consists of one-shot studies. Hence, it is difficult to see how the research can provide the basis for constructing a theoretically grounded elementary mathematics teacher education program. Nevertheless, it does illustrate some of the problems associated with preparing elementary teachers and reveals some of the concerns shared by mathematics educators involved in elementary mathematics teacher education. Missing from this research, perhaps because knowledge and attitudes are studied separately, is an attempt to consider the means by which elementary teachers construct mathematical knowledge and what attitudes emerge as a result of that construction. Kulm (1980), in a review of research on attitudes of preservice elementary teachers, concludes that additional research should be conducted on the relationship between teachers' attitudes and mathematical ability and students' attitudes.

Effective Teaching

Early research on teaching focused on teacher characteristics and their possible relationship to student learning. However, this line of research did not appear to be productive in the field of mathematics research. The limitations may have been a consequence of research design, or perhaps of the fact that the issues were not framed in such a way as to highlight the specific nature of mathematics and mathematics education.

Since the late 1960s researchers have shifted their attention from teacher characteristics to teacher behavior. A large number of process–product studies were conducted to establish relationships between specific teacher actions and student achievement. Reviews by Cooney (1980), Dessart and Frandsen (1973), Dunkin and Biddle (1974), Riedesel and Burns (1973), and Rosenshine and Furst (1971) suggest that research in the late 1960s and 1970s yielded some findings deserving of consideration as factors related to effective instruction. Some studies, (e.g., Ebmeier & Good, 1979) utilized results from descriptive and correlational studies to help design treatments in experimental studies, in order to link in a causal way teacher behavior and student achievement.

More recently Brophy and Good (1986) provide an extensive review of research on effective teaching that involved more than 200 studies. One of their comforting conclusions is that teachers do make a difference with regard to student achievement. Although the authors conclude that effective teaching consists of a complex set of interrelated teaching behaviors, they express the view that research on teaching is beginning to develop a basis for teacher education.

Indeed, one of the goals of research on teaching is the generation of general principles of teaching that can serve as a basis for the construction of teacher education programs. Nowhere is this more obvious than in Rosenshine's 1987 article, in which 11 skills are identified that Rosenshine concludes are characteristic of the effective teacher. In Rosenshine's view, effective teaching consists of using these skills in the following six well-defined steps: review and check previous work; present new material in small steps; guide practice; provide feedback and correctives; supervise independent practice; and review, both weekly and monthly. From such a research program, teacher training flows in what is perceived to be a natural way. That is, prospective teachers are taught these skills, given considerable opportunity to practice them, and provided a model of teaching based on the six steps. Rosenshine provides the following analysis:

Pre-service teachers should also have a great deal of guided practice and independent practice in applying these skills. In such training, they would study and practice how to teach various areas of explicit teaching such as lists (e.g., parts of a castle, parts of a plant, countries of South America), concepts (e.g., parts of speech, and distinguishing fact and opinion), and procedures (e.g., adding decimals, completing and balancing a chemical equation, computing the area of a rectangle). The same procedures of explicit presentation, guided practice, and independent practice would be used to teach these skills to preservice teachers. (p. 36)

Another directive for research in teacher education is suggested by the more general research agenda of Joyce and Showers (1980). They map out four potential dimensions of influence in the education of teachers with regard to skills of the kind singled out by the research on effective teaching: (a) awareness of the importance of the skill, (b) knowledge *about* the skill, (c) acquisition of the skill, (d) application of the skill in context. They then single out a number of elements in the training of teachers for affecting teaching skills: (a) presentation of theory (to influence the first dimension); (b) modeling the skill (to influence the first and second dimensions; (c) opportunities to practice in microteaching with feedback (to influence the third); and (d) coaching in the context of the classroom. Such a program might provide researchers who focus on effective teaching with the necessary perspective to better understand what influences student teachers to adopt desired strategies once they are engaged in their own teaching.

The problem of identifying the most salient variables to investigate is confounded by the multiplicity of cognitive and affective variables that potentially influence outcomes of the research. It is one thing, for example, to propose a linkage between modeling and informing people about the importance of knowledge of a skill; it is another thing, however, to determine what makes it possible for a teacher, particularly a novice, even to perceive what it is that is being modeled. An important research question, then, might be, What are the variables that affect the neophyte's ability to even perceive salient features of a teaching model?

Expert–Novice Teachers

There have been recent efforts to further refine the components of effective mathematics teaching by transporting the concepts of *expert* and *novice* as applied to such fields as the study of chess and of business. The purpose of such research is to provide a profile of what constitutes *expert teaching,* thereby providing a basis of training teachers to demonstrate the knowledge and performance that characterize the expert. Expert teachers are usually defined in terms of student growth on standardized achievement tests or in terms of the opinions of other teachers, supervisors, or administrators. Most of the research that involves mathematics has concentrated on the teaching of elementary or middle school mathematics (e.g., Leinhardt & Putnam, 1986).

A recent government report entitled *How the Experts Teach Math* (McKinney, 1986) briefly summarizes a significant amount of novice–expert research over a 6-year period. Teachers in both groups exhibit differential uses of time, orchestration of lessons, and content competence. In particular, experts make wiser use of time, organize lessons better, and have a better knowledge of content than do novices. In addition, experts far surpass novices in their explanations of why, how, and when mathematical concepts are used. Their lessons are clearer than those of novices, and their students are more frequently aware of what is expected of them. Further, it is not only these categories in isolation but also the manner in which they are integrated that differentiate the two groups. The disparity between experts and novices is one that can be quantified in a rather dramatic way. Thus, the research summary tells us:

1. Novices can take as long as 15 minutes to correct the prior day's homework; experts take 2 or 3 minutes.
2. Most expert teachers cover at least 40 problems a day through games, drills or written work. Novice teachers, on

the other hand, may cover only 6 or 7 (McKinney, 1986, p. 1).

Working from an information-processing paradigm, Leinhardt's (1988) approach to research on experts and novices involves making comparisons with respect to various components of the structure of a lesson. In doing so, she focused on *segments* and *routines* and on the more comprehensive notion of lesson *scripts*. Leinhardt found that expert teachers were better able to weave segments and routines together and had a richer array of scripts than did novice teachers. Expert teachers could call upon the scripts in a variety of contexts, thus enabling them to be more flexible. She also found that expert teachers could provide a richer array of representations of the concept of fraction, which also provided a basis for being more flexible during instruction.

What are the implications of such research for teacher education? To the extent that the research is valid and reliable, it suggests that we should employ, train, and reward teachers according to their potential and their ability to explain well, operate efficiently, and minimize confusion and that we should provide a basis for them to increase their flexibility in reacting to students. Accordingly, research in teacher education would focus on the extent to which programs produced teachers who could and would exhibit these characteristics in school settings. Of particular interest would be the identification of potent variables and effective techniques for training teachers.

There are other interesting questions in the area of research in teacher education that could be derived from the expert–novice research. Most obviously, we might wish to know not only what the salient differences are but also how they come about. Embedded in much of the literature on expert–novice teachers is the implication that some form of training might make the difference. It is conceivable that experience, rather than explicit training, is required. It could be that an appropriate school environment trains some teachers informally and over time to acquire the skills of the expert (e.g., Peterson, Fennema, Carpenter, & Loef, 1989). Such researchers might then wish to generate hypotheses about the nature of school contexts that could account for growth in some people and not in others.

Aspects of Teacher Education

Perhaps the work that is the most recognized among mathematics educators is that of Good, Grouws, and Ebmeier (1983) on active mathematics teaching, which focuses explicitly on developing a model for effective methods of teaching mathematics. What makes the work particularly noteworthy is that it is the product of a series of investigations and considers not only the question of effective teaching but also the question of how knowledge about effective teaching can influence teachers participating in a teacher-training program. Although intended to be used as a heuristic, the authors' program has typically been implemented as a algorithm that emphasizes a rather definite time allocation for class activities consisting of the following: review and practice on mental computation (8 minutes), devel-

opmental portion of the lesson (20 minutes), seatwork (15 minutes), and assignment of homework (2 minutes).

Good et al. developed a teacher-training program based on their major research conclusions on effective teaching. One of their puzzlements, however, is what it is that accounts for disparity in the implementation of the program beyond the training period. The authors observed that "most teachers who implemented the program obtained positive gains from students; however, it is not clear why some teachers implemented the program better than other" (p. 196). The question inherent in their observation is one that would trouble any mathematics teacher educator. Good et al. conclude that, "only more research that involves the developmental of more advanced training procedures as well as alternative instructional procedures will clarify this issue" (p. 196). It as an open question whether the issue of differential effects should be addressed by more advanced training techniques as suggested by the researchers, or whether what is missing is a fundamental understanding of why teachers gravitate to some aspects of training and not to others.

Another research project on teaching mathematics that has a teacher-training component is the one conducted by Peterson et al. (1989). Although Brophy and Good (1986) suggest that direct instruction is effective with respect to promoting mathematical outcomes that are of a lower order in nature, Peterson (1988) argues that achievement of higher order mathematical outcomes might require instruction that is less structured and affords greater student autonomy. Peterson describes a research program called *Cognitively-Guided Instruction* (CGI) that involves both quantitative methodologies, in an effort to understand how first-grade students' higher order thinking skills can be improved. One of the interesting features of the research is the feedback of the projects' findings to teachers in an effort to increase their knowledge and sensitivity to how to promote such achievement among first graders. Peterson provides the following description of this aspect of the program:

In addition, CGI teachers were *not* trained in specific techniques for altering their classrooms and curricula, Thus, in applying a CGI approach to 'educating' the teachers and working with them as 'thoughtful professionals,' who construct their own knowledge and understanding, we remained consistent with our theoretical framework drawn from cognitive science. However, the result will undoubtedly be large variations in the extent and degree to which CGI teachers change their curricula and teaching to incorporate CGI principles. Indeed, our preliminary observation of CGI teachers' classroom implementation suggested that this is the case. (p. 23)

Although the research presented by Peterson is not yet complete, preliminary results suggest a finding similar to that of Good et al. (1983), namely that, when teachers are provided knowledge about teaching, they use that information in a wide variety of ways, including minimally. Although Peterson's program seems less oriented to addressing the problem through more advanced training techniques, the program neglects to search for an understanding of why such effects occur in the first place.

Summary

In a review of research on the teaching and learning of mathematics, Romberg and Carpenter (1986) conclude that "'scientific' studies related to the teaching of mathematics have failed to provide teachers with a list of tested behaviors that will make them competent teachers and ensure that their students will learn" (p. 865). It follows from their conclusion that effective teaching models do not constitute a basis upon which to develop teacher education programs that can produce competent teachers who can insure that students learn. Still, reviews such as Driscoll's (1982) suggest that research on teaching has generated useful information about effective teaching methods and could potentially yield a basis for teacher education.

Research on teacher education from an analytic perspective focuses on the identification of salient variables involving various training techniques; the content, both mathematical and pedagogical, of the training; and the expected outcomes including the acquisition of knowledge and beliefs and the performance of teaching. Of particular interest is the identification of training techniques that produce teachers who can exhibit the knowledge and behavior associated with effective teachers (Cooney, 1980).

A CRITICAL REFLECTION ON ANALYTIC-BASED RESEARCH

The analytic perspective on mathematics teaching leads to research oriented to developing generalizations about teaching rooted in tested and established research paradigms. It appears that Brophy and Good (1986) are more optimistic than Romberg and Carpenter (1986) in terms of the existence and import of these generalizations (the latter referring specifically to mathematics education, the former to teaching more generally conceived), but this difference alone does not suggest the research is wrongheaded with respect to mathematics education. Indeed one gets the impression from reading various reviews of research on teaching that progress is a function of time and quantity, that is the magnitude of the vector is meager, but its direction is on target. Thus, it could be that more studies devoted specifically to the teaching of mathematics might yield greater optimism in mathematics education and, hence, influence research in mathematics teacher education.

There are assumptions, however, underlying much of the research cited in the previous sections that deserve examination as one questions what it means to be an effective teacher of mathematics. These are issues regarding the meaning of what constitutes mathematics, not unlike those debated in previous reform movements associated with Brownell, Dewey, and the behaviorists. Often these assumptions not only are implicit but also believed to be neutral, in that they have no bearing on the research. As much of the post-Kuhnian literature on philosophy of science persuasively argues, there is no such thing as value-free research even in the hard sciences (Feyerabend, 1975; Kuhn, 1970).

The first assumption has to do with a conception of mathe- matics and what one considers it to be and with how it is learned. The second assumption is one inherent in many forms of research on teaching, a form of the naturalistic fallacy. Finally, a possible circularity exists between assumptions and outcomes of the research. All three of these issues have relevance for how research in mathematics teacher education is conceived and conducted.

Conceptions of Mathematics

Many believe that one of the unique characteristics of mathematics is that it is a well-defined body of knowledge. Of all the disciplines, it has the reputation of being the least problematic with respect to the curriculum and the one in which the concept of order and sequence is often unquestioned. Mathematics is perceived of as the discipline within which there is consensus regarding what it is that is true and what counts for appropriate and adequate evidence in an argument.

Such a view of mathematics entices researchers to believe that testing for mathematical ability, competence, and achievement is relatively easy, as compared with other subjects. Identifying and defining effective teaching strategies should be less difficult to establish than in other fields. Accordingly, research on effective methods of teaching mathematics often embraces a naive view of mathematics and sets out to determine which teaching methods produce particular types of mathematical outcomes that often reflect lower cognitive demands such as the execution of standard computational procedures, the recognition of basic concepts, and the routine application of generalizations.

Such an orientation has considerable appeal. It simplifies research and allows the researcher to focus on questions of obvious importance to the public, particularly, how to increase students' standardized test scores. But the view is in sharp contrast with a conception of mathematics shared by many mathematics educators and mathematicians. Steen (1988), a former president of the Mathematical Association of America, contrasts two different views of mathematics in the following way:

> Many educated persons, especially scientists and engineers, harbor an image of mathematics as akin to a tree of knowledge: formulas, theorems, and results hang like ripe fruits to be plucked by passing scientists to nourish their theories. Mathematicians, in contrast, see their field as a rapidly growing rain forest, nourished and shaped by forces outside mathematics while contributing to human civilization a rich and ever-changing variety of intellectual flora and fauna. These differences in perception are due primarily to the steep and harsh terrain of abstract language that separates the mathematical rain forest from the domain of ordinary human activity. (p. 611)

Metaphorically, Steen has contrasted two conceptions of mathematics that underlie debates about what constitutes effective mathematics teaching and how research on the teaching of mathematics should proceed (e.g., Brophy, 1986; Confrey, 1986). From the first perspective, mathematics is viewed as a field within which one can gather objects that were developed independently from the gatherer. It follows that the responsibility of the teacher is to assist students in the process of harvesting. In contrast, the second conception emphasizes mathematics as a subject capable of being created and appreciated by both mathematicians and elementary pupils. Here the role of the teacher is to facilitate that creation. Clearly, these two conceptions of mathematics lead to quite different instructional responsibilities. Does the teacher enable students to pluck or to construct? Consequently, differences emerge over what constitutes effective teaching and, concomitantly, over what kind of research agenda one develops and follows.

The Naturalistic Fallacy

Much of the research on teacher effectiveness seems, in a disguised way, to commit what in philosophical circles is called a *naturalistic fallacy*. That is, one draws (usually without realizing it) the conclusion that what *ought* to be is derived from what *is* the case. Romberg and Carpenter (1986) imply such a fallacy exists when, in their review of research on the teaching and learning of school mathematics, they conclude that "[Even] when researchers find reasonable variables such as 'lesson development,' which are demonstrably effective, they are only effective within the traditional conception of teaching. They can only make current teaching more efficient or effective, they cannot make it radically different" (p. 865).

Though practicing educators frequently fault researchers on the grounds that the latter do not offer helpful prescriptions, the irony is that researchers frequently view fundamental categories and variables from the existing scene in a way that is consistent with the perspective of practitioners. For example, there is much that is taken for granted with regard to the concept of *schooling*. In most of the research we have depicted, the idea of a *lesson* is assumed. Within the concept of lesson, a great deal more is embedded. There is regularity and both wielding of and submission to authority on every level. The student *receives* a lesson from a teacher who *receives* a curriculum from coordinators and specialists in the field.

Further, much is assumed with regard to knowledge and how it is acquired. A great deal of the research on effective teaching attempts to honor problem solving, an emerging theme that has received considerable attention in the last decade (NCTM's *An Agenda for Action*, 1980, and *Curriculum and Evaluation Standards for Mathematics Education*, 1989). Notice, however, that the expert teacher covers *40* problems a day (McKinney, 1986). Even if we assume that, in elementary school, about an hour a day is devoted to mathematics (which is not the case in many elementary schools), then students are exposed to approximately a problem a minute!

Yet problem solving in the mathematics education community at large is touted as an activity designed to cultivate thinking, to encourage students to reflect upon heuristics of problem solving, and to create an independence of mind. What is needed to develop such an orientation toward the world? It is surely not coming up with answers to problems at the rate of approximately one per minute. Students must be given the opportunity to work on problems that are vaguely and poorly stated, as well as on those that have been formulated by the teacher or the text. They must have the opportunity to pose their own problems, as well as to work on those posed by others. They must have the occasion to think through why and if a problem is worth pursuing in the first place. Students must even be encouraged to pursue problems for an extended period of time that are frustrating and appear to be (and in fact might be) dead ends (see S. I. Brown, 1987; S. I. Brown & Walter, 1983).

What bearing does this research have on the findings that clarity, efficiency, and coherence are essential characteristics of effective teaching? It is important to recognize that research on teaching of any sort is necessarily contextual. It exists in the context of schools, with all the trappings of management and control, emphasis on students' performances on tests, rather specific and rigid views of lessons, and, often, a positivistic view of mathematics learning. Furthermore, the evaluation instruments themselves tend to entrench these traditional views, as it is difficult in the context of testing to capture the perspective that mathematics is man made and is the product of many false starts through the centuries.

Thus, we have an underlying circularity that encompasses much of our research when we try to identify characteristics of effective teaching. For indeed, the notions of clarity, efficiency, and orchestration not only are essential values of schooling, but also underlie the research methodology. One wonders what conclusions we as educators would be persuaded to reach if the opposites of these traits had emerged triumphant.

What we must realize is that, whatever characteristics we identify and associate with effective teaching, ultimately our findings reflect what we perceive schools and mathematics to be. The product of our research is not simply a set of findings that allows us to see the light and to understand in an unbiased way what ought to account for effective teaching. What we are doing is confirming our biases in a way that makes this realization exceedingly difficult, despite all of the objectivity and scientific paradigms that we bring to the research enterprise.

And so we come, again, to the question of what this research implies for research in mathematics teacher education. The apparent inadequacy of elementary teachers' knowledge of mathematics and the question of what and how attitudes develop suggest a research agenda in itself, not to mention the fact that virtually no research exists regarding the knowledge and attitudes of secondary teachers. Research related to effective teaching, including research on experts and novices, provides findings that are not definitive but that could be used as a partial basis for teacher education. What must be recognized, however, is that the basis for such a teacher education program carries with it certain implications for how mathematics, the teaching of mathematics, and schooling itself are conceived. This recognition deserves consideration and reflection from researchers who engage in such research.

RESEARCH BASED ON A HUMANISTIC PERSPECTIVE

Friend: What is the problem you are working on?
Sharon: I'm trying to divide 4266 by 17. But I'm stuck. I can't divide 17 into 16.

Friend: Show me what you have.
Sharon: (Displays the following work.)

$$\begin{array}{r} 251 \\ 17\overline{\smash{\big)}\,4266} \\ \underline{34} \\ 86 \\ \underline{85} \\ 16 \end{array}$$

You see 17 does not go into 16. It's too big. But 17 goes into 17 so I put a 1 up on top.
Friend: Now what?
Sharon: Well, I know my answer is too big.
Friend: What can you do?
Sharon: Since I had 16 instead of 17 as the last number, I have to subtract one as a remainder. I could write:

$$\begin{array}{r} 251 \quad (R{-}1) \\ 17\overline{\smash{\big)}\,4266} \end{array}$$

Friend: How would you check it?
Sharon: That's easy. Multiply 251 by 17 and subtract 1 from the answer.
Friend: That's beautiful. I love it! You just invented a new way of doing division that maybe no one ever thought about before.
Sharon: Stop! I don't want to do that anymore.
Friend: Why not?
Sharon: Show me the right way.
Friend: What do you mean?
Sharon: Show me the way they want me to do it in school.
Friend: Why?
Sharon: If I do my problems like that in school, the teacher will tell me that it's not right for me to do it that way. The teacher will tell me that maybe when I get older and understand a lot more I can do division that way. (S. I. Brown, 1984, pp. 1, 2).

We present this dialogue between a 9-year-old, intellectually alive youngster and her friend because it captures two categories that we see as fundamental to research from a humanistic perspective, namely, meaning and the social context of teaching and learning. Sharon created a nontrivial algorithm that represents a novel way of interpreting division. But she did so in a context in which she felt compelled to relinquish her mathematical discovery in favor of the social goal of maintaining an acceptable posture with the teacher and, most probably, with her peers as well. Indeed, issues related to the very goal of education are embedded in Sharon's perception of what schooling is about.

Although it would be a mistake to think that humanistic-based research is only about personal meanings or about the social context of schooling, these are the two categories that have emerged from existing research on teaching. Many researchers have addressed the need for studying the meanings that teachers ascribe to their experiences and to the importance of the social context of schooling in shaping those meanings (e.g., S. I. Brown & Cooney, 1986; Cobb, 1986; Erickson, 1986; Fenstermacher, 1986; Lerman, 1986; Munby, 1982; Nickson, 1981; Romberg & Carpenter, 1986; Schram, Wilcox, Lanier, Lappan, & Even, 1988; Shulman, 1986). We will examine these two areas of humanistic-based research on teaching and consider the implications for research in mathematics teacher education.

Teachers' Beliefs and Meaning Making

Many researchers have attested to the complexity of classroom teaching and to the difficulty teachers face in dealing with the sociocultural environment, as well as with the mathematical environment (e.g., Bauersfeld, 1980; Bishop, 1985; Floden & Clark, 1988). However, mathematics teachers often do not seem to appreciate the generative possibilities of this complexity, nor do they seem to take it into account in their teaching. Many speak of the cut-and-dried nature of mathematics, as if the discipline were composed of many disparate and already prepared parts, and tend to conceive of teaching mathematics as showing or telling students the proper techniques in the clearest way possible, thereby helping the children to reach the "correct" way of thinking of mathematics (Kesler, 1985; McGalliard, 1983). Neither teaching nor learning is seen as problematic, and an understanding of mathematics is tied only to successful performance on tests or homework: knowing *how* supersedes what appears to be the less important knowing *why*. Within this view is the belief that mathematics should be straightforward and that exploratory "messing around" is not an appropriate strategy for learning mathematics (Owens, 1987; Schoenfeld, 1983).

But the predictability of a cut-and-dried discipline is a double-edged sword. The use of routines reduces the complexity of the classroom, but it might also work against the aims of developing a rich conceptual understanding of mathematics (Bauersfeld, 1980). Quilter and Harper (1988), who investigated the reasons given by adults for their difficulties, fears, and inabilities to cope with mathematics on more than a rudimentary level, found that one-third of their informants "cited instrumental learning as the most important factor during their schooling leading to disaffection with mathematics. This disaffection was commonly related also to their perception of mathematics as a rigid subject" (p. 125).

An issue of great concern to many teachers is that of authority and the accompanying question of how to exercise authority in a way that maintains an appropriate learning environment. McNeil (1986) suggests that a contradiction exists between teachers' desire to help individual students and the bureaucracy and constraints in which teachers find themselves when trying to nurture that individuality. But there is another concern as well, one that involves the means by which mathematics is communicated in the classroom. This concern takes many forms, ranging from who is in control of the class to who determines class content, to whether and how calculators and computers are used, to what should be assessed and how that assessment should take place. A dualistic reliance on the legitimizing authority of the teacher and the textbook or the curriculum guide appears to outweigh any quest for personal *meaning making* of mathematics or of methods for teaching mathematics. Based on such reliance, some teachers expect a teacher education program to give them "a methods notebook so that when I go into my own math classroom and have to teach logarithms (for example), I'll be able to turn to a certain page and find a nice method for teaching them" (Meyerson, 1978, p. 130). Others "never ask (students) to do any (examples) that are not in the text" (Kesler, 1985, p. 88). Still others are unwilling or unable to deviate from the curriculum, even when adherence is not required by the school system (C. Brown, 1985). Such reliance on external authority tends to encourage a passive view of teaching and learning and can limit teachers' and students' beliefs about mathematics and about teaching mathematics.

Some research has dealt explicitly with trying to influence teachers' beliefs away from an authoritorian perspective on mathematics. Perry's (1970) scheme of intellectual growth provides a theoretical perspective on a person's relationship to authority. One can conceive of three stages of development: (a) the dualist, who sees authority as omniscient; (b) the multiplist, who sees legitimate uncertainty in authority; and (c) the relativist, who sees authority as dependent upon context. Meyerson (1977/1978) reports some success in moving preservice secondary teachers through these stages by having them reflect on their own meaning-making activities when doubt and paradox were introduced into previously unquestioned mathematical situations.

Schram et al. (1988) report findings from a mathematics course recently redesigned for prospective elementary teachers in which the instructor emphasized group work and problem-solving activities. In talking about the value of group work, the student Chris, who was enrolled in the course, alluded to what, for many students (Sharon, for example), could be an uncomfortable need to focus on satisfying an authority rather than on learning mathematics. The instructional techniques of the class allowed Chris to direct more of his energy to learning mathematics: "Maybe we've learned that's what you kinda have to do, sometimes just start making guesses and see what you get. Also, people are more relaxed in groups. They know each other. They don't care if you kinda screw up" (p. 18).

At issue here is more than just a view of what is considered appropriate classroom teaching. Along with a style of classroom management is conveyed a view that mathematics is nothing more than the propositions that make it up and that doing mathematics is no more than replicating exercises encountered in mathematics class. Such an attitude results in part because it is difficult for teachers to be leaders in the classroom and still pursue the kind of mathematical study that would rectify such a naive perspective.

Though teachers' beliefs about mathematics and the teaching of mathematics continue to form during their teaching experience (Ball, 1988; Bush, 1982/1983; Owens, 1987; Schram et al., 1988), at least some of their beliefs about mathematics and its teaching are in place before they begin their teacher education programs. Teachers thus are not *tabulae rasae* be-

fore they become involved in their formal preparation for teaching. They have lenses that dictate, or at least influence, much of what they encounter in teacher education. Duffy and Roehler (1986) suggest that innovations and ideas for teaching that are presented to teachers must pass through a number of filters such as their conceptions of teaching and their perceptions of the demands of schools. An idea that seems reasonable, and perhaps even exciting, when discussed in a teacher education class or in an inservice setting might not survive the filtering process, or, if it does, it might bear so little resemblance to what was discussed as to appear inappropriate for use in the classroom.

Inservice teachers' resistance to change and preservice and beginning teachers' reversion to teaching styles similar to those their own teachers used are legendary. The question of how teachers engage in meaning-making activities and how their beliefs about mathematics and the teaching of mathematics can be enriched is one of considerable interest in the field of mathematics education. Lappan et al. (1988) address this question of change, using a theory developed by Lewin (see Blanchard & Zigarmi, 1981). Lewin's general model for change consists of three phases: *unfreezing*, intended to motivate and make individuals or groups ready to change; *changing*, in which new patterns of behavior are learned; and *refreezing*, in which the new patterns are integrated into the person's repertoire.

Blanchard and Zigarmi (1981) suggest that, for effective change to occur, each of the phases must take place. Lappan et al. (1988) adapted Lewin's model for use in a 2-year study of change in middle school mathematics teachers. They were committed to helping teachers experience all three phases of the change process, in an attempt to help them adopt a more conceptual approach to teaching mathematics in the middle grades. Lappan et al. provide the following analysis:

> We conjectured that the first stage of teachers' change would be in the way they *thought* and *talked* about classroom instruction related to the project goals. This would be characterized by such things as using project language without any real understanding and/or belief. This would be followed by a change in the *teachers' actions* in the classroom. These actions would be at a surface level. For example, teachers might simply try increasing wait time, putting students physically in groups, or asking more questions. As the teacher began to move from *thinking* to *believing* that a conceptual focus has a payoff for students in learning mathematics, we expected to see a change in the *behaviors* that are more comprehensive than mere changes in acting. The teacher would then be able to provide a *purpose* for group work which would be communicated to the students. A teacher would not simply ask more questions, but the quality of the questions and the response encouraged from students would be more conceptually focused. (p. 8)

They found that the presentation of detailed teaching units in a 2-week summer workshop was sufficient to teach the teachers the project's units but not to enable transfer to other parts of the curriculum. They reported that this transfer and integration requires a substantial, long-term, staff-development program of at least 2 years' duration, including intellectual and emotional support in addition to any provision of materials.

Social Goals

Students to whom a reliance upon authority is communicated are likely to have goals that are more social than mathematical (Bauersfeld, 1980; Cobb, 1986). Finding an answer to a particular problem or seeking to emulate a procedure or algorithm demonstrated in mathematics class might have more to do with satisfying an authority or gaining approval than with making sense of mathematics. Cobb provides the following analysis:

Students' apparently bizarre [mathematical] behaviors frequently cannot be accounted for solely in terms of conceptual limitations. [There] is a need to move beyond the "purely cognitive." . . . Students reorganize their beliefs about mathematics to resolve problems that are primarily social rather than mathematical in origin. (p. 2)

Although Cobb was referring to the social goals of students, goals that are defined at least in part by the tone set by the teacher, the goals are not unrelated to how teachers define their goals and construct their views of life in the classroom. It makes little sense to interpret either students' goals or teachers' goals in isolation one from the other. Stephens and Romberg (1985) point this out explicitly in their analysis of how teachers interpret and teach an experimental mathematics program. The authors cite the following student and teacher remarks in pointing out how students' goals and expectations potentially influence teachers' goals and expectations:

Why are we doing this? Is this part of a games period? How are you going to assess what we are going to do in this activity? (Student remark) (p. 8)

They (students) expect a certain kind of approach to education in general, and that includes mathematics. Students expect the teacher to be in charge and to give clear directions, to give lots of work for students to do. There is little expectation that they will have to motivate themselves or show initiative in what they do. (Teacher remark) (p. 12)

(A difficulty is) setting the story and getting the students in the right frame of mind to do the lesson; that is, getting the students to accept a different form of teaching. (Teacher remark) (p. 16)

The case of Fred (C. Brown, 1985; Cooney, 1985) further illustrates how the social context of the classroom contributes to how mathematical activities become defined. Fred struggled with the conflict between his goals concerning students' experiences with mathematics and their expectations of school. In a remarkable effort for a first-year teacher, he tried to incorporate a problem-solving strategy into his teaching of a general mathematics class. He had students experiment with dice to help them appreciate probability and, eventually, insurance and mortality tables. But the method turned sour, as reflected in his own analysis of the students' reactions:

They only see me as wanting to play games. They feel I have enough cooked up to waste their time. Maybe not all of them but at least some of them felt "I am not going to participate in this class because you (referring to Fred) are just wasting my time." It is so ironic because if I was doing the types of things they wanted to do, they would be turning around in their seats and talking. So it's a no-win situation. (Cooney, 1985, p. 332.)

Although Fred felt a need to meet his general mathematics students "on their own level," he was unable to solve the problem of how to teach interesting mathematics at a lower academic level. The students complained that Fred was making a joke out of mathematics and that they were failing because he never got down to the serious work of adding, subtracting, multiplying, and dividing fractions and decimal numbers. Fred seemed never to have made any real connection between the mathematical problem solving he so dearly loved and pedagogical problem solving. Ultimately he retreated to teaching by the textbook.

Some research is beginning to deal with teachers' knowledge and beliefs and sociocultural contexts as they relate to mathematics teacher education programs. The National Center for Research on Teacher Education at Michigan State University is investigating the impact that various approaches or alternatives to teacher education have on teachers' knowledge, skills, and dispositions and the role that teacher education, as but one of many influences on teachers and their preparation, plays in relationship to other influences (D. L. Ball, personal communication, November 22, 1988). In conducting their investigation, researchers at the NCRTE are looking at samples of students in a broad range of teacher education programs across the United States. Specifically, the researchers are following teachers in these programs from the time they enter their teacher education programs through their first year out of the programs.

Virginia Polytechnic Institute and State University's Learning to Teach Mathematics project is concerned with both cognitive and sociocultural aspects of teacher education (H. Borko and R. Underhill, personal communications, November 15, 1988). This project has drawn researchers from a variety of backgrounds including educational anthropology and cognitive psychology, as well as mathematics education, in an attempt to understand how the knowledge and beliefs of student teachers develop and change during their last year of teacher education and their first year of teaching.

The goal of these projects is to provide the kind of background data on teachers and programs that will allow researchers to develop richer theoretical frameworks for research in mathematics teacher education. Although the work is very much *in progress*, it promises to contribute to the developing research base in mathematics teacher education.

Summary

Our review of the research conducted in the humanistic tradition shows that we are beginning to know more about how teachers construct meaning and view their professional life. What we are also finding out is just how little we know about how this information might affect mathematics teacher education programs. It is not enough to know that we must deal with different levels of development among students in teaching-methods courses; nor that the notion of authority is important to teachers and that it takes many forms; nor that teachers' beliefs and orientations influence their teaching. Of greater importance is how we use this information in reorganizing the way we think about designing and conducting teacher education programs.

Researchers who are involved in the study of meaning making and the teachers they work with are both telling us that such investigations are not only a form of research but also a form of teacher education (S. I. Brown & Cooney, 1986; Lappan et al., 1988; Meyerson, 1977/1978; Nespor, 1984). The teachers involved report that they think differently about such things as explanations and language use and are in fact engaged in the creation of meaning about these and other issues simply because they are being asked all sorts of questions by an investigator who is trying to understand the teacher's thinking and experience.

A CRITICAL REFLECTION ON HUMANISTIC-BASED RESEARCH

The best stories are those which stir people's minds, hearts, and souls and by doing so give them new insights into themselves, their problems, and their human condition. The challenge is to develop a human science that more fully serves this aim. The question then is not, "Is story telling science?" but "Can science learn to tell good stories?" (Mitroff & Kilmann, 1978, p. 93)

The question of the value of research from a humanistic perspective rests largely on whether one sees science as telling a story. Much of the research cited in the previous section consists of stories about individual teachers and students and about the meanings and goals that those individuals were involved with.

For the most part these stories were told by investigators who were themselves professional educators and who assumed that they had a common language with their informants. Though that assumption led to the ability to empathize with informants, it also had the drawback of pseudofamiliarity. That is, researchers operated on occasion as if they understood informants who used words and expressions like *problem solving*, *tests*, and *student ability*. However, the snare of the "immaculate perception" can prove to be troublesome, particularly for those committed to interpretive research. Munby (1982) states that:

The opportunities for running educational research upon the rails of the assumption of shared perception are legion. Responses children make to attitude and achievement tests are taken by us as having the meaning *we* attach to these; we assume that when we code a teacher's utterance to a class as a management one, then it was delivered as one and heard as one; and we traditionally accept that the meaning we retrieve from a statement in a transcribed interview is consistent with and equal to the meaning intended by its author. (p. 207)

Much of research in the humanistic tradition provides mechanisms for testing whether meaning has been adequately captured in a context that is more interactive than is the case with analytic research, but the possibility of misinterpretation still exists. Perhaps more of this kind of research should be done by outsiders who are well versed in anthropological strategies but who do not share a common language with mathematics teachers. Part of the problem lies with the difficulty of what Spradley (1979) calls making the familiar unfamiliar.

The Naturalist Fallacy Revisited

Many teachers and students have a dualistic orientation to mathematics and mathematics teaching. As with the constructs of clarity, efficiency, and coherence, is this interpretation just another case of the influence of paradigm? Do we see dualism only because we are attuned to it and find it to be an important theoretical construct? Might it not be that teachers' and students' orientations to mathematics are constrained by the school setting, by the time of day they have mathematics class, or even by equipment and room arrangements? It is difficult for the teacher who perceives that the school district requires strict adherence to a preset curriculum guide to consider unconventional approaches to teaching mathematics. Likewise, it is difficult to think about using manipulatives that need to be spread out or stacked, or to think about emphasizing group work, when the classroom is crowded with desks, some of which are bolted to the floor.

Other factors also contribute to teachers' orientations to teaching mathematics. Consider, for example, the fact that problem-solving episodes are rare occurrences in most classrooms, save the presentation of quick solutions to well-formulated problems stated in texts. Given that teachers are products of these classrooms and that they bring to teacher education a lack of experience with problem solving, it is not difficult to envision entrenchment and inertia with respect to the profession of teaching mathematics. It seems essential that we study the means by which we can help teachers develop and consider their belief systems, in order for them to have an informed basis for accepting, modifying, or rejecting whatever contemporary pronouncements exist with respect to teaching mathematics, whether those pronouncements are calls for problem solving or for repetitive practice to achieve mastery of basic skills.

Teachers' Theories and Conflicting Beliefs

Study of the meanings that mathematics teachers hold and attribute to their teaching and learning experiences is a rather new and relatively undefined undertaking in educational research. As with any new endeavor, particularly those involved in interpretation, the researcher needs a starting point and often imports constructs from existing work. Researchers studying teachers' beliefs and actions have often talked about incipient or personal *theories* as guiding rationales for the teacher. Bromme (1984) suggests that the use of theory when referring to teachers' action-relevant knowledge might be metaphorical. The implication is that, though there is something about teachers' beliefs and world views that is like scientists' theories, the differences are significant. Bromme suggests that part of the difference is functional. Theories in the natural sciences are intended to be rational, to take into account all information in a balanced and appropriate analysis. We have seen that this is not typically the case for teachers' subjective theories. To reduce the complexity of classroom interactions, decisions are often made on the basis of past experience, partial information, and incomplete understanding. Sometimes resulting inconsistencies suggest a selective, and perhaps distorted, perception of the events and actions that constitute the teaching experience. At the very least, we must be careful about conceiving of the knowledge teachers appear to draw upon for their teaching as theory.

It seems unreasonable to assume that teachers are so aware of their actions that they can see whatever discrepancies there are between those actions and their beliefs about mathematics and how it should be taught. In an interview that one of the authors conducted, a university mathematician indicated that he wanted his students to "see mathematics come alive"; he went on to say that he hoped he could accomplish this through carefully and thoroughly planned lectures. There is no reason to assume that one's beliefs are consistent and logically arranged, as if considerable thought had gone into the networking of the beliefs. Some beliefs are held in isolation from one another; that is, the belief in the importance of seeing mathematics come alive and the belief that life can be breathed into mathematics through the passive medium of hearing a lecture. Thus, beliefs can exist in separate clusters, segregated and protected from one another.

Students' and teachers' beliefs are often incompatible with the context within which they are supposedly realized. Though teachers frequently express the opinion that the primary goal of teaching mathematics is to increase students' reasoning abilities (Kesler, 1985; Thompson, 1982, 1984), pedagogy relying on lecture, on show-and-tell, or on other forms of *presenting* material will go far toward its realization. The belief that the goal of teaching school mathematics is to help children develop their mathematical power, to build their problem-solving skills, to develop their abilities to communicate mathematically, and to develop higher order reasoning skills (NCTM, 1989), is surely isolated from the belief that mathematics is a received body of knowledge, regardless of how aesthetically appealing that body of knowledge might be. To understand how these incompatible beliefs arise among those who teach mathematics, beliefs must be addressed in a holistic manner. Though ethnographic research as studied by anthropologists tends to explore culture in such a broad based manner (over significant time spans), researchers in mathematics education who have made use of ethnographic type strategies have tended to be more piecemeal (a legacy of the analytic tradition) than holistic in their efforts to understand the culture and the evaluation of its beliefs. Any attempt to study beliefs in isolation from the whole will fail to reveal the significance of problems associated with potentially conflicting beliefs.

CONCLUSION

We have considered the implications of two research paradigms for research in mathematics teacher education. We have indicated how they differ in not only fundamental assumptions about the nature and purpose of research but also their views of mathematics as a discipline and their vision of schooling. In closing, it is perhaps worth highlighting the linkages within and among these paradigms.

The analytic paradigm of research tends to strive for a sharp separation between investigator and subjects studied, tends to see incompatibility of theoretical perspectives as something to be adjudicated, and searches for scientifically based generalizations. Such research tends to view mathematics as a received body of knowledge and the context of education as relatively value free.

The humanistic paradigm views the investigator as implicated in the research, embraces logically competing theories, and is inclined to find value in a small number of subjects (informants), though there is disagreement regarding the potential to generalize findings. A humanistic perspective tends to view mathematics from a constructivist point of view, to consider the context of schooling as value laden and in need of sociopolitical analyses, even when the phenomenon being investigated would appear to be separable from such context.

Table 35-1 summarizes these distinctions. Though there are people on the fringes of each of the two paradigms who have no common language, there are potential crossovers. Significant conceptual and practical clarifications might be achieved if both camps were to carry on substantial dialogues. Although the scheme of Mitroff and Kilmann (1978) addresses the nature of research in each of the four paradigms developed, and although such an idealized scheme sharply partitions these paradigms, valuable research might flow not only from efforts of each side to find value in competing paradigms but also from efforts to establish impure forms.

The issue is not only one of comparing research assumptions (boxes [1] and [4]) in each of the paradigms. We need to encourage the advocates of competing paradigms to figure out what precisely they do assume about the nature of mathematics (boxes [2] and [5]) and the nature of schooling (boxes [3] and [6]). Consider, for example, the question of whether the nature of mathematics alone or whether the relationship of mathematics to the human mind creates the divide between constructivists and those who adopt a received view of mathematics. As Dewey so often pointed out, stalking dualisms might not only impel us to search for formerly denied intersections, but also reveal unexamined assumptions that are shared by each of the poles. Such clarification could have the beneficial effect of generating a more enticing set of research questions in mathematics teacher education, even if the investigators in each of the paradigms are not moved to modify their perspectives.

One of the issues that arises from such distinctions is that of collaboration. Some have argued that research would be enhanced if mathematics educators collaborated with educational psychologists who are more versed in general aspects of teaching (Brophy, 1986). Though there is value in communication among people from different academic perspectives, distinctions made earlier are also important. Suppose a subject-matter specialist in mathematics, who believes that mathematics

TABLE 35–1 Distinctions between analytic and humanistic approaches

Paradigm	Research	Mathematics	Schooling
Analytic	[1] detached	[2] received	[3] value free
Humanistic	[4] connected	[5] constructed	[6] value laden

is sequential in nature, deals only with truths in a deductive manner, and believes that mathematics is not a socially derived discipline, works with an expert–novice researcher of the sort described earlier. Such a collaboration would likely be blind to questions of meaning making, which is one of the primary emphases of the humanistic perspective.

What we need is some set of mechanisms by which specialists who cross not only disciplines, such as anthropologists, philosophers, and psychologists of different orientations, but also world views, so that we can learn to deliberate, become wiser about the range of issues around which we seek reconciliation or perhaps sharp separation (S. I. Brown & Rising, 1978; Schwab, 1971). In so doing, we will all become sensitive to the value-laden components of even the most neutral-appearing paradigm. We need to reflect upon our own research paradigms, recognizing aspects of the research that consist of competing paradigms and either honoring the distinctions or resolving the issues, so that the research avoids becoming a qualitative study with a quantitative mind-set or vice versa.

Although the humanistic tradition has tended to point out the implicit assumptions of the analytic school and has thus provided an enriched conception of what the field might be about, it has not gone far enough. The field still holds a vision of teacher education as consisting of course work in a number of different fields including foundations of education, mathematics, methods of teaching mathematics, and some sort of practicum in a school setting. Teachers who had been subjects in research on meaning making found out that they were not only *reacting* to questions we posed to them but also *transformed* by the dialogue. The research, thus, not only *investigated* but became a *form* of teacher education. This suggests the possibility of an entirely new conception of teacher education. Might we not substitute some course work in teacher education with experiences that borrow from and modify different conceptions of therapy, encounters in which teachers are not taught methodologies but are encouraged to find out what they believe to be important, problematic, and essential elements of their own mathematical knowledge, as well as that of their students (see S. I. Brown, 1982; S. I. Brown & Cooney, 1986; Schön, 1983).

In providing for such reflection, we need not necessarily separate the expression and development of incipient theories and beliefs from practice. It is important, however, that early practice be viewed not primarily as the acquisition of appropriate behaviors but rather as yet one more ingredient for reflection. We might profit by adopting a metaphor that has not been adequately exploited as a research agenda by teacher educators: the metaphor of *teacher as researcher*. What do different forms of practice do for the teacher as hypothesis generator and tester that go beyond acts of introspection alone?

As a field, we have tended to generate a rather narrow range of options to investigate. Much of the research prized by those in an analytic paradigm has a taken-for-granted orientation towards schooling, but those in the humanistic tradition have tended to be equally constricting in their limited perception of models for teacher education. What is needed by both groups is not only investigation of what already exists (whether in measurable quantities or not) but also creation of alternative visions of what might be, visions that expand what ought to be investigated, how it ought to be investigated, and who the clientele are that are to be served by that inquiry. If the field of mathematics education is now clamoring for a rebirth of inquisitiveness and exploration, and orientation consistent with the legacy of Brownell and Dewey and, more recently, the advocacy of problem solving and the NCTM standards (1989), then it is just that much more important that research in mathematics teacher education at least mirror that orientation. What is desired is the generation of both courage and wisdom to consider pedagogical problems in different lights and from different perspectives and to adopt agendas that are personally and intellectually alive for not only the researcher but also the constituents and eventual clientele.

References

Ball, D. L. (1988, April). *Prospective teachers' understandings of mathematics: What do they bring with them to teacher education?* Paper presented at the annual meeting of the American Educational Research Association, New Orleans.

Battista, M. T., Wheatley, G. H., & Talsma, G. (1982). The importance of spatial visualization and cognitive development for geometry learning in preservice elementary teachers. *Journal for Research in Mathematics Education, 13*, 332–340.

Bauersfeld, H. (1980). Hidden dimensions in the so-called reality of a mathematics classroom. *Educational Studies in Mathematics, 11*, 23–41.

Beberman, M. (1958). *An emerging program of secondary school mathematics.* Cambridge, MA: Harvard University Press.

Becker, J. R. (1986). Mathematics attitudes of elementary education majors. *Arithmetic Teacher, 33*, 50–51.

Begle, E. G. (1968). Curriculum research in mathematics. In H. J. Klausmeier & G. T. O'Hearn (Eds.), *Research and development toward the improvement of education* (pp. 44–48). Madison, WI: Dembar Educational Research Services.

Bestgen, B. J., Reys, R. E., Rybolt, J. F., & Wyatt, J. W. (1980). Effectiveness of systematic instruction on attitude and computational estimate skills of preservice elementary teachers. *Journal for Research in Mathematics Education, 11*, 124–136.

Bishop, A. (1985). The social construction of meaning: A significant development for mathematics education? *For the Learning of Mathematics, 5*(1), 24–28.

Bitter, G. D. (1980). Calculator teacher attitudes improved through inservice education. *School Science and Mathematics, 80*, 323–326.

Blanchard, K. H., & Zigarmi, P. (1981). Models for change in schools. In J. Price & J. Gawronski (Eds.), *Changing school mathematics: A responsive process* (pp. 36–51). Reston, VA: National Council of Teachers of Mathematics.

Bromme, R. (1984). On the limitations of the theory metaphor for the study of teachers' expert knowledge. In R. Halkes & J. K. Olson (Eds.), *Teacher thinking: A new perspective on persisting problems in education* (pp. 43–57). Lisse, The Netherlands: Swets & Zeitlinger.

Brophy, J. E. (1986). Teaching and learning mathematics: Where research should be going. *Journal for Research in Mathematics Education, 17,* 323–346.

Brophy, J. E., & Good, T. L. (1986). Teacher behavior and student achievement. In M. C. Wittrock (Ed.), *Handbook of research on teaching* (3rd ed., pp. 328–375). New York: Macmillan.

Brown, C. (1985). *A study of the socialization to teaching of a beginning secondary mathematics teacher.* Unpublished doctoral dissertation, University of Georgia, Athens.

Brown, C. A., Carpenter, T. P., Kouba, V. L., Lindquist, M. M., Silver, E. A., & Swafford, J. O. (1988a). Secondary school results for the fourth NAEP mathematics assessment: Algebra, geometry, mathematical methods, and attitudes. *Mathematics Teacher, 81,* 337–347, 397.

Brown, C. A., Carpenter, T. P., Kouba, V. L., Lindquist, M. M., Silver, E. A., & Swafford, J. O. (1988b). Secondary school results for the fourth NAEP mathematics assessment: Discrete mathematics, data organization and interpretation, measurement, number and operations. *Mathematics Teacher, 81,* 241–249.

Brown, S. I. (1982). On humanistic alternatives in the practice of teacher education. *Journal of Research and Development in Education, 15*(4), 1–14.

Brown, S. I. (Ed.). (1984). *Creative problem solving.* Albany, NY: State Education Department, Bureau of Curriculum Development.

Brown, S. I. (1987). *Student generations.* Arlington, MA: Consortium for Mathematics and Its Applications.

Brown, S. I., & Cooney, T. J. (1986). Stalking the dualism between theory and practice. In P. F. L. Verstappen (Ed.), *Second conference on systematic co-operation between theory and practice in mathematics education* (pp. 21–40). Lochem, The Netherlands: National Institute for Curriculum Development.

Brown, S. I., & Rising, G. (1978). Alternatives to chi-square. *Mathematics Teaching, 85,* 24–29.

Brown, S. I., & Walter, M. I. (1983). *The art of problem posing.* Hillsdale, NJ: Lawrence Erlbaum.

Brownell, W. A. (1944). The progressive nature of learning in mathematics. *Mathematics Teacher, 37,* 147–157.

Brownell, W. A. (1945). When is arithmetic meaningful? *Journal of Educational Research, 38,* 481–498.

Brownell, W. A. (1947). The place of meaning in the teaching of arithmetic. *Elementary School Journal, 47,* 256–265.

Bruner, J. (1960). *The process of education.* Cambridge, MA: Harvard University Press.

Bruner, J. (1966). *Toward a theory of instruction.* Cambridge, MA: Harvard University Press.

Bush, W. (1983). Preservice secondary mathematics teachers' knowledge about teaching mathematics and decision-making during teacher training (Doctoral dissertation, University of Georgia, 1982). *Dissertation Abstracts International, 43,* 2264A.

Carpenter, T. P., Corbitt, M. K., Kepner, H. S., Jr., Lindquist, M. M., & Reys, R. (1980). Results of the second NAEP mathematics assessment: Secondary school. *Mathematics Teacher, 73,* 329–338.

Carpenter, T. P., Lindquist, M. M., Matthews, W., & Silver, E. A. (1983). Results of the third NAEP mathematics assessment: Secondary school. *Mathematics Teacher, 76,* 652–659.

Carnegie Forum on Education and the Economy, Task Force on Teaching as a Profession. (1986). *A nation prepared: Teachers for the 21st century.* Washington, DC: Author.

Charles, R. (1980). Exemplification and characterization moves in the classroom teaching of geometry concepts. *Journal for Research in Mathematics Education, 11,* 10–21.

Cobb, P. (1986). Contexts, goals, beliefs, and learning mathematics. *For the Learning of Mathematics, 6*(2), 2–9.

Confrey, J. (1986). A critique of teacher effectiveness research in mathematics education. *Journal for Research in Mathematics Education, 17,* 347–360.

Cooney, T. J. (1980). Research on teaching and teacher education. In R. J. Shumway (Ed.), *Research in mathematics education* (pp. 433–474). Reston, VA: National Council of Teachers of Mathematics.

Cooney, T. J. (1985). A beginning teacher's view of problem solving. *Journal for Research in Mathematics Education, 16,* 324–336.

Cooney, T. J. (1988). The issue of reform: What have we learned from yesteryear? *Mathematics Teacher, 81,* 352–363.

Davis, R. B. (1967). *A modern mathematics program as it pertains to the interrelationships of mathematical content, teaching methods and classroom atmosphere* (Final report, USOE Project No. D-233). Syracuse, NY: Syracuse University and Webster College.

Dessart, D. J., & Frandsen, H. (1973). Research on teaching secondary-school mathematics. In R. M. W. Travers (Ed.), *Second handbook of research on teaching* (pp. 1177–1195). Chicago: Rand McNally.

Dewey, J. (1896). The psychology of number. *Science,* N. S. III, 286–289.

Dewey, J. (1898). Some remarks on the psychology of number. *Pedagogical Seminary,* V, 426–434.

Dewey, J., & McLellan, J. A. (1895). *The psychology of number and its applications to methods of teaching arithmetic* (International Education Series, Vol. XXXIII, W. T. Harris, Ed.). New York: D. Appleton & Co.

Driscoll, M. (1982). *Research within reach: Secondary school mathematics. A research-guided response to the concerns of educators.* Reston, VA: National Council of Teachers of Mathematics.

Duffy, G., & Roehler, L. (1986). Constraints on teacher change. *Journal of Teacher Education, 37*(1), 55–59.

Dunkin, M. J., & Biddle, B. J. (1974). *The study of teaching.* New York: Holt, Rinehart & Winston.

Eastman, P. M., & Barnett, J. C. (1979). Further study of the use of manipulatives with prospective teachers. *Journal for Research in Mathematics Education, 10,* 211–213.

Ebmeier, H., & Good, T. (1979). The effects of instructing teachers about good teaching on the mathematics achievement of fourth-grade students. *American Educational Research Journal, 16,* 1–16.

Eisenberg, T. A. (1977). Begle revisited: Teacher knowledge and student achievement in algebra. *Journal for Research in Mathematics Education, 8,* 216–222.

Erickson, F. (1986). Qualitative methods in research on teaching. In M. C. Wittrock (Ed.), *Handbook of research on teaching* (3rd ed., pp. 119–161). New York: Macmillan.

Fenstermacher, G. D. (1986). Philosophy of research on teaching: Three aspects. In M. C. Wittrock (Ed.), *Handbook of research on teaching* (3rd ed., pp. 37–49). New York: Macmillan.

Feyerabend, P. K. (1975). *Against Method.* London: New Left Books.

Fisher, L. C. (1988). Strategies used by secondary mathematics teachers to solve proportion problems. *Journal for Research in Mathematics Education, 19,* 157–168.

Floden, R. E., & Clark, C. (1988). Preparing teachers for uncertainty. *Teachers College Record, 89*(4), 505–524.

Galbraith, P. L. (1984). Attitudes to mathematics of beginning undergraduates and prospective teachers: Some implications for education. *Higher Education, 13,* 675–685.

Ginther, J. L., Pigge, F., & Gibney, T. C. (1987). Three decade comparison of elementary teachers' mathematics courses and understandings. *School Science and Mathematics, 87,* 587–597.

Good, T., Grouws, D., & Ebmeier, H. (1983). *Active Mathematics Teaching.* New York: Longman.

Graeber, A., Tirosh, D., & Glover, R. (1986). Perservice teachers' beliefs and performance on measurement and partitive division problems. In G. Lappan & R. Even (Eds.), *Proceedings of the Eighth Annual Meeting of the North American Chapter of the International Group for the Psychology of Mathematics Education* (pp. 262–267). East Lansing, MI: Michigan State University.

Heath, R. W., & Neilsen, M. A. (1974). The research basis for performance-based teacher education. *Review of Educational Research, 44,* 463–484.

Holmes Group. (1986). *Tomorrow's teachers.* East Lansing, MI: Author.

Joyce, B. R., & Showers, B. (1980). Improving inservice training: The message of research. *Educational Leadership, 37,* 379–385.

Kesler, R. (1985). *Teachers' instructional behavior related to their conceptions of teaching and mathematics and their level of dogmatism: Four case studies.* Unpublished doctoral dissertation, University of Georgia, Athens.

Kline, M. (1958). The ancients versus the moderns: A new battle of the books. *Mathematics Teacher, 51,* 418–427.

Kouba, V. L., Brown, C. A., Carpenter, T. P., Lindquist, M. M., Silver, E. A., & Swafford, J. O. (1988). Results of the fourth NAEP assessment of mathematics: Number, operations, and word problems. *Arithmetic Teacher, 35,* 14–19.

Kuhn, T. S. (1970). *The structure of scientific revolutions* (2nd ed.). Chicago: University of Chicago Press.

Kulm, G. (1980). Research on mathematics attitude. In R. J. Shumway (Ed.), *Research in Mathematics Education* (pp. 356–387). Reston, Va: National Council of Teachers of Mathematics.

Lakatos, I. (1978). *The methodology of scientific research programmes.* Cambridge: Cambridge University Press.

Lampert, M. (1986). Knowing, doing, and teaching multiplication. *Cognition and Instruction, 3,* 305–342.

Lappan, G., Fitzgerald, W., Phillips, E., Winter, M. J., Lanier, P., Madsen-Nason, A., Even, R., Lee, B., Smith, J., & Weinberg, D. (1988). *The middle grades mathematics project. The challenge: Good mathematics—taught well* (Final report to the National Science Foundation for Grant #MDR8318218). East Lansing, MI: Michigan State University.

Leinhardt, G. (1988). Expertise in instructional lessons: An example from fractions. In D. Grouws, T. Cooney, & D. Jones (Eds.), *Perspectives on research on effective mathematics teaching* (pp. 47–66). Reston, VA: National Council of Teachers of Mathematics.

Leinhardt, G., & Putnam, R. T. (1986). Research report: Profile of expertise in elementary school mathematics teaching. *Arithmetic Teacher, 34*(4), 28–29.

Lerman, S. (1986). *Alternative views of the nature of mathematics and their possible influence on the teaching of mathematics.* Unpublished doctoral dissertation, Centre for Educational Studies, Kings College, University of London.

Magoon, A. J. (1977). Constructivist approaches in educational research. *Review of Educational Research, 17,* 651–693.

Mayberry, J. (1983). The Van Hiele levels of geometric thought in undergraduate preservice teachers. *Journal for Research in Mathematics Education, 14,* 50–59.

McGalliard, W. (1983). Selected factors in the conceptual systems of geometry teachers: Four case studies (Doctoral Dissertation, University of Georgia, 1982). *Dissertation Abstracts International, 44,* 1364A.

McKillip, W. D. (1980). CBTE in elementary mathematics education. *Arithmetic Teacher, 28*(1), 24–27.

McKinney, K. (1986). How the experts teach math. In *Research in Brief.* Washington, DC: U.S. Department of Education, Office of Educational Research and Improvement.

McKnight, C. C., Crosswhite, F. J., Dossey, J. A., Kifer, E., Swafford, J. O., Travers, K. J., & Cooney, T. J. (1987). *The underachieving curriculum: Assessing U.S. school mathematics from an international perspective.* Champaign, IL: Stipes.

McNeil, L. M. (1986). *Contradictions of control: School structure and knowledge.* New York: Methuen/Routledge & Kegan Paul.

Meder, A. E., Jr. (1958). The ancients versus the moderns: A reply. *Mathematics Teacher, 51,* 428–433.

Meyerson, L. N. (1978). Conception of knowledge in mathematics: Interaction with and applications to a teaching methods course (Doctoral dissertation, State University of New York, Buffalo, 1977). *Dissertation Abstracts International, 38,* 733A.

Mitroff, I., & Kilmann, R. (1978). *Methodological approaches to social sciences.* San Francisco: Jossey-Bass.

Munby, H. (1982). The place of teachers' beliefs in research on teacher thinking and decision making, and an alternative methodology. *Instructional Science, 11,* 201–225.

National Commission on Excellence in Education. (1983). *A nation at risk: The imperative for educational reform.* Washington, DC: U.S. Government Printing Office.

National Council of Teachers of Mathematics (1980). *An agenda for action: Recommendations for school mathematics of the 1980s.* Reston, VA: Author.

National Council of Teachers of Mathematics (1989). *Curriculum and evaluation standards for school mathematics.* Reston, VA: Author.

Nespor, J. (1984). *The interaction of school context and teachers' beliefs* (R&D Report No. 8023). Austin, TX: University of Texas at Austin, The R&D Center for Teacher Education. (ERIC Document Reproduction Service No. ED 260 079).

Nichols, E. D. (1968). The many forms of revolution. In W. C. Seyfert (Ed.), *The continuing revolution in mathematics* (pp. 16–37). Washington, DC: National Council of Teachers of Mathematics.

Nickson, M. (1981). *Social foundations of the mathematics curriculum: A rationale for change.* Unpublished doctoral dissertation, Institute of Education, University of London.

Owens, J. (1987). *A study of four preservice secondary mathematics teachers' constructs of mathematics and mathematics teaching.* Unpublished doctoral dissertation, University of Georgia, Athens.

Perry, W. (1970). *Forms of intellectual and ethical development in the college years: A scheme.* New York: Holt, Rinehart & Winston.

Peterson, P. L. (1988). Teaching for higher-order thinking in mathematics: The challenge for the next decade. In D. Grouws, T. Cooney, & D. Jones (Eds.), *Perspectives on research on effective mathematics teaching* (pp. 2–26). Reston, VA: National Council of Teachers of Mathematics.

Peterson, P. L., Fennema, E., Carpenter, T. P., & Loef, M. (1989). Teachers's pedagogical content beliefs in mathematics. *Cognition and Instruction 6*(1), 1–40.

Piaget, J. (1952). *The child's conception of number.* New York: Humanities Press.

Piaget, J., Inhelder, B., & Szeminska, A. (1960). *The child's conception of geometry.* New York: Basic Books.

Polya, G. (1945). *How to solve it: A new aspect of mathematical method.* Princeton, NJ: Princeton University Press.

Polya, G. (1962). *Mathematical Discovery: On understanding, learning, and teaching problem solving* (Vol.I). New York: John Wiley and Sons.

Polya, G. (1965). *Mathematical Discovery: On understanding, learning, and teaching problem solving* (Vol.II). New York: John Wiley & Sons.

Quilter, D., & Harper, E. (1988). 'Why we didn't like mathematics, and why we can't do it.' *Educational Research, 30*(2), 121–134.

Riedesel, C. A., & Burns, P. C. (1973). Research on the teaching of elementary school mathematics. In R. M. W. Travers (Ed.), *Second handbook of research on teaching* (pp. 1149–1176). Chicago: Rand McNally.

Romberg, T. A., & Carpenter, T. P. (1986). Research on teaching and learning mathematics: Two disciplines of scientific inquiry. In M. C. Wittrock (Ed.), *Handbook of research on teaching* (3rd ed., pp. 850–873). New York: Macmillan.

Rosenshine, B. (1987). Explicit teaching and teacher training. *Journal of Teacher Education, 38*(3), 34–36.

Rosenshine, B., & Furst, N. (1971). Research teacher performance criteria. In B. O. Smith (Ed.), *Research in teacher education: A symposium* (pp. 37–72). Englewood Cliffs, NJ: Prentice-Hall.

Sarason, S. B. (1982). *The culture of the school and the problem of change* (2nd ed.). Boston: Allyn & Bacon.

Schoenfeld, A. (1983). Beyond the purely cognitive: Belief systems, social cognitions, and metacognitions as driving forces in intellectual performance. *Cognitive Science 7,* 329–363.

Schön, D. A. (1983). *The reflective practitioner: How professionals think in action.* New York: Basic Books.

Schram, P., Wilcox, S., Lanier, P., Lappan, G., & Even, R. (1988, April). *Changing mathematical conceptions of preservice teachers: A content and pedagogical intervention.* Paper presented at the annual meeting of the American Educational Research Association, New Orleans.

Schwab, J. (1971). The practical: Arts of eclectic. *School Review, 79,* 493–541.

Shulman, L. (1986). Those who understand: Knowledge growth in teaching. *Educational Researcher, 15*(2), 4–14.

Shulman, L. S., & Keislar, E. R. (Eds.). (1966). *Learning by discovery: A critical appraisal.* Chicago: Rand McNally.

Spradley, J. (1979). *The ethnographic interview.* New York: Holt, Rinehart & Winston.

Stake, R. E., & Easley, J. (Eds.). (1978). *Case studies in science education.* Urbana, IL: University of Illinois, Center for Instructional Research and Curriculum Evaluation.

Steen, L. (1988). The science of patterns. *Science, 240,* 611–616.

Stephens, W. M., & Romberg, T. A. (1985, April). *Reconceptualizing the role of the mathematics teacher.* Paper presented at the annual meeting of the American Educational Research Association, Chicago.

Thompson, A. (1982). *Teachers' conceptions of mathematics and mathematics teaching: Three case studies.* Unpublished doctoral dissertation, University of Georgia, Athens.

Thompson, A. (1984). The relationship of teachers' conceptions of mathematics and mathematics teaching to instructional practice. *Educational Studies in Mathematics, 15,* 105–127.

Wheeler, M. M., & Feghali, I. (1983). Much ado about nothing: Preservice elementary school teachers' concept of zero. *Journal for Research in Mathematics Education, 14,* 147–155.

·36·

SCIENCE TEACHER EDUCATION

Robert E. Yager and John E. Penick
THE UNIVERSITY OF IOWA

Although answers to current questions concerning science teacher education might not be found in the past, a look at the past could provide new insight into present problems, suggesting desirable strategies and actions. Too often research findings and experiences with new practices go unheeded because the questions and issues are not clear when out of context. Kettering's assertion that a problem well stated is a problem half solved becomes quite attractive as teacher education practices in the United States are called into serious question.

SCIENCE TEACHER EDUCATION IN HISTORICAL CONTEXT

The First Hundred Years

Prior to 1821, secondary education was primarily private schooling for persons preparing for the clergy and the law, and by 1800 it included science skill areas such as navigation, surveying, and agriculture. Teachers often had no formal preparation in science; there were no minimum standards, and the use of lay teachers was common. During the fifty years following the creation of the first public high school in Boston in 1821, numerous special science courses were available. Still, most teachers were poorly prepared, with large numbers being trained by the clergy. By 1870 and the emergence of the first normal schools, many science teachers began to teach after formal study of science in college. Designated qualifications for specific teaching assignments varied from state to state, with few common patterns or standards.

College instructional practices dominated the total high school preparation for all students. This domination influenced the science curriculum in schools. In 1872 Harvard University first established physics as a college entrance requirement and later added chemistry. Biology was born as a discipline by combining botany, physiology, and zoology. Each new university requirement for admission called for changes in the high school. Just prior to 1900, new calls for "science" in the school program were made, at a time when the 6-3-3 plan emerged and the curriculum became more standardized. The demand for college-trained science teachers was strong, but the supply remained inadequate.

The First Half of the Twentieth Century

Even as general science and junior high programs became common for all students, the emphasis in the science curriculum was upon mastery of factual information. At the upper high school grades, science was seen as important only as preparation for college. Most teachers completed a science teacher preparation program, but very few specialized in science for the junior high level. Many science teachers in junior high schools were reported to be poorly prepared in science. In addition, the methods component of their programs was very general and focused upon classroom techniques.

The 31st Yearbook of the National Society for the Study of Education, *A Program for Science Teaching* (Whipple, 1932), put forth as a central objective the building of learning exercises and instructions around broad scientific principles fundamental to understanding nature. In 1938 the Progressive Education Association, in its publication *Science in General Education*, asserted that science should contribute to students'

The authors wish to acknowledge the significant assistance and suggestions provided by two colleagues, namely, James P. Barufaldi (University of Texas–Austin) and Eugene L. Chiappetta (University of Houston). Not only did they provide their own input to written drafts, but they also assisted with a symposium related to this chapter at a meeting of the National Association for Research in Science Teaching. Participants in this symposium provided further reaction and input that affected the final draft.

(a) personal living, (b) immediate personal–societal relationships, (c) social–civic relationships, (d) economic relationships, and (e) reflective thinking. Studies conducted in the 1930s showed that the implementation of such objectives was rare and their impact negligible. Again, teachers were found to be poorly prepared in general. When well-prepared ones were found, they often were assigned so many diverse tasks that their effectiveness was impaired regardless of their preparation. Few students experienced science in any way other than as information to be mastered.

When World War II ended, the place of science in the school program had attained universal acceptance. Many statements of objectives appeared in *Education for All American Youth*, by the Educational Polices Commission of the National Education Association (National Education Association [NEA] 1944); *General Education in a Free Society* by the Committee on the Objectives of a General Education in a Free Society (1945); *Science Education in American Schools*, a publication of the National Society for the Study of Education (Henry, 1947); *Education for All American Youth: A Further Look*, by the Educational Policies Commission of the National Education Association and the American Association of School Administrators (NEA, 1952); and *Science in Secondary Schools Today*, a report of the National Association of Secondary School Principals (1953). The major focus was upon functional science experiences, those that provided skills and knowledge that students could use.

This era was characterized by many studies on the deplorable state of science teaching and by reports of committees proposing improvement of programs for the preparation of science teachers. One of the most significant studies was *The Preparation of High School Science and Mathematics Teachers* (Report No. 4, 1946), conducted by the Cooperative Committee on Science Teaching of the American Association for the Advancement of Science. Among other things, the report emphasized that "Blame for the inadequacy of our teaching of high school science and mathematics belongs with the American public, which fails to pay its teachers decently, and with the American colleges and universities, which have failed to prepare prospective teachers for the kind of teaching they should do" (American Association for the Advancement of Science [AAAS], 1946, p. 108). After a careful analysis of the problems, the committee recommended that:

1. A policy of certification in closely related subjects within broad areas of science and mathematics be established.
2. Approximately one-half of prospective teachers' four-year college program be devoted to courses in science (and/or mathematics).
3. Certificates to teach general science in 7th, 8th, and 9th grades be granted on the basis of broad preparation in all science subjects.
4. College and certification authorities should work toward five-year programs for preparation of high school science teachers.
5. Curriculum improvement in small high schools should go hand in hand with improvements in teacher preparation.(pp. 111–114)

As a proposal for implementation, it was suggested that "In colleges and universities, it is the first duty of the science departments to seek the cooperation of the departments of education" (p. 117). Although more than four decades have passed, the problems and current debates are remarkably similar.

In 1953 the National Science Foundation began a program for improvement of "Education in the Sciences" with the financing of two summer institutes for upgrading the science preparation of secondary school science teachers. The program was begun after studies by the foundation revealed serious inadequacies in the training of the majority of science teachers.

The Recent Past

It took the Soviet *Sputnik* launching in .1957 to move the American public and its leaders to propose major science curriculum projects and science teacher education initiatives. During the 25-year period following *Sputnik*, $2 billion were allocated for reforms. This first and most extensive federal intrusion into course improvement and teacher education saw the return of the college and professional scientific community to leadership roles in correcting school science problems. It also resulted in massive updating of course materials and the use of up-to-date content from college courses, especially those made available to inservice teachers by means of the NSF institute program. Unfortunately, in many respects, the revisions of course materials and the new efforts with inservice science teachers were conducted with little or no input from science teacher educators. Indeed, many considered the pre-*Sputnik* problems with respect to course content and teacher education to have been caused by science educators, rather than by scientists responsible for the science preparation included in teacher education programs.

After almost 20 years of intensive funding and effort, the public became disillusioned with science and science education in the 1970s, and funding levels declined in both curriculum efforts and teacher education. By 1976 concerns were so intense that all active curriculum projects at the national level were halted while studies of their appropriateness and validity were considered. Teacher education support was also terminated. President Carter established a task force that issued a report, *Science & Engineering Education for the 80s & Beyond* (National Science Foundation and U.S. Department of Education, 1980), which called for new federal initiatives, new directions, and new efforts. However, after President Reagan's inauguration in 1980, the report was ignored. Instead, the science education directorate at NSF was scaled down to the point that support for graduate student research in the sciences was the only program funded. It took President Reagan's National Commission on Excellence in Education and its report, *A Nation at Risk*, to reverse the situation early in 1983. Later the same year, the report of the National Science Board's Commission on Precollege Education in Mathematics, Science, and Technology, *Educating Americans for the 21st Century* (National Science Board, 1983), was released, calling for renewed national commitment to science education and the expenditure of $1.51 billion in the first year to correct the problem. This was a major reversal from no perceived problem and no funds just 3 years earlier.

The decade of the 1980s resulted in major concerns with improving science teacher education. Improved science teaching was widely recognized as a national concern, not unlike the situation in 1957 that resulted in attention, funding, and action to improve school science programs and teachers as a way of responding to the wounded national pride caused by Soviet space achievements. In the 1980s it was the perceived supremacy of other industrial nations, especially Japan, in the economic arena. Huge trade deficits, an ever larger national debt, and international relations were seen as problems that improved science education could help resolve. In a very real sense these concerns were greater than those that existed in the late 1950s, and there were more actions from more diverse segments of our society at work on improved science education than ever in our more than 200 years as a nation.

As is too often the case, perceived crisis and emergency situations result in clamors for immediate actions and correctives. Seldom do we take time for reflection, study, and comtemplation. Seldom is it a time in which the past is seen as providing signals for current actions. Surely a look at the research concerning science teacher education warrants such consideration, as we look to the last decade of the twentieth century and beyond.

The ROSES Report

Prior to 1968 no information had been collected to determine the nature of science teacher education in the United States, other than reports assembled by accrediting organizations. Earlier studies were plagued with one of two inadequacies, namely, focusing on a limited population or dealing with only one aspect of the teacher education program. The Research on Science Education Survey (ROSES) was the first national effort conducted by science educators concerning the status of science teacher education in the United States (Newton & Watson, 1968). Newton and Watson sought to study the nature of science teacher education in 922 U.S. colleges and universities, the number purporting in a national survey to offer such programs. In addition, extensive on-site visits were made to 37 colleges and universities in 22 states. These institutions were selected purposefully to assure a representative sample in terms of type of institution, size, and geography, and the visits included interviews with faculty, random samples of students, and observations of methods classes.

Newton and Watson report that:

1. The number of science teachers prepared each year was increasing (9,455 in 1966 to 10,100 in 1967), one-half being prepared in biology. Physics teachers were the only group showing a decline.
2. The course requirements for teaching science varied considerably from institution to institution and among the science disciplines; the requirements were highest for biology teachers, lowest for earth science.
3. Science methods instructors were distributed fairly evenly across academic ranks; about half had PhDs in science education, 23 percent in a science, and 30 percent in a general field of education.
4. There was general diversity among institutions concerning student teaching patterns; the most common was for full-time teaching in school for a period of 8 to 12 weeks.
5. Science education faculty listed the following attributes as essential to the prospective science teacher: knowledge of science, 17 percent; understanding of the nature of science, 14 percent; variety of pedagogical skills, 20 percent; familiarity with related teaching skills, 12 percent; affective qualities related to science, 13 percent.
6. Great interest existed with respect to "the" methods course in science teacher education. Following is an indication of words and topics instructors of secondary and elementary methods courses used in describing the nature of their methods courses; the first percentage being the perception of secondary instructors and the second being those of elementary instructors: methods of instruction (52 and 56 percent), planning (50 and 52 percent), objectives of science teaching (42 and 40 percent), evaluation (35 and 23 percent), study of curriculum (32 and 26 percent), science content (28 and 42 percent), and resources for teaching (27 and 31 percent).

   The variety of reported teaching techniques used in teaching methods was also of interest. Secondary and elementary methods instructors reported using the following techniques (again with the first number being percentage of secondary instructors and the second of elementary instructors): class discussion (51 and 31 percent), student laboratories (27 and 38 percent), student demonstrations (25 and 29 percent), mock teaching (21 and 17 percent), construction of teaching units (19 and 19 percent), and lecturing (11 and 11 percent).
7. The characteristics of science methods students were established as follows:
   a. The typical student was a male (61 percent), between 20 and 25 years of age (65 percent), single (71 percent), and from a household in which the father was either a businessman or a skilled laborer (39 percent).
   b. Most majored in the biological sciences (41 percent), followed by the physical sciences (21 percent).
   c. Only 50 percent reported that they definitely planned to teach high school science when they had completed the program.
8. Although the study of the "new" science courses supported with public funds might be expected to be an important part of the science methods classes, only about half of the methods instructors who responded to the questionnaire reported that they gave some attention to at least one of these courses. A much smaller number reported studying these courses intensively.

Newton and Watson end their 1968 report with the following comments:

It is possible to highlight a few of the most obvious trends in science education today. First, the diversity of programs in science education is very great. Whether one talks about methods courses, practice teaching arrangements, course requirements, or almost any other aspect of teacher preparation programs, there are examples of almost every conceivable pattern to be found somewhere in the nation. Second, the lack of basic, objective evidence on the effectiveness of teacher education programs is striking. The courses and programs described in the report are almost entirely acts of faith with little or no feedback or follow-up information to support the practices that institutions follow. In view of some of the student comments reported in the study, the demand for a further investigation of the effectiveness of these programs seems to be a critical priority. Finally, the isolation of science educators from their colleagues at other institutions seems to have some serious implications for programs for the preparation of science teachers. The chaos in the profession is probably one consequence of the inability of science educators to confer about and agree upon the goals and structure of the teacher preparation program in the sciences. The times call for a strong professional organization to assume a leadership role in the focusing of energy and efforts in science education. (p. 120)

Concerns at the end of the 1970s included the lack of general information regarding problems, the effects of past curriculum and teacher education correctives, and the current situation in U.S. schools. As a result, the National Science Foundation funded three status studies that were completed in 1978, each drawing from different data sources. The first of these was a review of all the research in science education during the 1955–1975 period (Helgeson, Blosser, & Howe, 1977). The second was a huge survey of materials and practices in K–12 science (Weiss, 1978). The third was a series of case studies conducted by trained observers who spent several months in each of 11 communities studying science education offerings and procedures (Stake & Easley, 1978).

As these status studies were nearing completion, NSF funded Project Synthesis (Harms & Yager, 1981) as a further effort to define the nature of science programs and teaching approaches. These researchers first considered the latest discoveries in science, the critical reports of school science, the recommendations of think tank groups, and the current materials and products of new curricular developments. This proactive synthesis was then compared with a retroactive synthesis of results from the three NSF status studies (what research said, what professionals said, and what trained observers reported to be occurring) with the results of the third assessment of science of the National Assessment of Educational Progress (NAEP, 1978). The NAEP results provided direct input from students in terms of their knowledge and their attitudes. The Project Synthesis report ended with several general recommendations including calls for:

1. A major redefinition and reformulation of goals for science education; a new rationale, a new focus, a new statement of purpose are needed.
2. A new conceptualization of the science curriculum to meet new goals; redesigns of courses, course sequences/articulation, and discipline alliances are needed.
3. New programs and procedures for the preparation, certification, assignment, and the continuing education of teachers; planned changes, continuing growth, and systems for peer support are needed.

4. New materials to exemplify new philosophy, new curriculum structure, new teacher strategies.
5. A means for translating new research findings into programs for affecting practice; a profession must have a philosophic basis, a research base, a means for changes to occur based on new information.
6. Renewed attention to the significance of evaluation in science education.
7. Much greater attention to development of systems for implementation and support for exemplary teaching and programs at the local level. (Harms & Yager, 1981, pp. 129–130)

Such studies and recommendations provided rich sources for ideas for science teacher education. They suggested the need for major changes in what was being done and the kind of team needed to accomplish the changes.

The NSF also funded a variety of other status studies. One was a study of graduate programs in science education that also considered teacher education programs in such colleges and universities. The *Council of Graduate Schools Directory* (1979) included 365 institutions. After three mailings and telephone contacts, a response rate of 90 percent was achieved. The study concluded that only 40 percent of the graduate institutions had graduate programs in science education. As with the ROSES study, visitations were made to nine of the largest centers to collect additional on-site study and to add to the questionnaires' database (Yager, 1980a; 1980b).

At the undergraduate level at these institutions it was found that:

1. The number of persons pursuing a science teaching major at graduate institutions dropped by 25 percent during the 1960–80 period while general enrollment of the students was increasing by 30 percent.
2. The number of faculty members in science education and the number of courses offered at a given institution increased from 1960–70 and leveled off during 1970–80.
3. Most faculty members at graduate institutions spend more time with undergraduate teacher education that with any other activity (an average of 31 percent time spent on teacher education responsibilities); teacher education was listed as the greatest interest of graduate faculty members.
4. Most instruction is associated with methods of teaching elementary and/or secondary science and student teaching supervision.
5. The science education faculty does not control the science teaching major except for the methods courses and some aspects of student teaching.

The status study ended with 10 generalizations:

1. Science education as a discipline grew swiftly from 1960–70 (and slowly from 1970–75) in terms of institutions offering programs, faculty employed, and graduates at all levels. Since 1975 there was a gradual decline in all categories.
2. Graduate programs changed little over a twenty year pe-

riod in spite of national guidelines adopted in 1966 and 1974 which suggested specific features; more advanced preparation in science represented half of the typical course requirements for graduate degrees.

3. Financial support for science education increased during the 1960–70 decade; the increase continued gradually until 1975; then there were declines. Major declines in support occurred with respect to externally funded projects and internal funding for graduate students.

4. Graduate faculty in science education had little commitment to personal research productivity; most had a greater commitment to specific research involving graduate students and their thesis/dissertation research; relatively few faculty members had prolonged and field-specific lines of research.

5. Faculty members of major centers for science education were fairly homogeneous as to sex, age, academic preparation, previous professional experience, teaching, and service responsibilities.

6. There was little agreement as to a definition for science education, a rationale or framework for the discipline, or a theory-base for research.

7. Relatively few science education programs existed as formal departments and/or centers; most were special programs within a larger curriculum and instruction unit. In recent years there was a trend to less autonomy for science education programs at graduate institutions.

8. Most research in science education was concerned with entry conditions for the study of science; a more recent emphasis was on the study of instruction and the results of instruction.

9. There was little attention to goals for the discipline; there were few attempts at defining science education in any way other than the science that is taught in schools and the preparation of teachers for such efforts.

10. There was a high level of professional isolation in the discipline of science education. There were few examples of cooperative research and all too few mechanisms for promoting professional dialogue. (Yager, 1980b, pp. vii–viii)

When the study was extended in 1985 by Iskander (1986), the declines in enrollments, offerings, and faculty had leveled off or were reversing. A greater focus on applied science was reported in a significant number of institutions, and many were incorporating experiences that extended into communities and provided the use of scientific information.

A status study of collegiate programs was extended to those existing in 4-year colleges (Yager & Bybee, in press), where a third of all science teachers are prepared. Brockway (1989) completed a study of the 28 institutions in Iowa with science teacher education programs. This study verified many of the generalities that arose from the Yager-Bybee national study. These small liberal arts colleges rarely have a specialized methods sequence taught by a faculty member with expertise and/or experience in science education. General methods courses are offered, and the student-teaching experience is supervised almost wholly by inservice teachers.

Another research effort funded by NSF at the beginning of the 1980s was a series of metanalyses (R. D. Anderson, 1983; R. D. Anderson, Kahle, Glass, & Smith, 1983). In one of these, Druva and Anderson (1983) identify 65 studies dealing with specific teaching behaviors as they related to student outcomes. Druva and Anderson were interested in studying science teacher background characteristics (e.g., gender, coursework completed, personality traits) and their relationships to teacher classroom behavior (e.g., questioning style), teacher orientation, and/or student outcomes (e.g., achievement, attitude toward science).

Druva and Anderson's work yielded 481 correlation coefficients, many resulting from a single study. They are also careful to emphasize that the absolute value of correlation coefficients was relatively low. Of 322 cells containing data in the teacher characteristics by teacher behavior matrix, only 31 had a correlation coefficient that reached or exceeded 0.5 in absolute value. In the case of the teacher characteristics by students' outcome matrix, only 6 of 242 cells had a correlation coefficient that reached or exceeded 0.5.

Druva and Anderson offer the following summary concerning their studies:

1. The largest correlation is found between teaching effectiveness and quantity of training a teacher has (both science and education).
2. The next most positive relationship is found between teaching effectiveness and positive attitude toward teaching.
3. The degree of association between teacher characteristics and student outcomes is much less than between teacher characteristics and teacher behavior.

Druva and Anderson also report a positive relationship between teacher education programs and what graduates do as teachers. Quality of science courses, education courses, and overall academic performance is positively associated with successful teachers (Druva & Anderson, 1983, p. 478). As a result of an analysis of research, Welch (1983) laments the fact that most factors studied concerning teaching effectiveness account for very little of what is involved in being effective. Studies seem to focus on what can be observed and easily measured, as opposed to on what is important.

Yager's studies of least and most effective science teachers identified by members of the National Science Supervisors Association complement Druva and Anderson's efforts. In a study of 159 least effective and 162 most effective 7–12 science teachers, the major difference was found to be the amount of institute-type experience that the inservice teacher had completed and, especially, the number of such in-service experiences that had been voluntarily elected (Yager, 1988; Yager, Hidayat, & Penick, 1988). Effective science teachers were found to be those seeking out new information, new teaching practices, and new materials. Apparently, the best science teachers seek to improve; they model good learning.

Although NSF involvement focused on curricular development and inservice teacher education, a small preservice program initiated in 1970 was the Undergraduate Pre-Service Teacher Education Program (UPSTEP). A wide variety of science teacher education programs were funded over a decade, with many providing only local impact and some subsidizing single-course developments in the whole array of courses required for science teaching. Some concentrated on preparing teachers for the elementary schools; others focused exclusively upon preparing secondary teachers. Unlike in many other NSF programs, evaluation was a critical component of each project. Some generalizable models evolved from the national effort with science teacher education, but few of the innovations were implemented at other institutions because of cost and the need to have relatively large numbers of science education students.

Some of the specific outcomes of the 1970–1975 UPSTEP projects supported by NSF include:

1. Effective preservice programs integrate science and education and often require five years.
2. Science faculties are important ingredients in program planning, teaching, and program administration.
3. The preparation of an effective science teacher involves more than providing a student with up-to-date content and some generalized teaching skills. Preservice teachers must focus on specific teaching strategies, have models as teachers, and appreciate teaching as an intellectual activity as well as a skill.
4. Effective programs involve master teachers, school and community leaders, and industrial representatives as well as college/university faculty members.
5. Teacher education can be evaluated; such evaluation should be used in improving existing programs.
6. It is important to be aware of advances in a variety of areas in addition to a major in a science area and science education; advances in computer technology, educational psychology, philosophy, sociology, and history of science must be included in model programs. (Yager, Lunetta, & Penick, 1980)

The position that federal involvement should be broader than provision of model materials, assistance with inservice updating, and research and analysis is again being advanced. However, the total number of UPSTEP programs supported prior to 1975 was low and the generalizable results few. Although no comprehensive evaluation of the UPSTEP program was undertaken independently, several evaluations of the individual models were undertaken. For example, Krajcik and Penick (in press) compared graduates of the Iowa UPSTEP program with a select group of teachers invited to a funded honors workshop. Even though Iowa graduates were less experienced and had completed fewer science courses, they had the same positive impact on student attitudes as did teachers in the honors workshop. This is in direct contrast with science teachers in general as evidenced by the last national assessments (Educational Testing Service, 1988b; Hueftle, Rakow, & Welch, 1983; NAEP, 1978).

During this same period the U.S. Office of Education funded nine programs for improving elementary science teacher education programs. However, no information is available concerning their effectiveness. Helgeson et al. (1977) reported that there was no follow-up research concerning the impact of these attempts at teacher education improvement.

Teacher Education Reforms

In the mid-1980s many reports called for reform in teacher education. Many of the recommendations from such reports have yet to affect science teacher education. And many are not unlike those produced at various intervals from the 1930s on. However, the current public clamor for reforms in science education has never been so great from the general U.S. public. Fairly recent surveys (Yager & Penick, 1986) indicate that in excess of 85 percent of the public is anxious for reforms in school science education; this includes science teacher education. It is an exciting and challenging time for science teacher education in the United States.

CURRENT ISSUES IN SCIENCE TEACHER EDUCATION

As the twentieth century moves to a close, many specific issues remain unresolved. These current issues can be divided into five questions for discussion and for relating them to current practices and research: (a) Who should teach science? (b) How should college science experiences for teachers be organized? (c) What should the education sequence be? (d) What are other important dimensions for a model program? (e) How can we insure that science teachers continue as learners?

Prospective Students for Science Teacher Education

With the disappearance of teachers colleges, there is no obvious college for prospective science teachers. Often at large universities persons considering teacher education programs are those not encouraged to pursue graduate degrees in basic sciences and those not gaining entrance to medicine, dentistry, or allied health fields. In smaller colleges science majors often consider teaching because there are few careers to pursue with a bachelor's degree, especially if they do not see themselves pursuing graduate or professional degrees at larger institutions.

More persons are being attracted to science teacher education programs than was the situation a few years ago (Iskander, 1986). This increase in numbers of students pursuing science teaching appears to be in response to the frequent reports of a severe shortage of science teachers, especially in chemistry and physics, and the lack of employment opportunities elsewhere.

But, how to attract better students for better reasons? Inservice teachers are quick to admit that they do not usually recommend science teaching as a desirable career for their own students. Instead they take great pride in the numbers they encourage for engineering, medicine, and the basic sciences. Many assume that the best secondary science teacher is one who has completed a science major at a college and who is willing to review this collegiate learning with students in schools. Elementary teachers are usually expected to take the same freshman science courses offered to science majors, digest this information, and produce a child's version of everything from acceleration to zoology. This means that a given teacher professes to teach in the science disciplines in which the most college coursework was completed. Texas has even gone so far as to limit credit in colleges, schools, and departments of education (Imig, 1988), which increases the opportunity for completing even more work in science. This situation tends to retain the *status quo* with respect to science content; teachers teach primarily for those students who show similar interests to their own.

The Science Experience for Science Teaching Majors

Obviously the best kind of science preparation depends upon the kind of science program envisioned for the school. Currently there is a major controversy concerning whether there is fundamental knowledge in science that everyone should know. Herbert Spencer (1911) wrote an essay entitled "What Knowledge Is of Most Worth?" For many this settled the argument that the task was an impossible one when the question was extended into the future, that is, through the lifetime of a student. Recently, Hirsch's best-selling book *Cultural Literacy: What Every American Needs to Know* (1987) gave new weight to the argument that someone can determine what every American student should know about the concepts of science (and every other discipline) and can determine where and when it should be taught to every student.

In science, another major project funded by the Carnegie Foundation of New York and the Mellon Foundation and administered by the American Association for the Advancement of Science is called Project 2061 (AAAS, 1988). Basic to this undertaking is the determination of the science concepts in each of several basic areas that every high school graduate should know. These statements of basic scientific concepts are then used to produce a single framework that outlines the general science attributes that every high school graduate should have. Later efforts concentrate on how this can be accomplished in schools.

Too many of these efforts at defining essential science concepts seem flawed. They are contrary to worldwide efforts to provide science for all, rather than just for future scientists. Many science educators feel we can best reach all through applying science, rather than through just learning it. This attempt to reach all learners, often called the science/technology/society (S/T/S) approach, is well documented in many countries, both developed and developing (Roy, 1987).

Dewey's conception (1938) of learning from direct experience and personal involvement supports the S/T/S framework and suggests the necessity of beginning with a problem that students identify and internalize. This focus invariably improves attitude and encourages creativity. More positive attitudes and greater creativity make it possible for most to enter the process and information domains, the starting points for traditional science teaching. Most would agree that teacher education programs must provide teachers-to-be with similar approaches and experiences with science. Although it is possible to start with information and skills for the college science major, this beginning point apparently is inappropriate for most.

Students from society at large identify problems related to

their lives. Almost invariably, current problems are related to science and technology. Technology, particularly, affects aspects of all lives most directly, including homes, clothing, transportation, communication, careers, leisure activities, food, and health. Technology in the curriculum was separated from science study during the 1960s. Now technology has become central, the means of connecting people to the world of science. The consideration of technology provides an opportunity for enhancing the interests of students and their creative skills in dealing with them.

The 1985 Yearbook of the Association for the Education of Teachers in Science focused upon resources and strategies for preparing science teachers for an S/T/S organization and the teaching strategies it requires (James, 1986). This yearbook states that broad field preparation is most appropriate for preparing science teachers for the kind of school science programs needed for the next decade and for the citizens and society of the future.

Obviously, some work in basic science is important, but perhaps not so important as it has been seen in the past for preparing students to teach science. More important than the information a teacher acquires about science is a teacher's knowing how to inquire, how to find answers, how to use material and human resources, and how to model these in a science classroom. Yet most students see their science teachers as information sources (NAEP, 1978; Yager & Bonnstetter, 1984; Yager & Penick, 1986). High school science teachers are rarely, if ever, seen as admitting to not knowing science information. To many teachers, administrators, and parents, the most effective science teachers are seen by their students as frequently not knowing (Bonnstetter, Penick, & Yager, 1983). As Secretary of Education William J. Bennett (1986) said, "We need a revolution in school science. There is probably no other subject whose teaching is so at odds with its true nature" (Bennett, 1986, p. 27).

Several of the exemplary elementary service programs described by the National Science Teachers Association (Penick, 1987) require that preservice elementary teachers complete courses similar to those of Ball State University, which include biological concepts for teachers; physical geography/earth science concepts for teachers; nutrition; physical science concepts for teachers; field experience in biology for teachers; astronomy materials for teachers; conservation for teachers; elements of human health; and global geography for teachers. These courses are specifically designed to give elementary teachers adequate and appropriate background and understanding to teach science as it should be taught. These classes provide considerable laboratory time and science modeling. In essence, they are both science and science methods courses.

A major problem continues to exist at most colleges with the nature of the collegiate science courses completed by most preservice teachers in terms of content organization and the teaching strategies employed. The NSF has recognized these problems and has mounted major projects designed to improve college science offerings. The Carnegie Foundation of New York has also funded another major project with the American Association for the Advancement of Science designed to study the problem of science teaching at the college level and to propose correctives (Champagne & Lovitts, 1988). Because typical

[handwritten margin note: Unknown → Do undergraduate content and methods in science prepare one for graduate work in science?]

high school programs are modeled after college programs, the improvement of college programs is all the more crucial.

University courses in science have remained fairly static for years. Of course, specialty courses are updated in terms of current research, but the course structure and teaching approach are traditional. The information that constitutes current understanding is presented, and laboratories are usually offered as places to learn specific procedures and to verify firsthand the explanations presented in text and lecture (Furhman, Lunetta, & Novick, 1982). Little is known about the appropriateness of such courses and teaching procedures in terms of preparation for further study in graduate school or professional school. However, there is mounting evidence that such courses provide poor preparation for K–12 teachers of science.

[handwritten margin note: A research void →]

Kracjik and Yager (1987) have shown that high-ability secondary school students who have not completed high school chemistry or physics can perform just as well in collegiate courses in their disciplines as students completing the high school courses. The research indicates that little would be lost if the advanced high school courses were to be altered considerably and made more appropriate for more students. In their current format, physics and chemistry courses are not so important as is generally assumed as preparation for standard study of science in college.

[handwritten margin note: ? No content advantage in AP courses]

The Science Education Sequence

Specialized science methods courses are available in the largest teacher education programs; sometimes they are distinguished according to science discipline and/or the particular teaching level. Many now focus on practicum experiences in schools, thus assuring that there is practice and direct experience to accompany theory and study. In many programs the methods offerings are multiple and have specific foci, often reflected in course titles that are more descriptive than "methods" (Brockway, 1989; Penick, 1987; Yager, 1980b). Smaller colleges with science teacher education programs rarely have a specialized methods course of any kind (Brockway, 1989; Yager & Bybee, in press).

In exemplary centers, clinical experiences, requiring more time and spaced throughout the program, provide a natural bridge to a full semester internship or student-teaching experience. The first clinical experience usually includes informal work with students over an entire semester. Later students work up to a full-time experience, often with four or more master teachers; include teaching at multiple grade levels; and provide direct experience in a variety of courses/disciplines for a variety of students in terms of interest and ability (Penick, Yager, & Berg, 1988). Several studies have shown clearly the advantage of clinical experiences prior to student teaching (Lunetta, 1975; Repicky & Hardy, 1975). Student teachers are able to begin actual teaching earlier and more successfully, hence are better able to assume full-time teaching positions. Lazarowitz, Barufaldi, and Huntsberger (1978) analyzed student teacher characteristics with respect to their attitudes concerning the basic skills of science. Such studies confirm the problems of separating the various facets of a science teacher

[handwritten margin note: Advantages of early field experiences]

education program without opportunities for synthesis and developing the necessary traits for teaching science.

In science education, there is ever-increasing agreement that student assessment must be more central to preparatory programs and that it must occur in multiple dimensions. Assessment is basic to science itself, and it is automatically extended to science teaching in exemplary programs (Bonnstetter et al., 1983; Penick, 1987). Assessment of science growth and learning should occur with would-be teachers as they prepare to deal with students in schools. Major dimensions to consider and to measure are:

1. *Knowing and understanding.* Knowledge of science includes facts, concepts, laws (principles), and existing hypotheses and theories being used by scientists. All of this vast amount of information is usually classified into such manageable topics as matter, energy, motion, animal behavior, and plant development. Assessing, understanding, and knowing, as opposed to retention of information, are important goals.

2. *Exploring and discovering.* Some processes of science are observing and describing, classifying and organizing, measuring and charting, communicating and understanding communications of others, predicting and inferring, hypothesizing and hypothesis testing, identifying and controlling variables, interpreting data, and constructing instruments and physical models. Such skills require instructional time and deserve attention as success with science instruction is considered.

3. *Imagining and creating.* Some of the human abilities important in this dimension are visualizing or producing mental images; combining objects and ideas in new ways, producing alternate or unusual uses for objects, solving problems and puzzles, fantasizing, pretending, dreaming, designing devices and machines, and producing unusual ideas. Increased student skills in this dimension are a desirable goal and an area for assessment.

4. *Feeling and valuing.* Human feelings and values inherent in decision-making skills are important in terms of assessment of preservice teachers and, later, their students, including developing positive attitudes toward science and science teachers, developing positive attitudes toward oneself, exploring human emotions, developing sensitivity to and respect for the feelings of other people, expressing personal feelings in constructive ways, making decisions about personal values, and making decisions about social and environmental issues. Enhanced student attitudes are an important goal and worthy of serious and continuous assessment efforts.

5. *Using and applying.* Teachers of students need to become sensitized to experiences they encounter that reflect ideas they have learned in science; some of which are identifying scientific concepts in everyday life experiences; applying science concepts and skills learned to everyday technological problems; understanding scientific and technological principles involved in household technological devices; using scientific processes to solve problems in everyday life; understanding and evaluating mass media reports of scien-

tific developments; making decisions related to personal health, nutrition, and life-style based on knowledge of scientific concepts, rather than on hearsay or emotions; and integrating science with other subjects. This could be the most important goal for science teaching and the most critical area for attention when assessing success.

Teachers who are comfortable and competent in these five domains actually inquire, seek information, and work toward resolving problems they identify. Experiences with assessment in these five dimensions with inservice teachers need to be provided in preservice programs if new science teachers are to model the desired behaviors for their students. Experience with assessing their own growth and, later, the growth of their students must be stressed.

Other Facets of a Model Program

There is more to a model science teacher education program than science and education sequences. A science teacher needs to consider the rationale for school science. Harms and Yager (1981) advance four justifications, or rationales, for science in their Project Synthesis effort:

1. *Science for meeting personal needs.* Science education should prepare individuals to use science for improving their own lives and for coping with an increasingly technological world.
2. *Science for resolving current societal issues.* Science education should produce informed citizens prepared to deal responsibly with science-related societal issues.
3. *Science for assisting with career choices.* Science education should give all students an awareness of the nature and scope of a wide variety of science- and technology-related careers open to those with varying aptitudes and interests.
4. *Science for preparing for further study.* Science education should allow students who are likely to pursue science academically, as well as professionally, to acquire the academic knowledge appropriate to their needs. (pp. 7–8)

Much of the current work dealing with teacher behaviors and their relationship to student achievement is of utmost importance in determining appropriate topics and activities in the professional sequence of topics. Yeany and Padilla (1986) have synthesized the research concerning teacher strategies that should be considered in the teaching sequence. Some of these strategies arise from Yeany's seminal work (1977), which dealt with systematic analysis of specific teaching styles. The analysis of videotaped model lessons proved to be a powerful tool in assessing teaching improvement. Further, the importance of using students as a source of data, not merely as the recipients of teacher information, was exemplified and used to improve teaching ability. Sunal (1978) reviewed studies and conducted some of his own that established the relationship of science skill performances of students to preservice teaching behaviors.

More recently, the work of Gallagher and Tobin (1987) has focused upon teacher management related to student engagement in science education classes. Their studies were based on case studies conducted in Australia. Students selected by teachers as "target students" were involved in specific class interactions; identifiable teacher behaviors tended to stimulate high formal reasoning abilities in the targeted students. Gallagher and Tobin offer the following conclusions from their studies.

1. Secondary science teachers equate task completion (coverage of content) with student learning.
2. A majority of class time is devoted to whole-class interaction during which the pace of instruction depends on the responses of 5–7 more able students.
3. Teachers hold different expectations of their students during class work and laboratory work.
4. The level of cognitive demand placed on students during science classes and laboratories is relatively low.
5. Students with poor achievement and motivation frequently are problematic to secondary science teachers who offer watered-down versions of regular classes to them.
6. Some disruptive behavior occurs in all classes—however, in most cases disruptions are relatively minor.
7. Preparations for examinations (both teacher developed and external examination) are continually reinforced by teachers as the purpose of instruction, class work, homework, and laboratory work. (p. 555)

Such observations of teaching in actual classroom settings provide powerful information that should influence actions and investigations for science teacher educators to use during preservice instruction. Such efforts provide ideas for developing new science teachers with different perceptions and skills than those observed in common practice.

Science Teachers as Continuous Learners

A persistent problem has been the gap between pre- and inservice science teacher education. The NSF support for teacher inservice from 1960–1975 focused on updating science preparation, in an attempt to narrow the gap. In fact, the NSF institute efforts often tended to deepen the problem, seemingly focusing on the shortcomings of typical college science offerings, especially the education sequence.

The model has been the sponge model. If a teacher can soak up enough current information, most problems disappear, because teachers merely communicate information to students and insist that they commit it to memory. What was not learned was a set of intellectual tools with which teachers could evaluate the instruction they provided (Lanier & Little, 1986). Brophy (1980) points out that the key to improvement has been concentration on knowledge about effective teaching and algorithms that teachers can learn and incorporate in their planning prior to teaching.

The research proves that effective science teachers must have a broader view of science and of education (Holdzkom & Lutz, 1984). They need to be in tune with the basic goals of science education in K–12 settings, and they must be prepared to deal with all students in efforts to meet such objectives

Enquiry - much hoopla
- little in practice

(Holdzkom & Lutz, 1984). New pictures are emerging as common objectives unfold and concerns are related (Hurd, 1986). Harty and Enochs (1985) have offered an excellent analysis of the form of inservice important for science teachers. They recommend that inservice programs:

1. Have a well defined, organized, and responsible governing mechanism;
2. Reflect the involvement of teachers in the needs-assessment, planning, designing and implementing processes;
3. Provide diverse, flexible offerings that address the current concerns of the practitioner and can be utilized readily in the classroom; and
4. Include an evaluation plan of the individual components of the program and the program's effect in the classroom. (p. 131)

Teachers have always thought in terms of content that includes both concepts and processes. Unfortunately, many teachers approach science processes as merely another set of commandments. Those educators who were involved in the programs of the 1960s found an emphasis on processes reassuring but often asked students to use them at the descriptive/information level—just more material to be learned. Perhaps the best known listing and treatment of science processes are those designed by AAAS scientists, who structured an entire elementary school program around them in the mid-1960s, *Science: A Process Approach* (AAAS, 1975). Teachers continue to find this program valuable and fascinating.

The content (or concept) versus process debate continues and is counterproductive at best. Science cannot be characterized by either content, the products produced by scientists, or process, behaviors that bring scientists to new understandings. Effective teacher education programs cannot be developed if the science preparation focuses on content mastery and the education component focuses on process. Teachers must learn to use the skills and processes of science to develop new knowledge of both science and teaching.

The problems of traditional teaching (practices of traditional teachers) are emphasized in the results of the science and mathematics assessment conducted by the National Assessment of Educational Progress (Educational Testing Service, 1988a, 1988b). Successful students learn rules by rote and perform tasks for which they see no use in their lives. Even the most successful and motivated students who continue their formal study of science are not really learning. Cognitive science studies reveal that as many as 80 percent of the physics majors at universities cannot relate the concepts and the problem skills they seem to know to any real-world situation. Even though successful as students, they hold naive theories and misconceptions about the real world (Champagne & Klopfer, 1984).

Physics Colloquium →

Hurd (1978) laments the fact that most attempts to present science as a series of processes fail. In reviewing the effect of presenting biology as experiences with scientific inquiry, Hurd observes:

The development of Enquiry skills as a major goal of instruction in biology appears to have had only a minimal effect on secondary school teaching. The rhetoric about enquiry and process teaching greatly exceeds both the research on the subject and the classroom practice. The validity of the enquiry goal itself could profit from more scholarly interchange and confrontation even if it is simply to recognize that science is not totally confined to logical processes and data-gathering. (p. 62)

Current issues relating science and society might be the best and most obvious items around which to organize the curriculum. Some of the most obvious are energy sources, water quality, draught, space exploration, pesticides, acid rain, and the greenhouse effect. Why struggle with artificial examples that illustrate the importance of concepts and processes when real ones are available? Impact is the justification for concepts and process, and impact comes from reality. If one thinks first of impact and uses it to uncover useful processes to derive important and useful concepts, motivation and a reason for knowing are provided. Important concepts are seen as useful and in a variety of contexts.

Yager (1987) provides a listing of science teaching approaches and a delineation of differences among the three:

Concept Mastery Approach
Identify and study chemistry as it relates to compounds, including asbestos.
Study concepts related to cancer including its causes, physiology, and cures.
Consider environmental problems in the community.
Combine information to consider the community issues involving asbestos removal from schools and its disposal near community water sources.

Process Approach
Formulate hypotheses and design laboratories to determine qualities of asbestos.
Review questions and simulate experiments related to cancer (i.e., uncontrolled cell division and resultant tissue/organ growth).
Observe, collect data, interpret information, and formulate explanations from environmental phenomena.
Assimilate information collected from direct inquiries and apply it and the techniques to the asbestos problem in the community.

Issue Approach
Identify current problems associated with deposition of large quantities of asbestos near the city water supply.
Identify necessary information and procedures to respond to the issue as it actually exists.
Use information and process procedures in an attempt to identify and resolve the specific community problem.
Review and discuss the concepts mastered and techniques used to resolve the issue. Establish these concepts and processes as valuable facets of science that are useful in terms of daily living and resolving societal problems. Communicate with appropriate individuals regarding these concepts and the proposed solutions. (p. 29)

A real situation requiring information and skills (concepts and processes) and the need to take action provides a powerful reason for students and future teachers to master concepts and to practice specific science processes. By being presented with the tools of science inquiry first, some students, by failing to learn the processes, lose before ever getting to the reason they were being taught. Identifying and using issues as organizers for science study assures that many students will learn information and practice skills through their own motivation and their own decision that knowing has value. So should it be with science teacher education.

The issues in science teacher education have never been so clear nor so numerous. Science educators at every major institution are at work developing and evaluating programs. New positions are being created. Never have times been more exciting for dealing with major unresolved issues.

PROMISING PRACTICES IN SCIENCE TEACHER EDUCATION

Since the ROSES report in 1968, several attempts have been made to study promising practices, to develop models, and to stimulate interest and dialogue in science teacher education. Many of these efforts have involved qualitative research techniques, especially use of case study techniques. Many of the efforts have been international ones. In some respects, much more attention has been directed to science teacher education in nations other than the United States, perhaps because of the much more common central control of school programs and teacher preparation outside the United States. Interest in fundamental improvements in science teacher education in the United States increased dramatically during the 1980s; similar efforts developed elsewhere in the world during the preceding decade. Much of this focus has been, as Heath (1986) puts it, on "developing teachers, not just techniques."

Meyer (1975) identifies two general trends of science teacher education. The first relates to the increasing awareness that preservice training is just a first cycle in a continuous process that must be supplemented by further cycles of inservice programs. And second, there exists growing dissatisfaction with what he calls the "end-on" approach, with which all the training in pedagogy is compressed into one year (sometimes) at the end of the professional study of science. "Concurrent" rather than "end-on" training programs are becoming more and more widespread in various countries.

Meyer reports that the concurrent approach has the following advantages:

- It provides the student with an early opportunity to develop a personal position and commitment on certain aspects of teaching and education.
- It provides an opportunity for students to find out whether they really wish to consider teaching as a career.
- It allows for closer integration between academic and education areas.
- It allows for greater flexibility in course structure.
- In certain cases the science academic programs are designed to be relevant to perceived teaching needs in terms of objectives, content and method. For example, in recent years environmental matters such as pollution, human ecology, and population studies have been emphasized. In approaching science more personally, some colleges are offering more individualized science courses based, for example, on audio-tutorials or on individual projects.

Tamir (1976) describes the Science Teacher Education Project (STEP) in Britain, an example of model teacher education practices in the interactional arena. He calls the British STEP program potentially the most effective approach available for the improvement of science teacher education. The key feature of this project was the formation of a community of tutors extending across many institutions who shared a common interest in improving their methods courses by adapting them to the needs of prospective science teachers. More than 200 tutors all over Britain participated by either contributing ideas and activities or trying and providing feedback on trial units. As a result of this cooperative effort, 160 activities were actually tried, of which 97 appeared in the final product. These activities can be characterized as follows:

1. They are concerned, not just with the content of science, but also with pedagogy, that is, methods of teaching and related aspects of psychology, sociology, and philosophy.
2. They involve students in the activities, for example, small-group discussion, analysis of tape recordings of parts of lessons, team planning, team teaching, writing, teaching small groups, testing children, testing oneself, observing/recording and analyzing classroom interactions, and role playing.
3. They are short, often not more than 1-1/2 hours, and sufficiently self-contained to be used independently of one another.
4. They carry a note on objectives, expressed in terms of qualities or skills that could be enhanced in students. Users are asked to look for behavioral symptoms of these qualities.
5. Many of them use resource materials such as films, videotapes, audiotapes, and slides. (p. 18)

A conscious effort has been made in the STEP project activities to show how theoretical matters bear on actual classroom practice. In reference to activities, the student is conceived of as being mentally active and emotionally sensitive, practicing skill and experiencing the results of doing so.

Tamir, Lunetta, and Yager (1978) identify nine basic "principles" for an idealized science teacher education program that emerged during the decade following the ROSES report:

1. Experiences in teacher education are planned for a span of several years and integrated with the total academic program.
2. The program consists of a broad curriculum that goes beyond the separate science disciplines.
3. The nature of science in a historical, philosophical, and social perspective is a central component.
4. The program is based upon stated objectives, generally expressed in performance terms that delineate a variety of instructional skills and competencies.
5. Experiences for improving communication and interpersonal relationships are included.
6. Preservice teachers are actively involved in a variety of teaching experiences, a significant number of these occurring with students in public schools.
7. Experiences are provided in evaluation and in the application of research to learning and teaching.

8. The preservice program is but a first step in a continuous cycle of professional growth and inservice education.
9. The program is based upon continuing evaluation of needs and program effectiveness and includes continuous assessment of the skills of individual preservice teachers. (p. 85)

In 1973 the Science, Mathematics, and Environmental Education Information Analysis Center, one of the U.S. Office of Education's ERIC centers, published a new volume entitled *In Search of Promising Practices in Science Teacher Education*. This volume was another response to Newton and Watson's ROSES report of 1968. The authors of the volume offered no analysis or summary. It was merely a report of the responses on a national survey of all teacher education institutions. A simple schema was used that took the form of an equation. It related elements of a teacher education program as follows:

$$\text{CONTENT} + \text{STRATEGY} \rightarrow$$
$$\text{OUTCOME(S)} = = = = = \text{EVIDENCE}$$

This report included 4 programs that were identified as K–12 programs, 20 as elementary, and 26 as secondary. The appendix included minimal information on 16 other programs in which reports and information were forwarded by contact persons who did not complete the survey form nor provide the specific information requested.

Although the report received attention and fairly wide distribution, its impact was negligible, probably because no analysis or summary was included and no criteria for excellence were developed. There was no attempt to provide a model or to reflect on some of the deficiencies or the correctives for problems cited in the ROSES report.

Stronck (1985) conducted a study of science teacher education in British Columbia and developed a series of recommendations for improvement. However, he notes that changes are typically slow to occur and then only if there is clear evidence of needed directions and general acceptance of the need for reform. More studies like Stronck's are needed in many states to offset perceived reforms being advocated by political leaders, most of which are not based upon any experimental or observational evidence.

In 1983 the National Science Teachers Association (NSTA) decided to extend its Search for Excellence in Science Education (SESE) program to include teacher education. Criteria for elementary science teacher education programs, secondary science teacher programs, and inservice programs for science teachers were developed by expert task forces appointed by NSTA and the Association for the Education of Teachers in Science. After a year of effort was expended in developing criteria for excellent programs, the following features were identified as the most significant (with differences between elementary and secondary programs occurring only with respect to science background):

A. Teachers should:
   – display positive attitudes toward science and science education.
   – recognize the inherent value of science in the lives of people.
   – be able to implement courses which meet the SESE criteria for excellence in elementary school science.
   – be committed to continuing professional self-improvement in science and science teaching.
B. With regard to background in science concepts and processes, the teacher's preparation will include:
   For elementary teachers:
   – 12 semester hours of study balanced among biology, physical science, and earth science, including appropriate laboratory experience.
   – content applicable to the elementary science curriculum; these courses should be designed to specifically serve the needs of preservice elementary school teachers.
   The secondary program will include:
   – specialization (i.e., preparation equivalent to the bachelor's level) in one of the following: Biology, Chemistry, Earth and Space Sciences, General Science, Physical Science, or Physics, as well as significant course work in at least two additional areas of science in each specialization offered.
   – supportive preparation in mathematics (to at least introductory calculus), the scientific and educational use/interpretation of statistics, and competency in a variety of computer applications to science teaching.
   – course work at least equivalent to a "minor" in that area (20 semester hours of carefully-selected course work) for teachers to teach in additional science areas.
   For both elementary and secondary teachers, an exemplary program will:
   – provide understanding of societal implications of science and technology.
   – prepare teachers to use such processes of science as observing, classifying, measuring, interpreting data, predicting, and experimenting.
C. With regard to preparation in science teaching approaches and strategies, the preservice teacher's preparation will provide the candidate with:
   – at least three semester hours of study devoted exclusively to science methods, such work ideally undertaken just prior to student teaching.
   – the knowledge and skills to work effectively with a wide range of student abilities, socio-economic, and ethnic backgrounds.
   – personal problem-solving and process skills, acquired through significant hands-on-experience.
   – the knowledge and skills to develop a classroom environment that promotes positive attitudes toward science.
   – the ability to use media, computers, and other technologies appropriately in classroom instruction.
   – the ability to use a variety of instructional strategies and materials, including local/community resources and personnel.
   – an understanding of how to insure safety in science activities.
   – an understanding of techniques for evaluating pupil progress which are congruent with instruction and which address the processes as well as the content of science.

D. The candidate's instructional program will be carefully organized to provide:
- significant field and laboratory experience; at least 30 percent of the candidate's science coursework should be based on direct experience in investigating phenomena using scientific equipment.
- opportunities throughout the program to teach science to children in schools; these experiences should begin with observation and tutoring and gradually proceed through various forms of small and large group instruction.
- student teaching which includes experience in both planning for and teaching science to elementary school students.
- significant contact with the kinds of facilities, equipment, instructional and library materials which are typical of outstanding science teaching/learning program.

- a continuous feedback process to keep the program current in both science and science education.
E. Faculty who serve in the preservice education of teachers in science should:
- have the qualifications, experience, and interest to provide high-quality instruction.
- have specific preparation in and experience with the teaching of science.
- model exemplary instructional design and practice in science teaching.
- keep current in science education research as well as science.
- model participation in professional associations in science education.
- maintain a close continuing association with cooperating elementary schools (National Science Teachers Association, 1987, pp. 34–37).

TABLE 36-1 Components of Two Model Programs

NEBRASKA-NUSTEP SECONDARY PROGRAM

	Phase I	Phase II	Science Methods	Student Teaching
Seminar	0 hours	0 hours	105 hours	30 hours
Focus	Meets with foundations courses	Meets with foundations courses	Research on effective teaching	Effective teaching
Field Experience	20 hours	20 hours	105 hours	16 weeks
Class size	15	20	18	10
Staff	1 Faculty, 4 Assistants			

Special Features: All students are involved systematically in science-fair judging and the Science Olympiad. The university provides a van for travel to one professional meeting in the region each semester. Students have access to a science curriculum library that is an official depository for all state-approved science curricula. A recent addition is a science education computer room where students analyze their classroom performance. In addition, a science education club, SEARCH, meets monthly, with pre- and inservice teachers attending. All students devote a minimum of 8 clock hours to a professional activity such as parent–teacher conferences, local inservice, search meetings, and professional meetings.

IOWA-UPSTEP SECONDARY PROGRAM

	Science Methods I: Elementary	Science Methods II: Middle School	Science Methods III: K–12	Student Teaching
Seminar	24 hours	60 hours	120 hours	30 hours
Focus	Elementary teaching, children, and curriculum	Self-evaluation, communication, cognitive development, middle/junior	Research on effective practice, K–12	Effective teaching
Field Experience	50 hours (elementary)	75 hours (middle/junior)	24 hours (secondary)	16 weeks
Class Size	15	15	14	14
Staff	4 Faculty (37 years experience in K–12 teaching) 1 Clinical Professor who teaches 1/2 times in local schools (10 years experience in K–12 teaching) 5 Assistants (33 years experience in K–12 teaching) 1 Secretary			

Special feature: Within the Science Education Center (a faculty of eight) all Iowa—UPSTEP students complete a 2-semester sequence in the history, philosophy, and sociology of science, as well as 2 semesters of applied science. As a result, all prospective teachers are enrolled for at least eight science education courses during their minimum of 4 semesters. The Science Education Center houses a library, a materials center, a computer facility, and a darkroom, in addition to four specialized laboratory and seminar rooms.

In 1985, seven preservice elementary programs were selected that best met the criteria. These programs are described in NSTA's *Focus on Excellence* series (Penick, 1987).

Although a search for model secondary programs was conducted by NSTA in 1986, only four programs were nominated from the 50 states, Of these, only the program at the University of Nebraska was selected as a national exemplar. The Nebraska program is very similar to the University of Iowa program, one of the four nominations. Both were originally funded by National Science Foundation UPSTEP funds; both include intensive seminars, extensive field components, expert supervision, and many related opportunities (see Table 36-1). All students are videotaped and audiotaped a number of times prior to student teaching, and, following the wellknown adage "the more they study the subject, the more they learn" (Fisher et al., 1978), the programs demand heavy involvement of student and faculty time.

A key point in the methods courses is *how* they are taught. As Weil and Murphy (1982) point out, because instructional processes make a significant contribution to student outcomes, we must design these to accomplish distinct objectives. Knowing that students copy their teachers' behaviors (H. H. Anderson & Brewer, 1946), methods instructors model the behaviors they wish preservice students to exhibit. Instructors consciously model questioning and responding behaviors and patterns, using a variety of techniques to make these planned behaviors more overtly visible to their students. Instructors recognize that preservice teachers have difficulty making the transition from being relatively passive students to being active, dynamic, and thoughtful teachers. As a result, instruction involves many concrete and abstract notions about teaching, reflecting an understanding of the developmental stages of becoming a teacher (Santmire & Friesen, 1984).

Both the Nebraska and Iowa programs produce teachers with a research-based rationale for teaching science (Penick & Yager, 1988). As Joyce and Showers (1983) put it: "Important skills cannot be used mindlessly, and principles need to be developed in the training setting concerning the appropriate use of the skill, how to modify it to fit the students, how to tell when it is working, and how to read one's own behavior and the behavior of the students to determine the degree to which it is effective" (p. 17–18). By doing so, students learn to approach teaching as they would science, by observing, analyzing, predicting, and testing. Seeing the cause-and-effect relationships in teaching and learning leads them to understand and apply Black's (1981) admonition that everything done in the classroom is important. Equally important, these programs work. Krajcik's comparison of Iowa UPSTEP graduates with teachers in exemplary programs revealed few differences and provided strong evidence that a teacher education program can produce exemplary teachers (Krajcik & Penick, in press).

In 1986 the National Science Foundation renewed interest in funding of model science teacher education programs. Seven institutions were selected from competitive proposals for the establishment of experimental centers for preparing science teachers for middle schools. Projects supported under this solicitation were expected to develop outstanding programs and materials that would substantially improve the preparation of middle/junior high school science or mathematics teachers in the specific institutions supported. Individually and collectively the projects were expected to serve as excellent models for other teacher-preparation institutions wishing to develop similar programs. Funding was to be maintained for at least 5 years. The emergence of major NSF funding and support promises to provide new information and new models for others to try.

The NSF also awarded major grants for improving science in the elementary and middle schools. These projects are all allied with a business, usually a publisher that has agreed to produce model materials for use in schools and to provide major assistance with teacher education activities.

The NSF has also moved to reinstitute its support for preservice programs. In the first 2 years more projects have been supported than during the decade following 1965. Unfortunately, these developments are too current to permit analysis and/or report of specific successes and failures. But, they do represent intentions and new commitments to improve science teacher education.

A fairly recent review of research was completed with funds from the National Institute of Education and the U.S. Department of Education as part of the Research Within Reach Project. In this report Bethel (1984) offers the following summary of research concerning science teacher education:

1. The most severe problem facing science education presently is the critical shortage of *qualified* science and mathematics teachers.
2. Many educators, including school principals, supervising teachers, and science educators, agree that beginning teachers lack competence in science subject matter.
3. Undergraduate courses by preservice teachers are the same as those usually taken by students preparing for graduate study or for professional schools.
4. Elementary preservice teachers are rarely required to take more science content than is required for the academic foundations component of their undergraduate program.
5. The college or university major for science teachers is not typically based on a content analysis of (present) school science, or, in other words, what the teacher is expected to teach.
6. While national science education organizations continue to refine their positions about teacher education, there is no mechanism for translating these positions and statements into science education courses that can improve the preparation and quality of preservice science teachers at both the elementary and secondary levels.
7. How teachers get trained in their profession affects both their teaching practices and their attitudes.
8. Science inquiry activities from the elementary science "alphabet" programs are effective in changing attitudes toward science and science inquiry teaching.
9. Training models used to instruct preservice teachers are effective in developing specific teaching behaviors such as observing students, evaluating students' classroom perfor-

mance in science, developing effective questioning strategies, and other behaviors related to teaching science in inquiry.

10. Neither elementary nor secondary school science teachers have been exposed to science courses where the teaching methodology emphasized inquiry and the development of concepts (Bethel, 1984, pp. 143–150).

Science teacher education seems poised for some major accomplishments. Public interest and support have never been greater; there has never been a time when there has been so much agreement concerning needs. The renewed NSF funding and that from other national agencies, the initiatives undertaken in almost every state, the involvement of professional societies, and the support and encouragement from business and industry groups all combine to make the current situation exciting and full of promise.

THE IMMEDIATE PROBLEM

In many respects the calls for reform and improvement have resulted in greater specificity of requirements and more college science preparation. As in the past, there are few calling for specific evidence that more is better. There is an inherent assumption that a science teacher with 100 semester hours of credit in science will be better than one with 50 semester hours. And yet there is no research to substantiate this, and there is some to suggest that science preparation above a certain level makes no difference (Yager et al., 1988).

In 1987 the National Science Teachers Association entered the science teacher certification arena. Their standards, higher than those of any state (Aldridge, 1984), have resulted in only 75 science teachers in the entire United States meeting the standards after one year. The organization offers its own certification as a means for qualifying teachers, to improve the profession and to gain greater prestige.

As with all disciplines, there is much that is known and many explanations that are currently accepted for use and practice. However, unlike in many other disciplines, many divisions and barriers remain to achieving the advances nearly all are urging. Teacher educators come from very diverse institutions with faculty, resources, students, and ties to research that are so varied that communication and collaboration are difficult

at best. Worst of all, there is no common agreement as to the basic meaning of science as a part of the education of all youth.

There are many signs that major impediments will be removed and that major new initiatives will prove valid and appropriate models for all. As we enter the last decade of the century, most of us have experienced great excitement; promise of future advances is abundant. But major unresolved issues still exist, including:

1. Who should become a science teacher?
   –Recruitment of high ability students
   –How can science teaching attract more first-choice people?
2. Should we prepare teachers of science disciplines or teachers of broad field science?
3. Do standard science courses provide a complete and accurate picture of science?
   –K–12 science as a prelude to post–high school science
   –University science courses: Who takes them? For what purpose?
4. Should we stress processes as a goal or the use of processes in thinking about and using science?
5. What is the relative need for science courses, versus courses and practicum experiences focusing on teaching methodology?
6. Should science study precede any study of teaching, or should it be integrated throughout the preparatory program?
7. How much technology should be included in science instruction?
8. What is the nature of an effective methods course?
9. What is the proper role and placement of clinical experience?
10. How can the gap between preservice and inservice programs be minimized?
11. Science teacher educators: How should they be prepared? What are minimal qualifications? What is their role? How can they best model desired behaviors?

Each of these issues represents both a barrier to success and an area in need of investigation and research. More information should yield better answers and appropriate resolutions. All will lead to enhanced teacher education in science.

References

Aldridge, B. G. (1984). Why NSTA should certify science teachers. *Science Teacher, 51*(5), 20–23.

American Association for the Advancement of Science. (1946). The preparation of high school science and mathematics teachers (Report No. 4 of the AAAS Cooperative Committee on Science Teaching). *School Science and Mathematics, 46*(400), 106–121.

American Association for the Advancement of Science. (1975). *Science: A process approach.* Washington, DC: Ginn & Co.

American Association for the Advancement of Science. (1988). *Project 2061: Education for a changing future.* Washington, DC: Author.

Anderson, H. H., & Brewer, J. E. (1946). Studies of teachers' classroom personalities, II: Effects of teachers' dominative and integrative contacts on children's classroom behavior. *Applied Psychology Monographs*, No. 8. Stanford, CA: Stanford University Press.

Anderson, R. D. (1983). A consolidation and appraisal of science meta-analyses. *Journal of Research in Science Teaching, 20*(5), 497–509.

Anderson, R. D., Kahle, S. R., Glass, G. V., & Smith, M. L. (1983). Science education: A meta-analysis of major questions. *Journal of Research in Science Teaching, 20*(5), 379–385.

Bennett, W. J. (1986). *First lessons: A report on elementary education in America* (Report No. 0-161-837). Washington, DC: U.S. Government Printing Office.

Bethel, L. J. (1984). Is there a shortage of science and mathematics teachers? Are new science teachers being prepared to enter the profession. In D. Holdzkom & P. B. Lutz (Eds.), *Research within reach: Science education* (pp. 143–157). Charleston, WV: Appalachia Educational Laboratory, Research and Development Interpretation Service.

Black, P. (1981). *Flawless consulting: A guide to getting your expertise used.* San Diego, CA: University Associates.

Bonnstetter, R. J., Penick, J. E., & Yager, R. E. (1983). *Teachers in exemplary programs: How do they compare?* Washington, DC: National Science Teachers Association.

Brockway, C. (1989). *The status of science teacher education in Iowa— 1988.* Unpublished doctoral dissertation, University of Iowa, Iowa City.

Brophy, J. E. (1980). *Teachers' cognitive activities and overt behaviors.* East Lansing, MI: Michigan State University, College of Education.

Champagne, A. B., & Klopfer, L. E. (1984). Research in science education: The cognitive psychology perspective. In D. Holdzkom & P. B. Lutz (Eds.), *Research within reach: Science education* (pp. 171–189). Charleston, WV: Appalachia Educational Laboratory, Research and Development Interpretation Service.

Champagne, A. B., & Lovitts, B. (1988). *The report of the project on liberal education and the sciences.* Washington, DC: American Association for the Advancement of Science.

Committee on the Objectives of a General Education in a Free Society. (1945). *General education in a free society.* Cambridge, MA: Harvard University.

Council of Graduate Schools directory. (1979). Princeton, NJ: Educational Testing Service.

Dewey, J. (1938). *Experience and education.* New York: Macmillan.

Druva, C. A., & Anderson, R. D. (1983). Science teacher characteristics by teacher behavior and by student outcome: A meta-analysis of research. *Journal of Research in Science Teaching, 20*(5), 467–479.

Educational Testing Service. (1988a). *The mathematics report card: Are we measuring up? Trends and achievement based on the 1986 national assessment* (Rep. No. 17-M-01). Princeton, NJ: National Assessment of Educational Progress.

Educational Testing Service. (1988b). *The science report card: Trends and achievement based on the 1986 national assessment* (Rep. No.17-S-01). Princeton, NJ: National Assessment of Educational Progress.

Fisher, C. W., Filby, N. A., Marliave, R., Cohen, L. S., Dishaw, M. M., Moore, J. E., & Berliner, D. C. (1978). *Teaching behaviors, academic learning time and student achievements: Final report of phase III-B, beginning teacher evaluation study* (Tech. Rep. No. V-1). San Francisco: Far West Laboratory for Education Research and Development.

Furhman, M., Lunetta, V. N., & Novick, S. (1982). Do secondary school laboratory tests reflect the goals of "new" science curricula? *Journal of Chemical Education, 49*(7), 563–565.

Gallagher, J. J., & Tobin, K. (1987). Teacher management and student engagement in high school science. *Science Education, 71*(4), 535–555.

Harms, N. C., & Yager, R. E. (Eds.). (1981). *What research says to the science teacher (Vol. 3).* Washington, DC: National Science Teachers Association.

Harty, H., & Enochs, L. G. (1985). Toward reshaping the inservice education of science teachers. *School Science and Mathematics, 85*(2), 125–135.

Heath, D. (1986). Developing teachers, not just techniques. In K. K. Zumwalt (Ed.), *Improving teaching* (1986 Yearbook of the ASCD, pp. 1–14). Alexandria, VA: Association for Supervision and Curriculum Development.

Helgeson, S. L., Blosser, P. E., & Howe, R. W. (1977). *The status of pre-college science, mathematics, and social science education: 1955–75.* Columbus, OH: Ohio State University, Center for Science and Mathematics Education.

Henry, N. B. (Ed.) (1947). *Science education in American schools.* Chicago: University of Chicago Press.

Hirsch, E. D. Jr. (1987). *Cultural literacy: What every American needs to know.* Boston: Houghton Mifflin.

Holdzkom, D., & Lutz, P. B. (Eds.). (1984). *Research within reach: Science education.* Charleston, WV: Appalachia Educational Laboratory, Research and Development Interpretation Service.

Hueftle, S. J., Rakow, S. J., & Welch, W. W. (1983). *Images of science: A summary of results from the 1981–82 national assessment in science.* Minneapolis: University of Minnesota, Minnesota Research and Evaluation Center.

Hurd, P. DeH. (1978). The golden age of biological education 1960–75. In W. V. Mayer (Ed.), *BSCS biology teacher's handbook* (3rd ed., pp. 28–98). New York: John Wiley & Sons.

Hurd, P. DeH. (1986). Perspectives for the reform of science education. *Phi Delta Kappan, 67*(5), 353–358.

Imig, D. G. (1988). Outrage in Texas. *American Association of Colleges for Teacher Education BRIEFS, 9*(8), 2.

Iskander, S. (1986). *The status of science education in the United States colleges and universities in 1985.* Unpublished master's thesis, University Iowa, Iowa City.

James, R. K. (Ed.). (1986). *Science, technology and society: Resources for science educators* (1985 Yearbook of the Association for the Education of Teachers in Science). Columbus, OH: SMEAC Information Reference Center.

Joyce, B. R., & Showers, B. (1983). *Power in staff development through research on training.* Alexandria, VA: Association for Supervision and Curriculum Development.

Krajcik, J. S., & Penick, J. E. (in press). Evaluation of a model science teacher education program. *Journal of Research in Science Teaching.*

Krajcik, J. S., & Yager, R. E. (1987). High school chemistry as preparation for college chemistry. *Journal of Chemical Education, 64*(5), 433–435.

Lanier, J., & Little, J. (1986). Research on teacher education. In M. C. Wittrock (Ed.), *Handbook of research on teaching* (3rd ed., pp. 527–569). New York: Macmillan.

Lazarowitz, R., Barufaldi, P. J., & Huntsberger, P. J. (1978). Student teachers' characteristics and favorable attitudes toward inquiry. *Journal of Research in Science Teaching, 15*(6), 559–566.

Lunetta. V. N. (1975). Field-based clinical experiences in science teacher education. *Science Education, 59*(4), 517–520.

Meyer, R. (1975, September). *Development in the training and retraining of school biology teachers.* Paper presented at the International Congress on the Improvement of Biology Education, Upsala, Sweden.

National Assessment of Educational Progress. (1978). *The third assessment of science, 1976–77.* Denver, CO: Author.

National Association of Secondary School Principals. (1953). *Science in secondary schools today: Reports of trends, issues, promising practices, problems and recommendations by more than fifty contributors.* (Guidance by committee on special bulletins of the NSTA). Washington, DC: Author.

National Commission on Excellence in Education. (1983). *A nation at risk: The imperative for educational reform.* Washington, DC: U.S. Government Printing Office.

National Education Association, Educational Policies Commission. (1944). *Education for all American youth.* Washington, DC: Author.

National Education Association. Educational Policies Commission. (1952). *Education for all American youth: A further look.* Washington, DC: National Education Association and American Association of School Administrators.

National Science Board, Commission on Precollege Education in Mathematics, Science and Technology. (1983). *Educating Americans for the 21st century.* Washington, DC: National Science Foundation.

National Science Foundation and U.S. Department of Education. (1980). *Science & engineering education for the 1980's & beyond.* Washington, DC: U.S. Government Printing Office.

National Science Teachers Association. (1987). *Criteria for excellence.* Washington, DC: Author.

Newton, D. E., & Watson, F. G. (1968). *The research on science education survey: The status of teacher education programs in the sciences, 1965–67.* Cambridge, MA: Authors.

Penick, J. E. (Ed.). (1987). *Focus on excellence: Preservice elementary teacher education in science, 4(2).* Washington DC: National Science Teachers Association.

Penick, J. E., & Yager, R. E. (1988). Science teacher education: A program with a theoretical and pragmatic rationale. *Journal of Teacher Education 39(6),* 59–64.

Penick, J. E., Yager, R. E., & Berg, C. (1988). The practicum in teacher education: The Iowa-UPSTEP example. *Teaching Education, 2(2),* 73–79.

Progressive Education Association. (1938). *Science in general education: Suggestions for science teachers in secondary schools and in lower divisions of colleges report.* New York: Author.

Repicky, P. A., & Hardy, H. (1975). Evaluation design elements for an early field-based experience in science education for preservice teachers. *Science Education, 59(4),* 531–537.

Roy, R. (1987). The nature and nurture of technological health. In *Ceramics and civilization: Vol. III. High technology ceramics: Past, present, and future* (pp. 351–370). Westerville, OH: American Ceramic Society.

Santmire, T., & Friesen, P. A. (1984). A developmental analysis of research on effective teacher-student interactions: Implications for teacher preparation. In R. L. Egbert & M. M. Kluender (Eds.), *Using research to improve teacher education* (pp. 28–53). Washington, DC: AACTE/ERIC Clearinghouse on Teacher Education.

Science, Mathematics, and Environmental Education Information Analysis Center. (1973). *In search of promising practices in science teacher education.* Columbus, OH: Author.

Spencer, H. (1911). What knowledge is of most worth? In *Essays on education and kindred subjects* (pp. 1–45). New York: E. P. Dutton.

Stake, R. E., & Easley, J. A. (1978). *Case studies in science education.* Urbana, IL: University of Illinois, Center for Instructional Research and Curriculum Evaluation.

Stronck, D. R. (1985). Recommendations of British Columbia science teachers for revising teacher education programs. *Science Education, 69(2),* 247–257.

Sunal, D. W. (1978). Relationship of science skill performance to preservice teaching behavior. *Science Education, 62(2),* 187–194.

Tamir, P. (1976). The Iowa-UPSTEP program in international perspective. *Technical Report #9, Technical Report Series.* Iowa City, IA: University of Iowa, Science Education Center.

Tamir, P., Lunetta, V. N., & Yager, R. E. (1978). Science teacher education: An assessment inventory. *Science Education, 62(1),* 85–94.

Weil, M. L., & Murphy, J. (1982). Instructional processes. In H. E. Mitzel (Ed.), *Encyclopedia of educational research* (pp. 890–917). New York: Free Press.

Weiss, I. R. (1978). *Report of the 1977 national survey of science, mathematics, and social studies education.* Washington, DC: U.S. Government Printing Office.

Welch, W. W. (1983). Research in science education: Review and recommendations. In National Institute of Education, *Teacher shortage in science & mathematics: Myths, realities & research* (pp. 8–14). Washington, DC: National Institute of Education.

Whipple, G. M. (Ed.). (1932). *A program for science teaching* (31st yearbook of the National Society for the Study of Education). Washington, DC: National Society for the Study of Education.

Yager, R. E. (1980a). *Case studies of nine graduate science education programs* (Tech. Rep. No. 22). Iowa City, IA: University of Iowa, Science Education Center.

Yager, R. E. (1980b). *Status study of graduate science education in the United States, 1960–1980.* Washington, DC: National Science Foundation.

Yager, R. E. (1987). Impact as an organizer. *Science Scope, 10(4),* 28–29.

Yager, R. E. (1988). Differences between most and least effective science teachers selected by science supervisors. *School Science and Mathematics, 88(4),* 301–307.

Yager, R. E., & Bonnstetter, R. J. (1984). Student perceptions of science teachers, classes, and course content. *School Science and Mathematics, 84(5),* 406–414.

Yager, R. E., & Bybee, R. W. (in press). Science teacher education in four-year colleges. *Science Education.*

Yager, R. E., Hidayat, E. M., & Penick, J. E. (1988). Features which separate least effective from most effective science teachers. *Journal of Research in Science Teaching, 25(3),* 165–177.

Yager, R. E., Lunetta, V. N., & Penick, J. E. (1980). *The Iowa-UPSTEP program: Final report.* Iowa City, IA: University of Iowa, Science Education Center.

Yager, R. E., & Penick, J. E. (1986). Public attitude toward science and science education. *Bulletin of Science, Technology, and Society, 6(6),* 535–540.

Yeany, R. H. (1977). The effects of model viewing with systematic strategy analysis on the science teaching styles of preservice teachers. *Journal of Research in Science Teaching, 14(3),* 209–222.

Yeany, R. H., & Padilla, M. J. (1986). Teaching science teachers to utilize better teaching strategies: A research synthesis. *Journal of Research in Science Teaching, 23(2),* 85–95.

·37·

SOCIAL STUDIES TEACHER EDUCATION

James A. Banks and Walter C. Parker

UNIVERSITY OF WASHINGTON, SEATTLE

After the fervor of the social studies reform movement of the 1960s and 1970s had waned and the enthusiasm for it had vanished, social studies educators were more convinced than ever that the classroom teacher had a cogent influence on the interpretation of curricular materials and on student learning (Project SPAN Staff and Consultants, 1982). They had witnessed the extent to which so-called teacher-proof and innovative curricular materials had been mediated and interpreted and sometimes rejected outright, by teachers and other practicing educators. The social studies reform movement was heavily influenced by Bruner (1960), curriculum theorists (Schwab, 1968), and social scientists (Morrissett, 1967). The hope and the belief, which became tenacious, were that learning theorists, social scientists, and other academicians could intellectualize the schools from a distance. Although the social studies reform movement invigorated the scholarly debate in the field and had a significant influence on teaching materials, social studies teaching remained highly resistant to its influence, as it has to most other educational innovations in the past (Cuban, 1984; Stake & Easley, 1978).

An interesting anomaly exists within social studies education. Although most scholars and practitioners in the field regard the teacher as central to student learning, the lack of attention devoted to the study of social studies teaching and to teacher education in social studies is conspicuous. Indeed, the fact that the field of social studies education lacks a cumulative body of coherent research on social studies teaching and teacher education is a major finding of this chapter.

This is not the first attempt to review the research on social studies teacher education and to derive implications for practice, research, and theory. In an earlier review, Grannis (1970) tried to determine how knowledge of subject matter influences the social studies teacher's effectiveness. He also examined how training influences aspects of teacher behavior. A more comprehensive review was undertaken by Tucker (1977). He reviewed research related to three concepts of social studies education: (a) social studies as academic disciplines, (b) social studies as personal development, and (c) social studies as social issues. Tucker also reviewed research derived from conceptions of competence, including models of teaching and teacher-training products.

Tucker's review of research was published in a book sponsored jointly by the National Council for the Social Studies (NCSS) and the Social Science Education Consortium (SSEC) (Hunkins, Ehman, Hahn, Martorella, & Tucker, 1977). The successor to this publication was edited by Stanley (1985). A chapter on teacher education was not included in the Stanley volume. Ochoa's (1981) review focused on the preparation of social studies teachers. She lamented the paucity of research. In her review of research on social studies teaching, Armento (1986) did not include a discussion of research on social studies teacher education.

The plan of this chapter is as follows: In the first part, the field of social studies teacher education is defined, and research questions for the review are derived. In the second, studies that shed light on the questions posed are reviewed. In the third, competing conceptions of quality in social studies teacher education are described and compared.

THE FIELD OF SOCIAL STUDIES TEACHER EDUCATION

The field of social studies teacher education consists of several major actors, programs, and learning environments: (a) college or university students who enter a social studies teacher education program (preservice teachers), (b) a teacher education curriculum; (c) a general studies and social science

The authors wish to thank professors Catherine Cornbleth (State University of New York, Buffalo), Carole L. Hahn (Emory University), and Peter H. Martorella (North Carolina State University) for their helpful comments.

curriculum, (d) teachers of preservice and inservice teachers, (e) teachers who have completed the social studies teacher education curriculum, and (f) public or private school students who have been taught by certified social studies teachers.

A social studies teacher education program is based on the assumption that the teacher-preparation curriculum students experience will change, in some significant ways, their (a) knowledge, (b) attitudes and values, (c) skills, and (d) perspectives. In other words, the knowledge, attitudes, pedagogical skills, and perspectives of students should be significantly different or refined when they complete a social studies teacher education program. Furthermore, the knowledge, attitudes, skills, and perspectives they acquire should have a positive influence on student achievement in the social studies.

A number of questions arise from this conception of social studies teacher education:

1. What are the characteristics of people who enter social studies teacher education programs?
2. What are the characteristics of the curriculum they experience?
3. What effects do the general, social science, and teacher education curricula have on their knowledge, attitudes and values, pedagogical skills, and perspectives?
4. How do social studies teachers influence the achievement, attitudes, values, and perspectives of their students?
5. What are the characteristics of teachers of social studies teachers?
6. What are the alternative conceptions of quality in social studies teacher education?

The meager and contradictory nature of the existing research does not allow us to answer each of these questions satisfactorily. Consequently, the questions do not constitute the organizing framework for this chapter. Rather, an effort is made to shed light on these questions within the broad topics considered.

REVIEW OF RESEARCH ON SOCIAL STUDIES TEACHER EDUCATION

In this section, empirical research on social studies teacher education is reviewed. Topics included are the selection and education of social studies teachers, the role of academic knowledge in social studies teaching, characteristics of social studies teachers and professors, and inservice education.

Selection and Education of Social Studies Teachers

Selection. Individuals who become social studies teachers at the elementary, junior high, and secondary levels are drawn from the same pool of students as other teacher education candidates. Their abilities, backgrounds, and experiences prior to admission to teacher education probably do not differ significantly from those of other teacher education applicants. Some evidence, however, does indicate that social studies teachers

are characterized by more diversity than are teachers in other subject areas (Project SPAN Staff and Consultants 1982).

There is no need to review here the litany of literature that documents and laments the aptitudes and abilities of teacher education candidates, compared with students in the college and university community at large. Both Kerr (1983) and Lanier and Little (1986) have discussed the range of abilities of teacher education candidates and the complex reasons why they often have lower scores on standardized tests and lower grade point averages than do students who enter other professional schools. The educational reform movement intensified after Kerr and Lanier and Little completed their studies and resulted in the tightening of entrance requirements in many teacher education programs, especially at research universities. At these universities, the grade point average requirement for teacher education applicants is sometimes equivalent to that for entrance to other professional schools (Gifford, 1984).

The criteria for admission to social studies teacher education programs parallel those for teacher education generally: grade point average, letters of endorsement, personal interviews, and previous experience with children (Howey, Yarger, & Joyce, 1978, pp. 38–39). As Ochoa (1981) points out in a discussion of these criteria, they have not been empirically demonstrated to be significantly related to teaching success and effectiveness. Since Ochoa made her observations and recommendation for the use of empirically demonstrated criteria for admission to social studies teacher education programs and suggested the need for the grade point average of applicants to be raised, a number of changes have taken place in admission criteria. Grade point averages for admission to many programs have been raised, and a bachelor's degree (or its equivalent) in an academic discipline is now required for admission to a number of teacher education programs.

State Requirements. Ochoa (1981) reviewed the state education requirements for social studies teachers. Both those for elementary teachers and the recommendations of national associations for social studies teachers were examined by Weible and Dumas (1986). These reviews indicate that elementary and secondary teachers are required by most states to complete courses in general education, which usually include some social science courses, and in professional education. The professional education sequence includes foundation and methods courses and student teaching. The range in the required numbers of semester hours in each of these components varies enormously across the 50 states. Secondary teachers also are required to acquire a certificate in a teaching field such as social science, history, geography, or psychology.

Both Ochoa and Weible and Dumas found that states establish minimum requirements for social studies teachers, whereas colleges, universities, and professional associations tend to exceed state requirements in their requirements and recommendations. Weible and Dumas, for example, found that only 17 of the 50 states specify that elementary teachers have a course in methods or materials for teaching social studies, and only 8 states have requirements in multicultural education. In its "Standards for the Preparation of Social Studies

Teachers," the National Council for the Social Studies (1988) recommends that both elementary and secondary teachers take a course in social studies methods. The national guidelines issued by the American Association of Colleges for Teacher Education recommend that all teacher education students have a strong component in multicultural education. The NCSS standards also recommend that multicultural components be a part of both the general studies and the history and social science components of the program requirement for social studies teachers.

Although only 17 states require elementary teachers to have a course in the methods or materials of the social studies, 38 have a course requirement for educational psychology, 23 for social foundations of education, 41 for teaching of reading, 20 the for teaching of mathematics, 18 for the teaching of science, and 20 for the teaching of English (Weible & Dumas, 1986). The differential state requirements for methods courses in the subject areas could indicate that state departments view and value differently the various subject areas.

Content of Methods Courses. Although nearly all secondary social studies teacher education students and many elementary teachers take a course in methods of teaching the social studies, there are few empirical data about the content of these courses or about their effects on teacher behavior in the classroom (Ochoa, 1981). A content analysis of a sample of currently used elementary and secondary social studies methods textbooks can provide important clues about the content of social studies methods courses.

Such an analysis was undertaken for this chapter. It was limited in two important ways: (a) The sample was selective, not random, and (b) a textbook gives only a partial view of what takes place in a course. However, the sample included 12 methods textbooks that the authors believed to be the most frequently used elementary and secondary methods texts. Also, the similarity found in these textbooks is striking and signals a high degree of consensus in the field about topics that should be included in a social studies methods course.

Categories for the content analysis were derived by analyzing seven of the books, randomly selected. To be included as a category, a topic had to be the subject of at least one chapter in a book. Eleven categories were derived in this way. An additional category was added when the total sample was analyzed. The 12 topical categories shown in Table 37-1 were derived and ordered with this procedure. As indicated, Goals/Rationale, Planning, Evaluation, Values Education, Thinking Skills/Inquiry,and Skills were the most frequently appearing topics. This analysis indicates that the social studies methods course is viewed primarily as a vehicle for dealing with pedagogy and instructional problems. Most of the textbooks did not deal extensively with issues related to the nature of the social science disciplines or with issues that help students take a critical and reflective view of schools and society. It is notable, for example, how little attention is devoted to the nature of the social science disciplines (ranked seventh) or to social issues (ranked sixth). Topics included in the secondary textbooks differed little from those in the elementary texts. However, the secondary texts included fewer topics and, surprisingly, no more discussion of the social science disciplines and social issues than did the elementary methods texts

Tucker and Joyce (1979) examined the views of a sample of social studies methods professors about practices and problems in teacher education, including the methods course. Some of the elementary methods professors viewed the emerging content in the social studies, such as energy, law, and globalism, as an opportunity to revitalize the social studies. Others viewed it as a challenge that might threaten the field's disciplinary purity. Most of the elementary professors viewed multicultural education as important, but only half described opportunities for this content in their courses. Tucker and Joyce concluded that there was an inconsistentcy between the professors' stated views on multicultural education and their practices. Few of the respondents had incorporated content about exceptional students into their courses. The elementary professors showed more interest in issues related to exceptional students than did the secondary professors.

An important qualitative case study of a block of elementary methods courses that included a social studies methods course revealed what might be true generally of such courses (Goodman, 1986b). The emphasis in these courses was on providing students with techniques of teaching that would enable them to "fit into" the existing structure of schools and on "being relevant" to the schools. Because the methods courses in the Goodman study focused on preparing teacher education students to adapt to the existing structure of schools, they did not challenge them to participate in school reform or to ask critical and reflective questions about school practice.

Role of Knowledge in Social Studies Teaching and Teacher Education

The ways that teachers' subject-matter knowledge influences teaching behavior and student learning are important and little studied in social studies teacher education. During periods of educational reform, when educators themselves are criticized, a frequently heard complaint is that teachers do not have sufficient grasp of the knowledge they are trying to teach their students (e.g., Cheney, 1987). Yet the ways that a teacher's knowledge of subject matter influence that teacher's peda-

TABLE 37–1. Analysis of Social Studies Methods Textbooks

Category (topic)	Frequency	Rank
Goals/rationale	12	1
Planning	11	2
Evaluation	10	3
Values education	10	3
Thinking skills/inquiry	9	4
Skills	8	5
Facts, concepts, generalizations	7	6
Social issues/concerns	7	6
Social science disciplines	6	7
Instruction	6	7
Reading in the social studies	5	8
Computers in the social studies	3	9

gogical behavior have not been sufficiently clarified and researched. Shulman (1986) pointed out that, although the general public and educational policymakers agree that quality teachers must be competent in the subjects they teach, the kinds of knowledge teachers need to teach effectively remain vague. He stated that teachers need three kinds of knowledge: subject-matter, pedagogical, and curricular.

Grannis (1970) concluded his review by stating that there is little relationship between a teacher's knowledge of subject matter and student achievement in elementary school subjects. At the secondary level, the only relationship found between teacher's knowledge and students' achievement was one for "bright" students in advanced mathematics, chemistry, and physics. Several researchers have approached the question by asking social studies teachers or supervisors to indicate whether knowledge of subject matter or pedagogical issues was more important in teaching, or which factor caused more problems in teaching. Cogan and Miner (1977) asked a sample of social studies supervisors to rank the 66 guidelines in the NCSS Curriculum Guidelines statements from most to least important. The five highest ranked guidelines deal with student learning activities and experiences. One of the lowest ranked guidelines states, "The program must include a careful selection from the disciplines of that knowledge which is of most worth" (p. 5).

Sowders (1982) found that a sample of secondary teachers, supervisors, and leaders in the social studies field placed greater emphasis on affective and participatory objectives in civics than on knowledge objectives. Cooperating teachers viewed knowledge of subject matter and teaching procedures as equally important and interdependent in a study by McMann and McMann (1984). Berryman and Schneider (1984) examined the views of social studies supervisors regarding the teaching skills of beginning teachers. They saw the most serious deficiencies of beginning teachers as factors related to pedagogy and not to subject matter. Russell and Morrow (1986) found that a sample of secondary social studies teachers and supervising principals viewed factors related to instruction and pedagogy as causing the most concern and problems for social studies teachers. Knowledge and selection of subject matter caused teachers the least concern.

Stahl and Matiya (1981) examined the question of the relationship between subject-matter competency and teaching in a different and more innovative way than the studies previously reported. Using a questionnaire to obtain their data, they compared the psychology courses taught by psychology teachers certified to teach social studies with courses taught by teachers of psychology who held certification in other subject areas. Stahl and Matiya concluded that the psychology course was taught and organized essentially the same by both groups, regardless of their certification or academic preparation. They also used identical teaching methods with the same frequency.

The Stanford Studies.
Shulman (1987) and his students at Stanford University (Grossman & Richert, 1988; Gudmundsdottir, 1987; Gudmundsdottir, Carey, & Wilson, 1985; McGraw, 1987; Wilson & Wineberg, n.d.; Wineburg, 1987) have examined the knowledge base of teaching with a series of ex-

tensive case studies of novice and experienced secondary school teachers. According to Shulman, the central question of this research is, What are the sources of the knowledge base for teaching? Some of their case studies have followed individuals from their teacher education program through their becoming beginning teachers. A theoretical model of pedagogical reasoning and action has emerged from their case studies (Shulman, 1987). It consists of "comprehension (of purposes, subject-matter structures, ideas within and outside the discipline), transformation, instruction, evaluation, reflection, and new comprehensions" (p. 15).

This research indicates that the subject-matter preparation of teachers has a strong influence on the way teachers conceptualize, organize, and teach social studies subjects. Through extensive interviews and observations of one or several teachers, their findings indicate that teachers use the disciplinary framework in which they were trained to view and structure the social studies courses they teach. For example, Gudmundsdottir et al. (1985) studied four student teachers to determine how their academic specialization influenced their organization of content and teaching. They concluded that prior content knowledge influences the ways student teachers in social studies organize and teach their classes. The social studies courses organized by the anthropology major in the study reflected anthropological perspectives. Those organized by teachers who majored in history and political science reflected those two disciplines. The other Stanford studies on knowledge and teaching (cited earlier) support the conclusion that secondary teachers' academic knowledge influences the way they conceptualize and organize their social studies courses.

Summary and Interpretation.
Data on the relationship between academic knowledge and teaching the social studies are sparse and conflicting, but promising. We can only interpret the summary of studies by Grannis (1970) to mean that teachers examined in the studies had a sufficient level of competency in the subject matters they taught. That could be why no relationship between subject-matter competency and student learning was found by the researchers. Common sense and "wisdom of practice" tell us that teachers cannot teach what they do not know. The tendency of social studies teachers, supervisors, and principals to consider pedagogical problems as more important than teachers' grasp of academic knowledge could have a number of meanings. It could mean that teachers, supervisors and principals, view social studies teachers as sufficiently prepared in academic subjects but lacking in skills needed to maintain classroom control, to motivate students, and to function in the school culture. It is logical that beginning teachers, fresh from the university, would be more competent in the academic subjects they had just studied than in the acts of teaching they had experienced only during student teaching. It is also possible that practicing educators value factors such as classroom control and management more highly than academic knowledge.

The findings of the Stahl and Matiya (1981) study and the studies by the Stanford team (e.g., Grossman & Richert, 1988; Gudmundsdottir et al. 1985) are inconsistent. One would hypothesize, based on the Stanford studies, that teachers who are certified in psychology would conceptualize and teach their courses differently from teachers who are students of other disciplines. There are several possible reasons why the Stahl and Matiya findings and those of the Stanford team are inconsistent. The teachers studied by the Stanford team were majors in a social science discipline such as history or anthropology. The teachers surveyed in the Stahl and Matiya study were certified in psychology but might have taken highly varying numbers of psychology courses, ranging from one or two to a major in psychology. The different research methods used in the Stahl and Matiya and the Stanford studies might account in part for their inconsistent findings. Most of the Stanford studies were observational case studies of from one to four teachers. The Stahl and Matiya study was a sample survey with a large sample: 554 teachers.

Subject-matter background could have different effects on novice and experienced teachers. Novice teachers, such as those in the Stanford studies, might be strongly influenced in teaching by their academic backgrounds, because they still have familiarity with and attachment to their disciplines and have not been socialized into the school culture. However, experienced teachers, such as those studied by Stahl and Matiya, might be more strongly influenced by the culture of the school, in which classroom management skills and textbooks, rather than a teacher's academic background, become the primary arbiters of the curriculum (Goodlad, 1984). Case studies such as those now conducted at Stanford, which follow teachers over a period of years, should help clarify the role of academic knowledge in social studies teaching.

Characteristics of Social Studies Teachers

Eslinger and Superka (1982) synthesized a number of studies describing the characteristics of social studies teachers. Relying heavily upon studies by Weiss (1978) and Wiley (1977), their review reveals that most elementary teachers do not feel well qualified to teach the social studies. They feel most qualified to teach reading and mathematics. As for secondary social studies teachers, most specialize in one social science discipline, devoting little attention to professional education. History appears to be the most frequent major for secondary social studies teachers, with few of them taking interdisciplinary courses. Elementary and secondary teachers do not indicate that "obtaining subject-matter information" is a major need.

The Eslinger and Superka (1982) review indicates that most junior and senior high social studies teachers teach only social studies courses and that they, like those in other subjects, "tend to run teacher-directed classrooms, making frequent use of lecture and discussion, textbooks, and worksheets" (p. 166). Social studies teachers view their role, like most other teachers, as socializing students into the existing society rather than as promoting social change. They also view the social studies primarily as history, geography, and government, devoting minor attention to social problems and self-awareness. However, few social studies teachers view the social studies as social science and critical inquiry (Shaver, Davis, & Helburn, 1979).

The three problems that high school social studies teachers perceive as most important in their work are (a) inadequate student reading abilities, (b) lack of student interest in the subject, and (c) lack of materials for individualizing instruction. Several of the studies that Eslinger and Superka reviewed indicate that social studies teachers are highly diverse and idiosyncratic in their perspectives, in how they teach, and in what they teach.

Several researchers have examined the perspectives of social studies teachers. Adler (1984) defines perspectives as "the meanings and interpretations which teachers give to their work and work situation. Unlike more abstract statements, perspectives are set in the concrete world of actual situations and have reference to particular behaviors" (p. 14). Using a case study approach, Adler examined the perspectives of four student teachers during their field experience. She concluded that social studies teaching is influenced by a variety of factors including beliefs about the social studies, ideas about what school is about, and past experiences. In a follow-up study, Goodman and Adler (1985) analyzed the perspectives of 16 elementary-level student teachers. They developed a typology for classifying the perspectives of the student teacher on social studies as a nonsubject, as human relations, as citizenship indoctrination, as school knowledge, as the integrative core of the elementary curriculum, and as education for action. The researchers also found that the institutional demands within the practicum sites strongly influenced teacher perspectives. Ross (1987) found that structural variables such as teacher education courses and field experiences appear to have little influence on teacher perspectives and belief systems in a preservice program.

Palonsky and Nelson (1980) studied the constraints on social studies teaching perceived by history/social studies education majors. Most of the students did all or part of their teaching assignments in classes in which chronological political history was taught. These preservice teachers noted serious limitations on the teaching and discussion of certain topics and issues in public high schools. Sex, religion, and race were mentioned most frequently as the topics that had the most limitations for discussion in the schools. Palonsky and Nelson conclude that "The effects of this atmosphere of informal censorship are pervasive and effective. . . . The norms of the school prevailed over the norms of the university" (p. 31).

Both the ideological orientations of preservice teachers and the constraints they see in the public school environment could help to explain the findings of Kickbusch (1987). He found that a sample of seven secondary social studies teachers exemplified a centrist position on citizenship education in their teaching and classroom discourse. The centrist position, which is dominant within social studies education, promotes citizenship transmission and is characterized by a focus on factual recitation and a study of dominant institutions. When teachers endorse critical theory, they treat students as "critical agents" and encourage them to view "existing institutions as representing choices from within a universe of choices" (Kickbusch, 1987, p. 176).

Professors in social studies education have devoted little attention to studying themselves. Only two studies were found (Shermis & Washburn, 1986; Tucker & Joyce, 1979). The study by Shermis and Washburn was limited to Indiana and consisted of a sample (N = 25) of NCSS College and University Faculty Assembly members. All the subjects were white males. Most were Christian, Anglo-Saxon, middle-aged, midwestern, and upwardly mobile. Only 12 percent indicated that the social sciences was one of their three areas of concentration in graduate school. Almost half (44 percent) of the respondents indicated that courses that involved the manipulation of quantitative data were some of the least desirable components of their graduate program. Most indicated that their students should learn the concepts and methods of the social science disciplines. Shermis and Washburn hypothesize that, because of the demographic, cultural, and social characteristics of the social studies professors they studied, these individuals probably are not likely to teach methods courses in a way that encourages students to raise questions about the status quo or that promotes social action.

Influence of Inservice Education on Teacher and Student Behavior and Attitudes

A number of experimental studies indicate that when teachers participate in academic inservice training programs, both their subject-matter knowledge and the achievement of their students increase. In a study conducted by Highsmith (1974), student achievement in economics was positively related to their teachers' participation in an inservice training program. Thornton and Vredeveld (1977) found that disseminating economic teaching materials to teachers positively influenced student achievement. They note that their approach, which emphasized materials and pedagogy, was as effective in influencing student achievement as were the more traditional inservice approaches that emphasize teaching economic content (Highsmith, 1974). Dawson (1978) found that the participation of teachers in two curriculum-development laboratories on economic knowledge had a positive effect on their knowledge and attitudes and on the economic knowledge of their students.

Walstad (1980) found that the achievement of students increased after they viewed "Trade-Offs," a television film for teaching economics to children, if their teachers had taken a 30-hour inservice course on basic economics. Walstad concludes that trained teachers probably used "Trade-Offs" more effectively than did untrained teachers. Tolbert (1981) found that the economic knowledge and attitudes of students of trained teachers did not differ significantly from those of students of untrained teachers in a study in which she used the "Trade-Offs" program. In a study by Pierce (1982), the teacher workshop participants neither experienced a gain in economic knowledge nor developed more positive attitudes toward economics. However, their students experienced a significant gain in economics knowledge and a positive attitude change toward economics. Teacher participation in an economics inservice program had a significant, though indirect, positive effect on both the economics achievement and opinions about economics of students in subsequent economics classes they taught (Schober, 1984).

Studies of the effects of inservice education in social science disciplines other than economics are sparse. Tetreault (1979) studied the effects of a 26-hour inservice training program on the inclusion of women in U.S. history and their students. She found that the attitudes in grades 8 and 11 toward males and females were significantly less stereotyped if their teachers had participated in the inservice program and used the classroom set of women's history materials. Hudgins (1980) found that a long-term inservice political science education program had no effect on the participants' knowledge of political science or selected instructional strategies. It did, however, positively influence their attitudes toward using those types of knowledge. In an inquiry-oriented 10-week training program for elementary teachers who taught social studies (Travis, 1980), teachers exhibited several changes in classroom interaction patterns, including the reduction of direct teacher emphasis. The inservice training also resulted in increased achievement for the students of the participants.

Summary

Individuals who enter social studies teacher education programs are similar to their peers in other programs. Professional associations recommend experiences for social studies teachers that far exceed the certification requirements of state departments of education. Few studies describe the content of social studies methods courses. The research that does exist indicates that these courses promote the socialization of teachers into the existing structure of schools rather than social change or institutional reform. The only study of methods professors found (Tucker & Joyce, 1979) indicates that their attitudes and perceptions are consistent with the socialization nature of methods courses.

Research on the effects of disciplinary knowledge on teaching and on student achievement is sparse and has inconsistent findings. However, it indicates that school practitioners view pedagogy and curriculum as more important concerns than subject-matter knowledge. Most secondary social studies teachers who are history teachers view their role the same way it is presented in methods courses: one of socializing students into the existing social and political structure. Social studies teachers also perceive ideological constraints in the public school that limit the attention they can devote to social issues, public controversy, and social change. Ideological consistency characterizes social studies methods professors, social studies teachers, and the public schools. Research indicates that inservice education can increase the subject-matter knowledge of teachers and the achievement of their students. Much of this research has been done in economics education.

COMPETING CONCEPTIONS OF QUALITY

It is the rare observer who contests the claim that the teacher education curriculum is "largely arbitrary, technical, fragmented, and without depth" (Lanier & Little, 1986, p. 554). Moreover, the teacher education faculty members are, as a group, often poor models of the instructional practices they preach. Faculty in academic departments avoid them, and graduates of their teacher-preparation programs seem largely dissatisfied (Borrowman, 1965; Cheney, 1987; Judge, 1982; Koerner, 1963; Lortie, 1975; Powell, 1976; Raths & Katz, 1982).

This deficit implies a vision of the good, which is the subject of this section. Indeed there are alternative visions, and three that are prominent today are described. Their respective priorities are preparing teachers to induct their students into a common body of cultural knowledge, equipping teachers with effective ways of teaching, and helping teachers examine critically what the activity of teaching actually is and might be (Parker, 1989). To help describe these conceptions, a few scholars will be highlighted as representatives of each, and the conceptions will be treated as though they were discrete categories with hard boundaries. Of course, this can be misleading, for there is ample diversity within these conceptions and much overlapping among them.

Cultural Induction

Since social studies per se were conceived in the first quarter of the twentieth century, there have been surges of conflict within and among groups of historians, social scientists, educators, and philosophers over control of the social studies curriculum. An early debate among historians over the usefulness of historical study pitted advocates of the mental disciplines and classics approaches against those who considered history a vehicle for social reform (e.g., Lynd, 1939; Robinson, 1912). Meanwhile, social scientists were forming associations of their own and arguing for separate courses in their various disciplines; John Dewey's ideas (1910, 1916) were generating enthusiasm for curricula relevant to contemporary conditions and needs; and experimental research was undermining the rationale for the mental disciplines approach (see Barr, Barth, & Shermis, 1977; Thorndike, 1913).

The flavor of those early debates was apparent again in the 1950s (e.g., Bestor, 1953) and is apparent again today. A group of scholars and politicians began arguing in the late 1980s that educators under the sway of both Dewey's philosophy and the social upheavals of the 1960s had lost history to the twin errors of instrumentalism and educational formalism. Diane Ravitch (1985, 1987) claims that social studies educators typically are more concerned with the instrumental value of knowledge for different groups of students than with providing a common core of historical studies for children. That concern, she charges, has resulted in today's wildly differentiated, utilitarian curriculum captured in ability grouping, tracking, expanding horizons, and the smorgasbord curriculum. The trend has been so popular, she argues, that those who have objected to it are "dismissed as reactionaries, out of touch with the times and with the findings of modern pedagogical science" (Ravitch, 1985, p. 128).

According to this conception of quality, another force helped to destroy the vision of inducting all children into a common body of historical knowledge. Instrumentalism divided the curriculum, but the new preoccupation with skills instruction conquered it. Hirsch (1987) calls this *educational formalism*. It "conceives of literacy as a set of techniques that can be developed by proper coaching and practice" and is "promulgated in our schools of education" (pp. 110, 112). The specific contents at hand matter little in this theory, Hirsch charges, so long as they are tied to students' prior knowledge. The skills emphasis, along with concomitant teaching methods meant to instruct children in their proper use, is buttressed by the popular argument that society is entering an information age in which knowing *how* to think is more important than having a particular network of information about which to think. Thus, priority on teaching the *processes* of learning has assumed a romantic, heroic dimension, as though it might rescue children from the parade of trivial facts foisted upon them by academics who insist that *what* you know is of primary importance. But the opposite is true, according to the inductionists. The distaste for memorization "is more pious than realistic" (Hirsch, 1987, p. 30); whatever the culture, children need to learn its fundamental information, without which even the best skills curriculum will leave then unable to thrive.

Citing low scores on an assessment of 17-year-old students' knowledge of history and literature, Cheney (1987) is explicit in affixing blame:

The culprit is "process"—the belief that we can teach our children *how* to think without troubling them to learn anything worth thinking about, the belief that we can teach them how to understand the world in which they live without conveying to them the events and ideas that have brought it into existence. (p. 5)

Once elevated to dogma in teacher-preparation programs, Cheney continues, the skills priority is not examined critically but inculcated as received truth into countless new teachers who come to believe that what matters is what a lesson enables students to *do*, not what it helps them to know. To the complaint that students do not know what the Reformation was or when the American Civil War took place, these now indoctrinated young educators can respond with confidence, "But they know how to look them up" (p. 22).

To summarize, at the core of this conception of what teacher preparation in social studies should be is the conviction that teachers mainly need to transmit to their students a common body of core academic knowledge; consequently, their preparation mainly needs to be concerned with studying the subjects they will teach. Time spent in pedagogy courses is considered, therefore, to be doubly wasteful: not only is it time spent away from strengthening their substantive knowledge base, but also it is time spent immersed in the mistaken ideas that caused the current mess in the first place.

Pedagogy

A competing vision of what teacher education in social studies should be centers on the pedagogic knowledge that will best bring about increased learning in social studies lessons. The pedagogues' emphasis generally is on instruction rather than curriculum, on pedagogy rather than the contents of instruction. The two are, however, related in means-to-end fashion: Because so many students fail to learn well so much of the curriculum at hand, teachers must use instructional practices that might increase student learning of that curriculum. The point is that content that is "taught" is often not "caught," and treating low scores on social studies assessments simply as a *curriculum* deficit misses this point altogether. Admittedly, students who do not know about the Reformation or the American Civil War might not have had lessons on these topics, but students who *have* had such lessons did not necessarily learn them.

Goodlad's analysis (1983, 1984) of a national sample of schools and classrooms displayed the logic of this conception quite well. Like Ravitch, Cheney, and Hirsch, he is alarmed that so little attention has been afforded the K–12 curriculum in recent decades. Among the consequences he documented is the absence of a common, comprehensive curriculum for students in the United States; that is, curricula are distributed undemocratically among the nation's schools. Apparently, the school one attends largely determines the knowledge to which one has access. At one senior high school, a student might take more social studies courses than vocational courses; attend another and the reverse could be the case.

However, Goodlad's analysis did not end there. He saw not one but two sides to the problem of access to knowledge. Sensitive to curricular problems across schools, he also concentrated on instructional problems within them. He asked, "Does each individual school provide those enrolled with a reasonably equal opportunity to acquire these learnings?" (1983, p. 787). With this question he took up the pedagogues' "taught but not caught" issue: "Covered" material is not necessarily learned, greater learning is associated with particular teaching practices, the occurrence of these teaching practices is not common in schools and generally declines after the primary grades, and their distribution within a school is to the disadvantage of children who are poor (Goodlad, 1984; see also Bloom, 1984; Joyce, Showers, & Rolheiser-Bennett, 1987; Oakes, 1985; Rosenshine & Stevens, 1986; Shaver et al., 1979). The priority within this conception of quality is the identification and propagation of those instructional practices likely to increase student learning, both within and across schools.

Two approaches to this priority can be identified among pedagogues. One includes myriad instructional practices thought likely, for one reason or another, to improve social studies education. Examples are reflective inquiry (Hunt & Metcalf, 1955; Newmann & Oliver, 1970), decision making (Engle, 1960), concept formation (Taba, 1966), questioning (Hunkins, 1972), discussion of moral dilemmas (Kohlberg, 1973), cooperative learning (Slavin, 1986), critical thinking (Beyer, 1985), and the several models of instruction described by Joyce and Weil (1986). These practices are not necessarily used by experienced teachers but, according to their proponents, *ought* to be. Teacher educators whose work falls into this category, many of them attuned to Dewey's progressivism and convinced that education is a moral undertaking, point beyond the school to societal problems and assert the potential of these practices to advance their solution.

In the second category are instructional practices advocated

because they are found in the repertoire of effective teachers. A diverse array of work is found here, too, from detailed accounts of effective teaching behaviors (Bloom, 1984) and instructional decision making (Clark & Peterson, 1986) to more encompassing attempts to characterize the "expert pedagogue" (Berliner, 1986; Shulman, 1987). Also in this category is Hunter's (1979) teacher decision-making model. The intent of Shulman's (1987) ambitious studies is to record and organize the actions and the reasoning, both pedagogic *and academic*, of exceptional teachers. From these data, he hopes to derive standards of practice in various subject areas to which teacher education and assessment can be directed. Shulman argues that this work is promising because it should identify teaching practices that are far richer than the effective behaviors found in the earlier work. Those behaviors (e.g., wait time, use of feedback and correction) were typically stripped away from the curricular material at hand, the ecology of the classroom, and teachers' reasoning about both. Agreeing, Rosenshine (1986) has since conceded, in a study of a social studies lesson on the *Federalist Papers*, that the effective behaviors identified in the process–product studies were most appropriate to instruction on *skills*, as contrasted with *understandings* of complex ideas.

To summarize, despite differences among them, these pedagogues are alike in their intent to prepare teachers who can and will engage in particular instructional practices. It is this intent that distinguishes them clearly from cultural inductionists. Although cultural inductionists lament the inadequacy of the social studies curriculum and the time squandered by preservice teachers in methods courses, the pedagogues lament the poor record of methods courses to propagate desirable ways of teaching.

Critical Rationality

A third vision argues that the dominant way of thinking in which teacher education is immersed was drawn not from the pedagogy of John Dewey, as cultural inductionists charge, but from the social-intellectual climate of American society at the turn of the twentieth century, from the philosophy of corporate management (Kliebard, 1975). Made explicit by Cubberley in 1916, the premise of the corporate management model of public schooling is as follows:

The specifications for manufacturing come from the demands of twentieth-century civilization, and it is the business of the school to build its pupils according to the specifications laid down. This demands good tools, specialized machinery, continuous measurement of production to see if it is according to specifications, the elimination of waste in manufacture, and a large variety in the output. (Cubberley, in Kliebard, 1975, p. 52).

Proponents of the third conception of quality in teacher education, here called *critical rationality*, would move educational thought from this production-driven, technical rationality to a critical rationality. According to this conception, both inductionists and pedagogues operate within a technocratic rationality and, therefore, fall short of teacher education's most important task: to free teachers from an uncritical acceptance of the present so that they might create classrooms that like-wise free their students.

The vision is emancipatory teacher education. The priority it places on critical inquiry stems from the need to scrutinize the existing educational regime, its conditions and assumptions. Without such scrutiny, it is argued, preservice and inservice teachers simply accept and adapt to the status quo, even though it does not emancipate but deadens and confines. Schooling, both precollegiate and collegiate, far from being the vehicle for cultural literacy envisioned in the first conception or the instrument of social reform hoped for by progressive pedagogues, is actually "more oriented to producing failure than to developing creative, critical minds that could be the basis for a more humanistic, democratic society" (Carnoy & Levin, 1985, p. 17). Teachers in preparation programs should be encouraged to contemplate this contradiction between the promise and reality of American schools, to inquire into its root causes, and to envision alternatives.

Summarized in two issues of *Social Education* (Nelson, 1985; Popkewitz, 1987a), this challenge to mainstream teacher education faults technocratic rationality on several closely related points. Most important, that rationality fails to acknowledge that teacher education is a political process, and that there are pervasive interests in teacher education other than producing effective teachers (Cherryholmes, 1987; Giroux, 1980; Giroux & McLaren, 1986; Popkewitz, 1987b). Teacher education is not the autonomous social agency it is thought to be by inductionists and pedagogues. Rather, the critics argue, it is embedded in the broader society, its institutions, power relations, and conflicts.

Yet teacher education manages to appear neutral. It accomplishes this by concentrating on methods and knowledge. Viewed from the standpoint of technical rationality, methods and knowledge *are* neutral phenomena. In fact, according to critical rationality, both are deeply invested. The "methodology madness" (Giroux, 1980, p. 9) rampant today, although defended as practical and sensible by more than a few pedagogues (e.g., Smith, 1980), is a conserving force. By narrow attention to the question of what methods are most effective, focus is fixed on the means, or technology, of teaching and kept away from questions that could change the status quo, questions like: What is the purpose of social studies education? Whose interests are served by it? Whose are not?

Knowledge, too, can be a conserving force. In analyses of reports published in 1986 on teacher education by the Holmes Group (1986) and the Carnegie Forum (1986), Cornbleth (1987) and Whitson (1988) found both to be pervaded by technical rationality. Within this rationality, knowledge is reified as certain, neutral, and separate from its moorings in history and practice. That it is not "discovered," like wealth by a lone miner panning for gold, but constructed, is not understood; nor is it noted that its construction is social and manifests the interests of dominant groups living in particular historical settings. Far from making new teachers competent, this epistemology, the argument goes, disables them.

How should teacher preparation in social studies be constructed according to this conception of quality? Mainly, it should seek the development of critical rationality in teachers,

"characterized by wide-ranging skepticism as well as grounding in logical argument and empirical data. It entails probing beneath surface appearance and questioning claims, evidence, and proposals" (Cornbleth, 1987, p. 516). Moreover, it entails linking the study of social foundations of education with the study of pedagogy, so that means can be aligned with ends, thus raising the question, What type of schooling—and what type of teaching practices—for what type of society? (see Wood, 1987). Although Dewey's (1910) reflective-inquiry process is likely to figure prominently in such a methods course, these critics would rescue it from the technical, step-by-step treatment pedagogues often afford it in methods texts. It would not merely be defined by expository techniques but also practiced and scrutinized as part of the fabric of the methods classroom and field experiences. In this way, teachers might master the principles and practices of a truly critical reflective inquiry, and it might then become the "lens through which preservice teachers conceptualize their practice" (Ross & Hannay, 1986, p. 12; see also Adler & Goodman, 1986; Cherryholmes, 1980; Goodman, 1986a; Parker, 1987; Zeichner & Teitelbaum, 1982). To summarize, teacher education ought to liberate preservice and inservice teachers from the unreflective, buzzword world of "competence," "excellence," "theory-versus-practice," and "effective teaching." It ought to introduce them to critical reflection, where skepticism is welcome, contrary conceptions are brought to the surface for comparison, and democratic interests in education are put first.

Summary

This section characterized alternative conceptions of quality in social studies teacher education. One would strengthen teachers' knowledge of the subject matter they are expected to teach; another would strengthen their knowledge of instructional practices that might help children, all children, learn that subject matter; a third would strengthen their ability and commitment to reflect critically on, rather than acquiesce to, the given world.

CONCLUSIONS AND RECOMMENDATIONS

The first part of this chapter raised the central questions of the social studies teacher education field, and the second reviewed selected studies that bear on the questions raised. The third described three conceptions of quality in the field. It is reasonable to conclude that there is a paucity of research conducted on this field and that there are conflicting visions of what constitutes good social studies teacher education. The research reviewed in this chapter indicates that the vision of the pedagogue is the dominant one in social studies education and that this vision is amply infused with notions of cultural induction. The content analysis of social studies methods textbooks conducted for this chapter, the study by Tucker and Joyce (1979), and the informative study by Goodman (1986a) indicate that social studies methods courses and methods professors are concerned primarily with helping teacher education students acquire the knowledge, skills, values, and perspectives they need to survive in the schools as they are currently structured and to socialize students so they will fit well into society's dominant social, cultural, and political systems.

The critical vision of social studies teacher education is largely absent from methods courses and the student-teaching component of social studies teacher education. Social studies teacher education students are rarely encouraged to reflect upon the social structure of society or to participate in school reform. They also perceive serious constraints on the discussion of social issues in their school settings when they are student teaching (Palonsky & Nelson, 1980). Consistent with this socializing conception of the social studies, teachers tend to view the social studies primarily as history, geography, and government and not as an interdisciplinary and decision-making subject that develops critical and reflective citizens of the commonwealth (Wiley, 1977). Shermis and Washburn (1986) questioned whether the social studies methods professors in their study could help students raise critical questions about a society in which they had benefited, experienced social mobility, and were deeply entrenched.

The Dilemma

There is a rich tradition of scholarship and social studies teaching materials designed to teach students to think critically about social issues. The first edition of Hunt and Metcalf's (1955) highly regarded methods text, which considered ways to promote reflective thought about social issues, was published a decade prior to the civil rights movement. Significant publications by Oliver and Shaver (1966) and Newmann and Oliver (1970) also considered ways in which teachers could teach students to engage in reflective and critical inquiry about the nature of society and schools. Newmann's book (1975) illustrated ways in which teachers could involve students in meaningful social action and in thinking reflectively about society. Yet this rich tradition related to social criticism and social action, as well as the newer radical criticism (e.g., Cherryholmes, 1980), apparently has had little influence on the professional component of social studies teacher education or on the way the social studies are taught in the schools.

Social studies teacher educators, even when they are committed to teaching reflective thinking and a critical view of U.S. society, face a dilemma. On the one hand, many appear to want reform and change in the schools; on the other hand, they want their students to experience success in the schools as they are currently structured. The research reviewed in this chapter suggests that methods professors usually opt to make their courses "relevant" to the schools at the expense of helping teacher education students become critical and reflective about school practices. The result is that most often social studies teachers education programs reinforce the status quo in both the society and the schools rather than becoming vehicles for social transformation.

The fact that the social studies often reinforce the dominant beliefs, myths, and explanations for existing social and class stratification and often do not deal with the survival issues and problems that many students experience in their daily lives (Hunt & Metcalf, 1968) might be why teachers state that a major problem in teaching the social studies is "lack of student interest" (Eslinger & Superka, 1982). The ethnic and class textures of the schools are changing rapidly as the nation experiences a rush of immigrants from distant lands, a high birthrate among some indigenous ethnic groups, and virtually zero population growth among the white population. The result is that, by the turn of the century, one out of three students in the nation's public schools will be an ethnic minority; many students in the nation's schools will also be poor. The number of ethnic minority teachers will have dropped from about 12 percent of the nation's teachers (in 1980) to about 5 percent in 2000. In many school districts, ethnic and language minorities will be distinct majorities, as they are today in most of the nation's large cities such as Seattle, Los Angeles, New York City, Chicago, and Washington, DC.

The changing cultural and class textures of the nation's public schools pose a special challenge to social studies teacher educators. Students who are victimized by class stratification and powerlessness need a social studies curriculum that empowers them to participate in reflective social action with the intent to make the nation's ideals more consistent with its realities (Banks, 1987). To meet this challenge, the professional component of social studies teacher education, including methods courses, must help preservice and inservice teachers to think critically about schools and society in addition to helping them acquire effective techniques for surviving and prospering in schools as they are now.

Research Possibilities

Social studies educators tend to be housed in curriculum and instruction departments or a similar division within a school or college of education. Coming largely from public school teaching careers, they usually have heavy teaching loads, low status within the college or school, and disproportionate responsibility for the teacher education program. Social studies is also a low priority within most funding agencies.

Because of the heavy responsibility they have for teacher education and teaching and because of their own orientation toward the practical, professors in social studies education are more likely to be involved in materials development such as textbook series and methods books than they are to be engaged in research that seems to have less direct application to practice. For these reasons, it is unlikely that the status of research in social studies education is likely to change unless social studies education professors can engage in research while they teach methods courses, observe student teachers, or prepare curricular materials.

They can engage in significant research. For example, using case study designs, social studies professors can observe how preservice teachers construct and use academic and pedagogic knowledge to plan lessons and units. In light of the persistent problem of depth versus breadth of content coverage in social studies (Newmann, 1988), it will be particularly helpful to understand how these teachers develop criteria for the selection and organization of content and how they cope with the ubiquitous pressure to cover yet more material. In light of another problem, the persistence of recitation (Goodlad, 1984), it would be helpful to understand how these teachers articulate those content decisions with instructional design decisions. What are their conceptions of more and less thoughtful lessons? How do they articulate higher order thinking with

decisions to cover more and less material? And, in light of the persistent separation of methods and social foundations courses, it would be helpful to understand how preservice teachers link planning and teaching to multicultural and social-class realities. It would also help to build an empirical base that compares teacher-preparation interventions in all three areas.

References

Adler, S. (1984). A field study of selected student teacher perspectives toward social studies. *Theory and Research in Social Education, 12,* 13–30.

Adler, S., & Goodman, J. (1986). Critical theory as a foundation for methods courses. *Journal of Teacher Education, 37*(4), 2–8.

Armento, B. J. (1986). Research on teaching social studies. In M. C. Wittrock (Ed.), *Handbook of research on teaching* (3rd ed., pp. 942–951). New York: Macmillan.

Banks, J. A. (1987). The social studies, ethnic diversity, and social change. *Elementary School Journal, 87*(5), 531–543.

Barr, R. D., Barth, J. L., & Shermis, S. S. (1977). *Defining the social studies* (Bulletin No. 51). Arlington, VA: National Council for the Social Studies.

Berliner, D. (1986). In pursuit of the expert pedagogue. *Educational Researcher, 15,* 5–13.

Berryman, C., & Schneider, D. O. (1984). Social studies teacher education: More academic content and less teaching methodology? *Social Education, 84,* 507–509.

Bestor, A. (1953). *Educational wastelands: The retreat from learning in our public schools.* Urbana, IL: University of Illinois Press.

Beyer, B. K. (1985). Critical thinking: What is it? *Social Education, 49,* 270–276.

Bloom, B. S. (1984). The two-sigma problem: The search for methods of group instruction as effective as one-to-one tutoring. *Educational Researcher, 13,* 4–16.

Borrowman, M. (Ed.). (1965). *Teacher education in America: A documentary history.* New York: Teachers College Press.

Bruner, J. S. (1960). *The process of education.* New York: Vintage.

Carnegie Forum on Education and the Economy, Task Force on Teaching as a Profession. (1986). *A nation prepared: Teachers for the 21st century.* Washington, DC: Author.

Carnoy, M., & Levin, H. M. (1985). *Schooling and work in the democratic state.* Stanford, CA: Stanford University Press.

Cheney, L. V. (1987). *The American memory: A report on the humanities in the nation's public schools.* Washington, DC: National Endowment for the Humanities.

Cherryholmes, C. H. (1980). Social knowledge and citizenship education: Two views of truth and criticism. *Curriculum Inquiry, 10,* 115–142.

Cherryholmes, C. H. (1987). The political project of tomorrow's teachers. *Social Education, 51,* 501–505.

Clark, C. M., & Peterson, P. L. (1986). Teachers' thought processes. In M. C. Wittrock (Ed.), *Handbook of research on teaching* (3rd ed., pp. 255–296). New York: Macmillan.

Cogan, J. J., & Miner, L. A. (1977). Social studies supervisors' ratings of the NCSS curriculum guidelines. *Theory and Research in Social Education, 5,* 1–9.

Cornbleth, C. (1987). Knowledge in curriculum and teacher education. *Social Education, 51,* 513–516.

Cuban, L. (1984). *How teachers taught: Consistency and change in American classrooms: 1890–1980.* New York: Longman.

Dawson, R. W. (1978). *A study of the impact of an economic curriculum development laboratory on junior high school social studies teachers and students.* Unpublished doctoral dissertation, Kansas State University of Agriculture and Applied Science, Manhattan.

Dewey, J. (1910). *How we think.* Boston: D. C. Heath.

Dewey, J. (1916). *Democracy and education.* New York: Macmillan.

Engle, S. H. (1960). Decision making: The heart of social studies instruction. *Social Education, 24,* 301–304, 306.

Eslinger, M. V., & Superka, D. P. (1982). Social studies teachers. In Project SPAN Staff and Consultants (Eds.), *The current state of social studies: A report of Project SPAN.* Boulder, CO: Social Science Education Consortium.

Gifford, B. M. (1984). *The good school of education: Linking knowledge, teaching and learning.* Berkeley, CA: University of California, School of Education.

Giroux, H. (1980). Teacher education and the ideology of social control. *Journal of Education, 162,* 5–27.

Giroux, H. A., & McLaren, P. (1986). Teacher education and the politics of engagement: The case for democratic schooling. *Harvard Educational Review, 56*(3), 213–238.

Goodlad, J. I. (1983). Access to knowledge. *Teachers College Record, 84*(4), 787–800.

Goodlad, J. I. (1984). *A place called school: Prospects for the future.* New York: McGraw-Hill.

Goodman, J. (1986a). Making early field experience meaningful: A critical approach. *Journal of Education for Teaching, 12,* 109–125.

Goodman, J. (1986b). University education courses and the professional preparation of teachers. *Teaching and Teacher Education, 2,* 341–353.

Goodman, J., & Adler, S. (1985). Becoming an elementary social studies teacher: A study of perspectives. *Theory and Research in Social Education, 13,* 1–20.

Grannis, J. C. (1970). The social studies teacher and research on teacher education. *Social Education, 34,* 291–301.

Grossman, P. L., & Richert, A. E. (1988). Unacknowledged knowledge growth: A re-examination of the effects of teacher education. *Teaching and Teacher Education, 4,* 53–62.

Gudmundsdottir, S. (1987, April). *Pedagogical content knowledge: Teachers' ways of knowing.* Paper presented at the annual meeting of the American Educational Research Association, Washington, DC.

Gudmundsdottir, S., Carey, N., & Wilson, S. (1985). *Role of prior subject matter knowledge in learning to teach social studies.* Paper presented at the annual meeting of the American Educational Research Association, Chicago.

Highsmith, R. (1974). A study to measure the impact of in-service institutes on the students of teachers who have participated. *Journal of Economic Education, 5,* 77–81.

Hirsch, E. D., Jr., (1987). *Cultural literacy: What every American needs to know*. Boston: Houghton Mifflin.

Holmes Group. (1986). *Tomorrow's teachers*. East Lansing, MI: Author.

Howey, K., Yarger, S., & Joyce, B. (1978). Reflections on preservice preparation: Impressions from the national survey. *Journal of Teacher Education, 29*(1), 38–40.

Hudgins, W. B. (1980). *An assessment of effects of a long-term inservice political education program on teacher knowledge and attitudes*. Unpublished doctoral dissertation, University of Georgia, Athens.

Hunkins, F. P. (1972). *Questioning strategies and techniques*. Boston: Allyn & Bacon.

Hunkins, F. P., Ehman, L. H., Hahn, C. L., Martorella, P. H., & Tucker, J. L. (1977). *Review of research in social studies education*. Washington, DC: National Council for the Social Studies.

Hunt, M., & Metcalf, L. (1955). *Teaching high school social studies*. New York: Harper & Row.

Hunt, M. P., & Metcalf, L. E. (1968). *Teaching high school social studies* (2nd ed.). New York: Harper & Row.

Hunter, M. (1979). Teaching as decision making. *Educational Leadership, 37*(1), 62–67.

Joyce, B., Showers, B., & Rolheiser-Bennett, C. (1987). Staff development and student learning: A synthesis of research on models of teaching. *Educational Leadership, 45*(2), 11–23.

Joyce, B. & Weil, M. (1986). *Models of teaching*. Englewood Cliffs, NJ: Prentice-Hall.

Judge, H. (1982). *American graduate schools of education: A view from abroad*. New York: Ford Foundation.

Kerr, D. H. (1983). Teaching competence and teacher education in the United States. In L. S. Shulman & G. Sykes (Eds.), *Handbook of teaching and policy* (pp. 126–149). New York: Longman.

Kickbusch, K. W. (1987). Civic education and preservice educators: Extending the boundaries of discourse. *Theory and Research in Social Education, 15*, 173–188.

Kliebard, H. M. (1975). Bureaucracy and curriculum theory. In W. Pinar (Ed.), *Curriculum theorizing: The reconceptualists* (pp. 51–69). Berkeley, CA: McCutchan.

Koerner, J. (1963). *The miseducation of American teachers*. Boston: Houghton Mifflin.

Kohlberg, L. (1973). Moral development and the new social studies. *Social Education, 37*, 369–375.

Lanier, J. E., & Little, J. W. (1986). Research on teacher education. In M. C. Wittrock (Ed.), *Handbook of research on teaching* (3rd ed., pp. 527–569). New York: Macmillan.

Lortie, D. (1975). *Schoolteacher: A sociological study*. Chicago: University of Chicago Press.

Lynd, R. S. (1939). *Knowledge for what: The place of social science in American culture*. Princeton, NJ: Princeton University Press.

McGraw, L. (1987). *The anthropologist in the classroom: Chris: A case study of a beginning social studies teacher*. Unpublished manuscript, Stanford University, Stanford, CA.

McMann, F. C., Jr., & McMann, C. J. (1984). Defining characteristics of social studies: A response of Ochoa's challenge. *The Social Studies, 75*, 36–41.

Morrissett, I. (Ed.). (1967). *Concepts and structure in the new social science curricula*. New York: Henry Holt.

National Council for the Social Studies. (1988). Standards for the preparation of social studies teachers. *Social Education, 52*, 10–12.

Nelson, J. L. (Ed.). (1985). The new criticism and social education. *Social Education, 49*, 368–405.

Newmann, F. M. (1975). *Education for citizen action*. Berkeley, CA: McCutchan.

Newmann, F. M. (1988). Can depth replace coverage in the high school curriculum? *Phi Delta Kappan, 69*, 345–348.

Newmann, F. M., & Oliver, D. W. (1970). *Clarifying public controversy: An approach to teaching social studies*. Boston: Little, Brown.

Oakes, J. (1985). *Keeping track: How schools structure inequality*. New Haven, CT: Yale University Press.

Ochoa, A. S. (1981). The education of social studies teachers. In H. D. Mehlinger & O. L. Davis (Eds.), *The social studies*, (80th yearbook of the National Society for the Study of Education, Part II, pp. 151–169). Chicago: University of Chicago Press.

Oliver, D. W., & Shaver, J. P. (1966). *Teaching public issues in the high school*. Boston: Houghton Mifflin.

Palonsky, S., & Nelson, J. (1980). Political restraint in the socialization of student teachers. *Theory and Research in Social Education, 7*, 19–34.

Parker, W. C. (1987). Teachers' mediation in social studies. *Theory and Research in Social Education, 15*, 1–22.

Parker, W. C. (1989). New directions in teacher education: Which direction? In J. A. Braun, Jr. (Ed.), *The reform of teacher education: Issues and new directions* (pp. 161–183). New York: Garland.

Pierce, R. H. (1982). *An assessment of an inservice workshop's effectiveness in preparing teachers to use an integrated instructional approach for economic education*. Unpublished doctoral dissertation, Ohio State University, Columbus.

Popkewitz, T. S. (Ed.). (1987a). Improving teaching and teacher education. *Social Education, 51*, 493–521.

Popkewitz, T. S. (1987b). Organization and power: Teacher education reforms. *Social Education, 51*, 496–500.

Powell, A. G. (1976). University schools of education in the twentieth century. *Peabody Journal of Education, 54*(1), 3–20.

Project SPAN Staff and Consultants. (Eds.). (1982). *The current state of social studies: A report of Project SPAN*. Boulder, CO: Social Science Education Consortium.

Raths, J., & Katz, L. (1982). The best of intentions for the education of teachers. *Journal of Education for Teaching, 8*, 275–283.

Ravitch, D. (1985). From history to social studies: Dilemmas and problems. In D. Ravitch (Ed.), *The schools we deserve* (pp. 112–132). New York: Basic Books.

Ravitch, D. (1987). Tot sociology. *American Scholar, 56*, 343–354.

Robinson, J. H. (1912). *The new history and the social studies*. New York: Macmillan.

Rosenshine, B. (1986). Unsolved issues in teaching content: A critique of a lesson on Federalist Paper No. 10. *Teaching and Teacher Education, 2*, 301–308.

Rosenshine, B., & Stevens, R. (1986). Teaching functions. In M. C. Wittrock (Ed.), *Handbook of research on teaching* (3rd ed., pp. 376–391). New York: Macmillan.

Ross, E. W. (1987). Teacher perspective development. A study of preservice social studies teachers. *Theory and Research in Social Education, 15*, 225–243.

Ross, E. W., & Hannay, L. M. (1986). Towards a critical theory of reflective inquiry. *Journal of Teacher Education, 37*(4), 9–15.

Russell, T. E., & Morrow, J. E. (1986). Reform in teacher education: Perceptions of secondary social studies teachers. *Theory and Research in Social Education, 14*, 325–330.

Schober, H. M. (1984). An anlysis of the impact of teacher training in economics. *Theory and Research in Social Education. 12*, 1–12.

Schwab, J. J. (1968). The concept of the structure of a discipline. In L. J. Herbert & W. Murphy (Eds.), *Structure in the social studies*. Washington, DC: National Council for the Social Studies.

Shaver, J. P., Davis, O. L., Jr., & Helburn S. W. (1979). The status of social studies education: Impressions from three NSF studies. *Social Education, 43,* 150–153.

Shermis, S. S., & Washburn, P. C. (1986). Social studies educators and their beliefs: Preliminary data from Indiana colleges. *Theory and Research in Social Education, 14,* 331–339.

Shulman, L. (1986). Paradigms and research programs in the study of teaching: A contemporary perspective. In M. C. Wittrock (Ed.), *Handbook of research on teaching* (3rd ed., pp. 3–36). New York: Macmillan.

Shulman, L. S. (1987). Knowledge and teaching: Foundations of the new reform. *Harvard Educational Review, 57,*(1), 1–22.

Slavin, R. E. (1986). *Using student team learning* (3rd ed). Baltimore: Johns Hopkins Team Learning Project.

Smith, B. O. (1980). *A design for a school of pedagogy.* Washington, DC: U.S. Government Printing Office.

Sowders, R. W. (1982). *The importance of civics/government objectives as viewed by secondary teachers, social studies curriculum supervisors, and leaders in the field.* Unpublished doctoral dissertation, University of Maryland, College Park.

Stahl, R. J., & Matiya, J. C. (1981). Teaching psychology in the high school: Does area of certification translate into different types of teachers and courses? *Theory and Research in Social Education, 9,* 55–86.

Stake, R. E., & Easley, J. A. (1978). *Case studies in science education.* Urbana, IL: University of Illinois, Center for Instructional Research and Curriculum Evaluation.

Stanley, W. B. (Ed.). (1985). *Review of research in social studies education, 1976–1983* (Bulletin 75). Washington, DC: National Council for the Social Studies.

Taba, H. (1966). *Teaching strategies and cognitive functioning in elementary school children.* Unpublished paper, Cooperative Research Bureau Project No. 2404, San Francisco State College.

Tetreault, M. K. T. (1979). *The inclusion of women in the United States history curriculum and adolescent attitudes toward sex-appropriate behavior.* Unpublished dissertation, Boston University, School of Education.

Thorndike, E. L. (1913). *Educational Psychology.* New York: Columbia University, Teachers College.

Thornton, D. L., & Vredeveld, G. M. (1977). Inservice education and its effects on secondary students: A new approach. *Journal of Economic Education, 8,* 93–99.

Tolbert, P. A. (1981). *Some effects of an economic inservice program on student learning and attitudes.* Unpublished doctoral dissertation, University of Georgia, Athens.

Travis, W. D. (1980). *The selected effects of an inservice training teaching skills program on the teaching performance of elementary school social studies teachers.* Unpublished doctoral dissertation, Boston University.

Tucker, J. L. (1977). Research on social studies teaching and teacher education. In F. P. Hunkins, C. L. Hahn, P. H. Martorella, & J. L. Tucker (Eds.), *Review of research in social studies education: 1970–1975* (pp. 97–135). Washington, DC: National Council for the Social Studies.

Tucker, J. L., & Joyce, W. W. (1979). *Social studies teacher education: Practices, problems, and recommendations.* Boulder, CO: Social Science Education Consortium.

Walstad, W. B. (1980). The impact of "trade-offs" and teacher training on economic understanding and attitudes. *Journal of Economic Education, 11,* 41–48.

Weible, T., & Dumas, W. (1986). Elementary teacher education and certification. In V. A. Atwood (Ed.), *Elementary school social studies: Research as a guide to practice—Bulletin No. 79* (pp. 137–145). Washington, DC: National Council for the Social Studies.

Weiss, I. R. (1978). *National survey of science, mathematics, and social studies education.* Washington, DC: National Science Foundation.

Whitson, J. A. (1988). The politics of "nonpolitical" curriculum: Heteroglossia and the discourse of "choice" and "effectiveness." In W. Pinar (Ed.), *Contemporary curriculum discourse* (pp. 279–330). Scottsdale, AZ: Gorsuch Scarisbrick.

Wiley, K. B. (1977). *The status of precollege science. mathematics, and social studies education: 1955–1975* (Vol. 3). Washington, DC: National Science Foundation.

Wilson, S. M., & Wineburg, S. S. (n.d.). *Peering at history from different lenses: The role of disciplinary perspectives in the teaching of American history.* Unpublished paper, Stanford University, Stanford, CA.

Wineburg, S. S. (1987). *From fieldwork to classwork: Cathy: A case study of a beginning social studies teacher.* Unpublished paper, Stanford University, Stanford, CA.

Wood, G. H. (1987). Social foundations: Introduction to democracy and education. *Teaching Education, 1,* 64–67.

Zeichner, K., & Teitelbaum, K. (1982). Personalized and inquiry-oriented teacher education: An analysis of two approaches to the development of curriculum for field-based experiences. *Journal of Education for Teaching, 8,* 98–117.

·38·

READING TEACHER EDUCATION

Donna E. Alvermann
UNIVERSITY OF GEORGIA

This chapter provides a framework for organizing and relating the research, theories, and practices in the field of reading teacher education. The first section describes three contrasting conceptions of reading teacher education and includes studies representative of the research within each domain. Subsequent sections describe the field's knowledge base, the distinctions drawn between experts and novices, and the extent of the research base for long-term professional development programs. A concluding section identifies the major issues and research needs in reading teacher education. Although reading teacher education is embedded within the larger domain of literacy teacher education, this chapter focuses solely on the preparation of elementary and secondary classroom teachers of reading, reading specialists, and allied professionals.

CONTRASTING CONCEPTIONS OF READING TEACHER EDUCATION

Historically, the preparation of teachers of reading has been influenced by three contrasting conceptions of teacher education: the traditional-craft approach, the competency-based approach, and the inquiry-oriented approach (Zeichner, 1983). In many ways these are false distinctions, for traces of each can be found in all three approaches. By focusing attention on three separate conceptions, however, it is possible to highlight their fundamental differences, especially as those differences relate to the research, theories, and practices of reading teacher education.

Traditional-Craft Reading Teacher Education

From its inception, preservice reading teacher education has been greatly influenced by the apprenticeship model of teaching, or by what Zeichner (1983) calls the traditional-craft concept of teacher education. A major assumption of this model is that novices develop an awareness of (and later emulate) what constitutes good reading practices by observing master teachers. At the inservice level of reading teacher education, the focus of the traditional-craft model shifts from mentoring novices to helping experienced teachers refine their craft. Here, the apprenticeship is not one of simply observing and emulating the master teacher, but rather one of adapting new paradigms for teaching reading or refining old ones.

The importance of the student teaching experience to preservice reading teacher education is well documented in each of three major studies that began with *The Torch Lighters* (Austin & Morrison, 1961). Sponsored by a grant from the Carnegie Corporation of New York and by the Graduate School of Education at Harvard University, Austin and Morrison surveyed the preservice education practices of 371 four-year institutions of higher learning and made 74 site visits. Their report drew attention to the central role of student teaching in the preparation of teachers of reading:

That the practice teaching experience [a footnote equated the term *practice teaching* with *student teaching* and *apprenticeship teaching*] is considered the heart of the teacher education program and the main integrating force in its operation is seen in testimony by college staff, cooperating teachers, and students. All agreed with the maxim, "Prac-

The author wishes to express her appreciation to the following persons who provided thoughtful reviews of an earlier draft of this chapter: Mark Conley (Michigan State University), Rosary Lalik (Virginia Polytechnical Institute), Donna Ogle (National College of Education), and Linda Vavrus (Stanford University).

tice is the best of all instructors." Such comments as "The practice teaching program is the most influencing experience prospective teachers are likely to have in college," and, "There is no course work equal in importance to that of practice teaching," are typical of the enthusiastic remarks made by the respondents. (p.74)

Despite the importance attributed to student teaching, Malone (1984) found only one experimental study that dealt directly with preservice field experiences in reading and that met the qualifications for inclusion in his meta-analysis of field experiences in teacher education.

The second Harvard-Carnegie reading study, *The First R*, (Austin & Morrison, 1963), was an attempt to investigate, among other questions, what beginning and experienced teachers valued in their teacher-preparation program. A questionnaire survey was conducted of all school systems located in U.S. cities and counties with a population of more than 10,000. In addition, interviews and elementary classroom observations were conducted in a representative sample of the surveyed school systems. As in the first study, the importance of student teaching was evident. Respondents labeled their student teaching experiences "real", "dynamic", or "meaningful" (p. 167). As a result of this positive finding, plus the finding that many school systems did not utilize the services of master teachers outside their own classrooms, Austin and Morrison recommended "that [master] teachers be relieved of classroom responsibilities for prescribed periods of time so that they can assist beginning and inexperienced teachers through demonstration lessons . . . conferences, and observations" (p. 238).

Of the 22 original recommendations made by Austin and Morrison (1961), none was considered more essential than the one specifying "that the colleges recruit, train, and certify cooperating teachers [who would] after training and college certification, serve in the capacity of associates to the college" (p. 152). Sixteen years later Morrison and Austin (1977) published *The Torch Lighters Revisited*, a follow-up to their original study. On the basis of data gathered from additional interviews and a 73.2 percent return rate of completed questionnaires that had been mailed to 220 institutions in 40 states (including the 74 original site visits), the authors concluded that a majority of their recommendations were being implemented. The one notable exception was in the recruitment, training, and certification of cooperating teachers, a factor deemed crucial to the success of the traditional-craft concept of reading teacher education.

There is some evidence that attention is currently being paid to the recruitment and training of cooperating teachers. For example, the Akron Intern Program, developed by JoAnne Vacca of Kent State University (Ambrose & Janes, 1987), began with a semester-long training institute for 50 master teachers in 1983. Its purpose was to prepare teachers to supervise elementary interns in the public schools. What started as a few building-level action plans involving teams of teachers and their principals evolved into a model program and then into a professional development center of the Holmes Group (1986) variety. Two major factors are credited with the success of the Akron Intern Program. Teachers took part in all decision making and helped establish a balance between institutional and

personal goals. Staff development activities were varied to accommodate changes in teachers' and principals' responses to their organizational and personal environments (J. L. Vacca, personal communication, October 30, 1987).

Competency-Based Reading Teacher Education

To complete most competency-based reading teacher education programs, students are required to demonstrate proficiencies in specific and observable skills associated with the effective teaching of reading. Modules are frequently the instructional vehicles for helping students meet a specified list of competencies. For example, a module on beginning reading instruction might require students to complete a set of competencies having to do with home and school influences on early reading, formal and informal readiness measures, and beginning reading materials. Typically, modules contain a preassessment, several learning activities, and a postassessment that includes both knowledge and performance-level tasks. Field experiences that involve students in teaching small groups of pupils are often part of the postassessment.

During the early 1970s, many reading faculties across the United States developed instructional modules that took into account preservice and inservice teachers' professional needs, learning styles, and learning rates. Today, the influence of competency-based reading teacher education is felt more commonly in teacher assessment programs at the state level than in teacher education programs at the university or college level. For example, Georgia's Reading Specialist Test (Flippo, Hayes, & Aaron, 1983), the Teacher Competency Test, and the Teacher Performance Assessment Instruments (Teacher Assessment Unit, 1987) are part of the Georgia Department of Education, which is charged with the licensing of teachers in that state.

Research conducted during the period in which competency-based reading teacher education was at its height reflected educators' concerns with demonstrating mastery of specific objectives. Two of the larger and longer term studies involved inservice, rather than preservice, teachers. L. M. Anderson, Evertson, and Brophy (1979) provided first-grade teachers with a manual containing 22 principles of effective small-group instruction that they were to master and use with their reading groups over a 6-month period. Intervention was minimal and prescriptive. Researchers met individually with teachers to describe the 22 principles early in the school year. A week later the researchers returned to test the teachers' mastery of the principles and to answer any concerns. At the end of the school year, pupils who had been in the treatment teachers' reading groups scored significantly higher on a standardized reading achievement test than pupils in the control teachers' groups.

Stallings (1980) provided secondary reading teachers with guidelines for asking questions, reacting to students' responses, and managing individual, small-group, and whole-class instruction. The guidelines were based on effective basic-skills instruction that she had observed in an earlier study (Stallings, Cory, Fairweather, & Needels, 1978). Students of teachers who received training in implementing the behaviorally oriented guidelines gained an average of 6 months more in reading achievement than students of teachers in the control group. Stallings' nationally validated training model, *The Process of Teaching Basic Reading Skills in Secondary Schools,* continues to serve as a teacher-training model for improving reading skills in the District of Columbia Public Schools (S. L. Anderson, 1984 and personal communication, September 17, 1987; Bush, 1984).

Inquiry-Oriented Reading Teacher Education

Currently, teachers' professional, or craft, knowledge is recognized as being far more complex than earlier research on the traditional-craft concept of teacher education would suggest (Zeichner, Tabachnick, & Densmore, 1987). Instead of focusing on what constitutes good reading practices, researchers presently are more interested in understanding how preservice and inservice teachers acquire knowledge and what implicit theories they use to guide their actions within different contexts (e.g., Hollingsworth, in press; Roehler, Duffy, Herrmann, Conley, & Johnson, 1988). In Shulman's words, the focus is on attempting "to make the implied more explicit so that it can be shared and deliberated upon" (1987b, p. 480).

Inquiry-oriented teacher education has been conceptualized in a variety of ways. Tom (1985) developed three dimensions, or continua, for exploring its various forms. One of those dimensions makes it possible to locate on a continuum the degree to which teaching is viewed as problematic. According to Tom, "To make teaching problematic is to raise doubts about what, under ordinary circumstances, appears to be effective or wise practice" (p. 37). Those who would limit the arena of the problematic to include only the teaching–learning process view inquiry-oriented teacher education much less comprehensively than those who would include, in addition to the teaching–learning process, the social, cultural, economic, and political aspects of schooling.

Although these two contrasting views of the way inquiry-oriented teacher education can be conceptualized are not the only ones, they are helpful in understanding two different approaches to inquiry-oriented reading teacher education. In the first approach, the emphasis is on helping teachers improve practice through reflecting on their past teaching or through making their implicit knowledge-in-action explicit. For example, teachers might be asked to consider how and under what conditions they would opt to modify or abandon a particular sequence of activities in a basal lesson. By making the teaching–learning process problematic, reading teacher educators encourage preservice and inservice teachers to consider alternatives to established practice. In the second approach, the arena of the problematic is greatly enlarged. Here, for example, the emphasis is on freeing teachers from established practices that are thought to be negatively influenced by social, cultural, economic, or political forces outside the teaching–learning process. Through this larger arena of the problematic, teachers are shown *what is denied* by the present practices and what reading instruction might become for all participants.

In short, . . . 'it doesn't have to be this way and together we can change it'" (Shannon, 1986, p. 407).

Research on inquiry-oriented reading teacher education is as diverse as the multifaceted conceptions of this approach would suggest. Nonetheless, within this diversity there are common strands or themes. For example, nearly all of the studies reported here have incorporated teacher decision making and reflection, either as part of an intervention or as a means for studying teachers' thought processes. Most have been long-term studies, some extending for a year or more. Thematically, the studies have been concerned with how teachers acquire knowledge of complex reading instructional strategies and what beliefs, or implicit theories of teaching, they use to guide their reading instruction.

Alternative instructional strategies and methods for adapting current basal practices have provided the foci for many of the studies. For example, the staff-development model for a yearlong teacher explanation project involving 20 third-grade teachers (Putnam, Roehler, & Duffy, 1987) offered an alternative to the traditional drill and practice instructional model associated with various basal reading skills. Although the model was deemed successful, the study raised several issues regarding how to train teachers to use new instructional methods, when to release responsibility for developing and teaching the strategy to the teachers, and how to avoid conflicts between experimental design needs and staff-development needs in classroom-based experimental studies. Another example of a study that investigated adapting current basal practices was a lesson-planning study (Lalik & Niles, in press; Niles & Lalik, 1987) in which preservice teachers' thinking was monitored as they engaged in an assignment to improve an existing basal workbook page. This study revealed the power of collaborative group learning.

Another group of researchers has investigated preservice and inservice teachers' implicit theories of teaching and how these theories were used to guide their reading instruction. One of the studies was a yearlong case study that documented an experienced kindergarten teacher's beliefs during her induction as a Chapter I reading teacher (Lalik & Pecic, 1986). A second study (Elbaz, 1981) documented how a secondary reading- and learning-skills teacher used her beliefs about teaching, subject matter, and school milieu to simplify the task of structuring classwork. A third study (Barr, 1987) accounted for a change in classroom dialogue about assigned readings by examining a high school English teacher's beliefs about sequencing curricular materials. Finally, a series of case studies (Alvermann & Hayes, 1989) chronicled five content area teachers' attempts to incorporate an intervention that challenged their beliefs about postreading discussions of assigned material.

In sum, the three contrasting conceptions of reading teacher education provide insights into how preservice and inservice teachers are taught pedagogical content knowledge (Shulman, 1987a) appropriate to their fields. In each model, whether traditional-craft, competency-based, or inquiry-oriented, there is a flow from teacher dependence to teacher independence and decision making. As Ogle (1989) has noted, moving from theory to practice requires careful structuring, so that a shared knowledge base can be translated into performance-based competencies, which in turn can provide the grist for reflection and inquiry. Although the traditional-craft and competency-based approaches to reading teacher education are more widespread, a growing interest in the inquiry-oriented approach promises new perspectives on how preservice and inservice teachers acquire knowledge and how their beliefs influence practice.

PREPARATION AND LICENSURE OF READING TEACHER EDUCATORS

The *Guidelines for the Specialized Preparation of Reading Professionals* (International Reading Association, 1986) lists the recommended competencies to be used by institutions engaged in preparing classroom teachers of reading, reading specialists, and allied professionals. These guidelines, which are also used by the National Council for Accreditation of Teacher Education (NCATE, 1987), encompass the current knowledge base for reading teacher education. This knowledge base consists broadly of knowledge about reading and pedagogical knowledge.

Three of the five groups of reading specialists who are classified in the guidelines have responsibility for educating classroom teachers of reading and other specialists in reading. The *reading professor* teaches undergraduate and graduate reading education courses at the college or university level. The *reading consultant/reading resource* teacher is responsible for providing leadership and staff development for classroom teachers, diagnostic-remedial specialists, and/or developmental reading–study skills specialists at the building level. The *reading coordinator/supervisor*, who is employed at the district or community level, is responsible for the supervision and professional development of classroom teachers, diagnostic-remedial specialists, developmental reading–study skills specialists, and reading consultants/reading resource teachers. The other two groups of reading specialists (diagnostic-remedial specialist and developmental reading-study skills specialist) are not responsible for teacher education.

Knowledge Base

Table 38-1 lists the six general areas of the knowledge base for the three groups of reading specialists just described. Although classroom teachers of reading, allied professionals, and reading specialists who do not have responsibility for teacher education are expected to acquire some of the same knowledge, their knowledge can be less extensive and deep than that of the reading specialists involved in reading teacher education.

Empirical support for a knowledge base in the preparation of all who plan to teach or supervise reading can be traced to the first quarter of this century, specifically to some of the early writings of William S. Gray, Dean of the College of Education, University of Chicago. As a member of the Committee on Economy of Time in Education (Whipple, 1919), Gray and five

TABLE 38–1. Knowledge Base for the Three Groups of Reading Specialists With Teacher Education Responsibilities

I. Linguistic and cognitive bases for reading
    A. Linguistics
    B. Psychology of language and cognition
    C. Language and cognitive development
II. Comprehension
    A. Literal/interpretive comprehension
    B. Critical/evaluative comprehension
    C. Reference and study skills
III. Word identification and vocabulary
    A. Word recognition
    B. Word meanings
IV. Appreciation and enjoyment
    A. Teaching the author's craft
    B. Developing lifelong reading habits
V. Diagnostic Teaching
    A. Assessing student needs
    B. Organizing classrooms for effective instruction
    C. Using effective teaching and learning approaches
    D. Instructing students with special reading needs
VI. Continuing program maintenance planning and improvement
    A. Interaction with other professionals, parents, and the community
    B. Curriculum development
    C. Staff development
    D. Conducting research

Note. From *Guidelines for the Specialized Preparation of Reading Professionals* (pp. 9–18) by International Reading Association, 1986, Newark, DE: Author. Copyright 1986 by International Reading Association. Adapted by permission.

other members "accepted the responsibility of gathering for one elementary school subject, the experimental data bearing on the most economical methods of learning that subject" (p. 8). Gray wrote on the subject of reading and included such topics as the development of reading ability, word recognition, and the improvement of comprehension. These topics are reflected in the current knowledge base.

Academic Preparation of Reading Specialists

Although concerns expressed during the first quarter of this century indicated a need for specialists who would take responsibility for supervising reading instruction in the schools (Smith, 1965), the move to train reading specialists did not gain widespread recognition until 1927. In that year, two influential books were published: *The Teaching and Supervision of Reading* (Gist & King, 1927) and *Supervision and Teaching of Reading* (Harris, Donovan, & Alexander, 1927). According to Smith (1965), however, it was Yoakam's (1937) chapter on reading supervision in Part I of the Thirty-Sixth Yearbook of the National Society for the Study of Education that gave direction to the academic preparation of reading supervisors.

By 1961, Gray's description of the academic preparation for supervising reading specialists and reading education professors looked very similar to that presently recommended by the Professional Standards and Ethics Committee of the International Reading Association. Table 38-2 lists the current recommended courses and credit hours for the preparation of the three groups of reading specialists with teacher education responsibilities.

With the exception of one course on college and adult reading programs, the academic preparation of reading specialists is heavily weighted toward elementary and secondary reading. Historically, reading teacher education has focused on the K–12 curriculum. With the rapid growth of college learning centers in the United States and Canada (Sullivan, 1980), however, reading teacher education programs experienced a demand for courses of study aimed directly at preparing college reading specialists. In a survey of 24 graduate reading programs, Eanet (1983) found that half did not offer a single course that directly addressed the issues of teaching college reading. Concern over the inadequate professional preparation of college reading teachers prompted a comprehensive review of the research literature in this area (Stahl, Gordon, & Brozo, 1984). On the basis of their review, Stahl et al. recommend that the academic preparation of college reading specialists include (a) an undergraduate program that emphasizes academic rather than pedagogical coursework (b) a knowledge of the theoretical base underlying college-level instructional skills, (c) a background in research methodology, and (d) a broad, working knowledge of administrative and counseling skills.

Licensure

Licensure is used synonymously with certification by many states (NCATE, 1987). However, members of the Teacher Assessment Project at Stanford University (Vavrus & Calfee,

1988) are working to enhance the professionalization of teaching by making a distinction between *licensure* (minimum competency for entry into the profession) and *certification* (recognition of excellence in teaching).

Historically, the licensing of reading teachers has reflected what is deemed acceptable in the way of literacy standards of the time. For example, in the early decades of nineteenth-century France, teachers who wished to work the seasonal fairs announced their subject specialties by placing one, two, or three feathers in their caps. One feather reportedly meant the individual was competent to teach reading, two, arithmetic, and three, Latin (Resnick & Resnick, 1980). Compared with today's standards for licensing teachers of reading, this earlier method seems quaint at best.

It is worth pointing out, however, that as late as 1968 no systematized method existed for defining the roles, responsibilities, and competencies of reading professionals in the United States (Austin, 1968). Further, with few exceptions, states did not require a course in the teaching of reading as a prerequisite for licensure. Describing some of the exceptions, Austin notes:

Indiana requires that persons teaching at the junior-high-school level (but not elementary or high-school levels) have a reading course as part of their preservice education. Since October 1, 1964, Pennsylvania has required a course in basic reading instruction for the issuance of a provisional college certificate which is necessary to teach academic subjects at the secondary level. . . . One state has made it mandatory for reading specialists to complete twenty-one credit hours of course work in reading for certification. However, at present no university in the state offers more than fifteen formal course hours in reading. (pp. 372–373)

TABLE 38–2. Academic Preparation for Reading Specialists With
Teacher Education Responsibilities

Reading Consultant/ Reading Resource Teacher	Reading Coordinator/Supervisor	Reading Professor
Minimum of 18–24 graduate credit hours in reading education courses from among: Language Arts Content Area Reading, Study and Thinking Skills Evaluation of Reading and Related Abilities Children's or Adolescent Literature Psychology of Reading Sociology of Reading Assessment of Reading Difficulties Correction of Reading and Related Deficiencies Clinical Practicum Internship Seminar in Reading Research College and Adult Reading Programs Reading and the Learning-disabled Student Teaching English As a Second Language	3–6 credit hours in supervision and administration courses and an additional 3–6 credit hours in specialized reading courses from among: Action Research and Program Evaluation in Reading Supervision and Organization of Reading Programs Internship in Clinical or Field-based Supervision	Should be prepared in coursework similar to that of other reading specialists. In addition, should be a graduate of an accredited doctoral program that prepares individuals to assess, interpret, and engage in research and development activities.

Note. From *Guidelines for the Specialized Preparation of Reading Professionals* (pp. 2–3) by International Reading Association, 1986, Newark, DE: Author, Copyright 1986 by International Reading Association. Adapted by permission.

Although conditions have improved since then, the need for institutions of higher learning, professional associations, and state departments of education to work cooperatively in establishing criteria for the uniform preparation and licensure of reading professionals continues to be addressed (see Dishner & Olson, 1989; Morris, 1988; Nicholson, 1979).

The licensing of secondary school teachers whose major responsibility is teaching the content of their respective subject areas has received considerable attention in the research literature since the mid-1920s (Austin & Morrison, 1961; Dishner & Olson, 1989; Gray, 1927; Herber & Nelson-Herber, 1984; D. W. Moore, Readence, & Rickelman, 1983; Morrison & Austin, 1977; Whipple, 1925). Yet, as Venezky (1986) has pointed out, few of the recommendations stemming from this literature have received more than casual recognition. A case in point is the slowness with which states have acted in requiring a course in the teaching of secondary reading as a prerequisite for licensing secondary teachers. In the early 1970s, four states and the District of Columbia required such a course in all academic areas (Estes & Piercey, 1973). Although the number of states that have followed suit has increased gradually over the intervening years (Bader, 1975; Mangieri & Kemper, 1979; Thomas & Simpson, 1979), by 1984 only 63 percent of them required a course in the teaching of reading for licensure in all secondary academic areas (Farrell & Cirrincione, 1984). A survey conducted in Australia in 1986 revealed that only 63 percent of all secondary teacher-training programs in that country reported having a compulsory course in the teaching of reading (Morris, 1988).

An issue that is gaining increasing attention is the licensing of individuals who provide supplementary reading instruction through learning center franchises (Stahl, 1987). The number of these centers increased significantly in the 1980s according to Robbins-Wilf (1987), whose doctoral dissertation remains one of the few well-documented studies on this phenomenon. In her study, services in New Jersey's learning centers are described as being primarily oriented toward remedial, corrective, and developmental reading instruction. In the absence of any state licensing procedures, Robbins-Wilf recommends that the first step in assuring quality instruction should involve requiring proper credentials for all staff members. At the time the study was conducted, only half of the respondents indicated that more than 80 percent of their staff held a bachelor's degree. Less than one-third said that more than 80 percent of their staff had graduate degrees. Similar findings from a study conducted in California (Seat, 1983) have begun to raise public awareness of the need to license individuals engaged in reading instruction in these private learning centers.

In summation, the knowledge base of reading teacher educators is drawn from various fields of study including linguistics, psychology, pedagogy, and sociology. Academic preparation has been focused largely on elementary and secondary classroom teachers of reading. With the growing demand for college reading specialists, however, there is need for an expanded knowledge base that includes courses directly related to teaching college reading. Currently, two other issues commanding attention are the need to ensure proper training in reading pedagogy prior to licensing secondary school teachers

and proper credentialing for all individuals who teach reading at private learning centers.

EXPERTS AND NOVICES

The rationale for studying expert and novice teachers of reading rests on the assumption that, through an understanding of their developing belief systems and practices, an improved knowledge base can be derived from which to draw implications for reading teacher education. According to Shulman (1987a, 1987b), codifying the emerging knowledge and actions of experienced and inexperienced teachers can lead to a knowledge base that is grounded in what he calls the "wisdom of practice." However, there are at least two problems with studying the development of reading teacher expertise. First, as Berliner (1986) has pointed out, the potential for confounding expertise with experience is great, especially as the terms are used interchangeably in the research literature. A second problem inherent in studying the development of reading teacher expertise is the tendency to overlook differences in the results obtained from policy-capturing studies (see Shulman, 1986) and those obtained from studies conducted in naturalistic settings. To avoid this problem, the two types of studies are addressed separately in the discussion that follows.

Policy-Capturing Studies

Policy-capturing studies in the literature on reading teacher education typically involve experts and novices in simulated cases and vignettes that focus on the match (or mismatch) between teachers' theoretical beliefs about reading instruction and their hypothetical implementation of those beliefs. The limited generalizability of policy-capturing studies in general has caused critics to question their validity (e.g., Cook-Gumperz & Gumperz, 1982; Mishler, 1979; Shake, 1984). Nonetheless, the results of several such studies are included here because they illustrate one approach to studying expert–novice differences in reading teacher education.

In the early 1980s, Duffy pointed out that little advantage had been taken of two rich and reciprocally informing communities of research. He described the communities as being research on reading and research on teaching, which he saw as "moving forward 'out of earshot' of each other" (1981, p. 113). Although researchers in both areas (e.g., Borko, Shavelson, & Stern, 1981; Harste & Burke, 1977; Kamil & Pearson, 1979) reasoned that teachers' theoretical orientations toward reading guided their instructional decisions, the empirical support for such an idea was missing (Pace & Powers, 1981).

In the intervening years, the results of research involving the relation of experts' and novices' theoretical orientations to reading instruction have been mixed. On the one hand, it appears that there is little relation between teachers' stated belief systems and their stated practices (Duffy & Anderson, 1984; P. J. Moore, 1983). In a study by Meyers and Ringler (1980), only the inexperienced teachers demonstrated consistency between their stated view of the reading process and their plan for diagnostically intervening in the hypothesized case study of a disabled reader. On the other hand, there is evidence to suggest that, not only do experienced teachers' beliefs about reading influence their decisions (Rupley & Logan, 1985), but also preservice and inservice teachers differ little in their understanding of how reading takes place and how reading ability develops (Kinzer, 1988).

The results of other policy-capturing studies suggest that situational factors play a large role in experts' and novices' conceptions of reading instruction. Experienced teachers (Borko & Niles, 1982) and teachers in their first year of elementary school teaching (Hoffman & O'Neal, 1984) in districts with basal reading programs tended to favor a basal and linear skills approach to reading instruction, whereas preservice teachers, who had not taught the basal program, favored a more natural language and interest-based approach to reading instruction (Borko & Niles, 1982). Preservice and inservice teachers in the Borko and Niles study also differed in their use of strategies for estimating students' mastery of the reading curriculum and for grouping students for instruction. In both cases the experienced teachers demonstrated more complex decision-making strategies.

Naturalistic Studies

The results of several naturalistic studies (Duffy & McIntyre, 1982; Durkin, 1979; Guzzetti, 1989; Morine-Dershimer, 1979), or studies conducted in what Duffy (1982, p. 295) calls "full classrooms," support the notion that teachers' theoretical orientations toward reading and decision making are constrained by commercially prepared materials, curriculum mandates, and a variety of classroom conditions. Despite these constraints, experienced as well as beginning teachers have been observed adapting content reading strategies (Guzzetti, 1989) and reading lessons (Blanton & Moorman, 1987; Borko, Eisenhart, Kello, & Vandett, 1984; Lalik & Pecic, 1986) to match their own theories of reading instruction.

A similar adaptability has been observed among first-year and preservice teachers. For example, in a yearlong case study involving two novice teachers, the researchers (Lalik, Borko, Pecic, Perry, & Livingston, 1985) found that both teachers, though they differed in how they perceived themselves as decision makers, supplemented the basal program to make it more consistent with their own views. In another study, Borko, Lalik, and Tomchin (1987) reported that student teachers enrolled in a yearlong field experience identified the changes they made in particular basal reading lessons as contributing to the success of those lessons. Although the student teachers indicated they would have liked to make further modifications in their instruction, they seemed content, like the novices in Alvermann's (1981) study, to wait until they were in charge of their own classrooms.

Other lines of research involving expert–novice differences include the investigation of effective content-area reading staff development programs (Conley, 1986a, 1986b) and the exploration of preservice teachers' knowledge structures (Roehler et al., 1988). Conley's work with experienced secondary teachers,

who were at different training levels of proficiency in a long-term staff-development model for teaching reading in content areas (see Herber & Nelson-Herber, 1984), documented how expertise in teaching influences adaptability. As teachers in Conley's studies reached higher levels of proficiency in applying the content-area reading strategies they were expected to learn, they also demonstrated greater willingness to adapt the strategies to meet their students' needs. Similarly, as reported by Roehler et al., patterns in preservice teachers' knowledge structures for teaching reading changed considerably in the context of specific instructional situations over a yearlong undergraduate teacher-preparation program.

In summary, the results of policy-capturing studies and studies conducted in natural settings on expert–novice differences can inform reading teacher education. However, the degree to which experienced and inexperienced teachers' stated beliefs match a set of hypothetical practices might be of less interest to reading teacher educators than knowledge of how these teachers' developing expertise influences adaptability in reading instruction in real classrooms.

PROFESSIONAL-DEVELOPMENT PROGRAMS IN READING TEACHER EDUCATION

Professional-development programs mirror the three conceptions of reading teacher education, though not as clearly as Table 38-3 would suggest. There are, of course, overlaps. For example, the competency-based staff-development program of the Kamehameha Early Education Program (KEEP) also shares features of the inquiry-oriented and traditional-craft conceptions of reading teacher education (Au et al., 1986). These overlaps in program areas are to be expected, especially if one considers that professional development is a process that evolves over time.

Table 38-3 reflects the conceptual variations in professional-development programs across four common approaches to reading instruction: basal reading, integrated language arts, compensatory reading, and secondary content-area reading. Within each of these approaches, programs are compared and contrasted in terms of their scope, goals, conceptions of teacher education, implementation procedures, and evaluation data.

Basal Reading Professional-Development Programs

All three programs in this area were concerned to varying degrees with modifying existing basal reading practices. The traditional-craft and inquiry-oriented approaches to staff development concentrated on changing teachers' cognitive structuring of tasks; the competency-based approach focused largely on changing teachers' behaviors and attitudes.

Project READ and the Teacher Explanation Project. The staff-development programs of Project READ (Calfee & Henry, 1986; Calfee, Henry, & Funderburg, 1988) and the Teacher Explanation Project (Putnam et al., 1987) differed in

TABLE 38–3. Professional-Development Programs Within Three Concepts of
Reading Teacher Education

Conceptions of Reading Teacher Education	Basal Reading	Integrated Language Arts	Compensatory Reading	Secondary Content-Area Reading
Traditional-craft	Project READ (Calfee & Henry, 1986; Calfee, Henry, & Funderburg, 1988)	Collaboration for School Improvement Project (Ogle, 1986)	STAR Reading Program (Smith-Burke & Ringler, 1986) Written Language Awareness (Taylor, Blum, & Logsdon, 1986)	Network of Secondary School Demonstration Centers for Teaching Reading in Content Areas (Herber & Nelson, 1983) Learning from Text Project (Singer & Bean, 1988)
Competency-based	Program to Improve Teacher Effectiveness in Reading Instruction (Miller & Ellsworth, 1985)	KEEP Reading Program (Au et al., 1986; Hao, 1988)	Oregon Direct Instruction Follow Through Program (Meyer, Gersten, & Gutkin, 1983; Meyer, 1988; Stallings & Kaskowitz, 1974)	Content Area Reading Program (CARP) (Askov & Dupuis, 1983)
Inquiry-oriented	Teacher Explanation Project (Putnam, Roehler, & Duffy, 1987	Metcalf Project (Tierney et al., 1988) Benchmark School (Gaskins, 1988)	Reading Recovery Program (Clay, 1987; Pinnell, 1987; Rentel & Pinnell, 1987)	Content Reading in Secondary Schools (CRISS) (Santa, 1986; 1988) Orange County (FL) Reading in Content Areas Program (Monahan, 1987)

scope and in the ways they were implemented but not in their goals. Both programs focused on helping teachers make independent decisions about how to use existing basal reading materials more effectively. Project READ, a schoolwide effort in Northern California, stressed the importance of having teachers design coherent reading lessons by using scripts, or general-purpose lesson frames, to analyze separate components of the basal lesson. In contrast, the Teacher Explanation Project, focused on individual teachers, rather than on an entire faculty. A team of educators from the Institute for Research on Teaching at Michigan State University worked individually with teachers to help them internalize procedures for recasting drill and practice-type skills into strategies that could be explained to low-ability readers.

Project READ was implemented through a traditional approach to teacher education. An introductory workshop presented teachers with the basic concepts and procedures of the program. At various times throughout the year, staff members visited the school to demonstrate specific program components, to observe and give feedback to teachers as they practiced new procedures, and to introduce additional information. At the end of the school year, staff members interviewed the teachers to determine the impact of the program on reading instruction.

The implementation of the staff-development program for

the Teacher Explanation Project shared several of the features typically associated with the inquiry-oriented approach to teacher education. For example, by treating instruction as problematic and worthy of inquiry, teachers were able to identify ways in which their current reading instructional practices were inappropriate for low-ability readers. As a result of the insights gained from inquiring into the nature of those practices, teachers were more willing to consider changing the way they taught their low-reading groups. Other features of the inquiry-oriented approach to teacher education included provision of opportunities for teachers and their coaches (the teacher educators in the project) to reflect, confront, and share new knowledge. The coaches gave support in various ways: by modeling explanation behavior, by intervening when teachers were unsuccessful in their attempts to internalize new explanation strategies, and by building a sense of teacher ownership in the project through gradually transferring responsibilities from themselves to the teachers.

Evaluation data for Project READ document some hurdles to be overcome in implementing a large-scale staff-development program, which is continuing. Past evaluations have shown that the use of a script to design lessons is a new concept for teachers and one that requires considerable preparation time. Teachers have also expressed a need for more guidance as they work toward making new procedures automatic. On the positive side, teachers have reported a sense of professional competence in taking charge of literacy instruction. Additionally, they have acknowledged a growing sense of professional camaraderie as a result of working together to improve reading instruction.

Evaluation data for the Teacher Explanation Project also suggest some problem areas. Time was a big constraint, and yet time is necessary for building ownership in a program, especially when the program requires teachers to restructure the way they have been accustomed to thinking about reading instruction. Timing, as well as time, was a problem (cf. Berliner, 1988). Complex interventions such as teacher explanation make it difficult to know the appropriate time to transfer responsibility from the teacher educator–coach to the teacher. Some positive effects that were noted include the teacher–coach relationship. Formal and informal coaching sessions contributed to teachers' success and their sense of commitment to the program. Another positive outcome was the learning that resulted from having teachers critique their own instructional effectiveness. Provision of time for teachers to reflect on their instructional decisions is a key element in developing expertise in pedagogy (Berliner, 1988; Shulman, 1987a).

Teacher Effectiveness in Reading Instruction. A 2-year program to improve teacher effectiveness in reading instruction (Miller & Ellsworth, 1985) was instituted in three small-to-medium-sized school districts in Kansas for the purpose of producing measurable differences in elementary teachers' knowledge, attitudes, and instructional behaviors. A basal reading series provided the core of the reading program in each district. Participants in the staff-development program were expected to improve their reading instruction in six areas: assessment, differentiated instruction, diverse use of instructional materials, directed reading activity, story discussion techniques, and recreational reading. The implementation sequence involved students in earning graduate credits for college courses that extended over 4 semesters. A strong competency-based component during the second and third semesters included demonstration teaching, supervised trials, and performance analysis. Evaluation data suggest that teachers who participated in the 2-year staff-development program were measurably more knowledgeable than nonparticipating teachers. However, selectivity in attitude changes and small subsamples in the observed classroom instructional behaviors made differences between participating and nonparticipating teachers difficult to interpret.

Integrated Language Arts Professional-Development Programs

The four professional-development programs described here are alike in several ways. All subscribe or subscribed to a holistic, language-based approach to teaching reading. To varying degrees, each enlists or enlisted the collaboration of teachers and researchers, and, in three of the programs, consultants and/or administrators are or were part of the collaborative effort. Finally, teachers in each program are or were involved in implementing theory-based curricula.

Collaboration for School Improvement and KEEP. The Collaboration for School Improvement (Ogle, 1986) and KEEP (Au, et al., 1986; Hao, 1988) are multisite professional-development programs. The Collaboration for School Improvement project, funded originally as a 4-year, basic skills grant from the U.S. Office of Education, involved faculty and staff from the National College of Education and multiple sites within the Zion, Illinois, School District, a small community with a large minority and highly transient population. The KEEP reading program, which originated in a laboratory school setting in Honolulu, currently serves low-achieving Hawaiian and part-Hawaiian students in seven public schools on three of the islands. A major goal of both of these programs was to implement an instructional-leadership model that would assist elementary teachers in developing their own language arts program.

In the Collaboration for School Improvement project, teams of principals and teachers were introduced to the theoretical underpinnings of several reading and writing strategies for the purpose of developing a shared knowledge base. This knowledge base was then translated into teaching strategies aimed at improving students' language arts. Initially, these teaching strategies were demonstrated by a master teacher on the project's staff (typically an advanced graduate student from the college or a teacher from the school district who had earned a master's degree from the college). After that, at monthly intervals, teachers were observed and given feedback as they adapted the various strategies to their own classroom situations. The project director coordinated staff development at the various sites and worked directly with the principals to learn how their leadership styles could be used in implementing the instructional-leadership model.

Although the KEEP instructional-leadership model initially had a strong competency-based orientation, it presently shares many features of the inquiry-oriented and traditional-craft conceptions of teacher education. For example, the yearlong training program for reading consultants consists of seminars, practicum experiences, and on-site training sessions in which teachers are given time to reflect on their current practices and how those practices can change over time. As consultants begin to interact with teachers, they model the type of small-group instructional techniques they expect teachers to use with children. Following a series of initial training workshops, consultants work with individual teachers to develop goals for instruction and classroom management of the numerous learning centers, which are essential to the KEEP reading program.

Evaluation data in the form of feedback from participants and formative measures administered periodically during the first 2 years of the Collaboration for School Improvement project demonstrated the positive impact the project had had on the Zion schools. However, the federal government withdrew funding from all basic-skills grants at the end of year two, thus cutting short the project. At the same time, Zion School District sustained a severe cutback in industrial tax dollars and entered a period of unrest between teachers and administrators due to stalled contract negotiations. Despite these setbacks, the project was approved by the school board for a third year, and the instructional-leadership model was implemented in one of the Chicago school districts. Currently, Zion School District has initiated a further collaboration with the faculty and staff of the National College of Education, this time with stronger emphasis on inquiry-oriented professional development (D. M. Ogle, personal communication, December 10, 1988).

Evaluation data for the KEEP reading program have come from experimentation, program evaluation, and qualitative studies. Research and program implementation are closely tied, sometimes becoming one and the same. For example, problems in implementing and disseminating the KEEP reading program are identified by the training and dissemination staff for formal study in one of the research departments in the laboratory school. To assure that research findings are incorporated into the program at each of the field sites, consultants use an essential-features coding checklist during their six observations of each teacher each year. The effectiveness of the program is measured by standardized reading-achievement tests and informal assessments.

Metcalf and Benchmark. The professional-development programs associated with the Metcalf Project (Tierney, Tucker, Gallagher, Crismore, & Pearson, 1988) and Benchmark School (Gaskins, 1988) are the results of long-term collaboration involving teachers, supervisors, administrators, and teacher educators/researchers. The Metcalf Project was a 3-year collaboration between teachers and researchers whose goal was to explore language arts instruction through an inquiry-oriented staff-development program that looked upon teaching as a continuing experiment. During the first year of the Metcalf Project, teachers' thinking and their practices were of primary interest. Emphasis was placed on understanding how teachers examined and made decisions about alternative reading and writing strategies, not on whether they actually adopted the strategies. In the second year of the project, the teachers and researchers became partners in several action research studies designed to make reading and writing instruction a problem-solving experience. In the final year of the project, the goal was to assure that the teachers became self-initiators, so that the project would maintain its momentum after the researchers left.

Benchmark School opened in 1970 as a private, ungraded school for intellectually bright children who had difficulty reading. Adapting instruction to the needs of these children is the primary focus of the school's inquiry-oriented professional-development program. Since its inception the Benchmark staff's professional growth has been attributed to four factors: climate, involvement, ownership, and knowledge. The climate is characterized by trust and administrative responsiveness to staff needs. Teachers at Benchmark are applauded for taking risks and for broadening the arena of the problematic (see Tom, 1985). They are involved in identifying instructional problems, field-testing alternative practices, and making decisions about which practices to implement. As a result of this action research approach to reading and writing instruction, teachers develop a sense of ownership in the practices that they decide to implement. Weekly research seminars in which supervisors and teachers meet to study topics of interest, a well-stocked professional library, and monthly inservice meetings that bring Benchmark staff in contact with literacy researchers from across the nation are a few of the features through which teachers acquire a shared knowledge base.

Evaluation data for both Metcalf and Benchmark professional-development programs suggest that teachers are willing to consider alternative reading and writing practices and to make changes in their instructional routines when they have been active participants in the change process. Collaborative action research is one means of assuring active involvement. In the Metcalf Project, the inquiry-oriented approach to teacher education enabled individual teachers, in collaboration with their university partners, to evaluate existing practices in light of current research and to make changes in those practices based upon the results of their action research projects. With a staff of 60, Benchmark School's approach to evaluation is somewhat different. In addition to the partnerships between individual teachers and supervisors (supervisors frequently serve as coaches or mentors to the teachers), there are regularly scheduled large-group meetings involving administrators and staff members for the purpose of obtaining input and engaging in problem-solving discussions.

Compensatory-Reading Professional-Development Programs

The professional-development components of compensatory-reading programs vary widely in quality and in the amount of invested effort. In summarizing some of the disappointing findings from the Educational Testing Service's nationwide survey of compensatory-reading programs, Drum and Calfee (1979) note, "It should have been more obvious from the beginning that robust inservice training programs were essential to the success of the Title I effort, as well as other compensatory programs" (p. 185). The professional-development programs described next are noteworthy for two reasons. *First,* they were robust in terms of their duration and/or usefulness as models for other staff-development programs. *Second,* they illustrate the difficulties encountered in attempting to interpret available evaluation data.

STAR and Written-Language Awareness. Structured Teaching in the Areas of Reading and Writing (STAR), a Title I reading program for grades 3–9, was developed by a teacher committee from East Harlem and teacher educators from New York University (Smith-Burke & Ringler, 1986). Like the STAR staff-development program, the Right-to-Read written-language-awareness program (Taylor, Blum, & Logsdon, 1986) was designed to enable teachers to implement a theory-based reading curriculum in low-income schools. Although the staff-development components of these two programs had similar goals, they differed in scope. The Title I staff-development program served teachers in 16 elementary and 4 junior high schools. The Right-to-Read staff-development program involved 13 prekindergarten and kindergarten teachers from mostly low-income Washington, DC, schools.

The traditional-craft conception of teacher education influenced the implementation of these two staff-development programs. In the case of STAR, university consultants provided workshop training for inservice trainers from the central administration, who in turn provided training in the schools for the Title I reading teachers. Later, the inservice trainers helped classroom teachers incorporate some of the STAR reading strategies into their regular reading and language programs. Staff development in the Right-to-Read program consisted of a 2-week summer workshop, monthly inservice meetings during the school year, and two consultant visits per month to each of the teachers' classrooms. The summer workshop and monthly inservice meetings were used to develop a theoretical base for creating a language- and print-rich environment. During classroom visits, the consultants observed teachers as they attempted to implement the written-language-awareness curriculum. Following each observed lesson, the consultants provided feedback to the teachers and helped them decide on alternative techniques.

Evaluation data for the two staff-development programs are difficult to interpret. On the one hand, it seems reasonable to conclude that the teacher-training component of STAR was a success. Evidence comes from the fact that, when two key administrators moved from the district, they took experienced STAR personnel to serve as teacher trainers in their new districts. On the other hand, it was the change in administration and a further reduction of central staff directly involved with the program that diminished the visibility of STAR. The evaluation data from the Right-to-Read project were also equivocal. Over the yearlong implementation period, there was an approximate 50-50 split between those teachers who completely adopted the language- and print-rich environment techniques and those who did so on a limited scale or not at all.

Follow Through and Reading Recovery. The contrasts are greater between the Oregon Direct Instruction Follow Through teacher-training program (Meyer, 1988; Meyer, Gersten, & Gutkin, 1983; Stallings & Kaskowitz, 1974) and the Reading Recovery training program (Clay, 1987; Pinnell, 1987; Rentel & Pinnell, 1987). Although the goal of both of these early-intervention programs is to reduce reading failure, the Follow Through training model reflects the competency-based conception of teacher education, whereas Reading Recovery reflects more of an inquiry-oriented approach to teacher education. The origin and scope of the two programs also vary. The Oregon Direct Instruction Follow Through model was developed in the United States and by 1983 had been implemented in 60 American cities and a number of foreign countries (Stallings & Stipek, 1986). The Reading Recovery model was developed in New Zealand and was implemented nationally in that country in 1983. By 1984, it had been implemented in Central Victoria, Australia, and Columbus, Ohio (Clay, 1987). Following a successful pilot program in Ohio, Reading Recovery was funded as a statewide program (Rentel & Pinnell, 1987). Presently, Ohio State University offers year-long residency training programs for individuals from within and outside the United States who wish to learn more about Reading Recovery.

Responsibility for the implementation of the Oregon Direct Instruction Follow Through training model is given to a project manager, who conducts either one-on-one training within individual teachers' classrooms or in small-group training outside of the classroom. This training can include demonstrations by the project manager or by a teacher trainer who has been trained by the manager. Training in the basic techniques of the program can be accomplished in a matter of hours, but weekly observations and technical assistance in individual teachers' classrooms are needed to assure that teachers and paraprofessionals are following the model. A teacher's manual and specially prepared DISTAR curricular materials assure uniformity in what, when, and how teachers teach and students perform.

Like Follow Through, the staff-development model for Reading Recovery does not separate training from practice. However, once Reading Recovery teachers have undergone a highly structured training program, they are enrolled in a year-long staff-development course (with follow-up support in subsequent years) for the purpose of involving them in decision-making and theory-building processes. During weekly seminars and through the facilitation of a teacher–leader, teachers (no more than 12 in a group) are challenged to make their implicit ideas about reading instruction and student learning explicit. This is accomplished in two ways. In the weekly seminars, teachers observe a member of their group instruct a child using a variety of reading and writing materials, including trade books. The observation is done through a one-way viewing window, which allows the observers to talk among themselves and to analyze what is happening according to the understandings they bring to the situation and in light of the new understandings they are developing about reading and writing instruction. A second way in which teachers learn to make their theories about reading and writing instruction explicit is through teaching lessons in their own classrooms during the teacher–leader's regularly scheduled classroom visits.

Evaluation data from the Oregon Direct Instruction Follow Through model of teacher training are available from several sources. Kennedy (1978) attributes the University of Oregon's nonadaptive policy toward program implementation as one factor that contributed to the success of the Direct Instruction model in New York City, where none of the other Follow Through models succeeded. Meyer, et al. (1983) note that the well-articulated teacher-training program of the Oregon Direct Instruction model made it suitable for school settings with high teacher turnover. Negative aspects of this model stemmed largely from teachers feeling rushed, overwhelmed, and ideologically at odds with the scripting and isolated-skills focus of the program, especially in the first year (Meyer, 1988).

Evaluation data from the Reading Recovery program are generally reported in terms of student achievement. One exception was a study conducted by Pinnell and Woolsey (1985) in which they assessed the impact of the model on teachers' professional development over a period of one year. Data from bimonthly reflection sessions, in-depth interviews, questionnaires, and classroom observations supported the program's goal of helping teachers make their implicit theories of reading and writing explicit through observation and discussion. Some specific findings include the facts that (a) teachers gained confidence in their ability to cope with the school district's accountability demands; (b) teachers generally moved from a skills orientation to literacy to a more holistic, integrated orientation; and (c) teachers more readily accepted responsibility for flexible decision making when it was grounded in their own theories of reading and writing instruction.

Secondary Content-Area Reading Professional-Development Programs

The five professional-development programs in secondary content-area reading that are discussed next are alike in several ways. They represent innovations or changes in the curricula of junior and senior high schools, which traditionally have not had well-articulated reading programs. The impetus for change in each case was either falling test scores or teacher dissatisfaction with students' abilities to learn from text. Each of the programs described is concerned with helping content-area teachers assume responsibility for teaching secondary school students how to learn from text. Each program also makes extensive use of peer training. The programs differ, however, in their approaches to inservice teacher education, particularly in terms of teacher involvement and ownership in the programs.

The Network and the Learning from Text Project. Developers of the Network of Secondary School Demonstration Centers for Teaching Reading in Content Areas (Herber & Nelson, 1983; Herber & Nelson-Herber, 1984) and the Learning from Text Project (Singer & Bean, 1988) shared two common goals. They were interested in developing inservice models that would enable content-areas teachers simultaneously to teach content and the reading processes necessary to learn the content. They were also interested in learning more about the staff-development process at the secondary school level. The two inservice models they developed differed greatly in scope but not in implementation procedures.

The Network of Secondary School Demonstration Centers included four school districts (three in New York and one in North Carolina) and two universities. The project was approved for 4 years under the National Basic Skills Program; however, legislation instituted in 1981 eliminated the Basic Skills Program, and funding for the Network ceased after 2 years. The staff-development model, which was the core of the Network, continues to exist. Elements of the model also can be found in Australia's Learning in Language Project, which grew out of the Effective Reading in Content Areas/Queensland Writing Project (Morris & Stewart-Dore, 1984; Stewart-Dore, 1986), and in a two-year inservice program developed by Wedman and Robinson (1988). The Learning from Text Project, a 4-year inservice model that began in 1982, involved a university professor, an assistant superintendent, a curriculum director, several reading specialists, and content representatives from the Anaheim Union High School District in California. District funds were used to support summer workshops and released time for teachers who participated in the Learning from Text Project during the school year.

Implementation procedures used in both the Network and the Learning from Text projects were based on the traditional-craft conception of teacher education. That is, teachers who were proficient in the theoretical orientations of the learning from text strategies and who could demonstrate those strategies in actual classroom situations were responsible for assisting other teachers who were less experienced in the approach. Time was set aside for teachers to practice and receive feedback on newly learned strategies. Released time for teachers to prepare materials that could be used in helping students become strategic readers was deemed essential to both projects. The existence of a common core of materials also assured that the information passed down from one generation of teacher trainers to the next was fairly consistent.

Evaluation data for the Network of Secondary School Demonstration Centers are available from two sources: the final report of the project (Herber & Nelson, 1983) and a qualitative study of the project's implementation at the North Carolina site (Whitford, 1987). According to the final report, despite the termination of federal funds to support the project, individual project sites continued to exist, and three additional sites had either replicated the staff-development model or were planning to become involved in such a replication. Data from the qualitative study suggested that, despite numerous obstacles resulting from organizational changes at the North Carolina school site, the staff-development program (though reduced in size) managed to become stabilized, partly as a result of teacher commitment.

Evaluation data on the Learning from Text Project are available for the summer workshops. These data were used in planning staff-development sessions during the year for department and school faculty. However, systematic data collections have not been completed for the other two components of the evaluation design, that is, school-level evaluation of the dissemination effort and classroom-level implementation.

CARP, CRISS, and Orange County (FL). The Content Area Reading Program (CARP) (Askov & Dupuis, 1983; Dupuis, Askov, & Lee, 1979) provides an interesting contrast to two other programs, Content Reading in Secondary Schools (CRISS) (Santa, 1986, 1988) and Orange County's (FL) Reading in Content Areas (Monahan, 1987). CARP, a competency-based, inservice program that began as a Pennsylvania Department of Education funded project and later received national funding under Title IV-C, existed for 5 years, and focused on competencies such as diagnosis and grouping, evaluation of materials, and teacher-directed instruction. The CRISS project, which was developed in the junior high and senior high school of Kalispell, Montana, has since become part of the National Diffusion Network. Its focus, like that of Orange County, has been on the development of a content reading program that is theoretically based and that actively involves teachers as researchers.

Implementation procedures typically reflect the developer's conception of teacher education. In the CARP model, the inservice program consisted of two 3-hour workshops each month. Teachers learned about a topic from a university professor in the first workshop and applied that information to the development of materials during the second workshop. A reading supervisor conducted the application workshop and then made classroom visits to check on teachers' competencies in using the materials that had been developed in the workshop. In the CRISS model, a 3-day workshop is presented by content area teachers from Kalispell, and in Orange County, reading resource teachers offer back-to-back hourly workshops during the school day to accommodate teachers' planning periods. Once teachers have had opportunities to try some of the new strategies with their classes, the CRISS and Orange County staff help them design action research projects to evaluate the effectiveness of their newly learned teaching strategies. The assumption is that, as a consequence of inquiring into a particular strategy's effectiveness, teachers will develop a sense of ownership in the strategy.

Evaluation data for CARP, overall, suggest that the program increased teachers' knowledge of reading skills and improved their attitude toward content-area reading instruction. No published evaluation data were available for the CRISS and Orange County staff-development models.

Summary

Professional-development programs in reading were grouped on the basis of (a) their relationship to four common approaches to reading instruction, and (b) their general membership in one of three contrasting conceptions of teacher education. Notwithstanding the limitations inherent in such groupings, two purposes were served by this classification scheme: variations in professional-development programs were highlighted, and the ties between theory and practice in reading teacher education were illustrated.

MAJOR ISSUES AND RESEARCH NEEDS

Reading teacher education lacks status as a topic in the field of reading research. In an exhaustive retrieval of research syntheses on a variety of reading topics, Guthrie, Seifert, and Mosberg (1983) located only one review on reading teacher education, and that one was in a practitioner's journal. Other topics such as text comprehension, reading acquisition, word recognition, instructional effects, program evaluation, and reading disability received from 21 to 34 reviews each.

Reading teacher education appears to rank low in teachers' views of research as well. Fitzgerald's (1984) survey of a representative sample of teachers enrolled in graduate reading courses in the United States and Canada revealed that teachers did not consider reading teacher preparation a viable research topic. In fact, it received no mention, whereas the teaching of reading and the study of physiological and psychological processes of reading received 44 percent and 40 percent of the mentions, respectively.

As a result of the reports from the Carnegie Forum on Education and the Economy (1986) and the Holmes Group (1986), it is unlikely that reading teacher education will remain the poor stepchild of reading research. The issues raised in those reports and in this chapter demand the research attention of reading teacher educators. To provide a focus for such attention, the final section of this chapter summarizes the issues raised in previous sections and points to future directions in the research on reading teacher education.

Issues in Reading Teacher Education

The first issue concerns a lack of empirical support for the traditional-craft conception of reading teacher education at the preservice level. As noted earlier, Malone (1984) could find only one experimental study that dealt directly with field experiences in reading and that met the criteria for inclusion in his meta-analysis. Although this model dominates the preservice reading programs in the United States, there is no evidence that it or any of its components, such as early field experiences and supervised practice teaching, provide the most effective means of educating teachers of reading (Blanton & Moorman, 1985; Hodges, 1982). The lack of information about early field experiences and the role of supervising and cooperating teachers is an issue that extends beyond reading teacher education (Ishler & Kay, 1981; Koehler, 1985). However, with the current interest in the "reflective practitioner" (Schön, 1983) and inquiry-oriented teacher education at the inservice level, it is particularly important to examine the traditional-craft conception of reading teacher education at the preservice level.

The second issue concerns the failure of the knowledge base and certain licensing practices to keep pace with current literacy demands. With the rapid growth of college learning centers, reading teacher education programs are faced with demands for courses that are not part of the regular curriculum. Eanet's (1983) survey, although small, points out the need to offer courses of study aimed directly at preparing college reading specialists. Rapid growth in other types of learning centers—the franchised reading centers springing up around the country—presents a different kind of problem. In the absence of state licensing guidelines for staff employed in these centers, there is the risk of inappropriate instruction and/or program development. Another problem area is the lack of uniform licensing procedures for secondary teachers who are responsible for helping students learn from text in all their academic subjects. Unless states require a course in the teaching of reading as a prerequisite for licensure at the secondary school level, progress in teaching reading across the curriculum will be slow.

The third issue concerns the lack of systematically reported evaluation data for many of the long-term professional-development programs in reading teacher education. Although plans for evaluation design might have been part of the programs initially, the results of the evaluation plans are typically incomplete or reported in terms of student achievement rather than of teacher learning and satisfaction. Perhaps the sheer magnitude of the problems encountered in implementing long-term profesional-development programs in reading has left little time for systematically gathering and reporting evaluation data. Whatever the reason, it is an issue whose time has come. If replicating program developers are to realize their potential as decision makers and change agents, they must have available valid and reliable results of the model programs in the field.

Directions for Research

One direction for future research is in the area of preservice reading teacher education. Studies are needed that examine the nature of the relationship between the master teacher and the apprentice or between the university/college supervisor and the preservice teacher (e.g., Hollingsworth, in press). Specifically, how does the master teacher influence the student teacher's development as a professional? Is there a reciprocal nature to that influence? How effective are field experiences in the traditional-craft conception of reading teacher education, as compared with other conceptions of teacher education? Is there a place for the university or college supervisor in early field experiences? To what degree do preservice teachers of reading share the same characteristics as those of their named "influential" teachers (Haggard, 1985; Ruddell & Haggard, 1982)? These and other related questions are in need of exploration if an empirical base is to be built for the apprenticeship model of learning to teach reading.

Effort also needs to be devoted to the development of inquiry-oriented models of reading teacher education. Their development should include preservice and inservice models. For example, more studies are needed like the one conducted by Beverstock, Bowman, Myers, Serebrin, and Smitten (1988) in which preservice teachers "set out to uncover the ways [they] made sense of their language clusters" (p. 1). Until recently, research was done *on* teachers, not *with* them. Researchers drew their questions primarily from the literature, and only rarely from classroom teachers. This no longer has to be the norm. In fact, calls have gone forth recently for research paradigms that offer greater sensitivity to classroom realities (Duffy, 1983; Shefelbine & Hollingsworth, 1987), for teachers to become researchers, and researchers to become teachers (Harste, 1988; Lapp, Flood, & Alvarez, 1988; Short, 1987), for professional-development models that assist teachers in reducing the disparity between intentions and actions (Richardson-Koehler & Fenstermacher, 1988; L. R. Roehler, personal communication, December 6, 1988; Smyth, 1982), and for program-evaluation designs that aim to improve, not prove (Nicholson, 1989; Tierney, 1987).

Finally, the examination of expert–novice differences needs to be context sensitive. Although findings from policy-capturing studies have their place in the research, more naturalistic studies are needed to assure ecological validity and to enhance potential for the transfer of results to real classrooms. In particular, studies are needed that examine how preservice and inservice teachers acquire knowledge and what implicit theories they use to guide their actions in different contexts (Shulman, 1987a, 1987b; Tierney & Gee, 1988). Theories of developmental stages in moving from novice to expert teacher of reading (Berliner, 1988; Hollingsworth, in press) also need to be tested. Likewise, there is a need for studies that clarify how novices and experts use their declarative knowledge about reading instruction to inform their procedural knowledge (Conley, 1986a; Roehler et al., 1988), for longitudinal case studies that trace how factors outside the teaching–learning process mediate teachers' beliefs and practices (Lalik & Pecic, 1986), and for classroom research that unites teachers and students as a community of learners (Beverstock et al., 1988; Carter & Tierney, 1988; Dillon, O'Brien, & Ruhl, 1988; Five, 1986).

References

Alvermann, D. E. (1981). The possible values of dissonance in student teaching experiences. *Journal of Teacher Education, 32*(3), 24–25.

Alvermann, D. E., & Hayes, D. A. (1989). Classroom discussion of content area reading assignments: An intervention study. *Reading Research Quarterly, 24,* 305–335.

Ambrose, R., & Janes, D. (1987, April). *School district and university collaboration: Kent State University–Akron Public School elementary education intern program.* Paper presented at the spring conference of the Ohio Confederation of Teacher Education Organizations, Dublin.

Anderson, L. M., Evertson, C. M., & Brophy, J. E. (1979). An experimental study of effective teaching in first-grade reading groups. *Elementary School Journal, 79*(4), 193–223.

Anderson, S. L. (1984). Teacher training techniques from four observational perspectives. *Journal of Classroom Interaction, 20,* 16–28.

Askov, E. N., & Dupuis, M. M. (1983). Results of a three-year study of teacher change through inservice in content area reading. In G. H. McNinch (Ed.), *Reading research to reading practice* (3rd yearbook of the American Reading Forum, pp. 110–112). Athens, GA: American Reading Forum.

Au, K. H., Crowell, D. C., Jordan, C., Sloat, K. C. M., Speidel, G. E., Klein, T. W., & Tharp, R. G. (1986). Development and implementation of the KEEP Reading Program. In J. Orasanu (Ed.), *Reading comprehension: From research to practice* (pp. 235–252). Hillsdale, NJ: Lawrence Erlbaum.

Austin, M. C. (1968). Professional training of reading personnel. In H.

M. Robinson (Ed.), *Innovation and change in reading instruction* (67th yearbook of the National Society for the Study of Education, Part II, pp. 357–396). Chicago: National Society for the Study of Education.

Austin, M. C., & Morrison, C. (1961). *The torch lighters: Tomorrow's teachers of reading.* Cambridge, MA: Harvard University Press.

Austin, M. C., & Morrison, C. (1963). *The first R: The Harvard report on reading in elementary schools.* New York: Macmillan.

Bader, L. A. (1975). Certification requirements in reading. *Journal of Reading, 19,* 237–240.

Barr, R. (1987). Classroom interaction and curricular content. In D. Bloome (Ed.), *Literacy and schooling,* (pp. 150–168). Norwood, NJ: Ablex.

Berliner, D. (1986). In pursuit of the expert pedagogue. *Educational Researcher, 15,* 5–13.

Berliner, D. C. (1988). *The development of expertise in pedagogy.* Unpublished manuscript, Stanford University, Center for Advanced Study in Behavioral Sciences, Stanford.

Beverstock, C., Bowman, P., Myers, J., Serebrin, W., & Smitten, B. (1988). *The "sense" preservice teachers make of their language arts/reading methods classes and field placement experience.* Unpublished manuscript, Indiana University, Bloomington.

Blanton, W. E., & Moorman, G. B. (1985). Field experiences: Aids or impediments to classroom reading instruction? *Reading Research and Instruction, 25,* 56–59.

Blanton, W. E., & Moorman, G. (1987). *The effects of knowledge on the instructional behavior of classroom reading teachers* (Research Report No. 6). Boone, NC: Appalachian State University, Center on Excellence in Teacher Education.

Borko, H., Eisenhart, M., Kello, M., & Vandett, N. (1984). Teachers as decision makers versus technicians. In J. A. Niles & L. A. Harris (Eds.), *Changing perspectives on research in reading/language processing and instruction* (33rd yearbook of the National Reading Conference, pp. 124–131). Rochester, NY: National Reading Conference.

Borko, H., Lalik, R., & Tomchin, E. (1987). Student teachers' understandings of successful and unsuccessful teaching. *Teaching and Teacher Education, 3,* 77–90.

Borko, H., & Niles, J. (1982). Factors contributing to teachers' judgments about students and decisions about grouping students for reading instruction. *Journal of Reading Behavior, 14,* 127–140.

Borko, H., Shavelson, R. J., & Stern, P. (1981). Teachers' decisions in the planning of reading instruction. *Reading Research Quarterly, 16,* 449–466.

Bush, M. M. (1984). The complexity of institutionalizing a program: Acquisition of training, observing, and computing capability. *Journal of Classroom Interaction, 20,* 6–15.

Calfee, R., & Henry, M. K. (1986). Project READ: An inservice model for training classroom teachers in effective reading instruction. In J. V. Hoffman (Ed.), *Effective teaching of reading: Research and practice* (pp. 199–229). Newark, DE: International Reading Association.

Calfee, R., Henry, M., & Funderburg, J. (1988). A model for school change. In S. J. Samuels & P. D. Pearson (Eds.), *Changing school reading programs* (pp. 121–141). Newark, DE: International Reading Association.

Carnegie Forum on Education and the Economy, Task Force on Teaching as a Profession. (1986). *A nation prepared: Teachers for the 21st century.* New York: Author.

Carter, M., & Tierney, R. (1988, December). *Reading and writing growth: Using portfolios in assessment.* Paper presented at the annual meeting of the National Reading Conference, Tucson.

Clay, M. (1987). Implementing Reading Recovery: Systematic adaptations to an educational innovation. *New Zealand Journal of Educational Studies, 22,* 35–58.

Conley, M. W. (1986a). The influence of training on three teachers' comprehension questions during content area lessons. *Elementary School Journal, 87,* 17–27.

Conley, M. W. (1986b). Teachers' conceptions, decisions, and changes during initial classroom lessons containing content reading strategies. In J. Niles & R. Lalik (Eds.), *Solving problems in literacy: Learners, teachers, and researchers* (35th yearbook of the National Reading Conference, pp. 120–126). Rochester, NY: National Reading Conference.

Cook-Gumperz, J., & Gumperz, J. J. (1982). Communicative competence in educational perspective. In L. C. Wilkinson (Ed.), *Communicating in the classroom* (pp. 13–24). New York: Academic Press.

Dillon, D. R., O'Brien, D. G., & Ruhl, J. D. (1988, December). *The construction of the social organization in one secondary content classroom: An ethnographic study of a biology teacher and his academic-track students.* Paper presented at the annual meeting of the National Reading Conference, Tucson.

Dishner, E. K., & Olson, M. W. (1989). Content area reading: A historical perspective. In D. Lapp, J. Flood, & N. Farnan (Eds.), *Content area reading and learning: Instructional strategies* (pp. 2–13). Englewood Cliffs, NJ: Prentice-Hall.

Drum, P. A., & Calfee, R. C. (1979). Compensatory reading programs, what are they like, and are they different? In R. C. Calfee & P. A. Drum (Eds.), *Teaching reading in compensatory classes* (pp. 172–191). Newark, DE: International Reading Association.

Duffy, G. G. (1981). Teacher effectiveness research: Implications for the reading profession. In M. L. Kamil (Ed.), *Directions in reading: Research and instruction* (30th yearbook of the National Reading Conference, pp. 113–136). Washington, DC: National Reading Conference.

Duffy, G. G. (1982). Response to Borko, Shavelson, and Stern: There's more to instructional decision-making in reading than the "empty classroom." *Reading Research Quarterly, 17,* 295–300.

Duffy, G. G. (1983). Should we adapt to them or them to us? Messages from research on teaching regarding the reading research to reading practice issue. In G. H. McNinch (Ed.), *Reading research to reading practice* (3rd yearbook of the American Reading Forum, pp. 87–89). Athens, GA: American Reading Forum.

Duffy, G. G., & Anderson, L. (1984). Teachers' theoretical orientations and the real classroom. *Reading Psychology, 5,* 97–104.

Duffy, G. G., & McIntyre, L. K. (1982). A naturalistic study of instruction assistance in primary grade reading. *Elementary School Journal, 83,* 15–23.

Dupuis, M. M., Askov, E. N., & Lee, J. W. (1979). Changing attitudes toward content area reading: The content area reading project. *Journal of Educational Research, 73,* 66–74.

Durkin, D. (1979). What classroom observations reveal about reading comprehension instruction. *Reading Research Quarterly, 14,* 481–533.

Eanet, M. G. (1983). Do graduate reading programs prepare college reading specialists? *Forum for Reading, 14,* 30–33.

Elbaz, F. (1981). The teacher's "practical knowledge": Report of a case study. *Curriculum Inquiry, 11,* 43–71.

Estes, T. H., & Piercey, D. (1973). Secondary reading requirements: Report on the states. *Journal of Reading, 17,* 20–24.

Farrell, R. J., & Cirrincione, J. M. (1984). State certification requirements in reading for content area teachers. *Journal of Reading, 28,* 152–158.

Fitzgerald, J. (1984). Teachers' views of reading research. *Reading World, 24,* 1–9.

Five, C. L. (1986). Fifth graders respond to a changed reading program. *Harvard Educational Review, 56*(4), 395–405.

Flippo, R. F., Hayes, D. A., & Aaron, R. L. (1983). Teacher competency testing and reading specialty preparation in Georgia. In G. H. McNinch (Ed.), *Reading research to reading practice* (3rd yearbook of the American Reading Forum, pp. 94–98). Athens, GA: American Reading Forum.

Gaskins, I. W. (1988). Helping teachers adapt to the needs of students with learning problems. In S. J. Samuels & P. D. Pearson (Eds.), *Changing school reading programs* (pp. 143–159). Newark, DE: International Reading Association.

Gist, A. S., & King, W. A. (1927). *The teaching and supervision of reading.* New York: Charles Scribner's Sons.

Gray, W. S. (1927). Summary of reading investigations: July 1, 1925 to June 30, 1926. *Elementary School Journal, 27,* 456–466, 495–510.

Guthrie, J. T., Seifert, M., & Mosberg, L. (1983). Research synthesis in reading: Topics, audiences, and citation rates. *Reading Research Quarterly, 19,* 16–27.

Guzzetti, B. J. (1989). From preservice to inservice: A naturalistic inquiry of beginning teachers' practices in content reading. *Teacher Education Quarterly, 16,* 65–71.

Haggard, M. R. (1985). Pre-teacher and influential teacher perceptions. *Teacher Education Quarterly, 12,* 64–72.

Hao, R. N. (1988). Research and development model for improving reading instruction. In S. J. Samuels & P. D. Pearson (Eds.), *Changing school reading programs* (pp. 95–118). Newark, DE: International Reading Association.

Harris, J. M., Donovan, H. L., & Alexander, T. (1927). *Supervision and teaching of reading.* Atlanta: Johnson.

Harste, J. C. (1988). Tomorrow's readers today: Becoming a profession of collaborative learners. In J. E. Readence & R. S. Baldwin (Eds.), *Dialogues in literacy research* (37th yearbook of the National Reading Conference, pp. 3–13). Chicago: National Reading Conference.

Harste, J., & Burke, C. (1977). A new hypothesis for reading teacher research: Both teaching and learning of reading are theoretically based. In P. D. Pearson (Ed.), *Reading: Theory, research, and practice* (26th yearbook of the National Reading Conference, pp. 32–40). Clemson, SC: National Reading Conference.

Herber, H. L., & Nelson, J. (1983). *A network of secondary school demonstration centers for teaching reading in content areas* (Final Report of the Basic Skills Improvement Program, Title II, Project No. 599AH00558). Syracuse, NY: Syracuse University, Reading and Language Arts Center.

Herber, H. L., & Nelson-Herber, J. (1984). Effective programs to help people become readers. In A. C. Purves & O. Niles (Eds.), *Becoming readers in a complex society* (83rd yearbook of the National Society for the Study of Education, Part I, pp. 174–208). Chicago: University of Chicago Press.

Hodges, C. (1982). Implementing methods: If you can't blame the cooperating teacher, who can you blame? *Journal of Teacher Education, 33*(6), 25–29.

Hoffman, J. V., & O'Neal, S. F. (1984). Curriculum decision making and the beginning teacher of reading in the elementary school classroom. In J. A. Niles & L. A. Harris (Eds.), *Changing perspectives on research in reading/language processing and instruction* (pp. 137–145). Rochester, NY: National Reading Conference.

Hollingsworth, S. (in press). Prior beliefs and cognitive change in learning to teach. *American Educational Research Journal.*

Holmes Group (1986). *Tomorrow's teachers.* East Lansing, MI: Author.

International Reading Association (1986). *Guidelines for the specialized preparation of reading professionals.* Newark, DE: Author.

Ishler, P., & Kay, R. S. (1981). A survey of institutional practice. In C. Webb, N. Gehrke, P. Ishler, & A. Mendoza (Eds.), *Exploratory field experiences in teacher education* (pp. 15–22). Reston, VA: Association of Teacher Educators.

Kamil, M., & Pearson, P. D. (1979). Theory and practice in teaching reading. *New York University Education Quarterly*, Winter, 10–16.

Kennedy, M. (1978). Findings from the Follow Through planned variation study. *Educational Researcher, 7*(6), 3–11.

Kinzer, C. K. (1988). Instructional frameworks and instructional choices: Comparisons between preservice and inservice teachers. *Journal of Reading Behavior, 20,* 357–377.

Koehler, V. (1985). Research on preservice teacher education. *Journal of Teacher Education, 36*(1), 23–30.

Lalik, R., Borko, H., Pecic, K., Perry, D., & Livingston, C. (1985, December). *Beginning teachers' use of basal manuals during reading and language arts instruction.* Paper presented at the annual meeting of the National Reading Conference, San Diego.

Lalik, R., & Niles, J. A. (in press). Student teachers' planning in collaborative groups: An examination of task structure. *Elementary School Journal.*

Lalik, R., & Pecic, K. (1986, December). *Learning to teach Chapter I reading: An examination of the belief/practice connections.* Paper presented at the annual meeting of the National Reading Conference, Austin.

Lapp, D., Flood, J., & Alvarez, D. (1988, December). *Preservice teachers, secondary classroom teachers and teacher educators: A model which promotes effective instruction and learning.* Paper presented at the annual meeting of the National Reading Conference, Tucson.

Malone, M. R. (1984). Project MAFEX: Report on preservice field experiences in reading education. In G. H. McNinch (Ed.), *Reading teacher education* (4th yearbook of the American Reading Forum, pp. 43–45). Carrollton, GA: American Reading Forum.

Mangieri, J. N., & Kemper, R. E. (1979). Reading: Another challenge for teacher education. *Journal of Teacher Education, 30*(6), 11–12.

Meyer, L. (1988). Research on implementation: What seems to work. In S. J. Samuels & P. D. Pearson (Eds.), *Changing school reading programs* (pp. 41–57). Newark, DE: International Reading Association.

Meyer, L. A., Gersten, R., & Gutkin, J. (1983). Direct instruction: A Project Follow Through success story. *Elementary School Journal, 84,* 241–252.

Meyers, R. S., & Ringler, L. (1980). Teacher interns' conceptualization of reading theory and practice. In M. L. Kamil & A. J. Moe (Eds.), *Perspectives on reading research and instruction* (29th yearbook of the National Reading Conference, pp. 238–242). Washington, DC: National Reading Conference.

Miller, J. W., & Ellsworth, R. (1985). The evaluation of a two-year program to improve teacher effectiveness in reading instruction. *Elementary School Journal, 85*(4), 485–495.

Mishler, E. G. (1979). Meaning in context: Is there any other kind? *Harvard Educational Review, 49,* 1–19.

Monahan, J. N. (1987). Secondary teachers do care! *Journal of Reading, 30,* 676–678.

Moore, D. W., Readence, J. E., & Rickelman, R. J. (1983). An historical exploration of content area reading instruction. *Reading Research Quarterly, 18,* 419–438.

Moore, P. J. (1983). Teachers' views on reading: Match or mismatch with materials. In J. Anderson & K. Lovett (Eds.), *Teaching reading and writing to every child* (pp. 116–124). Adelaide, South Australia: Australian Reading Association.

Morine-Dershimer, G. (1979). *Teacher plans and classroom reality: The South Bay Study, Part IV* (Research Series No. 60.). East Lansing, MI: Michigan State University, Institute for Research on Teaching.

Morris, A. (1988). Preparation of Australian secondary teachers in the teaching of reading: 1976–1986. *Australian Journal of Reading, 11*(1), 54–64.

Morris, A., & Stewart-Dore, N. (1984). *Learning to learn from text.* Sydney, Australia: Addison-Wesley.

Morrison, C., & Austin, M. C. (1977). *The torch lighters revisited.* Newark, DE: International Reading Association.

National Council for Accreditation of Teacher Education. (1987). *NCATE standards, procedures and policies for the accreditation of professional teacher education units.* Washington, DC: Author.

Nicholson, T. (1979). Training programmes for teachers of reading in New Zealand. *South Pacific Journal of Teacher Education, 7,* 116–119.

Nicholson, T. (1989). Using the CIPP model to evaluate reading instruction. *Journal of Reading, 32,* 312–318.

Niles, J. A., & Lalik, R. V. (1987). Learning to teach comprehension: A collaborative approach. In J. E. Readence & R. S. Baldwin (Eds.), *Research in literacy: Merging perspectives* (36th yearbook of the National Reading Conference, pp. 153–160). Rochester, NY: National Reading Conference.

Ogle, D. (1986). Collaboration for school improvement: A case study of a school district and a college. In J. Orasanu (Ed.), *Reading comprehension from research to practice* (pp. 287–301). Hillsdale, NJ: Lawrence Erlbaum.

Ogle, D. M. (1989). Implementing strategic teaching. *Educational Leadership, 46*(4), 47–48, 57–60.

Pace, A. J., & Powers, W. C. (1981). The relationship between teachers' behaviors and beliefs and students' reading. In J. R. Edwards (Ed.), *Language and literacy: The social psychology of reading*

(Vol. 1, pp. 99–115). Silver Spring, MD: Institute of Modern Languages.

Pinnell, G. S. (1987). Helping teachers see how readers read: Staff development through observation. *Theory into Practice, 26,* 51–58.

Pinnell, G. S., & Woolsey, D. (1985). *Report of a study of teacher co-researchers in a project to prevent reading failure* (Sponsored by a grant from the Research Foundation of the National Council of Teachers of English, Urbana, IL). Unpublished report submitted to NCTE and available from first author at Ohio State University.

Putnam, J., Roehler, L. R., & Duffy, G. G. (1987). *The staff development model of the teacher explanation project* (Occasional Paper No. 108). East Lansing, MI: Michigan State Universtiy, Institute for Research on Teaching.

Rentel, V. M., & Pinnell, G. S. (1987, December). *A study of practical reasoning in Reading Recovery instruction.* Paper presented at the meeting of the National Reading Conference, St. Petersburg Beach.

Resnick, D. P., & Resnick, L. B. (1980). The nature of literacy: An historical exploration. In M. Wolf, M. K. McQuillan, & E. Radwin (Eds.), *Thought, language and reading* (pp. 396–411). (Harvard Educational Review Reprint Series No. 14).

Richardson-Koehler, V., & Fenstermacher, G. (1988). *The use of practical arguments in staff development.* (ERIC Document Reproduction Service No. SP 030 047)

Robbins-Wilf, M. (1987). How do New Jersey's private reading service centers operate? *Reading Instruction Journal,* Fall, 23–28.

Roehler, L. R., Duffy, G. G., Herrmann, B. A., Conley, M., & Johnson, J., (1988). Knowledge structures as evidence of the 'Personal': Bridging the gap from thought to practice. *Journal of Curriculum Studies, 20,* 159–165.

Ruddell, R. B., & Haggard, M. R. (1982). Influential teachers: Characteristics and classroom performance. In J. A. Niles & L. A. Harris (Eds.), *New inquiries in reading research and instruction* (pp. 227–231). Rochester, NY: National Reading Conference.

Rupley, W. H., & Logan, J. W. (1985). Elementary teachers' beliefs about reading and knowledge of reading content: Relationships to decision about reading outcomes. *Reading Psychology, 6*(3–4), 145–156.

Santa, C. M. (1986). Content reading in secondary schools. In J. Orasanu (Ed.), *Reading comprehension: From research to practice* (pp. 303–317). Hilsdale, NJ: Lawrence Erlbaum.

Santa, C. M. (1988). Changing teacher behavior in content reading through collaborative research. In S. J. Samuels & P. D. Pearson (Eds.), *Changing school reading programs* (pp. 185–204). Newark, DE: International Reading Association.

Schön, D. A. (1983). *The reflective practitioner: How professionals think in action.* New York: Basic Books.

Seat, K. W. (1983). A model for program development and evaluation of private reading clinics (Doctoral dissertation, University of Southern California, 1982). *Dissertation Abstracts International, 43,* 2619A.

Shake, M. C. (1984, December). *Teachers as thinkers: A naturalistic study of teacher thinking and decision making.* Paper presented at the annual meeting of the National Reading Conference, St. Petersburg Beach.

Shannon, P. (1986). The role of the reading researcher in public schools: Researcher as outsider. In J. A. Niles & R. V. Lalik (Eds.), *Solving problems in literacy: Learners, teachers, and researchers* (pp. 406–409). Rochester, NY: National Reading Conference.

Shefelbine, J. L., & Hollingsworth, S. (1987). The instructional decisions of preservice teachers during a reading practicum. *Journal of Teacher Education, 38*(1), 36–42.

Short, K. G. (1987, December). *Collaborative research: New potentials for knowing.* Paper presented at the annual meeting of the National Reading Conference, St. Petersburg Beach.

Shulman, L. S. (1986). Paradigms and research programs in the study of teaching: A contemporary perspective. In M. C. Wittrock (Ed.), *Handbook of research on teaching* (3rd ed., pp. 3–36). New York: Macmillan.

Shulman, L. S. (1987a). Knowledge and teaching: Foundations of the new reform. *Harvard Educational Review, 57*(1), 1–22.

Shulman, L. S. (1987b). Sounding an alarm: A reply to Sockett. *Harvard Educational Review, 57,* 473–482.

Singer, H., & Bean, T. W. (1988). Three models for helping teachers to help students learn from text. In S. J. Samuels & P. D. Pearson (Eds.), *Changing school reading programs* (pp. 161–182). Newark, DE: International Reading Association.

Smith, N. B. (1965). *American reading instruction.* Newark, DE: International Reading Association.

Smith-Burke, M. T., & Ringler, L. H. (1986). STAR: Teaching reading and writing. In J. Orasanu (Ed.), *Reading comprehension: From research to practice* (pp. 215–234). Hillsdale, NJ: Lawrence Erlbaum.

Smyth, J. (1982). A teacher development approach to bridging the practice–research gap. *Curriculum Inquiry, 14,* 331–342.

Stahl, N. A., (1987). Big bucks or big problems: The implications of the franchise learning centers for reading professionals. *Georgia Journal of Reading, 12*(2), 2–6.

Stahl, N. A., Gordon, B., & Brozo, W. G. (1984). The professional preparation of college reading and study skills specialists. In G. H. McNinch (Ed.), *Reading teacher education* (4th yearbook of the American Reading Forum, pp. 47–50). Carrollton, GA: American Reading Forum.

Stallings, J. (1980). Allocated academic learning time revisited, or beyond time on task. *Educational Research, 8*(11), 11–16.

Stallings, J., Cory, R., Fairweather, J., & Needels, M. (1978). *A study of basic reading skills taught in secondary schools.* Menlo Park, CA: Stanford Research Institute.

Stallings, J., & Kaskowitz, D. (1974). *Follow Through classroom observation evaluation, 1972–1973.* Menlo Park, CA: Stanford Research Institute.

Stallings, J., & Stipek, D. (1986). Research on early childhood and elementary school teaching programs. In M. C. Wittrock (Ed.), *Handbook of research on teaching* (3rd ed., pp. 727–753). New York: Macmillan.

Stewart-Dore, N. (1986). Practising language across the curriculum: A secondary school case study. In M. L. Tickoo (Ed.), *Language in learning* (Anthology Series 16, pp. 131–148). Singapore: SEAMEO Regional Language Centre.

Sullivan, L. L. (1980). Growth and influence of the learning center movement. *New Directions for College Learning Assistance, 1,* 1–7.

Taylor, N. E., Blum, I. H., & Logsdon, D. M. (1986). The development of written language awareness: Environmental aspects and program characteristics. *Reading Research Quarterly, 21,* 132–149.

Teacher Assessment Unit. (1987). Division of Assessment, Evaluation, and Personnel, Georgia Department of Education, Atlanta, GA.

Thomas, K. J., & Simpson, M. (1979). Reading requirements and basic secondary teacher certification: An update. *Reading Horizons, 20,* 20–26.

Tierney, R. J. (1987, December). *Empowering student and teacher problem-solving in reading and writing: A university-school collaboration.* Paper presented at the annual meeting of the National Reading Conference, St. Petersburg Beach.

Tierney, R., & Gee, J. M. (1988, December). *Knowledge shifts in preservice teachers engaged in self-sponsored learning activities.* Paper presented at the annual meeting of the National Reading Conference, Tucson.

Tierney, R. J., Tucker, D. L. Gallagher, M. C., Crismore, A., & Pearson, P. D. (1988). The Metcalf Project: A teacher-researcher collaboration. In S. J. Samuels & P. D. Pearson (Eds.), *Changing school reading programs* (pp. 207–226). Newark, DE: International Reading Association.

Tom, A. R. (1985). Inquiring into inquiry-oriented teacher education. *Journal of Teacher Education, 36*(5), 35–44.

Vavrus, L. G., & Calfee, R. C. (1988, December). *A research strategy for assessing teachers of elementary literacy: The promise of performance portfolios.* Paper presented at the annual meeting of the National Reading Conference, Tucson.

Venezky, R. L. (1986). Steps toward a modern history of American reading instruction. In E. Z. Rothkopf (Ed.), *Review of Research in Education* (Vol. 13, pp. 129–167). Washington, DC: American Educational Research Association.

Wedman, J. M., & Robinson, R. (1988). Effects of extended inservice on secondary teachers' use of content reading instructional strategies. *Journal of Research and Development in Education, 21,* 65–70.

Whipple, G. M. (Ed.). (1919). *Fourth report of the Committee on Economy of Time in Education* (18th yearbook of the National Society for the Study of Education, Part II). Chicago: University of Chicago Press.

Whipple, G. M. (Ed.). (1925). *Report of the National Committee on Reading* (24th yearbook of the National Society for the Study of Education, Part I). Chicago: University of Chicago Press.

Whitford, B. L. (1987). Effects of organizational context on program implementation. In G. W. Noblit & W. T. Pink (Eds.), *Schooling in social context: Qualitative studies* (pp. 93–118). Norwood, NJ: Ablex.

Yoakam, G. A. (1937). The reorganization and improvement of instruction in reading through adequate supervision. In G. M. Whipple (Ed.), *The teaching of reading: A second report* (36th yearbook of the National Society for the Study of Education, Part I, pp. 419–438).Chicago: University of Chicago Press.

Zeichner, K. M. (1983). Alternative paradigms of teacher education. *Journal of Teacher Education, 34*(3), 3–9.

Zeichner, K. M., Tabachnick, B. R., & Densmore, K. (1987). Individual, institutional, and cultural influences on the development of teachers' craft knowlege. In J. Calderhead (Ed.), *Exploring teachers' thinking* (pp. 21–59). London: Cassell.

ENGLISH LANGUAGE ARTS TEACHER EDUCATION

Roy C. O'Donnell

UNIVERSITY OF GEORGIA

In his overview of research on teacher education, Richard L. Turner (Rehage, 1975) states that "the aim of research in teacher education is to optimize that portion of teacher work success attributable to teacher preparation" (p. 87). His schema for organizing information about teacher education includes four broad categories: selection, training, placement, and work success. The application of Turner's schema in a quest for research studies in the preparation of teachers of English language arts would result in the inclusion of only a few existing studies. In fact, of all the studies cited in Lanier and Little's review of research on teacher education in the third *Handbook of Research on Teaching* (Wittrock, 1986), not one places primary emphasis on the education of English teachers.

A computer search of the ERIC data base yielded 20,159 items related to teacher education and 5,369 items related to language arts, but there were only 206 items with both descriptors. Screening of these items to exclude those primarily related to reading (reviewed elsewhere in this volume) and those only peripherally related to language arts eliminated a large percentage of the total, leaving only a small number of items directly related to the preparation of teachers of the English language arts.

An informal poll of a selected sample of recognized leaders in English education asking them to identify studies that should not be omitted from this review confirmed the author's impression that significant research in the preparation of English teachers is not voluminous. Although there is very little research on English teacher preparation of the kind Turner describes, there is a considerable body of literature related to English teacher preparation, much of it produced in the decade of the 1960s.

THE STATUS OF ENGLISH TEACHER PREPARATION IN THE 1960s

In the aftermath of the *Sputnik* launching in 1957, the accumulated criticisms of progressivism and the life-adjustment approach to education found a focus, and the primacy of academic content of school subjects was reasserted. The resulting attempts to define the school subject called English were accompanied by a reexamination of standards of teacher preparation and certification. Federal agencies were quick to respond to requests for funds to support improved instruction in mathematics and the sciences, but the need for better English teaching was not obvious to them. To provide data in support of the effort to obtain funding for the humanities through extension of the National Defense Education Act, the National Council of Teachers of English (NCTE) conducted a comprehensive national survey of the status of English teaching, the results of which were published under the title, *The National Interest and the Teaching of English* (NCTE, 1961). Four of the seven goals for improving instruction in English cited in that report focus on teacher education: to educate teachers of English to the developmental and sequential nature of the study, to improve present preparatory programs for teachers of English, to improve the preparation of practicing teachers of English, and to recruit and prepare more teachers of English (p. 3).

The other three goals deal with the needs for defining the subject, providing support services, and encouraging research about the teaching of English. Suggested projects for improving teacher preparation include establishing regional centers for study and demonstration, supporting special confer-

The author thanks reviewers William H. Peters (Texas A&M University) and Robert E. Shafer (Arizona State University).

ences for teacher education personnel, establishing pilot programs in teacher education, supporting summer and yearlong institutes, and supporting large-scale experimental projects (pp. 5–8).

The report is buttressed by statistics showing that state certification regulations for teaching English in elementary and secondary schools were deplorably weak. Ten states allowed certification of elementary teachers without a bachelor's degree; 19 states specified no requirement in English for elementary certification; 21 reported no definite requirement of courses in reading, children's literature, or methods of teaching the language arts. The median number of semester hours of English required as minimum preparation of high school English teachers was 16–18, and 16 states required not more than 12 semester hours for the part-time teaching of English (p. 43). Only 4 states required English teachers to have as much as 30 semester hours in English. Requirements in professional education ranged from 16–36 semester hours for elementary teachers, with a median of 21. Requirements for secondary teachers ranged from 12–27, with a median of 18 (p. 46).

Questionnaire responses from 569 colleges and universities preparing elementary teachers showed similar weaknesses in degree requirements; 53 percent required from 0–6 semester hours in English, in addition to freshman-level courses; 39 percent required from 7–12 hours; 6.5 percent required from 13–18 hours; and only 2 percent required more than 18 hours (p. 52). Only 5 percent of the institutions required elementary teachers to have a course in the history and structure of English; 38.5 percent required a course in grammar and usage; and 20 percent required a course in composition beyond the freshman level (pp. 52–55). Sixty-nine percent required 5 hours or less in professional courses dealing with the methods of teaching reading and the language arts; 25 percent required from 6–10 hours; only 3 percent required over 11 semester hours.

The report also includes results of a survey of 374 institutions preparing high school English teachers: 34 percent required prospective English teachers to take 24 semester hours or less in English courses beyond the freshman level; 37 percent required 25–30 hours; and 14 percent required more than 30 semester hours. Twenty-five percent required a course in the history of the English language; 11 percent required a formal grammar review; 17 percent required a course in modern English grammar (pp. 66–68). Only 41 percent of the institutions required an advanced composition course (p. 70).

Slightly more than half required an English methods course. Only one-third of the methods courses devoted as much as 7 clock hours to teaching formal grammar; less than one-fourth devoted that much time to the teaching of English usage. Less than two-thirds of the methods courses devoted time to the teaching of composition, and less than two-thirds of that number allotted as much as 3 weeks to this important topic (pp. 72–73). Commenting on these data, the authors of the report wrote:

In short, most of the English majors who were graduated in June, 1960, and are now teaching in high school are simply not equipped to deal with problems of teaching the language and composition. . . .

Unhappily, what is true of the class of 1960 is no less true of the great body of teachers now in English classrooms. (p. 75)

The level of preparation in literature was found to be somewhat more adequate than that in language, but with notable deficiencies in the areas of world literature, contemporary literature, adolescent literature, and methods of literary criticism. The authors conclude, on the basis of the evidence presented, that there was a nationwide need for more highly qualified teachers of English (p. 86).

A subsequent study, *The National Interest and the Continuing Education of Teachers of English* (NCTE, 1964), reports that over 40 percent of those teaching in elementary schools at the time began full-time teaching without a baccalaureate degree and that 12 percent of the secondary English teachers began teaching without the degree. It was pointed out that, although 24 percent of the total instructional time in K–12 was spent on some form of instruction in English, with as much as 40 percent to 50 percent in the elementary grades, the average elementary teacher in the survey had devoted less than 8 percent of her or his college work to English, and almost half (49.5 percent) of all secondary teachers conducting English classes lacked majors in the subject (33 percent lacked even an English-related major such as speech or journalism, pp. 4–5). The typical elementary teacher in the survey had taught for approximately 9 years but had taken no English course in the past 6 years. Almost two-thirds of the secondary English teachers did not feel confident of their preparation in composition, and almost half were insecure in literature and language as well. Slightly over half considered themselves well prepared to teach literature; slightly more than a third, to teach composition; slightly more than half, to teach the English language. Only one-third felt well prepared to teach oral skills; and only one-tenth, to teach reading at the secondary level. Almost a third of the more experienced teachers reported not having taken an English course since certification or in the past 10 years. With an average of over 9 years of teaching experience, English teachers had completed an average of only .4 semester hours in composition and .7 hours in language (pp. 5, 6).

The report concludes with seven recommendations concerning the continuing education of teachers of English and language arts, the first two focusing on summer and year-round institutes on the content of English and on institutes and workshops on the specialized methods required to teach English in elementary and secondary schools (pp. 167–169).

The 1961 report on *The National Interest and the Teaching of English* includes a statement that had been formulated by the NCTE Standing Committee on Preparation and Certification of Teachers. This statement emphasizes the linguistic and literary content of English, as well as the science and art of teaching:

A Standard of Preparation to Teach English

I. The teacher of English should have a certain fundamental and specialized knowledge of the English language and its literature, together with certain abilities and skills which enable him to perform expertly in his discipline.

A. In language, he should have:

  1. A fundamental knowledge of the historical development and present character of the English language: phonology (phonetics and phonemics), morphology, syntax, vocabulary (etymology and semantics), the relations of language and society.

  2. A specialized knowledge of the English language which is appropriate to the teacher's particular field of interest and responsibility.

  3. An informed command of the arts of language—rhetoric and logic; ability to speak and write language which is not only unified, coherent, and correct but also responsible, appropriate to the situation, and stylistically effective.

B. In literature, he should have:

  1. A reading background of major literary works which emphasize the essential dignity of the individual man. This background:

    a. Implies a knowledge of major works, writers, forms, themes, and movements of the literature of the English-speaking people.

    b. Reflects intensive study of many literacy pieces.

    c. Includes familiarity with some of the standing literary works in English translation, or in the original language, of the Greek, Roman, Norse, Italian, French, Spanish, German, Slavic, and Oriental peoples.

  2. A specialized knowledge of whatever writers and literary works, forms, themes, media, and movements are appropriate to the teacher's particular field of interest and responsibility.

  3. An ability to analyze and evaluate independently the various forms of imaginative literature as well as the utilitarian forms of verbal expression, and the insight to use suitable critical approaches in order to discover their literary and human values.

II. The teacher of English should have certain abilities and knowledge which belong to the science and the art of teaching language and literature.

A. These abilities include:

  1. The ability to envision how his students may develop their potentialities through the study of language and literature.

  2. The ability to excite their interest and direct their learning.

  3. The ability to help them understand and use English practically and creatively.

  4. The ability to elevate their taste and critical powers.

  5. The ability to lead them to a perception of human problems and an appreciation of human values.

  6. The ability to evaluate their progress and the efficacy of their own methods.

B. These abilities presuppose not only the fundamental but also the specialized knowledge and skills of the English language and literature which the teacher needs to fulfill his professional responsibility.

C. These abilities imply knowledge of the philosophies of education and the psychologies of learning as they relate to the study and teaching of the English language and its literature. Such knowledge:

  1. Reveals how an individual unfolds and grows through his use and understanding of language and literature.

  2. Supplies the teacher with a variety of methods for use in teaching his students the skills and arts which are appropriate to their level of attainment in English.

  3. Informs the teacher of the relation which each phase or level has to the total school, college, and university program.

  4. Includes an awareness of the basic issues in the teaching of English. (pp. 40–42)

This statement was also included in *The Education of Teachers of English for American Schools and Colleges* (Grommon, 1963), prepared by NCTE's Commission on the English Curriculum under the editorship of Alfred H. Grommon. In his "A History of the Preparation of Teachers of English," published 5 years later in *English Journal* (April 1968), Grommon refers to this volume as, "by far the most comprehensive study yet attempted of the recruitment and the preservice and inservice education of teachers for elementary schools and teachers of English for secondary schools and colleges" (p. 513).

The Commission on the English Curriculum was composed of 38 specialists in English and in the teaching of English at all levels. The committee of specialists in elementary education formulated program recommendations for the general education, academic education, and professional education of teachers for elementary schools. Following a detailed analysis of what an elementary teacher does on a typical school day in teaching reading, literature, writing, speech, and listening, the committee presented sample programs from colleges and universities throughout the country, illustrating how preservice and inservice education of teachers contribute to their learning how to fulfill professional responsibilities.

In view of the large amount of time elementary teachers devote to teaching various aspects of the English language arts, the committee recommended that all students preparing to teach in the elementary school complete (a) a course in advanced composition (in addition to freshman English); (b) a course in the structure, historical development, and social functions of the English language; and (c) two courses in literature, one covering major American writers and the other English or world masterpieces. They also emphasized the significance of courses in speech (including oral interpretation and creative dramatics) and in children's literature and book selection. It was their opinion that prospective elementary school teachers should have enough undergraduate work in one academic area, and preferably in two, to be eligible later to pursue graduate courses in those areas (Grommon, 1963, pp. 90, 91). Similar proposals are still being advanced by advocates for reform of teacher education.

It was the committee's further recommendation that all candidates for teaching in elementary schools be required to complete a 5-year program. Throughout the last 2 or 3 years of the program, whether 4 or 5 years in length, candidates should acquire the professional knowledge, understanding, appreciation, and skills needed to contribute to the education of children. Detailed discussions of courses essential to a program of professional education, several sample programs, and specific recommendations for course content are included (Grommon, 1963, pp. 123–128).

The committee of specialists responsible for the secondary section recommended preparation in keeping, not only with the needs of present-day secondary schools, but also with foreseeable future needs. They advocated institutionwide committees on teacher education, to coordinate the full resources of the institutions and to further productive cooperation between academic departments and departments of education in such matters as appointing qualified faculty, planning courses and programs, and recruiting and advising students.

Without specific research findings to indicate that one particular program is significantly better than all others in preparing effective teachers of English, the committee offered several examples of existing patterns and recommended essential program elements. It was their view that at least 40 percent of the total program should be given over to general education, at least 40 percent to English and related courses, and no more than 20 percent to professional education (Grommon, 1963, p. 144). Major courses should provide coverage in the English language (history and structure, modern grammar, usage, and lexicography), composition (basic and advanced), and literature (English, American, world, contemporary, Shakespearean, literary criticism, and literature written for adolescents). Instruction in related subjects (speech, dramatics, and journalism) should also be provided (pp. 186, 187).

Preparation in professional education should include study of the psychological, social, and philosophical foundations of education, a practical course in methods of teaching, observation in schools, and practice teaching (Grommon, 1963, p. 144). Through courses and other experiences before assuming full responsibility for a classroom; the prospective teacher should acquire:

Essential understanding of human growth and development, especially the processes of learning and teaching, some knowledge of the nature and roles of public education in the United States, and some knowledge of and guided practice in using methods of teaching his subjects based upon research and a systematic study of English teachers' experience reported in the literature. (p. 357)

The specialists gave detailed descriptions of courses in methods of teaching English, in directed observations, and in supervised teaching. They also included extensive discussions and examples of inservice programs and of what colleges and universities might do when making follow-up studies of their graduates. Throughout the volume there is ample evidence of the specialists' awareness of the deficiencies identified in the two *National Interest* reports. There is also recognition of remaining problems including (a) lack of an adequate unifying theory of teacher education, (b) lack of persuasive research evidence of what the indispensable elements of an ideal program for preparing teachers of English might be, and (c) lack of a sure means of recruiting enough academically talented students for careers in teaching (Grommon, 1963, pp. 357–358).

THE ENGLISH TEACHER PREPARATION STUDY AND GUIDELINES

An important milestone in the development of standards for the preparation of English teachers was reached in 1968, when the English Teacher Preparation Study culminated in the publication of "Guidelines for the Preparation of English Teachers" (English Teacher Preparation Study, 1968). The study was conducted jointly by the National Association of State Directors of Teacher Education and Certification, the National Council of Teachers of English, and the Modern Language Association of America (MLA), with the cooperation of Western Michigan University and the financial support of the United States Office of Education. Between September 1965 and March 1967, a series of four regional conferences, a national meeting, and many consultations with interested agencies, organizations, institutions, and individuals were held. Throughout the study, successive drafts of the *Guidelines* were distributed widely for evaluation and reaction. Professors of English, professors of education, deans, state school officers, and classroom teachers were involved in drafting and refining the recommendations that resulted from the study. Most of the April 1968 issue of *English Journal* was devoted to the guidelines and related documents.

The *Guidelines*, reflecting the academic resurgence of the early 1960s, were intended to suggest desirable competencies for English teachers. They were to be used by state departments of education in evaluating programs for the preparation of teachers and by colleges and universities in developing and evaluating their teacher education programs and in recruiting and selecting good candidates for the teaching profession.

Recommendations focus on personal qualifications, skills, and kinds of knowledge contributing to effective teaching, including teacher's personality, general education, communication skills, and knowledge about and ability to teach English. Reflecting the definition formulated by the College Entrance Examination Board's Commission on English, the document divides the subject into language, literature, and composition; at the same time, it emphasizes the importance of the conception of English as a unified discipline.

The introductory paragraphs include the statement that:

Although English studies in American colleges and universities have emphasized chiefly the reading and appreciation of literature, the preparation of the elementary school teacher and of the secondary school teacher of English must include work in the English language, in composition, and in listening, speaking, reading, and writing, both to extend the teacher's own background and to prepare him to meet the full range of his obligations as a teacher of English. (English Teacher Preparation Study, 1968, p. 529).

Language, as used in the *Guidelines*, is defined as the structure and historical development of present-day English; *literature*, as chiefly British and American writing of distinction, "but also any other writing of distinction in English or in English translation" (p. 529); and *composition*, as oral and written composition and their relation to rhetorical theory. The phrase "the teacher of English at any level" is used throughout the document to include elementary school teachers, as well as specialists in English at the secondary school level. It is noted that elementary teachers, despite their many other professional obligations, spend some 40 percent to 60 percent of their time teaching English and related skills.

The introductory section also identifies two basic assumptions underlying the recommendations:

First, to teach the content of his subject effectively, the teacher not only must know the varied subject matter of English but also must understand how to communicate his knowledge and appreciation to his students; second, his preparation for teaching English should be based upon and supplemented by a background in the liberal arts and sciences, including psychology. (p. 530)

The *Guidelines* do not identify specific courses or ·course sequences, nor do they specify the exact number of credit hours required for adequate preparation to teach English. They do note, however, the consensus of those participating in the conferences that at least 15 semester hours in English above the freshman level would be required for the adequate preparation of elementary teachers and at least 36 for secondary teachers of English. They also note that "although the teacher of English incorporates journalism, dramatics, speech, and the teaching of reading skills into his teaching of English, he is not a specialist in these areas" (p. 530).

The document consists of six guidelines, all except the second beginning with the phrase "The teacher of English at any level should have. . . ." Guideline I deals with desirable personal qualities and general educational background; Guideline III with understanding and appreciation of a wide body of literature; Guideline IV with skills in listening, speaking, reading, writing, and understanding the nature of language and rhetoric; Guideline V with understanding the relationship of child and adolescent development to the teaching of English; and Guideline VI with methods of teaching English and the supervised teaching experience. Guideline II is divided into three parts:

A. The program in English for the elementary school teacher should provide a balanced study of language, literature, and composition above the level of freshman English. In addition, the program should require supervised teaching and English or language arts methods, including the teaching of reading, and it should provide for a fifth year of study.

B. The program in English for the secondary school teacher of English should constitute a major so arranged as to provide a balanced study of language, literature, and composition above the level of freshman English. In addition, the program should require supervised teaching and English methods, including the teaching of reading at the secondary level, and it should provide for a fifth year of study, largely in graduate courses in English and in English Education.

C. The teacher of English at any level should consider growth in his profession as a continuing process. (pp. 532–533)

Other items related to "Guidelines for the Preparation of Teachers of English" in the April 1968 issue of *English Journal* are "I: An Introduction to the English Teacher Preparation Study"; "II: Teacher Preparation and the English Classroom," including Grommon's "A History of Preparation of Teachers of English" (Grommon, 1968); "IV: Classic Statements on Teacher Preparation in English"; and "V: Certification Requirements to Teach English in Elementary or Secondary School—1967."

The certification requirements section, written by Eugene E. Slaughter (1968), updates his similar study published 4 years earlier (Slaughter, 1964, pp. 591–604). The data were obtained from 50 states, the District of Columbia, and Puerto Rico, and they were similar to the comprehensive studies of Stinnett, Frady, and Pershing (1967), and Woellner and Wood (1967). Summaries of data are presented in tabular form. Elementary-certificate requirements in semester hours are reported for each state for 1964 and 1967 as minimums in English (including speech, dramatics, and journalism), in professional education, and in reading methods, children's literature, and combined language arts. Requirements for the English area range from 6–24 hours, with 5 states reporting higher minimums and one state lower in 1967 than in 1964. Professional-education requirements range from 16–36 hours in 1964 and 16–40 hours in 1967. Six states reported higher minimums and four states lower in 1967 than in 1964. Most states did not report specific requirements in elementary school language arts, but they did indicate a requirement in the area.

Secondary certificate requirements in professional education range from 12–30 hours, with a median of 18 hours, for both years. Six states reported higher minimums and two states lower in 1967 than in 1964. The minimum in English (often including speech, dramatics, and journalism) required for teaching a full load of three or more English classes ranges from 12–40 hours, with a median of 24 hours, for both years. More specifically, in 1967, three states required a full-time teacher of English to have only 12 semester hours of college English; five states, 15 hours; two states, 16 hours; nine states, 18 hours; one state, 19 hours; two states, 20 hours; one state, 22 hours; 14 states, 24 hours; one state, 28 hours; eight states, 30 hours; five states, 36 hours; and one state, 40 hours. Five states showed an increase over 1964 requirements and six states showed a decrease.

The "Classic Statements on Teacher Preparation in English" include the 1958 NASDTEC Declaration of Policy on Teacher Education and Certification; an excerpt from the Basic Issues in the Teaching of English document (Basic Issues Conference Members, 1959); "A Standard of Preparation to Teach English" from *The National Interest and the Teaching of English* (NCTE, 1961); "Resolutions Adopted at a Seminar of English Department Chairmen" (Rogers, 1963); major recommendations for educating teachers of English for elementary and secondary schools from *The Education of Teachers of English* (Grommon, 1963); "Recommendations to Improve the Quality of Instruction" from *Freedom and Discipline in English* (College Entrance Examination Board, 1965); "Qualifications of Secondary School Teachers of English: A Preliminary Statement from the Illinois Statewide Curriculum Center for Preparation of Secondary School Teachers of English (Hook, 1965); and "Resolutions of the Anglo-American Conference on the Teaching and Learning of English" (Dixon, 1967; Muller, 1967). Although this conference, held at Dartmouth in the summer of 1966, is cited, its implications for the teaching of English and, subsequently, the preparation of English teachers are not fully reflected in the *Guidelines*.

Grommon's *A History of the Preparation of Teachers of English* covers a wider scope, ranging from the work of the Committee of Ten (1892–1894) to the professional contributions of Fred N. Scott (1903–1913), to the founding of NCTE (1911), to Hosic's *Reorganization of English in Secondary Schools* (1917), to the work of Walter Barnes (1918–1935), to the first NCTE curriculum commission under Wilbur Hatfield (1929–1940), to the second curriculum commission under Dora V. Smith (1946–1963), to the Conference on Basic Issues (1958), to the publication of *The Education of Teachers of English for American Schools and Colleges* (Grommon, 1963), to the work of NDEA Institutes for the Advanced Study of English (1965–1969), to the Dartmouth Conference (1966) and the English Teacher Preparation Study (1965–1967).

THE 1976 STATEMENT ON THE PREPARATION OF TEACHERS

Almost a decade later, the NCTE Standing Committee on Teacher Preparation and Certification issued *A Statement on the Preparation of Teachers of English and the Language Arts* (NCTE, 1976), in which they sought "to reaffirm those parts of the 1967 Guidelines that still apply, to strengthen the positions taken in the earlier Guidelines about the essentials of teacher education, and to reflect the changes that have taken place in our profession since 1967" (p. v). These changes included the growing emphasis on the process approach to education, as well as the emphasis on competency-based education. The *Statement* includes an introductory section, three major parts, and a 1974 NCTE resolution discouraging the use of competency-based teacher education programs.

The Introduction identifies some of the developments that must be taken into account in the preparation of teachers, including changes in the definition of English, changes in teacher education, changes in the teaching environment, and changes in the world at large. The authors of the *Statement* believed the tripod metaphor of English language, literature, and composition in the 1967 *Guidelines* had largely been replaced by a view of English as not only a body of knowledge and sets of skills and attitudes but also a process, or activity. They recognized a shift from the view of English as mainly an academic discipline whose mastery was a sign of intellectual development to the post-Dartmouth view that the use of English is also a means by which students grow towards emotional development. The latter view emphasizes how "students respond to their experiences and learn about their worlds, their feelings, their attitudes, and themselves by using language about these subjects" (NCTE, 1976, p. 1). It includes in English "whatever one does with language," perhaps even "whatever one does with symbols," and broadened the range of activities considered appropriate for English classrooms, to embrace dramatic activities, oral language, the media, and popular culture, as well as more literature written by minority writers and women. Recognition is also given to the question of whether the college

campus is the best place for the preparation of teachers, to the insistence on getting prospective teachers into the schools more and having them serve as apprentices in a variety of ways, and to the lack of research evidence to prove the superiority of field-based programs.

One change noted in the teaching environment is the shift away from government-supported projects designed to improve teaching materials and skills to those designed to assess accomplishments and enforce accountability. A related change is the increasing unionization of teachers and the perception of a climate of adversary relationships between teachers and their administrators and elected officials. Changes in the world at large include sharpened concern for preservation of the natural environment, population growth and mobility, technological advances, uneven distribution of resources, and claims for recognition from minority groups.

Part I of the *Statement* deals with "Qualifications Needed by Teachers of English" and is subdivided into Knowledge, Abilities, and Attitudes. It asserts that "the qualifications needed by individual teachers will vary according to the students they teach, but teachers at all levels, dealing with all kinds of children, need most of the same qualifications" (p. 5). Taking for granted that the education of teachers of English is a continuing process, the authors state that the process of acquiring the desired qualifications is not finished when the teacher attains certification but should continue throughout the teacher's professional life. Following the phrase that "Teachers of English need to know, and know how to draw on for their teaching, according to the needs and interests of their students" (p. 5) are items related to language acquisition, analysis of discourse, composing processes, reading, literature, nonprint media, resources for teaching, language in society, curriculum design, testing, and research. Abilities are grouped in relation to working with students, parents, and administrators; helping students create and respond to discourse; and helping students work with alternate (nonprint and nonverbal) forms of communication. Attitudes include those having to do with teachers' relationships to students as human beings, respect for the individual language and dialect of each student, desire to help students become familiar with diverse cultures, sensitivity to the impact of events and developments in the world outside the school, and commitment to continued professional growth.

Part II of the *Statement* enumerates "Experiences for Prospective Teachers That Will Help Them Develop the Necessary Qualifications." The authors make clear their assumption that there should be no single pattern in teacher education programs. They assert that "there are many paths to effective professional work in teaching, and prospective teachers should be encouraged to follow the path that most nearly suits their interests and abilities" (p. 9). In addition to a dozen kinds of experiences needed by all prospective teachers, five kinds of experiences needed by prospective English teachers are included:

1. gathering—and helping students in the schools to gather—materials that illuminate subjects of interest to students. In these experiences prospective teachers should seek out not

only recognized literary works but also journalistic writing (news stories, editorials, feature articles, advertisements), cartoons, photographs, films, records, tapes, and other materials appropriate to classroom situations. Ideally, prospective teachers should get this experience through working with classes having varied kinds of student populations.

2. engaging in varied language activities—and leading students in schools to engage in comparable activities. These activities should include *speaking* (e.g., in interpersonal communication, discussion, panel presentation, debate, role-playing exercise, dramatic enactment); *reading and reporting* about what has been found in materials read and seen; *conducting research* (not simply by reading) to collect data on subjects being studied; and *writing* (writing in varied forms: journals, narratives of personal experience, editorials, news stories, poetry, pieces of dialogue; using their own voices and assumed voices; addressing different audiences). Prospective teachers and their students should also have the experience of devising situations that invite a variety of language activities, and then engaging in the varied language activities, possible in those situations. Indeed, teachers should have the experience of drawing from students a variety of symbol-using activities, so that the students will come to understand the linguistic and nonlinguistic resources available to them.

3. leading classroom discussions by using questions that range from simple to abstract, helping students formulate for themselves questions at several levels of abstraction, and encouraging interchange between student and student.

4. observing and understanding the special problems exhibited by some students in reading, listening, writing, speaking; and finding appropriate means to help students improve in these activities.

5. doing, themselves, the activities they expect students to perform—e.g., keeping a journal, writing poetry, writing to different audiences in different voices, taking part in dramatic improvisations, making films—and analyzing at some point the processes they pass through in doing these things. (pp. 9–10)

These experiences were expected to enable prospective English teachers to discover what it means to understand and use language effectively and to design activities that could increase their students' power over language.

Part III of the *Statement* is devoted to "Issues for Discussion in the Planning of Programs for Preparing Teachers of English." It is in this section, as well as in the definition of English, that the difference between this *Statement* and the earlier *Guidelines* becomes most evident. Rather than offering suggested outlines or models of teacher education programs to guide program planners, the authors present some of the questions that planners must confront and try to resolve. The questions address the kinds of knowledge, skills, and attitudes prospective teachers need before student teaching and those needed before certification, as contrasted with those that can be left for later development during the teacher's active career. They also address the preferred blending of courses in English and courses in the teaching of English and, more specifically,

the balance in literature, language, reading, writing, and other areas, as well as the balance between on-campus and off-campus experiences. Other questions deal with the standards of admission and achievement, the extent of preservice teacher education programs, and the need for special preparation for teachers to deal with students with particular geographic, social, and economic backgrounds. The final group of questions addresses the personal and affective development of prospective teachers of English.

THE 1986 GUIDELINES FOR THE PREPARATION OF TEACHERS

The most recent document from the NCTE Standing Committee on Teacher Preparation and Certification is the 1986 *Guidelines for the Preparation of Teachers of English Language Arts* (NCTE, 1986). This document consists of an Introduction and two major parts. The Introduction explains the rationale for the revision of the 1976 *Statement*. Among the factors determining changes in emphasis are:

The increased use of standardized testing for both students and teachers; the growing influence of psycholinguistics and sociolinguistics on the teaching of English as a second language; pedagogy for exceptional students; recent developments in technology, especially the microcomputer and calls for "computer literacy"; a variety of learning theories in composition, accompanied by process-oriented approaches to the teaching of writing; influential literary theories developed since the "New Criticism"; research investigating connections between language and cognition; and the language-for-learning movement. (p. 1)

In addition, there is reference to the interest in educational reform documented in such reports as *High School: A Report on Secondary Education in America* (Boyer, 1983). *A Place Called School: Prospects for the Future* (Goodlad, 1984), *A Nation at Risk: The Imperative for Educational Reform* (National Commission on Excellence in Education, 1983), and *Horace's Compromise: The Dilemma of the American High School* (Sizer, 1984). Of particular significance for the preparation of English teachers is the acknowledgement in these reports of the centrality of language and literacy at all educational levels, as well as the recommendations for serious reconsideration of practices in teacher education.

Another element of the rationale for revision is the continuing redefinition of English and of teacher education. The 1986 *Guidelines* document largely reaffirms the view of English that the 1976 *Statement* presented, but it reflects the more recent emphasis on the integration of all language processes. The resulting holistic perspective on English,

in which the language arts are fully integrated, is rooted in contemporary research and theory which explore the relationships among linguistic, cognitive, and affective processes: the active and constructive nature of reading and listening, the interrelatedness of language with literature and composition study, and the centrality of language in learning. (p. 3)

Like the earlier documents, the 1986 publication takes for granted that the education of teachers is a continuing, lifelong process. Unlike them, it distinguishes between preservice and inservice education and advances recommendations for the essential elements of a preservice program of preparation. Following the lead of the 1976 *Statement*, it avoids suggesting any particular arrangement of program elements, and it does not delineate a specified number of courses of credit hours. Although the essential elements advanced generally apply to both elementary and secondary school teachers, distinctions are drawn between the two groups.

Part I, "Qualifications for Teachers of English Language Arts," identifies and defines the knowledge, pedagogical abilities, and attitudes English teachers must acquire and develop through preservice programs. The *Knowledge* portion discusses what teachers need to know about language development, composition and analysis of language, reading and literature, nonprint media, instructional media, evaluation and research. The *Pedagogy* section deals with instructional planning, performance, and assessment; instruction in oral and written language, reading, literature, nonprint media, and language for learning; and instructional uses of emerging technologies. The section on *Attitudes* attends to the concern for students, adaptability, and professional perspective. Each item has an annotation in which its rationale is presented, appropriate distinctions between elementary and secondary applications are made, and elaborations are provided.

Part II, "Experiences in Preparing Effective Teachers of English Language Arts," sets forth the kinds of campus-based and field-based learning experiences prospective teachers should have. Underlying the suggested experiences are the assumptions that prospective teachers of English language arts should "(a) experience in their college and university classes effective models of instruction, (b) analyze and evaluate the nature of effective teaching, and (c) witness and practice various aspects of effective teaching" (p. 5). Part II is intended as a guide to the development of programs to prepare prospective teachers who can translate what they have studied in their major courses into activities and experiences that will be effective and productive for their own students. These programs should prepare prospective teachers "in ways that will make them students of the teaching of English language arts throughout their teaching careers" (p. 17).

RECOMMENDATIONS OF THE COALITION OF ENGLISH ASSOCIATIONS

The ongoing redefinition of English, which will continue to have implications for the preparation of English teachers, reached another milestone in the meeting of the Coalition of English Associations in the summer of 1987. Strand A3 of the conference dealt with the English major. Noting changes in both the discipline of English and students, the participants recommended that students majoring in English read a variety of texts (literary, media, scientific, and theoretical) and engage in diverse types of writing.

They should be able to inquire into the complex functions of language, especially in relation to their own and other cultures; the ways in which

meanings are created; the nature of literature; the relationships between readers and texts, authors and texts, literature and society, and reading and writing in their experiential and historical dimensions. (Lloyd-Jones & Lunsford, 1989, p. 33)

Following the section on "Recommended Pedagogical Techniques," the report addresses "Teacher Education," suggesting that courses in English education emphasize learning, rather than teaching, and that they be extended with courses in learning theory and adolescent development. The report continues with the following statement:

The English major we propose, with its emphasis on how to do English rather than what English is, will better address the needs of preservice and inservice teachers. The models that college English instructors will offer teachers preparing to work at all levels (elementary, secondary, and tertiary) will place a self-conscious emphasis on the major issues. Teachers can thus see that addressing questions of sending and receiving messages in texts of all kinds will aid their students in realizing the power of language. The questions that teachers ask, in accord with this model, will become the following: "How do people learn from texts?"; "How does one read a text?"; "How does the teaching of texts in particular ways affect the ways students learn about them?"; "How does the classroom construct knowledge?" (Lloyd-Jones & Lunsford, 1989, p. 36)

How the recommendations of the coalition report will be translated into teacher education programs remains to be seen, but they will no doubt eventually be reflected in subsequent guidelines for the preparation of English teachers.

Although much of the literature reviewed up to this point is not the sort of thing usually considered research, it has obviously formed the information base for teacher education programs in English. And, because it represents the collective and distilled wisdom of English educators as a group, perhaps it should be regarded as a kind of research. At any rate, it is more voluminous and more influential than the body of literature defined by the more restrictive criteria laid down by Turner. The studies to which attention is directed next, however, come closer to the conventional definition of research.

SURVEYS OF PROFESSIONAL COMPETENCE

A wide-ranging, 5-year project to study ways to improve the preparation of English teachers was conducted during the 1960s by representatives of 20 Illinois institutions, under the direction of J. N. Hook. Known as the Illinois State-wide Curriculum Center for Preparation of Secondary School English Teachers (ISCPET), it was supported by funds from the United States Office of Education. An early product of the project was a preliminary list of qualifications of secondary school teachers of English, which was prepared as a working guide and was used in various subprojects. The list of qualifications was based upon the experience and observation of the institutional representatives; upon the recommendations of an advisory committee composed of 12 nationally known persons in English, speech, and education; and upon additional recommendations from Illinois authorities on certification, school administrators,

English consultants, department heads, and teachers. The list is arranged under five headings: Knowledge of Language, Knowledge and Skill in Written Composition, Knowledge and Skill in Literature, Knowledge and Skill in Oral Communication, and Knowledge and Skill in the Teaching of English. Specific items were listed under three quality levels: Minimal, Good, and Superior. The *minimal* level is intended to describe the competencies expected of teachers with an English minor or those with an English major but with less than average preparation or ability. The *good* level describes competencies of able or fairly able English majors. The *superior* level describes competencies to be expected of highly able teachers with very good or excellent college preparation, probably some graduate work, and some years of teaching experience. It was expected that institutions preparing secondary school teachers of English would attempt to produce graduates who would attain at least the *good* level (Hook, 1965).

The preliminary list was the basis of the Illinois Teacher Rating Scales (Forms A–F) developed by the project staff. Form G: For Experienced English Teachers was developed later for a study of *The Professional Competency of Illinois Secondary School English Teachers* (Crisp, 1968). Among the questions addressed in the study are, How do experienced secondary school English teachers evaluate themselves on given areas of knowledge in English and knowledge and skill in the teaching of English? What does actual teaching experience do to the self-evaluations of experienced English teachers? What does the level of college preparation do to these self-evaluations?

The rating scale was distributed to 600 Illinois teachers, randomly selected from the membership of the Illinois Association of Teachers of English and the secondary section of NCTE; 341 completed scales were returned. Overall, the respondents considered their professional competency in knowledge of English and Knowledge and Skill in Teaching English to be *Good.* A larger percentage of teachers with master's degrees than those with bachelor's degrees rated themselves *Superior.* The bachelor's-degree group considered their weakest area to be Knowledge and Skill in Teaching English; the master's degree group saw themselves as weakest in Knowledge of Language. Both groups considered their strongest category to be Knowledge and Skill in Oral Communication. Results of the survey indicated that the preparatory curriculum for prospective English teachers needed to include:

more courses in language, linguistics, and the application of linguistics to teaching English, literary criticism, theories of literary criticism, the history of rhetoric, and the development of English prose. More than the traditional two-semester sequence of courses in freshman composition needs to be offered. Further, courses in how to teach composition need to be offered. As well, courses in adolescent literature and courses on how to teach reading should be offered. (Crisp, 1968, p. 48).

The final report of the ISCPET project in 1969 (cited in Fagan & Laine, 1980) identifies several areas of inadequacy in teacher-preparation programs, as perceived by Illinois teachers. Topics cited by teachers of grades 7, 8, and 9 were: reading, composition, literature for adolescents, grammar, history of language, and related work in linguistics. Teachers of grades 10, 11, and 12 also cited grammar, language, and composition; and English department chairpersons cited language preparation in general.

A decade later, Fagan and Laine (1980) conducted a survey of Pennsylvania English teachers, questioning them about the professional effectiveness of their undergraduate programs in composition, history of the English language, grammar, literary criticism, literature for adolescents, linguistics, and reading. They also included an item on slow learners and the culturally different. Their questionnaire was mailed to 91 recent graduates of Pennsylvania State University's English Education program in December 1978. By the return deadline 2 months later, 45 usable returns had been received. Responses were tabulated and compared with the Illinois study. On a scale of 1 (*strongly disagree*) to 5 (*strongly agree*), responses on perceived adequacy of items were as follows: composition, 3.5; grammar, 3.7; adolescent literature, 3.3; reading, 3.0; linguistics, 3.1.

Comparison with data from the Illinois study showed that many of the teachers in both groups seemed dissatisfied with their undergraduate preparation (between 30 percent and 50 percent of the Illinois teachers and about 34 percent of the Pennsylvania teachers). With respect to differences in the programs teachers had completed, it was found that:

Prospective Illinois English teachers in 1969 followed a professional program characterized by a general methods course, possibly some reading and adolescent literature (about 25% of sampled respondents) possibly, some composition or teaching of composition (about 20% of respondents) a prescriptive grammar course, and survey courses in American, English, or period courses [and] prospective Pennsylvania English teachers in 1979 followed a professional program characterized by prescribed courses in: special methods, reading, adolescent literature, composition, linguistics (which included prescriptive, descriptive and transformational grammars); other prescribed courses with alternatives, that is, Milton or Chaucer; mass media analysis (Journalism) or mass media analysis (Theatre); speech communication, film, educational measurement and supporting courses in American or English literature. (Fagan & Laine, 1980, p. 70)

The researchers conclude that the Pennsylvania State English teacher preparation program, in comparison with the programs reflected in the Illinois study, was "more restrictive and specified; yet . . . broader in the sense that delivery systems and audiences for the contents of the discipline are intrinsic targets for the program" (p. 70).

The evaluation study by Moore (1976) of the preservice secondary English education program at the University of Georgia is perhaps representative of the best research on specific programs for English teacher preparation. Subjects for the study were 40 undergraduate students enrolled in the field center practicum in 1975 and 1976. The complete program consisted of three major components, the first of which included 20 quarter hours in the humanities, 20 hours in mathematics and science, 20 hours in social science, 6 hours in physical education, and 30 hours in courses related to the English major. The second component included major courses in composition, language, and literature, as well as an introductory education course with a human relations unit. The third component consisted of a two-quarter sequence in the public schools during which students completed courses in psychology, reading, curriculum, methods, and student teaching.

The program evaluation was based on the competencies of teacher candidates after they completed the program. Competencies were related to the specific objectives of the program and measured by five instruments: the *Minnesota Teacher Attitude Inventory*, the *Fundamental Interpersonal Relation Orientation—Behavior*, the *Teacher-Candidate Progress Report Form*, the *Department English Education Test*, and the *Inventory of Student Perception of Instruction*. The follow-up study included the rating of major and professional courses in the English education program and an evaluation of 10 first-year teachers who had completed the program in 1975.

Acceptance or rejection of hypotheses was based on differences between certain pretest and posttest mean scores and, in some instances, on the achievement of scores above a preset criterion. Correlations among measures were identified in an intercorrelation matrix. Results of the study included the following: (a) Although the teacher candidates showed negative changes in attitudes toward teaching, they showed significant development in leadership ability during the field experience, and, as rated by the supervisors, they showed growth in their teaching performance; (b) there were significant relationships among the various measures, but correlations were not high enough to justify any single measure as a predictor or criterion measure; (c) graduates of the program were rated as competent first-year teachers. In general, the results of Moore's study indicated that the teacher-preparation program made a significant contribution to the performance of teacher candidates and that they rated the program favorably (Moore, 1976, pp. 101–104).

In view of a maturing teaching force largely in place in the 1980s, the problem of how best to respond to the apparently increasing inservice needs of Ohio English teachers was addressed in a statewide survey by Mertz and Zidonis (1982). The survey included a random sample of English teachers and nonrandom samples of supervisors of secondary language arts and professors in English education. Major questions underlying questionnaire items were:

1. What parts of the secondary English program do these three groups rate as most important?
2. How do teachers of English rate their own preparation in a variety of teaching areas?
3. How do supervisors and professors rate teachers' preparation in these same areas?
4. In which areas of English do teachers, supervisors, and professors deem additional preparation desirable? (p. 279)

Using a 5-point scale, the researchers asked each respondent to make a judgment about teacher readiness to handle 27 components of the English curriculum and three general teaching abilities (individualizing instruction, using questioning strategies, and writing behavioral objectives). Teachers were asked to rate themselves, supervisors were asked to rate teachers in their districts, and professors were asked to rate graduates of their programs.

Teachers, supervisors, and professors were in substantial agreement about the important content of the secondary English curriculum; literature, language, writing, and reading appeared among the top five choices for all three groups. They also agreed that fiction is what teachers are best prepared to teach, with poetry being ranked somewhat lower. Teachers rated themselves well prepared to teach punctuation, spelling, and traditional grammar, but none of the three groups rated writing or language among their best-prepared areas. The areas of least preparation were mass media, minority literature, and dialect study. More than a third of the teachers selected as areas for further work developmental reading, critical viewing of television, individualized instruction, and filmmaking. Supervisors focused on needed work in reading, individualized instruction, questioning strategies, critical viewing of television, and writing of behavioral objectives. At least a third of the professors identified seven areas in which further preparation seemed desirable: adolescent literature, developmental reading, filmmaking, expository writing, dialects, critical viewing of television, and minority literature. This was the only group to place writing among the top five areas in need of additional preparation.

All of these surveys of professional competence relied heavily on subjective judgments of the respondents. Perhaps studies in the future will be able to relate objective criteria of performance to specific elements of teacher-preparation programs.

OTHER LITERATURE RELATED TO TEACHER PREPARATION

In addition to the items cited in the preceding pages, there are numerous books, articles, and conference papers related directly or indirectly to research in English teacher preparation. Prominent among them is the 76th Yearbook of the National Society for the Study of Education (Squire, 1977), which analyzes concerns and controversies in the teaching of English and summarizes much of what has been learned in 3 decades of curricular reform. Topics discussed include language and the nature of learning, essential language competencies, values in the English classroom, changing content in the English curriculum, evaluation of growth in English, future directions of English teaching, and changing patterns in teacher education. In the latter chapter, William A. Jenkins concludes that the repeated attempts to improve the preservice and inservice education of teachers of English have resulted in changed emphases, but the education of teachers, like their classroom teaching, remains much the same as it has been. Technology, teacher institutes, specialized training programs, and all other influences have failed to revolutionize education. "And yet," he says, "each innovation, each important new approach, has made a modicum of difference, produced a minuscule change, a barely perceptible leaning in a new direction" (p. 281).

A book with an international perspective on the teaching of English is *Timely Voices: English Teaching in the Eighties* (Arnold, 1983), which includes a chapter by Robert E. Shafer (pp. 154–173) on new perspectives for teacher education. Shafer states his view that teacher education reflects public attitudes toward education at any particular time and that, over the past several decades, these public attitudes have tended to insist that education be conservative, encouraging economical production and accountability. In teacher education of the future, he thinks we need to turn away from programs based on an industrial model. He says that we can best be accountable by restoring the 'caring elements" to teacher education programs, and he proposes the establishing of a personal growth model in teacher education in English.

Another significant work is the recent report of the Conference on English Education Commission on Research in Teacher Effectiveness (Peters, Grindstaff, Hanzelka, & Olson, 1987), which has obvious implications for teacher preparation. It is the intention of the report to provide preservice and inservice teachers with essential knowledge from teacher effectiveness research within the context of an organic field model of the teaching of English. The model proposed in the report offers a dynamic view of the interactions that occur in the English classroom. It attends to the necessary overlap of substance, skills, and process in the school subject called English and the importance of the context of community, policy, and profession in which teaching occurs.

An important contribution to the discussion of theoretical issues is Henry's (1986) article on the nature of English education and the critiques that article engendered. Having discussed, among other things, the nature of English as a discipline, changes in English, and changes in the concept of science, Henry concludes:

In sum, English education is composed of an "English" never sure of the nature of its substance, and an "education" uncertain of the soundness of the kind of science it believes English teaching needs. Under these conditions the foremost role of research in English education is to help explore this very paradox, and it is the role of English to point out to science where to spade. But only a large philosophical theory—such as transactionalism, phenomenology, the drama of conflict in a Universe of Discourse—can put the two in tandem. To date, such a philosophy has never been summoned up by a science of education alone or by English alone. (p. 32)

CONCLUSION

It is clear from the foregoing that research in the preparation of teachers of English language arts is an unfinished enterprise. Although a great deal of information can be gleaned from existing literature, there is an obvious need to update and expand the body of information about the current state of English teacher preparation and certification practices. Much has recently been written in the popular press about teachers who are unprepared to teach. The extent to which negative allegations about the preparedness of English teachers is true or false cannot be determined in the absence of accurate information. A new survey similar to those reported in the *National Interest* studies would be extremely helpful at this time. Alternatives to established patterns of teacher certification have recently received a great deal of attention. A comparison of minimum certification standards nationwide with the degree requirements in approved teacher education programs in colleges and universities would be interesting and valuable. The current efforts resulting from demands for assessment of teacher performance need to be coordinated and related to programs for the preservice and inservice preparation of English teachers. The interrelationships of English teacher preparation, recruiting and selection practices, job placement, and successful teaching performance in the classroom could be studied effectively in this context.

It should be a matter of grave concern to professionals in English education that the "remaining problems" identified by the authors of *The Education of Teachers of English* a quarter of a century ago still remain. Despite the minuscule changes and barely perceptible leanings in new directions that Jenkins mentions, until we have the kind of philosophical theory Henry calls for, we are not likely to find an "adequate unifying theory of teacher education," and lacking that, we cannot expect "persuasive research evidence of what the indispensable elements of an ideal program for preparing teachers of English might be." It is hoped, however, that building on the work already done, researchers will, in the near future, supply what is lacking.

References

Arnold, R. (1983). *Timely voices: English teaching in the eighties.* Melbourne, Australia: Oxford University Press.

Basic Issues Conference Members (1959). An articulated English program: A hypothesis to test *PMLA, 74*(4), part 2.

Boyer, E. L. (1983). *High school: A report on secondary education in America.* New York: Harper & Row.

College Entrance Examination Board, Commission on English. (1965). *Freedom and discipline in English: Report of the commission on English.* New York: Author.

Crisp, R. D. (1968). *The professional competency of Illinois secondary school English teachers: Interim report.* U.S. Department of Health, Education and Welfare.

Dixon, J. (1967). *Growth through English.* Reading, England: National Association of Teachers of English.

English Teacher Preparation Study. (1968). Guidelines for the preparation of teachers of English—1968. *English Journal, 57*(4), 528–536.

Fagan, E. R., & Laine, C. H. (1980). Two perspectives of undergraduate English teacher preparation. *Research in the Teaching of English, 14*(1), 67–72.

Goodlad, J. I. (1984). *A place called school: Prospects for the future.* New York: McGraw-Hill.

Grommon, A. H. (Ed.). (1963). *The education of teachers of English for American schools and colleges.* New York: Appleton-Century-Crofts.

Grommon, A. H. (1968). A history of the preparation of teachers of English. *English Journal, 57*(4), 484–524.

Henry, G. H. (1986). What is the nature of English education? *English Education, 18*(1), 4–41.

Hook, J. N. (1965). Qualifications of secondary school teachers of English: A preliminary statement. *College English, 27,* 166–169.

Hosic, J. F. (1917). *Reorganization of English in secondary schools* (Bureau of Education Bulletin, No. 2). Washington, DC: U.S. Government Printing Office.

Lloyd-Jones, R., & Lunsford, A. A. (1989). *The English Coalition Conference: Democracy through language.* New York: Modern Language Association.

Mertz, M. P., & Zidonis, F. (1982). Perceived preparation of Ohio English teachers. *Research in the Teaching of English, 16*(3), 279–284.

Moore, C. A. (1976). *Evaluation of the pre-service secondary English education program at the University of Georgia.* Unpublished doctoral dissertation, University of Georgia, Athens.

Muller, H. J. (1967). *The uses of English.* New York: Holt, Rinehart & Winston.

National Association of State Directors of Teacher Education and Certification. (1958). *Declaration of policy on teacher education and certification.* Sacramento, CA: Author.

National Commission on Excellence in Education (1983). *A nation at risk: The imperative for educational reform.* Washington, DC: U.S. Government Printing Office.

National Council of Teachers of English, Committee on National Interest. (1961). *The national interest and the teaching of English.* Champaign, IL: Author.

National Council of Teachers of English, Committee on National Interest. (1964). *The national interest and the continuing education of teachers of English.* Champaign, IL: Author

National Council of Teachers of English, Standing Committee on Teacher Preparation and Certification. (1976). *A statement on the preparation of teachers of English and the language arts.* Urbana, IL: Author.

National Council of Teachers of English, Standing Committee on Teacher Preparation and Certification. (1986). *Guidelines for the preparation of teachers of English language arts.* Urbana, IL: Author.

Peters, W. H., Grindstaff, F. L., Hanzelka, R. L., & Olson, M. C. (1987). *Effective English teaching: Conception, research, and practice.* Urbana, IL: National Council of Teachers of English.

Rehage, K. J. (Ed.). (1975). *Teacher education.* Chicago: University of Chicago Press.

Rogers, R. W. (1963). Resolutions adopted at a seminar of English department chairmen. *College English, 24,* 473–475.

Sizer, T. (1984). *Horace's compromise: The dilemma of the American high school.* Boston: Houghton Mifflin.

Slaughter, E. E. (1964). 1964 certification to teach English in the secondary school. *College English, 25,* 591–604.

Slaughter, E. E. (1968). Certification requirements to teach English in elementary or secondary school—1967. *English Journal, 57*(4), 551–564.

Squire, J. R. (Ed.) (1977). *The teaching of English.* Chicago: University of Chicago Press.

Stinnett, T. M. with Frady, E. N., & Pershing, G. E. (1967). *A manual on certification requirements for school personnel in the United States.* Washington, DC: National Education Association.

Wittrock, M. C. (Ed.). (1986). *Handbook of research on teaching* (3rd ed.). New York: Macmillan.

Woellner, E. H., & Wood, M. A. (1967). *Requirements for certification, 1967–68.* Chicago: University of Chicago Press.

· 40 ·

EDUCATING TEACHERS FOR LANGUAGE
MINORITY STUDENTS

Eugene E. Garcia

UNIVERSITY OF CALIFORNIA—SANTA CRUZ

The debate regarding the education of bilingual students in the United States has centered on the instructional use of the two languages of the bilingual. In schools, the broader issue has been the effective instruction of a growing population of ethnic minority students who do not speak English and, therefore, are considered candidates for special educational programming that takes into consideration this language difference. This issue has involved representatives of psychology, linguistics, sociology, politics, and education in cross-disciplinary dialogue. For a thorough discussion of these issues see August and Garcia (1988), Baker and deKanter (1983), Cummins (1979), Garcia (1983), Hakuta and Gould (1987), Rossell and Ross (1986), Troike (1981), Willig (1985). The central theme of these discussions is the specific instructional role of the native language. At one extreme of this discussion, it is recommended that the native language play a significant part in the non-English-speaking student's elementary school years, from 4–6 years, with a set standard of native-language mastery prior to immersion into the English curriculum. At the other extreme, immersion into an English curriculum is recommended early, as early as preschool, with minimal use of the native language and concern for English language leveling by instructional staff to facilitate understanding by the limited-English-speaking student.

Each of these disparate approaches argues that its implementation brings psychological, linguistic, social, political, and educational benefits. The *native-language* approach suggests that competencies in the native language, particularly as they relate to academic learning, provide important psychological and linguistic foundations for second-language learning and academic learning in general—"you really only learn to read once." Native-language instruction builds on social and cultural experiences and serves to politically empower students

from communities that have been historically limited in their meaningful participation in majority educational institutions. The *immersion* approach suggests that, the sooner a child receives instruction in English, the more likely he or she will be to acquire English proficiency—"more time on task, better proficiency." English proficiency in turn mitigates against educational failure, social separation and segregation, and, ultimately, economic disparity.

As this debate developed during the 1970s and 1980s, it became clear that the students who came to school speaking a language other than English received considerable attention in research, policy development, and practice. The Departments of Education and Health and Human Services, as well as private foundations, supported specific demographic studies and instructional research related to this population of students, preschool through college. The United States Congress authorized legislation targeted directly at these students on five separate occasions (1968, 1974, 1978, 1984, and 1988), and numerous states enacted legislation and developed explicit program guidelines. Moreover, federal district courts and the U.S. Supreme Court concluded adjudication proceedings that directly influenced the educational treatment of language minority students. This significant attention generated answers to some important questions that were unanswerable as late as the early 1980s. The following discussion will highlight these questions and their respective treatment in light of emerging information regarding bilingual language minority students.

DEFINING LANGUAGE MINORITY STUDENTS

The search for a comprehensive definition of "language minority student" reveals a variety of attempts. At one end of the continuum are general definitions such as "students who come from homes in which a language other than English is spoken." At the other end are highly operational definitions such as, "students who scored in the first quartile on a standardized test of English language proficiency." Regardless of the definition adopted, it is apparent that students vary widely in linguistic abilities. The language minority population in the United States continues to be linguistically heterogeneous, with over 100 distinct language groups. Even in the largest language minority ethnic group, some Hispanics are monolingual Spanish speakers, whereas others are bilingual to some degree. Other non-English-speaking minority groups in the United States are similarly heterogeneous. Not inconsequential is the related cultural attributes of these populations of students, which are not only *linguistically* distinct but also *culturally* distinct. Describing the typical language minority student, therefore, is highly problematic. In simple terms, the language minority student is one who (a) is characterized by substantive participation in a non-English-speaking social environment, (b) has acquired the normal communicative abilities of that social environment, and (c) is exposed to a substantive English-speaking environment, more than likely for the first time, during the formal schooling process.

Estimates of the number of language minority students have been compiled by the federal government on several occasions (Development Associates, 1984; O'Malley, 1981). These estimates differ because of the definition adopted for identifying these students, the particular measure utilized to obtain the estimate, and the statistical treatment utilized to generalize beyond the actual sample obtained. For example, O'Malley defines the language minority student population by utilizing a specific cutoff score on an English language proficiency test administered to a stratified sample of students. Development Associates estimates the population by utilizing reports from a stratified sample of local school districts. Therefore, estimates of language minority students have ranged between 1,300,000 (Development Associates, 1984) and 3,600,000 (O'Malley, 1981).

In 1976 the total number of language minority children aged 5–14 approximated 2.52 million, with a drop to 2.39 million in 1980 and a projected gradual increase to 3.40 million by the year 2000 (Waggoner, 1984). In 1983 this population was more conservatively estimated to be 1.29 million (Development Associates, 1984). This divergence in estimates reflects the procedures used to obtain language minority counts and estimates. These children reside throughout the United States, but distinct geographical clustering can be identified. About 62 percent of language minority children are found in Arizona, Colorado, California, New Mexico, and Texas (Development Associates, 1984; O'Malley, 1981; Waggoner, 1984). Of the estimated number of language minority children in 1978, 72 percent were of Spanish language background, 22 percent were of other European language backgrounds, 5 percent were of Asian background, and 1 percent were of American Indian background. However, such distributions will change, due to differential growth rates, and by the year 2000 the proportion of Spanish language background children is projected to be about 77 percent of the total (O'Malley, 1981). Estimates by Development Associates (1984) for students in grades K–6 indicate that 76 percent are of Spanish language background; 8 percent, Southeast Asian (e.g., Vietnamese, Cambodian, Hmong); 5 percent, other European; 5 percent, East Asian (e.g., Chinese, Korean); and 5 percent, other (e.g., Arabic, Navaho). For the national school-districts sample in the 19 most highly impacted states utilized by Development Associates, 17 percent of the total K–6 student population was estimated to be language minority in these states.

Regardless of differing estimates, a significant number of students from language backgrounds other than English attend United States schools. As this population increases steadily in the future, the challenge these students present to United States educational institutions will increase concomitantly.

Educational Programs Serving These Students

For a school-district staff with language minority students, there are many possible program options: e.g., Transitional Bilingual Education, Maintenance Bilingual Education, English-as-a-Second Language, Immersion, Sheltered English, and Submersion (General Accounting Office, 1987). Ultimately, school staffs reject program labels and focus instead on the following questions: (a) What are the native language (L1) and second language (L2) characteristics of the students, families, and communities to be served? (b) What model of instruction is desired? This involves the question of utilizing L1 and L2 as mediums of instruction as well as handling the actual instruction of L1 and L2. (c) What is the nature of the school and resources required to implement the desired instruction?

Programs for language minority students can be differentiated by the ways they utilize the native language and English during instruction. A recent report by Development Associates (1984) was based on a survey of 333 school districts in the 19 states serving over 80 percent of the language minority students in the United States. For grades K–5, they report the following salient features regarding the use of languages(s) during instruction: (a) 93 percent of the schools reported that the use of English predominated in their programs, and conversely, 7 percent indicated that the use of the native language predominated; (b) 60 percent of the sampled schools reported that instruction was in the native language and English; (c) 30 percent of the sampled schools reported minimal or no use of the native language during instruction.

Two-thirds of these schools have chosen to utilize some form of bilingual curriculum to serve this population of students. However, some one-third of them minimize or altogether ignore native-language use in their instruction of language minority students. Programs that serve Spanish-speaking background students have been characterized primarily as *Bilingual Transitional* education. These programs transition students from early grade, Spanish-emphasis instruction to later grade, *English-Emphasis* instruction and eventually to *English-Only* instruction.

Recent research in transition type programs suggests that language minority students can be served effectively. Effective schools organize and develop educational structures and processes that take into consideration both the broader aspects of effective schools reported for English-speaking students (Purkey & Smith, 1983) and the specific attributes relevant to language minority students (Carter & Chatfield, 1986; Garcia, 1988; Tikenoff, 1983). Of particular importance has been the positive effect of intensive instruction in the native language that focuses on literacy development (Wong-Fillmore & Valdez, 1986). Hakuta and Gould (1987) and Hudelson (1987) maintain that skills and concepts learned in the native language provide a basis for acquisition of new knowledge in the second language.

For the one-third of the students receiving little or no instruction in the native language, two alternative types of instructional approaches, English as a Second Language and Immersion, predominate. Each of these program types depends on the primary utilization of English during instruction but does not ignore the fact that the student served is limited in English proficiency. These programs are used in classrooms in which there is not a substantial number of students from one non-English-speaking group. These programs have been particularly influenced by recent theoretical developments regarding second-language acquisition (Chamot & O'Malley, 1986; Krashen, 1982), and indicate that effective second-language learning is best accomplished under conditions that simulate natural communicative interactions.

School-district staff have been creative in developing a wide range of programs for language minority students. They have answered the previously listed questions differentially for (a) different language groups (Spanish, Vietnamese, Chinese, etc.), (b) different grade levels within a school, (c) different language subgroups of students within a classroom and even different levels of language proficiency. The result has been a broad and, at times, perplexing variety of program models.

FEDERAL AND STATE POLICIES

The preceding has described who the language minority student is and how that student has been served. The analysis that follows deals with educational policy, *first*, federal legislation and legal initiatives and, *second*, state initiatives.

Federal Legislative Initiatives

The United States Congress set a minimum standard for the education of language minority students in public educational institutions in its passage of Title VI of the Civil Rights Act of 1964 and, subsequently, in the Equal Educational Opportunity Act of 1974 (EEOA), prohibiting discrimination by educational institutions on the basis of race, color, sex, or national origin. The EEOA was an effort by Congress to specifically define what constitutes a denial of constitutionally guaranteed equal educational opportunity. The EEOA provides in part:

No state shall deny equal educational opportunities to an individual on account of his or her race, color, sex, or national origin, by . . . the

failure by an educational agency to take appropriate action to overcome language barriers that impede equal participation by students in its instructional programs. (U.S. Congress, 1984)

This statute does not mandate specific educational treatment, but it does require public educational agencies to sustain programs to meet the language needs of their students.

As noted, the Congress of the United States on five occasions (1968, 1974, 1978, 1984, and 1988) passed specific legislation related to the education of language minority students. The Bilingual Education Act (BEA) of 1968 was intended to foster programs designed to meet the educational needs of low-income limited-English-speaking children. Grants were awarded to local educational agencies, institutions of higher education, or regional research facilities to (a) develop and operate bilingual education programs, native history and culture programs, early childhood education programs, adult education programs and programs to train bilingual aides; (b) make efforts to attract and retain as teachers individuals from non-English-speaking backgrounds; and (c) establish cooperation between the home and the school (August & Garcia, 1988).

Four major reauthorizations of the BEA have occurred since 1968: in 1974, 1978, 1984, and 1988. As a consequence of the 1974 amendments (PL 93–380), a bilingual education program was defined for the first time as "instruction given in, and study of English and to the extent necessary to allow a child to progress effectively through the education system, the native language" (Schneider, 1976, p. 56). The goal of bilingual education continued to be transition to English, rather than maintenance of the native language. Children no longer had to be from low-income backgrounds to participate. New programs were funded, including a graduate fellowship program for study in the field of training teachers for bilingual education programs and a program for the development, assessment, and dissemination of classroom materials.

In the bilingual education amendments of 1978 (Public Law 95–561), program eligibility was expanded to include students with limited English academic proficiency, as well as students with limited-English-speaking ability. Parents were given a greater role in program planning and operation. Teachers were required to be proficient in both English and the native language of the children in the program. Grant recipients were required to demonstrate how they would continue the program when federal funds were withdrawn.

The Bilingual Education Act of 1984 created new program options including special alternative instructional programs that did not require use of the child's native language. These program alternatives were expanded in 1988. State and local agency program staff were required to collect data, identify the population served, and describe program effectiveness.

Over $1 billion from the national government have been appropriated through Title VII legislation for educational activities aimed at language minority students (program development, program implementation, professional training, and research). In addition, other congressional appropriations (e.g., Vocational Education and Chapter I) explicitly target language minority students.

Federal Legal Initiatives

The 1974 United States Supreme Court decision in *Lau v. Nichols* (1974) is the landmark statement supporting the rights of language minority students. It requires language support for students with limited English proficiency.

[T]here is no equality of treatment merely by providing students with the same facilities, textbooks, teachers, and curriculum: for students who do not understand English are effectively foreclosed from any meaningful education. Basic English skills are at the very core of what these public schools teach. Imposition of a requirement that, before a child can effectively participate in the education program he must already have acquired those basic skills is to make a mockery of public education. We know that those who do not understand English are certain to find their classroom experiences wholly incomprehensible and in no way meaningful. (p. 27)

The Fifth Circuit *Castañeda v. Pickard* (1981) decision set three requirements that constitute an appropriate program for language minority students: (a) The program must be based on a sound educational theory; (b) the program must be "reasonably calculated to implement effectively" the chosen theory; and (c) the program must produce results in a reasonable time.

The courts have also required appropriate action to overcome language barriers. "Measures which will actually overcome the problem," are called for by the *U.S. v. Texas* court decision (1981), or "results indicating that the language barriers confronting students are actually being overcome" are mandated by the *Castañneda* court decision (1981). Therefore, local school districts and state education agencies have an obligation to assess the effectiveness of special language programs on an ongoing basis. Other court decisions have delineated minimum-staff professional-training attributes and the particular role of standardized tests.

State Initiatives

Through state legislation, 12 states mandate special educational services for language minority students, 12 states permit these services, and one state prohibits them. Twenty-six states have no legislation directly addressing language minority students (August & Garcia, 1988).

State programs for language minority students are characterized by the following policies: (a) Instructional programs allow or require instruction in a language other than English (17 states); (b) special qualifications are required for the certification of professional instructional staff (15 states); (c) school districts provide supplementary funds in support of educational programs (15 states); (d) a cultural component is required (15 states); and (e) parental consent is required for enrollment of students (11 states).

Six states (Arizona, Illinois, Indiana, Massachusetts, Rhode Island, and Texas) impose all of these requirements concurrently. Such a pattern demonstrates the continued attention of states to issues related to language minority students.

EFFECTIVE INSTRUCTION FOR LANGUAGE MINORITY POPULATIONS

The preceding review is most relevant to Hispanic students because they make up a projected 71 percent to 77 percent of the population of language minority students nationwide. These students are located in seven states (Arizona, California, Colorado, Florida, New Mexico, New York, and Texas) and are also concentrated within school sites, often making up 30 percent to 80 percent of individual elementary classroom populations in which they are found. Such a concentration has typically allowed the implementation of native-language instruction, although that has not always been the case (Ramirez, 1986). A report by Development Associates (1984) presents the results of a survey of 333 school districts in 19 targeted states, in an attempt to obtain a clearer picture of the nature of service to language minority students. For grades K–5, they report the following salient features regarding the use of language(s) during instruction: (a) eight separate treatments regarding the use of the native language were identified, ranging from use of the native language only to nonuse of the native language; (b) 93 percent of the schools reported that use of English predominated in their programs and 7 percent, conversely, indicated primary use of the native language; (c) 60 percent of the sampled schools reported that both the native language and English were utilized; (d) 30 percent of the sampled schools reported minimal use of the native language during instruction.

What seems clear from these data, although the source of the data is a self-report survey, is that the instruction of language minority students is not limited to the use of native-language instructional methodologies nor even bilingual methodologies. The fact that some 30 percent of children in the Developmental Associates sample received predominantly English language instruction is significant. It is also not a mere coincidence that some 30 percent of U.S. language minority students are non-Spanish-speaking. Although not precisely confirmed, it is likely that non-Spanish-speaking students are the primary consumers of non-native-language instructional practices. Two specific program types characterize this non-native-language form of instruction: *English as a Second Language* and *Immersion*. Each of these program types depends on the primary utilization of English but does not ignore the specific language liability of the student due to the lack of functioning English. However, with emphasis on English acquisition, these programs do not require instructional personnel who speak the native language of the student. Moreover, these programs are suited to classrooms in which there is no substantial concentration of students from one non-English language but, which, instead, a heterogeneous non-English student population (Ovando & Collier, 1985).

Both English as a Second Language and Immersion programs have been particularly influenced by recent theoretical developments regarding the teaching of a second language (Chamot & O'Malley, 1986; Krashen, 1982). These developments have suggested that effective second-language learning is best accomplished under conditions that simulate natural communicative interactions and minimize the formal instruction of linguistic structures, such as memorization drills and learning grammatical rules. Although English as a Second Language programs continue to involve pull-out sessions in which students are removed from the regular classroom to spend time on concentrated language-learning activities with specially trained educational staff, the recent theoretical and practice consensus is that such language-learning experiences should be communicative and centered around academic content areas (Chamot & O'Malley, 1986).

In Immersion programs all the instruction is in English; however, the English utilized by the instructional staff is directly monitored, so as to maximize the understanding of the particular non-English-speaking student. The intent of this English leveling is to insure the use of English by the instructional staff in authentic instructional situations and, at the same time, to emphasize communicative understanding. This practice rests on Krashen's (Krashen & Biber, 1988) hypothesis that second-language learning is positively related to linguistic exposure in the target language that is just beyond the learner's level of comprehension. That is, the degree to which linguistic input is comprehensible to the learner determines acquisition rate. Moreover, comprehensibility is hypothesized to be influenced by an "affective filter" (Krashen & Biber, 1988). This filter is characterized as being related to psychological attributes of the learner in the learning situation, such as the learner's anxiety level, motivation to learn, and self-confidence.

Other theoretical and empirical research regarding the social and cognitive influences on second-language learning is relevant to English as a Second Language and Immersion programs. Schumann (1976) found that children are more motivated to learn a second language if they do not perceive this learning process as alienation from their own culture. If a child belongs to a family whose integration pattern is preservation of the native language and culture rather than assimilation or acculturation, the child might be less motivated to acquire the second language. There could be less impetus for cultural group to assimilate or acculturate to American society if that group has its own segregated community or if the group's expected residence in the United States is perceived as temporary.

Not only is the individual's attitude toward the target culture important, but also the relationship between the two cultures influences second-language acquisition. Schumann (1976) hypothesizes that, the greater the social distance between the cultures, the greater the difficulty of the second-language learner in learning the target language, and, conversely, the smaller the social distance, the better the language-learning situation. Social distance is determined in part by the relative status of the two cultures. Two cultures that are politically, culturally, and technically equal in status have less social distance than two cultures whose relationship is characterized by dominance and subordination. In addition, there is less social distance if the cultures of the two groups are congruent.

A child motivated to learn a second language still needs certain social skills to facilitate her or his ability to establish and maintain contact with speakers of the target language. Wong-Fillmore (1976) and Wong-Fillmore and Valdez (1986) suggest that individual differences in the social skills of the child influence the rate of second-language acquisition. Second-language learners who seem most successful employ specific social strategies. They join a group and act as if they understand what's going on, even when they do not. They initiate interactions and pretend to know what is going on. As a result, they are included in conversations and activities. These learners give the impression with a few well-chosen words that they can speak the language. When children are willing to use whatever language they have, other children keep trying to communicate with them. These learners count on friends for help. The acquisition of language depends on the participation of both the learner and someone who already speaks the language—a friend. Friends help in several ways. They show faith in the learner's ability to learn the language, and, by including the learner in their activities, they made a real effort to understand what the learner is saying. They also provide the learner with natural linguistic input that he or she is able to understand.

Seliger (1977) also demonstrates that high-input generators are the most successful second-language learners. High-input generators are learners who place themselves in situations in which they are exposed to the target language and are willing to use it for communication; therefore, they receive the necessary input and the opportunity for practice.

With emphasis on cognitive variables related to second-language acquisition, Seliger (1984) and McLaughlin (1985) propose two different types of processes related to second-language learning. One such process calls for the learner to formulate hypotheses and revise those hypotheses on the basis of cognitive strategies. These strategies are considered universal and are likely based on innate language-specific cognitive mechanisms (McLaughlin, 1985). These processes include such strategies as overgeneralization, simplification, and hypothesis testing. A second type of process assists learners in meeting the engagement demands of a particular situation. These tactics are chosen deliberately to overcome temporary and immediate obstacles to learning a task. Second-language learners may choose to learn the grammar, seek out native speakers, memorize vocabulary items, and other techniques (Seliger, 1984). In each case, strategies and tactics are viewed as cognitive mechanisms that assist the learner in the acquisition of the second language.

Hakuta (1985) likens second-language learning to a problem-solving task. The learner uses numerous strategies, hunches, hypotheses, and related cognitive devices to solve the problem. This might include both knowledge-related symbolic perceptual representation, organization, and processing and utilization of such knowledge under differing circumstances to achieve different goals. Significantly, according to Hakuta, the learner can transfer all the cognitive knowledge related to the first language to solving the learning problem in the second language. The learner, having determined that language is symbolic; that it is made up of phonology, morphology, and syntax; that it must be communicative and structured around certain discourse rules, can rely on such information and related cognitive mechanisms to successfully address second-language learning. In addition, instructional staff can assist the second-language-learning enterprise by focusing on childrens' overall second-language-learning strategies and not concentrating on specific linguistic skill development.

From this review of second-language acquisition theory and research, second-language learning seems most effective under instructional conditions that (a) emphasize authentic communicative learning situations; (b) take into consideration the "comprehensibility" of English interaction; (c) minimize anxiety and frustration and allow second-language learners to take risks; (d) minimize linguistic and cultural segregation of second-language learners; and (e) maximize the utilization of basic cognitive mechanism.

Hammerly (1985) also suggests that it is useful to indicate that second-language learning is not (a) an intellectual exercise involving the understanding and memorization of grammar; (b) translation; (c) memorization of sentences; (d) mechanical conditioning; or (e) applying abstract rules.

Unfortunately, no large-scale body of research is presently available regarding effective instruction in English as a Second Language or Immersion Programs. Baker and deKanter (1983), and Hakuta and Gould (1987), Rossell and Ross (1986), Willig (1985), each discuss, in comparative terms, the effectiveness of native-language instruction versus English as a Second Language and/or Immersion. (Ramirez, 1986, reports preliminary data of a national study that is attempting to compare the instructional effectiveness of these diverse programs.) It is appropriate to conclude that these authors differ significantly regarding their recommendations to language minority educators. Yet they all agree that present research and evaluation studies are significantly flawed methodologically and, therefore, limit the confidence that can be placed in their conclusions. It is not the intent of this analysis to suggest that a best instructional strategy now exists for the effective schooling of language minority students. The intent is to review recent findings that have specifically reported effective instructional strategies. Such findings have been reported primarily for Hispanic language minority students who are receiving native-language instructional experiences. The absence of similar reports with other non-English-language students, and the absence of such data for English as a Second Language and Immersion Programs, underscores the need for such information but also limits the discussion of effective instructional characteristics in such programs. This limitation not only implies that such approaches are ineffective, but also suggests that needed information is unavailable. However, as Ramirez (1986) and Hakuta and Gould (1987) indicate, national comparative data related to alternative program treatment of language minority students (particularly Native Language Programs and Immersion programs) should be available in the near future.

SPECIFIC EFFECTIVE INSTRUCTIONAL PROGRAMS

Although it is difficult to identify specific programs that have served language minority programs effectively, recent efforts have been more successful. Unlike earlier reports (Troike,

1981) in which Title VII program-evaluation reports were reviewed to identify and describe effective programs, recent efforts have sought out effective programs and/or schools, then attempted to describe their organizational and instructional character (Carter & Chatfield, 1986; Tikenoff, 1983). The following sections describe specific schools that have been the focus of such studies. These schools are neither distributed evenly throughout the United States nor reflective of the broad range of program alternatives that serve language minority students. Instead, they again reflect the predominance of descriptive research that characterizes the native-language instructional programs serving Hispanic students. Moreover, they are located in regions of the country in which the researchers happened to reside and do not constitute a representative sample of effective schools serving language minority students.

Phoenix, Arizona, Schools

Attributes of effective schools specific to Hispanic language minority education received 2 years of investigatory attention from this author in a project funded by the Inter-University Program for Latino Research and the Social Research Council and conducted at Arizona State University. With a focus on academic learning, this research provided an in-depth investigation of schools serving Hispanic LEP students effectively. The primary goal of the project included the determination of organizational, instructional, and social characteristics of effective schools, their classrooms, and their professional personnel. The research was conducted by an interdisciplinary research team utilizing multimethodological approaches that provided a broad (macro) analysis of the schooling environment and a focused (micro) analysis of instruction. The research was done in collaboration with the Phoenix Elementary School District, the Glendale Elementary School District, and the Chandler Unified School District.

Procedure. Characteristics identified by Purkey and Smith (1983) and Carter and Chatfield (1986) associated with effective schools were assessed over a period of 2 years. This included a series of interviews, as well as an ethnographic description of the school environment and the surrounding community. Interviews and the ethnographic data were collected systematically over the study period in an effort to portray a 2-year comprehensive picture of effective schooling processes. More specifically, activities of students in instructional school contexts, as well as in home and community contexts, were systematically sampled over the period. These data addressed (a) instructional processes in literacy and math; (b) parental attitudes related to educational materials and educational assistance to students; (c) teacher and principal attitudes; (d) student performance on standardized language, cognitive, and metacognitive measure; (e) academic achievement.

Research Site and Population. The research sites in this study included three elementary schools and seven classrooms (grades K–6) in the Phoenix, Arizona, metropolitan area that had been nominated by local educational colleagues as effective schools and whose students were attaining at or above grade level on standardized measures of academic achievement. Classrooms selected to take part in the study included students from Spanish emphasis, English emphasis, and bilingual language instruction classrooms.

Results. The results of this study provide important insights regarding the school community, instruction, literacy development, academic achievement, and perspectives of the various constituent groups involved in the study. An analysis of the study site indicates several types of classrooms, each with individual linguistic and organizational characteristics, yet a high degree of commonality among them in several significant domains. It was evident that in each classroom the major emphasis was on insuring functional communication between teacher and students and between students and students. Classrooms were characterized by an integrated curriculum emphasizing thematic organization of instructional objectives with (a) student collaboration in almost all academic activity, (b) minimal individualized work tasks, and (c) a highly informal, almost familial, social and collaborative relationship between teachers and students.

Analyses of audio/videotapes of classroom instruction during literacy and mathematics lessons were conducted biweekly. Results of these analyses indicated that, for instruction related to literacy, teachers organized instruction in a manner that led students to interact with each other regarding the instructional topic. It was during these student–student discussions (occurring over 50 percent of the time) that higher order cognitive and linguistic discourse was observed. The data also indicated a trend to English language instruction, with lower grades emphasizing Spanish and upper grades emphasizing English concurrently, with a clear commitment to self-transitioning strategies such as the utilization of student–teacher and student–student dialogue journals.

Analyses of literacy in grades K–6 were conducted utilizing daily journal entries that allowed students to discuss topics of their choice with teachers on a daily basis. Results of these analyses indicate (a) a systematic progression of writing in the native language in the early grades; (b) writing in the second language emerging at or above the level observed in the first language; (c) generally, a high degree of conventional spelling, even in early grades and even when spelling was not an independent target in these classrooms; and (d) the quantitative and qualitative character of student journal entries directly related to the cognitive and linguistic nature of the teacher's responses.

Several cognitive and academic achievement measures were administered to students, and teachers were asked to rate academic success. Results indicated that (a) teachers in early grades did not assess academic achievement (as measured by academic achievement tests) as accurately as teachers in later grades; (b) average academic achievement in reading and mathematics for students in these classrooms was at or above grade level, with students scoring higher on mathematics measures; and (c) there was a positive predictive relationship between cognitive measures and mathematics academic achievement measures and between Spanish-language proficiency and English reading achievement.

Interviews with classroom teachers, school site principals, parents, and students were conducted to determine their perspectives and roles regarding education. Classroom teachers (average teaching experience of 6.7 years) were highly committed to the educational success of all their students; perceived themselves as instructional innovators utilizing new psychological and social theories to guide their instructional approaches (all were highly articulate regarding theory-to-practice issues); continued to be involved in professional-development activities including participation in small-group teacher networking; had a strong, demonstrated commitment to student–home communication (three teachers had developed a weekly mechanism for informally communicating student progress to parents); and felt they had the autonomy to create or change the curriculum implemented in their classrooms, even if it did not meet the precise guidelines established by the local or state education agency.

Principals (average administrative experience of 11.7 years) tended to be highly articulate regarding the curriculum and instructional strategies undertaken in their schools, were highly supportive of their instructional staff, and recognized the importance of teacher autonomy while being aware of the pressures to conform to district policies regarding the standardization of curriculum and the need for academic accountability.

Parents (average schooling of 7.1 years) expressed a high level of satisfaction with the educational experience of their children, indicated their own active support for educational efforts on behalf of their children (by assisting with homework, purchasing reading materials, etc.), and strongly supported their children's academic success as a basis for future economic mobility. The strategies for support by nonliterate parents were particularly interesting and involved insuring sibling/peer assistance with homework and reading to young children by inventing prose to match storybook pictures, among others.

The general impressions of investigators as they sifted through the data and interacted personally with the schools' various constituencies was that these schools did indeed serve all students well, academically and otherwise. That such schools succeed is not surprising, because they make schooling and exhilarating experience.

Carter and Chatfield (1986) provide one of the most detailed descriptions of an effective language minority school presently available in the literature. Their work began in 1981 as a California State Department of Education project to identify, describe, and disseminate information relevant to effective instructional programs throughout the State of California. In that project, J. Calvin Lauderbach School was identified, and descriptive research has been ongoing until this writing. Lauderbach is located in Chula Vista, California, a middle-sized city south of San Diego and just north of the Mexican–U.S. border. Of the 600 children who attend the school, half are Hispanic, one-third are Anglo, and the remainder are black, Filipino, Laotian, Japanese, or Guamanian. Almost all the Hispanic students' home language is Spanish, and over 50 percent are identified as limited English proficient by local language-testing criteria.

Lauderbach was considered effective primarily on indicators of student academic learning. Measures of academic achievement indicate that the low socioeconomic status, language minority students it serves are learning as well as middle-class English-proficient students. Carter and Chatfield summarize their project in this manner:

The district developed and Lauderbach utilizes a well-developed and quite specific curriculum continuum; a management system parallels this continuum. Goals and objectives are detailed, and grade-level expectations are clear. In most curricular areas rich Spanish-language materials supplement the English continuum. The management system is employed by the school to monitor student learning. Additionally, the district administers a carefully constructed, curricularly valid proficiency test at the fifth grade. Lauderbach students scored remarkably well on this test last year, as they do every year. Seventy-one percent of fifth graders passed all four subtests. This places Lauderbach ninth from the top among the 28 district schools. If one considers only the English only non-special-education children, Lauderbach scores second highest in the district with 90 percent passing all four subtests. Lauderbach students appear to be learning the basics as well as or better than those attending Chula Vista schools that have much higher socio-economic status indices. According to figures provided by the district, Lauderbach ranks twenty-second among the 28 schools in socio-economic status, as measured by the CAP SES scale. The school is in the lowest fourth of district schools in socio-economic status but in the top quartile in achievement as measured by district proficiency tests. Lauderbach children appear to be learning very well those things they are taught. (p. 209)

The school offers a comprehensive, team-taught, K–6 bilingual education program, with approximately 70 percent of the students participating in this program, with one-third of the students not being Hispanic, Collaborative teaching utilizing a Spanish teacher and an English insures integration of instructional responsibilities, planning, and curriculum implementation of Spanish and English instruction. The program receives the strong support of all the school staff and is highly regarded in the community. An individual learning plan is developed for each non-Spanish-speaking LEP student. As in the bilingual program, the student's native language is utilized to assist in concept and English language development. This is usually facilitated by using teacher aides who are native speakers of a variety of languages. Of particular significance are the presence of supportive administrative leadership and the staffwide concern for continual school improvement.

Conclusion

Summative evaluations of programs that use different approaches have run into difficulty on a number of fronts. Willig (1985), in a metanalysis of studies of the effectiveness of bilingual education, complained that:

Inadequacies of the research studies in general were reflected in research design, in the failure to document or describe the educational programs under scrutiny, in the statistical treatments of the data, and in the failure to equate the experimental and comparison groups on such characteristics as language proficiency and socioeconomic status. (p. 270)

Willig woefully concluded that "most research conclusions regarding the effectiveness of bilingual education reflect weaknesses of the research itself rather than effects of the actual programs" (p. 297).

The range of variability among the approaches chosen for research is instructive. It should be noted that almost all of the evaluation studies concentrate on the effectiveness of the programs in teaching students English, rather than on their overall academic development or factors outside of traditional measures of school success. Furthermore, the studies tend to observe children over only a limited duration, often no more than 2 years. The research defines its treatments and outcomes in strictly linguistic terms. At stake is the question of which approach would lead to faster and stronger acquisition of English. This question is a scientifically legitimate one, but it is dwarfed when compared with the outcomes that are of real long-term interest to society: the social and economic advancement of linguistic minority populations through education. A simple curriculum change regarding the language of instruction would solve the problem.

Christina Bratt Paulston (1980) expresses concern with the narrowness of the definition of program success in the following way:

It makes a lot more sense to look at employment figures upon leaving school, figures on drug addiction and alcoholism, suicide rates, and personality disorders, i.e., indicators which measures the social pathology which accompanies social injustice rather than in terms of language skills. . . . The dropout rate for American Indians in Chicago public schools is 95 percent; in the bilingual-bicultural Little Big Horn High School in Chicago the dropout rate in 1976 was 11 percent, and I find that figure a much more meaningful indicator for evaluation of the bilingual program than any psychometric assessment of students' language skills. (p. 41)

It is not always the case that English language proficiency has guided educational research with bilinguals. Funded in 1980, a federal study related to effective instruction, known as the Significant Bilingual Instructional Features Study, described the characteristics of successful programs serving bilingual students (Tikenoff, 1983). More recent research, particularly that of Carter and Chatfield (1986) and Krashen and Biber (1988) have followed this earlier example of describing the organizational and instructional attributes of schools and classrooms that produce academically bilingual students. However, even the most recent federal initiatives regarding program evaluation continue to look almost exclusively at English language skills as the primary outcome variable (Ramirez 1986).

CONCLUSIONS REGARDING BILINGUAL EDUCATION

Linguistic minority education in the United States has been driven by the obsession to make those who speak another language proficient in English. In 1974 (PL 93-380), Congress defined bilingual education as "instruction given in, and study of English and to the extent necessary to allow a child to progress effectively through the education system, the native language," and, in so doing, set the stage for the debate on how English proficiency should be achieved. Unfortunately, following the narrow interpretation that English proficiency is the prerequisite variable preventing linguistic minority students from achieving academic success has not led to the development of effective educational programs for these historically underserved populations. This is not to argue that English language proficiency is not an important goal of linguistic minority education but to acknowledge that it should take a more appropriate place among other valuable academic, social, psychological, and intellectual goals of schooling for linguistic minority students. Preparation of education professionals must also reflect this broader understanding.

IMPLICATIONS FOR PROFESSIONAL TRAINING

The preceding analysis has provided an overview of research, policy, and practice as they relate to the education of linguistic minority students of the United States. It is clear that a variety of programmatic efforts have been developed in response to this growing body of students. It has also become evident that professional education training, particularly for teachers, has not kept pace with the demand for specifically trained educational personnel with expertise in these new programmatic endeavors. However, it is not the case that training of such individuals has been completely ignored. The following discussion will provide an overview of activities in this domain. Although not exhaustive, the discussion should provide a foundation for understanding the types of issues relevant to training a competent linguistic minority teacher. It is appropriate to indicate that other views, some more detailed, are available (see Ada, 1986; Chu & Levy, 1984, 1988; Collier, 1985).

Linguistic Minority Education: An Instructional Innovation

In any discussion of professional training for linquistic minority education, it is important to note that such training is a relatively new enterprise. Not until the mid-1960s did substantial educational initiatives exist in this specialized arena. It was not until 1974 that the U.S. Congress authorized resources for training activities by institutions of higher education in this area of education. The recent nature of this innovation, much like similar developments in the field of special education, has spawned many new training programs that are still struggling to establish themselves as legitimate areas of training alongside longer standing programs in elementary and secondary education. This newness is complicated by the nature of the training-program content; that is, this new program must take a more multidisciplinary perspective. It must be concerned not only with subject matter and pedagogy, but also much more directly with language (native language and/or second language) and instruction for populations that are culturally different.

The 1980–1982 Teachers Language Skills Survey identified the need for 100,000 bilingual teachers if bilingual programs were implemented in schools in which LEP students from one language background were sufficiently concentrated to make such programs feasible. In 1982 there were an estimated 27,000 to 32,000 trained bilingual teachers, leaving 68,000 to 73,000 yet to be trained. Since 168 institutions of higher education graduate approximately 2,000 to 2,600 trained bilingual teachers each year (Blatchford, 1982), the shortage will continue. The Teachers Language Skills Survey reported that, of 103,000 teachers assigned to teach ESL, only 40 percent had received any training in the methods of doing so. It is estimated that at least 350,000 teachers currently need such specialized training (O'Malley, 1981; Waggoner, 1984).

Halcon (1981) and Development Associates (1984) report on the types of training that linguistic minority teachers working in the field have actually experienced. Less than 25 percent of such teachers report graduating from a specific program designed to meet their needs. Instead, most teachers in linguistic minority classrooms have participated in a variety of unsystematic university coursework, district workshops, and federally or state supported inservice training activities. Moreover, the average formal instructional experience of a teacher assigned major instructional responsibilities related to language minority students is less than 3.5 years. Further, less than 33 percent of instructors in linguistic minority classrooms or in related support roles hold the requisite state credentials (in those states where such credentials are available and in the majority of cases actually mandatory). Such data continue to suggest that linguistic minority education programs are staffed by professionals not directly trained for such programs who might be acquiring their expertise on the job. This situation indicates that the education of language minority students continues to be viewed as a temporary innovation. By their very nature, educational innovations do not have well-developed training strategies or institutional recognition; they must go through a developmental process to achieve the desired goals of status and permanence.

With respect to such a process, Chu and Levy (1984) describe the development of an innovative language minority teacher-training program at George Mason University. Their descriptive analysis suggests that several factors played a role in determining the development, implementation, and institutionalization of such innovations: (a) publicly evident active support by academic administrators (chairs, deans, etc.); (b) evident positive support by nonlinguistic minority training faculty; (c) a majority of regular tenure-track faculty (d) involvement of several types of professionals such as faculty from different departments (psychology, foreign languages) and from outside the university (district-level staff and special training consultants from federal and/or state agencies); (e) compatibility of the new program initiative with institutional priorities; (f) sufficient student demand to sustain the program without direct assistance from federal or state resources to cover tuition costs.

It is important to note that this program is still flourishing at George Mason University, just as similar programs are growing elsewhere, particularly in California, Florida, New York, and Texas. However, many will still consider such programs innovative and will continue to evaluate students on their effectiveness with children and youth. Ada (1986) asserts that the challenges faced by minority language teachers include the need to overcome a sense of isolation, to develop mastery of non-English languages, to learn language training pedagogy, to overcome a sense of powerlessness, and to acquire the ability to integrate theory and experience. She argues that linguistic minority teachers must be able to act creatively in their professional roles, and, to do so, they themselves must receive creative training. Teacher training must itself be liberating and validate teachers as conscientious, creative, and intellectual human beings. Professionals must have the ability to understand the societal forces that have influenced their own and their students' cultural identity in such a manner that they stop the passive acceptance of their circumstances and rise above them to take action. Chu and Levy (1984) identify the body of a linguistic minority teacher training program and Ada (1986) describes the soul of such a program.

Specific Professional-Training Issues

On the basis of the foregoing foundation of linguistic minority teacher training, it is proper to consider the actual content of such preparation. As with all training endeavors, it has always been incumbent upon the trainers to identify the desired end product of their efforts in some form of performance competencies. The literature abounds with numerous listings of such competencies (Collier, 1985). The most recent and most detailed is presented by Chu and Levy (1988). This list of competencies is derived from a review of federally and non–federally supported linguistic minority training programs presently operating within United States universities. It focuses on the intercultural competencies that serve as a foundation for the anticipated instructional success of a well-prepared linguistic minority educator. These competencies are presented in Table 40-1 and are organized into knowledge regarding theory, society, and classroom.

TABLE 40–1. Intercultural Competencies for Linguistic Minority Teacher

A. Theory
The graduates will
1. Know a variety of definitions of culture.
2. Know various views of cultural diversity (e.g., cultural deprivation vs. cultural difference).
3. Know various approaches to the study of culture.
4. Know various methods and techniques useful in the study of culture in school and community settings.
5. Know the concepts of cultural relativism, ethnocentrism, and cultural universals.
6. Know the concepts of enculturation, acculturation, assimilation, and biculturalism and how these concepts relate to the target group and majority culture.
7. Know the concepts of national culture, dominant culture, and minority culture and how these concepts relate to the target group and majority culture.
8. Know the concept of ethnicity.
9. Know basic ideas concerning the relationship between culture and education.
10. Know the role of the teacher as cultural transmitter and cultural broker in the context of bilingual education.
11. Avoid stereotyping in the presentation of cultural information by presenting it in a general comparative framework, i.e., with a global perspective.

B. Society
The graduates will
12. Know the historical development of diverse cultural group in the United States.
13. Know some positive and negative effects of cultural diversity in the historical and cultural development of the United States.
14. Know some distinctions between social-class characteristics and cultural attributes of target and mainstream cultural groups.
15. Know some similarities and differences between the majority and minority cultures and the potential conflict and opportunities they create for social groups.
16. Know key aspects of the contemporary life-styles of the target group and their compatibility with life-styles in the local community.
17. Know diverse, as well as common, cultural traditions within both the target and majority culural groups.
18. Know the past and present circumstances of the target group as they relate to the dominant culture in the United States and, when applicable, to the culture of the country of ancestry.
19. Know the patterns of migration, employment, education, and social mobility of the target group.
20. Know about past and current social, cultural, literary, and political development of significance to the target group.
21. Know about the contributions of the target group to the cultural development of the United States.
22. Know basic ideas concerning intercultural communication.
23. Have a positive attitude toward cultural diversity
24. Appreciate the contributions of minority groups to the cultural development of the United States.

C. Classroom
The graduates will
25. Know various methods and models of cross-cultural training and their applicability to bilingual education.
26. Know potential effects of cultural and socioeconomic variables on students' school-related attitudes, values, and behavior.
27. Know potential sources of conflict in cross-cultural interaction in the school setting and how to promote positive interaction.
28. Incorporate into curricular activities materials and other aspects of the instructional environment: (a) culture and history of target group's ancestry, (b) contributions of group to history and culture of United States, (c) contemporary life-styles of target group.
29. Encourage positive cross-cultural interaction through use of appropriate methods and techniques.
30. Demonstrate understanding of diverse verbal and nonverbal communication styles.
31. Demonstrate sensitivity to the cultural differences among students, parents, and instructional personnel and create an environment to develop such sensitivity in others.
32. Have a positive attitude toward cultural groups represented in the school.
33. Take the attitude that stereotyping is to be avoided.
34. Appreciate the cultural heritage of the target groups.

Note From "Multicultural Skills for Bilingual Teachers" by H. Chu and J. Levy, 1988, NABE *Journal*, 12, pp. 3 to 5. Copyright 1988 by National Association for Bilingual Education.

TABLE 40–2. NASDTEC Certification Standards*

Content Standards in Bilingual/Multicultural Education (B/M ED)	Possible IHE Course Offerings
1. Proficiency in L_1 and L_2 for effective teaching	Foreign language and English department courses
2. Knowledge of history and cultures of L_1 and L_2 speakers	Cross-cultural studies, multicultural education (ME), history and civilization, literature, ethnic studies
3. Historical, philosophical, and legal bases for B/M ED and related research	Foundations of BE (or introduction to BE)
4. Organizational models for programs and classrooms in B/M ED	Foundations of BE
5. L_2 methods of teaching (including ESL methodology)	Methods of teaching a second language
6. Communication with students, parents, and others in culturally and linguistically different communities	Cross-cultural studies, ME, school/community relations
7. Differences between L_1 and L_2; language and dialect differences across geographic regions, ethnic groups, social levels	Sociolinguistics, bilingualism

Content Standards in English for Speakers of Other Languages	Possible IHE Courses Offerings
1. Nature of language, language varieties, structure of English language	General linguistics; English phonology, morphology, and syntax
2. Demonstrated proficiency in spoken and written English	English department courses
3. Demonstrated proficiency in a second language	Foreign language courses
4. L_1 and L_2 acquisition process	Language acquisition
5. Effects of socio-cultural variables on language learning	Language acquisition, ME, cross-cultural studies, sociolinguistics
6. Language assessment, program development, implementation, and evaluation	Language assessment, program development, and evaluation

*These are supplemental standards to the NASDTEC professional education standards required of all teachers.

The most widely distributed cited list of competencies was developed and published in 1984 by the National Association of State Directors of Teacher Education and Certification. That list, presented in an abbreviated format in Table 40-2, was a result of combining previous competency lists developed by the Center for Applied Linguistics in 1974 and the Teachers of English to Speakers of Other Languages association in 1975. The list, although not as comprehensive as the Chu and Levy (1988) list, has served as a cornerstone of teacher-training programs in the United States. Articulation of these competencies has led to the development of coursework that attempts to address the domains identified. Collier (1985) provides a sample menu of courses likely to characterize today's linguistic minority teacher-training program (see Table 40-3).

Such specifications of competencies do not insure that teacher-training programs have developed the required expertise or the general support needed to implement the training. Very few teacher-training faculty have themselves received specific training in language minority education. In the University of California, Santa Cruz, which houses a well-respected program in linguistic minority education staffed by five faculty, not one member of the training faculty can point to graduate school experience directly related to this field. The

TABLE 40–3. Sample Courses in a Linguistic Minority Education Teacher Preparation Program

First and second language acquisition and bilingualism

Teaching native language arts

Methods of teaching a second language (e.g., ESL, SSL, VSL)

Methods of teaching content areas, both bilingually and through the second language

Multicultural education including teaching the culturally and linguistically different exceptional child

Program models, policy, school–community relations, and administrative issues in bilingual education and ESL

The phonology, morphology, and syntax of English

The phonology, morphology, and syntax of another language, in addition to English (for bilingual teachers)

Assessment in bilingual/ESL settings

Curriculum development in bilingual/ESL settings

Reading and research in foundations of education (anthropolgy, sociology, history, philosophy, psychology, social psychology related to the education of minority language students)

Use of instructional technology for teaching first and second languages and content areas

Note, From *University Models for ESL and Bilingual Teacher Training* (p. 86) by J.P. Collier, 1985, Rosslyn, VA: National Clearing house for Bilingual Education. Copyright 1985 by National Clearinghouse for Bilingual Education.

expertise, like that of classroom teachers, has been developed on the job, typically after graduate training and faculty experience in some indirectly related academic domain such as foreign languages, psychology, sociology, anthropology, or some other educational specialty.

In addition, it should be noted that linguistic minority education, as a general educational intervention, continues to be at the forefront of ideological debates, even within school faculty. Such debate, unfortunately, brings negative attention to developing program initiatives, hampers normal development, makes potential students chary about such programs and, in times of limited training resources, leads to withdrawal of resources dedicated to such controversial programs. (See August & Garcia, 1988, for a detailed discussion of federal training resource depletion since the beginning of the 1980s.) These circumstances have actually kept enrollment in training programs relatively below expectation, even as school districts increase their efforts to attract linguistic minority educational professionals. Presently, university programs do not even come close to meeting the demand. One demographic report in California concludes that every graduate of teacher-programs in the state will need to be a linguistic minority teacher for the next 4 years, in order to meet the estimated need for such teachers in the early 1990s. Such training is, of course, unlikely, even when detailed lists of competencies and related coursework have been identified.

Inservice Training

Recognizing that university programs are not, in the short term, able to meet the growing demand for linguistic minority teachers, extensive inservice training initiatives have become the typical vehicle for meeting these growing professional needs. In 1974 federal resources were dedicated to this inservice enterprise, and those resources have continued. Bilingual Education Service Centers conducted needs assessments on a regional basis and implemented regular inservice training activities from 1975 through 1982. In the late 1980s a smaller federally funded effort located in regional Multifunctional Resource Centers continued this activity. In addition, state offices of education in states highly affected by linguistic minority students have developed their own inservice training programs.

Significantly, local school districts have implemented extensive inservice programs to meet their particular needs in substantively increasing the linguistic minority expertise of their teaching personnel. One such program, in Denver, Colorado, exemplifies this inservice training activity. This urban district, highly affected by linguistic minority students, determined that its needs could be partially met by the professional development of its existent teaching staff. Several training presuppositions guided the development and implementation of the inservice training: (a) Teachers needed theoretical grounding and practical application of instruction reflecting that theory, (b) external consultants with linguistic minority expertise would work collaboratively over an extended period of time (4–6

years) with a cadre of local teachers, (c) a local teacher group demonstrating enhanced expertise would provide mentor support to their district colleagues, (d) development of new mentor groups at individual school sites would insure the systematic augmentation of linguistic minority expertise throughout the district. A recent analysis of this inservice strategy indicates that over 500 district teachers participated in this training from the mid 1980s to the late 1980s. Significant gains in service delivery to Denver's growing population of linguistic minority students has been documented. A corps of 100 linguistic minority mentors now exists in support of the over 500 linguistic minority teachers. This mentor corps continues to provide formal training experiences, classroom demonstrations, local site networking, and curricular leadership.

This alternative form of teacher training was born of immediate needs that could not be met through normal teacher-training channels. It demonstrates a useful and highly responsive solution to a problem many school districts face with respect to linguistic minority populations. This alternative form of training could be appropriate for enhancing the effectiveness of most educational professionals.

CONCLUSION

It seems clear that language minority students can be served effectively by schools and educational professionals. They can be served by schools organized to develop educational structures and processes that take into consideration both the broader attributes of effective schooling practices and the specific attributes relevant to language minority students (Carter & Chatfield, 1986; Garcia, 1988; Tikenoff, 1983). Effective classrooms exemplify instructional strategies that seem to build on socialization factors relevant to the student population. Effective instruction is characterized by emphasis on student-to-student communication regarding academic material. Such communication builds on culturally appropriate interaction strategies. It allows students to engage in instructional interactions that promote higher order linguistic and cognitive functioning.

Although the training of language minority education teachers is in a developmental period and in need of further clarifying research, it is clearly not its infancy. A serious body of literature addressing instructional practices, organization, and their effects is emerging. The training of professional innovators is a challenge for university and federal, state, and local educational agencies. The needs are great, and the production of competent professionals has lagged. However, professional organizations, credentialing bodies, and universities have responded with competencies, guidelines, and curricula. Local districts have also had to engage in substantial training endeavors. The challenge for all those engaged in teacher training is to consider the rapidly expanding literature regarding linguistic minority students, to evaluate its implications critically and to apply it in the best interests of teachers, children, and youth.

References

Ada, A. F. (1986). Creative education for bilingual teachers. *Harvard Educational Review, 56*(4), 386–394.

August, D., & Garcia, E. (1988). *Language minority education in the U.S.: Research policy and practice.* Springfield, IL: Charles C. Thomas.

Baker, K., & deKanter, A. A. (1983). An answer from research on bilingual education. *American Education, 19*(6), 40–48.

Carter, T. P., & Chatfield, M. L. (1986). Effective bilingual schools: Implications for policy and practice. *American Journal of Education, 95*(1), 200–234.

Castañeda v. Pickard. (1981). 648 F. 2d 989, 1007 (5th Cir. court, 1981) 103 S. Ct. 3321.

Chamot, A., & O'Malley, J. M. (1986). *A cognitive academic learning approach: An ESL content based curriculum.* Wheaton, MD: National Clearinghouse for Bilingual Education.

Chu, H., & Levy, J. (1984). Institutionalizing a bilingual training program: A case study of George Mason University. *NABE Journal, 8*(3), 41–54.

Chu, H., & Levy, J. (1988). Multicultural skills for bilingual teachers. *NABE Journal, 12*(2), 17–36.

Collier, J. P. (1985). University models for ESL and bilingual teacher training. In National Clearinghouse for Bilingual Education (Ed.), *Issues in English language development* (pp. 81–90). Rosslyn, VA: Editor.

Cummins, J. (1979). Linguistic interdependence and the educational development of bilingual children. *Review of Educational Research, 19,* 222–251.

Development Associates. (1984, December). *Final report: Descriptive study phase of the national longitudinal evaluation of the effectiveness of services for language minority limited English proficient students.* Arlington, VA: Author.

Garcia, E. (1983). *Bilingualism in early childhood.* Albuquerque, NM: University of New Mexico Press.

Garcia, E. (1988). Effective schooling for language minority students. In National Clearinghouse for Bilingual Education (Ed.), *New focus.* Arlington, VA: Editor.

General Accounting Office. (1987). *Research evidence on bilingual education* (GAO/PEMD-87-12BR). Washington, DC: Author.

Hakuta, K. (1985). *Mirror of language: The debate on bilingualism.* New York: Basic Books.

Hakuta, K., & Gould, L. J. (1987). Synthesis of research on bilingual education. *Educational Leadership, 44*(6), 38–45.

Halcon, J. (1981). Features of federal bilingual programs. *NABE Journal, 6*(1), 27–39.

Hudelson, S. (1987). The role of native language literacy in the education of language minority children. *Language Arts, 64*(8), 827–841.

Hammerly, H. (1985). *An integrated theory of language teaching.* Burnby, Canada: Second Language Publications.

Krashen, S. D. (1982). *Principles and practices in second language acquisition.* Oxford, England: Pergamon Press.

Krashen, S. D. & Biber, D. (1988). *On course: Bilingual education success in California.* Sacramento, CA: California Association for Bilingual Education.

Lau v. Nichols, 414, U.S. 563 (1974).

McLaughlin, B. (1985). *Second language acquisition in childhood: Vol. 2. School-age children.* Hillsdale, NJ: Lawrence Erlbaum.

National Association of State Directors of Teacher Education and Certification (1984). *NASDTEC Certification Standards.* Washington, DC: Author.

O'Malley, M. J. (1981). *Children's and services study: Language minority children with limited English proficiency in the United States.* Rosslyn, VA: National Clearinghouse for Bilingual Education.

Ovando, C. J., & Collier, V. P. (1985). *Bilingual and ESL classrooms: Teaching in multicultural contexts.* New York: McGraw-Hill.

Paulston, C. B. (1980). *Bilingual education: Theories and issues.* Rowley, MA: Newbury House.

Purkey, S. C., & Smith, M. S. (1983). Effective schools: A review. *Elementary School Journal, 83*(4), 426–452.

Ramirez, A. (1986). *Bilingualism through schooling.* Albany, NY: State University of New York Press.

Rossell, C., & Ross, J. M. (1986). *The social science evidence on bilingual education.* Boston: Boston University.

Schneider, S. G. (1976). *Revolution, reaction or reform: The 1974 Bilingual Education Act.* New York: Las Americas.

Schumann, J. H. (1976). Affective factors and the problem of age in second language acquisition. *Language Learning, 25,* 209–239.

Seliger, H. W. (1977). Does practice make perfect? A study of interactional patterns and L2 competence. *Language Learning, 27*(2), 263–278.

Seliger, H. W. (1984). Processing universals in second language acquisition. In F. R. Eckman, L. H. Bell, & D. Nelson (Eds.), *Universals of second language acquisition* (pp. 161–183). Rowley, MA: Newbury House.

Tikenoff, W. J. (1983). *Compatibility of the SBIF features with other research on instruction of LEP students* (SBIF-83-4.8/10). San Francisco: Far West Laboratory.

Troike, R. C. (1981). Synthesis of research in bilingual education. *Educational Leadership, 38*(6), 498–504.

United States Congress. (1984). *Equal Education Opportunities and Transportation of Students Act of 1974,* 294(f) .20 U.S.L.

U.S. v. Texas, 647 F. 2d 69 (9th Cir. 1981).

Waggoner, D. (1984). The need for bilingual education: Estimates from the 1980 census. *NABE Journal, 8*(2), 1–14.

Willig, A. C. (1985). A meta-analysis of selected studies on effectiveness of bilingual education. *Review of Educational Research, 55,* 269–317.

Wong-Fillmore, L. (1976). *The second time around: Cognitive and social strategies in second language acquisition.* Unpublished doctoral dissertation, Stanford University.

Wong-Fillmore, L., & Valdez, C. (1986). Teaching bilingual learners. In M. C. Wittrock (Ed.), *Handbook of research on teaching* (3rd ed. pp. 648–685). New York: Macmillan.

·41·

MUSIC TEACHER EDUCATION

Eunice Boardman

UNIVERSITY OF ILLINOIS-URBANA-CHAMPAIGN

Formal training in music instruction for teachers has existed in institutions of higher learning for at least a hundred years. During that period many books have been written and extensive research conducted proposing various ways to improve music instruction in the schools, including recommendations for curricular change and prescriptions for making use of specific methodologies. However, a cohesive body of research directly focused on how best to prepare the new teacher and to implement such recommendations still does not exist. This continues to be true in spite of the fact that concerns regarding the quality of preparation have been voiced almost as long as courses in music teaching have existed.

In the late 1930s, as a result of an extensive study of music teacher education practices, Edna McEachern noted, "To date, many school music teacher education institutions have admitted inadequately prepared students, and . . . continue to graduate mediocre school music teachers . . . truly a vicious circle" (1937, p. 116). In 1982, the same concerns were expressed, in almost the same words, "Students, inadequately educated at the public school level . . . enroll in ineffective *teacher training programs* . . . return to the public schools inadequately prepared . . . such a circle is indeed vicious" (Meske, 1982, p. 65).

Recommendations for change and improvement, of which there are many, seem to be primarily based on (a) views of practicing teachers, who base their advice on recollections of their own training experiences; (b) prescriptions made by leaders in the field (frequently the college professors responsible for that training), who seek to apply current theories about music, teaching, and learning to teacher training; and (c) re-

sponses by those in charge of developing teacher training curricula to outside pressures including state, regional, and federal agencies responsible for public education.

J. Anderson (1987) concludes that, in spite of stated desires to improve undergraduate teacher education, relatively few researchers have dealt specifically with these problems. Research that has been undertaken has been fragmented, sporadic, and isolated; few strands of research can be identified that build on a particular aspect of the music teacher training process and, thus, present a cohesive set of studies that provide clear direction. There are no longitudinal studies to help the educator of music teachers draw conclusions as to the relative value of recommended content, curricular sequence, or experiences. For example, since the early 1950s, music teacher education programs, in response to outside pressures, have been increasingly altered to include a substantial practicum element (Colwell, 1985). However, while the number of required hours of field experience has increased to over 300 in some states, and many statements stipulate the value of such experience, no studies exist in the field of music education that verify that this apprenticeship model results in better prepared beginning teachers. Some studies suggest that the constant contact with teachers and schools set in a particular mold may in fact limit the student teacher's perception of what can or should be accomplished within a school setting (P. Krueger, 1987). Anderson also observes a conflict as to the type of research needed: should research focus on improving the process of teacher training or on defining the competencies trainees should possess when beginning to teach? A survey of studies forces the conclusion that, for many researchers, the later

Appreciation is expressed to Anthony Barressi, contributing author of the section on historical perspective; David Nelson, contributing author of the section on the influences of governmental and nongovernmental agencies; and Gerald Olson, contributing author of the section on participants in the music teacher education process, all from the University of Wisconsin—Madison. Appreciation is also expressed to Roy Ernst (Eastman School of Music) and Mary Hoffman (University of Illinois) for their insightful reviews of the manuscript.

seems to be their concern. However, this chapter will primarily concentrate on research and other studies concerned with seeking information related to the first point.

An examination of studies, reports, and recommendations published since the mid-1960s dealing directly with improvement of music teacher preparation suggests that those concerned with improvement have concentrated on the influence of (a) philosophical views as to the role of education and music education in contemporary society, (b) contemporary theories of the psychology of learning as they affect content and structure of teacher education curricula, (c) decisions made by agencies outside the teacher education setting (whether pre- or in-service), and (d) these three forces as they affect a specific instructional level (i.e., elementary, secondary) or type of specialization (i.e., choral, instrumental, or general). These topics will serve as the organizing framework for the following summary of research in music teacher education. The authors have sought to be as comprehensive and complete in their reporting as possible, but the studies cited are selective and not intended to be an exhaustive list.

A HISTORICAL PERSPECTIVE

The rise of formal music teacher education in this country postdated by a number of years the inclusion of formal music education in schools. In colonial America, music education was, for the most part, accomplished on an informal basis within the home or in singing schools taught by itinerant teachers. Anyone who could afford the minimal fee could receive instruction to develop or improve musical and vocal skills, skills that were offered to improve church music performance (Britten, 1966). Teachers by avocation rather than by occupation, these singing-school instructors were trained, if at all, by other teachers or in classes taught by master teachers who often developed and published their own books (Birge, 1928).

The socially democratic spirit of the times was also evident in the transfer of singing-school practices to public education when Lowell Mason and other singing-school teachers instituted music programs in public schools, thus making music instruction readily available to all children (Britten, 1966). Along with the transfer of the teaching of singing to the public school setting, recognition of the need for more consistent teacher training emerged. To fit within the educational framework of the elementary school and to insure efficient instruction for all the students therein, a number of the early music educators sought philosophical and psychological underpinnings upon which to base instructional approaches and shared these assumptions with others entering the field. Such arguments formed the basis of the teacher-training programs of the time. Pestalozzi, freely interpreted, provided a methodological framework for Lowell Mason's instruction in the Boston Public Schools (Keene, 1982). As one of the first advocates of public music education, Mason's theories, influenced by Pestalozzi, affected teaching and teacher training in music during the early part of the nineteenth century, conveyed, in part, by the wide dissemination of his *Manual of Instruction* (Mason, 1834). The

Boston School Board accepted Mason's argument that music should be included in the curriculum because of its intellectual, moral, and physical value. From that time until at least the 1960s, school music programs continued to be influenced by educational philosophies based on rationales that were anything but aesthetic (Birge, 1928, pp. 41–56). Good personal hygiene, improved mental discipline, and vocational training were among the extramusical justifications that emerged as teachers sought to defend their programs in terms compatible with the educational goals of a developing nation. Not until the 1960s were personal enrichment and aesthetic value generally offered and accepted as prime reasons for music instruction in the schools (College Board, 1985).

While varied rationales were presented as arguments for including music in the school curriculum, they simultaneously influenced the content and structure of contemporary teacher education practices. Teacher training during the nineteenth century was accomplished primarily through conventions and summer normal institutes, where teachers were taught musical skills and pedagogical approaches. One of the first such institutes convened in 1853 (Keene, 1982). By the mid-century instructional materials in the form of music book series were available to assist teachers in instruction. Book companies such as American Book Company and Silver Burdett Company offered workshops on how to use their material, thereby supplying teachers with inservice opportunities for instructional improvement. One of the longest in operation was the American Institute of Normal Methods, established in 1884. Participants in this annual 3-week summer school operated by Silver, Burdett were awarded a diploma at the end of a 3-year course of study (Platt, 1982). Gradually, as universities assumed the responsibility for training music educators, extensive programs such as that of the American Institute were replaced by shorter workshops, a model that continues to this day. For nearly 40 years, however, these institutes served as one of the principal avenues through which school music teachers received instruction in music theory, performance, and methodology.

Along with these somewhat informal opportunities for instruction, formalized music teacher education as part of the normal-school curriculum began to appear in some educational institutions during the latter part of the nineteenth century. In schools devoted to the education of teachers, content similar to that presented in the conventions and institutes was taught to future music supervisors and classroom teachers. Toward the end of the century, as high school attendance began to increase, the need for teachers with specialized performance skills in instrumental and vocal music became essential. Partially in response to this need, some conservatories, colleges, and universities established music teacher education programs, introducing a European influence into American music education (Wager & McGrath, 1962). This influence took the form of the *performance paradigm* that stressed individual instruction of the talented and total dedication of the learner to the art form. Because this performance paradigm presented such a powerful instructional model, music teachers in the school setting were faced with a dilemma: whether to follow the artistic dictates of the performance setting or continue to seek to meet the traditional educational goals of the school, directed toward the growth and development of all students (Barresi, 1980).

Such conflicts have been at the heart of the controversy over the role of music in the schools and, thus, the form of music teacher education since its inception. From the early nineteenth century, when music study was introduced into the schools, music educators sought to defend music's place in the precollege curriculum and to structure pedagogical approaches on the ideologies of the time. Kliebard (1986) identifies four educational ideologies that have molded the curricular mainstream of American education during the twentieth century. The influence of each of these can, to a greater or lesser extent, be observed in parallel recommendations for music learning and teaching. The *humanist* ideology held that a core of subjects, classical in nature, should be taught to every student in the school. Mental discipline gained by the learner from such interactions with the curriculum was a major goal of followers of this ideology.

The *social efficiency* ideology was based upon the industrial model and sought to control society by scientifically assigning the student to a place therein that fit her or his abilities and then providing training to insure the success of the individual in later life. *Child study* ideologists advocated placing curricular emphasis upon the needs and interests of the child. Understanding of how the child thought and learned was a keystone of this curricular movement. Finally, the *social-meliorist* advocates, who gained prominence in the 1930s, viewed the school as the only hope for social change. Teachers were urged to devise curricula that would promote social awareness in students.

In the nineteenth century, music in the schools was defended on its ability to promote general goals of the curriculum; in the twentieth century this pattern continued, as support was sought in contemporary curricular ideologies for music education (as identified by Kliebard). Two of these ideologies, social efficiency and child-study, are reflected in the works of music psychologists and music educators. Musical intelligence and aptitude testing, as well as other behaviorial characteristics of the social efficiency movement found currency in the work of music psychologists including Kwalwasser (1927) and Seashore (1940) and music educators such as Gordon (1980). The work of the psychologists Piaget and Bruner, leaders in the study of cognitive and developmental factors implicit in the child-study ideology, has also been applied to music learning by music psychologists and educators. Some examples of such applications include studies conducted by Nelson (1987), Serafine (1988), and Zimmerman (1980).

The extent to which the profession has been deeply affected by both of these psychological strains can be observed in teacher education programs that involve future teachers in experiences and methodologies reflecting principles drawn from one or the other of these ideologies. *Education for Musical Growth* (Mursell, 1948), *Foundations and Principles of Music Education* (Leonhard & House, 1959), *Psychology of Music Teaching* (Gordon, 1971), and *Foundations of Music Education* (Abeles, Hoffer, & Klotman, 1981) are a few of the books written for future music teachers that reflect one or both of these strands.

Although in the early twentieth century European practices in training the artist were included in teacher-training institutions, in more recent decades methods for teaching music devised by foreign artists—such as those bearing the names of Suzuki, Orff, Dalcroze, and Kodaly—were imported to the United States and adapted to the requirements of American educational settings (Kowall, 1966, pp. 381–414; Landis & Carder, 1972). American proponents of these foreign imports sometimes claim that one or another of such approaches reflects behaviorist, cognitive, or developmental theories; however, it is impossible to find proof that such psychological underpinnings were ever the intent of the founders.

Perhaps the philosophical trend that has had the most profound influence upon teacher education in the latter part of this century is that relating to aesthetic education. The result of a continuing line of philosophical thought, with roots in the social-meliorist and child-study ideologies, this position's educational genesis appeared in the writings of John Dewey (Dewey, 1916). James Mursell, a leading figure in music education from the 1930s through the 1960s, acknowledged the influence of these ideologies when he maintained that the goal of music study in the schools should be to learn to "love music wisely. . . . thus the school music teacher should dedicate himself to the task of conveying the power and glory of music to all the children of our schools" (Mursell & Glenn, 1931, p. 369).

Charles Leonhard, a Mursell student and author of a widely influential book on music education principles and practices, further averred that music programs must develop musical responsiveness and understanding in every student and "take into account the nature of the aesthetic experience and the importance of aesthetic experience in the life of the human being" (Leonhard & House, 1959, pp. 2–3).

In more recent years, the most widely quoted advocate of the aesthetic education philosophy has been Bennett Reimer, whose impetus comes from the Mursell-Leonhard line. In his book, *Philosophy of Music Education*, Reimer (1970) synthesizes ideas drawn from the works of Leonard B. Meyer and Suzanne Langer, among others, and forges an aesthetic education position that many college and university music education departments have sought to incorporate into their teacher-preparation curricula. Although it would be naive to believe that the goal of aesthetic education has been fully achieved in American schools, it is certain that the philosophical ideal has influenced numerous contemporary music educators. Its influence on recommended teacher education practices can be observed in many teacher education textbooks such as *Principles and Problems of Music Education* (Regelski, 1975).

A number of conferences during the 1960s and 1970s were also influential in providing a philosophical basis for music education goals and, by implication, teacher education practices. In the early 1960s a group of musicologists, performing artists, composers, and a few music educators gathered at Yale University to discuss the state of music education in American primary and secondary schools. The final report of this Yale Seminar was critical of much of the school music repertoire, performance, and methodology (Palisca, 1964). In response to this criticism, an angered, yet chastened, music education professional organization, the Music Educators National Conference (MENC), organized its own conference in 1967. This conference, known as the Tanglewood Symposium, brought together artists, educators, psychologists, government personnel, and music industry representatives to review, discuss, and seek to improve music education in American schools. The published proceedings stressed the importance of musical experiences in the lives of all children; recommended the expansion of repertoire to include a wide variety of musical periods, styles, and cultures; and focused upon the importance of aesthetic growth, as well as skill development (R. Choate, 1968). As a result of Tanglewood, the MENC set up a task force to chart future directions for the profession. This Goals and Objectives project (GO) established a number of guidelines that have influenced music programs and teacher preparation for the past generation (Music Educators National Conference [MENC], 1970a).

The MENC also addressed issues of how students perceive and learn music in a series of conferences held in Ann Arbor, Michigan. Noted music education and psychological researchers gathered to review past research and recommend future studies that might affect the teaching and learning of music (MENC, 1981, 1983). Although the Ann Arbor conferences did not result in specific recommendations for teacher education, they alerted the profession to the importance of understanding how music is learned as the basis for determining how it should be taught. These conferences also influenced how many teachers reviewed and accomplished their work. Philosophical positions derived from these conferences caused teachers of teachers to alter their programs toward the preparation of music instructors who would place greater emphasis upon learning-centered goals (process) than upon performance-centered goals (product) (Leonhard, 1985a).

INFLUENCES OF GOVERNMENTAL AND NONGOVERNMENTAL AGENCIES

Traditionally, the roles of governmental and nongovernmental agencies in determining the content of music teacher education programs, certification policies, and certification procedures have been tightly interwoven (Poolos, 1968). Consequently, the very strong influences of state governmental agencies and, to a lesser degree, the roles of professional organizations (i.e., the National Association of Schools of Music [NASM] and MENC, as well as regional accrediting agencies) provide a basis for analyses of current practices and trends.

Collins (1970) reports that certification and licensing practices in music education are basically a twentieth-century phenomenon. This is partially due to the gradually increasing influence of teacher-training institutions that began during the post–Civil War years and the subsequent endorsements of music teaching as a speciality area by state certification agencies. The trend toward greater state influence culminated in the 1960s when a baccalaureate degree finally became the minimum requirement for music teacher certification in every state.

Wolfe (1972) notes that many of the characteristics of music

teacher certification remained constant between 1954 and 1972. This stability was coupled with a trend away from required credits in specific subject-matter areas to a more comprehensive approval by state agencies of the music teacher education curricula as submitted by individual institutions of higher education.

Erbes (1983), in a follow-up to Wolfe's study, surmised that the public's growing concern for competent, well-trained teachers would be reflected in a number of changes in music teacher education practices and trends during the period 1972–1983. However, his study concluded "that major trends in certification policies and academic requirements affecting music majors have not changed in a dramatic manner, nor have the procedures for program approval and accreditation been modified by various accrediting bodies and agencies" (p. 42). He did note that one significant change occurring during this period was "the increasing emphasis for continuing study in a planned program beyond the bachelor's degree as a means for obtaining advanced certification" (p. 42).

In his most recent study, Erbes (1986) finds little change in music teacher certification practices since 1983. However, he notes major changes "in the areas of certification renewal procedures and testing for admission and exit from teacher education programs prior to certification" (p. 1). He feels that the dominant trend has been toward increased testing for certification, with 13 states requiring the music education portion of the National Teacher Examination or a similarly designed test related to the music content area.

In critiquing these trends, Erbes (1984) points to a few of the potential weaknesses inherent in an increased use of preprofessional competency testing in music education. Although it is generally recognized that testing can determine an individual's subject-related knowledge, it does not offer important data regarding personal skills, ability to work with youth, or, perhaps most important for the field of music education, basic musicianship. Consequently, Erbes suggests four supplemental approaches: (a) early evaluation of music education candidates, (b) field experiences before student teaching, (c) continuing education, and (d) extended training for practicing teachers.

Finally, Erbes identifies the important role that regional accrediting agencies play in establishing reciprocity plans that have direct bearing on the formation of music teacher education programs. These agreements include programs established by the Interstate Agreement on Qualification of Educational Personnel, the National Association of State Directors of Teacher Education and Certification (1981, 1983), and the National Council for Accreditation of Teacher Education. Possible effects of recent recommendations for teacher education reform on certification have also been examined by Erbes (1987).

The National Association of Schools of Music (NASM) as the primary national professional organization, is the agency responsible for the accreditation of music curricula in higher education (NASM, 1986, p. 5). The NASM determines requirements for music teacher education in curricular structure, general studies, personal qualities, and musical competencies (i.e., conducting, performing, composing, and arranging) for all students, as well as specific competencies and experiences for each area of specialization. Teaching competencies and professional procedures for implementing the music teacher education program are prescribed.

In addition to its role as the certifying agency for schools of music, the NASM provides an important forum through which the profession can discuss current issues related to music teacher education. Recommendations by the NASM often provide a model from which the music teacher education profession derives standards in their lobbying efforts at the state level. Lobbying by these organizations is needed to assure that the curricular standards established by specific state departments of education are flexible enough to also provide time for the types of undergraduate experiences considered essential by these professional music teacher educators. Many college educators speak to the concern for this potential conflict (Leonhard, 1985b; Olson, 1979b). They express concern that the increasing number of professional education courses required at the undergraduate level could force a proportionate diminishing of requirements in music content, if total credits for graduation are to be maintained at a realistic number. Because the NASM dictates that a minimum of one-half of undergraduate degree credits be in music, the result, if both state certifying agency and professional-agency requirements are met, can be an ever upward spiral in the total number of hours required for graduation. Concerns related to the cost of multiple accreditation were also summarized in a study by Morgan (1987).

However, in spite of the oft-expressed concern that certifying agencies are dictating teacher education curricula, a study undertaken in 1977 concludes that, although four alternative certification plans were available in the state of Texas, the curricular designs of the Texas colleges studied remained almost identical (Funk, 1977).

PARTICIPANTS IN THE MUSIC TEACHER EDUCATION PROCESS

In *Music Teacher Education: Partnership and Process* (Olson, 1987), participants in the music teacher education process are identified as (a) the high school student anticipating a career in music education, (b) the undergraduate student preparing for such a career, (c) the college professor (including those in music, music education, professional education, and general education) directing the undergraduate's preparation, (d) the cooperating teacher involved in various aspects of the undergraduate's preparation, (e) the master teacher who continues to guide the novice teacher in inservice situations, and (f) those college professors directly involved in graduate programs in music education. The document proposes that these participants form a partnership and calls for "the establishment of strong bonds among this nation's elementary and secondary school music educators and college music and music education professors—bonds through which new ideas can flow and cooperative ventures can evolve" (p. 13). It also proposes an expanded view of the process through which one becomes a good

teacher, a process that begins prior to the college program of preparation and extends throughout an active career.

The MENC Task Force addresses the issue of recruitment, selection, and retention of music educators for the twenty-first century. Selection and retention was also the focus of some earlier research (Shellahamer, 1984); however, most studies have focused on procedures for identification, screening, and periodic evaluation of preservice and inservice music teachers. Among the factors selected for study have been attitudes (J. Anderson, 1974; Knab, 1975); predictors of success (J. Anderson, 1965); selected characteristics of prospective music educators (Doane, 1983; Froelich & L'Roy, 1985), including motivation (Caimi, 1979; Walker, 1977); and various personality characteristics (R. Krueger, 1976).

Krueger concluded that personality and motivation variables are related to music teaching success in fairly powerful ways. He also found that no study provided a significantly stable relationship between objective measures in terms of gain scores to the extent that any could be used as criteria for success. Knab (1975) compared attitudes of prospective music teachers with prospective performers and teachers in the field, concluding that there were differences among the three groups. He concluded that, with improvement of the instrument, such measures could be used with caution to screen and advise applicants. The need to be sensitive to the interests and needs of undergraduate music education majors, as a step toward improving teacher education practices, is stressed by Brand (1989).

The long-standing issue of competency-based teacher education is summarized by Mountford (1976), who synthesizes the studies undertaken between 1964 and 1974. This controversial approach, as a basis for teacher education curricula, has continued to be the subject of a number of studies since that time, most commonly through attempts to identify musical and extramusical competencies that should be possessed before one begins to teach. Most of these lists are the result of surveys to which public school music teachers, administrators, and/or college music educators responded. Among such studies conducted since Mountford's are those by Coleman (1979), Lofgren (1974), Parr (1976), Reeves (1980), Smith (1985), Stegall (1975), and Taylor (1980). Each dealt with the task of identification in slightly different ways, but Parr found 387 competencies to be essential! The wide variation in types of lists, from very general to very specific, makes it impossible to draw meaningful implications for curricular change from the research results. Perhaps in response to this dilemma, the development of valid competency-based tests as part of exit evaluation was addressed by Beazley (1981). Recommendations for screening, based on some of the previously cited research, are made by Brand (1987), who calls for procedures that ensure the best and the brightest are selected for admission into teacher education programs.

In light of some of these research findings, *Music Teacher Education: Partnership and Process* (Olson, 1987) makes specific recommendations regarding identification of potential teachers, confirmation of their potential for successful teaching, and encouragement of these students to seek a career in music teaching. Included is a listing of preferred personal, intellectual, musical, and instructional teacher attributes. Such summaries have been offered periodically by members of the profession, including one presented by Lehman at the Symposium on Music Teacher Education sponsored by Arizona State University in 1985 (Lehman, 1986).

Olson (1987) also calls for (a) establishing formal procedures for evaluating applications for admission to teacher certification programs in music; (b) involving partnership members in confirming the attributes and achievements of students who have been recruited for their potential for teaching; (c) evaluating applicants on the basis of personal, intellectual, musical and instructional attributes; (d) basing decisions on observed and recorded evaluations of a candidate's achievements or potential; and (e) establishing advising procedures and periodic record reviews between music education professors and music teacher candidates.

The school music educator, as a member of the partnership model, has a direct influence on the education of potential music teachers. Consequently, the attitudes and practices of inservice music teachers are often passed on to the preservice teacher through cooperative teaching ventures and master teaching programs (Abeles, 1987; P. Krueger, 1987). Some research exists concerning assessment of the quality of work in undergraduate studies and its relationship to music teaching effectiveness. Borkowski (1967), for example, concludes that quality of work in a number of undergraduate courses traditionally included in the music curriculum did not correlate positively with student achievement in classes taught by the teachers included in the study. Other research focused on similar aspects of education related to teaching effectiveness (Asmus, 1981; J. Choate, 1976; Cody, 1968; Franklin, 1968; Niemeyer, 1974). It should be noted that the influence of relationships investigated in most of these studies rarely exceeded 50 percent.

Other studies examined characteristics of a particular group of participants including desirable qualities of music administrators (Burden, 1985) and supervisors of student teachers (D'Arca, 1985). The relationship between some teacher characteristics and inservice growth has been identified by Taebel and Coker (1980) and Weerts (1977).

In many ways, *Music Teacher Education: Partnership and Process* represents an evolution of thought that had been proffered 15 years earlier in a publication developed by a similarly charged group, the MENC Commission on Teacher Education. That report, *Teacher Education in Music: Final Report* (Klotman, 1972), outlined 13 objectives as part of the Goals and Objective project. Among the 13, those most directly concerned with identification and training of teachers were:

1. List of competencies needed by music educators
2. Recommendations for musical, general, and professional education components for teacher education
3. Identification of innovative programs and practices in music teacher preservice and inservice activities
4. Survey of research and professional literature on evaluation of teacher education in music

5. Study of admission and retention policies
6. Preparation of standards and evaluation criteria
7. Recommendation of precollege experiences for potential music teachers
8. Publication of materials to promote improvement of music teacher education
9. Development of a statement of desired competencies for elementary classroom teachers of music.

As noted by Colwell (1985), the changes called for during the 1980s were for the reform of teacher education, which carried with it the implication that such reform must also extend to the reform of programs designed to prepare a professional cadre of university-level music educators. LeBlanc (1984), Lundquist (1987), and Mortenson (1988), among others, address this issue. Noting that "The Society for Music Teacher Education has selected as one of its major thrusts improvements in the instruction of college professors responsible for the preparation of school educators" (p. 112), Lundquist makes specific suggestions on how to provide more effective teachers of teachers in colleges and universities. Included in her suggestions are some instructional components that could prove to be effective additions to the preparation of doctoral students studying to be instructors of preservice music educators. Meske (1987) also urges that reform be initiated in areas affecting the training of the college music educator, including clearly defined and carefully implemented processes for recruitment, selection, training, and evaluation. The MENC, through the Report of the Graduate Commission on Teacher Education (Ball, 1982), has recognized that the doctoral component of graduate teacher education must include preparation for the teaching and administration of undergraduate teacher education programs.

CURRICULAR CONTEXTS AND MODELS

Historically, formal music teacher education has taken place within the context of four distinctive college and university settings: the music conservatory, the liberal arts college, the teachers college, and the research university. Traditionally, the preparation of music teachers varied according to the type of program carved out of the curriculum in each type of institution. In general, the music conservatory required a heavy percentage of music performance courses; the liberal arts college required a significant percentage of academic courses in music, as well as in the liberal studies; the teachers college required a large percentage of courses in professional and music education. The university assimilated faculty specialists from the other three unique settings. John (1979) reports that music teachers representing these unique backgrounds "formed a loose federation in establishing music faculties for American colleges and universities. . . . Each faction expected the newly created university music department to be structured similarly to their former school, an expectation that created a three-way, long-term confrontation" (pp. 58–59). The models for music teacher education programs were thus initially shaped from curricular space available for preparing music teachers within the philosophical framework of each type of institution.

Although the models for preservice teacher education are of necessity largely influenced by the standards provided by professional, regional, and state accrediting agencies, professional organizations in music education and education continue to seek ways of influencing teacher education curricula. During the late 1960s and early 1970s, MENC initiated a major effort to influence music teacher education, beginning with the formulation of the National Commission on Teacher Education. As part of the GO project of 1970, the commission identified a number of objectives, many of which were assigned to a continuing National Commission on Instruction (NCI). Among the objectives addressed by NCI were several that were particularly relevant to reform in undergraduate preparation of teachers. After specifying personal qualities, musical competencies, and professional qualities deemed necessary for music educators, NCI recommended critical changes in three important areas (National Commission on Instruction, 1974), which can be summarized as follows:

A. Musicianship
   1. That a 4-year sequential program in comprehensive musicianship become the basis for training of all undergraduate musicians, replacing fragmented courses in theory, ear training, history, and literature
   2. That students participate in a variety of ensemble experiences
   3. That a required senior recital be waived where demonstration of other musical strengths is more appropriate to the student's teaching goals
B. General Education
   1. That preservice music teachers be required to engage in a substantial amount of study outside music in such broad areas as natural science, social science, and the arts and humanities
   2. That courses offered by the music department be reexamined to ascertain how they can better relate the art of music to humanity's other concerns
C. Professional Education
   1. That all music methods courses be taught by successful music educators regularly engaged in teaching music students of ages appropriate to the specific course
   2. That each prospective music educator be involved throughout the college years, beginning with the first, with a program of in-school observation and participation in teaching–learning situations
   3. That steps be taken immediately to individualize music teacher education programs in music to include the establishment of procedures of admission and retention, counseling, and courses of study fitted to each student's particular needs, competencies, and professional aspirations

Undoubtedly the recommendations prepared by the NCI were strongly influenced by two other projects supported by MENC. The first of these was the Comprehensive Music Project (CMP) (MENC, 1965; Willoughby, 1971). This project was devoted to the promotion of an interdisciplinary study of music wherein insights gained from the study of music theory, history, and performance might be applied to all musical settings. Further, this movement redefined important skills for learners in music and called for the use of contemporary music and creative activities both in preparing music educators and for teaching music in the schools. The GO project, CMP, and NCI generated creative thinking regarding the preparation of music teachers, although none of the proposed programs appears to have affected lasting change in the manner in which music teachers are prepared (Mark, 1981, p. 61). Recognition that such change has not occurred lies in expressions of concern and recommendations for reform by other educators of the 1980s whose statements echo those of earlier decades (Hoffman, 1985; Lehman, 1987). In a more recent study, Schmidt (1989) concluded, after surveying 180 schools, that little consistency among programs occurred and that content and direction of programs did not consistently reflect recommendations frequently found in teacher education literature.

One reason for lack of substantive change could be the fact that systematic research into contexts and models for music teacher education has not been substantial. Frequently, attempts to redefine curricular content have been based on surveys of teachers in the field as to their opinions of their own undergraduate preparation including those conducted by Corbett (1977), Duvall (1970), Lacy (1985), Medley (1974), and Taylor (1970). Duvall found that, for the majority of duties identified as part of first-year band instruction, undergraduate preparation had been inadequate. Taylor also discovered that many respondents made pleas for improvement in general education as well as in methods courses, felt that techniques for classroom control were ignored, and believed that much of the student-teaching experience was inadequate.

Projects resulting in curricular innovation, reform, and change in a particular music education department have been the subject of many reports, of which a listing of nearly 40 can be found in a summary of research and literature in music teacher education prepared by Brandt (1985). Among these reports are those by Faulmann (1978) and Platt (1978). To encourage such innovation, the MENC Commission on Teacher Education identified exemplary programs in the early 1970s to be used as models for other departments (MENC, 1971a). Some attempts have been made to design procedures for program evaluation that could be adapted to local situations (Jessup, 1980). Positions on the nature of teacher preparation, coupled with recommendations for change, have frequently been offered by college educators (Benn, 1967; Hoffer, 1987; Hood, 1955; Leonhard, 1982; Meske, 1985). In spite of the continued pleas for change embedded in such positions, it is difficult to find evidence that the recommendations have widely affected undergraduate curricula.

Inservice education for practicing music teachers has been studied by several educators including Parkes (1988), who evaluated the effect of inservice training in comprehensive musicianship on teacher and student attitude. Olson (1979b) projected at least three reasons why teachers participate in music inservice education: (a) corrective—they elect inservice experiences to remedy deficiencies they perceive in their backgrounds and to renew and reinforce understandings at a deeper level, once teaching experience has accrued; (b) evaluative—they seek professional growth to develop skills of self-evaluation and reflection regarding teaching effectiveness, to enable long-term professional growth to continue; and (c) generative—they pursue opportunities for experiences that provide new content and critical thinking skills, so that they can develop the independent and creative judgments regarding learning and teaching needed to adapt to the variety of changes expected in a long career of music teaching. Inservice experiences to meet any or all of these three purposes, or simply to enable the individual to progress on career and salary ladders, can take one of two forms (or a combination): an informal process of continuing education through a variety of noncredit workshops and conferences or a formal plan for continued study leading to an advanced degree.

Inservice education has a long and rich tradition. In the latter half of the twentieth century, colleges and universities have continued that tradition by offering short-term workshops for inservice growth, based on the models begun in the nineteenth century. More recently, individual school districts have begun to plan and present their own inservice music activities specifically designed to meet local concerns. Another tradition that continues from the nineteenth century is the practice of state and national music educators' professional organizations planning and presenting annual inservice conferences and conventions. Many such sessions are designed by specialty subject areas, such as the Mid-West National Band and Orchestra Clinic, the American Choral Director's Association Regional and National Conferences, and the Society for General Music, held at regional and national conferences of the MENC. Increasingly, sessions sponsored by these various groups carry professional advancement credit; occasionally certain types of workshops also offer graduate credit. Although popular, no evaluative studies have been conducted on the efficacy of such intense studies nor on their lasting influence for change in teaching practice.

The second option for inservice education, which, although not as old as the activities just described, dates back to the early twentieth century, is the graduate program in music education. Graduate study in music education has become increasingly common over the past few decades, as many music teachers elect to place their professional-development experiences on a formal plan for advancement and states require advanced study for continuing certification and salary improvement. Although the MENC on Graduate Music Teacher Education (Ball, 1982) has offered some guidelines, the models for graduate study vary significantly, depending on the balance of music, music education, and professional education required for the master's and doctoral degree programs. Except for broad recommendations by NASM, few standards have been established for curricular structure of graduate programs at either the master's or the doctoral level (Hilton, 1978). The fact that recommendations rarely result in changed practice can be found in a recent study undertaken by Platt and McGuire (1988). This study sought to trace the frequency with which a single recommendation—to include the history of music education—has been incorporated into the curriculum. They con-clude that, in spite of the prevalence of the recommendation, inclusion of intensive study of the historical foundations of the profession is infrequent.

CONTENT AND EXPERIENCES OF TEACHER-PREPARATION PROGRAM

"Without methods courses, no music teacher education program can exist" (Leonhard, 1985a). Among the courses that make up the teacher education program, the methods class is considered the heart of the curriculum, the place where a synthesis of learnings acquired elsewhere in the educative sequence should occur, where a wedding of theory and practice must be achieved (Barresi, 1985). In spite of these assertions, commonly held by the profession, the amount of research focused on identification and evaluation of appropriate content and experiences within this crucial course is sparse. This neglect continues in spite of the fact that surveys covering over 50 years continue to report the same results: dissatisfaction by teachers with their undergraduate methods courses (McEachern, 1937; Taylor, 1970). Leonhard proposes that this dissatisfaction, frequently expressed in terms such as *irrelevant, too theoretical, unrealistic,* and *uninteresting,* could be eliminated if methods teachers applied the same principles of teaching and learning to their own courses that they seek to instill in the future public school music teacher (Leonhard, 1985b, p. 14). Similar proposals have been the theme of a number of papers (Austin, 1970; Brand, 1980, 1986; Erbes, 1977; Meske, 1986). Others who have also sought to apply principles drawn from research in learning theory to the development of viable undergraduate teacher education experiences include Dorman (1969), Glennon (1979), Mollard (1978), Mulligan (1973), Parker (1982), and Rosenthal (1982).

Although teacher educators continue to voice support for the principle that research results must be applied to practice, J. Anderson (1987) points out that this seldom occurs, citing the content of methods texts as an indicator of current thought as to important course content and direction. Perusal of a representative sampling of methods books published from the late 1950s on forces one to agree with Anderson. Actual research results are rarely cited, and it is difficult to identify the influence of commonly known research conclusions and recommendations for teaching practices within such texts. If references to research do occur, the citation is frequently to research in categories other than music education, such as child development or theories of learning. When music education references are made, more frequently they are to books and articles with general recommendations, rather than to the results of actual research. For example, one of the most extensively studied topics in elementary music education is the development of children's ability to sing accurately. A random survey of recent elementary music education texts reveals that, of those examined, although all include a section on vocal development, none make direct reference to this large body of research.

Although specific application of research might not be observable, perusal of tables of contents of representative methods textbooks from different decades does reflect shifts in philosophical positions and changing patterns of music education curricula. A popular book of the 1940s (Dykema & Gehrkens, 1941) is organized by typical classroom activities, with sections dealing with the music assembly, the vocal program, the band and orchestra classes, the piano study, the theory, the history and appreciation, the radio, the concerts and operettas, and it is reflective of the activities-oriented curricula of the period. In contrast, methods books of the 1970s reflect the movement to defend the inclusion of music in the schools on aesthetic grounds. In these books, topics such as "understanding the nature of music" are found, as well as chapters seeking to help the future teacher apply contemporary theories of perception, learning, and motivation to music teaching (Glenn, McBride, & Wilson, 1970). This trend toward presentation of contemporary learning theories and philosophical assumptions, with illustrations of possible implications for music, is contained in books of the 1980s. Within a particular text, certain theories and assumptions are emphasized. For example, Greer (1980) reveals the influence of the behaviorist school of educational psychology, as models for all organizations are presented. In contrast, Peters and Miller (1982) move closer to cognitive theories of learning as the basis of effective teaching, with topics such as "theories of musical learning and motivation" and the "cognitive, psychomotor and affective components of music learning and teaching" serving as chapter headings.

The largest number of methods textbooks focused on a specific speciality within the teacher education curriculum are those written for elementary general music methods classes. Examination of the changing nature of these texts reveals, among other trends, the influence of the methodologies imported from Europe, including those developed by Dalcroze, Kodaly, and Orff (Choksy, Abramson, Gillespie, & Woods, 1986). The influence of contemporary thinking in areas of cognition and child development, primarily as set forth in the writings of Piaget and Bruner, can also be observed in textbooks written for the future teacher of elementary general music, such as those by Bergethon, Meske, and Montgomery (1986); Hackett and Lindeman (1980); and Nye and Nye (1985).

Investigations based on incorporation of specific types of strategies purported to have a positive effect on the student music educator's behavior in the classroom make up a definitive portion of research studies focused on the methods class. Among the topics intensively studied are the use of videotapes, both as a way for students to observe teaching situations (McKenna, 1977; Stuart, 1977) and in microteaching settings as a vehicle for learning basic strategies (Gonzo & Forsyth, 1976; Stuart, 1978; Stuart & McKnight, 1980). Several studies have been undertaken to investigate the possibility of changing specific teaching behaviors, including the use of instructional language (DeNicola, 1986), strategies for reinforcing student behavior (Madsen & Duke, 1987), and developing qualities of effective teaching such as "intensity" (Cassidy, 1988; Madsen, Standley, & Cassidy, 1989). In a review of prior studies on the value of observational systems for the analysis of music teaching, Dorman (1969) concludes that the use of such techniques might help refine all behaviors.

Other topics that have been studied by music education researchers include consideration of piano proficiency requirements (March, 1988), the application of theories of management such as interaction analysis (Erbes, 1978; Froelich, 1981; Hicks, 1976), simulation techniques (Brand, 1976, 1977; Buehning & Schieman, 1983; Schleuter, 1986; Walters, 1972), and procedures for evaluation including self-evaluation (Hedrick, 1976; Yarbrough, 1987). As the use of technology, including computers, has expanded in the schools, recommendations for incorporating its use into the teacher-preparation program have also emerged (Miller, 1987; Peters, 1984; Saul 1976). Kneiter (1985) offers a specific list of experiences with technology that students in music education programs should encounter. In response to recent concern for the need to help children develop appropriate cognitive skills essential for effective musical learning, Pautz (1989) has shown how some of the approaches used with children can be used to help teachers improve thinking skills.

As the general field of education turns to new issues in response to changing needs in the schools, music educators reflect these concerns by incorporating recommendations for addressing such issues into the methods classes. Merrion's (1980) guidelines for solving classroom-management problems and Pogonowski's (1987) suggestions for helping student teachers apply thinking strategies to their own teaching are recent examples of responses to educational trends.

Various aspects of field experience have also served as topics for research studies (Bowman, 1987), although Grashel (1983), in a survey of such studies completed during the years 1962–1971, notes "the paucity of experimental research, the lack of focus and, in some cases, insufficient rigor" (p. 30). A variety of aspects of such experience have been considered, including evaluation of student teachers (Panhorst, 1971), ways of improving supervision of the student teacher (Verrastra, 1967, 1975), and attitudes about the student-teaching experience (Bennett, 1982; Dick, 1977; Erbes, 1971), as well as more general examinations and recommendations for the structure of field-based programs (Morten, 1975; Surplus 1968). Guides to the student-teaching experience have been proposed by Bauer (1968), Boney and Rhea (1970), and Madsen and Yarbrough (1985), the last of which is also designed as a guide for all preservice field experiences.

SPECIAL PROBLEMS IN MUSIC EDUCATION

A variety of special concerns have been identified by the profession and, thence, subjected to research since the late 1950s. One such problem that has received considerable attention is the music teaching preparation of the elementary classroom teacher who is responsible for teaching all subjects within a self-contained classroom setting. The MENC, in another project growing out of the GO projects, specified music competencies for this classroom teacher (MENC, 1971b). However, the controversy as to the role of the classroom teacher in the music classroom and, thus, the type of competencies needed has a long-standing history. Recognition of this controversy was most recently admitted by Ball (1986), who spoke for those who believe the primary role should be given to the specialist.

According to a survey completed by Sarvis (1969), approximately 75 percent of the institutions surveyed required prospective classroom teachers to complete some coursework in music education. Because of the dual problem of helping classroom teachers attain the essential musical competencies (music fundamentals) while acquiring basic methods for teaching music to children, most of the institutions surveyed by Sarvis indicated that the amount of time provided in the undergraduate program was inadequate. A number of researchers have sought to solve this problem in a variety of ways including organizing the students according to prior musical experience (McGlothlin, 1970), experimenting with teaching fundamentals and methods in combined or separated formats (Holt, 1973; Hudson, 1973; Morris, 1969; Slagle, 1967), and exploring different types of settings (Kelly, 1984; Moore, 1974). However, as with other aspects of music teacher education preparation, the limited amount of research makes it impossible to draw firm conclusions as to the most appropriate educational environment for classroom teachers. This conclusion is confirmed by a study conducted by Brown (1988). After surveying 80 institutions in the Great Lakes region he discovered that there was little agreement as to the content and approach to classroom teacher instruction.

Closely related to concerns about adequate preparation for elementary classroom teachers is the increasing recognition of the need to provide training for the teacher of pre-school-age children (Reilly, 1969). As an outgrowth of one of the GO projects, MENC published *Music in Early Childhood* (Andress, 1973), which provided guidelines for preschool teachers. However, as in other areas of teacher education, little specific research has been conducted regarding the preservice preparation of teachers in these areas.

In spite of the increasing recognition of the need to prepare teachers to work with special populations, little research has focused specifically on educating music teachers to work with the handicapped, children at risk, children in urban environments, or those belonging to minority populations. Educators have long recognized that the preparation of teachers for the culturally disadvantaged is fundamentally inadequate (Andrews, 1967). Both college educators and public school teachers speak to the urgent need for better preservice preparation for teachers beginning their teaching career in urban schools (MENC, 1970b). Some studies that address these problems are those by Sullivan (1982) and Lee (1970). A summary of the research conducted in relation to the urban child can be found in Hicks, Standifer, and Carter (1983), the first book to address the music educator directly on the problems and needs of the urban community.

Although numerous articles have been written regarding the importance of including multicultural music in the curriculum (McAllester, 1967), most do not speak directly to preparation of teachers. Three studies which do, include those conducted by Lundquist (1973), Montague (1988), and Mumford (1984). Several books provide suggestions for inclusion of music of a special cultural group, such as *Teaching Asian Musics in the Elementary and Secondary Schools* (W. Anderson, 1975) and *African Materials for Music Educators* (Reeder & Standifer, 1972). Two issues of the *Music Educators Journal* (MENC, 1972b, 1983) have been devoted to the music of various cultures and ways of incorporating their study into the classroom.

Research on how to help future music educators work with the mentally and physically handicapped is equally limited. Two special issues of the *Music Educators Journal* (MENC, 1972a, 1982) are devoted to the topic. Some textbooks are available (e.g., Graham, 1975; Nocera, 1979; Zinar, 1987). However few books or articles make specific suggestions concerning the experiences or knowledge that should be included in the undergraduate music education curriculum. Two authors who have addressed this issue directly are Lehr (1982) and Nocera (1972).

CONCLUSION

As a result of the survey of existing studies, two major problems are evident in teacher education research. *First*, such research is limited, sporadic, and fragmented. *Second*, recommendations that have been presented, and that can be defended by research results, have not been acted upon. The need for a complete reorientation of music education research practices is clearly defined by Reimer (1985), who avers that the profession cannot "go on doing research study after research study on topics irrelevant to or only remotely related to the central values of our field" (p. 11). The irrelevance and/or lack of application of many of our research findings is also emphasized by Colwell (1985) who, in a discussion of teacher education program evaluation, points out that "researchers have been unsuccessful in profiling the successful teacher. Good and poor teachers seem to exit from the same curriculum" (p. 39).

The conclusion is painfully apparent. College music educators, those who are primarily responsible for the quality of the music teacher education program, are (a) unable to draw useful information from existing research results and apply it to program and course reform because of pressures from various agencies; (b) unwilling to alter current practices, for any of a variety of reasons; or (c) unaware of existing information. The call for teacher education reform, recommendations for implementing that reform, and the profile of teacher education curricula remain depressingly similar over at least the past 50 years. Until those primarily responsible for initiating change are able to identify and overcome the possible reasons for the continuing inertia, additional research and recommendations for reform or expanded testing for desired competencies will provide no magic solutions.

Reimer's recommendations for revision of research practices in music education offer one direction. He calls for changes to involve (a) clustering research efforts around significant problems; (b) defining borders of these topics to ensure systematic research efforts; (c) developing studies that reflect all modalities—philosophical, historical, descriptive, and experimental; (d) initiating large-scale, long-term research; and (e) forging cooperative efforts among research universities (Reimer, 1985, pp. 15–19). Certainly such reorientation might help to answer some of the concerns already expressed. Of particular need are carefully designed longitudinal studies that seek to define the many parameters involved in the complex task of teaching as they are affected by particular undergraduate experiences. Conclusions tentatively drawn from past studies suggest that the most important characteristics are those related to personality, motivation, and other (so far) intangible qualities. If these conclusions are valid, the profession might need to recognize that certain crucial personal attributes cannot be taught, and, therefore, greater attention should be focused on developing viable tools that clearly identify teacher education applicants who already possess these significant characteristics.

A second conclusion that is difficult to avoid is the recognition that recommendations for organizing experiences to teach isolated components of the act will not provide the kind of drastic and lasting reform in teacher education that must occur. Until those in charge of conveying the knowledge and skills considered essential to successful teaching are ready to focus directly on *process*—how this knowledge and skill is to be conveyed within the college environment—instead of merely specifying a desired *product* by compiling lists of essential competencies, meaningful reform will simply not occur.

Issues that should be the focus of meaningful research into music teacher education are implicit in the recommendations of the report *Music Teacher Education: Partnership and Process* (Olson, 1987). This document addresses four major issues, each of which needs to be subjected to the type of research recommended by Reimer:

1. Selection and retention of candidates for music teacher education

2. Development of programs of music teacher preparation, with the central focus on laboratory experiences

3. Implementation of processes for professional development with concepts identified and practiced within the teacher-preparation program and extended through one's professional career

4. Preparation of teachers as an important element of the "partnership and process" model

A theme permeating the Olson (1987) document is that of cooperation by all agencies concerned with the quality of teaching and learning. Such cooperation must extend to the design and execution of viable research efforts that recognize the complexity of the teacher educating process.

Whether conducted by school districts, professional organizations, or colleges and universities, the contexts and models of music teacher education can be expected to change as significant change occurs in educational needs and practices in the twenty-first century. The report of the Holmes Group (1986) calls for revision in the undergraduate program of preparation, changes in the study of pedagogy and allied fields, and new relationships between universities and teachers in the nation's schools. The future can be expected to bring new alliances, new research, and new expectations for teacher preparation and inservice education. We in the music education profession must be prepared to respond to these demands by, as Reimer proposes, identifying the major issues in music teacher education and developing new models of research to seek answers to these issues. If we are not ready to look inward and objectively examine the quality of our own teaching within the teacher education program, the primary responsibility for such education could well pass to other agencies.

References

Abeles, H. (1987). The role of the master teacher in achieving professional excellence. *Music Educators Journal, 72*(6), 47–50.

Abeles, H., Hoffer, C., & Klotman, R. (1981). *Foundations of music education.* New York: Schirmer Books.

Anderson, J. (1965). The use of musical talent, personality and vocational interest factors in predicting success for student music teachers (Doctoral dissertation, University of Southern California). *Dissertation Abstracts, 26,* 6523A. (University Microfilms No. 66-567)

Anderson. J. (1974). An investigation of the teacher attitude of music education undergraduates and of the meaning they ascribe to selected educational concepts (Doctoral dissertation, University of Minnesota). *Dissertation Abstracts International,* 1975, 35, 4218A. (University Microfilms No. 75-152)

Anderson, J. (1987). The role of music research in teacher training programs. *Designs for Arts in Education, 88*(5), 42–44.

Anderson, W. (1975). *Teaching Asian musics in the elementary and secondary schools.* New York: Schirmer.

Andress, B. (1973). *Music in early childhood.* Reston, VA: Music Educators National Conference.

Andrews, F. (1967). The preparation of music educators for the culturally disadvantaged. *Music Educators Journal, 53*(6), 42–44.

Asmus, E. (1981). Course entry affect and its relationship to course grades in music education and music theory courses. *Journal of Research in Music Education, 29*(4), 257–64.

Austin, V. (1970). Is methods a d———y word? *Music Educators Journal, 56*(8), 49–51.

Ball, C. (Ed.). (1982). *Graduate music teacher education report.* Reston, VA: Music Educators National Conference.

Ball, C. (1986). Educating the specialist teacher of music. *Design for Arts in Education, 87*(6), 5–8.

Barresi, A. (1980). The artist and educator controversy. *Dialogue in Instrumental Music Education, 4*(2), 48–59.

Barresi, A. (1985). Summary report of the symposium on teacher education. *Dialogue in Instrumental Music Education, 9*(1), 14–21.

Bauer, H. (1968). A guide for the cooperating teacher in music (Doctoral dissertation, Columbia University). *Dissertation Abstracts International, 30,* 1192A. (University Microfilms No. 69-15,153)

Beazley, H. (1981). Development and validation of a music education competency test. *Journal of Research in Music Education, 29*(1), 5–10.

Benn, O. (1967). Objectives and responsibilities in teacher education. *Music Educators Journal, 53*(9), 42–45.

Bennett, B. (1982). Differential effects of initial early field experience on the concerns of preservice music teachers (Doctoral dissertation, University of Texas at Austin). *Dissertation Abstracts International*, 1983, *43*, 3878A. (University Microfilms No. DA83-09,114)

Bergethon, B., Meske, E., & Montgomery, J. (1986). *Musical growth in the elementary schools* (5th ed.). New York: Holt, Rinehart & Winston.

Birge, E. (1928). *History of public school music in the United States*. Washington DC: Music Educators National Conference.

Boney, J., & Rhea, L. (1970). *A guide to student teaching in music*. Englewood Cliffs, NJ: Prentice-Hall.

Borkowski, F. (1967). The relationship of quality of work in undergraduate music curricula to effectiveness of instrumental music teaching in the public schools (Doctoral dissertation, West Virginia University). *Dissertation Abstracts*, *28*, 1834A. (University Microfilms No. 67-11,778)

Bowman, A. (1987). Perspectives on becoming a secondary teacher: A prestudent teaching experience (Doctoral dissertation, Arizona State University). *Dissertation Abstracts International*, *48*, 3092A. (University Microfilms No. DA8802775).

Brand, M. (1976). Watch what you're learning to cope with behavior problems through video simulation. *Music Educators Journal*, *63*(3), 50–53.

Brand, M. (1977). Effectiveness of simulation techniques in teaching behavior management. *Journal of Research in Music Education*, *25*(2), 131–138.

Brand, M. (1980). An instrumental music education methods curriculum: An overview. *Dialogue in Instrumental Music Education*, *4*(2), 60–65.

Brand, M. (1986). Methods class: Key to improving music teacher education. *Music Educators Journal*, *76*(8), 6–28.

Brand, M. (1987). The best and the brightest: Screening prospective music teachers. *Music Educators Journal*, *73*(6), 33–36.

Brand, M. (1989). Toward a better understanding of undergraduate music education majors: Perry's perspective. *Council for Research in Music Education Bulletin*, *98*, 22–31.

Brandt, T. (1985). A selected bibliography of related research and literature in music teacher education. *Dialogue in Instrumental Music Education*, *9*(1), 23–49.

Britten, A. (1966). Music education: An American speciality. In *Perspectives in music education, source book III*. Washington, DC: Music Educators National Conference.

Brown, R. L. (1988). A descriptive study of college level music courses for elementary education majors at NASM institutions in the Western Great Lakes region of the United States (Doctoral dissertation, Michigan State University). *Dissertation Abstracts International*, *49*, 2959A. (University Microfilms No. DA89-13)

Buehning, W., & Schieman, E. (1983). Simulation can teach teachers. *Music Educators Journal*, *49*(5), 54–55.

Burden, F. (1985). The nature of the public school music administrator's work: Case studies on three selected Texas public school music administrators (Doctoral dissertation, University of Houston). *Dissertation Abstracts International*, *47*, 458A. (University Microfilms No. DA86-07010)

Caimi, F. (1979). An investigation of the relationships between certain motivational variables and selected criterion measures useful for estimating success at high school band directing (Doctoral dissertation, Pennsylvania State University). *Dissertation Abstracts International*, 1980, *40*, 5772A. (University Microfilms No. 80-10,031)

Cassidy, J. W. (1988). The effect of training in intensity on accuracy of instruction and effectiveness of delivery among preservice elementary education majors in a music setting (Doctoral dissertation, The Florida State University). *Dissertation Abstracts International*, *49*, 2140A. (University Microfilms No. DA88-22,442)

Choate, J. (1976). An analysis of the undergraduate curriculum and the subsequent professional involvement of selected instrumental music education graduates of Louisiana State University (Doctoral dissertation. Louisiana State University and Agricultural and Mechanical College). *Dissertation Abstracts International*, *37*, 3490A. (University Microfilms No. 76-28,794)

Choate, R. (1968). *Documentary report of the Tanglewood Symposium*. Washington, DC: Music Educators National Conference.

Choksy, L., Abramson, R., Gillespie, A., & Woods, D. (1986). *Teaching music in the twentieth century*. Englewood Cliffs, NJ: Prentice-Hall.

Cody, R. (1968). A study of college teacher preparation programs and certain secondary programs in music as reflected by opinions from secondary music teachers and administrators (Doctoral dissertation, East Texas State University). *Dissertation Abstracts International*, *29*, 1065A. (University Microfilms No. 68-14,498)

Coleman, H. (1979). Perceptions of music teacher competencies through a survey of public school music teachers in selected school districts: A positive response to accountability for higher education (Doctoral dissertation, Memphis State University). *Dissertation Abstracts International*, 1980, *40*, 3861A. (University Microfilms No. 80-01,179)

College Board EQuality Project. (1985). *Academic preparation for college: What students need to know and be able to do*. New York: Author.

Collins, C. (1970). Public school music certification in historical perspective (Doctoral dissertation, University of Michigan). *Dissertation Abstracts International*, 1971, *31*, 4196A. (University Microfilms No 71-4548)

Colwell, R. (1985). Toward reform in music teacher education. *Council for Research in Music Education*, *81*, 18–62.

Corbett, D. (1977). An analysis of the opinions of recent music education graduates from Kansas teacher training institutions regarding the adequacy of their preparation to teach music (Doctoral dissertation, University of Kansas). *Dissertation Abstracts International*, *38*, 4007A. (University Microfilms No. 77-28,853)

D'Arca, L. (1985). A comparative study of the qualifications, training, and function of supervisors of student teachers in music at selected midwestern colleges and universities (Doctoral dissertation, University of Missouri—Columbia). *Dissertation Abstracts International*, 1986, *47*, 458A. (University Microfilms No. DA86-07,900)

DeNicola, D. N. (1986). The development of an instructional language assessment instrument based upon the historical perspectives of Quintilian, Erasmus, and Herbart, and its use in analyzing the language behaviors of pre-service elementary and music education majors (Doctoral dissertation, The Florida State University). *Dissertation Abstracts International*, 1987, *47*, 2938A. (University Microfilms No. DA86-26,793)

Dewey, J. (1916). *Democracy and education*. New York: Macmillan.

Dick, R. (1977). Teacher role perception of music student teachers before and after student teaching at University of Northern Colorado (Doctoral dissertation, University of Northern Colorado). *Dissertation Abstracts International*, 1978, *38*, 6493A. (University Microfilms No. 78-5493)

Doane, C. (1983). The identification and assessment of selected characteristics of prospective music educators. *Contributions to Music Education*, *10*, 9–18.

Dorman, P. (1969). The relationship between an analysis of teaching incidents as described by undergraduate seniors majoring in music education in three New York State colleges and Taba's theoretical construction of the teaching–learning situation (Doctoral dissertation, State University of New York at Buffalo). *Dissertation Abstracts International*, *30*, 2398A. (University Microfilms No. 69-19,030)

Duvall. O. (1970). The responsibilities and preparation of graduates of Colorado institutions of higher education in their first year of teaching instrumental music in the state (Doctoral dissertation, University of Northern Colorado). *Dissertation Abstracts International*, 1971, *31*, 4197A. (University Microfilms No. 71-470)

Dykema, P., & Gehrkens, K. (1941). *The teaching and administration of high school music.* Boston: C. C. Birchard.

Erbes, R. (1971). Student teaching satisfaction. *Music Educators Journal, 58*(1), 40–43.

Erbes, R. (1977). An instrumental methods teaching lab. *Dialogue in Instrumental Music Education, 1*(1), 4–7.

Erbes, R. (1978). I used to direct my rehearsals like a drill sergeant . . . until I learned about interaction analysis. *Music Educators Journal, 65*(2), 50–53.

Erbes, R. (1983). *Certification practices and trends in music education 1972–1983.* Reston, VA: Music Educators National Conference.

Erbes, R. (1984). The revolution in teacher certification. *Music Educators Journal, 71*(3), 34–39.

Erbes, R. (1986). *Certification practices and trends in music education, 1985–1986.* Reston, VA: Music Educators National Conference.

Erbes, R. L. (1987). A new era in teacher certification. *Music Educators Journal, 73*(6), 42–46.

Faulmann, J. (1978). A curriculum innovation: The core program for music education classes. In M. L. Raiman (Ed.), *Midwest Symposium on Music Education: Proceedings, 1* (pp. 21–28). Tulsa, OK: University of Tulsa.

Franklin, A. (1968). The relationship between academic preparation and professional responsibilities of instrumental and choral instructors in South Carolina (Doctoral dissertation, Florida State University). *Dissertation Abstracts, 29*, 1555A. (University Microfilms No. 68-16,369)

Froelich, H. (1981). The use of systematic classroom observation in research on elementary general music teaching. *Council for Research in Music Education, 66*(7), 15–19.

Froelich, H., & L'Roy, D. (1985). An investigation of occupancy identity in undergraduate music education majors. *Council for Research in Music Education, 85*, 65–75.

Funk, R. (1977). An analysis of music teacher preparatory programs in selected Texas four-year colleges and universities (Doctoral dissertation, University of Texas—Austin). *Dissertation Abstracts International, 38*, 4008A. (University Microfilms No 77-29,030)

Gibson, R. (1986). *Critical theory and education.* London: Hodder & Stoughton.

Glenn, N., McBride, W., & Wilson, G. (1970). *Secondary school music.* Englewood Cliffs, NJ: Prentice-Hall.

Glennon, M. (1979). Carl Rogers–theory of facilitation as a basis for the preparation of student teachers in music education (Doctoral dissertation, Temple University). *Dissertation Abstracts International, 40*, 2532A. (University Microfilms No. 7924036)

Gonzo, C., & Forsythe, J. (1976). Developing and using videotapes to teach rehearsal techniques and principles. *Journal of Research in Music Education, 24*(1), 32–41.

Gordon, E. (1971). *The psychology of music teaching.* Englewood Cliffs, NJ: Prentice-Hall.

Gordon, E. (1980). *Learning sequences in music.* Chicago: G.I.A.

Graham, R. (1975). *Music for the exceptional child.* Reston, VA: Music Educators National Conference.

Grashel, J. (1983). Doctoral research in music student teaching: 1962–1971. *Council for Research in Music Education Bulletin, 78*, 24–32.

Greer, R. (1980). *Design for music learning: Introduction to teaching.* New York: Teachers College Press.

Hackett, P., & Lindeman, C. (1980). *The musical classroom.* Englewood Cliffs, NJ: Prentice-Hall.

Hedrick, G. (1976). The development of a verbal analysis system for self-evaluation of preservice music teachers (Doctoral dissertation, Florida State University). *Dissertation Abstracts International, 1977, 37*, 6334A. (University Microfilms No. 77-8590)

Hicks, C. (1976). The effect of training in interaction analysis on the verbal teaching behaviors and attitudes of prospective school instrumental music education students studying conducting (Doctoral dissertation, Michigan State University). *Dissertation Abstracts International, 1977, 37*, 5671A. (University Microfilms No. 77-5817)

Hicks, C, Standifer, J., & Carter, W. (1983). *Methods and perspectives in urban music education.* Fredrick, MD: University Publications of America.

Hilton, L. (1978). What should be the nature and function of graduate study in music education? In M. L. Raiman (Ed.), *Midwest Symposium on Music Education: Proceedings, 1* (pp. 22–29). Tulsa, OK: University of Tulsa.

Hoffer, C. (1987). Tomorrow's directions in the education of music teachers. *Music Educators Journal, 73*(6), 27–31.

Hoffman, M. (1985). *Teacher competence and the balanced music curriculum.* Reston, VA: Music Educators National Conference.

Holmes Group. (1986). *Tomorrow's teachers: A report of the Holmes group.* East Lansing, MI: Author.

Holt, D. (1973). An evaluation study of two units of instruction for providing prospective elementary teachers with an orientation to selected aspects of general music teaching and learning (Doctoral dissertation, The Ohio State University). *Dissertation Abstracts International, 1974, 34*, 4823A. (University Microfilms No. 74-3201)

Hood, M. (1955). Teacher training as part of college music study. *National Association of Schools of Music Bulletin, 40*, 128–139.

Hudson, L. (1973). A study of the effectiveness of teaching music fundamentals and methods to prospective elementary school classroom teachers using two different approaches within a course (Doctoral dissertation, Indiana University). *Dissertation Abstracts International, 1974, 34*, 4824A. (University Microfilms No. 74-1595)

Jessup, S. (1980). An application of Sage analysis in determining weaknesses in a program for training secondary music teachers (Doctoral dissertation, Brigham Young University). *Dissertation Abstracts International, 41*, 3936A. (University Microfilms No. 8106545)

John, R. (1979). Degrees, titles and college music teaching. *Music Educators Journal, 66*(2), 58–59.

Keene, J. (1982). *A history of music education in the United States.* Hanover, CN: University Press of New England.

Kelly, M. (1984). The differential effects of modeling and discrimination training on selected music teaching skills, confidence levels, and achievement among elementary education majors (Doctoral dissertation, Ohio State University). *Dissertation Abstracts International, 1985, 45*, 2434A. (University Microfilms No. DA84-26,419)

Kliebard, H. (1986). *The struggle for the American curriculum 1893–1958.* Boston: Routledge & Kegan Paul.

Klotman, R. (Ed.). (1972). *Teacher education in music: Final report.* Washington, DC: Music Educators National Conference.

Knab, R. (1975). The construction and validation of an instrument to measure attitudes of prospective music teachers (Doctoral dissertation, Indiana University). *Dissertation Abstracts International, 1976, 36*, 4096A. (University Microfilms No. 76-1888)

Kneiter, G. (1985). What are the implications of technology for teaching and learning in music education? In M. Vincent & E. Karjala (Eds.), *Music and technology.* Muncie, IN: Ball State University.

Kowall, B. (1966). Influences from abroad. In B. Kowall, (Ed.), *Perspectives in music education, source book III* (pp. 381–414). Washington, DC: Music Educators National Conference.

Krueger, P. (1987). The hidden curriculum of music student teaching: An ethnography. *Dialogue in Instrumental Music Education, 11*(1), 37–53.

Krueger, R. (1976). An investigation of personality and music teaching success. *Council for Research in Music Education, 47,* 16–25.

Kwalwasser, J. (1927). *Tests and measurements in music.* Boston: C. C. Birchard.

Lacy, L. C. (1985). A survey and evaluation of music teacher education program in selected, accredited black private colleges and universities in the United States (Doctoral dissertation, Ohio State University). *Dissertation Abstracts International,* 1986, *46,* 2610A. (University Microfilms No. DA85-26,204)

Landis, B., & Carder, P. (1972). *The eclectic curriculum in American music education: Contributions of Dalcroze, Kodaly and Orff.* Reston, VA: Music Educators National Conference.

LeBlanc, A. (1984). Making the tough decisions: Excellence in music teacher education. *Music Educators Journal, 70*(9), 36–38.

Lee, R. (1970). A study of teacher training experiences for prospective inner-city instrumental music teachers (Doctoral dissertation, University of Michigan). *Dissertation Abstracts International,* 1971, *31,* 4202A. (University Microfilms No. 71-4660)

Lehman, P. (1986). Teaching music in the 1990's. *Dialogue in Instrumental Music Education, 10*(1), 3–18.

Lehman, P. (1987). A view of tomorrow. *Proceedings of the 62nd Annual Meeting of the NASM* (pp. 209–220). Reston, VA: National Association of Schools of Music.

Lehr, J. (1982). Teacher training programs for exceptional classes. *Music Educators Journal, 68*(8), 46–48.

Leonhard, C. (1982). Music teacher education in the United States. *Symposium in Music Education* (pp. 233–248). Urbana-Champaign, IL: University of Illinois.

Leonhard, C. (1985a). Methods courses: An address presented to the symposium on teacher education. *Dialogue in Instrumental Education, 9*(1), 1–13.

Leonhard, C. (1985b). Toward reform in music teacher education. *Council for Research in Music Education, 81*(1), 10–17.

Leonhard, C., & House, R. (1959). *Foundations and principles of music education.* New York: McGraw-Hill.

Lofgren, N. R. (1974). A task-analysis approach to determine musical and extra-musical competencies of school music teachers (Doctoral dissertation, Baylor University). (University Microfilms No. 75-10,780)

Lundquist, B. (1973). Clinic-demonstration report—sound in time: Participation in three music processes, clinic-demonstration report—musical competencies for classroom teachers. The development of an intercultural base for broadening the conceptual framework of music (Doctoral dissertation, University of Washington). *Dissertation Abstracts International,* 1974, *34,* 6688A. (University Microfilms No. 74-2264)

Lundquist, B. (1987). Components of teacher preparation for music doctoral students. *Proceedings of the 62nd annual meeting of the NASM* (pp. 111–125). Reston, VA: National Association of Schools of Music.

Madsen, C. K., & Duke, R. A. (1987). The effect of teacher training on the ability to recognize need for giving approval for appropriate student behavior. *Council for Research in Music Education Bulletin, 91,* 103–109.

Madsen, C. K., Standley, J. M., & Cassidy, J. W. (1989). Demonstration and recognition of high and low contrasts in teacher intensity. *Journal of Research in Music Education, 37*(2), 85–92.

Madsen, C., & Yarbrough, C. (1985). *Competency based music education.* Raleigh, NC: Contemporary.

March, W. (1988). A study of piano proficiency requirements at institutions of higher education in the state of Oregon as related to the needs and requirements of public school music teachers (Doctoral dissertation, University of Oregon). *Dissertation Abstracts International, 49,* 1087A. (University Microfilms No. DA88-14,191)

Mark, M. (1981). The graduate music education program—education or training? *Dialogue in Instrumental Music Education, 5*(1), 12–15.

Mason, L. (1834). *Manual of the Boston Academy of Music, for instruction in the elements of vocal music on the system of Pestalozzi.* Boston: Carter and Hendee.

McAllester, D. (1967). Teaching the music teacher to use the music of his own culture. *International Music Educator, 16,* 538–541.

McEachern, E. (1937). A survey and evaluation of the education of school music teachers in the United States. In *Contributions to Education* (p. 116). New York: Columbia University, Teachers College, Bureau of Publications.

McGlothin, D. (1970). An investigation of the efficacy of ability grouping prospective teachers enrolled in elementary music methods and materials courses (Doctoral dissertation, University of Iowa). *Dissertation Abstracts International, 31,* 1312A. (University Microfilms No. 70-15,621)

McKenna, G. (1977). Videotape usage in pre-service instrumental music education: An on-site process. *Dialogue in Instrumental Music Education, 1*(2), 35–41.

Medley, G. (1974). An identification and comparison of competencies for the preservice education of secondary vocal music teachers in Texas (Doctoral dissertation, Texas Tech University). *Dissertation Abstracts International,* 1975, *35,* 5992A. (University Microfilms No. 75-7422)

Merrion, M. (1980). Guidelines on classroom management for beginning music educators. *Music Educators Journal, 66*(6), 47–49.

Meske, E. (1982). Educating the music teacher: Participation in a metamorphosis. *Symposium in Music Education* (pp. 249–265). Champaign-Urbana, IL: University of Illinois.

Meske, E. (1985). Teacher education, a wedding of theory and practice. *Bulletin of the Council for Research in Music Education, 81,* 65–73.

Meske, E. (1986). A process for improvement of undergraduate teacher training programs. *Dialogue in Instrumental Music Education, 10*(1), 19–37.

Meske, E. (1987). Teacher education reform and the college music educator. *Music Educators Journal, 73*(6), 22–26.

Miller, A. W. (1987). Feasibility of instruction in instrumental music education with an interactive videodisc adapted from existing media (Doctoral dissertation, University of Illinois at Urbana-Champaign). *Dissertation Abstracts International,* 1988, *48,* 1693A. (University Microfilms No. DA87-21,716)

Mollard, S. (1978). Open education: Guidelines for teacher preparation in music (Doctoral dissertation, Temple University). *Dissertation Abstracts International,* 1979, *39,* 6619A. (University Microfilms No. 79-09,976)

Montague, M. J. (1988). An investigation of teacher training in multicultural music education in selected universities and colleges (Doctoral dissertation, University of Michigan). *Dissertation Abstracts International, 49,* 2142A. (University Microfilms No. DA88-21,622)

Moore, R. (1974). The effect of differential teaching techniques on achievement, attitudes, and teaching skills in elementary music education (Doctoral dissertation, Florida State University). *Disserta-

tion Abstracts International, 1975, *35*, 5896A. (University Microfilms No. 75-7291)

Morgan, D. P. (1987). An analysis of the costs associated with regional and selected professional accreditation relationships at three southern higher education institutions (Doctoral dissertation, University of Alabama). *Dissertation Abstracts International*, 1988, *48*, 2819A. (University Microfilms No. DA88-1920)

Morris, E. (1969). A comparison of two texts for teaching the fundamentals of music and music methods to future elementary classroom teachers (Doctoral dissertation, Colorado State College.) *Dissertation Abstracts International*, 1970, *30*, 4482A. (University Microfilms No. 70-7152)

Morten, H. (1975). A suggested field-based teacher education program: Construction of modules for music education, their implementation and evaluation (Doctoral dissertation, University of South Dakota). *Dissertation Abstracts International*, *36*, 3479A. (University Microfilms No. 75-28,914)

Mortenson, G. C. (1988). But it's not in my job description: The varied roles of college teachers. *Music Educators Journal*, *74*(9), 26–30.

Mountford, R. (1976). Competency based teacher education: The controversy and a synthesis of related research in music from 1964 to 1974. *Council for Research in Music Education Bulletin*, *46*, 1–12.

Mulligan, M. (1973). An application of the principles of Carl Rogers and Jerome Bruner to a music methods course for elementary education majors (Doctoral dissertation, University of Colorado at Boulder). *Dissertation Abstracts International*, 1974, *34*, 7810A. (University Microfilms No. 74-12, 393)

Mumford, J. E. (1984). The effect on the attitudes of music education majors of direct experiences with Afro-American popular music ensembles: A case study (Doctoral dissertation, Indiana University). *Dissertation Abstracts International*, 1985, *45*, 3298A–3299A. (University Microfilms No. DA85-1451)

Mursell, J. (1948). *Education for musical growth*. Boston: Ginn.

Mursell, J., & Glenn, M. (1931). *The psychology of school music Teaching*. New York: W. W. Norton.

Music Educators National Conference. (1965). *Comprehensive musicianship, the foundation for college education in music*. Reston, VA: Author.

Music Educators National Conference. (1970a). *Goals and objectives for music education*. Reston, VA: Author.

Music Educators National Conference. (1970b). Teacher education: Stop sending innocents into battle unarmed. *Music Educators Journal*, *56*(95), 103–111.

Music Educators National Conference. (1971a). Innovative and exemplary programs in music teacher education: A progress report of Task Group III of the MENC Commission on teacher education. *Music Educators Journal*, *58*(2), 43.

Music Educators National Conference. (1971b). Music competencies for classroom teachers: An initial report from task group IV of the MENC commission on teacher education. *Music Educators Journal*, *57*, 40–41.

Music Educators National Conference. (1972a). Music in special education [Special issue]. *Music Educators Journal*, *58*(8).

Music Educators National Conference. (1972b). Music in world cultures [Special issue]. *Music Educators Journal*, *59*(2).

Music Educators National Conference. (1981, 1983). *Documentary report of the Ann Arbor Symposium: Application of psychology to the teaching and learning of music*. Reston VA: Author.

Music Educators National Conference. (1982). Music for every child: Teaching special students [Special issue]. *Music Educators Journal*, *68*(8).

Music Educators National Conference. (1983). The multicultural imperative [Special issue]. *Music Educators Journal*, *69*(9).

National Association of Schools of Music. (1986). *Handbook*. Reston VA: Author.

National Association of State Directors of Teacher Education and Certification. (1981, 1983). *Standards for Accreditation and Certification*. Salt Lake City, UT: Author.

National Commission on Instruction. (1974). *The school music program: Description and standards*. Reston, VA: Music Educators National Conference.

Nelson, D. (1987). An interpretation of the Piagetian model in light of the theories of Case. *Council for Research in Music Education Bulletin*, *92*, 23–34.

Niemeyer, V. (1974). An empirical investigation of selected teacher competencies and student achievement (Doctoral dissertation, Florida State University). *Dissertation Abstracts International*, 1975, *35*, 5993A. (University Microfilms No. 75-6294)

Nocera, S. (1972). Special education teachers need a special education. *Music Educators Journal*, *58*(8), 73–75.

Nocera, S. (1979). *Reaching the special learner through music*. Morristown, NJ: Silver Burdett.

Nye, R., & Nye, V. (1985). *Music in the elementary school* (5th ed.). Englewood Cliffs, NJ: Prentice-Hall.

Olson, G. (1979a). The dilemma in music teacher education. *Dialogue in Instrumental Music Education*, *2*, 38–42.

Olson, G. (1979b). Options for inservice growth by instrumental music teachers. *Dialogue in Instrumental Music Education*, *3*(1), 18–23.

Olson, G. (Ed.). (1987). *Music teacher education: Partnership and process*. Reston, VA: Music Educators National Conference.

Palisca, C. (Ed.). (1964). *Music in our schools: A search for improvement* (Report of the Yale Seminar on Music Education, OE-33033 Bulletin, No. 28). Washington, DC: U.S. Department of Health, Education and Welfare, Office of Education.

Panhorst, D. (1971). Current practices in the evaluation of student teachers in music. *Journal of Research in Music Education*, *19*(2), 204–208.

Parker, C. (1982). A model with four training components for preinternship teacher education in music (Doctoral dissertation, University of Washington). *Dissertation Abstracts International*, *43*, 582A. (University Microfilms No. DA82-18,259).

Parkes, M. B. (1988). The development and implementation of an inservice course in comprehensive musicianship for elementary band directors: Measurement of teacher attitude shift, student attitudes and student achievement (Doctoral dissertation, University of Rochester, Eastman School of Music). *Dissertation Abstracts International*, *49*, 1728A. (University Microfilms No. DA88-13,178).

Parr, J. (1976). Essential and desirable music and music teaching competencies for first-year band instructors in the public schools (Doctoral dissertation, University of Iowa). *Dissertation Abstracts International*, 1977, *37*, 7601A. (University Microfilms No. 77-13,124)

Pautz, M. (1989). Musical thinking in the teacher education classroom. In E. Boardman (Ed.), *Dimensions of musical thinking* (pp. 101–110). Reston, VA: Music Educators National Conference.

Peters, G. (1984). Teacher training and high technology. *Music Educators Journal*, *70*(5), 35–39.

Peters, G., & Miller, R. (1982). *Music teaching and learning*. New York: Longman.

Platt, M. (1978). Teacher education redesign in Ohio. In M. Raiman, (Ed.), *Midwest symposium on music education: Proceedings*, *1*, 7–14. Tulsa; OK: University of Tulsa.

Platt, M. (1982). The history and development of the American Institute of Normal Methods. In S. H. Barnes (Ed.), *A cross-section of research in music education*. Lanham, MD: University Press of America.

Platt, M., & McGuire, D. (1988). The incidence of history of music education teaching. *Bulletin of Historical Research in Music Education*, *9*(1), 23–60.

Pogonowski, L. (1987). Developing skills in critical thinking and problem solving. *Music Educators Journal*, *73*(6), 37–41.

Poolos, J. (1968). A survey of the influences that affect the music curriculum of state-supported universities (Doctoral dissertation, Florida State University). *Dissertation Abstracts*, 1969, 29,2294A. (University Microfilms No. 69-599)

Reeder, B., & Standifer, J. (1972). *Source book of African materials for music educators*. Reston, VA: Music Educators National Conference.

Reeves, J. (1980). Expected competencies for beginning music teachers by music supervisors, principals, college music educators and beginning music teachers: A comparative study (Doctoral dissertation, Catholic University of America). *Dissertation Abstracts International*, *40*, 6182A. (University Microfilms No. 8013223)

Regelski, T. (1975). *Principles and problems of music education*. Englewood Cliffs, NJ: Prentice-Hall.

Reilly, M. (1969). Preschool teachers need music. *Music Educators Journal*, *55*(8), 40–42.

Reimer, B. (1970). *A philosophy of music education*. Englewood Cliffs, NJ: Prentice-Hall.

Reimer, B. (1985). Toward a more scientific approach to music education research. *Council for Research in Music Education*, *83*, 1–21.

Rosenthal, R. (1982). A data-based approach to elementary general music teacher preparation (Doctoral dissertation, Syracuse University). *Dissertation Abstracts International*, 1983, *43*, 2920A. (University Microfilms No. DA82-29,036)

Sarvis, G. (1969). An investigation of the nature and conditions of music education courses in teacher training programs in selected universities in the United States (Doctoral dissertation, University of Oregon). *Dissertation Abstracts International*, 1970, *31*, 1124A. (University Microfilms No. 70-15,356)

Saul, T. (1976). Three applications of the computer in the education of music teachers (Doctoral dissertation, University of Rochester, Eastman School of Music). *Dissertation Abstracts International*, *37*, 1867A. (University Microfilms No. 76-21,655)

Schleuter, L. (1986). Simulation: Why and how for music education. *Update*, *4*(3), 17–20.

Schmidt, C. P. (1989). An investigation of undergraduate music education curriculum content. *Council for Research in Music Education Bulletin*, *99*, 42–55.

Seashore, C. (1940). *The psychology of music*. New York: Ronald.

Serafine, M. (1988). *Music as cognition*. New York: Columbia University Press.

Shellahamer, B. (1984). Selection and retention criteria in undergraduate music teacher education programs: Survey, analysis and implications. (Doctoral dissertation, Ohio State University). *Dissertation Abstracts International*, *45*, 1679A. (University Microfilms No. DA84-19,011)

Slagle, H. (1967). An investigation of the effect of seven methods of instruction on the musical achievement of elementary education majors (Doctoral dissertation, University of Illinois—Champaign). *Dissertation Abstracts*, 1968, *28*, 5098A. (University Microfilms No. 68-8226)

Smith, A. (1985). An evaluation of music teacher competencies identified by the Florida Music Educators Association and teacher assessment of undergraduate preparation to demonstrate those competencies (Doctoral dissertation, Florida State University). *Dissertation Abstracts International*, 1986, *47*, 115A. (University Microfilms No. DA86-05,792)

Stegall, J. (1975). A list of competencies for an undergraduate curriculum in music education (Doctoral dissertation, University of North Carolina at Chapel Hill). *Dissertation Abstracts International*, 1976, *37*, 1448A. (University Microfilms No. 76-20,076)

Stuart, M. (1977). The use of simulation and videotape recordings to increase error detection skills. *Dialogue in Instrumental Music Education*, *1*(2), 48–54.

Stuart, M. (1978). Microteaching: Feedback procedures for developing teaching skills in music. (1978). *Dialogue in Instrumental Music Education*, *2*(2), 50–69.

Stuart, M., & McKnight, P. (1980). Microteaching in music education. *Dialogue in Instrumental Music Education*, *4*(1), 26–39.

Sullivan, W. (1982). Preparing prospective music teachers to teach more effectively in urban schools (Doctoral dissertation, University of Cincinnati). *Dissertation Abstracts International*, *44*, 422A. (University Microfilms No. DA83-13,509)

Surplus, R. (1968). The role of student teaching in the preservice education of music majors (Doctoral dissertation, Columbia University. *Dissertation Abstracts*, 1969, *29*, 4357A. (University Microfilms No. 69-9919)

Taebel, D., & Coker, J. (1980). Teaching effectiveness in elementary classroom music: Relationships among competency measures, pupil product measures, and certain attribute variables. *Journal of Research in Music Education*, *28*(4), 250–264.

Taylor, B. P. (1980). The relative importance of various competencies needed by choral-general music teachers in elementary and secondary schools as rated by college supervisors, music supervisors and choral-general music teachers (Doctoral dissertation, Indiana University). *Dissertation Abstracts International*, *41*, 2990A. (University Microfilms No. 8101952)

Taylor, C. (1970). Opinion of music teachers regarding professional preparation in music education. *Journal of Research in Music Education*, *18*(4), 330–339.

Verrastra, R. E. (1967). Improving student-teacher supervision. *Music Educators Journal*, *54*, 81–83.

Verrastra, R. E. (1975). Verbal behavior analysis as a supervisory technique with student teachers of music. *Journal of Research in Music Education*, *23*, 171–185.

Wager, W., & McGrath, E. (1962). *Liberal education and music*. New York: Teachers College Press.

Walker, R. (1977). An investigation of the relationship of selected background and motivational varibles to achievement in the music curriculum of undergraduate music education majors at Mississippi State University (Doctoral dissertation, Mississippi State University). *Dissertation Abstracts International*, *38*, 4011A. (University Microfilms No. 77-28,567)

Walters, D. (1972). The development of simulated critical teaching situations for use in instrumental music teacher education (Doctoral dissertation, Michigan State University). *Dissertation Abstracts International*, 1973, *33*, 5024A. (University Microfilms No. 73-5511)

Weerts, R. (1977). The quality teacher and the problem of inservice growth for the instrumental music teacher. *Dialogue in Instrumental Music Education*, *1*(2), 55–63.

Willoughby, D. (Ed.). (1971). *Comprehensive musicianship and undergraduate music curricula*. Washington, DC: Music Educators National Conference.

Wolfe, I. (1972). *State certification of music teachers*. Washington, DC: Music Educators National Conference.

Yarborough, C. (1987). The relationship of behavioral self-assessment to the achievement of basic conducting skills. *Journal of Research in Music Education*, *35*(3), 183–189.

Yarbrough, C. (1987). The relationship of behavioral self-assessment to the achievement of basic conducting skills. *Journal of Research in Music Education*, *35*(3), 183.

Zimmerman, M. (1980). Developmental research and the music curriculum. In *Contributions to Symposium/80: The Bowling Green State University Symposium on Music Teaching and Research, 1* (pp. 192–219). Bowling Green, OH: Bowling Green State University.

Zinar, R. (1987). *Music activities for special children*. West Nyack, NY: Parker.

TEACHER EDUCATION FOR THE VISUAL ARTS

D. Jack Davis

UNIVERSITY OF NORTH TEXAS

Since art was first taught in the schools of America, there has been some form of art teacher preparation. Those individuals who realized the importance of an education in the visual arts for children and assumed the responsibility for delivering the instruction were prepared in the arts at some level, either formally or informally. The history of the teaching of art in the public schools of America reveals that teachers with varying degrees of preparation in the visual arts have assumed this responsibility.

At the elementary school level there have been two major groups of teachers: the art specialist teacher and the general classroom teacher. This dualism continues today and is an often debated issue in professional circles. At the secondary level, the visual arts are almost always taught by individuals who are art specialists and have certification in the visual arts. Even so, the range of preparation for the secondary teacher varies greatly. It can range from a professional degree in art, with a substantial portion of the degree devoted to courses in the visual arts, to a professional degree in education, with the number of courses in art substantially fewer and the number of courses in professional education and general education much greater.

Even though there is a great diversity in the preparation of individuals who deliver art instruction in the American schools, there are two major foci of teacher education in the visual arts: preparation of the art specialist teacher (professional art educator), who may teach at either the elementary or secondary level, and preparation of the non–art specialist teacher (elementary classroom teacher), who may teach only at the elementary level.

Within these two groups there are a range of teacher education activities. For the art specialist teacher, both elementary and secondary, these include preservice education with degrees in art and/or art education; inservice education such as workshops, short courses, and participation in professional art and art education conferences; and programs of graduate study in which teachers seek advanced degrees in art, art education, and/or professional education. For the non–art specialist teacher, the range of teacher-preparation activities includes preservice education, in which the student usually takes one or more courses in art and/or art education as part of the requirements for a degree in elementary education; inservice education, which includes workshops, short courses, and occasional participation in art and art education professional conferences; and graduate study in a field other than art, usually in professional education, which might include one or more support courses in art and/or art education.

HISTORICAL PERSPECTIVES

With these general parameters in mind, it is appropriate to consider briefly some historical perspectives on teacher education in the visual arts in America. Efforts at teaching the visual arts in the United States can be traced to the late 1700s and the early 1800s. However, it was not until 1870, when the Massachusetts legislature passed a law requiring that art be taught (Belshe, 1946; Logan, 1954), that "art instruction came more easily and at a faster tempo" (Belshe, 1946, pp. 28–29). Likewise, attention to teacher preparation in the visual arts was almost nonexistent until the last quarter of the nineteenth century, with the founding of the Massachusetts Normal Art School in 1873 (Logan, 1954). Wygant (1983) points out that drawing was "a part of the course of studies in the first normal schools established by Horace Mann in 1839. Before the Civil War, drawing was offered at normal schools in New Britain,

The assistance of Margaret O. Lucas (West Virginia University) and Gene A. Mittler (Texas Tech University) in reviewing drafts of this chapter is gratefully acknowledged.

Connecticut; Newark, New Jersey; Ypsilanti, Michigan; and at Oswego" (p. 127). The creation of the Massachusetts Normal Art School had a dramatic effect upon teacher preparation in the visual arts because, as Logan (1954) points out, "so many of its graduates initiated public-school drawing and art programs all over the country by the year 1900 . . . [i]ts curriculum. . . . served as the dominant pattern for teacher training in the arts up to the present time" (p. 72). It provided the theoretical base for art teacher training, which still exists today: "that the prospective art teacher needs a little training in many art activities" (Logan, 1954, p. 72).

Many teachers prior to this time and many after were prepared in art through study at professional art schools in both this country and Europe or through apprenticeship programs, which had long been popular models for education in the visual arts. Art education, or the pedagogical aspects of teaching art, was, no doubt, acquired through observations by the teachers in the professional art schools or the individuals to whom they were apprenticed. These teachers likely went into the public schools and taught as they were taught. This approach is clearly evident in the first curriculum of the Massachusetts Normal Art School, which was built around "painstaking drawing of geometrical problems, of perspective, or orthographic projection, of machines, building construction details, shadow projection, cast ornaments, human and animal forms from the cast, furniture details, designs to be derived from plant forms, and historical ornament" (Logan, 1954, p. 71).

The Oswego approach to teaching was also emerging during this time. This movement, which originated at the Oswego, New York, Normal School under the guidance of E. A. Sheldon, utilized materials such as charts, cards, picture sets, blocks, examples, and specimens. This approach to teaching, heavily employing illustrative objects, encouraged teachers of drawing to go beyond the limits of the exercise books that had been promoted by Walter Smith at the Massachusetts Normal Art School (Logan, 1954). According to Logan, "one of the first steps taken toward 'pictorial' or 'art' drawing as distinct from industrial drawing was the creation of 'type form' blocks as models for drawing lessons" (p. 89). The implications for teacher education in drawing are evident.

By 1900, the normal school had become a popular institution; however, teacher preparation programs also existed in universities and colleges, as well as in high schools. More than 90,000 students were enrolled in the normal schools alone, and drawing was taught to many of them during the course of their 2-year program, but, it was not a universal requirement (Wygant, 1983, p. 127). Wygant also points out that, by 1900, Walter Smith's "idea that drawing could be taught by the regular teachers in the high school had been rejected, but it was generally agreed that in the elementary grades, art instruction would be given more effectively by the classroom teacher than by a visiting art specialist" (p. 127).

By the end of the century another major teacher-training institution, Teachers College, Columbia University, was challenging the leadership of the Massachusetts Normal Art School. It extended the teacher preparation program from two years to four years and emphasized the relationship of the fine arts, the manual arts, and the crafts (Wygant, 1983). The influ-

ence of this institution extended well into the twentieth century, making strong contributions to teacher education through the work of individuals such as Arthur Wesley Dow, who first began to organize and articulate the elements and principles of design as we know and teach them today.

By the turn of the century, the new education based upon the child-study movement was influencing all of education including art teacher education. Such an approach to the teaching of art placed the emphasis upon the child, rather than upon the product produced by the child. Based upon European experience, especially in Germany, this philosophy of education was quickly adapted by art education. It is within this context that the first systematic research related to art education was conducted and reported. In 1883, G. Stanley Hall reported his study of the content of children's minds upon entering school, which included extensive information about color and visual concepts (Hall, 1883). This major change in educational philosophy made a significant impact upon the teaching of art, as well as upon the preparation of teachers of art.

This philosophy continued to develop into the second quarter of the twentieth century, manifesting itself in the Progressive Education Movement and the work of John Dewey. Dewey believed strongly in art and advocated learning through experience, a philosophy consistent with the freedom developing in the general field of art in this country and abroad.

Two other major events occurred in the second quarter of the twentieth century that influenced the teaching of art and subsequently the preparation of teachers of art in a significant manner. The first of these was the development of the Bauhaus in Germany and its subsequent move to the United States. Built upon the philosophy that a common core of knowledge and experience underscored education in all of the arts, both fine and applied, the Bauhaus philosophy played a major role in shaping the rapidly expanding art programs and curricula in America's colleges and universities, including the teacher education programs. This approach, which still dominates the curricula of art programs in higher education today, also shaped the programs and curricula of art teacher education programs.

The second event was the emergence of a philosophy of art supporting the notion that art permeates all aspects of everyday life. Gaining significant impetus through the Owatonna Art Education Project (Art in Everyday Life, conducted by the University of Minnesota during the 1930s), a strong influence even today is a belief that art is a part of everyday living. This project, along with several leaders in the fields of art education and applied arts and significant and influential publications (Faulkner, Ziegfeld, & Hill, 1941; Goldstein & Goldstein, 1925) in both fields, has had a strong impact upon the preparation of art teachers, both art-specialist teachers and classroom teachers.

With the beginning of the third quarter of the twentieth century, teacher education took some dramatic turns. With the returning veterans from World War II, college enrollments exploded and programs developed rapidly, building upon the philosophies introduced during the earlier part of the century. Teacher preparation was no exception; the growth of graduate programs in visual arts education was phenomenal. The growth of these programs and the emergence of a number of major figures in art education who were also major contributors to the literature (e.g., Viktor Lowenfeld and Manual Barkan) had a major impact. The leadership positions assumed by major graduate programs in visual arts education such as those at The Pennsylvania State University and The Ohio State University influenced teacher preparation in art education throughout the United States, as the graduates of these programs assumed faculty and leadership positions in institutions of higher education.

With the emergence of federal government support of educational activity in the 1960s, these graduate programs exerted even greater influence by assuming the leadership for staging major events focused on research and teaching in the visual arts. The Penn State Conference on Curriculum Development and Research impacted on teacher preparation in the visual arts in significant ways. As part of the Johnson administration's Elementary and Secondary Education Act of 1965, the roots of the aesthetic education program and its subsequent concerns for teacher preparation were nurtured. The Aesthetic Education program, developed by the Central Midwestern Regional Educational Laboratory (CEMREL), was a federally funded program of research and curriculum development in the arts begun in the late 1960s and continuing throughout the 1970s. The visual arts discipline was influenced greatly by its philosophy that all of the arts could be taught in an integrated and interrelated manner, with the aesthetic experience the central core.

Likewise, the development of events and directions in education in general had a major impact on teacher education in the visual arts. For example, the importance and influence of the general study of creativity on teacher preparation in the visual arts was great. Major figures in this movement such as E. Paul Torrance, Calvin Taylor, and J. P. Guilford were involved in important ways with visual arts education.

With its beginnings in the educational reform of the 1960s, which resulted from the *Sputnik* experience and its explorations, and its continuation through the aesthetic education movement of the 1970s, the educational reform activity of the 1980s influenced teacher education in the visual arts with a growing emphasis on the content of the discipline of art as a basis for education in the visual arts. The most influential activity in this arena was the emergence of discipline-based art education and the Getty Center for Education in the Arts. One of the most important activities in the Center's work is the inservice preparation of teachers and other school personnel. The major contributors to the literature who support this approach to art education are Eisner (n.d.) and Broudy (1987), prominent voices in the general literature of art education and, more specifically, in the literature on teacher preparation in the arts.

Several major reports of the field chronicle the events of the last half of the twentieth century and their impact on teacher preparation in the visual arts. In 1941 and again in 1965 the National Society for the Study of Education examined the status of art education (Hastie, 1965a; Whipple, 1941). The 1965 report was accompanied by the Report of the Commission on Art Education, which was established by the National Art Education Association (Hausman, 1965). The activities of the 1970s

and, particularly, the 1980s are manifested in a series of commissioned papers that appeared in the Summer 1987 issue of *The Journal of Aesthetic Education.* These major reviews of teacher education in the visual arts established a perspective on teacher preparation in that subject from various times from the mid-1950s on.

One of the first comprehensive reviews of art education and, more specifically, of teacher education in the visual arts was *Art in American Life and Education,* the 40th Yearbook of the National Society for the Study of Education (Whipple, 1941). One of the four major sections of the yearbook is devoted to "The Preparation of Teachers of Art." That 14-chapter section covers a range of topics: (a) aims and methods in training art teachers, (b) teacher education course requirements and curricular patterns including technical preparation, (c) preparation in art history and art education, (d) theory and practice of education, (e) courses other than art and education, (f) recommended experiences in addition to school and technical training, (g) graduate work for the art teacher, (h) preparation of the general classroom teacher for teaching art, (i) the teacher of art in colleges and universities, (j) training of college teachers of art history and appreciation, (k) preparation of the art supervisor, (l) rural art supervision, and (m) teacher's extension classes.

In the introduction to the yearbook, Thomas Munro points out:

It is difficult to generalize, because of the diverse conditions prevailing in different institutions and localities, but it seems fairly evident that various types of institution [sic] for preparing teachers have developed on very different lines, and that much dislocation had resulted in the field as a whole. Teachers of art in the colleges are being prepared with heavy or exclusive emphasis on the historical approach to art, with fairly good cultural background, but with little or no technique in the practice of art, and little or no study of educational methods. Teachers of art in the schools below college level are being prepared with some technique and some educational methods, but often with little art history or theory, and little general cultural background, as evidenced by the small number of courses required in literature, history and science. Teachers of professional art or craft instruction tend in their preparation to specialize on technique and to sacrifice all the other alternatives to some extent, except as they are forced to a broader preparation by certification requirements. (1941, p. 24)

When the National Society for the Study of Education addressed the field of art education some 25 years later (Hastie, 1965a), teacher education again received prominent attention, with 2 of the 14 chapters of the 1965 yearbook devoted to the topic. The elementary school classroom teacher and the art specialist teacher were the focus of the two chapters. The teaching of art was the sole responsibility of regular classroom teachers in well over half the schools in the United States. Mitchell (1965) notes that:

What children learn about art from these teachers during their formative years in the elementary schools will have deep, perhaps permanent, effects on their attitudes and attainments in art. For this, if for no other reason, the quality of art teaching by elementary-school teachers is vitally important. (p. 221)

In addressing both the preservice and continuing-education needs of the classroom teacher of art, Mitchell considers what the elementary classroom teacher needs to know about art and articulates a number of issues that need to be addressed through research. She takes the position that:

Art should be taught as a discipline at all levels and that it can best be learned when the learner acts as an artist at his own level of comprehension and understanding. Since elementary-school teachers will most likely teach art in terms of their own conceptions of its nature, values and purposes, as well as in terms of their understanding of children, they should learn in and about art as a discipline by acting as artists while they learn. (p. 229)

In the same yearbook, Hastie (1965b) addresses the issue of teacher preparation for the art-specialist teacher. Stating a concern of the time, he articulates a situation facing art teachers in the twenty-first century:

Art-teaching as a career has never been for the timid or complacent, for those who desire a comfortable, trouble-free, professional life. The nature of art and the values of those individuals who are attracted to the practice of its discipline quite often seem to be at odds with the immediate surface values and solutions to the problems of education in our society. The conventional interpretation of our national need—individuals who are productive in terms of modern technology, with marketable skills that will strengthen the economy and our defense capability—leaves out, to a large degree, those aspects of our common need that are fulfilled through experience and practice in art—aesthetic judgment, thoughtful self-expression, perceptive awareness, understanding of our heritage and the roots of our culture, and the desire to penetrate unknown realms in order to achieve something original. (pp. 244–245)

Outlining the qualities of the superior art teacher, Hastie examines the qualities and competencies expected of the teacher as an artist and those expected of the teacher as a person who teaches art, indicating how such a "teacher is similar to and different from the artist and from the teacher of other school subjects" (1965b, p. 273). He also projects a theoretical model of instruction for art teacher education involving "professionalized" experience or "professionalized" activities. The model involves "exploration and the predisposition to learn," the "structuring of knowledge for learning," the "sequence in which material is presented," the "form and pacing of reinforcement," the "nature and pacing of rewards," and the "interrelation of knowledge." In every instance, the learner is perceived to be an adult who is learning to teach art with the motivation, the sequence and structure of learning, the evaluation, and the total instructional procedures determined by the goal of the learner (pp. 258–272). Hastie concludes that "no single set of principles of instruction for art-teacher education can be drawn from present theory and research. The theory is too divergent and the research is too sparse" (p. 272).

At the same time the National Society for the Study of Education was examining art education the National Art Education Association formed a commission on art education to do essentially the same task. Fortunately, the two efforts were coordinated through the leadership of W. Reid Hastie, who was a past president of the association. The *Report of the Commis-*

sion on Art Education (Hausman, 1965) was published the same year as the society's. Part III addresses art teacher education, with one chapter devoted to the teacher of art (inservice education) and a second chapter devoted to the bases for art teacher preparation (preservice education).

Schultz (1965) points out that the "teacher's education does not end with receiving a college degree. A good teacher continues to learn about teaching as long as he is in the profession of helping others to learn" (p. 107). He points out that the content of art education is derived from two distinct fields, art and education, and he describes the artist's experience as it relates to the activity of teaching and the teaching of art in relation to how people learn.

In the second chapter of the report related to teacher preparation, Johnson (1965) deals with the preservice experience, pointing out that a curriculum that sets the stage for a prospective teacher's growth toward professional competence is based in both art and education, as contrasted with times past when art teachers prepared themselves by taking a series of courses in art and occasionally involved themselves in unrelated education methods courses. He states: "The basic content is planned (a) to develop deep aesthetic awareness, (b) to help the student gain knowledge of the broad scope and traditions of art, and (c) to relate the content of art to the nature of learning and human development" (p. 119).

Johnson advocates the idea that prospective teachers should have an opportunity to engage in depth in some aspect of art or art education. This concept was emerging in the literature at the time and was supported with some limited research efforts that examined the relative merits of the depth, versus the breadth, approach to teaching art (Beittel & Mattil, 1961). Johnson also supports the notion that the professional sequence in art education is essential in the preparation of an art teacher. He believes that "it is usually the student's experience in art education courses that ties together the whole of what he has learned in all his courses" (p. 123). Moreover, the professional sequence in art education courses helps establish the relevance of their content to the overall purposes of teaching. He states that the major emphasis in art education programs should be enabling the student:

To know himself—his strengths and weaknesses and his relationship to others

To gain insights into the nature of learning

To study the complex and vital dynamics of creative behavior

To translate the content of art into learning to meet the needs of those he will teach

To gain knowledge of school organization and the types of curriculum

To intern at the levels he expects to teach

To become oriented to independent study and research toward solving problems and improving the quality of his teaching. (p. 123)

A series of papers was commissioned by the Getty Center for Education in the Arts and published as the summer 1987 issue of the *The Journal of Aesthetic Education*. One of the 10 chapters in this special issue was devoted to teacher education and discipline-based art education (DBAE) (Sevigny, 1987). Recognizing the diversity of activities included in the arena of teacher education in art, this particular report focuses on the preparation of art-specialist teachers. While attempting to gain insights useful to the future development of DBAE, Sevigny (1987) investigated its antecedents. He concluded that "although the current disposition toward DBAE appears to be gaining favor, teacher educators have much to learn about the methods of teaching that are appropriate to DBAE. Many pedagogical issues still need clarification" (p. 117).

MAJOR CONCERNS AND RELATED RESEARCH

Through this historical overview of teacher education in the visual arts, it can readily be seen that several major factors have influenced the development of teacher education in the visual arts in the United States. Likewise, a number of persistent concerns and issues have confronted, and continue to confront, teacher education in the visual arts. These issues seem to center on three broad major areas: (a) content knowledge base, (b) professional knowledge base, and (c) conceptions of quality teacher education in the visual arts. Each of these areas will be addressed, with particular attention to current issues related to each.

Two primary sources review the published research relating to teacher education in the visual arts: a study by Strange (1940), which identifies and reviews the research literature between 1883 and 1939, and a study by D. J. Davis (1977), which reviews the published research relating to art and art education since 1940. A computer data-base search of ERIC; *Resources in Education; Current Index to Journals in Education*; and *Dissertation Abstracts* completed the review. Unfortunately, only a very small portion of the published research in art and art education has focused on the area of teacher education. Often the reported research has little direct application to the issues at hand.

Knowledge Base for Teacher Preparation in the Visual Arts

The identification of appropriate content for art education programs and, subsequently, for teacher education programs continues to be a major issue in the field. Historically, this was associated with the development of the subdisciplines of the field of art. Early programs focused entirely on drawing. With the evolution of the field, the areas of design, art history, art appreciation, and the crafts have each taken on increasing importance over the years. There has been changing emphasis in the disciplinary components, as evidenced by the teaching of the visual arts and subsequent teacher education efforts. There is general agreement among art educators today that the field of art is comprised of four major subdisciplines—art production, art history, art criticism, and aesthetics—but the relative emphasis of each of these in the education of the child and the preparation of the teacher remains controversial. The issue becomes even more complex with considerations of the rela-

tionship and balance of the disciplinary components in programs for non-art-specialist teachers. Unfortunately, research tells us very little about content and balance in teacher education programs for either group.

A limited number of research studies have attempted to examine various aspects of the four subdisciplines and their interrelationships, particularly as they relate to the preservice and inservice education of teachers (Armstrong, 1972; DuTerroil, 1979; Kerr 1985; Lawson, 1970; MacGregor, 1971; Mork-Morgan, 1976; Parramore, 1970; Pitluga, 1970; Schnyder, 1936; Walther, 1977). Content topics that were studied varied greatly and included issues related to aesthetics and criticism (DuTerroil, 1979; Kerr, 1985; MacGregor, 1971; Parramore, 1970) and studio processes and products (Armstrong, 1972; Lawson, 1970; Mork-Morgan, 1976). The studies by Armstrong and Kerr exemplify the two areas most studied: studio and criticism. Armstrong studied the characteristics of art products of preservice elementary teachers to determine if there was a difference between those who measured high in flexibility and those who measured low in flexibility. Differences were found on six items: texture, depth, unity, thickness of line, gradation of values, and abstractness. Kerr examined eight characteristics of art-critical discourse by isolating, analyzing, and exemplifying selections from the critical writing of contemporary art critics. Of particular concern was the role played by language in education in general and art education in particular.

Inferences about content can be drawn from studies that examined the teaching of art in colleges and universities, as well as the course requirements for art teachers (Ahrens, 1964; Arnold, 1976; Barclay, 1963; Beelke, 1954; R. Davis, 1986; De Francesco, 1943; Diffily, 1963; Frattallone, 1974; Goldwater, 1943; Hager & Ziegfeld, 1941; Leach, 1963; Manzella, 1956; Nateman, 1986; Perogallo, 1978; Sevigny, 1987; Wessel, 1964). In surveying the teaching of art in American colleges, Goldwater (1943) studied 50 institutions for the years 1900, 1914, 1920, 1925, 1930, 1933, 1937, and 1940. The study revealed an early classical emphasis in art programs, with a lack of balance between theory and practice, painting and the other arts, and various types of introductory, history, and studio courses. Manzella (1956) compared the number and kinds of art offerings in 50 colleges for the years 1940 and 1954. The comparison indicated a changing emphasis on art for the nonartist. He also observed increasing awareness of the educational values inherent in the practice of art on the part of liberal arts colleges, as well as increasing awareness of the importance of contemporary art as a study important to an understanding of the present. Perogallo (1978) conducted a trend analysis of selected art course offerings at institutions granting art education degrees. She found that:

semester hours of course work offered in major studio art and art education . . . maintained a constant rate of growth, semester hours offered in minor studio art . . . had a decreasing rate of growth, and semester hours offered in art history . . . had an irregular rate of growth for the time periods of this study. (p. 70)

Focusing on requirements for teachers of art, Hager and Ziegfeld (1941) examined the art, art education, education, and general academic requirements at 50 colleges and universities. They reported considerable lack of agreement as to what should be included in the programs of preparation. Beelke (1954) took a slightly different approach and analyzed the official bulletins and regulations issued by various state departments of education and public instruction. Finding vast differences in the definitions of a "certified art teacher," he concluded that certification standards needed to be improved. Arnold (1976) studied the "state of art teacher preparation programs in the United States in the 70's" (p. 27). He reports that requirements emphasized studio art, with the mean number of semester hours being 35.6. Art history requirements averaged 9.4 semester credits, and slightly more than half required a course in contemporary art or art criticism. R. Davis (1986) studied accredited historically black colleges and universities in the South in regard to current practices in art for elementary teacher preparation. He found that stronger emphasis was placed on the studio component than on the art history component in the preparation of art teachers for elementary schools. The curricula also revealed a disproportionate share of courses in humanistic and behavior studies. Sevigny (1987) reports that, although preservice programs for art specialist teachers have many unique qualities, "they share . . . a common structure that includes three major components," one of which is "academic preparation in the content areas of art" (p. 96). He reports that "between 1965 and 1970 the general structure of art education requirements remained stable" (p. 104). Examining undergraduate bulletins at 5-year intervals from 1974 until 1984, Sevigny (1987) reports that requirements have changed little, with studio art still dominating the curriculum and art history requirements still only nine credit hours. One-third of his sample still did not require any course in art criticism or aesthetics. He concludes that "apart from the gradual shifts in art education courses, the overall distribution of requirements in the four domains of study appears seemingly unchanged since Arnold's 1975 survey" (p. 109). From these studies, one can conclude that teacher education programs in art are still dominated by studio instruction, with nominal attention given to art appreciation/art history and almost no attention given to criticism and aesthetics. Contemporary concern with this issue has its roots in the 1960s. Reflective of this early thinking is Barkan's (1962) keystone piece, "Transition in Art Education." Even with the current movements in discipline-based art education, there is still a long way to go before a balanced approach to the visual arts is achieved in the teacher preparation programs of American colleges and universities and, subsequently, the art classrooms of America. Not to be overlooked are the teacher certification requirements and regulations placed upon institutions of higher education by state laws and state departments of education. Before institutions can change, these requirements and regulations must be modified or relaxed.

How the various subdisciplines are taught or interrelated is an even greater issue. The research literature is also limited in this arena. Certain implications can be derived from a small number of curriculum-related research studies (Brooks, 1974; Caldwell, 1960; Campsey, 1965; DeWolf, 1974; Earthrowl, 1979; Lindemann, 1956; Lott, 1970; Lucas, 1973; Maitland-

Gholson, 1986; Myers, 1985; Nichols, 1951; Rouse & Hubbard, 1970; Rozmajzl, 1976; Sawyer, 1966; Sykes, 1964; Whiting, 1938). Rouse and Hubbard (1970) advocate a structured approach to curriculum based upon existing research that includes six learning task categories: learning to perceive, learning the language of art, learning about artists and the ways they work, criticizing and judging art, learning to use art tools and materials, and building productive artistic abilities. Myers (1985) and Maitland-Gholson (1986) explored discipline-based art education from both a theoretical and practical point of view. This approach advocates balanced coverage of the four subdisciplines of art: production, art history, criticism, and aesthetics. The use of television instruction was explored by Lott (1970) and Sykes (1964). Various models for instructional delivery were projected by DeWolf (1974), Lucas (1973), and Nichols (1951), and particular learning strategies were examined by Brooks (1974), Caldwell (1960), Lindemann (1956), and Sawyer (1966).

Other inferences about teacher preparation can be derived from a small number of studies in a related area of inquiry that examines art teachers in practice, with particular emphasis upon whether or not the teachers had a background in art and, if so, how well they thought it equipped them for their jobs (Bachelor, 1984; Blackman, 1977; Colbert, 1984; Degge, 1987; Thompson, 1985). Blackman (1977) prepared a profile of art teachers in Louisiana public schools and found that the majority were Caucasian, female, and between the ages of 25 and 40; the majority felt that their college courses adequately prepared them for teaching. Bachelor's (1984) profile of fine-arts-specialist teachers in southern California elementary schools found fewer minorities and more males, as compared with teachers in general. Colbert's (1984) study showed that children below the age of 6 were being taught by teachers with less training in the visual arts. Closely related is an isolated study examining selected teacher characteristics of art student teachers (Danielson, 1971). Exploring the possibility of a commonalty of personality traits among art student teachers, Danielson concluded that it was feasible to measure student teacher characteristics prior to the student-teaching experience for purposes of predicting potential problem areas. She found art student teachers to be "disorganized and unsystematic; permissive child–centered in educational viewpoint; relatively uninvolved in the teaching process and relatively unimaginative; unstimulating and unfriendly (p. 47).

Thompson (1985) studied the nature and effect of an existential-phenomenological approach to educating art teachers. Proposing that initiation into a vocation should be gradual and transformative and that it alters the self, she offers a proposal for art teacher education that emphasizes a necessary dialectic between reflection and experiences and supportive elements such as time, contact, content, and community.

Because of the limited amount of research in this area, it is necessary to turn to philosophical positions for insight. The issues related to appropriate content are discussed extensively in the current literature on discipline-based art education (*Beyond Creating*, 1985; Crawford, 1987; Eisner, n.d.; Kleinbauer, 1987; Risatti, 1987; Spratt, 1987).

Professional Knowledge Base for Teacher Preparation in the Visual Arts

Aside from the general statistical information provided in the studies reported previously, research information regarding the professional knowledge base for teacher preparation in the visual arts is limited. An array of isolated studies exists including those on values and attitudes (Broudy & Mikel, 1979; Budhal, 1972; Holen, 1973; Koppitz, 1960; Lenard, 1978; Meehan, 1983; Neale, 1973; Parks, 1986; Pum, 1971; Qualls, 1980; Scamell, 1974; Seiferth & Samuel, 1979; Smith, 1974); on creativity (Burkhart, 1961; D. J. Davis & Torrance, 1965; Grossman, 1971; Sample, 1961); on self-concept (Kain, 1972); on student–teacher interaction and questioning strategies (Clements, 1964; Jones, 1965); on nonverbal strategies (Szekely, 1975; Victoria, 1970; Vislosky, 1969); on oral verbal fluency (Cornell, 1973); on open-mindedness (Pearson, 1971); on approaches to teaching studio (Eickhorst, 1973); on problems of beginning teachers (Carter, 1955); on role perceptions of cooperating teachers (Spence, 1970); and on the holding power of the teaching profession (Easterbrook, 1964). Attitude studies focus on perceptions of various approaches to teacher education, both preservice and inservice, as well as on the perception of attitudes about the teacher's ability to teach art and the aesthetic attitudes of key administrative personnel. Burkhart (1961) attempted to identify the attributes of creative behavior and personality structure in art and student teaching, and D. J. Davis and Torrance (1965) explored the values inservice teachers held in relation to the creative personality. Parks (1986) analyzed seven art education textbooks used in teacher education to determine if those who used them were being exposed to attitude formation and change information. Frequent references were made to the importance of attitudes to art learning, but only one text specifically discussed their relationships to the art classroom. In spite of frequent references to the importance of attitudes to art learning, none discussed what the attitudes were, where they come from, or how they could be effected. Student–teacher interaction and questioning strategies, particularly as they relate to evaluative dialogues in art, are also reported in the literature (Clements, 1964; Jones, 1965).

A number of issues in this arena demand consideration. Some of the more pressing ones are whether the curriculum and methodology courses and the observation/internship experiences are best taught as general professional education courses by professional educators or as courses specifically applied to the visual arts by art educators. Although the theoretical literature in art education would strongly suggest that this is best done by professional art educators, there is no research to support such contentions. There seems to be little question about who is responsible for courses that provide understanding about the learner (child/adolescent psychology) or the foundations and historical background of education. These are the responsibility of the professional educator. Questions also exist regarding how much professional education is needed to prepare an art teacher of high quality.

Although data exist indicating that a large part of the art instruction at the elementary level is conducted by non-art-specialist teachers, little information is available concerning the extent of their art preparation. A study of art in the elementary schools of Indiana by Carter and Fox (1950) found that a few schools made no provisions for art and far too many made very inadequate provisions. In the large schools, 40 percent of the classroom teachers were responsible for art instruction, and 60 percent shared the responsibility with a supervisor or a special teacher. No research indicates what configuration of art courses for preservice, non–art specialists is most desirable or most effective. Hastie (1954) studied the best practices in art education and art competencies necessary for elementary school teachers. He found that art educators subscribed to a curricular approach in which the needs, interests, and requests of the pupils were basic. These findings strongly support the child-centered approach dominating art education during this time. Barr-Johnson (1979) investigated staff-development plans in 67 Florida counties and identified 143 components for arts-related professional growth, which included working with art media as well as general teaching competencies such as classroom management, instructional methods, and program administration. The same issues regarding who should teach curriculum development and methodology courses in art for art-specialist teachers exist for the non-art-specialist teacher. The theoretical literature would strongly support the notion that these courses are best taught by professional art educators; however, there is a wide diversity of opinion regarding the content and structure of such courses.

The issue of administration of programs is another major concern in the field. Schwartz (1987) studied educators' perceptions of an instructional supervision system for implementing discipline-based art education, to determine whether teachers, principals, and supervisors perceive the system and its components as clear and useful. She found that the teaching behavior in the supervision system measures three constructs of DBAE instruction: content, curriculum, and context. The system was seen as clear and useful by each of the educator groups, with the items rated higher as years of experience in educational administration increased. Content and curriculum were rated lower as years in art education increased, and context items were rated higher. Hill (1986) stresses an approach to bridge the gap between theory and practice: the development of an aesthetic-education learning center that emphasizes aesthetic education as a way for classroom teachers to become change agents in the delivery of art in the school. There is not a clear position indicated in the research or theoretical literature on where such programs of instruction are most effectively administered. Some argue that these courses/programs should be a subdiscipline within a visual arts program; others suggest that these courses/programs are best administered through a college/department of education.

Conceptions of Quality Teacher Education in the Visual Arts

In addressing the concern for quality teacher education in the visual arts, at least four major issues arise: (a) the relationship and the responsibility of the art educator, the professional artist, and the professional general educator in teaching and teacher preparation in the visual arts, for both the art specialist teacher and the non–art specialist (classroom) teacher; (b) the appropriate entry level into practice for the art educator—undergraduate or graduate preparation; the professional degree in art, versus the liberal arts degree, as the basic preparation for teacher education in the visual arts; (c) the validation process of the basic preparation for teachers; and (d) the role of teacher education in bridging the gap between research and practice. In reviewing the research literature in art and art education, one finds no empirical research data that address these major issues. Consequently, the field is left with various philosophical positions to review and evaluate in determining what constitutes a quality teacher education experience in art education.

The relationship and responsibility of the art educator, the professional artist, and the professional educator in teaching and teacher preparation in the visual arts have been the source of debate for many years. There are those who feel that the prospective teacher, as well as the inservice teacher, should be taught in the same manner and by the same individuals as the professional artist. This is felt to be particularly appropriate for the art-specialist teacher. This position is supported by the belief that the content of the field—studio, art history, criticism, and aesthetics—is best learned from those individuals who are experts in the various subdisciplines. This position is frequently supported by the belief that the pedagogical considerations can then be added by the professional art educator and the professional general educator. This approach is particularly prevalent today in the form of discipline-based art education.

On the other hand, there are those who feel that the preparation of the prospective art teacher, as well as the continuing education of the inservice art teacher, should be the responsibility of the art educator who has preparation in both art and education. This position supports the notion that even the content of the field can best be provided to the prospective teacher and the inservice teacher by the art educator, who can interpret and present the content of the field in light of pedagogical considerations. Although this position was more popular in the 1940s and 1950s, many teacher educators who were prepared during this era still strongly support this position.

An integral part of this issue is related to the question of who should teach art in the elementary school, the art specialist or the non–art specialist. There is rarely a question of who should teach art at the secondary level; the favored position is clearly that this is the responsibility of the art-specialist teacher. Although art educators argue that art in the elementary school should be taught by art-specialist teachers, many school administrators and the reality of the situation support the notion that art can and will largely be taught by the non-art-specialist (classroom) teacher. There seems to be an emerging position that a quality art program in the elementary school demands both the art-specialist teacher and the nonart-specialist (classroom) teacher as well as the existence of external resources such as art museums, art councils, and human resources related to the arts. Built on the concept that each has a unique contribution to make to the visual arts education experience of each child, the position articulates a clearly defined role for the classroom teacher and suggests a redefinition of the traditional role of the art-specialist teacher. Simply stated, the position advocates that basic visual arts instruction should be a shared effort of the classroom teacher and the art-specialist teacher, with the classroom teacher assuming responsibility for the integration of art concepts and skills with other subject areas and the art-specialist teacher assuming responsibility for extending the basic instruction. Community resources or museum personnel support both the integrations and the extensions of basic instruction. If such a position is accepted, there are significant implications for both the preservice and inservice education of art-specialist teachers and classroom teachers.

The appropriate entry level into practice for the art educator has traditionally been undergraduate preparation, with proponents for both the professional degree in art and the liberal arts degree with a major in art as the framework for the basic preparation. With the emerging concern about the quality of teacher preparation, there has been growing interest in graduate-level preparation as a basis for initial teacher certification. The visual arts have been part of this concern; a growing number of programs are considering the fifth year (graduate study) an essential part of initial teacher certification.

Closely related to this issue is the validation process of the basic preparation for teachers. This has traditionally been in the hands of the institutions providing the preparation program, but there is growing emphasis upon external validation. Patterning after other professional areas such as law, medicine, architecture, and nursing that require an external validation or licensure process, many states are now requiring a similar process for teachers, to insure that preparation programs have provided their graduates with sufficient knowledge and skills for at least a minimal level of competence for practice. Such examinations generally cover the content or discipline competencies as well as pedagogical competencies.

The fourth major issue in both preservice and inservice teacher-preparation programs is the role of teacher educators in bridging the gap between research and practice. There is still a minimal research base that supports the basic working assumptions in art education, but the research that does exist is not often utilized. Rush and Lovano-Kerr (1982) point out that:

We like to think that art teachers and art researchers have a symbiotic relationship, with researchers purposefully and efficiently uncovering new information that teachers can use to enhance their effectiveness in the classroom. We cherish this image in our technological society; but while a direct link between research and product consumption may exist in the automotive industry, teaching is still an art, not a business, and researchers' discoveries don't always profit the classroom. The reasons for the misfit between teaching and research are several. There is a small body of research on art learning and even less on art teaching. There is little agreement between researcher and teacher on the relative values of basic and applied research. There is a lack of funding for researchers in the arts, which, for good or ill, leaves research priorities to be set by individual researchers rather than teachers or policy-making institutions. Research questions, therefore, have not always been of equal interest to both parties. (p. 11)

No doubt there are many reasons, including those articulated by Rush and Lovano-Kerr, for this gap between research and practice in the field of art education, not the least of which is communication. Although some paradigms for integrating the two exist in the field, other approaches should be considered. The teacher educator can play a key role in this endeavor because of his or her involvement in the preparation and education of both the researcher and the practitioner.

Improved communication between the two can be aided through education. The education of the researcher whose primary concerns are the problems of the field and appropriate methodologies to examine problems should focus either directly or indirectly on long-range improvement in teaching and learning in art or expanding the knowledge base essential for both. On the other hand, knowledge about research and its interpretations should be a more integral part of the education of the practitioner. The education of the practitioner should treat research as an essential and integral part of the field and not as a phenomenon in opposition to the very essence of the arts themselves. Perhaps more importantly, the practitioner must be educated to realize that the outcomes of research will not always be instantaneous. (D. J. Davis, 1987, p. 18)

Unfortunately, research data do not support, question, or negate any of the positions suggested in considering the concerns for quality teacher education. Practice will continue to be guided for the time being by philosophical position rather than by empirical evidence. Likewise, the research literature is void of data supporting particular teacher education programs, practices, and techniques in the preparation of visual arts teachers.

The research literature in the visual arts provides minimal guidance for the teacher educator. Major gaps in research related to teacher preparation in the visual arts need to be addressed. Within the broad areas of research interest outlined in this chapter are numerous specific and researchable problems. Research questions must be articulated so that they focus directly upon the issues and concerns before teacher educators; this will ultimately yield the data that will build bodies of knowledge that guide and support our working assumptions in educating the visual arts teacher. A research agenda must be articulated, and a commitment to pursing it must be a high priority.

References

Ahrens, H. W. (1964). Art programs in New Jersey state colleges: A survey of selected practices in the teaching of art in New Jersey state colleges with recommendations for improved programs. *Dissertation Abstracts, 26,* 3766. (University Microfilms No. 65-6595)

Armstrong, C. (1972). Art product characteristics of elementary education majors measuring high in flexibility. *Studies in Art Education, 13*(3), 43–61.

Arnold, R. (1976). The state of teacher education: An analysis of selected art teacher preparation programs in the United States. *Art Education, 29*(2), 27–29.

Bachelor, B. G. (1984). *Profile of specialist teachers in elementary schools: Fine arts.* Los Alamatos, CA: Southwest Regional Laboratory for Educational Research and Development.

Barclay, D. L. (1963). An evaluative study of a Wayne State University program for the preparation of art teachers. *Dissertation Abstracts, 25,* 2304. (University Microfilms No. 64-5095)

Barkan, M. (1962). Transition in art education. *Art Education, 15*(7), 12–18.

Barr-Johnson, V. (1979). What can an art teacher gain from inservice activities? *Art Education, 32,*(1), 13–16.

Beelke, R. G. (1954). A study of certification requirements for teachers of art in the United States. In M. Barkan (Ed.), *Research in art education* (Fifth yearbook of the National Art Education Association, pp. 28–77). Kutztown, PA: Kutztown State Teachers College.

Beittel, K. R., & Mattil, E. L. (1961). The effect of a "depth" vs a "breadth" method of art instruction at the ninth grade level. *Studies in Art Education, 3*(1), 75–87.

Belshe, F. B. (1946). A history of art education in the public schools of the United States. *Dissertation Abstracts, 25,* 3956. (University Microfilms No. 6502019)

Beyond creating: The place for art in American schools. (1985). Los Angeles: Getty Center for Education in the Arts.

Blackman, C. R. (1977). *Louisiana public school art teachers: Profile, preparation, and opinions.* Baton Rouge, LA: Louisiana State University, Bureau of Educational Materials and Research.

Brooks, R. L. (1974). A problematic approach to curriculum improvement for teacher preparation in art. *Dissertation Abstracts International, 35,* 2820A. (University Microfilms No. 74-24,833)

Broudy, H. S. (1987). *The role of imagery in learning.* Los Angeles: Getty Center for Education in the Arts.

Broudy, H. S., & Mikel, E. (1979). *Survey of aesthetic attitudes of key school personnel.* St. Louis: Central Midwestern Regional Educational Laboratory.

Budhal, L. P. (1972). An experimental study of selected attitudinal variables utilizing a visual mode in a presentation relative to art criticism for prospective elementary teachers. *Dissertation Abstracts International, 34,* 3198A. (University Microfilms No. 73-28,844)

Burkhart, R. C. (1961). The interrelationship of separate criteria for creativity in art and student teaching to form personality factors. *Studies in Art Education, 3,* 18–38.

Caldwell, E. J. (1960). Planning art education workshops: A guide for the coordinator. *Dissertation Abstracts, 1960,* 76.

Campsey, N. (1965). An analysis of the instructional effect of correlated language arts and art education projects, experienced during the junior year at Jersey City State College, on people now employed as public school elementary teachers. *Dissertation Abstracts, 26,* 889. (University Microfilms No. 65-8835)

Carter, M. R. (1955). A study of the problems of beginning art teachers as related to learning experiences in the methods courses and in student teaching at Indiana University. *Dissertation Abstracts, 16,* 915. (University Microfilms No. AAD0011198)

Carter, M. R., & Fox, W. H. (1950). Art in the elementary schools of Indiana. *Bulletin of the School of Education, Indiana University, 25,* 1–82.

Clements, R. D. (1964). Art student-teacher questioning. *Studies in Art Education, 6,* 14–19.

Colbert, C. B. (1984). Status of the visual arts in early education. *Art Education, 374,* 28–31.

Cornell, E. M. (1973). A study to determine the relationship of oral verbal fluency to desirability and to other variables in candidates for teaching positions in art. *Dissertation Abstracts International, 34*, 2434A. (University Microfilms No. 73-26,135)

Crawford, D. W. (1987). Aesthetics in discipline-based art education. *Journal of Aesthetic Education, 21*(2), 227–239.

Danielson, P. I. (1971). Selected teacher characteristics of art student teachers. *Studies in Art Education, 12*(2), 42–48.

Davis, D. J. (1977). Research trends in art and art education, 1883–1972. In S. S. Madeja (Ed.), *Arts and aesthetics: An agenda for the future* (pp. 109–147). St. Louis: Central, Midwestern Regional Educational Laboratory.

Davis, D. J. (1987). From research to practice. *Design for Arts in Education, 88*, 15–20.

Davis, D. J., & Torrance, E. P. (1965). How favorable are the values of art education to the creative personality? *Studies in Art Education, 6*, 42–53.

Davis, R. (1986). Current practices in art for the elementary teacher preparation in accredited historically black colleges and universities in the south. *Dissertation Abstracts International, 47*, 3640A. (University Microfilms No. DA86-27,696)

De Francesco, I. L. (1943). An evaluation of curricula for the preparation of teachers of art. *Dissertation Abstracts*, SO146

DeWolf, W. F. (1974). The development of a prototype teaching module to enable prospective art teachers to gain skills in the processes of communication in the teaching of art criticism. *Dissertation Abstracts International, 35*, 6547A. (University Microfilms No. 75-8044)

Degge, R. M. (1987). A descriptive study of community art teachers with implications for teacher preparation and cultural policy. *Studies in Art Education, 28*(3), 164–175.

Diffily, J. (1963). Course requirements for prospective teachers of art, 1941–1962: A comparison. *Studies in Art Education, 4*, 52–58.

DuTerroil, A. M. (1979). Diagnosis of aesthetic behavioral responses toward art among students in elementary teacher education programs. *Dissertation Abstracts International, 40*, 5694A. (University Microfilms No. 8009854)

Earthrowl, K. J. (1979). An interdisciplinary arts program for pre-service teacher training in elementary education. *Dissertation Abstracts International, 40*, 4361A. (University Microfilms No. 80-04,917)

Easterbrook, C. M. (1964). Pursuit of a quest: Mortalities along the way. A study of a selected group of variables relative to the holding power of the art teaching profession. *Dissertation Abstracts, 26*(8), 4478. (University Microfilms No. 65-7721)

Eickhorst, W. S. (1973). A study to compare two teaching approaches to a studio art experience for elementary education majors. *Dissertation Abstracts International, 34*, 199A. (University Microfilms No. 73-16,068)

Eisner, E. W. (n.d.). *The role of discipline-based art education in America's schools.* Los Angeles: Getty Center for Education in the Arts.

Faulkner, R., Ziegfeld, E., & Hill, G. (1941). *Art today.* New York: Henry Holt.

Frattallone, J. A. (1974). A comparison of undergraduate art teacher training programs in 17 midwestern states. *Dissertation Abstracts International, 35*, 6548A. (University Microfilms No. 75-5553)

Goldstein, H., & Goldstein, V. (1925). *Art in everyday life.* New York: Macmillan.

Goldwater, R. J. (1943). The teaching of art in the colleges of the United States. *College Art Journal, 2*, 3–31.

Grossman, M. (1971). Perceptual style, creativity, and various drawing abilities. *Studies in Art Education, 12*(3), 64–66.

Hager, W. E., & Ziegfeld, E. (1941). Course requirements for teach-

ers of art in fifty institutions. In G. M. Whipple (Ed.), *Art in American life and education* (pp. 335–343). Bloomington, IL: Public School Publishing Company.

Hall, G. S. (1883). The contents of children's minds on entering school. *Princeton Review*, 267.

Hastie, W. R. (1954). Current opinions concerning best practices in art for the elementary schools and for elementary school teacher preparation. In M. Barkan (Ed.), *Research in art education* (Fifth yearbook of the National Art Education Association, pp. 78–113. Kutztown, PA.: Kutztown State Teachers College.

Hastie, W. R., (Ed.). (1965a). *Art education* (64th yearbook of the National Society for the Study of Education). Chicago: University of Chicago Press.

Hastie, W. R. (1965b). The education of an art teacher. In W. R. Hastie (Ed.), *Art education* (64th yearbook of the National Society for the Study of Education, pp. 243–273). Chicago: University of Chicago Press.

Hausman, J. J. (Ed.). (1965). *Report of the commission on art education.* Washington, DC: National Art Education Association.

Hill, E. P. (1986). An inter-institutional plan for an aesthetic education learning center for the pre-service and in-service education of classroom teachers. *Dissertation Abstracts International, 47*, 1697A. (University Microfilm No. DA86-16,889)

Holen, M. C. (1973). A note on the attitudinal consistency of prospective art teachers toward the relationship of art to the individual, society, education, and the environment. *Studies in Art Education, 14*(2), 28–34.

Johnson, I. (1965). The bases for art teacher preparation. In J. J. Hausman (Ed.), *Report of the commission on art education* (pp. 119–125). Washington, DC: National Art Education Association.

Jones, L. H. (1965). Student and teacher interaction during evaluative dialogues in art. *Art Education, 18*, 13–15.

Kain, J. D. (1972). An experimental study of the relation of university coordinated clinical task assignment-activities to the self-concept of art education student teachers. *Dissertation Abstracts International, 33*, 3460A. (University Microfilms No. 72-32,302)

Kerr, G. J. (1985). Hermeneutics and art discourse: Implications for teachers. *Dissertation Abstracts International, 46*, 1168A. (University Microfilms No. DA85-14,019)

Kleinbauer, W. E. (1987). Art history in discipline-based art education. *Journal of Aesthetic Education, 21*(2), 205–215.

Koppitz, E. M. (1960). Teacher's attitude and children's performance on the Bender Gestalt Test and human figure drawings. *Journal of Clinical Psychology, 16*, 204–208.

Lawson, N. G. (1970). Process/product values held by teachers and students regarding the studio art component of art for elementary education majors in selected southeastern institutions of higher learning. *Dissertation Abstracts International, 31*, 5909A. (University Microfilms No. 71-13,504)

Leach, G. B. (1963). Art requirements in teacher training programs of southern colleges since 1900. *Dissertation Abstracts, 23*, 2437. (University Microfilms No. 63-27)

Lenard, R. (1978). A study of selected art administrators' attitudes on teacher preparation programs for culturally disadvantaged. *Dissertation Abstracts International, 39*, 5270A. (University Microfilms No. 79-05,089)

Lindemann, E. M. (1956). Analysis and proposals for special methods course in relation to total program preparing art teachers at New York University. *Dissertation Abstracts 1956*, 102.

Logan, F. M. (1954). *Growth of art in American schools.* New York: Harper & Brothers.

Lott, H. H. (1970). Televised art education for the elementary classroom teacher: Proposals for content in an ITV program. *Disserta-*

tion Abstracts International, 31, 1668A. (University Microfilms No. 70-19,693)

Lucas, M. O. (1973). A collaborative model for the preparation of art teachers of inner-city youth. *Dissertation Abstracts International, 34,* 4965A. (University Microfilms No. 74-4266)

MacGregor, N. P. (1971). The use of selected concepts of art criticism in the preparation of art teachers. *Dissertation Abstracts International, 32,* 1961A. (University Microfilms No. 71-27,514)

Maitland-Gholson, J. (1986). Theory, practice, teacher preparation, and discipline-based art education. *Visual Arts Research, 122,* 26–33.

Manzella, D. B. (1956). The teaching of art in the colleges of the United States. *College Art Journal, 25,* 241–251.

Meehan, M. L. (1983). Inservice teachers' predispositions and attitudes towards arts education impacted by unique workshop. *College Student Journal, 17*(1), 83–88.

Mitchell, C. (1965). The art education of elementary-school teachers. In W. R. Hastie (Ed.), *Art education,* (64th yearbook of the National Society for the Study of Education, pp. 221–242). Chicago: University of Chicago Press.

Mork-Morgan, M. E. (1976). A historical study of the theories and methodology of Arthur Wesley Dow and their contribution to teacher training in art education. *Dissertation Abstracts International, 37,* 6905A. (University Microfilms No. 77-9514)

Munro, T. (1941). Introduction. In G. M. Whipple (Ed.), *Art in American life and education* (40th yearbook of the National Society for the Study of Education, pp. 3–25). Chicago: University of Chicago Press.

Myers, S. A. (1985). *Disciplined-based art education for preservice elementary teachers.* Unpublished master's thesis, University of Arizona, Tucson.

Nateman, D. S. (1986). An historical examination of the development and revision of art teacher education and certification standards in Ohio between 1802 and 1974. *Dissertation Abstracts International, 47,* 1578A. (University Microfilms No. DA86-18,822)

Neale, J. L. (1973). An examination of an in-service course to effect change in teachers' attitudes toward teaching art: A study conducted in economically poor areas of Chicago. *Dissertation Abstracts International, 34,* 4064A. (University Microfilms No. 73-30,101)

Nichols, A. W. (1951). Development of a program for a college art museum as part of teacher education. *Dissertation Abstracts, 1951,* 170.

Parks, M. E. (1986). An analysis of attitude recognition, formation, and change concepts in selected art education textbooks. *Studies in Art Education, 27*(4), 198–208.

Parramore, H. M. (1970). Aesthetic perception and the skills of criticism of the visual arts in elementary teacher education: A teaching method. *Dissertation Abstracts International, 31,* 5913A. (University Microfilms No. 71-13,448)

Pearson, D. W. (1971). The relationship between open-mindedness in prospective art teachers and certain variables in teacher preparation. *Dissertation Abstracts International, 32,* 3141A. (University Microfilms No. 72-963)

Perogallo, A. M. (1978). Trend analysis of selected art course offerings at institutions granting art education degrees. *Studies in Art Education, 20*(1), 64–72.

Pitluga, G. E. (1970). Art teacher preparation and our visual environments: A new look at a continuing responsibility. *Dissertation Abstracts International, 32,* 5476A. (University Microfilms No. AAD72-01,255)

Pum, R. J. (1971). Differential characteristics of art-teaching majors and elementary-education majors in college; as measured by selected attitude, value, and personality factors. *Dissertation Abstracts International, 32,* 5659A. (University Microfilms No. 72-7515)

Qualls, G. S. (1980, November). *Children's attitudes toward art: An intervention program.* Paper presented at the meeting of the Mid-South Educational Research Association, New Orleans.

Risatti, H. (1987). Art criticism in discipline-based art education. *Journal of Aesthetic Education, 21*(2), 217–225.

Rouse, M. J., & Hubbard, G. (1970). Structured curriculum in art for the classroom teacher: Giving order to disorder. *Studies in Art Education, 11,* 14–26.

Rozmajzl, M. M. (1976). A design and trail of an interdisciplinary course in aesthetics for teacher education in music, visual art, and literature (Vol. 1 & 2). *Dissertation Abstracts International, 37,* 6425A. (University Microfilms No. 77-8019)

Rush, J. C., & Lovano-Kerr, J. (1982). Research for the classroom: An ecological impact statement. *Art Education, 35*(2), 11–23.

Sample, R. E. (1961). A comparison of the effects of two teaching methods on general creativity in teacher preparation for elementary art. *Dissertation Abstracts, 22,* 3940. (University Microfilms No. 62-1816)

Sawyer, J. R. (1966). Convergent and divergent instructional procedures used in the preparation of teachers of art. *Dissertation Abstracts, 27,* 3635A. (University Microfilms No. 67-5959)

Scamell, E. V. (1974). Some personality characteristics and value interests of elementary art teachers. *Dissertation Abstracts International, 36,* 234A. (University Microfilms No. 75-5661)

Schnyder, D. M. (1936). The essential elements in the preparation of teachers of art for the secondary schools. *Dissertation Abstracts, 1936,* 68. (University Microfilms No. 73-3402)

Schultz, H. A. (1965). The teacher of art. In J. J. Hausman (Ed.), *Report of the commission on art education* (pp. 107–117). Washington, DC: National Art Education Association.

Schwartz, K. A. (1987). Educators' perceptions of an instructional supervision system for discipline-based art education. *Dissertation Abstracts International, 48,* 368A. (University Microfilms No. DA87-11,646)

Seiferth, B., & Samuel, M. (1979). *A survey of attitudinal changes of student teachers in fine arts* (Report No. SOD12032). Carbondale: Southern Illinois University. (ERIC Document Reproduction Service No. ED 177 084)

Sevigny, M. J. (1987). Discipline-based art education and teacher education. *Journal of Aesthetic Education, 21*(2), 95–126.

Smith, J. W. (1974). Art attitudes of preservice elementary teachers as affected by a modular program in art. *Dissertation Abstracts International, 36,* 838A. (University Microfilms No. 75-16,447)

Spence, J. R. (1970). Role perceptions of selected cooperating teachers in art and implications for student teaching experiences. *Dissertation Abstracts International, 32,* 829A. (University Microfilms No. 71-21,806)

Spratt, F. (1987). Art production in discipline-based art education. *Journal of Aesthetic Education, 21*(2), 197–204.

Strange, M. (1940). *A summary of scientific investigations relating to art.* Unpublished master's thesis, Baylor University, Waco, TX.

Sykes, R. E. (1964). The effectiveness of closed-circuit television observation and of direct observation of children's art classes for implementing elementary teachers' training in art education. *Dissertation Abstracts, 25,* 2387. (University Microfilms No. 64-10,799)

Szekely, G. E. (1975). A system for training art teachers in the use of nonverbal classroom communication and interaction methods for NES children. *Dissertation Abstracts International, 36,* 4967A. (University Microfilms No. 76-3290)

Thompson, C. M. (1985). Origination and communion: Experience and reflection in the education of art teachers (phenomenology). *Dissertation Abstracts International, 47*, 3A. (University Microfilms No. DA86-11,150)

Victoria, J. J. (1970). The development of a typology of nonverbal behavior and observational procedures for the identification of nonverbal behavior of student-teachers of art. *Dissertation Abstracts International, 31,* 4610A. (University Microfilms No. 71-6369)

Vislosky, R. J. (1969). A comparative study of first-year art teachers' evaluations of the teacher preparation curricula in four Pennsylvania state colleges. *Dissertation Abstracts International, 30,* 4866A. (University Microfilms No. 70-7252)

Walther, J. M. (1977). The development of a program in ethnic art appreciation for teacher education. *Dissertation Abstracts International, 38,* 3117A. (University Microfilms No. 77-25,528)

Wessel, H. M. (1964). A comparative study of art education programs in the north central states. *Dissertation Abstracts, 25,* 5773. (University Microfilms No. 65-4681)

Whipple, G. M. (Ed.). (1941). *Art in American life and education* (40th yearbook of the National Society for the Study of Education). Chicago: University of Chicago Press.

Whiting, M. R. (1938). The use of art in the teaching of other subjects in the secondary schools, with implications for teacher training. *Dissertation Abstracts, 1938,* 70.

Wygant, F. (1983). *Art in American schools in the nineteenth century.* Cincinnati: Interwood Press.

·43·

PHYSICAL EDUCATION TEACHER EDUCATION

Linda L. Bain

CALIFORNIA STATE UNIVERSITY, NORTHRIDGE

The central question confronting teacher educators is how to prepare teachers who can and will conduct quality instructional programs in schools. This question is particularly urgent in physical education where widespread discontent and marginal status within schools seem to threaten the continued existence of physical education programs. Embedded in this central question about teacher education are issues of values (e.g., What is quality physical education?) and issues of effectiveness (e.g., What skills do teachers need and how can they best acquire them?). The breadth of these concerns accounts for the complexity and scope of research in physical education teacher education.

Teacher education, as evidenced by the contents of this *Handbook*, is a complex field in which scholars have addressed difficult issues involving normative and empirical questions. Teacher education in physical education has been informed and improved by the generic research on teaching and teacher education. Researchers in physical education have built upon this general body of knowledge, elaborating on ideas and examining their usefulness in the physical education setting. In addition to testing the generalizability of classroom research, physical education researchers have addressed issues unique to the teaching of that field.

This chapter will examine research related to teacher education in physical education. A complete understanding of this topic requires familiarity with several bodies of research including generic research on teaching and teacher education, research on motor learning, and research on teaching in physical education. However, this chapter will be limited to research dealing with teacher education in physical education. The first section of the chapter will provide a historical perspective on the development of physical education school programs and teacher education programs. The next section will

discuss the theoretical perspectives underlying teacher education research in physical education. The review of research will then be organized into three sections. The first will describe teacher educators and teacher education students in physical education. The second section will discuss research related to initial teacher education programs, and the third will focus on induction into schools and inservice education.

HISTORICAL PERSPECTIVE

An understanding of the unique concerns in the preparation of physical education teachers requires knowledge of the history of the field and of the contemporary circumstances affecting the world of the physical education teacher. Although a comprehensive review of the history of physical education is beyond the scope of this chapter, a brief examination will provide perspective for the discussion of teacher education in physical education.

Physical education has been taught in American schools since the 1820s, with considerable expansion occurring during the late 1800s. The first school physical education programs were gymnastics and exercise programs designed to contribute to health (Spears & Swanson, 1978). Sports and games were available in schools but only as extracurricular activities. In the early 1900s, influenced by progressive education and the American play movement, physical education programs shifted to an emphasis on sports and recreational activities presumed to contribute to the development of the whole child, an approach labeled *education through the physical* (Spears & Swanson, 1978).

Despite some residual influence of physical training programs, *education through the physical* emerged as the domi-

---

The author wishes to thank Hal Lawson (Miami University, Ohio), and Larry Locke (University of Massachusetts) for their thoughtful reviews and helpful suggestions.

nant curricular philosophy in physical education throughout the first half of the twentieth century (Lawson, 1988). The focus was on sports and games with periodic efforts to increase the attention given to fitness in response to concerns about the physical well-being of the population. The emphasis on the educational value of sports provided support for the expansion of interscholastic athletic programs, most of which are closely connected to the physical education program (Lewis, 1969).

The dominance of *education through the physical* perspective began to give way in the 1960s, and physical education entered a period marked by considerable debate regarding curricular content and goals. That debate was sparked by events occurring in physical education departments in colleges and universities.

Beginning in the late 1800s, the need for teachers of physical education in schools and for instructors in parks and playgrounds led to the establishment of programs for training teachers (Spears & Swanson, 1978; Ziegler, 1975). Most were one or 2-year, normal-school programs that included theoretical study of science (anatomy, physiology, anthropometry) and practical work in gymnastics and exercise. Gradually colleges and universities began to provide teacher-preparation programs. Because of the emphasis on health, many of these programs were directed by medical doctors. As the emphasis shifted from gymnastics to sports in the early 1900s, physicians were replaced by educationists and athletic coaches (Lewis, 1969).

These early programs provided a teaching major, not a liberal arts or academic major. That is, only students preparing to be teachers could major in physical education, and the coursework in these programs placed heavy emphasis on pedagogy, as well as on science. Many programs retained the normal-school view of teaching as a craft learned primarily through apprenticeship (Zeichner, 1983). Although the scientific base of physical education programs expanded throughout the twentieth century, physical education continued to be defined as a teaching field, not an academic major, until the 1960s.

The publication of a classic article by Franklin Henry (1964), "Physical Education as an Academic Discipline," marked a turning point. Physical educators began to talk about physical education as a disciplinary area focusing on the study of human movement and to offer academic majors to students seeking a liberal arts degree or preparing for a career other than teaching (Lawson, 1981; Spears & Swanson, 1978). In some cases these programs were renamed "sport science," "movement arts and sciences," or "kinesiology," to differentiate the academic major from teacher preparation. Although debate continues regarding whether physical education should be defined as a discipline or a profession (Bressan, 1979; Broekhoff, 1982; Hellison, 1987; Locke, 1977), most would now concur that the field encompasses more than teacher education. The expansion to include preparation for careers other than teaching has been reinforced by a constriction of employment opportunities and an oversupply of physical education teachers (Randall, 1986).

Several elements of this history influence contemporary teacher education in physical education. One is the continuing struggle to define the subject matter of the field (Jewett &

Bain, 1985). Physical education is marked by a lack of consensus, not only about the mission and goals of the field, but also about the nature of its subject matter. Some view the subject matter as the forms of motoric play (that is, sports, games, and dance). Others see the subject matter as the analysis and scientific study of human movement.

The various curricular models and definitions of subject matter have had differing impacts on schools and universities. Elementary school physical education programs teach basic movement skills and/or games and sports. Secondary school physical education programs teach sports and games and, to a lesser extent, fitness activities. Although a few school physical education programs have begun to teach movement analysis or the scientific aspects of fitness, most continue to teach sports. University physical education departments teach prospective physical education teachers the scientific study of movement. College students majoring in physical education often experience a discontinuity between their experiences in schools and what they are being taught in the university.

The struggle within universities to redefine the field as an academic area continues. Because of its history, physical education is frequently the only department on campus that delivers both subject-matter preparation and teacher education courses to its students. This dual responsibility facilitates the integration of content and pedagogy, but it has made more difficult the effort to attain recognition as an academic area of study. The dual role has also made the administrative location of physical education departments uncertain. Approximately half are located in colleges of education, whereas the others are in liberal arts or some other administrative unit (e.g., college of applied sciences or, in a few cases, college of health, physical education, and recreation). Regardless of location, departments of physical education often seem, at least partially, misfits.

To some extent, this feeling of being a misfit is related to the status of the field. Because physical education has not been viewed as an academic area, it has had marginal status in schools (Evans, 1988; Hendry, 1975a; O'Sullivan, 1989; Templin & Schempp, 1989) and universities (Goc-Karp, Kim, & Skinner, 1985). This marginality has recently been reflected in the omission of physical education from the educational reform literature of the 1980s (J. L. Taylor, 1986) and from the third edition of the *Handbook of Research on Teaching* (Wittrock, 1986).

The marginal status of physical education affects its teacher education programs. Physical education students often feel neglected or discriminated against in generic education courses. Within physical education departments, a microcosm of the university's pecking order can develop, with movement scientists seen as more prestigious than pedagogy specialists. Students learn to view the teaching of physical education as a low-status occupation, and many seek to maintain their feelings of self-worth by pursuing more prestigious career options (e.g., exercise specialist or sport manager) or by emphasizing coaching rather than teaching.

Physical education's relationship with athletics and coaching has a profound influence on the teaching of physical education. Because of the extensive interscholastic athletic programs in American schools, most middle and secondary school physical education teachers also are required to coach (Chu, 1984). Some of the literature suggests that teaching and coaching require different characteristics and abilities. Research indicates that employment as a teacher and coach causes role conflict and stress (Bain, 1983; Locke & Massengale, 1978). A major source of stress is the heavy time demands required to fulfill both roles. A frequent response to role conflict is that one of the roles is adopted as the major one. Because of the visibility and prestige associated with the coaching role, many physical education teachers exhibit greater commitment to coaching than to teaching. A significant problem confronting physical education teacher education programs is preparing students to both teach and coach and to deal with role conflict in ways that maintain the integrity of instructional and athletic programs. Issues related to teacher/coach role conflict will be discussed further in the sections describing teacher educators and teacher education students.

One other aspect of the history of physical education should be noted because of its continuing effects on teacher education programs. Until the passage of Title IX in the 1970s, physical education programs were generally segregated by sex. Although boys and girls might be taught together in the primary grades, separate programs were begun in the upper elementary grades. The content of the two programs differed, based on perceptions of gender-appropriate activities. Men and women teachers attended different teacher-preparation programs and tended to differ in program emphasis and teaching styles (Spears & Swanson, 1978). Athletic programs for boys and girls differed because of differences in community beliefs, state regulations, and district-level financial support. Perhaps because of more limited athletic programs for girls, women tended to devote greater time and attention to teaching physical education (VanderZwaag, 1981).

After the passage of Title IX in 1972 and its implementation in physical education and sport in 1978, physical education programs were required to be coeducational, with the exception of participation in contact sports. Although separate athletic programs for boys and girls were permitted, the programs were required to provide equal support and opportunity. The effects of Title IX on school physical education and on teacher education programs have been dramatic. Athletic programs for girls have expanded. Many school physical education programs are now coeducational, but that aspect of the law has been met with resistance by teachers who found it difficult to implement and resented the arbitrary nature of mandated change. Most university physical education programs are now coeducational. Separate men's and women's physical education departments have been merged. Male and female physical education faculty, many of whom were trained in separate departments, now share responsibility for preparing teachers to work in coeducational situations.

The recent merger of programs does not imply that issues of sex equity have been resolved. Patriarchal beliefs about gender are deeply embedded in sport and physical education and affect the perceptions and behaviors of teachers and students (Griffin, 1983, 1985a). Sport is "an important cultural practice that contributes to the definition and recreation [sic] of gender

inequality" (Theberge, 1985, p. 197). Some would argue that this contribution to the social construction of gender relations has been a primary, if unacknowledged, reason for the existence of sport and physical education programs in schools. Although increased sport participation by women has challenged male domination, women's quest for equality in sport remains contested and ambiguous (Messner, 1988). Griffin (1989a) suggests, "By framing the problem as one of simply providing equal access, we have failed to question the structure of sport and physical education and the sacred meaning they have in a male-dominated society" (p. 220).

Increasing attention is being given to the ways in which the sport culture shapes the experiences of physical education teachers as well as their students. Dodds (1989) suggests that those training to be physical education teachers may experience contradictions between espoused educational goals of opportunity for all and the view of sport widely endorsed in the society. When physical educators in Britain attempted to implement curricular changes intended to emphasize broad participation rather than competition, their efforts were strongly criticized by the media and political leaders as undermining the basic values of the society (Evans, 1988). Pollard (1988) suggests that the concept of competition is central to the legitimation of capitalism and to the definition of masculinity in Western culture.

The traditional definition of sport as a male domain is reinforced by the dominance of men in physical education. Despite the history of many strong women's physical education programs and leaders (Spears, 1979), current university physical education departments have a majority of male faculty and are likely to have a male department chair (Hoferek, 1980). Men are more likely to seek and attain publication of their work than are women, a fact that could be attributed to structural barriers inhibiting the scholarly productivity of female physical educators (Knoppers, 1989; Safrit, 1979, 1984; Schuiteman & Knoppers, 1987). Men tend to be concentrated in the more prestigious areas of the field such as exercise physiology and biomechanics, whereas women are more likely to be associated with lower status functions such as the social sciences or teacher education. The gender patterns within the department seem likely to reinforce the view of teaching as a low-status activity, primarily of interest to women, not men.

This picture portrayed in this brief analysis is that of a field in transition. Since the early 1950s physical education has moved from a sex-segregated program for the preparation of teachers to an interdisciplinary program for the study of human movement and the preparation for a range of professional occupations. Although a majority of students majoring in physical education continue to seek teacher certification, the teaching of physical education is viewed as a low-status occupation by those in physical education, as well as by others in education. Many of those pursuing teacher certification in physical education choose to do so because of what Lortie (1975) describes as convertibility (i.e., its usefulness as a step toward other occupations; in this case, coaching). Interpretation of the research on teacher education in physical education must be approached with an understanding of the circumstances and context within which such programs exist. Examination of the theoretical perspectives underlying teacher education research also is important.

THEORETICAL PERSPECTIVES

Although some of the research on teacher education in physical education has been atheoretical, much of the work seems to derive from one of two theoretical positions: behavior analysis or occupational socialization. Daryl Siedentop (1972, 1983b, 1985, 1986) is the primary spokesperson for the behavior analysis perspective and has been a major influence in establishing a natural science research tradition within physical education pedagogy (Siedentop, 1981, 1982). Although not all researchers within this tradition have explicitly endorsed behavior analysis, much of the research on teaching and teacher education shares the assumptions of causality and determinism and seeks to find lawlike generalizations about human behavior. Siedentop (1986) identifies the following as necessary characteristics of teacher education research based on a natural science of behavior:

First, the studies would have to focus on teacher behavior as a natural phenomenon studied for its own value rather than as an epiphenomenon studied only to infer something about other less accessible variables. . . . Second, the training intervention would have to be defined with sufficient specificity to allow for replication. And finally, the research design would have to allow for some internally valid means for attributing changes to the presence and absence of the training strategy. (p. 5)

The goal of such research is to identify procedures for developing effective training programs for teachers.

The occupational socialization perspective was first introduced into the physical education literature in the early 1970s (Burlingame, 1972; Pooley, 1972). Although a few scattered studies using this perspective followed, no programs of research comparable to those based on behavior analysis existed. In the early 1980s, Hal Lawson (1983b, 1983c, 1986, 1988) emerged as a spokesperson for the socialization approach, and a number of researchers began to employ this theoretical perspective. The growing volume of research examining the socialization of physical education teachers has been summarized by Templin and Schempp (1989).

Occupational socialization "includes all of the kinds of socialization that initially influence persons to enter the field of physical education and that later are responsible for their perceptions and actions as teacher educators and teachers" (Lawson, 1986, p. 107). Lawson suggests that this includes societal socialization, sport socialization, professional socialization, and organizational or bureaucratic socialization. Early research on socialization, including teacher socialization, has been criticized for adopting a deterministic view in which the individual is molded to fit the existing social structure (Lacey, 1987). Lawson (1983c) avoids this criticism by suggesting that socialization is "problematic, not automatic" and that "while institutions try to typecast individual actors and actions, people also try to transform institutions" (p. 4). The research based on the occu-

pational socialization perspective studies not just teachers' behaviors but also their characteristics, perceptions, and beliefs. Much of the research has employed psychometric or qualitative research methods. Some qualitative researchers are uncomfortable with the deterministic characteristics of early socialization research, but their work can be encompassed in the more interactive, dialectic version of the theory.

Behavior analysis research and occupational socialization research differ in goals and techniques. Lawson (1983a) compares the goals of the two basic approaches to research by saying, "researchers on teaching will look for generalizable laws derived from replicated findings, while researchers on teachers will look for time-bound forms of understanding that are often situation- and person-specific" (p. 353). Despite some debates about the relative merits of the two perspectives (Schempp, 1987, 1988; Siedentop, 1987), many believe that both research traditions have an important contribution to make to the field (Lawson, 1983a). Locke (1984), in his important review of physical education teacher education research from 1960 to 1984, describes the shift from "a largely atheoretical tradition" to work grounded in socialization or behavior analysis or related theories (p. 40). He reports valuable findings emanating from both lines of research.

In addition to the two dominant research traditions, a few physical education scholars are examining teacher education from a critical theory perspective (Bain, 1989; Bain & Jewett, 1987). Critical science views research as inherently political, inescapably tied to issues of power and legitimacy. Researchers in this paradigm seek to understand contextual constraints on human behavior and to use this information to empower those being researched. This form of research combines scholarship and advocacy, and is usually grounded in one of three theoretical perspectives: feminism, neo-marxism, or empowering pedagogy (Lather, 1986). Dewar (in press) summarizes the critical perspective as follows:

What I mean by alternative, critical pedagogies are those pedagogies that begin with the assumption that physical education programs and practices are socially constructed and historically produced. Recognition of this fact means that physical education is seen as an area of the curriculum where struggles over power and privilege are negotiated and contested. Understanding these struggles and making visible the various oppressions (sexism, racism, ageism, fat phobia, classism, heterosexism, able bodiedism, etc.) that are being struggled over allows us to begin to deconstruct *what* we do in physical education programs, *how* and *why* we do it, and social, moral and political implications of our actions and our decisions.

This chapter will summarize research derived from the behavior analysis, the occupational socialization, and the critical theory perspectives.

PARTICIPANTS IN TEACHER EDUCATION

Research describing participants in the teacher education process—teacher educators and teacher education students—is of interest primarily to those concerned with the occupational socialization of teachers. Most of the early work was atheoretical and focused on the personal attributes of physical education students or teachers (Locke, 1984; Sage, 1980). However, more recent work, grounded in socialization theory, has attempted to describe perceptions and experiences influencing choice of a career and subsequent performance of the role.

Teacher Education Students

Lortie (1975) describes occupational choice as a process by which the individual forms an impression of, and is attracted to or repelled by, a particular occupation. An important aspect of the process is the formation of the subjective warrant, which refers to "an individual's perceptions of the skills and abilities necessary for entry into, and performance of work in a specific occupation" (Dewar & Lawson, 1984, p. 15). The subjective warrant is formed through direct observation of members of the occupation and through information provided by others in one's social environment. In the case of teaching, potential recruits have years of direct observation on which to base their perceptions. The choice of occupation is made by comparing one's interests, aspirations, and abilities with the subjective warrant held for each of the occupations being considered. This stage of learning about and selecting an occupation also constitutes the beginning phase of acquiring the beliefs, values, and norms of the group, a process that is called *anticipatory socialization*.

Three reviews summarize research on occupational choice and anticipatory socialization in physical education (Dewar & Lawson, 1984; Lawson, 1983c; Templin, Woodford, & Mulling, 1982). The research includes descriptions of the subjective warrants held by potential recruits. Dewar (1984) found that the dominant view of physical education among high school students is that a career in physical education "involved playing games and learning how to teach them to others" (p. 6). Many of these students expressed a desire to reproduce their school physical education programs, a perspective described as *custodial orientation*. This subjective warrant was shared by many of Dewar's subjects, a group that included students attracted to careers in physical education, as well as students who had decided not to pursue such careers.

The decision regarding choice of career is affected by the attractors or benefits associated with the profession, as well as by the facilitators or influences on one's choice of occupation. The research indicates that physical education students, like other prospective teachers, choose their occupation because they enjoy working with others and they see their profession as providing a valuable service to society (Pooley, 1975; Templin et al., 1982).

Lortie (1975) suggests that some persons select teaching as a career because they become so attached to the schooling process that they wish to remain associated with it. This motive, which has been labeled *the continuation theme*, seems to be a strong influence on the career choice of physical education students. Many students have extensive past involvement in, and love for, sport and physical activity and seek to enter the

field to continue this association with sport (Dewar, 1984; Pooley, 1975; Templin et al., 1982). However, many of the recruits have a stronger association with athletic programs than with physical education. Evidence indicates that a desire to coach, not to teach, is often the primary motive for selecting physical education, especially for males (Bain & Wendt, 1983b; Chu, 1978; Sage, 1989; Segrave, 1980). Selecting physical education as a means of entry into another career (e.g., coaching or being professional athlete) indicates that the recruit views teaching, not as a primary commitment, but as a career contingency, a view that affects the student's response to the teacher education program. This frequent preference for coaching seems to be based on extensive experience in competitive sport and on the strong influence of coaches on career decisions.

Differential preference for the two roles seems to indicate that recruits into physical education have different subjective warrants for the occupations of teaching and coaching. Experienced teachers/coaches perceive the roles as distinct and separate, requiring different behaviors for success (Chu, 1980; Earls, 1981; Sage, 1989), and observation confirms differences in behavior in the two settings (Bain, 1978). However, Bain and Wendt (1983b) report that, although expressing differential preferences for teaching and coaching, undergraduate students seem to perceive the roles as requiring rather similar characteristics or abilities. This suggests that the anticipatory socialization process might not provide a thorough understanding of the two roles and that the recruits' preferences might primarily reflect the greater visibility and prestige associated with coaching, particularly in boys' and men's athletics.

Both gender and social class seem to have an effect on reasons for selecting physical education as a career. Women are more likely than men to value teaching more than coaching (Bain & Wendt, 1983b; Riggins, 1979; Segrave, 1980). Women are also more likely to select a career in physical education for humanitarian and altruistic reasons, rather than for extrinsic rewards (Segrave, 1980). However, Segrave notes that female students demonstrate a much less consistent pattern of role preference, and this inconsistency could reflect changes resulting from the growth of athletic opportunities for women. Social class also is related to reasons for selecting a career in physical education. Physical education recruits are generally from lower-middle- or lower-class families; the much smaller group of middle- and upper-class students who enter the field seems to endorse intrinsic rewards and humanitarian reasons to a greater extent than lower-class students (Segrave, 1980).

Because occupational choice involves comparing one's abilities, interests, and aspirations with the perceived requirements of a field, occupations tend to attract recruits who share certain characteristics. A majority of those entering teaching are women from middle-class or men from lower-middle-class backgrounds (Lanier & Little, 1986), a trend that also applies to physical education (Kenyon, 1965; Segrave, 1980). Evidence seems to indicate that persons from such backgrounds are conformist and value practical knowledge more than theoretical knowledge (Lanier & Little, 1986). Conservatism has been observed among teachers, but the evidence suggests that physical educators, especially males, are more conservative than other teachers (Hendry & Whiting, 1972; Kenyon, 1965; Locke, 1962; Sage, 1980).

The tendency toward conservatism seems closely related to identification with the coaching profession. Physical educators who aspire to advancement in coaching appear to be more traditional (Riggins, 1979) and to operate at lower levels of moral judgment (Henkel & Earls, 1985) than those with lower coaching aspirations. A number of scholars have proposed an interactionist interpretation of such data arguing "that the specific social situation and role expectancies have a major effect upon those personal characteristics which are evidenced by physical educator/coaches" (Sage, 1980, p. 118). Hendry (1975a, 1975b) found that other teachers expected the physical educator to achieve success in competitive sports, in order to bring prestige to the school. Physical educators felt great pressure to meet this expectation in order to survive in a role viewed as marginal to the goals of the institution. Sage (1987b) found that coaches viewed their job security as contingent upon a winning record. Edwards (1973) suggests that the conservatism and authoritarianism of coaches derives from institutional demands for accountability, which result in "limited control with complete liability" (p. 139). Because many physical education recruits have extensive experience in competitive sport, the athletic environment might foster development of conservative attitudes and values relatively early in their professional socialization.

Ease of entrance into the field could also be an important factor in career selection for some students. Lanier & Little (1986) indicate that, although teacher education does attract and retain persons of high ability, the data indicate that an excessive number of low-ability students are admitted into the field. The research suggests that a similar problem exists within physical education. The relatively low admission standards might attract recruits with mediocre academic records and low test scores (Locke, 1962; Templin et al., 1982), although there is some indication that female recruits have better academic records than male recruits (Dewar, 1984). The problem of low academic ability might be compounded in physical education by a tendency toward anti-intellectualism within the field (Sage, 1980). This anti-intellectualism seems to derive from a dualistic view of human beings and the perception that physical educators deal with the body, not the mind (Hendry & Whiting, 1972).

As noted previously, female physical educators differ from their male counterparts in several ways including social class, academic ability, attitudes toward teaching and coaching, and degree of conservatism. These differences seem to derive from the complex ways in which sport and physical education relate to the social construction of gender. Interest in the relationship between sport and gender has resulted in two types of research describing the attitudes and beliefs of physical educators. One line of work has viewed women physical educators as nontraditional women and has attempted to describe how they are perceived by themselves and others. Although such research has been inconsistent with regard to the contention that women in physical education differ significantly from other women, it has indicated that women's involvement in a male-identified field could lead others to stereotype them as masculine (Lenskyj, 1986; Thompson, 1983; Widdop & Widdop, 1975). Allegations of lesbianism have been used to intimidate women in physical education and have forced a silence within the profession regarding the lives of lesbian physical educators (Cobhan, 1982; Guthrie, 1982; Woods, 1989). That silence has recently been broken by efforts to deal with homophobia within the field (Gondola, 1988; Griffin, 1989b; Whitaker, 1988).

The second area of research to beliefs and gender has been the examination of physical educators' attitudes toward gender equality. Despite the general conservatism of physical educators, recent studies indicate that a substantial number of them express support for gender equality (Duquin, Bredemeier, Oglesby, & Greendorfer, 1984; Hoferek, 1982). This support was stronger among those who identified themselves as political liberals and among women, of whom 70 percent reported having experienced gender inequity in their professional lives (Duquin et al., 1984). Although the majority of physical educators expressed support for gender equality, most expressed little interest in political activism to pursue such equity. Within the largest professional organization, men believed that women's rights are being met, whereas women were mostly undecided on the issue (Oxendine, 1987).

Although socialization researchers have studied the characteristics of physical educators, in order to understand recruitment and anticipatory socialization, scholars employing the natural science paradigm have focused on "characteristics which relate in some predictable way to an aspect of teaching performance, or the training process" (Locke, 1984, p. 23). Although advocates of behavior analysis disdain psychometric research (Siedentop, 1986), others within the natural science paradigm have attempted to relate characteristics to performance.

One area of research has been the attempt to identify predictors of success that might be used as criteria for admission or retention in a physical education program. Martens (1987) summarizes this work, saying, "studies attempting to relate GPAs (particularly high school GPAs), interviews, physical qualities, and personality ratings to potential effectiveness in teaching physical education have met with limited success" (pp. 415–416). Limitations of the research include the use of student-teaching ratings as the measure of success and the restriction of the sample to students admitted to a program. Given the difficulty of identifying valid predictors of success, Martens suggests that selective admissions procedures might communicate program philosophy and improve the image of a program, but they cannot currently identify the best prospective teachers.

Another area of research has been the attempt to relate teacher characteristics not to overall success but to specific aspects of teaching performance. Some of this research has related psychological characteristics to particular teaching behaviors (Askew, 1979; Y. R. S. Smith, 1981). Although such research extends understanding of teaching performance, the relative stability of psychological characteristics makes it of limited practical value. In contrast, physical fitness is a modifiable characteristic that has received some attention. Barker (1986), in a study of elementary school physical education teachers, found that a teacher's personal involvement in fitness activities related to the emphasis on fitness in the elementary school curriculum. A more recent study also indicated that a teacher's level of fitness could influence students' attitudes toward exercise (Melville & Maddalozzo, 1988).

In general, examination of the relationship between teacher characteristics and teacher performance has not been a particularly useful line of research. The results have provided little promise of identifying effective selection criteria or suggesting training procedures. Dewar (1989) suggests that the topic of recruitment needs to be examined from a critical perspective that raises issues about who controls and defines good physical education teaching and how those definitions influence the "process by which individuals are selected for and allocated to careers in physical education" (p. 42).

Teacher Educators

One of the difficulties in describing teacher educators is defining the population. Because teacher education programs include general–liberal studies, coursework in the student's major and minor fields, and pedagogical coursework, many university faculty can be considered teachers of teachers (Lanier & Little, 1986). The situation within physical education is further confused by the fact that the physical education department frequently delivers part or all of the pedagogical coursework for its students. Because pedagogical specialists in physical education are generally located in the same department with content specialists, there often is a blurring of the two groups.

Three studies, one a survey of a national sample of elementary and secondary specialists (Metzler & Freedman, 1985) and two interview studies of selected groups of pedagogy faculty (Mitchell & Lawson, 1986; Williamson, 1988), provide some insight into physical education teacher educators. However, caution in making generalizations seems advisable, based on the relatively low return rate in the survey study (46 percent) and the small sample size (15) in each of the other two studies.

Metzler and Freedman (1985) found that faculty who identified themselves as elementary or secondary specialists had a wide variety of duties, usually only a small portion of which were directly preprofessional. Most had public school teaching experience, and approximately two-thirds had a doctoral degree. Although two-thirds of physical education faculty were male, 56 percent of the teacher education faculty were female. The male and female samples had very different profiles. The men were more likely to have a doctoral degree (71 percent to 36 percent), to publish more, and to have higher ranks and salaries. The women were more likely to work at smaller institutions.

Many physical education programs seem to hire experienced teachers, especially women, without advanced training to serve as teacher educators. Mitchell and Lawson's study (1986) indicated that those teach courses in curriculum, instruction, or supervision frequently had no formal training for these responsibilities, even if they held the doctoral degree. Successful experience as a physical education teacher is seen as sufficient qualification for teaching pedagogy courses. Williamson (1988) found that administrators frequently assigned student-teaching supervision to fill faculty members' schedules, regardless of training or experience, a practice that seemed to undermine the value of work undertaken by faculty in teacher education.

Lawson (1983c) suggests that the absence of a distinct group of teacher educators within physical education sends students an implicit message: "There are no pedagogical specialists, nor is there an agreed-upon, shared technical culture, and consequently, one person's view of teaching is as good as another's" (p. 11). This message of the lack of a scholarly basis for teaching is reinforced by the low rates of publication among physical education teacher educators. Only 35 percent have one or more refereed publications, in contrast with 76 percent of faculty in schools of education (Metzler & Freedman, 1985). Locke (1987) notes a low level of utilization of research in teacher education programs and proposes that it reflects "a pervasive uneasiness among professors about research" (p.18).

Williamson (1988) indicates that teacher educators' attitudes toward research seem to be shaped by institutional expectations, the nature of their doctoral training, and their role expectations at the time they were hired. Most see teaching as their priority and view interaction with students as their primary source of job satisfaction. In institutions where research is encouraged, faculty express frustration, senior faculty because of changing role expectations and junior faculty because of lack of time. Low publication rates might reflect the priority that teacher educators place on teaching and the wide range of other responsibilities they carry (Rog, 1979; Williamson, 1988).

Physical education teacher educators frequently have administrative and advisement duties, and approximately one-fifth of them also coach. Combined teaching and coaching responsibilities are especially prevalent at small schools. Faculty with dual assignments, especially those who prefer coaching only, might experience role conflict (Decker, 1986). One source of this conflict seems to be contradictory expectations communicated by departmental or institutional administrators.

In addition to role conflict, involvement in coaching might also contribute to the conservatism of physical education faculty. A 1969 survey by the Carnegie Commission on Higher Education indicates that physical education faculty ranked second only to agriculture faculty in degree of conservatism (cited in Sage, 1980). In part this could be due to the almost exclusive recruitment of physical education faculty from the ranks of public school teachers of physical education. However, Kenyon (1965) notes that those pursuing graduate study in physical education are somewhat less conservative and come from slightly higher social-class backgrounds than the undergraduate population. Faculty tendencies toward conservatism might be exacerbated by the circumstances of coaching, especially the institutional demand for total accountability for team performance (Massengale, 1974).

In summary, teacher educators in physical education are generally experienced teachers with no special training in pedagogy who have a wide range of job responsibilities. Although the influence of the characteristics of teacher educators on teacher education students is uncertain, it seems likely that they would reinforce a conservative view of physical education in the schools and a craft-apprenticeship view of teacher education. The growing number of doctoral programs in physical education with specializations in teaching and teacher education might change the profile of teacher educators in the future (Lawson, 1983a; Siedentop, 1982). However, the graduates of these programs are likely to be employed in larger research universities and might have little effect on most of the 700 institutions that certify physical education teachers.

PRESERVICE TEACHER EDUCATION PROGRAMS

Although teacher education can be viewed as a lifelong process including anticipatory socialization before entering college and continuing education throughout the teaching career, much of the attention of researchers has been directed to formal teacher education programs in colleges and universities. This attention has generally been piecemeal rather than systematic and has concentrated on selected aspects of the program (e.g., student teaching) while ignoring others (Locke, 1984). This review will discuss issues and summarize research related to three areas: program content, program design, and the hidden curriculum in physical education preservice teacher education programs.

Program Content

Shulman (1987) proposes that the knowledge base for teachers include seven categories of knowledge. Four of these categories include information appropriate for all teachers, regardless of subject-matter specialty: knowledge of learners and their characteristics; knowledge of educational contexts; knowledge of educational ends, purposes, and values; and general pedagogical knowledge. Because of space limitations, this chapter will not examine these categories, other than to note that general education coursework sometimes treats these topics in ways that make the special concerns of physical educators seem invisible. For example, courses on child development often omit motor development. Discussions of the social context of the school frequently ignore the role of athletics in school culture. Such omissions reinforce the marginality of physical education and sport within education.

Shulman identifies three categories of teacher knowledge that are specific to the subject area: content knowledge, curricular knowledge, and pedagogical-content knowledge. The recently adopted accreditation guidelines developed by the American Alliance for Health, Physical Education, Recreation and Dance for use by the National Council for Accreditation of Teacher Education include requirements in three comparable categories (Alliance for Health, Physical Education, Recreation and Dance, 1987). These categories provide a useful way to examine research related to program content in physical education teacher education.

Content Knowledge. Shulman suggests that the teacher is a member of a scholarly community who needs depth of understanding of the content field:

He or she must understand the structures of subject matter, the principles of conceptual organization, and the principles of inquiry that help answer two kinds of questions in each field: What are the important ideas and skills in this domain? and How are new ideas added and deficient ones dropped by those who produce knowledge in this area? (p. 9)

Within physical education, knowledge of the content field is usually interpreted as knowledge about movement and the ability to perform movement.

Two basic value positions underlie the debate about the selection and structure of disciplinary knowledge in preservice teacher education programs. One position is that the program ought to be designed to provide a comprehensive understanding of movement phenomena (Husman, Clarke, & Kelley, 1981; Lawson & Morford, 1979; Morford, Lawson, & Hutton, 1981). The other position is that disciplinary information ought to be selected and organized on the basis of its applicability to the teaching of sports, dance, and exercise (Enberg, Harrington, & Cady, 1981; Locke, 1977; Locke, Mand, & Siedentop, 1981; Siedentop, 1977).

Within this underlying dispute have been several other points of contention, including the extent to which information from various disciplinary perspectives should be integrated (Lawson & Morford, 1979) and the relative emphasis on various areas of disciplinary study. Several scholars have decried the deemphasis on philosophical and sociocultural examinations of movement within programs dominated by emphasis on the biological and behavioral bases of performance (Bressan, 1985; Hatfield, 1984; Hollands, 1984; Miller, 1984; Rees, 1984; Sage, 1987a). Arguments for inclusion of sociocultural studies have claimed applicability to teaching and appealed to the need for comprehensive understanding.

Because these questions about program content are normative as well as pragmatic, they cannot be resolved through value-free research. However, a few related research studies might provide some understanding of the issues. The continuing emphasis on teaching in undergraduate curricula is demonstrated by the high percentage of required coursework devoted to pedagogy (33 percent), compared with that devoted to disciplinary studies (13 percent) and performance courses (11 percent) (Murphy, 1980). The emphasis on the science of movement and the deemphasis on sociocultural studies has been confirmed by Southard (1982, 1983) in a survey of the courses offered and the beliefs of program directors at 546 institutions with physical education teacher education programs. Despite the apparent programmatic emphasis on the science of movement and on pedagogy, research testing physical educators' knowledge in these areas indicates that neither experienced teachers nor graduating seniors meet standards established by experts (Kelley & Lindsay, 1977, 1980).

Several explanations are possible for this failure to master basic content knowledge, including a mismatch between the curriculum and the test and poor quality instruction in disciplinary and pedagogy courses. Another explanation might relate to the contrast that Lawson (1985a) has drawn between the knowledge systems of researchers and practitioners. He suggests that practitioners prefer not scholarly, scientific knowledge, but working knowledge that blends selectively perceived, scientific knowledge with professional ideology and experiential knowledge. The tendency of physical education teachers to rely on peers as a primary source of information reflects the importance they give to practical knowledge (Campbell, 1988). Such an interpretation views practitioners not merely as consumers to information but also as active participants in the generation of knowledge. To understand the process by which content knowledge is taught and mastered it might be necessary to investigate the process by which students "reinvent" this knowledge for their own use.

Another area of considerable debate within physical education has been the number and type of movement performance courses that should be included in the program (Lawson & Pugh, 1981). Although physical education has been described as a performance-based field comparable to art and music, the role of performance in physical education seems to have been less adequately resolved, perhaps because sport and exercise classes do not have the cloak of the fine arts to provide respectability within the university environment. For some, performance courses are an integral part of content mastery, a process Arnold (1979) describes as education in movement as well as education about movement. Within this view, physical education majors, including those who are preparing to teach, should take courses in which performance is taught for its own sake. For others, performance courses are viewed as pedagogy courses rather than content courses; that is, only students who are preparing to teach are required to take them, and the focus is on how to teach the activity rather than on the development of personal skill. Some suggest that students need both types of performance courses. None of these groups has exhibited much unanimity regarding how many courses are required, which specific activities should be covered, or what level of performance expertise should be attained. This lack of consensus regarding performance courses indicates diverse views regarding definitions of the subject matter of physical education, views that are reflected in what Shulman calls *curricular knowledge*.

Curricular Knowledge. In addition to mastery of subject-matter content, prospective teachers need to understand the development and design of educational programs. Because of the absence in school physical education of two major mechanisms for controlling the curriculum, textbooks and standardized achievement tests, considerable autonomy exists regarding curriculum development. Although some states have mandated curricular content in physical education, most of the decision-making authority seems to rest at the local level. What has emerged are numerous curricular models that compete for support of teachers as curriculum planners (Jewett & Bain, 1985; Lawson, 1988). Although recent debates have raised the issue of a national curriculum in physical education (Bain, 1986; Lawson, 1985b; Loughrey, 1987), such a development seems unlikely at present.

The choice that confronts teacher educators is whether to expose preservice teachers to a range of models as a basis for subsequent teacher choice or to select one or two models and train students to implement them thoroughly. The choice is a complex one because the various curriculum models provide differing definitions of the content and purposes of physical education and involve differing conceptions of teacher expertise needed to implement the program.

Present research gives few clues as to which of these practices is more common or to the comparative effects of each approach. Several studies have examined the beliefs of university physical education faculty regarding the goals of physical education (Gordon, Thompson, & Alspaugh, 1973; LaPlante & Jewett, 1987; Rosentswieg, 1969; Speakman-Yearta, 1987), but this research has not examined endorsement of a specific curriculum model. More recent research suggests that beliefs about curriculum models are multidimensional rather than unidimensional; that is, faculty adopt an eclectic position in which they support part of several curriculum models (Caldwell, 1986; Caldwell & Bain, 1985).

Another way to examine present practice is through content analysis of textbooks. Barrett (1988) classified elementary school physical education textbooks published from 1917 to 1986 and found that they could be categorized in three groups, based on their treatment of subject matter. What this study suggests is that the selection of a textbook is likely to provide exposure to one view of curriculum but not to competing models. However, a few fairly recent textbooks have provided an overview of a range of curriculum models (Jewett & Bain, 1985; Lawson & Placek, 1981; Siedentop, Mand, & Taggart, 1986). Future research might examine whether this suggests a shift in the way in which curricular knowledge is viewed by teacher educators and presented to their students.

Pedagogical-Content Knowledge. Shulman (1987) describes pedagogical-content knowledge as "the capacity of a teacher to transform the content knowledge he or she possesses into forms that are pedagogically powerful and yet adaptive to the variations in ability and background presented by the students" (p. 15). Pedagogical-content knowledge seems to comprise the "shared technical culture" discussed in the teacher socialization literature (Lawson, 1983c; Lortie, 1975). Several forms of research have contributed to the identification of this technical culture. Research on teaching effectiveness has attempted to identify those teacher behaviors related to student achievement. However, Shulman (1987) notes that "Because the search has focused on generic relationships—teacher behaviors associated with student academic gains irrespective of subject matter or grade level—the findings have been much more closely connected with the management of classrooms than with the subtleties of content pedagogy" (p. 10). Another important source of knowledge has been descriptions of "the wisdom of practice" (p. 11).

Within physical education, approaches to the identification of pedagogical skills needed by prospective teachers have included research describing factors influencing the acquisition of motor skills, research on teaching effectiveness (Pieron, 1986), surveys of various groups to describe their perceptions of needed competencies (Hendry, 1972, 1975a; Kane, 1975; Weber, 1977), and interviews with or observations of distinctive teachers (Earls, 1981; Siedentop, 1989). A number of generic managerial and teaching skills seem applicable to physical education (Siedentop, 1983a). In addition, two aspects of pedagogical-content knowledge have received some attention: the design of learning tasks and observation/analysis of movement.

One aspect of pedagogical-content knowledge is the ability to design appropriate learning tasks for students. Until recently, research provided little assistance in preparing teachers for this responsibility. Much of the motor learning research on conditions of practice was of limited usefulness to teachers. Early research on teaching physical education focused primarily on the process, not the content, frequently failing even to identify the subject matter taught (Pieron, 1986; Vickers, 1987). Much attention was given to the amount of time on task provided for students, with little attention to the nature of those tasks (Dodds & Rife, 1983). However, more recent work has begun to describe the characteristics of the learning task and its impact on students (K. C. Graham, 1987; Rink & Werner, 1987; Tousignant & Siedentop, 1983). Although information about the nature of learning tasks is expanding, relatively little is known about how to prepare teachers to design appropriate tasks.

Instructional planning is often assumed to be the basis for effective task design, and practice in instructional planning is generally a major part of teacher education programs. Nevertheless, research indicates that physical education teachers do relatively little planning and that what planning they do focuses on activities rather than on learning outcomes (Placek, 1984). The model of planning used by teachers focuses on management and differs from the model emphasizing learning presented in teacher education programs (Goc-Karp & Zakrajsek, 1987). However, a study of seven effective elementary physical education teachers indicated that all prepared written plans focused on student learning; the major difference that emerged among the teachers was that more experienced teachers felt less dependent on written plans (Stroot & Morton, 1989). Research in laboratory settings indicates that experienced teachers use a wider range of instructional strategies aimed as skill acquisition than do novices (Housner & Griffey, 1985) and that planning practices of novice teachers relate to their teaching behaviors (Imwold et al., 1984; Twardy & Yerg, 1987). The research seems to indicate that teachers can develop expertise in planning and conducting physical education classes (Siedentop & Eldar, 1989). What is unclear from the research is whether practice in instructional planning is an effective procedure for teaching the design of learning tasks.

One aspect of instructional planning that has received considerable attention is the analysis of movement. Several comprehensive systems for movement analysis have been proposed (Barrett, 1985; Broer & Zernicke, 1979; Rink, 1985; Vickers, 1983). The assumption is that the training of teachers to use a comprehensive analysis system will improve their ability to design learning tasks, to observe movement performance, and to provide feedback to students. Limited research has examined these assumptions, but modest improvements in perception and diagnosis of selected skills through instruction in an analysis system have been replicated (Beveridge & Gangstead, 1988; Gangstead & Beveridge, 1984). However, the results leave unresolved the issue of whether training in a generic analysis system or in analysis of specific skills is more effective.

A number of studies examining proficiency in observation and analysis of movement have been reviewed by Armstrong (1986) and S. J. Hoffman (1983). Of interest to teacher educators is the role of training and experience in developing such expertise. Two types of experience have been presumed to be related to analytic skill: performance experience and teaching experience. Contradictory results have been obtained in research relating performance skill and movement analysis ability (Armstrong, 1986; Drummond, 1988; Vickers, 1986). Teaching experience has generally related positively to analytic proficiency. Evidence seems to indicate that it is experience teaching the specific skills, not overall teaching experience, that is important, but some conflicting results have been found (DeDeyn, 1987). Specialized training in movement analysis has produced improvements (F. I. Bell, 1987; Francis, 1986; Halverson, 1988; Kniffin, 1986; Wilkinson, 1986), but such an approach has not been compared with training in a generic analysis system.

Laboratory research on observation and analysis of movement does not address the issue of how well such skills transfer to the field setting. Barrett (1977, 1979, 1983) proposes a model for training teachers to observe in field settings, and she and her colleagues have done a series of studies examining what preservice teachers observe during early field experiences (Allison, 1987; Barrett, Allison, & Bell, 1987; R. Bell, Barrett, & Allison, 1985). Their studies indicate that, as students progress through a teacher education program emphasizing analysis of movement, they shift from noticing personal characteristics of students to focusing on observation of movement responses, although their later responses continue to include little attention to details of movement. These results seem consistent with Housner and Griffey's (1985) finding that experienced teachers focused more attention on individual student performance than did novices. What remains unknown is what combination of training and experience is needed to provide teachers and coaches with necessary observation and analysis skills.

Program Design

In addition to identifying the content of the program, teacher educators must make decisions about how that content will be organized and delivered to students. Several different models for the design of preservice teacher education programs have been proposed (H. A. Hoffman & Rink, 1985; Lawson, 1981). However, little research has examined the effectiveness of these various models. In part, this is because of the complexity of developing effective procedures for data-based program evaluation (Hawkins, Wiegand, & Bahneman, 1983). Examination of the program as a whole could also fail to identify those components contributing to its effectiveness. In addition, research related to a specific program could be difficult to generalize to other situations (McBride, 1984a; Paese, 1985). This might particularly be the case if the theoretical position underlying the program were unclear.

One theoretical basis for programs that has received some attention within physical education is the teacher concerns model developed by Fuller (1970). Fuller suggests that, as teachers develop, their concerns shift from those about personal survival (self) to those about teaching (task), to those about student learning (impact). She recommends that the teacher education program be organized so as to treat these concerns sequentially. Research on physical education preservice and inservice teachers has indicated that they differ from teachers in other areas, exhibiting less concern about impact on student learning (Boggess, McBride, & Griffey, 1985; McBride, Boggess, & Griffey, 1986; Wendt, Bain, & Jackson, 1981). Longitudinal research has indicated changes in concerns during the teacher education program, but the results have been conflicting (Boggess et al., 1985; Wendt & Bain, 1989; Wendt et al., 1981). At this point, the implications of concerns research for program design are unclear.

The apparent absence of concern for student learning among some physical education teachers has also been reflected in research on teacher planning (Placek, 1983). This has led some scholars to suggest that the development of teacher commitment to learning could be the central criterion for overall program success (Locke et al., 1981; Templin, 1985). George Graham (1987) used this criterion to identify three high-impact teacher education programs that he describes as sharing the following characteristics: (a) the faculty share a common view of program outcomes; (b) the students are provided with carefully structured teaching experiences designed to help them acquire "procedural knowledge" (Berliner, 1985); (c) the team of cooperating teachers in the schools are adherents of the model of physical education espoused at the university; and (d) the faculty spend considerable time working with students in laboratory experiences.

G. M. Graham's analysis highlights the central role assigned to laboratory and field experiences in physical education teacher education programs. A national survey revealed that 86 percent of such programs require field experiences before student teaching, with an average requirement of 68 hours (Placek & Silverman, 1983). However, the survey indicates that a small proportion of this time is spent teaching. Relatively little information is available regarding the effects of laboratory and early field experiences. A few studies examining microteaching in physical education indicate that it seems to be an effective means for teaching some teaching skills (G. M. Graham, 1973; Legos, 1978; M. S. Taylor, 1978). A case study of changes in teaching behaviors across a 2-year sequence of field experiences found that preservice teachers achieved high levels of desirable behaviors in their first teaching experiences (Gusthart & Rink, 1983). As students progressed to more complex teaching environments, some of these behaviors decreased, although the students maintained higher levels than have been reported for practicing teachers. The primary improvement was an increase in the ability to modify tasks for individuals within a group-instruction setting.

Although early field experiences have received little attention from researchers, student teaching has been the focus of much research within physical education (Dodds, 1985b, 1989; Locke, 1984). A growing body of work has examined student teaching as a socialization experience (Arrighi & Young, 1987; Schempp, 1983, 1985, 1986; Templin, 1979, 1981). During student teaching, students seem to become more concerned with control and discipline and to feel less responsible for student learning. The primary socializing agents during student teaching are the cooperating teacher and the students being taught. The university supervisor appears to be less influential because of the limited time spent in the setting and because the cooperating teacher and student teacher seem to have different perceptions and expectations than the supervisor (Gallemore, 1981; McBride, 1984b).

Several studies have explored the dynamics of the socialization process by describing the interactions among student teachers, cooperating teachers, and students. This research suggests that the student teacher attempts to mirror many of the behaviors of the cooperating teacher, perhaps because these practices seem to work with students in the local context (Embrey, 1987; Tinning & Siedentop, 1985). The influence of the cooperating teacher seems to be somewhat indirect, relying on tasks that are partially explicit and informal accountability mechanisms (Tinning & Siedentop, 1985). Perhaps because of lack of training in the supervisory process, cooperating teachers seem to provide minimal supervision of student teachers (Tannehill & Zakrajsek, 1988). Marrs and Templin (1983) suggest that the student teacher is not the passive recipient of values and behaviors but that the process of socialization involves a complex dialectical process. They conclude that "student teachers made conscious decisions about those cooperating teacher traits and behaviors that they chose to emulate, as well as those that they chose to ignore or reject" (p. 124).

Because of concerns about the effects of student teaching, some researchers have examined the effectiveness of various interventions during field experiences. One line of research has examined the effects of training teacher education students to use a systematic observation instrument, then using that instrument to provide feedback about teaching (Mancini, Wuest, & van der Mars, 1985). Such an approach has been an effective means of changing selected teaching behaviors. One aspect of the process that might need additional study is the type of suggestions for improvement that need to accompany the quantitative feedback (Hawkins, Wiegand, & Landin, 1985; Landin, Hawkins, & Wiegand, 1986). A second line of research has been the application of behavior analysis principles to the supervision of field experiences (Ocansey, 1988; Siedentop, 1981, 1986). Selected behaviors are targeted for change, and an intervention consisting of goals, explanatory materials, regular observation, feedback, and graphing is provided. Such interventions have been successful in producing changes in the targeted behaviors, and evidence indicates that university supervisors, cooperating teachers, peers, or students themselves can be trained to serve as change agents.

The question that remains is whether skills attained through field experiences are sustained after completion of the program. A number of factors seem to influence the transfer of skills from training to practice, including degree of initial mastery, context, and trainee acceptance or rejection of skills (Locke, 1984). Siedentop (1986) notes that behavioral and developmental theories make different assumptions regarding this problem. The developmental perspective assumes that what needs to be modified is some "inner essence which, once changed, is permanent" and that is reflected in behavior (pp. 12 to 13). The behavioral perspective assumes that generalization from training program to workplace requires bringing the behavior under the control of contingencies that will continue to be present in the workplace and that support the desired behavior. Neither the behavior analysis nor the socialization perspective seems to have resolved this issue.

It should be noted that many physical education programs seem to assume that one training program will prepare students to teach and to coach. Chu (1980, 1984) found that, despite high interest in coaching and perceived differences in the two roles, a low percentage of coursework relates specifically to coaching. He suggests that existing programs provide inadequate preparation for coaching but that the incorporation of coaching within physical education enables the field to draw students and resources without risking academic opposition by aligning openly with athletics.

Hidden Curriculum

The term *hidden curriculum* has been used in curriculum literature to refer to those aspects of schooling that are not part of the formal, explicit curriculum but that have an effect on students. The concept of the hidden curriculum has been used in physical education to analyze what occurs in schools (Bain, 1975, 1985b; Dodds, 1983) and in teacher education programs (Bain, 1985a; Dodds, 1985a). The hidden curriculum encompasses tacit messages associated with the rituals and routines of the program. One effect of research on the hidden curriculum is to raise these tacit meanings to a level of consciousness that permits their examination.

Analysis of program design is one way of studying the hidden curriculum. The ways in which teacher education programs are organized and conducted communicate a view of what knowledge is worth learning and of the characteristics of knowledge itself. Within physical education, the separation of theory and performance courses could be reinforcing a dualistic view of objective and subjective forms of knowing (Bain, 1985a). The labeling of courses as "motor learning and performance" employs a metaphor that compares the body to a machine (Charles, 1979; Lawson, 1984). Program design might also be communicating messages about the profession of teaching. The low priority that teacher education faculty give to research (Metzler & Freedman, 1985) might give the impression that research on teaching has little value for practice. The tendency to view the teaching of university faculty as an individual responsibility (Rog, 1979) could be reinforcing the perception of teaching as a career marked by isolation. The absence of specific training for coaching and the general lack of certification requirements for coaches (Sisley & Wiese, 1987) might be indicating that athletic experience is more important than professional training and expertise.

Physical education programs probably also communicate messages about social relationships. Although the sex segregation of physical education teacher education programs is now

gone, remnants remain of the pervasive sexism on which it was based. Areas traditionally associated with and taught by women, such as dance and elementary physical education, often are given only a peripheral role in the program. As in the university at large, women in physical education are frequently concentrated in the lower ranks and in the social sciences and methods courses. Racism is also a concern within the field of physical education. Blacks are highly visible as varsity athletes on most campuses but are conspicuously absent from the ranks for the professoriate in physical education (Pierro, 1975). Physical education departments and athletic programs often have an uneasy partnership that permits athletes majoring in physical education to stay eligible but not to graduate, a partnership that is clearly visible to students in teacher education programs. This compromise does not allow students with inadequate preparation to become certified to teach, but it often makes physical education a party to the exploitation of athletes, many of whom are black (Edwards, 1984).

Analysis of program design and demographics might provide some insight into the hidden curriculum, but such an approach runs the risk of providing an overly deterministic view of the process. This risk can be avoided by studying the lived culture of the teacher education program in order to examine how experiences are interpreted and meanings are negotiated within the program. Some recent research has used qualitative studies to examine students' experiences in physical education teacher education programs.

Several studies that focused on descriptions of the student-teaching experience seemed to indicate that student teachers were strongly influenced by the values and behaviors of cooperating teachers (Embrey, 1987; Templin, 1979; Tinning & Siedentop, 1985). Research examining physical education courses taken earlier in the program suggests that faculty and students have different perceptions of useful knowledge (Placek, 1985) and that students might focus more on completing course and program requirements than on becoming professionals (Steen, 1989). Graber (1989) found that teacher education students engaged in "studentship" behaviors such as shortcutting, cheating, colluding, and image projection to respond to the demands of the teacher education program. Such studentship behaviors enabled them to attain some control over their lives as students, a role much more immediate than their future role as teachers.

The research also suggests that students are powerfully presocialized by their past experiences in physical education and sport and that they use these experiences to accept or reject their training experiences selectively (Schempp, 1989). A teacher education program employing a personalized instruction system found that the shift in needed study habits and the absence of peer comparisons made some students resistant to the program (Tousignant & Brunelle, 1987). An effort to involve students in reflection about teaching found that few students actively resisted and that most acquiesced to the requirement to keep a journal, but only a few students were committed to the process of reflection (Gore, in press).

Dewar's (1987) study of the social construction of gender in a physical education program suggests that both program organization and structure and student's past experiences influence student reactions to the program. She found that program emphasis on applied knowledge useful in improving performance led students to value technical information in biological and behavioral courses and to question the value of socio-cultural courses that encouraged critical reflection on issues such as gender. Student responses to gender issues were also based on the ways in which they created and expressed their gender identities. The study indicates that the social construction of meaning involves a complex process in which students receive contradictory messages and both accommodate and resist the dominant cultural view. Research related to the hidden curriculum in teacher education requires examination of the implicit messages communicated by the program and of students' responses to those messages.

INSERVICE TEACHER EDUCATION

Preservice teacher education programs have received the most attention from researchers, but the process of teacher education continues throughout the teacher's career. Lawson (1983c) notes that occupational socialization includes both professional socialization, through which teachers learn the norms and practices of the profession, and bureaucratic socialization, which teaches them the rules and expectations of the school as an organization. The primary focus of preservice teacher education, with the possible exception of student teaching, is on professional socialization. Although some attention is given to the acquisition of professional skills in inservice education, a major component of the socialization process for the inservice teacher appears to be bureaucratic socialization. Learning to deal with the organizational realities of the school seems to be the primary task in the first few years of teaching, a period frequently labeled *the induction phase*.

Induction

The term *induction* can be used to describe the entire process by which the novice is brought into the profession (Lawson, 1983c). More frequently it is used to describe entry into the workplace, a use that may reflect the importance of bureaucratic socialization in learning to teach. A major task of new teachers is to learn the organizational culture of the school, which consists "primarily of deeply embedded assumptions, which are accepted and professed by veteran and powerful school personnel, about the school and its functions" (Lawson, 1989, p. 152). Little research has examined how this process occurs, but evidence seems to suggest that new teachers experience a reality shock as they move into their first teaching positions (Earls, 1981).

Many aspects of the instructional setting contribute to this reality shock, a number of which seem to be unique to physical education. The lack of adequate facilities and equipment, the large class sizes, and the lack of time for instruction are common problems (Locke & Griffin, 1986) that might reflect the lack of public support for physical education (Dodds & Locke,

1984) and its marginal status in the school (L. Bell, 1986; Hendry, 1975a). Teachers in inner-city schools often have particularly difficult teaching conditions in addition to dealing with multiracial student populations for which they have been inadequately prepared (Griffin, 1985b; Holmen & Parkhouse, 1981; Locke & Griffin, 1986; Parkhouse & Holmen, 1980). The expectation that most physical educators will coach results in heavy time demands and frequently interferes with teaching responsibilities (Chu, 1980; Earls, 1981; Sage, 1989). Physical education teachers are often isolated from other teachers, and receive little professional support or assistance (Griffin, 1985b; Locke & Griffin, 1986).

Perhaps because of this isolation, students seem to be a major socializing influence on the physical education teacher. Teachers base their planning on the selection of activities that will produce high levels of student involvement and enjoyment and low levels of student misbehavior (Goc-Karp & Zakrajsek, 1987; Placek, 1984; Templin, 1981) and judge their success as teachers on the basis of positive student responses (Arrighi, 1983; Earls, 1981; Placek, 1983; Placek & Dodds, 1988). The result seems to be that physical education teachers place relatively little emphasis on student achievement (Bain, 1976, 1978; Veal, 1988a) and conduct programs that do not reflect instructional practices recommended in the professional literature (Kneer, 1986). However, Veal (1988b) notes that the apparent deemphasis on achievement might not indicate that teachers do not care about learning but that they feel that student participation and effort are the only aspects of the learning process over which they have control.

Programs to assist new teachers with the transition to the workplace have been initiated in recent years (Bolam, 1987; Brooks, 1987). Although evidence regarding the effectiveness of induction programs is not conclusive and the high cost of such programs is an issue, many new programs are being initiated. Despite expressions of concern regarding the problems confronting beginning physical education teachers (Bain & Wendt, 1983a; Locke, 1979), no research examining the effectiveness of programs to assist new teachers has been conducted.

Inservice Programs

Although induction programs to assist beginning teachers are relatively new, inservice education programs designed to improve the effectiveness of teachers are a common practice in school systems. However, inservice activities are generally viewed as ineffective, and much of the research on inservice education has lacked an adequate theoretical foundation. Eraut (1987) describes four paradigms for inservice education that underly practice and research: (a) the defect approach, which attempts to improve effectiveness by using behavioral training to build skills that teachers lack; (b) the growth approach, which assumes that the purpose of inservice is not to repair inadequacy but to seek greater teacher fulfillment, primarily through reflection on experience; (c) a problem-solving approach, which uses inservice to address problems diagnosed by teachers; and (d) the change paradigm, which employs inservice education as a means to modify the educational system in response to changes in the larger society, changes not necessarily desired by all teachers. Although much of the research related to physical education inservice education has not consciously employed one of these paradigms, the categories provide a useful heuristic for reviewing the research.

Research on skill building with inservice physical education teachers has employed many of the same techniques as have been used with student teachers. Behavior analysis and systematic feedback have been used to change targeted teacher behaviors (Borys, 1986; Cusimano, 1987; Mancini, Clark, & Wuest, 1987; Ratliffe, 1986), and at least one study indicated that such changes are sustained over time (Mancini et al., 1987). Because intervention by an outside trainer is not always practical, some attention has been given to documenting the effectiveness of self-assessment techniques (Cusimano, 1987) and of observation and feedback by the school principal (Ratliffe, 1986, 1988). Intervention programs employing techniques other than systematic feedback also have been effective in changing targeted teacher behaviors such as teaching styles (Brockmeyer, 1987; Countiss, 1976).

In general, the research has indicated that inservice education that attempts to develop specific skills can effectively do so. However, a few studies have raised some issues about the effectiveness of this approach. Two studies attempting to increase student academic learning time (ALT-PE) by training teachers found that ALT-PE seemed to be more affected by the future nature of the activity than by teacher behaviors (Beamer, 1983; Whaley, 1980). Another study employing interaction analysis to change behaviors of teachers working with handicapped students concluded that "knowledge of results may not bring about change where there is resistance" (Gaudet, 1982).

A second category of research on inservice education in physical education combines the growth and problem-solving perspectives. Some of this research has attempted to identify teachers' perceptions of their inservice education needs (Earls, 1981; Oliver, 1987) and the factors influencing their professional development (Chandler, Lane, Bibik, & Oliver, 1988; Oliver, Bibik, Chandler, & Lane, 1988). Examples of inservice programs based on the growth and problem-solving approaches include the program-development networks initiated by Teachers College, Columbia University (Anderson, 1982, 1987, 1988) and by the University of Massachusetts (Griffin & Hutchinson, 1988). Projects conducted by these centers have demonstrated the effectiveness of teacher-initiated program-improvement efforts in solving technical problems identified by teachers (Schwager, 1986; Schwager & Doolittle, 1988).

The third area of inservice research deals with programs designed to bring about change in response to the societal circumstances. Perhaps the most visible efforts within physical education have been inservice education programs to promote equity, particularly sex equity (L. A. Bell, 1983; Dodds, 1982, 1986; Dunbar & O'Sullivan, 1986; Griffin, 1985a). Other examples include efforts to implement mainstreaming of handicapped children (Knowles, 1981; Knowles & Hord, 1981) and to promote major curricular change (Faucette, 1987; Faucette & Graham, 1986; Kirk, 1986b). This research indicates that inservice as a means to change is a complex process affected by the concerns of teachers and the social context of the school. Although specific examples of successful change efforts have been described, existing practice in physical education seems generally resistant to change.

Developing effective programs of inservice education requires an understanding of the career patterns of physical education teachers, including changes in teachers' beliefs and behaviors and the factors affecting career decisions (Boggess, 1986; Earls, 1981; Largey, 1981). Recent work indicates that the marginal status of physical education has a negative effect on teachers' career satisfaction (Evans, 1988; O'Sullivan, Stroot, & Tannehill, 1989; Templin, 1989). The decline of physical ability with age is also of concern to physical education teachers (Sikes, 1988). Many experienced teachers seek to leave physical education, although their ability to do so may be limited by others' view of them as nonacademic and, for women, by their gender (Evans & Williams, 1989). Little is known about how to help teachers deal with these problems and how to sustain teacher commitment and competence throughout a career.

SUMMARY AND IMPLICATIONS

In a recent analysis of physical education teacher education, Locke and Dodds (1984) conclude that "the condition of physical education in the public schools demonstrates the existence of serious problems in preparing teachers" (p. 92). They recognize that teacher education programs are not solely accountable for the problems in school physical education, but they suggest that teacher educators must assume some to the responsibility. Zeichner and Tabachnick (1981) summarize three views on the relative influence of schools and universities in the socialization of teachers. The prevailing view is that universities have a liberalizing effect on prospective teachers, but these progressive or liberal attitudes are "washed out" by school experience. An alternative view is that prospective teachers are socialized primarily through the internalization of beliefs based on observation of teachers before entering college and that teacher education has little, if any, effect on them. The third possibility is that teacher education institutions encourage students to affirm liberal slogans but that both universities and schools expose students to inherently conservative educational practice. Present evidence does not provide a conclusive answer to this issue, but physical education research seems to indicate that precollege experiences constitute a powerful socialization experience and that teacher education programs do little to modify students' perceptions of the profession. The research also suggests that the marginal status of physical education has a pervasive effect on recruitment and socialization of teachers, as well as on their job performance.

Programmatic Implications

The behavior analysis scholars attribute the ineffectiveness of teacher education programs to the absence of systematic training procedures to provide teachers with specific teaching skills (Locke, et al., 1981; Locke & Siedentop, 1980; Siedentop, 1985, 1986). They suggest that the usual lecture/discussion and field-experience approach is a weak treatment that enables prospective teachers to talk about teaching but does not help them to acquire or use teaching skills. Siedentop (1986) concludes that a number of training strategies have been demonstrated to be effective, given sufficient specificity and appropriate contingencies. A teacher education program incorporating these principles has been implemented at the Ohio State University (Taggart, 1988). However, despite a growing body of research based on the behavior analysis paradigm, the technical-training approach to physical education teacher education programs has not been widely implemented. Several reasons have been suggested including cost, inability of faculty to conduct such a program, and incompatibility of such a training program with the values and norms of the university. Siedentop (1985) suggests that, if universities cannot or will not develop effective training programs, the professional preparation of teachers might eventually move out of the universities and into the schools.

The occupational socialization perspective acknowledges the importance of acquiring teaching skills but sees them as part of a shared technical culture that includes knowledge, values, and skills (Lawson 1983b, 1983c, 1986). The role of the teacher education program is to identify and convey the shared technical culture and a professional ideology and to perform a gatekeeping function for entry into the profession. Lawson (1986, 1989) suggests that the absence of a shared technical culture has created problems for school physical education and teacher education and that improved teacher education programs require more uniform professional beliefs among physical educators. He recommends a model of teacher education that combines technical training of skills with a deliberative orientation that helps teachers define, as well as solve problems (Lawson, 1983a, 1984, 1986). He argues that this model will increase the professional competence and status of physical education teachers (Lawson, 1979, 1980, 1984).

A few physical educators have extended the notion of teacher deliberation to a call for critical inquiry as the basis for physical education practice and teacher education (Bain, 1988; Evans, 1986; Kirk, 1986a, 1989; Tinning, 1987, 1988). This approach emphasizes the political and ethical dimensions of teaching and sees teacher education as a process of critical reflection on the teaching act. Preservice and inservice teachers are involved in action research in which they attempt to improve educational practice through analysis, dialogue, and strategic action. This is combined with program components intended to help teachers "move beyond commonsense categories of thought in order to gain critical insight into the process of schooling" (Kirk, 1986a, p. 236). To date, a limited amount of research, primarily conducted in England and Australia, has described action research and critical inquiry in physical education (Almond & Thorpe, 1988; Evans, 1986;

Martinek & Butt, 1988; Schempp & Martinek, 1988; Tinning, 1987, 1988).

Research Implications

Future research related to physical education teacher education will continue to derive from the behavioral analysis, occupational socialization, and critical theory perspectives. The behavior analysis research will focus on training for more complex skills and on the maintenance and appropriate use of previously acquired skills (Siedentop, 1986; Siedentop & Eldar, 1989). The identification of complex teaching skills will emerge from research on teaching that is reexamining relationships between teaching behaviors and student responses (Godbout, Brunelle, & Tousignant, 1987; Rink & Werner, 1987). The teacher education research will examine what training techniques are needed to develop more complex skills and the ability to discriminate when to use them. The research on maintenance of skills will attempt to identify contingencies in the workplace that can be used to maintain teaching skills developed in the teacher education program. Specifically, the concern seems to be "to bring teacher behavior under the control of certain student behaviors rather than others, to have teacher behavior controlled by signs of academic progress among students" (Siedentop, 1986; p. 13).

Although the socialization researchers employ a different theoretical perspective, they too are concerned with understanding how the teacher education program can affect the practice of teachers. One focus of future research will be understanding how the subjective warrant is formed, how it changes during preservice education, and how it relates to a teacher's job performance. A second area that requires attention is the process of bureaucratic socialization that occurs upon entry into the workplace, with particular attention to how conflicts between professional and bureaucratic socialization are resolved. A third area that has received little attention but has important implications for inservice education is the examination of the career patterns of physical educators.

An increase in the use of qualitative research methods to study teacher education seems likely (Locke, 1986). The publication of tutorial information about qualitative methods in the *Journal of Teaching in Physical Education* (Earls, 1986) and in the *Research Quarterly for Exercise and Sport* (Locke, 1989) is an indication of the increasing use of these techniques in physical education. Qualitative methods are especially appropriate for socialization research that attempts to describe beliefs as well as behaviors. Naturalistic studies of how teacher education faculty and students interpret their experiences in teacher education programs seem particularly promising. Although behaviorists predominantly use quantitative research techniques, they might employ qualitative techniques in the theory-development stage to lead to identification of behaviorally oriented concepts and propositions that are testable and predictable. Qualitative methods have proven useful in exploring contingencies that control teacher and student behavior in school settings (Tinning & Siedentop, 1985; Tousignant & Siedentop, 1983).

Those scholars interested in critical theory also employ qualitative research methods, but with the assumption that research is a value-based, not a value-free, activity (Bain & Jewett, 1987). The purpose of critical science is to understand the patterns of belief and social conditions that restrict human action and to not only describe the world but also change it (Popkewitz, 1984). A goal of the research is to empower those being researched, that is, to provide them with the insight necessary to demystify and critique their own social circumstances and to choose actions to improve their lives (Lather, 1986). Because of the emphasis on empowerment within critical research and the use of action research as a pedagogical strategy, there is an interactive relationship between critical research and critical pedagogy. S. J. Smith (1982) argues that the strong behaviorist orientation of pedagogical research in physical education constitutes a hidden curriculum that works against the development of a critical pedagogy in physical education teacher education. He suggests that deterministic research denies human beings the fact of consciousness and the possibility of acting in a transformative capacity. Some would argue that the presumed value neutrality of behaviorist and socialization research limits its ability to do more than describe the status quo. Critical theory responds to this criticism by making value commitments explicit.

The issue of value positions seems important in a field of scholarship in which the improvement of practice is seen as a central commitment (Siedentop, 1983b). Such a commitment presumes a view of quality physical education. Crum (1986) suggests that researchers who wish to contribute to the improvement of pedagogical practice should address three research tasks:

1. The hermeneutic research task—dealing with the ideological clarification of the relationship between fundamental conceptions, sports education objectives, and criteria for the quality of sport pedagogy;
2. The descriptive-explanatory research task—dealing with the description and explanation of the empirical relationships between actual presage, process, product, and context variables of sport pedagogy;
3. The constructive research task—dealing with design, controlled implementation, and evaluation of sport pedagogical improvements. (p.215)

His analysis of sport pedagogy literature indicates that North American scholars tend to neglect the hermeneutic research task, an absence that obscures the theoretical basis of the empirical research. Hawkins (1987) concurs with the need for hermeneutics but suggests that, rather than the focus on clarification, criticism and debate of competing value positions should be the purpose. Although it is doubtful and perhaps undesirable that attention to the hermeneutic task would produce the "uniform professional orientations" Lawson recommends (1986; p. 113), the process of explaining and defending the assumptions and values underlying teacher education research and programs can serve to sharpen and strengthen the available alternatives.

References

American Alliance for Health, Physical Education, Recreation and Dance. (1987). *Physical Education NCATE Guidelines*. Reston, VA: Author.

Allison, P. C. (1987). What and how preservice physical education teachers observe during an early field experience. *Research Quarterly for Exercise and Sport, 58*(3), 242–249.

Almond, L., & Thorpe, R. (1988). Asking teachers to research. *Journal of Teaching in Physical Education, 7*(3),221–227.

Anderson, W. G. (1982). Working with inservice teachers: Suggestions for teacher educators. *Journal of Teaching in Physical Education, 1*(3), 15–21.

Anderson, W. G. (1987). Five years of program development: A retrospective. In G. T. Barrette, F. W. Feingold, C. R. Rees, & M. Pieron (Eds.), *Myths, models, & methods in sport pedagogy* (pp. 123–134). Champaign, IL: Human Kinetics.

Anderson, W. G. (1988). A school-centered collaborative model for program development. *Journal of Teaching in Physical Education, 7*(3), 176–183.

Armstrong, C. W. (1986). Research on movement analysis: Implications for the development of pedagogical competence. In M. Pieron & G. Graham (Eds.), *Sport pedagogy* (pp. 27–32). Champaign, IL: Human Kinetics.

Arnold, P. J. (1979). *Meaning in movement, sport and physical education*. London: Heinemann.

Arrighi, M. A. (1983). Physical education teachers' perceptions of their own success. In A. E. Jewett, M. M. Carnes, & M. Speakman (Eds.), *Proceedings of the third conference on curriculum theory in physical education*. (pp. 183–197). Athens, GA: University of Georgia.

Arrighi, M. A., & Young, J. C. (1987). Teacher perceptions about effective and successful teaching. *Journal of Teaching in Physical Education, 6*(2), 122–135.

Askew, J. A. (1979). A technique for identifying educational beliefs of preservice physical educators relative to student decision-making. *Dissertation Abstracts International, 39*, 4117A.

Bain, L. L. (1975). The hidden curriculum in physical education. *Quest, 24*, 92–101.

Bain, L. L. (1976). Description of the hidden curriculum in secondary physical education. *Research Quarterly, 47*(2), 154–160.

Bain, L. L. (1978). Differences in values implicit in teaching and coaching behaviors. *Research Quarterly, 49*(1), 5–11.

Bain, L. L. (1983). Teacher/coach role conflict: Factors influencing role performance. In T. J. Templin & J. K. Olson (Eds.), *Teaching in physical education* (pp. 94–101). Champaign, IL: Human Kinetics.

Bain, L. L. (1985a). The hidden curriculum in teacher education. In H. A. Hoffman & J. E. Rink (Eds.), *Physical education professional preparation: Insights and foresights* (pp. 132–142). Reston, VA: American Alliance for Health, Physical Education, Recreation and Dance.

Bain, L. L. (1985b). The hidden curriculum re-examined. *Quest, 37*(2), 145–153.

Bain, L. L. (1986, April). Risks of a national curriculum. Paper presented at the annual convention of the American Alliance for Health, Physical Education, Recreation and Dance, Cincinnati. (ERIC Document Reproduction Service No. ED 273 601)

Bain, L. L. (1988). Curriculum for critical reflection in physical education. In R. S. Brandt (Ed.), *Content of the curriculum*. Alexandria, VA: Association for Supervision and Curriculum Development.

Bain, L. L. (1989). Interpretive and critical research in sport and physical education. *Research Quarterly for Exercise and Sport, 60*(1), 21–24.

Bain, L. L., & Jewett, A. E. (1987). Future research and theory-building. *Journal of Teaching in Physical Education, 6*(3), 346–364.

Bain, L. L., & Wendt, J. C. (1983a). *Transition to teaching: A guide for the beginning teacher*. Reston, VA: American Alliance for Health, Physical Education, Recreation and Dance.

Bain, L. L., & Wendt, J. C. (1983b). Undergraduate physical education majors' perceptions of the roles of teacher and coach. *Research Quarterly for Exercise and Sport, 54*(2), 112–118.

Barker, W. A. (1986). The effect of teacher knowledge, involvement, and beliefs on content decisions of physical education teachers. *Dissertation Abstracts International, 47*, 2075A.

Barrett, K. R. (1977). We see so much but perceive so little: Why? In L. I. Gedvilas & M. E. Kneer (Eds.), *Proceedings of the NAPECW/NCPEAM national conference* (pp. 180–190). Chicago: University of Illinois at Chicago Circle.

Barrett, K. R. (1979). Observation of movement for teachers: A synthesis and implications. *Motor Skills: Theory Into Practice, 3*(2), 67–76.

Barrett, K. R. (1983). A hypothetical model of observing as a teaching skill. *Journal of Teaching in Physical Education, 3*(1), 22–31.

Barrett, K. R. (1985). The content of an elementary school physical education program and its impact on teacher preparation. In H. A. Hoffman & J. E. Rink (Eds.), *Physical education professional preparation: Insights and foresights* (pp. 9–25). Reston, VA: American Alliance for Health, Physical Education, Recreation and Dance.

Barrett, K. R. (1988). Two views. The subject matter of children's physical education. *Journal of Physical Education, Recreation & Dance, 59*(2), 42–46.

Barrett, K. R., Allison, P. C., & Bell, R. (1987). What preservice physical education teachers see in an unguided field experience: A follow-up study. *Journal of Teaching in Physical Education, 7*(1), 12–21.

Beamer, D. W. (1983). The effects of an inservice education program on the academic learning time of selected students in physical education. *Dissertation Abstracts International, 43*, 2593A.

Bell, F. I. (1987). The effects of two training programs on the ability of preservice physical education majors to observe the developmental steps in the overarm throw for force. *Dissertation Abstracts International, 48*, 1144A.

Bell, L. A. (1983). Change and resistance in schools: A case study follow-up and general systems analysis of the impact of a federal Title IX project in one school district. *Dissertation Abstracts International, 43*, 2508A.

Bell, L. (1986). Managing to survive in secondary school physical education. In J. Evans (Ed.)., *Physical education, sport and schooling* (pp. 95–116). London: Falmer Press.

Bell, R., Barrett, K. R., & Allison, P. C. (1985). What preservice physical education teachers see in an unguided, early field experience. *Journal of Teaching in Physical Education, 4*(2), 81–90.

Berliner, D. C. (1985). Laboratory settings and the study of teacher education. *Journal of Teacher Education, 36*(6), 2–8.

Beveridge, S. K., & Gangstead, S. K. (1988). Teaching experience and training in the sports skill analysis process. *Journal of Teaching in Physical Education, 7*(2), 103–114.

Boggess, T. E. (1986). A study of the implicit beliefs about curriculum and instruction of physical education teachers with varying years of experience. *Dissertation Abstracts International, 47*, 462A.

Boggess, T. E., McBride, R. E., & Griffey, D. C. (1985). The concerns of physical education student teachers: A developmental view. *Journal of Teaching in Physical Education, 4*(3), 202–211.

Bolam, R. (1987). Induction of beginning teachers. In M. J. Dunkin (Ed.), *The international encyclopidia of teaching and teacher education* (pp. 745–756). Elmsford, NY: Pergamon Press.

Borys, A. H. (1986). Development of a training procedure to increase pupil motor engagement time (MET). In M. Pieron & G. Graham (Eds.), *Sport pedagogy* (pp. 19–26). Champaign, IL: Human Kinetics.

Bressan, E. S. (1979). 2001: The profession is dead—was it murder or suicide? *Quest, 31*(1), 77–82.

Bressan, E. S. (1985). Teaching as a rational enterprise: A problem of neglect. In H. A. Hoffman & J. E. Rink (Eds.), *Physical education professional preparation: Insights and foresights* (pp. 26–31). Reston, VA: American Alliance for Health, Physical Education, Recreation and Dance.

Brockmeyer, G. A. (1987). Creativity in movement. *Journal of Teaching in Physical Education, 6*(3), 310–319.

Broekhoff, J. (1982). A discipline—who needs it? In *Proceedings, National Association for Physical Education in Higher Education* (Vol. III, pp. 28–35). Champaign, IL: Human Kinetics.

Broer, M. R., & Zernicke, R. F. (1979). *Efficiency of human movement* (4th ed.). Philadelphia: W. B. Saunders.

Brooks, D. M. (Ed.). (1987). *Teacher induction: A new beginning*. Reston, VA: Association of Teacher Educators. (ERIC Document Reproduction Service No. 279 607)

Burlingame, M. (1972). Socialization constructs and the teaching of teachers. *Quest, 18*, 40–56.

Caldwell, P. (1986). College physical educators' perceptions of physical education program objectives consistent with three curriculum theories. *Dissertation Abstracts International, 47*, 462A.

Caldwell, P., & Bain, L. L. (1985). The multidimensionality of curriculum models. In M. Carnes (Ed.), *Proceedings of the Fourth Conference on Curriculum theory in physical education* (pp. 223–239). Athens, GA.

Campbell, S. (1988). From research to practice: Functioning processes of knowledge dissemination in physical education. *Dissertation Abstracts International, 48*, 2276A.

Chandler, T. J. L., Lane, S. L., Bibik, J. M., & Oliver, B. (1988). The career ladder and lattice: A new look at the teaching career. *Journal of Teaching in Physical Education, 7*(2), 132–141.

Charles, J. M. (1979). Technocentric ideology in physical education. *Quest, 31*(2), 277–284.

Chu, D. (1978). A foundational study of the occupational induction of physical education teacher/coaches as it is affected by the organizational requirements of the training institution and its environment. *Dissertation Abstracts International, 39* 3860A.

Chu, D. (1980). Functional myths of educational organizations: College as career training and the relationship of formal title to actual duties upon secondary school employment. In V. Crafts (Ed.), *Proceedings, National Association for Physical Education in Higher Education* (Vol. II, pp. 36–46). Champaign: Human Kinetics.

Chu, D. (1984). Teacher/coach orientation and role socialization: A description and explanation. *Journal of Teaching in Physical Education, 3*(2), 3–8.

Cobhan, L. (1982). Lesbians in physical education and sport. In M. Cruikshank (Ed.), *Lesbian studies: Present and future* (pp. 179–186). Old Westbury, NY: Feminist Press.

Countiss, J. R. (1976). The effects of training in the spectrum of teaching styles on the attitudes and behaviors of in-service physical education teachers. *Dissertation Abstracts International, 37,* 175A.

Crum, B. (1986). Concerning the quality of the development of knowledge in sport pedagogy. *Journal of Teaching in Physical Education, 5*(4), 209–210.

Cusimano, B. E. (1987). Effects of self-assessment and goal setting on verbal behavior of elementary physical education teachers. *Journal of Teaching in Physical Education, 6*(2), 166–173.

Decker, J. I. (1986). Role conflict in teacher/coaches in small colleges. *Sociology of Sport Journal, 3*(4), 356–365.

DeDeyn, K. M. (1987). Error identification comparison between three modes of viewing a skill. *Dissertation Abstracts International, 47,* 2944A.

Dewar, A. M. (1984). *High school students' subjective warrants for physical education.* Paper presented at the Olympic Scientific Congress, Eugene, OR.

Dewar, A. M. (1987). The social construction of gender in a physical education programme. *Women's Studies International Forum, 10,* 453–466.

Dewar, A. M. (1989). Recruitment in physical education teaching: Toward a critical approach. In T. J. Templin & P. G. Schempp (Eds.), *Socialization into physical education: Learning to teach* (pp.39–58). Indianapolis, IN: Benchmark Press.

Dewar, A. M. (in press). Feminist pedagogy: Empowering who? For what? And why? In *Proceedings of the sixth conference on curriculum theory in physical education.* Athens, GA: University of Georgia.

Dewar, A. M., & Lawson, H. A. (1984). The subjective warrant and recruitment into physical education. *Quest, 36*(1), 15–25.

Dodds, P. (1982). Teaching equitably: An interim evaluation. Report for project TEAM [Teaching Equity Approaches in Massachusetts]. In M. Pieron & J. Cheffers (Eds.), *Studying the teaching in physical education* (pp. 251–258). Liège; Belgium: Association Internationale des Ecoles Supérieures d'Education Physique.

Dodds, P. (1983). Consciousness raising in curriculum: A teacher's model for analysis. In A. E. Jewett, M. M. Carnes, & M. Speakman (Eds.), *Proceedings of the third conference on curriculum theory in physical education* (pp. 213–234). Athens, GA: University of Georgia.

Dodds, P. (1985a). Are hunters of the function curriculum seeking quarks or snarks? *Journal of Teaching in Physical Education, 4*(2), 91–99.

Dodds, P. (1985b). Delusions of "Worth-it-ness": Field experiences in elementary physical education teacher education programs. In H. A. Hoffman & J. E. Rink (Eds.), *Physical education professional preparation: Insights and foresights* (pp. 90–109). Reston, VA: American Alliance for Health, Physical Education, Recreation and Dance.

Dodds, P. (1986). Stamp out the ugly "isms" in your gym. In M. Pieron & G. Graham (Eds.), *Sport pedagogy* (pp. 141–150). Champaign, IL: Human Kinetics.

Dodds, P. (1989). Trainees, field experiences, and socialization into teaching. In T. J. Templin & P. G. Schempp (Eds.), *Socialization into physical education: Learning to teach* (pp. 81–104). Indianapolis, IN: Benchmark Press.

Dodds, P., & Locke, L. F. (1984). Is physical education in American schools worth saving? Evidence, alternatives, judgment. In N. Struna (Ed.), *Proceedings, National Association for Physical Education in Higher Education,* Vol. 5 (pp. 76–90). Champaign, IL: Human Kinetics.

Dodds P., & Rife, F. (Eds.). (1983). Time to learn in physical education: History, completed research, and potential future for academic learning time in physical education. *Journal of Teaching in Physical Education Monograph 1.*

Drummond, J. L. (1988). The effects of experience on visual retention and observation strategies of specific sports skills. *Dissertation Abstracts International, 48,* 2015A.

Dunbar, R. R., & O'Sullivan, M. M. (1986). Effects of intervention on differential treatment of boys and girls in elementary physical education lessons. *Journal of Teaching in Physical Education, 5*(3), 166–175.

Duquin, M. E., Bredemeier, B. J., Oglesby, C., & Greendorfer, S. L. (1984). Teacher values: Political and social justice orientations of physical educators. *Journal of Teaching in Physical Education, 3*(2), 9–19.

Earls, N. (1981). Distinctive teachers' personal qualities, perceptions of teacher education, and realities of teaching. *Journal of Teaching in Physical Education, 1*(1), 59–70.

Earls, N. (Ed.). (1986). Naturalistic inquiry: Interactive research and the insider–outsider perspective [Special issue]. *Journal of Teaching in Physical Education, 6*(1).

Edwards, H. (1973). *Sociology of sport.* Homewood, IL: Dorsey Press.

Edwards, H. (1984). The black "dumb jock": An American sports tragedy. *College Board Review, 131,* 8–13.

Embrey, L. F. R. (1987). A physical education student teacher in an elementary school: A case study. *Dissertation Abstracts International, 47,* 3735A.

Enberg, M. L., Harrington, W., & Cady, L. V. (1981). Competency-based teacher preparation in physical education at Washington State University. In H. A. Lawson (Ed.), *Undergraduate physical education programs: Issues and approaches* (pp. 19–32). Reston, VA: American Alliance for Health, Physical Education, Recreation and Dance.

Eraut, M. (1987). Inservice teacher education. In M. J. Dunkin (Ed.), *The international encyclopedia of teaching and teacher education* (pp. 730–743). Elmsford, NY: Pergamon Press.

Evans, J. (Ed.). (1986). *Physical education, sport and schooling.* London: Falmer Press.

Evans, J. (Ed.). (1988). *Teachers, teaching and control in physical education.* London: Falmer Press.

Evans, J., & Williams, T. (1989). Moving up and getting out: The classed and gendered career opportunities of physical education teachers. In T. J. Templin & P. G. Schempp (Eds.), *Socialization into physical education: Learning to teach* (pp. 235–250). Indianapolis, IN: Benchmark Press.

Faucette, N. (1987). Teachers' concerns and participation styles during in-service education. *Journal of Teaching in Physical Education, 6*(4), 425–440.

Faucette, N., & Graham, G. (1986). The impact of principals on teachers during inservice education: A qualitative analysis. *Journal of Teaching in Physical Education, 5*(2), 79–90.

Francis, P. K. (1986). Developing selected observational skills in physical education teachers using an individualized learning program. *Dissertation Abstracts International, 47,* 1647A.

Fuller, F. F. (1970). *Personalized education for teachers: An introduction for teacher education.* Austin, TX: University of Texas.

Gallemore, S. L. (1981). Perceptions about the objectives of student teaching. *Research Quarterly for Exercise and Sport, 52,*(2), 180–190.

Gangstead, S. K., & Beveridge, S. K. (1984). The implementation and evaluation of a methodological approach to qualitative sport skill analysis instruction. *Journal of Teaching in Physical Education, 3*(2), 60–70.

Gaudet, E. (1982). The effect of interaction analysis in changing behaviors with the multiple handicapped. In M. Pieron & J. Cheffers (Eds.), *Studying the teaching in physical education* (pp. 167–178). Liège, Belgium: Association Internationale des Ecoles Supérieures d'Education Physique.

Goc-Karp, G., Kim, D. W., & Skinner, P. C. (1985). Professor and student perceptions and beliefs about physical education. *Physical Educator, 43*(3), 115–120.

Goc-Karp, G., & Zakrajsek, D. B. (1987). Planning for learning—theory into practice? *Journal of Teaching in Physical Education, 6*(4), 377–392.

Godbout, P., Brunelle, J., & Tousignant, M. (1987). Who benefits from passing through the program? In G. T. Barrette, R. S. Feingold, C. R. Rees, & M. Pieron (Eds.), *Myths, models, & methods in sport pedagogy* (pp. 183–198). Champaign, IL: Human Kinetics.

Gondola, J. C. (1988). Homophobia: The red herring in girls' and women's sports. In M. J. Adrian (Ed.), *National Coaching Institute applied research papers.* Champaign, IL: NAGWS.

Gordon, L. D., Thompson, M. M., & Alspaugh, J. W. (1973). The relative importance of various physical education objectives for grades K–2. *Research Quarterly, 44*(2), 192–196.

Gore, J. M. (in press). Pedagogy as "text" in physical education teacher education: Beyond the preferred reading. In D. Kirk & R. Tinning (Eds.), *Curriculum studies in physical education.* London: Falmer Press.

Graber, K. C. (1989). Teaching tomorrow's teachers: Professional preparation as an agent of socialization. In T. J. Templin & P. G. Schempp (Eds.), *Socialization into physical education: Learning to teach* (pp. 59–80). Indianapolis, IN: Benchmark Press.

Graham, G. M. (1973). The effects of a micro-teaching laboratory on the ability of teacher trainees to teach a novel motor skill to fifth-grade and sixth-grade children. *Dissertation Abstracts International, 34,* 3118A.

Graham, G. M. (1987). *The developing physical education teacher and coach: Empirical and research insights.* Paper presented at the meeting of the Association Internationale des Ecoles Supérieures d'Education Physique, Trois Rivières, Québec.

Graham, K. C. (1987). A description of academic work and student performance during a middle school volleyball unit. *Journal of Teaching in Physical Education, 7*(1),22–37.

Griffin, P. S. (1983). Gymnastics is a girls' thing: Participation and interaction patterns in middle school gymnastics classes. In T. J. Templin & J. K. Olson (Eds.), *Teaching in physical education* (pp. 71–85). Champaign, IL: Human Kinetics.

Griffin, P. S. (1985a). Teacher perceptions of and reactions to equity problems in a middle school physical education program. *Research Quarterly for Exercise and Sport, 56*(2), 103–110.

Griffin, P. S. (1985b). Teaching in an urban multiracial physical education program: The power of context. *Quest, 37*(2), 154–165.

Griffin, P. S. (1989a). Gender as a socializing agent in physical education. In T. J. Templin & P. G. Schempp (Eds.), *Socialization into physical education: Learning to teach* (pp. 219–234). Indianapolis, IN: Benchmark Press.

Griffin, P. S. (1989b, April). *Using participatory research to empower gay and lesbian educators.* Paper presented at the annual meeting of the American Educational Research Association, San Francisco.

Griffin, P. S., & Hutchinson, G. (1988). Second wind: A physical education program development network. *Journal of Teaching in Physical Education, 7*(3), 184–189.

Gusthart, J. L., & Rink, J. (1983). Teaching behavior through various levels of field experiences. *Journal of Teaching in Physical Education, 3*(1), 32–46.

Guthrie, S. P. (1982). *Homophobia: Its impact on women in sport and physical education.* Unpublished master's thesis, Calfornia State University, Long Beach.

Halverson, P. D. (1988). The effects of peer tutoring on sport skill analytic ability. *Dissertation Abstracts International, 48,* 2274A.

Hatfield, B. D. (1984). Psychological knowledge and its emerging role in the physical education curriculum. In N. Struna (Ed.), *Proceedings, National Association for Physical Education in Higher Education,* Vol. 5 (pp. 60–68). Champaign, IL: Human Kinetics.

Hawkins, A. (1987). On the role of hermeneutics in sport pedagogy: A reply to Crum. *Journal of Teaching in Physical Education, 6*(4), 367–372.

Hawkins, A., Wiegand, R., & Bahneman, C. (1983), Data-based evaluation of a physical education professional preparation program. In T. J. Templin & J. K. Olson (Eds.), *Teaching in physical education* (pp. 131–141). Champaign, IL: Human Kinetics.

Hawkins, A., Wiegand, R. L., & Landin, D. K. (1985). Cataloguing the collective wisdom of teacher educators. *Journal of Teaching in Physical Education, 4*(4), 241–255.

Hellison, D. R. (1987). Dreaming the possible dream: The rise and triumph of physical education. In J. D. Massengale (Ed.), *Trends toward the future in physical education* (pp. 137–151). Champaign, IL: Human Kinetics.

Hendry, L. B. (1972). The coaching sterotype. In H. T. A. Whiting (Ed.), *Readings in sport psychology.* London: Kimpton.

Hendry, L. B. (1975a). Survival in a marginal role: The professional identity of the physical education teacher. *British Journal of Sociology, 26*(1), 465–476.

Hendry, L. B. (1975b). The role of the physical education teacher. *Education Research, 17*(1), 115–121.

Hendry, L. B., & Whiting, H. T. A. (1972). General course and specialist physical education student characteristics. *Educational Research, 14*(2), 152–156.

Henkel, S. A., & Earls, N. F. (1985). The moral judgement of physical education teachers. *Journal of Teaching in Physical Education, 4*(3), 178–189.

Henry, F. (1964). Physical education as an academic discipline. *Journal of Health, Physical Education and Recreation, 37*(9), 32–33.

Hoferek. M. (1980). At the crossroad: Merger or ———? *Quest, 32*(1), 95–102.

Hoferek, M. J. (1982). Sex-role prescriptions and attitudes of physical educators. *Sex Roles, 8*(1), 83–98.

Hoffman, H. A., & Rink, J. E. (Eds.). (1985). *Physical education professional preparation: Insights and foresights.* Reston, VA: American Alliance for Health, Physical Education, Recreation and Dance.

Hoffman, S. J. (1983). Clinical diagnosis as a pedagogical skill. In T. J. Templin & J. K. Olson (Eds.), *Teaching in physical education* (pp. 35–45). Champaign, IL: Human Kinetics.

Hollands, R. G. (1984). The role of cultural studies and social criticism in the sociological study of sport. *Quest, 36*(1), 66–79.

Holmen, M. G., & Parkhouse, B. L. (1981). Relationship between working environment, self-concept, real–ideal self discrepancy, and functionality in physical education teachers. *Research Quarterly for Exercise and Sport, 52*(3), 311–323.

Housner, L. D., & Griffey, D. C. (1985). Teacher cognition: Differences in planning and interactive decision-making between experienced and inexperienced teachers. *Research Quarterly for Exercise and Sport, 56*(1), 45–53.

Husman, B. F., Clarke, D. H., & Kelley, D. L. (1981). A disciplinary model for a curriculum in kinesiological sciences. In H. A. Lawson (Ed.), *Undergraduate physical education programs: Issues and approaches* (pp. 55–62). Reston, VA: American Alliance for Health, Physical Education, Recreation and Dance.

Imwold. C. H., Rider, R. A., Twardy, B. M., Oliver, P. S., Griffin, M., & Arsenault, D. N. (1984). The effect of planning on the teaching behavior of preservice physical education teachers. *Journal of Teaching in Physical Education, 4*(1), 50–56.

Jewett, A. E., & Bain, L. L. (1985). *The curriculum process in physical education.* Dubuque, IA: William C. Brown.

Kane, J. E. (1975). Perceptions of personal characteristics by physical education teachers and coaches. In H. T. A. Whiting (Ed.), *Readings in sport psychology, 2*. London: Lepus.

Kelley, E., & Lindsay, C. (1977). Knowledge obsolescence in physical educators. *Research Quarterly, 48*(2), 463–474.

Kelley, E., & Lindsay, C. (1980). A comparison of knowledge obsolescence of graduating seniors and practitioners in the field of physical education. *Research Quarterly for Exercise and Sport, 51*(4), 636–644.

Kenyon, G. S. (1965). Certain psychosocial and cultural characteristics unique to prospective teachers of physical education. *Research Quarterly, 36*(1), 105–142.

Kirk, D. (1986a). A critical pedagogy for teacher education: Toward an inquiry-oriented approach. *Journal of Teaching in Physical Education, 5*(4), 230–246.

Kirk, D. (1986b). Health related fitness as an innovation in the physical education curriculum. In J. Evans (Ed.), *Physical education, sport and schooling* (pp. 167–182). London: Falmer Press.

Kirk, D. (1989). The orthodoxy in RT-PE and the research/practice gap: A critique and an alternative view. *Journal of Teaching in Physical Education, 8*(2), 123–130.

Kneer, M. E. (1986). Description of physical education instructional theory/practice gap in selected secondary schools. *Journal of Teaching in Physical Education, 5*(2), 91–106.

Kniffin, K. M. (1986). The effects of individualized videotape instruction on the ability of undergraduate physical education majors to analyze select sport skills. *Dissertation Abstracts International, 47*, 119A.

Knoppers, A. (1989). Productivity and collaborative patterns of physical educators. *Research Quarterly for Exercise and Sport, 60*(2), 159–165.

Knowles, C. J. (1981). Concerns of teachers about implementing individualized instruction in the physical education setting. *Research Quarterly for Exercise and Sport, 52*(1), 48–57.

Knowles, C. J., & Hord, S. M. (1981). The concerns-based adoption model: Tools for planning, personalizing and evaluating a staff development program. *Journal of Teaching in Physical Education, 1*(1), 24–37.

Lacey, C. (1987). Professional socialization of teachers. In M. J. Dunkin (Ed.), *The international encyclopedia of teaching and teacher education* (pp. 634–644). Elmsford, NY: Pergamon Press.

Landin, D. K., Hawkins, A., & Wiegand, R. L. (1986). Validating the collective wisdom of teacher educators. *Journal of Teaching in Physical Education, 5*(4), 252–271.

Lanier, J. E., & Little, J. W. (1986). Research on teacher education. In M. C. Wittrock (Ed.), *Handbook of research on teaching* (3rd ed., pp. 527–569). New York: Macmillan.

LaPlante, M. J., & Jewett, A. E. (1987). Content validation of the purpose dimension. *Journal of Teaching in Physical Education, 6*(3), 214–223.

Largey, D. L. (1981). Analysis of the relationship of selected variables to career longevity in physical education. *Dissertation Abstracts International, 42*, 2561A.

Lather, P. (1986). Issues of validity in openly ideological research: Between a rock and a soft place. *Interchange, 17*(4), 63–84.

Lawson, H. A. (1979). Paths towards professionalization. *Quest, 31*(2), 231–243.

Lawson, H. A. (1980). Beyond teaching and adhocracy: Increasing the sphere of influence and control for physical educationists. *Quest, 32*(1), 22–30.

Lawson, H. A. (Ed.). (1981). *Undergraduate physical education programs: Issues and approaches.* Reston, VA: American Alliance for Health, Physical Education, Recreation and Dance.

Lawson, H. A. (1983a). Paradigms for research on teaching and teach-

ers. In T. J. Templin & J. K. Olson (Eds), *Teaching in physical education* (pp. 339–358). Champaign, IL: Human Kinetics.

Lawson, H. A. (1983b). Toward a model of teacher socialization in physical education: Entry into schools, teachers' role orientations, and longevity in teaching (Part 2). *Journal of Teaching in Physical Education, 3*(1), 3–15.

Lawson, H. A. (1983c). Toward a model of teacher socialization in physical education: The subjective warrant, recruitment, and teacher education (Part 1). *Journal of Teaching in Physical Education, 2*(3), 3–16.

Lawson, H. A. (1984). Problem-setting for physical education and sport. *Quest, 36*(1), 48–60.

Lawson, H. A. (1985a). Knowledge for work in the physical education profession. *Sociology of Sport Journal, 2*(1), 9–24.

Lawson, H. A. (1985b). Research and development priories. In M. Carnes (Ed.), *Proceedings of the fourth conference on curriculum theory in physical education* (pp. 374–382). Athens, GA: University of Georgia.

Lawson. H. A. (1986). Occupational socialization and the design of teacher education programs. *Journal of Teaching in Physical Education, 5*(2), 107–116.

Lawson, H. A. (1988). Occupational socialization, cultural studies, and the physical education curriculum. *Journal of Teaching in Physical Education, 7*(4), 265–288.

Lawson, H. A. (1989). From rookie to veteran: Workplace conditions in physical education and induction into the profession. In T. J. Templin & P. G. Schempp (Eds.), *Socialization into physical education: Learning to teach* (pp. 145–164). Indianapolis, IN: Benchmark Press.

Lawson, H. A., & Morford, W. R. (1979). The crossdisciplinary structure of kinesiology and sports studies: Distinctions, implications, and advantages. *Quest, 31*(2), 222–230.

Lawson, H. A., & Placek, J. (1981). *Physical education in the secondary schools: Curricular alternatives.* Boston: Allyn & Bacon.

Lawson, H. A., & Pugh, D. L. (1981). Six significant questions about performance and performance courses. *Journal of Physical Education and Recreation, 52*(3), 59–61.

Legos, P. M. (1978). The effects of microteaching on the acquisition of teaching patterns and selected personality characteristics by preservice health and physical education teachers. *Dissertation Abstracts International, 39*, 2198A.

Lenskyj, H. (1986). *Out of bounds: Women, sport & sexuality.* Toronto, Ontario: The Women's Press.

Lewis, G. M. (1969). Adaptation of the sports program, 1906–1939: The role of accommodation in the transformation of physical education. *Quest, 12*, 34–46.

Locke, L. F. (1962). Performance of administration oriented male physical educators on selected psychological tests. *Research Quarterly, 33*(1), 418–429.

Locke, L. F. (1977). From research and the disciplines to practice and the profession: One more time. In L. I. Gedvilas & M. E. Kneer (Eds.), *Proceedings of the NAPECW/NCPEAM National Conference* (pp. 34–44). Chicago: University of Illinois at Chicago Circle.

Locke, L. F. (1979). Supervision, schools and student teaching: Why things stay the same. *Academy Papers, 13*, 65–74.

Locke, L. F. (1984). Research on teaching teachers: Where are we now? *Journal of Teaching in Physical Education Monograph 2.*

Locke, L. F. (1986). The future of research on pedagogy: Balancing on the cutting edge. *Academy Papers, 20*, 83–95.

Locke, L. F. (1987). Research and the improvement of teaching: The professor as the problem. In G. T. Barrette, R. S. Feingold, & C. R. Rees (Eds.), *Myths, models & methods in sport pedagogy* (pp. 1–26). Champaign, IL: Human Kinetics.

Locke, L. F. (1989). Qualitative research as a form of scientific inquiry in sport and physical education. *Research Quarterly for Exercise and Sport, 60*(1), 1–20.

Locke, L. F., & Dodds, P. (1984). Is physical education teacher education in American colleges worth saving? Evidence, alternatives, judgment. In N. Struna (Ed.), *Proceedings, National Association for Physical Education in Higher Education*, Vol. 5 (pp. 91–109). Champaign, IL: Human Kinetics.

Locke, L. F., & Griffin, P. (Eds.) (1986). Profiles of struggle. *Journal of Physical Education, Recreation and Dance, 57*(4), 32–63.

Locke, L. F., Mand, C. L., & Siedentop, D. (1981). The preparation of physical education teachers: A subject-matter-centered model. In H. A. Lawson (Ed.), *Undergraduate physical education programs: Issues and approaches* (pp. 33–54). Reston, VA: American Alliance for Health, Physical Education, Recreation and Dance.

Locke, L. F., & Massengale, J. (1978). Role-conflict in teacher-coaches. *Research Quarterly, 49*(2), 162–174.

Locke, L. F., & Siedentop, D. (1980). Beyond arrogance and ad hominem: A reply to Hal Lawson. *Quest, 32*(1), 31–43.

Lortie, D. (1975). *Schoolteacher: A sociological study.* Chicago: University of Chicago Press.

Loughrey, T. J. (1987). Professional derivation at the national level. In M. Carnes & P. Stueck (Eds.), *Proceedings of the fifth curriculum theory conference in physical education*(pp. 276–282). Athens, GA: University of Georgia.

Mancini, V. H., Clark, E. K., & Wuest, D. A. (1987). Short- and long-term effects of supervisory feedback on the interaction patterns of an intercollegiate field hockey coach. *Journal of Teaching in Physical Education, 6*(4), 404–410.

Mancini, V. H., Wuest, D. A., & van der Mars, H. (1985). Use of instruction and supervision in systematic observation in undergraduate professional preparation. *Journal of Teaching in Physical Education, 5*(1), 22–33.

Marrs, L. K., & Templin, T. J. (1983). Student teacher as social strategist. In T. J. Templin & J. K. Olson (Eds.), *Teaching in physical education* (pp. 118–128). Champaign, IL: Human Kinetics.

Martens, F. L. (1987). Selection of physical education students and success in student teaching. *Journal of Teaching in Physical Education, 6*(4), 411–424.

Martinek, T. J., & Butt, K. (1988). An application of an action research model for changing instructional practice. *Journal of Teaching in Physical Education, 7*(3), 214–220.

Massengale, J. D. (1974). Coaching as an occupational subculture. *Phi Delta Kappan, 56*(2), 140–142.

McBride, R. E. (1984a). An intensive study of a systematic teacher training model in physical education. *Journal of Teaching in Physical Education, 4*(1), 3–16.

McBride, R. E. (1984b). Perceived teaching and program concerns among preservice teachers, university supervisors, and cooperating teachers. *Journal of Teaching in Physical Education, 3*(3), 36–43.

McBride, R. E., Boggess, T. E., & Griffey, D. C. (1986). Concerns of inservice physical education teachers as compared with Fuller's concern model. *Journal of Teaching in Physical Education, 5*(3), 149–156.

Melville, D. S., & Maddalozzo, J. G. F. (1988). The effects of a physical educator's appearance of body fatness on communicating exercise concepts to high school students. *Journal of Teaching in Physical Education, 7*(4), 343–352.

Messner, M. A. (1988). Sports and male domination: The female athlete as contested terrain. *Sociology of Sport Journal, 5*(3), 197–211.

Metzler, M. W., & Freedman, M. S. (1985). Here's looking at you, Pete: A profile of physical education teacher education faculty. *Journal of Teaching in Physical Education, 4*(2), 123–133.

Miller, D. M. (1984). Philosophy: Whose business? *Quest, 36*(1), 26–36.

Mitchell, M. F., & Lawson, H. A. (1986). Career paths and role orientations of professors of teacher education in physical education. In M. Pieron & G. Graham (Eds.), *Sport pedagogy* (pp. 41–46). Champaign, IL: Human Kinetics.

Morford, W. R., Lawson, H. A., & Hutton, R. S. (1981). Undergraduate physical education: A cross-disciplinary model. In H. A. Lawson (Ed.), *Undergraduate physical education programs: Issues and approaches* (pp. 63–74). Reston, VA: American Alliance for Health, Physical Education, Recreation and Dance.

Murphy, R. D. (1980). Professional-discipline orientation in undergraduate curriculums for preparation of teachers of physical education, 1978–1980. *Dissertation Abstracts International, 41*, 2499A.

Ocansey, R. T. A. (1988). The effects of a behavioral model of supervision on the supervisory behaviors of cooperating teachers. *Journal of Teaching in Physical Education, 8*(1), 46–63.

Oliver, B. (1987). Teacher and school characteristics: Their relationship to the inservice needs of teachers. *Journal of Teaching in Physical Education, 7*(1), 38–45.

Oliver, B., Bibik, J. M., Chandler, T. J. L., & Lane, S. L. (1988). Teacher development and job incentives: A psychological view. *Journal of Teaching in Physical Education, 7*(2), 121–131.

O'Sullivan, M. (1989). Failing gym is like failing lunch or recess: Two beginning teachers' struggle for legitimacy. *Journal of Teaching in Physical Education, 8*(3), 227–242.

O'Sullivan, M., Stroot, S. A., & Tannehill, D. (1989). Elementary physical education specialists: A commitment to student learning. *Journal of Teaching in Physical Education, 8*(3), 261–265.

Oxendine, J. B. (1987). Alliance attitudes regarding human rights. *Journal of Physical Education, Recreation & Dance, 58*(2), 80–83.

Paese, P. C. (1985). Assessment of a teacher education program based on student intern performance. *Journal of Teaching in Physical Education, 5*(1), 52–58.

Parkhouse, B. L., & Holmen, M. G. (1980). Differences in job satisfaction among suburban and inner-city high school physical education faculty. *Research Quarterly for Exercise and Sport, 51*(4), 654–662.

Pieron, M. (1986). Analysis of the research based on observation of the teaching of physical education. In M. Pieron & G. Graham (Eds.), *Sport pedagogy* (pp. 193–202). Champaign, IL: Human Kinetics.

Pierro, A. A. (1975). A history of professional preparation in physical education in selected Negro colleges and universities to 1958. In E. F. Ziegler (Ed.), *A history of physical education and sport in the United States and Canada.* Champaign, IL: Stipes.

Placek, J. H. (1983). Conceptions of success in teaching: Busy, happy and good? In T. J. Templin & J. K. Olson (Eds.), *Teaching in physical education* (pp. 46–56). Champaign, IL: Human Kinetics.

Placek, J. H. (1984). A multi-case study of teacher planning in physical education. *Journal of Teaching in Physical Education, 4*(1), 39–49.

Placek, J. H. (1985). Teacher educators and students: The communication gap. In M. M. Carnes (Ed.), *Proceedings of the fourth conference on curriculum theory in physical education* (pp. 193–203). Athens, GA: University of Georgia.

Placek, J. H., & Dodds, P. (1988). A critical incident study of preservice teachers' beliefs about teaching success and nonsuccess. *Research Quarterly for Exercise and Sport, 59*(4) 351–358.

Placek, J. H., & Silverman, S. (1983). Early field teaching requirements in undergraduate physical education programs. *Journal of Teaching in Physical Education, 2*(3), 48–54.

Pollard, A. (1988). Physical education, competition and control in primary education. In J. Evans (Ed.), *Teachers, teaching and control in physical education* (pp. 109–124). London: Falmer Press.

Pooley, J. C. (1972). Professional socialization: A model of the pre-training phase applicable to physical education students. *Quest, 18*, 57–66.

Pooley, J. C. (1975). The professional socialization of physical education students in the United States and England. *International Review of Sport Sociology*, *3–4*, 97–108.

Popkewitz, T. S. (1984). *Paradigm and ideology in education research.* London: Falmer Press.

Randall, L. E. (1986). Employment statistics. A national survey in public school physical education. *Journal of Physical Education, Recreation & Dance*, *57*(1), 23–28.

Ratliffe, T. (1986). The influence of school principals on management time and student activity time for two elementary physical education teachers. *Journal of Teaching in Physical Education*, *5*(2), 117–125.

Ratliffe, T. (1988). Principal training for effective staff development. *Journal of Teaching in Physical Education*, *7*(3), 228–234.

Rees, R. C. (1984). Applying sociology to physical education: Who needs it? In N. Struna (Ed.), *Proceedings, National Association for Physical Education in Higher Education*, Vol. 5 (pp. 54–59). Champaign, IL: Human Kinetics.

Riggins, P. L, Jr. (1979). Assessing the teacher/coach behavior potential of undergraduate physical education majors: A social learning approach to the problem of occupational role conflict. *Dissertation Abstracts International*, *40*, 3188A.

Rink, J. E. (1985). *Teaching physical education for learning.* St. Louis: Times Mirror/Mosby.

Rink, J. E., & Werner, P. (1987). Student responses as a measure of teacher effectiveness. In G. T. Barrette, R. S. Feingold, C. R. Rees, & M. Pieron (Eds.), *Myths, models, & methods in sport pedagogy* (pp. 199–206). Champaign, IL: Human Kinetics.

Rog, J. A. (1979). Faculty attitudes toward teaching: A descriptive interview-based study of three departments of physical education. *Dissertation Abstracts International*, *40*, 1348A.

Rosentswieg, J. (1969). A ranking of the objectives of physical education. *Research Quarterly*, *40*(4), 783–787.

Safrit, M. (1979). Women in research in physical education. *Quest*, *32*(2), 158–171.

Safrit, M. (1984). Women in research in physical education: A 1984 update. *Quest*, *36*(2), 103–114.

Sage, G. H. (1980). Sociology of physical educator/coaches: Personal attributes controversy. *Research Quarterly for Exercise and Sport*, *51*(1), 110–121.

Sage, G. H. (1987a). The role of sport studies in sport pedagogy. In G. T. Barrette, R. S. Feingold, C. R. Rees, & M. Pieron (Eds.), *Myths, models, & methods in sport pedagogy* (pp. 29–40). Champaign, IL: Human Kinetics.

Sage, G. H. (1987b). The social world of high school athletic coaches: Multiple role demands and their consequences. *Sociology of Sport Journal*, *4*(3), 213–228.

Sage, G. H. (1989). Becoming a high school coach: From playing sports to coaching. *Research Quarterly for Exercise and Sport*, *60*(1), 81–92.

Schempp, P. G. (1983). Learning the role: The transformation from student to teacher. In T. J. Templin & J. K. Olson (Eds.), *Teaching in physical education* (pp. 109–117). Champaign, IL: Human Kinetics.

Schempp, P. G. (1985). Becoming a better teacher: An analysis of the student teaching experience. *Journal of Teaching in Physical Education*, *4*(3), 158–166.

Schempp, P. G. (1986). Physical education student teachers' beliefs in their control over student learning. *Journal of Teaching in Physical Education*, *5*(3), 198–203.

Schempp, P. G. (1987). Research on teaching in physical education: Beyond the limits of natural science. *Journal of Teaching in Physical Education*, *6*(2), 111–121.

Schempp, P. G. (1988). Exorcist II: A reply to Siedentop. *Journal of Teaching in Physical Education*, *7*(2), 79–81.

Schempp, P. G. (1989). Apprenticeship-of-observation and the development of physical education teachers. In T. J. Templin & P. G. Schempp (Eds.), *Socialization into physical education: Learning to teach* (pp. 13–38). Indianapolis, IN: Benchmark Press.

Schempp, P. G., & Martinek, T. J. (1988). Collaborative research in physical education. *Journal of Teaching in Physical Education*, *7*(3), 208–213.

Schuiteman, J., & Knoppers, A. (1987). An examination of gender differences in scholarly productivity among physical educators. *Research Quarterly for Exercise and Sport*, *58*(3), 265–272.

Schwager, S. M. (1986). Ongoing program development: Teachers as collaborators. *Journal of Teaching in Physical Education*, *5*(4), 272–279.

Schwager, S. M., & Doolittle, S. A. (1988). Teachers' reaction to activities in ongoing program development. *Journal of Teaching in Physical Education*, *7*(3), 240–249.

Segrave, J. O. (1980). Role preferences among prospective physical education teacher/coaches. In V. Crafts (Ed.), *Proceedings, National Association for Physical Education in Higher Education* (Vol. II, pp. 53–61). Champaign: Human Kinetics.

Shulman, L. S. (1987). Knowledge and teaching: Foundations of the new reform. *Harvard Educational Review*, *57*(1), 1–22.

Siedentop, D. (1972). Behavior analysis and teacher training. *Quest*, *18*, 26–32.

Siedentop, D. (1977). Motor learning and instructional design: Why the shotgun wedding? In L. I. Gedvilas & M. E. Kneer (Eds.), *Proceedings of the NAPECW/NCPEAM National Conference* (pp. 145–152). Chicago: University of Illinois at Chicago Circle.

Siedentop, D. (1981). The Ohio State University supervision research program summary report. *Journal of Teaching in Physical Education* (Introductory issue), 30–38.

Siedentop, D. (1982). Recent advances in pedagogical research in physical education. *Academy Papers*, *16*, 82–94.

Siedentop, D. (1983a). *Developing teaching skills in physical education.* Palo Alto, CA: Mayfield.

Siedentop, D. (1983b). Research on teaching in physical education. In T. J. Templin & J. K. Olson (Eds.), *Teaching in physical education* (pp. 3–15). Champaign, IL: Human Kinetics.

Siedentop, D. (1985). The great teacher education legend. In H. A. Hoffman & J. E. Rink (Eds.), *Physical education professional preparation: Insights and foresights* (pp. 48–57). Reston, VA: American Alliance for Health, Physical Education, Recreation and Dance.

Siedentop, D. (1986). The modification of teacher behavior. In M. Pieron & G. Graham (Eds.), *Sport pedagogy* (pp. 3–18). Champaign, IL: Human Kinetics.

Siedentop, D. (1987). Dialogue or exorcism? A rejoinder to Schempp. *Journal of Teaching in Physical Education*, *6*(4), 373–376.

Siedentop, D. (Ed.). (1989). The effective elementary specialist study, *Journal of Teaching in Physical Education Monograph*, *8*(3).

Siedentop, D., & Eldar, E. (1989). Expertise, experience, and effectiveness. *Journal of Teaching in Physical Education*, *8*(3), 254–260.

Siedentop, D., Mand, C., & Taggart, A. (1986). *Physical education: Teaching and curriculum strategies for grades 5 to 12.* Palo Alto, CA: Mayfield.

Sikes, P. J. (1988). Growing old gracefully? Age, identity, and physical education. In J. Evans (Ed.), *Teachers, teaching and control in physical education* (pp. 21–40). London: Falmer Press.

Sisley, B. L., & Wiese, D. M. (1987). Current status: Requirements for interscholastic coaches. *Journal of Physical Education, Recreation & Dance*, *58*(7), 73–85.

Smith, S. J. (1982). The hidden curriculum of pedagogical research in physical education. In M. L. Howell & J. E. Saunders (Eds.), *Proceedings of the VII Commonwealth and International Confer-*

ence on Sport, Physical Education, Recreation and Dance (Vol. 66, pp. 231–238).

Smith, Y. R. S. (1981). Analysis of selected processes associated with physical education student teachers' experiences. *Dissertation Abstracts International, 42,* 1536A.

Southard, D. (1982). A national survey: Sociology of sport within American college and university physical education professional preparation programs. In A. O. Dunleavy, A. W. Miracle, & C. R. Rees (Eds.), *Studies in the sociology of sport* (pp. 365–372). Ft. Worth, TX: Texas Christian University Press.

Southard, D. (1983). Importance of selected competencies and relationship to corresponding coursework in programs of teacher preparation. *Research Quarterly for Exercise & Sport, 54*(4), 383–388.

Speakman-Yearta, M. A. (1987). Cross-cultural comparisons of physical education purposes. *Journal of Teaching in Physical Education, 6*(3), 252–258.

Spears, B. (1979). Success, women, and physical education. In M. G. Scott & M. J. Hoferek (Eds.), *Women as leaders in physical education and sports* (pp. 5–19). Iowa City, IA: University of Iowa.

Spears, B., & Swanson, R. A. (1978). *History of sport and physical activity in the United States.* Dubuque, IA: William C. Brown.

Steen, T. B. (1986). A case study of teacher socialization in physical education during early training experiences: A qualitative analysis. *Dissertation Abstracts International, 46,* 2668A.

Stroot, S. A., & Morton, P. J. (1989). Blueprints for learning. *Journal of Teaching in Physical Education, 8*(3), 213–222.

Taggart, A. C. (1988). The systematic development of teaching skills: A sequence of planned pedagogical experiences. *Journal of Teaching in Physical Education, 8*(1), 73–86.

Tannehill, D., & Zakrajsek, D. (1988). What's happening in supervision of student teachers in secondary physical education. *Journal of Teaching in Physical Education, 8*(1), 1–12.

Taylor, J. L. (1986). Surviving the challenge. *Journal of Physical Education, Recreation & Dance, 57*(1), 69–72.

Taylor, M. S. (1978). The use of microteaching to aid preservice physical educators in the acquisition of a variety of teaching strategies as identified by the amount and kind of student decisions. *Dissertation Abstracts International, 38,* 5337A.

Templin, T. J. (1979). Occupational socialization and the physical education student teacher. *Research Quarterly, 50*(3), 482–493.

Templin, T. J. (1981). Student as socializing agent. *Journal of Teaching in Physical Education* (Introductory issue), 71–79.

Templin, T. J. (1985). Developing commitment to teaching: The professional. In H. A. Hoffman & J. E. Rink (Eds.), *Physical education professional preparation: Insights and foresights* (pp. 119–131). Reston, VA: American Alliance for Health, Physical Education, Recreation and Dance.

Templin, T. J. (1989). Running on ice: A case study of the influence of workplace conditions on a secondary school physical educator. In T. J. Templin & P. G. Schempp (Eds.), *Socialization into physical education: Learning to teach* (pp. 165–198). Indianapolis, IN: Benchmark Press.

Templin, T. J. (in press). Settling down: An examination of two women physical education teachers. In J. Evans (Ed.), *Teachers, teaching and control in the PE curriculum.* London: Falmer Press.

Templin, T. J., & Schempp, P. G. (Eds.). (1989). *Socialization into physical education: Learning to teach.* Indianapolis: Benchmark Press.

Templin, T. J., Woodford, R., & Mulling, C. (1982). On becoming a physical educator: Occupational choice and the anticipatory socialization process. *Quest, 34*(2), 119–133.

Theberge, N. (1985). Toward a feminist alternative to sport as a male preserve. *Quest, 37*(2), 193–202.

Thompson, D. K. (1983). Self-concept and role orientation of women physical education majors as perceived by themselves and the university community. *Dissertation Abstracts International, 43,* 3260A.

Tinning, R. I. (1987). Beyond the development of a utilitarian teaching perspective: An Australian case study of action research in teacher preparation. In G. T. Barrette, R. S. Feingold, C. R. Rees, & M. Pieron (Eds.), *Myths, models, & methods in sport pedagogy* (pp. 113–122). Champaign, IL: Human Kinetics.

Tinning, R. I. (1988). Student teaching and the pedagogy of necessity. *Journal of Teaching in Physical Education, 7*(2), 82–89.

Tinning, R., & Siedentop, D. (1985). The characteristics of tasks and accountability in student teaching. *Journal of Teaching in Physical Education, 4*(4), 286–299.

Tousignant, M., & Brunelle, J. (1987). Personalized instruction: A relief for some and a pain for others. In G. T. Barrette, R. S. Feingold, C. R. Rees, & M. Pieron (Eds.), *Myths, models, & methods in sport pedagogy* (pp. 215–224). Champaign, IL: Human Kinetics.

Tousignant, M., & Siedentop, D. (1983). A qualitative analysis of task structures in required secondary physical education classes. *Journal of Teaching in Physical Education, 3*(1), 47–57.

Twardy, B. M., & Yerg, B. J. (1987). The impact of planning on in-class interactive behaviors of preservice teachers. *Journal of Teaching in Physical Education, 6*(2), 136–148.

VanderZwaag, H. J. (1981). What the profession was once like: Physical education 1906–1970. *Academy Papers, 15,* 21–26.

Veal, M. L. (1988a). Pupil assessment issues: A teacher educator's perspective. *Quest, 40*(2), 151–161.

Veal, M. L. (1988b). Pupil assessment perceptions and practices of secondary teachers. *Journal of Teaching in Physical Education, 7*(4), 327–342.

Vickers, J. N. (1983). The role of expert knowledge structures in an instructional design model for physical education. *Journal of Teaching in Physical Education, 2*(3), 17–32.

Vickers, J. N. (1986). The resequencing task: Determining expert–novice differences in the organization of a movement sequence. *Research Quarterly for Exercise and Sport, 57*(3), 260–264.

Vickers, J. N. (1987). The role of subject matter in the preparation of teachers in physical education. *Quest, 39*(2), 179–184.

Weber, M. (1977). Physical education teacher role identification instrument. *Research Quarterly, 48*(2), 445–451.

Wendt, J. C., & Bain, L. L. (1989). Concerns of preservice and inservice physical educators. *Journal of Teaching in Physical Education, 8*(2), 177–180.

Wendt, J. C., Bain, L. L., & Jackson, A. S. (1981). Fuller's concerns theory as tested on prospective physical educators. *Journal of Teaching in Physical Education* (Introductory issue), 66–70.

Whaley, G. M. (1980). The effect of daily monitoring and feedback to teachers and students on academic learning time—physical education. (Doctoral dissertation, Ohio State University). *Dissertation Abstracts International, 41,* 1477A.

Whitaker, K. G. (1988). Homophobia in girls' and women's sports. In M. J. Adrian (Ed.), *National Coaching Institute Applied Research Papers.* Champaign, IL: NAGWS.

Widdop, J. H., & Widdop, V. (1975). A comparison of the personality traits of female teacher education and physical education students. *Research Quarterly, 46*(3), 274–281.

Wilkinson, S. (1986). Effects of a visual discrimination training program on the acquisition and maintenance of physical education student's volleyball skill analytic ability. *Dissertation Abstracts International, 47,* 1650A.

Williamson, K. M. (1988). *A phenomenological description of the professional lives and experiences of physical education teacher educators.* Unpublished doctoral dissertation, University of Massachusetts, Amherst.

Wittrock, M. C. (Ed.). (1986). *Handbook of research on teaching* (3rd ed.). New York: Macmillan.

Woods, S. (1989). *A phenomenological interview study of the experiences of lesbian physical education teachers.* Unpublished doctoral dissertation, University of Massachusetts, Amherst.

Zeichner, K. M. (1983). Alternative paradigms of teacher education. *Journal of Teacher Education, 34*(3), 3–9.

Zeichner, K. M., & Tabachnick, B. R. (1981). Are the effects of university teacher education "washed out" by school experience? *Journal of Teacher Education, 32*(3), 7–11.

Ziegler, E. F. (1975). A history of undergraduate professional preparation for physical education in the United States, 1861–1961. In E. F. Ziegler (Ed.), *A history of physical education and sport in the United States and Canada.* Champaign, IL: Stipes.

VOCATIONAL TEACHER EDUCATION

Frank C. Pratzner and Ray D. Ryan
THE OHIO STATE UNIVERSITY

The very foundations of vocational education in the United States of America have been and are continuing to be closely examined. The dynamics of these examinations are still occurring and will continue. This can be forecast because the very being of vocational education is dynamic and not static. The people served, the skills taught, and the delivery systems all change. To better understand these systems, their clients, and the subject matter and status of teacher education, it is necessary to understand the overall context of vocational education.

CONTEXT OF VOCATIONAL EDUCATION

Public vocational education must be understood within the context of the nation's public education system, as well as within the broad context of the vocational–technical education and job-training system, which requires the cooperative efforts of a variety of agencies and programs. Key among the providers of education and training for work are publicly funded secondary, postsecondary, and adult vocational education programs; apprenticeship systems; on-the-job training by business, industry, and trade unions; proprietary schools; military job training; and federally funded training programs such as those provided through the Job Training Partnership Act and the Job Corps.

Despite overlaps and gaps, each education and training agency or program has identifiable purposes and clientele. Collectively, they constitute a very significant enterprise, affecting millions of lives and spending billions of dollars annually. They differ from each other fundamentally in their goals, from remediating early socialization gaps to increasing profit margins. Their instructional strategies range from traditional classroom practices to on-the-job mentoring. They focus upon competen-

cies that range from literacy skills to job-ready technical proficiency, from personal development to work socialization, from basic assembly to mastery of complex state-of-the-art high technology. Their organizational structures range from federal, state, and local agencies or multicorporate companies to single programs in a school system or an entrepreneurial operation.

This enormous diversity in programs and services contributes to the broader goal of providing multiple service deliverers at the local level, so that individuals at different ages and stages of their lives have options that meet specific developmental and employment needs. Because these diverse programs have not been viewed by those who provide them or by others as components of an "articulated system" for work preparation, there has been little coordination or collaboration in their policies, practices, and services (Barnard, Leach, & Hofstrand, 1985; Taylor, Rosen, & Pratzner, 1982). Moreover, they do not share a common philosophy or approach to education and training.

Public-Sector Programs

Public secondary vocational education is offered in approximately 17,000 high schools in the nation (National Council on Employment Policy, 1982). Evans (1982) notes that four principal goals of vocational education are to "(a) provide the skilled workers needed by society, (b) increase the work-related options of trainees, (c) increase the face validity of general education and (d) enable trainees to improve their working conditions" (p. 267).

One of the more common organizational arrangements for providing secondary-level vocational education is as part of the comprehensive high school. The arrangement of general academic, college preparatory, and vocational offerings tends to

The authors gratefully acknowledge the assistance of W. R. Miller (University of Missouri—Columbia) for his comments on the draft of this chapter.

generate greater interaction among both students and faculty from all instructional areas. The amount of vocational education provided varies widely from one school to another, depending upon the number of students served, the resources available, and the interests of students and schools in the particular locality (Weber, Puleo, Kurth, Fisch, & Schaffner, 1988).

The separate-area vocational school, supported by a local school district or a group of school districts, is another organizational arrangement for vocational education. Students receive occupational preparation, as well as academic and related education, away from their neighborhood high schools. Area vocational schools have a broad base of support and, thus, are able to offer a wide variety of vocational programs.

Vocational education in the United States has developed as an adult enterprise. Little vocational education per se is available in American schools below the ninth-grade level. However, prevocational programs such as career education, industrial arts (technology education), and home economics are provided as part of the general education curriculum.

Secondary-level vocational education is virtually the only formal system of job preparation available to youth in this country. It is the mainstream system for youth to obtain education and training for work that requires less than a baccalaureate degree. All of the other major job-training programs such as those offered through apprenticeship, the military, employers, proprietary schools, and community colleges are adult programs. They are only available to adults or to older youth who have completed high school and/or are at least 17 or 18 years of age.

At the postsecondary level, vocational and technical programs are offered in 2-year community colleges, area vocational–technical schools, and technical institutes. Postsecondary enrollment increased sharply in the 1980s, as displaced and underemployed youth and adults sought more saleable skills in a rapidly changing labor market. In 1970, there were fewer than 1 million students in postsecondary programs; by 1984, there were over 10 million (National Center for Education Statistics, 1984).

Individualized instruction has facilitated *open-entry/open-exit* programs in many postsecondary schools. In the ideal form of such programs, students may enroll in and begin a program designed to meet their personal needs and occupational goals at any time during the school year. They proceed through the program at their own rates of learning and leave the program when they have achieved the required competencies. Open-entry/open-exit programs are now more common in postsecondary schools and private sector training programs, where compulsory school attendance laws are not a consideration.

Cooperative education programs have been highly successful. Students work part-time in business establishments and spend part of their time in school pursuing their general education and the vocational program. Training on the job is coordinated by school personnel. There are many groups throughout the country urging expansion of cooperative programs as a way of making education more relevant to students and broadening the impact of vocational and technical education.

Competency-based education is an important development

that has gained wide acceptance in vocational education (Finch, 1982). In this approach, performance objectives and standards are specified and agreed upon with students in advance of instruction. Each student then progresses systematically through an organized series of highly structured learning experiences, presented as learning packages or instructional modules. At each step, the student must demonstrate ability to perform the task before moving on to another learning assignment.

Numerous studies of performance- or competency-based teacher education were conducted throughout the 1970s. Cotrell, Chase, and Molnar (1972) identified 384 professional teacher competencies and launched a decade of research and development on CBTE. Weber et al. (1988) point out that, although competency-based instruction is quite prevalent, the available data provide few insights into the quality of the approaches or the extensiveness with which they have been implemented (p. xxi).

Adult vocational–technical programs constitute an important part of vocational education at both the secondary and postsecondary levels. In light of current economic and social trends, the occupational emphasis in adult education is not surprising. Millions of adults are finding that jobs are unavailable in expanding areas of the economy for which they are qualified. These adults must either change careers or upgrade their knowledge and skill levels.

A System in Transformation

Along with the rest of public education, vocational education is in a period of turmoil and rapid change. Compounding the reforms in the education system itself, profound and lasting changes are taking place in the nature of jobs and in the organization of work. Significant technological changes and quality of work-life developments are being implemented, to improve the productivity, quality, and international competitiveness of U.S. business and industry. Major social and demographic changes represent other factors shaping the way we live and work. These developments appear to have significant implications for vocational education and, in particular, for vocational teacher education (Levine & Rumberger, 1983; Pratzner & Russell, 1983, 1984; Sherman, 1983; Wirth, 1983a, 1983b).

Educational Dimensions of Change. American education is experiencing significant decentralization in the management of the educational enterprise. Authority and responsibility continue to increase at the local school level (Darling-Hammond & Berry, 1988; Mackenzie, 1982). Administrators and teachers are working more closely with parents and other interested stakeholders (e.g., school boards, employers, and district personnel). The major role of school administrators is becoming one of developing broad, visionary policies on the basis of extensive interactions with stakeholders.

Teaching is also becoming more complex and diverse than in the past. Teachers likely will continue to have more involvement with their students and the community, will be evaluated more frequently, and will have major responsibility for program reorientation (National Commission on Excellence in Education, 1983; National Commission for Excellence in Teacher Education, 1985; National Governors' Association, 1986).

The preparation of teachers will change drastically if the Carnegie Forum (1986) and the Holmes Group (1986) recommendations are implemented. For example, the move by major research institutions of higher education to require a 5-year preparation program has serious implications, especially for those areas of vocational education so reliant on work experience as a key criterion for teachers.

The major efforts underway to significantly upgrade the selection, preparation, certification, and remuneration of teachers will affect vocational education. Among the issues of particular concern to vocational education are the impact of higher standards for preparation and certification on the supply of new vocational teachers, what to do about nondegreed vocational teachers including those already teaching and those who might seek entry into vocational teaching from business and industry, how to rapidly update and upgrade vocational teacher preservice and inservice preparation, and how to attract and retain minority vocational teachers.

One consequence of the school reform and excellence movement is that the role and function of vocational education at the secondary school level has been called into serious question and a major reexamination is underway (e.g., Kadamus & Daggett, 1986; Lotto, 1986; Oakes, 1986; Pratzner, 1984, 1985; Pratzner & Russell, 1983; Ryan, 1984). This reexamination of high school vocational education has contributed, in turn, to the reappraisal of postsecondary-level vocational education and its articulation with secondary-level programs (National Commission on Secondary Vocational Education, 1985).

In spite of the uncertainty surrounding the appropriate role of vocational education in the high school, there is growing consensus that vocational education should give substantial attention to enhancing and reinforcing students' basic skills (e.g., Bennett, 1985; Carl D. Perkins Vocational Education Act, 1984; Levine & Rumberger, 1983; Lotto, 1983; National Academy of Sciences, 1984; National Commission on Secondary Vocational Education, 1985; Pratzner & Russell, 1983; Shields, 1984). The way this is to be done and the means for assessing the results are unclear (e.g., Mikulecky, 1986; Mikulecky, Ehlinger, & Meenan, 1987; Stern, Dayton, Paik, Weisberg, & Evans, 1988; Sticht, 1987; Sticht & Mikulecky, 1984). Moreover, the skills often called *basic* are expanding to include such areas as learning to learn, group process skills, problem solving, decision making, and critical thinking (Pratzner & Russell, 1984). Relatively little is known about the specific nature of these skills and the approaches and techniques needed for their effective practice, application, and enhancement (e.g., Bottoms, 1989; Bracey, 1983; Carnevale, Gainer, & Meltzer, 1988; Gainer, 1988; Resnick, 1987).

Economic/Technological Dimensions of Change. Uncertainty and disagreement exist about the nature of economic change and technological developments in the workplace and their impact on skill requirements and on the education and training needs of workers. However, two broad types of educational

consequences seem to be especially important for teacher preparation: (a) changes in the skills and skill levels of workers, resulting from sociotechnological (i.e., social, organizational, and technological) changes at work; and (b) changes in the workplace as a learning environment for continuing and recurrent education.

Clearly, more education and training for work will take place within business and industry in the future than was true in the past. Carnevale and Goldstein (1983) note that employee training by employers is already by far the largest system of adult education. Eurick (1985) estimates that corporations are spending $40 to $60 billion to train and educate nearly 8 million students/employees annually. He points out that this approaches the total annual expenditures of all of America's 4-year and graduate colleges and universities. Moreover, as noted by Carnevale and Goldstein (1983), Carnevale and Gainer (1988), Goldstein (1980), and Zemsky and Meyerson (1985), measurement problems and the lack of detailed company records systematically drive estimates of employee training below actual levels.

Given the current rate of technological change, the demographics of the labor force, and the changing attitudes and approaches to work of large segments of the work force, employers will be increasingly pressed to design and implement workplaces that function effectively as continuous learning environments. These increases in industry-specific training have important potential implications for vocational teacher preparation.

Sociodemographic Dimensions of Change. The effects of social and demographic changes on education and vocational education are many and are discussed extensively in the literature (e.g., Adams, Pratzner, Anderson, & Zimmerer, 1987; American Vocational Association, 1986; Thornton, 1984; Trafford, 1984; U.S. General Accounting Office, 1986; Young, 1985). Much less literature and concern is evident for the implications of such demographic changes as the aging of the U.S. population, the continuing rapid increases in all minority populations, the increases in nontraditional occupational roles, and the significant changes in life-styles and in the management and organization of work for vocational teacher preparation.

Our society is experiencing rapid increases in minority populations. Over one-third of new births are to minority parents. Thornton (1984) points out that 28.6 million blacks account for 12.1 percent of the population. Hispanic Americans, now numbering around 16 million, are expected to become the largest minority group in the 1990s. Asian Americans, the fastest growing group, jumped 128 percent in one decade to total 3.5 million in 1980.

Few educators are prepared to deal with the problems spawned by these demographic trends. In many of our urban areas "minority majorities" will increasingly occupy the classrooms. At the same time that standards of academic excellence and achievement are increasing, schools must find ways to insure effective learning by increasing numbers of black, Hispanic, and other minority youth who traditionally have not done well in academic settings. How these academically less able and dropout-prone students are best served and what role vocational education should play in quality education for these groups are unanswered questions of great concern (Friedenberg, 1987).

Along with the task of determining how best to serve the needs of an increasingly culturally diverse student body, schools are facing the difficult task of dealing with a significant dropout problem. Across the nation, more than one in every four students enrolling in the ninth grade drops out before high school graduation. Compared with white students, the dropout rate of black students is just under twice as great, and for Hispanic students it is twice as great (U.S. General Accounting Office 1986, p. 6). In some school systems, the dropout rate for Hispanic students approaches 70 percent. Dropouts experience higher unemployment rates and lower earnings throughout their lives, creating a potential future dual-class society. In effect, many of these individuals not only drop out of school, but also drop out of life (American Vocational Association, 1986).

Women, minorities, and the handicapped continue to experience higher unemployment rates than white males. The problem is exacerbated for teenagers, especially minority teenagers. For many historical reasons, women and minorities are crowded into specific kinds of occupations. Because of this situation, on the average, minority men earn less than majority men, and women earn about 63 percent of what men earn (U.S. General Accounting Office, 1986).

Lower birthrates, increased life expectancy, and aging of the baby boom generation are the causes of America's aging. By 1990, the number of people between the ages of 30 and 44 has been projected to have increased by 20 percent and to have reached a total of 60 million. This aging process may be the leading reason for decreased spending for elementary and secondary education, coupled with an increased need for adult education.

Workers with critical technical skills will be retiring at an increasingly rapid rate. For example, the average age of the nation's 300,000 machinists is 58, yet industry is presently training only one-fourth of the skilled machinists needed each year (American Vocational Association, 1986). Responses to these shortages need to be developed.

In general, the decline in labor force growth, the search for self-fulfillment, the increased levels of educational attainment, the increased numbers of two wage earners in a household with fewer children, the move toward more permanent part-time work, and the increased competition for fewer middle-management positions by the increasing numbers of people from the baby boom cohort are all signals of the changes occurring in the workplace. They provide powerful incentives for employers to be flexible in meeting the personal needs of workers and managers and they have important implications for vocational education and teacher preparation.

Because vocational education is part of the nation's educational system and a major component of its diverse employment and training system, vocational teacher education programs not only prepare vocational teachers for public school programs, but are also major suppliers of a variety of education and training specialists for vocational education and job training in the private sector. Consequently, vocational teacher preparation is not solely responsive to the needs or directions of the public education system. Needs, directions, and changes within any of the diverse agencies and programs that makeup the nation's education and job-training system can have significant implications for vocational teacher preparation.

Thus, for example, increases in private sector adult training and retraining resulting from significant technological change and major demographic shifts (Carnevale & Goldstein, 1983; Eurick, 1985) suggest that preparation of new types of vocational education and training specialists for the private sector is becoming a rapidly expanding market for vocational teacher preparation. To maintain a share of this growth market, vocational teacher preparation might need to develop new collaborative arrangements with other college and university departments or schools, to create new hybrid programs, approaches, and specialties for human resource development, human performance assessment, and training and development in business and industry (Pratzner, 1988). In addition to teacher preparation, substantive expertise and new, imaginative, and highly flexible management and instructional delivery systems might also be needed for teacher-preparation institutions to compete effectively with secondary-level area vocational schools and 2-year postsecondary vocational institutions for a share of the in-plant, specialized, employee training and retraining market.

VOCATIONAL EDUCATION TEACHERS

The formal preparation of vocational teachers has not followed a single track or approach. However, almost all states require prospective public vocational teachers to have from 3 to 6 years or more of full-time significant occupational experience prior to teaching. Many nondegreed vocational teachers enter teaching directly from business and industry (including the military) with extensive occupational skills and experience but with little or no pedagogical skills or preparation. This occurs primarily at the postsecondary level and in the private sector, where state licensing and teacher certification requirements beyond occupational competence are usually not a consideration.

Vocational teachers entering public secondary-level vocational education from business and industry might also enter teaching directly. But most states require vocational teachers to obtain from 16 to 200 clock hours of initial pedagogical instruction concurrent with their first year of teaching and additional hours of professional-skill development annually to maintain their state certification. Often this part-time instruction is provided by a college or university teacher education program, and the credits earned may be applied toward a baccalaureate degree in teaching. Alternatively, prospective vocational teachers coming from business and industry may enter a full-time baccalaureate-degree teacher education program prior to entering teaching.

Master's and doctoral degrees are typically required for vocational teacher educators in colleges and universities. But even today, college-level vocational teacher educators can be found with baccalaureate degrees only.

Vocational Teacher Characteristics

Three recent studies are especially important for vocational education and provide the major sources of data for this and subsequent sections of the chapter. The first is a survey by Pratzner (1987) of first-year vocational teachers' perceptions of their competencies and their preservice and inservice preparation for teaching. Included as beginning teachers was an unbiased national sample of 740 degreed and nondegreed vocational teachers from 24 states stratified and selected by geographic region. The teachers represented all of the major vocational service areas, and they had begun their first year of teaching in school year 1985–1986. Additionally, data were obtained from 69 of 114 vocational teacher education institutions in the 24 states surveyed, from 530 school administrators/mentors identified by beginning teachers as individuals who had the major responsibility and best opportunity to monitor their first-year teaching performance, and from the 50 state directors of vocational education.

The second study was a major vocational data-collection project conducted by Weber et al. (1988). This study collected systematic, national data on the content, processes, and outcomes of vocational education programs at the high school level. This national data base included observations of 893 classrooms in 120 high schools. The 120 schools constituted and unbiased, nationwide sample of high schools that offered two or more federally assisted vocational programs, with systematic variations in such factors as school size, type, and location; racial/ethnic mix of student body; economic status of community; and geographic characteristics. Each of the classrooms in the study was observed by one assigned observer on two different occasions (full periods on 2 different days during a one-week period). Then the data were accumulated over class periods into a single observational protocol per classroom. Included in this data base are data on a total of 267 variables for each of 2,251 teachers (737 observed teachers and 1,514 nonobserved teachers; 1,294 vocational teachers and 939 nonvocational teachers).

The third study focused on public postsecondary vocational education (Hollenbeck, Belcher, Dean, Rider, & Warmbrod, 1987). About 730 institutions were sampled, representing over 30 percent of all U.S. institutions offering public postsecondary vocational education. At each institution, responses were solicited from as many as 20 different individuals: administrators, instructors, placement directors, chairpersons, and students. Over 6,000 responses were received and used in the analyses. In addition to the survey, project staff spent from 3 to 5 days in each of 48 institutions located in 38 states interviewing staff, including instructors, and observing classroom instruction.

According to the Pratzner (1987) study of 740 beginning vocational teachers, approximately one-half of the teachers were male (362), one-half were female (354), and 24 did not report their sex. The large majority (86.2 percent) were white, 3.1 percent were Hispanic, and 3.1 percent were black. The remainder were American Indian ($n = 11$), Asian American ($n = 4$), or did not report their race ($n = 24$). Weber et al. (1988) report that 7 percent of their sample of 1,294 vocational teachers were black, and 5 percent were from other minority groups. Hollenbeck et al. (1987) found that the average percentage of 1,239 vocational instructors by racial/ethnic origin in postsecondary institutions was 91 percent white, 4.7 percent black, 1.6 percent Hispanic.

Interestingly, a national survey of college education majors by the American Association of Colleges for Teacher Education (1987) confirms that the racial mix of this study's sample of vocational teachers is also an accurate reflection of the racial mix for all education majors. It found that 5 percent of education students in the 1985–1986 academic year were black, whereas only 3 percent were Hispanic.

These data on race seem to be a reasonable reflection of conditions in the field of vocational teaching as a whole, and they highlight a serious problem: the lack of minority vocational teachers (Intergovernmental Advisory Council on Education, 1985). Unless a major minority recruitment and enrollment effort is made within the field, it is a problem that will grow increasingly more serious as the number of minority students in high school and in vocational programs rapidly increases in the years immediately ahead. Although such a recruitment effort is critical, it will also be increasingly more difficult in the future, as others within and outside education seek to extent their own minority recruitment and training programs and as minorities continue to broaden their employment opportunities and seek preparation for a wider range of jobs outside of education jobs with higher salaries and more prestige than teaching.

The average age of the beginning teachers was 33.2 years old and the ages ranged from 22 to 66 years old. This average age is probably somewhat higher than might be expected for beginning teachers in general and is probably accounted for by the fact that, as noted, most states require for certification 3–6 or more years of full-time work experience in the occupation to be taught. Even in the several teaching areas that typically do not require occupational experience (e.g., industrial arts, home economics), it is not unusual for teachers to come from full-time jobs in business and industry and, therefore, to be somewhat older than beginning teachers in general (Dugger, Fowler, Jones, & Starkweather, 1986).

The average age of the secondary school vocational teachers in the Weber et al. study was 43.8 years. The average for postsecondary vocational instructors in the Hollenbeck et al. study was 45.2 years.

Approximately 75 percent of the beginning teachers in the Pratzner study had completed bachelor's degrees or higher levels of education. Twenty-six percent ($n = 193$) were nondegreed vocational teachers who had completed some college, or perhaps a 2-year associate degree, but who had not earned the baccalaureate degree. Moreover, the health, trade and industrial (T&I), and technical occupations service areas had significantly more nondegreed teachers than the other service areas. Whereas 73 percent of the T&I teachers did not have degrees ($n = 108$), one-half of the technical teachers ($n = 17$) and health occupations teachers ($n = 25$) did not have degrees. Weber et al. report that 37 percent of the vocational teachers in their study had bachelor's degrees and 35 percent had master's degrees or higher. Hollenbeck et al. found that almost 21 percent of postsecondary instructors were nondegreed, 8 percent had bachelor's degrees, and about 71 percent had graduate credit or master's or higher degrees.

Most of the teachers in the Pratzner study were secondary school teachers. Almost 69 percent of those responding taught in comprehensive high schools (46.8 percent) and secondary-level area vocational schools (21.9 percent). However, analysis of variance of teachers' age by service area revealed that those who taught health, trade, and industrial subjects and technical occupations were predominantly postsecondary teachers and were significantly older than teachers in the other occupational service areas.

Almost all of the beginning teachers (98 percent) taught in public institutions, whereas only 2 percent taught in private institutions. At the beginning of their second year of teaching, the majority (95 percent) were teaching in the same school they had started at a year earlier. Nearly one-half of the teachers said they were certified and taught in three vocational areas: trade and industrial occupations ($n = 136$), consumer and homemaking education ($n = 93$), and business and office occupations ($n = 91$). The remaining half were spread across the other occupational service areas (agricultural education, $n = 67$; marketing and distributive education, $n = 27$; health occupations, $n = 48$; technical occupations, $n = 32$; industrial arts, $n = 65$; vocational special education, $n = 7$), or they were certified and taught in other related areas ($n = 61$). Twenty-seven were teaching without certification.

According to Hollenbeck et al., approximately 53 percent of postsecondary instructors were state certified to teach. Thirty-two percent said they were not required to and did not have state certification, and another 14.7 percent were not certified at all or were certified for less than one year.

The average length of time in their current jobs for postsecondary instructors was 8.9 years, and the average annual salary was $30,200. Weber et al. report that the average years of teaching experience for high school vocational teachers was 6.2 years, with an approximate average annual salary of $22,000 to $25,999. Although the average salary for high school vocational teachers was about the same as that for nonvocational high school teachers (Darling-Hammond & Berry, 1988; Weber et al., 1988), it was somewhat lower than that for postsecondary teachers. Approximately 37 percent of the 1,239 postsecondary instructors were covered under collective bargaining agreements. Comparable data for beginning and high school vocational teachers were not available.

In 1985–1986, beginning teachers taught an average of 84.3 students and 22.4 special needs students. However, the number of students taught differed significantly by service area. Analysis of variance revealed that industrial arts ($\overline{X} = 163.2$), consumer and homemaking ($\overline{X} = 111.3$), and business and office ($\overline{X} = 103.0$) teachers taught significantly more students than teachers in the other occupational service areas.

After one year of teaching, the study sample of beginning teachers' satisfaction with various aspects of teaching was mixed. On average, they were most satisfied with the administrative support they received, with class sizes, and with school facilities (see also Dugger et al., 1986). They were least satisfied with their opportunities for input into school decisions. They were also dissatisfied with the parental support they received, their opportunities for advancement, and the time they had available for preparation. Seventy-seven percent were either very satisfied or somewhat satisfied with their salaries. In spite of these dissatisfactions, when asked how long they anticipated remaining in teaching, almost half said they expected to remain from 2 to 10 years and the other half anticipated staying indefinitely.

Conversely, the aspects of teaching that beginning teachers liked most in their first year were the intrinsic aspects of the job, all clearly related to interactions and relationships with students. Other aspects of teaching or school facilities and personnel were not rated highly. Almost one-third said that seeing students grow and succeed was the thing they liked best about teaching ($n = 226$). Another one-fourth felt that helping, influencing, and working with young people was their favorite thing ($n = 183$). Thirteen percent ($n = 95$) reported that interaction and communication with students on a personal level was the thing they liked most about first-year teaching. These findings were consistent with those of the American Association of Colleges for Teacher Education survey (1987) which reported that 90 percent of education majors wanted to become teachers in order to help children grow and learn.

These findings on beginning vocational teacher job satisfaction and anticipated time in teaching are also consistent with the findings of the Metropolitan Life Insurance Companys' annual survey of the American teacher (1987). These data reveal that teacher morale rose significantly in 1987, with the number of teachers saying they were satisfied with their jobs rising from 81 to 85 percent. In addition, according to an article in the September 10, 1987, issue of *Teacher Education Reports*, the pollsters found that "the number now saying that they are likely to give up teaching within the next five years declined from 27 percent in 1986 to 22 percent this year" (p. 2). The article goes on to state that this change in attitude is "most marked among those young and new teachers with less than five years' experience. In 1986 the surveyors found that 39 percent of these teachers were contemplating a career change, but that number has plummeted by nearly half to 20 percent this year" (p. 2). Additionally, the AACTE survey of college education majors found that nearly half planned to teach for at least 10 years, whereas 27 percent said they planned to teach twice that long.

Vocational Teacher Testing and Certification

Teacher quality is receiving considerable attention from politicians, policymakers, and the general public. Kaplan (1985) observes that "the recruitment, performance, work habits, incentives, preparation, and quality of teachers have ignited attention and action throughout the nation. Scarcely a week passes without legislative or executive measures aimed at achieving excellence in the teaching profession" (p. 2). National polls have repeatedly shown that the great majority of the American public supports mandatory teacher competency testing for certification. For example, the 1986 Gallup poll of the public's attitude toward the public schools showed that "85 percent of the public favored requiring experienced teachers to pass a statewide test of basic competency in their subject areas. Three previous education polls showed across-the-board support for teacher competency testing" (Gallup & Clark, 1987, p. 27). Denham (1985) comments on the factors that have generated support for teacher competency testing, noting that "a recent loss of confidence in universities as providers of well-educated graduates, often coupled with suspicion that university teacher training programs are neither rigorous nor effective, has led about all of the fifty states to require competency tests for the credentialing of teachers" (p. 41).

Ishler (1985) observes that "competency testing of prospective teachers seems to be taking this country by storm." He goes on to note that "It is being viewed both as a quality assurance measure for the general public and as a way of demonstrating that teaching is indeed a profession since other professions already require successful completion of an examination prior to entry" (p. 27).

Although almost all states have implemented, or are in the process of implementing, some form of mandatory basic-skills competency testing for certification of regular academic teachers, little is known regarding states' initiatives and policies related to the certification of vocational teachers. Presently, there are no universal standards governing the certification of vocational teachers. There are wide variations in vocational teacher certification requirements not only among states, but also within states and across specific specialty areas and levels of instruction. These requirements are also different within states for degreed and nondegreed teachers. In general, states' requirements for the certification of nondegreed vocational teachers have been limited to documented evidence of basic education and a minimum amount of relevant occupational experience. On the other hand, candidates aspiring to teach in such areas as business education, industrial arts, and home economics must, in general, hold bachelor's degrees and have some amount of relevant occupational experience (Miller, 1982).

A fairly recent survey of state practices related to the certification of prospective vocational teachers (Milanovich, 1986) shows a national trend toward competency testing consistent with the trend in all areas of certification. The survey by Pratzner (1987) examined the patterns and practices of competency testing of vocational teachers for three primary purposes: (a) admission to teacher education programs, (b) graduation from teacher education programs, and (c) state certification. Data regarding the first two purposes were obtained by means of the mailed survey of 740 first-year vocational teachers and 69 colleges and universities offering undergraduate vocational teacher education programs in 24 selected states. Data regarding state-mandated competency testing requirements for the certification of vocational teachers across the 50 states were gathered from the state directors of vocational education through an electronic mail network.

Testing for Teacher Program Admission and Graduation

The finding regarding test requirements for vocational teacher education program admission show that the American College Test was the most popular test for admission during the 1980s (Pratzner, 1987). This was followed by the Scholastic Aptitude Test and the Pre-professional Skills Test. Although the National Teacher Examination Core Battery was used by only 20.7 percent of the institutions, its use relative to the early 1980s had almost doubled. The number of institutions reporting average minimum acceptable standards on these tests for admission was inadequate to draw any conclusions.

In general, these findings regarding test requirements for program admission are similar to those reported for the 18 member–institutions of the University Council for Vocational Education (Anderson, 1986). Seven of the 18 institutions (almost 39 percent) reported that "passing a competency test was required prior to admission to teacher education" (p. 7).

Apparently, most institutions do *not* require competency examinations for graduation. Among those requiring a competency test for graduation, no single test was used predominantly. However, almost half of the institutions (49.2 percent) used some part of the National Teacher Examination. Almost 19 percent used the NTE professional-knowledge test for graduation, whereas 17.4 percent used the NTE Core Battery.

These findings of little or no change in the type or rigor of program admission and graduation requirements from the early to mid-1980s are surprising in light of all the attention given to wide-ranging improvements and increased rigor in teacher education by a variety of prestigious state and national groups, starting with the National Commission on Excellence in Education and including, among others, the Carnegie Forum's Task Force on Teaching as a Profession, the Holmes Group, the two major teacher unions, and the American Association of Colleges for Teacher Education.

When asked how receptive they thought their institutions were to the recommendations of the Holmes Group, 47.8 percent of the respondents said they thought their institutions were receptive to them. Almost 22 percent said they were *not* receptive to them, and 30.4 percent did not respond to the question. Additionally, 72.1 percent of the teacher education institutions (or 61 of 69 institutions) said they had no plans to restructure preservice programs to include a fifth-year master's-degree program to improve preparation for teaching basic skills, and 68.3 percent said they did not plan a fifth-year master's-degree program to improve preparation for teaching special needs students. Whereas changes in teacher education policies and practices growing out of the reform debate and the Holmes Group recommendations might eventually improve the rigor of vocational teacher preparation, other equally compelling current practices work against this. For example, such practices as the heavy insistence on increased student full-time equivalent (FTE) production in many institutions might dissuade faculty and students from seeking appropriate and rigorous preparation outside their major departments and, thereby, contribute to mediocrity.

Testing for State Certification. Of the 50 states surveyed, 23 states (45 percent) indicated that basic-skills-competency testing was one of the state-mandated requirements for the certification of vocational teachers. Similarly, in 26 states (52 percent), occupational-competency testing was a certification requirement for vocational teachers. In 14 (28 percent) of the states surveyed, testing in both basic skills and occupational competency was required for vocational teacher certification (Pratzner, 1987). However, very few states were testing the pedagogical and professional teaching skills of prospective vocational teachers.

Results also indicated that six different tests were used by states for testing the basic-skills competencies of prospective vocational teachers. The National Teacher Examination Core Battery (34.8 percent of the states) and state-developed tests (30.4 percent) were the most frequently used instruments.

Another issue related to competency testing for vocational teachers is that of achieving an appropriate balance of academic skills, pedagogical skills and professional knowledge, and occupational skills. Raising basic-skills test requirements for vocational teachers could discourage competent craftpersons and technicians from high school teaching and push them toward teaching in the private sector or at the public postsecondary level, where certification and competency testing are presently not major issues or concerns. Moreover, minority teachers are underrepresented in the teaching profession, and a disproportionate number of minority candidates are failing tests for certification. The full impact of this is still unknown. However, a report by the U.S. Department of Education's Office of Educational Research and Improvement (1987), examining the impact of the teacher-testing phenomenon upon minority group members, finds that "there has been a drop in the supply of talented, well-educated minority teachers and this is occurring at a time when there is an increasing need for Black, Hispanic and Asian-American classroom instructors" (*Teacher Education Reports*, 1987, p. 5). Consequently, policymakers need to assess the full societal, cultural, and political impact of teacher competency testing before its full-blown implementation.

On the other hand, in today's workplace, where technology is expanding at an exponential rate, developing vocational education students' basic skills has become as important as developing their occupational skills. Therefore, the concept of integrating or infusing basic-skills preparation into vocational education is gaining more acceptance (Wirt, Muraskin, Goodwin, & Meyer, 1989; Pritz, 1988). To achieve this objective, vocational teachers with sound basic-skills preparation are needed. Consequently, basic skills, as well as occupational-competency testing, designed to insure that prospective vocational teachers can meet these challenges, seems highly desirable (Bottoms, 1989; Pratzner, 1987).

A critical concern closely related to the competency testing issue is the growing support for the requirement that all public school teachers have a 4-year liberal arts degree with a subject-matter major before entering a teacher-preparation program. "This requirement, which has been advocated strongly by two major reform groups in teacher education (the Carnegie Forum on Teaching [*sic*] and the Holmes Group) is favored by 72 percent of the public. Only 17 percent oppose it" (Gallup & Clark, 1987, p. 27). A poll of 1,513 adults and 202 top executives from 1,000 of the country's leading corporations was conducted for the Carnegie Forum on Education and the Economy by Louis Harris and Associates. Results revealed that "nearly 80 percent of the public and 68 percent of the business executives favored

the Forum's recommendation that teachers obtain a four-year college degree in the subject they plan to teach" (*Education Daily*, 1986). Also, according to the survey, most of the adults and top executives "believe teachers should be required to demonstrate full command of the subject they teach and the ability to communicate that knowledge to students" (p. 2).

Two conclusions seem to be important. First, although it would seem to be highly desirable for all teachers, including public school vocational teachers, to have a 4-year liberal arts degree, this would not appear to be sufficient for vocational teachers to acquire full command of the subject they will teach. High levels of occupational competence probably are best acquired through years of direct, on-the-job, work experience, which is a traditional and continuing requirement for vocational teacher certification. Whether or not they teach occupations that require less than a baccalaureate degree, to relate effectively with their academic colleagues and to meet increased public expectations and standards, all vocational teachers, especially at the secondary school level, will increasingly need to acquire 4-year baccalaureate degrees. It would seem that the traditional expectation and route into vocational teaching, including the combination of a 4-year baccalaureate degree with a balanced emphasis on teaching and a liberal education and 3–6 years of related occupational experience, should enable vocational teachers to develop the skills and knowledge in the three major areas necessary for teaching: basic skills, professional knowledge and pedagogical skills, and subject-matter specialty skills and knowledge.

Second, acquiring a liberal arts degree with a major in the subject they plan to teach might not be sufficient preparation for academic teachers to "demonstrate full command of the subject they teach and the ability to communicate that knowledge to students" (Pratzner, 1987, p. 31). Beyond the requirement of a liberal arts degree and pedagogical expertise, it seems essential that state certification requirements, as well as the major teacher reform groups, consider the need of all teachers, especially academic teachers, for significant amounts of practical, on-the-job, work experience in or related to their academic disciplines. Such discipline-related work experience should provide structured, real-world opportunities for the application and use of discipline-based knowledge and skills outside of strictly academic and school-based settings, thereby broadening teachers' command of the subjects they teach. Almost 70 years of experience in public vocational education and recent experiments with alternative routes into teaching (primarily in New Jersey) have shown that this could be a promising way to eventually reduce some of the abstractness and lack of relevance of much of current academic teaching and its detrimental effects on students. It might also help facilitate the integration of academic and vocational education.

Vocational Teacher Preparation

The average number of full-time education faculty, including vocational education, at the 69 institutions included in the Pratzner study was 63. The average number of full-time vocational education faculty was 10. On average, education faculties included 17 part-time faculty, of which 5 were in vocational education.

Nearly one-third of the institutions did not report student enrollment figures. For the two-thirds responding, the average full-time enrollment in teacher education, including vocational teacher education, was 366 students, and 166 students was the average part-time enrollment. The average full-time enrollment in all occupational service areas of vocational teacher education was 99 students, and the average part-time enrollment was 47 students.

As pointed out in a study of the 18 member institutions of the University Council for Vocational Education (Anderson, 1986), most institutions have experienced reduced demand for vocational education courses both on and off campus since the early 1980s. Moreover, the total number of undergraduate and doctoral students in vocational teacher education declined since this time, as has the number of full-time faculty and support staff (p. 849).

Most students entered the vocational teacher education program in either their junior year of college (44.9 percent) or their freshman year (30.4 percent). The average time required to complete the vocational teacher program was 3.6 years.

Almost all of the institutions (95.7 percent) were accredited by their respective states. Sixty-one percent had regional accreditation, and 84.1 percent were accredited by the National Council for Accreditation of Teacher Education. Six of the institutions were members of the University Council for Vocational Education, and 20 were members of the Holmes Group. Over three-fourths of the teacher education institutions offered industrial arts programs. Consumer and homemaking occupations, office occupations, and trade and industry programs were each offered by close to two-thirds of the institutions.

The business education program, offered by over 50 percent of the institutions, was by far the largest program in terms of average number of graduates ($\overline{X} = 20.1$). This was followed by agricultural programs ($\overline{X} = 15.5$), industrial arts programs ($\overline{X} = 11.0$), and office occupations programs ($\overline{X} = 10.7$).

Entry requirements changed little during this time (Pratzner, 1987). When most 1985 graduates entered teacher education programs entry requirements were about the same as those for 1981 and 1983. Most institutions did not require prior experiences working with youth or personal letters of recommendation for admission to their programs, and this had not changed since the early 1980s. The large majority of institutions used an average undergraduate cumulative grade point average (GPA) of 2.4 points for program admission then and in the early 1980s. Almost 48 percent of the institutions required an average of 3 years of work experience related to the vocational service area students intended to enter.

Although 80 percent of the institutions required a high school diploma for admission, almost 15 percent did *not* require one. Most of the institutions did *not* use high school class rank or high school GPA for their admission decisions. For the 25 percent of the institutions that did use high school GPA, the average GPA required was 2.0 points. This was the same as that required in the early 1980s.

There was no apparent change in the number of institutions requiring courses in communications and mathematics or in the average number of credits required in these courses for admission to teacher education programs. An average seven or eight credits were required in communication courses, and four or five credits in mathematics courses were required for program admission.

Almost 88 percent of the institutions ($n = 57$) required one or two additional courses in mathematics, and 71 percent required three or four additional courses in communications, as part of their vocational teacher education program. A course was defined as one that met for two to five classroom hours per week during one semester or quarter. Additionally, 64 percent required two or three courses in the humanities and fine arts, 62.5 percent required two or three courses in science, and 70 percent required two or three courses in the social sciences. Almost 59 percent required one course in computer skills, whereas 32 percent did not require computer skills courses. A comparison of the average number of courses actually taken in these academic areas by beginning vocational teachers with the institutional course requirements in the area shows that, in general, the beginning teachers met or exceeded the institutional requirements in each of the areas.

If it is assumed that a college course is equivalent to three college credits, then the courses taken and the institutional credit requirements in the five major academic areas for beginning vocational teachers can be compared with three other estimates of academic requirements. These three estimates are all based upon a study of college transcripts conducted by Galambos, Cornett, and Spitler (1985) for the Southern Regional Education Board. Although there was considerable variability among the 17 institutions included in the SREB study and among the 69 institutions in the Pratzner study, several trends can be noted.

First, in all academic areas, the average institutional requirements reported for the 69 institutions in the Pratzner study exceeded the average catalog requirements listed for the 17 SREB institutions. *Second*, on average, the number of credit hours reportedly taken by beginning vocational teachers in mathematics (7.2 credits) was about the same as the average number of mathematics credits taken either by academic teachers (6.0 credits) or arts and sciences majors (7.2 credits). However, it should be noted that Galambos et al. and a study of Texas institutions conducted by Galambos (1986) both found that lower level mathematics courses, remedial courses, and courses in mathematics explicitly designed for teachers help account for the average number of credits in mathematics for academic teachers. This could also be the case for beginning vocational teachers, but data were not collected regarding the exact nature of the courses or credits taken by them. The average number of English credits taken by beginning vocational teachers (10.2 credits) was slightly less than the average number of English credits taken by the academic teachers and the arts and sciences majors (11.3 and 11.8 average credits respectively).

In each of the other three academic areas, the academic teachers and arts and sciences majors in the SREB study, on average, greatly exceeded the beginning vocational teachers in average credits taken and in average institutional requirements. It seems clear that, in general, beginning vocational teachers did not pursue a rigorous liberal arts program. In general, they were considerably below academic teachers and arts and sciences majors in science, social science, and humanities credits required or earned. Moreover, T&I teachers took significantly fewer courses in these academic areas in their preservice preparation than any of the other beginning vocational teachers.

Clearly, vocational teacher education must improve the academic rigor of its programs and the quality of its students. It must achieve a more appropriate balance of preparation in academic and liberal arts, pedagogical and professional skills and knowledge, and occupational skills. Currently, a rigorous liberal arts component is missing. Moreover, because the concept of integrating and infusing basic skills into vocational teaching is gaining widespread acceptance, vocational teachers with sound basic-skills preparation are needed (Bottoms, 1989; Pratzner, 1987).

Preservice and inservice vocational programs need to be expanded and improved relative to teachers' preparation to teach basic skills and special student populations. At present, vocational teacher preservice preparation gives little or modest attention, at best, to these critical needs. Beginning teachers take very few courses, or even parts of courses, to prepare them for teaching basic skills and special needs students (Pratzner, 1987; Weber et al., 1988). Most teachers say they spend from one to 3 hours per week improving and reinforcing students' basic skills. The majority of beginning teachers do not rank basic skills among the top four skill areas they emphasize in their teaching. Whereas economically disadvantaged and handicapped students and students in programs nontraditional for their sex seem to be included to a limited extent in beginning vocational teachers' teaching, the large majority of teachers spend little or no time teaching retraining for adults, single parents and displaced homemakers, limited-English-proficient students, and incarcerated individuals.

The majority of beginning vocational teachers received no inservice preparation during their first year of teaching. The little amount of inservice preparation available to the few was generally judged by them as being only somewhat effective.

Apparently, such recent developments as so-called *induction year programs* and first-year mentoring and assistance programs for teachers are still things of the future in secondary-level vocational education. Teacher education institutions need to work more closely with local schools in the provision of inservice training to help meet beginning-teacher and local school needs (Hanes & Rowls, 1984) and, especially, to help reduce and ultimately eliminate the practice of nondegreed vocational teaching.

The *only* time beginning teachers considered desirable for receiving inservice preparation was professional days (i.e., release time or time when teachers would ordinarily be teaching). They overwhelmingly rejected mornings and afternoons outside the normal school day and weekends as possible times for inservice activities.

Regarding the desirability of different kinds of inservice providers, the Pratzner study revealed that the *most* desirable providers of inservice preparation were teachers with practical expertise in effective instructional methods. The next most desirable providers were training experts from business and industry, and finally university faculty with expertise in both vocational and special education. Conversely, there seems to be general agreement about and aversion to district-office and state department personnel as desirable providers of inservice preparation. This may be explained by the likelihood that few beginning teachers are familiar with district-office and state department services and expertise.

In general, inservice preparation for teaching basic skills seems to have received slightly more attention than inservice preparation for working with special needs students. This is also a little surprising, because federal vocational legislation has long emphasized the need for vocational education to improve access and services for special student populations, and it has only more recently emphasized improved basic-skills development of students.

In almost all cases, administrators rated a variety of inservice strategies for strengthening teachers' abilities in teaching basic skills and special student populations higher in effectiveness than did beginning teachers. The inservice strategies rated most highly effective by both teachers and administrators were (a) courses taken at a college or university that related directly to the teacher's needs; (b) first-year teacher-support teams (including mentor, administrator, vocational/area specialist); and (c) workshops or seminars for small groups of teachers.

The single experience rated most useful for teaching basic skills and special student populations by the largest percentage of teachers was student teaching. Formal inservice training was rated second in usefulness for teaching basic skills, and other activities such as volunteer work and personal contact with special needs individuals were also rated by a large percentage of the teachers as highly useful for teaching special needs students.

A large percentage of the teacher education institutions surveyed by Pratzner (1987) had already implemented a number of strategies to improve the preparation of vocational teachers to teach special needs students. For example, over 68 percent of the institutions had improved faculty awareness and development through workshops, seminars, and other programs; over 60 percent had added one or more courses on special education to the curriculum; and over 70 percent had redesigned existing methods courses to emphasize more strongly the teaching of special needs students. Still, many institutions seemed to have no plans to implement numerous strategies they judged to be effective or somewhat effective in preparation to teach special needs students.

RESEARCH CHALLENGE

Clearly, one of the greatest challenges facing vocational education is the paucity of high-quality research dealing with vocational teacher education. In preparing this chapter, the lack of available research on critical teacher education problems was apparent.

The 1962 issue of the *Review of Educational Research* on vocational, technical, and practical arts education ("Vocational," 1962) listed 10 studies in teacher education. In his review of research in vocational technical teacher education from 1962 to 1967, Moss (1967) concludes that, "with some exceptions, little has been done which materially contributes to the development of a science of teacher education. . . . At present, we are still operating programs primarily on the basis of tradition, conventional wisdom, and personal experience" (p. 26).

The period between 1967 and 1973 was no more fruitful according to Peterson (1973). He reviewed research on vocational teacher education for the period, and he concludes that it "was quite frequently the result of doctoral dissertations or graduate research fellows. Teacher educators are undoubtedly giving first priority to teaching responsibilities and research efforts have a secondary claim for time. . . . At best the research appears piecemeal and without reason or order" (pp. 27, 32).

Adamsky and Cotrell (1979) reviewed the vocational teacher education research from 1973 to 1979. They found that the majority of research studies dealt with identifying teachers' occupational competencies, experience and use of task-analytical approaches, and performance-based vocational teacher education, which continued to grow and spread throughout the states (p. V). However, they conclude that "vocational teacher education remains an ancillary activity, . . . research in this field remains sparse overall, and . . . there has not been much progress recently toward establishing vocational teacher education as an intellectual field within the broader area of educational research" (p. 25). This lack of high-quality research could be due in part to an overall decline in funding and other resources for educational research from the highs of the 1960s and early 1970s to the 1980s (Adamsky & Cotrell, 1979), to a lack of attention and support for vocational teacher education in recent federal vocational law, and to a lack of concensus on the appropriate role and direction of public vocational education in America (see Research, 1988).

A pervasive problem with much of the limited research that is available and a possible contributing reason for the lack of high-quality teacher education research is that it is often fragmented and narrowly focused. There is not a cumulative body of research guided by theory and focused on persistent problems of national significance in vocational teacher education (Cheek, 1988; Peterson, 1973). Instead, much of the available research is directed at state-level issues and concerns and/or it is narrowly focused on one of the five or six major occupational service areas within vocational education. Thus, it is extremely difficult, if not impossible, to systematically accumulate or synthesize research focused on a specific problem related to agricultural teacher education in Ohio with research on a specific problem of trade and industrial teachers in New Jersey. Often the occupational specialty focus and/or the state focus are necessary and desirable, but when either or both can be broadened, the potential application and usefulness of the research can also be expanded. In this way the research might be able to contribute better to the development of a cumulative body of research on persistent problems of national significance in vocational teacher education.

References

Adams, D. A., Pratzner, F. C., Anderson, B. H., & Zimmerer, M. E. (1987). Vocational teacher education in an era of change. *Vocational Education Journal, 62*, 24–27.

Adamsky, R. A., & Cotrell, C. J. (1979). *Vocational teacher education: A review of the research* (Info. Ser. No. 185). Columbus, OH: Ohio State University, National Center for Research in Vocational Education.

American Association of Colleges for Teacher Education. (1987). *Teaching and teachers: Facts and figures.* Washington, DC: Author.

American Vocational Association. (1986). *Critical issues facing vocational education.* Washington, DC: AVA Board of Directors.

Anderson, B. H. (1986). *The status of vocational teacher education in University Council for Vocational Education member institutions.* Fort Collins, CO: Colorado State University.

Barnard, W. S., Leach, J. A., & Hofstrand, R. K. (1985). A study of cooperation/collaboration among employment training systems. *Journal of Vocational Education Research, 10*, 13–34.

Bennett, W. J. (1985, December). Address of U.S. Secretary of Education to the Annual Convention of the American Vocational Association, Atlanta.

Bottoms, J. E. (1989). *Closing the gap between vocational and academic education* (Discussion paper for the National Assessment of Vocational Education). Washington, DC: U.S. Department of Education, National Assessment of Vocational Education.

Bracey, G. W. (1983). On the compelling need to go beyond minimum competency. *Phi Delta Kappan, 64*, 717–721.

Carl D. Perkins Vocational Education Act of 1984. (Public Law 98-524).

Carnegie Forum on Education and the Economy, Task Force on Teaching as a Profession. (1986). *A nation prepared: Teachers for the 21st century.* New York: Author.

Carnevale, A. P., & Gainer, L. J. (1988). *The learning enterprise.* Washington, DC: American Society for Training and Development.

Carnevale, A. P., Gainer, L. J., & Meltzer, A. S. (1988). *Workplace basics: The skills employers want.* Washington, DC: American Society for Training and Development.

Carnevale, A. P., & Goldstein, H. (1983). *Employee training: Its changing role and analysis of new data.* Washington, DC: American Society for Training and Development.

Cheek, J. G. (1988). Maintaining momentum in vocational education research. *Journal of Vocational Education Research, 13*, 1–17.

Cotrell, C., Chase, S., & Molnar, M. (1972). *Model curricula for vocational and technical teacher education: Report No. V. General objectives set II.* Columbus, OH: Ohio State University, National Center for Research in Vocational Education.

Darling-Hammond, L., & Berry, B. (1988). *The evolution of teacher policy.* Santa Monica, CA: RAND Corporation.

Denham, C. (1985). Initiatives in teacher education in the California state system. *Action in Teacher Education, 7*(1–2), 41–44.

Dugger, W. E., Fowler, F. S., Jones, A. H., & Starkweather, K. N. (1986). Results of the second survey of industrial, technical, and vocational teachers. *Technology Teacher, 46*, 9–14.

Education Daily, August 27, 1986.

Eurick, N. P. (1985). *Corporate classrooms: The learning business (Carnegie Foundation Special Report)*. Princeton, NJ: Princeton University Press.

Evans, R. N. (1982). Public secondary and postsecondary vocational education. In R. Taylor, H. Rosen, & F. Pratzner (Eds.). *Job Training for Youth*. Columbus, OH: Ohio State University, National Center for Research in Vocational Education.

Finch, C. R. (1982). Trade and industrial education. In H. E. Mitzel (Ed.), *Encyclopedia of Educational Research* (pp. 1937–1947). New York: Free Press.

Friedenberg, J. E. (1987). *The condition of vocational education for limited English-proficient persons in selected areas of the United States*. Columbus: Ohio State University, National Center for Research in Vocational Education.

Gainer, L. (1988). *ASTD update: Basic skills*. Washington, DC: American Society for Training and Development.

Galambos, E. C. (1986). *The baccalaureate program for teachers and other graduates of Texas universities: A transcript study*. Austin, TX: Select Committee on Higher Education.

Galambos, E. C., Cornett, L. M., & Spitler, H. D. (1985). *An analysis of transcripts of teachers and arts and science graduates*. Atlanta: Southern Regional Education Board.

Gallup, A. M., & Clark, D. L. (1987). The 19th annual Gallup poll of the public's attitude toward the public schools. *Phi Delta Kappan*, 69(1), 17–30.

Goldstein, H. (1980). *Training and education by industry*. Washington, DC: National Institute for Work & Learning.

Hanes, M. L., & Rowls, M. D. (1984). Teacher recertification: A survey of the states. *Phi Delta Kappan*, 66, 123–126.

Hollenbeck, K. M., Belcher, J. O., Dean, G. D., Rider, B. L., & Warmbrod, C. P. (1987). *Postsecondary occupational education delivery: An examination*. Columbus, OH: Ohio State University, National Center for Research in Vocational Education.

Holmes Group. (1986). *Tomorrow's teachers*. East Lansing, MI: Author.

Intergovernmental Advisory Council on Education. (1985). *A report to the President of the United States: Teacher preparation and retention*. Washington, DC: Author.

Ishler, R. E. (1985). Teacher competency testing Texas style. *Action in Teacher Education*, 7(1–2), 27–30.

Kadamus, J. A., & Daggett, W. R. (1986). *New directions for vocational education at the secondary level* (Info. Ser. No. 311). Columbus, OH: Ohio State University, National Center for Research in Vocational Education.

Kaplan, G. R. (1985). *Items for an agenda: Educational research and the reports on excellence*. Washington, DC: American Educational Research Association.

Levine, H. M., & Rumberger, R. W. (1983). *The educational implications of high technology*. Palo Alto, CA: Stanford University, Institute for Research on Educational Finance and Governance.

Lotto, L. S. (1983). *Building basic skills: Results from vocational education*. Columbus, OH: Ohio State University, National Center for Research in Vocational Education.

Lotto, L. S. (1986). Expectations and outcomes of vocational education: Match or mismatch. *Journal of Vocational Education Research*, 11, 41–60.

Mackenzie, D. E. (1982). Research for school improvement: An appraisal of some recent trends, *Educational Researcher*, 12, 5–17.

Metropolitan Life Insurance Co. (1987). *Survey of the American teacher 1987: Strengthening links between home and school*. New York: Author.

Mikulecky, L. (1986). *Job literacy research: Past results and new directions. Paper presented at the International Reading Association Conference, Anaheim, CA.

Mikulecky, L., Ehlinger, J., & Meenan, A. L. (1987). *Training for job literacy demands: What research applies to practice*. University Park: Pennsylvania State University, Institute for the Study of Adult Literacy.

Milanovich, N. J. (1986). Vocational-technical teacher certification: Where are we? And where are we going? In Institute for Research and Development in Occupational Education (Eds.), *Achieving excellence in vocational teacher education*. New York: City University of New York, Center for Advanced Study in Education, Institute for Research and Development in Occupational Education.

Miller, A. J. (1982). Certification: A question of validity. *Vocational Education Journal*, 57, 27–29.

Moss, J. (1967). *Review of research in vocational technical teacher education*. Minneapolis: University of Minnesota, Minnesota Research Coordination Unit in Occupational Education.

National Academy of Sciences. (1984). *High schools and the changing workplace: The employer's view*. Washington, DC: Author.

National Center for Education Statistics. (1984). *Preliminary VEDS data 1981–82*. Washington, DC: Author.

National Commission on Excellence in Education. (1983). *A nation at risk: The imperative for educational reform*. Washington, DC: U.S. Government Printing Office.

National Commission for Excellence in Teacher Education. (1985). *A call for change in teacher education*. Washington, DC: American Association of Colleges for Teacher Education.

National Commission on Secondary Vocational Education. (1985). *The unfinished agenda: The role of vocational education in the high school*. Columbus, OH: Ohio State University, National Center for Research in Vocational Education.

National Council on Employment Policy. (1982). *A vocational education policy for the 1980s*. Washington, DC: Author.

National Governor's Association. (1986). *Time for results: The governor's 1991 report on education*. Washington, DC: Author.

Oakes, J. (1986). Beneath the bottom line: A critique of vocational education research. *Journal of Vocational Education Research*, 11, 33–50.

Office of Educational Research and Improvement. (1987). *What's happening in teacher testing: An analysis of state teacher testing practices*. Washington, DC: Author.

Peterson, R. L. (1973). *Review and synthesis of research in vocational teacher education* (Info. Ser. No. 101). Columbus, OH: Ohio State University, National Center for Research in Vocational Education.

Pratzner, F. C. (1984). Redirection of vocational education in the comprehensive high school. *Journal of Industrial Teacher Education*, 21, 3–12.

Pratzner, F. C. (1985). The vocational education paradigm: Adjustment, replacement, or extinction? *Journal of Industrial Teacher Education*, 22, 6–19.

Pratzner, F. C. (1987). *Vocational teacher education: A survey of preservice and inservice preparation*. Columbus, OH: Ohio State University, National Center for Research in Vocational Education.

Pratzner, F. C. (1988). Vocational teacher education: Changes & challenges. *Journal of Industrial Teacher Education*, 26, 48–56.

Pratzner, F. C., & Russell, J. F. (1983). *The roles and functions of vocational education: Some current perspectives*. Columbus, OH: Ohio State University, National Center for Research in Vocational Education.

Pratzner, F. C., & Russell, J. F. (1984). *The changing workplace: Implications of quality of work life for vocational education*. Columbus, OH: Ohio State University, National Center for Research in Vocational Education.

Pritz, S. G. (1988). Basic skills: The new imperative. *Vocational Education Journal, 63*(2), 24–26.

Research in industrial and technical teacher education: Perspectives from the editorial board. (1988). *Journal of Industrial Teacher Education, 25*, 88–98.

Resnick, L. B. (1987). *Education and learning to think.* Washington, DC: National Academy Press.

Ryan, R. D. (1984). Delivery systems for vocational education. In W. R. Miller & L. West, *Reaching for excellence in education: Vocational education trends and priorities.* Columbia, MO: University of Missouri—Columbia.

Sherman, S. W. (Ed.). (1983). *Education for tomorrow's jobs.* Washington, DC: National Academy Press.

Shields, D. (1984). *The history and value of organized labor's linkage with vocational education.* Columbus, OH: Ohio State University, National Center for Research in Vocational Education.

Stern, D., Dayton, C., Paik, I., Weisberg, A., & Evans, J. (1988). Combining academic and vocational courses in an integrated program to reduce high school dropout rates: Second-year results from replications of the California peninsula academies. *Educational Evaluation and Policy Analysis, 10*(2), 161–170.

Sticht, T. G. (1987). *Functional context education.* San Diego, CA: Applied Behavioral and Cognitive Sciences.

Sticht, T. G., & Mikulecky, L. (1984). *Job-related basic skills: Cases and conclusions.* Columbus, OH: Ohio State University, National Center for Research in Vocational Education.

Taylor, R., Rosen, H., & Pratzner, F. C. (Eds.). (1982). *Job training for youth.* Columbus, OH: Ohio State University, National Center for Research in Vocational Education.

Teacher education reports. (1987, September). 9(17).

Thornton, J. (1984, March 19). 10 forces reshaping America: Force six, rise of minorities. *U.S. News and World Report*, p. 48.

Trafford, A. (1984, March 19). 10 forces reshaping America: Force five, women on the move. *U.S. News and World Report*, pp. 46–48.

U.S. General Accounting Office. (1986). *School dropouts: The extent and nature of the problem.* Washington, DC: Author.

Vocational, technical, and practical arts education [Special issue]. (1962). *Review of Educational Research, 32*(4).

Weber, J. M., Puleo, N. F., Kurth, P., Fisch, M., & Schaffner, D. (1988). *The dynamics of secondary vocational classrooms.* Columbus, OH: Ohio State University, National Center for Research in Vocational Education.

Wirt, J. G., Muraskin, L. D., Goodwin, D. A., & Meyer, R. H. (1989). *National assessment of vocational education: Summary of findings and recommendations.* Washington, DC: U.S. Department of Education, National Assessment of Vocational Education.

Wirt, A. G. (1983a, August). *New work & education: Sociotechnical work theory & school learning.* Paper presented at the meeting of the World Futures Society Conference, Washington, DC.

Wirth, A. G. (1983b). *Productive work in industry & schools: Becoming persons again.* Washington, DC: University Press of America.

Young, A. M. (1985, February). One-fourth of the adult labor force are college graduates. *Monthly Labor Review, 108*, 43–46.

Zemsky, R., & Meyerson, M. (1985). *Training practices: Education & training within the American firm.* Philadelphia: University of Pennsylvania, Higher Education Finance Research Institute.

·45·

BUSINESS TEACHER EDUCATION

Judith J. Lambrecht

UNIVERSITY OF MINNESOTA, TWIN CITIES CAMPUS

A person planning to teach business subjects today faces a wide array of possibilities regarding the students, subject areas, school levels, and sites at which business subjects are taught. The routes to certification and/or licensure to teach in these settings are equally diverse. The challenge in business teacher education is to provide viable paths for professional development and growth in settings that often require diverse technical skills and teaching competencies.

This chapter examines research and issues related to business teacher preparation by first providing a brief description of the broad field of business education and the purposes of business teacher preparation. The general nature of research related to business teacher education is followed by a description of characteristics of current business teacher preparation programs. The research supporting the subject matter and pedagogical content of these programs is discussed, followed by examination of the evaluation practices and standards available for judging the quality of these programs and/or their teacher products.

DEFINITION OF BUSINESS EDUCATION

Business education as a field is part of two worlds, worlds currently viewed separately because of funding and licensing requirements. Business education is provided to meet both general education and vocational education needs. The business education goals considered part of general education are considered appropriate for all students and citizens. Calhoun (1986) summarizes these as follows:

1. promoting career awareness and exploration of business careers

2. preparing students to be competent consumers of goods and services
3. providing a basic knowledge of economics and the free enterprise system
4. developing skills and knowledge needed in managing personal business affairs
5. furthering competencies of a business nature that have special supportive value in other professions
6. inspiring respect for the value and dignity of honest work
7. providing general business knowledge, skills, and understanding (pp. 4–5).

If these goals are appropriate for all persons, then explicit employment-preparation goals can be said to build upon these general business outcomes. The vocational education goals of business education extend these goals, in Calhoun's basic definition, as follows:

1. developing occupational competencies for obtaining a job and/or advancing in a career
2. helping adjust to occupational change
3. promoting career awareness and exploration preceding occupational preparation
4. establishing a foundation for further study of the field of business
5. providing knowledge and understanding of the free enterprise system, thereby developing more competent producers of goods and services (p. 4).

The various levels at which business education is offered are the focus of the definition of business education provided by Nanassy, Malsbary, and Tonne (1977):

Ordinarily, when speaking of programs in colleges or schools of business in universities or divisions of business in liberal arts colleges, the

The author wishes to express gratitude for the time Calfrey C. Calhoun (East Carolina University, Greenville) and J. Howard Jackson (Virginia Commonwealth University) gave to reading and commenting on the manuscript.

795

general term business administration will be used. We will reserve the term business education for those business programs and courses taught ordinarily at the secondary level, and "business teacher education" will be used to describe professional preparation. (p. 4)

The Policies Commission for Business and Economic Education publication, *This We Believe About the Mission of Business Education* (1977), notes that business education represents a broad and diverse discipline (perhaps field of study is a better term) that is included in all types of educational delivery systems: elementary and secondary schools, one- and 2-year schools and community colleges, and 4-year colleges and universities. Business education can begin at any level; it can be interrupted for varying periods of time; and it can be continued throughout the life of an individual. Business education includes education for office occupations, distributive and marketing occupations, business teaching, business administration, and economic understandings (p. 1).

The breadth of the field and the ambiguity of purpose of some offerings are captured in the basic definitions provided by Hopkins and Lambrecht (1984):

Today's business education includes a commitment to the economic education of all students (general education) as well as commitment for office occupations education (vocational education) for some students. When the model is studied, however, it is apparent that a currently popular purpose of business education (personal use) has not been included. Several of the business education courses are not easily categorized in the dual-purpose framework described. These include personal-use typewriting/keyboarding, personal use shorthand, and personal use recordkeeping when the content is skill oriented without the accompanying economics learning. Clientele are those students interested in developing personal-use skills related to business occupations. (p. 611)

Although discussion of the composition of business programs at various school levels is be included in this chapter, one caveat about the definition of business education is important with regard to teacher education. Business teacher education licensing has focused on the secondary level, and it is at this level, and this level only, that the multifaceted role of business education has been implemented. As expressed by Hopkins and Lambrecht (1984):

It is only at this level (upper-secondary), in most cases, that one would find courses that claim to provide for the development of personal-use skills, the development of occupational skills and intelligence, and the development of economic understanding and personal economic competence. At the same time, there are many who question whether the secondary program really achieves the vocational (occupational) education goals of developing intelligence and of developing an employable skill of business. Many would consider it prevocational at best with the success of a student finding employment much more a factor of the student's general intelligence and ability rather than the program completed. (p. 612)

PURPOSES

The purposes of business teacher education coincide with the general breadth of the field. Teaching licensure as provided by the various states is generally of two types: standard licensure for teaching in the secondary schools and vocational licensure for teaching in programs reimbursed by state and federal vocational funds. Vocational programs and their corresponding licensing requirements can be at either the secondary or postsecondary levels. Initial standard licensing in the past has generally required the completion of an undergraduate program; this is changing for those programs that have moved or are now moving to a postbaccalaureate degree requirement for standard, initial licensure.

In addition to initial licensing, business teacher education has been a provider of inservice teacher education and graduate coursework for the completion of advanced degrees. For many business programs, a new activity has been that of providing professional coursework, and perhaps certification, for persons providing training or human resource development services in industry. Although formal degree programs in training and development are just developing (T. M. Palmer, 1985), this is viewed as a growth area for business education (Duff & Merrier, 1984; Ownby, 1981).

RESEARCH

The purpose of this chapter is to review only the research that focuses on the preparation of business teachers. To permit attention to current issues and concerns, research completed since the late 1960s has been examined, though some research has built upon earlier studies.

One way to summarize the types of research being carried out in business education that concern teacher preparation is to examine the manuscript topics in the *NABTE Review*, an annual refereed publication of the National Association for Business Teacher Education. This is the premiere publication for examining important research and issues affecting both undergraduate and graduate teacher preparation.

The 209 manuscripts (excluding editorials and introductory statements to issue sections) that appeared in Volumes 1–15 (1973–1988) were categorized as relating specifically to business teacher education (BTE) or being concerned with business education (BE) in the sense of teaching at levels not directly related to teacher preparation. Articles were further classified as being primarily positions/critical reviews or data-based research reports. Data-based research reports were further categorized as being of four types: those identifying teaching content (subject), those examining teaching practices (pedagogy), evaluative research, and descriptive studies. Position/critical review papers were also classified as one of three broad types: those identifying teaching content (subject), those examining teaching practices (pedagogy), and general philosophical positions. Table 45-1 shows this tally.

Approximately 43 percent of the 221 manuscripts were concerned specifically with business teacher education. Half of these (50 articles) were data-based research reports, and, of these 50, 36 articles were descriptive status reports concerning business teacher education programs. These findings will be summarized shortly, but two points should be noted now. The National Association for Business Teacher Education has maintained a descriptive data base of programs in NABTE-member

TABLE 45–1 NABTE *Review* Articles, Volumes 1–15 (1973–1988)

	BE Research	BE Position	BTE Research	BTE Position	TOTAL	%
Philosophical/position		36		27	63	29
Subject matter	30	25	5	1	61	28
Pedagogy	13	10	4	16	43	19
Descriptive studies			36		36	16
Evaluation	13		5		18	8
Total manuscripts	56	71	50	44	221	
Percent of total	25	32	23	20	100	

institutions, and the *NABTE Review* has been the primary vehicle for publication of these cumulative histories of the field. Perhaps this gives an undue prominence to status reports in this publication.

Other than position papers related to various topics of general concern to business education, 28 percent of all the articles, the largest single group, related to identification of content for teaching. The volatile nature of business changes that have affected business employment requirements have caused business teacher educators to be concerned first with issues of what to teach. Questions about how to teach and about teaching effectiveness have been raised in relation to business subject areas which are more stable than office occupations or information systems employment preparation as a whole. (See Lambrecht, D'Onofrio, Jones, & Merrier [1981] for a review of research in the broader field of business education from 1968 through 1980.)

Limited formal research attention to business teacher education is further confirmed by Ober's (1982) analysis of doctoral research in business education from 1978–1980. A total of 21 studies (10 percent of the total) were devoted to teacher education, and 10 of these were surveys; none were experimental research. Thomas (1983) summarized the topics of articles in the *NABTE Review* and the *Delta Pi Epsilon Journal* during the 1977–1981 period and found four manuscripts on teacher education in the *Journal*. These two publications represent the major research-oriented, refereed journals in the field of business education. However, for both journals combined for 1977–1981, teacher education was the largest single topic category, 23 percent of the total of 151 articles tallied.

Since 1981, however, no articles have been included in the *Journal* concerning teacher education as a specific area for research attention. This could imply three possible situations now occurring in the field: (a) Concerns for the instructional consequences of rapid technological change continue to dominate as research questions; (b) factors having major impact on business teacher preparation are not sufficiently different from factors affecting other teaching fields for the business area to receive singular attention; or (c) concerns for business teacher preparation are submerged in the more general field of vocational education teacher preparation. For example, the study by Wardlow (1987), comparing student teacher evaluations for undergraduates in vocational education with undergraduates in other educational fields, includes business education students among the vocational education group. This is not easily detected, even by reading the research report, and undoubt-

edly other pertinent research related to business teacher education is implicit in more general research reports. The teacher education research receiving attention in this chapter relates primarily to business teachers in studies identified as such.

PROGRAM DESCRIPTION

Much of business teacher education research has focused on collecting descriptive program information. There has been general concern about the implications of enrollment declines, program locations in either a college of education or a college of business, general composition of the professional-education segment of the program, and program responses to technological change (Bortz, 1982; Bronner, 1983; Campbell & Horn, 1986; Gades, 1983; Golen & Lynch, 1987; Hopkins, 1986, 1987; Langford, Sink, & Weeks, 1978; Lewis & Freeman, 1986; Mahlman, 1983/1984, 1985; Schmidt, 1984, 1985).

Currently 250 institutions in the United States provide business teacher preparation by offering a bachelor's degree that meets the requirements of a "comprehensive" teaching license, or a license to teach the broadest range of business courses at the secondary level. This requirement of a 4-year degree is true internationally as well, but for teaching business administration and secretarial science at the vocational technical institute level, not necessarily the secondary level (Malone, 1982). Several studies (Beringson, 1966; Brinson, 1978; Hayes, 1965; Light, 1977) have documented the considerable diversity among the states regarding licensing standards. The *approved-program approach* is the most common. In it the state or accrediting agency approves specific teacher preparation programs, then the institution recommends individuals who have completed those programs. Other analyses of teacher-preparation programs concur in documenting the diversity among requirements when they conclude that, "The certification of classroom teachers in the U.S. is a mess" (Feistritzer, 1984, p. 36).

In the United States, programs offering business teacher preparation have reported at least 60 different program titles (Hopkins, 1987), the most common being Business Education and Business Education and Office Administration. Three-quarters (Gades, 1983) to four-fifths (Hopkins, 1987) to even 90 percent (Dorrell, Darsey, & White, 1982) of business teacher programs also offer preparation in Administrative Office Management. They teach the office-related courses that are part of the content preparation of business teachers.

This dual responsibility—business teacher preparation plus teaching of office-related content—is a major factor in collegiate business educators' preoccupation with technical content. They must focus their professional attention on both teaching content and providing a portion of the pedagogical preparation for future business teachers.

Current data on the number of specific methods courses for teaching business subjects in NABTE-member institutions indicates that 40 percent to 50 percent of the institutions offer two or more specific business methods courses, more than two being available in institutions with higher enrollments (Bortz, 1982; Mahlman, 1985). When more than one business methods course is offered, the division in subject matter is between the basic business/economics area and the office skills subjects. A third common separation of business content is a methods course in accounting. If accounting is not treated separately, it is likely to be part of the basic business/economics teaching-methods course. Business methods courses could be in addition to an introductory course in the principles of business education and a curriculum-development course (Bortz, 1982).

Supply of Business Teachers

The number of business teacher education programs decreased 18 percent between 1980 and 1986, from 305 to 250 institutions. Hopkins (1987) reports a marked decline in business teacher education programs in private institutions (1981–1982, 27% of responding institutions; 1985–1986, 12 percent). The annual supply of business teachers currently is approximately 1,500 graduates, a decline from the 3,175 graduates estimated in 1980 (Bortz, 1982). This trend is consistent with national trends of new teacher supply in general (Wells, 1986) and might justify the expectation of a teacher shortage with future increases in secondary school enrollments in the 1990s. Because the demand for business teachers, in particular, parallels the demand for entry-level business employees and the clerical/secretarial area continues to be one of growth, a shortage of business teachers is a reasonable projection (Gades, 1983).

Characteristics of Potential and Current Business Teachers

With regard to comparisons among teachers in similar fields, Swenson (1976/1977, 1978) attempted to validate Holland's theory of vocational choice when comparing business and marketing education majors. He found business education candidates more easily identifiable and personality type to be important in explaining academic achievement and academic satisfaction. Underwood and Davis (1985, 1987) also compared business and marketing education students and found differences, particularly between males and females. Males expressed greater concern for personal and professional advancement, whereas females showed greater concern for instructional issues and working conditions.

Groups of college students preparing for either business teaching or office administration were subjects in Hopson's (1984) study of career aspirations. The two groups were not compared directly, but both were found to have congruence between their career aspirations and their career expectations; in short, they were committed to the career goals of their chosen majors. Church's (1978) comparisons of business teachers, high school students, and employed office personnel on the basis of occupational aspirations, needs, and perceptions provided evidence that high school students with less exposure to actual office settings were most likely to differ from employed workers. When business ethics of high school business seniors, collegiate business teacher education seniors, and nonmanagerial workers were compared, age was the primary factor accounting for differences (Chapman, 1986).

Those factors leading to job satisfaction of employed teachers have been examined in several studies using the same instrument, the Minnesota Satisfaction and/or Minnesota Satisfactoriness Scales (Hadaway, 1978; Olson, 1974; Stitt, 1983). Teaching is a satisfying career when these opportunities exist (a) opportunity to do things for others; (b) opportunity to do things that do not conflict with one's conscience; (c) opportunity to keep busy at all times; and (d) opportunity to use one's own teaching methods.

Issue of Program Location

Two-thirds of undergraduate business teacher education programs are located in schools or colleges of business; the remainder are in schools or colleges of education (Hopkins, 1987; Mahlman, 1985). This is in contrast with the location of doctoral programs in business education; two-thirds of 49 such programs are located in schools or colleges of education (Golen & Lynch, 1987). A long-standing concern, or belief, regarding undergraduate business teacher preparation is that schools of business that are accredited by the American Assembly of Collegiate Schools of Business (AACSB) have more rigorous business content requirements. Langford et al. (1978) present this view as follows:

Survey responses and catalogue analysis for the years 1955, 1965, and 1975 make it clear that more business content is required and better coverage of the common body of knowledge is required when business education programs are located in business administration at schools where the business program is accredited by AACSB. . . . There has been a shift toward requiring better coverage of common body knowledge subjects during the 1955 to 1975 period in all areas except where the business education program is located in [a school of] education in an institution where the business program has not been accredited by AACSB. Serious deficiencies still exist, however, in the large number of business education programs not requiring coverage of production, computer science, and policy. (pp. 13–14)

A continuing issue in business teacher preparation is identifying and balancing two potentially different types of content knowledge: (a) the business content necessary to provide sound general business preparation (and legitimacy within the collegiate business community), and (b) the business content necessary to teach at the secondary level, especially when this includes both employment preparation and general education

G. R. Smith and Stoddard (1982) argue that such a balance can be found within the flexible program requirements of the AACSB accreditation standards. This debate has been continued in position papers by Bennett (1989) and Sapre (1989) on the issue of where business teacher preparation can best thrive, in a school of business or of education.

Comparison of teacher certification test scores of students in schools of business and outside such schools provide additional data. Bloodworth (1983) compared scores on the Georgia Teacher Certification Test (TCT) in Business, the National Teacher Examination for the Business Education area, and the Teacher Performance Assessment Instrument scores for students from business education programs. She concludes:

Students who complete programs housed outside schools, divisions, or departments of business score higher on the TCT and the NTE than students completing programs within a school, division, or department of business; however, the location of the business education program does not affect the on-the-job performance. (p. 75)

Standardized Testing for Licensure

The testing data compared by Bloodworth give one indication of increased external verification of teaching competencies through standardized testing. "Twenty-five states require testing for admission to teacher education programs. . . . Forty-one states require some form of testing prior to certification" (Wise & Darling-Hammond, 1986, p. 9). Because the validity of objective-format tests is being challenged, several states (11 in 1986) have implemented a performance-assessment program for beginning teachers. Such performance tests "will not be a test of discrete behavioral skills or a test of recall of presecribed responses. Instead, it will test the candidate's ability to exhibit skills related to effective teaching (Wise & Darling-Hammond, 1986, p. 22).

Of 1,986 respondents to the annual NABTE survey (Hopkins, 1987), 60 percent indicated that a state or national teacher examination was required for certification, with the National Teacher Examination the most common for both the business education area and general teaching. Further, the Pre-Professional Skills Test (PPST) was seen as "becoming increasingly popular as an admission tool" (p. 30). Widespread implementation of performance evaluation as a formal licensing requirement is not yet apparent.

Technological Responsiveness

A major preoccupation of all business teachers is maintaining up-to-date programs with regard to information-processing technology. Analysis of technology implementation within business teacher preparation programs has led to the judgment that a gap is developing where innovative leadership should exist. The convergence of several office automation technologies is not taking place as rapidly in collegiate institutions as it is in industry (Campbell & Horn, 1986; Grever & Zimmerman, 1986). Only the microcomputer was judged as having been adopted by teacher education programs, out of several technological possibilities.

Other survey data (Hopkins, 1987; Lewis & Freeman, 1986) confirm the addition of new courses within business teacher education programs that use microcomputer technology to teach business applications and the dropping of office skills courses using less current technology. Conspicuous for their absence in new course offerings are pedagogical courses related to technological teaching issues, though this does not imply that current offerings are not recognizing these teaching possibilities.

QUALITY INDICATORS

A major portion of business teacher education research has provided descriptive information about programs. This can be helpful for depicting the current status of the field and allowing professionals to judge whether the current state of affairs or any evident trends are desirable. Individuals can compare their programs to the normative data and ask whether it is favorable or unfavorable to differ from the norm. The descriptive data highlighted in the first part of this chapter do not provide evidence that the current status should be the preferred one. Different research questions need to be asked to establish appropriate program components and to assess program quality.

Program Development

Teacher preparation is generally accepted as having at least three components (not necessarily discrete components): general education, subject-matter content, and professional education. Teacher educators have the most control over specification of (if not teaching of) the subject-matter content and professional-education components. States may establish licensing requirements in terms of minimum numbers of courses or credits (or competencies) in a given area, but university programs generally may exceed these minimums.

Research in business teacher education has implicitly dealt with the following questions in specifying what business teachers need to know and what pedagogical preparation is necessary to support the teaching of this content:

1. To what extent can subject-matter competencies be separated from the teaching of pedagogical skills? Does the subject matter establish a fundamental context for the development of appropriate teaching practices?
2. What theoretical models support the description of either subject-matter or pedagogical competencies?
3. To what extent should the subject-matter content and pedagogical preparation differ for teachers at different school levels, elementary through collegiate, for business subjects? For preservice and inservice teachers?
4. How are the subject-matter and pedagogical competencies attained? Can collegiate, formal, institution-based instruction provide adequate content preparation? What roles do business employment or field-based teaching practice play?

Although these questions do not exhaust the possible queries about the preparation and licensing of business teachers, they permit the organization of existing research on business teacher preparation.

Subject-Matter Competencies. Business teachers at the secondary level have historically been licensed to teach all business subjects. Crank and Crank described the situation in 1977, and it can be restated today:

The philosophy still prevails in business teacher education programs that graduates of these programs should be able to teach all the business subjects in the high school. This situation is likely to continue, and the present period of declining enrollments may bring increasingly higher requirements for entry into the teaching profession. (p. 17)

Although high school business teachers are generally licensed to teach comprehensively, business teachers' evaluations of their teaching difficulties indicate that their preparation might not be balanced (Brinson, 1978; Clow, 1971; Hopkins, 1982; Johnson, 1976, 1979; Rucker, 1983/1984; Schenk, 1969). Several studies concur that, although breadth of content preparation is desired, there has been overemphasis on office occupations content and inadequate preparation for teaching in the basic business and economics areas. There is some irony in this lack of confidence or competency to teach the basic business subjects, because economics is the single common course or subject included in almost all teacher-preparation programs (Malone, 1982).

How can the breadth of business content requirements be clarified and delimited such that business teachers are adequately prepared? The need to provide this clarification has intensified since the late 1960s with the development and refinement of thinking related to competency-based teacher education. Few business teacher preparation programs were considered competency-based in 1981 (Uthe, 1981), and serious questions have been raised about the ability to implement what could become mechanistic skills-development approaches (Erickson, 1978; Woolschlager, 1979). Even so, the need has remained to objectively clarify the dimensions of quality necessary for effective teaching.

The essential attributes of CBTE presented in 1973 by Calhoun were reiterated in 1983 by Vaughan, with slight modification. A competency-based teacher education program has the following characteristics: (a) field centered, (b) individualized, (c) based on specific performance criteria, and (d) controlled by a consortium of colleges, professional teacher organizations, and schools (Calhoun, 1973). In 1983 the restatement maintained that five components should be present. (a) competencies to be demonstrated by the student (prospective teacher) are identified, (b) criterion levels are specified, (c) criterion tests are designed, (d) instructional strategies are planned, and (e) student and program evaluators are effected (Vaughan, 1983).

For competency-based teacher education programs to be individualized or student-paced may not be essential (Bryan, 1979), because more traditional instructional arrangements have produced positive outcomes favoring the use of instructional modules with performance-based assessment. The identification of the criterion measures, however, is as difficult in

professional teacher preparation as in any occupational field (Schmidt, 1981). It is costly, time consuming, and highly laden with value judgments about the quality of the performance and the causal link between teaching practice and eventual student achievement. Even so, the various levels of performance evaluation that are being applied to teachers, often legislated, are not being strongly opposed (Williams, 1985). The opportunity to upgrade the substance of teacher-preparation programs, as well as the image of the field, is a potentially positive outcome.

Vaughan's (1983) statement does not give as much prominence as Calhoun's to the consortium of professionals who monitor the process, but this feature probably has become more important than it was in 1973. Calhoun's position parallels Stiles's (1973) assertion that, "Professional specialists in each field should take responsibility for setting standards and judging qualifications for both entry and continuation in teaching" (p. 45). Such professional responsibility was judged essential to overcoming the inherent lack of validity in the approved-program approach to teacher licensing. Current efforts to certify teachers through mechanisms separate from their initial preparation, such as the Teacher Assessment Project (Shulman, 1987; Shulman & Sykes, 1986), reinforce this judgment.

The business teacher education literature is replete with research efforts to identify the competencies needed for effective teaching in business, the large majority of these studies being directed at specific content areas, not the broad field of business. The early 1970s was a period for active development of such competency identification. Several efforts focused on business teachers in general (Bryan, 1979; Byorek, 1978; Cook & Richey, 1972, 1979; Johnson, 1979). The office skills areas have been individually addressed: office education (Broder, 1974); secretarial (Rossetti, 1973); shorthand (Prather, 1974); skills subjects (Chaney, 1972); records management (Bennett, 1984); and typewriting (Hebert, 1973). The basic business and economics fields have been analyzed: entrepreneurship and small business (Zelinko, 1986); basic business (Brown, 1973; Haynes, 1987), economics (Hoggan, 1977; Manzer, 1984); business law (Wilkinson, 1979); and economics, accounting, and data processing as a group (Peterson, 1985). Accounting has been addressed separately (Funk, 1976; Norton, 1975; L. M. C. Smith, 1986), as have data processing (Armstrong, 1984; Lambrecht & McLean, 1977) and computer literacy or microcomputer applications (Hilgenfeld, 1983/1984; Lambrecht, 1986; Wentz, 1985). Gruber (1977, 1979) examined and found differences in the competencies required by business teachers in skill subjects, versus basic business subjects.

The business communications area has received little formal attention from teacher preparation (Switzer, 1982); teaching competencies can be identified, but those who teach in this area have generally acquired their expertise on the job (Dunning, 1982). Because business communications has been a major area for business teaching at the collegiate level, this lack of formal teacher preparation could be similar to other collegiate teaching fields. Subject-matter expertise is the primary job requisite, and professional teaching preparation is self-directed, informal, or does not exist.

It is easy to find diversity and lack of agreement about essential business teacher competencies (Clow, 1971). Although commonality of competency areas will be found in these lists, the level of specificity varies widely. Some lists limit competencies to a dozen broad areas; others have hundreds. Within single lists, the level of complexity and importance of the competencies varies: parallel level statements in one list include "write legibly and quickly on the chalkboard" and "develop specific evaluative criteria for measuring the effectiveness of individual and group activities" (Johnson, 1979).

Two generalizations can be derived from the competency-identification efforts. *First*, the specific subject-matter context is the most fundamental unit of attention, not business as a broad field. *Second*, the pedagogical competencies are inextricably embedded in the subject-matter context. Without the subject-matter frame of reference, the competencies take on the characteristics of personal teacher traits, such as "treats all students fairly," or topics of units, such as "organizing an occupational advisory committee." Such statements might, however, be useful. Similar statements have been developed for teachers as a professional group, described in terms of dispositions, skills, and knowledge (see *Minnesota's Vision for Teacher Education: Stronger Standards, New Partnerships*, 1986). It is apparent, however, that, when specific performances of teachers are the focus of attention, subject-matter gives such performance a meaningful context for behavioral and conceptual description, teacher involvement, and eventual development through reflective evaluation of performance outcomes.

The volatile content of several business fields makes the mix of teaching subject content with pedagogical content necessary or desirable, especially in teacher inservice education. This is particularly true in those areas of business affected most by technological changes, such as word processing (Dalton, 1981), office education in general (Sheahan, 1972; Sink, 1981), and accounting (L. M. C. Smith, 1986).

Theoretical Models for Competency Identification. Five possibly distinct rationales have been apparent in the competency-identification research in business teacher education. These are subject-matter reference, Cotrell Model, DACUM Model, Whitlock Model, and Steel and Stone Model, using the names applied by researchers who used such approaches.

Most developers started with the assumption that the *subject matter* itself is the major frame of reference. Even if the subject matter itself is not described in the competencies, the literature related to teaching a given subject content was judged to be the necessary source of the competency statements. A list of competencies was thus developed by reviewing this literature and organizing the competencies into categories that appeared meaningful. Different competency organizations have similar components, but the organization is unique to the specific project. For example, the competency organization by Byorek (1978) yielded nine areas for the 206 competencies generated: (a) instruction, (b) planning, (c) evaluation, (d) execution, (e) human relations, (f) administration and supervision, (g) guidance, (h) professional role, and (i) professional skills. In this case, Byorek was examining business education as a broad field. A similar literature-developed model related specifically to the secretarial area (Rossetti, 1973) yielded a seven-area

scheme for competency categorization that reflects a closer tie to the content area: (a) professional and community; (b) methodology and techniques of teaching; (c) understanding the student and the learning situation; (d) planning the curriculum; (e) selecting, developing, and using instructional materials; (f) organizing and managing the classroom; and (g) testing and evaluation.

Since its development in 1971, the Cotrell et al. (1972) list of 384 competencies in 10 categories has been the next most frequently used model for organizing competencies of vocational education teachers (Bryan, 1979; Calhoun, 1973; Cook & Richey, 1979; Hoggan, 1977). The 10 categories are (a) program planning, development, and evaluation; (b) instructional planning; (c) instructional execution; (d) instructional evaluation; (e) instructional management; (f) guidance; (g) school–community relations; (h) student vocational organizations; (i) professional role and development; and (j) coordination. Not all 384 Cotrell competencies have been applicable to all business programs, and the list has been modified for specific content areas. Vocational teachers, supervisors, and teacher educators were the original source of the teaching tasks that yielded the competencies.

The *DACUM* Model (Adams, 1974) could be considered similar to the Cotrell list in that its frame of reference has been curriculum development for employment preparation. However, the DACUM Model does not start with a list of competencies. It provides procedures for developing the competency list by using task analysis and evaluation according to frequency of performance and difficulty of learning. Zelinko (1986) used this model for identifying 130 tasks and 18 duty areas for small business owners, leading to competencies for teachers in each subject area.

A different model for identifying competencies applied by Brown (1973) and credited to Whitlock (1971) uses students as the source of examples of effective or ineffective teacher behavior, relying on student evaluation of teacher effectiveness as a valid measure. This differs from the other models in which teachers themselves have generally been the originating or validating source of judgments, using the Delphi research technique. In the Brown study, the resulting list from students of qualities/performances of effective basic business teachers was later validated by teachers, using the Delphi technique. The list of effective teaching behaviors developed by Brown is brief (19) and related specifically to the basic business classroom.

In contrast, the last model identified by Gruber (1979) when comparing effective teaching behavior of office skill versus basic business teachers is that developed by Steel and Stone (Stone & Henrie, 1979). This is a research-based attempt to avoid the frequently used laundry list of competencies and to focus specifically on teaching–learning skills, not the full range of teacher responsibilities. The result is a list of 14 learning process elements grouped into five clusters: (a) situational, (b) readiness, (c) ideational, (d) task, and (e) feedback. This analysis tool was able to differentiate between skill and basic business teachers and describe their effective teaching behaviors.

Differentiation Between Teacher Groups. Several of the research studies directed at competency identification focused not only on a single subject area, but also on the community college level (Falk, 1975; Funk, 1976; Long, 1977/1978; Robinson, 1974; Slaymaker, 1971). Frequently the purpose of the study was not only to determine necessary teacher competencies, but also to identify inservice educational needs of current teachers. Studies that have examined inservice needs have found that secondary and postsecondary teachers differ (Lambrecht, 1986). Other studies including both secondary and postsecondary teachers have concluded that the receptivity of business teachers to competency-based curricula differs by school level, with secondary teachers less receptive to the student-paced format (Slaugh & Thomas, 1987).

When inservice teacher preparation has been the separate focus of research, however, its structure and goals differ little from the concerns of preservice education (Santos, 1971; Summer, 1980; Vaughan, 1982, 1983). The audience is different, and methods of delivery are more varied with regard to location, timing, and length (Meell, 1985; Ryckman, 1982). Because of the maturity of the participants, wider target-audience participation in identifying content and goals for inservice education is possible and preferred (Kanu, 1983). However, teachers' perceived needs might not represent their actual needs (Falk, 1975; Lambrecht, 1986), and a wider range of advice than from teachers themselves is needed to determine inservice offerings.

Although no single study offers confirmation, the following are plausible assumptions about differences or similarities among business teacher groups:

1. At a single educational level (secondary school, community college, or vocational–technical institute) there is overlap in the preservice and inservice needs of teachers, but these three levels differ.
2. The community college and postsecondary technical institute teachers have more specialized subject-area requirements than secondary-level teachers. The expectation that teachers are responsible for the wide breadth of business content (at an introductory level) applies primarily at the secondary level.
3. Community college teachers are likely to achieve subject-matter specialization and differentiation from technical institute teachers through higher educational requirements (master's degree) and efforts directed at preparing students for both employment and transfer to 4-year universities (Slaymaker, 1971).
4. The technical institute business teacher can be differentiated from the community college teacher by two factors: greater focus on employment preparation as the outcome for students and extended work-experience requirement for teachers. Business teachers at this level tend to have at least 4-year degrees, but they might work in an environment that values practical work experience more than extended academic preparation. The curricular focus on employment needs might diminish the value of general education, which is less directly related to job needs. This would affect the type of person who is attracted to teaching at this level.

Where or How Competencies Should Be Attained. Although a 4-year degree has been implicitly assumed as a basic requirement of teacher licensing, this might be changing. The components of such a degree can be presented in several possible arrangements; 4 years might not be sufficient preparation, or a 4-year degree might be unnecessary.

Four years of teacher preparation might not be sufficient when business teachers must attain essential employment skills outside collegiate settings (Hopkins, 1987; Malone, 1982; Sink, 1981) or when a fifth year or master's degree is required for initial licensing, a goal being pursued by universities who are members of the Holmes Group (Murray, 1986). A vocational education teaching license for business teachers puts a premium on work experience and might permit teaching without any degree if work experience and specialized professional preparation are sufficient. However, studies of nondegreed teachers in vocational education show that business teachers are not a large part of this group (Pucel, Jensrud, & Persico, 1987).

Business teacher preparation might include not only a 4-year collegiate degree, but also two kinds of clinical or field experience: employment in a business occupation for which the teacher will later offer preparation, and student teaching or internship experience as part of professional preparation. This professional internship might be carried out after students obtain a baccalaureate degree.

Numerous models can and have been offered for integrating clinical teaching experiences into 4- or 5-year (even 6-year) degree programs (Binnion, 1975; Graf, 1987; Grunkemeyer, 1971; Pyke, 1971; Thomas, Mayer & Clinkscale, 1979). Five- or 6-year programs (or internships rather than student teaching) generally include the awarding of a master's degree. Extended programs have been justified because they provide greater professional preparation for teaching special populations of students, teaching experience in a greater variety of school settings, or an extended general educational background. Integration of formal, supervised work experience into the 4-year degree has also been recommended (Santos, Olinzock, & Salzman, 1980; Sink, 1981).

Business education research recommending extended programs is over a decade old. Current efforts to restructure teacher preparation are making similar extended-program recommendations, but the impetus is different. It goes beyond the need for longer, more diversified clinical experiences or preparation to serve special populations, even though this is still a key part of the rationale. Reports from the Holmes Group (1986) and the Carnegie Forum (1986) have focused on raising the intellectual rigor of teacher preparation, increasing entry requirements into the teaching field, and altering the structure of professional career development. There has been wide public support (Gallup & Clark, 1987) for the recommendation that teachers have a 4-year liberal arts degree with a major in some subject before entering teacher preparation.

Research is just now becoming available that addresses the implications of these recommendations for vocational education. Pratzner (1987, 1988) provides national follow-up data from beginning vocational education teachers (approximately

17 percent of whom completed collegiate majors in Business and Office Occupations Education) that report teachers' perceptions of their competencies for teaching basic skills and special student populations. He concludes the following with regard to vocational teachers' liberal arts preparation.

Thus, it would seem that preservice vocational teacher programs and teachers were not greatly different from their academic counterparts, or arts and science majors in general, in terms of their basic skills (math and English) requirements. However, it seems clear that, in general, the beginning vocational teachers did not pursue a rigorous liberal arts program. (Pratzner, 1988, p. 15)

However, he further concludes that "the expectation that all teachers will have at least a four-year Bachelor's degree in the liberal arts and an additional Master's degree in teaching, while desirable, will be extremely difficult to achieve throughout vocational education for several reasons" (p. 19). These reasons include the generally higher age of vocational teachers who have been required to obtain 3–6 years of full-time work experience in the occupations being taught and the presence of nondegreed teachers in some vocational fields. In short, although a 4-year baccalaureate degree was seen as desirable for all teachers, it was not sufficient, not even for academic teachers who could benefit from practical, on-the-job work experience related to their academic disciplines. Clearly, the issue of appropriate balance in teacher preparation has not been settled.

Work experience has been considered an essential part of business preparation (Brower, 1987; Holmes, 1977; Malone, 1982; J. J. Palmer, 1982, 1984). It is frequently required for a vocational license. However, work experience is not generally required for graduation from business teacher education programs (Bortz, 1982; Thoreson, 1972). Research on the value of work experience is mixed. Teachers value the experience (Colorado State University, 1976; Groneman, 1976; Schenk, 1969), but the amount or recency of related work experience of business teachers has not been shown to result in greater teaching effectiveness (Brooks, 1972; Brown, 1973; Ellis, 1969; Groneman, 1976; Holmes, 1977).

Burrow & Groneman (1976) recommend that, because length and recency of occupational experience show no relationship to teaching competency, these criteria should be minimized for vocational licensing purposes. Emphasis should be placed instead on the teaching competencies actually developed through work experience. Using Cotrell's competency areas, 32 competencies within the following two aspects of business teachers' responsibilities were found to be affected by work experience: (a) program planning, development, and evaluation; and (b) coordination of student work-experience programs. Ten purposes were identified as being accomplished by actual work experience (Groneman, 1976), and these provided an indication of the kinds of teaching competencies that result:

1. to secure specific knowledge and understanding of the nature and requirements of specific occupations

2. to integrate theory learned in school with actual practices on the job
3. to experience the actual stress, pressures, and frustrations that are a part of every job
4. to learn new technologies in business and industry
5. to develop, improve, and apply and/or integrate technical competencies of an occupation
6. to obtain information about current business standards
7. to obtain an overall picture of the organization of a business
8. to formulate realistic concepts of career opportunities
9. to develop interpersonal skills involving relationships with fellow workers and clients
10. to develop confidence in one's abilities and skills (p. 106)

These outcomes suggest that work-experience requirements do not supplant, but rather complement, the formal course-based instruction related to business content and skills. Likewise, formal coursework is not likely to be the source of these outcomes; genuine participation in the work force is necessary.

Program Assessment

Several of the studies cited have implicitly contained evaluative judgments of business teachers' needs/deficiencies and the program characteristics or processes that should respond to these needs. Current concerns for establishing and maintaining higher standards for teachers have focused greatest attention on student performance outcomes, particularly in the form of competency, performance-based models that have dominated the research literature.

Teacher Performance Assessments. Follow-up studies that have asked business teachers to evaluate their preparation could be considered product assessments (efforts to examine the results of the teacher-preparation process as judged by the teachers themselves). Strong links have not been established between different types of experiences (types and numbers of courses, students' characteristics, prior grades or student teaching evaluations) and current teacher performance (Carpenter, 1970; Lynch, 1973). For example, Bloodworth (1983) shows that graduating teachers' scores on the National Teacher Examination or the Teacher Certification Test in Business are unrelated to these same teachers' scores on the Teacher Performance Assessment Instrument.

Research has consistently shown that business teachers benefit from content-related methods classes (Clow, 1971; Montgomery, 1983; Schenk, 1969) and that common problem areas have persisted over the years: discipline or classroom management; providing for individual student differences; and evaluation/testing (Johnson, 1979; Montgomery, 1983; Morrison, 1971; Schenk, 1969; Wiggins, 1975).

Problems related to meeting the needs of diverse student populations are likely to continue. These generally have been addressed by special course requirements in such areas as special needs of exceptional students, teaching reading within content areas, and working in multicultural contexts (Hopkins, 1987; Uthe, 1981). Business teachers have benefited from focused instruction in reading (Walters, 1975), especially when the reading instruction was directly linked to later evaluation practices assessing demonstration of the learned techniques (Havercamp, 1983).

As an alternative to asking teachers to make judgments about their preparation, teaching performance can be evaluated by others such as supervisors and business teachers' own students. Various observation forms and procedures have been used, such as the Purdue Instructor Performance Indicator for secretarial teachers (Jurist, 1974) or a modification of Flanders' Interaction Analysis and Roberson's Code to incorporate nonverbal teaching behaviors in general business (Lynch, 1973). Selected facets of communicator style in collegiate business courses are related to student course evaluations of teaching effectiveness, as determined by the Norton Communicator Style Measure (Bednar & Clements, 1985; Brandenburg, 1985).

Legitimate questions continue to be raised about the validity and reliability of student evaluations of teacher performance (Lynch, 1979; Wilson & Wilson, 1978), particularly for different types of subject matter and by students of differing characteristics. For example, students' gender, age, and their purpose for taking a course have affected their judgments in different settings (Kourilsky & Cords, 1974; Long, 1977/1978). Kourilsky and Cords, in examining student course evaluations in economics, theorized that consumer orientation is different from investment orientation. Students seeking to attain specific occupational or professional goals might have an investment orientation and, therefore, offer more stringent judgments about value than those who take courses more casually as consumers.

Other research that has compared teaching-performance evaluations by students with those by supervisors has provided evidence for both conflicting judgments (Brooks, 1972; Lynch, 1973) and positive relationships (Brown, 1973, 1975). The two groups, students and supervisors, consider different factors in making their assessments.

The likely implication of such inconsistent outcomes is that performance evaluations will continue to be important, but no single evaluation instrument or source will be sufficient. Multiple assessments are necessary to make valid, equitable, and legal evaluations of teachers' on-the-job performance or to predict their likely future behavior.

Program Standards. Competency expectations identified for business teachers are also appropriate for their own teachers, business teacher educators. During their initial training, future teachers should be able to participate in the kinds of teaching – learning activities they will later be expected to use. Modeling effective business teaching behaviors is a reasonable expectation in business teacher education, because these educators frequently teach a portion of the business content, as well as handling the professional pedagogical training.

There is a gap in the business teacher education literature, however, in the area of how best to organize and deliver the pedagogical and clinical portions of the program. Earlier follow-up studies (Schenk, 1969; Sheahan, 1972) allowed teachers to indicate what they thought should be emphasized in teaching methods courses and also what they thought should be changed or emphasized in the student-teaching experience (Brinson, 1978; Schenk, 1969). Support was provided, for example, for choosing on-site cooperating teachers for their professional mentoring skills and for having a university subject-matter specialist supervise the clinical experience. Formal preclinical experiences have also been recommended that, in effect, extend the clinical portion of the teacher education program (Graf, 1987).

Missing from business teacher education research, however, are explicit analysis of how subject matter is transformed into instruction. This omission is not unique to business teacher education (Shulman, 1986). Shulman suggests that teachers need to possess a distinctive kind of content knowledge that facilitates the transfer of that content to give audiences of students. Given the strong link in business education between subject matter and teaching methodology, this extension of thinking could be a natural one.

The form of process evaluation that is more commonly used in business teacher education programs is the lens of scrutiny applied by the standards of professional organizations. Even those who argue that end-of-program teacher (student) competencies—products—are the ultimate evaluation of program quality recommend the specification of program standards—process assessments (Chaney & Simon, 1980).

Two national professional organizations exert this influence: the National Association for Business Teacher Education and the National Business Education Association. The *NABTE Standards for Business Teacher Education* (1982) parallels the accreditation standards developed by the American Assembly of Collegiate Schools of Business. Guidelines have been established for the broad content areas to be included in the foundational and specialized business studies portions of a 4-year program, each of which comprises approximately one-fourth of the program requirements.

Greater specificity of standards for program development and evaluation is provided by the *Business Teacher Education Curriculum Guide* (National Business Education Association, 1987), designed for the preparation of business teachers at all levels of instruction. The guide is designed to be competency based; it is the result of extensive task-force efforts to relate the competencies identified to research completed in the field. The guide states:

The primary responsibility of the business teacher is to provide effective instruction. This requires:

1. Mastery of the subject matter to be taught
2. Knowledge of the learning process
3. Competence in the use of a variety of instructional strategies
4. Effective interpersonal communication (p. vii).

The conceptual framework is a systems model that identifies inputs, processes and their determinants, and outputs of a teacher-preparation program. The outputs are educated professionals capable of performing the processes that describe effective teaching. The model can be applied to any educational program, but the competencies are intended for a business teacher audience. Eight major roles of business teachers are identified: (a) curriculum development, (b) instruction, (c) evaluation, (d) management, (e) guidance, (f) interpersonal relationships, (g) student organizations, and (h) professional development. A ninth separate section identifies the business subject-matter competencies necessary for successful teaching. These subject-matter competencies, in turn, have been drawn from the standards developed by the NBEA Model Curriculum Task Force (K–14) and the American Assembly of Collegiate Schools of Business.

In addition to these standards, the U.S. Department of Education has supported the development of *Standards for Excellence in Business Education* (Calhoun, Finch, & White, 1985), which establishes 247 standards in nine topical areas for the field as a whole. These qualitative standards describe program features, in contrast with the NBEA *Business Teacher Education Curriculum Guide* (1987), which describes competencies of persons. The program standards areas are the following:

1. Philosophy and Purpose
2. Organization and Administration
3. Curriculum and Instruction
4. Instructional Staff
5. Financial Resources
6. Instructional Support Systems
7. Public Relations
8. Student Development Services
9. Evaluation (Calhoun et al., 1985, p. 9)

Reflecting the concern in business education for maintaining relevant business content, the *Standards* contain an additional section of "Information Processing Instructional Standards." Six topical areas contain 188 standards. Of these, 113 relate to information-processing content.

This incorporation of instructional standards with broad program-development standards signifies the major impact technological changes have had and continue to have on business education. The directors of the Standards of Excellence study (Calhoun & Finch, 1984) maintain that business programs are typically "a) comprehensive in scope, b) reflect current and emerging trends and practices, and c) provide students with the skills and knowledge necessary to function effectively in the labor market" (p. 38). Although business education is comprehensive, the crucial updating needs are in the information-processing segments of that field: word processing and data processing.

Standards for Excellence in Business Education and *Business Teacher Education Curriculum Guide* provide essential tools for business education program development and assessment in both pre- and inservice teacher education. The broad range of professional participation in their development and validation by teachers at several instructional levels enhances their usability and credibility.

SUMMARY STATEMENT OF ISSUES AND NEEDED RESEARCH

The major collection of business teacher education research was completed during the early 1970s; the topics now receiving the most doctoral research attention are those related to identifying technological implications for teaching and relating these changes to specific content areas of business education. The impact is indirectly on teacher-preparation programs. However, it should be noted that the considerable early attention to competency-based education, including teacher education, only in the late 1980s resulted in formal statements from professional organizations regarding standards and curricula for the broad field of business education.

Now is perhaps the time for the following areas to receive visible research attention: examining the implications of extended teacher-preparation programs, using computing technology to deliver instruction, serving more diverse student groups, expanding the scope of teacher-preparation programs to include training in industry, and promoting independent learning.

Implications of Extended Teacher Education Programs

Movements to lengthen teacher-preparation periods will likely change the type of student being served by these programs and also remove some of the influence teacher educators have had over undergraduate preparation. How will this affect the subject-matter content preparation received by business teachers? Will even greater efforts be made to certify that necessary competencies have been attained, regardless of the source of such preparation? What guidance or assistance can prospective teachers be given about the appropriate source of business content preparation, particularly office skill preparation, which is necessary for employment and teacher licensing but which might not be available in a 4-year, collegiate-level institution?

One reason for extending teacher-preparation programs has been to increase the field-based, or clinical, portion of the program. How can such experiences be organized for business teachers so that different levels or types of teaching competencies are developed than were possible with less extensive or intensive student teaching or internship requirements? At present, research evidence in business teacher education does not suggest a need for longer student teaching. What, in short, is to be gained by postbaccalaureate, fifth-year, or master's level professional education programs?

Using Computing Technology to Deliver Instruction

All business teachers have been affected by the trend toward incorporating computing technology, especially microcomputers, into their curricula. Attention has been given to teaching the business applications of such technology. Relatively little attention has been given to delivering business instruction using this same computing technology. Business teacher education should provide a model of this potential for all business teachers. How do business teacher educators gain the expertise to use these tools effectively to deliver instruction? How can they build upon research in other content areas to make better use of newer instructional delivery systems?

Serving Diverse Student Populations

More diverse populations of students are being served by public schools. The needs of these special, exceptional, or multicultural groups of students will receive greater attention in the professional preparation of all teachers. Ways need to be found to recruit and prepare teachers from underrepresented minority groups. Further, the business employment needs of these student groups should receive the research attention of business educators. How do the needs of both these potential teachers and students differ from other social groups?

Expanding the Scope to Include Training in Industry

The preparation of human resource specialists or training and development specialists for business and industry has been identified as a growth area for teacher employment. How do the pedagogical and subject-matter needs of these professionals differ from other educators? How can this preparation be integrated into existing teacher-preparation programs?

Developing Independent Learners

Technological changes are an ever-present reminder that students at all levels need to prepare for lifelong retraining. Teachers, in particular, need to exemplify independent learning skills, both skills they use to keep their programs current and skills they impart to students who must also become independent learners in employment settings. Do current teaching conditions and inservice development opportunities encourage and reward initiative of this type? What array of inservice options would be most effective in encouraging continuous teacher growth?

References

Adams, R. E. (1974). Building competency models: One approach to occupational analysis. *Canadian Vocational Journal, 10,* 36–41, 54. (ERIC Document Reproduction Service No. EJ 108 659)

Armstrong, G. R. (1984). The identification of data processing competencies needed by secondary business data processing teachers (Doctoral dissertation, Temple University). *Dissertation Abstracts International, 45*(01), 152A. (University Microfilms No. 84-10, 119)

Bednar, D. A., & Clements, C. (1985). Relationships between communicator style and perceived teaching effectiveness in business classes. *Journal of Business Education, 60,* 356–359.

Bennett, J. C. (1984). Computer applications in records management: Implications for curriculum development. In *1984 National Research Conference Proceedings* (pp. 33–35). St. Peter, MN: Delta Pi Epsilon.

Bennett, J. C. (1989). Where business programs should be housed: The preferable home for business education programs is a school of business. *Business Education Forum 44*(2), 13–14.

Beringson, D. L. (1966). A study to determine the certification requirements to teach business education in the United States. Unpublished doctoral dissertation, University of North Dakota, Grand Forks.

Binnion, J. E. (1975). There is a way to do it better—find it. *NABTE Review, 3,* 85–92.

Bloodworth, K. G. (1983). Comparative analysis of teacher certification area scores, national teacher examinations area scores, and the teacher performance assessment instruments in business education (Doctoral dissertation, University of Georgia). *Dissertation Abstracts International, 44*(05), 1308A. (University Microfilms No. ADG83-2,0357)

Bortz, R. F. (1982). Courses and enrollments in business education: A market study for prospective authors. *NABTE Review, 9,* 13–16.

Brandenburg, M. (1985). Communicator style and its relationship to instructional effectiveness in collegiate business education (Doc-

toral dissertation, Oklahoma State University). *Dissertation Abstracts International, 47*(04), 1160A. (University Microfilms No. 86-11,510)

Brinson, A. V. (1978). A comprehensive analysis, classification, and synthesis of research findings on business teacher education, 1964–1969, with summary statements relating those findings to NABTE guidelines (Doctoral dissertation, Indiana University). *Dissertation Abstracts International, 39*(09), 5378A. (University Microfilms No. 79-05,988)

Broder, T. N. (1974). An identification of teaching competencies for office education (Doctoral dissertation, Wayne State University). *Dissertation Abstracts International, 35*(12), 7764A. (University Microfilms No. 75-13,299)

Bronner, M. (1983). The status of business education in the United States. *NABTE Review, 10,* 34–38.

Brooks, L. D. (1972). The relationship between related work experience of vocational office education teachers (Doctoral dissertation, University of Tennessee. *Dissertation Abstracts International, 32,* 4461A. (University Microfilms No. 72-5,417)

Brower, W. A. (1987). The education of business teachers 1987. *NABTE Review, 14,* 9–11.

Brown, B. J. (1973). *Qualities of an effective general business teacher.* Knoxville, TN: University of Tennessee, College of Business Administration, Center for Business and Economic Research.

Brown, B. J. (1975). The relationship between supervisor and student evaluations of teaching effectiveness of general business teachers. *NABTE Review, 3,* 48–54.

Bryan, F. S. (1979). Adapting a competency-based model for preparing vocational business teachers in the traditional class. *NABTE Review, 6,* 34–38.

Burrow, J., & Groneman, N. (1976). *The purposes of and competencies developed through occupational experience for vocational education teachers* (Final report of Vocational Education Research Project, Nebraska State Department of Education, Division of Vocational Education and Nebraska Research Coordinating Unit). Lincoln, NE: University of Nebraska.

Byorek, J. (1978). Competencies needed by secondary school business education teachers in the United States (Doctoral dissertation, New York University). *Dissertation Abstracts International*, 39(08), 4671A. (University Microfilms No. 78-24,072)

Calhoun, C. C. (1973). New approaches and trends in business teacher education in the south. *NABTE Review, 1*, 13–20.

Calhoun, C. C. (1986). *Managing the learning process in business education* (2nd ed.). Belmont, CA: Wadsworth.

Calhoun, C. C., & Finch, A. V. (1984). Business education program standards, a national study. In *1984 National Research Conference Proceedings* (pp. 36–38). St. Peter, MN: Delta Pi Epsilon.

Calhoun, C. C., Finch, A. V., & White, J. L. (1985). *Standards for excellence in business education*. Reston, VA: National Business Education Association.

Campbell, D. L., & Horn, C. J., Jr. (1986). Adoption of technology in business teacher education training institutions. *NABTE Review, 13*, 24–26.

Carnegie Forum on Education and the Economy, Task Force on Teaching as a Profession. (1986). *A nation prepared: Teachers for the 21st century*. New York: Author.

Carpenter, C. T. (1970). Study of the relationship of selected factors to the performance of business education graduates at Grambling College on the commons sections of the NTE (Doctoral dissertation, Indiana University). *Dissertation Abstracts International, 31*, 5900A. (University Microfilms No. 71-11,373)

Chaney, L. H. (1972). The development of an instrument for evaluating students' teachers of skills subjects in business (Doctoral dissertation, University of Tennessee). *Dissertation Abstracts International, 33*(05), 2211A. (University Microfilms No. 72-27,452)

Chaney, L., & Simon J. C. (1980). Evaluation in business teacher education. *NABTE Review, 7*, 57–60.

Chapman, P. H. (1986). Comparison of business ethical beliefs among high school senior business education students, college seniors in business education teacher training, and non-managerial office workers (Doctoral dissertation, University of South Carolina). *Dissertation Abstracts International, 47*(8), 2859A. (University Microfilms No. ADG86-26,263)

Church, O. D. (1978). *Aspirations, needs and perceptions by occupation and sex of office personnel, high school students, and teachers* (Final Report). Laramie, WY: University of Wyoming, College of Education. (ERIC Document Reproduction Service No. ED 155 306)

Clow, J. E. (1971). The relationship of methodology course learnings to student teaching and first-year teaching experience of business teachers (Doctoral dissertation, Northern Illinois University). *Dissertation Abstracts International, 33*(02), 643A. (University Microfilms No. 72-22,782)

Colorado State University. (1976). *The effect of vocational instructor's occupational experience and experience recency on instructor's attitude and proficiency* (Final Report: Vol. 2. Technical Report). Ft. Collins, CO: Author. (ERIC Document Reproduction Service No. ED 145 229)

Cook, F. S., & Richey, R. C. (1972). *Two VAE systems models: A model for a competency-based instructional system: The VAE accountability model* (Competency-Based Teacher Education Series No. 2). Detroit, MI: Wayne State University, Department of Vocational Education.

Cook, F. S., & Richey, R. C. (1979). Models for competency-based business teacher education. *NABTE Review, 6*, 30–34.

Cotrell, C., et al. (1972). *Model curricula for vocational and technical teacher education: Report No. V. General objectives, set II*. Columbus, OH: Ohio State University, Center for Vocational Education.

Crank, F., & Crank, D. (1977). Historical perspectives of education for business. In J. W. Crews & Z. S. Dickerson (Eds.), *Curriculum development in education for business* (National Business Education Association yearbook No. 15, pp. 1–18). Reston, VA: National Business Education Association.

Dalton, M. (1981). Preparing teachers of word processing. *NABTE Review, 8*, 35–36.

Dorrell, J., Darsey, N., & White, K. (1982). A study of shorthand and typewriting student placement testing practices of selected NABTE institutions. *NABTE Review, 9*, 21–25.

Duff, T. B., & Merrier, P. A. (1984). Business educators can be trainers. *NABTE Review, 11*, 40–42.

Dunning, D. G. (1982). A comparison of the stated educational preparation in certain knowledges and skills of business communication teachers with model requisites (Doctoral dissertation, Memphis State University).

Ellis, W. G. (1969). The relationship of related work experience to the teaching success of beginning business teachers (Doctoral dissertation, Pennsylvania State University). *Dissertation Abstracts International, 30*, 1072A. (University Microfilms No. 71-29,818)

Erickson, L. W. (1978). Competency-based business education. *NABTE Review, 5*, 35–40.

Falk, C. F. (1975). A study of the in-service education and supervision needs of community college business instructors in the state of Illinois (Doctoral dissertation, Northern Illinois University). *Dissertation Abstracts International, 36*(05), 2580A. (University Microfilms No. 75-23,117)

Feistritzer, C. E. (1984). *The making of a teacher: A report on teacher education and certification*. Washington, DC: National Center for Education Information.

Funk, J. A. (1976). An analysis of competencies needed by teachers of postsecondary introductory accounting with emphasis on junior college teaching (Doctoral dissertation, University of Houston). *Dissertation Abstracts International, 36*(09), 5754A. (University Microfilms No. 76-06,051)

Gades, R. E. (1983). A look at the current status of business education in NABTE institutions. *NABTE Review, 10*, 39–41.

Gallup, A. M., & Clark, D. L. (1987). The 19th annual Gallup poll of the public's attitude toward the public schools. *Phi Delta Kappan, 69*(1), 17–30.

Golen, S. P., & Lynch, D. H. (1987). The current status of doctoral programs in business education. *NABTE Review, 14*, 47–51.

Graf, D. (1987). Internship in business teacher education: A modular approach. *NABTE Review, 14*, 21–23.

Grever, J., & Zimmerman, H. L. (1986). How are we meeting the challenge of preparing teachers and students in business technology? In *1986 Golden Anniversary National Business Education Research Conference Proceedings* (pp. 69–72). St. Peter, MN: Delta Pi Epsilon.

Groneman, N. J. (1976). Purposes of teaching competencies developed through occupational experience for business and office education teachers (Doctoral dissertation, University of Nebraska). *Dissertation Abstracts International, 38*(01), 224A. (University Microfilms No. 77-14,620)

Gruber, J. L. (1977). The description of teaching competencies by selected secondary Utah business teachers (Doctoral dissertation, Utah State University). *Dissertation Abstracts International, 38*(12), 7112A. (University Microfilms No. 78-08,179)

Gruber, J. L. (1979). A description of teaching competencies by selected secondary Utah teachers. *NABTE Review*, 6, 25–28.

Grunkemeyer, F. B. (1971). Implications of internship programs for the preparation of secondary business education teachers (Doctoral dissertation, Ohio State University). *Dissertation Abstracts International*, 32(11), 6002A. University Microfilms No. 75-15,216)

Hadaway, F. (1978). Selected personal characteristics related to job satisfaction of public high school business teachers (Doctoral dissertation, University of Georgia). *Dissertation Abstracts International*, 39, 3999A. (University Microfilms No. 79-01,640)

Havercamp, M. F. (1983). An analysis of the relationship between preservice teacher training in reading methods and directed teaching performance. *NABTE Review*, 10, 25–30.

Hayes, H. M. (1965). An examination of the certification requirements for secondary school teachers of business education in the United States. (Doctoral dissertation, Northern Illinois University).

Haynes, T. (1987). A proposed experiential model for the teaching methods course in basic business education. NABTE Review, 14, 17–20.

Hebert, M. M. (1973). An analysis of competencies needed by typewriting teachers as perceived by business teachers and by authorities in business education (Doctoral dissertation, University of Houston). *Dissertation Abstracts International*, 34(08), 4960A. (University Microfilms No. 74-02,840)

Hilgenfeld, R. M. (1984). Computer literacy: A model plan for teacher education in the area of instructional applications of computers (Doctoral dissertation, University of Wyoming, 1983). *Dissertation Abstracts International*, 45(01), 153A. (University Microfilms No. 84-08751)

Hoggan, D. F. (1977). Economic understanding needed by secondary school distributive education teachers (Doctoral dissertation, Arizona State University). *Dissertation Abstracts International*, 38(11), 6482A. (University Microfilms No. 78-05,290)

Holmes Group. (1986). *Tomorrow's teachers*. East Lansing, MI: Author.

Holmes, L. B. (1977). Work experience required for certification of business teachers?—Yes and No! *NABTE Review*, 4, 53–57.

Hopkins, C. R. (1982). Basic business teacher education programs. In E. Jones (Ed.), *Revitalization of basic business education at all instructional levels* (National Business Education Yearbook, No. 20, pp. 147–153). Reston, VA: National Business Education Association.

Hopkins, C. R. (1986). Business education in the United States: 1984–1985 NABTE Survey Results. *NABTE Review*, 13, 4–12.

Hopkins, C. R. (1987). Business education in the United States: 1985–1986 NABTE Survey Results. *NABTE Review*, 14, 24–34.

Hopkins, C. R., & Lambrecht, J. J. (1985). Business education. In T. Husen & T. N. Postlewaite (Eds.), *International Encyclopedia of Education: Research and Studies* (Vol. 1, pp. 607–618). London: Pergamon Press.

Hopson, B. B. (1984). Career aspirations and expectations of senior women majoring in business teacher education or office administration (traditional occupations, nontraditional occupation, secretary) (Doctoral dissertation, University of Georgia). *Dissertation Abstracts International*, 45(09), 2735A. (University Microfilms No. ADG84-27,544)

Johnson, V. J. (1976). An analysis of congruence between competencies requisite for secondary school business education teachers and preparation received in teacher education programs in South Carolina. (Doctoral dissertation, University of South Carolina). *Dissertation Abstracts International*, 37(04), 1941A. (University Microfilms No. 76-21,903)

Johnson, V. J. (1979). Factors emanating from analyses of competencies. *NABTE Review*, 6, 45–49.

Jurist, R. G. (1974). An analysis of high school secretarial business education teacher performance (Doctoral dissertation, Rutgers—The State University). *Dissertation Abstracts International*, 35(06), 3588A. (University Microfilms No. 74-27,328)

Kanu, I. N. (1983). An analysis of job satisfaction and participation in in-service education programs of Wisconsin postsecondary business and office education teachers (Doctoral dissertation, University of Wisconsin). *Dissertation Abstracts International*, 45(01), 60A. (University Microfilms No. 84-02,030)

Kourilsky, M., & Cords, D. (1974). An investigation of what is measured by teacher evaluations in economics. *NABTE Review*, 2, 69–74.

Lambrecht, J. J. (1986). *Instructional microcomputer applications by business teachers in Minnesota*. St. Paul, MN: University of Minnesota, Department of Vocational and Technical Education.

Lambrecht, J. J., D'Onofrio, M. J., Jones, E. L., & Merrier, P. A. (1981). *Business and office education: Review and synthesis of research*. Columbus, OH: Ohio State University, National Center for Research in Vocational Education.

Lambrecht, J. J., & McLean, G. N. (1977). Content and methodology background and perceived competencies of data processing teachers. *NABTE Review*, 4, 25–28.

Langford, T. E., Sink, C. V., & Weeks, R. R. (1978). The business education department in a college of business administration. *NABTE Review*, 5, 9–15.

Lewis, S. D., & Freeman, G. L. (1986). Business education and office administration curricula in the 1980's: A curriculum study of NABTE member schools. In *1986 Golden Anniversary National Business Education Research Conference Proceedings* (pp. 7–9). St. Peter, MN: Delta Pi Epsilon.

Light, S. L. (1977). Business teacher certification: Yesterday, today, tomorrow. *NABTE Review*, 4, 48–52.

Long, W. (1978). A study of the importance of selected characteristics and competencies for community college business instructors (Doctoral dissertation, Northern Illinois University, 1977). *Dissertation Abstracts International*, 39(01), 76A. (University Microfilms No. 78-11, 182)

Lynch, D. H. (1973). Pre-service and other factors related to secondary business teacher performance. (Doctoral dissertation, Northern Illinois University). *Dissertation Abstracts International*, 34(09), 5782A. (University Microfilms No. 73-27,600)

Lynch, D. H. (1979). Student ratings of college teachers: Reliability, validity, and effect on instructor behavior. *NABTE Review*, 6, 19–24.

Mahlman, R. R. (1984). A study of the content of business methods courses offered at NABTE colleges and universities (Doctoral dissertation, Oklahoma State University, 1983). *Dissertation Abstracts International*, 45(03), 731A. (University Microfilms No. 84-14,170)

Mahlman, R. R. (1985). A study of the content of business methods courses offered in NABTE colleges and universities. *NABTE Review*, 12, 80–84.

Malone, P. L. (1982). An analysis of business teacher education in the SIEC (ISBE) countries: A status study (Europe, North and South American) (Doctoral dissertation, University of Nebraska). *Dissertation Abstracts International*, 43(06), 1939A. (University Microfilms No. 82-27,023)

Manzer, J. P. (1984). Promoting economic literacy: Issues, goals, and strategies. In *1984 National Research Conference Proceedings* (pp. 33–35). St. Peter, MN: Delta Pi Epsilon.

Meell, M. A. (1985). The impact of motivation strategies on staff development programs in education and training programs in business and industry: Implications for teacher education (Doctoral dissertation, University of Houston). *Dissertation Abstracts International, 47*(02), 507A. (University Microfilms No. 86-07,025)

Minnesota's vision for teacher education: Stronger standards, new partnerships (1986). (Report of the Task Force on Teacher Education for Minnesota's Future). St. Paul: Minnesota Board of Teaching, Minnesota Higher Education Coordinating Board.

Montgomery, F. H. (1983). A study of the teaching difficulties of beginning business education teachers throughout the United States (Doctoral dissertation, University of Georgia). *Dissertation Abstracts International, 44*(05), 1308A-1309A. (University Microfilms No. 83-20,364)

Morrison, J. L., Jr. (1971). An analysis of the effect of class socio-economic characteristics upon the discrepancy between student teacher preparation in business education and student teaching problems (Doctoral dissertation, Temple University). *Dissertation Abstracts International, 32*(04), 1963A. (University Microfilms No. 71-26,829)

Murray, F. B. (1986). Goals for the reform of teacher education: An executive summary of the Holmes Group Report. *Phi Delta Kappan, 68*(1), 28–32.

Nanassy, L. D., Malsbary, D. R., & Tonne, H. A. (1977). *Principles and trends in business education.* Indianapolis: Bobbs-Merrill.

National Association for Business Teacher Education. (1982). *Standards for business teacher education.* Reston, VA: Author.

National Business Education Association. (1987). *Business teacher education curriculum guide: Designed for the preparation of business teachers at all levels of instruction.* Reston, VA: Author.

Norton, C. T. (1975). An analysis of the competencies needed by bookkeeping/accounting teachers as perceived by authorities and teachers of bookkeeping/accounting (Doctoral dissertation, University of Houston). *Dissertation Abstracts International, 36*(05), 2600A. (University Microfilms No. 75-23,954)

Ober, S. (1982). An analysis of doctoral research in business education. *NABTE Review, 9,* 44–47.

Olson, H. L. T. (1974). The relationship between needs-reinforcer correspondence and job satisfaction of Minnesota secondary school office education teacher coordinators (Doctoral dissertation, University of Minnesota). *Dissertation Abstracts International, 35*(12), 7599A. (University Microfilms No. 75-12,032)

Ownby, A. C. (1981). Training and development for business: An added dimension to business education. *NABTE Review, 8,* 28–31.

Palmer, J. J. (1982). Office work environment expectations and perceptions of students, teachers, and workers (Doctoral dissertation, Arizona State University). *Dissertation Abstracts International, 43*(02), 345A. (University Microfilms No. 82-16,472)

Palmer, J. J. (1984). Work expectations of business students and teachers—How realistic? *NABTE Review, 11,* 37–39.

Palmer, T. M. (1985, November). *The preparation of training professionals.* Paper presented at the National Adult Education Conference, Milwaukee. (ERIC Document Reproduction Service No. ED 262 188)

Peterson, L. G. (1985). An assessment of perceived instructional needs and inservice training preferences of full-time accounting, data processing, and economics faculty in Michigan public community colleges (Doctoral dissertation, Michigan State University). *Dissertation Abstracts International, 46*(05), 1174A. (University Microfilms No. 85-13,933)

Policies Commission for Business and Economic Education. (1977). *This we believe about the mission of business education.* Reston, VA: Author.

Prather, H. (1974). An analysis of competencies needed by shorthand teachers as perceived by business teachers and by authorities in business education (Doctoral dissertation, University of Houston),

Dissertation Abstracts International, 35(07), 4307A. (University Microfilms No. 75-01,020)

Pratzner, F. C. (1987, December). *Vocational teacher education: Selected highlights from a survey of preservice and inservice preparation.* Paper presented at the meeting of the American Vocational Association, Las Vegas.

Pratzner, F. C. (1988, April). *Vocational teacher education and the Holmes Group: Selected highlights from a survey of preservice and inservice preparation.* Paper presented at the Ninth Annual Rupert N. Evans National Symposium, University of Illinois.

Pucel, D. J., Jensrud, Q., & Persico, J. (1987). *A career follow-up of non-education degreed postsecondary and adult vocational teachers.* St. Paul: University of Minnesota, Department of Vocational and Technical Education, Minnesota Research and Development Center for Vocational Education.

Pyke, W. (1971). Patterns of organization and characteristics of student teaching and internship programs in business teacher education (Doctoral dissertation, Northern Illinois University). *Dissertation Abstracts International, 33*(02), 651A. (University Microfilms No. 72-22,799)

Robinson, A. V., Jr. (1974). An identification of professional teaching competencies for community college business education (Doctoral dissertation, Wayne State University, Detroit). *Dissertation Abstracts International, 35*(12), 7625A. (University Microfilms No. 75-13,379)

Rossetti, A. D. (1973). Identification of teaching competencies for which additional information and/or understanding is needed by the secretarial business education teachers in the public secondary of New Jersey (Doctoral dissertation, Rutgers—The State University). *Dissertation Abstracts International, 34*(07), 4067A. (University Microfilms No. 74-01,646)

Rucker, J. D. (1984). An appraisal of the undergraduate business education program at Wayne State College based on a follow-up of the graduates from January, 1971, through December, 1981 (Doctoral dissertation, University of Nebraska, 1983). *Dissertation Abstracts International. 44*(09), 2659A. (University Microfilms No. 84-01,391)

Ryckman, L. A. (1982). Identification of in-service needs as related to performance tasks and related demographic factors by selected Michigan business and office education teachers (Doctoral dissertation, Michigan State University). *Dissertation Abstracts International, 43*(05), 1399A. (University Microfilms No. 82-24,478)

Santos, O., Jr. (1971). The applicability of innovative business in-service teaching methods, techniques, and devices to the in-service training of business education teachers (Doctoral dissertation, Ohio State University). *Dissertation Abstracts International, 32*(07), 3847A. (University Microfilms No. 72-04,633)

Santos, O., Jr., Olinzock, A. A., & Salzman, G. (1980). A systematic approach to occupational experience certification requirements for business teachers. *NABTE Review, 7,* 38–44.

Sapre, P. M. (1989). Where business education programs should be housed: Business education programs belong in a school of education. *Business Education Forum 44*(2), 14–15.

Schenk, R. L. (1969). Teaching difficulties of beginning business teachers in relation to secondary school enrollment (Doctoral dissertation, University of Nebraska). *Dissertation Abstracts International, 30*(09), 3841A. (University Microfilms No. 70-04,672)

Schmidt, B. J. (1981). Criterion-referenced measures: Their effectiveness in assessing business skills. *NABTE Review, 8,* 21–25.

Schmidt, B. J. (1984). Business education in the United States: 1982–1983 NABTE survey results. *NABTE Review, 11,* 50–55.

Schmidt, B. J. (1985). Business education in the United States: 1983–1984 NABTE survey results. *NABTE Review, 12,* 85–90.

Sheahan, P. H. (1972). An evaluation of the office practice course taught in Illinois high schools with implications for preparation of office practice teachers (Doctoral dissertation, Northern Illinois University). *Dissertation Abstracts International, 33*(02), 655A. (University Microfilms No. 72-22,804)

Shulman, L. C. (1986). Those who understand: Knowledge growth in teaching. *Educational Researcher, 15*(2), 4–14.

Shulman, L. C. (1987). Assessment for teaching: An initiative for the profession. *Phi Delta Kappan, 69*(1), 38–44.

Shulman, L. C., & Sykes, G. (1986). *A national board for teaching? In search of a bold standard* (A report for the task force on teaching as a profession). New York: Carnegie Corporation.

Sink, C. V. (1981). The status of teacher certification of NABTE institutions in the eastern business education association region. *NABTE Review, 8,* 7–8.

Slaugh, L. A. C., & Thomas, H. B. (1987). Perceived barriers to implementing Florida's competency-based business education curriculum. *Journal of Vocational Education Research, 12*(1), 53–70.

Slaymaker, S. T. (1971). A curriculum study to develop a graduate level junior college business teacher training program (Doctoral dissertation, University of Arkansas). *Dissertation Abstracts International, 32*(02), 827A. (University Microfilms No. 71-19,578)

Smith, L. M. C. (1986). Secondary school accounting teachers need electronic data processing instruction. *NABTE Review, 13,* 27–30.

Smith, G. R., & Stoddard, T. D. (1982). Reconciling the AACSB common body of knowledge requirements with business teacher education. *NABTE Review, 9,* 9–13.

Stiles, L. J. (1973). The professional license. *NABTE Review, 1,* 42–47.

Stitt, W. L. (1983). Relationship of selected personal attributes of business teacher educators to job satisfaction. *NABTE Review, 10,* 42–45.

Stone, D. R., & Henrie, B. (1979). A learning skills model for competency-based teacher education. *NABTE Review, 6,* 38–44.

Sumner, M. (1980). Improving instruction in collegiate business subjects: A challenge to business teacher educators. *NABTE Review, 7,* 53–56.

Swenson, D. H. (1977). Personality type as a factor in predicting academic achievement, satisfaction, success, and group membership of business and distributive education teacher candidates (Doctoral dissertation, Utah State University, 1976). *Dissertation Abstracts International, 37*(10), 6284A. (University Microfilms No. 77-08,491)

Swenson, D. H. (1978). Personality type as an academic predictor for business and distributive education teacher candidates. *NABTE Review, 5,* 85–89.

Switzer, S. K. (1982). Curriculum structure and content in business communication at National Association for Business Teacher Education member colleges and universities (Master of Business Education thesis, Central Michigan University). In *1984 National Research Conference Proceedings* (pp. 22–24). St. Peter, MN: Delta Pi Epsilon.

Thomas, E. G. (1983). An analysis of business education research articles. *NABTE Review, 10,* 55–58.

Thomas, E. G., Mayer, K. R., & Clinkscale, B. G. (1979). Implications of Public Law 94-142 for business teacher education. *NABTE Review, 6,* 51–58.

Thoreson, H. N. (1972). An analysis of current and recommended occupational experience requirements for certification of vocational business and office education teacher-coordinators in the United States (Doctoral dissertation, University of North Dakota). *Dissertation Abstracts International, 33*(12), 6780A. (University Microfilms No. 73-15,310)

Underwood, R., & Davis, R. (1985). A comparison of the perceived concerns of Indiana secondary school business and distributive education teachers. *NABTE Review, 12,* 65–70.

Underwood, R., & Davis, R. (1987). Concerns of prospective and experienced business and marketing education teachers: Implications for the profession. *NABTE Review, 14,* 39–43.

Uthe, E. F. (1981). Critical issues in business teacher education. *NABTE Review, 8,* 53–59.

Vaughan, R. T. (1982). The identification of certain competencies appropriate for secondary school business teachers (Doctoral dissertation, University of North Carolina at Greensboro). *Dissertation Abstracts International, 43*(03), 637A. (University Microfilms No. 82-18,680)

Vaughan, R. T. (1983). The identification of certain competencies appropriate for preservice and in-service secondary school business teachers. *NABTE Review, 10,* 22–24.

Walters, G. L. (1975). *The development and refinement of reading skills in business education.* (Monograph No. 128). Cincinnati, OH: South-Western Publishing.

Wardlow, G. (1987). The teaching performance of graduates of teacher education programs in vocational and technical education. *Journal of Vocational Education Research, 12*(3), 57–68.

Wells, L. C. (1986). Teacher supply and demand: A problem for Minnesota? *CURA Reporter, 16*(4), 5–8.

Wentz, J. E. (1985). The identification of computer competencies: Training guidelines for a teacher preparation program (Doctoral dissertation, University of Nevada). *Dissertation Abstracts International, 46*(06), 1602A. (University Microfilms No. 85-17,379)

Whitlock, G. (1971). *Evaluating instruction: Learning/perceptions.* Knoxville, TN: University of Tennessee, Learning Research Center.

Wiggins, E. (1975). An analysis of teaching strengths and weaknesses of black business teachers in the southeastern United States (Doctoral dissertation, University of Mississippi). *Dissertation Abstracts International, 36*(04), 2152A. (University Microfilms No. 75-21,560)

Wilkinson, K. L. (1979). Effective and ineffective teacher behavior as viewed by students in secondary business law classes. *Delta Pi Epsilon Journal, 21*(1), 1–11. (ERIC Document Reproduction Service No. ED 206 050)

Williams, L. B. (1985). A study of the impact of house bill 1706 on undergraduate business education programs leading to graduate vocational business teacher certification for the teaching of computer technology (Doctoral Dissertation, University of Oklahoma). *Dissertation Abstracts International, 46*(03), 686A. (University Microfilms No. 85-10,308)

Wilson, P. A., & Wilson, T. C. (1978, March). *What factors contribute to better instruction? Business students vs. other colleges.* Paper presented at the meeting of the American Education Research Association, Toronto, Canada. (ERIC Document Reproduction Service No. ED 153 009)

Wise, A. E., & Darling-Hammond, L. (1986). *Evaluating the teaching skills of beginning teachers.* Santa Monica, CA: RAND Corporation.

Woolschlager, R. B. (1979). Implications of new developments for business education in the 1980's. *NABTE Review, 6,* 12–18.

Zelinko, M. A. (1986). DACUM identification of the job duties and tasks of the small business owner/entrepreneur and to what degree the tasks are included in the marketing and distributive education teacher preparation programs in Pennsylvania (Doctoral dissertation, Temple University). *Dissertation Abstracts International, 47*(04), 1301A. (University Microfilms No. 86-11,949)

BROADENED PERSPECTIVES
OF TEACHER EDUCATION

CHOOSING A GOAL FOR PROFESSIONAL EDUCATION

Mary M. Kennedy

MICHIGAN STATE UNIVERSITY

In a pragmatic society such as ours, professional education is sometimes considered easier to justify than liberal education. Although liberal educators must defend vaguely defined outcomes such as intellectual liberation or broadened perspectives, professional educators often claim they are preparing people to do useful and socially important tasks. With the justification of utility comes the burden of accountability, for professional educators must develop and defend educational programs that assure that graduates can and will behave in particular ways.

The professional educator must, therefore, have a sense of what professional practice entails and of how education can influence practice. And, although educators usually know the general boundaries of practice, they cannot anticipate the particular demands that will be faced by any particular practitioner. Professional educators have devised two general strategies for responding to this problem. One is to develop, codify, and give to students as much knowledge as possible—knowledge about every conceivable situation they might ever encounter—so that they will be prepared for the maximum possible variety of situations. The other strategy is to prepare students to think on their feet, giving them both reasoning skills and strategies for analyzing and interpreting new situations, until they are sufficiently flexible and adaptable to accommodate the variety of situations they are likely to encounter.

The former strategy assumes that, even though particular situations are new, they are nonetheless examples of larger categories of situations and that there is a generally accepted best way to handle any given category of situation. Therefore, the role of professional educators is to provide students with knowledge of the generally accepted principles for handling each category. The latter strategy assumes either that best strategies have not yet been discovered or that they are too situation-specific ever to be prescribed, so that the practitioner should be able to create solutions on her or his own. Therefore, professional educators have a responsibility to provide as much analytic and reasoning skill as possible.

These two views of practice, and of the relationship between professional education and practice, tend to dominate thinking, not only about the technical aspects of practice, but also about the ethical aspects. When professional educators want to provide their students with a social conscience as well, with intellectual tools, they usually resort to these same two methods: Either they provide their students with as much knowledge as possible about the variety of ethical issues they will face, and provide guidance in solving these categories of ethical issues, or they provide some kind of sensitivity training that is expected to function like analytic experiences do, enhancing the students' sensitivity to client needs so that the students can decide for themselves the best course of action, based on the particular circumstances of each case.

Neither of these two strategies is sufficient by itself. Knowledge cannot be applied without thought, and thought cannot function without knowledge. Yet the educational implications of dual goals are extremely difficult to define. If codified knowledge is important, and there is a substantial body of it to learn, then professional educators are obligated to provide as much

The author is grateful to Arthur Elstein (University of Chicago School of Medicine) for his very helpful comments. This work was supported in part by the National Center for Research on Teacher Education, with a grant from Office of Research, U.S. Department of Education. The views expressed are the author's and should not be construed as representing those of the funding agency.

of that knowledge as possible. If, in contrast, independent thought is important, then educators are obligated *not* to reveal their own best thinking on an issue but instead to wait the painful time it takes for students to work these ideas out for themselves. The apparently contradictory conclusions implied by these two educational goals lead many educators to choose one or the other approach, rather than try to achieve both.

Moreover, each professional *field* must find its own solution to this tension: they emphasize the first goal, they emphasize the second goal, or they fail to reach consensus regarding the goal. The first section of this chapter describes two fields, medicine and engineering, in which educators emphasize the first goal and try to give students as much codified knowledge as possible. The second describes two others, law and architecture, in which educators emphasize the second goal and try to help students become independent thinkers. Each of these fields—medicine, engineering, law, and architecture—contains a small but vocal counterculture of educators who argue against the dominant view and for a better balance of the two goals. In the third section, several fields are described, one of which is teacher education, in which professional educators are so split between the two goals that no dominant view can be identified. Following these is a section in which the same tension is described as it applies to developing students' social consciences and a closing section that discusses the importance of a coherent view on this issue.

Before beginning, two caveats are in order. First, there is very little literature that describes average professional educational practices. Instead, literature in professional education tends to consist of (a) descriptions of particular innovations; (b) criticisms of the dominant goal, written by the counterculture in each profession; and (c) official statements of standards, or surveys of practices, that summarize course requirements but provide little detail regarding pedagogy. It is possible that all three of these sources reflect only the views of a small fraction of elite educators who choose to write about their work. Second, when a particular view dominates thought within a field, that view is rarely articulated, for it is taken for granted by members of the group. I have tended to rely on the literature of the countercultures within each profession as a means of learning the dominant views. Their accounts are likely to be biased.

THE GOAL OF PROVIDING AS MUCH CODIFIED KNOWLEDGE AS POSSIBLE

Virtually every profession has a body of knowledge it thinks is relevant, or even essential, for its members to know: physicians must know physiology; engineers, physics; teachers, learning theory; architects, construction engineering. The content deemed most relevant is reflected in a list of courses students are required to take. The number of such courses needed, and the volume of knowledge identified as necessary, varies considerably from one profession to another.

It has been argued that the possession of specialized knowledge is *the* defining characteristic of a profession (Cullen, 1978;

Shils, 1978) and that the volume of such knowledge available to each profession contributes to recognized status distinctions among the professions (Glazer, 1974). Yet the volume of codified knowledge taught to students is not strongly related to the level of their first professional degree. For example, library students take far fewer professional courses than do engineering students, but the librarian's first professional degree is a master's degree, whereas the engineer's is a bachelor's degree. And professional nurses receive their first professional degree in any of three ways: through an associate degree, a baccalaureate degree, or a hospital diploma.

The two professions with the most knowledge-oriented curricula, medicine and engineering, also exemplify this point: In the United States and Canada, medical education begins *after* students have completed their baccalaureate degrees, whereas engineering programs are provided *within* the baccalaureate degree. Engineering students encounter such a heavy dose of course requirements that they can rarely complete their bachelor's degree within the allotted 4 years, but medical students follow their bachelor's degree with 2 years of basic sciences and 2 years of clinical training. Among medical educators, these 4 years of basic and clinical sciences are called the *undergraduate* years, because virtually all physicians pursue further clinical specialization once they complete this 4-year sequence.

With few exceptions, the two "undergraduate" years of basic sciences in medical education include such subjects as anatomy, biochemistry, physiology, pharmacology, microbiology, and pathology (S. Abrahamson, 1981; Thorne, 1973b; M. P. Wilson & Smythe, 1983), whereas the 2 years of undergraduate clinical studies are organized around the "clinical disciplines": obstetrics–gynecology, medicine, surgery, pediatrics, psychiatry, and, sometimes, family practice or some other elective (Association of American Medical Colleges, 1984). Moreover, in addition to this 4-year undergraduate sequence, many students, whether encouraged by medical schools or not, also choose a science major for their bachelor's degree.

Medical students who do not study basic sciences for their bachelor's degrees actually take fewer courses in the codified knowledge of the medical profession than do engineering students, even though medical students' first professional degree is much higher. A 1955 study of engineering education (American Society for Engineering Education, 1955) recommends that 75 percent of the undergraduate curriculum be devoted to mathematics, basic sciences, and engineering courses, giving students 20 percent coursework in the humanities and 5 percent in electives. This contrasts with 50 percent in basic sciences in the medical student's "undergraduate" curriculum. Moreover, many engineering programs have been unable to maintain the balance proposed in 1955 and tend to require even more scientific or technical courses than this report recommends. By 1981 distribution had evolved so that only 13 percent of student coursework was devoted to humanities and social science; 63 percent to mathematics, science, and engineering, and 25 percent to electives. Even the electives that students chose tended to provide technical, prescriptive knowledge in areas such as accounting, finance, and technical writing (Gerstein, 1981). Despite its heavy emphasis on technical content, this curriculum was and is considered broad by most engineering educators.

Teacher preparation has not concentrated on codified, prescriptive knowledge to the degree that medicine and engineering have, but it tends to lean in this direction more than in the direction of independent thought and analysis. Teacher education courses are organized around disciplines, called *foundations*, and around techniques of practice, usually called *methods*. The first set of courses includes educational psychology, sociology of education, philosophy of education, and history of education. The second includes methods for teaching mathematics, methods for teaching reading, and so forth. In the 1960s, teacher education went through a competency-based reform effort, intended to provide teachers with a more prescriptive knowledge base. The movement failed, in part because teacher educators could not reach a consensus that such prescription was appropriate for teachers and in part because competencies could not be justified on the basis of research. Now, a body of research findings on effective teacher behaviors has developed that could form the basis for a more prescriptive teacher education curriculum (Brophy & Good, 1986; Gage, 1977, 1985; B. O. Smith, 1980; Watts, 1982). In light of these new findings, teacher education is experiencing a new movement toward codified and more prescriptive content in its curriculum (Evertson, Hawley, & Zlotnick, 1984; Gage, 1985; Gideonse, 1986).

Like the competency-based movement, this new movement in teacher education consists in part of defining the relevant content to be taught and in part of organizing the teacher education curriculum to assure that this content is included. In fact, interest in defining the knowledge base of teaching is currently so widespread that the American Association of Colleges for Teacher Education has sponsored a major effort to define the knowledge base (Reynolds, 1989; D. C. Smith, 1983) and the U. S. Department of Education has funded several teacher education programs to infuse their curricula with this research-generated knowledge base (Weil & Loucks-Horsley, 1987).

Even though the volume of codified knowledge is the mark most often associated with professional practice, and even though it is the goal most widely accepted by professional educators, a number of problems have arisen in medicine and engineering, where professional educators have overemphasized the knowledge-acquisition goal at the expense of independent thinking. These problems are listed in the following paragraphs.

One outcome of trying to provide as much knowledge as possible is that, as new content areas and new technologies are developed, new courses are continually added to the curriculum (Gerstein, 1981; Wilson & Smythe, 1983). Similarly, as new knowledge is generated within recognized areas, existing courses are expanded. Consequently, both medicine and engineering have become victims of their own expanding knowledge bases (Eichna, 1980). Once the available space is filled, curriculum revision depends on difficult zero-sum decisions: Adding a new course here or a new chapter there necessarily means eliminating another course or chapter elsewhere.

Even clinical time is converted to the goal of efficiently transmitting knowledge. In medicine, faculty–student clinical interactions consist almost entirely of faculty lectures (Foley, Smilansky, & Yonke, 1979), and engineering laboratory courses have almost disappeared from the curriculum (National Research Council, 1986). A recent report on the status of engineering education programs (National Research Council, 1986) refers to a tenuous balance of priorities, such that additional courses in any area would seriously threaten the remaining areas, because any addition necessarily means deleting something from one of the other areas. In medicine, the Association of American Medical Colleges (1981) criticizes politicians for adding their favorite topics, things like human nutrition, geriatrics, and human sexuality, to the list of medical school curricular requirements but was itself equally guilty by recommending the addition of information sciences such as computers to the medical curriculum (Association of American Medical Colleges, 1984).

Moreover, there are no rules for determining which content is most important. After all, the goal of the knowledge-oriented educator is to prepare the student for every possible contingency. When the curriculum is filled, as it quickly is, professional educators have no recourse but to add to its size, for they usually cannot agree on decision rules that enable some content to be removed from their list of important knowledge. The medical curriculum, for instance, which has been described as a relatively stable one that has not changed substantially since the early 1900s (E. M. Abrahamson, 1979; Lundmerer, 1985), actually varies considerably from one institution to another, because each program establishes its own criteria for content coverage in each subject. The time spent studying anatomy, for instance, ranges from 135 to 612 hours, depending on the institution. In physiology the range is 90–341 hours; in biochemistry, 55–272 hours; and in neuroscience, 18–210 hours (Association of American Medical Colleges, 1984). Ironically, despite these variations in content coverage, most medical educators feel there is not much room to maneuver within the medical school curriculum.

According to the counterculture in each field, this orientation also affects students negatively. In medicine, critics argue that the press for content coverage forces students to memorize vast sums of material, with little opportunity to meaningfully digest it; that the very act of memorizing facts can both inhibit thoughtful practice and promote survival ethics inappropriate for medical practitioners (Association of American Medical Colleges, 1984; Bishop, 1984; Eichna, 1980; Neame, 1984); and that the pace of clinical studies encourages students to learn to cope with death and disease through "gallows humor" (R. C. Fox, 1957), institutionalizing authority (Light, 1980), guarding their autonomy, and rejecting processes of accountability (Mizrahi, 1984).

In engineering, critics have argued that engineering graduates lack sound judgment and display disorganized thinking (Albright & Albright, 1981) and that they are learning only how to compute and not how to solve complex problems (Cowan, 1986). To solve these problems, some writers (e.g., Kemper, 1986) propose hiring more faculty who come from practitioner backgrounds (an argument that assumes the content could be taught in a way that simultaneously enhances thought and analysis), whereas others (e.g., Ernst, 1986) propose that students take more laboratory and design courses (an argument that assumes independent thought and analysis must be learned in a different environment).

But the strong tide of interest in covering all the knowledge available mitigates against widespread acceptance of these views. In 1984 the Association of American Medical Colleges sponsored a major review of medical education, which turned out to be critical of the volume of material students had to memorize and recommended altering both the curriculum and the student-evaluation procedures to attend more to the goal of independent learning and problem solving. They suggested that students be "active, independent learners and problem solvers rather than passive recipients of information" (pp. 2–3). The report generated considerable furor from medical educators, who perceived it as antiscience and, implicitly, not intellectually rigorous (Muller, 1985). Resistance was so strong that the association sponsored a second curriculum review panel whose ostensible purpose was to elaborate on the first report (Association of American Medical Colleges, 1985). The second report reads more like a second opinion than like an addendum to the first report. It says the second panel had been concerned about the recommendation for more attention to problem solving, for fear that such attention would lessen the importance of the codified knowledge base in science. After review, however, this panel decided that its fear was unfounded and that the authors of the first report were actually just trying to say that medical educators should not ignore these other aspects of student learning.

In these two fields, the emphasis on knowledge acquisition is so strong that a culture has become established in which content coverage is the primary criterion for success. Educators in these fields have come to see time spent solving problems as time *lost* from learning more content. There is a tendency, therefore, to resist proposals to attend to students' ability to make their own decisions, not only because these proposals would result in less time for learning codified content but also because they are perceived to make for a less rigorous program of study.

Because their cultural norms so strongly emphasize content coverage, medical and engineering educators who want to produce better decision makers tend to provide *separate content* rather than a *different way of learning the content that is already there*. For instance, Eck and Wilhelm (1979) propose giving engineering students slow-motion practice in decision making through an instructional strategy they call *guided design*. In guided design, decision-making steps constitute the content to be taught. Students are given a handout that lists decision-making steps and problems to solve using these steps.

In the 1950s and 1960s some medical educators did try to reform the medical curriculum radically. Two ideas dominated these reforms. One idea was to organize the codified knowledge so that it better reflected the contexts of practice, the organ systems, than the scientific disciplines from which it arose (e.g., Association of American Medical Colleges, 1984; Barrows, 1985; Rosse, 1974). Such a strategy would make the knowledge more relevant and more meaningful to students and, consequently, more likely to be remembered. The second was to encourage students to take a more active role in their own learning by having them establish their own study agenda (Barrows & Tamblyn, 1980; Eichna, 1985; Neufeld & Barrows, 1974; Neufeld & Chong, 1985). These reforms still retained the model of the practitioner as someone who applies known solutions to recognizable categories of situations; that is, the reason for organizing knowledge around the contexts of practice, rather than around the basic scientific disciplines, was to promote better retention, and the reason for encouraging self-study was to assure that students would continue to seek out new content throughout their careers as it became available.

The most radical and widely recognized reform occurred at Case Western Reserve in 1954, when the entire basic sciences curriculum was reorganized around the organ systems, rather than around the scientific disciplines, and each course was taught by a committee representing the various relevant disciplines. Moreover, students learned through problems that required them to seek out knowledge in order to find solutions. In this way, students established their own study agendas. But, over time, the program devolved back toward the more traditional approach to medical education (G. Williams, 1980). In 1968 a curriculum revision eliminated the bridge between basic and clinical sciences, reduced laboratory time, and eliminated self-study projects. By 1977, the syllabus had grown to 3,000 pages, and a self-study committee established for accreditation review said that the students concentrated on memorizing its contents rather than using the variety of learning resources that had been designed to foster self-directed, problem-oriented learning (G. Williams, 1980).

THE GOAL OF ENHANCING INDEPENDENT THOUGHT AND ANALYSIS

Educators who emphasize independent thought and analysis more than the possession of codified content tend to hold a different model of the relationship between education and practice. Rather than trying to provide an a priori solution to every possible future problem, they are more inclined to provide extensive practice in analyzing situations and establishing situation-specific goals based on these analyses. Perhaps the most significant feature of this model is the assumption that goals can legitimately vary from one situation to another. The educator who believes codified knowledge can be applied to most situations also necessarily assumes there is an agreed-upon goal. Without prior agreement on goals, it would not be possible to define the appropriate knowledge in advance (Schön, 1983). But, if situations can be resolved in a variety of ways, then the ideal practitioner is someone who can, upon encountering a new situation, generate alternative goals, develop hypotheses, conduct mental experiments, and try other alternatives. In the process, *both* means *and* ends are experimentally varied, until a satisfactory solution is obtained.

Architecture and law are fields in which faculty tend to assume that independent thought and analysis are the most important goals of professional education. These educators provide students with plenty of time to practice their profession's analytic strategies. Student lawyers study almost exclusively by analyzing appellate court decisions, through which they acquire the principles of law, and student architects participate in a series of studio design courses in which they practice designing a variety of architectural structures.

Law school generally follows a baccalaureate degree and extends schooling for 3 additional years. Though not universal, the most notable feature of law schools is their reliance on what they call the Socratic method of teaching. In the typical law school, students analyze appellate court decisions in an effort to reconstruct the reasoning that went into them. They argue about alternative precedents that could be applied to the cases and about the merits of different arguments that were made. It is this immersion into a way of thinking that marks the success of legal educators. They concentrate on appellate cases because these cases deal exclusively with the principles of law, whereas jurisdictional cases deal with both the law and the particular facts of the case at hand. If they reviewed jurisdictional cases, students would have to consider not only the principles of law but also such issues as whether the witnesses were truthful, whether evidence was valid, and so forth. The appellate case provides students with an opportunity for purely legal reasoning.

The law curriculum, like engineering and medical curricula, consists of a series of relatively predictable course titles, organized around the contexts in which law is practiced: contracts, torts, criminal law, constitutional law, taxes and administrative law, and so forth (Boyak, 1980; Thorne, 1973a). Legal educators are so convinced of the importance of their analytic teaching strategy that arguments about the law curriculum tend to be over the amount of *time* students need to study law (2 years versus 3), rather than over the *content* of the courses they take. At issue is how much guided practice in legal analysis is needed before students are ready to practice as professionals.

Architects generally take a 5-year Baccalaureate of Architecture degree. The first 2 years of their program are similar to the first 2 years of any other baccalaureate degree, and the last 3 years focus on professional education. During these last 3 years, students generally take one studio design course each term, along with other courses introducing them to various content areas (Cole, 1980). The bulk of the architecture curriculum, including the studio design courses, consists of electives, and architecture educators defend this approach to curriculum by pointing out that architectural knowledge is artistic knowledge; it does not accumulate in the way that scientific knowledge does (Guttman, 1985).

By the time architecture students graduate, nearly half of their professional curriculum has been studio design (Allen, 1980). Studio design is generally assumed to be at the center of all architecture schools, and it has been argued that an architecture school is as good as its studio design courses (Wines, 1984). There is some debate among architect educators about the nature and purposes of these studios, however. Some want studio to give students practice in pure design (Guttman, 1985; Wines, 1984), whereas others argue that design should be integrated with construction (McSheffrey, 1985) and with other social issues (Copeland, 1984; Stea, 1981). In the integrated versions, students design buildings that respond to a set of real constraints: a particular landscape, a particular function the building is to serve, a particular client concern. Taken together, these constraints define The Problem, and the students' task is to develop A Solution. As students develop their solutions, they might study the architectural styles of a particular period, read about strategies for designing particular kinds of buildings, read social science studies about the population who will use the building (e.g., the elderly), or visit local examples of similar buildings and observe their use. The nature of architecture is such that many solutions are possible to any given problem, and the criteria for evaluating solutions are difficult to define. When students complete their work, they must present their solutions along with the findings from their research, and they must justify their designs not only to their classmates but also to a jury (Hurrt, 1985).

It has been argued that teacher education should adopt independent thought and analysis as its primary goal. Just as legal educators want their students to think like lawyers and architecture educators want their students to be innovative and creative, contemporary teacher educators have borrowed Schön's (1983) language and want their teachers to be "reflective." Reflection is an ongoing process that enables teachers to continually learn from their own experiences by considering alternative interpretations of situations, generating and evaluating goals, and examining experiences in light of alternative goals and hypotheses (Dewey, 1904/1965; Schwab, 1978; Zeichner & Liston, 1987).

But this concept of practice lacks the cultural support that it enjoys in law and in architecture. In both law and architecture, analytic activity is associated with a culture of individualism: architects are supposed to create unique styles, and lawyers are supposed to be competitive. The culture of teaching is not one that values individualism or competition. Rather than teachers being encouraged to debate rigorously, differences in viewpoint are glossed over with aphorisms like "You have to find out what works for you" that tend to trivialize the significance of differences in view. Moreover, the intellectual products of architects and lawyers are available for public scrutiny in buildings and in legal records, so that lawyers and architects have ways of demonstrating their work, of being recognized for their independent contributions, and of being criticized for their failures. In contrast, the intellectual products of teachers' work are not publicly available. Neither their successes nor their failures can be scrutinized by their peers.

Nor is it clear that teacher educators should promote independent thought, at least to the extreme that it is promoted in architecture and law, for concentrating on this goal at the expense of transmitting codified knowledge can lead to problems.

One problem occurs when educators decide that some particular content *is* important. When architect educators want to introduce particular content, for instance, they have difficulty doing so in a curriculum designed to enhance independent thought and analysis. Cole (1980) points out that, because studio design courses are purposely holistic, they do not enable architecture educators to teach any particular design principles or techniques. If architecture educators ask students to practice making buildings more energy efficient, they automatically decrease students' attention to other design issues and, thereby, diminish the value of the design studio as a vehicle for learning to balance numerous concerns when designing buildings. Yet if students do not learn to take energy efficiency into account, architecture educators have failed to produce the kind of graduates they should be producing. So the very strength of the architecture curriculum—its holistic studio design—is also its greatest weakness, for it does not permit any particular issues to be highlighted.

Cole (1980) proposes solving this problem by incorporating concerns such as energy efficiency into the set of constraints that define the studio design problem. But such a solution raises other issues, for the entire set of studio design courses is loosely connected, with design constraints varying randomly from studio to studio. Introducing particular constraints into the system could upset the entire array in a way that would interfere with its decision-making orientation. This solution could assure that students take particular issues into account, but it could not assure that they learn particular content that they might need to know.

Another problem with programs oriented toward independent thought and analysis is that these programs lack structure. Because these educators are more interested in the quality of the student's experiences than in the transmission of content, no, or very few, courses are required. Consequently, educators are accused of offering programs with nothing more than random sequences of experiences (Cramton, 1982), and they must routinely defend themselves against critics who wonder how their programs can be justified if nothing is required (Guttman, 1985; Schwartz, 1982). Cardoza (1977) suggests that the ambiguous curriculum makes it difficult for law students to tell if they are learning whatever it is they are supposed to be learning, and Rappaport (1984) criticizes studio designs for their inefficiency, pointing out that there is no evidence of their effectiveness. Porter (1979) argues that architecture has no conceptual map of the field, suggesting that the current mode of instruction enhances the "mysterious judgment" aspect of design. Moreover, professors in both fields have been accused of idiosyncratic standards such that students mainly learn to adapt to the particular views of particular professors (Porter, 1979; Rappaport, 1984). Even in law clinics, according to Condlin (1983), professors argue for subliminal preferences and use their authority at their own convenience to suppress discussions.

Another criticism of these programs is that they negatively affect students' sense of social conscience. In law, for instance, Dvorkin, Himmenstein, and Lesnick (1981) argue that the emphasis on relevance in legal reasoning suggests implicitly to students that nonlaw issues must not be relevant because they are never dealt with in the classroom. Similarly, E. M. Abrahamson (1979) suggests that the cherished goal of getting students to think like lawyers could mean that they no longer think like humanitarians, Cramton (1978) deplores the emphasis on hard facts and cold logic, and Pipkin (1979) argues that the latent curriculum produces a hierarchy of tasks such that intellectual tasks are valued over emotive, ethical, or aesthetic tasks, and analysis is valued over sensitive discussion or lecture.

Moreover, students adopt these values and can become so intrigued by their intellectual task that they lose their sense of social purpose and, consequently, lack an adequate social conscience (Payton, 1985; Sutton, 1984). One result of law school norms is that students perceive courses dealing with issues of professional responsibility, introduced into law curricula following the Watergate episode, less intellectually rigorous and consequently less important (Pipkin, 1979). The analogous situation in architecture occurs when students think that any design compromise necessarily demeans their artistic creations, even when the compromises are asked for by their clients. R. D. Fox (1984) points out that there are many satisfactory solutions to any given problem and that it is possible to negotiate on certain points without jeopardizing the entire design, but students often see their artistic designs as *thwarted* by clients, rather than seeing the clients' desires as legitimate parts of The Problem (Guttman, 1985). Similar myopic vision can occur among lawyers when, for instance, they advise clients according to what is legally justifiable, with no regard for whether their proposal is actually in the clients' best economic or personal interests (Payton, 1985).

Students might also adopt the view that codified knowledge is of less importance than their own analytic thought processes. In architecture, students' lack of interest in construction became such a serious issue in the 1970s that a major symposium was held several years ago to analyze this problem and to generate solutions to it (Wagner, 1981). Participants bemoaned the fact that architecture students were not interested in engineering, and they wished students would envision themselves as master builders. Though clients tend to judge architects by their technical results, architects judge each other by their aesthetic results, thus further reinforcing the view that technical issues are not important. Several participants at this conference felt this anticonstruction view emanated from the 1940s, when architecture educators began to view engineering as too vocational to be included in professional education. Other participants argued that construction was indeed vocational and that it did not belong in a professional education. Here is a case, then, where a particular body of knowledge was perceived to be useful for architects to know but was not perceived to be sufficiently intellectually rigorous to meet their standard for university work. Consequently, professional educators found themselves at odds over their role in providing this knowledge to students.

Finally, in part because of educators' orientation toward thought and analysis and against content coverage, employers often claim graduates do not know enough about basic principles and techniques of their fields. Architecture graduates are said to lack knowledge of the principles of construction (McSheffrey, 1985) and law graduates to lack knowledge of how to prepare legal briefs (Payton, 1985). Porter (1979) even argues that, because architecture graduates do not have adequate scientific and technical knowledge, more and more buildings are being built without their help: Public housing projects are designed by social engineers, and airports are built on the basis of complex mathematical models of traffic patterns with which architects are not familiar.

Law schools have been severely criticized for their inattention to the techniques of practicing law (Clare, 1976; Cramton,

1982; Littlejohn, 1980; Roark, 1978). These criticisms crescendoed in the 1970s and 1980s, after Chief Justice Warren E. Burger publicly criticized the competence of lawyers practicing in the federal courts (Burger, 1973; Jacobson, 1979). A New York commission formed to review the situation recommended that any lawyer wanting to practice before the Second Circuit Court should be required to take a specific set of courses (Clare, 1976). The recommendation stimulated a storm of controversy among law educators and lawyers. Law-school deans who testified before this commission resisted the idea of requiring particular content on the grounds that their purpose was to teach students to think like lawyers and that no specific course content was necessarily relevant to that goal.

In other arenas, law educators have also argued against teaching specific skills. Cardoza (1977), for instance, argues that practical techniques can be learned in the doing, but those professional qualities of most importance can develop only through participation in penetrating analyses. Rohan (1976) tells the story of a law professor's response to an irate father. The father complained that his son had not learned to draw up a particular kind of document, and the father had to teach his son himself. The professor asked how long it took to teach this, and the father estimated about 5 minutes. The professor then said, "I thought so. You see, we are teaching our students things which you couldn't teach him in a lifetime."

THE PROBLEM OF AMBIVALENCE

In the professions just described, educators have reached a remarkable consensus in their views about the nature of professional practice and the way in which professional education contributes to practice. In each case, that agreement focused attention on *either* knowledge acquisition *or* independent thought, so that attention to the other goal became the province of a small counterculture within each profession. In other professions, educators fall into yet another kind of difficulty, for they are unable to agree on a requisite knowledge base or an appropriate pedagogy for their profession. Educators in these professions lack strong cultural norms regarding what counts in their fields. Included in this set of professions are social work, nursing, librarianship, and journalism.

Social work educators offer two professional degrees, a bachelor's (BSW) and a master's (MSW). Until the late 1960s, the MSW was the first professional degree. But in 1969, the National Association of Social Workers began admitting BSW practitioners to membership in the association, and in 1970 the Council of Social Work Educators began accrediting BSW programs (Dinerman, 1981; Guran & Williams, 1973). Recognition of the BSW as the first professional degree occurred partly because employing agencies could not afford MSW-degreed people, and so they were hiring people with bachelor's degrees in other fields and giving them full social work responsibilities. Because most professions are under continual pressure to raise their first professional degrees, either to enhance their profession's status or to provide space for more content, social work is unusual in lowering its first professional degree (Cohen & Wagner, 1982).

Both BSW and MSW curricula include courses in five areas: human behavior and social environment, research methods, social welfare policy, social work practice, and field experiences. Courses in human behavior and social environment are analogous to foundation courses in education, and social work practice courses are analogous to methods courses. Apparently, the number of credits and the content offered in these five areas are highly variable across programs, and content on ethics is scattered unsystematically throughout the curriculum (Dinerman, 1981). The Council on Social Work Education requires students to take 300 clock hours of field experiences, either concentrated in blocks of full-time work (S. J. Wilson, 1981) or spread over 30 weeks at 2 or 3 days a week (Council on Social Work Education, 1984).

Prior to the 1960s, social work educators assumed their graduates would engage in *casework*, that is, they would help individual clients make social or psychological adjustments (Goldstein, 1980). In keeping with that assumption, curricular guidelines emphasized the growth and development of individuals, and curricular content was driven primarily by personality theories. But in the 1960s, questions were raised about whether the primary task of the social worker was to help the individual adapt to the situation or to help the individual *change* the situation. Social workers and social work educators began to construe social workers as professional change agents. In 1962 the curricular guidelines were altered to refer to human growth and the *social environment*, rather than to human growth and development, and in 1969 all curricular requirements were removed in favor of a general goal of professional values and a commitment to serving people (Guran & Williams, 1973). The field continues today to be divided between these two professional roles (Goldstein, 1980).

Social work educators are plagued by disputes about the role that codified knowledge can play in social work. One regularly finds articles in which research and theory are disparaged for their potential to jeopardize the genuineness of social worker–client relations. Bierter (1977), for instance, argues that the goal of science is to explain phenomena with principles that are independent of time and place but that the social worker's role is to experience each conversation as a unique encounter. When social workers use theories to guide their conversations, they can fail to connect a client's problems to his or her particular time, place, and personality. Gelfand (1982) argues for the importance of divergent thinking in social work and suggests that the field overemphasizes logical thinking, and Reid (1979) pleads for social workers not to view people as puzzles, because that view mechanizes and alienates them.

Nursing programs are offered through three different degrees, and the curricula, even within a given degree, are extremely varied. Baccalaureate-degree nursing (Bachelor of Science in Nursing/BSN) programs also vary in the proportion of professional versus arts and sciences courses that are required. On average, nursing courses compose 43 percent of the curriculum (Quiring & Gray, 1979). This variation in content and volume occurs in part because nurse educators cannot agree on what knowledge is critical to nursing. Scales (1985) argues that what is needed is a conception of nursing as a profession. For instance, human beings, the objects of nursing care, can be thought of as biological, psychological, social, or spiritual beings. Similarly, the nursing process can be construed as interpersonal, supporting, assisting, problem solving, adaptative, behavioral, or health care: And the goal of nursing can be construed as equilibration, adaptation, repatterning of health, self-care, health restoration, health maintenance, or health promotion. Developing an appropriate curriculum requires nurse educators to sort through all of these issues.

This confusing array of possibilities is apparent in the variety of curricula being proposed or implemented by nurse educators. Greaves (1984) proposes that the curriculum be organized around specific kinds of nursing interventions: preventative, restorative, adaptive, and maintenance, and King (1986) includes courses in historical and philosophical foundations of nursing, theories of nursing, ethical and legal dimensions of nursing, role and function of the professional nurse. In the late 1970s, Quiring and Gray (1979) surveyed BSN program directors and found extreme variability among their curricula. One program, for instance, included courses on adult illness, child illness, maternal–child illness, psychosocial illness, and community health; another included courses on the nurse in relation to the individual, the family, and the community; another provided courses on minor and major health issues and health care systems; and yet another provided courses on process adaptation, tools, synthesis, chronicity, and complex situations.

A major argument within nursing education today concerns the most appropriate degree for nurses to obtain. The American Nurses Association has formally adopted the BSN as the degree of choice, but the field contains strong opposition to this degree. Faculty in BSN programs are working to establish role distinctions between BSN nurses and others, arguing that the nurse with a BSN is a professional, whereas the nurse with a 2-year associate degree in nursing is a technician (Kramer, 1981), and that BSN nurses are more capable of leadership or more accountable (McClosky, 1981). Critics of this movement accuse college programs of being ivory towered (Dexter & Liadig, 1980). They argue that nurses do not need any professional education at all; that all they need is social conscience (Nichols, 1987); that overeducated nurses cannot or will not do the work that is needed; that they are more assertive, expect higher salaries, expect better working conditions, and only want to supervise (Grace, 1983).

Library schools are also troubled by ambiguities about both degree and content. In the not-so-distant past, library schools provided a more detailed curriculum than they now do. The core curriculum included book selection, cataloging and classification, reference, administration, and history of books and libraries. Students first completed a baccalaureate degree in a field of study of their own choosing, then completed a one-year program that led to a second baccalaureate degree in library science. Later, if they wanted, they could return for another one-year program that would yield a master's degree in library science. In the early 1950s, these two one-year degrees were collapsed into a single one-year master's degree (Bidlack, 1981). In the 1960s, library faculty began to question their core courses, and eventually most library schools stopped requiring courses (Marco, 1978). Today, most master's degrees consist of a one-year program with no required courses. The American Library Association's accreditation standards do not delineate a library curriculum but, instead, describe broad substantive goals such as emphasizing the significance of the subjects taught and reflecting the findings of research (American Library Association, 1975).

One reason the curricular content of library schools is difficult to define is that the profession itself is becoming increasingly diversified. Many students do not become librarians but, instead, information specialists (Bidlack, 1981). In response to these changes in the field, some 38 percent of library schools now carry the term *information sciences* in their titles (Stuart, 1981). But diversification makes it particularly difficult to identify a body of codified knowledge that is relevant to such diverse occupations. Garrison (1978) argues the need to move course content away from specific techniques and toward general principles, on the grounds that the diversity of professional occupations renders the teaching of specific techniques no longer practicable. In a related move, the American Library Association specified that, for accreditation, courses should stress understanding rather than rote learning of facts (American Library Association, 1975). Thus, Garrison advocates a change in emphasis as a means of offering applied knowledge, but the American Library Association recommends a similar move as a way of making course content more intellectually rigorous.

Finally, journalism suffers from ambiguity of purpose. Journalism has traditionally been, and continues to be, a baccalaureate-level degree that permits students to specialize in such diverse areas as advertising, public relations, mass communication, and sometimes even interpersonal communication (White, 1986). Journalism students must take a curriculum that includes at least 75 percent liberal arts courses and are expected to limit their journalism courses to 25 percent of their curriculum. Typical courses within journalism include reporting, feature writing, history of journalism, journalism ethics, sociology, organization or psychology of journalism, law of libel, and comparative journalism (Lindley, 1975).

But the journalism professoriate cannot agree on critical professional content or pedagogy. In his examination of the field, Lindley (1975) found several approaches to journalism education. One approach emphasized the principles and techniques of communication; another emphasized humanities, because journalism shapes tastes; and yet another emphasized social sciences, because journalists transmit knowledge. The field is also split in regard to what its core courses should emphasize. In a recent survey of journalism educators, Blanchard and Christ (1985) found a variety of approaches to core course requirements for journalism degrees. Some schools required no core courses; some required courses that emphasized scientific or technical knowledge, topics like newswriting and communication law; some emphasized thinking and analysis through case studies or practice in "researching" sources; and some provided exposure to issues of social conscience through courses that presented journalism in a broader social context.

Teacher educators also fall within this group of ambivalent professional educators. As we indicated above, some teacher educators envision the ideal teacher as someone who knows the research findings regarding pedagogy and can apply these principles to each situation encountered; others argue that teaching practices cannot be prescribed and envision, instead, an ideal teacher who can analyze each new situation, recognizing, for instance, a unique teachable moment when children are suddenly open to an otherwise difficult idea. Although some might argue that such divergent views stimulate creative program development, B. O. Smith (1980) argues that the current disunity in teacher education is merely confusing, and Watts (1982) refers to it as chaos.

In fact, in none of these fields is ambivalence productive. Rather than promoting balanced attention to the two main goals of professional education, ambivalence stimulates endless debates about the nature of the professional task and a tendency to overly abstract and idealized characterizations of the work.

Nurse educators, for instance, in their desire to develop an ideal conception of the nurse's role, have developed an excessive passion for theory and have almost severed their ties with practice. Their efforts to define their curriculum are tied to efforts to define a nursing role that is substantially different from the role most nurses actually assume when they are employed. When nursing students have learned idealized models of practice rather than real ones and have had little guided clinical experience, many were unable to adjust to the demands of practice (Brudney, 1987; Dexter & Liadig, 1980). Dropout rates within the profession are extremely high within the first 18 months and can be as high as 70 percent within the first 5 years (Brudney, 1987). In an ethnographic study of beginning nurses, Kramer (1974) found that nurses encountered *reality shock*, a variant of culture shock, when they left their ivory-towered educational setting and entered real hospitals. In school, they had learned to value high-quality care, such that each patient received comprehensive, sympathetic attention. But the demands of hospitals require numerous compromises.

White (1986) argues that most journalism courses are also overly theoretical. He claims they have no bearing on practice and that journalism students are not curious in a profound way but, rather, in a restless way. Journalists, he argues, enjoy trivial pursuit, and taking theoretical courses does not alter their inherent makeup. Under the assumption that theory stands in opposition to practice, White advocates journalism courses that are less theoretical and more applied.

THE ANALOGOUS PROBLEM IN THE AREA OF SOCIAL CONSCIENCE

Just as professional educators try to provide their students with the intellectual tools needed for their work, they also try to provide them with an appropriate sense of their professional responsibilities to their clients and to society as a whole. Professional educators encounter two central problems in their efforts to develop students' social consciences. One is that attention to the intellectual tools of the profession necessarily limits, and can even inhibit, the development of appropriate social consciences; that is, the strong press to acquire a large volume of codified knowledge, or to become more intellectually facile, can yield students whose social consciences are atrophied as a result of these intense intellectual experiences. As we have seen, educators in medicine, engineering, law, and architecture have all encountered this dilemma.

The second problem is that it is not clear whether or how students' social consciences can be influenced. If the nature of the profession's intellectual task is difficult to define, the nature of its social conscience is even more difficult to define. One view holds that social conscience derives from knowledge that can be given to students and that the educator's task is to assure that students learn the requisite knowledge and skills associated with a social conscience. Another view holds social conscience to be a matter of character and argues that developing a social conscience is not a matter of adding new knowledge or skill but, rather, of providing experiences that inspire students to construct their own social consciences.

Consistent with their view that all professional education resides in content, medical educators and engineering educators also tend to assume that the route to social conscience is through additional course content covering social issues. Each field provides courses in professional ethics, and each contains a minority of educators who advocate courses in the humanities as a means of producing practitioners with a stronger sense of social conscience (Graham, 1980; Pellagrino, 1977, 1978; Walton, 1985). In fact, there now exists an organization in medical education whose goal is to introduce more humanities courses into the curriculum. Similarly, engineering educators have heard arguments for students taking more humanities courses (Poruch & Benzon, 1983) and for programs offering more interdisciplinary courses, where engineering faculty and humanities faculty teach together (Goulter, 1985; Hodges & Lichter, 1980). Engineering schools have responded only halfheartedly to proposals to add more humanities courses to the curriculum (Turmeau, 1982), in part because they evaluate humanities courses from a utilitarian frame of reference (Hodges & Lichter, 1980) and in part because they perceive these courses to be less intellectually rigorous (Goulter, 1985). Consequently, advisors often denigrate humanities courses, so that, even when students take these courses, they do not expect to benefit from them.

Social work educators, like medical educators, tend to view social conscience as knowledge. One way they try to enhance social conscience is by incorporating a specific view about the profession and its social role into the body of content knowledge to be taught. When Griffin and Eure (1985) surveyed BSW program directors to learn what they perceived to be the most important content for social workers to learn, they included three kinds of content: knowledge, skills, and values. A value might be, "respect for variations in personal life-styles" or "a belief in the right of access to services." These education outcomes, explicitly geared to the students' social conscience, constituted about 10 percent of the content social work program directors identified as most important. In addition, some of the items labeled *knowledge* also had a value-laden component. Among the knowledge items program directors identified as important were understanding "the strengths of minority families and minority cultures," "inherent inequalities in social service delivery for special groups including minorities, women and the aged," and "the legitimacy of social work at the societal level." In addition to providing "right" ways of thinking about social issues, social work educators also provide specific training in behaviors associated with right social positions. Thus Keefe (1979) designed an empathy training course in which he taught the specific behaviors of empathy.

By far the most common strategy for developing students' social conscience is providing them with courses in the humanities, a strategy that offers the advantage of deferring the issue to other faculty. Often, the argument for requiring a bachelor's degree as a prerequisite for entering professional school is that students need a strong liberal education in order to have the personal attributes required of a professional. When the BSW became the professional degree for social work, social work educators had to decide the extent to which they would permit professional courses to replace general education courses. In a fascinating series of letters to the editor of *Social Work*, social work educators argued their myriad positions: that humanities are more helpful in learning to deal with people than social sciences are (R. L. Williams, 1977); that humanities make no contribution at all (Kilman, 1977); that new BSW practitioners will have taken so few humanities courses that they will be technicians rather than contemplative minds (Brull, 1977); that an intellectual education is no guarantee of a humanistic one (Shatz, 1977); and that liberal arts students also spend their second 2 years in a single discipline and, so, are no more liberally educated than are BSW students (Constable, 1977).

Although teacher educators give as much lip service to social conscience as other professional educators do, they have fewer agreed-upon strategies for achieving this goal. Courses in professional ethics are nearly nonexistent in teacher education, and humanities courses are assumed to provide teachers with content to teach rather than with social consciences. Instead, like social workers, teachers obtain their social consciences through foundations courses, courses with titles such as "school and society" or "teaching the disadvantaged child."

THE IMPORTANCE OF COHERENCE IN PROFESSIONAL EDUCATION

The most compelling arguments for professional-education strategies are based on the nature of practice. Medical and engineering educators argue that their students need to apply codified knowledge to situations in a prescribed way, and law and architecture educators argue that their students need to be independent thinkers, interpreting the situations they encounter in a variety of ways. Educators of social workers, nurses, librarians, journalists, and teachers cannot reach consensus on the nature of their graduates' work. Regardless of the agreement that is reached, educators in virtually all fields assume that the essence of practice is *either* the application of technical knowledge *or* independent thought and that the role of professional education is to enhance the practitioner's ability to do that one thing well. Moreover, professional educators seem to assume that these two goals are mutually exclusive, so that enhancing one automatically hinders the other. The memory tasks imposed on students in knowledge-oriented curricula

are presumed not only to *replace* time to think and analyze but actually to *hinder* the capacity for independent thought. Practice in problem solving is often argued not only to *limit* the volume of knowledge that can be conveyed to students but also actually to *stultify* students' interest in learning such content. Rarely does any group of professional educators entertain the possibility that providing more knowledge might actually facilitate problem solving or that providing problem-solving skills might help students find the knowledge they need when it is time to apply it.

The history of professional education provides some explanations for these patterns. Professional preparation has evolved in most cases from apprenticeships to university degrees, and part of the rationale for this evolution was that practice required a deeper and more intellectual preparation than mere training in a smattering of technical skills. The argument, in other words, focused on the intellectual nature of the knowledge or skill required, rather than on its utility. This history places professional educators in a unique position: Their reason for being is based on the utility of their programs, but their reason for being *in a university* is based on the intellectual rigor of their programs. So, just as professional educators must balance between, or choose between, the goal of giving students knowledge and the goal of helping students learn to reason on their own, they must also balance between, or choose between, the standard of intellectual rigor and the standard of utility.

The resolution of the standards dilemma contributes to the resolution of the goals dilemma, for educators have developed separate rationales for each goal that renders each by itself both useful and rigorous. Thus, by selecting one or the other of the goals, rather than a dual goal, professional educators can solve the apparent tension between intellectual rigor and utility. In medicine and engineering, both academic rigor and utility are measured by the volume of knowledge students acquire. The more knowledge students get, the more rigorous the program. And the more knowledge they get, the more prepared they are for the myriad situations they will face in practice. Thus the two standards not only reinforce each other, they reinforce the prevailing view of practice as the application of codified knowledge, and they reinforce the prevailing goal of professional education to give students as much knowledge as possible.

Just as medical educators view the problem-solving curriculum as less rigorous, because it diminishes the volume of content that can be covered, so law and architecture educators view content coverage as less rigorous, because it is not as intellectually demanding as analysis. And they view content as less useful as well. Law educators remind their critics that information does not last over time (Sovern, 1976), and architect educators say that excessive theorizing can destroy the intuitive sense students should be developing (Guttman, 1985). Though these arguments are based in part on an assessment of the nature of professional practice, they are also based, to some extent, on expedience. For instance, although it is reasonable to argue that relevant codified knowledge should be given to practitioners, the volume of such knowledge available is a matter of judgment. Legal knowledge, for instance, does not accrue in the same way that scientific knowledge accrues, but there is nevertheless a continually expanding data base of legal precedents and laws for budding lawyers to know about. Yet legal educators resist the notion that their task should be to assure that their students have absorbed all of this content.

Alternatively, to the extent that professional practice is perceived to be ambiguous, professional educators might argue that they need to provide extensive training in decision making. But ambiguity is also in the eye of the beholder, for medical complications sometimes place physicians in highly problematic situations, and many architectural tasks are, in fact, quite routine. Yet, despite their tenuous premises, each line of reasoning, whether it focuses on the volume of knowledge or on independent thought and analysis, is strengthened by its own internal consistency, and each resists regular attacks by the profession's counterculture. Though the two lines of reasoning are different, each enables educators to define practice, to define their own educational goals, to define the standards of academic rigor and utility, and to do all of these things in ways that are compatible.

There are many ways in which practitioners who graduate from these tightly argued programs differ from graduates of programs in which educators are ambivalent. One difference has to do with income: Generally speaking, physicians, engineers, lawyers, and architects all earn more than social workers, nurses, librarians, journalists, or teachers. Another difference has to do with gender: The former professions are dominated by males, the latter by females. Still another difference has to do with the work environment. Practitioners in the former fields have traditionally been self-employed, whereas those in the latter fields have tended to be employed by public agencies. The extent of these differences varies by profession, and varies over time, but these general patterns still contribute to differences in social status among professions and to reams of literature on the sociology of professions.

But there is another important difference between these groups, and that has to do with the perceived intellectual demands of their practices. A coherent "package" of views, regardless of whether the view is that practice requires volumes of knowledge or that it requires independent thought and analysis, enables both educators and practitioners to share a coherent set of beliefs and values and, thereby, to develop unified professional standards, guidelines, and curricula. Even if their educational practices fail to provide students with the full complement of intellectual tools they need, they provide clear intellectual identities. These intellectual identities, in turn, generate a public perception that practitioners really do possess a special kind of expertise that justifies a special status. Professions without such strongly shared views do not have clear intellectual identities, and their work is often not perceived as having a particularly demanding intellectual character. The choice between providing volumes of knowledge and fostering independent thought and analysis is a hard one to make, for either option necessarily means that students do not receive all the intellectual tools they need. But the failure to choose denies students an intellectual identity and, consequently, all of the social and personal benefits that accompany that identity.

References

Abrahamson, E. M. (1979). Law, humanities and the hinterlands. *Journal of Legal Education, 33,* 27–42.

Abrahamson, S. (1981). Education for health professions: problems and prospects. In M. Boaz (Ed.), *Issues in higher education and the professions in the 1980s* (pp. 41–59). Littleton, CO: Libraries Unlimited.

Albright, R. J., & Albright, L. G. (1981). Developing professional qualities in engineering students. *Engineering Education, 71,* 677–679.

Allen, E. (1980). Things learned in lab. *Journal of Architectural Education 34*(2), 22–25.

American Library Association. (1975). *Standards for accreditation.* Chicago: Author.

American Society for Engineering Education. (1955). *The report of the committee on evaluation of engineering education.* Washington, DC: Author.

Association of American Medical Colleges. (1981). Graduate medical education: Proposals for the eighties. *Journal of Medical Education, 56*(9, Part 2, Suppl.).

Association of American Medical Colleges. (1984). Physicians for the twenty-first century (Report of the project panel on the General Professional Education of the Physician and College Preparation in Medicine). Washington, DC: Author.

Association of American Medical Colleges. (1985). *Commentary on the report on the general professional education of the physician and college preparation in medicine.* Washington, DC: Author.

Barrows, H. S. (1985). *How to design a problem-based curriculum for the preclinical years.* New York: Springer.

Barrows, H. S., & Tamblyn, R. M. (1980). *Problem-based learning: An approach to medical education.* New York: Springer.

Bidlack, R. E. (1981). Issues in education for librarianship. In M. Boaz (Ed.), *Issues in higher education and the professions in the 1980s* (pp. 117–128). Littleton, CO: Libraries Unlimited.

Bierter, W. (1977). The dangers of allowing social work to be invaded by science. *International Social Science Journal, 29,* 789–794.

Bishop, J. M. (1984). Infuriating tensions: Science and the medical student. *Journal of Medical Education, 59,* 91–102.

Blanchard, R. O., & Christ, W. G. (1985). In search of the unit core: Commonalities in curricula. *Journalism Educator, 40*(3), 28–33.

Boyak, D. C. (1980). A conceptual approach to legal education: An alternative curriculum. In E. T. Byrne & D. E. Wolfe (Eds.), *New directions for experiential learning: Developing experiential learning programs for professional education* (No. 8, pp. 27–36). San Francisco: Jossey-Bass.

Brophy, J., & Good, T. L. (1986). Teacher behavior and student achievement. In M. C. Wittrock (Ed.), *Handbook of research on teaching* (3rd ed., pp. 328–375). New York: Macmillan.

Brudney, J. F. (1987, October 26). Deaconess Program offers RNs chance to be interns. *Boston Globe.*

Brull, H. F. (1977). Liberal arts and social work education. *Social Work, 22,* 65–66.

Burger, W. E. (1973). The special skills of advocacy: Are specialized training and certification of advocates essential to our system of justice? *Fordham Law Review, 42,* 234.

Cardoza, M. H. (1977). [Untitled article]. In B. A. Boley (Ed.), *Crossfires in professional education: Students, the professions, and society* (pp. 39–55). Elmsford, NY: Pergamon Press.

Clare, R. L., Jr. (1976). Incompetence and the responsibility of courts and law schools. *St. John's Law Review, 50,* 463–472.

Cohen, M. D., & Wagner, D. (1982). Social work professionalism: Reality and illusion. In C. Derber (Ed.), *Professionals as workers* (pp. 141–164). Boston: G. K. Hall.

Cole, R. J. (1980). Teaching experiments integrating theory and design. *Journal of Architectural Education, 34*(2), 10–14.

Condlin, R. J. (1983). Clinical education in the seventies: An appraisal of the decade. *Journal of Legal Education, 33,* 604–612.

Constable, R. T. (1977). [Letter to the editor]. *Social Work, 22,* 248.

Copeland, L. G. (1984). Architecture education: Balancing the practicalities with the humanities. *Architectural Record, 172,* 45, 47.

Council on Social Work Education. (1984). *Summary information on master of social work programs: 1984.* New York: Author.

Cowan, J. (1986). Are we neglecting real analytic skills in engineering education? *European Journal of Engineering Education, 11*(1), 67–73.

Cramton, R. C. (1978). The ordinary religion of the law school classroom. *Journal of Legal Education, 29,* 247–263.

Cramton, R. C. (1982). The current state of the law curriculum. *Journal of legal education, 32,* 321–335.

Cullen, J. (1978). *The structure of professionalism.* New York: Petrocelli.

Dewey, J. (1965). The relation of theory to practice in education. In M. L. Borrowman (Ed.), *Teacher education in America: A documentary history* (pp. 140–171). New York: Teachers College Press. (Original work published 1904)

Dexter, P., & Liadig, J. (1980). Breaking the education/service barrier. *Nursing Outlook, 28*(3), 179–182.

Dinerman, M. (1981). *Social work curriculum at the baccalaureate and masters level.* New York: Lois and Samuel Silberman Fund.

Dvorkin, E., Himmenstein, J., & Lesnick, H. (1981). *Becoming a lawyer: A humanistic perspective on legal education and professionalism.* St. Paul: West.

Eck, R. W., & Wilhelm, W. J. (1979). Guided design: An approach to education for the practice of engineering. *Engineering Education, 70,* 191–197, 219.

Eichna, L. W. (1980). Medical school education, 1975–1979: A student's perspective. *New England Journal of Medicine, 303,* 727–734.

Eichna, L. W. (1985). A medical school curriculum for the 1980's. *New England Journal of Medicine, 308,* 18–21.

Ernst, E. W. (1986). The undergraduate engineering laboratory. *Engineering Education, 76,* 163–165.

Evertson, C., Hawley, W. O., & Zlotnick, M. (1984). *The characteristics of effective teacher preparation programs: A review of research.* Nashville, TN: Vanderbilt University, Peabody College.

Foley, R., Smilansky, J., & Yonke, A. (1979). Teacher–student interactions in a medical clerkship. *Journal of Medical Education, 54,* 622–662.

Fox, R. C. (1957). Training for uncertainty. In R. K. Merton, G. G. Reader, & P. L. Kendall (Eds.), *The student-physician* (pp. 207–241). Cambridge, MA: Harvard University Press.

Fox, R. D. (1984). Architectural education: A student's long path into Arcadia. *Architectural Record, 172,* 53, 55.

Gage, N. L. (1977). *The scientific basis of the art of teaching.* New York: Teachers College Press.

Gage, N. L. (1985). *Hard gains in the soft sciences: The case of pedagogy.* Bloomington, IN: Phi Delta Kappa.

Garrison, G. (1978). Needed: A core curriculum for a diversifying profession. *Journal of Education for Librarianship, 19,* 179–183.

Gelfand, B. (1982). Creative imagination: The forgotten ingredient in social work practice. *Social Casework, 63,* 499–503.

Gerstein, M. (1981). Engineering and engineering education in the 1980s. In M. Boaz (Ed.), *Issues in higher education and the professions in the 1980s* (pp. 74–81). Littleton, CO: Libraries Unlimited.

Gideonse, H. D. (1986). Blackwell's commentaries, engineering's handbooks, and Merck's manuals: What would a teacher's equivalent be? *Educational Evaluation and Policy Analysis, 8,* 316–323.

Glazer, N. (1974). The schools of the minor professions. *Minerva, 12,* 346–364.

Goldstein, E. G. (1980). Knowledge base of clinical social work. *Social Work, 25,* 173–178.

Goulter, I. C. (1985). How effective is the humanities and social sciences component? *Engineering Education, 75,* 215–217.

Grace, H. K. (1983). Nursing. In C. H. McGuire, R. P. Foley, A. Gorr, & R. W. Richards (Eds.), *Handbook of health professions education* (pp. 92–112). San Francisco: Jossey-Bass.

Graham, P. (1980). The place of the humanities in medical education. *Liberal Education, 66,* 388–393.

Greaves, F. (1984). *Nurse education and the curriculum: A curricular model.* London: Croom Helm.

Griffin, J. E., & Eure, G. K. (1985). Defining the professional foundation in social work education. *Journal of Social Work Education, 21*(3), 73–91.

Guran, A., & Williams, D. (1973). Social work education. In E. C. Hughes (Ed.), *Education for the professions of medicine, law, theology, and social welfare* (pp. 201–247). New York: Carnegie Foundation for the Advancement of Teaching.

Guttman, R. (1985). Educating architects: Pedagogy and the pendulum. *The Public Interest, 80,* 67–91.

Hodges, M. P., & Lichter, B. D. (1980). The union of theory and practice. *American Society for Engineering Education, 70,* 816–821.

Hurrt, S. (1985). Architecture education: The design studio—another opinion in defense of the obvious and the not so obvious. *Architectural Record, 173,* 49–55.

Jacobson, R. L. (1979). Bar unit urges law schools to shift emphasis. *Chronicle of Higher Education, 18*(15), 6.

Keefe, T. (1979). The development of empathic skill: A study. *Journal of Education for Social Work, 15*(2), 30–37.

Kemper, J. D. (1986). Preparation for the teaching of engineering. *Engineering Education, 76,* 154–156.

Kilman, K. (1977). [Letter to the editor]. *Social Work, 22,* 249.

King, I. M. (1986). *Curriculum and instruction in nursing: Concepts and process.* Norwalk, CT: Appleton-Century-Crofts.

Kramer, M. (1974). *Reality shock: Why nurses leave nursing.* St. Louis: C. V. Mosby.

Light, D. W. (1980). *Becoming psychiatrists: The professional transformation of self.* New York: McGraw-Hill.

Lindley, W. R. (1975). *Journalism and higher education: The search for academic purpose.* Stillwater, OK: Journalistic Services.

Littlejohn, B. (1980). The law school's role in lawyer competence. *Trial, 16*(4), 10–11.

Lundmerer, K. M. (1985). *Learning to heal: The development of American medical education.* New York: Basic Books.

Marco, G. A. (1978). Recent adventures of the American core curriculum. *UNESCO Bulletin for Libraries, 32,* 279–283.

McClosky, J. C. (1981). The effects of nursing education on job effectiveness: An overview of the literature. *Research in Nursing and Health, 4,* 355–373.

McSheffrey, G. R. (1985). Architectural education: Construction is essential to the design process. *Architectural Record, 173,* 55–57.

Mizrahi, T. (1984). Managing medical mistakes: Ideology, insularity, and accountability among internists-in-training. *Social Science Medicine, 19,* 135–146.

Muller, S. (1985). Medicine: A learned profession? *Journal of Medical Education, 60,* 85–91.

National Research Council. (1986). *Engineering undergraduate education.* Washington, DC: National Academy Press.

Neame, R. L. B. (1984). The preclinical course of study: Help or hindrance? *Journal of Medical Education, 59,* 699–707.

Neufeld, V. R., & Barrows, H. S. (1974). The "McMaster Philosophy": An approach to medical education. *Journal of Medical Education, 49,* 1040–1050.

Neufeld, V. R., & Chong, J. P. (1985). Problem-based professional education in medicine. In S. Goodlad (Ed.), *Education for the professions: Quis custodiet . . . ?* (pp. 249–256). Guildford, England: NFER-Nelson.

Nichols, S. (1987, June 18). Critical: Proposed legislation shakes up state nurses. *Lansing State Journal,* 3a.

Payton, S. (1985). Is thinking like a lawyer enough? *University of Michigan Journal of Law Reform, 18,* 233–250.

Pellagrino, E. D. (1977). [Untitled article]. In B. A. Boley (Ed.), *Crossfires in professional education: Students, the professions, and society* (pp. 1–17). Elmsford, NY: Pergamon Press.

Pellagrino, E. D. (1978). Humanities and human values in medical education. *National Forum, 58,* 13–17.

Pipkin, R. M. (1979). Law school instruction in professional responsibility: A curricular paradox. *American Bar Foundation Research Journal, 247,* 274.

Porter, W. (1979). Architectural education in the university context: dilemmas and directions. *Journal of Architectural Education, 32*(3), 3–7.

Poruch, D., & Benzon, W. (1983). Educating engineers: The usefulness of humanities. *ADE Bulletin, 75,* 18–21.

Quiring, J. D., & Gray, G. T. (1979). Is baccalaureate education based on a patchwork curriculum? *Nursing Outlook, 27*(11), 708–713.

Rappaport, A. (1984). Architect education: There is an urgent need to reduce or eliminate the dominance of the studio. *Architectural Record, 172,* 100–105.

Reid, S. (1979). Undergraduate and social work education and the liberal tradition. *Journal of Education for Social Work, 15*(2), 38–44.

Reynolds, M. (Ed.). (1989). *Knowledge base for the beginning teacher.* Elmsford, NY: Pergamon Press.

Roark, A. C. (1978). Burger urges law schools to provide on-the-job training in courtrooms. *Chronicle of Higher Education, 16*(13), 3.

Rohan, P. J. (1976). Legal education and training for the profession: An overview. *St. John's Law Review, 50,* 494–501.

Rosse, C. (1974). Integrated versus discipline-oriented instruction in medical education. *Journal of Medical Education, 49,* 995–998.

Scales, F. S. (1985). *Nursing curriculum: Development, structure, function.* Norwalk, CT: Appleton-Century-Crofts.

Schön, D. A. (1983). *The reflective practitioner: How professionals think in action.* New York: Basic Books.

Schwab, J. J. (1978). Education and the structure of the disciplines. In I. Westbury & N. J. Wilkof (Eds.), *Science, curriculum, and liberal education: Selected essays* (pp. 229–272). Chicago: University of Chicago Press.

Schwartz, M. I. (1982). The reach and limits of legal education. *Journal of Legal Education, 32,* 543–568.

Shatz, E. (1977). [Letter to the editor]. *Social Work, 22,* 248–249.

Shils, E. (1978). The order of learning in the United States from 1865 to 1920: The ascendancy of the universities. *Minerva, 16,* 159–195.

Smith, B. O. (1980). Pedagogical education: How about reform? *Phi Delta Kappan, 62*(2), 87–91.

Smith, D. C. (Ed.). (1983). *Essential knowledge for beginning educators.* Washington, DC: American Association of Colleges for Teacher Education, and ERIC Clearinghouse on Teacher Education.

Sovern, M. I. (1976). A better-prepared bar—the wrong approach. *St. John's Law Review, 50,* 473–478.

Stea, D. (1981). Some thoughts on the past, present and future of architecture education. In M. Boaz (Ed.), *Issues in higher education and the professions in the 1980s* (pp. 66–73). Littleton, CO: Libraries Unlimited.

Sutton, S. E. (1984). Architectural education: Should behavioral studies be integrated into the design studio? *Architectural Record, 172,* 43–47.

Stuart, R. D. (1981). Great expectations: Library and information science education at the crossroads. *Library Journal, 106,* 1989–1992.

Thorne, B. (1973a). Professional education in law. In E. C. Hugnes (Ed.), *Education for the professions of medicine, law, theology, and social welfare* (pp. 101–168). New York: Carnegie Foundation for the Advancement of Teaching.

Thorne, B. (1973b). Professional education in medicine. In E. C. Hughes (Ed.), *Education for the professions of medicine, law, theology, and social welfare* (pp. 17–100). New York: Carnegie Foundation for the Advancement of Teaching.

Turmeau, W. A. (1982). Engineering degree curricula for the future. *Higher Education, 11,* 397–403.

Wagner, W. F. (Ed.). (1981). The engineering education of the architect: How much does the architect really need to know? *Architectural Record, 169,* 82–89.

Walton, H. (1985). Overview of themes in medical education. In S. Goodlad (Ed.), *Education for the professions: Quis custodiet . . . ?* (pp. 41–55). Guildford, England: NFER-Nelson.

Watts, D. (1982). Can campus-based preservice teacher education survive? Part II; Professional knowledge and professional studies. *Journal of Teacher Education, 33,*(2), 37–41.

Weil, M., & Loucks-Horsley, S. (1987). *Guidelines for documentation and assessment for teacher education demonstration projects.* Andover, MA: The Network.

White, S. (1986). Why journalism schools? *The Public Interest, 82,* 39–57.

Williams, G. (1980). *Western Reserve's experiment in medical education and its outcome.* New York: Oxford University Press.

Williams, R. L. (1977). [Letter to the editor]. *Social Work, 22,* 249.

Wilson, M. P., & Smythe, C. McD. (1983). Medicine. In C. H. McGuire, R. P. Foley, A. Gorr, & R. W. Richards (Eds.), *Handbook of health professions education* (pp. 20–50). San Francisco: Jossey-Bass.

Wilson, S. J. (1981). *Field instruction: Techniques for supervisors.* New York: Free Press.

Wines, J. (1984). Architectural education: A vivid challenge to the status quo. *Architectural Record, 172,* 51–57.

Zeichner, K. M., & Liston, D. P. (1987). Teaching student teachers to reflect. *Harvard Educational Review, 57,* 23–48.

· 47 ·

IMPLICATIONS OF PSYCHOLOGICAL RESEARCH ON STUDENT LEARNING AND COLLEGE TEACHING FOR TEACHER EDUCATION

Paul R. Pintrich

THE UNIVERSITY OF MICHIGAN

Teachers, like all individuals, learn and develop over the course of their careers. They begin their careers as relatively novice student teachers in college and, over time, become expert educational professionals. There are many models of this developmental progression of teachers (e.g., Feiman-Nemser, 1983; Lortie, 1975), as well as numerous instructional models of how to facilitate or shape this developmental sequence (e.g., Lanier & Little, 1986; Woolfolk, 1989). This chapter will discuss the two general issues of teacher development and teacher education from the perspective of the literature on learning and teaching in the college classroom. Given that most students, regardless of age, begin their formal teaching careers in college classrooms when they enroll in teacher-preparation programs (Lanier & Little, 1986), the literature on learning and teaching in college classrooms (e.g., Chickering, 1981) should be relevant to models of teacher development and teacher education. In addition, many college students are still in their late adolescence (18–21 years of age); therefore, the literature on adolescent and adult thinking (e.g., Adelson, 1980; Merriam & Cunningham, 1989; Salthouse, 1982) should be useful for building a conceptual framework. Accordingly, the psychological research on student learning and development provides a solid foundation for a discussion of teacher learning and development (e.g., Chickering, 1981; Sprinthall

& Thies-Sprinthall, 1983). In addition, research on college teaching (e.g., Dunkin, 1986; McKeachie, 1986; McKeachie, Pintrich, Lin, & Smith, 1986; Menges, 1981) suggests a number of fruitful directions for both research and pedagogy in teacher education. More important, recent research on the psychology of instruction suggests the need to integrate models of instruction with models of student learning and development that are not only theoretically driven and empirically supported but also ecologically valid (Pintrich, Cross, Kozma, & McKeachie, 1986; Resnick, 1983).

The general purpose of this chapter is to review the psychological literature on college learning and teaching and delineate the implications of this research for teacher learning and development, as well as for teacher education. A comprehensive review of the college learning and teaching literature is beyond the scope of this chapter. The chapter will focus on integration and synthesis of the research, to suggest common themes, and draw implications for teacher development and teacher education. The review is organized into three sections, with the first two guided by two general questions. *First,* What does the psychological literature on college student learning and development have to offer teacher educators as they attempt to conceptualize the novice-to-expert developmental progression of teachers? *Second,* What does the research on

Preparation of this chapter was facilitated by a Spencer Fellowship from The National Academy of Education. The author thanks the editorial consultants for this chapter, Michael J. Dunkin and Robert J. Menges, who provided a number of very helpful suggestions. In addition, colleagues at The University of Michigan, Wilbert J. McKeachie, Phyllis Blumenfeld, Janet Lawrence, and Malcolm Lowther, provided useful comments. Finally, special thanks goes to Elisabeth De Groot and Linda Weller-Ferris for providing helpful comments and invaluable bibliographic assistance. The chapter could not have been completed without their help.

college teaching have to offer teacher educators as they attempt to design and implement instructional programs to facilitate teacher learning and development? The third section attempts to summarize the common themes and implications that have been discussed and suggests future directions for research.

PSYCHOLOGICAL MODELS OF THE COLLEGE LEARNER

There are two important questions for understanding any developmental progression, including the development of teachers from novice student teachers to expert educational professionals. They are What develops? and How does this development occur? A general social-cognitive perspective will be used to address these two questions vis-à-vis teacher development. The cognitive aspect of the perspective implies that teachers are active thinkers, decision makers, reflective practitioners, information processors, problem solvers, and rational human beings (cf. Borko, 1989; Carter & Doyle, 1989; Clark & Peterson, 1986; Kagan, 1988; P. Peterson, 1988; Shavelson & Stern, 1981; Shulman, 1986). Given this cognitive focus, the question of what develops will be discussed in terms of the development of teacher *knowledge* and *cognitive skills*. It is assumed that, over the course of their careers, teachers develop in their knowledge of subject-matter content and curriculum, their knowledge of pedagogical methods and classroom management practices, and their understanding of children's development, learning, and motivation (e.g. Shulman, 1986, 1987). At the same time, teachers must be able to enact and use this knowledge in their classroom teaching. Consequently, they also develop their cognitive skills in self-regulation and metacognition, as well as their thinking, reasoning, and problem-solving skills for teaching (e.g., Clark & Peterson, 1986; P. Peterson, 1988; P. Peterson & Comeaux, 1989; Shavelson & Stern, 1981). Although current research in developmental and instructional psychology often pits knowledge and skill-based explanations of learning against one another (e.g., Glaser, 1984; Pintrich et al., 1986), contributions from both perspectives will be reviewed in this chapter.

At the same time, the social aspect of the general social-cognitive perspective implies that cognitive knowledge and skills are embedded in a social context that includes the individual and the individual's interactions and relationships with others. Accordingly, besides the more academic and content-related knowledge and skills, teachers also develop knowledge about themselves (e.g., beliefs about their own knowledge and skills) and others (e.g., attributions for others' behavior), as well as coping skills in managing intrapersonal and interpersonal issues (Cantor & Kihlstrom, 1987). In addition, another important aspect of the social-cognitive analysis of teacher development is teacher motivation. Most of the current models of teacher thinking emphasize knowledge and cognition and tend to ignore motivational components, paralleling recent cognitive research on student learning (Pintrich et al., 1986). However, because it is important to integrate motivational and

cognitive components in comprehensive models of student learning (Pintrich, 1988a; Pintrich et al., 1986), models of teacher development and learning should be no exception. It is assumed that teachers' beliefs about themselves in terms of their perceptions of self-efficacy and competence, their goals and values for teaching, and their affective reactions to teaching will influence and interact with their more cognitive knowledge and skills (Pintrich, 1988a). Accordingly, the hot cognitions of *self-beliefs and motivation* must be considered along with the cold cognitions of knowledge and cognitive skills (cf. Sternberg, 1985; Zajonc, 1980) in addressing the issue of what develops in teacher development.

In terms of the *process* of development, there are a variety of general perspectives on the nature of developmental change, ranging from mechanistic behavioral models that emphasize environmental and situational influences, through organismic models that stress the role of individual characteristics, to hybrid models (i.e., organismic-contextual models) that attempt to integrate both personal and environmental influence (Lerner, 1986). It is beyond the scope of this chapter to address the conundrum of the person–environment issue in detail; rather, a general person–environment interactional model (e.g., Corno & Snow, 1986) is assumed to be an adequate compromise. This interactional assumption is reflected in the emphasis of the social-cognitive perspective on, not only the cognitive and motivational beliefs and processes that individuals use to construct their interpretations of different situations, but also the actual life tasks and social contexts that individuals confront that help shape their cognition, motivation, and behavior. In addition, because it is assumed that these life tasks and contexts change with age, a developmental approach is important for understanding teacher development. Taken together, these assumptions imply that a general cognitive, developmental, and social-interactionist model is a valid approach to conceptualizing teacher development.

There are numerous approaches to learning and development that have relevance for developing a model of the teacher as a learner. Four general research traditions will be discussed: the cognitive style literature, the classic developmental literature, the cognitive and information-processing literature, and the motivational literature. These different traditions vary in their assumptions about the nature of learning and development, have assigned differential importance to a variety of psychological constructs, and have different implications for conceptualizing teacher learning and development.

Individual Differences as the Focus of Development: Research on Cognitive Styles

The cognitive style literature has a long history in psychology, dating back to German typology theories of the 1920s and psychodynamically based ego psychology (Cantor & Kilhstrom, 1987; Kogan, 1983). More recently, cognitive-style constructs have been heavily researched in educational psychology. Cognitive-style models are a classic representation of the focus on individual differences in psychological theories, as opposed to more experimental approaches (Cronbach, 1957, 1975). As with most theories and research traditions that emphasize individual differences, cognitive-style models assume that individuals can be described by certain psychological characteristics, traits, or styles that influence the way they perceive, organize, and react to different environmental stimuli. It is beyond the scope of this chapter to summarize all the research on the vast number of cognitive and personality styles that have been identified and studied such as, field dependence–independence, reflectivity–impulsivity, cognitive complexity–simplicity, introversion–extroversion, concrete–abstract, and leveling–sharpening. For reviews of this work see Claxton and Murrell (1987), Kogan (1983), Kolb (1981), Messick (1976), and Witkin and Goodenough (1981). At a theoretical level, however, there are two general orientations to cognitive styles that have important implications for understanding teacher development.

The traditional personality orientation, often an older view, characterizes cognitive styles as relatively stable personality traits of the individual that are consistently expressed in most situations. For example, cognitive-style models that are popular in the higher education literature, such as the ego development models of Loevinger (1976) and Weathersby (1981), the Jungian-derived Myers-Briggs typology (Myers & McCaulley, 1985), and J. L. Holland's (1966) personality and vocational typology, all propose that individuals can be classified in terms of their dominant cognitive styles or personality traits. These cognitive styles or personality traits (i.e., introversion–extroversion, abstract–concrete, reflective–impulsive) are then assumed to guide and direct the individual's interactions with the environment. Although there are a variety of ways to assess cognitive style (see Kogan, 1983), in a typical study a group of students or adults are given a self-report instrument that requires them to respond to a series of questions regarding their preferred or normative mode of responding to different situations (e.g., I tend to think of all the options before doing a task). These responses are then used to categorize individuals into groups (e.g., reflective–impulsive), and the groups are compared in terms of their behavior in different situations or on different tasks (e.g., performance on tests of cognitive abilities or nature of interaction in small groups).

One implication of this approach for teacher development is the expectation that two student teachers, one classified as reflective, the other as impulsive, when confronted with the same classroom discipline problem would react quite differently as a function of their relative reflectivity–impulsivity style and that these differences would be consistent and stable over time and in different situations. Accordingly, one teacher would continue to act in a generally reflective fashion, and the other would continue to be impulsive over the course of a teaching career. In addition, this general approach often assumes that occupations and careers, as well as college majors (or academic disciplines), can be characterized in terms of the most dominant cognitive styles inherent in the nature of the work and the most dominant personality styles of individuals in these careers or disciplines (e.g., Myers & McCaulley, 1985). Following this logic of typing both individuals and occupations, this general approach often suggests that individuals should be matched to their occupations on the basis of compatibility be-

tween their cognitive style and the cognitive style most representative of the occupation (Claxton & Murrell, 1987). One implication of this approach for teacher education is that the selection of teachers could be based on assessment of student teachers in terms of their dominant cognitive styles, which could then be matched with the most representative cognitive style of successful teachers in the profession.

Although the general idea of matching students to the educational task is an important one in education (Corno & Snow, 1986), the traditional personality approach to cognitive styles has a number of limitations. This approach has been justly criticized on a variety of grounds including problems in the reliability and validity of the measurement instruments for assessing cognitive and personality styles, difficulty in specifying the theoretical nature of the personality constructs in relation to other constructs such as cognitive skills and abilities, difficulty in establishing actual empirical relationships to achievement and instruction, and lack of generality of the findings across different studies, tasks, situations, and cultures (e.g., Baron, 1982; Cantor & Kihlstrom, 1987; Corno & Snow, 1986; Cronbach, 1975; Cronbach & Snow, 1977; Laboratory of Comparative Human Cognition [LCHC], 1983; Magnusson & Endler, 1977; Messick, 1984; Mischel, 1968, 1973, 1979). Although there is continuing controversy over the nature of personality traits and the situational and cross-situational stability of behavior (e.g., Allen & Potkay, 1981; Epstein & O'Brien, 1985; Epstein & Teraspulsky, 1986; Gangestad & Synder, 1985; Mischel & Peake, 1982), most current research in personality and social psychology eschews traditional models that characterize individuals in terms of stable personality traits (e.g., Cantor & Kihlstrom, 1987). Accordingly, models that conceptualize cognitive styles as traits of individuals that are stable across different domains (i.e., academic, work, personal, social) are less likely to be useful for conceptualizing teacher development or guiding teacher education.

In contrast with the traditional approach, modern personality theory and research has moved in the direction of conceptualizing personality variables in terms of process-oriented, dynamic characteristics of individuals, rather than stable, enduring traits. This modern approach also emphasizes the importance of situational characteristics in determining an individual's behavior. In line with this orientation, more recent conceptualizations of cognitive styles stress the cognitive and information-processing nature of styles, rather than the trait or personality aspect of styles. In this research, cognitive styles are defined as information-processing regularities related to underlying personality characteristics (Corno & Snow, 1986; Messick, 1984). As Corno and Snow point out, cognitive styles are conceptually at the overlap between individual differences in intellectual abilities and personality characteristics. These consistencies in information processing are different from cognitive abilities because they focus on the mode of cognition (how), not the content (what) or level (how much) of cognition (cf. Sternberg, 1985). In addition, Messick (1984) proposes that cognitive styles reflect propensities of the individual, rather than actual cognitive competencies in terms of cognitive skills. In the same way, this propensity aspect differentiates cognitive styles from cognitive strategies. The use of different cognitive strategies is assumed to be a function of student choice and control, as well as of the nature of task demands (cf. Brown, Bransford, Ferrara, & Campione, 1983; Weinstein & Mayer, 1986), whereas cognitive styles are assumed to be applied to different tasks in a rather spontaneous, unconscious, and consistent manner (Messick, 1984).

In line with this more recent approach to cognitive styles, researchers have identified individual differences in college students' information-processing patterns for learning academic material, especially learning from text material. This research typically involves examining college students' cognitive processes and learning strategies for different academic tasks in college courses (i.e., studying a textbook, writing an essay, taking notes, preparing for an exam) through the use of detailed interviews, think-aloud protocols, and self-report questionnaires. For example, Marton and Saljo (1976a, 1976b) found two information-processing patterns in college students' approach to text learning: surface and deep processing. Surface processors concentrated on completing the reading and focused on the facts and details of the text. Deep processors attempted to discover the aims of the author and focused on the organization and meaning of the text. A number of other researchers have found similar patterns, such as Ausubel's (1963) distinction between rote and meaningful learning; Entwistle, Hanley, and Hounsell's (1979) identifying, reproducing, and understanding types of learning; Pask's (1976) serialists or operation learners and wholists or comprehension learners; Schmeck's (1983) shallow-reiterative and deep-elaborative learners; and Siegel and Siegel's (1965) factual and conceptual learners.

Although there are some theoretical differences among these various conceptions of a learner's cognitive style, it is more crucial to keep in mind the important distinction between a surface and a deep-processing orientation to learning and studying, regardless of the actual label (Entwistle & Marton, 1984). Researchers in Great Britain and Sweden have continued to explore the surface versus deep-processing difference with students in higher education settings (Marton, Hounsell, & Entwistle, 1984) and suggest that these two general-information-processing styles represent individuals' goals and intentions for studying, as well as their actual learning and studying strategies. In addition, this research suggests that these orientations to learning and studying interact in a dynamic manner with differences in course content and context (e.g., Ramsden, 1984; Saljo, 1984). In contrast with the personality view of cognitive styles as stable traits of an individual that are not under the control of the learner nor particularly sensitive to situational demands, this conceptualization of surface–deep processing proposes a more constructivist view of the learner in which individuals attempt to derive meaning from the course material in line with their intentions and purposes, their use of cognitive strategies, and the nature of the academic task and context (Entwistle, 1984; cf. Brown et al., 1983).

In line with Corno and Snow's (1986) conceptualization of cognitive styles as representing both cognitive and personality characteristics, this general-information-processing style seems to include two basic components: motivational (the student's goal for the task) and cognitive (the strategy used to accomplish the task). These two components appear to work together to determine how the student accomplishes the task. For example, surface processors seem to have a completion or learn-the-facts goal that leads them to use rote rehearsal strategies. This orientation to learning and studying results in students focusing on learning course material to do well on examinations or assignments in the class, not to deepen their understanding of the course content. In contrast, deep processors seem to have a goal of truly understanding the course content in a meaningful way, which leads them to use more elaborative and metacognitive strategies (Marton et al., 1984). The use of cognitive strategies such as paraphrasing or summarizing and metacognitive strategies such as comprehension monitoring should result in better integration of the new course material with their prior content and personal knowledge (Weinstein & Mayer, 1986).

In line with this conception of cognitive styles, teacher education courses and programs should attempt to facilitate the adoption of a deep-processing orientation to learning by students. The surface–deep conceptualization would suggest that student teachers who adopt a deep-processing approach to course work in pedagogy would be more likely to change their conceptions of teaching and learning than student teachers who adopt a surface orientation. At the same time, this approach suggests that students who maintain a surface orientation to learning might have difficulty with teacher education courses if tasks are used that require more than rote rehearsal of facts. For example, a teacher education course in which case methods are used to engage students in the process of discussing and integrating personal knowledge of teaching with different philosophical, psychological, and empirical approaches to educational practice could be very difficult for students who remain committed to a surface orientation. In fact, these students might express a great deal of dissatisfaction with and resentment of this course, in comparison with other college courses that do not make the same cognitive demands.

Although the motivational and cognitive components of the surface–deep processing style might not be under the control of the learner in some definitions of cognitive styles (Messick, 1984), it seems likely that students can adopt different motivational goals and cognitive strategies for different academic tasks, courses, and domains of study (Dweck & Elliott, 1983; Dweck & Leggett, 1988; McKeachie, Pintrich, Lin, & Smith, 1986; Pintrich, 1988a, 1988b). Consequently, it seems useful to unpack the different motivational and cognitive components of cognitive styles to provide a more dynamic, sophisticated, and multivariate analysis of student learning. If students do select different motivational goals for different academic tasks, courses, and domains of study, they might employ different cognitive and metacognitive strategies. At the same time, students' facility in using different cognitive strategies might influence their adoption of different motivational goals. In addition, different types of academic tasks might invoke different types of motivational and cognitive patterns (Doyle, 1983; Pintrich, 1989). Most of the work on cognitive styles tends to elide these important distinctions, to provide simple and heuristic descriptions of student learning. The research on the surface–deep cognitive style is an exception by virtue of its focus on the potential links between the information-processing patterns of students and their motivational orientation. In addition, this work characterizes students in global terms that provide useful prototypes for college instructors to think about as they plan and teach their courses. At the same time, however, these global terms can be readily overgeneralized by practitioners in ways not intended by researchers (e.g., assuming that a surface or deep-processing style is a stable trait of a student that is relevant across a variety of tasks, domains, and courses). Consequently, it might be more prudent to investigate the different motivational and cognitive components of student learning, to provide the necessary depth of analysis and sophistication for building a comprehensive and dynamic model of student learning.

Stages and Structures as the Focus of Development: Classic Development Models

Many developmental models have been proposed as descriptions of human development. There are, however, two basic models that characterize most of the classic developmental models: the organismic and the contextual (Lerner, 1986). A third general model, the mechanistic, is not discussed here but is reflected in some of the information-processing models and descriptions of cognition presented in a later section.

Organismic Models. The organismic model assumes that the individual organism is the focus of development and that the developmental changes that take place are a function of the organism's active construction and organization of the environment. In addition, the general-organismic approach assumes that developmental changes conform to an epigenetic pattern described by qualitative and discontinuous growth (Lerner, 1986). Accordingly, aspects of individuals' cognition or personality at higher levels of development are qualitatively different and distinct from their cognition or personality at lower levels of development. The higher levels of development are characterized by the emergence of distinctly new functions or structures that cannot be reduced or explained in terms of the characteristics operative at lower levels of development. The levels of development are characterized, not by having more or less of some skill or process, but in terms of new structures, organizations, or functions. For example, a qualitative-organismic view of teacher development would suggest that expert teachers do not just have more knowledge and skills than novice teachers, but also that their knowledge and skills are organized in a qualitatively different fashion. In addition, although not a central assumption of all organismic theories, many organismic models propose or describe an end point or final stage of development. For example, students' cognition develops toward a final stage of formal operations (e.g., Inhelder & Piaget, 1958) or toward a stage of dialectical operations (e.g., Basseches, 1986; Riegel, 1973).

The classic developmental and organismic model of cognition is Piaget's theory of cognitive development (e.g., Inhelder & Piaget, 1958). This model is concerned with describing the development of the formal and logical aspects of thinking, not with the content of individuals' thinking. The model describes four stages of cognitive development, with the fourth stage, formal operations, being of most interest and relevance for this chapter. The hallmarks of formal operational thinking (cf. Flavell, 1985; Keating, 1980) are (a) abstract thinking, ability to think about possibilities, thinking not constrained by concrete reality; (b) propositional thinking, ability to think about logical relations among ideas, concepts, propositions, and cognitive operations; (c) combinatorial thinking, ability to generate all possible combinations of ideas and cognitive operations; (d) hypothetical-deductive thinking, ability to think scientifically including definition and control of variables, generating, testing, and revising hypotheses; (e) ability to think ahead, planning for problem solution including problem definition, strategy selection, and revision; (f) ability to be metacognitive, thinking about cognitive processes, memory, learning, language, and so on; (g) ability to be self-reflective about not just cognitive processes but also a range of topics such as identity, existence, morality, and personal relationships.

Of course, a teacher's skill in all of these cognitive operations is relevant to teacher learning and development. It seems likely that expert teachers are able to think ahead and plan, that they are able to generate and test hypotheses about students and their own teaching behavior, that they are able to be metacognitive and reflect on their own thinking and teaching (cf. Clark & Peterson, 1986; P. Peterson, 1988; Shulman, 1986). Accordingly, the traditional formal operations proposed by Piagetian theory should be important components in our models of teacher learning and development. However, the classic Piagetian description of cognitive development is a strong structural-stage formalization (Kohlberg & Armon, 1984), and strong stage models that propose very general stages of cognition have been criticized on logical, theoretical, and empirical grounds as being inadequate representations of how cognition develops (e.g., Brainerd, 1978; Flavell, 1971, 1982; Gelman & Baillargeon, 1983; Keating, 1980).

In terms of research on adolescent thinking, there are difficulties in the operational definition and assessment of formal operations (Keating, 1980). These formal operations are typically assessed by interviewing students regarding their strategies for solving a variety of Piagetian-type tasks such as conservation, the balance beam problem, the pendulum problem and their reasoning on syllogisms or the creation of combinations. These tasks are decontextualized and often do not accurately reflect students' knowledge as demonstrated on academic or school tasks (Keating, 1980; King, 1986; LCHC, 1983). Formal operations are theoretically achieved in adolescence; yet empirical studies show that, depending on the sample of students and tasks involved, the actual percentage of individuals who actually display thinking representative of the stage of formal operations can vary from zero to 100 percent, with most estimates in the 40 percent to 70 percent range (Keating, 1980; King, 1986; Neimark, 1983).

Besides this problem of postulating a stage of development that many adults do not seem to attain, the problem of intraindividual differences in the level of reasoning, depending on the domain assessed, remains a major one for any strong stage model (in Piagetian terms, the problem of horizontal decalage). For example, DeLisi and Staudt (1980) found that physics, political science, and English majors were more likely to display formal operational reasoning on problems relevant to their major when presented with the traditional pendulum problem, a political socialization problem, or a literary analysis problem. This type of domain specificity of reasoning suggests that students' thinking might depend more on their knowledge in a particular subject area and on the type of task presented to them than on any broad general logical structure such as a stage of formal operations (cf. Brown et al., 1983; Gelman & Baillargeon, 1983; Glaser, 1984).

This criticism of general stage models from a domain-specificity view of cognition parallels the criticism of traditional personality and trait models from a situational-specificity view of behavior (e.g., Cantor & Kihlstrom, 1987). Accordingly, models of teacher learning and development might need to incorporate some of the psychological constructs of general stage models (e.g., the cognitive operations that are proposed as indicators of formal operations) in terms of describing what develops, but current research and theory suggest avoiding strong and general stage formulations when describing how developmental progression might occur in teacher development.

There have been several other descriptions of students' thinking that build upon the basic Piagetian framework. In the moral-development domain, Kohlberg's cognitive-developmental theory of moral reasoning is based on interviews and in-depth analysis of students' reactions to standard moral dilemmas (i.e., the Heinz dilemma) and includes six stages of moral judgment (Kohlberg, 1976). Thinking at the different stages reflects qualitatively different ways of reasoning about moral issues, including the nature of social arrangements; the organization and function of rules, regulations, and norms in societal institutions; and the rights, responsibilities, and duties of an individual vis-à-vis society. The theory suggests that thinking about these issues develops from a focus on power, authority, and individual interest to reasoning that takes into consideration the necessity of rules and regulations for the maintenance of the social system. The final level of development involves relativistic reasoning about individual rights and the social system, as well as universal ethical principles such as equality of human rights (Rest, 1983). Although the theory has been criticized on theoretical and empirical grounds (cf. Gibbs, 1977, 1979; Gilligan, 1982; Kurtines & Greif, 1974; Rest, 1983), the issues raised are important in understanding students' and teachers' norms and values for teaching and learning. Shulman (1986) suggests that teachers have propositional knowledge of the norms of teaching that concern issues of justice, equity, and fairness that are central to their practice. In addition, Tom (1984) has suggested that teaching involves moral decision making and behavior. Accordingly, how individuals reason about these issues can be important to our understanding of teacher development.

Another developmental model that addresses some of the same issues and has enjoyed great popularity in the higher education literature is Perry's (1970, 1981) model of college student development. In contrast with Piaget's and Kohlberg's emphasis on the logic of students' reasoning, Perry's concern was with the content of college students' reasoning about the intellectual and moral relativism often encountered in the course of a college education. In his original research he interviewed 140 students from the Harvard and Radcliffe classes of 1958, 1962 and 1963 about their college experience. Perry based his description of the stages that characterize college student development on 84 men that he was able to interview over the 4 years of college. He suggested that students move through nine stages, or positions, throughout their 4 years of college. The stages and transitions are quite detailed (see Perry, 1970, 1981), but the initial positions describe students who are moral and intellectual absolutists and believe that there are correct solutions for every moral and intellectual problem and rely on authorities to teach them the proper answers. For example, one implication of this stage model for teacher education is that students at these initial stages might demand that their instructors tell them the one correct way to teach content or handle discipline problems.

The middle positions in Perry's scheme are characterized by the discovery of relativistic answers to problems and contextual reasoning about issues. In these stages authorities are perceived as other individuals who have beliefs and opinions that could be helpful to the student in understanding the moral and intellectual issues, but authorities' beliefs might be challenged on contextual and relativistic grounds. Teachers and students at these stages might challenge inservice development specialists or college instructors on the grounds that research on teaching is meaningless or that instructors' experiences are not relevant to them and decide that good pedagogical practice depends only on an individual's personal experience and opinion.

The final stages in the Perry model describe students as developing a set of personal values that they become committed to as an expression of their own identity. This personal commitment helps them cope with the relativity inherent in many intellectual and moral issues and allows them to move away from absolutism and idealism to the pragmatic considerations and commitments of adulthood (Labouvie-Vief, 1982). Teachers and students in these later stages would be able to make commitments to their own pedagogical practice but would also be aware that there are other approaches that have value. Teachers at these levels would be open to new ideas, albeit their adoption of new concepts would be informed and shaped by their own knowledge and commitments.

As Perry (1981) points out, his stage model is a constructivist model and focuses on how students make meaning out of their college experience, in particular how they come to build their own frameworks for evaluating knowledge and integrate these epistemological frameworks with their own personal and moral identities. The general trends described by the model relate to a number of different domains of psychological development including constructivist views of students' epistemological beliefs (e.g., Posner, Strike, Hewson, & Gertzog, 1982), identity development (e.g., Cantor & Kihlstrom, 1987), and moral development (e.g., Gilligan, 1981, 1982). However, Perry's model is a very general-stage model and seems to assume that the general-stage descriptions and transitions he postulates apply across a variety of domains and contexts. As has been noted previously, very general-trait or stage models are open to the criticism of the domain or situational specificity of knowledge and behavior (e.g., DeLisi & Staudt, 1980). Accordingly, in line with this chapter's more contextual perspective on development, Perry's model provides an important foundation for understanding college student development, but the different domains implicated in his model must be explored in more detail and, perhaps, without the disadvantages inherent in a strong stage formalization (cf. Flavell, 1982; Kohlberg & Armon, 1984).

A more recent model of adolescent and adult development that builds on some of Perry's ideas is the Reflective Judgment Model (King, Kitchener, Davison, Parker, & Wood, 1983; Kitchener, 1983, 1986; Kitchener & King, 1981). The model describes the development of individuals' beliefs and assumptions about the nature of knowledge or forms of epistemic cognition (Kitchener, 1986). This includes individuals' understandings about what can and cannot be known (e.g., how a child learns), how they can come to know something (e.g., through experience, research, intuition), and how certain they can be in their knowledge (e.g., absolutely, probabilistically). These assumptions about the nature of knowledge influence how individuals justify their beliefs, as well as identify and define problems, seek solutions, and revise their problem-solving behavior (Kitchener, 1986; cf. Arlin, 1986; Posner et al., 1982). The model proposes that there are seven stages characterizing the different levels of epistemic cognition. Individuals in the first stage believe that reality can be understood through direct observation, that there is no uncertainty in this knowledge, and that, therefore, there is no need to justify one's beliefs. Stages two and three reflect a move away from absolutist beliefs, although there is still an assumption of a true reality, and differences in perceptions of reality are due to false claims or uncertainty. Direct observation and knowledgeable authorities provide a means of deciding among competing claims in these stages. In stages four and five reality is seen as subjective, depending on individuals' perceptions and experience. Accordingly, in this world view, beliefs are not certain and can only be developed through reliance on data, logic, and rules of inquiry that are applicable to a specific context. In the final two stages, there is a move away from the purely relativistic thinking of stages four and five to belief that reality is constructed through personal interpretations but that there are appropriate methods (e.g., personal evaluation of the opinions of experts, critical inquiry or synthesis) for evaluating the evidence for different world views. This leads to the development of a personal world view that acknowledges that some claims about reality are better or more complete than others (Kitchener, 1986).

This model, with its focus on epistemic beliefs, provides a useful conceptualization of one aspect of thinking that is relevant to teacher development. It provides a more detailed description of some of the issues concerning the nature of students' epistemological beliefs that have been implicated in other models of student learning and conceptual change (e.g., Posner et at., 1982). The Reflective Judgment Model, however, says little about the cognitive operations that might be required to move through the proposed stages. Recent empirical research by Basseches (1980, 1984, 1986) on dialectical thinking might provide a description of some of the cognitive

operations necessary for the development of epistemic beliefs. The centerpiece of this research is the concept of the dialectic and dialectical modes of thought and development as originally suggested by Riegel (1973, 1975, 1976). Dialectical thought and reasoning includes the ability to look for and recognize examples of the dialectic inherent in competing principles, models, and theories, and the ability to use dialectical logic to analyze different systems of knowledge and theories in terms of their context and relationships to each other (Basseches, 1986). Basseches (1980, 1984, 1986) provides a psychological framework for the 24 types of schemata, or cognitive operations, that can be employed in dialectical thinking. Commons, Richards, & Kuhn (1982) and Richards & Commons (1984) have also developed a formal system of cognitive operations that describes how individuals go beyond Piaget's formal operations to reason, not just about variables or sets of variables, but about systems of thought or fields of thought (paradigms).

An adaptation of an example from Basseches (1986) provides a concrete illustration of how the ideas of dialectical thought and reflective judgment may be used to characterize student thinking in a teacher education context. Julie, Karen, and Janet are all preparing to become teachers, but are feeling very frustrated; they believe their teacher education experience is destroying their love for teaching. Julie is confused, not understanding why she has to take so many hours of practical classroom experience or all the education courses. Moreover, she is confused by all the contradictions in what she reads, what her college instructors tell her, and what she hears from her cooperating teachers. She thinks that teacher trainees would learn more and be less confused if they were able to develop their own program of education that would be more relevant to their own backgrounds, experience, and needs. At the same time, she assumes that the program was designed by teacher education experts who have a rationale for the program, so she resigns herself to putting in her time.

Karen, in contrast, is angry. She resents having to take all the stupid education courses that contradict each other, followed by different collaborating teachers telling her to forget what she learned in her coursework. She believes that all the ideas and theories in teacher education classes are arbitrary and subjective and does not believe that anyone's teaching can be evaluated objectively. She thinks her instructors and collaborating teachers are just using their power to recommend certification to make her conform to their own personal beliefs and values about teaching. However, she does want certification, so she cynically decides to just give people what they want to hear, even when she has to continually contradict herself in different settings.

Janet starts to analyze the problem in terms of the contradictions inherent in a teacher education program between the two functions of certification and education. She realizes that a certification function is partially determined by state or national standards and that these requirements are most often met by specifying a standard sequence of courses and minimum number of hours in classroom settings. At the same time, she realizes that the educational function is best determined by what she is actually asked to do in those courses and classroom settings. In addition, she realizes that how she will be evaluated in her courses and her classroom experiences can vary as a function of school or classroom contexts, as well as of individual differences in her instructors and supervisors (e.g., a more theoretical focus in her college instructors, in contrast with a more pragmatic focus in her classroom supervisors). Nevertheless, she is able to make a commitment to her goal of learning as much as she can from these different experiences, well aware of some of the reasons for the subjectivity and contradictions inherent in the system.

The example of these three students touches upon many of the ideas of Basseches (1986), Kitchener (1986), and Perry (1970). Although the issues of the subjectivity of knowledge and commitment reflect some of Perry's and Kitchener's concerns, Basseches tries to focus more on the actual cognitive operations necessary to reason like Janet. Accordingly, in his framework of 24 dialectical operations he proposes that students must be able to recognize the existence of contradictions (between different courses in a program) and try to resolve them in a systematic way involving dialectical reasoning (e.g., thesis-antithesis-synthesis), that students examine systems (e.g., a teacher education program) in terms of their functions and structures, and that students understand the influence of context on forms of knowledge (e.g., the context of the university setting versus the classroom setting). Taken together, these models of epistemic belief development and dialectical thought provide a useful conceptualization for discussing how teachers might develop their beliefs about teaching and learning.

Teachers, especially novice teachers, are confronted with an overwhelming amount of data on teaching and learning from a variety of sources, such as research-based data from educational psychology and other educational courses or workshops; from authorities such as collaborating teachers, university supervisors of field experience and other teacher educators, and peers; and from past experience in school as a student and present experience as a teacher. In addition, beyond diversity of content, the information is organized in a variety of forms, systems, and paradigms. Teachers must be able to sift through all this information, judging the relative merits of the information and evaluating the source, and begin to develop a belief system about teaching and learning. Often these different sources present contradictory information, as in the research on classroom management that suggests quick pacing to reduce discipline problems and the research on wait-time that suggests waiting for a response to a question (Shulman, 1986), and teachers have to be able to reconcile these views. More important, teachers, especially novices, often have to reconcile the formalistic and scientific approach to teaching and learning fostered in their university training with the more subjective and pragmatic approach encountered in the schools (e.g., Griffin, 1989).

Given this description of some of the learning tasks that teachers confront, the developmental models that describe epistemic belief development and dialectical thinking are addressing appropriate issues for conceptualizing teacher development. The descriptions provided by these models are very useful for beginning to specify an important aspect of teacher knowledge, epistemological beliefs and theories, and its role

in teacher development and education. At the same time, as has been noted previously, the formalization of a strong structural-stage view is probably not warranted (Brainerd, 1978; Flavell, 1971, 1982; Gelman & Baillargeon, 1983). Accordingly, concepts from these models can be used to develop a more domain-specific and dynamic view of teacher development.

Contextual and Life-Span Models. In contrast with the organismic approach that focuses on the structure of the individual's thought, the contextual approach focuses on the context or environment in which the individual exists and the individual's relationship to the context. This approach assumes that the historical event (also called the life event, the life task) or, simply put, the nature of the individual's interactions in different situations over the course of the life span, is the crucial aspect of development. Given that individuals are engaged in many interactions and situations over time, change is assumed to be a fundamental fact of development. Development is not static or uniform but, rather, characterized by constant change. Accordingly, contextual models of development must focus on describing and explaining the nature of the changes and the change processes (Lerner, 1986).

The life-span approach to human development is the best exemplar of a contextual model. There are a number of assumptions or themes that appear in most life-span approaches (e.g., Abeles, 1987; Baltes & Schaie, 1973; Featherman, 1983):

1. Developmental change is a lifelong process not limited to certain ages.
2. Developmental change can be both quantitative and qualitative.
3. Developmental change is multidimensional. Changes occur in many domains including biological, social, and psychological.
4. Developmental change is multidirectional. There can be different patterns and trajectories of development, depending on the domain and the individual. Developmental change is not necessarily directed toward a particular end point or state.
5. Developmental change is multidetermined. There are many different causes of development including biological, social, psychological, physical, and historical events. There are complex interactions between these different determinants, so that similar changes in different individuals can have different causes.
6. Individuals are active constructors and organizers of their own life histories. Accordingly, developmental change is not just a function of the different life events the individual encounters, but also a dialectical process among the multiple environmental determinants of change and the individual's personal construal of these determinants.

Some of the most popular life-span approaches conceptualize development as evolving over time in terms of both the objective events (physical, social, biological) that occur at certain chronological ages or stages in the development of the individual and the more subjective, psychological issues that these events seem to evoke in individuals (e.g., Erikson, 1963; Levinson, 1978; Neugarten, 1968; Veroff & Veroff, 1980). Obviously, as Brim and Ryff (1980) point out, biological events (normative changes in hormonal levels over the life span); social role changes in marital, career, and family status; and physical events (changes in the physical environment as a function of relocation, physical injuries or illness, changes in physical appearance) are all objective events that individuals must cope with as they develop. These events provide one aspect of the context that helps shape individuals' lives.

More important, however, from a social-cognitive view, it is important to understand the psychological issues evoked by these objective events and how individuals interpret and construct meaning for them vis-à-vis their own development (Labouvie-Vief, 1981). This constructivist approach has suggested that life tasks (Cantor & Kihstrom, 1987), or current concerns (Klinger, 1977), or personal projects (Little, 1983), or life themes (Csikszentmihalyi, 1985) are more personal construals of the general life events and psychological issues experienced by individuals. An important aspect of this conceptualization is that the notion of a task includes an individual's representation of both a goal for the task and a strategy for solving the task (cf. Doyle, 1983; Carter & Doyle, 1989). Accordingly, this approach includes both motivational and cognitive components.

In addition, the social context and culture provide a general framework for these tasks, but individuals might generate their own life tasks in an idiosyncratic pattern (Cantor & Kihlstrom, 1987). In this constructivist view, an individual's life tasks don't necessarily follow a prescribed, universal pattern of development (e.g., identity and generativity issues might be resolved before intimacy issues). For example, in a study of college students, Cantor and her colleagues (see Cantor & Kihlstrom, 1987) found that students could identify a number of concerns that were personally demanding and that guided their activities. These included academic goals (doing well, getting organized) and social goals (making friends, being on one's own, and establishing an identity). As Cantor & Kilhstrom point out, these concerns reflect normative life tasks (achievement, intimacy, independence) that would be predicted by most life-span approaches (e.g., Erikson, 1963; Veroff & Veroff, 1980). However, the life-task approach, in line with the assumptions of a life-span contextual approach, differs in assuming that individuals will define these issues somewhat differently and seek different strategies for solution. For example, some students defined independence in terms of coping without parental support, whereas others concentrated on more practical matters such as money management. In addition, students had very different problem-solving strategies as a function of their personal construal of college life tasks (Cantor & Kihlstrom, 1987).

The application of the life-task approach to teacher development seems to be a very promising avenue for research. It seems clear that there are general-developmental stages where certain issues or concerns are paramount for the development of a teacher. For example, Feiman-Nemser (1983) suggests that there are four general stages: (a) a pretraining stage, which takes place before any formal educational courses are taken; (b) a preservice phase, which involves teacher education courses and student teaching; (c) an induction phase, which involves the first year or so of teaching; and (d) an inservice phase, which involves the later years after the teacher has mastered the basics of teaching. Fuller (1969) found that the concerns of teachers differ, depending on these phases. She found that students in the pretraining phase were characterized by a real absence of concern about teaching. Their concerns seemed to reflect the general concerns of college students, not the concerns specific to teaching. In the preservice and induction phases, Fuller found that teachers were concerned about their competence as teachers in terms of both discipline and instruction, as well as about the nature of their role as teacher and authority figure and their relationship to the institution of schooling. Finally, in the later phase, more experienced teachers expressed less concern about self-related issues of competence and role and more concern about others, specifically student progress and development and evaluating their teaching in terms of student gain. Veenman (1984), in a review of studies concerning beginning teachers' perceived problems, found eight general concerns, including discipline, motivation, individual differences and problems of students, assessment and organization of student work, teaching materials and supplies, and relationships with parents.

These concerns might set the normative parameters for teachers, but a life-task approach would suggest that individuals will define these concerns somewhat differently and attempt to solve them with different strategies. For example, consider two student teachers, both struggling with their role as authority figure and the issue of discipline. One might cope with this concern by adopting the goal of wanting the students' respect as an adult and use a strategy of becoming overly strict and authoritarian and acting in accordance with the old dictum, "don't smile until Christmas." The other student teacher might attempt to resolve this issue by adopting the goal of becoming the students' friend and become overly solicitous. In the same fashion, more experienced teachers who are attempting to cope with generativity issues in general (e.g., Erikson, 1963; Veroff & Veroff, 1980) and evaluating their teaching in terms of student development (Fuller, 1969) might adopt different goals and strategies for coping with these concerns. For example, some teachers might become more involved in working directly with students on extracurricular activities and on other student-development concerns, whereas others might choose to go on to administration or other duties. The important assumption underlying this approach is that individuals' personal construals of normative life issues and problems are central to understanding their development. Accordingly, it is important to consider how teachers view the problems and issues that confront them over the developmental course of their careers and attempt to understand what goals and strategies they adopt as they go about their daily teaching tasks. Certainly, more research is needed on these issues from a developmental and social-cognitive life-task approach.

Although this life-task approach, specifically, and the life-span contextual approach, in general, have important implications for conceptualizing teacher development, the general paradigm does have some drawbacks. The general contextual approach can be very dispersive theoretically (Lerner, 1986;

Pepper, 1942) in terms of allowing for the generation of an infinite number of unique individual interpretations of life tasks, goals, and strategies, as well as any number of contextually bound findings. In contrast with some of the traditional trait or stage models that might be improperly overgeneralized to different individuals and situations, an extreme constructivist and contextualist approach can become mired in an overwhelming focus on individual and contextual or situational differences in cognition, motivation, and behavior, which could preclude any attempt to construct a generalizable and useful theory of teacher learning and development. Accordingly, efforts to develop a model of teacher learning and development must continually negotiate between the Scylla of overly simplistic or deterministic trait and stage models and the Charybdis of overly indeterminate and dispersive contextual models.

Student Knowledge and Cognition as the Focus of Development: Cognitive and Information-Processing Models

Recent developments in cognitive psychology that stress the importance of the learner's prior knowledge or knowledge base and general-information-processing theories of cognition have important implications for teacher learning and development. Paralleling the discussion of trait, stage, and contextual models, the issue of the relative generality or domain specificity of students' cognition remains a continuing problem for current conceptualizations of student knowledge and cognition.

Knowledge Structure Models. In recent years educational and instructional psychologists have emphasized the importance of students' domain-specific knowledge and the organization of that knowledge for learning (Ausubel, 1963, 1968; Gagne, 1985; Glaser, 1984; Greeno, 1978, 1980; Pintrich, 1988a; Pintrich et al., 1986). This research focuses on how subject-matter knowledge is organized (content structure) and how students' representations or cognitive structures for the subject matter influence learning. Both content structures and cognitive structures are assumed to be based on the propositional relationships between concepts (i.e., words, symbols). The structure of the material to be learned and the students' cognitive representations of the material seem to influence learning (McKeachie et al., 1986).

Content structure is assumed to be reflected in a body of instructional material such as lectures, textbooks, syllabi, handouts, and exams (Phillips, 1983; Shavelson, 1981; Shavelson & Geeslin, 1975). The nature of this structure should influence what students can learn and recall from it. For example, Donald (1983) studied the content structures in 16 university courses representing different disciplines and found that the key concepts were often organized by a superordinate–subordinates relationship. She also found that natural science, humanities, and social sciences courses differed in the nature of the relationships. Natural science courses showed greater use of dependency or causal relationships among key concepts, whereas social science and humanities courses showed greater use of similarity relationships (McKeachie et al., 1986). The

work of Kintsch and van Dijk (1978) and Meyer (1975, 1977) in reading suggests that the content structure of a text is an important factor influencing recall, comprehension, and learning. This research suggests that how the information to be learned is organized (the materials or text factor in the Brown et al., 1983, tetrahedral model) influences student learning. The idea of developing a content structure representation for material to be learned has been used successfully in assessment of reading (e.g., Wixson & Peters, 1987) and should be useful for teacher assessment. More generally, the notion of content structure has been used in curriculum development to organize the knowledge to be learned, to sequence the content, and to suggest appropriate teaching strategies (e.g., Novak & Gowin, 1984; Stewart, 1980, 1982, 1984).

One implication of this work on knowledge structures for teacher education is the necessity of developing a content structure representation of the knowledge base for teaching to guide curriculum development, instruction, and assessment (Shulman, 1986). For example, Shulman (1987) and P. Peterson and Comeaux (1989) outline the beginnings of a taxonomy for describing the knowledge teachers should acquire over the course of their careers. Shulman (1987) proposes that teachers could acquire seven categories of knowledge: knowledge of a content area, general pedagogical knowledge, content-specific pedagogical knowledge, knowledge of learners, knowledge of curriculum, knowledge of educational contexts, and knowledge of educational goals. Of course, the actual content within these seven categories and the relationships between the categories and the content still need to be specified before this could be considered a formal content structure of the knowledge base for teacher education. However, the categories can be used to develop a teacher education curriculum and select the content of the courses in the curriculum, as well as to guide teacher assessment (P. Peterson & Comeaux, 1989; Shulman, 1987).

The development of a content structure of a specific domain of knowledge is an external representation of the relevant knowledge base. However, students' actual representations of that content structure in terms of internal cognitive structures are very important for learning. A large number of experimental and correlational studies have examined the role of students' cognitive representations of knowledge in learning. There are descriptive studies that compare experts' and novices' representations of knowledge in a particular domain (e.g., chess, physics, mathematics) and assume that these different representations are responsible for the differences in performance between experts and novices. Other studies examine how novice and expert representations are related to actual performance in a domain or examine the effects of an intervention to improve students' representations (see Gagné, 1985). Accordingly, students' cognitive representations and structures have been used as both independent and dependent variables in these studies. There is no one accepted method for assessing cognitive structures, and different researchers, using different theories, have developed a number of methods to assess students' representations of the content, such as, detailed interviews, concept maps or diagrams of the relationships, coding of written responses on essays, word associations, card sorting, and simple tests (see McKeachie et al., 1986, for a review). Although there are a number of methodological issues in the study and assessment of cognitive structures that need to be resolved (e.g., Phillips, 1983; Shavelson, 1983), in terms of implications for teacher education, the construct has been and will continue to be a very important idea (e.g., Shulman, 1986, 1987).

As a hypothetical construct, cognitive structures are assumed to be mental represenations of the different kinds of knowledge and information in an individual's long-term memory (Ausubel, 1963; Ausubel, Novak, & Hanesian, 1978; Shavelson, 1972, 1974). There are, however, a wide variety of theoretical and conceptual approaches to defining these mental representations (Rumelhart & Norman, 1988). Some theorists have considered cognitive structures to be schemata (e.g., Rumelhart & Ortony, 1977; Spiro, 1977). "Cognitive structures (schemata) are cumulative, holistic, assimilative blends of information" (Spiro, 1977, p. 137). According to Mandler (1985), a schema is "a category of mental structures that stores and organizes past experience and guides our subsequent perception and experience" (p. 36). The script notion has also been proposed as another representation of individuals' knowledge about events (Abelson, 1981). Other theorists (e.g., Anderson, 1985; Gagne, 1985; Greeno, 1978; Shavelson, 1981) have proposed that students' knowledge can be categorized into two types, declarative (e.g., knowing that, knowing about something) and procedural (knowing how to do something). Declarative knowledge is defined as the actual concepts and the propositional networks that characterize the relationships among these concepts. Procedural knowledge is defined as the intellectual skills, production systems, and heuristic rules or principles for processing information (Anderson, 1985; Gagne, 1985; Greeno, 1978; Shavelson, 1981). Regardless of the label and the conceptual underpinings, a great deal of research in a number of domains (e.g., chess playing, problem solving, mathematics and science learning, reading, writing) demonstrates that students' knowledge and beliefs about the content to be learned influence a wide variety of cognitive processes including memory, comprehension, deduction and induction, problem representation, and problem solution (e.g., Anderson, 1985; Gagne, 1985; Posner et al., 1982).

Given the importance of students' knowledge representations for cognitive processing of information in general, teachers' prior knowledge and beliefs about teaching should be equally important for teacher learning and development. The general-knowledge-structure approach to expert–novice thinking has been used as a foundation for much of the recent work in conceptualizing teacher thinking (Clark & Peterson, 1986; Shulman, 1986, 1987). For example, studies of expert and novice teachers suggest that expert teachers have highly organized knowledge structures for teaching that focus on the lesson structures, routines, and activities needed to teach specific content and to have students work on that content (e.g., Carter, Sabers, Cushing, Pinnegar, & Berliner, 1987; Leinhardt & Greeno, 1986). These knowledge structures then serve to facilitate the processing of information and problem solving in planning or interactive teaching (Borko, 1989).

P. Peterson and Comeaux (1989) use the distinction between declarative and procedural knowledge to discuss two types of representations teachers might have of the seven categories of knowledge proposed by Shulman (1987). For example, novice or beginning teachers might know about specific classroom-management strategies (declarative knowledge about general pedagogical techniques) but not understand how to use them in a classroom (procedural knowledge). Moreover, teachers need to know when and why to use these classroom-management strategies in their actual practice. This type of metacognitive, or conditional, knowledge about when and why to use certain kinds of knowledge is an important type of knowledge that differs from declarative and procedural knowledge (cf. Paris, Lipson, & Wixson, 1983; P. Peterson & Comeaux, 1989).

Accordingly, in terms of what develops, not only does knowledge develop in the seven domains suggested by Shulman (1987), but also the manner in which this knowledge is represented (i.e., declarative, procedural, metacognitive, and conditional) should develop over a teacher's career. In fact, as P. Peterson & Comeaux (1989) imply, there could be some utility in teacher education and teacher assessment programs' adopting a model that assumes a general developmental progression from declarative knowledge to procedural, metacognitive, and conditional knowledge. For example, preservice education classes at the college level might best be suited to providing students with declarative knowledge about general pedagogical techniques, knowledge of learners, and other domains of teacher knowledge. In contrast, clinical experience in the classroom seems best suited to offering opportunities for student teachers to develop procedural knowledge and metacognitive and conditional knowledge in the different domains. Following this model, teacher assessments would be designed to examine the different types of knowledge teachers should acquire at different points in their careers (P. Peterson & Comeaux, 1989).

Besides these general curricular and assessment issues, the research on knowledge structure has implications for instruction at the individual course level. First, the content structure idea suggests that it is important for the college instructor to have a relatively well defined representation of the course content to aid in designing instruction and assessment (cf. Novak & Gowin, 1984). For example, the work of my colleagues at the National Center for the Improvement of Postsecondary Teaching and Learning at The University of Michigan (e.g., Naveh-Benjamin & Lin, 1988; Naveh-Benjamin, McKeachie, Lin, & Tucker, 1986) suggests that these content structures can be used to design assessments of student learning in specific courses that will show development from the beginning to the end of the term (cf. West & Pines, 1985). Moreover, this research has shown that these content structures can be explicitly taught to college students and seem to help them learn the course material, in comparison with students in the same course with whom the content structure framework was not used (Naveh-Benjamin & Lin, 1988).

In addition, the idea that students enter the course with a variety of cognitive representations of the course content that influence their learning implies that college instructors need to be aware of these representations and design their instruction accordingly. This suggests the need for college instructors to assess students' entering beliefs and cognitive representations of the course content. This is especially relevant in the area of education, where college students entering preservice education programs have spent 12–14 years in school and have a great deal of tacit knowledge about teaching and learning. Students' prior knowledge could be relatively well entrenched and conflict with the knowledge about teaching and learning presented in education courses. Students' prior beliefs, naive conceptions, and misconceptions about teaching and learning can result in difficulties for the teacher in terms of instruction and for the students in terms in learning the material and changing their conceptions of teaching and learning.

The literature on conceptual change (e.g., Posner et al., 1982; West & Pines, 1985) suggests some ways of teaching to help overcome these difficulties such as, use of anomalies, analogies, metaphors, case studies, and laboratory exercises, but it is crucial that the instructor understand what the students' prior conceptions of teaching and learning are and work to change them, rather than assume that all students have the same conceptions or that their conceptions are not relevant for learning. Finally, some of the research on conceptual change (e.g., Posner et al., 1982) applies the notion of paradigmatic change in scientific fields (e.g., Kuhn, 1970) to individual student learning. This research suggests that instruction should change not only the content of student's knowledge about teaching and learning, but also their epistemological and metaphysical beliefs about the nature of teaching and learning (cf. Bassesches, 1986; Kitchener, 1986; Perry, 1970). In other words, the goal for education courses would be to change students' paradigms or world views for thinking about teaching and learning. For example, students might be philosophically committed to an explanatory model for student learning that is predicated on personal experience and intuition. This type of explanatory model or paradigm might conflict with other scientific, empirical, psychological, or educational paradigms for explaining student learning. Accordingly, instructors would need to be aware of these differences and help students resolve the differences as part of instruction in their classes (cf. Feiman-Nemser & Buchmann, 1989).

The knowledge structure construct has also been applied to knowledge about the self, not just knowledge about science concepts, mathematics algorithms, or beliefs about teaching and learning. Markus (1977) and her colleagues (Markus & Nurius, 1986; Markus & Wurf, 1987) suggest that knowledge and information about the self can be organized in a fashion similar to cognitive structures about content. For example, encoded in our memory is knowledge about what our thoughts, affect, and behavior were in past situations, and this self-knowledge can be used to guide us in new situations. In addition, just as different cognitive representations or different aspects of prior knowledge can be evoked by the nature of the material to be learned, different concepts of the self (i.e., achieving self, nurturing self, competitive self, anxious self) can be evoked by different situations (Markus & Wurf, 1987). The model assumes that individuals develop these different self-representations through experience and, more important, through self-reflection. This conceptualization of self and self-knowledge

allows for a more dynamic, less static view of the self-concept by acknowledging both the stability of our self-knowledge in terms of our autobiographical memories and personal narratives and the potential for change in self-knowledge as a function of experience in different situations and our self-reflection on this experience. In addition, this conceptualization attempts to reconcile the person–environment problem by recognizing the situational specificity of our access to self-knowledge and the dynamic interplay between the self-knowledge that is acitivated in a specific situation and our behavior in the situation (Cantor & Kihlstrom, 1987).

This dynamic approach to the self-concept seems to have a number of implications for teacher education. First, it suggests that student teachers and experienced teachers can have multiple "possible selves" (Markus & Nurius, 1986) that can be activated in different situations. For example, the self-as-teacher that is activated in a one-on-one tutoring situation, versus a group lecture situation, could be very different, with repercussions for actual instructional behavior. In the same fashion, interactions with different students can evoke differential self-knowledge and behavior, or, in the case of student teachers, interactions with different supervising teachers and classes can activate different selves and behavior. This model of the dynamic self-concept proposes a mechanism by which the active self mediates and provides continuity between the personal characteristics of the individual and the environmental demands of the situation. For example, this type of role for self-concept helps explain individual differences in teacher feedback as a function of both personal characteristics and situational characteristics, for example, different activity structures such as recitation and seatwork (see Bossert, 1979).

Second, this model gives a central role to self-reflection, linking it to a number of other conceptualizations of teaching (e.g., Dewey, 1963; Kennedy, 1987; Schön, 1983, 1987; Wildman & Niles, 1987). Of course, the model recognizes the difficulty individuals might have in making inferences about the self, given the biased judgmental heuristics that might be operating (Nisbett & Ross, 1980). If individuals have difficulty perceiving themselves accurately, it might be difficult for them to make changes in their behavior in order to adapt to the situation (Cantor & Kihlstrom, 1987). For example, teachers who are not very self-reflective or accurate in their self-perceptions of teaching might have difficulty recognizing their relative strengths and weaknesses. Furthermore, it might be difficult to improve their teaching behavior as their inaccurate self-perceptions become more stable over time.

Information-Processing Strategies, Metacognition, and Self-Regulation. The previous section stressed the role of knowledge in learning. Although the content and structure of knowledge are important, they might not be sufficient for all learning or problem solving (Pintrich, 1988a; Pintrich et al., 1986). In fact, most knowledge-based models or expertise models never clarify exactly how people acquire their knowledge and expertise. The research on expertise has focused on comparing experts to novices at one point in time, but it has not addressed the developmental process by which the experts constructed and acquired their rich knowledge base. The work on general-information-processing strategies, metacognition, and self-regulation suggests some potential ways individuals might acquire and use their knowledge.

Weinstein & Mayer (1986) propose four main components of information processing that are similar to other models of information processing (cf. Corno & Mandinach, 1983; Sternberg, 1985): selection, acquisition, construction, and integration. The selection component concerns the control of attention to certain stimuli or information in the environment and the transfer of that information to working memory. Corno and Mandinach label this phase *alertness and selectivity*. The acquisition phase involves the transfer of information from working memory to long-term memory for permanent storage. In the construction phase the student actively builds connections among ideas in working memory. Mayer (1984) and Bransford (1979) refer to this process of construction as *schema development*, which results in the new information being held together by a coherent outline or organization (Weinstein & Mayer, 1986). The integration phase involves connecting prior knowledge with incoming information (cf. Corno & Mandinach's *connection component*). These aspects of information processing should be related to the acquisition and retrieval of students' knowledge structures.

In addition, most information-processing theories propose some type of metacognitive or self-regulatory function as an important aspect of information processing. The term *metacognition* is a popular one used by a variety of researchers in cognitive, educational, and instructional psychology. As Brown et al. (1983) point out, the term has a number of definitions, making it a "fuzzy" concept. It is most often used to refer to two aspects of cognitive life: the awareness of and knowledge about cognition and the control and regulation of cognition (Brown et al., 1983; Flavell, 1979; P. Peterson, 1988). The awareness aspect of metacognition refers to learners' knowledge of person, task, and strategy variables that influence performance. According to Flavell, awareness of person variables refers to knowledge about the self in terms of cognitive performance (e.g., knowing that you are a fast reader or a poor writer). This aspect of metacognition is closely related to motivational constructs such as perceived competence and self-concept (cf. Cantor & Kihlstrom, 1987; Markus & Nurius, 1986). Task-variable knowledge includes information about the difficulty of various tasks and the different demands of academic tasks. Strategy-variable knowledge concerns learners' knowledge about different strategies and how to use them, that is, declarative and procedural knowledge (cf. Flavell, 1979; Paris et al., 1983). As P. Peterson (1988) points out, teachers' metacognitive knowledge about classroom learning and teaching is an important component of the knowledge base for teaching.

Although knowledge about person, task, and strategy variables in teaching is important, the control and regulation aspect of metacognition seems to be crucial for teacher development. Brown et al. (1983) note that there are three general processes that make up metacognitive control activities: planning, monitoring, and self-regulation. These activities are closely related to metacognitive knowledge, although they can be distinguished theoretically. Planning activities include setting goals for the task, skimming to get an overview, generating questions or foreshadowing problems, and doing a task analysis of the problem. All these activities help the individual to actually use cognitive strategies and complete a project. In addition, they help to activate, or to prime, relevant aspects of prior knowledge that make organization and comprehension of the material easier. Brown et al. (1983) summarize various planning models that have been suggested by cognitive psychologists. Much of the research on planning, and metacognition in general, suggests that good learners engage in more planning and more metacognitive activities than poor learners (cf. Pressley, 1986).

Monitoring and self-regulation activities are an essential aspect of metacognitive control (Bandura, 1986; Cantor & Kihlstrom, 1987; Corno, 1986; Weinstein & Mayer, 1986). Monitoring activities include tracking of attention as one performs a task and self-testing to insure proper understanding and completion. Self-regulation activities involve changing behavior to better suit the task, based on feedback from the monitoring activities. For example, just as a thermostat monitors temperature and then starts or stops the heating or cooling process to regulate the temperature, metacognitive activities help learners monitor and regulate their cognition and behavior. This continuous adjustment and fine-tuning of cognition is an important component of metacognition (Brown et al., 1983).

Another aspect of self-regulation and metacognition is the volitional control of these metacognitive activities. Corno (1986), drawing on the work of Bandura (1986), Kuhl (1987), and Vygotsky (1962), suggests that individuals' ability to control a wide variety of personal and environmental conditions results in better cognitive engagement and achievement. For example, beside the attentional, encoding, and information-processing control strategies mentioned, Corno suggests that students must be able to control their motivation (e.g., set up internal goals and incentive systems to regulate behavior), to control their emotional responses (e.g., anxiety, elation), and to control distractions in the environment (e.g., other students). These control strategies represent students' volition, or will, to accomplish the task and are assumed to protect the individuals' intentions from self-induced distractions such as anxious thoughts or environmentally induced distractions (Corno, 1986). These control strategies help students adapt to the environment, as well as change the environment to fit their needs (cf. Bandura, 1986; Sternberg, 1985).

These metacognitive and self-regulatory functions are crucial for teachers as they coordinate content and pedagogical knowledge while teaching, as well as manage a classroom and react to individual differences among students (Gallimore, Dalton, & Tharp, 1986). For example, the literature on teacher planning and thinking (e.g., Clark & Peterson, 1986) demonstrates the key role in teaching of the metacognitive activities of planning (i.e., preparing lesson plans), monitoring (i.e., assessing student motivation and comprehension of a lesson while teaching) and self-regulating (e.g., changing instructional behavior as a function of feedback from students on a lesson). It is interesting to note that an analysis of teacher behavior from a metacognitive and self-regulatory view of cognition suggests how a lesson plan can serve as an external support or scaffold (see Palinscar & Brown, 1984) to guide teacher instructional behavior, especially a novice teacher's behavior. As teachers become more experienced and skilled at both teaching and self-regulation of their teaching, they internalize the knowledge and skills needed to teach effectively and do not need these external supports. Accordingly, most experienced teachers do not develop detailed written lesson plans (Clark & Peterson, 1986). In contrast, the novice teacher usually does not have all the teaching knowledge or skills readily accessible and might need external supports (i.e., lesson plan, lecture notes) for guidance. Accordingly, the concept of metacognitive control and self-regulation of cognition provides a psychological rationale for the emphasis on the development of lesson plans for novice teachers.

The other control processes outlined by Corno (1986) might also be a source of differences between expert and novice teachers. For example, some novice teachers might not have developed the self-regulating or coping skills to control some common emotional responses to student teaching (i.e., anxiety, fear, shame, embarrassment) that might interfere with effective teaching performance (cf. Bandura, 1986). In addition, as Corno (1986) suggests for students, the self-regulating skill of being able to control their attention and behavior in the face of numerous distractions would seem to be crucial for teachers also. The research on classroom management has shown that expert teachers know which distractions from teaching (i.e., student misbehavior, visitors, deviations from the lesson plan) they should attend to and which can be ignored (e.g., Brophy & Good, 1986). In contrast, novice teachers often become so immersed in their lesson that they do not allow any distractions to alter their behavior, or they often become so overwhelmed with distractions that they lose control of the lesson. This suggests that the declarative and procedural knowledge about classroom management (the what and how of managing a classroom) is necessary but not sufficient for becoming a good teacher. It is also necessary that teachers actually regulate their own cognition and behavior, in effect manage themselves, as they proceed to manage and instruct a group of students. Finally, another aspect of self-control or management that is relevant for both novice and expert teachers is the setting up of internal goals and incentive systems to control their own motivation for teaching (Bandura, 1986; Corno, 1986). Teaching, in general, and learning to teach, especially, are difficult tasks and fraught with many motivational and emotional highs and lows (cf. Wildman, Niles, Maliaro, & McLaughlin, 1989). Teachers who are able to find ways to continually motivate themselves, to maintain their will to teach, should be better able to cope with the demands of teaching.

Intelligence, Thinking, and Problem-Solving Models. The classic area of intelligence has probably shown more signs of change since the late 1970s than in any period since Thurstone and Spearman introduced factorial studies of intelligence. Paralleling the research on cognitive styles, recent research on intelligence has been revitalized by cognitive information-processing approaches that stress the dynamic aspects of thinking and problem solving, in contrast with theories of intelligence that focus on static individual differences in aptitude (Pintrich et al., 1986). The traditional, differential approach to intelligence is best represented by the psychometric paradigm. Psychometric theories of intelligence have attempted to define intelligence by focusing on the number and relationships of factors or latent traits of individuals that explain performance, particularly performance in school (Sternberg, 1985). Psychometric theories represent individual differences among people in terms of a set of latent factors or traits. These factors are assumed to underlie the individual differences in performance on intelligence tests. Most psychometric theories differ only in the number of factors proposed as a source of variation (e.g., the general "g" factor versus multiple factors). For example, Guilford (1982) proposes 150 factors underlying intelligence, but more recent adaptations of general theories focus on crystallized abilities, fluid or analytic abilities, and spatial-visualization abilities (Snow & Lohman, 1984). Snow and Lohman suggest that crystallized abilities are evoked by familiar tasks and environments, and unusual tasks or instructional techniques requiring analysis or decontextualization demand fluid ability. Differences between the types of tasks or environment can result in attribute-treatment-interactions between instruction and learners.

In line with this task differentiation view, Gardner (1983) suggests that intelligence varies across different domains or symbol systems such as language, music, mathematics, and physical coordination (kinesthetic). This approach highlights the fact that the components measured in traditional intelligence tests emphasize the symbol systems used in schools, predominantly the verbal symbol system. In contrast, Gardner proposes that intelligence is a set of abilities that facilitates the solution of problems or the production of products appropriate in specific domains (Walters & Gardner, 1986). Accordingly, intelligence is not defined by a single, unitary, general "g" factor but by a variety of intelligences specific to particular domains. The seven domains that Gardner (1983) identifies include musical, bodily-kinesthetic (athletic skill), logical-mathematical, linguistic (verbal), spatial (including artistic skill), interpersonal (relating to others), and intrapersonal (self-knowledge and reflection). The model provides a useful way of conceptualizing individual differences in different domains without proposing an unwieldy number of factors. In addition, it seems clear that teachers must have skills, not just in the linguistic and logical-mathematical domains, but also in the interpersonal and intrapersonal domains.

Another approach to intelligence that stresses the dynamic processes involved in intelligence, rather than static traits of individuals, is the information-processing model proposed by Sternberg (1985, 1988). Sternberg proposes an ambitious triarchic theory of intelligence that attempts to integrate and synthesize most of the research on intelligence. As such, the triarchic theory is both metatheoretical and theoretical. The three subtheories in his overall theory are the componential, the experiential, and the contextual.

The componential subtheory represents Sternberg's (1985) attempt to specify the mechanisms, or cognitive processes, responsible for intelligent performance on tasks. The componential subtheory is closest to traditional psychometric and cognitive psychological approaches to intelligence. Sternberg defines a component as an "elementary information process that operates upon internal representations of objects or symbols" (Sternberg, 1985, p. 97). Components can be classified according to three general functions: (a) Metacomponents are higher order cognitive processes used in planning, monitoring, and decision making, essentially the same metacognitive and self-regulatory skills discussed in the preceding section; (b) performance components are cognitive processes used in the execution of a task such as, the inductive reasoning processes of encoding information, making inferences, and mapping relationships used in solving analogies; and (c) knowledge-acquisition components are cognitive processes used to learn new information such as, encoding relevant information and combining information in relevant ways.

These three types of components (metacomponents, performance, and knowledge-acquisition) are most closely related to intelligent performance on academic tasks and the types of tasks that appear on intelligence tests. In Sternberg's model, these components represent students' general analytic ability. Students who score high on standardized intelligence tests and other aptitude measures such as the Scholastic Aptitude Test and the Graduate Record Exam are able to recruit, employ, and regulate the cognitive processes that are important for success on these tasks. These three components of intelligence are relevant to good performance in teaching and might even be necessary (e.g., Kerr, 1983; Lanier & Little, 1986; Vance & Schlechty, 1982), but they might not be sufficient for excellent teaching. As Sternberg notes, there are other aspects of the learner that are important for success in life that do not depend on the analytical aspects of the componential model. These other aspects are part of Sternberg's experiential and contextual subtheories.

The experiential component involves students' ability to be creative and to synthesize disparate experiences in new, insightful ways. This means being able to go beyond the information given. Specifically, the experiential component involves students' ability to adapt to novel tasks and situational demands, as well as the ability to automatize cognitive processes (Sternberg, 1985, 1988). An important aspect of intelligent performance is students' ability to confront novel tasks and to use prior knowledge and present skills in successfully completing the tasks. This aspect of intelligence is readily applicable to preservice teachers. For example, college students who have high standardized test scores or high grade point averages in their liberal arts coursework, measures indicative of the componential and analytic aspects of intelligence, must be able to adapt these skills to the new and difficult tasks inherent in becoming a teacher. It is clear from both research and experience that not all students high in the componential aspects of intelligence are able to make the transition and become effective teachers. Accordingly, the experiential subtheory suggests another aspect of intelligence beyond high standardized test scores (cf. Lanier & Little, 1986) that is relevant to our conceptualization of teacher development.

The other aspect of experiential intelligence concerns students' ability to automatize cognitive processes that are required on specific academic tasks as the students gain more experience with the tasks. For example, reading is a compli-

cated task that requires a variety of cognitive processes. The more students are able to automatize some of the cognitive processes involved (e.g., word recognition), the more they are able to devote attention to more complex cognitive aspects of reading such as comprehension monitoring (Sternberg, 1985). In a similar fashion, this ability to automatize some cognitive processes is crucial for teaching. For example, if teachers are cognitively engaged in processing some aspect of the content being taught (e.g., retrieving the rule for conjugation of an irregular verb in French and then proceeding to conjugate the verb, executing the algorithm for an algebra problem, recalling the formula for a chemistry problem), they will be less able to monitor and regulate their general instructional behavior and to manage and regulate a classroom. The lack of automatization of certain types of knowledge and skills might underlie the oft-heard complaint about student teachers lacking knowledge in their content areas. It could be that student teachers not only lack the pedagogical knowledge to teach a specific content (e.g., Shulman, 1986), but also do not have the specific content knowledge in a form that is automatized and readily available for flexible use. Although the experiential intelligence subtheory is less well defined and researched than the componential subtheory, it seems clear that the ability to deal with a variety of novel tasks and to automatize various cognitive processes is crucial for successful teacher development.

The third subtheory, contextual intelligence, concerns students' ability to adapt to and manipulate the environment. In more colloquial terms, it involves students' street smarts, or practical intelligence. In Sternberg's view, adaptation to the environment is one aspect of the contextual subtheory. It is also important, however, for students to be able to select and shape the environment to fit their needs. Wagner and Sternberg (1985, 1986) propose that practical intelligence consists of individuals' tacit knowledge about how to manage themselves, manage others, and manage their careers. They assume that much of this knowledge is not taught directly but that individuals learn tacit knowledge through experience. In their studies of academic psychologists and business managers, Wagner and Sternberg (1985, 1986) found that tacit-knowledge scores correlated positively with success measures (promotions, salary increases, and other markers). The ability to manage oneself in ways appropriate to the environmental context of one's occupation is similar to Gardner's (1983) intrapersonal intelligence and should be a crucial skill for teachers. Teachers, especially preservice teachers, must be able to reflect on their strengths and weaknesses and to develop strategies to overcome their deficiencies (Sternberg & Caruso, 1985). The ability to manage others, in Wagner and Sternberg's model of practical intelligence, parallels the interpersonal intelligence proposed by Gardner (1983). Again, teachers must interact with a large number of students in an appropriate fashion. In addition, just as in any work situation, teachers must be able to work effectively with other teachers, their principal, and other school staff. These aspects of social competence are important components of intelligence and should be related to teacher development (Sternberg & Caruso, 1985).

Besides these models of general intellectual skills, other research on problem solving and reasoning has suggested a number of general cognitive processes that should be related to teacher development. For example, the psychological research on problem solving (e.g., Mayer, 1983; Newell & Simon, 1972), although somewhat limited in application because it often has not used ecologically valid tasks, has suggested general problem-solving heuristics, such as means–ends analysis, working forward, working backward, and reasoning by analogy, that should be relevant for teacher development such as teacher planning (Clark & Peterson, 1986). More recently, the research on inference and judgmental heuristics (e.g., J. H. Holland, Holyoak, Nisbett, & Thagard, 1986; Nisbett & Ross, 1980; Tversky & Kahneman, 1974) has pointed up important implications for teacher thinking (cf. Clark & Peterson, 1986). This research assumes that all individuals are intuitive scientists and are constantly seeking to understand and make sense of their world (e.g., why this event happened to me, why that person did that). To do this, individuals, similarly to scientists, attempt to assess covariation between events, assign causality, predict future events, and build their own theories about the phenomena of interest (Nisbett & Ross, 1980). Of course, this does not mean that individuals follow normative principles of statistical reasoning or hypothetical-deductive thinking as suggested by Piaget (J. H. Holland et al., 1986). In fact, Nisbett and Ross summarize a large number of studies suggesting that most adults are prone to making inferential errors in many situations, due to the combination of certain types of information-processing strategies (i.e., the availability and representative heuristics, the vividness criterion) and the specific knowledge structure evoked by the situation. However, it does appear that college students can be taught to use certain types of general statistical reasoning heuristics (e.g., the law of large numbers) that can be used to overcome some of these inferential errors (Fong, Krantz, & Nisbett, 1986; Nisbett, Krantz, Jepson, & Kunda, 1983), although the problem of generalizability across different domains still remains (J. H. Holland et al., 1986).

All of these general reasoning heuristics are assumed to be generalizable to a large number of tasks, situations, and contexts, in contrast with the content-specific knowledge structures, which are only relevant for particular domains or tasks. The issue of domain specificity of knowledge versus the use of general reasoning strategies is unlikely to be resolved in the near future. In fact, recent reviews of the literature (e.g., Alexander & Judy, 1988; Garner & Alexander, 1989) have suggested that it is more important to examine how domain-specific knowledge interacts with strategic knowledge. For example, Campione and Armbruster (1985) suggest that individuals have access to both very specific knowledge and general heuristics. They suggest that general strategies are rather weak in problem-solving power, in comparison with specific knowledge, but general heuristics can be useful for beginning to solve novel tasks when there is little specific knowledge available for problem solution. This could be especially relevant for novice teachers; hence the emphasis on improving the general-aptitude levels in teacher education programs (Lanier & Little, 1986).

More recent work on mental models (e.g., Gentner & Stevens, 1983; J. H. Holland et al., 1986; Johnson-Laird, 1983) provides another attempt at an intermediate position in this debate. It assumes that an individual's reasoning is not just dependent on domain-specific knowledge, nor strictly reliant on syntactic rules of formal logic. The research suggests that individuals build internal cognitive models of external reality that they are then able to manipulate, change, and experiment on, using certain types of general rules, or heuristics, that are defined in terms of the goals and types of relationships defined by the model. These mental models represent both domain-specific knowledge (e.g., what an individual teacher knows about students) and general rules or strategies for operating on this knowledge (e.g., rules for making causal inferences or attributions about student performance). The power of the mental-model construct comes from combining domain-specific knowledge with general heuristics within one system, thereby avoiding the problems of inert knowledge (e.g. knowing many facts but not knowing how to use them to solve problems) and empty process skills (e.g., knowing general heuristics but lacking the content knowledge to solve specific problems). The work on mental models seems to provide one useful way of conceptualizing teacher knowledge and should generate a number of research studies on the development of teachers' mental models for teaching and learning.

There are several implications of this research for teacher development and education. Teachers make many valid and invalid inferences and judgments about students (e.g., Johnny can't learn because he is not motivated, he comes from a bad home), instruction (e.g., the lesson didn't work because the students are not ready for this material), and classroom management (e.g., I don't need any rules because this is an advanced placement class). Teachers who are aware of some of the difficulties of making social judgments (e.g., Nisbett & Ross, 1980), who are taught to think more scientifically (e.g., control variables in assessing causality), and who learn to use statistical reasoning heuristics could be more likely to avoid some of the problems of fallacious reasoning. At the same time, these general statistical and scientific reasoning strategies are more likely to be used by teachers if not taught in the abstract such as in general courses in statistics or research methods. They need to be embedded in an array of knowledge structures or mental models about students, instruction, and classroom management (e.g., Cheng, Holyoak, Nisbett, & Oliver, 1986). In the same fashion, students need to encounter knowledge about students, instruction, and classroom management in a context in which they are asked to think, reason, and solve problems with the content knowledge, not just passively record the knowledge (e.g., lecture courses in child development or educational psychology). Accordingly, it is not enough to teach general heuristics to teachers, nor is it enough to tell teachers the domain-specific knowledge about teaching and learning. Teacher education must develop ways of involving students in courses and tasks (e.g., the case study method) that facilitate the integration of knowledge about teaching and learning with general cognitive heuristics, or strategies, for thinking and problem solving.

Values, Beliefs, and Affects as the Focus of Development: Motivational Components of Student Learning

Cognitive models of student learning are very relevant and useful for conceptualizing teacher development, but they tend to ignore or avoid questions about individuals' intentions, purposes, goals, needs, and motivation. The rather cold image of teachers as decision makers and processors of information about teaching and learning that is implied by most cognitive models needs to be complemented by the image of teachers with a variety of thoughts and feelings about themselves and their environment. These thoughts and feelings about self and the environment are assumed to be related to two types of motivational behaviors: choice of activity (e.g., what people choose to do) and level or strength of the activity (e.g., how long someone will persist at an activity, how hard she or he will try). Most motivational constructs and theories are designed to explain choice and activity level of an individual's behavior.

Although there are many models of motivation that could be relevant to student learning (see Weiner, 1980, for a review of general motivational models), a general expectancy-value model serves as a useful framework for analyzing the research on motivational components (McKeachie et al., 1986; Pintrich, 1988a). The model is an adaptation of Eccles's (1983) expectancy-value model, with additions and refinements added to integrate different motivational components. Recent cognitive reformulations of general-expectancy-value models have made the role of individuals' perceptions of themselves and the tasks they confront in classrooms central to achievement dynamics (e.g., Dweck & Elliott, 1983; Eccles, 1983; Nicholls, 1984; Weiner, 1986). Three general components seem to be important in these different models: (a) beliefs about the importance and value of the task (value components), (b) beliefs about one's ability or skill to perform the task (expectancy components), and (c) feelings about the self or emotional reactions to the task (affective components). These three general components are assumed to interact with one another to influence individuals' choice of activities to engage in, their persistence at the tasks, and the nature of their involvement in the tasks.

Value Components. Value components of the model incorporate individuals' goals for engaging in tasks and their beliefs about the importance, utility, or interest of a task. Essentially, these components concern the question, Why am I doing this task? These components should be related to choice of activities as well as persistence at a task (Eccles, 1983). Although there are a variety of different conceptualizations of value, two basic components seem relevant: goal orientation and task value.

Goal orientation. All motivational theories posit some type of goal, purpose, or intentionality to human behavior, although these goals range from relatively accessible and conscious ones, as in attribution theory, to relatively inaccessible and unconscious ones, as in psychodynamic theory (Zukier, 1986). In more recent cognitive reformulations of achievement motivation theory, goals are assumed to be cognitive representations of the different purposes students adopt in different achievement situations (Dweck & Elliott, 1983; Dweck & Leggett, 1988; Ford, 1986). A number of researchers have discussed goal orientation (e.g., Ames & Ames, 1984; Covington & Beery, 1976; Dweck & Elliott, 1983; Ford, 1986; Nicholls, 1984) using alternative terms and definitions, but one of the main distinctions that seems to be most crucial is between intrinsic and extrinsic goal orientation. Harter (1981) distinguishes between students who offer intrinsic rationales such as mastery, challenge, learning, and curiosity from students who are more oriented to extrinsic considerations such as grades, rewards, and approval from others. These intrinsic and extrinsic orientations parallel to some extent Dweck & Elliott's (1983) distinction between learning and performance goals and Nicholls's (1984) task-involved versus ego-involved orientations. Covington & Beery (1976) also suggest that some students are not necessarily intrinsically motivated for challenge or mastery, but are motivated to increase, or at least protect, their self-worth and self-esteem. This self-worth motive is similar to Nicholls's concern with students who are ego-involved in a task (e.g., involved to show how smart they are rather than to learn the material). It seems likely that individuals who adopt a more intrinsic orientation not only try harder or persist longer, but also recruit more effective strategies for learning or problem solving (Pintrich, 1989). For example, Elliott & Dweck (1988) found that students who adopted a learning goal used more effective strategies to solve a laborabory-concept learning task. In the same fashion, teachers who adopt more intrinsic, or task-involved, goals might be more willing to try different teaching strategies and be more open to evaluation and assessment (e.g., less ego-involved and threatened).

These two different goal orientations are often thought to be extremes on a bipolar continuum from intrinsic to extrinsic (cf. Harter, 1981). However, more recent research on internal and external beliefs about control (an expectancy component) suggests that students differ along both internal and external dimensions (e.g., Harter, 1985). Accordingly, individuals could have varying beliefs along two related dimensions of internal and external control (cf. Connell, 1985). These two dimensions could be orthogonal theoretically but are probably correlated for most individuals. Extending this analysis to intrinsic and extrinsic goals suggests that individuals could have both intrinsic and extrinsic rationales for engaging in a task. For example, a college student could choose to be a teacher for both intrinsic reasons such as concern for child development and desire to improve the educational system and the extrinsic reason that it appears to be a relatively easy career to enter and in which to obtain a position (cf. Lanier & Little, 1986).

The intrinsic and extrinsic analysis of goals has been extended to the work setting by a number of researchers (e.g., Maehr & Braskamp, 1986; Vroom, 1964). This work suggests that individuals can become involved in their work as a function of different goals that range along a continuum from intrinsic to extrinsic. The most intrinsic goals include mastery or concern for excellence, but there are also ego goals, which are less intrinsic (being better than others in terms of competition, social comparison). Social goals are somewhat more extrinsic and include getting along with others and winning social approval. Finally, the most extrinsic goals are financial- and social-recognition goals (Maehr & Braskamp, 1986). In addition, in keeping with a developmental approach, the strength or salience of these goals can vary at different points in an individual's career, with intrinsic goals being more important at certain ages than extrinsic goals (e.g., Maehr & Kleiber, 1981; Wigfield & Braskamp, 1985). This implies that younger and older teachers may not be more or less motivated in some absolute sense but are motivated in different ways by their adoption of different goals. Accordingly, teacher education programs need to understand the differential goals teachers might adopt, as well as to be aware that these goals can change over the course of a teacher's career.

Task value. Task value was originally conceived of as the value an individual attached to success or failure on a task. This value was defined in relation to task difficulty and the probability of success by Atkinson (1964) in his achievement motivation theory. However, as Eccles (1983) points out, task value can be conceived of in more subjective, broader, and individualistic terms (cf. Parsons & Goff, 1978; Raynor, 1974; Spenner & Featherman, 1978). This more subjective focus includes the characteristics of the task, as well as the needs and goals of the student. Three components of task value have been proposed by Eccles (1983) as important in achievement dynamics: the individual's perception of the importance of the task, the intrinsic value or the intrinsic interest in the task, and the utility value of the task for future goals. These three value components could be rather parallel in children and college students, but they can vary significantly in adults (Wlodkowski, 1988).

The importance component of task value refers to individuals' perception of the task's importance or salience for them. The perceived importance of a task is related to a general goal orientation, but importance could vary by goal orientation. An individual's orientation might guide the general direction of behavior, but value might relate to the strength or intensity of the behavior. For example, a student teacher might believe that success in a particular course is very important (or unimportant) to him or her, regardless of the intrinsic or extrinsic goals. That is, the student might see success in the course as learning the material or getting a good grade, but she or he might still attach differential importance to these goals. Importance should be related to individuals' persistence at a task, as well as to their choice of task.

Student interest in the task is another aspect of task value. Interest is assumed to be individuals' general attitude toward or liking of the task. In an educational setting this includes their interest in the course content and their reactions to the other characteristics of the course such as the instructor (cf. Wlodkowski, 1988). Interest in the task is partially a function of individuals' preferences, as well as of aspects of the task (e.g., Malone, 1981). Interest is assumed to be related to choice of activity and level of involvement.

In contrast with the means or process motivational dynamic of interest, utility value refers to the ends, or instrumental motivation, of the student (Eccles, 1983). Utility value is determined by individuals' perception of the usefulness of the task for them. For teachers this might include beliefs that the

course (educational psychology, teaching methods) or workshop (teacher burnout, M. Hunter's teaching program) will be useful for them in the classroom immediately, in the classroom in the future, or just in life in general. At a task level, student teachers might perceive different course assignments (e.g., construction of lesson and unit plans, analysis of case studies, construction of essay and multiple-choice examinations, writing of term papers) as more or less useful and decide to become more or less cognitively engaged in the task.

Expectancy Components. Expectancy components are generally more familiar and more researched than value components (Parsons & Goff, 1978). Expectancy components include individuals' beliefs about their ability to perform a task, their judgments of self-efficacy and control, and their expectations of success at the task. Essentially, these components concern the question, Can I do this task?

Control beliefs. There have been a number of constructs and theories proposed about the role of control beliefs for motivational dynamics. For example, early work on locus of control (e.g., Lefcourt, 1976; Rotter, 1966) found that students who believed they were in control of their behavior and could influence the environment tended to achieve at higher levels. De Charms (1968) and Deci (1975) discuss perceptions of control in terms of students' belief in self-determination. De Charms (1968) coined the terms *origins* and *pawns* to describe students who believed they were able to control their actions and students who believed others controlled their behavior. More recently, Connell (1985) suggests that there are three aspects of control beliefs: an internal source, an external source or powerful others, and an unknown source. Students who believe in internal sources of control are assumed to perform better than students who believe powerful others (e.g., teachers, parents) are responsible for their success or failure or students who don't know who or what is responsible for the outcomes.

The same logic would apply to teachers. If teachers, especially student teachers, believe that others (e.g., the students in the class) are really in control of the classroom environment, they might be less willing to persist and put forth effort in difficult situations, and teaching performance could suffer. The importance of control beliefs is highlighted by some of the difficulties inherent in the student teacher–supervising teacher relationship, because the student teacher does not really have full control of the curriculum, the instructional materials, or the general organization of the classroom and might have difficulties adapting to this situation. Student teachers might give up trying in these situations, with subsequent decrements in teaching performance. In the same fashion, teachers often perceive lack of control or control by unknown others in issues of curriculum, textbook selection, class composition, and other educational matters which results in debilitating feelings and lack of motivation (e.g., Freedman, Jackson, & Boles, 1983).

The overriding message of all these models is that a general pattern of perception of internal control results in positive outcomes (i.e., higher achievement, higher self-esteem), whereas sustained perceptions of external control result in negative outcomes. Reviews of research in this area are somewhat conflicting, however. For example, Stipek and Weisz (1981), in a review of research on perceived control and academic achievement, conclude that there is little relationship between perceptions of control and elementary students' academic achievement. In contrast, Findley and Cooper (1983), in a larger review that included studies of college students and adults, found a small but significant positive relationship between perception of internal control and academic achievement. Findley and Cooper also found evidence of a curvilinear relationship between perceptions of internal control and achievement. They found that the relationship was strongest for young adolescents (e.g., junior high school students) and weakest for elementary students (first through third grades) and college students. This curvilinear relationship by age could be responsible for the conflicting findings of previous reviews, if they did not sample or analyze by age of subject. In addition, Findley and Cooper found that the positive relationship was stronger for males than females. These findings suggest that, for college students, the relationship between perceptions of internal control and achievement might not be straightforward.

Almost all the models concerned with internal perceptions of control automatically assume that higher levels of internal control result in positive outcomes. However, this might not necessarily be the case. There could be times when perceptions of internal control are debilitating (Covington & Beery, 1976). Harter (1985) proposes a refinement of the general internal–external orientation with the construct of beneffectance. The neologism *beneffectance*, coined by Greenwald (1980), was formed by combining effectance motivation (White, 1959) and beneficence, meaning *good outcomes*. Harter proposes that beneffectance involves the individual's tendency to attribute successful outcomes to internal causes and attribute unsuccessful outcomes to external causes. This hedonic bias should result in more positive outcomes. As expected, students who tend to have a high level of beneffectance, tend to perform better on academic tasks and have higher expectancies for future success (Harter, 1985). Given the facts that teachers cannot control all aspects of their job and that research seems to suggest that attempting to control the uncontrollable is a poor coping strategy (Langer, 1975), the beneffectance construct might offer a more reasonable view of the role of control beliefs for teachers.

Self-efficacy beliefs. Self-efficacy has been defined as individuals' beliefs about their performance capabilities in a particular domain (Bandura, 1982, 1986; Schunk, 1985). The construct of self-efficacy includes individuals' judgments about their ability to accomplish certain goals or tasks by their actions in specific situations (Schunk, 1985). This approach implies a relatively situational or domain-specific construct, rather than a global personality trait. In an achievement context, it includes students' confidence in their cognitive skills to perform the academic task. In addition, it is important to distinguish these perceptions of efficacy from students' beliefs about outcome. As Schunk (1985) points out, outcome expectations refer to individuals' belief concerning their ability to influence outcomes, that is, their belief that the environment is responsive to their actions. This belief that outcomes are contingent on their behavior leads individuals to have higher expectations for

success and should lead to more persistence. When individuals do not perceive a contingency between their behavior and outcomes, this can lead to passivity, anxiety, lack of effort, and lower achievement, often labeled *learned helplessness* (cf. Abramson, Seligman, & Teasdale, 1978; Kuhl, 1987; Weiner, 1980; Wortman & Brehm, 1975). These beliefs are distinct from individuals' self-appraisals of their ability to master the task (Bandura, 1986; Schunk, 1985). Accordingly, beliefs about self-efficacy and outcome can vary. For example, student teachers might believe that they have the capability to teach well but, at the same time, expect to do poorly because the class is impossible or the supervising teacher is difficult to satisfy. These beliefs about the classroom situation would lead the student teachers to expect a lower outcome than their self-efficacy beliefs would predict. Ashton (1985) has developed a model of teacher efficacy that attempts to outline the potential sources of teacher efficacy beliefs and the role of efficacy beliefs in teacher behavior. For example, Sparks (1988) found that experienced teachers' perceptions of their self-efficacy for teaching was correlated with their use of instructional strategies presented in an inservice program.

Expectancy for success beliefs. Expectancy for success is defined as individuals' beliefs about their probability of success (or failure) on a particular task. As Eccles (1983) points out, there is a long history in motivational research of the importance of expectancies for academic performance, task persistence, and task choice (e.g., Atkinson, 1964; Covington & Omelich, 1979a, 1979b; Dweck & Elliott, 1983; Feather, 1969; Lewin, 1938; Veroff, 1969). Expectancies can be specific or general. For example, teachers can believe a specific lesson will not go well because they did not prepare it very well (a specific short-term expectancy). A more generalized expectancy would be teachers' beliefs about their students in terms of achievement over the course of the year. An even more generalized expectancy would include teachers' beliefs about their relative success or failure as teachers. These expectancy beliefs are closely tied to individuals' actual behavior in terms of choice and persistence (Weiner, 1986). It seems obvious that, if teachers do not expect to succeed at a particular task (teaching a specific concept, working with a difficult student), they will be unlikely to persist at the task or they will attempt to avoid that task in the future (cf. Clark & Peterson, 1986).

These expectancy beliefs have been closely tied to the nature of individuals' attributions for past performance (Weiner, 1979, 1985, 1986). Attributional theory proposes that the causal attributions an individual makes for success or failure mediate future expectancies, not the actual success or failure event. A large number of studies have shown that individuals who tend to attribute success to internal and stable causes like ability or skill tend to expect to succeed in the future. In contrast, individuals who attribute their success to external or unstable causes (e.g., ease of the task) do not expect to do well in the future. For failure situations, the positive motivational pattern consists of attributing failure to external and unstable causes (difficult task, lack of effort), and the negative motivational pattern consists of attributing failure to internal and stable causes (e.g., ability, skill). This general attributional approach has been applied to numerous situations, and the motivational dynamics seem to be remarkably robust and similar (Weiner, 1979, 1985, 1986).

In addition, some researchers suggest that individuals have relatively stable and consistent attributional patterns across domains (e.g., Fincham & Cain, 1986; C. Peterson & Seligman, 1987). These attributional patterns seem to predict individuals' performance over time. For example, if teachers consistently attribute their success to their own skill and ability as teachers, it would be predicted that they would continually expect success with future classes of students. In contrast, if teachers consistently attribute success to other causes (e.g., excellent students, luck), their expectations might not be as high for future classes. There has been research on attributional retraining in achievement situations (e.g., Foersterling, 1985) that suggests that teaching individuals to make appropriate attributions for failure on school tasks (i.e., effort attributions instead of ability attributions) can facilitate future achievement. In the same fashion, detrimental patterns of teachers' attributions for their own performance could be changed through staff-development efforts. Of course, there are a variety of issues to consider in attributional retraining, including the specification of which attributional patterns are actually dysfunctional, the relative accuracy of the new attributional pattern, and the issue of only attempting to change a motivational component instead of the cognitive skill that might be important for performance (cf. Blumenfeld, Pintrich, Meece, & Wessels, 1982; Weiner, 1986). All of these issues will have to be resolved in future research on teachers' attributional patterns for their own behavior.

Affective Components. Affective components include students' emotional reactions to the task and their performance (i.e., anxiety, pride, shame) and their more emotional needs in terms of self-worth or self-esteem, affiliation, and self-actualization (cf. Covington & Beery, 1976; Veroff & Veroff, 1980). Affective components address the basic question, How does the task make me feel?

Anxiety. There is a long history of research on test anxiety and its relationship to academic performance that suggests how anxiety might be related to teacher performance. Anxiety about performance is often conceptualized as a function of lack of skills or as a mediator of attention that interferes with performance (McKeachie, 1984). Tobias (1985) proposes a cognitive capacity model that attempts to synthesize the cognitive-skills-deficit model of test anxiety (e.g., Benjamin, McKeachie, Lin, & Holinger, 1981; Culler & Holahan, 1980) with the attentional-interference model (e.g., Wine, 1971). Tobias suggests that these two models are complementary, rather than mutually exclusive. His model assumes that students have a limited cognitive capacity to process information at any one time. The model also proposes that access to cognitive skills tends to increase the amount of cognitive capacity available to the student for any one task, whereas, in a complementary but inverse fashion, the interference components decrease the cognitive capacity available. If this is so, then the cognitive skills should reduce the cognitive demands on the student when the student is performing the task, and interfering thoughts should increase cognitive demands. For example, if students are well prepared for the task, their cognitive capacity is free to deal with any interfering anxious thoughts that arise in the situation. In the context of teaching, the model suggests that teachers who are well-prepared in terms of a good lesson plan (or more generally, very experienced) will have more cognitive capacity available to deal with any anxiety-arousing thoughts. Novice teachers, who could be especially prone to anxious thoughts about teaching, would then need to be even more well prepared, in order to have the cognitive capacity available to cope with the cognitive interference generated by the anxious thoughts. This model demonstrates how cognitive and motivational components can work together to influence performance. In addition, it supports the importance of having well-prepared lesson, unit, and classroom-management plans for novice teachers.

Other affective reactions. Besides anxiety, other affective reactions can influence choice and persistence behavior. Weiner (1979, 1985, 1986), in his attributional analysis of emotion, suggests that certain types of emotions (e.g., anger, pity, shame, pride, guilt) are dependent on the types of attributions individuals make for their successes and failures. For example, this research suggests that a teacher tends to feel pity for a student who did poorly on an examination because of some uncontrollable reason (e.g., death in family) and is more likely to help that student in the future. In contrast, a teacher is more likely to feel anger at a student who did poorly through a simple lack of effort and to be less willing to help that student in the future. These attributional patterns can also be applied to the self. For example, it is likely that, for teachers to experience pride in the work of their students, they have to attribute some responsibility for the students' success to their own instructional efforts. The attributional analysis of motivation and emotion proposed by Weiner (1979, 1985, 1986) has had an enormous influence on conceptualizations of student and teacher motivation in the classroom and provides useful insights for integrating the emotional reactions of teachers into a general model of teacher development.

Emotional needs. The issue of an individual's emotional needs (e.g., for affiliation, power, self-worth, self-esteem, self-actualization) is related to the motivational construct of goal orientation, although the needs component is assumed to be less cognitive, more affective, and, perhaps, less accessible to the individual. There have been a number of models of emotional needs suggested (e.g., Maslow, 1970; Veroff & Veroff, 1980; Wlodkowski, 1988), but the need for self-worth, or self-esteem, seems particularly relevant for teachers. Research on student learning shows that self-esteem, or sense of self-worth, has often been implicated in models of school performance (e.g., Covington & Beery, 1976). Covington (1984) suggests that individuals are always motivated to establish, maintain, and promote a positive self-image. Given that this hedonic bias is assumed to be operating at all times, individuals might develop a variety of coping strategies to maintain self-worth, but, at the same time, these coping strategies might actually be self-defeating. Covington and his colleagues (e.g., Covington,

1984; Covington & Berry, 1976; Covington & Omelich, 1979a, 1979b) document how several of these strategies can have debilitating effects on student performance. Many of these poor coping strategies hinge on the role of effort and the fact that effort can be a double-edged sword (Covington & Omelich, 1979a). Students who try harder increase the probability of their success but also increase their risk of having to make an ability attribution for failure, followed by a drop in expectancy for success and self-worth (Covington, 1984).

There are several classic failure-avoiding tactics that demonstrate the power of the motive to maintain a sense of self-worth. One strategy is to choose easy tasks. As Covington (1984) notes, individuals choose tasks that insure success, although the tasks do not really test their actual skill levels. Teachers might choose this strategy by maintaining their teaching style, even if relatively ineffective, instead of attempting to change. A second failure-avoiding strategy involves procrastination. For example, a teacher who does not prepare a lesson in advance because of lack of time, can, if the lesson is successful, attribute it to superior teaching skill. On the other hand, this type of procrastination maintains an individual's sense of self-worth because, if the lesson is not successful, the teacher can attribute it to lack of time, not poor teaching skill. This effort-avoiding coping strategy could be especially appealing to novice teachers, who might have some self-doubts about their teaching skills, resulting in procrastination and a propensity to avoid adequate lesson preparation. Of course, inadequate lesson preparation increases the probability of a poor lesson, especially when coupled with the difficulties associated with anxiety arousal and lack of self-regulatory skills for a novice teacher. However, as noted, a failed lesson that was inadequately prepared allows the novice to attribute the poor lesson to other factors, not to poor teaching skill, thereby maintaining self-worth.

RESEARCH ON COLLEGE TEACHING

The psychological models of the learner presented in the first section focused on the description of individual characteristics such as knowledge structures, thinking skills, and motivation, not on the environmental characteristics that can influence the process of teacher learning and development. However, a good description of the learner is necessary for the construction of a psychology of instruction (Pintrich et al., 1986; Resnick, 1983). Given the discussion of student cognition and motivation and its implications for teacher learning and development, it seems crucial that teacher education programs strive to facilitate both teacher cognition and motivation. What characteristics of college classrooms might facilitate active involvement in learning so that both cognition and motivation would be improved? There are a number of excellent reviews of the research on college teaching (e.g., Dunkin, 1986; Eble, 1988; McKeachie, 1980, 1986; McKeachie et al., 1986; Menges, 1981) that have addressed the issue in terms of different features of college classrooms such as class size and of instructional methods such as lecture, discussion, and laboratory methods. A review of this literature is beyond the scope of this

chapter, but some key dimensions of college classrooms and academic work will be suggested as promising avenues for research and practice in teacher education. These dimensions include the academic tasks students are asked to perform, the reward and goal structures of the class, the instructional method used, and the instructor's behavior.

Academic Tasks in College Classrooms

As noted, recent work in cognitive psychology has stressed the importance of task characteristics in determining students' reactions to and cognitions for school tasks (e.g., Brown et al., 1983; Doyle, 1983; Marton et al., 1984). The task that students are asked to perform is assumed to have a potent influence on their learning. In this sense, the task organizes and guides students' information processing. In addition, the task is one of the means by which the curriculum is actually enacted by the instructor and the student. The task becomes the mediating link between the students and the instructor and curriculum (Blumenfeld, Mergendoller, & Swarthout, 1987; Doyle, 1983). The task construct assumes that different features of the task can engender the use of different cognitive and metacognitive strategies by the student. In addition, task features should engage different motivational orientations of students. Crooks (1988) summarizes a variety of these cognitive and motivational effects of academic tasks and evaluation procedures.

There are a number of important dimensions of tasks that can influence student motivation and cognition in the college classroom but two that seem crucial are content and product. These dimensions can be distinguished at a theoretical level, and it is assumed that they could be orthogonal to one another, although in actual practice they might be confounded. Content refers to the nature of the actual material that students have to learn (the content structure discussed earlier). Brown et al. (1983), in their tetrahedral model, discuss how the complexity and difficulty of the material to be learned influences students' use of cognitive strategies. In addition, the difficulty level and familiarity of the material can influence students' perceptions of efficacy and expectancy. Finally, the appeal or interest level of the material can evoke students' interest or value for the task (Blumenfeld et al., 1987). At the college level, the content dimension has often been conceptualized as a function of instructor characteristics, in particular the quality of lectures and discussion. There are a number of studies on the effects of the content and style of a lecture (e.g., the Dr. Fox effect) on student learning and satisfaction (see Dunkin, 1986, for a review), but these studies usually do not examine what students have to do in these courses. The task construct assumes that what students are asked to read, what types of assignments they are asked to complete, and how these assignments are graded can have a more important influence on their motivation and cognition than lecture style (McKeachie et al., 1986).

Accordingly, the content dimension would be reflected in the nature of the readings for the course (e.g., level of difficulty, primary versus secondary sources) and the nature of the content covered in the exams and other assignments for the course. For example, two educational psychology courses could cover the same basic material, but in one course students read a fairly easy textbook, whereas in the other course students read a more sophisticated textbook supplemented with primary source material written by eminent educational psychologists and educators. This simple difference could result in quite different motivational and cognitive outcomes. It is important to note that the difficulty level of the material to be read (e.g., easy textbook versus more difficult primary source) might be confounded with the appeal of the material (e.g., less interesting text versus more interesting primary source), so that separating these content dimensions in actual classroom tasks can be difficult. In any event, much more research similar to that on science learning (e.g., West & Pines, 1985) is needed on the relationships between the content of teacher education programs and the logical structure of this content and teachers' cognition and motivation.

Besides the actual material to be learned, the product dimension has been discussed by most researchers concerned with tasks (cf. Blumenfeld et al., 1987; Brown et al., 1983; Doyle, 1983). This dimension involves the actual production of some response to the task (e.g., the answers on an examination, a laboratory report, an essay or term paper). A student analyzing a case study of an instructional problem for an educational psychology class has a very different product to create from a student writing a term paper about instruction. Students who have to take a multiple-choice examination are faced with a different kind of production task from students who are asked to take an essay exam. These products can influence the type of cognitive and metacognitive strategies involved in completing the task (Doyle, 1983). For example, multiple-choice questions that only tap recall of material place very different demands on students' information-processing skills from exams or case studies that require application, analysis, or synthesis of material. This product dimension can be quite varied in teacher education programs; yet it might have important influences on teacher development. For example, preparation of a portfolio of teaching materials for evaluation might result in different outcomes from taking a multiple-choice examination or being rated by a supervisor (P. Peterson & Comeaux, 1989). Accordingly, it is important that research on teacher education courses and programs examine very carefully the nature of the products that teachers are asked to produce during their training and the relationship to teacher motivation and cognition. For example, what happens to student cognition and motivation when case study analyses are required in teacher education courses instead of recall of information on multiple-choice exams?

At the same time, this focus on academic tasks must be supplemented by a constructivist view that suggests that students' perceptions of the task are just as important aspects of the task as any objective criteria. For example, instructors might perceive their essay questions as requiring critical analysis of different theoretical interpretations, whereas students might see the essay questions as simple recall of instructors' theoretical orientations. This does not mean that certain features of classroom tasks cannot be identified, but it does suggest the importance of tapping individuals' perceptions of tasks as well (Marton et al., 1984). Accordingly, the academic-task construct can help conceptualize the classroom environment at a level where

features of the classroom that have main effects in a nomothetic view can be identified, as well as gauge individual perceptions of tasks that describe individual differences in an idiographic view of classroom research (cf. Cantor & Kihlstrom, 1987).

Reward and Goal Structures of College Classrooms

The task is also embedded in a classroom context that can influence an individual's motivation and cognition. Two important dimensions of the classroom context that help to define how a task is experienced by students are the reward structure and the goal structure of the task. These two social organizations of the task help to define the social or interactive relationships among students concerning their independence or interdependence. These two constructs are often used interchangeably but can be distinguished theoretically. Reward structure refers to how rewards (e.g., grades) are distributed among students. In contrast, goal structure refers to how the task is designed to be accomplished by the students. As Good & Brophy (1987) note, these two dimensions can be orthogonal to one another, although in practice some configurations are more probable than others.

Reward structures can be independent, cooperative, or competitive. Independent reward structures would assign grades based only on a student's performance in relation to some set standard (as in criterion-referenced or mastery-based systems) or in relation to the individual's past performance (e.g., improvement over time). The student's grade does not depend on how other students in class perform. A cooperative reward structure would assign grades on the basis of some type of interdependence among cooperative groups. (See Slavin, 1983, for a summary of different methods.) For example, two students might write one laboratory report or a small group of students might complete one group project, and these products would be given one grade, with all students in the group receiving the same grade. In contrast, a competitive reward structure makes students' grades dependent on other students' performance. The most common example of this is grading on a curve where there are some explicit or implicit requirements regarding the number of As, Bs, Cs, and lower grades that are distributed to students. These curves can vary from very strict curves that do not consider the relative level of students' performance to curves that are somewhat flexible, depending on student performance. In contrast with cooperative structures where student grades are interdependent but in a positive fashion, competitive reward structures force students' grades to be linked negatively, with some students receiving better grades than others regardless of relative performance, which can have detrimental effects (McKeachie, 1986). In general, the research suggests that cooperative reward structures have positive effects on student motivation and can facilitate performance (e.g., Johnson, Maruyama, Johnson, Nelson, & Skon, 1981; Slavin, 1983). The use of cooperative reward structures could be useful in some situations for teacher training, although there are issues of individual accountability in terms of grades or salary increases that might mitigate against its wholesale use.

In contrast with the reward structure, the goal structure of a task concerns how the task is designed to be completed by the students. Goal structures can be individualistic, cooperative, or competitive. Most college classroom goal structures are probably individualistic. Most students work alone when studying for an examination or writing a paper. However, students might make studying for an examination cooperative by arranging to study together, or, to make the goal structure of studying more cooperative and interdependent, divide up the material to be studied so that each student in the group is responsible for different sections of the material. Another example of a cooperative goal structure occurs when students are required by the instructor to work together on a labatory or group project. In this case, the goal structure requires the students to complete the project by working together. These goal structures, however, can be orthogonal to how the students' product is graded. Students studying together could still take an examination that was graded on a competitive reward structure (e.g., a curve), or students working together on a group project might have to produce individual reports that could be graded under an independent or competitive reward structure. Although a competitive goal structure, where students actually compete while performing the task, might be unusual in college classrooms, there could be situations that are somewhat competitive. For example, in class discussions, students might compete with one another for recognition and quality of ideas presented to the group. Of course, this type of competition might be fostered by the instructor's competitive reward structure for the discussion, where only certain individuals or ideas are recognized. As noted, the use of cooperative goal structures can have positive influences on student motivation and performance (e.g., Slavin, 1983). Cooperative goal structures can be used in teacher education programs in a variety of ways to promote interaction and interdependence among teachers. For example, the use of study groups in education classes to analyze cases would be similar to law and business school practices. Curriculum-development efforts and teacher improvement programs can be made more cooperative in terms of their goal structures (if not their reward structures) to facilitate teacher involvement (Weinshank, Trumbull, & Daly, 1983).

Instructional Methods in College Classrooms

The structural variables of task, reward, and goal structures can have important influences on motivational and cognitive outcomes. However, the actual instructional methods that are used to convey content information can have a major influence on what students learn in college classrooms. Lectures are often used in college courses, due to the large class size. Lectures might not be the most effective way to teach students problem-solving skills directly (Dunkin, 1986; Menges, 1981), but some research (see McKeachie, 1986) suggests that lectures can be very useful for providing students with information not available in readings or for integrating information from a variety of sources. In addition, lectures can be used by the instructor to actually model particular ways of thinking about the information that might be helpful to students when they attempt to understand and think about the information on

their own. Both roles of information provider and model thinker can be very important for instructors in education courses. If there is a body of pedagogical knowledge that most students do not have personal knowledge of and that might not be represented in text materials (Shulman, 1987), this information needs to be conveyed to students. At the same time, this information needs to be provided to students in a manner that will facilitate their own thinking about the material. Because it is doubtful that the institutional constraints on class size are going to disappear soon and, therefore the lecture format will remain, more research is needed on how to make the lecture method an active learning situation for students in college courses.

Nevertheless, research on teaching problem solving and thinking skills suggests that discussion methods that involve more teacher–student and student–student interaction are better than lectures for promoting critical thinking in college students (e.g., Dunkin, 1986; Fischer & Grant, 1983; Mann et al., 1970; Menges, 1981; McKeachie, 1986; Smith, 1977). In addition, discussions can promote student involvement and motivation (McKeachie, 1986). If teacher education programs want to encourage students to think actively and critically about the content of their courses, it seems crucial that teacher education courses have opportunities for discussion. Although actual personal contact is probably the most desirable, there might be ways of using computer conferences, student study groups, and exchange of student logs and journals to facilitate discussion.

Laboratories are believed to be important in teaching problem solving in the sciences, but there is some evidence that they only achieve problem-solving goals if taught with special emphasis on problem solving. Although reviews of research on laboratory teaching find that laboratory courses are effective in improving skills in handling apparatus, laboratories generally are not very effective in teaching scientific method and problem solving (Bligh, Jacques, & Piper, 1980; Shulman & Tamir, 1973). The exceptions to this general finding (e.g., Lawrenz, 1985) point to the importance of developing understanding, rather than teaching problem solutions by going through a routine series of steps. The answer to the question of whether the laboratory is superior to the lecture–demonstration in developing understanding and problem-solving skills probably depend on the extent to which understanding of concepts and a general problem-solving orientation are emphasized, as opposed to cookbook methods. In the same fashion, teacher education courses or workshops that offer rather formulaic procedures for solving complex educational problems probably do not facilitate teacher thinking or problem-solving behavior. This might encourage teachers to apply the procedures or material discussed in the course in rather routine, unreflective manner, much as college students do when taught scientific procedures in a routine way.

Instructor Behavior in College Classrooms

Although these different instructional methods can have influence on student motivation and cognition, what the instructor actually says and does in the college classroom is also important. Dunkin (1986) suggests that the research on teaching behaviors in higher education parallels, to some extent, the work at the elementary and secondary level. It appears that the level of question-asking and the general level of discourse in college classrooms are rather low in terms of cognitive complexity, although this might be changed by the use of different instructional materials and strategies (Dunkin, 1986). The research on the development of knowledge structures suggest several strategies to improve the level of cognitive complexity of the classroom. For example, the development of knowledge structures can be facilitated by (a) presenting the structure and organization of instructional materials in a meaningful way, including the use of advance organizers; (b) requiring students to actively organize the learning material through the use of concept maps or other restructuring methods; (c) activating the learners' cognitive structure and linking the instructional material to students' knowledge structures; (d) using analogies, metaphors, and examples to help students map new structures onto old structures; and (e) employing confrontational techniques and Socratic methods to expose the inadequacy of students' representations, not just of the actual content, but also of their epistemological beliefs (Ausubel, 1977; Champagne, Gunstone, & Klopfer, 1985; Geva, 1983; Glaser, 1984; Holley & Dansereau, 1984; McKeachie et al., 1986; Novak, 1985; Novak & Gowin, 1984; Posner et al., 1982; Strike & Posner, 1982; West & Pines, 1985).

These suggestions for teacher behavior are based on knowledge structure views of learning, but other suggestions for teacher behavior can be generated from research on metacognition, self-regulation, and problem solving including (a) explicitly demonstrating, modeling, and explaining the desired cognitive process, regardless of the instructional method used (lecture or discussion); (b) explictly teaching for transfer by using multiple tasks and contexts; (c) selecting tasks appropriate for students' level of competence and providing appropriate support for problem solution; and (d) actively seeking methods (e.g., logs, journals, learning pairs, small groups) that help students verbalize and make explicit their own thinking processes (e.g., Brookfield, 1986, 1987; Palinscar & Brown, 1984; Paris, Wixson, & Palinscar, 1986; Nickerson, Perkins, & Smith, 1985). These suggestions are not all necessarily easy to implement, especially in large college classes, but they provide some examples of behaviors that instructors might be able to use to improve student learning.

CONCLUSIONS AND FUTURE DIRECTIONS FOR RESEARCH

The review of the psychological literature on student learning and development and college teaching has suggested a number of important concepts that can be used to develop a model of teacher learning and development and that suggests implications for teacher education. Of course, much more research remains to be done on specific applications of the concepts to teacher development and education, but the outlines of a framework for conceptualizing teacher learning and development are emerging, although there may be no overarching grand theory. In terms of the original question, what develops, the following four items provide the beginnings of a taxonomy to direct future research and theory.

Teachers' Knowledge. As has been pointed out by many researchers (e.g., Clark & Peterson, 1986; P. Peterson, 1988; Shulman, 1986, 1987), teachers' knowledge of their content area, their knowledge of pedagogical practices, and their knowledge of isses in child development, learning, and motivation develops over time. However, much of this work has been cross-sectional, comparing experts and novices, and has not been longitudinal in terms of tracing individuals' knowledge development over time. Consequently, there is a little research on how expert teachers actually acquire their wealth of knowledge and use it appropriately in their classrooms. In addition, there is little guidance from this research on why all experienced teachers don't develop into experts. Why do some teachers with as much teaching experience and formal education as expert teachers never become expert, effective teachers? Some of these questions could be addressed by longitudinal studies of the novice–expert progression of teachers.

In addition, research on adolescent and adult thinking suggests that teachers' epistemological knowledge will develop (e.g., Basseches, 1986; Kitchener, 1986; Perry, 1970). Moreover, this research suggests that teachers' epistemological and metaphysical beliefs about the nature of inquiry, the construction of new knowledge, and judgments about reality (e.g., Posner et al., 1982) can influence what and how they learn from teacher education courses and professional-development seminars. Research is needed on how these beliefs influence the learning of teachers in teacher education courses. Finally, teachers' knowledge about themselves (e.g., self-schemas and metacognitive knowledge of person variables) is important to consider in relation to their content knowledge and their actual behavior. The research suggests that this type of self-knowledge can influence their skill in coping with the demands of teaching and their ability to learn how to use new teaching strategies. The notion of the dynamic self-concept promises to be a powerful idea in social psychology in general, helping to resolve the person–situation debate. The idea has some intriguing applications for teacher development and should be an area of active research interest.

Teachers' Reasoning, Problem-Solving, and Thinking Skills. The development of knowledge in the various domains noted is an important aspect of teacher development, but, at the same time, how teachers actively use that knowledge to solve instructional and management problems implicates problem-solving and thinking skills. It seems clear from the discussion that many problem-solving and thinking skills are domain-specific and contextualized. For example, a mathematics teacher with excellent problem-solving skills in mathematics isn't necessarily able to generalize those skills to the domains of classroom management or interpersonal interactions with colleagues. Accordingly, teachers have to be trained to think and solve problems in a variety of domains, not just in their content area domains. Research is needed that addresses the issues of transfer of knowledge across domains of teacher education courses and the activation and use of this knowledge in the classroom. Of course, the domain specificity of knowledge, versus the general reasoning problem, will continue to be a recurring issue in cognitive psychology and in research on teacher thinking in different domains. Models will have to be developed for teacher thinking that attempt to resolve this issue (i.e., adaptations of the mental model research).

Teachers' Metacognitive Control and Self-Regulation of Cognition and Behavior. The ability to control and regulate one's own thought and behavior is crucial in many aspects of life, and teaching is no exception. Teachers must continually monitor and regulate their teaching behavior as they work with pupils. Teachers' ability to reflect and think about their own teaching is an important component of self-regulation. Although many writers and researchers have discussed the importance of self-reflection and self-regulation of cognition and behavior, there is still a need for more research on the empirical linkages between self-reflection and metacognition and actual teaching behavior. In addition, research is needed on the efficacy of various methods and strategies that can be used in teacher education and professional-development programs to foster self-reflection and self-regulation.

Teachers' Motivational Goals, Values, and Beliefs. The cognitive components just mentioned are important because teaching involves a great deal of cognitive activity. At the same time, contrary to some positions on academic cognition (cf., Brown et al., 1983), the cognitions that are involved in teaching are not cold, effortful, or isolated cognitive activities. Metacognition and self-regulation implicate beliefs about the self as important components of thinking. In addition, teachers' goals and values for teaching, as well as their affect, can influence not only their behavior but also their cognition. There has been very little research on the interactions between motivation and cognition in general. Although this is changing (see Pintrich, 1989), there is still a great need for research on how teachers' motivation and cognition interact to influence behavior.

These four general domains of teacher knowledge, thinking and problem solving, metacognition and self-regulation, and motivation comprise a good foundation for research and model building in teacher learning and development. There is still much research to be done in particular on the interrelationships among the domains and how teacher education programs can be designed and implemented to facilitate teacher development in these domains. For example, what are the relationships among teacher knowledge, thinking, self-regulation, and motivation? How do teacher life goals influence their acquisition of knowledge, their use of thinking strategies, and their self-regulatory skill? How do teachers' general epistemological beliefs about learning and teaching and their self-beliefs influence their acquisition of new knowledge on learning and teach-

ing and their willingness to use this knowledge in the classroom? Research is needed, not only to define and describe these domains carefully and clarify their role in effective teaching, but also to provide a more comprehensive, sophisticated, and dynamic view of teachers that better reflects an integration of cognitive and motivational components of human behavior. Given a better description of the learner, instructional programs can be better designed to facilitate learning and development.

Besides the specification and clarification of these four domains, there are several other themes that are important to consider in future research efforts on teacher learning and development and teacher education. First, as implied by the emphasis on teacher cognition and motivation, a general constructivist paradigm could be the most fruitful approach to pursue for research. Accordingly, not only will the focus be on exploring general nomothetic relationships among teacher cognition, motivation, and behavior, but also individual differences in these relationships will be of interest. For example, how do different teachers construe the instructional or motivational problems that confront them? Given differences in perceptions of problems, what goals, knowledge, and strategies do teachers then activate to solve the problems? To complement this focus on individual differences, models will have to be developed to include ways of conceptualizing different contexts, domains, and tasks as the sites for teacher cognition, motivation, and behavior (cf. Carter & Doyle, 1989). Finally, in terms of conceptualizing the process of development, life-span developmental concerns, including general developmental issues and personal construals of these issues, must be addressed by these models. Although it appears that strong structural-stage formulations might not be useful, the life-span approach suggests a number of principles that could guide research on the process of teacher development. Accordingly, models for teacher development will have to allow for individual, contextual, and developmental variation but not be so dispersive theoretically as to be useless for generalization or as guides to practice. Finding an appropriate level of specificity and generality for models of teacher development will be a persistent problem in the future.

Finally, given the emphasis on cognition and motivation and the active, constructive role of teachers in making meaning for themselves, our teacher education and professional-development programs will have to develop teaching methods and strategies that foster active engagement in the task of becoming a teacher. There have been some general strategies suggested for teaching, but they need to be developed in the context and content of teacher education programs. Accordingly, there is a great deal of curricular and instructional development work that remains to be done in this area (cf. Schlechty & Whitford, 1989). Nevertheless, it seems likely that lectures or workshops that simply convey information and leave teachers in a passive role will tend to be less useful for teacher development than other methods that actively engage teachers in the learning process. Of course, there is still a great deal of empirical research to do on teaching methods to foster active engagement, but this is a goal for all teachers and teacher educators to strive for in their own practice.

References

Abeles, R. P. (1987). *Life-span perspectives and social psychology.* Hillsdale, NJ: Lawrence Erlbaum.

Abelson, R. P. (1981). Psychological status of the script concept. *American Psychologist, 36,* 715–729.

Abramson, L. Y., Seligman, M. E. P., & Teasdale, J. D. (1978). Learned helplessness in humans: Critique and reformulation. *Journal of Abnormal Psychology, 87,* 49–74.

Adelson, J. (1980). *Handbook of adolescent psychology.* New York: John Wiley & Sons.

Allen, B. P., & Potkay, C. R. (1981). On the arbitrary distinction between states and traits. *Journal of Personality and Social Psychology, 41,* 916–928.

Ames, C., & Ames, R. (1984). Systems of student and teacher motivation: Towards a qualitative definition. *Journal of Educational Psychology, 76,* 535–556.

Alexander, P., & Judy, J. (1988). The interaction of domain-specific and strategic knowledge in academic performance. *Review of Educational Research, 58,* 375–404.

Anderson, J. R. (1985). *Cognitive psychology and its implications.* San Francisco: W. H. Freeman.

Arlin, P. K. (1986). Problem finding and young adult cognition. In R. A. Mines & K. S. Kitchener (Eds.), *Adult cognitive development: Methods and models* (pp. 22–32). New York: Praeger.

Ashton, P. (1985). Motivation and the teacher's sense of efficacy. In R. Ames & C. Ames (Eds.), *Research on motivation in education: The classroom milieu* (pp. 141–171). Orlando, FL: Academic Press.

Atkinson, J. W. (1964). *An introduction to motivation.* Princeton, NJ: Van Nostrand.

Ausubel, D. P. (1963). *The psychology of meaningful verbal learning.* New York: Grune & Stratton.

Ausubel, D. P. (1968). *Educational psychology: A cognitive view.* New York: Holt, Rinehart, & Winston.

Ausubel, D. P. (1977). The facilitation of meaningful verbal learning in the classroom. *Educational Psychologist, 12,* 162–178.

Ausubel, D. P., Novak, J. D., & Hanesian, H. (1978). *Educational psychology: A cognitive view.* New York: Holt, Rinehart, & Winston.

Baltes, P. B., & Schaie, K. W. (1973). *Life-span developmental psychology.* New York: Academic Press.

Bandura, A. (1982). Self-efficacy mechanisms in human agency. *American Psychologist, 37,* 122–148.

Bandura, A. (1986). *Social foundations of thought and action: A social cognitive theory.* Englewood Cliffs, NJ: Prentice-Hall.

Baron, J. (1982). Personality and intelligence. In R. Sternberg (Ed.), *Handbook of human intelligence* (pp. 308–351). Cambridge: Cambridge University Press.

Basseches, M. (1980). Dialectical schemata: A framework for the empirical study of the development of dialectical thinking. *Human Development, 23,* 400–421.

Basseches, M. (1984). *Dialectical thinking and adult development.* Norwood, NJ: Ablex.

Basseches, M. (1986). Dialectical thinking and young adult cognitive development. In R. A. Mines & K. S. Kitchener (Eds.), *Adult cognitive development: Methods and models* (pp. 33–56). New York: Praeger.

Benjamin, M., McKeachie, W. J., Lin, Y. G., & Holinger, D. P. (1981). Test anxiety: Deficits in information processing. *Journal of Educational Psychology, 73,* 816–824.

Bligh, D., Jacques, P., & Piper, P. W. (1980). *Methods and techniques of teaching in postsecondary education.* Paris, France: UNESCO.

Blumenfeld, P. C., Mergendoller, J. R., & Swartout, D. W. (1987). Task as a heuristic for understanding student learning and motivation. *Journal of Curriculum Studies, 19,* 135–148.

Blumenfeld, P. C., Pintrich, P. R., Meece, J., & Wessels, K. (1982). The formation and role of self-perceptions of ability in elementary classrooms. *Elementary School Journal, 82,* 401–420.

Borko, H. (1989). Research on learning to teach: Implications for graduate teacher preparation. In A. E. Woolfolk (Ed.), *Research perspectives on the graduate preparation of teachers* (pp. 69–87). Englewood Cliffs, NJ: Prentice-Hall.

Bossert, S. (1979). *Tasks and social relationships in classrooms.* Cambridge: Cambridge University Press.

Brainerd, C. J. (1978). The stage question in cognitive-developmental theory. *Behavioral and Brain Sciences, 2,* 173–213.

Bransford, J. D. (1979). *Human cognition: Learning, understanding and remembering.* Belmont, CA: Wadsworth.

Brim, O. G., & Ryff, C. D. (1980). On the properties of life events. In P. B. Baltes & O. G. Brim (Eds.), *Life-span development and behavior* (pp. 368–388). New York: Academic Press.

Brookfield, S. D. (1986). *Understanding and facilitating adult learning.* San Francisco: Jossey-Bass.

Brookfield, S. D. (1987). *Developing critical thinkers.* San Francisco: Jossey-Bass.

Brophy, J. E., & Good, T. L. (1986). Teacher behavior and student achievement. In M. C. Wittrock (Ed.), *Handbook of research on teaching* (3rd ed., pp. 328–375). New York: Macmillan.

Brown, A. L., Bransford, J. D., Ferrara, R. A., & Campione, J. C. (1983). Learning, remembering, and understanding. In J. H. Flavell & E. M. Markman (Eds.), *Handbook of child psychology: Cognitive development* (Vol. 3, pp. 77–166). New York: John Wiley & Sons.

Campione, J. C., & Armbruster, B. B. (1985). Acquiring information from texts: An analysis of four approaches. In J. W. Segal, S. F. Chipman, & R. Glaser (Eds.), *Thinking and learning skills* (Vol. 1, pp. 317–359). Hillsdale, NJ: Lawrence Erlbaum.

Cantor, N., & Kihlstrom, J. (1987). *Personality and social intelligence.* Englewood Cliffs, NJ: Prentice-Hall.

Carter, K., & Doyle, W. (1989). Classroom research as a resource for the graduate preparation of teachers. In A. E. Woolfolk (Ed.), *Research perspective on the graduate preparation of teachers* (pp. 51–68). Englewood Cliffs, NJ: Prentice-Hall.

Carter, K., Sabers, D., Cushing, K., Pinnegar, S., & Berliner, D. C. (1987). Processing and using information about students: A study of expert, novice, and postulant teachers. *Teaching and Teacher Education, 3,* 147–157.

Champagne, A. B., Gunstone, R. F., & Klopfer, L. E. (1985). Effecting changes in cognitive structures among physics students. In L. H. T. West & A. L. Pines (Eds.), *Cognitive structure and conceptual change* (pp. 163–187). New York: Academic Press.

Cheng, P. W., Holyoak, K. J., Nisbett, R. E., & Oliver, L. M. (1986). Pragmatic versus syntactic approaches to training deductive reasoning. *Cognitive Psychology, 18,* 293–328.

Chickering, A. W. (1981). *The modern American college.* San Francisco: Jossey-Bass.

Clark, C. M., & Peterson, P. L. (1986). Teachers' thought processes. In M. C. Wittrock (Ed.), *Handbook of research on teaching* (3rd ed., pp. 255–296). New York: Macmillan.

Claxton, C. S., & Murrell, P. H. (1987). *Learning styles: Implications for improving educational practices* (ASHE-ERIC Higher Education Report No. 4). Washington, DC: Association for the Study of Higher Education.

Commons, M. L., Richards, F. A., & Kuhn, D. (1982). Systematic and metasystematic reasoning: A case for levels of reasoning beyond Piaget's stage of formal operations. *Child Development, 53,* 1058–1069.

Connell, J. P. (1985). A new multidimensional measure of children's perceptions of control. *Child Development, 56,* 1018–1041.

Corno, L. (1986). The metacognitive control components of self-regulated learning. *Contemporary Educational Psychology, 11,* 333–346.

Corno, L., & Mandinach, E. B. (1983). The role of cognitive engagement in classroom learning and motivation. *Educational Psychologist, 18,* 88–108.

Corno, L., & Snow, R. E. (1986). Adapting teaching to individual differences among learners. In M. C. Wittrock (Ed.), *Handbook of research on teaching* (3rd ed., pp. 605–629). New York: Macmillan.

Covington, M. (1984). The motive for self-worth. In R. Ames & C. Ames (Eds.), *Research on motivation in education: Student motivation* (pp. 77–113). Orlando, FL: Academic Press.

Covington, M., & Beery, R. (1976). *Self-worth and school learning.* New York: Holt, Rinehart & Winston.

Covington, M. V., & Omelich, C. L. (1979a). Are causal attributions causal? A path analysis of the cognitive model of achievement motivation. *Journal of Personality and Social Psychology, 37,* 1487–1504.

Covington, M. V., & Omelich, C. L. (1979b). Effort: The double-edged sword in school achievement. *Journal of Educational Psychology, 71,* 169–182.

Cronbach, L. (1957). The two disciplines of scientific psychology. *American Psychologist, 12,* 671–684.

Cronbach, L. (1975). Beyond the two disciplines of scientific psychology. *American Psychologist, 30,* 116–127.

Cronbach, L., & Snow, R., (1977). *Aptitudes and instructional methods.* New York: Irvington.

Crooks, T. (1988). The impact of classroom evaluation practices on students. *Review of Educational Research, 58,* 438–481.

Csikszentmihalyi, M. (1985). Emergent motivation and the evolution of the self. In D. A. Kleiber & M. Maehr (Eds.), *Advances in motivation and achievement: Motivation and adulthood* (pp. 93–119). Greenwich, CT: JAI Press.

Culler, R. E., & Holahan, C. J. (1980). Test anxiety and academic performance: The effects of study and related behaviors. *Journal of Educational Psychology, 72,* 16–20.

de Charms, R. (1968). *Personal causation.* New York: Academic Press.

Deci, E. L. (1975). *Intrinsic motivation.* New York: Plenum.

DeLisi, R., & Staudt, J. (1980). Individual differences in college students' performance on formal operations tasks. *Journal of Applied Developmental Psychology, 1,* 108–208.

Dewey, J. (1963). *Experience and education.* New York: Macmillan.

Donald, J. G. (1983). Knowledge structures: Methods for exploring course content. *Journal of Higher Education, 54,* 31–41.

Doyle, W. (1983). Academic work. *Review of Educational Research, 53,* 159–199.

Dunkin, M. J. (1986). Research on teaching in higher education. In M. C. Wittrock (Ed.), *Handbook of research on teaching* (3rd. ed., pp. 754–777). New York: Macmillan.

Dweck, C. S., & Elliott, E. S. (1983). Achievement motivation. In E. M. Heatherington (Ed.), *Handbook of child psychology: Socialization, personality, and social development,* (Vol. 4, pp 643–691). New York: John Wiley & Sons.

Dweck, C. S., & Leggett, E. L. (1988). A social-cognitive approach to motivation and personality. *Psychological Review, 95(2),* 256–273.

Eble, K. E. (1988). *The craft of teaching: A guide to mastering the professor's art.* San Francisco: Jossey-Bass.

Eccles, J. (1983). Expectancies, values, and academic behaviors. In J. T. Spence (Ed.), *Achievement and achievement motives* (pp. 75–146). San Francisco: W. H. Freeman.

Elliott, E. S., & Dweck, C. S. (1988). Goals: An approach to motivation and achievement. *Journal of Personality and Social Psychology, 54,* 5–12.

Entwistle, N. (1984). Contrasting perspectives on learning. In F. Marton, D. Hounsell, & N. Entwistle (Eds.), *The experience of learning* (pp. 1–18). Edinburgh, Scotland: Scottish Academic Press.

Entwistle, N., Hanley, M., & Hounsell, D. (1979). Identifying distinctive approaches to studying. *Higher Education, 8,* 3655–3680.

Entwistle, N., & Marton, F. (1984). Changing conceptions of learning and research. In F. Marton, D. Hounsell, & N. Entwistle (Eds.), *The experience of learning* (pp. 211–236). Edinburgh, Scotland: Scottish Academic Press.

Epstein, S., & O'Brien, E. J. (1985). The person-situation debate in historical and current perspective. *Psychological Bulletin, 98(3),* 513–537.

Epstein, S., & Teraspulsky, L. (1986). Perception of cross-situational consistency. *Journal of Personality and Social Psychology, 50(6).* 1152–1160.

Erickson, E. H. (1963). *Childhood and society* (2nd ed.). New York: W. W. Norton.

Feather, N. T. (1969). Attribution of responsibility and valence of success and failure in relation to initial confidence and task performance. *Journal of Personality and Social Psychology, 13,* 129–144.

Featherman, D. L. (1983). Life-span perspectives in social science research. In P. B. Baltes & O. G. Brim (Eds.), *Life-span development and behavior* (pp. 1–57). New York: Academic Press.

Feiman-Nemser, S. (1983). Learning to teach. In L. S. Shulman & G. Sykes (Eds.), *Handbook of teaching and policy* (pp. 150–170). New York: Longman.

Feiman-Nemser, S., & Buchmann, M. (1989). Describing teacher education: A framework and illustrative findings from a longitudinal study of six students. *Elementary School Journal, 89,* 365–377.

Fincham, F. D., & Cain, K. M. (1986). Learned helplessness in humans: A developmental analysis. *Developmental Review, 6,* 301–333.

Findley, M., & Cooper, H. (1983). Locus of control and academic achievement: A review of the literature. *Journal of Personality and Social Psychology, 44,* 419–427.

Fischer, C. G., & Grant, G. F. (1983). Intellectual levels in college classrooms. In C. L. Ellner & C. P. Barnes (Eds.), *Studies of college teaching* (pp. 47–60). Lexington, MA: D. C. Heath.

Flavell, J. H. (1971). Stage-related properties of cognitive development. *Cognitive Development, 2,* 421–453.

Flavell, J. H. (1979). Metacognition and cognitive monitoring: A new area of cognitive-developmental inquiry. *American Psychologist, 34,* 906–911.

Flavell, J. H. (1982). Structures, stages, and sequences in cognitive development. In W. A. Collins (Ed.), *Minnesota symposia on child psychology* (pp. 1–28). Hillsdale, NJ: Lawrence Erlbaum.

Flavell, J. H. (1985). *Cognitive development.* Englewood Cliffs, NJ: Prentice-Hall.

Foersterling, F. (1985). Attributional retraining: A review. *Psychological Bulletin, 98,* 495–512.

Fong, G. T., Krantz, D. H., & Nisbett, R. E. (1986). The effects of statistical training on thinking about everyday problems. *Cognitive Psychology, 18,* 253–292.

Ford, M. E. (1986). For all practical purposes: Criteria for defining and evaluating practical intelligence. In R. J. Sternberg & R. K. Wagner (Eds.), *Practical intelligence* (pp. 183–200). Cambridge: Cambridge University Press.

Freedman, S., Jackson, J., & Boles, K. (1983). Teaching: An imperilled "profession." In L. S. Shulman & G. Sykes (Eds.), *Handbook of teaching and policy* (pp. 261–299). New York: Longman.

Fuller, F. F. (1969). Concerns of teachers: A developmental conceptualization. *American Educational Research Journal, 6,* 207–226.

Gagné, E. D. (1985). *The cognitive psychology of school learning.* Boston: Little, Brown.

Gallimore, R., Dalton, S., & Tharp, R. (1986). Self-regulation and interactive teaching: The effects of teaching conditions on teachers' cognitive activity. *Elementary School Journal, 86,* 613–631.

Gangestad, S., & Snyder, M. (1985). "To carve nature at its joints": On the existence of discrete classes in personality. *Psychological Review, 92,*(3), 317–349.

Gardner, H. (1983). *Frames of mind: The theory of multiple intelligence.* New York: Basic Books.

Garner, R., & Alexander, P. (1989). Metacognition: Answered and unanswered questions. *Educational Psychologist, 24,* 143–158.

Gelman, R., & Baillargeon, R. (1983). A review of some Piagetian concepts. In J. H. Flavell and E. M. Markman (Eds.), *Handbook of child psychology: Cognitive development* (Vol. 3, pp. 167–230). New York: John Wiley & Sons.

Gentner, D., & Stevens, A. (1983). *Mental models.* Hillsdale, NJ: Lawrence Erlbaum.

Geva, E. (1983). Facilitating reading comprehension through flow-charting. *Reading Research Quarterly, 18,* 384–405.

Gibbs, J. C. (1977). Kohlberg's stages of moral judgment: A constructive critique. *Harvard Educational Review, 47,* 43–61.

Gibbs, J. C. (1979). Kohlberg's moral stage theory: A Piagetian revision. *Human Development, 22,* 89–112.

Gilligan, C. (1981). Moral development. In A. W. Chickering (Ed.), *The modern American college* (pp. 139–157). San Francisco: Jossey-Bass.

Gilligan, C. (1982). *In a different voice: Psychological theory and women's development.* Cambridge, MA: Harvard University Press.

Glaser, R. (1984). Education and thinking: The role of knowledge. *American Psychologist, 39,* 93–105.

Good, T. L., & Brophy, J. E. (1987). *Looking in classrooms.* New York: Harper & Row.

Greeno, J. G. (1978). A study of problem solving. In R. Glaser (Ed.), *Advances in instructional psychology* (pp. 13–75). Hillsdale, NJ: Lawrence Erlbaum.

Greeno, J. G. (1980). Psychology of learning, 1960–1980: One participant's observations. *American Psychologist, 35,* 713–728.

Greenwald, A. G. (1980). The totalitarian ego: Fabrication and revision of personal history. *American Psychologist, 35,* 603–618.

Griffin, G. (1989). A descriptive study of student teaching. *Elementary School Journal, 89,* 343–364.

Guilford, J. P. (1982). Cognitive psychology's ambiguities: Some suggested remedies. *Psychological Review, 89,* 48–59.

Harter, S. (1981). A new self-report scale of intrinsic versus extrinsic orientation in the classroom: Motivational and informational components. *Developmental Psychology, 17,* 300–312.

Harter, S. (1985). Competence as a dimension of self-evaluation: Toward a comprehensive model of self-worth. In R. L. Leahy (Ed.), *The development of the self* (pp. 95–121). New York: Academic Press.

Holland, J. H., Holyoak, K. J., Nisbett, R. E., & Thagard, P. R. (1986). *Induction: Processes of inference, learning, and discovery.* Cambridge, MA: MIT Press.

Holland, J. L. (1966). *The psychology of vocational choice.* Waltham, MA: Ginn.

Holley, C. D., & Dansereau, D. F. (1984). *Spatial learning strategies: Techniques, applications, and related issues.* New York: Academic Press.

Inhelder, B., & Piaget, J. (1958). *The growth of logical thinking from childhood to adolescence.* New York: Basic Books.

Johnson, D. W., Maruyama, G., Johnson, R., Nelson, D., & Skon, L. (1981). The effects of cooperative, competitive and individualistic goals structures on achievement: A meta-analysis. *Psychological Bulletin, 89,* 47–62.

Johnson-Laird, P. N. (1983). *Mental models.* Cambridge, MA: Harvard University Press.

Kagan, D. (1988). Teaching as clinical problem solving: A critical examination of the analogy and its implications. *Review of Educational Research, 58,* 482–505.

Keating, D. P. (1980). Thinking processes in adolescence. In J. Adelson (Ed.), *Handbook of adolescent psychology* (pp. 211–246). New York: John Wiley & Sons.

Kennedy, M. (1987). Inexact sciences: Professional education and the development of expertise. In E. Z. Rothkopf (Ed.), *Review of research in education* (Vol. 14, pp. 133–167). Washington, DC: American Educational Research Association.

Kerr, D. H. (1983). Teaching competence and teacher education in the United States. In L. S. Shulman & G. Sykes (Eds.), *Handbook of teaching and policy* (pp. 126–149). New York: Longman.

King, P. M. (1986). Formal reasoning in adults: A review and critique. In R. A. Mines & K. S. Kitchener (Eds.), *Adult cognitive development: Methods and models* (pp. 1–21). New York: Praeger.

King, P. M., Kitchener, K. S., Davison, M. L., Parker, C. A., & Wood, P. K. (1983). The justification of beliefs in young adults: A longitudinal study. *Human Development, 26,* 106–116.

Kintsch, W., & van Dijk, T. A. (1978). Toward a model of text comprehension and production. *Psychological Review, 85,* 363–394.

Kitchener, K. S. (1983). Cognition, metacognition, and epistemic cognition: A three-level model of cognitive processing. *Human Development, 26,* 222–232.

Kitchener, K. S. (1986). The reflective judgment model: Characteristics, evidence, and measurement. In R. A. Mines & K. S. Kitchener (Eds.), *Adult cognitive development: Methods and models* (pp. 76–91). New York: Praeger.

Kitchener, K. S., & King, P. M. (1981). Reflective judgment: Concepts of justification and their relationship to age and education. *Journal of Applied Developmental Psychology, 2,* 89–116.

Klinger, E. (1977). *Meaning and void: Inner experience and the incentives in people's lives.* Minneapolis: University of Minnesota Press.

Kogan, N. (1983). Stylistic variation in childhood and adolescence: Creativity, metaphor, and cognitive style. In J. H. Flavell & E. M. Markman (Eds.), *Handbook of child psychology: Cognitive development* (Vol. 3, pp. 695–706). New York: John Wiley & Sons.

Kohlberg, L. (1976). Moral stages and moralization. In T. Lickona (Ed.), *Moral development and behavior: Theory, research and social issues* (pp. 2–15). New York: Holt, Rinehart & Winston.

Kohlberg, L., & Armon, C. (1984). Three types of stage models used in the study of adult development. In. M. L. Commons, F. A. Richards, & C. Armon (Eds.), *Beyond formal operations: Late adolescent and adult cognitive development* (pp. 383–394). New York: Praeger.

Kolb, D. A. (1981). Learning styles and disciplinary differences. In A. W. Chickering (Ed.), *The modern American college* (pp. 232–255). San Francisco: Jossey-Bass.

Kuhl, J. (1987). Feeling versus being helpless: Metacognitive mediation of failure-induced performance deficits. In F. E. Weinert & R. H. Kluwe (Eds.), *Metacognition, motivation, and understanding* (pp. 217–235). Hillsdale: NJ: Lawrence Erlbaum.

Kuhn, T. S. (1970). *The structure of scientific revolutions (2nd ed.).* Chicago: University of Chicago Press.

Kurtines, W., & Greif, E. (1974). The development of moral thought:

Review and evaluation of Kohlberg's approach. *Psychological Bulletin, 81,* 453–470.

Laboratory of Comparative Human Cognition. (1983). Culture and cognitive development. In W. Kessen (Ed.), *Handbook of child psychology: History, theory, and methods* (Vol. 1, pp. 295–356). New York: John Wiley & Sons.

Labouvie-Vief, G. (1981). Proactive and reactive aspects of constructivism: Growth and aging in life-span perspective. In R. M. Lerner & N. A. Busch-Rossnagel (Eds.), *Individuals as producers of their own development: A life-span perspective* (pp. 197–230). New York: Academic Press.

Labouvie-Vief, G. (1982). Dynamic development and mature autonomy: A theoretical prologue. *Human Development, 25,* 161–191.

Langer, E. J. (1975). The illusion of control. *Journal of Personality and Social Psychology, 32,* 311–328.

Lanier, J. E., & Little, J. W. (1986). Research on teacher education. In M. C. Wittrock (Ed.), *Handbook of research on teaching* (3rd ed., pp. 527–569). New York: Macmillan.

Lawrenz, F. (1985). Aptitude-treatment effects of laboratory grouping methods for students of differing reasoning ability. *Journal of Research in Science Teaching, 22,* 279–287.

Lefcourt, H. (1976). *Locus of control: Current trends in theory and research.* Hillsdale, NJ: Lawrence Erlbaum.

Leinhardt, G., & Greeno, J. G. (1986). The cognitive skill of teaching. *Journal of Educational Psychology, 78,* 75–95.

Lerner, R. (1986). *Concepts and theories of human development.* New York: Random House.

Levinson, D. J. (1978). *The seasons of a man's life.* New York: Ballantine.

Lewin, K. (1938). *The conceptual representation and the measurement of psychological forces.* Durham, NC: Duke University Press.

Little, B. (1983). Personal projects: A rationale and methods for investigation. *Environmental Behavior, 15,* 273–309.

Loevinger, J. (1976). *Ego development: Conceptions and theories.* San Francisco: Jossey-Bass.

Lortie, D. (1975). *Schoolteacher: A sociological study.* Chicago: University of Chicago Press.

Maehr, M. L., & Braskamp, L. A. (1986). *The motivation factor: A theory of personal investment.* Lexington, MA: D. C. Heath.

Maehr, M. L., & Kleiber, D. A. (1981). The graying of achievement motivation. *American Psychologist, 36,* 781–793.

Magnusson, D., & Endler, N. (1977). *Personality at the crossroads: Current issues in interactional psychology.* Hillsdale, NJ: Lawrence Erlbaum.

Malone, T. W. (1981). Toward a theory of intrinsically motivating instruction. *Cognitive Science, 5,* 333–370.

Mandler, G. (1985). *Cognitive psychology: An essay in cognitive science.* Hillsdale, NJ: Lawrence Erlbaum.

Mann, R. D., Arnold, S. M., Binder, J., Cytrynbaum, S., Newman, B. M., Ringwald, B., Ringwald, J., & Rosenwein, R. (1970). *The college classroom: Conflict, change, and learning.* New York: John Wiley & Sons.

Markus, H. (1977). Self-schemata and processing information about the self. *Journal of Personality and Social Psychology, 35,* 63–78.

Markus, H., & Nurius, P. (1986). Possible selves. *American Psychologist, 41,* 954–969.

Markus, H., & Wurf, E. (1987). The dynamic self-concept: A social psychological perspective. *Annual Review of Psychology, 38,* 299–337.

Marton, F., Hounsell, D., & Entwistle, N. (1984). *The experience of learning.* Edinburgh, Scotland: Scottish Academic Press.

Marton, F., & Saljo, R. (1976a). On qualitative differences in learning: I. Outcomes and process. *British Journal of Educational Psychology, 46,* 4–11.

Marton, F., & Saljo, R. (1976b). On qualitative differences in learning: II. Outcome as a function of the learners' conceptions of the task. *British Journal of Educational Psychology, 46,* 115–127.

Maslow, A. (1970). *Motivation and personality.* New York: Harper & Row.

Mayer, R. E. (1983). *Thinking, problem solving, and cognition.* San Fransisco: W. H. Freeman.

Mayer, R. E. (1984). Aids to prose comprehension. *Educational Psychologist, 19,* 30–42.

McKeachie, W. J. (1980). *Learning, cognition, and college teaching: New directions for teaching and learning.* San Francisco: Jossey-Bass.

McKeachie, W. J. (1984). Does anxiety disrupt information processing or does poor information processing lead to anxiety? *International Review of Applied Psychology, 33,* 187–203.

McKeachie, W. J. (1986). *Teaching tips: A guidebook for the beginning college teacher.* Boston: D. C. Heath.

McKeachie, W. J., Pintrich, P. R., Lin, Y. G., & Smith, D. (1986). *Teaching and learning in the college classroom: A review of the research literature.* Ann Arbor, MI: University of Michigan, National Center for Research to Improve Postsecondary Teaching and Learning.

Menges, R. J. (1981). Instructional methods. In A. W. Chickering (Ed.), *The modern American college* (pp. 556–581). San Francisco: Jossey-Bass.

Merriam, S., & Cunningham, P. (1989). *Handbook of adult and continuing education,* San Francisco; Jossey-Bass.

Messick, S. (1976). *Individuality in learning: Implications of cognitive style and creativity for human development.* San Francisco: Jossey-Bass.

Messick, S. (1984). The nature of cognitive styles: Problems and promise in educational practice. *Educational Psychology, 19*(2), 59–74.

Meyer, B. J. F. (1975). *The organization of prose and its effect on memory.* Amsterdam: North Holland.

Meyer, B. J. F. (1977). What is remembered from prose: A function of passage structure. In R. O. Freedle (Ed.), *Discourse production and comprehension* (pp. 307–336). Norwood, NJ: Ablex.

Mischel, W. (1968). *Personality and assessment.* New York: John Wiley & Sons.

Mischel, W. (1973). Towards a cognitive social learning reconceptualization of personality. *Psychological Review, 80,* 252–283.

Mischel, W. (1979). On the interface of cognition and personality: Beyond the personality and situation debate. *American Psychologist, 34,* 740–754.

Mischel, W., & Peake, P. K. (1982). Beyond deja vu in the search for cross-situational consistency. *Psychological Review, 89,* 730–755.

Myers, I. B., & McCaulley, M. H. (1985). *The Myers-Briggs Manual: A guide to the development and use of the Myers-Briggs Type Indicator.* Palo Alto, CA: Consulting Psychologists Press.

Naveh-Benjamin, M., & Lin, Y. A. (1988, August). *The effects of explicitly teaching an instructor's knowledge structure on students' cognitive structures.* Paper presented at the meeting of the American Psychological Association, Atlanta.

Naveh-Benjamin, M., McKeachie, W. J., Lin, Y. A., & Tucker, D. G. (1986). Inferring students' cognitive structures and their development using the "ordered tree technique." *Journal of Educational Psychology, 78,* 130–140.

Neimark, E. D. (1983). Adolescent thought: Transition to formal operations. In B. B. Wolman (Ed.), *Handbook of developmental psychology* (pp. 486–502). Englewood, Cliffs, NJ: Prentice-Hall.

Neugarten, B. L. (1968). *Middle age and aging.* Chicago: University of Chicago Press.

Newell, A., & Simon, H. A. (1972). *Human problem solving.* Englewood Cliffs, NJ: Prentice-Hall.

Nicholls, J. (1984). Achievement motivation: Conceptions of ability, subjective experience, task choice, and performance. *Psychological Review, 91(3),* 328–346.

Nickerson, R. S., Perkins, D. N., Smith, E. E. (1985). *The teaching of thinking.* Hillsdale, NJ: Lawrence Erlbaum.

Nisbett, R. E., Krantz, D. H., Jepson, C., & Kunda, Z. (1983). The use of statistical heuristics in everyday reasoning. *Psychological Review, 90,* 339–363.

Nisbett, R. E., & Ross, L. (1980). *Human inference: Strategies and shortcomings of social judgement.* Englewood Cliffs, NJ: Prentice-Hall.

Novak, J. D. (1985). Metalearning and metaknowledge strategies to help students learn how to learn. In L. H. T. West & A. L. Pines (Eds.), *Cognitive structure and conceptual change* (pp. 189–209). New York: Academic Press.

Novak, J. D., & Gowin, D. B. (1984). *Learning how to learn.* Cambridge: Cambridge University Press.

Palincsar, A. S., & Brown, A. L. (1984). Reciprocal teaching of comprehension-fostering and monitoring activities. *Cognition and Instruction, 1,* 117–175.

Paris, S. G., Lipson, M., & Wixson, K. (1983). Becoming a strategic reader. *Contemporary Educational Psychology, 8,* 293–316.

Paris, S. G., Wixson, K. K., & Palincsar, A. S. (1986). Instructional approaches to reading comprehension. In E. Rothkopf (Ed.), *Review of research in education* (Vol. 13, pp. 91–128). Washington, DC: American Educational Research Association.

Parsons, J. E., & Goff, S. B. (1978). Achievement and motivation: Dual modalities. *Journal of Educational Psychology, 13,* 93–96.

Pask, G. (1976). Styles and strategies of learning. *British Journal of Educational Psychology, 46,* 128–148.

Pepper, S. (1942). *World hypotheses.* Berkley, CA: University of California Press.

Perry, W. G. (1970). *Forms of intellectual and ethical development in the college years: A scheme.* New York: Holt, Rinehart & Winston.

Perry, W. G. (1981). Cognitive and ethical growth: The making of meaning. In A. W. Chickering (Ed.), *The modern American college* (pp. 76–116). San Francisco: Jossey-Bass.

Peterson, C., & Seligman, M. E. P. (1987). Helplessness and attributional style in depression. In F. E. Weinert & R. H. Kluwe (Eds.), *Metacognition, motivation, and understanding* (pp. 185–216). Hillsdale, NJ: Lawrence Erlbaum.

Peterson, P. (1988). Teachers' and students' cognitional knowledge for classroom teaching and learning. *Educational Researcher, 17,* 5–14.

Peterson, P., & Comeaux, M. (1989). Assessing the teacher as a reflective professional: New perspectives on teacher evaluation. In A. E. Woolfolk (Ed.), *Research perspectives on the graduate preparation of teachers* (pp. 132–152). Englewood Cliffs, NJ: Prentice-Hall.

Phillips, D. C. (1983). On describing a student's cognitive structure. *Educational Psychologist, 18,* 59–74.

Pintrich, P. R. (1988a). A process-oriented view of student motivation and cognition. In J. Stark & L. Mets (Eds.), *Improving teaching and learning through research. New Directions for Institutional Research* (Vol. 57, pp. 65–79). San Francisco: Jossey-Bass.

Pintrich, P. R. (1988b). Student learning and college teaching. In R. E. Young & K. E. Eble (Eds.), *College teaching and learning: Preparing for new commitments. New Directions for Teaching and Learning* (Vol. 33, pp. 71–86). San Francisco: Jossey-Bass.

Pintrich, P. R. (1989). The dynamic interplay of student motivation and cognition in the college classroom. In M. Maehr and C. Ames (Eds.), *Advances in motivation and achievement: Motivation-enhancing environments* (Vol. 6, pp. 117–160). Greenwich, CT: JAI Press.

Pintrich, P. R., Cross, D., Kozma, R., & McKeachie, W. J. (1986).

Instructional psychology. *Annual Review of Psychology, 37,* 611–651.

Posner, G. J., Strike, K. A., Hewson, P. W., & Gertzog, W. A. (1982). Accommodation of a scientific conception: Toward a theory of conceptual change. *Science Education, 66,* 211–227.

Pressley, M. (1986). The relevance of the good strategy user model to the teaching of mathematics. *Educational Psychologist, 21,* 139–161.

Ramsden, P. (1984). The context of learning. In F. Marton, D. Hounsell, & N. Entwistle (Eds.), *The experience of learning* (pp. 144–164). Edinburgh, Scotland: Scottish Academic Press.

Raynor, J. O. (1974). Future orientation in the study of achievement motivation. In J. W. Atkinson & J. O. Raynor (Eds.), *Motivation and achievement* (pp. 121–154). Washington, DC: V. H. Winston & Sons.

Resnick, L. B. (1983). Toward a cognitive theory of instruction. In S. Paris, G. Olson, & H. Stevenson (Eds.), *Learning and motivation in the classroom* (pp. 5–38). Hillsdale, NJ: Lawrence Erlbaum.

Rest, J. R. (1983). Morality. In J. H. Flavell & E. M. Markman (Eds.), *Handbook of child psychology: Vol. 3. Cognitive development* (pp. 556–629). New York: John Wiley & Sons.

Richards, F. A., & Commons, M. L. (1984). Systematic, metasystematic, and cross-paradigmatic reasoning: A case for stages of reasoning beyond formal operations. In M. L. Commons, F. A. Richards, & C. Armon (Eds.). *Beyond formal operations: Late adolescent and cognitive development* (pp. 92–140). New York: Praeger.

Riegel, K. F. (1973). Dialectic operations: The final period of cognitive development. *Human Development, 16,* 346–370.

Riegel, K. F. (1975). Toward a dialectical theory of development. *Human Development, 18,* 50–64.

Riegel, K. F. (1976). The dialectics of human development. *American Psychologist, 31,* 689–700.

Rotter, J. B. (1966). Generalized expectancies for internal versus external control reinforcement. *Psychological Monographs, 80,* 1–28.

Rumelhart, D. E., & Norman, D. A. (1988). Representation in memory. In R. C. Atkinson, R. Herrnstein, G. Lindzey, & R. D. Luce (Eds.), *Stevens handbook of experimental psychology* (pp. 511–587). New York: John Wiley & Sons.

Rumelhart, D. E., & Ortony, A. (1977). The representation of knowledge in memory. In R. C. Anderson, R. J. Spiro, & W. E. Montague (Eds.), *Schooling and the acquisition of knowledge* (pp. 99–136). Hillsdale, NJ: Lawrence Erlbaum.

Saljo, R. (1984). Learning from readings. In F. Marton, D. Hounsell, & N. Entwistle (Eds.), *The experience of learning* (pp. 71–89). Edinburgh, Scotland: Scottish Academic Press.

Salthouse, T. A. (1982). *Adult cognition: An experimental psychology of human aging.* New York: Springer-Verlag.

Schlechty, P., & Whitford, B. (1989). Systematic perspectives on beginning teacher programs. *Elementary School Journal, 89,* 441–449.

Schmeck, R. (1983). Learning styles of college students. In R. F. Dillon & R. R. Schmeck (Eds.), *Individual differences in cognition* (pp. 233–279). New York: Academic Press.

Schön, D. E. (1983). *The reflective practitioner: How professionals think in action.* New York: Basic Books.

Schön, D. E. (1987). *Educating the reflective practitioner.* San Francisco: Jossey-Bass.

Schunk, D. H. (1985). Self-efficacy and classroom learning. *Psychology in the Schools, 22,* 208–223.

Shavelson, R. J. (1972). Some aspects of the correspondence between content structure and cognitive structure in physics instruction. *Journal of Educational Psychology, 63,* 225–234.

Shavelson, R. J. (1974). Methods for examining representations of a subject matter structure in students' memory. *Journal of Research in Science Teaching, 11,* 231–250.

Shavelson, R. J. (1981). Teaching mathematics: Contributions of cognitive research. *Educational Psychologist, 16*, 23–44.

Shavelson, R. J. (1983). On quagmires, philosophical and otherwise: A reply to Phillips. *Educational Psychologist, 18*, 81–87.

Shavelson, R. J., & Geeslin, W. E. (1975). A method for examining subject-matter structure in instructional material. *Journal of Structural Learning, 4*, 199–218.

Shavelson, R. J., & Stern, P. (1981). Research on teachers' pedagogical thoughts, judgments, decisions, and behavior. *Review of Educational Research, 51*, 455–498.

Shulman, L. S. (1986). Those who understand: Knowledge growth in teaching. *Educational Researcher, 15*(2), 4–14.

Shulman, L. S. (1987). Knowledge and teaching: Foundations of the new reform. *Harvard Educational Review, 57*, 1–22.

Shulman, L. S., & Tamir, P. (1973). Research on teaching in the natural sciences. In R. N. W. Travers (Ed.), *Second handbook of research on teaching* (pp. 1098–1148). Chicago: Rand McNally.

Siegel, L., & Siegel, L. C. (1965). Educational set: A determinant of acquisition. *Journal of Educational Psychology, 56*, 1–12.

Slavin, R. (1983). *Cooperative learning.* New York: Longman.

Smith, D. G. (1977). College classroom interactions and critical thinking. *Journal of Educational Psychology, 69*, 180–190.

Snow, R. E., & Lohman, D. F. (1984). Toward a theory of cognitive aptitude for learning from instruction. *Journal of Educational Psychology, 76*, 347–377.

Sparks, G. (1988). Teachers' attitudes toward change and subsequent improvements in classroom teaching. *Journal of Educational Psychology, 80*, 111–117.

Spenner, K., & Featherman, D. L. (1978). Achievement ambitions. *Annual Review of Sociology, 4*, 373–420.

Spiro, R. (1977). Remembering information from text: The "state of schema" approach. In R. C. Anderson, R. Spiro, & W. Montague (Eds.), *Schooling and the acquisition of knowledge.* Hillsdale, NJ: Lawrence Erlbaum.

Sprinthall, N. A., & Thies-Sprinthall, L. (1983). The teacher as an adult learner: A cognitive-developmental view. In G. A. Griffin (Ed.), *Staff development* (82nd yearbook of the National Society for the Study of Education Part II, pp. 13–35). Chicago: University of Chicago Press.

Sternberg, R. J. (1985). *Beyond IQ: A triarchic theory of human intelligence.* New York: Cambridge University Press.

Sternberg, R. J. (1988). *The triarchic mind: A new theory of human intelligence.* New York: Viking Penguin.

Sternberg, R. J., & Caruso, D. R. (1985). Practical modes of knowing. In E. Eisner (Ed.), *Learning and teaching the ways of knowing* (84th yearbook of the National Society for the Study of Education, pp. 133–158). Chicago: University of Chicago Press.

Stewart, J. (1980). Techniques for assessing and representing information in cognitive structure. *Science Education, 64*, 223–235.

Stewart, J. (1982). Two aspects of meaningful problem solving in science. *Science Education, 66*, 731–749.

Stewart, J. (1984). The representation of knowledge: Curricular and instructional implications for science teaching. In C. D. Holley & D. F. Dansereau (Eds.), *Spatial learning strategies: Techniques, applications, and related issues* (pp. 235–253). New York: Academic Press.

Stipek, D., & Weisz, J. (1981). Perceived personal control and academic achievement. *Review of Educational Research, 51*, 101–137.

Strike, K. A., & Posner, G. J. (1985). A conceptual change view of learning and understanding. In L. H. T. West & A. L. Pines (Eds.), *Cognitive structure and conceptual change* (pp. 211–231). New York: Academic Press.

Tobias, S. (1985). Test anxiety: Inference, defective skills, and cognitive capacity. *Educational Psychologist, 20*, 135–142.

Tom, A. (1984). *Teaching as a moral craft.* New York: Longman.

Tversky, A., & Kahneman, D. (1974). Judgment under uncertainty: Heuristics and bias. *Science, 185*, 1124–1131.

Vance, V. S., & Schlechty, P. C. (1982). The distribution of academic ability in the teaching force: Policy implications. *Phi Delta Kappan, 64*(1), 2–27.

Veenman, S (1984). Perceived problems of beginning teachers. *Review of Educational Research, 54*, 143–178.

Veroff, J. (1969). Social comparison and the development of achievement motivation. In C. P. Smith (Ed.), *Achievement-related motives in children* (pp. 46–101). New York: Russell Sage.

Veroff, J., & Veroff, J. B. (1980). *Social incentives: A life-span developmental approach.* New York: Academic Press.

Vroom, V. H. (1964). *Work and motivation.* New York: John Wiley & Sons.

Vygotsky, L. S. (1962). *Thought and language.* New York: John Wiley & Sons.

Wagner, R. K., & Sternberg, R. J. (1985). Practical intelligence in real-world pursuits: The role of tacit knowledge. *Journal of Personality and Social Psychology, 48*, 436–458.

Wagner, R. K., & Sternberg, R. J. (1986). Tacit knowledge and intelligence in the everyday world. In R. J. Sternberg & R. K. Wagner (Eds.), *Practical intelligence: Nature and origins of competence in the everyday world* (pp. 51–83). Cambridge: Cambridge University Press.

Walters, J. M., & Gardner, H. (1986). The theory of multiple intelligence: Some issues and answers. In R. J. Sternberg & R. K. Wagner (Eds.), *Practical intelligence: Nature and origins of competence in the everyday world* (pp. 163–182). Cambridge: Cambridge University Press.

Weathersby, R. (1981). Ego development. In A. Chickering (Ed.), *The modern American college* (pp. 51–75). San Francisco: Jossey-Bass.

Weiner, B. (1979). A theory of motivation for some classroom experiences. *Journal of Educational Psychology, 71*, 3–25.

Weiner, B. (1980). *Human motivation.* New York: Holt, Rinehart & Winston.

Weiner, B. (1985). An attributional theory of achievement motivation and emotion. *Psychological Review, 92*(4), 548–573.

Weiner, B. (1986). *An attributional theory of motivation and emotion.* New York: Springer-Verlag.

Weinshank, A. B., Trumbull, E. S., & Daly, P. L. (1983). The role of the teacher in school change. In L. S. Shulman & G. Sykes (Eds.), *Handbook of teaching and policy* (pp. 300–314). New York: Longman.

Weinstein, C., & Mayer, R. (1986). The teaching of learning strategies. In M. C. Wittrock (Ed.), *Handbook of research on teaching* (3rd ed., pp. 315–327). New York: Macmillan.

West, L. H. T., & Pines, A. L. (1985). *Cognitive structure and conceptual change.* New York: Academic Press.

White, R. W. (1959). Motivation reconsidered: The concept of competence. *Psychological Review, 66*, 297–333.

Wigfield, A., & Braskamp, L. A. (1985). Age and personal investment in work. In D. A. Kleiber & M. L. Maehr (Eds.), *Advances in motivation and achievement* (Vol. 4, pp. 297–331). Greenwich, Conn.: JAI Press.

Wildman, T. M., & Niles, J. A. (1987). Reflective teachers: Tensions between abstractions and realities. *Journal of Teacher Education, 38*(4), 25–31.

Wildman, T., Niles, J., Maliaro, S., & McLaughlin, R. (1989). Teaching and learning to teach: The two roles of beginning teachers. *Elementary School Journal, 89*, 471–493.

Wine, J. (1971). Test anxiety and direction of attention. *Psychological Bulletin, 76*, 92–104.

Witkin, H. A., & Goodenough, D. R. (1981). *Cognitive styles: Essence and origins: Field dependence and field independence.* New York: International Universities Press.

Wixson, K. K., & Peters, C. W. (1987). Comprehension assessment: Implementing an interactive view of reading. *Educational Psychologist, 22,* 333–356.

Wlodkowski, R. J. (1988). *Enhancing adult motivation to learn.* San Francisco: Jossey-Bass.

Woolfolk, A. E. (1989). *Research perspectives on the graduate preparation of teachers.* Englewood Cliffs, NJ: Prentice-Hall.

Wortman, C. B., & Brehm, J. W. (1975). Response to uncontrollable outcomes: An integration of reactance theory and the learned helplessness model. In L. Berkowitz (Ed.), *Advances in experimental social psychology* (pp. 227–336). New York: Academic Press.

Zajonc, R. B. (1980). Feeling and thinking: Preferences need no inferences. *American Psychologist, 35,* 151–175.

Zukier, H. (1986). The paradigmatic and narrative modes in goal-guided inference. In R. M. Sorrentino & E. T. Higgins (Eds.), *Handbook of motivation and cognition: Foundations of social behavior* (pp. 465–502). New York: Guilford Press.

· 48 ·

COMPARATIVE TEACHER EDUCATION: ILLUSTRATIONS FROM ENGLISH-SPEAKING COUNTRIES

Beverly Lindsay

UNIVERSITY OF GEORGIA

> Teacher education may ... prove to be a particularly illuminating theme through which to approach cross-national studies. [It has been] suggested that the main purpose of comparative study is to generate supranational laws. An ... equally respectable task [is] the clarification of what is peculiar to a culture. Taken together, these two points ... indicate a ... stage of analysis, or more correctly of synthesis. (Judge, 1988, pp. 153–154, 156)

Scholars and policymakers are often tempted to focus on issues particular to their respective societies. The preceding quote suggests that perhaps teacher education is an especially beneficial and timely topic to examine cross-nationally. Comprehending what is unique and generic could help in the quest to analyze and synthesize features that might be applicable in individual educational settings.

Indeed, since the early nineteenth century, part of the stock-in-trade of comparative education has been the description and examination of educational developments in other societies. The purpose is to learn, to borrow ideas, and even to introduce reforms. In discussing education in England, Wat-

son asserts that problems of curriculum innovation, multicultural provisions, and examination reforms are not dissimilar from those encountered in other developed nations (1985, pp. 2–3). Issues and problems can be strikingly similar; resolution of issues in light of particular sociocultural, political, and economic realities is the challenge.

The overall purpose of this chapter is to provide a critical overview of teacher education and training for secondary schools by devoting special attention to select teacher education models in three English-speaking countries: England, Australia, and Kenya. All were influenced historically by England through the English educational system and various so-

The author expresses appreciation to Suzanne Shafer and Witold Tulasiewicz for their insightful critiques, which enhanced her understanding of cross-cultural issues in teacher education. Also appreciated are the comments and assistance of George Eshiwani, Michael Korir-Koech, and Janie White.

cioeconomic and political practices. In addition, all are undertaking critical national appraisals and reforms. To achieve this purpose, the major parameters encompass (a) analyzing some overarching purposes of secondary and teacher education in relation to sociopolitical and economic purposes of the respective countries and in light of historical and contemporary conditions; (b) explicating the structure and curriculum of secondary schools and teacher education programs for such schools; (c) presenting and critiquing methods of assessment of secondary students and those in college or university teacher education programs; (d) examining the interactive processes between public (federal and state or provincial) and college or university policies that affect teacher education programs; and (e) synthesizing ongoing applied or policy research issues that might evince components of alternate paradigms for teacher education.

After discussing such parameters for the several countries, the chapter concludes by reexamining generic and culture-specific motifs, which have cross-national implications, among these countries and the United States. Throughout this overview, illustrations focus primarily on initial diploma or baccalaureate degree programs for preservice secondary teachers. The numerous complexities and variations of primary teacher education programs, graduate degree programs, and inservice training in three countries are simply beyond the scope of a single chapter.

TEACHER EDUCATION IN ENGLAND

Purposes of Secondary and Teacher Education

According to various writers, the mid-1940s ushered in a new era of education in England (Bruce, 1985, pp. 164–165; Holmes, 1985, p. 1; Jones, 1985 pp. 24–27). The ending of World War II provided the opportunity for more attention to be devoted to education. Emerging salient issues that were linked to education during the next 20 or so years included developing and strengthening economic and political relations with other Western nations and within the colonies, preparing a domestic work force, and presenting the opportunity for some form of secondary education for all youth. To most educators and many political leaders, the provision of secondary education for all youth was the primary issue. However, it was clearly linked to the other salient issues.

Redeveloping the economic structure and its various components was a central issue immediately after World War II. This meant producing a domestic work force capable of meeting the demands for rebuilding a domestic industrial society and forging economic linkages with other developed nations while simultaneously extracting economic benefits from the colonies. Although not always explicitly stated, there was an emerging consensus among various education policymakers that different types of education for students could help address these and other societal goals. In fact, four prewar reports on education contributed to this consensus. In this light, the 1944 Education Act should be examined.

This act was based on the view that three stages of education—primary, secondary, and further—should be available to students on the basis of academic ability and *not* parents' ability to pay. The massive introduction of the "eleven-plus" examination at the conclusion of primary education was designed to determine students' ability and aptitude to attend one of three secondary schools: grammar, secondary modern, or technical. A liberal education, steeped in the arts and sciences, would be appropriate for future business, industrial, and government leaders through grammar schools. The secondary modern school was an extension of general education. For most others, educational training of a vocational or technical nature through technical schools would enable them to fit efficiently into various occupational niches (Holmes, 1985, p. 2). In essence, the perpetuation of English class and cultural distinctions would be transmitted through the educational system.

This act also brought education under the purview of the Minister of Education; but each Local Education Authority (LEA) was to provide satisfactorily for all the stages, or levels, of education including teacher education, which led to diplomas (not university degrees). The minister was empowered to insure that there were sufficient facilities for training teachers for service in schools and colleges and, as necessary, to require local authorities to maintain or assist any teacher-training college. In short, a demarcation existed between national or central government's responsibility for education and those at the local level, who had independent authority for training, curriculum, and education administration (Bruce, 1985, pp. 164–165; E. King, 1973, pp. 187, 190–191). The result has often been tension between the two levels of control, particularly in teacher education.

By the 1960s and 1970s, numerous economic and sociopolitical changes had occurred domestically and internationally that affected the English educational system. The immigration of various ethnic and racial groups changed the demographic profile of the workplace and the schools. By the late 1970s, about 5 percent of the population were recent immigrants, with the Irish, West Indians, and Indians constituting the largest groups (Watson, 1985, p. 67). The decline of direct extraction of economic resources from independent nations (that is, former colonies), and the increased demands by the indigenous work force to participate more fully in the democratic process were other prominent examples of changes (Bruce, 1988, pp. 383–384). Hence, it became necessary for the educational system to address such changes, as highlighted by several major reports of the national government.

From the 1940s to the 1980s, several major reports were issued by the Ministry of Education that addressed issues pertaining to secondary education and teacher training. The 1963 Newsom Report, *Half Our Future* (Ministry of Education, 1963), stirred national attention by revealing how social handicaps permanently blight the educational prospects of secondary students in low-income districts (E. King, 1973, p. 200). The 1967 Plowden Report, *Children and Their Primary Schools*, also received extensive coverage. It focused on primary age children and educational and social problems (Ministry of Education, 1967). Although the Robbins Committee report on higher education (1963) focused on universities, it also addressed problems of colleges of further education and teachers' colleges, that is, the two major components of the binary system of higher education. Ensuring initiatives to establish and upgrade standards was a central focus of this report (E. King, 1973, pp. 232, 235). In this regard, other educational institutions (now higher education institutions such as polytechnics) could provide courses leading to degrees awarded by the Council for National Academic Awards, established as a result of the Robbins Report. This report led to extensive expansion in further education due to the need for more high-level manpower needs and to meet the rising aspirations of the general population.

The 1972 James Report on *Teacher Education and Training* initially focused on the remoteness of teacher education from the needs of the field, particularly after teachers had taught for several years. Post–teacher education and inservice programs were called for (Judge, 1984, pp. 5, 9). The 1977 Taylor Report called for more participation by educators, parents, and students in school and university affairs (Halls, 1985, p. 34). The 1981 interim report by the Rampton Committee (Committee of Inquiry Into the Education of Children from Ethnic Minority Groups, 1981) and the 1988 Swann Committee Report (Committee of Inquiry into the Education of Children from Ethnic Minority Groups) focused on ethnic and racial minorities in the schools (Ministry of Education, 1988). Changes in curriculum that addressed various demographic needs were discussed.

Structure and Curriculum of Secondary Schools and Teacher Education Programs

The 1944 Education Act led, as indicated, to the solidification of a tripartite secondary school system: grammar (academic), secondary modern (general), and technical (vocational) schools. These types of publicly funded schools largely existed until the mid-1960s. Since Circular 10/65 (issued by the Department of Education and Science in 1965), comprehensive, grammar, and technical schools exist in most parts of England. However, the real emergence of comprehensive schools occurred in the 1970s. The elitism perpetuated through the multifaceted approach should now be lessened through comprehensive schools. The key distinction between the two periods is observed through attempts to broaden access to secondary education without adverse effects of tracking students into a particular type of school and curriculum. (Under the old system, secondary school selections were usually made at age 11, with limited opportunities for change at 13 and 15 or 16 years of age.) Comprehensive schools, offering academic and vocational curriculum, enroll children from 11 to 18 in one of several secondary models (Holmes, 1985, p. 16). The vast majority of secondary students now attend some type of comprehensive secondary school, whereas through the mid-1960s only about 25 percent of the students attended secondary grammar schools, which provided the education needed for college or university study (Holmes, 1985, p. 16; Judge, 1984, p. 3). Since the 1940s, private schools (public schools in the English sense) have provided a 4–6 year academic curriculum potentially leading to a university education. In this regard, private and grammar schools are analogous.

In several ways, the dual system of secondary education was reflected in a similar structure for teacher education and training. Teachers for grammar or academic schools pursued initial higher education and subsequent teacher training through degrees and programs in universities. In 1970 only about 13 percent of the 207 teacher education sites (including those in Wales) were situated in universities. Other teachers usually studied in teacher-training colleges or colleges of technology, later colleges of advanced education. Vocational or technical teachers for secondary education studied in polytechnic institutions (Judge, 1984, p. 6). In the 1980s, the number of sites and the internal structure and content of teacher education programs changed significantly.

By 1982, the balance had shifted in the sites and the curriculum of teacher education programs. The shift occurred, to a considerable extent, because of the reduction in the number of sites by the Department of Education and Science. Declining enrollments, precipitated by shifting demographic patterns, were taken into account in planning site reductions. University teacher education sites still accounted for 27 sites, the same figure as in the early 1970s. Essentially, major site reductions occurred in the heterogeneous nonuniversity sector. University students earned baccalaureate degrees, and then those wishing to become teachers pursued professional education courses and practica. Consecutive, rather than concurrent, teacher education was the model at the universities. In the mid-1980s, 54 percent of new teachers were educated in this manner, compared with 22 percent in the late 1970s (Judge, 1984, p. 7; Lynch & Plunkett, 1973, pp. 40–41).

Variations of this model spread to other sites offering baccalaureate degrees, including polytechnic institutes and colleges of higher education. During the 1970s the baccalaureate in education (BEd) emerged as the major "concurrent" route into teaching, particularly in what had formerly been the nonuniversity sector (Bruce, 1985, p. 167). In the late 1980s, the baccalaureate in arts or science, with a major in education, was also present. The salient feature of teacher education programs is the emphasis on the study of academic subjects, not just education courses, when acquiring a baccalaureate degree.

An illustration of this can be noted at the University of Exeter in its typical teacher-preparation program for intending secondary teachers. For example, students registering for science education study additional science (and mathematics) courses, whereas those registering for physical education study English or drama, French, history, mathematics, or science education. For the baccalaureate in education, a 4-year program is undertaken consisting of courses in educational studies each year. During the first year, visits are made to schools to complement the study of the professional aspects of subject teaching. During the second year, professional-education studies continue with a period of teaching practice. In the third and fourth years, there are separate yet overlapping programs of teaching in educational studies, with a long teaching practice (University of Exeter, 1987, p. 53).

Under the rubric of education courses, distinctions may be made among educational studies (educational foundations such as sociology and psychology of education and learning theory and testing); subject methods courses (curriculum), which integrate content and methods; and professional studies (including practica and internships or student teaching).

Although these practices were emerging in the 1970s and 1980s, continuing educational and societal conditions indicated the need for alterations in the structure and curriculum. One example focused on the changing ethnic, racial, and class composition of secondary schools and the subsequent need for teacher training to address such populations. A second example focused on the changing qualifications in the vocations and professions that should be addressed in some fashion in secondary education. A third example concerned the growing emphasis on the distinctions and the integrations of subject matter or content *and* pedagogy. Such illustrations will be explored more fully in the sections on Public and Higher Education Policies and Policy Research Issues.

Methods of Assessment

Broadfoot (1985, pp. 7–8) states that public examinations are a peculiarly English disease, given the scale of the enterprise. Examinations are formalized procedures, distinct from the classroom, that enable successful candidates to receive certificates or diplomas. That is, certification appears to be a salient feature of such examinations. Through the 1970s, secondary students in academic tracks in comprehensive schools and grammar schools took the General Certificate of Education (GCE) *Ordinary*, or O level, examination after approximately 4 years of study. This examination focused on several subjects. If successful on this examination, students could take the *Advanced*, or A level, examination about 2 years later wherein they generally concentrated on two or three subjects to qualify for higher education. From 1965 onward, the Certificate of Secondary Education (CSE) was taken by students in other tracks who were not *qualified* to take the O level examination. The CSE students would leave secondary schools with a certificate, rather than a failure on the O level examinations. For students who achieved a *Grade One* on the CSE, the certificate was equivalent to the O level examinations.

Proponents of the examinations emphasize the need for ritual and competition fostered by the examinations. Moreover, they contend that motivation is enhanced, standards are maintained, and a fair selection mechanism is available. If mechanisms could be devised to use the examinations for assessment and evaluation (two major purposes of examinations), still another benefit might be noted. Evidence does not suggest that examinations were consistently utilized in this fashion. In fact, considerable criticism emerged regarding the several forms of secondary examinations, although the CSE was clearly introduced to provide an opportunity for a certificate for all students. Some of the criticisms focused on the social bias in favor of white middle-class students, to the exclusion of working-class and racial minority students; the inaccuracies and poor predictability of the examinations; the overemphasis on an academic approach to learning; and the considerable incurred expenses (Broadfoot, 1985, p. 9). When preparing for and taking

the examination, students could be "cooled out" of the academic courses in comprehensive schools and eventually out of academic postsecondary options (Holmes, 1985, p. 19).

In 1986, a new examination leading to the General Certification of Secondary Education (GCSE) was introduced for 16-year olds. This examination replaced the GCE and the CSE. Its proponents assert that it is a "fair" method of assessing knowledge and skills garnered in secondary schools (Watson, 1985, p. 3). Given the recent introduction of the GCSE, comprehensive test data results are not available. For teacher education programs, examination issues highlight questions such as the relative importance of teaching a variety of facets of a subject or confining instruction to the official examination syllabi to help students prepare for and take examinations. Individual teacher assessments might become peripheral when there is overemphasis on external examinations. Perhaps the GCSE will actually provide an avenue for teachers to teach subjects and critical skills without an external examination as the looming concern. Skeptics abound.

Within baccalaureate degree teacher-preparation programs, assessments focus on several areas. Assessments and examinations are in the various academic subjects, education courses, and teaching practice. Students are assessed by lectures in their individual academic and education subjects throughout their programs. In concurrent teacher education programs, practica and student teaching are integral components. For example, at the University of Exeter, the following is observed. During the first year, students visit schools, observe classes, and engage in limited teaching. Five weeks of teaching practice are required during the second year, and an entire 10-week term during the third year. A professional-development project focusing on some aspect of school is required and might develop from the teaching practice. During the extensive teaching practice, a local school teacher (usually a teaching tutor or supervisor) and a university lecturer evaluate student performance. Extensive examinations throughout the final year are divided between the academic and education courses and are read by local and external readers (University of Exeter, 1987, pp. 52–53).

For students who hold baccalaureate degrees, a consecutive teacher education program leading to the Post Graduate Certificate in Education may be undertaken. A year of study with a concentration in education courses and teaching practice comprises the majority of the program. Again, for assessment purposes, the local teacher and university lecturer assess the teaching practice. Special options or projects may also be undertaken, for example, on curriculum design or teaching practices in other countries.

The methods of assessing students and content in secondary schools and teacher-preparation programs raise several fundamental research questions. *First,* to what extent is there a clear nexus between the curriculum and assessments in teacher-preparation programs and what students actually teach in secondary schools? For example, Judge (1988, pp. 156–158) asks whether mastery of a subject, ascertained through examinations, is all that is required as preparation for teaching that subject? A different focus emerges when examining assessments of academic subjects and professional education or pedagogy. For instance, assessing potential teachers' knowledge of multiracial and multi-ethnic students is distinct from knowing if the teacher can work effectively with diverse secondary students. In short, what is the relationship between the conceptual or theoretical underpinnings of a teacher-preparation program and the world of practice?

Second, how might the curriculum per se of teacher education programs be examined? Is there a quality blend of professional or clinical experiences through practica and student teaching with intellectual rigor (Judge, 1984, p. 8)? Or does the pendulum swing too far in one direction, so that teachers know how to teach but not what to teach? Are they less certain, for example, about the content of course syllabi? In another vein, what is the hidden or subtle curriculum of teacher-preparation programs, and how can its latent affects be ascertained? For example, despite the Rampton and Swann Committee Reports on the educational needs of different racial groups in England, does the curriculum overlook such needs or convey the impression that all children have similar needs (Jones, 1985, pp. 26–27)?

Third, to what extent can teacher-preparation programs help potential teachers assess the multiple needs of secondary students? Although some academic skills are assessed through formal examinations during the fourth and sixth years of secondary schools, how are social and interpersonal skills assessed? How might improvements in one set of skills complement those in other areas?

Public and Higher Education Policies

The preceding discussion of the structure, curriculum, and methods of assessment in secondary schools and teacher-preparation programs provided clues regarding the development and refinement of public and higher education policies. Some problems and issues that were identified in the discussion of such factors are considered by the government, higher education institutions, and secondary teachers.

In September 1987, the Conservative government's proposed bill introduced what some scholars term the most radical educational measure since the 1944 Education Act. This legislation was introduced several months after the general election wherein Conservatives made educational reform a key issue. Educational reform was to be the first step in the massive overhaul of public welfare and social services. This bill was introduced and became an act in 1988, due to considerable efforts by conservative legislators who wanted the central government to address educational problems that were not being addressed by educators and Local Education Authorities. The role of the central government through the Department of Education and Science would be increased dramatically (McLean, 1988, pp. 1–2; Miller, 1988a, pp. 1–2; 1988b, pp. 1–3; University of Exeter, 1988, p. 1). Opponents asserted that innovation would be stifled by drastically curtailing the powers of the LEAs. A notable example is the Inner London Education Authority (ILEA), which has often been in the forefront of plans for innovations.

Several main stipulations for preuniversity education are included in the act. *First,* there is to be a uniform national curriculum consisting of programs, subjects, and student-attainment targets, which would account for up to 80 percent of pupil time during the compulsory schooling up to age 16. (English public schools are exempt from the national curriculum.) Nationally controlled assessment based upon the national curriculum would be undertaken at select ages from 7 to 16. *Second,* parents can generally have more choice of the school their children attend. Appeals can be made to the Department of Education and Science to alter the admission levels of individual schools. *Third,* individual schools can opt out of Local Education Authority control. *Fourth,* schools may obtain control over internal budgets, including teachers salaries. New powers are to be acquired by the Department of Education and Science (DES) in the determination of curriculum, the testing of students, and the more direct intervention with LEAs (McLean, 1988, pp. 17–19; Miller, 1988b, pp. 5–7). Part of this direct intervention in the curriculum and schools is also an attempt to address the need to provide skilled youth for the increasing demands of a technological and information society and to provide viable employment skills for young adults.

Although teacher education per se was not an initial direct focus of the Education Bill, shifting policy emphases prior to 1987 (upgrading teacher qualifications and acquiring skills very relevant to schools) became evident. From 1985 onward, teacher education institutions were regulated closely by the Department of Education and Science, and it established the national Council for the Accreditation of Teacher Education (CATE). Composed of DES-appointed administrators, teacher trainers, LEA officials, and practicing teachers, CATE advises the Department of Education and Science regarding the *approval* of teacher education courses and programs in universities and the public sector. Approval criteria focus on academic subjects and educational and professional studies including practical experiences in school settings. Educational studies should teach a range of material to enable potential students to work with multiple racial and ethnic groups and to help guard against preconceptions based on gender. The *validation* of the academic merit of courses, programs, and awarding of degrees would still be retained by colleges and universities (Department of Education and Science, 1984, pp. 18–21, 24–26).

Teacher education programs, as part of colleges and universities, were affected by main act provisions regarding higher and further education. In this aspect, major features encompassed:

the restatement of the functions of further and higher education previously . . . under local authority control, and the delegation to the governing bodies of further education colleges; the management of colleges' budget and of responsibility for the appointment and dismissal of staff; the establishment of a University Funding Council to replace the University Grants Committee; [and] new arrangements in relation to academic tenure. (Miller, 1988b, p. 8)

Academic autonomy was essentially left intact. However, components of the act are still under discussion, so academic autonomy might be eroded further.

Within the higher education sector, considerable opposition to the preuniversity and postsecondary provisions is being voiced. In several aspects, the concerns are similar to those of primary and secondary educators. The issues include teacher autonomy, freedom of choice by parents in affecting school curriculum and structure, and local versus national control. Indeed, this last factor appears to be the heart of the debate at all levels and across all types of institutions. The National Association of Teachers in Higher and Further Education and advisors to previous Ministers of Education contend, on the one hand, that the control of central government would increase enormously (McLean, 1988, pp. 21–22; Miller, 1988b, pp. 10–11). On the other hand, others assert that the loss of autonomy and control would not be comparable to that at the preuniversity level. For example, the CATE should have independent autonomy from the national government when reviewing teacher education courses and programs based upon criteria established by professional educators and university faculty. Moreover, the nature of academic freedom in universities, which house nearly one-third of the teacher education programs, provides another mechanism for considerable autonomy (Judge, 1984, p. 6).

The task for teacher education institutions might be designing comprehensive programs that encompass curriculum and practical experiences in response to the changes of the national government as they directly affect secondary education. Providing future teachers with the skills to work in a restricted environment in secondary schools, to respond creatively to the needs of diverse students, and to conduct individual student assessments while teaching the national curriculum (which is the basis of assessment for all 16 year olds) are basic challenges for teacher education programs.

Policy Research Issues

Salient policy research issues focus on internal and external conditions during an era of national reform and transitions within education institutions per se. An initial internal policy research issue for higher education is establishing a mission or direction in light of external sociopolitical conditions, whether through legislative and executive decisions by the national government or through the changing demographic profile of secondary students, and the scholarly *raison d'être* of colleges and universities. What is the *balance* between these two missions or goals? For example, ascertaining the knowledge base for preservice teachers and instruction therein would be part of the scholarly mission of teacher education. Yet this base should be integrally related to the world of practice for secondary teachers that is affected by sociopolitical conditions.

A second internal policy issue focuses on evaluation and assessment, that is, assessments and evaluations for students *and* program evaluation including the structure and curriculum of programs. To what extent might structural changes within the program affect student evaluations? For example, if sociocultural foundations of education courses are taught each year (a change in the curriculum structure of educational studies), might this be reflected in students' increased comprehension of classroom dynamics, which can be assessed during field experiences and practice teaching?

To what degree, should teacher-training colleges and faculties, as part of higher education, seek to be at the forefront in establishing external policies? That is, what are the *interactive* processes between public policies and those developed internally by teacher education professionals? A professor of education from Cambridge University stated that the recommendations and policies that were developed that established the Council for the Accreditation of Teacher Education and the subsequent criteria that were developed for evaluating teacher education programs and courses were only marginally based upon systematic research findings (Tulasiewicz, 1988, Interview). Yet research conducted by teacher education professors could provide the underpinnings for policies that directly affected teacher education programs.

TEACHER EDUCATION IN AUSTRALIA

Purposes of Secondary and Teacher Education

Until the middle of this century, the historical, cultural and political roots of Australia grew primarily out of English traditions. Indeed, it has been stated that Australians perceived themselves as part of the British Empire. Although Australia became independent in 1901, its overall economic and political development was closely linked to that of England through the 1940s, when approximately 90 percent of the residents were of British descent (Inglis, 1986, p. 424; Ogilvie, 1981, p. 328). An Australian national-cosmopolitan view slowly emerged after the World War II, due, in part, to the perceived inability of England to defend Australia from attack and the American "invasion" of the 1940s (Ogilvie, 1981, p. 329). Part of this perspective meant forging economic linkage with other Commonwealth countries, and enhancing domestic economic and political progress.

From the mid-1940s to the mid-1970s, this national-cosmopolitan perspective suggested an increasingly significant role for education. The federal government's involvement was increased with the passage of the 1945 Commonwealth Education Act, which established the Commonwealth Office of Education, which later became the Department of Education and, finally, in 1987 the Department of Employment, Education and Training. This last name change reflects the linkages among employment, education, and training. In 1959, the Australian Universities Act created a Universities Commission; in 1964 the Martin Report (Committee on the Future of Tertiary Education in Australia, 1964) initiated the binary decision, through differential funding, between universities and colleges of education. The 1967 capital grants for teachers colleges was passed, and the 1974 act created the Schools Commission. By the 1970s, several major demographic and economic changes had occurred that would be reflected in the secondary and higher education system.

The demographic changes were evinced through migration patterns and increases in the aboriginal population. From 1947 to 1986, the population increased from 7 to 16 million. Early migrants were primarily from Great Britain and other European nations, due to measures such as the Immigration Restriction Acts (the White Australian Policy), which were altered in the late 1940s but really not abandoned until the 1970s. By 1977 and 1978, for example, 40 percent of the migrants were from Europe. The Middle East, Asia, and South America were the areas of origin of the new immigrants. Approximately 20 percent of the migrants and their children, from 60 plus linguistic groups, could not speak English upon arrival in Australia (Education News, 1981, p. 246; Inglis, 1986, pp. 445–446; Shafer, 1983, pp. 418–420).

By the mid-1980s, the aboriginal population totaled approximately 160,000, or 1 percent of the population. This apparent growth, stemming from increased fertility and persons who identified themselves as aborigines, belied the view that the aborigines were a dying race. This most disadvantaged group (given their deplorable health, welfare, economic, and education conditions) in the society was "granted" full citizenship rights via the 1967 referendum. Through this referendum, responsibilities regarding aboriginal affairs were transferred from the state to the federal level (Inglis, 1986, p. 425; Shafer, 1983, p. 416).

Providing education for indigenous minorities and immigrants, as well as for children of working-class Australians (whose secondary school completion rates were often under 30 percent), was a fundamental challenge to the preuniversity and higher education system. The industrial community and other employers also challenged the education sector to provide a skilled labor force. Yet the burgeoning demographic increases helped contribute to a teacher shortage in the late 1950s and 1960s, which, ironically, became a surplus by the mid-1970s. In short, massive social, economic, and political changes emerged that necessitated comprehensive examinations of education, especially secondary and higher education and teacher training, through several major commissions and reports.

The 1973 Karmel Report, *Schools in Australia*, (Interim Committee for the Australian Schools Commission, 1973) highlights the role of social and cultural variables in relation to instruction and educational outcomes. This report helped contribute to an expansion of educational inputs or provisions for various ethnic and racial groups. The development of alternate and novel curricula and teaching methods through the short-lived national Curriculum Development Centre was one method of providing changes in schools and teacher-training sites (Inglis, 1986, pp. 426–427; Karmel, 1985, pp. 282–283; Keeves, 1987, p. 156). The Williams Report of 1979 (Committee of Inquiry into Education and Training, 1979) emphasizes that universities should concentrate on "most able" students and on graduate studies and research. The unique roles of professional schools were examined, including faculties of education in universities and colleges (Beswick, 1987, pp. 218–219). Colleges of Advanced Education (CAEs) could train persons for select professions (R. King & Young, 1986, pp. 110–111).

More particular attention was devoted to teacher education through the Auchmuty Report of 1980 (National Inquiry into Teacher Education, 1980), which examines the role of practical teaching skills and research on teaching and pedagogy (Beswick, 1987, p. 219). The most recent report of the Joint Review of Teacher Education, *Improving Teacher Education*, (1986) presents several recommendations to improve teaching in schools with a high proportion of socioeconomically disadvantaged students; to implement projects in secondary schools and colleges to increase the participation of women in science and mathematics; to endorse the development and provision of programs designed to enhance the recruitment and preparation of aboriginal teachers; and to review preservice teacher education institutions and programs (pp. 61–63). There were a series of federal and state reports that led to the establishment of the Australian Advisory Committee on Research and Development in Education and its successor, the Education Research and Development Committee (ERDC), which focused on national research concerns. Declining economic circumstances led to the disbanding of the ERDC in the early 1980s (Turney, 1987, pp. 179–180). The Tertiary Education Commission Report of 1981 provides a rationale for merging and consolidating colleges of advanced education, including teacher education programs, among institutions (Foster, 1987, p. 75; Harman, 1986, pp. 572–574). This has largely occurred, and distinctions between colleges of advanced education (CAEs) and universities are blurred.

The National Aboriginal Education Commission issued a report in 1981 that addresses special measures to increase aboriginal participation in higher and teacher education. Teacher-training efforts would be particularly concentrated in the 1985–1988 period, to help reach a target of 1,000 aboriginal teachers by 1990. In 1982, there were only 220 aboriginal teacher education graduates (Inglis, 1986, p. 426; National Aboriginal Education Committee, 1981). The target of training 1,000 aboriginal teachers by 1990 is probably unattainable.

Structure and Curriculum of Secondary Schools and Teacher Education Programs

Secondary schools in Australia are organized into a dual system of public (government) and private (nongovernment) education. The largest types of private schools are those affiliated with Catholic and Protestant churches, although both private and public types receive public funds. Comprehensive public secondary schools provide 5–6 years of education to grade 12 in a variety of academic, vocational, and technical subjects. The curriculum may be viewed in terms of core academic subjects and elective subjects. Private schools provide an academic curriculum through the same levels for approximately 25 percent of the students. Compulsory schooling is required until age 15.

The Australian tertiary education system historically consisted of universities, colleges of advanced education, and technical and further education (TAFE). The binary system of higher education refers to universities and colleges of advanced education, the two sectors that prepare secondary teachers. They were funded by the federal government through the Commonwealth Tertiary Education Commission, now the National Board of Employment, Education, and Training; yet they are administered by state governments (Harman, 1986, p. 570; Joint Review of Teacher Education, 1986, p. 12). There is considerable overlap between universities and CAEs (and between CAEs and TAFE). For example, in the early 1980s about 70 percent of the CAE students were enrolled in baccalaureate or postgraduate programs, rather than in diploma ones, which had been the situation historically. Moreover, mergers have reduced the number of CAEs (from 73 in 1981 to 47 in 1986) while increasing their comprehensiveness and depth (Harman, 1986, pp. 568–570).

Preservice teacher education programs for secondary schools typically occur in one of two forms, concurrent or end-on, as in England. Under the concurrent models, a 4-year degree program incorporates general academic and professional teacher-preparation courses including practical experiences. Under the end-on model, a one-year, concentrated, teacher education program, consisting primarily of professional education courses and a teaching practicum, is pursued after completing an undergraduate degree or perhaps a 3-year, non-teacher education diploma (Joint Review of Teacher Education, 1986, p. 12). At the University of New England, for example, during the 4-year degree program, the student takes general academic subjects in the first year; educational courses (foundations, curriculum, and social psychology) and two specialization subjects (the major) in the second year; and specialization subjects, education courses, and a practicum during the third and fourth years (University of New England, 1987, pp. vii–ix).

As discussed in the previous section, various demographic, economic, and social changes produced a varied profile of secondary students and those who entered higher education. For example, in New South Wales, only 8 percent of aboriginal students completed secondary school. Only 38 percent of aboriginal entrants in teacher education programs completed them (Inglis, 1986, p. 430; Scott, 1985, p. 190). Moreover, secondary teachers are needed in critical fields such as mathematics, science, and English as a second language and to teach in isolated geographical areas (Joint Review of Teacher Education, 1986, pp. 4–5). Such changes underscored the need for alterations in the structure and curriculum of secondary schools and teacher-training programs. The responses of the government and education community to such changes will be discussed later.

Methods of Assessment

Individual classroom assessments are used as students are generally promoted from one grade to the next. Grade repetition is relatively rare, but there is often ability grouping within grades. At the end of the tenth year of secondary education, the Year 10 examination is administered, and the resulting School Certificate is the credential for transferring to the world of work or for completing 2 additional years of secondary education. At the end of the twelfth year, the Higher School Certificate (HSC) is awarded after successful completion of another examination. Generally, external assessments are used for traditional academic subjects, which, in turn, are used to ascertain direct admission into colleges and universities (Holmes, 1979, pp. 71–72; Review Committee on Quality of Education in Australia, 1985, pp. 91–94). The examinations for the Higher School Certificate have pervasive influence on the whole secondary curriculum and usually serve as the overriding criterion for successful learning, as viewed by potential employers and higher education institutions (D'Urso & Smith, 1981, p. 46). Hence, new student assessments after Year 12 based upon collaborative efforts of several local schools, as a viable alternative to the traditional HSC, are not viewed as favorably as those from external assessments.

The retention rates and entrance rates to colleges and universities between public and private schools illustrate significant distinctions. For example, from 1972 to 1982, the retention rates in public secondary schools increased by only 1.4 percent, or from 27.6 percent to 29 percent. During this period, retention rates in Catholic schools increased by 12.3 percent, to 47.5 percent, whereas the retention rates in non-Catholic private schools moved from 86.5 percent to 89.9 percent, an increase of 3.4 percent. Less than 40 percent of the entrants to universities were from public schools. In short, the academic private schools consistently retained a much higher percentage of their students who later entered colleges and universities after completing the Higher School Certificate (R. King & Young, 1986, pp. 101, 105). This is comparable to a similar phenomenon in England.

For university and CAE students in concurrent degree programs, cumulative assessments occur in the various individual subjects or classes. Unlike in the English system of education, comprehensive examinations are not administered for the overall major areas of study; cumulative assessment is the norm. The teaching practica are evaluated each year by a university or CAE lecturer in conjunction with a local supervising teacher. Successful completion of the practicum is mandatory for teacher certification. Similar to the concurrent program, individual faculty who teach end-on courses devise cumulative assessments for individual classes, and the teaching practicum is evaluated by the university faculty and local supervising teacher.

Turney (1987, pp. 191–194) identifies several research issues and problems associated with assessments of teaching practica. Handling disruptive students who need discipline, addressing the needs of multiracial and multicultural students, and facilitating the learning processes of students with disabilities are all practical problems that confront the student teacher during the practicum. Might the practicums be extended or the structure altered to allow ample time to address such needs? Or should methods and curriculum courses attempt to incorporate such issues into their content? In one study, students stated that microteaching, individualized programs, and human relations training might be used in conjunction with teaching practica (Turney, 1987, p. 197). In essence, integrating theory and practice is as fundamental an issue as it is in England.

The report of the Joint Review of Teacher Education (1986, p. 42) stresses the need to examine preservice teacher education programs in a manner similar to current assessments of other academic disciplines in higher education. Issues of content and effective delivery to students and other sectors of the education community are to be examined. For instance, the role of multicultural education is generally recognized for teacher training (Keeves, 1987, p. 147). Should this area be subject specific or permeate various components of the overall curriculum for preservice teachers?

The role of teacher education programs in addressing attrition rates of secondary students, particularly special populations such as aboriginals, where the completion rate is well below 10 percent, is another research and evaluation issue (Inglis, 1986, pp. 431–432). For example, how might various assessments be used for different populations in secondary schools and teacher education? For all secondary students, the blend of cumulative or continuous classroom evaluations by individual teachers with the content of the Year 10 and Year 12 examinations could be analyzed. Considerable emphasis on the external Higher School Certificate has an overwhelming effect on the secondary curriculum and assessments, so that constructive feedback and corrective procedures are not always provided to students after classroom teachers administer tests (D'Urso & Smith, 1981, p. 46; Keeves, 1987, p. 158). Perhaps the ultimate issue is conducting appropriate assessments in light of individual student needs and those of the society (Karmel, 1985, pp. 287–289).

Public and Higher Education Policies

An understanding of the distinct and interrelated roles, functions, and responsibilities of the federal and state governments and higher education institutions, particularly those for teacher education, is essential to this analysis. As stated previously, the federal government provides primary funding (about 85 percent) for the higher education system, although such institutions were established by state legislation and are legally responsible to a state minister and government (Harman, 1986, pp. 569–570; *Higher Education: A Policy Discussion Paper*, 1987, p. 75). In select areas such as aboriginal education, the federal government has overall responsibility. For preservice teacher education, as part of the higher education system, recurrent grants are now allocated through the National Board of Employment, Education, and Training to institutions that determine the detailed distribution of available resources among particular activities. Historically, the federal government has not been involved directly in teacher education, although state involvement has been notable (particularly for CAEs for primary teacher training) in course advisory and accreditation processes (Joint Review of Teacher Education, 1986, p. 17). Program structure, curriculum content, and assessments are the responsibility of the individual colleges and universities.

Due to its finding responsibilities, the Commonwealth government exerts influence on structural changes in higher education through mergers, monitors teacher supply and demand, and approves (or disapproves) courses in higher education that fall within declared classes of new teaching developments. Nevertheless, universities normally maintain autonomy through final decisions on courses. Federal funding is not reappropriated because of university decisions on a few courses. At the state level, the Australian Council on Tertiary Awards, comprised of state and national representatives, is responsible for teacher program accreditation (Joint Review of Teacher Education, 1986, pp. 15, 17–19). The state education depart-

ments also address preservice teacher education by evaluating education programs, including recommendations that all teacher-training programs last at least 4 years; devising methods to attract mature people from a broad cross-section of the community into teacher education; and emphasizing the vital role of the teaching practicum in providing preteaching practical experiences (p. 33).

According to the Minister for Employment, Education, and Training, recent and ongoing mergers *and* critical assessments and recommendations for funding in light of national economic needs are designed to permit flexibility at the institutional level. Determining course offerings, research priorities, and exit criteria through local institutional measures should be enhanced (*Higher Education*, 1987, pp. 27–28, 43). Despite such statements, the higher education community has expressed grave concerns, because economic rationales appear to be the guiding principles. The major universities might not be affected unduly, but CAEs and smaller institutions are in more precarious positions because their size and educational profile are not often broad enough to enable them to continue separate institutional status. Moreover, many faculty in higher education express uneasiness in view of proposals to introduce a ratio of 1 : 10 (of nontenured to tenured staff) at the level of lecturer (equivalent to an assistant professor) and above. In essence, the percentage of fixed-term appointments would also be increased. The conditions of work and morale are declining (*Higher Education* 1987, pp. 27–29, 59, 61; McCulloch & Nichols, 1987, pp. 24–25).

Policy Research Issues

Significant policy research issues encompass the following: (a) content of preservice teacher education programs, (b) mergers and cooperative agreements, (c) centralization and decentralization, (d) special populations, and (e) parameters for research and evaluation in teacher education.

Defining the content of preservice teacher education in relation to the transition, or induction to, actual classroom teaching raises several internal institutional policy considerations. To what extent should an integrative or wholistic approach to teacher education theory and practice be utilized? Or should discrete courses or modules emphasize the facets of theory and practice (Barrie, 1981, pp. 85, 86; Keeves, 1987, p. 160)? When defining the content of programs, institutional means should also be ascertained and utilized to alter policies and procedures. Redesigning the structure and curriculum in response to changes in new technology and the world of work are illustrations of areas where policies and procedures could be altered (Davis, 1981, p. 83).

Policies of the federal and state government produced mergers among various CAEs and between universities and CAEs. Although there were varying degrees of resistance to these mergers (Harman, 1986, pp. 571–572), a practical internal policy issue is developing cooperative agreements among programs and formerly distinct institutions. The key policy and procedural issue is "how to make the mergers work", given that they are a reality. What types of evaluations might be undertaken to alter or enhance internal arrangements?

The issue of mergers and amalgamations highlights the larger issue of centralization versus decentralization, especially in a time of economic constraint. Mergers, reduced funding to the state development program for teachers, and new directions to state Professional Development Program committees could be seen as indexes of national policy decision making. Such national policies "illustrate a move away from the devolutionary principle of encouraging the local identification of needs and the shaping of policy to meet those needs. These moves represent a return to centralisation and to determination of needs at a national level" (Foster, 1987, pp. 75–76).

Special populations most often include racial and ethnic minorities. A range of policy and practical research issues can be cited. The recognition and reexamination of distinctions between the needs of indigenous aboriginal secondary students and preservice teachers and those of recent immigrants to Australia are issues. For example, basic access to secondary and teacher education are salient issues for the former group, whereas diverse linguistic differences are basic issues for the latter groups. This recognition has fiscal policy implications in an era of scarce resources (Inglis, 1986, p. 433; Karmel, 1985, p. 282). Issues of access to, and retention in teacher education programs are of continuous concern for special populations, especially as observed in various government policy statements such as the one to prepare 1,000 aboriginal teachers by 1990 (Joint Review of Teacher Education, 1986, p. 80). The task for universities and CAEs is to help design internal policies, for example, cost-efficient support mechanisms, to lessen attrition among aboriginal students.

Various federal and state government papers and reports highlight the need for further research and evaluation on various aspects of teacher education programs (*Higher Education*, 1987; Joint Review of Teacher Education, 1986). Yet, as in other areas of higher education, research funds are not increasing for teacher education. Hence, the identification of priority research areas and the coordination of research on teacher education assume more paramountcy, especially when bodies such as the Education Research and Development Committee have been disbanded in the mid-1980s (Turney, 1987, pp. 179, 200–201). (The ERDC was the successor to the Australian Advisory Committee on Research and Development, which funded research on teacher education.) Nevertheless, a range of quantitative and qualitative studies are still needed on issues such as the critical skills needed by beginning teachers, the alternate patterns of teacher preparation, the role of practica, and the relationships between teaching and learning (Keeves, 1987, pp. 147–148, 170). Such studies should provide innovative directions for theory and practice for institutional programs and help establish alternate government policies designed to enhance teacher education at the state and federal levels.

TEACHER EDUCATION IN KENYA

Purposes of Secondary and Teacher Education

Prior to Kenya's independence in December of 1963, the country was a colony of Great Britain. As such, it was molded in the English fashion and reflected political and economic initiatives of the British Parliament. During colonialism, the education system functioned primarily for the benefit of the colonial rulers, rather than of Africans. Operating under the colonial motto that the "master's children were to remain masters in the government," the colonial rulers determined the level and type of education that Africans would receive. Thus, during this period, the government educated Africans only to provide the needed support services of a laboring and clerical class. The educational system developed by the British government clearly reflected a segregationist policy. In sum, the three racial groups (African, Asian, and European) would be trained to maintain their respective social statuses, with Europeans trained as supervisors and leaders and Africans trained as servants and laborers (Cheru, 1987, p. 34).

There were some efforts to enlighten Africans through missionary schools and centers where Kenyans were taught to read the Bible, thereby assisting in the spread of Christianity. However, neither the missionary schools nor the colonial education system made an attempt to link African education to development problems or indigenous cultural heritage (Andambi, 1984, p. 2; Rono, 1988, p. 6). Indeed, some Africans believed the missionary schools to be merely cooperating with European settlers by providing a second-rate education intended to force Africans into roles of semirural laborers (Cheru, 1987, p. 34).

As a former British colony, Kenya's education system evolved from English foundations, such as the 1925 Memorandum on Educational Policy in Tropical Africa and the 1944 Education Act. The latter established three levels of schools—primary, secondary, and further—with major examinations at the conclusion of primary school to determine the type of secondary education. The 1944 Educational Act, in variations, transferred to Africa but did not generally provide secondary education for large numbers of Africans (Lindsay, 1980, p. 276; Rono, 1988; p. 6). Specifically, the educational system was designed to limit access to secondary education via stringent examinations and high African dropout rates. Thus, only 2 of every 100 African children entered secondary school (Cheru, 1987, p. 41). Moreover, the English envisioned continued colonial domination; so few Kenyans with secondary education moved into professional or white collar employment that would contribute to national development. Even as late as 1964 there was a shortage of Africans practicing domestically in professions: 36 doctors, 20 electrical engineers, 17 university professors, and 7 economists. Despite the limited access to education and lack of high level manpower, Kenyans and other Africans continued to envisage formal education as a means to an independent country and status equivalent to Europeans.

After independence in 1963, the government began a continual review of the educational system. The 1964 *Report of the Education Commission* (Education Commission, 1964), better known as the Ominde Report, was most influential in the review process. The Ominde Report addressed various educational problems and stressed the changing sociopolitical objectives of education. As a result, several national educational aims were identified: national unity, national development, individual development and self-fulfillment, social equality, respect for and development of cultural heritage, and international consciousness (Cheru, 1987, p. 7; Jomo Kenyatta Foundation, 1973, pp. 1–3). These aims had significant implications for Kenya's diverse ethnic groups, and, in an attempt to achieve national equality, the newly independent Kenyan government abolished racial schools. A further recommendation of the Ominde Report was the development of universal primary education, which would actually be implemented in 1980.

Kenya's independence and the Ominde Report set the stage for the First Development Decade. Objectives and goals for this first decade were developed and covered an array of economic, social, and educational fields as presented in national development plans and annual reports published respectively by the Ministry of Economic Planning and Development and the Ministry of Education (Sifuna, 1983, p. 481). Within the educational realm, priority was given to secondary and tertiary education. Factors that influenced the importance given to secondary education included the need to create and increase a high-level national "elite" who would replace foreign personnel who had directed administrative and commercial tasks; the need to expand technical education and increase personnel in fields like agriculture; and the sociopolitical pressure from the community to expand long-denied higher education. Thus, Kenya's immediate education goals were to produce local workers and education for national development. The scarcity of secondary schools, however, proved to be a critical hindrance to these goals. In 1974 only 58,638 (or 25 percent) of students who were qualified to attend secondary school were admitted. Of the 25 percent, 32,885 (or 56 percent) were admitted into unaided schools. The remaining 168,362 (or 75 percent) left school without any prospect for further education or employment (Cheru, 1987, p. 53).

Kenya's secondary school system was expanded by self-help initiatives and *harambee* schools. Citizens indicated their determination to provide educational facilities by adopting the Kiswahili phrase *harambee*, meaning "let us pull together." Although the government provides modest funds for harambee education, the citizens make major financial contributions including local manpower for building school facilities. In fact, citizens have contributed to the establishment of more than one-half of Kenya's secondary schools (Hill, 1974, p. 117; Korir-Koech, 1986, p. 6). For example, in 1966 there were 206 government-maintained secondary schools and 336 harambee secondary schools. By 1977 the corresponding figures rose to 444 and 1,042, respectively (Cheru, 1987, 9. 62). Yet harambee schools generally provided an education inferior to that of government schools.

During the first 10–15 years of Kenya's independence, school leavers and parents saw education as a means to social and economic advancement. The expansion of secondary and tertiary education prepared workers for entry into prestigious white-collar jobs (Sifuna, 1983, p. 484). However, as the number of graduates increased and the number of job opportunities decreased, school leavers were finding themselves displaced at home in rural areas and facing unemployment in urban centers.

The educational system, especially the curriculum, was held at fault. The curriculum was criticized as being too narrow, emphasizing rote learning through certificate accumulation, lacking practical and creative activities, and catering to the minority who proceed beyond primary education (Andambi, 1984, p. 8). As these criticisms were voiced, the minister of education called for changes in the curriculum and established a committee to examine educational policies. This committee produced the 1976 *Report of the National Committee on Educational Objectives and Policy*, also known as the Gacathi Report (National Committee on Educational Objectives and Policy, 1976).

The Gacathi Report proposed reform for primary education that included 9 years of primary education, strengthened facilities, new examinations, new curriculum, and teacher retraining. This report reiterated that "the optimal objectives and structure of the first cycle of education (pre-primary, primary, junior secondary) implies designing the most favorable structure which is guided by the nation's economic, social, and cultural values" (p. 50). The implications of the report for secondary education and teacher training lie in the facts that educational emphasis was placed on basic primary education rather than on secondary education, thus moving secondary education and associated teacher training from the center.

Structure and Curriculum of Secondary Schools and Teacher Education Programs

Prior to independence, Kenya's educational focus had been on primary education. For example, in 1948 the educational structure consisted of 6 years of primary and 6 years of secondary education. Ominde points out that by 1962:

further changes had taken place, mainly in connection with the primary section of the African system. There were thus two major systems, the African with its eight year primary course, and the rest, including European, Asian and Arab, with a seven year primary structure. (1967, pp. 289–290)

After independence there was a change from 8 years of primary education for Africans to 7 years in the 7-6-3 plan. Under the 7-6-3 structure, students received 7 years of primary (standards 1–7), 6 years of secondary (Forms I–VI), and 3 years of university education. At this time secondary education was greatly expanded and major curriculum changes were implemented. Changes were also made in the teaching methods and the subjects. For example, modern mathematics was introduced, and Kiswahili was no longer compulsory in primary schools. From primary to university levels, emphasis was placed on academic rather than practical skills (Andambi, 1984, p. 7).

Recommendations of the Gacathi Report in 1976 and the University Task Force in 1981 led to the restructuring of Kenya's educational system. In January of 1985, Kenya shifted from a 7-6-3 model to the present 8-4-4 model, which encompasses 8 years of primary, 4 years of secondary, and 4 years of university education. The rationales provided for the new 8-4-4 model included responding to the needs of the country and its people, providing a more relevant curriculum, establishing a more equitable distribution of educational resources, emphasizing technical and vocational training, providing appropriate assessment and evaluation, increasing opportunities for further education and training, and fostering a sense of national unity (Ministry of Education, Science and Technology, 1984, pp. 1–2).

Under the new educational system, the 4-year secondary cycle began in 1986, with Forms V and VI being phased out by 1989. Teacher education programs now require students to take a minimum of 4 years to obtain their first degree. The exception is the last Form VI students of the former system, who will spend 3 years on similar courses (Rono, 1988, p. 14). Thus, in 1990 two groups of students will be considered for admission to the universities, the Form IV students of the 8-4-4 system and the Form VI students of the 7-6-3 system.

Kenyatta University is charged with responsibility for all degree, undergraduate and postgraduate, teacher-training programs. Kenya Science Teachers College also prepares secondary teachers who earn diplomas. Curriculum for the Bachelor of Education degree offered by Kenyatta University contains four components: academic studies, educational studies, pedagogical studies, and practical studies. The academic studies area involves subject disciplines, with courses offered in science, arts, and education (Ministry of Education, Science and Technology, 1984, p. 10). Foundations for educational studies are divided into educational administration, planning and curriculum development, educational communication and technology, and physical education and games (Ayot, 1980, p. 3). Pedagogical methods are designed to address the needs of the teacher in the classroom situation. Courses such as teaching strategies, unit and lesson planning, classroom organization, and methods in educational communication are offered to strengthen teacher skills. The practical-studies component is aimed at providing initial confidence and competence in the art of teaching. Practical studies employ techniques such as peer teaching, microteaching, in-college practice, demonstration teaching, and block teaching practice (Ayot, 1980, p. 4). Similar curricular groupings are offered at Kenya Science Teachers College.

The patterns of training in teacher education programs produced considerable debate. The pedagogical methods proposed in the divergent philosophies of academicians and education policymakers sometimes clashed with particular time and financial limitations. Attempts to reconcile these differences usually led to training patterns in preservice teacher education programs that were either end-on or concurrent (Ayot, 1980, pp. 4–5). These patterns are similar to those in England and Australia. Neither the end-on nor the concurrent pattern is guaranteed to be effective; the key is to develop programs in which the focus is on professional competence, rather than merely on training in concepts and academic fields.

The structure and curriculum of Kenya's secondary education and teacher-training programs were reformed to emphasize the production of highly skilled manpower. This reform reflected Kenya's Second Development Plan, which focused on producing sufficient numbers of people to work in rural and urban settings capable of supporting a high rate of economic growth. This plan for reform through basic education and rural development is quite sound but has accomplished little (Sifuna, 1983, p. 490). There are continuing indications of the need to alter the educational structure and curriculum. Initial indicators of the need to alter the educational structure encompassed a preoccupation with examinations and crowded classrooms, both of which lead to a restricted teaching role. The preoccupation with examinations, especially the Certificate of Primary Education, is understandable in light of the 7-6-3 system. Under this structure, technical and vocational education were not strong postprimary options, putting pressure on students to secure places in secondary schools.

In terms of life chances, students felt compelled to pass the Certificate of Primary Education examination, although it led to repeating. Primary students who repeat standards contribute to crowded classrooms where the teacher–pupil ratio can be as high as 1 to 50. It has been estimated that 35 percent to 40 percent of primary students in the upper standards repeated, later contributing to more crowded secondary schools (Lindsay, 1980, p. 282; Somerset, 1974, pp. 150–151). Such space and content constraints often left teachers unable to devote time to developing and introducing innovative pedagogical methods in secondary schools.

The complications caused by space and content constraints can be further compounded by the lack of educational resources. For example, at a high school in Kisumu there is no school library; only one laboratory which serves Forms I through VI; and an inadequate water system (Otieno, 1985). Training teachers to produce students who are expected to proceed to the university without necessary resources undoubtedly requires specialized curriculum and methods.

Another indicator of the need for educational reform is youth unemployment. Secondary schools failed to equip those leaving with the skills required in the labor market, especially in the area of technology. In fact, harambee institutes of technology were a direct response to the problem of unemployment among secondary school leavers (Keller, 1975). School leavers, being educated but unemployable, attributed this problem to the "white-collar mentality" that encourages youngsters to set their sights on a limited number of civil service and management jobs and reject agricultural or manual work (Cheru, 1987, p. 140).

Although the aforementioned examples are curriculum or program-design issues of pre–higher education, they have direct implications for teacher education. For example, the secondary curriculum would need to be altered (with considerable input from teacher educators) in an effort to work toward national development and simultaneously to increase postschool chances. It would also be necessary to train and prepare secondary teachers to work in diverse and often inadequate secondary settings.

Methods of Assessment

After independence, Kenya, Uganda, and Tanzania collectively assessed secondary students on the basis of two examinations. The East African Certificate Examination was administered after 4 years, and the East African Advanced Certificate Examination after 6 years, of secondary education. During the 1970s each country began administering separate examinations. Administration of two national examinations continued under the Kenyan 7-6-3 and 8-4-4 systems. Students who successfully completed secondary education under the 7-6-3 system were administered the Kenya Certificate of Education Examination, which was offered for the last time in 1987, and the Kenya Advanced Certificate of Education Examination, which was offered for the last time in 1989. The Kenya Junior Secondary Examination, which was offered after 2 years of secondary education for potential primary school educators, has also been eliminated from the 8-4-4 system, being administered for the last time in 1985.

Students of the new 8-4-4 system were offered the Kenya Certificate of Secondary Education Examination (KCSE) for the first time in 1989. It was administered to students recruited to Form I in 1986 who completed 4 years of secondary education in 1989 (Ministry of Education, Science and Technology, 1984, p. 15). The KCSE covers all subjects prescribed in the secondary curriculum: communication (English, Kiswahili, and foreign languages); mathematics; science (physical and biological); humanities (geography, history, government, religious education, social education, and ethics); applied education (agriculture, industrial education, business education, home science, art, and music); and physical education. As in England and Australia, performance on these external assessments is used to determine admission into universities and colleges.

The revisions in Kenya's methods of assessment at the secondary level occurred for several reasons. As Kenya began to emphasize universal primary education in the Second Development Decade, societal demand for secondary education increased. As the number of secondary school leavers increased quickly, the capacities of universities were subsequently diminished. This imbalance forced higher education authorities to limit university entrance (Timar, 1983, p. 406). Thus, secondary examinations became a screening device used primarily for the purpose of selecting university applicants. Indeed, some developing countries tried to curb enthusiasm for higher education by making the secondary school examinations more difficult (Timar, 1983, p. 406). Such action certainly restricts the equitable distribution of educational resources.

The methods of assessment for teacher education programs are quite encompassing. During the 1970s and early 1980s, for example, Kenya Science Teachers College evaluated students on the basis of annual examinations, special projects or independent study, and teaching practice (Lindsay, 1974, p. 87). If a student failed an examination, the course was repeated, and the examination was administered again a year later. Similarly, if the student was judged unsatisfactory in teaching practice, a one-year provisional certificate was awarded, and reevaluation occurred after one year.

Assessment of teacher education students at Kenyatta University means yearly comprehensive subject examinations with external readers, as well as comprehensive examinations with external readers in the final year (Bakuli, 1988). The preservice student teaching lasts 12 weeks and is evaluated by faculty observations (Eshiwani, 1988). The yearly examinations are administered under the auspices of the University Senate. The minimum pass is often 40 percent in a specific content area. If a student fails one subject area but receives a pass on all other subjects, the student can proceed. If the student fails two subjects, supplemental examinations are administered. If supplemental examinations are not passed, the student may repeat the year, but only one time (Bakuli, 1988). (It should be noted that assessment at Kenya Science Teachers College and Kenyatta University are in a transitional state in light of structural changes.)

Research issues regarding assessments concentrate on several areas. First, a primary concern is the lack of well-articulated and substantive documents outlining the processes and procedures to be used in the implementation of assessment programs (Korir-Koech, 1986, p. 10). For example, individual teacher assessments of secondary school students might be used to identify the potential of individuals in terms of future education or employment. A plan for pupil assessment has been formulated and consists of continuous assessment by the Ministry of Education, Science and Technology through the schools and an external examination by the Kenya National Examination Council. This plan, however, tends to be vague, and the relative weights of the continuous assessment and the examinations are not clearly delineated (Rono, 1988, p. 16). Moreover, the role of continuous assessment in and of itself is a technical process that requires well-defined plans and professional training. Teachers and heads of schools are required to report on each student's overall progress from one term to another, as an integral part of the 8-4-4 system. However, the manner in which this assessment is incorporated into the credentialing system, as well as its feasibility, have not been well researched (Korir-Koech, 1986, p. 11).

A second research issue involves the assessment and evaluation of teacher-training programs. Two of the major flaws in current training programs are the lack of skills analysis and the lack of feedback strategies for preservice teachers (Koinage, 1980, p. 5). A successful program requires the differentiation and analysis of teacher roles and the matching of those roles with the skills necessary to perform them. Teacher-training programs train students in higher education settings, observe them in practica, and then certify them to teach. This sequence maintains no contact between the preservice educator and the new inductees. The subsequent transition of the inductee to the world of work is probably not very smooth.

The problems generated by this lack of feedback and evaluation are often further compounded by the erroneous assumption that the teacher's roles are interchangeable; hence a third research concern (Koinage, 1980, p. 4). Teachers' roles and skills are not necessarily the same for all types and levels of teaching, that is, they are not interchangeable. Yet teacher-training programs and procedures have not changed over the years, despite new aims, goals, and objectives of various educational structures. This type of training, which lacks feedback and evaluation, has led to the provision of the same skills, year after year, and to various sets of students in teacher-training programs. Various skills and competencies are seldom differentiated.

A key to proper evaluation in Kenya's educational setting is applied research, which is a fourth issue. It has been suggested that the most important role that research in teacher education could play would be to identify the relationship that exists between given variables such as curriculum, examination, and assessment *and* teacher training (Koinage, 1980, p. 8). This research activity should be conducted in a scientific manner, with data collection, derivation of generalizations, and application to a variety of educational problems.

Public and Higher Education Policies

Kenya's Ministry of Basic Education and Ministry of Higher Education merged in 1983 to become the Ministry of Education, Science and Technology, thereby stressing the relationships of education, science, and technology to national development (Ministry of Education, Science and Technology, 1984, p. 22). The restructured ministry accepted the recommendations of the Presidential Working Party of the Second University (also known as the McKay Report [Ministry of Education, 1981]), which included implementing the 8-4-4 educational model. This was to be one of Kenya's most comprehensive educational reformations. The effects of such reforms are especially visible in the expanded role of the government via the ministry. The pending full implementation of the 8-4-4 plan manifested needs such as expanding teacher-training programs to produce more qualified teachers, addressing problems of unemployment as the number of secondary and university graduates increased, and supplementing physical facilities at all levels. These needs were reflected in particular policy considerations in the areas of curriculum, assessment, and teacher education.

Policies regarding curriculum at the primary and secondary level are to be determined by the ministry. Alterations for preuniversity education in the new educational system include a uniform national curriculum. This curriculum was designed and developed to teach useful skills through practical subjects and provides a heavier dose of technical education (Ministry of Education, Science and Technology, 1984, p. v). This curriculum policy decision, which will be implemented at a national level, will influence the curriculum at teacher-training institutes.

Another policy issue at the preuniversity level focuses on nationally controlled assessment of pupils on a continuous basis. To what extent is this general policy clearly articulated and disseminated to school administrators and teachers throughout the country? Although seminars and workshops were conducted, it is still difficult to ascertain how the policy translates into practice.

The 8-4-4 system also calls for the altering of teacher education programs. Most obvious is the change from a 3-year degree in higher education to a 4-year one. This will be an internal policy issue for universities as they are left to design and develop their own basic degree courses of study (Ministry of Education, Science and Technology, 1984, p. 8). A double-standard policy goes into effect in 1990, as two groups of students apply for admission to the university. The last group of students under the 7-6-3 system will be required to complete

only 3 years of university education to obtain a degree, whereas the first group of 8-4-4 students must complete 4 years of university training to obtain a degree, as noted earlier.

Higher education policies at teacher education colleges and universities will invariably be affected by the new methods of assessment and evaluation, as well as by the curriculum modifications. Selection for teacher-training colleges and universities will be based on the new KCSE, which, in turn, should reflect efficiency of learning under the new curriculum.

Policy Research Issues

An initial policy research issue concerns the equitable distribution of educational resources for all students, regardless of place of origin, race, or creed. In fact, this was an original rationale for shifting to the 8-4-4 educational structure. Kenya is a multi-ethnic country, and it is difficult to insure that the more than 30 ethnic groups throughout the country benefit from the changes. For example, will more educational resources be allocated in certain areas? There are indications that certain regions within Kenya lack the necessary resources. Coast, Northeastern, and Rift Valley provinces often do not have the same educational resources as other provinces (Cheru, 1987, p. 61). For example, in 1985 the Northeastern Region, composed of the districts of Garissa, Mandera, and Wajir, recruited only 48 primary teachers for a province that has 87 schools (Ministry of Education, Science and Technology, 1984, pp. 1, 35–37). Furthermore, the Coast province has employed the highest percentage of untrained teachers.

A second policy research issue address the 8-4-4 model as an altered component of the North American, primarily U.S. model. When this model has been fully implemented in Kenya, "it will have similar elements as that of the U.S.A. where each state/district is responsible for minimum standards, financing and administering its education" (Korir-Koech, 1986, p. 16). It is crucial to the success of the new system that it be sufficiently adapted to the Kenyan context. It has been noted that adapted systems that were inherited or borrowed from industrialized countries led to expansion of formal schools in developing countries but were accompanied by lack of qualitative improvements (Sifuna, 1983, p. 486).

The assumption that national development can be achieved through education and the 8-4-4 program and curriculum gives rise to a third policy issue. This assumption infers discovering and maintaining a balance among vocational, academic, and pedagogical subjects and components. The new system is geared toward developing rural areas through agricultural productivity in a country where agriculture provides employment and income for 80 percent of the population. Reevaluation will be necessary to determine if the curriculum provides the skills and knowledge to enhance national development, rather than cater to the 20 percent of urban pupils with "purely" academic interests (Ministry of Education, Science and Technology, 1984, p. vi).

A fourth policy research issue involves the transition to the teaching profession. Once preservice training has been completed, students are certified to teach. Little contact is maintained with educators or trainers, providing minimal feedback and making the transition to teaching a self-adjusting one (Koinage, 1980, p. 5). Research should address teacher effectiveness at regular intervals after certification, and inservice training could be provided. Similar policy research issues were evident in England and Australia.

A fifth policy research issue is research per se. Educational research in Kenya, as in most developing countries, is fairly limited and must be expanded. Research is necessary to provide a theoretical base for the behavior and learning of students in educational settings. As in developed countries, what is the relationship between methods of teaching secondary students and learning (Koinage, 1980, p. 22)? Quite crucial is the necessity for continuous research to ascertain the changing functions of the new 8-4-4 structure in relation to teacher education for national development. It is, after all, secondary and teacher education that provide most skilled human resources for national development.

GENERIC AND CULTURE-SPECIFIC TEACHER EDUCATION MOTIFS

In the preceding analysis of teacher education in three English-speaking countries, culture-specific and generic motifs emerged. These patterns may be broadly grouped into categories external to teacher education and formal schooling; internal to educational institutions; and requiring careful synthesis of interactive processes between internal and external conditions. The prominent patterns that surfaced are sociopolitical and economic conditions, national reports and initiatives, examinations and curriculum, multiracial and cultural groups, locus of control of teacher education and other education programs, and policy research pertaining to teacher education.

Sociopolitical and economic issues may be envisioned as generic external conditions affecting secondary and teacher education programs. For the three countries, use of education to enhance domestic and international economic conditions was expressed by the business community and government via the national ministry or department that addressed education. In England and Australia, this meant producing secondary and teacher education graduates who could contribute to the skilled and professional work force, which would enable the countries to maintain and enhance domestic and international economic conditions. In Kenya, a developing country, this meant establishing basic conditions so individual citizens and the nation benefit economically. Part of the endeavor in Kenya, as witnessed in Australia, also entailed renaming the Ministry of Education the Ministry of Education, Science and Technology. In both countries, science, technology, and education are more closely linked to economic development.

In several instances, the national governments commissioned major reports and initiatives in response to broad economic and sociopolitical changes. Accountability was a theme continually echoed in England and Australia (Karmel, 1985,

pp. 279, 282), as the reports and initiatives addressed modes of improving the quality of education and the product, that is, the student. Kenyan reports usually concentrated on providing universal and comprehensive education for secondary students and those in teacher education programs. Hence, the recent University Task Force, in conjunction with the Ministry of Education, Science and Technology, established the mechanisms for restructuring the entire Kenyan education system along the American model. The purpose was to provide comprehensive education for all, so that students who exited at each level could contribute to national development.

Major reports and initiatives in the United States echo variations of the accountability theme; for example, *A Nation at Risk* (National Commission on Excellence in Education, 1983), *A Nation Prepared: Teachers for the Twenty-first Century* (Carnegie Forum on Education and the Economy, 1986), and various state reports such as *Improving Undergraduate Teacher Education Programs in Georgia* (External Review Committee for the Improvement of Teacher Education in Georgia, 1986). Moreover, external bodies that specifically evaluate and accredit teacher education programs emphasize excellence and quality of graduates as means of accountability to the profession of teacher educators. The new standards and criteria of the American National Council for Accreditation of Teacher Education and the recently created Council for the Accreditation of Teacher Education in England are illustrations.

Examinations and curriculum for secondary schools and teacher education programs evince the interactive processes between external societal conditions and internal educational programs and structures. In England, the content and focus of the terminal examinations for secondary students, which are administered externally, permeate the entire secondary curriculum. The fairly recent introduction of the GCSE resulted in one comprehensive examination at the end of 4 years of secondary school based upon a national core curriculum. The negative distinctions between the O and the Certificate of Secondary Education might be mitigated. Nevertheless, secondary teachers and teacher educators still express concerns about requiring students to study a national curriculum.

In Australia, the Higher School Certificate is administered externally for those who wish to pursue higher education in universities or teacher education colleges. Similar to England, the external HSC heavily influences the general secondary curriculum and does not permit enough flexibility for individual classroom teachers. The situation was not vastly different in Kenya when examinations were administered at the conclusion of four or six years of secondary education. Under the new Kenyan educational structure, an examination is administered after 4 years of secondary education (as in England with the new GCSE) covering academic and vocational courses that should have been taught in the curriculum. Although there are mixed views regarding the content of a national curriculum in Kenya, there is a consensus that a national curriculum might help ensure similar educational provisions throughout the country.

For the three countries, examinations and assessments of

preservice teachers are largely determined by college or university requirements and faculty in the teacher education program. Therefore, the interactive processes between internal and external processes might be less than those of secondary school assessments and curriculum. Helping intending teachers to respond to the practical realities of secondary school is the mode wherein interactive processes can be witnessed.

The curricula for preservice teacher education programs in England, Australia, and Kenya have historically presented a strong concentration in academic subjects, but this area is now receiving increased attention in the United States. The integration of pedagogy and professional education courses, a historical emphasis in the United States, is now being stressed in the three other English-speaking countries. Teacher education programs and universities in these countries are reasserting their academic right to assess and certify their graduates, and external bodies in the United States are pointing to international reports and establishing certification tests for graduating preservice teachers. For instance, the State Department of Education in Georgia administers the Teacher Certification Test (TCT), which all teachers must pass in their teaching field before being certified by the state. Ironically, the contention is voiced that some teacher education programs are now "teaching for the TCT," a cry similar to that often heard in England and Kenya about terminal secondary examinations.

Multiracial and multi-ethnic groups are a significant portion of the population in the three countries. In the United States, such secondary students are often termed "at risk" because of their high potential for becoming dropouts. High attrition rates were also witnessed in the several international settings. For example, secondary completion rates for aboriginal students are below 10 percent, and in teacher education programs, which draw from a limited pool, the rate is below 40 percent. In some inner-city London schools, completion rates for West Indian males are below 30 percent. Devising components of teacher education curriculum and structures that respond to the needs of special populations is an ongoing educational research issue for higher education. A delicate balance between the special needs of racial and ethnic minority students that helps insure equality *and* quality programs must be maintained in light of sound educational practices and the vociferous statements of critics of educational equality.

Contentions regarding equality assume a different posture in the developing country of Kenya, where race is usually a constant factor. However, small ethnic groups and those located in isolated rural areas often do not have equality of educational opportunity. Equipping potential teachers to address the needs of such special populations in Kenya is a concern for teacher education programs. In short, a synthesis of interactive processes must be taken into account, so the external societal conditions confronting special populations are addressed in teacher education.

Perhaps looking at perspectives regarding locus of control is the clearest way to analyze interactive processes between educational institutions and external bodies such as the Department or Ministry of Education. Central versus decentralized authority appears to be the matter of concern in England.

Under provisions of the 1988 Education Act, the authority of the national Department of Education and Science would be increased, whereas that of Local Education Authorities would be decreased. Classroom teachers, for example, would have less influence on curriculum and student assessments because the overall parameters of these areas would be established by the Department of Education and Science. While national control should not permeate teacher education programs to the extent of that in pre-university education, the challenge for higher education is preparing intending teachers to work effectively in milieux where teacher influence will likely continue to decrease.

In Australia, recent mergers among colleges of advanced education and universities highlight the issue of locus of control. Although the Australian federal government views the mergers as efficient responses to shifting economic constraints, higher education faculty often perceive a lack of participation in decision making and policy formulation. The Kenyan universities that encompass secondary teacher preparation and one other secondary diploma program are national in scope. Hence, local versus national control is not manifested in ways comparable to Australia and England.

In the United States, education is primarily a state or private responsibility, despite the fact that federal regulations govern various aspects of local education. Research funding in higher and teacher education is often a federal responsibility, and the general foci of such research is established by national funding agencies. Affirmative action is also a major federal responsibility, although this federal role is decreasing under Republican presidents. Overall, direct federal control tends to be absent in curriculum and assessment areas. Such issues are determined by the college or university and/or the state teacher certification agency. In contrast with those in England and Australia, American educational reformers and minority scholars advocate central federal control of key structural educational components. History has clearly portrayed the absence of state and local educational provisions for special populations. Federal intervention has mitigated some educational neglect, thereby providing the rationale for centralized control of select issues.

Arrays of research and evaluation themes pertaining to teacher education were presented: the relationship between theory and practice, the transition to the world of work, skill development for preservice teachers to work effectively with multiracial and multi-ethnic populations, and student and program assessments and evaluations. Yet the identification and clear recognition of policy research issues elucidate both interactive processes between external social conditions and those in education institutions within a specific country *and* fundamental cross-national motifs. Policy research issues pertaining to teacher education, whether ascertaining the role of teacher education faculty in developing national policies or devising innovative techniques to respond to national policies, must constantly take into account international trends and culture-specific conditions. Perhaps supranational laws will not be developed, but clarification and comprehension of similar patterns in other nations might be used on the home front.

References

Andambi, M. (1984). *The launching of the 8-4-4 education system* (Review of Literature). Nairobi, Kenya: Kenyatta University College, Bureau of Educational Research.

Ayot, H. O. (1980). *Teacher education in a changing society* (Seminar Paper No. 2040). Nairobi, Kenya: Kenyatta University College, Bureau of Educational Research.

Bakuli, D. (1988, October). Telephone interview with professor from the University of Nairobi, Kenya, in Amherst, Massachusetts.

Barrie, J. (1981). The debate on integrating studies. In S. D'Urso & R. Smith (Eds.), *Changes, issues and prospects in Australian education* (pp. 85–90). St. Lucia, Queensland, Australia: University of Queensland Press.

Beswick, D. (1987). Trends in higher education. In J. P. Keeves (Ed.), *Australian education: Review of recent research.* Sydney: Allen & Unwin.

Broadfoot, P. (1985). Comparative perspectives on the reform examinations. In K. Watson (Ed.), *Key issues in education: Comparative perspectives* (pp. 7–17). London: Croom Helm.

Bruce, M. (1985). Teacher education since 1944: Providing the teachers and controlling the providers. *British Journal of Educational Studies, 33*(2), 164–172.

Bruce, M. (1988). Making the grade or marking time? *Phi Delta Kappan, 69*(5), 383–384.

Carnegie Forum on Education and the Economy, Task Force on Teaching as a Profession (1986). *A nation prepared: Teachers for the 21st century.* New York: Author.

Cheru, F. (1987). *Independence, underdevelopment and unemployment in Kenya.* Lanham, MD: University Press of America.

Committee of Inquiry into Education and Training. (1979). *Report of the Committee of Inquiry into Education and Training* (Williams Report). Canberra, Australia: Australian Government Publishing Service.

Committee of Inquiry into the Education of Children from Ethnic Minority Groups (1981). *West Indian children in our schools* (Rampton Report). London: Her Majesty's Stationery Office.

Committee on the Future of Tertiary Education in Australia (1964). *Tertiary Education in Australia: Report to the Australian Universities Commission* (Martin Report). Melbourne, Australia: Government Printer.

Davis, E. (1981). Curriculum for the 1980s. In S. D'Urso & R. Smith (Eds.), *Changes, issues and prospects in Australian education* (pp. 79–84). St. Lucia, Queensland, Australia: University of Queensland Press.

Department of Education and Science. (1984). *Initial teacher training: Approval of courses.* London: Author.

D'Urso, S., & Smith, R. (1981). *Changes, issues and prospects in Australian education.* St. Lucia, Queensland, Australia: University of Queensland Press.

Education Commission. (1964). *Report of the Education Commission* (Ominde Report). Nairobi, Kenya: Government Printer.

Education News. (1981). Galbally on education and after. In S. D'Urso & R. Smith (Eds.), *Changes, issues and prospects in Australian education* (pp. 245–249). St. Lucia, Queensland, Australia: University of Queensland Press.

Eshiwani, G. S. (1988). *Teacher education in Kenya* (Personal communication). Kenyatta University, Nairobi, Kenya.

External Review Committee for the Improvement of Teacher Education in Georgia. (1986). *Improving undergraduate teacher education programs in Georgia.* Atlanta: University System of Georgia.

Foster, L. (1987). *Australian education: A sociological perspective.* Englewood Cliffs, NJ: Prentice-Hall.

Halls, W. D. (1985). Democratization in secondary and higher education: Some comparative viewpoints. In K. Watson (Ed.), *Key issues in education: Comparative perspectives* (pp. 18–37). London: Croom Helm.

Harman, G. (1986). Restructuring higher education systems through institutional mergers: Australian experience, 1981–1983. *Higher Education, 15,* 567–586.

Higher education: A policy discussion paper. (1987). Canberra: Australian Government Publishing Service.

Hill, M. (1974). Harambee schools in Kitui. *Kenya Education Review, 1* (4), 61–68.

Holmes, B. (1979). *International guide to education systems.* Paris: United National Educational, Scientific and Cultural Organization.

Holmes, B. (1985). *Equality and freedom in education: A comparative study.* London: Allen & Unwin.

Inglis, C. (1986). Australia. *Education and Urban Society, 18*(4), 423–436.

Interim Committee for the Australian Schools Commission. (1973). *Schools in Australia* (Karmel Report). Canberra, Australia: Australian Government Publishing Service.

James Report. (1972). *Teacher Education and Training.* London: Her Majesty's Stationery Office.

Joint Review of Teacher Education. (1986). *Improving teacher education.* Canberra, Australia: Author.

Jomo Kenyatta Foundation. (1973). *Curriculum guides for secondary schools* (vol. 2). Nairobi, Kenya: Author.

Jones, C. (1985). Education in England and Wales: A national system locally administered. In B. Holmes (Ed.), *Equality and freedom in education: A comparative study* (pp. 24–62). London: Allen & Unwin.

Judge, H. (1984, September). *Teacher education in England and Wales.* Paper presented at the meeting of the National Commission for Excellence in Teacher Education, Minneapolis.

Judge, H. (1988). Cross-national perceptions of teachers. *Comparative Education Review, 32*(2), 143–158.

Karmel, P. (1985). Quality and equality in education. *Australian Journal of Education, 29*(3), 279–293.

Keeves, J. (1987). *Australian education: Review of recent research.* Sydney, Australia: Allen & Unwin.

Keller, E. (1975). The role of self help in education for development: The Harambee school movement in Kenya. In M. Holden, Jr. & D. Dresang (Eds.), *What government does* (pp. 209–231). Beverly Hills, CA: Sage.

King, E. (1973). *Other schools and ours.* London: Holt, Rinehart & Winston.

King, R., & Young, R. (1986). *A systematic sociology of Australian education.* Sydney, Australia: Allen & Unwin.

Koinage, J. K. (1980). *The role of research in teacher education in Kenya.* Nairobi, Kenya: Kenyatta University College.

Korir-Koech, M. (1986, March). *Restructuring Kenya's educational system: Implications of following the United States model.* Paper presented at the annual conference of the Comparative and International Education Society, Toronto.

Lindsay, B. (1974). *Kenyan higher education institutions and their social responsibility.* Unpublished doctoral dissertation, University of Massachusetts, Amherst.

Lindsay, B. (1980). Educational testing in Kenya. *Journal of Negro Education, 49*(3), 274–288.

ABOUT THE CONTRIBUTORS

Donna E. Alvermann is Associate Professor in Reading Education and a Fellow in the Institute for Behavioral Research at the University of Georgia. Prior to receiving her PhD in Reading Education from Syracuse University, she taught in the public schools of Texas and New York. She teaches and supervises preservice teachers enrolled in their first field-based reading methods course, teaches graduate-level research courses, and serves as a consultant to state boards of education and school systems throughout the United States.

Theodore E. Andrews is Director, Professional Education for the Superintendent of Public Instruction, State of Washington. He is responsible for administering the Teacher Assistance Program and developing the Model Assessment Programs for the state of Washington. For 8 years he served as president of Andrews-Bryant Inc., a consulting firm located in Washington, DC. Prior to that he was the Director of the Multi-State Consortium on Performance-Based Teacher Education while with the New York State Education Department. He has conducted research in teacher assessment, competency-based teacher education, adult learning, and state certification programs.

Linda L. Bain is Professor of Kinesiology and Physical Education and Dean of the School of Communication and Professional Studies at California State University, Northridge. Her specialty is physical education curriculum theory and design, and her research has focused on the hidden curriculum in physical education and on the socialization of teachers and coaches.

Deborah Loewenberg Ball is Assistant Professor of Teacher Education at Michigan State University and Senior Researcher with the National Center for Research on Teacher Education. Her research focuses on the role of subject-matter knowledge in teaching mathematics, how teachers' knowledge of subject matter interacts with other domains of knowledge in teaching mathematics, and how teachers learn to teach or change their teaching of mathematics. She teaches undergraduate and graduate courses in the Department of Teacher Education; she also teaches third-grade mathematics in a local school. She is interested in helping to forge new relationships between schools and the university and among teachers, teacher educators, and researchers.

James A. Banks is Professor of Education at the University of Washington, Seattle. He is a former Chairman of Curriculum and Instruction and a Past President of the National Council for the Social Studies. Professor Banks is a specialist in social studies and multicultural education and has published widely in these fields. His books include *Teaching Strategies for the Social Studies* (3rd ed.), *Teaching Strategies for Ethnic Studies* (4th ed.), *Multiethnic Education: Theory and Practice* (2nd ed.), and (with Cherry A. McGee Banks) *Multicultural Education: Issues and Perspectives*.

Susan Barnes is an Assistant Dean in the School of Education and a member of the Curriculum and Instruction faculty at Southwest Texas State University. She formerly served as the Director of Teacher Education and the Director of Programs for Teacher Appraisal for the Texas Education Agency. She also served as the Assistant Director of the Research in Teacher Education Program at the Research and Development Center for Teacher Education at The University of Texas at Austin. Her research interests include induction, teacher evaluation, and the study of teaching.

Theresa M. Bey is Associate Professor of Instructional Supervision in the Department of Curriculum and Supervision at the University of Georgia. She has consulted with teachers and administrators across the United States. Her research interests include the training of mentor teachers, teacher effectiveness, and student underachievement. She is active in the Association of Teacher Educators and serves as Chair of the Commission on the Role and Preparation of Mentor Teachers.

Eunice Boardman is Director of the School of Music and Professor of Music and Education at the University of Illinois—Urbana—Champaign. Her primary research interest is in the application of learning theory to music instruction for young children. Recent publications include *Holt Music* (an elementary textbook series for kindergarten through eighth grade) and *Musical Growth in the Elementary Schools*. She is currently editing a book, *Dimensions of Musical Thinking*, for the Music Educators National Conference. In 1986–1987 she served as the Chair of the Society for Music Teacher Education.

Kathryn M. Borman is Associate Dean of Graduate Studies and Research, and Professor of Education and Sociology in the College of Education, University of Cincinnati. She is Past President of the American Educational Studies Association and Co-editor of its new journal, *Educational Foundations*. She has had a career-long interest in the role of educational foundations in the preparation of teachers. Her current research agenda includes the transition from school to work for adolescents. She and a number of her colleagues are investigating influences on literacy learning of urban black and Appalachian elementary school students through a regents' sponsored program, The Center for Research on Literacy and Schooling in the College of Education.

Douglas Brooks is Chair/Professor of the Department of Teacher Education in the School of Education and Allied Professions, Miami University, Oxford, Ohio. He received the PhD from Northwestern University in Educational Psychology. His research has explored novice–expert teacher verbal and nonverbal behavioral expression. He was editor of the 1987 ATE National Commission on Induction monograph, *Teacher Induction: A New Beginning*, and guest editor of Kappa Delta Pi's award-winning theme issue of *The Record*, "Teaching: The First Year." His research program has utilized videotape technology and influenced the development of preservice programs that apply this technology to teacher preparation.

Stephen I. Brown is Professor of Philosophy of Education and Mathematics Education at the State University of New York at Buffalo. He has served on the editorial boards of a number of prestigious journals. He is the author of *Some "Prime" Comparisons* and *Student Generations*, editor of *Creative Problem Solving*, co-author (with Marion Walter) of *The Art of Problem Posing*, and co-editor (with Mary E. Finn) of *Readings in Progressive Education: A Movement and its Professional Journal*. He was the recipient of a John Dewey Senior Fellowship during the 1986–1987 academic year.

Margret Buchmann is Senior Researcher of the Institute for Research on Teaching and Professor in the Department of Teacher Education at Michigan State University. With a background in philosophy and sociology, she has conducted conceptual and empirical work on the contributions of formal knowledge and experience in teaching and learning to teach. Her current research interests include the foundations of teacher education curriculum and conceptions of teacher thinking, knowledge, and judgment. Her work on knowledge utilization and research communication, teaching knowledge and the teaching role, practical arguments and contemplation has appeared in numerous books and journals inside and outside the United States.

Paul R. Burden is Associate Professor and Assistant Head of the Division of Teacher Education at Kansas State University. He is editor of the *Journal of Staff Development*, author of *Establishing Career Ladders for Teaching*, co-author of *Developing Career Ladders in Teaching*, and author of several book chapters and journal articles.

William I. Burke is Associate Dean for Teacher Education at the University of North Carolina—Chapel Hill. He received his EdD from the University of Florida. At the University of North Carolina he has developed several experimental teacher education programs. His major research activity is the development of a longitudinal data base for teacher education. Prior to his appointment to the University of North Carolina, he directed a Teacher Corps project and an Upward Bound project and served as an elementary and high school teacher and principal.

Kathy Carter is Assistant Professor in Teaching and Teacher Education at the University of Arizona. She is an Advisory Editor of the *Elementary School Journal* and has served on several committees of the American Educational Research Association. Her articles have appeared in numerous journals. Her current work focuses on studies of teachers' knowledge and the development of a case literature for teacher education.

David L. Clark is William Clay Parrish, Jr., Professor of Education in the Curry School of Education, University of Virginia. His research and writing are primarily in the areas of policy studies and organizational theory. He serves as Executive Director of the National Policy Board on Educational Administration and Co-director of the Policy Studies Center of the University Council for Educational Administration. His most recent publications are *An Assessment of Changes in Federal Education Policy During the Reagan Administration*, *Paradoxical Choice Options in Organizations* (both with T. A. Astuto), and *Renouncing Bureaucracy: A Democratic Structure for Leadership in Schools* (with J. M. Meloy).

Renee T. Clift is Assistant Professor of Curriculum and Instruction at the University of Houston. Her research interests include the process of learning to teach and the factors that influence that process. She has been involved in the development of a preservice teacher education curriculum that encourages reflective inquiry through interdepartmental collaboration and collaboration with public schools. Research on this program has been supported by an OERI grant. This endeavor led to a second project supported by a Danforth Foundation grant in school site-based management that encourages teachers and administrators to collaborate for the improvement of teaching. Her recent publications include *Touch the Future: Teach!* (with W. R. Houston, H. J. Freiberg, and A. R. Warner), *Encouraging Reflective Practice: An Examination of Issues and Exemplars* (co-edited with W. R. Houston and M. Pugach), and journal articles on collaboration in teacher education.

Thomas J. Cooney is Professor of Mathematics Education at the University of Georgia. Dr. Cooney has co-authored two methods texts and a geometry text and authored numerous publications on research, mathematics teaching, and teacher education. He is co-editor of three monographs on research on teaching mathematics; issue editor of the NCTM yearbook, *Mathematics Teaching and Learning in the 1990's*; and a frequent speaker at national and international meetings including the last four international Congresses on Mathematical Education. He is past president of the School Science and Mathematics Association, former NSF program manager for research in science education, a member of the United States Commission on Mathmatical Instruction, and a member of the task force that developed NCTM's recent *Curriculum and Evaluation Standards for School Mathematics*. He has conducted research with Stephen Brown on mathematics teachers' beliefs from a humanistic perspective.

Dean C. Corrigan is Professor and former Dean of the College of Education, Texas A&M University. Previously, he served as Dean of Education at the University of Maryland and the University of Vermont. His vita includes more than 100 scholarly publications. He is Past President of the American Association of Colleges for Teacher Education, Past Chairman of the National Council for the Accreditation of Teacher Education, President of the National Association of Colleges and Schools of Education in State Universities and Land Grant Colleges, and member of the Executive Committee of the Holmes Group. He served as a member of the Select Committee on Public Education in Texas, currently serves as a member of the National Committee for Economic Development Subcommittee on Business and Schools, and has been named to a 3-year term on the National Technology Medal Nomination Committee by the Secretary of Commerce.

Among his honors, he was cited as "Educator of the Year" by the Maryland Association of Teacher Educators in 1978 and, 4 years earlier, received the "Distinguished Leader Award" from the national Association of Teacher Educators. He was awarded the Ted Booker Memorial Award as Outstanding Educator in Texas for 1983–1984 by the Texas Society of College Teachers of Education.

Ronald G. Corwin is Professor of Sociology at The Ohio State University, where he has taught since receiving his PhD from the University of Minnesota. He also taught at Teachers College, Columbia University, and in 1967 was appointed Acting Director for Basic Research, U.S. Office of Education. He has served as Associate Editor of *Sociology of Education* and Chair of the Sociology of Education Section of the American Educational Research Association. Author of *The Organization-Society Nexus* (Greenwood Press, 1987), he is currently editor of the annual series, *Research in Sociology of Education and Socialization* (JAI Press). His other books include *Militant Professionalism, Reform and Organizational Survival*, and *A Sociology of Education*. In 1976, he was ranked by specialists in his field among individuals who have made "the greatest contributions to the growth and development of the sociology of education over the past 25 years."

James R. Craig received his PhD in experimental psychology from Iowa State University in 1969 and currently is Professor of Psychology at Western Kentucky University. His professional interests are in the development of evaluation techniques and procedures and in the application of evaluation procedures in a variety of situations such as evaluating youth drug abuse prevention programs, assessing teacher effectiveness, and determining training program outcomes. He recently served as the Director of Research for the Kentucky Career Ladder Commission, and he has provided a variety of evaluation services to local, state, and national organizations. He is co-author of *Methods of Psychological Research* and *Methods of Psychological Research* (2nd ed).

Donald R. Cruickshank is Professor of Teacher Education at The Ohio State University, where he teaches doctoral courses in teacher education. His scholarship has primarily focused on teacher problems and teacher clarity. Related development and research activities have made contributions to knowledge with regard to the use of simulations, protocol materials, and reflective teaching in teacher education. His most recent book is *Research That Informs Teaching and Teacher Education*. He has been a Senior Fulbright Scholar in Australia and Brazil.

Linda Darling-Hammond is Professor, Teachers College, Columbia University, and formerly Director of the RAND Corporation's Education and Human Resources Program. Her professional interests focus on educational research and policy analysis. She has conducted numerous studies of the effects of educational policies on state and local education agencies, on classroom teaching, and on the working conditions of teachers. Her recent work includes studies of teacher evaluation and selection practices, teacher supply and demand, development of educational indicators, and teacher competency testing policies.

She has been Director of the National Urban Coalition's Excellence in Education Program, where she conducted research on exemplary city school programs and urban school finance issues. She has served as a Visiting Professor in Temple University's Graduate School of Education and as Associate Editor of *Cross Reference: A Journal of Public Policy and Multi-Cultural Education*, and she currently serves as At-Large member of the AERA Council, member of the editorial advisory boards for *Educational Researcher* and the *American Journal of Education*, and member of the National Academy of Education.

She began her career as a public school teacher and was cofounder of a preschool and day care center. She received her B.A. magna cum laude from Yale University and her doctorate in urban education, with highest distinction, from Temple University. She was the recipient of the Phi Delta Kappa George E. Walk Award for the most outstanding dissertation in the field of education in 1978 and of the American Educational Research Association's Research Review Award in 1985.

D. Jack Davis is Professor of Art and Vice Provost/Associate Vice President for Academic Affairs at the University of

North Texas. He is President of the Texas Art Education Association and a Former Board Member and Director of the Higher Education Division of the National Art Education Association. His work on research trends in art and art education and curriculum development and evaluation in art has appeared in numerous journal articles and edited works.

Christopher J. Dede is Professor of Educational Foundations at the University of Houston—Clear Lake and Director of its Advanced Knowledge Transfer Project. He founded the Education Section of the World Future Society and initiated America's first and third graduate degree programs in futures research. Under the sponsorship of the U.S. Information Agency, he conducted workshops in nine countries on the future of American education. For a year, he was a Policy Fellow in strategic planning at the National Institute of Education. His other major professional focus is artificial intelligence applications to education, which has led to Visiting Scientist positions at MIT and at NASA.

Walter Doyle is Professor in the College of Education at the University of Arizona. He was Associate Editor of the *Elementary School Journal* and the *American Educational Research Journal*, and Vice President of Division K (Teaching and Teacher Education) of the American Educational Research Association. He is a specialist in classroom research, with interests in the areas of classroom management, academic work, curriculum theory, and teacher education pedagogy. His publications include *Focus on Teaching* (with Tom Good), "Academic Work" in the *Review of Educational Research*, "Content Representation in Teachers' Definitions of Academic Work" in the *Journal of Curriculum Studies*, and "Classroom Management" in the *Handbook of Research on Teaching* (3rd ed.).

Roy A. Edelfelt is a Clinical Professor at the University of North Carolina at Chapel Hill and partner in Edelfelt Johnson, a free-lance education enterprise. He holds an EdD from Teachers College, Columbia University. After public school teaching, he taught at the State University of New York at Oneonta, St. Cloud State College in Minnesota, and Michigan State University. He is a former executive secretary of the National Commission on Teacher Education and Professional Standards and staff associate in the National Education Association's Division of Instruction and Professional Development. He is the author of numerous articles and has written or edited several pamphlets and books.

Sharon Feiman-Nemser is Professor of Teacher Education at Michigan State University and Senior Researcher at the National Center for Research on Teacher Education. Since receiving her doctorate at Teachers College, Columbia University, she has been directly involved in the study and practice of teacher education and the education of educators. She directed the MST program at the University of Chicago, developed the required introductory course at Michigan State, pioneered descriptive/analytic research on teacher centers, learning to teach, and the preservice curriculum. Her publications include "Pitfalls of Experience in Learning to Teach," "The Cultures of Teaching," and *Teacher Centers: What Place in Education?*

Robert E. Floden is Professor of Teacher Education and Educational Psychology and Assistant to the Dean for Graduate Studies in the College of Education, Michigan State University. He is also Associate Director of the National Center for Research on Teacher Education, where he is studying teachers' learning and the academic purposes and character of teacher education. Recent publications include "Preparing Teachers for Uncertainty" (with C. M. Clark) in *Teachers College Record* and "Instructional Leadership at the District Level: A Closer Look at Autonomy and Control" (with Porter, Alford, Freeman, Irwin, Schmidt, and Schwille) in the *Educational Administration Quarterly*.

H. Jerome Freiberg is Professor of Curriculum and Instruction in the College of Education at the University of Houston. He is Director, Institute for Research on Urban Schooling and editor of the *Journal of Classroom Interaction*. He directed a Teacher Corps project from 1976 to 1982 and has been the principal investigator and director of nearly $2 million in research and training grants. He is the President of the Classroom Observation Special Interest Group for the American Educational Research Association. He has published in more than 50 books, in chapters, in monographs, and in journals. His latest books are *Touch the Future: Teach!* (with W. R. Houston, R. T. Clift, and A. R. Warner) and *Images of Reflection in Teacher Education* (edited with H. C. Waxman, J. C. Vaughan, and M. Weil).

Gary R. Galluzzo is Associate Professor of Teacher Education at Western Kentucky University. He did his graduate work at Syracuse University. His primary research interests include program development and program evaluation in teacher education and the development of beginning teachers. He is a member of the Research and Information Committee of the American Association of Colleges for Teacher Education and a coresearcher on the Research About Teacher Education Project.

Eugene Garcia is Chairperson of the Board of Studies in Education and Professor of Education and Psychology at the University of California, Santa Cruz. He received his BA from the University of Kansas and served as a Post Doctoral Fellow in Human Development at Harvard University and as a National Research Council Fellow. He has been a faculty member at the University of Utah; the University of California, Santa Barbara; and Arizona State University. He was editor of *NABE Journal* and is the author of *Bilingualism in Early Childhood; Language Minority Education in the United States*, and the editor of *Advances in Bilingual Education Research, Language and Literacy Research in Bilingual Education*, and *The Mexican American Child*.

Mark B. Ginsburg is Director of the Institute for International Studies in Education and Associate Professor in the Comparative Sociology of Education, Administrative and Policy Studies Department, University of Pittsburgh. His research interests focus on the occupational and political socialization of teachers, the ideology and practice of educators as workers and political actors, and the connections between education and unequal class, race, and gender relations. Recent publications include *Contradictions in Teacher Education and Society: A Critical Analysis.*

Carl D. Glickman is Director of the Program for School Improvement and Professor of Curriculum and Supervision at the University of Georgia. His research focuses on shared governance of instruction, developmental levels of school improvement, and the school as the center of action research. He serves on several national commissions dealing with the restructuring of schools and is the author of books and articles on instructional leadership, supervision, and school reform. The second edition of his book *Supervision of Instruction: A Developmental Approach* has been recently published.

Jennifer M. Gore, Doctoral student in the Department of Curriculum and Instruction, University of Wisconsin—Madison, was formerly a lecturer at the University of Queensland, Australia. Her interests include teacher socialization and reflective teaching. Her doctoral research is aimed at clarifying the currently fragmented and ambiguous discourses of critical and feminist pedagogies.

Carl A. Grant is Professor in the Department of Curriculum and Instruction and Chair of the Department of Afro-American Studies at the University Wisconsin—Madison. His major professional interests include multicultural education; race, social class and gender, and school life; and preservice and inservice education. Among his books are *Making Choices for Multicultural Education: Five Approaches to Race, Class and Gender*, and *After the School Bell Rings* (both with Christine Sleeter), *Preparing for Reflective Teaching, Bringing Teaching to Life*, and *Community Participation in Education.* His forthcoming book (with Christine Sleeter) is *Turning on Learning.*

Edith Guyton is Director of Educational Field Experience at Georgia State University. She has served as Chairperson of the National Field Directors Forum and President of her state and regional ATE. Her primary research interests are in the areas of field experiences, mentoring, induction and alternative certification programs, and teacher education standards. She was coordinator of mentor education and research director for the Georgia Alternative Certification Institute, 1988–1989.

Martin Haberman, Professor of Education, University of Wisconsin—Milwaukee, is a teacher educator. In addition to very extensive publications, media involvement, and research production, he has played a significant role in shaping almost every major development in teacher education: MAT programs, the original model on which the National Teacher Corps was based, the Trainers of Teacher Trainers Program, NDEA Institutes, Professional Development Centers, Alternative Certification Programs and, currently, a range of pre- and inservice programs. Most recently, he has worked with AFT units developing teacher education programs to be offered under the aegis of urban teachers' unions.

His primary focus is on preparing teachers for urban schools at both the pre- and inservice levels. His work can be characterized by several constant themes: broadening access to better educational opportunities, making the content of programs more multicultural, and involving classroom teachers as the senior partners in teacher preparation and school-improvement efforts. In January, 1989, he received an honorary doctorate from Rhode Island College.

Willis D. Hawley, is Professor of Education and Political Science and former Dean of Peabody College of Vanderbilt University. He received the PhD, with distinction, from the University of California, Berkeley. He taught at Yale and Duke universities before going to Vanderbilt in 1980. He is the author or co-author of *Nonpartisan Elections and the Case for Party Politics, Theoretical Perspectives on Urban Politics, Strategies for Effective School Desegregation—Lessons from Research, Good Schools, The Politics of Government Reorganization,* and *New Directors for Teacher Education in the United States.* He has published numerous articles and contributed to books dealing with teacher education, school reform, urban politics, political learning, organizational change, and educational policy. He has edited several books, including *The Search for Community Power; Improving the Quality of Urban Management; The Courts, Social Science and School Desegregation;* and *The Consequences of School Desegregation.*

He served as Director of Education Studies, President's Reorganization Project, Executive Office of the President of the United States; consultant to numerous public agencies including the U.S. Office of Management and Budget, the U.S. Department of Health, Education and Welfare, the U.S. Senate Committee on Labor and Human Resources, the U.S. Department of Education; and many state and local governments.

W. Robert Houston is Professor and Associate Dean for Academic Affairs, College of Education, University of Houston, where he is concerned primarily with teacher education. He has been principal investigator of 24 major multi-year externally funded, research and development projects that have explored competency-based teacher education, teacher centers, needs assessment for staff development, school-based teacher educators, mid-life career changes into teaching, and reflective inquiry in teacher education. He has authored or co-authored 37 books, nearly 100 chapters and journal articles, 67 research reports and monographs, and 38 multimedia training programs. He has consulted and spoken on teacher education, competency-based education, and elementary mathematics education, working with schools, state departments, and universities in 42 states and 17 foreign countries.

He has been a teacher and administrator in elementary and secondary schools, as well as at the university level at Michigan State University and the University of Houston. He received the BS and the MEd degrees from North Texas State University and the EdD from The University of Texas.

In 1975, The University of Texas honored him as the

outstanding education alumnus of the year. All four Texas teacher education organizations have honored him by bestowing their annual award for distinguished contributions to education: Texas Association of Teacher Educators (1978), Texas Cooperative Teacher Center Network (1982), Texas Society of College Teachers of Education (1987), and Texas Association of Colleges for Teacher Education (1988). Other awards for educational contributions were from District IV, Texas State Teachers Association (1981) and American Council of Life Insurance (1982), and in 1979 the TC-TCN honored him as its founder. During 1985–1986, he was President of the national Association of Teacher Educators. He has been president of several state organizations and a member of national committees and commissions.

Kenneth R. Howey is Professor of Education at The Ohio State University. His research and development interests focus on the education of teachers, both preservice preparation and continuing professional development. He is the research editor of the *Journal of Teacher Education* and the chair of the AACTE committee, which is conducting the longitudinal Research About Teacher Education (RATE) studies. He is the author or co-author of over 90 publications concerned with teacher education, including six books.

Leslie Huling-Austin is the Director of the LBJ Institute for the Improvement of Teaching and Learning at Southwest Texas State University, where she also teaches in the Secondary Education Program. She has done extensive research and writing focused on beginning teachers and teacher-induction programs and has served as a member of the Association of Teacher Educators' national Commission on the Induction Process. Prior to joining the faculty at SWTU, she was Director of the Strategies for Improving Teacher Education Program at the Research and Development Center for Teacher Education at The University of Texas at Austin. In this capacity she coordinated a national Teacher Induction Network and managed a national collaborative teacher induction study involving 26 institutions. Her other research interests are in the areas of school improvement and the educational change process.

Doug Jones is currently project director of the NSF-sponsored research project "Learning to Teach Mathematics: The Evolution of Novice Teachers' Instructional Decisions and Actions" at Virginia Polytechnic Institute and State University. He is also pursuing a doctorate in mathematics education at the University of Georgia. His research interests include the characterization of mathematics teachers' claims (their beliefs and knowledge) and the reciprocal influence of these claims and the teachers' instruction. He has made presentations about mathematics education and mathematics teacher education at various regional, national, and international conferences. He is co-author of various articles related to teaching mathematics and to research in mathematics education, and he has served as a reviewer for the *Journal for Research in Mathematics Education* and *Theory and Research in Social Education*.

Mary M. Kennedy is Director of the National Center on Teacher Education and a professor at Michigan State University. Before joining the center, her research was oriented mainly toward policy-making audiences. She has conducted research on policies related to the effect of evaluation and testing requirements on school districts, education for the disadvantaged, special education, and dissemination of effective practices. She has a continuing interest in the role of evaluation and research in improving educational policies and practices, and she has written extensively on the contributions of research to practice and to thought.

Thomas W. Kopp is Assistant Professor of Instructional Technology in the Teacher Education Department of Miami University. He received his PhD in Instructional Design from Syracuse University in 1982. A researcher in the area of human motivation in instructional design, he is the author of several articles on the use of technology to stimulate learner curiosity and attention. Dr. Kopp recently co-authored a chapter entitled "An Application of the ARCS Model of Motivational Design" that appeared in the award winning book *Instructional Theories in Action*, edited by Charles Reigeluth. He currently serves on the International Board of Standards for Training, Performance, and Instruction. He has extended his explorations of the applications of instructional design theory into the corporate sector, where he currently serves on the International Board of Standards for Training, Performance, and Instruction.

Theodore J. Kowalski is Dean of Teachers College and Professor of Curriculum at Ball State University. Prior to coming to Ball State, he was a public school teacher, a principal, and a superintendent. He has taught at Purdue and Saint Louis universities, serving as director of educational leadership studies at Saint Louis University. The author of many books, chapters, and articles, he is author of *Organizing and Planning Adult Education* and coauthor of *Case Studies on Teaching*. Dean Kowalski serves on the editorial boards of three professional journals and on several boards of directors of professional organizations.

Judith J. Lambrecht is Professor of Business Education in the Department of Vocational and Technical Education at the University of Minnesota, St. Paul. Her teaching and research is related to preparing business teachers to teach office systems and office technology. She is former editor of *The Delta Pi Epsilon Journal* and co-author of *Business and Office Education: Review and Synthesis of Research*.

Beverly Lindsay is the Associate Dean for Academic Affairs and Professor at the College of Education, University of Georgia, and President of the Comparative and International Education Society of America. Her PhD is in Administration and Management and her EdD is in Comparative Sociology of Education. She was an American Council on Education Fellow and Senior Researcher at the National Institute of Education, where she was a staff consultant to the National Commission on Excellence in Education, which produced *A Nation at Risk*. She was also the Special Assistant to the Vice President for Academic Services, Pennsylvania State University, where she held a graduate faculty appointment. Over 45 of her publications have appeared in refereed journals and academic publications. Her original anthologies are *African Migration and National Development* and *Comparative Perspectives of Third World Women: The Impact of Race, Sex, and Class*. Her research focuses on comparative sociology of education and public policies in developing countries and the United States.

Susan Loucks-Horsley is Program Director for Teacher Development at The Regional Laboratory for Educational Improvement of the Northeast and Islands and Associate Director of The National Center for Improving Science Education. Her research and development interests include innovation and change, staff development, and program improvement. Codeveloper of the Concerns-Based Adoption Model while at the Texas Research and Development Center for Teacher Education, her focus on narrowing the gap between research and practice has resulted in two recent publications: *An Action Guide to Improvement* and *Continuing to Learn: A Guidebook for Teacher Development*.

G. Williamson McDiarmid, Associate Professor of Teacher Education at Michigan State University, is Associate Director of the National Center for Research on Teacher Education. Formerly at the Center for Cross-Cultural Studies at the University of Alaska-Fairbanks, he has taught at both the elementary and secondary levels in the United States and abroad. Currently, he teaches both undergraduate and graduate courses in teacher education. His interest in the knowledge teachers possess and how they come to acquire that knowledge includes the role that liberal arts education plays in their understanding of specific subject matter. McDiarmid's work also focuses on how to increase teachers' capacity to assist culturally different students in understanding subject matter in ways that such students find meaningful.

D. John McIntyre is Professor of Curriculum and Instruction and Director of the Teaching Skills Laboratory at Southern Illinois University at Carbondale. His research interests include teachers' reflective thinking, teaching contexts, instructional supervision, and teacher education practices. He was a recipient of the Association of Teacher Educators' Research in Teacher Education Award in 1986 and is a former executive board member of the association.

Robert F. McNergney is Associate Professor of Educational Studies and Director of the Commonwealth Center for the Education of Teachers, University of Virginia and James Madison University. His research interests include teacher evaluation and teacher–student interaction. He was the first Secretary of Division K (Teaching and Teacher Education) in the American Educational Research Association. He writes a regular column (with Martin Haberman) for *NEA Today* called "Research Clues." He is co-author of *Teacher*

Development (with Carol Carrier) and editor of *Guide to Classroom Teaching*.

Kim Kenneth Metcalf is Assistant Professor of Elementary and Secondary Education at Southwest Missouri State University. His research and scholarly interests include general teacher education, field laboratory, clinical experiences in professional education, and professional skill development. His dissertation involved the development and field testing of a regimen intended to make teachers more clear in their presentations.

Roy C. O'Donnell is Professor of Language Education and Department Chairman at the University of Georgia. He has served as Chairman of the Committee on Research, National Council of Teachers of English, Trustee of the NCTE Research Foundation, and President of the National Conference on Research in English. He is the author of numerous journal articles and research reports on language learning and teaching and a former editor of *Research in the Teaching of English*.

Walter C. Parker is Associate Professor of Social Studies Education and Director of the Center for the Study of Civic Intelligence at the University of Washington in Seattle. His work on thoughtful learning in social studies, citizenship education, and teachers' mediation of curriculum innovations has appeared in numerous journals. His forthcoming book is *Planning the Social Studies Curriculum: Toward Civic Virtue*.

John E. Penick is Professor of Science Education and Director of Secondary Science Teaching at the University of Iowa. Author or co-author of more than 160 articles and chapters, he received the ATES Outstanding Science Educator award in 1987. He has also received two Ohaus Awards from NSTA for Innovations in College Science Teaching, a Distinguished Alumni Award from Florida State University, and an award for Best Paper Which Interprets Theory for Practice from AETS in 1978. He has been associate editor of *The Journal of Research in Science Teaching* and editor of thirteen volumes of *The Focus on Excellence* series from NSTA. The 1989 president of the National Association of Biology Teachers, his interests are classroom teaching analysis and science teacher education.

Bruce A. Peseau is Professor and Program Chairman, Administration of Higher Education at the University of Alabama. His current research projects include analysis of resources and productivity in teacher education programs; identification of peer programs with cluster analysis; systems modeling of preparation programs; and computer applications in educational management. He has published more than 50 book chapters and articles.

Paul R. Pintrich is Assistant Professor in the Department of Curriculum, Teaching, and Psychological Studies, School of Education, University of Michigan, Ann Arbor. He is Codirector of the Program on Teaching and Learning Strategies for the National Center for Research to Improve Postsecondary Teaching and Learning. The Teaching and Learning

Program is investigating the role of student disciplinary knowledge, cognition, and motivation in different college and university settings. In addition, he is examining the relationships among adolescents' motivation, learning strategies, and metacognition in junior high school classrooms. He has published in numerous professional journals.

Chris Pipho is Director of the Information Clearinghouse at the Education Commission of the States. In this position he supervises the tracking of state education policy issues in all 50 states and writes and speaks extensively on state legislative activities. He also writes the "Stateline" column for *Phi Delta Kappan*.

Frank C. Pratzner is Associate Professor and Senior Research Specialist at the National Center for Research in Vocational Education, The Ohio State University. His major research interests are vocational teacher education, the role and function of vocational education, transferable skills, and job analysis for curriculum development. He is assistant editor of the *Journal of Industrial Teacher Education* and a member of the editorial board of the *Journal of Vocational Education Research*.

Maynard C. Reynolds is Professor of Educational Psychology (in the Special Education Program unit), University of Minnesota. He is a former President of the International Council for Exceptional Children and received that group's highest award, the J. E. Wallace Wallin Award, in 1971. He headed a federally funded Leadership Training Institute in special education for several years, beginning in the late 1960s, and later directed a National Support System for the Dean's Grant Projects involving 240 colleges and universities. He is editor of the AACTE publication *Knowledge Base for Beginning Teachers*, co-author of *Adaptive Mainstreaming*, and author/editor of 18 other books, all relating to special education.

Robert A. Roth is Professor of Education and Chair of the Department of Teacher Education, California State University, Long Beach. The author of over 100 publications, his current areas of study include induction support programs for beginning teachers, analysis and application of NCATE, teacher stress factors as correlates of personality type, clinical supervision, and communication models. He is a Distinguished Member and Past President of the Association of Teacher Educators.

Ray D. Ryan is Executive Director of the National Center for Research in Vocational Education, The Ohio State University. He has held academic appointments at The Ohio State University, Arizona State University, and the University of Nevada—Las Vegas. Other positions have included the State Director of Vocational Education and Deputy Superintendent of Public Instruction for the Arizona State Department of Education and Deputy Superintendent of Public Instruction in Nevada. He has been a member of several boards and advisory bodies.

Walter G. Secada is Assistant Professor of Curriculum and Instruction, University of Wisconsin—Madison and Research Associate at the Wisconsin Center for Educational Research. His research interests include equity in education and bilingual education. An associate editor of the *Journal for Research in Mathematics Education*, he is editor of the book *Equity in Education* and has written chapters in *Dimensions of Thinking and Cognitive Instruction* and the forthcoming *Handbook of Research on Teaching and Learning Mathematics*.

John Sikula is President of the national Association of Teacher Educators and one of two Associate Editors of this *Handbook*. He has served as Dean of the Graduate School of Education at California State University, Long Beach since 1984 and was the founding president of the State of California Association of Teacher Educators. He was founding editor of *Action in Teacher Education*, ATE's national journal, and served from 1978 to 1988, and he was Chair of the Blue Ribbon Task Force that analyzed commission reports in *Visions of Reform*. He has authored or coauthored more than 150 publications including 8 books and monographs, 11 chapters and research reports, and 60 journal articles in 35 different journals.

Philip L. Smith is Professor of Educational Psychology at the University of Wisconsin—Milwaukee. His primary research interests are in the areas of research methodology and applied testing and measurement. His work has been published in numerous national journals and books. He serves on the editorial staff of several journals in educational measurement.

Dennis Sparks is Executive Director of the National Staff Development Council and executive editor of the *Journal of Staff Development*. He has served as director of a federally funded teacher center, codirector of an alternative high school, and classroom teacher. His professional interests include research on effective teaching, adult learning, and planning for school improvement.

Jane Stallings is currently the Chairperson of the Curriculum and Instruction Department and director of the Houston Center for Effective Teaching in the College of Education, University of Houston. She is best known for her work in classroom research, which links observed instructional strategies to student behavioral outcomes. Findings from this research formed the basis for a teacher education program that requires teachers and/or student teachers to analyze their own observed behavior and set goals for improvement. In 1987, she initiated a school/college partnership with the Houston Independent School District in which college supervisors, student teachers, and supervising teachers observed and met in weekly seminars. She is the author of *Learning to Look: A Handbook for Observation and Models of Teaching*.

Alan R. Tom is Professor of Education and coordinator of the Division of Teaching and Teacher Education at the University of Arizona. He is the author of *Teaching as a Moral Craft* and has published articles in a variety of areas in teacher education, including program design, program accreditation, supervision, and the relationship of research and teaching practice. His forthcoming book, *Redesigning Teacher Education*, explores the issues that an education faculty ought to consider when rethinking the professional curriculum for prospective teachers.

Wayne J. Urban is Research Professor of Educational Foundations and Professor of History at Georgia State University. He is the author of *Why Teacher Organized* and is finishing a biography of the noted black educator, Horace Mann Bond. He is a past president of the History of Education Society and has just completed a term as vice president of Division F, History and Historiography, of the American Educational Research Association.

Linda Valli is Assistant Professor and Director of Teacher Education at the Catholic University of America in Washington, DC. She is the author of *Becoming Clerical Workers*, a critical social analysis of gender, schooling, and workplace relations, and is editing the forthcoming *Curriculum Differentiation: Interpretive Studies of U.S. Secondary Schools* with Reba Page. Her primary areas of interest include gender issues in education, school cultures, and reflective teaching.

Hersholt C. Waxman is Associate Dean for Research and Associate Professor in Curriculum and Instruction at the University of Houston. He received his doctorate in educational research and evaluation from the University of Illinois at Chicago and a postdoctoral fellowship from the Learning Research and Development Center, University of Pittsburgh. He is president of the Southwest Educational Research Association. He has been involved in many nationally funded, school-based, research projects in the areas of effective classroom instruction and learning environments and has published many articles in journals and books, including his most recent, *Images of Reflection in Teacher Education*.

Robert E. Yager is Professor of Science Education in the Science Education Center at the University of Iowa. He has authored over 300 manuscripts, directed over 100 teacher institutes and special programs, headed test centers for using new curriculum materials, and directed over 70 PhD dissertations. He has been president of the National Science Teachers Association, the Association for the Education of Teachers in Science, the National Association for Research in Science Teaching, the School Science and Mathematics Association, the National Association of Biology Teachers, and Section Q of the American Association for the Advancement of Science and has served on numerous committees, boards, and task forces.

Sam J. Yarger is Professor and Dean of the School of Education, University of Wisconsin—Milwaukee. He has been an elementary school teacher and principal, school psychologist, and member of the faculties at the University of Toledo and Syracuse University. His research interests are primarily in program development and research in teacher education at the inservice and preservice levels. He has authored or co-authored nearly 50 research reports, books, monographs, chapters, and articles. He teaches both graduate and undergraduate courses in educational psychology, child development, classroom observation, and teacher education policy. He serves on numerous commissions and boards, most recently as a member of the board of directors of the American Association of Colleges for Teacher Education.

Kenneth M. Zeichner, Professor in the Department of Curriculum and Instruction, University of Wisconsin—Madison, is also a Senior Researcher with the National Center for Research in Teacher Education at Michigan State University. He is engaged primarily in the study of teacher education, with particular interest in how teachers learn to teach. His articles on these subjects have been published widely in this country and abroad. He is currently working on a book (with coauthor Dan Liston), *Teacher Education and the Conditions of Schooling*.

Nancy L. Zimpher is Associate Professor, College of Education at The Ohio State University. She offers graduate instruction in the area of professional development for teachers. Her research interests and publications focus on inquiry into the nature of initial programs of teacher preparation, entry-year programs, and characteristics of teacher mentors and purposes and formats of staff development for teachers in schools. She is a member of the Research and Information Task Force of the American Association of Colleges for Teacher Education, which conducts longitudinal studies of teacher preparation; is the book review editor for the *Journal of Teacher Education*; and chairs the membership committee of Division K of the American Educational Research Association.

INDEXES

NAME INDEX

889

SUBJECT INDEX